SOCIAL SECURITY LEGISLATION 2007

VOLUME III: ADMINISTRATION, ADJUDICATION AND THE EUROPEAN DIMENSION

AUSTRALIA
Law Book Co.
Sydney

CANADA and USA
Carswell
Toronto

HONG KONG
Sweet & Maxwell Asia

NEW ZEALAND
Brookers
Auckland

SINGAPORE and MALAYSIA
Sweet & Maxwell Asia
Singapore and Kuala Lumpur

SOCIAL SECURITY LEGISLATION 2007

General Editor
David Bonner, LL.B, LL.M

VOLUME III: ADMINISTRATION, ADJUDICATION AND THE EUROPEAN DIMENSION

Commentary By

Mark Rowland, LL.B.
Social Security Commissioner

Robin White, M.A., LL.M.
Professor of Law, University of Leicester
Deputy Social Security Commissioner

Consultant Editor
Child Poverty Action Group

LONDON
SWEET & MAXWELL
2007

Published in 2007 by
Sweet & Maxwell Limited of
100 Avenue Road, Swiss Cottage,
London NW3 3PF
http://www.sweetandmaxwell.co.uk
Typeset by Servis Filmsetting Ltd, Manchester
Printed and bound in England by
MPG Books Ltd, Bodmin, Cornwall

No natural forests were destroyed to make this product.
Only farmed timber was used and re-planted.

A catalogue record for this book is
available from the British Library

ISBN 9 781 847 032 607

All rights reserved. Crown Copyright Material is reproduced with the permission of the Controller of HMSO and the Queen's Printer for Scotland.

No part of this publication may be reproduced or transmitted in any form or by any means, or stored in any retrieval system of any nature without prior written permission, except for permitted fair dealing under the Copyright, Designs and Patents Act 1988, or in accordance with the terms of a licence issued by the Copyright Licensing Agency in respect of photocopying and/or reprographic reproduction. Application for permission for other use of copyright material including permission to reproduce extracts in other published works shall be made to the publishers. Full acknowledgment of author, publisher and source must be given.

Application for permission for other use of copyright material controlled by the publisher shall be made to the publishers. Material is contained in this publication for which publishing permission has been sought, and for which copyright is acknowledged. Permission to reproduce such material cannot be granted by the publishers and application must be made to the copyright holder.

Commentators have asserted their moral rights under the Copyright, Designs and Patents Act 1988 to be identified as the authors of the commentary in this Volume.

©
Sweet & Maxwell Limited
2007

CHILD POVERTY ACTION GROUP

The Child Poverty Action Group (CPAG) is a charity, founded in 1965, which campaigns for the relief of poverty in the United Kingdom. It has a particular reputation in the field of welfare benefits law derived from its legal work, publications, training and parliamentary and policy work, and is widely recognised as the leading organisation for taking test cases on social security law.

CPAG is therefore ideally placed to act as Consultant Editor to this 4-volume work—**Social Security Legislation 2007**. CPAG is not responsible for the detail of what is contained in each volume, and the authors' views are not necessarily those of CPAG. The Consultant Editor's role is to act in an advisory capacity on the overall structure, focus and direction of the work.

For more information about CPAG, its rights and policy publications or training courses, its address is 94 White Lion Street, London, N1 9PF (telephone: 020 7837 7979—website: *http://www.cpag.org.uk*).

FOREWORD

The volumes which make up the Social Security Legislation with the accompanying commentary have become an indispensable part of the tribunal decision making process. I am glad to be able, once again, to commend them and their sister publications to all those who are involved in any way in administrative decision making or who might have cause to come before our tribunals. Once again we have at our disposal a readily available source of some of the most complex legislation in any jurisdiction with a clear exposition of its meaning and interpretation. I am grateful to all those who have taken the time and effort to compile these volumes and present them for publication.

His Honour Michael Harris
President of Appeals Tribunals

PREFACE

Administration, Adjudication and the European Dimension is Volume III of the four volume series, *Social Security Legislation 2007*. The companion volumes are: Bonner, Hooker and White, *Vol. I: Non Means Tested Benefits;* Wood, Poynter, Wikeley and Bonner, *Vol. II: Income Support, Jobseeker's Allowance, State Pension Credit and the Social Fund*; and Wikeley and Williams, *Vol. IV: Tax Credits, Child Trust Funds and Employer-Paid Social Security Benefits*.

Each of the volumes in the series provides a legislative text, clearly showing the form and date of amendments, and commentary up to date to April 12, 2007.

Though this has been a relatively quiet year in terms of legal change, there remain a myriad of minor amendments to legislation, as well as clarifications in Commissioners and court decisions on important points of social security law. Among the current lively issues are the impact of European Community Law on entitlement to benefits of migrants from the new Member States, as well as the status of special non-contributory benefits which has been argued at the Luxembourg Court. Issues relating to decisions and appeals continue to throw up complex points which can perplex even the experts.

As always, revising and updating the legislative text and commentary has required considerable flexibility on the part of the publisher and a great deal of help from a number of sources, including CPAG as advisory editor to the series, for which we express sincere thanks. Particular mention must be made here of the debt owed by all of us to John Mesher, who began the provision of annotated legislation for tribunals, has given wise advice on the development of this series, and who happily remains on call as consultant in respect of Vol.II.

To maximise space for explanatory commentary we have provided lists of definitions only where the commentary to the provision is substantial, or where reference to definitions is essential for a proper understanding. Users of this book should always check whether particular words or phrases they are called on to apply have a particular meaning ascribed to them in legislation. Generally the first or second regulation in each set of regulations contains definitions of key terms (check the "Arrangement of Regulations" at the beginning of each set for an indication of the subject matter covered by each regulation or Schedule). There are also definition or "interpretation" sections in each of the Acts (check the "Arrangement of Sections" at the beginning of each Act for an indication of the subject matter covered by each section or Schedule).

In the last edition we had to omit the index for reasons of reducing page length. Having listened carefully to the view of users, we are very pleased that Sweet & Maxwell have felt able to respond by reinstating it in this edition.

Users of the series, and its predecessor works, have over the years provided valuable comments which have invariably been helpful to the editors in

Preface

ensuring that the selection of legislative material for inclusion and the commentary upon it reflect the sorts of difficulties encountered in practice. In doing so, readers have thus helped to shape the content of each of the volumes in the current series. We hope that readers will maintain that tradition. Please write to the General Editor of the series, David Bonner, Faculty of Law, University of Leicester, University Road, Leicester, LE1 7RH, who will pass on any comments received to the appropriate commentator.

Our gratitude must also go to the President of the Appeal Tribunals and his staff for continuing the tradition of help and encouragement.

Mark Rowland
Robin White

CONTENTS

	Page
Foreword	vii
Preface	ix
Using this book, using legal authority and finding other sources of information	xiii
Table of Cases	xxi
Table of Social Security Commissioners' Decisions	xxxvii
Table of Abbreviations	xliii

PART I   STATUTES

	Paras
Race Relations Act 1976	1.1
Forfeiture Act 1982	1.12
Social Security Administration Act 1992	1.23
Welsh Language Act 1993	1.239
Pension Schemes Act 1993	1.247
Employment Tribunals Act 1996	1.249
Social Security (Recovery of Benefits) Act 1997	1.253
Social Security Act 1998	1.335
Social Security Contributions (Transfer of Functions, etc.) Act 1999	1.544
Welfare Reform and Pensions Act 1999	1.555
Child Support, Pensions and Social Security Act 2000	1.560
Social Security Fraud Act 2001	1.568
Tax Credits Act 2002	1.577
Gender Recognition Act 2004	1.599
Civil Partnership Act 2004	1.631

PART II   REGULATIONS
SECTION A—SOCIAL SECURITY

The Social Security (Breach of Community Order) Regulations 2001	2.1
The Social Security (Claims and Payments) Regulations 1987	2.32
The Social Security (Claims and Information) Regulations 1999	2.260
The Social Security Commissioners (Procedure) Regulations 1999	2.279
The Social Security and Child Support (Decisions and Appeals) Regulations 1999	2.339
The Social Security (General Benefit) Regulations 1982	2.571
The Social Security (Incapacity Benefit Work-focused Interviews) Regulations 2003	2.578
The Social Security (Jobcentre Plus Interviews) Regulations 2002	2.599
The Social Security (Jobcentre Plus Interviews for Partners) Regulations 2003	2.618
The Social Security (Loss of Benefit) Regulations 2001	2.635
The Social Security (Medical Evidence) Regulations 1976	2.659

The Social Security (Notification of Change of Circumstances)
    Regulations 2001   2.677
The Social Security (Payments on Account, Overpayments and
    Recovery) Regulations 1988   2.684
The Social Security Act 1998 (Prescribed Benefits)
    Regulations 2006   2.723
The Social Security (Quarterly Work-Focused Interviews for
    for Certain Lone Parents) Regulations 2004   2.726
The Employment Protection (Recoupment of Jobseeker's
    Allowance and Income Support) Regulations 1996   2.737
The Social Security (Recovery of Benefits) Regulations 1997   2.752
The Social Security (Work-focused Interviews for Lone
    Parents) and Miscellaneous Amendments Regulations 2000   2.769
The Social Security (Working Neighbourhoods) Regulations 2004   2.785

       Section B—Child Benefit and Guardian's Allowance
Child Benefit and Guardian's Allowance (Administration)
    Regulations 2003   2.786
The Child Benefit and Guardian's Allowance (Administrative
    Arrangements) Regulations 2003   2.849
The Child Benefit and Guardian's Allowance (Decisions and
    Appeals) Regulations 2003   2.855

       PART III   EUROPEAN COMMUNITY LAW

European Communities Act 1972   3.1
Extracts from the EC Treaty   3.17
Council Regulation (EEC) No.1612/68   3.56
Directive 2004/38/EC   3.60
Council Regulation (EEC) No.1408/71   3.110
Council Regulation (EEC) No.574/72   3.308
Council Regulation (EC) No. 859/2003   3.442
Council Directive 79/7   3.450

       PART IV   HUMAN RIGHTS LAW

Human Rights Act 1998   4.01

USING THIS BOOK, USING LEGAL AUTHORITY AND FINDING OTHER SOURCES OF INFORMATION

Introduction

This book is not designed as an introduction to, or general textbook on, the law relating to social security. Inevitably some familiarity with the social security system has been assumed. This note is designed to assist readers who are not lawyers—and also those lawyers who are not familiar with this particular field of law—by identifying the sources of social security law and showing how to find them. Volume IV also deals with income tax law, and its version of this section contains additional comments about that.

Primary sources of social security law

Social security law is based on legislation, consisting of *Acts of Parliament*, which are primary legislation and are also known as statutes, and *statutory instruments*, which are secondary or delegated legislation made by ministers acting under powers conferred by primary legislation and are also known as regulations (or, occasionally, orders). Another source of the law lies in *judicial decisions*, made, in this context, principally by Social Security Commissioners who hear appeals from appeal tribunals although some decisions of the courts are also relevant. Such judicial decisions provide authoritative interpretation of the legislation. The precise mixture of the three sources differs from benefit to benefit.

The scope of this book and the status of the commentary

This book contains an up-to-date text of the principal statutes and statutory instruments relevant to the work of appeal tribunals and Commissioners. It also contains a commentary on that legislation, referring to relevant decisions of Commissioners and the courts. The commentary aims to help readers understand the legislation and its implications. The focus in decision-making, however, must remain on the actual words of the legislation as applied by the Commissioners and courts, because the commentary merely reflects the opinion of the commentator on what the law is.

Finding a particular section in a statute

Statutes consist of numbered sections (sometimes grouped in Parts, which may in turn be divided into Chapters) and they often have schedules at the end.

Suppose you wanted to find section 94 of the Social Security Contributions and Benefits Act 1992. Sometimes the word "section" is abbreviated to "s."; so you could refer to the Social Security Contributions and Benefits Act 1992, s.94.

To find this provision, you can use the contents pages to find where

Using this Book

provisions of the Social Security Contributions and Benefits Act 1992 are printed. You can also use the running heads at the top of each page; the header on the left-hand page gives the name of the Act while the header on the right-hand page gives the year and chapter number (abbreviated "c.") as well as the section dealt with on that page. The chapter number simply indicates the order in the Parliamentary year of the statute; the Social Security Contributions and Benefits Act 1992 is chapter 4, meaning that it was the fourth statute to be passed by Parliament in 1992.

After the text of the section comes a note of the AMENDMENTS made to the provision, reference to relevant DEFINITIONS, and the commentary, which appears under the heading GENERAL NOTE. Where the section is re-enacted in consolidating legislation, that is, legislation drawing together all the amendments over time in a new statute, the DERIVATION, or source, of the provision is also given so that you can see where the provision originally appeared. This can be helpful in considering any decisions of Commissioners or the courts on the earlier form of the provision.

Finding a particular regulation

Statutory instruments consist of numbered regulations (or articles where the statutory instrument is in the form of an order rather than being a set of regulations) and, like statutes, they sometimes have schedules at the end.

Suppose you wanted to find regulation 26 of the Social Security (Incapacity for Work) (General) Regulations 1995. Sometimes the word "regulation" is abbreviated to "reg."; so you could refer to the Social Security (Incapacity for Work) (General) Regulations 1995, reg.26.

To find this provision, use the contents pages to find the Social Security (Incapacity for Work) (General) Regulations 1995. Then move forward within the regulations until you find the one you want. Again the running headers at the top of each page will assist you. The header on the right-hand page gives the statutory instrument number, that is the year of publication and the number, as in SI 1995/311, indicating that these regulations were the 311th statutory instrument made by Ministers and approved by Parliament in 1995.

As with statutes, after the text of the regulation comes a note of the AMENDMENTS made to the provision, reference to relevant DEFINITIONS, and the commentary which appears under the heading GENERAL NOTE Where the regulation is re-enacted in consolidating regulations, that is, legislation drawing together all the amendments made over time in a new set of regulations, the DERIVATION or source, of the provision is also given so that you can see where the provision originally appeared. This can be helpful in considering any decisions of Commissioners or the courts on the earlier form of the provision.

Commissioners' decisions

Both reported and unreported decisions of Commissioners are important sources of guidance on the interpretation and application of legislation relating to social security benefits and their administration. Where relevant, these are binding on both decision-makers and on tribunals. The binding nature of Commissioners' decisions is discussed below. A single Commissioner hears most appeals, though the Chief Commissioner does occasionally direct that three Commissioners sitting together should hear

Using this Book

cases of special importance. This is then known as a Tribunal of Commissioners.

Reported decisions

About 40 to 50 decisions a year are selected to be "reported". Selection used to be a decision of the Chief Commissioner acting alone. Later he made his selection on advice from a committee of Commissioners, but, since 2002, selection of decisions to report has been the task of an Editorial committee chaired by the Chief Commissioner. Decisions are selected for reporting only if they are of general importance and command the assent of at least a majority of Commissioners. They are published in biennial bound volumes by The Stationery Office and in looseleaf form (contact Margaret Drummond, Print Solutions, Room B0202, Benton Park Road, Newcastle-upon- Tyne NE98 1YX (tel. 0191 225 5422)) and on the world wide web (*http://www.dwp.gov.uk/advisers/docs/commdecs/index.asp*) by the Department for Work and Pensions (replacing the DSS). They can also be accessed via the Commissioners' website (*http://www.osscsc.gov.uk*). These decisions are available in all tribunal venues and can be consulted in local social security offices, and some main libraries.

Reported decisions are renumbered with the initial letter "R" for "reported". *R(IB) 1/00* was the first decision on incapacity benefit to be reported in 2000. A decision of a Tribunal of Commissioners is often identified by adding a letter "T" in brackets after the reference, as in *R(IB) 2/99(T)*. Scottish decisions are not specifically identified as such.

Unreported decisions

Reported decisions are selected from a greater body of decisions in the cases dealt with by the Commissioners. Those not reported are known as unreported decisions but still have precedential value. Each Commissioner's decision is given a file number in the Commissioners' Office, which is a unique identification number. From 1997 cases have been registered consecutively by number within a calendar year, without a separate range of numbers for each benefit. Prior to 1995, there was a separate range of numbers for each benefit. So Commissioner's decision *CU/23/1992* is the 23rd case on unemployment benefit registered in 1992. The letters "CU" indicate that the decision is that of a Commissioner (C) and that the benefit in question is unemployment benefit (U). Between 1995 and 1997, there had been a change of approach, reflecting computerisation. The system of numbering consecutively within benefits in a particular year ceased. The lettering system remained the same, but the number after the letters, as in *CU 7328/1995*, indicated that this was the 7328th case on any benefit registered since the beginning of 1995.

Scottish decisions have an "S" after the "C" (e.g. *CSI/26/98*) and, until the Welsh office of the Commissioners was closed, Welsh decisions could be identified as having a "W" after the "C". The "W" will be added again in 2005.

Until the end of 2001, some 100 decisions a year were "starred" because it was considered that they raised points of significance or interest and deserved wider circulation. They did not, however, acquire any enhanced precedential status from being starred. The practice of starring was discontinued from the start of 2002. Instead decisions that Commissioners believe should have wider currency are available on the Commissioners' new website (*http://www.osscsc.gov.uk*). Some decisions are selected as of particular interest and highlighted for a time in the Most Recent Decisions part of the Decisions section of that website. As with "starring", however, a decision does not gain enhanced precedential status through "highlighting".

Other sources of/on Commissioners' decisions

There are a number of other sources of valuable information or commentary on Commissioners' decisions, whether reported or unreported: see in particular publications such as the *Journal of Social Security Law*, CPAG's *Welfare Rights Bulletin, Legal Action* and the *Adviser*. As far as online resources go there is little to beat Rightsnet (*http://www.rightsnet.org.uk*). This site contains a wealth of resources for people working in the welfare benefits field but of special relevance in this context are the "Briefcase" area which contains summaries of Commissioners' Decisions (with links to the full decision on the Commissioners' website (*http://www.osscsc.gov.uk*)) and the Commissioners' Decisions section of the "Toolkit" area.

What does it mean to say that a case is binding?

Reference to decisions being binding means that where a similar point is raised in a later case before an adjudicating authority bound by the decision, that adjudicating authority must accept the interpretation of the law contained in the decision. So a Commissioner's decision explaining what a term in a particular regulation means, lays down the definition of that term in much the same way as if the term had been defined in the regulations themselves. The decision may also help in deciding what the same term means when it is used in a different set of regulations, provided that the term appears to have been used in a similar text.

Appeals to the Commissioners are now available only on points of law, but before April 1987 appeals were available on points of fact as well as law. Care should be taken in reading older decisions to appreciate that some were concerned with fact rather than law, though the reported decisions invariably contain points of general application. Relevant decisions of the Commissioners and the courts are explained in the commentary to the statutory provisions in this volume, together with guidance on their significant for decision-making in the tribunals. Users of the book should remember that it is the decision itself which is binding and not the explanation of it in the commentary; that is merely the opinion of the commentator.

Using Commissioners' decisions: the hierarchy of authority

Although the Chief Commissioner has directed that, so far as possible, reference should be made to reported decisions only, the legal position is that all decisions of Commissioners are binding on decision-makers and tribunals. Where there is a conflict, a decision of a Tribunal of Commissioners should be preferred to a decision of a single Commissioner and a reported decision should generally be preferred to an unreported decision (*R(I) 12/75(T)*), unless the unreported decision was the later decision and the Commissioner expressly decided not to follow the earlier reported decision (see the Northern Ireland decision, *R 1/00(FC)*). Decisions of Commissioners are not binding on other Commissioners.

Using this Book

However, a single Commissioner will always follow a decision of a Tribunal of Commissioners and will generally follow a decision of another single Commissioner (*R(I) 12/75(T)*). A Tribunal of Commissioners will generally follow a decision of another such Tribunal but is not bound to do so (*R(U) 4/88(T)*).

There are separate Commissioners in Northern Ireland considering legislation that is often indistinguishable from the legislation in Great Britain. Decisions of Northern Ireland Commissioners are not binding in Great Britain (*R(SB) 1/90(T)*) but are persuasive. Such decisions are included in the decisions published on the website of the Great Britain Commissioners but the selection of decisions to be reported is made by the Chief Commissioner in Northern Ireland. Looseleaf publication by The Stationery Office and on the world wide web by the Department for Social Development (*http://www.dsdni.gov.uk*) is separate from the publication of Great Britain decisions. So was the publication of bound volumes by The Stationery Office until 1999. From 2000, reported Northern Ireland decisions are included in the same bound volumes as reported decisions of Commissioners in Great Britain. References to decisions of Northern Ireland Commissioners can always be distinguished from references to decisions of Commissioners in Great Britain because the former are numbered differently with the letters identifying the type of benefit always being in brackets after the numbers, as in *C12/98(IS)*, which has been reported as *R1/00(IS)*. Unreported decisions of the Northern Ireland Commissioners can be found on the Department for Social development website at *http://www.dsdni.gov.uk*.

Using Commissioners' decisions at Tribunals and before the Commissioners

Decision-makers and claimants are entitled to assume that tribunals and Commissioners have immediate access to reported decisions of Commissioners and they need not provide copies, although it may sometimes be helpful to do so. However, where either a decision-maker or a claimant intends to rely on an unreported decision, it will be necessary to provide a copy of the decision to the tribunal or Commissioner. A copy of the decision should also be provided to the other party before the hearing because otherwise it may be necessary for there to be an adjournment to enable that party to take advice on the significance of the decision.

Decisions of the Courts

Decisions of the superior courts in Great Britain and Northern Ireland on questions of legal principle are almost invariably followed by decision-makers, tribunals and Commissioners, even when they are not strictly binding because the relevant court was in a different part of the United Kingdom or exercised a parallel—but not superior—jurisdiction (see the note to section 14 of the Social Security Act 1998 in Part I of this volume).

Decisions of the courts on social security matters are generally included among the reports of Commissioners' decisions. So, for example, *R(I) 1/00* contains Commissioner's decisions *CSI 12/98*, the decision of the Court of Session upholding the Commissioner's decision and the decision of the

House of Lords in *Chief Adjudication Officer v Faulds*, reversing the decision of the Court of Session. Decisions issued in recent years by the higher courts in the United Kingdom (e.g., the High Court, the Court of Appeal, the Court of Session and the House of Lords) and some decisions of tribunals are also published free on the website of the British and Irish Legal Information Institute (*http://www.bailii.org*), often within hours of delivery. Some of them can also be found in the various series of law reports familiar to lawyers (in particular, in the *Law Reports*, the *Weekly Law Reports*, the *All England Law Reports*, the *Industrial Cases Reports* and the *Family Law Reports*. Sweet and Maxwell's online subscription service *Westlaw* is another valuable source (*http://www.westlaw.co.uk*), as is Smith Bernal's *Casetrack* (*http://www.casetrack.com*) and Lexis Nexis' *Lexis* (*http://www.lexis.com*).

European Community Law

The European Community is part of the European Union. European Community Law affecting social security is covered in Part III of this volume.

The European Union has two courts: the Court of Justice of the European Communities, and the Court of First Instance. Decision-makers, tribunals and Commissioners are under a duty by reason of Article 10 (ex.5) of the EC Treaty to apply decisions of the Luxembourg courts, where relevant to cases before them, in preference to other authorities binding on them.

Decisions of the Court of Justice of the European Communities come in two parts: the Opinion of the Advocate General and the decision of the Court. It is the decision of the Court which is binding. The Court is assisted by hearing the Opinion of the Advocate General before itself coming to a conclusion on the issue before it. The Court does not always follow its Advocate General. Where it does, the Opinion of the Advocate General often elaborates the arguments in greater detail than the single collegiate judgment of the Court. No dissenting judgments appear in reports from the Court of Justice.

Decisions of the Luxembourg courts, together with legislation of the European Union, are published in English on the world wide web at *http://eur-lex.europa.eu/en/index.htm*.

The European Convention on Human Rights, the Strasbourg Court and the Human Rights Act 1998

The Court of Human Rights in Strasbourg is quite separate from the Luxembourg courts and serves a different purpose: interpreting and applying the European Convention on Human Rights, which is incorporated into United Kingdom law by the Human Rights Act 1998. From October 2, 2000, public authorities, including courts, Commissioners, tribunals and decision-makers (the Secretary of State) must act in accordance with the incorporated provisions of the Convention, unless statute prevents this. They must take into account the Strasbourg case law. They are required to interpret legislation, so far as is possible to do so, to give effect to the incorporated Convention rights. Any court or tribunal may declare secondary legislation incompatible with those rights and, in certain circumstances, invalidate it. Only the higher courts can declare a provision of primary legislation to be incompatible with those rights, but no court or tribunal can invalidate primary legislation.

Using this Book

The work of the Court and the impact of the Human Rights Act 1998 on social security are discussed in Part IV of this volume.

Judgments of the Court of Human Rights are made by majority, and separate concurring or dissenting judgments are included with the decision of the majority where the Court is not unanimous.

Decisions of the Court of Human Rights are available on the world wide web at *http://www.echr.coe.int*.

Official guidance on Social Security Law

The law has been translated into a more civil servant friendly format. Prior to the decision-making and appeals changes made by the Social Security Act 1998, guidance on benefits and their administration was set out in the thirteen volume *Adjudication Officers Guide (AOG)* published by The Stationery Office. This has now been replaced by a fourteen volume *Decision Makers Guide (DMG)*. This is available on the world wide web at *http://www.dwp.gov.uk/publications/dwp/dmg/index.asp*.

The coverage of the DMG is as follows:

Volume 1	Decision Making and Appeals
Volume 2	International Subjects
Volume 3	Subjects Common to all Benefits
Volume 4	Jobseeker's Allowance and Income Support
Volume 5	Jobseeker's Allowance and Income Support
Volume 6	Jobseeker's Allowance and Income Support
Volume 7	Jobseeker's Allowance and Income Support
Volume 8	No longer issued
Volume 9	No longer issued
Volume 10	Benefits for Incapacity, Disability and Maternity
Volume 11	Industrial Injuries Benefits
Volume 12	Widow's Benefit and Retirement Pension
Volume 13	State Pension Credit
Volume 14	State Pension Credit

It should be noted that the DMG is not binding on tribunals and Commissioners; it is internal guidance for the use of decision-makers within the Department.

Child Benefit and Guardian's Allowance are now administered by HM Revenue and Customs, as are tax credits. A range of useful material can be found on its website at *http://www.hmrc.gov.uk/practitioners/index.shtml*.

Unofficial guidance on Social Security Law

There are a large number of guides. CPAG's *Welfare Benefits Handbook*, published annually each spring, is unrivalled as a practical and comprehensive introduction from the claimant's viewpoint.

TABLE OF CASES

Abbas v Secretary of State for Work and Pensions [2005] EWCA Civ 652, CA (Civ Div) 1.376
Abdirahman, Abdirahman and Uluslow v Secretary of State for Work and Pensions, CA 3.31
Achterberg-te Riele v Sociale Verzekeringsbank Amsterdam (C–48/88) [1989] E.C.R. 1963; [1990] 3 C.M.L.R. 323, ECJ (2nd Chamber) 3.454
Adoui v Belgium (115/81); Cornuaille v Belgium (116/81) [1982] E.C.R. 1665; [1982] 3 C.M.L.R. 631, ECJ 3.37
Akewushola v Secretary of State for the Home Department; sub nom Akewushola v Immigration Officer (Heathrow) [2000] 1 W.L.R. 2295; [2000] 2 All E.R. 148; [1999] Imm. A.R. 594; [1999] I.N.L.R. 433, CA (Civ Div) 2.508
Akram v Adam [2004] EWCA Civ 2762; [2005] 1 W.L.R. 2762; [2005] 1 All E.R. 741; [2005] C.P. Rep. 14; [2005] H.L.R. 14; [2005] L. & T.R. 9; [2004] 50 E.G. 84 (C.S.); (2005) 102(5) L.S.G. 28; (2004) 148 S.J.L.B. 1433; [2004] N.P.C. 182; [2005] 1 P. & C.R. DG13, CA (Civ Div) 2.508
Aldewereld RL v Staatssecretarisvan Financien (C–60/93) [1994] E.C.R. I–2991, ECJ (5th Chamber) 3.142
Ali v Secretary of State for the Home Department [2006] EWCA Civ 484; [2006] 3 C.M.L.R. 10; [2006] Eu. L.R. 1045; [2006] Imm. A.R. 532; [2006] I.N.L.R. 537; [2006] E.L.R. 423; (2006) 103(20) L.S.G. 25; (2006) 150 S.J.L.B. 606, CA (Civ Div) 3.31
Allen v Allen [1986] 2 F.L.R. 265; [1986] Fam. Law 268, CA (Civ Div) 1.141
Arbetsmarknadsstyrelsen v Rydergärd (C–215/00) [2002] E.C.R. I–1817, ECJ (5th Chamber) 3.238
Arcaro, Criminal Proceedings against (C–168/95) [1997] All E.R. (EC) 82; [1996] E.C.R. I–4705; [1997] 1 C.M.L.R. 179; [1998] Env. L.R. 39, ECJ 3.23
Armstrong v First York Ltd [2005] EWCA Civ 277; [2005] 1 W.L.R. 2751; [2005] C.P. Rep. 25; [2005] R.T.R. 19, CA (Civ Div) 1.380
Aston Cantlow and Wilmcote with Billesley Parochial Church Council v Wallbank; sub nom Wallbank v Aston Cantlow and Wilmcote with Billesley Parochial Church Council [2003] UKHL 37; [2004] 1 A.C. 546; [2003] 3 W.L.R. 283; [2003] 3 All E.R. 1213; [2003] H.R.L.R. 28; [2003] U.K.H.R.R. 919; [2003] 27 E.G. 137 (C.S.); (2003) 100(33) L.S.G. 28; (2003) 153 N.L.J. 1030; (2003) 147 S.J.L.B. 812; [2003] N.P.C. 80, HL 4.16
Atlanta Fruchthandelsgesellschaft mbH v Bundesamt fur Ernahrung und Forstwirtschaft (C–465/93) [1996] All E.R. (E.C.) 31; [1995] E.C.R. I–3761; [1996] 1 C.M.L.R. 575, ECJ 3.53
B v Secretary of State for Work and Pensions [2005] EWCA Civ 929; [2005] 1 W.L.R. 3796, CA (Civ Div) 1.87, 1.93, 2.387
Bangs v Connex South Eastern Ltd; sub nom Connex South Eastern Ltd v Bangs [2005] EWCA Civ 14; [2005] 2 All E.R. 316; [2005] I.C.R. 763; [2005] I.R.L.R. 389; (2005) 149 S.J.L.B. 148, CA (Civ Div) 2.498
Banks v Theatre Royal de la Monnaie (C–178/97); sub nom Banks v Theatre Royale de la Monnaie (C–178/97) [2000] Q.B. 865; [2000] 3 W.L.R. 1069; [2000] All E.R. (EC) 324; [2000] E.C.R. I–2005; [2000] 2 C.M.L.R. 754; [2000] C.E.C. 256, ECJ (5th Chamber) 3.147
Barke v SEETEC Business Technology Centre Ltd [2005] EWCA Civ 578; [2005] I.C.R. 1373; [2005] I.R.L.R. 633, CA (Civ Div) 2.498
Baron v Secretary of State for Social Services, *The Times*, March 25, 1985, CA (Civ Div) 2.498
Barrow v United Kingdom (App.42735/02), unreported, August 2006, ECHR 4.66, 4.78
Baumbast v Secretary of State for the Home Department (C–413/99) [2002] E.C.R. I–7091; [2002] 3 C.M.L.R. 23; [2003] I.C.R. 1347; [2003] I.N.L.R. 1, ECJ 3.31, 3.37

xxi

Table of Cases

Beaney (Deceased), Re; sub nom Beaney v Beaney [1978] 1 W.L.R. 770; [1978] 2 All E.R. 595; (1977) 121 S.J. 832, Ch D 1.96
Begum (Runa) v Tower Hamlets LBC; sub nom Tower Hamlets LBC v Begum (Runa) [2003] UKHL 5; [2003] 2 A.C. 430; [2003] 2 W.L.R. 388; [2003] 1 All E.R. 731; [2003] H.R.L.R. 16; [2003] U.K.H.R.R. 419; 14 B.H.R.C. 400; [2003] H.L.R. 32; [2003] B.L.G.R. 205; 2003 Hous. L.R. 20; [2003] A.C.D. 41; (2003) 100(13) L.S.G. 28; (2003) 147 S.J.L.B. 232; [2003] N.P.C. 21, HL 2.541, 4.56
Belgium v Humbel (263/86) [1988] E.C.R. 5365; [1989] 1 C.M.L.R. 393, ECJ 3.31
Bellinger v Bellinger [2003] UKHL 21; [2003] 2 A.C. 467; [2003] 2 W.L.R. 1174; [2003] 2 All E.R. 593; [2003] 1 F.L.R. 1043; [2003] 2 F.C.R. 1; [2003] H.R.L.R. 22; [2003] U.K.H.R.R. 679; 14 B.H.R.C. 127; (2003) 72 B.M.L.R. 147; [2003] A.C.D. 74; [2003] Fam. Law 485; (2003) 153 N.L.J. 594; (2003) 147 S.J.L.B. 472, HL 4.68
Beltekian v Westminster City Council [2004] EWCA Civ 1784; [2005] A.C.D. 76, CA (Civ Div) 1.361, 1.382, 2.353, 2.442, 2.905
Bergemann v Bundesanstalt für Arbeit (236/87) [1988] E.C.R. 5125; [1990] 1 C.M.L.R. 525, ECJ (1st Chamber) 3.241
Bestuur van de Nieuwe Algemene Bedrijfsvereniging v Warmerdam-Steggerda (C–388/87) [1989] E.C.R. 1203; [1991] 2 C.M.L.R. 86, ECJ (6th Chamber) 3.241
Bestuur van de Sociale Verzekeringsbank v Cabanis-Issarte (C–308/93) [1996] E.C.R. I–2097; [1996] 2 C.M.L.R. 729, ECJ 3.118
Bickel, Criminal Proceedings against (C–274/96); sub nom Re Bickel (C–274/96); Criminal Proceedings against Franz (C–274/96) [1998] E.C.R. I–7637; [1999] 1 C.M.L.R. 348; [1999] C.E.C. 119, ECJ 3.67
Bidar. See R. (on the application of Bidar) v Ealing LBC
Blaik v Chief Adjudication Officer. See R(SB)6/91 .... 3.458
Bosman. See Union Royale Belge des Sociétés de Football Association (ASBL) v Bosman
Bozzone v Office de Securite Sociale d'Outre-Mer (C–87/76) [1977] E.C.R. 687; [1977] 2 C.M.L.R. 604, ECJ 3.122
Bramhill v Chief Adjudication Officer (C–420/92) [1994] E.C.R. I–3191; [1995] 2 C.M.L.R. 35, ECJ (5th Chamber) 3.466
Brown v Secretary of State for the Home Department, LTA 97/6885/J 2.488
— v Secretary of State for Work and Pensions [2006] EWCA Civ 89 .... 2.691
Bullerwell v United Kingdom (Admissibility) (48013/99) (2003) 36 E.H.R.R. CD76, ECHR 4.58
Burns v Secretary of State for Social Services, 1985 S.C. 143; 1985 S.L.T. 351, IH (1 Div) 1.14
Butterfield (on behalf of James William Butterfield) (Deceased) v Secretary of State for Defence [2002] EWHC 2247, QBD (Admin) 2.492
CG v Austria (17371/90) (1994) 18 E.H.R.R. CD51, Eur Comm HR 4.68
CILFIT Srl v Ministero della Sanita (283/81); sub nom CILFIT Srl v Ministro della Sanita (283/81) [1982] E.C.R. 3415; [1983] 1 C.M.L.R. 472, ECJ 3.53
Caisse Regionale d'Assurance Maladie (Lille) v Diamente Palermo (Toia) (C–237/78) [1979] E.C.R. 2645; [1980] 2 C.M.L.R. 31, ECJ 3.120
Calvin v Carr [1980] A.C. 574; [1979] 2 W.L.R. 755; [1979] 2 All E.R. 440; (1979) 123 S.J. 112, PC (Aus) 1.85
Campbell v Secretary of State for Work and Pensions [2005] EWCA Civ 989, CA (Civ Div) 1.215, 2.541
Campus Oil Ltd v Minister for Industry and Energy (72/83) [1984] E.C.R. 2727; [1984] 3 C.M.L.R. 544, ECJ 3.52
Carpenter v Secretary of State for the Home Department (C–60/00) [2003] Q.B. 416; [2003] 2 W.L.R. 267; [2003] All E.R. (EC) 577; [2002] E.C.R. I–6279; [2002] 2 C.M.L.R. 64; [2003] 2 F.C.R. 711; [2002] I.N.L.R. 439, ECJ 3.31
— v Secretary of State for Work and Pensions; sub nom Carpenter v Social Security Commissioner [2003] EWCA Civ 33; [2003] A.C.D. 52, CA (Civ Div) 2.492, 2.498
Centre Public d'Aide Sociale, Courcelles v Lebon (316/85) [1987] E.C.R. 2811; [1989] 1 C.M.L.R. 337, ECJ 3.37
Chateignier v Office National de l'Emploi (ONEM) (C–346/05) [2007] 1 C.M.L.R. 20, ECJ 3.120
Chen v Secretary of State for the Home Department (C–200/02); Zhu v Secretary of State for the Home Department (C–200/02) [2005] Q.B. 325; [2004] 3 W.L.R. 1453; [2005] All E.R. (EC) 129; [2004] E.C.R. I–9925; [2004] 3 C.M.L.R. 48; [2004] C.E.C. 503; [2004] Imm. A.R. 754; [2005] I.N.L.R. 1, ECJ 3.31

Table of Cases

Chief Adjudication Officer v Foster [1993] A.C. 754; [1993] 2 W.L.R. 292; [1993] 1
  All E.R. 705; [1993] C.O.D. 259; (1993) 137 S.J.L.B. 36, HL 4.22
— v McKiernon. *See* R(I)2/94 .... 2.375
— v Sherriff, Court of Appeal, May 4, 1995, *The Times*, May 10, 1995 .... 1.96, 1.99
— v Twomey (C–215/90) [1992] E.C.R. I–1823; [1992] 2 C.M.L.R. 571, ECJ (5th
  Chamber) 3.164
Chief Supplementary Benefit Officer v Leary [1985] 1 W.L.R. 84; [1985] 1 All E.R.
  1061; (1984) 81 L.S.G. 3596; (1984) 128 S.J. 852, CA (Civ Div) 1.100
Coccioli v Bundesanstalt für Arbeit (C–139/78) [1979] E.C.R. 991; [1979] 3 C.M.L.R.
  144, ECJ 3.238
Collins v Secretary of State for Work and Pensions (C–138/02) [2005] Q.B. 145; [2004]
  3 W.L.R. 1236; [2004] All E.R. (EC) 1005; [2004] E.C.R. I–2703; [2004] 2
  C.M.L.R. 8; [2004] C.E.C. 436; [2005] I.C.R. 37, ECJ 3.31, 3.57
Commission of the European Communities v Belgium (No.1) (149/79); sub nom Re
  Public Employees (No.1) (149/79) [1980] E.C.R. 3881; [1981] 2 C.M.L.R. 413,
  ECJ 3.37
— v — (C–229/89); sub nom Re Unemployed Heads of Households [1991] E.C.R.
  I–2205; [1993] 2 C.M.L.R. 403; [1991] I.R.L.R. 393, ECJ 3.458
— v Germany (205/84); sub nom Insurance Services, Re (205/84) [1986] E.C.R. 3755;
  [1987] 2 C.M.L.R. 69, ECJ 3.37
Cooke v Glenrose Fish Co [2004] I.C.R. 1188; [2004] I.R.L.R. 866, EAT 2.485, 2.508
— v Secretary of State for Social Security; sub nom Cooke v Social Security
  Commissioner [2001] EWCA Civ 734; [2002] 3 All E.R. 279, CA (Civ Div) ... 2.373,
  2.376, 2.380
Coppola v Insurance Officer (C–150/82) [1983] E.C.R. 43; [1983] 3 C.M.L.R. 586,
  ECJ (3rd Chamber) 3.162
Couronne v Crawley BC; Bontemps v Secretary of State for Work and Pensions [2006]
  EWHC 1514, QBD (Admin) 4.09, 4.84
Cowan v Trésor Public (186/87) [1989] E.C.R. 195; [1990] 2 C.M.L.R. 613, ECJ 3.37
Daalmeijer v Bestuur van de Sociale Verzekeringsbank (C–245/88) [1991] E.C.R.
  I–555; [1992] 3 C.M.L.R. 510, ECJ 3.143
De Cubber v Belgium (A/86); sub nom De Cubber v Belgium (9186/80) (1985) 7
  E.H.R.R. 236, ECHR 4.59
De Cuyper v Office National de l'Emploi (ONEM) (C–406/04) [2006] All E.R. (EC)
  947; [2006] E.C.R. I–6947; [2006] 3 C.M.L.R. 44; [2006] C.E.C. 937; [2007]
  I.C.R. 317, ECJ 3.31
Deghillage v Caisse Primaire d'Assurance Maladie (28/85) [1986] E.C.R. 991; [1987]
  2 C.M.L.R. 812, ECJ (1st Chamber) 3.214
Delaney v Delaney [1990] 2 F.L.R. 457; [1991] F.C.R. 161; [1991] Fam. Law 22;
  (1990) 154 J.P.N. 693, CA (Civ Div) 1.141
Denson v Secretary of State for Work and Pensions [2004] EWCA Civ 462 .... 2.446
Department for Work and Pensions v Richards. *See* R. v Richards (Michael)
Deumeland v Germany (A/120); sub nom Deumeland v Germany (9384/81) (1986) 8
  E.H.R.R. 448, ECHR 4.55, 4.56, 4.58
Di Paolo v Office National de l'Emploi (C–76/76) [1977] E.C.R. 315; [1977] 2
  C.M.L.R. 59, ECJ 3.241
Directeur Regional de la Securité Sociale de Nancy v Gillard (9/78) [1978] E.C.R.
  1661; [1978] 3 C.M.L.R. 554, ECJ 3.122
Dombo Beheer BV v Netherlands (A/274-A) (1994) 18 E.H.R.R. 213, ECHR 4.57, 4.62
Douglas v North Tyneside MBC. *See* R. (on the application of Douglas) v North
  Tyneside MBC
Drake v Chief Adjudication Officer (C–150/85) [1987] Q.B. 166; [1986] 3 W.L.R.
  1005; [1986] 3 All E.R. 65; [1986] E.C.R. 1995; [1986] 3 C.M.L.R. 43; (1987)
  84 L.S.G. 264; (1986) 130 S.J. 923, ECJ (4th Chamber) 3.454, 3.456
Duggan v Chief Adjudication Officer, *The Times*, December 19, 1988, CA (Civ Div) 1.99
Dunbar v Plant [1998] Ch. 412; [1997] 3 W.L.R. 1261; [1997] 4 All E.R. 289; [1998]
  1 F.L.R. 157; [1997] 3 F.C.R. 669; [1998] Fam. Law 139; (1997) 94(36) L.S.G.
  44; (1997) 141 S.J.L.B. 191, CA (Civ Div) 1.14, 1.18
Dyer v Watson; K (A Juvenile) v HM Advocate; sub nom HM Advocate v JK; Procurator
  Fiscal, Linlithgow v Watson; HM Advocate v K (A Juvenile); K v Lord Advocate
  [2002] UKPC D 1; [2004] 1 A.C. 379; [2002] 3 W.L.R. 1488; [2002] 4 All E.R.
  1; 2002 S.C. (P.C.) 89; 2002 S.L.T. 229; 2002 S.C.C.R. 220; [2002] H.R.L.R. 21;
  [2002] U.K.H.R.R. 542; 2002 G.W.D. 5-153, PC (Sc) 4.24, 4.58

Table of Cases

Eagil Trust Co v Pigott-Brown [1985] 3 All E.R. 119, CA (Civ Div) 2.498
Eagle Star Insurance v Department for Social Development, CA (NI) 1.256, 1.278
Elo v Finland (App.30742), ECHR 4.61
Emmott v Minister for Social Welfare (C–208/90); Emmott v Attorney General
  (C–208/90) [1991] E.C.R. I–4269; [1991] 3 C.M.L.R. 894; [1993] I.C.R. 8;
  [1991] I.R.L.R. 387, ECJ 3.13
English v Emery Reimbold & Strick Ltd; DJ&C Withers (Farms) Ltd v Ambic
  Equipment Ltd; Verrechia (t/a Freightmaster Commercials) v Commissioner of
  Police of the Metropolis [2002] EWCA Civ 605; [2002] 1 W.L.R. 2409; [2002] 3
  All E.R. 385; [2002] C.P.L.R. 520; [2003] I.R.L.R. 710; [2002] U.K.H.R.R. 957;
  (2002) 99(22) L.S.G. 34; (2002) 152 N.L.J. 758; (2002) 146 S.J.L.B. 123, CA (Civ
  Div) 2.498
Esfandiari v Secretary of State for Work and Pensions; Latif v Secretary of State for Work
  and Pensions; Nessa (Hawarun) v Secretary of State for Work and Pensions; Nessa
  (Momirun) v Secretary of State for Work and Pensions [2006] EWCA Civ 282;
  [2006] H.R.L.R. 26, CA (Civ Div) 4.16, 4.84
Ettl v Austria (A/117); sub nom Ettl v Austria (9273/81) (1988) 10 E.H.R.R. 255,
  ECHR 4.63
Evans v Secretary of State for Social Security. See R(I)5/94 .... 2.492, 2.498
Fabrizii v Office National des Pensions (C–113/92) ECJ (2nd Chamber) [1993] E.C.R.
  I–6707, ECJ (2nd Chamber) 3.203
Feldbrugge v Netherlands (A/99); sub nom A v Netherlands (8562/79) (1986) 8
  E.H.R.R. 425, ECHR 4.55, 4.56
Fellinger v Bundesanstalt für Arbeit, Nurnberg (C–67/79) [1980] E.C.R. 535; [1981]
  1 C.M.L.R. 471, ECJ (1st Chamber) 3.236
Firma Foto Frost v Hauptzollamt Lübeck-Ost (314/85) [1987] E.C.R. 4199; [1988] 3
  C.M.L.R. 57, ECJ 3.53
Fitzwilliam Executive Search Ltd (t/a Fitzwilliam Technical Services) v Bestuur van het
  Landelijk Instituut Sociale Verzekeringen (C–202/97) [2000] Q.B. 906; [2000] 3
  W.L.R. 1107 (Note); [2000] All E.R. (EC) 144; [2000] E.C.R. I-883; [2000] 1
  C.M.L.R. 708; [2000] C.E.C. 175, ECJ 3.147
Flannery v Halifax Estate Agencies Ltd (t/a Colleys Professional Services) [2000] 1
  W.L.R. 377; [2000] 1 All E.R. 373; [2000] C.P. Rep. 18; [1999] B.L.R. 107; (1999)
  11 Admin. L.R. 465; (1999) 15 Const. L.J. 313; (1999) 96(13) L.S.G. 32; (1999)
  149 N.L.J. 284; [1999] N.P.C. 22, CA (Civ Div) 2.498
Fonds Voor Arbeidsongevallen v Madeleine de Paep (C–196/90) [1991] E.C.R. I–4815,
  AGO 3.142
Foster v British Gas Plc (C–188/89) [1991] 1 Q.B. 405; [1991] 2 W.L.R. 258; [1990]
  3 All E.R. 897; [1990] E.C.R. I-3313; [1990] 2 C.M.L.R. 833; [1991] I.C.R. 84;
  [1990] I.R.L.R. 353, ECJ 3.10
Franklin v Chief Adjudication Officer, *The Times*, December 29, 1995, CA (Civ Div) ... 1.97
Gaumain-Cerri v Kaufmannische Krankenkasse-Pflegekasse (C–502/01) [2004]
  E.C.R. I–6483; [2004] 3 C.M.L.R. 27, ECJ (2nd Chamber) 3.122
Gaygusuz v Austria (17371/90) (1997) 23 E.H.R.R. 364, ECHR 4.78
Ghaidan v Godin-Mendoza; sub nom Mendoza v Ghaidan; Ghaidan v Mendoza;
  Godin-Mendoza v Ghaidan [2004] UKHL 30; [2004] 2 A.C. 557; [2004] 3 W.L.R.
  113; [2004] 3 All E.R. 411; [2004] 2 F.L.R. 600; [2004] 2 F.C.R. 481; [2004]
  H.R.L.R. 31; [2004] U.K.H.R.R. 827; 16 B.H.R.C. 671; [2004] H.L.R. 46; [2005]
  1 P. & C.R. 18; [2005] L. & T.R. 3; [2004] 2 E.G.L.R. 132; [2004] Fam. Law 641;
  [2004] 27 E.G. 128 (C.S.); (2004) 101(27) L.S.G. 30; (2004) 154 N.L.J. 1013;
  (2004) 148 S.J.L.B. 792; [2004] N.P.C. 100; [2004] 2 P. & C.R. DG17, HL 4.11,
                                                                                 4.80, 4.83
Giagounidis v Reutlingen (C–376/89) [1991] E.C.R. I–1069; [1993] 1 C.M.L.R. 537,
  ECJ (6th Chamber) 3.29
Gillies v Secretary of State for Work and Pensions; sub nom Secretary of State for Work
  and Pensions v Gillies [2006] UKHL 2; [2006] 1 W.L.R. 781; [2006] 1 All E.R.
  731; 2006 S.C. (H.L.) 71; 2006 S.L.T. 77; 2006 S.C.L.R. 276; [2006] I.C.R. 267;
  (2006) 9 C.C.L. Rep. 404; (2006) 103(9) L.S.G. 33; (2006) 150 S.J.L.B. 127;
  2006 G.W.D. 3-66, HL 1.346, 2.458, 4.62
Gillow v United Kingdom (A/109); sub nom Gillow v United Kingdom (9063/80)
  (1989) 11 E.H.R.R. 335, ECHR 4.77
Giménez Zaera v Instituto Nacional de la Seguridad Social (C126/86) [1987] E.C.R.
  3697; [1989] 1 C.M.L.R. 827, ECJ (6th Chamber) 3.19

Table of Cases

Golder v United Kingdom (A/18) (1979–80) 1 E.H.R.R. 524, ECHR 4.60
Goodwin v United Kingdom (28957/95) [2002] I.R.L.R. 664; [2002] 2 F.L.R. 487; [2002] 2 F.C.R. 577; (2002) 35 E.H.R.R. 18; 13 B.H.R.C. 120; (2002) 67 B.M.L.R. 199; [2002] Fam. Law 738; (2002) 152 N.L.J. 1171, ECHR 4.68
Graham v Secretary of State for Social Security (C–92/94); Chief Adjudication Officer v Graham; sub nom Secretary of State for Social Security v Graham [1995] All E.R. (E.C.) 736; [1995] E.C.R. I–2521; [1995] 3 C.M.L.R. 169; [1996] I.C.R. 258, ECJ (6th Chamber) 3.464
Gray v Adjudication Officer (C–62/91) [1992] E.C.R. I–2737; [1992] 2 C.M.L.R. 584, ECJ (3rd Chamber) 3.235
— v Barr [1971] 2 Q.B. 554; [1971] 2 W.L.R. 1334; [1971] 2 All E.R. 949; [1971] 2 Lloyd's Rep. 1; (1971) 115 S.J. 364, CA (Civ Div) 1.14
Griffiths v British Coal Corp [2001] EWCA Civ 336; [2001] 1 W.L.R. 1493; [2001] P.I.Q.R. Q11; (2001) 60 B.M.L.R. 188, CA (Civ Div) 1.334
Grzelczyk v Centre Public d'Aide Sociale d'Ottignies Louvain la Neuve (C–184/99) [2003] All E.R. (EC) 385; [2001] E.C.R. I–6193; [2002] 1 C.M.L.R. 19; [2002] I.C.R. 566, ECJ 3.31
Gül v Regierungsprasident Dusseldorf (131/85) [1986] E.C.R. 1573; [1987] 1 C.M.L.R. 501, ECJ (4th Chamber) 3.37
HP Bulmer Ltd v J Bollinger SA (No.2) [1974] Ch. 401; [1974] 3 W.L.R. 202; [1974] 2 All E.R. 1226; [1974] 2 C.M.L.R. 91; [1974] F.S.R. 334; [1975] R.P.C. 321; (1974) 118 S.J. 404, CA (Civ Div) 3.52
Haackert v Pensionsversicherungsanstalt der Angestellten (C–303/02) [2004] E.C.R. I–2195, ECJ 3.464
Hampshire CC v Beer t/a Hammer Trout Farm. *See* R. (on the application of Beer (t/a Hammer Trout Farm)) v Hampshire Farmers Markets Ltd
Harris v Secretary of State for Social Security, SSTRF 96/0469/B, CA (Civ Div) 3.134
Harrison's Settlement; Ropner v Ropner; Re Ropner's Settlement; Re Williams Will Trust; sub nom Harrison v Harrison [1955] Ch. 260; [1955] 2 W.L.R. 256; [1955] 1 All E.R. 185; (1955) 99 S.J. 74, CA 2.506
Hassall v Secretary of State for Social Security [1995] 1 W.L.R. 812; [1995] 3 All E.R. 909; [1995] R.T.R. 316; [1995] P.I.Q.R. P292; (1995) 92(8) L.S.G. 41; (1995) 139 S.J.L.B. 57, CA (Civ Div) 1.256
Hatungimana v Secretary of State for the Home Department [2006] EWCA Civ 231, CA (Civ Div) 2.498
Hepple v Adjudication Officer (C–196/98) [2000] All E.R. (EC) 513; [2000] E.C.R. I–3701; [2000] 3 C.M.L.R. 271; [2000] C.E.C. 351, ECJ 3.464
Heylens. *See* Union Nationale des Entraineurs et Cadres Techniques Professionnels du Football (UNECTEF) v Heylens
Hinchy v Secretary of State for Work and Pensions [2005] UKHL 16; [2005] 1 W.L.R. 967; [2005] 2 All E.R. 129; (2005) 102(17) L.S.G. 32; (2005) 149 S.J.L.B. 299, HL 1.92, 1.93, 1.94
Hirvisari v Finland, unreported, 2001, ECHR 2.498
Hobbs v United Kingdom (63684/00); Richard v United Kingdom (63475/00); Walsh v United Kingdom (63484/00); Green v United Kingdom (63468/00) [2006] S.T.I. 2506, ECHR 4.13
Hockenjos v Secretary of State for Social Security [2001] EWCA Civ 624; [2001] 2 C.M.L.R. 51; [2001] I.C.R. 966, CA (Civ Div) 3.456, 3.458
Hodgson v Armstrong [1967] 2 Q.B. 299; [1967] 2 W.L.R. 311; [1967] 1 All E.R. 307; (1966) 110 S.J. 907, CA 2.66
Hoeckx v Openbaar Centrum voor Maatschappelijik Welzijn (249/83); sub nom: Hoeckx v Centre Public d'Aide Sociale de Kalmthout (249/83) [1985] E.C.R. 973; [1987] 3 C.M.L.R. 638, ECJ (2nd Chamber) 3.136
Höfner v Macrotron GmbH (C–41/90) [1991] E.C.R. I–1979; [1993] 4 C.M.L.R. 306; (1991) 135 S.J.L.B. 54, ECJ (6th Chamber) 3.37
Homan v A1 Bacon Co Ltd [1996] I.C.R. 721, EAT 2.746
Hoppe v Germany (28422/95) [2003] 1 F.L.R. 384; [2003] 1 F.C.R. 176; (2004) 38 E.H.R.R. 15; [2003] Fam. Law 159, ECHR 2.321
Hosse v Land Salzburg (C–286/03) [2006] All E.R. (EC) 640; [2006] E.C.R. I–1771; [2006] 2 C.M.L.R. 52; [2006] C.E.C. 553, ECJ 3.136
Houghton (Intestacy), Re; sub nom Houghton v Houghton [1915] 2 Ch. 173, Ch D 1.14
Howker v Secretary of State for Work and Pensions [2002] EWCA Civ 1623; [2003] I.C.R. 405; (2003) 100(2) L.S.G. 32, CA (Civ Div) 1.206

Table of Cases

Hughes v Chief Adjudication Officer (C–78/91) [1992] E.C.R. I–4839; [1992] 3 C.M.L.R. 490; [1993] 1 F.L.R. 791; [1993] Fam. Law 477, ECJ (5th Chamber) 3.136, 3.456
Hulley v Thompson [1981] 1 W.L.R. 159; [1981] 1 All E.R. 1128; (1981) 125 S.J. 47, DC 1.141
Institut National d'Assurances Sociales pour Travailleurs Independants (INASTI) v Hervein (C–393/99); Institut National d'Assurances Sociales pour Travailleurs Independants (INASTI) v Lorthiois (C–394/99) [2002] E.C.R. I–2829; [2002] 2 C.M.L.R. 16, ECJ 3.111
Insurance Officer v McCaffrey [1984] 1 W.L.R. 1353; [1985] 1 All E.R. 5; (1985) 82 L.S.G. 203; (1984) 128 S.J. 836, HL 1.26, 1.33, 2.39
Ioannidis. *See* Office National de l'Emploi v Ioannidis
Ireland v United Kingdom (A/25) (1979–80) 2 E.H.R.R. 25, ECHR 4.48
Irish Creamery Milk Suppliers Association v Ireland (36/80) [1981] E.C.R. 735; [1981] 2 C.M.L.R. 455, ECJ 3.52
JS (A Minor) (Declaration of Paternity), Re [1981] Fam. 22; [1980] 3 W.L.R. 984; [1980] 1 All E.R. 1061; (1980) 10 Fam. Law 121; (1980) 124 S.J. 881, CA (Civ Div) 2.102
Jackson v Chief Adjudication Officer (C–63/91); Cresswell v Chief Adjudication Officer (C–64/91) [1993] Q.B. 367; [1993] 2 W.L.R. 658; [1993] 3 All E.R. 265; [1992] E.C.R. I–4737; [1992] 3 C.M.L.R. 389; [1993] Fam. Law 477, ECJ 3.456
Jacobs v Norsalta [1977] I.C.R. 189; (1976) 11 I.T.R. 206, EAT 2.492
Jasim v Secretary of State for the Home Department [2006] EWCA Civ 342, CA (Civ Div) 2.498
Jauch v Pensionsversicherungsanstalt der Arbeiter (C–215/99) [2001] E.C.R. I–1901, ECJ 3.136
Johnson v Chief Adjudication Officer (No.1) (C–31/90) [1993] Q.B. 252; [1991] E.C.R. I-3723; [1991] 3 C.M.L.R. 917; [1993] I.C.R. 204, ECJ (5th Chamber) ... 3.454
— v — (No.2) (C410/92) [1995] All E.R. (E.C.) 258; [1994] E.C.R. I–5483; [1995] 1 C.M.L.R. 725; [1995] I.C.R. 375; [1995] I.R.L.R. 157, ECJ 3.13
Jones v Chief Adjudication Officer; Sharples v Chief Adjudication Officer [1994] 1 W.L.R. 62; [1994] 1 All E.R. 225; (1993) 137 S.J.L.B. 188, CA (Civ Div) 1.97
Julius v Lord Bishop of Oxford; sub nom R. v Bishop of Oxford; Julius v Bishop of Oxford (1879–80) L.R. 5 App. Cas. 214, HL 2.373
K (A Child) (Secure Accommodation Order: Right to Liberty), Re; sub nom W BC v DK; W BC v AK [2001] Fam. 377; [2001] 2 W.L.R. 1141; [2001] 2 All E.R. 719; (2001) 165 J.P. 241; [2001] 1 F.L.R. 526; [2001] 1 F.C.R. 249; [2001] H.R.L.R. 13; (2001) 3 L.G.L.R. 39; [2001] A.C.D. 41; [2001] Fam. Law 99; (2001) 165 J.P.N. 585; (2000) 97(48) L.S.G. 36; (2000) 144 S.J.L.B. 291, CA (Civ Div) 4.13
Kamasinski v Austria (A/168); sub nom Kamasinski v Austria (9783/82) (1991) 13 E.H.R.R. 36, ECHR 2.483
Kaske v Landesgeschaftsstelle des Arbeitsmarktservice Wien (C–277/99) [2002] E.C.R. I–1261, ECJ 3.126
Kay v Lambeth LBC; Gorman v Lambeth LBC; Constantine v Lambeth LBC; Barnett v Lambeth LBC; Cole v Lambeth LBC; Dymny v Lambeth LBC; Price v Leeds City Council; sub nom Leeds City Council v Price; Lambeth LBC v Kay [2006] UKHL 10; [2006] 2 A.C. 465; [2006] 2 W.L.R. 570; [2006] 4 All E.R. 128; [2006] 2 F.C.R. 20; [2006] H.R.L.R. 17; [2006] U.K.H.R.R. 640; 20 B.H.R.C. 33; [2006] H.L.R. 22; [2006] B.L.G.R. 323; [2006] 2 P. & C.R. 25; [2006] L. & T.R. 8; [2006] 11 E.G. 194 (C.S.); (2006) 150 S.J.L.B. 365; [2006] N.P.C. 29, HL 4.09
Kerr v Department for Social Development [2004] UKHL 23; [2004] 1 W.L.R. 1372; [2004] 4 All E.R. 385; [2004] N.I. 397, HL (NI) 1.379, 1.380, 2.82, 2.380, 2.705
Kersbergen-Lap v Raad van Bestuur van het Uitvoeringsinstituut Werknemersverzekeringen (C–154/05) [2006] E.C.R. I–6249; [2006] All E.R. (EC) 973, ECJ 3.136
Khalil v Bundesanstalt für Arbeit (C–95/99); Chaaban v Bundesanstalt fur Arbeit (C–96/99); Osseili v Bundesanstalt für Arbeit (C–97/99); Nasser v Landeshauptstadt Stuttgart (C–98/99); Addou v Land Nordrhein Westfalen (C–180/99) [2001] E.C.R. I–7413; [2001] 3 C.M.L.R. 50, ECJ 3.120
Klass v Germany (A/28) (1979–80) 2 E.H.R.R. 214, ECHR 4.19
Knoch v Bundesanstalt für Arbeit (C–102/91) [1992] E.C.R. I–4341, ECJ (4th Chamber) 3.241
Kraska v Switzerland (A/254-B) (1994) 18 E.H.R.R. 188, ECHR 4.57
Krasniqi v Chief Adjudication Officer [1999] C.O.D. 154, CA (Civ Div) 3.120

Table of Cases

Kuusijärvi v Riksforsakringsverket (C–275/96) [1998] E.C.R. I–3419, ECJ ....:.. 3.143
Land, dec, Re [2006] EWHC 2069 (Ch); [2007] 1 W.L.R. 1009 .... 1.14
Lang v Devon General [1987] I.C.R. 4; (1986) 83 L.S.G. 2653; (1986) 136 N.L.J. 893, EAT 2.66
Larusai v Secretary of State for Work and Pensions [2003] EWHC 371, QBD (Admin) 1.100, 2.704
Lawal v Northern Spirit Ltd [2003] UKHL 35; [2004] 1 All E.R. 187; [2003] I.C.R. 856; [2003] I.R.L.R. 538; [2003] H.R.L.R. 29; [2003] U.K.H.R.R. 1024; (2003) 100(28) L.S.G. 30; (2003) 153 N.L.J. 1005; (2003) 147 S.J.L.B. 783, HL .. 1.346, 4.62
Lawrie-Blum v Land Baden-Wurttemberg (C–66/85) [1986] E.C.R. 2121; [1987] 3 C.M.L.R. 389; [1987] I.C.R. 483, ECJ 3.37
Lebon. *See* Centre Public d'Aide Sociale, Courcelles v Lebon
Leclère v Caisse Nationale des Prestations Familiales (C–43/99) [2001] E.C.R. I–4265; [2001] 2 C.M.L.R. 49, ECJ 3.136
Leeds City Council v Price; sub nom Price v Leeds City Council [2005] EWCA Civ 289; [2005] 1 W.L.R. 1825; [2005] 3 All E.R. 573; [2005] U.K.H.R.R. 413; [2005] H.L.R. 31; [2005] B.L.G.R. 782; [2005] 2 P. & C.R. 26; [2005] J.P.L. 1241; [2005] 12 E.G. 218 (C.S.); (2005) 102(19) L.S.G. 33; (2005) 149 S.J.L.B. 359; [2005] N.P.C. 41, CA (Civ Div) 4.16
Lenoir v Caisse d'Allocations Familiales des Alpes-Maritimes (C–313/86) [1988] E.C.R. 5391; [1990] 1 C.M.L.R. 543, ECJ 3.136
Levin v Staatssecretaris van Justitie (53/81); sub nom Levin v Secretary of State for Justice (53/81) [1982] E.C.R. 1035; [1982] 2 C.M.L.R. 454, ECJ 3.19, 3.37
Levy v Secretary of State for Work and Pensions [2006] EWCA Civ 890, CA (Civ Div) 2.66, 2.347, 2.508
Lloyd v McMahon [1987] A.C. 625; [1987] 2 W.L.R. 821; [1987] 1 All E.R. 1118; 85 L.G.R. 545; [1987] R.V.R. 58; (1987) 84 L.S.G. 1240; (1987) 137 N.L.J. 265; (1987) 131 S.J. 409, HL 2.508
Lloyds Bank Plc v Waterhouse [1993] 2 F.L.R. 97; (1991) 10 Tr. L.R. 161; [1991] Fam. Law 23, CA (Civ Div) 1.99
Locabail (UK) Ltd v Bayfield Properties Ltd (Leave to Appeal); Locabail (UK) Ltd v Waldorf Investment Corp (Leave to Appeal); Timmins v Gormley; Williams v Inspector of Taxes; R. v Bristol Betting and Gaming Licensing Committee Ex p. O'Callaghan [1999] EWCA Civ 3004; [2000] Q.B. 451; [2000] 2 W.L.R. 870; [2000] 1 All E.R. 65; [2000] I.R.L.R. 96; [2000] H.R.L.R. 290; [2000] U.K.H.R.R. 300; 7 B.H.R.C. 583; (1999) 149 N.L.J. 1793; [1999] N.P.C. 143, CA (Civ Div) 1.346
Lombardo v Italy (A/249-B) (1996) 21 E.H.R.R. 188, ECHR 4.56
Lowther v Chatwin; sub nom Chatwin v Lowther [2003] EWCA Civ 729; [2003] P.I.Q.R. Q5, CA (Civ Div) 1.334
M v Secretary of State for Work and Pensions; Langley v Bradford MDC; sub nom Secretary of State for Work and Pensions v M [2006] UKHL 11; [2006] 2 A.C. 91; [2006] 2 W.L.R. 637; [2006] 4 All E.R. 929; [2006] 2 F.L.R. 56; [2006] 1 F.C.R. 497; [2006] H.R.L.R. 19; [2006] U.K.H.R.R. 799; 21 B.H.R.C. 254; [2006] Fam. Law 524; (2006) 150 S.J.L.B. 363, HL 4.83
— v United Kingdom. *See* PM v United Kingdom
McDermott v Minister for Social Welfare (286/85) [1987] E.C.R. 1453; [1987] 2 C.M.L.R. 607, ECJ 3.13
McMenamin v Adjudication Officer (C–119/91) [1992] E.C.R. I–6393; [1993] 1 C.M.L.R. 509, ECJ (5th Chamber) 3.243
Magill v Weeks. *See* Porter v Magill
Manning v Revenue and Customs Commissioners [2006] S.T.C. (S.C.D.) 588; [2006] S.T.I. 1920, Sp Comm 4.84
Marleasing SA v La Comercial Internacional de Alimentacion SA (C–106/89) [1990] E.C.R. I–4135; [1993] B.C.C. 421; [1992] 1 C.M.L.R. 305, ECJ (6th Chamber) ... 3.23
Martinez Sala v Freistaat Bayern (C–85/96) [1998] E.C.R. I–2691, ECJ 3.25, 3.31
Meyers v Chief Adjudication Officer (C–116/94) [1995] E.C.R. I–2131 .... 3.456
Micheletti v Delegacion del Gobierno en Cantabria (C–369/90) [1992] E.C.R. I–4239, ECJ 3.29
Millar (David Cameron) v Dickson; Stewart v Heywood; Payne v Heywood; Tracey v Heywood; Marshall v Ritchie [2001] UKPC D 4; [2002] 1 W.L.R. 1615; [2002] 3 All E.R. 1041; 2002 S.C. (P.C.) 30; 2001 S.L.T. 988; 2001 S.C.C.R. 741; [2001] H.R.L.R. 59; [2001] U.K.H.R.R. 999; 2001 G.W.D. 26-1015, PC (Sc) 2.458

xxvii

Table of Cases

Miller v Secretary of State for Work and Pensions, 2002 G.W.D. 25-861, IH (Ex Div) ... 2.321
Mitchell v Laing, 1998 S.C. 342; 1998 S.L.T. 203; 1998 S.C.L.R. 266; 1997 G.W.D. 40-2035, IH (1 Div) 1.294, 1.334
Molenaar v Allgemeine Ortskrankenkasse Baden-Württemberg (C–160/96) [1998] E.C.R. I–843, ECJ 3.122, 3.136
Molenbroek v Bestuur van de Sociale Verzekeringsbank (C–226/91) [1992] E.C.R. I–5943, ECJ (2nd Chamber) 3.458
Morina v Secretary of State for Work and Pensions [2007] EWCA Civ 749 ...... 1.399, ... 1.412, 2.344, 2.446, 2.478
Morrell v Secretary of State for Work and Pensions [2003] EWCA Civ 526, CA (Civ Div) 1.92
Mulvey v Secretary of State for Social Security, 1997 S.C. (H.L.) 105; 1997 S.L.T. 753; 1997 S.C.L.R. 348; [1997] B.P.I.R. 696; 1997 G.W.D. 11-488, HL 1.125, 1.224
Murru v Caisse Regionale d'Assurance Maladie de Paris (2/72) [1972] E.C.R. 333; [1972] C.M.L.R. 888, ECJ 3.203
National Assistance Board v Parkes; sub nom Stopher v National Assistance Board [1955] 2 Q.B. 506; [1955] 3 W.L.R. 347; [1955] 3 All E.R. 1; (1955) 99 S.J. 540, CA 1.141
Neal v Bingle [1998] Q.B. 466; [1998] 2 W.L.R. 57; [1998] 2 All E.R. 58; [1998] P.I.Q.R. Q1; (1998) 40 B.M.L.R. 52; (1997) 94(34) L.S.G. 29; (1997) 141 S.J.L.B. 190, CA (Civ Div) 1.257, 2.749
Nemec v Caisse Regionale d'Assurance Maladie du Nord-Est (C–205/05) [2007] 1 C.M.L.R. 29, ECJ (2nd Chamber) 3.222
Nielsen v Denmark (A/144); sub nom Nielsen v Denmark (10929/84) (1989) 11 E.H.R.R. 175, ECHR 4.19
Nikula, Re (C–50/05) [2006] E.C.R. I–7029, ECJ 3.184
Nimmo v Alexander Cowan & Sons Ltd [1968] A.C. 107; [1967] 3 W.L.R. 1169; [1967] 3 All E.R. 187; 1967 S.C. (H.L.) 79; 1967 S.L.T. 277; 3 K.I.R. 277; (1967) 111 S.J. 668, HL 1.379
Ninni-Orasche v Bundesminister für Wissenschaft, Verkehr und Kunst (C–413/01) [2004] All E.R. (EC) 765; [2003] E.C.R. I-13187; [2004] 1 C.M.L.R. 19, ECJ (6th Chamber) 3.57
Noij v Staatssecretaris van Financien (C–140/88) [1991] E.C.R. I–387; [1992] 3 C.M.L.R. 737, ECJ 3.143
Norris v Ireland (A/142); sub nom Norris v Ireland (10581/83) (1991) 13 E.H.R.R. 186, ECHR 4.19
Office National de l'Emploi v Ioannidis (C–258/04) [2006] All E.R. (EC) 926; [2005] E.C.R. I–8275; [2005] 3 C.M.L.R. 47; [2006] C.E.C. 960, ECJ (1st Chamber) 3.37
Ophelia, The [1916] 2 A.C. 206, PC (UK) 1.98
PM v United Kingdom (6638/03); sub nom M v United Kingdom (6638/03) [2005] S.T.C. 1566; [2005] 3 F.C.R. 101; (2006) 42 E.H.R.R. 45; 18 B.H.R.C. 668; 7 I.T.L. Rep. 970, ECHR 4.46
Page and Davis v Chief Adjudication Officer, *The Times*, July 4, 1991, CA (Civ Div) 1.91
Paletta v Brennet AG (C–45/90) [1992] E.C.R. I–3423; [1995] 2 C.M.L.R. 163, ECJ 3.195
Partridge v Adjudication Officer (C–297/96) [1998] E.C.R. I–3467; [1998] 3 C.M.L.R. 941, ECJ (3rd Chamber) 3.136
Pearson v United Kingdom, unreported, August 2006, ECHR 4.66, 4.78
Perez Naranjo v Caisse Regionale d'Assurance Maladie (CRAM) Nord Picardie (C–265/05), ECJ 3.136
Perry v Chief Adjudication Officer [1999] 2 C.M.L.R. 439, CA (Civ Div) 3.122, 3.136
Peterbroeck Van Campenhout & Cie SCS v Belgium (C–312/93) [1996] All E.R. (E.C.) 242; [1995] E.C.R. I–4599; [1996] 1 C.M.L.R. 793, ECJ 3.13
Petroni v Office National des Pensions pour Travailleurs Salaries (ONPTS) (24/75) [1975] E.C.R. 1149, ECJ 3.42
Pinna v Caisse d'Allocations Familiales de la Savoie (41/84) [1986] E.C.R. 1; [1988] 1 C.M.L.R. 350, ECJ 3.42
Piscitello v Instituto Nazionale della Previdenza Sociale (139/82) [1983] E.C.R. 1427; [1984] 1 C.M.L.R. 108, ECJ (3rd Chamber) 3.134
Plewa v Chief Adjudication Officer [1995] 1 A.C. 249; [1994] 3 W.L.R. 317; [1994] 3 All E.R. 323; (1994) 91(30) L.S.G. 32; (1994) 138 S.J.L.B. 152, HL 1.83
Poirrez v France (40892/98) (2005) 40 E.H.R.R. 2, ECHR 4.78
Poplar Housing & Regeneration Community Association Ltd v Donoghue; sub nom Donoghue v Poplar Housing & Regeneration Community Association Ltd; Poplar

Table of Cases

Housing & Regeneration Community Association Ltd v Donaghue [2001] EWCA Civ 595; [2002] Q.B. 48; [2001] 3 W.L.R. 183; [2001] 4 All E.R. 604; [2001] 2 F.L.R. 284; [2001] 3 F.C.R. 74; [2001] U.K.H.R.R. 693; (2001) 33 H.L.R. 73; (2001) 3 L.G.L.R. 41; [2001] B.L.G.R. 489; [2001] A.C.D. 76; [2001] Fam. Law 588; [2001] 19 E.G. 141 (C.S.); (2001) 98(19) L.S.G. 38; (2001) 98(23) L.S.G. 38; (2001) 145 S.J.L.B. 122; [2001] N.P.C. 84, CA (Civ Div) 4.11, 4.16

Porter v Magill; Weeks v Magill; Hartley v Magill; England v Magill; Phillips v Magill; sub nom Magill v Weeks; Magill v Porter [2001] UKHL 67; [2002] 2 A.C. 357; [2002] 2 W.L.R. 37; [2002] 1 All E.R. 465; [2002] H.R.L.R. 16; [2002] H.L.R. 16; [2002] B.L.G.R. 51; (2001) 151 N.L.J. 1886; [2001] N.P.C. 184, HL 4.62

Post Office Counters Ltd v Mahida [2003] EWCA Civ 1583, CA (Civ Div) 1.98, 1.380

Posthuma van Damme v Bestuur van de Bedrijfsvereniging voor Detailhandel, Ambachten en Huisvrouwen (C–280/94) [1996] E.C.R. I–179, ECJ (6th Chamber) 3.454

Poyser and Mills' Arbitration, Re; sub nom Poyser v Mills [1964] 2 Q.B. 467; [1963] 2 W.L.R. 1309; [1963] 1 All E.R. 612; (1963) 107 S.J. 115, QBD 2.498

Pretore di Salo v Persons Unknown (C–14/86); sub nom Criminal Proceedings against a Person or Persons Unknown (C–14/86) [1987] E.C.R. 2545; [1989] 1 C.M.L.R. 71, ECJ (5th Chamber) 3.52

Pretto v Italy (A/71) (1984) 6 E.H.R.R. 182, ECHR 4.58

Quinn v Department for Social Development [2004] N.I.C.A. 22 .... 2.498

— v A (Complainant's Sexual History); sub nom — v A (No.2); — v Y (Sexual Offence: Complainant's Sexual History) [2001] UKHL 25; [2002] 1 A.C. 45; [2001] 2 W.L.R. 1546; [2001] 3 All E.R. 1; [2001] 2 Cr. App. R. 21; (2001) 165 J.P. 609; [2001] H.R.L.R. 48; [2001] U.K.H.R.R. 825; 11 B.H.R.C. 225; [2001] Crim. L.R. 908; (2001) 165 J.P.N. 750, HL 4.11

— v Adjudication Officer Ex p. Golding; sub nom R. v Secretary of State for Social Security Ex p. Golding [1996] N.P.C. 107, CA (Civ Div) 2.236

— v Bouchereau (Pierre Roger) (30/77) [1978] Q.B. 732; [1978] 2 W.L.R. 251; [1981] 2 All E.R. 924; [1977] E.C.R. 1999; [1978] E.C.R. 1999; (1978) 66 Cr. App. R. 202; [1977] 2 C.M.L.R. 800; (1978) 122 S.J. 79, ECJ 3.37

— v Chief National Insurance Commissioner Ex p. Connor [1981] Q.B. 758; [1981] 2 W.L.R. 412; [1981] 1 All E.R. 769; [1980] Crim. L.R. 579; (1980) 124 S.J. 478, QBD 1.14

— v Deputy Industrial Injuries Commissioner Ex p. Moore [1965] 1 Q.B. 456; [1965] 2 W.L.R. 89; [1965] 1 All E.R. 81; (1964) 108 S.J. 1030, CA 1.379

— v Higher Education Funding Council Ex p. Institute of Dental Surgery [1994] 1 W.L.R. 242; [1994] 1 All E.R. 651; [1994] C.O.D. 147, DC 2.498

— v International Stock Exchange of the United Kingdom and the Republic of Ireland Ltd Ex p. Else (1982) Ltd; — v International Stock Exchange of the United Kingdom and the Republic of Ireland Ltd Ex p. Thomas [1993] Q.B. 534; [1993] 2 W.L.R. 70; [1993] 1 All E.R. 420; [1993] B.C.C. 11; [1993] B.C.L.C. 834; [1993] 2 C.M.L.R. 677; (1994) 6 Admin. L.R. 67; [1993] C.O.D. 236, CA (Civ Div) 3.52

— v Lambert (Steven); R. v Ali (Mudassir Mohammed); R. v Jordan (Shirley) [2001] UKHL 37; [2002] 2 A.C. 545; [2001] 3 W.L.R. 206; [2001] 3 All E.R. 577; [2002] 1 All E.R. 2; [2001] 2 Cr. App. R. 28; [2001] H.R.L.R. 55; [2001] U.K.H.R.R. 1074; [2001] Crim. L.R. 806; (2001) 98(33) L.S.G. 29; (2001) 145 S.J.L.B. 174, HL 4.11, 4.44

— v Medical Appeal Tribunal (Midland Region) Ex p. Carrarini [1966] 1 W.L.R. 883; (1966) 110 S.J. 509, DC 2.492

— v Medical Appeal Tribunal (North Midland Region) Ex p. Hubble [1959] 2 Q.B. 408; [1959] 3 W.L.R. 456; [1959] 3 All E.R. 40; (1959) 103 S.J. 562, CA 1.379

— v Richards (Michael); sub nom Department for Work and Pensions v Richards [2005] EWCA Crim 491; [2005] 2 Cr. App. R. (S.) 97; [2005] Crim. L.R. 582; (2005) 149 S.J.L.B. 357, CA (Crim Div) 2.704

— v Saunders (Vera Ann) (C–175/78) [1980] Q.B. 72; [1979] 3 W.L.R. 359; [1979] 2 All E.R. 267; [1979] E.C.R. 1129; [1979] 2 C.M.L.R. 216; (1979) 123 S.J. 674, ECJ 3.37

— v Secretary of State for Health Ex p. Richardson (C–137/94) [1995] All E.R. (E.C.) 865; [1995] E.C.R. I–3407; [1995] 3 C.M.L.R. 376; [1996] I.C.R. 471, ECJ (6th Chamber) 3.456, 3.464

— v Secretary of State for Social Security Ex p. Cullen; R. v Secretary of State for Social Security Ex p. Nelson [1997] C.O.D. 405, CA (Civ Div) 2.85, 2.176

xxix

Table of Cases

— v — Ex p. Equal Opportunities Commission (C–9/91) [1992] 3 All E.R. 577; [1992] E.C.R. I–4297; [1992] 3 C.M.L.R. 233; [1992] I.C.R. 782; [1992] I.R.L.R. 376, ECJ 3.464
— v — Ex p. Grant, High Court, July 31, 1997 .... 2.687
— v — Ex p. Moore; R. v Secretary of State for Social Security Ex p. Rouse, CA (Civ Div) 2.541
— v — Ex p. Sarwar; R. v Secretary of State for Social Security Ex p. Getachew; R. v Secretary of State for Social Security Ex p. Urbanek [1997] 3 C.M.L.R. 648, CA (Civ Div) 2.687
— v — Ex p. Smithson (Florence Rose) (C–243/90) [1992] E.C.R. I–467; [1992] 1 C.M.L.R. 1061, ECJ (6th Chamber) 3.456
— v — Ex p. Sutton (C–66/95) [1997] All E.R. (EC) 497; [1997] E.C.R. I–2163; [1997] 2 C.M.L.R. 382; [1997] C.E.C. 1110; [1997] I.C.R. 961; [1997] I.R.L.R. 524, ECJ 3.461
— v — Ex p. Taylor; R. v Secretary of State for Social Security Ex p. Chapman [1997] B.P.I.R. 505; [1996] C.O.D. 332, QBD 1.125
— v — (C–382/98) [2000] All E.R. (EC) 80; [1999] E.C.R. I–8955; [2000] 1 C.M.L.R. 873; [2000] C.E.C. 3; [2000] I.C.R. 843, ECJ (6th Chamber) 3.456, 3.464
— v Secretary of State for Social Services Ex p. Britnell; sub nom Britnell v Secretary of State for Social Services [1991] 1 W.L.R. 198; [1991] 2 All E.R. 726; (1991) 135 S.J. 412, HL 1.100
— v — Ex p. Child Poverty Action Group [1990] 2 Q.B. 540; [1989] 3 W.L.R. 1116; [1989] 1 All E.R. 1047; (1989) 86(41) L.S.G. 41; (1989) 133 S.J. 1373, CA (Civ Div) 2.81
— v Secretary of State for the Home Department [2002] E.C.R. I–7091 .... 3.37
— v — Ex p. Mehta; sub nom Mehta v Secretary of State for the Home Department [1975] 1 W.L.R. 1087; [1975] 2 All E.R. 1084; (1975) 119 S.J. 475, CA (Civ Div) 2.514
— v — Ex p. Saleem; sub nom R. v Immigration Appeal Tribunal Ex p. Saleem; Saleem v Secretary of State for the Home Department [2001] 1 W.L.R. 443; [2000] 4 All E.R. 814; [2000] Imm. A.R. 529; [2000] I.N.L.R. 413, CA (Civ Div) 2.347
— v Secretary of State for Transport Ex p. Factortame Ltd (C–221/89) [1992] Q.B. 680; [1992] 3 W.L.R. 288; [1991] 3 All E.R. 769; [1991] 2 Lloyd's Rep. 648; [1991] E.C.R. I-3905; [1991] 3 C.M.L.R. 589; (1991) 141 N.L.J. 1107, ECJ 3.9
— v — (No.2) [1991] 1 A.C. 603; [1990] 3 W.L.R. 818; [1991] 1 All E.R. 70; [1991] 1 Lloyd's Rep. 10; [1990] 3 C.M.L.R. 375; (1991) 3 Admin. L.R. 333; (1990) 140 N.L.J. 1457; (1990) 134 S.J. 1189, HL 2.687
— v — (No.5) ..... [2000] 1 A.C. 524; [1999] 3 W.L.R. 1062; [1999] 4 All E.R. 906; [1999] 3 C.M.L.R. 597; [2000] Eu. L.R. 40; (1999) 96(43) L.S.G. 32; [1999] N.P.C. 126, HL 3.12
— v Social Security Commissioner Ex p. Snares [1997] C.O.D. 403, QBD 2.687, 3.14
— v — Ex p. Bibi, unreported, May 23, 2000 .... 2.492
— v West London Supplementary Benefits Appeal Tribunal Ex p. Clarke [1975] 1 W.L.R. 1396; [1975] 3 All E.R. 513; (1975) 119 S.J. 743, DC 1.136
— v Wicks (Peter Edward) [1998] A.C. 92; [1997] 2 W.L.R. 876; [1997] 2 All E.R. 801; (1997) 161 J.P. 433; (1997) 9 Admin. L.R. 349; [1997] 2 P.L.R. 97; [1997] J.P.L. 1049; (1997) 161 J.P.N. 628; (1997) 94(35) L.S.G. 34; (1997) 147 N.L.J. 883; (1997) 141 S.J.L.B. 127; [1997] N.P.C. 85, HL 1.85
— (on the application of Alconbury Developments Ltd) v Secretary of State for the Environment, Transport and the Regions. *See* R. (on the application of Holding & Barnes Plc) v Secretary of State for the Environment, Transport and the Regions
— (on the application of Anderson) v Secretary of State for the Home Department; sub nom — v Secretary of State for the Home Department Ex p. Anderson; — v Secretary of State for the Home Department Ex p. Taylor; R. (on the application of Taylor) v Secretary of State for the Home Department [2002] UKHL 46; [2003] 1 A.C. 837; [2002] 3 W.L.R. 1800; [2002] 4 All E.R. 1089; [2003] 1 Cr. App. R. 32; [2003] H.R.L.R. 7; [2003] U.K.H.R.R. 112; 13 B.H.R.C. 450; (2003) 100(3) L.S.G. 31; (2002) 146 S.J.L.B. 272, HL 4.11
— (on the application of Asha Foundation) v Millennium Commission [2003] EWCA Civ 88; [2003] A.C.D. 50; (2003) 100(11) L.S.G. 31, CA (Civ Div) 2.498
— (on the application of Balding) v Secretary of State for Work and Pensions [2007] EWHC 759 (Admin), DC 1.83

Table of Cases

— (on the application of Beer (t/a Hammer Trout Farm)) v Hampshire Farmers Markets Ltd; sub nom Hampshire CC v Beer (t/a Hammer Trout Farm) [2003] EWCA Civ 1056; [2004] 1 W.L.R. 233; [2004] U.K.H.R.R. 727; [2003] 31 E.G. 67 (C.S.); (2003) 100(36) L.S.G. 40; (2003) 147 S.J.L.B. 1085; [2003] N.P.C. 93, CA (Civ Div) 4.16
— (on the application of Bidar) v Ealing LBC (C–209/03) [2005] Q.B. 812; [2005] 2 W.L.R. 1078; [2005] All E.R. (EC) 687; [2005] E.C.R. I-2119; [2005] 2 C.M.L.R. 3; [2005] C.E.C. 607; [2005] E.L.R. 404, ECJ 3.31
— (on the application of Carson) v Secretary of State for Work and Pensions; R. (on the application of Reynolds) v Secretary of State for Work and Pensions; sub nom Carson v Secretary of State for Work and Pensions [2005] UKHL 37; [2006] 1 A.C. 173; [2005] 2 W.L.R. 1369; [2005] 4 All E.R. 545; [2005] H.R.L.R. 23; [2005] U.K.H.R.R. 1185; 18 B.H.R.C. 677, HL 4.82, 4.84
— (on the application of Douglas) v North Tyneside MBC; sub nom Douglas v North Tyneside MBC [2003] EWCA Civ 1847; [2004] 1 W.L.R. 2363; [2004] 1 All E.R. 709; [2004] H.R.L.R. 14; [2004] U.K.H.R.R. 425; [2004] E.L.R. 117; [2004] A.C.D. 25; (2004) 154 N.L.J. 56; (2004) 148 S.J.L.B. 58, CA (Civ Div) 4.88
— (on the application of H) v Secretary of State for Work and Pensions; R. (on the application of D) v Secretary of State for Work and Pensions [2004] EWHC 1097; [2004] 3 C.M.L.R. 11, QBD (Admin) 3.38
— (on the application of Holding & Barnes Plc) v Secretary of State for the Environment, Transport and the Regions; R. (on the application of Premier Leisure UK Ltd) v Secretary of State for the Environment, Transport and the Regions; R. (on the application of Alconbury Developments Ltd) v Secretary of State for the Environment, Transport and the Regions; Secretary of State for the Environment, Transport and the Regions v Legal & General Assurance Society Ltd; sub nom — v Secretary of State for the Environment, Transport and the Regions Ex p. Holdings & Barnes Plc [2001] UKHL 23; [2003] 2 A.C. 295; [2001] 2 W.L.R. 1389; [2001] 2 All E.R. 929; [2002] Env. L.R. 12; [2001] H.R.L.R. 45; [2001] U.K.H.R.R. 728; (2001) 3 L.G.L.R. 38; (2001) 82 P. & C.R. 40; [2001] 2 P.L.R. 76; [2001] J.P.L. 920; [2001] 20 E.G. 228 (C.S.); (2001) 98(24) L.S.G. 45; (2001) 151 N.L.J. 727; (2001) 145 S.J.L.B. 140; [2001] N.P.C. 90, HL 2.541
— (on the application of Hooper) v Secretary of State for Work and Pensions; R. (on the application of Withey) v Secretary of State for Work and Pensions; R. (on the application of Naylor) v Secretary of State for Work and Pensions; R. (on the application of Martin) v Secretary of State for Work and Pensions; sub nom Hooper v Secretary of State for Work and Pensions [2005] UKHL 29; [2005] 1 W.L.R. 1681; [2006] 1 All E.R. 487; [2005] 2 F.C.R. 183; [2005] H.R.L.R. 21; [2005] U.K.H.R.R. 717; [2005] Pens. L.R. 337, HL 4.11, 4.16, 4.19, 4.22, 4.81, 4.83
— (on the application of Howes) v Social Security Commissioner [2007] EWHC 559 (Admin) 2.513
— (on the application of Limbuela) v Secretary of State for the Home Department; R. (on the application of Tesema) v Secretary of State for the Home Department; R. (on the application of Adam) v Secretary of State for the Home Department [2005] UKHL 66; [2006] 1 A.C. 396; [2005] 3 W.L.R. 1014; [2007] 1 All E.R. 951; [2006] H.R.L.R. 4; [2006] H.L.R. 10; (2006) 9 C.C.L. Rep. 30; (2005) 102(46) L.S.G. 25; (2005) 149 S.J.L.B. 1354, HL 3.38, 4.48
— (on the application of M) v Secretary of State for Work and Pensions [2006] EWHC 1761, QBD (Admin) 4.84
— (on the application of Nahar) v Social Security Commissioners; sub nom R. (on the application of Nahar) v Secretary of State for Work and Pensions [2002] EWCA Civ 859; [2002] A.C.D. 105, CA (Civ Div) 1.362
— (on the application of Roberts) v Parole Board; sub nom Roberts v Parole Board [2005] UKHL 45; [2005] 2 A.C. 738; [2005] 3 W.L.R. 152; [2006] 1 All E.R. 39; [2005] H.R.L.R. 38; [2005] U.K.H.R.R. 939; (2005) 155 N.L.J. 1096, HL 2.472
— (on the application of Steele) v Birmingham City Council [2005] EWCA Civ 1824; [2006] 1 W.L.R. 2380; [2007] 1 All E.R. 73; [2006] I.C.R. 869; [2006] B.P.I.R. 856; [2006] R.V.R. 120, CA (Civ Div) 1.83
— (on the application of Thompson) v Law Society [2004] EWCA Civ 167; [2004] 1 W.L.R. 2522; [2004] 2 All E.R. 113; (2004) 101(13) L.S.G. 35; (2004) 154 N.L.J. 307; (2004) 148 S.J.L.B. 265, CA (Civ Div) 2.321, 4.61
— (on the application of Viggers) v Pensions Appeal Tribunal [2006] EWHC 1066; [2006] A.C.D. 80, QBD 2.498

Table of Cases

— (on the application of Wall) v Appeals Service and Benefits Agency [2003] EWHC 465 Admin 4.62
Raad van Arbeid v Brusse (101/83) [1984] E.C.R. 2223; [1985] 2 C.M.L.R. 633, ECJ (1st Chamber) 3.158
Racal Communications Ltd, Re; sub nom Re Company (No.00996 of 1979) [1981] A.C. 374; [1980] 3 W.L.R. 181; [1980] 2 All E.R. 634, HL 1.85
Ragazzoni v Caisse de Compensation Pour Allocations Familiales 'Assubel' (C–134/77) [1978] E.C.R. 963; [1979] 3 C.M.L.R. 67, ECJ 3.243
Ramrath v Ministre de la Justice (C–106/91); sub nom Ramrath v Minister of Justice (C–106/91) [1992] E.C.R. I–3351; [1995] 2 C.M.L.R. 187; [1992] 3 C.M.L.R. 173, ECJ (6th Chamber) 3.37
Rand v East Dorset HA (Deduction of Benefits) [2001] P.I.Q.R. Q1; [2000] Lloyd's Rep. Med. 377, QBD 1.256
Raulin v Minister van Onderwijs en Wetenschappen (C–357/89) [1992] E.C.R. I–1027; [1994] 1 C.M.L.R. 227, ECJ 3.37
Reibold v Bundesanstalt für Arbeit (C–216/89) [1990] E.C.R. I–4163, ECJ 3.241
Reyners v Belgium (2/74) [1974] E.C.R. 631; [1974] 2 C.M.L.R. 305, ECJ 3.37
Rheinmühlen-Dusseldorf v Einfuhr- und Vorratsstelle für Getreide und Futtermittel (166/73) [1974] E.C.R. 33; [1974] 1 C.M.L.R. 523, ECJ 3.52
Richards v Secretary of State for Work and Pensions (C–423/04) [2006] All E.R. (EC) 895; [2006] E.C.R. I–3585; [2006] 2 C.M.L.R. 49; [2006] C.E.C. 637; [2006] I.C.R. 1181; [2006] 2 F.L.R. 487; [2006] 3 F.C.R. 229; [2006] Pens. L.R. 123; [2006] Fam. Law 639, ECJ (1st Chamber) 3.458
Rijksdienst voor Arbeidsvoorziening v van Gestel (C–454/93) [1995] E.C.R. I–1707; [1996] 1 C.M.L.R. 437; (1996) 93(20) L.S.G. 31, ECJ (6th Chamber) 3.158
Rijksdienst voor Sociale Zekerheid v Herbosch Kiere NV (C–2/05) [2006] E.C.R. I–1079, ECJ 3.147
Ringeisen v Austria (No.1) (A/13) (1979–80) 1 E.H.R.R. 455, ECHR 4.55
Roberts v Parole Board. See R. (on the application of Roberts) v Parole Board
Rodriguez v Landesversicherungsanstalt Rheinprovinz (C–113/96) [1998] E.C.R. I–2482; [1999] 1 C.M.L.R. 129, ECJ (5th Chamber) 3.126
Rönfeldt v Bundesversicherungsanstalt fur Angestellte (C–227/89) [1991] E.C.R. I–323, AGO 3.126
Ruiz-Mateos v Spain (A/262) (1993) 16 E.H.R.R. 505, ECHR 4.57
Rydqvist v Secretary of State for Work and Pensions [2002] EWCA Civ 947; [2002] 1 W.L.R. 3343; [2002] I.C.R. 1383; (2002) 146 S.J.L.B. 247, CA (Civ Div) 2.468
S (Children) (Care Order: Implementation of Care Plan), Re; Re W (Children) (Care Order: Adequacy of Care Plan); sub nom Re W and B (Children) (Care Plan), Re; W (Children) (Care Plan) [2002] UKHL 10; [2002] 2 A.C. 291; [2002] 2 W.L.R. 720; [2002] 2 All E.R. 192; [2002] 1 F.L.R. 815; [2002] 1 F.C.R. 577; [2002] H.R.L.R. 26; [2002] U.K.H.R.R. 652; [2002] B.L.G.R. 251; [2002] Fam. Law 413; (2002) 99(17) L.S.G. 34; (2002) 146 S.J.L.B. 85, HL 4.11
S (FC), Re; Re S and Re W. See Re S (Children) (Care Order: Implementation of Care Plan)
Saker v Secretary of State for Social Services, CA (Civ Div) 2.375
Salesi v Italy (A/257-E) (1998) 26 E.H.R.R. 187, ECHR 4.56
Schuler-Zgraggen v Switzerland (A/263) [1994] 1 F.C.R. 453; (1993) 16 E.H.R.R. 405, ECHR 4.56, 4.61
Scrivner v Chief Adjudication Officer [1990] 1 C.M.L.R. 637, CA (Civ Div) 3.417
Secretary of State for Defence v Pensions Appeal Tribunals (England and Wales); sub nom R. (on the application of Secretary of State for Defence) v President of the Pensions Appeal Tribunals [2004] EWHC 141; [2004] 2 All E.R. 159, QBD (Admin) 2.508
Secretary of State for Social Security v Graham. See Graham v Secretary of State for Social Security
— v Scully; sub nom R. v Secretary of State for Social Security Ex p. Scully [1992] 1 W.L.R. 927; [1992] 4 All E.R. 1, CA (Civ Div) 1.355
— v Thomas (C–328/91); sub nom Thomas v Secretary of State for Social Security; Thomas v Chief Adjudication Officer (C–328/91) [1993] Q.B. 747; [1993] 3 W.L.R. 581; [1993] 4 All E.R. 556; [1993] E.C.R. I–1247; [1993] 3 C.M.L.R. 880; [1993] I.C.R. 673; [1993] I.R.L.R. 292, ECJ (6th Chamber) 3.463
— v Walter. See Walter v Secretary of State for Social Security
Secretary of State for Social Services v Solly [1974] 3 All E.R. 922, CA (Civ Div) .. 1.87, 1.163

Table of Cases

Secretary of State for Work and Pensions v Adams [2003] EWCA Civ 796, CA (Civ Div) 1.368
— v Bhakta [2006] EWCA Civ 65; (2006) 103(10) L.S.G. 26, CA (Civ Div) 1.353, 2.92
— v Bobezes [2005] EWCA Civ 111; [2005] 3 All E.R. 497, CA (Civ Div) 3.59, 3.120
— v Cunningham, 2005 1 S.C. 19; 2004 S.L.T. 1007; 2004 G.W.D. 25-546, IH (Ex Div) 1.346, 2.458
— v Nelligan; sub nom Secretary of State for Work and Pensions v Nelligen [2003] EWCA Civ 555; [2004] 1 W.L.R. 894; [2003] 4 All E.R. 171; (2003) 100(26) L.S.G. 38; (2003) 153 N.L.J. 667, CA (Civ Div) 1.26
— v Walker-Fox; sub nom Walker-Fox v Secretary of State for Work and Pensions [2005] EWCA Civ 1441; [2006] Eu. L.R. 601, CA (Civ Div) 3.13, 3.122
Shackell v United Kingdom (App.45851/99), unreported, April 27, 2000, ECHR 4.81
Shallow v Shallow [1979] Fam. 1; [1978] 2 W.L.R. 583; [1978] 2 All E.R. 483; (1977) 121 S.J. 830, CA (Civ Div) 1.141
Sharples v Chief Adjudication Officer. *See* Jones v Chief Adjudication Officer
Sheridan v Stanley Cole (Wainfleet) Ltd. *See* Stanley Cole (Wainfleet) Ltd v Sheridan
Simmenthal SpA v Amministrazione delle Finanze dello Stato (70/77) [1978] E.C.R. 1453; [1978] 3 C.M.L.R. 670, ECJ 3.53
Skalka v Sozialversicherungsanstalt der Gewerblichen Wirtschaft (C–160/02) [2004] E.C.R. I–5613, ECJ 3.136
Snares v Adjudication Officer (C–20/96) [1997] All E.R. (E.C.) 886; [1997] E.C.R. I-6057; [1998] 1 C.M.L.R. 897, ECJ 3.136
South Buckinghamshire DC v Porter (No.2); sub nom South Buckinghamshire DC v Secretary of State for Transport, Local Government and the Regions [2004] UKHL 33; [2004] 1 W.L.R. 1953; [2004] 4 All E.R. 775; [2005] 1 P. & C.R. 6; [2004] 4 P.L.R. 50; [2004] 28 E.G. 177 (C.S.); (2004) 101(31) L.S.G. 25; (2004) 148 S.J.L.B. 825; [2004] N.P.C. 108, HL 2.498
Southwark LBC v Kofi-Adu [2006] EWCA Civ 281; [2006] H.L.R. 33; [2006] N.P.C. 36, CA (Civ Div) 1.379
Sporrong & Lonnroth v Sweden (A/52) (1983) 5 E.H.R.R. 35, ECHR 4.89
Stanley Cole (Wainfleet) Ltd v Sheridan; sub nom Sheridan v Stanley Cole (Wainfleet) Ltd [2003] EWCA Civ 1046; [2003] 4 All E.R. 1181; [2003] I.C.R. 1449; [2003] I.R.L.R. 885; (2003) 100(38) L.S.G. 33, CA (Civ Div) 4.61
Stansbury v Datapulse Plc; sub nom Stansby v Datapulse Plc [2003] EWCA Civ 1951; [2004] I.C.R. 523; [2004] I.R.L.R. 466; [2004] U.K.H.R.R. 340; (2004) 101(6) L.S.G. 32; (2004) 148 S.J.L.B. 145, CA (Civ Div) 4.62
Stec v United Kingdom (65731/01) (2006) 43 E.H.R.R. 47; 20 B.H.R.C. 348, ECHR (Grand Chamber) 2.39, 4.09, 4.16, 4.76, 4.77, 4.78, 4.90
Steen (Volker) v Deutsche Bundespost (C–332/90) [1992] E.C.R. I–341, AGO 3.37
Steenhorst-Neerings v Bestuur van de Bedrijfsvereniging voor Detailhandel, Ambachten en Huisvrouwen (C–338/91) [1993] E.C.R. I–5475; [1995] 3 C.M.L.R. 323; [1994] I.R.L.R. 244, ECJ 3.13
Stinco v Istituto Nazionale della Previdenza Sociale (INPS) (C–132/96) [1998] E.C.R. I–5225, ECJ (6th Chamber) 3.417
Stretch v United Kingdom (44277/98) (2004) 38 E.H.R.R. 12; [2004] B.L.G.R. 401; [2004] 1 E.G.L.R. 11; [2004] 03 E.G. 100; [2003] 29 E.G. 118 (C.S.); [2003] N.P.C. 125, ECHR 4.89
Stubbings v United Kingdom (22083/93) [1997] 1 F.L.R. 105; [1997] 3 F.C.R. 157; (1997) 23 E.H.R.R. 213; 1 B.H.R.C. 316; [1997] Fam. Law 241, ECHR 4.78
Sulak v Turkey (1996) 84 D.R. 101 .... 4.88
Swaddling v Adjudication Officer (C–90/97) [1999] All E.R. (EC) 217; [1999] E.C.R. I–1075; [1999] 2 C.M.L.R. 679; [1999] C.E.C. 184; [1999] 2 F.L.R. 184; [1999] Fam. Law 382, ECJ (5th Chamber) 3.122
Swaddling v Adjudication Officer (C–90/97) [1999] All E.R. (EC) 217; [1999] E.C.R. I–1075; [1999] 2 C.M.L.R. 679; [1999] C.E.C. 184; [1999] 2 F.L.R. 184; [1999] Fam. Law 382, ECJ (5th Chamber) 3.136
Szoma v Secretary of State for Work and Pensions [2005] UKHL 64; [2006] 1 A.C. 564; [2005] 3 W.L.R. 955; [2006] 1 All E.R. 1; [2006] Imm. A.R. 48; [2006] I.N.L.R. 88; (2005) 102(43) L.S.G. 31, HL 3.445
Telemarsicabruzzo SpA v Circostel (C–320/90); Telemarsicabruzzo SpA v Ministero delle Poste e Telecomunicazioni (C–320/90) [1993] E.C.R. I–393, ECJ 3.53
Ten Holder v Nieuwe Algemene Bedrijfsvereniging (302/84) [1986] E.C.R. 1821; [1987] 2 C.M.L.R. 208, ECJ (3rd Chamber) 3.143

Table of Cases

Testa v Bundesanstalt für Arbeit, Nuremberg (C–41/79); Maggio v Bundesanstalt für Arbeit, Nuremberg (C–121/79); Vitale v Bundesanstalt für Arbeit, Nuremberg (C–796/79) [1981] E.C.R. 1979; [1980] E.C.R. 1979; [1981] 2 C.M.L.R. 552, ECJ 3.238
Teuling v Bedrijfsvereniging voor de Chemische Industrie (C–30/85); sub nom: Teuling v Bedrijfsvereniging voor de Chemische Industrie (C–30/85) [1987] E.C.R. 2497; [1988] 3 C.M.L.R. 789, ECJ (6th Chamber) 3.458
Thelen v Bundesanstalt für Arbeit (C–75/99) [2000] E.C.R. I–9399, ECJ (6th Chamber) 3.126
Thévenon v Landesversicherungsanstalt Rheinland Pfalz (C–475/93) [1995] E.C.R. I–3813, ECJ 3.127
Thomas v Secretary of State for Social Security. *See* Secretary of State for Social Security v Thomas
Toosey v Chief Adjudication Officer (C–287/92) [1994] E.C.R. I–279; [1994] 2 C.M.L.R. 745, ECJ (1st Chamber) 3.241
Trojani v Centre Public d'Aide Sociale de Bruxelles (CPAS) (C–456/02) [2004] All E.R. (EC) 1065; [2004] E.C.R. I–7573; [2004] 3 C.M.L.R. 38; [2005] C.E.C. 139, ECJ 3.31
Tsfayo v United Kingdom (60860/00) [2007] B.L.G.R. 1, ECHR 4.58
Turpeinen, Proceedings Brought by (C–520/04) [2007] 1 C.M.L.R. 28; [2006] S.T.I. 2458, ECJ (1st Chamber) 3.31
Union Nationale des Entraineurs et Cadres Techniques Professionnels du Football (UNECTEF) v Heylens (222/86) [1987] E.C.R. 4097; [1989] 1 C.M.L.R. 901, ECJ 3.37
Union Royale Belge des Sociétés de Football Association (ASBL) v Bosman (C–415/93); sub nom Royal Club Liegois SA v Bosman (C–415/93); Union des Associations Européennes de Football (UEFA) v Bosman (C–415/93) [1996] All E.R. (EC) 97; [1995] E.C.R. I–4921; [1996] 1 C.M.L.R. 645; [1996] C.E.C. 38, ECJ 3.37
Van Gemert-Derks v Bestuur van de Nieuwe Industriele Bedrijfsvereniging (C–337/91) [1993] E.C.R. I–5435; [1995] 1 C.M.L.R. 773, ECJ 3.458
Venables v News Group Newspapers Ltd; Thompson v News Group Newspapers Ltd [2001] Fam. 430; [2001] 2 W.L.R. 1038; [2001] 1 All E.R. 908; [2001] E.M.L.R. 10; [2001] 1 F.L.R. 791; [2002] 1 F.C.R. 333; [2001] H.R.L.R. 19; [2001] U.K.H.R.R. 628; 9 B.H.R.C. 587; [2001] Fam. Law 258; (2001) 98(12) L.S.G. 41; (2001) 151 N.L.J. 57; (2001) 145 S.J.L.B. 43, Fam Div 4.68
Von Colson v Land Nordrhein-Westfahlen (C–14/83); Harz v Deutsche Tradax GmbH (C–79/83) [1984] E.C.R. 1891; [1986] 2 C.M.L.R. 430, ECJ 3.23
W (China) and X (China) v Secretary of State for the Home Department [2006] EWCA Civ 1494 .... 3.31
Walder v Bestuur de Sociale Verzekeringsbank (82/72) [1973] E.C.R. 599, ECJ 3.126
Walker v United Kingdom (Admissibility) (37212/02) (2004) 39 E.H.R.R. SE4, ECH 4.13
— v —, unreported, August 2006, ECHR 4.66, 4.78
Walsh v Chief Adjudication Officer (Consent Order), January 19, 1995, CA 2.154
Walter v Secretary of State for Social Security; sub nom Secretary of State for Social Security v Walter [2001] EWCA Civ 1913; [2002] 1 C.M.L.R. 27; [2002] I.C.R. 540; [2002] E.L.R. 296; (2002) 99(6) L.S.G. 31, CA (Civ Div) 3.458
Wandsworth LBC v Michalak; sub nom Michaelek v Wandsworth LBC; Michalak v Wandsworth LBC [2002] EWCA Civ 271; [2003] 1 W.L.R. 617; [2002] 4 All E.R. 1136; [2003] 1 F.C.R. 713; [2002] H.L.R. 39; [2002] N.P.C. 34, CA (Civ Div) 4.80
Webb v EMO Air Cargo (UK) Ltd (Reference to ECJ) [1993] 1 W.L.R. 49; [1992] 4 All E.R. 929; [1993] 1 C.M.L.R. 259; [1993] I.C.R. 175; [1993] I.R.L.R. 27; (1992) 142 N.L.J. 1720; (1993) 137 S.J.L.B. 48, HL 4.11
White v Chief Adjudication Officer [1986] 2 All E.R. 905; (1986) 83 L.S.G. 1319; (1986) 130 S.J. 448, CA (Civ Div) 2.338
Williams v Devon CC [2003] EWCA Civ 365; [2003] C.P. Rep. 47; [2003] P.I.Q.R. Q4, CA (Civ Div) 1.280, 1.296
Willis v United Kingdom (36042/97) [2002] 2 F.L.R. 582; [2002] 2 F.C.R. 743; (2002) 35 E.H.R.R. 21; [2002] Fam. Law 661, ECHR 4.81, 4.96
Wilson v First County Trust Ltd (No.2); sub nom Wilson v Secretary of State for Trade and Industry [2003] UKHL 40; [2004] 1 A.C. 816; [2003] 3 W.L.R. 568; [2003]

Table of Cases

4 All E.R. 97; [2003] 2 All E.R. (Comm) 491; [2003] H.R.L.R. 33; [2003]
U.K.H.R.R. 1085; (2003) 100(35) L.S.G. 39; (2003) 147 S.J.L.B. 872, HL .. 4.13, 4.44
Wingrave v United Kingdom (App.40029/02), April 8, 2003 and May 18, 2004,
ECHR 4.62
Wirth v Landeshauptstadt Hannover (C–109/93) [1993] E.C.R. I–6447, ECJ (5th
Chamber) 3.31, 3.37
Wisely v John Fulton (Plumbers) Ltd; Wadey v Surrey CC [2000] 1 W.L.R. 820; [2000]
2 All E.R. 545; 2000 S.C. (H.L.) 95; 2000 S.L.T. 494; 2000 S.C.L.R. 693; [2000]
P.I.Q.R. Q306; (2000) 97(22) L.S.G. 43; (2000) 144 S.J.L.B. 197; 2000 G.W.D.
13-487, HL 1.298
Wood v Secretary of State for Work and Pensions [2003] EWCA Civ 53, CA (Civ
Div) 1.367, 1.376, 2.373, 2.375
X v Sweden (App.434/58), June 30, 1959, 2 Y.B. 354 .... 4.57
— v United Kingdom (App.3860/68) (1970) 30 C.D. 70 .... 4.58
— v — (App.4288/69) (1970) 13 Y.B. 892 .... 4.89
Yunying Jia v Migrationsverket, January 9, 2007 .... 3.31
Zalewska v Department for Social Development, NI CA 3.31
Zuckerfabrik Suderdithmarschen AG v Hauptzollamt Itzehoe (C–143/88) Zuckerfabrik
Soest GmbH v Hauptzollamt Paderborn (C–92/89) [1991] E.C.R. I–415; [1993]
3 C.M.L.R. 1; (1991) 135 S.J.L.B. 6, ECJ 3.53

TABLE OF SOCIAL SECURITY COMMISSIONERS' DECISIONS

C1/89(WB) 1.97	CDLA/5413/1999 .... 2.347, 2.508, 4.56,
C2/89(CB) 1.97	4.57, 4.61, 4.62
C12/98(IS) 2.119	CDLA/5419/1999 .... 2.498
C50/90–00(DLA) 3.59	CDLA/5469/1999 .... 2.373
C3/00–01(IS) 2.123	CDLA/6336/1999 .... 1.94
C3/00–01(IS)(T) 2.123	CDLA/9/2001 .... 2.373, 2.435
C28/001–01(IB)(T) 4.62	CDLA/557/2001 .... 2.492
C2/01–02(CRS) 1.278	CDLA/572/2001 .... 2.499
C12/2003–04(DLA) 2.98	CDLA/1000/2001 .... 1.389
C1/05–06(WB) 4.68	CDLA/1338/2001 .... 4.44
C2/05–06(WB) 4.68	CDLA/2335/2001 .... 2.423
C3/05–06(WB) 4.68	CDLA/3364/2001 .... 2.377
C5/05–06(IB) 4.61	CDLA/3432/2001 .... 4.62
C6/05–06(IS) 3.31	CDLA/3848/2001 .... 2.98
C8/06–07(IB) 2.373, 4.86	CDLA/3875/2001 .... 2.377
CA/303/92 .... 1.96	CDLA/3908/2001 .... 2.373
CA/171/1993 .... 2.85	CDLA/4895/2001 .... 2.513
CA/1014/1999 .... 1.88, 2.154, 2.345, 2.429	CDLA/5167/2001 .... 2.423
CA/4297/2004 .... 2.498	CDLA/705/2002 .... 2.373
CA/2650/2006 .... 2.394	CDLA/1761/2002 .... 4.62
CA/3800/2006 .... 2.373, 2.416	CDLA/2748/2002 .... 2.483, 4.57
CAF/4200/2005 .... 1.378	CDLA/3768/2002 .... 2.704
CAF/857/2006 .... 2.343	CDLA/4331/2002 .... 2.98
CCR/4/1993 .... 1.286	CDLA/5574/2002 .... 2.315, 2.502
CCR/8023/1995 .... 1.271	CDLA/402/2003 .... 3.134
CCR/3396/2000 .... 2.497, 2.498	CDLA/1807/2003 .... 2.498
CCR/4307/2000 .... 1.256, 1.278	CDLA/2115/2003 .... 2.377
CCR/2046/2002 .... 1.256	CDLA/2462/2003 .... 2.487
CCR/2231/2003 .... 1.279	CDLA/2807/2003 .... 2.164
CCR/3425/2003 .... 1.279, 1.380	CDLA/3323/2003 .... 2.354
CCR/3391/2005 .... 1.275, 2.399	CDLA/3440/2003 .... 2.435
CCR/1022/2006 .... 1.256	CDLA/1823/2004 .... 1.93, 2.387
CCR/2232/2006 .... 1.256, 1.285	CDLA/2014/2004 .... 1.380
CCS/910/1999 .... 2.333	CDLA/2429/2004 .... 2.492
CCS/2064/1999 .... 2.514	CDLA/2999/2004 .... 1.354, 1.364, 2.725
CCS/6302/1999 .... 2.347	CDLA/1707/2005 .... 1.382, 2.343
CCS/1306/2001 .... 4.44	CDLA/2379/2005 .... 1.346, 4.62
CCS/1626/2002 .... 2.498	CDLA/393/2006 .... 2.343
CCS/5515/2002 .... 2.435, 2.442	CDLA/1480/2006 .... 2.466
CCS/3749/2003 .... 1.380	CDLA/2328/2006 .... 1.93, 2.150
CCS/3757/2004 .... 1.380, 2.462	CF/667/1997 .... 3.247
CCS/1495/2005 .... 1.380	CF/3662/1999 .... 3.120
CCS/2288/2005 .... 2.347	CF/3565/2001 .... 2.541, 4.62
CCS/1876/2006 .... 2.492	CF/1727/2006 .... 3.142
CDLA/913/1994 .... 2.687	CFC/2766/2003 .... 1.92, 1.93
CDLA/1596/1996 .... 2.40	CG/065/1989 .... 1.87, 1.88
CDLA/14895/1996 .... 2.98	CG/449/1994 .... 1.94
CDLA/1389/1997 .... 2.504	CG/5425/1995 .... 3.454
CDLA/3680/1997 .... 2.492	CG/622/1998 .... 1.97
CDLA/4110/1997 .... 2.504	CG/1567/1998 .... 1.97
CDLA/5793/1997 .... 2.498	CG/2112/1998 .... 1.97
CDLA/1552/1998 .... 2.492	CG/160/1999 .... 1.94
CDLA/1820/1998 .... 2.373	CG/4494/1999 .... 1.93, 1.94, 1.96, 1.99
CDLA/1347/1999 .... 2.466, 2.472	CG/5631/1999 .... 1.94

xxxvii

Table of Social Security Commissioners' Decisions

CG/2888/2000	1.94	CIB/3074/2003	1.380
CG/1467/2001	4.11	CIB/3838/2003	1.380
CG/1259/2002	4.81	CIB/3925/2003	1.93
CG/2965/2002	4.83	CIB/4193/2003	2.466
CG/3049/2002	1.98	CIB/763/2004	2.387
CG/734/2003	4.83	CIB/1009/2004	2.492
CG/2973/2004	2.66, 2.347, 2.508	CIB/1509/2004	2.380
CG/1614/05	4.84	CIB/2058/2004	2.492
CH/5125/2002	4.79	CIB/4253/2004	1.380, 2.462
CH/5126/2002	4.79	CIB/1599/2005	2.387
CH/5128/2002	4.79	CIS/8/1990	2.43
CH/5129/2002	4.79	CIS/156/1990	1.97
CH/5130/2002	4.79	CIS/159/1990	1.99
CH/3439/2004	2.353	CIS/375/1990	2.43
CH/2553/2005	2.315, 2.498	CIS/616/1990	1.126
CH/3314/2005	3.31	CIS/620/1990	2.111
CH/687/2006	2.343	CIS/222/1991	1.99
CH/1400/2006	3.31	CIS/427/1991	2.380
CH/1821/2006	1.378	CIS/465/1991	2.176
CH/2484/2006	2.502, 3.31	CIS/625/1991	1.116
CI/06–07(IS)	1.85	CIS/638/1991	2.154
CI/141/1987	2.506	CIS/136/1992	1.100
CI/343/1988	2.498	CIS/137/1992	1.100
CI/636/1993	2.498	CIS/442/1992	1.100
CI/1327/1998	2.456	CIS/734/1992	1.88
CI/5199/1998	2.498	CIS/759/1992	2.48, 2.66, 2.347
CI/3887/1999	2.506	CIS/812/1992	2.154
CI/5880/1999	4.62	CIS/102/1993	1.97
CI/4421/2000	4.62	CIS/332/1993	1.88
CI/1021/2001	1.379	CIS/501/1993	3.52
CI/1547/2001	1.376, 2.373, 2.431	CIS/645/1993	1.92
CI/1800/01	1.364	CIS/026/1994	1.82
CI/1802/2001	2.498, 2.498	CIS/288/1994	2.236
CI/954/2006	1.365, 2.373, 2.431	CIS/642/1994	2.154
CIB/13368/1996	3.464	CIS/674/1994	1.97
CIB/15663/1996	1.380	CIS/5206/1995	2.236
CIB/17533/1996	2.662	CIS/7009/1995	2.176
CIB/3013/1997	2.504	CIS/12016/1996	2.176
CIB/4497/1998	2.497, 2.498, 2.498	CIS/12032/1996	1.96
CIB/4563/1998	1.206	CIS/12082/1996	1.117, 3.417
CIB/303/1999	2.347, 2.508	CIS/13742/1996	1.89, 1.99
CIB/4243/1999	3.122	CIS/14025/1996	1.94
CIB/5227/1999	2.508	CIS/15146/1996	2.236
CIB/230/2000	3.458	CIS/619/1997	1.89, 1.99
CIB/1972/2000	2.380	CIS/771/1997	3.52
CIB/2338/2000	1.355, 1.376, 2.375, 2.380	CIS/1055/1997	1.84
		CIS/1423/1997	2.145
CIB/2620/2000	2.456	CIS/2447/1997	1.99
CIB/3179/2000	2.380	CIS/2498/1997	1.94
CIB/3667/2000	2.380	CIS/610/1998	2.121, 2.123
CIB/4471/2000	3.195	CIS/849/1998	2.117
CIB/378/2001	2.380	CIS/1721/1998	2.123
CIB/563/2001	2.498	CIS/2057/1998	2.115, 2.119, 2.121
CIB/3427/2001	4.62	CIS/2132/1998	2.498
CIB/3933/2001	3.458	CIS/3749/1998	2.123
CIB/3985/2001	2.380, 4.62	CIS/3994/1998	2.123
CIB/4791/2001	2.294, 2.295	CIS/4437/1998	2.513
CIB/313/2002	1.356, 2.380, 2.395	CIS/5117/1998	1.92
CIB/2751/2002	2.467, 2.486, 4.54	CIS/5131/1998	1.94
CIB/3645/2002	4.62	CIS/5321/1998	1.379
CIB/3654/2002	4.62	CIS/1148/1999	1.94
CIB/460/2003	2.452	CIS/1340/1999	2.146
CIB/2805/2003	2.48	CIS/1769/1999	1.96

Table of Social Security Commissioners' Decisions

CIS/2428/1999	1.353	CIS/3573/2005	3.31
CIS/4316/1999	1.117	CIS/3605/2005	1.84
CIS/4354/1999	2.123	CIS/3875/2005	3.31
CIS/5848/1999	1.94	CIS/3890/2005	3.37
CIS/5899/1999	1.99	CIS/624/2006	1.376, 1.378, 2.375, 2.439, 2.496
CIS/6249/1999	2.373		
CIS/1777/2000	2.704	CIS/1462/2006	1.85
CIS/2292/2000	2.492	CIS/1757/2006	4.09
CIS/0155/2001	1.115	CIS/1867/2006	1.93
CIS/157/2001	2.114	CJSA/1136/1998	2.124
CIS/825/2001	3.59	CJSA/3121/1998	2.118
CIS/2291/2001	2.704	CJSA/3994/1998	2.117
CIS/2345/2001	2.497, 2.498	CJSA/4890/1998	3.458
CIS/4248/2001	2.466	CJSA/935/1999	4.68
CIS/4769/2001	4.83	CJSA/1423/1999	1.90
CIS/5140/2001	1.92	CJSA/3979/1999	2.63
CIS/203/2002	1.84	CJSA/4065/1999	3.57
CIS/362/2002	1.84	CJSA/69/2001	2.41, 2.541
CIS/540/2002	4.62	CJSA/3659/2001	2.127
CIS/758/2002	2.39	CJSA/5100/2001	4.54, 4.62
CIS/764/2002	1.84, 1.100, 1.117	CJSA/5101/2001	4.60, 4.62
CIS/1887/2002	1.93	CJSA/232/2003	4.78
CIS/4220/2002	4.58	CJSA/580/2003	2.123
CIS/4422/2002	1.93	CJSA/4383/2003	2.128
CIS/4848/2002	1.95	CJSA/3084/2004	2.123
CIS/4884/2002	2.123	CJSA/0743/2006	2.127
CIS/4901/2002	2.66, 2.127	CJSA/1703/2006	1.378
CIS/5048/2002	1.115	CJSA/3960/2006	2.127
CIS/0170/2003	1.84	CM/449/1990	2.492
CIS/242/2003	1.88	CP/1074/1997	2.102
CIS/306/2003	2.66, 2.347	CP/3643/2001	1.26
CIS/362/2003	1.84	CP/4762/2001	4.96
CIS/1010/2003	2.117	CP/5084/2001	4.76, 4.83, 4.84
CIS/1870/2003	4.84	CP/0281/2002	4.96
CIS/1965/2003	4.84	CP/518/2003	4.79, 4.84
CIS/2303/2003	4.84	CP/3447/2003	2.49
CIS/2305/2003	4.84	CP/3833/2003	1.248
CIS/2624/2003	4.84	CP/0428/2004	3.458
CIS/3173/2003	2.50	CP/3017/2004	2.102
CIS/3228/2003	1.84, 1.356	CP/4104/2004	2.65
CIS/3280/2003	2.92	CPC/389/2004	1.356
CIS/3535/2003	1.358	CPC/206/2005	2.343
CIS/4167/2003	2.111	CPC/2920/2005	3.31
CIS/4348/2003	1.93, 2.150	CPC/4177/2005	3.456
CIS/488/2004	3.134	CS/371/49	2.166
CIS/579/2004	2.128	CS/366/1993	1.100
CIS/1124/2004	2.92	CS/343/1994	2.502
CIS/1344/2004	2.547	CS/1753/2000	2.487
CIS/1491/2004	3.134	CS/1952/2001	2.292, 2.295
CIS/1616/2004	4.84	CS/3202/2002	2.466, 2.486
CIS/1840/2004	2.92	CSA/248/2002	2.98
CIS/2042/2004	1.93	CSB/53/1981	1.100
CIS/2337/2004	1.29, 2.114	CSB/64/1986	1.99
CIS/3438/2004	2.46	CSB/0677/1986	1.93
CIS/4088/2004	1.376	CSB/957/1987	1.96
CIS/4434/2004	1.84, 2.387	CSB/790/1988	1.97
CIS/840/2005	1.376	CSB/1093/1989	1.84, 1.96
CIS/1216/2005	2.492	CSB/1272/1989	1.84
CIS/1363/2005	2.344, 2.478	CSB/329/1990	1.79
CIS/2559/2005	3.31	CSB/083/1991	1.100
CIS/2680/2005	3.31	CSB/18/1992	1.97
CIS/3182/2005	3.31	CSB/108/1992	1.92
CIS/3315/2005	3.31	CSB/168/1993	2.154, 2.176

Table of Social Security Commissioners' Decisions

CSB/61/1995	2.176	LA18/01–02(DLA)	2.292
CSB/15394/1996	2.508	R1/01(CRS)	1.256, 1.278
CSB/574/1997	2.508	R1/01(IS)(T)	2.123
CSCR/1/1995	1.286	R1/02(IB)	1.379, 2.466
CSCS/1/1995	1.276	R1/04(IB)	2.380
CSDLA/5/1995	2.472	R1/04(SF)	1.379, 2.81, 2.380
CSDLA/90/1998	2.492, 2.492	R1/05(CRS)	1.256
CSDLA/303/1998	2.508	R1/05(DLA)	2.375
CSDLA/71/1999	2.293, 2.514	R1/06(CRS)	1.256
CSDLA/536/1999	2.513	R002/01(IS)	2.118
CSDLA/551/1999	2.497, 2.498	R2/01(IB)	2.498
CSDLA/1019/1999	4.44, 4.62	R2/04(DLA)	2.498
CSDLA/101/2000	2.329	R2/05	1.353
CSDLA/300/2000	2.298	R3/01(IB)	2.498
CSDLA/531/2000	2.497	R3/02(IB)	2.315, 2.498
CSDLA/1207/2000	2.297	R3/04(IB)	2.466
CSDLA/1282/2001	1.88, 2.150, 2.154	R6/94(IS)	1.97
CSDLA/866/2002	2.462, 2.492	R(A)1/72	2.498
CSDLA/91/2003	4.62	R(A)1/75	1.96
CSDLA/606/2003	4.62	R(A)4/81	2.375
CSDLA/765/2004	2.373	R(A)2/83	2.380
CSDLA/364/2005	1.346	R(A)4/89	2.472
CSDLA/242/2006	2.95	R(A)1/90	2.373
CSDLA/637/2006	2.373	R(A)2/94	3.456
CSG/357/1997	1.100	R(A)1/95	1.93, 1.96
CSHC/729/2003	2.487	R(A)1/97	2.85
CSI/74/1991	2.506	R(A)1/99	3.136
CSI/146/2003	2.459	R(A)2/06	1.93, 2.345, 2.387, 2.429
CSIB/973/1999	4.22		
CSIB/501/2003	2.380	R(CR)1/95	1.256
CSIB/439/2004	2.503	R(CR)1/96	1.256
CSIB/404/2005	2.485	R(CR)1/01	1.256
CSIS/045/1990	1.84	R(CR)1/02	1.256, 1.278, 1.285
CSIS/065/1991	1.60, 2.662	R(CR)2/02	1.278
CSIS/48/1992	2.48, 2.66, 2.347	R(CR)1/03	1.256, 1.278
CSIS/61/1992	2.127	R(CR)2/03	1.271, 1.278, 1.279, 1.285, 1.296, 2.766
CSIS/66/1992	2.47		
CSIS/7/1994	1.99	R(CR)3/03	1.256
CSIS/98/1994	2.236	R(CR)4/03	1.256, 1.260
CSIS/8/1995	1.100	R(CR)1/04	1.278
CSIS/174/1996	1.84	R(CR)2/04	1.256, 1.271, 1.278, 1.280, 1.294, 1.296, 1.303, 1.334, 2.762
CSIS/399/2001	1.84		
CSIS/400/2001	1.84		
CSIS/460/2002	4.24, 4.44	R(CS)5/02	2.478
CSIS/815/2004	2.123	R(CS)3/04	2.343
CSIS/345/2004	1.92	R(CS)4/04	2.446
CSJSA/0125/2004	4.84	R(CS)2/06	3.445
CSS/33/1990	1.94	R(DLA)2/98	2.452
CSS/36/1992	1.271	R(DLA)2/99	3.134
CSSB/621/1988	1.84	R(DLA)3/99	1.380
CSSB/316/1989	1.84	R(DLA)4/99	2.687, 3.14
CSSB/517/1989	1.84	R(DLA)5/99	2.687, 3.14, 3.136
CSSB/6/1995	1.163	R(DLA)3/01	1.353
CSU/03/1991	1.92	R(DLA)6/01	2.373, 2.375
CTC/1061/2001	2.62	R(DLA)4/02	4.68
CTC/2979/2001	2.373	R(DLA)6/02	2.373
CTC/5401/2002	1.97	R(DLA)1/03	1.367, 1.376, 2.373, 2.375, 4.56
CTC/4025/2003	1.92		
CTC/2090/2004	1.379	R(DLA)7/04	2.346, 2.458, 4.62
CTC/3543/2004	2.345	R(DLA)3/05	2.347
CTC/0031/2006	4.59	R(DLA)4/05	1.45, 1.353, 2.92, 2.98, 2.102
CU/94/1994	2.39		
CU/2604/1999	2.165	R(DLA)1/06	2.373

Table of Social Security Commissioners' Decisions

R(DLA)2/06	2.482	R(IB)1/02	3.162, 3.195
R(DLA)3/06	1.380, 2.488	R(IB)4/02	2.347, 2.498
R(DLA)5/06	1.346, 2.458, 4.62	R(IB)3/03	1.206
R(DLA)2/07	2.691	R(IB)6/03	2.492, 2.498
R(F)1/72	1.378, 1.381	R(IB)2/04	1.84, 1.368, 1.376,
R(F)1/94	3.253		1.378, 1.380, 1.382, 1.383,
R(F)1/98	3.253		2.98, 2.349, 2.373, 2.377,
R(F)2/99	1.99		2.380, 2.395, 2.435,
R(FC)2/90	3.14, 4.24		2.442, 2.496
R(FC)1/91	1.352	R(IB)5/04	3.458
R(FC)2/98	3.456	R(IB)1/05	2.387, 2.396
R(FC)3/98	2.343	R(IB)2/05	2.380
R(FG)1/04	1.14, 1.20	R(IB)4/05	1.93
R(FP)1/05	1.14, 1.18	R(IB)5/05	1.383
R(G)2/79	1.14	R(IB)7/05	1.380
R(G)1/82	1.355	R(IS)5/91	2.154
R(G)1/83	1.14	R(IS)7/91	1.84, 2.165
R(G)1/84	1.18	R(IS)10/91	3.456
R(G)2/84	1.18	R(IS)5/92	1.100
R(G)3/84	1.14	R(IS)11/92	1.98, 1.380
R(G)1/88	1.14, 1.20	R(IS)4/93	2.81
R(G)1/90	1.20	R(IS)7/94	1.97
R(G)2/90	1.14	R(IS)14/94	2.696
R(G)3/90	1.18	R(IS)14/95	2.223, 2.236
R(G)1/91	1.18, 1.20	R(IS)2/96	1.84
R(G)2/94	3.464	R(IS)9/96	1.100
R(G)1/98	1.18	R(IS)14/96	1.96, 1.99
R(G)1/03	1.368	R(IS)16/96	1.97
R(G)1/04	4.81	R(IS)2/97	1.84, 2.375, 2.380
R(G)2/04	4.11, 4.81	R(IS)4/98	3.57
R(G)1/06	4.84	R(IS)12/98	3.57
R(G)2/06	2.66, 2.347, 2.508	R(IS)4/99	3.122, 3.136
R(H)1/04	2.343	R(IS)6/99	3.122, 3.136
R(H)2/04	2.343	R(IS)11/99	1.379, 2.298, 2.498, 2.513
R(H)3/04	1.378	R(IS)15/99	3.120
R(H)9/04	1.352	R(IS)5/00	1.88
R(H)1/05	4.09	R(IS)3/01	2.117, 2.123
R(H)3/05	1.380, 2.81, 2.541, 4.56	R(IS)3/02	4.44
R(H)8/05	1.361, 1.382, 2.353,	R(IS)6/02	3.417
	2.442, 2.905	R(IS)5/03	1.88, 1.93
R(H)6/06	1.378	R(IS)6/03	1.92
R(H)1/07	1.377	R(IS)1/04	4.58
R(I)56/54	2.375, 2.398	R(IS)2/04	4.58
R(I)18/61	2.498	R(IS)3/04	2.67, 2.145
R(I)30/61	2.498	R(IS)5/04	2.498
R(I)4/65	1.379	R(IS)6/04	2.39, 2.41, 2.541, 4.44,
R(I)13/65	2.492		4.56, 4.62
R(I)14/74	2.506	R(IS)12/04	4.13, 4.22, 4.83
R(I)3/75	2.377	R(IS)14/04	1.115, 1.376, 1.387, 2.67
R(I)2/83	2.146	R(IS)15/04	1.361, 1.382, 2.349,
R(I)2/88	2.375		2.353, 2.354, 2.442,
R(I)4/91	2.456		2.905, 4.63
R(I)2/94	2.375	R(IS)16/04	2.117, 2.127
R(I)5/94	2.492, 2.498	R(IS)17/04	1.379
R(I)7/94	1.377	R(IS)1/05	2.705
R(I)4/02	2.498	R(IS)6/05	3.59, 3.120
R(I)5/02	1.353, 1.376, 2.343, 2.431	R(IS)7/05	1.94
R(I)3/03	2.498	R(IS)12/05	1.376
R(I)4/03	1.365	R(IS)13/05	1.84, 1.356
R(I)1/04	2.498	R(IS)1/06	3.116
R(I)2/06	2.498	R(IS)3/06	3.13, 3.122
R(IB)1/01	2.402	R(IS)4/06	1.99
R(IB)2/01	2.402	R(IS)6/06	4.78, 4.84

xli

Table of Social Security Commissioners' Decisions

R(IS)7/06	1.353, 2.92	R(S)2/98	1.353
R(IS)8/06	3.122	R(SB)3/81	1.99
R(IS)9/06	1.93, 2.387	R(SB)1/82	1.381
R(IS)10/06	2.67	R(SB)21/82	1.87, 1.93, 1.96, 1.99, 1.100, 1.163
R(IS)11/06	4.16, 4.84		
R(IS)12/06	4.84	R(SB)19/83	2.347, 2.508
R(JSA)3/02	3.458	R(SB)23/83	1.87
R(JSA)3/03	2.749	R(SB)28/83	1.91, 1.93, 1.163
R(JSA)4/03	3.458	R(SB)29/83	2.81
R(JSA)2/04	1.376	R(SB)34/83	1.88
R(JSA)3/06	3.31	R(SB)42/83	1.381
R(M)2/78	2.498	R(SB)43/83	1.86, 1.100
R(M)6/86	2.498	R(SB)54/83	1.94
R(M)1/87	2.514	R(SB)55/83	2.347, 2.508
R(M)1/89	2.315, 2.502	R(SB)9/84	2.40, 2.49, 2.115, 2.154
R(M)1/96	2.380, 2.498	R(SB)18/84	1.126
R(P)1/55	1.381	R(SB)20/84	1.100
R(P)2/57	2.574	R(SB)25/84	2.146
R(P)2/73	2.108	R(SB)40/84	1.96
R(P)1/84	1.18	R(SB)6/85	1.100
R(P)1/88	1.14	R(SB)9/85	1.91, 1.92, 1.100
R(P)3/93	2.165	R(SB)10/85(T)	1.100
R(P)1/95	3.456	R(SB)15/85	1.100
R(P)1/96	3.456, 3.465	R(SB)18/85	1.91, 1.92
R(P)2/96	3.466	R(SB)28/85	1.116, 1.119
R(P)2/03	1.26	R(SB)11/86	1.100
R(P)1/04	1.248, 1.371, 2.405, 2.435, 2.464	R(SB)15/87	1.93, 1.94, 1.97, 1.99
		R(SB)8/88	2.155
R(P)1/06	4.86	R(SB)5/89	2.39
R(P)2/06	4.84	R(SB)8/89	2.65
R(P)1/07	3.558	R(SB)13/89	1.99
R(S)9/51	1.60	R(SB)3/90	1.92, 1.97, 1.99
R(S)1/55	2.380	R(SB)5/90	2.154
R(S)7/56	2.146	R(SB)1/91	1.100, 3.417
R(S)9/56	2.574	R(SB)3/91	1.100, 3.417
R(S)1/63	2.39	R(SB)5/91	1.82
R(S)2/63	2.166	R(SB)6/91	3.52, 3.458
R(S)1/71	2.574	R(SB)10/91	2.343
R(S)8/79	2.574	R(SB)2/92	1.91
R(S)4/82	1.379	R(SB)1/93	2.47
R(S)1/83	1.353	R(SB)2/93	2.343
R(S)8/85	2.338	R(SB)1/94	2.176
R(S)3/89	2.333	R(SB)1/96	1.87
R(S)3/90	2.111	R(TC)1/05	2.367, 2.446
R(S)2/91	1.33, 1.92	R(U)9/60	2.39, 2.541
R(S)3/92	3.164	R(U)2/79	2.39
R(S)2/93	3.52	R(U)7/83	2.39
R(S)5/93	1.355	R(U)4/86	3.241
R(S)7/94	3.241	R(U)3/88	2.492
R(S)1/95	3.454	R(U)3/89	2.508
R(S)2/95	3.464	R(U)1/02	2.165

TABLE OF ABBREVIATIONS USED IN THIS SERIES

2002 Act	Tax Credits Act 2002
AA	Attendance Allowance
A.C.	Appeal Cases
A.C.D.	Administrative Court Digest
ADHD	Attention Deficit Hyperactivity Disorder
Adjudication Regulations	Social Security (Adjudication) Regulations 1986
Admin.L.R.	Administrative Law Reports
All E.R.	All England Law Reports (Butterworths)
All E.R. (EC)	All England Law Reports European Cases
AMA	Adjudicating Medical Authority
AO	Adjudication Officer
AOG	*Adjudication Officers' Guide*
Attendance Allowance Regulations	Social Security (Attendance Allowance) Regulations 1991
BAMS	Benefits Agency Medical Service
B.H.R.C.	Butterworths Human Rights Cases
B.L.G.R.	Butterworths Local Government Reports
Blue Books	*The Law Relating to Social Security*, Vols 1–11
B.M.L.R.	Butterworths Medico-Legal Reports
B.P.I.R.	Bankruptcy and Personal Insolvency Reports
B.T.C.	British Tax Cases
CAA 2001	Capital Allowance Act 2001
CAB	Citizens Advice Bureau
CAO	Chief Adjudication Officer
CBA	Child Benefit Act 1975
CBJSA	Contribution-based Jobseeker's Allowance
C.C.L. Rep.	Community Care Law Reports
CCM	Claimant Compliance Manual
CCN	New Tax Credits Claimant Compliance Manual
C.E.C.	European Community Cases
CERA	Cortical Evoked Response Audiogram
Ch.	Chancery Law Reports
Child Benefit Regulations	Child Benefit (General) Regulations 2006
Claims and Payments Regulations 1979	Social Security (Claims and Payments) Regulations 1979

xliii

Table of Abbreviations used in this Series

Claims and Payments Regulations 1987	Social Security (Claims and Payments) Regulations 1987
C.M.L.R.	Common Market Law Reports
C.O.D.	Crown Office Digest
Commissioners Procedure Regulations	Social Security Commissioners (Procedure) Regulations 1999
Computation of Earnings Regulations 1978	Social Security Benefit (Computation of 1978 Earnings) Regulations 1978
Computation of Earnings Regulations 1996	Social Security Benefit (Computation of 1996 Earnings) Regulations 1996
Const.L.J.	Construction Law Journal
Council Tax Benefit Regulations	Council Tax Benefit (General) Regulations 1992 (SI 1992/1814)
CP	Carer Premium
CPAG	Child Poverty Action Group
C.P.L.R.	Civil Practice Law Reports
CPR	Civil Procedure Rules
C.P.Rep.	Civil Procedure Reports
Cr.App.R.	Criminal Appeal Reports
Cr.App.R.(S)	Criminal Appeal Reports (Sentencing)
CRCA	Commissioners for Revenue and Customs Act 2005
Crim.L.R.	Criminal Law Review
Crim.L.R.	Criminal Law Review
CRU	Compensation Recovery Unit
CSA 1995	Child Support Act 1995
CS(NI)O	Child Support (Northern Ireland) Order 1995
CSO	Child Support Officer
CSPSSA	Child Support, Pensions and Social Security Act 2000
CTC	Child Tax Credit
DAT	Disability Appeal Tribunal
DCP	Disabled Child Premium
Decisions and Appeals Regulations 1999	Social Security and Child Support (Decision and Appeals) Regulations 1999
Dependency Regulations	Social Security Benefit (Dependency) Regulations 1977
Disability Working Allowance Regulations	Disabnility Working Allowance (General) Regulations 1991
DLA	Disability Living Allowance
DLADAA 1991	Disability Living Allowance and Disability Allowance Act 1991
DM	Decision Maker
DMA	Decision-making and Appeals
DMG	*Decision-Makers Guide*
DMP	Delegated Medical Practitioner

Table of Abbreviations used in this Series

DPTC	Disabled Person's Tax Credit
DSDNI	Department for Social Development, Northern Ireland
DSS	Department of Social Security
DTI	Department of Trade and Industry
DWA	Disability Working Allowance
DWP	Department for Work and Pensions
EAA	Extrinsic Allergic Alveolitis
ECHR	European Court of Human Rights
E.C.R.	European Court Reports
ECSMA Agreement	European Convention on Social and Medical Assistance
EEA	European Economic Area
E.G.	Estates Gazette
E.H.R.R.	European Human Rights Reports
E.L.R.	Education Law Reports
EMA	Education Maintenance Allowance
EMO	Examining Medical Officer
EMP	Examining Medical Practitioner
ERA	Evoked Response Audiometry
ERA 1996	Employment Rights Act 1996
ER(NI)O	Employers Rights (Northern Ireland) Order 1996
Eur. L. Rev.	European Law Review
FA	Finance Act
Fam.Law	Family Law
Family Credit Regulations	Family Credit (General) Regulations 1987
FAS	Financial Assistance Scheme
FIS	Family Income Supplement
Fixing and Adjustment of Rates (Amendment) Regulations 1998	Child Benefit and Social Security (Fixing and Adjustment of Rates) (Amendment) Regulations 1998
Fixing and Adjustment of Rates Regulations 1976	Child Benefit and Social Security (Fixing and Adjustment of Rates) Regulations 1976
F.L.R.	Family Law Reports
GA Regulations	Social Security (Guardian's Allowance) Regulations 1975
General Benefit Regulations	Social Security (General Benefit) Regulations 1982
General Regulations	Statutory Maternity Pay (General) Regulations 1986
G.P.	General Practitioner
Graduated Retirement Benefit Regulations 2005	Social Security (Graduated Retirement Benefit) Regulations 2005
GRP	Graduated Retirement Pension
G.W.D.	Green's Weekly Digest

Table of Abbreviations used in this Series

HASSASSA	Health and Social Services and Social Security Adjudication Act 1983
HCD	House of Commons Debates
HCWA	House of Commons Written Answers
H.L.R.	Housing Law Reports
HMRC	Her Majesty's Revenue and Customs
HNCIP	(Housewives') Non-Contributory Invalidity Pension
Hospital In-Patients Regulations	Social Security (Hospital In-Patients) Regulations 1975
Housing Benefit Regulations	Housing Benefit (General) Regulations 1987 (SI 1987/1971)
HPP	Higher Pensioner Premium
HRA 1998	Human Rights Act 1998
H.R.L.R.	Human Rights Law Reports
HSE	Health and Safety Executive
IB	Incapactity Benefit
IB Regulations	Social Security (Incapacity Benefit) Regulations 1994
IBS	Irritable Bowel Syndrome
ICA	Invalid Care Allowance
I.C.R.	Industrial Cases Reports
ICTA	Income and Corporation Taxes Act 1988
IIAC	Industrial Injuries Advisory Council
I.L.J.	Industrial Law Journal
Imm.A.R.	Immigration Appeals Reports
Incapacity for Work Regulations	Social Security (Incapacity for Work) (General) Regulations 1995
Income Support Regulations	Income Support (General) Regulations 1987
Increases for Dependents Regulations	Social Security Benefit (Dependency) Regulations 1977
IND	Immigration and Nationality Directorate of the Home Office
I.N.L.R	Immigration and Nationality Law Reports
Invalid Care Allowance Regulations	Social Security (Invalid Care Allowance) Regulations 1976
IPPR	Institute of Public Policy Research
I.R.L.R.	Industrial Relations Law Reports
IS	Income Support
ISAs	Individual Savings Accounts
ITA	Income Tax Act 2007
ITEPA	Income Tax (Earnings and Pensions) Act 2003
ITTOIA	Income Tax (Trading and Other Income Act 2005)
ITS	Independent Tribunal Service
IWA	Social Security (Incapacity for Work) Act 1994

Table of Abbreviations used in this Series

IW (Dependants) Regs	Social Security (Incapacity for Work) (Dependants) Regulations
IW (General) Regulations	Social Security (Incapacity for Work) (General) Regulations 1995
IW (Transitional) Regulations	Social Security (Incapacity for Work) (Transitional) Regulations 1995
IVB	Invalidity Benefit
J.P.	Justice of the Peace
JSA	Jobseeker's Allowance
JSA 1995	Jobseekers Act 1995
JSA Regulations	Jobseeker's Allowance Regulations 1996
JSA (Transitional) Regulations	Jobseeker's Allowance (Transitional) Regulations 1996
JS(NI)O	Jobseekers (Northern Ireland) Act 1995
J.S.W.F.L.	Journal of Social Welfare and Family Law
J.S.W.L.	Journal of Social Welfare Law
J.S.S.L.	Journal of Social Security Law
K.I.R.	Knights Industrial Reports
LEL	Lower Earnings Limit
Ll.L.Report	Lloyds' Law Report
Lloyd's Rep.	Lloyd's Law Reports
L.S.G.	Law Society Gazette
LTAHAW	Living Together As Husband And Wife
L.&T.R.	Landlord and Tenant Reports
MA	Maternity Allowance
MAF	Medical Assessment Framework
MAT	Medical Appeal Tribunal
Maternity Benefit Regulations	Social Security (Maternity Benefit) Regulations 1975
Medical Evidence Regulations	Social Security (Medical Evidence) Regulations 1976
NCIP	Non-Contributory Invalidity Pension
NDPD	Notes on the Diagnosis of Prescribed Diseases
NI	National Insurance
N.I.	Northern Ireland Law Reports
NIC	National Insurance Contribution
N.L.J.	New Law Journal
N.P.C.	New Property Cases
Ogus, Barendt and Wikeley	A. Ogus, E. Barendt and N. Wikeley, *The Law of Social Security* (4th ed., Butterworths, 1995)
OPA	Overseas Pensions Act 1973
OPB	One Parent Benefit
OPSSAT	Office of the President of the Social Security Appeals Tribunal

Table of Abbreviations used in this Series

Overlapping Benefits Regulations	Social Security (Overlapping Benefits) Regulations 1979
Overpayments Regulations	Social Security (Payments on account, Overpayments and Recovery) Regulations
P.	Probate, Divorce and Admiralty
PAYE	Pay as You Earn
PCA	Personal Capability Assessment
P.&C.R.	Property, Planning & Compensation Reports
P.D.	Practice Direction
PD	Prescribed Disease
PPF	Pension Protection Fund
Pens.L.R.	Pension Law Reports
Persons Abroad Regulations	Social Security Benefit (Persons Abroad) Regulations 1975
Persons Residing Together Regulations	Social Security Benefit (Persons Residing Together) Regulations 1977
PIE	Period of Interruption of Employment
PILON	Pay in Lieu of Notice
PIW	Period of Incapacity for Work
P.L.R.	Planning Law Reports
Polygamous Marriage Regulations	Social Security and Family Allowances (Polygamous Marriages) Regulations 1975 (SI 1975/561)
PPF	Pension Protection Fund
Prescribed Diseases Regulations	Social Security (Industrial Injuries) (Prescribed Diseases) Regulations 1985
PTA	Pure Tone Audiometry
Q.B.	Queen's Bench
Recoupment Regulations	Social Security (Recoupment) Regulations 1990
REA	Reduced Earnings Allowance
RMO	Regional Medical Officer
RSI	Repetitive Strain Injury
R.T.R.	Road Traffic Reports
SAP	Statutory Adoption Pay
SAYE	Save As You Earn
S.C.	Session Cases
S.C.(H.L.)	Session Cases (House of Lords)
S.C.(P.C.)	Session Cases (Privy Council)
S.C.C.R.	Scottish Criminal Case Reports
S.C.L.R.	Scottish Civil Law Reports
SDA	Severe Disablement Allowance
SDP	Severe Disability Premium
SERPS	State Earnings-Related Pension Scheme
Severe Disablement Allowance	Social Security (Severe Disablement Regulations Allowance) Regulations 1984

Table of Abbreviations used in this Series

S.J.	Solicitors' Journal
S.J.L.B.	Solicitors' Journal Law Brief
S.L.T.	Scots Law Times
SMP	Statutory Maternity Pay
SPC	State Pension Credit
SPCA	State Pension Credit Act 2002
SPCA(NI)	State Pension Credit Act (Northern Ireland) 2002
SPP	Statutory Paternity Pay
SPP and SAP (Administration) Regulations 2002	Statutory Paternity Pay and Statutory Adoption Pay (Administration) Regulations 2002
SPP and SAP (General) Regulations 2002	Statutory Paternity Pay and Statutory Adoption Pay (General) Regulations 2002
SPP and SAP (National Health Service Employees) Regulations 2002	Statutory Paternity Pay and Statutory Adoption Pay (National Health Service Employees) Regulations 2002
SPP and SAP (Weekly Rates) Regulations 2002	Statutory Paternity Pay and Statutory Adoption Pay (Weekly Rates) Regulations 2002
SSA	Social Security Act
SSAA	Social Security Administration Act 1992*
SSAC	Social Security Advisory Committee
SSAT	Social Security Appeal Tribunal
SSCBA	Social Security Contributions and Benefits Act 1992*
SSCB(NI)	Social Security Contributions and Benefits (Northern Ireland) Act 1992
SS(CP)A	Social Security (Consequential Provisions) Act 1992
SSHBA	Social Security and Housing Benefits Act 1982
SS(MP)A	Social Security (Miscellaneous Provisions) Act 1977
SSP	Statutory Sick Pay
SSPA	Social Security Pensions Act 1975
S.T.C.	Simon's Tax Cases
S.T.C. (S.C.D.)	Simon's Tax Cases: Special Commissioners Decisions
STIB	Short-term Incapacity Benefit
S.T.I.	Simon's Tax Intelligence
TC	Tax Cases
TCA	Tax Credits Act
TC (Claims and Notifications) Regs	Tax Credit (Claims and Notifications) Regulations 2002
TCGA	Taxation of Chargeable Gains Act 1992
TCTM	Tax Credits Technical Manual
TMA	Taxes Management Act 1970
U.K.H.R.R.	United Kingdom Human Rights Reports

xlix

Table of Abbreviations used in this Series

Unemployment, Sickness and Invalidity Benefit Regs	Social Security (Unemployment, Sickness and Invalidity Benefit) Regulations 1983
USI Regulations	Social Security (Unemployment, Sickness and Invalidity Benefit) Regulations 1983
VERA 1992	Vehicle Excise and Registration Act 1992
WFTC	Working Family Tax Credit
White Paper	Jobseeker's Allowance, Cm.2687 (October 1994)
Widow's Benefit and Retirement Pensions Regulations	Social Security (Widow's Benefit and Retirement Pensions) Regulations 1979
Wikeley, Annotations	N. Wikeley, "Annotations to Jobseekers Act 1995 (c.18)" in *Current Law Statutes Annotated* (1995)
Wikeley, Ogus and Barendt	Wikeley, Ogus and Barendt, *The Law of Social Security* (5th ed., Butterworths, 2002)
W.L.R.	Weekly Law Reports
Workmen's Compensation Acts	Workmen's Compensation Acts 1925 to 1945
WRPA	Welfare Reform and Pensions Act 1999
WRP(NI)O	Welfare Reform and Pensions (Northern Ireland) Order 1999
WTC	Working Tax Credit
WTC (Entitlement and Maximum Rate) Regulations 2002	Working Tax Credit (Entitlement and Maximum Rate) Regulations 2002
W.T.L.R.	Wills & Trusts Law Reports

* Where the context makes it seem more appropriate, these could also be referred to as Contributions and Benefits Act 1992, Administration Act 1992 (AA 1992).

PART I

STATUTES

Race Relations Act 1976

(1976 c.24) (as amended)

Arrangement of Sections

1. Racial discrimination.
2. Discrimination by way of victimisation.
3. Meaning of "racial grounds", "racial group" etc.
19B. Discrimination by public authorities.
19C. Exceptions or further exceptions form section 19B for judicial legislative acts etc.
19D. Exceptions from section 19B for certain acts in immigration and nationality cases.
19E. Monitoring of exception in relation to immigration and nationality cases.
19F. Exceptions from section 19B for decisions not to prosecute etc.

An Act to make fresh provision with respect to discrimination on racial grounds and relations between people of different racial groups; and to make in the Sex Discrimination Act 1975 amendments for bringing provisions in that Act relating to its administration and enforcement into conformity with the corresponding provisions in this Act.

Racial discrimination

1.—(1) A person discriminates against another in any circumstances relevant for the purposes of any provision of this Act if—
  (a) on racial grounds he treats that other less favourably than he treats or would treat other persons; or
  (b) he applies to that other a requirement or condition which he applies or would apply equally to persons not of the same racial group as that other but—
      (i) which is such that the proportion of persons of the same racial group as that other who can comply with it is considerably smaller than the proportion of persons not of that racial group who can comply with it; and
      (ii) which he cannot show to be justifiable irrespective of the colour, race, nationality or ethnic or national origins of the person to whom it is applied; and
      (iii) which is to the detriment of that other because he cannot comply with it.

[¹ (1A) A person also discriminates against another if, in any circumstances relevant for the purposes of any provision referred to in subsection (1B), he applies to that other a provision, criterion or practice which he applies or would apply equally to persons not of the same race or ethnic or national origins as that other, but—
  (a) which puts or would put persons of the same race or ethnic or national origins as that other at a particular disadvantage when compared with other persons,
  (b) which puts that other at that disadvantage, and

(c) which he cannot show to be a proportionate means of achieving a legitimate aim.
(1B) The provisions mentioned in subsection (1A) are—
(a) Part II;
(b) sections 17 to 18D;
(c) section 19B, so far as relating to—
  (i) any form of social security;
  (ii) health care;
  (iii) any other form of social protection; and
  (iv) any form of social advantage;
  which does not fall within section 20;
(d) sections 20 to 24;
(e) sections 26A and 26B;
(f) sections 76 and 76ZA; and
(g) Part IV, in its application to the provisions referred to in paragraphs (a) to (f).
(1C) Where, by virtue of subsection (1A), a person discriminates against another, subsection (1)(b) does not apply to him.]
(2) It is hereby declared that, for the purposes of this Act, segregating a person from other persons on racial grounds is treating him less favourably than they are treated.

AMENDMENT

1. The Race Relations Act 1976 (Amendment) Regulations 2003 (SI 2003/1626), reg.3 (July 19, 2003).

Discrimination by way of victimisation

2.—(1) A person ("the discriminator") discriminates against another person ("the person victimised") in any circumstances relevant for the purposes of any provision of this Act if he treats the person victimised less favourably than in those circumstances he treats or would treat other persons, and does so by reason that the person victimised has—
(a) brought proceedings against the discriminator or any other person under this Act; or
(b) given evidence or information in connection with proceedings brought by any person against the discriminator or any other person under this Act; or
(c) otherwise done anything under or by reference to this Act in relation to the discriminator or any other person; or
(d) alleged that the discriminator or any other person has committed an act which (whether or not the allegation so states) would amount to a contravention of this Act,
or by reason that the discriminator knows that the person victimised intends to do any of those things, or suspects that the person victimised has done, or intends to do, any of them.
(2) Subsection (1) does not apply to treatment of a person by reason of any allegation made by him if the allegation was false and not made in good faith.

Meaning of "racial grounds", "racial group" etc.

3.—(1) In this Act, unless the context otherwise requires—
"racial grounds" means any of the following grounds, namely colour, race nationality or ethnic or national origins;

"racial group" means a group of persons defined by reference to colour, race, nationality or ethnic or national origins, and references to a person's racial group refer to any racial group into which he falls.

(2) The fact that a racial group comprises two or more distinct racial groups does not prevent it from constituting a particular racial group for the purposes of this Act.

(3) In this Act—
(a) references to discrimination refer to any discrimination falling within section 1 or 2; and
(b) references to racial discrimination refer to any discrimination falling within section 1,
and related expressions shall be construed accordingly.

(4) A comparison of the case of a person of a particular racial group with that of a person not of that group under section 1(1) [¹ or (1A)] must be such that the relevant circumstances in the one case are the same, or not materially different, in the other.

AMENDMENT

1. The Race Relations Act 1976 (Amendment) Regulations 2003 (SI 2003/1626), reg.4 (July 19, 2003).

[¹ Harassment

3A.—(1) A person subjects another to harassment in any circumstances relevant for the purposes of any provision referred to in section 1(1B) where, on grounds of race or ethnic or national origins, he engages in unwanted conduct which has the purpose or effect of—
(a) violating that other person's dignity, or
(b) creating an intimidating, hostile, degrading, humiliating or offensive environment for him.

(2) Conduct shall be regarded as having the effect specified in paragraph (a) or (b) of subsection (1) only if, having regard to all the circumstances, including in particular the perception of that other person, it should reasonably be considered as having that effect.]

AMENDMENT

1. The Race Relations Act 1976 (Amendment) Regulations 2003 (SI 2003/1626), reg.5 (July 19, 2003).

[¹ Discrimination by public authorities

[**19B.**—(1) It is unlawful for a public authority in carrying out any functions of the authority to do any act which constitutes discrimination.

[² (1A) It is unlawful for a public authority to subject a person to harassment in the course of carrying out any functions of the authority which consist of the provision of—
(a) any form of social security;
(b) healthcare;
(c) any other form of social protection; or
(d) any form of social advantage,
which does not fall within section 20.]

(2) In this section "public authority"—
(a) includes any person certain of whose functions are functions of a public nature; but

(b) does not include any person mentioned in subsection (3).
(3) The persons mentioned in this subsection are—
(a) either House of Parliament;
(b) a person exercising functions in connection with proceedings in Parliament;
(c) the Security Service;
(d) the Secret Intelligence Service;
(e) the Government Communications Headquarters; and
(f) any unit or part of a unit of any of the naval, military or air forces of the Crown which is for the time being required by the Secretary of State to assist the Government Communications Headquarters in carrying out its functions.
(4) In relation to a particular act, a person is not a public authority by virtue only of subsection (2)(a) if the nature of the act is private.
(5) This section is subject to sections 19C to 19F.
(6) Nothing in this section makes unlawful any act of discrimination which—
(a) is made unlawful by virtue of any other provision of this Act; or
(b) would be so made but for any provision made by or under this Act.]

AMENDMENTS

1. This section was inserted by the Race Relations (Amendment) Act 2000 (c.34) s.1 (April 2, 2001).
2. The Race Relations Act 1976 (Amendment) Regulations 2003 (SI 2003/1626), reg.20 (July 19, 2003).

GENERAL NOTE

1.7   The Race Relations (Amendment) Act 2000 extended the prohibition of racial discrimination to "public authorities". This includes the statutory authorities who make the initial decisions in relation to benefit claims. Note that there are special provisions in s.19B in relation to judicial and legislative acts. It may be that claimants will assert that they have been victims of racial discrimination in decisions relating to their benefit entitlement which tribunals and Commissioners will need to address.

[1 Exceptions or further exceptions from section 19B for judicial and legislative acts etc.

1.8   [19C.—(1) Section 19B does not apply to—
(a) any judicial act (whether done by a court, tribunal or other person); or
(b) any act done on the instructions, or on behalf, of a person acting in a judicial capacity.
(2) Section 19B does not apply to any act of, or relating to, making, confirming or approving any enactment or Order in Council or any instrument made by a Minister of the Crown under an enactment.
(3) Section 19B does not apply to any act of, or relating to, making or approving arrangements, or imposing requirements or conditions, of a kind [2 excepted by] section 41.
(4) Section 19B does not apply to any act of, or relating to, imposing a requirement, or giving an express authorisation, of a kind mentioned in section 19D(3) in relation to the carrying out of [3 immigration functions].
(5) In this section—
[3 "immigration functions"] has the meaning given in section 19D; and
"Minister of the Crown" includes the National Assembly for Wales and a member of the Scottish Executive.]

(1976, c.24, s.19C) (as amended)

AMENDMENTS

1. This section was inserted by the Race Relations (Amendment) Act 2000 (c.34) s.1 (April 2, 2001).
2. The Race Relations Act 1976 (Amendment) Regulations 2003 (SI 2003/1626) reg.21 (July 19, 2003).
3. The Nationality, Immigration and Asylum Act 2002 (Consequential and Incidental Provisions) Order 2003 (SI 2003/1016) (April 4, 2003).

[¹ Exception from section 19B for certain acts in immigration and nationality cases

[**19D.**—(1) Section 19B does not make it unlawful for a relevant person to discriminate against another person on grounds of nationality or ethnic or national origins in carrying out [immigration functions].

(2) For the purposes of subsection (1), "relevant person" means—
 (a) a Minister of the Crown acting personally; or
 (b) any other person acting in accordance with a relevant authorisation.

(3) In subsection (2), "relevant authorisation" means a requirement imposed or express authorisation given—
 (a) with respect to a particular case or class of case, by a Minister of the Crown acting personally;
 (b) with respect to a particular class of case—
   (i) by any of the enactments mentioned in subsection (5); or
   (ii) by any instrument made under or by virtue of any of those enactments.

[² (4) In subsection (1) "immigration functions" means functions exercisable by virtue of any of the enactments mentioned in subsection (5).

(5) Those enactments are—
 (a) the Immigration Acts [³ (within the meaning of section 44 of the Asylum and Immigration (Treatment of Claimants, etc.) Act 2004) excluding sections 28A to 28K of the Immigration Act 1971 (c 77) so far as they relate to offences under Part III of that Act and excluding section 14 of the Asylum and Immigration (Treatment of Claimants, etc.) Act 2004];
 (b) the Special Immigration Appeals Commission Act 1997 (c 68);
 (c) provision made under section 2(2) of the European Communities Act 1972 (c 68) which relates to immigration or asylum; and
 (d) any provision of Community law which relates to immigration or asylum.]]

AMENDMENTS

1. This section was inserted by the Race Relations (Amendment) Act 2000 (c.34) s.1 (April 2, 2001).
2. Substituted by the Nationality, Immigration and Asylum Act 2002, s.6(1), (3) (November 7, 2002).
3. The Asylum and Immigration (Treatment of Claimants, etc.) Act 2004 (Commencement No. 2) Order 2004 (SI 2004/2999) (December 1, 2004).

[¹ Monitoring of exception in relation to immigration and nationality cases

[**19E.**—(1) The Secretary of State shall appoint a person who is not a member of his staff to act as a monitor.

(2) Before appointing any such person, the Secretary of State shall consult the Commission.

(3) The person so appointed shall monitor, in such manner as the Secretary of State may determine—
- (a) the likely effect on the operation of the exception in section 19D of any relevant authorisation relating to the carrying out of [²immigration functions] which has been given by a Minister of the Crown acting personally; and
- (b) the operation of that exception in relation to acts which have been done by a person acting in accordance with such an authorisation.

(4) The monitor shall make an annual report on the discharge of his functions to the Secretary of State.

(5) The Secretary of State shall lay a copy of any report made to him under subsection (4) before each House of Parliament.

(6) The Secretary of State shall pay to the monitor such fees and allowances (if any) as he may determine.

(7) [². . .]]

AMENDMENTS

1. This section was inserted by the Race Relations (Amendment) Act 2000 (c.34) s.1 (April 2, 2001).

2. Nationality, Immigration and Asylum Act 2002, s.6 (November 7, 2002).

[¹ **Exceptions from section 19B for decisions not to prosecute etc.**

19F. *Omitted.*

AMENDMENT

1. This section was inserted by the Race Relations (Amendment) Act 2000 (c.34) s.1 (April 2, 2001).

Forfeiture Act 1982

(1982 c.34)

ARRANGEMENT OF SECTIONS

1. The "forfeiture rule"
2. *Omitted.*
3. *Omitted.*
4. Commissioner to decide whether rule applies to social security benefits
5. Exclusion of murder
6. *Omitted.*
7. *Omitted.*

An Act to provide for relief for persons guilty of unlawful killing from forfeiture of inheritance and other rights; to enable such persons to apply for financial provision out of the deceased's estate; to provide for the question whether pension and social security benefits have been forfeited to be determined by the Social Security Commissioners; and for connected purposes.

[13th July 1982]

(1982 c.34, s.1)

1.—(1) In this Act, the "forfeiture rule" means the rule of public policy which in certain circumstances precludes a person who has unlawfully killed another from acquiring a benefit in consequence of the killing.

(2) References in this Act to a person who has unlawfully killed another include a reference to a person who has unlawfully aided, abetted, counselled or procured the death of that other and references in this Act to unlawful killing shall be interpreted accordingly.

GENERAL NOTE

There is a general rule of English law that a person should not benefit from his wrongdoing. In particular, the forfeiture rule has the effect that, in certain circumstances, a person who has unlawfully killed another forfeits his or her right to any benefit that might otherwise have been acquired as a result of the death, e.g. an inheritance under a will or an indemnity under an insurance policy. In *R. v National Insurance Commissioner, Ex p. Connor* [1981] Q.B. 758 (also reported as an appendix to *R(G) 2/79*), the forfeiture rule was applied to prevent a woman convicted of the manslaughter of her husband from obtaining entitlement to widow's benefit. A Tribunal of Commissioners subsequently held that it also applied to entitlement to a Category B retirement pension based on a victim's contribution record (*R(P) 1/88*). The same rule applies in Scotland (*Burns v Secretary of State for Social Services* [1985] S.L.T. 351 (also reported as an appendix to *R(G) 1/83*)).

There is an "unlawful killing" where death is the direct consequence of "criminal conduct", including aiding and abetting suicide, which is a crime under the Suicide Act 1961 even though suicide itself is not (*Dunbar v Plant* [1998] Ch. 412). It follows that the forfeiture rule applies in any case of manslaughter, including manslaughter on the ground of diminished responsibility (*R(FP) 1/05*, in which it was held that *R(G) 3/84* must now be regarded as wrongly decided, and *In re Land, decd.* [2006] EWHC 2069 (Ch); [2007] 1 W.L.R. 1009), and presumably also applies to causing death by dangerous driving. It also follows that the forfeiture rule applies if the killing was abroad, provided that the death was the direct consequence of what would have been a crime in Great Britain (*R(G) 1/88*). Subs.(2) recognises that acting as an accessory to a crime may be enough to cause the forfeiture rule to apply and, in *R(FG) 1/04*, it was held that a person convicted under s.4 of the Offences against the Person Act 1861 of soliciting to murder was likely to have "counselled . . . the death of [the victim]" for the purposes of the subsection. The forfeiture rule does not apply where a person is of unsound mind to the extent of being incapable of committing a crime (*Re Houghton, Houghton v Houghton* [1915] 2 Ch. 173).

It is not necessary that the claimant have been convicted of any crime, provided that the Commissioner is satisfied that he or she committed one (*Gray v Barr* [1970] 2 Q.B. 626, where a shotgun with which the victim was being threatened went off accidentally and the perpetrator was acquitted of manslaughter after a summing up that was "remarkable for failing to draw the jury's attention to the formidable evidence against [him]"). However, a Commissioner would be slow to go behind an acquittal and it has been held that the criminal standard of proof should be applied in such a case (*R(G) 2/90*). A Commissioner would probably be even slower to go behind a conviction but, in *R(FP) 1/05*, there was left open the possibility of finding in another case that a conviction of manslaughter on the grounds of diminished responsibility had been inappropriate and that a verdict of not guilty by reason of insanity would have been the correct one.

Section 4 of this Act permits a Commissioner to modify the forfeiture rule so that it does not apply with its full force, but s.5 provides that it cannot be modified in a case of murder.

2. *Omitted.*
3. *Omitted.*

Forfeiture Act 1982

Commissioner to decide whether rule applies to social security benefits

1.17

4.—(1) Where a question arises as to whether, if a person were otherwise entitled to or eligible for any benefit or advantage under a relevant enactment, he would be precluded by virtue of the forfeiture rule from receiving the whole or part of the benefit or advantage, that question shall (notwithstanding anything in any relevant enactment) be determined by a Commissioner.

[²(1A) Where a Commissioner determines that the forfeiture rule has precluded a person (in this section referred to as "the offender") who has unlawfully killed another from receiving the whole or part of any such benefit or advantage, the Commissioner may make a decision under this subsection modifying the effect of that rule and may do so whether the unlawful killing occurred before or after the coming into force of this subsection.

(1B) The Commissioner shall not make a decision under subsection (1A) above modifying the effect of the forfeiture rule in any case unless he is satisfied that having regard to the conduct of the offender and of the deceased and to such other circumstances as appear to the Commissioner to be material, the justice of the case requires the effect of the rule to be so modified in that case.

(1C) Subject to subsection (1D) below, a decision under subsection (1A) above may modify the effect of the forfeiture rule in either or both of the following ways—
  (a) so that it applies only in respect of a specified proportion of the benefit or advantage;
  (b) so that it applies in respect of the benefit or advantage only for a specified period of time.

(1D) Such a decision may not modify the effect of the forfeiture rule so as to allow any person to receive the whole or any part of a benefit or advantage in respect of any period before the commencement of this subsection.

(1E) If the Commissioner thinks it expedient to do so, he may direct that his decision shall apply to any future claim for a benefit or advantage under a relevant enactment, on which a question such as is mentioned in subsection (1) above arises by reason of the same unlawful killing.

(1F) It is immaterial for the purposes of subsection (1E) above whether the claim is in respect of the same or a different benefit or advantage.

(1G) For the purposes of obtaining a decision whether the forfeiture rule should be modified the Secretary of State may refer to a commissioner for review any determination of a question such as is mentioned in subsection (1) above that was made before the commencement of subsections (1A) to (1F) above (whether by a Commissioner or not) and shall do so if the offender requests him to refer such a determination.

(1H) Subsections (1A) to (1F) above shall have effect on a reference under subsection (1G) above as if in subsection (1A) the words "it has been determined" were substituted for the words "a Commissioner determines".]

(2) Regulations under this section may make such provisions as appears to [¹the Lord Chancellor] to be necessary or expedient for carrying this section into effect; and (without prejudice to the generality of that) the regulations may, in relation to the question mentioned in subsection (1) above or any determination under that subsection [² or any decision under subsection (1A) above]—

(1982 c.34, s.4)

(a) apply any provision of any relevant enactment, with or without modifications, or exclude or contain provisions corresponding to any such provisions; and
(b) make provisions for purposes corresponding to those for which provisions may be made by regulations under [⁶ section 16 of the Social Security Act 1998] (matters relating to adjudication)].

(3) The power to make regulations under this section shall be exercisable by statutory instrument which shall be subject to annulment in pursuance of a resolution of either House of Parliament.

(4) [⁴ Section 175(3) to (5) of the Social Security Contributions and Benefits Act 1992] (provision about extent of power to make regulations) shall apply to the power to make regulations conferred by this section as it applies to the power to make regulations conferred by that Act, but as if for references to that Act there were substituted references to this section.

(5) In this section—
"Commissioner" has the same meaning as in the [⁶ Chapter II of Part 1 of the Social Security Act 1998]; and
"relevant enactment" means any provision of the following and any instrument made by virtue of such a provision:
the Personal Injuries (Emergency Provisions) Act 1939.
the Pensions (Navy, Army, Air Force and Mercantile
Marine) Act 1939,
the Polish Resettlement Act 1947.
[⁴ . . .],
[³ the Social Security Acts 1975 to 1991],
[⁴ the Social Security Contributions and Benefits Act 1992],
[⁷ section 1 of the Armed Forces (Pensions and Compensation) Act 2004,]
[⁵ the Pension Schemes Act 1993]
and any other enactment relating to pensions or social security prescribed by regulations under this section.

AMENDMENTS

1. SI 1984/1818, art.3 (January 1, 1985).
2. Social Security Act 1986, s.76 (July 25, 1986).
3. Statutory Sick Pay Act 1991, s.3(1)(c) (February 12, 1991).
4. Social Security (Consequential Provisions) Act 1992, ss.3 and 4 and Sch.2, para.63.
5. Pension Schemes Act 1993, Sch.8, para.15 (February 7, 1994).
6. Social Security Act 1998, Sch.7, para.11 (July 5, 1999).
7. Armed Forces (Pensions and Compensation) Act 2004, s.7(1) (April 6, 2005).

DEFINITIONS

"Commissioner"—see subs.(5).
"forfeiture rule"—see s.1(1).
"offender"—see subs.(1A).
"relevant enactment—see subs.(5).

GENERAL NOTE

Subss.(1A) to (1H) were added after a Tribunal of Commissioners held that subs.(1) gave Commissioners power only to decide whether the forfeiture rule applied and did not give them any power to modify it *(R/G) 1/84, R(G) 2/84, R(P) 1/84)*. Whenever a claimant's entitlement to a social security benefit under a

1.18

"relevant enactment" (see subs.(5)) arises at least partly in consequence of the death of someone the claimant has killed, there is likely to arise the question whether the killing was unlawful and the forfeiture rule applies. The Secretary of State or other authority responsible for determining entitlement to benefit is then bound to refer the case to a Commissioner so that the Commissioner can decide under subs.(1) whether the forfeiture rule does apply (see the note to s.1) and, if so, whether it should be modified under subs.(1A).

The forfeiture rule cannot be modified in a case of murder (see s.5). However, the Act recognises that in other cases the forfeiture rule is capable of being unduly harsh and so a Commissioner may modify the effect of the rule. The paramount consideration when considering modification is the culpability of the claimant (*Dunbar v Plant* [1998] Ch. 412). A Commissioner has a broad discretion and may even decide that the forfeiture rule should have no effect at all, although that will be rare (*R(G) 1/98*, holding *R(G) 3/90* to have been implicitly overruled). Equally, though, a Commissioner may decline to modify the effect of the forfeiture rule. In *R(G) 1/91*, the Commissioner refused to modify the rule where the Court of Appeal had quashed a conviction for murder and substituted a verdict of manslaughter on the ground of diminished responsibility because the trial judge had failed adequately to address the jury in relation to two written medical reports put to a defence witness in cross-examination when the prosecution had failed to call the authors of the reports to give evidence. The Commissioner, who was not bound by the same rules of evidence, held that the weight of evidence was against a finding of diminished responsibility and pointed to a finding of murder, although he acknowledged that s.5 did not apply because the claimant did not actually stand convicted of murder. In *R(FP) 1/05*, where the claimant's plea of guilty to manslaughter on the ground of diminished responsibility had been accepted, the Commissioner considered the claimant's culpability to be low but he still refused to modify the forfeiture rule because only 47p pw was at stake and he considered that the effect of the forfeiture rule was not harsh but was just.

Modification is usually in the form of an order directing that the forfeiture rule will have effect only for a certain period or that it will have effect only to reduce benefit by a certain proportion or both (subs.(1C)). For regulations made under this section, see the Social Security Commissioners (Procedure) Regulations 1999 and, in particular, regs 14, 15 and 29. A Social Security Commissioner determining a forfeiture question arising under either of the 1939 Acts, the 1947 Act or the 2004 Act mentioned in subs.(5) is known as a "Pensions Appeal Commissioner" (*ibid.* reg.4(3)).

Exclusion of murderers

1.19   **5.**—Nothing in this Act or in any order made under section 2 or referred to in section 3(1) of the Act [¹ or in any decision made under section 4(1A) of this Act] shall affect the application of the forfeiture rule in the case of a person who stands convicted of murder.

AMENDMENT

1. Social Security Act 1986, s.76(4) (July 25, 1986).

DEFINITION

"forfeiture rule"—see s.1(1).

GENERAL NOTE

1.20   This section was applied in *R(G) 1/90*. Note that it applies only if the claimant has actually been convicted of murder, although if a Commissioner is satisfied that the actions of the claimant amounted to murder notwithstanding the lack of a conviction, the Commissioner would be likely to refuse to exercise the power of modification conferred by s.4(1A) anyway (see, for instance, *R(G) 1/91*). In *R(G) 1/88*, the claimant

(1982 c.34, s.5)

was convicted of homicide in Germany where the killing took place and the Commissioner held that it was necessary to consider whether the claimant's actions would have amounted to murder had the killing taken place in Great Britain. A conviction for soliciting to murder, contrary to s.4 of the Offences against the Person Act 1861, does not amount to a conviction for murder, even though it may be tantamount to finding the claimant was an accessory to murder which, in many cases, would mean that he or she could in fact have been convicted of murder *(R(FG) 1/04)*.

6. Omitted.
7. Omitted.

Social Security Administration Act 1992

(1992 c.5)

Arrangement of Sections

Part I

Claims for and Payments and General Administration of Benefit Section

Necessity of Claim

1. Entitlement to benefit dependent on claim.
2. Retrospective effect of provisions making entitlement to benefit dependent on claim.
2A. Claim or full entitlement to certain benefits conditional on work-focused interview.
2B. Supplementary provisions relating to work-focused interviews.
2C. Optional work-focused interviews.

Bereavement benefits

3. Late claims for widowhood benefit where death is difficult to establish.
4. Treatment of payments of benefit to certain widows.

Claims and payments regulations

5. Regulations about claims for and payments of benefit.

Community charge benefits etc.†

6. *Omitted.*
7. Relationship between community charge benefits† and other benefits.
7A. Sharing of functions as regards certain claims and information.

†*Unreliable heading. (Council tax benefit replaced community charge benefits w.e.f. 1.4.93.)*

Industrial injuries benefit

8. Notification of accidents, etc.

9. Medical examination and treatment of claimants.
10. Obligations of claimants.

Disabled person's tax credit

11. Initial claims and repeat claims.

The social fund

12. Necessity of application for certain payments.

Child benefit

13. Necessity of application for child benefit.

Statutory sick pay

14. Duties of employees etc. in relation to statutory sick pay.

Statutory maternity pay

15. Duties of women etc in relation to statutory maternity pay.

Payments in respect of mortgage interest etc.

15A. Payment out of benefit of sums in respect of mortgage interest etc.

Emergency payments

16. Emergency payments by local authorities and other bodies.

PART II

ADJUDICATION

17.–70. *Repealed.*

PART III

OVERPAYMENTS AND ADJUSTMENTS OF BENEFIT

Misrepresentation etc.

71. Overpayments—general.
71ZA. Overpayments out of social fund.

Jobseeker's allowance

71A. Recovery of jobseeker's allowance: severe hardship cases.

Misrepresentation etc. (continued)

72. Special provision as to recovery of income support.

(1992 c.5)

Adjustments of benefits

73. Overlapping benefits—general.
74. Income support and other payments.
74A. Payment of benefit where maintenance payments collected by Secretary of State.

Housing benefit

75. *Omitted.*

Community charge benefits†

76. *Omitted.*
77. *Omitted.*

†*Unreliable heading. (Council tax benefit replaced community charge benefits w.e.f. 1.4.93.)*

Social fund awards

78. Recovery of social fund awards.

Northern Ireland payments

79. Recovery of Northern Ireland payments.

Adjustment of child benefit

80. Child benefit—overlap with benefits under legislation of other member States.

Part IV

Recovery from Compensation Payments

81–104. *Repealed.*

Part V

Income Support and the Duty to Maintain

105. Failure to maintain—general.
106. Recovery of expenditure on benefit from person liable for maintenance.
107. Recovery of expenditure on income support: additional amounts and transfer of orders.
108. Reduction of expenditure on income support: certain maintenance orders to be enforceable by the Secretary of State.
109. Diversion of arrested earnings to Secretary of State—Scotland.

Social Security Administration Act 1992

PART VI

ENFORCEMENT

110.–121. *Omitted.*

PART VII

PROVISION OF INFORMATION

Inland Revenue

122. *Omitted.*

Persons employed or formerly employed in social security administration or adjudication

123. *Omitted.*

The Registration Service

124. Provisions relating to age, death and marriage.
125. Regulations as to notification of deaths.

Personal representatives—income support and supplementary benefit

126. Personal representatives to give information about the estate of a deceased person who was in receipt of income support or supplementary benefit.
126A. *Omitted.*

Housing benefit

127. *Repealed.*

Community charge benefits

128. *Repealed.*

Expedited claims for housing and council tax benefit

128A. *Repealed.*

Statutory sick pay and other benefits

129. Disclosure by Secretary of State for purpose of determination of period of entitlement to statutory sick pay.
130. Duties of employers—statutory sick pay and claims for other benefits.

(1992 c.5)

Statutory maternity pay and other benefits

131. Disclosure by Secretary of State for purpose of determination of period of entitlement to statutory maternity pay.
132. Duties of employers—statutory maternity pay and claims for other benefits.

Maintenance proceedings

133. Furnishing of addresses for maintenance proceedings, etc.

PART VIII

ARRANGEMENTS FOR HOUSING BENEFIT AND COMMUNITY CHARGE BENEFITS† AND RELATED SUBSIDIES

134.–140. *Omitted.*

PART IX

ALTERATION OF CONTRIBUTIONS ETC.

141.–149. *Omitted.*

PART X

REVIEW AND ALTERATION OF BENEFITS

150.–154. *Omitted.*

PART XI

COMPUTATION OF BENEFITS

155. Effect of alteration of rates of benefit under Parts II to V of Contributions and Benefits Act.
155A. Power to anticipate pensions up-rating order.
156. Up-rating under section 150 above of pensions increased under section 52(3) of the Contributions and Benefits Act.
157. Effect of alteration of rates of child benefit.
158. Treatment of excess benefit as paid on account of child benefit.
159. Effect of alteration in the component rates of income support.
159A. Effect of alteration of rates of a jobseeker's allowance.
159B. Effect of alterations affecting state pension credit.
160. Implementation of increases in income support due to attainment of particular ages.
160A. Implementation of increases in income-based jobseeker's allowance due to attainment of particular ages.

17

Social Security Administration Act 1992

Part XII

Finance

161.–166. *Omitted.*
167. The social fund.
168. Allocations from social fund.
169. Adjustments between social fund and other sources of finance.

Part XIII

Advisory Bodies and Consultation

The Social Security Advisory Committee and the Industrial Injuries Advisory Council

170. The Social Security Advisory Committee.
171. The Industrial Injuries Advisory Council.
172. Functions of Committee and Council in relation to regulations.
173. Cases in which consultation is not required.
174.–176. *Omitted.*

Part XIV

Social Security Systems Outside Great Britain

Co-ordination

177. Co-ordination with Northern Ireland.

Reciprocity

178. Reciprocal arrangements with Northern Ireland—income-related benefits and child benefit.
179. Reciprocal agreements with countries outside the United Kingdom.
179A. Exchange of information with overseas authorities.

Part XV

Miscellaneous

Travelling expenses

180. *Omitted.*

(1992 c.5)

Offences

181. *Omitted.*
182. *Omitted.*

National Insurance Numbers

Industrial injuries and diseases

182c. Requirement is apply for National Insurance Number
183. *Omitted.*
184. *Omitted.*

Workmen's compensation etc.

185. *Omitted.*

Supplementary benefit etc.

186. Application of provisions of Act to supplementary benefit etc.

Miscellaneous

187. Certain benefit to be inalienable.
188. *Omitted.*

PART XVI

GENERAL

Subordinate legislation

189. Regulations and orders—general.
190. Parliamentary control of orders and regulations.

Supplementary

191. Interpretation—general.
192. Short title, commencement and extent.

SCHEDULES:

1. Claims for benefit made or treated as made before 1st October 1990.
2.–9. *Omitted.*
10. Supplementary benefit etc.

Social Security Administration Act 1992

Part I

Claims for and Payments and General Administration of Benefit

Necessity of claim

Entitlement to benefit dependent on claim

1.—(1) Except in such cases as may be prescribed, and subject to the following provisions of this section and to section 3 below, no person shall be entitled to any benefit unless, in addition to any other conditions relating to that benefit being satisfied—
  (a) he makes a claim for it in the manner, and within the time, prescribed in relation to that benefit by regulations under this Part of this Act; or
  (b) he is treated by virtue of such regulations as making a claim for it.
[[2](1A) No person whose entitlement to any benefit depends on his making a claim shall be entitled to the benefit unless subsection (1B) below is satisfied in relation both to the person making the claim and to any other person in respect of whom he is claiming benefit.
(1B) This subsection is satisfied in relation to a person if—
  (a) the claim is accompanied by—
    (i) a statement of the person's national insurance number and information or evidence establishing that that number has been allocated to the person; or
    (ii) information or evidence enabling the national insurance number that has been allocated to the person to be ascertained; or
  (b) the person makes an application for a national insurance number to be allocated to him which is accompanied by information or evidence enabling such a number to be so allocated.
(1C) Regulations may make provision disapplying subsection (1A) above in the case of—
  (a) prescribed benefits;
  (b) prescribed descriptions of persons making claims; or
  (c) prescribed descriptions of persons in respect of whom benefit is claimed,
or in other prescribed circumstances.]
(2) Where under subsection (1) above a person is required to make a claim or to be treated as making a claim for a benefit in order to be entitled to it—
  (a) if the benefit is a [[3] . . .] [[3]bereavement payment, the person] shall not be entitled to it in respect of a death occurring more than 12 months before the date on which the claim is made or treated as made; and
  (b) if the benefit is any other benefit except disablement benefit or reduced earnings allowance, the person shall not be entitled to it in respect of any period more than 12 months before that date,
except as provided by section 3 below.
(3) Where a person purports to make a claim on behalf of another—
  (a) for an attendance allowance by virtue of section 66(1) of the Contributions and Benefits Act; or

(1992 c.5, s.1)

  (b) for a disability living allowance by virtue of section 72(5) or 73(12) of that Act,

that other shall be regarded for the purposes of this section as making the claim, notwithstanding that it is made without his knowledge or authority.

  (4) In this section and in section 2 below "benefit" means—

    (a) benefit as defined in section 122 of the Contributions and Benefits Act;

[¹(aa) a jobseeker's allowance;] and

[⁴(ab) state pension credit;] and

    (b) any income-related benefit.

  (5) This section (which corresponds to section 165A of the 1975 Act, as it had effect immediately before this Act came into force) applies to claims made on or after 1st October 1990 or treated by virtue of regulations under that section or this section as having been made on or after that date.

  (6) Schedule 1 to this Act shall have effect in relation to other claims.

AMENDMENTS

  1. Jobseekers Act 1995, Sch.2, para.38 (October 7, 1996).
  2. Social Security Administration (Fraud) Act 1997, s.19 (December 1, 1997).
  3. Welfare Reform and Pensions Act 1999, Sch.8, para.16 (April 24, 2000).
  4. State Pension Credit Act 2002, s.11 and Sch.1, paras 1–2. (April 7, 2003).

DERIVATION

Social Security Act 1975, s.165A.

DEFINITIONS

  "the 1975 Act"—see s.191.
  "claim"—*ibid.*
  "disablement benefit"—*ibid.*
  "the Contributions and Benefits Act"—*ibid.*
  "income-related benefit"—*ibid.*
  "prescribe"—*ibid.*

GENERAL NOTE

Subs. (1)

The general rule is that there cannot be entitlement to benefit unless a claim is made for it. But note that this is a general rule, not a universal one. The general rule is subject to special cases for which special provision is made, and to the provisions of this section. "Benefit" for the purposes of this section is defined in para.(4). Section 1 applies to claims made on or after October 1, 1990. Schedule 1 deals with earlier claims.

The introduction of the predecessor of s.1 was precipitated by the decision of the House of Lords in *Insurance Officer v McCaffrey* [1984] 1 W.L.R. 1353 that (subject to an express provision to the contrary) a person was entitled to benefit if he met the conditions of entitlement even though he had not made a claim for that benefit. Claiming went to payability, not entitlement. This was contrary to the long-standing assumption of the Department and was corrected with effect from September 2, 1985.

Section 3, which is excluded from the operation of s.1, deals with late claims for bereavement benefit where the death of the spouse is difficult to establish.

Secretary of State for Work and Pensions v Nelligan, R(P)2/03 [2003] EWCA Civ 555, Judgment of April 15, 2003, is the Court of Appeal's decision on the appeal

Social Security Administration Act 1992

against the Commissioner's decision in *CP/3643/2001*. The Commissioner had concluded that s.43(5) of the Contributions and Benefits Act 1992 contained an exception to the general rule that there must always be a claim for benefit. He decided that a married woman does not need to claim *both* a Category A *and* a Category B pension in order to obtain payment of the latter. The Court of Appeal allowed the appeal. It concluded that s.43(5) only applied where there had been a claim for *both* a Category A *and* a Category B retirement pension. There was no derogation from the general principle in s.1 of the Administration Act 1992. The Court of Appeal considered that s.43 was about making a choice between two competing entitlements rather than about establishing entitlement to benefit.

Subss. (1A)–(1C)

1.27 These provisions were inserted by s.19 of the Social Security Administration (Fraud) Act 1997 and came into force on December 1, 1997. The effect of subss.(1A) and (1B) is to impose an additional condition of entitlement to benefit where subs.(1)(a) applies (i.e. in the normal case). Claimants will not be entitled to benefit unless when making a claim they provide a national insurance (NI) number, together with information or evidence to show that it is theirs, or provide evidence or information to enable their NI number to be traced, or apply for a NI number and provided sufficient information or evidence for one to be allocated to them. This requirement for an NI number applies to both claimants and any person for whom they are claiming, except in prescribed circumstances (subs.(1C)). See reg.2A of the Income Support Regulations, and the Jobseeker's Allowance Regulations, for who is exempt and note the different dates from which this requirement bites for these benefits.

Subs. (2)

1.28 This provision imposes an overall limit of 12 months to the entitlement to benefit before the date of claim. Not all benefits are caught by subs.(1) and there is a further exclusion in para.(b). Regulation 19 of and Sch.4 to the Claims and Payments Regulations impose the ordinary time-limits for claiming and since April 1997 allow the limits in the cases of income support, JSA, family credit and disability working allowance (and their successor benefits) to be extended for a maximum of three months only in tightly defined circumstances. The test of good cause has been abandoned. Where there is such an extension, the claim is then treated as made on the first day of the period for which the claim is allowed to relate (reg.6(3)). Although the drafting is not at all clear, the reference in subs.(2) to the 12-month limit from the date on which the claim is made or is treated as made seems to make the limit start from the date fixed by reg.6(3). However, reg.19(4) prevents an extension of the time-limit for the benefits covered by reg.6(3) leading to entitlement earlier than three months before the actual date of claim. But the restriction seems to stem from that regulation and not from s.1(2), or the earlier forms set out in Sch.1.

Note that from April 1997 the time limit for claiming social fund maternity and funeral payments is three months (Claims and Payments Regulations, reg.19(1) and Sch.4, paras 8 and 9) and there is no longer any provision allowing claims for these payments to be made outside this time limit.

Subs. (3)

1.29 Subsection (3) deals with a particular situation which may arise in connection with claims to attendance allowance and disability living allowance. In general, there is no objection to claims being made by someone on behalf of another person, though the Department will require a clear indication that the agent is acting with the express authority of the person claiming.

Subs. (4)

This subsection contains the definition of "benefit" for the purposes of the section.

(1992 c.5, s.1)

The starting point is the definition of benefit in s.122 of the Contributions and Benefits Act, which (so far as current benefits are concerned) refers to benefits under Pts II to V of the Contributions and Benefits Act. That brings in the following contributory benefits: incapacity benefit, sickness benefit, invalidity benefit, maternity allowance, benefits for widows and widowers, Category A and B retirement pensions, child's special allowance, and graduated retirement benefit; as well as the following non-contributory benefits: attendance allowance, severe disablement allowance, carer's allowance, disability living allowance, guardian's allowance, and Category C and D retirement pensions. Part IV of the Contributions and Benefits Act provides for increases of certain benefits for dependants, while Part V relates to benefit for industrial injuries. Specific provisions of para.(4) add Jobseeker's Allowance, State pension credit, and any income-related benefit.

Though fairly comprehensive, this list does not include child benefit and winter fuel payments. On the latter see *CIS/2337/2004*, para.9. This does not mean that claims are not required for those benefits (indeed provision is made for claims elsewhere in the social security legislation), but it does mean that s.1 does not apply in relation to entitlement to benefit being dependent upon a claim.

It can be argued that the form of decision will differ depending upon whether a claim is a condition of entitlement. It is at least arguable that, if a claim is not a condition of entitlement and no claim has been made but a person claims to be entitled to the benefit, any decision should be in the form that there is a nil award. By contrast, if an adverse decision is made because no claim has been made where a claim is a condition of entitlement, then the form of the decision should be that there is no entitlement. This fine distinction is unlikely to impress those seeking a benefit, but may assist in drawing a distinction between the majority of cases where s.1 makes a claim a condition of entitlement, and the much smaller class of cases where s.1 does not apply.

Subs.(5)

There were a number of different versions of the section from which this section is derived and subs.(5) indicates that this section is limited to claims made on or after October 1, 1990. Schedule 1 sets out the earlier variations of the section. In many cases concerning claims to benefit care will need to be taken to apply the law as at the date of the claim. There is a particular risk of error where appeals are being reheard after the considerable delays inherent in successful appeals. Obviously, as time goes by this risk will diminish and eventually disappear.

1.30

Retrospective effect of provisions making entitlement to benefit dependent on claim

2.—(1) This section applies where a claim for benefit is made or treated as made at any time on or after 2nd September 1985 (the date on which section 165A of the 1975 Act (general provision as to necessity of claim for entitlement to benefit), as originally enacted, came into force) in respect of a period the whole or any part of which falls on or after that date.

(2) Where this section applies, any question arising as to—
 (a) whether the claimant is or was at any time (whether before, on or after 2nd September 1985) entitled to the benefit in question, or to any other benefit on which his entitlement to that benefit depends; or
 (b) in a case where the claimant's entitlement to the benefit depends on the entitlement of another person to a benefit, whether that other person is or was so entitled,
shall be determined as if the relevant claim enactment and any regulations made under or referred to in that enactment had also been in force, with any necessary modifications, at all times relevant for the purpose of determining the entitlement of the claimant, and, where applicable, of the other

1.31

Social Security Administration Act 1992

person, to the benefit or benefits in question (including the entitlement of any person to any benefit on which that entitlement depends, and so on).

(3) In this section "the relevant claim enactment" means section 1 above as it has effect in relation to the claim referred to in subsection (1) above.

(4) In any case where—
   (a) a claim for benefit was made or treated as made (whether before, on or after 2nd September 1985, and whether by the same claimant as the claim referred to in subsection (1) above or not), and benefit was awarded on that claim, in respect of a period falling wholly or partly before that date; but
   (b) that award would not have been made had the current requirements applied in relation to claims for benefit, whenever made, in respect of periods before that date; and
   (c) entitlement to the benefit claimed as mentioned in subsection (1) above depends on whether the claimant or some other person was previously entitled or treated as entitled to that or some other benefit,
then, in determining whether the conditions of entitlement to the benefit so claimed are satisfied, the person to whom benefit was awarded as mentioned in paragraphs (a) and (b) above shall be taken to have been entitled to the benefit so awarded, notwithstanding anything in subsection (2) above.

(5) In subsection (4) above "the current requirements" means—
   (a) the relevant claim enactment, and any regulations made or treated as made under that enactment, or referred to in it, as in force at the time of the claim referred to in subsection (1) above, with any necessary modifications; and
   (b) subsection (1) (with the omission of the words following "at any time") and subsections (2) and (3) above.

DERIVATION

1.32   Social Security Act 1975, s.165B.

DEFINITIONS

"the 1975 Act"—s.191.
"benefit"—see s.1(1).
"claim"—see s.191.
"claimant"—*ibid.*

GENERAL NOTE

1.33   There are a number of benefits where entitlement can depend on whether a person was entitled to a benefit at some earlier date (e.g. on reaching pensionable age). While the predecessor of s.1 clearly governed such questions from September 2, 1985, onwards, it was arguable that in relation to earlier dates the *McCaffrey* principle (see note to s.1(1) above) had to be applied. *R(S) 2/91* decided that that argument was correct. The predecessor of s.2 was inserted by the Social Security Act 1990 to reverse the effect of that decision and to do so retrospectively back to September 2, 1985.

The form of s.2 is complex and the retrospective effects are difficult to work out. It only applies to claims made or treated as made on or after September 2, 1985 (subs.(1)). Thus very late appeals or very long good causes for late claim might not be affected. Then on any such claim if a question of entitlement at any other date arises (including dates before September 2, 1985) that question is to be decided according to the principle of s.1 as it was in force at the relevant time (subs.(2)). The only exception to this is that if for any period benefit has been awarded following

(1992 c.5, s.2)

a claim, that beneficiary is to be treated as entitled to that benefit even though under the current requirements he would not be (subs.(4)).

[1 Claim or full entitlement to certain benefits conditional on work-focused interview.

2A.—(1) Regulations may make provision for or in connection with—
(a) imposing, as a condition falling to be satisfied by a person who—
  (i) makes a claim for a benefit to which this section applies, and
  (ii) is under the age of 60 at the time of making the claim,
  a requirement to take part in a work-focused interview;
(b) imposing, at a time when—
  (i) a person under that age and entitled to such a benefit, and
  (ii) any prescribed circumstances exist,
  a requirement to take part in such an interview as a condition of that person continuing to be entitled to the full amount which is payable to him in respect of the benefit apart from the regulations.
(2) The benefits to which this section applies are—
(a) income support;
(b) housing benefit;
(c) council tax benefit;
(d) widow's and bereavement benefits falling within section 20(1)(e) and (ea) of the Contributions and Benefits Act (other than a bereavement payment);
(e) incapacity benefit;
(f) severe disablement allowance; and
(g) [2 carer's allowance].
(3) Regulations under this section may, in particular, make provision—
(a) for securing, where a person would otherwise be required to take part in interviews relating to two or more benefits—
  (i) that he is only required to take part in one interview, and
  (ii) that any such interview is capable of counting for the purposes of all those benefits;
(b) for determining the person by whom interviews are to be conducted;
(c) conferring power on such persons or the designated authority to determine when and where interviews are to take place (including power in prescribed circumstances to determine that they are to take place in the homes of those being interviewed);
(d) prescribing the circumstances in which persons attending interviews are to be regarded as having or not having taken part in them;
(e) for securing that the appropriate consequences mentioned in subsection (4)(a) or (b) below ensue if a person who has been notified that he is required to take part in an interview—
  (i) fails to take part in the interview, and
  (ii) does not show, within the prescribed period, that he had good cause for that failure;
(f) prescribing—
  (i) matters which are or are not to be taken into account in determining whether a person does or does not have good cause for any failure to comply with the regulations, or
  (ii) circumstances in which a person is or is not to be regarded as having or not having good cause for any such failure.

1.34

(4) For the purposes of subsection (3)(e) above the appropriate consequence of a failure falling within that provision are—
- (a) where the requirement to take part in an interview applied by virtue of subsection (1)(a) above, that as regards any relevant benefit either—
  - (i) the person in question is to be regarded as not having made a claim for the benefit, or
  - (ii) if (in the cases of an interview postponed in accordance with subsection (7)) that person has already been awarded the benefit, his entitlement to the benefit is to terminate immediately;
- (b) where the requirement to take part in an interview applied by virtue of subsection (1)(b) above, that the amount payable to the person in question in respect of any relevant benefit is to be reduced by the specified amount until the specified time.

(5) Regulations under this section may, in relation to any such reduction, provide—
- (a) for the amount of the reduction to be calculated in the first instance by reference to such amount as may be prescribed;
- (b) for the amount as so calculated to be restricted, in prescribed circumstances, to the prescribed extent;
- (c) where the person in question is entitled to two or more relevant benefits, for determining the extent, and the order, in which those benefits are to be reduced in order to give effect to the reduction required in his case.

(6) Regulations under this section may provide that any requirement to take part in an interview that would otherwise apply to a person by virtue of such regulations—
- (a) is, in any prescribed circumstances, either not to apply or not to apply until such time as is specified;
- (b) is not to apply if the designated authority determines that an interview—
  - (i) would not be of assistance to that person, or
  - (ii) would not be appropriate in the circumstances,
- (c) is not to apply until such time as the designated authority determines, if that authority determines that an interview—
  - (i) would not be of assistance to that person, or
  - (ii) would not be appropriate in the circumstances,
  until that time;

and the regulations may make provision for treating a person in relation to whom any such requirement does not apply, or does not apply until a particular time, as having complied with that requirement to such extent and for such purposes as are specified.

(7) Where—
- (a) a person is required to take part in an interview by virtue of subsection (1)(a), and
- (b) the interview is postponed by or under regulations made in pursuance of subsection (6)(a) or (c),

the time to which it is postponed may be a time falling after an award of the relevant benefit to that person.

(8) In this section—
"the designated authority" means such of the following as may be specified, namely—

(1992 c.5, s.2A)

  (a) the Secretary of State,
  (b) a person providing services to the Secretary of State,
  (c) a local authority,
  (d) a person providing services to, or authorised to exercise any function of, any such authority;
"interview" (in subsections (3) to (7)) means a work-focused interview;
"relevant benefit", in relation to any person required to take part in a work-focused interview, means any benefit in relation to which that requirement applied by virtue of subsection (1)(a) or (b) above;
"specified" means prescribed by or determined in accordance with regulations;
"work-focused interview", in relation to a person, means an interview conducted for such purposes connected with employment or training in the case of that person as may be specified;
and the purposes which may be specified include purposes connected with a person's existing or future employment or training prospects or needs, and (in particular) assisting or encouraging a person to enhance his employment prospects.]

AMENDMENTS

1. This section was added by the Welfare Reform and Pensions Act 1999, ss.57–58 with effect from November 11, 1999.

2. The Regulatory Reform (Carer's Allowance) Order 2002 (SI 2002/1457), art.1 (September 1, 2002 for the purpose of making regulations; April 1, 2003 for all other purposes).

[1 Full entitlement to certain benefits conditional on work-focused interview for partner

2AA.—(1) Regulations may make provision for or in connection with imposing, at a time when—

  (a) a person ("the claimant") who—
    (i) is under the age of 60, and
    (ii) has a partner who is also under that age,
  is entitled to a benefit to which this section applies at a higher rate referable to his partner, and
  (b) prescribed circumstances exist,

a requirement for the partner to take part in a work-focused interview as a condition of the benefit continuing to be payable to the claimant at that rate.

(2) The benefits to which this section applies are—
  (a) income support;
  (b) an income-based jobseeker's allowance other than a joint-claim jobseeker's allowance;
  (c) incapacity benefit;
  (d) severe disablement allowance; and
  (e) invalid care allowance.

(3) For the purposes of this section a benefit is payable to a person at a higher rate referable to his partner if the amount that is payable in his case—
  (a) is more than it would be if the person concerned was not a member of a couple; or
  (b) includes an increase of benefit for his partner as an adult dependant of his.

1.35

(4) Regulations under this section may, in particular, make provision—
(a) for securing, where the partner of the claimant would otherwise be required to take part in work-focused interviews relating to two or more benefits—
   (i) that the partner is required instead to take part in only one such interview; and
   (ii) that the interview is capable of counting for the purposes of all those benefits;
(b) in a case where the claimant has more than one partner, for determining which of those partners is required to take part in the work-focused interview or requiring each of them to take part in such an interview;
(c) for determining the persons by whom work-focused interviews are to be conducted;
(d) conferring power on such persons or the designated authority to determine when and where work-focused interviews are to take place (including power in prescribed circumstances to determine that they are to take place in the homes of those being interviewed);
(e) prescribing the circumstances in which partners attending work-focused interviews are to be regarded as having or not having taken part in them;
(f) for securing that if—
   (i) a partner who has been notified of a requirement to take part in a work-focused interview fails to take part in it, and
   (ii) it is not shown (by him or by the claimant), within the prescribed period, that he had good cause for that failure,
the amount payable to the claimant in respect of the benefit in relation to which the requirement applied is to be reduced by the specified amount until the specified time;
(g) prescribing—
   (i) matters which are or are not to be taken into account in determining whether a partner does or does not have good cause for any failure to comply with the regulations; or
   (ii) circumstances in which a partner is or is not to be regarded as having or not having good cause for any such failure.

(5) Regulations under this section may, in relation to a reduction under subsection (4)(f), provide—
(a) for the amount of the reduction to be calculated in the first instance by reference to such amount as may be prescribed;
(b) for the amount as so calculated to be restricted, in prescribed circumstances, to the prescribed extent;
(c) where the claimant is entitled to two or more benefits in relation to each of which a requirement to take part in a work-focused interview applied, for determining the extent to, and the order in, which those benefits are to be reduced in order to give effect to the reduction required in his case.

(6) Regulations under this section may provide that any requirement to take part in a work-focused interview that would otherwise apply to a partner by virtue of the regulations—
(a) is, in any prescribed circumstances, either not to apply or not to apply until the specified time;

(1992 c.5, s.2AA)

(b) is not to apply if the designated authority determines that such an interview would not be of assistance to him or appropriate in the circumstances;
(c) is not to apply until such time as the designated authority determines (if that authority determines that such an interview would not be of assistance to him or appropriate in the circumstances until that time);

and the regulations may make provision for treating a partner to whom any such requirement does not apply, or does not apply until a particular time, as having complied with that requirement to such extent and for such purposes as are specified.

(7) In this section—

[2 "couple" has the meaning given by s.137(1) of the Contributions and Benefits Act;]

"designated authority" means such of the following as may be specified, namely—
(a) the Secretary of State,
(b) a person providing services to the Secretary of State,
(c) a local authority, and
(d) a person providing services to, or authorised to exercise any function of, a local authority;

"partner" means a person who is a member of the same couple as the claimant;

"specified" means prescribed by or determined in accordance with regulations;

and

"work-focused interview" has the same meaning as in section 2A above.]

AMENDMENTS

1. Inserted by the Employment Act 2002, s.49 (July 5, 2003).
2. Civil Partnership Act 2004, s.254 and Sch.24, para.55 (December 5, 2005).

[1 Supplementary provisions relating to work-focused interviews

2B.—(1) Chapter II of Part I of the Social Security Act 1998 (social security decisions and appeals) shall have effect in relation to relevant decisions subject to and in accordance with subsections (3) to (8) below (and in those subsections "the 1998 Act" means that Act).

(2) For the purposes of this section a "relevant decision" is a decision made under regulations under section 2A above that a person—
(a) has failed to comply with a requirement to take part in an interview which applied to him by virtue of the regulations, or
(b) has not shown, within the prescribed period mentioned in section 2A(3)(e)(ii) above, that he had good cause for such a failure.

[3 (2A) For the purposes of this section a "relevant decision", in relation to regulations under section 2AA above, is a decision that—
(a) the partner of a person entitled to a benefit has failed to comply with a requirement to take part in an interview which applied to the partner by virtue of the regulations, or
(b) it has not been shown within the prescribed period mentioned in section 2AA(4)(f)(ii) above that the partner had good cause for such a failure.]

1.36

(3) Section 8(1)(c) of the 1998 Act (decisions falling to be made under or by virtue of certain enactments are to be made by the Secretary of State) shall have effect subject to any provisions of regulations under section 2A [4 or 2AA] above by virtue of which relevant decisions fall to be made otherwise than by the Secretary of State.

(4) For the purposes of each of sections 9 and 10 of the 1998 Act (revision and supersession of decisions of Secretary of State) any relevant decision made otherwise than by the Secretary of State shall be treated as if it were such a decision made by the Secretary of State (and accordingly may be revised by him under section 9 or superseded by a decision made by him under section 10).

(5) Subject to any provisions of regulations under either section 9 or 10 of the 1998 Act, any relevant decision made, or (by virtue of subsection (4) above) treated as made, by the Secretary of State may be—
- (a) revised under section 9 by a person or authority exercising functions under regulations under section 2A [4 or 2AA] above other than the Secretary of State, or
- (b) superseded under section 10 by a decision made by such a person or authority,

as if that person or authority were the Secretary of State.

(6) Regulations shall make provision for conferring (except in any prescribed circumstances) a right of appeal under section 12 of the 1998 Act (appeal to appeal tribunal) against—
- (a) any relevant decision, and
- (b) any decision under section 10 of that Act superseding any such decision,

whether made by the Secretary of State or otherwise.

(7) Subsections (4) to (6) above apply whether—
- (a) the relevant decision, or
- (b) (in the case of subsection (6)(b)) the decision under section 10 of the 1998 Act,

is as originally made or has been revised (by the Secretary of State or otherwise) under section 9 of that Act; and regulations under subsection (6) above may make provision for treating, for the purposes of section 12 of that Act, any decision made or revised otherwise than by the Secretary of State as if it were a decision made or revised by him.

(8) Section 12 of the 1998 Act shall not apply to any decision falling within subsection (6) above except in accordance with regulations under that subsection.

(9) In [2. . .]
- (b) section 72(6) of the Welfare Reform and Pensions Act 1999 (supply of information),

any reference to information relating to social security includes any information supplied by a person for the purposes of an interview which he is required to take part in by virtue of section 2A [4 or 2AA] above.

(10) In this section "interview" means a work-focused interview within the meaning of section 2A above.]

AMENDMENTS

1. Welfare Reform and Pensions Act 1999, s.57 (November 11, 1999).
2. Employment Act 2002 (2002 c.22) s.54 and Sch.8 (November 24, 2002).
3. Employment Act 2002 (2002 c.22) s.54 and Sch.7 (July 5, 2003).
4. Employment Act 2002 (2002 c.22) s.53 and Sch.7 (July 5, 2003).

(1992 c.5, s.2C)

[¹ **Optional work-focused interviews**

2C.—(1) Regulations may make provision for conferring on local authorities functions in connection with conducting work-focused interviews in cases where such interviews are requested or consented to by persons to whom this section applies.

(2) This section applies to[³ . . .] [³ —
- (a) persons making claims for or entitled to any of the benefits listed in section 2A(2) above or any prescribed benefit; and
- (b) partners of persons entitled to any of the benefits listed in section 2AA(2) above or any prescribed benefit;]

and it so applies regardless of whether such persons have, in accordance with regulations under section 2A [³ or 2AA] above, already taken part in interviews conducted under such regulations.

(3) The function which may be conferred on a local authority by regulations under this section include functions relating to—
- (a) the obtaining and receiving of information for the purposes of work-focused interviews conducted under the regulations;
- (b) the recording and forwarding of information supplied at, or for the purposes of, such interviews;
- (c) the taking of steps to identify potential employment or training opportunities for persons taking part in such interviews.

(4) Regulations under this section may make different provision for different areas or different authorities.

(5) In this section "work-focused interviews", in relation to a person to whom this section applies, means an interview conducted for such purposes connected with employment or training in the case of such a person as may be prescribed; and the purposes which may be so prescribed include—
- (a) purposes connected with the existing or future employment prospects or needs of such a person, and
- (b) (in particular) assisting or encouraging such a person to enhance his employment prospects.]

1.37

AMENDMENTS

1. This section was added by the Welfare Reform and Pensions Act 1999, ss.57–58 with effect from November 11, 1999.
2. Employment Act 2002, s.54 and Sch.8 (November 24, 2002).
3. Employment Act 2002, s.53 and Sch.7 (July 5, 2003).

[¹*Bereavement benefits*

Late claims for bereavement benefit where death is difficult to establish

3.—(1) This section applies were a person's spouse [³ or civil partner] has died or may be presumed to have died on or after the appointed day and the circumstances are such that—
- (a) more than 12 months have elapsed since the date of death; and
- (b) either—

1.38

Social Security Administration Act 1992

(i) the spouse's [³ or civil partner] body has not been discovered or identified or, if it has been discovered and identified, the surviving spouse [³ or civil partner] does not know that fact; or

(ii) less than 12 months have elapsed since the surviving spouse [³ or civil partner] first knew of the discovery and identification of the body.

(2) Where this section applies, notwithstanding that any time prescribed for making a claim for a bereavement benefit in respect of the death has elapsed, then—

(a) in any case falling within paragraph (b)(i) of subsection (1) above where it has been decided under section 8 of the Social Security Act 1998 that the spouse [³ or civil partner] has died or is presumed to have died, or

(b) in any case falling within paragraph (b)(ii) of subsection (1) above where the identification was made not more than 12 months before the surviving spouse [³ or civil partner] first knew of the discovery and identification of the body,

such a claim may be made or treated as made at any time before the expiration of the period of 12 months beginning with the date on which that decision was made or, as the case may be, the date on which the surviving spouse [³ or civil partner] first knew of the discovery and identification.

(3) If, in a case where a claim for a bereavement benefit is made or treated as made by virtue of this section, the claimant would, apart from subsection (2) of section 1 above, be entitled to—

(a) a bereavement payment in respect of the spouse's [³ or civil partner's] death more than 12 months before the date on which the claim is made or treated as made; or

(b) any other bereavement benefit in respect of his or her death for a period more than 12 months before that date,

then, notwithstanding anything in that section, the surviving spouse [³ or civil partner] shall be entitled to that payment or, as the case may be, to that other benefit [² . . .].

(4) In subsection (1) above "the appointed day" means the day appointed for the coming into force of sections 54 to 56 of the Welfare Reform and Pensions Act 1999.]

AMENDMENTS

1. This section was added by the Welfare Reform and Pensions Act 1999, ss.57–58 with effect from November 11, 1999.
2. Tax Credits Act 2002, s.60 and Sch.6 (April 6, 2003).
3. Civil Partnership Act 2004, s.254 and Sch.24, para.56 (December 5, 2005).

SAVING

1.39   Article 3 of The Tax Credits Act 2002 (Commencement No.3 and Transitional Provisions and Savings) Order 2003 (SI 2003/938) provides:

"Saving provision

3.—(1) Notwithstanding the coming into force of the specified provisions, the Contributions and Benefits Act and the Administration Act shall, in cases to which paragraph (2) applies, subject to paragraph (3), continue to have effect from the commencement date as if those provisions had not come into force.

(1992 c.5, s.3)

(2) This paragraph applies where a person—
(a) is entitled to a relevant increase on the day before the commencement date; or
(b) claims a relevant increase on or after the commencement date and it is subsequently determined that he is entitled to a relevant increase in respect of a period which includes the day before the commencement date.

(3) The provisions saved by paragraph (1) shall continue to have effect until—
(a) subject to sub-paragraph(c), where a relevant increase ceases to be payable to a person to whom paragraph (2) applies for a period greater than 58 days beginning with the day on which it was last payable, on the day 59 days after the day on which it was last payable; or
(b) in any other case, subject to sub-paragraph (c), on the date on which entitlement to a relevant increase ceases;
(c) where regulation 6(19) or (23) of the Social Security (Claims and Payments) Regulations 1987 applies to a further claim for a relevant increase, on the date on which entitlement to that relevant increase ceases.

(4) In this article—
'the commencement date' means 6th April 2003;
'a relevant increase' means an increase under section 80 or 90 of the Contributions and Benefits Act;
'the specified provisions' means the provisions of the 2002 Act which are brought into force by article 2."

GENERAL NOTE
Subs.(4)
The appointed day referred to in this subsection is April 24, 2000.

1.40

Treatment of payments of benefit to certain widows

4. In any case where—
(a) a claim for widow's pension or a widowed mother's allowance is made, or treated as made, before 13th July 1990 (the date of the passing of the Social Security Act 1990); and
(b) the Secretary of State has made a payment to or for the claimant on the ground that if the claim had been received immediately after the passing of that Act she would have been entitled to that pension or allowance, or entitled to it at a higher rate, for the period in respect of which the payment is made,

the payment so made shall be treated as a payment of that pension or allowance, and, if and to the extent that an award of the pension or allowance, or an award at a higher rate, is made for the period in respect of which the payment was made, the payment shall be treated as made in accordance with that award.

1.41

DERIVATION
SSA 1990, s.21(1) and Sch.6, para.27(2).

1.42

Social Security Administration Act 1992

Claims and payments regulations

Regulations about claims for and payments of benefit

1.43   **5.**—(1) Regulations may provide—
   (a) for requiring a claim for a benefit to which this section applies to be made by such person, in such manner and within such time as may be prescribed;
   (b) for treating such a claim made in such circumstances as may be prescribed as having been made at such date earlier or later than that at which it is made as may be prescribed;
   (c) for permitting such a claim to be made, or treated as if made, for a period wholly or partly after the date on which it is made;
   (d) for permitting an award on such a claim to be made for such a period subject to the condition that the claimant satisfies the requirements for entitlement when benefit becomes payable under the award;
   (e) [³ for any such award to be revised under section 9 of the Social Security Act 1998, or superseded under section 10 of that Act, if any of those requirements are found not to have been satisfied;]
   (f) for the disallowance on any ground of a person's claim for a benefit to which this section applies to be treated as a disallowance of any further claim by that person for that benefit until the grounds of the original disallowance have ceased to exist;
   (g) for enabling one person to act for another in relation to a claim for a benefit to which this section applies and for enabling such a claim to be made and proceeded within the name of a person who has died;
   (h) for requiring any information or evidence needed for the determination of such a claim or of any question arising in connection withsuch a claim to be furnished by such person as may be prescribed in accordance withthe regulations;
   [⁵ (hh) for requiring such persons as may be prescribed to furnish any information or evidence needed for a determination whether a decision on an award of benefit to which this section applies—
      (i) should be revised under section 9 of the Social Security Act 1998; or
      (ii) should be superseded under section 10 of that Act;]
   (i) for the person to whom, time when and manner in which a benefit to which this section applies is to be paid and for the information and evidence to be furnished in connection with the payment of such a benefit;
   (j) for notice to be given of any change of circumstances affecting the continuance of entitlement to such a benefit or payment of such a benefit;
   (k) for the day on which entitlement to such a benefit is to begin or end;
   (l) for calculating the amounts of such a benefit according to a prescribed scale or otherwise adjusting them so as to avoid fractional amounts or facilitate computation;
   (m) for extinguishing the right to payment of such a benefit if payment is not obtained within such period, not being less than 12 months, as may be prescribed from the date on which the right is treated under the regulations as having arisen;

(1992 c.5, s.5)

(n) [³. . .]
(nn) [². . .]
(o) [³. . .]
(p) for the circumstances and manner in which payments of such a benefit may be made to another person on behalf of the beneficiary for any purpose, which may be to discharge, in whole or in part, an obligation of the beneficiary or any other person;
(q) for the payment or distribution of such a benefit to or among persons claiming to be entitled on the death of any person and for dispensing withstrict proof of their title;
(r) for the making of a payment on account of such a benefit—
   (i) where no claim has been made and it is impracticable for one to be made immediately;
   (ii) where a claim has been made and it is impracticable for the claim or an appeal, reference, review or application relating to it to be immediately determined;
   (iii) where an award has been made but it is impracticable to pay the whole immediately.

(2) This section applies to the following benefits—
(a) benefits as defined in section 122 of the Contributions and Benefits Act;
[¹(aa) a jobseeker's allowance;]
[⁶(ab) state pension credit;]
(b) income support;
(c) [⁹ . . .];
(d) [⁹ . . .];
(e) housing benefit;
(f) any social fund payments such as are mentioned in section 138(1)(a) or (2) of the Contributions and Benefits Act;
(g) child benefit; and
(h) Christmas bonus.

(3) The reference in subsection (1)(h) above to information or evidence needed for the determination of a claim includes a reference to information or evidence required by a rent officer under section 121 of the Housing Act 1988.

[⁷ (3A) The references in paragraphs (h) and (hh) of subsection (1) above to information or evidence needed for the determination of a claim or of any question arising in connection with a claim or (as the case may be) for a determination whether a decision on an award should be revised or should be superseded, includes, in the case of state pension credit, a reference to information or evidence as to the likelihood of future changes in a person's circumstances which is needed for determining—
(a) whether a period should be specified as an assessed income period under section 6 of the State Pension Credit Act 2002 in relation to any decision; and
(b) if so, the length of the period to be so specified.]

(4) Subsection (1)(n) above shall have effect in relation to housing benefit as if the reference to the Secretary of State were a reference to the authority paying the benefit.

(5) Subsection (1)(g), (i), (l), (p) and (q) above shall have effect as if statutory sick pay [⁸,] statutory maternity pay [⁸, statutory paternity pay and statutory adoption pay] were benefits to which this section applies.

[⁵(6) As it has effect in relation to housing benefit subsection (1)(p) above authorises provision requiring the making of payments of benefit to another person, on behalf of the beneficiary, in such circumstances as may be prescribed.]

AMENDMENTS

1. Jobseekers Act 1995, Sch.2, para.39 (October 7, 1996).
2. Social Security Act 1998, Sch.6, para.5(1) (May 21, 1998). This amendment applies from May 21, 1998 until s.21(2)(d) of the 1998 Act comes into force.
3. Social Security Act 1998, Sch.8 (July 5, 1999).
4. Social Security Act 1998, s.74 (March4, 1999).
5. Housing Act 1996, s.120 (with unlimited retrospective effect, so with effect from July 1, 1992).
6. State Pension Credit Act 2002, s.11 and Sch.1 (July 2, 2002 for the purpose of making regulations only).
7. State Pension Credit Act 2002, s.11 and Sch.1 (July 2, 2002 for the purpose of making regulations only).
8. Employment Act 2002, s.53 and Sch.7 (December 8, 2002).
9. Tax Credits Act 2002, s.60 and Sch.6 (April 8, 2003).

DERIVATION

1.44   Subss.(1) and (2): Social Security Act 1986, s.51(1) and (2).

DEFINITIONS

"the Contributions and Benefits Act"—see s.191.
"prescribed"—*ibid*.

GENERAL NOTE

1.45   An argument was put in *R(DLA) 4/05* concerning the relationship of reg.13C of the Claims and Payments Regulations (further claim for and award of disability living allowance—the provision which permits a continuation claim for a disability living allowance to be made during the last six months of the current award) with s.5. The Tribunal of Commissioners responded:

"Although at first sight regulation 13C(2)(b) may appear to provide a power to make an award, that is not so. Regulation 13C can best be understood by looking at the enabling provisions in section 5 of the 1992 Act. Section 5(1)(c) authorises the making of a regulation that permits a claim to be made in advance. Section 5(1)(d) authorises the making of a regulation that permits an award on such a claim to be made subject to a condition. It does not authorise the making of a regulation that permits an award to be made in advance because it is unnecessary to do so. The power to make an award follows from the duty to determine a claim, imposed on the Secretary of State by sections 1 and 8(1) of the 1998 Act. One can see that regulation 13C(1) is made under section 5(1)(c), regulation 13C(2)(a) is made under section 5(1)(b), regulation 13C(2)(b) is made under section 5(1)(d) and regulation 13C(3) is made under section 5(1)(e). Thus, what regulation 13C(2)(b) permits is not the making of an award in the light of the prospective claim but the imposition of a condition on the award that is required to be made by the 1998 Act. The word 'accordingly' [in reg.13C(2)(b)] therefore means no more than 'on that claim' and its only significance is that it links paragraph (2)(b) with paragraphs (1) and (2)(a) so that, in conformity with the enabling provision (giving effect to the word "such" in both places where it occurs

(1992 c.5, s.5)

in section 5(1)(d)), the condition may be imposed only on an award made on a renewal claim made in advance and treated as made on the renewal date." (para.16.)

6. *Omitted.*

Community charge benefits, etc.

Relationship between community charge benefits and other benefits

7.—(1) Regulations may provide for a claim for one relevant benefit to be treated, either in the alternative or in addition, as a claim for any other relevant benefit that may be prescribed.

(2) Regulations may provide for treating a payment made or right conferred by virtue of regulations—
(a) under section 5(1)(r) above; or
(b) under section 6(1)(r) to (t) above,
as made or conferred on account of any relevant benefit that is subsequently awarded or paid.

(3) For the purposes of subsections (1) and (2) above relevant benefits are—
(a) any benefit to which section 5 above applies; and
(b) [¹council tax benefit].

AMENDMENT

1. Local Government Finance Act 1992, Sch.9, para.13 (April 1, 1993).

DERIVATION

Social Security Act 1986, s.51B.

DEFINITIONS

"claim"—see s.191.
"prescribed"—*ibid.*

GENERAL NOTE

Subs.(1)
See Claims and Payments Regulations, Sch.1.

Subs.(2)
See the Social Security (Payments on account, Overpayments and Recovery) Regulations, regs 5–8.

[¹ Sharing of functions as regards certain claims and information

7A.—(1)Regulations may, for the purpose of supplementing the persons or bodies to whom claims for relevant benefits may be made, make provision—
(a) as regards housing benefit or council tax benefit, for claims for that benefit to be made to—
(i) a Minister of the Crown, or

Social Security Administration Act 1992

　　　　(ii) a person providing services to a Minister of the Crown;
　(b) as regards any other relevant benefit for claims for that benefit to be made to—
　　　　(i) a local authority,
　　　　(ii) a person providing services to a local authority, or
　　　　(iii) a person authorised to exercise any function of a local authority relating to housing benefit or council tax benefit.
(2) Regulations may make provision for or in connection with—
(a) the forwarding by a relevant authority of—
　　　　(i) claims received by virtue of any provision authorised by subsection (1) above, and
　　　　(ii) information or evidence supplied in connection with making such claims (whether supplied by persons making the claims or by other persons);
(b) the receiving and forwarding by a relevant authority of information or evidence relating to social security [3 or work] matters supplied by, or the obtaining by a relevant authority of such information or evidence from—
　　　　(i) persons making, or who have made, claims for a relevant benefit, or
　　　　(ii) other persons in connection with such claims,
　　including information or evidence not relating to the claim or benefit in question;
(c) the recording by a relevant authority of information or evidence relating to social security matters supplied to, or obtained by, the authority and the holding by the authority of such information or evidence (whether as supplied or obtained or recorded);
(d) the giving of information or advice with respect to social security matters by a relevant authority to persons making, or who have made, claims for a relevant benefit.
(3) In paragraphs (b) and (d) of subsection (2) above—
(a) references to claims for as relevant benefit are to such claims whether made as mentioned in subsection (1)(a) or (b) above or not; and
(b) references to persons who have made such claims include persons to who awards of benefit have been made on the claims.
(4) Regulations under this section may make different provision for different areas.
(5) Regulations under any other enactment may make such different provision for different areas as appears to the Secretary of State expedient on connection withany exercise by regulations under this section of the power conferred by subsection (4) above.
(6) In this section—
(a) "benefit" includes child support or a war pension (any reference to a claim being read, in relation to child support, as a reference to an application [2 (or an application treated as having been made)] under the Child Support Act 1991 for a maintenance assessment [2 maintenance assessment]);
(b) "local authority" means an authority administering housing benefit or council tax benefit;
(c) "relevant authority" means—
　　　　(i) a Minister of the Crown,
　　　　(ii) a person providing services to a Minister of the Crown,

(1992 c.5, s.7A)

     (iii) a local authority,
     (iv) a person providing services to a local authority, or
     (v) a person authorised to exercise any function of a local authority relating to housing benefit or council tax benefit;
  (d) "relevant benefit" means housing benefit, council tax benefit or any other benefit prescribed for the purposes of this section;
[³ (e) "social security or work matters" means matters relating to—
     (i) social security, child support or war pensions, or
     (ii) employment or training;]
and in this subsection "war pension" means a war pension within the meaning of section 25 of the Social Security Act 1989 (establishment and functions of war pensions committees).]

AMENDMENTS

1. Welfare Reform and Pensions Act 1999, s.71 (November 11, 1999).
2. Child Support, Pensions and Social Security Act 2000, s.26 and Sch.3, para.12 (March 3, 2003 for certain purposes only: see SI 2003/192).
3. Employment Act 2002, s.53 and Sch.7 (November 24, 2002).

Industrial injuries benefit

Notification of accidents, etc.

8. Regulations may provide—   1.52
(a) for requiring the prescribed notice of an accident in respect of which industrial injuries benefit may be payable to be given within the prescribed time by the employed earner to the earner's employer or other prescribed person;
(b) for requiring employers—
     (i) to make reports, to such person and in such form and within such time as may be prescribed, of accidents in respect of which industrial injuries benefit may be payable;
     (ii) to furnish to the prescribed person any information required for the determination of claims, or of questions arising in connection with claims or awards;
     (iii) to take such other steps as may be prescribed to facilitate the giving notice of accidents, the making of claims and the determination of claims and of questions so arising.

DERIVATION

SSA 1975, s.88.   1.53

GENERAL NOTE

   The regulations made under this section are the Claims and Payment Regulations 1979, regs 24 and 25. The provisions of the regulations are, of course, significant in trying to ensure that the adjudicating authorities have access to a record of the circumstances surrounding an industrial accident, and the opportunity to put questions to the employer. Entries in the accident book are not always illuminating, but it is in the interests of the employees that they give the fullest possible contemporaneous account of the accident, particularly where its effects may be slow to emerge (as, sometimes, in head or back injuries).   1.54

Social Security Administration Act 1992

Medical examination and treatment of claimants

1.55   **9.**—(1) Regulations may provide for requiring claimants for disablement benefit—
  (a) to submit themselves from time to time to medical examination for the purpose of determining the effect of the relevant accident, or the treatment appropriate to the relevant injury or loss of faculty;
  (b) to submit themselves from time to time to appropriate medical treatment for the injury or loss of faculty.

(2) Regulations under subsection (1) above requiring persons to submit themselves to medical examination or treatment may—
  (a) require those persons to attend at such places and at such times as may be required; and
  (b) with the consent of the Treasury provide for the payment by the Secretary of State to those persons of travelling and other allowances (including compensation for loss of remunerative time).

DERIVATION

1.56   SSA 1975, s.89.

DEFINITION

"medical examinations," "medical treatment": see s.191.

GENERAL NOTE

1.57   The regulations referred to are the Claims and Payments Regulations 1979, reg.26.

Obligations of claimants

1.58   **10.**—(1) Subject to subsection (3) below, regulations may provide for disqualifying a claimant for the receipt of industrial injuries benefit—
  (a) for failure without good cause to comply with any requirement of regulations to which this subsection applies (including in the case of a claim for industrial death benefit, a failure on the part of some other person to give the prescribed notice of the relevant accident);
  (b) for wilful obstruction of, or other misconduct in connection with, any examination or treatment to which he is required under regulations to which this subsection applies to submit himself, or in proceedings under this Act for the determination of his right to benefit or to its receipt,

or for suspending proceedings on the claim or payment of benefit as the case may be, in the case of any such failure, obstruction or misconduct.

(2) The regulations to which subsection (1) above applies are—
  (a) any regulations made by virtue of section 5(1)(h), (i) or (l) above, so far as relating to industrial injuries benefit; and
  (b) regulations made by virtue of section 8 or 9 above.

(3) Regulations under subsection (1) above providing for disqualification of the receipt of benefit for any of the following matters, that is to say—
  (a) for failure to comply withthe requirements of regulations under section 9(1) or (2) above;
  (b) for obstruction of, or misconduct in connection with, medical examination or treatment, shall not be made so as to disentitle a claimant to benefit for a period exceeding 6 weeks on any disqualification.

(1992 c.5, s.10)

DERIVATION

SSA 1975, s.90(2)–(4) as amended.

GENERAL NOTE

In *R(S)9/51* it was held that a deeply held personal conviction that a claimant's religious beliefs require him or her to refuse to have a medical examination amounted to good cause for refusal to do so. Mere prejudice or distaste for the process will not alone suffice. But the decision did go on to point out the possible consequential difficulties of meeting the burden of proof for entitlement to benefit if the refusal to submit to a medical examination resulted in their being no, or little, medical evidence available. Much would depend on the cogency of the other evidence available which might be sufficient to establish incapacity without full medical evidence. See also *CSIS/065/1991* discussed in the annotations to reg.2 of the Medical Evidence Regulations.

[¹Disabled person's tax credit]

Initial claims and repeat claims

[² . . .]

AMENDMENTS

1. Tax Credits Act 1999, Sch.1 (October 5, 1999).
2. Repealed by Tax Credits Act 2002, s.60 and Sch.6 (April 8, 2003).

DERIVATION

Social Security Act 1986, s.27B(1)–(3).

The social fund

Necessity of application for certain payments

12.—(1) A social fund payment such as is mentioned in section 138(1)(b) of the Contributions and Benefits Act may be awarded to a person only if an application for such a payment has been made by him or on his behalf in such form and manner as may be prescribed.

(2) The Secretary of State may by regulations—
(a) make provision with respect to the time at which an application for such a social fund payment is to be treated as made;
(b) prescribe conditions that must be satisfied before any determination in connection with such an application may be made or any award of such a payment may be paid;
(c) prescribe circumstances in which such an award becomes extinguished.

DERIVATION

Social Security Act 1986, s.33(1) and (13).

Social Security Administration Act 1992

DEFINITIONS
"the Contributions and Benefits Act"—see s.191.
"prescribed"—*ibid.*

GENERAL NOTE

Subs. (1)

1.65 This provision applies to the "ordinary" social fund, not to funeral or maternity payments or cold weather payments. See the Social Fund (Applications) Regulations.

Subs. (2)

1.66 See the Social Fund (Miscellaneous Provisions) Regulations.

Child benefit

Necessity of application for child benefit

1.67 **13.**—(1) Subject to the provisions of this Act, no person shall be entitled to child benefit unless he claims it in the manner, and within the time, prescribed in relation to child benefit by regulations under section 5 above.

[¹ (1A) No person shall be entitled to child benefit unless subsection (1B) below is satisfied in relation to him.

(1B) This subsection is satisfied in relation to a person if—
(a) his claim for child benefit is accompanied by—
(i) a statement of his national insurance number and information or evidence establishing that that number has been allocated to him; or
(ii) information or evidence enabling the national insurance number that has been allocated to him to be ascertained; or
(b) he make an application for a national insurance number to be allocated to him which is accompanied by information or evidence enabling such a number to be so allocated.

(1C) Regulations may make provision disapplying subsection (1A) above in the case of—
(a) prescribed descriptions of persons making claims, or
(b) prescribed descriptions of children [² or qualifying young persons] in respect of whom child benefit is claimed,
or in other prescribed circumstances.]

(2) Except where regulations otherwise provide, no person shall be entitled to child benefit for any week on a claim made by him after that week if child benefit in respect of the same child [² or qualifying young person] has already been paid for that week to another person, whether or not that other person was entitled to it.

AMENDMENTS

1. Welfare Reform and Pensions Act 1999, s.69 (May 15, 2000).
2. Child Benefit Act 2005, Sch.1, Pt 1, para.20 (April 10, 2006).

DERIVATION

1.68 CBA 1975, s.6.

(1992 c.5, s.13)

GENERAL NOTE

There is a general bar on receiving child benefit if it has already been paid to someone else in respect of the same child even though that other person was not entitled to it.

The rules relating to claims for and payments of child benefit are now to be found in the Claims and Payments Regulations 1987.

See notes to reg.14A of the Child Benefit (General) Regulations 1976 for an escape route from the application of the rule in subs.(2).

1.69

Statutory sick pay

Duties of employees etc. in relation to statutory sick pay

14.—(1) Any employee who claims to be entitled to statutory sick pay from his employer shall, if so required by his employer, provide such information as may reasonably be required for the purpose of determining the duration of the period of entitlement in question or whether a period of entitlement exists as between them.

(2) The Secretary of State may by regulations [¹ made with the concurrence of the Inland Revenue] direct—
(a) that medical information required under subsection (1) above shall, in such cases as may be prescribed, be provided in a prescribed form;
(b) that an employee shall not be required under subsection (1) above to provide medical information in respect of such days as may be prescribed in a period of incapacity for work.

(3) Where an employee asks an employer of his to provide him with a written statement, in respect of a period before the request is made, of one or more of the following—
(a) the days within that period which the employer regards as days in respect of which he is liable to pay statutory sick pay to that employee;
(b) the reasons why the employer does not so regard the other days in that period;
(c) the employer's opinion as to the amount of statutory sick pay to which the employee is entitled in respect of each of those days,
the employer shall, to the extent to which the request was reasonable, comply with it within a reasonable time.

1.70

AMENDMENT

1. Transfer of Functions Act 1999, Sch.3 (April 1, 1999).

DERIVATION

SSA 1981, s.17(2)–(3).

1.71

Statutory maternity pay

Duties of women, etc., in relation to statutory maternity pay

15.—(1) A woman shall provide the person who is liable to pay her statutory maternity pay—

1.72

43

Social Security Administration Act 1992

(a) with evidence as to her pregnancy and the expected date of confinement in such form and at such time as may be prescribed; and
(b) where she commences work after her confinement but within the maternity pay period, with such additional information as may be prescribed.

[¹(1A) Any regulations for the purposes of subsection (1) above must be made with the concurrence of the Inland Revenue.]

(2) Where a woman asks an employer or former employer of hers to provide her with a written statement, in respect of a period before the request is made, of one or more of the following—
(a) the weeks within that period which he regards as weeks in respect of which he is liable to pay statutory maternity pay to the woman,
(b) the reasons why he does not so regard the other weeks in that period, and
(c) his opinion as to the amount of statutory maternity pay to which the woman is entitled in respect of each of the weeks in respect of which he regards himself as liable to make a payment,

the employer or former employer shall, to the extent to which the request was reasonable, comply with it within a reasonable time.

AMENDMENT

1. Transfer of Functions Act 1999, Sch.3 (April 1, 1999).

DERIVATION

1.73   SSA 1986, s.49 and Sch.4, paras 6 and 7.

[¹*Payments in respect of mortgage interest etc.*

Payment out of benefit of sums in respect of mortgage interest etc.

1.74   **15A.**—(1) This section applies in relation to cases where—
(a) mortgage interest is payable to a qualifying lender by a person ("the borrower") who is entitled, or whose partner, former partner or qualifying associate is entitled, to income support [² or an income-based jobseeker's allowance]; and
(b) a sum in respect of that mortgage interest is or was brought into account in determining the applicable amount for the purposes of income support [² or an income-based jobseeker's allowance] in the case of the borrower or the partner, former partner or qualifying associate;

and any reference in this section to "the relevant beneficiary" is a reference to the person whose applicable amount for the purposes of income support [² or an income-based jobseeker's allowance] is or was determined as mentioned in paragraph (b) above.

[³ (1A) This section also applies in relation to cases where—
(c) mortgage interest is payable to a qualifying lender by a person (also referred to as "the borrower") who is, or whose partner, or former partner or qualifying associate is, entitled to state pension credit; and
(d) a sum in respect of that mortgage interest is or was brought into account in determining the appropriate minimum guarantee for the

(1992 c.5, s.15A)

purposes of state pension credit in the case of the borrower or the partner, former partner or qualifying associate;
and any reference in this section to "the relevant beneficiary" includes a reference to the person whose appropriate minimum guarantee for the purposes of state pension credit is or was determined as mentioned in paragraph (b) above.]

(2) Without prejudice to paragraphs (i) and (p) of section 5(1) above, regulations may, in relation to cases where this section applies, make provision—

- (a) requiring that, in prescribed circumstances, a prescribed part of any relevant benefits [³ (other than state pension credit)] to which the relevant beneficiary is entitled shall be paid by the Secretary of State directly to the qualifying lender and applied by that lender towards the discharge of the liability in respect of the mortgage interest;
- [³ (aa) authorising or requiring that, in prescribed circumstances, a prescribed part of any state pension credit to which the relevant beneficiary is entitled may (or, as the case may be, shall) be paid by the Secretary of State directly to the qualifying lender and shall be applied by that lender towards the discharge of the liability in respect of the mortgage interest;]
- (b) for the expenses of the Secretary of State in administering the making of payments under the regulations to be defrayed, in whole or in part, at the expense of qualifying lenders, whether by requiring them to pay prescribed fees or by deducting and retaining a prescribed part of the payments that would otherwise be made to them under the regulations or by such other method as may be prescribed;
- (c) for requiring a qualifying lender, in a case where by virtue of paragraph (b) above the amount of the payment made to him under the regulations is less than it would otherwise have been, to credit against the liability in respect of the mortgage interest (in addition to the payment actually made) an amount equal to the difference between—
  - (i) the payment that would have been so made, apart from paragraph (b) above; and
  - (ii) the payment actually made;
  and, in any such case, for treating the amount so credited as properly paid on account of benefit due to the relevant beneficiary;
- (d) for enabling a body which, or person who, would otherwise be a qualifying lender to elect not to be regarded as such for the purposes of this section, other than this paragraph;
- (e) for the recovery from any body or person—
  - (i) of any sums paid to that body or person by way of payment under the regulations that ought not to have been so paid; or
  - (ii) of any fees or other sums due from that body or person by virtue of paragraph(b) above;
- (f) for cases where the same person is the borrower in relation to mortgage interest payable in respect of two or more different loans; and
- (g) for any person of a prescribed class or description who would otherwise be regarded for the purposes of this section as the borrower in relation to any mortgage interest not to be so regarded, except for the purposes of this paragraph;

but the Secretary of State shall not make any regulations under paragraph (b) above unless he has consulted with such organisations representing qualifying lenders likely to be affected by the regulations as he considers appropriate.

Social Security Administration Act 1992

(3) The bodies and persons who are "qualifying lenders" for the purposes of this section are—

[4 (a) a deposit taker;]
  (b) [4 . . .]
[4 (c) an insurer;]
  (d) any county council, [5 county borough council,] district council . . . or London Borough Council,
  (e) the Common Council of the City of London,
[6 (ee) any council constituted under section 2 of the Local Government etc (Scotland) Act 1994]
  (f) the Council of the Isles of Scilly,
  (g) any new town corporation,
and such bodies or persons not falling within the above paragraphs as may be prescribed.

(4) In this section—

[3 "appropriate minimum guarantee" has the meaning given by section 2(3) of the State Pension Credit Act 2002;]

[4 "deposit taker" means—
(a) a person who has permission under Part 4 of the Financial Services and Markets Act 2000 to accept deposits, or
(b) an EEA firm of the kind mentioned in paragraph 5(b) of Schedule 3 to that Act which has permission under paragraph 15 of that Schedule (as a result of qualifying for authorisation under paragraph 12 of that Schedule) to accept deposits;

"insurer" means—
(a) a person who has permission under Part 4 of the Financial Services and Markets Act 2000 to effect and carry out contracts of insurance, or
(b) an EEA firm of the kind mentioned in [paragraph 5(d)] of Schedule 3 to that Act which has permission under paragraph 15 of that Schedule (as a result of qualifying for authorisation under paragraph 12 of that Schedule) to effect and carry out contracts of insurance;]

"mortgage interest" means interest on a loan which is secured by a mortgage of or charge over land, or (in Scotland) by a heritable security, and which has been taken out to defray money applied for any of the following purposes, that is to say—
(a) acquiring any residential land which was intended, at the time of the acquisition, for occupation by the borrower as his home;
(b) carrying out repairs or improvements to any residential land which was intended, at the time of taking out the loan, for occupation by the borrower as his home;
(c) paying off another loan; or
(d) any prescribed purpose not falling within paragraphs (a) to (c) above;
but interest shall be regarded as mortgage interest by virtue of paragraph (c) above only to the extent that interest on that other loan would have been regarded as mortgage interest for the purposes of this section had the loan not been paid off;

"partner" means—
    (a) any person [7 who is married to, or a civil partner of, the borrower] and who is a member of the same household as the borrower; or
    (b) any person [7 who is neither married to, nor a civil partner of, the borrower but who lives together with the borrower as husband and

wife or as if they were civil partners], otherwise than in prescribed circumstances;

and "former partner" means a person who has at some time been, but no longer is, the borrower's partner;

"qualifying associate", in relation to the borrower, means a person who, for the purposes of income support [³ or an income-based jobseeker's allowance], [, an income-based jobseeker's allowance or state pension credit,] falls to be treated by regulations under Part VII of the Contributions and Benefits Act [² or (as the case may be) under the Jobseekers Act 1995 [³ or the State Pension Credit Act 2002],] as responsible for so much of the expenditure which relates to housing costs (within the meaning of those regulations) as consists of any of the mortgage interest payable by the borrower, and who falls to be so treated because—

(a) the borrower is not meeting those costs, so that the person has to meet them if he is to continue to live in the dwelling occupied as his home; and

(b) the person is one whom it is reasonable, in the circumstances, to treat as liable to meet those costs;

"relevant benefits" means such of the following benefits as may be prescribed, namely—

(a) benefits, as defined in section 122 of the Contributions and Benefits Act;

[² (aa) a jobseeker's allowance;]

(b) income support;

[³ (c) state pension credit;]

"residential land" means any land which consists of or includes a dwelling.

[⁴ (4A) The definitions of "deposit taker" and "insurer" in subsection (4) must be read with—

(a) section 22 of the Financial Services and Markets Act 2000;

(b) any relevant order under that section; and

(c) Schedule 2 to that Act.]

(5) For the purposes of this section, regulations may make provision—

(a) as to circumstances in which residential land is or is not to be treated as intended for occupation by the borrower as his home; or

(b) as to circumstances in which persons are to be treated as being or not being members of the same household.]

[⁷ (4B) For the purposes of this section, two people of the same sex are to be regarded living together as if they were civil partners if, but only if, they would be regarded together as husband and wife were they instead two people of the opposite sex.]

AMENDMENTS

1. Social Security (Mortgage Interest Payments) Act 1992, s.1 and Sch., para.1 (July 1, 1992; the equivalent amendment to the Social Security Act 1986 came into force on March 16, 1992).

2. Jobseekers Act 1995, Sch.2, para.40 (October 7, 1996).

3. State Pension Credit Act 2002, s.14 and Sch.2 (July 2, 2002 for the purpose only of making regulation; fully in force October 6, 2003).

4. The Financial Services and Markets Act 2000 (Consequential Amendments and Repeals) Order 2001 (SI 2001/3649) (October 6, 2003).

5. Local Government (Wales) Act 1994, Sch.8, para.11 (April 1, 1996).

6. Local Government etc. (Scotland) Act 1994, Sch.13, para.175 (April 1, 1996).

7. Civil Partnership Act 2004, s.254 and Sch.24, para.57 (December 5, 2005).

Social Security Administration Act 1992

DEFINITION

"Contributions and Benefits Act"—see s.191.

GENERAL NOTE

1.75 Section 15A authorises the regulations which set out the meat of the scheme for direct payment to lenders of the element of housing costs in income support, and from October 7, 1996, income-based JSA, to cover mortgage interest and supplies some basic definitions. The main provisions are in Sch.9A to the Claims and Payments Regulations.

Emergency payments

Emergency payments by local authorities and other bodies

1.76 **16.**—(1) The Secretary of State may make arrangements—
(a) with a local authority to which this section applies; or
(b) with any other body,
for the making on his behalf by members of the staff of any such authority or body of payments on account of benefits to which section 5 above applies in circumstances corresponding to those in which the Secretary of State himself has the power to make such payments under subsection (1)(r) of that section; and a local authority to which this section applies shall have power to enter into any such arrangements.

(2) A payment under any such arrangements shall be treated for the purposes of any Act of Parliament or instrument made under an Act of Parliament as if it had been made by the Secretary of State.

(3) The Secretary of State shall repay a local authority or other body such amount as he determines to be the reasonable administrative expenses incurred by the authority or body in making payments in accordance with arrangements under this subsection.

(4) The local authorities to which this section applies are—
(a) a local authority as defined in section 270(1) of the Local Government Act 1972, other than a parish or community council;
(b) the Common Council of the City of London; and
(c) a local authority as defined in section 235(1) of the Local Government (Scotland) Act 1973.

DERIVATION

1.77 Social Security Act 1988, s.8.

PART II

ADJUDICATION

GENERAL NOTE

1.78 The whole of Pt II of the Social Security Administration Act 1992 is repealed by the Social Security Act 1998 in order to give effect to the policy proposals outlined in the Government's Consultation Paper, *Improving Decision Making and Appeals in Social Security*, Cm 3328. The theme of the proposals is to modernise the administration of the social security system. The emphasis is placed on simplifying organisational structures, defining responsibilities and streamlining procedures. The Consultation Paper points to 13 different types of decision-maker involved in the determination of claims to benefit. In particular, the split between adjudication officers' and Secretary of State's decisions is criticised for causing confusion for both Departmental staff and claimants, especially where one individual officer is simply acting in different capacities. The lack of a right of appeal from Secretary of State decisions creates further anomalies.

The proliferation of decision-makers at the appeals level is also seen as inflexible and cumbersome. The distinctive jurisdictions of Social Security Appeal Tribunals, Disability Appeal Tribunals, Medical Appeal Tribunals, Child Support Appeal Tribunals and Vaccine Damage Tribunals are felt to impose rigid, categorical boundaries. The rectification of manifest errors in tribunal decisions requires a ponderous trek to the Commissioners.

The remedial measures, however, go far beyond those necessary to tackle complexity and delay. Greater managerial control is the order of the day. Thus, the division between adjudication officer's and Secretary of State's decisions is resolved by abolishing adjudication officers and having all decisions on and in relation to claims taken in the name of the Secretary of State by decision makers. In this way, the prerogative of adjudication officers' to "act independently of Agency Managers, Chief Executives and Ministers when making decisions", which is evidently treated by the Consultation Paper as a problem, is bluntly terminated. Similarly to disappear are the Chief Adjudication Officer, who is responsible for monitoring and promoting standards of administrative decision-making, and the Central Adjudication Service, which serve as a source of relatively policy-free guidance on the interpretation and application of the law. At the appeals level, the clock is turned back 15 years, to before the days of the Independent Tribunal Service (and its precursor, the Office of the President of Social Security Appeal Tribunals). The administration of the appeals system is to revert to the Department through the mechanism of an appeals agency headed by a Chief Executive accountable to the Minister. The ITS as such will be replaced by The Appeals Service—a dualistic body comprising the appeals agency and a judicial arm headed by a President.

The transition from the old administrative and tribunal arrangements to the new has been phased in benefit by benefit during the course of 1999. The timetable is:—

June 1, 1999:	Child Support
July 5, 1999:	Disablement Benefit
	Reduced Earnings Allowance
	Retirement Allowance
	Child Benefit & Guardians Allowance
September 6, 1999:	Incapacity Benefit
	Severe Disablement Allowance
	Retirement Benefit
	Widows Benefit
	Maternity Allowance
October 5, 1999:	Family Credit renamed working families' tax credit
	Disability Working Allowance renamed disabled person's tax credit
October 18, 1999:	Jobseeker's Allowance
	Disability Living Allowance
	Attendance Allowance
	Invalid Care Allowance
November 29, 1999:	All other benefits, including:—
	Income Support and social fund payments

On and from each transition date all claims or pending appeals in relation to the particular benefit converted on that date will be dealt with under the new arrangements. A series of commencement orders gave effect to the transitional measures.

However, the intended simplification of responsibility for decision-making fragments with the introduction of the Social Security Contributions (Transfer of Functions, etc.) Act 1999, which moves responsibility for deciding most of the contribution questions vested in the Secretary of State by s.17 Social Security Administration Act 1992 to the Board of Inland Revenue with corresponding rights of appeal to the tax appeal commissioners.

PART III

OVERPAYMENTS AND ADJUSTMENTS OF BENEFIT

Misrepresentation etc.

Overpayments—general

1.79

71.—(1) Where it is determined that, whether fraudulently or otherwise, any person has misrepresented, or failed to disclose, any material fact and in consequence of the misrepresentation or failure—
    (a) a payment has been made in respect of a benefit to which this section applies; or
    (b) any sum recoverable by or on behalf of the Secretary of State in connection with any such payment has not been recovered,
the Secretary of State shall be entitled to recover the amount of any payment which he would not have made or any sum which he would have received but for the misrepresentation or failure to disclose.

[1(2) Where any such determination as is referred to in subsection (1) above is made, the person making the determination shall [2 in the case of the Secretary of State or a tribunal, and may in the case of a Commissioner or court]—
    (a) determine whether any, and if so what, amount is recoverable under that subsection by the Secretary of State, and
    (b) specify the period during which that amount was paid to the person concerned.]

(3) An amount recoverable under subsection (1)(above is in all cases recoverable from the person who misrepresented the fact or failed to disclose it.

(4) In relation to cases where payments of benefit to which this section applies have been credited to a bank account or other account under arrangements made with the agreement of the beneficiary or a person acting for him, circumstances may be prescribed in which the Secretary of State is to be entitled to recover any amount paid in excess of entitlement; but any such regulations shall not apply in relation to any payment unless before he agreed to the arrangements such notice of the effect of the regulations as may be prescribed was given in such manner as may be prescribed to the beneficiary or to a person acting for him.

(5) Except where regulations otherwise provide, an amount shall not be recoverable under [3. . .] regulations under subsection (4) above unless—
    (a) the determination in pursuance of which it was paid has been reversed or varied on an appeal or [2 has been revised under section 9 or super-seded under section 10 of the Social Security Act 1998]; and

(b) it has been determined on the appeal or [² under that section] that the amount is so recoverable.

[⁴(5A) Except where regulations otherwise provide, an amount shall not be recoverable under subsection (1) above unless the determination in pursuance of which it was paid has been reversed or varied on an appeal or [² has been revised under section 9 or superseded under section 10 of the Social Security Act 1998].]

(6) Regulations may provide—
  (a) that amounts recoverable under subsection (1) above or regulations under subsection (4) above shall be calculated or estimated in such manner and on such basis as may be prescribed;
  (b) for treating any amount paid to any person under an award which is subsequently determined was not payable—
    (i) as properly paid; or
    (ii) as paid on account of a payment which it is determined should be or should have been made, and for reducing or withholding any arrears payable by virtue of the subsequent determination;
  (c) for treating any amount paid to one person in respect of another as properly paid for any period for which it is not payable in cases where in consequence of the subsequent determination—
    (i) the other person is himself entitled to a payment for that period; or
    (ii) a third person is entitled in priority to the payee to a payment for that period in respect of the other person, and for reducing or withholding any arrears payable for that period by virtue of the subsequent determination.

(7) Circumstances may be prescribed in which a payment on account by virtue of section 5(1)(r) above may be recovered to the extent that it exceeds entitlement.

(8) Where any amount paid [⁸, other than an amount paid in respect of child benefit or guardian's allowance,] is recoverable under—
  (a) subsection (1) above;
  (b) regulations under subsection (4) or (7) above; or
  (c) section 74 below,
it may, without prejudice to any other method of recovery, be recovered by deduction from prescribed benefits.

(9) Where any amount paid in respect of a [¹¹ couple] is recoverable as mentioned in subsection (8) above, it may, without prejudice to any other method of recovery, be recovered, in such circumstances as may be prescribed, by deduction from prescribed benefits payable to either of them.

(10) Any amount recoverable under the provisions mentioned in subsection (8) above—
  (a) if the person from whom it is recoverable resides in England and Wales and the county court so orders, shall be recoverable by execution issued from the county court or otherwise as if it were payable under an order of that court; and
  (b) if he resides in Scotland, shall be enforced in like manner as an extract registered decree arbitral bearing a warrant for execution issued by the sheriff court of any sheriffdom in Scotland.

[⁵(10A) Where—
  (a) a jobseeker's allowance is payable to a person from whom any amount is recoverable as mentioned in subsection (8) above; and

Social Security Administration Act 1992

(b) that person is subject to a bankruptcy order,

a sum deducted from that benefit under that subsection shall not be treated as income of his for the purposes of the Insolvency Act 1986.

(10B) Where—
(a) a jobseeker's allowance is payable to a person from whom any amount is recoverable as mentioned in subsection (8) above; and
(b) the estate of that person is sequestrated,

a sum deducted from that benefit under that subsection shall not be treated as income of his for the purposes of the Bankruptcy (Scotland) Act 1985.]

(11) This section applies to the following benefits—
(a) benefits as defined in section 122 of the Contributions and Benefits Act;
[6(aa) subject to section 71A below, a jobseeker's allowance;]
[9(ab) state pension credit;]
(b) [7. . .] income support;
(c) [10 . . .]
(d) [10 . . .]
(e) any social fund payments such as are mentioned in section 138(1)(a) or (2) of the Contributions and Benefits Act; and
(f) child benefit."

[11 (12) In this section, "couple" has the meaning given by section 137(1) of the Contributions and Benefits Act.]

AMENDMENTS

1. Social Security (Overpayments) Act 1996, s.1(2) (for determination made after July 24, 1996).
2. Social Security Act 1998, Sch.7 (July 5, 1999).
3. Social Security (Overpayments) Act 1996, s.1(3) (for determinations made after July 24, 1996).
4. Social Security (Overpayments) Act 1996, s.1(4) (for determinations made after July 24, 1996).
5. Jobseekers Act 1995, s.32(1) (October 7, 1996).
6. Jobseekers Act 1995, Sch.2 (October 7, 1996).
7. Jobseekers Act 1995, Sch.3 (October 7, 1996).
8. Tax Credits Act 2002, s.51 and Sch.4 (February 26, 2003 for the purpose of making regulations only; April 1, 2003 for the purpose of transfer of functions only; for remaining purposes date to be appointed).
9. State Pension Credit Act 2002, s.14 and Sch.2 (July 2, 2002 for the purposes of making regulations only; fully in force October 6, 2003).
10. Tax Credits Act 2002, s.60 and Sch.6 (April 8, 2003).
11. Civil Partnership Act 2004, s.254 and Sch.24, para.58 (December 5, 2005).

DERIVATION

1.80   Social Security Act 1986, s.53.

GENERAL NOTE

This general note is structured under the following headings:
Regulations: para.**1.81**
Limitation periods: para.**1.82**
When does s.71 apply?: para.**1.83**
The requirement for revision or supersession: para.**1.84**
The test to be applied: para.**1.86**
Any person: para.**1.87**
Appointees: para.**1.88**
Overpayments involving spouses: para.**1.89**

(1992 c.5, s.71)

Recoverability decisions against a claimant's estate where there are no duly constituted personal representatives: para.**1.90**
Whether fraudulently or otherwise: para.**1.91**
Misrepresents: para.**1.92**
Fails to disclose: para.**1.93**
Mental capacity: para.**1.96**
Material fact: para.**1.97**
Missing documents: para.**1.98**
Causation: para.**1.99**
The amount of the overpayment which is recoverable: para.**1.100**
Automated credit transfers: para.**1.101**
Tax credits: substitution of subs.(8)–(9): para.**1.102**
Welfare Reform and Pensions Act 1999: para.**1.103**
A useful book: para.**1.104**

Regulations
The regulations referred to in this section are the Social Security (Payments on Account, Overpayments and Recovery) Regulations 1988, para. 2.684 below.

1.81

Limitation periods
Arguments that overpayments are not recoverable because of the application of the limitation periods applicable to the recovery of debts in actions before the courts are destined to fail. In *R(SB)5/91* the Commissioner said,

1.82

> "The plain fact is that section 9(1) of the Limitation Act 1980 simply has no application to proceedings before the adjudicating authorities. But when the amount of the overpayment has been *finally* determined by them, as in this case it is by my decision (unless it is proposed to take the matter on appeal to the Court of Appeal) then, and then only, for the purposes of recovery of the overpayment by action in the Courts, time begins to run." (para.7.)

In *CIS/026/1994* the claimant sought a review of the overpayment decision on the grounds that the Secretary of State was no longer able to seek recovery of the overpaid benefit because more than six years had passed and any action in a court would be barred by the operation of s.9(1) of the Limitation Act 1980, and that this constituted a relevant change of circumstances. The overpayment was at the time of the application being recovered at the rate of £5 per week from the claimant's retirement pension. The Commissioner regarded the applications as wholly misconceived (as had the tribunal). The Commissioner confirmed that, so far as relevant to social security payments, "the Limitation Acts take away only the remedy by action or by set-off and that they leave the right otherwise untouched. The social security adjudicating authorities are not concerned with and have no jurisdiction in respect of remedies by action or set-off." (para.5.)

When does s.71 apply?
The predecessor to the section replaced the misrepresentation/non-disclosure test formerly contained in s.20 of the Supplementary Benefits Act 1976 which applied to supplementary benefit and the due care and diligence test in s.119 of the Social Security Act 1975 which applied to non-means tested benefits. Following a series of cases, it has been finally established by the House of Lords in *Plewa v Chief Adjudication Officer* [1994] 2 W.L.R. 317 that where the overpayment spans periods before and after April 6, 1987 (the date s.53 of the Social Security Act 1986 came into force) the relevant test prior to April 6, 1987 must be applied to the overpayment in respect of that period, and the new test applied to the period starting on April 6, 1987. Only where the whole of the period of the overpayment is on or after April 6, 1987 is the new test alone applied to the issue of recoverability.

1.83

The view of the Court of Appeal in *R. (Steele) v Birmingham CC and the Secretary of State for Work and Pensions* [2005] EWCA Civ 1824, that s.71 is the *only* route by which the Secretary of State can recover an overpayment of benefit seemingly settles,

53

for the moment at least, an area which has been the subject of some dispute over the years, namely whether the Secretary of State could seek to recover the overpayment under the common law without invoking s.71.

The effect of bankruptcy on recovery of overpayments of benefit was considered in *R (Balding) v Secretary of State for Work and Pensions* [2007] EWHC (Admin) 759. A decision that an overpayment of income support was recoverable from Balding had been made before he was adjudged to be bankrupt. The Administrative Court ruled that the liability was a 'contingent liability' under the Insolvency Act 1986, and Balding was therefore not liable to repay the overpayment when he was discharged from bankruptcy. It is understood that the Secretary of State is seeking to appeal the decision.

The requirement for revision or supersession

1.84   The first requirement in overpayment cases is for a variation of the decision awarding benefit to be made either on review, supersession or appeal. Without such a variation, there is no power to recover overpayments: s.71(5A). The only exception to this rule is found in reg.12 of the Overpayments Regulations (see below). Tribunals usually deal with cases where there has been a revision of the initial determination. However, a common ground upon which appeals to the Commissioner concerning overpayment decisions have succeeded is the failure of the tribunal to consider whether grounds for review within s.71(5A) exist: see *R(IS) 7/91*. In a number of unreported decisions (*CSSB/621/1988, CSSB/316/1989, CSSB/517/1989* and *CSIS/118/1990*), Commissioners exhort tribunals to remember that revision is a prerequisite to recovery under s.71. Where the overpayments span a number of years, every decision over that period must be identified and revised before the overpayment is recoverable: see para.6 of *CSIS/45/1990*.

In *CIS/4434/2004* the Commissioner held that the section generally requires that the review of entitlement and the determination that there has been a recoverable overpayment must happen at the same time. The Social Security (Overpayments) Act 1996 has amended s.71 to reverse the effect of that decision. There is still a requirement that there must have been a review of benefit entitlement and a decision that there is a recoverable overpayment, but these need not take place at the same time.

In *R(IS) 13/05* the Commissioner confirmed that a decision that a couple is living together as husband and wife is not a decision which meets the requirements of s.71(5A), and a decision that an overpayment is recoverable cannot be based on such a determination. Such a decision is commonly only the first step in revising or superseding a person's entitlement to benefit. It is the ensuing decisions on which an overpayment decision must be founded.

In *CIS/1055/1997* the Commissioner holds that the determination referred to is a recovery determination (and not an entitlement determination). The new provisions apply to recovery determinations made after July 24, 1996 regardless of the date of any entitlement determination (including the entitlement determination which resulted in there having been an overpayment of benefit). In *CSIS/174/1996* the Commissioner indicated that in his view the determination must be that of an adjudication officer and could not be a decision of a tribunal correcting an earlier omission. The Commissioner considers that best practice is for the review decision itself to be put before the tribunal and not simply a summary of it in the written submission to the tribunal. This is considered essential where the claimant puts in issue any of its terms.

In *CSB/1272/1989* the Commissioner considers whether a tribunal could use its powers to determine questions first arising in the course of the appeal to correct a failure by an adjudication officer to review the award of benefit as required by what was then s.53(4) of the Social Security Act 1986. That decision attracted some cautionary comments in *CSB/1093/1989*. The issue is now largely academic since the power to determine questions first arising in the course of the appeal has not been re-enacted in the Social Security Act 1998. There will be little alternative but to set aside any decision where there has not been a review as required by the section.

(1992 c.5, s.71)

The nature of the evidence which an adjudication officer was expected to produce to demonstrate that there has been a review was considered in *R(IS)2/96*. The Commissioner holds that a computer print-out is not sufficient by itself to establish that a review has taken place (though it might, if the output is intelligible and records that a proper determination had taken place), since there must be some human interaction with the computer to convert computer-based information into a review decision. The Commissioner notes that the computer print-out in issue in the case was, by itself, unintelligible. However, verbal evidence to interpret the print-out, or submission of a copy of a letter informing the claimant of the decision which contained sufficient detail might suffice to show that there had been a review and revision of entitlement. Failure to provide such evidence would mean that the adjudication officer had failed to meet the burden of proof in overpayment cases.

In *CIS/362/2002* the Commissioner re-affirms that recovery is conditional on a valid revision or supersession of the decision awarding benefit. Defects of form might be correctable by tribunals and Commissioners, but not defects of substance. In this case, the relevant decision "was so defective in substance as to be invalid as a supersession in relation to the relevant period.": (para.12). In *CIS/764/2002* the same Commissioner clarified his views on this issue as follows:

"In a supersession case not involving overpayment recoverability an appeal tribunal may, if the relevant evidence is available, conduct or perfect a defective decision taken by the Secretary of State, providing that the defects in the Secretary of State's decision are not so great that it must be said that the decision is invalid, rather than merely defective. In my judgment that is the line to be drawn, not a line between defects of substance and defects of form. That is what I said recently in paragraph 12 of decision *CIS/362/2002* [and] was consistent with the Tribunal of Commissioners' decision *R(IS) 2/97*. I did not say there, as Mr Miller suggested in his written submission dated 20 August 2002, that no defects of substance could be corrected. I referred to 'defects of substance which rendered the purported review invalid' and to a decision being 'so defective in substance as to be invalid as a supersession'. Defects merely of form may always be corrected by an appeal tribunal. Defects of substance may be corrected, providing that they are not so great as to render the decision invalid. In a case where the decision under appeal combines an overpayment recoverability decision with a supersession decision, that general approach is not displaced, for the reasons given in paragraph 41 of decision *CSIS/399/2001* and *CSIS/400/2001*. It may be different if the overpayment recoverability decision is taken separately from the supersession decision and is appealed on its own." (para.11.)

R(IB) 2/04 considered the scope of the general power to make review and supersession decisions under ss.9 and 10 of the 1998 Act, and concluded that tribunals had powers to remedy defects in decisions save where they were so serious as to render the decision in issue wholly incoherent. In general a Secretary of State's decision which altered the original decision with effect from the date of the original decision should be treated as a review under s.9 and a Secretary of State's decision which altered the decision from a later date should be treated as a supersession under s.10. This broad interpretation of a tribunal's powers has not removed all the difficulties in relation to the procedural requirements in relation to overpayments decisions. In *CIS/362/2003*, the Commissioner had noted that the test for remedying defects in overpayments cases may be stricter than in other cases.

This issue is further explored in *CIS/3228/2003*. The case concerned a decision that there had been a £6,018.53 overpayment of income support, which had arisen when the claimant had failed to disclose the receipt of a residence order allowance. After an adjournment before the tribunal, the Secretary of State had produced a certificate indicating that on December 11, 2001 a decision had been made superseding the award of income support from January 4, 1996 but purporting to revise the claimant's entitlement arising from a decision of January 4, 1996. However, the submission to the tribunal stated that all decisions awarding income support from

January 4, 1996 were superseded, whereas the certified decision related only to the first decision awarding benefit.

There was no dispute that the proper process for complying with s.71(5) required a decision *revising* all the decisions awarding benefit; these would take effect from the date of the decisions which were revised. But a supersession decision on the grounds of ignorance of fact could only take effect from the date of the supersession decision. The Secretary of State's representative conceded that the certified decision was defective in that it certified a supersession decision rather than a revision decision.

The Commissioner concludes that a certified record of a decision is conclusive evidence of the decision (para.13). However, in the light of the decision of the Tribunal of Commissioners in *R(IB) 2/04* it was open to a tribunal to regard the decision as a revision rather than a supersession:

> 16. In my judgment, a tribunal's power to overlook mere defects of form in decisions made under section 9 or section 10 of the 1998 Act is not limited to cases where a supersession decision or a decision which has been revised under section 9 is under appeal to the tribunal. In *CIS/764/2002* Mr Commissioner Mesher held that defects of substance in a decision which were not so great as to affect its validity could be corrected by a tribunal if the supersession decision and the overpayment recoverability decision were both under appeal. Although the Commissioner reserved the position in relation to such cases where an overpayment recoverability decision is taken separately from the supersession decision and is appealed on its own, he did not suggest that it was necessary for the supersession decision to be under appeal in order for the tribunal to have power to ignore errors which did not affect the substance of the decision.
>
> 17. If the decision in this case recorded in the certified record is taken at face value, it changed the decision awarding income support as from the date on which the awarding decision took effect, and could therefore only have been a revision decision under section 9 of the 1998 Act. The record of the decision gave a valid ground for the making of such a decision, namely that the decision awarding benefit was made in ignorance of a material fact. The tribunal was not called on to exercise any jurisdiction over the decision altering entitlement to benefit, other than to determine whether a valid decision had been made which complied with the requirements of section 71(5A) of the Administration Act. On the basis that the certified record of the decision taken on 11 December 2001 was correct in recording a decision which removed benefit from the date of the award, I do not consider that the erroneous description of the decision as a supersession decision prevented the tribunal from regarding it as a valid revision decision.

However, although the tribunal could have treated the supersession decision as a revision decision, there remained defects which rendered the overpayment not recoverable in that the decision did not alter all the decisions awarding benefit (only the first decision), and the decision failed to specify the amounts of the revised entitlement. On the latter point the Commissioner says:

> 20. . . . . . I consider that a decision awarding a claimant benefit of a stated amount can only be effectively revised if it is replaced by a new decision which also specifies the amount of benefit (if any) to which the claimant is entitled, in the light of the fact which was not taken into account when the original decision was made. A revision decision to the effect that an earlier decision awarding benefit of a specified amount has been "revised", but which does not state the amount of the revised entitlement is, in my judgment inchoate. If a revision (or supersession) decision resulting in an overpayment is made separately from a recovery decision, it will therefore be necessary for the claimant's revised benefit entitlement to be calculated as part of the revision decision before a valid overpayment recoverability decision can be made under section 71(1).

(1992 c.5, s.71)

In this case, the Secretary of State appears to have been hoist with his own petard in certifying a decision. That is conclusive and cannot be revisited. Although it could be treated as a valid revision decision, if it remained defective for not referring to all relevant decisions awarding benefit, and if it failed to specify the amount of the revised entitlement, it could not ground recovery of overpaid benefit.

In *CIS/0170/2003* a different Commissioner took the same view, noting further that there could not be a supersession decision based upon change of circumstances where the claimant's circumstances had not changed. It is not a change of circumstances where something new which has been in existence for a long time comes to the notice of the Secretary of State. In this decision, the Commissioner warns tribunals against being too ready to substitute revision decisions for faulty supersession decisions. In many cases, there will be insufficient evidence (especially where one or both parties is not present) and the tribunal must take care not simply to "construct a narrative" to borrow a phrase from *CIS/3228/2003*. Furthermore, where computer printouts are provided under the Generalised Matching Service, these must be accompanied by full explanations of the significance of the various codes used. Otherwise there is a real risk of making findings of fact which no reasonable tribunal could make.

The outcome is that there will remain scope for arguments to be put before tribunals that the procedural requirements for recovery of overpaid benefit have not been met.

CIS/3605/2005 was concerned with the application of s.71(5A) in a case in which the amount of income support to which the claimant was entitled had reduced following the cessation of child benefit. Complications arose when that entitlement had been resurrected for a number of periods. The claimant argued that the revision decision had been made in ignorance of the true position on the dates for which child benefit had been awarded and so was invalid. The Commissioner concluded:

"10. It seems to me that the claimant's argument confuses the concepts of correctness and validity. The Secretary of State had statutory power to make the decision of 14th August 2002, even if it was based on an inaccurate understanding of the facts. It was subject to supersession, revision, and appeal, but until one of those events took place it was, in law, a valid decision, and satisfied the requirements of section 71(5A) for the purposes of a recoverability decision.

11. This approach is consistent with the jurisprudence of the House of Lords in administrative law. Thus, a decision which might traditionally have been regarded as void is nevertheless to be treated as having legal effect until a court has decided that it is void (*Re Racal Communications Ltd* [1980] 2 All ER 634) and an order may be void for one purpose and valid for another (*Calvin v Carr* [1980] AC 574; *R v Wicks* [1998] AC 92)."

CIS/764/2002 and *CIS/3228/2003*, on the need for revision or supersession of all decisions authorising payment of benefit during a period of alleged overpayment, have been followed in *CIS/203/2002* (a post-*Hinchy* decision of August 24, 2006).

The Secretary of State must present all the evidence

Generally in overpayment cases, the burden is on the Secretary of State to establish all the facts which justify a conclusion that an overpayment is recoverable. The absence of a representative of the Secretary of State in tribunals can present difficulties, and tribunals will need to consider whether it is fair to both parties to adjourn with directions for the submission of further evidence where the evidence presented in the papers on behalf of the Secretary of State is incomplete.

1.85

In *C1/06-07(IS)*, a Commissioner in Northern Ireland stresses the importance of the Department's presenting documentary evidence in support of key matters on which the decision to recover overpaid benefit is based. In this case, it was two forms through which the Department claimed to have notified the claimant that he had been found capable of work. Had the claimant disclosed the content of these decisions the overpayment of income support in issue could not have occurred. The Commissioner said,

"26. . . . In general terms I consider that the Department should supply copies or pro formas of relevant notifications in recoverability cases. In cases where notification is an issue the tribunal should ask to see at least pro formas of these documents if they have not been furnished."

A similar point on the need for the Secretary of State to present all the evidence to the tribunal was made by the Commissioner in *CIS/1462/2006*, a case in which there was a possible trust which meant that the claimant had no beneficial interest in certain resources. The Commissioner also criticises (in paras 18–20) in strong terms the failure of the Secretary of State to ensure representation in cases, such as this, which are of some complexity. He also noted that the burden of proof rests with the Secretary of State.

The test to be applied

1.86 The test laid down in subs.(1) requires a number of conditions to be satisfied. Where:

(a) any person

(b) whether fraudulently or otherwise

(c) misrepresents, or

(d) fails to disclose

(e) a material fact

(f) and this results in an overpayment of benefit for any period

the amount of the overpayment is recoverable from the person misrepresenting or failing to disclose that material fact.

It is for the Department to prove on the balance of probabilities the facts which justify the recovery of the overpayment: *R(SB)43/83*. Appeals involving overpayments require fastidious attention to the facts which are often hotly disputed. In such disputes having regard to where the burden of proof lies is particularly important.

Any person

1.87 The person making the misrepresentation or failing to disclose need not be the claimant. It can be anyone. In *R(SB)21/82* recovery was sought from the claimant's wife; and in *R(SB)23/83* it was the claimant's personal representative. It had been made clear in *Secretary of State for Social Services v Solly* [1974] 3 All E.R. 922 that recovery from the estate of a deceased person was possible. However, tribunals are not the place in which which objections to liability by the executor on the grounds, for example, that the estate has already been distributed are to be resolved. Those are matters concerning a decision to pursue recovery (which were reserved under the old adjudication system for the Secretary of State) rather than liability for the overpayment, and may need adjudication in court: *R(SB)1/96*.

Non-disclosure by someone other than the claimant requires some clear evidence of responsibility on that person to disclose information. In *R(SB)21/82* the Commissioner said that the non-disclosure must have occurred "in circumstances in which, at least, disclosure by the person was reasonably to be expected." Following the decision of the Court of Appeal in *B v Secretary of State* (see below at para.1.93), it is eminently arguable that the source of the obligation is much higher than this, namely that recovery from a third party can only succeed where a legal obligation to disclose can be established.

In *CG/065/1989* the adjudication officer had sought recovery (in addition to recovery from the claimant) from two solicitors who had acted for the claimant. The Commissioner advises that where recovery is sought from more than one party, a tribunal should deal with the recoverability of the overpayment from each of the parties covered by the adjudication officer's decision. It will not be enough to decide only that the overpayment is recoverable from the claimant.

Appointees
Special considerations can arise where recovery is sought from an appointee. 1.88
In *CG/065/1989*, a case concerning recovery from solicitor appointees, the Commissioner contemplated recovery being available from both the claimant and any appointee. In *CIS/734/1992* the Commissioner held that there could be no recovery from the claimant by reason of the appointee's misrepresentation or failure to disclose, but there could be recovery from the appointee. In *CIS/332/1993* the acts of the appointee, when acting as such, are treated as acts of the claimant and so recovery is only available from the claimant (or the claimant's estate) and not the appointee (paras 22–24). Reliance is placed, in part, on an analogy with the situation in *R(SB)34/83*, which concerned a failure to disclose material facts by a receiver appointed by the Court of Protection, and where the resulting overpayment was recoverable from the claimant's estate rather than from the receiver personally. The Commissioner notes that the decision in *CIS/734/1992*, which was predicated on the claimant's lack of capacity because of his mental state, meant that it would be inappropriate to impute to him any failure to disclose or misrepresentation of the appointee. But it is, of course, of the essence of an appointment that the claimant is for some reason unable to act. Are distinctions based on physical and mental capacity appropriate when reg.33 of the Claims and Payments Regulations under which such appointments are made speaks of the appointee exercising any right to which the claimant may be entitled? The Commissioner acknowledges that the matter is one of extreme difficulty.

In *R(IS)5/00* a different Commissioner describes the distinction between a person in their capacity as appointee and in their personal capacity as "puzzling and metaphysical". In upholding the decision of a tribunal that an overpayment was recoverable from an appointee who was the mother of the claimant and had failed to disclose increases in the claimant's savings, the Commissioner appears to differ from the view that the capacity in which a person acts affects the person from whom the overpayment is recoverable.

There is logic in both positions. The first Commissioner is making the point that an appointee's acts are those of the claimant who is unable to act for himself or herself. If a person is acting as appointee, then the recovery should be from the claimant. The second Commissioner reflects the realities of daily life by noting that a person in the position of appointee will almost certainly not make clear distinctions in the capacity in which they are dealing with the Department. If they should have disclosed something such as an increase in savings, then recovery can be sought from them as well as from the claimant.

The decision of the Tribunal of Commissioners in *R(IS)5/03* was handed down on October 28, 2002. The principal point in issue related to the liability of appointees for overpayments of benefit under s.71(3) of the Social Security Administration Act 1992. The appeal had been referred to a Tribunal of Commissioners in order to resolve the conflict between *CIS/332/1993* and *R(IS) 5/00*.

The overpayment had arisen when income support continued in payment at the previous rate when the costs of the claimant's accommodation in a nursing home was met wholly by the health authority. The claimant's mother was her appointee under an appointment made by the Secretary of State for all benefit purposes. The appointee had failed to inform the Department that the costs of her daughter's accommodation in a nursing home were fully met by the health authority.

The Tribunal of Commissioners draws on the common law relating to agency, but recognises that the social security context requires certain modification to the common law rules applicable in a contractual situation. This is justified, in particular, because normal agency principles come into play where the principal has delegated authority to an agent. In the social security context, no such delegation exists, since it is the payer (the Secretary of State) who authorises another to act on behalf of persons unable to act for themselves. The benefit recipient, where reg.33 of the Claims and Payments Regulations applies, is not a party to the delegation of powers. It had been argued by the appellant and CPAG that to render the appointee personally liable would produce a situation in which, for example, social workers might be unwilling to undertake responsibilities as appointees to the disadvantage of benefit recipients. The Tribunal of Commissioners in preferring the principles set out in *R(IS) 5/00*, and concluding that *CIS/332/1993* is wrongly decided, mollified the impact of their decision by finding that there are exceptions to the liability of an appointee. Generally, both the claimant and the appointee will be liable for overpayments resulting from misrepresentations or failure to disclose. There are two exceptions to this rule. The first is that only the appointee will be liable for the overpayment if the appointee has retained the benefit instead of paying it to or applying it for the benefit of the claimant. The second exception is that the appointee will not be liable if the appointee has acted with "due care and diligence". This will avoid an appointee becoming personally liable where the appointee makes a wholly innocent representation, because some change in the claimant's affairs has not been made known to the appointee, and the appointee has not failed to exercise the powers of appointee in such a manner that the appointee could be held to be at fault.

The resurrection of a due care and diligence test in relation to certain overpayments where appointees have been appointed (failure to take due care and diligence to avoid overpayment used to be the test for recovery of non-means tested benefits under repealed s.119 of the Social Security Act 1975) would seem likely to generate a new line of case law which may draw on the old authorities, and might not be as straightforward as the Tribunal thinks. The Tribunal refers (in para.61) to the use of due care and diligence in making a representation, and this is more limited than the old notion of due care and diligence to avoid an overpayment.

Despite the inevitable intricacies which always seem to arise in the manifold scenarios in which overpayments of benefits arise, this decision now makes it clear that the starting point is that both the claimant and any appointee are liable for overpayments of benefit subject to the two qualifications set out in the tribunal's decision.

The issue has also been considered in some detail in the context of a disability living allowance claim by a Deputy Commissioner in Scotland in *CSDLA/1282/2001*. In this case an overpayment of a disability living allowance arose as a result of the failure to disclose that the claimant had been admitted to hospital. At the material time the claimant's son held a Power of Attorney in respect of his mother's affairs, but had not been made an appointee by the Secretary of State under reg.33 of the Claims and Payments Regulations. There had been disclosure to the local office in relation to the claimant's entitlement to income support and retirement pension, and the child benefit she was receiving for her grand-daughter, but there had been no notification to the DLA Unit. In remitting the case for a rehearing, the Deputy Commissioner concludes, (1) following *CA/1014/1999*, that a person holding a power of attorney is not an appointee for the purposes of reg.33 of the Claims and Payments Regulations; (2) that benefit was not receivable by the son and so he was under no duty to inform the Benefits Agency of changes of circumstances under reg.32 of the Claims and Payments Regulations; and (3) that it was not open to the decision-maker to seek recovery from the son where he held a Power of Attorney but had not been made an appointee by the Secretary of State. *CA/1014/1999* has been followed and discussed in *CSDLA/1282/2001* and *CIS/242/2003*.

A useful article on the appointee system can be found at Lowery, R and Lundy, L, "The Social Security Appointee System" [1994] J.S.W.F.L. 313.

Overpayments involving spouses

1.89 In *CIS/619/1997* the Commissioner follows *CIS/13742/1996* in holding that s.71 requires a review of the claims of both husband and wife before reg.13 of the Overpayments Regulations can be used to offset benefit payable to one spouse against an overpayment that is recoverable from the other spouse. Tribunals faced with such cases should have regard to these two decisions in dealing with an appeal before them. The Commissioner also questions the propriety of inclusion in papers relating to the wife's appeal of details concerning the husband where she had maintained throughout that she was living separately from her husband. He suggests that there might be breach of confidentiality in relation to the husband's affairs, and appears to urge that such cases may be ones in which consideration would need to be given to disclosure of the husband's affairs to the tribunal as distinct from disclosure to the claimant. He recognises that this in turn gives rise to issues touching on the requirement to provide a fair hearing from the claimant and of natural justice.

Recoverability decisions against a claimant's estate where there are no duly constituted personal representatives

In *CJSA/1423/1999* the Commissioner held that the Secretary of State has no power under s.71 to seek recovery from the estate of a deceased claimant where there are no duly constituted personal representatives. The Secretary of State is not, however, without any powers in such circumstances, since "he could have made application to the High Court for a limited grant of administration under section 116 of the Supreme Court Act 1981. The court can apparently make a limited grant of that kind for a variety of purposes." (para.38.)

1.90

Whether fraudulently or otherwise

The wording makes clear that there is no need to prove any fraudulent intent. Wholly innocent mistakes by claimants can result in recoverable overpayments: *R(SB)28/83*; *R(SB)9/85*; and *R(SB)18/85*. Innocent misrepresentations are easy to imagine. But it may be better to think of non-fraudulent failures to disclose rather than innocent failures, since non-disclosures involve some breach of a duty to disclose. In *R(SB)28/83* it was suggested that the duty to disclose extends to matters relevant to the claim to benefit which a person with reasonable diligence would have been aware.

1.91

This interpretation of the section is confirmed by the Court of Appeal in *Page and Davis v Chief Adjudication Officer*, published as a supplement to *R(SB)2/92*, where Dillon LJ said:

"The whole burden of the phrase 'whether fraudulently or otherwise' must be . . . that it is to apply even if the misrepresentation is not fraudulent, in other words, if it is innocent. No other construction makes any sense, in my view, of this particular subsection."

Misrepresents

Misrepresentation is founded on positive and deliberate action: *R(SB)9/85*, and may be oral or in writing, or even in some cases arise from conduct such as the cashing of a giro-cheque. As noted above the reason why the statement represented to the Department is incorrect is irrelevant. If a statement has been made, whether written or oral (*R(SB)18/85*) which is untrue, it is a misrepresentation whatever the explanation for the incorrect information proffered. A misrepresentation in a written document may be qualified by an oral statement; it is often asserted by claimants that the form does not accurately reflect everything that was said. While generally claimants bear responsibility for the contents of forms, if it is accepted that an oral qualification has not been properly noted, this may preclude the written representation from being a misrepresentation: *R(SB)18/85*.

1.92

Questions can arise as to whom the misrepresentation is addressed. Most representations will be made to the Department, but it is sometimes argued that the misrepresentation was made, for example, to the Post Office. Does this constitute a misrepresentation for the purposes of s.71?

A written misrepresentation may also be qualified or modified when that written communication is read in conjunction with other written communications which should be before the decision-maker in making the decision which resulted in the overpayment of benefit: *R(SB)2/91*, paras 10–13. In such cases, it goes without saying that careful findings of fact are vital. Tribunals should call for originals (or clear copies) of statements signed by persons which are claimed to be the misrepresentation on which an overpayment decision is founded.

Rather more complex than cases where a claimant argues that they have qualified the contents of a misrepresentation in some way in completing the form on which the claim is based are those cases where the claimant argues that they have qualified the contents of a current claim by information contained in an earlier claim. These situations are much less likely to lead to the overpayment not being recoverable. So in *CSB/108/1992* a claimant, who misrepresented that he did not have an army pension believing that it was not relevant to a claim to supplementary benefit and who sought to rely on statements which appear to have been made by him in connection with claims for unemployment benefit and sickness benefit, did not succeed in escaping a liability to repay overpaid supplementary benefit. The Commissioner indicated that the contemporaneity of the oral qualifications was crucial.

In *R(SB)3/90* the Commissioner holds that there can still be a misrepresentation of a material fact even where there has been an earlier disclosure of that fact (para.11). Although disclosure prevents any recovery of an overpayment based on the failure to disclose head, a misrepresentation by declaration on a claim form that a claimant had no money coming in when superannuation payments from a former employer were in payment, receipt of which had previously been disclosed, overrides that disclosure. The Commissioner specifically states that the Department is entitled to rely on statements in the current claim form and is under no duty to check back to see whether those statements are consistent withearlier disclosures. So it remains incumbent on claimants to be meticulous in their completion of claim forms even after a course of dealing with the Department. The reasoning of the Commissioner in *R(SB) 3/90* is implicitly approved by the Court of Appeal in *Morrell v Secretary of State for Work and Pensions* [2003] EWCA Civ 526, *R(IS)6/03*, at paras 38–48.

CSU/03/1991 adds a gloss to *R(SB)3/90*. *CSU/03/1991* was a case in which two forms had been submitted by the claimant containing conflicting information about the claimant's pension position. When he initially claimed unemployment benefit, he disclosed on Form UB461 the correct amount of his pension expressed as a weekly amount, but a few days later he erred in recording on Form UB81(PEN) the pension as £293.75 per *year* rather than per *month*. The claimant's argument was that in considering his claim the adjudication officer should have had both documents before him or her, that this would have indicated the error and no overpayment would have resulted. The adjudication officer sought to argue that he or she was not required to check back to see whether any inconsistent information was given in earlier documents. The Commissioner held that something had clearly gone wrong in the Department; both documents should have been before the adjudication officer in determining this claim and the adjudication officer could not rely on *R(SB)3/90* as the basis for recovering the overpayment of benefit which resulted from the adjudication officer's reliance on the incorrect figure on the Form UB81(PEN).

In *CIS/5140/2001* the Commissioner applied the principle established in *R(SB)3/90* to a variant of the facts of that case. The claimant had received money from her mother each month to help her with her payments of rent to her landlord. The Department sought recovery of an overpayment of benefit arising because that income (and the Commissioner concludes that it was properly categorised as income in the circumstances of the case) was not taken into account in determining the amount of income support payable. There were two periods in issue, separated by a period during which the Department could not seek recovery because it knew of the true facts. The recovery for the second period was sought because the claimant had repeated the misrepresentation about her income in completing a review form. The Commissioner concludes that the Department was entitled to rely on the statements about income in the review form to ground recovery based upon a misrepresentation of fact despite their prior knowledge of the true position.

In *CIS/5117/1998*, the Commissioner addresses the question of the extent to which silence can constitute a misrepresentation. The claim form for income support had been completed by an officer of the Department, and read back to him. The form indicated that the claimant was married and living with his wife. None of the questions about his wife, and in particular about her earnings or other income, had been answered. The tribunal found as a fact that the claimant had not been asked questions about his wife's earnings or other income by the Department's officer. An overpayment decision went on appeal to the tribunal which found that there had been no misrepresentation or failure to disclose in the circumstances of this case. The adjudication officer appealed. The Commissioner upheld the tribunal; the only substantial issue was whether or not the claimant made a misrepresentation by his silence when he made the claim on which the award of income support was based.

The Commissioner concludes that *R(SB)18/85* applied to this case. The claimant answered all the questions put to him by the officer of the Department, and the form was not read over to the claimant in its entirety. In these circumstances, says the Commissioner, the claimant's "misrepresentation" that the information on the form was complete "was qualified by the fact that he had supplied all the information for which he had been asked" in circumstances where the officer had given him no opportunity to answer the relevant questions about his wife's earnings, gave no indication that such matters might be material to benefit entitlement, and did not read back the entries on the claim form to confirm their correctness.

The facts of this case are unusual, and appear to represent a failure by the Department to follow its own recommended procedures. But, where such unusual circumstances are established, the claimant's silence does not amount to a misrepresentation. In so far as *CIS/645/1993* suggests that silence as to material facts known to the claimant amounts to a misrepresentation, that decision must be read as referring to a deliberate decision to say nothing on a matter known to be material.

In *Hinchy v Secretary of State for Work and Pensions* [2003] EWCA Civ 138 (February 20, 2003), the Court of Appeal touched on but did not resolve the question of whether misrepresentation provided a separate basis for seeking to recover an overpayment where the claimant signed a declaration in an order book in circumstances where the Secretary of State and his officials are to be treated as knowing a material fact. The Court did suggest that it would be odd if a representation to the Post Office "would amount to a misrepresentation causing the payment" (Aldous LJ at para.33) Carnwath LJ expressed his reservations more clearly, "I would need some persuasion that the signing of the declaration, without more, is sufficient to found a claim under section 71, in any case where it turns out for some reason the entitlement had not arisen or had changed." (para.47)

There is no comment on this aspect of the case in the decision of the House of Lords in this case, which is discussed below.

In *CTC/4025/2003*, the Commissioner considered an appeal by a claimant against whom a decision seeking to recover overpaid tax credits had been made. The claimant had responded to a question on the claim form "Do you have a partner with whom you normally live?" in the negative. At the time a marriage of very short duration was in difficulties and the claimant and her husband were living apart. However, the effect of reg.9(1) of the Family Credit (General) Regulations was that the husband and wife were to be treated as members of the same household for the purposes of claims to Working Families Tax Credit. The Commissioner rejects the argument originally put to the tribunal (and which the Secretary of State conceded in the submission to the Commissioner involved "quite a leap") that because the regulations treated the claimant and her husband as members of the same household, she must have misrepresented the facts by saying that she was not living with a partner. The overpayments were not recoverable from her.

The appeal in *CFC/2766/2003* concerned entitlement to working families tax credit. Shortly before the claim was made, the claimant disposed of significant amounts of capital. When the claim was made, the claimant correctly reported capital of no more than £2,500. When the capital disposal came to light, the Department sought recovery of an overpayment of the tax credit on the grounds that the claimant had misrepresented the position in relation to their capital. But the claimant had not done so. There was no question asking about capital they once had but no longer have.

CSIS/0345/2004 concerned a claimant who had misrepresented her income. When the claimant claimed income support, she had not disclosed sick pay received from her employer under income protection insurance offered by the employer. She

Social Security Administration Act 1992

claimed not to have done so on the basis of advice from an officer of the Department to the effect that such income was not relevant to entitlement to income support. The Commissioner notes that, where recovery of overpayments is sought on the grounds of misrepresentation, the reason for the misrepresentation is irrelevant. The sole issue was, accordingly, whether (assuming that the tribunal accepted that there had been the course of dealing put forward by the claimant) the representation on the claim form could be regarded as qualified by the earlier disclosure of receipt of the sick pay when the enquiry was made. The Commissioner said,

" . . ., even if . . . the disclosure was clearly made in terms of 'sick pay', the connection between such a prior general enquiry and the later determination made on the claim once the form was actually submitted, was much too remote for there to be any reasonable expectation that a link would be made and the disclosure taken into account. The concept of a prior disclosure qualifying a later written representation, so that the latter is no longer to be regarded as an incorrect one, must be restricted to very special circumstances; otherwise, the rationale behind recoverability based even on *innocent* misrepresentation, that it was positive and deliberate action upon which a decision maker must be entitled to rely, would be subverted." (para.29).

Fails to disclose

1.93 The notion of a failure to disclose is more open ended than that of a misrepresentation. The case law is complicated and can be confusing. The interpretation of s.71 in this context may be in a state of flux at the moment, and some long-established principles have recently been questioned by the Commissioners and the courts.

The discussion will accordingly be discussed under three headings:
(a) The nature of the duty to disclose
(b) Disclosure to whom and the continuing duty to disclose
(c) Disclosure at an office displaying the **one** logo

(a) the nature of the duty to disclose

The starting point is that the legislation uses the term "fails to disclose", which is not the same as "does not disclose". One of the most quoted extracts from a Commissioner's decision is that in *R(SB) 21/82* that a failure to disclose "necessarily imports the concept of some breach of obligation, moral or legal—i.e. that non-disclosure must have occurred in circumstances in which . . . disclosure by the person in question was reasonably to be expected" (para.4(2)). It should, however, be remembered that this decision involved recovery from someone other than the claimant. Both Commissioners and judges in the courts have taken the view that the duty to disclose will, in most cases, be a legal one rather than a moral one: see *Hinchy v Secretary of State for Work and Pensions* [2005] UKHL 16, para.39 (dissenting opinion of Lord Scott); para 53 (opinion of Baroness Hale) and the Tribunal of Commissioners in *CIS/4348/2003*, paras 16–17 (though this is without prejudice to arguments on a moral duty to disclose).

The emerging consensus appears to be that the duty to disclose is either inherent in the recoverability scheme established by s.71, or can be found, in particular, in reg.32 of the Claims and Payments Regulations: see *Hinchy v Secretary of State for Work and Pensions* [2005] UKHL 16, paras 19 to 22 (opinion of Lord Hoffmann); para.40 (dissenting opinion of Lord Scott); and para.54 (opinion of Baroness Hale); and the Tribunal of Commissioners in *CIS/4348/2003*, paras 22–32.

Regulation 32 of the Claims and Payments Regulations contains two duties. The first duty is for benefit recipients to provide such certificates, documents and information affecting the right to benefit as the Secretary of State or the Board of Inland Revenue may require. The second duty is to notify the Secretary of State or the Board of any change of circumstances which benefit recipients might "reasonably be expected to know might affect the right to benefit, or to its receipt, as soon as reasonably practicable after its occurrence, by giving notice in writing . . . of any such change to the appropriate office."

(1992 c.5, s.71)

Note that the duty to provide information required by the Secretary of State or the Board of Inland Revenue under the first head of reg.32 is an unqualified duty, whereas the duty to notify changes of circumstances is qualified by the requirement that the claimant might reasonably be expected to know that the change of circumstances is relevant to continuing benefit entitlement.

The decision of the Tribunal of Commissioners in *CIS/4348/2003* of October 12, 2004 affirmed on appeal to the Court of Appeal as B v *Secretary of State for Work and Pensions*, judgment of July 20, 2005 [2005] EWCA Civ 929 reported as *R(IS) 9/06* (leave to appeal to the House of Lords was refused—the claimant has now made an application to the European Courts of Human Rights alleging a violation of human rights), overturns some leading authorities of long standing in ruling, in essence, that there is no over-riding requirement applying in every case that disclosure must be reasonably expected of the claimant before an overpayment of benefit can be recovered on the grounds of the failure to disclose. However, the detail is rather more complex than this simple statement suggests.

The facts in the appeal before the Tribunal of Commissioners can be simply stated. The claimant has a learning disability. She was a lone parent in receipt of income support and received an allowance for her children. When they were taken into care, she did not disclose this fact despite clear indications in documentation she received from the Department that this was a specific change of circumstances that required disclosure. The tribunal had accepted that she would not have understood the meaning of what was written in the order book, and presumably also in other written communications from the Department. The issue was whether the mental capacity of the claimant was such as to prevent the Secretary of State from seeking recovery of the overpayment of income support (para.8).

The Tribunal of Commissioners begins by examining the relevant principles before considering the conflicting Commissioners' decisions. The following matters were accepted as common ground:
  (i) There can be a wholly innocent failure to disclose, exemplified by those who do not disclose some material fact because they do not appreciate that it is a material fact.
  (ii) Persons cannot fail to disclose for the purposes of s.71 a matter unless it is known to them. Whether a matter is known to someone is determined by applying a subjective test.
  (iii) A material fact for the purposes of s.71 is a fact which is objectively material to the decision to award benefit.
  (iv) Failure to disclose is not the same as mere non-disclosure. "It imports a breach of some obligation to disclose" (para.13).

Where the obligation to disclose comes from was more contentious. The Tribunal of Commissioners reject the importing of insurance law obligations; these flow from a common law duty, whereas in the social security context, there are "specific duties of disclosure set out in a statutory scheme in respect of benefits." (para.15). The Tribunal of Commissioners expresses some difficulty with the concept of breach of a "moral" obligation to disclose (to which reference is made in *R(SB) 21/82*) and could not envisage a case where it would be necessary to rely on a moral duty as distinct from a legal duty to disclose. However, the appeal before them turned on the nature of the legal duty to disclose and the Tribunal of Commissioners does not consider the issue further.

The duty to disclose is not found in s.71; that section presupposes a duty but does not impose it (para.20). The duty is to be found in reg.32 of the Claims and Payments Regulations. The Tribunal of Commissioners was concerned with the version of this regulation in force prior to its amendment by SI 2003/1050, but does not regard the amendment made by the 2003 amending regulations as affecting the substance of the provisions. The reasoning adopted is expressly stated to apply to the current version of the reg.32.

Reg.32 contains two duties. The first duty required a claimant to furnish information on request material to any decision relating to entitlement to or payment of benefit (this is contained in reg.32(1) and (1A) of the current version). The second duty required a claimant to notify a change of circumstances affecting the continuance of entitlement to benefit (this is contained in reg.32(1B) of the current version). The two duties are "entirely distinct" (para.30).

For further discussion of the nature of the duties under reg. 32(1A) and (1B), see *CDLA/2328/2006* discussed in the General Note to reg. 32 of the Claims and Payments Regulations.

The first duty is not qualified in any way, but the second duty is. It requires notification of changes of circumstances as soon as reasonably practicable which claimants might reasonably be expected to know might affect the continuance of entitlement to benefit or the payment of benefit. The Tribunal of Commissioners expressly reject the argument that the words qualifying the second duty also inform the first duty.

Some of the s.71 case law is relevant to the proper construction of reg.32. First, one cannot fail to furnish information or notify a change of circumstances unless the information or change of circumstances is known (para.32(a)). Secondly, where information is requested by the Secretary of State under the first duty, any view the claimant might have as to the relevance of the information to benefit entitlement does not arise.

In the context of meeting the obligation set out in the first duty, no question arises concerning the mental capacity of the person required to furnish the information. It is not open to claimants to argue that they were unable to respond to an unambiguous request because, as a result of mental incapacity, they did not understand the request (para.34). The consequences of failing to disclose information in breach of the first duty in reg.32 are to be found in s.71:

> "That provides simply that, where there was a breach of the obligation to disclose any material fact under regulation 32(1), whether fraudulent or innocent, then the Secretary of State shall be entitled to recover any overpayment that results." (para.36).

The Tribunal of Commissioners then considers whether, on basic principles, s.71 can be said to import a notion that disclosure is only required where it can reasonably be expected of the claimant:

> ". . . even had we been persuaded that the duty to disclose sufficient to enable recovery of overpayments arose from section 71 itself, we would not have been persuaded that the duty was restricted to circumstances in which the claimant could reasonably have been expected to disclose it. That construction is simply impermissible in context. We would have held that in respect of any duty arising under section 71—as with the duty actually arising under regulation 32(1)—the subjective opinion or appreciation of the claimant as to materiality has no part to play in the scope of the duty." (para.42).

The Tribunal of Commissioners then turns to the well-established line of authority which had adopted the approach that the test did involve consideration of whether disclosure was reasonably to be expected of the claimant. The leading authority is, of course, *R(SB) 21/82*, which has been cited in many Commissioners' decisions including three decisions of Tribunals of Commissioners: *R(SB) 15/87; CG/4494/1999;* and *R(IS) 5/03*. The Tribunal of Commissioners concludes that successive decisions of Commissioners have been misled by the importation into s.71 of qualifying words from the then-equivalent of the second duty in reg.32 in *R(SB) 21/82*. The Tribunal of Commissioners says that, "On the most generous view, the words do not represent a possible construction of s.71." (para.52). The Tribunal of Commissioners further concludes that the issue has "never been the subject of any analysis or full argument" (para.58). The Tribunal of Commissioners concludes,

> "59. We do not resile from the fact that, in adopting the proper construction of the relevant statutory provisions, we are changing the direction of the law by abandoning a supposed but erroneous requirement in respect of recovery cases to which regular reference has been made over the years. However, having the law

(1992 c.5, s.71)

properly applied cannot of itself be unfairly prejudicial, even if that law is adverse to the interests of a particular person. We do not see any way in which claimants could be unfairly prejudiced by the benefit system adopting the proper construction of these statutory provisions now. They cannot for example possibly have organised their affairs on the basis that R(SB) 21/82 is good law, with the result that they would suffer a detriment if the position were changed now. There seems to us to be no reason to perpetuate error now by slavish adherence to previous decisions.

60. For these reasons, insofar as previous decisions of Commissioners (including Tribunals of Commissioners) are inconsistent with the reasoning of this decision, they must be treated as wrongly decided."

The Tribunal of Commissioner refer specifically to *R(A) 1/95*. The Tribunal agrees that mental capacity is relevant as to whether the claimant knew of the matter not disclosed, and that mental capacity is not relevant to the issue of whether there was a failure to disclose. However, they disapprove of the reasoning in paragraph 6 of this decision, partly because they cannot deduce any proper explanation of the passage from *R(SB) 21/82* to which the Commissioner makes reference, and partly because it relies upon an insurance analogy which the Tribunal of Commissioners does not consider to be helpful in this context of recovery of overpayments.

The Tribunal of Commissioners goes on to consider what protection there is for claimants whose capacity may affect their ability to handle their affairs. Two protections are identified. First, there is the possibility that an appointee is appointed to act on their behalf. The Tribunal of Commissioners notes that, where no appointment has been made, "the higher courts have in the past taken a fairly robust approach to submission based on a lack of capacity" (para.64). Secondly, there is the possibility that the Secretary of State will exercise the discretion not to recover the overpayment in the particular circumstances of any given case, though the Tribunal comments that it is not "aware of any published guidelines on the exercise of this discretion." (para.65).

The decision is bound to reverberate through the system for some time. It is certain to generate appeals to the Commissioner on its application in the variety of circumstances in which overpayments of benefit arise. The following points should be borne in mind in applying the decision:

(1) This decision should be the starting point in any overpayment case involving a failure to disclose.
(2) The decision does not equate the words "failed to disclose" with "did not disclose". There must still be some breach of duty.
(3) It remains the case that there can be no failure to disclose some fact or matter which is not known to the person (though there can, of course, be a misrepresentation in relation to such a matter: see, for example, *CIS/2042/2004*).
(4) The legal duty can be found in reg.32 of the Claims and Payments Regulations.
(5) Where the first duty in reg.32 is in issue, it follows that the adjudicating authorities will need to identify with some clarity where the requirement to furnish information came from. In the case before the Commissioners, this was straightforward. The information provided to the claimant in connection with her claim required her to notify the Secretary of State if her children ceased to live with her or were taken into care. It is submitted that it will not be enough to convert the first duty into some general duty to furnish information to the Secretary of State. There are bound to be cases where the requirement to furnish information is rather less clear cut, and will need to be explored with some care.
(6) If the case falls within the second duty, then there is a requirement that the change of circumstances is one which claimants might reasonably be expected to know might affect the continuance of entitlement or the payment of benefit. There will also be a temporal question to consider: whether the claimant notified the Secretary of State of the change as soon as reasonably practicable.

The *Hinchy* judgment in the House of Lords (see below) expressly states that it is concerned with a different question from that raised in the decision of the Tribunal of Commissioners.

CFC/2766/2003 was decided after *CIS/4348/2003*, and concerned a situation where it was alleged that the claimant had failed to disclose spending of capital prior to her first claim for benefit. As noted above in the section on misrepresentation, her answers on the claim form did not constitute misrepresentations as she was only asked what her current level of capital was. Moreover, on the face of it neither of the duties under regulation 32(1) discussed in *CIS/4348/2003* would apply as the loss of the capital was not a change in circumstances since the claim had been made nor had the claimant been asked by the Secretary of State to provide information about changes in her capital prior to the date of claim. This may have provided the basis for Commissioner Howell distinguishing *CIS/4348/2003*, but his comments perhaps suggest a deeper unease with the correctness of that decision. On failure to disclose he directed the tribunal to whom he referred the case back that:

". . . it is not of course necessary for the Board to prove that the failure of disclosure was other than innocent, and I further direct the tribunal that, as is well settled law, the principal question is whether disclosure was reasonably to be expected of the claimant in all the circumstances. That long established principle was laid down and confirmed by two Commissioners of unquestionable learning and experience, Mr I Edwards-Jones QC and Mr J S Watson QC, in the (reported) cases **R(SB) 21/82** and **R(SB) 28/83**, has since been followed and applied as good law and practical sense on countless occasions by Commissioners and tribunals over the last 20 years and more, and should at least for the present continue to be applied in the context of facts such as these, notwithstanding the doubts voiced in quite a different context by a recent tribunal of Commissioners in case CIS/4348/2003."

A different Commissioner has also commented on the ambit of *CIS/4348/2003* in *CDLA/1823/2004*. The Commissioner indicates that the Tribunal of Commissioners was dealing with cases where disclosure had not been made despite being required by clear and unambiguous instructions. In many cases, the situation will not be as clear cut. In such cases, the Commissioner considers that whether there has been a failure to disclose "must inevitably be determined by considering whether the Secretary of State could reasonably have expected the claimant to disclose or notify that fact." (para.9.) A tribunal would need to consider how a reasonable claimant would have construed any instruction to report changes in circumstances or some other instruction. In the case before him, there was no evidence as to the instructions given to the claimant.

In *R (IB) 4/05* the Commissioner follows the decision in *CIB/3925/2003* to the effect that the advice given to recipients of incapacity benefit about exempt work are couched in terms which do not *require* notification to the Department before undertaking such work, though it was accepted that undertaking the work without giving the required notice had the result that entitlement to incapacity benefit ceased. The advice to benefit recipients could not be said to be "unambiguous" such that non-disclosure of undertaking such work could ground recovery of any overpayment of incapacity benefit.

This approach is confirmed in the decision of the Court of Appeal in *Hooper v Secretary of State for Work and Pensions* [2007] EWCA Civ 495, reported as *R(IB) 4/07*, which concerned an overpayment that had arisen when a recipient of incapacity benefit had started work without notifying the Secretary of State. The Commissioner had taken the view that a direction in a factsheet given to the claimant that "you should tell the office . . . before you start work" constituted a requirement because it was a "polite way of wording an instruction". The Court of Appeal disagreed. There was no reason why the language used could not be clearer in indicating a formal requirement to notify by using the word "must" rather than "should". Dyson LJ said, "The context is not one which demanded politeness at the expense of clarity." (para. 57). In the course of his judgment, Dyson J expressly approves the reasoning of Commissioners Mesher and Howell in *CIB/3925/2003* and *R(IB) 4/05*.

(1992 c.5, s.71)

In *CIS/1887/2002*, the Commissioner ruled that there can be no failure to disclose where both benefits in question were being handled by the same local office, even where the benefits were being handled by different sections of that local office. The claimant submitted a claim for both income support and incapacity benefit to the same office. Income support was awarded, and an award of incapacity benefit was subsequently made. The claimant did not tell the local office of this award, and his income support continued to be paid resulting in a substantial overpayment of that benefit.

The Commissioner, following *CSB/0677/1986* concluded:

"21. It is also in my judgment a principle established beyond question that for the purposes of section 71 there is no 'failure to disclose' where the material fact in question is already known to the person or office to whom, under the principle laid down by the House of Lords in *Hinchy*, notification would otherwise have to be made. This too I take to be axiomatic and not called in question by anything said in the recent decision of their Lordships. It may be the kind of point Lord Hoffmann had in mind when he said 'a disclosure which would be thought necessary only by a literal-minded pedant . . . need not be made', though perhaps a true pedant would be the least likely to think disclosure necessary in such circumstances, taking the (accurate) view that there can be no question of 'disclosure' to a person or entity of something that he or it knows already.

"22. In my judgment the question of liability under section 71 is concluded in favour of the claimant, and against the Department's view as accepted by the tribunal, by the fact that all questions affecting both of the interconnected benefits involved in this case were being dealt with by the single local benefits office at the same address; and there was nothing in any of the correspondence, literature or other evidence put before the tribunal to show that the staff from time to time dealing with the relevant incapacity benefit and income support questions were separately identified to the claimant or any else as different 'offices'; or that the need to track down and notify any separate individual or section of individuals within that same office at the same address was either reasonably to be expected mf the claimant or in any way brought to his attention. On the contrary, all the material before the tribunal pointed to the opposite conclusion, and that has been reinforced by the further submissions and explanations of the system in such an office provided for me for the purposes of this appeal."

In *CIS/4422/2002* the Commissioner has followed the approach adopted in *CIS/1887/2002* in ruling that, in situations where a claimant's benefit is being dealt with inside the same local office, this "does not mean that the claimant has gratuitously to notify it of the actions of its own staff." (para. 1). In this case ". . . there was no evidence of any requirement on [the claimant] to send any separate notification to any separately identified section of staff working within what was otherwise presented to him as a single local office of the Department for Work and Pensions . . ." (para. 10). The overpayment was accordingly not recoverable.

In *CIS/1996/2006* and *CIS/2125/2006* the Commissioner alludes to the negative consequences of the decision in *B v Secretary of State* in noting that there can be no obligation on a claimant's partner to disclose, and so, if the partner was the only person who knew the material fact, there can be no failure to disclose. The pertinent paragraph of the decision reads:

"As the submissions . . . on behalf of the Secretary of State in each of these appeals are right to concede, the tribunal's findings of facts and reasons were insufficient to show how the duty of disclosure it placed on the appellant arose. Moreover in my judgment the tribunal misdirected itself in holding that the facts could bring him within regulation 32(1B) of the Claims and Payments regulations at all. That provision, as the decision rightly said, imposes a duty; but a person in this appellant's position is not one of the people on whom that duty is expressed to be imposed. An income support claimant's partner, whose details have to be

Social Security Administration Act 1992

included in the claim, does not thereby become another claimant; is not a 'beneficiary' (an expression which is undefined, but in this context must mean a person with some entitlement to the relevant benefit); or a person 'by whom' the benefit awarded, not to the partner but to the claimant in his or her own right, is receivable. Nor is the income support under such an award receivable by the claimant in any sense as agent for or 'on behalf of' a partner merely because that partner's existence and resources are disclosed in the claim and taken into account in calculating the applicable amount, and thus the net overall level of benefit, appropriate to the *claimant* on the claim and any resulting award." (para. 14).

In *R(A) 2/06*, the Commissioner considered the extent to which oral representations by an officer of the Department can have an impact on the statutory duty to disclose. The case concerned a claimant with an appointee who was in a care home. When the local authority took over the payment of the care home fees, no disclosure was made and attendance allowance continued to be paid resulting in an overpayment of that benefit. In the run-up to the change of legislation which resulted in the local authority payment of the care home fees, the daughter (who was the appointee) was visited by a Customer Liaison Manager. In evidence, the appointee said that the Customer Liaison Manager "told me that the visit . . . would initiate any action required with regard to my mother's benefit changes when council funding started and there was no need for me to take any further action." (para.6 of the Decision.)

The Commissioner concludes that *R(IS) 5/03* has survived the Court of Appeal's decision in *B v Secretary of State*. He also accepts that a particular duty to provide information is capable of being modified by an oral representation made by an officer of the Department, though it will be vital that careful findings of fact are made about such representations and their context. Finally, the Secretary of State must present evidence to show any duty to disclose; such a duty will not be implied and any assumption made by the Secretary of State that there is a duty to disclose is likely to be challenged in overpayment cases.

In *CIS/1867/2006* the claimant sought to rely on telephone advice that the capital limit for income support purposes was £8,000. The claimant, in fact, had capital in excess of £3,000 but below £8,000. As a result of its non-disclosure there was an overpayment of income support. The Commissioner concludes in deciding the case himself that the telephone advice was not given in response to disclosure of possession of capital, and did not relieve the claimant of the obligation to read the disclosure requirements in the back of her payment book. In the course of his decision, the Commissioner indicates that the Secretary of State must, in such cases, provide a copy of the instructions as to disclosure given to a claimant, and must indicate that the diminishing capital rule has been applied (paras 7 and 8 of the decision).

(b) disclosure to whom and the continuing duty to disclose

1.94 Compliance with the duty to disclose, and the continuing duty to disclose, have proved to be contentious issues, which have required a decision of the House of Lords to resolve. That decision has reversed the decision of the Court of Appeal and re-affirmed the long-standing authorities of the Commissioners in *R(SB) 54/83* and *R(SB) 15/87*, reaffirmed by a Tribunal of Commissioners in *CG/449/1999*. It will be helpful to set out the decision of the House of Lords in *Hinchy* v *Secretary of State for Work and Pensions* [2005] UKHL 16, reported as *R(IS) 7/05*, before setting out some of the detail of the circumstances claimants may face.

The facts were straightforward. The claimant had been in receipt of disability living allowance (awarded for a fixed period of five years) which had passported her to entitlement to a severe disability premium as part of her income support. Her claim for renewal of the disability living allowance was unsuccessful. The claimant did not disclose to the Department that her disability living allowance had ended. Though she ceased to be entitled to the severe disability premium, it continued in payment for some time. The Department sought recovery of the overpaid income support on the grounds that the claimant had failed to disclose the termination of the award of her disability living allowance. There was a clear instruction (though quite how clear this was is questioned by two of their Lordships: Lord Scott in his dissent and Baroness Hale in her opinion allowing the appeal) in the documentation given to the claimant requiring her to notify the Department if there was any change in her overall benefit entitlement. It transpired at the appellate stages of the case that there was a postcard notification system in operation between the disability living allowance centre and the local office administering the income support, and that the local office had received notice of the fixed term award at its outset, which had triggered the award of the severe disability premium.

The claimant challenged the recoverability claim on two grounds. Both were subsequently determined on the facts (and so could not ground an appeal), but the appeal before the Commissioner raised the question of whether a person could fail to disclose (within the meaning given to that phrase in s.71) some fact which was already known to the Secretary of State for Work and Pensions. After reviewing the duty of disclosure in s.71 and reg.32 of the Claims and Payments Regulations, Lord Hoffmann, giving the lead opinion in the House of Lords, considered that the line of authority established in the Commissioners' decisions reflected the realities of benefit administration, and went on to say:

"32. . . . The claimant is not concerned or entitled to make any assumptions about the internal administrative arrangements of the department. In particular, she is not entitled to assume the existence of infallible channels of communication between one office and another. Her duty is to comply with what the Tribunal called the 'simple instruction' in the order book. . . . For my part, I would approve the principles stated by the Commissioners in *R(SB) 15/87* and *CG/4494/99*. The duty of the claimant is the duty imposed by regulation 32 or implied by section 71 to make disclosure to the person or office identified to the claimant as the decision maker. The latter is not deemed to know anything which he did not actually know."

Baroness Hale agreed, noting that there was nothing intrinsically wrong in requiring disclosure from the claimant of information known to one part of the Department which may or may not be known to another part of the Department. Baroness Hale has some reservations about whether the requirement to disclose the termination of the disability living allowance was made sufficiently clear in this case, but concedes that this goes to findings of fact rather than a question of law.

Lord Scott dissented essentially on the ground that the instructions the claimant had received did not impose on her an obligation to inform the local office that her disability living allowance award had come to an end. He also appears to accept that the local office had actual knowledge (as distinct from deemed knowledge) of the duration of the award of disability living allowance by reason of its receipt of the notification of its award at its outset.

Accordingly the existing authorities remain determinative of when and how disclosure must be made, and would suggest the following propositions:

(i) A personal disclosure to an officer in the local office administering the award of benefit is complete disclosure and absolves the person from further disclosure even if it is not acted on by the department and the claimant continues to receive benefit or suffers no reduction in benefit: *R(SB) 15/87*. Subsequent statements when signing for benefit are not misrepresentations because the representation made is that there has been no change subsequent to the disclosure. This proposition is approved by the Commissioner in *CIS/14025/1996*, para.6. The words of the Commissioners in *R(SB) 15/87* spell out exactly who the officer should be to whom the disclosure is made:

"We accept that a claimant cannot be expected to identify the precise person or persons who have the handling of the claim. His duty is best fulfilled by disclosure to the local office where his claim is being handled whether in the claim form or otherwise in terms that make sufficient reference to his claim to enable the matter disclosed to be referred to the proper person. If he does this, it is difficult . . . to visualise any circumstances in which a further duty to disclose the same matter can arise. In the case of a [supplementary benefit or income support] claimant required to be available for employment who is directed . . . to deliver or send his claim to the relevant unemployment benefit office for onward transmission to the department, disclosure on the claim form submitted must also be regard as fulfilling the duty."

But disclosure to the Post Office where benefit is collected will not amount to disclosure to the Department: *CSS/33/1990*, para.6.

(ii) A continuing obligation to disclose will exist where a claimant (or someone acting on the claimant's behalf) has disclosed to an officer of the Department either not in the local office or not in the section of that office administering the benefit. Such disclosure will initially be good disclosure provided that the claimant acted reasonably in thinking that the information would be brought to the attention of the relevant officer. But if subsequent events suggest that the information has not reached that officer, then it might well be considered reasonable to expect a claimant to disclose again in a way more certain to ensure that the information is known to the relevant benefit section. How long it will be before a subsequent disclosure is required will vary depending on the particular facts of each case.

The above paragraph is approved by the Commissioner in *CIS/14025/1996*, para.6. He notes that in such circumstances it is the practice of the Department to expect a further disclosure after the second payment following the first disclosure, and says he would "not cavil with such an approach", though each case must be considered on its own facts. The stronger the claimant's belief that the information would be passed to the adjudication officer (or now decision-maker), the longer it is reasonable to wait before a second disclosure is made.

(iii) The disclosure need not be in writing though it will normally be reduced to written form in the Department and signed by the person making the disclosure: see reg.32 of the Claims and Payments Regulations. Nor need it be made by the claimant in person. Where the information is proffered by someone acting on behalf of the claimant, it must be reasonable for that person to act as the claimant's delegate (this should be presumed if the claimant has asked to delegate to act) and it must be made clear that the delegate is acting on behalf of the claimant and in connection with the claimant's claim to benefit. Note that there are suggestions in para.29 of *R(SB) 15/87* that the disclosure may well be complete even if the information was given in the course of some entirely separate transaction if (1) the information was given to the relevant benefit office, (2) the claimant knew the information had been given, and (3) it was reasonable for the claimant to believe it was unnecessary for him to take any action himself. Casual or incidental disclosure is not good enough. Careful findings of fact will be needed because it seems quite common for the delegate to be also at the office in connection with his or her own claim to benefit. What remains unclear is whether such delegated disclosure removes the continuing obligation to disclose. The matter may depend on findings of fact about the delegated disclosure. The clearest evidence that the information has been disclosed in full and in connection with the claimant's claim to benefit at the relevant local office would certainly justify a conclusion that the disclosure was complete and would relieve the claimant of any continuing obligation to disclose just as if the disclosure had been made personally.

In *CIS/14025/1996*, para.7, the Commissioner comments as follows on this proposition:

"Finally Bonner implies that it might be different in certain circumstances, depending on the dicta in para 29 . . . of *R(SB) 15/87*. That paragraph however

(1992 c.5, s.71)

concerns the disclosure *on behalf of* another person. Thus disclosure may be made *on behalf of* the claimant:

(a) if the information was given to the relevant office;
(b) the claimant knew that the information had been given and;
(c) it was reasonable for the claimant to believe that it was unnecessary for him to take any action himself.

That does not, in my view, go to the adequacy of the disclosure made; it only goes to whether disclosure by one person can be said to have been disclosure on behalf of another. In this context disclosure, as it were, by chance of 'casual or incidental' is not disclosure on behalf of a claimant. While I have relied on the general principles set out in Bonner above, I dissent from the particular view expressed concerning para 29 of *R(SB)15/87*."

(iv) There appears to be a difficulty over written disclosures posted to the Department. Can the claimant rely on something akin to the presumption that a posted letter arrives in the ordinary course of post contained in s.7 of the Interpretation Act 1978 unless the contrary is proved. This is probably a case where the continuing obligation to disclose exists because subsequent events may indicate that the postal disclosure has not been effective. The difficulty relates to issues of evidence and proof: must the Department rebut the presumption that the letter was delivered or can they simply say that they have no record of receipt and that it is for the claimant to ensure that his or her disclosure arrives? The former will probably be more difficult than the latter since it would be proper to inquire as to the incidence of letters going stray after arriving at the Department.

In *CIS/5848/1999* the Commissioner addresses the issue of when *separate* notifications of circumstances to the Secretary of State are required. The scenario is a familiar one. A claimant, with children, claimed income support for herself and her children; unusually she was not in receipt of child benefit when she claimed income support but she also claimed that benefit. When she claimed that benefit she disclosed that she was also an income support claimant. Income support was paid without deduction of child benefit. The overpayment which resulted from this came to light about six months later; the Commissioner says, "the probable explanation is either a belated putting-together of information already in the possession of the Secretary of State in different places in the department's records, or a belated realisation, on the part of those responsible for calculating her income support, of the significance of the information they already had." The appeal tribunal upheld an overpayment decision. The adjudication officer's case was based upon a failure to disclose receipt of payments of child benefit. The claimant argued, and the Commissioner found on the balance of probabilities, that the claimant's child benefit award was duly communicated by the child benefit centre to the officials concerned with calculating her income support entitlement. That says the Commissioner was sufficient to dispose of the appeal in favour of the claimant; their failure to recalculate the benefit was not caused by the claimant's lack of a separate notification of the same piece of information. The issues of when a beneficiary is fixed with knowledge of a change which must be reported to the Department, and of whether notification is required when the Department holds the information continue to prove troublesome.

In *CDLA/6336/1999* the claimant, who was in receipt of a disability living allowance and income support, was admitted to hospital having taken an overdose of medication. That part of the Department dealing with her income support award was notified by means of an in-patient certificate issued by the admitting hospital. The information later found its way to the DLA Unit, which reviewed and revised the claimant's award of a disability living allowance and raised a recoverable overpayment. The Commissioner concluded that, although delivery of the information to the office handling the income support did not, of itself, constitute good disclosure, it was necessary to consider the rules on disclosure on behalf of the claimant. There was some evidence that the claimant had told the hospital that the Benefits Agency needed to be told of her admission to hospital and that this had been done. There needed to be a careful consideration of whether (a) the information was given to the relevant officer; (b) the claimant knew that the information had been given; and (c) it was reasonable for the claimant to believe that it was unnecessary to take action himself or herself in all the circumstances of the case. The Commissioner indicates that condition (a) would be met if the notification to the local office was made in circumstances where it was reasonable to assume that it would be passed to the DLA Unit; that would be met if the notification contained an implied or express request that the DLA Unit be notified and if there was some general practice of the local office passing on the information in the circumstances presented by the claimant. Much would turn on the facts of the particular case. The Commissioner rejected an argument that recovery could be based on misrepresentation, since, if the disclosure had been made in accordance with the tests set out above, there would, in the particular circumstances of the case, be no continuing duty to disclose and any representation that any material facts had been reported would be factually true and not a misrepresentation.

In *CG/160/1999* a Commissioner considered the question of knowledge in the context of an overpayment which had arisen when an entitlement to an invalid care allowance had ceased because the person being cared for ceased to be entitled to the requisite rate of the care component of a disability living allowance. The Commissioner concludes that it did not help the claimant that the reduction of the care component from the middle rate to the lowest rate was within the knowledge of the Department as a whole, since the tribunal had found that the claimant was aware of the need to report any reduction in the rate of disability living allowance to which her mother (for whom she was caring) was entitled.

Before the Commissioner, it was argued that the tribunal had made no finding of fact as to whether the claimant actually knew of the reduction in her mother's benefit. The decision contains a helpful discussion of the concept of "constructive knowledge". This was not an issue which arose in the Court of Appeal decisions in *Sharples*, which concerned knowledge of assets of another person, or in *Franklin*, which concerned a change in the mortgage interest rate. The Commissioner accepted that having the theoretical means of knowledge is not enough to fix a person with constructive knowledge (para.10); rather the test is "whether it is reasonable to expect a claimant to have made enquiries, or to have kept making enquiries, about material facts" (para.10). The Commissioner remitted the case for a fresh hearing because the tribunal had made no finding of fact on whether the claimant did or did not know of the change in her mother's disability living allowance award. He was also critical of the tribunal's allowing a case such as this to proceed as a "paper" hearing.

In *CIS/5131/1998* and *CIS/1148/1999* a Commissioner considered whether the ability of the Department to check by data matching what benefits a claimant was receiving could preclude the recovery of an overpayment of benefit which had resulted from a failure to disclose a benefit by the claimant; he did so in the light of the Commissioners' decisions in *CIS/2498/1997* and *CIS/5848/1999*. The Commissioner declined to draw quite such sweeping conclusions on the impact of easier means of communication within the Department than the Commissioners in the cases cited. In any event, it was not part of the claimant's case that the Department should have known about his benefit position; he had argued that there was an oral qualification to the written form, but the tribunal had not accepted his evidence in that regard.

A number of these issues was addressed by a Tribunal of Commissioners in two cases: *CG/4494/1999* and *CG/5631/1999*. The main decision is *CG/4494/1999*; the purpose of the calling a Tribunal of Commissioners was to determine whether *CIS/2498/1997* and *CIS/5848/1999* were rightly decided.

CG/4494/1999 concerned an overpayment of invalid care allowance which had arisen when entitlement to that benefit had ceased because the person being cared for ceased to be entitled to an attendance allowance. It was argued that the

(1992 c.5, s.71)

overpayment was recoverable because the claimant to the invalid care allowance had failed to disclose the termination of entitlement to the attendance allowance. The tribunal had found that the amount was recoverable but on the basis that the claimant had misrepresented, rather than failed to disclose, a material fact. The claimant did not speak, read or write English.

The key issue was that the Department knew of the cessation of attendance allowance; it was argued for the claimant that if the Secretary of State knew the relevant fact, then any overpayment would not be causally linked to the misrepresentation. It was further argued that "if anybody of any authority in the Department knew about the cessation of attendance allowance the the Minister had the appropriate knowledge." (para.11.) This argument was rejected by the tribunal, as was a similar argument based on the wording of regs 20 and 32 of the Claims and Payments Regulations. What was key was knowledge by that part of the Department responsible for administering the particular benefit.

The Tribunal of Commissioners then comments on *CIS/2498/1997* and determines that it should not be followed. A similar conclusion is drawn in respect of the *obiter* remarks of the Commissioner in *CIS/5848/1999*, though in para.20 of their decision, the Commissioners note,

" . . . we were favoured by Mr Drabble [counsel for the Department] with an account of the steps taken and being taken by the Department to relate internally decisions by one benefit team to the work of another. We do not think it is likely to be helpful to record what those steps are since they are not matters which affect the law or our interpretation of it. . . . All that we would say is that we are heartened to hear that what Mr Commissioner Howell Q.C. hoped might happen has begun to occur."

The tribunal also spends some time considering the plea of *non est factum* having regard to the claimant's inability to read, speak or write English. The Tribunal of Commissioners affirms that there are three conditions for a plea of *non est factum* to succeed:

1. The claimant was under a disability (which might include illiteracy).

2. The document signed was fundamentally, radically or totally different from that which the person thought they were signing.

3. The person signing the document was not careless in doing so, and took such precautions as ought to have been taken in all the circumstances to ascertain the content and significance of the document.

The case was remitted for consideration by a fresh tribunal on this issue, though the Tribunal of Commissioners expresses its agreement with the proposition that if the claimant had the capacity to make the claim, then she had the capacity to make a representation about it.

The other decision of the Tribunal of Commissioners is *CG/5631/1999*. In addition to certain issues which were identical with those raised in *CG/4494/1999*, a further issue arose in this appeal which required a separate decision; the decision is an exception to the general principle laid down in *CG/4494/1999*. Indeed in *CG/2888/2000* it is described as an "important exception". The Commissioner in this case notes that the principle established in *CG/4494/1999* "does not apply where an automatic computer interface exists between two parts of the Department." (para.9). The Commissioner indicates that the decision in *CG/5361/ 1999* is not limited only to the interface in relation to (1) disability living allowance or attendance allowance, and (2) invalid care allowance. The Commissioner continues,

"It must apply between any two parts of the Department if the two conditions behind that decision are met. First, the need to link the information about the two benefits or allowances arises where the receipt of one benefit or of a specific amount of that benefit is conditional in law upon the receipt (or non-receipt) of another benefit (or of a specific amount of the second benefit). Second, the two parts of the Department dealing with the two benefits have in place an automatic computer interface between their systems so that a change in one benefit by one part of the Department is notified in the ordinary course of events by the computer interface to the other part of the Department." (para.10.)

It appears to have been established in this case that there is an automatic computer link between the Child Benefit Centre and those responsible for survivor's benefits. There will remain problematic evidential issues (and responses to enquiries may be more likely to be forthcoming at Commissioner level than at tribunal level), since it seems that the computer systems within the Department for sharing and passing information are many and various, and change from time to time. The position is further complicated by frequent restructuring of the Department.

So, where does *CG/4494/1999* leave the authorities in relation to recoverability of overpayments? The answer would appear to be: much as before. The advent of computerised data systems with easy national access has not yet reached the point where the possibility of data matching within the Department will provide much protection for claimants where overpayments arise because of the inter-relationship of conditions of entitlement to different benefits. It remains safest to disclose information to the office handling the particular benefit, preferably in writing rather than relying upon an officer of the Department to reduce the disclosure to writing. It would probably be overly optimistic to conclude that the decision breathes new life into the plea of *non est factum* in the social security context. In cases of lack of knowledge of English, this will, in virtually all cases, be known to the claimant and will trigger the requirement of care (for example, appropriate use of interpretation or explanation in the first language) under the third condition identified by the Commissioners. This is likely to ensure that the claimant will not be able to argue that the document signed was fundamentally different from what claimants think they are deciding.

There may be special considerations which arise where claims are made by those aged 60 or more (the current "qualifying age" under the State Pension Credit Act 2002) by virtue of reg.4(6C) and 4(6CC) of the Claims and Payments Regulations. Where these paragraphs apply, disclosure to the local authority or other authority referred to in reg.4(6B) may well be good disclosure.

(c) Disclosure at an office displaying the **one** *logo*

1.95 *CIS/4848/2002* raises a point which may be of very practical significance in overpayments cases. The claimant had made disclosure that he and his partner were living together as husband and wife when they attended what they described as a "One Stop Shop." Only when the appeal came before the Commissioner was it established that the claimant had not attended a One Stop Shop but an office of the Department displaying the **one** logo. The distinction proved to be crucial. One Stop Shops or One Stop Offices are run by local councils, and are concerned with all matters for which council have responsibility. There is no requirement for such offices to pass on information relating to social security entitlements. By contrast, offices displaying the **one** logo are a form of one stop shop where there is a mandatory requirement that an office of a participating local authority *shall* pass on information relating to social security benefits administered by the Department except where it relates solely to benefits administered by the local authority. Clearly disclosure that two people are living together as husband and wife relates to a number of social security benefits administered by the Department. It followed that disclosure to the office displaying the **one** logo was good disclosure to the Department. There was accordingly no recoverable overpayment.

Mental capacity

1.96 As noted above, questions of mental capacity have been raised both in relation to misrepresentations and failures to disclose. The issue is not without difficulty even though some basic guidance is contained in the case law reported above.

(1992 c.5, s.71)

CSB/1093/1989 explores in some detail issues concerning mental capacity in overpayments cases. The particular question addressed was the extent to which claimants are entitled to escape the normal consequences of material misrepresentations by contending that they were mentally incapacitated at the time when they signed the relevant document.

The case concerned an overpayment of supplementary benefit which had arisen when, over a period of six months, the claimant misrepresented that her son was still a member of the family for benefit purposes when he had left school and had undertaken a Youth Training Scheme. It was argued on behalf of the claimant that her mental condition, combined with effects of anti-depressant drugs, was such that she could not be held responsible for putting her signature to the declarations in connection with the benefit claim. There is a discussion of the possibility of pleading *non est factum* (that the mind did not go with the pen with the result that the signature is to be treated as not having been made). The Commissioner stresses the narrow nature of the defence of *non est factum* and the difficulty of applying the doctrine to the realities of a modern social security system. The Commissioner indicates at paras 17 and 18 that he believes that the case of *Re Beaney, deceased* [1978] 1 W.L.R. 770, which was not concerned with social security at all, might be of assistance to tribunals. Mrs Beaney was an old lady whose health had been deteriorating for some time. She executed a transfer of a house to her eldest daughter in circumstances where all parties present at the signing of the document, including a solicitor who was an old friend of Mrs Beaney's late husband, thought that she understood what she was doing. Medical evidence, however, was that she had advanced senile dementia and her mental state was such that she could not have understood what she was doing. The two younger children sought a declaration that the transfer was void for want of capacity. The judge stated in his judgment that the degree or extent of understanding required in respect of any instrument is relative to the particular transaction which it is to effect. The more trivial the transaction, the lower the requisite degree of understanding. The Commissioner indicates that regard must be had to this test and that the key question is whether a claimant at the time of signing realised that he or she was signing a document in connection with a claim to benefit which could result in the payment of benefit. If the answer is negative, then s.71 cannot be applied to that claimant.

In difficult cases all the evidence will need to be considered over the period under review. So lucid letters written by the claimant about benefit in the relevant period will be relevant evidence of capacity. The most important evidence will be that of expert medical witnesses, whose views are to be preferred, as in *Re Beaney*, to the views of witnesses who are without medical qualifications.

In *Chief Adjudication Officer v Sheriff*, Court of Appeal, May 4, 1995, *The Times*, May 10, 1995 was reported as *R(IS)14/96*. The Court of Appeal concluded that, even where a receiver has been appointed by the Court of Protection, a claimant who signs a claim form for benefit is capable of making a misrepresentation as to the facts upon which payment of benefit is based. Nor can such a person defeat a claim to repayment of overpaid benefit by arguing that he or she lacked capacity to make a representation. Nourse L.J. said:

> "If the representor need not know of the material fact misrepresented, I cannot see why it should make any difference if she does not know that she is making a representation. That no doubt would make the misrepresentation more innocent. But it would not take it outside s.53(1) [now s.71(1)]. So that can be no ground for saying that the misrepresentation was not made by the claimant."

Millett L.J. put it even more bluntly:

> "... it does not avail a recipient of benefit from whom the Secretary of State seeks repayment of benefit on the ground that he misrepresented a material fact to deny that he had mental capacity to make the representation."

The discussion on the extent to which mental incapacity will enable a person to escape the consequences of a failure to disclose must now be read in the light of the

Social Security Administration Act 1992

decision in *B v Secretary of State* [2005] EWCA Civ 929, where the Court of Appeal ruled that "the statutory meaning of 'failed to disclose' admits of no qualification in favour of claimants who do not appreciate that they have an obligation to disclose something once they are aware of it . . ." (para. 44).

R(IS) 4/06 is authority for four propositions. First, even if the doctrine of *non est factum* applied to social security, which was doubtful, there was no evidence that the form was fundamentally different from the form the claimant thought he was signing and he could reasonably have taken precautions to ascertain its contents and significance (*Lloyds Bank Plc v Waterhouse* [1993] 2 FLR 97 followed) (paras 9 to 23). Secondly, there is a difference between acting deliberately and acting dishonestly or fraudulently and it is possible for a claimant to make an innocent misrepresentation by omission (paras 30 and 31). Thirdly, the language of the declaration signed by the claimant could not be read other than as a guarantee that the form had been completed in a way that accurately set out all details that might affect entitlement to the benefit claimed and hence as a misrepresentation and not a failure to disclose (*Chief Adjudication Officer v Sherriff* (reported as *R(IS) 14/96*) followed) (para. 39). Finally, in the present case there was no ambiguity or contradiction in the information in the claim form as there was in *CIS/222/1991*, but simply an incompleteness which did not require further investigation by the adjudication officer before deciding the claim and (following *Duggan v Chief Adjudication Officer* (reported as the Appendix to *R(SB) 13/89*)) any failure to investigate by the decision-maker did not relieve the claimant of responsibility for the overpayment (paras 42 to 47).

Material fact

1.97 The fact misrepresented or not disclosed must be "material". This will usually be determined by consideration of issues of causation (see below). But it seems right that a representation by a claimant that he or she is entitled to benefit, being a question of law, should only be treated as a material fact in so far as it amounts to a representation that the circumstances justifying the award of the benefit have not changed: see *CIS/156/1990* discussed below. However, if a claimant who made a representation that they were entitled to benefit when they *knew* they were not, such a representation would become a misrepresentation of fact since the claimant knew the representation of entitlement to be untrue.

In *R(SB) 3/90* the Commissioner holds that there can still be a misrepresentation of a material fact even though there has been an earlier disclosure of that fact (para.11) (discussed above).

However, where the misrepresentation in issue is the result of the signing of a declaration to the effect that the claimant has reported any fact affecting payment, great care will need to be taken by tribunals in considering whether there are good grounds for recovery. In *CSB/790/1988* the Commissioner held that the declaration made, for example, each time a person receives payment from a payment book is simply a declaration that the claimant had reported facts she understood should be reported as a result of reading the instructions in the order book. The declaration was held merely to guard against failure to disclose material facts and was of no assistance on the issue of misrepresentation. The key passage in the Commissioner's decision reads:

"The declaration on the order books . . . is as follows:

'I declare that I have read and *understand* all the instructions in this order book, that I have *correctly* reported any fact which could affect the amount of my payment and that I am entitled to the above sum.' (my emphasis).

What was the representation made in that declaration? It seems to me that it was no more than that the claimant had reported any fact she understood should be reported, as a result of reading the instructions, and imports the claimant's belief as to whether or not she had already informed 'the issuing office' of her child benefit. It was a representation as to what she believed. . . The point turns on what was actually represented and not whether the representation was innocent or otherwise." (para.10.)

(1992 c.5, s.71)

Two cases from Northern Ireland (where the requirements for recovery of overpayments are the same), *C1/89(WB)* and *C2/89(CB)*, concerned the receipt of child benefit for a child who had left school in circumstances where the claimant was not aware of this. Recovery was sought in reliance on a misrepresentation alleged to have been made when the claimant signed the order book to the effect that her circumstances had not changed. The Commissioner in Northern Ireland refused to accept that such a declaration could be converted into a misrepresentation of material fact. The Commissioner says that "a misrepresentation of material fact must be just that". So it will be important for tribunals to ask themselves what material fact has been misrepresented by the signing of a particular statement. These decisions get perilously close to saying that declarations made to the best of a person's knowledge and belief do not amount to misrepresentations. Again tribunals will need to take considerable care not to jump to the conclusion that the circumstances in which a misrepresentation is made are not relevant to the issue of recovery under s.71. Decisions should also be clear as to the exact nature of the material fact the subject of the misrepresentation.

In *CSB/329/1990* the Commissioner was faced with a situation in which an elderly Asian who spoke little English continued to sign orders to the effect that there had been no change in his circumstances when two non-dependants had moved into his home. The Commissioner noted that he was in no way bound by the Northern Ireland decisions and was not disposed to follow them since they could not be reconciled with well-known decisions of the Commissioners in Great Britain (at para.5).

Perhaps the starting point today is the decisions of the Court of Appeal on July 1, 1993, in *Jones v Chief Adjudication Officer* and *Sharples v Chief Adjudication Officer*, reported at *R(IS) 7/94*.

On the same day, Jones had claimed unemployment benefit from the Department of Employment and income support from the Department of Health and Social Security. Unemployment benefit was put in payment first, from December 13, 1988. Jones received regular giro cheques. Income support was subsequently put in payment without taking into account the payment of unemployment benefit, and so there was an overpayment of income support. Jones had signed a declaration to the effect that he had reported any fact to the Department of Health and Social Security which would affect the amount of his payment and that he was entitled to the sum in the order. He did not report the award of unemployment benefit to the Department of Health and Social Security. On appeal to the Commissioner, the Commissioner held that the overpayment was recoverable because Jones had misrepresented a material fact in signing the declaration in the order book. Jones appealed to the Court of Appeal on the grounds that a representation that material facts had been correctly reported was not itself a representation of a material fact and that a representation that he was entitled to the benefit was a representation of law and not of fact.

Sharples claimed supplementary benefit. On the claim form he had indicated that neither he nor his partner had any life insurance or endowment policies, and had confirmed that as far as he was aware, the information on the form was true and complete. Sharples had made this statement unaware that his partner had such assets. Supplementary benefit was in fact overpaid. The Commissioner held that there was a recoverable overpayment in that Sharples had misrepresented a material fact in completing the forms. Sharples appealed on the grounds that he had only represented the facts to the best of his knowledge and that he was unaware of the policies held by his partner when he completed the form.

By a majority of 2–1, Jones lost his appeal. The reasoning of the judges in the majority differs. Stuart Smith L.J. held that, by signing the order book, Jones had represented that he had correctly reported any facts of which he knew which could affect his benefit entitlement. That was a representation of a material fact "since unless the statement is true the claimant is not entitled to the amount of benefit claimed." Stuart Smith L.J. also considered that Jones had failed to disclose a material fact, since he knew he was in receipt of unemployment benefit and must have known that the payment of unemployment benefit had an effect on the amount of income support payable. Dillon L.J. considered that the claimant was not entitled to qualify the representation by the addition of a qualification that he was reporting facts "in so far as disclosure could reasonably be expected of me". Evans L.J. dissented holding that a declaration of entitlement to the sum paid was a representation of law. It was only a representation of fact in so far as the claimant was confirming that he or she was the person entitled to receive the payable order.

In *Sharples*, the Court of Appeal was unanimous in concluding that the terms of the declaration which was qualified by the words indicating that the information given was to the best of the claimant's knowledge were such that there was no misrepresentation since Sharples did not know of the policies owned by his partners.

CTC/5401/2002 concerned an overpayment of tax credit. The claimant had responded to questions on the claim form concerning whether or not he had a job by indicating that he did not. He was a supply teacher, and, although he did not work on the day he completed the claim form, he was under contract at the time to provide sessional teaching for the education authority. The terms of the declaration he had signed were 'to the best of my knowledge and belief'. The Commissioner concludes that the proper question to ask is not merely whether the claimant believed that his answers were true, but also to consider whether he believed that (in this case) the Inland Revenue would take the same view. The Commissioner says:

> "The Inland Revenue are entitled to ask in a claim form broad questions in a non-technical form with a view to determining later whether the technical criteria for entitlement to a tax credit are satisfied. A person who provides a narrower answer because he believes that is all that is technically relevant does so at his own peril. Of course, if he is correct, there is no question of an overpayment arising. Further, if the answers on the form are qualified in the way they were on this form, he may avoid having to repay and overpayment caused by an answer that is wrong because it is based on too narrow a construction of the question, provided he genuinely believed that the narrow construction given by him to the question is not the one intended by the Inland Revenue and he knows that the answer is also not a correct and complete answer to the broad question being asked, he must repay any overpayment arising because the answer is too narrow." (para.9.)

The terms of declarations are not the same in all circumstances, and it will be absolutely essential to make precise findings of fact as to the terms of any declaration signed by claimants. The qualification in the declaration signed by Sharples is no longer used. But even where there are no qualifying words, it may be appropriate to read them in. In *Franklin v Chief Adjudication Officer*, reported as *R(IS) 16/96*, the Court of Appeal ruled on December 13, 1995 that a declaration in the terms, "I declare that I have read and understood all the instructions in the order book, that I have correctly reported any facts which could affect the amount of any payment and I am entitled to the above sum", should be construed as a declaration that the claimant had reported all material facts known to her. She had been unaware of a reduction in the mortgage interest applicable to her, which had resulted in there being an overpayment of housing costs as part of her income support.

In *CIS/102/1993* the Commissioner supports the view both that a representation that a claimant is entitled to a payment of benefit is a representation of law and not of fact, and that there can be a representation of material fact by conduct where a person continues to cash orders in an order book knowing that their entitlement to benefit has been reviewed and revised so as to withdraw the entitlement. In a Northern Ireland decision, *R6/94(IS)*, the Commissioner holds at para.9 that any person who signs an order book declaration of entitlement knowing full well that there is no entitlement to the benefit payable misrepresents a material fact.

In *CSB/18/1992* and *CIS/674/1994* the Commissioner followed the *Jones* and *Franklin* approach. In the latter case the Commissioner draws a helpful distinction between responses to specific questions, where ignorance of the true facts does not prevent recovery on the grounds of a misrepresentation of a material fact, and responses to non-specific questions where knowledge of the true facts is a prerequisite to the making of the representation. In other words, it will be essential in every case to articulate what it is that the claimant has misrepresented.

A further limitation on the ambit of the representation made by signing the declaration on a payable order is suggested, obiter, by the Commissioner in *CG/662/1998*, *CG/1567/1998* and *CG/2112/1998*. In these cases, an indefinite award of invalid care allowance had been made to the claimant in respect of care for a person who had been awarded a disability living allowance for a fixed period. Contrary to the instruction at the back of the order book, the claimant had not reported the non-renewal of the award of the disability living allowance and an overpayment of invalid care allowance occurred. The Commissioner decides on the basis of the majority decision in *Jones* that by signing the order book declaration, the claimant had misrepresented that he had correctly reported any fact that could affect the amount of benefit payable. The relevant fact was the end of the award of the disability living allowance and its non-renewal. However, he went on to suggest that the representation made by signing the declaration was limited not only to facts known to the claimant, as in *Jones*, but also to facts that had not already been reported on the signatory's behalf or otherwise. But this is subject to the conditions set out in para.29 of *R(SB)15/87*, namely:

"(a) the information was given to the relevant benefit office;
(b) the claimant was aware that the information had been so given; and
(c) in the circumstances it was reasonable for the claimant to believe that it was unnecessary for him to take action himself."

In his view these conditions had to be strictly applied. Thus, on the facts of these cases, while the existence of *accurate* information in the computer system might be enough to satisfy (a) (it was accepted that the ICA Unit both knew that disability living allowance had been awarded for a fixed period and had the means of knowing—through the Benefits Agency's computer records—that a renewal claim had not been successful to the required extent), (b) was not satisfied because the claimant could not have known, at the time he signed the order book, whether or not the information was accurate. In addition (c) was not met because the Benefits Agency was perfectly entitled to ask the claimant to report facts as a means of checking the accuracy of information held on computer and the fact that the Agency apparently did not use the computer at all in these circumstances did not make it reasonable for the claimant not to follow the instruction in the order book.

The view expressed by the Commissioner is *obiter* and did not assist the claimant in this case but might apply on other facts. For example, if the claimant could show that he knew that the appropriate benefit office had the correct information, it might well be reasonable for him to take no further action, depending on the particular circumstances of the case.

Missing documents

Arguments concerning missing documents are often raised in appeals concerning overpayments. *R(IS)11/92* now provides detailed guidance on the principles to be applied in such cases. In this case the Commissioner confronts what he describes as "a certain mythology" building up around the old prize case *The Ophelia* [1915] P. 129 and [1916] 2 A.C. 206. *The Ophelia* concerned the practice of "spoliation of documents" that is the deliberate destruction of documents and the presumption that the contents of the documents destroyed by their holder are contrary to their claims. The case has been relied upon before a number of tribunals to found an argument that where the Department has destroyed documents they hold, the contents of those documents are to be presumed to be helpful to the claims made by claimants.

The Commissioner at para.23 reviews the evidence before him concerning the "weeding" of files. The information in that paragraph is no more than the Commissioner's findings of fact in the case on the evidence given to him and should not be taken as reflecting universal practice. In every case, it will be important for tribunals to hear some evidence on what the practices adopted in the particular office having the conduct of the claim. What does seem clear, however, is that there is a

1.98

Social Security Administration Act 1992

general practice of weeding files after 18 months of documents which appear no longer to have relevance to any current claim.

The Commissioner then turns his attention to the implications of the doctrine of spoliation in *The Ophelia* for tribunals and states a number of important propositions:

- The case seems to have passed out of current thinking (para.28). *The Ophelia* is not a binding authority, but is only of persuasive authority. It is, however, not to be lightly disregarded if the principle it enshrines accords with common sense in the social security jurisdiction (para.29).

- The assertion that *The Ophelia* supports the proposition that documents which have been destroyed by the Department must be presumed to support the claimant's case is mythology. Spoliation had a technical meaning and is not the same as simple destruction. The key distinction is between deliberate destruction of documents *with the intention of destroying evidence*, and the deliberate destruction of documents *where there is no such intention*. Adverse presumptions come into place only in the former context (para.30).

- There is no such thing as "The Ophelia principle"; it is merely a case illustrating the application of a principle of evidence applicable in the prize jurisdiction. The underlying principle, however, remains good law. Reliance on the rule that destroyed documents must be construed against the destroyer of those documents depends on the establishment of some reprehensible act or omission by the destroyer (paras 31 and 32).

The Commissioner goes on to note that that where documents have been destroyed, then a tribunal will need to rely on secondary evidence concerning the contents of the destroyed documents; such evidence might be oral or written. Tribunals can, of course, admit any evidence which they regard as relevant and helpful.

The Commissioner summarised his conclusion on *The Ophelia* in Appendix III of the decision; paras (3) and (4) bear quotation:

"(3) The strong presumptions which are to be drawn against a party who destroys documents *only* fall to be drawn where the documents were destroyed with the intention of destroying evidence. (The intention to destroy evidence will, of course, be almost impossible to establish where the destroying party is aware of copies of the destroyed documents.) Where there is no such intention, the only detriment to which the destroying party lays himself open is the loss of the corroboration which the documents might have afforded him.

(4) Accordingly, in the social security jurisdiction *no* presumptions fall to be drawn where the Department of Social Security has destroyed documents withthe intention of clearing storage space or simply because no point can be seen in retaining such documents."

For a case concerning missing documents and proof of an amount owed in a different context, see *Post Office Counters Ltd v Mahida* [2003] EWCA Civ 1583, where the Court of Appeal indicated that a party which had destroyed documents which they knew were vital to a claim they were making and which they had reason to believe were in contention, might well find themselves unable to rely upon secondary evidence to prove their claim. The circumstances in issue concerned irregularities in the accounting by a sub-postmistress in relation to benefit payments, which the Post Office was seeking to recover. Part of the evidence was material from the Department of Social Security in Northern Ireland. Original documents had been destroyed in accordance with standard "weeding" policy.

Tribunals should have regard to where the burden of proof lies in cases with a history. In overpayments cases, it is for the decision-maker to show that the grounds for recovering any overpayment exist. This in turn generally required the decision maker to show that there is evidence which will ground a revision on review.

CG/3049/2002 conerned a substantial overpayment of widow's benefit which was claimed on the basis that the claimant had failed to disclose that she was living with a man as husband and wife. Her argument was that she had informed the Department of her situation when she applied for widow's benefit. She argued that if the claim form had asked about her living arrangements, she would have disclosed the factual situation accurately. The form could not be found. In remitting the case for a rehearing, the Commissioner indicated that the responsibilities of tribunals following the decision in *R(IS) 11/92* is to seek to reconstruct the claim form. The Commissioner directs the new tribunal in the following terms:

"As the whole case then depends on what the claim form did or did not say, the tribunal should do its best, following *R(IS) 11/92* to reconstruct the form. That might, for example, involve taking evidence on oath or affirmation from the claimant about the full circumstances of the claim, and also seeing and putting to her a copy of the claim form that would have been used in 1997. And the tribunal must also bear in mind that if there is no evidence, it should not guess. The critical question is: are the submission and assertions of either party just guesswork, or are they something more than that? In weighing the evidence and the lack of it, the tribunal must have the principle of equality of arms in mind (under article 6 of the European Convention on Human Rights). It should not make assumptions that the Department is less likely to have made a mistake than the claimant unless it has evidence for that. If the tribunal cannot establish what was in the claim form then, to repeat the words of Commissioner Mitchell, it should leave the tree lying where it fell." (para.14.)

Causation

Under s.71 the overpayment must be "in consequence of the misrepresentation or failure to disclose" and so there must be a clear causal connection between the misrepresentation or failure to disclose and the overpayment: *R(SB)3/81*, *R(SB)21/82* and *R(SB)15/87*. So, for example, if a clear finding of fact could be made that an overpayment was the result of an administrative error by the Department unconnected with any misrepresentation or failure to disclose, there would be no causal link between the misrepresentation or failure to disclose and the overpayment, which would not be recoverable. But it seems that failure of an administrative procedure for notification between benefit sections will not break the chain of causation: *CSB/64/1986*. Arguments that a breakdown of internal communication between parts of the Department have caused the overpayment, have been met with the consistent arguments that the test of causation is whether, if the claimant had disclosed or not misrepresented a material fact, the Secretary of State would have made payment of the benefit. If the answer is that he would not, then the necessary causal connection is made: *R(SB)3/90* and *Duggan v Chief Adjudication Officer*, appendix to *R(SB)13/89*. But if it can be shown that the inter-office communication system did operate (that is, that there was actual rather than deemed knowledge) but was not then used to initiate any reviews, there would be a break in the chain of causation: *R(SB)15/87* and *CIS/159/1990* and *CSIS/7/1994*. See also *CIS/5899/1999* discussed in relation to the obligation to disclose material facts.

The scope of *Duggan* where there has been an error or neglect by an adjudication officer is discussed in *CIS/2447/1997*. The claimant stated on her income support claim form in November 1993 that her partner was not working. In October 1995 it came to light that he had always been in full-time work. The claimant's income support award had been reviewed in March 1994 following the birth of her son. It was argued that any overpayment after that review resulted not from the misrepresentation on the claim form but from the adjudication officer's negligence. This was because the adjudication officer had failed to identify any basis for the claimant's continued entitlement to income support after that time. She was no longer exempted from the condition of being available for work on the ground of pregnancy and she was not a single parent. The tribunal rejected this argument, holding that the circumstances were not distinguishable from those in *Duggan*. The Court of Appeal's decision in that case was closely related to its particular facts. It had not laid down a general rule that, whatever the extent or nature of the error by an adjudication officer,

1.99

Social Security Administration Act 1992

it did not remove the causative effect of some earlier failure to disclose or misrepresentation by a claimant. All the circumstances of the case had to be looked at. For example, if in the present case, the claimant had later told the income support office that she had won £10,000 and the adjudication officer had mistakenly determined that that did not affect entitlement to income support, the continued payment of benefit could not be said to have as even one of its causes the initial misrepresentation that her partner was not in full-time work. However, the actual facts of this case did not fall into that category. The information that her baby had been born would not on its own have inevitably led to to the conclusion that entitlement to income support would cease. Even though the claimant might have become a person required to be available for work, her entitlement to income support would only have ceased if she had, for example, refused to make herself available for work. The adjudication officer's failure to investigate such issues was an *additional*, but not the *sole*, cause of the overpayment and, as such, did not break the chain of causation between the initial misrepresentation and the overpayment. As had been noted in *R(F)2/99* adjudicating bodies have no jurisdiction to apportion responsibility for overpayments between a number of parties on the basis of a number of causes of the overpayment. This is, however, something the Secretary of State might take into account in determining whether to seek recovery of all or part of a recoverable overpayment.

An example of an error by the adjudication officer which did exonerate the claimant can be found in *CIS/222/1991*. The Commissioner holds that if the claimant's answers on the claim form were plainly inconsistent and ambiguous, this put the adjudication officer on notice to investigate the position. If this was not done, any overpayment was not recoverable as it was due to error on the part of the Department rather than a misrepresentation by the claimant. Here the information *on the claim form* should have triggered investigation by the adjudication officer, but the adjudication officer chose not to resolve those conflicts before awarding benefit.

Note that if income support is paid while a claimant is waiting for a decision on entitlement for another benefit and arrears of the other benefit are paid for this period, any excess income support cannot be recovered under this section, since it does not result from a failure to disclose. But s.74 and the Overpayments Regulations will operate to allow the excess to be deducted from the arrears of the other benefit or recovered from the recipient.

The situation dealt with in *CIS/13742/1996* is a particular illustration of the fact that the overpayment has to result from the misrepresentation or failure to disclose. The claimant and her partner (who were now separated) had each claimed benefit as single people while they were living together as husband and wife (and had thus been paid more benefit in total than that to which they would have been entitled had they claimed as a couple). The adjudication officer decided that the total amount of the overpayment was recoverable from the claimant. However the Commissioner holds that this was incorrect. Any overpayment to the partner was not due to any action or failure to act on the part of the claimant but due to the fact that he had held himself out as a single person. Thus the claimant was not the cause of the overpayment to the partner and as a result recovery of any such overpayment could not be sought from her. But had the claimant herself been overpaid benefit? From November 21, 1983 the claimant could have claimed benefit in respect of herself and her family (up to November 21, 1983 the claim could only have been made by her partner). Thus if the claimant could show that such a claim would have been successful, there would be no question of an overpayment because she would have received less benefit than she was entitled to. If, however, she could not have qualified as the claimant for the family, she would be liable to repay *all* the benefit that she had received in the relevant period. The Commissioner did, however, comment that in his view it would be inequitable for the Secretary of State to require her to repay more than the amount of the actual excess benefit paid.

The question of recovery of an overpayment from one member of a couple where both had been claiming income support separately was also considered in *CIS/619/1997*. The Commissioner agrees with *CIS/13742/1996* that unless there had

(1992 c.5, s.71)

been a review of the decision awarding benefit to the other member of the couple (in this case the husband), the overpayment, and any offset against it under the Overpayments Regulations could only be considered in connection with the claimant's own claim. It was therefore incumbent on the tribunal to ascertain the position on the husband's claim (which they had not done). See now also *CG/4494/1999* discussed above in para.1.94.

The amount of the overpayment which is recoverable

It is for the Secretary of State to determine the amount of the overpayment and this must be checked by tribunals. 1.100

In *CS/366/1993* the Commissioner gives advice on the level of proof of payment of a benefit recovery of which is being sought. This is an issue which can come up in overpayment appeals, when a claimant either directly or indirectly puts in issue whether they have ever received the money which the adjudication officer, or now decision-maker, says is recoverable. The Commissioner reminds tribunals that the burden of proof is on the balance of probabilities. Where there is evidence of entitlement to and payment of benefit, that may be sufficient to show that the benefit was paid. It certainly is in the absence of any challenge by the claimant. Equally, no higher burden will lie with the adjudication officer if the claimant does not adduce evidence that he or she did not receive the benefit, but simply asked the adjudication officer to prove that the benefit was paid.

A schedule showing how the overpayment is calculated is normally included in the appeal papers, but great care must be taken in simply adopting these, especially if there is any variation of the decision under appeal. The tribunal may, for example, find that an overpayment is recoverable for a different period. This will affect the amount recoverable. The need for tribunals to state expressly the sum which is recoverable and how it is calculated was stressed in *R(SB)9/85*. This advice was repeated in *R(SB)11/86* where the Commissioner helpfully approves the practice of leaving a difficult recalculation to the adjudication officer *provided that* it is made clear that the claimant or the adjudication officer may refer the matter back to the tribunal in the event of any particular difficulty or disagreement arising. The approach tribunals should adopt is to recalculate benefit in the light of the facts as found by them to determine the amount of the overpayment: *R(SB)20/84* and *R(SB)10/85(T)*. In *R(SB)11/86* it was held that underpayments of benefit during the relevant period could be taken into account, but this may need to be qualified in the light of reg.13 of the Overpayments Regulations.

A controversial question under the pre-April 1987 law was how far it was possible to take account of underpayments of benefit against the overpayment. Regulation 13(b) of the Overpayments Regulations provides that from the gross amount of the overpayment is to be deducted any additional amount of income support which should have been awarded on the basis of the claim as originally presented or with the addition of the facts misrepresented or not disclosed. This allows a somewhat more extensive set-off than under the old law. *R(IS)9/96* holds that reg.13 makes it mandatory for an adjudication officer to consider the question of a possible underpayment of benefit of income support when calculating the overpayment. A tribunal must also consider the question of any offset before it reaches a decision on the recoverability of the overpayment; it cannot merely decide that an overpayment is recoverable and then refer the question of any offset back to the adjudication officer: *CSG/357/1997*.

R(IS)5/92 confirms that the reg.13(b) deduction from the amount of the overpayment is not limited to the period after the beginning of the overpayment but can go back to the date of claim. In addition, *CSIS/8/1995* points out that the overpayment may relate to an entirely different benefit. Again, there need be no connection between the respective periods. But the examination of the additional amount which would have been payable must be based on the claim as originally presented, or with the addition of the material facts misrepresented or not disclosed. In *R(IS)5/92* the Commissioner construes "claim as presented" in reg.13(b) as including facts that would be discovered by "any reasonable enquiry . . . prompted by the claim form."

This is applied in *CIS/136/1992* to require the adjudication officer to consider an award of income support on hardship grounds. *CIS/137/1992* points out that reg.13 is concerned with deductions from an overpayment and so only comes into play after the overpayment had been calculated. The review which results in a decision as to the amount of benefit that ought to have been paid is therefore to be carried out without any fetter being imposed by reg.13.

Another problem now dealt with by regulations arises when the misrepresentation or failure to disclose is of capital resources. If it emerged that a claimant who had been in receipt of income support or family credit for a few years throughout had capital of £1 over the limit, it would be most unfair to require repayment of the whole amount of benefit. If the capital had been properly taken into account, so that benefit was not initially awarded, the capital would immediately have been reduced below the limit in order to provide for living expenses. So the Commissioner applied the "diminishing capital" principle: *CSB/53/1981*, *Chief Supplementary Benefit Officer v Leary*, appendix to *R(SB)6/85* and *R(SB)15/85*. The position is now governed by reg.14 of the Overpayments Regulations. This provides for the reduction of the figure of capital resources at quarterly intervals from the beginning of the period of the overpayment period by the amount overpaid in income support, income-based jobseeker's allowance, working families tax credit or disabled person's tax credit in the previous quarter. No other reduction of the actual amount of capital resources is allowed: reg.14(2). Under the Commissioners' approach the notional reduction had to be made week by week. It will be considerably easier to make the calculation at 13-week intervals, but the tendency will be for smaller reductions of the overpayment to be produced.

It is for the decision-maker to prove the existence of the amount of capital taken into account in calculating an overpayment: *R(SB)21/82*. Here, sums had suddenly appeared in building society accounts and there was no evidence where they had come from. The Commissioner commends the adoption of a lower figure of overpayment rather than a higher one based on the assumption that the capital assets had not been possessed before any evidence existed about them. The Commissioner in *R(SB)43/83* agrees strongly on the burden of proof, but points out that if the person concerned was alive and failed to give any proper explanation of the origin of such sums, adverse inferences could be drawn against them, enabling the adjudication officer to discharge the burden of proof. He goes on to hold that the estate of a deceased person should be in the same position. Therefore, a heavy responsibility devolved on the executor to make every reasonable enquiry as to the origin of the money. But if after such efforts there was no evidence where the money came from the burden of proof on the adjudication officer would not have been discharged.

Care needs to be taken by tribunals in the way in which matters relating to the amount of the overpayment are handled. As noted above, *R(SB)11/86* helpfully approved the practice of giving directions for the recalculation of the overpayment, while making it clear that either party is free to return to the tribunal for a determination by the tribunal of any disputed issue. *CSB/083/1991* illustrates how things can go wrong. A tribunal concluded that there had been a recoverable overpayment but went on to say, "The amount of overpayment is therefore recoverable. Actual amount to be rechecked, and this matter is therefore adjourned."

The claimant took issue with the decision on recoverability and appealed to the Commissioner who held that the determination of the tribunal did not constitute a decision and consequently the Commissioner was without jurisdiction. It is unclear whether a decision which followed more closely the guidance in *R(SB)11/86* would constitute a decision. On the one hand, all the ingredients to convert the directions into a decision would be present, but on the other, the possibility of the parties returning to the tribunal suggests that there is not yet a final determination of all the relevant issues before the tribunal. A claimant who continued to dispute the recoverability of any overpayment is not in a good position to agree a recalculation of the overpayment. Those receiving applications for leave to appeal in such cases may

(1992 c.5, s.71)

need to consider carefully whether there is a full decision of the tribunal which will attract a right of appeal.

In *CIS/442/1992* the Commissioner reminds tribunals of the proper procedure to follow when the calculation of the amount of the overpayment is initially left for determination by the parties. Where reference back to the tribunal is necessary, then that reference should be to the same tribunal which dealt with the issue of liability (para.5). Should it prove necessary to refer the case back to a differently constituted tribunal, then both the issue of liability and the issue of calculation will need to be considered at the adjourned hearing (para.7). A different tribunal should only hear the case if satisfied that it is not practicable to reconvene the original tribunal (para.7).

An argument was raised that s.53(1A) of the SSA 1986 (now s.71(2) of the Administration Act) outlawed the practice of remitting the calculation of the amount of the overpayment in the manner set out in *R(SB)11/86*. The Commissioner concludes that this argument is misplaced and that the new subsection did nothing to disturb "the existing practice of remitting matters of quantification" (para.8).

In *CIS/764/2002* the Commissioner says,

"I conclude in the present case (although the issue may need eventually to be argued out in some other case) that when there has been an abatement under section 74(2) of the Social Security Administration Act 1992, the relevant amount of income support is to be treated as if had not been paid as income support. Therefore it cannot be touched by a subsequent decision about the recoverability of an overpayment of income support under section 71. I rest that on the overall context of sections 71 and 74, if the conclusion is not required by regulations 5 and 13(a) of the Payments Regulations." (para.22.)

The Commissioner had concluded that the requirements of regs 5 and 13(a) of the Payments on Account Regulations required the same result: see para.20 of the decision.

In *R. v Secretary of State for Social Security, Ex p. Britnell* [1991] 1 W.L.R. 198, the House of Lords held that the power in reg.20 of the Overpayments Regulations to apply the recovery provisions of s.71 to any amount recoverable under any enactment repealed by the Social Security Act 1986 as if it was an amount recoverable under s.71 was valid and wide enough to encompass recovery of overpaid unemployment benefit in 1973–74 from a subsequent entitlement to supplementary benefit.

Note that in certain circumstances duplicated benefit may be recovered from a benefit due in another Member State of the European Union: *R(SB)1/91* and *R(SB)3/91*.

For a case concerned with the off-setting of working families tax credit to which the claimant is entitled against an overpayment of income support, see *Larusai v Secretary of State for Work and Pensions* [2003] EWHC 371 (Admin) which is discussed in the annotations to reg.13 of the Payments on account etc Regulations.

Automated credit transfers
Subsection (4) provides an independent ground for recovering overpayments resulting from the use of payments to a bank account or other similar account. Recovery will only be available if the claimant received, before agreeing to such method of payment, notice in the form specified in reg.11 of the Overpayments Regulations. These overpayments arise most often in cases of child benefit.

1.101

Tax credits: substitution of subss. (8)–(9)
Section 71(8)–(9) is, with effect from October 5, 1999, by virtue of s.2 and Pt IV, para.10 of Sch.2 to the Tax Credits Act 1999 to be read as follows in any case where the overpayment was made in respect of tax credits:

1.102

"(8) An amount recoverable under subsection (1) above in any year of assessment—

Social Security Administration Act 1992

(a) shall be treated for the purposes of Part VI of the Taxes Management Act 1970 (collection and recovery) as if it were tax charged in an assessment and due and payable;

(b) shall be treated for the purposes of section 203(2)(a) of the Income and Corporation Taxes Act 1988 (PAYE) as if it were an underpayment of tax for a previous year of assessment.

(8A) Where—

(a) an amount paid in respect of a claim is recoverable under subsection (1) above; and

(b) a penalty has been imposed under section 9(1) of the Tax Credits Act 1999 (penalties for fraud etc.) on the ground that a person fraudulently or negligently made an incorrect statement or declaration in connection withthat claim,

the amount shall carry interest at the rate applicable from the date on which it becomes recoverable until payment.

(9) The rate applicable for the purposes of subsection (8A) above shall be the rate from time to time prescribed under section 178 of the Finance Act 1989 for those purposes."

See *Larusai v Secretary of State for Work and Pensions* [2003] EWHC 371 (Admin) discussed in the annotations to reg.13 of the Payments on account, etc. Regulations for the relationship between working families tax credit and benefits administered by the Department in relation to recovery of overpayments of benefits administered by the Department.

Welfare Reform and Pensions Act 1999

1.103　Note that s.68 of the Welfare Reform and Pensions Act 1999 provides that certain overpayments of benefit are not to be recoverable. In dealing with overpayments the provisions of that section should be checked to determine whether they exclude recovery.

A useful book

1.104　A detailed, but now somewhat dated, guide on overpayments is P. Stagg, *Overpayments and Recovery of Social Security Benefits* (Legal Action Group, 1996), ISBN 0 905 09973 7.

[¹ Overpayments out of social fund

1.105　**71ZA.**—(1) Subject to subsection (2) below, section 71 above shall apply in relation to social fund payments to which this section applies as it applies in relation to payments made in respect of benefits to which that section applies.

[²(2) Section 71 above as it so applies shall have effect as if the following provisions were omitted, namely—

(a) in paragraph (a) of subsection (5) and subsection (5A), the words "reversed or varied on an appeal or";

(b) in paragraph (b) of subsection (5), the words "appeal or"; and

(c) subsections (7), (10A) and (10B).]

(3) This section applies to social fund payments such as are mentioned in section 138(1)(b) of the Contributions and Benefits Act.]

AMENDMENTS

1. Social Security Act 1998, s.75(1) (October 5, 1998).
2. Note that until ss.9, 10 and 38 of the 1998 Act come into force, subs.(2) is substituted by para.8 of Sch.6 to the Act.

(1992 c.5, s.71ZA)

General Note

Section 75(2) of the Social Security Act 1998 provides that s.71ZA applies to social fund overpayment decisions made on or after October 5, 1998.

1.106

Recovery of jobseeker's allowance: severe hardship cases

71A.—(1) Where—

(a) a severe hardship direction is revoked; and
(b) it is determined by [² the Secretary of State] that—
   (i) whether fraudulently or otherwise, any person has misrepresented, or failed to disclose, any material fact; and
   (ii) in consequence of the failure or misrepresentation, payment of a jobseeker's allowance has been made during the relevant period to the person to whom the direction related,

[² the Secretary of State] may determine that [² he] is entitled to recover the amount of the payment.

(2) In this section—

"severe hardship direction" means a direction given under section 16 of the Jobseekers Act 1995; and

"the relevant period" means—

(a) if the revocation is under section 16(3)(a) of that Act, the period beginning with the date of the change of circumstances and ending with the date of the revocation; and
(b) if the revocation is under section 16(3)(b) or (c) of that Act, the period during which the direction was in force.

(3) Where a severe hardship direction is revoked, the Secretary of State may certify whether there has been misrepresentation of a material fact or failure to disclose a material fact.

(4) If the Secretary of State certifies that there has been such misrepresentation or failure to disclose, he may certify—

(a) who made the misrepresentation or failed to make the disclosure; and
(b) whether or not a payment of jobseeker's allowance has been made in consequence of the misrepresentation or failure.

(5) If the Secretary of State certifies that a payment has been made, he may certify the period during which a jobseeker's allowance would not have been paid but for the misrepresentation or failure to disclose.

(6) A certificate under this section shall be conclusive as to any matter certified.

(7) Subsections (3) and (6) to (10) of section 71 above apply to a jobseeker's allowance recoverable under subsection (1) above as they apply to a jobseeker's allowance recoverable under section 71(1) above.

(8) The other provisions of section 71 above do not apply to a jobseeker's allowance recoverable under subsection (1) above.]

1.107

Amendments

1. Jobseekers Act 1995, s.18 (October 7, 1996).
2. Social Security Act 1998, Sch.7, para.82 (October 18, 1999).

General Note

Section 16 of the Jobseekers Act 1995 enables the Secretary of State to direct that a person under the age of 18 is to qualify for JSA in order to avoid severe hardship. The direction may be revoked on the ground of change of circumstances (s.16(3)(a))

1.108

or on the ground that the young person has failed to pursue an opportunity, or rejected an offer, of training without good cause (s.16(3)(b)) or on the ground that mistake as to or ignorance of a material fact led to the determination that severe hardship would result if JSA was not paid (s.16(3)(c)). A special provision is needed for recovery in cases of misrepresentation or failure to disclose because the revocation of the direction is not a review which can found action under s.71 and it appears that it does not enable the decision on entitlement to JSA to be reviewed for any period before the date of the revocation. Note that the Secretary of State's certificate is conclusive on almost every issue (subs.(3)–(6)). The provisions of s.71 about the mechanics of recovery apply.

Special provision as to recovery of income support

1.109   **72.** [1. . .]

AMENDMENT

1. Repealed by Jobseekers Act 1995, Sch.3 (October 7, 1996).

Overlapping benefits—general

1.110   **73.**—(1) Regulations may provide for adjusting benefit as defined in section 122 of the Contributions and Benefits Act [1, or a contribution-based jobseeker's allowance] which is payable to or in respect of any person, or the conditions for [2 receipt of that benefit] where—
   (a) there is payable in his case any such pension or allowance as is described in subsection (2) below; or
   (b) the person is, or is treated under the regulations as, undergoing medical or other treatment as an in-patient in a hospital or similar institution.

(2) Subsection (1)(a) above applies to any pension, allowance or benefit payable out of public funds (including any other benefit as so defined, whether it is of the same or a different description) which is payable to or in respect of—
   (a) the person referred to in subsection (1);
   (b) that person's [4 wife, husband or civil partner];
   (c) any [5 . . .] dependent of that person; or
   (d) the [4 wife, husband or civil partner] of any adult dependant of that person.

(3) Where but for regulations made by virtue of subsection (1)(a) above two persons would both be entitled to an increase of benefit in respect of a third person, regulations may make provision as to their priority.

[3(4) Regulations may provide for adjusting—
   (a) benefit as defined in section 122 of the Contributions and Benefits Act; or
   (b) a contribution-based jobseeker's allowance,
payable to or in respect of any person where there is payable in his case any such benefit as is described in subsection (5) below.]

(5) Subsection (4) above applies to any benefit payable under the legislation of any member State other than the United Kingdom which is payable to or in respect of—
   (a) the person referred to in that subsection;
   (b) that person's [4 wife, husband or civil partner];
   (c) any [4 . . .] dependent of that person; or
   (d) the [4 wife, husband or civil partners] of any adult dependant of that person.

(1992 c.5, s.73)

AMENDMENTS

1. Jobseekers Act 1995, Sch.2, para.49(2)(a) (June 11, 1996).
2. Jobseekers Act 1995, Sch.2, para.49(2)(b) (June 11, 1996).
3. Jobseekers Act 1995, Sch.2, para.49(3) (June 11, 1996).
4. Civil Partnership Act 2004, s.254 and Sch.24, para.59 (December 5, 2005).
5. Child Benefit Act 2005, Sch.1, Pt 1, para.21 (April 10, 2006).

DERIVATION

SSA 1975, s.85 as amended. 1.111

GENERAL NOTE

See the Hospital In-Patients Regulations and Overlapping Benefits Regulations. 1.112

Income support and other payments

74.—(1) Where— 1.113
(a) a payment by way of prescribed income is made after the date which is the prescribed date in relation to the payment; and
(b) it is determined that an amount which has been paid by way of income support [². . .] [², an income-based jobseeker's allowance or state pension credit] would not have been paid if the payment had been made on the prescribed date,
the Secretary of State shall be entitled to recover that amount from the person to whom it was paid.

(2) Where—
(a) a prescribed payment which apart from this subsection falls to be made from public funds in the United Kingdom or under the law of any other member State is not made on or before the date which is the prescribed date in relation to the payment; and
(b) it is determined that an amount ("the relevant amount") has been paid by way of income support [². . .] [², an income-based jobseeker's allowance or state pension credit] that would not have been paid if the payment mentioned in paragraph (a) above had been made on the prescribed date,
then—
   (i) in the case of a payment from public funds in the United Kingdom, the authority responsible for making it may abate it by the relevant amount; and
   (ii) in the case of any other payment, the Secretary of State shall be entitled to receive the relevant amount out of the payment.

(3) Where—
(a) a person (in this subsection referred to as A) is entitled to any prescribed benefit for any period in respect of another person (in this subsection referred to as B); and
(b) either—
   (i) B has received income support [¹or an income-based jobseeker's allowance] for that period; or
   (ii) B was, during that period, a member of the same family as some person other than A who received income support [¹ or an income-based jobseeker's allowance] for that period; and
(c) the amount of the income support [¹or an income-based jobseeker's allowance] has been determined on the basis that A has not made

91

Social Security Administration Act 1992

> payments for the maintenance of B at a rate equal to or exceeding the amount of the prescribed benefit,

the amount of the prescribed benefit may, at the discretion of the authority administering it, be abated by the amount by which the amounts paid by way of income support [¹or an income-based jobseeker's allowance] exceed what it is determined that they would have been had A, at the time the amount of the income support [¹or an income-based jobseeker's allowance] was determined, been making payments for the maintenance of B at a rate equal to the amount of the prescribed benefit.

(4) Where an amount could have been recovered by abatement by virtue of subsection (2) or (3) above but has not been so recovered, the Secretary of State may recover it otherwise than by way of abatement—
- (a) in the case of an amount which could have been recovered by virtue of subsection (2) above, from the person to whom it was paid; and
- (b) in the case of an amount which could have been recovered by virtue of subsection (3) above, from the person to whom the prescribed benefit in question was paid.

(5) Where a payment is made in a currency other than sterling, its value in sterling shall be determined for the purposes of this section in accordance with regulations.

AMENDMENTS

1. Jobseekers Act 1995, Sch.2, para.50 (October 7, 1996).
2. State Pension Credit Act 2002, s.14 and Sch.2 (July 2, 2002 for the purposes of making regulations only; fully in force October 6, 2003).

DERIVATION

1.114 Social Security Act 1986, s.27.

DEFINITION

"prescribed"—see s.191.

GENERAL NOTE

1.115 Most of this section was originally, in substance, s.12 of the Supplementary Benefits Act 1976. There are changes in form from the old s.12, but the overall aim is the same, to prevent a claimant from getting a double payment when other sources of income are not paid on time. This is an important provision, which is often overlooked. It now extends to income-based JSA as well as to income support. In *R(IS) 14/04* the Commissioner confirms that there is an appeal against a determination that there is a recoverable overpayment under this section to an appeal tribunal under the Social Security Act 1998 in the following terms:

> ". . . a determination made by the Secretary of State under section 74(1) that a particular amount of income support has been paid to the claim but would not have been so paid had he received his prescribed income payments at the prescribed date, and in consequence is legally recoverable from him under the terms of section 74(1), is an appealable decision within the jurisdiction of the tribunal under section 12 Social Security Act 1998. The appeal does not however extend to any subsequent question of whether or how to enforce any liability so established, which is an administrative or discretionary matter for the Secretary of State." (para.21.)

The determination of appeals under s.74 will be a much more technical matter than appeals under s.71. The question which arises under this section is whether there has been a payment of a prescribed benefit which would not have been made had prescribed income been paid to the claimant on the prescribed date.

(1992 c.5, s.74)

In *CIS/0155/2001* the Commissioner was called upon to consider whether a tribunal had any jurisdiction to control the way the Secretary of State exercises the jurisdiction to seek recovery of an overpayment arising under s.74. The Commissioner concludes that the appropriate way in which to challenge the way in which the discretion to recover had been exercised in this case was by application for judicial review, and that any consideration of such questions was outside the jurisdiction of the tribunal (and indeed the Commissioner). The decision is expressed to be without prejudice to the position after November 29, 1999 when certain provisions of the Administration Act 1992 were replaced by new provisions in the Social Security Act 1998.

CIS/5048/2002 illustrates the limitations of this section. The claimant had been receiving income support for herself and her husband. The claimant's husband had applied for, and was awarded, incapacity benefit for himself which he had not disclosed to his wife. The result was an overpayment of income support, which the Secretary of State sought to recover under s.74. The Commissioner ruled on the appeal:

"10. Two subsections of section 74 were invoked in the submission to the tribunal, subsections (2) and (4). Subsection (2) allows, on the facts of this case, an abatement of the incapacity benefit paid to the husband. It does not authorise any deduction from the claimant. There is nothing in the subsection that allows recovery from 'the other' member of a married or unmarried couple (other than joint claimants). For the record, I indicated in a direction that I do not see how section 74(3) could be applied here either, and the secretary of state's representative has not disputed this. As I noted in those directions, there is in any event no mention of subsection (3) anywhere in the papers. Subsection (4) applies where an abatement could have been made under subsection (2) or subsection (3) but has not been made. As applied with subsection (2) it allows recovery from the person from whom the abatement could have been retained the husband, not the claimant. So neither of the preconditions for subsection (4) to be applicable to the claimant are present. The decision of the tribunal therefore cannot stand. Equally, neither can the decision of the Secretary of State.

11. I have not considered whether section 74(1) could apply to the claimant because it has not been put in issue. The secretary of state's representative makes the suggestion, which I agree is the best way forward in this case, that the appropriate action is for me to set aside the decision of the Secretary of State and refer the matter back to the Secretary of State. That I do. The Secretary of State can make further decisions about overpayment if he so decides, and those decisions will have their own rights of appeal. He will note the comments of the solicitors about the inapplicability of section 71 to the claimant."

Subs. (1)

Prescribed income is defined in reg.7(1) of the Social Security (Payments on account, Overpayments and Recovery) Regulations 1988 ("the Overpayments Regulations") as any income which is to be taken into account under Pt V of the Income Support (General) Regulations or Pt VIII of the Jobseeker's Allowance Regulations. The prescribed date under reg.7(2) is, in general, the first day of the period to which that income relates. If as a result of that income being paid after the prescribed date, more income support or income-based JSA is paid than would have been paid if the income had been paid on the prescribed date, the excess may be recovered. Note that the right to recover is absolute and does not depend on lack of care on the claimant's part, or on the effect of this section having been pointed out. That approach is confirmed in *CIS/625/1991*, where the Commissioner rejected the argument that there had to be an investigation of what an adjudication officer would in practice have done if the income had been paid on time. An example would be where a claimant has not been paid part-time earnings when they were due and as a result has been paid income support on the basis of having no earnings. Once the

1.116

Social Security Administration Act 1992

arrears of wages are received, the excess benefit would be recoverable. Late payment of most social security benefits is covered in subss.(2) and (4), but can also come within subs.(1). For instance, if a claim is made for child benefit and while a decision is awaited income support is paid without any deduction for the amount of the expected child benefit, then if arrears of child benefit are eventually paid in full (i.e. the abatement procedure of subs.(2) does not work) the "excess" income support for the period covered by the arrears is recoverable under subs.(1) or (4).

It is essential that the dates on which prescribed income was due to be paid and on what dates due payments would have affected income support entitlement should be determined: *R(SB) 28/85* and *CIS/625/1991*.

Subs.(2)

1.117   Prescribed payments are listed in reg.8(1) of the Overpayments Regulations and include most social security benefits, training allowances and social security benefits from other E.C. countries. As under the excess income support or JSA, if the abatement mechanism breaks down, the Secretary of State may recover the excess under subs.(4). Under s.71(8)(c), amounts may be recovered by deduction from most benefits.

In *CIS/12082/1996* and *CIS/4316/1999* the same Commissioner ruled that Article 111 of E.C. Reg.574/72 does not preclude the application of s.74(2). *CIS/4316/1999* illustrates the application of s.74(2) in the context of the complex rules for determining entitlement to retirement pension where contributions have been made in more than one Member State of the European Union.

In *CIS/764/2002* the Commissioner says,

"I conclude in the present case (although the issue may need eventually to be argued out in some other case) that when there has been an abatement under section 74(2) of the Social Security Administration Act 1992, the relevant amount of income support is to be treated as if had not been paid as income support. Therefore it cannot be touched by a subsequent decision about the recoverability of an overpayment of income support under section 71. I rest that on the overall context of sections 71 and 74, if the conclusion is not required by regulations 5 and 13(a) of the Payments Regulations." (para.22.)

The Commissioner had concluded that the requirements of regs.5 and 13(a) of the Payments on Account Regulations required the same result: see para.20 of the decision.

Subs.(4)

1.118   See notes to subss.(2) and (3).

Subs.(5)

1.119   *R(SB) 28/85* had revealed problems in valuing a payment of arrears in a foreign currency which might cover quite a long period during which exchange rates varied. This provision authorises regulations to be made to deal with the conversion. See reg.10 of the Payments Regulations, which appears to require the actual net amount received to be taken into account, reversing the effect of *R(SB) 28/85*.

[1 **Payment of benefit where maintenance payments collected by Secretary of State**

1.120   **74A.**—(1) This section applies where—
  (a) a person ("the claimant") is entitled to a benefit to which this section applies;
  (b) the Secretary of State is collecting periodical payments of child or spousal maintenance made in respect of the claimant or a member of the claimant's family; and

(1992 c.5, s.74A)

(c) the inclusion of any such periodical payment in the claimant's relevant income would, apart from this section, have the effect of reducing the amount of the benefit to which the claimant is entitled.

(2) The Secretary of State may, to such extent as he considers appropriate, treat any such periodical payment as not being relevant income for the purposes of calculating the amount of benefit to which the claimant is entitled.

(3) The Secretary of State may, to the extent that any periodical payment collected by him is treated as not being relevant income for those purposes, retain the whole or any part of that payment.

(4) Any sum retained by the Secretary of State under subsection (3) shall be paid by him into the Consolidated Fund.

(5) In this section—
"child" means a person under the age of 16;
"child maintenance", "spousal maintenance" and "relevant income" have such meaning as may be prescribed;
[2 "couple" has the meaning given by section 137(1) of the Contributions and Benefits Act;]
"family" means—
(a) [2 couple];
(b) a [2 couple] and a member of the same household for whom one of them is, or both are, responsible and who is a child or a person of a prescribed description;
(c) except in prescribed circumstances, a person who is not a member of a [2 couple] and a member of the same household for whom that person is responsible and who is a child or a person of a prescribed description;
[2 . . .]

(6) For the purposes of this section, the Secretary of State may by regulations make provision as to the circumstances in which—
(a) persons are to be treated as being or not being members of the same household;
(b) one person is to be treated as responsible or not responsible for another.

(7) The benefits to which this section applies are income support, an income-based jobseeker's allowance and such other benefits (if any) as may be prescribed.]

AMENDMENT

1. Child Support Act 1995, s.25 (October 1, 1995).
2. Civil Partnership Act 2004, s.254 and Sch.24, para.60 (December 5, 2005).

GENERAL NOTE

See reg.2 of the Social Security Benefits (Maintenance Payments and Consequential Amendments) Regulations 1996 for definitions of "child maintenance", "spousal maintenance" and "relevant income" and regs 3–5 for other points of interpretation.

Where maintenance payments are being collected on behalf of an income support or income-based JSA claimant or any member of the family, s.74A provides for part or the whole of those payments to be retained by the Secretary of State, in which case they will be disregarded for the purpose of calculating the claimant's benefit. See regs 55A and 60E of the Income Support Regulations and regs 119 and 127 of the Jobseeker's Allowance Regulations.

75.–77. *Omitted.*

Social Security Administration Act 1992

Social fund awards

Recovery of social fund awards

78.—(1) A social fund award which is repayable shall be recoverable by the Secretary of State.

(2) Without prejudice to any other method of recovery, the Secretary of State may recover an award by deduction from prescribed benefits.

(3) The Secretary of State may recover an award—
   (a) from the person to or for the benefit of whom it was made;
   (b) where that person is a member of a [³ couple], from the other member of the couple;
   (c) from a person who is liable to maintain the person by or on behalf of whom the application for the award was made or any person in relation to whose needs the award was made.

[¹(3A) Where—
   (a) a jobseeker's allowance is payable to a person from whom an award is recoverable under subsection (3) above; and
   (b) that person is subject to a bankruptcy order,
a sum deducted from that benefit under subsection (2) above shall not be treated as income of his for the purposes of the Insolvency Act 1986.

(3B) Where—
   (a) a jobseeker's allowance is payable to a person from whom an award is recoverable under subsection (3) above; and
   (b) the estate of that person is sequestrated,
a sum deducted from that benefit under subsection (2) above shall not be treated as income of his for the purposes of the Bankruptcy (Scotland) Act 1985.]

(4) Payments to meet funeral expenses may in all cases be recovered, as if they were funeral expenses, out of the estate of the deceased, and (subject to section 71 above) by no other means.

[³ (5) In this section "couple" has the meaning given by section 137(1) of the Contributions and Benefits Act.]

(6) For the purposes of this section—
   (a) a man shall be liable to maintain his wife [³ or civil partner] and any children of whom he is the father; and
   (b) a woman shall be liable to maintain her husband [³ or civil partner] and any children of whom she is the mother;
   (c) a person shall be liable to maintain another person throughout any period in respect of which the first-mentioned person has, on or after 23rd May 1980 (the date of the passing of the Social Security Act 1980) and either alone or jointly with a further person, given an undertaking in writing in pursuance of immigration rules within the meaning of the Immigration Act 1971 to be responsible for the maintenance and accommodation of the other person; and
   (d) "child" includes a person who has attained the age of 16 but not the age of 19 and in respect of whom either parent, or some person acting in place of either parent, is receiving income support [² or an income-based jobseeker's allowance].

(7) Any reference in subsection (6) above to children of whom the man or the woman is the father or mother shall be construed in accordance with section 1 of the Family Law Reform Act 1987.

(8) Subsection (7) above does not apply in Scotland, and in the application of subsection (6) above to Scotland any reference to children of whom the man or the woman is the father or the mother shall be construed as a reference to any such children whether or not their parents have ever been married to one another.

(9) A document bearing a certificate which—
(a) is signed by a person authorised in that behalf by the Secretary of State; and
(b) states that the document apart from the certificate is, or is a copy of, such an undertaking as is mentioned in subsection (6)(c) above,

shall be conclusive of the undertaking in question for the purposes of this section; and a certificate purporting to be so signed shall be deemed to be so signed until the contrary is proved.

AMENDMENTS

1. Jobseekers Act 1995, s.32(2) (October 7, 1996).
2. Jobseekers Act 1995, Sch.2, para.51 (October 7, 1996).
3. Civil Partnership Act 2004, s.254 and Sch.24, para.61 (December 5, 2005).

DERIVATIONS

Subss.(1)–(3): Social Security Act 1986, s.33(5)–(7).
Subs.(4): 1986 Act, s.32(4).
Subs.(5): 1986 Act, s.33(12).
Subss.(6)–(9): 1986 Act, ss.26(3)–(6) and 33(8).

1.124

DEFINITION

"prescribed"—see s.191.

GENERAL NOTE

Subss. (1)–(3)
These provisions give the framework for recovery of social fund loans. See the Social Fund (Recovery by Deductions from Benefits) Regulations 1988.

1.125

Income support and JSA are prescribed benefits for the purposes of subs.(2) (reg.3(a) and (c) of the Social Fund (Recovery by Deductions from Benefits) Regulations). In *Mulvey v Secretary of State for Social Security, The Times*, March 20, 1997, the House of Lords on March 13, 1997 held that where deductions were being made from benefit under subs.(2) when the claimant was sequestrated (the Scottish equivalent of a declaration of bankruptcy), the Secretary of State was entitled to continue to make the deductions. If that were not so, the gross benefit would become payable to the claimant, who would thus gain an immediate financial advantage from sequestration, a result which Parliament could not have intended.

"Prior to sequestration the [claimant] had no right to receive by way of income support more than her gross entitlement under deduction of such sum as had been notified to her by the [Secretary of State] prior to payment of the award by the [Secretary of State]. This was the result of the statutory scheme and she could not have demanded more. The [Secretary of State's] continued exercise of a statutory power of deduction after sequestration was unrelated thereto and was not calculated to obtain a benefit for him at the expense of other creditors. The only person who had any realistic interest in the deductions was the [claimant] from which it follows that the [Secretary of State] was not seeking to exercise any right against the permanent trustee." (Lord Jauncey)

The view of the Inner House of the Court of Session was thus approved. See the notes in the 1996 edition for the earlier decisions in *Mulvey*.

English bankruptcy law is not the same as Scottish sequestration law. However, in *R. v Secretary of State for Social Security, Ex p. Taylor and Chapman*, The Times, February 5, 1996, Keene J. reached the same conclusion as the Inner House in *Mulvey* in relation to the effect of s.285(3) of the Insolvency Act 1986 in these circumstances. The deductions in *Chapman* were not being made under subs.(2) but from the claimant's retirement pension under s.71(8) in order to recover an overpayment of income support, but it was accepted that the position was the same in both cases. Keene J. rejected a submission by the Secretary of State that the operation of s.285(3) was precluded in this situation, but held that it did not prevent the deductions under subs.(2) and s.71(8) being made. The Secretary of State was not seeking to go against "the property of the bankrupt" within the terms of s.285(3) as the claimants' entitlement under the 1992 Act was to the net amount of benefit. In *Mulvey* (above) Lord Jauncey said this about the contrary argument:

> "Even more bizarre would be the situation where overpayments obtained by fraud were being recovered by deduction from benefits. On sequestration the fraudster would immediately receive the gross benefit. It is difficult to believe that Parliament can have intended such a result."

Note that s.32 of the Jobseekers Act 1995 amends both ss.78 and 71 to provide that amounts deducted under subs.(2) or s.71(8) from JSA payable to a bankrupt person are not to be treated as income for the purposes of the Insolvency Act 1986 and the Bankruptcy (Scotland) Act 1985 (in effect giving preference to the DSS over other creditors, although the House of Lords in *Mulvey* rejected such a comparison).

Subs. (4)

1.126   Subsection (4) contains an important provision for the recovery of any payment for funeral expenses out of the estate of the deceased. Regulation 8 of the Social Fund Maternity and Funeral Expenses (General) Regulations lists sums to be deducted in calculating the amount of a funeral payment. These include assets of the deceased which are available before probate or letters of administration have been granted. The old reg.8(3)(a) of the Single Payments Regulations required the deduction of the value of the deceased's estate, but since it might take some time for the estate to become available, the provision in subs.(4) is preferable.

The funeral payment is to be recovered as if it was funeral expenses. Funeral expenses are a first charge on the estate, in priority to anything else (see *R(SB) 18/84*, paras 8 and 10, for the law in England and Scotland). *CIS/616/1990* decides that the right to recover is given to the Secretary of State. The adjudication officer (and the tribunal) has no role in subs.(4).

The only other method of recovery is under s.71, which applies generally where there has been misrepresentation or a failure to disclose and does depend on a review of entitlement by an adjudication officer followed by a determination of an overpayment.

Subss. (6)–(9)

1.127   See the notes to s.105.

Northern Ireland payments

Recovery of Northern Ireland payments

1.128   79. Without prejudice to any other method of recovery—
(a) amounts recoverable under any enactment or instrument having effect in Northern Ireland and corresponding to an enactment or

(1992 c.5, s.79)

     instrument mentioned in section 71(8) above shall be recoverable by deduction from benefits prescribed under that subsection;
- (b) amounts recoverable under any enactment having effect in Northern Ireland and corresponding to section 75 above shall be recoverable by deduction from benefits prescribed under subsection (4) of that section; and
- (c) awards recoverable under Part III of the Northern Ireland Administration Act shall be recoverable by deduction from benefits prescribed under subsection (2) of section 78 above and subsection (3) of that section shall have effect in relation to such awards as it has effect in relation to such awards out of the social fund under this Act.

DERIVATIONS

Paragraph (a): Social Security Act 1986, s.53(7A). 1.129
Paragraph (b): 1986 Act, s.29(8).
Paragraph (c): 1986 Act, s.33(8A).

DEFINITIONS

"the Northern Ireland Administration Act"—see s.191.
"prescribed"—*ibid*.

Child benefit—overlap with benefits under legislation of other member States

80. Regulations may provide for adjusting child benefit payable in respect of any child [¹ or qualifying young person] in respect of whom any benefit is payable under the legislation of any member State other than the United Kingdom. 1.130

DERIVATION

CBA 1975, s.4A. 1.131

AMENDMENT

1. Child Benefit Act 2005, Sch.1, Pt 1, para.22 (April 10, 2006).

PART IV

RECOVERY FROM COMPENSATION PAYMENTS

GENERAL NOTE ON PART IV

Part IV has been repealed with effect from October 6, 1997 by the Social Security (Recovery of Benefits) Act 1997 (c.27), which re-enacts the provisions of Pt IV with significant amendments. It applies to all compensation schemes in respect of any accident, injury or disease settled on or after October 6, 1997. Two sets of implementing regulations have been promulgated: the Social Security (Recovery of Benefits) Regulations 1997 (SI 1997/2205) and the Social Security (Recovery of Benefits) (Appeals) Regulations 1997 (SI 1997/2237). The relevant primary and secondary legislation can be found in this volume. 1.132

Social Security Administration Act 1992

Part V

Income Support and the Duty to Maintain

Failure to maintain—general

105.—(1) If—
(a) any person persistently refuses or neglects to maintain himself or any person whom he is liable to maintain; and
(b) in consequence of his refusal or neglect income support [¹or an income-based jobseeker's allowance] is paid to or in respect of him or such a person,
he shall be guilty of an offence and liable on summary conviction to imprisonment for a term not exceeding 3 months or to a fine of an amount not exceeding level 4 on the standard scale or to both.

(2) For the purposes of subsection (1) above a person shall not be taken to refuse or neglect to maintain himself or any other person by reason only of anything done or omitted in furtherance of a trade dispute.

(3) [¹Subject to sub-section (4) below,] subsections (6) to (9) of section 78 above shall have effect for the purposes of this Part of this Act as they have effect for the purposes of that section.

[¹(4) For the purposes of this section, in its application to an income-based jobseeker's allowance, a person is liable to maintain another if that other person is his or her spouse [² or civil partner].]

Amendments

1. Jobseekers Act 1995, Sch.2, para.53 (October 7, 1996).
2. Civil Partnership Act 2004, s.254 and Sch.24, para.62 (December 5, 2005).

Derivation

Social Security Act 1986, s.26.

General Note

Subs. (1)
The criminal offence created by subs.(1) of refusing or neglecting to maintain oneself is at first sight rather extraordinary, but it is only committed if as a consequence income support or income-based JSA is paid. Prosecution is very much a last resort after the ordinary sanctions against voluntary unemployment have been used. In 1984–85 there were none (NACRO, *Enforcement of the Law Relating to Social Security*, para.8.6). Prosecution of those who refuse or neglect to maintain others is more common.

Liability to maintain
Under subs.(3), liability to maintain another person for the purposes of Pt V is tested, except in relation to income-based JSA, according to s.78(6)–(9). Both men and women are liable to maintain their spouses and children. This liability remains in force despite the enactment of the Child Support Act 1991, with the result that the Department retains its power to enforce that liability under ss.106–108. But although this power remains, in practice the Department does not enforce the liability to maintain children now that the Child Support Agency has acquired this role. Note also that since April 5, 1993, the courts have not had power to make new orders for maintenance for children (s.8(3), Child Support Act 1991). Under subs.(4) the only liability to maintain which is relevant to s.105 for the purposes of income-based JSA is the liability of one spouse to maintain the other.

(1992 c.5, s.105)

The definition of child goes beyond the usual meaning in s.137 of the Contributions and Benefits Act of a person under 16 to include those under 19 who count as a dependant in someone else's income support entitlement (s.78(6)(d)). The effect of the reference in s.78(4) to s.1 of the Family Law Reform Act 1987 is that in determining whether a person is the father or mother of a child it is irrelevant whether the person was married to the other parent at the time of the birth or not. If a married couple divorce, their liability to maintain each other ceases for the purposes of Pt V, but the obligation to maintain their children remains. This then is the remnant of the old family means-test that used to extend much wider until the Poor Law was finally "abolished" by the National Assistance Act 1948. For the enforcement of this liability, see ss.106–108, and for a criminal offence, subs.(1).

Section 78(6)(c) was new in 1980. In *R. v W. London SBAT, Ex p. Clarke* [1975] 1 W.L.R. 1396, the court had held that the sponsor of an immigrant was under no obligation to maintain the immigrant for supplementary benefit purposes. This position is now reversed, and s.78(9) provides for conclusive certificates of an undertaking to maintain to be produced. The liability to maintain is enforced under s.106. The SBC policy struck down in *Clarke*'s case had deemed the immigrant to be receiving the support from his sponsor even where it was not forthcoming. This is not now the case. It is only a resource when actually received.

Recovery of expenditure on benefit from person liable for maintenance

106.—(1) Subject to the following provisions of this section, if income support is claimed by or in respect of a person whom another person is liable to maintain or paid to or in respect of such a person, the Secretary of State may make a complaint against the liable person to a magistrates' court for an order under this section.

(2) On the hearing of a complaint under this section the court shall have regard to all the circumstances and, in particular, to the income of the liable person, and may order him to pay such sum, weekly or otherwise, as it may consider appropriate, except that in a case falling within section 78(6)(c) above that sum shall not include any amount which is not attributable to income support (whether paid before or after the making of the order).

(3) In determining whether to order any payments to be made in respect of income support for any period before the complaint was made, or the amount of any such payments, the court shall disregard any amount by which the liable person's income exceeds the income which was his during that period.

(4) Any payments ordered to be made under this section shall be made—
(a) to the Secretary of State in so far as they are attributable to any income support (whether paid before or after the making of the order);
(b) to the person claiming income support or (if different) the dependant; or
(c) to such other person as appears to the court expedient in the interests of the dependant.

(5) An order under this section shall be enforceable as a magistrates' court maintenance order within the meaning of section 150(1) of the Magistrates' Court Act 1980.

(6) In the application of this section to Scotland, subsection (5) above shall be omitted and for the references to a complaint and to a magistrates' court there shall be substituted respectively references to an application and to the sheriff.

1.137

(7) On an application under subsection (1) above a court in Scotland may make a finding as to the parentage of a child for the purpose of establishing whether a person is, for the purposes of section 105 above and this section, liable to maintain him.

DERIVATION

1.138   Social Security Act 1986, s.24.

DEFINITION

"child"—see ss.105(3) and 78(b).

GENERAL NOTE

1.139   This section gives the Department an independent right to enforce the liability to maintain in s.78(6), which now covers both spouses and children, by an order in the magistrates' court, providing that income support has been claimed or paid for the person sought to be maintained.

Children

1.140   From April 1993 the Child Support Act 1991 has introduced an entirely new system of determining and enforcing the liability of parents to maintain children, through the Child Support Agency. This book does not deal with that system, for which, see Jacobs and Douglas, *Child Support Legislation*. But the Department's rights under s.106 remain in force not only between spouses, but also as between parents and children. It is not clear in what circumstances action against a parent may be taken under s.106 rather than through the Child Support Agency. The Department has said that they do not intend to use the s.106 power in relation to children, and this seems to be implicit in the Income Support Special Circumstances Guide, paras 6000–6014. The Child Support Agency phased in applications for child support maintenance for income support claimants. It was originally intended that all income support claimants would have been required to apply under s.6 of the Child Support Act 1991 by April 1996; however, there have been some delays in taking on cases. Despite the delays, claimants receiving maintenance under a court order or an arrangement with liable relative officers were given priority by the Child Support Agency and so there should no longer be any cases where maintenance for dependent children is still being dealt with by the Benefits Agency. Benefit may only be reduced for failure to comply with obligations under s.6, not for failure to co-operate in relation to the liability to maintain in s.78(6). Note also that since April 5, 1993, the courts have not had the power to make new orders for maintenance for children (s.8(3), Child Support Act 1991).

Spouses

1.141   The usual procedure was last described in detail in Chapter 13 of the *Supplementary Benefits Handbook* (1984 ed.) and will presumably continue to apply, since it was repeated in essence in the DSS *Guide to Income Support*, although there were some administrative changes. The current Income Support Guide does not contain the liable relative procedure. This apparently is now in an internal guide called "Residual Liable Relatives and Proceedings Guide". The most common situation is where a breakdown of marriage leads to separation or divorce and the woman claims income support. The same procedures can apply if it is the man who claims benefit. If there has already been a divorce then there is no liability to maintain between the ex-spouses. If there has merely been a separation then the wife is entitled to benefit as a single person, but there will be an investigation of the circumstances to ensure that the separation is genuine. If the husband is already paying maintenance under a court order or the wife has taken proceedings herself which are reasonably advanced, no approach to the husband will be made by the Department.

Otherwise, the wife will be asked for information about the whereabouts of the liable relative (although producing the information cannot be made a condition of receiving benefit) and he will be contacted as soon as possible. The husband is asked to pay as much as he can, if possible enough to remove the need for income support to be paid to the wife and any children.

In deciding what level of payment is acceptable on a voluntary basis, it is understood that the following formula is used as a starting point. The income support personal allowances and premiums for the man are taken, plus rent, or mortgage payments, council tax and 15 per cent of his net wage. If the man has a new partner, two calculations are done—one as if the man was single and the other using joint incomes. The lower figure is then taken. The excess over this amount is regarded as available to be used as maintenance. But this is only a basis for discussion and payment of a lesser sum may be agreed, particularly if there are other essential expenses. Clearly there is scope for negotiation here. Thus if the man himself is receiving income support he would not be expected to pay anything.

If the husband is unwilling to make a payment voluntarily, although the Department believe that he has sufficient income, then legal proceedings may be considered. The first step will be to see if the wife will take action. The official policy is that the wife will merely be advised on the advantages of taking proceedings herself (that she may get enough maintenance to lift her off benefit and that an order for maintenance will continue if she ceases to be entitled to income support, as by working full-time). The first advantage is likely to be real in only a small minority of cases and the force of the second has been reduced by the introduction of the procedure in s.107(3)–(14). The choice should be left entirely to the woman. A wife may of course take proceedings herself even though the Department has accepted voluntary payments from the husband.

The courts have refused to adopt the "liable relative formula" in private proceedings by wives or ex-wives (*Shallow v Shallow* [1979] Fam. 1) and will only have regard to the man's subsistence level. By this they mean the ordinary scale rates of benefit plus housing costs. A more realistic approach may have been presaged by *Allen v Allen* [1986] 2 F.L.R. 265, where the Court of Appeal used the long-term scale rate (now disappeared) as a yardstick. In *Delaney v Delaney* [1990] 2 F.L.R. 457, the Court of Appeal accepted the principle that where the man had insufficient resources after taking account of his reasonable commitments to a new family to maintain his former wife and family properly, a maintenance order should not financially cripple him where the wife is entitled to social security benefits. But no calculation of the man's income support level was made.

If the wife does not take proceedings, then the Department may. The court is to have regard to all the circumstances, in particular the husband's resources, and may order him to pay whatever sum is appropriate (subs.(2)). Presumably, the same principles will govern the amount of an order as in a private application. There were some new provisions in s.107(1) in cases where the order included amounts for children, but it is not at all clear how these interacted with the general test of appropriateness under subs.(2). Note that since April 5, 1993 the courts have not had the power to make new orders for maintenance for children (s.8(3) Child Support Act 1991). The wife's adultery or desertion or other conduct is only a factor to be taken into account, not a bar to any order. Nor is the existence of a separation agreement under which the wife agrees not to claim maintenance a bar (*National Assistance Board v Parkes* [1955] 2 Q.B. 506). Although *Hulley v Thompson* [1981] 1 W.L.R. 159 concerned only the liability to maintain children, because there had been a divorce, it showed that not even a consent order under which the man transferred the matrimonial home to his ex-wife and she agreed to receive no maintenance for herself or the children, barred the statutory liability to maintain the children. However, it seems that the existence of the order could be taken into account in deciding what amount it is appropriate for the man to pay.

Proceedings by the Department are relatively rare. In 1979 there were only 431 (SBC Annual Report for 1979 (Cmnd. 8033), para.8.30).

Social Security Administration Act 1992

Recovery of expenditure on income support: additional amounts and transfer of orders

107.—(1) In any case where—
  (a) the claim for income support referred to in section 106(1) above is or was made by the parent of one or more children in respect of both himself and those children; and
  (b) the other parent is liable to maintain those children but, by virtue of not being the claimant's husband or wife [² or civil partner], is not liable to maintain the claimant,
the sum which the court may order that other parent to pay under subsection (2) of that section may include an amount, determined in accordance with regulations, in respect of any income support paid to or for the claimant by virtue of such provisions as may be prescribed.

(2) Where the sum which a court orders a person to pay under section 106 above includes by virtue of subsection (1) above an amount (in this section referred to as a "personal allowance element") in respect of income support by virtue of paragraph 1(2) of Schedule 2 to the Income Support (General) Regulations 1987 (personal allowance for lone parent) the order shall separately identify the amount of the personal allowance element.

(3) In any case where—
  (a) there is in force an order under subsection (2) of section 106 above made against a person ("the liable parent") who is the parent of one or more children, in respect of the other parent or the children; and
  (b) payments under the order fall to be made to the Secretary of State by virtue of subsection (4)(a) of that section; and
  (c) that other parent ("the dependent parent") ceases to claim income support,
the Secretary of State may, by giving notice in writing to the court which made the order and to the liable parent and the dependent parent, transfer to the dependent parent the right to receive the payments under the order, exclusive of any personal allowance element, and to exercise the relevant rights in relation to the order, except so far as relating to that element.

(4) Notice under subsection (3) above shall not be given (and if purportedly given, shall be of no effect) at a time when there is in force a maintenance order made against the liable parent—
  (a) in favour of the dependent parent or one or more of the children; or
  (b) in favour of some other person for the benefit of the dependent parent or one or more of the children;
and if such a maintenance order is made at any time after notice under that subsection has been given, the order under section 106(2) above shall cease to have effect.

(5) In any case where—
  (a) notice is given to a magistrates' court under subsection (3) above,
  (b) payments under the order are required to be made by any method of payment falling within section 59(6) of the Magistrates' Courts Act 1980 (standing order, etc.), and
  (c) the clerk to the justices for the petty sessions area for which the court is acting decides that payment by that method is no longer possible,
the clerk shall amend the order to provide that payments under the order shall be made by the liable parent [¹ to the justices' chief clerk for the court.]

(1992 c.5, s.107)

(6) Except as provided by subsections (8) and (12) below, where the Secretary of State gives notice under subsection (3) above, he shall cease to be entitled—
  (a) to receive any payment under the order in respect of any personal allowance element; or
  (b) to exercise the relevant rights, so far as relating to any such element, notwithstanding that the dependent parent does not become entitled to receive any payment in respect of that element or to exercise the relevant rights so far as so relating.

(7) If, in a case where the Secretary of State gives notice under subsection (3) above, a payment under the order is or has been made to him wholly or partly in respect of the whole or any part of the period beginning with the day on which the transfer takes effect and ending with the day on which the notice under subsection (3) above is given to the liable parent, the Secretary of State shall—
  (a) repay to or for the liable parent so much of the payment as is referable to any personal allowance element in respect of that period or, as the case may be, the part of it in question; and
  (b) pay to or for the dependent parent so much of any remaining balance of the payment as is referable to that period or part;
and a payment under paragraph (b) above shall be taken to discharge, to that extent, the liability of the liable parent to the dependent parent under the order in respect of that period or part.

(8) If, in a case where the Secretary of State has given notice under subsection (3) above, the dependent parent makes a further claim for income support, then—
  (a) the Secretary of State may, by giving a further notice in writing to the court which made the order and to the liable parent and the dependent parent, transfer back from the dependent parent to himself the right to receive the payments and to exercise the relevant rights; and
  (b) that transfer shall revive the Secretary of State's right to receive payment under the order in respect of any personal allowance element and to exercise the relevant rights so far as relating to any such element.

(9) Subject to subsections (10) and (11) below, in any case where—
  (a) notice is given to a magistrates' court under subsection (8) above, and
  (b) the method of payment under the order which subsists immediately before the day on which the transfer under subsection (8) above takes effect differs from the method of payment which subsisted immediately before the day on which the transfer under subsection (3) above (or, as the case may be, the last such transfer) took effect,
the clerk to the justices for the petty sessions area for which the court is acting shall amend the order by reinstating the method of payment under the order which subsisted immediately before the day on which the transfer under subsection (3) above (or, as the case may be, the last such transfer) took effect.

(10) The clerk shall not amend the order under subsection (9) above if the Secretary of State gives notice in writing to the clerk, on or before the day on which notice under subsection (8) above is given, that the method of payment under the order which subsists immediately before the day on which the transfer under subsection (8) above takes effect is to continue.

Social Security Administration Act 1992

(11) In any case where—
(a) notice is given to a magistrates' court under subsection (8) above,
(b) the method of payment under the order which subsisted immediately before the day on which the transfer under subsection (3) above (or, if there has been more than one such transfer, the last such transfer) took effect was any method of payment falling within section 59(6) of the Magistrates' Courts Act 1980 (standing order, etc.), and
(c) the clerk decides that payment by that method is no longer possible,
the clerk shall amend the order to provide that payments under the order shall be made by the liable parent [¹ to the justices' chief executive for the court.]

(12) A transfer under subsection (3) or (8) above does not transfer or otherwise affect the right of any person—
(a) to receive a payment which fell due to him at a time before the transfer took effect; or
(b) to exercise the relevant rights in relation to any such payment;
and, where notice is given under subsection (3), subsection (6) above does not deprive the Secretary of State of his right to receive such a payment in respect of any personal allowance element or to exercise the relevant rights in relation to such a payment.

(13) For the purposes of this section—
(a) a transfer under subsection (3) above takes effect on the day on which the dependent parent ceases to be in receipt of income support in consequence of the cessation referred to in paragraph (c) of that subsection, and
(b) a transfer under subsection (8) above takes effect on—
    (i) the first day in respect of which the dependent parent receives income support after the transfer under subsection (3) above took effect, or
    (ii) such later day as may be specified for the purpose in the notice under subsection (8).
irrespective of the day on which notice under the subsection in question is given.

(14) Any notice required to be given to the liable parent under subsection (3) or (8) above shall be taken to have been given if it has been sent to his last known address.

(15) In this section—
"child" means a person under the age of 16, notwithstanding section 78(6)(d) above;
"court" shall be construed in accordance with section 106 above;
"maintenance order"—
(a) in England and Wales, means—
    (i) any order for the making of periodical payments or for the payment of a lump sum which is, or has at any time been, a maintenance order within the meaning of the Attachment of Earnings Act 1971;
    (ii) any order under Part III of the Matrimonial and Family Proceedings Act 1984 (overseas divorce) for the making of periodical payments or for the payment of a lump sum;
    [² (iii) any order under Schedule 7 to the Civil Partnership Act 2004 for the making of periodical payments or for the payment of a lump sum;]

(1992 c.5, s.107)

(b) in Scotland, has the meaning given by section 106 of the Debtors (Scotland) Act 1987, but disgarding paragraph (h) (alimentary bond or agreement);

"the relevant rights", in relation to an order under section 106(2) above, means the right to bring any proceedings, take any steps or do any other thing under or in relation to the order which the Secretary of State could have brought, taken or done apart from any transfer under this section.

AMENDMENTS

1. Access to Justice Act 1999, Sch.13, paras 167 and 168 (April 1, 2001).
2. Civil Partnership Act 2004, s.254 and Sch.24, para.63 (December 5, 2005).

DERIVATION

Social Security Act 1986, s.24A, as amended by the Maintenance Enforcement Act 1991, s.9, with effect from April 1, 1992 (Maintenance Enforcement Act 1991 (Commencement) (No.2) Order 1992 (SI 1992/455)). 　1.143

GENERAL NOTE

The predecessors of this section and s.108 formed one of the central strategic objectives of the Social Security Act 1990 (HC *Hansard*, April 3, 1990, Vol.170, col. 1137 (Tony Newton); HL *Hansard*, April 20, 1990, Vol.518, col. 234 (Lord Henley)), but were only introduced at the Report stage in the Commons. They therefore received relatively little Parliamentary discussion due to the operation of the guillotine. The Government carried out a general review of the maintenance system, based on a survey of work in United Kingdom courts and DSS offices and study of overseas systems, and produced radical proposals in *Children Come First* (Cm. 1264), now embodied in the Child Support Act 1991 from April 1993. But action had already been taken to tighten up the assessment of an absent parent's ability to pay maintenance for his family on income support. The new provisions were regarded as desirable in the short term to improve the effectiveness of the present system, pending the more radical reform (HC *Hansard*, March 28, Vol.170, col. 566). However, ss.107 and 108 remain in force despite the implementation of the Child Support Act. 　1.144

Section 107 contains two elements. The first relates to the situation where a lone parent is receiving income support, but the absent parent of the child(ren) is not liable to maintain the parent under s.78(6) because the parents are not or are no longer married. Where the Department seeks its own order against the absent parent, courts are empowered to take into account income support relating to the lone parent in calculating the amount to be paid for the child(ren) and the Department may of course take this into account in negotiating voluntary agreements. The second is to allow a Department order to be transferred to the lone parent when that person comes off income support, rather than the lone parent having to obtain a separate private maintenance order. Note that since April 5, 1993, the courts have not had the power to make new orders for maintenance for children (s.8(3) Child Support Act 1991).

Subss. (1) and (2)

These provisions comprise the first element identified above. They apply when both of conditions (a) and (b) in subs.(1) are satisfied. Under para.(a), s.106 gives the Department power to obtain an order against a person who is liable to maintain a claimant of income support or a person included in the family for claiming purposes. Section 78(6) defines liability to maintain for this purpose. There is a liability to maintain a spouse and any children. Under s.78(6)(d) "child" includes a person aged 16–18 (inclusive) who is still a member of the claimant's family for income support purposes (e.g. because still in full-time education). However, s.107(15) provides that for the purposes of s.107 "child" is restricted to a person under the age of 16. Thus, lone parent claimants whose children are all over 15 will 　1.145

fall outside this provision. Under para.(b), the absent parent must not be married to the lone parent, so that the obligation to maintain under s.78(6) is only in respect of the child(ren). If both these conditions are met, a court may include whatever amount the regulations determine in respect of the income support paid for the lone parent. The Income Support (Liable Relatives) Regulations specify in general the children's personal allowances, family premium, lone parent premium (now the higher rate of family premium), disabled child premium and the carer premium in respect of care for a child.

The intention was said to be that the regulation-making power "will be used to specify that once having looked at the allowances and premiums that are paid because there are children, the court should also have regard to the income support personal allowance paid for the mother" (HC *Hansard*, March 28, 1990, Vol.170, col. 567). The Liable Relatives Regulations provide that if the liable parent has the means to pay in addition to the amounts already specified, a court order may include some or all of the dependent parent's personal allowance.

It was said that in a private maintenance order for children the court could take account of the parent's care costs and that social security law was thus being brought into line with family law. However, there was nothing as specific as s.107 in family law. The existing power of the court on orders sought by the Department was already wide and it is not clear how much real difference the new powers made. Under s.106(2) the court may order payment of such sum as it may consider appropriate. The assumption seems to be that not only could the personal allowance for a child under 16 be considered under this provision, but also the family premium (paid to all claimants with a child or young person (16–18) in the family) and the additional lone parent premium (now the higher rate of family premium). If such amounts can be considered under the existing law (and they might be considered to reflect the care costs of the lone parent) there seems no reason why the court could not also consider some part of the parent's personal allowance if that was considered "appropriate." However, s.107(1) and the Liable Relatives Regulations make the position clear, which should be an advantage.

It is notable that the court retains a discretion as to what amounts to consider and that the overriding factor under s.106(2) is what is appropriate. Under para.1 of Sch.2 to the Income Support (General) Regulations 1987 the personal allowance for a lone parent aged under 18 or over 24 is the same as for a single person with no dependants. There is only a difference (currently £10.50 p.w.) for those aged 18–24.

Subsection (2) provides that if the lone parent's personal allowance under Sch.2 is covered by the order, this element must be separately identified. This has no bearing on subs.(1), but is relevant to the procedure set up by subss.(3)–(14).

Subss. (3)–(15)

1.146   These provisions contain the once-important procedure allowing the transfer of a Department's order to the lone parent on coming off income support. The conditions for transfer under subs.(3) are that in such a case (remembering that "child" is defined to cover only those under 16 (subs.(15)) the Secretary of State gives notice to the court which made the order and to both the parents. Then the right to enforce or apply for variation of the order (apart from any personal allowance element identified under subs.(2)) is transferred to the lone parent (known as "the dependent parent"). Thus, the personal allowance element, which is of no net benefit to the lone parent while she is on income support, is removed at the point when its value would actually be felt by the lone parent. The Department can no longer enforce the personal allowance element of the order (subs.(6)). Under subs.(13)(a) the transfer takes effect on the day on which the dependent parent ceases to receive income support in consequence of ceasing to claim. This is a peculiar way of putting things. If the dependent parent's circumstances change (e.g. her capital goes over the cut-off limit or she starts full-time work) her entitlement to income support may be terminated on review by the adjudication officer under s.25. She may well then choose not to claim income support again, as it would be a useless exercise. The dependent parent could with

(1992 c.5, s.107)

some strain be said to cease to claim income support and so to satisfy subs.(3)(c), but the cessation of receipt of income support is not in consequence of the cessation of claiming but of the review and revision by the adjudication officer.

Subsection (3) is not to apply if a private maintenance order (see subs.(15) for definition) is in existence, and if the dependent parent obtains one after a transfer the right to enforce the Department's order disappears (subs.(4)).

If, after a transfer, the dependent parent makes another claim for income support (presumably only while still having children under 16), the Secretary of State may by giving notice to all parties re-transfer to the Department the right to enforce the order and revive the personal allowance element on the dependent parent becoming entitled to income support (subss.(8) and (13)(b)). Presumably, the revival of the personal allowance element depends on the conditions of subss.(1) and (2) being met at the date of revival.

Reduction of expenditure on income support: certain maintenance orders to be enforceable by the Secretary of State

108.—(1) This section applies where—
  (a) a person ("the claimant") who is the parent of one or more children is in receipt of income support either in respect of those children or in respect of both himself and those children; and
  (b) there is in force a maintenance order made against the other parent ("the liable person")—
    (i) in favour of the claimant or one or more of the children, or
    (ii) in favour of some other person for the benefit of the claimant or one or more of the children,
and in this section "the primary recipient" means the person in whose favour that maintenance order was made.

(2) If, in a case where this section applies, the liable person fails to comply with any of the terms of the maintenance order—
  (a) the Secretary of State may bring any proceedings or take any other steps to enforce the order that could have been brought or taken by or on behalf of the primary recipient; and
  (b) any court before which proceedings are brought by the Secretary of State by virtue of paragraph (a) above shall have the same powers in connection with those proceedings as it would have had if they had been brought by the primary recipient.

(3) The Secretary of State's powers under this section are exercisable at his discretion and whether or not the primary recipient or any other person consents to their exercise; but any sums recovered by virtue of this section shall be payable to or for the primary recipient, as if the proceedings or steps in question had been brought or taken by him or on his behalf.

(4) The powers conferred on the Secretary of State by subsection (2)(a) above include power—
  (a) to apply for the registration of the maintenance order under—
    (i) section 17 of the Maintenance Orders Act 1950;
    (ii) section 2 of the Maintenance Orders Act 1958; or
    (iii) the Civil Jurisdiction and Judgments Act 1982; [² or
    (iv) Council Regulation (EC) No 44/2001 of 22nd December 2000 on jurisdiction and the recognition and enforcement of judgments in civil and commercial matters; and]
  (b) to make an application under section 2 of the Maintenance Orders (Reciprocal Enforcement) Act 1972 (application for enforcement in reciprocating country).

Social Security Administration Act 1992

(5) Where this section applies, the prescribed person shall in prescribed circumstances give the Secretary of State notice of any application—
  (a) to alter, vary, suspend, discharge, revoke, revive, or enforce the maintenance order in question; or
  (b) to remit arrears under that maintenance order;
and the Secretary of State shall be entitled to appear and be heard on the application.

(6) Where, by virtue of this section, the Secretary of State commences any proceedings to enforce a maintenance order, he shall, in relation to those proceedings, be treated for the purposes of any enactment or instrument relating to maintenance orders as if he were a person entitled to payment under the maintenance order in question (but shall not thereby become entitled to any such payment).

(7) Where, in any proceedings under this section in England and Wales, the court makes an order for the whole or any part of the arrears due under the maintenance order in question to be paid as a lump sum, the Secretary of State shall inform [¹ the Legal Services Commission] of the amount of that lump sum if he knows—
  (a) that the primary recipient either—
    (i) received legal aid under the Legal Aid Act 1974 in connection with the proceedings in which the maintenance order was made, or
    (ii) was an assisted party, within the meaning of the Legal Aid Act 1988, in those proceedings, or
    [¹(iii) received services funded by the Legal Services Commission as part of the Community Legal Service; and]
  (b) that a sum remains unpaid on account of the contribution required of the primary recipient—
    (i) under section 9 of the Legal Aid Act 1974 in respect of those proceedings, or
    (ii) under section 16 of the Legal Aid Act 1988 in respect of the costs of his being represented under Part IV of that Act in those proceedings, [¹ or
    (iii) by virtue of section 10 of the Access to Justice Act 1999 in respect of services funded by the Legal Services Commission as part of the Community Legal Service.]

(8) In this section "maintenance order" has the same meaning as it has in section 107 above but does not include any such order for the payment of a lump sum.

AMENDMENTS

1. Access to Justice Act 1999, Sch.4, para.48 (April 1, 2000)
2. The Civil Jurisdiction and Judgments Order 2001 (SI 2001/3929), art.5 and Sch.3 (March 1, 2002).

DERIVATION

1.148 Social Security Act 1986, s.24B.

GENERAL NOTE

1.149 Section 108 enables the Department to enforce certain private maintenance orders in favour of lone parent claimants of income support. Only lone parents are covered by subs.(1)(a), and not mere separated or divorced spouses, but the maintenance order may be in favour either of the parent or the child(ren) or both. The Secretary of State may at his discretion and without the consent of the lone parent take steps (including those specified in subs.(5)) to enforce the order as if he were the person entitled to payment under the order (subss.(2), (3) and (6)). But any sums recovered are payable to the primary recipient under the order (subss.(3) and (6)). Under subs.(5) regulations may specify who has to inform the Department of applications to vary, suspend etc. the private order or to remit arrears. Regulation 3 of the Income Support (Liable Relatives) Regulations specifies various court officials. The Secretary of State is given the right to be heard on any such application, but has no power to make such an application, e.g. to increase the amount of an order. This is because subs.(2) only operates when there is a failure to comply with the terms (i.e. the existing terms) of the order.

Subsection (7) requires the Secretary of State to inform the Legal Aid Commission when a lump sum of arrears is to be paid when the Commission might be able to recover a contribution out of the lump sum.

Overall s.108 is a powerful weapon for the Department to enforce the payment of maintenance orders. If the lone parent has her own order, which is not being paid, income support will make up the shortfall. There is thus no great incentive for the lone parent to go through all the hassle of enforcement, and there may be other circumstances making her reluctant to take action. The Department will have no such inhibitions.

The Secretary of State predicted that the amount of maintenance recovered by the Department in respect of lone parents on income support would rise to about £260 million in 1990–91, having gone up from £155 million in 1988–89 to £180 million in 1989–90 (HC *Hansard*, March 28, 1990, Vol.170, col. 571). The predicted increase was partly based on the provisions now contained in ss.107 and 108 and partly on giving greater priority and resources to such work, with changes in the administrative guidance. These changes are to point up the need to stress to lone parents on benefits the advantages of reflecting the absent parent's proper responsibilities in the maintenance arrangements from the outset and also to indicate that the "normal expectation" should be that a lone parent will co-operate in establishing where responsibility lies. It is, however, recognised that there may be circumstances in which lone parents will not wish to name the father of a child. The White Paper, *Children Come First*, proposed reductions in the lone parent's benefit if she declines without good cause to take maintenance proceedings. The Child Support Act 1991 imposes such an obligation only in relation to applications under the Act.

Diversion of arrested earnings to Secretary of State—Scotland

109.—(1) Where in Scotland a creditor who is enforcing a maintenance order or alimentary bond or agreement by a current maintenance arrestment or a conjoined arrestment order is in receipt of income support, the creditor may in writing authorise the Secretary of State to receive any sums payable under the arrestment or order until the creditor ceases to be in receipt of income support or in writing withdraws the authorisation, whichever occurs first.

1.150

(2) On the intimation by the Secretary of State—
  (a) to the employer operating the current maintenance arrestment; or
  (b) to the sheriff clerk operating the conjoined arrestment order;
of an authorisation under subsection (1) above, the employer or sheriff clerk shall, until notified by the Secretary of State that the authorisation has ceased to have effect, pay to the Secretary of State any sums which would otherwise be payable under the arrestment or order to the creditor.

Social Security Administration Act 1992

Derivation

1.151 Social Security Act 1986, s.25A.

1.152 **Part VI.** *Omitted.*

General Note

1.153 Note that s.67 and Sch.6 to the Child Support, Pensions and Social Security Act 2000 make substantial amendments to Pt VI of this Act with effect from April 2, 2001.

1.154 **121E.–123.** *Omitted.*

Part VII

Information

The Registration Service

Provisions relating to age, death and marriage

1.155 **124.**—(1) Regulations made by the Registrar General under section 20 of the Registration Service Act 1953 or section 54 of the Registration of Births, Deaths and Marriages (Scotland) Act 1965 may provide for the furnishing by superintendent registrars and registrars, subject to the payment of such fee as may be prescribed by the regulations, of such information for the purposes—
    (a) of the provisions of the Contributions and Benefits Act to which this section applies;
[¹(aa) of the provisions of Parts I and II of the Jobseekers Act 1995;]
[³(ab) of the provisions of the State Pension Credit Act 2002; and]
    (b) the provisions of this Act so far as they have effect in relation to matters arising under those provisions,
including copies or extracts from the registers in their custody, as may be so prescribed.

(2) This section applies to the following provisions of the Contributions and Benefits Act—
    (a) Parts I to VI except section 108;
    (b) Part VII, so far as it relates to income support and [⁵ . . .];
    (c) Part VIII, so far as it relates to any social fund payment such as is mentioned in section 138(1)(a) or (2);
    (d) Part IX;
    (e) Part XI; and
    (f) Part XII.

(3) Where the age, marriage or death of a person is required to be ascertained or proved for the purposes mentioned in subsection (1) above, any person—
    (a) on presenting to the custodian of the register under the enactments relating to the registration of births, marriages and deaths, in which particulars of the birth, marriage or death (as the case may be) of the

(1992 c.5, s.124)

first-mentioned person are entered, a duly completed requisition in writing in that behalf; and
(b) on payment of a fee of [² £3.50] in England and Wales and [⁴ £8.50] in Scotland,

shall be entitled to obtain a copy, certified under the hand of the custodian, of the entry of those particulars.

(4) Requisitions for the purposes of subsection (3) above shall be in such form and contain such particulars as may from time to time be specified by the Registrar General, and suitable forms of requisition shall, on request, be supplied without charge by superintendent registrars and registrars.

(5) In this section—
(a) as it applies to England and Wales—
"Registrar General" means the Registrar General for England and Wales; and
"superintendent registrar" and "registrar" mean a superintendent registrar or, as the case may be, registrar for the purposes of the enactments relating to the registration of births, deaths and marriages; and
(b) as it applies to Scotland—
"Registrar General" means the Registrar General of Births, Deaths and Marriages for Scotland;
"registrar" means a district registrar, senior registrar or assistant registrar for the purposes of the enactment relating to the registration of births, deaths and marriages in Scotland.

AMENDMENTS

1. Jobseekers Act 1995, Sch.2, para.59 (October 7, 1996).
2. The Registration of Births, Deaths and Marriages (Fees) Order 2002 (SI 2002/3076), art.1 (April 1, 2003; this Order specifies a fee of £7 where the certificate is issued by a superintendent registrar or any other custodian of the register).
3. State Pension Credit Act 2002, s.14 and Sch.2 (July 2, 2002 for the purpose of making regulations only; fully in force October 6, 2003).
4. The Registration of Births, Deaths and Marriages (Fees) (Scotland) Order 2002 (SSI 2002/389) (October 1, 2002).
5. Tax Credits Act 2002, s.60 and Sch.6 (April 8, 2003).

DERIVATION

Social Security Act 1975, s.160.

1.156

DEFINITIONS

"the Contributions and Benefits Act"—see s.191.
"prescribed"—*ibid.*

[¹ Provisions relating to civil partnership: England and Wales

124A.—(1) Regulations made by the Registrar General under section 36 of the Civil Partnership Act 2004 may provide for the furnishing by registration authorities, subject to the payment of the prescribed fee, of such information for the purposes mentioned in section 124(1) above as may be so prescribed.

1.157

(2) Where the civil partnership of a person is required to be ascertained or proved for those purposes, any person—

113

(a) on presenting to the registration authority for the area in which the civil partnership was formed a request in the prescribed manner in that behalf, and
(b) on payment of the prescribed fee,

shall be entitled to obtain a certified copy of such entries in the register as are prescribed by regulations made under section 36 of the 2004 Act.

(3) "The prescribed fee" means any fee prescribed under section 34(1) of the 2004 Act.

(4) "The prescribed manner" means—
(a) in accordance with any regulations made under section 36 of the 2004 Act, and
(b) in such form as is approved by the Registrar General for England and Wales,

and forms for making a request under subsection (2) shall, on request, be supplied without charge by registration authorities.]

AMENDMENT

1. Civil Partnership Act 2004 (Overseas Relationships and Consequential etc. Amendments) Order 2005 (SI 2005/3129), Sch.1, para.4 (December 5, 2005).

[¹ Provisions relating to civil partnership: Scotland

1.158

124B.—(1) Where the civil partnership of a person is required to be ascertained or proved for the purposes mentioned in section 124(1) above, any person, on presenting to a district registrar a request in the approved manner in that behalf, shall be entitled to obtain a copy, certified by the registrar, of the entry in the civil partnership register of the particulars of the civil partnership.

(2) "The approved manner" means in such form and containing such particulars as may be approved by the Registrar General for Scotland.

(3) Forms for making a request under subsection (1) shall, on request, be supplied without charge by district registrars.

(4) "Civil partnership register" has the same meaning as in Part 3 of the Civil Partnership Act 2004.]

AMENDMENT

1. Civil Partnership Act 2004 (Overseas Relationships and Consequential etc. Amendments) Order 2005 (SI 2005/3129), Sch.1, para.4 (December 5, 2005).

Regulations as to notifications of deaths

1.159

125.—(1) Regulations [³made with the concurrence of the Inland Revenue] may provide that it shall be the duty of any of the following persons—
(a) the Registrar General for England and Wales;
(b) the Registrar General of Births, Deaths and Marriages for Scotland;
(c) each registrar of births and deaths,

to furnish the Secretary of State, [³or the Inland Revenue, for the purposes of their respective functions] under the Contributions and Benefits Act [¹, the Jobseekers Act 1995] [²the Social Security (Recovery of Benefits) Act 1997] [⁴, the Social Security Act 1998] [⁵, the State Pension Credit Act 2002] and this Act and the functions of the Northern Ireland Department under any Northern Ireland legislation corresponding to

(1992 c.5, s.125)

[¹any of those Acts], with the prescribed particulars of such deaths as may be prescribed.

(2) The regulations may make provision as to the manner in which and the times at which the particulars are to be furnished.

AMENDMENTS

1. Jobseekers Act 1995, Sch.2, para.60 (October 7, 1996).
2. Social Security (Recovery of Benefits) Act 1997, s.33 and Sch.3, para.5 (October 6, 1997).
3. Social Security Contributions (Transfer of Functions, etc.) Act 1999, s.1(1) and Sch.1, para.25 (April 1, 1999).
4. Social Security Act 1998, s.86 and Sch.7 (dates as for implementation of SSA 1998 for various benefits as set out on para.1.88 of this volume).
5. State Pension Credit Act 2002, s.14 and Sch.2 (July 2, 2002 for the purpose of making regulations only; fully in force October 6, 2003).

DERIVATION

Social Security Act 1986, s.60.

1.160

DEFINITIONS

"the Contributions and Benefits Act"—see s.191.
"the Northern Ireland Department"—*ibid.*
"prescribed"—*ibid.*

Personal representatives—income support and supplementary benefit

Personal representatives to give information about the estate of a deceased person who was in receipt of income support or supplementary benefit

126.—(1) The personal representatives of a person who was in receipt of income support [¹, an income-based jobseeker's allowance] [², state pension credit] or supplementary benefit at any time before his death shall provide the Secretary of State with such information as he may require relating to the assets and liabilities of that person's estate.

1.161

(2) If the personal representatives fail to supply any information within 28 days of being required to do so under subsection (1) above, then—
   (a) the appropriate court may, on the application of the Secretary of State, make an order directing them to supply that information within such time as may be specified in the order; and
   (b) any such order may provide that all costs (or, in Scotland, expenses) of and incidental to the application shall be borne personally by any of the personal representatives.

(3) In this section "the appropriate court" means—
   (a) in England and Wales, a county court;
   (b) in Scotland, the sheriff;
and any application to the sheriff under this section shall be made by summary application.

Social Security Administration Act 1992

AMENDMENTS

1. Jobseekers Act 1995, Sch.2, para.61 (October 7, 1996).
2. State Pension Credit Act 2002, s.14 and Sch.2 (July 2, 2002 for the purpose of making regulations only; fully in force October 6, 2003).

DERIVATION

1.162   Social Security Act 1986, s.27A.

GENERAL NOTE

1.163   Under s.71(3) an overpayment which would have been recoverable from a person may be recoverable from that person's estate (*Secretary of State for Social Services v Solly* [1974] 3 All E.R. 922, *CSSB 6/1995*). Section 126 provides a specific obligation for the estate to provide information about the assets in it. However, s.126 only applies to the estates of income support, income-based JSA or supplementary benefit claimants. It does not apply to all benefits. Nor does it apply to anyone other than a recipient of income support, JSA or supplementary benefit. Sometimes a person other than a recipient may become liable to recovery by making a misrepresentation or failing to disclose a material fact: *R(SB) 21/82* and *R(SB) 28/83*. See the note to s.71(3).

1.164   **126A.** *Omitted.*

1.165   **127.–128A.** *Repealed by Sch.2 to the Social Security Administration (Fraud) Act 1997 (July 1, 1997).*

Statutory sick pay and other benefits

Disclosure by Secretary of State for purpose of determination of period of entitlement to statutory sick pay

1.166   **129.** Where the Secretary of State considers that it is reasonable for information held by him to be disclosed to an employer, for the purpose of enabling that employer to determine the duration of a period of entitlement under Part XI of the Contributions and Benefits Act in respect of an employee, or whether such a period exists, he may disclose the information to that employer.

DERIVATION

1.167   SSHBA 1982, s.17(1).

Duties of employers—statutory sick pay and claims for other benefits

1.168   **130.**—(1) Regulations may make provision requiring an employer, in a case falling within subsection (3) below to furnish information in connection with the making, by a person who is, or has been, an employee of that employer, of a claim for—
(a) [¹ short-term incapacity benefit];
(b) a maternity allowance;
(c) [¹ long-term incapacity benefit];
(d) industrial injuries benefit; or
(e) [³ . . .]

(1992 c.5, s.130)

(2) Regulations under this section shall prescribe—
(a) the kind of information to be furnished in accordance with the regulations;
(b) the person to whom information of the prescribed kind is to be furnished; and
(c) the manner in which, and period within which, it is to be furnished.

(3) The cases are—
(a) where, by virtue of paragraph 2 of Schedule 11 to the Contributions and Benefits Act or of regulations made under paragraph 1 of that Schedule, a period of entitlement does not arise in relation to a period of incapacity for work;
(b) where a period of entitlement has come to an end but the period of incapacity for work which was running immediately before the period of entitlement came to an end continues; and
(c) where a period of entitlement has not come to an end but, on the assumption that—
   (i) the period of incapacity for work in question continues to run for a prescribed period; and
   (ii) there is no material change in circumstances, the period of entitlement will have ended on or before the end of the prescribed period.

(4) Regulations [² made with the concurrence of the Inland Revenue]—
(a) may require employers to maintain such records in connection with statutory sick pay as may be prescribed;
(b) may provide for—
   (i) any person claiming to be entitled to statutory sick pay; or
   (ii) any other person who is a party to proceedings arising under Part XI of the Contributions and Benefits Act,
   to furnish to the Secretary of State [²or the Inland Revenue (as the regulations may require)] within a prescribed period, any information required for the determination of any question arising in connection therewith; and
(c) may require employers who have made payments of statutory sick pay to furnish to the Secretary of State [²or the Inland Revenue (as the regulations may require)] such documents and information, at such times, as may be prescribed.

AMENDMENTS

1. Social Security (Incapacity for Work) Act 1994, Sch.1 (April 13, 1995).
2. Transfer of Functions Act 1999, Sch.1 (April 1, 1999).
3. Welfare Reform and Pensions Act 1999, Sch.1, para.39 (November 3, 2000).

DERIVATION

SSHBA 1982, ss.9, 17 and 18.

1.169

Disclosure by Secretary of State for purpose of determination of period of entitlement to statutory maternity pay

131. Where the Secretary of State considers that it is reasonable for information held by him to be disclosed to a person liable to make payments of statutory maternity pay for the purpose of enabling that person to determine—

1.170

(a) whether a maternity pay period exists in relation to a woman who is or has been an employee of his; and
(b) if it does, the date of its commencement and the weeks in it in respect of which he may be liable to pay statutory maternity pay, he may disclose the information to that person.

DERIVATION

1.171   SSA 1986, s.49.

Duties of employers—statutory maternity pay and claims for other benefits

1.172   **132.**—(1) Regulations may make provision requiring an employer in prescribed circumstances to furnish information in connection with the making of a claim by a woman who is or has been his employee for—
(a) a maternity allowance;
(b) [1 short-term incapacity benefit];
(c) [1 long-term incapacity benefit under section 30A], 40 and 41 of the Contributions and Benefits Act; or
(d) [3 . . .].
(2) Regulations under this section shall prescribe—
(a) the kind of information to be furnished in accordance with the regulations;
(b) the person to whom information of the prescribed kind is to be furnished; and
(c) the manner in which, and period within which, it is to be furnished.
(3) Regulations [2 made with the concurrence of the Inland Revenue]
(a) may require employers to maintain such records in connection with statutory maternity pay as may be prescribed;
(b) may provide for—
   (i) any woman claiming to be entitled to statutory maternity pay; or
   (ii) any other person who is a party to proceedings arising under Part XII of the Contributions and Benefits Act,
to furnish to the Secretary of State [2 or the Inland Revenue (as the regulations may require)], within a prescribed period, any information required for the determination of any question arising in connection therewith; and
(c) may require persons who have made payments of statutory maternity pay to furnish to the Secretary of State [2 or the Inland Revenue (as the regulations may require)] such documents and information, at such time, as may be prescribed.

AMENDMENTS

1. Social Security (Incapacity for Work) Act 1994, Sch.1 (April 13, 1995).
2. Transfer of Functions Act 1999, Sch.1 (April 1, 1999).
3. Welfare Reform and Pensions Act 1999, Sch.13, Pt IV (November 3, 2000).

DERIVATION

1.173   SSHBA, 1982, s.49.

(1992 c.5, s.133)

Maintenance proceedings

Furnishing of addresses for maintenance proceedings, etc.

133. The Secretary of State may incur expenses for the purpose of furnishing the address at which a man or woman is recorded by him as residing, where the address is required for the purpose of taking or carrying on legal proceedings to obtain or enforce an order for the making by the man or woman of payments—
  (a) for the maintenance of the man's wife or former wife, or the woman's husband or former husband; or
  (b) for the maintenance or education of any person as being the son or daughter of the man or his wife or former wife, or of the woman or her husband or former husband.

1.174

DERIVATION

SSA 1975, s.161.

1.175

134.–154. *Omitted.*

1.176

PART XI

COMPUTATION OF BENEFITS

Effect of alteration of rates of benefit under Parts II to V of Contributions and Benefits Act

155.—(1) This section has effect where the rate of any benefit to which this section applies is altered—
  (a) by an Act subsequent to this Act;
  (b) by an order under section 150 or 152 above; or
  (c) in consequence of any such Act or order altering any maximum rate of benefit;
and in this section "the commencing date" means the date fixed for payment of benefit at an altered rate to commence.

(2) This section applies to benefit under Part II, III, IV or V of the Contributions and Benefits Act.

(3) Subject to such exceptions or conditions as may be prescribed, where—
  (a) the weekly rate of a benefit to which this section applies is altered to a fixed amount higher or lower than the previous amount; and
  (b) before the commencing date an award of that benefit has been made (whether before or after the passing of the relevant Act or the making of the relevant order),
except as respects any period falling before the commencing date, the benefit shall become payable at the altered rate without any claim being made for it in the case of an increase in the rate of benefit or any review of the award in the case of a decrease, and the award shall have effect accordingly.

1.177

Social Security Administration Act 1992

(4) Where—
(a) the weekly rate of a benefit to which this section applies is altered; and
(b) before the commencing date (but after that date is fixed) an award is made of the benefit,

the award either may provide for the benefit to be paid as from the commencing date at the altered rate or may be expressed in terms of the rate appropriate at the date of the award.

(5) Where in consequence of the passing of an Act, or the making of an order, altering the rate of disablement pension, regulations are made varying the scale of disablement gratuities, the regulations may provide that the scale as varied shall apply only in cases where the period taken into account by the assessment of the extent of the disablement in respect of which the gratuity is awarded begins or began after such day as may be prescribed.

(6) Subject to such exceptions or conditions as may be prescribed, where—
(a) for any purpose of any Act or regulations the weekly rate at which a person contributes to the cost of providing for a child [2 or qualifying young person], or to the maintenance of an adult dependant, is to be calculated for a period beginning on or after the commencing date for an increase in the weekly rate of benefit; but
(b) account is to be taken of amounts referable to the period before the commencing date,

those amounts shall be treated as increased in proportion to the increase in the weekly rate of benefit.

(7) So long as sections 36 and 37 of the National Insurance Act 1965 (graduated retirement benefit) continue in force by virtue of regulations made under Schedule 3 of the Social Security (Consequential Provisions) Act 1975 or under Schedule 3 to the Consequential Provisions Act, regulation may make provision for applying the provisions of this section—

[1(a) to the amount of graduate retirement benefit payable for each unit of graduated contributions,
(b) To increased of such benefit under any provisions made by virtue of section 24(1)(b) of the Social Security Pensions Act 1975 or section 62(1)(a) of the Contributions and Benefits Act, and
(c) to any addition under section 37(1) of the National Insurance Act 1965 (addition to weekly rate of retirement pension for widows and widowers) to the amount of such benefit].

AMENDMENTS

1. Pensions Act 1995, s.131(3) (July 19, 1995).
2. Child Benefit Act 2005, Sch.1, Pt 1, para.23 (April 10, 2006).

DERIVATION

1.178 SSA 1986, s.64.

[1Power to anticipate pensions up-rating order

1.179 155A.—(1) This section applies where a statement is made in the House of Commons by or on behalf of the Secretary of State which specifies—
(a) the amounts by which he proposes, by an order under section 150 above, to increase—
(i) the weekly sums that are payable by way of retirement pension [2 or shared additional pension]; or

(1992 c.5, s.155A)

(ii) the amount of graduated retirement benefit payable for each unit of graduated contributions; and
(b) the date of which he proposes to bring the increases into force ("the commencing date").

(2) Where before the commencing date and after the date on which the statement is made, an award is made of a retirement pension [³, a shared additional pension] or a graduated retirement benefit, the award may provide for the pension or benefit to be paid as from the commencing date at the increased rate or may be expressed in terms of the rate appropriate at the date of the award.

AMENDMENTS

1. Social Security Act 1998, s.76 (November 16, 1998).
2. Welfare Reform and Pensions Act 1999, Sch.12, para.25(3) (December 1, 2000).
3. Welfare Reform and Pensions Act 1999, Sch.12, para.25(3) (December 1, 2000).

Up-rating under sections 150 above of pensions increased under section 52(3) of the Contributions and Benefits Act.

[¹**156.**—(1) This section applies in any case where a person is entitled to a Category A retirement pension with an increase, under section 52(3) of the Contributions and Benefits Act, in the additional pension on account of the contributions of a spouse [² or civil partner] who had died.

(2) Where in the case of any up-rating order under section 150 above—
(a) The spouse's [² or civil partner's] final relevant year is the tax year preceding the tax year in which the up-rating order comes into force, but
(b) The person's final relevant year was an earlier tax year,
then the up-rating order shall not have effect in relation to that part of the additional pension which is attributable to the spouse's [² or civil partner] contributions.

(3) Where in the case of any up-rating order under section 150 above—
(a) The person's final relevant year is the tax year preceding the tax year in which the up-rating order comes into force, but
(b) The spouse's [² or civil partner's] final relevant year was an earlier tax year,
Then the up-rating order shall not have effect in relation to that part of the additional pension which is attributable to the person's contributions.]

AMENDMENTS

1. Pensions Act 1995, s.130(1) (July 19, 1995).
2. Civil Partnership Act 2004, s.254 and Sch.24, para.66 (December 5, 2005).

DERIVATION

SSPA 1975, s.23(2A).

Effect of alteration of rates of child benefit

157.—(1) Subsections (3) and (4) of section 155 above shall have effect where there is an increase in the rate or any of the rates of child benefit as they have effect in relation to the rate of benefit to which that section applies.

(2) Where in connection with child benefit—
(a) any question arises in respect of a period after the date fixed for the commencement of payment of child benefit at an increased rate—

Social Security Administration Act 1992

  (i) as to the weekly rate at which a person is contributing to the cost of providing for a child [¹ or qualifying young person]; or
  (ii) as to the expenditure that a person is incurring in respect of a child [¹ or qualifying young person]; and
 (b) in determining that question account falls to be taken of contributions made or expenditure incurred for a period before that date,
the contributions made or expenditure incurred before that date shall be treated as increased in proportion to the increase in the rate of benefit.

DERIVATION

 CBA 1975, s.5(6).

AMENDMENT

1.183 1. Child Benefit Act 2005, Sch.1, Pt 1, para.24 (April 10, 2006).

Treatment of excess benefit as paid on account of child benefit

1.184 **158.**—(1) In any case where—
 (a) any benefit as defined in section 122 of the Contributions and Benefits Act or any increase of such benefit ("the relevant benefit or increase") has been paid to a person for a period in respect of a child [¹ or qualifying young person]; and
 (b) subsequently child benefit for that period in respect of the child [¹ or qualifying young person] becomes payable at a rate which is such that, had the relevant benefit or increase been awarded after the child benefit became payable, the rate of the relevant benefit or increase would have been reduced,
then, except in so far as regulations otherwise provide, the excess shall be treated as paid on account of child benefit for that period in respect of the child [¹ or qualifying young person].
 (2) In subsection (1) above "the excess" means so much of the relevant benefit or increase as is equal to the difference between—
 (a) the amount of it which was paid for the period referred to in that subsection; and
 (b) the amount of it which would have been paid for that period if it had been paid at the reduced rate referred to in paragraph (b) of that subsection.

DERIVATION

1.185 SS(MP)A 1977, s.17(4).

AMENDMENT

 1. Child Benefit Act 2005, Sch.1, Pt 1, para.25 (April 10, 2006).

GENERAL NOTE

1.186 This provision avoids increases of benefits overlapping with, in particular, increase of child benefit. See also paras (4) and (5) of reg.2 of the Fixing and Adjustment of Rates Regulations.

Effect of alteration in the component rates of income support

1.187 **159.**—(1) Subject to such exceptions and conditions as may be prescribed, where—

(1992 c.5, s.159)

    (a) an award of income support is in force in favour of any person ("the recipient"); and
    (b) there is an alteration in any of the relevant amounts, that is to say—
        (i) any of the component rates of income support;
        (ii) any of the other sums specified in regulations under Part VII of the Contributions and Benefits Act; or
        (iii) the recipient's benefit income; and
    (c) the alteration affects the computation of the amount of income support to which the recipient is entitled,
then subsection (2) or (3) below (as the case may be) shall have effect.

(2) Where, in consequence of the alteration in question, the recipient becomes entitled to an increased or reduced amount of income support ("the new amount"), then, as from the commencing date, the amount of income support payable to or for the recipient under the award shall be the new amount, without any further decision of [1the Secretary of State], and the award shall have effect accordingly.

(3) Where, notwithstanding the alteration in question, the recipient continues on and after the commencing date to be entitled to the same amount of income support as before, the award shall continue in force accordingly.

(4) In any case where—
    (a) there is an alteration in any of the relevant amounts; and
    (b) before the commencing date (but after that date is fixed) an award of income support is made in favour of a person,
the award either may provide for income support to be paid as from the commencing date, in which case the amount shall be determined by reference to the relevant amounts which will be in force on that date, or may provide for an amount determined by reference to the amounts in force at the date of the award.

(5) In this section—
"alteration" means—
    (a) in relation to—
        (i) the component rates of income support; or
        (ii) any other sums specified in regulations under Part VII of the Contributions and Benefits Act,
their alteration by or under any enactment whether or not contained in that Part; and
    (b) in relation to a person's benefit income, the alteration of any of the sums referred to in section 150 above—
        (i) by any enactment; or
        (ii) by an order under section 150 or 152 above,
to the extent that any such alteration affects the amount of his benefit income;
"benefit income", in relation to any person, means so much of his income as consists of—
    (a) benefit under the Contributions and Benefits Act, other than income support; or
    (b) a war disablement pension or war widow's pension;
"the commencing date" in relation to an alteration, means the date on which the alteration comes into force in the case of the person in question;
"component rate", in relation to income support, means the amount of—
    (a) the sum referred to in section 126(5)(b)(i) and (ii) of the Contributions and Benefits Act; or

Social Security Administration Act 1992

  (b) any of the sums specified in regulations under section 135(1) of that Act; and

"relevant amounts" has the meaning given by subsection (1)(b) above.

AMENDMENT

1. SI 1999/3178, Sch.1 (November 29, 1999).

DERIVATION

1.188 Social Security Act 1986, s.64A.

DEFINITIONS

"the Contributions and Benefits Act"—see s.191.
"war disablement pension"—*ibid.*
"war widow's pension"—*ibid.*

GENERAL NOTE

1.189 The general rule under s.159 is that if there is an alteration in the prescribed figures for personal allowances, premiums, the relevant sum (i.e. assumed "strike pay" in trade dispute cases), or any social security benefits which count as income for income support purposes (subss.(1) and (5)), then any consequent change in the amount of income support which is payable takes effect automatically without the need for a decision by an adjudication officer (subs.(2)). Thus no right of appeal arises against the change in the amount, although the claimant can always request a review of the decision awarding benefit, as altered under s.159.

[¹ Effect of alteration of rates of a jobseeker's allowance

1.190 **159A.**—(1) This section applies where—
 (a) an award of a jobseeker's allowance is in force in favour of any person ("the recipient"); and
 (b) an alteration—
  (i) in any component of the allowance, or
  (ii) in the recipient's benefit income,
 affects the amount of the jobseeker's allowance to which he is entitled.
 (2) Subsection (3) applies where, as a result of the alteration, the amount of the jobseeker's allowance to which the recipient is entitled is increased or reduced.
 (3) As from the commencing date, the amount of the jobseeker's allowance payable to or for the recipient under the award shall be the increased or reduced amount, without any further decision of [² the Secretary of State]; and the award shall have effect accordingly.
 (4) In any case where—
 (a) there is an alteration of a kind mentioned in subsection (1)(b); and
 (b) before the commencing date (but after that date is fixed) an award of a jobseeker's allowance is made in favour of a person,
the award may provide for the jobseeker's allowance to be paid as from the commencing date, in which case the amount of the jobseeker's allowance shall be determined by reference to the components applicable on that date, or may provide for an amount determined by reference to the components applicable at the date of the award.
 (5) In this section—
"alteration" means—
 (a) in relation to any component of a jobseeker's allowance, its alteration by or under any enactment; and

(b) in relation to a person's benefit income, the alteration of any of the sums referred to in section 150 above by any enactment or by an order under section 150 above, to the extent that any such alteration affects the amount of the recipient's benefit income;

"benefit income", in relation to a recipient, means so much of his income as consists of—
(a) benefit under the Contributions and Benefits Act; or
(b) a war disablement pension or war widow's pension;

"the commencing date" in relation to an alteration, means the date on which the alteration comes into force in relation to the recipient;

"component", in relation to a jobseeker's allowance, means any of the sums specified in regulations under the Jobseekers Act 1995 which are relevant in calculating the amount payable by way of a jobseeker's allowance.]

AMENDMENTS

1. Jobseekers Act 1995, s.24 (October 7, 1996).
2. Social Security Act 1998, Sch.7, para.96 (October 18, 1999).

DEFINITIONS

"the Contributions and Benefit Act"—see s.191.
"war disablement pension"—*ibid.*
"war widow's pension—*ibid.*

GENERAL NOTE

This section has the same effect for income-based JSA as s.159 does for income support.

1.191

[1 Effect of alterations affecting state pension credit]

159B.—(1) Subject to such exceptions and conditions as may be prescribed, subsection (2) or (3) below shall have effect where—
(a) an award of state pension credit is in force in favour of any person ("the recipient"); and
(b) an alteration—
  (i) in any component of state pension credit,
  (ii) in the recipient's benefit income,
  (iii) in any component of a contribution-based jobseeker's allowance, or
  (iv) in the recipient's war disablement pension or war widow's or widower's pension, affects the computation of the amount of state pension credit to which he is entitled.

(2) Where, as a result of the alteration, the amount of state pension credit to which the recipient is entitled is increased or reduced, then, as from the commencing date, the amount of state pension credit payable in the case of the recipient under the award shall be the increased or reduced amount, without any further decision of the Secretary of State; and the award shall have effect accordingly.

(3) Where, notwithstanding the alteration, the recipient continues on and after the commencing date to be entitled to the same amount of state pension credit as before, the award shall continue in force accordingly.

(4) Subsection (5) below applies where a statement is made in the House of Commons by or on behalf of the Secretary of State which specifies—

1.192

Social Security Administration Act 1992

 (a) in relation to any of the items referred to in subsection (1)(b)(i) to (iv) above, the amount of the alteration which he proposes to make by an order under section 150 or 152 above or by or under any other enactment; and

 (b) the date on which he proposes to bring the alteration into force ("the proposed commencing date").

(5) If, in a case where this subsection applies, an award of state pension credit is made in favour of a person before the proposed commencing date and after the date on which the statement is made, the award—

 (a) may provide for state pension credit to be paid as from the proposed commencing date at a rate determined by reference to the amounts of the items specified in subsection (1)(b)(i) to (iv) above which will be in force on that date; or

 (b) may be expressed in terms of the amounts of those items in force at the date of the award.

(6) In this section—

"alteration" means—

 (a) in relation to any component of state pension credit, its alteration by or under any enactment;

 (b) in relation to a person's benefit income, the alteration of any of the sums referred to in section 150 above by any enactment or by an order under section 150 or 152 above to the extent that any such alteration affects the amount of his benefit income;

 (c) in relation to any component of a contribution-based jobseeker's allowance, its alteration by or under any enactment; and

 (d) in relation to a person's war disablement pension or war widow's or widower's pension, its alteration by or under any enactment;

"benefit income", in relation to a person, means so much of his income as consists of benefit under the Contributions and Benefits Act;

"the commencing date", in relation to an alteration, means the date on which the alteration comes into force in relation to the recipient;

"component"—

 (a) in relation to contribution-based jobseeker's allowance, means any of the sums specified in regulations under the Jobseekers Act 1995 (c 18) which are relevant in calculating the amount payable by way of a jobseeker's allowance;

 (b) in relation to state pension credit, means any of the sums specified in regulations under section 2, 3 or 12 of the State Pension Credit Act 2002;

"war disablement pension" means—

 (a) any retired pay, pension or allowance granted in respect of disablement under powers conferred by or under—

  (i) the Air Force (Constitution) Act 1917 (c 51);

  (ii) the Personal Injuries (Emergency Provisions) Act 1939 (c 82);

  (iii) the Pensions (Navy, Army, Air Force and Mercantile Marine) Act 1939 (c 83);

  (iv) the Polish Resettlement Act 1947 (c 19); or

  (v) Part 7 or section 151 of the Reserve Forces Act 1980 (c 9); or

 (b) without prejudice to paragraph (a), any retired pay or pension to which [² any of paragraphs (a) to (f) of that section 641(1) of the Income Tax (Earnings and Pensions) Act 2003] applies;

"war widow's or widower's pension" means—

(a) any widow's or widower's pension or allowance granted in respect of a death due to service or war injury and payable by virtue of any enactment mentioned in paragraph (a) of the definition of "war disablement pension"; or
(b) a pension or allowance for a widow or widower granted under any scheme mentioned in [² section 641(1)(e) or (f) of the Income Tax (Earnings and Pensions) Act 2003.]

AMENDMENTS

1. Inserted by State Pensions Credit Act 2002, s.14 and Sch.2 (July 2, 2002 for the purpose of making regulations only; fully in force October 6, 2003).
2. Income Tax (Earnings and Pensions) Act 2003, s.722, Sch.6, Pt 2, paras 186, 188(1), (3). (Income Tax (Earnings and Pensions) Act 2003, s.722, Sch.6, Pt.2, paras 186, 188(1), (3).

Implementation of increases in income support due to attainment of particular ages

160.—(1) This section applies where—
(a) an award of income support is in force in favour of a person ("the recipient"); and
(b) there is a component which becomes applicable, or applicable at a particular rate, in his case if he or some other person attains a particular age.

(2) If, in a case where this section applies, the recipient or other person attains the particular age referred to in paragraph (b) of subsection (1) above and, in consequence—
(a) the component in question becomes applicable, or applicable at a particular rate, in the recipient's case (whether or not some other component ceases, for the same reason, to be applicable, or applicable at a particular rate, in his case; and
(b) after taking account of any such cessation, the recipient becomes entitled to an increased amount of income support,
then, except as provided by subsection (3) below, as from the day on which he becomes so entitled, the amount of income support payable to or for him under the award shall be that increased amount, without any further decision of [¹ the Secretary of State], and the award shall have effect accordingly.

(3) Subsection (2) above does not apply in any case where, in consequence of the recipient or other person attaining the age in question, some question arises in relation to the recipient's entitlement to any benefit under the Contributions and Benefits Act, other than—
(a) the question whether the component concerned, or any other component, becomes or ceases to be applicable, or applicable at a particular rate, in his case; and
(b) the question whether, in consequence, the amount of his income support falls to be varied.

(4) In this section "component", in relation to a person and his income support, means any of the sums specified in regulations under section 135(1) of the Contributions and Benefits Act.

AMENDMENT

1. SI 1999/3178, Sch.1 (November 29, 1999).

DERIVATION

1.194   Social Security Act 1986, s.64B.

DEFINITION

"the Contributions and Benefits Act"—see s.191.

GENERAL NOTE

1.195   Section 160 extends the process begun by s.159 of taking routine adjustments in the amount of income support out of the ordinary mechanism of review.

[¹Implementation of increases in income-based jobseeker's allowance due to attainment of particular ages

1.196   **160A.**—(1) This section applies where—
   (a) an award of an income-based jobseeker's allowance is in force in favour of a person ("the recipient"); and
   (b) a component has become applicable, or applicable at a particular rate, because he or some other person has reached a particular age ("the qualifying age")

(2) If, as a result of the recipient or other person reaching the qualifying age, the recipient becomes entitled to an income-based jobseeker's allowance of an increased amount, the amount payable to or for him under the award shall, as from the day on which he becomes so entitled, be that increased amount, without any further decision of [² the Secretary of State]; and the award shall have effect accordingly.

(3) Subsection (2) above does not apply where, in consequence of the recipient or other person reaching the qualifying age, a question arises in relation to the recipient's entitlement to—
   (a) a benefit under the Contributions and Benefits Act; or
   (b) a jobseeker's allowance.

(4) Subsection (3)(b) above does not apply to the question—
   (a) whether the component concerned, or any other component, becomes or ceases to be applicable, or applicable at a particular rate, in the recipient's case; and
   (b) whether, in consequence, the amount of his income-based jobseeker's allowance falls to be varied.

(5) In this section "component", in relation to a recipient and his jobseeker's allowance, means any of the amounts determined in accordance with regulations made under section 4(5) of the Jobseekers Act 1995.]

AMENDMENTS

1. Jobseekers Act 1995, s.25 (October 7, 1996).
2. Social Security Act 1998, Sch.7, para.98 (October 18, 1999).

DEFINITION

"the Contributions and Benefits Act"—see s.191.

GENERAL NOTE

1.197   See s.160.

(1992 c.5, s.161)

PART XII

FINANCE

161.–166. *Omitted.*

The social fund

167.—(1) The fund known as the social fund shall continue in being by that name.

(2) The social fund shall continue to be maintained under the control and management of the Secretary of State and payments out of it shall be made by him.

(3) The Secretary of State shall make payments into the social fund of such amounts, at such times and in such manner as he may with the approval of the Treasury determine.

(4) Accounts of the social fund shall be prepared in such form, and in such manner and at such times, as the Treasury may direct, and the Comptroller and Auditor General shall examine and certify every such account and shall lay copies of it, together with his report, before Parliament.

(5) The Secretary of State shall prepare an annual report on the social fund.

(6) A copy of every such report shall be laid before each House of Parliament.

DERIVATIONS

Subs.(1): Social Security Act 1986, s.32(1).
Subss.(2)–(6): 1986 Act, s.32(5)–(7B).

Allocations from social fund

168.—(1) The Secretary of State shall allocate amounts for payments from the social fund such as are mentioned in section 138(1)(b) of the Contributions and Benefits Act in a financial year.

(2) The Secretary of State may specify the amounts either as sums of money or by reference to money falling into the social fund on repayment or partial repayment of loans, or partly in the former and partly in the latter manner.

(3) Allocations—
(a) may be for payments by [¹ a particular appropriate officer or group of appropriate fund officers],
(b) may be for different amounts for different purposes;
(c) may be made at such time or times as the Secretary of State considers appropriate; and
(d) may be in addition to any other allocation to the same officer or group of officers or for the same purpose.

(4) The Secretary of State may at any time re-allocate amounts previously allocated, and subsections (2) and (3) above shall have effect in relation to a re-allocation as they have effect in relation to an allocation.

(5) The Secretary of State may give general directions to [¹ appropriate officers] or groups of [¹ appropriate officers], or to any class of [¹ appropriate

officers], with respect to the control and management by [¹ appropriate officers] or groups of [¹ appropriate officers] of the amounts allocated to them under this section.

[¹(6) In this section "appropriate officer" means an officer of the Secretary of State who, acting under his authority, is exercising functions of the Secretary of State in relation to payments from the social fund such as are mentioned in section 138(1)(b) of the Contributions and Benefits Act.]

AMENDMENT

1. Social Security Act 1998, Sch.7, para.103 (November 29, 1999).

DERIVATION

1.202 Social Security Act 1986, s.32(8A)–(8E).

DEFINITION

"the Contributions and Benefits Act"—see s.191.

Adjustments between social fund and other sources of finance

1.203 **169.**—(1) There shall be made—
(a) out of the social fund into the Consolidated Fund or the National Insurance Fund;
(b) into the social fund out of money provided by Parliament or the National Insurance Fund,

such payments by way of adjustment as the Secretary of State determines (in accordance with any directions of the Treasury) to be appropriate in consequence of any enactment or regulations relating to the repayment or offsetting of a benefit or other payment under the Contributions and Benefits Act [¹ or the State Pension Credit Act 2002].

(2) Where in any other circumstances payments fall to be made by way of adjustment—
(a) out of the social fund into the Consolidated Fund or the National Insurance Fund; or
(b) into the social fund out of money provided by Parliament or the National Insurance Fund,

then, in such cases or classes of cases as may be specified by the Secretary of State by order, the amount of the payments to be made shall be taken to be such, and payments on account of it shall be be made at such times and in such manner, as may be determined by the Secretary of State in accordance with any direction given by the Treasury.

AMENDMENT

1. State Pension Credit Act 2002, s.14 and Sch.2 (July 2, 2002 for the purpose of making regulations only; fully in force October 6, 2003).

DERIVATION

1.204 Social Security Act 1986, s.85(11) and (12).

DEFINITION

"the Contributions and Benefits Act"—see s.191.

(1992 c.5, s.170)

Part XIII

Advisory Bodies and Consultation

The Social Security Advisory Committee and the Industrial Injuries Advisory Council

The Social Security Advisory Committee

170.—(1) The Social Security Advisory Committee (in this Act referred to as "the Committee") constituted under section 9 of the Social Security Act 1980 shall continue in being by that name—
  (a) to give (whether in pursuance of a reference under this Act or otherwise) advice and assistance to the Secretary of State in connection with the discharge of his functions under the relevant enactments;
  (b) to give (whether in pursuance of a reference under this Act or otherwise) advice and assistance to the Northern Ireland Department in connection with the discharge of its functions under the relevant Northern Ireland enactments; and
  (c) to perform such other duties as may be assigned to the Committee under any enactment.

(2) Schedule 5 to this Act shall have effect with respect to the constitution of the Committee and the other matters there mentioned.

(3) The Secretary of State may from time to time refer to the Committee for consideration and advice such questions relating to the operation of any of the relevant enactments as he thinks fit (including questions as to the advisability of amending any of them).

(4) The Secretary of State shall furnish the Committee with such information as the Committee may reasonably require for the proper discharge of its functions.

(5) In this Act—
"the relevant enactments" means—
  (a) the provisions of the Contributions and Benefits Act [1, this Act and the Social Security (Incapacity for Work) Act 1994], except as they apply to industrial injuries benefit and Old Cases payments;
[2 (aa) the provisions of the Jobseekers Act 1995;] and
[3 (ab) section 10 of the Child Support Act 1995;]
[4 (ac) the provisions of the Social Security (Recovery of Benefits) Act 1997; and]
[5 (ad) the provisions of Chapter II of Part I of the Social Security Act 1998 and section 72 of that Act;]
[6 (ae) sections 60, 72 and 79 of the Welfare Reform and Pensions Act 1999;]
[7 (af) section 42, sections 62 to 65 and sections 68 to 70 of the Child Support Pensions and Social Security Act 2000 and Schedule 7 to that Act;]
[8 (ag) sections 7 to 11 of the Social Security Fraud Act 2001;]
[9 (ah) the provisions of the State Pension Credit Act 2002;]

1.205

Social Security Administration Act 1992

(b) the provisions of Part II of Schedule 3 to the Consequential Provisions Act, except as they apply to industrial injuries benefit; and

"the relevant Northern Ireland enactments" means—

(a) the provisions of the Northern Ireland Contributions and Benefits Act and the Northern Ireland Administration Act, except as they apply to Northern Ireland industrial injuries benefit and payments under Part I of Schedule 8 to the Northern Ireland Contributions and Benefits Act; and

[^{2} (aa) any provisions in Northern Ireland which correspond to provisions of the Jobseekers Act 1995; and]

[^{3} (ab) any enactment corresponding to section 10 of the Child Support Act 1995 having effect with respect to Northern Ireland; and]

[^{4} (ac) any provisions in Northern Ireland which correspond to provisions of the Social Security (Recovery of Benefits) Act 1997; and]

[^{5} (ad) any provisions in Northern Ireland which correspond to provisions of Chapter II of Part I of the Social Security Act 1998 and section 72 of that Act;]

[^{6} (ae) any provisions in Northern Ireland which correspond to sections 60, 72 and 79 of the Welfare Reform and Pensions Act 1999;]

[^{7} (af) any provisions in Northern Ireland which correspond to section 42, any of sections 62 to 65, 68 to 70 of the Child Support, Pensions and Social Security Act 2000 or Schedule 7 to that Act; and]

[^{8} (ag) any provisions in Northern Ireland which correspond to sections 7 to 11 of the Social Security Fraud Act 2001, and]

[^{9} (ah) any provisions in Northern Ireland which correspond to provisions of the State Pension Credit Act 2002; and]

(b) the provisions of Part II of Schedule 3 to the Social Security (Consequential Provisions) (Northern Ireland) Act 1992, except as they apply to Northern Ireland industrial injuries benefit; and

[^{10} (c) section 32(6) of the Pension Schemes (Northern Ireland) Act 1993;]

and in this definition—

(i) "Northern Ireland Contributions and Benefits Act" means the Social Security Contributions and Benefits (Northern Ireland) Act 1992;

(ii) "Northern Ireland industrial injuries benefit" means benefit under Part V of the Northern Ireland Contributions and Benefits Act other than under Schedule 8 to that Act.

AMENDMENTS

1. Social Security (Incapacity for Work) Act 1994, Sch.1, para.51 (April 13, 1995).
2. Jobseekers Act 1995, Sch.2, para.67 (April 22, 1996).
3. Child Support Act 1995, Sch.3, para.20 (October 6, 1997).
4. Social Security (Recovery of Benefits) Act 1997, Sch.3, para.8 (October 6, 1997).
5. Social Security Act 1998, Sch.7, para.104 (March 4, 1999).
6. Welfare Reform and Pensions Act 1999, Sch.12, para.81 (November 11, 1999).
7. Child Support, Pensions and Social Security Act 2000, s.73 (December 1, 2000).
8. Social Security Fraud Act 2001, s.12 (April 1, 2002).
9. State Pension Credit Act 2002, Sch.2, para.20 (July 2, 2002 for the purpose of making regulations only; fully in force October 6, 2003).
10. Pension Schemes (Northern Ireland) Act 1993, Sch.7, para.26 (February 7, 1994).

(1992 c.5, s.170)

GENERAL NOTE

In *Howker v Secretary of State for Work and Pensions* [2002] EWCA Civ. 1623, *R(IB)3/03* the Court of Appeal (hearing the appeal against the decision in *CIB/4563/1998*, confirmed the jurisdiction of Commissioners (and presumably also tribunals) to invalidate subordinate legislation. The circumstances of this case involved the Secretary of State through his official misleading the Social Security Advisory Committee by presenting information which was obviously incorrect which resulted in the securing of the agreement of the Committee to the proposed changes. The Court of Appeal concluded that it was manifest that the procedure intended by Parliament for the making of regulations had not been observed and so the regulations as made were invalid for failure to comply with the requirements of s.172. See annotation to reg.27(b) of the Incapacity for Work General Regulations in Vol. I for the substance of the Court's decision.

1.206

The Industrial Injuries Advisory Council

171.—(1) The Industrial Injuries Advisory Council (in this Act referred to as "the Council") constituted under section 62 of the National Insurance (Industrial Injuries) Act 1965 shall continue in being by that name.

1.207

(2) Schedule 6 to this Act shall have effect with respect to the constitution of the Council and the other matters there mentioned.

(3) The Secretary of State may from time to time refer to the Council for consideration and advice such questions as he thinks fit relating to industrial injuries benefit or its administration.

(4) The Council may also give advice to the Secretary of State on any other matter relating to such benefit or its administration.

Functions of Committee and Council in relation to regulations

172.—(1) Subject—
(a) to subsection (3) below; and
(b) to section 173 below,
where the Secretary of State proposes to make regulations under any of the relevant enactments, he shall refer the proposals, in the form of draft regulations or otherwise, to the Committee.

1.208

(2) Subject—
(a) to subsection (4) below; and
(b) to section 173 below, where the Secretary of State proposes to make regulations relating only to industrial injuries benefit or its administration, he shall refer the proposals, in the form of draft regulations or otherwise, to the Council for consideration and advice.

(3) Subsection (1) above does not apply to the regulations specified in Part I of Schedule 7 to this Act.

(4) Subsection (2) above does not apply to the regulations specified in Part II of that Schedule.

(5) In relation to regulations required or authorised to be made by the Secretary of State in conjunction with the Treasury, the reference in subsection (1) above to the Secretary of State shall be construed as a reference to the Secretary of State and the Treasury.

Cases in which consultation is not required

173.—(1) Nothing in any enactment shall require any proposals in respect of regulations to be referred to the Committee or the Council if—

1.209

Social Security Administration Act 1992

    (a) it appears to the Secretary of State that by reason of the urgency of the matter it is inexpedient so to refer them; or

    (b) the relevant advisory body have agreed that they shall not be referred.

(2) Where by virtue only of subsection (1)(a) above the Secretary of State makes regulations without proposals in respect of them having been referred, then, unless the relevant advisory body agrees that this subsection shall not apply, he shall refer the regulations to that body as soon as practicable after making them.

(3) Where the Secretary of State has referred proposals to the Committee or the Council, he may make the proposed regulations before the Committee have made their report or, as the case may be the Council have given their advice, only if after the reference it appears to him that by reason of the urgency of the matter it is expedient to do so.

(4) Where by virtue of this section regulations are made before a report of the Committee has been made, the Committee shall consider them and make a report to the Secretary of State containing such recommendations with regard to the regulations as the Committee thinks appropriate; and a copy of any report made to the Secretary of State on the regulations shall be laid by him before each House of Parliament together, if the report contains recommendations, with a statement—

    (a) of the extent (if any) to which the Secretary of State proposes to give effect to the recommendations; and

    (b) in so far as he does not propose to give effect to them, of his reasons why not.

(5) Except to the extent that this subsection is excluded by an enactment passed after 25th July 1986, nothing in any enactment shall require the reference to the Committee or the Council of any regulations contained in either—

    (a) a statutory instrument made before the end of the period of 6 months beginning with the coming into force of the enactment under which those regulations are made; or

    (b) a statutory instrument—

        (i) which states that it contains only regulations made by virtue of, or consequential upon, a specified enactment; and

        (ii) which is made before the end of the period of 6 months beginning with the coming into force of that specified enactment.

(6) In relation to regulations required or authorised to be made by the Secretary of State in conjunction with the Treasury, any reference in this section to the Secretary of State shall be construed as a reference to the Secretary of State and the Treasury.

(7) In this section "regulations" means regulations under any enactment, whenever passed.

1.210   **174.–176.** *Omitted.*

(1992 c.5, s.177)

Part XIV

Social Security Systems Outside Great Britain

Co-ordination

Section 177: *repealed by the Northern Ireland Act 1998, Sch.15 (December 2, 1999).*

Section 178: *repealed by the Northern Ireland Act 1998, Sch.15 (December 2, 1999).*

Reciprocal agreements with countries outside the United Kingdom

179.—(1) For the purpose of giving effect—
 (a) to any agreement with the government of a country outside the United Kingdom providing for reciprocity in matters relating to payments for purposes similar or comparable to the purposes of legislation to which this section applies, or
 (b) to any such agreement as it would be if it were altered in accordance with proposals to alter it which, in consequence of any change in the law of Great Britain, the government of the United Kingdom has made to the other government in question,
Her Majesty may by Order in Council make provision for modifying or adapting such legislation in its application to cases affected by the agreement or proposed alterations.

(2) An Order made by virtue of subsection (1) above may, instead of or in addition to making specific modifications or adaptions, provide generally that legislation to which this section applies shall be modified to such extent as may be required to give effect to the provisions contained in the agreement or, as the case may be, alterations in question.

(3) The modifications which may be made by virtue of subsection (1) above include provisions—
 (a) for securing that acts, omissions and events having any effect for the purposes of the law of the country in respect of which the agreement is made have a corresponding effect for the purposes of this Act, [¹ the Jobseeker's Act 1995], [² Chapter II of Part I of the Social Security Act 1998] [³ Part II of the Social Security Contributions (Transfer of Functions, etc.) Act 1999] [⁵, Part III of the Social Security Contributions (Transfer of Functions etc.) (Northern Ireland) Order 1999] [⁶, the State Pension Credit Act 2002] and the Contributions and Benefits Act (but not so as to confer a right to double benefit);
 (b) for determining, in cases where rights accrue under such legislation and under the law of that country, which of those rights is to be available to the person concerned;
 (c) for making any necessary financial adjustments.

(4) This section applies—
 (a) to the Contributions and Benefits Act;
 (aa) [¹ to the Jobseeker's Act 1995];

Social Security Administration Act 1992

    (ab) [² to Chapter II of Part I of the Social Security Act 1998];
    (ac) [³ to Part II of the Social Security Contributions (Transfers of Functions, etc.) Act 1999]; and
[⁴(ad) to Part III of the Social Security Contributions (Transfer of Functions etc.) (Northern Ireland) Order 1999;]
[⁵(ae) to the State Pension Credit Act 2002; and]
    (b) to this Act,
except in relation to the following benefits—
        (i) community charge benefits;
        (ii) payments out of the social fund;
        (iii) Christmas bonus;
        (iv) statutory sick pay; and
        (v) statutory maternity pay.

    (5) The power conferred by subsection (1) above shall also be exercisable in relation to regulations made under the Contributions and Benefits Act or this Act and concerning—
    (a) income support;
[¹(aa) jobseeker's allowance];
[⁵(ab) state pension credit];
    (b) [⁶ . . .];
    (c) [⁶ . . .];
    (d) housing benefit; or
    (e) child benefit.

AMENDMENTS

1. Jobseekers Act 1995, Sch.2 (April 22, 1996).
2. Social Security Act 1998, Sch.7 (July 5, 1999).
3. Transfer of Functions Act 1999, Sch.7 (April 1, 1999).
4. Social Security Contributions (Transfer of Functions etc.) (Northern Ireland) Order 1999 (April 1, 1999).
5. State Pension Credit Act 2002, s.14 and Sch.2 (July 2, 2002 for the purpose of making regulations only; fully in force October 6, 2003).
6. Tax Credits Act 2002, s.60 and Sch.6 (April 8, 2003).

DERIVATION

1.214   SSA 1975, s.143 as amended and CBA 1975, s.15 as amended.

GENERAL NOTE

1.215   For details of current reciprocal arrangements, see annotations to s.113, of the Contributions and Benefits Act 1992.

For a discussion on how s.179 acts to modify other social security provisions, see *Compbell v Secretary of State for Work and Pensions* [2005] EWCA Civ 989.

[¹ Exchange of information with overseas authorities]

1.216   **179A.**—(1) This section applies where it appears to the Secretary of State—
    (a) that there are arrangements in force for the exchange of relevant information between him and any authorities in a country outside the United Kingdom ("the overseas country"); and
    (b) that the arrangements and the law in force in the overseas country are such as to ensure that there are adequate safeguards in place against any improper use of information disclosed by the Secretary of State under this section.

(1992 c.5, s.179A)

(2) For the purpose of facilitating the carrying out by authorities in the overseas country of any function relating to anything corresponding to, or in the nature of, a social security benefit, the Secretary of State may make any such disclosure of relevant information to authorities in the overseas country as he considers necessary to give effect to the arrangements.

(3) It shall be the duty of the Secretary of State to take all such steps as may be reasonable for securing that relevant information disclosed to him in accordance with the arrangements is not used for any purpose for which its use is not expressly or impliedly authorised by or under the arrangements.

(4) This section does not apply where provision is in force under section 179 above for giving effect to the arrangements in question.

(5) The purposes for which information may be required to be disclosed to the Secretary of State under section 122D above or section 116D of the Northern Ireland Administration Act (information required from authorities administering housing benefit or council tax benefit) shall be deemed to include the further disclosure of that information in accordance withthis section.

(6) In this section "relevant information" means any information held by the Secretary of State or any authorities in a country outside the United Kingdom for the purposes of any functions relating to, or to anything corresponding to or in the nature of, a social security benefit.]

AMENDMENT

1. Inserted by the Social Security Fraud Act 2001, ss.1 and 5 (February 14, 2003).

PART XV

MISCELLANEOUS

180.–182B. *Omitted.* 1.217

National insurance numbers

[1 Requirement to apply for national insurance number

182C.—(1) Regulations may make provision requiring a person to apply for a national insurance number to be allocated to him. 1.218

[2(1A) Regulations under subsection (1) above may require the application to be made to the Secretary of State or to the Inland Revenue.]

(2) An application required by regulations under subsection (1) above shall be accompanied by information or evidence enabling such a number to be allocated.]

AMENDMENTS

1. Social Security Administration (Fraud) Act 1997, Sch.1, para.9 (July 1, 1997).
2. Social Security Contributions (Transfer of Functions, etc.) Act 1999, s.1(1) and Sch.1, para.31 (April 1, 1999).

General Note

1.219   See subss.(1A)–(1C) of s.1, inserted by s.19 of the Social Security Administration (Fraud) Act, which make having, or applying for, a national insurance number a condition of entitlement to benefit in most cases.

1.220   **183.–185.** *Omitted.*

Supplementary benefit etc.

Applications of provisions of Act to supplementary benefit etc.

1.221   **186.** Schedule 10 to this Act shall have effect for the purposes of making provision in relation to the benefits there mentioned.

Miscellaneous

Certain benefit to be inalienable

1.222   **187.**—(1) Subject to the provisions of this Act, every assignment of or charge on—

(a) benefit as defined in section 122 of the Contributions and Benefits Act;
[^{1}(aa) a jobseeker's allowance;]
[^{2}(ab) state pension credit;]
(b) any income-related benefit; or
(c) child benefit,

and every agreement to assign or charge such benefit shall be void; and, on the bankruptcy of a beneficiary, such benefit shall not pass to any trustee or other person acting on behalf of his creditors.

(2) In the application of subsection (1) above to Scotland—

(a) the reference to assignment of benefit shall be read as a reference to assignation, "assign" being construed accordingly;
(b) the reference to a beneficiary's bankruptcy shall be read as a reference to the sequestration of his estate or the appointment on his estate of a judicial factor under section 41 of the Solicitors (Scotland) Act 1980.

(3) In calculating for the purposes of section 5 of the Debtors Act 1869 or section 4 of the Civil Imprisonment (Scotland) Act 1882 the means of any beneficiary, no account shall be taken of any increase of disablement benefit in respect of a child or of industrial death benefit.

Amendments

1. Jobseekers Act 1995, Sch.2, para.72 (October 7, 1996).
2. State Pension Credit Act 2002, s.14 and Sch.2 (July 2, 2002 for the purposes of making regulations only; fully in force October 6, 2003).

Derivations

1.223   Social Security Act 1975, s.87.
"the Contributions and Benefits Act"—see s.191.
"income-related benefit"—*ibid.*

(1992 c.5, s.187)

GENERAL NOTE

The House of Lords in *Mulvey v Secretary of State for Social Security*, *The Times*, March 20, 1997 dealt with the part of s.187(1) providing that, on bankruptcy or sequestration of a beneficiary, benefit does not pass to the trustee in bankruptcy. It held that the purpose was "to make clear beyond peradventure that the permanent trustee [the Scottish equivalent of the trustee in bankruptcy] could have no interest in any entitlement of a debtor to receive any of the social security benefits to which it applied" (Lord Jauncey). The Secretary of State's obligation to make payment of benefit is owed to the beneficiary and cannot be owed to the trustee in bankruptcy or permanent trustee. See the notes to s.78(2) for the situation where deductions are being made from benefit for the repayment of social fund loans or the recovery of overpayments.

1.224

188. *Omitted.*

1.225

PART XVI

GENERAL

Subordinate legislation

189.—(1) Subject to [. . .[1]] [[2]any Provision proving for an order or regulations to be made by the Treasury or the Inland Revenue and to] any [[8] . . .] express provision of this Act, regulations and orders under this Act shall be made by the Secretary of State.

1.226

(2) [. . .[1]]

(3) Powers under this Act to make regulations or orders are exercisable by statutory instrument.

(4) Except in the case of regulations under section [. . .[1]] 175 above and in so far as this Act otherwise provides, any power conferred by this Act to make an Order in Council, regulations or an order may be exercised—
 (a) either in relation to all cases to which the power extends, or in relation to those cases subject to specified exceptions, or in relation to any specified cases or classes of case;
 (b) so as to make, as respects the cases in relation to which it is exercised—
  (i) the full provision to which the power extends or any less provision (whether by way of exception or otherwise);
  (ii) the same provision for all cases in relation to which the power is exercised, or different provision for different cases or different classes of case or different provision as respects the same case or class of case for different purposes of this Act;
  (iii) any such provision either unconditionally or subject to any specified condition;
and where such a power is expressed to be exercisable for alternative purposes it may be exercised in relation to the same case for any or all of those purposes; and powers to make an Order in Council, regulations or an order for the purposes of any one provision of this Act are without prejudice to powers to make regulations or an order for the purposes of any other provision.

(5) Without prejudice to any specific provision in this Act, a power conferred by this Act to make an Order in Council, regulations or an order [. . .[1]] includes power to make thereby such incidental, supplementary, consequential or transitional provision as appears to Her Majesty, or the authority making the regulations or order, as the case may be, to be expedient for the purposes of the Order in Council, regulations or order.

(6) Without prejudice to any specific provisions in this Act, a power conferred by any provision of this Act, except section 14, [. . .[1]], 130 and 175, to make an Order in Council, regulations or an order includes power to provide for a person to exercise a discretion in dealing with any matter.

(7) Any power conferred by this Act to make orders or regulations relating to housing benefit or [[3] council tax benefit] shall include power to make different provision for different areas [[4] or different authorities].

[[7] (7A) Without prejudice to the generality of any the preceding provisions of this section, regulations under any of sections 2A to 2C and 7A above may provide for all or any of the provisions of the regulations to apply only in relation to any area or areas specified in the regulations.]

(8) An order under section [[5] 140B, 140C] 150, 152, [[6] 165(4)(a)] or 169 above [. . .[7]] shall not be made [[8] by the Secretary of State] without the consent of the Treasury.

(9) Any powers of the Secretary of State under any provision of this Act, except under sections 80, 154, . . . to make any regulations or order, where the power is not expressed to be exercisable with the consent of the Treasury, shall if the Treasury so direct be exercisable only in conjunction withthem.

(10) Where the Lord Chancellor proposes to make regulations under this Act, other than under section 24 above, it shall be his duty to consult the Secretary of State with respect to the proposal.

(11) A power under any of section 179 above to make provision by regulations or Order in Council for modifications or adaptations of the Contributions and Benefits Act or this Act shall be exercisable in relation to any enactment passed after this Act which is directed to be construed as one withthem, except in so far as any such enactment relates to a benefit in relation to which the power is not exercisable; but this subsection applies only so far as a contrary intention is not expressed in the enactment so passed, and is without prejudice to the generality of any such direction.

(12) Any reference in this section or section 190 below to an Order in Council, or an order or regulations, under this Act includes a reference to an Order in Council, an order or regulations made under any provision of an enactment passed after this Act and directed to be construed as one with this Act; but this subsection applies only so far as a contrary intention is not expressed in the enactment so passed, and without prejudice to the generality of any such direction.

AMENDMENTS

1. Social Security Act 1998, Sch.7 (September 6, 1999).
2. Transfer of Functions Act 1999, Sch.3 (April 1, 1999).
3. Local Government Finance Act 1992, Sch.9 (April 1, 1993).
4. Social Security Administration (Fraud) Act 1997, Sch.1 (July 1, 1997).
5. Housing Act 1996, Sch.13 (April 1, 1997).
6. Social Security (Recovery of Benefits) Act 1997, Sch.3 (October 6, 1997).
7. Welfare Reform and Pensions Act 1999, Sch.12, paras 79 and 82 (November 11, 1999).

(1992 c.5, s.189)

8. Tax Credits Act 2002, s.60 and Sch.6 (February 26, 2003 for the purpose of making regulations in relation to child benefit and guardian's allowance; April 1, 2003 for remaining purposes).

GENERAL NOTE

In accordance with s.2(1) of the Tax Credits Act 1999, this section is to be read, in relation to tax credit, as if references to the Secretary of State were references to the Treasury or, as the case may be, the Board.

1.227

DERIVATIONS

SSA 1975, ss.113, 133, 166 and 168 as amended.
Parliamentary control of orders and regulations.

190.—(1) Subject to the provision of this section, a statutory instrument containing (whether alone or with other provisions)—
  (a) an order under section 141, 143 [. . .⁶], 145, [. . .²], 150, 152, or 162(7) above; or
[⁷(aza) any order containing provision adding any person to the list of persons falling within section 109B(2A) above; or]
[⁸(aa) the first regulations to be made under section 2A;]
[⁹ (ab) the first regulations to be made under section 2AA;]
  (b) regulations under section [. . .³] [⁴122B(1)(b) or] 154 above,
shall not be made unless a draft of the instrument has been laid before Parliament and been approved by a resolution of each House of Parliament.

(2) Subsection (1) above does not apply to a statutory instrument by reason only that it contains regulations under section 154 above which are to be made for the purpose of consolidating regulations to be revoked in the instrument.

(3) A statutory instrument—
  (a) which contains (whether alone or with other provisions) orders or regulations made under this Act by the Secretary of State [⁵, the Treasury or the Inland Revenue]; and
  (b) which is not subject to any requirement that a draft of the instrument be laid before and approved by a resolution of each House of Parliament,
shall be subject to annulment in pursuance of a resolution of either House of Parliament.

(4) A statutory instrument—
  (a) which contains (whether alone or with other provisions) regulations made under this Act by the Lord Chancellor; and
  (b) which is not subject to any requirement that a draft of the instrument be laid before and approved by a resolution of each House of Parliament,
shall be subject to annulment in pursuance of a resolution of either House of Parliament.

1.228

AMENDMENTS

1. Social Security Act 1998, Sch.7 (8 September, 1998).
2. Social Security Act 1998, Sch.7 (April 6, 1999).
3. Social Security (Recovery of Benefits) Act 1997, Sch.3 (October 6, 1997).
4. Social Security Administration (Fraud) Act 1997, Sch.1 (July 1, 1997).
5. Transfer of Functions Act 1999, Sch.3 (April 1, 1999).
6. Welfare Reform and Pensions Act 1999, Sch.13 (April 6, 2000).

Social Security Administration Act 1992

7. Social Security Fraud Act 2001, s.20 (February 26, 2002).
8. Welfare Reform and Pensions Act 1999, Sch.12, paras 79 and 83 (November 11, 1999).
9. Employment Act 2002, s.53 and Sch.7 (July 5, 2003).

GENERAL NOTE

1.229   In accordance with s.2(1) of the Tax Credits Act 1999, this section is to be read, in relation to tax credit, as if references to the Secretary of State were references to the Treasury or, as the case may be, the Board.

DERIVATION

1.230   SSA 1975, s.167 as amended and CBA 1975, s.22.

Supplementary

Interpretation—general

1.231   **191.** In this Act, unless the context otherwise requires—
"the 1975 Act" means the Social Security Act 1975;
"the 1986 Act" means the Social Security Act 1986;
"benefit" means benefit under the Contributions and Benefits Act [¹and includes a jobseeker's allowance] [¹⁹ and state pension credit];
[²"billing authority" has the same meaning as in Part I of the Local Government Finance Act 1992;]
"Christmas bonus" means a payment under Part X of the Contributions and Benefits Act;
"claim" is to be construed in accordance with "claimant";
"claimant" (in relation to contributions under Part I and to benefit under Parts II to IV of the Contributions and Benefits Act) means—
  (a) a person whose right to be excepted from liability to pay, or to have his liability deferred for, or to be credited with, a contribution, is in question;
  (b) a person who has claimed benefit;
and includes, in relation to an award or decision a beneficiary under the award or affected by the decision;
"claimant" (in relation to industrial injuries benefit) means a person who has claimed such a benefit and includes—
  (a) an applicant for a declaration under [³ section 29 of the Social Security Act 1998] that an accident was or was not an industrial accident; and
  (b) in relation to an award or decision, a beneficiary under the award or affected by the decision;
"Commissioner" means the Chief Social Security Commissioner or any other Social Security Commissioner and includes a tribunal of 3 Commissioners constituted under section 57 above;
[. . .⁴]
"the Consequential Provisions Act" means the Social Security (Consequential Provisions) Act 1992;
[⁵"contribution" means a contribution under Part I of the Contributions and Benefit Act;]

(1992 c.5, s.191)

[⁶"contribution-based jobseeker's allowance" has the same meaning as in the Jobseekers Act 1995;]
"contributions card" has the meaning assigned to it by section 114(6) above;
"the Contributions and Benefits Act" means the Social Security Contributions and Benefits Act 1992;
[⁷"council tax benefit Scheme" shall be construed in accordance with section 139(1) above;]
"disablement benefit" is to be construed in accordance with section 94(2)(a) of the Contributions and Benefits Act;
"the disablement questions" is to be construed in accordance with section 45 above;
"dwelling" means any residential accommodation, whether or not consisting of the whole or part of a building and whether or not comprising separate and self-contained premises;
[⁹"financial year" has the same meaning as in the Local Government Finance Act 1992;]
"5 year general qualification" is to be construed in accordance with section 71 of the Courts and Legal Services Act 1990;
"housing authority" means a local authority, a new town corporation, Scottish Homes or the Development Board for Rural Wales;
"house benefit scheme" is to be construed in accordance with section 134(1) above;
[¹"income-based jobseeker's allowance" has the same meaning as in the Jobseekers Act 1995;]
"income-related benefit" means—
  (a) income support;
  (b) [⁸ working families tax credit]
  (c) [⁸ disabled person's tax credit]
  (d) housing benefit; and
  [²(e) council tax benefit];
"industrial injuries benefit" means benefit under Part V of the Contributions and Benefits Act, other than under Schedule 8;
[¹⁰"Inland Revenue" means the Commissioners of Inland Revenue]
. . .¹⁰;
. . .¹¹;
"local authority" means—
  (a) in relation to England . . .¹², the council of a district or London borough, the Common Council of the City of London or the Council of the Isles of Scilly;
[¹¹(aa) in relation to Wales, the council of a county or county borough;] and
  (b) in relation to Scotland [¹²a council constituted under section 2 of the Local Government etc. (Scotland) Act 1994];
"medical examination" includes bacteriological and radiographical tests and similar investigations, and "medically examined" has a corresponding meaning;
"medical practitioner" means—
  (a) a registered medical practitioner; or
  (b) a person outside the United Kingdom who is not a registered medical practitioner, but has qualifications corresponding (in the Secretary of State's opinion) to those of a registered medical practitioner;

143

"medical treatment" means medical, surgical or rehabilitative treatment (including any course of diet or other regimen), and references to a person receiving or submitting himself to medical treatment are to be construed accordingly;

[15 "money purchase contracted-out scheme" has the same meaning as in section 8(1)(a)(ii) of the Pensions Act;]

"new town corporation" means—
  (a) in relation to England and Wales, a development corporation established under the New Towns Act 1981 or the Commission for the New Towns; and
  (b) in relation to Scotland, a development corporation established under the New Towns (Scotland) Act 1968;

[20 "the Northern Ireland Department" means the Department for Social Development but—
  (a) in section 122 and sections 122B to 122E also includes the Department of Finance and Personnel; and
  (b) in sections 121E, 121F, 122, 122ZA, 122C and 122D also includes the Department for Employment and Learning;]

"the Northern Ireland Administration Act" means the Social Security (Northern Ireland) Administration Act 1992;

"occupational pension scheme" has the same meaning as in [15section 1] of the Pensions Act;

"the Old Cases Act" means the Industrial Injuries and Diseases (Old Cases) Act 1975;

"Old Cases payments" means payments under Part I of Schedule 8 to the Contributions and Benefits Act;

[17"pensionable age" has the meaning given by the rules in paragraph 1 of Schedule 4 to the Pensions Act 1995];

"the Pensions Act" means the [15Pension Schemes Act 1993];

"personal pension scheme" has the meaning assigned to it by [15section 1 of the Pensions Act] [15and "appropriate", in relation to such a scheme, shall be construed in accordance with section 7(4) of that Act]

"prescribe" means prescribe by regulations;

"President" means the President of social security appeal tribunals; disability appeal tribunals and medical appeal tribunals;

"rate rebate", [. . .18] and "rent allowance" shall be construed in accordance with section 134 above;

[. . .18]

[19 "state pension credit" means state pension credit under the State Pension Credit Act 2002;]

"tax year" means the 12 months beginning with 6th April in any year;

"10 year general qualification" is to be construed in accordance with section 71 of the Courts and Legal Services Act 1990; and

"widows benefit" has the meaning assigned to it by section 20(1)(e) of the Contributions and Benefits Act.

AMENDMENTS

  1. Jobseekers Act 1995, Sch.2 (April 22, 1996).
  2. Local Government Finance Act 1992, Sch.9 (March 6, 1992).
  3. Social Security Act 1998, Sch.7 (July 7, 1999).
  4. Social Security (Recovery of Benefits) Act 1997, Sch.3 (October 6, 1997).
  5. Social Security Administration (Fraud) Act 1997, Sch.1 (July 1, 1997).

(1992 c.5, s.191)

    6. Jobseekers Act 1995, Sch.2 (April 22, 1996).
    7. Housing Benefit Act 1996, Sch.13 (April 1, 1997).
    8. Tax Credits Act 1999, Sch.1 (October 5, 1999).
    9. Local Government Finance Act 1992, Sch.9 (March 6, 1992).
    10. Transfer of Functions Act 1999, Sch.1 (April 1, 1999).
    11. Social Security (Incapacity for Work) Act 1994, Sch.1 (April 13, 1995).
    12. Local Government etc. (Scotland) Act 1994, Sch.14 (April 1, 1996)
    13. Local Government (Wales) Act 1994, Sch.16 (April 1, 1996).
    14. Local Government etc. (Scotland) Act 1994, Sch.13 (April 1, 1996)
    15. Pension Schemes Act 1993, Sch.8 (February 7, 1994).
    16. Social Security Administration (Fraud) Act, Sch.1 (July 1, 1997).
    17. Pensions Act 1995, Sch.4 (July 19, 1995).
    18. Housing Act 1996, Sch.13 (April 1, 1997).
    19. State Pension Credit Act 2002, s.14 and Sch.2 (July 2, 2002 for the purpose of making regulations only; fully in force October 6, 2003).
    20. Employment Act 2002, s.53 and Sch.7 (September 9, 2002).

DERIVATIONS

SSA 1975, s.168 and Sch.20. 1.232
Short title, commencement and extent.

192.—(1) This Act may be cited as the Social Security Administration Act 1992. 1.233

(2) This Act is to be read, where appropriate, with the Contributions and Benefits Act and the Consequential Provisions Act.

(3) The enactments consolidated by this Act are repealed, in consequence of the consolidation, by the Consequential Provisions Act.

(4) Except as provided in Schedule 4 to the Consequential Provisions Act, this Act shall come into force on 1st July 1992.

(5) The following provisions extend to Northern Ireland—
[. . .¹];
[²]
section 170 (with Schedule 5);
section 177 (with Schedule 8);
and this section.

(6) Except as provided by this section, this Act does not extend to Northern Ireland.

AMENDMENTS

    1. Social Security Act 1998, Sch.7 (October 5, 1999).
    2. Social Security (Recovery of Benefits) Act 1997, Sch.3 (October 6, 1997).

SCHEDULES

SCHEDULE 1

CLAIMS FOR BENEFIT MADE OR TREATED AS MADE BEFORE 1ST OCTOBER 1990 1.234

Claims made or treated as made on or after 2nd September 1985 and before 1st October 1986

    1. Section 1 above shall have effect in relation to a claim made or treated as made on or after 2nd September 1985 and before 1st October 1986 as if the following subsections were substituted for subsections (1) to (3)—

    "(1) Except in such cases as may be prescribed, no person shall be entitled to any benefit unless, in addition to any other conditions relating to that benefit being satisfied—

(a) he makes a claim for it—
  (i) in the prescribed manner; and
  (ii) subject to subsection (2) below, within the prescribed time; or
(b) by virtue of a provision of Chapter VI of Part II of the 1975 Act or of regulations made under such a provision he would have been treated as making a claim for it."

"(2) Regulations shall provide for extending, subject to any prescribed conditions, the time within which a claim may be made in cases where it is not made within the prescribed time but good cause is shown for the delay.

(3) Notwithstanding any regulations made under this section, no person shall be entitled to any benefit (except disablement benefit or industrial death benefit) in respect of any period more than 12 months before the date on which the claim is made."

Claims made or treated as made on or after 1st October 1986 and before 6th April 1987

2. Section 1 above shall have effect in relation to a claim made or treated as made on or after 1986 and before 6th April 1987 as if the subsections set out in paragraph 1 above were substituted for subsections (1) to (3) but with the insertion in subsection (3) of the words "reduced earnings allowance" after the words "disablement benefit".

Claims made or treated as made on or after 6th April 1987 and before 21st July 1989

3. Section 1 above shall have effect in relation to a claim made or treated as made on or after 6th April 1987 and before 21st July 1989, as if—
(a) the following subsection were substituted for subsection (1)—

"(1) Except in such cases as may be prescribed, no person shall be entitled to any benefit unless, in addition to any other conditions relating to that benefit being satisfied—
  (a) he makes a claim for it in the prescribed manner and within the prescribed time; or
  (b) by virtue of regulations made under section 51 of the 1986 Act he would have been treated as making a claim for it."; and
(c) there were omitted—
  (i) from subsection (2), the words "except as provided by section 3 below"; and
  (ii) subsection (3).

Claims made or treated as made on or after 21st July 1989 and before 13th July 1990

4. Section 1 above shall have effect in relation to a claim made or treated as made on or after 21st July 1989 and before 13th July 1990 as if there were omitted—
(a) from subsection (1), the words "and subject to the following provisions of this section and to section 3 below";
(b) from subsection (2), the words "except as provided by section 3 below"; and
(c) subsection (3).

Claims made or treated as made on or after 13th July 1990 and before 1st October 1990

5. Section 1 above shall have effect in relation to a claim made or treated as made on or after 13th July 1990 and before 1st October 1990 as if there were omitted—
(a) from subsection (1), the words "the following provisions of this section and to";
(b) subsection (3)

GENERAL NOTE

1.235　See annotations to s.1

1.236　**Schedules 2.–9.** *Omitted.*

SCHEDULE 10　　　　　　　　　　Section 186

SUPPLEMENTARY BENEFIT ETC.

Interpretation

1.237　**1.** In this Schedule—

"the former National Insurance Acts" means the National Insurance Act 1946 and the National Insurance Act 1965; and

(1992 c.5, Sch.10)

"the former Industrial Injuries Acts" means the National Insurance (Industrial Injuries) Act 1946 and the National Insurance (Industrial Injuries) Act 1965.

Claims and payments

2.—(1) Section 5 above shall have effect in relation to the benefits specified in subparagraph (2) below as it has effect in relation to the benefits to which it applies by virtue of subsection (2).

(2) The benefits mentioned in sub-paragraph (1) above are benefits under—
  (a) the former National Insurance Acts;
  (b) the former Industrial Injuries Acts;
  (c) the National Assistance Act 1948;
  (d) the Supplementary Benefit Act 1966;
  (e) the Supplementary Benefits Act 1976;
  (f) the Family Income Supplements Act 1970.

Adjudication

3.—(1) [[1] Sections 8 to 18, 29 to 31 and 39 of the Social Security Act 1998] and [[3] sections 124 to 124B] above shall have effect for the purposes of the benefits specified in paragraph 2(2) above as they have effect for the purposes of benefit within the meaning of section 122 of the Contributions and Benefits Act other than attendance allowance, disability living allowance and disability working allowance.

(2) Procedure regulations made under section 59 above [[1] section 16 of the Social Security Act 1998] by virtue of sub-paragraph(1) may make different provision in relation to each of the benefits specified in paragraph 2(2) above.

Overpayments etc.

4.—(1) Section 71 above shall have effect in relation to the benefits mentioned in paragraph 2(2) above as it has effect in relation to the benefits to which it applies by virtue of subsection (11).

(2) Section 74 above shall have effect in relation to supplementary benefit as it has effect in relation to income support.

(3) The reference to housing benefit in section 75 above includes a reference to housing benefits under Part II of the Social Security and Housing Benefits Act 1982.

Inspection

5. [[2] Part VI of this Act shall have effect as if the following Acts were included in the Acts comprised in the relevant social security legislation]—
  (a) the Supplementary Benefits Act 1976,
  (b) the Family Income Supplements Act 1970.

Legal proceedings

6. Section 116 above shall have effect as if any reference to this Act in that section included—
  (a) the National Assistance Act 1948;
  (b) the Supplementary Benefit Act 1966;
  (c) the Supplementary Benefits Act 1976;
  (d) the Family Income Supplements Act 1970.

AMENDMENTS

1. Social Security Act 1998, s.86 and Sch.7 (November 29, 1999 except in relation to housing benefit, council tax benefit or decisions to which the Transfer of Functions Act 1999 applies).
2. Child Support, Pensions and Social Security Act 2000, s.67 and Sch.6 (April 2, 2001).
3. Civil Partnership Act 2004 (Overseas Relationships and Consequential etc. Amendments) Order 2005 (SI 2005/3129), Sch.1, para.4 (December 5, 2005).

DERIVATION

Social Security Act 1986, Sch.7.

1.238

DEFINITION

"the Contributions and Benefits Act"—see s.191.

Welsh Language Act 1993

(1993 c.38)

ARRANGEMENT OF SECTIONS

PART II

WELSH LANGUAGE SCHEMES

Duty to prepare schemes

1.239   5.   Duty of notified public bodies to prepare schemes.

PART III

MISCELLANEOUS

Welsh in legal proceedings

22.   Use of Welsh in legal proceedings.
23.   Oaths and affirmations.

Statutory names, forms etc.

26.   Powers to prescribe Welsh forms.
27.   Provisions supplementary to sections 25 and 26.

An Act to establish a Board having the function of promoting and facilitating the use of the Welsh language, to provide for the preparation by public bodies of schemes giving effect to the principle that in the conduct of public business and the administration of justice in Wales the English and Welsh languages should be treated on a basis of equality, to make further provision relating to the Welsh language, to repeal certain spent enactments relating to Wales, and for connected purposes.

[21st October 1993]

1–4. *Omitted.*

(1993 c.38, s.5)

PART II

WELSH LANGUAGE SCHEMES

Duty to prepare schemes

Duty of notified public bodies to prepare schemes

5.—(1) Every public body to which a notice is given under section 7 below and which—
 (a) provides services to the public in Wales, or
 (b) exercises statutory functions in relation to the provision by other public bodies of services to the public in Wales,
shall prepare a scheme specifying the measures which it proposes to take, for the purpose mentioned in subsection (2) below, as to the use of the Welsh language in connection with the provision of those services, or of such of them as are specified in the notice.

(2) The purpose referred to in subsection (1) above is that of giving effect, so far as is both appropriate in the circumstances and reasonably practicable, to the principle that in the conduct of public business and the administration of justice in Wales the English and Welsh languages should be treated on a basis of equality.

(3) In preparing a scheme under this Part of this Act a public body shall have regard to any guidelines issued by the Board under section 9 below.

6.–21. *Omitted.*

GENERAL NOTE

The "Board" is the Welsh Language Board established under Part I of this Act. Sections 6 to 21 make provision for the Board to give guidelines as to the form and content of schemes and for their preparation, approval and subsequent revision. Provision is also made for the handling of complaints about non-compliance. The government departments and agencies responsible for the administration of benefits and tax credits all have schemes, as does the Tribunals Service.

1.240

1.241

PART III

MISCELLANEOUS

Welsh in legal proceedings

Use of Welsh in legal proceedings

22.—(1) In any legal proceedings in Wales the Welsh language may be spoken by any party, witness or other person who desires to use it, subject

1.242

in the case of proceedings in a court other than a magistrates' court to such prior notice as may be required by rules of court; and any necessary provision for interpretation shall be made accordingly.

(2) Any power to make rules of court includes power to make provision as to the use, in proceedings in or having a connection with Wales, of documents in the Welsh language.

Oaths and affirmations

1.243

23. The Lord Chancellor may make rules prescribing a translation in the Welsh language of any form for the time being prescribed by law as the form of any oath or affirmation to be administered and taken or made by any person in any court, and an oath or affirmation administered and taken or made in any court in Wales in the translation prescribed by such rules shall, without interpretation, be of the like effect as if it had been administered and taken or made in the English language.

GENERAL NOTE

1.244

This applies only to proceedings in courts and not to proceedings before appeal tribunals or Commissioners. However, as appeal tribunals and Commissioners have the power to administer oaths and as the practice is to use the forms of oath and affirmation prescribed for use in courts, it can be expected that the translations in the Welsh language prescribed for use in courts will also be used in proceedings before appeal tribunals and the Commissioners.

24. *Omitted.*

Statutory names, forms etc.

25. *Omitted.*

Powers to prescribe Welsh forms

1.245

26.—(1) This section applies where an Act of Parliament specifies, or confers power to specify,—
  (a) the form of any document, or
  (b) any form of words,
which is to be or may be used for an official or public purpose or for any other purpose where the consequences in law of any act depend on the form used.

(2) Where the Act itself specifies the form of the document or the form of words, the appropriate Minister may by order prescribe—
  (a) a form of the document in Welsh, or partly in Welsh and partly in English or, as the case may be,
  (b) a form of words in Welsh,
for use in such circumstances and subject to such conditions as may be prescribed by the order.

(3) Where the Act confers a power to specify the form of the document or the form of words, the power shall include power to prescribe—

(a) separate forms of the document, or separate forms of words, in Welsh and in English, and
(b) in the case of a document, a form partly in Welsh and partly in English,

for use in such circumstances and subject to such conditions as may be prescribed by the instrument by which the power is exercised.

(4) Where the powers conferred by this section are exercised in relation to the form of a document or a form of words, a reference in an Act or instrument to the form shall, so far as may be necessary, be construed as (or as including) a reference to the form prescribed under or by virtue of this section.

(5) This section shall not apply in relation to a provision which—
(a) confers, or gives power to confer, a name on any body, office or place, or
(b) requires specified words to be included in the name of any body, office or place.

Provisions supplementary to sections 25 and 26

27.—(1) Anything done in Welsh by virtue of section 26 above shall have the like effect as if done in English.

(2) Any provision authorising—
(a) the use of a document or words to the like effect as a document or words of which another version is prescribed by virtue of section 26 above, or
(b) the adaptation of a document or words of which another version is so prescribed,

shall apply in relation to both versions.

(3) The powers to make orders under sections 25(1) and 26(2) above shall be exercisable by statutory instrument, which shall be laid before Parliament after being made.

(4) References in sections 25 and 26 above to an Act of Parliament include references to Acts passed after this Act; and in those sections "the appropriate Minister" in relation to any Act means—
(a) in the case of provisions for the execution of which in Wales a Minister other than the Secretary of State is responsible, that Minister, and
(b) in any other case, the Secretary of State.

(5) Any question arising under paragraphs (a) and (b) of subsection (4) above shall be determined by the Treasury; and in that subsection "Minister" includes the Treasury, the Commissioners of Customs and Excise and the Commissioners of Inland Revenue.

28.–33. *Omitted.*

Pension Schemes Act 1993

Pension Schemes Act 1993

(1993 c.48)

ARRANGEMENT OF SECTIONS

170.   Decisions and appeals

An Act to consolidate certain enactments relating to pension schemes with-amendments to give effect to recommendations of the Law Commission and the Scottish Law Commission

[5th November 1993]

[1 Decisions and appeals

1.247   **170.**—(1) Section 2 (use of computers) of the Social Security Act 1998 ("the 1998 Act") applies as if, for the purposes of subsection (1) of that section, this Act were a relevant enactment.
   [2(2) It shall be for an officer of the Inland Revenue—
   (a) to make any decision that falls to be made under or by virtue of Part III of this Act, other than a decision which under or by virtue of that Part falls to be made by the Secretary of State;
   (b) to decide any issue arising in connection with payments under section 7 of the Social Security Act 1986 (occupational pension schemes becoming contracted out between 1986 and 1993); and
   (c) to decide any issue arising by virtue of regulations made under paragraph 15 of Schedule 3 to the Social Security (Consequential Provisions) Act 1992 (continuing in force of certain enactments repealed by the Social Security Act 1973).
   (3) In the following provisions of this section a "relevant decision" means any decision which under subsection (2) falls to be made by an officer of the Inland Revenue, other than a decision under section 53 or section 54.
   (4) Sections 9 and 10 of the 1998 Act (revisions of decisions and decisions superseding earlier decisions) apply as if—
   (a) any reference in those sections to a decision of the Secretary of State under section 8 of that Act included a reference to a relevant decision; and
   (b) any other reference in those sections to the Secretary of State were, in relation to a relevant decision, a reference to an officer of the Inland Revenue.
   (5) Regulations may make provision—
   [3(a) generally with respect to the making of relevant decisions;
   (b) with respect to the procedure to be adopted on any application made under section 9 or 10 of the 1998 Act by virtue of subsection (4); and
   (c) generally withrespect to such applications, revisions under section 9 and decisions under section 10;]
but may not prevent such a revision or decision being made without such an application.
   (6) Section 12 of the 1998 Act (appeal to appeal tribunal) applies as if, for the purposes of subsection (1)(b) of that section, a relevant decision

were a decision of the Secretary of State falling within Schedule 3 to the 1998 Act.

(7) The following provisions of the 1998 Act (which relate to decisions and appeals)—
sections 13 to 18,
sections 25 and 26,
section 28, and
Schedules 4 and 5,
shall apply in relation to any appeal under section 12 of the 1998 Act by virtue of subsection (6) above as if any reference to the Secretary of State were a reference to an officer of the Inland Revenue.]]

AMENDMENTS

1. Social Security Act 1998, s.86(1) and Sch.7, para.131 (March 4, 1999).
2. Social Security Contributions (Transfer of Functions, etc.) Act 1999, s.16 (April 1, 1999).
3. Welfare Reform and Pensions Act 1999, Sch.11, para.22.

GENERAL NOTE

A former employee may be entitled to both a state pension and one or more private pensions. The Social Security Contributions and Benefits Act 1992 provides for a Category A retirement pension, the state pension, consisting of a basic pension and an additional pension under either the former State Earnings-Related Pension Scheme or, from 2002, the new "second state pension" scheme. However, employees have been able to "contract out" of the liability to make contributions for an additional pension provided they were making contributions to an approved occupational or personal pension scheme. The Pensions Schemes Act 1993, provides for guaranteed minimum pensions from contracted-out occupational pension schemes. See Vol.1 of this work for both Acts.

Over a working life, a person may have contributed both to an additional pension under one or both of the state schemes and to one or more occupational or personal pension schemes. Where a guaranteed minimum pension is payable under an occupational scheme to a person entitled to an additional pension under the State Earnings-Related Pension Scheme, overlap is avoided by s.46 of the 1993 Act which provides for an adjustment to the Category A retirement pension. This involves the determination of a number of questions, some of which are to be determined by the Secretary of State and some of which are allocated to the Her Majesty's Revenue and Customs (to whom the functions of the Commissioners for Inland Revenue have been transferred by the Commissioners for Revenue and Customs Act 2005, s.5(2)) by this section. In *R(P) 1/04*, the Commissioner held that it was for the Secretary of State to determine entitlement to a Category A retirement pension and to identify the occupational pension schemes relevant to that entitlement, for the Inland Revenue to determine entitlement to a guaranteed minimum pension in respect of each occupational pension scheme and for the Secretary of State to aggregate the guaranteed minimum pensions and decide on the amount of any reduction of the Category A retirement pension under s.46 of the 1993 Act.

Section 170(6) and (7) provides for appeals against decisions of Her Majesty's Revenue and Customs relating to guaranteed minimum pensions to be heard by appeal tribunals and Social Security Commissioners, rather than the tax commissioners who hear most appeals from such decisions. However, it was pointed out in *R(P) 1/04* that there can be no appeal until a formal decision is issued and that the Inland Revenue did not always issue a formal decision unless a calculation was disputed. In those circumstances, as any dispute was likely to be raised first in a challenge to the final decision issued by the Secretary of State, it

1.248

was suggested that it might be necessary for the Secretary of State or an appeal tribunal to refer a question to the Inland Revenue for formal determination even though regs 11A and 38A of the Social Security and Child Support (Decisions and Appeals) Regulations 1999 did not strictly apply.

Perhaps surprisingly, an appeal against a refusal to issue a contracting-out or appropriate scheme certificate is one type of case that falls, by virtue of this section, within the jurisdiction of appeal tribunals. However, where a question arises as to whether a particular claimant was in contracted-in or contracted-out employment for the purpose of ascertaining his entitlement to a pension, it arises as part of a question as to his liability to pay contributions or as to what contributions have been paid and so is a question falling within the jurisdiction of the tax commissioners by virtue of s.8(1)(c) or (e) of the Social Security Contributions (Transfer of Functions, etc.) Act 1999 (*CP/3833/2003*).

Employment Tribunals Act 1996

(1996 c.17)

Arrangement of Sections

16. Power to provide for recoupment of benefits.
17. Recoupment: further provisions.

An Act to consolidate enactments relating to industrial tribunals and the Employment Appeal Tribunal.

[22nd May 1996]

General Note

1.249 This Act started life as the Industrial Tribunals Act 1996 but was given its new short title by s.1(2) of the Employment Rights (Dispute Resolution) Act 1998, which also renamed the tribunals themselves, with effect from August 1, 1998.

Power to provide for recoupment of benefits

1.250 **16.**—(1) This section applies to payments which are the subject of proceedings before [¹ employment tribunals] and which are—
  (a) payments of wages or compensation for loss of wages,
  (b) payments by employers to employees under sections 146 to 151, sections 168 to 173 or section 192 of the Trade Union and Labour Relations (Consolidation) Act 1992,
  (c) payments by employers to employees under —
      (i) Part III, V, VI or VII,
      (ii) section 93, or
      (iii) Part X,
           of the Employment Rights Act 1996, or
  (d) payments by employers to employees of a nature similar to, or for a purpose corresponding to the purpose of, payments within paragraph (b) or (c),

and to payments of remuneration under a protective award under section 189 of the Trade Union and Labour Relations (Consolidation) Act 1992.

(2) The Secretary of State may by regulations make with respect to payments to which this section applies provision for any or all of the purposes specified in subsection (3).

(3) The purposes referred to in subsection (2) are—
(a) enabling the Secretary of State to recover from an employer, by way of total or partial recoupment of jobseeker's allowance or income support—
   (i) a sum not exceeding the amount of the prescribed element of the monetary award, or
   (ii) in the case of a protective award, the amount of the remuneration,
(b) requiring or authorising an [1employment tribunal] to order the payment of such a sum, by way of total or partial recoupment of either benefit, to the Secretary of State instead of to an employee, and
(c) requiring an [1employment tribunal] to order the payment to an employee of only the excess of the prescribed element of the monetary award over the amount of any jobseeker's allowance or income support shown to the tribunal to have been paid to the employee and enabling the Secretary of State to recover from the employer, by way of total or partial recoupment of the benefit, a sum not exceeding that amount.

(4) Regulations under this section may be framed—
(a) so as to apply to all payments to which this section applies or to one or more classes of those payments, and
(b) so as to apply to both jobseeker's allowance and income support, or to only jobseeker's allowance or income support.

(5) Regulations under this section may—
(a) confer powers and impose duties on [1 employment tribunals] or [2 . . .] other persons,
(b) impose on an employer to whom a monetary award or protective award relates a duty—
   (i) to furnish particulars connected with the award, and
   (ii) to suspend payments in pursuance of the award during any period prescribed by the regulations,
(c) provide for an employer who pays a sum to the Secretary of State in pursuance of this section to be relieved from any liability to pay the sum to another person,
[2 (cc) provide for the determination by the Secretary of State of any issue arising as to the total or partial recoupment in pursuance of the regulations of a jobseeker's allowance, unemployment benefit or income support,
(d) confer on an employee a right of appeal to an appeal tribunal constituted under chapter I of Part I of the Social Security Act 1998 against any decision of the Secretary of State on any such issue, and]
(e) provide for the proof in proceedings before [1 employment tribunals] (whether by certificate or in any other manner) of any amount of jobseeker's allowance or income support paid to an employee.

(6) Regulations under this section may make different provision for different cases.

Employment Tribunals Act 1996

AMENDMENTS

1. Employment Rights (Dispute Resolution) Act 1998, s.1(2) (August 1, 1998).
2. Social Security Act 1998, Sch.7, para.147 (October 18, 1999).

DEFINITIONS

"income-based jobseeker's allowance"—see s.17(4).
"monetary award"—see s.17(3).
"the prescribed element"—*ibid.*

GENERAL NOTE

1.251 See the Employment Protection (Recoupment of Jobseeker's Allowance and Income Support) Regulations 1996.

Recoupment: further provisions

1.252 **17.**—(1) Where in pursuance of any regulations under section 16 a sum has been recovered by or paid to the Secretary of State by way of total or partial recoupment of jobseeker's allowance or income support—
   (a) no sum shall be recoverable under Part III or V of the Social Security Administration Act 1992, and
   (b) no abatement, payment or reduction shall be made by reference to the jobseeker's allowance or income support recouped.

(2) Any amount found to have been duly recovered by or paid to the Secretary of State in pursuance of regulations under section 16 by way of total or partial recoupment of jobseeker's allowance shall be paid into the National Insurance Fund.

(3) In section 16—

"monetary award" means the amount which is awarded, or ordered to be paid, to the employee by the tribunal or would be so awarded or ordered apart from any provision of regulations under that section, and

"the prescribed element", in relation to any monetary award, means so much of that award as is attributable to such matters as may be prescribed by regulations under that section.

(4) In section 16 "income-based jobseeker's allowance" has the same meaning as in the Jobseekers Act 1995.

Social Security (Recovery of Benefits) Act 1997

(1997 C.27)

ARRANGEMENT OF SECTIONS

Introductory

1.253   1. Cases in which this Act applies.
      2. Compensation payments to which this Act applies.
      3. "The relevant period".

(1997 c.27)

Certificates of recoverable benefits

4. Applications for certificates of recoverable benefits.
5. Information contained in certificates.

Liability of person paying compensation

6. Liability to pay Secretary of State amount of benefits.
7. Recovery of payments due under section 6.

Reduction of compensation payment

8. Reduction of compensation payment.
9. Section 8: supplementary.

Reviews and appeals

10. Review of certificates of recoverable benefits.
11. Appeals against certificates of recoverable benefits.
12. Reference of questions to medical appeal tribunal.
13. Appeal to Social Security Commissioner.
14. Reviews and appeals: supplementary.

Courts

15. Court orders.
16. Payments into court.
17. Benefits irrelevant to assessment of damages.

Reduction of compensation: complex cases

18. Lump sum and periodical payments.
19. Payments by more than one person.

Miscellaneous

20. Amounts overpaid under section 6.
21. Compensation payments to be disregarded.
22. *Omitted.*
23. Provision of information.
24. Power to amend Schedule 2.

Provisions relating to Northern Ireland

25.–27. *Omitted.*

General

28. The Crown.
29. General interpretation.
30. Regulations and orders.

Social Security (Recovery of Benefits) Act 1997

31. *Omitted.*
32. Power to make transitional, consequential etc. provisions.
33. *Omitted.*
34. Short title, commencement and extent.

SCHEDULES:

Schedule 1—Compensation payments.
 Part I—Exempted payments.
 Part II—Power to disregard small payments.
Schedule 2—Calculation of compensation payment.
Schedule 3—*Omitted.*
Schedule 4—*Omitted.*

An Act to re-state, with amendments, Part IV of the Social Security Administration Act 1992.

[19th March 1997]

GENERAL NOTE

1.254 This Act provides for the recovery from those who cause personal injury or disease of benefits paid to those who are injured or made ill. As the long title says, the Act is to "re-state, with amendments," Pt IV of the Social Security Act 1992, which was a true consolidation measure and re-enacted s.22 of, and Sch.4 to, the Social Security Act 1989 which first introduced a scheme like this for recovering benefits. This Act is not a consolidation measure because, while a number of the provisions are the same as under the old schemes, the amendments make some fundamental changes.

The Compensation Recovery Unit of the Department for Work and Pensions at Durham House, Washington, Tyne and Wear NE38 7SF (tel: 0191–489 2266) publish a free guide to the procedure. A person making a compensation payment in consequence of an accident injury or disease (whether voluntarily or pursuant to a court order or agreement or otherwise—see s.1(3)—unless the payment is exempt—see s.1(2) and Sch.1) *must* apply under s.4 to the Compensation Recovery Unit for a "certificate of recoverable benefits" *before* making the payment. Under s.5, that certificate should specify the amount of relevant benefits (listed in col.2 of Sch.2) paid, or expected to be paid within the "relevant period" (which will end when the compensation payment is made if the maximum period of five years has not already elapsed—see s.3), *in respect of* the accident, injury or disease (see the definition of "recoverable benefit" in s.1(4)(c) which refers back to s.1(1)(b)). The compensator must then pay to the Secretary of State a sum equal to the total amount of those recoverable benefits (s.6) and pay to the victim the compensation payment. Certain parts of the compensation payment may be reduced to reflect the benefits received by the victim during the "relevant period" (s.8), but benefits paid after that period must be ignored in the assessment of damages (s.17).

Sections 10–14 provide for reviews of, and appeals against, certificates of recoverable benefits.

Introductory

Cases in which this Act applies

1.255 **1.**—(1) This Act applies in cases where—
 (a) a person makes a payment (whether on his own behalf or not) to or in respect of any other person in consequence of any accident, injury or disease suffered by the other, and
 (b) any listed benefits have been, or are likely to be, paid to or for the other during the relevant period in respect of the accident, injury or disease.

(1997 c.27, s.1)

(2) The reference above to a payment in consequence of any accident, injury or disease is to a payment made—
  (a) by or on behalf of a person who is, or is alleged to be, liable to any extent in respect of the accident, injury or disease, or
  (b) in pursuance of a compensation scheme for motor accidents;
but does not include a payment mentioned in Part I of Schedule 1.
(3) Subsection (1)(a) applies to a payment made—
  (a) voluntarily, or in pursuance of a court order or an agreement, or otherwise, and
  (b) in the United Kingdom or elsewhere.
(4) In a case where this Act applies—
  (a) the "injured person" is the person who suffered the accident, injury or disease,
  (b) the "compensation payment" is the payment within subsection (1)(a), and
  (c) "recoverable benefit" is listed benefit which has been or is likely to be paid as mentioned in the subsection (1)(b).

DEFINITIONS

"compensation scheme for motor accidents"—see s.29.
"listed benefit"—*ibid.*
"payment"—*ibid.*
"the relevant period"—see s.3.

GENERAL NOTE

In *Rand v East Dorset Health Authority* [2001] P.I.Q.R. Q1, this Act was held not to apply where parents of a child were awarded damages in respect of the defendants' negligence in failing to inform them before the child's birth that the child would be suffering from Down's Syndrome. It had been claimed that the child would have been aborted had the parents received the information and the damages had been awarded purely for economic loss resulting from negligent mis-statement and so were not awarded "in consequence of any accident, injury or disease suffered by the [parents]". That decision was distinguished in *R(CR) 4/03*, which was also a case of medical negligence. There, a doctor was alleged to have failed to recognise symptoms of diabetes in a woman in an advanced stage of pregnancy. It was claimed that, had the symptoms been detected, the condition would have been confirmed and an emergency Caesarean section could have been performed with a high chance of the child being born alive. As it was, the child died *in utero* and labour had to be induced and the mother suffered a major depressive episode. Compensation was claimed not only under the Fatal Accidents Act 1976 (which compensation is exempt under reg.2 of the Social Security (Recovery of Benefits) Regulations 1997) but also for the mother's psychiatric injury. The case was settled. The Commissioner held that compensation was paid in consequence of an accident, injury or disease suffered by the mother. However, he commented that the phrase "accident, injury or disease" was an "odd one" because it was not clear how benefits might be paid in respect of an accident if there was neither injury nor disease. He suggested that there might be little difference between an "accident" and an "injury" in this context.

The crucial question in most cases arising under this Act is whether listed benefits have been paid "in respect of" the accident, injury or disease within the meaning that phrase has in subs.(1)(b), so as to fall within the scope of the term "recoverable benefit" as defined in subs.(4)(c).

For a benefit to be paid "in respect of" an accident, injury or disease, the accident, injury or disease must be an effective cause of the payment of benefit and an accident may cease to be an effective cause of disablement if its effects have worn off and been replaced by the effects of a worsening pre-accident condition (*R(CR) 1/01*). In *R(CR)*

1.256

3/03, it was held that only benefits the payment of which was caused by the relevant disease were paid "in respect of" the disease and that ordinary principles of causation applied, having regard to the conditions of entitlement to each benefit. A relevant accident, injury or disease could therefore cease to be an effective cause of the payment of benefit even if its effects had not worn off. It was enough merely for it to be shown that the benefit would have been paid due to a pre-existing condition even if the relevant disease had not been developed. In that case, the claimant was paid compensation in respect of asbestos–induced disease but the evidence was that the claimant was suffering from other, longer-standing, conditions that contributed to his disablement and were getting worse. The Commissioner found the claimant would have become incapable of work from a certain date even if he had not suffered from the asbestos-induced disease and therefore that the asbestos-induced disease ceased to be a cause of the payment of benefits paid in respect of incapacity from that date, although it had accelerated the onset of incapacity. In relation to disability living allowance, he found that the asbestos-related disease had been a contributory factor in the claimant's entitlement to the mobility component throughout that part of the "relevant period" for which it had been paid but that it had never been a contributory factor in the claimant's entitlement to the care component. Thus, part of the incapacity benefits listed in the original certificate of recoverable benefits and all of the care component of disability living allowance were not recoverable but the rest of the incapacity benefits and all of the mobility component were recoverable.

Conversely, where the other cause of disablement arises *after* the relevant accident, benefit that would have been paid as a result of the relevant accident if the other cause had not arisen is attributable to the relevant accident, whereas benefit that would not have been paid but for the other cause of disablement is attributable to that other cause. In *R(CR) 2/04*, the claimant had returned to work for another employer after the relevant accident, even though he was still suffering from some minor disablement, and then suffered a second industrial accident, following which he was incapable of work again. The Commissioner found that the incapacity was initially attributable to the second accident because the claimant would have been able to continue working but for that accident. However, the effects of that accident then wore off and the effects of the relevant accident worsened and the Commissioner found that there came a time when the claimant would have been incapable of work due to the relevant accident even if the second accident had not occurred so that the payment of benefits became attributable to the relevant accident again.

Where a claimant undergoes a medical operation as a result of an accident, injury or disease and the operation causes further disablement, benefits paid in consequence of that further disablement will have been paid "in respect of" the accident (*CCR/2046/ 2002*). The same applied where the claimant suffered a psychological reaction due to stress caused by a misdiagnosis due to the misreading of an X-ray that was required by the relevant accident, although it was suggested that the result might have been different if it had been proved that the misdiagnosis had been due to negligence (*CCR/4307/2000*).

Where there has been medical negligence, compensation may be paid in respect of any injury or disease caused by the negligence. In *CCR/1022/2006*, it was pointed out that it is important to distinguish between the effects of the accident, injury or disease that led to the claimant being admitted to hospital and the effects of the medical negligence that occurred while he was a patient there. "The question for the tribunal was whether, had there not been the delay in arranging the MRI scan and therefore a delay in surgery, the appellant would have qualified for disability living allowance at the rate at which it was awarded or at a lower rate. If the answer was 'yes', the benefit was to that extent not recoverable."

However, where a claimant had accepted £50,000 in respect of a claim that injuries from a particular date were due solely to medical negligence, it was necessary to adopt a consistent approach and the claimant was not entitled to argue that the injuries he had suffered after that date were entirely due to the accident that had led him to be hospitalised rather than to the medical negligence (*CCR/2232/2006*).

(1997 c.27, s.1)

The need for consistency between the approach taken by a party to court proceedings and the approach taken by the same party in proceedings under this Act is not confined to medical negligence cases and such consistency is expected from compensators as well as from claimants. In *CCR/2658/2006*, where a compensator settled a claim made on the basis that psychiatric injury was due to a particular cause, the compensator was not entitled to argue that the injury was due to a cause not covered by the claim and that the compensator was therefore not in fact liable in respect of the injury in consequence of which the compensation was paid. Attention was drawn to the word "alleged" in s.1(2)(a). Compensators must therefore pay careful attention to the certificate of recoverable benefits when deciding whether to compromise a case that could be defended. It is important to note that the principal issue in both *CCR/2232/2006* and *CCR/2658/2006* was whether the compensation had been paid in respect of a particular injury (in circumstances where it could not plausibly be claimed to have been paid in respect of some other injury or damage), rather than whether the benefits listed in the certificate of recoverable benefits were paid in respect of the injury. The issue therefore did not fall within the scope of the right of appeal conferred by s.11.

Benefits that ought not to have been paid at all—because they were paid under a mistake of fact or medical opinion or law, whether deliberately induced by the claimant or not—cannot be said to have been paid "in respect of" an accident, injury or disease *(R(CR) 1/02*, a decision of a Tribunal of Commissioners, and *Eagle Star Insurance v Department for Social Development*, a decision of the Court of Appeal in Northern Ireland reported as R1/01(CRS)). It follows that, if it is shown that benefit was paid at too high a rate, only that part of the benefit properly paid was paid "in respect of" the accident, injury or disease *(R(CR) 1/03)*. See further the note to s.11.

However, in *R1/05(CRS)*, it was held that benefits paid as a result of bureaucratic delay between the date of a medical examination and a consequent supersession decision do not necessarily cease to be recoverable.

There is no provision for reducing the amount of recoverable benefit because some other benefit would have been paid to the claimant if the relevant accident or injury had not occurred or the relevant disease had not been developed. Furthermore, income support is paid "in respect of" an accident if it is paid on the basis of the claimant being incapable of work due to the accident, even if the claimant would have been paid income support on some other basis if the accident had not happened (*Hassall v Secretary of State for Social Security* [1995] 1 W.L.R. 812 (also reported as *R(CR) 1/95)*). Where a claimant might be at risk of having compensation reduced under s.8 in respect of post-accident benefits paid in place of pre-accident benefits, he or she may need to include a claim for the loss of the pre-accident benefits in the claim for compensation (*ibid.* and *Neal v Bingle* [1998] Q.B. 466), although this is less of a problem under this Act than it was under the legislation it replaced. In *R1/06 (CRS)*, the Commissioner followed *Hassall* when deciding that the whole of income support awarded during the relevant period on the grounds of incapacity caused by the accident was recoverable notwithstanding that part of it was attributable to dependants acquired by the claimant after the relevant accident. It would not have been necessary for benefit to be paid in respect of the dependants if the accident had not occurred. In *R(CR) 1/96*, the claimant was a hairdresser injured in a road accident. She was awarded income support on the basis of incapacity for work and later, after she became capable of light work, on the basis that she was available for work, although she was still unfit for work as a hairdresser. The Commissioner held that the income support paid on the basis of the claimant's availability for work was paid "otherwise than in consequence of the accident". It is suggested that this part of the decision is based on a misreading of *Hassall* and would probably not be followed by a Commissioner if the issue were to arise again. *Hassall* was concerned with income support paid on the basis of availability for work *before* the accident but there seems no reason why such a benefit should not be recoverable when a claimant has lost employment as the result of an accident, particularly as jobseeker's allowance, which has replaced income support when a claimant is capable of, and available for, work is clearly listed in Sch.2. However, the issue may not

Social Security (Recovery of Benefits) Act 1997

arise for determination because, in practice, the Secretary of State seldom seeks recovery of jobseeker's allowance (see *R(CR) 2/04* at para.19).

There may be a question as to whether benefit paid in consequence of a disease for a period before the beginning of the "relevant period" is recoverable (see the note to s.3).

Compensation payments to which this Act applies

1.257   **2.** This Act applies in relation to compensation payments made on or after the day on which this section comes into force, unless they are made in pursuance of a court order or agreement made before that day.

DEFINITION

"compensation payment"—see s.1(4)(b).

GENERAL NOTE

1.258   By virtue of the Social Security (Recovery of Benefits) Act 1997 (Commencement Order) 1997 (SI 1997/2085), this section came into force on October 6, 1997. Where a court order or agreement was made before that date, the recovery provisions of Pt IV of the Social Security Administration Act 1992 continue to apply, unless the accident or injury occurred before January 1, 1989 (or, in the case of a disease, benefit was claimed before January 1, 1989), in which case benefits will not be recoverable by the Secretary of State at all (see s.81(7) of the 1992 Act). Regulation 12 of the Social Security (Recovery of Benefits) Regulations 1997 makes transitional provision for cases arising under the 1992 Act.

"The relevant period"

1.259   **3.**—(1) In relation to a person ("the claimant") who has suffered any accident, injury or disease, "the relevant period" has the meaning given by the following subsections.

(2) Subject to subsection (4), if it is a case of accident or injury, the relevant period is the period of five years immediately following the day on which the accident or injury in question occurred.

(3) Subject to subsection (4), if it is a case of disease, the relevant period is the period of five years beginning with the date on which the claimant first claims a listed benefit in consequence of the disease.

(4) If at any time before the end of the period referred to in subsection (2) or (3)—
  (a) a person makes a compensation payment in final discharge of any claim made by or in respect of the claimant and arising out of the accident, injury or disease, or
  (b) an agreement is made under which an earlier compensation payment is treated as having been made in final discharge of any such claim,
the relevant period ends at that time.

DEFINITIONS

"claimant"—see subs.(1).
"compensation payment"—see s.1(4)(b).
"listed benefit"—see s.29.

GENERAL NOTE

1.260   Subsection (2) identifies the beginning of the "relevant period" if the compensation is paid in consequence of an accident or injury and subs.(3) identifies the beginning of the "relevant period" if compensation is paid in consequence of a disease.

It was observed in *R(CR) 4/03* that this section implies that "accident" and "injury" are indistinguishable in this Act in cases where the injury is due to an accident, because subs.(2) clearly envisages them occurring on the same specific date, rather than contemplating the injury being the, possibly long-standing and possibly delayed, result of an accident. It was also observed that this section requires a distinction to be drawn between an "injury" and a "disease" and that that might not always be straightforward. It may be noted that the Social Security (Industrial Injuries) (Prescribed Diseases) Regulations 1985 in fact include prescribed injuries as well as diseases (see also s.108(1)(b) of the Social Security Contributions and Benefits Act 1992). It is unclear when the "relevant period" begins if a disease is caused by an accident and benefit in respect of the disease is not claimed until some time after the date of the accident.

If s.1(1)(b) and (4)(c) and subs.(3) of this section are all read literally, it appears that there is a possibility of more than five years' worth of benefit being recovered where compensation is paid in consequence of a disease. That is because the "relevant period" appears to run from the date of claim, rather than the date from which benefit is awarded. Typically, arrears of disablement benefit in respect of a prescribed disease are paid in respect of a period of three months before the date of claim, although the payment of those arrears is obviously made after that date and within the "relevant period". It may be arguable that one or more of the provisions should not be read literally on the basis that it is unlikely that it was intended that more than five years' worth of benefit should be recoverable, although the counter-argument is that the possibility of arrears being caught should have been obvious to the draftsman and could easily have been avoided if it was unintended.

Subsections (2) and (3) provide for a "relevant period" of five years but subs.(4) shortens it if compensation is paid sooner. As benefits payable after the "relevant period" are not recoverable (s.1(1)(b) and (4)(c)) and are ignored in the calculation of damages (s.17), it is likely to be in the interests of a compensator and, usually, a claimant to settle a claim for compensation as soon as possible.

Certificates of recoverable benefits

Applications for certificates of recoverable benefits

4.—(1) Before a person ("the compensator") makes a compensation payment he must apply to the Secretary of State for a certificate of recoverable benefits.

1.261

(2) Where the compensator applies for a certificate of recoverable benefits, the Secretary of State must—
(a) send to him a written acknowledgement of receipt of his application, and
(b) subject to subsection (7), issue the certificate before the end of the following period
(3) The period is—
(a) the prescribed period, or
(b) if there is no prescribed period, the period of four weeks,
which begins with the day following the day on which the application is received.

(4) The certificate is to remain in force until the date specified in it for that purpose.

Social Security (Recovery of Benefits) Act 1997

(5) The compensator may apply for fresh certificates from time to time.

(6) Where a certificate of recoverable benefits ceases to be in force, the Secretary of State may issue a fresh certificate without an application for one being made.

(7) Where the compensator applies for a fresh certificate while a certificate ("the existing certificate") remains in force, the Secretary of State must issue the fresh certificate before the end of the following period.

(8) The period is—
  (a) the prescribed period, or
  (b) if there is no prescribed period, the period of four weeks,
which begins with the day following the day on which the existing certificate ceases to be in force.

(9) For the purposes of this Act, regulations may provide for the day on which an application for a certificate of recoverable benefits is to be treated as received.

DEFINITIONS

"compensator—see subs.(1).
"compensation payment"—see s.1(4)(b).
"existing certificate"—see subs.(7).
"prescribed—see s.29.
"recoverable benefit"—see s.1(4)(c).
"regulations"—see s.29.

GENERAL NOTE

1.262   No period has yet been prescribed for the purposes of subss.(3)(a) or (8)(a). By virtue of s.21, the consequence of the Secretary of State failing to issue a certificate of recoverable benefits within the specified period is that no benefits are recoverable and the victim is entitled to the full compensation without deduction. However, for s.21 to apply, the application for the certificate of recoverable benefits must have been accurate and it must have been acknowledged. The Compensation Recovery Unit asks compensators to tell them if an acknowledgement has not been received within 10 days.

In practice, potential compensators are asked to notify the Compensation Recovery Unit of any *claim* for compensation by sending form CRU1 within 14 days of the claim being received. This enables the Unit to start collecting the relevant information from the offices responsible for the payment of benefits. The Unit sends to the potential compensator a form CRU4 which serves as an acknowledgement of the notification and is also the form the compensator must use to obtain the certificate of recoverable benefits. Form CRU4 can also be used by a compensator to obtain, for the purposes of negotiation with the victim, an informal indication of the benefits that have been paid, although the Unit stresses that the accuracy of such an indication depends on how much information they have to hand at that time and a formal certificate of recoverable benefits issued later may be based on more up-to-date information. The victim is, of course, entitled to that information as well and can obtain it directly from the office or offices responsible for payment.

Subs.(9)

1.263   See reg.7(2) of the Social Security (Recovery of Benefits) Regulations 1997.

Information contained in certificates

1.264   **5.**—(1) A certificate of recoverable benefits must specify, for each recoverable benefit—

(1997 c.27, s.5)

(a) the amount which has been or is likely to have been paid on or before a specified date, and
(b) if the benefit is paid or likely to be paid after the specified date, the rate and period for which, and the intervals at which, it is or is likely to be paid.

(2) In a case where the relevant period has ended before the day on which the Secretary of State receives the application for the certificate, the date specified in the certificate for the purposes of subsection (1) must be the day on which the relevant period ended.

(3) In any other case, the date specified for those purposes must not be earlier than the day on which the Secretary of State received the application.

(4) The Secretary of State may estimate, in such manner as he thinks fit, any of the amounts, rates or periods specified in the certificate.

(5) Where the Secretary of State issues a certificate of recoverable benefits, he must provide the information contained in the certificate to—

(a) the person who appears to him to be the injured person, or
(b) any person who he thinks will receive a compensation payment in respect of the injured person.

(6) A person to whom a certificate of recoverable benefits is issued or who is provided with information under subsection (5) is entitled to particulars of the manner in which any amount, rate or period specified in the certificate has been determined, if he applies to the Secretary of State for those particulars.

DEFINITIONS

"benefit"—see s.29.
"compensation payment"—see s.1(4)(b).
"injured person"—see s.1(4)(a).
"recoverable benefit"—see s.1(4)(c).
"the relevant period"—see s.3.

GENERAL NOTE

Note that only "recoverable" benefits should be specified on the certificate and, by virtue of s.1(1)(b) and (4)(c), that means benefits listed in col.2 of Sch.2 that have been, or are likely to be, paid to or for the victim during the relevant period *in respect of* the accident, injury or disease. Thus, not all benefits paid, or to be paid, during the relevant period should be specified in the certificate; only those that are attributable to the accident, injury or disease are recoverable. See the note to s.1.

For reviews of, and appeals against, certificates of recoverable benefits, see ss.10–14.

1.265

Liability of person paying compensation

Liability to pay Secretary of State amount of benefits

6.—(1) A person who makes a compensation payment in any case is liable to pay to the Secretary of State an amount equal to the total amount of the recoverable benefits.

1.266

(2) The liability referred to in subsection (1) arises immediately before the compensation payment or, if there is more than one, the first of them is made.

(3) No amount becomes payable under this section before the end of the period of 14 days following the day on which the liability arises.

(4) Subject to subsection (3), an amount becomes payable under this section at the end of the period of 14 days beginning with the day on which a certificate of recoverable benefits is first issued showing that the amount of recoverable benefit to which it relates has been or is likely to have been paid before a specified date.

DEFINITIONS

"amount of the recoverable benefits"—see s.9(4)(b).
"compensation payment"—see s.1(4)(b).
"recoverable benefit"—see s.1(4)(c).

GENERAL NOTE

1.267   The compensator may recoup some of the payment by reducing under s.8 the amount of compensation paid to the victim. However, the additional cost of benefits paid to the victim during the relevant period falls on the compensator. The compensator may not appeal against the certificate of recoverable benefits until the compensation has been paid (s.11(3)).

Recovery of payments due under section 6

1.268   7.—(1) This section applies where a person has made a compensation payment but—
   (a) has not applied for a certificate of recoverable benefits, or
   (b) has not made a payment to the Secretary of State under section 6 before the end of the period allowed under that section.
(2) The Secretary of State may—
   (a) issue the person who made the compensation payment with a certificate of recoverable benefits, if none has been issued, or
   (b) issue him with a copy of the certificate of recoverable benefits or (if more than one has been issued) the most recent one,
and (in either case) issue him with a demand that payment of any amount due under section 6 be made immediately.
(3) The Secretary of State may, in accordance with subsections (4) and (5), recover the amount for which a demand for payment is made under subsection (2) from the person who made the compensation payment.
(4) If the person who made the compensation payment resides or carries on business in England and Wales and a county court so orders, any amount recoverable under subsection (3) is recoverable by execution issued from the county court or otherwise as if it were payable under an order of that court.
(5) If the person who made the payment resides or carries on business in Scotland, any amount recoverable under subsection (3) may be enforced in like manner as an extract registered decree arbitral bearing a warrant for execution issued by the sheriff court of any sheriffdom in Scotland.
(6) A document bearing a certificate which—
   (a) is signed by a person authorised to do so by the Secretary of State, and
   (b) states that the document, apart from the certificate, is a record of the amount recoverable under subsection (3),
is conclusive evidence that that amount is so recoverable.
(7) A certificate under subsection (6) purporting to be signed by a person authorised to do so by the Secretary of State is to be treated as so signed unless the contrary is proved.

(1997 c.27, s.7)

DEFINITIONS

"compensation payment"—see s.1(4)(b).
"payment"—see s.29.
"recoverable benefit"—see s.1(4)(c).

GENERAL NOTE

This section provides a simple way of recovering not only sums due under s.6 from compensators who have followed the proper procedures but also sums due from those who have failed to apply for a certificate of recoverable benefits at all. For reviews of, and appeals against, certificates issued under s.7(2)(a), see ss.10–14.

1.269

Reduction of compensation payment

Reduction of compensation payment

8.—(1) This section applies in a case where, in relation to any head of compensation listed in column 1 of Schedule 2—
  (a) any of the compensation payment is attributable to that head, and
  (b) any recoverable benefit is shown against that head in column 2 of the Schedule.
(2) In such a case, any claim of a person to receive the compensation payment is to be treated for all purposes as discharged if—
  (a) he is paid the amount (if any) of the compensation payment calculated in accordance with this section, and
  (b) if the amount of the compensation payment so calculated is nil, he is given a statement saying so by the person who (apart from this section) would have paid the gross amount of the compensation payment.
(3) For each head of compensation listed in column 1 of the Schedule for which paragraphs (a) and (b) of subsection (1) are met, so much of the gross amount of the compensation payment as is attributable to that head is to be reduced (to nil, if necessary) by deducting the amount of the recoverable benefit or, as the case may be, the aggregate amount of the recoverable benefits shown against it.
(4) Subsection (3) is to have effect as if a requirement to reduce a payment by deducting an amount which exceeds that payment were a requirement to reduce that payment to nil.
(5) The amount of the compensation payment calculated in accordance with this section is—
  (a) the gross amount of the compensation payment, and
  (b) the sum of the reductions made under subsection (3),
(and, accordingly, the amount may be nil).

1.270

DEFINITIONS

"amount of the recoverable benefit"—see s.9(4)(b).
"compensation payment"—see s.1(4)(b).
"gross amount of the compensation payment"—see s.9(4)(a).
"payment"—see s.29.
"recoverable benefit"—see s.1(4)(c).

Social Security (Recovery of Benefits) Act 1997

GENERAL NOTE

1.271   Under the scheme replaced by this Act, the compensation payment was reduced by the whole amount of benefits paid within the relevant period in respect of the accident, injury or disease, even if the compensation had been awarded solely in respect of pain and suffering (*CSS/36/1992*). The effect was that the compensator almost always passed the entire cost of the recovery of benefits on to the injured person. This could produce unfair results, because the claimant's compensation for pain and suffering was eroded, particularly in two types of cases. The first was where the benefits were paid in respect of, say, a need for personal care (i.e. where the care component of disability living allowance was paid) for which the claimant had not claimed compensation because, say, the care was provided by a spouse free of charge. To some extent this could be avoided by claimants inventing new and cumbersome claims for loss based on the effects of the legislation for recovery of benefits. The second was a less tractable problem, which arose because most claims for compensation are settled and there is likely to be an element of compromise. If a claim for loss of earnings was settled on the basis that was inconsistent with the basis of a claim for benefits, the recovery of benefits from the claimant could appear disproportionate (*CCR/8023/1995*). Whether that was unfair or not depended on whether or not the basis of settlement more accurately reflected the truth than the basis of the claim for benefit, but there could obviously be unfairness where there was a genuine compromise of the claim for compensation but the real burden of repaying the Secretary of State fell wholly on the claimant, rather than being shared by the compensator.

Under the new scheme, the compensator bears the cost of the alleged wrongdoing, being able to pass the cost on to the claimant only to the extent that he has paid relevant compensation to the claimant. Schedule 2 sets out three relevant heads of compensation (lost earnings, cost of care and loss of mobility) and sets out beside each of them the benefits in respect of which a deduction may be made under this section. Where a court makes an award of damages, it must quantify the amount allowed in respect of each of the heads of compensation set out in Sch.2 (s.15(2)). It is then for the compensator to make the appropriate deduction under s.8. Disputes as to the proper amount to be deducted under s.8 are not unusual. The legislation does not make explicit provision for the resolution of such disputes. Presumably, if the parties have become aware in the course of pre-trial negotiations that there is an issue as to the operation of s.8, the court can be asked to deal with that issue at the same time as assessing damages. What is quite clear is that the issue is to be determined by a court and not on an appeal to a tribunal under s.11 (*R(CR) 2/03* and also *R(CR) 2/04* in which it was suggested that the issue could be determined in enforcement proceedings if it has not been dealt with by the judge at trial).

Where a payment into court is made, the compensator must state whether any deduction has been made under this section (see the note to s.16). Where a case is settled without there being a payment into court, the parties will no doubt have had regard to the operation of this section in reaching the settlement but it will usually be presumed that there was no reduction under this section unless the agreement expressly records such a reduction. It is important to the parties to record such a reduction if it is intended that the claimant should bring an appeal before a tribunal challenging the recoverability of benefits, because a claimant has a right of appeal only if there has been a reduction (see s.11(2)(b)). Otherwise only the compensator has a right of appeal. The question of who should bear the cost or risk of such an appeal can be a matter to be taken into account in negotiating a settlement but the settlement must be worded appropriately if it is to have the intended effect. Section 11(3) provides that an appeal may be brought only after the claim giving rise to the compensation payment has been disposed of, so that the Secretary of State does not get caught up in arguments between the claimant and the compensator as to the amount of compensation and the proper application of s.8. Where an application for review or an appeal by either party is success-

(1997 c.27, s.8)

ful in a case where there was a reduction of the compensation payment under this section, the refund is made to the compensator who must make a new calculation under this section (reg.11(4) and (5) of the Social Security (Recovery of Benefits) Regulations 1997). This has the effect that a compensator has no practical interest in appealing where the compensation payment has been reduced by the whole amount of recoverable benefits (*R(CR) 2/03*). The compensator has an interest only to the extent to which the amount of recoverable benefits *has not* been reflected in a reduction under this section, just as a claimant has an interest only to the extent to which the amount of recoverable benefits *has* been reflected in a reduction. Where, following a review or appeal, a compensator is obliged to make a further payment to the Secretary of State in a case where there was a reduction under this section, there are limited circumstances in which the reduction may be recalculated and the claimant may be required to make a refund to the compensator (*ibid.*, reg.11(6) and (7)).

Although neither s.8 nor Sch.2 refers to the period in respect of which recoverable benefits may be taken into account, it was suggested in *R(CR) 2/04* that benefits should be deducted under s.8 only in so far as they are payable in respect of the period for which compensation in respect of the relevant head of damages has been paid. The Commissioner also suggested that the calculation under s.8 should be made *before* the amount of compensation is reduced to take account of contributory negligence. However, as he also held that the proper operation of s.8 was a matter for the courts and not for tribunals or Commissioners, those suggestions are obiter dicta.

Section 8: supplementary

9.—(1) A person who makes a compensation payment calculated in accordance with section 8 must inform the person to whom the payment is made—
   (a) that the payment has been so calculated, and
   (b) of the date for payment by reference to which the calculation has been made.

(2) If the amount of a compensation payment calculated in accordance with section 8 is nil, a person giving a statement saying so is to be treated for the purposes of this Act as making a payment within section 1(1)(a) on the day on which he gives the statement.

(3) Where a person—
   (a) makes a compensation payment calculated in accordance with section 8, and
   (b) if the amount of the compensation payment so calculated is nil, gives a statement saying so,

he is to be treated, for the purpose of determining any rights and liabilities in respect of contribution or indemnity, as having paid the gross amount of the compensation payment.

(4) For the purposes of this Act—
   (a) the gross amount of the compensation payment is the amount of the compensation payment apart from section 8, and
   (b) the amount of any recoverable benefit is the amount determined in accordance with the certificate of recoverable benefits.

1.272

DEFINITIONS

"compensation payment"—see s.1(4)(b).
"gross amount of the compensation payment"—see subs.(4)(a).
"payment"—see s.29.
"recoverable benefit"—see s.1(4)(c).

Social Security (Recovery of Benefits) Act 1997

Reviews and appeals

Review of certificates of recoverable benefits

1.273   10.—[¹(1) Any certificate of recoverable benefits may be reviewed by the Secretary of State—
   (a) either within the prescribed period or in prescribed circumstances; and
   (b) either on an application made for the purpose or on his own initiative.]
(2) On a review under this section the Secretary of State may either—
   (a) confirm the certificate, or
   (b) (subject to subsection (3)) issue a fresh certificate containing such variations as he considers appropriate[¹ or
   (c) revoke the certificate.]
(3) The Secretary of State may not vary the certificate so as to increase the total amount of the recoverable benefits unless it appears to him that the variation is required as a result of the person who applied for the certificate supplying him with incorrect or insufficient information.

AMENDMENT

1. Social Security Act 1998, Sch.7, para.149 (March 4, 1999 for the making of regulations, November 29, 1999 for other purposes).

DEFINITIONS

"amount of the recoverable benefits"—see s.9(4)(b).
"prescribed"—see s.29.
"recoverable benefit"—see s.1(4)(c).
"regulations"—see s.29.

1.274   GENERAL NOTE

Subs. (1)

1.275   Note that the Social Security Act 1998 does not abolish the concept of review in this context. No period has been prescribed, so an application for review may be made at any time. The circumstances in which a decision may be reviewed are prescribed by reg.9 of the Social Security and Child Support (Decisions and Appeals) Regulations 1999 and are very broad. However, there is no right of appeal against a refusal to review a certificate of recoverable benefits so that it may be unwise to apply for a review instead of appealing if that might cause the time for appealing to expire, although pursuing that alternative course of action might be regarded as a reason for admitting a late appeal and subs.(3) provides protection on a review that is lacking on an appeal. Moreover, it is unnecessary to make a separate application for review before appealing because reg.9(d) of the 1999 Regulations provides that a decision may be reviewed if "a ground of appeal is satisfied under section 11 of the 1997 Act". In *CCR/3391/2005*, it was said that the Secretary of State should always consider reviewing a decision against which an appeal has been brought, so as to prevent unnecessary appeals reaching tribunals. "In effect, a submission to a tribunal should be an explanation for the Secretary of State not reviewing the decision in the light of the grounds of appeal." That approach is particularly necessary where the appellant has provided on the appeal evidence that was not before the Secretary of State either when the certificate of recoverable benefits was issued or when the benefits concerned were awarded so that there is a factual issue upon which the Secretary of State has not previously made a decision.

Subs. (3)

1.276   This is an important provision. Once a certificate has been issued, it cannot be varied on review so as to increase the amount of recoverable benefits unless the

(1997 c.27, s.10)

person who applied for the certificate (the compensator) caused the error. Where the compensator has provided incorrect or insufficient information as a result of being given incorrect or insufficient information by a claimant who knew it to be incorrect or insufficient and who provided it with intent to limit the amount of a reduction under s.8, the compensator may be able to recover from the claimant some or all of the additional money due to the Secretary of State (reg.11(6) and (7) of the Social Security (Recovery of Benefits) Regulations 1997). As the Secretary of State has only four weeks in which to issue the certificate (s.4(3)(b) and (8)(b)), it may occasionally be impossible to obtain accurate information and resort may be had to estimation (s.5(4)). If lack of information or an inaccurate estimate results in a calculation that turns out to be unfavourable to the Secretary of State, he is nevertheless bound by it until the certificate expires under s.4(4). However, any new certificate issued in respect of a later period may list the benefit omitted from the earlier one. Furthermore, subs.(3) does not prevent the amount of recoverable benefits from being increased on an appeal (*CSCS/1/1995*).

Appeals against certificates of recoverable benefits

11.—(1) An appeal against a certificate of recoverable benefits may be made on the ground—
   (a) that any amount, rate or period specified in the certificate is incorrect, or
   (b) that listed benefits which have been, or are likely to be, paid otherwise than in respect of the accident, injury or disease in question have been brought into account [¹ or
   (c) that listed benefits which have not been, and are not likely to be, paid to the injured person during the relevant period have been brought into account, or
   (d) that the payment on the basis of which the certificate was issued is not a payment within section 1(1)(a)].
(2) An appeal under this section may be made by—
   (a) the person who applied for the certificate of recoverable benefits, or
[¹(aa) (in a case where the certificate was issued under section 7(2)(a)) the person to whom it was so issued, or]
   (b) (in a case where the amount of the compensation payment has been calculated under section 8) the injured person or other person to whom the payment is made.
(3) No appeal may be made under this section until—
   (a) the claim giving rise to the compensation payment has been finally disposed of, and
   (b) the liability under section 6 has been discharged.
(4) For the purposes of subsection (3)(a), if an award of damages in respect of a claim has been made under or by virtue of—
   (a) section 32A(2)(a) of the Supreme Court Act 1981,
   (b) section 12(2)(a) of the Administration of Justice Act 1982, or
   (c) section 51(2)(a) of the County Courts Act 1984,
(orders for provisional damages in personal injury cases), the claim is to be treated as having been finally disposed of.
(5) Regulations may make provision—
   (a) as to the manner in which, and the time within which, appeals under this section may be made,
   (b) as to the procedure to be followed where such an appeal is made, and
   (c) for the purpose of enabling any such appeal to be treated as an application for review under section 10.
(6) [¹ . . .]

1.277

Social Security (Recovery of Benefits) Act 1997

AMENDMENT

1. Social Security Act 1998, Sch.7, para.150 and Sch.8 (November 29, 1999).

DEFINITIONS

"compensation payment"—see s.1(4)(b).
"injured person"—see s.1(4)(a).
"listed benefit"—see s.29.
"payment"—*ibid.*
"recoverable benefit"—see s.1(4)(c).
"regulations"—see s.29.

GENERAL NOTE

Subs.(1)

1.278 Any appeal is heard by an appeal tribunal constituted under the Social Security Act 1998 (see ss.12 and 29), with a further right of appeal to a Social Security Commissioner on a point of law (see ss.13 and 29).

It is not easy to see the distinction between paras (a) and (c), save perhaps that para.(a) more clearly allows a challenge to the Secretary of State's view as to the appropriate "relevant period". Both paragraphs appear to permit an appeal based on a dispute as to the amount of benefit actually paid to the claimant.

Paragraph (b) permits an appeal where there is a dispute as to whether benefit was paid "in respect of" the relevant accident, injury or disease (see the note to s.1). This is the ground on which most appeals are brought. The burden of proving that benefit was paid otherwise than in respect of the relevant accident, injury or disease is placed on the appellant but the Secretary of State can be expected to provide a prima facie justification for the inclusion of the benefits in the certificate in the first place (*CCR/4307/2000*) and an adverse inference may be drawn if he fails to do so. A tribunal considering an appeal under this section is entitled to reach a decision that is inconsistent with the decision awarding benefit because benefit that ought not to have been awarded cannot be said to have been awarded "in respect of" the relevant accident, injury or disease (*R(CR) 1/02*, a decision of a Tribunal of Commissioners, and *Eagle Star Insurance v Department for Social Development* (reported as *R1/01 (CRS)*), a decision of the Court of Appeal in Northern Ireland). Similarly, a tribunal is entitled to find that benefit was paid at too high a rate (*R(CR) 1/03*). In *C2/01–02(CRS)*, a Commissioner in Northern Ireland held that it was not the tribunal's function to substitute their judgment for the authority who awarded benefit and that the question was whether benefit had reasonably been awarded. Thus, if the awarding authority could properly have awarded benefit in respect of the relevant accident, injury or disease on the evidence before them and there is no new evidence, it will be impossible to show that benefit was awarded otherwise than in respect of the accident, injury or disease. However, in many cases a tribunal considering an appeal under s.11 will have before them evidence that was not before the authority awarding benefit and in those circumstances the tribunal's judgment will be the only one that can be applied. Where benefit may be awarded on a number of different bases and it is being alleged that benefit ought not to have been awarded or that the disablement justifying the award was not caused by the relevant accident, injury or disease, it is important for the tribunal to be able to infer from the evidence on which basis the benefit in question was actually awarded because only then is it possible to determine whether the claimant's circumstances justified that award. For instance, it is a gross over-simplification to believe that incapacity benefit is paid because a person is actually incapable of work. Establishing that the claimant was in fact capable of work may not demonstrate a lack of entitlement. The personal capability assessment is applicable to most claimants of incapacity benefit and an argument that a claimant ought not to have been treated as satisfying that assessment on account of the relevant accident, injury or disease requires evidence focused on the activities considered in such an assessment. Before a personal capability assessment is actually made, a

(1997 c.27, s.11)

claimant is usually treated as incapable of work under reg.28 of the Social Security (Incapacity for Work) (General) Regulations 1995 (see Vol.I of this work) on the basis of medical certificates provided by a doctor. In *R(CR) 2/02*, it was suggested by the Tribunal of Commissioners that as long as a claimant was providing such certificates referring to the relevant disease, benefit was properly awarded in respect of that disease whether or not the claimant was actually incapable of work or would actually have satisfied a personal capability assessment. Doubtless, there would be exceptions where, for instance, a claimant was working and so was required to be treated as capable of work under reg.16 of the 1995 Regulations. It may also be arguable that, where a claimant had obtained the medical certificate by misleading his doctor as to the severity of his or her condition or, perhaps, where the doctor plainly ought not to have given a certificate, benefit can be said not to have been properly paid in respect of the relevant accident, injury or disease but, given that a medical certificate merely certifies that the claimant was advised not to work and is not actually a certificate that the person is incapable of work (see Sch.1 to the Social Security (Medical Evidence) Regulations 1976), it will not be easy to demonstrate that a certificate was inappropriate. However, *R(CR) 2/02* was distinguished in *R(CR) 1/04*. In the latter case, incapacity benefit had been awarded pending the carrying out of a personal capability assessment on the basis of medical certificates supplied by the claimant's doctor, which referred to an eye injury sustained when a fire extinguisher had gone off accidentally. The Commissioner found that the eye injury caused by the fire extinguisher had in fact had no disabling effect on the claimant after a week and that the disablement was the result of a pre-existing condition in the claimant's eye and, later, from both that cause and a depressive illness. In those circumstances, he held that the incapacity benefit had not been paid "in respect of" the relevant accident, notwithstanding that the claimant had been deemed to be incapable of work on the strength of the medical certificates. Some claimants are not required to satisfy the personal capability assessment and are treated as being incapable of work under reg.10 or reg.27 of the 1995 Regulations. Again, a submission that benefit was not properly awarded would have to focus on the terms of those regulations.

Paragraph (d) permits an appeal where there is a dispute as to whether the Act applies at all because, for instance, it is claimed that compensation was not paid "in consequence of any accident, injury or disease" (see the note to s.1). If this paragraph is read with para. (b), it is plain that a claimant or compensator is also entitled to argue that a payment of compensation was not paid in respect of a particular injury and that benefits paid in respect of that injury should not have been brought into account. However, such an argument can be advanced only where it can be shown that the compensation was in fact paid in respect of some other injury or damage. Thus, in *CCR/2232/2006*, where the claimant had received £50,000 damages on the basis that injuries after a particular date were due solely to medical negligence, he was not entitled to argue on an appeal under this section that the injury was due to the accident that led to him being hospitalised rather then to the medical negligence and, in *CCR/2658/2006*, where a compensator settled a claim made on the basis that psychiatric injury was due to a particular cause, the compensator was not entitled to argue that the injury was due wholly to a cause not covered by the claim for compensation.

Note that no appeal lies under this section against a compensator's decision to make a reduction under s.8. Any dispute about such a reduction must be determined by the court seised of the claim for compensation, either when compensation is assessed or in enforcement proceedings. A claimant should not accept a payment into court or an offer of settlement if he or she is not prepared to accept that s.8 has been applied reasonably or at least that the net award of compensation is adequate (see *R(CR) 2/03* and *R(CR) 2/04*).

Subs.(2)

A compensator always has a right of appeal but in fact has no interest in appealing insofar as the amount of compensation was reduced under s.8, due to the effect of

1.279

reg.11(5) of the Social Security (Recovery of Benefits) Regulations 1997 which requires the recalculation of the s.8 reduction if the appeal is successful (*R(CR) 2/03*). An injured person has a right of appeal only if there has been a s.8 reduction. In any appeal under this section, any other person who could have appealed is made a party to the proceedings (see the definition of "party to the proceedings" in reg.1(3) of the Social Security and Child Support (Decisions and Appeals) Regulations 1999). In *CCR/3425/2003*, the Commissioner said that, as a claimant was entitled to be a party to a compensator's appeal only where there had been a deduction under s.8, it was to be inferred that the right to respond arose because the claimant might be entitled to a refund from the compensator under reg.11(5) of the 1997 Regulations, rather than because the Secretary of State might decide to revise or supersede an award of benefit, if the compensator was successful. Accordingly, as the claimant did not support the compensator's appeal and did not seek a refund, he had suffered no material loss when he had been misled by a letter from the Department suggesting that he need not attend the hearing. If both the claimant and the compensator appeal, the Compensation Recovery Unit should inform the clerk to the appeal tribunal and ask for the appeals to be heard together (*CCR/2231/2003*).

Subs. (3)

1.280 An appeal cannot be brought until after the compensation claim has been fully disposed of and the s.6 payment has been paid to the Secretary of State. A claim is not finally disposed of until any appeal against a court's order or judgment is determined (*Williams v Devon CC* [2003] EWCA Civ. 365 (*The Times*, March 26, 2003)) and so presumably the reference to the s.6 payment having been made must include any further payments required under reg.9 of the Social Security (Recovery of Benefits) Regulations 1997 in the event of a claimant's appeal being successful and requiring a further payment of compensation to be made. Generally, payment of compensation is made following the settlement of a claim, which implies agreement by the claimant as to the net amount of compensation to be paid after any reduction under s.8. However, where a court assesses compensation, it is not obliged at that stage to assess the appropriate amount of any reduction under s.8. That is left to the compensator. It was suggested in *R(CR) 2/04* that if the claimant wishes to challenge the amount of a s.8 reduction, he or she can do so in enforcement proceedings brought on the basis that the compensator has not fully satisfied the court's judgment.

See reg.31(3) of the Social Security and Child Support (Decisions and Appeals) Regulations 1999 for the time within which an appeal to a tribunal must be brought.

Subs. (5)

1.281 See regs 29, 31(3) and (4), 32–34, 38–40, 42–51 and 53–57 of the Social Security and Child Support (Decisions and Appeals) Regulations 1999. Note that reg.29(6) has been made under subs.(5)(c). Note also that a tribunal considering an appeal under this section has no express power either to refer the victim for examination or to examine him themselves because the primary legislation contains no power equivalent to s.20 of the Social Security Act 1998 under which regs 41 and 52 of the 1999 Regulations are made.

Reference of questions to medical appeal tribunal

1.282 **12.**—[[1](1) The Secretary of State must refer an appeal under section 11 to an appeal tribunal.]

(2) [[1]. . .]

(3) In determining [[1] any appeal under section 11], the tribunal must take into account any decision of a court relating to the same, or any similar, issue arising in connection with the accident, injury or disease in question.

(4) On [[1] an appeal under section 11 an appeal tribunal] may either—
   (a) confirm the amounts, rates and periods specified in the certificate of recoverable benefits, or

(1997 c.27, s.12)

   (b) specify any variations which are to be made on the issue of a fresh certificate under subsection (5) [¹ or

   (c) declare that the certificate of recoverable benefits is to be revoked.]

(5) When the Secretary of State has received [¹the decision of the tribunal on the appeal under section 11, he must in accordance with that decision] either—

   (a) confirm the certificate against which the appeal was brought, or

   (b) issue a fresh certificate [¹ or

   (c) revoke the certificate.]

(6) [¹ . . .]

(7) Regulations [¹ . . .] may (among other things) provide for the nondisclosure of medical advice or medical evidence given or submitted following a reference under subsection (1).

(8) [¹ . . .]

AMENDMENT

1. Social Security Act 1998, Sch.7, para.151 and Sch.8 (November 29, 1999).

DEFINITIONS

"appeal tribunal"—see s.29.
"recoverable benefit"—see s.1(4)(c).
"regulations"—see s.29.

GENERAL NOTE

The reference in the heading to a "medical appeal tribunal" has become an anachronism now that such tribunals have been replaced by the appeal tribunals introduced by the Social Security Act 1998.

1.283

Subs. (1)

An appeal under s.11(1)(b) must be heard by a tribunal consisting of a legally qualified panel member and a medically qualified panel member, whereas appeals under s.11(1)(a), (c) or (d) are heard by a legally qualified panel member sitting alone (reg.36 of the Social Security and Child Support (Decisions and Appeals) Regulations 1999). What happens if an appeal is brought under both para.(b) and one of the other paragraphs is unclear. Note that the primary legislation includes no provision equivalent to s.20 of the Social Security Act 1998. Therefore, even when the tribunal includes a medically qualified panel member, the tribunal has no express power to examine the victim, although there is also no express prohibition on such an examination. Presumably the victim could consent to an examination. There is not even any express power to refer a victim for examination but it is difficult to see any objection to there being such a reference, provided the victim were to consent and some arrangement could be made for the payment of an examining doctor.

1.284

Subs. (3)

Note that the tribunal need only "take into account" any decision of a court; it is not bound by such a decision. This is partly because it would be unfair on the Secretary of State to be bound by a decision in proceedings to which he was not a party (*R(CR) 1/02*). Most proceedings before courts are settled and do not result in reasoned decisions but claimants and compensators are expected to act before a tribunal in a manner that is consistent with the way they have settled a case or, in the case of a claimant, have claimed benefits. Thus a tribunal should be slow to accept an argument advanced by a compensator that is inconsistent with a section 8 deduction that it has made, unless the claimant agrees that the deduction

1.285

should not have been made, and, equally, a tribunal should be slow to accept an argument advanced by a claimant that is inconsistent with the basis on which compensation was obtained or benefits were claimed (*R(CR) 2/03*). Where a claimant had accepted £50,000 in respect of a claim that injury in respect of which benefits had been paid was due solely to medical negligence, he was not entitled to argue that the benefits were paid otherwise than in respect of that injury (*CCR/2232/2006*).

Similarly, where a compensator had settled a claim made on the basis that psychiatric injury was due to a particular cause, the compensator was not entitled to argue that the injury was due wholly to a cause not covered by the claim for compensation (*CCR/2658/2006*).

Subs. (4)

1.286 In *CCR/4/1993* and *CSCR/1/1995*, Commissioners held that, on appeals, the Secretary of State was entitled to refer to the tribunal questions which related to benefits that were not on the original "certificates of total benefit" (the forerunners of certificates of recoverable benefits). In the first case the Commissioner held that, on an appeal, all matters were at large. In the second case, the Commissioner took a narrower approach and held that a tribunal were strictly confined to the issues referred to them by the Secretary of State but that, in that case, the new benefits were within the scope of the reference. The Commissioner noted the contrast between the position on appeal and the limitation, now contained in s.10(3), with respect to reviews and warned of the perils of appealing.

Under the new legislation as amended, what are before the tribunal by virtue of subs.(1) are the "appeal" under s.11 and all matters that can fairly be said to arise within that appeal—and within the jurisdiction of the tribunal bearing in mind its constitution (see the note to subs.(1) above). There is no provision in this Act equivalent to s.12(8)(a) of the Social Security Act 1998, but it is suggested that the approach should be the same: the tribunal may deal with issues not expressly raised by the notice of appeal but are not bound to do so, provided they exercise that discretion judicially.

Subs. (7)

1.287 See reg.42 of the Social Security and Child Support (Decisions and Appeals) Regulations 1999.

Appeal to Social Security Commissioner

1.288 **13.**—(1) An appeal may be made to a Commissioner against any decision of [¹ an appeal tribunal] under section 12 on the ground that the decision was erroneous in point of law.

(2) An appeal under this section may be made by—
(a) the Secretary of State,
(b) the person who applied for the certificate of recoverable benefits,
[¹(bb) (in a case where that certificate was issued under section 7(2)(a)) the person to whom it was issued, or]
(c) (in a case where the amount of the compensation payment has been calculated in accordance with section 8) the injured person or other person to whom the payment is made.

(3) [¹Subsections (7) to (12) of section 14 of the Social Security Act 1998] apply to appeals under this section as they apply to appeals under that section.

(4) [¹. . .]

AMENDMENT

1. Social Security Act 1998, Sch.7, para.152 and Sch.8 (November 29, 1999).

(1997 c.27, s.13)

DEFINITIONS

"appeal tribunal"—see s.29.
"Commissioner"—*ibid.*
"compensation payment"—see s.1(4)(b).
"injured person"—see s.1(4)(a).

GENERAL NOTE

Subs. (1)
For the scope of the phrase "erroneous in point of law", see the note to s.14 of the Social Security Act 1998.

The terms of s.15 of the 1998 Act are wide enough to permit an appeal to an appropriate court against a decision of a Commissioner given under this section.

1.289

Subs. (3)
Section 14(10) of the Social Security Act 1998 provides that an appeal may be brought only with the leave of a tribunal chairman or a Commissioner and s.14(11) enables procedure regulations to be made as to the time within which applications for leave must be made (see reg.58 of the Social Security and Child Support (Decisions and Appeals) Regulations 1999 and the Social Security Commissioners (Procedure) Regulations 1999).

1.290

Reviews and appeals: supplementary

14.—(1) This section applies in cases where a fresh certificate of recoverable benefits is issued as a result of a review under section 10 or an appeal under section 11.

1.291

(2) If—
(a) a person has made one or more payments to the Secretary of State under section 6, and
(b) in consequence of the review or appeal, it appears that the total amount paid is more than the amount that ought to have been paid,

regulations may provide for the Secretary of State to pay the difference to that person, or to the person to whom the compensation payment is made, or partly to one and partly to the other.

(3) If—
(a) a person has made one or more payments to the Secretary of State under section 6, and
(b) in consequence of the review or appeal, it appears that the total amount paid is less than the amount that ought to have been paid,

regulations may provide for that person to pay the difference to the Secretary of State.

(4) Regulations under this section may provide—
(a) for the re-calculation in accordance with section 8 of the amount of any compensation payment,
(b) for giving credit for amounts already paid, and
(c) for the payment by any person of any balance or the recovery from any person of any excess,

and may provide for any matter by modifying this Act.

DEFINITIONS

"compensation payment"—see s.1(4)(b).
"payment"—see s.29.

Social Security (Recovery of Benefits) Act 1997

"recoverable benefit"—see s.1(4)(c).
"regulations"—see s.29.

GENERAL NOTE

1.292 See reg.11 of the Social Security (Recovery of Benefits) Regulations 1997.

Courts

Court orders

1.293 **15.**—(1) This section applies where a court makes an order for a compensation payment to be made in any case, unless the order is made with the consent of the injured person and the person by whom the payment is to be made.

(2) The court must, in the case of each head of compensation listed in column 1 of Schedule 2 to which any of the compensation payment is attributable, specify in the order the amount of the compensation payment which is attributable to that head.

DEFINITIONS

"compensation payment"—see s.1(4)(b).
"injured person"—see s.1(4)(a).

GENERAL NOTE

Subs. (2)

1.294 A court hearing a case within five years of a relevant accident must specify the amount of the compensation awarded that was attributable to any particular head in col.1 of Sch.2 in respect of the whole five-year period, because the court cannot know when payment of the sum awarded will actually be made (*Mitchell v Laing*, 1998 S.C. 342). Nonetheless, the compensator was to deduct only those benefits that had been paid or were due to be paid up until the date of the payment of the sum awarded by the court.

The court's view must be taken into account by any tribunal considering an appeal against a certificate of recoverable benefits (see s.12(3)) and, presumably, also by the Secretary of State considering a review (see reg.9(d) of the Social Security and Child Support (Decisions and Appeals) Regulations 1999). However, the principal purpose of s.15(2) is to enable s.8 to be operated properly. There is no express requirement to state the period in respect of which each head of the compensation is paid (which, it has been suggested in *R(CR) 2/04*, is a material fact limiting the amount of any deduction under s.8) but that information will usually be clear from the court's reasoning.

Payments into court

1.295 **16.**—(1) Regulations may make provision (including provision modifying this Act) for any case in which a payment into court is made.

(2) The regulations may (among other things) provide—
   (a) for the making of a payment into court to be treated in prescribed circumstances as the making of a compensation payment,
   (b) for application for, and issue of, certificates of recoverable benefits, and
   (c) for the relevant period to be treated as ending on a date determined in accordance with the regulations.

(1997 c.27, s.16)

(3) Rules of court may make provision governing practice and procedure in such cases.

(4) This section does not extend to Scotland.

Definitions

"compensation payment"—see s.1(4)(b).
"recoverable benefit"—see s.1(4)(c).
"payment"—see s.29.
"prescribed"—*ibid.*
"regulations"—*ibid.*
"relevant period"—see s.3.

General Note

Subss. (1) and (2)
Regulation 8 of the Social Security (Recovery of Benefits) Regulations 1997 provides that a payment into court is treated as a compensation payment under the Social Security (Recovery of Benefits) Act 1997 and a current certificate of recoverable benefits must be lodged with it (reg.8(1)). However, the liability of the compensator under s.6 of the Act to pay the Secretary of State the recoverable benefits does not arise until notice has been given that all or part of the payment into court has been paid to the victim (reg.8(2)). If the payment into court is accepted by the victim within 21 days, the "relevant period" under s.3 is taken to have ended on the date the money, or the last part of it, was paid into court (reg.8(3)). If, however, the case is settled after that 21 days have expired and the money is paid to the victim by consent in satisfaction of the claim, the "relevant period" is taken to have ended on the date on which the application to the court for the payment is made (reg.8(4)). If all or part of the money in court is paid to the victim following an order of the court, the "relevant period" is taken to have ended on the date of the order (reg.8(5)). If the whole of the payment into court is returned to the defendant, the making of the payment into court ceases to be treated as the making of a compensation payment and there is no liability to pay anything to the Secretary of State (reg.8(7)).

1.296

Subs. (3)
See CPR. r.36.23 and PD 36, para.10. Rule 36.23 provides—
"(1) This rule applies where a payment to a claimant following acceptance of a Part 36 offer or Part 36 payment into court would be a compensation payment as defined in section 1 of the Social Security (Recovery of Benefits) Act 1997.
(2) A defendant to a money claim may make an offer to settle the claim which will have the consequences set out in this Part, without making a Part 36 payment if—
   (a) at the time he makes the offer he has applied for, but not received, a certificate of recoverable benefit; and
   (b) he makes a Part 36 payment not more than 7 days after he receives the certificate.
(Section 1 of the 1997 Act defines 'recoverable benefit').
(3) A Part 36 payment notice must state—
   (a) the amount of gross compensation;
   (b) the name and amount of any benefit by which that gross amount is reduced in accordance with section 8 and Schedule 2 to the 1997 Act; and
   (c) that the sum paid in is the net amount after deduction of the amount of benefit.
(4) For the purposes of rule 36.20, a claimant fails to better a Part 36 payment if he fails to obtain judgment for more than the gross sum specified in the Part 36 payment notice.
(4A) For the purposes of rule 36.20(1)(c), where the court is determining whether the claimant has failed to obtain a judgment which is more advantageous

Social Security (Recovery of Benefits) Act 1997

than the Part 36 offer made under rule 36.2A, the amount of any lump sum paid into court which it takes into account is to be the amount of the gross sum specified in the Part 36 payment notice.
(5) Where—
   (a) a Part 36 payment has been made; and
   (b) application is made for the money remaining in court to be paid out, the court may treat the money in court as being reduced by a sum equivalent to any further recoverable benefits paid to the claimant since the date of payment into court and may direct payment out accordingly."

The effect of failing to "better a Part 36 payment" is usually that the claimant has to pay costs incurred by the defendant from the latest date the payment into court could have been accepted without the permission of the court. Rules 36.23(4) and, now, (4A) could therefore cause injustice in a case where the claimant was content to settle the case on the defendant's estimate of gross compensation but considered that the net sum paid in was too small because s.8 had not been applied properly. This was recognised in *Williams v Devon CC* [2003] EWCA Civ.365 (*The Times*, March 25, 2003), where it as held that a defendant's miscalculation of the amount to be deducted under s.8 could justify the court exercising its discretion under r.36.20 not to award the defendant his costs even though the claimant had not obtained judgment for more than the gross amount of compensation. *Williams* makes it clear that the claimant must be content with the amount of the s.8 reduction, or at least be content with the net amount of compensation, *before* deciding to accept the Pt 36 payment (see also *R(CR) 2/03* and *R(CR) 2/04* which confirm that there is no right of appeal to a tribunal against the amount of a s.8 reduction).

Benefits irrelevant to assessment of damages

1.297

17. In assessing damages in respect of any accident, injury or disease, the amount of any listed benefits paid or likely to be paid is to be disregarded.

DEFINITION

"listed benefit"—see s.29.

GENERAL NOTE

1.298

Benefits are disregarded not only when assessing damages but also when calculating interest on the damages, so that recoverable benefits are not to be deducted from damages for loss of earnings before calculating the interest due (*Wisely v John Fulton (Plumbers) Ltd, Wadey v Surrey CC* [2000] 1 W.L.R. 820 (HL)).

Reduction of compensation: complex cases

Lump sum and periodical payments

1.299

18.—(1) Regulations may make provision (including provision modifying this Act) for any case in which two or more compensation payments in the form of lump sums are made by the same person to or in respect of the injured person in consequence of the same accident, injury or disease.
(2) The regulations may (among other things) provide—
   (a) for the re-calculation in accordance with section 8 of the amount of any compensation payment,
   (b) for giving credit for amounts already paid, and

(1997 c.27, s.18)

(c) for the payment by any person of any balance or the recovery from any person of any excess.

(3) For the purposes of subsection (2), the regulations may provide for the gross amounts of the compensation payments to be aggregated and for—

(a) the aggregate amount to be taken to be the gross amount of the compensation payment for the purposes of section 8,

(b) so much of the aggregate amount as is attributable to a head of compensation listed in column 1 of Schedule 2 to be taken to be the part of the gross amount which is attributable to that head;

and for the amount of any recoverable benefit shown against any head in column 2 of that Schedule to be taken to be the amount determined in accordance with the most recent certificate of recoverable benefits.

(4) Regulations may make provision (including provision modifying this Act) for any case in which, in final settlement of the injured person's claim, an agreement is entered into for the making of—

(a) periodical compensation payments (whether of an income or capital nature), or

(b) periodical compensation payments and lump sum compensation payments.

(5) Regulations made by virtue of subsection (4) may (among other things) provide—

(a) for the relevant period to be treated as ending at a prescribed time,

(b) for the person who is to make the payments under the agreement to be treated for the purposes of this Act as if he had made a single compensation payment on a prescribed date.

(6) A periodical payment may be a compensation payment for the purposes of this section even though it is a small payment (as defined in Part II of Schedule 1).

DEFINITIONS

"amount of any recoverable benefit"—see s.9(4)(b).
"compensation payment"—see s.1(4)(b).
"gross amount of the compensation payment"—see s.9(4)(a).
"injured person"—see s.29.
"recoverable benefit"—see s.1(4)(c).
"payment"—see s.29.
"prescribed"—*ibid.*
"regulations"—*ibid.*
"the relevant period"—see s.3.

GENERAL NOTE

Subss. (1)–(3)
See reg.9 of the Social Security (Recovery of Benefits) Regulations 1997. **1.300**

Subss. (4)–(6)
See reg.10 of the Social Security (Recovery of Benefits) Regulations 1997. **1.301**

Payments by more than one person

19.—(1) Regulations may make provision (including provision modifying this Act) for any case in which two or more persons ("the compensators") **1.302**

make compensation payments to or in respect of the same injured person in consequence of the same accident, injury or disease.

(2) In such a case, the sum of the liabilities of the compensators under section 6 is not to exceed the total amount of the recoverable benefits, and the regulations may provide for determining the respective liabilities under that section of each of the compensators.

(3) The regulations may (among other things) provide in the case of each compensator—
- (a) for determining or re-determining the part of the recoverable benefits which may be taken into account in his case,
- (b) for calculating or re-calculating in accordance with section 8 the amount of any compensation payment,
- (c) for giving credit for amounts already paid, and
- (d) for the payment by any person of any balance or the recovery from any person of any excess.

DEFINITIONS

"amount of any recoverable benefit"—see s.9(4)(b).
"compensation payment"—see s.1(4)(b).
"compensator"—see subs.(1).
"injured person"—see s.1(4)(a).
"recoverable benefit"—see s.1(4)(c).
"payment"—see s.29.
"regulations"—*ibid.*
"the relevant period"—see s.3.

GENERAL NOTE

1.303   See reg.9 of the Social Security (Recovery of Benefits) Regulations 1997. Note that the liability for benefits paid before the making of the first compensation payment generally falls on the compensator who makes that payment and there is no provision for apportionment as such. Compensators therefore need to co-operate among themselves to ensure that the burden of making payments to the Secretary of State is shared appropriately. Note also that no provision can be made for cases where a claimant's disablement is attributable to two successive accidents caused by the negligence or breach of statutory duty of different compensators. The payment of benefits in consequence of the disablement must therefore be attributed solely to one accident or the other so that only one of the compensators is liable to make payments to the Secretary of State (*R(CR) 2/04* and see the note to s.1 for how the attribution is to be made).

Miscellaneous

Amounts overpaid under section 6

1.304   **20.**—(1) Regulations may make provision (including provision modifying this Act) for cases where a person has paid to the Secretary of State under section 6 any amount ("the amount of the overpayment") which he was not liable to pay.

(2) The regulations may provide—
- (a) for the Secretary of State to pay the amount of the overpayment to that person, or to the person to whom the compensation payment is made, or partly to one and partly to the other, or

(b) for the receipt by the Secretary of State of the amount of the overpayment to be treated as the recovery of that amount.

(3) Regulations made by virtue of subsection (2)(b) are to have effect in spite of anything in section 71 of the Social Security Administration Act 1992 (overpayments—general).

(4) The regulations may also (among other things) provide—
(a) for the re-calculation in accordance with section 8 of the amount of any compensation payment,
(b) for giving credit for amounts already paid, and
(c) for the payment by any person of any balance or the recovery from any person of any excess.

(5) This section does not apply in a case where section 14 applies.

DEFINITIONS

"compensation payment"—see s.1(4)(b).
"payment"—see s.29.
"regulations"—*ibid.*
"the amount of the overpayment"—see subs.(1).

GENERAL NOTE

No regulations have been made under this section. 1.305

Compensation payments to be disregarded

21.—(1) If, when a compensation payment is made, the first and second conditions are met, the payment is to be disregarded for the purposes of sections 6 and 8. 1.306

(2) The first condition is that the person making the payment—
(a) has made an application for a certificate of recoverable benefits which complies with subsection (3), and
(b) has in his possession a written acknowledgement of the receipt of his application.

(3) An application complies with this subsection if it—
(a) accurately states the prescribed particulars relating to the injured person and the accident, injury or disease in question, and
(b) specifies the name and address of the person to whom the certificate is to be sent.

(4) The second condition is that the Secretary of State has not sent the certificate to the person, at the address, specified in the application, before the end of the period allowed under section 4.

(5) In any case where—
(a) by virtue of subsection (1), a compensation payment is disregarded for the purposes of sections 6 and 8, but
(b) the person who made the compensation payment nevertheless makes a payment to the Secretary of State for which (but for subsection (1)) he would be liable under section 6,
subsection (1) is to cease to apply in relation to the compensation payment.

(6) If, in the opinion of the Secretary of State, circumstances have arisen which adversely affect normal methods of communication—
(a) he may by order provide that subsection (1) is not to apply during a specified period not exceeding three months, and

(b) he may continue any such order in force for further periods not exceeding three months at a time.

DEFINITIONS

"compensation payment"—see s.1(4)(b).
"injured person"—see s.29.
"payment"—see s.29.
"prescribed—*ibid.*
"recoverable benefit"—see s.1(4)(c).

GENERAL NOTE

1.307   If a certificate of recoverable benefits is not issued within four weeks (subject to subs.(6)) following receipt and acknowledgement of a full and accurate application, the Secretary of State loses his right of recovery. It is clear from subs.(4) that the late issue of a certificate will not do. However, if the compensator makes a payment to the Secretary of State in error – perhaps in reliance on an expired certificate – the Secretary of State is not obliged to pay it back because the dispensation under this section ceases to apply (subs.(5)). For the date on which an application is treated as received, see reg.7(2) of the Social Security (Recovery of Benefits) Regulations 1997 which is made under s.4(9).

Subs.(3)

1.308   For the prescribed particulars, see reg.7(1) of the Social Security (Recovery of Benefits) Regulations 1997.

Subs.(4)

1.309   The period allowed under s.4(3) and (8) is four weeks, but see s.21(6).

Subs.(5)

1.310   It is not clear whether the Secretary of State can, by issuing an out of time certificate, insist on obtaining more than the payment made by the compensator or whether he is confined to accepting what has been sent, which is likely to have been based on an earlier certificate.

1.311   **22.** *Omitted.*

Provision of information

1.312   **23.**—(1) Where compensation is sought in respect of any accident, injury or disease suffered by any person ("the injured person"), the following persons must give the Secretary of State the prescribed information about the injured person—
(a) anyone who is, or is alleged to be, liable in respect of the accident, injury or disease, and
(b) anyone acting on behalf of such a person.
(2) A person who receives or claims a listed benefit which is or is likely to be paid in respect of an accident, injury or disease suffered by him, must give the Secretary of State the prescribed information about the accident, injury or disease.
(3) Where a person who has received a listed benefit dies, the duty in subsection (2) is imposed on his personal representative.
(4) Any person who makes a payment (whether on his own behalf or not)—

(a) in consequence of, or

(b) which is referable to any costs (in Scotland, expenses) incurred by reason of,

any accident, injury or disease, or any damage to property, must, if the Secretary of State requests him in writing to do so, give the Secretary of State such particulars relating to the size and composition of the payment as are specified in the request.

(5) The employer of a person who suffers or has suffered an accident, injury or disease, and anyone who has been the employer of such a person at any time during the relevant period, must give the Secretary of State the prescribed information about the payment of statutory sick pay in respect of that person.

(6) In subsection (5) "employer" has the same meaning as it has in Part XI of the Social Security Contributions and Benefits Act 1992.

(7) A person who is required to give information under this section must do so in the prescribed manner, at the prescribed place and within the prescribed time.

(8) Section 1 does not apply in relation to this section.

DEFINITIONS

"employer"—see subs.(6).
"injured person"—see subs.(1) (and subs.(8), disapplying s.1).
"listed benefit"—see s.29.
"payment"—*ibid.*
"prescribed"—*ibid.*
"the relevant period"—see s.3.

GENERAL NOTE

Subs.(1)
See reg.3 of the Social Security (Recovery of Benefits) Regulations 1997.   1.313

Subs.(2)
See reg.4 of the Social Security (Recovery of Benefits) Regulations 1997.   1.314

Subs.(5)
See reg.5 of the Social Security (Recovery of Benefits) Regulations 1997.   1.315

Subs.(7)
See reg.6 of the Social Security (Recovery of Benefits) Regulations 1997.   1.316

Power to amend Schedule 2

24.—(1) The Secretary of State may by regulations amend Schedule 2.   1.317

(2) A statutory instrument which contains such regulations shall not be made unless a draft of the instrument has been laid before and approved by resolution of each House of Parliament.

DEFINITION

"regulations"—see s.29.

Social Security (Recovery of Benefits) Act 1997

Provisions relating to Northern Ireland

25.–27. *Omitted.*

General

The Crown

28. This Act applies to the Crown.

GENERAL NOTE

This is effectively a new provision because s.104 of the Social Security Administration Act 1992 was never brought into force (see Social Security (Consequential Provisions) Act 1992, Sch.4, para.3).

General interpretation

29. In this Act—
[1"appeal tribunal" means an appeal tribunal constituted under Chapter I of Part I of the Social Security Act 1998,]
"benefit" means any benefit under the Social Security Contributions and Benefits Act 1992, a jobseeker's allowance or mobility allowance,
[1"Commissioner" has the same meaning as in Chapter II of Part I of the Social Security Act 1998 (see section 39),]
"compensation scheme for motor accidents" means any scheme or arrangement under which funds are available for the payment of compensation in respect of motor accidents caused, or alleged to have been caused, by uninsured or unidentified persons,
"listed benefit" means a benefit listed in column 2 of Schedule 2,
"payment" means payment in money or money's worth, and related expressions are to be interpreted accordingly,
"prescribed" means prescribed by regulations, and
"regulations" means regulations made by the Secretary of State.

AMENDMENT

1. Social Security Act 1998, Sch.7, para.153 (November 29, 1999).

Regulations and orders

30.—(1) Any power under this Act to make regulations or an order is exercisable by statutory instrument.

(2) A statutory instrument containing regulations or an order under this Act (other than regulations under section 24 or an order under section 34) shall be subject to annulment in pursuance of a resolution of either House of Parliament.

(3) Regulations under section 20, under section 24 amending the list of benefits in column 2 of Schedule 2 or under paragraph 9 of Schedule 1 may not be made without the consent of the Treasury.

(4) Subsections (4), (5), (6) and (9) of section 189 of the Social Security Administration Act 1992 (regulations and orders—general) apply for the purposes of this Act as they apply for the purposes of that.

DEFINITIONS

"benefit"—see s.29.
"regulations"—*ibid.*

31. *Omitted.*

Power to make transitional, consequential etc. provisions

32.—(1) Regulations may make such transitional and consequential provisions, and such savings, as the Secretary of State considers necessary or expedient in preparation for, in connection with, or in consequence of—
 (a) the coming into force of any provision of this Act, or
 (b) the operation of any enactment repealed or amended by a provision of this Act during any period when the repeal or amendment is not wholly in force.
(2) Regulations under this section may (among other things) provide—
 (a) for compensation payments in relation to which, by virtue of section 2, this Act does not apply to be treated as payments in relation to which this Act applies,
 (b) for compensation payments in relation to which, by virtue of section 2, this Act applies to be treated as payments in relation to which this Act does not apply, and
 (c) for the modification of any enactment contained in this Act or referred to in subsection (1)(b) in its application to any compensation payment.

DEFINITIONS

"compensation payment"—see s.1(4)(b).
"payment"—see s.29.
"regulations"—*ibid.*

GENERAL NOTE

See reg.12 of the Social Security (Recovery of Benefits) Regulations 1997.

33. *Omitted.*

Short title, commencement and extent

34.—(1) This Act may be cited as the Social Security (Recovery of Benefits) Act 1997.
(2) Sections 1 to 24, 26 to 28 and 33 are to come into force on such day as the Secretary of State may by order appoint, and different days may be appointed for different purposes.
(3) Apart from sections 25 to 27, section 33 so far as it relates to any enactment which extends to Northern Ireland, and this section this Act does not extend to Northern Ireland.

GENERAL NOTE

Some regulation-making powers were brought into force on September 3, 1997 but the main provisions of the Act came into force on October 6, 1997 (see the Social Security (Recovery of Benefits) Act 1997 (Commencement Order) 1997 (SI 1997/2085)).

Social Security (Recovery of Benefits) Act 1997

SCHEDULES

Schedule 1

Compensation Payments

Part I

Exempted payments

1.329

1. Any small payment (defined in Part II of this Schedule).

2. Any payment made to or for the injured person under section 35 of the Powers of Criminal Courts Act 1973 or section 249 of the Criminal Procedure (Scotland) Act 1995 (compensation orders against convicted persons).

3. Any payment made in the exercise of a discretion out of property held subject to a trust in a case where no more than 50 per cent. by value of the capital contributed to the trust was directly or indirectly provided by persons who are, or are alleged to be, liable in respect of—
   (a) the accident, injury or disease suffered by the injured person, or
   (b) the same or any connected accident, injury or disease suffered by another.

4. Any payment made out of property held for the purposes of any prescribed trust (whether the payment also falls within paragraph 3 or not).

5. Any payment made to the injured person by an insurance company within the meaning of the Insurance Companies Act 1982 under the terms of any contract of insurance entered into between the injured person and the company before—
   (a) the date on which the injured person first claims a listed benefit in consequence of the disease in question, or
   (b) the occurrence of the accident or injury in question.

6. Any redundancy payment falling to be taken into account in the assessment of damages in respect of an accident, injury or disease.

7. So much of any payment as is referable to costs.

8. Any prescribed payment.

Part II

Power to disregard small payments

1.330

9.—(1) Regulations may make provision for compensation payments to be disregarded for the purposes of sections 6 and 8 in prescribed cases where the amount of the compensation payment, or the aggregate amount of two or more connected compensation payments, does not exceed the prescribed sum.

(2) A compensation payment disregarded by virtue of this paragraph is referred to in paragraph 1 as a "small payment".

(3) For the purposes of this paragraph—
   (a) two or more compensation payments are "connected" if each is made to or in respect of the same injured person and in respect of the same accident, injury or disease, and
   (b) any reference to a compensation payment is a reference to a payment which would be such a payment apart from paragraph 1.

Definitions

"compensation payment"—see s.1(4)(b) and para.9(3)(b).
"connected"—see para.9(3)(a).
"injured person"—see s.1(4)(a).
"listed benefit" –see s.29.
"payment"—*ibid.*
"prescribed"—*ibid.*
"regulations"—*ibid.*
"small payment"—see para.9.

General Note

1.331

For exempted trusts and payments prescribed for the purposes of paras 4 and 8, see reg.2 of the Social Security (Recovery of Benefits) Regulations 1997.

(1997 c.27, Sch.1)

No regulations have been made under para.9. Under the former legislation, payments not exceeding £2,500 were disregarded. Now, general damages for pain and suffering are protected, because benefits can be recovered only from compensation for loss of earnings, care or loss of mobility, and so there is not considered to be a need for a general exemption for small claims.

SCHEDULE 2

CALCULATION OF COMPENSATION PAYMENT

(1) Head of compensation	(2) Benefit
1. Compensation for earnings lost during the relevant period	Disability working allowance
	Disablement pension payable under section 103 of the 1992 Act
	Incapacity benefit
	Income support
	Invalidity pension and allowance
	Jobseeker's allowance
	Reduced earnings allowance
	Severe disablement allowance
	Sickness benefit
	Statutory sick pay
	Unemployability supplement
	Unemployment benefit
2. Compensation for cost of care incurred during the relevant period	Attendance allowance
	Care component of disability living allowance
	Disablement pension increase payable under section 104 or 105 of the 1992 Act
3. Compensation for loss of mobility during the relevant period.	Mobility allowance
	Mobility component of disability living allowance

1.332

Notes

1.—(1) References to incapacity benefit, invalidity pension and allowance, severe disablement allowance, sickness benefit and unemployment benefit also include any income support paid with each of those benefits on the same instrument of payment or paid concurrently with each of those benefits by means of an instrument for benefit payment.

(2) For the purpose of this Note, income support includes personal expenses addition, special transitional additions and transitional addition as defined in the Income Support (Transitional) Regulations 1987.

2. Any reference to statutory sick pay—
  (a) includes only 80 per cent. of payments made between 6th April 1991 and 5th April 1994, and
  (b) does not include payments made on or after 6th April 1994.

3. In this Schedule "the 1992 Act" means the Social Security Contributions and Benefits Act 1992.

1.333

DEFINITIONS

"compensation payment"—see s.1(4)(b).
"payment"—*ibid.*
"the relevant period"—see s.3.

GENERAL NOTE

In *R(CR) 2/04*, the Commissioner commented that disablement pension was not, strictly speaking, paid in respect of loss of earnings.

In *Lowther v Chatwin* [2003] EWCA Civ 729, the claimant had to close her business due to injuries sustained in an accident. She had been trading at a loss but had been

1.334

able to pay 5/7ths of her business rent from the income of the business. She claimed damages in respect of her continuing liability to her landlord. The judge awarded her 5/7ths of the rent settlement and he held that that compensation was not for loss of earnings but for the destruction of the business. The Court of Appeal held that it was "compensation for earnings lost" and that the compensator was therefore entitled to deduct from that compensation the amount of relevant benefits paid to the claimant.

"Compensation for earnings lost" includes interest on damages for loss of earnings (*Griffiths v British Coal Corp* [2001] EWCA Civ 336 (*The Times*, March 13, 2001).

Given the way that ss.6 and 8 operate together, compensation for lost earnings presumably includes compensation for loss of *potential* earnings in the case of a person who was not employed at the time of a relevant accident or who was in temporary employment only. A benefit is recoverable only if it was paid "in respect of" the relevant accident, injury or disease (see the note to s.1).

"Compensation for cost of care" includes damages for services in the nature of care and domestic assistance given gratuitously, because the object of the legislation is to avoid double recovery as well as avoiding loss to the Secretary of State who had become liable to pay the benefits (*Griffiths v British Coal Corp* [2001] EWCA Civ 336; [2001] 1 W.L.R. 1493).

"Compensation for loss of mobility" in para.3, col.1 refers only to compensation for patrimonial (i.e. financial) loss, such as the cost of fares for journeys by bus or taxi, and does not refer to any element of solatium (i.e. compensation for pain and suffering or loss of amenity) (*Mitchell v Laing*, 1998 S.C. 342).

Schedules 3 and 4: Omitted.

Social Security Act 1998

(1998 c.14)

ARRANGEMENT OF SECTIONS

PART I

DECISIONS AND APPEALS

CHAPTER I

GENERAL

Decisions

1.335

1. Transfer of functions to Secretary of State.
2. Use of computers.
3. Use of information.

Appeals

4. Unified appeal tribunals.
5. President of appeal tribunals.
6. Panel for appointment to appeal tribunals.
7. Constitution of appeal tribunals.

(1998 c.14)

CHAPTER II

SOCIAL SECURITY DECISIONS AND APPEALS

Decisions

8. Decisions by Secretary of State.
9. Revision of decisions.
10. Decisons superseding earlier decisions.
10A. Reference of issues by Secretary of State to Inland Revenue.
11. Regulations with respect to decisions.

Appeals

12. Appeal to appeal tribunal.
13. Redetermination etc. of appeals by tribunal.
14. Appeal from tribunal to Commissioner.
15. Appeal from Commissioner on point of law.

Procedure etc.

16. Procedure.
17. Finality of decisions.
18. Matters arising as respects decisions.

Medical examinations

19. Medical examination required by Secretary of State.
20. Medical examination required by appeal tribunal.

Suspension and termination of benefit

21. Suspension in prescribed circumstances.
22. Suspension for failure to furnish information etc.
23. Termination in cases of failure to furnish information.
24. Suspension and termination for failure to submit to medical examination.

Appeals dependent on issues falling to be decided by Inland Revenue

24A. Appeals dependent on issues falling to be decided by Inland Revenue.

Decisions and appeals dependent on other cases

25. Decisions involving issues that arise on appeal in other cases.
26. Appeals involving issues that arise on appeal in other cases.

Social Security Act 1998

Cases of error

27. Restrictions on entitlement to benefit in certain cases of error.
28. Correct of errors and setting aside of decisions.

Industrial accidents

29. Decision that accident is an industrial accident.
30. Effect of decision.

Other special cases

31. Incapacity for work.
32. Industrial diseases.
33. Christmas bonus.

Housing benefit and council tax benefit

34. and 35. *Omitted.*

Social fund payment

36. to 38. *Omitted.*

Supplemental

39. Interpretation etc. of Chapter II.

CHAPTER III

OTHER DECISIONS AND APPEALS

40. to 47. *Omitted.*

PART II

CONTRIBUTIONS

48. to 66. *Omitted.*

PART III

BENEFITS

67. to 76. *Omitted.*

(1998 c.14)

Part IV

Miscellaneous and Supplemental

77. Pilot schemes.
78. *Omitted.*
79. Regulations and orders.
80. Parliamentary control of regulations.
81. Reports by Secretary of State.
82. *Omitted.*
83. *Omitted.*
84. Interpretation: general.
85. *Omitted.*
86. *Omitted.*
87. Short title, commencement and extent.

Schedules:

Schedule 1—Appeal tribunals: supplementary provisions.
Schedule 2—Decisions against which no appeal lies.
Schedule 3—Decisions against which an appeal lies.
  Part I—Benefit decisions.
  Part II—Contribution decisions.
Schedule 4—Social Security Commissioners.
Schedule 5—Regulations as to procedure: provision which may be made.
Schedule 6—*Omitted.*
Schedule 7—*Omitted.*
Schedule 8—*Omitted.*

An Act to make provision as to the making of decisions and the determination of appeals under enactments relating to social security, child support, vaccine damage payments and war pensions; to make further provision with respect to social security; and for connected purposes.

[21st May 1998]

Part I

Decisions and Appeals

Chapter I

General

Decisions

Transfer of functions to Secretary of State

1.336

1. The following functions are hereby transferred to the Secretary of State, namely—

Social Security Act 1998

(a) the functions of adjudication officers appointed under section 38 of the Social Security Administration Act 1992 ("the Administration Act");
(b) the functions of social fund officers appointed under section 64 of that Act; and
(c) the functions of child support officers appointed under section 13 of the Child Support Act 1991 ("the Child Support Act").

GENERAL NOTE

1.337   This is a transitional provision, transferring existing cases to the new system brought into effect under Chapter II. For the functions of adjudication officers, see s.20 of the Social Security Administration Act 1992 and s.9(6) of the Jobseekers Act 1995. Essentially, all questions arising on, or in connection with, a claim for benefit, other than those already reserved to the Secretary of State, were referred to adjudication officers. At first sight unifying the roles seems a major simplification but in fact it has not made a great deal of difference. The main practical distinction between adjudication officers' decisions and Secretary of State's decisions were that the former were appealable and the latter were not (except in a few cases). Now all decisions are made by the Secretary of State but provision is made for some decisions to be unappealable (Sch.2 to the Act and Sch.2 to the Social Security and Child Support (Decisions and Appeals) Regulations 1999) whereas others are appealable (s.12(1) and Sch.3 to the Act). Those that are unappealable are more or less the same decisions that were made by the Secretary of State under the old legislation; those that are appealable are generally the decisions formerly made by adjudication officers (but see the note to s.8(5)).

So far as they relate to working families' tax credit and disabled person's tax credit (both now abolished), the functions were further transferred to an officer of the Inland Revenue from October 5, 1999 (Tax Credits Act 1999, s.2(1)(b) and Sch.2, para.5(a)). From April 6, 2003, functions relating to child benefit and guardian's allowance were also transferred to the Commissioners of Inland Revenue (Tax Credits Act 2002, s.50(1) and (2)(e)). The functions of the Commissioners of Inland Revenue and officers of Inland Revenue have now been transferred to the Commissioners for Her Majesty's Revenue and Customs and officers of Revenue and Customs (Commissioners for Revenue and Customs Act 2005, ss.5 and 7).

Use of computers

1.338   **2.**—(1) Any decision, determination or assessment falling to be made or certificate falling to be issued by the Secretary of State under or by virtue of a relevant enactment, or in relation to a war pension, may be made or issued not only by an officer of his acting under his authority but also—
(a) by a computer for whose operation such an officer is responsible; and
(b) in the case of a decision, determination or assessment that may be made or a certificate that may be issued by a person providing services to the Secretary of State, by a computer for whose operation such a person is responsible.

(2) In this section "relevant enactment" means any enactment contained in—
(a) Chapter II of this Part;
(b) the Social Security Contributions and Benefits Act 1992 ("the Contributions and Benefits Act");
(c) the Administration Act;
(d) the Child Support Act;
(e) the Social Security (Incapacity for Work) Act 1994;

(1998 c.14, s.2)

(f) the Jobseekers Act 1995 ("the Jobseekers Act");
(g) the Child Support Act 1995; [¹ . . .]
(h) the Social Security (Recovery of Benefits) Act 1997 [¹ or
(i) the State Pension Credit Act 2002.]
(3) In this section and section 3 below "war pension" has the same meaning as in section 25 of the Social Security Act 1989 (establishment and functions of war pensions committees).

AMENDMENT

1. State Pension Credit Act 2002, Sch.1, para.5 and Sch.3 (July 2, 2002 for the purpose of exercising any power to make regulations or orders and April 7, 2003 for other purposes).

DEFINITIONS

"the Administration Act"—see s.84.
"the Child Support Act"—*ibid*.
"relevant enactment"—see subs.(2).
"war pension"—see subs.(3).

GENERAL NOTE

This section applies as though the Pension Schemes Act 1993 were a relevant enactment (Pension Schemes Act 1993, s.170(1)).

1.339

Use of information

3.—(1) Subsection (2) below applies to information relating to social security, child support or war pensions [¹, or employment or training] which is held—
(a) by the Secretary of State or the Northern Ireland Department; or
(b) by a person providing services to the Secretary of State or the Northern Ireland Department in connection with the provision of those services.
(2) Information to which this subsection applies—
(a) may be used for the purposes of, or for any purposes connected with, the exercise of functions in relation to social security, child support or war pensions [¹, or employment or training]; and
(b) may be supplied to, or to a person providing services to, the Secretary of State or the Northern Ireland Department for use for those purposes.
(3) [¹ . . .]
(4) In this section "the Northern Ireland Department" means the Department of Health and Social Services for Northern Ireland [¹ of for the Department for Employment and learning in Northern Ireland].

1.340

AMENDMENT

1. Employment Act 2002, Sch.6, paras 1 and 4 (September 9, 2002).

DEFINITIONS

"the Administration Act"—see s.84.
"the Northern Ireland Department"—see subs.(4).
"war pension"—see s.2(3).

Social Security Act 1998

Appeals

Unified appeal tribunals

1.341
4.—(1) Subject to the provisions of this Act—
  (a) the functions of social security appeal tribunals, disability appeal tribunals and medical appeal tribunals constituted under Part II of the Administration Act;
  (b) the functions of child support appeal tribunals established under section 21 of the Child Support Act; and
  (c) the functions of vaccine damage tribunals established by regulations made under section 4 of the Vaccine Damage Payments Act 1979 ("the Vaccine Damage Payments Act"),
are hereby transferred to appeal tribunals constituted under the following provisions of this Chapter.
  (2) Accordingly appeals under—
  (a) section 12 below;
  (b) section 20 of the Child Support Act, as substituted by section 42 below;
  (c) section 4 of the Vaccine Damage Payments Act, as substituted by section 46 below; and
  (d) section 11 of the Social Security (Recovery of Benefits) Act 1997,
shall be determined by appeal tribunals so constituted (in the following provisions of this Chapter referred to as "appeal tribunals").

DEFINITIONS

"the Administration Act"—see s.84.
"the Child Support Act"—*ibid*.
"the Vaccine Damage Payments Act"—*ibid*.

GENERAL NOTE

1.342
Like s.1, this is a transitional provision, bringing existing cases into the new system established under Chapter II. As with the changes wrought by s.1, the changes made by this section are not quite as dramatic as they might appear at first sight. Tribunals are unified in name but reg.36 of the Social Security and Child Support (Decisions and Appeals) Regulations 1999 provides that the composition of the tribunal is determined by the subject matter of the appeal. More importantly, the flexibility that one might hope for under a unified tribunal is somewhat reduced because it is far more difficult than it was before for tribunals to draw together all outstanding issues concerning a claimant and deal with them all at once. Everything must first be the subject of a decision by the Secretary of State and then be the subject of a separate appeal. The Secretary of State has no power to refer outstanding questions to a tribunal dealing with another case concerning the same claimant and tribunals no longer have an express power to deal with matters first arising before them (as there was in s.36 of the Social Security Administration Act 1992). See the note to s.12 for further discussion of the significance of these changes.

President of appeal tribunals

1.343
5.—(1) The Lord Chancellor may, after consultation with the Lord Advocate, appoint a President of appeal tribunals.
  (2) A person is qualified to be appointed President if—
  (a) he has a 10 year general qualification (construed in accordance with section 71 of the Courts and Legal Services Act 1990); or

(1998 c.14, s.5)

(b) he is an advocate or solicitor in Scotland of at least 10 years' standing.

(3) Schedule 1 to this Act shall have effect for supplementing this section.

DEFINITION

"appeal tribunal"—see s.4(2).

GENERAL NOTE

By the Transfer of Functions (Lord Advocate and Secretary of State) Order 1999, SI 1999/678, art.2(1) and Schedule, the functions of the Lord Advocate under this section are transferred to the Secretary of State.

1.344

Panel for appointment to appeal tribunals

6.—(1) The Lord Chancellor shall constitute a panel of persons to act as members of appeals tribunals.

(2) Subject to subsection (3) below, the panel shall be composed of such [³ persons appointed by the Lord Chancellor].

(3) The panel shall include persons possessing such qualifications as may be prescribed by regulations made with the concurrence of the Lord Chancellor.

[³ (3A) As part of the selection process for the appointment of a medical practitioner as a member of the panel, the Judicial Appointments Commission shall consult the Chief Medical Officer.]

(4) The numbers of persons appointed to the panel, and the terms and conditions of their appointments, shall be determined by the Lord Chancellor with the consent of the Secretary of State.

(5) A person may be removed from the panel by the Lord Chancellor on the ground of incapacity or misbehaviour [³; but the Lord Chancellor may remove such a person only with the concurrence of the appropriate senior judge].

[³ (5A) The appropriate senior judge is the Lord Chief Justice of England and Wales, unless the person to be removed exercises functions wholly or mainly in Scotland, in which case it is the Lord President of the Court of Session.]

(6) In this section "the Chief Medical Officer" means—
(a) in relation to England, the Chief Medical Officer of the Department of Health;
(b) in relation to Wales, the Chief Medical Officer of the [² National Assembly for Wales]; and
(c) in relation to Scotland, the Chief Medical Officer of the [¹ Scottish Administration]

1.345

DEFINITIONS

"appeal tribunal"—see s.4(2).
"Chief Medical Officer"—see subs.(5).
"prescribed"—see s.84.

AMENDMENTS

1. Scotland Act 1998 (Consequential Modifications) (No.1) Order 1999 (SI 1999/1042), art.5 and Sch.3, Pt I, para.4.
2. National Assembly for Wales (Transfer of Functions) Order 2000 (SI 2000/253), art.7 and Sch.5, para.3 (February 16, 2000).
3. Constitutional Reform Act 2005, Sch.4, paras 271 and 272 (April 3, 2006).

General Note

Subs. (3).

1.346
By reg.35 of, and Sch.3 to, the Social Security and Child Support (Decisions and Appeals) Regulations 1999, panel members must be lawyers, doctors, accountants or people other than doctors who are experienced in dealing with the needs of disabled persons. Other lay people no longer have a part to play in tribunals.

Quite a number of medically qualified panel members also work as examining medical practitioners providing reports for use by the Secretary of State when determining claims. In *Gillies v Secretary of State for Work and Pensions* [2006] UKHL 2; [2006] 1 W.L.R. 781 (also reported as *R(DLA) 5/06*), the House of Lords considered whether it was proper for a person who acted as an examining medical practitioner in some cases to sit as a member of a tribunal when reports of other examining medical practitioners were being challenged by claimants. Lord Hope of Craighead pointed out that the "fair-minded and informed observer" by whose standards fairness is to be judged must be taken to be neither complacent nor unduly sensitive or suspicious and to be able distinguish between what is relevant and what is irrelevant and decide what weight should be given to facts that are relevant. He then said:

"18. . . . A fair-minded observer who had considered the facts properly would appreciate that professional detachment and the ability to exercise her own independent judgment on medical issues lay at the heart of [the examining medical practitioner's] relationship with the [Benefits] Agency. He would also appreciate that she was just as capable of exercising those qualities when sitting as a medical member of a disability appeal tribunal. So there is no basis for a finding that there was a reasonable apprehension of bias on the ground that Dr Armstrong had a predisposition to favour the interests of the Benefits Agency. . . .

"20. . . . The fair-minded observer would understand that there was a crucial difference between approaching the issues which the tribunal had to decide with a predisposition in favour of the views of the EMP, and drawing upon her medical knowledge and experience when testing those views against the other evidence. He would appreciate, looking at the matter objectively, that he knowledge and experience could cut both ways as she would be just as well placed to spot the weaknesses in these reports as to spot their strengths. He would have no reason to think, in the absence of other facts indicating the contrary, that she would not apply her medical knowledge and experience in just the same impartial way when she was sitting as a tribunal member as she would when she was acting as an EMP.

"21. . . . The observer would appreciate that Dr Armstrong's experience of working as an EMP would be likely to be of benefit to her, and through her to the other tribunal members, when she was evaluating the EMP report. The exercise of her independent judgment, after all, was the function that she was expected to perform as the tribunal's medical member. Her experience in the preparation of these reports was an asset which was available, through her, for the other tribunal members to draw upon when they were considering the whole of the evidence. . . .

"23. The fact is that the bringing of experience to bear when examining evidence and reaching a decision upon it has nothing to do with bias. The purpose of disqualification on the ground of apparent bias is to preserve the administration of justice from anything that might detract from the basic rules of fairness. One guiding principle is to be found in the concept of independence. . . . There is no suggestion that that principle was breached in this case. The other principle is to be found in the concept of impartiality – that justice must not only be done but be seen to be done. This too has at its heart the need to maintain public confidence in the integrity of the administration of justice. Impartiality consists in the absence of a predisposition to favour the interests of either side in the dispute. Therein lies the integrity of the adjudication system. But its integrity is not compromised by the use of specialist knowledge or experience when the judge or tribunal member is examining the evidence."

Lord Rodger of Earlsferry pointed out that the approach adopted on behalf of the claimant in that case might lead to an argument that a member of a tribunal who was disabled should be disqualified on the ground that they would be likely to be partial to the disabled person claiming benefit. He also said that "the position might have been different if there had been any reason to suppose that the [examining medical practitioners] were a close-knit group sharing an esprit de corps". Baroness Hale made a similar point and emphasised that the Tribunal of Commissioners (CSDLA/1019/1999) had rejected the suggestion that an examining medical practitioner was a "Benefits Agency doctor" rather than an independent expert adviser. Doctors frequently have to review each others' decisions. She further observed that the Benefits Agency had no particular interest in the outcome of any individual case and was not realistically in a position to influence the doctor's decision one way or the other. Accordingly, the House of Lords held that there was no apparent bias.

There is, nonetheless, a difficulty that must arise if some examining medical practitioners sit also as members of tribunals. Inevitably, there will be cases where the report of such an examining medical practitioner has to be considered by a tribunal, the chairman or disability qualified panel member of which know the examining medical practitioner because he or she has been the medically qualified member of a tribunal on which they have sat on a previous occasion. In *Secretary of State for Work and Pensions v Cunningham*, 2004 S.L.T. 1007 (also reported as *R(DLA) 7/04*) the issue was whether there was apparent bias when a tribunal had to consider a report by an examining medical practitioner who had sat 22 times as a member of a tribunal with the chairman and 14 times with the member of the tribunal with a disability qualification. The Court of Session held that there was an apprehension of bias applying *Lawal v Northern Spirit Ltd* [2003] UKHL 35; [2003] I.C.R. 856, in which the House of Lords held there to have been apparent bias where one party to proceedings before the Employment Appeal Tribunal was represented by a barrister who had previously sat as a part-time judge of that tribunal with the lay members before whom he was appearing. *Cunningham* was cited in argument in *Gillies* but is not mentioned in the speeches of the House of Lords. It is suggested that a case like *Cunningham* turns not on whether examining medical practitioners are "a close-knit group sharing an esprit de corps" but on whether the tribunal is. As a tribunal must work together in a way that examining medical practitioners do not, *Cunningham* can be distinguished from *Gillies* and it is suggested that it is unaffected by the later case. In *Cunningham*, the Court of Session declined to give guidance as to how often a member of a tribunal has to have sat with an examining medical practitioner before there is apparent bias. In *CSDLA/364/2005*, decided before the House of Lords' decision in *Gillies*, it was held that a chairman was disqualified from hearing an appeal if he had sat with the examining medical practitioner only once. However, that decision was not followed in *CDLA/2379/2005* and was subsequently reversed by the Court of Session, without reasons, when the claimant withdrew her opposition to the Secretary of State's appeal. In *CDLA/2379/2005*, the Commissioner referred to *Locabail (UK) Ltd v Bayfield Properties Ltd* [1999] EWCA Civ 3004; [2000] Q.B. 451 in which it was suggested that each case had to be determined on its facts, that any doubts had to be resolved in favour of recusal and that "[t]he greater the passage of time between the event relied on as showing a danger of bias and the case in which the objection is raised, the weaker (other things being equal) the objection will be" but held that there was a reasonable apprehension of bias where the chairman of the tribunal had sat on a tribunal with the examining medical practitioner whose report was being considered on three occasions, the last being three and a half months before the relevant hearing. The practical answer to the problem revealed in these cases is for those responsible for tribunals to ensure that medically qualified panel members who are also examining medical practitioners do not sit in the areas where they usually act as examining medical practitioners, so that

Social Security Act 1998

they only rarely sit with other members who might subsequently have to consider their reports.

Constitution of appeal tribunals

1.347
7.—(1) Subject to subsection (2) below, an appeal tribunal shall consist of one, two or three members drawn by the President from the panel constituted under section 6 above.

(2) The member, or (as the case may be) at least one member, of an appeal tribunal must—
   (a) have a general qualification (construed in accordance with section 71 of the Courts and Legal Services Act 1990); or
   (b) be an advocate or solicitor in Scotland.

(3) Where an appeal tribunal has more than one member—
   (a) the President shall nominate one of the members as chairman;
   (b) decisions shall be taken by a majority of votes; and
   (c) unless regulations otherwise provide, the chairman shall have any casting vote.

(4) Where it appears to an appeal tribunal that a matter before it involves a question of fact of special difficulty, then, unless regulations otherwise provide, the tribunal may require one or more experts to provide assistance to it in dealing withthe question.

(5) In subsection (4) above "expert" means a member of the panel constituted under section 6 above who appears to the appeal tribunal concerned to have knowledge or experience which would be relevant in determining the question of fact of special difficulty.

(6) Regulations shall make provision with respect to—
   (a) the composition of appeal tribunals;
   (b) the procedure to be followed in allocating cases among differently constituted tribunals; and
   (c) the manner in which expert assistance is to be given under subsection (4) above.

(7) Schedule 1 to this Act shall have effect for supplementing this section.

DEFINITIONS

"appeal tribunal"—see s.4(2).
"expert"—see subs.(5).

GENERAL NOTE

Subss.(2) and (3)

1.348
In *Improving decision making and appeals in Social Security* (Cm 3328), para.5.5, it was suggested that there was no need for every tribunal to have a lawyer among its members. However, the legislation as enacted does require a lawyer who must be a barrister, solicitor or advocate but who need not be of any particular seniority. There is no requirement that the legally qualified member of a two or three person tribunal should be the chairman although that is the invariable practice at the moment.

Subs.(6)

1.349
See regs 36 and 50 of the Social Security and Child Support (Decisions and Appeals) Regulations 1999 and regs 9 and 16 of the Tax Credits (Appeals) (No.2) Regulations 2002.

(1998 c.14, s.8)

CHAPTER II

SOCIAL SECURITY DECISIONS AND APPEALS

Decisions

Decisions by Secretary of State

8.—(1) Subject to the provisions of this Chapter, it shall be for the Secretary of State—
  (a) to decide any claim for a relevant benefit;
  (b) to decide any claim for a social fund payment mentioned in section 138(1)(b) of the Contributions and Benefits Act; [¹ and]
  (c) subject to subsection (5) below, to make any decision that falls to be made under or by virtue of a relevant enactment; [¹ . . .]
  (d) [¹ . . .]
(2) Where at any time a claim for a relevant benefit is decided by the Secretary of State—
  (a) the claim shall not be regarded as subsisting after that time; and
  (b) accordingly, the claimant shall not (without making a further claim) be entitled to the benefit on the basis of circumstances not obtaining at that time.
(3) In this Chapter "relevant benefit" [² . . .] means any of the following, namely—
  (a) benefit under Parts II to V of the Contributions and Benefits Act;
  (b) a jobseeker's allowance;
[³(bb) state pension credit;]
  (c) income support;
  (d) [⁴ . . .];
  (e) [⁴ . . .];
  (f) a social fund payment mentioned in section 138(1)(a) or (2) of the Contributions and Benefits Act;
  (g) child benefit;
  (h) such other benefit as may be prescribed.
(4) In this section "relevant enactment" means any enactment contained in this Chapter, the Contributions and Benefits Act, the Administration Act, the Social Security (Consequential Provisions) Act 1992 [³, the Jobseekers Act [³ or the State Pension Credit Act 2002], other than one contained in—
  (a) Part VII of the Contributions and Benefits Act so far as relating to housing benefit and council tax benefit;
  (b) Part VIII of the Administration Act (arrangements for housing benefit and council tax benefit and related subsidies).
(5) [¹ Subsection (1)(c) above does not include any decision which under section 8 of the Social Security Contributions (Transfer of Functions, etc.) Act 1999 falls to be made by an officer of the Inland Revenue.]

AMENDMENTS

1. Social Security Contributions (Transfer of Functions, etc.) Act 1999, Sch.7, para.22 (April 1, 1999).

Social Security Act 1998

2. Welfare Reform and Pensions Act 1999, s.88 and Sch.13 (April 6, 2000).
3. State Pension Credit Act 2002, Sch.1, para.6 (July 2, 2002 for the purpose of exercising any power to make regulations or orders and April 7, 2003 for other purposes).
4. Tax Credits Act 2002, Sch.6 (April 8, 2003, subject to a saving in respect of outstanding questions concerning work families' tax credit and disabled person's tax credit—see Tax Credits Act 2002 (Commencement No.4, Transitional Provisions and Savings) Order 2003 (SI 2003/962), art.3(1)–(3)).

DEFINITIONS

"the Administration Act"—see s.84.
"claim"—by virtue of s.39(2), see s.191 of the Social Security Administration Act 1992.
"claimant"—see s.39(1) and, by virtue of s.39(2), see s.191 of the Social Security Administration Act 1992.
"the Contributions and Benefits Act"—see s.84.
"Inland Revenue"—by virtue of s.39(2), see s.191 of the Social Security Administration Act 1992 but note that the Inland Revenue has been merged into Her Majesty's Revenue and Customs by the Commissioners for Revenue and Customs Act 2005.
"the Jobseekers Act"—see s.84.
"prescribed"—*ibid.*
"relevant enactment"—see subs.(4).
"relevant benefit"—see subs.(3).

GENERAL NOTE

1.351   This section makes general provision for initial decisions by the Secretary of State. However, by Tax Credits Act 1999, s.2(1)(b) and Sch.2, para.5(b)(i), the functions of making initial decisions in respect of working families' tax credit and disabled person's tax credit (both now abolished) were transferred to officers of the Inland Revenue. By s.50(2)(e) of the Tax Credits Act 2002, the Secretary of State's functions under this Act relating to child benefit and guardian's allowance were transferred to the Board of Inland Revenue with effect from April 7, 2003. The Inland Revenue has now been merged into Her Majesty's Revenue and Customs, by the Commissioners for Revenue and Customs Act 2005.

Subs.(1)

1.352   Where another body has made a decision on a question relevant to a claim for benefit, it is not necessary for the Secretary of State to consider that question from scratch as though the other decision did not exist, provided the other body made a considered decision on the point. He is entitled, in the absence of anything to compel a contrary conclusion, to regard the existence of that decision as satisfactory evidence *(R(H) 9/04)* of the facts found by that body. However, he is not bound to reach the same conclusion as the other body and must take account of any new evidence or any contrary submission made by the claimant. Thus, an immigration adjudicator's decision accepting, contrary to the argument of the Home Secretary, that the claimant was validly married, was persuasive but not binding on the Secretary of State for Work and Pensions or a tribunal or a Commissioner determining a claim for widow's pension *(R. (Nahar) v Social Security Commissioners* [2001] EWHC 1049 (Admin). Although there was an appeal, the decision of the adjudicator had by then been set aside by the immigration appeal tribunal and so the point did not arise before the Court of Appeal [2002] EWCA Civ 859.) The same approach applies in relation to decisions of tax inspectors *(R(FC) 1/91).*

(1998 c.14, s.8)

Subs.(2)
This subsection is disapplied in industrial disease cases where there has been recrudescence (see reg.12A of the Social Security and Child Support (Decisions and Appeals) Regulations 1999).

Paragraph (a) refers to a "claim" but in this context that is not to be read as being in contradistinction to, say, a supersession. The purpose of para.(a), read with s.12(8)(b) is to reverse the effect of *R(S) 1/83* and *R(S) 2/98*, in which it was held that a tribunal was entitled to take account of changes of circumstances occurring after the decision under appeal, on the basis that the claim made by the claimant subsisted until finally disposed of by the decision of the tribunal.

Paragraph (b) is not well drafted. The point being made in para.(a) is that a claim is effective only until it is decided *by the Secretary of State* (although benefit may then be awarded indefinitely or for a specified period in the future) and para.(b) is intended to make it clear that the consequence is that a change of circumstances taking place after the date of decision cannot give rise to entitlement under the original claim. This means that if a claimant appeals against the Secretary of State's decision, the tribunal cannot award benefit on the basis of a change of circumstances that has taken place between the Secretary of State's decision and its own decision. If no benefit was awarded on the initial claim, a new claim must, as para.(b) makes clear, be made if the claimant wishes to take advantage of the change of circumstances. That a decision refusing benefit cannot be superseded on the ground of a change of circumstances has been confirmed by a Tribunal of Commissioners in *R(I) 5/02*.

An assessment of disablement is a freestanding decision made under s.8(1)(c) and is appealable by virtue of reg.26 of the Social Security (Decisions and Appeals) Regulations 1999. In *R(I) 5/02*, the Tribunal of Commissioners held that a final assessment of disablement that had originally been made under s.47 of the Social Security Administration Act 1992 for a period that had come to an end could be superseded (having regard to para.4(1) of Sch.12 to the Social Security Act 1998 (Commencement No.8 and Savings and Consequential and Transitional Provisions) Order 1999) because it had continuing effect. However, they expressly declined to say whether the same approach would apply to an assessment originally made under s.8(1)(c). It is suggested that it would not, because such an assessment has no effect after the period for which it has been made comes to an end. What is required is an entirely new assessment made on a new claim for disablement benefit.

However, para.(b) overlooks the possibility that a claim may be decided some while after the date of claim and may be made in respect of a period beginning before the date of claim. In some cases a claimant will have been entitled to benefit in respect of the early part of the period for which it is claimed but, by reason of a change of circumstances, will have ceased to be entitled to benefit by the time the Secretary of State gives his decision. Read literally, para.(b) would require the claimant to be refused benefit altogether in such a case because, on the basis of circumstances obtaining at the date of decision, he or she would not qualify. However, it is suggested that the word "accordingly" shows that para.(b) merely makes provision for the natural consequence of para.(a) and should be read to the effect that the claimant shall not be entitled to the benefit on the basis of circumstances not obtaining at *or before* the date of decision. This approach is consistent with that taken in *CIS/2428/1999* in the context of s.12(8)(b). In that case, it was pointed out that a literal interpretation of s.12(8)(b) would prevent a tribunal from taking account of a cause for a late claim which existed before the claim was made and had ceased to exist before the Secretary of State's decision on the claim. The Commissioner considered that that would be absurd and would prevent adjudication on a case falling within reg.19(5) of the Social Security (Claims and Payments) Regulations 1987. He held that a circumstance "obtains" at the date of decision if it is a circumstance, whenever it occurred, that is relied on by a claimant in justifying a late claim.

1.353

In *R(DLA) 4/05*, a Tribunal of Commissioners held that para.(b) precluded the Secretary of State from taking account of an anticipated change of circumstances, even on a claim made in advance. However, they held that it did not preclude the Secretary of State from having regard to the effect on entitlement to benefit on the mere passage of time. Therefore, he can make an advance decision on a renewal claim taking into account the fact that by the renewal date the qualifying period for a particular rate of benefit will have elapsed or the claimant will have attained a certain age. Prediction is also permitted where entitlement to benefit at the date of decision depends on what is "likely" to happen in the future (*R(DLA) 3/01*). Otherwise, where the Secretary of State anticipates a change of circumstances, he must either defer making a decision or make a decision ignoring the expected change but possibly marking the case for future consideration of revision or supersession. *R(DLA) 4/05* has been followed by a Tribunal of Commissioners in Northern Ireland (*R 2/05 (DLA)*). In *Secretary of State for Work and Pensions v Bhakta* [2006] EWCA Civ 65 (reported as *R(IS) 7/06*), the Court of Appeal approved *R(DLA) 4/05*. *Bhakta* was a case where the claimant intended to reside in the United Kingdom but had not become habitually resident in the United Kingdom at the date of the Secretary of State's decision only because a sufficient period of residence had not yet elapsed. The Court held that the Secretary of State could, under reg.13 of the Social Security (Claims and Payments) Regulations 1987, have made an advance award of income support from the date on which habitual residence had been likely to be established on the assumption that there would be no change in the claimant's circumstances. Regulation 13 has been amended with effect from May 23, 2007 so as to exclude that class of case (and all claims by "persons from abroad") from the scope of the regulation (see reg. 2(2)(c) of the Social Security, Housing Benefit and Council Tax Benefit (Miscellaneous Amendments) Regulations 2007 (SI 2007/1331)), but the principle confirmed in *Bhakta* remains good in other contexts.

Subs.(3)

1.354
It having been pointed out that the lack of any reference in subs.(3) to mobility allowance meant that there was no power to revise or supersede a decision relating to mobility allowance so as to be able to recover an overpayment (*CDLA/2999/2004*), the Social Security Act 1998 (Prescribed Benefits) Regulations 2006 prescribe a number of benefits payable under the Social Security Act 1995 and the Supplementary Benefits Act 1976. The benefits prescribed were all abolished before the 1998 Act came into force and are unemployment benefit, sickness benefit, invalidity benefit, attendance allowance (as paid to those under 65), mobility allowance and supplementary benefit.

The provisions of Chapter II of Part I of the 1998 Act are applied to decisions under ss.2 and 3 of the Age-Related Payments Act 2004, not by virtue of regulations made under this subsection but by s.5(5) of the 2004 Act.

Subs.(5)

1.355
Under s.8(1)(e) of the Social Security Contributions (Transfer of Functions, etc.) Act 1999 and the Commissioners for Revenue and Customs Act 2005, it is for Her Majesty's Revenue and Customs to determine whether contributions of a particular class have been paid in respect of any period.

However, the question whether a person is entitled to "credits" is a matter for the Secretary of State (Sch.3, para.17 to the Social Security Act 1998, *CIB/2338/2000*) and so is the question whether a person is entitled to home responsibilities protection (Sch.3, para.16). It also appears that any dispute as to which is the relevant contribution year in respect of any claim is a matter for the Secretary of State, so that the effect of *Secretary of State for Social Security v Scully* [1992] 1 W.L.R. 927 (reported also as *R(S) 5/93*) is reversed and the effect of *R(G) 1/82* is restored. The Secretary of State's decisions are appealable under s.12.

(1998 c.14, s.9)

Revision of decisions

9.—(1) Subject to section 36(3) below, any decision of the Secretary of State under section 8 above or section 10 below may be revised by the Secretary of State—
  (a) either within the prescribed period or in prescribed cases or circumstances; and
  (b) either on an application made for the purpose or on his own initiative;
and regulations may prescribe the procedure by which a decision of the Secretary of State may be so revised.

(2) In making a decision under subsection (1) above, the Secretary of State need not consider any issue that is not raised by the application or, as the case may be, did not cause him to act on his own initiative.

(3) Subject to subsections (4) and (5) and section 27 below, a revision under this section shall take effect as from the date on which the original decision took (or was to take) effect.

(4) Regulations may provide that, in prescribed cases or circumstances, a revision under this section shall take effect as from such other date as may be prescribed.

(5) Where a decision is revised under this section, for the purpose of any rule as to the time allowed for bringing an appeal, the decision shall be regarded as made on the date on which it is so revised.

(6) Except in prescribed circumstances, an appeal against a decision of the Secretary of State shall lapse if the decision is revised under this section before the appeal is determined.

DEFINITION

"prescribed"—see s.84.

GENERAL NOTE

This section applies to decisions under ss.2 and 3 of the Age-Related Payments Act 2004 (see s.5(5) of the 2004 Act). In relation to child benefit and guardian's allowance, the functions of the Secretary of State under this section were transferred with effect from April 7, 2003 to the Board of Inland Revenue (Tax Credits Act 2002, s.50(2)(e)). The functions of the Secretary of State in relation to the former working families' tax credit and disabled person's tax credit were similarly transferred to officers of the Inland Revenue from October 5, 1999 (Tax Credit Act 1999, s.2(1)(b) and Sch.2). The Inland Revenue has now been merged into Her Majesty's Revenue and Customs, by the Commissioners for Revenue and Customs Act 2005.

This section also applies to most decisions of Her Majesty's Revenue and Customs made under s.170(2) of the Pensions Schemes Act 1993, by virtue of s.170(4).

Provision is made within the Social Security and Child Support (Decisions and Appeals) Regulations 1999 for decisions under the 1993 and 1999 Acts but separate regulations have been made in respect of child benefit and guardian's allowance (see the Child Benefit and Guardian's Allowance (Decisions and Appeals) Regulations 2003).

Subs.(1)

Under the Social Security Administration Act 1992, provision was made for the "review" of decisions. Such reviews are replaced by "revisions" under s.9 and "supersessions" under s.10. Note that only a decision of the Secretary of State may be revised whereas a decision of the Secretary of State *or* of a tribunal or a Commissioner may be superseded. Apart from that, there is little that can be gleaned from the primary legislation as to the difference between revision and supersession. The most obvious distinction between the two concepts probably lies in the date from which the new decision takes effect. Where a decision is revised, the revised decision has effect from the effective date (or what should have been the effective date) of the original decision (see s.9(3)). On a supersession, the new decision takes effect from the date on which it is made and does not affect any past period, subject to limited provision for backdating in some cases (s.10(5)). A related distinction is that there is no appeal under s.12 against a refusal to revise under s.9. Formally, there is only a right of appeal against the original decision but s.9(5) extends the time for appealing against the original decision if it is revised, although not always if there is a refusal to revise (see the annotation to subs.(5)). By contrast, an appeal may be brought under s.12 against any decision under s.10. Beyond all that, no indication is given by the primary legislation as to the circumstances in which a revision of a decision is more appropriate than a supersession or vice versa. For that information, one must look at regs 3 and 4 of the Social Security and Child Support (Decisions and Appeals) Regulations 1999 and regs 5–11 of the Child Benefit and Guardian's Allowance (Decisions and Appeals) Regulations 2003 relating to revisions and at reg.6 of the 1999 Regulations and reg.13 of the 2003 Regulations relating to supersession. There would still be some overlap between the two procedures if it were not for reg.3(9) of the 1999 Regulations and reg.5(3) of the 2003 Regulations, which have the effect that supersession is always the appropriate procedure where there has been a change of circumstances since the Secretary of State's decision, and for reg.6(3) of the 1999 Regulations and reg.15 of the 2003 Regulations, which provide that a decision that may be revised cannot be superseded (save in limited circumstances where the revision could not take into account a further ground of supersession).

Happily, an application for supersession may be treated as an application for revision and vice versa (regs 3(10) and 6(5) of the 1999 Regulations and regs 7(1)(a) and 14(1)(a) of the 2003 Regulations), so that it is not fatal if claimants or their advisors do not fully understand the difference when making the application.

Despite, or perhaps because of, this flexibility, experience shows that decisions are not always issued in the correct form. Indeed, it is often Departmental practice to issue decisions that state the outcome without stating whether the decision is a revision or supersession. It has been suggested that that is not necessarily improper when the decision is first issued to the claimant but that the decision ought nonetheless to have been made in the appropriate form so that, if there is a request for reasons or an appeal, the true basis of the decision can be explained (*CIB/313/2002*). However, strong criticisms have been made of the Secretary of State's failure in many circumstances to record any decision at all in the proper form (see *CPC/3891/2004* and *R(IS) 13/05*). Even where a decision is made in terms of a revision or supersession, there are occasions when the wrong type of decision is issued. This is unfortunate because the distinction between revision and supersession is very important when an appeal is lodged. While an appeal following a revision or refusal to revise lies against the original decision, an appeal following a supersession or refusal to supersede lies against the later decision. It is particularly important for a decision terminating an award to be issued in the correct form if the Secretary of State or Her Majesty's Revenue and Customs intends subsequently to make a decision to the effect that there has been a recoverable overpayment, because s.71(5A) of the Social Security Administration Act 1992 generally requires there to have been a revision or supersession before an overpayment can be recovered (*CIS/3228/2003, R(IS) 13/05*). Section 71(5A) recognises that, unless an award is either revised or else superseded on a ground that makes the supersession retrospective by virtue of reg.7 of the 1999 Regulations or reg.16 of the 2003 Regulations, the original award still governs entitlement in respect of the period before the decision terminating it was made and it cannot be shown that any benefit was overpaid.

For the circumstances in which an appeal tribunal may give a decision in terms of supersession on an appeal following a revision or refusal to revise and vice versa, see the note to s.12(2). It is suggested that many of the difficulties identified would be removed if grounds for revision under reg.3(4) and (5) to (8) of the Social Security and

(1998 c.14, s.9)

Child Support (Decisions and Appeals) Regulations 1999 and regs 8 to 11 of the Child Benefit and Guardian's Allowance (Decisions and Appeals) Regulations 2003 were instead grounds for supersession. In deciding whether revision or supersession was the more appropriate remedy, the draftsmen of the Regulations appear to have placed too much emphasis on the date from which a decision is effective and too little on the lack of an appropriate right of appeal against a decision given in terms of revision and the lack of any express provision for correcting on appeal a decision-maker's mistaken choice as to the appropriate procedure for making a change to an earlier decision.

Section 9(1) provides that "any decision . . . under section 8 above or section 10 below" may be revised. However, in s.12(1) there is reference to "any decision . . . under section 8 or 10 above (whether as originally made or as revised under section 9 above)" and similar words referring to section 9 are to be found in s.10(1)(a). Do those references to s.9 in ss.10 and 12 suggest that references to decisions under ss 8 and 10 normally include decisions that have been revised? Or does the fact that there are references to s.9 in ss.10 and 12 but none in s.9 itself suggest that a decision that has already been revised cannot be revised again? In *CIS/3535/2003*, the Deputy Commissioner preferred the former approach and said, obiter, that a decision that has already been revised may be revised again and that the time for bringing an application under reg.3(1) of the Social Security and Child Support (Decisions and Appeals) Regulations 1999 starts again from the date the revision is notified.

Subs.(2)

Note that the Secretary of State "need not", but nonetheless may, consider additional issues. On an appeal following a revision or refusal to revise, the decision under appeal is the original decision (see subs.(5) read with s.12(1)). The tribunal's duty to consider issues is determined by the issues raised by the appeal (see s.12(8)(a)) rather than by the issues raised by the earlier application for revision because they are not obliged to consider independently the merits of the revisions or refusal to revise, at any rate where the revision or application for revision was made under reg.3(1) or (3) of the Social Security and Child Support (Decisions and Appeals) Regulations 1999.

1.359

Subs.(4)

See reg.5 of the Social Security and Child Support (Decisions and Appeals) Regulations 1999 and reg.12 of the Child Benefit and Guardian's Allowance (Decisions and Appeals) Regulations 2003 which provide that the principal exception to the general rule is where a ground for the revision is that the original decision was made effective from the wrong date in the first place.

1.360

Subs.(5)

This allows a claimant to appeal against a revised decision. Note, however, that an application for a revision of a decision of the Secretary of State has the effect of automatically extending the time for appealing only where the application is brought under reg.3(1) or (3) of the Social Security and Child Support (Decisions and Appeals) Regulations 1999 (see reg.31(2)(a)). In other cases, it will generally be wise for any person asking for a revision to lodge an appeal at the same time so that, if the decision is not revised, the claimant will not have to bring a late appeal. The fact that a claimant was waiting for a decision on an application for revision may be regarded as a compelling reason for admitting an appeal late under reg.32 of the Social Security and Child Support (Decisions and Appeals) Regulations 1999, but a claimant would be unwise to take that for granted. If, the claimant having lodged both an application for revision and an appeal, the decision is not revised, the appeal will proceed. If the decision is revised, the appeal will lapse under subs.(6) only if the revised decision is more advantageous to the claimant that the original decision. This subsection then applies to such a case, enabling the claimant to appeal against the decision as revised. If the original decision is revised otherwise than to the advantage of the claimant, the appeal will not lapse but the claimant will be given another month to make representations in the light of the revision.

1.361

Social Security Act 1998

In a case where an application for revision is made otherwise than under reg.3(1) and (3) of the Social Security and Child Support (Decisions and Appeals) Regulations 1999 and more than 13 months has elapsed since the original decision, so that no appeal may be brought against it, there is no way of challenging by way of an appeal a refusal to revise the decision (see *R(IS) 15/04* and *Beltekian v Westminster CC* [2004] EWCA Civ 1784 (reported as *R(H) 8/05*), in which no attempt appears to have been made to argue that subs.(5) should be read as including a refusal to revise in the same way that s.12(9) must be read as referring to a refusal to supersede). Recourse must be had to judicial review. See the note to reg.31 of the 1999 Regulations for further discussion of the problems caused by the lack of any reference in the primary legislation to refusals to revise.

Subs. (6)

1.362   See reg.30 of the Social Security and Child Support (Decisions and Appeals) Regulations 1999 and reg.27 of the Child Benefit and Guardian's Allowance (Decisions and Appeals) Regulations 2003.

Decisions superseding earlier decisions

1.363   **10.**—(1) Subject to [¹ subsection (3)] and section 36(3) below, the following, namely—

(a) any decision of the Secretary of State under section 8 above or this section, whether as originally made or as revised under section 9 above; and

(b) any decision under this Chapter of an appeal tribunal or a Commissioner,

may be superseded by a decision made by the Secretary of State, either on an application made for the purpose or on his own initiative.

(2) In making a decision under subsection (1) above, the Secretary of State need not consider any issue that is not raised by the application or, as the case may be, did not cause him to act on his own initiative.

(3) Regulations may prescribe the cases and circumstances in which, and the procedure by which, a decision may be made under this section.

(4) [¹ . . .]

(5) Subject to subsection (6) and section 27 below, a decision under this section shall take effect as from the date on which it is made or, where applicable, the date on which the application was made.

(6) Regulations may provide that, in prescribed cases or circumstances, a decision under this section shall take effect as from such other date as may be prescribed.

AMENDMENT

1. Social Security Contributions (Transfer of Functions, etc.) Act 1999, Sch.7, para.23 (April 1, 1999).

DEFINITIONS

"appeal tribunal"—see s.39(1).
"Commissioner"—*ibid.*
"prescribed"—see s.84.

GENERAL NOTE

1.364   Transitional provisions in the various commencement orders bringing this Act into force (see the note to s.87), provide for the supersession under this section of decisions

(1998 c.14, s.10)

made by the various adjudicating authorities that existed under earlier legislation and, in *CI/1800/01*, the Commissioner construed a reference to adjudicating medical authorities as including medical appeal tribunals so as to enable a claimant to apply for supersession of a decision of a medical appeal tribunal that had continuing effect. However, in *CDLA/2999/2004*, the Commissioner declined to find any power to supersede an award of mobility allowance (which was a benefit that was replaced by the mobility component of disability living allowance in April 1992) made by an adjudication officer in 1986.

The practical effect of *CDLA/2999/2004* has now substantially been reversed by the Social Security Act 1998 (Prescribed Benefits) Regulations 2006, which prescribes mobility allowance (and certain other benefits) for the purposes of s.8(3)(h) of this Act, and by the Social Security Act 1998 (Commencement Nos. 9 and 11) (Amendment) Order 2006 (SI 2006/2540), which amends transitional provisions relating to the replacement of sickness and invalidity benefit by incapacity benefit and to the replacement of attendance allowance for people under 65 and mobility allowance by disability living allowance.

This section applies to decisions under ss.2 and 3 of the Age-Related Payments Act 2004 (see s.5(5) of the 2004 Act).

In relation to child benefit and guardian's allowance, the functions of the Secretary of State under this section were transferred with effect from April 7, 2003 to the Board of Inland Revenue (Tax Credits Act 2002, s.50(2)(e)). The functions of the Secretary of State in relation to the former working families' tax credit and disabled person's tax credit were similarly transferred to officers of the Inland Revenue from October 5, 1999 (Tax Credit Act 1999, s.2(1)(b) and Sch.2). The Inland Revenue has now been merged into Her Majesty's Revenue and Customs, by the Commissioners for Revenue and Customs Act 2005.

This section also applies to most decisions of Her Majesty's Revenue and Customs made under s.170(2) of the Pensions Schemes Act 1993, by virtue of s.170(4).

Provision is made within the Social Security and Child Support (Decisions and Appeals) Regulations 1999 for decisions under the 1993 and 1999 Acts but separate regulations have been made in respect of child benefit and guardian's allowance.

Subs.(1)

For the distinction between revision and supersession, see the note to s.9(1). Note that an application for supersession may be treated as an application for revision and vice versa (regs 3(10) and 6(5) of the Social Security and Child Support (Decisions and Appeals) Regulations 1999 and regs 7(1)(a) and 14(1)(a) of the Child Benefit and Guardian's Allowance (Decisions and Appeals) Regulations 2003).

Also, under reg. 6(5), the provision of information to the Secretary of State may be treated as an application for supersession. There are no other provisions specifying what constitutes an application for supersession. In *CI/954/2006*, the Commissioner doubted that giving information to a medical adviser during an examination was to be treated as an application for supersession, although the Secretary of State could have superseded on his own motion in the light of the information.

Often departmental procedures require a claimant to complete a claim form for what is really a supersession rather than a claim. This can lead to confusion. One example is the practice of requiring claimants of income support who move to a new address to complete a new claim. If this is not done promptly, a claimant may find that there is a gap in benefit payments that is not subsequently made up. The grounds upon which benefit is withheld in those circumstances may be somewhat dubious. In *CI/954/2006*, it was pointed out that where a claimant is in receipt of disablement benefit and suffers another industrial accident, a claim in respect of the subsequent accident may have to be treated in the alternative as an application for supersession of the original award, because, following *R(I) 4/03*, aggregation of assessments of disablement is an alternative to the making of two separate awards. One practical difference is that claims may be backdated but supersessions in those

1.365

Social Security Act 1998

circumstances cannot, which the Commissioner suggested is anomalous. The Commissioner also pointed out that an application for supersession of an assessment of disablement needed to be treated also as an application for supersession of the underlying award if proper effect was to be given to any supersession of the assessment of disablement (see the annotations to regs 6 and 26 of the 1999 Regulations, below).

Subs. (2)

1.366 On an appeal against a supersession or refusal to supersede, it is doubtful that a tribunal may refuse to consider an issue raised by the appeal merely because it was not raised on the original application for supersession or, as the case may be, did not cause the Secretary of State to act on his own initiative. However, where an issue is not raised by an appeal, the fact that it was not raised before the Secretary of State either may be a factor the tribunal should take into account when deciding whether to consider the issue on the appeal (see s.12(8)(a)).

Subs. (3)

1.367 See regs 6 and 8 of the Social Security and Child Support (Decisions and Appeals) Regulations 1999 and regs 13 and 14 of the Child Benefit and Guardian's Allowance (Decisions and Appeals) Regulations 2003.

Where a person applies for supersession and the Secretary of State decides that the case and circumstances are not among those prescribed by reg.6 of the 1999 Regulations (or, equally, reg.13 of the 2003 Regulations), it has now been established that the Secretary of State may issue a decision refusing to supersede the original decision, rather than superseding it but without making any change (see *Wood v Secretary of State for Work and Pensions* [2003] EWCA Civ 53 (reported as *R(DLA) 1/03)*). It is not entirely clear whether he may still, as an alternative approach, supersede the original decision without making any change, but the distinction is of little practical importance. See the note to reg.6 of the 1999 Regulations.

Subs. (5)

1.368 In *R(IB) 2/04*, the Tribunal of Commissioners decided that where a claimant has applied for supersession in order to obtain an increase of benefit but the Secretary of State supersedes the award so as to reduce entitlement, the supersession is made on the Secretary of State's own initiative and not on the claimant's application. Therefore, subject to the effect of any regulations made under subs.(6), it is effective from the date of the decision and not the date of the claimant's application. Similarly, where the Secretary of State's supersession decision is not less favourable than the original decision but the claimant appeals and the tribunal not only does not allow the appeal but also makes a decision even less favourable than the original decision, the tribunal's decision is usually effective from the date of the Secretary of State's supersession decision. See paras 95 to 97 of the Tribunal's decision.

Where a decision has been made that invalid care allowance is not payable because incapacity benefit is in payment and reg.4 of the Social Security (Overlapping Benefits) Regulations 1977 precluded the payment of both benefits, a decision to resume payment of invalid care allowance after payment of incapacity benefit ceases is a decision under s.8 and not a supersession under s.10 (*Secretary of State for Work and Pensions v Adams* [2003] EWCA Civ 796 (reported as *R(G) 1/03)*). This means that, where there has been a delay in reinstating payment of invalid care allowance, the decision is nonetheless automatically effective from the date when payment of incapacity benefit ceased, rather than from a later date determined by s.10(5).

Subs. (6)

1.369 See reg.7 of, and Sch.3A to, the Social Security and Child Support (Decisions and Appeals) Regulations 1999 and reg.16 of the Child Benefit and Guardian's Allowance (Decisions and Appeals) Regulations 2003.

(1998 c.14, s.10A)

[¹*Reference of issues by Secretary of State to Inland Revenue*

References of issues by Secretary of State to Inland Revenue

10A.—(1) Regulations may make provision requiring the Secretary of State, where on consideration of any claim or other matter he is of the opinion that there arises any issue which under section 8 of the Social Security Contributions (Transfer of Functions, etc.) Act 1999 falls to be decided by an officer of the Inland Revenue, to refer the issue to the Inland Revenue.

Regulations under this section may—
(a) provide for the Inland Revenue to give the Secretary of State a preliminary opinion on any issue referred to them,
(b) specify the circumstances in which an officer of the Inland Revenue is to make a decision under section 8 of the Social Security Contributions (Transfer of Functions, etc.) Act 1999 on a reference by the Secretary of State,
(c) enable or require the Secretary of State, in specified circumstances to deal with any other issue arising on consideration of the claim or other matter pending the decision of the referred issue, and
(d) require the Secretary of State to decide the claim or other matter in accordance with the decision of an officer of the Inland Revenue on the issue referred to them, or in accordance with any determination of the tax appeal Commissioners made on appeal from their decision.]

AMENDMENT

1. Social Security Contributions (Transfer of Functions, etc.) Act 1999, Sch.7, para.24 (July 5, 1999).

DEFINITIONS

"claim"—by virtue of s.39(2), see s.191 of the Social Security Administration Act 1992.
"Inland Revenue"—*ibid*, but note that the Inland Revenue has been merged into Her Majesty's Revenue and Customs by the Commissioners for Revenue and Customs Act 2005.
"tax appeal Commissioners"—see s.39(1).
"prescribed"—see s.84.

GENERAL NOTE

See reg.11A of the Social Security and Child Support (Decisions and Appeals) Regulations 1999.
Some decisions fall to be made by Her Majesty's Revenue and Customs by virtue of s.170 of the Pensions Schemes Act 1993 (rather than by virtue of s.8 of the Social Security Contributions (Transfer of Functions, etc.) Act 1999) but the Secretary of State may nevertheless refer to Her Majesty's Revenue and Customs issues for determination under the 1993 Act notwithstanding that regulations under this section do not apply (*R(P) 1/04*).

Regulations with respect to decisions

11.—(1) Subject to the provisions of this Chapter and the Administration Act, provision may be made by regulations for the making of any decision by the Secretary of State under or in connection with the current legislation, or the former legislation, including a decision on a claim for benefit.

Social Security Act 1998

(2) Where it appears to the Secretary of State that a matter before him involves a question of fact requiring special expertise, he may direct that in dealing with that matter he shall have the assistance of one or more experts.

(3) In this section—

"the current legislation" means the Contributions and Benefits Act, the Jobseekers Act [1, the Social Security (Recovery of Benefits) Act 1997 or the State Pension Credit Act 2002];

"expert" means a person appearing to the Secretary of State to have knowledge or experience which would be relevant in determining the question of fact requiring special expertise;

"the former legislation" means the National Insurance Acts 1965 to 1974, the National Insurance (Industrial Injuries) Acts 1965 to 1974, the Social Security Act 1975 and Part II of the Social Security Act 1986.

AMENDMENT

1. State Pension Credit Act 2002, ss.11 and 21 and Sch.1, para.7 and Sch.3 (July 2, 2002 for the purpose of exercising any power to make regulations or orders and April 7, 2003 for other purposes).

DEFINITIONS

"the Administration Act"—see s.84.
"benefit"—by virtue of s.39(2), see s.191 of the Social Security Administration Act 1992.
"claim"—*ibid*.
"Contributions and Benefits Act"—see s.84.
"the current legislation"—see subs.(3).
"expert"—*ibid*.
"the former legislation"—*ibid*.
"the Jobseeker's Act"—see s.84.

GENERAL NOTE

1.373   In relation to the former working families' tax credit and disabled person's tax credit, the power to make regulations was transferred to the Commissioners of Inland Revenue and the other functions of the Secretary of State were transferred to officers of the Inland Revenue, with effect from October 5, 1999 (Tax Credits Act 1999, s.2(1)(b) and Sch.2, paras 5(b)(iii) and 8(a)). In relation to child benefit and guardian's allowance, powers and functions were similarly transferred to the Inland Revenue by the Tax Credits Act 2002 (see s.50(2)(e)). The Inland Revenue has now been merged into Her Majesty's Revenue and Customs, by the Commissioners for Revenue and Customs Act 2005.

Subs. (1)

See reg.28 of the Social Security and Child Support (Decisions and Appeals) Regulations 1999.

Appeals

Appeal to appeal tribunal

1.374   **12.**—(1) This section applies to any decision of the Secretary of State under section 8 or 10 above (whether as originally made or as revised under section 9 above) which—

(a) is made on a claim for, or on an award of, a relevant benefit, and does not fall within Schedule 2 to this Act; [¹ or]
(b) is made otherwise than on such a claim or award, and falls within Schedule 3 to this Act; [¹ . . .]
(c) [¹ . . .]

[¹ (2) In the case of a decision to which this section applies, the claimant and such other person as may be prescribed shall have a right to appeal to an appeal tribunal, but nothing in this subsection shall confer a right of appeal in relation to a prescribed decision, or a prescribed determination embodied in or necessary to a decision.]

(3) Regulations under subsection (2) above shall not prescribe any decision or determination that relates to the conditions of entitlement to a relevant benefit for which a claim has been validly made or for which no claim is required.

(4) Where the Secretary of State has determined that any amount is recoverable under or by virtue of section 71 or 74 of the Administration Act, any person from whom he has determined that it is recoverable shall have the same right of appeal to an appeal tribunal as a claimant.

(5) In any case where—
(a) the Secretary of State has made a decision in relation to a claim under Part V of the Contributions and Benefits Act; and
(b) the entitlement to benefit under that Part of that Act of any person other than the claimant is or may be, under Part VI of Schedule 7 to that Act, affected by that decision,

that other person shall have the same right of appeal to an appeal tribunal as the claimant.

(6) A person with a right of appeal under this section shall be given such notice of a decision to which this section applies and of that right as may be prescribed.

(7) Regulations may make provision as to the manner in which, and the time within which, appeals are to be brought.

(8) In deciding an appeal under this section, an appeal tribunal—
(a) need not consider any issue that is not raised by the appeal; and
(b) shall not take into account any circumstances not obtaining at the time when the decision appealed against was made.

(9) The reference in subsection (1) above to a decision under section 10 above is a reference to a decision superseding any such decision as is mentioned in paragraph (a) or (b) of subsection (1) of that section.

AMENDMENT

1. Social Security Contributions (Transfer of Functions, etc.) Act 1999, Sch.7, para.25 (April 1, 1999).

DEFINITIONS

"the administration Act"—see s.84.
"appeal tribunal"—see s.39(1).
"claim"—by virtue of s.39(2), see s.191 of the Social Security Administration Act 1992.
"claimant"—see s.39(1) and, by virtue of s.39(2), see s.191 of the Social Security Administration Act 1992.
"the Contributions and Benefits Act"—see s.84.
"prescribed"—*ibid.*
"relevant benefit"—see s.8(3).

Social Security Act 1998

General Note

1.375 This section provides only for appeals against decisions made by the Secretary of State under ss.8 and 10 of this Act. However, it applies to decisions under ss.2 and 3 of the Age-Related Payments Act 2004 by virtue of s.5(5) of the 2004 Act) and is also applied to other decisions of the Secretary of State by reg.9 of the Social Security (Work-focused Interviews for Lone Parents) Miscellaneous Amendments Regulations 2000, reg.15 of the Social Security (Jobcentre Plus Interviews) Regulations 2002, reg.14 of the Social Security (Jobcentre Plus Interviews for Partners) Regulations 2003, reg.12 of the Social Security (Incapacity Benefit Work-focused Interviews) Regulations 2003, reg.15 of the Social Security (Working Neighbourhoods) Regulations 2004 and, until April 29, 2007, reg.9 of the Social Security (Quarterly Work-focused Interviews for Certain Lone Parents) Regulations 2004, all of which are concerned with decisions that claimants have failed without good cause to attend interviews.

It is applied in a substantially modified form (see Vol.IV) to appeals brought by virtue of s.63 of the Tax Credits Act 2002 against decisions made by Her Majesty's Revenue and Customs in connection with tax credits including the determination of certain penalties.

It also applies—with only the modification that references to the Secretary of State are to be construed as references to the Board of Inland Revenue or to an officer of the Inland Revenue—so as to provide for appeals against decisions relating to child benefit and guardian's allowance (by virtue of the Tax Credits Act 2002, Sch.4, para.50), against decisions relating to the former working families' tax credit and disabled person's tax credit (by virtue of the Tax Credits Act 1999, Sch.2, para.21), against penalties imposed under s.9(1), (3)(a) or (5)(a) of the 1999 Act (by virtue of Sch.4, para.3(2) of the 1999 Act) and against decisions given under s.170 of the Pension Schemes Act 1993 in respect of retirement pensions (by virtue of s.170(6) of the 1993 Act). The Inland Revenue has now been merged into Her Majesty's Revenue and Customs, by the Commissioners for Revenue and Customs Act 2005.

Quite separate rights of appeal to appeal tribunals are given under s.4 of the Vaccine Damage Payments Act 1979 (in respect of vaccine damage payments— see Volume I of this work), under s.14 of the Child Support Act 1991 (in respect of child support maintenance—not within the scope of this work), under ss.11 and 12 of the Social Security (Recovery of Benefits) Act 1997 (in respect of the recovery of benefits from those making compensation payments in respect of personal injury), under ss.7 and 8 of the Road Traffic (NHS Charges) Act 1999 (in respect of the recovery of National Health Service costs from those making compensation payments in respect of personal injury incurred before January 29, 2007—not within the scope of this work), under para.6 of Sch.7 to the Child Support, Pensions and Social Security Act 2000 (in respect of housing benefit and council tax benefit—not within the scope of this work), under ss 157 and 158 of the Health and Social Care (Community Health and Standards) Act 2003 (in respect of the recovery of National Health Service costs from those making compensation in respect of personal injury incurred on or after January 29, 2007 – not within the scope of this work) and under reg.10(2B) of the Employment Protection (Recoupment of Jobseeker's Allowance and Income Support) Regulations 1996 (in respect of the recovery of benefits from those making compensation payments in employment tribunal proceedings).

Separate rights of appeal to appeal tribunals are also given under ss.21(9), 22 and 23 of the Child Trust Funds Act 2004, as modified by s.24 of that Act, but subss. (7) and (8)(b) of the 1998 Act are applied to such appeals by reg.6 of the Child Trust Funds (Non-tax Appeals) Regulations 2005 (see Vol.IV).

Further information about appeal tribunals, including practical information about appealing, may be obtained from the website of the Tribunals Service at *http://www.appeals-service.gov.uk*.

Subs. (1)

1.376 This section provides only for appeals against decisions under ss.8 and 10 of this Act (but see the note above). Challenges to decisions under s.9 are brought by appealing against the original decision rather than the s.9 decision. The phrase "decision . . . under section . . . 10" includes a decision to refuse to supersede (*Wood v Secretary of State for Work and Pensions* [2003] EWCA Civ 53 (reported as *R(DLA) 1/03)*), notwithstanding the terms of subs.(9).

There cannot be an appeal unless there has been a decision under s.8 or s.10 and so a tribunal had no jurisdiction to consider a challenge to the Secretary of State's failure to exercise his power to make a winter fuel payment without a claim (*R(IS) 12/05*). In *CIS/4088/2004*, the Commissioner considered that there must have been a decision refusing to make a payment in circumstances where the claimant had previously received a winter fuel payment and it was erroneously believed within the Department for Work and Pensions that no further payment could be made in the absence of a claim after the claimant had ceased to be entitled to incapacity benefit but that decision was doubted in *CIS/840/2005*.

The scope of a tribunal's jurisdiction must depend on the scope of the decision which is the subject of the appeal. Paragraph (a) provides for an appeal against any decision made *on* a claim or award. Section 20(1)(a) and (b) of the Social Security Administration Act 1992 drew a distinction between a "claim" and a "question" and s.36 expressly enabled a tribunal to deal with any question first arising before them and not previously considered by an adjudication officer. The new legislation does not use the terms "claim" and "question" and there is no provision similar to the old s.36. However, it is suggested that this may not make much difference. In *CIB/2338/2000*, the Commissioner held that the only type of "decision" that could be appealed was an "outcome" decision which is "a useful expression to refer to decisions that have, in crude terms, an impact on a claimant's pocket". He pointed out that an appeal lay only against decisions under ss.8 and 10. Section 8(1)(a) and (b) provides only that the Secretary of State shall "decide any claim". Section 8(1)(c) provides for the making of "any decision that falls to be made under or by virtue of any enactment" but the Commissioner did not construe that as referring to the individual determinations that are the building blocks of a decision on a claim for benefit. He understood it to refer to the making of decisions in relation to, say, crediting of earnings for contributions purposes. Section 10 refers to the supersession of decisions under s.8 or decisions of tribunals or Commissioners on appeal against from s.8 decisions. Therefore, there is no appeal against a decision on what used to be called a "question". In *CIB/2338/2000*, that meant that there was no appeal solely against the determination that the claimant was incapable of work; the appeal was against the consequential decision that he was not entitled to a "credit". This approach, which was endorsed by a Tribunal of Commissioners in *R(IB) 2/04*, makes it unnecessary for there to be a provision equivalent to the old s.36 expressly providing for a tribunal to deal with an issue that has not been considered by a decision-maker, because it is implicit that, if a tribunal has rejected a ground upon which the decision-maker has made an "outcome decision", it is necessary (subject to s.12(8)(a)) for the tribunal to consider such other issues as are necessary in order to substitute its own "outcome decision" for the decision-maker's. However, this is all subject to two qualifications. First, Sch. 3 to the Act and reg.26 of the Social Security and Child Support (Decisions and Appeals) Regulations 1999 make provision for appeals to be brought against certain freestanding decisions that are not "outcome decisions". Secondly, there are circumstances in which a tribunal is not obliged to substitute an "outcome decision" for one under appeal but may, in effect, remit the case to the Secretary of State or Her Majesty's Revenue and Customs (*CIS/624/2006*, discussed in more detail in the annotation to subs.(2) below).

Accurately identifying the scope of the appeal may be very important in some cases. For instance, where a person is in receipt of income support on the basis that he or she is incapable of work, that person will usually be in receipt also of incapacity benefit or "credits". A decision to the effect that he or she is not incapable of work will usually be made for the purposes of an "outcome decision" in relation to incapacity benefit or "credits". By virtue of reg.10 of the Social Security and Child Support (Decisions and Appeals) Regulations 1999, that determination will be conclusive for the purposes

Social Security Act 1998

of the income support claim. If the claimant wishes both to challenge the determination that he or she is not incapable work and to suggest that the entitlement to income support should continue on another ground, it will be necessary for there to be an appeal against both "outcome decisions". In order to determine the scope of an appeal, it may be necessary to consider the terms of the form or letter of appeal as well as the notice of decision because, if another decision-maker has dealt with the consequences of the first decision, a claimant may have appealed against both decisions in the same letter of appeal.

By virtue of s.12(1)(b) there is a right of appeal against an assessment of disablement for industrial disablement benefit, as a freestanding decision (see para.9 of Sch.3 to the Act and reg.26 of the Social Security and Child Support (Decisions and Appeals) Regulations 1999). In *R(I) 5/02*, the Tribunal of Commissioners held that a tribunal considering such an appeal had no jurisdiction to consider a refusal of benefit consequent upon the assessment of disablement. It is not clear how the two decisions were notified to the claimant in that case but it has been suggested that an appeal against an assessment of disablement should be treated as being also an appeal against the refusal of benefit, unless the Secretary of State is prepared to treat it as an application for revision of the refusal of benefit (*CI/1547/2001*). This is because, if there is no appeal against the refusal of benefit, it would have to be revised or superseded to give effect to a successful appeal in respect of the assessment of disablement. It does not appear that any such revision or supersession could be effective from the beginning of the period of assessment if action for revision or supersession is taken only after the tribunal's decision. There are other circumstances where a decision against one decision should be taken to be also an appeal against another decision, even where the other decision is implicit and has not actually been recorded. Thus, in *R(JSA) 2/04*, it was held that, where a claimant seeks benefit for the period between the end of one award and a new claim, an appeal against a refusal to backdate the new claim must sometimes be treated as being also an appeal against the termination of that previous award, because the latter may be the decision that is really being challenged. In *Abbas v Secretary of State for Work and Pensions* [2005] EWCA Civ 652, where the claimant had made a continuation claim for disability living allowance and the Secretary of State's response was to supersede the existing award and terminate it before it had originally been due to end, it was necessary for the appeal against the supersession decision to be treated also as an appeal against a disallowance of the continuation claim because otherwise, if the claimant showed that she satisfied the conditions for entitlement to disability living allowance, benefit could not be awarded in respect of any period after the original renewal date.

A *lacuna* in subs.(1) was explored in *R(IS) 14/04*, where the claimant had purported to appeal to an appeal tribunal against a decision to the effect that benefit was recoverable from him under s.74 of the Social Security Administration Act 1992. The Commissioner agreed with the tribunal that a right of appeal could not arise under subs.(1)(b) because there was no reference in Sch.3 to decisions under s.74 of the 1992 Act, although paras 5 and 6 of the Schedule refer to recoverability decisions made under s.71 of the 1992 Act and subs.(4) shows that it is intended that claimants should be entitled to appeal against decisions under either s.71 or s.74. He concluded that the right of appeal arose under subs.(1)(a) because the decision under s.74 "is sufficiently related to the award of income support on which the excess payment has been made".

Subs. (2)

1.377
For regulations made under this subsection, see regs 25 and 27 of the Social Security and Child Support (Decisions and Appeals) Regulations 1999, reg.3 of the Tax Credits (Appeals) (No. 2) Regulations 2002 and regs 24 and 25 of the Child Benefit and Guardian's Allowance (Decisions and Appeal) Regulations 2003.

Although an appeal to a tribunal must be lodged at an "appropriate office" administered by the Secretary of State or other body from whom the appeal is to be brought (see reg. 33 of the 1999 Regulations and reg. 31 of the 2003 Regulations), the Secretary of State is not entitled to refuse to refer the case to a tribunal if he considers

(1998 c.14, s.12)

that the tribunal has no jurisdiction to hear it. It is for the tribunal to determine whether it has jurisdiction to hear a case *(R(I) 7/94)* and, if the Secretary of State were to refuse to refer an appeal lodged at an office of the Department for Work and Pensions to the tribunal, it would be open to the tribunal to consider whether it had jurisdiction and, if it had, to determine the appeal without the appeal having been passed to it by the Secretary of State *(R(H) 1/07)*.

The powers of a tribunal

An appeal to a tribunal is a rehearing *(R(F) 1/72)*; it is not just a review of the decision under appeal. The tribunal stands in the shoes of the decision-maker and has the power to consider any issue and make any decision the decision-maker could have made *(R(IB) 2/04)*. Therefore, where the Secretary of State has a broad discretion, e.g. as to the period of disqualification for jobseeker's allowance to be imposed when a person leaves his employment voluntarily without just cause, the tribunal has to substitute its own judgment for that of the Secretary of State, rather than merely considering whether the Secretary of State has acted reasonably *(CJSA/1703/2006, R(AF)3/07)*.

1.378

In *R(H) 6/06*, it was said that "a right of appeal against an exercise of discretion that is non-justiciable because the relevant considerations cannot be discerned must be limited to points of law". A discretion is non-justiciable only if the relevant considerations are policy matters requiring "essentially non-legal judgments" *(R(H) 3/04)* and legislation does not normally confer a right of appeal to a tribunal against such a decision unless it expressly limits the right to points of law. If legislation appears to confer such a right in respect of a non-justiciable decsion, there may arise questions as to the construction or validity of the legislation, as in *R(H) 6/06*. In *CH/1821/2006*, the Commissioner pointed out that the mere fact that different people might legitimately exercise their judgment differently on the same facts does not make the judgment a discretion and, if there is a discretion, does not make it non-justiciable. It has not been suggested that any appeal under s.12 is capable of raising a non-justiciable issue.

There is nothing in s.12 to indicate what powers a tribunal has when it allows an appeal, and it is therefore open to a tribunal to set aside a decision and, in effect, to remit the case to the original decision-maker where that appears to be more appropriate than substituting its own decision. Examples are where the decision under appeal was made without jurisdiction or where a recoverability decision should have been made against a person who is not a party to the appeal *(R(H) 6/06)* or where issues first arise in the course of an appeal *(CIS/624/2006*, where it was made clear that the tribunal must nonetheless deal with the issues originally raised in the appeal). Thus, although an appeal to a tribunal normally lies only against an "outcome decision" *(R(IB) 2/04)*, a tribunal hearing an appeal against an "outcome decision" is not always obliged to substitute another such decision. The Tribunal of Commissioners said, at para.48 of *CIS/624/2006* –

> "When an appeal against an outcome decision raises one issue on which the appeal is allowed but it is necessary to deal with a further issue before another outcome decision is substituted, a tribunal may set aside the original outcome decision without substituting another outcome decision, provided it deals with the original issue raised by the appeal and substitutes a decision on that issue. The Secretary of State must then consider the new issue and decide what outcome decision to give. In that outcome decision, he must give effect to the tribunal's decision on the original issue unless, at the time he makes the outcome decision, he is satisfied that there are grounds on which to supersede the tribunal's decision so as, for instance, to take account of any changes of circumstances that have occurred since he made the decision that was the subject of the appeal to the tribunal. Because his decision is an outcome decision, the claimant will have a right of appeal against it."

The Tribunal of Commissioners gave the following additional guidance at para. 55(2) –

"Where a tribunal, having dealt with the issues originally raised in an appeal, is not able immediately to give an outcome decision, it must decide whether to adjourn or whether to remit the question of entitlement to the Secretary of State. The technical difficulty of the outstanding issues and the likelihood of a further appeal if the entitlement question is remitted will be relevant considerations. The tribunal should consider whether the Secretary of State would be in a better position to decide the issue and to seek further information from the claimant. It may have to balance the desirability of a decision being made as quickly as possible against the desirability of it being made as accurately as possible, given that an appeal on a point of fact will not lie against a decision of the tribunal on any fresh issue. The wishes of the parties should be taken into account."

The inquisitorial role of the tribunal and the burden of proof

1.379 It has long been recognised that proceedings before tribunals are inquisitorial rather than adversarial and this has been confirmed by the House of Lords in *Kerr v Department for Social Development* [2004] UKHL 23; [2004] 1 W.L.R. 1372 (also reported as an appendix to *R1/04(SF)*), where some of the consequences of this approach were considered. Baroness Hale of Richmond said:

"61. Ever since the decision of the Divisional Court in *R. v Medical Appeal Tribunal (North Midland Region), Ex p. Hubble* [1958] 2 Q.B. 228, it has been accepted that the process of benefits adjudication in inquisitorial rather than adversarial. Diplock J. as he then was said this of an industrial injury benefit claim at p.240:

'A claim by an insured person to benefit under the Act is not truly analogous to a *lis inter partes*. A claim to benefit is a claim to receive money out of the insurance funds . . . Any such claim investigation to determine whether any, and if so, what amount of benefit is payable out of the fund. In such an investigation, the minister or insurance officer is not a party adverse to the claimant. If analogy be sought in the other branches of the law, it is to be found in an inquest rather than an action.'

62. What emerges from all this is a co-operative process of investigation in which both the claimant and the department play their part. The department is the one which knows what questions it needs to ask and what information it needs to have in order to determine whether the conditions of entitlement have been met. The claimant is the one who generally speaking can and must supply that information. But where the information is available to the department rather than the claimant, then the department must take the necessary steps to enable it to be traced.

63. If that sensible approach is taken, it will rarely be necessary to resort to concepts taken from adversarial litigation such as the burden of proof. The first question will be whether each partner in the process has played their part. If there is still ignorance about a relevant matter then generally speaking it should be determined against the one who has not done all that they reasonably could to discover it. As Mr Commissioner Henty put it in *CIS/5321/1998*: 'a claimant must to the best of his or her ability give such information to the AO as he reasonably can, in default of which a contrary inference can always be drawn.' The same should apply to information which the department can reasonably be expected to discover for itself."

In that particular case the claimant had been unable to tell the department whether either his brother or sister, with whom he had lost contact, was in receipt of relevant benefits. The department could have discovered that information had they had the brother's and sister's dates of birth, which the claimant could have given them but for which the department never asked. It was held that the department could not rely on their failure to ask questions which would have led to the right answer to defeat the claim.

Where all relevant questions have been asked and there are still things unknown, it was held in *Kerr* that it has to be decided who should bear the consequences of the collective ignorance. If the ignorance concerns a matter relevant to conditions of entitlement, the claimant has to bear the consequences but if the ignorance concerns an exception to those conditions, the department must bear the consequences. In *Kerr*, the claimant was prima facie entitled to a funeral payment but would not be entitled if his brother or sister was not receiving benefit or had capital. The ignorance as to whether they were receiving benefit or had capital was therefore ignorance concerning an exception to entitlement and the department had to bear the burden and pay the claim. Lord Hope of Craighead set out, at para.[16], the following basic principles to be applied where the information available to a decision-maker falls short of what is needed for a clear decision one way or the other.

> "(1) Facts which may reasonably be supposed to be within the claimant's own knowledge are for the claimant to supply at each stage in the inquiry.
> (2) But the claimant must be given a reasonable opportunity to supply them. Knowledge as to the information that is needed to deal with his claim lies with the department, not with him.
> (3) So it is for the department to ask the relevant questions. The claimant is not to be faulted if the relevant questions to show whether or not the claim is excluded by the Regulations were not asked.
> (4) The general rule is that it is for the party who alleges an affirmative to make good his allegation. It is also a general rule that he who desires to take advantage of an exception must bring himself within the provisions of the exception. As Lord Wilberforce observed, exceptions are to be set up by those who rely on them: *Nimmo v Alexander Cowan & Sons Ltd* [1968] A.C. 107, 130."

It is suggested that the tribunal in *Kerr* would not necessarily have been obliged to determine the case in the claimant's favour when the case first came before them. The inquisitorial role of tribunals obliges them to ask questions that the Secretary of State should have asked but has not (*R(IS) 11/99*). It would have been open to the tribunal to ask the claimant whether he knew the dates of birth of his brother and sister and, if the answer was in the affirmative, to give the department the opportunity of investigating the matter further. However, the question whether to adjourn in those circumstances is a matter within the discretion of the tribunal and the department cannot expect always to be given a chance to do something it could perfectly well have done earlier. By the time *Kerr* reached the courts, it was doubtless felt to be a bit late for the department to be making further enquiries.

Kerr was decided in the context of a claim. It is suggested, however, that it is reasonably clear that, on an appeal against a supersession decision made on the Secretary of State's own initiative, it is the Secretary of State who must bear the burden of ignorance as to whether there are grounds for supersession because it is he who must assert that there are grounds for supersession.

The effect of the tribunal having an inquisitorial role was also considered by a Tribunal of Commissioners in *R(IS) 17/04*. In 2002, the Secretary of State had superseded awards of benefit from 1988, amounting to some £30,000. The claimant appealed and the Secretary of State made a written submission and produced a considerable amount of evidence. A tribunal chairman directed that a presenting officer attend the hearing to put the Secretary of State's case. In the event, two investigating officers attended as witnesses but there was no presenting officer and a short adjournment established that none would attend. On the basis that the burden of proof lay on the Secretary of State and that the written material was not sufficient in the light of the specific direction that there be a presenting officer, the tribunal allowed the claimant's appeal without putting to her the Secretary of State's case. The Tribunal of Commissioners held the tribunal to have erred. The written material had been sufficient to raise a case for the claimant to answer and the inquisitorial role of the tribunal required the tribunal "to ascertain and determine the true amount of social security benefit to which the claimant was properly entitled", which, once the tribunal had decided not to adjourn, entailed putting the case raised by the Secretary of State's written material to the claimant and enabling her representative to question the witnesses. The Tribunal of Commissioners rejected a submission that a tribunal could not act fairly if it "descended into the arena" and they referred to another decision of a Tribunal of Commissioners, *R(S) 4/82*, where it was said that it was legitimate for a tribunal to put questions, even probing questions, to a claimant to deal with the obvious points that arose on an appeal. However, questions from a tribunal have to be put carefully and phrased neutrally and a tribunal chairman must avoid the risk described in *Southwark LBC v Kofi-Adu* [2006] EWCA Civ 281 that his descent into the arena "may so hamper his ability properly to evaluate and weigh the evidence before him as to impair his judgment, and may *for that reason* render the trial unfair" (emphasis of the Court of Appeal). Plainly it is better that the Secretary of State be represented in highly contentious or complex cases and the Tribunal of Commissioners recorded both the Secretary of State's declared policy "to appear by way of a presenting officer at every tribunal hearing where the tribunal had made a direction requiring a presenting officer to attend" and the Secretary of State's acceptance of a recommendation of the National Audit Office that he should himself identify complex cases where spending money on presenting officers might achieve greater financial savings.

The Tribunal of Commissioners cited with approval *CI/1021/2001*, where it was held that a tribunal is not entitled to rely upon a "failure to discharge the burden of proof as a substitute for a proper enquiry where there is evidence that there is something into which there needs to be an enquiry". A similar approach led a Tribunal of Commissioners in Northern Ireland to hold a tribunal to have erred when, at a "paper hearing", they had incomplete evidence that raised important issues it could not answer and they failed to adjourn in order to give the claimant the opportunity of attending *(R1/02(IB))*. However, it does not follow from *R(IS) 17/04* that decision-making bodies need make no effort to present evidence to a tribunal. In *CTC/2090/2004*, the Board of Inland Revenue failed to provide any evidence to a tribunal on the question whether the claimant or his ex-wife had the main responsibility for their daughter. That was important because it determined which of the parents was entitled to child tax credit. Both of the parents had claimed child tax credit and it had been awarded to the claimant's ex-wife. The Board did not ask for an adjournment and did not even send an officer to the hearing. The tribunal heard evidence from the claimant as to which parent had the main responsibility for the child and allowed his appeal. The Board appealed on the ground that its position was neutral and that as child tax credit could not be awarded to both parents, the tribunal's inquisitorial jurisdiction required it to summons the claimant's ex-wife to provide evidence against the claimant in her interest. The Commissioner gave that argument short shrift. Being neutral did not justify inactivity on the Board's part. In the light of *Kerr*, it had been the Board's duty to investigate the cases of both parents properly and avoid inconsistent decisions, which clearly meant enquiring themselves into the question of which parent had the main responsibility. However, the tribunal's decision would not be binding on the claimant's ex-wife and the tribunal had been entitled to assume that the Board was content for the claimant's appeal to be determined without information being obtained from his ex-wife. In other words, the tribunal's inquisitorial duty in respect of the father's claim had been satisfied by obtaining relevant evidence from him.

What, however, is made plain in *R(IS) 17/04* is that the inquisitorial role of the tribunal is not brought into play only for the purpose of assisting a claimant. A tribunal is part of the machinery for determining the true entitlement of a claimant. It follows that a tribunal is at liberty to follow its own view of a case even if that does not coincide with the view of either the claimant or the Secretary of State (*R. v Deputy Industrial Injuries Commissioner, Ex p. Moore* [1965] 1 Q.B. 456 (C.A.) (also reported as an appendix to *R(I) 4/65)*).

Evidence

1.380   It may be arguable that the emphasis in *Kerr* on the duty of the department to cooperate in the investigation of cases has some implications for the standard of evidence that should be expected from the department so far as its own records are concerned. In *R(IS) 11/92*, the Commissioner held that no adverse inference was to be drawn against the department where it had destroyed documents in a general "weeding" programme rather with any specific intention of destroying evidence. However, it may be suggested that a tribunal should not be quick to disbelieve a claimant where the department's inability to produce contrary evidence is due to the reckless weeding of documents that should have been seen to be relevant to foreseeable proceedings. Even more is that true when documents have been destroyed while a case has been pending. In *Post Office Counters Ltd v Mahida* [2003] EWCA Civ 1583, the Court of Appeal held a judge to have erred in allowing the Post Office to rely on secondary evidence when the defendant's ability to challenge it had been undermined by the Post Office's own loss or destruction of original documents before proceedings were brought but when proceedings might have been contemplated. On the other hand, secondary evidence of the terms of a decision is acceptable where there were plainly grounds for a decision that produced the outcome that had been achieved, particularly as the law generally presumes, in the absence of evidence to the contrary, that that which ought to have been done has in fact been done (*CIB/3838/2003*). Similarly, it may be inferred from a record that a document has been "issued" that it was actually posted (*Secretary of State for Work and Pensions v Roach* [2007] EWCA Civ 1746 (reported as *R(CS) 4/07*)).

In *CCS/3757/2004*, the Commissioner points out that a failure to provide evidence does not necessarily justify the drawing of an adverse inference against the person who should have provided the evidence. All the circumstances and the other evidence that is available must be considered. It may be particularly relevant to consider whether the failure to produce evidence might have been due to it being unfavourable to the party concerned. In many cases, a failure to produce evidence merely justifies a conclusion that there is no, or no adequate, evidence on a particular point, which will then fall to be determined against the person who bears the "burden of collective ignorance" (see *Kerr*, above). That is not quite the same as drawing an adverse inference, which involves making a positive finding against the party concerned. However, the effect will be much the same in many cases and, where it is not, it will often be appropriate to draw an adverse inference, which *Kerr* makes clear is permissible. Thus, for instance, a claimant's failure to produce evidence of the amount of her income following a clear request may well justify a positive finding that she receives income at a level that makes her ineligible for benefit (*R(H) 3/05*). *CCS/3757/2004*, however, emphasises the need to consider any other evidence in the case before going so far as to draw an adverse inference. Note, also, that providing evidence late is unlikely to justify the drawing of an adverse inference, unless it justifies ignoring the evidence altogether (see *CIB/4253/2004*).

Tribunals are not bound by the common law rules of evidence and so, in *CDLA/2014/2004*, a tribunal erred in refusing to allow a disability consultant to give evidence of his opinion. However, it does not follow that those rules of evidence have no relevance at all. Tribunals have no power to override any privilege of a witness not to give evidence, such as the privilege attaching to solicitor-client communications and the privilege against self-incrimination. Furthermore, the common law rules of evidence may be relevant in the evaluation of evidence because the considerations which have led to the evidence being inadmissible often mean that it has little weight. Thus, in *CDLA/2014/2004*, there might have been good reasons for treating the disability consultant's evidence with caution, but it was wrong to refuse to consider it at all. Similarly, in *R(IB) 7/05*, the Commissioner held that it was not necessary for the Secretary of State to follow the certification procedure under s.7 of the under the Electronic Communications Act 2000 when there was a challenge to the authenticity of an electronic signature. In *CCS/3749/2003*, it was held that a tribunal should refuse to consider any information about proceedings relating to children of a court sitting in private (because use of the information by a party is potentially a contempt of court) but was entitled to hear evidence about ancillary relief proceedings that had taken in place in private. See also *CCR/3425/2003*. In *CCS/1495/2005*, it was pointed out that it is very easy to obtain the permission of a family court to use court documents that are really relevant to an issue before a tribunal.

In *R(DLA) 3/99*, the Commissioner held that it was wrong for a tribunal to accept evidence of an examining medical practitioner on the basis that it must normally prevail over other evidence, even though in practice, once a proper weighing exercise had been carried out without giving an examining medical practitioner's evidence any special weight, the examining medical practitioner's evidence might be accepted in the majority of cases. Equally, a tribunal is not entitled to arrive at a view of the credibility of the claimant and then, as a separate exercise, consider whether that finding might be shifted by the expert evidence available; "The evidence has to be looked at as a whole" (*AJ (Cameroon) v Secretary of State for the Home Department* [2007] EWCA Civ 373). Even where an expert's evidence is found convincing, a tribunal is entitled to accept evidence from a blameless and honest witness that conflicts with it and conclude that, although it cannot identify an error in the expert's evidence, some such error must exist (*Armstrong v FirstYork Ltd* [2005] EWCA Civ 277; [2005] 1 W.L.R. 2751). In *CIB/3074/2003*, the Commissioner suggested that a distinction could be drawn in some cases between the weight to be given to clinical findings of an examining medical officer and the weight to be given to his or her assessment as to the claimant's capabilities in the light of those findings.

"13. In *CIB/15663/1996*, deputy Commissioner Fellner (as she then was) stated that a tribunal was entitled to give full weight to an examining medical officer's findings. A tribunal should of course give full weight to all the evidence, but may often be justified in regarding clinical findings of an examining medical officer as reliable, although even clinical findings should not be regarded as conclusive and may in some cases be displaced by other evidence. However, the impact of any given degree of loss of function will vary from claimant to claimant. In some cases (such as incontinence) a clinical examination will often give very little indication of the extent of impairment of the activities which need to be considered in carrying out the personal capability assessment, although in such cases the examining medical practitioner will often be able to make an informed assessment of the degree of impairment on the basis of the claimant's medical history and other evidence of functional ability. The examining medical officer's choice of a descriptor will therefore generally require the exercise of judgment to a greater or lesser degree, and a tribunal may therefore not necessarily give the same weight to an examining medical officer's choice of descriptors as it does to clinical findings on examination."

In *R(DLA) 3/06*, the foster parent and appointee of the 12-year old claimant, who was alleged to have learning difficulties and behavioural problems, did not arrange for her to attend the hearing to give oral evidence, despite a summons. The Tribunal of Commissioners said:

"[W]e consider the approach of the tribunal to the child claimant – in summonsing the child to give evidence, and then in drawing an adverse inference from the fact that she did not attend (despite the view of the local authority, her carer and a clinical psychologist that her attendance might have an adverse effect upon her) – was inappropriate and unlawful as breaching the claimant's right to a fair hearing."

The Tribunal of Commissioners gave general guidance as to the circumstances in which a child's evidence should be heard (see the note to reg.49 of the Social Security and Child Support (Decisions and Appeals) Regulations 1999).

Correcting procedural errors by the Secretary of State

1.381   In *R(IB)2/04*, a Tribunal of Commissioners considered in depth the jurisdiction of tribunals and the extent to which tribunals are limited, or not limited, by the terms of the decision against which an appeal has been brought. They noted that s.12 makes no positive provision at all as to a tribunal's powers so that those powers must be found by a process of implication. They therefore considered the case law

(1998 c.14, s.12)

on adjudication before the 1998 Act came into force (in particular, *R(F) 1/72*, *R(P) 1/55*, *R(SB) 1/82* and *R(SB) 42/83*). That led to the conclusion that an appeal to an appeal tribunal under s.12 is by way of rehearing. At paragraph 24, the Tribunal said:

> "As a matter of principle, on such an appeal the tribunal may make any decision which the officer below could have made on the legal questions before that officer. That principle encompasses dealing with new questions so as to reach the right result on an appeal, within the limit that the appeal tribunal has no jurisdiction (in the absence of express legislation to that effect) to determine questions which fall outside the scope of that which the officer below could have done on the proper legal view of the issues before him, by way of a claim or an application or otherwise."

They pointed out, at para.31, that s.12(8)(a) reinforces that approach because it is implicit in that provision that an appeal tribunal is not limited to considering issues actually raised by the parties.

Against that background, the Tribunal considered three issues concerning the powers of tribunals: whether supersession decisions can be substituted for revision decisions and vice versa, whether defects in supersession decisions can be remedied, and whether a tribunal can make a decision less favourable to a claimant than the decision under appeal. (Other issues considered by the Tribunal are noted in the annotations to regs 3 and 6 of the Social Security and Child Support (Decisions and Appeals) Regulations 1999).

Can supersession decisions be substituted for revision decisions and vice versa?

1.382

The Tribunal's decision on this issue is based on their view of the nature of appeals following supersession decisions under s.10 and revision decisions under s.9. In the former case, the appeal is, both in form and in substance, an appeal against the decision to supersede or not to supersede. Where there has been a revision or a refusal to revise, any appeal is, in form, against the original decision because s.12(1) does not provide for an appeal against the decision under s.9 but reg.31(2) of the Social Security and Child Support (Decisions and Appeals) Regulations 1999 extends the time for appealing against the earlier decision as revised or, where the revision or non-revision was under regs 3(1) or (3), not revised. If there is a refusal to revise under, say, reg.3(5)(a) on the ground of "official error", the time for appealing is not extended which may have the consequence that the refusal to revise cannot be challenged save by way of judicial review (*R(IS)15/04*, approved by the Court of Appeal in *Beltekian v Westminster CC* [2004] EWCA Civ 1784 (reported as *R(H) 8/05*)). However, where a claimant is entitled to appeal following a refusal to revise a decision on the ground of "official error", he or she must show that the original decision did arise from an official error if the appeal is to be allowed. Therefore, the Tribunal held at para.40 of *R(IB)2/04*, an appeal following a revision or refusal to revise is, in substance, an appeal against the decision under s.9, even if in form it is an appeal against the original decision.

The parties nonetheless argued that the legislation did not allow a tribunal to give a supersession decision on appeal from a revision decision and vice versa, although counsel for the claimants submitted that it should readily be implied that a revision decision included a refusal to supersede and that a supersession decision included a refusal to revise. However, the Tribunal considered that the result of taking the approach advocated by the parties had too often been absurd. At para.50, they said:

> "The meaning of a statutory provision which is so clear that it admits only one possible construction cannot be altered or departed from by reference to the consequences, however inconvenient or anomalous. However, in our judgement the statutory provisions relevant to this issue fail by some margin to reach the degree of clarity which would bring that principle into play. In these circumstances, in ascertaining the legislature's intention, it is quite proper to have regard to the potential consequences of possible alternative constructions, in the context of the statutory scheme as a whole. In the field of benefit decisions and appeals

procedure, we consider it proper, in construing the relevant provisions, to assume that the legislature did not intend to create a scheme which would be likely to lead to impracticable or indeed absurd results in a significant number of cases. On the contrary, we proceed on the basis that the legislature intended the provisions relating to decisions and appeals (and in particular those relating to provisions changing the effect of a previous decision) to form at least a reasonably workable scheme."

Having given examples of some of the more absurd consequences of the parties' submissions, the Tribunal held, at para.55:

"In our judgment, if an appeal tribunal decides that the Secretary of State's decision under Section 9 or Section 10 changing or refusing to change a previous decision was wrong then (subject to the restriction in Section 12(8)(b), if relevant) it has jurisdiction to make the revision or supersession decision which it considers the Secretary of State ought to have made, even if that means making a decision under Section 9 when the Secretary of State acted only under Section 10, and vice versa."

They rejected the need to resort to the theory of implied decisions on the ground that "the 1998 legislation could not have been intended to involve consideration of such arid technicalities and complications" (para.59). However, in *R(IS) 15/04*, the same Tribunal, sitting a few weeks later resiled somewhat from what they had said in both para.55 and para.59 of *R(IB) 2/04*. In *R(IS) 15/04* (subsequently approved by the Court of Appeal in *Beltekian v Westminster CC* [2004] EWCA Civ 1784 (reported as *R(H) 8/05*)), the Secretary of State had expressly both superseded and refused to revise a decision. The claimant appealed but was out of time for appealing against the original decision and so was unable to challenge the refusal to revise although he could challenge the supersession. The Tribunal of Commissioners held that the appeal tribunal had had no jurisdiction to substitute a revision for the supersession, saying, at para.78:

"It seems to us, in those circumstances, if an appeal tribunal were permitted to substitute a revision decision for the supersession decision, that would in effect be to permit by the back door what is not permitted by the front door, namely an appeal against the refusal to revise."

Obscurely, they added that "[i]t would have been a different matter if the Secretary of State had not made a decision (whether express or implied) on the issue of revision for official error". It is not clear why they took that view, which, strictly speaking, is obiter, particularly as it is not clear what they meant by an implied decision, given their rejection of the theory in *R(IB) 2/04*. It is suggested that the theory of implied decisions would always treat a decision in terms of supersession as an implied refusal to revise, even if the issue of official error had not expressly been considered, because it is a precondition of any supersession decision that there are no grounds for revision (see reg.6(3) of the Social Security and Child Support (Decisions and Appeals) Regulations 1999, which allows only a technical exception to that general rule). However, in *CDLA/1707/2005*, the Deputy Commissioner applied the approach of the Tribunal of Commissioners and substituted for a refusal to supersede an award of benefit a decision revising the award on the ground of "official error".

Can defects in supersession decisions be remedied?

1.383
The Tribunal of Commissioners in *R(IB) 2/04* held that an appeal tribunal can remedy defects in a decision such as failing to acknowledge that an existing decision needed superseding, failing to state the grounds of supersession or relying on the wrong grounds of supersession.

"72. . . . there may be some decisions made by the Secretary of State which have so little coherence or connection to legal powers that they do not amount to decisions under Section 10 at all. . . .

(1998 c.14, s.12)

73. If, however, the Secretary of State's decision was made under Section 10 (as to which, see paragraph 76 below), . . . the appeal tribunal has jurisdiction, on appeal, to decide whether the outcome arrived at by that decision (i.e. either to change or not to change the original decision) was correct. . . .

76. In our judgment a decision should generally be regarded as having been made under Section 10, regardless of the form in which it may be expressed, if it has the effect of terminating an existing entitlement from the date of the decision (or from some later date than the effective date of the original decision). . . . Similarly, a decision should generally be regarded as having been made under Section 9 if it changes the original decision with effect from the effective date of that decision."

The implication of the Tribunal's decision appears to be that an appeal tribunal should limit its decision to holding that the Secretary of State's decision was invalid only in cases where the Secretary of State's decision is completely incoherent and the nature of the decision cannot be implied or where the Secretary of State had no power to make any decision at all. Another implication of a tribunal being entitled to correct defects in decisions of the Secretary of State is that it will often be unnecessary for a tribunal to consider the exact nature of the decision of the Secretary of State that is under appeal; it will usually be enough to consider what he *should* have decided (*CIS/624/2006*).

The Tribunal went on to say, at para.82, that it is necessary for an appeal tribunal chairman to "perfect" or "recast" a defective decision in the tribunal's decision notice only "if either (i) the decision as expressed is wrong in some material respect (e.g. states an incorrect ground of appeal) or (ii) there is likely to be some particular practical benefit to the claimant or to the adjudication process in future in reformulating the decision". However, if a statement of reasons is requested, giving reasons for the tribunal's decision is likely to involve explaining how any defects in the Secretary of State's decision were approached.

The ability of a tribunal to correct defects in a decision of the Secretary of State means that, where the Secretary of State wrongly applied the personal capability assessment as amended by regulations that had been held to be ultra vires, the tribunal was entitled to substitute a decision by applying the unamended test (*R(IB)5/05*).

Can a tribunal make a decision less favourable to a claimant than a supersession decision under appeal?

The Tribunal held that an appeal tribunal could make a decision less favourable to a claimant than a supersession decision under appeal. This followed both from the Tribunal's view as to the nature of an appeal to an appeal tribunal and from the terms of s.12(8)(a), implicitly providing that a tribunal may consider issues not raised by the parties. However, the Tribunal made two important comments at paras 94 and 97 of their decision.

1.384

Firstly, a tribunal must consciously exercise the discretion in s.12(8)(a) to consider a point not raised by the parties and, if a statement of reasons is requested, must explain in that statement why the discretion was exercised in the manner it was. For the points to be taken into account when exercising the discretion, see the annotation to s.12(8)(a) below.

Secondly, where the tribunal's decision is even less favourable to the claimant than the original decision that was the subject of the supersession decision under appeal, the tribunal's decision is "effectively the exercise by the tribunal of the Secretary of State's power to supersede 'on his own initiative' " and so, by virtue of s.10(5), the decision is usually effective from the date of the Secretary of State's decision under appeal rather than from the date of the claimant's application for supersession.

1.385

Subs.(3)

See the note to Sch.2 to the Social Security and Child Support (Decisions and Appeals) Regulations 1999 in which it is suggested that either much of that schedule is ultra vires or else this subsection is of no practical effect.

1.386

225

Subs. (4)

1.387
Although this subsection assumes that a claimant has a right of appeal against a decision under either s.71 or s.74 of the 1992 Act, only decisions under s.71 are mentioned in Sch.3. However, in *R(IS)14/04*, the Commissioner held that a claimant was entitled to appeal against a decision under s.74 by virtue of subs.(1)(a) of this section, rather than subs.(1)(b).

Subs. (7)

1.388
See regs 31–33 of the Social Security and Child Support (Decisions and Appeals) Regulations 1999, and regs 28–32 of the Child Benefit and Guardian's Allowance (Decisions and Appeals) Regulations 2003 and reg.4 of the Child Trust Funds (Appeals) Regulations 2005.

Subs. (8)(a)

1.389
In *CDLA/1000/2001*, it was held that the question whether an issue is "raised by the appeal" is to be determined by reference to the substance of the appeal and not just the wording of the letter of appeal. The claimant was in receipt of the mobility component of disability living allowance and was seeking the care component. The Commissioner decided that, as the claimant had attributed some of his care needs to the arthritis that caused his mobility difficulties, it was impossible for the tribunal to consider the care component without also considering the basis of the award of the mobility component. Therefore, the claimant's entitlement to the mobility component was raised by his appeal in respect of the care component. The Commissioner also held that the claimant had no preserved right to the protection formerly accorded to life awards of one component when a claimant had sought the other. That protection had been swept away when Pt II of the Social Security Administration Act 1992 was repealed by the Social Security Act 1998.

Paragraph (a) confers a discretion. In *CI/531/2000*, the Commissioner considered a standard submission by the Secretary of State in appeals relating to the diagnosis of industrial diseases in which it was said that the only issue before the tribunal was the diagnosis question and that, if the tribunal decided that question in the claimant's favour, it was not possible for them to go on and consider whether to award benefit. The Commissioner held the submission to be wrong in law but that the discretion to consider other issues must be exercised judicially. He pointed out that it was often desirable to deal with disablement at the same time as diagnosis but he said that natural justice required that the claimant (and, it can be added, the Secretary of State) be warned that disablement would also be considered and that when a tribunal dealt with a factual issue that had not previously been considered, the result was that the claimant was deprived of any appeal on the facts (and, it may be added, any application for revision under reg.3(1)(b) of the Social Security and Child Support (Decisions and Appeals) Regulations 1999). However, as already noted in relation to subs.(1), it was held in *CIB/2338/2000* that appeals lie only against "outcome decisions" and not against determinations of mere "questions". It follows that, in any case where a claimant has claimed disablement benefit, a determination that he or she is not suffering from a prescribed disease will be a determination made for the purpose of deciding that disablement benefit is not payable and any challenge to the determination will be made in an appeal against the refusal of benefit. If, on such an appeal, a tribunal decides that the claimant *was* suffering from the prescribed disease at the date the Secretary of State's decision was given, can the tribunal refuse to go on and determine all the other issues that must be determined if a decision is to be made as to whether or not to award benefit? No doubt they can adjourn and give the parties the opportunity of considering the other issues, but is it necessary for them to substitute an "outcome decision" for the one they have held to be wrong? The conclusion reached in *CI/531/2000* suggests that the implication of subs.(8)(a) is that a tribunal has a discretion as to whether to substitute an "outcome decision" for one they have found was wrong or alternatively merely to set aside the decision-maker's "outcome decision", determine the specific issue raised on the appeal and then refer the case back to the Secretary of State to make a fresh "outcome decision" in the light of their determination. It may be thought unhelpful that the legislation nowhere specifies exactly what the tribunal's powers are (compare s.14(8) in relation to Commissioners). However, it has long been common practice for tribunals and Commissioners to determine contentious issues that the parties have wanted determined and leave other matters for the first instance decision-maker to determine later and it seems unlikely that it was intended to prohibit that practice.

A slightly different approach was taken in *CIS/3535/2003*, where the claimant was told that a refusal of a social fund funeral payment, against which she had appealed, had been revised although the amount of the payment had not been quantified. The Deputy Commissioner observed that the concept of an "outcome decision" was not mentioned in the legislation and he held that the revision was effective and caused the outstanding appeal to lapse under s.9(6). This case is probably distinguishable from *CIS/3228/2003*, in which it was held that a purported revision that did not quantify entitlement was an insufficient basis for a decision that an overpayment was recoverable.

In *R(IB)2/04* at paras 93 and 94, the Tribunal of Commissioners held that, where an appeal tribunal is minded to make a decision less favourable to the claimant than the one under appeal and the respondent has not invited them to make such a decision, the appeal tribunal must address their minds to the power conferred by subs.(8)(a) not to consider the issue. The discretion is one to be exercised judicially, taking into account all the circumstances of the particular case. Furthermore, the tribunal's decision is likely to be held to be erroneous in point of law if the statement of reasons does not show that there has been a conscious exercise of the discretion.

"In exercising the discretion, the appeal tribunal must of course have in mind, in particular, two factors. First, it must bear in mind the need to comply with Article 6 of the Convention and the rules of natural justice. This will involve, at the very least, ensuring that the claimant has had sufficient notice of the tribunal's intention to consider superseding adversely to him to enable him properly to prepare his case. The fact that the claimant is entitled to withdraw his appeal any time before the appeal tribunal's decision may also be material to what Article 6 and the rules of natural justice demand. Second, the appeal tribunal may consider it more appropriate to leave the question whether the original decision should be superseded adversely to the claimant to be decided subsequently by the Secretary of State. This might be so if, for example, deciding that question would involve factual issues which do not overlap those raised by the appeal, or if it would necessitate an adjournment of the hearing."

The same approach is required where a tribunal takes a new point against the Secretary of State. In *CH/3009/2002*, a decision had been made on a claim that could have been treated also as an application for the revision of a decision terminating an earlier award. The Commissioner held that, although it followed from *R(IB)2/04* that the tribunal had the power to give a decision in terms of revision, the question of revision could be left to the Secretary of State. Thus, subs.(8)(a) can be seen as providing an alternative course of action to the adjournment that will sometimes be required where a new point is taken, although the Commissioner deciding *CH/3009/2002* did comment that, depending on the terms of the Secretary of State's decision, it might not be possible for a claimant to get the case back before a tribunal given the decision of the Tribunal of Commissioners in *R(IS)15/04* (subsequently approved by the Court of Appeal in *Beltekian v Westminster CC* [2004] EWCA Civ 1784 (reported as *R(H) 8/05*)). It is suggested that the position might be no different if there were an adjournment because the Secretary of State could presumably make a decision before the tribunal was reconvened.

In considering how the discretion conferred by para.(a) should be exercised, a tribunal ought to have regard (among other things) to the adequacy of any alternative action that the claimant or Secretary of State might take to have the new issue taken into account and, if it is not obvious, ought to draw attention to that alternative action

(*CDLA/15961/1996*). If an entirely new point is being taken at a hearing, it is necessary for the parties to have the opportunity of dealing with it but that does not necessarily mean there must be an adjournment because it ought to be possible for most points to be adequately considered immediately. If a party has deliberately chosen not to attend, the question whether there should be an adjournment so that he or she may consider the new point may be more complicated. There are three options: to refuse to consider the new point, to consider it immediately or to adjourn. A lot will depend on the nature of the issue and whether any advance notice was given of it, as well as the possibility of applying for a revision or supersession on the new ground. A wise appellant who wishes to raise a new point will give both the tribunal and the Secretary of State notice as soon as possible. However, if the Secretary of State chooses not to be represented at a hearing, it may be thought that he can hardly complain about not being allowed to comment on any evidence the claimant may give.

Subs.(8)(a) implies a power to consider new issues but makes it clear that there are limits to the extent to which the inquisitorial role of a tribunal imposes a duty to consider such issues. As was said by a Tribunal of Commissioners in *R(SB) 2/83*,

> "Everything will depend on the circumstances in any given instance. We would be slow to convict a tribunal of failure to identify an uncanvassed factual point in favour of the claimant in the absence of the most obvious and clear cut circumstances."

In particular, where a claimant has an apparently competent representative, it is not always necessary for a tribunal to explore matters not raised by the representative (see *CSDLA/336/2000*, in which the Commissioner reviews the authorities and emphasises the summary nature of proceedings before tribunals). Thus, in *CSIB/160/2000*, the representative identified the descriptors in issue on the all work test and the tribunal were entitled to assume that the representative knew the claimant's case and so therefore the tribunal did not err in not considering other descriptors. In *CH/2484/2006*, the Deputy Commissioner said that "it would be unrealistic – especially in a case like this where both parties were represented – to expect tribunals to read every clause of a tenancy agreement in case a representative fails to rely on a clause which might be helpful to his case". He also said –

> "To the extent that the local authority is dissatisfied with the outcome of this case, that perhaps highlights the need for thorough preparation of a local authority's factual case in advance of tribunal hearings, so that all the points can be raised there. Even the most thoroughly prepared appeal to a Commissioner is not an adequate substitute for doing so, for the reason that, however strongly a Commissioner might doubt the factual correctness of a tribunal decision . . ., the Commissioner's doubts are irrelevant in the absence of an error of law. And it will seldom be an error of law for a tribunal to fail to deal with a point that a local authority representative has not raised before it."

Even less is a tribunal required to investigate issues when a representative has declined to make submissions on them having been given a specific opportunity to do so (*CSIB/588/1998*).

However, sometimes issues raised by the evidence but overlooked by otherwise competent professional representatives are so fundamental that a tribunal will err in not dealing with them. That was the case in *R4/01(IS)*, a decision of a Tribunal of Commissioners in Northern Ireland. The claimant's executor had appealed to a tribunal against a decision that £63,735.31 had been overpaid to the claimant and was recoverable from her estate because the claimant had failed to disclose capital assets in the form of land. The executor was represented by counsel. The case was argued on the basis that there had been disclosure but it was stated that, although the legal interest in the land was vested in the claimant, the land had been regarded as belonging to her brother. The Tribunal of Commissioners held that that clearly raised the question whether the claimant had any beneficial interest in the land and that the appeal tribunal had erred in failing to consider that issue notwithstanding that it had not been raised by counsel representing the executor. The issue had been fundamental to the appeal. However, the Tribunal of Commissioners also said that an appeal tribunal must have a reasonable expectation that important and fundamental issues will be brought to its attention by professional representatives. Given the professional representation, if the issue of the property being regarded as belonging to the brother had not been mentioned by a witness at the hearing itself, the appeal tribunal would have been entitled to conclude it had been dropped.

The Court of Appeal in Northern Ireland has, in *Mongan v Department for Social Development* [2005] NICA 16 (reported as *R3/05 (DLA)*), taken a similar approach to that taken by Commissioners and the approach taken in *Mongan* has been expressly endorsed by the Court of Appeal in England and Wales (*Secretary of State for Work and Pensions v Hooper* [2007] EWCA Civ 495 (reported as *R(IB) 4/07*). In *Mongan*, the Court held that the identical wording of the Northern Ireland equivalent of s.12(8)(a) suggests "that the tribunal would not be absolved of the duty to consider relevant issues simply because they have been neglected by the appellant or her legal representatives and that it has a role to identify what issues are at stake on the appeal even if they have not been clearly or expressly articulated by the appellant." There is no duty "to exhaustively trawl the evidence to see if there is any remote possibility of an issue being raised by it" but issues "clearly apparent from the evidence" must be considered.

"[17] Whether an issue is sufficiently apparent from the evidence will depend on the particular circumstances of each case. Likewise, the question of how far the tribunal must go in exploring such an issue will depend on the specific facts of the case. The more obviously relevant an issue, the greater will be the need to investigate it. An extensive enquiry into an issue will not invariably be required. Indeed, a perfunctory examination of the issue may often suffice. It appears to us, however, that where a higher rate of benefit is claimed and the facts presented to the tribunal suggest that an appellant might well be entitled to a lower rate, it will normally be necessary to examine the issue, whether or not it has been raised by the appellant or her legal representatives.

[18] In carrying out their inquisitorial function, the tribunal should have regard to whether the party has the benefit of legal representation. It need hardly be said that close attention should be paid to the possibility that relevant issues might be overlooked where the appellant does not have legal representation. Where an appellant is legally represented the tribunal is entitled to look to the legal representative for elucidation of the issues that arise. But this does not relieve them of the obligation to enquire into potentially relevant matters. A poorly represented party should not be placed at any greater disadvantage than an unrepresented party."

In that case, the claimant had sought the higher rate of the mobility component of disability living allowance but the Court held that the arguments and evidence presented to the tribunal were such that it should have been alert to the need to investigate entitlement to the lower rate of the mobility component, whether or not that question was raised by the claimant's solicitor.

On the other hand, in *CDLA/4099/2004*, the Commissioner held that a tribunal had not erred in law in failing to deal with an issue when the claimant had an adequate alternative remedy. The claimant had applied for supersession of an award of disability living allowance. The application was treated as effective from the date it was received and, on appeal, the case was argued before the tribunal on that basis because the claimant's representative wrongly considered that an award of benefit for a period before the application could be considered on a subsequent application for revision. In fact, the tribunal could, by virtue of s.12(8)(a), have considered entitlement to benefit during that earlier period (because reg.7(6) of the Social Security and Child Support (Decisions and Appeals) Regulations 1999 would have applied if the claimant's proposed argument in respect of that earlier period had been accepted). However, the Commissioner held that the tribunal had not been *bound* to consider entitlement during that earlier period because the claimant still had an adequate alternative remedy in a further application for supersession.

Subs. (8) (b)

1.390   By contrast with para.(a), para.(b) confers no discretion. In the light of reg.3(9) of the Social Security and Child Support (Decisions and Appeals) Regulations 1999 and s.9(5) of the Act, when a decision has been revised under s.9, "the time when the decision appealed against was made" must refer to the date on which the original decision was made. Paragraph (b) is therefore consistent with the approach that any change of circumstances requires a new claim or a supersession under s.10 and it reverses the effect of *R(S)2/98*. Note, however, that para.(b) does not apply where the appeal was brought before May 21, 1998 when this Act received the Royal Assent and Sch.6, para.3 (which made transitory provision preventing social security appeal tribunals and disability appeal tribunals from taking account of circumstances not obtaining at the date of the decision under appeal) came into force. In such a case, a tribunal must still consider the claimant's entitlement to benefit throughout the period to the date of its decision or down to the date from which another decision is effective (*CIB/213/1999*).

Note also that para.(b) does not prevent a tribunal having regard to evidence that was not before the Secretary of State and came into existence after the decision was made or to evidence of events after the decision under appeal was made for the purpose of drawing inferences as to the circumstances obtaining when, or before, the decision was made (*R(DLA) 2/01, R(DLA) 3/01*). This creates particular difficulties where entitlement to benefit depends on a prognosis. Thus, in *R(DLA) 3/01*, the claimant would be entitled to disability living allowance only if she was likely to satisfy the relevant conditions for six months. She was recovering from an operation. The Commissioner held that, in such a case, a tribunal was entitled to take account of the actual rate of recovery, even though the evidence of that arose after the date of the decision under appeal, provided that the fact that the claimant had not recovered as quickly as originally expected merely reflected the natural vagaries of an uncertain recovery process. Untoward circumstances arising after the date of the decision had to be disregarded, whether that operated to the claimant's advantage or to her disadvantage. Thus the fact that a claimant recovering from a heart attack developed pneumonia after the Secretary of State's decision was made would have to be ignored. So too would a dramatic improvement in a claimant's condition due to the use of a new drug. A similar case came before a Commissioner in *CDLA/2878/2000*. The claimant was a nurse who became incapacitated due to a slipped disc. She claimed disability living allowance on August 31, 1999, had a successful operation on December 17, 1999 and was able to return to work on February 14, 2000. The tribunal said simply that disability living allowance could not be awarded because there was no evidence that the claimant could have satisfied the conditions of entitlement from February 14, 2000, which was less than six months from the date of claim. The Commissioner set aside the tribunal's decision on the ground that the tribunal had not considered whether, at the date of claim, it had been likely that she would cease to satisfy the conditions of entitlement within six months. He directed the new tribunal to determine that likelihood on the basis of what was known at the date of claim.

A contention that subs.(8)(b) did not apply to changes of circumstances occurring between the date of a decision made in advance and the date from which the decision was effective was rejected by a Tribunal of Commissioners in *R(DLA) 4/05* who pointed out that s.8(2)(b) precluded the Secretary of State from taking account of any such change of circumstances that he might anticipate. However, they stressed that they were not disagreeing with the approach taken in *R(DLA) 3/01* and also that the Secretary of State (when making an advance award) could take account of the effects of the mere passage of time, such as the claimant attaining a certain age or the qualifying period for a benefit being completed. Consequently, a tribunal may take account of the effect of the mere passage of time after the date of the Secretary of State's decision in any case where the Secretary of State could have made an advance award of disability allowance under reg.13A of the Social Security (Claims and Payments) Regulations 1987. In *Secretary of State for Work and Pensions v Bhakta* [2006] EWCA Civ 65 (reported as *R(IS) 7/06*), the Court of Appeal approved

R(DLA) 4/05 and applied it to an income support case where an advance award could have been made under reg.13. The case was one where the only reason that the claimant had not been found by the Commissioner to be habitually resident at the date of the Secretary of State's decision was that a sufficient period of residence had not elapsed by that date. Reg.13 has been amended with effect from May 23, 2007 so as to exclude that class of case (and all claims by "persons from abroad") from the scope of the regulation (see reg.2(2)(c) of the Social Security, Housing Benefit and Council Tax Benefit (Miscellaneous Amendments) Regulations 2007 (SI 2007/1331)), but the principle confirmed in *Bhakta* remains good in other contexts. *R(DLA) 4/05* has also been followed by a Tribunal of Commissioners in Northern Ireland (*R3/05 (DLA)*).

In *CDLA/3293/2000*, a case where the claimant had appealed against a decision of the Secretary of State to make no award of disability living allowance, the Commissioner held that s.12(8)(b) did not preclude a tribunal from using hindsight to fix the length of an award that they considered should be made. However, in *CDLA/3722/2000*, a tribunal was held not entitled to do that where the award would be for less than the minimum period of six months. At the time of the Secretary of State's decision she was likely to satisfy the conditions for disability living allowance for six months. In fact, she had a course of treatment and got better much earlier than had been expected. The Commissioner held that the tribunal were obliged to turn a blind eye to the improvement and the Secretary of State would not be able to supersede the decision so as to prevent benefit being paid for longer than the claimant's condition merited. The Commissioner deciding *R(DLA) 3/01* observed that s.12(8)(b) required tribunals to indulge in the sort of artificial exercise that is frowned upon in modern courts where judges are not expected to close their eyes to reality and he referred to *Charles v Hugh James Jones and Jenkins (a firm)* [2000] 1 All E.R. 289, 299–301. Section 12(8)(b) is of particular importance in disablement benefit cases where tribunals can usually themselves examine the claimant (see reg.52 of the Social Security and Child Support (Decisions and Appeals) Regulations 1999) and must be careful to distinguish between those of their findings that are relevant to circumstances obtaining at the time of the decision under appeal and those that are not.

In *CIS/2428/1999*, it was pointed out that a literal interpretation of s.12(8)(b) would prevent a tribunal from taking account of a cause for a late claim which existed before the claim was made and had ceased to exist before the Secretary of State's decision on the claim. The Commissioner considered that that would be absurd and would prevent adjudication on a case falling within reg.19(5) of the Social Security (Claims and Payments) Regulations 1987. He extended the principle behind *R(DLA) 3/01* and held that a circumstance "obtains" at the date of decision if it is a circumstance, whenever it occurred, that is relied on by a claimant in justifying a late claim. The principle has been further extended in *CJSA/2375/00*. In that case, the claimant had failed to attend two courses and had been disqualified from jobseeker's allowance for two weeks in respect of the first failure and four weeks in respect of the second failure. The disqualification for four weeks was permitted only because there had been a previous disqualification. The claimant appealed against both disqualifications and the appeals came before two different tribunals. The appeal against the first disqualification was allowed. The second appeal was dismissed and the claimant appealed to the Commissioner. The Commissioner said that, following the decision of the first tribunal, the Secretary of State should have revised the second disqualification under reg.3(6) of the Social Security and Child Support (Decisions and Appeals) Regulations 1999, so as to reduce the period to two weeks. However, as the Secretary of State had not done so, the second tribunal should have reduced the period, notwithstanding that the decision of the first tribunal had been given after the Secretary of State's decision on the second disqualification. The Commissioner said:

"In a case like this, an appeal tribunal is entitled to take account of any factor known to it that relates to a past period or past event that was relevant to the decision under appeal, even if the position at the date of the hearing is different from that at the date of the decision. This gives section 12(8)(b) a sensible operation. It allows an appeal tribunal to substitute a decision on factors relevant to the period the Secretary of State had considered. But it prevents the tribunal from trespassing into the period after that date by taking account of factors that are only relevant to that later period.

I repeat that I have not defined the words used in section 12(8)(b). I have simply tried to give them a sensible operation in circumstances like those involved in this case. I emphasise that I have been concerned in this decision with past periods or events. I have not been concerned with cases where the Secretary of State has had to speculate on the likely future course of events, such as the qualifying period for a disability living allowance, which I considered in [*R(DLA) 3/01*]".

Similar contortions were required in *CJSA/2472/2005*. In this case, entitlement to jobseeker's allowance had been terminated on the ground that the claimant had to be treated as not being available for work because the restrictions he had put on his availability were more restrictive than those recorded in his jobseeker's agreement. He had already, before the termination of his entitlement to benefit, applied for a variation of his jobseeker's agreement. That application had been only partially successful and the claimant had appealed against both the variation of his jobseeker's agreement and the termination of his entitlement to jobseeker's allowance. The Commissioner held that the Secretary of State, a tribunal or a Commissioner may direct that a varied jobseeker's agreement be given retrospective effect so that it has effect from the date of the application for variation. The consequence of the Commissioner allowing the claimant's appeal in respect of the jobseeker's agreement and making such a direction in that case was that, if the claimant signed the varied agreement, the circumstances obtaining at the date of the decision in respect of entitlement to jobseeker's allowance would be changed, affecting the operation of s.12(8)(b). He therefore adjourned the appeal in respect of entitlement to jobseeker's allowance in order to give the claimant the opportunity to sign the varied jobseeker's agreement, pointing out that the Secretary of State would be able to revise the termination of entitlement if the agreement were signed.

Section 12(8)(b) would be unobjectionable if, like s.12(8)(a), it said "need not" instead of "shall not". As it is, it introduces an unwelcome element of technicality into appeals to tribunals that were once supposed to be user-friendly. As the cases demonstrate, this is particularly so where "outcome decisions" in respect of entitlement are dependent on other decisions. In less complex cases, the remedy for a claimant is to make a new claim, or application for supersession, whenever there is an event that might be regarded as a new circumstance. There may be some cases where the wise claimant will make such claims or applications at regular intervals while an appeal is pending. The Secretary of State would then be obliged to make separate decisions on each claim or application (because the power to refer claims or applications to a tribunal so that they can be considered with a pending appeal has been abolished) and there would be a separate right of appeal against each decision. However, experience suggests that claimants do not consider new claims or applications to be necessary while an appeal is pending, even though some of the literature provided to them makes the suggestion, and so the reality may be that claimants lose benefit that they would undoubtedly have been entitled to but for s.12(8)(b).

Note that where a claimant does make a new claim or application for supersession pending an appeal, the Secretary of State is now empowered to revise the decision made on that claim or application in the light of the decision given on appeal (reg.3(5A) of the Social Security and Child Support (Decisions and Appeals) Regulations 1999). This makes it unnecessary for claimants to lodge repeated appeals based on the same grounds, but it remains necessary to lodge a further appeal if the point in issue arises out of a change of circumstances since the decision that was the subject of the original appeal.

(1998 c.14, s.12)

Of course, s.12(8)(b) can work in a claimant's favour if there has been a new circumstance since the decision under appeal that would have reduced his or her entitlement to benefit. It may well be that the Secretary of State could not supersede the tribunal's decision (see the note to reg.6(2)(a) of the Social Security and Child Support (Decisions and Appeals) Regulations 1999). See *CDLA/3722/2000*, mentioned above. Giving effect to the tribunal's decision in the claimant's favour might, in some cases, give rise to an overpayment that was recoverable under s.71 of the Social Security Administration Act 1992 on the basis that the change of circumstances should have been disclosed to the Secretary of State so that the decision under appeal could have been superseded before the appeal was heard. However, in a case where the Secretary of State had refused benefit altogether in the decision under appeal and benefit had then been awarded by the tribunal on the basis of their findings as to the circumstances obtaining at the date of the Secretary of State's decision, it seems unlikely that there would have been any duty on the claimant to disclose any changes of circumstances while the appeal was pending. Even if the Secretary of State does have power to supersede a tribunal's decision in the light of a change of circumstances arising before the decision was given, another problem facing the Secretary of State may be continued ignorance of the new circumstance. He does not always send a representative to tribunal hearings and he does not usually ask for a copy of the record of proceedings or a full statement of the tribunal's findings and reasoning. Unless a tribunal refers in the short decision notice, recorded under reg.53(1) of the Social Security and Child Support (Decisions and Appeals) Regulations 1999, to a change of circumstances mentioned at the hearing, the Secretary of State may remain ignorant of it for ever and, of course, the tribunal will have been obliged by s.12(8)(b) to ignore the change when awarding benefit.

An element of discretion in s.12(8)(b) might make it much easier to do justice.

Subs. (9)

In *Wood v Secretary of State for Work and Pensions* [2003] EWCA Civ 53 (reported as *R(DLA) 1/03*), the Court of Appeal overruled *R(DLA) 6/02* and held that the phrase "a decision superseding" should be read as "a decision taken pursuant to the power to supersede", so as to permit an appeal against a refusal to supersede. Rix LJ conceded that that left this subsection as "a fairly redundant provision".

1.391

Redetermination etc. of appeals by tribunal

13.—(1) This section applies where an application is made to a person under section 14(10)(a) below for leave to appeal from a decision of an appeal tribunal.

1.392

(2) If the person considers that the decision was erroneous in point of law, he may set aside the decision and refer the case either for redetermination by the tribunal or for determination by a differently constituted tribunal.

(3) If each of the principal parties to the case expresses the view that the decision was erroneous in point of law, the person shall set aside the decision and refer the case for determination by a differently constituted tribunal.

[¹(4) In this section and section 14 below "the principal parties" means—
(a) the persons mentioned in subsection (3)(a) and (b) of that section, and
(b) where applicable, the person mentioned in subsection (3)(d) and such a person as is first mentioned in subsection (4) of that section.]

AMENDMENT

1. Social Security Contributions (Transfer of Functions, etc.) Act 1999, Sch.7, para.26 (April 1, 1999).

Social Security Act 1998

DEFINITIONS

"appeal tribunal"—see s.39(1).
"the principal parties"—see subs.(4).

GENERAL NOTE

1.393 This section is applied in a modified form to appeals under s.63 of the Tax Credits Act 2002 and the Child Trust Funds Act 2004 (see Vol.IV).

Subs. (1)

1.394 At first sight, s.13 appears to be a useful provision allowing a decision to be set aside when the person who was, or who chaired, a tribunal realises, in the light of a challenge or otherwise on reconsideration of the case, that the decision was erroneous in point of law. However, under reg.58(6) of the Social Security and Child Support (Decisions and Appeals) Regulations 1999, applications for leave to appeal may be considered by full-time, legally qualified panel members where the tribunal that gave the decision was, or was chaired by, a part-time, legally qualified panel member. In practice, *all* applications are considered by full-time panel members and the effect of s.13 is that they routinely sit as a court of appeal from their part-time colleagues. Whether that is how s.13 was intended to operate seems doubtful but it does speed up the processing of challenges to unsatisfactory decisions.

A decision may not be set aside under this section once the application for leave to appeal has been determined and leave has been either granted or refused (*CF/6923/1999* but see *CIB/2949/200*, where the Commissioner suggested that this might have been too broadly expressed). Nor may a decision be set aside under this section if the legally qualified panel member has no power to grant leave to appeal due to the application being too late or there being no statement of reasons (see the annotation to reg.58(1) of the Social Security and Child Support (Decisions and Appeals) Regulations 1999). Therefore, where the Secretary of State sought a statement of reasons within the prescribed time but the request was not acted upon immediately and the chairman was subsequently unable to provide a statement of reasons, the setting aside of the tribunal's decision under s.13(2) was invalid and so was the consequent decision of another tribunal (*CDLA/1685/2004*). The Commissioner allowed the claimant's appeal against the second decision but suggested that the Secretary of State should apply to a Commissioner for leave to appeal against the first decision, as a Commissioner is not precluded from granting leave to appeal by the lack of a statement of reasons.

In *CIB/4193/2003*, a decision made at a paper hearing was set aside and a new paper hearing was arranged without that being made clear to the claimant who had decided that she wanted to attend the second hearing. The Commissioner set aside the second decision and suggested that claimants should be given an opportunity to ask for an oral rehearing when a decision is set aside under s.13.

Subs. (2)

1.395 Subsection (2) is cast in discretionary terms. In principle, one would expect a panel member to obtain the views of both parties before exercising the power to set aside rather than grant or dismiss the application for leave to appeal to a Commissioner. If the respondent agreed that the decision was erroneous in point of law, subs.(3) would be brought into play and the panel member would be bound to set the decision aside. However, it appears that the Secretary of State and Her Majesty's Revenue and Customs have waived any right to be consulted on a claimant's application for leave to appeal (because having to respond would create additional work, although it is difficult to see why the amount of work should be great if only cases where the panel member was minded to set aside were referred for comment) and are content for any decision to be set aside if the panel member thinks it right to do so. It is not usual for panel members to ask claimant applicants whether they have any objection to a decision being set aside under this provision instead of leave to appeal being granted. Generally, of course, a claimant applicant would be quite content to have a decision set aside but, in a case where

(1998 c.14, s.13)

there is more than one possible error of law in a tribunal's decision, a claimant may prefer to have leave to appeal and have a major issue of law resolved by a Commissioner rather than have the decision set aside on some minor point and have to argue the major point before another tribunal with the probability of a later appeal to a Commissioner. The purpose of this section is plainly to avoid unnecessary appeals to Commissioners but panel members need to be careful to avoid setting aside decisions when that will prolong litigation, rather than shorten it. Applications by the Secretary of State create different problems because claimants are less likely to agree to a setting aside. It is a breach of the rules of natural justice not to seek a claimant's view before setting aside a decision that was in his or her favour (*CIS/4533/2001*). If there is active opposition to a setting aside and there is a serious point of law to be determined, it is suggested that the panel member should grant leave to appeal rather than set aside the decision. To do otherwise, would be to usurp the function of the Commissioner. However, there are cases where there has been an obvious procedural error or a tribunal has obviously overlooked a material statutory provision or important piece of evidence so that the only possible conclusion is that the tribunal's decision is erroneous in point of law. In such cases, it is hard to see what objection there could be to a setting aside under subs.(2), but a panel member needs to be sure the error really is clear. If, despite a claimant's opposition, or simple failure to comment, a decision is set aside, it is suggested that a brief reason should be given (for the benefit of the tribunal who must rehear the case as well as the parties). There is no appeal to a Commissioner against a setting aside under this subsection (*CIS/4533/2001*) but a person anxious to rely on the decision set aside could apply for judicial review of the setting aside.

Unlike subs.(3), subs.(2) permits a case to be referred back to the same tribunal as made the decision that has been set aside. That is not necessarily unfair but it was held to be unfair in the particular circumstances of the case in *CDLA/1312/2006* in light of the view the tribunal had expressed about the utility of certain medical evidence and its implied rejection of the claimant's evidence and also of the view expressed by the legally qualified panel member to the effect that the first decision had been carefully reasoned apart from two particular points, given that the purpose of the referral was that there should be a complete rehearing and that the legally qualified panel member had no power to give binding guidance. The Commissioner suggested that the power to refer a case back to the same tribunal should be exercised "only in the plainest cases, where there is some positive reason for doing so". Otherwise, there is a risk of the decision of the second tribunal being set aside on appeal on the ground that there was no fair hearing. If a case is referred to a differently constituted tribunal, it is usual for the decision that has been set aside to be included in the papers. That is not inappropriate. Even if their findings of fact cannot be relied upon, issues identified by the first tribunal may well be of assistance to the new tribunal, although it must be careful not to be influenced by the discredited findings (*Swash v Secretary of State for the Home Department* [2006] EWCA Civ 1093; [2007] 1 W.L.R. 1264). There may, however, be special circumstances in which the legally qualified panel member setting the first decision aside considers that the interests of justice require the case to be heard by a tribunal that has not seen that decision and he or she will be able to issue appropriate directions to ensure that that happens (*ibid.*).

Regulation 57 of the Social Security and Child Support (Decisions and Appeals) Regulations 1999 and reg.25 of the Tax Credits (Appeals) (No.2) Regulations 2002 give an additional power to set aside a decision where a relevant document has gone astray or a person failed to attend the hearing in circumstances where there may have been an injustice without there actually being an error of law. See also s.28(2) for the possibility of an implied further power to set aside decisions to avoid injustice.

Subs. (3)

This subsection does not apply to tax credit appeals or child trust fund appeals. It is a bizarre provision. It would be wholly unobjectionable if it provided a *power* to set aside a decision rather than imposing a *duty* to do so, although it might be

1.396

Social Security Act 1998

thought that there are few cases not falling within subs.(2) in which a decision should be set aside merely because the parties consent. It is the mandatory terms of the section (in contrast to s.14(7)) which creates the difficulty. The tribunal will have been, or will have included, a lawyer. It is very rare for any of the principal parties to be represented by a lawyer before a tribunal. Yet if the parties express the view, no matter how unreasonably, that the tribunal has erred *in law*, their view prevails and the decision of the tribunal *must* be set aside. The readiness of the Secretary of State's representatives to agree with unmeritorious grounds of appeal advanced by claimants on appeals to Commissioners has been criticised (see, for instance, *CSIB/611/1999*, *CSDLA/737/1999* and *CSDLA/868/1999*) and the quality of submissions is unlikely to be much better at tribunal level. It is not even necessary for the parties to agree on the error of law. A tribunal may have steered carefully between two extreme views advanced by the parties, all to no avail. If redetermining tribunals took the same approach and the parties remained stubborn, the litigation could go on for ever unless action were taken to avoid this subsection coming into play. Happily, such action is possible through the simple expedient of not seeking the views of the other principal parties when an application for leave to appeal is received.

In practice, that is what happens. Indeed, it is possible that it was originally intended that the panel member would seek the views of the principal parties other than the applicant only if a setting aside under subs.(2) was contemplated. Then, if the other parties agreed that the decision was erroneous in point of law, subs.(3) would have enabled the decision to be set aside without further consideration. However, as has been noted, the Secretary of State has waived his right to express views on a proposed setting aside under subs.(2) following a claimant's application for leave to appeal. The effect is that the duty to set aside a decision under subs.(3) very seldom arises. When it does, it is usually because the panel member is already contemplating setting aside the decision under subs.(2). One exception is when both parties seek leave to appeal at the same time and the panel member has to consider both aplications together, although even then there is the possibility that one party will not only raise no point of law but will also fail positively to assert that there is an error of law in the tribunal's decision. In *CIB/4427/2002*, a panel member was criticised for not setting a decision aside instead of granting leave to appeal when, following the claimant's application for leave to appeal to a Commissioner, based on the conduct of a member of the tribunal, the presenting officer of the Benefits Agency stated (in circumstances that are not clear from the Commissioner's decision) that he too considered the tribunal's decision to be erroneous in point of law due to the member's conduct. While the Commissioner held he could give no remedy in respect of the breach of subs.(3), he gave short shrift to the Secretary of State's opposition to the appeal on its merits. In Northern Ireland, a Tribunal of Commissioners has held that, where a legally qualified panel member has erred in failing to set aside a decision under s.13(3), a Commissioner should usually remedy the defect by setting the decision aside under s.14(7), at any rate where the parties consent and there are no compelling reasons for not doing so (*R1/04(DLA)*).

If a cross-application is received after an application by the other party has been determined, the decision cannot be set aside under this subsection (*CF/6923/1999*) but, if either party is given leave to appeal, it will be open to the Commissioner to set the decision aside summarily under s.14(7).

Appeal from tribunal to Commissioner

1.397

14.—(1) Subject to the provisions of this section, an appeal lies to a Commissioner from any decision of an appeal tribunal under section 12 or 13 above on the ground that the decision of the tribunal was erroneous in point of law.

(2) [¹ . . .]

(1998 c.14, s.14)

(3) [¹ . . .] An appeal lies under this section at the instance of any of the following—
- (a) the Secretary of State;
- (b) the claimant and such other person as may be prescribed;
- (c) in any of the cases mentioned in subsection (5) below, a trade union; and
- (d) a person from whom it is determined that any amount is recoverable under or by virtue of section 71 or 74 of the Administration Act.

(4) In a case relating to industrial injuries benefit an appeal lies under this section at the instance of a person whose entitlement to benefit is, or may be, under Part VI of Schedule 7 to the Contributions and Benefits Act, affected by the decision appealed against, as well as at the instance of any person or body such as is mentioned in subsection (3) above.

(5) The following are the cases in which an appeal lies at the instance of a trade union—
- (a) where the claimant is a member of the union at the time of the appeal and was so immediately before the matter in question arose;
- (b) where that matter in any way relates to a deceased person who was a member of the union at the time of his death;
- (c) where the case relates to industrial injuries benefit and the claimant or, in relation to industrial death benefit, the deceased, was a member of the union at the time of the relevant accident.

(6) Subsections [¹. . .] (3) and (5) above, as they apply to a trade union, apply also to any other association which exists to promote the interests and welfare of its members.

(7) If each of the principal parties to the appeal expresses the view that the decision appealed against was erroneous in point of law, the Commissioner may set aside the decision and refer the case to a tribunal with directions for its determination.

(8) Where the Commissioner holds that the decision appealed against was erroneous in point of law, he shall set it aside and—
- (a) he shall have power—
  - (i) give the decision which he considers the tribunal should have given, if he can do so without making fresh or further findings of fact; or
  - (ii) if he considers it expedient, to make such findings and to give such decision as he considers appropriate in the light of them; and
- (b) in any other case he shall refer the case to a tribunal with directions for its determination.

(9) Subject to any direction of the Commissioner, a reference under subsection (7) or (8)(b) above shall be to a differently constituted tribunal.

(10) No appeal lies under this section without the leave—
- (a) of the person who constituted, or was the chairman of, the tribunal when the decision was given or, in a prescribed case, the leave of such other person as may be prescribed; or
- (b) subject to and in accordance with regulations, of a Commissioner.

(11) Regulations may make provision as to the manner in which, and the time within which, appeals are to be brought and applications made for leave to appeal.

(12) Schedule 4 to this Act shall have effect with respect to the appointment, remuneration and tenure of office of Commissioners and other matters relating to them.

Amendment

1. Social Security Contributions (Transfer of Functions, etc.) Act 1999, Sch.7, para.27 (April 1, 1999).

Definitions

"the Administration Act"—see s.84.
"appeal tribunal"—see s.39(1).
"claimant"—see s.39(1) and, by virtue of s.39(2), see s.191 of the Social Security Administration Act 1992.
"Commissioner"—see s.84.
"the Contributions and Benefits Act"—*ibid.*
"industrial injuries benefit"—by virtue of s.39(2), see s.191 of the Social Security Administration Act 1992.
"prescribed"—see s.84.
"principal parties"—see s.13(4).

General Note

1.398

This section provides for an appeal against a decision made by an appeal tribunal where the right of appeal to the tribunal arose under s.12 of this Act, including a case where the right of appeal under that section was conferred by another enactment.

In *R(JSA) 3/03*, it has been held that an appeal also lies under this section against a decision given by an appeal tribunal under reg.10(2B) of the Employment Protection (Recoupment of Jobseeker's Allowance and Income Support) Regulations 1996 (in respect of the recovery of benefits from those making compensation payments in employment tribunal proceedings).

Quite separate rights of appeal from an appeal tribunal to a Social Security Commissioner are given by s.13 of the Social Security (Recovery of Benefits) Act 1997 (in respect of the recovery of benefits from those making compensation payments in respect of personal injury), by para.8 of Sch.7 to the Child Support, Pensions and Social Security Act 2000 (in respect of housing benefit and council tax benefit—not within the scope of this work) and by s.159 of the Health and Social Care (Community Health and Standards) Act 2003 (in respect of the recovery of National Health Service costs from those making compensation in respect of personal injury incurred on or after January 29, 2007 – not within the scope of this work). There is no right of appeal to a Social Security Commissioner against a decision of an appeal tribunal under the Child Support Act 1991 (in respect of which appeals are heard by Child Support Commissioners) or under the Vaccine Damage Act 1979 or the Road Traffic (NHS Charges) Act 1999 (in respect of which appeals are heard by the High Court or, in Scotland, the Court of Session).

In relation to cases where the original decision was made by Her Majesty's Revenue and Customs (i.e. cases under s.170 of the Pension Schemes Act 1993 or cases concerning the former working families' tax credit or disabled person's tax credit or, now child benefit or guardian's allowance), this section applies with the modification that references to the Secretary of State are to be read as references to Her Majesty's Revenue and Customs (Pensions Schemes Act 1993, s.170(7), Tax Credits Act 1999, Sch.2, para.21 and Sch.4, para.3(2), Tax Credits Act 2002, Sch.4, para.15 and Commissioners for Revenue and Customs Act 2005, s.4(1)).

This section is also applied in a slightly more modified form to appeals brought against decisions made by appeal tribunals by virtue of s.63 of the Tax Credits Act 2002 and under the Child Trust Funds Act 2004 (see Vol.IV).

Commissioners also hear appeals from Pensions Appeal Tribunals under s.6A of the Pensions Appeal Tribunals Act 1943. Such appeals concern disability and death benefits under war pension schemes and the Armed Forces Compensation Scheme and are beyond the scope of this work.

The only first-instance jurisdiction of Commissioners arises under the Forfeiture Act 1982.

(1998 c.14, s.14)

The Commissioners have two offices, at 3rd Floor, Procession House, 55 Ludgate Hill, London EC4M 7JW and at George House, 126 George Street, Edinburgh EH2 4HH. Most appeals to Commissioners are dealt with by way of written submissions (see regs 18–20 and 23(1) of the Social Security Commissioners (Procedure) Regulations 1999) but claimants may ask for oral hearings (regs 23 and 24 of the 1999 Regulations). Oral hearings usually take place in London or Edinburgh (cases from the far north of England being heard in Edinburgh when that is more convenient although English law is applied) but the Commissioners also regularly travel to sit at law courts in Cardiff and various places in the north of England (usually Bury, Darlington and either Doncaster or Leeds) and in North Wales. Video links are also available from a number of centres in England and Wales. If a claimant is disabled and would have great difficulty in travelling to one of the usual centres, it is possible to ask the Commissioners' office to arrange a hearing in a more local court building.

Commissioners have no power to award costs to successful claimants or to the Secretary of State (see *R(FC) 2/90*).

Nor is community legal service funding (legal aid) generally available for proceedings before Commissioners in England and Wales, although s.6(8)(b) of the Access to Justice Act 1999 enables the Lord Chancellor to authorise the Legal Services Commission to fund representation in England and Wales either in specified circumstances or in an individual case. A Public Interest Advisory Panel considers individual cases and their views are taken into account when funding is considered (see *http://www.legalservices.gov.uk/civil/guidance/public_interest_reports.asp*). The Panel has regard not only to the legal significance of the issues raised by a case but also their importance in terms of benefiting a significant number of claimants so that the case can be said to have a wider public interest. If a significant number of other claimants might benefit from a ruling favourable to the claimant in the prospective test case, the fact that other claimants might be disadvantaged by the ruling will not be considered to deprive the case of its wider public interest. Grants of funding under these provisions are rare. There has only been one year in which more than five grants have been made for proceedings before Commissioners.

In Scotland, the position is different and legal aid under the Legal Aid (Scotland) Act 1986 is available for representation before a Commissioner in cases where any appeal against the Commissioner's decision under s.15 of the Social Security Act 1998 would lie to the Court of Session (Civil Legal Aid (Scotland) Regulations 2002, regs 4(k) and 47). Entitlement to legal aid depends on the claimant's means but any benefit recovered or preserved in the proceedings before the Commissioner is not taken into account when calculating the amount of the claimant's net liability to the Legal Aid Fund (*ibid.*, reg.33(a)(xi)).

A copy of any funding notice issued by the Legal Services Commission or, in Scotland, a copy of a legal aid certificate, must be sent to the Commissioners' office (see reg.8A of the Social Security Commissioners (Procedure) Regulations 1999).

The Commissioners have websites where further information, including practical information about appealing and copies of their decisions, may be obtained (*http://www.osscsc.gov.uk* and *http://www.ossc-scotland.org.uk*).

Subs.(1)

The reference to s.13 is to the decision of the tribunal redetermining a case following the setting aside under that section of an earlier decision. There is no right of appeal against a decision under that section to set aside, or not to set aside, an earlier decision (*CIS/4533/2001*). Nor is there a right of appeal against a determination under reg. 56 or 57 of the Social Security and Child Support (Decisions and Appeals) Regulations 1999 to correct or set aside, or not to correct or set aside, a decision of a tribunal (see reg. 57A(2)). Indeed, although decisions of legally qualified panel members made under the 1999 Regulations are decisions of the tribunal (*Morina v Secretary of State for Work and Pensions* [2007] EWCA Civ 749), there is no right of appeal against such, or at least most such, decisions. In some cases, this is because a determination of a legally qualified panel member is regarded as inherently unappealable on the ground

1.399

that having a right of appeal would defeat the purpose of, say, refusing to admit a late appeal to a tribunal or striking out an appeal to a tribunal (*ibid.*). In those cases, the only remedy lies in an application to the Administrative Court, or, in Scotland, the Court of Session, for judicial review. In other cases, it is because the determination of the legally qualified panel member is merely a "determination of any matter along the way leading to a decision" such as a refusal to postpone a hearing. In those cases – and cases where full tribunals make similar determinations such as refusals to adjourn – there is no right of appeal because such a right is unnecessary (*Carpenter v Secretary of State for Work and Pensions* [2003] EWCA Civ 33 (reported as *R(IB)* 6/03). If, say, a refusal to adjourn is unfair, it can make the final decision of the tribunal on the substantive issues erroneous in point of law and so justify an appeal against the final decision (*R. v Medical Appeal Tribunal (Midland Region), Ex p. Carrarini* [1966] 1 W.L.R. 883 (also reported as an appendix to *R(I)* 13/65)).

Point of Law

1.400   An appeal to a Commissioner lies only on a "point of law". Commissioners may therefore be expected to resist any attempt by an appellant to present an appeal on facts as raising questions of law, even if they have grave doubts about the decision under appeal. No appeal on a question of law should be allowed to be turned into a rehearing of parts of the evidence (*Yeboah v Crofton* [2002] I.R.L.R. 634). However, once a Commissioner is satisfied that a decision is erroneous in point of law, he or she is entitled to determine any outstanding questions of fact (see subs.(8)(a)(ii)).

The meaning of "point of law" was considered by the Court of Appeal in *Nipa Begum v Tower Hamlets LBC* [2000] 1 W.L.R. 306 in a case where a homeless person appealed to the county court under s.204 of the Housing Act 1996 against a decision of a housing authority. An appeal lay "on any point of law arising from" such a decision and the Court of Appeal held that the county court had powers akin to those available on an application for judicial review in the High Court and so could quash a decision on the ground of procedural error, lack of vires, irrationality or inadequacy of reasons as well as for straightforward errors of legal interpretation.

In *R(A)* 1/72 and *R(IS)* 11/99, Commissioners had made similar lists of errors that would amount to errors of law, rather than of fact. More recently, in *R(I)* 2/06, a Tribunal of Commissioners has referred to the judgment of the Court of Appeal in *R (Iran) v Secretary of State for the Home Department* [2005] EWCA Civ 982, offering a "brief summary of the points of law that will most often be encountered in practice". These were—

"(i) Making perverse or irrational findings on a matter or matters that were material to the outcome ('material matters');
(ii) Failing to give reasons or any adequate reasons for findings on material matters;
(iii) Failing to take into account and/or resolve conflicts of fact or opinion on material matters;
(iv) Giving weight to immaterial matters;
(v) Making a material misdirection of law on any material matter;
(vi) Committing or permitting a procedural or other irregularity capable of making a material difference to the outcome or the fairness of proceedings;
(vii) Making a mistake as to a material fact which could be established by objective and uncontentious evidence, where the appellant and/or his advisers were not responsible for the mistake, and where unfairness resulted from the fact that a mistake was made.

"Each of these grounds for detecting any error of law contains the word 'material' (or 'immaterial'). Errors of law of which it can be said that they would have made no difference to the outcome do not matter."

(In *R(I)* 2/06, The Tribunal of Commissioners omitted point (vii) as not relevant to the appeals under consideration, but it may be relevant in other cases.) The seven points identified by the Court of Appeal and the issue of "materiality" are considered in more detail below.

Challenging findings of fact

The Court of Appeal's points (i), (iii), (iv) and (vii) show the limited grounds on which findings of fact may be challenged.   **1.401**

The Court emphasised what a demanding concept "perversity" was and so did the Tribunal of Commissioners, citing *Murrell v Secretary of State for Social Services* (reported as an appendix to *R(I) 3/84*) in which it was said that an assessment of disablement is perverse only if it is "so wildly wrong that it can be set aside". A finding of fact is also perverse if "was wholly unsupported by any evidence" (*Iran*) or it is based on a misunderstanding that "is plain and incontrovertible and where there is no room for difference about it" (*Braintree DC v Thompson* [2005] EWCA Civ 178, a housing benefit case in which the Court of Appeal said that a Deputy Commissioner had not been entitled to substitute his view of the facts for the view of the tribunal). It is particularly difficult to show that a decision is perverse where it required an element of judgment (such as, for instance, whether the claimant was virtually unable to walk). In *Moyna v Secretary of State for Work and Pensions* [2003] UKHL 44, [2003] 1 W.L.R. 1929 (also reported as *R(DLA) 7/03*), Lord Hoffman, with whom the other members of the House of Lords agreed, said:

> "In any case in which a tribunal has to apply a standard with a greater or lesser degree of imprecision and to take a number of factors into account, there are bound to be cases in which it will be impossible for a reviewing court to say that the tribunal must have erred in deciding the case either way: see *George Mitchell (Chesterhall) Ltd v Finney Lock Seeds Ltd* [1983] 2 A.C. 803, 815–816."

If perversity is not shown, it is usually necessary to show some flaw in the reasoning instead, either because it a finding is irrational (i.e. there is something illogical in the reasoning leading to it) or because the tribunal has failed to take into account a relevant matter or has given weight to an irrelevant matter. In order to show that any of these errors has been made, it is necessary to analyse the tribunal's statement of reasons. On the other hand, merely pointing to a different analysis of the evidence from that adopted by the tribunal is not sufficient to show an error of law (*Secretary of State for Work and Pensions v Roach* [2007] EWCA Civ 1746 (reported as *R(CS) 4/07*)).

Although tribunals may be found to have erred in the way they have dealt with the evidence before them, Commissioners have pointed out that tribunals cannot be criticised for not taking account of evidence that was not before them at all. In *CDLA/7980/1995*, the Commissioner said that –

> "Finality is another important principle. Parties cannot demand a rehearing simply because, at the original hearing, they failed to adduce the right evidence, failed to ask the right questions or failed to advance the right arguments."

However, the Court of Appeal's point (vii) in the *Iran* case is a limited exception to this approach, derived from *E v Secretary of State for the Home Department* [2004] EWCA Civ 49; [2004] 2 W.L.R. 1351. The strictness of the requirements listed in point (vii) for finding a mistake of fact to be an error of law has been emphasised in *Shehu v Secretary of State for the Home Department* [2004] EWCA Civ 854, where the material evidence could, with reasonable diligence, have been obtained and adduced before the tribunal and the lack of the evidence did not make the decision unfair. Where neither those conditions nor the traditional grounds identified in points (i), (iii) and (iv) are met, the only remedy for a mistake of fact made by a tribunal is an application for supersession under regulation 6(2)(c) of the Social Security and Child Support (Decisions and Appeals) Regulations 1999 or reg.13(2)(c) of the Child Benefit and Guardian's Allowance (Decisions and Appeals) Regulations 2003. The value of that remedy may be limited by the date from which any supersession can be effective.

Challenging misdirections of law

It is much more obvious that a misdirection of law (e.g. the tribunal misunderstanding or overlooking a regulation or making a mistake about the law of property),   **1.402**

Social Security Act 1998

the Court of Appeal's point (v) in the *Iran* case, is an error of law. It is also a misdirection of law for a tribunal to rely upon a regulation that is ultra vires (*Foster v Chief Adjudication Officer* [1993] A.C. 754 (also reported as *R(IS) 22/93*)) or is inconsistent with European Community law (see s.2(4) of the European Communities Act 1972).

Inadequate reasons

1.403   The standard of reasoning required from tribunals by the Court of Appeal's point (ii) and the requirement to resolve conflicts (see point (iii)) is considered in detail in the note to reg.53(4) of the Social Security and Child Support (Decisions and Appeals) Regulations 1999. The reasons should be sufficient to avoid "substantial doubt as to whether the [tribunal] erred in law" on any of the other grounds identified in the *Iran* case, but they "need refer only to the main issues in the dispute, not to every consideration" (*South Bucks DC v Porter (No.2)* [2004] UKHL 33; [2004] 1 W.L.R. 1953 at [36]. In the *Iran* case itself, the Court of Appeal referred to *Eagil Trust Co Ltd v Pigott-Brown* [1985] 3 All E.R. 119, 122, where Griffiths L.J. said that, "if it be that the judge has not dealt with a particular argument but it can be seen that there are grounds on which he would have been entitled to reject it, this court should assume that he acted on those grounds unless the appellant can point to convincing reasons leading to a contrary conclusion."

Procedural and other irregularities

1.404   Whether a breach of procedural rules renders a decision invalid or erroneous in point of law is to be determined by considering whether the legislature intended that to be the effect of such a breach (*R. v Soneji* [2005] UKHL 49; [2006] 1 A.C. 340). Therefore, not every procedural error entitles a party to have a decision set aside on appeal. It largely depends on whether there was any unfairness as a result of the breach. This is point (vi) in the *Iran* case.

The old distinction between "mandatory" and "directory" requirements is no longer regarded as helpful. Instead, it is necessary to consider the language of the legislation and the legislator's intention against the factual situation and seek to do what is just in all the circumstances. This involves considering whether the procedural requirement is satisfied by "substantial" compliance with it and, if so, whether there has in fact been such substantial compliance or whether non-compliance had been waived. If there has not been sufficient compliance and non-compliance has not been waived, consideration should also be given to the intended consequence of non-compliance because it does not necessarily follow from an applicant's failure to comply with a procedural requirement that the application is a nullity (*R. v Secretary of State for the Home Department, Ex p. Jeyeanthan* [2000] 1 W.L.R. 354). Tribunals have no express power to waive irregularities (unlike Commissioners – see reg.27 of the Social Security Commissioners (Procedure) Regulations 1999) but this approach suggests that they have an implied power.

Consideration must be given to whether the breach of procedural rules might have made any difference to the decision of the tribunal or whether a party to the proceedings has lost anything (such as the opportunity of advancing a particular argument on appeal) as a result of the breach, so that a rehearing is the only way of remedying the breach. For this reason, a breach of the requirement to keep a record of proceedings will render a decision of a tribunal erroneous in point of law if the lack of a record of proceedings makes it difficult to determine whether or not the tribunal has provided an adequate statement of reasons (*CDLA/16902/1996*). On the other hand, a failure to provide any summary of reasons in a decision notice will not render the decision erroneous in point of law because the remedy is to apply for a full statement of reasons (*CIB/4497/1998*). The most commonly relied upon breach is a breach of the statutory duty to give reasons for a decision (see the note to reg.53(4) of the Social Security and Child Support (Decisions and Appeals) Regulations 1999), although this is considered in the *Iran* case to be an entirely separate type of error of law, perhaps because there would be a common law duty to give reasons even if the legislation imposed no duty.

When considering breaches of procedural rules, fairness is judged by reference to the three "rules of natural justice", which are that every party should have a proper opportunity to present his or her case, that there should be no bias and that a decision should be based on the evidence. Even where there is no breach of a statutory provision, breach of the rules of natural justice will amount to at least an irregularity. The scope of the rules is fairly broad but it has nonetheless been suggested that Commissioners ought to express their decisions in terms of the parties' right to a fair hearing under Art.6(1) of the European Convention on Human Rights rather than in terms of the rules of natural justice which are apt to be misunderstood (*CJSA/5100/2001* and the linked cases *CIB/2751/2002 and CS/3202/2002*) even if the practical differences are not great. In *CSDLA/773/2004*, the Commissioner disagreed and said that the issue was whether there had been a breach of the rules of natural justice and that any assertion that a convention right had been breached had to be raised as a separate issue. It is suggested that that goes too far in the opposite direction and that, while a Commissioner is entitled to focus on the questions whether a tribunal listened fairly to the contentions of both sides and whether it was biased, those questions must now be considered in the light of Art.6 of the Convention.

In *R. v Secretary of State for the Home Department, Ex p. Al-Mehdawi* [1990] 1 A.C. 876 it was said to be incorrect to state simply that a party to a dispute who has not been heard through no fault of his own has been denied justice. In that case, notice of the hearing had been given to the party's solicitors but they had wrongly addressed their letter telling the party of the hearing. Although the House of Lords accepted that a decision of a tribunal may be erroneous in point of law where the tribunal has been entirely blameless but there had been some fault on the part of the other party, they held that there was no error of law in that case because the solicitors had had notice. Service on a solicitor was also treated as service on a claimant in *Tkachuk v Secretary of State for Work and Pensions* [2007] EWCA Civ 515 (reported as *R(IS) 3/07*). However, in social security cases, notices of hearings and decisions are usually sent both to the claimant and any representative. In *CCS/6302/1999*, a decision was set aside because a party had not received notice of the appeal due to the Child Support Agency failing to tell the clerk to the tribunal of his change of address. In *CIB/5227/1999*, the claimant simply did not receive the letter from the clerk inviting him to seek an oral hearing and there was no fault on the part of either the tribunal or the Benefits Agency. The Commissioner distinguished *Al-Mehdawi* and did not base his decision to allow the appeal on there having been any fault of anyone (although presumably the failure of the letter to arrive was attributable to someone). He just said that there had been a fundamental unfairness about the proceedings before the tribunal. That was not so in *CIB/4533/1999*, where the claimant's representative had not been sent notice of the hearing but notice was sent to the claimant, who made a mistake about the date and appeared three days late. It was held that the claimant had not been denied a hearing, notwithstanding the lack of notice to his representative, and his appeal to the Commissioner was dismissed.

It is not necessarily a breach of the rules of natural justice for a tribunal to cite Commissioners' decisions that were not mentioned during the course of the proceedings before the tribunal. The question is whether the proceedings were unfair and that depends on whether it might reasonably be considered that the case has been decided on a basis that could not have been anticipated by the parties so that they did not have a proper opportunity of addressing the tribunal on the relevant issues (*Sheridan v Stanley Cole (Wainfleet) Ltd* [2003] EWCA Civ 1046; [2003] 4 All E.R. 1181).

The rule against bias was considered in detail in *Locabail (UK) Ltd v Bayfield Properties Ltd* [1999] EWCA Civ 3004; [2000] Q.B. 451. It has the effect that, where a member of a tribunal has any direct personal interest, apart from the most trivial, in the outcome of proceedings, he or she is automatically disqualified from hearing the case, irrespective of his or her knowledge of the interest. In cases where there is no direct personal interest, the question is whether the circumstances would lead a fair-minded and informed observer to conclude that there was a real possibility that the tribunal was biased, in the sense that the tribunal member might unfairly regard with favour or disfavour a party in the proceedings (*Porter v Magill* [2001] UKHL 67; [2002] 2 A.C. 357) and, on appeal, it will be relevant whether the tribunal member knew of the connection with the party because, if he or she did not, no favour or disfavour would have been shown. It was stressed in *CS/1753/2000* that the issue was whether there was a likelihood of bias, not whether there was actual bias. Appearances are therefore important and a decision may be set aside if a tribunal member gives the appearance of having fallen asleep (*Stansby v Datapulse* [2003] EWCA Civ 1951; [2004] I.C.R. 523) but, in *Locobail* itself, it was stressed that "[t]he mere fact the a judge, earlier in the same case or in a previous case, had commented adversely on a party or witness, or found the evidence of a party or witness to be unreliable, would not without more found a sustainable objection". On the other hand, in *CCS/1876/2006*, the Commissioner made the point that the mere fact that a tribunal chairman is not bound to recuse himself when he has previously decided a case against a party before him does not mean that he is not entitled to arrange for the appeal to be heard by another chairman if he considers it desirable do so in order to strengthen the party's confidence in the fairness of the procedures and undue expense will not be involved.

In *Lawal v Northern Spirit Ltd* [2003] UKHL 35; [2003] I.C.R. 856, the House of Lords held there to have been apparent bias where a party was represented by a barrister who had previously sat as a part-time judge with lay members of the Employment Appeal Tribunal before whom he was appearing. *Lawal* was followed in *Secretary of State for Work and Pensions v Cunningham* [2004] S.L.T. 1007 (also reported as *R(DLA) 7/04*), where a tribunal had relied on a medical report by an examining medical practitioner with whom two members of the tribunal had sat previously and the Court of Session held there had been apparent bias. On the other hand, in *Gillies v Secretary of State for Work and Pensions* [2006] UKHL 2; [2006] 1 W.L.R. 781, it was held by the House of Lords that there was no appearance of bias merely because a member of a tribunal also acted as an examining medical practitioner for the Secretary of State. (For further discussion of *Cunningham* and *Gillies*, see the note to s.6.) A long-standing personal friendship with a witness will also give rise to an appearance of bias and a judge was wrong to take into account the inconvenience to the parties in having to adjourn when he refused to recuse himself. "There was either a real possibility of bias, in which case the judge was disqualified by the principle of judicial impartiality, or there was not, in which case there was no valid objection to trial by him." (*AWG Group Ltd v Morrison* [2006] EWCA Civ 6; [2006] 1 W.L.R. 1163 at [20]). Friendship with an advocate will not give rise to an appearance of bias unless the advocate is "a domestic partner of the judge or any other person of either sex in a close personal relationship with the judge" or "a companion or employee of the judge and who lives in the judge's household" (*Guide to Judicial Conduct*, para. 7.2.8, which also says that a judge should not try a case in which his or her spouse, children, children-in-law or other close relative living in the judge's household is an advocate).

A party can waive the right to object to the lack of independence of a member of a tribunal but any such waiver must be voluntary, informed and unequivocal (*Millar v Dickson* [2001] UKPC D4; [2002] 1 W.L.R. 1615). However, in *CSDLA/ 444/2002*, it was pointed out, referring to *CS/343/1994* and *CDLA/2050/2002*, that, if objection to the constitution of a tribunal is not taken *before* a hearing, a party does run a substantial risk of being taken to have waived the right to object. It was held that the claimant in *CSDLA/444/2002* had not waived the right to object to the members of the tribunal. Although her lay representative had been aware of a relevant decision of a Tribunal of Commissioners on the point, she could not have been expected fully to understand the legal issues involved. The Court of Session did not consider the question of waiver when dismissing the appeal against the Commissioner's decision (*Cunningham* (see above)).

The materiality of errors

In the *Iran* case, the Court of Appeal stressed the point that only "material" errors of law are important. An error is not material only if the tribunal "would have been *bound* to have reached the same conclusion, notwithstanding the error of law", given findings it made that are not tainted by the error (*Detamu v Secretary of State for the Home Department* [2006] EWCA Civ 604). Errors that would make no difference may be ignored and Commissioners have often simply dismissed an appeal despite identifying an error of law because the identified error would have made no difference. On the other hand, Commissioners frequently set aside decisions on the ground of error of law only to substitute a decision to the same effect as the tribunal's. This is not necessarily inconsistent. It has to be borne in mind that, in social security cases, the Secretary of State has wide, but not unlimited, powers to supersede a decision of a tribunal or a Commissioner on the ground of mistake of fact or change of circumstances and the way in which a decision is expressed may well affect those powers. It may therefore be important for a Commissioner to correct an error made by a tribunal even though the correction has no immediate effect on the amount of benefit payable to the claimant.

1.405

Precedent

Decisions of the Commissioners on matters of legal principle are binding on tribunals and the Secretary of State, as are decisions of the superior courts. Where there are conflicting Commissioners' decisions, a reported decision should generally be followed in preference to an unreported decision (*R(I) 12/75*). Generally, where one decision has been carefully considered in a later decision and not followed, the later decision should be followed (*R(IS) 13/01*, applying *Colchester Estates (Cardiff) v Carlton Industries Plc* [1986] Ch. 80) and it has been held in a Northern Ireland case that that applies even if the earlier decision was reported and the later was not (*R1/00(FC)*). Decisions of Northern Ireland Commissioners are not strictly binding in Great Britain but are highly persuasive (*R(SB) 1/90*). A single Commissioner will usually follow a decision of another single Commissioner and will always follow a decision of a Tribunal of Commissioners appointed under s.16(7) (*R(I) 12/75*). A Tribunal of Commissioners will usually follow the decision of another Tribunal but will not always do so if satisfied that it was wrong (*R(U) 4/88*). A Commissioner in England and Wales is bound by a decision of the High Court given on judicial review of a Commissioner's decision but otherwise is not strictly bound by a decision of the High Court, although he or she will rarely depart from a decision of a single High Court judge and will always follow a decision of a divisional court as a matter of comity (*R(IS) 15/99*, disagreeing with *R(S) 1/96*). A Tribunal of Commissioners may, on rare occasions, decline to follow a decision of a divisional court (*R(SB) 52/83*). In *R(AF) 1/07*, the Commissioner followed *Chief Supplementary Benefit Officer v Leary* [1985] 1 W.L.R. 84 (also reported as an appendix to *R(SB) 6/85*) in holding that, where a Commissioner exercises a jurisdiction equivalent to that previously exercised by a single judge of the High Court on a statutory appeal, the Commissioner is not bound by the decisions made by judges on such appeals. Single Commissioners approach such cases in the same way as they approach decisions of other single Commissioners, normally following them "in the interests of comity and to secure certainty and avoid confusion on questions of legal principle" but recognising that "a slavish adherence to this could lead to the perpetuation of error" and departing from them when there is a good reason for doing so (*R(I) 12/75*). Commissioners in England and Wales applying the law of England and Wales are bound by decisions of the Court of Appeal and will always, as a matter of comity and practicality, follow decisions of the Court of Session or the Court of Appeal in Northern Ireland that are not in conflict with decisions of the Court of Appeal, although they are not strictly bound by them (*Clarke v Frank Staddon Ltd* [2004] EWCA Civ 422, *R(SB) 1/90* and *R(IB) 4/04*). Similarly, Commissioners in Scotland applying the law of Scotland are bound by decisions of the Court of Session and, subject to that, will always follow decisions of the Court

1.406

of Appeal in England and Wales or the Court of Appeal in Northern Ireland. Should there ever be a conflict between decisions of the Court of Appeal and the Court of Session, Commissioners and tribunals in England and Wales would follow the Court of Appeal and Commissioners and tribunals in Scotland would follow the Court of Session and the Secretary of State's decision-makers would also have to make different decisions depending on which side of the border the cases arose. Presumably steps would be taken, by way of an appeal to the House of Lords or by legislation, to remove the conflict as rapidly as possible. All Commissioners are bound by decisions of the House of Lords. Strictly speaking, only the reasoning vital to the decision of a court is binding and other comments are not but, where those other comments are made after full argument and expressly for the purpose of giving guidance, they should be followed by Commissioners except in quite exceptional circumstances (*R(IB)4/04*). Similarly, a decision of the Court of Appeal refusing leave to appeal to that Court is not a full decision for these purposes and, while reasons given by the Court of Appeal for refusing leave are not to be disregarded lightly, their value as precedent must be assessed taking account of all relevant factors, in particular whether the Court heard substantial argument and whether the reasons were given fully (*CCS/2567/1998*, applying *Clark v University of Humberside and Lincolnshire* [2000] 1 W.L.R. 1988, and see also *R(IS) 15/96*). Decisions of the European Court of Human Rights must be taken into account (Human Rights Act 1998, s.2) but do not take precedence over a binding decision of a domestic court unless the decision of the domestic court predates, and cannot survive, the coming into force of the Human Rights Act 1998 (*Kay v Lambeth LBC* [2006] UKHL 10; [2006] 2 W.L.R. 570). Decisions of the European Court of Justice determine European Union law, which takes precedence over domestic law (European Communities Act 1972, s.2(4)) and so such decisions are always binding. Where domestic legislation is inconsistent with European Union legislation or European Union directives having direct effect, tribunals and Commissioners must disapply the domestic legislation (*R. (Manson) v Ministry of Defence* [2005] EWCA Civ 1678; [2006] I.C.R. 355, *R(JSA) 4/03*).

Subs. (3)

1.407
Where the original decision was made by the Board of Inland Revenue, or an officer of the Board, the reference to the Secretary of State must be read as a reference to Her Majesty's Revenue and Customs (see the beginning of this note). The only exercise of the power in subs.(3)(b) to make regulations is to be found in reg.58A of the Social Security and Child Support (Decisions and Appeals) Regulations 1999 and so not everyone mentioned in reg.25 of those Regulations as having a right of appeal to a tribunal is given an express right of appeal to a Commissioner. This may be due to a difference of opinion between the Secretary of State and the Lord Chancellor as to the necessity of making such express provision in some instances and, although it appears to be a regrettable oversight in other instances, in practice Commissioners admit appeals brought by people who were entitled to appeal to the tribunal by virtue of reg.25.

Subs. (7)

Unlike s.13(3), this subsection confers a discretionary power on a Commissioner. Note that the power arises only after leave to appeal has been granted. Note also that the power can only be exercised when the case is to be referred to another tribunal. There is no provision allowing a decision to be set aside summarily and for the Commissioner then to give a final decision, even if the parties are agreed as to the decision to be given. This is presumably because the Commissioner is expected, in such a case, to satisfy himself or herself that the parties' submissions are correct, following which it is not unduly burdensome to issue a short decision to that effect.

A setting aside under this subsection does not necessarily imply that the Commissioner is satisfied that the decision under appeal was erroneous in point of

(1998 c.14, s.14)

law. The point of this provision is to enable a decision to be set aside without the Commissioner having to go into the case in the depth necessary to make that judgement. The Commissioner will therefore wish to be able to rely substantially on the parties' submissions. The Secretary of State's representatives have in the past been criticised for submitting too readily that a decision is erroneous in point of law on the ground that the reasoning is inadequate (*CSIB/596/1999, CSIB/611/1999, CSDLA/505/1999*). It was said in *CDLA/4102/1999* that a party submitting that a tribunal have failed to give reasons for accepting a piece of evidence should state what contradictory evidence there was and explain why the lack of reasoning is of significance. It was also suggested in *CDLA/4102/1999* that it was not appropriate for a decision to be set aside under this subsection in a case where there was a serious dispute of law between the parties upon which the tribunal rehearing the case ought to be given guidance. The Secretary of State's representative was criticised for ignoring such a dispute and submitting that the tribunal's decision should be set aside under this subsection on a ground that would have been immaterial if the tribunal had not erred in their approach to a more important issue in the case.

A setting aside under this subsection should not be cited as authority for any proposition of law (*CI/3596/2001*).

Subs. (8)

Where a Commissioner's decision would be to the same effect as the tribunal's, the Commissioner may take the view that any error on the part of the tribunal was not of sufficient substance for the tribunal's decision to be found to be erroneous in point of law at all (*CSDLA/257/1996, C55/99-00(IB), R(I) 2/06*). Certainly courts will generally dismiss an appeal on a point of law where satisfied that the result of decision under appeal was correct even if the decision was otherwise flawed. However, it can be important to substitute a decision based on correct reasoning if there is any possibility of there being a subsequent application for supersession and Commissioners therefore often set aside a decision only to substitute a decision to the same effect.

1.408

Commissioners should identify outstanding issues of fact or law before referring a case to another tribunal, because otherwise a tribunal is likely to find its role unclear (*Secretary of State for Work and Pensions v Menary-Smith* [2006] EWCA Civ 1689). To like effect, a Tribunal of Commissioners said in *R(IB) 2/07* that it was wrong to suggest that a Commissioner allowing an appeal necessarily had to refer a case to another tribunal, just because no witness had attended to give evidence before the Commissioner and there was a dispute between the parties as to the decision that should be substituted for one that had been set aside. Neither party in that case had suggested there was any material evidence not recorded in the papers or that anything turned on a dispute about that evidence. If the evidence was not in issue, the dispute between the parties was likely to be one of law that a Commissioner should resolve. Similarly, where a tribunal's findings of primary fact are adequate and the reasoning supporting those findings is also adequate, it is wrong to suggest that a Commissioner should refer the case to another tribunal to identify grounds for supersession. The Commissioner can perform that exercise himself under subs.(8)(a)(i) without making new findings of primary fact (*CDLA/4217/2001*). Moreover, a successful appellant cannot insist on a Commissioner referring a case to another tribunal under para.(8)(b) so that the tribunal can consider a factual case entirely different from the one presented to the tribunal whose decision has been set aside if the Commissioner is able, under para.(8)(a)(i) to give the decision the first tribunal should have given on the basis of its findings of fact, especially if the claimant was legally represented before the first tribunal (*CH/2484/2005*, a decision of a Tribunal of Commissioners subsequently upheld by the Court of Appeal, without reference to this point, in *Abdirahman v Secretary of State for Work and Pensions* [2007] EWCA Civ 657).

If a case is referred to a differently constituted tribunal, it is usual for the decision that has been set aside to be included in the papers. That is not inappropriate. Even if their findings of fact cannot be relied upon, issues identified by the first tribunal may well be of assistance to the new tribunal, although it must be careful not to be influenced by the discredited findings (*Swash v Secretary of State for the Home Department* [2006] EWCA Civ 1093; [2007] 1 W.L.R. 1264). There may, however, be special circumstances in which the Commissioner setting the first decision aside considers that the interests of justice require the case to be heard by a tribunal that has not seen that decision and he or she will be able to issue appropriate directions to ensure that that happens (*ibid.*).

If a decision of a tribunal has been superseded while an appeal against a Commissioner's decision has been pending, it is necessary to consider the effect of the supersession on the appeal or vice versa. If the supersession was under reg.6(2)(c) (ignorance of, or mistake as to, fact), there may be circumstances in which the appeal to the Commissioner should be treated as having lapsed, particularly if the supersession has given the claimant all that he or she seeks on the appeal. If the appeal is not treated as having lapsed and is allowed, the supersession decision is generally allowed to stand, and the decision to be made by a Commissioner or another tribunal following the setting aside of the first tribunal's decision is made in respect of a period ending immediately before the supersession took effect. This approach was held in *R(DLA)2/04* to be justifiable where the parties are content with the outcome of the supersession or where it is plain that supersession would have been appropriate whatever the outcome of the appeal because there had been an obvious change of circumstances or, perhaps, new medical evidence justifying supersession under reg.6(2)(g) of the Social Security and Child Support (Decisions and Appeals) Regulations 1999 in an incapacity benefit case. In *R(DLA)2/04* itself, the claimant had both appealed against and applied for supersession of a decision of a tribunal. The appeal was successful and a Commissioner had referred the case to another tribunal. The application for supersession had failed and the claimant's appeal came before the same tribunal as the remitted appeal. The new tribunal made an award on the remitted appeal and did not limit it on account of the failed supersession application. No award was made on the supersession appeal. On further appeals, the Commissioner held that that was the correct approach where, as in that case, the application for supersession had been under reg.6(2)(c) (error of fact). He advanced three rules:

"1. An application for supersession that results in a refusal to supersede the original decision does not terminate the period under consideration on an appeal against the original decision.
2. Live proceedings arising out of an application for supersession based on ignorance of, or a mistake as to, a material fact lapse when the decision to be superseded is set aside on appeal (provided that there is no further appeal in respect of the original decision).
3. Live proceedings arising out of an application for supersession based on a change of circumstances do not lapse when the decision to be superseded is set aside on appeal (but the application may have to be treated as an application for supersession of a different decision or, perhaps, as a new claim, depending on the circumstances)."

The second and third rules arise because a tribunal or Commissioner hearing an appeal against the original decision must correct any error of fact in the original decision but, by virtue of s.12(8)(b), must not take account of any subsequent change of circumstances. In *CDLA/3948/2002*, a different Commissioner also held that a supersession of a tribunal's decision became ineffective when the Commissioner set the tribunal's decision aside. Latham L.J. considered that approach to be correct and refused leave to appeal (*Farrington v Secretary of State for Work and Pensions* [2004] EWCA Civ 435).

It has been said in *CDLA/3323/2003* that where a Commissioner sets aside a decision of a tribunal awarding benefit for a fixed period, the period in issue before the Commissioner or a tribunal to whom the case is remitted is not necessarily limited

(1998 c.14, s.14)

by the fact that there has been a decision on a renewal claim, although the award on the renewal claim must be treated as having lapsed if an award on the original claim is made in respect of the same period and any benefit paid as a result of the renewal claim must be treated as having been paid on account of the decision eventually made on the earlier claim.

Subs. (10)

Regulation 58(6) of the Social Security and Child Support (Decisions and Appeals) Regulations 1999 is made under this subsection.

1.409

Leave to appeal may be granted on grounds other than those raised by the parties (*Krasniqi v Secretary of State for the Home Department* [2006] EWCA Civ 391). Nonetheless, a Commissioner considering an application for leave to appeal is not bound to trawl through the papers looking for grounds of appeal that have not been advanced by the applicant (*R. (Anayet Begum) v Social Security Commissioner* [2002] EWHC 401 (Admin). The same approach has been taken in the Court of Session in *Mooney v Secretary of State for Work and Pensions*, 2004 S.L.T. 1141 (also reported *sub. nom. Mooney v Social Security Commissioner* as *R(DLA) 5/04*). In that case, it was unsuccessfully argued that a Commissioner should have granted leave to appeal on the ground that a tribunal had failed to ask a claimant certain questions. Lord Brodie regarded it as significant that the claimant had failed to aver that the questions would have elicited any favourable evidence and also that the claimant had been represented and his representative had failed to adduce the evidence).

Once a legally qualified panel member has refused leave to appeal, it is not open to that panel member or another to grant leave to appeal (*R(U) 10/55*) and the only remedy is to make an application to a Commissioner. A Commissioner's refusal of leave to appeal is also final but it may be set aside where the conditions of reg.31 of the Social Security Commissioners (Procedure) Regulations 1999 are satisfied (*R(U) 3/89*).

Where a Commissioner refuses leave to appeal against a decision of a tribunal, no appeal lies against the refusal of leave but it may be challenged by way of an application for judicial review (*Bland v Chief Supplementary Benefit Officer*) [1983] 1 W.L.R. 262 (also reported as *R(SB) 12/83*). It has been made plain in relation to refusals by circuit judges of leave to appeal against decisions of district judges that applications for permission to apply for judicial review of refusals of leave to appeal should generally be dismissed summarily on the ground that Parliament has put in place an adequate system for reviewing the merits of district judge's decisions (*R. (Sivasubramaniam) v Wandsworth CC (Lord Chancellor's Department intervening)* [2003] EWCA Civ 1738; [2003] 1 W.L.R. 475). In *R. (Sinclair Gardens Investments (Kensington) Ltd) v Lands Tribunal* [2005] EWCA Civ 1305, leave to appeal to the Lands Tribunal from a Leasehold Valuation Tribunal had been refused by a surveyor member of the Lands Tribunal rather than a legally qualified member. The Court of Appeal dismissed an appeal from a refusal of judicial review of the refusal of leave and explicitly made the point that it followed from *Sivasubramaniam* that a refusal of leave to appeal would not necessarily be quashed on judicial review because it was erroneous in point of law. "It would also have to be established that the error was sufficiently grave to justify the case being treated as exceptional. . . . A possible example would be if the Lands Tribunal, despite being aware of the position, refused, without any good reason, permission to appeal on a difficult point of law of general application, which had been before a number of different LVTs which had taken different views on it, and which cried out for a definitive answer in the public interest." The Court also confirmed that reasons for refusing leave to appeal need not necessarily amount to more than expressing agreement with the lower tribunal. In *Gibson v Secretary of State for Work and Pensions* [2004] EWHC 561 (Admin) and *R. (Thomas) v Benefits Agency* [2004] EWHC 1352 (Admin) (both of which cases, despite their titles, involved applications for leave to apply for judicial review of Commissioners' refusals of leave to appeal from tribunals), Richards J.

similarly suggested that the *Sivasubramaniam* approach might also apply to judicial review of a Commissioner's decision, although he did consider the applications on a broader basis before dismissing them. However, the approach taken in *Sinclair Gardens* may not be applicable in respect of Commissioners because the relevant right of appeal to the Lands Tribunal, like the right of appeal to a circuit judge in *Sivasubramaniam*, was not restricted to points of law, whereas the right of appeal to a Commissioner usually is. In this context, the proper test is that suggested by the Court of Appeal in *R. v Social Security Commissioner, Ex p. Pattni* [1993] Fam. Law 213, where it was said that judicial review lay only in "the plainest possible case" where there was a clear error of law on the part of the Commissioner and that, if a judge considering an application for leave had any doubt as to whether there was such a clear error of law, he should adjourn the application in order to obtain the respondents' views *before* determining the application for leave. This represented some tightening up of the approach taken in *R. v Secretary of State for Social Services, Ex p. Connolly* [1986] 1 W.L.R. 421. In practice, it is suggested, an applicant must now show that the Commissioner was *probably* wrong, rather than merely showing that he or she was *possibly* wrong. Moreover, if an applicant for judicial review is seeking to argue that a Commissioner erred in refusing leave to appeal on grounds that were not raised in the application for leave to appeal that was rejected by the Commissioner, the point must be both obvious and have strong prospects of success and there must also be no other reasons that would have justified the refusal of leave (*Donnelly v Secretary of State for Work and Pensions* [2007] CSOH 01).

Where a Commissioner in England refuses leave to appeal in a case that arose in Scotland, or vice versa, both the Court of Session in Scotland and the High Court in England have jurisdiction to consider an application for judicial review. Nonetheless, it is open to a respondent to ask a court to decline jurisdiction on the ground that it would have been more appropriate to bring the proceedings in the other court. In *Tehrani v Secretary of State for the Home Department* [2006] UKHL 47; [2006] 3 W.L.R. 699, where such an issue arose in an immigration case, it was held that the appropriate court would normally be the court in the part of the United Kingdom where the adjudicator (the equivalent of an appeal tribunal) sat. However, there is probably a broader discretion to consider all the circumstances in a social security case, because the House of Lords relied by analogy on the statutory provision providing that the appropriate court on an appeal from the Immigration Appeal Tribunal depended on where the adjudicator sat, whereas s.15(4) of the Social Security Act 1998 is less prescriptive.

Subs. (11)

1.410 See reg.58 of the Social Security and Child Support (Decisions and Appeals) Regulations 1999 and regs 9–13 of the Social Security Commissioners (Procedure) Regulations 1999.

Appeal from Commissioner on point of law

1.411 **15.**—(1) Subject to subsections (2) and (3) below, an appeal on a question of law shall lie to the appropriate court from any decision of a Commissioner.

(2) No appeal under this section shall lie from a decision except—
   (a) with the leave of the Commissioner who gave the decision or, in a prescribed case, with the leave of a Commissioner selected in accordance with regulations; or
   (b) if he refuses leave, with the leave of the appropriate court.

(3) An application for leave under this section in respect of a Commissioner's decision may only be made by—
   (a) a person who, before the proceedings before the Commissioner were begun, was entitled to appeal to the Commissioner from the decision to which the Commissioner's decision relates;

(b) any other person who was a party to the proceedings in which the first decision mentioned in paragraph (a) above was given;

(c) any other person who is authorised by regulations to apply for leave; and regulations may make provision with respect to the manner in which and the time within which applications must be made to a Commissioner for leave under this section and with respect to the procedure for dealing with such applications.

(4) On an application to a Commissioner for leave under this section it shall be the duty of the Commissioner to specify as the appropriate court—
  (a) the Court of Appeal if it appears to him that the relevant place is in England or Wales;
  (b) the Court of Session if it appears to him that the relevant place is in Scotland; and
  (c) the Court of Appeal in Northern Ireland if it appears to him that the relevant place is in Northern Ireland,

Except that if it appears to him, having regard to the circumstances of the case and in particular to the convenience of the persons who may be parties to the proposed appeal, that he should specify a different court mentioned in paragraphs (a) to (c) above as the appropriate court, it shall be his duty to specify that court as the appropriate court.

(5) In this section—

"the appropriate court", except in subsection (4) above, means the court specified in pursuance of that subsection;

"the relevant place", in relation to an application for leave to appeal from a decision of a Commissioner, means the premises where the person or authority whose decision was the subject of the Commissioner's decision usually exercises his or its functions.

DEFINITIONS

"appropriate court"—see subs.(5).
"Commissioner"—see s.39(1).
"prescribed"—see s.84.
"relevant place"—see subs.(5).

GENERAL NOTE

This re-enacts ss.24 and 34(5) of the Social Security Administration Act 1992 but it clearly provides for a right of appeal against *any* decision of a Commissioner and not just a decision given under s.14. It therefore applies to decisions under s.13 of the Social Security (Recovery of Benefits) Act 1997 and under s.4 of the Forfeiture Act 1982. This is an improvement because it was arguable that the general right of appeal against Commissioners' decisions introduced by s.14 of the Social Security Act 1980 was lost in the 1992 consolidation and that appeals could then be brought only against decisions given under ss.23 and 34 of the 1992 Act, although no-one ever took the point. Nevertheless, reg.8 of the Tax Credits (Appeals) Regulations 2002 makes express provision in respect of tax credit appeals (as did the Tax Credits Act 1999, Sch.4, para.3(2)). So too do s.6D of the Pensions Appeal Tribunals Act 1943, para.9 of Sch.7 to the Child Support, Pensions and Social Security Act 2000 and reg.10 of the Child Trust Funds (Non-tax Appeals) Regulations 2005. However, the history of the legislation suggests that those provisions are all unnecessary.

For what amounts to a question of law, see the note to s.14(1). A decision of a Commissioner to refuse leave to appeal to a Commissioner is not a "decision" against which an appeal lies under this section. Instead, any challenge must be made

1.412

by way of an application for judicial review (*Bland v Chief Supplementary Benefit Officer* [1983] 1 W.L.R. 262, also reported as *R(SB) 12/83*). Although s.56 of the Access to Justice Act 1999 allows the Lord Chancellor to make an order requiring appeals in England and Wales to be heard by a court other than the Court of Appeal, no such order has been made in respect of appeals from Commissioners.

Leave to appeal must be obtained. If the Commissioner refuses leave, it is still necessary for him or her to identify the "appropriate court" so that an application for leave (known as "permission" in the Court of Appeal), may be made to that court. For the procedure for applying to the Commissioner for leave, see reg.33 of the Social Security Commissioners (Procedure) Regulations 1999. Note that the three-month time limit for making an application to the Commissioner may be extended by the Commissioner, under reg.5(2)(a), but if he or she refuses to do so, the time cannot be extended by the "appropriate court", although the Commissioner's refusal could be challenged by way of an application for judicial review (*White v Chief Adjudication Officer* [1986] 2 All E.R. 905, also reported as an appendix to *R(S) 8/85*). For the procedure in the Court of Appeal, see CPR Pt 52. An application for permission to appeal or an appeal must be brought within six weeks of the Commissioner's refusal or grant of leave being sent to the parties (PD 52, para.21.5), although the court has a general power under (CPR r.52.6) to extend time limits. For the procedure in the Court of Session, see R.C. 290 and 293B.

It is explained in *Practice Direction (Court of Appeal (Civil Division))* [1999] 1 W.L.R. 1027 that, in an ordinary case, permission to appeal to the Court of Appeal should be refused only if it is considered that the applicant has "no real prospect" of success, although, exceptionally, the Court will grant permission even if not so satisfied because there is an issue which they consider should, in the public interest, be considered by the Court. Examples are where a case raises questions of great public interest or questions of general policy or where authority binding on the Court of Appeal may call for reconsideration. However, s.55 of the Access to Justice Act 1999 provides that, where an appeal has been made to a county court or the High Court, a further appeal to the Court of Appeal lies only where the appeal would raise an important point of principle or practice or there is some other compelling reason for the Court of Appeal to hear it. In *Cooke v Secretary of State for Social Security* [2001] EWCA Civ 734 (reported as *R(DLA) 6/01*), it was pointed out that an appeal against a decision of a Commissioner was also a second appeal and it was held that, although s.55 did not apply, a robust attitude to the prospect of success criterion ought to be adopted on applications for leave from Commissioners. In particular, it was suggested that, given the Commissioners' expertise, the Court should take "an appropriately modest view . . . of how likely it is that the Commissioner will have got it wrong". The practical effect may be that, unless there is an important point of principle or practice, it will be necessary to persuade a Judge hearing an application for permission to appeal that the Commissioner was *probably* wrong, rather than *possibly* wrong. A Commissioner considering an application for leave to appeal should take the same approach (*Fryer-Kelsey v Secretary of State for Work and Pensions* [2005] EWCA Civ 511 (also reported as *R(IB) 6/05*). A Commissioner does not usually give reasons for refusing leave to appeal as the simple implication is that he or she considers that the applicant has no real prospect of overturning the decision for which full reasons will have been given. If an application is made to the Court of Appeal and is refused, the *Practice Direction* states that the Court will give short reasons. Where leave is granted, the Court may also identify, for the benefit of the parties and the Court hearing the appeal, a reason for granting leave, but it cannot be assumed that the Court has not accepted that there are other issues to be decided as well as the one identified. It is possible for a respondent to apply for a grant of leave by the Court to be set aside but the onus is a heavy one and such applications are discouraged. See CPR r.52.3.

It was made plain in *McAllister v Secretary of State for Work and Pensions* (2003) S.L.T. 1195 that, before allowing an appeal against a decision of a person or body exercising statutory powers, the Court of Session in Scotland requires to be satisfied that there are proper grounds for doing so. Therefore a written argument must be submitted, on the basis of which the Court will decide whether the case should be listed for hearing. In England and Wales, the Court of Appeal readily allows appeals by consent, without considering their merits. It is arguable that that is not appropriate in public law cases and that the Court of Session's approach is preferable, but the contrary argument is that experience shows that decisions given when there is no real dispute between the parties are often unsatisfactory because the opposing points of view are not fully explored. There have been a small number of instances when Commissioners' decisions have been set aside by the Court of Appeal without the Court considering the merits of the appeal. Although such a decision given by the Court of Appeal is not binding on anyone other than for the purposes of that particular case (*R(FC) 1/97*), it can create difficulties because the fact that the Commissioner's decision has been set aside plainly means that that too cannot be regarded as binding, although the Commissioner's reasoning may still be regarded as persuasive. The law is thus left uncertain.

In a different context, the Court of Appeal took a robust approach in *Secretary of State for Work and Pensions v DH (a child)* [2004] EWCA Civ 16 (reported as *R(DLA) 1/04*). They refused to consider on its merits an opposed appeal, brought by the Secretary of State on grounds that had not been advanced before the Commissioner despite the Commissioner having given a clear opportunity by indicating his provisional views. The Court said that the case did not appear to raise any new point of principle and that, in a case concerned with the mere application of established principles, it was "of the utmost value, on an appeal from a specialist tribunal, to have the considered views of the points at issue of that specialist tribunal before testing them on appeal". They were not impressed by the argument that the Commissioner's decision would remain as an unfortunate precedent, saying that if the issue was that important it was because there were many other similar cases and therefore the Secretary of State would be able to find another case in which to advance his arguments before a Commissioner and, if necessary, the Court.

Because an appeal lies against "any decision" rather than "any judgment or order", it is possible for an appeal to be brought by an appellant who does not wish to disturb the result of the Commissioner's decision, although leave to appeal will be given only if it is sought to challenge a ruling on a discrete point of general significance (*Morina v Secretary of State for Work and Pensions* [2007] EWCA Civ 749). It is arguable that a Commissioner should not grant leave in such a case but should let the appropriate court decide whether leave should be given, particularly as such an appeal might not be resisted and the court might therefore wish to consider the desirability of there being an advocate to the court.

Where the claimant is the appellant, the respondent will be either the Secretary of State for Work and Pensions or Her Majesty's Revenue and Customs (*not* the Social Security Commissioner). The Solicitor to the Department for Work and Pensions will accept service on behalf of the Secretary of State. His address is New Court, Carey Street, London WC2A 2LS.

Procedure etc.

Procedure

16.—(1) Regulations ("procedure regulations") may make any such provision as is specified in Schedule 5 to this Act.

(2) Procedure regulations prescribing the procedure to be followed in cases before a Commissioner shall provide that any hearing shall be in public except in so far as the Commissioner for special reasons otherwise directs.

(3) It is hereby declared—
(a) that the power to prescribe procedure includes power to make provision as to the representation of one person, at any hearing of a case, by another person whether having professional qualifications or not; and

1.413

Social Security Act 1998

(b) that the power to provide for the procedure to be followed in connection with the making of decisions by the Secretary of State includes power to make provision with respect to the formulation of the matters to be decided, whether on a reference under section 117 of the Administration Act or otherwise.

(4) *Omitted.*

(5) *Omitted.*

(6) If it appears to a Commissioner that a matter before him involves a question of fact of special difficulty, he may direct that in dealing with that matter he shall have the assistance of one or more experts. In this subsection "expert" means a person appearing to the Commissioner to have knowledge or experience which would be relevant in determining the question of fact of special difficulty.

(7) If it appears to the Chief Commissioner (or, in the case of his inability to act, to such other of the Commissioners as he may have nominated to act for the purpose) that—

(a) an application for leave under section 14(10)(b) above; or

(b) an appeal,

falling to be heard by one of the Commissioners involves a question of law of special difficulty, he may direct that the application or appeal be dealt with, not by that Commissioner alone, but by a tribunal consisting of any three or more of the Commissioners.

If the decision of the tribunal is not unanimous, the decision of the majority shall be the decision of the tribunal; and the presiding Commissioner shall have a casting vote if the votes are equally divided.

(8) Where a direction is given under subsection (7)(a) above, section 14(10)(b) above shall have effect as if the reference to a Commissioner were a reference to such a tribunal as is mentioned in subsection (7) above.

(9) Except so far as it may be applied in relation to England and Wales by procedure regulations, Part I of the Arbitration Act 1996 shall not apply to any proceedings under this Chapter.

DEFINITIONS

"the Administration Act"—see s.84.
"Commissioner"—see s.39(1).
"the Contributions and Benefits Act"—see s.84.
"prescribe"—*ibid.*
"procedure regulations"—see subs.(1).

GENERAL NOTE

1.414   This section, apart from subss.(3)(b), (4) and (5), is applied to tax credit appeals and to child trust fund appeals (see Vol.IV).

Subss. (1)–(3)

See the Social Security and Child Support (Decisions and Appeals) Regulations 1999, the Child Benefit and Guardian's Allowance (Decisions and Appeals) Regulations 2003, the Social Security Commissioners (Procedure) Regulations 1999. Regulations in respect of appeal tribunals are made by the Secretary of State (s.79(1)). Regulations in respect of Commissioners are made by the Lord Chancellor after consultation with the Scottish Ministers (s.79(2)). In *CIS/1363/2005*, it was held that there is no power in this section to make regulations conferring the function of making procedural decisions on a legally qualified panel member rather than a tribunal, with the result that a decision of a legally qualified panel member striking out an appeal is to be treated as a decision of a tribunal and an appeal lies against it under s. 14. At the time of going to press, a challenge to that decision has been heard by the Court of Appeal and judgment is awaited.

Subss. (4) and (5)
These subsections are to be repealed by the Social Security Contributions (Transfer of Functions, etc.) Act 1999, Sch.7, para.28, presumably at the same time as the only provisions that would have given them practical effect and which have never been brought into force.

1.415

Subs. (6)
There is no longer any general power to sit with assessors but the possibility of doing so is preserved for Commissioners by this subsection. There is no provision allowing the scope of the assistance given under this subsection to be limited by regulations as there is in s.7(6)(c).

1.416

Subss. (7) and (8)
The power to appoint a Tribunal of Commissioners to hear an appeal has been extended to enable a Tribunal to hear an application. It has also been provided that a tribunal may consist of more than three Commissioners, reflecting the fact that three no longer represent even a sizeable proportion of Commissioners, whereas in 1948 they would have represented a majority. Tribunals are often appointed to hear cases giving rise to issues about which single Commissioners have disagreed. A decision of a Tribunal usually settles the dispute because a decision of a Tribunal of Commissioners will always be followed by single Commissioners (*R(I) 12/75*), although not always by another Tribunal (*R(U) 4/88*).

1.417

Finality of decisions

17.—(1) Subject to the provisions of this Chapter, any decision made in accordance with the foregoing provisions of this Chapter shall be final; and subject to the provisions of any regulations under section 11 above, any decision made in accordance with those regulations shall be final.

(2) If and to the extent that regulations so provide, any finding of fact or other determination embodied in or necessary to such a decision, or on which such a decision is based, shall be conclusive for the purposes of—
  (a) further such decisions;
  (b) decisions made under the Child Support Act; and
  (c) decisions made under the Vaccine Damage Payments Act.

1.418

DEFINITIONS

"the Child Support Act"—see s.84.
"the Vaccine Damage Payments Act"—see s.84.

GENERAL NOTE

This section is applied, with substantial modifications, to decisions of appeal tribunals or Commissioners on tax credit appeals and child trust fund cases (see Vol.IV).

1.419

Subs. (1)
This re-enacts s.60(1) of the Social Security Administration Act 1992. Decisions are "final" subject to appeals and revisions or supersesssions. Therefore, it is not possible to sue the Secretary of State in negligence in respect of a decision (*Jones v Department of Employment* [1989] Q.B. 1) although an action could lie in misfeasance. That does not prevent the Department for Work and Pensions being sued in respect of bad advice. The finality of decisions does not prevent decisions being challenged by way of judicial review (*R. v Medical Appeal Tribunal, Ex p. Gilmore* [1957] 1 Q.B. 574, a decision made

1.420

Social Security Act 1998

before there was a right of appeal from a medical appeal tribunal to a Commissioner) although the reluctance of the High Court to allow such challenges when there is a statutory right of appeal means that they are confined to exceptional cases.

Subs. (2)

1.421   See reg.10 of the Social Security and Child Support (Decisions and Appeals) Regulations 1999 (in relation to decisions as to whether or not a person is incapable of work) and reg.5(2) and 6(1) of the Social Security (Industrial Diseases) (Prescribed Diseases) Regulations 1985 (in relation to whether or not a person has been suffering from a prescribed disease). Note that there is no express provision re-enacting s.60(2) of the 1992 Act which provided that, as a general rule, a finding in one decision was *not* conclusive for the purpose of any other decision. However, it is suggested that such an express provision is not necessary and that, in the absence of any rule of evidence to the contrary, a person or body making a decision is entitled to rely on an earlier finding but is not bound to do so. If that were not the approach to be taken in the absence of any express provision, subs.(2) would be unnecessary. Thus, as was pointed out in *CIB/3327/2004*, although a decision as to whether or not a person is incapable of work that is made on a claim for incapacity benefit is conclusive for the purposes of credits in respect of incapacity for work (by virtue of reg.10 of the 1999 Regulations), a decision as to whether or not a person is engaged in remunerative work made on a claim for jobseeker's allowance is not conclusive for the purposes of credits in respect of involuntary unemployment.

There is no power to make decisions under this Act conclusive for the purpose of decisions under the Social Security (Recovery of Benefits) Act 1997. Therefore, a tribunal considering an appeal under s.11 of that Act is entitled to find that benefit was not paid in respect of an accident, even if that conclusion is inconsistent with the benefit having been awarded at all (*R(CR) 1/02*). Similarly, *CIS/1330/2002* holds that a finding of fact within a decision as to a claimant's entitlement to benefit is not conclusive for the purposes of a decision as to whether an overpayment has been made and is recoverable. Again, it was held in *CIS/3605/2005* that an erroneous decision on entitlement was a valid revision or supersession decision for the purposes of s. 71(5A) of the Social Security Administration Act 1992, so as to enable the Secretary of State to recover an overpayment, but was not conclusive as to the amount of the overpayment, with the result that only the amount actually overpaid was recoverable. This approach was applied in *CA/2650/2006*, where a tribunal had found a claimant not to be ordinarily resident in Great Britain from October 27, 2003, when she had moved abroad, and had upheld a decision superseding her award of attendance allowance from that date. On an appeal against a second tribunal decision to the effect that an overpayment from October 27, 2003 to January 4, 2004 was recoverable from the claimant, the Commissioner found that she had ceased to be ordinarily resident in Great Britain only from January 4, 2004 (even though she was also resident abroad) and so she had not been overpaid benefit as a result of any failure to disclose a material fact. Accordingly, he allowed her appeal. However, under the law as it then stood, the first tribunal ought to have superseded her award only from the date of supersession in February 2004. The Commissioner pointed out that, even if the claimant had in fact ceased to be ordinarily resident in Great Britain on October 27, 2003, the first tribunal would have wrongly decided that she had not been entitled to attendance allowance from then until January 4, 2004, but that decision was final by virtue of s.17(1) of the Social Security Act 1998. Moreover, if she had ceased to be ordinarily resident, she would have actually been overpaid during that period because, had she reported the fact that she had moved overseas straightaway, her award would have been terminated immediately. He considered that, in those circumstances, he would have been bound to find that there had been an overpayment and that it was recoverable, despite the first tribunal's error. That suggestion is, strictly speaking, obiter dicta and the Commissioner did not consider whether a supersession that is technically defective (as opposed to being based on an erroneous finding of fact) might be found to be ineffective for the purposes of s.71(5A) so that, even though there was an overpayment, the overpayment would not be recoverable.

Note that s.29(2) makes an industrial accident declaration conclusive for the purposes of any claim for industrial injuries benefit in respect of that accident. That provision is not applied in respect of the onset of industrial diseases. However, in *Secretary of State for Work and Pensions v Whalley* [2002] EWCA Civ 166 (reported as *R(I) 2/03*), the Court of Appeal held that a finding as to the date of onset of an industrial disease made in the context of a claim for disablement benefit was binding in respect of a later claim for reduced earnings allowance. The Court appears to have accepted an argument advanced by the Secretary of State that s.60(1) of the 1992 Act made the finding binding and that s.60(2) was concerned only with "preliminary matters such as the precise symptoms displayed at any particular time". This is, in effect, an argument that was rejected by the Tribunal of Commissioners in *R(CR) 1/02*. *Whalley* was considered in *R(I) 2/04*, in which it was held that the reason that a finding as to a date of onset of an industrial disease is conclusive lies in reg.6(1) of the Social Security (Industrial Injuries) (Prescribed Diseases) Regulations 1985 rather than in s.17. It was pointed out that in *Whalley* the issue had been whether a finding that the claimant was *not* suffering from a prescribed disease so that there was *no* date of onset was conclusive and that that had turned on the finality of a decision on a diagnosis question under the pre-1998 Act system of adjudication, which in turn had precluded a finding in a later claim for disablement pension that there had been an earlier date of onset. In *R(I) 5/04*, it was held that, while a finding that a claimant had suffered from a prescribed disease from a particular date was conclusive as to the date of onset by virtue of reg.6(1) of the 1985 Regulations, a finding that the claimant had *not* been suffering from a prescribed disease was not conclusive under the new system of adjudication in the context of the legislation then in force, but was merely final in respect of the period up to the date of the decision of the Secretary of State in which the finding was made. However, reg.5(2) of the 1985 Regulations was introduced with effect from March 18, 2005 to reverse *R(I) 5/04* by providing that a negative finding is now also conclusive.

Matters arising as respects decisions

18.—(1) Regulations may make provision as respects matters arising—
  (a) pending any decision under this Chapter of the Secretary of State, an appeal tribunal or a Commissioner which relates to—
    (i) any claim for a relevant benefit; [1 or]
    (ii) any person's entitlement to such a benefit or its receipt; [1 or]
    (iii) [1 . . .]
    (iv) [1 . . .]
  (b) out of the revision under section 9 above or on appeal of any such decision.

(2) Regulations under subsection (1) above as it applies to child benefit may include provision as to the date from which child benefit is to be payable to a person in respect of a child [2 or qualifying young person] in a case where, before the benefit was awarded to that person, child benefit in respect of the child [2 or qualifying young person] was awarded to another person.

AMENDMENTS

1. Social Security Contributions (Transfer of Functions, etc.) Act 1999, Sch.7, para.29 (April 1, 1999).
2. Child Benefit Act 2005, Sch.1, para.26 (April 10, 2006).

Social Security Act 1998

DEFINITIONS

"appeal tribunal"—see s.39(1).
"claim"—by virtue of s.39(2), see s.191 of the Social Security Administration Act 1992.
"Commissioner"—see s.39(1).
"relevant benefit"—see s.8(3).

Medical examinations

Medical examination required by Secretary of State

1.423 **19.**—(1) Before making a decision on a claim for a relevant benefit, or as to a person's entitlement to such a benefit [¹ . . .], the Secretary of State may refer the person—
   (a) in respect of whom the claim is made; or
   (b) whose entitlement is at issue,
to a medical practitioner for such examination and report as appears to the Secretary of State to be necessary for the purpose of providing him with information for use in making the decision.
   (2) Subsection (3) below applies where—
   (a) the Secretary of State has exercised the power conferred on him by subsection (1) above; and
   (b) the medical practitioner requests the person referred to him to attend for or submit himself to medical examination.
   (3) If the person fails without good cause to comply with the request, the Secretary of State shall make the decision against him.

AMENDMENT

1. Social Security Contributions (Transfer of Functions, etc.) Act 1999, Sch.7, para.30 (April 1, 1999).

DEFINITIONS

"claim"—by virtue of s.39(2), see s.191 of the Social Security Administration Act 1992.
"medical examination"—*ibid*.
"medical practitioner"—*ibid*.
"relevant benefit"—see s.8(3).

GENERAL NOTE

Subss.(1) and (2)

1.424 This section must be distinguished from reg.19 of the Social Security and Child Support (Decisions and Appeals) Regulations 1999. Under this section, the Secretary of State refers the claimant for examination and report but it is the *medical practitioner* who requests attendance for, or submission to, a medical examination. The penalty imposed by subs.(3) is imposed for failing to comply with the medical practitioner's request. This section, therefore, appears to be for the purpose of obtaining a report—it being for the medical practitioner to decide whether an examination is necessary. Under reg.19, it is the Secretary of State who requires the claimant to attend the examination and the penalty for failure to do so is different. These distinctions reflect the different purposes of the two provisions. Section 19 makes provision for the obtaining of a report for the purpose of determining a claim whereas reg.19 makes provision for obtaining a report for the purpose of determining whether an award should be revised or superseded.

(1998 c.14, s.19)

In *CDLA/4127/2003*, the Secretary of State conceded that a full-time medical practitioner had gone too far in not only drawing the attention of a part-time examining medical practitioner to apparent contradictions and other failings in his report, which was originally favourable to the claimant in certain respects, but also in suggesting alterations that made the report unfavourable. The Commissioner further observed that difficulties were created by the fact that the examining medical practitioner had declared his original findings and opinions to be correct to the best of his knowledge but he had not made any such declaration in respect of his amendments or explained why the particular amendments made were justified despite the original declaration. On the claimant's appeal, the tribunal relied on the corrected report on the ground that it was "objective", without making any comment on the significance of the amendments. It was held that they had erred in law in exercising their inquisitorial role selectively, asking probing question of the claimant but not, even rhetorically, of the Secretary of State. Submissions to tribunals sometimes refer to s.19 when the terms of the decision suggest that it was made under reg.19. The consequence is that the submissions do not address the correct issues and relevant evidence is not placed before tribunals. See *CDLA/5167/2001* for an example. The Social Security (Incapacity for Work) (General) Regulations 1995 continue to contain yet another similar power and associated penalty for failure to comply. Note also that this section applies only to references by the Secretary of State: separate provision is made under s.20 for references required to assist tribunals.

A medical practitioner is entitled to decline to examine a person in the absence of a chaperon but, in such a case, even if the medical practitioner completes a report on the basis of informal observations and a lengthy conversation with the claimant, there has been no examination within the terms of this section. In *CDLA/4208/2004*, the Commissioner criticised a tribunal for referring to opinions formed by a doctor in those circumstances as "clinical findings".

Subs. (3)

What the decision is, depends on what the question was. It may be a decision to reject a whole claim but it may be a decision to award benefit but on a basis less favourable to the claimant than would otherwise have been the case. The claimant will usually be able to appeal against the decision (and apply for revision under s.9) and will be entitled to argue that he did have good cause for failing to comply with the request. He or she would also be entitled to argue that the decision was less favourable than was required by subs.(3), having regard to what was really in issue. The other remedy open to a claimant is to make a new claim (if benefit was not awarded) or make a new application for a supersession (if there is some continuing entitlement). The consequence will be to raise the question again and the Secretary of State (or Majesty's Revenue and Cusoms) will be obliged to make a new decision, which he will not be able to make under subs.(3) unless the claimant has failed without good cause to comply with a new request to attend for, or submit to, a medical examination.

1.425

Medical examination required by appeal tribunal

20.—(1) This section applies where an appeal has been brought under section 12 above against a decision on a claim for a relevant benefit, or as to a person's entitlement to such a benefit [1 . . .].

1.426

(2) An eligible person may, if prescribed conditions are satisfied, refer the person—

(a) in respect of whom the claim is made; or
(b) whose entitlement is at issue,

to a medical practitioner for such examination and report as appears to the eligible person to be necessary for the purpose of providing an appeal tribunal with information for use in determining the appeal.

259

Social Security Act 1998

In this subsection "eligible person" means a person who is eligible to be appointed as the sole member of an appeal tribunal, or to be nominated as the chairman of such a tribunal.

(3) At a hearing before an appeal tribunal, except in prescribed cases or circumstances, the tribunal—
  (a) may not carry out a physical examination of the person mentioned in subsection (2) above; and
  (b) may not require that person to undergo any physical test for the purpose of determining whether he satisfies the condition mentioned in section 73(1)(a) of the Contributions and Benefits Act.

AMENDMENT

1. Social Security Contributions (Transfer of Functions, etc.) Act 1999, Sch.7, para.31 (April 1, 1999).

DEFINITIONS

"appeal tribunal"—see s.39(1).
"claim"—by virtue of s.39(2), see s.191 of the Social Security Administration Act 1992.
"the Contributions and Benefits Act"—see s.84.
"medical examination"—by virtue of s.39(2), see s.191 of the Social Security Administration Act 1992.
"medical practitioner"—*ibid*.
"prescribed"—see s.84.
"relevant benefit"—see s.8(3).

GENERAL NOTE

Subs.(2)

1.427
A reference may be made only in circumstances set out in reg.41 of the Social Security and Child Support (Decisions and Appeals) Regulations 1999. Note that it is not a tribunal who has the power to refer, but an "eligible person" who will in practice be a legally qualified panel member. There is no statutory penalty for failing to attend for, or submit to, a medical examination required by an "eligible person" or requested by a medical practitioner making a report under this section. Such a penalty is unnecessary as it is open to the tribunal to draw such inferences from the failure as appear proper when deciding the medical issues arising before them.

It is not the practice for tribunals to obtain reports from the claimant's own doctors as a matter of course. However, claimants sometimes expect that that will be done. In *R(M) 2/80*, the claimant's consultant wrote suggesting that the Mobility Allowance Unit obtain medical evidence from his department. They did not do so. The Commissioner held that the claimant should have been told that her consultant's suggestion would not be followed up and that it would be up to her to obtain any further evidence if she so wished. Similar approaches were taken in *CI/13/1986* and *CA/133/1988*. These decisions were applied in *CIB/16604/1996* where the claimant wrote in his letter of appeal that "you are quite free to check my hospital and [doctor's] records". Neither the claimant nor the adjudication officer attended the hearing before the tribunal. The Commissioner held that there had been a breach of the rules of natural justice because the claimant reasonably believed that the tribunal would have before them his medical records and he was therefore prevented from providing relevant evidence in the sense that he could not reasonably be expected to produce evidence he thought the tribunal already had. That case was distinguished in *CIB/5030/1998* because there was evidence before the Commissioner that the Independent Tribunal Service issued a leaflet making it

(1998 c.14, s.20)

clear that claimants' doctors would not automatically be approached by the Benefits Agency, the Department of Social Security or the tribunal. The Commissioner held that it was not reasonable for the claimant to believe that the tribunal would have before them evidence from his doctors. That was so even though the claimant said that he had misunderstood the leaflet and thought he had only to give his consent. The Commissioner considered that there was no basis for that misunderstanding.

Subs.(3)

See reg.52 of the Social Security and Child Support (Decisions and Appeals) Regulations 1999. In *CDLA/433/1999*, it was held that carrying out a physical examination in breach of the forerunner of this subsection was not an error of law rendering a decision liable to be set aside but relying on evidence from the examination would have been. Observing a claimant during a hearing is not a physical examination or test (*R(DLA) 1/95*). In *R4/99(IB)*, the Commissioner in Northern Ireland said that a tribunal were entitled to use all their senses, including sight, in assessing evidence before them. In *R1/01(IB)*, a Tribunal of Commissioners in Northern Ireland adopted both those views. They held that the phrase "may not carry out a physical examination" suggests some formal process beyond mere observing and that a tribunal is not prohibited from looking at an injury if it is either readily visible or if the claimant wishes them to see it. They said that the tribunal had erred in simply rejecting the claimant's request to look at his knee. The tribunal should either have acceded to the request or else they should have given the claimant the opportunity of obtaining alternative evidence. A tribunal should not simply refuse such a request, unless they consider the evidence unnecessary or irrelevant. The Tribunal of Commissioners said that the legislation prohibits an appeal tribunal from asking to see a part of the claimant's body but it does not prevent the claimant from asking the tribunal to look. Nor does it prevent the tribunal from looking at what they can see without making any request. However, they are not entitled to do more than observe and, except in a case to which reg.52 of the Social Security and Child Support (Decisions and Appeals) Regulations 1999 applies, a medically qualified panel member ought not to accede to a request to feel a lump or manipulate a limb. If such evidence is necessary, the tribunal should adjourn in order to obtain a report. However, in *R(DLA) 5/03*, the Commissioner noted the distinction between a "physical examination" and a "physical test" and held that the prohibition on tests for the purpose of determining whether a claimant is unable, or virtually unable, to walk did not prevent a tribunal from asking a claimant to demonstrate activities for other purposes. He further said that a tribunal might be entitled to draw inferences from a refusal to comply with such a request, depending on the reasonableness of the request and any reasons given by the claimant for not complying. In *R(IB) 2/06*, it was held that examining x-rays is not a "physical examination" but that a tribunal was entitled to decline to look at x-rays on the ground that it did not have the expertise to analyse them. However, in such a case, the tribunal was obliged to consider whether to adjourn to obtain a report, which would involve considering whether it was likely that such a report would assist the tribunal in determining the point in issue before it.

1.428

Suspension and termination of benefit

Suspension in prescribed circumstances

21.—(1) Regulations may provide for—
(a) Suspending payments of a relevant benefit, in whole or in part, in prescribed circumstances;
(b) the subsequent making in prescribed circumstances of any or all of the payments so suspended.

1.429

Social Security Act 1998

(2) Regulations made under subsection (1) above may, in particular, make provision for any case where—
   (a) it appears to the Secretary of State that an issue arises whether the conditions for entitlement to a relevant benefit are or were fulfilled;
   (b) it appears to the Secretary of State that an issue arises whether a decision as to an award of a relevant benefit should be revised (under section 9 above) or superseded (under section 10 above);
   (c) an appeal is pending against a decision of an appeal tribunal, a Commissioner or a court; or
   (d) an appeal is pending against the decision given in a different case by a Commissioner or a court, and it appears to the Secretary of State that if the appeal were to be determined in a particular way an issue would arise whether the award of a relevant benefit (whether the same benefit or not) in the case itself ought to be revised or superseded.

(3) For the purposes of subsection (2) above, an appeal against a decision is pending if—
   (a) an appeal against the decision has been brought but not determined;
   (b) an application for leave to appeal against the decision has been made but not determined; or
   (c) in such circumstances as may be prescribed, an appeal against the decision has not been brought (or, as the case may be, an application for leave to appeal against the decision has not been made) but the time for doing so has not yet expired.

(4) [1 . . .]

AMENDMENT

1. Social Security Contributions (Transfer of Functions, etc.) Act 1999, Sch.7, para.32 (April 1, 1999).

DEFINITIONS

"appeal tribunal"—see s.39(1).
"Commissioner"—*ibid.*
"prescribed"—s.84.
"relevant benefit"—see s.8(3).

GENERAL NOTE

1.430   See regs 16 and 20 of the Social Security and Child Support (Decisions and Appeals) Regulations 1999 and regs 18 and 21 of the Child Benefit and Guardian's Allowance (Decisions and Appeals) Regulations 2003.

Suspension for failure to furnish information etc.

1.431   **22.**—(1) The powers conferred by this section are exercisable in relation to persons who fail to comply with information requirements.

(2) Regulations may provide for—
   (a) suspending payments of a relevant benefit, in whole or in part;
   (b) the subsequent making in prescribed circumstances of any or all of the payments so suspended.

(3) In this section and section 23 below "information requirement" means a requirement, made in pursuance of regulations under subsection (1)(hh) of section 5 of the Administration Act, to furnish information or evidence needed for a determination whether a decision on an award of benefit

(1998 c.14, s.22)

to which that section applies should be revised under section 9 or superseded under section 10 above.

[¹ (4) Subsection (3A) of section 5 of the Administration Act (which glosses paragraph (hh) in the case of state pension credit) shall apply in relation to subsection (3) above as it applies in relation to paragraph (hh) of subsection (1) of that section.]

AMENDMENT

1. State Pension Credit Act 2002, Sch.1, para.8 (July 2, 2002 for the purpose of exercising any power to make regulations or orders and October 6, 2003 for other purposes).

DEFINITIONS

"the Administration Act"—see s.84.
"information requirement"—see subs.(3).
"prescribed"—see s.84.
"relevant benefit"—see s.8(3).

GENERAL NOTE

See reg.17 of the Social Security and Child Support (Decisions and Appeals) Regulations 1999 and reg.19 of the Child Benefit and Guardian's Allowance (Decisions and Appeals) Regulations 2003.

1.432

Termination in cases of failure to furnish information

23. Regulations may provide that, except in prescribed cases or circumstances, a person—
  (a) whose benefit has been suspended in accordance with regulations under section 21 above and who subsequently fails to comply withan information requirement; or
  (b) whose benefit has been suspended in accordance with regulations under section 22 above for failing to comply with such a requirement,
shall cease to be entitled to the benefit from a date not earlier than the date on which payments were suspended.

1.433

DEFINITIONS

"information requirement"—see s.22(3).
"prescribed"—see s.84.

GENERAL NOTE

See reg.18 of the Social Security and Child Support (Decisions and Appeals) Regulations 1999 and reg.20 of the Child Benefit and Guardian's Allowance (Decisions and Appeals) Regulations 2003.

1.434

Suspension and termination for failure to submit to medical examination

24. Regulations may make provision—
  (a) enabling the Secretary of State to require a person to whom a relevant benefit has been awarded to submit to medical examination;
  (b) for suspending payments of benefit, in whole or in part, in a case of a person who fails to submit himself to a medical examination to which he is required to submit in accordance with regulations under paragraph(a) above;
  (c) for the subsequent making in prescribed circumstances of any or all of the payments so suspended;

1.435

Social Security Act 1998

 (d) for entitlement to the benefit to cease, except in prescribed cases or circumstances, from a date not earlier than the date on which payments were suspended.

DEFINITIONS

"medical examination"—by virtue of s.39(2), see s.191 of the Social Security Administration Act 1992.
"prescribed"—see s.84.
"relevant benefit"—see s.8(3).

GENERAL NOTE

1.436   See reg.19 of the Social Security and Child Support (Decisions and Appeals) Regulations 1999.

[¹*Appeals dependent on issues falling to be decided by Inland Revenue*

Appeals dependent on issues falling to be decided by Inland Revenue

1.437   **24A.**—(1) Regulations may make provision for an appeal tribunal or Commissioner, where on any appeal there arises any issue which under section 8 of the Social Security Contributions (Transfer of Functions, etc.) Act 1999 falls to be decided by an officer of the Inland Revenue, to require the Secretary of State to refer the issue to the Inland Revenue.

(2) Regulations under this section may—
 (a) provide for the appeal to be referred to the Secretary of State pending the decision of the Inland Revenue,
 (b) enable or require the Secretary of State, in specified circumstances, to deal with any other issue arising on the appeal pending the decision on the referred issue, and
 (c) enable the Secretary of State, on receiving the decision of an officer of the Inland Revenue, or any determination of the tax appeal Commissioners made on appeal from his decision—
  (i) to revise his decision,
  (ii) to make a decision superseding his decision, or
  (iii) to refer the appeal to the appeal tribunal or Commissioner for determination.]

AMENDMENT

1. Social Security Contributions (Transfer of Functions, etc.) Act 1999, Sch.7, para.33 (July 5, 1999).

DEFINITIONS

"appeal tribunal"—see s.39(1).
"Commissioner"—*ibid.*
"Inland Revenue"—by virtue of s.39(2), see s.191 of the Social Security Administration Act 1992 but note that the Inland Revenue has been merged into Her Majesty's Revenue and Customs by the Commissioners for Revenue and Customs Act 2005.
"tax appeal Commissioners"—see s.39(1).

GENERAL NOTE

1.438   See reg.38A of the Social Security and Child Support (Decisions and Appeals) Regulations 1999.

(1998 c.14, s.25)

Decisions and appeals dependent on other cases

Decisions involving issues that arise on appeal in other cases

25.—(1) This section applies where—
  (a) a decision by the Secretary of State falls to be made under section 8, 9 or 10 above in relation to a particular case; and
  (b) an appeal is pending against the decision given in another case by a Commissioner or a court (whether or not the two cases concern the same benefit).

(2) In a case relating to a relevant benefit, the Secretary of State need not make the decision while the appeal is pending if he considers it possible that the result of the appeal will be such that, if it were already determined, there would be no entitlement to benefit.

(3) If the Secretary of State considers it possible that the result of the appeal will be such that, if it were already determined, it would affect the decision in some other way—
  (a) he need not, except in such cases or circumstances as may be prescribed, make the decision while the appeal is pending;
  (b) he may, in such cases or circumstances as may be prescribed, make the decision on such basis as may be prescribed.

(4) Where the Secretary of State acts in accordance with subsection (3)(b) above, following the determination of the appeal he shall if appropriate revise his decision (under section 9 above) in accordance with that determination.

(5) For the purposes of this section, an appeal against a decision is pending if—
  (a) an appeal against the decision has been brought but not determined;
  (b) an application for leave to appeal against the decision has been made but not determined; or
  (c) in such circumstances as may be prescribed, an appeal against the decision has not been brought (or, as the case may be, an application for leave to appeal against the decision has not been made) but the time for doing so has not yet expired.

(6) In paragraphs (a), (b) and (c) of subsection (5) above, any reference to an appeal, or an application for leave to appeal, against a decision includes a reference to—
  (a) an application for, or for leave to apply for judicial review of the decision under section 31 of the Supreme Court Act 1981; or
  (b) an application to the supervisory jurisdiction of the Court of Session in respect of the decision.

1.439

DEFINITIONS

"appeal tribunal"—see s.39(1).
"Commissioner"—*ibid.*
"prescribed"—see s.84.
"relevant benefit"—see s.8(3).

GENERAL NOTE

Subs. (1)
This section applies only where a decision falls to be made by the Secretary of State (or, in relation to decisions under s.170 of the Pension Schemes Act 1993 or

1.440

in respect of child benefit or guardian's allowance, Her Majesty's Revenue and Customs—see s.170(7) of the 1993 Act (if it is not construed too literally) and ss.50(2)(e) and 51 of, and Sch.4, para.15 to, the Tax Credits Act 2002). See s.26 where a decision falls to be made by a tribunal or Commissioner. No appeal lies against a decision under this section (see Social Security and Child Support (Decisions and Appeals) Regulations 1999, Sch.2, para.7 and Child Benefit and Guardian's Allowance (Decisions and Appeals) Regulations 2003 Sch.2, para.4).

"Court" is not defined for the purposes of this section (compare s.27(7)) but the context in which the word appears limits its scope. There must be an appeal pending against a decision "in another case" of a Commissioner or a court. This includes an application for judicial review of a Commissioner's decision (see subs.(6)) but not an application for judicial review of a decision of the Secretary of State or Her Majesty's Revenue and Customs or, in a housing benefit case, a local authority. However, an appeal to the Court of Appeal against a decision of the High Court, or to the Inner House of the Court of Session from a decision of the Outer House, on judicial review of the Secretary of State, Her Majesty's Revenue and Customs or a local authority would appear to be caught. A renewed application for leave to apply for judicial review made to the Court of Appeal is probably not caught. A reference to the European Court of Justice by a Commissioner is certainly not caught. The words in parenthesis tend to suggest that the court must be concerned with some sort of social security benefit as does the general context of the provision and the need to have some sort of practical boundary. Otherwise, it might be suggested that, say, an appeal to the House of Lords from a decision of the Court of Appeal dealing with the meaning of the word "misrepresentation" in a marine insurance policy was a relevant appeal (because it might possibly assist with the understanding of that word in s.71 of the Social Security Administration Act 1992).

Subss.(2) and (3)

1.441   The Secretary of State (or Her Majesty's Revenue and Customs) must consider two separate issues. The first is whether a possible result of the appeal would affect the decision before him. The Secretary of State would be a party to most such appeals and it is to be hoped that he does not indulge in too much wishful thinking. The word "possible" is broad. And what is the meaning of "result of the appeal"? Is it confined to the ratio decidendi or is it sufficient that the Secretary of State considers that there might be some useful obiter dicta? The second issue the Secretary of State (or Her Majesty's Revenue and Customs) must consider is whether he should not make the decision or should decide it in accordance with subs.(3)(b) or whether he should ignore the fact that there is an appeal pending. He has a broad discretion and much will depend on such circumstances as the number of cases, the amount of money at stake, hardship to the claimants and the degree of probability that the court's decision will provide significant assistance with the determination of the cases before him.

For regulations under subs.(3)(b), see reg.21(1)–(3) of the Social Security and Child Support (Decisions and Appeals) Regulations 1999 and reg.22(1)–(3) of the Child Benefit and Guardian's Allowance (Decisions and Appeals) Regulations 2003.

Subs.(4)

1.442   The revision usually has effect from the same date as the original decision (see s.9(3)).

Subs.(5)

1.443   See reg.21(4) of the Social Security and Child Support (Decisions and Appeals) Regulations 1999 and reg.22(4) of the Child Benefit and Guardian's Allowance (Decisions and Appeals) Regulations 2003.

Appeals involving issues that arise on appeal in other cases

1.444   **26.**—(1) This section applies where—

(a) an appeal ("appeal A") in relation to a decision under section 8, 9 or 10 above is made to an appeal tribunal, or from an appeal tribunal to a Commissioner; and

(b) an appeal ("appeal B") is pending against a decision given in a different case by a Commissioner or a court (whether or not the two appeals concern the same benefit).

(2) If the Secretary of State considers it possible that the result of appeal B will be such that, if it were already determined, it would affect the determination of appeal A, he may serve notice requiring the tribunal or Commissioner—

(a) not to determine appeal A but to refer it to him; or

(b) to deal withthe appeal in accordance with subsection (4) below.

(3) Where appeal A is referred to the Secretary of State under subsection (2)(a) above, following the determination of appeal B and in accordance with that determination, he shall if appropriate—

(a) in a case where appeal A has not been determined by the tribunal, revise (under section 9 above) his decision which gave rise to that appeal; or

(b) in a case where appeal A has been determined by the tribunal, make a decision (under section 10 above) superseding the tribunal's decision.

(4) Where appeal A is to be dealt with in accordance with this subsection, the appeal tribunal or Commissioner shall either—

(a) stay appeal A until appeal B is determined; or

(b) if the tribunal or Commissioner considers it to be in the interests of the appellant to do so, determine appeal A as if—

(i) appeal B had already been determined; and

(ii) the issues arising on appeal B had been decided in the way that was most unfavourable to the appellant.

In this subsection "the appellant" means the person who appealed or, as the case may be, first appealed against the decision mentioned in subsection (1)(a) above.

(5) Where the appeal tribunal or Commissioner acts in accordance with subsection (4)(b) above, following the determination of appeal B the Secretary of State shall, if appropriate, make a decision (under section 10 above) superseding the decision of the tribunal or Commissioner in accordance withthat determination.

(6) For the purposes of this section, an appeal against a decision is pending if—

(a) an appeal against the decision has been brought but not determined;

(b) an application for leave to appeal against the decision has been made but not determined; or

(c) in such circumstances as may be prescribed, an appeal against the decision has not been brought (or, as the case may be, an application for leave to appeal against the decision has not been made) but the time for doing so has not yet expired.

(7) In this section—

(a) the reference in subsection (1)(a) above to an appeal to a Commissioner includes a reference to an application for leave to appeal to a Commissioner; and

(b) any reference in paragraph (a), (b) or (c) of subsection (6) above to an appeal, or to an application for leave to appeal, against a decision includes a reference to—

> > (i) an application for, or for leave to apply for, judicial review of the decision under section 31 of the Supreme Court Act
> > (ii) an application to the supervisory jurisdiction of the Court of Session in respect of the decision.
>
> (8) Regulations may make provision supplementing that made by this section.

DEFINITIONS

> "appeal tribunal"—see s.39(1).
> "Commissioner"—*ibid*.
> "prescribed"—see s.84.

1.445 GENERAL NOTE

Subs. (1)
See the note to s.25(1) for the meaning of "court". See also subss.(6) and (7).

Subs. (2)

1.446 It is for the Secretary of State (or, in relation to decisions under s.170 of the Pension Schemes Act 1993 or in respect of child benefit or guardian's allowance, Her Majesty's Revenue and Customs—see s.170(7) of the 1993 Act (if it is not construed too literally) and ss.50(2)(e) and 51 of, and Sch.4, para.15 to, the Tax Credits Act 2002) to identify both appeal B and appeal A although there is no reason why one notice may not be issued in respect of several appeals A (see reg.21 of the Social Security Commissioners (Procedure) Regulations 1999). As in s.25(2) and (3), the Secretary of State (or Her Majesty's Revenue and Customs) must first make a judgment as to the possible effects of the decision in appeal B and must then consider whether to serve notice under this subsection. It will not always be appropriate to do so. If the Secretary of State does decide to issue the notice, he must go on to decide whether the tribunal should be required to refer appeal A to him under para.(a) or to deal with the appeal in accordance with subs.(4) under para.(b). Which option is appropriate will depend on the circumstances of the case. It may be thought to be unobjectionable that there be specific provision as to the way appeals should be handled while the decision in a "test case" is awaited, but to be highly objectionable that the decision as to the appropriate procedure should lie wholly in the hands of the Secretary of State who is a party in appeal A and is usually a party in appeal B. The perception that this provision was desirable appears to have arisen out of an occasion when the then President of social security appeal tribunals directed tribunals to determine a vast number of appeals notwithstanding the fact that an appeal against a Commissioner's decision was pending in the courts. This resulted in some thousands of extra appeals being brought before the Commissioners. It may be thought that this is unlikely to be repeated. In practice the Secretary of State is very often content to allow tribunals and Commissioners to manage blocks of "lookalike" cases without resorting to serving a notice under this section and where a notice is served it is usually after consultation with the President of appeal tribunals and the Chief Commissioner. There can be an advantage to a claimant in having a notice served under this section where a tribunal or Commissioner might award some benefit on appeal A even if that appeal is determined on the basis that appeal B is determined adversely to the claimant. The claimant is then not deprived of that benefit while appeal B is awaiting final determination. It might be better if the legislation merely allowed the Secretary of State to seek a general direction in respect of a block of similar cases from the President of appeal tribunals (or a senior legally qualified panel member) or a Commissioner. As it is, any challenge to the Secretary of State's judgment must be by way of an application for judicial review.

(1998 c.14, s.26)

Subs. (3)
Presumably para.(b) exists in case appeal A was decided in ignorance of the notice requiring it not to be determined. The decision is not rendered ineffective and so operates until it is superseded. It is not clear what happens if either party appeals against it.

Subs. (4)
It is for the tribunal or Commissioner to decide whether para.(a) or para.(b) should apply in any particular case. Paragraph (b) is unlikely to be used a great deal unless either the claimant asks for it to be used or else the tribunal or Commissioner is fairly sure that the decision on appeal B is unlikely to assist the claimant. A judgment as to what is the most unfavourable way in which the issues arising on appeal B might be decided requires that the tribunal or Commissioner be given considerable information about the appeal, including pleadings, so that it can be established what the issues really are.

Subs. (5)
The supersession is effective from the date from which the tribunal or Commissioner's decision would have been effective had it been decided in accordance with the decision in "Appeal B", the test case (reg.7(33) of the Social Security and Child Support (Decisions and Appeals) Regulations 1999).

Subs. (6)
See reg.22 of the Social Security and Child Support (Decisions and Appeals) Regulations 1999 and reg.23 of the Child Benefit and Guardian's Allowance (Decisions and Appeals) Regulations 2003.

Subs. (8)
See reg.21 of the Social Security Commissioners (Procedure) Regulations 1999. There is no equivalent provision in the Social Security and Child Support (Decisions and Appeals) Regulations 1999.

Cases of error

Restrictions on entitlement to benefit in certain cases of error

27.—(1) Subject to subsection (2) below, this section applies where—
(a) the effect of the determination, whenever made, of an appeal to a Commissioner or the court ("the relevant determination") is that the adjudicating authority's decision out of which the appeal arose was erroneous in point of law; and
(b) after the date of the relevant determination a decision falls to be made by the Secretary of State in accordance with that determination (or would, apart from this section, fall to be so made)—
  (i) in relation to a claim for benefit;
  (ii) as to whether to revise, under section 9 above, a decision as to a person's entitlement to benefit; or
  (iii) on an application made under section 10 above for a decision as to a person's entitlement to benefit to be superseded.
(2) This section does not apply where the decision of the Secretary of State mentioned in subsection (1)(b) above—
(a) is one which, but for section 25(2) or (3)(a) above, would have been made before the date of the relevant determination; or

(b) is one made in pursuance of section 26(3) or (5) above.

(3) In so far as the decision relates to a person's entitlement to a benefit in respect of—

(a) a period before the date of the relevant determination; or

(b) in the case of a widow's payment, a death occurring before that date,

it shall be made as if the adjudicating authority's decision had been found by the Commissioner or court not to have been erroneous in point of law.

(4) In deciding whether a person is entitled to benefit in a case where his entitlement depends on his having been entitled to the same or some other benefit before attaining a particular age, subsection (3) above shall be disregarded for the purpose only of deciding whether he was so entitled before attaining that age.

(5) Subsection (1)(a) above shall be read as including a case where—

(a) the effect of the relevant determination is that part or all of a purported regulation or order is invalid; and

(b) the error of law made by the adjudicating authority was to act on the basis that the purported regulation or order (or the part held to be invalid) was valid.

(6) It is immaterial for the purposes of subsection (1) above—

(a) where such a decision as is mentioned in paragraph (b)(i) falls to be made, whether the claim was made before or after the date of the relevant determination;

(b) where such a decision as is mentioned in paragraph (b)(ii) or (iii) falls to be made on an application under section 9 or (as the case may be) 10 above, whether the application was made before or after that date.

(7) In this section—

"adjudicating authority" means—

(a) the Secretary of State;

(b) any former officer, tribunal or body; or

(c) any officer, tribunal or body in Northern Ireland corresponding to a former officer, tribunal or body;

"benefit" means—

(a) benefit under Parts II to V of the Contributions and Benefits Act, other than Old Cases payments;

(b) benefit under Part II of the Social Security Act 1975 (in respect of a period before July 1, 1992 but not before April 6, 1975);

(c) benefit under the National Insurance Act 1946 or 1965, or the National Insurance (Industrial Injuries) Act 1946 or 1965 (in respect of a period before April 6, 1975);

(d) a jobseeker's allowance;

[¹ (dd) state pension credit;]

(e) any benefit corresponding to a benefit mentioned in [¹ paragraphs (a) to (dd) above]; and

(f) any income-related benefit;

"the court" means the High Court, the Court of Appeal, the Court of Session, the High Court or Court of Appeal in Northern Ireland, the House of Lords or the Court of Justice in the European Community;

"former officer, tribunal or body" means any of the following, that is to say—

(a) an adjudication officer or, in the case of a decision given on a reference under section 21(2) or 25(1) of the Administration Act, a

(1998 c.14, s.27)

social security appeal tribunal, a disability appeal tribunal or a medical appeal tribunal;
(b) an adjudicating medical practitioner appointed under section 49 of that Act or a specially qualified adjudicating medical practitioner appointed in accordance with regulations under section 62(2) of that Act; or
(c) the National Assistance Board, the Supplementary Benefits Commission, the Attendance Allowance Board, a benefit officer, an insurance officer or a supplement officer.

(8) For the purposes of this section, any reference to entitlement to benefit includes a reference to entitlement—
(a) to any increase in the rate of a benefit; or
(b) to a benefit, or increase of benefit, at a particular rate.

(9) The date of the relevant determination shall, in prescribed cases, be determined for the purposes of this section in accordance with any regulations made for that purpose.

(10) Regulations made under subsection (9) above may include provision—
(a) for a determination of a higher court to be treated as if it had been made on the date of a determination of a lower court or a Commissioner; or
(b) for a determination of a lower court or a Commissioner to be treated as if it had been made on the date of a determination of a higher court.

AMENDMENT

1. State Pension Credit Act 2002, Sch.1, para.9 (July 2, 2002 for the purposes of exercising any power to make regulations or orders and October 6, 2003 for other purposes).

DEFINITIONS

"adjudicating authority"—see subs.(7).
"the Administration Act"—see s.84.
"appeal tribunal"—see s.39(1).
"benefit"—see subs.(7).
"claim"—by virtue of s.39(2), see s.191 of the Social Security Administration Act 1992.
"Commissioner"—see s.39(1).
"the Contributions and Benefits Act"—see s.84.
"the court"—see subs.(7).
"former officer, tribunal or body"—*ibid.*
"income-related benefit"—by virtue of s.39(2), see s.191 of the Social Security Administration Act 1992.
"Old Cases payments"—*ibid.*
"prescribed"—see s.84.
"the relevant determination"—see subs.(1).

GENERAL NOTE

In so far as they apply to child benefit and guardian's allowance, the Secretary of State's functions under this section were transferred to the Board of Inland Revenue (Tax Credit Act 2002, s.50(2)(e)) and are now exercised by Her Majesty's Revenue and Customs (Commissioners for Revenue and Customs Act 2005).

1.453

Subs. (1)

The Secretary of State is an adjudicating authority but an appeal tribunal is not (see subs.(7)). As the question for a Commissioner or court is whether an *appeal tribunal* has erred in law, it may not always be easy to tell whether the effect of the

1.454

Social Security Act 1998

Commissioner's or court's determination is that the Secretary of State's decision was erroneous in point of law. See also subss.(5) and (6).

Paragraph (b) is in broad terms but it is suggested that, although s.27 would apply to revision under reg.3(5)(b) of the Social Security and Child Support (Decisions and Appeals) Regulations 1999 (mistake of fact too favourable to the claimant), it would not apply to the related decisions under s.71 of the Social Security Administration Act 1992 as to the amount of the overpayment or the Secretary of State's entitlement to recover the overpayment. Nor does it apply to decisions under the Social Security (Recovery of Benefits) Act 1997. Where successive Commissioners' decisions have held a departmental practice to be wrong, it is the first such decision that is "the relevant determination", even where Commissioners have differed as to their reasoning (*R(I)1/03*, a decision of a Tribunal of Commissioners).

Subs.(3)

1.455 This subsection has the effect that any decision of a Commissioner or court that is unfavourable to the Secretary of State is only prospective in its effect in other cases. Such a provision is not necessarily unreasonable to the extent that it does not require existing decisions in respect of earlier periods to be reversed but this one takes the principle to extremes by requiring the Secretary of State to continue giving erroneous decisions in respect of the period before the Commissioner's or court's decision after the error has been discovered. This is done so that all claimants are treated equally unfavourably in respect of that period. The perceived need for the provision may arise from the general power to revise at any time a decision arising from an official error (reg.3(5)(a) of the Social Security and Child Support (Decisions and Appeals) Regulations 1999). The corollary is that any supersession as a result of the Commissioner's or court's determination is effective from the date of that determination (reg.7(6)) which tends to operate to the advantage of claimants although it is not entirely clear when supersession would be appropriate rather than revision on the ground of official error in this context. Most, if not all, of the objections to s.27 would be removed if it operated only in relation to the power to revise decisions on the ground of official error and did not catch other claims and applications where the conventional time limits (much more restrictive than when the forerunner of s.27 was first introduced in 1990) adequately limit the extent to which an unexpected decision could apply retrospectively.

Subs.(5)

1.456 This is logical but may be thought to reinforce the view that subs.(3) is objectionable. Parliament has here not only ratified in advance decisions made, presumably in good faith, in excess of powers; it has also enabled (and required) the Secretary of State to continue making decisions (in respect of past periods) in excess of those powers once he knows the limits of the powers. This is despite the fact that Parliament could not have known the extent to which the powers would be exceeded. Henry VIII could hardly have asked for more.

Subs.(7)

1.457 Note that an appeal tribunal is not an "adjudicating authority". Quite why a social security appeal tribunal giving a decision on a reference should have been included as a "former tribunal" is unclear because there was no reason to suppose that their view of the law would necessarily be consistent with that held by the Department of Social Security. Perhaps the draftsman had a particular case in mind. The inclusion of disability appeal tribunals and medical appeal tribunals is even more obscure as there was no power to refer cases to them under the provisions cited. The inclusion of the Court of Appeal in Northern Ireland in the definition of "court" is interesting as a decision of that court is not, strictly speaking, binding in Great Britain. Such a decision is, however, highly persuasive and should usually be followed. The implication is that, if the Secretary of State does decide to follow a decision of the Court of Appeal in Northern Ireland, the decision before him "falls

(1998 c.14, s.27)

to be made . . . in accordance with" the decision of the court for the purpose of subs.(1).

Subss. (9) and (10)
No regulations have yet been made under these powers.   1.458

Correction of errors and setting aside of decisions

28.—(1) Regulations may make provision with respect to—   1.459
   (a) the correction of accidental errors in any decision or record of a decision made under any relevant enactment; and
   (b) the setting aside of any such decision in a case where it appears just to set the decision aside on the ground that—
      (i) a document relating to the proceedings in which the decision was given was not sent to, or was not received at an appropriate time by, a party to the proceedings or a party's representative or was not received at an appropriate time by the body or person who gave the decision; or
      (ii) a party to the proceedings or a party's representative was not present at a hearing related to the proceedings.

[¹ (1A) In subsection (1) "decision" does not include any decision made by an officer of the Inland Revenue, other than a decision under or by virtue of Part III of the Pensions Schemes Act 1993.]

(2) Nothing in subsection (1) above shall be construed as derogating from any power to correct errors or set aside decisions which is exercisable apart from regulations made by virtue of that subsection.

(3) In this section "relevant enactment" means any enactment contained in—
   (a) this Chapter;
   (b) the Contributions and Benefits Act;
   (c) the Pension Schemes Act 1993;
   (d) the Jobseekers Act; [² . . .]
   (e) the Social Security (Recovery of Benefits) Act 1997; [² or
   (f) the State Pension Credit Act 2002.

AMENDMENTS

1. Social Security Contributions (Transfer of Functions, etc.) Act 1999, Sch.7, para.34 (July 5, 1999).
2. State Pension Credit Act 2002, Sch.1, para.10 and Sch.3 (July 2, 2002 for the purposes of exercising any power to make regulations or orders and April 7, 2003 for other purposes).

DEFINITIONS

"Contributions and Benefits Act"—see s.84.
"Inland Revenue"—by virtue of s.39(2), see s.191 of the Social Security Administration Act 1992 but note that the Inland Revenue has been merged into Her Majesty's Revenue and Customs by the Commissioners for Revenue and Customs Act 2005.
"the Jobseekers Act"—see s.84.
"prescribed"—see s.84.
"relevant enactment"—see subs.(3).

General Note

1.460 This section is applied, with a different definition of "relevant enactment" in subs.(3), to decisions of appeal tribunals and Commissioners relating to tax credit appeals and child trust fund appeals (see Vol.IV).

Subs. (1)

1.461 See regs 56–57A of the Social Security and Child Support (Decisions and Appeals) Regulations 1999 and regs 30–32 of the Social Security Commissioners (Procedure) Regulations 1999.

Subs. (2)

1.462 Other powers include those to be found in s.13 but this subsection (which is derived from s.70(2) of the Social Security Administration Act 1992 which contained no equivalent to s.13 of this Act) may contemplate a more general implied power to correct or set aside decisions where it is necessary to do so in the interests of justice. See further the note to reg.57 of the Social Security and Child Support (Decisions and Appeals) Regulations 1999.

Industrial accidents

Decision that accident is an industrial accident

1.463 **29.**—(1) Where, in connection with any claim for industrial injuries benefit, it is decided that the relevant accident was or was not an industrial accident—

(a) an express declaration of that fact shall be made and recorded; and

(b) subject to subsection (3) below, a claimant shall be entitled to have the issue whether the relevant accident was an industrial accident decided, notwithstanding that his claim is disallowed on other grounds.

(2) Subject to subsection (3) and section 30 below, any person suffering personal injury by accident shall be entitled, if he claims the accident was an industrial accident—

(a) to have that issue decided; and

(b) to have a declaration made and recorded accordingly,

notwithstanding that no claim for benefit has been made in connection with which the issue arises; and this Chapter shall apply for that purpose as if the issue had arisen in connection with a claim for benefit.

(3) The Secretary of State, an appeal tribunal or a Commissioner (as the case may be) may refuse to decide the issue whether an accident was an industrial accident, if satisfied that it is unlikely to be necessary to decide the issue for the purposes of any claim for benefit and this Chapter shall apply as if any such refusal were a decision on the issue.

(4) Subject to sections 9 to 15 above, any declaration under this section that an accident was or was not an industrial accident shall be conclusive for the purposes of any claim for industrial injuries benefit in respect of that accident.

(5) Where subsection (4) above applies—

(a) in relation to a death occurring before April 11, 1988; or

(b) for the purposes of section 60(2) of the Contributions and Benefits Act, it shall have effect as if at the end there were added the words "whether or not the claimant is the person at whose instance the declaration was made".

(6) For the purposes of this section (but subject to section 30 below), an accident whereby a person suffers personal injury shall be deemed, in relation to him, to be an industrial accident if—
(a) it arises out of and in the course of his employment;
(b) that employment is employed earner's employment for the purposes of Part V of the Contributions and Benefits Act; and
(c) payment of benefit is not under section 94(5) of that Act precluded because the accident happened while he was outside Great Britain.

(7) A decision under this section shall be final except that sections 9 and 10 above apply to a decision under this section that an accident was or was not an industrial accident as they apply to a decision under section 8 above if, but only if, the Secretary of State is satisfied that the decision under this section was given in consequence of any wilful non-disclosure or misrepresentation of a material fact.

DEFINITIONS

"appeal tribunal"—see s.39(1).
"benefit—by virtue of s.39(2), see s.191 of the Social Security Administration Act 1992.
"claim"—*ibid.*
"claimant"—see s.39(1) and, by virtue of s.39(2), see s.191 of the Social Security Administration Act 1992.
"Commissioner"—see s.39(1).
"Contributions and Benefits Act"—see s.84.
"industrial injuries benefit"—by virtue of s.39(2), see s.191 of the Social Security Administration Act 1992.

GENERAL NOTE

This section re-enacts s.44 of the Social Security Administration Act 1992 with only minor changes. It provides for the Secretary of State to make a declaration that a person has suffered an industrial accident, whether or not there has been a claim for benefit and whether or not any claim has any prospects of success on other grounds, although, under subs.(3), the Secretary of State (or a tribunal or Commissioner) may refuse to determine that question if it is unlikely there will ever be a claim for benefit.

1.464

A determination that there was or was not an industrial accident is conclusive for the purposes of later claims for benefit (unless it is set aside on appeal or is revised or superseded). However, it is important to note that this section is expressed to be subject to s.30, so that a decision under this section which implies that a person has suffered personal injury as a result of an accident does not require anyone to find that the claimant has suffered disablement as a result of the injury even though the two decisions may appear, in the circumstances of the case, to contradict one another.

The usual rights of appeal apply to declarations under this section, but the power to revise or supersede such decisions is strictly limited, by subs.(7), to cases of *wilful* non-disclosure or misrepresentation of a material fact.

An appeal tribunal hearing an appeal from a decision given under subs.(2) is constituted by a legally-qualified panel member sitting alone (see the note to reg.36 of the Social Security and Child Support (Decisions and Appeals) Regulations 1999).

Social Security Act 1998

Where the Secretary of State has decided that a claimant has not suffered an industrial accident and the claimant appeals against that decision, a tribunal may exercise the power conferred by subs.(3) to refuse to decide the issue on the ground that it is unlikely to be relevant to any claim to benefit (*CI/1297/2002*). That refusal to decide the issue must replace the Secretary of State's decision, and will make an important difference if the tribunal is wrong and there ever is a claim for benefit, because the Secretary of State's decision would have been conclusive by virtue of subs.(4).

Effect of decision

30.—(1) A decision (given under subsection (2) of section 29 above or otherwise) that an accident was an industrial accident is to be taken as determining only that paragraphs (a), (b) and (c) of subsection (6) of that section are satisfied in relation to the accident.

(2) Subject to subsections (3) and (4) below, no such decision is to be taken as importing a decision as to the origin of any injury or disability suffered by the claimant, whether or not there is an event identifiable as an accident apart from any injury that may have been received.

(3) A decision that, on a particular occasion when there was no event so identifiable, a person had an industrial accident by reason of an injury shall be treated as a decision that, if the injury was suffered by accident on that occasion, the accident was an industrial accident.

(4) A decision that an accident was an industrial accident may be given, and a declaration to that effect be made and recorded in accordance with section 29 above, without its having been found that personal injury resulted from the accident.

(5) Subsection (4) above has effect, subject to the discretion under section 29(3) above, to refuse to decide the issue if it is unlikely to be necessary for the purposes of a claim for benefit.

DEFINITIONS

"benefit"—by virtue of s.39(2), see s.191 of the Social Security Administration Act 1992.
"claim"—*ibid*.
"claimant"—see s.39(1) and, by virtue of s.39(2), see s.191 of the Social Security Administration Act 1992.

GENERAL NOTE

This section replaces s.60(3) of the Social Security Administration Act 1992. The drafting of the new provision is a great improvement. The overall effect is the same. A finding that there has been an industrial accident does not prevent it from being found that there has been no loss of faculty resulting from the accident even if the two decisions appear to be inconsistent. This is so even in a case where a person suffers a heart attack and the only "accident" found was the heart attack itself. Another decision-maker is still entitled to hold that the heart attack was not the result of an accident. This provision was first introduced by the National Insurance Act 1972 to reverse the effect of *Jones v Secretary of State for Social Services* [1972] A.C. 944 (also reported as an appendix to *R(I) 3/69*). It is less important than it used to be now that all material decisions are made by the Secretary of State and there is no longer the old division of jurisdiction between adjudication officers and adjudicating medical authorities. However, it still has significance where a declaration is made under s.29(2) (i.e. otherwise than in the course of determining a claim to benefit) or where different decision-makers deal with the question whether there was an industrial accident and the question whether the claimant suffers a loss of faculty as a result of the accident (e.g. where a tribunal reverses a decision to the effect that there was no industrial accident but does not go on and deal with the other questions arising on the claim). In *CI/105/1998*, it was pointed out that, quite apart from cases where the accident is indistinguishable from the injury suffered, there are cases where an indication that an accident was one giving rise to personal injury is a necessary part of a decision-maker's reasoning because it may help to explain why a declaration is made in respect of that alleged cause of the injury rather than another. However, it was also made clear that the effect of the forerunner of this section was that any view as to causation expressed when making the decision that an accident was an industrial accident could be only provisional.

Other special cases

Incapacity for work

31.—(1) Regulations may provide that a determination that a person is disqualified for any period in accordance with regulations under section 171E of the Contributions and Benefits Act shall have effect for such purposes as may be prescribed as a determination that he is to be treated as capable of work for that period, and vice versa.

(2) Provision may be made by regulations for matters of such descriptions as may be prescribed to be determined by the Secretary of State, notwithstanding that other matters fall to be determined by another authority.

(3) Nothing in this section shall be taken to prejudice the generality of the power conferred by section 17(2) above.

1.467

DEFINITIONS

"Contributions and Benefits Act"—see s.84.
"prescribed"—*ibid.*

GENERAL NOTE

Subs.(1)
This subsection replaces s.61A(2) of the Social Security Administration Act 1992. See reg.10 of the Social Security and Child Support (Decisions and Appeals) Regulations 1999.

1.468

Subs.(2)
See reg.11 of the Social Security and Child Support (Decisions and Appeals) Regulations 1999.

1.469

Industrial diseases

32. Regulations shall provide for applying the provisions of this Chapter, subject to any prescribed additions or modifications, in relation to decisions made or falling to be made under sections 108 to 110 of the Contributions and Benefits Act.

1.470

DEFINITIONS

"Contributions and Benefits Act"—see s.84.
"prescribed"—*ibid.*

GENERAL NOTE

1.471   See the Social Security (Industrial Injuries) (Prescribed Diseases) Regulations 1985 as amended by Art.4(8) of and Sch.8 to the Social Security Act 1998 (Commencement No.8 and Savings and Consequential and Transitional Provisions) Order 1999.

Christmas bonus

1.472   **33.**—(1) A decision by the Secretary of State that a person is entitled or not entitled to payment of a qualifying benefit in respect of a period which includes a day in the relevant week shall be conclusive for the purposes of section 148 of the Contributions and Benefits Act.

(2) In this section, expressions to which a meaning is assigned by section 150 of that Act have that meaning.

DEFINITIONS

"Contributions and Benefits Act"—see s.84.
"qualifying benefit"—by virtue of subs.(2), see s.150 of the Social Security Contributions and Benefits Act 1992.
"relevant week"—*ibid*.

GENERAL NOTE

1.473   This replaces s.67 of the Social Security Administration Act 1992.

Housing benefit and council tax benefit

1.474   **34.–35.** *Omitted.*

Social fund payments

1.475   **36.–38.** *Omitted.*

Supplemental

Interpretation etc. of Chapter II

1.476   **39.**—(1) In this Chapter—
"appeal tribunal" means an appeal tribunal constituted under Chapter I of this Part;
[2 "claimant", in relation to a joint-claim couple claiming a joint-claim jobseeker's allowance (within the meaning of the Jobseekers Act 1995), means the couple or either member of the couple;]
"Commissioner" [1 (except in the expression "tax appeal Commissioners")] means the Chief Social Security Commissioner or any other Social Security Commissioner, and includes a tribunal of three or more Commissioners constituted under section 16(7) above;

(1998 c.14, s.39)

"relevant benefit" has the meaning given by section 8(3) above;

[¹ "tax appeal Commissioners" means the Commissioners for the general purposes of the income tax appointed under section 2 of the Taxes Management Act 1970 or the Commissioners for the special purposes of the Income Tax Acts appointed under section 4 of that Act.]

(2) Expressions used in this Chapter to which a meaning is assigned by section 191 of the Administration Act have that meaning in this Chapter.

(3) Part II of the Administration Act, which is superseded by the foregoing provisions of this Chapter, shall cease to have effect.

AMENDMENTS

1. Social Security Contributions (Transfer of Functions, etc.) Act 1999, Sch.7, para.35 (April 1, 1999).
2. Welfare Reform and Pensions Act 1999, Sch.7, para.17 (March 19, 2001).

DEFINITION

"the Administration Act"—see s.84.

GENERAL NOTE

This section is applied, with some modifications to the definitions, for the purposes of tax credit appeals and child trust fund appeals (see Vol.IV). 1.477

CHAPTER III

OTHER DECISIONS AND APPEALS

40.–47. *Omitted.* 1.478

PART II

CONTRIBUTIONS

48.–66. *Omitted.* 1.479

PART III

BENEFITS

67.–76. *Omitted.* 1.480

279

Social Security Act 1998

Part IV

Miscellaneous and Supplemental

Pilot schemes

77.—(1) Any regulations to which this subsection applies may be made so as to have effect for a specified period not exceeding 12 months.

(2) Any regulations which, by virtue of subsection (1) above, are to have effect for a limited period are referred to in this section as "a pilot scheme".

(3) A pilot scheme may provide that its provisions are to apply only in relation to—
  (a) one or more specified areas of localities;
  (b) one or more specified classes of person;
  (c) persons selected—
    (i) by reference to prescribed criteria; or
    (ii) on a sampling basis,

(4) A pilot scheme may make consequential or transitional provision with respect to the cessation of the scheme on the expiry of the specified period.

(5) A pilot scheme ("the previous scheme") may be replaced by a further pilot scheme making the same, or similar, provision (apart from the specified period) to that made by the previous scheme.

(6) In so far as a pilot scheme would, apart from this subsection, have the effect of—
  (a) treating as capable of work any person who would not otherwise be so treated; or
  (b) reducing the total amount of benefit that would otherwise be payable to any person,
it shall not apply in relation to that person.

(7) Subsection (1) above applies to—
  (a) regulations made under section 171D of the Contributions and Benefits Act (incapacity for work: persons treated as incapable of work); and
  (b) in so far as they are consequential on or supplementary to any such regulations, regulations made under any of the provisions mentioned in subsection (8) below.

(8) The provisions are—
  (a) subsection (5)(a) of section 22 of the Contributions and Benefits Act (earnings factors);
  (b) section 30C of that Act (incapacity benefit);
  (c) [1 . . .];
  (d) subsection (1)(e) of section 124 of that Act (income support) and, so far as relating to income support, subsection (1) of section 135 of that Act (the applicable amount);
  (e) Part XIIA of that Act (incapacity for work);
  (f) section 61A of the Administration Act and section 31 above (incapacity for work).

(9) A statutory instrument containing (whether alone or with other provisions) a pilot scheme shall not be made unless a draft of the instrument has been laid before Parliament and approved by a resolution of each House of Parliament.

(1998 c.14, s.77)

AMENDMENT

1. Welfare Reform and Pensions Act 1999, Sch.13, Pt IV (April 6, 2001).

DEFINITIONS

"the Administration Act"—see s.84.
"the Contributions and Benefits Act"—*ibid.*
"prescribed"—*ibid.*

78. *Omitted.* 1.482

Regulations and orders

79.—(1) Subject to [¹ subsections (2) and (2A) below and paragraph 6 of Schedule 4 to this Act, regulations under this Act shall be made by the Secretary of State. 1.483

(2) Regulations with respect to proceedings before the Commissioners (whether for the determination of any matter or for leave to appeal to or from the Commissioners) shall be made by the Lord Chancellor; and where the Lord Chancellor proposes to make regulations under this Act it shall be his duty to consult the Lord Advocate with respect to the proposal.

[¹ (2A) Subsection (1) has effect subject to any provision providing for regulations to be made by the Treasury or the Commissioners of Inland Revenue.]

(3) Powers under this Act to make regulations or orders are exercisable by statutory instrument.

(4) Any power conferred by this Act to make regulations or orders may be exercised—
  (a) either in relation to all cases to which the power extends, or in relation to those cases subject to specified exceptions, or in relation to any specified cases or classes of case;
  (b) so as to make, as respects the cases in relation to which it is exercised—
    (i) the full provision to which the power extends or any less provision (whether by way of exception or otherwise);
    (ii) the same provision for all cases in relation to which the power is exercised, or different provision for different cases or different classes of case or different provision as respects the same case or class of case for different purposes of this Act;
    (iii) any such provision either unconditionally or subject to any specified condition;
and where such a power is expressed to be exercisable for alternative purposes it may be exercised in relation to the same case for any or all of those purposes.

(5) Powers to make regulations for the purposes of any one provision of this Act are without prejudice to powers to make regulations for the purposes of any other provision.

(6) Without prejudice to any specific provision in this Act, a power conferred by this Act to make regulations includes power to make thereby such incidental, supplementary, consequential or transitional provision as appears to the authority making the regulations to be expedient for the purposes of those regulations.

Social Security Act 1998

(7) Without prejudice to any specific provisions in this Act, a power conferred by any provision of this Act to make regulations includes power to provide for a person to exercise a discretion in dealing with any matter.

(8) Any power conferred by this Act to make regulations relating to housing benefit or council tax benefit shall include power to make different provision for different areas or different authorities.

(9) In this section "Commissioner" has the same meaning as in Chapter II of Part I.

AMENDMENTS

1. Tax Credits Act 2002, Sch.4, para.13 (February 26, 2003).

GENERAL NOTE

Subs. (2)

By the Transfer of Functions (Lord Advocate and Secretary of State) Order 1999, SI 1999/678, art.2(1) and Schedule, the function of the Lord Advocate under this subsection was transferred to the Secretary of State. It was then treated as being exercisable in or as regards Scotland by the Scotland Act 1998) (Functions Exercisable in or as Regards Scotland) Order 1999 (SI 1999/1748, art.3 and Sch.1, para.19 and was transferred to the Scottish Ministers by the Scotland Act 1998 (Transfer of Functions to the Scottish Ministers etc.) Order 1999 (SI 1999/1750), art.2 and Sch.1.

The functions of the Commissioners of Inland Revenue have been transferred to the Commissioners for Her Majesty's Revenue and Customs (Commissioners for Revenue and Customs Act 2005, s.5(2)(a)).

This section applies in relation to regulations for child trust fund appeals, with the modification that subss. (2A) and (8) are omitted (see Vol.IV).

Parliamentary control of regulations

80.—(1) Subject to the provisions of this section, a statutory instrument containing (whether alone or with other provisions) regulations under—
  (a) section 7, 12(2) or 72 above; or
  (b) paragraph 12 of Schedule 1, paragraph 9 of Schedule 2 or paragraph 2 of Schedule 5 to this Act,
shall not be made unless a draft of the instrument has been laid before Parliament and been approved by a resolution of each House of Parliament.

(2) A statutory instrument—
  (a) which contains (whether alone or with other provisions) regulations made under this Act by the Secretary of State [¹, the Treasury or the Commissioners of Inland Revenue]; and
  (b) which is not subject to any requirement that a draft of the instrument be laid before and approved by a resolution of each House of Parliament,
shall be subject to annulment in pursuance of a resolution of either House of Parliament.

(3) A statutory instrument—
  (a) which contains (whether alone or with other provisions) regulations made under this Act by the Lord Chancellor; and
  (b) which is not subject to any requirement that a draft of the instrument be laid before and approved by a resolution of each House of Parliament,

shall be subject to annulment in pursuance of a resolution of either House of Parliament.

AMENDMENT

1. Tax Credits Act 2002, Sch.4, para.14 (February 26, 2003).

Reports by Secretary of State

81.—(1) The Secretary of State shall prepare, either annually or at such times or intervals as may be prescribed, a report on the standards achieved by the Secretary of State in the making of decisions against which an appeal lies to an appeal tribunal constituted under Chapter I of Part I.

(2) A copy of every such report shall be laid before each House of Parliament.

1.486

DEFINITION

"prescribed"—see s.84.

82. *Omitted.* 1.487

83. *Omitted.* 1.488

Interpretation: general

84. In this Act—
"the Administration Act" means the Social Security Administration Act 1992;
"the Child Support Act" means the Child Support Act 1991;
"the Contributions and Benefits Act" means the Social Security Contributions and Benefits Act 1992;
"the Jobseekers Act" means the Jobseekers Act 1995;
"the Vaccine Damage Payments Act" means the Vaccine Damage Payments Act 1979;
"prescribe" means prescribe by regulations.

1.489

85. *Omitted.* 1.490

86. *Omitted.* 1.491

Short title, commencement and extent

87.—(1) This Act may be cited as the Social Security Act 1998.
(2) This Act, except—
(a) sections 66, 69, 72 and 77 to 85, this section and Schedule 6 to this Act; and
(b) subsection (1) of section 50 so far as relating to a sum which is chargeable to tax by virtue of section 313 of the Income and Corporation Taxes Act 1988, and subsections (2) to (4) of that section,

1.492

Social Security Act 1998

shall come into force on such day as may be appointed by order made by the Secretary of State; and different days may be appointed for different provisions and for different purposes.

(3) An order under subsection (2) above may make such savings, or such transitional or consequential provision, as the Secretary of State considers necessary or expedient—
- (a) in preparation for or in connection with the coming into force of any provision of this Act; or
- (b) in connection with the operation of any enactment repealed or amended by a provision of this Act during any period when the repeal or amendment is not wholly in force.

(4) This Act, except—
- (a) section 2 so far as relating to war pensions;
- (b) sections 3, 15, 45 to 47, 59, 78 and 85 and this section; and
- (c) section 86 and Schedules 7 and 8 so far as relating to enactments which extend to Northern Ireland,

does not extend to Northern Ireland.

(5) The following provisions of this Act extend to the Isle of Man, namely—
- (a) in section 4, subsections (1)(c) and (2)(c);
- (b) sections 6 and 7 and Schedule 1 so far as relating to appeals under the Vaccine Damage Payments Act;
- (c) sections 45 to 47 and this section;
- (d) paragraphs 5 to 10 of Schedule 7 and section 86(1) so far as relating to those paragraphs; and
- (e) section 86(2) and Schedule 8 so far as relating to the Vaccine Damage Payments Act.

DEFINITION

"Vaccine Damage Payments Act"—see s.84.

GENERAL NOTE

Subss. (2) and (3)

1.493
The following commencement orders have been made: SI 1998/2209, SI 1998/2708, SI 1999/418, SI 1999/526, SI 1999/528, SI 1999/1055, SI 1999/1510, SI 1999/1958, SI 1999/2422, SI 1999/2739, SI 1999/2860 and SI 1999/3178. The main provisions relating to social security adjudication were brought into effect at different times, depending on the benefit in issue, according to the following time-table:

Industrial injuries benefit; Guardian's allowance; Child benefit; Pension Schemes Act 1993—July 5, 1999 (see, primarily, SI 1999/1958).

Retirement pension; Widow's benefit; Incapacity benefit; Severe disablement allowance; Maternity allowance—September 6, 1999 (see, primarily, SI 1999/2422).

Working families' tax credit; Disabled person's tax credit—October 5, 1999 (see, primarily, SI 1999/2739).

Attendance allowance; Disability living allowance; Invalid care allowance; Jobseeker's allowance; Credits of contributions or earnings; Home responsibilities protection; Vaccine damage payments—October 18, 1999 (see, primarily, SI 1999/2860).

All other purposes (including income support)—November 29, 1999 (see, primarily, SI 1999/3178).

(1998 c.14, Sch.1)

SCHEDULES

Schedule 1

Appeal Tribunals: Supplementary Provisions

Tenure of office

1.—(1) Subject to the following provisions of this paragraph, the President of appeal tribunals shall hold and vacate office in accordance with the terms of his appointment.

(2) The President shall vacate his office on the day on which he attains the age of 70, but subject to section 26(4) to (6) of the Judicial Pensions and Retirement Act 1993 (power to authorise continuance in office up to the age of 75).

(3) The President may be removed from office by the Lord Chancellor [⁴, with the concurrence of the Lord Chief Justice and the Lord President of the Court of Session,] on the ground of incapacity or misbehaviour.

(4) Where the Lord Chancellor proposes to exercise a power conferred on him by subparagraph (3) above, it shall be his duty to consult the Lord Advocate with respect to the proposal.

1.494

Remuneration etc.

2. The Secretary of State may pay, or make such payments towards the provision of, such remuneration, pensions or allowances to or in respect of the President as he may determine.

3. The Secretary of State may pay, or make such payments towards the provision of, such remuneration, pensions or allowances to or in respect of any person appointed under this Chapter to act as a member of an appeal tribunal, or as an expert to such a tribunal, as he may determine.

4.—(1) The Secretary of State may pay—
  (a) to any person required to attend at any proceedings under section 12 of this Act [³, section 20 of the Child Support Act or paragraph 6 of Schedule 7 to the Child Support, Pensions and Social Security Act 2000]; or
  (b) to any person required under this Part (whether for the purposes of this Part or otherwise) to attend for or to submit himself to medical or other examination or treatment,

such travelling and other allowances as he may determine.

(2) In this paragraph references to travelling and other allowances including references to compensation for loss of remunerative time but such compensation shall not be paid to any person in respect of any time during which he is in receipt of remuneration under paragraph 3 above.

5.—(1) Subject to sub-paragraph (2) below, the Secretary of State may pay such other expenses in connection with the work of any person or tribunal appointed or constituted under any provision of this Part as he may determine.

(2) Expenses are not payable under sub-paragraph (1) above in connection with the work of a tribunal presided over by a Social Security Commissioner.

1.495

Officers and staff

6. The Secretary of State may appoint such officers and staff as he thinks fit for the President and for appeal tribunals.

1.496

Functions of President

7. The President shall ensure that appropriate steps are taken by an appeal tribunal to secure the confidentiality, in such circumstances as may be prescribed, of any prescribed material or any prescribed classes or categories of material.

8.—(1) The President shall, after the requisite consultation, arrange such training for persons appointed to the panel constituted under section 6 above as he considers appropriate.

(2) In sub-paragraph (1) above "the requisite consultation" means—
  (a) except in the case of medical practitioners, consultation with the Secretary of State;
  (b) in the case of such practitioners, consultation with the Chief Medical Officers of the Department of Health, the [² National Assembly for Wales] and the [¹ Scottish Administration].

9. The President shall supply the Secretary of State with such reports and other information with respect to the carrying out of the functions of appeal tribunals as the Secretary of State may require.

10. Each year the President shall make to the Secretary of State a written report, based on the cases coming before appeal tribunals, on the standards achieved by the Secretary of State

1.497

Social Security Act 1998

Clerks to appeal tribunals

1.498   11. The Secretary of State may by regulations provide—
(a) for clerks to be assigned to service appeal tribunals; and
(b) for clerks so assigned to be responsible for summoning members of the panel constituted under section 6 above to serve on such tribunals.

Delegation of certain functions of appeal tribunals

1.499   12.—(1) The Secretary of State may by regulations provide—
(a) for officers authorised by the Secretary of State to make any determinations which fall to be made by an appeal tribunal and which do not involve the determination of any appeal, application for leave to appeal or reference;
(b) for the procedure to be followed by such officers in making such determinations;
(c) for the manner in which such determinations by such officers may be called in question.
(2) A determinations which would have the effect of preventing an appeal, application for leave to appeal or reference being determined by an appeal tribunal is not a determination of the appeal, application or reference for the purposes of sub-paragraph (1) above.

Certificates

1.500   13. A document bearing a certificate which—
(a) is signed by a person authorised in that behalf by the Secretary of State; and
(b) states that the document, apart from the certificate, is a record of a decision of an appeal tribunal or of an officer of the Secretary of State,
shall be conclusive evidence of the decision; and a certificate purporting to be so signed shall be deemed to be so signed unless the contrary is proved.

AMENDMENTS

1. Scotland Act 1998 (Consequential Modifications) (No.1) Order 1999 (SI 1999/1042), art.5 and Sch.3, Pt I, para.4.
2. National Assembly for Wales (Transfer of Functions) Order 2000 (SI 2000/253), art.7 and Sch.5, para.3 (February 16, 2000).
3. Child Support, Pensions and Social Security Act 2000, Sch.7, para.22(2).
4. Constitutional Reform Act 2005, Sch.4, paras 271 and 273 (April 3, 2006).

DEFINITIONS

"appeal tribunal"—see s.39(1).
"the Child Support Act"—see s.84.
"prescibed"—*ibid.*

GENERAL NOTE

Para.1

1.501   By the Transfer of Functions (Lord Advocate and Secretary of State) Order 1999, SI 1999/678, art.2(1) and Sch., the function of the Lord Advocate under sub-para.(4) is transferred to the Secretary of State. It was then treated as being exercisable in or as regards Scotland by the Scotland Act 1998 (Functions Exercisable in or as Regards Scotland) Order 1999 (SI 1999/1748), art.3 and Sch.1, para.19 and was transferred to the Scottish Ministers by the Scotland Act 1998 (Transfer of Functions to the Scottish Ministers etc.) Order 1999 (SI 1999/1750), art.2 and Sch.1.

Para.11

1.502   See reg.37 of the Social Security and Child Support (Decisions and Appeals) Regulations 1999 and reg.10 of the Tax Credits (Appeals) (No.2) Regulations 2002.

(1998 c.14, Sch.1)

Para.12
See regs 46–48 of the Social Security and Child Support (Decisions and Appeals) Regulations 1999. 1.503

Schedule 2

Decisions Against Which No Appeal Lies

Jobseeker's allowance for persons under 18

1. In relation to a person who has reached the age of 16 but not the age of 18, a decision— 1.504
   (a) whether section 16 of the Jobseekers Act is to apply to him; or
   (b) whether to issue a certificate under section 17(4) of that Act.

Christmas bonus

2. A decision whether a person is entitled to payment under section 148 of the Contributions and Benefits Act. 1.505

Priority between persons entitled to [³ carer's allowance]

3. A decision as to the exercise of the discretion under section 70(7) of the Contributions and Benefits Act. 1.506

Priority between persons entitled to child benefit

4. A decision as to the exercise of the discretion under paragraph 5 of Schedule 10 to the Contributions and Benefits Act. 1.507

Persons treated as if present in Great Britain

5. A decision whether to certify, in accordance with regulations made under section 64(1), 71(6), 113(1) or 119 of the Contributions and Benefits Act, that it is consistent with the proper administration of that Act to treat a person as though he were present in Great Britain. 1.508

[¹ Work-focused interviews

5A. A decision terminating or reducing the amount of a person's benefit made in consequence of any decision made under regulations under section 2A [⁴ or 2AA] of the Administration Act (work-focused interviews).] 1.509

Alteration of rates of benefit

6. A decision as to the amount of benefit to which a person is entitled, where it appears to the Secretary of State that the amount is determined by— 1.510
   (a) the rate of benefit provided for by law; or
   (b) an alteration of a kind referred to in—
      (i) section 159(1)(b) of the Administration Act (income support); [² . . .]
      (ii) section 159A(1)(b) of that Act (jobseeker's allowance) [² or
      (iii) section 129B(1)(b) of that Act (state pension credit).]

Increases in income support due to attainment of particular ages

7. A decision as to the amount of benefit to which a person is entitled, where it appears to the Secretary of State that the amount is determined by the recipient's entitlement to an increased amount of income support or income-based jobseeker's allowance in the circumstances referred to in section 160(2) or 160A(2) of the Administration Act. 1.511

Reduction in accordance with reduced benefit direction

8. A decision to reduce the amount of a person's benefit in accordance with a reduced benefit direction (within the meaning of section 46 of the Child Support Act). 1.512

Power to prescribe other decisions

9. Such other decisions as may be prescribed. 1.513

Social Security Act 1998

AMENDMENTS

1. Welfare Reform and Pensions Act 1999, s.81 and Sch.11, para.87 (November 11, 1999).
2. State Pension Credit Act 2002, s.11 and Sch.1, para.11 (July 2, 2002 for the purpose of exercising any power to make regulations or orders and October 6, 2003 for all other purposes).
3. Regulatory Reform (Carer's Allowance) Order 2002 (SI 2002/1457), Art.2(1) and Sch., para.3(b) September 2002 for the purposes of exercising powers to make subordinate legislation and October 28, 2002 for all other purposes).
4. Employment Act 2002. s.53 and Sch.7, para.51 (July 5, 2003).

DEFINITIONS

"the Administration Act"—see s.84.
"benefit"—by virtue of reg.39(2), see s.191 of the Social Security Administration Act 1992.
"the Child Support Act"—see s.84.
"the Contributions and benefits Act"—*ibid.*
"the Jobseekers Act"—*ibid.*
"prescribed"—*ibid.*

GENERAL NOTE

Para.6

1.514 A decision under reg.22A of the Income Support (General) Regulations 1987, reducing the amount of income support payable to a person while an appeal against a decision that the claimant is capable of work is pending, is not a decision on the "rate of benefit" within para.6(a). Therefore, there is a right of appeal against such a decision (*Re Smyth's Application* [2001] N.I. 393, QBD (NI), in which Kerr J. considered the equivalent provision in the Social Security (Northern Ireland) Order 1998).

Para.9

1.515 See Sch.2 to the Social Security and Child Support (Decisions and Appeals) Regulations 1999 and Sch.2 to the Child Benefit and Guardian's Allowance (Decisions and Appeals) Regulations 2003.

SCHEDULE 3

DECISIONS AGAINST WHICH AN APPEAL LIES

PART I

BENEFIT DECISIONS

Entitlement to benefit without a claim

1.516 1. In such cases or circumstances as may be prescribed, a decision whether a person is entitled to a relevant benefit for which no claim is required.
2. If so, a decision as to the amount to which he is entitled.

Payability of benefit

1.517 3. A decision whether a relevant benefit (or a component of a relevant benefit) to which a person is entitled is not payable by reason of—
   (a) any provision of the Contributions and Benefits Act by which the person is disqualified for receiving benefit;
   (b) regulations made under section 72(8) of that Act (disability living allowance);
   (c) regulations made under section 113(2) of that Act (suspension of payment); [[1] . . .]
   (d) section 19 of the Jobseekers Act (jobseeker's allowance);
   [[1](e) section 62 or 63 of the Child Support, Pensions and Social Security Act 2000;] [[2] or
   (f) section 7, 8 or 9 of the Social Security Fraud Act 2001.]

(1998 c.14, Sch.3)

Payments to third parties

4. Except in such cases or circumstances as may be prescribed, a decision whether the whole or part of a benefit to which a person is entitled is, by virtue of regulations, to be paid to a person other than him. 1.518

Recovery of benefits

5. A decision whether payment is recoverable under section 71 or 71A of the Administration Act. 1.519

6. If so, a decision as to the amount of payment recoverable. 1.520

Industrial injuries benefit

7. A decision whether an accident was an industrial accident for the purposes of industrial injuries benefit. 1.521

Jobseekers' agreements

8. A decision in relation to a jobseeker's agreement as proposed to be made under section 9 of the Jobseekers Act, or as proposed to be varied under section 10 of that Act. 1.522

[³ *State pension credit*

8A. A decision whether to specify a period as an assessed income period under section 6 of the State Pension Credit Act 2002. 1.523

8B. If so, a decision as to the period to be so specified.

8C. A decision whether an assessed income period comes to an end by virtue of section 9(4) or (5) of that Act.

8D. If so, a decision as to when the assessed income period so ends.]

Power to prescribe other decisions

9. Such other decisions relating to a relevant benefit as may be prescribed. 1.524

PART II

CONTRIBUTIONS DECISIONS

Paragraphs **10.–15.** *Omitted.* 1.525

16. A decision whether a person was (within the meaning of regulations) precluded from regular employment by responsibilities at home.

17. A decision whether a person is entitled to be credited with earnings or contributions in accordance with regulations made under section 22(5) of the Contributions and Benefits Act.

Paragraphs **18.–29.** *Omitted.*

AMENDMENTS

1. Child Support, Pensions and Social Security Act 2000, s.66 and Sch.9, Pt V (October 15, 2001).
2. Social Security Fraud Act 2001, s.12(2).
3. State Pension Credit Act 2002, Sch.1, para.12 (July 2, 2002 for the purpose of exercising any power to make regulations or orders and October 6, 2003 for other purposes).

DEFINITIONS

"the Administration Act"—see s.84.

"benefit"—by virtue of reg.39(2), see s.191 of the Social Security Administration Act 1992.

"claim"—*ibid.*

"the Child Support Act"—see s.84.

"the Contributions and benefits Act"—*ibid.*

"industrial injuries benefit"—by virtue of s.39(2), see s.191 of the Social Security Administration Act 1992.

"the Jobseekers Act"—s.84.

Social Security Act 1998

"prescribed"—*ibid.*
"relevant benefit"—see s.8(3).

GENERAL NOTE

Para. 3

1.526 A decision under art.13(2) of the Convention on Social Security between Great Britain and Jamaica that a person is not permanently incapacitated for work is not a decision under s.113 of the Social Security Contributions and Benefits Act 1992 disqualifying a person from benefit, even though it may lead to such a decision, and therefore it does not fall within para.3(a) (*Campbell v Secretary of State for Work and Pensions* [2005] EWCA Civ 989).

Para. 5

Notwithstanding the omission from para.5 of any reference to s.74 of the Administration Act, an appeal lies against a decision that benefit is recoverable under that section (*R(IS) 14/04*).

Para. 9

Regulation 26 of the Social Security and Child Support (Decisions and Appeals) Regulations 1999 is made under para.9.

Paras 10 to 29

Paragraphs 10–15 and 18–29 have never been brought into force and are all to be repealed by the Social Security Contributions (Transfer of Functions, etc.,) Act 1999, Sch.7, para.36 but so far the repealing provision has been brought into effect only in respect of para.23 (twice! See SI 1999/527 and SI 1999/1662). The jurisdictions which would have been conferred on appeal tribunals are instead transferred to the tax commissioners. Paragraphs 16 and 17, on the other hand, introduce new rights of appeal to appeal tribunals where none existed before 1999. In *CIB/3327/2004*, the Commissioner commented on the lack of arrangements within the Department for Work and Pensions for proper decisions to be made in respect of the crediting of earnings or contributions. In particular, it appeared that such decisions as were made did not include information about the new right of appeal conferred by para.17. Arrangements have been made under s.17 of the Social Security Contributions (Transfer of Functions, etc.) Act 1999 for Her Majesty's Revenue and Customs to make decisions on behalf of the Secretary of State in respect of matters falling within the scope of para.16 and in respect of some matters falling within the scope of para.17. These arrangements appear not to cover decisions relating to the crediting of earnings or contributions in respect of unemployment or incapacity for work, although *CIB/3327/2004* reveals some confusion among staff as to the division of responsibility between the Department for Work and Pensions and Her Majesty's Revenue and Customs.

SCHEDULE 4

SOCIAL SECURITY COMMISSIONERS

Appointment

1.527 **1.**—(1) Her Majesty may from time to time appoint, from among persons who have a 10 year general qualification or advocates or solicitors in Scotland of at least 10 years' standing—
    (a) a Chief Social Security Commissioner; and
    (b) such number of other Social Security Commissioners as Her Majesty thinks fit.
(2) If the Lord Chancellor considers that, in order to facilitate the disposal of the business of Social Security Commissioners, he should make an appointment in pursuance of this sub-paragraph, he may appoint—
    (a) a person who has a 10 year general qualification; or
    (b) an advocate or solicitor in Scotland of at least 10 years' standing; or
    (c) a member of the bar of Northern Ireland or solicitor of the Supreme Court of Northern Ireland of at least 10 years' standing,

(1998 c.14, Sch.4)

to be a Social Security Commissioner (but to be known as a deputy Commissioner) for such period or on such occasions as the Lord Chancellor thinks fit.

(3) In this paragraph "10 year general qualification" shall be construed in accordance with section 71 of the Courts and Legal Services Act 1990.

Remuneration etc.

2. The Lord Chancellor shall pay to a Commissioner such salary or other remuneration, and such expenses incurred in connection with the work of a Commissioner or any tribunal presided over by a Commissioner, as he may determine.

1.528

3.—(1) The Lord Chancellor or, in Scotland, the Secretary of State may pay to any person who attends any proceedings under section 14 of this Act [² , under section 6A of the Pensions Appeal Tribunals Act 1943] [¹ or under paragraph 8 of Schedule 7 to the Child Support, Pensions and Social Security Act 2000] such travelling and other allowances as he may determine.

(2) In this paragraph the reference to travelling and other allowances includes a reference to compensation for loss of remunerative time.

Tenure of office

4.—(1) Commissioners shall vacate their offices on the day on which they attain the age of 70, but subject to section 26(4) to (6) of the Judicial Pensions and Retirement Act 1993 (power to authorise continuance in office up to the age of 75).

1.529

(2) Nothing in sub-paragraph (1) above or in section 13 or 32 of the Judicial Pensions Act 1981 (which relate to pensions for Commissioners) shall apply to a person by virtue of his appointment in pursuance of paragraph 1(2) above.

5.—(1) A Commissioner may be removed from office by the Lord Chancellor on the ground of incapacity or misbehaviour.

[³ (1A) The Lord Chancellor may remove a person under sub-paragraph (1) only with the concurrence of the appropriate senior judge.

(2A) The appropriate senior judge is the Lord Chief Justice of England and Wales, unless the person exercises functions wholly or mainly in Scotland, in which case it is the Lord President of the Court of Session.]

(2) Nothing in sub-paragraph (1) above applies to a Commissioner appointed before May 23, 1980.

Delegation of functions

6. The Lord Chancellor may by regulations provide—
 (a) for officers authorised by the Lord Chancellor or, in Scotland, by the Secretary of State to make any determinations which fall to be made by Commissioners;
 (b) for the procedure to be followed by such officers in making such determinations;
 (c) for the manner in which such determinations by such officers may be called in question.

1.530

Certificates

7. A document bearing a certificate which—
 (a) is signed by a person authorised in that behalf by the Secretary of State; and
 (b) states that the document, apart from the certificate, is a record of a decision of a Commissioner,
shall be conclusive evidence of the decision; and a certificate purporting to be so signed shall be deemed to be so signed unless the contrary is proved.

1.531

Supplemental

8. Where the Lord Chancellor proposes to exercise a power conferred on him by paragraph 1(2), 5(1) or 6 above, it shall be his duty to consult the Lord Advocate with respect to the proposal.

1.532

AMENDMENTS

1. Child Support, Pensions and Social Security Act 2000, Sch.7, para.22(3).
2. Armed Forces (Pensions and Compensation) Act 2004, s.7(2).
3. Constitutional Reform Act 2005, Sch.4, paras 271 and 274 (April 3, 2006).

DEFINITION

"Commissioner"—see s.39(1)

Social Security Act 1998

General Note

1.533   This Schedule is applied to tax credit appeals and child trust fund appeals (see Vol.IV).

Para.6

1.534   See reg.7 of the Social Security Commissioners (Procedure) Regulations 1999.

Para.8

1.535   By the Transfer of Functions (Lord Advocate and Secretary of State) Order 1999, SI 1999/678, art.2(1) and Schedule, the function of the Lord Advocate under this paragraph is transferred to the Secretary of State. It was then treated as being exercisable in or as regards Scotland by the Scotland Act 1998 (Functions Exercisable in or as Regards Scotland) Order 1999 (SI 1999/1748, art.3 and Sch.1, para.19 and was transferred to the Scottish Ministers by the Scotland Act 1998 (Transfer of Functions to the Scottish Ministers etc.) Order 1999 (SI 1999/1750), art.2 and Sch.1.

Schedule 5

Regulations as to Procedure: Provision Which may be Made

1.536   1. Provision prescribing the procedure to be followed in connection with—
   (a) the making of decisions or determinations by the Secretary of State, an appeal tribunal or a Commissioner; and
   (b) the withdrawal of claims, applications, appeals or references falling to be decided or determined by the Secretary of State, an appeal tribunal or a Commissioner.

2. Provision as to the striking out or reinstatement of proceedings.

3. Provision as to the form which is to be used for any document, the evidence which is to be required and the circumstances in which any official record or certificate is to be sufficient or conclusive evidence.

4. Provision as to the time within which, or the manner in which—
   (a) any evidence is to be produced; or
   (b) any application, reference or appeal is to be made.

1.537   5. Provision for summoning persons to attend and give evidence or produce documents and for authorising the administration of oaths to witnesses.

1.538   6. Provision with respect to the procedure to be followed on appeals to and in other proceedings before appeal tribunals.

1.539   7. Provision for authorising an appeal tribunal consisting of two or more members to proceed with any case, with the consent of the claimant, in the absence of any member.

1.540   8. Provision for empowering an appeal tribunal to give directions for the disposal of any purported appeal which the tribunal is satisfied that it does not have jurisdiction to entertain.

1.541   9. Provision for the non-disclosure to a person of the particulars of any medical advice or medical evidence given or submitted for the purposes of a determination.

Definitions

"appeal tribunal"—see s.39(1).
"Commissioner"—*ibid.*

General Note

1.542   This Schedule is applied, with modifications, for the purposes of tax credits appeals (see Vol.IV) and, with references to the Board substituted for references to the Secretary of State, to child benefit and guardian's allowance decisions and appeals (Tax Credits Act 2002, Sch.4, para.15).

See the Social Security and Child Support (Decisions and Appeals) Regulations 1999, the Child Benefit and Guardian's Allowance (Decisions and Appeals) Regulations 2003 and the Social Security Commissioners (Procedure) Regulations 1999.

Schedules 6 to 8

1.543   Omitted.

(1999 c.2)

Social Security Contributions (Transfer of Functions, etc.) Act 1999

(1999 c.2)

ARRANGEMENT OF SECTIONS

PART I

GENERAL

1.–7. *Omitted.*

PART II

DECISIONS AND APPEALS

8. Decisions by officers of Board.
9.–16. *Omitted.*
17. Arrangement for discharge of decision-making functions.
18. and 19. *Omitted.*

PART III

MISCELLANEOUS AND SUPPLEMENTAL

20.–26. *Omitted.*
27. Interpretation.
28. Short title, commencement and extent.

SCHEDULES

Omitted.

An Act to transfer from the Secretary of State to the Commissioners of Inland Revenue or the Treasury certain functions relating to national insurance contributions, the National Insurance Fund, statutory sick pay, statutory maternity pay or person schemes and certain associated functions relating to benefits; to enable functions relating to any of those matters in respect of Northern Ireland to be transferred to the Secretary of State, the Commissioners of Inland Revenue or the Treasury; to make further provision, in connection with the functions transferred, as to the powers of the Commissioners of Inland Revenue, the making of decisions and appeals; to provide that rebates payable in respect of members of money purchase contracted-out pension schemes are to be payable out of the National Insurance Fund; and for connected purposes.

[25th February 1999]

Social Security Contributions (Transfer of Functions, etc.) Act 1999

PART I

GENERAL

1.545 **1.–7.** *Omitted.*

PART II

DECISIONS AND APPEALS

Decisions by officers of Board

1.546 **8.**—(1) Subject to the provisions of the Part, it shall be for an officer of the Board—
 (a) to decide whether for the purposes of Parts I to V of the Social Security Contributions and Benefits Act 1992 a person is or was an earner and, if so, the category of earners in which he is or was to be included,
 (b) to decide whether a person is or was employed in employed earner's employment for the purposes of Part V of the Social Security Contributions and Benefits Act 1992 (industrial injuries),
 (c) to decide whether a person is or was liable to pay contributions of any particular class and, if so, the amount that he is or was liable to pay,
 (d) to decide whether a person is or was entitled to pay contributions of any particular class that he is or was not liable to pay and, if so, the amount that he is or was entitled to pay,
 (e) to decide whether contributions of a particular class have been paid in respect of any period,
 (f) subject to and in accordance with regulations made for the purposes of this paragraph by the Secretary of State with the concurrence of the Board, to decide any issue arising as to, or in connection with, entitlement to statutory sick pay or statutory maternity pay,
 (g) to make any other decision that falls to be made under Part XI of the Social Security Contributions and Benefits Act 1992 (statutory sick pay) or Part XII of that Act (statutory maternity pay),
 (h) to decide any question as to the issue and content of a notice under subsection (2) of section 121C of the Social Security Administration Act 1992 (liability of directors etc. for company's contributions),
 (i) to decide any issue arising under section 27 of the Jobseekers Act 1995 (employment of long-term unemployed; deductions by employers), or under any provision of regulations under that section, as to—
  (i) whether a person is or was an employee or employer of another,
  (ii) whether an employer is or was entitled to make any deduction from his contributions payments in accordance with regulations under section 27 of that Act,
  (iii) whether a payment falls to be made to an employer in accordance with those regulations,

(iv) the amount that falls to be so deducted or paid, or
(v) whether two or more employers are, by virtue of regulations under section 27 of that Act, to be treated as one,
(j) [¹ . . .],
(k) to decide whether a person is liable to a penalty under—
   (i) paragraph 7A(2) or 7B(2)(h) of Schedule 1 to the Social Security Contributions and Benefits Act 1992, or
   (ii) section 113(1)(a) of the Social Security Administration Act 1992,
(l) to decide the [¹ . . .] or penalty payable under any of the provisions mentioned in [¹ paragraph k] above, and
(m) to decide such issues relating to contributions, other than the issues specified in paragraphs (a) to (l) above or in paragraphs 16 and 17 of Schedule 3 to the Social Security Act 1998, as may be prescribed by regulations made by the Board.

(2) *Omitted.*
(3) *Omitted.*
(4) *Omitted.*

AMENDMENT

1. Child Support, Pensions and Social Security Act 2000, s.76(6) and Sch.9, Pt VIII.

DEFINITIONS

"the Board"—see s.27, but note that the functions of the Board have been transferred to Her Majesty's Revenue and Customs by the Commissioners for Revenue and Customs Act 2005.
"contributions"—see s.27.

GENERAL NOTE

This section provides for a number of matters previously determined by the Secretary of State for Social Security to be determined by the Board of Inland Revenue (see s.27), whose functions have now been transferred to the Commissioners for Her Majesty's Revenue and Customs by s.5(2) of the Commissioners for Revenue and Customs Act 2005. They are mainly concerned with contributions and employment status (which is important for entitlement to industrial injuries benefits (see para.(b)), but also include statutory sick pay and statutory maternity pay (see paras (f) and (g)). Entitlement to statutory sick pay and statutory maternity pay had been determined by adjudication officers, until the Social Security Act 1998 transferred that function to the Secretary of State by provisions that never came fully into force because they were overtaken by this Act. Sections 9–14 of this Act make provision for decisions by Her Majesty's Revenue and Customs and appeals to the tax appeal commissioners which are beyond the scope of this volume, but see Vol.IV.

The questions listed in s.8(1) are *not* to be decided by the Secretary of State (see s.8(5) of the Social Security Act 1998) and therefore do not fall within the jurisdiction of appeal tribunals. However, although it was for the Inland Revenue to consider whether a person is or was in employed earner's employment, the Commissioner in *CI/7507/1999* accepted a submission by the Secretary of State that the question whether a person was to be *treated* as having been an employed earner for the purposes of the industrial injuries scheme was a matter for the Secretary of State and, on appeal, for an appeal tribunal. If that is the construction to be given to s.8(1)(b), presumably the same approach must be taken to s.8(1)(a), although questions relating to the payment of contributions will be matters for Her Majesty's Revenue and Customs by virtue of s.8(1)(c)–(e) and regulations made under s.8(1)(m). *CI/7507/1999* was distinguished in *R(JSA)8/02*, where the Commissioner held that the question whether a person was to be *treated* as having

1.547

paid contributions (where contributions had been deducted from her salary but not passed on to the Inland Revenue) was a question to be determined by the Inland Revenue. Where, following a claim for retirement pension, there is a dispute between the Secretary of State and a claimant as to whether employment he had been in was contracted-out or contracted-in employment, it arises as part of a question as to his liability to pay contributions or as to what contributions have been paid and so is a question falling within the jurisdiction of Her Majesty's Revenue and Customs by virtue of s.8(1)(c) or (e) (*CP/3833/2003*). Therefore any appeal lies to the tax commissioners and not to an appeal tribunal, notwithstanding that appeals against refusals of contracting-out certificates lie to appeal tribunals by virtue of s.170 of the Pension Schemes Act 1993.

Questions relating to "home responsibilities protection" and the crediting of contributions or earnings remain matters for the Secretary of State by virtue of the combined effect of s.8(1)(m) of this Act and s.8(1)(c) of the Social Security Act 1998. Note, however, that s.17 permits the Secretary of State to make arrangements for Her Majesty's Revenue and Customs to discharge his decision-making functions in relation to those matters.

1.548   **9.–16.** *Omitted.*

Arrangements for discharge of decision-making functions

1.549   **17.**—(1) The Secretary of State may make arrangements with the Board for any his functions under Chapter II of Part I of the Social Security Act 1998 in relation to—
(a) a decision whether a person was (within the meaning of regulations) precluded from regular employment by responsibilities at home, or
(b) a decision whether a person is entitled to be credited with earnings or contributions in accordance with regulations made under section 22(5) of the Social Security Contributions and Benefits Act 1992,
to be discharged by the Board or by officers of the Board.

(2) No such arrangements shall effect the responsibility of the Secretary of State or the application of Chapter II of Part I of the Social Security Act 1998 in relation to any decision.

(3) *Omitted.*

DEFINITIONS

"the Board"—see s.27, but note that the functions of the Board have been transferred to Her Majesty's Revenue and Customs by the Commissioners for Revenue and Customs Act 2005.
"contributions"—see s.27.

GENERAL NOTE

Questions about home responsibilities protection and the crediting of earnings or contributions are questions that are relevant to a person's contributions record, but they are nonetheless decisions within the jurisdiction of the Secretary of State and there are rights of appeal to tribunals (see the Social Security Act 1998, Sch.3, paras 16 and 17). Despite this, decisions about home responsibilities protection are made by Her Majesty's Revenue and Customs under an arrangement under this section. So too are most decisions about "credits" other than those related to incapacity for work or availability for work, which are made by the Secretary of State because a person claiming benefit on the ground of incapacity for work or availability for work is usually treated also as claiming "credits".

1.550   **18.–19.** *Omitted.*

(1999 c.2, s.20)

Part III

Miscellaneous and Supplemental

20.–26. *Omitted.* 1.551

Interpretation

27. In this Act, unless a contrary intention appears— 1.552
"the Board" means the Commissioners of Inland Revenue;
"contributions" means contributions under Part I of the Social Security Contributions and Benefits Act 1992.

General Note

"the Board" 1.553
The functions of the Commissioners of Inland Revenue have now been transferred to the Commissioners for Her Majesty's Revenue and Customs by s.5(2) of the Commissioners for Revenue and Customs Act 2005.

Short title, commencement and extent

28.—(1) This Act may be cited as the Social Security Contributions (Transfer of Functions, etc.) Act 1999. 1.554
(2) *Omitted.*
(3) *Omitted.*

Welfare Reform and Pensions Act 1999

(1999 c.30)

Arrangement of Sections

Part I to IV (*omitted*)

Part V

Welfare

Chapter I

Social Security Benefits

52.–67. *Omitted.*

Miscellaneous

1.555 68. Certain overpayments of benefit not to be recoverable.
69.–70. *Omitted.*

Supplementary

71. *Omitted.*
72. Supply of information for certain purposes.
73.–91. *Omitted.*

Certain overpayments of benefit not to be recoverable

1.556 **68.**—(1) An overpayment to which this section applies shall not be recoverable from the payee, whether by the Secretary of State or a local authority, under any provision made by or under Part III of the Administration Act (overpayments and adjustments of benefit).

(2) This section applies to an overpayment if—
   (a) it is in respect of a qualifying benefit;
   (b) it is referable to a decision given on a review that there has been an alteration in the relevant person's condition, being a decision to which effect is required to be given as from a date earlier than that on which it was given;
   (c) the decision was given before June 1, 1999; and
   (d) the overpayment is not excluded by virtue subsection (6).

(3) In subsection (2)(b) the reference to a decision on a review that there has been an alteration in the relevant person's condition is a reference to a decision so given that that person's physical or mental condition either was at the time when the original decision was given, or has subsequently become, different from that on which that decision was based, with the result—
   (a) that he did not at that time, or (as the case may be) has subsequently ceased to, meet any of the conditions contained in the following provisions of the Contributions and Benefits Act, namely—
      (i) section 64 (attendance allowance),
      (ii) section 72(1) or (2) (care component of disability living allowance), and
      (iii) section 73(1) or (2) (mobility component of that allowance); or
   (b) that he was at that time, or (as the case may be) has subsequently become, capable of work in accordance with regulations made under section 171C(2) of that Act (the all work test).

(4) For the purposes of this section "qualifying benefit" means—
   (a) attendance allowance;
   (b) disability living allowance;
   (c) any benefit awarded wholly or partly by reason of a person being (or being treated as being) in receipt of a component of disability living allowance or in receipt of attendance allowance;
   (d) incapacity benefit;
   (e) any benefit (other than incapacity benefit) awarded wholly or partly by reason of a person being (or being treated as being) in receipt of any benefit falling within paragraph (c), (d) or (e).

(1999 c.2, s.68)

(5) For the purposes of this section—
  (a) "review" means a review taking place by virtue of section 25(1)(a) or (b), 30(2)(a) or (b) or 35(1)(a) or (b) of the Administration Act;
  (b) "the relevant person", in relation to a review, means the person to whose entitlement to a qualifying benefit or to whose incapacity for work the review related; and
  (c) "the original decision", in relation to a review, means the decision as to any such entitlement or incapacity to which the review related.

(6) An overpayment is excluded by virtue of this subsection if (before or after the passing of this Act)—
  (a) the payee has agreed to pay a penalty in respect of the overpayment under section 115A of the Administration Act,
  (b) the payee has been convicted of any offence (under section 111A or 112(1) or (1A) of that Act or otherwise) in connection with the overpayment, or
  (c) proceedings have been instituted against the payee for such an offence and the proceedings have not been determined or abandoned.

(7) Nothing in this section applies to an overpayment to the extent that it was recovered from the payee (by any means) before February 26, 1999.

(8) In this section—
"benefit" includes any amount included in—
  (a) the applicable amount in relation to an income-related benefit (as defined by section 135(1) of the Contributions and Benefits Act), or
  (b) the applicable amount in relation to a jobseeker's allowance (as defined by section 4(5) of the Jobseekers Act 1995);
"income-related benefit" has the meaning given by section 123(1) of the Contributions and Benefits Act;
"overpayment" means an amount of benefit paid in excess of entitlement;
"the payee", in relation to an overpayment, means the person to whom that amount was paid.

COMMENCEMENT

November 11, 1999.

GENERAL NOTE

The purpose of this provision is to give an amnesty to certain benefit holders held to have been overpaid benefit in the circumstances set out in subs.(2). The section is replete with difficulty. Subsection (1) says that the overpayment is not to be recoverable; quite what this means in the context of the section is not clear. Subsection (6) refers to circumstances which take the overpayment out of the scope of subs.(2). There are both issues of timing and of culpability in the section which it is difficult to understand. Clearly subs.(6) is intended to exempt culpable overpayments from the amnesty, but the drafting is obscure.

1.557

Supply of information for certain purposes

72.—(1) The Secretary of State may by regulations make such provision for or in connection with any of the following matters, namely—
  (a) the use by a person within subsection (2) of social security information held by that person,
  (b) the supply (whether to a person within subsection (2) or otherwise) of social security information held by a person within that subsection,

1.558

(c) the relevant purposes for which a person to whom such information is supplied under the regulations may use it, and

(d) the circumstances and extent (if any) in and to which a person to whom such information is supplied under the regulations may supply it to another person (whether within subsection (2) or not),

as the secretary of State considers appropriate in connection with any provision to which subsection (3) applies or in connection with any scheme or arrangements to which subsection (4) applies.

(2) The persons within this subsection are—

(a) a Minister of the crown,

(b) a person providing services to, or designated for the purposes of this section by an order of, a Minister of the Crown;

(c) a local authority (within the meaning of the Administration Act); and

(d) a person providing services to, or authorised to exercise any function of, any such authority.

(3) This subsection applies to any provision made by or under—

(a) any of the sections of the Administration Act inserted by section 57, 58 or 71 of this Act,

[[1] (aa) section 2AA of the Administration Act,]

(b) section 60 of this Act, or

(c) the Jobseekers Act 1995.

(4) This subsection applies to—

(a) any scheme designated by regulations under subsection (1), being a scheme operated by the Secretary of State (whether under arrangements with any other person or not) for any purposes connected withemployment or training in the case of persons of a particular category or description;

(b) any arrangements of a description specified in such regulations, being arrangements made by the Secretary of State for any such purposes.

(5) Regulations under subsection (1) may, in particular, authorise information supplies to a person under the regulations—

(a) to be used for the purpose of amending or supplementing other information held by that person; and

(b) if it is so used, to be supplied to any other person, and used for any purpose, to whom or for whom that other information could be supplied or used.

(6) In this section—

"relevant provisions" means purposes connected with—

(a) social security, child support or war pensions, or

(b) employment or training;

"social security information" means information relating to social security, child support or war pensions;

and in this subsection "war pensions" means war pensions within the meaning of section 25 of the Social Security Act 1989 (establishment and functions of war pensions committees).

(7) Any reference in this section to purposes connected with employment or training includes purposes connected with the existing or future employment or training prospects or needs of persons, and (in particular) assisting or encouraging persons to enhance their employment prospects."

COMMENCEMENT

November 11, 1999.

(1999 c.2, s.72)

AMENDMENT

1. Employment Act 2002, s.53 and Sch.7 (July 5, 2003).

GENERAL NOTE

Subs.(3)
Sections 57 and 58 inserted ss.2A–2C into the Administration Act. Section 71 inserted s.7A into the Administration Act. Section 60 concerns special schemes for claimants for jobseeker's allowance.

1.559

Child Support, Pensions and Social Security Act 2000

(2000 C.19)

ARRANGEMENT OF SECTIONS

PART III

SOCIAL SECURITY

Loss of benefit

62. Loss of benefit for breach of community order.
63. Loss of joint-claim jobseeker's allowance.
64. Information provision.
65. Loss of benefit regulations.
66. *Omitted.*

1.560

An Act to amend the law relating to child support; to amend the law relating to occupational and personal pensions and war pensions; to amend the law relating to social security benefits and social security administration; to amend the law relating to national insurance contributions; to amend Part III of the Family Law Reform Act 1969 and Part III of the Family Law Act 1986; and for connected purposes.

[28th July 2000]

GENERAL NOTE TO SECTIONS 62–66

Except as set out below, ss.62–66 of the Child Support, Pensions and Social Security Act 2000 ("CSPSSA 2000") were brought into effect for certain pilot areas of England on October 15, 2001 by the Child Support, Pensions and Social Security Act 2000 (Commencement No.10) Order 2001 (SI 2001/2619). As there is at present no pilot area in Scotland, s.62(11) and subss.(3), (4)(b), 7(d), (9) and (11) of s.64 (which are included in the text below for the sake of completeness) have yet to be brought into force.

For an analysis of ss.62–66, see the General Note to Social Security (Breach of Community Order) Regulations 2001 (SI 2001/1395), below.

Sections 7–12 of the Social Security (Fraud) Act 2001 contain similar "loss of benefit" provisions for people convicted of two separate benefit offences within three years.

1.561

Child Support, Pensions and Social Security Act 2000

Part III

Social Security

Loss of benefit

Loss of benefit for breach of community order

1.562   **62.**—(1) If—
(a) a court makes a determination that a person ("the offender") has failed without reasonable excuse to comply with the requirements of a relevant community order made in respect of him,
(b) the Secretary of State is notified in accordance with regulations under section 64 of the determination, and
(c) the offender is a person with respect to whom the conditions for any entitlement to a relevant benefit are or become satisfied,
then, even though those conditions are satisfied, the following restrictions shall apply in relation to the payment of that benefit in the offender's case.

(2) Subject to subsections (3) to (5), the relevant benefit shall not be payable in the offender's case for the prescribed period.

(3) Where the relevant benefit is income support, the benefit shall be payable in the offender's case for the prescribed period as if the applicable amount used for the determination under section 124(4) of the Social Security Contributions and Benefits Act 1992 of the amount of the offender's entitlement for that period were reduced in such manner as may be prescribed.

(4) The Secretary of State may by regulations provide that, where the relevant benefit is jobseeker's allowance, any income-based jobseeker's allowance shall be payable, during the whole or a part of the prescribed period, as if one or more of the following applied—
(a) the rate of the allowance were such reduced rate as may be prescribed;
(b) the allowance were payable only if there is compliance by the offender with such obligations with respect to the provision of information as may be imposed by the regulations;
(c) the allowance were payable only if the circumstances are otherwise such as may be prescribed.

(5) Where the relevant benefit is a payment under section 2 of the Employment and Training Act 1973 (under which training allowances are payable), that benefit shall not be payable for the prescribed period except to such extent (if any) as may be prescribed.

(6) Where the determination by a court that was made in the offender's case is quashed or otherwise set aside by the decision of that or any other court, all such payments and other adjustments shall be made in his case as would be necessary if the restrictions imposed by or under this section in respect of that determination had not been imposed.

(7) The length of any period prescribed for the purposes of any of subsections (2) to (5) shall not exceed twenty-six weeks.

(8) In this section—
"income-based jobseeker's allowance" and "joint-claim jobseeker's allowance" have the same meanings as in the Jobseekers Act 1995;
"relevant benefit" means—
(a) income support;

(2000 c.19, s.62)

    (b) any jobseeker's allowance other than joint-claim jobseeker's allowance;
    (c) any benefit under the Social Security Contributions and Benefits Act 1992 (other than income support) which is prescribed for the purposes of this section; or
    (d) any prescribed payment under section 2 of the Employment and Training Act 1973 (under which training allowances are payable);
"relevant community order" means—
  [¹(a) a community punishment order;
    (b) a community rehabilitation order;
    (c) a community punishment and rehabilitation order;]
    (d) such other description of community order within the meaning of the Powers of Criminal Courts (Sentencing) Act 2000 as may be prescribed for the purposes of this section; or
    (e) any order falling in England and Wales to be treated as an order specified in paragraphs (a) to (d).

(9) In relation to a relevant benefit falling within paragraph (d) of the definition of that expression in subsection (8), references in this section to the conditions for entitlement to that benefit being or becoming satisfied with respect to any person are references to there having been or, as the case may be, the taking of a decision to make a payment of such benefit to that person.

(10) In relation to any time before the coming into force of the Powers of Criminal Courts (Sentencing) Act 2000, the reference to that Act in subsection (8) shall be taken to be a reference to Part I of the Criminal Justice Act 1991.

(11) In the application to Scotland of this section—
    (a) in subsection (1) after the word "excuse" insert "(or, in the case of a probation order, failed)";
    (b) for paragraph (b) of that subsection substitute—

      "(b) the Secretary of State is notified in accordance with an Act of Adjournal made under section 64 of the determination"; and

    (c) in subsection (8)—
      (i) in the definition of relevant benefit, paragraph (d) does not apply in the case of any payment made by or on behalf of the Scottish Ministers; and
      (ii) in the definition of relevant community order, for paragraphs (c) to (e) substitute—
  [¹(ii) in the definition of relevant community order, for paragraphs (a) to (e) substitute—
"(a) a community service order;
    (b) a probation order;
    (c) such other description of order made under the Criminal Procedure (Scotland) Act 1995 as may be prescribed for the purposes of this section; or
    (d) any order falling in Scotland to be treated as an order specified in paragraphs (a) to (c)."]

AMENDMENT

1. Criminal Justice and Courts Act 2000, Sch.7, paras 205 and 206 (April 1, 2001).

DEFINITIONS

"income-based jobseeker's allowance"—by virtue of subs.(8), see Jobseeker's Act 1995, s.1(4).
"joint-claim jobseeker's allowance"—*ibid.*
"offender"—see subs.(1).
"prescribed"—see s.65(1).
"relevant benefit" see subs.(8)
"relevant community order" *ibid.*

GENERAL NOTE

1.563 See the General Note to the Social Security (Beach of Community Order) Regulations 2001 below.

Subs.(8) and (11) were amended by the Criminal Courts and Justice Act 2000 on April 1, 2001 (i.e. before they were in force) (see the Criminal Courts and Justice Act 2000 (Commencement No.4) Order 2001 (SI 2001/919)). Subs.(11) is not yet in force (see the General Note to Sections 62–66 above).

The Powers of Criminal Courts (Sentencing) Act 2000 came into force on August 25, 2000 (three months after it received Royal Assent (see s.168(1) of that Act). Therefore although subs.(10) was brought into force on October 15, 2001 it has no practical effect.

Loss of joint-claim jobseeker's allowance

1.564 **63.**—(1) Subsections (2) and (3) shall have effect, subject to the other provisions of this section, where—
   (a) the conditions for the entitlement of any joint-claim couple to a joint-claim jobseeker's allowance are or become satisfied at any time; and
   (b) the restriction in subsection (2) of section 62 would apply in the case of at least one of the members of the couple if the entitlement were an entitlement of that member to a relevant benefit.

(2) The allowance shall not be payable in the couple's case for so much of the prescribed period as is a period for which—
   (a) in the case of each of the members of the couple, the restriction in subsection (2) of section 62 would apply if the entitlement were an entitlement of that member to a relevant benefit; or
   [1(b) that restriction would apply in the case of one of the members of the couple and the other member of the couple—
      (i) is subject to sanctions for the purposes of section 20A of the Jobseekers Act 1995 (denial or reduction of joint-claim jobseeker's allowance); or
      (ii) is a person in whose case the restriction in subsection (2) of section 8 of the Social Security Fraud Act 2001 (loss of benefit for offenders) would apply if the entitlement were an entitlement to a sanctionable benefit (within the meaning of that section).]

(3) For any part of the period for which subsection (2) does not apply, the allowance—
   (a) shall be payable in the couple's case as if the amount of the allowance were reduced to an amount calculated using the method prescribed for the purposes of this subsection; but
   (b) shall be payable only to the member of the couple who is not the person in relation to whom the court has made a determination.

(4) The Secretary of State may by regulations provide in relation to cases to which subsection (2) would otherwise apply that joint-claim jobseeker's

allowance shall be payable in a couple's case, during the whole or a part of so much of the prescribed period as falls within paragraph (a) or (b) of that subsection, as if one or more of the following applied—
  (a) the rate of the allowance were such reduced rate as may be prescribed;
  (b) the allowance were payable only if there is compliance by each of the members of the couple with such obligations with respect to the provision of information as may be imposed by the regulations;
  (c) the allowance were payable only if the circumstances are otherwise such as may be prescribed.
  (5) Subsection (6) of section 20A of the Jobseekers Act 1995 (calculation of reduced amount) shall apply for the purposes of subsection (3) above as it applies for the purposes of subsection (5) of that section.
  (6) Subsection (6) of section 62 shall apply for the purposes of this section in relation to any determination relating to one or both members of the joint-claim couple as it applies for the purposes of that section in relation to the determination relating to the offender.
  (7) The length of any period prescribed for the purposes of subsection (2) or (3) shall not exceed twenty-six weeks.
  (8) In this section—
    "joint-claim couple" and "joint-claim jobseeker's allowance" have the same meanings as in the Jobseekers Act 1995; and
    "relevant benefit" has the same meaning as in section 62.

AMENDMENT

1. Social Security Fraud Act 2001, s.12(1) (April 1, 2002).

DEFINITIONS

"joint-claim couple"—by virtue of subs.(8), see Jobseeker's Act 1995, s.(4).
"joint-claim jobseeker's allowance"—*ibid.*
"prescribed—see s.65(1).
"relevant benefit"—by virtue of subs.(8), see s.62(8).

Information provision

64.—(1) A court in Great Britain shall, before making a relevant community order in relation to any person, explain to that person in ordinary language the consequences by virtue of sections 62 and 63 of a failure to comply with the order.

1.565

  (2) The Secretary of State may by regulations require the [¹chief officer of a local probation board], or such other person as may be prescribed, to notify the Secretary of State at the prescribed time and in the prescribed manner—
    (a) of the laying by [² an officer of a local probation board] of any information that a person has failed to comply with the requirements of a relevant community order;
    (b) of any such determination as is mentioned in section 62(1);
    (c) of such information about the offender, and in the possession of the person giving the notification, as may be prescribed; and
    (d) of any circumstances by virtue of which any payment or adjustment might fall to be made by virtue of section 62(6) or 63(6).
  (3) The High Court of Justiciary may, by Act of Adjournal, make provision requiring the clerk of the court in which any proceedings are commenced that could result in a determination of a failure to comply with a

relevant community order to notify the Secretary of State at such time and in such manner as may be specified in the Act of Adjournal of—
   (a) the commencement of the proceedings;
   (b) any such determination made in the proceedings;
   (c) such information about the offender as may be so specified; and
   (d) any circumstances by virtue of which any payment or adjustment might fall to be made by virtue of section 62(6) or 63(6).
   (4) Where it appears to the Secretary of State that—
   (a) the laying of any information that has been laid in England and Wales, or
   (b) the commencement of any proceedings that have been commenced in Scotland,
could result in a determination the making of which would result in the imposition by or under one or both of sections 62 and 63 of any restrictions, it shall be the duty of the Secretary of State to notify the person in whose case those restrictions would be imposed, or (as the case may be) the members of any joint-claim couple in whose case they would be imposed, of the consequences under those sections of such a determination in the case of that person, or couple.
   (5) A notification required to be given by the Secretary of State under subsection (4) must be given as soon as reasonably practicable after it first appears to the Secretary of State as mentioned in that subsection.
   (6) The Secretary of State may by regulations make such provision as he thinks fit for the purposes of sections 62 to 65 of this Act about—
   (a) the use by a person within subsection (7) of information relating to community orders or social security;
   (b) the supply of such information by a person within that subsection to any other person (whether or not within that subsection); and
   (c) the purposes for which a person to whom such information is supplied under the regulations may use it.
   (7) The persons within this subsection are—
   (a) the Secretary of State;
   (b) a person providing services to the Secretary of State;
   (c) a person employed or appointed by a probation committee;
   (d) a person employed by a council constituted under section 2 of the Local Government etc. (Scotland) Act 1994.
   (8) Regulations under subsection (6) may, in particular, authorise information supplied to a person under the regulations—
   (a) to be used for the purpose of amending or supplementing other information held by that person; and
   (b) where so used, to be supplied to any other person to whom, and used for any purpose for which, the information amended or supplemented could be supplied or used.
   (9) The explanation given to the offender by the court in pursuance of subsection (1) shall be treated as part of the explanation required to be given to the offender for the purposes of section 228(5) or 238(4) of the Criminal Procedure (Scotland) Act 1995.
   (10) In this section "relevant community order" has the same meaning as in section 62.
   (11) For the purposes of this section proceedings that could result in such a determination as is mentioned in subsection (3) are commenced in Scotland when, and only when, a warrant to arrest the offender or to cite

the offender to appear before a court is issued under section 232(1) or 239(4) of the Criminal Procedure (Scotland) Act 1995.

AMENDMENTS

1. Criminal Justice and Courts Act 2000, Sch.7, paras 205 and 207(a) (April 1, 2001).
2. Criminal Justice and Courts Act 2000, Sch.7, paras 205 and 207(b) (April 1, 2001).
3. Criminal Justice and Courts Act 2000, Sch.7, paras 205 and 207(c) (April 1, 2001).

DEFINITIONS

"prescribed"—see s.65(1).
"relevant community order"—by virtue of subs.(10), see s.62(8).

GENERAL NOTE

Subss.(2) (7)(c) and (10) were amended by the Criminal Courts and Justice Act 2000 on April 1, 2001 (i.e. before they were in force) (see the Criminal Courts and Justice Act 2000 (Commencement No.4) Order 2001 (SI 2001/919). Subss.(3), (4)(b), 7(d), (9) and (11) are not yet in force (see the General Note to Sections 62–66).

For a discussion of "local probation boards" see the General Note to reg.1 of the Social Security (Breach of Community Order) Regulations 2001 (SI 2001/1395) below.

Loss of benefit regulations

65.—(1) In the loss of benefit provisions "prescribed" means prescribed by or determined in accordance with regulations made by the Secretary of State.

(2) Regulations prescribing a period for the purposes of any of the loss of benefit provisions may contain provision for determining the time from which the period is to run.

(3) Regulations under any of the loss of benefit provisions shall be made by statutory instrument which (except in the case of regulations to which subsection (4) applies) shall be subject to annulment in pursuance of a resolution of either House of Parliament.

(4) A statutory instrument containing (whether alone or with other provisions)—
(a) a provision prescribing the manner in which the applicable amount is to be reduced for the purposes of section 62(3),
(b) a provision prescribing the manner in which an amount of jointclaim jobseeker's allowance is to be reduced for the purposes of section 63(3)(a),
(c) a provision the making of which is authorised by section 62(4) or 63(4),
(d) a provision prescribing benefits under the Social Security Contributions and Benefits Act 1992 as benefits that are to be relevant benefits for the purposes of section 62, or
(e) a provision that any description of order is to be a relevant community order for the purposes of that section,

shall not be made unless a draft of the instrument has been laid before, and approved by a resolution of, each House of Parliament.

1.566

(5) Subsections (4) to (6) of section 189 of the Social Security Administration Act 1992 (supplemental and incidental powers etc.) shall apply in relation to any power to make regulations that is conferred by the loss of benefit provisions as they apply in relation to the powers to make regulations that are conferred by that Act.

(6) The provision that may be made in exercise of the powers to make regulations that are conferred by the loss of benefit provisions shall include different provision for different areas.

(7) Where regulations made under section 62(8) prescribe a description of order made under the Criminal Procedure (Scotland) Act 1995 as a relevant community order for the purposes of that section, the regulations may make such modifications of that section as appear to the Secretary of State to be necessary in consequence of so prescribing.

(8) In this section "the loss of benefit provisions" means sections 62 to 64 of this Act.

DEFINITION

"the loss of benefit provisions"—see subs.(8).

Appeals relating to loss of benefit

66. *Omitted.*

Social Security Fraud Act 2001

(2001 c.11)

ARRANGEMENT OF SECTIONS

Loss of benefit provisions

7. Loss of benefit for commission of benefit offences.
8. Effect of offence on joint-claim jobseeker's allowance.
9. Effect of offence on benefits for members of offender's family.
10. Power to supplement and mitigate loss of benefit provisions.
11. Loss of benefit regulations
12. *Omitted.*
13. Interpretation of sections 7 to 12.

Loss of benefit provisions

Loss of benefit for commission of benefit offences

7.—(1) If—
 (a) a person ("the offender") is convicted of one or more benefit offences in each of two separate sets of proceedings,
 (b) the benefit offence, or more of the benefit offences, of which he is convicted in the later proceedings is one committed within the period

(2001 c.11, s.7)

of three years after the date, or any of the dates, on which he was convicted of a benefit offence in the earlier proceedings,
(c) the later set of proceedings has not been taken into account for the purposes of any previous application of this section or section 8 or 9 in relation to the offender or any person who was then a member of his family,
(d) the earlier set of proceedings has not been taken into account as the earlier set of proceedings for the purposes of any previous application of this section or either of those sections in relation to the offender or any person who was then a member of his family, and
(e) the offender is a person with respect to whom the conditions for an entitlement to a sanctionable benefit are or become satisfied at any time within the disqualification period,

then, even though those conditions are satisfied, the following restrictions shall apply in relation to the payment of that benefit in the offender's case.

(2) Subject to subsections (3) to (5), the sanctionable benefit shall not be payable in the offender's case for any period comprised in the disqualification period.

(3) Where the sanctionable benefit is income support, the benefit shall be payable in the offender's case for any period comprised in the disqualification period as if the applicable amount used for the determination under section 124(4) of the Social Security Contributions and Benefits Act 1992 (c. 4) of the amount of the offender's entitlement for that period were reduced in such a manner as may be prescribed.

(4) The Secretary of State may by regulations provide that, where the sanctionable benefit is jobseeker's allowance, any income-based jobseeker's allowance shall be payable, during the whole or a part of any period comprised in the disqualification period, as if one or more of the following applied—
(a) the rate of the allowance were such reduced rate as may be prescribed;
(b) the allowance were payable only if there is compliance by the offender with such obligations with respect to the provision of information as may be imposed by the regulations;
(c) the allowance were payable only if the circumstances are otherwise such as may be prescribed.

[1 (4A) The Secretary of State may be regulations provide that, where the sanctionable benefit is state pension credit, the benefit shall be payable in the offender's case for any period comprised in the disqualification period as if the rate of benefit were reduced in such manner as may be prescribed.]

(5) The Secretary of State may by regulations provide that, where the sanctionable benefit is housing benefit or council tax benefit, the benefit shall be payable, during the whole or a part of any period comprised in the disqualification period, as if one or both of the following applied—
(a) the rate of the benefit were reduced in such manner as may be prescribed;
(b) the benefit were payable only if the circumstances are such as may be prescribed.

(6) For the purposes of this section the disqualification period, in relation to the conviction of a person of one or more benefit offences in each of two separate sets of proceedings, means the period of thirteen weeks beginning with such date, falling after the date of the conviction in the later set of

Social Security Fraud Act 2001

proceedings, as may be determined by or in accordance with regulations made by the Secretary of State.

(7) Where—
(a) the conviction of any person of any offence is taken into account for the purposes of the application of this section in relation to that person, and
(b) that conviction is subsequently quashed,

all such payments and other adjustments shall be made as would be necessary if no restriction had been imposed by or under this section that could not have been imposed if the conviction had not taken place.

(8) In this section—

"benefit offence" means—
(a) any post-commencement offence in connection with a claim for a disqualifying benefit;
(b) any post-commencement offence in connection with the receipt or payment of any amount by way of such a benefit;
(c) any post-commencement offence committed for the purpose of facilitating the commission (whether or not by the same person) of a benefit offence;
(d) any post-commencement offence consisting in an attempt or conspiracy to commit a benefit offence;

"disqualifying benefit" means (subject to any regulations under section 10(1)—
(a) any benefit under the Jobseekers Act 1995 (c. 18) or the Jobseekers (Northern Ireland) Order 1995 (S.I. 1995/2705 (N.I. 15));
[¹ (aa) any benefit under the State Pension Credit Act 2002 or under any provision having effect in Northern Ireland corresponding to that Act;]
(b) any benefit under the Social Security Contributions and Benefits Act 1992 (c. 4) or the Social Security Contributions and Benefits (Northern Ireland) Act 1992 (c. 7) other than—
 (i) maternity allowance;
 (ii) working families' tax credit;
 (iii) disabled person's tax credit; and
 (iv) statutory sick pay and statutory maternity pay;
(c) any war pension;

"sanctionable benefit" means (subject to subsection (11) and to any regulations under section 10(1)) any disqualifying benefit other than—
(a) joint-claim jobseeker's allowance;
(b) any retirement pension;
(c) graduated retirement benefit;
(d) disability living allowance;
(e) attendance allowance;
(f) child benefit;
(g) guardian's allowance;
(h) a payment out of the social fund in accordance with Part 8 of the Social Security Contributions and Benefits Act 1992;
(i) a payment under Part X of that Act (Christmas bonuses).

(9) For the purposes of this section—
(a) the date of a person's conviction in any proceedings of a benefit offence shall be taken to be the date on which he was found guilty of that offence in those proceedings (whenever he was sentenced); and

(b) references to a conviction include references to a conviction in relation to which the court makes an order for a conditional discharge or a court in Scotland makes a probation order and to a conviction in Nothern Ireland.

(10) In this section references to any previous application of this section or section 8 or 9—
  (a) include references to any previous application of a provision having an effect in Northern Ireland corresponding to provision made by this section, or either of those sections; but
  (b) do not include references to any previous application of this section, or of either of those sections, the effect of which was to impose a restriction for a period comprised in the same disqualification period.

(11) In its application to Northern Ireland this section shall have effect as if references to a sanctionable benefit were references only to a war pension.

AMENDMENT

1. State Pension Credit Act 2002, Sch.2, para.45 (July 2, 2002 for the purpose of exercising any power to make regulations or orders and October 6, 2003 for other purposes).

DEFINITIONS

"benefit offence"—see subs.(8).
"benefit"—see s.13.
"disqualification period"—see subs.(6).
"disqualifying benefit"—see subs.(8).
"family"—by virtue of s.13, see s.137(1) of the Social Security Contributions and Benefits Act 1992.
"income-based jobseeker's allowance"—by virtue of s.13, see s.1(4) of the Jobseekers Act 1995.
"joint-claim jobseeker's allowance"—*ibid.*
"offender"—see subs.(1).
"post-commencement offence"—see s.13.
"prescribed"—see s.11(1).
"sanctionable benefit"—see subs.(8).
"state pension credit"—see s.13.
"war pension"—by virtue of s.13, see s.25 of the Social Security Act 1989.

GENERAL NOTE

This section provides for the loss of a "sanctionable benefit" benefit for 13 weeks by people who, having been convicted of a benefit offence, are subsequently convicted of another benefit offence that was committed within three years of the date of the earlier conviction (i.e. the date he or she was found guilty, even if sentence was passed much later—see subs.(9)(a)). Very few people are convicted twice of benefit offences committed within such a short time. Section 8 makes provision in respect of joint-claim jobseeker's allowance and s.9 allows the penalty to fall on another member of the offender's family where that other person is claiming an income-related benefit that takes account of the offender's membership of the family. Benefit offences are offences in connection withthe obtaining of almost any social security benefit (including housing benefit and council tax benefit), other than maternity allowance, tax credits or statutory sick pay or statutory maternity pay. However, the term "sanctionable benefit" does not include retirement pensions or certain benefits for the disabled or for children. Further details are set out in regulations (see the Social Security (Loss of Benefit) Regulations 2001).

1.570

Effect of offence on joint-claim jobseeker's allowance

8.—(1) Subsections (2) and (3) shall have effect, subject to the other provisions of this section, where—
  (a) the conditions for the entitlement of any joint-claim couple to a joint-claim jobseeker's allowance are or become satisfied at any time; and
  (b) the restriction in subsection (2) of section 7 would apply in the case of at least one of the members of the couple if the entitlement were an entitlement of that member to a sanctionable benefit.

(2) The allowance shall not be payable in the couple's case for so much of any period comprised in the disqualification period as is a period for which—
  (a) in the case of each of the members of the couple, the restriction in subsection (2) of section 7 would apply if the entitlement were an entitlement of that member to a sanctionable benefit; or
  (b) that restriction would so apply in the case of one of the members of the couple and the other member of the couple—
    (i) is subject to sanctions for the purposes of section 20A of the Jobseekers Act 1995 (c. 18) (denial or reduction of joint-claim jobseeker's allowance); or
    (ii) is a person in whose case the restriction in subsection (2) of section 62 of the Child Support, Pensions and Social Security Act 2000 (c. 19) would apply if the entitlement were an entitlement to a relevant benefit (within the meaning of that section).

(3) For any part of any period comprised in the disqualification period for which subsection (2) does not apply, the allowance—
  (a) shall be payable in the couple's case as if the amount of the allowance were reduced to an amount calculated using the method prescribed for the purposes of this subsection; but
  (b) shall be payable only to the member of the couple who is not the person by reference to whose convictions section 7 would apply.

(4) The Secretary of State may by regulations provide in relation to cases to which subsection (2) would otherwise apply that joint-claim jobseeker's allowance shall be payable in a couple's case, during the whole or a part of so much of any period comprised in the disqualification period as falls within paragraph (a) or (b) of that subsection, as if one or more of the following applied—
  (a) the rate of the allowance were such reduced rate as may be prescribed;
  (b) the allowance were payable only if there is compliance by each of the members of the couple with such obligations with respect to the provision of information as may be imposed by the regulations;
  (c) the allowance were payable only if the circumstances were otherwise such as may be prescribed.

(5) Subsection (6) of section 20A of the Jobseekers Act 1995 (c. 18) (calculation of reduced amount) shall apply for the purposes of subsection (3) above as it applies for the purposes of subsection (5) of that section.

(6) Where—
  (a) the conviction of any member of a couple for any offence is taken into account for the purposes of the application of this section in relation to that couple, and
  (b) that conviction is subsequently quashed,

(2001 c.11, s.8)

all such payments and other adjustments shall be made as would be necessary if no restriction had been imposed by or under this section that could not have been imposed had the conviction not taken place.

DEFINITIONS

"disqualification period"—by virtue of s.13, see s.7(6).
"joint-claim couple"—by virtue of s.13, see s.1(4) of the Jobseekers Act 1995.
"joint-claim jobseeker's allowance"—*ibid.*
"prescribed"—see s.11(1).
"sanctionable benefit"—by virtue of s.13, see s.7(8).

Effect of offence on benefits for members of offender's family

9.—(1) This section applies to— 1.572
(a) income support;
(b) jobseeker's allowance;
[¹ (bb) state pension credit;]
(c) housing benefit; and
(d) council tax benefit.

(2) The Secretary of State may by regulations make provision in accordance with the following provisions of this section in relation to any case in which—
  (a) the conditions for entitlement to any benefit to which this section applies are or become satisfied in the case of any person ("the offender's family member");
  (b) that benefit falls to be paid in that person's case for the whole or any part of a period comprised in a period ("the relevant period") which is the disqualification period in relation to restrictions imposed under section 7 in the case of a member of that person's family; or
  (c) that member of that family ("the offender") is a person by reference to whom—
    (i) the conditions for the entitlement of the offender's family member to the benefit in question are satisfied; or
    (ii) the amount of benefit payable in the case of the offender's family member would fall (apart from any provision made under this section) to be determined.

(3) In relation to cases in which the benefit is income support, the provision that may be made by virtue of subsection (2) is provision that, in the case of the offender's family member, the benefit shall be payable for the whole or any part of any period comprised in the relevant period as if the applicable amount used for the determination under section 124(4) of the Social Security Contributions and Benefits Act 1992 (c.4) of the amount of the offender's entitlement for that period were reduced in such manner as may be prescribed.

(4) In relation to cases in which the benefit is jobseeker's allowance, the provision that may be made by virtue of subsection (2) is provision that, in the case of the offender's family member, any income-based jobseeker's allowance shall be payable, during the whole or a part of any period comprised in the relevant period, as if one or more of the following applied—
  (a) the rate of the allowance were such reduced rate as may be prescribed;
  (b) the allowance were payable only if there is compliance by the offender or the offender's family member, or both of them, with such

obligations with respect to the provision of information as may be imposed by the regulations;
(c) the allowance were payable only if the circumstances are otherwise such as may be prescribed.

[¹ (4A) In relation to cases in which the benefit is state pension credit, the provision that may be made by virtue of subsection (2) is provision that, in the case of the offender's family member, the benefit shall be payable for the whole or any part of any period comprised in the relevant period as if the rate of the benefit were reduced in such manner as may be prescribed.]

(5) In relation to cases in which the benefit is housing benefit or council tax benefit, the provision that may be made by virtue of subsection (2) is provision that, in the case of the offender's family member, the benefit shall be payable, during the whole or a part of any period comprised in the relevant period, as if one or both of the following applied—
(a) the rate of the benefit were reduced in such manner as may be prescribed;
(b) the benefit were payable only if the circumstances are such as may be prescribed.

(6) Where—
(a) the conviction of any member of a person's family for any offence is taken into account for the purposes of any restriction imposed by virtue of any regulations under this section, and
(b) that conviction is subsequently quashed,

all such payments and other adjustments shall be made in that person's case as would be necessary if no restriction had been imposed that could not have been imposed had the conviction not taken place.

AMENDMENT

1. State Pension Credit Act 2002, Sch.2, para.46 (July 2, 2002 for the purpose of exercising any power to make regulations or orders and October 6, 2003 for other purposes).

DEFINITIONS

"benefit"—see s.13.
"disqualifying benefit"—see subs.(8).
"family"—by virtue of s.13, see s.137(1) of the Social Security Contributions and Benefits Act 1992.
"income-based jobseeker's allowance"—by virtue of s.13, see s.1(4) of the Jobseekers Act 1995.
"the offender"—see subs.(2)(c).
"the offender's family member"—see subs.(2)(a).
"prescribed"—see s.11(1).
"the relevant period"—see subs.(2)(b).
"state pension credit"—see s.13.

Power to supplement and mitigate loss of benefit provisions

1.573   **10.**—(1) The Secretary of State may by regulations provide for any social security benefit to be treated for the purposes of sections 7 to 9—
(a) as a disqualifying benefit but not a sanctionable benefit; or
(b) as neither a sanctionable benefit nor a disqualifying benefit.

(2001 c.11, s.10)

(2) The Secretary of State may by regulations provide for any restriction in section 7, 8 or 9 not to apply in relation to payments of benefit to the extent of any deduction that (if any payment were made) would fall, in pursuance of provision made by or under any enactment, to be made from the payments and paid to a person other than the offender or, as the case may be, a member of his family.

(3) In this section "social security benefit" means—
  (a) any benefit under the Social Security Contributions and Benefits Act 1992 (c.4) or the Social Security Contributions and Benefits (Northern Ireland) Act 1992 (c.7); [[1] . . .]
  (b) any benefit under the Jobseekers Act 1995 (c. 18) or the Jobseekers (Northern Ireland) Order 1995 (S.I. 1995/2705 (N.I. 15));
[[1] (bb) any benefit under the State Pension Credit Act 2002 or under any provision having effect in Northern Ireland corresponding to that Act; or]
  (c) any war pension.

AMENDMENT

1. State Pension Credit Act 2002, Sch.2, para.47 and Sch.3 (July 2, 2002 for the purpose of exercising any power to make regulations or orders and October 6, 2003 for other purposes).

DEFINITIONS

"benefit"—see s.13.
"disqualifying benefit"—see s.7(8).
"family"—by virtue of s.13, see s.137(1) of the Social Security Contributions and Benefits Act 1992.
"sanctionable benefit"—by virtue of s.13, see s.7(8).
"war pension"—by virtue of s.13, see s.25 of the Social Security Act 1989.

Loss of benefit regulations

11.—(1) In sections 7 to 10 "prescribed" means prescribed by or determined in accordance with regulations made by the Secretary of State.

(2) Regulations under any of the provisions of sections 7 to 10 small be made by statutory instrument which (except in the case of regulations to which subsection (3) applies) shall be subject to annulment in pursuance of a resolution of either House of Parliament.

(3) A statutory instrument containing (whether alone or with other provisions)—
  (a) a provision by virtue of which anything is to be treated for the purposes of section 7 as a disqualifying benefit but not a sanctionable benefit,
  (b) a provision prescribing the manner in which the applicable amount is to be reduced for the purposes of section 7(3) or 9(3),
  (c) a provision the making of which is authorised by section 7(4) [[1], (4A)] or (5), 8(4) or 9(4) [[1], (4A)] or (5), or
  (d) a provision prescribing the manner in which the amount of joint-claim jobseeker's allowance is to be reduced for the purposes of section 8(3)(a),
shall not be made unless a draft of the instrument has been laid before, and approved by a resolution of, each House of Parliament.

1.574

(4) Subsections (4) to (6) of section 189 of the Administration Act (supplemental and incidental powers etc.) shall apply in relation to a power to make regulations that is conferred by any of the provisions of sections 7 to 10 as they apply in relation to the powers to make regulations that are conferred by that Act.

(5) The provision that may be made in exercise of the powers to make regulations that are conferred by sections 7 to 10 shall include different provision for different areas.

AMENDMENT

1. State Pension Credit Act 2002, Sch.2, para.48 (July 2, 2002 for the purpose of exercising any power to make regulations or orders and October 6, 2003 for other purposes).

DEFINITION

"the Administration Act", by virtue of s.18, means the Social Security Administration Act 1992.

Consequential amendments

12. *Omitted.*

Interpretation of Sections 7 to 12

13.—In this section and sections 7 to 12—
"benefit" includes any allowance, payment, credit or loan;
"disqualification period" has the meaning given by section 7(6);
"family" has the same meaning as in Part 7 of the Social Security Contributions and Benefits Act 1992 (c. 4);
"income-based jobseeker's allowance", "joint-claim jobseeker's allowance" and "joint-claim couple" have the same meanings as in the Jobseekers Act 1995 (c. 18);
"post-commencement offence" means any criminal offence committed after the commencement of section 7;
"sanctionable benefit" has the meaning given by section 7(8);
[1 "state pension credit" means state pension credit under the State Pension Credit Act 2002;]
"war pension" has the same meaning as in section 25 of the Social Security Act 1989 (c. 24) (establishment and functions of war pensions committees).

AMENDMENT

1. State Pension Credit Act 2002, Sch.2, para.49 (July 2, 2002 for the purpose of exercising any power to make regulations or orders and October 6, 2003 for other purposes).

(2002 c.21)

Tax Credits Act 2002

(2002 c. 21)

Arrangement of Sections

Part 1

Tax Credits

1.–48.   *Omitted.*

Part 2

Child Benefit and Guardian's Allowance

Transfer of functions etc.

49.   Functions transferred to Treasury.
50.   Functions transferred to Board.
51.–52. *Omitted.*
53.   General functions of Commissioners for Revenue and Customs.
54.   Transitional provisions.
55.–57. *Omitted.*

Part 3

Supplementary

Information etc.

58.   Administrative arrangements.
59.   *Omitted.*

Other supplementary provisions

60.–64. *Omitted.*
65.   Regulations, orders and schemes.
66.   Parliamentary etc. control of instruments.
67.   Interpretation.
68.–70. *Omitted.*

Schedules 1.–6. *Omitted.*

Tax Credits Act 2002

An Act to make provision for tax credits; to amend the law about child benefit and guardian's allowance; and for connected purposes.

[8th July 2002]

GENERAL NOTE

1.578   Part 1 of the Act provides for child tax credit and working tax credit which are dealt within Vol.IV of this work.

Part 2 of the Act transfers functions relating to child benefit and guardian's allowance from the Department for Work and Pensions to the Treasury and the Board of Inland Revenue which has now been merged into Her Majesty's Revenue and Customs. Those benefits remain social security benefits despite the change in responsibility for them and administration and adjudication remain under the Social Security Administration Act 1992 and the Social Security Act 1998, although new secondary legislation has been made.

1.579   **1.–48.** *Omitted.*

PART 2

CHILD BENEFIT AND GUARDIAN'S ALLOWANCE

Transfer of functions etc.

Functions transferred to Treasury

1.580   **49.**—(1) The functions of the Secretary of State under—
(a) section 77 of the Social Security Contributions and Benefits Act 1992 (c.4) (guardian's allowance: Great Britain),
(b) Part 9 of that Act (child benefit: Great Britain), except section 142(1)(c) and (2) and paragraphs 5 and 6(1) of Schedule 10,
(c) section 80 of the Social Security Administration Act 1992 (c.5) (overlap with benefits under legislation of other member States: Great Britain), and
(d) section 72 of the Social Security Act 1998 (c.14) (power to reduce child benefit for lone parents: Great Britain),
are transferred to the Treasury.

(2) The functions of the Northern Ireland Department under—
(a) section 77 of the Social Security Contributions and Benefits (Northern Ireland) Act 1992 (c.7) (guardian's allowance: Northern Ireland),
(b) Part 9 of that Act (child benefit: Northern Ireland), except section 138(1)(c) and (2) and paragraphs 5 and 6(1) of Schedule 10,
(c) section 76 of the Social Security Administration (Northern Ireland) Act 1992 (c.8) (overlap with benefits under legislation of other member States: Northern Ireland), and
(d) Article 68 of the Social Security (Northern Ireland) Order 1998 (1998/1506 (N.I. 10)) (power to reduce child benefit for lone parents: Northern Ireland),
are transferred to the Treasury.

(3) The functions of the Secretary of State under Part 10 of the Social Security Administration Act 1992 (c.5) (review and alteration of benefits:

Great Britain) so far as relating to child benefit and guardian's allowance are transferred to the Treasury.

(4) The functions of the Northern Ireland Department under sections 132 to 134 of the Social Security Administration (Northern Ireland) Act 1992 (c. 8) (review and alteration of benefits: Northern Ireland) so far as relating to child benefit and guardian's allowance are transferred to the Treasury.

AMENDMENT

1. Child Benefit Act 2005, s.3 and Sch.2, Pt. 1 (April 10, 2006).

DEFINITION

"the Northern Ireland Department": see s.67.

GENERAL NOTE

This section transfers policy responsibility for child benefit and guardian's allowance (i.e. making the regulations as to entitlement and fixing the rates) from the Secretary of State for Work and Pensions to the Treasury.

1.581

Functions transferred to Board

50.—(1) The functions of the Secretary of State and the Northern Ireland Department under the provisions specified in subsection (2), so far as relating to child benefit and guardian's allowance, are transferred to the Board.

1.582

(2) The provisions referred to in subsection (1) are—
  (a) the Social Security Contributions and Benefits Act 1992 (c.4),
  (b) the Social Security Administration Act 1992, except Part 13 (advisory bodies and consultation: Great Britain),
  (c) the Social Security Contributions and Benefits (Northern Ireland) Act 1992 (c. 7),
  (d) the Social Security Administration (Northern Ireland) Act 1992, except Part 12 (advisory bodies and consultation: Northern Ireland),
  (e) Chapter 2 of Part 1 of the Social Security Act 1998 (c.14) (social security decisions and appeals: Great Britain),
  (f) Chapter 2 of Part 2 of the Social Security (Northern Ireland) Order 1998 (1998/1506 (N.I. 10)) (social security decisions and appeals: Northern Ireland), and
  (g) any subordinate legislation made under any of the provisions specified in section 49 or any of the preceding provisions of this subsection.

(3) This section has effect subject to section 49.

DEFINITIONS

"the Board": see s.67, but note that the functions of the Board have been transferred to Her Majesty's Revenue and Customs by the Commissioners for Revenue and Customs Act 2005.

"the Northern Ireland Department": *ibid.*

GENERAL NOTE

While s.49 transfers policy responsibility for child benefit and guardian's allowance to the Treasury, this section transfers operational responsibility (i.e. administration and adjudication) from the Secretary of State for Work and Pensions to the

1.583

Board of Inland Revenue, whose functions have now been transferred to Her Majesty's Revenue and Customs by the Commissioners for Revenue and Customs Act 2005. The primary legislation governing administration and adjudication remains the same (subject to consequential amendments made by s.51 and Sch.4 and repeals under s.60 and Sch.6) but the Board made new subordinate legislation (see the Child Benefit and Guardian's Allowance (Administrative Arrangements) Regulations 2003, the Child Benefit and Guardian's Allowance (Administration) Regulations 2003 and the Child Benefit and Guardian's Allowance (Decisions and Appeals) Regulations 2003).

Consequential amendments

51. *Omitted.*
52. *Omitted*

[¹ General functions of Commissioners for Revenue and Customs

53.—The Commissioners for Her Majesty's Revenue and Customs shall be responsible for the payment and management of child benefit and guardian's allowance.]

AMENDMENT

1. Commissioners for Revenue and Customs Act 2005, s.50 and para.90 of Sch.4 (April 18, 2005).

Transitional provisions

54.—(1) Any function covered by section 49 which is a function of making subordinate legislation may be exercised by the Treasury at any time after the passing of this Act if the subordinate legislation made in the exercise of the function comes into force after the commencement of that section.

(2) Any function covered by section 50 which is a function of making subordinate legislation may be exercised by the Board at any time after the passing of this Act if the subordinate legislation made in the exercise of the function comes into force after the commencement of that section.

(3) Nothing in section 49 or 50 affects the validity of anything done by or in relation to the Secretary of State or the Northern Ireland Department before its commencement.

(4) Anything (including legal proceedings) relating to any functions transferred by section 49, or any property, rights or liabilities transferred by section 52(1), which is in the course of being done or carried on by or in relation to the Secretary of State or the Northern Ireland Department immediately before the transfer may be continued by or in relation to the Treasury.

(5) Anything (including legal proceedings) relating to any functions transferred by section 50, or any property, rights or liabilities transferred by section 52(2), which is in the course of being done or carried on by or in relation to the Secretary of State or the Northern Ireland Department immediately before the transfer may be continued by or in relation to the Board.

(6) Anything done by the Secretary of State or the Northern Ireland Department for the purposes of or in connection with any functions transferred by section 49, or any property, rights or liabilities transferred by section 52(1), which is in effect immediately before the transfer has effect afterwards as if done by the Treasury.

(7) Anything done by the Secretary of State or the Northern Ireland Department for the purposes of or in connection with any functions transferred by section 50, or any property, rights or liabilities transferred by section 52(2), which is in effect immediately before the transfer has effect afterwards as if done by the Board.

(8) The Treasury is substituted for the Secretary of State or the Northern Ireland Department in any subordinate legislation, any contracts or other documents and any legal proceedings relating to any functions transferred by section 49, or any property, rights or liabilities transferred by section 52(1), made or commenced before the transfer.

(9) The Board are substituted for the Secretary of State or the Northern Ireland Department in any subordinate legislation, any contracts or other documents and any legal proceedings relating to any functions transferred by section 50, or any property, rights or liabilities transferred by section 52(2), made or commenced before the transfer.

(10) Any order made under section 8 of the Electronic Communications Act 2000 (c.7) which—

(a) modifies provisions relating to child benefit or guardian's allowance, and

(b) is in force immediately before the commencement of this subsection,

is to continue to have effect for the purposes of child benefit and guardian's allowance, despite subsection (7) of that section, until regulations made by the Board under section 132 of the Finance Act 1999 (c.16) which are expressed to supersede that order come into force.

DEFINITIONS

"the Board": see s.67, but note that the functions of the Board have been transferred to Her Majesty's Revenue and Customs by the Commissioners for Revenue and Customs Act 2005.

"the Northern Ireland Department": *ibid.*

GENERAL NOTE

Subsections (1) and (2) came into force on the passing of the Act (s.61), but the remaining provisions of this Part came into force for the purpose of making subordinate legislation on February 26, 2003, for the purpose of the transfer of functions on April 1, 2003 and for the purpose of entitlement to payment of child benefit and guardian's allowance on April 7, 2003 (Tax Credits Act 2002 (Commencement No.2) Order 2003).

1.588

Subs. 10

The Social Security (Electronic Communications) (Child Benefit) Order 2002 remains in force.

1.589

55.–57. *Omitted.*

1.590

Tax Credits Act 2002

PART 3

SUPPLEMENTARY

Information etc.

Administrative arrangements

1.591   **58.**—(1) This section applies where regulations under—
(a) section 4 or 6 of this Act,
(b) section 5 of the Social Security Administration Act 1992 (c.5), or
(c) section 5 of the Social Security Administration (Northern Ireland) Act 1992 (c.8),
permit or require a claim or notification relating to a tax credit, child benefit or guardian's allowance to be made or given to a relevant authority.
(2) Where this section applies, regulations may make provision—
(a) for information or evidence relating to tax credits, child benefit or guardian's allowance to be provided to the relevant authority (whether by persons by whom such claims and notifications are or have been made or given, by the Board or by other persons),
(b) for the giving of information or advice by a relevant authority to persons by whom such claims or notifications are or have been made or given, and
(c) for the recording, verification and holding, and the forwarding to the Board or a person providing services to the Board, of claims and notifications received by virtue of the regulations referred to in subsection (1) and information or evidence received by virtue of paragraph (a),
(3) "Relevant authority" means—
(a) the Secretary of State,
(b) the Northern Ireland Department, or
(c) a person providing services to the Secretary of State or the Northern Ireland Department.

DEFINITIONS

"the Board"—see s.67, but note that the functions of the Board have been transferred to Her Majesty's Revenue and Customs by the Commissioners for Revenue and Customs Act 2005.
"relevant authority"—see subs.(3).
"tax credit"—by virtue of s.67, see s.1(2).

GENERAL NOTE

1.592   See the Child Benefit and Guardian's Allowance (Administrative Arrangements) Regulations 2003.

59. *Omitted.*

Other supplementary provisions

60.–64. *Omitted.*

Regulations, orders and schemes

65.—(1) Any power to make regulations under sections 3, 7 to 13, 42 and 43, and any power to make regulations under this Act prescribing a rate of interest, is exercisable by the Treasury.

(2) Any other power to make regulations under this Act is exercisable by the Board.

(3) Subject to subsection (4), any power to make regulations, orders or schemes under this Act is exercisable by statutory instrument.

(4) The power—
  (a) of the Department of Health, Social Services and Public Safety to make schemes under section 12(5), and
  (b) of the Northern Ireland Department to make orders under section 62(1),
is exercisable by statutory rule for the purposes of the Statutory Rules (Northern Ireland) Order 1979 (S.I. 1979/1573 (N.I. 12)).

(5) Regulations may not be made under section 25 or 26 in relation to appeals in Scotland without the consent of the Scottish Ministers.

(6) Regulations may not be made under section 39(6) or 63(8) without the consent of the Lord Chancellor and the Scottish Ministers.

(7) Any power to make regulations under this Act may be exercised—
  (a) in relation to all cases to which it extends, to all those cases with prescribed exceptions or to prescribed cases or classes of case,
  (b) so as to make as respects the cases in relation to which it is exercised the full provision to which it extends or any less provision (whether by way of exception or otherwise),
  (c) so as to make the same provision for all cases in relation to which it is exercised or different provision for different cases or classes of case or different provision as respects the same case or class of case for different purposes,
  (d) so as to make provision unconditionally or subject to any prescribed condition,
  (e) so as to provide for a person to exercise a discretion in dealing with any matter.

(8) Any regulations made under a power under this Act to prescribe a rate of interest may—
  (a) either themselves specify a rate of interest or make provision for any such rate to be determined by reference to such rate or the average of such rates as may be referred to in the regulations,
  (b) provide for rates to be reduced below, or increased above, what they otherwise would be by specified amounts or by reference to specified formulae,
  (c) provide for rates arrived at by reference to averages to be rounded up or down,
  (d) provide for circumstances in which alteration of a rate of interest is or is not to take place, and
  (e) provide that alterations of rates are to have effect for periods beginning on or after a day determined in accordance with the regulations in relation to interest running from before that day as well as from or from after that day.

(9) Any power to make regulations or a scheme under this Act includes power to make any incidental, supplementary, consequential or transitional

provision which appears appropriate for the purposes of, or in connection with, the regulations or scheme.

DEFINITIONS

"the Board"—see s.67, but note that the functions of the Board have been transferred to Her Majesty's Revenue and Customs by the Commissioners for Revenue and Customs Act 2005.
"prescribe"—see s.67.

Parliamentary etc. control of instruments

1.594

66.—(1) No regulations to which this subsection applies may be made unless a draft of the instrument containing them (whether or not together with other provisions) has been laid before, and approved by a resolution of, each House of Parliament.

(2) Subsection (1) applies to—
(a) regulations prescribing monetary amounts that are required to be reviewed under section 41,
(b) regulations made by virtue of subsection (2) of section 12 prescribing the amount in excess of which charges are not taken into account for the purposes of that subsection, and
(c) the first regulations made under sections 7(8) and (9), 9, 11, 12 and 13(2).

(3) A statutory instrument containing—
(a) regulations under this Act,
(b) a scheme made by the Secretary of State under section 12(5), or
(c) an Order in Council under section 52(7),

is (unless a draft of the instrument has been laid before, and approved by a resolution of, each House of Parliament) subject to annulment in pursuance of a resolution of either House of Parliament.

(4) A statutory instrument containing a scheme made by the Scottish Ministers under section 12(5) is subject to annulment in pursuance of a resolution of the Scottish Parliament.

(5) A statutory rule containing a scheme made by the Department of Health, Social Services and Public Safety under section 12(5) is subject to negative resolution within the meaning of section 41(6) of the Interpretation Act (Northern Ireland) 1954 (c. 33 (N.I.)).

Interpretation

1.595

67.—In this Act—
"the Board" means the Commissioners of Inland Revenue,
"modifications" includes alterations, additions and omissions, and "modifies" is to be construed accordingly,
"the Northern Ireland Department" means the Department for Social Development in Northern Ireland,
"prescribed" means prescribed by regulations, and
"tax credit" and "tax credits" have the meanings given by section 1(2).

GENERAL NOTE

1.596

"the Board"
The functions of the Commissioners of Inland Revenue have now been transferred to the Commissioners for Her Majesty's Revenue and Customs by s.5(2) of the Commissioners for Revenue and Customs Act 2005.

(2002 c.21, s.68)

68.–70. *Omitted.*

Schedules 1.–6. *Omitted.*

Gender Recognition Act 2004

(2004 c.7)

ARRANGEMENT OF SECTIONS

13. Social security benefits and pensions.
25. Interpretation

Schedule 5

An Act to make provision for and in connection with change of gender.

COMMENCEMENT

Certain formalities provisions entered into force on Royal Assent, but the whole Act entered into force on April 4, 2005: The Gender Recognition Act 2004 (Commencement) Order 2005 (SI 2005/54).

GENERAL NOTE

This Act makes provision, for the first time, for recognition of a change of gender identity for a transsexual. It follows judgments of the European Court of Human Rights against the United Kingdom finding violations of Convention rights in *Goodwin v United Kingdom* (App. 28957/95), Judgment of July 11, 2002, (2002) 35 E.H.R.R. 18, and *I v United Kingdom* (App. 25680/94), Judgment of July 11, 2002, (2003) 36 E.H.R.R. 53.

The scheme introduced by the Act is essentially a system of recognition of gender identity through the issue of a gender recognition certificate. The qualifying conditions for such a certificate are that the applicant (1) has or has had gender dysphoria; (2) has lived in the acquired gender for at least two years; and (3) intends to continue to live in the acquired gender until death. There is no requirement that an applicant has undergone gender reassignment surgery. Provision is made for recognition of a change of gender identity under the law of another country.

Provision is made for two types of certificate: an interim certificate and a full certificate. Unmarried applicants can only receive full certificates, whereas married applicants can only receive interim certificates. Matrimonial law is amended so that the issue of an interim certificate constitutes a ground for a marriage to be declared a nullity provided that proceedings are begun within six months of issue of the certificate. A court declaring a marriage a nullity under this ground must also issue a full gender recognition certificate.

The effect of the full certificate is to be found in s.9 which provides that a person's gender becomes for all purposes the acquired gender, although it does not affect things done or events occurring before the certificate is issued. This general principle is made subject to the express provisions of this Act and any other enactment. It is destined to become known as the "section 9 principle".

The Act contains a range of provisions seeking to work out the practical implications of the issue of a gender recognition certificate. Section 13 and Sch.5 concern social security benefits and pensions. These provisions are concerned only with old age and survivors benefits. The operation of the provisions of the section 9 principle

325

Social security benefits and pensions

1.602   **13.** Schedule 5 (entitlement to benefits and pensions) has effect.

GENERAL NOTE

1.603   The provisions of the Schedule constitute a set of free-standing rules rather than amendments to the Contributions and Benefits Act (and its counterparts elsewhere in the United Kingdom). They apply where a person holds a full gender recognition certificate. Perhaps unsurprisingly where the change of gender identity is from female to male, the rules applicable to men apply. These are, of course, generally less favourable in the field of old age and survivors benefits because of the age discrimination still operative in this area of social security. However, where the change of identity is from male to female, the position is less straightforward. Provision is made for entitlement to a retirement pension at age 60, but generally in relation to entitlement to benefits based on a spouse's national insurance contributions, there is no automatic passport to these.

Interpretation

1.604   **25.** In this Act—
"the acquired gender" is to be construed in accordance with s.1(2),
"approved country or territory" has the meaning given by s.2(4),
"the appointed day" means the day appointed by order under s.26,
"chartered psychologist" means a person for the time being listed in the British Psychological Society's Register of Chartered Psychologists,
"enactment" includes an enactment contained in an Act of the Scottish Parliament or in any Northern Ireland legislation,
"full gender recognition certificate" and "interim gender recognition certificate" mean the certificates issued as such under s.4 or 5 and "gender recognition certificate" means either of those sorts of certificate,
"gender dysphoria" means the disorder variously referred to as gender dysphoria, gender identity disorder and transsexualism,
"Gender Recognition Panel" (and "Panel") is to be construed in accordance with Sch.1,
"subordinate legislation" means an Order in Council, an order, rules, regulations, a scheme, a warrant, bye-laws or any other instrument made under an enactment, and
"UK birth register entry" has the meaning given by s.10(2).

SCHEDULE 5

BENEFITS AND PENSIONS

PART I

INTRODUCTORY

1.605   1. This Schedule applies where a full gender recognition certificate is issued to a person.

(2004 c.7, Sch.5)

Part II

State Benefits

Introductory

2.—(1) In this Part of this Schedule "the 1992 Act" means—
  (a) in England and Wales and Scotland, the Social Security Contributions and Benefits Act 1992 (c. 4), and
  (b) in Northern Ireland, the Social Security Contributions and Benefits (Northern Ireland) Act 1992 (c. 7).

(2) In this Part of this Schedule "the Administration Act" means—
  (a) in England and Wales and Scotland, the Social Security Administration Act 1992 (c. 5), and
  (b) in Northern Ireland, the Social Security Administration (Northern Ireland) Act 1992 (c. 8).

(3) Expressions used in this Part of this Schedule and in Part 2 of the 1992 Act have the same meaning in this Part of this Schedule as in Part 2 of the 1992 Act.

1.606

Widowed mother's allowance

3.—(1) If (immediately before the certificate is issued) the person is, or but for section 1 of the Administration Act would be, entitled to a widowed mother's allowance under section 37 of the 1992 Act (allowance for woman whose husband died before 9th April 2001)—
  (a) the person is not entitled to that allowance afterwards, but
  (b) (instead) subsections (2) to (5) of section 39A of the 1992 Act (widowed parent's allowance) apply in relation to the person.

(2) If (immediately before the certificate is issued) the person is (actually) entitled to a widowed mother's allowance, the entitlement to widowed parent's allowance conferred by sub-paragraph (1) is not subject to section 1 of the Administration Act.

1.607

General Note

This paragraph applies in the case of a female to male transsexual. If, immediately prior to the issue of the certificate, the person was (or would be but for having made a claim) entitled to widowed mother's allowance, entitlement to that benefit ceases on issue of the certificate, but the man becomes entitled to claim a widowed parent's allowance under the specified provisions of the Contributions and Benefits Act. If, however, widowed mother's allowance has been claimed and awarded, then the benefit converts to widowed parent's allowance without the need for a claim.

1.608

Widow's pension

4. If (immediately before the certificate is issued) the person is entitled to a widow's pension under section 38 of the 1992 Act (pension for woman whose husband died before 9th April 2001), the person is not entitled to that pension afterwards.

1.609

General Note

This paragraph applies in the case of a female to male transsexual. Since there is no equivalent pension under the bereavement benefits scheme (a widower's pension), the entitlement to the widow's pension ceases on issue of the certificate.

1.610

Widowed parent's allowance

5. If (immediately before the certificate is issued) the person is, or but for section 1 of the Administration Act would be, entitled to a widowed parent's allowance by virtue of subsection (1)(b) of section 39A of the 1992 Act (allowance for man whose wife died before 9th April 2001), subsections (2) to (5) of that section continue to apply in relation to the person afterwards.

1.611

GENERAL NOTE

1.612 Widowed parent's allowance is predominantly a gender neutral benefit, and the provision here is simply for entitlement to widowed parent's allowance to continue where a man has claimed in respect of a bereavement before April 2001. However, women in receipt of widowed mother's allowance have the potential right to move on to widow's pension, but no provision is made for transfer in a relevant case from widowed parent's allowance to widowed mother's allowance.

Long-term incapacity benefit etc.

1.613 6. If (immediately before the certificate is issued) the person is entitled to incapacity benefit, or a Category A retirement pension, under—
    (a) section 40 of the 1992 Act (long-term incapacity benefit etc. for woman whose husband died before 9th April 2001), or
    (b) section 41 of the 1992 Act (long-term incapacity benefit etc. for man whose wife died before that date),
the person is not so entitled afterwards.

GENERAL NOTE

1.614 The effect of these provisions is at first surprising. Sections 40 and 41 make provision respectively for widow and widowers which enabled a person incapable of work at the time of the bereavement to claim incapacity benefit even though the contribution conditions were not satisfied. On reaching pensionable age, the incapacity benefit would convert into a Category A retirement pension if the person was not otherwise entitled to retirement pension. For both male to female, and female to male, transsexuals, the entitlement to incapacity benefit on this basis ceases. This would appear to be because the principle adopted throughout the Schedule would seem to be to treat all those holding a gender recognition certificate as if they had been bereaved *after* April 2001. Sections 40 and 41 apply only where the person was bereaved before April 2001.

Category A retirement pension

1.615 7.—(1) Any question—
    (a) whether the person is entitled to a Category A retirement pension (under section 44 of the 1992 Act) for any period after the certificate is issued, and
    (b) (if so) the rate at which the person is so entitled for the period,
is to be decided as if the person's gender had always been the acquired gender.
(2) Accordingly, if (immediately before the certificate is issued) the person—
    (a) is a woman entitled to a Category A retirement pension, but
    (b) has not attained the age of 65,
the person ceases to be so entitled when it is issued.
(3) And, conversely, if (immediately before the certificate is issued) the person—
    (a) is a man who has attained the age at which a woman of the same age attains pensionable age, but
    (b) has not attained the age of 65,
the person is to be treated for the purposes of section 44 of the 1992 Act as attaining pensionable age when it is issued.
(4) But sub-paragraph (1) does not apply if and to the extent that the decision of any question to which it refers is affected by—
    (a) the payment or crediting of contributions, or the crediting of earnings, in respect of a period ending before the certificate is issued, or
    (b) preclusion from regular employment by responsibilities at home for such a period.
(5) Paragraph 10 makes provision about deferment of Category A retirement pensions.

GENERAL NOTE

1.616 The general principle in sub-paragraph (1) is an exception to the section 9 principle, because for these purposes the person's acquired gender is treated as though it has always been the person's gender. So a female to male transsexual who changes gender between the ages of 60 and 65 ceases to be entitled to any Category A retirement pension awarded, whereas a male to female transsexual who changes gender between the ages of 60 and 65 is treated for the purposes of determining entitlement to a Category A retirement pension as though she attained pensionable age on the date of issue of the certificate, but not before. There is no retrospectivity of entitlement.

Category B retirement pension etc.

8.—(1) Any question whether the person is entitled to—
 (a) a Category B retirement pension (under section 48A, 48B, 48BB or 51 of the 1992 Act), or
 (b) an increase in a Category A retirement pension under section 51A or 52 of the 1992 Act (increase in Category A retirement pension by reference to amount of Category B retirement pension),
for any period after the certificate is issued is (in accordance with section 9(1)) to be decided as if the person's gender were the acquired gender (but subject to sub-paragraph (4)).

(2) Accordingly, if (immediately before the certificate is issued) the person is a woman entitled to—
 (a) a Category B retirement pension, or
 (b) an increase in a Category A retirement pension under section 51A or 52 of the 1992 Act,
the person may cease to be so entitled when it is issued.

(3) And, conversely, if (immediately before the certificate is issued) the person—
 (a) is a man who has attained the age at which a woman of the same age attains pensionable age, but
 (b) has not attained the age of 65,
the person is to be treated for the purposes of sections 48A, 48B and 48BB of the 1992 Act as attaining pensionable age when it is issued.

(4) But a person who is a man (immediately before the certificate is issued) is not entitled to a Category B retirement pension under section 48B of the 1992 Act for any period after it is issued if the person—
 (a) attains (or has attained) the age of 65 before 6th April 2010, and
 (b) would not have been entitled to a Category B retirement pension under section 51 of the 1992 Act for that period if still a man.

(5) Paragraph 10 makes provision about deferment of Category B retirement pensions.

GENERAL NOTE

These rather complex provisions reflect the four different routes to entitlement to a Category B retirement pension coupled with the change which will come into effect in 2010 under which men will begin to acquire entitlement to Category B retirement pension. The general principle adopted in relation to acquisition of entitlement to a Category B retirement pension is that any question of entitlement after the issue of a gender recognition certificate is to be determined by applying the rules applicable to persons of the acquired gender. That means that if the acquired gender is that of a woman, the rules applicable to women are applied to the claimant, and, if the acquired gender is that of a man, the rules applicable to men are applied to the claimant. In both cases no concessions to the change of gender identity are made. The exception is sub-paragraph (4) which limits the ability of a male to female transsexual acquiring entitlement under s.48B of the Contributions and Benefits Act.

Shared additional pension

9.—(1) Any question—
 (a) whether the person is entitled to a shared additional pension (under section 55A of the 1992 Act) for any period after the certificate is issued, and
 (b) (if so) the rate at which the person is so entitled for the period,
is to be decided on the basis of the person attaining pensionable age on the same date as someone of the acquired gender (and the same age).

(2) Accordingly, if (immediately before the certificate is issued) the person—
 (a) is a woman entitled to a shared additional pension, but
 (b) has not attained the age of 65,
the person ceases to be so entitled when it is issued.

(3) And, conversely, if (immediately before the certificate is issued) the person—
   (a) is a man who has attained the age at which a woman of the same age attains pensionable age, but
   (b) has not attained the age of 65,
the person is to be treated for the purposes of section 55A of the 1992 Act as attaining pensionable age when it is issued.
(4) Paragraph 10 makes provision about deferment of shared additional pensions.

Deferment of pensions

1.620   **10.**—(1) The person's entitlement to—
   (a) a Category A retirement pension,
   (b) a Category B retirement pension, or
   (c) a shared additional pension,
is not to be taken to have been deferred for any period ending before the certificate is issued unless the condition in sub-paragraph (2) is satisfied.
(2) The condition is that the entitlement both—
   (a) was actually deferred during the period, and
   (b) would have been capable of being so deferred had the person's gender been the acquired gender.

GENERAL NOTE

1.621   The principle applied here is that there can be no notional deferment of pension on recognition of a change of gender identity.

Category C retirement pension for widows

1.622   11. If (immediately before the certificate is issued) the person is entitled to a Category C retirement pension under section 78(2) of the 1992 Act, the person is not entitled to that pension afterwards.

GENERAL NOTE

1.623   It would be surprising if this provision proves problematic in operation, since it relates (a) to persons who attained pensionable age before July 5, 1948, and (b) to the wives and widows of such persons. A change of gender identity from woman to man results in the loss of the entitlement.

Graduated retirement benefit: Great Britain

1.624   **12.**—(1) The provision that may be made by regulations under paragraph 15 of Schedule 3 to the Social Security (Consequential Provisions) Act 1992 (c. 6) (power to retain provisions repealed by Social Security Act 1973 (c. 38), with or without modification, for transitional purposes) includes provision modifying the preserved graduated retirement benefit provisions in consequence of this Act.
(2) "The preserved graduated retirement benefit provisions" are the provisions of the National Insurance Act 1965 (c. 51) relating to graduated retirement benefit continued in force, with or without modification, by regulations having effect as if made under that paragraph.

Graduated retirement benefit: Northern Ireland

1.625   **13.**—(1) The provision that may be made by regulations under paragraph 15 of Schedule 3 to the Social Security (Consequential Provisions) (Northern Ireland) Act 1992 (c. 9) (corresponding power for Northern Ireland) includes provision modifying the Northern Ireland preserved graduated retirement benefit provisions in consequence of this Act.
(2) "The Northern Ireland preserved graduated retirement benefit provisions" are the provisions of the National Insurance Act (Northern Ireland) 1966 (c. 6 (N.I.)) relating to graduated retirement benefit continued in force, with or without modification, by regulations having effect as if made under that paragraph.

Part 3

Occupational Pension Schemes

General Note

The Schedule does not make any rules about occupational pension schemes, but it does have to deal with the provisions guaranteeing those in receipt of occupational pensions the guaranteed minimum pension, and preserved equivalent pension benefits.

1.626

Guaranteed minimum pensions etc.: Great Britain

14.—(1) In this paragraph "the 1993 Act" means the Pension Schemes Act 1993 (c. 48); and expressions used in this paragraph and in that Act have the same meaning in this paragraph as in that Act.

1.627

(2) The fact that the person's gender has become the acquired gender does not affect the operation of section 14 of the 1993 Act (guaranteed minimum) in relation to the person, except to the extent that its operation depends on section 16 of the 1993 Act (revaluation); and sub-paragraphs (3) and (5) have effect subject to that.

(3) If (immediately before the certificate is issued) the person is a woman who is entitled to a guaranteed minimum pension but has not attained the age of 65—
  (a) the person is for the purposes of section 13 of the 1993 Act and the guaranteed minimum pension provisions to be treated after it is issued as not having attained pensionable age (so that the entitlement ceases) but as attaining pensionable age on subsequently attaining the age of 65, and
  (b) in a case where the person's guaranteed minimum pension has commenced before the certificate is issued, it is to be treated for the purposes of Chapter 3 of Part 4 of the 1993 Act (anti-franking) as if it had not.

(4) But sub-paragraph (3)(a) does not—
  (a) affect any pension previously paid to the person, or
  (b) prevent section 15 of the 1993 Act (increase of guaranteed minimum where commencement of guaranteed minimum pension postponed) operating to increase the person's guaranteed minimum by reason of a postponement of the commencement of the person's guaranteed minimum pension for a period ending before the certificate is issued.

(5) If (immediately before the certificate is issued) the person is a man who—
  (a) has attained the age of 60, but
  (b) has not attained the age of 65,
the person is to be treated for the purposes of section 13 of the 1993 Act and the guaranteed minimum pension provisions as attaining pensionable age when it is issued.

(6) If at that time the person has attained the age of 65, the fact that the person's gender has become the acquired gender does not affect the person's pensionable age for those purposes.

(7) The fact that the person's gender has become the acquired gender does not affect any guaranteed minimum pension to which the person is entitled as a widow or widower immediately before the certificate is issued (except in consequence of the operation of the previous provisions of this Schedule).

(8) If a transaction to which section 19 of the 1993 Act applies which is carried out before the certificate is issued discharges a liability to provide a guaranteed minimum pension for or in respect of the person, it continues to do so afterwards.

(9) "The guaranteed minimum pension provision" means so much of the 1993 Act (apart from section 13) and of any other enactment as relates to guaranteed minimum pensions.

Guaranteed minimum pensions etc.: Northern Ireland

15.—(1) In this paragraph "the 1993 Act" means the Pension Schemes (Northern Ireland) Act 1993 (c. 49); and expressions used in this paragraph and in that Act have the same meaning in this paragraph as in that Act.

1.628

(2) The fact that the person's gender has become the acquired gender does not affect the operation of section 10 of the 1993 Act (guaranteed minimum) in relation to the person, except to the extent that its operation depends on section 12 of the 1993 Act (revaluation); and sub-paragraphs (3) and (5) have effect subject to that.

(3) If (immediately before the certificate is issued) the person is a woman who is entitled to a guaranteed minimum pension but has not attained the age of 65—
  (a) the person is for the purposes of section 9 of the 1993 Act and the guaranteed minimum pension provisions to be treated after it is issued as not having attained pensionable age (so that the entitlement ceases) but as attaining pensionable age on subsequently attaining the age of 65, and
  (b) in a case where the person's guaranteed minimum pension has commenced before the certificate is issued, it is to be treated for the purposes of Chapter 3 of Part 4 of the 1993 Act (anti-franking) as if it had not.

(4) But sub-paragraph (3)(a) does not—
  (a) affect any pension previously paid to the person, or
  (b) prevent section 11 of the 1993 Act (increase of guaranteed minimum where commencement of guaranteed minimum pension postponed) operating to increase the person's guaranteed minimum by reason of a postponement of the commencement of the person's guaranteed minimum pension for a period ending before the certificate is issued.

(5) If (immediately before the certificate is issued) the person is a man who—
  (a) has attained the age of 60, but
  (b) has not attained the age of 65,
the person is to be treated for the purposes of section 9 of the 1993 Act and the guaranteed minimum pension provisions as attaining pensionable age when it is issued.

(6) If at that time the person has attained the age of 65, the fact that the person's gender has become the acquired gender does not affect the person's pensionable age for those purposes.

(7) The fact that the person's gender has become the acquired gender does not affect any guaranteed minimum pension to which the person is entitled as a widow or widower immediately before the certificate is issued (except in consequence of the operation of the previous provisions of this Schedule).

(8) If a transaction to which section 15 of the 1993 Act applies which is carried out before the certificate is issued discharges a liability to provide a guaranteed minimum pension for or in respect of the person, it continues to do so afterwards.

(9) "The guaranteed minimum pension provision" means so much of the 1993 Act (apart from section 9) and of any other enactment as relates to guaranteed minimum pensions.

Equivalent pension benefits: Great Britain

1.629   16.—(1) The provision that may be made by regulations under paragraph 15 of Schedule 3 to the Social Security (Consequential Provisions) Act 1992 (c. 6) (power to retain provisions repealed by Social Security Act 1973 (c. 38), with or without modification, for transitional purposes) includes provision modifying the preserved equivalent pension benefits provisions in consequence of this Act.

(2) "The preserved equivalent pension benefits provisions" are the provisions of the National Insurance Act 1965 (c. 51) relating to equivalent pension benefits continued in force, with or without modification, by regulations having effect as if made under that paragraph.

Equivalent pension benefits: Northern Ireland

1.630   17.—(1) The provision that may be made by regulations under paragraph 15 of Schedule 3 to the Social Security (Consequential Provisions) (Northern Ireland) Act 1992 (c. 9) (corresponding power for Northern Ireland) includes provision modifying the Northern Ireland preserved equivalent pension benefits provisions in consequence of this Act.

(2) "The Northern Ireland preserved equivalent pension benefits provisions" are the provisions of the National Insurance Act (Northern Ireland) 1966 (c. 6 (N.I.)) relating to equivalent pension benefits continued in force, with or without modification, by regulations having effect as if made under that paragraph.

(2004 c.33)

Civil Partnership Act 2004

(2004 c.33)

An Act to make provision for and in connection with civil partnership.

Part 1

Introduction

Civil partnership

1.—(1) A civil partnership is a relationship between two people of the same sex ("civil partners")—
   (a) which is formed when they register as civil partners of each other—
       (i) in England or Wales (under Part 2),
       (ii) in Scotland (under Part 3),
       (iii) in Northern Ireland (under Part 4), or
       (iv) outside the United Kingdom under an Order in Council made under Chapter 1 of Part 5 (registration at British consulates etc. or by armed forces personnel), or
   (b) which they are treated under Chapter 2 of Part 5 as having formed (at the time determined under that Chapter) by virtue of having registered an overseas relationship.

(2) Subsection (1) is subject to the provisions of this Act under or by virtue of which a civil partnership is void.

(3) A civil partnership ends only on death, dissolution or annulment.

(4) The references in subsection (3) to dissolution and annulment are to dissolution and annulment having effect under or recognised in accordance with this Act.

(5) *Omitted.*

1.631

General Note

The Civil Partnership Act 2004 entered into force on December 5, 2005, and received widespread publicity. The Act applies to the whole of the United Kingdom, though there are different legislative provisions in the Act relating to England and Wales (Pt 2), Scotland (Pt 3) and Northern Ireland (Pt 4). The purpose of the Act is to enable same sex-couples to secure legal recognition of their relationship through the formal status of civil partnership. This is obtained through a process of registration. The conditions for entering a civil partnership are fourfold: (1) the parties are of the same sex; (2) neither party is already lawfully married or a member of a civil partnership; (3) the parties are not within the prohibited degrees of relationship; and (4) both parties are aged 16 or more. The fourth condition is subject to some regional variations since in England and Wales, and Northern Ireland additional consent is needed for a civil partnership if the parties are aged 16 but under 18.

Unsurprisingly, many amendments to social security law are required to accommodate recognition of this new relationship. These amendments are recorded in in the relevant substantive provisions.

There is a helpful explanatory memorandum to the new legislation at http://www.opsi.gov.uk/acts/en2004/2004en33.htm.

1.632

Civil Partnership Act 2004

See also Jones, S, *The Civil Partnership Act 2004 and Social Security Law* [2005] JSSL 119.

246.—Interpretation of statutory references to stepchildren etc.

1.633
(1) In any provision to which this section applies, references to a stepchild or step-parent of a person (here, "A"), and cognate expressions, are to be read as follows—

A's stepchild includes a person who is the child of A's civil partner (but is not A's child);

A's step-parent includes a person who is the civil partner of A's parent (but is not A's parent);

A's stepdaughter includes a person who is the daughter of A's civil partner (but is not A's daughter);

A's stepson includes a person who is the son of A's civil partner (but is not A's son);

A's stepfather includes a person who is the civil partner of A's father (but is not A's parent);

A's stepmother includes a person who is the civil partner of A's mother (but is not A's parent);

A's stepbrother includes a person who is the son of the civil partner of A's parent (but is not the son of either of A's parents);

A's stepsister includes a person who is the daughter of the civil partner of A's parent (but is not the daughter of either of A's parents).

(2) For the purposes of any provision to which this section applies—

"brother-in-law" includes civil partner's brother,

"daughter-in-law" includes daughter's civil partner,

"father-in-law" includes civil partner's father,

"mother-in-law" includes civil partner's mother,

"parent-in-law" includes civil partner's parent,

"sister-in-law" includes civil partner's sister, and

"son-in-law" includes son's civil partner.

GENERAL NOTE

1.634
With effect from May 11, 2006 The Civil Partnership Act 2004 (Relationships Arising Through Civil Partnership) Order 2006 (SI 2006/1121) applies s.246 to the entry in column (A) of para. 7 of Pt 3 of Sch. 1(employment by father etc.) to the Social Security Categorisation of Earners) Regulations 1978.

PART II

REGULATIONS

SECTION A

SOCIAL SECURITY

NOTE

References to 1992 Acts in pre-1992 Regulations

Some regulations made under pre-1992 legislation remain in force. They naturally contain references to provisions in that earlier legislation but, where provisions of the Social Security Contributions and Benefits Act 1992 or the Social Security Administration Act 1992 have replaced those earlier provisions, those references are deemed to be references to the equivalent provisions of the 1992 Acts.

In order to be as helpful as possible to users of this volume, the authors have, wherever practicable, inserted in square brackets reference to the relevant provisions of the 1992 legislation.

However, some of the older regulations contain many references to legislation which has either been repealed or is only of significance to those able to retain an entitlement to a defunct benefit. In these cases, reference has generally been left to the earlier legislation. Equally, in some regulations, it was considered that it might mislead if the interpretation regulation was amended.

Readers should therefore note that the material appearing in square brackets is the authors' amendment to include reference to the 1992 legislation. Such amendments have no official standing. All other references to legislation are as they appear in the current version of the regulations printed in this volume.

The Social Security (Breach of Community Order) Regulations 2001

(SI 2001/1395)

Made 5th April 2001
Coming into force 15th October 2001

Whereas a draft of this instrument was laid before Parliament in accordance with section 65(4) of the Child Support, Pensions and Social Security Act 2000 and approved by resolution of each House of Parliament.

2.1

Now therefore, the Secretary of State for Social Security, in exercise of the powers conferred upon him by sections 62(2) to (5) and (8), 63(2) to (4), 64(2), (6) and (8) and 65(1) and (2) of the Child Support, Pensions and Social Security Act 2000 and section 189(4) of the Social Security Administration Act 1992, and of all other powers enabling him in that behalf, which is made before the end of a period of 6 months beginning with the coming into force of sections 62 to 65 of the Child Support, Pensions and Social Security Act, by this Instrument, hereby makes the following Regulations:

GENERAL NOTE

These regulations implement the "loss of benefit provisions", which are defined in s.65(8) of CSPSSA 2000 as meaning in ss.62–64 of that Act. Under the Child Support, Pensions and Social Security Act 2000 (Commencement No.10) Order 2001 (SI 2001/2619), the provisions are being implemented progressively. At present they only apply to "any person who, as a result of a relevant community order . . . being made in relation to him, falls to be supervised by an officer of the local probation board for any of the probation areas of Derbyshire, Hertfordshire, Teesside and West Midlands" (see art.2(2)(a) of the Commencement Order). Note that, by art.2(2)(b) of the Commencement Order it is also necessary for a relevant community order to have been made under s.64(1) (which requires offenders to have been warned before the order is made of the loss of benefit consequences of failing to comply with it—see below). The loss of benefit provisions therefore do not apply where the community order was made before October 15, 2001—the date on which s.64(1) came into force—even if the failure to comply occurred after that date.

2.2

The scheme established by the loss of benefit provisions is as follows:

The rules apply to people who have been convicted of a criminal offence and sentenced to a *relevant community order*. Under s.62(1)(a) and (b), loss of benefit is a sanction applied to a person where a court decides that s/he has failed, without reasonable excuse, to comply with the requirements of a relevant community order and the Secretary of State is notified of that determination under s.64. Such person is referred to as "the offender".

"Relevant community order" is defined by s.62(8) as meaning a community punishment order (formerly a community service order), a community rehabilitation order (formerly a probation order), a community punishment and rehabilitation order (formerly a combination order), and "any order falling in England and Wales to be treated as" such an order. There is power to prescribe any other community order within the Powers of Criminal Courts (Sentencing) Act 2000 as being a relevant community order but no such prescription has yet been made. Therefore, at least at present, failure to comply with the requirements of an exclusion order, a curfew order, a drug treatment and testing order, an attendance centre order, a supervision order, an action plan order or a drug abstinence order does not incur

339

a community sentence sanction. Regulations under s.62(8) which add to the definition of "relevant community order" require an affirmative resolution of both Houses of Parliament—see s.65(4)(e).

Under s.62(1)(c) the loss of benefit provisions apply where the conditions of entitlement to a *relevant benefit* "are or become satisfied" by the offender. Subject to the provisions of reg.3 below, it therefore does not seem to matter whether the offender first becomes entitled to such a benefit before or after the court determines that s/he has failed to comply with the community order. Where the "relevant benefit" is a training allowance (see below), the reference in s.62(1) to satisfying the conditions of entitlement are to be read as references to "there having been or, as the case may be, the taking of a decision to make payment of such benefit" (see s.62(9)). This is because training allowances are discretionary in nature and there is therefore no "entitlement" to them.

Relevant benefit is defined in s.62(8) as being income support and "any jobseeker's allowance other than joint-claim jobseeker's allowance" (for which equivalent provision is made in s.63). The reference to *any* jobseeker's allowance demonstrates that both contribution-based and income-based jobseeker's allowance are included. Contribution-based jobseeker's allowance is the only contributory benefit currently affected by the provisions, although head (c) of the definition contains a power—as yet unexercised—for the Secretary of State to prescribe any benefit under SSCBA 1992 (other than income support) as a relevant benefit. There is also power—in head (d) of the definition—to prescribe as a relevant benefit any type of training allowance under s.2 of the Employment and Training Act 1973. That power has been exercised to make reg.2(1) below. Regulations under s.62(8) which prescribe benefits under SSCBA 1992 as relevant benefits require an affirmative resolution of both Houses of Parliament—see s.65(4)(d).

The effect of the loss of benefit provisions is, by virtue of s.62(1), that even though the conditions of entitlement to the relevant benefit are satisfied, restrictions apply "in relation to the payment of that benefit in the offender's case". It may be important in some contexts to note that the provisions are therefore concerned with the payability of benefit and (other than in the case of a training allowance—see above) do not appear to affect the underlying entitlement to the benefit concerned.

Official guidance refers to the restriction on payability imposed by s.62(1) (and also by s.63(2) and (3)—see below) as a "community sentence sanction". Although the phrase does not appear in the legislation, it will be convenient to use it in this Note and the Notes to the individual regulations.

The precise nature of the community sentence sanction is dealt with in subss. (2)–(5). The general rule, in subs.(2), is that for a *prescribed period* (which, under subs.(7) cannot exceed 26 weeks but is otherwise defined in reg.3 below) the relevant benefit is not payable. However:

(a) under subs.(3), if the relevant benefit is income support, it is payable at a reduced rate (see reg.4 below);

(b) under subs.(4), if the relevant benefit is *income-based* (i.e. not contribution-based) jobseeker's allowance, the Secretary of State has power to prescribe that payment should only be made in certain circumstances and/or at a reduced rate and/or only if the offender complies with requirements as to the provision of information. This power has been used to make the rules on hardship in Pt III of the regulations;

(c) under subs.(5), if the relevant benefit is a training allowance, the Secretary of State has power to make regulations allowing payment "to such extent (as any) as may be prescribed". This power has been used to make reg.2(2) below.

Section 63 makes similar provision in the case of a joint-claim jobseeker's allowance. For this benefit, the rules have to take into account the possibilities that, at any given time:

(a) both members have failed to comply with a relevant community order;

(b) one member of a joint-claim couple has failed to comply with a relevant community order and the other is subject to a labour market sanction under s.20A of the Jobseekers Act 1995;

(c) one member of a joint-claim couple has failed to comply with a relevant community order but the order is not subject to any type of sanction.

The effect of s.63 is to modify the rules in s.62 so that (subject to the regulations on "hardship" made under s.63(4)):

(a) where both members of the couple are subject to a sanction (whether community sentence or labour-market) joint-claim jobseeker's allowance is not payable during the prescribed period (see s.63(2));

(b) where one member of the couple is subject to a community sentence sanction and the other is not subject to any sanction, benefit is paid at a reduced rate to the member who is not subject to the sanction (see s.63(3)). By s.63(5) the Secretary of State's regulation-making powers are the same as under s.20A(6) of the Jobseekers Act 1995 (see Vol.II) in relation to labour-market sanctions. Reg.5 below, made under those powers, is identical in effect to reg.74B of the Jobseeker's Allowance Regulations (see Vol.II): if the non-sanctioned member is entitled to contribution-based jobseeker's allowance, benefit is paid to her/him at the appropriate "personal rate" under s.4(1) of the Jobseekers Act 1995. Otherwise, benefit is paid as if the non-sanctioned member were a single claimant.

Note finally that if the determination that the offender has failed to comply with the relevant community order without reasonable excuse is quashed or set aside, arrears of relevant benefit are to be paid so as to put the claimant (or, in the case of a joint claim for jobseeker's allowance, claimants) in the same position as if the community sentence sanction had not been imposed (see s.62(6) and s.63(6)).

Sections 62–63 are supplemented by ss.64–66.

Section 64 is headed "information provision". It imposes different obligations on the people and institutions involved in the process of criminal justice to notify one another, and the claimant, of information which might be relevant to the imposition of a community sentence sanction. Thus:

(a) under subs.(1) the court which makes the relevant community order must explain to the claimant "in ordinary language" the consequence by virtue of ss.62 and 63 of a failure to comply with it;

(b) under subs.(2) the Secretary of State may make regulations requiring chief officers of local probation boards to notify him when a probation officer refers an offender to court for failure to comply with a relevant community order, of a determination by the court that the offender has so failed to comply, of any circumstances which might give rise to a payment of arrears under ss.62(6) or 63(6) and such other information about the offender "as may be prescribed";

(c) under subss.(4) and (5), if the Secretary of State becomes aware that proceedings are being taken which could lead to a determination that the offender has failed to comply with a relevant community order, he must notify the offender (or in a case of a joint-claim couple, both members of that couple even if only one of them is an offender) as soon as reasonable practicable, that a community sentence sanction will be imposed if such a determination is made;

There are also powers to regulate the exchange of information between the Secretary of State, his contractors and local probation boards and the use to which such information is put.

Section 65 makes supplementary provision relating to the regulation-making powers of the Secretary of State.

The Social Security (Breach of Community Order) Regulations 2001

Section 66 establishes a right to appeal to an Appeal Tribunal by adding ss.62 and 63 to the list in para.3 of Sch.3 to the Social Security Act 1998.

For the sake of completeness, it will also be convenient to note here the amendments to the Social Security and Child Support (Decisions and Appeals) Regulations 1999 ("the Decisions and Appeals Regulations") made by reg.2(2) of the Social Security (Breach of Community Order) (Consequential Amendments) Regulations 2001 (SI 2001/1711). They are to the following effect:

(a) reg.2(2)(b) of SI 2001/1711 inserts a new para.(i) into reg.6(2) of the Decisions and Appeals Regulations providing that the making by a court of an order within s.62(1) of CSPSSA is a ground for the supersession of a decision to award income support or jobseeker's allowance. By reg.2(2)(c), reg.7 of the Decisions and Appeals Regulations is amended to ensure that the superseding decision takes effect in accordance with reg.3 below.

(b) reg.2(2)(a) of SI 2001/1711 inserts a new para.(8A) in reg.3 of the Decisions and Appeals Regulations. This provides that the quashing or setting aside of an order within s.62(1) is a ground for revision of the decision to impose the community sentence sanction.

PART I

GENERAL

Citation, commencement and interpretation

2.3   **1.**—(1) These Regulations shall be cited as the Social Security (Breach of Community Order) Regulations 2001 and shall come into force on 15th October 2001.

(2) In these Regulations, unless the context otherwise requires—

"the Act" means the Child Support, Pensions and Social Security Act 2000;

"the Benefits Act" means the Social Security Contributions and Benefits Act 1992;

"the Jobseekers Act" means the Jobseekers Act 1995;

"the Income Support Regulations" means the Income Support (General) Regulations 1987;

"the Jobseeker's Allowance Regulations" means the Jobseeker's Allowance Regulations 1996;

"local probation board" means a local probation board established under section 4 of the Criminal Justice and Court Services Act 2000;

"offender" means the person in respect of whom a court has made a determination in accordance with section 62(1)(a) of the Act;

"prescribed period" means the period in respect of which the restrictions on payment of a relevant benefit apply in accordance with sections 62 and 63 of the Act and shall be interpreted in accordance with regulation 3.

(3) Expressions used in these Regulations which are defined either for the purposes of the Jobseekers Act or for the purposes of the Jobseeker's Allowance Regulations shall, except where the context otherwise requires, have the same meaning as for the purposes of that Act or, as the case may be, those Regulations.

(4) In these Regulations, unless the context otherwise requires, a reference—
(a) to a numbered regulation is to the regulation in these Regulations bearing that number;
(b) in a regulation to a numbered paragraph is to the paragraph in that regulation bearing that number.

General Note

This regulation establishes a number of definitions for the purposes of the regulations which follow. Most of these are self explanatory.

Local probation boards are corporate bodies established under s.4 of, and Sch.1 to, the Criminal Justice and Court Services Act 2000 with effect from April 1, 2001 (see the Criminal Justice and Court Services Act 2000 (Commencement No.4 Order) 2001 (SI 2001/919)). They are part of the National Probation Service for England and Wales which, under s.1, exists for the purposes of ensuring that courts are given assistance in sentencing and of the supervision and rehabilitation of people charged with or convicted of offences. This latter purpose includes giving effect to community orders, supervising those released from prison on licence and providing approved accommodation. There are 42 local areas each with its own board. With one exception, these areas are the same as police areas. The exception is the London area which covers both the Metropolitan Police District and City of London Police Area. Under s.5 the function of a local probation board is to arrange for sufficient provision to be made in its area for the purposes listed in s.1 and, under s.5(1)(b), "to make arrangements for ensuring the performance of any functions conferred by virtue of . . . any enactment on officers of the board. The wording in s.5(1)(b) is clearly apt to include the obligations imposed on officers of local probation boards by s.64 of CSPSSA 2000.

Description of a prescribed payment for the purposes of section 62(8) of the Act and the extent to which it is payable in accordance with section 62(5) of the Act

2.—(1) A prescribed payment for the purposes of paragraph (d) of the definition of "relevant benefit" in section 62(8) of the Act is a payment of a training allowance made to an individual pursuant to arrangements under section 2 of the Employment and Training Act 1973 in respect of that individual's participation in—
(a) the programme known as Work-Based Learning for Adults;
(b) one of the employment programmes specified in regulation 75(1)(a)(ii) of the Jobseeker's Allowance Regulations or the training scheme specified in regulation 75(1)(b)(ii) of those Regulations;
(c) the Intensive Activity Period within the meaning of regulation 75(1)(a)(iv) of those Regulations; or
(d) the Intensive Activity Period for 50 plus as defined in regulation 1(3) of those Regulations.

(2) In accordance with section 62(5) of the Act, where section 62(2) of the Act applies, the payment prescribed in paragraph (1) shall be payable for the prescribed period only to the extent of any part of that payment that is within the meaning of—
(a) sub-paragraph (a), (b), (c) or (d) of paragraph 14 of Schedule 7 to the Jobseeker's Allowance Regulations; or
(b) paragraph 60 of Schedule 7 to those Regulations.

The Social Security (Breach of Community Order) Regulations 2001

General Note

Regulation 2(1) lists the types of training allowance under s.2 of the Employment and Training Act 1973 which are to count as relevant benefits under head (d) of the definition in s.62(8). Other payments under s.2 cannot be restricted as part of a community sentence sanction.

Regulation 2(2) is made under s.62(5). The effect is that where the recipient of one of the types of training allowance listed in reg.2(1) is subject to a community sentence sanction to the element of the payment which reflects the underlying JSA entitlement is not paid. However, the elements of the allowance which are listed in paras 14 or 60 of Sch.17 to the Jobseeker's Allowance Regulations (see Vol.II) remain in payment. Those elements are travelling expenses, living away from home allowances, training premiums, certain child care expenses and certain mandatory top-up payments.

Prescribed period

3.—(1) Subject to paragraphs (5) and (6), in relation to a restriction under section 62(2) of the Act applying in respect of a jobseeker's allowance, the prescribed period shall be—
  (a) where the offender was entitled to a jobseeker's allowance on the examination day, the period of four weeks commencing on the operative day;
  (b) where the offender claims a jobseeker's allowance after the examination day but before the final day, the period commencing on the first day of the first benefit week after the examination day on which the offender is entitled to a jobseeker's allowance and ending on the last day of the benefit week which ends on, or immediately before, the final day.

(2) Subject to paragraphs (5) and (6), in relation to a restriction under section 62(2) of the Act applying in respect of a payment prescribed in regulation 2, the prescribed period shall be the period of four weeks commencing on the operative day.

(3) Subject to paragraphs [¹ (5), (6) and (6A)], in relation to a restriction under section 62(3) of the Act (income support), the prescribed period shall be—
  (a) where the offender was entitled to income support on the examination day, the period of four weeks commencing on the operative day;
  (b) where the offender claims income support after the examination day but before the final day, the period commencing on the first day of the first benefit week after the examination day on which the offender is entitled to income support and ending on the last day of the benefit week which ends on, or immediately before, the final day.

(4) Subject to paragraphs (5) and (6), in relation to a restriction under section 63(1) of the Act (joint-claim jobseeker's allowance), the prescribed period shall be—
  (a) where a joint-claim couple of which at least one member is an offender is entitled to a joint-claim jobseeker's allowance on the examination day, the period of four weeks commencing on the operative day;
  (b) where an offender is a member of a joint-claim couple which claims a joint-claim jobseeker's allowance after the examination day but before the final day, the period commencing on the first day of the

(SI 2001/1395, reg.3)

first benefit week after the examination day on which the joint-claim couple is entitled to a joint-claim jobseeker's allowance and ending on the last day of the benefit week which ends on, or immediately before, the final day.

(5) Where the offender is aged 17 on the examination day but attains the age of 18 before the last day of the period prescribed in paragraphs (1) to (4), the prescribed period shall be the period commencing on the first day of the benefit week commencing immediately after the day on which the offender attains the age of 18 and ending on the last day of the period prescribed in paragraphs (1) to (4).

(6) Where the offender is aged 59 on the examination day but attains the age of 60 before the final day, the prescribed period shall be the period commencing on the first day of the period prescribed in paragraphs (1) to (4) and ending on the last day of the benefit week ending immediately before the day on which the offender attains the age of 60.

[1 (6A) For the purposes of paragraph (3), the prescribed period shall not include any week in respect of which a payment of income support is subject to a restriction imposed pursuant to section 7 or 9 of the Social Security Fraud Act 2001.]

(7) In this regulation—
"benefit week"—
  (a) in relation to income support, shall have the same meaning as in regulation 2(1) of the Income Support Regulations;
  (b) in relation to a jobseeker's allowance, shall have the same meaning as in regulation 1(3) of the Jobseeker's Allowance Regulations;
  (c) in relation to a payment referred to in regulation 2, means—
    (i) where the offender is also entitled to income support on the examination day, the relevant benefit week under (a) above;
    (ii) where the offender is also entitled to a jobseeker's allowance on the examination day, the relevant benefit week under (b) above;
    (iii) where the offender is in receipt of such a payment on the examination day but is not entitled to, or in receipt of, income support or jobseeker's allowance on that day, the period of seven days ending on the day which corresponds with the day of the week which is the last day of the period in respect of which that payment is made;
"the examination day" means the day on which the Secretary of State, pursuant to a notification made to him that a determination has been made as mentioned in section 62(1)(a) of the Act, examines his records to ascertain whether the offender is, on that day, entitled to a relevant benefit or whether he is a member of a joint-claim couple who are, on that day, entitled to a joint-claim jobseeker's allowance;
"the final day" means the day before the day which is four weeks after the examination day;
"the operative day" means the first day of the first benefit week following the date of the Secretary of State's decision—
  (a) in relation to a relevant benefit, that that benefit shall not be payable or that it shall be reduced pursuant to section 62 of the Act;
  (b) in relation to a joint-claim jobseeker's allowance, that that allowance shall not be payable or that it shall be reduced pursuant to section 63 of the Act.

The Social Security (Breach of Community Order) Regulations 2001

AMENDMENT

1. Social Security (Loss of Benefit) (Consequential Amendments) Regulations 2002 (SI 2002/490), reg.11 (April 1, 2002).

GENERAL NOTE

2.8 This regulation defines the length of the *prescribed period* under s.62(2), i.e. the period during which the community sentence sanction is to apply.

The starting point is the concept of the *examination day* which is defined in reg.3(7). This is the day on which an officer acting on behalf of the Secretary of State examines the Department's records following a notification from the local probation board under reg.19 in order to determine whether the offender is entitled to a relevant benefit (or is one of a couple entitled to a joint-claim jobseeker's allowance). If the answer to that question is yes, the prescribed period is a period of *four weeks* beginning on the *operative day*—see regs 3(1)(a), (2) and (3)(a).

The "operative day" is the first day of the benefit week immediately following the Secretary of State's decision to impose a community sentence sanction. Where the offender is entitled to IS or JSA, "benefit week" has the same meaning as in the Income Support Regulations or, as the case may be, the Jobseeker's Allowance Regulations. However, if the offender is in receipt of one of the prescribed types of training allowance and is not also entitled to either IS or JSA "benefit week" means (in effect) the seven day period in respect of which that allowance is normally paid.

In most cases, the day of the Secretary of State's decision will, presumably, be the same as the examination day but there is no requirement that the two must necessarily be the same nor does there appear to be requirement that the decision to impose a sanction must be taken within a certain number of days or weeks of, or within a reasonable time of, the examination day.

Regs 3(1)(b), and (3)(b) deal with the position where an offender is not entitled to IS or JSA on the examination day but subsequently claims one of those benefits. In such a case, the prescribed period—and therefore also the sanction—begins on the first day of first benefit week for which the offender becomes entitled to benefit and ends on the last day of the benefit week which ends on, or immediately before the *final day*. The "final day" is defined by reg.3(7) as the day before the day which is four weeks after the examination day. An offender who does not become entitled to a relevant benefit until after the final day is not subject to a community sentence sanction.

Appeals concerning the application of regs 3(1)(b), and (3)(b) may present particular practical difficulties for tribunals. The correct sanction period will depend on when the Department first examined its records following notification by the local probation board that an order within s.62(1) has been made. However, by definition, the claimant will not have been entitled to either IS or JSA on that date and therefore no decision will have been made following that examination. It is unclear at present what records will be kept of the carrying out of an examination which does not lead to a decision. It is suggested that as the issue in such an appeal will be whether someone who is *Ex hypothesi* entitled to benefit should be disqualified for payment, the burden of proof is on the Secretary of State to establish on a balance of probabilities the length of the prescribed period which he asserts to be appropriate. In a case where the examination day for which the Secretary of State contends is substantially after the Department would ordinarily have received notice under reg.19 (see below) from the local probation board, the tribunal may—at least in the absence of an explanation for the delay—conclude it is more likely that the records were first examined reasonably quickly after the reg.19 notification would have been received in the ordinary course of the post.

All the above rules are subject to the exceptions established by paras (5) and (6) which affect, respectively, 17-year-olds who turn 18 and 59-year-olds who turn 60 in the four weeks between the examination day and the final day. In the former case,

(SI 2001/1395, reg.3)

the sanction begins at the beginning of the first benefit week immediately following the 18th birthday and ends on the day when it would have ended if the offender had at all material times been 18. In the latter, the sanction begins under the usual rules but ends on the last day of the benefit week immediately before the 60th birthday.

PART II

REDUCED AMOUNTS

Reduction of income support

4.—(1) Subject to paragraphs (3) and (4), any payment of income support which falls to be made to an offender in respect of any week in the prescribed period shall be reduced—
   (a) where the offender or any other member of his family is pregnant or seriously ill, by a sum equal to 20%;
   (b) in any other case, by a sum equal to 40%,
   of the relevant amount applicable on the first day of the prescribed period under paragraph 1(1) of Schedule 2 to the Income Support Regulations in respect of a single claimant for income support.

(2) For the purposes of paragraph (1)(a), whether or not a person is a member of the offender's family shall be determined in accordance with section 137(1) of the Benefits Act and Part III of the Income Support Regulations.

(3) Payment shall not be reduced under paragraph (1) below 10 pence per week.

(4) A reduction under paragraph (1) shall, if it is not a multiple of 5p, be rounded to the nearest such multiple or, if it is a multiple of 2.5p but not of 5p, to the next lower multiple of 5p.

(5) Where the rate of income support payable to an offender changes, the rules set out above for a reduction in the benefit payable shall be applied to the new rates and any adjustment to the reduction shall take effect from the beginning of the first benefit week to commence for the offender following the change.

GENERAL NOTE

Reg.4 is broadly self-explanatory. Where the relevant benefit is IS, it is normally reduced by 40 per cent but if the offender or a member of his family is pregnant or seriously ill the reduction is 20 per cent. The reduction is applied to "any payment of income support" and therefore, it would seem, to premiums, housing costs and, in an appropriate case, residential allowances as well as the basic personal allowance. Note also that what is reduced is the payment "which falls to be made *to the offender*" (emphasis added) which means that the personal allowances paid in respect of other members of the claimant's family will also be reduced where the offender is the claimant. However, the regulation does not state that a reduction should be made in income support which is payable to someone else *in respect of* of the offender and there may therefore be some scope for certain couples (e.g, where both are retired, or incapable of work or otherwise within the categories listed in Sch.1B to the Income Support Regulations) to "swap" claimants to that payment of benefit "falls to be made to" the offender's partner. This is particularly so, given that the offender is bound to have some notice of the possibility that a court order within s.62(1) will be made. Claimants considering this course (and advisers suggesting it to them) should ensure that the termination of the existing claim by the offender will not lead to the loss of transitional protection which would have been of greater value than the avoidance of the sanction.

As with reg.145 of the Jobseeker's Allowance Regulations, the circumstances in which a person is "seriously ill" for the purposes of eligibility for the lower, 20 per cent, reduction are not defined.

Reduction of joint-claim jobseeker's allowance

2.11   **5.**—(1) In respect of any part of the prescribed period for which section 63(2) of the Act does not apply but subject to paragraph (2), the reduced rate of joint-claim jobseeker's allowance payable to the member of that couple who is not the offender for the prescribed period shall be—
   (a) in any case in which the member of the couple who is not the offender satisfies the conditions set out in section 2 of the Jobseekers Act (contribution-based conditions), a rate equal to the amount calculated in accordance with section 4(1) of that Act;
   (b) in any case where the couple are a couple in hardship for the purposes of regulation 12, a rate equal to the amount calculated in accordance with regulation 17;
   (c) in any other case, a rate calculated in accordance with section 4(3A) of the Jobseekers Act save that the applicable amount shall be the amount determined by reference to paragraph 1(1) of Schedule 1 to the Jobseeker's Allowance Regulations which would have been the applicable amount had the member of the couple who is not the offender been a single claimant.

(2) Paragraph (1) shall only apply to the extent that the member of the joint-claim couple who is not the offender is not also subject to sanctions for the purposes of section 20A of the Jobseekers Act.

GENERAL NOTE

2.12   The effect of reg.5 is noted in the General Note at the beginning of these Regulations. Its effect is equivalent to the effect of reg.74B of the Jobseeker's Allowance Regulations in relation to labour market sanctions (see Vol.II).

PART III

HARDSHIP

Meaning of "person in hardship"

2.13   **6.**—(1) In this Part of these Regulations, a "person in hardship" means, for the purposes of regulation 7, an offender, other than an offender to whom paragraph (3) or (4) applies where—
   (a) she is a single woman who is pregnant and in respect of whom the Secretary of State is satisfied that, unless a jobseeker's allowance is paid, she will suffer hardship;
   (b) he is a single person who is responsible for a young person, and the Secretary of State is satisfied that, unless a jobseeker's allowance is paid, the young person will suffer hardship;

(SI 2001/1395, reg. 6)

(c) he is a member of [² a couple] where—
  [² (i) at least one member of the couple is a woman who is pregnant; and]
  (ii) the Secretary of State is satisfied that, unless a jobseeker's allowance is paid, she will suffer hardship;
(d) he is a member of a polygamous marriage and—
  (i) one member of the marriage is pregnant; and
  (ii) the Secretary of State is satisfied that, unless a jobseeker's allowance is paid, she will suffer hardship;
(e) he is a member of [² a couple] or of a polygamous marriage where—
  (i) one or both members of the couple, or one or more members of the polygamous marriage, are responsible for a child or young person; and
  (ii) the Secretary of State is satisfied that, unless a jobseeker's allowance is paid, the child or young person will suffer hardship;
(f) he has an award of a jobseeker's allowance which includes or would, if a claim for a jobseeker's allowance from him were to succeed, have included in his applicable amount a disability premium and the Secretary of State is satisfied that, unless a jobseeker's allowance is paid, the person who would satisfy the conditions of entitlement to that premium would suffer hardship;
(g) he suffers, or his partner suffers, from a chronic medical condition which results in functional capacity being limited or restricted by physical impairment and the Secretary of State is satisfied that—
  (i) the suffering has already lasted, or is likely to last, for not less than 26 weeks; and
  (ii) unless a jobseeker's allowance is paid to the offender, the probability is that the health of the person suffering would, within 2 weeks of the Secretary of State making his decision, decline further than that of a normally healthy adult and that person would suffer hardship;
(h) he does, or his partner does, or in the case of an offender who is married to more than one person under a law which permits polygamy, at least one of those persons does, devote a considerable portion of each week to caring for another person who—
  (i) is in receipt of an attendance allowance or the care component of disability living allowance at one of the two higher rates prescribed under section 72(4) of the Benefits Act;
  (ii) has claimed either attendance allowance or disability living allowance, but only for so long as the claim has not been determined, or for 26 weeks from the date of claiming, whichever is the earlier; or
  (iii) has claimed either attendance allowance or disability living allowance and has an award of either attendance allowance or the care component of disability living allowance at one of the two higher rates prescribed under section 72(4) of the Benefits Act for a period commencing after the date on which that claim was made, and the Secretary of State is satisfied, after taking account of the factors set out in paragraph (5), in so far as they are appropriate to the particular circumstances of the case, that the person providing the care will not be able to continue doing so unless a jobseeker's allowance is paid to the offender;

The Social Security (Breach of Community Order) Regulations 2001

    (i) he is a person or is the partner of a person to whom section 16 of the Jobseekers Act applies by virtue of a direction issued by the Secretary of State, except where the person to whom the direction applies does not satisfy the requirements of section 1(2)(a) to (c) of that Act;

    (j) he is a person—
- (i) to whom section 3(1)(f)(iii) of the Jobseekers Act (persons under the age of 18) applies, or is the partner of such a person; and
- (ii) in respect of whom the Secretary of State is satisfied that the person will, unless a jobseeker's allowance is paid, suffer hardship; or

    (k) he is a person—
- (i) who, pursuant to the Children Act 1989, was being looked after by a local authority;
- (ii) with whom the local authority had a duty, pursuant to that Act, to take reasonable steps to keep in touch; or
- (iii) who, pursuant to that Act, qualified for advice and assistance from a local authority,

but in respect of whom head (i), (ii) or, as the case may be, (iii) above had not applied for a period of three years or less as at the date on which he complies with the requirements of regulation 9; and

- (iv) as at the date on which he complies with the requirements of regulation 9, is under the age of 21.

(2) Except in a case to which paragraph (3) or (4) applies, an offender shall, for the purposes of regulation 8, be deemed to be a person in hardship where, after taking account of the factors set out in paragraph (5) in so far as they are appropriate to the particular circumstances of the case, the Secretary of State is satisfied that he or his partner will suffer hardship unless a jobseeker's allowance is paid to him.

(3) In paragraphs (1) and (2), the offender shall not be deemed to be a person in hardship—

    (a) where he is entitled, or his partner is entitled, to income support or where he or his partner fall within a category of persons prescribed for the purpose of section 124(1)(e) of the Benefits Act; or

    (b) during any period in respect of which it has been determined that a jobseeker's allowance is not payable to him pursuant to section 19 of the Jobseekers Act (circumstances in which a jobseeker's allowance is not payable).

(4) Paragraph (1)(h) shall not apply in a case where the person being cared for resides in a [¹ care home, an Abbeyfield Home or an independent hospital].

(5) Factors which, for the purposes of paragraphs (1) and (2), the Secretary of State is to take into account in determining whether the offender is a person in hardship are—

    (a) the presence in the offender's family of a person who satisfies the requirements for a disability premium specified in paragraphs 13 and 14 of Schedule 1 to the Jobseeker's Allowance Regulations or for a disabled child premium specified in paragraph 16 of that Schedule to those Regulations;

    (b) the resources which, without a jobseeker's allowance, are likely to be available to the offender's family, the amount by which these resources fall short of the amount applicable in his case in accordance

(SI 2001/1395, reg.6)

with regulation 11 (applicable amount in hardship cases), the amount of any resources which may be available to members of the offender's family from any person in the offender's household who is not a member of his family, and the length of time for which those factors are likely to persist;
(c) whether there is a substantial risk that essential items, including food, clothing, heating and accommodation, will cease to be available to the claimant or to a member of the offender's family, or will be available at considerably reduced levels and the length of time those factors are likely to persist.

(6) In determining the resources available to the offender's family under paragraph (5)(b), any training premium or top-up payment paid pursuant to the Employment and Training Act 1973 shall be disregarded.

AMENDMENTS

1. Social Security (Care Homes and Independent Hospitals) Regulations 2005 (SI 2005/2687), reg.14(2) (October 24, 2005).
2. Civil Partnership (Pensions, Social Security and Child Support) (Consequential, etc. Provisions) Order 2005 (SI 2005/2877), Sch.3, para.33(2) (December 5, 2005).

GENERAL NOTE

Regulation 6 defines the phrase "person in hardship" for the purposes of regs 7 and 8. The definition is almost identical to the definition in reg.140 of the Jobseeker's Allowance Regulations for the purposes of that benefit. Readers are referred to the commentary to that regulation in Vol.II.

2.14

Circumstances in which an income-based jobseeker's allowance is payable to an offender who is a person in hardship

7.—(1) This regulation applies to a person in hardship within the meaning of regulation 6(1) and is subject to the provisions of regulations 9 and 10.

2.15

(2) An income-based jobseeker's allowance shall be payable to a person in hardship even though section 62(2) of the Act prevents payment of a jobseeker's allowance to him but the allowance shall be payable only if and for so long as he satisfies the conditions for entitlement to an income-based jobseeker's allowance.

GENERAL NOTE

Where the offender satisfies the conditions of entitlement of an income-based jobseeker's allowance and s/he, or a member of her/his family is a "person in hardship" as defined in reg.6(1), that allowance remains payable despite the community sentence sanction. However, payment is at the reduced rates set out in reg.11. Payment is also subject to the offender's applying for the hardship payment on a (signed) approved form (reg.9) and providing information as to the circumstances of the person who is claimed to be "in hardship". Where the offender or family member is a "person in hardship" as defined by reg.6(2), reg.8 below applies.

2.16

Further circumstances in which an income-based jobseeker's allowance is payable to an offender who is a person in hardship

8.—(1) This regulation applies to a person in hardship within the meaning of regulation 6(2) and is subject to the provisions of regulations 9 and 10.

2.17

(2) An income-based jobseeker's allowance shall be payable to a person in hardship even though section 62(2) of the Act prevents payment of a jobseeker's allowance to him but the allowance—

The Social Security (Breach of Community Order) Regulations 2001

(a) shall not be payable under this paragraph in respect of the first 14 days of the prescribed period; and
(b) shall be payable thereafter only if and for so long as he satisfies the conditions for entitlement to an income-based jobseeker's allowance.

GENERAL NOTE

Offenders who are entitled to income-based jobseeker's allowance and who are, or who have a family member who is, a "person in hardship" as defined in reg.6(2) are not entitled to a hardship payment for the first two weeks of the sanction period. Thereafter benefit is paid on the same basis as in reg.7.

Conditions for payment of income-based jobseeker's allowance

2.18

9.—(1) An income-based jobseeker's allowance shall not be payable in accordance with regulation 7 or 8 except where the offender has—
(a) furnished on a form approved for the purpose by the Secretary of State or in such other form as he may in any particular case approve, a statement of the circumstances he relies upon to establish entitlement under regulation 6(1), or, as the case may be 6(2); and
(b) signed the statement.
(2) The completed and signed form shall be delivered by the offender to such office as the Secretary of State may specify.

GENERAL NOTE

See the General Note to reg.7 above.

Provision of information

2.19

10. For the purposes of section 62(4)(b) of the Act, the offender shall provide to the Secretary of State information as to the circumstances of the person alleged to be in hardship.

GENERAL NOTE

See the General Note to reg.7 above.

Applicable amount in hardship cases

2.20

11.—(1) The weekly applicable amount of a person to whom an income-based jobseeker's allowance is payable in accordance with this Part shall be reduced by a sum equivalent to 40% or, in a case where the offender or any other member of his family is either pregnant or seriously ill, 20% of the following amount—
(a) where the offender is a single claimant aged not less than 18 but less than 25 or a member of a couple or polygamous marriage where one member is aged not less than 18 but less than 25 and the other member or, in the case of a polygamous marriage each other member, is a person under 18 who is not eligible for an income-based jobseeker's allowance under section 3(1)(f)(iii) of the Jobseekers Act or is not subject to a direction under section 16 of that Act, the amount specified in paragraph 1(1)(d) of Schedule 1 to the Jobseeker's Allowance Regulations;
(b) where the offender is a single claimant aged not less than 25 or a member of a couple or a polygamous marriage (other than a member

(SI 2001/1395, reg.11)

of a couple or polygamous marriage to whom subparagraph (a) applies) at least one of whom is aged not less than 18, the amount specified in paragraph 1(1)(e) of Schedule 1 to the Jobseeker's Allowance Regulations.

(2) A reduction under paragraph (1) shall, if it is not a multiple of 5p, be rounded to the nearest such multiple or, if it is a multiple of 2.5p but not of 5p, to the next lower multiple of 5p.

GENERAL NOTE

This is the equivalent of reg.145 of the Jobseeker's Allowance Regulations 1996 (see Vol.II). Benefit is reduced by 40 per cent of the basic personal allowance for a single claimant or by 20 per cent of that amount if the offender or a member of her/his family is pregnant or seriously ill. The latter phrase is, again, undefined.

PART IV

HARDSHIP FOR JOINT-CLAIM COUPLES

Meaning of "couple in hardship"

12.—(1) In this Part of these Regulations, a "couple in hardship" means, for the purposes of regulation 13, a joint-claim couple, other than a couple to whom paragraph (3) or (4) applies, who are claiming a joint-claim jobseeker's allowance jointly where at least one member of that couple is an offender and where—

 (a) [2 at least one member of the couple is a woman who is pregnant] and the Secretary of State is satisfied that, unless a joint-claim jobseeker's allowance is paid, she will suffer hardship;

 (b) one or both members of the couple are members of a polygamous marriage, one member of the marriage is pregnant and the Secretary of State is satisfied that, unless a joint-claim jobseeker's allowance is paid, she will suffer hardship;

 (c) the award of a joint-claim jobseeker's allowance includes, or would, if a claim for a jobseeker's allowance from the couple were to succeed, have included in their applicable amount a disability premium and the Secretary of State is satisfied that, unless a jointclaim jobseeker's allowance is paid, the member of the couple who would have caused the disability premium to be applicable to the couple would suffer hardship;

 (d) either member of the couple suffers from a chronic medical condition which results in functional capacity being limited or restricted by physical impairment and the Secretary of State is satisfied that—

  (i) the suffering has already lasted or is likely to last, for not less than 26 weeks; and

  (ii) unless a joint-claim jobseeker's allowance is paid, the probability is that the health of the person suffering would, within two weeks of the Secretary of State making his decision, decline further than that of a normally healthy adult and the member of the couple who suffers from that condition would suffer hardship;

2.21

The Social Security (Breach of Community Order) Regulations 2001

(e) either member of the couple, or where a member of that couple is married to more than one person under a law which permits polygamy, one member of that marriage, devotes a considerable portion of each week to caring for another person who—
   (i) is in receipt of an attendance allowance or the care component of disability living allowance at one of the two higher rates prescribed under section 72(4) of the Benefits Act;
   (ii) has claimed either attendance allowance or disability living allowance, but only for so long as the claim has not been determined, or for 26 weeks from the date of claiming, whichever is the earlier; or
   (iii) has claimed either attendance allowance or disability living allowance and has an award of either attendance allowance or the care component of disability living allowance at one of the two higher rates prescribed under section 72(4) of the Benefits Act for a period commencing after the date on which that claim was made, and the Secretary of State is satisfied, after taking account of the factors set out in paragraph (5) in so far as they are appropriate to the particular circumstances of the case, that the person providing the care will not be able to continue doing so unless a joint-claim jobseeker's allowance is paid; or
(f) section 16 of the Jobseekers Act applies to either member of the couple by virtue of a direction issued by the Secretary of State, except where the member of the joint-claim couple to whom the direction applies does not satisfy the requirements of section 1(2)(a) to (c) of that Act;
(g) section 3A(1)(e)(ii) of the Jobseekers Act (member of joint-claim couple under the age of 18) applies to either member of the couple and the Secretary of State is satisfied that unless a joint-claim jobseeker's allowance is paid, the couple will suffer hardship; or
(h) one or both members of the couple is a person—
   (i) who, pursuant to the Children Act 1989, was being looked after by a local authority;
   (ii) with whom the local authority had a duty, pursuant to that Act, to take reasonable steps to keep in touch; or
   (iii) who, pursuant to that Act, qualified for advice or assistance from a local authority,
   but in respect of whom head (i), (ii) or, as the case may be, (iii) above had not applied for a period of three years or less as at the date on which the requirements of regulation 16 are complied with; and
   (iv) as at the date on which the requirements of regulation 16 are complied with, that member is, or both of those members are, under the age of 21.

(2) Except in a case to which paragraph (3) or (4) applies, a joint-claim couple shall, for the purposes of regulation 14, be deemed to be a couple in hardship where the Secretary of State is satisfied, after taking account of the factors set out in paragraph (5) in so far as they are appropriate to the particular circumstances of the case, that the couple will suffer hardship unless a joint-claim jobseeker's allowance is paid.

(3) In paragraph (1) and (2), a joint-claim couple shall not be deemed to be a couple in hardship—

(a) where one member of the couple is entitled to income support or falls within a category of persons prescribed for the purposes of section 124(1)(e) of the Benefits Act; or
(b) during a period in respect of which it has been determined that both members of the couple are subject to sanctions for the purposes of section 20A of the Jobseekers Act (denial or reduction of joint-claim jobseeker's allowance).

(4) Paragraph (1)(e) shall not apply in a case where the person being cared for resides in a [¹ care home, an Abbeyfield Home or an independent hospital].

(5) Factors which, for the purposes of paragraphs (1) and (2), the Secretary of State is to take into account in determining whether a joint-claim couple will suffer hardship are—
(a) the presence in the joint-claim couple of a person who satisfies the requirements for a disability premium specified in paragraphs 20H and 20I of Schedule 1 to the Jobseeker's Allowance Regulations;
(b) the resources which, without a joint-claim jobseeker's allowance, are likely to be available to the joint-claim couple, the amount by which these resources fall short of the amount applicable in their case in accordance with regulation 17 (applicable amount in hardship cases for joint-claim couples), the amount of any resources which may be available to the joint-claim couple from any person in the couple's household who is not a member of the family and the length of time for which those factors are likely to persist;
(c) whether there is a substantial risk that essential items, including food, clothing, heating and accommodation, will cease to be available to the joint-claim couple, or will be available at considerably reduced levels, the hardship that will result and the length of time those factors are likely to persist.

(6) In determining the resources available to the offender's family under paragraph (5)(b), any training premium or top-up payment paid pursuant to the Employment and Training Act 1973 shall be disregarded.

AMENDMENTS

1. Social Security (Care Homes and Independent Hospitals) Regulations 2005 (SI 2005/2687), reg.14(3) (October 24, 2005).
2. Civil Partnership (Pensions, Social Security and Child Support) (Consequential, etc. Provisions) Order 2005 (SI 2005/2877), Sch.3, para.33(3) (December 5, 2005).

GENERAL NOTE

This regulation makes provision corresponding to reg.6 for joint-claim couples. See also the commentary to reg.140 of the Jobseeker's Allowance Regulations 1996.

Circumstances in which a joint-claim jobseeker's allowance is payable where a joint-claim couple is a couple in hardship

13.—(1) This regulation applies where a joint-claim couple is a couple in hardship within the meaning of regulation 12(1) and is subject to the provisions of regulations 15 and 16.

(2) A joint-claim jobseeker's allowance shall be payable to a couple in hardship even though section 63(2) of the Act prevents payment of a joint-claim jobseeker's allowance to the couple or section 63(3) of the Act

2.22

reduces the amount of a joint-claim jobseeker's allowance payable to the couple but the allowance shall be payable only if and for so long as—
(a) the joint-claim couple satisfy the other conditions of entitlement to a joint-claim jobseeker's allowance; or
(b) one member satisfies those conditions and the other member comes within any paragraph in Schedule A1 to the Jobseeker's Allowance Regulations (categories of members not required to satisfy conditions in section 1(2B)(b) of the Jobseekers Act).

GENERAL NOTE

This regulation makes provision corresponding to reg.7 for joint-claim couples.

Further circumstances in which a joint-claim jobseeker's allowance is payable to a couple in hardship

2.23

14.—(1) This regulation applies to a couple in hardship falling within regulation 12(2) and is subject to the provisions of regulations 15 and 16.
(2) A joint-claim jobseeker's allowance shall be payable to a couple in hardship even though section 63(2) of the Act prevents payment of a joint-claim jobseeker's allowance to them or section 63(3) of the Act reduces the amount of a joint-claim jobseeker's allowance payable to them but the allowance—
(a) shall not be payable under this paragraph in respect of the first 14 days of the prescribed period; and
(b) shall be payable thereafter only if and for so long as the conditions of entitlement to a joint-claim jobseeker's allowance are satisfied or where one member satisfies those conditions and the other member comes within any paragraph in Schedule A1 to the Jobseeker's Allowance Regulations (categories of members not required to satisfy conditions in section 1(2B)(b) of the Jobseekers Act).

GENERAL NOTE

This regulation makes provision corresponding to reg.8 for joint-claim couples.

Conditions for payment of a joint-claim jobseeker's allowance

2.24

15.—(1) A joint-claim jobseeker's allowance shall not be payable in accordance with regulation 13 or 14 except where either member of the couple has—
(a) furnished on a form approved for the purpose by the Secretary of State or in such other form as he may in any particular case approve, a statement of the circumstances he relies upon to establish entitlement under regulation 12(1) or, as the case may be 12(2); and
(b) signed the statement.
(2) The completed and signed form shall be delivered by a member of the couple to such office as the Secretary of State may specify.

GENERAL NOTE

This regulation makes provision corresponding to reg.9 for joint-claim couples.

Provision of information

2.25

16. For the purposes of section 63(4)(b) of the Act, a member of the couple shall provide to the Secretary of State information as to the circumstances of the alleged hardship of the couple.

(SI 2001/1395, reg.17)

GENERAL NOTE

This regulation makes provision corresponding to reg.10 for joint-claim couples.

Applicable amount of joint-claim couple in hardship cases

17.—(1) The weekly applicable amount of a couple to whom a jointclaim jobseeker's allowance is payable in accordance with this Part shall be reduced by a sum equivalent to 40% or, in a case where a member of the joint-claim couple is either pregnant or seriously ill or where a member of the joint-claim couple is a member of a polygamous marriage and one of those members is either pregnant or seriously ill, 20% of the following amount—
  (a) where one member of the joint-claim couple or of the polygamous marriage is aged not less than 18 but less than 25 and the other member or, in the case of a polygamous marriage, each other member, is a person under 18 to whom section 3A(1)(e)(ii) of the Jobseekers Act applies or is not subject to a direction under section 16 of that Act, the amount specified in paragraph 1(1)(d) of Schedule 1 to the Jobseeker's Allowance Regulations;
  (b) where one member of the joint-claim couple or of the polygamous marriage (other than a member of a couple or polygamous marriage to whom sub-paragraph (a) applies) at least one of whom is aged not less than 18, the amount specified in paragraph 1(1)(e) of Schedule 1 to the Jobseeker's Allowance Regulations.
(2) A reduction under paragraph (1) shall, if it is not a multiple of 5p, be rounded to the nearest such multiple or, if it is a multiple of 2.5p but not of 5p, to the next lower multiple of 5p.

GENERAL NOTE

This regulation makes provision corresponding to reg.11 for joint-claim couples.

PART V

INFORMATION

Notification at the time of the laying of the information

18. As soon as practicable after an information has been laid in England and Wales which could result in a determination the making of which would result in the imposition by or under one or both of sections 62 and 63 of the Act of any restrictions, the chief officer of the local probation board or other person acting on his behalf shall notify the Secretary of State in writing of—
  (a) the full name, address and date of birth of the person to whom the information relates;
  (b) the Probation Service Offender Reference Number relating to that person;
  (c) the date on which a court imposed the requirement to comply with the requirements of the relevant community order in respect of which the information was laid; and
  (d) the court at which it will be determined whether or not there has been a failure, without reasonable excuse, to comply with the requirements of a relevant community order.

The Social Security (Breach of Community Order) Regulations 2001

GENERAL NOTE

Regulation 18 is made under s.64(2)(a) of CSPSSA 2000. In England and Wales, the laying of an information by an officer of the local parole board is the first stage in the process which might lead to a court making an order that the offender has failed, without reasonable excuse, to comply with the requirements of a relevant community order. Notification to the Secretary of State is required at this stage so that he may comply with his duty to notify the claimant (or the claimant and her/his partner in the case of a joint claim couple) under s.64(4).

Notification at the time of making the determination

2.28 19. As soon as practicable after a court has determined that there has been a failure, without reasonable excuse, to comply with the requirements of a relevant community order, the chief officer of the local probation board or other person acting on his behalf shall notify the Secretary of State in writing of—
  (a) the full name, address and date of birth of the person to whom the determination relates;
  (b) the Probation Service Offender Reference Number relating to that person; and
  (c) the date on which, and the place at which, the court determined that there had been a failure, without reasonable excuse, to comply with the requirements of a relevant community order.

GENERAL NOTE

Reg.19 is made under s.64(2)(b) of CSPSSA 2000. Its purpose is self-evident: if the Secretary of State is not notified that an order within s.62 has been made, he cannot arrange for the imposition of the sanction required by that section.

Notification where determination is set aside

2.29 20. As soon as practicable after a court has quashed or set aside a determination by that or any other court that there has been a failure, without reasonable excuse, to comply with the requirements of a relevant community order, the chief officer of the local probation board or other person acting on his behalf shall notify the Secretary of State in writing of—
  (a) the full name, address and date of birth of the person to whom the determination relates;
  (b) the date on which, and the place at which, a court had determined that there had been a failure, without reasonable excuse, to comply with the requirements of a relevant community order;
  (c) the Probation Service Offender Reference Number relating to that person; and
  (d) the date on which, and the place at which, that or any other court quashed or set aside the determination that there had been a failure, without reasonable excuse, to comply with the requirements of a relevant community order.

GENERAL NOTE

Regulation 20 is made under s.64(2)(c) of CSPSSA 2000. Again its purpose is self-evident: if the court decision which led to the imposition of the sanction is quashed or set aside, the Secretary of State needs to know that fact so that payment

(SI 2001/1395, reg.20)

of benefit may, in an appropriate case, be reinstated in full and so that the payment of arrears required by ss.62(6) and 63(6) can be made.

Use or supply of information for other purposes

21. Information relating to community orders or social security which is either held by the Secretary of State as at the date on which these Regulations come into force or which subsequently comes into existence, may be used or supplied by the Secretary of State, in so far as it relates to sections 62 to 65 of the Act, for the purposes of research, monitoring or evaluation or for the purpose of maintaining statistics.

GENERAL NOTE

Regulation 21 is made under s.64(6) to (8) of CSPSSA 2000. It confirms that information held by the Secretary of State in relation to the operation of the loss of benefit provisions may be used for research, for monitoring and evaluation of the operation of those provisions and for statistical purposes.

The Social Security (Claims and Payments) Regulations 1979 (SI 1979/628) can now be found in Volume I, since they relate solely to claims of industrial injuries benefit.

The Social Security (Claims and Payments) Regulations 1987

(SI 1987/1968) (AS AMENDED)

ARRANGEMENTS OF REGULATIONS

PART I

General

1. Citation and commencement
2. Interpretation

PART II

Claims

3. Claims not required for entitlement to benefit in certain cases
4. Making a claim for benefit
4A. Further provisions as to claims
4B. Forwarding claims and information
5. Amendment and withdrawal of claim
6. Date of claim
7. Evidence and information
8. Attendance in person
9. Interchange with claims for other benefits
10. Claim for incapacity benefit or severe disablement allowance where no entitlement to statutory sick pay or statutory maternity pay
11. Special provisions where it is certified that a woman is expected to be confined or where she has been confined
12. Self-certified claims for first 7 days of a spell of incapacity for work (*revoked*)

359

The Social Security (Claims and Payments) Regulations 1987

13. Advance claims and awards
13A. Advance award of disability living allowance
13B. Advance claim for and award of disability working allowance
13C. Further claim for and award of disability living allowance
14. Advance claim for and award of maternity allowance
15. Advance notice of retirement and claim for and award of pension
15A. Cold weather payments (*revoked*)
16. Date of entitlement under an award for the purpose of payability of benefit and effective date of change of rate
17. Duration of awards
18. Duration of disallowance (*revoked*)
19. Time for claiming benefit

PART III

Payments

20. Time and manner of payment: general provision
20A. Payment a presentation of an involvement for payment benefit
21. Direct credit transfer
22. Long term benefits
23. Child benefit and guardians's allowance
24. Incapacity benefit, maternity allowance and severe disablement allowance
25. Payment of attendance allowance and constant attendance allowance at a daily rate
26. Income support
26A. Jobseeker's allowance
27. Working families tax credit and disabled person's tax credit
28. Fractional amounts of benefit
29. Payments to persons under age 18
30. Payments on death
30A. Payment of arrears of joint-claim jobseekers allowance where the nominated person can no longer be traced
31. Time and manner of payments of industrial injuries gratuities
32. Information to be given and changes to be notified

PART IV

Third Parties

33. Persons unable to act
34. Payment to another person on the beneficiary's behalf
34A. Deductions of mortgage interest which shall be made from benefit and paid to qualifying lenders
35. Deductions which may be made from benefit and paid to third parties
35A. *Revoked*
36. Payment to a partner as alternative payee

PART V

Extinguishment

37. Suspension in individual cases (*revoked*)
37A. Suspension in identical cases (*revoked*)

(SI 1987/1968) (as amended)

37AA. Withholding of benefit in prescribed circumstances (*revoked*)
37AB. Payment of withheld benefit (*revoked*)
37B. Withholding payment of arrears of benefit (*revoked*)
38. Extinguishment of right to payment of sums by way of benefit where payment is not obtained within the prescribed period.

Part VI

Mobility Component of Disability Living Allowance and Disability Living Allowance for Children

42. Cases where allowance not to be payable
43. Children
44. Payment of disability living allowance on behalf of a beneficiary
45. Power for the Secretary of State to terminate an arrangement
46. Restriction on duration of arrangements by the Secretary of State

Part VII

Miscellaneous

47. Instruments of payment, etc and instruments for benefit payment
48. Revocations

SCHEDULES

1. PART I—Benefit claims and other benefit which may be treated as if claimed in addition or in the alternative
PART II—Interchange of claims for child benefit with claims for other benefits
2. Special provisions relating to claims for unemployment benefit during period connected with public holidays
3. Duration of disallowance (*revoked*)
4. Prescribed times for claiming benefit
5. Miscellaneous provisions which vary the prescribed times under Schedule 4 (*revoked*)
6. Days for payment of long term benefits
7. Manner and time of payment, effective date of change of circumstances and commencement of entitlement in income support cases
8. Election to have child benefit paid weekly
9. Deductions from benefit and direct payment to third parties
9A. Deductions of mortgage interest from benefit and payment to qualifying lenders
9B. Deductions from benefit in respect of child support maintenance and payment to persons with care
9C. Electronic communication
10. Revocation (not reproduced)

Whereas a draft of this instrument was laid before Parliament and approved by resolution of each House of Parliament:

Now therefore, the Secretary of State for Social Services, in exercise of the powers conferred by sections 165A and 166(2) of the Social Security Act 1975, section 6(1) of the Child Benefit Act 1975, sections 21(7), 51(1)(a) to (s), 54(1) and 84(1) of the Social Security Act 1986 and, as regards the revocations set out in Schedule 10 to this instrument, the powers specified in that Schedule, and all other powers enabling him in that behalf by this instrument which contains only regulations made under the

The Social Security (Claims and Payments) Regulations 1987

sections of the Social Security Act 1986 specified above and provisions consequential on those sections and which is made before the end of a period of 12 months from the commencement of those sections, makes the following Regulations:

PART I

GENERAL

Citation and commencement

2.33 1. These Regulations may be cited as the Social Security (Claims and Payments) Regulations 1987 and shall come into operation on 11th April 1988.

Interpretation

2.34 2.—(1) In these Regulations, unless the context otherwise requires—
[20 . . .];
[27 "the 1992 Act" means the Social Security Administration Act 1992;]
[23 "the 2000 Act" means the Electronic Communications Act 2000;]
[22 "the 2002 Act" means the State Pension Credit Act 2002;]
[22 "advance period" means the period specified in regulation 4E(2);]
[17 "appropriate office" means an office of the Department for Work and Pensions [or, in the case of a Crown servant posted overseas or his partner, a Regimental Administrative Office, Unit Personnel Office, Personnel Management Squadron Office, British Embassy, High Commission or Consulate;]
[15 "bereavement allowance" means an allowance referred to in section 39B) of the Contributions and Benefits Act;
"bereavement benefit" means a benefit referred to in section 20(1)(ea) of the Contributions and Benefits Act;]
[21 "the Board means the Commissioners of Inland Revenue; and references to "the Board" in these regulations have effect only with respect to working families tax credit;]
[11 "claim for asylum" has the same meaning as in the Asylum and Immigration Appeals Act 1993;]
"claim for benefit" includes—
  (a) an application for a declaration that an accident was an industrial accident;
  (b) [3. . .]
  (c) an application for [14a revision under section 9 of the Social Security Act 1998 or a supersession under section 10 of that Act] a decision for the purpose of obtaining any increase of benefit [6in respect of a child or adult dependant under the Social Security Act 1975 or an increase in disablement benefit under section 60 (special hardship), 61 (constant attendance), 62 (hospital treatment allowance) or 63 (exceptionally severe disablement) of the Social Security Act 1975], but does not include any other application for [14a revision under section 9 of the Social Security Act 1998 or a supersession under section 10 of that Act] of a decision;

(SI 1987/1968, reg. 2) (as amended)

[¹⁵ "Contributions and Benefits Act" means the Social Security Contributions and Benefits Act 1992;]

[²⁵ "couple" means—
(a) a man and woman who are married to each other and are members of the same household;
(b) a man and woman who are not married to each other but are living together as husband and wife;
(c) two people of the same sex who are civil partners of each other and are members of the same household; or
(d) two people of the same sex who are not civil partners of each other but are living together as if they were civil partners, and for the purposes of paragraph (d), two people of the same sex are to be regarded as living together as if they were civil partners if, but only if, they would be regarded as living together as husband and wife were they instead two people of the opposite sex;]

[¹⁷ "Crown servant posted overseas" means a person performing the duties of any office or employment under the Crown in right of the United Kingdom who is, or was prior to his posting, ordinarily resident in the United Kingdom;]

[¹³ " 'disabled person's tax credit' and 'working families' tax credit" shall be construed in accordance with section 1(1) of the Tax Credits Act 1999]

[²³ "electronic communication" has the same meaning as in section 15(1) of the 2000 Act;]

[²² "guarantee credit" is to be construed in accordance with sections 1 and 2 of the 2002 Act;]

[²⁶ . . .]

[¹⁰ "the Jobseekers Act" means the Jobseekers Act 1995;
"jobseeker's allowance" means an allowance payable under Part I of the Jobseekers Act;
"the Jobseeker's Allowance Regulations" means the Jobseeker's Allowance Regulations 1996;]

[¹⁶ "joint-claim couple" and "joint-claim jobseeker's allowance" have the same meaning in these Regulations as they have in the Jobseekers Act by virtue of section 1(4) of that Act;]

"long-term benefits" means any retirement pension, [²⁴ a shared additional pension] a widowed mother's allowance, a widow's pension, [¹⁵widowed parent's allowance, bereavement allowance,] attendance allowance, [⁵disability living allowance], [¹⁹ carer's allowance], [¹². . .], any pension or allowance for industrial injury or disease and any increase in any such benefit;

[²⁵ . . .];

"partner" means one of a [²⁵ couple]; [⁴. . .]

[⁹ "pension fund holder" means with respect to a personal pension scheme or retirement annuity contract, the trustees, managers or scheme administrators, as the case may be, of the scheme or contract concerned;]

[⁹ "personal pension scheme" has the same meaning as in section 1 of the Pension Schemes Act 1993 in respect of employed earners and in the case of self-employed earners, includes a scheme approved by the Board of Inland Revenue under Chapter IV of Part XIV of the Income and Corporation Taxes Act 1988;]

[²² "qualifying age" has the same meaning as in the 2002 Act by virtue of section 1(6) of that Act;]

The Social Security (Claims and Payments) Regulations 1987

[[11] "refugee" means a person recorded by the Secretary of State as a refugee within the definition in Article 1 of the Convention relating to the Status of Refugees done at Geneva on 28th July 1951 as extended by Article 1(2) of the Protocol relating to the Status of Refugees done at New York on 31st January 1967;]

[[20] "relevant authority" means a person within section 72(2) of the Welfare Reform and Pensions Act 1999;]

[[9] "retirement annuity contract" means a contract or trust scheme approved under Chapter III of Part XIV of the Income and Corporation Taxes Act 1988;]

[[24] "shared additional pension" means a shared additional pension under section 55A of the Contributions and Benefits Act;]

[[22] "state pension credit" means state pension credit under the 2002 Act;]

[[25] . . .]

"week" means a period of 7 days beginning with midnight between Saturday and Sunday.

[[15] "widowed parent's allowance" means an allowance referred to in section 39A of the Contributions and Benefits Act;]

(2) Unless the context otherwise requires, any reference in these Regulations to—

(a) a numbered regulation, Part or Schedule is a reference to the regulation, Part or Schedule bearing that number in these Regulations and any reference in a regulation to a numbered paragraph is a reference to the paragraph of that regulation having that number;

(b) a benefit includes any benefit under the Social Security Act 1975 [SSCBA], child benefit under Part I of the Child Benefit Act 1975, income support [[22] state pension credit] [[7], family credit and disability working allowance under the Social Security Act 1986 [SSCBA] and any social fund payments such as are mentioned in section 32(2)(a) [[1]and section 32(2A)] of that Act [SSCBA, s.138(1)(a) and (2)] [[10]and a jobseeker's allowance under Part I of the Jobseekers Act].

[[10](2A) References in regulations 20, 21 (except paragraphs (3) and (3A)), 29, 30, 32 to 34, 37 (except paragraph (1A)), 37A, 37AA (except paragraph (3)), 37AB, 37B, 38 and 47 to "benefit", "income support" or "a jobseeker's allowance", include a reference to a back to work bonus which, by virtue of regulation 25 of the Social Security (Back to Work Bonus) Regulations 1996, is to be treated as payable as income support or, as the case may be, as a jobseeker's allowance [[24] and a shared additional pension].]

(3) For the purposes of the provisions of these Regulations relating to the making of claims every increase of benefit under the Social Security Act 1975 [SSCBA] shall be treated as a separate benefit [[12]. . .].

[[22] (4) In these Regulations references to "beneficiaries" include any person entitled to state pension credit.]

AMENDMENTS

1. The Social Security (Common Provisions) Miscellaneous Amendments Regulations 1988 (SI 1988/1725), reg.3 (November 7, 1988).

2. Transfer of Functions (Health and Social Security) Order 1988 (SI 1988/1843), art.3(4) (November 28, 1988).

3. The Social Security (Medical Evidence, Claims and Payments) Amendment Regulations 1989 (SI 1989/1686), reg.3 (October 9, 1989).

4. The Social Security (Miscellaneous Provisions) Amendment Regulations 1991 (SI 1991/2284), reg.5 (November 1, 1991).

(SI 1987/1968, reg. 2) (as amended)

5. The Social Security (Claims and Payments) Amendment Regulations 1991 (SI 1991/2741), reg.2(a) (February 3, 1992).
6. The Social Security (Miscellaneous Provisions) Amendment Regulations 1992 (SI 1992/247), reg.9 (March 9, 1992).
7. The Social Security (Claims and Payments) Amendment Regulations 1991 (SI 1991/2741), reg.2(b) (March 10, 1992).
8. The Social Security (Claims and Payments) Amendment (No.4) Regulations 1994 (SI 1994/3196), reg.2 (January 10, 1995).
9. Income-related benefit Schemes and Social Security (Claims and Payments) (Miscellaneous Amendments) Regulations 1995 (SI 1995/2303), reg.10(2) (October 2, 1995).
10. The Social Security (Claims and Payments) (Jobseeker's Allowance Consequential Amendments) Regulations 1996 (SI 1996/1460), reg.2(2) (October 7, 1996).
11. The Income Support and Social Security (Claims and Payments) (Miscellaneous Amendments) Regulations 1996 (SI 1996/2431), reg.7(a) (October 15, 1996).
12. The Social Security (Claims and Payments) Amendment Regulations 1999 (SI 1999/2358), reg.2 (September 20, 1999) and The Child Benefit, Child Support and Social Security (Miscellaneous Amendments) Regulations 1996 (SI 1996/1803), reg.18 (April 7, 1997).
13. The Tax Credits (Claims and Payments) (Amendment) Regulations 1999 (SI 1999/2572), reg.3 (October 5, 1999).
14. The Social Security Act 1998 (Commencement No.9 and Savings and Consequential and Transitional Provisions) Order 1999 (SI 1999/2422), Sch.7 (September 6, 1999).
15. The Social Security (Benefits for Widows and Widowers) (Consequential Amendments) Regulations 2000, reg.9 (SI 2000/1483) (April 9, 2001).
16. The Social Security (Joint Claims: Consequential Amendments) Regulations 2000 (SI 2000/1982), reg.2(2) (March 19, 2001).
17. Tax Credits (Miscellaneous Amendments No.4) Regulations 2002 (SI 2002/696), reg.2 (July 23, 2002).
18. Social Security (Electronic Communications) (Child Benefit) Order 2002 (SI 2002/1789), art.2 (October 28, 2002); revoked with effect from December 1, 2003.
19. The Social Security Amendment (Carer's Allowance) Regulations 2002 (SI 2002/2497), Sch.2 (October 28, 2002).
20. Social Security Act 1998, Sch.6 (November 29, 1999).
21. Tax Credits (Claims and Payments) (Amendment) Regulations 1999 (SI 1999/2572), reg.3 (October 5, 1999).
22. State Pension Credit (Consequential, Transitional and Miscellaneous Provisions) Regulations 2002, SI 2002/3019, reg.3 (April 7, 2003).
23. The Social Security (Electronic Communications) (Carer's Allowance) Order 2003 (SI 2003/2800), reg.2 (December 1, 2003).
24. The Social Security (Shared Additional Pension) (Miscellaneous Amendments) Regulations 2005 (SI 2005/1551) (July 6, 2005).
25. The Civil Partnership (Pensions, Social Security and Child Support) (Consequential etc. Provisions) Order 2005 (SI 2005/2887) (December 5, 2005).
26. The Social Security (Miscellaneous Amendments) (No.2) Regulations 2006 (SI 2006/832), reg.2 (April 10, 2006).
27. The Social Security (Claims and Payments) Amendment (No. 2) Regulations 2006 (SI 2006/3188) (December 27, 2006).

GENERAL NOTE

Section 15(1) of the Electronic Communications Act 2000 defines "electronic communication" as follows:

2.35

" 'electronic communication' means a communication transmitted (whether from one person to another, from one device to another or from a person to a device or vice versa)—

The Social Security (Claims and Payments) Regulations 1987

(a) by means of a telecommunication system (within the meaning of the Telecommunications Act 1984); or
(b) by other means but while in an electronic form;"

PART II

CLAIMS

Claims not required for entitlement to benefit in certain cases

3. It shall not be a condition of entitlement to benefit that a claim be made for it in the following cases—
(a) In the case of a Category C retirement pension where the beneficiary is in receipt of—
  (i) another retirement pension under the Social Security Act 1975; or
  (ii) widow's benefit under Chapter 1 of Part II of that Act; or
  (iii) benefit by virtue of section 39(4) of that Act corresponding to a widow's pension or a widowed mother's allowance;
  (iv) bereavement benefit under Part II of the Contributions and Benefits Act;]
(b) in the case of a Category D retirement pension where the beneficiary—
  (i) was ordinarily resident in great Britain on the day on which he attained 80 years of age; and
  (ii) is in receipt of another retirement pension under the Social Security Act 1975;
(c) age addition in any case;
(d) in the case of a Category A or B retirement pension—
  (i) where the beneficiary is a woman over the age of 65 and entitled to a widowed mother's allowance [⁶ or widowed parent's allowance], on her ceasing to be so entitled; or
  (ii) where the beneficiary is a woman under the age of 65 and in receipt of widow's pension [⁶ or bereavement allowance], on her attaining that age
(e) [¹in the case of retirement allowance]
(f) [². . .]
(g) [³ in the case of a jobseeker's allowance where—
  (i) that allowance has previously been claimed and an award made;
  (ii) the Secretary of State has directed under regulation [⁴ 16(2) of the Social Security and Child Support (Decisions and Appeals) Regulations 1999] that payment under that award be suspended for a definite or indefinite period on the ground that a question arises whether the conditions for entitlement to that allowance are or were fulfilled or the award ought to be revised under [⁴ section 9 of the Social Security Act 1998 or superseded under section 10 of that Act]
  (iii) subsequently that suspension expires or is cancelled in respect of a part only of the period for which it has been in force;
  (iv) it is then determined that the award should be revised [⁴ or superseded] to the effect that there was no entitlement to the allowance in respect of all or any part of the period between the start of the period over which the award has been suspended and the date when the suspension expires or is cancelled; and

(SI 1987/1968, reg. 3) (as amended)

      (v) there are no other circumstances which cast doubt on the claimant's entitlement.]
  (h) [⁵ in the case of income support where the beneficiary—
      (i) is a person to whom regulation [⁸ . . .] [⁷ or 6(5)] of the Income Support (General) Regulations 1987 (persons not treated as engaged in remunerative work) applies;
      (ii) was in receipt of an income-based jobseeker's allowance on the day before the day on which he was first engaged in the work referred to in sub-paragraph (a) of [⁷ those paragraphs] and
      (iii) would satisfy the conditions of entitlement to income support (apart from the condition of making a claim would apply in the absence of this paragraph) only by virtue of regulation [⁸ . . . [⁷ . . .] regulation 6(6)] of those regulations.]
[⁹ (i) in the case of a shared additional pension where the beneficiary is in receipt of a retirement pension of any category.]

AMENDMENTS

1. The Social Security (Claims and Payments on Account, Overpayments and Recovery) Amendment Regulations 1989 (SI 1989/136), reg.3 (April 10, 1989).
2. The Social Security (Claims and Payments) Amendment (No.2) Regulations 1994 (SI 1994/2943), reg.2 (April 13, 1995).
3. The Social Security (Claims and Payments) (Jobseeker's Allowance Consequential Amendments) Regulations 1996 (SI 1996/1460), reg.2(3) (October 7, 1996).
4. The Social Security Act 1998 (Commencement No.11 and Transitional Provisions) Order 1989 (SI 1999/2860), Sch.3 (October 18, 1999).
5. The Social Security (Miscellaneous Amendments) (No.2) Regulations 1999 (SI 1999/2556), reg.7, (October 4, 1999).
6. The Social Security (Benefits for Widows and Widowers) (Consequential Amendments) Regulations 2000 (SI 2000/1483), reg.9 (April 9, 2001).
7. The Social Security (Miscellaneous Amendments) Regulations 2001 (SI 2001/488), reg.11 (April 9, 2001).
8. Social Security (Back to Work Bonus and Lone Parent Run-on) (Amendment and Revocation) Regulations 2003 (SI 2003/1589), reg.5 (October 25, 2004).
9. The Social Security (Shared Additional Pension) (Miscellaneous Amendments) Regulations 2005 (SI 2005/1551) (July 6, 2005).

GENERAL NOTE

On the meaning of "ordinarily resident" see annotation to reg.5 of the Persons Abroad Regulations in Vol.1

2.37

The Training for Work (Scottish Enterprise and Highlands and Islands Enterprise Programmes) Order 1993 (SI 1993/498) provides that for the purpose of these regulations, a person using facilities under the training programmes to which the Order refers are treated as participating in arrangments for training under s.2(3) of the Enterprise and New Towns (Scotland) Act 1990 and payments made to persons on those programmes are treated as payments in respect of training. See also, to the same effect, the Training for Work (Miscellaneous Provisions) October 1993 (SI 1993/348).

Making a claim for benefit

4.—(1) [¹³ Subject to paragraphs (10) and (11), every] claim for benefit [⁷other than a claim for income support or jobsseeker's allowance] shall be made in writing on a form approved by the Secretary of State [³for the purpose of the benefit for which the claim is made], or in such other

2.38

manner, being in writing, as the Secretary of State [8 or the Board] may accept as sufficient in the circumstances of any particular case.

[7 (1A) In the case of a claim for income support or jobseeker's allowance, the claim shall—
- (a) be made in writing on a form approved by the Secretary of State for the purpose of the benefit for which the claim is made;
- (b) unless any of the reasons specified in paragraph (1B) applies, be made in accordance with the instructions on the form; and
- (c) unless any of the reasons specified in paragraph (1B) applies, include such information and evidence as the form may require in connection with the claim.

(1B) The reasons referred to in paragraph (1A) are—
- (a) [10 subject paragraph (IBA)—
  - (i) the person making the claim is unable to complete the form in accordance with the instructions or to obtain the information or evidence it requires because he has a physical, learning, mental or communication difficulty; and
  - (ii) it is not reasonably practicable for the claimant to obtain assistance from another person to complete the form or obtain the information or evidence;

or
- (b) the information or evidence required by the form does not exist;

or
- (c) the information or evidence required by the form can only be obtained at serious risk of physical or mental harm to the claimant, and it is not reasonably practicable for the claimant to obtain the information or evidence by other means;

or
- (d) the information or evidence required by the form can only be obtained from a third party, and it is not reasonably practicable for the claimant to obtain such information or evidence from such third party;

or
- (e) the Secretary of State is of the opinion that the person making the claim [10or, in the case of claim for a jobseeker's allowance by a joint-claim couple, either member of that couple,] has provided sufficient information or evidence to show that he is not entitled to the benefit for which the claim is made, and that it would be inappropriate to require the form to be completed or further information or evidence to be supplied.

[10 (1BA) In the case of a joint-claim couple claiming a jobseeker's allowance jointly, paragraph (1B)(a) shall not apply to the extent that it is reasonably practicable for a member of a joint-claim couple to whom that sub-paragraph applies to obtain assistance from the other member of that couple.]

(1C) If a person making a claim is unable to complete the claim form or supply the evidence or information it requires because one of the reasons specified in sub-paragraphs (a) to (d) of paragraph (1B) applies, he may so notify an appropriate office by whatever means.]

[18 (1D) In calculating any period of one month for the purposes of paragraph (7) and regulation 6(1A)(b), there shall be disregarded any period commencing on a day on which a person is first notified of a decision that he failed to take part in a work-focused interview and ending on a day on

(SI 1987/1968, reg. 4) (as amended)

which he was notified that that decision has been revised so that the decision as revised is that he did take part.]

(2) [⁸In the case of a claim for working families' tax credit, where a married or unmarried couple is included in the family, the claim shall be made by whichever partner they agree should so claim.

(2A) Where, in a case to which paragraph (2) applies, the partners are unable to agree which of them should make the claim, the Board may in their discretion determine that the claim shall be made by the partner who, on the information available to the Board at the time of their determination, is in their opinion mainly caring for the children.]

(3) [⁵Subject to paragraph (3C),] in the case of a [¹⁶ couple], a claim for income support shall be made by whichever partner they agree should so claim or, in default of agreement, by such one of them as the Secretary of State shall in his discretion determine.

[²(3A) In the case of a married or unmarried couple where both partners satisfy the conditions set out in [⁸ section 129(1) of the Social Security Contributions and Benefits Act 1992], a claim for [⁸ disabled persons tax credit] shall be made by whichever partner they agree should so claim, or in default of agreement, by such one of them as [⁸ the Board] shall determine.]

[⁴(3B) For the purposes of income-based jobseeker's allowance—
   (a) in the case of a [¹⁶ couple], a claim shall be made by whichever partner they agree should so claim or, in default of agreement, by such one of them as the Secretary of State shall in his discretion determine;
   (b) [¹⁰ (b) where there is no entitlement to a contribution-based jobseeker's allowance on a claim made—
       (i) by a member of a joint-claim couple, he subsequently claims a joint-claim jobseeker's allowance with the other member of that couple, the claim made by the couple shall be treated as having been made on the date on which the member of that couple made the claim for a jobseeker's allowance in respect of which there was no entitlement to contribution-based jobseeker's allowance;
       (ii) by one partner and the other partner wishes to claim income-based jobseeker's allowance, the claim made by that other partner shall be treated as having been made on the date on which the first partner made his claim;]
   (c) where entitlement to income-based jobseeker's allowance arises on the expiry of entitlement to contribution-based jobseeker's allowance consequent on a claim made by one partner and the other partner then makes a claim—
       (i) the claim of the first partner shall be terminated; and
       (ii) the claim of the second partner shall be treated as having been made on the day after the entitlement to contribution-based jobseeker's allowance expired.]

[⁵(3C) In the case of a claim for income support for a period to which [⁹ regulation 21ZB(2)] of the Income Support (General) Regulations 1987 (treatment of refugees) refers, the claim shall be made by the refugee or in the case of a [¹⁶ couple] both of whom are refugees, by either of them.]

(4) Where one of a [¹⁶ couple] is entitled to income support under an award and, with his agreement, his partner claims income support that entitlement shall terminate on the day before that claim is made or treated as made.

The Social Security (Claims and Payments) Regulations 1987

[⁶(5) Where a person who wishes to make a claim for benefit and who has not been supplied with an approved form of claim notifies an appropriate office (by whatever means) of his intention to make a claim, he [¹⁰or if he is a member of a joint-claim couple, either member of that couple] shall be supplied, without charge, with such form of claim by such person as the Secretary of State [⁸ or the Board] may appoint or authorise for that purpose.]

[⁴(6) [¹² Subject to paragraphs (6A) to (6D),] A person wishing to make a claim for benefit shall—
   (a) if it is a claim for a jobseeker's allowance, unless the Secretary of State otherwise directs, attend in person at an appropriate office or such other place, and at such time, as the Secretary of State may specify in his case in a [¹⁰notification under regulation 23 or 23A] of the Jobseeker's Allowance Regulations;
   (b) if it is a claim for any other benefit, deliver or send the claim to an appropriate office.]

[¹² (6A) Paragraphs (6B) and (6C) apply in relation to a person—
   (a) who has attained the qualifying age and makes a claim for—
       (i) an attendance allowance, a bereavement benefit, a carer's allowance, a disability living allowance or incapacity benefit; or
       (ii) a retirement pension of any category [¹⁵ or a shared additional pension] for which a claim is required or a winter fuel payment for which a claim is required under regulation 3(1)(b) of the Social Fund Winter Fuel Payment Regulations 2000;
   (b) who has not yet attained the qualifying age and makes a claim for a retirement pension [¹⁵ or a shared additional pension] in advance in accordance with regulation 15(1); [¹⁷ . . .]
   (c) who has attained the qualifying age and makes a claim for income support in respect of a period before 6th October 2003 [¹⁷; or
   (d) who has not attained the qualifying age and who makes a claim for a disability living allowance or a carer's allowance.]

(6B) A person to whom paragraph (6A) applies may make a claim by sending or delivering it to, or by making it in person at—
   (a) an office designated by the Secretary of State for accepting such claims; [¹⁷ . . .]
   (b) the offices of—
       (i) a local authority administering housing benefit or council tax benefit;
       (ii) a person providing to such an authority services relating to housing benefit or council tax benefit; or
       (iii) a person authorised to exercise any function of a local authority relating to housing benefit or council tax benefit,
   if the Secretary of State has arranged with the local authority or person specified in head (ii) or (iii) for them to receive claims in accordance with this sub-paragraph, provided that the claim is made on a form which is approved by the Secretary of State for the purpose.

(6C) Where a person to whom paragraph (6A) applies makes a claim in accordance with paragraph (6B)(b), on receipt of the claim the local authority or other person specified in that sub-paragraph—
   (a) shall forward the claim to the Secretary of State as soon as reasonably practicable;
   (b) may receive information or evidence relating to the claim supplied by—
       (i) the person making, or who has made, the claim; or

(SI 1987/1968, reg.4) (as amended)

(ii) other persons in connection with the claim,
and shall forward it to the Secretary of State as soon as reasonably practicable;
(c) may obtain information or evidence relating to the claim from the person who has made the claim, but not any medical information or evidence except for that which the claimant must provide in accordance with instructions on the form, and shall forward the information or evidence to the Secretary of State as soon as reasonably practicable;
(d) may record information or evidence relating to the claim supplied or obtained in accordance with sub-paragraphs (b) or (c) and may hold the information or evidence (whether as supplied or obtained or as recorded) for the purpose of forwarding it to the Secretary of State; and
(e) may give information and advice with respect to the claim to the person who makes, or who has made, the claim.

[^{14} (6CC) Paragraphs (6C)(b) to (e) apply in respect of information, evidence and advice relating to any claim by a person to whom paragraph (6A) applies, whether the claim is made in accordance with paragraph (6B)(b) or otherwise.]

(6D) The benefits specified in paragraph (6A) are relevant benefits for the purposes of section 7A of the Social Security Administration Act 1992.]

(7) If a claim [^{7} other than a claim for income support or jobseeker's allowance,] is defective at the date when it is received [^{12} in an appropriate office, or other office specified in paragraph (6B) where that paragraph applies,] or has been made in writing but not on the form approved for the time being, the Secretary of State [^{8} or the Board] may refer the claim to the person making it or, as the case may be, supply him with the approved form, and if the form is received properly completed within one month, or such longer period as the Secretary of State [^{8} or the Board] may consider reasonable, from the date on which it is so referred or supplied, the Secretary of State shall treat the claim as if it has been duly made in the first instance.

[^{10} (7A) In the case of a claim for income support, if a defective claim is received, the Secretary of State shall advise the person making the claim of the defect and of the relevant provisions of regulation 6(1A) relating to the date of claim.

(7B) In the case of a claim for a jobseeker's allowance, if a defective claim is received, the Secretary of State shall advise—
(a) in the case of a claim made by a joint-claim couple, each member of the couple of the defect and of the relevant provisions of regulation 6(4ZA) relating to the date of that claim;
(b) in any other case, the person making the claim of the defect and of the relevant provisions of regulation 6(4A) relating to the date of claim.]

(8) A claim, other than a claim for income support or jobseeker's allowance, which is made on the form approved for the time being is, for the purposes of these Regulations, properly completed if completed in accordance with the instructions on the form and defective if not so completed.

[^{8}(8A) Where—
(a) the Board determine under paragraph (2A) that a claim for working families' tax credit shall be made by the partner who in their opinion is mainly caring for the children,

The Social Security (Claims and Payments) Regulations 1987

(b) a claim for working families' tax credit is made by that partner on the form approved for the time being, and
(c) the claim is not completed in accordance with the instructions on the form by reason only that, in consequence of the other partner not agreeing which of them should make the claim, it has not been signed by the other partner

the Board may in their discretion treat that claim as completed in accordance with the instructions on the form for the purposes of paragraph (8), notwithstanding that it has not been signed by the other partner in accordance with those instructions.]

(9) In the case of a claim for income support or jobseeker's allowance, a properly completed claim is a claim which meets the requirements of paragraph (1A) and a defective claim is a claim which does not meet those requirements.]

[[11] (10) This regulation shall not apply to a claim for state pension credit.]

[[13] (11) A claim for graduated retirement benefit [[15], or a shared additional pension] or retirement pension may be made by telephone call to the telephone number specified by the Secretary of State, unless the Secretary of State directs, in any particular case, that the claim must be made in writing.

(12) A claim made by telephone in accordance with paragraph (11) is defective unless the Secretary of State is provided, during that telephone call, with all the information he requires to determine the claim.

(13) Where a claim made by telephone is defective, the Secretary of State may refer the claim to the person making it.

(14) If the person corrects the defect within one month, or such longer period as the Secretary of State considers reasonable, of the date he referred the claim to the person, the Secretary of State shall treat the claim as if it have been duly made in the first instance.]

AMENDMENTS

1. The Social Security (Miscellaneous Provisions) Amendment Regulations 1990 (SI 1990/2208), reg.8 (December 5, 1990).
2. The Social Security (Claims and Payments) Amendment Regulations 1991 (SI 1991/2741), reg.3 (February 3, 1992).
3. The Social Security (Miscellaneous Provisions) Amendment Regulations 1992 (SI 1992/247), reg.10 (March 9, 1992).
4. The Social Security (Claims and Payments) (Jobseeker's Allowance Consequential Amendments) Regulations 1996 (SI 1996/1460), reg.2(4) (October 7, 1996).
5. The Income Support and Social Security (Claims and Payments) (Miscellaneous Amendments) Regulations 1996 (SI 1996/2431), reg.7(b) (October 15, 1996).
6. The Social Security (Miscellaneous Amendments) (No.2) Regulations 1997 (SI 1997/793), reg.2(4) (April 7, 1997).
7. The Social Security (Miscellaneous Amendments) (No.2) Regulations 1997 (SI 1997/793), reg.2 (October 6, 1997).
8. The Tax Credits (Claims and Payments) (Amendment) Regulations 1999 (SI 1999/2572), reg.4 (October 5, 1999).
9. The Social Security (Immigration and Asylum) Consequential Amendments Regulations 2000 (SI 2000/636), (April 3, 2000).
10. The Social Security (Joint Claims: Consequential Amendments) Regulations 2000 (SI 2000/1982), reg.2(3) (March 19, 2001).
11. State Pension Credit (Consequential, Transitional and Miscellaneous Provisions) Regulations 2002 (SI 2002/3019), reg.4 (April 7, 2003).

(SI 1987/1968, reg.4) (as amended)

12. The Social Security (Claims and Payments and Miscellaneous Amendments) Regulations 2003 (SI 2003/1632), reg.2(2) (July 21, 2003).
13. The Social Security (Claims and Payments on account, Overpayments and Recovery) Amendment Regulations 2005 (SI 2005/34), reg.2 (May 2, 2005).
14. The Social Security, Child Support and Tax Credits (Miscellaneous Amendments) Regulations 2005 (SI 2005/337), reg.7 (March 18, 2005).
15. The Social Security (Shared Additional Pension) (Miscellaneous Amendments) Regulations 2005 (SI 2005/1551) (July 6, 2005).
16. The Civil Partnership (Pensions, Social Security and Child Support) (Consequential etc. Provisions) Order 2005 (SI 2005/2887) (December 5, 2005).
17. The Social Security (Miscellaneous Amendments) (No.2) Regulations 2006 (SI 2006/832) (April 10, 2006).
18. The Social Security (Work-focused Interviews) Regulations 2000 (SI 2000/897), (April 3, 2000).

DEFINITIONS

"appropriate office"—see reg.2(1).
"benefit"—see reg.2(2).
"claim for benefit"—see reg.2(1).
"jobseeker's allowance"—*ibid*.
"married couple"—*ibid*.
"partner"—*ibid*.
"refugee"—*ibid*.
"unmarried couple"—*ibid*.

GENERAL NOTE

Introduction

Section 1 of the Administration Act requires a claim to be submitted for any benefit to which the section applies except where regulations otherwise prescribe (see reg.3), as a condition of entitlement to benefit. This largely removes the effect of the decision of the House of Lords in *Insurance Officer v McCaffrey* [1984] 1 W.L.R. 1353, though some doubt remained in relation to entitlement prior to September 2, 1985, when the first version of s.1 was implemented. This is now resolved by s.2.

The claims system is largely predicated on a system of written claims, but recent amendments now make provision for telephone claims in respect of retirement pension and graduated retirement pension. See annotations to paras (11) to (14) below.

A fine line used to be drawn between the responsibilities of the Secretary of State and the adjudicating authorities under this regulation. It has been consistently held that it is for the Secretary of State to say whether a document (not in the prescribed form) is acceptable as "sufficient in the circumstances of the particular case," but the duty lies on the adjudicating authorities to decide whether such a document is a claim for benefit: *R(U)9/60* and *R(S)1/63*. It may be significant that in both these cases the Commissioner concluded that a document accepted by the Secretary of State did not constitute a claim for benefit. It is sometimes argued that the Secretary of State's authority under para.(1) extends to determining the date of the claim. This is not so. The sole issue reserved for the Secretary of State under para.(1) is whether the *form* of the claim (if not on a prescribed form) is acceptable as a claim. It is left for decision makers and tribunals to determine the date of the claim and what has been claimed once the Secretary of State has determined that it is in acceptable form: *R(SB)5/89* confirmed in *CU/94/1994*. This distinction now largely disappears with the abolition of adjudication officers.

The issue of whether tribunals have jurisdiction to consider the decision of the Secretary of State as to when a claim was validly made where it is initially defective has been considered in cases *R(IS) 6/04* and *CIS/758/2002*. The Commissioner, in *R(IS) 6/04*, ruled that the absence of a right of appeal was incompatible with Art.6

2.39

The Social Security (Claims and Payments) Regulations 1987

of the European Convention, and so disapplied the provision in Schedule 2 to the Decisions and Appeals Regulations in so far as it was necessary to do so in order to ensure that the claimant was entitled to appeal against a decision as to whether or when a claim had been validly made in accordance with this regulation. This has restored the position to that which previously applied before the SSA 1998 entered into force: see *R(U)9/60*.

On the substance of what is required for a valid claim, the Commissioner has this to say:

"I do not think an over-literal approach should be taken in this context: if, for example, all the figures required to determine entitlement are supplied and identified sufficiently clearly when the claimant submits his claim, either in answers recorded on the claim form itself or in annexed documents to which those answers expressly or impliedly refer, then it would in my judgment be open to a tribunal to hold on the facts that there has been no *material* failure such as to render the claim and the information supplied with it incomplete, even if admittedly the claimant has not complied with the instructions to the letter by repeating the actual figures in the boxes on the form itself. In addition, it seems to have been regarded as a defect fatal to the *claim* that he only gave details of his bank, and not of a Post Office, in the part of the form that asked him about the method of *payment* he preferred if benefit was in due course awarded." (para.54.)

and:

"I direct the tribunal that for this purpose they should concern themselves only with the matters and information necessary to determine entitlement to the benefit claimed. It seems to me that both sides are right in saying, as Mr Wright submits and Mr Spencer very fairly agrees in the most recent written submissions, that the requirements in regulation 4(1A)(b)–(c) strictly concern the information and evidence required in connection with the *claim* so as to enable it to be determined; not such things as the administrative arrangements for payment of any benefit that may subsequently be awarded on that claim. Thus even though it is of course convenient and sensible for the claimant to be asked about these at the same time and to put them on the same form, the omission of such additional details as the Post Office, needed (if at all) only for payment purposes (and as Mr Spencer points out, not in any event crucial or binding so far as the Secretary of State is concerned, under regulation 20 of the Claims and Payments regulations) does not render an otherwise complete claim defective." (para.56.)

CIS/758/2002 added a gloss on this case in relation to defective claims for income support or a jobseeker's allowance, namely that the mandatory four week time limit for correcting defects on the claim form is not contrary to Convention rights protected by the Human Rights Act 1998 when compared with the longer discretionary time limit allowed for correcting defects in claims for other benefits. This is said to be because income support and income-based jobseeker's allowance are not possessions for the purposes of the protection of property rights under Art.1 of Protocol 1 of the European Convention, although that proposition is almost certainly no longer good law following the decision of the Grand Chamber in the *Stec* case: see annotations to Article 1 of Protocol 1 at para. 4.88.

Once a claim has been made, it may only be withdrawn before it has been adjudicated upon by an adjudication officer (now decision maker): *R(U)2/79* and *R(U)7/83* and see reg.5(2).

Para.(1)

2.40   Note that from October 6, 1997, para.(1) no longer applies to claims for income support and JSA, for which see paras (1A)–(1C).

For other benefits, para.(1) provides that claims must be made in writing, normally on an official form, although the Secretary of State may accept some other kind of written claim. In such a case, under para.(7), the Secretary of State may require the

(SI 1987/1968, reg.4) (as amended)

claimant to fill in the proper form. If this is done in the proper time the claim is treated as duly made in the first instance. It no longer seems possible for an oral claim to be accepted, but see below on telephone claims. However, see reg.6(1)(aa) for the position when a claimant contacts an office with a view to making a claim.

Note also *R(SB) 9/84* where a Tribunal of Commissioners holds that where a claim has been determined, the Secretary of State must be deemed, in the absence of any challenge at the time, to have accepted that the claim was made in sufficient manner. See the notes to reg.33. See also *CDLA/1596/1996* in which the Commissioner set aside the tribunal's decision because they had failed to consider whether they should refer to the Secretary of State the question whether the claimant's application for review should be treated as a claim under para.(1).

Paras (1A)–(1C)
These provisions, together with the new reg.6(1A) and (4A)–(4AB), introduce the so-called "onus of proof" changes for claims for income support and JSA from October 6, 1997. The aim is to place more responsibility on claimants for these benefits to provide information and evidence to support their claim (see the DSS's Memorandum to the Social Security Advisory Committee (SSAC) annexed to the Committee's report (Cm. 3586) on the proposals). SSAC supported this principle but considered that it was "premature to introduce penalties for failure to provide information when it is more likely that the current problems lie more with the forms and procedures than with dilatory or obstructive claimants". As the Committee pointed out, the current claim forms are lengthy, complex and difficult for many people to understand, and moreover in the past told claimants not to delay sending in the claim form even if they had not got all the required information. Furthermore, since income support and income-based JSA are basic subsistence benefits, claimants have every incentive to cooperate in providing all the information needed to get an early payment. Thus SSAC's main recommendation was that the claim forms and guidance to claimants should first be revised and tested "before introducing new penalties, which together with the proposed changes to backdating rules [see reg.19], will only serve to complicate the social security system and penalise the most disadvantaged claimants". But this recommendation was rejected by the Government, although the final form of the regulations did take limited account of some of SSAC's other recommendations.

2.41

Under the rules, in order for a claim for income support or JSA to be validly made, it must be in writing on a properly completed approved form (there is no longer any provision for the Secretary of State to accept any other kind of written claim) and all the information and evidence required by the form must have been provided (para.(1A)). However, the requirement to complete the form fully or to provide the required evidence does not apply in the circumstances set out in para.(1B). The list in para.(1B) is exhaustive and there is no category of analogous circumstances. If any of sub-paras (a)–(d) of para.(1B) do apply, the person can inform an appropriate office (defined in reg.2(1)) "by whatever means" (e.g. verbally or through a third party) (para.(1C)). Note that the obligation to provide information and evidence only relates to that required by the claim form; if a claim is accepted as validly made it will still be open to the Department to seek further information if this is required in order to decide the claim, but this will not alter the date of claim.

See reg.6(1A) for the date of claim for an income support claim and reg.6(4A)–(4AB) for the date of claim for JSA claims (and note the differences).

Thus the major effect of these new rules is that there is now a requirement to produce the specified information and evidence *before* a claim is treated as having been made (although see reg.6(1A) and (4A)–(4AB) for the date of claim). Whether the necessary evidence has been produced or whether a claimant is exempt under para.(1B) will, however, now be subject to appeal to a tribunal, on the application, by analogy, of the principle established in *R(IS) 6/04*. The contrary position which has been set out in earlier editions and was approved by the Commissioner in *CJSA/69/2001* would seem to be inconsistent with the approach adopted in *R(IS) 6/04*.

Note also s.1(1A) of the Administration Act, under which claimants will not be entitled to benefit unless they satisfy requirements relating to the provision of national insurance numbers.

Paras (2) and (2A)

2.42 In working families' tax credit cases, if a couple is involved, the claim may be made by either partner.

Para. (3)

2.43 In income support cases, where a couple is involved, either partner can be the claimant, except in the case of a refugee under para.(3C). There is a free choice. If the couple cannot jointly agree who should claim, the Secretary of State is to break the tie. There are still some differences in entitlement according to which partner is the claimant, particularly since only the claimant is required to be available for work. In addition, head (b) of para.12(1) of Sch.2 to the Income Support Regulations (disability and higher pensioner premium) can only be satisfied by the claimant. But there is now no long-term rate and the full-time employment of either partner excludes entitlement to income support. See reg.7(2). Under the Income Support (Transitional) Regulations transitional protection is lost if the claimant for the couple changes. *CIS 8/1990* and *CIS 375/1990* challenged this rule on the grounds that it was indirectly discriminatory against women (since in 98 per cent of couples (at that time) the man was the claimant). Following the European Court of Justice's decision in the *Cresswell* case that income support is not covered by EC Directive 79/7 on equal treatment for men and women in social security (see the notes to reg.36 of the Income Support Regulations), the claimants could not rely on European law. The Commissioner also rejects a submission that the Sex Discrimination Act 1975 prevented the discriminatory effect of regs 2 and 10 of the Transitional Regulations. Paragraph (4) below deals with changes of partner.

Para. (3A)

2.44 Under para.(3A), if both partners in a couple satisfy the conditions of entitlement for a disabled person's tax credit, they may choose which one of them is to claim. If they cannot choose, the Secretary of State makes the decision.

Para. (3B)

2.45 Sub-paragraph (a) applies the normal income support rule for couples to income-based JSA. Sub-paragraphs (b) and (c) make provision about the deemed date of the claim for income-based JSA by one partner when a claim for contribution-based JSA by the other partner fails or entitlement comes to an end.

Para. (3C)

2.46 Where one of a couple is a refugee, the claim for income support must be made by that partner. If both are refugees, there is a free choice.

CIS/3438/2004 concerned a claim for income support by a Turkish woman admitted to the United Kingdom as a refugee. She claimed income support on August 6, 2003 enclosing a letter from the Home Office dated July 16, 2003 acknowledging her refugee status. She had also been instructed to provide the Department with details of any support provided to her as an asylum seeker by the Home Office. She did not include such a letter with her claim form because she did not have such a letter. It did not exist because it had not at that time been provided by the Home Office. The required information was subsequently obtained and provided to the Department. The claim for income support made on August 6, 2003 was rejected on the ground that the claimant had failed to comply with the requirement in reg.4(1A) to "include such information and evidence as the form may require in connection with the claim." The tribunal upheld the decision refusing the claim. The Commissioner concludes that there was no proper basis for finding a claimant, in these circumstances, to be in breach of reg.4(1A) by not submitting a document which she did not have at the time with the claim form. While it would be proper to

(SI 1987/1968, reg.4) (as amended)

require submission of the information, it was an error of law to treat the claim which had been made as a nullity.

Para. (4)
If there is a change of claimant within a couple in the middle of a continuing income support claim, the claims are not to overlap. The change is a matter of a new claim for benefit, not review as it was for supplementary benefit *(R(SB) 1/93)*. In *CSIS 66/1992* the Commissioner rejects the argument that para.(4) combined with s.20(9) of the Social Security Act 1986 (SSCBA s.134(2)) meant that a change of claimant could not be backdated. If the claimant could show good cause for her delay in claiming, regs 19(2) and 6(3) enabled her claim to be backdated to the date from which she had good cause (subject to the then what was then a 12-month limit in reg.19(4)). Duplication of payment could be avoided by the AO reviewing the claimant's husband's entitlement for any past period in respect of which the claimant was held to be entitled to benefit and applying reg.5(1) and (2), Case 1, of the Payments Regulations. By becoming the claimant the wife qualified for a disability premium. There is a specific provision in para.19 of Sch.7 to the Income Support Regulations for arrears of a disability premium in these circumstances.

2.47

Para. (5)
Reg. 4(5) imposes a duty on the Department to provide a claim form in the circumstances set out there. The effect of a failure by the Department to comply with that duty is considered in *R (IS) 4/07*, which also reviews the earlier authorities on the point. The specific issue raised was whether a breach of reg. 4(5) results in suspension of the operation of the time limits for claiming. The Commissioner concludes that it does not. However, the provisions of reg. 19 on backdating would be available to a claimant who sought to have a claim backdated in such circumstances.

2.47.1

Para. (6)
The claim, except in the case of JSA, must be delivered or sent to the appropriate office, though increasing provision is now being made for telephone or electronic claims.

2.48

In *CSIS 48/1992* the Commissioner considered the effect of para.(6) in the light of s.7 and s.23 of the Interpretation Act 1978. He concludes that the effect of these provisions is that a claim for a social security benefit is a document authorised by an Act to be served by post, which is presumed to have been delivered in the ordinary course of post unless this is proved not to have been the case. The tribunal should therefore have considered whether it accepted that the claim had been posted, and, if so, whether the presumption of delivery had been rebutted by the adjudication officer. *CSIS 48/1992* has been followed in *CIS 759/1992*.

In *CIB/2805/2003* the Deputy Commissioner rules that, having regard to s.7 of the Interpretation Act 1978, the onus is on the Secretary of State to prove that a letter arrives at a date later than the date it should have been received in the ordinary course of post. This would involve producing some evidence of practice in the Department about date stamping incoming post. This was particularly important in this case since the letter in issue had been posted during the Easter holiday period. In such cases, the use of reg.19(7)(c), which deals with adverse postal conditions may be relevant: see annotations to that provision.

For JSA, a claimant wishing to make an initial claim must normally go in person to the nearest Job Centre to obtain a claim pack from the new jobseeker receptionist. An appointment will then be made for the claimant to return, usually within five days, for a new jobseeker interview. This is all part of the concept of "active signing". The claim will be treated as made on the date of the first attendance, if it is received properly completed within a month (reg.6(1)(aa) and (4A)).

Paras (7) and (8)
Paragraph (7), which does not apply to claims for income support or JSA (for which see para.(7A)), deals with written claims not made on the proper form (for which,

2.49

see para.(1)), and situations where the proper form is not completed according to the instructions (see para.8)). The Secretary of State may simply treat this as an ineffective attempt to claim, but also has power to refer the form back to the claimant. Then there is one month (extendable by the Secretary of State) to complete the form properly, in which case the claim is treated as made on the date of the original attempt to claim (see reg.6(1)(b)). Note also *R(SB) 9/84*; see the note to para.(1).

CP/3447/2003 concerned a claim for an adult dependency increase to a retirement pension for the claimant's wife. The claimant had made his claim for retirement pension at the proper time in advance of his 65th birthday indicating on the claim form that he wished to claim the increase for his wife. Adult dependency increase is, by virtue of reg.2(3) of the Claims and Payments Regulations, treated as a separate benefit requiring a separate claim. The Department failed to pick up the statement in the retirement pension claim form and did not send the claimant a further form to complete. In the following year, the claimant wrote to ask whether he was getting the increase after a query on his tax return. The required form was then issued to him. He completed it and it was clear that he should have been receiving the increase all along. The Secretary of State refused to pay it back to the start of the retirement pension on the grounds that the claim was received following the enquiry and could only be backdated three months from that date. By the time the appeal came before the tribunal, the Secretary of State accepted that the decision was wrong. The issue turned on the proper interpretation of reg.4(7). In particular, what was the date on which the claim was made 'in the first instance' in this case. Was it the date on which the claimant wrote his letter asking about his entitlement to the increase of his wife, or was it the indication in his original claim form for retirement pension indicating that he wanted the increase for his wife?

The Commissioner concluded,

"In those circumstances, given that (a) a claim in writing for the increase is now accepted as having been made in the first instance by the claimant in early 1999 as part of the original claim for his pension, and (b) the Secretary of State did in fact exercise his powers in regulation 4(7) to supply the claimant with the approved form which was returned duly completed well within the month stipulated, the conditions under which the Secretary of State is bound to treat the claim as if it had been duly made "in the first instance" are in my judgment satisfied in reference to the *original* date of claim in 1999, not just the enquiry letter the following year. Since the requirement to treat the claim as duly made "in the first instance" is mandatory once the conditions are met, there is no further exercise of discretionary or administrative judgment for the Secretary of State to make under regulation 4(7) before the effect in terms of entitlement to benefit can be properly determined. Although it was only in response to the further enquiry that the form was eventually supplied the Secretary of State could not in my judgment possibly rely on that as an argument for saying that the existence of the first claim should be ignored, when the failure to supply the form in the first instance was admittedly an administrative error by his own local officials and should never have happened at all." (para.15).

The Commissioner does, however, note that in so finding in the particular circumstances of this case, he is not to be taken as pronouncing as a matter of general principle that ticking boxes on a form in the expectation of receiving a further form ought in every case to constitute making a claim in writing for the benefit in question. (para.14).

Para.(7A)

2.50 There are special rules in reg.4 where the benefit claimed is income support. In *CIS/3173/2003*, the claimant had contacted an office of the Department with a view to making a claim for income support on October 14, 2002, and she had subsequently completed an income support claim form on October 24, 2002, but did not include payslips with that form. These were required since she declared that she was doing "therapeutic work" (actually work accepted as permitted for the purposes of

(SI 1987/1968, reg.4) (as amended)

incapacity benefit). The Department contacted the claimant on December 18, 2002 regarding the missing payslips. These were provided on December 19, 2002. The decision maker awarded income support only from December 19, 2002. The tribunal upheld that decision. The Commissioner also concludes that there was no entitlement until December 19, 2002. He concludes that the claim form sent in without the accompanying payslips was a defective claim under sub-para.(7A) with the consequences stated there, but that reg.6(1A) makes provision only for one month's leeway in providing the information or evidence required to cure the defect. More than one month had passed here, and accordingly no claim which complied with the requirement of reg.4(1A) was made until December 19, 2002. It did not matter that the Department had not requested the payslips earlier. The Commissioner has granted leave to appeal in this case.

Paras (7A), (7B) and (9)
If a claim for income support or JSA is defective (on which see para.(9)), the Secretary of State will simply advise the claimant of the defect and of the rules in reg.6(1A) (for income support claims) or reg.6(4A) (for JSA claims) as appropriate. It will then be up to the claimant to comply with those provisions if he is in a position to do so. 2.51

Paras (11) to (14)
These paragraphs make provision, in a system which has previously been based upon a requirement for written claims, for telephone claims for retirement pension and graduated retirement pension. Telephone claims will take the form of an interview between an officer of the Department and the claimant whose answers will be input directly into the Department's computer system. A decision on the claim may be made on the spot, since entitlement to pensions can very often be determined easily by reference to information already held in Departmental records. These paragraphs make provision for telephone claims, but reserve the Secretary of State's power to insist upon a written claim. Provision is also made for treating a telephone claim as a defective claim and allowing a period for the defect to be remedied. 2.52

[¹ Further provisions as to claims

4A.—(1) Where a claimant resides in both— 2.53
(a) the area of a local authority specified in Part I or II of Schedule 1 to the Social Security (Claims and Information) Regulations 1999; and
(b) a postcode district identified in Part I or II of Schedule 2 to the Social Security (Claims and Information) Regulations 1999,
any claim for a benefit to which paragraph (2) applies may be made to any office displaying the **one** logo(a) (whether or not that office is situated within the area of the local authority in which the claimant resides).
(2) The benefits to which this paragraph applies are—
(a) a jobseeker's allowance;
(b) income support;
(c) incapacity benefit;
(d) [² carer's allowance];
(e) severe disablement allowance;
(f) widow's benefit;
(g) bereavement benefits;
(h) disability living allowance.
(3) A claim made in accordance with paragraph (1), other than a claim for income support or a jobseeker's allowance, shall be made in writing on a form approved by the Secretary of State for the purpose of the benefit to

The Social Security (Claims and Payments) Regulations 1987

which the claim is made, or in such other manner, being in writing, as the person to whom the claim is made may accept as sufficient in the circumstances of the particular case.

(4) In the case of a claim for income support or a jobseeker's allowance, the provisions of regulation 4(1A) to (1C) shall apply.

(5) In its application to the area of any authority specified in Part I or II of Schedule 1 to the Social Security (Claims and Information) Regulations 1999, the "appropriate office" in these Regulations includes also an office of an authority or person to whom claims may be made in accordance with paragraph (1).

(6) In these Regulations, a "participating authority" means any local authority or person to whom claims may be made in accordance with paragraph (1).

AMENDMENTS

1. This regulation inserted by The Social Security (Claims and Information) Regulations 1999 (SI 1999/3108), reg.5 (November 29, 1999).
2. The Social Security Amendment (Carer's Allowance) Regulations 2002 (SI 2002/2497), Sch.2 (October 23, 2002).

Forwarding claims and information

2.54   **4B.**—(1) A participating authority may—
(a) record information or evidence relating to any social security matter supplied by or obtained from a person at an office displaying the **one** logo, whether or not the information or evidence is supplied or obtained in connection with the making of a claim for benefit;
(b) give information or advice with respect to any social security matter to persons who are making, or have made, claims for any benefit to which regulation 4A(2) applies [² or for state pension credit.]
(2) A participating authority shall forward to the Secretary of State—
(a) any claim for benefit, other than a claim for housing benefit or council tax benefit, together with any information or evidence supplied to the authority in connection with that claim; and
(b) any information or evidence relating to any other social security matter, except where the information or evidence relates solely to housing benefit or council tax benefit given to the authority by a person making a claim for, or who has claimed, a benefit to which regulation 4A(2) applies.]

AMENDMENTS

1. This regulation inserted by The Social Security (Claims and Information) Regulations 1999 (SI 1999/3108), reg.5 (November 29, 1999)
2. State Pension Credit (Consequential, Transitional and Miscellaneous) Regulations 2002 (SI 2002/3019), reg.4 (April 7, 2003).

[¹ Electronic claims for benefit

2.55   **4ZC.**—(1) Any claim for benefit in relation to which this regulation applies, and any certificate, notice, information or evidence given in connection with that claim, may be made or given by means of an electronic communication, in accordance with the provisions set out in Schedule 9ZC.

(SI 1987/1968, reg.4ZC) (as amended)

(2) This regulation applies in relation to carer's allowance [², attendance allowance, disability living allowance, graduated retirement benefit, retirement pension and shared additional pension].]

AMENDMENTS

1. The Social Security (Electronic Communications) (Carer's Allowance) Order 2003 (SI 2003/2800), reg.2 (December 1, 2003).
2. The Social Security (Electronic Communications) (Miscellaneous Benefits) Order 2005 (SI 2005/3321) (January 30, 2006).

[¹ Electronic claims for benefit

4C.—(1) Any claim for benefit in relation to which this regulation applies, and any certificate, notice, information or evidence given in connection with that claim, may be made or given by means of an electronic communication, in accordance with the provisions set out in Schedule 9C.

(2) This regulation applies in relation to child benefit.]

AMENDMENT

1. Inserted by the Social Security (Electronic Communications) (Child Benefit) Order 2002 (SI 2002/1789), art.3 (October 28, 2002).

[¹ Making a claim for state pension credit

4D.—(1) A claim for state pension credit need only be made in writing if the Secretary of State so directs in any particular case.

(2) A claim is made in writing either—
(a) by completing and returning in accordance with the instructions printed on it a form approved or provided by the Secretary of State for the purpose; or
(b) in such other written form as the Secretary of State accepts as sufficient in the circumstances of the case.

(3) A claim for state pension credit may be made in writing whether or not a direction is issued under paragraph (1) and may also be made [⁵ . . .] in person at an appropriate office [³ . . .].

[³ (3A) A claim made in writing may also be made at an office designated by the Secretary of State for accepting claims for state pension credit.]

(4) A claim made in writing may also be made at the offices of—
(a) a local authority administering housing benefit or council tax benefit;
(b) a person providing [² to such an authority services relating to housing benefit or council tax benefit]; or
(c) a person authorised to exercise any function of a local authority relating to housing benefit or council tax benefit [² if the Secretary of State has arranged with the local authority or person specified in sub-paragraph (b) or (c) for them to receive claims in accordance with this paragraph].

[³ (5) Where a claim is made in accordance with paragraph (4), the local authority or other specified person—
(a) shall forward the claim to the Secretary of State as soon as reasonably practicable;
(b) may receive information or evidence relating to the claim supplied by the person making, or who has made, the claim to another person, and shall forward it to the Secretary of State as soon as reasonably practicable;

(c) may obtain information or evidence relating to the claim from the person who has made the claim and shall forward it to the Secretary of State as soon as reasonably practicable;
(d) may record information or evidence relating to the claim supplied or obtained in accordance with sub-paragraph (b) or (c) and may hold the information or evidence (whether as supplied or obtained or as recorded) for the purpose of forwarding it to the Secretary of State; and
(e) may give information and advice with respect to the claim to the person who makes, or has made, the claim.]

[3 (5A) Paragraph (5)(b) to (e) applies in respect of information, evidence and advice relating to any claim for state pension credit, whether it is made in accordance with paragraph (4) or otherwise.]

(6) A claim for state pension credit made in person [5 . . .] is not a valid claim unless a written statement of the claimant's circumstances, provided for the purpose by the Secretary of State, is approved by the person making the claim.

[5 (6A) A claim for state pension credit may be made by telephone call to the telephone number specified by the Secretary of State.

(6B) Where the Secretary of State, in any particular case, directs that the person making the claim approves a written statement of his circumstances, provided for the purpose by the Secretary of State, a claim made by telephone is not a valid claim unless the person complies with the direction.

(6C) A claim made by telephone in accordance with paragraph (6A) is defective unless the Secretary of State is provided, during that telephone call, with all the information he requires to determine the claim.

(6D) Where a claim made by telephone in accordance with paragraph (6A) is defective, the Secretary of State is to provide the person making it with an opportunity to correct the defect.

(6E) If the person corrects the defect within one month, or such longer period as the Secretary of State considers reasonable, of the date the Secretary of State last drew attention to the defect, the Secretary of State shall treat the claim as if it had been duly made in the first instance.]

(7) A [4 couple] may agree between them as to which partner is to make a claim for state pension credit, but in the absence of an agreement, the Secretary of State shall decide which of them is to make the claim.

(8) Where one member of a [4 couple] ("the former claimant") is entitled to state pension credit under an award but a claim for state pension credit is made by the other member of the couple, then, if both members of the couple confirm in writing that they wish the claimant to be the other member, the former claimant's entitlement shall terminate on the last day of the benefit week specified in paragraph (9).

(9) That benefit week is the benefit week of the former claimant which includes the day immediately preceding the day the partner's claim is actually made or, if earlier, is treated as made.

(10) If a claim for state pension credit is defective when first received, the Secretary of State is to provide the person making it with an opportunity to correct the defect.

(11) If that person corrects the defect so that the claim then satisfies the requirements of paragraph (2) and does so within 1 month [6 or such longer period as the Secretary of State considers reasonable] of the date the Secretary of State last drew attention to the defect, the claim shall be treated as having been properly made on the date—

(SI 1987/1968, reg. 4D) (as amended)

(a) the defective claim was first received by the Secretary of State or the person acting on his behalf; or
(b) if regulation 4F(3) applies, the person informed an appropriate office [¹ or other office specified in regulation 4F(3)] of his intention to claim state pension credit.

(12) [⁵ Paragraph (6E) and (11) do] not apply in a case to which regulation 4E(3) applies.

(13) State pension credit is a relevant benefit for the purposes of section 7A of the Social Security Administration Act 1992.]

AMENDMENTS

1. Inserted by The State Pension Credit (Consequential, Transitional and Miscellaneous) Regulations 2002 (SI 2002/3019), reg.4 (April 7, 2003).
2. The Social Security (Claims and Payments and Miscellaneous Amendments) Regulations 2003 (SI 2003/1632) reg.2 (July 21, 2003).
3. The Social Security, Child Support and Tax Credits (Miscellaneous Amendments) Regulations 2005 (SI 2005/337) reg.7 (March 18, 2005).
4. The Civil Partnership (Pensions, Social Security and Child Support) (Consequential etc. Provisions) Order 2005 (SI 2005/2887) (December 5, 2005).
5. The Social Security (Miscellaneous Amendments) (No. 2) Regulations 2006 (SI 2006/832) (July 24, 2006).
6. The Social Security (Miscellaneous Amendments) (No.3) Regulations 2006 (SI 2006/2377) (October 2, 2006).

[¹ Making a claim before attaining the qualifying age

4E.—(1) A claim for state pension credit may be made, and any claim made may be determined, at any time within the advance period.

(2) The advance period begins on the date which falls 4 months before the day on which the claimant attains the qualifying age and ends on the day before he attains that age.

(3) A person who makes a claim within the advance period which is defective may correct the defect at any time before the end of the advance period.]

AMENDMENT

1. Inserted by the State Pension Credit (Consequential, Transitional and Miscellaneous) Regulations 2002 (SI 2002/3019), reg.4 (April 7, 2003).

[¹ Making a claim after attaining the qualifying age: date of claim

4F.—(1) This regulation applies in the case of a person who claims state pension credit on or after attaining the qualifying age.

(2) The date on which a claim is made shall, subject to paragraph (3), be—
(a) where the claim is made in writing and is not defective, the date on which the claim is first received—
  (i) by the Secretary of State or the person acting on his behalf; or
  (ii) in a case to which regulation 4D(4) relates, in the office of a person specified therein;
(b) where the claim is not made in writing but is otherwise made in accordance with regulation 4D(3) [⁴ or (6A)] and is not defective, the date the claimant provides details of his circumstances by telephone to, or in person at, the appropriate office or other office

The Social Security (Claims and Payments) Regulations 1987

designated by the Secretary of State to accept claims for state pension credit; or
(c) where a claim is initially defective but the defect is corrected under regulation [⁴ 4D(6E) or (11)], the date the claim is treated as having been made under that regulation.
(3) If a [³ person wishing to make a claim]—
(a) informs [³ (by whatever means) an appropriate office [², or other office designated by the Secretary of State for accepting claims for state pension credit or the office of the person specified in regulation 4(D)] of his intention to claim state pension credit; and
(b) subsequently makes the claim in accordance with regulation 4D within 1 month of complying with sub-paragraph (a), or within such longer period as the Secretary of State may allow,
the claim may, where in the circumstances of the particular case it is appropriate to do so, be treated as made on the day the claimant first informed [² an office specified in subparagraph (a)] of his intention to claim the credit.]

AMENDMENTS

1. Inserted by the State Pension Credit (Consequential, Transitional and Miscellaneous) Regulations 2002 (SI 2002/3019), reg.4 (April 7, 2003).
2. The Social Security (Claims and Payments and Miscellaneous Amendments) Regulations 2003 (SI 2003/1632), reg.2 (July 21, 2003).
3. Social Security (Housing Benefit, Council Tax Benefit, State Pension Credit and Miscellaneous Amendments) Regulations 2004 (SI 2004/2327), reg.8 (October 6, 2004).
4. The Social Security (Miscellaneous Amendments) (No. 2) Regulations 2006 (SI 2006/832) (July 24, 2006).

GENERAL NOTE

2.60   The amendments to reg.4 of the Claims and Payments Regulations are significant in that they may provision for much greater co-operation between the Department and local authorities in relation to the receipt of claims for benefits administered by these agencies. To date the only developments under the new arrangements heralded by s.7A of the Administration Act 1992 (added by the Welfare Reform and Pensions Act 1999) has been the introduction of **one** offices.

The new arrangements only apply to claims by those who have attained the age of 60 to retirement pension, incapacity benefit, bereavement benefits, carer's allowance, attendance allowance, disability living allowance, winter fuel payments and income support. Claims by this group to these benefits may be directed to an office designated by the Secretary of State for accepting such claims. In relation to benefits administered by the Department, the party receiving the claim s under a duty to forward the claim to the Department as soon as reasonably practicable.

Amendment and withdrawal of claim

2.61   **5.**—(1) A person who has made a claim may amend it at any time by notice in writing received in an appropriate office [¹ except where the claim was made by telephone, in accordance with regulation 4(11) [² or 4D(6A)], where the amendment may be made by telephone,] before a determination has been made on the claim, and any claim so amended may be treated as if it had been so amended in the first instance.

(SI 1987/1968, reg.5) (as amended)

(2) A person who has made a claim may withdraw it at any time before a determination has been made on it, by notice to an appropriate office, and any such notice of withdrawal shall have effect when it is received.

AMENDMENTS

1. The Social Security (Claims and Payments and Payments on account, Overpayments and Recovery) Amendment Regulations 2005 (SI 2005/34), reg.2 (May 2, 2005).
2. The Social Security (Miscellaneous Amendments) (No. 2) Regulations 2006 (SI 2006/832) (July 24, 2006).

DEFINITION

"appropriate office"—see reg.2(1).

GENERAL NOTE

Para. (1)

An issue arose in *CTC/1061/2001* on the meaning of reg.5. The claimant had claimed a disabled person's tax credit, reporting that he worked as a private hire driver. He answered a question about the amount of usage of the car for private purpose and responded that he used it 50 per cent for private purposes; he later said he had intended to indicate that he used the car for 50 per cent of the time and five per cent or less was for private purposes. The Secretary of State argued that this was irrelevant since a claim could not be altered after it had been determined. The tribunal accepted the argument. The Commissioner notes that there is nothing in reg.5 which prevents a claimant from seeking to explain an answer in a way which is different from how the decision-maker interpreted it. He goes on to raise the question whether there might be a difference for the purpose of reg.5(1) between a claim and evidence on a claim, but does not seek to answer the question.

Regulation 5(1) would appear to be drafted sufficiently widely that it would encompass an amendment not only to the claim, but also to the evidence on which the claim is based. The underlying purpose of the regulation appears to be to ensure that the decision is based on full circumstances obtaining when the claim is determined. So, for example, a claimant might wish to include new members of his family to the claim, or correct an error on the claim form which has just been notices. Both would appear to be within reg.5(1).

2.62

Para. (2)

In *CJSA/3979/1999* the Commissioner explores the possibility of a claimant's being able to withdraw a claim where there has been an award of benefit for an indefinite period. The Commissioner concludes,

"If the original claim is for an indefinite period, so that the award is for an indefinite period, I do not think that the claim can later be converted into one for a definite period. The original claim cannot be unmade or amended. . . . However, it does not necessarily follow from that that a claim cannot be withdraw for a prospective period even though there is a current indefinite award. In a sense there has already been an adjudication on that period through the making of an indefinite award, but only in a fairly technical sense. If a claimant unequivocally says that he wishes his claim to stop at the current date or that he wishes to withdraw his claim for the future, why should that not be given effect? Some regard should be had for the autonomy of claimants. . . . I conclude that even where there is a current award of benefit, a claimant may with-draw a claim on a prospective basis." (para.24.)

2.63

The Social Security (Claims and Payments) Regulations 1987

But the Commissioner goes on to indicate that the termination of the indefinite award should be the subject of adjudication in order to ensure that the withdrawal is properly made and not, for example, the result of coercion or improper inducement. In the case before the Commissioner, one issue raised was whether the claimant had been coerced into withdrawing a claim to JSA by threats to investigate whether he had been working for certain periods prior to those in respect of which he was interviewed.

Date of claim

2.64   **6.**—(1) [³Subject to the following provisions of this regulation] [²⁹ or regulation 6A (claims by persons subject to work-focused interviews)] the date on which a claim is made shall be—

(a) in the case of a claim which meets the requirements of regulation 4(1), the date on which it is received in an appropriate office;

[¹²(aa) in the case of a claim for—

[³⁰ . . .]

[³⁰ . . .]

jobseeker's allowance if first notification is received before 6th October 1997; or

income support if first notification is received before 6th October 1997;

which meets the requirements of regulation 4(1) and which is received in an appropriate office within one month of first notification in accordance with regulation 4(5), whichever is the later of—

(i) the date on which that notification is received; and

(ii) the first date on which that claim could have been made in accordance with these Regulations;]

(b) in the case of a claim which does not meet the requirements of regulation 4(1) but which is treated, under regulation 4(7) as having been duly made, the date on which the claim was received in an appropriate office in the first instance.

[²³ (c) in the case of a claim made by telephone in accordance with regulation 4(11), the date of that telephone call;

(d) in the case of a claim made by telephone which is defective but which is treated, under regulation 4(14) as having been duly made, the date of that telephone call.]

[²¹ (1ZA) In the case of a claim made in accordance with regulation 4(6B)—

(a) paragraph (1) shall apply in relation to a claim received at an office specified in that regulation as it applies in relation to a claim received at an appropriate office; and

(b) paragraph (1A) shall apply in relation to an office specified in that regulation as it applies in relation to an appropriate office.]

[¹³ (1A) In the case of claim for income support—

(a) subject to the following sub-paragraphs, the date on which a claim is made shall be the date on which a properly completed claim is received in an appropriate office or the first day in respect of which the claim is made if later;

(b) where a properly completed claim is received in an appropriate office within one month of first notification of intention to make that claim, the date of claim shall be the date on which that notification is deemed to be made or the first day in respect of which the claim is made if later;

(SI 1987/1968, reg. 6) (as amended)

    (c) a notification of intention to make a claim will be deemed to be made on the date when an appropriate office receives—
        (i) a notification in accordance with regulation 4(5); or
        (ii) a defective claim.]

[[18a] (1B) Subject to paragraph (1C), in the case of a claim for working families' tax credit or disabled person's tax credit which meets the requirements of regulation 4(1) and which is received in an appropriate office within one month of first notification in accordance with regulation 4(5)—
    (a) where the claimant is entitled to that credit on the date on which that notification is received ("the notification date") and the first day of the period in respect of which that claim is made is on or before the notification date, the date on which a claim is made shall be the notification date; or
    (b) where the claimant is not entitled to that credit on the notification date but becomes so entitled before the date on which the claim is received, the date on which the claim is received, the date on which a claim is made shall be—
        (i) the date on which the claimant becomes so entitled, or
        (ii) if later, the first day of the period in respect of which the claim is made provided that it is not later than the date on which the claim is received.

(1C) Paragraph (1B) shall not apply in the case of a claim which is received in an appropriate office—
    (a) in the case of working families' tax credit, within the period specified opposite that credit at paragraphs (a) or (aa) in column (2) of Schedule 4(**a**); or
    (b) in the case of disabled person's tax credit, within the period specified opposite that credit in paragraphs (a) or (b) in column (2) of Schedule 4.]

[[18b] unless the previous award of working families' tax credit or disabled person's tax credit was terminated by virtue of regulation 49ZA of the Family Credit (General) Regulations 1987 or regulation 54A of the Disability Working Allowance (General) Regulations 1991.]

[[27] (1D) Subject to paragraph (1E) and without prejudice to the generality of paragraph (1), where a properly completed claim for incapacity benefit is received in an appropriate office within one month of the claimant first notifying such an office, by whatever means, of his intention to make that claim, the date of claim shall be the date on which that notification is made or the first day in respect of which the claim is made if later.

(1E) For the purposes of paragraph (1D), a person who has attained the qualifying age may notify his intention and may send or deliver his claim to an office specified in regulation 4(6B)]

(2) [[1]...]

[[1](3) In the case of a claim for income support, [[14] working families' tax credit, disabled person's tax credit] [[12]or jobseeker's allowance][[5]...], where the time for claiming is extended under regulation 19 the claim shall be treated as made on the first day of the period in respect of which the claim is, by reason of the operation of that regulation, timeously made.

(4) Paragraph (3) shall not apply when the time for claiming income support [[14] working families' tax credit, disabled person's tax credit] or jobseeker's allowance]] has been extended under regulation 19 and the

The Social Security (Claims and Payments) Regulations 1987

failure to claim within the prescribed time for the purposes of that regulation is for the reason only that the claim has been sent by post.]

[[18] (4ZA)Where a member of a joint-claim couple notifies the employment officer (by whatever means) that he wishes to claim a jobseeker's allowance jointly with the other member of that couple, the claim shall be treated as made on the relevant date specified in accordance with paragraphs (4ZB) to (4ZD).

(4ZB) Where each member of a joint-claim couple is required to attend under regulation 4(6)(a)—
- (a) if each member subsequently attends for the purpose of jointly claiming a jobseeker's allowance at the time and place specified by the employment officer and complies with the requirements of paragraph (4AA)(a), the claim shall be treated as made on whichever is the later of the first notification of intention to make that claim and the first day in respect of which the claim is made;
- (b) if, without good cause, either member fails to attend for the purpose of jointly claiming a jobseeker's allowance at either the time or the place so specified or does not comply with the requirements of paragraph (4AA)(a), the claim shall be treated as made on the first day on which a member of the couple attends at the specified place and complies with the requirements of paragraph (4AA)(a).

(4ZC) Where only one member of the couple is required to attend under regulation 4(6)(a)—
- (a) subject to the following sub-paragraphs, the date on which the claim is made shall be the date on which a properly completed claim is received in an appropriate office or the first day in respect of which the claim is made, if later, provided that the member of the couple who is required to attend under regulation 4(6)(a) does so attend;
- (b) where a properly completed form is received in an appropriate office within one month of first notification of intention to make that claim, the date of claim shall be the date of that notification;
- (c) if, without good cause, the member of the couple who is required to attend under regulation 4(6)(a) fails to attend for the purpose of making a claim at either the time or place so specified or does not comply with the requirements of paragraph (4AA), the claim shall be treated as made on the first day on which that member does attend at that place and does provide a properly completed claim.

(4ZD) Where, as at the day on which a member of a joint-claim couple ("the first member") notifies the employment officer in accordance with paragraph (4ZA), the other member of that couple is temporarily absent from Great Britain in the circumstances specified in regulation 50(6B) of the Jobseeker's Allowance Regulations, the date on which the claim is made shall be the relevant date specified in paragraph (4ZB) or (4ZC) but nothing in this paragraph shall treat the claim as having been made on a day which is more than three months after the day on which the first member notified the employment officer in accordance with paragraph (4ZA).

[[13](4A) Where a person [[18]who is not a member of a joint-claim couple] notifies the Secretary of State (by whatever means) that he wishes to claim a jobseeker's allowance—

(SI 1987/1968, reg. 6) (as amended)

(a) if he is required to attend under regulation 4(6)(a)—
   (i) if he subsequently attends for the purpose of making a claim for that benefit at the time and place specified by the Secretary of State and complies with the requirements of paragraph (4AA) [¹⁸(b)], the claim shall be treated as made on whichever is the later of first notification of intention to make that claim and the first day in respect of which the claim is made;
   (ii) if, without good cause, he fails to attend for the purpose of making a claim for that benefit at either the time or place so specified, or does not comply with the requirements of paragraph (4AA) [¹⁸(b)], the claim shall be treated as made on the first day on which he does attend at that place and does provide a properly completed claim;
(b) if under regulation 4(6)(a) the Secretary of State directs that he is not required to attend—
   (i) subject to the following sub-paragraph, the date on which the claim is made shall be the date on which a properly completed claim is received in an appropriate office or the first day in respect of which the claim is made if later;
   (ii) where a properly completed claim is received in an appropriate office within one month of first notification of intention to make that claim, the date of claim shall be the date of that notification.

[¹⁸ (4AA) Unless the Secretary of State otherwise directs, a properly completed claim for shall be provided—
(a) in a case to which paragraph (4ZA) applies, at or before the time when a member of the joint-claim couple is first required to attend for the purpose of making a claim for a jobseeker's allowance;
(b) in any other case, at or before the time when the person making the claim for a jobseeker's allowance is required to attend for the purpose of making a claim.]

(4AB) The Secretary of State may direct that the time for providing a properly completed claim may be extended to a date no later than the date one month after the date of first notification of intention to make that claim.]

(4B) Where a person's entitlement to a jobseeker's allowance has ceased in any of the circumstances specified in regulation 25(1)(a), (b) or (c) of the Jobseeker's Allowance Regulations (entitlement ceasing on a failure to comply) and—
(a) where he had normally been required to attend in person, he shows that the failure to comply which caused the cessation of his previous entitlement was due to any of the circumstances mentioned in regulation 30(c) or (d) of those Regulations, and no later than the day immediately following the date when those circumstances cease to apply he makes a further claim for jobseeker's allowance; or
(b) where he had not normally been required to attend in person, he shows that he did not receive the notice to attend and he immediately makes a further claim for jobseeker's allowance,

that further claim shall be treated as having been made on the day following that cessation of entitlement.

(4C) Where a person's entitlement to a jobseeker's allowance ceases in the circumstances specified in regulation 25(1)(b) of the Jobseeker's Allowance Regulations (failure to attend at time specified) and that person makes a further claim for that allowance on the day on which he failed to attend at the time specified, that claim shall be treated as having been made on the following day.]

[¹¹(4D) In the case of a claim for income support to which regulation 4(3C) (claim by refugee) refers, the claim shall be treated as made [¹⁵ on the date on which his claim for asylum was recorded by the Secretary of State as having been made.]

[²(5) Where a person submits a claim for attendance allowance [⁶or disability living allowance or a request under paragraph (8)] by post and the arrival of that [⁶claim or request] at an appropriate office is delayed by postal disruption caused by industrial action, whether within the postal service or elsewhere, the [⁶claim or request] shall be treated as received on the day on which it would have been received if it had been delivered in the ordinary course of post.]

[³(6) Where—
(a) on or after 9th April 1990 a person satisfies the capital condition in section 22(6) of the Social Security Act 1986 [SSCBA, s.134(1)] for income support and he would not have satisfied that condition had the amount prescribed under regulation 45 of the Income Support (General) Regulation 1987 been £6,000; and
(b) a claim for that benefit is received from him in an appropriate office not later than 27th May 1990;
the claim shall be treated as made on the date [⁴not later than 5th December 1990] determined in accordance with paragraph (7).

(7) For the purpose of paragraph (6), where—
(a) the claimant satisfies the other conditions of entitlement to income support on the date on which he satisfies the capital condition, the date shall be the date on which he satisfies that condition;
(b) the claimant does not satisfy the other conditions of entitlement to income support on the date on which he satisfies the capital condition, the date shall be the date on which he satisfies the conditions of entitlement to that benefit.]

[⁶(8) [⁸Subject to paragraph (8A [²¹ and (8B)]),] where—
(a) a request is received in an appropriate office for a claim form for disability living allowance or attendance allowance; and
(b) in response to the request a claim form for disability living allowance or attendance is issued from an appropriate office; and
(c) within the time specified the claim form properly completed is received in an appropriate office,
the date on which the claim is made shall be the date which the request was received in the appropriate office.

[⁸(8A) Where, in a case which would otherwise fall within paragraph (8), it is not possible to determine the date when the request for a claim form was received in an appropriate office because of a failure to record that date, the claim shall be treated as having been made on the date 6 weeks before the date on which the properly completed claim form is received in an appropriate office.]

[²¹ (8B) In the case of a claim for disability living allowance or attendance allowance made in accordance with regulation 4(6B), paragraphs (8) and (8A) shall apply in relation to an office specified in that regulation as they apply in relation to an appropriate office.]

(9) [⁹In paragraph (8) and (8A)]—

(SI 1987/1968, reg. 6) (as amended)

"a claim form" means a form approved by the Secretary of State under regulation 4(1); "properly completed" has the meaning assigned by regulation 4(8);

"the time specified" means 6 weeks from the date on which the request was received or such longer period as the Secretary of State may consider reasonable.]

[⁷(10) Where a person starts a job on a Monday or Tuesday in any week and he makes a claim for [¹⁴ disabled person's tax credit] in that week the claim shall be treated as made on the Tuesday of that week.

(11) [¹⁴ . . .]

[¹² (12) [¹⁴ . . .] Where a person has claimed [¹⁴ disabled person's tax credit] and that claim ("the original claim") has been refused, and a further claim is made in the circumstances specified in paragraph (13), that further claim shall be treated as made—

(a) on the date of the original claim; or
(b) on the first date in respect of which the qualifying benefit was payable, whichever is the later.

(13) The circumstances referred to in paragraph (12) are that—

(a) the original claim was refused on the ground that the claimant did not qualify under section 129(2) of the Contributions and Benefits Act;
(b) at the date of the original claim the claimant had made a claim for a qualifying benefit and that claim had not been determined;
(c) after the original claim had been determined, the claim for the qualifying benefit was determined in the claimant's favour; and
(d) the further claim for [¹⁴ disabled person's tax credit] was made within three months of the date that the claim for the qualifying benefit was determined.

(14) [¹⁴ . . .]

(15) In paragraphs (12) and (13) "qualifying benefit" means any of the benefits referred to in section 129(2) of the Contributions and Benefits Act.

[¹⁶ (16) Where a person has claimed a relevant benefit and that claim ("the original claim") has been refused in the circumstances specified in paragraph (17), and a further claim is made in the additional circumstances specified in paragraph (18), that further claim shall be treated as made—

(a) on the date of the original claim; or
(b) on the first date in respect of which the qualifying benefit was payable, whichever is the later.

(17) The circumstances referred to in paragraph (16) are that the ground for refusal was—

(a) in the case of severe disablement allowance, that the claimant's disablement was less than 80 per cent;
(b) [²⁷ . . .];
(c) in any case, that the claimant [¹⁹, a member of his family or the disabled person] had not been awarded a qualifying benefit.

(18) The additional circumstances referred to in paragraph (16) are that—

[¹⁹(a) a claim for the qualifying benefit was made not later than 10 working days after the date of the original claim and the claim for the qualifying benefit had not been decided;
(b) after the original claim had been decided the claim for the qualifying benefit had been decided in favour of the claimant, a member or his family or the disabled person; and]

(c) the further claim was made within three months of the date on which the claim for the qualifying benefit was decided.

(19) Where a person has been awarded a relevant benefit and that award ("the original award") has been terminated in the circumstances specified in paragraph (20), and a further claim is made in the additional circumstances specified in paragraph (21), that further claim shall be treated as made—
- (a) on the date of termination of the original award; or
- (b) on the first date in respect of which the qualifying benefit [19 is [28 awarded or] re-awarded],

whichever is the later.

[28 (20) The circumstances referred to in paragraph (19) are—
- (a) that the award of the qualifying benefit has itself been terminated or reduced by means of a revision, supersession, appeal or termination of an award for a fixed period in such a way as to affect the original award; or
- (b) at the date the original award was terminated the claimant's claim for a qualifying benefit had not been decided.]

(21) The additional circumstances referred to in paragraph (19) are that—
- (a) after the original award has been terminated the claim for the qualifying benefit is decided in [19 favour of the claimant, a member of his family or the disabled person]; and

[28 (b) the further claim is made within three months of the date on which the qualifying benefit is awarded following a claim, whether initially, on revision or on appeal, or re-awarded following revision, supersession, appeal or further claim when an award for a fixed period expires, whether benefit is re-awarded when the further claim is decided or following a revision of, or an appeal against, such a decision.]

(22) In paragraphs (16) to (21) [19 . . .] [27, (30) and (33)]—

"relevant benefit" means any of the following, namely—
- (a) benefits under Parts II to V of the Contributions and Benefits Act except incapacity benefit;
- (b) income support;
- (c) a jobseeker's allowance;
- (d) a social fund payment mentioned in section 138(1)(a) or (2) of the Contributions and Benefits Act;
- (e) child benefit;
- [24 (f) state pension credit]

"qualifying benefit" means—
- (a) in relation to severe disablement allowance, the highest rate of the care component of disability living allowance;
- (b) in relation to invalid care allowance, any benefit referred to in section 70(2) of the Contributions and Benefits Act;
- (c) in relation to a social fund payment in respect of maternity or funeral expenses, any benefit referred to in regulation 5(1)(a) or 7(1)(a) of the Social Fund Maternity and Funeral Expenses (General) Regulations 1987;
- (d) any other relevant benefit which [19, when it is awarded or reawarded,] has the effect of making another relevant benefit payable or payable at an increased rate;

(SI 1987/1968, reg.6) (as amended)

"the disabled person" means the person for whom the invalid care allowanced claimant is caring in accordance with section 70(1)(a) of the Contributions and Benefits Act.

[[19] "family" has the same meaning as in section 137(1) of the Contributions and Benefits Act or, as the case may be, section 35(1) of the Jobseekers Act [[24], and in the case of state pension credit "member of his family" means the other member of a couple where the claimant is a member of a [[25] . . .] couple].]

(23) Where a person has ceased to be entitled to incapacity benefit, and a further claim for that benefit is made in the circumstances specified in paragraph (24), that further claim shall be treated as made—
  (a) on the date on which entitlement to incapacity benefit ceased; or
  (b) on the first date in respect of which the qualifying benefit was payable,
whichever is the later.

(24) The circumstances referred to in paragraph (23) are that—
  (a) entitlement to incapacity benefit ceased on the ground that the claimant was not incapable of work;
  (b) at the date that entitlement ceased the claimant had made a claim for a qualifying benefit and that claim had not been decided;
  (c) after entitlement had ceased, the claim for the qualifying benefit was decided in the claimant's favour; and
  (d) the further claim for incapacity benefit was made within three months of the date on which the claim for the qualifying benefit was decided.

(25) In paragraphs (23) and (24) "qualifying benefit" means any of the payments referred to in regulation 10(2)(a) of the Social Security (Incapacity for Work) (General) Regulations 1995.

(26) In paragraph [[27] (18)(a) and (c), 21(a), (24) and (30) and in paragraph (18)(b)] where the word appears for the second time, "decided" includes the making of a decision following a revision, supersession or an appeal, whether by the Secretary of State, an appeal tribunal, a Commissioner or the court.]

(27) Where a claim is made for [[14] working families' tax credit or disabled person's tax credit], and—
  (a) the claimant had previously made a claim for income support or jobseeker's allowance ("the original claim");
  (b) the original claim was refused on the ground that the claimant or his partner was in remunerative work; and
  (c) the claim for [[14] working families' tax credit or disabled person's tax credit] was made within 14 days of the date that the original claim was determined,
that claim shall be treated as made on the date of the original claim, or, if the claimant so requests, on a later date specified by the claimant.

(28) Where a claim is made for income support or jobseeker's allowance, and—
  (a) the claimant had previously made a claim for [[20] working tax credit] ("the original claim");
  (b) the original claim was refused on the ground that the claimant or his partner was not in remunerative work [[20] for the purposes of that tax credit]; and
  (c) the claim for income support or jobseeker's allowance was made within 14 days of the date that the original claim was determined,
that claim shall be treated as made on the date of the original claim, or, if the claimant so requests, on a later date specified by the claimant.]

(29) In the case of a claim for an increase of severe disablement allowance or of invalid care allowance in respect of a child or adult dependant, [17 paragraph (16) and (19)] shall apply to the claim as if it were a claim for severe disablement allowance or, as the case may be, invalid care allowance.

[19 (30) Where—
  (a) a claimant was awarded income support or income-based jobseeker's allowance ("the original award");
  (b) the original award was termination and not later than 10 working days after the termination, the claimant, a member of his family or the disabled person claimed a qualifying benefit; and
  (c) the claimant makes a further claim for income support or income-based jobseeker's allowance within 3 months of the date on which the claim for the qualifying benefit was decided,
the further claim shall be treated as made on the date of termination of the original award or the first date in respect of which the qualifying benefit is awarded, whichever is the later.]

[22 (31) Subject to paragraph (32), where—
  (a) a person—
    (i) has attained pensionable age, but for the time being makes no claim for a Category A retirement pension; or
    (ii) has attained pensionable age and has a spouse [26 or civil partner] who has attained pensionable age, but for the time being makes no claim for a Category B retirement pension;
  (b) in accordance with regulation 50A of the Social Security (Contributions) Regulations 2001, (Class 3 contributions: tax years 1996–97 to 2001–02) the Commissioners of Inland Revenue subsequently accept Class 3 contributions paid after the due date by the person or, in the case of a Category B retirement pension, the spouse [26 or civil partner];
  (c) in accordance with regulation 6A of the Social Security (Crediting and Treatment of Contributions, and National Insurance Numbers) Regulations 2001 the contributions are treated as paid on a date earlier than the date on which they were paid; and
  (d) the person claims a Category A or, as the case may be, a Category B retirement pension,
the claim shall be treated as made on—
  (i) 1st October 1998; or
  (ii) the date on which the person attained pensionable age in the case of a Category A retirement pension, or, in the case of a Category B retirement pension, the date on which the person's spouse [26 or civil partner] attained pensionable age,
whichever is later.

(32) Paragraph (31) shall not apply where—
  (a) the person's entitlement to a Category A or B retirement pension has been deferred by virtue of section 55(2)(a) of the Contributions and Benefits Act (increase of retirement pension where entitlement is deferred); or
  (b) the person's nominal entitlement to a Category A or B retirement pension is deferred in pursuance of section 36(4) and (7) of the National Insurance Act 1965 (increase of graduated retirement benefit where entitlement is deferred),
nor where sub-paragraph (a) and (b) both apply.]

(SI 1987/1968, reg.6) (as amended)

[²⁷ (33) Where a person makes a claim for a carer's allowance within 3 months of a decision made—
(a) on a claim;
(b) on revision or supersession; or
(c) on appeal whether by an appeal tribunal, a Commissioner or the court,
awarding a qualifying benefit to the disabled person, the date of claim is the first day in respect of which that qualifying benefit is payable.]

AMENDMENTS

1. The Social Security (Claims and Payments) Amendment Regulations 1988 (SI 1988/522), reg.2 (April 11, 1988).
2. The Social Security (Medical Evidence, Claims and Payments) Amendment Regulations 1989 (SI 1989/1686), reg.4 (October 9, 1989).
3. The Social Security (Claims and Payments) Amendment Regulations 1990 (SI 1990/725), reg.2 (April 9, 1990).
4. The Social Security (Miscellaneous Provisions) Amendment Regulations 1990 (SI 1990/2208), reg.9 (December 5, 1990).
5. The Social Security (Miscellaneous Provisions) Amendment Regulations 1991 (SI 1991/2284), reg.6 (November 1, 1991).
6. The Social Security (Claims and Payments) Amendment Regulations 1991 (SI 1991/2741), reg.4 (February 3, 1992).
7. The Social Security (Claims and Payments) Amendment Regulations 1991 (SI 1991/2741), reg.4 (March 10, 1992).
8. The Social Security (Claims and Payments) Amendment (No.3) Regulations 1993 (SI 1993/2113), reg.3 (September 27, 1993).
9. The Social Security (Claims and Payments) Amendment Regulations 1994 (SI 1994/2319), reg.2 (October 3, 1994).
10. The Social Security (Claims and Payments) (Jobseeker's Allowance Consequential Amendments) Regulations 1996 (SI 1996/1460), reg.2(5) (October 7, 1996).
11. The Income Support and Social Security (Claims and Payments) (Miscellaneous Amendments) Regulations 1996 (SI 1996/2431), reg.7(c) (October 15, 1996).
12. The Social Security (Miscellaneous Amendments) (No.2) Regulations 1997 (SI 1997/793), reg.3 (April 7, 1997).
13. The Social Security (Miscellaneous Amendments) (No.2) Regulations 1997 (SI 1997/793), reg.3(3) and (5) (October 6, 1997).
14. The Tax Credits (Claims and Payments) (Amendment) Regulations 1999 (SI 1999/2572), reg.5 (October 5, 1999).
15. The Social Security (Immigration and Asylum) Consequential Amendments Regulations 2000 (SI 2000/636), reg.5 (April 3, 2000).
16. The Social Security and Child Support (Miscellaneous Amendments) Regulations 2000 (SI 2000/1596), reg.3(a) (June 19, 2000).
17. The Social Security and Child Support (Miscellaneous Amendments) Regulations 2000 (SI 2000/1596), reg.3(b) (June 19, 2000).
18. The Social Security (Joint Claims: Consequential Amendments) Regulations 2000 (SI 2000/1982), reg.2(4) (March 19, 2001).
18a. The Tax Credits (Claims and Payments) (Amendment) Regulations 2001 (SI 2001/567) (April 10, 2001).
18b. The Tax Credits (Claims and Payments) Amendment (No.3) Regulations 2001 (SI 2001/892) (April 10, 2001)
19. The Social Security (Claims and Payments and Miscellaneous Amendments) Regulations 2002 (SI 2002/428), reg.2 (April 2, 2002).
20. The Social Security (Working Tax Credit and Child Tax Credit) (Consequential Amendments) Regulations 2003 (SI 2003/455), Sch.4 (April 1, 2003).
21. The Social Security (Claims and Payments and Miscellaneous Amendments) Regulations 2003 (SI 2003/1632), reg.2 (July 21, 2003).

The Social Security (Claims and Payments) Regulations 1987

22. Social Security (Retirement Pensions) Amendment Regulations 2004 (SI 2004/2283), reg.2 (September 27, 2004).
23. The Social Security (Claims and Payments and Payments on account, Overpayments and Recovery) Amendment Regulations 2005 (SI 2005/34), reg.2 (May 2, 2005).
24. The Social Security, Child Support and Tax Credits (Miscellaneous Amendments) Regulations 2005 (SI 2005/337), reg.7 (March 19, 2005).
25. The Social Security (Civil Partnerships) (Consequential Amendments) Regulations 2005 (SI 2005/2878) (December 5, 2005).
26. The Civil Partnership (Pensions, Social Security and Child Support) (Consequential etc. Provisions) Order 2005 (SI 2005/2877) (December 5, 2005).
27. The Social Security (Miscellaneous Amendments) (No.2) Regulations 2006 (SI 2006/832) (April 10, 2006).
28. The Social Security (Miscellaneous Amendments) (No.3) Regulations 2006 (SI 2006/2377) (October 2, 2006).
29. The Social Security (Work-focused Interviews) Regulations 2000 (SI 2000/897) (April 3, 2000).
30. The Tax Credits (Claims and Payments) (Amendment) Regulations 2001 (SI 2001/567) (April 10, 2001).

DEFINITIONS

"appropriate office"—see reg.2(1).
"claim for asylum"—*ibid*.
"claim for benefit"—*ibid*.
"jobseeker's allowance"—*ibid*.

GENERAL NOTE

Introduction

2.65   Claims are not made until received in any appropriate office.

R(SB)8/89 concerns the date of a claim for a single payment of supplementary benefit, but, since the date of claims for most benefits is also the date of receipt in the office of the Department, the decision is directly in point in relation to these benefits. The Commissioner's comments are worth quoting at length since the determination of the date of claim is often an issue arising on appeals:

"In order for the claim to be made it is not alone necessary for the claimant to despatch the form but it is also necessary for the office of the Department to receive it. In my judgment if the office of the Department puts it out of its power to receive the claim by closing its offices and also arranging with the Post Office not to deliver mail on the days upon which the office is closed, then it put it out of its power to receive the claim. It may be that the claim can be received by the office of the Department whether such office is open or closed, but it cannot be received in circumstances where the Department arranges that mail should not be delivered. In her submission to me the adjudication officer now concerned refers to no deliveries being made by the Post Office on days upon which the office of the Department are [*sic*] closed. It will be a question of fact for the new tribunal to find whether such is by arrangement between the Department and Post Office and then to consider whether the Department has put it out of its power to receive claims on a Saturday. If they come to the conclusion that it did and find that in the normal course of delivery on that day then such is the date of claim." (para.7.)

Where claim packs are sent out for disability living allowance and attendance allowance, it is not the practice of the Department (in contrast to the position where enquiries are made about other benefits) to follow the matter up if no completed claim is returned. The Claims and Payments Regulations clearly do not require such action, but it is understood that a number of welfare rights units are concerned that

(SI 1987/1968, reg.6) (as amended)

the variation in practice may operate to the disadvantage of claimants. It is, of course, the receipt of a completed claim (or at least some document which can be regarded as a claim under reg.4) which constitutes a claim under the regulations.

Establishing whether a person has claimed, and, if so, the date of a claim can arise with some frequency before tribunals. In *CP/4104/2004* the Commissioner reminds tribunals of the need to check on both departmental policies of destruction of documents and available computer records in assessing whether a claimant has made a claim. It may be necessary to receive evidence as to what a computer printout actually means. The core advice is not to accept unquestioningly assertions by the Department that it has no record of a claim or enquiry. In the case before the Commissioner that assertion was made to the tribunal, but on further enquiry turned out not to be the correct position.

Para. (1)

2.66 A properly completed claim on the proper form is made on the date that it is received in a benefit office.

There are now many complications around this basic rule following the introduction of JSA and the severe restriction on the backdating of claims under reg.19 from April 1997.

R(SB) 8/89 holds that if the Department puts it out of its power to receive a claim, as by closing its office and arranging with the Post Office not to deliver mail, e.g. on a Saturday, then if that day is the day on which the claim would have been delivered, it is the date of claim. It can be said that by making the arrangement with the Post Office the Department constitute the Post Office bailees of the mail (see *Hodgson v Armstrong* [1967] Q.B. 299 and *Lang v Devon General Ltd* [1987] I.C.R. 4). The Commissioner does not deal expressly with the situation where the office is closed, but there is no arrangement about the mail, e.g. if an office is closed on a Saturday and the Saturday and Monday mail is all stamped with the Monday date in the office. Here, principle would suggest that if it can be shown that in the normal course of the post delivery would have been on the Saturday, then the Saturday is the date of receipt and the date of claim. If a claimant proves a delivery by hand when the office is closed, the date of delivery is the date of receipt.

Note also *CIS/4901/2002* relating to arrangements between the Department and the Post Office for the handling of mail, which is reported in more detail in the annotations to reg.19.

Levy v Secretary of State for Work and Pensions [2006] EWCA Civ 890, reported as *R(G) 2/06* considered the applicability to social security claims of the rebuttable presumption in s.7 of the Interpretation Act 1978 that a letter put in the post is delivered to its addressee. The Court of Appeal ruled that reg.6(1) was not ultra vires. The next question was whether s.7 of the Interpretation Act 1978 applied. Dyson LJ (with whom Hallett and Pill LJJ agreed) concluded that the provision has no application in this context. Even if s.7 did apply, its application would appear to be excluded by the words "unless the contrary intention appears" in s.7 of the Interpretation Act. The Court of Appeal concludes that "It is plain that regulation 6(1) requires that the claim be received in fact and not merely that it be sent." (para. 32 of the judgment). It follows that *CIS/306/2003* and *CG/2973/2004* correctly analyse the legal position and that *CSIS/48/1992* and *CIS/759/1992* are wrong in so far as they suggest otherwise.

Para. (1A)

2.67 This provides that the date of claim for an income support claim will be the date a properly completed claim (i.e. one that complies with reg.4(1A)) is received (or the first day claimed for, if later). But if such a claim is received within one month of the date that the person first contacted the Department with a view to making a claim, or a previous defective claim (i.e. one that does not comply with reg.4(1A)), the date of claim will be the date of that initial contact or defective claim (or the first day claimed for, if later). Thus if more than a month elapses before the claimant

The Social Security (Claims and Payments) Regulations 1987

complies with the requirements of reg.4(1A), the date of claim will be the date of that compliance (unless the rules on backdating apply: see reg.19(4)–(7)). See further the note to reg.4(1A)–(1C).

In *R(IS) 10/06* the Commissioner considers whether there is any priority in the claims covered by reg.6(1A)(c). He concludes:

> "16. On further consideration, I now realise that I was wrong to be concerned about the absence of any specified priority between the two heads of reg.6(1A)(c). 17. This only appears puzzling if the heads in that provisions are read in isolation from subparagraph (b). Subparagraph (c) is expressed as a deeming provision. Its function, though, is more akin to a definition. It sets out the circumstances in which a person is tread as notifying an intention to make a claim. If heads (i) and (ii) are read into paragraph (b), it reads:
>
>> 'where a properly completed claim is received in an appropriate office within one month of first notification of intention to make that clauim, *which may be shown by (i) a notification in accordance with regulation 4(5) or (ii) a defective claim*, the date of claim shall be the date on which that notification is deemed to be made or the first day in respect of which the claim is made if later.'
>
> Set out like that, no issue of priority arises. The claimant is given a choice to rely on one month from the date of notification or from the date of defective claim."

It is worth noting that the view of the Department is that this decision conflicts with *R(IS) 14/04* (which, the Department contends, holds that the one-month period runs from the *first* point of contact; that is, the request for the claim form or the submission of the defective claim form), and argues that the *R(IS) 14/04* should be followed in preference to *R(IS) 10/06*.

In *R(IS) 3/04* the Commissioner rules that it is not possible for a valid claim to income support to be made where a claimant dies having given notification of intention to make a claim but not having perfected the claim before his death by completing and submitting a claim form. The case concerned a situation in which the claim was completed and submitted by the executor of the claimant's will.

Para. (3)

2.68 For these benefits, if the time for claiming is extended under reg.19, the claim is treated as made at the beginning of the period for which the claim is deemed to be in time. Initial claims for working families tax credit and disabled person's tax credit and claims for income support and JSA have to be made on the first day of the period claimed for (Sch.4, paras 6, 7 and 11).

Para. (4)

2.69 The interaction of this provision with others is far from clear. It does not look as though it can apply directly in a case where the decision maker has extended the time for claiming by up to a month under reg.19(6). If the claim is not actually made (i.e. received: para.(1)) within the extended period, the claim is not timeously made and para.(3) above does not apply anyway. Postal delay is not a circumstance listed in reg.19(5) (replacing the old good cause rule), but may be relevant to the reasonableness of the delay in claiming. See also reg.19(7).

Paras (4A)–(4AB)

2.70 In the case of JSA, if the person attends the Job Centre for the purpose of making a claim when required to do so and provides a properly completed claim (i.e. with all the necessary information: see reg.4(1A) and (9)), the date of claim will be the date the person first contacted the Job Centre (or the first day claimed for, if later) (para.(4)(a)(i) and (4AA)). Note the *discretion* to extend the time for delivery of a properly completed claim form under para.(4AB); unlike income support (and JSA postal signers) the month's allowance to return the fully completed claim form is not automatic. Note also para.(4A)(a)(ii) which provides that if the person fails to

(SI 1987/1968, reg.6) (as amended)

comply with these requirements without good cause the date of claim will be the date that he does comply. Thus if the person does have good cause for not so complying, presumably para.(4A)(a)(i) will apply when he does attend and does provide a fully completed claim form (and note the discretion in relation to the claim form under para.(4AB)). For claimants who are not required to attend the Job Centre in person (i.e. who are allowed to apply by post), their claim will be treated as made on the day they first contacted the Job Centre with a view to making a claim (or on the first day claimed for, if later) if a properly completed claim is received within one month, or the date the properly completed claim is received if more than one month has elapsed (para.(4A)(b)). See further the note to reg.4(1A)–(1C)).

Paras (4B) and (4C)
These paragraphs deal with certain cases where entitlement to JSA has ceased because of a failure to attend the Job Centre or to provide a signed declaration of availability and active search for employment, so that a new claim is necessary.

2.71

Para. (4D)
These are special rules for claims by refugees.

2.72

Paras (6) and (7)
These provisions create a special rule on the increase of the capital limit for income support to £8,000. Where, from April 9, 1990, a claimant has capital of more than £6,000 but not more than £8,000, a claim made before May 28, 1990, can be back-dated to the date on which all the conditions of entitlement are satisfied.

2.73

Para. (10)
Where a claimant starts work on a Monday or Tuesday and makes a claim for disability working allowance at any time in that week (i.e. Sunday to Saturday), the claim is treated as made on the Tuesday.

2.74

Paras (12)–(15)
Where a claim for disabled persons tax credit is disallowed on the ground that a qualifying benefit is not payable, although a claim for that benefit has been made, and later the qualifying benefit is awarded, a fresh claim for the tax credit made within three months of the award of the qualifying benefit is to be treated as made on the date of the original claim (or the date from which the qualifying benefit is awarded, if later). This rule is made necessary by the restrictions from April 1997 on the backdating of claims under reg.19 and on the effect of reviews.

2.75

Paras (31) and (32)
These provisions 'get around' the twelve month limitation on back-dating set out in s.1(2) of the Administration Act in relation to claims for retirement pension. They enable claimants to go back as far as October 1, 1998 in certain circumstances. The Explanatory Memorandum to the regulations indicates that the intended beneficiaries of the provisions are those who did not receive notice that their contribution records were deficient for the tax years 1996/97 to 2002/02 because the annual Deficiency Notice procedure which identifies such cases and advises customers of the need to consider making voluntary contributions to make good the shortfall did not take place in those years.

2.78

Claims by persons subject to work-focused interviews

[¹**6A.**—[² (1) This regulation applies to any person who is required to take part in a work-focused interview in accordance with regulations made under section 2A(1)(a) of the Social Security Administration Act 1992.]

2.79

(2) Subject to the following provisions of this regulation, where a person takes part in a work-focused interview, the date on which the claim is made shall be—

The Social Security (Claims and Payments) Regulations 1987

    (a) in a case where—
        (i) the claim made by the claimant meets the requirements of regulation 4(1), or
        (ii) the claim made by the claimant is for income support and meets the requirements of regulation 4(1A),
    the date on which the claim is received in the appropriate office.
    (b) in a case where a claim does not meet the requirements of regulation 4(a) but is treated, under regulation 4(7), as having been duly made, the date on which the claim was treated as received in the appropriate office in the first instance;
    (c) in a case where—
        (i) first notification of intention to claim income support is made to an appropriate office, or
        (ii) a claim for income support is received in an appropriate office which does not meet the requirements of regulation 4(1A),
[5 (d) without prejudice to sub-paragraphs (a) and (b), where a properly completed claim for incapacity benefit is received in an appropriate office within one month of the claimant first notifying such an office, by whatever means, of his intention to make that claim, the date of claim shall be the date on which that notification is made or the first day in respect of which the claim is made if later.]
the date of notification of, as the case may be, the date the claim is first received where the properly complete claim form is received within 1 month of notification or the date the claim is first received, or the day on which a properly completed claim form is received where these requirements are not met.

    (3) In a case where a decision is made that a person is regarded as not having made a claim for any benefit because he failed to take part in a work-focused interview but subsequently claims such a benefit, in applying paragraph (2) to that claim no regard shall be had to any claim regarded as not having been made in consequence of that decision.

    (4) Paragraph (2) shall not apply in any case where a decision has been made that the claimant has failed to take part in a work-focused interview.

    [4 (5) In regulation 4 and this regulation, "work-focused interview" means an interview which [. . .] [is conducted for such purposes connected with employment or training as are specified under section 2A of the Social Security Administration Act 1992.]

AMENDMENTS

    1. Regulation inserted by The Social Security (Work-focused Interviews) Regulations 2000 (SI 2000/897) (April 3, 2000).
    2. The Social Security (Jobcentre Plus Interviews) Regulations 2001 (SI 2001/3210) (October 22, 2001).
    3. Social Security (Jobcentre Plus Interviews) Regulations 2002 (SI 2002/1703), Sch.2, (September 30, 2002).
    4. Social Security (Working Neighbourhoods) Regulations 2004 (SI 2004/959), reg.22 (April 26, 2004).
    5. The Social Security (Miscellaneous Amendments) (No.2) Regulations 2006 (SI 2006/832) (April 10, 2006).

Evidence and information

2.80   **7.**—(1) [3Subject to paragraph (7),] every person who makes a claim for benefit shall furnish such certificates, documents, information and evidence in connection with the claim, or any question arising out of it, as may be

(SI 1987/1968, reg. 7) (as amended)

required by the Secretary of State [⁴ or the Board] and shall do so within one month of being required to do so or such longer period as the Secretary of State [⁵Board] may consider reasonable.

[⁶ (1A) A claimant shall furnish such information and evidence as the Secretary of State may require as to the likelihood of future changes in his circumstances which is needed to determine—
(a) whether a period should be specified as an assessed income period under section 6 of the 2002 Act in relation to any decision; and
(b) if so, the length of the period to be so specified.

(1B) The information and evidence required under paragraph (1A) shall be furnished within 1 month of the Secretary of State notifying the claimant of the requirement, or within such longer period as the Secretary of State considers reasonable in the claimant's case.

(1C) In the case of a claimant making a claim for state pension credit in the advance period, time begins to run for the purposes of paragraphs (1) and (1B) on the day following the end of that period.]

(2) [³Subject to paragraph (7),] where a benefit may be claimed by either of two partners or where entitlement to or the amount of any benefit is or may be affected by the circumstances of a partner, the Secretary of State may require the partner other than the [⁵claimant to do either or both of the following, within one month of being required to do so or such longer period as the Board may consider reasonable—
(a) to certify in writing whether he agrees to the claimant making or, as the case may be, that he confirms the information given about his circumstances;
(b) to furnish such certificates, documents, information and evidence in connection with the claim, or any question arising out of it, as the Board may require.]
claimant to certify in writing whether he agrees to the claimant making the claim or, as the case may be, that he confirms the information given about his circumstances [⁴working families tax credit or disabled persons tax credit].

(3) In the case of a claim for [⁴working families' tax credit] or [⁴disabled person's tax credit], the employer of the claimant or, as the case may be, of the partner shall [⁴within one month of being required to do so or such longer period as the Board may consider reasonable] furnish such certificates, documents, information and evidence in connection with the claim or any question arising out of it as may be required by the Secretary of State [⁴Board].

[² (4) In the case of a person who is claiming [⁴ disabled person's tax credit, working families' tax credit], [⁶ jobseeker's allowance or state pension credit] where that person or any partner is aged not less than 60 and is a member of, or a person deriving entitlement to a pension under, a personal pension scheme, or is a party to, or a person deriving entitlement to a pension under, a retirement annuity contract, he shall where the [⁵ Board so require, within one month of being required to do so or such longer period as the Board may consider reasonable] Secretary of State so requires furnish the following information—
(a) the name and address of the pension fund holder;
(b) such other information including any reference or policy number as is needed to enable the personal pension scheme or retirement annuity contract to be identified.

(5) Where the pension fund holder receives from the Secretary of State [⁵Board] a request for details concerning the personal pension scheme or

401

The Social Security (Claims and Payments) Regulations 1987

retirement annuity contract relating to a person or any partner to whom paragraph (4) refers, the pension fund holder shall [5, within one month of the request or such longer period as the Board may consider reasonable] provide the Secretary of State [5Board] with any information to which paragraph (6) refers.

(6) The information to which this paragraph refers is—
  (a) where the purchase of an annuity under a personal pension scheme has been deferred, the amount of any income which is being withdrawn from the personal pension scheme;
  (b) in the case of—
    (i) a personal pension scheme where income withdrawal is available, the maximum amount of income which may be withdrawn from the scheme; or
    (ii) a personal pension scheme where income withdrawal is not available, or a retirement annuity contract, the maximum amount of income which might be withdrawn from the fund if the fund were held under a personal pension scheme where income withdrawal was available,

calculated by or on behalf of the pension fund holder by means of tables prepared from time to time by the Government Actuary which are appropriate for this purpose.]

[3(7) Paragraphs (1) and (2) do not apply in the case of jobseeker's allowance.]

[4(8) Every person providing childcare in respect of which a claimant to whom regulation 46A of the Family Credit (General) Regulations 1987 applies is incurring relevant childcare charges, including a person providing childcare on behalf of a school, local authority, childcare scheme or establishment within paragraph (2)(b), (c) or (d) of that regulation, shall furnish such certificates, documents, information and evidence in connection with the claim made by the claimant, or any question arising out of it, as may required by the Board, and shall do so within one month of being required to do so or such longer period as the Board may consider reasonable.

(9) In paragraph (8) "relevant childcare charges" has the meaning given by regulation 46A(2) of the Family Credit (General) Regulations 1987.]

AMENDMENTS

1. The Social Security (Claims and Payments) Amendment Regulations 1991 (SI 1991/2741), reg.5 (March 10, 1992).
2. Income-related Benefit Schemes and Social Security (Claims and Payments) (Miscellaneous Amendments) Regulations 1995 (SI 1995/2303), reg.10(3) (October 2, 1995).
3. The Social Security (Claims and Payments) (Jobseeker's Allowance Consequential Amendments) Regulations 1996 (SI 1996/1460), reg.2(6) (October 7, 1996).
4. The Tax Credits (Claims and Payments) (Amendment) Regulations 1999 (SI 1999/2572), reg.6 (October 5, 1999).
5. For tax credits purposes only: The Tax Credits (Claims and Payments) (Amendment) Regulations 1999 (SI 1999/2572), reg.6 (October 5, 1999).
6. State Pension Credit (Consequential, Transitional and Miscellaneous) Regulations 2002 (SI 2002/3019), reg.4 (April 7, 2003).

DEFINITIONS

"benefit"—see reg.2(2).
"claim for benefit"—see reg.2(1).

(SI 1987/1968, reg.7) (as amended)

"jobseeker's allowance"—*ibid.*
"partner"—*ibid.*
"pension fund holder"—*ibid.*
"personal pension scheme"—*ibid.*
"retirement annuity contract"—*ibid.*

GENERAL NOTE

From time to time, decision makers have suggested that a person is not entitled to benefit because they have failed to furnish the Secretary of State with information within the one month referred to in reg.7(1). *R(IS)4/93* was just such a case. The adjudication officer decided that the claimant was not entitled to income support because the claimant had failed—inter alia to provide sufficient evidence as to the amount of capital held. The tribunal confirmed the adjudication officer's decision and the claimant appealed to the Commissioner.

2.81

Deputy Commissioner Mesher (as he then was) concluded that both the adjudication officer and the tribunal had misunderstood the operation of reg.7(1). Drawing on the reasoning of the Court of Appeal in *R. v Secretary of State for Social Services Ex p. Child Poverty Action Group* [1990] 2 Q.B. 540, the Deputy Commissioner explains that reg.7(1) is concerned with the responsibilities of the Secretary of State to collect information so that the Secretary of State can submit a claim to an adjudication officer for determination:

"Once such a submission is made, it is simply irrelevant whether or not the claimant has satisfied the Secretary of State under reg.7(1) of the Claims and Payments Regulations or whether or not the claimant has furnished sufficient information for the Secretary of State to refer the claim to the adjudication officer. Those matters are entirely for the Secretary of State [see para.11 of *R(SB)29/83*]. Once the claim is submitted to him under section 98(1) [now s.20(1) of the Administration Act], the adjudication officer's duty is to take it into consideration and, so far as practicable, dispose of it within 14 days of its submission (Social Security Act 1975, s.99(1)) [now s.21(1) of the Administration Act]. As decided by the Court of Appeal in the passage quoted above, the adjudication officer has the power to make further investigations or call for further evidence before determining the claim. Or he may determine the claim on the evidence currently available, especially if he considers that the claimant has already had a reasonable opportunity of producing the required information or evidence." (para.13.)

The Deputy Commissioner goes on to advise that adjudication officers and tribunals when presented with a claim for determination (whether initially or on appeal) must focus on the "essential elements of entitlement directly" in the light of the evidence available. Since claimants generally have the burden of showing on the balance of probabilities that they meet the conditions of entitlement, the absence of information from the claimant will often result in a finding against them.

The Deputy Commissioner does not spell out how tribunals should proceed if the absence of information means that the tribunal cannot make any findings of fact. There will be cases where there is insufficient information to find positively some fact which results in there being no entitlement. In these rare cases where a claimant's reluctance to participate defeats the inquisitorial jurisdiction of tribunals, it is open to the tribunal to decide the matter purely on the burden of proof. In such cases the proper approach is for the tribunal:

— to record no findings of fact, or perhaps only those that are proved, *avoiding* the inclusion of reference to those issues on which facts cannot be found

— to record in the decision that the claimant is not entitled to the benefit on the claim made on such and such a day because they have not proved on the balance of probabilities that they meet the conditions of entitlement for the benefit

The Social Security (Claims and Payments) Regulations 1987

— to explain fully in the reasons for the decision what the relevant conditions of entitlement are and why the tribunal is unable to make findings of fact on all the material issues.

R(IS) 4/93 has been referred to and disapproved by the Court of Appeal in Northern Ireland in *Kerr v Department for Social Development* [2002] N.I.C.A. 32, Judgment of July 4, 2002. That decision went an appeal to the House of Lords. The decision of the House of Lords in *Kerr v Department for Social Development*, [2004] UKHL 23; [2004] 1 W.L.R. 1372 (appendix to *R1/04(SF)*) was handed down on May 6, 2004. The discussion in the House of Lords broadened from the considerations which had taken place in the courts below. The comments, in particular of Baroness Hale, on the decision-making process are discussed in detail in the annotations to s.12, Social Security Act 1998. The House of Lords dismissed the appeal. In their opinions, no mention is made of *R(IS) 4/93* which had been disapproved in the reasons of the Court of Appeal. Notwithstanding the absence of any comment, its authority must be considerably weakened by the dismissal of the appeal. However, it is suggested that it will still provide some useful guidance in those cases where, despite the best endeavours of the adjudicating authorities to collect all the evidence needed to determine a claim for benefit, they remain short of evidence on key matters. For a discussion of the similar provisions in relation to the adjudication of housing benefit and council tax benefit claims see the decision of the Tribunal of Commissioners in *R(H) 3/05*.

In *CIS/51/2007* and *CIB/52/2007* the Commissioner comments on the relationship between regs 4–6A, and reg. 7. The context was a claim which left some uncertainty about the claimant's identity (the national insurance number provided did not correspond to the identity of the claimant) and the correctness of his address (enquiries to the address given had resulted in denials that the claimant had ever lived there). The Commissioner notes that there are requirements for making a claim under the regulations, which are a matter of form and procedure, and that these should be distinguished from "the obvious and universal necessity for any person making such a claim to substantiate it by showing he meets the qualifying conditions for entitlement". This is a matter of fact and evidence (para. 8). The provisions of reg.7(1) apply only to those who have made something that can be identified as a procedurally effective claim. That is determined by applying the rules in reg. 4 to 6A. A claim which raises questions about the identity of the claimant may be a claim. Establishing identity is a matter of fact and evidence. If claimants cannot establish these matters, then they have failed to comply with the reasonable evidence requirements, and it will be appropriate to determine that they have not met the conditions of entitlement.

Attendance in person

2.82   8.—(1)[^{1}. . .]

(2) Every person who makes a claim for benefit [^{1} (other than a jobseeker's allowance)] shall attend at such office or place and on such days and at such times as the Secretary of State [^{2} or the Board] may direct, for the purpose of furnishing certificates, documents, information and evidence under regulation 7, if reasonably so required by the Secretary of State [^{2} or the Board].

AMENDMENTS

1. The Social Security (Claims and Payments) (Jobseeker's Allowance Consequential Amendments) Regulations 1996 (SI 1996/1460), reg.2(7) (October 7, 1996).

2. The Tax Credits (Claims and Payments) (Amendment) Regulations 1999 (SI 1999/2572), reg.20 (October 5, 1999).

(SI 1987/1968, reg.8) (as amended)

DEFINITIONS

"benefit"—see reg.2(2).
"claim for benefit"—see reg.2(1).

GENERAL NOTE

There seems now to be no direct sanction for a failure to comply with reg.8(2) in relation to benefits other than JSA. For JSA obligations, see reg.23 of the Jobseeker's Allowance Regulations.

Interchange with claims for other benefits

9.—(1) Where it appears that a person who has made a claim for benefit specified in column (1) of Part I of Schedule 1 may be entitled to the benefit specified opposite to it in column (2) of that Part, any such claim may be treated by the Secretary of State [¹ or the Board] as a claim alternatively, or in addition, to the benefit specified opposite to it in that column.

(2) Where it appears that a person who has claimed any benefit specified in Part II of Schedule 1 in respect of a child may be entitled to child benefit in respect of the same child, the Secretary of State may treat the claim alternatively, or in addition, for the benefit in question as a claim by that person for child benefit.

(3) Where it appears that a person who has claimed child benefit in respect of a child may be entitled to any benefit specified in Part II of Schedule 1 [². . .] in respect of the same child, the Secretary of State may treat the claim for child benefit as a claim alternatively, or in addition, by that person for the benefit in question specified in that Part.

(4) Where it appears that a person who has made a claim for benefit other than child benefit is not entitled to it, but that some other person may be entitled to an increase of benefit in respect of him, the Secretary of State may treat the claim as if it were a claim by such other person for an increase of benefit in respect of the claimant.

(5) Where it appears that a person who has made a claim for an increase of benefit other than child benefit in respect of a child or adult dependant is not entitled to it but that some other person may be entitled to such an increase of benefit in respect of that child or adult dependant, the Secretary of State may treat the claim as if it were a claim by that other person for such an increase.

(6) Where it appears that a person who has made a claim for a guardian's allowance in respect of any child is not entitled to it, but that the claimant or the wife or husband of the claimant, may be entitled to an increase of benefit for that child, the Secretary of State may treat the claim as if it were a claim by the claimant or the wife or husband of the claimant for an increase of benefit for that child.

[³ (7) In determining whether he [¹ or they] should treat a claim alternatively or in addition to another claim (the original claim) under this regulation the Secretary of State shall treat the alternative or additional claim, whenever made, as having been made at the same time as the original claim.]

AMENDMENTS

1. The Tax Credits (Claims and Payments) (Amendment) Regulations 1999 (SI 1999/2572), regs 20 and 22 (October 5, 1999).

The Social Security (Claims and Payments) Regulations 1987

2. The Child Benefit, Child Support and Social Security (Miscellaneous Amendments) Regulations 1996 (SI 1996/1803), reg.19 (April 7, 1997).
3. The Social Security (Miscellaneous Provisions) Amendment Regulations 1992 (SI 1992/247), reg.12 (March 9, 1992).

GENERAL NOTE

2.85   This invaluable provision removes some of the rigour of ensuring that a claimant chooses the right benefit to claim and is not prejudiced by making a mistaken choice. The regulation now also covers interchange of claims for child benefit with claims for other benefits. There was originally some doubt over whether a decision to treat a claim as one in the alternative was for the adjudicating authorities or the Secretary of State. Note that, with the introduction of incapacity benefit, the arrangement whereby claims for unemployment benefit may be treated as claims for one of the sickness benefits has been ended.

In *R. v Secretary of State for Social Security Ex p. Cullen and Nelson* (*The Times*, May 16, 1997 reported as *R(A) 1/97*), the Court of Appeal confirmed the decision of Harrison J. in *Cullen* (November 16, 1996) and reversed the decision of the Commissioner in *Nelson* (*CA 171/1993*). In both cases, unsuccessful claims for supplementary benefit had been made prior to April 11, 1988. At that time, the 1979 Claims and Payments Regulations allowed the Secretary of State to treat a claim for supplementary benefit as in the alternative a claim for attendance allowance. The Claims and Payments Regulations 1987, which came into effect on April 11, 1988, contained no such power. In 1991 (*Cullen*) and 1993 (*Nelson*) claims for attendance allowance were made and it was sought to have the supplementary benefit claims treated as claims for attendance allowance. The Court of Appeal held that the Secretary of State had no power to do so, so that the Commissioner in *CA/171/1993* was wrong to refer the question to the Secretary of State for determination. Once the 1979 Regulations were revoked, the Secretary of State could no longer exercise a power which no longer existed. As the Secretary of State had only had a discretion under the 1979 Regulations whether or not to treat a supplementary benefit claim as in the alternative a claim for attendance allowance, the claimants had no accrued rights which were preserved on the revocation of the 1979 Regulations under s.16 of the Interpretation Act 1978.

[¹ Claim for incapacity benefit or severe disablement allowance where no entitlement to statutory sick pay or statutory maternity pay]

2.86   **10.**—(1) Paragraph (2) applies to a claim for incapacity benefit or severe] disablement allowance for a period of incapacity for work of which the claimant gave his employer a notice of incapacity under regulation 7 of the Statutory Sick Pay (General) Regulations 1982, and for which he has been informed in writing by his employer that there is no entitlement to statutory sick pay.

(2) A claim to which this paragraph applies shall be treated as made on the date accepted by the claimant's employer as the first day of incapacity, provided that he makes the claim—
  (a) within the appropriate time specified in paragraph 2 of Schedule 4 beginning with the day on which he is informed in writing that he was not entitled to statutory sick pay; or
  (b) [² . . .]

(3) Paragraph (4) applies to a claim for maternity allowance for a pregnancy or confinement by reason of which the claimant gave her employer notice of absence from work under [section 164(4) of the Social Security Contributions and Benefits Act 1992] and regulation 23 of the Statutory Maternity Pay (General) Regulations 1986 and in respect of which she has

(SI 1987/1968, reg.10) (as amended)

been informed in writing by her employer that there is no entitlement to statutory maternity pay.

(4) A claim to which this paragraph applies shall be treated as made on the date when the claimant gave her employer notice of absence from work or at the beginning of the 14th week before the expected week of confinement, whichever is later, provided that she makes the claim—
  (a) within three months of being informed in writing that she was not entitled to statutory maternity pay; or
  (b) [² . . .]

AMENDMENTS

1. The Social Security (Claims and Payments) Amendment (No.2) Regulations 1994 (SI 1994/2943), reg.3 (April 13, 1995).
2. The Social Security (Miscellaneous Amendments) (No.2) Regulations 1997 (SI 1997/793), reg.4 (April 7, 1997).

Special provisions where it is certified that a woman is expected to be confined or where she has been confined

11.—(1) Where in a certificate issued or having effect as issued under the Social Security (Medical Evidence) Regulations 1976 it has been certified that it is to be expected that a woman will be confined, and she makes a claim for maternity allowance in expectation of that confinement any such claim may, unless the Secretary of State otherwise directs, be treated as a claim for [¹ incapacity city benefit] or severe disablement allowance made in respect of any days in the period beginning with either—
  (a) the beginning of the 6th week before the expected week of confinement; or
  (b) the actual date of confinement, whichever is the earlier, and ending in either case on the 14th day after the actual date of confinement.

(2) Where, in a certificate issued under the Social Security (Medical Evidence) Regulations 1976 it has been certified that a woman has been confined and she claims maternity allowance within [² three months] of that date, her claim may be treated in the alternative or in addition as a claim for incapacity benefit or severe disablement allowance for the period beginning with the date of her confinement and ending 14 days after that date.

2.87

AMENDMENTS

1. The Social Security (Claims and Payments) Amendment (No.2) Regulations 1994 (SI 1994/2943), reg.4 (April 13, 1995).
2. The Social Security (Miscellaneous Amendments) (No.2) Regulations 1997 (SI 1997/793), reg.5 (April 7, 1997).

GENERAL NOTE

In *R(S)1/74* the Commissioner held that a similarly worded predecessor to this regulation which made similar, though not identical, provision neither confers title to sickness benefit nor restricts the right to it. The regulation does no more than define the period for which, having made an unsuccessful claim to maternity allowance, a woman may be treated as having made a claim to incapacity benefit. There is nothing to prevent her seeking to prove incapacity for some period or periods additional to that to which her claim is taken to relate.

2.88

The Social Security (Claims and Payments) Regulations 1987

2.89 *Regulation 12 revoked by The Social Security (Claims and Payments on account, Overpayments and Recovery) Amendment Regulations 1989 (SI 1989/136) (February 27, 1989).*

Advance claims and awards

2.90 13.—(1) Where, although a person does not satisfy the requirements for entitlement to a benefit on the date on which the claim is made, the [⁶ Secretary of State] is of the opinion that unless there is a change of circumstances he will satisfy those requirements for a period beginning on a day ("the relevant day") not more than 3 months after the date on which the claim is made, then [⁶ Secretary of State] may—
  (a) treat the claim as if made for a period beginning with the relevant day; and
  (b) award benefit accordingly, subject to the condition that the person satisfies the requirements for entitlement when benefit becomes payable under the award.
  (2) [⁶ A decision pursuant to paragraph (1)(b) to award benefit may be revised under section 9 of the Social Security Act 1998] if the requirements for entitlement are found not to have been satisfied on the relevant day.
  (3) [⁵ Subject to paragraph (4), paragraphs (1) and (2) do not] apply to any claim for maternity allowance, attendance allowance [⁷ disabled person's tax credit], [⁸ state pension credit] retirement pension or increase, [⁹ a shared additional pension] [⁷ working families' tax credit] [² disability living allowance], or any claim within regulation 11(1)(a) or (b)
  [¹(4) Paragraphs (1) and (2) of this regulation shall apply to a claim for [⁷ working families' tax credit] made—
  (a) on or after 10th March 1992 and before 7th April 1992;
  (b) in respect of a period beginning on or after 7th April 1992; and
  (c) by a person who, if he is a member of a married or unmarried couple, he or the other member of the couple, is engaged and normally engaged in remunerative work for not less than 16 but less than 24 hours a week on the date the claim is made.
  (5) In paragraph (4)(c) "remunerative work" and "engaged and normally engaged in remunerative work" shall be construed in accordance with regulations 4 and 5 respectively of the Family Credit (General) Regulations 1987 [³ save that in their application to paragraph 4(c) those regulations shall be read as though for the words "not less than 24 hours" there were substituted the words "not less than 16 hours but less than 24 hours"].]
  [⁵ (6) Where a person claims [⁷ working families' tax credit or disabled person's tax credit] but does not satisfy the requirements for entitlement to that benefit on the date on which the claim is made, and the adjudicating authority is of the opinion that he will satisfy those requirements for a period beginning on a day not more than 3 days after the date on which the claim is made, the adjudicating authority may treat the claim as if made for a period beginning with that day, and award benefit accordingly.]
  [⁷ Where on or after 7th September 1999 but before 5th October 1999 a person claims family credit or disability working allowance but does not satisfy the requirements for entitlement to that benefit on the date on which the claim is made, and the adjudicating authority is of the opinion that he will satisfy the requirements for working families' tax credit or disabled person's tax credit for a period beginning on 5th October 1999, the

(SI 1987/1968, reg.13) (as amended)

claim shall be treated by the adjudicating authority as a claim made on 5th October for a period starting on that date.

(8) Where on or after 20th September 1999 but before 2nd October 1999 a person claims working families' tax credit or disabled person's tax credit, the claim shall be treated by the adjudicating authority as a claim made on 5th October 1999 for a period starting on that date or on such later date as is specified in the claim.]

AMENDMENTS

1. The Social Security (Miscellaneous Provisions) Amendment Regulations 1991 (SI 1991/2284), reg.7 (November 1, 1991).
2. The Social Security (Claims and Payments) Amendment Regulations 1991 (SI 1991/2741) (SI 1991/2741), reg.6(a) (February 3, 1992).
3. The Social Security (Miscellaneous Provisions) Amendment Regulations 1992 (SI 1992/247), reg.13 (March 9, 1992).
4. The Social Security (Claims and Payments) Amendment Regulations 1991 (SI 1991/2741), reg.6(b) (March 10, 1992).
5. The Social Security (Claims and Payments) Amendment Regulations 1994 (SI 1994/2319), reg.3 (October 3, 1994).
6. The Social Security Act 1998 (Commencement No.9, and Savings and Consequential and Transitional Provisions) Order 1999 (SI 1999/2422), Sch.7 (September 6, 1999).
7. The Tax Credits (Claims and Payments) (Amendment) Regulations 1999 (SI 1999/2572), reg.7 (October 5, 1999).
8. State Pension Credit (Consequential, Transitional and Miscellaneous) Regulations 2002 (SI 2002/3019), reg.6 (April 7, 2003).
9. The Social Security (Shared Additional Pension) (Miscellaneous Amendments) Regulations 2005 (SI 2005/1551) (July 6, 2005).

DEFINITIONS

"adjudicating authority"—see reg.2(1).
"benefit"—see reg.2(2).
"married couple"—see reg.2(1).
"unmarried couple"—*ibid.*

GENERAL NOTE

Paragraphs (1) and (2) contain a useful power in income support and social fund maternity and funeral expenses cases, to make awards in advance, subject to review if circumstances change. Paragraph (1) gives a wide discretion (*CIS/459/1994*).

The general rule in para.(3) is that the power in paras (1) and (2) does not apply to family credit, but para.(4) allowed advance claims immediately in advance of the change in the number of qualifying hours from 24 to 16 in April 1992. See also para.(6).

The power in paras (1) and (2) does not apply to disabled person's tax credit (para.(3)), but see reg.13B for claims in advance of the start of the scheme, and para.(6).

From October 1994, para.(6) allows family credit and disability working allowance and now working families' tax credit and disabled person's tax credit claims to be made up to three days in advance.

Para.(1)

In joined cases *CIS/3280/2003*, *CIS/1124/2004* and *CIS/1840/2004* (which were "habitual residence" cases), an issue arose as to the proper interpretation of reg.13(1) and (2). The Tribunal of Commissioners in *R(DLA) 4/05* observed that the language of the similarly worded provision in reg.13A and 13C suggested that

2.91

2.92

The Social Security (Claims and Payments) Regulations 1987

the mere passage of time could not constitute a change of circumstances for the purposes of those regulations. The question in *CIS/3280/2003*, *CIS/1124/2004* and *CIS/1840/ 2004* was whether the passage of time in the case of a claim for income support which initially failed because the claimant was not considered to be habitually resident in Great Britain could constitute a change of circumstances. The Secretary of State argued that reg.13 had no application because being habitually resident is not a condition of entitlement to benefit. He argued that the effect of the claimant's not being habitually resident was that the claimant satisfied the conditions of entitlement but that the effect of her not being habitually resident was that she was treated as a person from abroad whose applicable amount was nil. The Commissioner, however, inclines to the view that reg.13 "should be construed so as to apply where a claimant's applicable amount is nil." (para.22). This would enable the Secretary of State (or a tribunal on appeal) to make an advance award effective from the date on which it would appear that the requirement of habitual residence would mean that the claimant was no longer to be treated as a person from abroad. Ultimately, the Commissioner did not need to take a firm view on this issue, since he found that reg.6(2)(a)(ii) of the Decisions and Appeals Regulations allowed the passage of time to be treated as a change of circumstances, which would enable a supersession decision to be made so as to award income support at a higher rate than nil when the habitual residence requirement was met.

CIS/1840/2004 has been upheld in the Court of Appeal as *The Secretary of State for Work and Pensions v Bhakta* [2006] EWCA Civ 65, reported as *R(IS) 7/06.*

Note that The Social Security, Housing Benefit and Council Tax Benefit (Miscellaneous Amendments) Regulations 2007, SI 2007/1331 (which entered into force on May 23, 2007) reverse the effect of the *Bhakta* decision. The amendments, in essence, insert a provision that excludes persons from abroad from making an advance claim for income support, income-based jobseeker's allowance, state pension credit, housing benefit, and council tax benefit.

Advance award of disability living allowance

2.93

[¹ **13A.**—(1) Where, although a person does not satisfy the requirement for entitlement to disability living allowance on the date on which the claim is made, the [² Secretary of State] is of the opinion that unless there is a change of circumstances he will satisfy those requirements for a period beginning on a day ("the relevant day" not more than 3 months after the date on which the claim is made, then [² the Secretary of State] may award disability living allowance from the relevant day subject to the condition that the person satisfies the requirements for entitlement on the relevant day.

(2) Where a person makes a claim for disability living allowance on or after 3rd February 1992 and before 6th April 1992 the adjudicating authority may award benefit for a period beginning on or after 5th April 1992 being a day not more than three months after the date on which the claim was made, subject to the condition that the person satisfies the requirements for entitlement when disability living allowance becomes payable under the award.

(3) [² A decision pursuant to paragraph (1) or (2) to award benefit may be revised under section 9 of the Social Security Act 1998] if the requirements for entitlement are found not to have been satisfied when disability living allowance becomes payable under the award.]

AMENDMENTS

1. The Social Security (Claims and Payments) Amendment Regulations 1991 (SI 1991/2741), reg.7 (February 3, 1992).

2. The Social Security Act 1998 (Commencement No.11 and Transitional Provisions) Order 1999 (SI 1999/2860), Sch.3 (October 18, 1999).

(SI 1987/1968, reg.13A) (as amended)

GENERAL NOTE

In *CSDLA/852/2002,* and repeated in *CSDLA/553/2005* the Commissioner explains: 2.94

"4. Regulation 13A thus permits an award of DLA where a claim is made no more than three months before the date from which the award takes effect, if the DM considers that by that date the claimant will satisfy the three months qualifying period for DLA and is then likely so to satisfy the qualifying conditions for a further six-month period. The claim subsists until the matter is determined by the DM (s.8(2)(a) of the Social Security Act 1998).
5. A claim is to be treated as being continuously made until it is determined. Therefore, although Regulation 13A only benefits the claimant if the claim is made within the relevant three-month period, it applies provided that the DLA conditions in question are satisfied by the date of the Secretary of State's decision under appeal and seemed likely to continue for both the three-month qualifying period and the six-month prospective period, so that the Secretary of State could then have made an advance award.
6. The issue for the tribunal was, therefore, whether . . . when the claim was decided by the Secretary of State (and beyond which circumstances could not be taken because of section 12(8)(b) of the Social Security Act 1998), circumstances existed, (even if proved by later evidence not available to the DM at the time) which justified an award under regulation 13A."
See also *CSDLA/242/2006.*

[¹ Advance claim for and award of disability working allowance

13B.—(1) Where a person makes a claim for disability working allowance 2.95
on or after 10th March 1992 and before 7th April 1992 the adjudicating authority may—
(a) treat the claim as if it were made for a period beginning on 7th April 1992; and
(b) An award benefit accordingly, subject to the condition that the person satisfies the requirements for entitlement on 7th April 1992.
(2) An award under paragraph (1)(b) shall be reviewed by the adjudicating authority if the requirements for entitlement are found not to have been satisfied on 7th April 1992.]

AMENDMENT

The Social Security (Claims and Payments) Amendment Regulations 1991 (SI 1991/2741), reg.7(2) (March 10, 1992).

DEFINITION

"adjudicating authority"—see reg.2(1).

GENERAL NOTE

This allowed an advance claim in the few weeks immediately before the start of 2.96
the scheme on April 7, 1992.

[¹ Further claim for and award of disability living allowance or attendance allowance

13C.—(1) A person entitled to an award of disability living allowance 2.97
or attendance allowance may make a further claim for disability living allowance or attendance allowance, as the case may be, during the period of 6 months immediately before the existing award expires.]

The Social Security (Claims and Payments) Regulations 1987

AMENDMENTS

1. The Social Security, Child Support and Tax Credits (Miscellaneous Amendments) Regulations 2005 (SI 2005/337), reg.7 (March 18, 2005).

GENERAL NOTE

2.98   This permits a continuation claim for disability living allowance to be made during the last six months of an existing award. The following authorities relate to the version of reg.13C which was in force prior to March 18, 2005.

In *CDLA/14895/1996*, it was held that reg.13C(2) should not be applied until it has been considered whether, if the claim were treated as an application for review under s.30(13) of the Social Security Administration Act 1992, there would be grounds for review. If there are grounds for review, the existing award should be reviewed. Otherwise, the claim should be treated as a renewal claim, effective only from the end of the existing award.

The relationship of this regulation and the prohibition on tribunals of considering circumstances obtaining after the date of claim under s.12(8)(b) of the Social Security Act 1998 was considered in *CDLA/3848/2001*, where the Commissioner said,

> "In my judgment it is implicit in Reg.13C of the 1987 Regulations that circumstances occurring between the date of a decision on a renewal claim and the renewal date can (and therefore must) be taken into account by an appeal tribunal.
> . . .
> Regulation 13C(2), having stated that the Secretary of State may treat the claim as if made on the renewal date, goes on to provide that he may 'award benefit accordingly.' That means that the task of a decision maker (and appeal tribunal on appeal) is to determine whether the conditions for disability living allowance will be (or were) satisfied *on the renewal date*. It is in my view implicit that circumstances which occur between the date of the decision maker's decision and the renewal date can be taken into account by an appeal tribunal. It cannot have been the intention of s.12(8)(b) and Reg.13C, read together, that an appeal tribunal is prevented from taking into account changes in circumstances relevant to the very issue which it has to decide. If it were to ignore such changes, the effect of its decision would not be to 'award benefit accordingly' (i.e. on the basis of a claim treated as made on the renewal date)."

A Scottish Commissioner agreed with this reasoning in deciding an appeal relating to a claim for an attendance allowance, where there is no corresponding provision. Though disability living allowance and attendance allowance are separate benefits, there is no logical reason why there should not be similar provision in relation to renewal claims. However, there is not. The Commissioner in *CSA/248/2002* had to decide the effect of a tribunal's only deciding matters down to the date of the decision, and whether this had constituted an error of law. The Commissioner concluded that the renewal claim could be competently made in advance of the expiry of the existing award (paras 12–13). But the Commissioner found himself compelled to conclude that s.12(8)(b) did apply to the renewal of an attendance allowance claim (para.19).

In *CDLA/4331/2002*, it was held that, when hearing an appeal from a decision on a renewal claim effective from the claimant's 16th birthday, a tribunal is required to determine the appeal on the basis that that the claimant was 16, even if she was only 15 at the date of the Secretary of State's decision. The approach taken was different from that in *CDLA/3848/2001*, but the result was the same on the facts of the case. In *C12/2003–04 (DLA)*, a Commissioner in Northern Ireland expressly disagreed with *CDLA/3848/2001* and concluded that the Secretary of State was not entitled to refuse benefit at all until the date from which the renewal claim would have been effective. A tribunal, faced with an appeal against a disallowance of a renewal claim made before the date from which a new award would have been effective,

(SI 1987/1968, reg.13C) (as amended)

therefore had no power to do more than set aside the Secretary of State's decision as having been made without jurisdiction, leaving the Secretary of State to make a new decision.

This conflict of authority has now been resolved in a decision of a Tribunal of Commissioners in *R(DLA)4/05*. The Tribunal of Commissioners departs from the reasoning in both *CDLA/3848/2001* and *C12/2003–04 (DLA)*. *CDLA/3848/2001* had failed to take into account that effect had to be given to the provisions of ss.8(2)(b) and 12(8)(b) of the Social Security Act 1998 in the context of renewal claims. This precluded the Secretary of State from taking into account any circumstances not obtaining at the date of the decision. This meant that the Secretary of State had to determine the renewal claim on the basis of circumstances existing at the time the decision was made. In so doing they dissent from paras 106–107 of another decision of a Tribunal of Commissioners in *R(IB)2/04* (see below) which had indicated that renewal claims required prediction. The later Tribunal of Commissioners concludes that this part of the earlier decision was made without full argument and consideration of the implications of s.8(2)(b). They consider that, if a change of circumstances before the renewal date is anticipated, best practice would be to defer the making of the decision until closer to the renewal date in order to know whether the anticipated change had indeed materialised. The Tribunal's disagreement with the Northern Ireland decision in that reg.13C(2)(b) only permits the imposition of a condition in the case of an advance award that all the conditions of entitlement exist as at the renewal date. So the Secretary of State did have power to disallow a renewal claim before the renewal date.

The earlier decision of the Tribunal of Commissioners in *R(IB)2/04* had, in its third issue, addressed the question of whether the power to revise in reg.13C(3) is a freestanding one, or whether reg.3 of the Decisions and Appeals Regulations needs to be established before a decision on a renewal claim can be altered under reg.13C(3). The Tribunal of Commissioners concludes that there is no need for a ground for revision under reg.3 of the Decisions and Appeals Regulations to exist to trigger a reg.13C(3) revision. However, in the usual case where the issue concerns the condition of the claimant at the renewal date, "it can be exercised only on the ground that the claimant's condition has either improved between the date of decision and the renewal date to a greater extent than anticipated by the decision maker or has not deteriorated during that period to the extent anticipated by the decision maker." (para.13 of the summary of conclusions on issues of law.' This conclusion must, however, now be read in the light of the decision of the Tribunal of Commissioners in the later decision referred to above.

[¹ Advance claims for an awards of state pension credit

13D.—(1) Paragraph (2) applies if—
(a) a person does not satisfy the requirements for entitlement to state pension credit on the date on which the claim is made; and
(b) the Secretary of State is of the opinion that unless there is a change of circumstances he will satisfy those requirements—
 (i) where the claim is made in the advance period, when he attains the qualifying age; or
 (ii) in any other case, within 4 months of the date on which the claim is made.

(2) Where this paragraph applies, the Secretary of State may—
(a) treat the claim as made for a period beginning on the day ("the relevant day") the claimant—
 (i) attains the qualifying age, where the claim is made in the advance period; or
 (ii) is likely to satisfy the requirements for entitlement in any other case; and

2.99

413

The Social Security (Claims and Payments) Regulations 1987

(b) if appropriate, award state pension credit accordingly, subject to the condition that the person satisfies the requirements for entitlement on the relevant day.

(3) An award under paragraph (2) may be revised under section 9 of the Social Security Act 1998 if the claimant fails to satisfy the conditions for entitlement to state pension credit on the relevant day.]

AMENDMENT

1. Inserted by the State Pension Credit (Consequential, Transitional and Miscellaneous Provisions) Regulations 2002 (SI 2002/3019), reg.6 (April 7, 2003).

Advance claim for and award of maternity allowance

2.100   **14.**—(1) Subject to the following provisions of this regulation, a claim for maternity allowance in expectation of confinement, or for an increase in such an allowance in respect of an adult dependent, and an award on such a claim, may be made not earlier than 14 weeks before the beginning of the expected week of confinement.

(2) A claim for an increase of maternity allowance in respect of an adult dependant may not be made in advance unless, on the date when made, the circumstances relating to the adult dependant concerned are such as would qualify the claimant for such an increase if they occurred in a period for which she was entitled to a maternity allowance.

Advance notice of retirement and claim for and award of pension

2.101   **15.**—(1) A claim for a retirement pension of any category, and for any increase in any such pension, [6 or a shared additional pension] and an award on such a claim, may be made at any time not more than 4 months before the date on which the claimant will, subject to the fulfilment of the necessary conditions, become entitled to such a pension.

(2) [1. . . .]
(3) [1. . . .]
(4) [1. . . .]

[2 (5) Where a person claims a Category A or Category B retirement pension and is, or but for that claim would be, in receipt of [3 incapacity benefit] [4. . .] for a period which includes the first day to which the claim relates, then if that day is not the appropriate day for the payment of retirement pension in his case, the claim shall be treated as if the first day of the claim was instead the next following such pay day.

(6) Where the spouse of such a person as is mentioned in paragraph (5) above claims a Category A or Category B retirement pension and the first day of that claim is the same as the first day of the claim made by that person, the provisions of that paragraph shall apply also to the claim made by the spouse [7 or civil partner].]

(7) For the purposes of facilitating the determination of a subsequent claim for a Category A, B or C retirement pension, a person may at any time not more than 4 months before the date on which he will attain pensionable age, and notwithstanding that he [5 intends to defer his entitlement to a Category A or Category B retirement pension] at that date, submit particulars in writing to the Secretary of State in a form approved by him for that purpose with a view to the determination (in advance of the claim) of any question under the Act relating to that person's title to such a

(SI 1987/1968, reg.15) (as amended)

retirement pension [⁵. . .] and subject to the necessary modifications, the provisions of these regulations shall apply to any such particulars.

AMENDMENTS

1. Social Security Act 1986 (October 1, 1989).
2. The Social Security (Abolition of Earnings Rule) (Consequential) Regulations 1989 (SI 1989/1642), reg.2(2) (October 1, 1989).
3. The Social Security (Claims and Payments) Amendment (No.2) Regulations 1994 (SI 1994/2943), reg.5 (April 13, 1995).
4. The Social Security (Claims and Payments) (Jobseeker's Allowance Consequential Amendments) Regulations 1996 (SI 1996/1460), reg.2 (October 7, 1996).
5. The Social Security (Abolition of Earnings Rule) (Consequential) Regulations 1989 (SI 1989/1642), reg.2(3) (October 1, 1989).
6. The Social Security (Shared Additional Pension) (Miscellaneous Amendments) Regulations 2005 (SI 2005/1551) (July 6, 2005).
7. The Civil Partnership (Pensions, Social Security and Child Support) (Consequential etc. Provisions) Order 2005 (SI 2005/2877) (December 5, 2005).

GENERAL NOTE

In *CP/1074/1997* a Commissioner had to consider the proper approach to be taken to the determination of a date of birth in relation to a claim for retirement pension. The claimant had been born in the Punjab, and his year of birth had been consistently stated on a number of documents as 1931, but there was no clear evidence of the day he was born in that year. On September 13, 1995 he made a claim for retirement pension, but the adjudication officer treated his date of birth as December 31, 1931 and concluded that the claim made on September 13, 1995 could not be accepted. This would have required the claimant to have been born no later than January 13, 1931 in order to be within the four months provided for in reg.15(1). The claimant adduced evidence that he had been born on December 18, 1930, but his was not accepted by the tribunal. In dealing with the appeal the Commissioner addresses a number of arguments put forward on behalf of the claimant. The Commissioner accepted that the claimant did not need to prove a particular date of birth, merely that he had reached retirement age by a particular date. He did not, however, accept a second argument which was based on the application of a mathematical approach to the evidential test of the balance of probabilities. The claimant argued that as each day passed in the year in which it was accepted that a person was born, it became more probable that the person had been born by that day in the year. By the beginning of July it could therefore be said that it was more probable than not that the claimant had been born by that date. In such circumstances, the practice of the adjudication officer in using the last day of the year as the date of birth was an error of law. The Commissioner rejects this argument, citing *Re JS (a minor)* [1980] 1 All E.R. 1061, for the proposition that the concept of evidential probability is not the same as the mathematical concept. The Commissioner approves the proposition in that case that the civil burden of proof requires the party on whom the burden falls to "satisfy the court that it is reasonably safe in all the circumstances of the case to act on the evidence before the court, bearing in mind the consequences which will follow". The Commissioner finally notes that this may not, in every case where a date of birth in the year is not known, result in the choice of the last day in the year. Regard must be had to all the evidence available at the time the decision is made in determining which date in the year is to be selected as the date by which the person was born.

In *CP/3017/2004* the Commissioner held, applying *R(DLA) 4/05* by analogy, that there is a power to disallow an advance claim made under reg.15(1) for an increase of retirement pension for a wife up to four months before a claimant might become entitled to the pension (para.7). However, the Commissioner considers,

2.102

The Social Security (Claims and Payments) Regulations 1987

" . . . in some cases where there was likely to be a significant change of circumstances before the start date of the period covered by a claim, it might well be good practice to defer making a decision until it was known whether that change had actually materialised. It seems to me that the present case is one where that course should have been taken. It was plain from the evidence provided that the claimant's wife's earnings fluctuated a great deal from one pay period to another. And the nature of the case is different from that of a person suffering some potentially disabling or incapacitating condition, where in most cases there can be a sensible prediction about how the condition might progress in the future. It was simply unknown on 3 March 2004 what the claimant's wife's earnings might be in the week prior to 31 May 2004. Quite apart from the doubts that I explain below about the averaging process carried out by the officer, it would have been better to have waited until close to 28 May 2004 and then considered the current evidence about the wife's earnings. I do not think that there would have been any difficulty in making an advance decision on the claimant's own retirement pension entitlement, but deferring the decision on the increase. However, that did not happen."

Cold weather payments

2.103   **15A.** [¹. . .]

Amendment

1. Social Security (Miscellaneous Provisions) Amendment Regulations 1991 (SI 1991/2284), reg.8 (November 1, 1991).

General Note

2.104   Claims for cold weather payments are no longer necessary or possible.

[¹ [²Advance claim for pension following deferment

2.105   **15B.** Where a person's entitlement to a Category A or Category B retirement pension or a shared additional pension is deferred in accordance with section 55(3) of the Contributions and Benefits Act (pension increase or lump sum where entitlement to retirement pension is deferred) or section 55C(3) (pension increase or lump sum where entitlement to shared additional pension is deferred) thereof (as the case may be) a claim for—
  (a) a Category A or Category B retirement pension;
  (b) any increase in that pension;
  (c) a shared additional pension,
may be made at any time not more than 4 months before the day on which the period of deferment, within the meaning of section 55(3) or section 55C(3) (as the case may be), ends.]]

Amendments

1. Orginally marked by the Social Security (Claims and Payments) Amendment Regulations 2005 (SI 2005/455), reg.2 (April 6, 2005).
2. The Social Security (Shared Additional Pension) (Miscellaneous Amendments) Regulations 2005 (SI 2005/1551) (July 6, 2005).

General Note

2.106   This additional regulation regularises what has been operational practice in allowing those who claim a deferred retirement pension to do so four months in advance of the date on which they wish to claim their pension. The purpose of the advance

(SI 1987/1968, reg.15B) (as amended)

claims provisions is to ensure that the retirement pension is put into payment on the due date without any delays.

There are further amendments to deal with the administrative arrangements needed to support the ability to take a lump sum rather than an increase in pension, and to extend the time limit for claiming but these changes do not take effect until 2006, though certain transition provisions come into effect in July 2005.

Date of entitlement under an award for the purpose of payability of benefit and effective date of change of rate

16.—(1) For the purpose only of determining the day from which benefit is to become payable, where a benefit other than one of those specified in paragraph (4) is awarded for a period of a week, or weeks, and the earliest date on which entitlement would otherwise commence is not the first day of a benefit week entitlement shall begin on the first day of the benefit week next following.

[1 (1A) Where a claim for [6 working families' tax credit] is made in accordance with paragraph 7(a) [2 or (aa)] of Schedule 4 for a period following the expiration of an existing award of family credit [6 or disabled person's tax credit], entitlement shall begin on the day after the expiration of that award.

(1B) Where a claim for [6 working families' tax credit or disabled person's tax credit] is made on or after the date when an up-rating order is made under [6 section 150 of the Social Security Administration Act 1992], but before the date when that order comes into force, and—

(a) an award cannot be made on that claim as at the date it is made but could have been made if that order were then in force, and

(b) the period beginning with the date of claim and ending immediately before the date when the order came into force does not exceed 28 days,

entitlement shall begin from the date the up-rating order comes into force.]

[2 (1C) Where a claim for [6 disabled person's tax credit] is made in accordance with paragraph 11(a) or (b) of Schedule 4 for a period following the expiration of an existing award of [6 disabled person's tax credit or working families' tax credit], entitlement shall begin on the day after the expiration of that award.]

(2) Where there is a change in the rate of any benefit to which paragraph (1) applies the change, if it would otherwise take effect on a day which is not the appropriate pay day for that benefit, shall take effect from the appropriate pay day next following.

[1 (3) For the purposes of this regulation the first day of the benefit week—

(a) in the case of child benefit [5 and guardian's allowance] is Monday,

(b) in the case of [6 disabled person's tax credit or working families' tax credit] is Tuesday, and

(c) in any other case is the day of the week on which the benefit is payable in accordance with regulation 22 (long-term benefits).]

(4) The benefits specified for exclusion from the scope of paragraph (1) are [4 jobseeker's allowance], [3 incapacity benefit], maternity allowance, [1. . .], severe disablement allowance, income support [6, state pension credit] [1. . .] and any increase of those benefits.

2.107

AMENDMENTS

1. The Social Security (Claims and Payments) Amendment Regulations 1988 (SI 1988/522), reg.3 (April 11, 1988).

The Social Security (Claims and Payments) Regulations 1987

2. The Social Security (Claims and Payments) Amendment Regulations 1991 (SI 1991/2741), reg.9 (March 10, 1992).
3. The Social Security (Claims and Payments) Amendment (No.2) Regulations 1994 (SI 1994/2943), reg.6 (April 13, 1995).
4. The Social Security (Claims and Payments) (Jobseeker's Allowance Consequential Amendments) Regulations 1996 (SI 1996/1460), reg.2(9) (October 7, 1996).
5. The Social Security (Claims and Payments) Amendment Regulations 1999 (S.I. 1999, No.2358), reg.2 (September 20, 1999).
6. State Pension Credit (Consequential, Transitional and Miscellaneous Provisions) Regulations 2002, (SI 2002/3019), reg.7 (April 7, 2003).

DEFINITIONS

"benefit"—see reg.2(2).
"jobseeker's allowance"—see reg.2(1).
"week"—*ibid.*

GENERAL NOTE

2.108   This regulation restates in part the rules formerly contained in reg.16(10) of the Claims and Payments Regulations 1979. In *R(P)2/73* it was held that the effect of a similarly worded predecessor to reg.16(10) was not just to make benefit payable from the next pay day but to make it begin on that day. The Commissioner made clear, though, that the regulation was concerned with "payability not title". The new wording does not appear wholly to resolve the difficulty, since para.(1) is prefaced by the intention only to concern itself with payability, though later the word "entitlement" is used. Presumably that means "entitlement to payment of benefit" and not title to the benefit itself. There are occasions where title to the benefit arising on an earlier date than the first date of payment has significant consequences.

[¹ Date of entitlement under an award of state pension credit for the purpose of payability and effective date of change of rate

2.109   **16A.**—(1) For the purpose only of determining the day from which state pension credit is to become payable, where the credit is awarded from a day which is not the first day of the claimant's benefit week, entitlement shall begin on the first day of the benefit week next following.

(2) In the case of a claimant who—
(a) immediately before attaining the qualifying age was entitled to income support or income-based jobseeker's allowance and is awarded state pension credit from the day on which he attains the qualifying age; or
(b) was entitled to an income-based jobseeker's allowance after attaining the qualifying age and is awarded state pension credit from the day which falls after the date that entitlement ends,
entitlement to the guarantee credit shall, notwithstanding paragraph (1), begin on the first day of the award.

(3) Where a change in the rate of state pension credit would otherwise take effect on a day which is not the first day of the claimant's benefit week, the change shall take effect from the first day of the benefit week next following.

(4) For the purpose of this regulation, "benefit week" means the period of 7 days beginning on the day on which, in the claimant's case, state pension credit is payable in accordance with regulation 26B.]

(SI 1987/1968, reg.16A) (as amended)

AMENDMENT

1. State Pension Credit (Consequential, Transitional and Miscellaneous Provisions) Regulations 2002 (SI 2002/3019), reg.7 (April 7, 2003).

Duration of awards

17.—(1) Subject to the provisions of this regulation and of section [¹37ZA(3) of the Social Security Act 1975 (disability living allowance) and section] 20(6) [² and (6F)] of the Social Security Act 1986 [⁴ working families' tax credit and disabled person's tax credit] [SSCBA, ss.71(3), 128(3) and 129(6)] a claim for benefit shall be treated as made for an indefinite period and any award of benefit on that claim shall be made for an indefinite period.

[³ (1A) Where an award of income support or an income-based jobseeker's allowance is made in respect of [⁷ a couple] and one member of the couple is, at the date of claim, a person to whom section 126 of the Contributions and Benefits Act or, as the case may be, section 14 of the Jobseekers Act applies, the award of benefit shall cease when the person to whom section 126 or, as the case may be, section 14 applies returns to work with the same employer.]

(2) [³. . .]

(3) [⁶ Except in the case of claims for and awards of state pension credit,] if [³. . .] it would be inappropriate to treat a claim as made and to make an award for an indefinite period (for example where a relevant change of circumstances is reasonably to be expected in the near future) the claim shall be treated as made and the award shall be for a definite period which is appropriate in the circumstances.

(4) In any case where benefit is awarded in respect of days subsequent to the date of claim the award shall be subject to the condition that the claimant satisfies the requirements for entitlement [⁵. . .]

(5) The provisions of Schedule 2 shall have effect in relation to claims for [³ᵃ jobseeker's allowance] made during periods connected with public holidays.

2.110

AMENDMENTS

1. The Social Security (Claims and Payments) Amendment Regulations 1991 (SI 1991/2741), reg.10 (February 3, 1992).
2. The Social Security (Claims and Payments) Amendment Regulations 1991 (SI 1991/2741), reg.10 (March 10, 1992).
3. The Social Security (Claims and Payments) (Jobseeker's Allowance Consequential Amendments) Regulations 1996 (SI 1996/1460), reg.2(10) (October 7, 1996).
4. The Tax Credits (Claims and Payments) (Amendment) Regulations 1999 (SI 1999/2572), regs 24 & 25 (October 5, 1999).
5. The Social Security Act 1998 (Commencement No.12 and Consequential and Transitional Provisions) Order 1999 (SI 1999/3178), Sch.6 (November 29, 1999).
6. State Pension Credit (Consequential, Transitional and Miscellaneous Provisions) Regulations 2002 (SI 2002/3019), reg.8 (April 7, 2003).
7. The Civil Partnership (Pensions, Social Security and Child Support) (Consequential etc. Provisions) Order 2005 (SI 2005/2877) (December 5, 2005).

DEFINITIONS

"benefit"—see reg.2(2).
"claim for benefit"—see reg.2(1).

"jobseeker's allowance"—*ibid.*
"the Jobseekers Act"—*ibid.*

GENERAL NOTE

2.111　In general awards are to be made for an indefinite period (para.1), subject to revision or supersession where the claimant's circumstances change such that the entitlement is reduced or removed. An award of benefit can only be terminated by supersession. In *CIS/4167/2003* the Commissioner queries whether terminations of indefinite awards have always been accompanied by the required supersession decision. In the case before him an award had been closed without the making of a supersession decision in circumstances where this suggested possible standard practice.

Paragraph (3) deals with short-term situations and allows awards for a fixed period, except in the case of state pension credit.

The effect of para.(1) is that awards of most benefits are now made for an indefinite period. Entitlement only ceases where there has been a revision or supersession which establishes that the conditions of entitlement are no longer met. In earlier times, there was a distinct tendency on reviews for adjudication officers to argue that it was for the claimant to establish continuing entitlement to the benefit, whereas the true position was that, where an indefinite award had been made, it was for the decision maker to show that there were good grounds to revise or supersede the award: see generally *R(S) 3/90*.

In *CIS/620/1990*, the Commissioner stressed that the requirements of reg.17 were not a mere technicality. An indefinite award of benefit can only be terminated on review if it its shown on review (under the earlier legislation) that the conditions of entitlement cease to be met. In any other circumstances the original award continues. Any purported subsequent award of benefit cannot overlap with the earlier award. Indeed there would be no jurisdiction to make a subsequent award since the matter is *res judicata:* see paras 8 and 11 of *CIS/620/1990*.

The power to review or supersede an award of benefit will arise under s.9 (revision, which takes effect from the operative date of the decision being revised) or s.10 (supersession, which takes effect from the date of the supersession decision) of the Social Security Act 1998. There must be grounds on which the decision maker can determine that the conditions of entitlement have ceased to exist. Some are specific to certain benefits while others are more general in application. Reference should be made to the annotations to ss.9 and 10 of the 1998 Act, as well as to Pt II of the Decisions and Appeals Regulations and the commentary on these regulations, if any issue under reg.17 arises.

2.112　*Regulation 18 revoked by The Social Security (Claims and Payments) (Jobseeker's Allowance Consequential Amendments) Regulations 1996 (SI 1996/1460) (October 7, 1996).*

[¹ **Time for claiming benefit**

2.113　**19.**—(1) Subject to the following provisions of this regulation, the prescribed time for claiming any benefit specified in column (1) of Schedule 4 is the appropriate time specified opposite that benefit in column (2) of that Schedule.

(2) The prescribed time for claiming the benefits specified in paragraph (3) is three months beginning with any day on which, apart from satisfying the condition of making a claim, the claimant is entitled to the benefit concerned.

(3) The benefits to which paragraph (2) applies are—
(a) child benefit;
(b) guardian's allowance;

(SI 1987/1968, reg.19) (as amended)

(c) [¹³ . . .];
(d) invalid care allowance or carer's allowance;
(e) maternity allowance;
(f) [¹³ . . .];
[¹⁰ (ff). . .]
(g) widow's benefit;
[¹¹ (ga) subject to paragraphs (3A) and (3B), bereavement benefit;]
(h) [¹¹ . . .] any increase in any benefit (other than income support or jobseeker's allowance) in respect of a child or adult dependant.

[⁸ (3A) The prescribed time for claiming a bereavement payment [¹¹ within the meaning of section 36 of the Contributions and Benefits Act] is 12 months beginning with the day on which, apart from satisfying the condition of making a claim, the claimant is entitled to such a payment.]

[¹¹ (3B) The time prescribed for claiming a bereavement benefit in respect of the day on which the claimant's spouse [¹² or civil partner] has died or may be presumed to have died where—
(a) less than 12 months have elapsed since the day of the death; and
(b) the circumstances are as specified in section 3(1)(b) of the Social Security Administration Act 1992 (death is difficult to establish),
is that day and the period of 12 months immediately following that day if the other conditions of entitlement are satisfied.]

(4) Subject to paragraph (8), in the case of a claim for income support, jobseeker's allowance, [³ working families' tax credit or disabled persons' tax credit], where the claim is not made within the time specified for that benefit in Schedule 4, the prescribed time for claiming the benefit shall be extended, subject to a maximum extension of three months, to the date on which the claim is made, where—
(a) any [⁷ one or more] of the circumstances specified in paragraph (5) applies or has applied to the claimant; and
(b) as a result of that circumstance or those circumstances the claimant could not reasonably have been expected to make the claim earlier.

(5) The circumstances referred to in paragraph (4) are—
(a) the claimant has difficulty communicating because—
  (i) he has learning, language or literacy difficulties; or
  (ii) he is deaf or blind,
  and it was not reasonably practicable for the claimant to obtain assistance from another person to make his claim;
(b) except in the case of a claim for jobseeker's allowance, the claimant was ill or disabled, and it was not reasonably practicable for the claimant to obtain assistance from another person to make his claim;
(c) the claimant was caring for a person who is ill or disabled, and it was not reasonably practicable for the claimant to obtain assistance from another person to make his claim;
(d) the claimant was given information by an officer of the [³ Department for Work and Pensions] [or in a case to which regulation 4A applies, a representative of a relevant authority] or the Board which led the claimant to believe that a claim for benefit would not succeed;
(e) the claimant was given written advice by a solicitor or other professional adviser, a medical practitioner, a local authority, or a person working in a Citizens Advice Bureau or a similar advice agency, which led the claimant to believe that a claim for benefit would not succeed;

(f) the claimant or his partner was given written information about his income or capital by his employer or former employer, or by a bank or building society, which led the claimant to believe that a claim for benefit would not succeed;
(g) the claimant was required to deal with a domestic emergency affecting him and it was not reasonably practicable for him to obtain assistance from another person to make his claim; or
(h) the claimant was prevented by adverse weather conditions from attending the appropriate office.

(6) In the case of a claim for income support jobseeker's allowance, [³working families' tax credit or disabled person's tax credit] [⁷ where the claim is not made within the time specified for that benefit in Schedule 4, the prescribed time for claiming the benefit shall be extended, subject to a maximum extension of one month, to the date on which the claim is made, where—
(a) any one or more of the circumstances specified in paragraph (7) applies or has applied to the claimant; and
(b) as a result of that circumstance or those circumstances the claimant could not reasonably have been expected to make the claim earlier.]

(7) The circumstances referred to in paragraph (6) are—
(a) the appropriate office where the claimant would be expected to make a claim was closed and alternative arrangements were not available;
(b) the claimant was unable to attend the appropriate office due to difficulties with his normal mode of transport and there was no reasonable alternative available;
(c) there were adverse postal conditions;
(d) the claimant [⁷ or, in the case of income support jobseeker's allowance, the claimant or his partner] was previously in receipt of another benefit, and notification of expiry of entitlement to that benefit was not sent to the claimant [⁷ or his partner, as the case may be,] before the date that his entitlement expired;
[⁹ (e) in the case of a claim for working families' tax credit, the claimant had previously been entitled, or the partner of the claimant had previously been entitled in relation to the claimant, to income support or jobseeker's allowance and the claim for working families' tax credit was made within one month of—
   (i) the expiry of entitlement to income support ignoring any period in which entitlement resulted from the person entitled not being treated as engaged in remunerative work by virtue of regulation 6(2) and (3) of the Income Support (General) Regulations 1987; or
   (ii) the expiry of entitlement to jobseeker's allowance;]
(f) except in the case of a claim for family credit or disability working allowance, the claimant had ceased to be a member of a married or unmarried couple within the period of one month before the claim was made; [² . . .]
(g) during the period of one month before the claim was made a close relative of the claimant had died, and for this purpose "close relative" means partner, parent, son, daughter, brother or [² sister; or]
[⁹ (h) in the case of a claim for disabled person's tax credit, the claimant had previously been entitled to income support, jobseeker's allowance,

(SI 1987/1968, reg.19) (as amended)

    incapacity benefit or severe disablement allowance and the claim for disabled person's tax credit was made within one month of—
      (i) the expiry of entitlement to income support ignoring any period in which entitlement resulted from the claimant being treated as engaged in remunerative work by virtue of paragraphs (2) and (3) or paragraph (5) and (6) of the Income Support (General) Regulations 1987; or
      (ii) the expiry of entitlement to jobseeker's allowance, incapacity benefit or severe disablement allowance;
 (ha) in the case of a claim for disabled person's tax credit, the partner of the claimant had previously been entitled in relation to the claimant to income support or jobseeker's allowance, and the claim for disabled person's tax credit was made within one month of—
      (i) the expiry of entitlement to income support ignoring any period in which entitlement resulted from the partner of the claimant not being treated as engaged in remunerative work by virtue of paragraphs (2) and (3) or paragraph (5) and (6) of the Income Support (General) Regulations 1987; or
      (ii) the expiry of entitlement to jobseeker's allowance;]
[6 (i) in the case of a claim for a jobseeker's allowance by a member of a joint-claim couple where the other member of that couple failed to attend at the time and place specified by the Secretary of State for the purposes of regulation 6.]
[14 (j) the claimant was unable to make telephone contact with the appropriate office where he would be expected to notify his intention of making a claim because the telephone lines to that office were busy or inoperative.]

  (8) This regulation shall not have effect with respect to a claim to which [4 regulation 21ZB] of the Income Support (General) Regulations 1987 (treatment of refugees) applies.]

AMENDMENTS

1. The Social Security (Miscellaenous Amendments) (No.2) Regulations 1997 (SI 1997/793), reg.6 (April 7, 1997).
2. The Social Security (Claims and Payments and Adjudication) Amendment (No.2) Regulations 1997 (SI 1997/2290), reg.6 (October 13, 1997).
3. The Secretaries of State for Education and Skills and for Work and Pensions Order 2002 (SI 2002/1397), art.18, (September 30, 2002).
4. The Social Security (Immigration and Asylum) Consequential Amendments Regulations 2000 (SI 2000/636), reg 5 (April 3, 2000).
5. The Social Security (Benefits for Widows and Widowers) (Consequential Amendments) Regulations 2000 (SI 2000/1483), reg.9 (April 9, 2001).
6. The Social Security (Joint Claims: Consequential Amendments) Regulations 2000 (SI 2000/1982), reg.2(5) (March 19, 2001).
7. The Social Security (Claims and Payments and Miscellaneous Amendments) Regulations 2002 (SI 2002/428), reg.3 (April 2, 2002).
8. The Social Security (Claims and Payments and Miscellaneous Amendments) (No.3) Regulations 2002 (SI 2002/2660), reg.2 (April 1, 2003).
9. The Tax Credits Schemes (Miscellaneous Amendments No.4) Regulations 2000 (SI 2000/2978), reg.10 (November 28, 2000).
10. Social Security (Claims and Payments) Amendment (No.2) Regulations 2004 (SI 2004/1821), reg.2(a) (October 6, 2004).
11. Social Security (Claims and Payments) Amendment (No.2) Regulations 2005 (SI 2005/777), reg.2 (April 11, 2005).

12. The Social Security (Civil Partnerships) (Consequential Amendments) Regulations 2005 (SI 2005/2878) (December 5, 2005).
13. The Social Security (Claims and Payment) Regulations 2005 (SI 2005/455), reg.3 (April 6, 2006).
14. The Social Security (Miscellaneous Amendments) (No.3) Regulations 2006 (SI 2006/2377) (October 2, 2006).

DEFINITIONS

"appropriate office"—see reg.2(1).
"jobseeker's allowance"—*ibid*.
"married couple"—*ibid*.
"partner"—*ibid*.
"unmarried couple"—*ibid*.

GENERAL NOTE

Introduction

2.114   Regulation 19 was completely re-drafted in April 1997 to remove references to good cause and with it decades of case law. Administrative complexity in dealing with back-dated claims was said to justify the new approach introduced in 1997. New case law is now emerging which suggests that the more limited grounds for back-dating may not be quite as restrictive as appears at first sight. It remains true that appeals concerning back-dating require a meticulous attention to fact-finding and careful attention to the words of reg.19 as interpreted in Commissioners' decisions.

There are now broadly two groups of benefits: those which must be claimed on the day in respect of which the situation giving rise to the claim first occurs, and those where a three months time limit is allowed for claiming. There are also two groups of benefits where issues of backdating arise.

The first group of benefits is income support, jobseeker's allowance whether income-based or contribution-based, working families' tax credit, and disabled person's tax credit. For this first group, there are two possible extensions available. They may be backdated for up to three months if the conditions set out in paras (4) and (5) are met. If the conditions are met, the backdating is mandatory. There is also the possibility of an extension of the time limit for claiming for up to one month if a different set of conditions set out in paras (6) and (7) are met.

The second group of benefits is child benefit, guardian's allowance, carer's allowance, maternity allowance, bereavement benefit, certain widowhood benefits (see para.(3)(h)), and increases of benefit (other than income support and jobseeker's allowance) in respect of a child or adult dependent. Those benefits listed in Sch. 4 for which the time limit is three months can also be included in this second group: incapacity benefit; disablement benefit and increases; reduced earnings allowance; and social fund payment for funeral expenses. For these benefits there is a three month time limit for claiming, which means that whatever the reasons for any delay in claiming, they can be backdated for up to three months.

The regulation does not apply to claims within reg.21ZB of the Income Support General Regulations. These set out special rules for claims for income support for a person who has submitted a claim for asylum on or after April 3, 2000 and is treated as a refugee. See commentary on the regulation in Vol.II.

Regulation 19 can only apply where there is a claim which is properly constituted for the purposes of reg.4: *CIS/157/2001*.

Note that reg.19 does not apply to claims for winter fuel payments: *CIS/2337/2004*, para.19.

Para. (1): the time limits

2.115   Paragraph (1) sets out the time limits for those benefits listed in Sch.4 to the regulations. These include income support.

(SI 1987/1968, reg.19) (as amended)

If a claimant signs an ordinary income support claim form which contains no question asking from what date benefit is claimed, the claim will be interpreted as a claim for an indefinite period from the date on which the claim is made. If claimants wish to claim for a past period, that must be expressly stated: *R(SB)9/84*, para.11. But note that in *CIS/2057/1998* the Commissioner accepted that a claimant who had put on her claim form "disabled—aged 16" had indicated an intention to claim income support from her 16th birthday. If, before a decision is made on an ordinary claim, a claimant indicates a wish to claim for a past period, that can operate as an amendment of the original claim taking effect on the original date. But if, after there has been a decision on the claim, the claimant indicates such a wish (as often happens when the original claim has been successful), it is generally assumed that such a claim can only be treated as a fresh claim on the date on which it is made, and that any question of back-dating under reg.19(4) has to be assessed according to that date of claim.

Paras (2) and (3): benefits for which the time limit for claiming is three months
The prescribed time for claiming the benefits listed in para.(3) is three months beginning the any day of potential entitlement. The contrast between this formulation of backdating and the technique adopted for income-related benefits may be important. If the claimant was entitled to the benefit (apart from the requirement to make a claim for the benefit) where the three-month time limit applies, the payment of benefit can be backdated for three months without any reason being shown for the delay in claiming. 2.116

Paras (4) and (5): claims for income support, jobseeker's allowance, working families' tax credit and disabled person's tax credit
(1) Introduction: Although it is common to speak of the backdating of claims, it should be appreciated that the technique adopted in para.(4) is to extend the time for claiming for a past period forward from the first day of that period. There is an immediate problem in the working of the three month time limit. If, on May 31 in any year, a claim is made for income support for the period from February 1 to May 30 in that year, it appears that the time for claiming for the whole period cannot be extended under para.(4) because to do so would go beyond the maximum period of three months permitted under the regulation. It does not matter that one of the listed circumstances has made it reasonable for the claim not to have been made earlier. The claim could be amended before a decision is made on it so as to make it a claim from March 1 to May 30, that is, the maximum permitted period of backdating. 2.117

It follows that it would be good practice for decision-makers in dealing with a claim which inevitably breaks the maximum period of backdating not to decide the claim, but to invite the claimant to amend the period claimed for.

An alternative approach would be for a decision-maker to treat a claim for an extension of the time limit for claiming beyond three months as being a claim for the maximum permitted period. It seems likely that most claimants, if asked, would say that they would prefer this approach if the alternative was the total rejection of the claim for an extension of the time limit for claiming.

Although reg.5(1) only provides for a claim to be amended before a determination of it, it does not explicitly state that a claim may not be amended after a determination has been made. Thus if an amendment is made before, or even at, an appeal hearing, it is suggested that a tribunal would be able to deal with the claim for an extension, as amended. Since the tribunal is conducting a complete rehearing of all the issues under appeal, it may also wish to consider whether to treat the claim as simply being a claim for the maximum period allowed for an extension whatever period was initially requested by the claimant. It certainly seems doubtful that the intention was that only claims for extensions of up to three months could be considered under para.(4). This view is supported by *CJSA/3994/1998* where the Deputy Commissioner held that a claimant who had asked for his claim to be backdated for nearly a year should be treated as asking for the time for his making his claim to be extended to the maximum permitted by the regulations.

The Social Security (Claims and Payments) Regulations 1987

In *R(IS) 16/04*, the Commissioner follows the approach adopted in *CIS/849/1998* and *CJSA/3994/1998* (the correctness of which was conceded by the Secretary of State) to the effect that a claim can be taken as including a claim for a period starting with the earliest date which would make the claim in time.

Note too that *R(IS) 3/01* holds that the maximum period of extension should be calculated backwards from the date of actual claim, not forwards from the first day of the period expressly claimed for.

In *R(IS) 16/04*, the Commissioner rules that the question of reasonableness under regs 19(4)(b) and 19(6)(b) can only be asked in relation to each particular period of claim, and not the totality of any delay. The Commissioner gives as an example the position of a claimant who delays making a claim for income support for several months, but who then makes a claim. Just after he posts the claim form, there is a strike by postal workers which holds up delivery of the claim for some weeks. The fact that the claimant could have claimed earlier than he did should not defeat his reliance on adverse postal conditions in relation to the claim he actually made.

For an interesting case concerning the position of jurors and benefits, see *CIS/1010/2003*.

2.118 *(2) The test to be satisfied under paras (4) and (5):* There are two questions which must be answered before there can be an extension of the time for claiming. The first is that one of the circumstances listed in para.(5) has applied to the claimant. There is no condition that the circumstances must have applied *throughout* the period claimed for or continues to apply at the date of claim. Such considerations may come in under the second question, which is whether as a result of the circumstances or a combination of them, the claimant could not reasonably have been expected to make the claim earlier. This approach is explicitly set out in the reported Northern Ireland decision *R002/01(IS)*. Thus, if a claimant who has been affected, for example, by illness delays unreasonably after recovery from the illness in making the claim, the request for an extension of the time limit for claiming will fail on the second ground. Such a claim could also fail if there has been unreasonable delay at some earlier stage before one of the listed circumstances applies.

Just as careful findings of fact were the secret of good decision-making under the old good cause rules, so too similar attention to detail will be required under the rules introduced in 1997. This will include findings of fact on key dates, and precision in making findings about what a claimant has been told and by whom.

Note that the list of circumstances set out in para.(5) is exhaustive, and there is no category of analogous circumstances to deal with meritorious cases which were not foreseen by the draftsman: *CJSA/3121/1998*, para.9. Ignorance of one's rights or of the procedure for claiming, whether reasonable or otherwise, does not feature in the circumstances listed in para.(5).

Finally, since the maximum period of backdating is now three months (previously it was 12 months), will this change the qualitative nature of the decision-making? Perhaps not, when the restrictive grounds on which the Secretary of State can extend the period to one month as set out in paras (6) and (7) are considered.

2.119 *(3) Paras (5)(a), (b), (c) and (g): reasonable practicability of obtaining assistance:* Several of the paragraphs provide, in addition to a primary set of circumstances, a further requirement, namely that "it was not reasonably practicable for the claimant to obtain assistance from another person to make his claim". In *CIS/2057/1998*, the Commissioner points out that the question is whether it is reasonable practicable for the claimant to seek assistance from another person to make the claim, not whether it is reasonable practicable for another person to take the initiative in offering assistance.

The corresponding words of the Northern Ireland regulations have been considered by the Chief Commissioner in Northern Ireland. In *C12/98 (IS)* the Chief Commissioner notes, having regard to the two-stage test set out in para.(4), that:

(SI 1987/1968, reg.19) (as amended)

" 'reasonably practicable for him to obtain assistance' . . . must mean something other than 'can reasonably have been expected to make the claim earlier', otherwise there would be no need for the two sub-paragraphs to consist of different terminology in qualifying reasonableness." (para.11.)

The Chief Commissioner adds:

" . . . I accept that [the adjudication officer] is correct in submitting that regulation 19(5)(b) places an obligation on a sick or disabled person to seek assistance with his or her claim unless it is not practicable for him to obtain it; but while it might be more likely that someone who suffers a mental health problem could satisfy the provisions of regulation 19(4) and (5), it is necessary for the Adjudicating Authorities to look at the circumstances of each case and they are not entitled to make an assumption that a person suffering from a mental health problem would automatically be unable to seek assistance from another person to make a claim."

The circumstances in which it will and will not be reasonably practicable to obtain assistance from another person are so varied that, once again, full and careful findings or fact are the key to good decision making in all claims involving consideration of this issue.

(4) Para.(5)(a): difficulty communicating: This sub-para. concerns difficulties of communication arising because a person has learning, language or literacy difficulties, or because a person is deaf or blind. The words "deaf" or "blind" are not defined and so should be given their ordinary meaning, namely and respectively a person without hearing and a person without sight. Those who are hearing impaired or visually impaired may not be properly described as deaf or blind, but might well fall within the scope of someone who has difficulty communicating because of learning, language or literacy difficulties. Note that those who are deaf and blind must have difficulty communicating as a result of that disability and, additionally, must show that it was not reasonably practicable to obtain assistance from another person to make the claim. This is certainly an area where the qualification of *reasonable* practicability will be important.

In *CIS/2057/1998* the claimant had learning difficulties. She made a claim for income support which was awarded. Later her mother requested on her behalf that benefit be backdated to her sixteenth birthday (no-one had been appointed to act on behalf of the claimant). The tribunal erred in taking the view that the claimant had a supportive family who should have taken the initiative in finding out about her benefit entitlement. The proper approach was to determine (and the Commissioner so found) whether the claimant came within sub-para.(a)(i) and then to ask whether it was reasonably practicable for her to obtain assistance, not whether it was reasonably practicable for her family to provide it.

2.120

(5) Para.(5)(b): illness and disability: This sub-paragraph does not apply to claims for jobseeker's allowance. It deals with those many situations in which a person's delay is caused by illness or disability. In *CIS/610/1998* (discussed below in relation to sub-para.(d)) the Commissioner noted that the tribunal should have investigated the nature of the claimant's illness and whether this prevented him from queuing.

2.121

The first determination is the nature and dates of the person's illness or disability. The illness or disability must be compounded by its not being reasonably practicable for the claimant to obtain assistance from another person to make the claim.

(6) Para.(5)(c): caring responsibilities: This sub-para. offers an escape route for those with caring responsibilities. The situation in which the sub-para. applies are likely to be (but not expressed exclusively to be) situations where a period of intensive caring arises, or perhaps where another carer becomes unavailable and the claimant has stepped in to help. It is easy to think of circumstances where the circumstances will be satisfied, but also easy to think of rather more marginal cases. The sub-para.

2.122

427

The Social Security (Claims and Payments) Regulations 1987

also requires the claimant to show that it was not reasonably practicable to obtain assistance from another person to make the claim.

2.123   *(7) Para.(5)(d): information from an officer of the Department leading a claimant to believe that a claim for benefit would not succeed:* This has proved to be a troublesome provision which the Department sought to argue was much narrower in its scope than its interpretation by the Commissioners. Note that there is no requirement that the claimant's belief that a claim would not succeed was reasonable in all the circumstances. But an unreasonably held belief might result in the claimant's failing the test in para.(4)(b).

A very common problem is the gap in benefit which often occurs when claimants transfer from jobseeker's allowance to income support because they have become incapable of work. It was thus perhaps predictable that the first Commissioners' decisions on the 1997 backdating rules would stem from this issue.

In *CIS/610/1998* the claimant, who had been claiming a jobseeker's allowance, took a Form Med. 3 issued by his GP to the Benefits Agency. There was a queue so he approached a security guard. The guard advised him that he did not need to fill in any forms, took his medical certificate, and wrote his national insurance number in a logging-in book. A week later the claimant received an incapacity benefit claim form through the post. He completed it and took it to the Benefits Agency. While in the queue, he was advised by another claimant that he needed to complete an income support claim form with his incapacity benefit claim form. He checked this advice when he reached the counter and then submitted claims for both benefits. The adjudication officer refused to backdate the claim for income support. The matter came before the Commissioner for consideration.

The Commissioner concluded on the facts of this case that the security guard was an "officer of the Department". The information supplied by the guard to the claimant could have left the claimant with the impression that he did not need to make another claim in connection with his transfer from a jobseeker's allowance to income support, and that in that sense any new claim would not succeed.

In *CIS/1721/1998* the claimant was given an incapacity benefit claim form when she went to the Job Centre with a medical certificate after fracturing her wrist. Two weeks later her claim for incapacity benefit was refused and she was advised to claim income support. The adjudication officer refused to backdate the claim.

The Commissioner accepts that the implication of the advice to claim incapacity benefit was that the claimant would be entitled to that benefit and not to income support. He considered that this was a reasonable belief on her part (incapacity benefit, if payable, would have exceeded her income support applicable amount). The Commissioner also took account of reg.4(5). The official to whom she produced the medical certificate should have supplied her with an income support claim form. A failure to supply this form would also have led her to believe that there was no entitlement to income support.

CIS/3749/1998 expands on this point. The Commissioner states that claimants were entitled by reason of reg.4(5) to assume that they had been given the right forms for the benefits they requested, and, if they were not, sub-para.(d) should clearly be considered. The claimant in this case had been receiving an income-based jobseeker's allowance, so there was at least a reasonable possibility that a claim for incapacity benefit would fail for lack of contributions. The Commissioner also drew attention to the fact that a failure to provide the right form bought reg.4(7A) into effect which would give the Secretary of State a discretion at accept a late claim.

In *CIS/3994/1998* (followed in *CSIS/815/2004*) the claimant had received advice that he was not entitled to income support on making two enquiries of the Department. That advice seemed to be correct in the light of the evidence of what the claimant had told the Department when he telephoned. The tribunal had ruled that this was not enough to bring the claimant within sub-para.(5)(d) in that the information he had received was reasonable. The Deputy Commissioner could find no such qualification in the sub-para.; the claimant had made an enquiry and

(SI 1987/1968, reg.19) (as amended)

had received information which caused him not to make a claim for income support sooner than he did. He was entitled to have the time limit for claiming extended.

In a Northern Ireland decision of a Tribunal of Commissioners in *R1/01(IS)(T)* (unreported reference *C3/00–01 (IS)(T)*), the tribunal had to decide whether a New Deal adviser was an "officer of the Department". The claimant was a 59-year old married man who had been claiming income-based JSA for a number of years, when he was told he was being sent on the New Deal scheme. The claimant obtained a medical certificate that he was incapable of work. He presented this at the Jobseekers Section, his claim to JSA was terminated, but he was not advised to claim income support. The claimant later claimed income support and sought to have the claim back-dated. The tribunal notes that the Northern Ireland legislation refers to "an officer of the Department" whereas the Great Britain legislation refers to "an officer of the Department of Social Security or of the Department for Education and Employment". In Northern Ireland New Deal advisers are not officers of the Department of Social Development. Thus, they are covered by the legislation applicable in Great Britain, but not that in Northern Ireland. The tribunal doubted whether this distinction was intended.

The second question was whether a failure to give advice can be said to come within these provisions. The tribunal concluded that the giving of information required "the transfer of factual data from an officer to a claimant" (para.35). The regulation requires the giving of information to lead the claimant to believe that a claim for benefit will not succeed; it is not enough that the information left the claimant in ignorance of the possibility of claiming a different benefit. The tribunal says it must actually have led him to believe that a claim would not succeed.

The tribunal goes on to find that the information referred to in sub-para.(d) does not need to relate in some way to the benefit that is claimed late. Information about one claim or benefit could lead a claimant to believe that a claim for another benefit would not succeed.

The fourth issue addressed by the tribunal was whether the test is an objective or subjective one. The tribunal agreed with the conclusions of a Great Britain Commissioner in *R(IS)3/01* (the report of *CIS/4354/1999*) that adjudicating authorities,

"may legitimately test whether or not it believes a claimant's evidence about what he was led to believe by what reason a person in the claimant's circumstances might have been led to believe." (para.18).

In *R(IS)3/01* the Commissioner had held that the words of reg.19(5)(d) "are not to be given any artificially restricted meaning" (para.14). The information to which the regulation refers is not limited to information given in respect of the claim in question, but could include information concerning the ending of entitlement to some other benefit (paras 13–18).

In *CIS/4884/2002* the Commissioner was considering a tribunal's decision following a paper hearing in which they had concluded that the claimant, who had been told to apply for incapacity benefit which had delayed his claim for income support to which he was actually entitled, had not received "advice that a claim for income support would not succeed." In concluding that the tribunal had erred in law, the Commissioner warns of the need to take care to avoid looseness of language, since the receipt of advice is different from the receipt of information. Indeed the Commissioner doubts the correctness of the Northern Ireland Commissioners as expressed in this regard in *C3/00–01 (IS)* The Commissioner goes on to advise,

"In my judgment the correct approach to regulation 19(5)(d) is that adopted by the Commissioner in report decision *R(IS)3/01*. The wording that 'the claimant was given information ... which led the claimant to believe' needs to be given a practical, not an artificially restricted meaning, and it is not necessary for this purpose that what the claim was told by a departmental official should have referred *expressly* to the benefit afterwards sought to be claimed, if for example the information was that some different benefit was available which, if correct, would

The Social Security (Claims and Payments) Regulations 1987

have made such a claim beside the point. Whether the claimant was given such information, and what he was or was not actually led to believe about the possibility of putting in a concurrent claim just in case, are matters of fact that need to be determined by the tribunal on the actual evidence; tested if necessary by cross-examination to resolve any doubt or dispute about what actually took place, or what the claimant afterwards says he believed at the time. Only when those facts have been clearly identified can a tribunal say if the condition in regulation 19(5)(d) has been met, and (if it has) then go on to assess as a matter of objective reasonableness whether the claimant also meets the further condition in regulation 19(4)(b) that he could not reasonably have been expected to make the claim earlier (not even one day earlier) than the date he did." (para.7.)

The Commissioner in *CJSA/580/2003* also followed the approach which had been adopted by Commissioners in Great Britain.

A rather unusual set of circumstances arose in *CJSA/3084/2004*. The claimant attended at an office of the Department to claim a jobseeker's allowance. He completed a form. This transpired to be not a claim form but a locally-used preliminary questionnaire (whose format frequently changed) which the Secretary of State conceded before the Commissioner gave the impression that a claim was being made. In allowing the backdating of a claim for a jobseeker's allowance, the Commissioner says:

"9. The point of law that emerged during the hearing before me of the application for leave to appeal, and which the tribunal did not consider is as follows. Regulation 19(5)(d) refers, not to advice, but to information. Reference was made to decisions by Commissioners in *R(IS) 3/01* and *CIS 4884 2002*. If a claimant has been led to believe that he has made a claim, but he has not in fact made a claim, and because no decision has been received therefore believes that the claim has not succeeded, that seems to me to amount to having been given information which led him to believe that a subsequent real or effective claim would also not succeed."

2.124 *(8) Para.(5)(e) and (f): written advice or information leading the claimant to believe that a claim to benefit would not succeed:* Sub-paragraph (e) is concerned with written advice given by knowledgeable advisers other than officers of the Department which also leads that claimant to believe that a claim for benefit would not succeed, while sub-para.(f) is concerned with written information from an employer or former employer, or a bank or a building society about income or capital which leads claimant to believe that a claim for benefit would not succeed. The additional requirement here is that the claimant must have received "written advice" or "written information". There may be significance in the use of the words "advice" and "information"; sub-para.(e) requires the advice to have led the claimant to believe that a claim for benefit would not succeed, whereas sub-para.(f) simply requires "information". So in the latter case, a bank statement may suffice. Quite what the limits of written advice and information are remains to be tested. Would oral advice backed up by a written file note setting out the advice be sufficient? That would appear to be a forced interpretation of the sub-para., which appears to suggest that the advice has been reduced to writing and given to the claimant. But it is suggested that a claimant should be able to rely on the sub-para. if they were given a document which they have lost. Here the issue will be whether the decision-maker accepts their account of the contents of the written advice. That is a matter of the claimant's credibility rather than substance. Not every advice agency keeps file copies of written advice to their clients.

CJSA/1136/1998 considers the requirement that the advice must be in writing. The claimant had been dismissed and was advised by his trade union official not to claim any benefit until the reasons for his dismissal had been investigated through his employer's appeal procedures. This advice was confirmed in writing in a letter produced by the tribunal hearing in January 1998. The Commissioner states that the reason the sub-para. required the advice to be in writing was to avoid any doubt or argument as to the contents of that advice. If before the decision made by the decision-maker or tribunal, the advice was confirmed in writing, these difficulties were avoided and the advice amounted to written advice for the purposes of the sub-para. The reasoning is questionable since the wording of the provision appears to require the written advice to be what leads the claimant to believe that a claim will not succeed. The Commissioners' approach could also raise difficulties now that tribunals cannot take account of any circumstances not obtaining at the time when the decision appealed against was made: s.12(8)(b), SSA 1998.

The group of advisers within the sub-paragraph is drawn widely, and covers a wide range of agencies.

As with sub-para.(5)(d), there is no requirement that the claimant's belief that a claim would not succeed was reasonable in all the circumstances. But an unreasonably held belief might result in the claimant's failing the test in para.(4)(b).

(9) Para.(5)(g): domestic emergencies: These circumstances are rather surprisingly included in para.(5) when they might more appropriately be included within the Secretary of State's discretion, since it is difficult to think of circumstances which would meet the requirements of the sub-para. which would last more than a month. Perhaps the distinction originally lay in the mandatory nature of the extension where para.(5) is satisfied compared with the discretionary nature of the extension in para.(7), but if that is the distinction, there are circumstances listed in para.(7) which should also be in para.(5). The extension in para.(6) is mandatory following the April 2002 amendment.

2.125

(10) Para.(5)(h): adverse weather conditions: Again these circumstances will usually be of very limited duration save in the more remote parts of the country, and the circumstances seem more appropriate for determination under the Secretary of State's decision-making under para.(6).

2.126

(11) Paras (6) and (7): the decision-maker's one-month decision: As originally drafted, this was the Secretary of State's discretion to extend the time limit for claiming up to one month and applies to claims for income support, jobseeker's allowance, working families' tax credit and disabled person's tax credit. The Secretary of State could extend the time limit for claiming for any period up to a maximum of one month,

2.127

- if the Secretary of State considered that to do so would be consistent with the proper administration of benefit, and
- any of the circumstances in para.(7) applied.

The April 2002 amendment makes this a mandatory list of special circumstances which justify a one month extension to the time limit for claiming. The reference to consistency with the proper administration of benefit happily disappears. Once again the list is exhaustive and has no category of analogous circumstances.

In *CJSA/3659/2001* the Commissioner notes that decisions under reg.19(6) and (7), which contain the requirement that the Secretary of State in the circumstances set out in these paragraphs extend the time limit for claiming to one month, are within the jurisdiction of tribunals. This flows from the provision in para.5(a) of Sch.2 to the Decisions and Appeals Regulations which excludes from the list of Secretary of State's decisions against which no appeal lies a decision under reg.19 as to the time for claiming benefit. This is drafted widely enough to bring within the tribunal's jurisdiction not only the matters in reg.19(4) and (5), but also those in reg.19(6) and (7). It follows that tribunals must consider both sets of rules relating to extension of the time limit for claiming.

Note in relation to these provisions, reg.6(1)(aa) and (1A) for the automatic allowance of one month to return the claim forms in the cases mentioned there, and note the discretionary rule in reg.6(4B) in relation to claims for a jobseeker's allowance.

It would seem that the principle of *CSIS/61/1992* still applies that in every case where a claim is made outside the time limit specified in Sch.4, the Secretary of State should consider the use of the operation of the extension under para.(6) before the claim is referred to a decision-maker for decision. If this has not been done, a tribunal may decide to adjourn for the matter to be considered. There may also be cases where information comes to light in the hearing which makes it appropriate to adjourn to enable the decision maker to re-consider the matter.

It is sometimes argued that the circumstances envisaged in sub-para.(7)(a) are exceptional, as when an office closes unexpectedly due to flooding or industrial action. It is submitted that this is to apply too narrow an interpretation to the words. The sub-para. surely covers situations where a claim would need to be made on a Saturday, but the office is closed and the claim is submitted on the following Monday.

There has been a decision on reg.19(7)(b), which may be limited to some rather special facts: *CSJSA/0811/2006*. It concerned a claimant's lack of funds to pay the ferry fare from Islay to the mainland. He argued that this meant that he was unable to attend the appropriate office due to difficulties with his normal mode of transport and there was no reasonable alternative available. The Deputy Commissioner, in remitting the appeal for determination a new tribunal, considered that "difficulties" in this context could include an inability to pay. He then addressed the issue of whether there was any reasonable alternative, and interpreted the regulation here as referring to reasonable alternative transport. Finally, it was necessary to consider whether the claimant could reasonably have been expected to make the claim earlier than he did. Here the issue was whether earlier claim by telephone was a reasonable course of action for the claimant to have taken. This would require consideration of any enquiry made by the claimant about telephone claims, and whether the claimant did as much as could reasonably be expected of him. If, having done that, he remained ignorant of the possibility of a telephone claim, then he would not fall foul of the provision in reg. 19(6)(b).

In *CIS/4901/2002* the Commissioner considered what is meant by the term "adverse postal conditions" as used in reg.19(7)(c), but ultimately decided the case on different grounds. The circumstances of the case were that the claimant had received some claim forms in the post but no reply paid envelope had been provided. The forms were completed and mailed to the Department in an envelope provided by the claimant to which he affixed a single first class stamp. However, the correct postage was more than this. It was not received by the Department. A second claim was made and benefit paid from a later date; the claimant sought to have this claim backdated to the date of an enquiry made of the Jobcentre about his benefit entitlement which had resulted in his being advised to claim income support or incapacity benefit, and in his being sent the first set of forms. Eventually, the first set of forms was returned to the claimant by the Post Office endorsed by the Revenue Protection Section indicating that insufficient postage had been attached to the letter. Some £0.77 needed to be paid for the forms to be delivered. A second endorsement was to the effect that the package had "not [been] called for." It was established that there was, in relation to the Benefit Office to which the claimant had sent the first set of forms, an arrangement under which the Post Office adopted a different policy from that which normally applies in relation to under-stamped mail. The normal practice is to advise the addressee that mail awaits them and is available on payment of the amount of the underpayment plus handling fee. The practice which it was accepted should have been adopted in this case was for the forms to have been delivered and for the amount of the underpayment to be included in a bulk surcharge arrangement with the Department. It would seem to flow from the detailed reasoning of the Commissioner in the case that he would accept that there might be an argument to bring the failure of such arrangements within the ambit of the phrase "adverse postal conditions." However, he decided the case on the basis that the Post Office in holding the first set of claim forms was the bailee for the Department and so the original forms are to be treated as being in the hands of the Department between the date of its receipt until they were returned to the claimant. This was sufficient to ground entitlement to the benefit from the earlier date.

In *R(IS) 16/04*, the Commissioner accepts that delays in post arriving over the Christmas period constitute adverse postal conditions within para.(7)(c).

In *CJSA/3960/2006*, the Deputy Commissioner ruled that a delay of two working days beyond the maximum period within which a letter should have been delivered constituted "adverse postal conditions". The mere fact of the delay established that there were adverse postal conditions. A second issue arose in the case on the interpretation of the words "before the date that his entitlement expired" in reg. 19(7)(d). The Deputy Commissioner ruled that a decision that a person was not entitled to income support from February 4, 2006 meant that the claimant's entitlement ended on February 3, 2006, since "her entitlement expired on the very last moment of the Friday but before the very first moment of the Saturday." (para. 20).

In *CJSA/0743/2006* the Commissioner ruled that the words "another benefit" in reg. 19(7)(d) referred to a different benefit. He said, "I consider that the natural meaning of the work in that context is 'different'" (para. 9).

(12) para. (8) CJSA/4383/2003 concerns the relationship of the 28 day time limit for claiming income support by asylum seekers who have received notification that they have been accepted as having refugee status under reg.21ZB(2) of the Income Support General Regulations. Provided income support is claimed within this time limit, the award can be backdated to the date of the asylum application. Because of delays inherent in the determination of such claims, this can be a very substantial period. In the appeal before the Commissioner, the issue arose as to whether a person within the ambit of reg.21ZB(2) lost all ability to use the provisions of reg.19(4) and (5) to seek backdating of a claim for income support. The Secretary of State had argued that the reg.19(8) had this effect. The Commissioner disagreed for the following reasons:

2.128

"17. . . . In my view this is to misunderstand the legislative framework. The starting point is section 1 of the Social Security Administration Act 1992, which (in virtually all cases) requires a claim to be made as a precondition of entitlement to benefit. Section 5 of the 1992 Act then grants the Secretary of State various regulation-making powers in relation to claims. In the exercise of these powers, the Social Security (Claims and Payments) Regulations 1987 have been made. Regulation 19(1) of, and Schedule 4 to, those Regulations sets out the basic rules for claiming various benefits and the time limits that apply. Thus the general rule is that claims for income support or jobseeker's allowance must be made on 'the first day of the period in respect of which the claim is made'. Regulation 19(4) and (5) then provide, by way of exception to this general principle, that the prescribed period for claiming these benefits can be extended for up to three months if 'good cause', as defined by the Regulations, can be established.

18. However, regulation 19(4) is expressly stated to be subject to regulation 19(8). The purpose of regulation 19(8) is to provide that those claimants who can avail themselves of regulation 21ZB are not to be caught by the standard limit of three months on backdating entitlement to income support. A successful applicant for asylum, who claims arrears of income support within 28 days of receiving the Home Office's notification, is a person who makes 'a claim to which regulation 21ZB [. . .] of the Income Support (General) Regulations 1987 (treatment of refugees) applies'. In that situation regulation 19(8) then provides that 'this regulation' (i.e. the normal three month rule) 'shall not have effect'. In other words, the claim for arrears of benefit, if made within the 28 day time limit, may be backdated by many more than three months and indeed right back to the date of the asylum application. This is supported by regulation 6(4D) of the 1987 Regulations, which deems the claim so made to have been made actually at the much earlier date when asylum was applied for – see the obiter opinion of Mrs Deputy Commissioner Rowley in *CIS/579/2004* (at paragraph 43.4).

The Social Security (Claims and Payments) Regulations 1987

19. In my view, therefore, there are not two entirely separate and mutually exclusive regimes, which appears to be the Secretary of State's contention. The correct position in law is that a person in the claimant's situation may be able to make a claim for backdated benefit in accordance with regulation 19(4) and (5). Just because he is a successful applicant for asylum does not take him out of that regime. However, if he had made his claim within 28 days of the Home Office letter, he might have his entitlement to benefit backdated to the date of his original application for asylum, by virtue of regulation 21ZB, regardless of the normal three month rule in regulation 19(4)."

PART III

PAYMENTS

[¹ Time of payment: general provision

2.129   **20.** Subject to regulations 21 to 26B, benefit shall be paid in accordance with an award as soon as is reasonably practicable after the award has been made.]

AMENDMENT

1. Inserted by The Social Security (Miscellaneous Amendments) (No.2) Regulations 2006 (SI 2006/832), reg.2 (April 10, 2006).

DEFINITION

"benefit"—see reg.2(2).

2.130   **20A.**—[¹ . . .]

AMENDMENT

1. The Social Security (Miscellaneous Amendments) (No.2) Regulations 2006 (SI 2006/832), reg.2 (April 10, 2006).

Direct credit transfer

2.131   **21.**—[⁹ (1) Subject to the provisions of this regulation, benefit may, by an arrangement between the Secretary of State and the person claiming or entitled to it [¹⁰ or person appointed under regulation 33 or specified in regulation 33(1)(c) or (d)], be paid by way of direct credit transfer into a bank or other account—
   (a) In the name of the person entitled to benefit, or his spouse or partner, or a person acting on his behalf, or
   (b) In the joint names of the person entitled to benefit and his spouse or partner, or the person entitled to benefit and a person acting on his behalf.]
   (2) [⁹ . . .]
   (3) [²Subject to paragraph (3A)] benefit shall be paid in accordance with paragraph (1) within seven days of the last day of each successive period of entitlement [⁹ . . .] [⁷or, so far as concerns working familiar tax credit, within such time as the Board may direct]

(SI 1987/1968, reg.21) (as amended)

[²(3A) Income Support shall be paid in accordance with paragraph (1) within 7 days of the time determined for the payment of income support in accordance with Schedule 7.]

[⁶(3B) Where child benefit is payable in accordance with paragraph (1), [⁹ an arrangement under that paragraph] shall also have effect for any guardian's allowance to which the claimant is entitled and that allowance shall be paid in the same manner as the child benefit due in his case.

(3C) Where guardian's allowance is payable in accordance with paragraph (1), [⁹ an arrangement under that paragraph] shall also have effect for the child benefit to which the claimant is entitled and that child benefit shall be paid in the same manner as the guardian's allowance which is due in his case.]

(4) In respect of benefit which is the subject of an arrangement for payment under this regulation, the Secretary of State [⁷or the Board] may make a particular payment by credit transfer otherwise than is provided by paragraph (3) [²or (3A)] if it appears to him [⁷or them] appropriate to do so for the purpose of—

(a) paying any arrears of benefit, or
(b) making a payment in respect of a terminal period of an award or for any similar purpose.

(5) The arrangement for benefit to be payable in accordance with this regulation may be terminated—

(a) by the person entitled to benefit or a person acting on his behalf by notice in writing delivered or sent to an appropriate office or
(b) by the Secretary of State [⁷or the Board] if the arrangement seems to him [⁷or them] to be no longer appropriate to the circumstances of the particular case.

[⁸ (5A) In relation to payment of a joint-claim jobseeker's allowance, references in this regulation to the person entitled to benefit shall be construed as references to the member of the joint-claim couple who is the nominated member for the purposes of section 3B of the Jobseekers Act.]

(6) [⁵. . .]

AMENDMENTS

1. The Social Security (Miscellaneous Provisions) Amendment Regulations 1992 (SI 1992/247), reg.15 (March 9, 1992).

2. The Social Security (Claims and Payments) Amendment (No.2) Regulations 1993 (SI 1993/1113), reg.2 (May 12, 1993).

3. The Social Security (Claims and Payments) Amendment Regulations 1994 (SI 1994/2319), reg.4 (October 3, 1994).

4. The Social Security (Claims and Payments) Amendment Regulations 1994 (SI 1994/2319), reg.8 (April 13, 1995).

5. The Social Security (Claims and Payments) Amendment Regulations 1996 (SI 1996/672), reg.2(3) (April 4, 1996).

6. The Social Security (Claims and Payments) Amendment Regulations 1999 (SI 1999/2358), reg.2 (September 20, 1999).

7. The Tax Credits (Claims and Payments) (Amendment) Regulations 1999 (SI 1999/2572), regs 20, 23 & 24 (October 5, 1999).

8. The Social Security (Joint Claims: Consequential Amendments) Regulations 2000 (SI 2000/1982), reg.2(6) (March 19, 2001).

9. The Social Security (Claims and Payments and Miscellaneous Amendments) (No.2) Regulations 2002 (SI 2002/2441), reg.2 (April 6, 2003).

10. The Social Security (Miscellaneous Amendments) (No.2) Regulations 2006 (SI 2006/832), reg.2 (April 10, 2006).

The Social Security (Claims and Payments) Regulations 1987

DEFINITIONS
"appropriate office"—see reg.2(1).
"partner"—*ibid.*

GENERAL NOTE

2.132   Until May 12, 1993, it was not possible for income support to be paid by direct credit transfer.

[¹ Delayed payment of lump sum

2.133   **21A.**—(1) The regulation applies where—
(a) a person ("P") is entitled to a lump sum under, as the case may be—
   (i) Schedule 5 to the Contributions and Benefits Act (pensions increase or lump sum where entitlement to retirement pension is deferred);
   (ii) Schedule 5A to that Act (pension increase or lump sum where entitlement to share additional pension is deferred); or
   (iii) Schedule 1 to the Social Security (Graduated Retirement Benefit) Regulations 2005 (further provisions replacing section 36(4) of the National Insurance Act 1965: increases of graduated retirement benefit and lump sums);
or
(b) the Secretary of State decides to make a payment on account of such a lump sum.

(2) Subject to paragraph (3), for the purposes of section 7 of the Finance (No. 2) Act 2005 (charge to income tax of lump sum), P may elect to be paid the lump sum in the tax year ("the later year of assessment") next following the tax year which would otherwise be the applicable year of assessment by virtue of section 8 of that Act (meaning of "applicable year of assessment" in section 7).

(3) P may not elect in accordance with paragraph (2) ("a tax election") unless he elects on the same day as he chooses a lump sum in accordance with, as the case may be—
(a) paragraph A1 or 3C of Schedule 5 to the Contributions and Benefits Act;
(b) paragraph 1 of Schedule 5A to that Act;
(c) paragraph 12 or 17 of Schedule 1 to the Social Security (Graduated Retirement Benefit) Regulations 2005,
or within a month of that day.

(4) A tax election may be made in writing to an office specified by the Secretary of state for accepting such elections or, except where in any particular case the Secretary of State directs that the election must be made in writing, it may be made by telephone call to the number specified by the Secretary of State.

(5) If P makes a tax election, payment of the lump sum, or any payment on account of the lump sum, shall be made in the first month of the later year of assessment or as soon as reasonably practicable after that month, unless P revokes the tax election before the payment is made.

(6) If P makes no tax elections in accordance with paragraph (2) and (3), or revokes a tax election, payment of the lump sum or any payment on account of the lump sum shall be made as soon as reasonably practicable after P—
(a) elected for a lump sum, or was treated as having so elected; or

(SI 1987/1968, reg.21A) (as amended)

   (b) revoked a tax election.

  (7) If P dies before the beginning of the later year of assessment—

   (a) any tax election in respect of P's lump sum shall cease to have effect; and

   (b) no person appointed under regulation 30 to act on P's behalf may make a tax election.

  (8) In this regulation "the later year of assessment" has the meaning given by section 8(5) of the Finance (No. 2) Act 2005.]

AMENDMENT

1. The Social Security (Deferral of Retirement Pensions, Shared Additional Pension and Graduated Retirement Benefit) (Miscellaneous Provisions) Regulations 2005 (SI 2005/2677) (April 6, 2006).

Long term benefits

22.—[5 (1) Subject to the provisions of this regulation and regulation 25(1), long term benefits may be paid at intervals of four weeks, or weekly in advance.

(1A) Disability living allowance shall be paid at intervals of four weeks.]

(2) Where the amount of long-term benefit payable is less than [4 £5.00] a week the Secretary of State may direct that it shall be paid (whether in advance or in arrears) at such intervals as may be specified not exceeding 12 months.

(3) Schedule 6 specifies the days of the week on which the various long term benefits are payable.

2.134

AMENDMENTS

1. The Social Security (Claims and Payments) Amendment Regulations 1991 (SI 1991/2741), reg.12(a) (February 3, 1992).

2. The Social Security (Claims and Payments) Amendment Regulations 1991 (SI 1991/2741), reg.12(b) (February 3, 1992).

3. The Social Security (Claims and Payments) Amendment (No.4) Regulations 1994 (SI 1994/3196), reg.5 (January 10, 1995).

4. The Social Security (Claims and Payments and Adjudication) Amendment Regulations 1996 (SI 1996/2306), reg.22(2) (October 7, 1996).

5. The Social Security (Claims and Payments and Miscellaneous Amendments) (No.2) Regulations 2002 (SI 2002/2441), reg.2 (April 6, 2003).

[1 Child benefit and guardian's allowance.]

23.—(1) Subject to the provisions of this regulation [3 . . .], child benefit shall be payable as follows:—

   (a) in a case where a person entitled to child benefit elects to receive payment weekly in accordance with the provisions of Schedule 8, child benefit shall be payable weekly from the first convenient date after the election has been made;

   (b) in any other case child benefit shall be payable in the last week of each successive period of four weeks of the period of entitlement.

(2) Subject to paragraph (3) and regulation 21, child benefit payable weekly or four-weekly shall be payable on Mondays or Tuesdays (as the Secretary of State may in any case determine) [2 by means of serial orders or on presentation of an instrument for benefit payment]

2.135

The Social Security (Claims and Payments) Regulations 1987

(3) In such cases as the Secretary of State may determine, child benefit shall be payable otherwise than—
  (a) by means of serial order [²or on presentation of an instrument for benefit payment,]
  (b) on Mondays or Tuesdays, or
  (c) at weekly or four-weekly intervals,
and where child benefit is paid at four-weekly intervals in accordance with paragraph (1)(b) the Secretary of State shall arrange for it to be paid weekly if satisfied that payment at intervals of four weeks is causing hardship.

[¹ (3A) Where a claimant for child benefit is also entitled to guardian's allowance, that allowance shall be payable in the same manner and at the same intervals as the claimant's child benefit under this regulation.]

(4) The Secretary of State shall take steps to notify persons to whom child benefit is payable of the arrangements he has made for payment so far as those arrangements affect such persons.

AMENDMENTS

1. The Social Security (Claims and Payments) Amendment Regulations 1999 (SI 1999/2358), reg.2(5) (September 20, 1999).
2. The Social Security (Claims and Payments) Amendment (No.4) Regulations 1994 (SI 1994/3196), reg.6 (January 10, 1995).
3. The Social Security (Claims and Payments and Miscellaneous Amendments) (No.2) Regulations 2002 (SI 2002/2441), reg.2 (April 1, 2003).

[¹ Incapacity benefit, maternity allowance and severe disablement allowance

2.136

24.—(1) Subject to [³ . . .] paragraphs (2) [²(3) and (3A)], incapacity benefit and severe disablement allowance shall be paid fortnightly in arrears unless, in any particular case, the Secretary of State arranges otherwise.

(2) Subject to [³ . . .] [² paragraphs (3) and (3A)], incapacity benefit and severe disablement allowance shall be paid weekly in arrears where—
  (a) immediately before 13th April 1995 a person was entitled to sickness benefit, invalidity benefit or severe disablement allowance and—
    (i) in the case of severe disablement allowance, there has been no break in the entitlement to that benefit on or after that date;
    (ii) in the case of sickness benefit and invalidity benefit, there has been no break in the entitlement to incapacity benefit on or after that date;
  (b) a claim for incapacity benefit or severe disablement allowance is made on or after 13th April 1995 and immediately before the date of the claim income support on the grounds of incapacity for work was being paid weekly.

(3) If the weekly amount of incapacity benefit or severe disablement allowance is less than £1.00 it may be paid in arrears at intervals of 4 weeks.

[² (3A) Where the amount of incapacity benefit payable after reduction for pension payments under section 30DD of the Social Security Contributions and Benefits Act 1992 (including any reduction for other purposes) is less than £5.00 per week, the Secretary of State may direct that it shall be paid (whether in advance or arrears) at such intervals as may be specified not exceeding 12 months.]

(SI 1987/1968, reg.24) (as amended)

(4) Maternity allowance shall be paid on Friday in the week for which it is payable unless in any particular case the Secretary of State arranges otherwise.]

AMENDMENTS

1. Reg.24 substituted by The Social Security (Claims and Payments) Amendment (No.2) Regulations 1994 (SI 1994/2943), reg.9 (April 13, 1995); words in heading to and certain words in regulation deleted by The Social Security (Claims and Payments) (Jobseeker's Allowance Consequential Amendments) Regulations 1996 (SI 1996/1460), reg.2(13) (October 7, 1996).
2. The Social Security (Incapacity Benefit) Miscellaneous Amendments Regulations 2000 (SI 2000/3210), reg.3 (April 6, 2001).
3. The Social Security (Claims and Payments and Miscellaneous Amendments) (No.2) Regulations 2002 (SI 2002/2441), reg.2 (April 8, 2003).

Payment of attendance allowance and constant attendance allowance at a daily rate

25.—(1) Attendance allowance [¹or disability living allowance] [². . .] shall be paid in respect of any person, for any day falling within a period to which paragraph (2) applies, at the daily rate (which shall be equal to ⅐th of the weekly rate) and attendance allowance [¹ or disability living allowance] [². . .] payable in pursuance of this regulation shall be paid weekly or as the Secretary of State may direct in any case.

2.137

(2) This paragraph applies to any period which—
(a) begins on the day immediately following the last day of the period during which a person was living in [³ a hospital specified in or other accommodation provided as specified in regulations made under [section 72(8) of the Social Security Contributions and Benefits Act 1992] ("specified hospital or other accommodation")]; and
(b) ends—
   (i) if the first day of the period was a day of payment, at midnight on the day preceding the [³ 4th] following day of payment, or
   (ii) if that day was not a day of payment, at midnight on the day preceding the [³ 5th] following day of payment, or
   (iii) if earlier, on the day immediately preceding the day on which [³ he next lives in specified hospital or other accommodation],
if on the first day of the period it is expected that, before the expiry of the period of [³ 28 days] beginning with that day, he will return to [³ specified hospital or other accommodation].

(3) An increase of disablement pension under [section 104 of the Social Security Contributions and Benefits Act 1992] where constant attendance is needed ("constant attendance allowance") shall be paid at a daily rate of 1/7th of the weekly rate in any case where it becomes payable for a period of less than a week which is immediately preceded and immediately succeeded by periods during which the constant attendance allowance was not payable because regulation 21(1) of the Social Security (General Benefit) Regulations 1982 applied.

AMENDMENTS

1. The Social Security (Claims and Payments) Amendment Regulations 1991 (SI 1991/2741), reg.13(a) (April 6, 1992).

The Social Security (Claims and Payments) Regulations 1987

2. The Social Security (Disability Living Allowance and Claims and Payments) Amendment Regulations 1996 (SI 1996/1436), reg.3 (July 31, 1996).
3. The Social Security (Claims and Payments) Amendment Regulations 1991 (SI 1991/2741), reg.13(b)–(f) (April 6, 1992).

Income support

2.138   **26.**—(1) [³ Subject to regulation 21 (direct credit transfer), Schedule 7] shall have effect for determining the [⁶ . . .] time at which income support is to be paid, [. . .⁵] and the day when entitlement to income support is to begin.
(2) [⁶ . . .]
[² (3) [⁶ . . .].]
(4) Where the entitlement to income support is less than 10 pence or, in the case of a beneficiary to whom [¹ section 23(a)] of the Social Security Act 1986 [SSCBA, s.126] applies, £5, that amount shall not be payable unless the claimant is also entitled to payment of any other benefit with which income support [²may be paid] under arrangements made by the Secretary of State.

AMENDMENTS

1. The Social Security (Claims and Payments) Amendment Regulations 1988 (SI 1988/522), reg.6 (April 11, 1988).
2. The Social Security (Claims and Payments and Payments on account, Overpayments and Recovery) Amendment Regulations 1989 (SI 1989/136), reg.2 (February 27, 1989).
3. The Social Security (Claims and Payments) Amendment (No.2) Regulations 1993 (SI 1993/1113), reg.3 (May 12, 1993).
4. The Social Security Act 1998 (Commencment No.12 and Consequential and Transitional Provisions) Order 1999 (SI 1999/3178), Sch.6 (November 29, 1999).
5. The Social Security and Child Support (Miscellaneous Amendments) Regulations 2000 (SI 2000/1596), reg.4(1) (June 19, 2000).
6. The Social Security (Miscellaneous Amendments) (No.2) Regulations 2006 (SI 2006/832), reg.2 (April 10, 2006).

[¹ Jobseeker's allowance

2.139   **26A.**—(1) Subject to the following provisions of this regulation, jobseeker's allowance shall be paid fortnightly in arrears unless in any particular case or class of case the Secretary of State arranges otherwise.
(2) The provisions of paragraph 2A of Schedule 7 (payment of income support at times of office closure) shall apply for the purposes of payment of a jobseeker's allowance as they apply for the purposes of payment of income support [⁵ . . .]
(3) Where the amount of a jobseeker's allowance is less than £1.00 a week the Secretary of State may direct that it shall be paid at such intervals, not exceeding 13 weeks, as may be specified in the direction.
(4) [. . .⁴].
(5) [. . .⁴].
(6) [. . .⁴].
(7) [. . .⁴].
(8) [. . .⁴].

AMENDMENTS

1. The Social Security (Claims and Payments) (Jobseeker's Allowance Consequential Amendments) Regulations 1996 (SI 1996/1460), reg.2(14) (October 7, 1996).

(SI 1987/1968, reg.26A) (as amended)

2. The Social Security (Miscellaneous Amendments) (No.4) Regulations 1998 (SI 1998/1174), reg.8(3)(a) (June 1, 1998).
3. The Social Security Act 1998 (Commencement No.12 and Consequential and Transitional Provisions) Order 1999 (SI 1999/3178), Sch.6 (November 29, 1999).
4. The Social Security and Child Support (Miscellaneous Amendments) Regulations 2000 (SI 2000/1596), reg.4(2) (June 19, 2000).
5. The Secretaries of State for Education and Skills and for Work and Pensions Order 2002 (SI 2002/1397), art.18 (June 27, 2002).

DEFINITIONS

"jobseeker's allowance"—see reg.2(1).
"the Jobseeker's Allowance Regulations"—*ibid.*
"partner"—*ibid.*
"week"—*ibid.*

[¹ State pension credit

26B.—(1) Except where paragraph (2) applies, state pension credit shall be payable on Mondays, but subject, [² to regulation 21 where payment is by direct credit transfer].

(2) State pension credit shall be payable—
 (a) if retirement pension is payable to the claimant, on the same day as the retirement pension is payable; or
 (b) on such other day of the week as the Secretary of State may, in the particular circumstances of the case, determine.

(3) [² . . .]

(4) State pension credit paid [² otherwise than in accordance with regulation 21] shall be paid weekly in advance.

(5) Where the amount of state pension credit payable is less than £1.00 per week, the Secretary of State may direct that it shall be paid at such intervals, not exceeding 13 weeks, as may be specified in the direction.

(6) [² . . .]

(7) [² . . .].]

2.140

AMENDMENTS

1. Inserted by State Pension Credit (Consequential, Transitional and Miscellaneous Provisions) Regulations 2002 (SI 2002/3019), reg.9 (April 7, 2003).
2. The Social Security (Miscellaneous Amendments) (No.2) Regulations 2006 (SI 2006/832), reg.2 (April 10, 2006).

[¹ [² Working families' tax credit and disabled persons' tax credit]]

27.—(1) Subject to regulation 21 [³and paragraph (1A)] [²working families' tax credit] and [²disabled persons' tax credit] shall be payable in respect of any benefit week on the Tuesday next following the end of that week by means of a book of serial orders [³or on presentation of an instrument for benefit payment] unless in any case the Secretary of State arranges [⁴ Board arrange] otherwise.

[⁵ (1A) Subject to paragraph (2), where an amount of [² working families' tax credit] and [² disabled persons' tax credit] becomes payable which is at a weekly rate of note more than £4.00, that amount shall, if the Secretary of State so directs [⁴ Board so direct], be payable as soon as practicable by means of a single payment; except that if that amount represents an

2.141

The Social Security (Claims and Payments) Regulations 1987

increase in the amount of either of those benefits which has previously been paid in respect of the same period, this paragraph shall apply only if that previous payment was made by means of a single payment.]

(2) Where the entitlement to [²working families' tax credit] and [² disabled persons' tax credit] is less than 50 pence a week that amount shall not be payable.]

AMENDMENTS

1. Reg.27 substituted by The Social Security (Claims and Payments) Amendment Regulations 1991 (SI 1991/2741), reg.14 (April 6, 1992).
2. The Tax Credits (Claims and Payments) (Amendment) Regulations 1999 (SI 1999/2752), regs 24 and 25 (October 5, 1999).
3. The Social Security (Claims and Payments) Amendment (No.3) Regulations 1993 (SI 1993/2113), reg.3(4) (October 25, 1993).
4. For tax credits purposes only, these words are substitue for the words "Secretary of State arranges": The Tax Credits (Claims and Payments) (Amendment) Regulations 1999 (SI 1999/2572), reg.12(a) (October 5, 1999).
5. The Social Security (Claims and Payments) Amendment (No.3) Regulations 1993 (SI 1993/2113), reg.3(4) (October 25, 1993).

Fractional amounts of benefit

[¹ **28.**—(1) Subject to paragraph (2),] where the amount of any benefit payable would, but for this regulation, include a fraction of a penny, that fraction shall be disregarded if it is less than half a penny and shall otherwise be treated as a penny.

[¹ (2) Where the amount of any maternity allowance payable would, but for this regulation, include a fraction of a penny, that fraction shall be treated as a penny.]

AMENDMENT

1. Social Security (Claims and Payments) Amendment (No.2) Regulations 2002 (SI 2002/1950), reg.2 (September 2, 2002).

DEFINITION

"benefit"—see reg.2(2).

[¹ Payments to persons under age 18

29.—Where benefit is paid to a person under the age of 18 (whether on his own behalf or on behalf of another) [² . . .] [² a direct credit transfer under regulation 21 into any such person's account, or the receipt by him of a payment made by some other means] shall be sufficient discharge to the Secretary of State [³ or the Board].]

AMENDMENTS

1. The Social Security (Claims and Payments etc.) Amendment Regulations 1996 (SI 1996/672), reg.2(4) (April 4, 1996).
2. Social Security (Claims and Payments and Miscellaneous Amendments) (No.2) Regulations 2002 (SI 2002/2441), reg.6 (October 23, 2002).
3. The Tax Credits (Claims and Payments) (Amendment) Regulations 1999 (SI 1999/2572), reg.30 (October 5, 1999).

(SI 1987/1968, reg.29) (as amended)

DEFINITION

"benefit"—see reg.2(2).

Payments on death

30.—(1) On the death of a person who has made a claim for benefit, the Secretary of State [¹or the Board] may appoint such person as he [¹or they] may think fit to proceed with the claim [¹⁵ and any related issue of revision, supersession or appeal].

(2) Subject to [¹² paragraphs (4) and (4A)], any sum payable by way of benefit which is payable under an award on a claim proceeded with under paragraph (1) may be paid or distributed by the Secretary of State to or amongst persons over the age of 16 claiming as personal representatives, legatees, next of kin, or creditors of the deceased (or, where the deceased was illegitimate, to or amongst other persons over the age of 16), and the provisions of regulation 38 (extinguishment of right) shall apply to any such payment or distribution; and—

(a) [¹³ a direct credit transfer under regulation 21 into any such person's account, or the receipt by him of a payment made by some other means,] shall be a good discharge to the Secretary of State [¹or the Board] for any sum so paid; and

(b) where the Secretary of State is satisfied [¹or the Board is satisfied] that any such sum or part thereof is needed for the benefit of any person under the age of 16, he [¹or they] may obtain a good discharge therefor by paying the sum or part thereof to a person over that age who satisfies the Secretary of State [¹or the Board] that he will apply the sum so paid for the benefit of the person under the age of 16.

(3) Subject to paragraph (2), any sum payable by way of benefit to the deceased, payment of which he had not obtained at the date of his death, may, unless the right thereto was already extinguished at that date, be paid or distributed to or amongst such persons as are mentioned in paragraph (2), and regulation 38 shall apply to any such payment or distribution, except that, for the purpose of that regulation, the period of 12 months shall be calculated from the date on which the right to payment of any sum is treated as having arisen in relation to any such person and not from the date on which that right is treated as having arisen in relation to the deceased.

(4) Paragraphs (2) and (3) shall not apply in any case unless written application for the payment of any such sum is made to the Secretary of State [¹or the Board] within 12 months from the date of the deceased's death or within such longer period as the Secretary of State [¹or the Board] may allow in any particular case.

[¹² (4A) In a case where a joint-claim jobseeker's allowance has been awarded to a joint-claim couple and one member of the couple dies, the amount payable under that award shall be payable to the other member of that couple.]

(5) [¹⁶ Subject to paragraphs (5A) to [¹⁸ (5G),] where the conditions specified in paragraph (6) are satisfied, a claim may be made on behalf of the deceased to any benefit other than [²jobseeker's allowance,] income support, [¹⁴, state pension credit] [³working families' tax credit or disabled person's tax credit] or a social fund payment such as is mentioned in section

2.144

The Social Security (Claims and Payments) Regulations 1987

32(2)(a) [⁴and section 32(2A)] of the Social security Act 1986 [⁵, or reduced earnings allowance or disablement benefit], to which he would have been entitled if he had claimed it in the prescribed manner and within the prescribed time.

[¹⁸ (5A) Subject to paragraphs (5B) to (5G), a claim may be made in accordance with paragraph (5) on behalf of the deceased for a Category A or Category B retirement pension or graduated retirement benefit provided that the deceased was not married or in a civil partnership on the date of his death.

(5B) But, subject to paragraphs (5C) to (5G), a claim may be made in accordance with paragraph (5) on behalf of the deceased for a Category A or Category B retirement pension or graduated retirement benefit where the deceased was a married woman or a civil partner on the date of death if the deceased's widower or surviving civil partner was under pensionable age on that date and due to attain pensionable age before 6th April 2010.

(5C) Where a claim is made for a shared additional pension under paragraph (5) or for a retirement pension or graduated retirement benefit under paragraphs (5) and (5A) or (5B), in determining the benefit to which the deceased would have been entitled if he had claimed within the prescribed time, the prescribed time shall be the period of three months ending on the date of his death and beginning with any day on which, apart from satisfying the condition of making a claim, he would have been entitled to the pension or benefit.

(5D) Paragraph (5E) applies where, throughout the period of 12 months ending with the day before the death of the deceased person, his entitlement to a Category A or a Category B retirement pension, shared additional pension or graduated retirement benefit was deferred in accordance with, as the case may be—
 (a) section 55 of the Contributions and Benefits Act (pension increase or lump sum where entitlement to retirement pension is deferred);
 (b) section 55C of that Act (pension increase or lump sum where entitlement to shared additional pension is deferred); or
 (c) section 36(4A) of the National Insurance Act 1965(c) (deferment of graduated retirement benefit).

(5E) Where a person claims under paragraph (5) or under paragraphs (5) and (5A) or (5B) the deceased shall be treated as having made an election in accordance with, as the case may be—
 (a) paragraph A1(1)(a) of Schedule 5 to the Contributions and Benefits Act (electing to have an increase of pension), where paragraph (5D)(a) applies;
 (b) paragraph 1(1)(a) of Schedule 5A to that Act (electing to have an increase of a shared additional pension) where paragraph (5D)(b) applies; or
 (c) paragraph 12(1)(a) of Schedule 1 to the Social Security (Graduated Retirement Benefit) Regulations 2005 (electing to have an increase of benefit), where paragraph (5D)(c) applies.

(5F) Paragraph (5G) applies where—
 (a) the deceased person was a widow, widower or surviving civil partner ("W") who was married to, or in a civil partnership with, the other party of the marriage or civil partnership ("S") when S died;

(SI 1987/1968, reg.30) (as amended)

(b) throughout the period of 12 months ending with the day before S's death, S's entitlement to a Category A or a Category B retirement pension or graduated retirement benefit was deferred in accordance with, as the case may be, paragraph (5D)(a) or (c); and

(c) W made no statutory election in consequence of the deferral.

(5G) Where a person claims under paragraphs (5) and (5A) the deceased ("W") shall be treated as having made an election in accordance with, as the case may be—

(a) paragraph 3C(2)(a) of Schedule 5 to the Contributions and Benefits Act (electing to have an increase of pension), where paragraph (5D)(a) applies; or

(b) paragraph 17(2)(a) of Schedule 1 to the Social Security (Graduated Retirement Benefit) Regulations 2005 (electing to have an increase in benefit), where paragraph (5D)(c) applies.]

(6) [⁶Subject to the following provisions of this regulation,] the following conditions are specified for the purposes of paragraph (5)—

(a) Within six months of the death an application must have been made in writing to the Secretary of State for a person, whom the Secretary of State thinks fit to be appointed to make the claim, to be so appointed;

(b) a person must have been appointed by the Secretary of State to make the claim;

(c) there must have been no longer period than six months between the appointment and the making of the claim.

[⁷(6A) Where the conditions specified in paragraph (6B) are satisfied, a person may make a claim for reduced earnings or disablement benefit, including any increase under [section 104 or 105 of the Social Security Contributions and Benefits Act 1992], in the name of a person who had died.

(6B) [⁸Subject to the following provisions of this regulation,] the conditions specified for the purposes of paragraph (6A) are—

(a) that the person who had died would have been entitled to the benefit claimed if he had made a claim for it in the prescribed manner and within the prescribed time;

(b) that within 6 months of a death certificate being issued in respect of the person who has died, the person making the claim has applied to the Secretary of State to be made an appointee of the person who has died

[⁹(ba) that person has been appointed by the Secretary of State to make the claim]

(c) the claim is made within six months of the appointment.]

[¹⁰(6C) Subject to paragraph (6D), where the Secretary of State certifies that to do so would be consistent with the proper administration of the Social Security Contributions and Benefits Act 1992 the period specified in paragraphs (6)(a) and (c) and (6B)(b) and (c) shall be extended to such period, not exceeding 6 months, as may be specified in the certificate.

(6D)(a) Where a certificate is given under paragraph (6C) extending the period specified in paragraph (6)(a) or (6B)(b), the period specified in paragraph (6)(c) or (6B)(c) shall be shortened by a period corresponding to the period specified in the certificate;

(b) no certificate shall be given under paragraph (6C) which would enable a claim to be made more than 12 months after the date of death (in a case falling within paragraph (6)) or the date of a death

445

certificate being issued in respect of the person who has died (in a case falling within paragraph (6B)); and

(c) in the application of sub-paragraph (b) any period between the date when an application for a person to be appointed to make a claim is made and the date when that appointment is made shall be disregarded.]

(7) A claim made in accordance with paragraph (5) [[11]or paragraph (6A)] shall be treated, for the purposes of these regulations, as if made by the deceased on the date of his death.

(8) The Secretary of State [[1]or the Board] may dispense with strict proof of the title of any person claiming in accordance with the provisions of this regulation.

(9) In paragraph (2) "next of kin" means—
 (a) in England and Wales, the persons who would take beneficially on an intestacy; and
 (b) in Scotland, the persons entitled to the moveable estate of the deceased on intestacy.

AMENDMENTS

1. The Tax Credits (Claims and Payments) (Amendment) Regulations 1999 (SI 1999/2572), regs 13, 20 and 22 (October 5, 1999).
2. The Social Security (Claims and Payments) (Jobseeker's Allowance Consequential Amendments) Regulations 1996 (SI 1996/1460), reg.2(15) (October 7, 1996).
3. The Tax Credits (Claims and Payments) (Amendments) Regulations 1999 (SI 1999/2572), regs 24 and 25 (October 5, 1999).
4. The Social Security (Claims and Payments) Amendment Regulations 1991 (SI 1991/2741), reg.15 (March 10, 1992).
5. The Social Security (Common Provisions) Miscellaneous Amendments Regulations 1988 (SI 1988/1725), reg.3(6) (November 7, 1988).
6. The Social Security (Claims and Payments) Amendment (No.3) Regulations 1993 (SI 1993/2113), reg.3(5)(a) (September 27, 1993).
7. Paras (6A) and (6B) inserted by The Social Security (Miscellaneous Provisions) Amendment Regulations 1990 (SI 1990/2208), reg.11(3) (December 5, 1990).
8. The Social Security (Claims and Payments) Amendment (No.3) Regulations 1993 (SI 1993/2113), reg.3(5)(a) (September 29, 1993).
9. The Social Security (Claims and Payments) Amendment Regulations 1994 (SI 1994/2319), reg.5 (October 3, 1994).
10. Paras (6C) and (6D) inserted by The Social Security (Claims and Payments) Amendment (No.3) Regulations 1993 (SI 1993/2113), reg.3(5)(b) (September 27, 1993).
11. The Social Security (Miscellaneous Provisions) Amendment Regulations 1990 (SI 1990/2208), reg.11(4) (December 5, 1990).
12. The Social Security (Joint Claims: Consequential Amendments) Regulations 2000 (SI 2000/1982), reg.2(7) (March 19, 2001).
13. Social Security (Claims and Payments and Miscellaneous Amendments) (No.2) Regulations 2002 (SI 2002/2441), reg.7, (October 23, 2002).
14. State Pension Credit (Consequential, Transitional and Miscellaneous Provisions) Regulations 2002 (SI 2002/3019), reg.10 (April 7, 2003).
15. The Social Security, Child Support and Tax Credits (Miscellaneous Amendments) Regulations 2005 (SI 2005/337), reg.7 (March 18, 2005).
16. The Social Security (Claims and Payments) Amendment Regulations 2005 (SI 2005/455), reg.4 (April 6, 2006).

(SI 1987/1968, reg.30) (as amended)

17. The Social Security (Shared Additional Pension) (Miscellaneous Amendments) Regulations 2005 (SI 2005/1551), reg.3 (April 6, 2006).

18. The Social Security (Retirement Pensions and Graduated Retirement Benefit) (Widowers and Civil Partnership) Regulations 2005 (SI 2005/3078), reg.4 (April 6, 2006).

GENERAL NOTE

Note the decisions referred to in the annotations to reg.33.

2.145

It would seem that the power of appointment in reg.30(1) on the death of the claimant is a separate appointment from that under reg.33. It would follow that where a claimant has an appointee under reg.33 and dies, there should at least be confirmation of continuation of the appointment under reg.33 to enable the appointee to act under reg.30. The better course, since there are specific requirements in the regulation, would be for a separate appointment to be made.

In *CIS/1423/1997* the Commissioner holds, at para.21 of his decision, that the plain words of reg.30 do not allow the Secretary of State to appoint a person to represent the claimant or their estate in the context of a decision for the recoverability of an overpayment from the claimant's estate.

Note that paras (4)–(7) contain a special power of appointment to enable *a claim* to be made after a person's death.

R(IS)3/04 discusses aspects of reg.30 at paras 14–17 of the decision. The Commissioner notes that reg.30(5) is the only provision permitting claims to be made in respect of deceased persons, and reg.30(5) expressly does not apply to income support.

Death of claimant pending appeal to the Commissioner

It sometimes happens that the claimant dies while the appeal is pending before the Commissioner. In such cases the surviving partner may not wish to take on an appointment enabling the matter to continue, and there may be no personal representatives because there is no estate. The result is that, where there is a claimant's appeal, there is no one who can withdraw the appeal. In such circumstances, the practice of the Commissioners is to treat the appeal as abated: see *R(S)7/56*, *R(1)2/83* and *R(SB)25/84*. For all practical purposes the matter is then closed, though the possibility remains that the matter could be revived on application. This could happen if, for example, the Secretary of State chose to appoint someone to act for the deceased claimant. The most likely appointee would be the Official Solicitor, but is difficult to imagine circumstances in which it would be appropriate to take such action. In overpayment cases, care should be taken to ensure that the Benefits Agency has given an assurance that it will not seek recovery from the estate before treating an appeal as abated, since abatement of a claimant's appeal without such an assurance would not preclude recovery against the estate.

2.146

The use of the abatement procedure is not appropriate where the appellant is the adjudication officer. In such cases, the proper course of action is for the adjudication officer to withdraw the appeal: *R(1)2/83*, para.6.

In *CIS/1340/1999* the Commissioner was considering an appeal involving a substantial overpayment of benefit in which the claimant had died since filing the appeal. No executors or administrators were appointed, and the claimant's husband did not respond to an invitation by the Department to consider applying to be the claimant's appointee. The Commissioner comments on the reference in these annotations that care should be taken to obtain an assurance that the Benefits Agency will not seek to recover the overpayment from the estate before treating the appeal as abated. He states that he does not consider that proposition to flow from the cases, and that *R(I)2/83* is merely authority for the proposition that, where such an assurance is available in an overpayment case, it may be appropriate to dismiss the appeal rather than merely declare it abated. At para.20, he says,

"But I see no reason why, before declaring the appeal abated or indeed striking it out, I should require an assurance to be sought from the Secretary of State that recovery of the overpayment will not be pursued. So long as the original decision of the adjudication officer stands the Secretary of State should be entitled to recover the overpayment. If he does so and there is anyone who has an interest in ensuring that it is not recovered, that person will be able to take steps to have the appeal reinstated." (para.20)

The appeal was declared abated.

[¹ Payment of arrears of joint-claim jobseeker's allowance where the nominated person can no longer be traced

30A. Where—
(a) an award of joint-claim jobseeker's allowance has been awarded to a joint-claim couple;
(b) that couple ceases to be a joint-claim couple; and
(c) the member of the joint-claim couple nominated for the purposes of section 3B of the Jobseekers Act cannot be traced,
arrears on the award of joint-claim jobseeker's allowance shall be paid to the other member of the former joint-claim couple.]

AMENDMENT

1. The Social Security Amendment (Joint Claims) Regulations 2001 (SI 2001/518), reg.5 (March 19, 2001).

Time and manner of payments of industrial injuries gratuities

31.—(1) This regulation applies to any gratuity payable under [Part V of the Social Security Contributions and Benefits Act 1992].

[² (1A) In the case of a person who made a claim for benefit in accordance with regulation 4A(1), a change of circumstances may be notified to a relevant authority at any office to which the claim for benefit could be made in accordance with that provision.]

(2) Subject to the following provisions of this regulation, every gratuity shall be payable in one sum.

(3) A gratuity may be payable by instalments of such amounts and at such times as appear reasonable in the circumstances of the case to the adjudicating authority awarding the gratuity if—
(a) the beneficiary to whom the gratuity has been awarded is, at the date of the award, under the age of 18 years, or
(b) in any other case, the amount of the gratuity so awarded (not being a gratuity payable to the widow of a deceased person on her remarriage) exceeds £52 and the beneficiary requests that payments should be made by instalments.

(4) An appeal shall not be brought against any decision that a gratuity should be payable by instalments or as to the amounts of any such instalments or the time of payment.

(5) Subject to the provisions of regulation 37 (suspension), a gratuity shall—
(a) if it is payable by equal weekly instalments, be paid in accordance with the provisions of regulation 22 insofar as they are applicable; or

(SI 1987/1968, reg.31) (as amended)

(b) in any case, be paid by such means as may appear to the Secretary of State to be appropriate in the circumstances.

AMENDMENTS

1. The Social Security Act 1998 (Commencement No.12 and Consequential and Transitional Provisions) Order 1999 (SI 1999/3178), Sch.6 (November 29, 1999).
2. The Social Security (Claims and Information) Regulations 1999 (SI 1999/3108) (November 29, 1999).

[⁵ Information to be given and changes to be notified

32.—(1) Except in the case of a jobseeker's allowance, every beneficiary and every person by whom or on whose behalf, sums by way of benefit are receivable shall furnish in such manner and at such times as the Secretary of State may determine such information or evidence as the Secretary of State may require for determining whether a decision on the award of benefit should be revised under section 9 of the Social Security Act 1998 or superseded under section 10 of that Act.

(1A) Every beneficiary and every person by whom, or on whose behalf, sums by way of benefit are receivable shall furnish in such manner and at such times as the Secretary of State may determine such information or evidence as the Secretary of State may require in connection with payment of the benefit claimed or awarded.

(1B) Except in the case of a jobseeker's allowance, every beneficiary and every person by whom or on whose behalf sums by way of benefit are receivable shall notify the Secretary of State of any change of circumstances which he might reasonably be expected to know might affect—

(a) the continuance of entitlement to benefit; or
(b) the payment of benefit

as soon as reasonably practicable after the change occurs by giving notice [⁸ of the change to the appropriate office—

    (i) in writing or by telephone (unless the Secretary of State determines in any particular case that notice must be in writing or may be given otherwise than in writing or by telephone; or
    (ii) in writing if in any class of class he requires written notice (unless he determines in any particular case to accept notice given otherwise than in writing)]]

[⁷ (1C) In the case of a person who made a claim for benefit in accordance with regulation 4A(1), a change of circumstances may be notified to a relevant authority at any office to which the claim for benefit could be made in accordance with that provision.]

(2) Where any sum is receivable on account of an increase of benefit in respect of an adult dependant, the Secretary of State may require the beneficiary to furnish a declaration signed by such dependant confirming the particulars respecting him, which have been given by the claimant.

[²(3) In the case of a person who is claiming income support, state pension credit [³or a jobseeker's allowance], where that person or any partner is aged not less than 60 and is a member of, or a person deriving entitlement to a pension under, a personal pension scheme, or is a party to, or a person deriving entitlement to a pension under, a retirement annuity contract, he shall where the Secretary of State so requires furnish the following information—

(a) the name and address of the pension fund holder;
(b) such other information including any reference or policy number as is needed to enable the personal pension scheme or retirement annuity contract to be identified.

(4) Where the pension fund holder receives from the Secretary of State a request for details concerning a personal pension scheme or retirement annuity contract relating to a person or any partner to whom paragraph (3) refers, the pension fund holder shall provide the Secretary of State with any information to which paragraph (5) refers.

(5) The information to which this paragraph refers is—
(a) where the purchase of an annuity under a personal pension scheme has been deferred, the amount of any income which is being withdrawn from the personal pension scheme;
(b) in the case of—
   (i) a personal pension scheme where income withdrawal is available, the maximum amount of income which may be withdrawn from the scheme; or
   (ii) a personal pension scheme where income withdrawal is not available, or a retirement annuity contract, the maximum amount of income which might be withdrawn from the fund if the fund were held under a personal pension scheme where income withdrawal was available,

calculated by or on behalf of the pension fund holder by means of tables prepared from time to time by the Government Actuary which are appropriate for this purpose.]

[⁶ (6) This regulation shall apply in the case of state pension credit subject to the following modifications—
(a) at the end of an assessed income period, the information and evidence required to be notified in accordance with this regulation includes information and evidence as to the likelihood of future changes in the claimant's circumstances needed to determine—
   (i) whether a period should be specified as an assessed income period under section 6 of the 2002 Act in relation to any decision; and
   (ii) if so, the length of the period to be so specified; and
[⁹ (b) except to the extent that sub-paragraph (a) applies, changes to an element of the claimant's retirement provision need not be notified if—
   (i) an assessed income period is current in his case;
   (ii) the time limit set out in sub-paragraph (c) has not expired; or
   (iii) the Secretary of State grants, or has granted, such longer period as he considers reasonable under sub-paragraph (c) and that period has not expired; and
(c) the information and evidence required under sub-paragraph (a) shall be furnished within one month of the date on which the Secretary of State notifies the claimant of the requirement or within such longer period as the Secretary of State considers reasonable.]

AMENDMENTS

1. The Social Security (Miscellaneous Provisions) Amendment (No.2) Regulations 1992 (SI 1992/2595), reg.4 (November 16, 1992).

(SI 1987/1968, reg.32) (as amended)

2. Income-related benefit Schemes and Social Security (Claims and Payments) (Miscellaneous Amendments) Regulations 1995 (SI 1995/2303), reg.10(4) (October 2, 1995).
3. The Social Security (Claims and Payments) (Jobseeker's Allowance Consequential Amendments) Regulations 1996 (SI 1996/1460), reg.2(16) (October 7, 1996).
4. The Tax Credits (Claims and Payments) (Amendment) Regulations 1999 (SI 1999/2572), reg.14 (October 5, 1999).
5. The Social Security and Child Support (Miscellaneous Amendments) Regulations 2003 (SI 2003/1050), reg.2 (May 5, 2003).
6. State Pension Credit (Consequential, Transitional and Miscellaneous Provisions) Regulations 2002 (SI 2002/3019), reg.11 (April 7, 2003).
7. The Social Security (Claims and Payments and Miscellaneous Amendments) Regulations 2003 (SI 2003/1632), reg.2 (July 21, 2003).
8. The Social Security (Notification of Change of Circumstances) Regulations 2003, SI 2003/3209, reg.2 (January 6, 2004).
9. The State Pension Credit (Transitional and Miscellaneous Provisions) Amendment Regulations 2003 (SI 2003/2274) (October 6, 2003).

DEFINITIONS

"appropriate office"—see reg.2(1).
"beneficiary"—see Social Security Act 1975, Sch.20.
"benefit"—see reg.2(2).
"jobseeker's allowance"—see reg.2(1).
"pension fund holder"—*ibid.*
"personal pension scheme"—*ibid.*
"retirement annuity contract"—*ibid.*

GENERAL NOTE

A Tribunal of Commissioners in *CIS/4348/2003* ruled that the duty to disclose under s.71 of the Administration Act flowed from the provisions of reg.32. Note that the duty applies to beneficiaries and "every person by whom or on whose behalf, sums by way of benefit are receivable". The latter group includes appointees under reg.33.

The Tribunal of Commissioners draws a clear distinction between the two duties set out in reg.32. There is a duty in regs 32(1) and (1A) to notify the Secretary of State or Board of Inland Revenue of any matter where the Secretary of State or the Board has given unambiguous directions for the disclosure of the matter. There is no question of deciding in such cases whether disclosure was reasonably to be expected to the claimant. Any failure to disclose such information will render any overpayment of benefit resulting from the failure to disclose recoverable.

By contrast the duty in reg.32(1B) is to notify changes of circumstances which e benefit recipient might reasonably be expected to know might affect the continuance of entitlement to benefit or the payment of benefit. The Tribunal of Commissioners concludes that it is only in these cases that it is necessary to consider whether disclosure by the claimant was in all the circumstances reasonably to be expected.

The distinction may be easier to make in theory than in practice, but, given the different consequences of failure to disclose under the two separate duties, it will be necessary to consider very carefully the source of any obligation to provide the Secretary of State or Her Majesty's Revenue and Customs with information and the specificity of that information. So, a requirement to disclose that children are no longer living with the claimant but had been taken into care (as was the case in *CIS/4348/2003*) which is clearly set out in documentation given to the claimant, will give rise to the duty to disclose under the first duty. Arguments about the claimant's

2.150

capacity are not relevant. By contrast, failure to disclose some unspecified set of circumstances which might affect benefit entitlement will fall under the second duty, and will require consideration of whether disclosure in all the circumstances of the case could reasonably be expected of the claimant.

In *CDLA/2328/2006* the Commissioner said,

" . . . There is nothing wrong in a tribunal relying on one paragraph rather than the other. The duties under paragraphs (1A) and (1B) are cumulative. The tribunal was entitled to rely on either duty. A finding that a claimant was in breach of paragraph (1B) is not rendered wrong in law just because the claimant was also in breach of paragraph (1A). What the tribunal must do is to rely on one or the other and make clear which." (para.20)

In interpreting the duty under paragraph (1A), the Commissioner stresses the distinction between information gathering and decision making. The claimant is required to report facts which might show that entitlement is affected. It is then for the decision maker to decide whether to investigate further, if necessary, and to make a decision on whether entitlement is in fact affected by the change in circumstances. The Commissioner says,

"23. The interpretation of the duties must reflect their nature and purpose. So the duty to report 'if things get easier for you' is not a duty to report 'if you believe that you are no longer virtually unable to walk'. Nor does this duty necessarily require a comparison between the claimant's abilities and disabilities at the time of the original award and those current at the time when the Secretary of State says a change should have been reported. That comparison does not arise until the later decision-making stage. The notes deal only with the earlier information-gathering stage. It is important not to confuse the issue whether the claimant failed to report a change of circumstances (an information-gathering question) and the issue whether that change was material to his entitlement (a decision-making question).

24. The duty does not set the focus of comparison on the time of the original award. If it did, it would become increasingly burdensome as time passes. In this case it would require the claimant to remember precisely how disabled he had been 18 years previously. The duty, like all the duties, is continuously speaking. It is to report if at any time things are easier for the claimant. That means easier by reference to the preceding period. Obviously that has to be applied in a reasonable time frame. It would not be necessary to report if a claimant were feeling a bit better today than yesterday. The test has to be applied over a period that is sufficient to show overall a sustained improvement or deterioration, taking account of any usual variation. This is not precise, but that is because it is a matter of judgment for each case."

On the interpretation of paragraph (1B) the Commissioner says,

"28. ... If the Secretary of State has issued an instruction to the claimant or to claimants generally, that will found a duty under paragraph (1A) and there should be no need to rely on paragraph (1B). There may be circumstances in which the Secretary of State could not rely on paragraph (1A) and could only rely on the instructions under paragraph (1B), but I have not been able to imagine one. But, assuming that this is possible, I accept that the notes issued by the Secretary of State are relevant under paragraph (1B). The instructions they contain may inform what is reasonable to expect a claimant to know. It would usually be reasonable for a claimant to know the contents of those instructions. (I do not exclude the possibility that it may not be reasonable for the claimant to know everything that is in the Secretary of State's notes. For example, this may, perhaps, not be reasonable on account of the claimant's mental state.) And the notes may be so comprehensive that, in a particular case, there is no need to consider anything else. But the duty under paragraph (1B) is defined by the terms of that paragraph. The instructions given to claimants do not define that duty. They are merely evidence of what it was reasonable to expect the claimant to know. And the duty to report may be wider than any instructions given by the Secretary of State. For example, it may be reasonable for the claimant to realise from questions in a claim pack that a particular matter is relevant to entitlement, even if the notes issued by the Secretary of State do not specifically refer to them.

29. For completeness, I will mention that the focus under paragraph (1B) is different from that under paragraph (1A). There the duty refers to entitlement, but only whether the claimant might reasonably be expected to know a change of circumstances *might* affect entitlement. It is not necessary for the claimant to understand the actual impact that a change will have, but the focus is different from that appropriate to the duty imposed under paragraph (1A). A comparison with his disablement at the time of the award may be justified. But it is also possible to envisage cases in which a claimant ought reasonably to realise that a change of circumstances might affect entitlement without undertaking a comparison with the time of the award. For example, a claimant's mobility may improve to such an extent that no reasonable person would consider that the claimant was virtually unable to walk."

Note that there is no general requirement that the form of disclosure must be in writing, though any disclosure will often be reduced to writing and signed by the claimant.

In *CSDLA/1282/2001* the Deputy Commissioner held that, where there was no appointment by the Secretary of State under reg.33, but there was a Power of Attorney, then benefit was not receivable by the person holding the Power of Attorney, and accordingly that person was under no duty to provide information under reg.32.

[¹ Information given electronically

32ZA.—(1) Where this regulation applies a person may given any certificate, notice, information or evidence required to be given and in particular may give notice or any change of circumstances required to be notified under regulation 32 by means of an electronic communication, in accordance with the provisions set out in Schedule 9ZC.

(2) This regulation applies in relation to carer's allowance.]

2.151

AMENDMENT

1. The Social Security (Electronic Communications) (Carer's Allowance) Order 2003 SI 2003/2800, reg.2 (December 1, 2003).

[¹ Information given electronically

32A.—(1) Where this regulation applies a person may give any certificate, notice, information or evidence required to be given and in particular may give notice of any change of circumstances required to be notified under regulation 32 by means of an electronic communication, in accordance with the provisions set out in Schedule 9C.

(2) This regulation applies in relation to child benefit.]

2.152

AMENDMENT

1. Social Security (Electronic Communications) (Child Benefit) Order 2002 (SI 2002/1789), art.4 (October 28, 2002).

The Social Security (Claims and Payments) Regulations 1987

Part IV

Third Parties

Persons unable to act

2.153

33.—(1) Where—
(a) a person is, or is alleged to be, entitled to benefit, whether or not a claim for benefit has been made by him or on his behalf; and
(b) that person is unable for the time being to act; and either
(c) no receiver has been appointed by the Court of Protection with power to claim, or as the case may be, receive benefit on his behalf; or
(d) in Scotland, his estate is not being administered by [4 a judicial factor or any guardian acting or appointed under the Adults with Incapacity (Scotland) Act 2004 who has power to claim or, as the case may be, receive benefit on his behalf],
the Secretary of State [2 or the Board] may, upon written application made to him by a person who, if a natural person, is over the age of 18, appoint that person to exercise, on behalf of the person who is unable to act, any right to which that person may be entitled and to receive and deal on his behalf with any sums payable to him.

[4 (1A) Where a person has been appointed under [5 regulation 82(3) of the Housing benefit Regulations 2006, regulation 63(3) of the Housing benefit (Persons who have attained the qualifying age for state pension credit) Regulations 2006, regulation 68(3) of the Council Tax Benefit Regulations 2006, or regulation 52(3) of the Council Tax benefit (Persons who have attained the qualifying age for state pension credit) Regulations 2006] by a relevant authority within the meaning of those Regulations to act on behalf of another in relation to a benefit claim or award, the Secretary of State may, if the person agrees, treat him as if he had appointed him under paragraph (1).]

(2) Where the Secretary of State has made [2 or the Board have made] an appointment [4, or treated an appointment as made,] under paragraph (1)—
(a) he [2 or they] may at any time revoke it;
(b) the person appointed may resign his office after having given one month's notice in writing to the Secretary of State [2 or the Board] of his intention to do so;
(c) any such appointment shall terminate when the Secretary of State is notified [2 or the Board are notified] that a receiver or other person to whom paragraph (1)(c) or (d) applies has been appointed.

(3) Anything required by these regulations to be done by or to any person who is for the time being unable to act may be done by or to the receiver, [4 judicial factor or] guardian, if any, or by or to the person appointed under this regulation or regulation 43 [1(disability living allowance for a child)] and [3 . . .] [3 a direct credit transfer under regulation 21 into the account of any person so appointed, or the receipt by him of a payment made by some other means] shall be a good discharge to the Secretary of State [2 or the Board] for any sum paid.

Amendments

1. The Social Security (Claims and Payments) Amendment Regulations 1991 (SI 1991/2741), reg.16 (February 3, 1992).

(SI 1987/1968, reg.33) (as amended)

2. The Tax Credits (Claims and Payments) (Amendment) Regulations 1999 (SI 1999/2572), regs 15, 20, 22 and 23 (October 5, 1999).
3. Social Security (Claims and Payments and Miscellaneous Amendments) (No.2) Regulations 2002 (SI 2002/2441), reg.8 (October 23, 2002).
4. The Social Security, Child Support and Tax Credits (Miscellaneous Amendments) Regulations 2005 (SI 2005/337), reg.7 (March 18, 2005).
5. The Housing Benefit and Council Tax Benefit (Consequential Provisions) Regulations 2006 (SI 2006/217), Sch.2, para.2 (March 6, 2006).

DEFINITIONS

"benefit"—see reg.2(2).
"claim for benefit"—see reg.2(1).

GENERAL NOTE

2.154

Even if no appointment has been made, a claim made by a person unable to act, or by an "unauthorised person" on their behalf, is still valid (*CIS/812/1992*, applying para.8 of *R(SB) 9/84* where a Tribunal of Commissioners holds that in the absence of any challenge at the time the Secretary of State must be deemed to have accepted that the claim was made in sufficient manner). In *Walsh v CAO* (Consent Order, January 19, 1995) the Court of Appeal also applied *R(SB)9/84* when setting aside *CIS/638/1991* in which the Commissioner had held that a claim made on behalf of a person unable to act by a person who had not been formally appointed was a nullity.

Note that any subsequent appointment has retrospective effect (*R(SB)5/90*).

In *CIS/642/1994* the claimant's husband was her appointee under reg.33. She died before the tribunal hearing. The Commissioner holds that the tribunal decision was a nullity because there had been no appointment under reg.30 (deceased persons). Appointments under reg.30 were a distinct and different form of appointment from reg.33 appointments. He dissents from para.8 of *R(SB) 9/84* and repeats his view (see *CIS/638/1991*) that it is open to adjudication officers and tribunals (and Commissioners) to determine that a claim is a nullity in cases where a person is unable to act and there has been no valid appointment. This is out of step with the current weight of authority.

CIS/812/1992 also confirms that, in relation to the pre-April 1997 form of the rules for backdating claims, if there has been no appointment it is only necessary to decide whether the claimant has good cause for a late claim; it is not necessary to consider the reasonableness of the failure to claim of a person who has been acting informally on his behalf. The Commissioner declines to follow paras 12 and 13 of *R(IS)5/91* since this could not be reconciled with paras 9 and 10 of *R(SB)9/84* (which was a Tribunal of Commissioners' decision). See also *CSB/168/1993* which takes a similar view and contains a useful summary of the authorities on this issue.

Under the current form of reg.19(5) the test is also of the claimant's personal circumstances, if there is no appointee, but those circumstances sometimes expressly include whether there is anyone who could help the claimant.

The Secretary of State's normal practice in making appointments is not to make an appointment generally but to limit it to a specific benefit: see *R(IS)5/91*. *R(IS)5/91* concerned the effect of an appointment for supplementary benefit purposes on a subsequent income support claim following the 1988 changes. There is some doubt whether such a limited appointment has survived the changes brought about then. There is now a single regulation governing appointments, and some argue that, at a consequence appointments are for all benefits. Tribunals do, however, continue to see appointments limited to certain benefits. The message is that the scope of the appointment needs to be considered in every case where it is relevant, though in the absence of any limiting conditions, there is a strong case for considering that it applies to all benefits.

Where a claimant has died, the Secretary of State may appoint a person to act: *R(SB)8/88*. Unless the Secretary of State does so, the tribunal has no jurisdiction to proceed in the absence of action by a personal representative under a grant of probate or letters of administration.

In *CSDLA/1282/2001,* the Deputy Commissioner concludes, following *CA/1014/1999*, that a person holding a Power of Attorney is not a person made an appointee under reg.33: see para.18.

In *R(SB)5/90*, Commissioner Goodman clarifies the decision in *R(SB)8/88* in holding that the appointment of a person to act by the Secretary of State operates retrospectively. Thus, so far as tribunals are concerned, an appointment after the date of the appeal but before the date of the hearing will be sufficient to ground jurisdiction. The power of appointment is to be found in reg.30(1).

Note that the power of appointment under this regulation is a separate power of appointment from that under reg.30 which arises on the death of the claimant, or where a claim is made after death, a potential claimant.

On the liability of appointees in respect of overpayments of benefit, see the discussion in the notes to s.71 of the Administration Act.

The practice of the Secretary of State in making appointments under reg.33 appears to vary. Since April 1988 there has been a single regulation governing appointments and the regulation is drafted in sufficiently wide terms to encompass a single appointment to cover all social security benefits; it covers "any sums payable to him". Previously there were separate sets of regulations covering means-tested and non-means-tested benefits, and it was the interaction of the sets of regulations which was primarily in issue in *R(IS)5/91*. The experience of tribunals appears to be that in some cases the appointment is for all benefits, and in other cases it is limited to particular benefits. Indeed, in some cases it is not clear what the scope of the appointment is, as when a claimant asks for an appointment in relation to a particular benefit and the appointment is made in general terms. The nature of the appointment seldom seems to be an issue upon which the appeal turns.

See also annotation to reg.30.

Payment to another person on the beneficiary's behalf

2.155

34.—[³ (1) Except in a case to which paragraph (2) applies,] the Secretary of State [² or the Board] may direct that benefit may be paid, wholly or in part, to [¹ another natural person] on the beneficiary's behalf if such a direction as to payment appears to the Secretary of State [² or the Board] to be necessary for protecting the interests of the beneficiary, or any child or dependant in respect of whom benefit is payable.

[³ (2) The Secretary of State may direct that a joint-claim jobseeker's allowance shall be paid wholly or in part to a natural person who is not a member of the joint-claim couple who is the nominated member for the purposes of section 3B of the Jobseekers Act if such a direction as to payment appears to the Secretary of State to be necessary for protecting the interests of the other member of that couple or, as the case may be, both members of that couple.]

AMENDMENTS

1. The Social Security (Miscellaneous Provisions) Amendment (No.2) Regulations 1992 (SI 1992/2595), reg.5 (January 4, 1993).

2. The Tax Credits (Claims and Payments) (Amendment) Regulations 1999 (SI 1999/2572), reg.20 (October 5, 1999).

3. The Social Security (Joint Claims: Consequential Amendments) Regulations 2000 (SI 2000/1982), reg.2(8) (March 19, 2001).

(SI 1987/1968, reg.34) (as amended)

DEFINITIONS

"beneficiary"—see Social Security Act 1975, Sch.20.
"benefit"—see reg.2(2).
"child"—see 1986 Act, s.20(11).

[¹ Deductions of mortgage interest which shall be made from benefit and paid to qualifying lenders

34A.—(1) [² In relation to cases to which section 15A(1) or (1A) of the Social Security Administration Act 1992] (payment out of benefit of sums in respect of mortgage interest etc.) applies and in the circumstances specified in Schedule 9A, such part of any relevant benefits to which a relevant beneficiary is entitled as may be specified in that Schedule shall be paid by the Secretary of State directly to the qualifying lender and shall be applied by that lender towards the discharge of the liability in respect of that mortgage interest.

[³ (1A) Paragraph (1) shall only apply in relation to a relevant beneficiary who is entitled to state pension credit where he is entitled to a guarantee credit.]

(2) The provisions of Schedule 9A shall have effect in relation to mortgage interest payments.]

2.156

AMENDMENTS

1. The Social Security (Claims and Payments) Amendment Regulations 1992 (SI 1992/1026), reg.3 (May 25, 1992).
2. State Pension Credit (Consequential, Transitional and Miscellaneous Provisions) Regulations 2002 (SI 2002/3019), reg.12 (April 7, 2003).
3. The State Pension Credit (Consequential, Transitional and Miscellaneous Provisions) (No. 2) Regulations 2002 (SI 2002/3197) (April 7, 2003).

DEFINITIONS

"qualifying lender"—see Administration Act, s.15A(3).
"relevant beneficiary"—see Administration Act, s.15A(1).
"relevant benefits"—see Administration Act, s.15A(4).

[¹ Deductions of mortgage interest which may be made from benefits and paid to qualifying lenders in other cases

34B.—(1) In relation to cases to which section 151A(1A) of the Social Security Administration Act 1992 applied (others than those referred to in regulation 34A(1A))—
   (a) in the circumstances specified in paragraph 2A(1) of Schedule 9A; and
   (b) in either of the further circumstances specified in paragrpag 2A(2) of that Schedule,
such part of any relevant benefits to which a relevant beneficiary is entitled as may be paid by the Secretary of State directly to the qualifying lender and shall be applied by that lender towards the discharge of the liabilityn in respect of that interest.

(2) The provisions of Schedule 9A shall have effect in relation to mortgage interest payments made under this regulation.]

2.157

The Social Security (Claims and Payments) Regulations 1987

AMENDMENT

1. The State Pension Credit (Consequential, Transitional and Miscellaneous Provisions) (No. 2) Regulations 2002 (SI 2002/3197) (April 7, 2003).

[¹ [³Deductions which may be made from benefit and paid to third parties

2.158　　**35.**—(1) Except as provided for in regulation 34A and Schedule 9A, deductions] may be made from benefit and direct payments may be made to third parties on behalf of a beneficiary in accordance with the provisions of Schedule 9 [⁴ and Schedule 9B].

(2) Where a social fund payment for maternity or funeral expenses [²or expenses for heating which appear to the Secretary of State to have been or to be likely to be incurred in cold weather] is made, wholly or in part, in respect of a debt which is, or will be, due to a third person, [⁵ . . .] [⁵ payment may be, and in the case of funeral expenses shall be, made to that person and where an instrument of payment is made to that person it may be sent to the beneficiary].

AMENDMENTS

1. The Social Security (Claims and Payments) Amendment Regulations 1988 (SI 1988/522), reg.7 (April 11, 1988).
2. The Social Security (Common Provisions) Miscellaneous Amendments Regulations 1988 (SI 1988/1725), reg.3 (November 7, 1988).
3. The Social Security (Claims and Payments) Amendment Regulations 1992 (SI 1992/1026), reg.4 (May 25, 1992).
4. The Social Security (Claims and Payments) Amendment Regulations 2001 (SI 2001/18), reg.2 (January 31, 2001).
5. Social Security (Claims and Payments and Miscellaneous Amendments) (No.2) Regulations 2002 (SI 2002/2441), reg.9 (April 8, 2003).

DEFINITIONS

"beneficiary"—see Social Security Act 1975, Sch.20.
"benefit"—see reg.2(2).

GENERAL NOTE

Child support payments

2.159　　Regulation 35 and Sch.9 make provision for various deductions from benefit to be paid to third parties. These include payments in lieu of child support payments, which are at the bottom of the list of priorities. A new Sch.9B was introduced dealing specifically with child support maintenance and payments to persons with care. But the relationship between Sch.9B deductions and those arising under Sch.9 is not spelled out, so that it is unclear whether flat rate child support liabilities take precedence over other deductions from benefit under Sch.9.

The policy response appears to be that child support deductions from a range of benefits will set apart from the rest of the direct payments scheme rather than take precedence over them. So child support deductions will, as a matter of policy rather than law, be taken without regard to other Sch.9 deductions. Administrative arrangements will ensure that where only one of a child support deduction and another deduction can be taken, priority will be given to the child support deduction. The provisions of Sch.9B kick in in April 2002, although Sch.9B was inserted in January 2001. It is said to be the intention that existing child support cases will continue to be dealt with under the provisions of Sch.9 with conversion to the new scheme at some later common date.

(SI 1987/1968, reg.35) (as amended)

This is all a most unsatisfactory way of sorting out deficiencies in the clarity of the legislative scheme.

Regulation 35A revoked by The Social Security (Care Homes and Independent Hospitals) Regulations 2005 (SI 2005/2687) (October 24, 2005).

Payment to a partner as alternative payee

36.—[³(1)] [¹ Except where a wife has elected in accordance with regulation 6A of the Social Security (Guardian's Allowances) Regulation 1975 (prescribed manner of making an election under section 77(9) of the Social Security Contributions and Benefits Act 1992) that guardian's allowance is not to be paid to her husband,] where one of a married or unmarried couple residing together is entitled to child benefit [² working families' tax credit, disabled person's tax credit][¹ or guardian's allowance] the Secretary of State [² or the Board] may make arrangements whereby that benefit as well as being payable to the person entitled to it, may, in the alternative, be paid to that person's partner on behalf of the person entitled.

[³ (2) Where a person is entitled to a winter fuel payment within the meaning of the Social Fund Winter Fuel Payment Regulations 2000 and—
  (a) that person is one [⁴ member of a] couple of a member of a polygamous marriage;
  (b) the other member of that couple or another member of that marriage ("the other person") is in receipt of income support or an income-based jobseeker's allowance; and
  (c) both members of the couple or marriage are living together within the meaning of regulation 1(3)(b) of those Regulations,
the Secretary of State may pay the winter fuel payment to the other person on behalf of the person entitled notwithstanding that the other person has not yet attained the ago of 60 in the qualifying week.]

AMENDMENTS

1. The Social Security (Claims and Payments) Amendment Regulations 1999 (SI 1999/2358), reg.2(6) (September 20, 1999).
2. The Tax Credits (Claims and Payments) (Amendment) Regulations 1999(SI 1999/2752), regs 20, 24 and 25 (October 5, 1999).
3. The Social Security (Claims and Payments and Miscellaneous Amendments) (No.3) Regulations 2002 (SI 2002/2660), reg.2 (November 2, 2002).
4. The Civil Partnership (Pensions, Social Security and Child Support) (Consequential etc. Provisions) Order 2005 (SI 2005/2877) (December 5, 2005).

Regulation 36A revoked by The Social Security (Claims and Payments) Amendment Regulations 1991 (SI1991/2741), reg.18 (April 6, 1992).

PART V

[¹ . . .] EXTINGUISHMENT

AMENDMENT

1. Words in heading omitted by The Social Security Act 1998 (Commencement No.8, and Savings and Consequential and Transitional Provisions) Order 1999 (SI 1999/1958), Sch.9 (July 5, 1999).

The Social Security (Claims and Payments) Regulations 1987

2.163 Regulations 37–37B revoked by *The Social Security Act 1998 (Commencement No. 8, and Savings and Consequential and Transitional Provisions) Order 1999 (SI1999/1958), Sch.9 (July 5, 1999).*

Extinguishment of right to payment of sums by way of benefit where payment is not obtained within the prescribed period

2.164 **38.**—(1) [¹Subject to paragraph (2A), the right to payment of any sum by way of benefit shall be extinguished] where payment of that sum is not obtained within the period of 12 months from the date on which the right is to be treated as having arisen; and for the purposes of this regulation the right shall be treated as having arisen—
  (a) in relation to any such sum contained in an instrument of payment which has been given or sent to the person to whom it is payable, or to a place approved by the Secretary of State [⁴ or the Board] for collection by him (whether or not received or collected as the case may be)—
    (i) on the date of the said instrument of payment, or
    (ii) if a further instrument of payment has been so given or sent as a replacement, on the date of the last such instrument of payment;
[³(aa) [⁸ . . .];]
  (b) in relation to any such sum to which sub-paragraph (a) does not apply, where notice is given (whether orally or in writing) or is sent that the sum contained in the notice is ready for collection on the date of the notice or, if more than one such notice is given or sent, the date of the first such notice;
[⁷ (bb) in relation to any such sum which the person entitled to it and the Secretary of State have arranged to be paid by means of direct credit transfer into a bank or other account, on the due date for payment of the sum;]
  (c) in relation to any such sum to which [³none of (a), [⁸ . . .] or [⁷ (b) or (bb) apply], on such date as the Secretary of State determines [⁴ or the Board determine].

(2) The giving or sending of an instrument of payment under paragraph (1)(a), or of a notice under paragraph (1)(b), shall be effective for the purposes of that paragraph, even where the sum contained in that instrument, or notice, is more or less than the sum which the person concerned has the right to receive.

[¹(2A) Where a question arises whether the right to payment of any sum by way of benefit has been extinguished by the operation of this regulation and the [⁵ Secretary of State] is satisfied that—
  (a) [⁵ he] first received [⁴ or the Board first received] written notice requesting payment of that sum after the expiration of 12 months; and
  (b) from a day within that period of 12 months and continuing until the day the written notice was given, there was good cause for not giving the notice; and
[²(c) [⁵. . .] either—
    (i) [⁵. . .] no instrument of payment has been given or sent to the person to whom it is payable and [⁵. . .] no payment has been made under the provisions of regulation 21 ([⁶ direct] credit transfer); or
    (ii) that such instrument has been produced to [⁵ the Secretary of State] and [⁵. . .] no further instrument has been issued as a replacement,]

(SI 1987/1968, reg.38) (as amended)

the period of 12 months shall be extended to the date on which the [⁵ Secretary of State] decides that question, and this regulation shall accordingly apply as though the right to payment had arisen on that date.]

(3) For the purposes of paragraph (1) the date of an instrument of payment is the date of issue of that instrument or, if the instrument specifies a date which is the earliest date on which payment can be obtained on the instrument and which is later than the date of issue, that date.(4) This regulation shall apply to a person authorised or appointed to act on behalf of a beneficiary as it applies to a beneficiary.(5) This regulation shall not apply to the right to a single payment of any industrial injuries gratuity or in satisfaction of a person's right to graduated retirement benefit.

AMENDMENTS

1. The Social Security (Medical Evidence, Claims and Payments) Amendment Regulations 1989 (SI 1989/1686), reg.7 (October 9, 1989).
2. Social Security (Claims and Payments) Amendment (No.3) Regulations 1993 (SI 1993/2113), reg.3(8) (September 27, 1993).
3. Social Security (Claims and Payments Etc.) Amendment Regulations 1996 (SI 1996/672), reg.2(5) (April 4, 1996).
4. The Tax Credits (Claims and Payments) (Amendment) Regulations 1999(SI 1999/2572), reg.20 (October 5, 1999).
5. The Social Security Act 1998 (Commencement No.9, and Savings and Consequential and Transitional Provisions) Order 1999 (SI 1999/2422), Sch.7 (September 6, 1999).
6. Social Security (Claims and Payments and Miscellaneous Amendments) (No.2) Regulations 2002 (SI 2002/2441), reg.10 (April 8, 2003).
7. The Social Security, Child Support and Tax Credits (Miscellaneous Amendments) Regulations 2005 (SI 2005/337), reg.7 (March 18, 2005).
8. The Social Security (Miscellaneous Amendments) (No.2) Regulations 2006 (SI 2006/832), reg.2 (April 10, 2006).

DEFINITIONS

"beneficiary"—see Social Security Act 1975, Sch.20.
"benefit"—see reg.2(2).
"instrument for benefit payment"—see reg.2(1).

GENERAL NOTE

In *CDLA/2807/2003* the Commissioner said,

"It seems to me quite impossible to say in circumstances where the operative decision is that no benefit is payable that any right to payment, let alone a right to payment of any amount that has been quantified, is in existence. There could be no right to payment until that decision has been altered in some way. Regulation 38 simply cannot have any operation in such circumstances."

In *CU/2604/1999*, the Commissioner said, 2.165

"The subject of regulation 38 is the 'right to payment of any sum'. The regulation sets out various rules for ascertaining the date on which that right is to be treated as having arisen. This includes the rule in regulation 38(1)(c). However, there must *first* be a right to payment of a *sum*. The word 'sum' means something otherwise it could have been omitted and left the provision meaning something slightly different. . . . In my view, if the amount has not been quantified, there is no 'sum', even if there has been identified a basis for quantifying it. Contrary to what has been argued on behalf of the Secretary of State, the fact that the tribunal later quantified the amount does not affect the fact it had not bee quantified at the time when the adjudication officer sought to extinguish the right to payment. If there is no sum, then the right to payment of it cannot arise, and cannot be extinguished under regulation 38." (para.17.)

In *CDLA/2609/2002*, the Commissioner offers a helpful overview of reg.38:

"15. I start with the overall scheme of regulation 38 of the Claims and Payments Regulations. It is concerned not with payment of benefit in a general sense, but with the extinguishment of a 'right to payment of any sum by way of benefit' (regulation 38(1)). The basic condition for such extinguishment is that 'payment of that sum is not obtained within the period of 12 months from the date on which the right is to be treated as having arisen'. Mr Commissioner Levenson has in decision *CU/2604/1999* (in the papers under that reference, but now reported as *R(U)1/02*) stressed that some meaning must be given to the word 'sum'. So he held there that where a Commissioner had decided that unemployment benefit was payable to a claimant for a specified period, without quantifying the amount of benefit, there was no sum identified to which a right of payment attached which could be extinguished. Likewise, it seems to me that some weight must be attached to the use of the term 'any sum by way of benefit' and to the test being in terms of 'obtaining' payment of such a sum. The use of language does not point towards a situation where benefit of a sufficiently ascertainable amount has been merely been awarded by a decision on entitlement and payability, so that the Secretary of State is under an obligation to pay the benefit as soon as reasonably practicable (Claims and Payments Regulations, regulation 20). It points towards a situation where a particular sum has been allocated to the claimant and some steps along the administrative process of making payment have been taken, leaving the claimant with some relatively mechanical steps to take to 'obtain' payment.

16. That view is also consistent with the provisions of subparagraphs (a) to (b) of regulation 38(1), which define the dates on which the right to payment of a sum by way of benefit is to be treated as having arisen in certain circumstances. The rules are that: where the claimant has been given or sent an instrument of payment or an instrument has been made available for collection, the right arises on the date of the instrument or any replacement instrument (subparagraph (a)); where a sum is payable by means of an instrument for benefit payment (see regulation 20A), the right arises on the first date on which payment could be obtained by that means (subparagraph (aa)); and, where subparagraph (a) does not apply and notice is given or sent that the sum is available for collection, the right arises on the date that the notice is sent (subparagraph (b)). It makes perfect sense to say in all those situations that a right to payment of the particular sum by way of benefit had arisen and that, if the claimant does not take the other necessary steps to get paid (even in a situation, for instance, where a letter gets lost in the post), payment has not been obtained. The final provision in regulation 38(1), the crucial provision in this case, is subparagraph (c), under which the right to payment is to be treated as having arisen:

'(c) in relation to any such sum to which none of (a), (aa) or (b) apply, on such date as the Secretary of State determines or the [Board of Inland Revenue] determine.'

17. It is plainly arguable that subparagraph (c) does not give the Secretary of State an unfettered discretion to choose any date whatsoever, but must be interpreted in accordance with the overall scheme and scope of regulation 38(1) and by reference to the circumstances of subparagraphs (a) to (b). It is true that regulation 38(2A) on good cause is drafted on the assumption that regulation 38(1) can apply in a case where no instrument of payment was given or sent to the claimant, but I do not think that that undermines what I have said above. Miss Topping submitted that, although subparagraph (c) might exclude irrational or completely unreasonable choices, it certainly allowed the Secretary of State to determine that a right to payment of a sum by way of benefit arose on the date on which a weekly payment

(SI 1987/1968, reg.38) (as amended)

of benefit would have been made in the ordinary course of things, even though no administrative steps at all had actually been taken towards making payment."

It is a common feature of social security benefit that the right to payment of benefit does not survive a delay of more than twelve months in obtaining payment of it. The determination of the date on which the right to payment is treated as arising may be crucial and is a matter for the Secretary of State (or Board of the Inland Revenue as appropriate).

Only where reg.38(2A) applies does any issue for the adjudicating authorities arise. Then it is only whether the right to payment has been extinguished, but it will still be for the Secretary of State to determine "whether there should be a replacement instrument." (para.7.)

Cases in which the claimant says that no giro was received are governed by *R(IS) 7/91* under which questions of payment were held not to be questions relating to the award of benefit.

Unravelling those matters which are for the adjudicating authorities and those matters which do not attract a right of appeal will become more complicated under the new system under which there adjudication officers have been abolished and all decisions are taken by the Secretary of State with some attracting a right of appeal and others not.

Note that *R(P)3/93* was concerned with the version of this regulation in force until September 27, 1993, and has no application to the present version of the regulation.

Good cause
The test of good cause is the test which formerly existed under the replaced reg.19 of the Claims and Payments Regulations. Reference to the 1996 edition of *Non Means Tested Benefits: The Legislation* contains a detailed account of the case law, but the classic definition of good cause is that found in *R(S)2/63:*

2.166

"In Decision *CS371/49* the Commissioner said " 'Good cause' " means, in my opinion, some fact which, having regard to all the circumstances (including the claimant's state of health and the information which he had received and that which he might have obtained) would probably have caused a reasonable person of his age and experience to act (or fail to act) as the claimant did.' This description of good cause has been quoted in countless cases. It has stood the test of time. In our judgment it is correct. The word 'fact' of course includes a combination of events happening either simultaneously or in succession."

PART VI

[¹Mobility Component of Disability Living Allowance and Disability Living Allowance for Children]

Amendment

1. The Social Security (Claims and Payments) Amendment Regulations 1991 (SI 1991/2741), reg.19(a) (February 3, 1992).

Regulations 39–41 revoked by The Social Security (Claims and Payments) Amendment Regulations 1991 (SI 1991/2741), reg.19(b) (February 3, 1992).

2.167

Cases where allowance not to be payable

42.—(1) Subject to the provisions of this regulation, [¹disability living allowance by virtue of entitlement to the mobility component] shall not be

2.168

The Social Security (Claims and Payments) Regulations 1987

payable to any person who would otherwise be entitled to it in respect of any period—
  (a) during which that person has the use of an invalid carriage or other vehicle provided by the Secretary of State under section 5(2) of and Schedule 2 to the National Health Service Act 1977 or section 46 of the National Health Service (Scotland) Act 1978 which is a vehicle propelled by petrol engine or by electric power supplied for use on the road and to be controlled by the occupant; or
  (b) in respect of which that person has received, or is receiving, any payment—
    (i) by way of grant under the said section 5(2) and Schedule 2 or section 46 towards the costs of running a private car, or
    (ii) of mobility supplement under the Naval, Military and Air Forces etc., (Disablement and Death) Service Pensions Order 1983 or the Personal Injuries (Civilians) Scheme 1983 or under the said Order by virtue of the War Pensions (Naval Auxiliary Personnel) Scheme 1964, the Pensions (Polish Forces) Scheme 1964, the War Pensions (Mercantile Marine) Scheme 1964 or an Order of Her Majesty in relation to the Home Guard dated 21st December, 1964 or 22nd December, 1964 or in relation to the Ulster Defence Regiment dated 4th January, 1971,
or any payment out of public funds which the Secretary of State is satisfied is analogous thereto.

(2) A person who has notified the Secretary of State that he no longer wishes to use such an invalid carriage or other vehicle as if referred to in paragraph (1)(a) and has signed an undertaking that he will not use it while it remains in his possession awaiting collection, shall be treated, for the purposes of this regulation, as not having the use of that invalid carriage or other vehicle.

(3) Where a person in respect of whom [[1]disability living allowance] is claimed for any period has received any such payment as referred to in paragraph (1)(b) for a period which, in whole or in part, covers the period for which the allowance is claimed, such payment shall be treated as an aggregate of equal weekly amounts in respect of each week in the period for which it is made and, where in respect of any such week a person is treated as having a weekly amount so calculated which is less than the weekly rate of [[1] mobility component of disability living allowance to which, apart from paragraph (1), he would be entitled], any allowance to which that person may be entitled for that week shall be payable at a weekly rate reduced by the weekly amount so calculated.

(4) In a case where the Secretary of State has issued a certificate to the effect that he is satisfied—
  (a) that the person in question either—
    (i) has purchased or taken on hire or hire-purchase; or
    (ii) intends to purchase or take on hire or hire-purchase a private car or similar vehicle ("the car") for a consideration which is more than nominal, on or about a date (not being earlier than 13th January, 1982) specified in the certificate ("the said date");
  (b) that that person intends to retain possession of the car at least during, and to learn to drive it within, the period of 6 months or greater or lesser length of time as may be specified in the certificate ("the said period") beginning on the said date; and

(SI 1987/1968, reg.42) (as amended)

(c) that the person will use [¹ disability living allowance by virtue of entitlement to the mobility component] in whole or in part during the said period towards meeting the expense of acquiring the car, paragraph (1)(a) shall not apply, and shall be treated as having never applied, during a period beginning on the said date and ending at the end of the said period or (if earlier) the date on which the Secretary of State cancels the certificate because that person has parted with possession of the car or for any other reason.

AMENDMENT

1. The Social Security (Claims and Payments) Amendment Regulations 1991 (SI 1991/2741), reg.20 (February 3, 1992).

Children

43.—(1) In any case where a claim for [¹disability living allowance] for a child is received by the Secretary of State, he shall, in accordance with the following provisions of this regulation, appoint a person to exercise, on behalf of the child, any right to which he may be entitled under the [Social Security Contributions and Benefits Act 1992] in connection with [¹disability living allowance] and to receive and deal on his behalf with any sums payable by way of [¹that allowance].

(2) Subject to the following provisions of this regulation, a person appointed by the Secretary of State under this regulation to act on behalf of the child shall—

(a) be a person with whom the child is living; and
(b) be over the age of 18 [² or, if the person is a parent of the child and living with him, be over the age of 16]; and
(c) be either the father or mother of the child, or, if the child is not living with either parent, be such other person as the Secretary of State may determine; and
(d) have given such undertaking as may be required by the Secretary of State as to the use, for the child's benefit, of any allowance paid.

(3) For the purpose of paragraph (2)(a), a person with whom a child has been living shall, subject to paragraph (4) and to the power of the Secretary of State to determine in any case that the provisions of this paragraph should not apply, be treated as continuing to live with that child during any period—

(a) during which that person and the child are separated but such separation has not lasted for a continuous period exceeding [¹12 weeks]; or
(b) during which the child is absent by reason only of the fact that he is receiving full-time education at a school; or
(c) during which the child is absent and undergoing medical or other treatment as an in-patient in a hospital or similar institution; or
(d) during such other period as the Secretary of State may in any particular case determine:

Provided that where the absence of the child under (b) has lasted for a continuous period of 26 weeks or the child is absent under (c), that person shall only be treated as continuing to live with that child if he satisfies the Secretary of State that he has incurred, or has undertaken to incur, expenditure for the benefit of the child of an amount not less than the allowance payable in respect of such period of absence.

2.169

(4) Where a child in respect of whom an allowance is payable, is, by virtue of any provision of an Act of Parliament—
  (a) committed to, or received into the care of, a local authority; or
  (b) subject to a supervision requirement and residing in a residential establishment under arrangements made by a local authority in Scotland;
any appointment made under the foregoing provisions of this regulation shall terminate forthwith:

Provided that, when a child is committed to, or received into, care or is made subject to a supervision requirement for a period which is, and when it began was, not intended to last for more than [[1]12 weeks] the appointment shall not terminate by virtue of this paragraph until such period has lasted for 8 weeks.

(5) In any case where an appointment on behalf of any child in the care of, or subject to a supervision requirement under arrangements made by, a local authority is terminated in accordance with paragraph (4), the Secretary of State may, upon application made to him by that local authority or by an officer of such authority nominated for the purpose by that authority, appoint the local authority or nominated officer thereof or appoint such other person as he may, after consultation with the local authority, determine, to exercise on behalf of the child any right to which that child may be entitled under the Act in connection with the allowance and to receive and deal on his behalf with any sums payable to him by way of [[1]disability living allowance] for any period during which he is in the care of, or, as the case may be, subject to a supervision requirement under arrangements made by, that authority.

(6) Where a child is undergoing medical or other treatment as an inpatient in a hospital or similar institution and there is no other person to whom [[1]disability living allowance] may be payable by virtue of an appointment under this regulation, the Secretary of State may, upon application made to him by the district health authority [[1] National Health Service Trust] [[3] NHS Foundation Trust] or, as the case may be, social services authority, controlling the hospital or similar institution in which the child is an in-patient, or by an officer of that authority [[1] or Trust] nominated for the purpose by the authority, appoint that authority [[1] or Trust] or the nominated officer thereof or such other person as the Secretary of State may, after consultation with that authority [[1] or Trust], determine, to exercise on behalf of the child any right to which that child may be entitled in connection with the allowance and to receive and deal on his behalf with any sums payable to him by way of [[1] disability living allowance] for any period during which he is an in-patient in a hospital or similar institution under the control of that authority [[1] or Trust].

(7) For the purpose of this regulation—
"district health authority" means, in relation to England and Wales a District Health Authority within the meaning of the National Health Service Act 1977 and, in relation to Scotland, a Health Board within the meaning of the National Health Services (Scotland) Act 1978;
[[2] "child" means a person under the age of 16;]
"child's father" and "child's mother" include a person who is a child's father or mother by adoption or would be such a relative if an illegitimate child had been borne legitimate;

(SI 1987/1968, reg.43) (as amended)

"hospital or similar institution" means any premises for the reception of and treatment of person suffering from any illness, including any mental disorder, or of persons suffering from physical disability and any premises used for providing treatment during convalescence or for medical rehabilitation;

"local authority" means, in relation to England and Wales, a local authority as defined in the Local Government Act 1972 and, in relation to Scotland, a local authority as defined in the Local Government (Scotland) Act 1973;

"social services authority" means—
  (a) in relation to England and Wales, the social services committee established by a local authority under section 2 of the Local Authority Social Services Act 1970; and
  (b) in relation to Scotland, the social work committee established by a local authority under section 2 of the Social Work (Scotland) Act 1968.

AMENDMENTS

1. The Social Security (Claims and Payments) Amendment Regulations 1991 (SI 1991/2741), reg.21 (February 3, 1992).
2. The Social Security, Child Support and Tax Credits (Miscellaneous Amendments) Regulations 2005 (SI 2005/337), reg.7 (March 18, 2005).
3. The Health and Social Care (Community Health and Standards) Act 2003 (Suplementary and Consequential Provisions) (NHS Foundation Trusts) Order 2004 (SI 2004/696), Art.3 and Sch.3 (March 11, 2004).

Payment of [¹ disability living allowance] on behalf of a beneficiary

44.—(1) Where, under arrangements made or negotiated by Motability, an agreement has been entered into by or on behalf of a beneficiary in respect of whom [¹ disability living allowance is payable by virtue of entitlement to the mobility component at the higher rate] for the hire or hire-purchase of a vehicle, the Secretary of State may arrange that any [¹ disability living allowance by virtue of entitlement to the mobility component at the higher rate payable] to the beneficiary shall be paid in whole or in part on behalf of the beneficiary in settlement of liability for payments due under that agreement.

2.170

(2) Subject to regulations 45 and 46 an arrangement made by the Secretary of State under paragraph (1) shall terminate at the end of whichever is the relevant period specified in paragraph (3), in the case of hire, or paragraph (4), in the case of a hire-purchase agreement.

(3) In the case of hire the relevant period shall be—
  (a) where the vehicle is returned to the owner at or before the expiration of the [³ . . .] term of hire, the period of the [³ . . .] term; or
  (b) where the vehicle is retained by or on behalf of the beneficiary with the owner's consent after the expiration of the original term of hire [³, other than where sub-paragraph (d) applies,], the period of the original term; or
  (c) where the vehicle is retained by or on behalf of the beneficiary otherwise than with the owner's consent after the expiration of the original term of hire or its earlier termination, whichever is the longer of the following periods—

The Social Security (Claims and Payments) Regulations 1987

(i) the period ending with the return of the vehicle to the owner; or
(ii) the period of the original term of hire.
[³; or
(d) where the original term of hire is extended by an agreed variation of the agreement, the period of the extended term.]
(4) In the case of a hire-purchase agreement, the relevant period shall be—
(a) the period ending with the purchase of the vehicle; or
(b) where the vehicle is returned to the owner or is repossessed by the owner under the terms of the agreement before the completion of the purchase, the original period of the agreement.
[²(5) In this regulation "Motability" means the company, set up under that name as a charity and originally incorporated under the Companies Act 1985 and subsequently incorporated by Royal Charter].

AMENDMENTS

1. The Social Security (Claims and Payments) Amendment Regulations 1991 (SI 1991/2741), reg.22 (February 3, 1992).
2. The Social Security (Miscellaneous Provisions) Amendment Regulations 1990 (SI 1990/2208), reg.13 (December 5, 1990).
3. The Social Security, Child Support and Tax Credits (Miscellaneous Amendments) Regulations 2005 (SI 2005/337), reg.7 (March 18, 2005).

Power for the Secretary of State to terminate an arrangement

2.171 **45.** The Secretary of State may terminate an arrangement for the payment of [¹disability living allowance by virtue of entitlement to the mobility component at the higher rate] on behalf of a beneficiary under regulation 44 on such date as he shall decide—
(a) if requested to do so by the owner of the vehicle to which the arrangement relates, or
(b) where it appears to him that the arrangement is causing undue hard-ship to the beneficiary and that it should be terminated before the end of any of the periods specified in regulation 44(3) or 44(4).

AMENDMENT

1. The Social Security (Claims and Payments) Amendment Regulations 1991 (SI 1991/2741), reg.23 (February 3, 1992).

Restriction on duration of arrangements by the Secretary of State

2.172 **46.** The Secretary of State shall end an arrangement for the payment of [¹ disability living allowance by virtue of entitlement to the mobility component at the higher rate] on behalf of a beneficiary made under regulation 44, where he is satisfied that the vehicle to which the arrangement relates has been returned to the owner, and that the expenses of the owner arising out of the hire or hire-purchase agreement have been recovered following the return of the vehicle.

(SI 1987/1968, reg.47) (as amended)

Part VII

Miscellaneous

[¹ **Instruments of payment**

47.—(1) Instruments of payment issued by the Secretary of State shall remain his property.

(2) Any person having an instrument of payment shall, on ceasing to be entitled to the benefit to which the instrument relates, or when so required by the Secretary of State, deliver it to the Secretary of State or such other person as he may direct.]

Amendment

1. Inserted by The Social Security (Miscellaneous Amendments) (No.2) Regulations 2006 (SI 2006/832), reg.2 (April 10, 2006).

Revocations

48. The regulations specified in column (1) of Schedule 10 to these regulations are hereby revoked to the extent mentioned in column (2) of that Schedule, in exercise of the powers specified in column (3).

Savings

49. [¹...]

Amendment

1. The Social Security (Miscellaneous Provisions) Amendment (No.2) Regulations 1992 (SI 1992/2595), reg.6 (November 16, 1992).

General Note

Regulation 49 maintained in force regulations about claims and reviews relating to supplementary benefit and family income support. See *CIS/465/1991*. Because its terms led to the mistaken impression that the substantive terms of the schemes survived the repeal of the Supplementary Benefits Act 1976 and the Family Income Supplements Act 1970 by the Social Security Act 1986, reg.49 has been revoked from November 16, 1992. See *R(SB) 1/94*. It is not immediately apparent that reg.49 was necessary in order to allow claims to be made for supplementary benefit for periods prior to April 11, 1988, and reviews of entitlement for such periods to be carried out. Therefore its revocation may have no effect on such matters. See Sch.10 to the Administration Act. However, *CSB 168/1993* is to the contrary.

In *CIS/12016/1996* a Commissioner, after a detailed review of the legal issues, concluded that from November 16, 1992, it has been impossible for an effective claim to be made for supplementary benefit. This was in spite of the powerful argument that an underlying entitlement to supplementary benefit for a period before April 11, 1988, and the right to pursue a remedy in respect of that entitlement could be preserved by s.16(1) of the Interpretation Act 1978 on the revocation of the supplementary benefit legislation. The reason was that any remedy protected would be under reg.3(1) of the Supplementary Benefit (Claims

The Social Security (Claims and Payments) Regulations 1987

and Payments) Regulations 1981, which required a claim for weekly supplementary benefit to be made in writing on a form approved by the Secretary of State or in such other manner as the Secretary of State accepted as sufficient. In *CIS/12016/1996* the claim was made in a letter in July 1993. By that date, the Secretary of State had no power to accept the manner of claim as sufficient, because the 1981 Regulations no longer existed. Since the Secretary of State's power was discretionary, the claimant had no accrued right which could be preserved by s.16(1). It had been held in *R. v Secretary of State for Social Security Ex p. Cullen* (November 21, 1996), now confirmed by the Court of Appeal (*The Times*, May 16, 1997, and see the notes to reg.9) that the hope of having a discretion to treat a claim for supplementary benefit as in the alternative a claim for attendance allowance was not preserved by s.16(1) as an accrued right. The same had to apply to the power to accept claims as made in sufficient manner.

Note also *CIS/7009/1995* which confirms that it was not possible to make a late claim for National Assistance after the start of the supplementary benefit scheme on November 24, 1966. There were no savings provisions to enable claims for National Assistance to succeed after that date (see *CSB 61/1995*).

SCHEDULE 1

Part I

Benefit Claimed and Other Benefit Which May be Treated as if Claimed in Addition or in the Alternative

2.177

Benefit claimed (1)	Alternative benefit (2)
[¹ Incapacity benefit]	[¹ Severe disablement allowance]
[² . . .]	[² . . .]
Severe disablement allowance	[¹ Incapacity benefit]
[² . . .]	[² . . .]
[¹ Incapacity benefit for a woman]	[¹ Maternity allowance]
Severe disablement allowance for a woman	Maternity allowance
Maternity allowance	[¹ Incapacity benefit or severe disablement allowance]
A retirement pension of any category	Widow's benefit [⁹ or bereavement benefit]
A retirement pension of any category	A retirement pension of any other category [³ or graduated retirement benefit]
[¹ An increase of incapacity benefit]	An increase of severe disablement allowance
Attendance allowance	An increase of disablement pension where constant attendance is needed
An increase of disablement pension where constant attendance is needed	Attendance allowance [⁴ or disability living allowance]
An increase of severe disablement allowance	[¹ An increase of incapacity benefit]
Income support	[⁵ . . .] [⁴ . . .] or [¹⁰ carer's allowance]
[⁶ Widow's benefit [⁹ or bereavement benefit]]	[⁶ A retirement pension of any category or graduated retirement benefit]
[⁴ Disability living allowance]	[⁴ Attendance allowance or an increase of disablement pension where constant attendance is needed]

470

(SI 1987/1968, Sch.1) (as amended)

[⁴ Attendance allowance or an increase of disablement pension where constant attendance is needed]

[⁴ Disability living allowance]

[⁷ Disabled person's tax credit]

[⁷ Working families' tax credit]

[⁷ Working families' tax credit]

[⁷ Disabled person's tax credit]

In this part of this Schedule—
(a) Reference to an increase of any benefit (other than an increase of disablement pension where constant attendance is needed) are to an increase of that benefit in respect of a child or adult dependant;
(b) "widow's benefit" means widow's benefit under [Part II of the Social Security Contributions and Benefits Act 1992] and benefit by virtue of section [78(9)] of that Act corresponding to a widow's pension or a widowed mother's allowance.

PART II

INTERCHANGE OF CLAIMS FOR CHILD BENEFIT WITH CLAIMS FOR OTHER BENEFITS

[⁸ . . .]
Guardian's allowance
Maternity allowance claimed after confinement
Increase of child dependant by virtue of [sections 80 and 90 of the Social Security Contributions and Benefits Act 1992], or regulations made under [section 78(9)] of that Act.

AMENDMENTS

1. The Social Security (Claims and Payments) Amendment (No.2) Regulations 1994 (SI 1994/2943), reg.10 (April 13, 1995).
2. The Social Security (Claims and Payments) (Jobseeker's Allowance Consequential Amendments) Regulations 1996 (SI 1996/1460), reg.2 (October 7, 1996).
3. The Social Security (Claims and Payments) Amendment Regulations 1988 (SI 1988/522), reg.8 (April 11, 1988).
4. The Social Security (Claims and Payments) Amendment Regulations 1991 (SI 1991/2741), reg.25 (February 3, 1992).
5. The Social Security (Miscellaneous Provisions) Amendment (No.2) Regulations 1992 (SI 1992/2595), reg.7 (November 16, 1992).
6. The Social Security (Miscellaneous Provisions) Amendment Regulations 1990 (SI 1990/2208), reg.14 (December 5, 1990).
7. The Tax Credits (Claims and Payments) (Amendment) Regulations 1999 (SI 1999/2572), regs 24 and 25 (October 5, 1999).
8. The Child Benefit, Child Support and Social Security (Miscellaneous Amendments) Regulations 1996 (SI 1996/1803), reg.20 (April 7, 1997).
9. The Social Security (Benefits for Widows and Widowers) (Consequential Amendments) Regulations 2000 (SI 2000/1483), reg.9 (April 9, 2001).
10. The Social Security Amendment (Carer's Allowance) Regulations 2002 (SI 2002/2497), Sch.2 (October 28, 2002).

SCHEDULE 2   **Regulation 17(5)**

SPECIAL PROVISIONS RELATING TO CLAIMS FOR [¹JOBSEEKER'S ALLOWANCE] DURING PERIODS CONNECTED WITH PUBLIC HOLIDAYS

1.—(1) In this Schedule—
(a) "public holiday" means, as the case may be, Christmas Day, Good Friday or a Bank Holiday under the Banking and Financial Dealings Act 1971 or in Scotland local holidays; and "Christmas and New Year holidays" and "Good Friday and Easter Monday" shall be construed accordingly and shall in each case be treated as one period;
(b) "office closure" means a period during which an [¹ office of the Department for Education an Employment] or associated office is closed in connection with a public holiday;

The Social Security (Claims and Payments) Regulations 1987

    (c) in computing any period of time Sundays shall not be disregarded.

  (2) Where any claim for [¹a jobseeker's allowance] is made during one of the periods set out in paragraph (3), the following provisions shall apply—

    (a) a claim for [¹a jobseeker's allowance] may be treated by [² the Secretary of State as a claim for that benefit for period, to be specified in his decision, not exceeding 35 days after the date of the claim where that claim is made during the period specified in sub-paragraph (a) of paragraph (3), or 21 days after the date of claim where the claim is made during the period specified in either sub-paragraph (b) or (c) of paragraph (3);

    (b) on any claim so treated, benefit may be awarded as if the provisions of paragraph (4) of regulation 17 applied.

  (3) For the purposes of paragraph (2) the periods are—

    (a) in the case of Christmas and New Year holidays, a period beginning with the start of the 35th day before the first day of office closure and ending at midnight between the last day of office closure and the following day;

    (b) in the case of Good Friday and Easter Monday, a period beginning with the start of the 16th day before the first day of the office closure and ending at midnight between the last day of office closure and the following day;

    (c) in the case of any public holiday, a period beginning with the start of the 14th day before the first day of office closure and ending at midnight between the last day of office closure and the following day.

AMENDMENTS

1. The Social Security (Claims and Payments) (Jobseeker's Allowance Consequential Amendments) Regulations 1996 (SI 1996/1460), reg.2 (October 7, 1996).

2. The Social Security Act 1998 (Commencement No.11 and Transitional Provisions) Order 1999 (SI 1999/2860), Sch.3 (October 18, 1999).

2.180 *Schedule 3 revoked by The Social Security (Claims and Payments) (Jobseeker's Allowance Consequential Amendments) Regulations 1996 (SI 1996/1460), reg.2 (October 7, 1996).*

SCHEDULE 4

PRESCRIBED TIME FOR CLAIMING BENEFIT

2.181

Description of benefit (1)	Prescribed time for claiming benefit (2)
1. [¹ Jobseeker's allowance]	[¹ The first day of the period in respect of which the claim is made]
[² **2.** Incapacity benefit or severe disablement allowance]	[² The day in respect of which the claim is made and period of [³ 3 months] immediately following it.]
3. Disablement benefit (not being an increase of benefit)	As regards any day on which, apart from satisfying the condition of making a claim, the claimant is entitled to benefit, that day and the period of 3 months immediately following it.
4. Increase of disablement benefit under section 61 (constant attendance), or 63 (exceptionally severe disablement) of the Social Security Act 1975.	As regards any day which apart form satisfying the conditions that there is a current award of disablement benefit and the making of a claim, the claimant is entitled to benefit, that day and the period of 3 months immediately following it.
5. Reduced earnings allowance	As regards any day on which apart from satisfying the conditions that there is an assessment of disablement of not less than one percent. and the making of a claim, the claim is entitled to the allowance, that day and the period of 3 months immediately following it.
6. Income support	The first day of the period in respect of which the claim is made.

(SI 1987/1968, Sch.4) (as amended)

7. [⁴ Working families' tax credit]

    (a) Where [⁴ working families' tax credit] has previously been claimed and awarded the period beginning 28 days before and ending 14 days after the last day of that award;

    [⁵ (aa) where [⁴ disabled person's tax credit] has previously been claimed and awarded the period beginning 42 days before and ending 14 days after the last day of that award of [⁴ disabled person's tax credit]]

    (b) Subject to [⁵ (a) and (aa)], the first day of the period in respect of which the claim is made;

    (c) where a claim for [⁴ working families' tax credit] is treated as if made for a period beginning with the relevant day by virtue of regulation 13 of these Regulations, the period beginning on 10th March 1992 and ending on 6th April 1992]

8. Social fund payment in respect of maternity expenses

[⁷ The period beginning 11 weeks before the first day of the expected week of confinement and ending three months after—

    (a) the actual date of confinement; or

    (b) in the case of an adopted child, the date of the adoption order; or

    (c) in the case of a child in respect of whom an order has been granted pursuant to section 30 of the Human Fertilisation and Embryology Act, the date of that Order.]

9. Social fund payment in respect of funeral expenses

[⁸ The period beginning with the date of death and ending 3 months after the date of the funeral.]

9A. [⁹ . . .]

10. Increase of disablement benefit under [¹⁰ section 60 of the Social Security Act 1975 on grounds of special hardship or] section 62 of the Social Security Act 1975 on the grounds of receipt of hospital treatment.

A regards any day on which, apart form satisfying the conditions that there is a current award of disablement benefit and the making of a claim, the claimant is entitled to benefit, that day and the period 3 months immediately following it.

[¹¹ 11. [¹² Disabled person's tax credit]

    (a) Where [¹² disabled person's tax credit] has previously been claimed and awarded the period beginning 42 days before and ending 14 days after the last day of that award;

    (b) where [¹² working families' tax credit] has previously been claimed and awarded the period beginning 28 days before and ending 14 days after the last day of that award of [¹² working families' tax credit];

    (c) subject to (a) and (b), the first day of the period in respect of which the claim is made;

    (d) where a claim for [¹² disabled person's tax credit] is made by virtue of regulation 13B(1), the period beginning on 10th March 1992 and ending on 6th April 1992.]

The Social Security (Claims and Payments) Regulations 1987

[¹³ 12. State pension credit. As regards any day on which, apart from satisfying the condition of making a claim, the claimant is entitled to benefit, that day and the period of 12 months immediately following it.]

[¹⁴ 13. Retirement pension of any category As regards any day on which apart from satisfying the condition of making a claim, the claimant is entitled to the pension, that day and the period of 12 months immediately following it.]

[¹⁴ 14. Graduated retirement benefit As regards any day on which, apart from satisfying the condition of making a claim, the claimant is entitled to benefit, that day and the period of 12 months immediately following it.]

[¹⁵ 15. Shared additional pension As regards any day on which, apart from satisfying the condition of making a claim, the claimant is entitled to the pension, that day and the period of 12 months immediately following it.]

For the purposes of this Schedule—

"actual date of confinement" means the date of the issue of the child or, if the woman is confined of twins or a greater number of children, the date of the issue of the last of them; and

"confinement" means labour resulting in the issue of a living child, or labour after 28 weeks of pregnancy resulting in the issue of a child whether alive or dead.

AMENDMENTS

1. The Social Security (Claims and Payments) (Jobseeker's Allowance Consequential Amendments) Regulations 1996 (SI 1996/460), reg.2 (October 7, 1996).
2. The Social Security (Claims and Payments) Amendment (No.2) Regulations 1994 (SI 1994/2943), reg.12 (April 13, 1995).
3. The Social Security (Miscellaneous Provisions) (No.2) Regulations 1997 (SI 1997/793), reg.7 (April 7, 1997).
4. The Tax Credits (Claims and Payments) (Amendment) Regulations 1999 (SI 1999/2572), regs 24 and 25 (October 5, 1999).
5. The Social Security (Claims and Payments) Amendment Regulations 1991 (SI 1991/2741), reg.26 (March 10, 1992).
6. The Social Security (Miscellaneous Provisions) Amendment Regulations 1991 (SI 1991/2284), reg.10 (November 1, 1991).
7. The Social Security (Social Fund and Claims and Payments) (Miscellaneous Amendments) Regulations 1997 (SI 1997/792), reg.8 (April 7, 1997).
8. The Social Security (Claims and Payments and Adjudication) Amendment Regulations 1996 (SI 1996/2306), reg.6 (October 7, 1996).
9. The Social Security (Miscellaneous Provisions) Amendment Regulations 1991 (SI 1991/2284), reg.11 (November 1, 1991).
10. The Social Security (Claims and Payments) Amendment Regulations 1988 (SI 1988/522), reg.9 (April 11, 1988).
11. The Social Security (Claims and Payments) Amendment Regulations 1991 (SI 1991/2741), reg 26(b) (March 10, 1992).
12. The Tax Credits (Claims and Payments) (Amendment) Regulations 1999 (SI 1999/2572), regs 24 and 25 (October 5, 1999).
13. Social Security (Claims and Payments) Amendment (No.2) Regulations 2004 (SI 2004/1821), reg.2(a) (October 6, 2004).
14. The Social Security (Claims and Payments) Amendment Regulations 2005 (SI 2005/455), reg.5 (April 6, 2006).
15. The Social Security (Shared Additional Pension (Miscellaneous Amendments) Regulations 2005 (SI 2005/1551), reg.3 (April 6, 2006).

(SI 1987/1968, Sch.4) (as amended)

GENERAL NOTE

Sometimes there is a need to be very precise about dates. *CIB/2805/2003* was just such a case. The Deputy Commissioner notes that the formulation used in relation to incapacity benefit (and, it should be noted, in relation to several other benefits) is to specify the time limit by reference to the day of claim and a period of three months immediately following it. The Deputy Commissioner rules that this means that the claimant gets the day of claim and a full three months immediately following the date in respect of which the claim is made. This gave the claimant two more days than the Secretary of State had calculated.

2.182

Schedule 5 revoked by The Social Security (Claims and Payments and Adjudication) Amendment Regulations 1996 (SI 1996/2306), reg.7 (October 7, 1996).

2.183

SCHEDULE 6   Regulation 22(3)

DAYS FOR PAYMENT OF LONG TERM BENEFITS

[¹ Attendance allowance and disability living allowance
   1. Subject to the provisions of regulation 25 (payment of attendance allowance, constant attendance allowance and the care component of a disability living allowance at a daily rate) attendance allowance shall be payable on Wednesdays, except that the Secretary of State may in a particular case arrange for either allowance to be payable on any other day of the week and where it is in payment to any person and the day on which it is payable is changed, it shall be paid at a daily rate of 1/7th of the weekly rate in respect of any of the days for which payment would have been made but for that change.]
   2. [². . .]

2.184

Industrial injuries benefit
   3. Any pension or allowance under [Part V of the Social Security Contributions and Benefits Act 1992], including any increase, shall be payable on Wednesdays.

2.185

[⁵Carer's allowance]
   4. [⁵carer's allowance] shall be payable on Mondays, except that where a person is entitled to that allowance in respect of a severely disabled person by virtue of regulation 3 of the Social Security (Invalid Care Allowance) Regulations 1976 the [⁵carer's allowance] shall be payable on Wednesdays.

2.186

Retirement pension
   5. Retirement pension shall be payable on Mondays, except that—
    (a) where a person became entitled to a retirement pension before September 28, 1984, that pension shall be payable on Thursdays;
 [³(b) where—
      (i) a woman was entitled to a widow's benefit, or
      (ii) a man or a woman was entitled to a bereavement benefit,
    immediately before becoming entitled to a retirement pension, that pension shall be payable on [⁴ . . .] [⁴ the day of the week which has become the appropriate day for payment of such a benefit to him in accordance with paragraph 6];]
    (c) where a woman becomes entitled to a retirement pension immediately following the payment to her husband of an increase of retirement pension in respect of her, the retirement pension to which she becomes entitled shall be payable on the same days as those upon which the retirement pension of the husband is payable;
    (d) the Secretary of State may, notwithstanding anything contained in the foregoing provisions of this paragraph, arrange for retirement pension to be payable on such other day of the week as he may [⁴ . . .] [⁴ where payment is by credit transfer, or in the circumstances of any particular case, determine];
    (e) where, in relation to any person, any particular day of the week has become the appropriate day of the week for the payment of retirement pension, that day shall thereafter remain the appropriate day in his case for such payment.

2.187

The Social Security (Claims and Payments) Regulations 1987

2.187.1

Shared additional pension

[⁶ **5A.** Shared additional pension shall be payable on Mondays, except that—
  (a) where a retirement pension is payable to the claimant, it shall be payable on the same day as the retirement pension; or
  (b) the Secretary of State may, notwithstanding the provisions of sub-paragraph (a), arrange for a shared additional pension to be payable on such other day of the week as he may, in the circumstances of any particular case, determine.]

2.188

Widowed mother's allowance and widow's pension

6. Widowed mother's allowance [³ widowed parents allowance, bereavement allowance] and widow's pension shall be payable on [⁴ on . . .]—
  (a) Tuesdays, or
  (b) such other day of the week as the Secretary of State may determine, where payment is by direct credit transfer, or in the circumstances of any particular case,
and where, in relation to any person, any particular day of the week has become the appropriate day of the week for payment of such an allowance or pension, that day shall thereafter remain the appropriate day of such payment in his case.]

7. [¹. . .]

AMENDMENTS

2.189

1. The Social Security (Claims and Payments) Amendment Regulations 1991 (SI 1991/2741), reg.27 (April 6, 1992).
2. The Social Security (Claims and Payments) Amendment Regulations 1999 (SI 1999/2358), reg.2 (September 20, 1999).
3. The Social Security (Benefits for Widows and Widowers) (Consequential Amendments) Regulations 2000 (SI 2000/1483), reg.9 (April 9, 2001).
4. Social Security (Claims and Payments and Miscellaneous Amendments) (No.2) Regulations 2002 (SI 2002/2441), reg.11 (October 23, 2002).
5. The Social Security Amendment (Carer's Allowance) Regulations 2002 (SI 2002/2497), Sch.2 (October 28, 2002).
6. The Social Security (Shared Additional Pension) (Miscellaneous Amendments) Regulations 2005 (SI 2005/1551) (July 6, 2005).

SCHEDULE 7   **Regulation 26**

[¹⁵ TIME OF PAYMENT AND COMMENCEMENT OF ENTITLEMENT IN INCOME SUPPORT CASES]

2.190

Manner of payment

1. Except as otherwise provided in these Regulations income support shall be paid in arrears in accordance with the award.]

2.191

Time of payment

2. Income support shall be paid in advance where the claimant is—
  (a) in receipt of retirement pension; or
  (b) over pensionable age and not in receipt of [⁹. . .] [⁷incapacity benefit or severe disablement allowance and is not a person to whom section 126 of the Social Security Contributions and Benefits Act 1992 (trade disputes) applies] unless he was in receipt of income support immediately before the trade dispute began; or
  (c) in receipt of widow's benefit [¹³or bereavement benefit] and is not [¹⁴ . . .] providing or required to provide medical evidence of incapacity for work; or
  (d) a person to whom [¹section 23(a)] of the Social Security Act 1986 [SSCBA, s.127] applies, but only for the period of 15 days mentioned in that subsection.

2.192

[²**2A.**—(1) For the purposes of this paragraph—
  (a) "public holiday" means, as the case may be, Christmas Day, Good Friday or a Bank Holiday under the Banking and Financial Dealings Act 1971 or in Scotland local holidays, and
  (b) "office closure" means a period during which an office of the Department of Social Security or associated office is closed in connection with a public holiday.

(2) Where income support is normally paid in arrears and the day on which the benefit is payable by reason of paragraph 3 is affected by office closure it may for that benefit week be

(SI 1987/1968, Sch. 7) (as amended)

paid wholly in advance or partly in advance and partly in arrears and on such a day as the Secretary of State may direct.

(3) Where under this paragraph income support is paid either in advance or partly in advance and partly in arrears it shall for any other purposes be treated as if it was paid in arrears.]

[³3. (1) Subject to [⁷sub-paragraph (1A) and to] any direction given by the Secretary of State in accordance with sub-paragraph (2), income support in respect of any benefit week shall, if the beneficiary is entitled to a relevant social security benefit or would be so entitled but for failure to satisfy the contribution conditions or had not exhausted his entitlement, be paid on the day and at the intervals appropriate to payment of that benefit.

2.193

[⁷(1A) Subject to sub-paragraph (2), where income support is paid to a person on the grounds of incapacity for work, that entitlement commenced on or after 13th April 1995, and no relevant social security benefit is paid to that person, the income support shall be paid fortnightly in arrears.]

(2) The Secretary of State may direct that income support in respect of any benefit week shall be paid at such intervals and on such days as he may in any particular case or class of case determine.

3A.—(1) Income support for any part-week shall be paid in accordance with an award on such day as the Secretary of State may in any particular case direct.

2.194

(2) In this paragraph, "part-week" has the same meaning as it has in Part VII of the Income Support (General) Regulations 1987.]

4.[¹In this Schedule]—

2.195

"benefit week" means, if the beneficiary is entitled to a relevant social security benefit or would be so entitled but for failure to satisfy the contribution conditions or had not exhausted his entitlement, the week corresponding to the week in respect of which that benefit is paid, and in any other case a period of 7 days beginning or ending with such day as the Secretary of State may direct;

[¹"Income Support Regulations" means the Income Support (General) Regulations 1987;] and

"relevant social security benefit" means [⁹. . .] [⁷incapacity benefit], severe disablement allowance, retirement pension [¹² bereavement benefit] or widow's benefit.

Payment of small amounts of income support

5. Where the amount of income support is less than £1.00 a week the Secretary of State may direct that it shall be paid at such intervals as may be specified not exceeding 13 weeks.

2.196

Commencement of entitlement to income support

6.—(1) Subject to sub-paragraphs (3) and (4), in a case where income support is payable in arrears entitlement shall commence on the date of claim.

2.197

(2) [¹Subject to sub-paragraphs (2A) and (3)], in a case where, under paragraph 2, income support is payable in advance entitlement shall commence on the date of claim if that day is a day for payment of income support as determined under paragraph 3 but otherwise on the first such day after the date of claim.

[¹(2A) Where income support is awarded under regulation 17(3) for a definite period which is not a benefit week or a multiple of such a week entitlement shall commence on the date of claim.

(3) In a case where regulation 13 applies, entitlement shall commence on the day which is the relevant day for the purposes of that regulation [⁵ except where income support is paid in advance, when entitlement shall commence on the relevant day, if that day is a day for payment as determined under paragraph 3 but otherwise on the first day for payment after the relevant day].]

(4) [¹. . .]

[⁹(5) If a claim is made by a claimant within 3 days of the date on which he became resident in a resettlement place provided pursuant to section 30 of the Jobseekers Act or at a centre providing facilities for the rehabilitation of alcoholics or drug addicts, and the claimant is so resident for the purposes of that rehabilitation, then the claim shall be treated as having been made on the day the claimant became so resident.]

(6) Where, in consequence of a further claim for income support such as is mentioned in sub-paragraph 4(7) of Schedule 3 to the Income Support (General) Regulations 1987, a claimant is treated as occupying a dwelling as his home for a period before moving in, that further claim shall be treated as having been made on the date from which he is treated as so occupying the dwelling or the date of the claim made before he moved in to the dwelling and referred to in that sub-paragraph, whichever is the later.

7. [. . .¹²].

2.198

The Social Security (Claims and Payments) Regulations 1987

AMENDMENTS

1. The Social Security (Claims and Payments) Amendment Regulations 1988 (SI 1988/522), reg.10 (April 11, 1988).
2. Transfer of Functions (Health and Social Security) Order 1988 (SI 1988/1843); The Social Security (Claims and Payments and Payments on account, Overpayments and Recovery) Amendment Regulations 1989 (SI 1989/136), reg.2(b) (February 27, 1989).
3. The Social Security (Medical Evidence, Claims and Payments) Amendment Regulations 1989 (SI 1989/1686), reg.8 (October 9, 1989).
4. The Social Security (Miscellaneous Provisions) Amendment Regulations 1990 (SI 1990/2208), reg.15 (December 5, 1990).
5. The Enterprise (Scotland) Consequential Amendments Order 1991 (SI 1991/387), art.2 and Sch.(April 1, 1991).
6. The Social Security (Miscellaneous Provisions) Amendment Regulations 1992 (SI 1992/247), reg.17 (March 9, 1992).
7. The Social Security (Claims and Payments) Amendment (No.2) Regulations 1994 (SI 1994/2943), reg.14 (April 13, 1995).
8. The Social Security (Claims and Payments etc.) Amendment Regulations 1996 (SI 1996/672), reg.2(6) (April 4, 1996).
9. The Social Security (Claims and Payments) (Jobseeker's Allowance Consequential Amendments) Regulations 1996 (SI 1996/1460), reg.2(24) (October 7, 1996).
10. The Social Security (Miscellaneous) Amendment (No.4) Regulations 1998 (SI 1998/1174), reg.8(3)(b) (June 1, 1998).
11. The Social Security Act 1998 (Commencement No.12 and Consequential and Transitional Provisions) Order 1999 (SI 1999/3178), Sch.6 (November 29, 1999).
12. The Social Security and Child Support (Miscellaneous Amendments) Regulations 2000 (SI 2000/1596), reg.5 (June 19, 2000).
13. The Social Security (Benefits for Widows and Widowers) (Consequential Amendments) Regulations 2000 (SI 2000/1483), reg.9 (April 9, 2001).
14. The Social Security, Child Support and Tax Credits (Miscellaneous Amendments) Regulations 2005 (SI 2005/337), reg.7 (March 18, 2005).
15. The Social Security (Miscellaneous Amendments) (No.2) Regulations 2006 (SI 2006/832), reg.2 (April 10, 2006).

GENERAL NOTE

Para.2

2.199   These categories of claimant are paid income support in advance. Apart from pensioners and most widows, those returning to work after a trade dispute are covered.

Paras 3 and 4

2.200   Where a claimant meets the conditions of entitlement for one of the benefits listed as a "relevant social security benefit," the income support benefit week, pay-day and interval of payment is the same as for that benefit. Thus, those incapable of work are paid fortnightly in arrears (reg.24(1)), although under reg.24 the Secretary of State can arrange payment of incapacity benefit at other intervals (e.g. weekly), in which case income support follows suit. Otherwise the benefit week is to be defined by the Secretary of State. Income support paid for a definite period under reg.17(3) need not be in terms of benefit weeks. Paragraph 3A provides that payments for part-weeks may be made as the Secretary of State directs.

Para.6

2.201   The general rule for income support paid in arrears is that entitlement begins on the date of claim. The first payment on the pay day at the end of the first benefit week (or the second benefit week in the case of the unemployed) can thus be

(SI 1987/1968, Sch.7) (as amended)

precisely calculated to include the right number of days. Payments can then continue on a weekly basis.

If income support is paid in advance, then, as for supplementary benefit, entitlement begins on the next pay day following the claim or coinciding with the date of claim.

Where the award is for a definite period under reg.17(3) entitlement begins with the date of claim (sub-para.(2A)). Sub-paragraph (3) deals with the special case of advance awards. Sub-paragraphs (5) and (6) cover other special cases.

2.202

SCHEDULE 8   Regulation 23(1)(a)

ELECTION TO HAVE CHILD BENEFIT PAID WEEKLY

1. A person to whom benefit is payable for an uninterrupted period beginning before and ending after March 15, 1982 may make an election, in accordance with paragraph 3, that benefit be payable weekly after that date, if either—
   (a) he makes the election before the end of the 26th week from the day on which benefit was payable for the first four weeks in respect of which the Secretary of State made arrangements for four-weekly payment to the person entitled in accordance with regulation 21 or regulation 23(1)(b); or
   (b) he was absent from Great Britain on the March 15, 1982 for one of the reasons specified in paragraph 4 and he makes the election before the end of the 26th week of the period beginning with the first week in respect of which benefit became payable to him in Great Britain on his return.

2.203

2. Subject to paragraph 5, a person entitled to benefit may make an election, in accordance with paragraph 3, that benefit be paid weekly if he satisfies either of the following conditions—
   (a) he is a lone parent within the meaning set out in regulation 2(2) of the Child Benefit and Social Security (Fixing and Adjustment of Rates) Regulations 1976, or]
   (b) he, or his spouse residing with him or the person with whom he is living as husband and wife, is receiving income support, [²an incomed-based jobseeker's allowance], [³ or payment in accordance with an award of family credit or disability working allowance which was awarded with effect for a date falling before 5th October 1999.]

2.204

3. An election for benefit to be payable weekly under paragraphs 1 or 2 shall be effected by giving notice in writing to the Secretary of State delivered or sent to the appropriate office and shall be made when it is received.

2.205

4. An election may not be made under paragraph 1(b) unless the person's absence abroad on the March 15, 1982 was by reason of his being—
   (a) a serving member of the forces, as defined by regulation 1(2) of the Social Security (Contributions) Regulations 1979, or
   (b) the spouse of such a member, or
   (c) a person living with such a member as husband and wife.

2.206

5. Every person making an election for benefit to be paid weekly under paragraph 2 shall furnish such certificates, documents and such other information of facts as the Secretary of State may, in his discretion, require, affecting his right to receive payment of benefit weekly and in particular shall notify the Secretary of State in writing of any change of circumstances which he might reasonably be expected to know might affect the right to receive payment of benefit weekly, as soon as reasonably practicable after the occurrence thereof.

2.207

6. Where a person makes an election, in accordance with this regulation, for benefit to be paid weekly, it shall continue to be so payable—
   (a) in the case of an election under paragraph 1, so long as that person remains continually entitled to benefit, or
   (b) in the case of an election under paragraph 2, so long as that person remains continually entitled to benefit and the conditions specified in that paragraph continue to be satisfied.

2.208

7. A person who has made an election that benefit be payable weekly may cancel it at any time by a notice in writing delivered or sent to the appropriate office; and effect shall be given to such a notice as soon as is convenient.

2.209

AMENDMENTS

1. The Child Benefit, Child Support and Social Security (Miscellaneous Amendments) Regulations 1996 (SI 1996/1803), reg.21 (April 7, 1997).

479

The Social Security (Claims and Payments) Regulations 1987

2. The Social Security (Claims and Payments) (Jobseeker's Allowance Consequential Amendments) Regulations 1996 (SI 1996/1460), reg.2 (October 7, 1996).

3. The Social Security and Child Support (Tax Credits) Consequential Amendments Regulations 1999 (SI 1999/2566), Sch.8 (September 5, 1999).

SCHEDULE 9   **Regulation 35**

DEDUCTIONS FROM BENEFIT AND DIRECT PAYMENT TO THIRD PARTIES

Interpretation

2.210

1. [[20]—(1)] In this Schedule—

[[11]"the Community Charges Regulations" means the Community Charges (Deductions from Income Support (No.2) Regulations 1990;
"the Community Charges (Scotland) Regulations" means the Community Charges (Deductions from Income Support) (Scotland) Regulations 1989;]

[[21]"contribution-based jobseeker's allowance" means any contribution-based jobseeker's allowance which does not fall within the definition of "specified benefit";]

["the Council Tax Regulations" mean the Council Tax (Deductions from Income Support) Regulations 1993;]

"family" in the case of a claimant who is not a member of a family means that claimant [[31] and for the purposes of state pension credit "a family" comprises the claimant, his partner, any additional partner to whom section 12(1)(c) of the 2002 Act applies and any person who has not attained the age of 19, is treated as a child for the purposes of section 142 of the Contributions and Benefits Act and lives with the claimant or the claimant's partner;];

[[11]"the Fines Regulations" means the Fines (Deductions from Income Support) Regulations 1992;]

[[6]"5 per cent of the personal allowance for the single claimant aged not less than 25" means where the percentage is not a multiple of 5 pence the sum obtained by rounding that 5 per cent to the next higher such multiple;

[[35] "hostel" means a building—
  (a) in which there is provided for persons generally, or for a class of persons, accommodation, otherwise than in separate and self-contained premises, and either board or facilities of a kind set out in paragraph 4A(1)(d) below adequate to the needs of those persons and—
  (b) which is—
    (i) managed by or owned by a housing association registered with the Housing Corporation established by the Housing Act 1964;
    (ii) managed or owned by a housing association registered with Scottish Homes established by the Housing (Scotland) Act 1988;
    (iii) operated other than on a commercial basis and in respect of which funds are provided wholly or in part by a government department or a local authority; or
    (iv) managed by a voluntary organisation or charity and provides care, support or supervision with a view to assisting those persons to be rehabilitated or resettled within the community, and
  (c) which is not—
    (i) a care home;
    (ii) an independent hospital; or
    (iii) an establishment run by the Abbeyfield Society including all bodies corporate or incorporated which are affiliated to that Society, and
  (d) in sub-paragraph (b)(iv) above, "voluntary organisation" shall mean a body the activities of which are carried out otherwise than for profit, but shall not include any public or local authority;]

"housing authority" means a local authority, a new town corporation, Scottish Homes or the Rural Development Board for Rural Wales;]

[[36] "the Housing Benefit Regulations" mean the Housing Benefit Regulations 2006;
"the Housing Benefit (State Pension Credit) Regulations" mean the Housing benefit (Persons who have attained the qualifying age for state pension credit) Regulations 2006;]

(SI 1987/1968, Sch.9) (as amended)

[20"housing costs" means any housing costs met under—
  (a) Schedule 3 to the Income Support Regulations but—
    (i) excludes costs under paragraph 17(1)(f) of that Schedule (tents and tent sites); and
    (ii) includes costs under paragraphs 17(1)(a) (ground rent [34...]) and 17(1)(c) (rentcharges) of that Schedule but only when they are paid with costs under paragraph 17(1)(b) of that Schedule (service charges); or
  (b) Schedule 2 to the Jobseeker's Allowance Regulations but—
    (i) excludes costs under paragraph 16(1)(f) of that Schedule (tents and tent sites); and
    (ii) includes costs under paragraphs 16(1)(a) (ground rent and feu duty) and 16(1)(c) (rentcharges) of that Schedule but only when they are paid with costs under paragraph 16(1)(b) of that Schedule (service charges);]
[31 (c) Schedule II to the State Pension Credit Regulations but—
    (i) excludes costs under paragraph 13(1)(f) of that Schedule (tents and sites); and
    (ii) includes costs under paragraphs 13(1)(a) (ground rent and feu duty) and 13(1)(c) (rent charges) of that Schedule but only when they are paid with costs under paragraph 13(1)(b) of that Schedule (service charges);]
[34...]
"the Income Support Regulations" means the Income Support (General) Regulations 1987;
"miscellaneous accommodation costs" has the meaning assigned by paragraph 4(1);
[20"mortgage payment" means the aggregate of any payments which fall to be met under—
  (a) Schedule 3 to the Income Support Regulations in accordance with paragraphs 6 to 10 of that Schedule (housing costs to be met in income support) on a loan which qualifies under paragraph 15 or 16 of that Schedule, but less any amount deducted under paragraph 18 of that Schedule (non-dependant deductions); or
  (b) Schedule 2 to the Jobseeker's Allowance Regulations in accordance with paragraphs 6 to 9 of that Schedule (housing costs to be met in jobseeker's allowance) on a loan which qualifies under paragraph 14 or 15 of that Schedule, but less any amount deducted under paragraph 17 of that Schedule (non-dependant deductions),
[31 or
  (c) Schedule II to the State Pension Credit Regulations in accordance with paragraph 7 of that Schedule (housing costs to be met in state pension credit) on a loan which qualifies under paragraph 11 or 12 of that Schedule, but less any amount deducted under paragraph 14 of that Schedule (non-dependant deductions),]
as the case may be.]
"personal allowance for a single claimant aged not less than 25 years" means the amount specified [31 in connection with income support and state pension credit] in [6paragraph 1(1)(e)] of column 2 of Schedule 2 to the Income Support Regulations [20or, [31 in connection with jobseeker's allowance], paragraph 1(1)(e) of Schedule 1 to the Jobseeker's Allowance Regulations];
[2...]
"rent" has the meaning assigned to it in the Housing Benefit Regulations and, for the purposes of this Schedule
  (a) includes any water charges which are paid with or as part of the rent;
  (b) where in any particular case a claimant's rent includes elements which would not otherwise fall to be treated as rent, references to rent shall include those elements; and
  (c) references to "rent" include references to part only of the rent; and
[17"specified benefit" means—
[34 (a) income support or, where in respect of any period it is paid together with any incapacity benefit or severe disablement allowance—
    (i) in a combined payment;
    (ii) in part to the beneficiary and in part to another person in accordance with regulation 34; or
    (iii) by means of two or more instruments of payment,
  income support and incapacity benefit or severe disablement allowance if the income support alone is insufficient for the purposes of this Schedule;]
  (b) [30....]
  (c) subject to sub-paragraph (2), jobseeker's allowance;]

481

The Social Security (Claims and Payments) Regulations 1987

[³⁴ (d) state pension credit or, where in respect of any period it is paid together with any retirement pension, incapacity benefit or severe disablement allowance—
  (i) in a combined payment; or
  (ii) in part to the beneficiary and in part to another person in accordance with regulation 34; or
  (iii) by means of two or more instruments of payment,
  state pension credit and retirement pension, incapacity benefit or severe disablement allowance if the state pension credit alone is insufficient for the purposes of this Schedule;]
[²³but does not include any sum payable by way of child maintenance bonus in accordance with section 10 of the Child Support Act 1995) and the [²⁴Social Security (Child Maintenance Bonus)] Regulations 1996;]]
[⁸"water charges" means charges for water or sewerage under Chapter I of Part V of the Water Industry Act 1991;]
[⁶"water undertaker" means a company which has been appointed under section 11(1) of the Water Act 1989 to be the water or sewerage undertaker for any area in England and Wales.]
[²⁰(2) For the purposes of the definition of "specified benefit" in sub-paragraph (1), "jobseeker's allowance" means—
  (a) income-based jobseeker's allowance; and
  (b) in a case where, if there was no entitlement to contribution-based jobseeker's allowance, there would be entitlement to income-based jobseeker's allowance at the same rate, contribution-based jobseeker's allowance.]

General

2.211 **2.**—(1) The specified benefit may be paid direct to a third party in accordance with the following provisions of this Schedule in discharge of a liability of the beneficiary or his partner to that third party in respect of—
  (a) housing costs;
  (b) miscellaneous accommodation costs;
  [⁶(bb) hostel payments;]
  (c) service charges for fuel, and rent not falling within head (a) above;
  (d) fuel costs; [¹⁰. . .]
  (e) water charges; [¹⁰ and
  (f) payments in place of payments of child support maintenance under section 43(1) of the Child Support Act 1991 and regulation 28 of the Child Support (Maintenance Assessments and Special Cases) Regulations 1992.]
  (2) No payment to a third party may be made under this Schedule unless the amount of the beneficiary's award of the specified benefit is not less than the total of the amount otherwise authorised to be so paid under this Schedule plus 10 pence.
  (3) A payment to be made to a third party under this Schedule shall be made, at such intervals as the Secretary of State may direct, on behalf of and in discharge (in whole or in part) of the obligation of the beneficiary or, as the case may be, of his partner, in respect of which the payment is made.

Housing costs

2.212 **3.**—(1) Subject to [⁷sub-paragraphs (4) to (6)] and paragraph 8, where a beneficiary who has been awarded the specified benefit or his partner is in debt for any item of housing costs which continues to be applicable to the beneficiary in the determination of his applicable amount [³¹ or appropriate minimum guarantee], the [²⁵Secretary of State] may, if in [²⁷ his] opinion it would be in the interests of the family to do so, determine that the amount of the award of the specified benefit ("the amount deductible") calculated in accordance with the following sub-paragraphs shall be paid in accordance with sub-paragraph 2(3).
  (2) [⁷Subject to sub-paragraphs (2A) and (3)], the amount deductible shall be such weekly aggregate of the following as is appropriate:—
    (a) in respect of any debt to which sub-paragraph (1) applies, or where the debt owed is in respect of an amount which includes more than one item of housing costs, a weekly amount equal to 5 per cent. of the personal allowance for a single claimant aged not less than 25 [¹. . .] for such period as it is necessary to discharge the debt, so however that in aggregate the weekly amount calculated under this sub-paragraph shall not exceed 3 times that 5 per cent;
    (b) for each such debt—
      (i) in respect of mortgage payments, the weekly amount of the mortgage payment in that case; and

(SI 1987/1968, Sch.9) (as amended)

      (ii) for any other housing item, the actual weekly cost necessary in respect of continuing needs for the relevant items,
and the [²⁵Secretary State] may direct that, when the debt is discharged, the amount determined under sub-paragraph (b) shall be the amount deductible.

[⁷(2A) Where a payment falls to be made to a third party in accordance with this Schedule, and—
- (a) more than one item of housing costs falls to be taken into account in determining the beneficiary's applicable amount; and
- (b) in accordance with [¹⁶paragraph 4(8) or (11) or] [¹⁵paragraph 18] of Schedule 3 to the Income Support Regulations [²⁰or, as the case may be, paragraph 4(8) or (11) or paragraph 17 of Schedule 2 to the Jobseeker's Allowance Regulations] [³¹ or paragraph 5(9) or (12) or paragraph 14 of Schedule II to the State Pension Credit Regulations] an amount is not allowed or a deduction falls to be made from the amount to be met by way of housing costs,

then in calculating the amount deductible, the weekly aggregate amount ascertained in accordance with sub-paragraph (2) shall be reduced by an amount determined by applying the formula—

$$C \times \frac{B}{A}$$

where—
- A = housing costs;
- B = the item of housing costs which falls to be paid to a third party under this Schedule;
- C = the sum which is not allowed or falls to be deducted in accordance with [¹⁵paragraph 4(8) or (11) or paragraph 18] of Schedule 3 to the Income Support Regulations. [²⁰or, as the case may be, paragraph 4(8) or (11) or paragraph 17 of Schedule 2 to the Jobseeker's Allowance Regulations][³¹ or paragraph 5(9) or (12) or paragraph 14 of Schedule II to the State Pension Credit Regulations]]

(3) Where the aggregate amount calculated under sub-paragraph (2) is such that paragraph 2(2) would operate to prevent any payment under this paragraph being made that aggregate amount shall be adjusted so that 10 pence of the award is payable to the beneficiary.

(4) Sub-paragraph (1) shall not apply to any debt which is either—
- (a) in respect of mortgage payments and the beneficiary or his partner has in the preceding 12 weeks paid sums equal to [⁸or greater than] 8 week's mortgage payments due in that period; or
- (b) for any other item of housing costs and is less than half the annual amount due to be paid by the beneficiary or his partner in respect of that item,

unless, in either case, in the opinion of the adjudicating authority it is in the overriding interests of the family that paragraph (1) should apply.

[⁷(5) No amount shall be paid pursuant to this paragraph in respect of mortgage interest in any case where a specified part of relevant benefits—
- (a) is required to be paid directly to a qualifying lender under regulation 34A and Schedule 9A; or
- (b) would have been required to be paid to a body which, or a person who, would otherwise have been a qualifying lender but for an election given under paragraph 9 of Schedule 9A not to be regarded as such.

(6) In sub-paragraph (5), "specified part" and "relevant benefits" have the meanings given to them in paragraph 1 of Schedule 9A.]

Miscellaneous accommodation costs

[⁹4.—(1) Where an award of income support [³², jobseeker's allowance or state pension credit]—
- (a) [³² in the case of income support] is made to a person [³⁵ residing in a care home, an Abbeyfield Home or an independent hospital] as defined in regulation [²⁸ 2(1)] of the Income Support Regulations [²⁰ or [³² in the case of jobseeker's allowance], regulation 1(3) of the Jobseeker's Allowance Regulations], or]

[³² (b) is made—
- (i) [³⁵ . . .]
- (ii) to person who is in accommodation provided under section 3(1) of, and Part II of the Schedule to, the Polish Resettlement Act 1947 (provision by the Secretary of State of accommodation in camps) except where that person is in receipt of state pension credit; or
- (iii) [³⁵ . . .]

2.213

The Social Security (Claims and Payments) Regulations 1987

(iv) in the case of an award of state pension credit, to a person who is in accommodation provided within the meaning of regulation 15(7) of the State Pension Credit Regulations,]

[32 or to a person who is only temporarily absent from such accommodation] the [25 Secretary of State] may determine that an amount of the specified benefit shall be paid direct to the person or body to whom the charges in respect of that accommodation are payable, [32 or to a person who is only temporarily absent from such accommodation] but, [32 except in a case where accommodation is provided under section 3(1) of, and Part II of the Schedule to, the Polish Resettlement Act 1947] or where the accommodation is [²run by a voluntary organisation either for purposes similar to the purposes for which resettlement units are provided] or which provides facilities for alcoholics or drug addicts, only if the adjudicating authority is satisfied that the beneficiary has failed to budget for the charges and that it is in the interests of the family.

[32 (2) Subject to sub-paragraphs (3) and (3A), the amount of any payment of income support, jobseeker's allowance or state pension credit to a third party determined under sub-paragraph (1) shall be—
  (a) in a case where the beneficiary is not in accommodation [35 . . .] as specified in regulation 15(7)(d) of the State Pension Credit Regulations,
    an amount equal to the award of income support, jobseeker's allowance, or guarantee credit payable to the claimant but excluding an amount, if any, which when added to any other income of the beneficiary as determined in accordance with regulation 28 of the Income Support Regulations, regulation 93 of the Jobseeker's Allowance Regulations or regulation 17 of the State Pension Credit Regulations will equal the amount prescribed in respect of personal expenses in sub-paragraph (2A); and
  (b) in any other case, the amount of the award of income support, jobseeker's allowance or guarantee credit, excluding the amount allowed by sub-paragraph (2A) in respect of personal expenses.

(2A) The amount in respect of personal expenses where a beneficiary is in accommodation referred to in paragraphs 4(1)(a) or (b) shall be—
  (a) for a single person the sum of [40 £20.45];
  (b) for a couple where both members of the couple are in such accommodation, [40 £20.45]; for each member;
  (c) for a member of a polygamous marriage where more than one member is in such accommodation, [40 £20.45]; for each member in such accommodation.

(3) This sub-paragraph shall apply where an award is made of—
  (a) income support calculated in accordance with Part VII of the Income Support Regulations (calculation of income support for part-weeks); or
  (b) jobseeker's allowance calculated in accordance with Part XI of the Jobseeker's Allowance Regulations (part-weeks); or
  (c) state pension credit for a period of less than a week calculated under regulation 13A of the State Pension Credit Regulations (part-weeks), or a part week payment of state pension credit calculated otherwise.

(3A) Where sub-paragraph (3) applies then the amount of any payment to a third party determined under sub-paragraph (1) shall be an amount calculated in accordance with sub-paragraph (2)(a) or (b) as appropriate except that in respect of—
  (a) the income of the beneficiary, if any; and
  (b) the amount allowed for personal expenses by sub-paragraph (2A) above,
the amount shall be the amount used in the calculation under the provisions listed in sub-paragraph (3)(a), (b) or (c), divided by 7 and multiplied by the number of days in the part-week and no payment shall be made to a third party where the Secretary of State certifies it would be impracticable to do so in that particular case.]

(4) Where the amount calculated under sub-paragraph [32 (2) or (3A) is such that paragraph 2(2) would operate to prevent any payment under this paragraph being made the amount shall be adjusted so that 10 pence of the award is payable to the beneficiary.]

[⁶**Hostel payments**

2.214   4A.—(1) This paragraph applies to a beneficiary if—
  (a) he has been awarded specified benefit; and
  (b) he or his partner has claimed housing benefit in the form of a rent rebate or rent allowance; and
  (c) he or his partner is resident in a hostel; and
  (d) the charge for that hostel includes a payment, whether direct or indirect, for one or more of the following services—
    (i) water;
    (ii) a service charge for fuel;

(SI 1987/1968, Sch.9) (as amended)

    (iii) meals;
    (iv) laundry;
    (v) cleaning (other than communal areas).

(2) Subject to sub-paragraph (3) below, where a beneficiary [[8] ...] has been awarded specified benefit the [[25] Secretary of State] may determine that an amount of specified benefit shall be paid to the person or body to whom the charges referred to in subparagraph (1)(d) above are or would be payable.

(3) The amount of any payment to a third party under this paragraph shall be either—
  (a) the aggregate of the amounts determined by a housing authority in accordance with the provisions specified in sub-paragraph (4); or
  (b) if no amount has been determined under paragraph (a) of this sub-paragraph, an amount which the adjudicating authority estimates to be the amount which is likely to be so determined.

[[36] (4) The provisions referred to in sub-paragraph (3)(a) above are regulation 12(6) of, and paragraphs 1(a)(ii) and (iv), 2, 3, 4 and either 6(1)(b) or 6(2) or 6(3) or 6(4) of Schedule 1 to, the Housing Benefit Regulations or, as the case may be, the Housing Benefit (State Pension Credit) Regulations;]

(5) [[36] ...]

[[20](6) Where—
  (a) an award of income support is calculated in accordance with regulation 73(1) of the Income Support Regulations (calculation of income support for part-weeks); or
  (b) an award of jobseeker's allowance is calculated in accordance with regulation 150(1) of the Jobseeker's Allowance Regulations (amount of a jobseeker's allowance payable),
the amount of any payment of income support or, as the case may be, jobseeker's allowance payable to a third party determined under sub-paragraph (2) above shall be an amount calculated in accordance with sub-paragraph (3)(a) or (b) above divided by 7 and multiplied by the number of days in the part-week, and no payment shall be made to a third party under this sub-paragraph where the Secretary of State certifies that it would be impracticable to do so in that particular case.]]

Service charges for fuel, and rent not falling within paragraph 2(1)(a)

5.—(1) Subject to paragraph 8, this paragraph applies to a beneficiary if—
  (a) he has been awarded the specified benefit; and
  (b) he or his partner is entitled to housing benefit in the form of a rent rebate or rent allowance; and
  (c) he or his partner has arrears of rent which equal or exceed four times the full weekly rent payable and—
    (i) there are arrears of rent in respect of at least 8 weeks and the landlord has requested the Secretary of State to make payments in accordance with this paragraph; or
    (ii) there are arrears of rent in respect of less than 8 weeks and in the opinion of the [[25] Secretary of State] it is in the overriding interests of the family that payments shall be made in accordance with this paragraph.

2.215

(2) For the purposes of sub-paragraph (1) arrears of rent do not include—
  (a) the 20 per cent of eligible rates excluded from a rent allowance under [[36] regulation 70 of the Housing Benefit Regulations or, as the case may be, regulation 50 of the Housing benefit (State Pension Credit) Regulations] (maximum housing benefit); or
  (b) any amount falls to be deducted when assessing a person's rent rebate or rent allowance under regulation 63 of those Regulations (non-dependants).

(3) Subject to sub-paragraph (4), the adjudicating authority shall determine that a weekly amount of the specified benefit awarded to the beneficiary shall be paid to his or his partner's landlord if—
  (a) he or his partner is entitled to housing benefit and in calculating that benefit a deduction is made under [[36] regulation 12(3) of the Housing Benefit Regulations or, as the case may be, the Housing Benefit (State Pension Credit) Regulations] in respect of either or both of water charges or service charges for fuel; and
  (b) the amount of the beneficiary's award is not less than the amount of the deduction, and the amount to be paid shall be equal to the amount of the deduction.

(4) [[36] ...].

[[20](5) A determination under this paragraph shall not be made without the consent of the beneficiary if the aggregate amount calculated in accordance with sub-paragraphs (3) and (6) exceeds [[38] a sum calculated in accordance with paragraph 8(4);]

[[31] (5A) [[38] ...]]

485

(6) In a case to which sub-paragraph (1) applies the adjudicating authority may determine that a weekly amount of the specified benefit awarded to that beneficiary equal to 5 per cent. of the personal allowance for a single claimant aged not less than 25 [6 . . .] shall be paid to his landlord until the debt is discharged.

[8(7) Immediately after the discharge of any arrears of rent to which sub-paragraph (1) applies and in respect of which a determination has been made under sub-paragraph (6) the adjudicating authority may, if satisfied that it would be in the interests of the family to do so, direct that an amount, equal to the amount by which the eligible rent is to be reduced by virtue of [36 regulation 12(3) of the Housing Benefit Regulations or, as the case may be, the Housing Benefit (State Pension Credit) Regulations] in respect of charges for water or service charges for fuel or both, shall be deductible.]

Fuel costs

2.216   **6.**—(1) [31 Subject to sub-paragraphs (6) and (6A)] and paragraph 8, where a beneficiary who has been awarded the specified benefit or his partner is in debt for any item of mains gas or mains electricity [13including any charges for the reconnection of gas or disconnection or reconnection of electricity] ("fuel item") to an amount not less than the rate of personal allowance for a single claimant aged not less than 25 and continues to require that fuel, the [5 Secretary of State], if in its opinion it would be in the interests of the family to do so, may determine that the amount of the award of the specified benefit ("the amount deductible") calculated in accordance with the following paragraphs shall be paid to the person or body to whom payment is due in accordance with paragraph 2(3).

(2) The amount deductible shall, in respect of any fuel item, be such weekly aggregate of the following as is appropriate:—

[6(a) in respect of each debt to which sub-paragraph (1) applies ("the original debt"), a weekly amount equal to 5 per cent of the personal allowance for a person aged not less than 25 for such period as is necessary to discharge the original debt, but the aggregate of the amounts, calculated under this paragraph shall not exceed twice 5 per cent of the personal allowance for a single claimant aged not less than 25;]

(b) except where current consumption is paid for by other means (for example prepayment meter), an amount equal to the estimated average weekly cost necessary to meet the continuing needs for that fuel item, varied, where appropriate, in accordance with sub-paragraph (4)(a).

(3) [6 . . .]

(4) Where an amount is being paid direct to a person or body on behalf of the beneficiary or his partner in accordance with a determination under sub-paragraph (1) and [27 a decision which embodies that determination falls to be reviewed]—

(a) where since the date of that determination the average weekly cost estimated for the purpose of sub-paragraph (2)(b) has either exceeded or proved insufficient to meet the actual cost of continuing consumption so that in respect of the continuing needs for that fuel item the beneficiary or his partner is in credit or, as the case may be, a further debt has accrued, the adjudicating authority may determine that the weekly amount calculated under that paragraph shall, for a period of 26 weeks [8or such longer period as may be reasonable in the circumstances of the case], be adjusted so as to take account of that credit or further debt;

(b) where an original debt in respect of any fuel item has been discharged the adjudicating authority may determine that the amount deductible in respect of that fuel item shall be the amount determined under sub-paragraph (2)(b).

(5) [6 . . .]

[20(6) Subject to paragraph 8, a determination under this paragraph shall not be made without the consent of the beneficiary if the aggregate amount calculated in accordance with sub-paragraph (2) exceeds [38 a sum calculated in accordance with paragraph 8(4).]

[31 [38 . . .]]

(7) [6 . . .]

[6**Water charges**

2.217   **7.**—(1) This paragraph does not apply where water charges are paid with rent; and in this paragraph "original debt" means the debt to which sub-paragraph (2) applies, [13 including any disconnection or reconnection charges and any other costs (including legal costs) arising out of that debt].

(2) Where a beneficiary or his partner is liable, whether directly or indirectly, for water charges and is in debt for those charges, the [25 Secretary of State] may determine, subject to paragraph 8, that a weekly amount of the specified benefit shall be paid either to a water

(SI 1987/1968, Sch.9) (as amended)

undertaker to whom that debt is owed, or to the person or body authorised to collect water charges for that undertaker, [8 but only if [27 the Secretary of State] is satisfied that the beneficiary or his partner has failed to budget for those charges, and that it would be in the interests of the family to make the determination.]

(3) Where water charges are determined by means of a water meter, the weekly amount to be paid under sub-paragraph (2) shall be the aggregate of—
  (a) in respect of the original debt, an amount equal to 5 per cent of the personal allowance for a single claimant aged not less than 25 years; and
  (b) the amount which the [25 Secretary of State] estimates to be the average weekly cost necessary to meet the continuing need for water consumption.

(4) Where the sum estimated in accordance with sub-paragraph (3)(b) proves to be greater or less than the average weekly cost necessary to meet continuing need for water consumption so that a beneficiary or his partner accrues a credit, or as the case may be a further debt, the adjudicating authority may determine that the sum so estimated shall be adjusted for a period of 26 weeks [8 or such longer period as may be reasonable in the circumstances of the case] to take account of that credit or further debt.

(5) Where water charges are determined other than by means of a water meter the weekly amount to be paid under sub-paragraph (2) shall be the aggregate of—
  (a) the amount referred to in sub-paragraph (3)(a); and
  (b) an amount equal to the weekly cost necessary to meet the continuing need for water consumption.

(6) Where the original debt in respect of water charges is discharged, the [25 Secretary of State] may direct that the amount deductible shall be—
  (a) where water charges are determined by means of a water meter, the amount determined under sub-paragraph (3)(b) taking into account any adjustment that may have been made in accordance with sub-paragraph (4); an
  (b) in any other case, the amount determined under sub-paragraph (5)(b).

(7) Where the beneficiary or his partner is in debt to two water undertakers—
  (a) only one weekly amount under sub-paragraph (3)(a) or (5)(a) shall be deducted; and
  (b) a deduction in respect of an original debt for sewerage shall only be made after the whole debt in respect of an original debt for water has been paid; and
  (c) deductions in respect of continuing charges for both water and for sewerage may be made at the same time.

[20 (8) Subject to paragraph 8 (maximum amount of payments to third parties), a determination under this paragraph shall not be made without the consent of the beneficiary if the aggregate amount calculated in accordance with sub-paragraphs (3), (4), (5) and (6) exceeds [38 a sum calculated in accordance with paragraph 8(4).]

[31 [38 . . .]]

[10 Payments in place of payments of child support maintenance

7A.—[12(1) Subject to paragraph (2), where [26 the Secretary of State] (within the meaning of section 13 of the Child Support Act 1991) has determined that section 43 of that Act and regulation 28 of the Child Support (Maintenance Assessments and Special Cases) Regulations 1992 (contribution to maintenance by deduction from benefit) apply in relation to a beneficiary or his partner, the [25 Secretary of State] shall (subject to paragraph 8), if it is satisfied that there is sufficient specified benefit in payment, determine that a weekly amount of that benefit shall be deducted by the Secretary of State for transmission to the person or persons entitled to it.]

2.218

(2) Not more than one deduction shall be made under [12sub-paragraph (1)] in any one benefit week as defined in paragraph 4 of Schedule 7.

(3) [18Subject to sub-paragraph (4),] the amount of specified benefit to be paid under this paragraph shall be the amount prescribed by regulation 28(2) of the Child Support (Maintenance Assessments and Special Cases) Regulations 1992 for the purposes of section 43(2)(a) of the Child Support Act 1991 [18 . . .].]

[18(4) Where, apart from the provisions of this sub-paragraph, the provisions of paragraphs 8(1) and 9 would result in the maximum aggregate amount payable equalling 2 times 5 per cent of the personal allowance for a single claimant aged not less than 25 years, the amount of specified benefit to be paid under this paragraph shall be one half of the amount specified in sub-paragraph (3).]

[21Arrears of child support maintenance

7B.—(1) Where a beneficiary is entitled to contribution-based jobseeker's allowance and an arrears notice has been served on the beneficiary, the Secretary of State may request in writing

2.219

The Social Security (Claims and Payments) Regulations 1987

that an amount in respect of arrears of child support maintenance be deducted from the beneficiary's jobseeker's allowance.

(2) Where a request is made in accordance with sub-paragraph (1), the [25 Secretary of State] shall determine that an amount in respect of the arrears of child support maintenance shall be deducted from the beneficiary's jobseeker's allowance for transmission to the person entitled to it.

(3) Subject to sub-paragraphs (4) and (5), the amount to be deducted under subparagraph (2) shall be the weekly amount requested by the Secretary of State, subject to a maximum of one-third of the age-related amount applicable to the beneficiary under section 4(1)(a) of the Jobseekers Act.

(4) No deduction shall be made under this paragraph where a deduction is being made from the beneficiary's contribution-based jobseeker's allowance under the Community Charges Regulations, the Community Charges (Scotland) Regulations, the Fines Regulations or the Council Tax Regulations.

(5) Where the sum that would otherwise fall to be deducted under this paragraph includes a fraction of a penny, the sum to be deducted shall be rounded down to the next whole penny.

(6) In this paragraph—

"arrears notice" means a notice served in accordance with regulation 2(2) of the Child Support (Arrears, Interest and Adjustment of Maintenance Assessments) Regulations 1992; and

"child support maintenance" means such periodical payments as are referred to in section 3(6) of the Child Support Act 1991.]

[39 **Eligible loans**

2.220

7C. —(1) In this paragraph—

"borrower" means a person who has, either solely or jointly, entered into a loan agreement with an eligible lender in respect of an eligible loan and who is, for the time being, entitled to an eligible benefit;

"eligible lender" means—

(a) a body registered under section 1 of the Industrial and Provident Societies Act 1965 (societies which may be registered);

(b) a credit union within the meaning of section 1 of the Credit Unions Act 1979 (registration under the Industrial and Provident Societies Act 1965);

(c) a charitable institution within the meaning of section 58(1) of the Charities Act 1992 (interpretation of Part II);

(d) a body entered on the Scottish Charity Register under section 3 of the Charities and Trustee Investment (Scotland) Act 2005 (Scottish Charities Register),which, except for a credit union, is licensed under the Consumer Credit Act 1974 and which may be determined by the Secretary of State as an appropriate body to which payments on behalf of the borrower may be made in respect of loans made by that body;

"eligible loan" means a loan made by a lender, who is at that time an eligible lender, to a borrower except a loan—

(a) which is secured by a charge or pledge;

(b) which is for the purpose of business or self-employment; or

(c) which was made by means of a credit card;

"loan agreement" means an agreement between the eligible lender and the borrower in respect of an eligible loan.

(2) In this paragraph "eligible benefit" means—

(a) carer's allowance;

(b) the following contributory benefits—

(i) incapacity benefit;

(ii) retirement pension; or

(c) the following benefits—

(i) income support;

(ii) jobseeker's allowance;

(iii) state pension credit.

(3) Where the conditions set out in sub-paragraph (4) are met the Secretary of State may deduct a sum from an eligible benefit to which the borrower is entitled equal to 5 per cent. of the personal allowance for a single borrower aged not less than 25 and pay that sum to the eligible lender towards discharge of the sum owing under the loan agreement at the date of the application.

(4) The conditions referred to in sub-paragraph (3) are—

(a) the borrower has failed to make payments as agreed with the eligible lender for a period of 13 weeks before the date of the application and has not resumed making payments;

(SI 1987/1968, Sch.9) (as amended)

    (b) the borrower has given his written permission to the eligible lender to provide to the Secretary of State personal data within the meaning of section 1 of the Data Protection Act 1998 (basic interpretive provisions);
    (c) the eligible lender has agreed that no interest or other charge will be added to the amount owed at the date of the application;
    (d) no sum is being deducted under this paragraph;
    (e) no sum is being deducted from the borrower's eligible benefit under section 71(8) of the 1992 Act (overpayments-general) at the date of the application; and
    (f) no sum is being deducted from the borrower's eligible benefit under section 78 of the 1992 Act (recovery of social fund awards) at the date of the application.

(5) The Secretary of State shall notify the borrower and the eligible lender in writing of a decision to make a deduction under this paragraph.

(6) The Secretary of State may make deductions under this paragraph only if the borrower is entitled to an eligible benefit throughout any benefit week.

(7) The Secretary of State shall not make deductions from a benefit mentioned in sub-paragraph (2)(a) where the borrower is in receipt of another eligible benefit unless that benefit is one mentioned in sub-paragraph (2)(b) and is insufficient to enable the deduction to be made or is a benefit mentioned in sub-paragraph (2)(c) and the amount is insufficient to meet the deduction plus 10 pence.

(8) The Secretary of State shall not make deductions from a benefit mentioned in sub-paragraph (2)(b) where the borrower is in receipt of a benefit mentioned in sub-paragraph (2)(c) unless the amount of that benefit is insufficient to meet the deduction plus 10 pence.

(9) The Secretary of State shall cease making deductions from an eligible benefit if—
    (a) there is no longer sufficient entitlement to an eligible benefit to enable him to make the deduction;
    (b) entitlement to all eligible benefits has ceased;
    (c) a sum is deducted from the borrower's eligible benefit under section 71(8) of the 1992 Act;
    (d) an eligible lender notifies the Secretary of State that he no longer wishes to accept payments by deductions;
    (e) the borrower's liability to make payment in respect of the eligible loan has ceased;
    (f) the lender has ceased to be an eligible lender; or
    (g) the borrower no longer resides in Great Britain.

(10) The sums deducted from an eligible benefit by the Secretary of State under this paragraph shall be paid to the eligible lender.

(11) The Secretary of State shall notify the borrower in writing of the total of sums deducted by him under any application—
    (a) on receipt of a written request for such information from the borrower; or
    (b) on the termination of deductions.

(12) Where a deduction is made under this paragraph from a specified benefit, paragraph 8 (maximum amount of payment to third parties) is to have effect as if—
    (a) in sub-paragraph (1) for "and 7A" there were substituted", 7A and 7C"; and
    (b) in sub-paragraph (2) for "and 7"there were substituted", 7 and 7C.]

Maximum amount of payments to third parties

8.—(1) The maximum aggregate amount payable under [19paragraphs] 3(2)(a), 5(6), 6(2)(a)[6, 7(3)(a)[11, 7(5)(a) and 7A]] [22. . .] [11, and [34 regulation 5 of the Council Tax Regulations and regulation 4 of the Fines Regulations] shall not exceed an amount equal to 3 times 5 per cent. of the personal allowance for a single claimant aged not less than 25 years.

(2) The maximum [5aggregate] amount payable under [6paragraphs 3(2)(a), 5, 6 and 7] shall not without the consent of the beneficiary, exceed [38 a sum calculated in accordance with sub-paragraph (4).]

[31 (2A) In the case of state pension credit, the maximum aggregate amount payable under paragraphs 3(2)(a), 5, 6, and 7 shall not, without the consent of the beneficiary, exceed a sum equal to 25 per cent. of the appropriate minimum guarantee less any housing costs under Schedule II to the State Pension Credit Regulations which may be applicable in the particular case.]

(3) [22. . .]

[38 (4) The sum referred to in sub-paragraph (2) is—
    (a) where the claimant or partner does not receive child tax credit, 25 per cent of—
        (i) in the case of income support, the applicable amount for the family as is awarded under sub-paragraphs (a) to (d) of regulation 17(1) (applicable amounts) or sub-paragraphs (a) to (e) of regulation 18(1) (polygamous marriages) of the Income Support Regulations;

The Social Security (Claims and Payments) Regulations 1987

    (ii) in the case of jobseeker's allowance, the applicable amount for the family as is awarded under paragraphs (a) to (e) of regulation 83 (applicable amounts) or sub-paragraphs (a) to (f) of regulation 84(1) (polygamous marriages) of the Jobseeker's Allowance Regulations; or
    (iii) in the case of state pension credit, the appropriate minimum guarantee less any housing costs under Schedule 2 to the State Pension Credit Regulations 2002 which may be applicable in the particular case; or
 (b) where the claimant or his partner receives child tax credit, 25 per cent of the sum of—
    (i) the amount mentioned in sub-paragraphs (a)(i) to (iii), which applies to the claimant;
    (ii) the amount of child benefit awarded to him or his partner by the Board under Part 2 of the Tax Credits Act 2002; and
    (iii) the amount of child tax credit awarded to him or his partner by the Board under section 8 of that Act.]

Priority as between certain debts

2.222   [[119]**9.**—(1A) Where in any one week—
 (a) more than one of the paragraphs 3 to 7A [[39] or 7C] are applicable to the beneficiary; or
 (b) one or more of those paragraphs are applicable to the beneficiary and one or more of the following provisions, namely, [[22]. . .] [[34] regulation 3 of the Community Charges Regulations, regulation 3 of the Community Charges (Scotland) Regulations, regulation 4 of the Fines Regulations and regulation 5 of the Council Tax Regulations] also applies; and
 (c) the amount of the specified benefit which may be made to third parties is insufficient to meet the whole of the liabilities for which provision is made;
the order of priorities specified in sub-paragraph (1)(B) shall apply.
  (1B) The order of priorities which shall apply in sub-paragraph (1)(A) is—
 (za) [[22]. . .]
 (a) any liability mentioned in paragraph 3 (housing costs);
 (b) any liability mentioned in paragraph 5 (service charges for fuel and rent not falling within paragraph 2(1)(a));
 (c) any liability mentioned in paragraph 6 (fuel costs);
 (d) any liability mentioned in paragraph 7 (water charges);
 (e) any liability mentioned in [[34] regulation 3 of the Community Charges Regulations (deductions from income support etc.), regulation 3 of the Community Charges (Scotland) Regulations (deductions from income support etc.) or any liability mentioned in regulation 5 of the Council Tax Regulations (deduction from debtor's income support etc.)];
 (f) any liability mentioned in [[34] regulation 4 of the Fines Regulations (deductions from offender's income support etc.)];
 (g) any liability mentioned in paragraph 7A (payments in place of payments of child support maintenance).]
 [[39] (h) any liability mentioned in paragraph 7C (liability in respect of loans).]
  (2) As between liability for items of housing costs liabilities in respect of mortgage payments shall have priority over all other items.
  (3) As between liabilities for items of gas or electricity the [[25] Secretary of State] shall give priority to whichever liability it considers it would, having regard to the circumstances and to any requests of the beneficiary, be appropriate to discharge.
  (4) [[6]. . .]

AMENDMENTS

  1. The Social Security (Claims and Payments) Amendment Regulations 1988 (SI 1988/522), reg.11 (April 11, 1988).
  2. The Social Security (Claims and Payments and Payments on account, Overpayments and Recovery) Amendment Regulations 1989 (SI 1989/136), reg.2(7) (February 27, 1989).
  3. The Social Security (Claims and Payments and Payments on account, Overpayments and Recovery) Amendment Regulations 1989 (SI 1989/136), reg.2(7) (April 10, 1989).
  4. The Social Security (Medical Evidence, Claims and Payments) Amendment Regulations 1989 (SI 1989/1686), reg.9 (October 9, 1989).

(SI 1987/1968, Sch.9) (as amended)

5. The Social Security (Miscellaneous Provisions) Amendment Regulations 1990 (SI 1990/2208), reg.16 (December 5, 1990).

6. The Social Security (Miscellaneous Provisions) Amendment Regulations 1991 (SI 1991/2284), regs 12 to 20 (November 1, 1991).

7. The Social Security (Claims and Payments) Amendment Regulations 1992 (SI 1992/1026), reg.5 (May 25, 1992).

8. The Social Security (Miscellaneous Provisions) Amendment (No.2) Regulations 1992 (SI 1992/2595), reg.8 (November 16, 1992).

9. The Social Security (Miscellaneous Provisions) Amendment (No.2) Regulations 1992 (SI 1992/2595), Sch.1, para.8 (April 1, 1993).

10. The Social Security (Claims and Payments) Amendment Regulations 1993 (SI 1993/478), reg.2 (April 1, 1993).

11. The Deductions from Income Support (Miscellaneous Amendments) Regulations 1993 (SI 1993/495), reg.2 (April 1, 1993).

12. The Social Security (Claims and Payments) Amendment (No.3) Regulations 1993 (SI 1993/2113), reg.3 (September 27, 1993).

13. The Social Security (Claims and Payments) Amendment Regulations 1994 (SI 1994/2319), reg.7 (October 3, 1994).

14. The Social Security (Claims and Payments) Amendment (No.2) Regulations 1994 (SI 1994/2943), reg.15 (April 13, 1995).

15. The Social Security (Income Support and Claims and Payments) Amendment Regulations 1995 (SI 1995/1613), reg.3 and Sch.2 (October 2, 1995).

16. The Social Security (Income Support, Claims and Payments and Adjudication) Amendment Regulations 1995 (SI 1995/2927), reg.3 (December 12, 1995).

17. The Social Security (Claims and Payments etc.) Amendment Regulations 1996 (SI 1996/672), reg.2(7) (April 4, 1996).

18. The Child Support (Maintenance Assessments and Special Cases) and Social Security (Claims and Payments) Amendment Regulations 1996 (SI 1996/481), reg.5 (April 8, 1996).

19. The Child Support (Maintenance Assessments and Special Cases) and Social Security (Claims and Payments) Amendment Regulations 1996 (SI 1996/481), reg.6 (April 8, 1996).

20. The Social Security (Claims and Payments) (Jobseeker's Allowance Consequential Amendments) Regulations 1996 (SI 1996/1460), reg.2(26) (October 7, 1996).

21. The Social Security (Jobseeker's Allowance Consequential Amendments) (Deductions) Regulations 1996 (SI 1996/2344), reg.25 (October 7, 1996).

22. The Social Security and Child Support (Miscellaneous Amendments) Regulations 1997 (SI 1997/827), reg.7(2) (April 7, 1997).

23. The Social Security (Child Maintenance Bonus) Regulations 1996 (SI 1996/3195), reg.16(2) (April 7, 1997).

24. The Social Security (Miscellaneous Amendments) Regulations 1997 (SI 1997/454), reg.8(10) (April 6, 1997).

25. The Social Security Act 1998 (Commencement No.11 and Transitional Provisions) Order 1999 (SI 1999/2860), Sch.3 (October 18, 1999).

26. The Social Security Act 1998 (Commencement No.7 and Consequential and Transitional Provisions) Order 1999 (SI 1999/1510), Sch.4 (June 1, 1999).

27. The Social Security Act 1998 (Commencement No.12 and Consequential and Transitional Provisions) Order 1999 (SI 1999/3178), Sch.6 (November 29, 1999).

28. The Social Security Amendment (Residential Care and Nursing Homes) Regulations 2002 (SI 2002/398), reg.2(2) (April 8, 2002).

29. The Social Security Amendment (Residential Care and Nursing Homes) Regulations 2002 (SI 2002/398), reg.2(3) (April 8, 2002).

30. Social Security (Claims and Payments and Miscellaneous Amendments) (No.2) Regulations 2002 (SI 2002/2441), reg.12 (October 23, 2002).

31. State Pension Credit (Consequential, Transitional and Miscellaneous Provisions) Regulations 2002 (SI 2002/3019), reg.14 (April 7, 2003).

The Social Security (Claims and Payments) Regulations 1987

32. The Social Security (Third Party Deductions and Miscellaneous Amendments) Regulations 2003 (SI 2003/2325), reg.2 (October 6, 2003).
33. The Social Security (Claims and Payments) Amendment Regulations 2004 (SI 2004/576), (April 12, 2004 of first benefit pay day thereafter).
34. Social Security (Claims and Payments) Amendment (No.2) Regulations 2005 (SI 2005/777), reg.3 (April 11, 2005).
35. The Social Security (Care Homes and Independent Hospitals) Regulations 2005 (SI 2005/2687) (October 24, 2005).
36. The Housing Benefit and Council Tax Benefit (Consequential Provisions) Regulations 2006 (SI 2006/217), Sch.2, para.2 (March 6, 2006).
37. The Social Security (Miscellaneous Amendments) (No.2) Regulations 2006 (SI 2006/832), reg.2 (April 10, 2006).
38. The Social Security (Miscellaneous Amendments) (No.3) Regulations 2006 (SI 2006/2377) (October 2, 2006).
39. The Social Security (Claims and Payments) Amendment (No. 2) Regulations 2006 (SI 2006/3188) (December 27, 2006).
40. The Social Security Benefits Up-rating Regulations 2007 (SI 2007/775) (April 9, 2007).

DEFINITIONS

"adjudicating authority"—see reg.2(1).
"beneficiary"—see Social Security Act 1975, Sch.20.
"family"—see 1986 Act, s.20(11) (SSCBA, s.137(1)).
"instrument for benefit payment"—see reg.2(1).
"jobseeker's allowance"—*ibid.*
"partner"—*ibid.*
"qualifying lender"—see Administration Act, s.15A(3).
Note that these references are only to phrases defined outside Sch.9 itself. See para.1 for definitions special to Sch.9.

GENERAL NOTE

2.223   The provisions for part of weekly benefit to be diverted direct to a third party are of great importance in determining the actual weekly incomes of claimants. There have been changes in the provisions on fuel and water charges and Sch.9A now deals specifically with payments of mortgage interest.

On deductions in respect of rent arrears under para.5(6), *R(IS) 14/95* holds that the arrears must be proved, at least where these are disputed. In addition, the existence of an arguable counterclaim in possession proceedings is a matter that an adjudicating authority might properly take into account in deciding whether to exercise the discretionary power to make deductions under para.5(6).

See annotations to reg.35 for comment on the precedence to be accorded to child support payments and the relationship between Sch.9 and Sch.9B.

[¹ SCHEDULE 9A

DEDUCTIONS OF MORTGAGE INTEREST FROM BENEFIT AND PAYMENT TO QUALIFYING LENDERS

Interpretation

2.224   **1.** In this Schedule—
[⁹. . .]

"Income Support Regulations" means the Income Support (General) Regulations 1987;
[⁷"relevant benefits" means—
   [¹⁹ (a)   income support, or income support and any incapacity benefit or severe disablement allowance where—

(SI 1987/1968, Sch.9A) (as amended)

      (i) either benefit is paid with income support in a combined payment in respect of any period; and
      (ii) the income support alone is insufficient for the purpose of this Schedule;]
  (b) [[16]....]
  (c) income-based jobseeker's allowance;] [[17] and
[[19] (d) state pension credit, or state pension credit and any retirement pension, incapacity benefit or severe disablement allowance where—
      (i) one of those benefits is paid with state pension credit in a combined payment in respect of any period; and
      (ii) the state pension credit alone is insufficient for the purpose of this Schedule;]
[[10]but does not include any sum payable by way of child maintenance bonus in accordance with section 10 of the Child Support Act 1995 and the [[11]Social Security (Child Maintenance Bonus)] Regulations 1996;]]
"specified part" shall be construed in accordance with paragraph 3.

Specified circumstances for the purposes of Regulation 34A

[[5]2. The circumstances referred to in regulation 34A are that— 2.225
[[8](a) [[17] the amount to be met under—
    (i) Schedule 3 to the Income Support Regulations; or
    (ii) Schedule 2 to the Jobseeker's Allowance Regulations; or
    (iii) Schedule II to the State Pension Credit Regulations,]
by reference to the standard rate [[21] . . .] and, in the case of income support, to any amount payable in accordance with paragraph 7 of Schedule 3 to the Income Support Regulations;] and
(b) the relevant benefits to which a relevant beneficiary is entitled are payable in respect of a period of 7 days or a multiple of such a period.]

[[23] Specified circumstances for the purposes of Regulation 34B

2A.—(1) The circumstances referred to in regulation 34B are that— 2.226
(a) the relevant beneficiary is entitled to a savings credit as construed in accordance with sections 1 and 3 of the 2002 Act and not to a guarantee credit; and
(b) sub-paragraphs (a) and (b) of paragraph 2 apply.
(2) The further circumstances referred to in that regulation are that —
(a) the relevant beneficiary has requested the Secretary of State in writing to make such payments to the qualifying lender; or
(b) the Secretary of State has determined that it would be in the relevant beneficiary's interests, or in the interests of his family to make such payment to the qualifying lender.
(3) In making the determination referred to in sub-paragraph (2)(b), the Secretary of State shall have regard to whether or not the relevant beneficiary is in arrears with his payments to the qualifying lender.
(4) For the purposes of sub-paragraph (2)(b), "a family" comprises the relevant beneficiary, his partner, any additional partner to whom section 12(1)(c) of the 2002 Act applies and any person who has not attained the age of 19, is treated as a child for the purposes of section 142 of the Contributions and Benefits Act and lives with the relevant beneficiary or the relevant beneficiary's partner.]

Specified Part of Relevant Benefit

3. [[5](1) Subject to the following provisions of this paragraph, the part of any relevant 2.227
benefits which, as determined by the [[14] Secretary of State in accordance with regulation 34A, shall be paid] directly to the qualifying lender ("the specified part") is[[8], in the case of income support,] a sum equal to the amount of mortgage interest to be met in accordance with paragraphs 6 and 8 to 10 of Schedule 3 to the Income Support Regulations (housing costs) together with an amount (if any) determined under paragraph 7 of that Schedule (transitional protection) [[8]or, in the case of jobseeker's allowance, a sum equal to the amount of mortgage interest to be met in accordance with paragraphs 6 to 9 of Schedule 2 to the Jobseeker's Allowance Regulations].]
  [[17] (1A) Subject to the following provisions of this paragraph, the part of state pension credit which, as determined by the Secretary of State in accordance with regulation 34A, shall be paid directly to the qualifying lender, is a sum equal to the amount of mortgage interest to be met under paragraph 7 of Schedule II to the State Pension Credit Regulations.]
  (2) [[5]. . .]

The Social Security (Claims and Payments) Regulations 1987

(3) Where, in determining a relevant beneficiary's applicable amount for the purposes of income support [⁸or income-based jobseeker's allowance [¹⁷ or a relevant beneficiary's appropriate minimum guarantee in state pension credit]]—
   (a) a sum in respect of housing costs is brought into account in addition to a sum in respect of mortgage interest; and
   (b) in accordance with [⁵paragraph 4(8) or (11) or paragraph 18] of Schedule 3 to the Income Support Regulations [⁸or, as the case may be, [¹⁷ paragraph 5(9) or (12) or paragraph 14 of Schedule II to the State Pension Credit Regulations or] paragraph 4(8) or (11) or paragraph 17 of Schedule 2 to the Jobseeker's Allowance Regulations] an amount is not allowed or a deduction falls to be made from the amount to be met under [⁸either of those Schedules],
then the specified part referred to in [¹⁷ sub-paragraph (1) or (1A)] of this paragraph is the mortgage interest minus a sum calculated by applying the formula—

$$C \times \frac{B}{A}$$

[⁵where—
A = housing costs within the meaning of paragraph 1 of Schedule 3 to the Income Support Regulations [⁸or, as the case may be, [¹⁷ paragraph 1 of Schedule II to the State Pension Credit Regulations or] paragraph 1 of Schedule 2 to the Jobseeker's Allowance Regulations];
B = the housing costs to be met in accordance with paragraphs 6 and 8 to 10 of Schedule 3 to the Income Support Regulations (housing costs) together with an amount (if any) determined under paragraph 7 of that Schedule (transitional protection) [⁸or, as the case may be, [¹⁷ paragraph 7 of Schedule II to the State Pension Credit Regulations or] paragraphs 6 to 9 of Schedule 2 to the Jobseeker's Allowance Regulations]; and
C = the sum which is not allowed or falls to be deducted in accordance with paragraph 18 of Schedule 3 to the Income Support Regulations [⁸or, as the case may be, [¹⁷ paragraph 5(9) or (12) or paragraph 14 of Schedule II to the State Pension Credit Regulations or] paragraph 4(8) or (11) or paragraph 17 of Schedule 2 to the Jobseeker's Allowance Regulations].]

(4) [¹⁷ Except where the relevant benefit is state pension credit,] Where a payment is being made under a policy of insurance taken out by a beneficiary to insure against the risk of his being unable to maintain repayments of mortgage interest to a qualifying lender, then the amount of any relevant benefits payable to that lender shall be reduced by a sum equivalent to so much of the amount payable under the policy of insurance as represents payments in respect of mortgage interest.

(5) [⁹. . .]
(6) [⁹. . .]
(7) [⁵. . .]

(8) Where the amount of any relevant benefits to which a relevant beneficiary is entitled is less than the sum which would, but for this sub-paragraph, have been the specified part, then the specified part shall be the amount of any relevant benefits to which the relevant beneficiary is entitled less 10p.

[¹⁵ (9) In the case of a person to whom regulation 6(5) of the Income Support Regulations applies, no part of any relevant benefit shall be paid directly by the Secretary of State to a qualifying lender.]

[¹⁷ (10) In sub-paragraph (1), the relevant benefits do not include in the case of state pension credit so much of any additional amount which is applicable in the claimant's case under Schedule II to the State Pension Credit Regulations (housing costs) in respect of a period before the decision awarding state pension credit was made.]

Direct payment: more than one loan

4.—(1) This paragraph applies where the borrower is liable to pay mortgage interest in respect of two or more different loans.

[⁵(2) Subject to the following provisions of this paragraph, the Secretary of State shall pay to the qualifying lender or, if there is more than one qualifying lender, to each qualifying lender—
   (a) a sum equal to the mortgage interest determined by reference to paragraph 12 of Schedule 3 to the Income Support Regulations [⁸or, as the case may be, paragraph 11 of Schedule 2 to the Jobseeker's Allowance Regulations] (standard rate) in respect of each loan made by that lender, plus

(SI 1987/1968, Sch.9A) (as amended)

    (b) any amount payable in accordance with paragraph 7 of Schedule 3 to the Income Support Regulations (transitional protection) attributable to the particular loan;
    [⁹. . .]
    (c) any additional amount attributable to a particular loan which may, under paragraph 3(5), have been taken into account in calculating the specified part.]

(3) If, by virtue of deductions made under either paragraph 3(2) or 3(3), the specified part is less than the amount payable by the borrower in respect of mortgage interest, then the sum payable under sub-paragraph (2)(a) shall be minus such proportion of the sum subtracted under those sub-paragraphs as is attributable to the particular loan.

(4) Paragraph 3(4) shall apply to reduce the amount payable to a qualifying lender mentioned in sub-paragraph (2) above as it applies to reduce the amount of any relevant benefits payable to a qualifying lender under paragraph 3.

(5) Where the specified part is the part referred to in paragraph 3(8), the Secretary of State shall pay the specified part directly to the qualifying lenders to whom mortgage interest is payable by the borrower in order of the priority of mortgages or (in Scotland) in accordance with the preference in ranking of heritable securities.

Relevant benefits
    5. [⁷. . .]   2.229

Time and manner of payments
    6. Payments to qualifying lenders under regulation 34A and this Schedule shall be made in arrears at intervals of 4 weeks.   2.230

Fees payable by qualifying lenders
    7. For the purposes of defraying the expenses of the Secretary of State in administering the making of payments under regulation 34A and this Schedule a qualifying lender shall pay to the Secretary of State a fee of [¹⁷. . . [²⁴ £0.47]] in respect of each payment made under regulation 34A and this Schedule.   2.231

Qualifying lenders
    8. The following bodies and persons shall be qualifying lenders—   2.232
    (a) the Housing Corporation;
    (b) Housing for Wales;
    (c) [²² Communities Scotland]
    (d) the Development Board for Rural Wales; and
    (e) any body incorporated under the Companies Act 1985 whose main objects include the making of loans secured by a mortgage of or a charge over land or (in Scotland) by a heritable security.

Election not to be regarded as a qualifying lender
    9.—(1) A body which, or a person who, would otherwise be a qualifying lender may elect not to be regarded as such for the purposes of these Regulations by giving notice of election under this paragraph to the Secretary of State in accordance with sub-paragraphs (2) and (3).   2.233

(2) Subject to sub-paragraph (3), notice of election shall be given in writing—
    (a) in the case of the financial year 1992 to 1993, before 23rd May 1992 and shall take effect on that date; and
    (b) in the case of any other financial year, before 1st February in the preceding year and shall take effect on 1st April following the giving of the notice.

(3) A body which, or a person who, becomes a qualifying lender during a financial year and who wishes to elect not to be regarded as such for the purposes of these Regulations shall give notice of election in writing within a period of six weeks from the date on which the person or body becomes a qualifying lender.

(4) Regulation 34A shall not apply to a body which, or a person who, becomes a qualifying lender during a financial year for a period of six weeks from the date on which the person or body became a qualifying lender unless, either before the start of that period or at any time during that period, the person or body notifies the Secretary of State in writing that this sub-paragraph should not apply.

The Social Security (Claims and Payments) Regulations 1987

(5) A body which, or a person who, has made an election under this paragraph may revoke that election by giving notice in writing to the Secretary of State before 1st February in any financial year and the revocation shall take effect on the 1st April following the giving of the notice.

(6) Where a notice under this paragraph is sent by post it shall be treated as having been given on the day it was posted.

Provision of information

2.234   10.—(1) A qualifying lender shall provide the Secretary of State with information relating to—
(a) the mortgage interest payable by a borrower;
(b) the amount of the loan;
(c) the purpose for which the loan is made;
(d) the amount outstanding on the loan on which the mortgage interest is payable;
(e) any change in the amount of interest payable by the borrower;
at the times specified in sub-paragraphs (2) and (3).

[^{17} (2) Subject to sub-paragraph (4), the information referred to in heads (a), (b), (c) and (d) of sub-paragraph (1) shall be provided at the request of the Secretary of State when a claim for—
(a) income support or income-based jobseeker's allowance is made and a sum in respect of mortgage interest is to be brought into account in determining the applicable amount; or
(b) state pension credit is made and a sum in respect of housing costs is applicable in the claimant's case in accordance with regulation 6(6)(c) of the State Pension Credit Regulations.]

(3) [^{12}Subject to sub-paragraph (4),] the information referred to in heads (d) and (e) of sub-paragraph (1) shall be provided at the request of the Secretary of State—
(a) when a claim for income support [^{17} state pension credit] [^{8}or income-based jobseeker's allowance] ceases to be paid to a relevant beneficiary; and
(b) once every 12 months notwithstanding that, in relation to head (d), the information may already have been provided during the period of 12 months preceding the date of the Secretary of State's request.

[^{12}(4) Where a claimant or his partner is a person to whom either paragraph 1A of Schedule 3 to the Income Support (General) Regulations 1987 (housing costs) or paragraph 1A of Schedule 2 to the Jobseeker's Allowance Regulations 1996 (housing costs) refers, the information to which sub-paragraphs (2) and (3)(b) refer shall be provided at the request of the Secretary of State on the anniversary of the date on which the housing costs in respect of mortgage interest were first brought into account in determining the applicable amount of the person concerned.]

Recovery of sums wrongly paid

2.235   11.—(1) Where sums have been paid to a qualifying lender under regulation 34A which ought not to have been paid for one or both of the reasons mentioned in sub-paragraph (2) of this paragraph, the qualifying lender shall, at the request of the Secretary of State, repay the sum overpaid.

(2) The reasons referred to in sub-paragraph (1) of this paragraph are—
(a) that—
    (i) the rate at which the borrower pays mortgage interest has been reduced [^{5} or the rate [^{18} determined in accordance with] paragraph 12 of Schedule 3 to the Income Support Regulations [^{8}or, as the case may be, paragraph 11 of Schedule 2 to the Jobseeker's Allowance Regulations] (standard rate) has been reduced] or the amount outstanding on the loan has been reduced, and
    (ii) as a result of this reduction the applicable amount of the relevant beneficiary has also been reduced, but
    (iii) no corresponding reduction was made to the specified part; or
(b) subject to paragraph (3), that the relevant beneficiary has ceased to be entitled to any relevant benefits.

(3) A qualifying lender shall only repay sums which ought not to have been paid for the reason mentioned in sub-paragraph (2)(b) of this paragraph if the Secretary of State has requested that lender to repay the sums within a period of 4 weeks starting with the last day on which the relevant beneficiary was entitled to any relevant benefits.]

(SI 1987/1968, Sch.9A) (as amended)

AMENDMENTS

1. The Social Security (Claims and Payments) Amendment Regulations 1992 (SI 1992/1026), reg.6 and Sch. (May 25, 1992).
2. The Social Security (Claims and Payments) Amendment (No.3) Regulations 1993 (SI 1993/2113), reg.3 (September 27, 1993).
3. The Social Security (Claims and Payments) Amendment (No.3) Regulations 1994 (SI 1994/2944), reg.2 (April 1, 1995).
4. The Social Security (Claims and Payments) Amendment (No.2) Regulations 1994 (SI 1994/2943), reg.16 (April 13, 1995).
5. The Social Security (Income Support and Claims and Payments) Amendment Regulations 1995 (SI 1995/1613), reg.3 and Sch.2 (October 2, 1995).
6. The Social Security (Claims and Payments) Amendment (No.2) Amendment Regulations 1996 (SI 1996/2988), reg.2 (April 1, 1997).
7. The Social Security (Claims and Payments etc.) Amendment Regulations 1996 (SI 1996/672), reg.2(8) (April 4, 1996).
8. The Social Security (Claims and Payments) (Jobseeker's Allowance Consequential Amendments) Regulations 1996 (SI 1996/1460), reg.2(27) (October 7, 1996).
9. The Social Security and Child Support (Miscellaneous Amendments) Regulations 1997 (SI 1997/827), reg.7(3) (April 7, 1997).
10. The Social Security (Child Maintenance Bonus) Regulations 1996 (SI 1996/3195), reg.16(2) (April 7, 1997).
11. The Social Security (Miscellaneous Amendments) Regulations 1997 (SI 1997/454), reg.8(10) (April 6, 1997).
12. The Social Security (Miscellaneous Amendments) (No.4) Regulations 1997 (SI 1997/2305), reg.5 (October 22, 1997).
13. The Social Security (Claims and Payments) Amendment Regulations 2002 (SI 2002/355), reg.2 (April 1, 2002).
14. The Social Security (Claims and Payments) Amendment Regulations 2000 (SI 2000/1366), reg.2, (June 14, 2000).
15. The Social security (Miscellaneous Amendments) Regulations 2001 (SI 2001/488), reg.11 (April 9, 2001).
16. Social Security (Claims and Payments and Miscellaneous Amendments) (No.2) Regulations 2002 (SI 2002/2441), reg.13 (October 23, 2002).
17. The Social Security (Claims and Payments) Amendment Regulations 2004 (SI 2004/576), (April 12, 2004 or first benefit pay day thereafter).
18. Social Security (Housing Costs Amendments) Regulations 2004 (SI 2004/2825), reg.3(b), (November 28, 2004).
19. Social Security (Claims and Payments) Amendment (No.2) Regulations 2005 (SI 2005/777), reg.4 (April 11, 2005).
20. The Social Security (Claims and Payments) Regulations 2006 (SI 2006/551) (April 1, 2006).
21. The Social Security (Housing Costs Amendments) Regulations 2004 (SI 2004/2825) (November 28, 2005).
22. The Social Security (Miscellaneous Amendments) (No.4) Regulations 2006, (SI 2006/2378) (October 1, 2006).
23. The State Pension Credit (Consequential, Transitional and Miscellaneous Provisions) (No. 2) Regulations 2002 (SI 2002/3197) (April 7, 2003).
24. The Social Security (Claims and Payments) Amendment Regulations 2007 (SI 2007/541) (April 1, 2007).

DEFINITIONS

"instrument for benefit payment"—see reg.2(1).
"jobseeker's allowance"—*ibid*.
"mortgage interest"—see Administration Act, s.15A(4).

The Social Security (Claims and Payments) Regulations 1987

"qualifying lender"—see Administration Act, s.15A(3).
"relevant beneficiary"—see Administration Act, s.15A(1).

GENERAL NOTE

2.236 Paragraph 11 only authorises recovery of overpaid interest in the circumstances specified in sub-paras (2) and (3).

In previous editions of this book it was suggested that it was not clear who decides that the interest has been overpaid, and that it was certainly arguable that this is the type of decision that should be made by an adjudication officer, now decision maker. *CIS 288/1994* and *CSIS 98/1994* hold that any decision regarding the recovery of any overpayment of mortgage interest from a qualifying lender is a matter for the Secretary of State, not the adjudication officer. The mortgage interest payment provisions are outside the scope of s.71 of the Administration Act (*CSIS 98/1994*). But in *CIS 5206/1995* the Commissioner reaches the opposite conclusion. He points out that under s.20 of the Administration Act all questions arising on claims or awards of benefit are to be determined by adjudication officers, unless reserved to the Secretary of State (or other bodies). The question of whether the Secretary of State was *entitled to* recover a payment under para.11 (which required consideration of whether the conditions in para.11(2) were satisfied and also required calculation of the amount of the overpayment) was not reserved by para.11 (or any other provision) to the Secretary of State. It therefore fell to be determined by an adjudication officer. Once it had been determined that an overpayment was recoverable, the Secretary of State then had the discretion as to whether to request the lender to repay the sum to him. The process of adjudication was thus the same as that under s.71 of the Act, even though the circumstances in which recovery could be sought were different. Furthermore, where any question of recovery under para.11 arose, the claimant's award must first be reviewed and revised under s.25 (as had been accepted by the Court of Appeal in *Golding*, see below). If not, the Secretary of State would be bound to pay any overpayment recovered from the lender to the claimant, since the money recovered represented part of the benefit due to the claimant. There is thus a conflict between these decisions but *CIS 5206/1995* is cogently argued and it is suggested that it is to be preferred.

Note also that under para.3(1) the amount that will be paid to the qualifying lender by the Secretary of State under reg.34A (the "specified part") is defined by reference to the amount of mortgage interest met in the income support or JSA assessment. Thus, if the claimant disputes the amount that has been awarded for mortgage interest, or maintains that there are no grounds for reviewing the amount of an existing award, he will have a right of appeal to a tribunal in the normal way.

In *R. v Secretary of State for Social Security Ex p. Golding, The Times*, March 15, 1996, there had been an overpayment of mortgage interest because the claimant's interest rate had reduced. Recovery of the overpayment was implemented by withholding current payments due to the claimant's building society. Brooke J. accepted the claimant's contention that the effect of sub-para.(2)(iii) was that the Secretary of State could only recover an overpayment where an adjudication officer had decided under sub-para.(2)(ii) that a claimant's applicable amount should be reduced but the amount paid to the lender had not changed. Thus the Secretary of State could not recover the overpayment from the lender under para.11 in respect of the period before the adjudication officer's decision. Paragraph 11 only applied to overpayments made after that decision (i.e. as a result of the decision not being implemented). The result of this decision would have been that in effect recovery of any overpayment would be governed by s.71 of the Administration Act (since it would normally be the period between the reduction in the interest rate and the adjudication officer's review decision that would be in issue, assuming the adjudication officer's decision was implemented promptly).

(SI 1987/1968, Sch.9A) (as amended)

The Court of Appeal on July 1, 1996 reversed Brooke J.'s decision. It was held that in sub-para.(2)(ii), the applicable amount means the amount as determined by the adjudication officer's assessment current at the date when the question is asked. Thus, once there had been a review with retrospective effect of Mr Golding's entitlement to take account of the reduction in interest rates, there was a reduction for that retrospective period in his applicable amount, so that sub-para.(2)(ii) was met. Sub-paragraph (2)(iii) was also met, because the "specified part" actually paid to the lender in that past period could not be reduced. Therefore the overpayment was repayable by the lender. The Court of Appeal rejected Mr Golding's argument that the condition in sub-para. (1) that the sums "ought not to have been paid" was not met, because the sums were paid under the current adjudication officer's assessment. The provisions were to be interpreted so as to be consistent with the clear statutory intention of dealing with the built-in problem under the direct payment scheme of annual retrospective notification of interest rate changes under para.10. Note the circumstances in which there can be no review on a reduction in interest rates where the claimant's liability remains constant (Adjudication Regulations, reg.63(7)).

The Court of Appeal did express concern over the method of recovery adopted by the Secretary of State, who had not asked the lender to repay the overpayment, but had made deductions from the amounts of mortgage interest currently being paid direct to the lender. The concern was that that might put the claimant into arrears. The Secretary of State accepted that he could only use the set-off method if it did not adversely affect the position of the claimant. The Court of Appeal considered that that would only be so if each deduction was accompanied in the lender's accounting system by a corresponding credit to the claimant's interest account. The Department has apparently carried out a review of the arrangements for recovery of overpayments from lenders.

It should be noted that para.11 only applies where the overpayment has occurred for the reasons specified in sub-para.(2) and not, for example, where it is due to an incorrect amount of capital being taken into account.

Until April 1997, deductions could be made from a claimant's benefit in respect of mortgage interest arrears under para.3(5) (the April 1996 rate was £2.40). This is no longer possible if the lender is covered by the mortgage payments direct scheme. *CIS 15146/1996* holds that it was for the adjudication officer to decide whether such deductions were to be made and that a decision to alter the amount of a deduction had to be made by way of review, as this was not one of the up-rating changes which took effect automatically under s.159 of the Act without the need for a review decision. Furthermore, it was necessary to investigate whether there were in fact mortgage arrears, as the existence of arrears had to be proved in order to justify the deduction (see *R(IS)14/95* which had adopted the same approach in relation to deductions under para.5 of Sch.9). Adjudication officers and tribunals were not limited to determining whether there was sufficient income support in payment to sustain the direct payment.

SCHEDULE 9B

DEDUCTIONS FROM BENEFIT IN RESPECT OF CHILD SUPPORT MAINTENANCE AND PAYMENT TO PERSONS WITH CARE

Interpretation
1. In this Schedule—

"the Act" means the Child Support Act 1991,
"beneficiary" means a person who has been awarded a specified benefit and includes each member of a joint-claim couple awarded joint-claim jobseeker's allowance,
"maintenance" [², except in paragraph 3,] means maintenance which a non-resident parent is liable to pay under the Act at a flat rate of child support maintenance (or would be so liable but for a variation having been agreed to), and that rate applies (or would have

2.237

The Social Security (Claims and Payments) Regulations 1987

applied) because he falls within paragraph 4(1)(b) or (c) or 4(2) of Schedule 1 to the Act, and includes such maintenance payable at a transitional rate in accordance with Regulations made under section 29(3)(a) of the Child Support, Pensions and Social Security Act 2000,

"specified benefit" means either a benefit, pension or allowance mentioned in section 5(2) of the Social Security Administration Act 1992 and which is prescribed for the purpose of paragraph 4(1)(b) or (c) of Schedule 1 to the Act or a war disablement pension or a war widow's pension within the meaning of section 150(2) of the Social Security Contributions and Benefits Act 1992.

Deductions

2.238   **2.**—(1) Subject to paragraphs 5 and 6, the Secretary of State may deduct from a specified benefit awarded to a beneficiary, an amount equal to the amount of maintenance which is payable by the beneficiary (or in the case of income support [³, state pension credit] or income-based jobseeker's allowance, payable either by the beneficiary or his partner) and pay the amount deducted to or among the person or persons with care in discharge (in whole or in part) of the liability to pay maintenance.

(2) A deduction may only be made from one of the specified benefits in any one week.

(3) No deduction may be made unless the amount of the relevant specified benefit is not less than the total of the amounts to be deducted under this Schedule plus 10 pence.

Arrears

2.239   **3.**—(1) Except where income support [³, state pension credit] or income-based jobseeker's allowance is payable to the beneficiary or his partner, the Secretary of State may deduct the sum of £1 per week from a specified benefit which the beneficiary has been awarded and, subject to sub-paragraph (2), pay the amount deducted to or among the person or persons with care in discharge (in whole or in part) of the beneficiary's liability to pay arrears of maintenance.

(2) Deductions made under sub-paragraph (1) may be retained by the Secretary of State in the circumstances set out in regulation 8 of the Child Support (Arrears, Interest and Adjustment of Maintenance Assessments) Regulations 1992.

[² (3) In sub-paragraph (1) "maintenance" means child support maintenance as defined by section 3(6) of the Act—

(a) before the amendment of the definition of such maintenance by section 1(2)(a) of the Child Support, Pensions and Social Security Act 2000;

(b) after the amendment of the definition; or

(c) both before and after the amendment of the definition,

and includes maintenance payable at a transitional rate in accordance with regulations made under section 29(3)(a) of that Act.]

Apportionment

2.240   **4.** Where maintenance is payable to more than one person with care, the amount deducted shall be apportioned between the persons with care in accordance with paragraphs 6, 7 and 8 of Schedule 1 to the Act.

Flat rate maintenance

2.241   **5.**—(1) This sub-paragraph applies where the beneficiary and his partner are each liable to pay maintenance at a flat rate in accordance with paragraph 4(2) of Schedule 1 to the Act and either of them has been awarded income support [³, state pension credit] or income-based jobseeker's allowance.

(2) Where sub-paragraph (1) applies, an amount not exceeding £5 may be deducted in respect of the sum of both partners' liability to pay maintenance, in the proportions described in regulation 4(3) of the Child Support (Maintenance Calculations and Special Cases) Regulations 2000 and shall be paid in discharge (in whole or in part) of the respective liabilities to pay maintenance.

Flat rate maintenance (polygamous marriage)

2.242   **6.**—(1) This sub-paragraph applies where two or more members of a polygamous marriage are each liable to pay maintenance at a flat rate in accordance with paragraph 4(2) of Schedule 1 to the Act and any member of the polygamous marriage has been awarded income support [³, state pension credit] or income-based jobseeker's allowance.

(2) Where sub-paragraph (1) applies, an amount not exceeding £5 may be deducted in respect of the sum of all the members' liability to pay maintenance, in the proportions described in regulation 4(3) of the Child Support (Maintenance Calculations and Special Cases) Regulations 2000 and shall be paid in discharge (in whole or in part) of the respective liabilities to pay maintenance.

(SI 1987/1968, Sch.9B) (as amended)

(3) In this paragraph "polygamous marriage" means any marriage during the subsistence of which a party to it is married to more than one person and the ceremony of marriage took place under the law of a country which permits polygamy.

Notice
7. When the Secretary of State commences making deductions, he shall notify the beneficiary in writing of the amount and frequency of the deduction and the benefit from which the deduction is made and shall give further such notice when there is a change to any of the particulars specified in the notice.

2.243

General
8. A deduction made in accordance with this Schedule is a deduction by way of recovery for the purposes of regulation 40(3) of the Income Support (General) Regulations 1987 and regulation 103(3) of the Jobseeker's Allowance Regulations 1996."

2.244

AMENDMENTS

1. The Social Security (Claims and Payments) Amendment Regulations 2001 (SI 2001/18), reg.2 (January 31, 2001).
2. Social Security (Claims and Payments) Amendment (No.2) Regulations 2002 (SI 2002/1950), reg.3 (entry into force tied to entry into force of s.43 of the Child Support Act 1991 as substituted by s.21 of the Child Support, Pensions and Social Security Act 2000: March 3, 2003 in relation to certain cases, see SI 2003/192; date to be appointed for remaining cases: see Child Support, Pensions and Social Security Act 2000, s.86(2)).
3. State Pension Credit (Consequential, Transitional and Miscellaneous Provisions) Regulations 2002, SI 2002/3019, reg.14 (April 7, 2003).

GENERAL NOTE

This schedule empowers the Secretary of State to deduct an amount in respect of certain child support maintenance liabilities from certain social security benefits where the person in receipt of the benefit is a non-resident parent. That sum is than paid to the person with the care of the child.

2.245

Regulation 3 of the amending regulations (SI 2001/18) contain a transitional provision as follows:

"No deductions shall be made under paragraph 7A or 7B of Schedule 9 to the Claims and Payments Regulations in respect of maintenance to which Schedule 9B applies."

See annotations to reg.35 for comment on the precedence to be accorded to child support payments and the relationship between Sch.9 and Sch.9B.

[¹ SCHEDULE 9ZC **Regulations 4ZC and 32ZA**

ELECTRONIC COMMUNICATION

PART 1

INTRODUCTION

Interpretation
1. In this Schedule "official computer system" means a computer system maintained by or on behalf of the Secretary of State for the sending, receiving, processing or storing of any claim, certificate, notice, information or evidence.

2.246

The Social Security (Claims and Payments) Regulations 1987

Part 2

Electronic Communication—General Provisions

Conditions for the use of electronic communication

2.247

2.—(1) The Secretary of State may use an electronic communication in connection with claims for, and awards of, carer's allowance [² attendance allowance, disability living allowance, graduated retirement benefit, retirement pension and shared additional pension.].

(2) A person other than the Secretary of State may use an electronic communication in connection with the matters referred to in sub-paragraph (1) if the conditions specified in sub-paragraphs (3) to (6) are satisfied.

(3) The first condition is that the person is for the time being permitted to use an electronic communication by an authorisation given by means of a direction of the Secretary of State.

(4) The second condition is that the person uses an approved method of—
  (a) authenticating the identity of the sender of the communication;
  (b) electronic communication;
  (c) authenticating any claim, certificate, notice, information or evidence delivered by means of an electronic communication; and
  (d) subject to sub-paragraph (7), submitting to the Secretary of State any claim, certificate, notice, information or evidence.

(5) The third condition is that any claim, certificate, notice, information or evidence sent by means of an electronic communication is in a form approved for the purpose of this Schedule.

(6) The fourth condition is that the person maintains such records in written or electronic form as may be specified in a direction given by the Secretary of State.

(7) Where the person uses any method other than the method approved by the Secretary of State, of submitting any claim, certificate, notice, information or evidence, that claim, certificate, notice, information or evidence shall be treated as not having been submitted.

(8) In this paragraph "approved" means approved by means of a direction given by the Secretary of State for the purposes of this Schedule.

Use of intermediaries

2.248

3. The Secretary of State may use intermediaries in connection with—
  (a) the delivery of any claim, certificate, notice, information or evidence by means of an electronic communication; and
  (b) the authentication or security of anything transmitted by such means,
and may require other persons to use intermediaries in connection with those matters.

Part 3

Electronic Communication—Evidental Provisions

Effect of delivering information by means of electronic communication

2.249

4.—(1) Any claim, certificate, notice, information or evidence which is delivered by means of an electronic communication shall be treated as having been delivered, in the manner or form required by any provision of these Regulations, on the day the conditions imposed—
  (a) by this Schedule; and
  (b) by or under an applicable enactment,
are satisfied.

(2) The Secretary of State may, by a direction, determine that any claim, certificate, notice, information or evidence is to be treated as delivered on a different day (whether earlier or later) from the day provided for in sub-paragraph (1).

(3) Information shall not be taken to have been delivered to an official computer system by means of an electronic communication unless it is accepted by the system to which it is delivered.

Proof of identify of sender or recipient of information

2.250

5. If it is necessary to prove, for the purpose of any legal proceedings, the identity of—
  (a) the sender of any claim, certificate, notice, information or evidence delivered by means of an electronic communication to an official computer system; or
  (b) the recipient of any such claim, certificate, notice, information or evidence delivered by means of an electronic communication from an official computer system,
the sender or recipient, as the case may be, shall be presumed to be the person whose name is recorded as such on that official computer system.

(SI 1987/1968, Sch.92C) (as amended)

Proof of delivery of information

6.—(1) If it is necessary to prove, for the purpose of any legal proceedings, that the use of an electronic communication has resulted in the delivery of any claim, certificate, notice, information or evidence this shall be presumed to have been the case where—
   (a) any such claim, certificate, notice, information or evidence has been delivered to the Secretary of State, if the delivery of that claim, certificate, notice, information or evidence has been recorded on an official computer system; or
   (b) any such certificate, notice, information or evidence has been delivered by the Secretary of State, if the delivery of that certificate, notice, information or evidence has been recorded on an official computer system.

(2) If it is necessary to prove, for the purpose of any legal proceedings, that the use of an electronic communication has resulted in the delivery of any such claim, certificate, notice, information or evidence, this shall be presumed not to be the case, if that claim, certificate, notice, information or evidence delivered to the Secretary of State has not been recorded on an official computer system.

(3) If it is necessary to prove, for the purpose of any legal proceedings, when any such claim, certificate, notice, information or evidence sent by means of an electronic communication has been received, the time and date of receipt shall be presumed to be that recorded on an official computer system.

2.251

Proof of content of information

7. If it is necessary to prove, for the purpose of any legal proceedings, the content of any claim, certificate, notice, information or evidence sent by means of an electronic communication, the content shall be presumed to be that recorded on an official computer system.]

2.252

AMENDMENTS

1. The Social Security (Electronic Communications) (Carer's Allowance) Order 2003 SI 2003/2800, reg.2 (December 1, 2003).

2. The Social Security (Electronic Communications) (Miscellaneous Benefits) Order 2005 (SI 2005/3321) (January 30, 2006).

[¹ SCHEDULE 9C   Regulations 4C and 32A

ELECTRONIC COMMUNICATION

PART 1

INTRODUCTION

Interpretation

1. In this Schedule "official computer system" means a computer system maintained by or on behalf of the Secretary of State for the–
   (a) sending or receiving of any claim, certificate, notice, information or evidence; or
   (b) processing or storing of any claim, certificate, notice, information or evidence.

2.253

PART 2

ELECTRONIC COMMUNICATION - GENERAL PROVISIONS

Conditions for the use of electronic communication

2.—(1) The Secretary of State may use an electronic communication in connection with claims for, and awards of, child benefit and elections under regulation 6A of the Social Security (Guardian's Allowances) Regulations 1975 (prescribed manner of making an election).

(2) A person other than the Secretary of State may use an electronic communication in connection with the matters referred to in sub-paragraph (1) if the conditions specified in sub-paragraphs (3) to (6) are satisfied.

(3) The first condition is that the person is for the time being permitted to use an electronic communication by an authorisation given by means of a direction of the Secretary of State.

(4) The second condition is that the person uses an approved method of–

2.254

The Social Security (Claims and Payments) Regulations 1987

(a) authenticating the identity of the sender of the communication;
(b) electronic communication;
(c) authenticating any claim, certificate, notice, information or evidence delivered by means of an electronic communication; and
(d) subject to sub-paragraph (7), submitting to the Secretary of State any claim, certificate, notice, information or evidence.

(5) The third condition is that any claim, certificate, notice, information or evidence sent by means of an electronic communication is in a form approved for the purpose of this Schedule.

(6) The fourth condition is that the person maintains such records in written or electronic form as may be specified in a direction given by the Secretary of State.

(7) Where the person uses any method other than the method approved by the Secretary of State, of submitting any claim, certificate, notice, information or evidence, that claim, certificate, notice, information or evidence shall be treated as not having been submitted.

(8) In this paragraph "approved" means approved by means of a direction given by the Secretary of State for the purposes of this Schedule.

Use of intermediaries

2.255

3. The Secretary of State may use intermediaries in connection with–
(a) the delivery of any claim, certificate, notice, information or evidence by means of an electronic communication; and
(b) the authentication or security of anything transmitted by such means, and may require other persons to use intermediaries in connection with those matters.

Part 3

Electronic Communication – Evidential Provisions

Effect of delivering information by means of electronic communication

2.256

4. —(1) Any claim, certificate, notice, information or evidence which is delivered by means of an electronic communication shall be treated as having been delivered, in the manner or form required by any provision of these Regulations, on the day the conditions imposed–
(a) by this Schedule; and
(b) by or under an applicable enactment,
are satisfied.

(2) The Secretary of State may, by a direction, determine that any claim, certificate, notice, information or evidence is to be treated as delivered on a different day (whether earlier or later) from the day provided for in sub-paragraph (1).

Proof of identity of sender or recipient of information

2.257

5. If it is necessary to prove, for the purpose of any legal proceedings, the identity of–
(a) the sender of any claim, certificate, notice, information or evidence delivered by means of an electronic communication to an official computer system; or
(b) the recipient of any such claim, certificate, notice, information or evidence delivered by means of an electronic communication from an official computer system, the sender or recipient, as the case may be, shall be presumed to be the person recorded as such on that official computer system.

Proof of delivery of information

2.258

6. —(1) If it is necessary to prove, for the purpose of any legal proceedings, that the use of an electronic communication has resulted in the delivery of any claim, certificate, notice, information or evidence this shall be presumed to have been the case where–
(a) any such claim, certificate, notice, information or evidence has been delivered to the Secretary of State, if the delivery of that claim, certificate, notice, information or evidence has been recorded on an official computer system; or
(b) any such certificate, notice, information or evidence has been delivered by the Secretary of State, if the delivery of that certificate, notice, information or evidence has been recorded on an official computer system.

(2) If it is necessary to prove, for the purpose of any legal proceedings, that the use of an electronic communication has resulted in the delivery of any such claim, certificate, notice, information or evidence, this shall be presumed not to be the case, if that claim, certificate, notice, information or evidence delivered to the Secretary of State has not been recorded on an official computer system.

(3) If it is necessary to prove, for the purpose of any legal proceedings, when any such claim, certificate, notice, information or evidence sent by means of an electronic communication has

(SI 1987/1968, Sch.9C) as amended

been received, the time of receipt shall be presumed to be that recorded on an official computer system.

Proof of content of information

7. If it is necessary to prove, for the purpose of any legal proceedings, the content of any claim, certificate, notice, information or evidence sent by means of an electronic communication, the content shall be presumed to be that recorded on an official computer system.]

2.259

AMENDMENT

1. Inserted by The Social Security (Electronic Communications) (Child Benefit) Order 2002 (SI 2002/1789) (October 28, 2002).

The Social Security (Claims and Information) Regulations 1999

(SI 1999/3108)

ARRANGEMENT OF REGULATIONS

1. Citation and commencement
2. Interpretation
3. Work-focused interview
4. Additional function of local authorities
5. Further provision as to claims
6. War pensions and child support
7. Holding information
8. Provision of information
9. Claims for Housing Benefit (*omitted*)
10. Consequential amendments to the Housing Benefit Regulations (*omitted*)
11. Claims for Council Tax Benefit (*omitted*)
12. Consequential amendments to the Council Tax Benefit Regulations (*omitted*)
13. Information
14. Purposes for which information may be used
15. Information supplied
16. Partners of claimants on jobseeker's allowance
17. Partners of claimants
18. Consequentials (*omitted*)

2.260

SCHEDULES (*OMITTED*)

The Secretary of State for Social Security, in exercise of the powers conferred upon him by sections 2C, 7A, 189(1), (4) and (5) and 1919 of the Social Security Administration Act 1992 and sections 72 and 83(1) and (4) to (8) of the Welfare Reform and Pensions Act 1999 and of all other powers enabling him in that behalf, after consultation in respect of provisions in these Regulations relating to housing benefit and council tax benefit with organisations appearing to him to be representative of the authorities concerned, by this instrument, which contains only regulations made by virtue of or consequential upon sections 58, 71 and 72 of the Welfare Reform and Pensions Act 1999 and which is made before the end of a period of 6 months beginning with the coming into force of those provisions, hereby makes the following Regulations:

505

The Social Security (Claims and Information) Regulations 1999

Citation and commencement

2.261 **1.** These Regulations may be cited as the Social Security (Claims and Information) Regulations 1999 and shall come into force on 29th November 1999.

Interpretation

2.262 **2.** In these Regulations,—
"the Act" means the Welfare Reform and Pensions Act 1999;
"the Child Support Acts" means the Child Support Act 1991 and the Child Support Act 1995;
"the Council Tax Benefit Regulations" means the Council Tax Benefit (General) Regulations 1992;
"the Housing Benefit Regulations" means the Housing Benefit (General) Regulations 1987;
"relevant authority" means a person within section 72(2) of the Act.

Work-focused interview

2.263 **3.** A work-focused interview is an interview conducted for any or all of the following purposes—
  (a) assessing a person's prospects for existing or future employment (whether paid or voluntary);
  (b) assisting or encouraging a person to enhance his prospects of such employment;
  (c) identifying activities which the person may undertake to strengthen his existing or future prospects of such employment;
  (d) identifying current or future employment or training opportunities suitable to the person's needs; and
  (e) identifying educational opportunities connected with the existing or future employment prospects or needs of the person.

Additional functions of local authorities

2.264 **4.**—(1) A local authority to whom Part I of Schedule 1 to these Regulations applies may conduct a work-focused interview with, or provide assistance to, a person to whom paragraphs (2) and (3) apply, where the interview or assistance is requested or consented to by that person.
  (2) This paragraph applies to a person who resides in a postcode district identified in Part I of Schedule 2 to these Regulations.
  (3) This paragraph applies to any person making a claim for, or entitled to, any benefit specified in paragraph (4) and applies whether or not a person has had an interview in accordance with regulations made under section 2A of the Administration Act(d).
  (4) The benefits specified in this paragraph are—
  (a) income support;
  (b) housing benefit;
  (c) council tax benefit;
  (d) widow's benefit;
  (e) bereavement benefits;

(f) incapacity benefit;
(g) severe disablement allowance;
(h) [² carer's allowance];
(i) a jobseeker's allowance;
(j) disability living allowance.

(5) For the purposes of paragraph (1), the request or consent may be made or given to—
   (a) the local authority conducting the interview or giving the assistance;
   (b) any person who, or authority which, may be specified as a designated authority for the purposes of section 2A(8) of the Administration Act; or
   (c) a person designated an employment officer for the purposes of section 9 of the Jobseekers Act 1995.

(6) For the purposes of carrying out functions under paragraph (1), a local authority may in particular—
   (a) obtain and receive information or evidence for the purpose of any work-focused interview to be conducted with that person;
   (b) arrange for the work-focused interview to be conducted by one of the following—
      (i) the Secretary of State;
      (ii) a person providing services to the Secretary of State; or
      (iii) a person providing services to, or authorised to exercise any function of, the local authority;
   (c) forward information supplied for the purpose of a work-focused interview to any person or authority conducting that interview;
   (d) take steps to identify potential employment or training opportunities for persons taking part in work-focused interviews;
   (e) [¹ . . .];
   (f) take steps to identify—
      (i) obstacles which may hinder a person in taking up employment or training opportunities;
      (ii) educational opportunities which may assist in reducing or removing such obstacles; and
   (g) record information supplied at a work-focused interview.

AMENDMENTS

1. The Social Security (Work-focused Interviews for Lone Parents) and Miscellaneous Amendments Regulations 2000 (SI 2000/1926), Sch.2 (August 14, 2000).

2. The Social Security Amendment (Carer's Allowance) Regulations 2002 (SI 2002/2497), Sch.2 (October 28, 2002).

Further provisions as to claims

Amends Claims as Payments Regulations 1987; the changes are incorporated in these regulations.

War Pensions and Child Support

6.—(1) Where a person resides in the area of an authority to which Part I or II of Schedule 1 to these Regulations refers, he may make a claim for a

The Social Security (Claims and Information) Regulations 1999

war pension, or submit an application under the Child Support Acts to any office [¹ of a relevant authority] displaying the **one** logo (whether or not that office is situated within the area of the local authority in which the person resides).

(2) Any change of circumstances arising since a claim or application was made in accordance with paragraph (1) may be reported to the office to which that claim or application was made.

(3) The areas to which this paragraph refers are those areas which are within both—
- (a) the area of a local authority identified in Part I or II of Schedule 1 to these Regulations, and
- (b) a postcode area identified in Part I or II of Schedule 2 to these Regulations.

(4) A person making a claim or application to a participating authority in accordance with paragraph (1) shall comply with any requirements for the time being in force in relation to—
- (a) claims for war pensions or applications under the Child Support Acts;
- (b) the provision of information and evidence in support of such claims or applications,

as if those requirements also applied to the participating authority.

(5) A participating authority shall forward to the Secretary of State—
- (a) any claim for a war pension or application under the Child Support Acts made in accordance with this regulation;
- (b) details of changes of circumstances reported to the authority in accordance with this regulation; and
- (c) any information or evidence—
    - (i) given to the authority by the person making a claim or application or reporting the change of circumstances; or
    - (ii) which is relevant to the claim or application or the change reported and which is held by the authority.

(6) For the purpose of this regulation, a "participating authority" means any authority or person to whom a claim or application may be made or change of circumstances reported in accordance with paragraphs (1) and (2).

Amendment

1. The Social Security (Work-focused Interviews for Lone Parents) and Miscellaneous Amendments Regulations 2000 (SI 2000/1926), Sch.2 (August 14, 2000).

Holding information

7. A relevant authority to whom information or evidence relating to social security matters is supplied or by whom such information or evidence is obtained, including information obtained under regulation 8(2), may—
- (a) make a record of that information or evidence; and
- (b) hold the information or evidence, whether as supplied or as recorded.

Provision of information

8.—(1) A relevant authority may give information or advice to any person, or to a person acting on his behalf, concerning—

(a) a claim he made, or a decision given on a claim he made, for a social security benefit or a war pension;
(b) an application he made, or a decision given on an application he made, under the Child Support Acts.

(2) For the purpose of giving information or advice in accordance with paragraph (1), a relevant authority may obtain information held by any other relevant authority.

9. Claims for Housing Benefit

Amends the Housing Benefit Regulations 2.269

10. Consequential Amendments to the Housing Benefit Regulations

Further amends the Housing Benefit Regulations 2.270

11. Claims for Council Tax Benefit

Amends the Council Tax Benefit Regulations 2.271

12. Consequential Amendments to the Council Tax Benefit Regulations

Further amends to the Council Tax Benefit Regulations 2.272

Information

13.—(1) A relevant authority which holds social security information may— 2.273
 (a) use that information—
  (i) in connection with arrangements known as the New Deal and made under section 2 of the Employment and Training Act 1973(**a**);
  (ii) for any purpose to which regulations 3, 4 and 6 of these Regulations, or any regulations inserted by these Regulations, apply; or
  (iii) for purposes connected with the employment or training of the persons to whom it relates;
 (b) supply the information—
  (i) to any other relevant authority to enable that authority to carry out a work-focused interview or any function conferred upon it by these Regulations or by regulations inserted by these Regulations;
  (ii) in so far as relevant for the purpose for which it is being provided, to any person in respect of whom the person undertaking the work-focused interview is notified has a vacancy or is about to have a vacancy in his employment or at his place of employment;
  (iii) to any person (an "employment zone provider") to whom payments are made by the Secretary of State in accordance with section 60(5)(c)(i) of the Act (special schemes for claimants for jobseeker's allowance);
  (iv) to any other relevant authority in connection with any scheme operated by, or any arrangements made by, the authority for purposes connected with employment or training;

The Social Security (Claims and Information) Regulations 1999

    (v) to any other relevant authority in connection with arrangements made under section 2 of the Employment and Training Act 1973 and known as the New Deal.

(2) An employment zone provider may supply to any other relevant authority information relating to any person participating in a scheme for which he receives a payment under section 60(5)(c)(i) of the Act where the information may be relevant to the person's benefit entitlement.

(3) Where the work-focused interview is undertaken by a relevant authority other than the authority which obtained the information, then the authority supplying the information shall, for the purposes of that interview, supply any other social security information held by them.

(4) A relevant authority which holds social security information may supply that information to any other relevant authority for the purposes of research, monitoring or evaluation in so far as it relates to any purpose specified in paragraph (5).

(5) The purposes specified in this paragraph are—
(a) work-focused interviews;
(b) any purpose for which regulations 3, 4 and 6 of these Regulations, or any regulations inserted by these Regulations, applies;
(c) any scheme or arrangements made by the Secretary of State connected with employment or training; and
(d) section 60 of the Act.

Purposes for which information may be used

2.274   **14.**—(1) The purposes for which information supplied in connection with matters referred to in paragraph (2) may be used are for—
(a) the processing of any claim for a social security benefit or a war pension or for an application for a maintenance assessment under the Child Support Act 1991;
(b) the consideration of any application for employment by a person to whom information is supplied in connection with any employment opportunity;
(c) the consideration of the training needs of the person who supplied the information;
(d) any purpose for which a work-focused interview may be conducted;
(e) the prevention, detection, investigation or prosecution of offences relating to social security matters.

(2) The matters referred to in this paragraph are—
(a) work-focused interviews; or
(b) any other provision in or introduced by these Regulations.

Information supplied

2.275   **15.** Information supplied to a person or authority under these Regulations—
(a) may be used for the purposes of amending or supplementing information held by the person or authority to whom it is supplied; and
(b) if it is so used, may be supplied to another person or authority, and used by him or it for any purpose, to whom or for which that other information could be supplied or used.

(SI 1999/3108, reg.16)

Partners of claimants on jobseeker's allowance

16.—(1) The social security information specified in paragraph (2) may be supplied by a relevant authority to the partner of a claimant for a jobseeker's allowance where—
  (a) the allowance has been in payment to the claimant, or would have been in payment to him but for section 19 of the Jobseekers Act 1995 (circumstances in which jobseeker's allowance is not payable) for a period of six months or more;
  (b) the allowance remains in payment or would be in payment but for that section; and
  (c) the partner is being invited to attend the office of the relevant authority for purposes connected with employment or training.
  (2) The information which may be supplied is—
  (a) that jobseeker's allowance is in payment to the claimant or would be in payment to him but for section 19 of the Jobseekers Act; and
  (b) that payment has been made to the claimant or would have been so made but for section 19, for a period of at least six months.
  (3) In this regulation, "partner" has the same meaning as in the Jobseeker's Allowance Regulations 1996 by virtue of section 1(3) of those Regulations.

Partners of claimants

17.—(1) The social security information specified in paragraph (4) may be supplied by a relevant authority to the partner of a claimant for a qualifying benefit where [¹ . . .] [¹ one or more of the qualifying benefits has been payable to the claimant for at least six months.]
  (2) The qualifying benefits are—
  (a) a jobseeker's allowance;
  (b) income support;
  (c) incapacity benefit;
  (d) severe disablement allowance;
  (e) [² carer's allowance]
  (3) [¹ . . .]
  (4) The information which may be supplied is—
  (a) that a qualifying benefit is or has been payable to the claimant;
  (b) the period for which the qualifying benefit has been payable.
  (5) In this regulation, [³ "partner"] means one member of [³ a couple] of which the claimant is also a member [³, and "couple" has the same meaning as in regulation 1(3) of the Jobseeker's Allowance Regulations 1996"].

AMENDMENTS

1. The Social Security (Claims and Information and Work-focused Interviews for Lone Parents) Amendment Regulations 2001 (SI 2001/1189), reg.2 (April 23, 2001).
2. The Social Security Amendment (Carer's Allowance) Regulations 2002 (SI 2002/2497), Sch.2 (October 28, 2002).
3. The Civil Partnership (Pensions, Social Security and Child Support) (Consequential etc. Provisions) Order 2005 (SI 2005/2877) (December 5, 2005).

Consequentials

18. *Omitted.*

Social Security Commissioners (Procedure) Regulations 1999

Social Security Commissioners (Procedure) Regulations 1999

(SI 1999/1495)

Arrangement of Regulations

Part I

General Provisions

1. Citation and commencement
2. Revocation
3. Transitional provisions
4. Interpretation
5. General powers of a Commissioner.
6. Transfer of proceedings between Commissioners
7. Delegation of functions to authorised officers
8. Manner of and time for service of notices, etc.
8A. Funding of legal services

Part II

Applications For Leave to Appeal, Appeals and References

9. Application to a Commissioner for leave to appeal
10. Notice of application to a Commissioner for leave to appeal
11. Determination of applications.
12. Notice of appeal
13. Time limit for appealing after leave obtained
14. References under the Forfeiture Act 1982.
15. Further provisions relating to references under the Forfeiture Act 1982
16. Acknowledgement of a notice of appeal or a reference and notification to each respondent

Part III

Procedure

17. Represenation
18. Respondent's written observations
19. Written observations in reply
20. Directions
21. Procedure on linked case notice from the Secretary of State
22. Non-disclosure of medical evidence
23. Requests for hearings
24. Hearings
25. Summoning of witnesses
26. Withdrawal of applications for leave to appeal, appeals and references
27. Irregularities

(SI 1999/1495)

Part IV

Decisions

28. Determinations and decisions of a Commissioner
29. Procedure after determination of a forfeiture rule question
30. Correction of accidental errors in decisions
31. Setting aside of decisions on certain grounds
32. Provisions common to regulations 30 and 31

Part V

Applications for Leave to Appeal to the Appellate court

33. Application to a Commissioner for leave to appeal to the Appellate court

The Lord Chancellor, in exercise of the powers conferred by sections 14 to 16, 28, 79(2) and 84 of, and Schedules 4 and 5 to, the Social Security Act 1998, section 4(2) of the Forfeiture Act 1982 and of all other powers enabling him in that behalf, after consultation with the Lord Advocate and, in accordance with section 8 of the Tribunals and Inquiries Act 1992, with the Council on Tribunals, makes the following Regulations, a draft of which has, in accordance with section 80(1) of the Social Security Act 1998 been laid before and approved by resolution of each House of Parliament—

Part 1

General Provisions

Citation and commencement

1. These Regulations may be cited as the Social Security Commissioners (Procedure) Regulations 1999 and shall come into force on June 1, 1999.

2.280

Revocation

2. The following Regulations are revoked to the extent that they relate to proceedings before the Social Security Commissioners—
   (a) the Social Security Commissioners Procedure Regulations 1987;
   (b) the Social Security Commissioners Procedure (Amendment) Regulations 1992; and
   (c) the Social Security (Adjudication) and Commissioners Procedure and Child Support Commissioners (Procedure) Amendment Regulations 1992; and

2.281

Definition

"proceedings"—see reg.4(1).

Social Security Commissioners (Procedure) Regulations 1999

Transitional provisions

2.282
3.—(1) Subject to paragraphs (2) to (3), these Regulations shall apply to all proceedings before the Commissioners on or after June 1, 1999.

(2) In relation to any appeal or application for leave to appeal from any social security, disability or medical appeal tribunal constituted under Part II of the Social Security Administration Act 1992 these Regulations shall have effect with the modifications that—
- (a) "appeal tribunal" includes a reference to any such tribunal;
- (b) "chairman" includes a reference to a person authorised to deal with applications for leave to appeal under the Social Security (Adjudication) Regulations 1995;
- (c) "Secretary of State" includes a reference to an adjudication officer;
- (d) "section 14(7) of [1 the 1998 Act]" includes a reference to sections 23(6A) and 48(4A) of the Social Security Administration Act 1992, as modified by paragraph 4 of Schedule 6 to [1 the 1998 Act];
- (e) "42 days" shall be substituted for "one month" in regulations 9(2) and 13(1); and
- (f) under regulation 9 a Commissioner may for special reasons accept an application for leave to appeal even though the applicant has not sought to obtain leave to appeal from the chairman.

(3) Any transitional question arising under any application, appeal or reference in consequence of the coming into force of these Regulations shall be determined by a Commissioner who may for this purpose give such directions as he may think just, including modifying the normal requirements of these Regulations in relation to the application, appeal or reference.

AMENDMENT

1. (Social Security Commissioners (Procedure) Regulations 2001 (SI 2001/1095), reg.2 (July 2, 2001).

DEFINITIONS

"the chairman"—see reg.4(1) as modified by reg.3(2)(b).
"Commissioner"—see reg.4(1).
"proceedings"—*ibid*.

Interpretation

2.283
4.—[2(1)] In these Regulations, unless the context otherwise requires—
[4 "the 1943 Act" means the Pensions Appeal Tribunals Act 1943;]
[2 "the 1998 Act"] means the Social Security Act 1998;
[2 "the 2000 Act" means the Child Support, Pensions and Social Security Act 2000;]
[4 "appeal tribunal" means -
- (i) an appeal tribunal constituted under Chapter 1 of Part 1 of the 1998 Act; or
- (ii) a Pensions Appeal Tribunal;]

"authorised officer" means an officer authorised by the Lord Chancellor, or in Scotland by the Secretary of State, in accordance with paragraph 6 of Schedule 4 to [2 the 1998 Act] [4 or section 6D(2) of the 1943 Act];

[¹ "the Board" means the Commissioners of Inland Revenue;]
"the chairman" for the purposes of regulations 9 and 10 means—
  (i) the person who was the chairman or sole member of the appeal tri-bunal which gave the decision against which leave to appeal is being sought; or
  (ii) any other person authorised to deal with applications for leave to appeal to a Commissioner against that decision under [² section 14 of the 1998 Act [⁴, section 6A of the 1943 Act] or paragraph 8 of Schedule 7 to the 2000 Act];
[³ "child benefit" means child benefit under Part 9 of the Social Security Contributions and Benefits Act 1992;]
[⁴ "Commissioner" means the Chief Social Security Commissioner or any other Social Security Commissioner appointed under the 1998 Act, and includes a tribunal of—
  (i) three or more Commissioners constituted under section 16(7) of the 1998 Act or paragraph 10(5) of Schedule 7 to the 2000 Act; and
  (ii) two or more Commissioners constituted under section 6D(5) of the 1943 Act or section 16(7) of the 1998 Act;]
"forfeiture rule question" means any question referred to in section 4(1) or 4(1A) to 4(1H) of the Forfeiture Act 1982;
[³ "funding notice" means the notice or letter from the Legal Services Commission confirming that legal services are to be funded;
"guardian's allowance" means guardian's allowance under section 77 of the Social Security Contributions and Benefits Act 1992;
"legal aid certificate" means the certificate issued by the Scottish Legal Aid Board confirming that legal services are to be funded;]
"legally qualified" means being a solicitor or barrister, or in Scotland, a solicitor or advocate;
[³ "Legal Services Commission" means the Legal Services Commission established under section 1 of the Access to Justice Act 1999;
"live television link" means a television link or other audio and video facilities which allow a person who is not physically present at an oral hearing to see and hear proceedings and be seen and heard by all others who are present (whether physically present or otherwise);]
"month" means a calendar month;
"office" means an Office of the Social Security Commissioners;
"party" means a party to the proceedings;
[² "person affected" means, subject to paragraph (2), a person who is a person affected under regulation 3 of the Housing Benefit and Council Tax (Decisions and Appeals) Regulations 2001 provided that he is an appellant against the appeal tribunal's decision or was a party to the appeal tribunal proceedings;]
"proceedings" means any proceedings before a Commissioner, whether by way of an application for leave to appeal to, or from, a Commissioner, by way of an appeal or reference, or otherwise;
[² "relevant authority" has the same meaning as in paragraph 1(1) of Schedule 7 to the 2000 Act;]
"respondent" means—
  [² (i) any person or organisation other than the applicant, appellant or person making the reference who is one of the principal parties as defined in section 13 of the 1998 Act,

Social Security Commissioners (Procedure) Regulations 1999

(ii) any other person taking part in the proceedings in accordance with section 14 of the 1998 Act or as a person affected or as a relevant authority or at the direction or with the leave of the Commissioner,
(iii) the Secretary of State in any case where he is not otherwise a respondent and has given notice to the Commissioner of his wish to be joined as a party to the proceedings;]
[4 (iv) in the case of an application or appeal under the 1943 Act, the person with a right to appeal under section 6A(2) of that Act other than the applicant or appellant.]
[3 "Scottish Legal Aid Board" means the Scottish Legal Aid Board established under section 1 of the Legal Aid (Scotland) Act 1986;]
"summons", in relation to Scotland, corresponds to "citation" and regulation 25 shall be construed accordingly;
[1 "tax credits" means working families' tax credit and disabled person's tax credit, construing those terms in accordance with section 1(1) of the Tax Credits Act 1999.]
[2 (2) For the purpose of paragraph 8(2)(c) of Schedule 7 to the 2000 Act "person affected" shall be construed in accordance with regulation 3 of the Housing Benefit and Council Tax Benefit (Decisions and Appeals) Regulations 2001 and for the purpose of paragraph 8(3) of Schedule 7 to the 2000 Act "person affected" shall have the meaning given in paragraph (1).]
[4 (3) A Commissioner is to be known as a "Pensions Appeal Commissioner"—
(a) where an application or appeal is made to a Commissioner under the 1943 Act;
(b) in respect of the determination of a forfeiture rule question, where the relevant enactment for the purposes of section 4(5) of the Forfeiture Act 1982 is—
    (i) the Personal Injuries (Emergency Provisions) Act 1939;
    (ii) the Pensions (Navy, Army, Air Force and Mercantile Marine) Act 1939;
    (iii) the Polish Resettlement Act 1947; or
    (iv) the Armed Forces (Pensions and Compensation) Act 2004.]

AMENDMENTS

1. Social Security Commissioners (Procedure) (Amendment) Regulations 2000 (SI 2000/2854), reg.3 (November 10, 2000).
2. Social Security Commissioners (Procedure) Regulations 2001 (SI 2001/1095), reg.3 (July 2, 2001).
3. Social Security and Child Support Commissioners (Procedure) (Amendment) Regulations 2005 (SI 2005/207), reg.2(3) (February 28, 2005).
4. Social Security Commissioners (Procedure) (Amendment) Regulations 2005 (SI 2005/870), reg.2 (April 6, 2005).

GENERAL NOTE

2.284   Regulation 3(2) modifies the definitions in para.(1) in respect of appeals, and applications for leave to appeal, from decisions of the various tribunals constituted under the Social Security Administration Act 1992, which were replaced by appeal tribunals constituted under the Social Security Act 1998.

The definition of "the Board" must be read in the light of the Commissioners for Revenue and Customs Act 2005. Section 5(2)(a) vests all the functions of the former

(SI 1999/1495, reg.4)

Commissioners of Inland Revenue in the Commissioners for Her Majesty's Revenue and Customs and s.4(1) provides that the Commissioners and the officers of Revenue and Customs may together be referred to as Her Majesty's Revenue and Customs.

The definition of "tax credits" refers only to tax credits under the Tax Credits Act 1999, payment of which ceased in 2003. Procedural rules for appeals and applications in respect of tax credits under the Tax Credits Act 2002 are to be found in the Social Security Commissioners (Procedure) (Tax Credits Appeals) Regulations 2002.

General powers of a Commissioner

5.—(1) Subject to the provisions of these Regulations, a Commissioner may adopt any procedure in relation to proceedings before him.

(2) A Commissioner may—
(a) extend or abridge any time limit under these Regulations (including, subject to regulations 9(3) and 13(2), granting an extension where the time limit has expired);
(b) expedite, postpone or adjourn any proceedings.

(3) Subject to paragraph (4), a Commissioner may, on or without the application of a party, strike out any proceedings for want of prosecution or abuse of process.

(4) Before making an order under paragraph (3), the Commissioner shall send notice to the party against whom it is proposed that it should be made giving him an opportunity to make representations why it should not be made.

(5) A Commissioner may, on application by the party concerned, give leave to reinstate any proceedings which have been struck out in accordance with paragraph (3) and, on giving leave, he may give directions as to the conduct of the proceedings.

(6) Nothing in these Regulations shall affect any power which is exercisable apart from these Regulations.

DEFINITIONS

"Commissioner"—see reg.4(1).
"party"—*ibid*.
"proceedings"—*ibid*.

Transfer of proceedings between Commissioners

6. If it becomes impractical or inexpedient for a Commissioner to continue to deal with proceedings which are or have been before him, any other Commissioner may rehear or deal with those proceedings and any related matters.

DEFINITIONS

"Commissioner"—see reg.4(1).
"proceedings"—*ibid*.

Delegation of functions to authorised officers

7.—(1) The following functions of Commissioners may be exercised by legally qualified authorised officers, to be known as legal officers to the Commissioners—

(a) giving directions under regulations 8 and 20;
(b) determining requests for or directing hearings under regulation 23;
(c) summoning witnesses, and setting aside a summons made by a legal officer, under regulation 25;
(d) postponing a hearing under regulation 5;
(e) giving leave to withdraw or reinstate applications, appeals or references under regulation 26;
(f) waiving irregularities under regulation 27 in connection with any matter being dealt with by a legal officer;
(g) extending or abridging time, directing expedition, giving notices, striking out and reinstating proceedings under regulation 5.

(2) Any party may, within 14 days of being sent notice of the direction or order of a legal officer, make a written request to a Commissioner asking him to reconsider the matter and confirm or replace the direction or order with his own, but, unless ordered by a Commissioner, a request shall not stop proceedings under the direction or order.

DEFINITIONS

"authorised officer"—see reg.4(1).
"Commissioner"—*ibid.*
"party"—*ibid.*
"proceedings"—*ibid.*
"summons"—*ibid.*

Manner of and time for service of notices, etc.

8.—(1) A notice to or other document for any party shall be deemed duly served if it is—
(a) delivered to him personally; or
(b) properly addressed and sent to him by prepaid post at the address last notified by him for this purpose, or to his ordinary address; or
[¹ (ba) subject to paragraph (1A), sent by email; or]
(c) served in any other manner a Commissioner may direct.
[¹ (1A) A document may be served by email on any party if the recipient has informed the person sending the email in writing -
(a) that he is willing to accept service by email;
(b) of the email address to which the documents should be sent; and
(c) if the recipient wishes to so specify, the electronic format in which documents must be sent.]
(2) A notice to or other document for a Commissioner shall be [¹ –
(a) delivered to the office in person;
(b) sent to the office by prepaid post;
(c) sent to the office by fax; or
(d) where the office has given written permission in advance, sent to the office by email].
(3) For the purposes of any time limit, a properly addressed notice or other document sent by prepaid post, fax or email is effective from the date it is sent.

AMENDMENT

1. Social Security and Child Support Commissioners (Procedure) (Amendment) Regulations 2005 (SI 2005/207), reg.2(4) (February 28, 2005).

(SI 1999/1495, reg. 8)

DEFINITIONS

"Commissioner"—see reg.4(1).
"office"—*ibid*.
"proceedings"—*ibid*.

[¹ Funding of legal services

8A. If a party is granted funding of legal services at any time, he shall -
(a) where funding is granted by the Legal Services Commission, send a copy of the funding notice to the office;
(b) where funding is granted by the Scottish Legal Aid Board, send a copy of the legal aid certificate to the office; and
(c) notify every other party that funding has been granted.]

AMENDMENT

1. Social Security and Child Support Commissioners (Procedure) (Amendment) Regulations 2005 (SI 2005/207), reg.2(5) (February 28, 2005).

DEFINITIONS

"funding notice"—see reg.4(1).
"legal aid certificate"—*ibid*.
"Legal Services Commission"—*ibid*.
"office"—*ibid*.
"party"—*ibid*.
"Scottish Legal Aid Board"—*ibid*.

GENERAL NOTE

In his *Practice Memorandum No. 5*, the Chief Commissioner states that, where the Commissioners' office receives a copy of a funding notice or legal aid certificate, it will send a copy to all the other parties in the case and, therefore, sending a copy of a funding notice or legal aid certificate to the office will be regarded as adequate notification to the other parties.

PART II

APPLICATIONS FOR LEAVE TO APPEAL, APPEALS AND REFERENCES

Application to a Commissioner for leave to appeal

9.—(1) An application to a Commissioner for leave to appeal against the decision of an appeal tribunal may be made only where the applicant has sought to obtain leave from the chairman and leave has been refused or the application has been rejected.

(2) Subject to paragraph (3) an application to a Commissioner shall be made within one month of notice of the refusal or rejection being sent to the applicant by the appeal tribunal.

(3) A Commissioner may for special reasons accept a late application or an application where the applicant failed to seek leave from the chairman within the specified time, but did so on or before the final date.

(4) In paragraph (3) the final date means the end of a period of 13 months from the date on which the decision of the appeal tribunal or, if

later, any separate statement of the reasons for it, was sent to the applicant by the appeal tribunal.

DEFINITIONS

"appeal tribunal"—see reg.4(1).
"the chairman"—*ibid*.
"Commissioner"—*ibid*.
"final date"—see para.(4).
"month"—see reg.4(1).

GENERAL NOTE

Para.(1)

2.292 In *LA18/01–02(DLA)*, a Commissioner in Northern Ireland held that a tribunal chairman had no jurisdiction to consider an application made after "the final date" and therefore could not "reject" the application. The consequence was that the application to the Commissioner was simply invalid. She appears to have thought that, otherwise, she would have to admit the application made to her for consideration because it had been made to her within one month of what the tribunal chairman had described as a "rejection". However, it is suggested that the preferable view is that the application to the Commissioner may have been valid, because it was properly made under para.(2), but that it was bound to be rejected also by her because para.(3) implies that an application may be accepted in circumstances where the application to the tribunal chairman was not made within the specified time *only* if the application to the chairman was made on or before the "final date" and only if the Commissioner finds special reasons for accepting it. In other words, para.(3) qualifies para.(2). This is what was decided in *CS/1952/2001*. In that case, the Commissioner held that an application is "rejected" by a tribunal chairman where the chairman has no jurisdiction to accept it because the applicant has not obtained a statement of reasons and that, as the application to the chairman was made after the "final date", the Commissioner too was obliged to reject it. The difference between the two approaches is unimportant in most cases but the approach in *CS/1952/2001* makes it clearer that the Commissioner is entitled to determine any question as to whether or not the application to the chairman was in fact made on or before the final date. It may be arguable that the Commissioner could waive under reg.27 the requirement to apply first to a tribunal chairman, particularly in a case where the application to the chairman was bound to fail because, for instance, the applicant had not obtained a statement of reasons or in a case where the applicant would miss the "final date".

Para.(2)

2.293 The date the application is made is the date on which it is sent (see reg.8(3)). In *CSDLA/1207/2000*, the Commissioner said that a Commissioner "would find it difficult to accept a document as sent on a particular date simply on the say so of the claimant, his representative or the Secretary of State, particularly where the matter is critical". It is not clear what further evidence he would have required. Time may be extended under para.(3) but the mere fact that delay is only one or two days will not necessarily guarantee an extension (*CSDLA/71/1999*).

Para.(3)

2.294 If the tribunal chairman has accepted, on the ground that there are "special reasons", a late application made to him or her under reg.58(5) of the Social Security and Child Support (Decisions and Appeals) Regulations 1999, and the application to the Commissioner is made within the one month allowed by para.(2),

(SI 1999/1495, reg. 9)

it is unnecessary for the Commissioner to consider whether there were "special reasons" *(CIB/4791/2001)*. For the meaning of "special reasons", see the note to reg.58(5) of the Social Security and Child Support (Decisions and Appeals) Regulations 1999.

Para. (4)
The "final date" is the day *after* the last day allowed by reg.58(5) of the Social Security and Child Support (Decisions and Appeals) Regulations 1999 for an application to the tribunal chairman *(CIB/4791/2001)*. In *CS/1952/2001*, the claimant had not applied to the tribunal chairman for a statement of reasons. The Commissioner held that, in such a case, the 13 months runs from the date the applicant was given or sent the decision notice.

2.295

Notice of application to a Commissioner for leave to appeal

10.—(1) An application to a Commissioner for leave to appeal shall be made by notice in writing, and shall contain—
  (a) the name and address of the applicant;
  (b) the grounds on which the applicant intends to rely;
  (c) if the application is made late, the grounds for seeking late acceptance; and
  (d) an address for sending notices and other documents to the applicant.
(2) The notice in paragraph (1) shall have with it copies of—
  (a) the decision against which leave to appeal is sought;
  (b) if separate, the written statement of the appeal tribunal's reasons for it; and
  (c) the notice of refusal or rejection sent to the applicant by the appeal tribunal.
(3) Where an application for leave to appeal is made [1 by the Secretary of State, the Board or a relevant authority, the applicant] shall send each respondent a copy of the notice of application and any documents sent with it when they are sent to the Commissioner.

2.296

AMENDMENT

1. Social Security Commissioners (Procedure) Regulations 2001 (SI 2001/1095), reg.4 (July 2, 2001).

DEFINITIONS

  "appeal tribunal"—see reg.4(1).
  "the Board"—*ibid*.
  "Commissioner"—*ibid*.
  "relevant authority"—*ibid*.
  "respondent"—*ibid*.

GENERAL NOTE

Para. (1)
An application must contain the grounds. Thus, in *CSDLA/1207/2000* where the claimant's representative faxed a letter without grounds and also posted the letter with the grounds, the fax was not a valid application but the letter was.

2.297

Para. (2)
A failure to send a copy of the tribunal's statement of reasons with the notice of hearing is an irregularity. Irregularities may be waived under reg.27. If an appellant

2.298

Social Security Commissioners (Procedure) Regulations 1999

has no statement of reasons because he or she failed to apply for one within the prescribed time, the tribunal's decision cannot be challenged on the ground of inadequacy of reasons (*R(IS) 11/99*). In *CSDLA/300/2000* there was no statement of the tribunal's reasons and the applicant alleged inadequacy, endeavouring to base the argument on the decision notice. The Commissioner declined to waive the irregularity arising from the breach of reg.10(2)(b) and therefore refused even to accept the application for consideration.

Determination of application

2.299

11.—(1) The office shall send written notice to the applicant and each respondent of the determination of an application for leave to appeal to a Commissioner.

(2) Subject to a direction by a Commissioner, where a Commissioner grants leave to appeal under regulation 9—
 (a) notice of appeal shall be deemed to have been sent on the date when notice of the determination is sent to the applicant; and
 (b) the notice of application shall be deemed to be a notice of appeal sent under regulation 12.

(3) If a Commissioner grants an application for leave to appeal he may, with the consent of the applicant and each respondent, treat and determine the application as an appeal.

DEFINITIONS

"Commissioner"—reg.4(1).
"office"—*ibid*.
"respondent"—*ibid*.

Notice of appeal

2.300

12.—(1) Subject to regulation 11(2), an appeal shall be made by notice in writing and shall contain—
 (a) the name and address of the appellant;
 (b) the date on which the appellant was notified that leave to appeal had been granted;
 (c) the grounds on which the appellant intends to rely;
 (d) if the appeal is made late, the grounds for seeking late acceptance; and
 (e) an address for sending notices and other documents to the appellant.

(2) The notice in paragraph (1) shall have with it copies of—
 (a) the notice informing the appellant that leave to appeal has been granted;
 (b) the decision against which leave to appeal has been granted; and
 (c) if separate, the written statement of the appeal tribunal's reasons for it.

DEFINITION

"appeal tribunal"—see reg.4(1).

GENERAL NOTE

2.301

As reg.11(2) is invariably applied when a Commissioner grants leave, this regulation applies only where a chairman grants leave.

(SI 1999/1495, reg.13)

Time limit for appealing after leave obtained

13.—(1) Subject to paragraph (2), a notice of appeal shall not be valid unless it is sent to a Commissioner within one month of the date on which the appellant was sent written notice that leave to appeal had been granted.

(2) A Commissioner may for special reasons accept a late notice of appeal.

DEFINITIONS

"appeal"—see reg.4(1).
"Commissioner"—*ibid.*
"month"—*ibid.*

GENERAL NOTE

As reg.11(2) is invariably applied when a Commissioner grants leave, this regulation applies only where a chairman grants leave.

References under the Forfeiture Act 1982

14.—(1) For the purposes of section 4(5) of the Forfeiture Act 1982, [² the 1998 Act] shall be prescribed as a relevant enactment.

[² (2) Where a forfeiture rule question arises,—
(a) the Board in cases concerning [³ child benefit or guardian's allowance],
(b) the relevant authority, in cases concerning housing benefit or council tax benefit, or
(c) the Secretary of State in any other case,
shall refer it to the Commissioner to determine, and shall notify the person in relation to whom the question arises that such a reference has been made.]

(3) [³ A reference under this regulations or under regulation 15(2) shall] be made in writing and shall include—
(a) a statement of the question for determination by the Commissioner and the relevant facts;
(b) the grounds upon which the reference is made; and
(c) the address for sending notices and other documents to [² the Secretary of State, the Board or the relevant authority] [¹ as appropriate] and to each respondent.

AMENDMENTS

1. Social Security Commissioners (Procedure) (Amendment) Regulations 2000 (SI 2000/2854), reg.5 (November 10, 2000).
2. Social Security Commissioners (Procedure) Regulations 2001 (SI 2001/1095), reg.5 (July 2, 2001).
3. Social Security and Child Support Commissioners (Procedure) (Amendment) Regulations 2005 (SI 2005/207), reg.2(6) (February 28, 2005).

DEFINITIONS

"the 1998 Act"—see reg.4(1).
"the Board"—*ibid.*
"child benefit"—ibid.
"Commissioner"—*ibid.*

"forfeiture rule question"—*ibid.*
"guardian's allowance"—ibid.
"relevant authority"—*ibid.*
"respondent"—*ibid.*

Further provisions relating to references under the Forfeiture Act 1982

2.305 15.—(1) [¹ Section 16(7) of the 1998 Act [³, section 6D(5) of the 1943 Act] and paragraph 10(5) of Schedule 7 to the 2000 Act] (tribunal of Commissioners to deal with cases involving questions of law of special difficulty) shall apply in relation to a forfeiture rule question as it applies [¹ in relation to an appeal under [³ one of] those Acts].

[² (2) Where the party who referred the forfeiture rule question to a Commissioner under regulation 14(2)—
 (a) considers that the decision should be superseded; or
 (b) has received a written application for supersession from the person in relation to whom the decision was made,
that party shall refer the decision to a Commissioner to determine whether it should be superseded, and shall notify the person to whom the forfeiture rule question relates that the reference has been made.

(3) A Commissioner may supersede any decision on a forfeiture rule question, whether as originally made or as superseded, if—
 (a) the decision was erroneous in point of law;
 (b) the decision was made in ignorance of, or was based on a mistake as to, some material fact; or
 (c) there has been a relevant change in circumstances since the decision was made.

(4) A determination by a Commissioner under this regulation shall take effect from the date on which it is made, or from such other date as a Commissioner may direct.]

AMENDMENTS

1. Social Security Commissioners (Procedure) Regulations 2001 (SI 2001/1095), reg.6 (July 2, 2001).
2. Social Security and Child Support Commissioners (Procedure) (Amendment) Regulations 2005 (SI 2005/207), reg.2(7) (February 28, 2005).
3. Social Security Commissioners (Procedure) (Amendment) Regulations 2005 (SI 2005/870), reg.3 (April 6, 2005).

DEFINITIONS

"the 1943 Act"—see reg.4(1).
"the 1998 Act"–*ibid.*
"the 2000 Act"—*ibid.*
"Commissioner"—*ibid.*
"forfeiture rule question"—*ibid.*

Acknowledgement of a notice of appeal or a reference and notification to each respondent

2.306 16. The office shall send—
 (a) to the appellant or other person making the reference, an acknowledgement of the receipt of the notice of appeal or the reference;
 (b) to each respondent, a copy of the notice of appeal or the reference.

(SI 1999/1495, reg.16)

DEFINITIONS

"office"—see reg.4(1).
"respondent"—*ibid.*

GENERAL NOTE

In practice, whenever there is an appeal from a decision of a tribunal, the Office of the Social Security and Child Support Commissioners obtains the tribunal file from the clerk to the tribunal and a complete bundle of papers is made up from that file and copied to each party.

2.307

PART III

PROCEDURE

Representation

17. A party may conduct his case himself (with assistance from any person if he wishes) or be represented by any person whom he may appoint for the purpose.

2.308

DEFINITION

"party"—see reg.4(1).

GENERAL NOTE

Representatives other than solicitors, barristers and advocates are expected to provide written authority to act, signed by the party. In *CSDLA/2/2001*, two different representatives, each purporting to be acting on behalf of the same claimant, lodged separate applications for leave to appeal. The Commissioner said that a representative should obtain a fresh mandate from a claimant before sending an application for leave to appeal to a Commissioner, rather than relying on a mandate obtained before a tribunal hearing. Furthermore, the representative ought to discuss the case with the claimant and obtain specific instructions to apply for leave to appeal.

See also the note to reg.49(8) of the Social Security and Child Support (Decisions and Appeals) Regulations 1999.

2.309

Respondent's written observations

18.—(1) A respondent may submit to a Commissioner written observations on an appeal or reference within one month of being sent written notice of it.
 (2) Written observations shall include—
 (a) the respondent's name and address and address for sending documents;
 (b) in the case of observations on an appeal, a statement as to whether or not he opposes the appeal, and
 (c) in any case, the grounds upon which the respondent proposes to rely.
 (3) The office shall send a copy of any written observations from a respondent to every other party.

2.310

Social Security Commissioners (Procedure) Regulations 1999

[¹ (4) Where there is more than one respondent, the order of and time for written observations shall be as directed by a Commissioner under regulation 20.]

AMENDMENT

1. Social Security Commissioners (Procedure) Regulations 2001 (SI 2001/1095), reg.7 (July 2, 2001).

DEFINITIONS

"Commissioner"—see reg.4(1).
"month"—*ibid.*
"office"—*ibid.*
"party"—*ibid.*
"respondent"—*ibid.*

GENERAL NOTE

2.311   See the note to reg.19.

Written observations in reply

2.312   **19.**—(1) Any party may submit to a Commissioner written observations in reply within one month of being sent written observations under regulation 18.

(2) The office shall send a copy of any written observations in reply to every other party.

(3) Where—
   (a) written observations have been received [¹ . . .] under regulation 18; and
   (b) each of the principal parties expresses the view that the decision appealed against was erroneous in point of law,

a Commissioner may make an order under [¹ section 14(7) of the 1998 Act [², section 6A(3) of the 1943 Act] or paragraph 8(3) of Schedule 7 to the 2000 Act] setting aside the decision and may dispense with the procedure in paragraphs (1) and (2).

AMENDMENTS

1. Social Security Commissioners (Procedure) Regulations 2001 (SI 2001/1095), reg.8 (July 2, 2001).
2. Social Security Commissioners (Procedure) (Amendment) Regulations 2005 (SI 2005/870), reg.4 (April 6, 2005).

DEFINITIONS

"the 1943 Act"—see reg.4(1).
"the 1998 Act"—*ibid.*
"the 2000 Act"—*ibid.*
"Commissioner"—*ibid.*
"month"—see *ibid.*
"office"—see *ibid.*
"party"—*ibid.*
"principal parties"—see s.13(4) of the Social Security Act 1998. In relation to housing benefit and council tax benefit, see para.7(4) of Sch.7 to the Child Support, Pensions and Social Security Act 2000.

(SI 1999/1495, reg.19)

General Note

Regulations 18 and 19 make provision for sequential observations. However, where a Commissioner considering an application for leave to appeal or giving case management directions on an appeal identifies what appears to be an obvious ground for allowing an appeal, the parties may be directed under reg.20 to indicate simultaneously whether they have any objection to the tribunal's decision being set aside on that ground. If no objection is received, the Commissioner determines the appeal when the responses are received or the time for responding has expired. This shortens the time taken to determine uncontentious appeals. If an objection of substance is received, the Commissioner obtains further observations in response.

Directions

20.—(1) Where a Commissioner considers that an application, appeal or reference made to him gives insufficient particulars to enable the question at issue to be determined, he may direct the party making the application, appeal or reference, or any respondent, to furnish any further particulars which may be reasonably required.

(2) In the case of an application for leave to appeal, or an appeal from an appeal tribunal, a Commissioner may, before determining the application or appeal, direct the tribunal to submit a statement of such facts or other matters as he considers necessary for the proper determination of that application or appeal.

(3) At any stage of the proceedings, a Commissioner may, on or without an application, give any directions as he may consider necessary or desirable for the efficient despatch of the proceedings.

(4) Without prejudice to regulations 18 and 19, or to paragraph (3), a Commissioner may direct any party before him to make any written observations as may seem to him necessary to enable the question at issue to be determined.

(5) An application under paragraph (3) shall be made in writing to a Commissioner and shall set out the direction which the applicant seeks.

(6) Unless a Commissioner shall otherwise determine, the office shall send a copy of an application under paragraph (3) to every other party.

Definitions

"appeal tribunal"—see reg.4(1).
"Commissioner"—*ibid*.
"office"—*ibid*.
"party"—*ibid*.
"proceedings"—*ibid*.
"respondent"—*ibid*.

General Note

Para. (2)
A Commissioner will often obtain statements from the tribunal when an appeal is based on allegations about the conduct of a hearing before the tribunal, provided the allegation is sufficiently particularised to merit investigation at all (*R(M) 1/89*). However, statements will not be obtained if the allegation is adequately supported by other evidence, unless fairness to the members of the tribunal requires them to be afforded an opportunity to comment in a case where the allegation amounts to one of personal misconduct (*CDLA/5574/2002*).

Social Security Commissioners (Procedure) Regulations 1999

A statement obtained under para.(2) cannot amount to a statement of reasons within the terms of reg.53(4) of the Social Security and Child Support (Decisions and Appeals) Regulations 1999 and para.(2) should not be used for a "fishing expedition" where the applicant or appellant has not obtained a statement of reasons and cannot demonstrate a prima facie case that the tribunal has erred in law (*R3/02(IB)*, a decision of a Tribunal of Commissioners in Northern Ireland). Similarly, in *CH/2553/2005*, the Commissioner expressed "grave doubts as to the propriety of Commissioners directing tribunals to provide statements of reasons, save perhaps in exceptional cases", pointing out that the usual remedy for a breach of the duty to provide reasons for a decision is the setting aside of the decision and that if there is a mere power to provide a late statement of reasons, "one consideration for a legally qualified panel member will be whether he has sufficient recollection of the case and a Commissioner cannot substitute his own judgment on that issue".

Para. (3)

2.316 Case management directions are usually issued when leave to appeal is granted by a Commissioner or upon receipt of an appeal in which a tribunal chairman has granted leave to appeal. Such directions often shorten the procedure required under regs 18 and 19 (see the note to reg.19). However, case management directions may be issued at any stage of the proceedings. They commonly require submissions to be made on specific issues or for specific written or documentary evidence to be produced. For the power to issue a summons requiring attendance in person, see reg.25.

Procedure on linked case notice from the Secretary of State

2.317 **21.** Any notice from the Secretary of State [¹ or the Board] to a Commissioner under section 26 of [² the 1998 Act] (Appeal involving issues that arise on appeal in other cases) shall be sent by notice in writing signed by or on behalf of the Secretary of State [¹ or by or on behalf of the Board] and shall identify, by its file reference or the names of the parties involved, each appeal or application to which it relates.

AMENDMENTS

1. Social Security Commissioners (Procedure) (Amendment) Regulations 2000 (SI 2000/2854), reg.6 (November 10, 2000).
2. Social Security Commissioners (Procedure) Regulations 2001 (SI 2001/1095), reg.8 (July 2, 2001).

DEFINITIONS

"the 1998 Act"—see reg.4(1).
"the Board"—*ibid.*
"Commissioner"—*ibid.*
"party"—*ibid.*

Non-disclosure of medical evidence

2.318 **22.**—(1) Where, in any proceedings, there is before a Commissioner medical evidence relating to a person which has not been disclosed to that person and in the opinion of the Commissioner the disclosure to that person of that evidence would be harmful to his health, such evidence shall not be disclosed to that person.
(2) Evidence such as is mentioned in paragraph (1)—
(a) shall not be disclosed to any person acting for or representing the person to whom it relates,

(b) in a case where a claim for benefit is made by reference to the disability of a person other than the claimant and the evidence relates to that other person, shall not be disclosed to the claimant or any person acting for or representing the claimant,

unless the Commissioner considers that it is in the interests of the person to whom the evidence relates to disclose it.

(3) Non-disclosure under paragraphs (1) or (2) does not preclude the Commissioner from taking the evidence concerned into account for the purpose of the proceedings.

DEFINITIONS

"claimant"—see s.39(1) of the Social Security Act 1998.
"Commissioner"—see reg.4(1).
"proceedings"—*ibid*.

GENERAL NOTE

See the note to reg.42 of the Social Security and Child Support (Decisions and Appeals) Regulations 1999.

Requests for hearings

23.—(1) Subject to paragraphs (2), (3) and (4), a Commissioner may determine any proceedings without a hearing.

(2) Where a request for a hearing is made by any party, a Commissioner shall grant the request unless he is satisfied that the proceedings can properly be determined without a hearing.

(3) Where a Commissioner refuses a request for a hearing, he shall send written notice to the person making the request, either before or at the same time as making his determination or decision.

(4) A Commissioner may, without an application and at any stage, direct a hearing.

DEFINITIONS

"Commissioner"—see reg.4(1).
"party"—*ibid*.
"proceedings"—*ibid*.

GENERAL NOTE

The European Convention on Human Rights does not require a second tier tribunal such as a Commissioner to hold an oral hearing where there has been an opportunity to have an oral hearing before the first tier tribunal (*Hoppe v Germany* [2003] F.L.R. 384). At common law a case can be determined without an oral hearing unless that would be unfair because, for instance, oral evidence is required or the case is complex (*R. (Thompson) v Law Society* [2004] EWCA Civ 167 [2004] 1 W.L.R. 2522). The test under reg.23(2) may be slightly different but it is suggested that a Commissioner is entitled to refuse a request for an oral hearing where oral evidence would be irrelevant and there is no reason to suppose that oral argument could make any difference to the outcome.

A Commissioner who is minded to reject a claimant's appeal despite the fact that it has been supported by the Secretary of State is not bound to direct an oral hearing if no request for a hearing has been made (*Miller v Secretary of State for Work and Pensions*, 2002 G.W.D. 25–861, IH).

Hearings

24.—(1) This regulation applies to any hearing of an application, appeal or reference to which these Regulations apply.

(2) Subject to paragraph (3), the office shall give reasonable notice of the time and place of any hearing before a Commissioner.

(3) Unless all the parties concerned agree to a hearing at shorter notice, the period of notice specified under paragraph (2) shall be at least 14 days before the date of the hearing.

(4) If any party to whom notice of a hearing has been sent fails to appear at the hearing, the Commissioner may proceed with the case in that party's absence, or may give directions with a view to the determination of the case.

(5) Any hearing before a Commissioner shall be in public, unless the Commissioner for special reasons directs otherwise.

(6) Where a Commissioner holds a hearing the following persons or organisations shall be entitled to be present and be heard—

(a) the person or organisation making the application, appeal or reference;
(b) the claimant;
[4 (ba) in the case of an application or appeal under the 1943 Act, the respondent]
(c) the Secretary of State [1 or, in proceedings concerning tax credits, the Board];
(d) a trade union, employers' association or other association which would have had a right of appeal under [2 the 1998 Act];
(e) [3 . . .];
(f) a person from whom it is determined that any amount is recoverable under or by virtue of [2 sections 71, 74, 75 or 76] of the Social Security Administration Act 1992; [2 . . .]
[2 (ff) in cases concerning housing benefit or council tax benefit, the relevant authority and any person affected; and]
(g) with the leave of a Commissioner, any other person.

[3 (6A) Subject to the direction of a Commissioner -
(a) any person or organisation entitled to be present and be heard at a hearing; and
(b) any representatives of such a person or organisation,
may be present by means of a live television link.

(6B) Any provision in these Regulations which refers to a party or representative being present is satisfied if the party or representative is present by means of a live television link.]

(7) Any person entitled to be heard at a hearing may—
(a) address the Commissioner;
(b) with the leave of the Commissioner, give evidence, call witnesses and put questions directly to any other person called as a witness.

(8) Nothing in these Regulations shall prevent a member of the Council on Tribunals or of the Scottish Committee of the Council in his capacity as such from being present at a hearing before a Commissioner which is not held in public.

AMENDMENTS

1. Social Security Commissioners (Procedure) (Amendment) Regulations 2000 (SI 2000/2854), reg.7 (November 10, 2000).

2. Social Security Commissioners (Procedure) Regulations 2001 (SI 2001/1095), reg.10 (July 2, 2001).

(SI 1999/1495, reg.24)

3. Social Security and Child Support Commissioners (Procedure) (Amendment) Regulations 2005 (SI 2005/207), reg.2(8) and (9) (February 28, 2005).
4. Social Security Commissioners (Procedure) (Amendment) Regulations 2005 (SI 2005/870), reg.5 (April 6, 2005).

DEFINITIONS

"the 1943 Act"—see reg.4(1).
"the 1998 Act"—*ibid*.
"the Board"—*ibid*.
"claimant"—see s.39(1) of the Social Security Act 1998.
"Commissioner"—see reg.4(1).
"live television link"—*ibid*.
"office"—*ibid*.
"party"—*ibid*.
"person affected"—*ibid*.
"relevant authority"—*ibid*.
"tax credits"—*ibid*.

Summoning of witnesses

25.—(1) Subject to paragraph (2), a Commissioner may summon any person to attend a hearing as a witness, at such time and place as may be specified in the summons, to answer any questions or produce any documents in his custody or under his control which relate to any matter in question in the proceedings.

(2) A person shall not be required to attend in obedience to a summons under paragraph (1) unless he has been given at least 14 days' notice before the date of the hearing or, if less than 14 days, has informed the Commissioner that he accepts such notice as he has been given.

(3) Upon the application of a person summoned under this regulation, a Commissioner may set the summons aside.

(4) A Commissioner may require any witness to give evidence on oath and for this purpose an oath may be administered in due form.

2.323

DEFINITIONS

"Commissioner"—see reg.4(1).
"proceedings"—*ibid*.
"summons"—*ibid*.

GENERAL NOTE

See the note to reg.43 of the Social Security and Child Support (Decisions and Appeals) Regulations 1999.

2.324

Withdrawal of applications for leave to appeal, appeals and references

26.—(1) At any time before it is determined, an applicant may withdraw an application to a Commissioner for leave to appeal against a decision of an appeal tribunal by giving written notice to a Commissioner.

(2) At any time before the decision is made, the appellant or person making a reference to a Commissioner may withdraw his appeal or reference with the leave of a Commissioner.

2.325

(3) A Commissioner may, on application by the party concerned, give leave to reinstate any application, appeal or reference which has been withdrawn in accordance with paragraphs (1) and (2) and, on giving leave, he may make directions as to the conduct of the proceedings.

DEFINITIONS

"appeal tribunal"—see reg.4(1).
"Commissioner"—*ibid.*
"party"—*ibid.*
"proceedings"—*ibid.*

GENERAL NOTE

2.326　Note that a Commissioner's approval is not required if an application for leave to appeal is to be withdrawn, whether it is an application for leave to appeal to a Commissioner or an application for leave to appeal to the Court of Appeal or Court of Session (see reg.33(5)).

Irregularities

2.327　**27.** Any irregularity resulting from failure to comply with the requirements of these Regulations shall not by itself invalidate any proceedings, and the Commissioner, before reaching his decision, may waive the irregularity or take steps to remedy it.

DEFINITIONS

"Commissioner"—see reg.4(1).
"proceedings"—*ibid.*

PART IV

DECISIONS

Determinations and decisions of a Commissioner

2.328　**28.**—(1) The determination of a Commissioner on an application for leave to appeal shall be in writing and signed by him.

(2) The decision of a Commissioner on an appeal or reference shall be in writing and signed by him and, unless it was a decision made with the consent of the parties or an order setting aside a tribunal's decision under [¹ section 14(7) of the 1998 Act [², section 6A(3) of the 1943 Act] or paragraph 8(3) of Schedule 7 to the 2000 Act], he shall include the reasons.

(3) The office shall send a copy of the determination or decision and any reasons to each party.

(4) Without prejudice to paragraphs (2) and (3), a Commissioner may announce his determination or decision at the end of a hearing.

(SI 1999/1495, reg.28)

AMENDMENTS

1. Social Security Commissioners (Procedure) Regulations 2001 (SI 2001/1095), reg.11 (July 2, 2001).
2. Social Security Commissioners (Procedure) (Amendment) Regulations 2005 (SI 2005/870), reg.6 (April 6, 2005).

DEFINITIONS

"the 1943 Act"—see reg.4(1).
"the 1998 Act"—*ibid.*
"the 2000 Act"—*ibid.*
"Commissioner"—*ibid.*
"office"—*ibid.*
"party"—*ibid.*

GENERAL NOTE

A decision given by consent without reasons has effect in the particular proceedings in which it is made but is not binding authority in any other case. Therefore, the Secretary of State was wrong to rely upon directions given in such a decision when making a written submission to a Commissioner (*CSDLA/101/2000*).

2.329

Procedure after determination of a forfeiture rule question

29. A Commissioner who has determined a forfeiture rule question shall remit the case to the [² the Secretary of State, the Board or a relevant authority] [¹, as appropriate,] for any necessary determination on entitlement to benefit to be made in the light of the decision on the forfeiture rule question.

2.330

AMENDMENTS

1. Social Security Commissioners (Procedure) (Amendment) Regulations 2000 (SI 2000/2854), reg.8 (November 10, 2000).
2. Social Security Commissioners (Procedure) Regulations 2001 (SI 2001/1095), reg.12 (July 2, 2001).

DEFINITIONS

"the Board"—see reg.4(1).
"Commissioner"—*ibid.*
"forfeiture rule question"—*ibid.*
"relevant authority"—*ibid.*

Correction of accidental errors in decisions

30.—(1) Subject to regulations 6 and 32, the Commissioner who gave the decision may at any time correct accidental errors in any decision or record of a decision.

(2) A correction made to, or to the record of, a decision shall become part of the decision or record, and the office shall send a written notice of the correction to any party to whom notice of the decision has been sent.

2.331

DEFINITIONS

"Commissioner"—see reg.4(1).
"decision"—see reg.32(1).

"office"—see reg.4(1).
"party"—*ibid*.

Setting aside decisions on certain grounds

2.332   **31.**—(1) Subject to regulations 6 and 32, on an application made by any party, the Commissioner who gave the decision in proceedings may set it aside where it appears just to do so on the ground that—
(a) a document relating to the proceedings was not sent to, or was not received at an appropriate time by, a party or his representative or was not received at an appropriate time by the Commissioner; or
(b) a party or his representative was not present at a hearing before the Commissioner, [¹ . . .]
(c) [¹ . . .]
(2) An application under this regulation shall be made in writing to a Commissioner within one month from the date on which the office gave written notice of the decision to the party making the application.
(3) Unless the Commissioner considers that it is unnecessary for the proper determination of an application made under paragraph (1), the office shall send a copy of it to each respondent, who shall be given a reasonable opportunity to make representations on it.
(4) The office shall send each party written notice of a determination of an application to set aside a decision and the reasons for it.

AMENDMENT

1. Social Security and Child Support Commissioners (Procedure) (Amendment) Regulations 2005 (SI 2005/207), reg.2(10) (February 28, 2005).

DEFINITIONS

"Commissioner"—see reg.4(1).
"decision"—see reg.32(1).
"month"' see reg.4(1).
"office"—*ibid*.
"party"—*ibid*.
"proceedings"—*ibid*.
"respondent"—*ibid*.

GENERAL NOTE

Para.(1)

2.333   It is a general principle that final decisions of courts cannot be set aside save for the purpose of correcting accidental errors "which cannot really be disputed" and this approach was adopted in relation to Commissioners' decisions in *R(S) 3/89*. It is based on the view that it is in the interests of justice that there be finality to litigation. In *CCS/910/1999*, the Commissioner, following the analogy with the courts suggested in *R(S) 3/89*, drew a distinction between final decisions, which should be set aside only rarely, and refusals of leave to appeal which might more readily be set aside where a Commissioner recognised that he or she had overlooked a statutory provision or had based a decision on a misunderstanding of the evidence or where the applicant produced further evidence after the decision had been given which he or she could not reasonably have been expected to produce earlier. Subpara.(c), which provided for the setting aside of a decision where "there has been some other procedural irregularity or mishap" has been revoked from March 18, 2005. See the note to reg.57 of the Social Security and Child Support (Decisions and Appeals) Regulations 1999 for the possible implications.

(SI 1999/1495, reg.31)

Para. (2)
The time can be extended (see reg.5(2)(a)).

Para. (3)
A Commissioner will usually regard it as necessary to obtain the views of the other parties unless he or she is minded to dismiss the application, in which case it is likely to be unnecessary.

Provisions common to regulations 30 and 31

32.—(1) In regulations 30 and 31, the word "decision" shall include determinations of applications for leave to appeal, orders setting aside tribunal decisions under [¹ section 14(7) of the 1998 Act [², section 6A(3) of the 1943 Act] or paragraph 8(3) of Schedule 7 to the 2000 Act] and decisions on appeals and references.

(2) There shall be no appeal against a correction or a refusal to correct under regulation 30 or a determination given under regulation 31.

AMENDMENTS

1. Social Security Commissioners (Procedure) Regulations 2001 (SI 2001/1095), reg.13 (July 2, 2001).
2. Social Security Commissioners (Procedure) (Amendment) Regulations 2005 (SI 2005/870), reg.7 (April 6, 2005).

DEFINITIONS

"the 1943 Act"—see reg.4(1).
"the 1998 Act"—*ibid*.
"the 2000 Act"—*ibid*.

PART V

APPLICATIONS FOR LEAVE TO APPEAL TO THE APPELLATE COURT

Application to a Commissioner for leave to appeal to the Appellate Court

33.—(1) Subject to paragraph (2), an application to a Commissioner under [¹ section 15 of the 1998 Act [³, section 6C of the 1943 Act] or paragraph 9 of Schedule 7 to the 2000 Act] leave to appeal against a decision of a Commissioner shall be made in writing, stating the grounds of the application, within three months from the date on which the applicant was sent written notice of the decision.

[² (2) Where—
(a) any decision or record of a decision is corrected under regulation 30; or
(b) an application for a decision to be set aside under regulation 31 is refused for reasons other than that the application was made outside the period specified in regulation 31(2),
the period specified in paragraph (1) shall run from the date on which written notice of the correction or refusal of the application to set aside is sent to the applicant.

Social Security Commissioners (Procedure) Regulations 1999

(3) Regulation 33 of the Social Security (Claims and Payments) Regulations 1987 [¹, [⁴ regulation 82(2) to (6) of the Housing Benefit Regulations 2006, regulation 63(2) to (6) of the Housing Benefit (Persons who have attained the qualifying age for state pension credit) Regulations 2006, regulation 68(2) to (6) of the Council Tax Benefit Regulations 2006 and regulation 52(2) to (6) of the Council Tax Benefit (Persons who have attained the qualifying age for state pension credit) Regulations 2006]] (persons unable to act) shall apply to the right of appeal conferred by [¹ section 15 of the 1998 Act or paragraph 9 of Schedule 7 to the 2000 Act] (appeal from Commissioner on point of law) [¹ as they apply] to rights arising under the Social Security Acts generally.

[¹ (4) A person in respect of whom a forfeiture rule question arises and—
 (a) the Board, in cases concerning [² child benefit or guardian's allowance],
 (b) the relevant authority, in cases concerning housing benefit or council tax benefit, or
 (c) the Secretary of State, in any other case,
shall be authorised to apply for leave to appeal from a Commissioner's decision on a forfeiture rule question.]

(5) Regulations 26(1) and 26(3) shall apply to an application to a Commissioner for leave to appeal from a Commissioner's decision as they apply to the proceedings in that regulation.

AMENDMENTS

1. (Social Security Commissioners (Procedure) Regulations 2001 (SI 2001/1095), reg.14 (July 2, 2001).
2. Social Security and Child Support Commissioners (Procedure) (Amendment) Regulations 2005 (SI 2005/207), reg.2(11) and (12) (February 28, 2005).
3. Social Security Commissioners (Procedure) (Amendment) Regulations 2005 (SI 2005/870), reg.8 (April 6, 2005).
4. Housing Benefit and Council Tax Benefit (Consequential Provisions) Regulations 2006 (SI 2006/217), Sch.2, para.15 (March 6, 2006).

DEFINITIONS

"the 1943 Act"—see reg.4(1).
"the 1998 Act"—*ibid*.
"the 2000 Act"—*ibid*.
"Commissioner"—*ibid*.
"forfeiture rule question"—*ibid*.
"month"—*ibid*.
"proceedings"—*ibid*.
"tax credit"—*ibid*.

GENERAL NOTE

2.338   The three-month time limit may be extended by the Commissioner under reg.5(2)(a) but if the Commissioner refuses to do so, the court cannot extend the time (*White v Chief Adjudication Officer* [1986] 2 All E.R. 905 (also reported as an appendix to *R(S) 8/85*)). It would be necessary to challenge the Commissioner's refusal by way of an application for judicial review. For the criteria for granting leave to appeal and the procedure for renewing an application in the court, see the note to s.15 of the Social Security Act 1998.

(SI 1999/991)

Social Security and Child Support (Decisions and Appeals) Regulations 1999

(SI 1999/991)

Arrangement of Regulations

Part I

General

1. Citation, commencement and interpretation.
2. Service of notices or documents.

2.339

Part II

Revisions, Supersessions and Other Matters (Social Security and Child Support)

Chapter I

Revisions

3. Revision of decisions.
3A. *Omitted.*
4. Late application for a revision.
5. Date from which a decision revised under section 9 takes effect.
5A. *Omitted.*

Chapter II

Supersessions

6. Supersession of decisions.
6A. *Omitted.*
6B. *Omitted.*
7. Date from which a decision superseded under section 10 takes effect.
7A. Definitions for the purposes of regulations 3(5)(c), 6(2)(g), 7(2)(c) and (5).
7B. *Omitted.*

7C. *Omitted.*
8. Effective date for late notifications of change of circumstances.

CHAPTER III

OTHER MATTERS

9. Certificates of recoverable benefits.
9A. Correction of accidental errors.
10. Effect of a determination as to capacity for work.
11. Secretary of State to determine certain matters.
11A. Issues for decision by officers of Inland Revenue.
12. Decisions of the Secretary of State relating to industrial injuries benefits.
12A. Recrudescence of a prescribed disease.
13. Income support and social fund determinations on incomplete evidence.
14. Effect of alteration in the component rates of income support and jobseeker's allowance.
15. Jobseeker's allowance determinations on incomplete evidence.

PART III

SUSPENSION, TERMINATION AND OTHER MATTERS

CHAPTER I

SUSPENSION AND TERMINATION

16. Suspension in prescribed cases.
17. Provision of information or evidence.
18. Termination in cases of failure to furnish information or evidence.
19. Suspension and termination for failure to submit to medical examination.
20. Making of payments which have been suspended.

CHAPTER II

OTHER MATTERS

21. Decisions involving issues that arise on appeal in other cases.
22. Appeals involving issues that arise in other cases.
23. *Omitted.*
24. *Omitted.*

(SI 1999/991)

PART IV

RIGHTS OF APPEAL AND PROCEDURE FOR BRINGING APPEALS

CHAPTER I

GENERAL

General appeals matters not including child support appeals

25. Other persons with a right of appeal.
26. Decisions against which an appeal lies.
27. Decisions against which no appeal lies.
28. Notice of decision against which appeal lies.
29. Further particulars required relating to certificate of recoverable benefits appeals or applications.

General appeals matters including child support appeals

30. Appeal against a decision which has been revised.
31. Time within which an appeal is to be brought.
32. Late appeals.
33. Making of appeals and applications.
34. Death of a party to an appeal.

PART V

APPEAL TRIBUNALS FOR SOCIAL SECURITY CONTRACTING OUT OF PENSIONS, VACCINE DAMAGE AND CHILD SUPPORT

CHAPTER I

THE PANEL AND APPEAL TRIBUNALS

35. Persons appointed to the panel.
36. Composition of appeal tribunals.
37. Assignment of clerks to appeal tribunals: function of clerks.

Chapter II

Procedure in Connection with Determination and Referrals of Appeals

38. Consideration and determination of appeals and referrals.
38A. Appeals raising issues for decision by officers of Inland Revenue.
39. Choice of hearing.
40. Withdrawal of appeal or referral.
41. Medical examination required by appeal tribunal.
42. Non-disclosure of medical advice or evidence.
43. Summoning of witnesses and administration of oaths.
44. *Omitted.*
45. *Omitted.*

Chapter III

Striking Out Appeals

46. Appeals which may be struck out.
47. Reinstatement of struck out appeals.
48. *Revoked.*

Chapter IV

Oral Hearings

49. Procedure at oral hearings.
50. Manner of providing expert assistance.
51. Postponement and adjournment.
52. Physical examination at oral hearings.

Chapter V

Decisions of Appeal Tribunals and Related Matters

Appeal tribunals decisions

53. Decisions of appeal tribunals.
54. Late applications for statement of reasons of tribunal decision.
55. Record of tribunal proceedings.
56. Correction of accidental errors.
57. Setting aside decisions on certain grounds.
57A. Provisions common to regulations 56 and 57.
57AA. Service of decision notice by electronic mail.
57B. Interpretation of Chapter V.

(SI 1999/991)

Applications for leave to appeal to Commissioner (not including child support)

58. Applications for leave to appeal to a Commissioner from an appeal tribunal.
58A. Appeal to a Commissioner by a partner.

PART VI

REVOCATIONS

59. Revocations.

SCHEDULES

Schedule 1 Provisions conferring powers exercised in making these Regulations.
Schedule 2 Decisions against which no appeal lies.
Schedule 3 Qualifications of Persons Appointed to the Panel.
Schedule 3A Date from which superseding decision takes effect where a claimant is in receipt of Income Support or Jobseeker's Allowance.
Schedule 3B Date on which change of circumstances takes effect where claimant entitled to State Pension Credit.
Schedule 4 Revocations.

Whereas a draft of this Instrument was laid before Parliament in accordance with section 80(1) of the Social Security Act 1998 and approved by resolution of each House of Parliament;

Now, therefore, the Secretary of State for Social Security, in exercise of powers set out in Schedule 1 to this Instrument and of all other powers enabling him in that behalf, with the concurrence of the Lord Chancellor in so far as the Regulations are made under section 6(3) of the Social Security Act 1998, by this Instrument, which contains only regulations made by virtue of, or consequential upon, those provisions of the Social Security Act 1998 and which is made before the end of the period of six months beginning with the coming into force of those provisions, after consultation with the Council on Tribunals in accordance with section 8 of the Tribunals and Inquiries Act 1992, hereby makes the following Regulations:

PART I

GENERAL

Citation, commencement and interpretation

1.—(1) These Regulations may be cited as the Social Security and Child Support (Decisions and Appeals) Regulations 1999.

(2) These Regulations shall come into force—

2.340

(a) in so far as they relate to child support and for the purposes of this regulation and regulation 2 on 1st June, 1999;
(b) in so far as they relate to—
 (i) industrial injuries benefit, guardian's allowance and child benefit; and
 (ii) a decision made under the Pension Schemes Act 1993 by virtue of section 170(2) of that Act;
on 5th July, 1999;
(c) in so far as they relate to retirement pension, widow's benefit, incapacity benefit, severe disablement allowance and maternity allowance, on 6th September, 1999;
(d) in so far as they relate to [³ working families' tax credit and disabled person's tax credit], on 5th October, 1999;
(e) in so far as they relate to attendance allowance, disability living allowance, invalid care allowance, jobseeker's allowance, credits of contributions or earnings, home responsibilities protection and vaccine damage payments, on 18th October, 1999; and
(f) for all remaining purposes, on 29th November, 1999.

(3) In these Regulations, unless the context otherwise requires—

"the Act" means the Social Security Act 1998;

"the 1997 Act" means the Social Security (Recovery of Benefits) Act 1997;

[⁶ "the Arrears, Interest and Adjustment of Maintenance Assessments Regulations" means the Child Support (Arrears, Interest and Adjustment of Maintenance Assessments) Regulations 1992;]

[¹⁰ "assessed income period" is to be construed in accordance with sections 6 and 9 of the State Pension Credit Act;]

"the Claims and Payments Regulations" means the Social Security (Claims and Payments) Regulations 1987;

"appeal" means an appeal to an appeal tribunal;

[¹ "the Board" means the Commissioners of Inland Revenue;]

"claimant" means—
(a) any person who is a claimant for the purposes of section 191 of the Administration Act [¹⁰ section 35(1) of the Jobseekers Act or section 17(1) of the State Pension Credit Act] or any other person from whom benefit is alleged to be recoverable; and
(b) any person subject to a decision of [¹ an officer of the Board] under the Pension Schemes Act 1993;

"clerk to the appeal tribunal" means a clerk assigned to the appeal tribunal in accordance with regulation 37;

[¹⁶ "couple" means—
(a) a man and a woman who are married to each other and are members of the same household;
(b) a man and a woman who are not married to each other but are living together as husband and wife;
(c) two people of the same sex who are civil partners of each other and are members of the same household; or
(d) two people of the same sex who are not civil partners of each other but are living together as if they were single partners,
and for the purposes of paragraph (d), two people of the same sex are to be regarded as living together as if they were single partners if, but only if, they would be regarded as living together as husband and wife were they instead two people of the opposite sex.]

(SI 1999/991, reg. 1)

"the date of notification" means—
(a) the date that notification of a decision of the Secretary of State [³ or an officer of the Board] is treated as having been given or sent in accordance with regulation 2(b); or
(b) in the case of a social fund payment arising in accordance with regulations made under section 138(2) of the Contributions and Benefits Act—
  (i) the date seven days after the date on which the Secretary of State makes his decision to make a payment to a person to meet expenses for heating;
  (ii) where a person collects the instrument of payment at a post office, the date the instrument is collected;
  (iii) where an instrument of payment is sent to a post office for collection but is not collected and a replacement instrument is issued, the date on which the replacement instrument is issued; or
  (iv) where a person questions his failure to be awarded a payment for expenses for heating, the date on which the notification of the Secretary of State's decision given in response to that question is issued;
[¹⁷ "the Deferral of Retirement Pensions etc. Regulations" means the Social Security (Deferral of Retirement Pensions, Shared Additional Pension and Graduated Retirement Benefit) (Miscellaneous Provisions) Regulations 2005;]
[⁹ "designated authority" means—
(a) the Secretary of State;
(b) a person providing services to the Secretary of State;
(c) a local authority;
(d) a person providing services to, or authorised to exercise any functions of, any such authority.]
[⁴ "family" has the same meaning as in section 137 of the Contributions and Benefits Act;]
"financially qualified panel member" means a panel member who satisfies the requirements of paragraph 4 of Schedule 3;
[¹⁷ "the Graduated Retirement Benefit Regulations" means the Social Security (Graduated Retirement Benefit) Regulations 2005;]
"the Income Support Regulations" means the Income Support (General) Regulations 1987;
"the Jobseeker's Allowance Regulations" means the Jobseeker's Allowance Regulations 1996;
[⁶ "a joint-claim couple" has the same meaning as in section 1(4) of the Jobseekers Act 1995;
"a joint-claim jobseeker's allowance" has the same meaning as in section 1(4) of the Jobseekers Act 1995;]
"legally qualified panel member" means a panel member who satisfies the requirements of paragraph 1 of Schedule 3;
[⁷ "the Breach of Community Order Regulations" means the Social Security (Breach of Community Order) (Consequential Amendments) Regulations 2001;]
[⁵ "the Maintenance Calculation Procedure Regulations" means the Child Support (Maintenance Calculation Procedure) Regulations 2000;

Social Security and Child Support (Decisions and Appeals) Regs 1999

"the Maintenance Calculations and Special Cases Regulations" means the Child Support (Maintenance Calculations and Special Cases) Regulations 2000;]
"medically qualified panel member" means a panel member who satisfies the requirements of paragraph 2 of Schedule 3;
[15 . . .]
[8 "official error" means an error made by—
  (a) an officer of the Department for Work and Pensions or the Board acting as such which no person outside the Department or the Inland Revenue caused or to which no person outside the Department or the Inland Revenue materially contributed;
  (b) a person employed by a designated authority acting on behalf of the authority, which no person outside that authority caused or to which no person outside that authority materially contributed,
but excludes any error of law which is shown to have been an error by virtue of a subsequent decision of a Commissioner or the court;]
[12 "out of jurisdiction appeal" means an appeal brought against a decision which is specified in—
  (a) Schedule 2 to the Act or a decision prescribed in regulation 27 [10 *regulation 25 of the Child Benefit and Guardian's Allowance (Decisions and Appeals) Regulations 2003*] (decision against which no appeal lies); or
  (b) paragraph 6(2) of Schedule 7 to the Child Support, Pensions and Social Security Act 2000 (appeal to appeal tribunal) or a decision prescribed in regulation 16 of the Housing Benefit and Council Tax Benefit (Decisions and Appeals) Regulations 2001 (decision against which no appeal lies);]
"panel" means the panel constituted under section 6;
"panel member" means a person appointed to the panel;
"panel member with a disability qualification" means a panel member who satisfies the requirements of paragraph 5 of Schedule 3;
[8 "partner" means—
  (a) where a person is a member of [16 a couple] the other member of that couple; or
  (b) where a person is polygamously married to two or more members of his household, any such member;]
"party to the proceedings" means the Secretary of State [3 or, as the case may be, the Board or an officer of the Board,] and any other person—
  (a) who is one of the principal parties for the purposes of sections 13 and 14;
  (b) who has a right of appeal to an appeal tribunal under section 11(2) of the 1997 Act, section 20 of the Child Support Act [6 . . .] [13, section 2B(6) of the Administration Act] or section 12(2);
"President" means the President of appeal tribunals appointed under section 5;
"referral" means a referral of an application for a departure direction to an appeal tribunal under section 28D(1)(b) of the Child Support Act;
[6 except where otherwise provided "relevant person" means—
  (a) a person with care;
  (b) a non-resident parent;
  (c) a parent who is treated as a non-resident parent under regulation 8 of the Maintenance Calculations and Special Cases Regulations;

(d) a child, where the application for a maintenance calculation is made by that child under section 7 of the Child Support Act,

in respect of whom a maintenance calculation has been applied for, or has been treated as applied for under section 6(3) of that Act, or is or has been in force;]

[5 "relevant credit" means a credit of contributions or earnings resulting from a decision in accordance with regulations made under section 22(5) of the Contributions and Benefits Act;]

[10 "state pension credit" means the benefit payable under the State Pension Credit Act;

"State Pension Credit Act" means the State Pension Credit Act 2002;

"State Pension Credit Regulations" means the State Pension Credit Regulations 2002;]

[3 "tax credit" means working families' tax credit or disabled person's tax credit, construing those terms in accordance with section 1(1) of the Tax Credits Act 1999;]

[2 "the Transfer Act" means the Social Security Contributions (Transfer of Functions, etc.) Act 1999.]

[7 "the Variations Regulations" means the Child Support (Variations) Regulations 2000;]

[14 "work focused-interview" means an interview in which a person is required to take part in accordance with regulations made under section 2A or 2AA of the Administration Act;]

[1 (3A) In these Regulations as they relate to any decision made under the Pension Schemes Act 1993 by virtue of section 170(2) of that Act, any reference to the Secretary of State is to be construed as if it were a reference to an officer of the Board.]

(4) In these Regulations, unless the context otherwise requires, a reference—

(a) to a numbered section is to the section of the Act bearing that number;
(b) to a numbered Part is to the Part of these Regulations bearing that number;
(c) to a numbered regulation or Schedule is to the regulation in, or Schedule to, these Regulations bearing that number;
(d) in a regulation or Schedule to a numbered paragraph is to the paragraph in that regulation or Schedule bearing that number;
(e) in a paragraph to a lettered or numbered sub-paragraph is to the sub-paragraph in that paragraph bearing that letter or number.

AMENDMENTS

1. Social Security Contributions (Transfer of Functions, etc.) Act 1999 (Commencement No.2 and Consequential and Transitional Provisions) Order 1999 (SI 1999/1662), art.3(2) (July 5, 1999).

2. Social Security and Child Support (Decisions and Appeals) Amendment (No.3) Regulations 1999 (SI 1999/1670), reg.2(2) (July 5, 1999).

3. Tax Credits (Decisions and Appeals) (Amendment) Regulations 1999 (SI 1999/2570), regs 3 and 4 (October 5, 1999). Note that amendments made by these regulations only have effect with respect to tax credit (reg.1(2) of the Amendment Regulations).

4. Social Security and Child Support (Miscellaneous Amendments) Regulations 2000 (SI 2000/1596), reg.14 (June 19, 2000).

5. Social Security Amendment (Joint Claims) Regulations 2001 (SI 2001/518), reg.4(a) (March 19, 2001).

Social Security and Child Support (Decisions and Appeals) Regs 1999

6. Child Support (Decisions and Appeals) (Amendment) Regulations 2000 (SI 2000/3185), reg.2 (various dates as provided in reg.1(1)).
7. Social Security (Breach of Community Order) (Consequential Amendments) Regulations 2001 (SI 2001/1711), reg.2(2)(a) (October 15, 2001).
8. Social Security and Child Support (Decisions and Appeals) (Miscellaneous Amendments) Regulations 2002 (SI 2002/1379), reg.2 (May 20, 2002).
9. Social Security (Jobcentre Plus Interviews) Regulations 2002 (SI 2002/1703), Sch.2, para.6(a) (September 30, 2002).
10. State Pension Credit (Consequential, Transitional and Miscellaneous Provisions) Regulations 2002 (SI 2002/3019), reg.16 (April 7, 2003).
11. Child Benefit and Guardian's Allowance (Decisions and Appeals) Regulations 2003 (SI 2003/916), reg.36 (April 7, 2003). Note that this amendment replaces the words "regulation 27" only so far as the definition relates to child benefit and guardian's allowance. See the annotation to this definition.
12. Social Security and Child Support (Miscellaneous Amendments) Regulations 2003 (SI 2003/1050), reg.3(1) (May 5, 2003).
13. Social Security (Jobcentre Plus Interviews for Partners) Regulations 2003 (SI 2003/1886), reg.15(2) (April 12, 2004).
14. Social Security (Working Neighbourhoods) Regulations 2004 (SI 2004/959), reg.24(2) (April 26, 2004).
15. Social Security, Child Support, and Tax Credits (Decisions and Appeals) Amendment Regulations 2004 (SI 2004/3368), reg.2(2) (December 21, 2004).
16. Civil Partnership (Consequential Amendments) Regulations 2005 (SI 2005/2878), reg.8(2) (December 5, 2005).
17. Social Security (Deferral of Retirement Pensions, Shared Additional Pension and Graduated Retirement Benefit) (Miscellaneous Provisions) Regulations 2005 (SI 2005/2677), reg.9(2) (April 6, 2006).

DEFINITIONS

"appeal tribunal"—see s.39(1) of the Social Security Act 1998.
"the Child Support Act"—see s.84 of the Social Security Act 1998.
"Commissioner"—see s.39(1) of the Social Security Act 1998.
"the Contributions and Benefits Act"—see s.84 of the Social Security Act 1998.

GENERAL NOTE

Para.(3)

2.341   The definitions of "the Claims and Payments Regulations" and the "Breach of Community Order Regulations" are out of sequence due to drafting errors.

"the Board"

2.342   The definition of "the Board" must be read in the light of the Commissioners for Revenue and Customs Act 2005. Section 5(2)(a) vests all the functions of the former Commissioners of Inland Revenue in the Commissioners for Her Majesty's Revenue and Customs and s.4(1) provides that the Commissioners and the officers of Revenue and Customs may together be referred to as Her Majesty's Revenue and Customs.

"official error"

2.343   The definition of "official error" is important because it is a ground for revision under reg.3, whereas a mistake of fact or law that is not an "official error" is a ground of supersession under reg.6 and a supersession is usually effective from a later date than a revision.

Only clear and obvious mistakes amount to errors in this context and a failure to elucidate facts not disclosed by a claimant is unlikely to suffice (*R(SB) 10/91* and *R(SB) 2/93*). There is also no "official error" where a decision is made without investigating a possible discrepancy in the evidence or on incomplete evidence, partly because in such cases a claimant is likely to have contributed to any error (*R(H) 1/04*,

(SI 1999/991, reg.1)

R(H) 2/04). Adjudication officers under the pre-1998 Act system of adjudication were "officers of the Department . . . acting as such" and so an error by an adjudication officer can constitute an "official error" (*R(CS) 3/04*, not following *R(I) 5/02*).

Since it was decided in *CDLA/1707/2005* that a tribunal is entitled to substitute a revision for a supersession or refusal to supersede (see the annotation to s.12(2) of the Social Security Act 1998, above), there have been a number of new decisions on the meaning of "official error". In *CDLA/393/2006*, the Commissioner regarded the adjudication officer's reliance on the claim form without obtaining further evidence as "a failure in the proper standards of administration" but found that the claimant's mother had contributed to the error by the way in which she had completed the claim form. There was therefore no "official error". He said that "in judging what was a material contribution a common sense approach should be taken, rather than a highly refined analysis of causation" and that the way the claim form had been completed should not be seen as merely the setting for the adjudication officer's error. In *CH/687/2006*, the claimant was overpaid housing benefit because the amount of her partner's incapacity benefit changed due to the length of time he had been incapable of work. The Deputy Commissioner reviewed the cases and held that there was no official error. Although the local authority had known that the incapacity benefit in payment when the award was made was only short-term incapacity benefit, which would inevitably be replaced by a higher rate if the claimant's partner continued to be incapable of work, the local authority had been entitled to presume that any change in the rate of incapacity benefit would be reported to it. This can therefore be seen as another case where the claimant contributed to the error. In *CPC/206/2005*, the Commissioner stated that the term "official error" is not confined to errors of law but said that it "involves more than merely taking a decision that another decision-maker with the same information would not take". He considered that it would not be helpful further to explain what the term meant. However, he found an official error in the case because "no Secretary of State or decision-maker acting reasonably could have [made the decision under appeal]". That would have been an error of law and it is perhaps difficult to envisage an official error that would not be an error of law in its public law sense (see the annotation to s.14(1) of the Social Security Act 1998, above). An "official error" is not revealed merely because a decision made some time ago in the light of current medical opinion is shown to have been wrong as a result of a change in medical opinion (*CAF/857/2006*). There will merely have been a mistake of fact justifying supersession.

The concluding words of the amended definition are imprecise. It is arguable that they apply only where there was an appeal relating to the particular claimant in respect of whom the relevant error was made but it is suggested that it is more probable that the draftsman had in mind a case where the official was acting in accordance with a general Departmental misunderstanding of the law and that the case before the Commissioner or court need not have directly involved the particular claimant in respect of whom the error was made. The jurisprudential difficulties arising because Commissioners and courts only declare the law to be as it has always been and because the misunderstanding may not have been shared by anyone outside the Department are familiar ones. An order made by a Court by consent is not a "decision" for these purposes (*R(FC) 3/98*).

"out of jurisdiction appeal"

This definition is important because an "out of jurisdiction appeal" may be struck out under reg.46. However, it was observed in *CIS/1363/2005* that the definition enables a decision against which there is no appeal by virtue of Sch.2 to the Act or reg.27 of, and Sch.2 to, these Regulations to be struck out but it does not enable an appeal to be struck out on the ground that there is no right of appeal for any other reason. In that case, it was arguable that the decision made by the Secretary of State was not within the scope of s.8 of the 1998 Act and that that was the reason why no appeal lay under s.12. The Court of Appeal did not comment on this issue when allowing an appeal against the Commissioner's decision. (*Morina v Secretary of State for Work and Pensions* [2007] EWCA Civ 749).

2.344

Social Security and Child Support (Decisions and Appeals) Regs 1999

The reference to reg.25 of the 2003 Regulations replaced the reference to reg.27 in the previous version of this definition. It has been presumed that it remains effective despite the substitution of the present definition.

"party to the proceedings"

2.345   In *CA/1014/1999*, it was held that, where the Secretary of State had decided that an overpayment was recoverable from a claimant but had made no decision in respect of the claimant's appointee, the claimant's appointee was not a "party to the proceedings" against whom the tribunal could make a recoverability decision, even though the appointee had brought the proceedings on behalf of the claimant (and had an express right of appeal under reg.25). However, in *CTC/3543/2004*, the same Commissioner held that, where Her Majesty's Revenue and Customs had made a decision to the effect that a tax credit was recoverable from both the husband and the wife, the husband was a "party to the proceedings" before the tribunal even though only his wife had appealed (although acting through her husband).

Where the Secretary of State has made a decision that an overpayment is recoverable from both a claimant and the claimant's appointee, an appeal brought by the appointee should be treated as an appeal brought on behalf of both the claimant and the appointee unless it is clear that an appeal on behalf of only one of them was intended (*R(A) 2/06*). Even if an appeal by only one of them is intended, *CA/1014/1999* is clearly distinguishable and whichever has not appealed will be a "party to the proceedings", as in *CTC/3543/2004*.

Service of notices or documents

2.346   **2.** Where, by any provision of the Act [3, of the Child Support Act] or of these Regulations—

(a) any notice or other document is required to be given or sent to the clerk to the appeal tribunal or to an officer authorised by the Secretary of State [1 or to an officer of the Board], that notice or document shall be treated as having been so given or sent on the day that it is received by the clerk to the appeal tribunal or by an officer authorised by the Secretary of State [1 or by an officer of the Board], as the case may be, and

(b) any notice (including notification of a decision of the Secretary of State [2 or of an officer of the Board] or other document is required to be given or sent to any person other than the clerk to the appeal tribunal [1 or an officer] authorised by the Secretary of State [1 or an officer of the Board], as the case may be, that notice or document shall, if sent by post to that person's last known address, be treated as having been given or sent on the day that it was posted.

AMENDMENTS

1. Tax Credits (Decisions and Appeals) (Amendment) Regulations 1999 (SI 1999/2570), reg.5 (October 5, 1999). Note that amendments made by these regulations only have effect with respect to tax credit (reg.1(2) of the Amendment Regulations).

2. Tax Credits (Decisions and Appeals) (Amendment) Regulations 2000 (SI 2000/127), reg.2 (February 14, 2000). This amendment has effect with respect only to tax credit (reg.1(2) of the amending Regulations).

3. Child Support (Decisions and Appeals) (Amendment) Regulations 2000 (SI 2000/3185), reg.3 (various dates as provided by reg.1(1)).

(SI 1999/991, reg.2)

DEFINITIONS

"the Act"—see reg.1(3).
"the Board"—*ibid.*
"the Child Support Act"—see s.39(1) of the Social Security Act 1998.
"clerk to the appeal tribunal"—see reg.1(3).

GENERAL NOTE

This regulation re-enacts reg.1(3) of the Social Security (Adjudication) Regulations 1995.

In *R(IB)4/02*, it was held that, where a document had, under reg.53(4) as then in force, to be sent to a chairman or member of a tribunal rather than to a clerk, para.(a) did not apply. Paragraph (b) applied instead so that the document was sent when posted and not when it was received. Regulation 53(4) has been amended so as to reverse the effect of that decision but the reasoning still holds good when a document must be sent to anyone not mentioned in para.(a). A document may be sent by fax and is received for the purposes of reg.2(a) when it is successfully transmitted to, and received by, a fax machine, irrespective of when it is actually collected from the fax machine *(R(DLA)3/05)*. Furthermore, the faxed request for a statement of reasons in that case was received by the clerk to the appeal tribunal when received at the tribunal venue, even though the clerk did not visit that venue until some days later. The Commissioner said that it would have been different if the venue had been a casual venue, such as local authority premises. Here, it was a dedicated venue and the fax number had been given to representatives precisely to enable them to communicate with the clerk. There was nothing in any document issued with the decision notice to indicate that the request for a statement of reasons had to be addressed to a different place.

In *CG/2973/2004*, the Commissioner applied *CIB/303/1999* (see below) in holding there to have been a breach of the rules of natural justice where a tribunal had not received medical evidence sent by the claimant in support of an application for a postponement. The tribunal's decision was therefore erroneous in point of law, notwithstanding reg.2(a). Having set aside the tribunal's decision, the Commissioner considered the main issue in the case, which was whether the claimant had made a claim for benefit on a certain date. A claim is generally effective only when received. The position is therefore similar to that under reg.2(a), relating to documents to be sent to a clerk to a tribunal. The Commissioner accepted that the claimant had posted a claim form but found that it was more likely to have been lost in the post before it reached the building where it was to be opened than lost in that building or subsequently. Strictly speaking, it was therefore unnecessary for him to consider whether, the claimant having succeeded in showing that the form had been posted, the burden of proving that the letter was lost after arrival at that building rested on her or whether the burden of proving that it was lost before then rested on the Secretary of State. However, having heard full legal argument, he said that the burden would have lain on the claimant to prove delivery so that, if it had been impossible to say where the letter was more likely to have been lost, the claimant would still have failed. He preferred *CIS/306/2003* to *CSIS/48/1992* and *CIS/759/1992*. An appeal against the Commissioner's decision was dismissed (*Levy v Secretary of State for Work and Pensions* [2006] EWCA Civ 890 (reported as *R(G) 2/06)*).

The "last known address" to which documents must be sent for para.(b) to apply need not be the person's last known *residence* because the concepts are different. Moreover, the sender must consider the address to be reliable and, if he does not, should take reasonable steps to see whether a more reliable one exists *(CCS/2288/2005)*. This approach exists to aid the innocent claimant and not the one who has failed to take reasonable steps to keep the relevant authority aware of his whereabouts. Generally, an authority is entitled to rely on a claimant to inform it of any move.

Under para.(b), notices sent by officials to claimants are deemed to be given or sent when they are posted. For most purposes, they are therefore taken to have been

2.347

received. However, it is to be noted that reg.57 draws a distinction between "sent" and "received" and a decision of a tribunal may therefore be set aside if it is accepted that a notice of hearing, or a direction from the clerk to a tribunal, was not in fact received by a claimant even though it was properly posted. An application under reg.57 is generally the appropriate procedure to be followed in such a case, rather than an appeal *(R(SB) 19/83)*.

A provision similar to reg.2(b) was held to be invalid in *R. v Secretary of State for the Home Department Ex p. Saleem* [2001] 1 W.L.R. 443 but Commissioners have distinguished that case on the ground that there was no remedy in the regulations under consideration in that case where a document was not in fact received *(CCS/6302/1999* and *CIB/303/1999)*. Regulation 57 provides such a remedy here where documents relating to a hearing before a tribunal have gone astray and there are also provisions for extending the time for appealing when notices of decisions are not received.

In *R(SB) 55/83*, it was held that an application under what is now reg.57 was the *only* remedy when a tribunal heard a case in a claimant's absence because he or she did not receive notice of the hearing. However, recently Commissioners have declined to follow that decision. In *CDLA/5413/1999*, the Commissioner referred to the European Convention on Human Rights. In *CIB/303/1999*, where there had been a refusal to set aside the tribunal decision, the Commissioner applied *Ex p. Saleem* and held that the right of appeal to a Commissioner could not be ousted by the provision of an alternative remedy in a case where the other remedy had proved ineffective. There was a breach of the rules of natural justice or an analogous error of law, notwithstanding that the tribunal had not been at fault, and the claimant was entitled to have the decision set aside on appeal. The Commissioner did, however, endorse what was said in *R(SB) 19/83* and repeated that an application under what is now reg.57 was the procedure to be preferred where a party does not receive notice of a hearing.

PART II

REVISIONS, SUPERSESSIONS AND OTHER MATTERS SOCIAL SECURITY AND CHILD SUPPORT

CHAPTER I

REVISIONS

Revision of decisions

2.348   **3.**—(1) Subject to the following provisions of this regulation, any decision of the Secretary of State [³ or the Board or an officer of the Board] under section 8 or 10 ("the original decision") may be revised by him [³ or them] if—
[¹⁰(a) he or they commence action leading to revision within one month of the date of notification of the original decision; or
  (b) an application for a revision is received by the Secretary of State or the Board or an officer of the Board at the appropriate office—
    (i) subject to regulation 9A(3), within one month of the date of notification of the original decision;
    (ii) where a written statement is requested under paragraph(1)(b) of regulation 28 and is provided within the period specified in head (i), within 14 days of the expiry of that period;

(SI 1999/991, reg.3)

  (iii) where a written statement is requested under paragraph(1)(b) of regulation 28 and is provided after the period specified in head (i), within 14 days of the date on which the statement is provided; or

  (iv) within such longer period as may be allowed under regulation 4.]

(2) Where the Secretary of State [3 or the Board or an officer of the Board] requires further evidence or information from the applicant in order to consider all the issues raised by an application under paragraph (1)(b) ("the original application"), he [³ or they] shall notify the applicant that further evidence or information is required and the decision may be revised—

 (a) where the applicant provides further relevant evidence or information within one month of the date of notification or such longer period of time as the Secretary of State [³ or the Board or an officer of the Board] may allow; or

 (b) where the applicant does not provide such evidence or information within the time allowed under sub-paragraph (a), on the basis of the original application.

(3) In the case of a payment out of the social fund in respect of maternity or funeral expenses, a decision under section 8 may be revised where the application is made—

 (a) within one month of the date of notification of the decision, or if later

 (b) within the time prescribed for claiming such a payment under regulation 19 of, and Schedule 4 to, the Claims and Payments Regulations, or

 (c) within such longer period of time as may be allowed under regulation 4.

(4) In the case of a decision made under the Pension Schemes Act 1993 by virtue of section 170(2) of that Act, the decision may be revised at any time by [² an officer of the Board] where it contains an error.

[¹⁰ (4A) Where there is an appeal against an original decision (within the meaning of paragraph (1)) within the time prescribed in regulation 31, or in a case to which regulation 32 applies within the time prescribed in that regulation, but the appeal has not been determined, the original decision may be revised at any time.]

(5) A decision of the Secretary of State [³ Board or an officer of the Board] under section 8 or 10—

 (a) which arose from an official error; or

 (b) [¹ except in the case of a disability decision or an incapacity benefit decision where there has been an incapacity determination (whether before or after the decision)] where the decision was made in ignorance of, or was based upon a mistake as to, some material fact and as a result of that ignorance of or mistake as to that fact, the decision was more advantageous to the claimant than it would otherwise have been but for that ignorance or mistake,

[³ *(bb) which was made in ignorance of, or was based on a mistake as to some material fact,*]

 (c) [¹ where the decision is a disability benefit decision, or is an incapacity benefit decision where there has been an incapacity determination (whether before or after the decision), which was made in ignorance of, or was based upon a mistake as to, some material fact in relation to a disability determination embodies in or necessary to the disability benefit decision, or the incapacity determination, and—

Social Security and Child Support (Decisions and Appeals) Regs 1999

> > (i) as a result of that ignorance or mistake as to that fact the decision was more advantageous to the claimant than it would otherwise have been but for that ignorance or mistake and,
> > (ii) the Secretary of State is satisfied that at the time the decision was made the claimant or payee knew or could reasonably have been expected to know of the fact in question and that it was relevant to the decision,]
>
> may be revised at any time by the Secretary of State [³ *by the Board or an officer of the Board at any time not later than the end of the period of six years immediately following the date of the decision or, where ignorance of the material fact referred to in sub-paragraph (b) was caused by the fraudulent or negligent conduct of the claimant, not later than the end of the period of twenty years immediately following the date of the decision.*]

[¹⁰ (5A) Where—
(a) the Secretary of State or the Board or an officer of the Board, as the case may be, makes a decision under section 8 or 10, or that decision is revised under section 9, in respect of a claim or award ("decision A") and the claimant appeals against decision A;
(b) decision A is superseded or the claimant makes a further claim which is decided ("decision B") after the claimant made the appeal but before the appeal results in a decision by an appeal tribunal ("decision C"); and
(c) the Secretary of State or the Board or an officer of the board, as the case may be, would have made decision B differently if he or they had been aware of decision C at the time he or they made decision B,

decision B may be revised at any time.]

(6) A decision of the Secretary of State under section 8 or 10 that a jobseeker's allowance is not payable to a claimant for any period in accordance with section 19 [⁶ or 20A] of the Jobseekers Act may be revised at any time by the Secretary of State.

[⁵ (6A) A relevant decision within the meaning of section 2B (2) [¹³ or (2A)] of the Administration Act may be revised at any time if it contains an error.]

[⁹ (7) Where—
(a) the Secretary of State or an officer of the Board makes a decision under section 8 or 10 awarding benefit to a claimant ("the original award"); and
(b) an award of another relevant benefit or an increase in the rate of another relevant benefit is made to the claimant or a member of his family for a period which includes the date on which the original award took effect,

the Secretary of State or an officer of the Board, as the case may require, may revise the original award.]

[¹⁴ (7ZA) Where—
(a) the Secretary of State makes a decision under section 8 or 10 awarding income support or state pension credit to a claimant ("the original award");
(b) the claimant has a non-dependant within the meaning of regulation 3 of the Income Support Regulations or a person residing with him within the meaning of paragraph 1(1)(a)(ii), (b)(ii) or (c)(iii) of Schedule I to the State Pension Credit Regulations ("the non-dependant");

(c) but for the non-dependant—
  (i) a severe disability premium would be applicable to the claimant under regulation 17(1)(d) of the Income Support Regulations; or
  (ii) an additional amount would be applicable to the claimant as a severe disabled person under regulation 6(4) of the State Pension Credit Regulations; and
(d) after the original award the non-dependant is awarded benefit which—
  (i) is for a period which includes the date on which the original award took effect; and
  (ii) is such that a severe disability premium becomes applicable to the claimant under paragraph 13(3)(a) of Schedule 2 to the Income Support Regulations or an additional amount for severe disability becomes applicable to him under paragraph 2(2)(a) of Schedule I to the State Pension Credit Regulations,
the Secretary of State may revise the original award.]

[[10] (7A) Where a decision as to a claimant's entitlement to a disablement pension under section 103 of the Contributions and Benefits Act is revised by the Secretary of State, or changed on appeal, a decision of the Secretary of State as to the claimant's entitlement to reduced earnings allowance under paragraph 11 or 12 of Schedule 7 to that Act may be revised at any time provided that the revised decision is more advantageous to the claimant than the original decision.]

[[14] (7B) A decision under regulation 22A of the Income Support Regulations (reduction in applicable amount where the claimant is appealing against a decision which embodies a determination that he is not incapable of work) may be revised if the appeal is successful [[16] or lapses].

(7C) Where a person's entitlement to income support is terminated because of a determination that he is not incapable of work and [[16] the decision which embodies that determination is revised or] he subsequently appeals the decision [[16] which embodies] that determination and is entitled to income support under regulation 22A of the Income Support Regulations, the decision to terminate entitlement may be revised.]

[[15] (7D) Where—
(a) a person elects for an increase of—
  (i) a Category A or Category B retirement pension in accordance with paragraph A1 or 3C of Schedule 5 to the Contributions and Benefits Act (pension increase or lump sum where entitlement to retirement pension is deferred);
  (ii) a shared additional pension in accordance with paragraph 1 of Schedule 5A to that Act (pension increase or lump sum where entitlement to shared additional pension is deferred); or, as the case may be,
  (iii) graduated retirement benefit in accordance with paragraph 12 or 17 of Schedule 1 to the Graduated Retirement Benefit Regulations (further provisions replacing section 36(4) of the National Insurance Act 1965: increases of graduated retirement benefit and lump sums);
(b) the Secretary of State decides that the person or his partner is entitled to state pension credit and takes into account the increase of pension or benefit in making or superseding that decision; and
(c) the person's election for an increase is subsequently changed in favour of a lump sum in accordance with regulation 5 of the Deferral

of Retirement Pensions etc. Regulations or, as the case may be, paragraph 20D of Schedule 1 to the Graduated Retirement Benefit Regulations,

the Secretary of State may revise the state pension credit decision.

(7E) Where—
(a) a person is awarded a Category A or Category B retirement pension, shared additional pension or, as the case may be, graduated retirement benefit;
(b) an election is made, or treated as made, in respect of the award in accordance with paragraph A1 or 3C of Schedule 5 or paragraph 1 of Schedule 5A to the Contributions and Benefits Act or, as the case may be, in accordance with paragraph 12 or 17 of Schedule 1 to the Graduated Retirement Benefit Regulations; and
(c) the election is subsequently changed in accordance with regulation 5 of the Deferral of Retirement Pensions etc. Regulations or, as the case may be, paragraph 20D of Schedule 1 to the Graduated Retirement Benefit Regulations,

the Secretary of State may revise the award.]

[[16] (7F) A decision under regulation 17(1)(d) of the Income Support Regulations that a person is no longer entitled to a disability premium because of a determination that he is not incapable of work may be revised where the decision which embodies that determination is revised or his appeal against the decision is successful.]

(8) A decision of the Secretary of State [[3] or the Board of an officer of the Board] which is specified in Schedule 2 to the Act or is prescribed in regulation 27 (decisions against which no appeal lies) may be revised at any time.

[[7] (8A) Where a court makes a determination which results in a restriction being imposed pursuant to section 62 or 63 of the Child Support, Pensions and Social Security Act 2000 (loss of benefit provisions) and that determination is quashed or set aside by that or any other court, a decision of the Secretary of State under section 8(1)(a) or 10 made in accordance with regulation 6(2)(i) may be revised at any time.]

[[8] (8B) Where a court convicts a person of an offence, that conviction results in a restriction being imposed under section 7, 8 or 9 of the Social Security Fraud Act 2001 (loss of benefit provisions) and that conviction is quashed or set aside by that or any other court, a decision of the Secretary of State under section 8(1)(a) or 10 made in accordance with regulation 6(2)(j) or (k) may be revised at any time.]

[[4] (9) Paragraph (1) shall not apply in respect of—
(a) a relevant change of circumstances which occurred since the decision [[12] had effect] [[14] or, in the case of an advance award under regulation 13, 13A or 13C of the Claims and Payments Regulations, since the decision was made,] or where the Secretary of State has evidence or information which indicates that a relevant change of circumstances will occur; nor
(b) a decision which relates to an attendance allowance or a disability living allowance where the person is terminally ill, within the meaning of section 66(2)(a) of the Contributions and Benefit Act, unless an application for revision which contains an express statement that the person is terminally ill is made either by—
   (i) the person himself; or

(SI 1999/991, reg.3)

      (ii) any other person purporting to act on his behalf whether or not that other person is acting with his knowledge or authority, but where such an application is received a decision may be so revised notwithstanding that no claim under section 66(1) or, as the case may be, 72(5) or 73(12) of that Act has been made.]

  (10) The Secretary of State [³ or the Board] may treat an application for a supersession as an application for a revision.

  (11) In this regulation and regulation 7, "appropriate office" means

(a) the office of the [¹⁰ Department for Work and Pensions] the address of which is indicated on the notification of the original decision; or

(b) in the case of a person who has claimed jobseeker's allowance, the office specified by the Secretary of State in accordance with regulation 23 of the Jobseeker's Allowance Regulations [²; or

(c) in the case of a contributions decision which falls within Part II of Schedule 3 to the Act, any National Insurance Contributions office of the Board or any office of the [¹⁰ Department for Work and Pensions]; or

(d) in the case of a decision made under the Pension Schemes Act 1993 by virtue of section 170(2) of that Act, any National Insurance Contributions office of the Board;] [³ or

(e) in the case of a person who has claimed working families' tax credit or disabled person's tax credit, a Tax Credits Office, the address of which is indicated on the notification of the original decision;] [⁵ or

[¹¹(f) in the case of a person who is, or would be, required to take part in a work-focused interview, an office of the Department for Work and Pensions which is designated by the Secretary of State as a Jobcentre Plus Office or an office of a designated authority which displays the **one** logo.]

AMENDMENTS

1. Social Security and Child Support (Decisions and Appeals) Amendment (No.2) Regulations 1999 (SI 1999/1623), reg.2 (July 5, 1999).

2. Social Security Contributions (Transfer of Functions, etc.) Act 1999 (Commencement No.2 and Consequential and Transitional Provisions) Order 1999 (SI 1999/1662), art.3(3) (July 5, 1999).

3. Tax Credits (Decisions and Appeals) (Amendment) Regulations 1999 (SI 1999/2570), reg.6 (October 5, 1999). Note that amendments made by these regulations only have effect with respect to tax credit (reg.1(2) of the Amendment Regulations). In the case of para.(5) the amendments are substituted in relation to tax credit; for this reason the substituted words in relation to tax credit are shown in italics.

4. Social Security and Child Support (Decisions and Appeals), Vaccine Damage Payments and Jobseeker's Allowance (Amendment) Regulations 1999 (SI 1999/2677), reg.6 (October 18, 1999).

5. Social Security (Work-focused Interviews) Regulations 2000 (SI 2000/897), reg.16(5) and Sch.6, para.3 (April 3, 2000).

6. Social Security (Joint Claims: Consequential Amendments) Regulations 2000 (SI 2000/1982), reg.5(a) (March 19, 2001).

7. Social Security (Breach of Community Order) (Consequential Amendments) Regulations 2001 (SI 2001/1711), reg.2(2)(b) (October 15, 2001).

8. Social Security (Loss of Benefit) (Consequential Amendments) Regulations 2002 (SI 2002/490), reg.8(a) (April 1, 2002).

9. Social Security (Claims and Payments and Miscellaneous Amendments) Regulations 2002 (SI 2002/428), reg.4(2) (April 2, 2002).

Social Security and Child Support (Decisions and Appeals) Regs 1999

10. Social Security and Child Support (Decisions and Appeals) (Miscellaneous Amendments) Regulations 2002 (SI 2002/1379), reg.3(e), (May 20, 2002).
11. Social Security (Jobcentre Plus Interviews) Regulations 2002 (SI 2002/1703), Sch.2, para.6(b) (September 30, 2002).
12. Social Security and Child Support (Miscellaneous Amendments) Regulations 2003 (SI 2003/1050), reg.3(2) (May 5, 2003).
13. Social Security (Jobcentre Plus Interviews for Partners) Regulations 2003 (SI 2003/1886, reg.15(3) (April 12, 2004).
14. Social Security, Child Support and Tax Credits (Miscellaneous Amendments) Regulations 2005 (SI 2005/337), reg.2(2) (March 18, 2005).
15. Social Security (Deferral of Retirement Pensions, Shared Additional Pension and Graduated Retirement Benefit) (Miscellaneous Provisions) Regulations 2005 (SI 2005/2677), reg.9(3) (April 6, 2006).
16. Social Security (Miscellaneous Amendments) (No.2) Regulations 2006 (SI 2006/832), reg.5(2) (April 10, 2006).

DEFINITIONS

"the Administration Act"—see s.84 of the Social Security Act 1998.
"appeal"—see reg.1(3).
"appropriate office"—see para.(11).
"the Board"—see reg.1(3).
"claimant"—*ibid.*
"the Claims and Payments Regulations"—*ibid.*
"the Contributions and Benefits Act"—see s.84 of the Social Security Act 1998.
"the date of notification"—see reg.1(3).
"the Deferral of Retirement Pensions etc. Regulations"—*ibid.*
"designated authority"—*ibid.*
"disability benefit decision"—see reg.7A(1).
"disability determination"—*ibid.*
"family"—see reg.1(3).
"the Graduated Retirement Benefit Regulations"—*ibid.*
"incapacity benefit decision"—see reg.7A(1).
"incapacity determination"—*ibid.*
"the Jobseekers Act"—see s.84 of the Social Security Act 1998.
"the Jobseeker's Allowance Regulations"—see reg.1(3).
"official error"—*ibid.*
"original decision"—see para.(1).
"payee"—see reg.7A(1).
"relevant benefit"—see s.39(1) of the Social Security Act 1998.
"tax credit"—see reg.1(3).
"work-focused interview"—*ibid.*

GENERAL NOTE

2.349   This regulation provides for the circumstances in which a decision may be revised under s.9 of the Social Security Act 1998, whereas reg.6 provides for the circumstances in which a decision may be superseded under s.10. There are three main distinctions between revision and supersession. Firstly, only decisions of the Secretary of State may be revised, whereas not only decisions of the Secretary of State but also decisions of tribunals and Commissioners may be superseded. Secondly, revisions have effect from the date from which the decision being revised was effective (see s.9(3) of the Social Security Act 1998) unless a mistake was made in respect of that date, in which case the correct date is used (reg.5). Supersessions are usually effective from a later date (s.10(5) or reg.7). Thirdly, there is no right of appeal to a tribunal against a decision to revise or not to revise, whereas there is a right of appeal under s.12 against a decision to supersede or not to supersede. Instead, a decision

(SI 1999/991, reg.3)

to revise and, in limited circumstances, a decision not to revise, extends the time for appealing against the decision that has been revised (see reg.31(2)).

The first and third of these distinctions give rise to considerable problems where there is an appeal to a tribunal and the tribunal considers that a decision expressed as a revision should have been expressed as a supersession or vice versa. These problems were explored by a Tribunal of Commissioners in *R(IB)2/04* and *R(IS)15/04* (see the annotations to s.12 of the Social Security Act 1998 and to reg.31(2)). It is arguable that many of the problems are caused by the wide scope of reg.3, which appears to be based on the premise that if it is intended that a new decision should take place from the same date as the decision that is being reconsidered, the new decision must be expressed as a revision rather than a supersession. That approach is unnecessary, as appears to be accepted where it is desired that a new decision given on reconsideration of a decision of a tribunal or Commissioner should take effect from the same date as the original decision, because provision can be made by regulations under s.10(6) for a supersession to take effect from the same date as the decision that has been superseded (see reg.7(5)). If the grounds for revision contained in paras (4) and (5) to (8B) were instead grounds for supersession, many of the problems identified by the Tribunal of Commissioners would be removed. That would leave revision available only for cases where a decision is looked at again within a month or so of its being made or pending an appeal. It is only in those circumstances that the first and third of the distinctions drawn above suggest that revision is more appropriate than supersession.

In addition to the circumstances outlined in this regulation, decisions in respect of advance claims may be revised under regs 13(2), 13A(3) and 13C(3) of the Social Security (Claims and Payments) Regulations 1987 (*R(IB)2/04* at paras 106 and 107). A further power to revise is conferred by s.25(4) of the Social Security Act 1998 in respect of decisions made while a test case is pending before a Commissioner or court.

Paras (1)–(3)
These allow a decision to be put right "on any ground" where the claimant applies for a revision within one month of the original decision being notified (but note the extension of time permitted where there has been a correction or request for reasons (see para.(1)(b)) or under para.(3)(b) in the case of a social fund payment or under reg.4). They also allow revision where the Secretary of State notices the error within that time. Note that the time for appealing against the original decision runs from the date the decision is revised *or is not revised* following an application under these paragraphs (reg.31(2)), so that a claimant is not prejudiced by seeking a revision before appealing.   2.350

A decision may now be revised under para.(4A) at any time while an appeal is pending against it. This makes it possible to avoid a tribunal hearing altogether where the Secretary of State is prepared to concede the case in its entirety.   2.351

Para.(4A)
This allows the Secretary of State to revise any decision while an appeal is pending in circumstances where it has not been, or could not be, revised under para.(1) or (3). The effect is that the appeal lapses under s.9(6) unless the revised decision is no more advantageous to the appellant than the decision that has been revised (see reg.30).   2.352

Para.(5)
Normally, a decision based on a mistake of law or fact made by the Secretary of State can only be superseded under reg.6(2)(b) unless the error is detected in time to allow revision under paras (1)–(3). Supersession will be effective only from the date the application was made (see s.10(5) of the Social Security Act 1998). Paragraph (5) provides for such a decision to be revised rather than superseded where either there has been an official error or else there has been an overpayment   2.353

(which might be recoverable under s.71 of the Social Security Administration Act 1992) due to a mistake of fact). In effect, the time limit is removed because revisions generally take effect from the same date as the original decision (see s.9(3) of the Social Security Act 1998).

"Official error" is defined in reg.1. In *R(IS)15/04* (subsequently approved by the Court of Appeal in *Beltekian v Westminster CC* [2004] EWCA Civ 1784 (reported as *R(H)8/05*)), the Tribunal of Commissioners noted that a claimant might wish to assert that there were grounds for revision for "official error", whereas a claimant would not wish to rely on para.(5)(b) or (c). Consequently, a claimant might wish to challenge a refusal to revise under para.(5)(a) but, due to the limitations of reg.31(2), might be unable to do so save by way of an application for judicial review. The burden of proving that there was an "official error" lies on the claimant where it is he who is applying for revision, but it is for the Secretary of State to produce evidence of the supersession or revision that is in issue before the tribunal (*CH/3439/2004*).

Note that para.(5)(c) protects claimants of disability benefits or incapacity benefits from the full rigour of para.(b) and effectively prevents there from being a recoverable overpayment where a claimant could not reasonably have known a fact of which the Secretary of State was ignorant, or as to which he made a mistake, or could not reasonably have known that it was relevant. It does not protect the claimant who reasonably did not know that the Secretary of State was ignorant of, or had made a mistake as to, an obviously relevant fact of which he was aware, but that is presumably because in such cases any overpayment is unlikely to be recoverable anyway due to the lack of any misrepresentation or failure to disclose a material fact.

Para. (5A)

2.354   This enables the Secretary of State to apply a tribunal's decision to any decision made while the appeal was pending, thus making it unnecessary for the claimant to appeal against the further decisions. The paragraph was required because, since the Social Security Act 1998 came into force, it has not been possible to refer to the tribunal questions arising while an appeal is pending or simply not to determine the questions on the basis that the tribunal could deal with all issues down to the date of decision. Although the Tribunal of Commissioners in *R(IS)15/04*, considered that para.(5)(a) was the only part of reg.3, other than paras. (1) to (3) upon which a claimant might wish to rely, it was suggested in *CDLA/3323/2003* that para.(5A) is another provision. The Commissioner held that he was not precluded by "decision B" from making a decision on an appeal from "decision C" that covered the same period as "decision B", in case the Secretary of State declined to revise "decision B" and the claimant was left without any remedy because the time for appealing had expired. He held that "decision B" lapsed in the light of his new award.

Para. (6)

2.355   In *CJSA/2375/2000*, the claimant was twice disqualified for failing to attend training courses. The second disqualification was for four weeks because there had been the previous disqualification. An appeal against the first disqualification was allowed by a tribunal. The Commissioner, hearing an appeal against a decision by a tribunal dismissing an appeal against the second disqualification said that the Secretary of State should have revised the second disqualification under para.(6) following the first tribunal's decision, in order to reduce the period to two weeks.

Para. (7)

2.356   There are many instances where an award of benefit affects entitlement to another benefit awarded earlier. If the second award is made in respect of a period which includes the date from which a decision in respect of the first benefit took effect, that earlier decision is revised under this paragraph. If entitlement under the second award arises only after that date, the earlier decision is superseded under reg.6(2)(e)

(SI 1999/991, reg.3)

instead. Note that the earlier decision must have resulted in an "award" of benefit. It is suggested that that does not include a refusal of benefit, because the same term is used in sub-para.(b) in relation to the second decision and it is fairly clear that only an increase in entitlement under the second decision, and not a decrease in entitlement, gives rise to a revision under this paragraph. Where a decision in respect of one benefit is affected by a decision in respect of another benefit that is *less* favourable to a claimant, neither this paragraph nor reg.6(2)(e) applies and any consequent revision or supersession must be made under some other provision.

Para. (7ZA)
This enables an award of income support or state pension credit to be revised in circumstances where the award was made while a non-dependant was awaiting determination of a claim for benefit and, as a result of a favourable decision on the non-dependant's claim, the first claimant becomes entitled to a severe disability premium.

2.357

Para. (7A)
This enables a decision as to entitlement to reduced earnings allowance to be revised in favour of the claimant following a favourable revision of, or a successful appeal against, a decision in respect of disablement benefit.

2.358

Paras (7B) and (7C)
Decisions about capacity for work are, in practice, always made in the context of entitlement to incapacity benefit or credits. A person who has been entitled to income support on the ground of incapacity for work and is then found not to be incapable of work for the purposes of incapacity benefit or credits is likely to have the award of income support terminated but, if he or she appeals against the incapacity determination, a fresh award of income support will be made at a reduced rate until the appeal is determined. These paragraphs have the effect that, if the appeal is successful or lapses because the incapacity determination is revised, the income support decisions may be revised. Paragraph (7F) has the same effect in a case where a claimant in receipt of income support has been found not to be incapable of work but remains entitled to income support on other grounds (e.g. being a single parent) at a lower rate due to the loss of the disability premium.

2.359

Paras (7D) and (7E)
Where entitlement to certain pensions has been deferred, the claimant may elect to have either an increase in the pension or a lump sum. These paragraphs enable awards of state pension credit and the relevant pensions to be revised following a change in such an election.

2.360

Para. (7F)
See the note to paras (7B) and (7C).

2.361

Para. (8)
See the note to reg.6(2)(d).

2.362

Para. (9)
Similarly, on an appeal against a decision as revised, it is not possible for the appeal tribunal to have regard to any change of circumstances arising between the date of the original decision and the date of revision (*R(CS) 1/03*).

2.363

Para. (10)
An application for supersession may be treated as an application for revision. Regulation 6(5) provides that an application for revision may be treated as an application for supersession.

2.364

For the powers of an appeal tribunal to treat a revision as a refusal to supersede and vice versa, see the note to s.12 of the Social Security Act 1998.

3A. *Omitted*

Late application for a revision

4.—(1) The time limit for making an application for a revision specified in regulation 3(1) or (3) [² or 3A(1)(a)] may be extended where the conditions specified in the following provisions of this regulation are satisfied.

(2) An application for an extension of time shall be made by [² the relevant person,] the claimant or a person acting on his behalf.

(3) An application shall—
(a) contain particulars of the grounds on which the extension of time is sought and shall contain sufficient details of the decision which it is sought to have revised to enable that decision to be identified; and
(b) be made within 13 months of the date of notification of the decision which it is sought to have revised [³, but if the applicant has requested a statement of the reasons in accordance with regulation 28(1)(b) the 13 month period shall be extended by—
  (i) if the statement is provided within one month of the notification, an additional 14 days; or
  (ii) if it is provided after the elapse of a period after the one month ends, the length of that period and an additional 14 days.]

(4) An application for an extension of time shall not be granted unless the applicant satisfies the Secretary of State [¹ or the Board or an officer of the Board] that—
(a) it is reasonable to grant the application;
(b) the application for revision has merit; and
(c) special circumstances are relevant to the application and as a result of those special circumstances it was not practicable for the application to be made within the time limit specified in regulation 3 [² or 3A].

(5) In determining whether it is reasonable to grant an application, the Secretary of State [¹ or the Board or an officer of the Board] shall have regard to the principle that the greater the amount of time that has elapsed between the expiration of the time specified in regulation 3(1) and (3) [² and regulation 3A(1)(a)] for applying for a revision and the making of the application for an extension of time, the more compelling should be the special circumstances on which the application is based.

(6) In determining whether it is reasonable to grant the application for an extension of time, no account shall be taken of the following—
(a) that the applicant or any person acting for him was unaware of or misunderstood the law applicable to his case (including ignorance or misunderstanding of the time limits imposed by these Regulations); or
(b) that a Commissioner [², a Child Support Commissioner] or a court has taken a different view of the law from that previously understood and applied.

(7) An application under this regulation for an extension of time which has been refused may not be renewed.

AMENDMENTS

1. Tax Credits (Decisions and Appeals) (Amendment) Regulations 1999 (SI 1999/2570), reg.7 (October 5, 1999). Note that amendments made by these

(SI 1999/991, reg.4)

regulations only have effect with respect to tax credit (reg.1(2) of the Amendment Regulations).

2. Child Support (Decisions and Appeals) (Amendment) Regulations 2000 (SI 2000/3185), reg.6 (various dates as provided by reg.1(1)).

3. Social Security, Child Support and Tax Credits (Miscellaneous Amendments) Regulations 2005 (SI 2005/337), reg.2(3) (March 18, 2005).

DEFINITIONS

"the Board"—see reg.1(3).
"claimant"—*ibid*.
"Commissioner"—see s.39(1) of the Social Security Act 1998.
"the date of notification"—see reg.1(3).
"relevant person"—*ibid*.

GENERAL NOTE

Para.(1)
It was held in *R(TC)1/05* that a tribunal did not have jurisdiction to consider whether the Inland Revenue ought, under reg.4, to have extended the time for applying for revision. In that case, the relevant decision was made on April 22, 2002, the claimant sought reconsideration on November 11, 2002 and the Inland Revenue refused to extend the time for applying for revision and therefore refused to revise the decision on November 25, 2002. The claimant appealed. There is no right of appeal against a revision or refusal to revise and so the appeal had to be treated as an appeal against the decision of April 22, 2002. The time for appealing against a decision is not extended under reg.31 when the application for revision is made late and time is not extended under reg.4. In those circumstances (and subject to the possibility that the decision of April 22, 2002 had not been sent to the claimant), the appeal should have been treated as having been late and therefore invalid, unless a legally qualified panel member extended, under reg.32, the time for appealing. On the facts of *R(TC)1/05*, it made no difference whether the time for applying for revision was extended under reg.4 or whether the time for appealing was extended under reg.31, but the Commissioner pointed out that the test for extending the time for applying for revision is now different from that for extending the time for appealing. He also pointed out that the thirteen-month absolute time limit for appeals (see reg.32(1)) means that in some cases an appeal could be valid only if the time for applying for revision had been extended. It seems regrettable that a tribunal should not have the power to determine whether the Secretary of State ought to have extended time under reg.4, especially as the exercise the Secretary of State is required to perform is not all that simple and a considerable amount of money may turn on it.

2.367

Para.(6)(b)
See the note to reg.32(8)(b) which is in similar terms.

2.368

Date from which a decision revised under section 9 takes effect

5.—[² (1)] Where, on a revision under section 9, the Secretary of State [¹ or the Board or an officer of the Board] decides that the date from which the decision under section 8 or 10 ("the original decision") took effect was erroneous, the decision under section 9 shall take effect on the date from which the original decision would have taken effect had the error not been made.

[² (2) Where—
(a) a person attains pensionable age, claims a retirement pension after the prescribed time for claiming and the Secretary of State decides ("the original decision") that he is not entitled because—

2.369

Social Security and Child Support (Decisions and Appeals) Regs 1999

        (i) in the case of a Category A retirement pension, the person has not satisfied the contribution conditions; or
        (ii) in the case of a Category B retirement pension, the person's spouse [³ or civil partner] has not satisfied the contribution conditions;
    (b) in accordance with regulation 50A of the Social Security (Contributions) Regulations 2001(Class 3 contributions: tax years 1996–97 to 2001–02) the Board subsequently accepts Class 3 contributions paid after the due date by the claimant or, as the case may be, the spouse [³ or civil partner];
    (c) in accordance with regulation 6A of the Social Security (Crediting and Treatment of Contributions, and National Insurance Numbers) Regulations 2001 the contributions are treated as paid on a date earlier than the date on which they were paid; and
    (d) the Secretary of State revises the original decision in accordance with regulation 11A(4)(a),
the revised decision shall take effect from—
        (i) 1st October 1998; or
        (ii) the date on which the claimant attained pensionable age in the case of a Category A pension, or, in the case of a Category B pension, the date on which the claimant's spouse [³ or civil partner] attained pensionable age,
whichever is later."

AMENDMENTS

1. Tax Credits (Decisions and Appeals) (Amendment) Regulations 1999 (SI 1999/2570), reg.8 (October 5, 1999). Note that amendments made by these regulations only have effect with respect to tax credit (reg.1(2) of the Amendment Regulations).
2. Social Security (Retirement Pensions) Amendment Regulations 2004 (SI 2004/2283), reg.3 (September 27, 2004).
3. Civil Partnership (Consequential Amendments) Regulations 2005 (SI 2005/2878), reg.8(3) (December 5, 2005).

DEFINITION

"the Board"—see reg.1(3).

GENERAL NOTE

2.370   These paragraphs provide the exceptions to the general rule in s.9(3) of the Social Security Act 1998 that a revision takes effect from the same date as the original decision that has been revised.

Para.(1) deals with the obvious case where the effective date of the original decision was wrong.

Para.(2) is linked to reg.6(31) and (32) of the Social Security (Claims and Payments) Regulations 1987 and deals with a problem caused by the failure from 1996 to 2003 to inform contributors of deficiencies in their contribution records so that they could pay voluntary Class 3 contributions to make up the deficit. By regulation 50A of the Social Security (Contributions) Regulations 2001, claimants are being allowed to pay their contributions very late. Regulation 6(31) of the 1987 Regulations enables a late claim based on those contributions to be made and this amendment allows an earlier decision disallowing a claim to be revised with effect from October 1, 1998 or the date the claimant or, where appropriate, the claimant's spouse [or civil partner] reached pensionable age. Without these amendments, the new claim or the revision

(SI 1999/991, reg. 5)

might be effective from a much later date and that might be unfair because, having discovered about the deficiency, the claimant might have delayed claiming on what was then a correct understanding that there was nothing that could be done about it.

5A. *Omitted*

CHAPTER II

SUPERSESSIONS

Supersession of decisions

6.—(1) Subject to the following provisions of this regulation, for the purposes of section 10, the cases and circumstances in which a decision may be superseded under that section are set out in paragraphs (2) to (4).

(2) A decision under section 10 may be made on the Secretary of State's [² or the Board's] own initiative or on an application made for the purpose on the basis that the decision to be superseded—
- (a) is one in respect of which—
    - (i) there has been a relevant change of circumstances since the decision [¹¹ had effect [¹⁵ or, in the case of an advance award under regulation 13, 13A or 13C of the Claims and Payments Regulations, since the decision was made]; or
    - (ii) it is anticipated that a relevant change of circumstances will occur;
- (b) is a decision of the Secretary of State [² or the Board or an officer of the Board] other than a decision to which sub-paragraph (d) refers and—
    - (i) the decision was erroneous in point of law, or it was made in ignorance of, or was based upon a mistake as to, some material fact; and
    - (ii) an application for a supersession was received by the Secretary of State [² or the Board], or the decision by the Secretary of State [² or the Board] to act on his [² or their] own initiative was taken, more than one month after the date of notification of the decision which is to be superseded or after the expiry of such longer period of time as may have been allowed under regulation 4;
- [¹¹ (c) is a decision of an appeal tribunal or of a Commissioner—
    - (i) that was made in ignorance of, or was based upon a mistake as to, some material fact; or
    - (ii) that was made in accordance with section 26(4)(b), in a case where section 26(5) applies;]
- (d) is a decision which is specified in Schedule 2 to the Act or is prescribed in regulation 27 (decisions against which no appeal lies); [¹¹ . . .]
- [⁵ (e) is a decision where—
    - (i) the claimant has been awarded entitlement to a relevant benefit; and

563

Social Security and Child Support (Decisions and Appeals) Regs 1999

(ii) [⁹ subsequent to the first day of the period to which that entitlement relates], the claimant or a member of his family becomes entitled to [⁹ . . .] another relevant benefit or an increase in the rate of another relevant benefit;]

[¹⁵ (ee) is an original award within the meaning of regulation 3(7ZA) and sub-paragraphs (a) to (c) and (d)(ii) of regulation 3(7ZA) apply but not sub-paragraph (d)(i);]

[³ (f) is a decision that a jobseeker's allowance is payable to a claimant where that allowance ceases to be payable by virtue of section 19(1) of the Jobseekers Act [⁶ or ceases to be payable or is reduced by virtue of section 20A(5) of that Act];]

[¹ (g) is an incapacity benefit decision where there has been an incapacity determination (whether before or after the decision) and where, since the decision was made, the Secretary of State has received medical evidence following an examination in accordance with regulation 8 of the Social Security (Incapacity for Work) (General) Regulations 1995 from a doctor referred to in paragraph (1) of that regulation;] [⁴ [¹¹ . . .]

(h) is one in respect of a person who—
  (i) is subsequently the subject of a separate decision or determination as to whether or not he took part in a work-focused interview;
  (ii) had been held not to have taken part in a work-focused interview but who had, subsequent to the decision to be superseded, attained the age of 60 or ceased to reside in an area in which there is a requirement to take part in a work-focused interview [¹³ or, in the case of a partner who was required to take part in a work-focused interview [¹⁴ in accordance with regulations made under section 2AA of the Administration Act, ceased to be a partner for the purposes of those regulations or is no longer a partner to whom the requirement to take part in a work-focused interview under those regulations applies];]

[⁷ (i) is a decision of the Secretary of State that a jobseeker's allowance or income support is payable to a claimant where the Secretary of State is notified that a court has made a determination which results in a restriction being imposed pursuant to section 62 or 63 of the Child Support, Pensions and Social Security Act 2000;]

[⁸ (j) is a decision of the Secretary of State that a sanctionable benefit is payable to a claimant where that benefit ceases to be payable or falls to be reduced under section 7 or 9 of the Social Security Fraud Act 2001 and for this purpose "sanctionable benefit" has the same meaning as in section 7 of that Act;

(k) is a decision of the Secretary of State that a joint-claim jobseeker's allowance is payable where that allowance ceases to be payable or falls to be reduced under section 8 of the Social Security Fraud Act 2001;]

[¹⁰ (l) is a relevant decision for the purposes of section 6 of the State Pension Credit Act and—
  (i) on making that decision, the Secretary of State specified a period as the assessed income period; and
  (ii) that period has ended or is about to end;]

[¹² (m) is a relevant decision for the purposes of section 6 of the State Pension Credit Act in a case where—

(i) the information and evidence required under regulation 32(6)(a) of the Claims and Payments Regulations has not been provided in accordance with the time limits set out in regulation 32(6)(c) of those Regulations;

(ii) the Secretary of State was prevented from specifying a new assessed income period under regulation 10(1) of the State Pension Credit Regulations; and

(iii) the information and evidence required under regulation 32(6)(a) of the Claims and Payments Regulations has since been provided;]

[15 (n) is a decision by an appeal tribunal confirming a decision by the Secretary of State terminating a claimant's entitlement to income support because he no longer falls within the category of person specified in paragraph 7 of Schedule 1B to the Income Support Regulations (persons incapable of work) and a further appeal tribunal subsequently determines that he is incapable of work;]

[16 (o) is a decision that a person is entitled to state pension credit and—
  (i) the person or his partner makes, or is treated as having made, an election for a lump sum in accordance with—
    (aa) paragraph A1 or 3C of Schedule 5 to the Contributions and Benefits Act;
    (bb) paragraph 1 of Schedule 5A to that Act; or, as the case may be,
    (cc) paragraph 12 or 17 of Schedule 1 to the Graduated Retirement Benefit Regulations;
    or
  (ii) such a lump sum is repaid in consequence of an application to change an election for a lump sum in accordance with regulation 5 of the Deferral of Retirement Pensions etc. Regulations or, as the case may be, paragraph 20D of Schedule 1 to the Graduated Retirement Benefit Regulations.]

(3) A decision which may be revised under regulation 3 may not be superseded under this regulation except where—

(a) circumstances arise in which the Secretary of State [2 or the Board or an officer of the Board] may revise that decision under regulation 3; and

(b) further circumstances arise in relation to that decision which are not specified in regulation 3 but are specified in paragraph (2) or (4).

(4) Where the Secretary of State requires [2 or the Board require] further evidence or information from the applicant in order to consider all the issues raised by an application under paragraph (2) ("the original application"), he [2 or they] shall notify the applicant that further evidence or information is required and the decision may be superseded—

(a) where the applicant provides further relevant evidence or information within one month of the date of notification or such longer period of time as the Secretary of State [2 or the Board] may allow; or

(b) where the applicant does not provide such evidence or information within the time allowed under sub-paragraph (a), on the basis of the original application.

(5) The Secretary of State [2 or the Board] may treat an application for a revision or a notification of a change of circumstances as an application for a supersession.

Social Security and Child Support (Decisions and Appeals) Regs 1999

(6) The following events are not relevant changes of circumstances for the purposes of paragraph (2)—
(a) the repayment of a loan to which regulation 66A of the Income Support Regulations or regulation 136 of the Jobseeker's Allowance Regulations applies;
(b) [15 . . .]
[3 (c) the fact that a person has become terminally ill, within the meaning of section 66(2)(a) of the Contributions and Benefits Act, unless an application for supersession which contains an express statement that the person is terminally ill is made either by—
(i) the person himself; or
(ii) any other person purporting to act on his behalf whether or not that other person is acting with his knowledge or authority;
and where such an application is received a decision may be so superseded notwithstanding that no claim under section 66(1) or, as the case may be, 72(5) or 73(12) of that Act has been made.]

(7) In paragraph (6)(b), "nursing home" and "residential care home" have the same meanings as they have in regulation 19 of the Income Support Regulations.

[10 (8) In relation to the assessed income period, the only change of circumstances relevant for the purposes of paragraph (2)(a) is that the assessed income period ends in accordance with section 9(4) of the State Credit Pension Act or the regulations made under section 9(5) of that Act.]

AMENDMENTS

1. Social Security and Child Support (Decisions and Appeals) Amendment (No.2) Regulations 1999 (SI 1999/1623), reg.2 (July 5, 1999).
2. Tax Credits (Decisions and Appeals) (Amendment) Regulations 1999 (SI 1999/2570), reg.9 (October 5, 1999). Note that amendments made by these regulations only have effect with respect to tax credit (reg.1(2) of the Amendment Regulations).
3. Social Security and Child Support (Decisions and Appeals), Vaccine Damage Payments and Jobseeker's Allowance (Amendment) Regulations 1999 (SI 1999/2677), reg.7 (October 18, 1999).
4. Social Security (Work-focused Interviews) Regulations 2000 (SI 2000/897), reg.16(5) and Sch.6, para.4 (April 3, 2000).
5. Social Security and Child Support (Miscellaneous Amendments) Regulations 2000 (SI 2000/1596), reg.16 (June 19, 2000).
6. Social Security (Joint Claims: Consequential Amendments) Regulations 2000 (SI 2000/1982), reg.5(b) (March 19, 2001).
7. Social Security (Breach of Community Order) (Consequential Amendments) Regulations 2001 (SI 2001/1711), reg.2(2)(c) (October 15, 2001).
8. Social Security (Loss of Benefit) (Consequential Amendments) Regulations 2002 (SI 2002/490), reg.8(b) (April 1, 2002).
9. Social Security (Claims and Payments and Miscellaneous Amendments) Regulations 2002 (SI 2002/428), reg.4(3) (April 2, 2002).
10. State Pension Credit (Consequential, Transitional and Miscellaneous Provisions) Regulations 2002 (SI 2002/3019), reg.17 (April 7, 2003).
11. Social Security and Child Support (Miscellaneous Amendments) Regulations 2003 (SI 2003/1050), reg.3(3) (May 5, 2003).
12. State Pension Credit (Transitional and Miscellaneous Provisions) Amendment Regulations 2003 (SI 2003/2274), reg.5(2) (October 6, 2003).
13. Social Security (Jobcentre Plus Interviews for Partners) Regulations 2003 (SI 2003/1886), reg.15(4) (April 12, 2004).

(SI 1999/991, reg.6)

14. Social Security (Working Neighbourhoods) Regulations 2004 (SI 2004/959), reg.24(3) (April 26, 2004).

15. Social Security, Child Support and Tax Credits (Miscellaneous Amendments) Regulations 2005 (SI 2005/337), reg.2(4) (March 18, 2005).

16. Social Security (Deferral of Retirement Pensions, Shared Additional Pension and Graduated Retirement Benefit) (Miscellaneous Provisions) Regulations 2005 (SI 2005/2677), reg.9(4) (April 6, 2006).

DEFINITIONS

"the Act"—see reg.1(3).
"appeal tribunal"—*ibid*.
"assessed income period"—*ibid*.
"the Board"—*ibid*.
"claimant"—*ibid*.
"Commissioner"—see s.39(1) of the Social Security Act 1998.
"the Contributions and Benefits Act"—see s.84 of the Social Security Act 1998.
"the date of notification"—see reg.1(3).
"the Deferral of Retirement Pensions etc. Regulations"—*ibid*.
"family"—*ibid*.
"the Graduated Retirement Benefit Regulations"—*ibid*.
"incapacity benefit decision"—see reg.7A(1).
"incapacity determination"—*ibid*.
"the Income Support Regulations"—see reg.1(3).
"the Jobseekers Act"—see s.84 of the Social Security Act 1998.
"the Jobseeker's Allowance Regulations"—see reg.1(3).
"a joint-claim jobseeker's allowance"—*ibid*.
"nursing home"—see para.(7).
"payee"—see reg.7A(1).
"relevant benefit"—see s.39(1) of the Social Security Act 1998.
"residential care home"—see para.(7).
"State Pension Credit Act"—see reg.1(3).
"work-focused interview"—*ibid*.

GENERAL NOTE

Para.(1)

This regulation is made under s.10(3) of the Social Security Act 1998.

In *Wood v Secretary of State for Work and Pensions* [2003] EWCA Civ 53 (reported as *R(DLA) 1/03*), the Court of Appeal overruled *R(DLA) 6/02* and held that a decision may be superseded only if one of the conditions in paras (2)–(4) is satisfied. If a claimant has applied for supersession and the conditions are not met, the Secretary of State must refuse to supersede. That is the natural meaning of the provisions but the Tribunal of Commissioners deciding *R(DLA) 6/02* had thought it necessary to give a strained construction to reg.6 because they understood s.12(9) of the 1998 Act precluded an appeal against a refusal to supersede, which would have been unfair. The majority of the Court of Appeal acknowledged that it was difficult to give both reg.6 and s.12(9) a literal construction but they preferred to give an extended construction to s.12(9), holding that there is an appeal against a refusal to supersede, and to take a more literal approach to reg.6, which certainly makes it easier to apply reg.6.

Where a decision is superseded and then the superseding decision is itself superseded, the body making that third decision must be satisfied that there are grounds for superseding the first decision as well as the second decision if the outcome is to be different from that of the first decision (*R(DLA) 1/06*).

It was held by a Tribunal of Commissioners in *R(IB)2/04*, adopting at para.10(4) a suggestion made by Rix L.J. in *Wood*, that the ground of supersession which is

2.373

Social Security and Child Support (Decisions and Appeals) Regs 1999

found to exist must form the basis of the supersession in the sense that the original decision can only be altered in a way which follows from that ground. This overrules *R(A)1/90*, although no reference was made to that decision by the Tribunal of Commissioners.

However, there is still a question whether the use of the word "may" in paras (1) and (2) means that the Secretary of State need not supersede even if he finds that one of the conditions in paras (2) to (4) is satisfied. In *Wood*, Rix L.J. regarded a superseded decision as an altered decision, which might imply that supersession of an award necessarily implied a change in the claimant's entitlement so that there was no scope for supersession without there being a different outcome. Such an approach would be rather different from that taken in the context of reviews under earlier legislation (see the note to para.(2)(a)(i) below). But, now that it has been established that there is a right of appeal against a refusal to supersede, there is no practical difference between a refusal to supersede and a decision to supersede "at the same rate", at least at the time the decision is given. There may be a difference later to the extent that, if there is a later supersession, the nature of an earlier decision may determine which decision must be superseded but, even then, it is difficult to see how the outcome in terms of entitlement to benefit could be affected. It may well be that there are two or more perfectly acceptable legal analyses, each producing the same practical result and any one of which can properly be applied without the decision-maker erring in law.

There may be no practical difference between a refusal to supersede and a supersession "at the same rate" but, in *CIS/6249/1999*, the Commissioner decided that the Secretary of State had a limited discretion to refuse to supersede even where grounds of supersession existed and any supersession would result in a change in entitlement. Although a power may appear discretionary, there is often a duty to exercise it in a particular way in order that the purpose for which the power is given is not frustrated (*Julius v Lord Bishop of Oxford* (1880) L.R. 5 App. Cas. 214) and therefore the Secretary of State is for practical purposes normally bound to supersede a decision if the conditions for supersession are met and would result in a change of entitlement. However, in *CIS/6249/1999*, there was a competing duty not to abuse power by reviewing an award of income support in respect of a period in the past in circumstances where the claimant would have been unfairly prejudiced. The facts of the case illustrate the operation of the principle. The claimant was an asylum seeker entitled to "urgent cases" payments of income support to which he was not entitled if he had any capital in the form of liquid assets. In October 1995, he had been paid almost £900, representing about 11 weeks' arrears of income support, which he paid into a bank. As long as it remained in his bank, that sum should have disentitled him from income support. In October 1996, he told a visiting officer that he still had £787 but benefit continued in payment until 1998, when a decision was made disentitling him from February 25, 1998. In principle, the claimant had not been entitled to income support from October 1995, but there was no question of the overpayment being recoverable as the Benefits Agency had known he had the money in October 1995. On the other hand, deciding that the claimant had not been entitled to income support throughout the period from October 1995 to February 1998 would have prevented the claimant from being paid any benefit in the future because the claimant would have been unable to show he was entitled to benefit immediately before February 5, 1996 and would have been deprived of the transitional protection given to asylum seekers in receipt of benefit at that date. Had benefit been stopped in October 1995, when it should have been, the claimant would undoubtedly have qualified for benefit again before February 5, 1996. The Commissioner considered that reviewing entitlement before February 25, 1998 would have been so unfair as to be an abuse of power. The same approach would presumably be appropriate in respect of supersession.

CIS/6249/1999 was distinguished (and to some extent its correctness was doubted) in *C8/06-07(IB)*, where it was held that it was not an abuse of power for a decision to be superseded retrospectively in a case where the claimant had sought advice from the Department for Social Development about working while claiming incapacity benefit

(SI 1999/991, reg. 6)

but had not been advised that he was required to give notice of any work in writing. The claimant had acted honestly at all times but, as the Commissioner observed, there was no question of the recovery of any overpaid benefit and she considered that any unfairness to the claimant did not outweigh the public interest in ensuring that a correct decision as to entitlement was made. It is not clear from the decision whether the claimant had in fact lost anything to which he would have been entitled had he not received the wrong advice except, presumably, credited contributions during the material period in the past. If a loss of entitlement in the past meant a loss of current entitlement because different contribution years had to be taken into account, that was not recorded. However, the Commissioner did point out that the claimant might have a remedy in the courts if he had suffered any loss.

Although it appears necessary first to determine whether one of the cases in para.(2) applies and then determine what the outcome should be, the two stages need not be kept rigidly apart. In *CDLA/5469/1999*, the Deputy Commissioner pointed out that the fact that a tribunal must, as a first step *in their deliberations*, ask themselves whether there are grounds for supersession does not translate into a rule of practice that the question whether grounds for supersession exist must be treated as a preliminary issue *in the hearing*. In most cases involving ignorance or mistake as to a material fact, he suggests, the tribunal should, after the hearing, first ask itself simply what the facts are that are material to the issue to be decided. Only then should it ask whether the original decision was made in ignorance of any of those facts. If the answer is yes, it can then give its own decision on the basis of the facts found. In *CSDLA/765/2004*, the Commissioner took the opposite approach and suggested that a hearing should initially be restricted to taking evidence relevant to a ground of supersession, but that was not followed in *CSDLA/637/2006*, where the Commissioner said:

"It is sensible rather that a tribunal hears all the evidence, including what is potentially relevant to current entitlement, but without yet making a final determination with respect to that, in order to compare present circumstances with those which surrounded the original award."

Indeed, it may be a legitimate inference from a finding that the claimant does not satisfy the conditions of entitlement to benefit that an earlier award was based on a mistake of law or fact or that that there has been a change of circumstances so that the earlier award may be superseded (*CDLA/1820/1998*), although that applies only where no reasonable person could find the conditions of entitlement currently to be satisfied. It is then appropriate to presume that the ground of supersession is the one least unfavourable to the claimant (*Cooke v Secretary of State for Social Security* [2001] EWCA Civ 734 (reported as *R(DLA) 6/01*)). In *CSDLA/637/2006*, however, the Commissioner pointed out that drawing such an inference did not imply that an original award made by a tribunal, as opposed to the Secretary of State, could be superseded, because an error of law is not a ground for superseding a tribunal's decision. She rejected the Secretary of State's contention that it should be presumed that the earlier tribunal had not erred in law and she consequently upheld a decision to the effect that grounds for supersession had not been made out.

The Secretary of State may supersede a decision either on an application or on his own initiative. Where he considers a claimant's application for supersession but reduces entitlement rather than increasing it, he must be treated as having superseded the original decision on his own initiative, rather than on the claimant's application (*R(IB)2/04* at para.95). That is necessary to avoid the claimant being unfairly prejudiced in respect of the date from which the decision is effective under s.10(5) of the 1998 Act. For the same reason, where a claimant appeals against a decision made on his or her application for supersession and a tribunal makes a decision that is less favourable to the claimant than the decision that is being superseded, the decision will be effective from the date on which it would have been effective if the Secretary of State had acted on his own initiative (*R(IB)2/04* at para.97). It has been held that if the Secretary of State considers a case on his own motion but decides not to change the award, he is bound nonetheless to issue a decision refusing to revise or supersede the decision, or revising or superseding it "at the same rate" (*CTC/2979/2001*). However, that was doubted in *CDLA/705/2002* and, in *CI/1547/2001*, it was said that the Secretary of State was nearly always bound to issue a decision on a claimant's application but need not do so when considering a case on his own motion. If a decision is given simply in terms of a new award without supersession being mentioned but in circumstances where the new award could be made only on supersession, the defect can be cured by a tribunal giving the decision in the correct form (*R(IB)2/04* at para.76). However, if the tribunal never discover that the decision should have been a supersession, because they are unaware that there was an award current when the decision was made, the tribunal's decision may well be set aside because it is impossible to infer that circumstances justifying a different outcome on supersession were made out (*CDLA/9/2001*).

Section 10(3) permits regulations to be made prescribing the procedure by which a supersession may be made, but no regulation has been made prescribing the form of an application and the question whether a letter amounts to an application for supersession does not fall within the exclusive jurisdiction of the Secretary of State. A letter providing information about a change of circumstances will often imply a request for supersession (see para.(5)) but not all letters to the Department carry a clear implication to that effect and it may sometimes be difficult to determine whether, in reconsidering a decision, the Secretary of State is acting on his own initiative or in response to an application. This would not matter were it not for the impact the distinction may have on the date from which the application is effective (see s.10(5) of the Social Security Act 1998). It is doubtful whether giving information to a medical advisor during a medical examination amounts to an application for supersession, even though a notification of a change of circumstances may be treated as an application for supersession under para. (5), but the Secretary of State can made a supsersession decision of his own motion when the information is passed to him (*CI/954/2006*).

A final assessment of disablement made under the legislation replaced by the 1998 Act implies that there was no disablement after the end of the award, and so has ongoing effect and requires supersession as well as a new claim for benefit (*R(I) 5/02*), whereas an assessment under the 1998 Act carries no such implication and, after it expires, requires just a new claim.

Save in the many instances where reg.7 or Schs 3A or 3B provide otherwise, a supersession is effective from the date on which it was made, if the supersession was made on the Secretary of State's own initiative, or on the date of application when the suppression was made on the application of a claimant or other interested person (s.10(5) of the 1998 Act). In *CI/1547/2001*, it was suggested that all appeals against assessment decisions should also be treated as appeals against the consequent entitlement decisions because the provisions for supersession and revision, are too limited, having regard to the dates from which they are effective, to deal satisfactorily with the consequences of a successful appeal on assessment alone. In *CI/954/2006*, the Commissioner made the same point in respect of an application to supersede an assessment of disablement. He also held that, where a person who had been awarded disablement benefit suffered another industrial accident, a claim for disablement benefit in respect of the second accident might have to be treated in the alternative as an application for supersession of the first award and he pointed out that there is an anomolous difference in the extent to which a claim and an application for supersession can be backdated.

Note that payment of benefit may be suspended under reg.16 while consideration is being given to superseding an award. In a case where payment of attendance allowance was terminated on supersession, because a local authority was paying care home fees, but the claimant was in dispute with a financial adviser and it was possible that money to pay the fees retrospectively would be forthcoming, payment ought merely to have been suspended (*CA/3800/2006*). It made a difference because, if payments were superseded, it was not possible to reinstate them from the date they were terminated by way of a further supersession.

(SI 1999/991, reg. 6)

Even if an award of benefit is a possession within Art.1 of Protocol 1 to the European Convention on Human Rights, its removal under the provisions for supersession is not in breach of the Convention (*CDLA/3908/2001*).

Para. (2)

There is some degree of overlap between the sub-paras (e.g. (a)(i) and (e)) but this is not of particular significance. It is suggested that where two sub-paras apply, the person applying for, or initiating, the supersession is entitled to have the benefit of the more advantageous of the two as determined under reg.7 or Schs 3A or 3B (which provide numerous exceptions to the general rule under s.10(5) that a supersession is effective from the date it is made or the application for it was made). 2.374

Para. (2)(a)(i)

In *R(I) 56/54*, the Commissioner said: "A relevant change of circumstances postulates that the decision has ceased to be correct". This means that only an award may be superseded on the ground of change of circumstances. A decision that a claimant is not entitled to benefit at all may not be superseded on that ground. Instead, the claimant must make a new claim. *R(I)56/54* also suggests that a change of circumstances is relevant only if it would result in a different "outcome decision". The same approach was taken in *Wood v Secretary of State for Work and Pensions* [2003] EWCA Civ 53 (reported as *R(DLA) 1/03*) but the Court did not refer to *Saker v Secretary of State for Social Services, The Times*, Jaunary 16, 1988 (reported as an appendix to *R(I) 2/88*) in which Nicholls L.J. considered what might amount to a "material" fact for the purposes of a provision similar to para.(2)(b)(i) and said that a fact was material "if it was one which, had it been known to the medical board, would have called for serious consideration by the board and might well have affected its decision". On the other hand, in *CIB/2338/2000*, the Commissioner said that the "subtleties based on the *Saker* decision, under which a change maybe relevant without justifying a different outcome, have no place in the scheme of adjudication under the 1998 Act". In practical terms there is probably nothing to choose between the *Wood* approach and the *Saker* approach because a refusal to supersede has the same effect as a supersession "at the same rate". In other words, properly applied, both approaches produce the same outcome. 2.375

A new medical opinion is not itself a change of circumstances but a new medical report may reveal not only a new opinion but also new clinical findings which would show a change of circumstances (*R(IS) 2/97* and *Cooke v Secretary of State for Social Security* [2001] EWCA Civ 734 (reported as *R(DLA) 6/01*)). A lessening of care needs is itself a change of circumstances (*R1/05(DLA)*). A change in legislation is a change of circumstances (*R(A) 4/81*) but an unexpected decision of a court (or a Commissioner) is not (*Chief Adjudication Officer v McKiernon*, reported as *R(I)2/94*). Paragraph (6) makes further provision as to matters that are not relevant changes of circumstances. It is suggested that, at least in some contexts, the passage of time may be a material change of circumstances for the purposes of permitting supersession, e.g. the passing of the end of a qualifying period, and that in other cases it may be reasonable to presume there to have been a change of circumstances where time has passed, e.g. in some cases involving mental health factors.

Although reg.6(2)(a)(i) enables the Secretary of State to supersede a decision on the ground that there has been a change of circumstances "since the decision had effect", a Tribunal of Commissioners has suggested that it would be improper for the Secretary of State to supersede on that ground where the decision being superseded was that of a tribunal and, because the change of circumstances occurred before the decision under appeal and the tribunal was well aware of it, the tribunal could have taken it into account notwithstanding section 12(8)(b) of the Social Security Act 1998 but did not do so (*CIS/624/2006*). "The Secretary of State should abide by a tribunal's decision in such circumstances." If he considers that the change of circumstances has not properly been taken into account, his remedy is to appeal.

See reg.7(2) for the date from which the supersession is effective.

Para. (2) (a) (ii)

2.376 Section 8(2) of the Social Security Act 1998 provides that, when the Secretary of State makes a decision on a claim, he is precluded from taking account of circumstances not obtaining at the date of his decision. There is no equivalent provision in s.10 in respect of supersessions and this head expressly permits the Secretary of State to anticipate a change of circumstances. This is obviously a useful provision allowing the Secretary of State to act immediately to make the appropriate adjustment when a claimant informs him that his circumstances are about to change. However, it raises some interesting questions. For instance, what ground of supersession would there be if the anticipated change of circumstances did not take place? Perhaps supersession or revision on the ground of mistake of fact would be appropriate? More problematic is that a tribunal is precluded by s.12(8)(b) from having regard to any change of circumstances not obtaining at the date of the Secretary of State's decision and would therefore apparently be bound to ignore the change of circumstances that the Secretary of State had anticipated, even if the tribunal found that the change of circumstances had occurred. Also, the amendment to this head made in respect of advance awards does not apply to an award made on supersession under this very head so that it might be difficult to supersede a decision in the light of an unanticipated change of circumstances occurring between the date of supersession and the date from which the supersession was effective.

Para. (2) (b) and (c)

2.377 Paragraph (2)(b)(ii) exists to prevent there from being any overlap between supersession under para.(b) and revision under reg.3(1). A decision ought not to be superseded under sub-paras (b) or (c) so as to produce a different outcome if correcting the error of fact does not itself justify a different decision *(R(IB)2/04)*. Ignorance or mistake must be as to a primary fact and not merely as to an inference or conclusion of fact. Thus, a decision cannot be superseded simply on the ground that the Secretary of State now takes a different view of the case. "He must go further and assert and prove that the inference might not have been drawn, if the determining authority had not been ignorant of some specific fact of which it could have been aware, or had not been mistaken as to some specific fact which it took into consideration" *(R(I) 3/75)*. It may be particularly difficult to show that a tribunal made a mistake of fact if neither party obtained a full statement of reasons and it may be equally difficult to show that a tribunal was ignorant of a material fact if neither party obtained a record of proceedings which would include a note of evidence. In *CDLA/3875/2001* and *CDLA/2115/2003*, the Commissioners commented on the consequence of keeping inadequate records of Secretary of State's decisions. Lack of evidence as to the basis on which an adjudication officer's decision was made had made it impossible for the Secretary of State to point to an error in the decision that he wished to supersede.

A tribunal should hesitate before superseding the decision of an earlier tribunal for error of fact, where the issue must have been considered by the earlier tribunal if it was doing its job properly *(CDLA/3364/2001)*. The tribunal should consider what the consequences may be and should obtain the parties' views. A copy of the statement of the earlier tribunal's reasons should also be obtained if one was issued.

Para. (2) (d)

2.378 This appears to overlap with reg.3(8) and therefore to be of no effect by virtue of para.(3).

Para. (2) (e)

2.379 The new decision has effect from the date on which entitlement arises to the other benefit or to an increase in the rate of that other benefit (reg.7(7)). If entitlement to the other benefit, or to an increase in the rate of that other benefit, arises on or before the date from which the decision being reconsidered was effective, the decision is revised under reg.3(7) instead of being superseded.

(SI 1999/991, reg.6)

Para.(2)(g)
For the meaning of "incapacity benefit decision" and "incapacity determination", see reg.7A.

In *R(IB) 2/05*, the claimant had twice been referred for medical examinations after being awarded incapacity benefit. On the first occasion he satisfied the personal capability assessment and on the second occasion he did not. Following the second examination, the Secretary of State issued a decision purporting to supersede the original award. The Commissioner declined to rule on a submission that there should have been a supersession decision after the first medical examination because the grounds for supersession under reg.6(2)(g) are such that it made no difference whether there should already have been a supersession of the original award or even whether there had been a supersession of that award. On any view, there must have been a decision that could properly be superseded under reg.6(2)(g) and it was unnecessary further to identify the decision.

It has long been held that the obtaining of a new medical opinion does not itself amount to a change of circumstances justifying supersession under para.(2)(a)(i) (formerly a review) although a new medical report might include clinical findings revealing that there had been a change of circumstances (*R(IS) 2/97, Cooke v Secretary of State for Social Security* [2001] EWCA Civ 734 (reported as *R(DLA) 6/01*)). This sub-para. provides that obtaining a report is in itself grounds for supersession. In *CIB/2338/2000*, it was said that this sub-para. was unnecessary because, on a proper understanding of para.(2)(a)(i), it was always possible to identify a relevant change of circumstances in those cases where there was justification for terminating an award. However, it is suggested that there is a clear purpose underlying this sub-para. In *Cooke v Secretary of State for Social Security*, it was pointed out that, in the absence of a provision like para.(2)(g), a decision terminating an award following receipt of a medical report could be based either on the ground that there had been a change of circumstances (see para.(2)(a)(i)) or on the ground that benefit should never have been awarded in the first place (see para.(2)(b)). It was at least theoretically necessary to decide which of those grounds applied and, if there had been a change of circumstances, determine the date of the change, because that would determine the date from which the new decision would be effective which in turn would determine whether there had been any potentially reoverable overpayment, although the necessity was avoided if the Secretary of State made it clear that there was no intention to recover any payment. The advantage of superseding a decision under para.(2)(g) is that it is unnecessary to identify a change of circumstances since, or an error in, the decision being superseded because, in the absence of any specific provision in reg.7, the new decision is effective from the date it is made (s.10(5) of the Social Security Act 1998). It is to be noted that para.(2)(g) does not oust the power to supersede under, say, para.(2)(a)(i) in an incapacity benefit or credit case. Regulation 7(2)(c), which was amended at the same time as reg.6(2)(g) was introduced, makes specific provision as to the date from which decisions under para.(2)(a)(i) are effective in such cases.

One consequence of it being unnecessary to find a specific change of circumstances since, or error in, an earlier decision is that it may be less important to consider the evidence lying behind the decision being superseded. However, where a claimant submits that his or her condition is unchanged since an earlier personal capability assessment, the findings made an earlier assessment may well be relevant (*R(S)1/55*) as evidence of the claimant's present condition, particularly if the condition is variable and any examination is likely to be only a snapshot (*CIB/2338/2000*). Commissioners were therefore highly critical of a rumoured proposal to destroy all records of personal capability assessments so that they were not available to decision-makers or tribunals concerned with subsequent supersessions (*CIB/1972/2000, CIB/3667/2000, CIB/378/2001, CIB/3179/2000*). In *CIB/3985/2001*, it was held that, where a claimant had stated that his condition had not changed since he had previously satisfied a personal capability assessment, the Secretary of State ought to make the report on that assessment available because the claimant had identified that as relevant evidence and was unable to produce it himself. Where the Secretary of State had not produced that

2.380

evidence, the tribunal had to proceed on the basis that they had before them an implied request for an adjournment. That meant they had to consider whether the evidence was potentially relevant, in the light of the other evidence before them and, in the circumstances of the case under consideration, the tribunal erred in law in failing to adjourn and direct the Secretary of State to produce the evidence. There was nothing to suggest that the earlier assessments had ceased to be relevant because, for instance, there had been a supervening operation or injury. In those circumstances, it was not sufficient for the tribunal to rely on the new assessment when the claimant's argument was that earlier assessments would show it to be incomplete and insufficient. The need to provide a tribunal with proper information about the adjudication history behind a decision, explaining the basis of previous awards and the grounds upon which the last award has been superseded, has again been emphasised by a Tribunal of Commissioners in Northern Ireland in *R1/04(IB)*.

Another consequence of it being unnecessary to find a change of circumstances since, or error in, an earlier decision is that a decision-maker is entitled to make a different judgement on the same facts so that, even if a tribunal accept that a claimant's condition has not changed since an earlier favourable assessment and they cannot identify an error of fact or law in that earlier decision, they may decide that the claimant is not entitled to benefit. Nonetheless, the burden of proving grounds for supersession always lies on the person seeking supersession so that, where a claimant has been entitled to incapacity benefit, it is for the Secretary of State to justify terminating the award by superseding it under reg.6(2)(g). However, it is pointed out in *CIB/1509/2004* that the burden of proof must be considered in two stages. For reg.6(2)(g) to apply at all, the Secretary of State must have received the necessary medical evidence following an appropriate medical examination. On an appeal to a tribunal, it is plainly for the Secretary of State to produce that evidence but he invariably does so and therefore that is not usually a live issue. The second stage is considering whether the claimant still satisfies the conditions for entitlement to benefit and so continues to be entitled to benefit notwithstanding that the requirements of reg.6(2)(g) are met. The Commissioner referred to *Kerr v Department for Social Development* [2004] UKHL 23; [2004] 1 W.L.R. 1372 (also reported as an appendix to *R1/04(SF)* (see the annotation to s.12 of the Social Security Act 1998), where Baroness Hale talked of "a co-operative process of investigation" (para.62) and said that "it will rarely be necessary to resort to concepts taken from adversarial litigation such as the burden of proof" (para.63). A tribunal must have regard to all the evidence produced in the investigation and decide the case on the balance of probabilities. The Commissioner followed *CIS/427/1991* in holding that the burden of proof is relevant only (a) if there is no relevant evidence on an issue (despite an adequate investigation) or (b) if the evidence on the issue is so evenly balanced that it is impossible to determine where the balance of probabilities lies. When superseding a decision on his own initiative, the burden of proof lies on the Secretary of State at both stages so that, in the few cases when it is relevant at the second stage, the case should be decided in favour of the claimant. Normally there is sufficient evidence to enable a tribunal to form a clear view one way or the other. That evidence includes the earlier decision and so, where it is decided to supersede it to the disadvantage of the claimant, it may be necessary for a tribunal's reasons to refer to the earlier decision *(R(M) 1/96)*. Decisions that appear inconsistent and are not adequately explained tend to bring the adjudication system into disrepute *(R(A) 2/83)*.

In *CIB/313/2002* and *R(IB)2/04* at para.125, Commissioners have suggested that reg.6(2)(g) is applicable only where the award to be superseded was based on a personal capability assessment (see the definition of "incapacity determination" in reg.7A) and that where, for instance, an award was based on deemed incapacity under reg.28 of the Social Security (Incapacity for Work) (General) Regulations 1995, the proper basis for supersession was reg.6(2)(a)(i). However, in neither case was the point determined because the result would have been the same whichever provision was applied. In *CSIB/501/2003* (subsequently approved by the Court of Appeal in *Hooper v Secretary of State for Work and Pensions* [2007] EWCA Civ 495 (reported as

(SI 1999/991, reg. 6)

R(IB) 4/07)), it was held that a decision to award invalidity benefit could not be "an incapacity benefit decision" and therefore could not be superseded under reg.6(2)(g). Presumably it could have been superseded under reg.6(2)(a)(i) but the Deputy Commissioner left such issues to be considered by the Secretary of State.

Para. (5)
An application for revision may be treated as an application for supersession. Regulation 3(10) provides that an application for supersession may be treated as an application for revision. For the power of an appeal tribunal to treat a supersession as a refusal to revise and vice versa, see the note to s.12 of the Social Security Act 1998.

2.381

6A. *Omitted.* 2.382
6B. *Omitted.* 2.383

Date from which a decision superseded under section 10 takes effect

7.—[⁴ (1) This regulation— 2.384
[¹² (a) is, except for [¹⁴ paragraphs (2)(b), (29) and (30)], subject to Schedules 3A and 3B; and]
(b) contains exceptions to the provisions of section 10(5) as to the date from which a decision under section 10 which supersedes an earlier decision is to take effect.]
(2) Where a decision under section 10 is made on the ground that there has been, or it is anticipated that there will be, a relevant change of circumstances since the decision [¹⁴ had effect] [¹⁹ or, in the case of an advance award, since the decision was made], the decision under section 10 shall take effect—
[⁴ (a) from the date the change occurred or, where the change does not have effect until a later date, from the first date on which such effect occurs where—
  (i) the decision is advantageous to the claimant; and
  (ii) the change was notified to an appropriate office within one month of the change occurring or within such longer period as may be allowed under regulation 8 for the claimant's failure to notify the change on an earlier date;]
(b) where the decision is advantageous to the claimant and the change was notified to an appropriate office more than one month after the change occurred or after the expiry of any such longer period as may have been allowed under regulation 8—
  (i) in the case of a claimant who is in receipt of income support [¹², jobseeker's allowance or state pension credit] and benefit is paid in arrears, from the beginning of the benefit week in which the notification was made;
  (ii) in the case of a claimant who is in receipt of income support [¹², jobseeker's allowance or state pension credit] and benefit is paid in advance and the date of notification is the first day of a benefit week from that date and otherwise, from the beginning of the benefit week following the week in which the notification was made; or
  (iii) in any other case, the date of notification of the relevant change of circumstances; or
[⁷(bb) where the decision is advantageous to the claimant and is made on the Secretary of State's own initiative, from the date on which the Secretary of State commenced action with a view to supersession;]

[²³ (bc) where the decision is advantageous to the claimant and is made in connection with the cessation of payment of a carer's allowance, the day after the last day for which that allowance was paid;]
  (c) where the decision is not advantageous to the claimant—
    (i) [⁴ . . .]
    [¹(ii) in the case of a disability benefit decision, or an incapacity benefit decision where there has been an incapacity determination (whether before or after the decision), where the Secretary of State is satisfied that in relation to a disability determination embodied in or necessary to the disability benefit decision, or the incapacity determination, the claimant or payee failed to notify an appropriate office of a change of circumstances which regulations under the Administration Act required him to notify, and the claimant or payee, as the case may be, knew or could reasonably have been expected to know that the change of circumstances should have been notified,
      (aa) from the date on which the claimant or payee, as the case may be, ought to have notified the change of circumstances, or
      (bb) if more than one change has taken place between the date from which the decision to be superseded took effect and the date of the superseding decision, from the date on which the first change ought to have been notified, or
    (iii) [²² . . .]
    [²¹(iv) in the case of a disability benefit decision, where the change of circumstances is not in relation to the disability determination embodied in or necessary to the disability benefit decision, from the date of the change; or
    (v) in any other case, except in the case of a decision which supersedes a disability benefit decision, from the date of the change.]

(3) For the purposes of paragraphs (2) and (8) "benefit week" has the same meaning as in regulation 2(1) of the Income Support Regulations or, as the case may be, regulation 1(3) of the Jobseeker's Regulations [¹² or regulation 1(2) of the State Pension Credit Regulations].

(4) In paragraph (2) a decision which is to the advantage of the claimant includes a decision specified in regulation 30(2)(a) to (f).

[⁷ (5) Where the Secretary of State supersedes a decision made by an appeal tribunal or a Commissioner on the grounds specified in regulation 6(2)(c) [¹⁴ (i)] (ignorance of, or mistake as to, a material fact), the decision under section 10 shall take effect, in a case where, as a result of that ignorance of or mistake as to material fact, the decision to be superseded was more advantageous to the claimant than it would otherwise have been and which either—
  (a) does not relate to a disability benefit decision or an incapacity benefit decision where there has been an incapacity determination; or
  (b) relates to a disability decision or an incapacity benefit decision where there has been an incapacity determination, and the Secretary of State is satisfied that at the time the decision was made the claimant or payee knew or could reasonably have been expected to know of the fact in question and that it was relevant to the decision.
from the date on which the decision of the appeal tribunal or the Commissioner took, or was to take, effect.]

(SI 1999/991, reg. 7)

(6) Any decision made under section 10 in consequence of a decision which is a relevant determination for the purposes of section 27 shall take effect as from the date of the relevant determination.

[[19] (6A) Where—
- (a) there is a decision which is a relevant determination for the purposes of section 27 and the Secretary of State makes a benefit decision of the kind specified in section 27(1)(b);
- (b) there is an appeal against the determination;
- (c) after the benefit decision payment is suspended in accordance with regulation 16(1) and (3)(b)(ii); and
- (d) on appeal a court, within the meaning of section 27, reverses the determination in whole or in part,

a consequential decision by the Secretary of State under section 10 which supersedes his earlier decision under sub-paragraph (a) shall take effect from the date on which the earlier decision took effect.]

[[21] (7) A decision which is superseded in accordance with regulation 6(2)(e) or (ee) shall be superseded—
- (a) subject to sub-paragraph (b), from the date on which entitlement arises to the other relevant benefit referred to in regulation 6(2)(e)(ii) or (ee) or to an increase in the rate of that other relevant benefit; or
- (b) where the claimant or his partner—
  - (i) is not a severely disabled person for the purposes of section 135(5) of the Contributions and Benefits Act (the applicable amount) or section 2(7) of the State Pension Credit Act (guarantee credit)
  - (ii) by virtue of his having—
    - (aa) a non-dependant as defined by regulation 3 of the Income Support Regulations; or
    - (bb) a person residing with him for the purposes of paragraph 1 of Schedule 1 to the State Pension Credit Regulations whose presence may not be ignored in accordance with paragraph 2 of that Schedule,

    at the date the superseded decision would, but for this sub-paragraph, have had effect,

  from the date on which the claimant or his partner ceased to have a non-dependant or person residing with him or from the date on which the presence of that person was first ignored.]

[[22] (7A) Where a decision is superseded in accordance with regulation 6(2)(o), the superseding decision shall take effect from the day on which a lump sum, or a payment on account of a lump sum, is paid or repaid if that day is the first day of the benefit week but, if it is not, from the next following such day.]

[[3] (8) A decision to which regulation 6(2)(f) applies shall take effect—
- (a) where section 19(2) [[8] or 20A(3)] of the Jobseekers Act applies, as from the beginning of the period specified in regulation 69 of the Jobseeker's Allowance Regulations; or
- (b) where section 19(3) [[8] or 20A(4)] of the Jobseekers Act applies, as from the beginning of the period determined in accordance with that subsection.]

[[4] (9) A decision relating to attendance allowance or disability living allowance which is advantageous to the claimant and which is made under

section 10 on the basis of a relevant change of circumstances shall take effect from—
[¹⁴ (a) where the decision is made on the Secretary of State's own initiative—
  (i) the date on which the Secretary of State commenced action with a view to supersession; or
  (ii) subject to paragraph (30), in a case where the relevant circumstances are that there has been a change in the legislation in relation to attendance allowance or disability living allowance, the date on which that change in the legislation had effect;]
(b) where—
  (i) the change is relevant to the question of entitlement to a particular rate of benefit; and
  (ii) the claimant notifies the change before a date one month after the satisfied the conditions of entitlement to that rate or within such longer period as may be allowed under regulation 8,
the first pay day (as specified in Schedule 6 to the Claims and Payments Regulations) after he satisfied those conditions;
(c) where—
  (i) the change is relevant to the question of whether benefit is payable; and
  (ii) the claimant notifies the change before a date one month after the change or within such longer period as may be allowed under regulation 8,
the first pay day (as specified in Schedule 6 to the Claims and Payments Regulations) after the change occurred; or
(d) in any other case, the date of the application for the superseding decision.]

(10) A decision as to an award of incapacity benefit, which is made under section 10 because section 30B(4) of the Contributions and Benefits Act applies to the claimant, shall take effect as from the date on which he became entitled to the highest rate of the care component of disability living allowance.

(11) A decision as to an award of incapacity benefit or severe disablement allowance, which is made under section 10 because the claimant is to be treated as incapable of work under regulation 10 of the Social Security (Incapacity for Work) (General) Regulations 1995 (certain persons with a severe condition to be treated as incapable of work), shall take effect as from the date he is to be treated as incapable of work.

(12) Where this paragraph applies, a decision under section 10 may be made so as to take effect as from such date not more than eight weeks before—
(a) the application for supersession; or
(b) where no application is made, the date on which the decision under section 10 is made,
as is reasonable in the particular circumstances of the case.

(13) Paragraph (12) applies where—
(a) the effect of a decision under section 10 is that there is to be included in a claimant's applicable amount an amount in respect of a loan which qualifies under—
  (i) paragraph 15 or 16 of Schedule 3 to the Income Support Regulations; or

(ii) paragraph 14 or 15 of Schedule 2 to the Jobseeker's Allowance Regulations; [¹² or
(iii) paragraph 11 or 12 of Schedule II to the State Pension Credit Regulations; and]
(b) that decision could not have been made earlier because information necessary to make that decision, requested otherwise than in accordance with paragraph 10(3)(b) of Schedule 9A to the Claims and Payments Regulations (annual requests for information), had not been supplied to the Secretary of State by the lender.

(14) Subject to paragraph (23), where a claimant is in receipt of income support and his applicable amount includes an amount determined in accordance with Schedule 3 to the Income Support Regulations (housing costs), and there is a reduction in the amount of eligible capital owing in connection with a loan which qualifies under paragraph 15 or 16 of that Schedule, a decision made under section 10 shall take effect—
(a) on the first anniversary of the date on which the claimant's housing costs were first met under that Schedule; or
(b) where the reduction in eligible capital occurred after the first anniversary of the date referred to in sub-paragraph (a), on the next anniversary of that date following the date of the reduction.

(15) Where a claimant is in receipt of income support and payments made to that claimant which fall within paragraph 29 or 30(1)(a) to (c) of Schedule 9 to the Income Support Regulations have been disregarded in relation to any decision under section 8 or 10 and there is a change in the amount of interest payable—
(a) on a loan qualifying under paragraph 15 or 16 of Schedule 3 to those Regulations to which those payments relate; or
(b) on a loan not so qualifying which is secured on the dwelling occupied as the home to which those payments relate,
a decision under section 10 which is made as a result of that change in the amount of interest payable shall take effect on whichever of the dates referred to in paragraph (16) is appropriate in the claimant's case.

(16) The date on which a decision under section 10 takes effect for the purposes of paragraph (15) is—
(a) the date on which the claimant's housing costs are first met under paragraph 6(1)(a), 8(1)(a) or 9(2)(a) of Schedule 3 to the Income Support Regulations; or
(b) where the change in the amount of interest payable occurred after the date referred to in sub-paragraph (a), on the date of the next alteration in the standard rate following the date of that change.

(17) In paragraph (16), "standard rate" has the same meaning as it has in paragraph 1(2) of Schedule 3 to the Income Support Regulations.

[¹² (17A) For the purposes of state pension credit—
(a) paragraph (14) shall apply as if the reference to—
(i) "income support and his applicable amount" was a reference to "state pension credit and his appropriate minimum guarantee";
(ii) "Schedule 3 to the Income Support Regulations" was a reference to "Schedule II to the State Pension Credit Regulations"; and
(iii) "paragraph 15 or 16" was a reference to "paragraph 11 or 12";
(b) paragraphs (15) to (17) shall not apply.]

[¹⁶ (17B) Paragraph 17C applies where—

(a) a claimant is awarded state pension credit;
(b) the claimant or his partner is aged 65 or over;
(c) his appropriate minimum guarantee (as defined by the State Pension Credit Act) includes housing costs determined in accordance with Schedule II to the State Pension Credit Regulations; and
(d) after the date from which sub-paragraph (c) applies—
  (i) a non-dependant (as defined in that Schedule) begins to reside with the claimant; or
  (ii) a non-dependant's income increases and this affects the applicable amount of the claimant's housing costs.

(17C) In the circumstances specified in paragraph (17B) a decision made under section 10 shall take effect—
(a) where there is more than one change of the kind specified in paragraph (17B)(d) in respect of the same non-dependant within the same 26 week period, 26 weeks after the date on which the first such change occurred; and
(b) in any other circumstances, 26 weeks after the date on which a change specified in paragraph (17B)(d) occurred.]

(18) Subject to paragraph (24) and, except in a case to which paragraph (23) applies, where a claimant is in receipt of a jobseeker's allowance and his applicable amount includes an amount determined in accordance with Schedule 2 to the Jobseeker's Allowance Regulations (housing costs), and there is a reduction in the amount of eligible capital owing in connection with a loan which qualifies under paragraph 14 or 15 of that Schedule, a decision under section 10 made as a result of that reduction shall take effect—
(a) on the first anniversary of the date on which the claimant's housing costs were first met under that Schedule; or
(b) where the reduction in eligible capital occurred after the first anniversary of the date referred to in sub-paragraph (a), on the next anniversary of that date following the date of the reduction.

(19) Where a claimant is in receipt of a jobseeker's allowance and payments made to that claimant which fall within paragraph 30 or 31(1)(a) to (c) of Schedule 7 to the Jobseeker's Allowance Regulations have been disregarded in relation to any decision under section 8 or 10 and there is a change in the amount of interest payable—
(a) on a loan qualifying under paragraph 14 or 15 of Schedule 2 to those Regulations to which those payments relate; or
(b) on a loan not so qualifying which is secured on the dwelling occupied as the home to which those payments relate,
any decision under section 10 which is made as a result of that change in the amount of interest payable shall take effect on whichever of the dates referred to in paragraph (20) is appropriate in the claimant's case.

(20) The date on which a decision under section 10 takes effect for the purposes of paragraph (19) is—
(a) the date on which the claimant's housing costs are first met under paragraph 6(1)(a), 7(1)(a) or 8(2)(a) of Schedule 2 to the Jobseeker's Allowance Regulations; or
(b) where the changes in the amount of interest payable occurred after the date referred to in sub-paragraph (a), on the date of the next alteration in the standard rate following the date of that change.

(21) In paragraph (20), "standard rate" has the same meaning as it has in paragraph 1(2) of Schedule 2 to the Jobseeker's Allowance Regulations.

(SI 1999/991, reg. 7)

(22) Where—
(a) a claimant was paid benefit in respect of October 6, 1996 in accordance with an award of income support;
(b) that claimant's applicable amount includes an amount determined in accordance with Schedule 3 to the Income Support Regulations (housing costs);
(c) that claimant is treated as having been awarded a jobseeker's allowance by virtue of regulation 7 of the Jobseeker's Allowance (Transitional Provisions) Regulations 1996 (jobseeker's allowance to replace income support and unemployment benefit); and
(d) a decision is made under section 10 in consequence of a reduction in the amount of eligible capital owing in connection with a loan which qualifies under paragraph 15 or 16 of Schedule 3 to the Income Support Regulations,

the decision under section 10 referred to in sub-paragraph (d) shall take effect on the next anniversary of the date on which housing costs were first met which occurs after the reduction.

[13 (23) Where, in any case to which paragraph (14), (17A), [16 . . .] or (18) applies, a claimant has been continuously in receipt of, or treated as having been continuously in receipt of income support, a jobseeker's allowance or state pension credit, or one of those benefits followed by the other, and he or his partner continues to receive any of those benefits, the anniversary to which those paragraphs refer shall be—
(a) in the case of income support or jobseeker's allowance, the anniversary of the earliest date on which benefit in respect of those mortgage interest costs became payable;
(b) in the case of state pension credit, the relevant anniversary date determined in accordance with paragraph 7 of Schedule II to the State Pension Credit Regulations.]

(24) Where—
(a) it has been determined that the amount of a jobseeker's allowance payable to a young person is to be reduced under regulation 63 of the Jobseeker's Allowance Regulations because paragraph (1)(b)(iii), (c), (d), (e) or (f) of that regulation (reduced payments under section 17 of the Jobseekers Act) applied in his case; and
(b) the decision made in consequence of sub-paragraph (a) falls to be superseded by a decision under section 10 because the Secretary of State has subsequently issued a certificate under section 17(4) of the Jobseekers Act with respect to the failure in question,

the decision under section 10 shall take effect as from the same date as the decision made in consequence of sub-paragraph (a) has effect.

[5 [17 (25) In a case where a decision ("the first decision") has been made that a person failed without good cause to take part in a work-focused interview, the decision under section 10 shall take effect as from—
(a) the first day of the benefit week to commence for that person following the date of the first decision; or
(b) in a case where a partner has failed without good cause to take part in a work-focused interview [18 in accordance with regulations made under section 2AA of the Administration Act]—
  (i) the first day of the benefit week to commence for the claimant [18 (meaning the person who has been awarded benefit within section 2AA(2) of the Administration Act at a higher

Social Security and Child Support (Decisions and Appeals) Regs 1999

rate referable to that partner)] following the date of the first decision; or

(ii) if that date arises five days or less after the day on which the first decision was made, as from the first day of the second benefit week to commence for the claimant following the date of the first decision.]

(26) In paragraph (25), "benefit week" means any period of 7 days corresponding to the week in respect of which the relevant social security benefit is due to be paid.]

[⁹ (27) A decision to which regulation 6(2)(i) applies shall take effect from the beginning of the period specified—
- (a) subject to sub-paragraphs (d) and (e), in relation to jobseeker's allowance—
    - (i) in regulation 3(1)(a) of the Breach of Community Order Regulations;
    - (ii) in regulation 3(1)(b) of those regulations;
- (b) subject to sub-paragraphs (d) and (e), in relation to income support—
    - (i) in regulation 3(3)(a) of the Breach of Community Order Regulations;
    - (ii) in regulation 3(3)(b) of those regulations;
- (c) subject to sub-paragraphs (d) and (e), in relation to a joint-claim jobseeker's allowance—
    - (i) in regulation 3(4)(a) of the Breach of Community Order Regulations;
    - (ii) in regulation 3(4)(b) of those regulations;
- (d) in regulation 3(5) of the Breach of Community Order Regulations;
- (e) in regulation 3(6) of the Breach of Community Order Regulations.]

[¹⁰ (28) A decision to which regulation 6(2)(j) or (k) applies shall take effect from the first day of the disqualification period prescribed for the purposes of section 7 of the Social Security Fraud Act 2001.]

[¹² (29) [¹⁵ Subject to paragraphs (29A) and (29B), a] decision to which regulation 6(2)(1) (state pension credit) refers shall take effect from the day following the day on which the assessed income period ends if that day is the first day of the claimant's benefit week, but if it is not, from the next following such day.]

[¹⁵ (29A) A decision to which regulation 6(2)(l) applies, where—
- (a) the decision is advantageous to the claimant; and
- (b) the information and evidence required under regulation 32(1) of the Claims and Payments Regulations has not been provided within the period allowed under that regulation,

shall take effect from the day the information and evidence required under that regulation is provided if that day is the first day of the claimant's benefit week, but, if it is not, from the next following such day.

(29B) A decision to which regulation 6(2)(l) applies, where—
- (a) the decision is disadvantageous to the claimant; and
- (b) the information and evidence required under regulation 32(1) of the Claims and Payments Regulations has not been provided within the period allowed under that regulation,

shall take effect from the day after the period allowed under that regulation expired.

(29C) Except where there is a change of circumstances during the period in which the Secretary of State was prevented from specifying a new assessed income period under regulation 10(1) of the State Pension Credit Regulations, a decision to which regulation 6(2)(m) applies shall take effect from the day on which the information and evidence required under regulation 32(6)(a) of the Claims and Payments Regulations was provided.]

[[14] (30) Where a decision is superseded in accordance with regulation 6(2)(a)(i) and the relevant circumstances are that there has been a change in the legislation in relation to a relevant benefit, the decision under section 10 shall take effect from the date on which that change in the legislation had effect.

(31) Where a decision is superseded in accordance with regulation 6(2)(a)(ii) and the relevant circumstances are that—
(a) a personal capability assessment has been carried out in the case of a person to whom section 171C(4) of the Contributions and Benefits Act applies; and
(b) the own occupation test remains applicable to him under section 171B(3) of that Act,

the decision under section 10 shall take effect on the day immediately following the day on which the own occupation test is no longer applicable to that person.

(32) For the purposes of paragraph (31)—
(a) "personal capability assessment" has the same meaning as in regulation 24 of the Social Security (Incapacity for Work) (General) Regulations 1995;
(b) "own occupation test" has the same meaning as in section 171B(2) of the Contributions and Benefits Act.

(33) A decision to which regulation 6(2)(c)(ii) applies shall take effect from the date on which the appeal tribunal or the Commissioner's decision would have taken effect had it been decided in accordance with the determination of the Commissioner or the court in the appeal referred to in section 26(1)(b).]

[[19] (34) A decision which supersedes a decision specified in regulation 6(2)(n) shall take effect from the effective date of the Secretary of State's decision to terminate income support which was confirmed by the decision specified in regulation 6(2)(n).]

AMENDMENTS

1. Social Security and Child Support (Decisions and Appeals) Amendment (No.2) Regulations 1999 (SI 1999/1623), reg.4 (July 5, 1999).

2. Tax Credits (Decisions and Appeals) (Amendment) Regulations 1999 (SI 1999/2570), reg.10 (October 5, 1999). Note that amendments made by these regulations only have effect with respect to tax credit (reg.1(2) of the Amendment Regulations).

3. Social Security and Child Support (Decisions and Appeals), Vaccine Damage Payments and Jobseeker's Allowance (Amendment) Regulations 1999 (SI 1999/2677), reg.8 (October 18, 1999).

4. Social Security Act 1998 (Commencement No.12 and Consequential and Transitional Provisions) Order 1999 (SI 1999/3178), art.3(19) and Sch.19, para.1 (November 29, 1999).

5. Social Security and Child Support (Decisions and Appeals) Amendment Regulations 2000 (SI 2000/119), reg.2 (February 17, 2000).

6. Social Security (Work-focused Interviews) Regulations 2000 (SI 2000/897), reg.16(5) and Sch.6, para.5 (April 3, 2000).

7. Social Security and Child Support (Miscellaneous Amendments) Regulations 2000 (SI 2000/1596), reg.17 (June 19, 2000).

8. Social Security (Joint Claims: Consequential Amendments) Regulations 2000 (SI 2000/1982), reg.5(c) (March 19, 2001).
9. Social Security (Breach of Community Order) (Consequential Amendments) Regulations 2001 (SI 2001/1711), reg.2(2)(d) (October 15, 2001).
10. Social Security (Loss of Benefit) (Consequential Amendments) Regulations 2002 (SI 2002/490), reg.8(c) (April 1, 2002).
11. Social Security (Claims and Payments and Miscellaneous Amendments) Regulations 2002 (SI 2002/428), reg.4(4) (April 2, 2002).
12. State Pension Credit (Consequential, Transitional and Miscellaneous Provisions) Regulations 2002 (SI 2002/3019), reg.18 (April 7, 2003).
13. State Pension Credit (Consequential, Transitional and Miscellaneous Provisions) (No.2) Regulations 2002 (SI 2002/3197), reg.6 (April 7, 2003).
14. Social Security and Child Support (Miscellaneous Amendments) Regulations 2003 (SI 2003/1050), reg.3(5) (May 5, 2003).
15. State Pension Credit (Transitional and Miscellaneous Provisions) Amendment Regulations 2003 (SI 2003/2274), reg.5(3) (October 6, 2003).
16. State Pension Credit (Miscellaneous Amendments) Regulations 2004 (SI 2004/647), reg.2 (April 5, 2004).
17. Social Security (Jobcentre Plus Interviews for Partners) Regulations 2003 (SI 2003/1886), reg.15(5) (April 12, 2004).
18. Social Security (Working Neighbourhoods) Regulations 2004 (SI 2004/959), reg.24(4) (April 26, 2004).
19. Social Security, Child Support and Tax Credits (Miscellaneous Amendments) Regulations 2005 (SI 2005/337), reg.2(5) (March 18, 2005).
20. Social Security (Housing Benefit, Council Tax Benefit, State Pension Credit and Miscellaneous Amendments) Regulations 2004 (SI 2004/2327), reg.4 (April 4, 2005).
21. Social Security (Deferral of Retirement Pensions, Shared Additional Pension and Graduated Retirement Benefit) (Miscellaneous Provisions) Regulations 2005 (SI 2005/2677), reg.9(5) (April 6, 2006).
22. Social Security (Miscellaneous Amendments) (No.2) Regulations 2006 (SI 2006/832), reg.5(3) (April 10, 2006).
23. Social Security (Miscellaneous Amendments) (No.3) Regulations 2006 (SI 2006/2377), reg.3(2) (October 2, 2006).

DEFINITIONS

"appeal tribunal"—see reg.1(3).
"appropriate office"—see reg.3(11).
"assessed income period"—see reg.1(3).
"benefit week"—see para.(3).
"the Board"—see reg.1(3).
"the Breach of Community Order Regulations"—*ibid*.
"claimant"—*ibid*.
"the Claims and Payments Regulations"—*ibid*.
"Commissioner"—see s.39(1) of the Social Security Act 1998.
"the Contributions and Benefits Act"—see s.84 of the Social Security Act 1998.
"disability benefit decision"—see reg.7A(1).
"disability determination"—*ibid*.
"incapacity benefit decision"—*ibid*.
"incapacity determination"—*ibid*.
"the Income Support Regulations"—see reg.1(3).
"the Jobseekers Act"—see s.84 of the Social Security Act 1998.
"the Jobseeker's Allowance Regulations"—see reg.1(3).
"a joint-claim jobseeker's allowance"—*ibid*.
"payee"—see reg.7A(1).
"standard rate"—see paras(17) and (21).

(SI 1999/991, reg.7)

"state pension credit"—see reg.1(3).
"State Pension Credit Regulations"—*ibid*.
"work-focused interview"—*ibid*.

GENERAL NOTE

This regulation is not quite as complicated as it looks at first sight. As is explained in para.(1), the regulation provides exceptions to the general rule that a supersession decision takes effect from the date it is made or, where applicable, the date the application for supersession was made (s.10(5) of the Social Security Act 1998). The structure of the regulations is as follows:

Para.(1):	Introductory.
Paras (2)–(4):	Supersession for change of circumstances.
Para.(5):	Supersession of a tribunal or Commissioner's decision for error of fact.
Para.(6) and 6(A):	Supersession following a test case.
Para.(7):	Supersession following an award of another relevant benefit.
Para.(7A):	Supersession following a change in election whether to receive an increase in pension or a lump sum following a deferral of pension.
Para.(8):	Supersession of an award of jobseeker's allowance following a finding of voluntary unemployment.
Para.(9):	Supersession advantageous to claimant of an award of attendance allowance or disability living allowance.
Para.(10):	Supersession of an award of short-term incapacity benefit to increase the rate following an award of the highest rate of the care component of disability living allowance.
Para.(11):	Supersession of an award of incapacity benefit following a determination that the claimant is to be treated as incapable of work because he or she is suffering from a severe condition.
Paras (12) and (13):	Supersession in an income support or jobseeker's allowance case where information about housing costs was not supplied to the Secretary of State by a lender.
Para.(14):	Supersession in an income support case where there has been a reduction in the amount of eligible capital owing in respect of a loan.
Paras (15)–(17):	Supersession in an income support case where the claimant has been receiving payments under an insurance policy in respect of housing costs and there has been a change in the amount of interest payable.
Para.(17A):	Supersession in a state pension credit case where there has been a reduction in the amount of eligible capital owing in respect of a loan.
Paras (17A)–(17C):	Supersession in a state pension credit case where a nondependant commences residing with the claimant or has an increase in income.
Para.(18):	Supersession in a jobseeker's allowance case where there has been a reduction in the amount of eligible capital owing in respect of a loan.
Paras (19)–(21):	Supersession in a jobseeker's allowance case where the claimant has been receiving payments under an insurance costs in respect of housing costs and there has been a change in the amount of interest payable.
Para.(22):	Supersession in case where a claimant was transferred from income support to jobseeker's allowance on October 6, 1996 and there has been a reduction in the amount of eligible capital owing in respect of a loan.

2.385

Para.(23):	Supplementary to paras (14)–(18) in a case where a person has been in receipt of more than one of income support, jobseeker's allowance and state pension credit.
Para.(24):	Supersession in a case where the claimant is a young person and was receiving a reduced amount of jobseeker's allowance on account of failing to complete a course and the Secretary of State has issued a certificate stating that the claimant had good cause for failing to complete the course.
Paras (25)–(26):	Supersession following a determination that the claimant has failed without good cause to take part in a work-focused interview.
Para.(27):	Supersession in order to reduce benefit because an offender has breached a community order.
Para.(28):	Supersession in order to remove benefit because a person has been convicted of benefit offences.
Paras (29)–(29)B:	Supersession in a state pension credit case on the ending of an assessed income period.
Para.(29C):	Supersession where late provision of information or evidence has delayed the specification of a new assessed income period.
Para.(30):	Supersession following a change in relevant legislation.
Paras (31)–(32):	Supersession following a personal capability assessment carried out before the all work test becomes applicable.
Para.(33):	Supersession of a decision determined by a tribunal or Commissioner under s.26 of the Social Security Act 1998 while a test case was pending.
Para.(34):	Supersession of a decision of a tribunal in relation to income support where another tribunal has subsequently decided that the claimant is incapable of work.

Note that Sch.3A makes further provision for income support and jobseeker's allowance cases and Sch.3B makes further provision for state pension credit cases.

Para.(1)

2.386   Section 10(5) of the Social Security Act 1998 provides that a supersession decision takes effect from the date it is made or, where applicable, the date the application for supersession was made. Schedule 3A provides further refinement for income support and jobseeker's allowance cases as does Sch.3B for state pension credit cases. Where a case is not covered by this regulation or by Sch.3A or Sch.3B, s.10(5) applies.

Para.(2)

2.387   A supersession on the ground of change of circumstances advantageous to the claimant is effective from the date of the change if the change is notified within a month (or such longer period as is allowed under reg.8) but is otherwise effective only from the date of notification. Where the change is not advantageous to the claimant, the supersession is generally effective from the date of change or, in the case of incapacity and disability cases, from the date when the change should have been reported. See reg.7A for definitions material to para.(2)(c). Presumably, para.(2) does not apply to those attendance allowance and disability living allowance cases where para.(9) applies or, indeed, to any cases where any of paras (10)–(34) applies.

Regulation 7(2)(c) is concerned to ensure that an appropriate effective date is fixed where the effect of a supersession due to a change of circumstances is that benefit has been overpaid and the overpayment is likely to be recoverable under s.71 of the Social Security Administration Act 1992. (Regulation 3(5)(b) and (c) makes similar provision by way of revision where the original decision was made in ignorance of, or on a mistake as to, a material fact). Section 71(5A) of the 1992 Act

(SI 1999/991, reg. 7)

provides that an overpayment can generally be recovered only if a decision has properly been given in terms of revision or supersession, a point reiterated in *CIS/4434/2004*. If the decision is in terms of supersession, there will only be an overpayment if the date from which the supersession is effective is before the date on which payment ceased. It is therefore not surprising that the question whether a claimant has "failed to notify" a change of circumstances for the purposes of reg.7(2)(c)(ii) was found in *CDLA/1823/2004* to be similar to the familiar question whether a person has "failed to disclose" a change of circumstances for the purposes of s.71. The Commissioner noted that the phrase "regulations under the Administration Act" refers to regulation 32 of the Social Security (Claims and Payments) Regulations 1987, which was considered in some detail in the context of s.71 by the Court of Appeal in *B v Secretary of State for Work and Pensions* [2005] EWCA Civ 929; [2005] 1 W.L.R. 3796 (also reported as *R(IS) 9/06*). He suggested that there will be a failure to notify a change of circumstances if there is a breach of clear and unambiguous instructions, as was the position in *R(IS) 9/06* but that otherwise the issue is likely to be whether the Secretary of State could reasonably have expected the claimant to notify him of the material fact. Determining the question whether reg.7(2)(c)(ii) applies may, therefore, require some evidence as to the instructions given to the claimant. See also *R(A) 2/06*. The practice of dealing with the recovery of overpayments separately from decisions as to entitlement may lead to the same complex issues of fact being considered twice.

The application of head (ii) is particularly important in relation to attendance allowance, disability living allowance, severe disablement allowance and industrial injuries disablement benefit because heads (ii), (iv) and (v) have the combined effect that supersessions are not retrospective where the change of circumstances relates to a "disability determination" as defined in reg.7A, except where the claimant both was required to notify the change of circumstances and knew or could reasonably have been expected to know that the change of circumstances should be notified. This means that, except where the claimant has clearly been at fault, there is no overpayment and so any question of the recoverability of an overpayment simply does not arise.

The revocation of reg.7(2)(c)(iii) and its replacement with heads (iv) and (v), which contain no exceptions in respect of incapacity determinations, deals with the anomalies revealed in such incapacity benefit cases as *R(IB) 1/05* and *CIB/763/2004*, where there had been changes of circumstances but no failure by the claimant to disclose them (so that head (ii) did not apply) but the Commissioner found that head (iii) did not apply either. Now, any supersession will be effective from the date of the change of circumstances by virtue of head (v). That, of course, will be at least as early as the date applicable under head (ii) and it might seem odd at first sight that a supersession may be effective from an earlier date when there has been no failure to disclose a change of circumstances than where there has been. However, this only acts to the disadvantage of a claimant where a payment of benefit has not already been made. If it has already been made, it will not be recoverable due to the lack of a failure to disclose the change of circumstances. If the payment has not already been made, there are obvious reasons why the supersession should take effect from the date of the change so that only the benefit to which the claimant is properly entitled is paid.

However, there may still be some difficulties in incapacity cases due to the practice of determining that a person is incapable of work in the contest of "credits" and then relying on that determination when determining entitlement to income support (see reg.10). In *CIB/1599/2005*, the claimant was in receipt of income support on the basis of a decision, made for the purposes of incapacity credits, that he was incapable of work. He failed to inform the social security office that he had taken some casual employment. The Commissioner held that reg.7(2)(c)(ii) did not apply because the claimant was not required by "regulations under the Administration Act" to notify his change of circumstances. Regulation 32 of the Social Security (Claims and Payments) Regulations 1987 applies only to benefit cases and not to "credits" cases. That meant that the "credits" decision could not be superseded with effect from a date before it was made. Given the terms of reg.10, that in turn

Social Security and Child Support (Decisions and Appeals) Regs 1999

presumably also limited the scope for superseding the award of income support retrospectively, although the Commissioner expressed no view on that issue.

Para. (5)

2.388 This provides consistency between, on the one hand, revision and supersession of decisions of the Secretary of State on the ground of error of fact (under regs 3(5) and 6(2)(b)) and, on the other hand, supersession of decisions of appeal tribunals and Commissioners on the ground of error of fact (under reg.6(2)(c)).

Para. (9)

2.389 Supersessions of decisions concerning attendance allowance and disability living allowance on the ground of changes of circumstances which are disadvantageous to claimants are dealt with under para.(2)(c). This paragraph deals with supersessions on the grounds of changes of circumstances that are advantageous to the claimant. It is difficult to envisage a situation in which para.(9)(c) can operate because if the claimant was not entitled to any benefit before the change occurred, a claim would have been appropriate rather than a supersession (*R(I) 56/54*). Perhaps its use is envisaged in cases where a claimant becomes terminally ill during the qualifying period, although it is arguable that, even then, a new claim would be appropriate. Paragraph (9)(b) is in terms similar to para.(2)(b) with variations that seem designed merely to take account of the qualifying periods for attendance allowance and disability living allowance and to require the supersession to be effective from the first pay day after the claimant qualifies for the new rate.

Paras (12)–(23)

2.390 These are all concerned with changes in housing costs and contain provisions similar to those previously found in regs 63 and 63A of the Social Security (Adjudication) Regulations 1995.

[¹ Definitions for the purposes of regulations 3(5)(c), 6(2)(g) [², 7(2)(c) and (5)] and ancillary provisions

2.391 **7A.**—(1) For the purposes of regulations 3(5)(c), 6(2)(g) [², 7(2)(c) and (5)]—

"disability benefit decision" means a decision to award a relevant benefit embodied in or necessary to which is a disability determination,

"disability determination" means—

(a) in the case of a decision as to an award of an attendance allowance or a disability living allowance, whether the person satisfies any of the conditions in section 64, 72(1) or 73(1) to (3), as the case may be, of the Contributions and Benefits Act,

(b) in the case of a decision as to an award of severe disablement allowance, whether the person is disabled for the purpose of section 68 of the Contributions and Benefits Act, or

(c) in the case of a decision as to an award of industrial injuries benefit, whether the existence or extent of any disablement is sufficient for the purposes of section 103 or 108 of the Contributions and Benefits Act or for the benefit to be paid at the rate which was in payment immediately prior to that decision;

"incapacity benefit decision" means a decision to award a relevant benefit [² or relevant credit] embodied in or necessary to which is a determination that a person is or is to be treated as incapable of work under Part XIIA of the Contributions and Benefits Act,

"incapacity determination" means a determination whether a person is incapable of work by applying the [² personal capability assessment] in

(SI 1999/991, reg. 7A)

regulation 24 of the Social Security (Incapacity for Work) (General) Regulations 1995 or whether a person is to be treated as incapable of work in accordance with regulation 10 (certain persons with a severe condition to be treated as incapable of work) or 27 (exceptional circumstances) of those Regulations, and

"payee" means a person to whom a benefit referred to in paragraph (a), (b) or (c) of the definition of "disability determination", or a benefit referred to in the definition of "incapacity benefit decision" is payable.

(2) Where a person's receipt of or entitlement to a benefit ("the first benefit") is a condition of his being entitled to any other benefit, allowance or advantage ("a second benefit") and a decision is revised under regulation 3(5)(c) or a superseding decision is made under regulation 6(2) to which regulation 7(2)(c)(ii) applies, the effect of which is that the first benefit ceases to be payable, or becomes payable at a lower rate than was in payment immediately prior to that revision or supersession, a consequent decision as to his entitlement to the second benefit shall take effect from the date of the change in his entitlement to the first benefit.]

AMENDMENTS

1. Social Security and Child Support (Decisions and Appeals) Amendment (No.2) Regulations 1999 (SI 1999/1623), reg.5 (July 5, 1999).
2. Social Security and Child Support (Miscellaneous Amendments) Regulations 2000 (SI 2000/1596), reg.18 (June 19, 2000).

DEFINITIONS

"Contributions and Benefits Act"—see s.84 of the Social Security Act 1998.
"relevant benefit"—see s.39(1) of the Social Security Act 1998.
"relevant credit"—see reg.1(3).

7B. *Omitted.*	2.392
7C. *Omitted.*	2.393

GENERAL NOTE

"disability determination"
In *CA/2650/2006*, the Commissioner held that the reference to s.64 of the Contributions and Benefits Act (which has a different structure from that in ss. 72 and 73) in head (a) of the definition of "disability determination" refers only to "determinations whether the conditions set out in section 64(2) and (3) were satisfied (and possibly extending to age and non-entitlement to DLA)" and so does not extend to determinations as to residence or presence. 2.394

"incapacity benefit decision"
An award of invalidity benefit, a forerunner of incapacity benefit, cannot be an "incapacity benefit decision", notwithstanding transitional provisions (*Hooper v Secretary of State for Work and Pensions* [2007] EWCA Civ 495 (reported as *R(IB) 4/07)*). 2.394.1

"incapacity determination"
In *CIB/313/2002* and *R(IB) 2/04* (at para.125), a single Commissioner and then a Tribunal of Commissioners left open the question whether there was an "incapacity determination" when it was determined that a person should be treated as having satisfied the personal capability assessment under reg.28 of the 1995 Regulations. In *R(IB) 1/05*, a single Commissioner decided that such a determination was an "incapacity determination", but his decision on that point did not make any difference to the ultimate result of the appeal before him. Although *R(IB) 1/05* is likely to be followed, the point may therefore still be arguable. However, as illustrated by all three of those decisions, it is seldom, if ever, of any practical significance. 2.395

Social Security and Child Support (Decisions and Appeals) Regs 1999

Effective date for late notifications of change of circumstances

2.396
8.—(1) For the purposes of regulation 7(2) [² and (9)], a longer period of time may be allowed for the notification of a change of circumstances in so far as it affects the effective date of the change where the conditions specified in the following provisions of this regulation are satisfied.

(2) An application for the purposes of regulation 7(2) [² or (9)] shall be made by the claimant or a person acting on his behalf.

(3) The application referred to in paragraph (2) shall—
 (a) contain particulars of the relevant change of circumstances and the reasons for the failure to notify the change of circumstances on an earlier date; and
 (b) be made within 13 months of the date the change occurred.

(4) An application under this regulation shall not be granted unless the Secretary of State is satisfied [¹ or the Board are satisfied] that—
 (a) it is reasonable to grant the application;
 (b) the change of circumstances notified by the applicant is relevant to the decision which is to be superseded; and
 (c) special circumstances are relevant to the application and as a result of those special circumstances it was not practicable for the applicant to notify the change of circumstances within one month of the change occurring.

(5) In determining whether it is reasonable to grant the application, the Secretary of State [¹ or the Board] shall have regard to the principle that the greater the amount of time that has elapsed between the date one month after the change of circumstances occurred and the date the application for the purposes of regulation 7(2) [² or (9)] is made, the more compelling should be the special circumstances on which the application is based.

(6) In determining whether it is reasonable to grant an application, no account shall be taken of the following—
 (a) that the applicant or any person acting for him was unaware of, or misunderstood, the law applicable to his case (including ignorance or misunderstanding of the time limits imposed by these Regulations); or
 (b) that a Commissioner or a court has taken a different view of the law from that previously understood and applied.

(7) An application under this regulation which has been refused may not be renewed.

AMENDMENTS

1. Tax Credits (Decisions and Appeals) (Amendment) Regulations 1999 (SI 1999/2570), reg.11 (October 5, 1999). Note that amendments made by these regulations only have effect with respect to tax credit (reg.1(2) of the Amendment Regulations).
2. Social Security and Child Support (Decisions and Appeals) Amendment Regulations 2000 (SI 2000/119), reg.3 (February 17, 2000).

DEFINITIONS

 "the Board"—see reg.1(3).
 "claimant"—*ibid.*

(SI 1999/991, reg. 8)

GENERAL NOTE

Para. (6)(b)
See the note to reg.32(8)(b) which is in similar terms.

CHAPTER III

OTHER MATTERS

Certificates of recoverable benefits

9. A certificate of recoverable benefits may be reviewed under section 10 of the 1997 Act where the Secretary of State is satisfied that—
   (a) a mistake (whether in computation of the amount specified or otherwise) occurred in the preparation of the certificate;
   (b) the benefit recovered from a person who makes a compensation payment (as defined in section 1 of the 1997 Act) is in excess of the amount due to the Secretary of State;
   (c) incorrect or insufficient information was supplied to the Secretary of State by the person who applied for the certificate and in consequence the amount of benefit specified in the certificate was less than it would have been had the information supplied been correct or sufficient; or
   (d) a ground for appeal is satisfied under section 11 of the 1997 Act.

DEFINITIONS

"the 1997 Act"—see reg.1(3).
"appeal"—*ibid.*

GENERAL NOTE

These grounds of review are very wide. In *CCR/3391/2005*, the Commissioner suggested that the Secretary of State should always consider reviewing a decision against which an appeal has been brought, so that unnecessary cases do not reach tribunals. Regulation 9(d) may have been drafted with such an approach in mind. A submission to a tribunal would then, in effect, be an explanation for the Secretary of State not reviewing the decision in the light of the grounds of appeal. Where the appellant is the compensator, grounds of appeal are often accompanied by a considerable amount of new evidence obtained in the course of defending the compensation proceedings. Considering a review is, in such circumstances, the first opportunity the Secretary of State has to take such evidence into account.

[¹ Correction of accidental errors

9A.—(1) Accidental errors in a decision of the Secretary of State or an officer of the Board under a relevant enactment within the meaning of section 28(3), or in any record of such a decision, may be corrected by the Secretary of State or an officer of the Board, as the case may be, at any time.
   (2) A correction made to, or to the record of, a decision shall be deemed to be part of the decision, or of that record, and the Secretary of State or an officer of the Board shall give a written notice of the correction as soon as practicable to the claimant.

Social Security and Child Support (Decisions and Appeals) Regs 1999

(3) In calculating the time within which an application can be made under regulation 3(1)(b) for a decision to be revised, or the time within which an appeal may be brought under regulation 31(1), there shall be disregarded any day falling before the day on which notice was given of the decision or to the record thereof under paragraph (2).]

AMENDMENT

1. Social Security and Child Support (Decisions and Appeals) (Miscellaneous Amendments) Regulations 2002 (SI 2002/1379), reg.4 (May 20, 2002).

DEFINITIONS

"appeal"—see reg.1(3).
"the Board"—*ibid*.
"claimant"—*ibid*.

Effect of a determination as to capacity for work

2.401   10. A determination (including a determination made following a change of circumstances) whether a person is, or is to be treated as, capable or incapable of work which is embodied in or necessary to a decision under Chapter II of Part I of the Act or on which such a decision is based shall be conclusive for the purposes of any further such decision.

DEFINITION

"the Act"—see reg.1(3).

GENERAL NOTE

2.402   This re-enacts reg.19 of the Social Security (Incapacity for Work) (General) Regulations 1995. Note that a decision that a person is *not*, or is not to be treated as, incapable of work is not of continuing effect. Consequently, it operates to allow supersession of any award of benefit current at the time it is made but it does not operate so as to prevent a person from making a new claim or a further application for supersession, although reg.28 of the 1995 Regulations may not apply while a new assessment is arranged (*R(IB)1/01* and *R(IB)2/01*). See the Social Security Act 1998 (Commencement No.9, and Savings and Consequential and Transitional Provisions) Order 1999, Sch.14, paras 15–17 for transitional provisions relating to determinations as to capacity for work.

Secretary of State to determine certain matters

2.403   11. Where, in relation to a determination for any purpose to which Part XIIA of the Contributions and Benefits Act applies, an issue arises as to—
(a) whether a person is, or is to be treated as, capable or incapable of work in respect of any period; or
(b) whether a person is terminally ill,
that issue shall be determined by the Secretary of State, notwithstanding that other matters fall to be determined by another authority.

DEFINITION

"the Contributions and Benefits Act"—see s.84 of the Social Security Act 1998.

[1 Issues for decision by officers of Inland Revenue

2.404   11A.—(1) Where, on consideration of any claim or other matter, it appears to the Secretary of State that an issue arises which, by virtue of

(SI 1999/991, reg.11A)

section 8 of the Transfer Act, falls to be decided by an officer of the Board, he shall refer that issue to the Board.

(2) Where—
(a) the Secretary of State has decided any claim or other matter on an assumption of facts—
  (i) as to which there appeared to him to be no dispute, but
  (ii) concerning which, had an issue arisen, that issue would have fallen, by virtue of section 8 of the Transfer Act, to be decided by an officer of the Board; and
(b) an application for revision or an application for supersession [² or an appeal] is made in relation to the decision of that claim or other matter; and
(c) it appears to the Secretary of State on [² receipt of the application or appeal] that such an issue arises,

he shall refer that issue to the Board.

(3) Pending the final decision of any issue which has been referred to the Board in accordance with paragraph (1) or (2) above, the Secretary of State may—
(a) determine any other issue arising on consideration of the claim or other matter or, as the case may be, of the application,
(b) seek a preliminary opinion of the Board on the issue referred and decide the claim or other matter or, as the case may be, the application in accordance with that opinion on that issue; or
(c) defer making any decision on the claim or other matter or, as the case may be, the application.

(4) On receipt by the Secretary of State of the final decision of an issue which has been referred to the Board in accordance with paragraph (1) or (2) above, the Secretary of State that—
(a) in a case to which paragraph (3)(b) above applies—
  (i) consider whether the decision ought to be revised under section 9 or superseded under section 10, and
  (ii) if so, revise it, or, as the case may be, make a further decision which supersedes it; or
(b) in a case to which paragraph (3)(a) or (c) above applies, decide the claim or other matter or, as the case may be, the application,

in accordance with the final decision of the issue so referred.

(5) In paragraphs (3) and (4) above "final decision" means the decision of an officer of the Board under section 8 of the Transfer Act or the determination of any appeal in relation to that decision.]

AMENDMENTS

1. Social Security and Child Support (Decisions and Appeals) Amendment (No.3) Regulations 1999 (SI 1999/1623), reg.2(3) (July 5, 1999).

2. Social Security and Child Support (Decisions and Appeals) (Miscellaneous Amendments) Regulations 2002 (SI 2002/1379), reg.5 (May 20, 2002).

DEFINITIONS

"appeal"—see reg.1(3).
"the Board"—*ibid.*
"claim"—by virtue of s.39(2) of the Social Security Act 1998, see s.191 of the Social Security Administration Act 1992.
"final decision"—see para.(5).
"the Transfer Act"—see reg.1(3).

General Note

2.405   Some decisions fall to be made by officers of the Inland Revenue by virtue of s.170 of the Pensions Schemes Act 1993 (rather than by virtue of s.8 of the Social Security Contributions (Transfer of Functions, etc.) Act 1999) but the Secretary of State may refer to officers of the Inland Revenue issues for determination under the 1993 Act notwithstanding that this regulation does not apply (*R(P)1/04*).

Decision of the Secretary of State relating to industrial injuries benefit

2.406   **12.**—(1) This regulation applies where, for the purpose of a decision of the Secretary of State relating to a claim for industrial injuries benefit under Part V of the Contributions and Benefits Act an issue to be decided is—

(a) the extent of a personal injury for the purposes of section 94 of that Act;

(b) whether the claimant has a disease prescribed for the purposes of section 108 of that Act or the extent of any disablement resulting from such a disease; or

(c) whether the claimant has a disablement for the purposes of section 103 of that Act or the extent of any such disablement.

(2) In connection with making a decision to which this regulation applies, the Secretary of State may refer an issue, together with any relevant evidence or information available to him, including any evidence or information provided by or on behalf of the claimant, to a medical practitioner who has experience in such of the issues specified in paragraph (1) as are relevant to the decision, for such report as appears to the Secretary of State to be necessary for the purpose of providing him with information for use in making the decision.

(3) In making a decision to which this regulation applies, the Secretary of State shall have regard to (among other factors)—

(a) all relevant medical reports provided to him in connection with that decision; and

(b) the experience, in such of the issues specified in paragraph (1) as are relevant to the decision, of any medical practitioner who has provided a report, including a medical practitioner who has provided a report following an examination required by the Secretary of State under section 19.

Definitions

"claimant"—see reg.1(3).
"industrial injuries benefit"—by virtue of s.39(2) of the Social Security Act 1998, see s.191 of the Social Security Administration Act 1992.
"medical practitioner"—*ibid.*

General Note

2.407   Adjudicating medical authorities have been abolished and so all decisions which an adjudication officer would, or might, have referred to such authorities under the Social Security Administration Act 1992 are now decided by the Secretary of State on the basis of medical advice. In practice, this does not make much difference in most cases but it does remove one level of decision-making in diagnosis and recrudescence cases where adverse decisions could be made by an adjudication officer and there was then a right of appeal to an adjudicating medical authority under reg.48 of the Social Security (Adjudication) Regulations 1995.

(SI 1999/991, reg.12)

See s.30 of the Social Security Act 1998 for the effect of an earlier declaration that the claimant has suffered personal injury by accident.

[¹ Recrudescence of a prescribed disease

12A.—(1) This regulation applies to a decision made under sections 108 to 110 of the Contributions and Benefits Act where a disease is subsequently treated as a recrudescence under regulation 7 of the Social Security (Industrial Injuries) (Prescribed Diseases) Regulations 1985.

(2) Where this regulation applies Chapter II of Part I of the Act shall apply as if section 8(2) did not apply.]

AMENDMENT

1. Social Security and Child Support (Miscellaneous Amendments) Regulations 2000 (SI 2000/1596), reg.19 (June 19, 2000).

DEFINITION

"the Contributions and Benefits Act"—see s.84 of the Social Security Act 1998.

Income support and social fund determinations on incomplete evidence

13.—(1) Where, for the purpose of a decision under section 8 or 10—
[¹ (a) a determination falls to be made by the Secretary of State as to what housing costs are to be included in—
   (i) a claimant's applicable amount by virtue of regulation 17(1)(e) or 18(1)(f) of, and Schedule 3 to, the Income Support Regulations; or
   (ii) a claimant's appropriate minimum guarantee by virtue of regulation 6(6)(c) and Schedule II to the State Pension Credit Regulations; and]
(b) it appears to the Secretary of State that he is not in possession of all of the evidence or information which is relevant for the purposes of such a determination,
he shall make the determination on the assumption that the housing costs to be included in the claimant's [¹ applicable amount or, as the case may be, appropriate minimum guarantee are those] that can be immediately determined.

(2) Where, for the purpose of a decision under section 8 or 10—
(a) a determination falls to be made by the Secretary of State as to whether—
   (i) in relation to any person, the applicable amount falls to be reduced or disregarded to any extent by virtue of section 126(3) of the Contributions and Benefits Act (persons affected by trade disputes);
   (ii) for the purposes of regulation 12 of the Income Support Regulations, a person is by virtue of that regulation to be treated as receiving relevant education; or
   (iii) in relation to any claimant, the applicable amount includes severe disability premium by virtue of regulation 17(1)(d) or 18(1)(e), and paragraph 13 of Schedule 2 to, the Income Support Regulations; and

(b) it appears to the Secretary of State that he is not in possession of all of the evidence or information which is relevant for the purposes of such a determination,

he shall make the determination on the assumption that the relevant evidence or information which is not in his possession is adverse to the claimant.

[¹ (3) Where, for the purposes of a decision under section 8 or 10—
(a) a determination falls to be made by the Secretary of State as to whether a claimant's appropriate minimum guarantee includes an additional amount in accordance with regulation 6(4) of, and paragraph 1 of Schedule I to, the State Pension Credit Regulations; and
(b) it appears to the Secretary of State that he is not in possession of all the evidence or information which is relevant for the purpose of such a determination,

he shall make the determination on the assumption that the relevant evidence or information which is not in his possession is adverse to the claimant.]

AMENDMENT

1. State Pension Credit (Consequential Transitional and Miscellaneous Provisions) Regulations 2002 (SI 2002/3019), reg.19 (April 7, 2003).

DEFINITIONS

"claimant"—see reg.1(3).
"the Contributions and Benefits Act"—see s.84 of the Social Security Act 1998.
"the Income Support Regulations"—see reg.1(3).
"State Pension Credit Regulations"—*ibid.*

[¹ Retirement pension after period of deferment

13A.—(1) This regulation applies where—
(a) a person claims a Category A or Category B retirement pension, shared additional pension or, as the case may be, graduated retirement benefit;
(b) an election is required by, as the case may be—
  (i) paragraph A1 or 3C of Schedule 5 to the Contributions and Benefits Act (pension increase or lump sum where entitlement to retirement pension is deferred);
  (ii) paragraph 1 of Schedule 5A to that Act (pension increase or lump sum where entitlement to shared additional pension is deferred); or, as the case may be,
  (iii) paragraph 12 or 17 of Schedule 1 to the Graduated Retirement Benefit Regulations (further provisions replacing section 36(4) of the National Insurance Act 1965: increases of graduated retirement benefit and lump sums); and
(c) no election is made when the claim is made.

(2) In the cicumstances specified in paragraph (1) the Secretary of State may decide the claim before any election is made, or is treated as made, for an increase or lump sum.

(3) When an election is made, or is treated as made, the Secretary of State shall revise the decision which he made in pursuance of paragraph (2).]

AMENDMENT

1. Social Security (Deferral of Retirement Pensions, Shared Additional Pension and Graduated Retirement Benefit) (Miscellaneous Provisions) Regulations 2005 (SI 2005/2677), reg.9(6) (April 6, 2006).

(SI 1999/991, reg.13A)

DEFINITIONS

"the Contributions and Benefits Act"—see s.84 of the Social Security Act 1998.
"the Graduated Retirement Benefit Regulations"—see reg.1(3).

Effect of alteration in the component rates of income support and jobseeker's allowance

14.—(1) Section 159 of the Administration Act (effect of alteration in the component rates of income support) shall not apply to any award of income support in force in favour of a person where there is applicable to that person—
  (a) any amount determined in accordance with regulation 17(2) to (7) of the Income Support Regulations; or
  (b) any protected sum determined in accordance with Schedule 3A or 3B of those Regulations; or
  (c) any transitional addition, personal expenses addition or special transitional addition applicable under Part II of the Income Support (Transitional) Regulations 1987 (transitional protection).

(2) Where section 159 of the Administration Act does not apply to an award of income support by virtue of paragraph (1), a decision under section 10 may be made in respect of that award for the sole purpose of giving effect to any change made by an order under section 150 of the Administration Act.

(3) Section 159A of the Administration Act (effect of alterations in the component rates of jobseeker's allowance) shall not apply to any award of a jobseeker's allowance in force in favour of a person where there is applicable to that person any amount determined in accordance with regulations 87 of the Jobseeker's Allowance Regulations.

(4) Where section 159A of the Administration Act does not apply to an award of a jobseeker's allowance by virtue of paragraph (3), a decision under section 10 may be made in respect of that award for the sole purpose of giving effect to any change made by an order under section 150 of the Administration Act.

[1 (5) Section 159B of the Administration Act (effect of alterations affecting state pension credit) shall not apply to any award of state pension credit in favour of a person where in relation to that person the appropriate minimum guarantee includes an amount determined under paragraph 6 of Part III of Schedule I to the State Pension Credit Regulations.

(6) Where section 159B of the Administration Act does not apply to an award of state pension credit by virtue of paragraph (5), a decision under section 10 may be made in respect of that award for the sole purpose of giving effect to any change made to an award under section 150 of the Administration Act.]

AMENDMENT

1. State Pension Credit (Consequential Transitional and Miscellaneous Provisions) Regulations 2002 (SI 2002/3019), reg.20 (April 7, 2003).

DEFINITIONS

"the Administration Act"—see s.84 of the Social Security Act 1998.
"the Income Support Regulations"—see reg.1(3).
"the Jobseeker's Allowance Regulations"—*ibid.*

Social Security and Child Support (Decisions and Appeals) Regs 1999

"state pension credit"—*ibid*.
"State Pension Credit Regulations"—*ibid*.

[¹ Termination of award of income support or jobseeker's allowance

2.412

14A.—(1) This regulation applies in a case where an award of income support or a jobseeker's allowance ("the existing benefit") exists in favour of a person and, if that award did not exist and a claim was made by that person or his partner for a jobseeker's allowance or, as the case may be, income support ("the alternative benefit"), an award of the alternative benefit would be made on that claim.

(2) In a case to which this regulation applies, if a claim for the alternative benefit is made the Secretary of State may bring to an end the award of the existing benefit if he is satisfied that an alternative benefit will be made on that claim.

(3) Where, under paragraph (2), the Secretary of State brings an award of the existing benefit to an end he shall do so with effect from the day immediately preceding the first day on which an award of the alternative benefit takes effect.

(4) Where an award of a jobseeker's allowance is made in accordance with the provisions of this regulation, paragraph 4 of Schedule 1 to the Jobseeker's Act (waiting days) shall not apply.]

AMENDMENT

1. Social Security and Child Support (Decisions and Appeals) (Miscellaneous Amendments) Regulations 2002 (SI 2002/1379), reg.6 (May 20, 2002).

DEFINITIONS

"the alternative benefit"—see para.(1).
"the Jobseekers Act"—see s.84 of the Social Security Act 1998.

Jobseeker's allowance determinations on incomplete evidence

2.413

15. Where, for the purpose of a decision under section 8 or 10—
(a) a determination falls to be made by the Secretary of State as to whether—
(i) in relation to any person, the applicable amount falls to be reduced or disregarded to any extent by virtue of section 15 of the Jobseekers Act (persons affected by trade disputes); or
(ii) for the purposes of regulation 54(2) to (4) of the Jobseeker's Allowance Regulations (relevant education), a person is by virtue of that regulation, to be treated as receiving relevant education; and
(b) it appears to the Secretary of State that he is not in possession of all of the evidence or information which is relevant for the purposes of such a determination.
he shall make the determination on the assumption that the relevant evidence or information which is not in his possession is adverse to the claimant.

DEFINITIONS

"claimant"—see reg.1(3).
"the Jobseekers Act"—see s.84 of the Social Security Act 1998.
"the Jobseeker's Allowance Regulations"—see reg.1(3).

(SI 1999/991, reg.16)

15A.–15D. *Omitted.*

Part III

Suspension, Termination and Other Matters

Chapter I

Suspension and Termination

Suspension in prescribed cases

16.—(1) Subject to paragraph (2), the Secretary of State [¹ or the Board] may suspend payment of a relevant benefit, in whole or in part, in the circumstances prescribed in paragraph (3).

(2) The Secretary of State shall suspend payment of a jobseeker's allowance in the circumstances prescribed in paragraph (3)(a)(i) or (ii) where the issue or one of the issues is whether a person, who has claimed a jobseeker's allowance, is or was available for employment or whether he is or was actively seeking employment.

(3) The prescribed circumstances are that—
(a) it appears to the Secretary of State [¹ or the Board] that—
  (i) an issue arises whether the conditions for entitlement to a relevant benefit are or were fulfilled;
  (ii) an issue arises whether a decision as to an award of a relevant benefit should be revised under section 9 or superseded under section 10;
  (iii) an issue arises whether any amount paid or payable to a person by way of, or in connection with a claim for, a relevant benefit is recoverable under section 71(overpayments), 71A (recovery of jobseeker's allowance: severe hardship cases) or 74 (income support and other payments) of the Administration Act or regulations made under any of those sections; or
  (iv) the last address notified to him [¹ or them] of a person who is in receipt of a relevant benefit is not the address at which that person is residing; or
(b) an appeal is pending against—
  (i) a decision of an appeal tribunal, a Commissioner or a court;
  (ii) a decision given in a different case by a Commissioner or a court, and it appears to the Secretary of State [¹ or the Board] that, if the appeal were to be determined in a particular way, an issue would arise as to whether the award of a relevant benefit (whether the same benefit or not) in the case itself ought to be revised or superseded.

[²(4) For the purposes of section 21(3)(c) an appeal is pending where a decision of an appeal tribunal, a Commissioner or a court has been made and the Secretary of State—
(a) is awaiting receipt of that decision or (in the case of an appeal tribunal decision) is considering whether to apply for a statement of the

Social Security and Child Support (Decisions and Appeals) Regs 1999

reasons for it, or has applied for such a statement and is awaiting receipt thereof; or

(b) has received that decision or (in the case of an appeal tribunal decision) the statement of the reasons for it, and is considering whether to apply for leave to appeal, or where leave to appeal has been granted, is considering whether to appeal;

and the Secretary of State shall give written notice of his proposal to make a request for a statement of the reasons for a tribunal decision, to apply for leave to appeal, or to appeal, as soon as reasonably practicable.]

AMENDMENTS

1. Tax Credits (Decisions and Appeals) (Amendment) Regulations 1999 (SI 1999/2570), reg.12 (October 5, 1999). Note that amendments made by these regulations only have effect with respect to tax credit (reg.1(2) of the Amendment Regulations).

2. Social Security and Child Support (Miscellaneous Amendments) Regulations 2000 (SI 2000/1596), reg.20 (June 19, 2000).

DEFINITIONS

"the Administration Act"—see s.84 of the Social Security Act 1998.
"appeal tribunal"—see reg.1(3).
"the Board"—*ibid.*
"Commissioner"—see s.39(1) of the Social Security Act 1998.
"relevant benefit"—*ibid.*

GENERAL NOTE

2.416
There is no appeal against a decision under reg.16 (see Sch.2, para.24). The claimant must wait until a decision is made as to entitlement. Regulation 18 makes proision for the termination of entitlement if information is not provided and reg.20 makes provision for the reinstatement of payments.

In *CA/3800/2006*, a claimant entitled to attendance allowance had been paying her own nursing home fees. However, she got into financial difficulties because her money had been badly invested by a financial adviser and the local authority started paying the fees. The claimant was in dispute with her financial adviser and eventually recovered a substantial sum that required her to reimburse the local authority for the fees it had paid. It was held that it had been inappropriate to supersede the award of attendance allowance so as to terminate payment when the local authority started paying the fees because it was impossible to reinstate the payments with effect from the date they had been terminated on a supersession following the reimbursement of the local authority. Instead, because the claimant had been in dispute with her financial adviser, the Secretary of State should merely have suspended payment on the ground that an issue within the scope of reg.16(3)(a)(ii) had arisen. The Commissioner revised the first supersession on the ground of "official error" so that payments could be reinstated from the date they had been stopped.

Provision of information or evidence

2.417
17.—(1) This regulation applies where the Secretary of State requires information or evidence for a determination whether a decision awarding a relevant benefit should be—

(a) revised under section 9; or
(b) superseded under section 10.

(2) For the purposes of paragraph (1), the following persons must satisfy the requirements of paragraph (4)—

(SI 1999/991, reg.17)

(a) a person in respect of whom payment of a benefit has been suspended in the circumstances prescribed in regulation 16(3)(a);
(b) a person who has made an application for a decision of the Secretary of State to be revised or superseded;
(c) a person who fails to comply with the provisions of regulation 32(1) of the Claims and Payments Regulations in so far as they relate to documents, information or facts required by the Secretary of State;
(d) a person who qualifies for income support by virtue of paragraph 7 of Schedule 1B to the Income Support Regulations;
(e) a person whose entitlement to benefit is conditional upon his being, or being treated as, incapable of work.

(3) The Secretary of State shall notify any person to whom paragraph (2) refers of the requirements of this regulation.

(4) A person to whom paragraph (2) refers must either—
(a) supply the information or evidence within—
  (i) a period of one month beginning with the date on which the notification under paragraph (3) was sent to him; or
  (ii) such longer period as he satisfies the Secretary of State is necessary in order to enable him to comply with the requirement; or
(b) satisfy the Secretary of State within the period of time specified in sub-paragraph (a)(i) that either—
  (i) the information or evidence required of him does not exist; or
  (ii) that it is not possible for him to obtain it.

(5) The Secretary of State may suspend the payment of a relevant benefit, in whole or in part, to any person to whom paragraph (2)(b) to (e) applies who fails to satisfy the requirements of paragraph (4).

(6) In this regulation, "evidence" includes evidence which a person is required to provide in accordance with regulation 2 of the Social Security (Medical Evidence) Regulations 1976.

DEFINITIONS

"the Claims and Payments Regulations"—see reg.1(3).
"evidence"—see para.(6).
"the Income Support Regulations"—see reg.1(3).
"relevant benefit"—see s.39(1) of the Social Security Act 1998.

GENERAL NOTE

2.418   A different version of this regulation (reproduced in editions of this work up to 2005) was enacted by reg.13 of the Tax Credits (Decisions and Appeals) (Amendment) Regulations 1999 (SI 1999/2570) with effect from October 5, 1999 in respect of working families' tax credit and disabled person's tax credit, payable under the Tax Credits Act 1999 until 2003.

Termination in cases of failure to furnish information or evidence

2.419   **18.**—(1) Subject to paragraphs (2), (3) and (4), the Secretary of State shall decide that where a person—
(a) whose benefit has been suspended in accordance with regulation 16 and who subsequently fails to comply with an information requirement made in pursuance of regulation 17; or
(b) whose benefit has been suspended in accordance with regulation 17(5),

that person shall cease to be entitled to that benefit from the date on which payment was suspended except where entitlement to benefit ceases on an earlier date other than under this regulation.

(2) Paragraph (1)(a) shall not apply where not more than one month has elapsed since the information requirement was made in pursuance of regulation 17.

(3) Paragraph (1)(b) shall not apply where not more than one month has elapsed since the first payment was suspended in accordance with regulation 17.

(4) Paragraph (1) shall not apply where benefit has been suspended in part under regulation 16 or, as the case may be, regulation 17.

GENERAL NOTE

2.420   A different version of this regulation (reproduced in editions of this work up to 2005) was enacted by reg.13 of the Tax Credits (Decisions and Appeals) (Amendment) Regulations 1999 (SI 1999/2570) with effect from October 5, 1999 in respect of working families' tax credit and disabled person's tax credit, payable under the Tax Credits Act 1999 until 2003.

Suspension and termination for failure to submit to medical examination

2.421   **19.**—(1) Except where regulation 8 of the Social Security (Incapacity for Work) (General) Regulations 1995 applies (where a question arises as to whether a person is capable of work), the Secretary of State [¹or the Board] may require a person to submit to a medical examination by a medical practitioner where that person is in receipt of a relevant benefit, and either—
   (a) the Secretary of State considers [¹or the Board consider] it necessary to satisfy himself [¹or themselves] as to the correctness of the award of the benefit, or of the rate at which it was awarded; or
   (b) that person applies for a revision or supersession of the award and the Secretary of State considers [¹ or the Board consider] that the examination is necessary for the purpose of making his [¹ or their] decision.

(2) The Secretary of State [¹ or the Board] may suspend payment of a relevant benefit in whole or in part, to a person who fails, without good cause, on two consecutive occasions to submit to a medical examination in accordance with requirements under paragraph (1) except where entitlement to benefit is suspended on an earlier date other than under this regulation.

(3) Subject to paragraph (4), the Secretary of State [¹ or the Board] may determine that the entitlement to a relevant benefit of a person, in respect of whom payment of such a benefit has been suspended under paragraph (2), shall cease from a date not earlier than the date on which payment was suspended except where entitlement to benefit ceases on an earlier date other than under this regulation.

(4) Paragraph (3) shall not apply where not more than one month has elapsed since the first payment was suspended under paragraph (2).

AMENDMENT

1. Tax Credits (Decisions and Appeals) (Amendment) Regulations 1999 (SI 1999/2570), reg.14 (October 5, 1999). Note that amendments made by these

regulations have effect only with respect to tax credit under the Tax Credit Act 1999 (reg.1(2) of the Amendment Regulations).

DEFINITIONS

"the Board"—see reg.1(3).
"medical examination"—by virtue of s.39(2) of the Social Security Act 1998, see s.191 of the Social Security Administration Act 1992.
"medical practitioner"—*ibid*.
"relevant benefit"—see s.39(1) of the Social Security Act 1998.

GENERAL NOTE

Whereas s.19 of the Social Security Act 1998 provides for the obtaining of a report for the purpose of determining a claim, this regulation provides for the obtaining of a report for the purpose of deciding whether an award should be revised or superseded. In *CDLA/2335/2001*, the claimant's award of disability living allowance was terminated because he had failed to attend two consecutive appointments for medical examinations. The claimant's appeal to a tribunal was dismissed and he appealed to a Commissioner. The Commissioner criticised the submission provided to the tribunal on behalf of the decision-maker, which had failed to include any reference to the statutory provision under which the award had been terminated. The Secretary of State conceded that the relevant provision was reg.19 and that the conditions for terminating an award of benefit under para.(3) were not met because, contrary to para.(2), benefit had been suspended before there had been any suggestion that the claimant should attend an appointment for an examination and, contrary to para.(4), more than a month had elapsed since the suspension. The Secretary of State's representative explained that the automated system used to generate decisions was unable to generate a decision in conformity with reg.19 and the decision-maker had used the "least inappropriate" code available. The claimant had said that, following the termination of the award of benefit, he had offered to attend a medical examination but that offer had been rebuffed. The Commissioner observed that a termination under reg.19(3) is effective only until the claimant makes a new claim and that, if the claimant had made such an offer, he should have been told he could make a new claim and that a medical examination would then be arranged.

A decision under reg.19(3) cannot be justified merely because there has been a purported suspension under reg.19(2). The conditions for such a suspension must actually have been satisfied (*CDLA/5167/2001*).

2.422

Making of payments which have been suspended

20.—(1) Subject to paragraphs (2) and (3), payment of a benefit suspended in accordance with regulation 16 [¹ or 17] shall be made where—
  (a) in a case to which regulation 16(2) or (3)(a)(i) to (iii) applies, the Secretary of State is satisfied [² or the Board are satisfied] that the benefit suspended is properly payable and no outstanding issues remain to be resolved;
  (b) in a case to which regulation 16(3)(a)(iv) applies, the Secretary of State is satisfied [² or the Board are satisfied] that the has [² or they have] been notified of the address at which the person is residing;
  (c) [³ . . .];
  (d) [¹ in a case to which regulation 17(5) applies, the Secretary of State is satisfied that the benefit is properly payable and the requirements of regulation 17(4) have been satisfied.]

2.423

Social Security and Child Support (Decisions and Appeals) Regs 1999

[² (d) *in a case to which regulation 18(1) applies, the Board are satisfied that the benefit suspended is properly payable and the requirements of regulation 17(2), (4), (5) or (7) have been satisfied.*]

[³ (2) Where regulation 16(3)(b)(i) applies, payment of a benefit suspended shall be made if the Secretary of State—
  (a) does not, in the case of a decision of an appeal tribunal, apply for a statement of the reasons for that decision within the period of one month specified in regulation 53(4);
  (b) does not, in the case of a decision of an appeal tribunal, a Commissioner or a court, make an application for leave to appeal and (where leave to appeal is granted) make the appeal within the time prescribed for the making of such applications and appeals;
  (c) withdraws an application for leave to appeal or the appeal; or
  (d) is refused leave to appeal, in circumstances where it is not open to him to renew the application for leave or to make a further application for leave to appeal.

(3) Where regulation 16(3)(b)(ii) applies, payment of a benefit suspended shall be made if the Secretary of State, in relation to the decision of a Commissioner or the court in a different case—
  (a) does not make an application for leave to appeal and (where leave to appeal is granted) make the appeal within the time prescribed for the making of such applications and appeals;
  (b) withdraws an application for leave to appeal or the appeal; or
  (c) is refused leave to appeal, in circumstances where it is not open to him to renew the application for leave or to make a further application for leave to appeal.]

(4) Payment of benefit which has been suspended in accordance with regulation 19 for failure to submit to a medical examination shall be made where the Secretary of State is satisfied [² or the Board are satisfied] that it is no longer necessary for the person referred to in that regulation to submit to a medical examination.

AMENDMENTS

1. Social Security and Child Support (Decisions and Appeals) Amendment (No.2) Regulations 1999 (SI 1999/1623), reg.6 (July 5, 1999).
2. Tax Credits (Decisions and Appeals) (Amendment) Regulations 1999 (SI 1999/2570), reg.15 (October 5, 1999). Note that amendments made by these Regulations have effect only with respect to tax credit under the Tax Credit Act 1999 (reg.1(2) of the Amendment Regulations). There are thus two forms of para.(1)(d) as the second form is only substituted for the purposes of tax credit.
3. Social Security and Child Support (Miscellaneous Amendments) Regulations 2000 (SI 2000/1596), reg.21 (June 19, 2000).

DEFINITIONS

"appeal tribunal"—see s.39(1) of the Social Security Act 1998.
"the Board"—see reg.1(3).
"Commissioner"—see s.39(1) of the Social Security Act 1998.
"medical examination"—by virtue of s.39(2) of the Social Security Act 1998, see s.191 of the Social Security Administration Act 1992.

(SI 1999/991, reg.21)

CHAPTER II

OTHER MATTERS

Decisions involving issues that arise on appeal in other cases

21.—(1) For the purposes of section 25(3)(b) (prescribed cases and circumstances in which a decision may be made on a prescribed basis) a case which satisfies the condition in paragraph (2) is a prescribed case.

(2) The condition is that the claimant would be entitled to the benefit to which the decision which falls to be made relates, even if the appeal in the other case referred to in section 25(1)(b) were decided in a way which is the most unfavourable to him.

(3) For the purposes of section 25(3)(b), the prescribed basis on which the Secretary of State [¹ or the Board] may make the decision is as if—
  (a) the appeal in the other case which is referred to in section 25(1)(b) had already been determined; and
  (b) that appeal had been decided in a way which is the most unfavourable to the claimant.

(4) The circumstance prescribed under section 25(5)(c), where an appeal is pending against a decision for the purposes of that section, even though an appeal against the decision has not been brought (or, as the case may be, an application for leave to appeal against the decision has not been made) but the time for doing so has not yet expired, is where the Secretary of State [¹ or the Board—
  (a) certifies in writing that he is [¹, or certify in writing that they are,] considering appealing against that decision; and
  (b) considers [¹, or consider,] that, if such an appeal were to be determined in a particular way—
    (i) there would be no entitlement to benefit in a case to which section 25(1)(a) refers; or
    (ii) the appeal would affect the decision in that case in some other way.

2.424

AMENDMENT

1. Tax Credits (Decisions and Appeals) (Amendment) Regulations 1999 (SI 1999/2570), reg.16 (October 5, 1999). Note that amendments made by these regulations only have effect with respect to tax credit under the Tax Credit Act 1999 (reg.1(2) of the Amendment Regulations).

DEFINITIONS

"the Board"—see reg.1(3).
"claimant"—*ibid.*

Appeals involving issues that arise in other cases

22. The circumstance prescribed under section 26(6)(c), where an appeal is pending against a decision in the case described in section 26(1)(b) even though an appeal against the decision has not been brought (or, as the case may be, an application for leave to appeal against the decision has not been made) but the time for doing so has not yet expired, is where the Secretary of State [¹ or the Board—

2.425

Social Security and Child Support (Decisions and Appeals) Regs 1999

  (a) certifies in writing that he is [¹, or certify in writing that they are,] considering appealing against that decision; and
  (b) considers [¹, or consider,] that, if such an appeal were already determined, it would affect the determination of the appeal described in section 26(1)(a).

AMENDMENT

1. Tax Credits (Decisions and Appeals) (Amendment) Regulations 1999 (SI 1999/2570), reg.17 (October 5, 1999). Note that amendments made by these regulations only have effect with respect to tax credit under the Tax Credit Act 1999 (reg.1(2) of the Amendment Regulations).

DEFINITION

"the Board"—see reg.1(3).

2.426   **23.** *Omitted.*

2.427   **24.** *Omitted.*

PART IV

RIGHTS OF APPEAL AND PROCEDURE FOR BRINGING APPEALS

CHAPTER I

GENERAL

General appeals matters not including child support appeals

Other persons with a right of appeal

2.428   **25.** For the purposes of [³ section 12(2)], the following other persons have a right to appeal to an appeal tribunal—
  [² (ai) any person who has been appointed by the Secretary of State or the Board under regulation 30(1) of the Claims and Payments Regulations (payments on death) to proceed with the claim of a person who has made a claim for benefit and subsequently died;
  (aii) any person who is appointed by the Secretary of State to claim benefit on behalf of a deceased person and who claims the benefit under regulation 30(5) and (6) of the Claims and Payments Regulations;
  (aiii) any person who is appointed by the Secretary of State to make a claim for reduced earnings allowance or disablement benefit in the name of a person who has died and who claims under regulation 30(6A) and (6B) of the Claims and Payments Regulations;]
  (a) any person appointed by the Secretary of State [¹ or the Board] under regulation 33(1) of the Claims and Payments Regulations (persons unable to act) to act on behalf of another;

(SI 1999/991, reg. 25)

  (b) any person claiming attendance allowance or disability living allowance on behalf of another under section 66(2)(b) of the Contributions and Benefits Act or, as the case may be, section 76(3) of that Act (claims on behalf of terminally ill persons);

  (c) in relation to a pension scheme, any person who, for the purposes of Part X of the Pension Schemes Act 1993, is an employer, member, trustee or manager by virtue of section 146(8) of that Act.

AMENDMENTS

1. Tax Credits (Decisions and Appeals) (Amendment) Regulations 1999 (SI 1999/2570), reg.18 (October 5, 1999). Note that amendments made by these regulations only have effect with respect to tax credit under the Tax Credit Act 1999 (reg.1(2) of the Amendment Regulations).
2. Social Security and Child Support (Decisions and Appeals) (Miscellaneous Amendments) Regulations 2002 (SI 2002/1379), reg.7 (May 20, 2002).
3. Social Security, Child Support and Tax Credits (Decisions and Appeals) Regulations 2004 (SI 2004/3368), reg.2(3) (December 21, 2004).

DEFINITIONS

"appeal"—see reg.1(3).
"appeal tribunal"—see s.39(1) of the Social Security Act 1998.
"the Board"—see reg.1(3).
"the Claims and Payments Regulations"—*ibid.*
"the Contributions and Benefits Act"—see s.84 of the Social Security Act 1998.

GENERAL NOTE

In *CA/1014/1999*, an appointee appealed on behalf of a claimant against a decision that an overpayment was recoverable from the claimant. It was held that the tribunal were not entitled to consider whether it was recoverable from the appointee, who was not a "party to the proceedings" as that term is defined in reg.1. However, where an appeal is brought against a decision that an overpayment is recoverable from both the claimant and the appointee, the appeal will generally be regarded as having been brought on behalf of both of them and, even if it is not, both will be parties to the proceedings (*R(A) 2/06*).

2.429

Decisions against which an appeal lies

26. An appeal shall lie to an appeal tribunal against a decision made by the Secretary of State [¹ or an officer of the Board]—

  (a) as to whether a person is entitled to a relevant benefit for which no claim is required by virtue of regulation 3 of the Claims and Payments Regulations; or

  (b) as to whether a payment be made out of the social fund to a person to meet expenses for heating by virtue of regulations made under section 138(2) of the Contributions and Benefits Act (payments out of the social fund); [² or

  (c) under Schedule 6 to the Contributions and Benefits Act (assessment of extent of disablement) in relation to sections 103 (disablement benefit) and 108 (prescribed diseases) of that Act for the purposes of industrial injuries benefit under Part V of that Act;] [³ or

  (d) under section 59 of, and Schedule 7 to, the Welfare Reform and Pensions Act 1999 (couples to make joint-claim for jobseeker's

2.430

Social Security and Child Support (Decisions and Appeals) Regs 1999

allowance) where one member of the couple is working and the Secretary of State has decided that both members of the couple are not engaged in remunerative work].

AMENDMENTS

1. Tax Credits (Decisions and Appeals) (Amendment) Regulations 1999 (SI 1999/2570), reg.19 (October 5, 1999). Note that amendments made by these regulations only have effect with respect to tax credit under the Tax Credit Act 1999 (reg.1(2) of the Amendment Regulations).
2. Social Security and Child Support (Miscellaneous Amendments) Regulations 2000 (SI 2000/1596), reg.22 (June 19, 2000).
3. Social Security Amendment (Joint Claims) Regulations 2001 (SI 2001/518), reg.4(b) (March 19, 2001).

DEFINITIONS

"appeal"—see reg.1(3).
"appeal tribunal"—see s.39(1) of the Social Security Act 1998.
"the Board"—see reg.1(3).
"the Claims and Payments Regulations"—*ibid.*
"the Contributions and Benefits Act"—see s.84 of the Social Security Act 1998.
"relevant benefit"—see s.89(1) of the Social Security Act 1998.

GENERAL NOTE

2.431   Paragraph (c) enables there to be an appeal against an assessment of disablement independently of any appeal against a decision awarding, or refusing to award, benefit. This creates difficulties. In *CI/1547/2001*, it was suggested that all appeals against assessment decisions should also be treated as appeals against the consequent entitlement decisions because the provisions for supersession and revision are too limited, having regard to the dates from which they are effective, to deal satisfactorily with the consequences of a successful appeal on assessment alone. For the same reason, an application to supersede an assessment of disablement should generally be treated as also an application to supersede the underlying award (*CI/954/2006*).

A final assessment of disablement made under the legislation replaced by the Social Security Act 1998 Act implies that there was no disablement after the end of the award, and so has ongoing effect and requires supersession of the assessment as well as a new claim for benefit (*R(I) 5/02*), whereas an assessment under the 1998 Act carries no such implication and, after it expires, requires just a new claim.

Decisions against which no appeal lies

2.432   **27.**—(1) No appeal lies to an appeal tribunal against a decision set out in Schedule 2.

(2) In paragraph (1) and Schedule 2, "decision" includes determinations embodied in or necessary to a decision.

(3) An appeal made against a decision specified in paragraph (1) may be struck out in accordance with regulation 46.

DEFINITIONS

"appeal"—see reg.1(3).
"appeal tribunal"—see s.39(1) of the Social Security Act 1998.
"decision"—see para.(2).

(SI 1999/991, reg.27)

GENERAL NOTE

See note to Sch.2.

Notice of decision against which appeal lies

28.—(1) A person with a right of appeal under the Act or these Regulations against any decision of the Secretary of State [¹ or the Board or an officer of the Board] shall—
  (a) be given written notice of the decision against which the appeal lies;
  (b) be informed that, in a case where that written notice does not include a statement of the reasons for that decision, he may, within one month of the date of notification of that decision, request that the Secretary of State [¹ or the Board or an officer of the Board] provide him with a written statement of the reasons for that decision; and
  (c) be given written notice of his right of appeal against that decision.

(2) Where a written statement of the reasons for the decision is not included in the written notice of the decision and is requested under paragraph (1)(b), the Secretary of State [¹ or the Board or an officer of the Board] shall provide that statement within 14 days of receipt of the request [² or as soon as practicable afterwards].

AMENDMENTS

1. Tax Credits (Decisions and Appeals) (Amendment) Regulations 1999 (SI 1999/2570), reg.20 (October 5, 1999). Note that amendments made by these regulations only have effect with respect to tax credit (reg.1(2) of the Amendment Regulations).
2. Social Security, Child Support and Tax Credits (Miscellaneous Amendments) Regulations 2005 (SI 2005/337), reg.2(6) (March 18, 2005).

DEFINITIONS

"the Act"—see reg.1(3).
"appeal"—*ibid*.
"the Board"—*ibid*.
"the date of notification"—*ibid*.

GENERAL NOTE

Para. (1)
There may be circumstances in which a failure to comply with the duties imposed by this regulation may invalidate the decision altogether. However, in *R(P) 1/04*, it was held that a failure to issue notice of a decision simply had the effect that the time for appealing against the decision did not start to run. The same is true where a decision is issued but it incorrectly tells the claimant that benefit has been awarded for life when it has been awarded only for a limited period. The decision is valid but time for appealing runs from when the claimant is informed of the true nature of the decision (*CDLA/3440/2003*). It is suggested that, where a decision is issued, a failure to provide the information required by sub-para.(c) also has the effect that the decision is valid but that the time for appealing against it does not start to run. If that is so, the time for appealing would run from when the claimant does become aware of his rights. This is a necessary approach because reg.32(8)(a) makes it impossible to obtain an extension of time for appealing on the ground of ignorance of the time limits for appealing. Any dispute as to whether an appeal is in time should be resolved by a ruling under reg.31(4). A different approach has been taken in child support cases where the interests of a third party entitled to rely on

the decision have to be taken into account and time has been held to run from the date of a decision even though the parties have been misled into thinking they had no right of appeal (*CCS/5515/2002*). However, even though time for appealing does not start to run, the decision itself is not invalidated by a failure to give proper notice of it in the correct form. It is arguable that a statement of reasons only counts as such for the purposes of sub-para.(b) if it is adequate but the adequacy of a statement of reasons is very much a matter of judgment and depends on the issues arising in the particular case. However, a request made under para.(1)(b) extends the time for appealing but, presumably, only if it is properly made and the notice really does not include an adequate statement of reasons. Accordingly, the cautious claimant will treat any purported statement of reasons as being adequate for the purpose and will ensure that the appeal is lodged within the usual one month time limit, even if a fuller explanation is expected in the Secretary of State's submission to the tribunal.

A failure to refer to the fact that a decision is a supersession can, like most other defects, be cured by a tribunal giving a decision in the proper form (*R(IB)2/04*). On the other hand, if a tribunal does not realise that a decision under appeal was, or should have been, a supersession rather than a decision on a new claim, the tribunal's decision is liable to be set aside if it is impossible to infer that any ground for altering the decision on supersession was made out (*CDLA/9/2001*).

Further particulars required relating to certificate of recoverable benefits appeals or applications

2.436

29.—(1) An appeal or application under the 1997 Act relating to a certificate of recoverable benefits shall, in addition to any requirements imposed by regulations, include also the following particulars—

(a) in the case of an appeal, the date of the certificate of recoverable benefits or the decision by the Secretary of State on review against which the appeal is brought, the question under section 11 of the 1997 Act to which the appeal relates and a summary of the arguments relied upon by the appellant to support his contention that the certificate is wrong;

(b) in the case of an application for an extension of time under regulation 32, in relation to the appeal which it is proposed to bring, the particulars required under sub-paragraph (a) together with particulars of the special circumstances on which the application is based.

(2) Where the appeal or the application for an extension of time is made by a person to whom a compensation payment has been made, a copy of the statement given to that person under section 9 of the 1997 Act or if that statement was not in writing, a written summary of it, shall be sent with that appeal or application.

(3) Where it appears to the Secretary of State that an appeal or application does not contain the further particulars required under paragraph (1) or is not accompanied by a written statement or summary as required under paragraph (2) he may direct the appellant or applicant to provide such particulars or such a statement or summary.

(4) Where paragraph (3) applies, the time specified for making the appeal or application may be extended by such period, not exceeding 14 days from the date of the Secretary of State's direction under paragraph (3), as the Secretary of State may determine.

(5) Where further particulars or a written statement or summary are required under paragraph (3) they shall be sent to or delivered to the Compensation Recovery Unit of the [² Department for Work and Pensions] at

(SI 1999/991, reg.29)

[¹Durham House, Washington, Tyne and Wear, NE38 7SF] within such period as the Secretary of State may direct.

(6) The Secretary of State may treat any appeal relating to the certificate of recoverable benefits as an application for review under section 10 of the 1997 Act.

AMENDMENTS

1. (Social Security (Recovery of Benefits) (Miscellaneous Amendments) Regulations 2000 (SI 2000/3030), reg.3 (December 4, 2000)).
2. Social Security and Child Support (Decisions and Appeals) (Miscellaneous Amendments) Regulations 2002 (SI 2002/1379), reg.8 (May 20, 2002).

DEFINITIONS

"the 1997 Act"—see reg.1(3).
"appeal"—*ibid.*

General appeals matters including child support appeals

Appeal against a decision which has been [² replaced or] revised

30.—(1) An appeal against a decision of the Secretary of State [¹ or the Board or an officer of the Board] shall not lapse where the decision [² is treated as replaced by a decision under section 11 of the Child Support Act by section 28F(5) of that Act, or is revised under section 16 of that Act] or section 9 before the appeal is determined and the decision as [² replaced or] revised is not more advantageous to the appellant than the decision before it was [² replaced or] revised.

(2) Decisions which are more advantageous for the purposes of this regulation include decisions where—
(a) any relevant benefit paid to the appellant is greater or is awarded for a longer period in consequence of the decision made under section 9;
(b) it would have resulted in the amount of relevant benefit in payment being greater but for the operation of any provision of the Administration Act or the Contributions and Benefits Act restricting or suspending the payment of, or disqualifying a claimant from receiving, some or all of the benefit;
(c) as a result of the decision, a denial or disqualification for the receiving of any relevant benefit, is lifted, wholly or in part;
(d) it reverses a decision to pay benefit to a third party;
[³(dd) it reverses a decision under section 29(2) that an accident is not an industrial accident;]
(e) in consequence of the revised decision, benefit paid is not recoverable under section 71, 71A or 74 of the Administration Act or regulations made under any of those sections, or the amount so recoverable is reduced; or
(f) a financial gain accrued or will accrue to the appellant in consequence of the decision.

(3) Where a decision as [² replaced under section 28F(5) of the Child Support Act, or as revised under section 16 of that Act] or under section 9

2.437

Social Security and Child Support (Decisions and Appeals) Regs 1999

is not more advantageous to the appellant than the decision before it was [² replaced or] revised, the appeal shall be treated as though it had been brought against the decision as [² replaced or] revised.

(4) The appellant shall have a period of one month from the date of notification of the decision as [² replaced or] revised to make further representations as to the appeal.

(5) After the expiration of the period specified in paragraph (4), or within that period if the appellant consents in writing, the appeal to the appeal tribunal shall proceed except where, in the light of the further representations from the appellant, the Secretary of State [¹ or the Board or an officer of the Board] further revises his [¹, or revise their,] decision and that decision is more advantageous to the appellant than the decision before it was [² replaced or] revised.

AMENDMENTS

2.438   1. Tax Credits (Decisions and Appeals) (Amendment) Regulations 1999 (SI 1999/2570), reg.21 (October 5, 1999). Note that amendments made by these regulations only have effect with respect to tax credit under the Tax Credit Act 1999 (reg.1(2) of the Amendment Regulations).

2. Child Support (Decisions and Appeals) (Amendment) Regulations 2000 (SI 2000/3185), reg.11 (various dates as provided by reg.1(1)).

3. Social Security, Child Support and Tax Credits (Miscellaneous Amendments) Regulations 2005 (SI 2005/337), reg.2(7) (March 18, 2005).

DEFINITIONS

"the Administration Act"—see s.84 of the Social Security Act 1998.
"appeal"—see reg.1(3).
"the Board"—*ibid*.
"the Child Support Act"—see s.84 of the Social Security Act 1998.
"the Contributions and Benefits Act"—*ibid*.
"the date of notification"—see reg.1(3).
"relevant benefit"—see s.39(1) of the Social Security Act 1998.

GENERAL NOTE

2.439   Paragraph (1) provides an exception to the general rule that an appeal lapses when the decision under appeal is revised (see s.9(6) of the Social Security Act 1998). It makes it unnecessary for the claimant to submit a fresh appeal where the decision under appeal is replaced by a decision that is no more favourable to the claimant. Paragraph (2), however, makes it clear that a fresh appeal will be required where the new decision is only partially favourable to a claimant as well as when it is wholly favourable. In *CIS/624/2006*, a decision was made in 2003 to the effect that the claimant was not entitled to income support from 17 May 2002. When the claimant appealed, the decision was revised and income support was paid in respect of the period from 17 May 2002 to 31 July 2002. It was held that reg.30(2)(a) did not require the appeal to be treated as having lapsed in respect of the period from 1 August 2002. The Tribunal of Commissioners said —

". . . where a period before the date of the original decision is in issue and a revision affects only part of that period, it seems to us that there are many circumstances in which it can be appropriate to regard the decision as being more advantageous to the appellant only in respect of that part of the period and not the remainder of the period. This is particularly so where the Secretary of State knows very well that the revision does not deal with the main issue raise by the appeal and that it would be a waste of time to treat the appeal as having lapsed and to require the appellant to start all over again."

(SI 1999/991, reg.30)

The new subpara.(dd) appears to have effect only in relation to industrial accident declarations made otherwise than in the course of a claim for benefit. It is probably meant to apply not only to cases where the reversed decision was to the effect that an accident was not an industrial accident but also to cases where it was to the effect that an alleged industrial accident was not an accident at all or did not even take place.

30A. *Omitted.*

Time within which an appeal is to be brought

31.—(1) Where an appeal lies from a decision of the Secretary of State [¹ or the Board or an officer of the Board] to an appeal tribunal, except in the case of a decision of the Secretary of State under section 3 or 3A of the Vaccine Damage Payments Act, the time within which that appeal must be brought is, subject to the following provisions of this Part—

[²(a) subject to regulation 9A(3), within one month of the date of notification of the decision against which the appeal is brought;
 (b) where a written statement of the reasons for that decision is requested and provided within the period specified in subparagraph (a), within 14 days of the expiry of that period; or
 (c) where a written statement of the reasons for that decision is requested but is not provided within the period specified in subparagraph (a), within 14 days of the date on which the statement is provided.]

(2) Where the Secretary of State [¹ or the Board or an officer of the Board]—
 (a) revises, or following an application for a revision under regulation 3(1) or (3) [³, 3A(1) or regulation 17(1)(a) of the Child Support (Maintenance Assessment Procedure) Regulations 1992]. does not revise, a decision under section 16 of the Child Support Act or under section 9, or
 (b) supersedes a decision under section 17 of the Child Support Act or under section 10,
the period of one month specified in paragraph (1) shall begin to run from the date of notification of the revision or supersession of the decision, or following an application for a revision under regulation 3(1) or (3) [³, 3A(1) or regulation 17(1)(a) of the Child Support (Maintenance Assessment Procedure) Regulations 1992], the date the Secretary of State [¹ or the Board or an officer of the Board] issues a notice that he is [¹ or they are] not revising the decision.

(3) An appeal against a certificate of recoverable benefits must be brought—
 (a) not later than one month after the date a person making a compensation payment discharges his liability under section 6 of the 1997 Act;
 (b) where the certificate is reviewed by the Secretary of State [¹ or the Board or an officer of the Board] in accordance with regulations made under section 11(5)(c) of the 1997 Act, not later than one month after the date the certificate is confirmed, or, as the case may be, a fresh certificate is issued; or
 (c) where an agreement is made under which an earlier compensation payment is treated as having been made in final discharge of a claim made by or in respect of an injured person and arising out of the

Social Security and Child Support (Decisions and Appeals) Regs 1999

accident, injury or disease, not later than one month after the date of that agreement.

(4) Where a dispute arises as to whether an appeal was brought within the time limit specified in this regulation, the dispute shall be referred to, and be determined by, a legally qualified panel member.

(5) The time limit specified in this regulation for bringing an appeal may be extended in accordance with regulation 32.

AMENDMENTS

1. Tax Credits (Decisions and Appeals) (Amendment) Regulations 1999 (SI 1999/ 2570), reg.22 (October 5, 1999). Note that amendments made by these regulations only have effect with respect to tax credit (reg.1(2) of the Amendment Regulations).
2. Social Security and Child Support (Decisions and Appeals) (Miscellaneous Amendments) Regulations 2002 (SI 2002/1379), reg.9 (May 20, 2002).
3. Social Security, Child Support and Tax Credits (Miscellaneous Amendments) Regulations 2005 (SI 2005/337), reg.2(8) (March 18, 2005).

DEFINITIONS

"the 1997 Act"—see reg.1(3).
"appeal"—*ibid.*
"appeal tribunal"—see s.39(1) of the Social Security Act 1998.
"the Board"—see reg.1(3).
"the Child Support Act"—see s.84 of the Social Security Act 1998.
"the Contributions and Benefits Act"—*ibid.*
"the date of notification"—see reg.1(3).
"the Vaccine Damage Payments Act"—see s.84 of the Social Security Act1998.

GENERAL NOTE

Para. (2)

2.442–
2.443

There is no right of appeal against a decision under s.9 of the Social Security Act 1998 to revise or not revise an earlier decision. This paragraph allows most s.9 decisions effectively to be challenged by extending the time for appealing against the decision that has been revised or not revised. However, it does not apply to refusals to revise, except where there was an application under regs 3(1) or (3) or 3A(1) of these Regulations or reg.17 of the Child Support (Maintenance Assessment Procedure Regulations 1992.

The reference to reg.3A(1) (which is also concerned only with child support decisions and is therefore not reproduced in this work) is interesting because reg.3A(1) is much broader in its scope than reg.3(1) and includes revision for "official error" which, in social security cases, falls under reg.3(5)(a). The consequence is that, in child support cases to which reg.3A applies, the time limit for appealing against a decision that has not been revised for "official error" is extended under reg.31(2) but the same is not true in social security cases. In *R(IS) 15/04* (subsequently approved by the Court of Appeal in *Beltekian v Westminster CC* [2004] EWCA Civ 1784 (reported as *R(H) 8/05*). a Tribunal of Commissioners held that it followed that there was no way of challenging a refusal to revise in a social security case, if it was too late to appeal against the original decision, other than by way of an application for judicial review. This is most unsatisfactory. The Tribunal pointed out that claimants would not wish to apply for revision under reg.3(5) except on the ground of "official error" because the other grounds for revision result in decisions less favourable to the claimant than the decision that has been revised. However, claimants might well apply for supersession under reg.3(5A), (6), (7) to (7F), (8A) or (8B) and so the problem is not confined to "official error" cases.

(SI 1999/991, reg.31)

Where it is still possible to appeal against the original decision following a refusal to revise, the Tribunal held in *R(IB)2/04* at para.39 that the appeal can succeed only if it can be shown that the decision should have been revised. Otherwise, as was pointed out in *CCS/5515/2002*, late appeals could easily be brought by making entirely unmeritorious applications for revision.

Late appeals

32.—(1) The time within which an appeal must be brought may be extended where the conditions specified in paragraphs (2) to (8) are satisfied, but no appeal shall in any event be brought more than one year after the expiration of the last day for appealing under regulation 31.

(2) An application for an extension of time under this regulation shall be made in accordance with regulation 33 and shall be determined by a legally qualified panel member [¹, except that where the Secretary of State or the Board, as the case may be, consider that the conditions in paragraphs (4)(b) to (8) are satisfied, the Secretary of State or the Board, as the case may be, may grant the application].

(3) An application under this regulation shall contain particulars of the grounds on which the extension of time is sought, including details of any relevant special circumstances for the purposes of paragraph (4).

[¹ (4) An application for an extension of time shall not be granted unless—
 (a) the panel member is satisfied that, if the application is granted, there are reasonable prospects that the appeal will be successful; or
 (b) the panel member, the Secretary of State or the Board, as the case may be, are satisfied that it is in the interests of justice for the application to be granted.]

(5) For the purposes of paragraph (4) it is not in the interests of justice to grant an application unless the panel member [¹, the Secretary of State or the Board, as the case may be,] is satisfied that—
 (a) the special circumstances specified in paragraph (6) are relevant to the application; or
 (b) some other special circumstances exist which are wholly exceptional and relevant to the application.
and as a result of those special circumstances, it was not practicable for the application to be made within the time limit specified in regulation 31.

(6) For the purposes of paragraph (5)(a), the special circumstances are that—
 (a) the applicant or a [¹ partner] or dependant of the applicant has died or suffered serious illness;
 (b) the applicant is not resident in the United Kingdom; or
 (c) normal postal services were disrupted.

(7) In determining whether it is in the interests of justice to grant the application, [¹ regard shall be had] to the principle that the greater the amount of time that has elapsed between the expiration of the time within which the appeal is to be brought under regulation 31 and the making of the application for an extension of time, the more compelling should be the special circumstances on which the application is based.

(8) In determining whether it is in the interests of justice to grant an application, no account shall be taken of the following—
 (a) that the applicant or any person acting for him was unaware of or misunderstood the law applicable to his case (including ignorance

2.444

or misunderstanding of the time limits imposed by these Regulations); or

(b) that a Commissioner or a court has taken a different view of the law from that previously understood and applied.

(9) An application under this regulation for an extension of time which has been refused may not be renewed.

(10) The panel member who determines an application under this regulation shall record a summary of his decision in such written form as has been approved by the President.

(11) As soon as practicable after the decision is made a copy of the decision shall be sent or given to every party to the proceedings.

DEFINITIONS

"appeal"—see reg.1(3).
"the Board"—*ibid*.
"Commissioner"—see s.39(1) of the Social Security Act 1998.
"legally qualified panel member"—see reg.1(3).
"panel member"—*ibid*.
"partner"—*ibid*.
"party to the proceedings"—*ibid*.
"President"—*ibid*.

AMENDMENT

1. Social Security and Child Support (Decisions and Appeals) (Miscellaneous Amendments) Regulations 2002 (SI 2002/1379), reg.10 (May 20, 2002).

GENERAL NOTE

2.445   These very stringent conditions are similar to those imposed under reg.3 of the Social Security (Adjudication) Regulations 1995 but para.(5)(a) is new and the test of practicality imposed by para.(5) is simpler than the previous test but no more generous.

Para. (1)

2.446   The absolute time limit prohibiting the bringing of appeals more than a year late is not incompatible with the European Convention on Human Rights (*Denson v Secretary of State for Work and Pensions* [2004] EWCA Civ 462 (reported as *R(CS) 4/04*). Nonetheless, it can work injustice, particularly in a case where an unrepresented claimant has been challenging the wrong decision and nobody tells him or her until it is too late which decision it is that must be challenged if he or she is to succeed in obtaining the benefit sought.

Although a determination by a legally qualified panel member is a decision of a tribunal, there is no right of appeal to a Commissioner against a determination that there is no jurisdiction to hear an appeal to a tribunal brought more than a year out of time (*Morina v Secretary of State for Work and Pensions* [2007] EWCA Civ 749).

In *R(TC) 1/05*, there was no evidence that anyone had considered whether there were grounds for admitting a late appeal, perhaps because the appeal had been proceeding on the basis that it was an in-time appeal against a supersession decision whereas, on a proper analysis, the supersession had been a refusal to revise so that the appeal was against an earlier decision and the circumstances were such that time had not been extended by virtue of reg.31(2). There was also a suggestion that notice of the original decision had not been sent to the claimant so that the appeal was not late at all. The Commissioner considered that the tribunal's brief reasons suggested that if the chairman had considered whether to extend the time for appealing, he would have refused. However, the Commissioner held the decision was invalid because, if the appeal had been late and there was no extension of time, the tribunal had had no jurisdiction to hear the appeal. The claimant was entitled to have the question of an extension of time properly considered. Had the chairman clearly refused an extension of time, the Commissioner said that it appeared that he would have had no jurisdiction to consider an appeal against that refusal, notwithstanding that there appeared to be no clear finding that notice of the decision under appeal had ever been issued. However, it is suggested that, if the tribunal had declined jurisdiction on the ground that time had not been extended, the refusal to accept jurisdictions would have been appealable and a failure to record a finding as to whether notice of the original decision had been issued might have led to the appeal being allowed. In an ordinary case, of course, the question of extending time is considered by a legally qualified panel member before the case is listed for hearing by a tribunal and, in many cases, a tribunal cannot be composed only of a legally qualified panel member.

The Commissioner also pointed out that, whereas under reg.32(2) the Secretary of State or Inland Revenue can consider whether the conditions in reg.32(4)(b) to (8) are satisfied, only a legally qualified panel member can consider whether the condition in reg.32(4)(a) is satisfied.

Para. (2)

The Secretary of State or the Board may decide that a late appeal should be admitted under para.(4)(b) (but not under para.(4)(a)). Presumably it is not expected that a tribunal will then object. It is not clear what the tribunal could do if it did object. It may be arguable that the decision of the panel member is a decision of an appeal tribunal for the purpose of permitting an appeal to be brought against it under s.14 of the Social Security Act 1998.

2.447

Para. (4)

The new form of reg.32(4)(a) bestows a fairly broad discretion on a legally qualified panel member to grant an extension of time and makes it unnecessary for him or her to consider the narrow conditions of reg.32(4)(b) to (8) in a meritorious case.

2.448

Para. (8)(a)

If a claimant is ignorant of the time limit for appealing because the Secretary of State failed to provide the information required by reg.28(1)(c), it is arguable that time for appealing has not started to run. Section 12(6) of the Social Security Act 1998 requires that information to be given. If this is correct, it is unnecessary for the claimant to apply for an extension of time for appealing (which might be difficult in the light of para.(8)(a)) and, instead, should apply for a ruling under reg.31(4).

2.449

Para. (8)(b)

Understood by whom? Presumably not the applicant because the view must also be different from that previously applied. But is it the understanding of the Department for Work and Pensions as a whole that matters or of the particular local office or of the panel member considering the application? Whatever the answer, it is not easy to see what sub-para.(b) adds to sub-para.(a).

2.450

Making of appeals and applications

33.—(1) An appeal, or an application for an extension of time for making an appeal to an appeal tribunal shall be in writing either on a form approved for the purpose by the Secretary of State [² or the Board] or in such

2.451

Social Security and Child Support (Decisions and Appeals) Regs 1999

other format as the Secretary of State accepts [² or the Board accepts] as sufficient for the purpose and shall—
- (a) be signed by—
  - (i) the person who, under [³ section 4(1) of the Vaccine Damage Payments Act], section 20 of the Child Support Act [⁷. . .], section 11(2) of the 1997 Act or section 12(2), has a right of appeal; or
  - (ii) where the person in head (i) has provided written authority to a representative to act on his behalf, by that representative;
- (b) be sent or delivered to an appropriate office;
- (c) contain particulars of the grounds on which it is made; and
- (d) contain sufficient particulars of the decision, the certificate of recoverable benefits or the subject of the application, as the case may be, to enable that decision, certificate or subject of the application to be identified.

(2) In this regulation, "an appropriate office" means—
- (a) in the case of an appeal under the 1997 Act against a certificate of recoverable benefits, the Compensation Recovery Unit of the [⁸ Department for Work and Pensions] at [⁶ Durham House, Washington, Tyne and Wear, NE38 7SF];
- (b) in the case of an appeal against a decision relating to a jobseeker's allowance, an office of the [⁸ Department for Work and Pensions the address of which was indicated on the notification of the decision which is subject to appeal];
- (c) in the case of a contributions decision which falls within Part II of Schedule 3 to the Act, any National Insurance Contributions office [¹ of the Board, or any office of the [⁸ Department for Work and Pensions];

[¹(cc) in the case of a decision made under the Pension Schemes Act 1993 by virtue of section 170(2) of that Act, any National Insurance Contributions office of the Board;]
- (d) in the case of an appeal under section 20 of the Child Support Act [⁷. . .] an office of the Child Support Agency; [². . .]

[²(dd) in the case of an appeal against a decision relating to working families' tax credit or disabled person's tax crdit, a Tax Credits Office of the Board;]

[⁴(ddd) in a case where the decision appealed against was a decision arising from a claim to a designated office, an office of a designated authority;] and
- (e) in any other case, an office of the [⁸ Department for Work and Pensions the address of which was indicated on the notification of the decision which is subject to appeal].

(3) A form which is not completed in accordance with the instructions on the form—
- (a) except where paragraph (4) applies, does not satisfy the requirements of paragraph (1), and
- (b) may be returned by the Secretary of State [² or the Board] to the sender for completion in accordance with those instructions.

(4) Where the Secretary of State is satisfied [² or the Board are satisfied] that the form, although not completed in accordance with the instructions on it, includes sufficient information to enable the appeal or application to proceed, he [² or they] may treat the form as satisfying the requirements of paragraph (1).

(SI 1999/991, reg.33)

(5) Where an appeal or application is made in writing otherwise than on the approved form ("the letter"), and the letter includes sufficient information to enable the appeal or application to proceed, the Secretary of State [2 or the Board] may treat the letter as satisfying the requirements of paragraph (1).

(6) Where the letter does not include sufficient information to enable the appeal or application to proceed, the Secretary of State [2 or the Board] may request further information in writing ("further particulars") from the person who wrote the letter.

[8 (7) Where a person to whom a form is returned, or from whom further particulars are requested, duly completes and returns the form or sends the further particulars, if the form or particulars, as the case may be, are received by the Secretary of State or the Board within—

(a) 14 days of the date on which the form was returned to him by the Secretary of State or the Board, the time for making the appeal shall be extended by 14 days from the date on which the form was returned;
(b) 14 days of the date on which the Secretary of State's or the Board's request was made, the time for making the appeal shall be extended by 14 days from the date of the request; or
(c) such longer period as the Secretary of State or the Board may direct, the time for making the appeal shall be extended by a period equal to that longer period directed by the Secretary of State or the Board.]

(8) Where a person to whom a form is returned or from whom further particulars are requested does not complete and return the form or send further particulars within the period of time specified in paragraph (7)—

(a) the Secretary of State [2 or the Board] shall forward a copy of the form, or as the case may be, the letter, together with any other relevant documents or evidence to a legally qualified panel member, and
(b) the panel member shall determine whether the form or the letter satisfies the requirement of paragraph (1), and shall inform the appellant or applicant and the Secretary of State [2 or the Board] of his determination.

(9) Where—

(a) a form is duly completed and returned or further particulars are sent after the expiry of the period of time allowed in accordance with paragraph (7), and
(b) no decision has been made under paragraph (8) at the time the form or the further particulars are received by the Secretary of State [2 or the Board],

that form or further particulars shall also be forwarded to the legally qualified panel member who shall take into account any further information or evidence set out in the form or further particulars.

[8 (10) The Secretary of State or the Board may discontinue action on an appeal where the appeal has not been forwarded to the clerk to an appeal tribunal or to a legally qualified panel member and the appellant or an authorised representative of the appellant has given written notice that he does not wish the appeal to continue.]

AMENDMENTS

1. Social Security Contributions (Transfer of Functions, etc.) Act 1999 (Commencement No.2 and Consequential and Transitional Provisions) Order 1999 (SI 1999/1662), art.3(4) (July 5, 1999).

Social Security and Child Support (Decisions and Appeals) Regs 1999

2. Tax Credits (Decisions and Appeals) (Amendment) Regulations 1999 (SI 1999/2570), reg.23 (October 5, 1999). Note that amendments made by these regulations only have effect with respect to tax credit under the Tax Credit Act 1999 (reg.1(2) of the Amendment Regulations).
3. Social Security and Child Support (Decisions and Appeals), Vaccine Damage Payments and Jobseeker's Allowance (Amendment) Regulations 1999 (SI 1999/2677), reg.9 (October 18, 1999).
4. Social Security (Work-focused Interviews) Regulations 2000 (SI 2000/897), reg.16(5) and Sch.6, para.6 (April 3, 2000).
5. Social Security and Child Support (Miscellaneous Amendments) Regulations 2000 (SI 2000/1596), reg.23 (June 19, 2000).
6. Social Security (Recovery of Benefits) (Miscellaneous Amendments) Regulations 2000 (SI 2000/3030), reg.4 (December 4, 2000).
7. Child Support (Consequential Amendments and Transitional Provisions) Regulations 2001 (SI 2001/158), reg.4(4) (various dates as provided in reg.1(3)).
8. Social Security and Child Support (Decisions and Appeals) (Miscellaneous Amendments) Regulations 2002 (SI 2002/1379), reg.11 (May 20, 2002).

DEFINITIONS

"the Act"—see reg.1(3).
"the 1997 Act"—*ibid*.
"appeal"—*ibid*.
"appeal tribunal"—see s.39(1) of the Social Security Act 1998.
"an appropriate office"—see para.(2).
"the Board"—see reg.1(3).
"the Child Support Act"—see s.84 of the Social Security Act 1998.
"clerk to the appeal tribunal"—see reg.1(3).
"designated authority"—*ibid*.
"legally qualified panel member"—*ibid*.
"tax credit"—*ibid*.
"the Vaccine Damage Payments Act"—see s.84 of the Social Security Act 1998.

GENERAL NOTE

Para. (1)

2.452
At first sight it is surprising that it should be the Secretary of State who decides whether the appeal is in a sufficient format, but it is implicit in paras (4) and (5) that a technically deficient appeal should be allowed to proceed provided that it includes sufficient information to make that possible and the final decision not to admit an appeal is made by a legally qualified panel member under para.(8).

A typed name can amount to a signature when it has been adopted by the person concerned through his or her signing another document or taking some other active step in an appeal (*R(DLA) 2/98*). In *CIB/460/2003*, the claimant's mother, who had not been appointed to act on behalf of the claimant, signed the appeal. No-one had objected and the claimant himself had signed the form issued by the clerk under reg.39(1), asking him, among other things, whether he wanted to withdraw his appeal. He had said "no". The Commissioner rejected a submission made on behalf of the Secretary of State to the effect that the appeal was not valid.

Death of a party to an appeal

2.453
34.—(1) In any proceedings, on the death of a party to those proceedings (other than the Secretary of State [¹ or the Board]), the Secretary of State [¹ or the Board] may appoint such person as he thinks [¹ or they think] fit to proceed with the appeal in the place of such deceased party.

(SI 1999/991, reg.34)

(2) A grant of probate, confirmation or letters of administration to the estate of the deceased party, whenever taken out, shall have no effect on an appointment made under paragraph (1).

(3) Where a person appointed under paragraph (1) has, prior to the date of such appointment, taken any action in relation to the appeal on behalf of the deceased party, the effective date of appointment by the Secretary of State [¹ or the Board] shall be the day immediately prior to the first day on which such action was taken.

AMENDMENT

1. Tax Credits (Decisions and Appeals) (Amendment) Regulations 1999 (SI 1999/2570), reg.24 (October 5, 1999). Note that amendments made by these regulations only have effect with respect to tax credit under the Tax Credit Act 1999 (reg.1(2) of the Amendment Regulations).

DEFINITIONS

"appeal"—see reg.1(3).
"the Board"—*ibid.*

PART V

APPEAL TRIBUNALS FOR SOCIAL SECURITY CONTRACTING OUT OF PENSIONS, VACCINE DAMAGE AND CHILD SUPPORT

CHAPTER I

THE PANEL AND APPEAL TRIBUNALS

Persons appointed to the panel

35. For the purposes of section 6(3), the panel shall include persons with the qualifications specified in Schedule 3.

2.454

DEFINITION

"panel"—see reg.1(3).

Composition of appeal tribunals

36.—(1) Subject to the following provisions of this regulation, an appeal tribunal [². . .] shall consist of a legally qualified panel member.

2.455

[¹ (2) Subject to [² paragraphs (3) to (5) [³ and(8)], an appeal tribunal shall consist of a legally qualified panel member and—
  (a) a medically qualified panel member where—
    (i) the issue, or one of the issues, raised on the appeal is whether the [² personal capability assessment] is satisfied, or
    (ii) the appeal is made under section 11(1)(b) of the 1997 Act; or
  (b) one medically qualified panel member or two such members or one medically qualified panel member and an additional member drawn from the panel for the purposes described in paragraph (5) below where—

(i) the issue, or one of the issues, raised on the appeal [² (not being an appeal where the only issue is whether there should be a declaration of an industrial accident under section 29(2))] relates to either industrial injuries benefit under Part V of the Contributions and Benefits Act or severe disablement allowance under section 68 of that Act; or
(ii) the appeal is made under section 4 of the Vaccine Damage Payments Act."]

(3) An appeal tribunal shall consist of a financially qualified panel member and a legally qualified panel member where—
 (a) the issue raised, or one of the issues raised on appeal or referral, relates to child support or a relevant benefit; and
 (b) the appeal or referral may require consideration by members of the appeal tribunal of issues which are, in the opinion of the President, difficult and which relate to—
  (i) profit and loss accounts, revenue accounts or balance sheets relating to any enterprise;
  (ii) an income and expenditure account in the case of an enterprise not trading for profit; or
  (iii) the accounts of any trust fund.

(4) Where the composition of an appeal tribunal would fall to be prescribed under both paragraphs (2) and (3), it shall consist of a medically qualified panel member, a financially qualified panel member and a legally qualified panel member.

(5) Where the composition of an appeal tribunal is prescribed under [¹paragraph (1), (2)(a)] [³ or (3)]], the President may determine that the appeal tribunal shall include such an additional member drawn from the panel constituted under section 6 as he considers appropriate for the purposes of providing further experience for that additional member or for assisting the President in the monitoring of standards of decision making by panel members.

(6) An appeal tribunal shall consist of a legally qualified panel member, a medically qualified panel member and a panel member with a disability qualification in any appeal which relates to an attendance allowance or a disability living allowance under Part III of the Contributions and Benefits Act or [² a disabled person's tax credit] under section 129 of that Act.

[¹(7) In paragraph (2)(a)(i) above, "[² personal capability assessment]" has the meaning it bears in regulation 2(1) of the Social Security(Incapacity for Work) (General) Regulations 1995.]

[² (8) A person shall not act as a medically qualified panel member of an appeal tribunal in any appeal if he has at any time advised or prepared a report upon any person whose medical condition is relevant to the issue in the appeal, or has at any time regularly attended such a person.

(9) [³ . . .]]

AMENDMENTS

1. Social Security and Child Support (Decisions and Appeals) (Amendment) Regulations 1999 (SI 1999/1466), reg.2 (June 1, 1999).
2. Social Security and Child Support (Miscellaneous Amendments) Regulations 2000 (SI 2000/1596), reg.24 (June 19, 2000).

(SI 1999/991, reg.36)

3. Social Security, Child Support and Tax Credits (Decisions and Appeals) Regulations 2004 (SI 2004/3368), reg.2(4) (December 21, 2004).

DEFINITIONS

"the 1997 Act"—see reg.1(3).
"appeal"—*ibid.*
"appeal tribunal"—see s.39(1) of the Social Security Act 1998.
"the Contributions and Benefits Act"—see s.84 of the Social Security Act 1998.
"financially qualified panel member"—see reg.1(3).
"legally qualified panel member"—*ibid.*
"medically qualified panel member"—*ibid.*
"panel member"—*ibid.*
"panel member with a disability qualification"—*ibid.*
"personal capability assessment"—see para.(7).
"President"—see reg.1(3).
"relevant benefit"—see s.39(1) of the Social Security Act 1998.
"tax credit"—see reg.1(3).
"the Vaccine Damage Payments Act"—see s.84 of the Social Security Act 1998.

GENERAL NOTE

The general rule established by para.(1) is that a tribunal consists of a single lawyer but para.(2) provides for tribunals consisting of a lawyer and one or two doctors, para.(3) provides for tribunals consisting of a lawyer and an accountant, para.(4) provides for tribunals consisting of a lawyer, a doctor and an accountant and para.(6) provides for tribunals consisting of a lawyer, a doctor and a person with experience of dealing with the needs of disabled persons either in a professional or voluntary capacity or because they are themselves disabled.

2.456

There is no statutory requirement that the lawyer should be the chairman of a tribunal with more than one member but that is the invariable practice. Nor is there any longer any statutory provision requiring, where practical, a member of the tribunal to be of the same sex as the claimant. Nonetheless, in *CIB/2620/2000*, the Commissioner held that there might be some:

"exceptional cases where the absence of a tribunal member of the same sex as the claimant may inhibit the presentation or understanding of the claimant's case to such an extent that there will be a breach of the requirements of natural justice and of Article 6 of the European Convention on Human Rights if the tribunal is not reconstituted. It is obviously sensible to have a female member of the tribunal, if possible, in a case such as this one; raising as it does sensitive issues relating to a female medical condition. If a claimant specifically raises as an issue the absence from the tribunal of a member of the same sex, it will also be necessary for the tribunal to consider whether there is a real possibility of an injustice if the tribunal is not reconstituted. The repeal of s.46(1) [of the Social Security Administration Act 1992] means that there is no longer a need for the tribunal to consider in every case whether it is practicable for the tribunal to include a member of the same sex as the claimant, but a tribunal will nevertheless be under a duty to raise the matter of its own motion if there is a genuine reason to believe that in the circumstances of the particular case the absence of such a member may lead to injustice."

However, in the case before him, no point had been taken before the tribunal as to the absence of a woman and, although the case was concerned with a female medical condition, the examining medical officer's report was not disputed and the tribunal was not required to investigate any further the effect on the claimant of that condition. Accordingly, a fair-minded and informed observer would not have concluded that there was a real possibility of the hearing having been unfair due to the lack of a woman member of the tribunal and the Commissioner rejected that particular ground of appeal.

Earlier legislation provided for social security appeal tribunals, medical appeal tribunals, child support appeal tribunals and disability appeal tribunals and the distinctions now drawn in the composition of appeal tribunals can be traced back to the distinctions between those tribunals. However, while similar jurisdictional issues can arise, the need for single cases to be considered by more than one tribunal has gone because a tribunal with a doctor among its members is not confined solely to medical issues. Thus, in *CI/1327/1998*, it was pointed out that *R(I) 4/91* had ceased to have any application because the diagnosis question and the prescription question in industrial disease cases may be determined by the same tribunal.

Para. (2)

2.457
The unsatisfactory experiment of having medical assessors in incapacity benefit cases has been abandoned in favour of having a doctor as a member of a tribunal. Some cases previously heard by a medical appeal tribunal are now heard by a tribunal with only one medical member but some continue to have two. The fact that all cases concerning disablement benefit now include a doctor is generally to be welcomed, although there may be a few cases where the need for a doctor is not immediately obvious. There is often an advantage in having a doctor considering whether a person has suffered an industrial accident and there is even more advantage in having that issue considered at the same time as the question whether the claimant has suffered a loss of faculty as the result of an accident. Note, however, that an appeal in respect of an industrial accident declaration under s.29(2) of the Social Security Act 1998, where there has been *no* claim for benefit, must be considered by a tribunal without a medical member (although s.30 limits the effect of such a decision). Given reg.26(c), it is perhaps odd that the same approach is not now taken where declarations are sought under s.29(1) within claims for benefit. Note also, that the circumstances in which the medical member or members of a tribunal may physically examine a claimant are limited by reg.52. As the power to examine a claimant is no longer related to the constitution of the tribunal, tribunals have to consider in each case whether or not they are entitled to examine the claimant.

This paragraph must be read as requiring a medically qualified panel member to sit on an appeal against a decision that the claimant's incapacity for work was no longer due to an industrial accident so that she ceased to be entitled to incapacity benefit under reg.17 of the Social Security (Incapacity Benefit) (Transitional) Regulations 1995 by virtue of reg.21 (*CIB/3236/2006*).

Para. (6)

2.458
It is not inappropriate for a doctor who acts as an examining medical practitioner preparing reports to sit as a medically qualified panel member (*Gillies v Secretary of State for Work and Pensions* [2006] UKHL 2; [2006] 1 W.L.R. 781 (also reported as *R(DLA) 5/06*), but it may be inappropriate for a chairman or disability qualified panel member to sit on a tribunal considering a medical report compiled by a doctor with whom they have sat on previous occasions (*Secretary of State for Work and Pensions v Cunningham*, 2004 S.L.T. 1007 (also reported as *R(DLA) 7/04*). In practice, therefore, medically qualified panel members do not sit in the areas where they act as examining medical practitioners. See further the annotation to s.6 of the Social Security Act 1998. It is open to a claimant to ask a member of a tribunal to stand down if he or she fears that there will be bias, whether conscious or unconscious, but that will usually mean that there will have to be an adjournment, particularly if the request is made on the day of the hearing. A claimant may waive the right to object to the apparent lack of independence of a member of the tribunal, but the waiver must be voluntary, informed and unequivocal (*Millar v Dickson* [2001] UKPC D4; [2002] 1 W.L.R. 1615). See further the note on procedural and other regularities in the annotation to s.14(1) of the 1998 Act.

In *CSI/146/2003*, the Commissioner said that there was no obligation on the President to ensure that a medically qualified panel member sitting on any particu-

(SI 1999/991, reg.36)

lar case was a specialist in the field of medicine relevant to the case. It was pointed out that there is not always such a specialist on the panel and, in any event, even if a case is unusual, any medically qualified panel member will ordinarily be able to deal adequately with competing views. If a specialist's report is necessary, it is open to a tribunal to ask the parties to obtain a relevant opinion or to obtain one themselves under s.20 of the Social Security Act 1998.

Para. (8)
It would be rare for a person's medical condition not to be relevant in any case where a medically qualified panel member was sitting. Even where that is so, it might be undesirable for such a panel member who had advised or prepared a report on the claimant to sit hearing an appeal by that claimant. The panel member might, for instance, have had reason to form a view as to the claimant's veracity.

Assignment of clerks to appeal tribunals: function of clerks

37. The Secretary of State shall assign a clerk to service each appeal tribunal and the clerk so assigned shall be responsible for summoning members of the panel constituted under section 6 to serve on the tribunal.

DEFINITIONS

"appeal tribunal"—see s.39(1) of the Social Security Act 1998.
"panel"—see reg.1(3).

CHAPTER II

PROCEDURE IN CONNECTION WITH DETERMINATION OF APPEALS AND REFERRALS

Consideration and determination of appeals and referrals

38.—(1) The procedure in connection with the consideration and determination of an appeal or a referral shall, subject to the following provisions of these Regulations, be such as a legally qualified panel member shall determine.

(2) A legally qualified panel member may give directions requiring a party to the proceedings to comply with any provision of these Regulations and may at any stage of the proceedings, either of his own motion or on a written application made to the clerk to the appeal tribunal by any party to the proceedings, give such directions as he may consider necessary or desirable for the just, effective and efficient conduct of the proceedings and may direct any party to the proceedings to provide such particulars or to produce such documents as may be reasonably required.

(3) Where a clerk to the appeal tribunal is authorised to take steps in relation to the procedure of the tribunal he may give directions requiring any party to the proceedings to comply with any provision of these Regulations.

DEFINITIONS

"appeal"—see reg.1(3).
"clerk to the appeal tribunal"—*ibid.*
"legally qualified panel member"—*ibid.*
"party to the proceedings"—*ibid.*
"referral"—*ibid.*

2.459

2.460

2.461

General Note

2.462   The wide power conferred by para.(2) to make directions must be exercised judicially. Thus, a legally qualified panel member is not generally entitled to subvert the decision of a tribunal to adjourn for a medical report by directing that the case be relisted without the report. On the other hand, if the case is relisted and no point is taken about the absence of the report, the Commissioner may decide that the final decision is not erroneous in point of law (*CSDLA/866/2002*).

Where a claimant has failed to produce evidence within the time allowed in a direction but produces it at a hearing before a tribunal, the tribunal may be entitled to refuse to admit the evidence. However, it must act proportionately, having regard to the purposes for which the time limit was placed in the direction and the prejudice caused by the failure to comply with it *(CIB/4253/2004)*. Where the evidence can easily be absorbed at the hearing by the tribunal and any other party, it is unlikely to be appropriate to refuse to admit it. A failure to comply at all with a direction to produce evidence does not always justify the drawing of an adverse inference, although it may well do so (*CCS/3757/2004*).

If an appellant is given due warning, an appeal may be struck out under reg.46(1)(c) for failure to comply with a direction.

[¹Appeals raising issues for decision by officers of Inland Revenue

2.463   **38A.**—(1) Where, [² a person has appealed to an appeal tribunal and it appears to the appeal tribunal, or a legally qualified panel member,] that an issue arises which, by virtue of section 8 of the Transfer Act, falls to be decided by an officer of the Board, that tribunal [² or legally qualified panel member, as the case may be] shall—

(a) refer the appeal to the Secretary of State pending the decision of that issue by an officer of the Board; and

(b) require the Secretary of State to refer that issue to the Board;

and the Secretary of State shall refer that issue accordingly.

(2) Pending the final decision of any issue which has been referred to the Board in accordance with paragraph (1) above, the Secretary of State may revise the decision under appeal, or make a further decision superseding that decision, in accordance with his determination of any issue other than one which has been so referred.

(3) On receipt by the Secretary of State of the final decision of an issue which has been referred in accordance with paragraph (1) above, he shall consider whether the decision under appeal ought to be revised under section 9 or superseded under section 10, and—

(a) if so, revise it or, as the case may be, make a further decision which supersedes it; or

(b) if not, forward the appeal to the appeal tribunal which shall determine the appeal in accordance with the final decision of the issue so referred.

(4) In paragraphs (2) and (3) above, "final decision" has the same meaning as in regulation 11A(3) and (4).]

Amendments

1. Social Security and Child Support (Decisions and Appeals) Amendment (No.3) Regulations 1999 (SI 1999/1670), reg.2(4) (July 5, 1999).

2. Social Security and Child Support (Decisions and Appeals) (Miscellaneous Amendments) Regulations 2002 (SI 2002/1379), reg.12 (May 20, 2002).

(SI 1999/991, reg.38A)

DEFINITIONS

"appeal"—see reg.1(3).
"appeal tribunal"—see s.39(1) of the Social Security Act 1998.
"the Board"—see reg.1(3).
"final decision"—by virtue of para.(4), see reg.11A(5).
"legally qualified panel member"—see reg.1(3).
"the Transfer Act"—*ibid.*

GENERAL NOTE

Some decisions fall to be made by officers of the Inland Revenue by virtue of s.170 of the Pensions Schemes Act 1993 (rather than by virtue of s.8 of the Social Security Contributions (Transfer of Functions, etc.) Act 1999) but the tribunal or legally qualified panel member may refer to officers of the Inland Revenue issues for determination under the 1993 Act notwithstanding that this regulation does not apply (*R(P) 1/04*). It might be necessary to adjourn the hearing before the tribunal while the question was being decided and procedures akin to those laid down in paras (2) and (3) could be followed.

2.464

[¹ Choice of hearing

39.—(1) Where an appeal or a referral is made to an appeal tribunal the appellant and any other party to the proceeding shall notify the clerk to the appeal tribunal, on a form approved by the Secretary of State, whether he wishes to have an oral hearing of the appeal or whether he is content for the appeal or referral to proceed without an oral hearing.

(2) Except in the case of a referral, the form shall include a statement informing the appellant that, if he does not notify the clerk to the appeal tribunal as required by paragraph (1) within the period specified in paragraph (3), the appeal may be struck out in accordance with regulation 46(1).

(3) Notification in accordance with paragraph (1)—
 (a) if given by the appellant or a party to the proceedings other than the Secretary of State, must be sent or given to the clerk to the appeal tribunal within 14 days of the date on which the form is issued to him; or
 (b) if given by the Secretary of State, must be sent or given to the clerk—
  (i) in the case of an appeal, within 14 days of the date on which the form is issued to the appellant; or
  (ii) in the case of a referral, on the date of referral,
  or within such longer period as the clerk may direct.

(4) Where an oral hearing is requested in accordance with paragraphs (1) and (3) the appeal tribunal shall hold an oral hearing unless the appeal is struck out under regulation 46(1).]

(5) The chairman, or in the case of an appeal tribunal that has only one member, that member, may of his own motion direct that an oral hearing of the appeal or referral be held if he is satisfied that such a hearing is necessary to enable the tribunal to reach a decision.

2.465

AMENDMENT

1. Social Security, Child Support and Tax Credits (Decisions and Appeals) Regulations 2004(SI 2004/3368), reg.2(5) (December 21, 2004).

DEFINITIONS

"appeal"—see reg.1(3).
"appeal tribunal"—see s.39(1) of the Social Security Act 1998.

"clerk to the appeal tribunal"—see reg.1(3).
"party to the proceedings"—*ibid.*
"referral"—*ibid.*

GENERAL NOTE

2.466　The new paras (1) to (4) were substituted for the old in 2004 in order to enable the form on which a party may opt for an oral hearing to be issued by the Secretary of State rather than by the clerk. This speeds the process up as the Secretary of State can issue that form to the claimant with a copy of the papers at the same time as sending the papers to the tribunal. The form can still be issued by the clerk if it has not already been issued. A clerk cannot simply rely on an indication in the appellant's letter of appeal that a hearing is not wanted (*R3/04(IB)*). If an appellant does not return the form, the appeal is liable to be struck out altogether under reg.46(1)(d).

There are many cases where a claimant really has no realistic prospects of success unless he or she attends an oral hearing and gives evidence. Even though claimants are advised in general terms that the chances of success may be greater at an oral hearing, it may be thought that the mere fact that they are offered the choice will suggest to many that a paper hearing is a not a foolish option. Paragraph (5) recognises that there are cases where justice requires an oral hearing. In *CDLA/1347/1999*, it was said that, if a tribunal considering an appeal on the papers was wholly unable to do justice without there being an oral hearing, it ought to adjourn the proceedings, and direct that there be one but that, otherwise, a tribunal was generally entitled to take the view that a claimant who had rejected the option of an oral hearing having had notice of the issues in the case had had an adequate opportunity to put his case and had lost the chance of strengthening it by giving oral evidence. In *R1/02(IB)*, a Tribunal of Commissioners in Northern Ireland set aside a decision of a tribunal who did not adjourn in the face of incomplete evidence raising questions that they could not answer. In *CIS/4248/2001*, the Commissioner held that an oral hearing should have been directed in a case where an apparently unrepresented claimant had opted for a paper hearing of an appeal against a decision that income support amounting to some £10,000 had been overpaid and was recoverable from her, in circumstances where the claimant had put forward a case that was tenable if she was believed.

> "A very great deal of money was at stake. Oral evidence would have assisted the tribunal's assessment of honesty, which was central to the case. She had not, as far as could be seen, had the benefit of advice from anyone with experience of tribunals. Those are all factors that suggest that justice required an oral hearing in this case."

At a "paper hearing", or indeed any hearing not attended by a claimant, it will always be an error of law for a tribunal to remove an award that has already been made unless the claimant has been given specific notice (in the sense of being focussed on their own particular case) that this is under consideration (*CDLA/1480/2006*).

When a decision is set aside by a Commissioner and referred to another tribunal, it is the invariable practice to hold an oral hearing. However, in *CIB/4193/2003*, the Commissioner noted that that was not the practice where a decision was set aside by a legally qualified panel member under s.13 of the Social Security Act 1998 and he suggested that claimants should be given a fresh opportunity to ask for an oral hearing. He commented that some claimants might reassess their prospects of success at a "paper hearing" once they had lost a case and had to apply for leave to appeal. On the facts of the case, he held that there had been a breach of the rules of natural justice because the claimant had been inadvertently misled into not asking for the oral hearing she wanted.

(SI 1999/991, reg.39)

In *CIB/2751/2002 and CS/3202/2002*, the Commissioner considered the difficulties that arise on a request for a domiciliary hearing, where a refusal to allow such a hearing may require the determination of the very issues that arise on the appeal itself. He said that fairness may require that a claimant who is refused a domiciliary hearing is given a further opportunity to provide evidence, perhaps by being visited by an expert appointed under s.7(4) of the Social Security Act 1998, who could then give evidence to the tribunal under reg.50. It is suggested, however, that the reality may be that a domiciliary hearing would not be refused where the legally qualified panel member believed that the claimant might not be able to attend a hearing at an ordinary venue. Virtual inability to walk does not usually preclude travelling in a car, perhaps driven by a relative, or use of a taxi. The greater need may therefore be that, where a domiciliary hearing is refused, it should be made clear to the claimant that it is considered that he or she could attend a hearing at an ordinary venue and should speak to the clerk about any special arrangements that might be necessary to enable him or her to do so. If it becomes apparent to a clerk that the claimant's difficulties are greater than was originally understood, the issue can always be referred back to the legally qualified panel member.

Withdrawal of appeal or referral

40.—(1) An appeal may be withdrawn by the appellant or an authorised representative of the appellant and a referral may be withdrawn by the Secretary of State [¹the Board or an officer of the Board], as the case may be, either—

(a) at an oral hearing; or

(b) at any other time before the appeal or referral is determined, by giving notice in writing of withdrawal to the clerk to the appeal tribunal.

(2) If an appeal or a referral is withdrawn (as the case may be) in accordance with paragraph (1)(a), the clerk to the appeal tribunal shall send a notice in writing to any party to the proceedings who is not present when the appeal or referral is withdrawn, informing him that the appeal or referral (as the case may be) has been withdrawn.

(3) If an appeal or a referral is withdrawn (as the case may be) in accordance with paragraph (1)(b), the clerk to the appeal tribunal shall send a notice in writing to every party to the proceedings informing them that the appeal or referral (as the case may be) has been withdrawn.

2.467

AMENDMENT

1. Tax Credits (Decisions and Appeals) (Amendment) Regulations 1999 (SI 1999/2570), reg.25 (October 5, 1999). Note that amendments made by these regulations only have effect with respect to tax credit under the Tax Credit Act 1999 (reg.1(2) of the Amendment Regulations).

DEFINITIONS

"appeal"—see reg.1(3).
"the Board"—*ibid*.
"clerk to the appeal tribunal"—*ibid*.
"party to the proceedings"—*ibid*.
"referral"—*ibid*.

GENERAL NOTE

Once an appeal has been withdrawn a tribunal has no jurisdiction to consider it, even if the Secretary of State's representative gives his consent (*Rydqvist v Secretary of*

2.468

Social Security and Child Support (Decisions and Appeals) Regs 1999

State for Work and Pensions [2002] EWCA Civ 947; [2002] 1 W.L.R. 3343). However, it is open to the would-be appellant to submit a new appeal. In *Rydqvist*, the would-be appellant had not submitted a new appeal or asked that any document be treated as a new appeal and the Court of Appeal observed that he would in any event have had to satisfy the conditions necessary for the admission of a late appeal. The tribunal could not be taken to have accepted a late appeal. As the Secretary of State may now admit a late appeal (see reg.32(2) above), consent given by the Secretary of State to consider a withdrawn appeal might now in some circumstances be construed as the acceptance of a late appeal, in which case the tribunal would have jurisdiction.

Medical examination required by appeal tribunal

2.469

41.—For the purposes of section 20(2) (medical examination required by appeal tribunal) the prescribed condition which must be satisfied is that the issue, or one of the issues, raised on the appeal—
  (a) is whether the claimant satisfies the conditions for entitlement to—
    (i) the care component of a disability living allowance specified in section 72(1) and (2) of the Contributions and Benefits Act;
    (ii) the mobility component of a disability living allowance specified in section 73(1), (8) and (9) of that Act;
    (iii) an attendance allowance specified in section 64 and 65(1) of that Act;
    (iv) a [²disabled person's tax credit] specified in section 129(1)(b) of that Act;
    (v) [¹. . .]; or
    (vi) severe disablement allowance under section 68 of that Act;
  (b) relates to the period throughout which the claimant is likely to satisfy the conditions for entitlement to an attendance allowance or a disability living allowance;
  (c) is the rate at which an attendance allowance is payable;
  (d) is the rate at which the care component or the mobility component of a disability living allowance is payable;
([¹(dd) is whether a person is incapable of work for the purposes of the Contributions and Benefits Act;]
  (e) [¹. . .];
  (f) relates to the extent of a person's disablement and its assessment in accordance with Schedule 6 to the Contributions and Benefits Act;
  (g) is whether the claimant suffers a loss of physical or mental faculty as a result of the relevant accident for the purposes of section 103 of the Contributions and Benefits Act;
  (h) relates to any disease or injury prescribed for the purposes of section 108 of the Contributions and Benefits Act; or
  (i) relates to any payment arising under, or by virtue of a scheme having effect under, section 111 of, and Schedule 8 to, the Contributions and Benefits Act (workmen's compensation).

AMENDMENTS

1. Social Security and Child Support (Decisions and Appeals) Amendment (No.3) Regulations 1999 (SI 1999/1670), reg.2(5) (July 5, 1999).
2. Tax Credits (Decisions and Appeals) (Amendment) Regulations 1999 (SI 1999/2570), reg.26 (October 5, 1999). Note that amendments made by these regulations only have effect with respect to tax credit (reg.1(2) of the Amendment Regulations).

(SI 1999/991, reg.41)

DEFINITIONS

"appeal"—see reg.1(3).
"appeal tribunal"—see s.39(1) of the Social Security Act 1998.
"claimant"—see reg.1(3).
"the Contributions and Benefits Act"—see s.84 of the Social Security Act 1998.
"medical examination"—by virtue of s.39(2) of the Social Security Act 1998, see s.191 of the Social Security Administration Act 1992.
"tax credit"—see reg.1(3).

GENERAL NOTE

These are the only circumstances in which a tribunal may refer a person for medical examination (although it is just arguable that s.7(4) of the Social Security Act 1998 and reg.50 are in broad enough terms to permit an examination in other cases). See reg.52 for the circumstances in which the tribunal may themselves carry out an examination.

2.470

Non-disclosure of medical advice or evidence

42.—(1) Where, in connection with [1 . . .] an appeal or referral there is [1 . . .] medical advice or medical evidence relating to a person which has not been disclosed to him and in the opinion of [1 a legally qualified panel member] the disclosure to that person of that advice or evidence would be harmful to his health, such advice or evidence shall not be required to be disclosed to that person.

(2) Advice or evidence such as is mentioned in paragraph (1) shall not be disclosed to any person acting for or representing the person to whom it relates or, in a case where a claim for benefit is made by reference to the disability of a person other than the claimant and the advice or evidence relates to that other person, shall not be disclosed to the claimant or any person acting for or representing him, unless [1 a legally-qualified panel member] is satisfied that it is in the interests of the person to whom the advice or evidence relates to do so.

(3) A tribunal shall not be precluded from taking into account for the purposes of the determination advice or evidence which has not been disclosed to a person under the provisions of paragraph (1) or (2).

2.471

AMENDMENT

1. Social Security and Child Support (Miscellaneous Amendments) Regulations 2000 (SI 2000/1596), reg.25 (June 19, 2000).

DEFINITIONS

"appeal"—see reg.1(3).
"claimant"—*ibid*.
"legally qualified panel member"—*ibid*.
"referral"—*ibid*.

GENERAL NOTE

In *R(A) 4/89*, the Attendance Allowance Board withheld from a claimant "additional information" supplied by a doctor who in effect said that when he arrived outside the claimant's house the claimant was sitting with her back to a window but

2.472

when he went in the claimant was lying on a couch claiming to be unable to respond to the doctor's questions. The doctor was therefore implying that the claimant was a fraud. The Commissioner held that this was not "medical evidence", but was factual evidence and that, in any event, the power to withhold evidence that was prejudicial, rather than helpful, to a claimant should be exercised with caution. He held the Board to have erred in law because it was common fairness to let the claimant be aware of the allegation that he was a fraud. It is difficult to see how evidence of the sort considered in that case could possibly be harmful to the claimant's health. A doctor's wish to avoid embarrassment is not a ground for withholding evidence.

In *CSDLA/5/1995*, there was withheld evidence that the child claimant was not seriously ill but that her mother, who was acting on her behalf, was suffering from Munchausen By Proxy Syndrome. The Deputy Commissioner pointed out that the fact a senior medical officer was of the view that disclosure would cause "considerably difficulty and distress" did not mean that it would be harmful to the health of any person. However, more fundamentally, he held that, while a claimant was not necessarily entitled to see the whole evidence in the case:

". . . no adversarial dispute should be decided against a party on the basis of evidence not disclosed to them unless that party has been given sufficient indication of the gist of that evidence to give them a proper opportunity to put forward their case."

He added that non-disclosure to a representative must be considered "quite separately to, and perhaps even more cautiously than, non-disclosure to a claimant" and that the regulation should be operated "in a manner consistent with the principles of natural justice". Further, he held that a claimant to whom material is not being disclosed should be told that fact, and the tribunal's record of reasons should refer to it and no part of that reasoning should not be disclosed to the claimant.

In *CDLA/1347/1999*, the Commissioner disagreed with that approach, holding that the statutory provision expressly authorised a breach of the rules of natural justice and that, in exercising the discretion to withhold evidence, a tribunal should consider whether the authorised breach would be a lesser evil than revealing the information. If minded to reveal evidence that had been withheld on medical advice, he suggested that it might be prudent to give the medical advisor the opportunity of justifying the advice before revealing the evidence. The Commissioner also agreed with a suggestion that, if reasons for a decision were being given, withheld evidence should be referred to in a supplementary statement of reasons given to the Secretary of State (and the claimant's representative if the evidence had been revealed to him or her) but not given to the claimant. That would have the effect that, in the event of an appeal, the Commissioner would know how the evidence had been approached.

In *CDLA/1347/1999* (as in *R(A) 4/89*), the withheld evidence was not even "medical advice or medical evidence". In *CSDLA/5/95*, the evidence was undoubtedly "medical evidence" but it is not clear why it was regarded as harmful. Indeed, in most cases concerning attendance allowance or disability living allowance, this regulation will not give rise to great problems because evidence that a claimant is seriously ill, which is the sort of evidence that would normally be withheld, is evidence that is likely to assist the claimant rather than the reverse. It is in cases concerning disablement benefit, where causation is often in issue, that the problem arises most acutely. There, if a tribunal are satisifed that evidence should be withheld but would be likely to be contested by a claimant if he or she knew of it, it is suggested that they should take care to ensure that it is properly tested by, for example, obtaining a second opinion. If proceedings cannot properly be adversarial, they must be truly inquisitorial. Indeed, if there were contradictory evidence and the claimant would be likely to contest the withheld evidence, a tribunal might well be particularly slow to conclude that reg.42 should be applied and might choose either to disclose the evidence or else to disregard it.

(SI 1999/991, reg.42)

The amendments enable a legally qualified panel member to consider as a preliminary issue, before the hearing, whether non-disclosure is appropriate and, if so, whether steps should be taken to minimise the potential unfairness. Provided the risk of harm to the claimant is properly balanced against his right to a fair hearing, there is unlikely to be a breach of the European Convention on Human Rights, particularly if the claimant has a representative to whom disclosure has been made (see *R. (Roberts) v Parole Board* [2005] UKHL 45; [2005] 2 A.C. 738).

Summoning of witnesses and administration of oaths

43.—(1) A chairman, or in the case of an appeal tribunal which has only one member, that member, may by summons, or in Scotland, by citation, require any person in Great Britain to attend as a witness at a hearing of an appeal, application or referral at such time and place as shall be specified in the summons or citation and, subject to paragraph (2), at the hearing to answer any question or produce any documents in his custody or under his control which relate to any matter in question in the appeal, application or referral but—
(a) no person shall be required to attend in obedience to such summons or citation unless he has been given at least 14 days' notice of the hearing or, if less than 14 days' notice is given, he has informed the tribunal that the notice given is sufficient; and
(b) no person shall be required to attend and give evidence or to produce any document in obedience to such summons or citation unless the necessary expenses of attendance are paid or tendered to him.

(2) No person shall be compelled to give any evidence or produce any document or other material that he could not be compelled to give or produce on a trial of an action in a court of law in that part of Great Britain where the hearing takes place.

(3) In exercising the powers conferred by this regulation, the chairman, or in the case of an appeal tribunal which has only one member, that member, shall take into account the need to protect any matter that relates to intimate personal or financial circumstances, is commercially sensitive, consists of information communicated or obtained in confidence or concerns national security.

(4) Every summons or citation issued under this regulation shall contain a statement to the effect that the person in question may apply in writing to a chairman to vary or set aside the summons or citation.

(5) A chairman, or in the case of an appeal tribunal which has only one member, that member, may require any witness, including a witness summoned under the powers conferred by this regulation, to give evidence on oath or affirmation and for that purpose there may be administered an oath or affirmation in due form.

DEFINITIONS

"appeal"—see reg.1(3).
"appeal tribunal"—see s.39(1) of the Social Security Act 1998.
"referral"—see reg.1(3).

GENERAL NOTE

The power to summons witnesses is not backed by any power to punish for non-compliance. A summons issued under this regulation therefore amounts to no more than a very formal request. This would not have mattered had RSC, Ord.38, r.19 remained in force because that enabled the High Court to issue a subpoena in aid of a tribunal who could not themselves compel attendance and a failure to comply with it would have been punishable in the High Court as contempt of court. CPR r.34.4 now enables the High Court to issue a summons in aid of a tribunal but only if the tribunal has no power to issue a summons itself. In the light of this regulation, it seems doubtful that a summons can be issued by the High Court in aid of an appeal tribunal constituted under the Social Security Act 1998. The Civil Procedure Rule Committee probably did not contemplate the possibility of a tribunal having the power to issue an unenforceable summons.

44. *Omitted.*

45. *Omitted.*

Chapter III

Striking Out Appeals

Appeals which may be struck out

46.—(1) Subject to paragraphs (2) and (3), an appeal may be struck out by the clerk to the appeal tribunal—
  (a) where it is an out of jurisdiction appeal and the appellant has been notified by the Secretary of State that an appeal brought against such a decision may be struck out;
  (b) for want of prosecution including an appeal not made within the time specified in these Regulations; [1 . . .]
  (c) [1 . . .] for failure of the appellant to comply with a direction given under these Regulations where the appellant has been notified that failure to comply with the direction could result in the appeal being struck out [1; or]
  [1 (d) for failure of the appellant to notify the clerk to the appeal tribunal, in accordance with regulation 39, whether or not he wishes to have an oral hearing of his appeal.]
  (2) Where the clerk to the appeal tribunal determines to strike out the appeal, he shall notify the appellant that his appeal has been struck out and of the procedure for reinstatement of the appeal as specified in regulation 47.
  (3) The clerk to the appeal tribunal may refer any matter for determination under this regulation to a legally qualified panel member for decision by the panel member rather than the clerk to the appeal tribunal.
  (4) [1 . . .]

AMENDMENT

1. Social Security, Child Support and Tax Credits (Decisions and Appeals) Regulations 2004 (SI 2004/3368), reg.2(6) (December 21, 2004).

DEFINITIONS

  "appeal"—see reg.1(3).
  "clerk to the appeal tribunal"—*ibid.*
  "legally qualified panel member"—*ibid.*
  "out of jurisdiction appeal"—*ibid.*

(SI 1999/991, reg.46)

General Note

It has been held by the Court of Appeal that, although a decision of a legally qualified panel member must be treated as a decision of a tribunal, no appeal lies to a Commissioner against the striking out of an appeal or a refusal to reinstate a struck out appeal (*Morina v Secretary of State for Work and Pensions* [2007] EWCA Civ 749, reversing *CIS/1365/2005*). The Court of Appeal did not comment on the Commissioner's observation in *CIS/1363/2005* that the definition of "out of jurisdiction appeal" enables a decision excluded from the scope of s.12 of the Social Security Act 1998 by virtue of Sch.2 to the Act or Sch.2 to these Regulations to be struck out but does not enable an appeal to be struck out on the ground that it does not fall within the scope of s.12 (or any other provision conferring a right of appeal) for any other reason.

Following the decision in *R(CS)5/02*, the power to strike out a "misconceived appeal" has been removed. Now an appeal that the Secretary of State considers is misconceived is simply listed for hearing. If it is indeed misconceived, it will be dismissed.

Reinstatement of struck out appeals

47.—[¹ (1) The clerk to the appeal tribunal may reinstate an appeal which has been struck out in accordance with regulation [² 46(1)(d)] where—
  (a) the appellant has made representations to him, or as the case may be, further representations in support of his appeal with reasons why he considers that his appeal should not have been struck out;
  (b) the representations are made in writing within one month of the order to strike out the appeal being issued; and
  (c) the clerk is satisfied in the light of those representations that there are reasonable grounds for reinstating the appeal
      but if the clerk is not satisfied that there are reasonable grounds for reinstatement a legally qualified panel member shall consider whether the appeal should be reinstated in accordance with paragraph (2).]

[¹ (2)] A legally qualified panel member may reinstate an appeal which has been struck out in accordance with regulation 46 [² . . .] where—
  (a) the appellant has made representations, or as the case may be, further representations in support of his appeal with reasons why he considers that his appeal should not have been struck out, to the clerk to the appeal tribunal, in writing within one month of the order to strike out the appeal being issued, and the panel member is satisfied in the light of those representations that there are reasonable grounds for reinstating the appeal;
  (b) [² . . .]
  (c) the panel member is satisfied that the appeal is not an appeal which may be struck out under regulation 46; or
  (d) the panel member is satisfied that notwithstanding that the appeal is one which may be struck out under regulation 46, it is not in the interests of justice for the appeal to be struck out.

Amendments

1. Social Security and Child Support (Decisions and Appeals) (Miscellaneous Amendments) Regulations 2002 (SI 2002/1379), reg.13, (May 20, 2002).

2. Social Security, Child Support and Tax Credits (Decisions and Appeals) Regulations 2004 (SI 2004/3368), reg.2(7) (December 21, 2004).

Social Security and Child Support (Decisions and Appeals) Regs 1999

DEFINITIONS

"appeal"—see reg.1(3).
"clerk to the appeal tribunal"—*ibid*.
"legally qualified panel member"—*ibid*.
"panel member"—*ibid*.

2.480 **48.** [¹ . . .]

AMENDMENT

1. Social Security, Child Support and Tax Credits (Decisions and Appeals) Regulations 2004 (SI 2004/3368), reg.2(8) (December 21, 2004).

CHAPTER IV

ORAL HEARINGS

Procedure at oral hearings

2.481 **49.**—(1) Subject to the following provisions of this Part, the procedure for an oral hearing shall be such as the chairman, or in the case of an appeal tribunal which has only one member, such as that member, shall determine.

(2) Except where paragraph (3) applies, not less than 14 days notice (beginning with the day on which the notice is given and ending on the day before the hearing of the appeal is to take place) of the time and place of any oral hearing of an appeal shall be given to every party to the proceedings, and if such notice has not been given to a person to whom it should have been given under the provisions of this paragraph the hearing may proceed only with the consent of that person.

(3) Any party to the proceedings may waive his right to receive not less than 14 days notice of the time and place of any oral hearing by giving notice to the clerk to the appeal tribunal.

(4) If a party to the proceedings to whom notice has been given under paragraph (2) fails to appear at the hearing the chairman, or in the case of an appeal tribunal which has only one member, that member, may, having regard to all the circumstances including any explanation offered for the absence, proceed with the hearing notwithstanding his absence, or give such directions with a view to the determination of the appeal as he may think proper.

(5) If a party to the proceedings has waived his right to be given notice under paragraph (2) the chairman, or in the case of an appeal tribunal which has only one member, that member, may proceed with the hearing notwithstanding his absence.

[¹ (6) An oral hearing shall be in public except where the chairman, or in the case of an appeal tribunal which has only one member, that member, is satisfied that it is necessary to hold the hearing, or part of the hearing, in private—
  (a) in the interests of national security, morals, public order or children;
  (b) for the protection of the private or family life of one or more parties to the proceedings; or
  (c) in special circumstances, because publicity would prejudice the interests of justice.

(SI 1999/991, reg. 49)

(7) At an oral hearing—
 (a) any party to the proceedings shall be entitled to be present and be heard; and
 (b) the following persons may be present by means of a live television link—
  (i) a party to the proceedings or his representative or both; or
  (ii) where an appeal tribunal consists of more than one member, a tribunal member other than the chairman,
provided that the person who constitutes or is the chairman of the tribunal gives permission [²...]]

(8) A person who has the right to be heard at a hearing may be accompanied and may be represented by another person whether having professional qualifications or not and, for the purposes of the proceedings at the hearing, any such representative shall have all the rights and powers to which the person whom he represents is entitled.

(9) The following persons shall also be entitled to be present at an oral hearing (whether or not it is otherwise in private) but shall take no part in the proceedings—
 (a) the President;
 (b) any person undergoing training as a chairman or [²...] member of an appeal tribunal or as a clerk to an appeal tribunal;
 (c) any person acting on behalf of the President in the training or supervision of panel members or in the monitoring of standards of decision-making by panel members;
 (d) with the leave of the chairman, or in the case of an appeal tribunal which has only one member, with the leave of that member, [²...] any other person; and
 (e) a member of the Council on Tribunals or of the Scottish Committee of the Council on Tribunals.

(10) Nothing in paragraph (9) affects the rights of any person mentioned in sub-paragraphs (a) and (b) of that paragraph at any oral hearing where he is sitting as a member of the tribunal or acting as its clerk, and nothing in this regulation prevents the presence at an oral hearing of any witness.

(11) Any person entitled to be heard at an oral hearing may address the tribunal, may give evidence, may call witnesses and may put questions directly to any other person called as a witness.

(12) For the purpose of arriving at its decision an appeal tribunal shall, and for the purpose of discussing any question of procedure may, notwithstanding anything contained in these Regulations, order all persons not being members of the tribunal, other than the person acting as clerk to the appeal tribunal, to withdraw from the hearing except that—
 (a) a member of the Council on Tribunals or of the Scottish Committee of the Council on Tribunals, the President or any person mentioned in paragraph (9)(c); and
 (b) with the leave of the chairman, or in the case of an appeal tribunal which has only one member, with the leave of that member, any person mentioned in paragraph (9)(b) or (d),
main remain present at any such sitting.

[¹ (13) In this regulation "live television link" means a live television link or other facilities which allow a person who is not physically present at an oral hearing to see and hear proceedings and be seen and heard by those physically present.]

Social Security and Child Support (Decisions and Appeals) Regs 1999

AMENDMENTS

1. Social Security and Child Support (Decisions and Appeals) (Miscellaneous Amendments) Regulations 2002 (SI 2002/1379), reg.14 (May 20, 2002).
2. Social Security, Child Support and Tax Credits (Miscellaneous Amendments) Regulations 2005 (SI 2005/337), reg.2(9) (March 18, 2005).

DEFINITIONS

"appeal" see reg.1(3).
"appeal tribunal"—see s.39(1) of the Social Security Act 1998.
"clerk to the appeal tribunal"—see reg.1(3).
"live television link"—see para.(13).
"panel member"—see reg.1(3).
"party to the proceedings"—*ibid.*
"President"—*ibid.*

GENERAL NOTE

Para.(1)

2.482
The legally qualified panel member has considerable latitude in deciding how a hearing will be conducted but it must be fair. If the rules of natural justice (which effectively guarantee a fair hearing) are broken, the decision of the tribunal is liable to be set aside on appeal on the ground that it is erroneous in point of law. See further the annotation to s.14(1) of the Social Security Act 1998.

A tribunal is entitled to take account of all that it sees and hears at a hearing but if it sees something that appears important, fairness generally requires that the party concerned should be given an opportunity of commenting on what the tribunal has seen. In *R(DLA) 2/06*, the Commissioner cautioned tribunals against giving too much weight to observations of a claimant's apparent well-being that might be unrepresentative and so be unreliable as evidence of his health generally. Giving a claimant an opportunity to comment enables the claimant to put the observation into a broader context. However, the Commissioner also pointed out that, where an observation merely confirms a conclusion that the tribunal would have reached anyway, a failure to invite the claimant to comment on it will not render the decision erroneous in pint of law although, unless a chairman makes clear what significance a recorded observation had in the tribunal's reasoning when he or she is writing the statement of reasons, it is likely to be assumed that it must have had an effect on the decision. The Commissioner also said that a chairman did not have to ask precise questions amounting to a cross-examination of the claimant but could ask an open question that gave a claimant the opportunity to comment. He said—

"...the chairman did not point out to the claimant the significance of the observations that the tribunal had made. But the claimant must have realised this. He had presented his claim on the basis of pain and exhaustion and the observations were clearly directly relevant to that."

What is important is whether, taking the hearing as a whole, the claimant has an adequate opportunity to address the issues raised by any significant observations.

2.483
In *CDLA/2748/2002*, the Commissioner held that a tribunal was required to consider the adequacy of an interpreter appointed by the Appeals Service and referred to *Kamasinski v Austria* [1991] 13 EHRR 36, where the Court ruled, at para.74, that para.(3)(e) of Art.6 to the European Convention on Human Rights:

"... does not go so far as to require a written translation of all items of written evidence or official documents in the procedure. The interpretive assistance provided should be such as to enable the defendant to understand the case against

(SI 1999/991, reg. 49)

him and to defend himself, notably by being able to put before the court his version of events.

In view of the need for the right guaranteed by paragraph (3)(e) to be practical and effective, the obligation of the competent authorities is not limited to the appointment of the interpreter but, if they are put on notice in the particular circumstances, may also extend to a degree of subsequent control over the adequacy of the interpretation provided."

Article 6(3) applies only to criminal proceedings and so the Commissioner accepted that that ruling did not apply directly, but he nonetheless held that the general approach to interpretation at tribunal hearings should be guided by that ruling.

Para. (2)

The previously inadequate period of notice required has been doubled to 14 days.   2.484

Para. (4)

In *Cooke v Glenrose Fish Co* [2004] I.C.R. 1188, the Employment Appeal Tribunal suggested that an employment tribunal should always at least consider telephoning an appellant who has failed to appear before proceeding in his absence and should ordinarily do so where there was an indication that the appellant had been intending to appear at the hearing because, for instance, solicitors were on the record. An oversight can then be rectified. However, the Employment Appeal Tribunal also held that employment tribunals were entitled to take a robust approach and generally to proceed to hear cases where there was an unexplained absence, because any injustice could be put right on review. The provision in these regulations equivalent to a review would be reg.57(1)(b), which permits the setting aside of a decision where a party or his representative was not present at a hearing. The Appeal Tribunal remarked that "it would appear to be a necessary concomitant of the more stringent attitude encouraged by [the President] that there be the less stringent attitude on a review if a party who has not attended comes forward with a genuine and full explanation and shows that the original hearing was not one from which he deliberately absented himself".   2.485

Where a claimant sent a message to a representative to say she would not be attending a hearing and wished the tribunal to proceed in her absence and the representative made no application for an adjournment, a Commissioner declined to hold the tribunal to have erred in not adjourning (*CSIB/404/2005*). However, he set the tribunal's decision aside for failure to deal adequately with questions concerning the claimant's mental health, even though it was difficult to see how the tribunal could have allowed the claimant's appeal on the evidence before it. That may suggest that, where the claimant's presence is really required to establish the facts and the non-attendance might have been attributable, at least in part, to the claimant's mental health, a tribunal really should consider whether an adjournment would be in the interests of justice, just as they would if the claimant had not asked for a hearing (see the annotation to reg.39). Of course, a tribunal is entitled to take into account the fact that the claimant has asked for a hearing and then failed to attend it in considering whether justice requires an adjournment and whether attendance in the future is likely.

Para. (6)

In *CIB/2751/2002 and CS/3202/2002*, the Commissioner considered how domiciliary hearings might be affected by para.(6). He suggested that it might be possible to hold a public hearing near a claimant's home rather than actually in it. Given that few people other than those invited by the parties ever watch tribunal hearings, the problems raised may be more theoretical than real but the legislation does require them to be addressed. The answer may be that, where a domiciliary hearing in a claimant's home is necessary, it will always be justifiable to hold the hearing in private in order to protect the claimant's private or family life. Presumably a claimant who has asked for an oral hearing can be taken to have waived his rights to privacy to the extent necessary to allow the hearing to take place with other parties being present.   2.486

Social Security and Child Support (Decisions and Appeals) Regs 1999

Para. (8)

2.487 A party has a right to be represented by any person (subject to their proper behaviour). Thus a chairman erred in refusing to hear submissions by what he described as a "McKenzie friend" and it was an error of law for him to insist that the claimant specify at the beginning of the hearing whether the person accompanying her was going to act as a representative in the conventional sense (*CS/1753/2000*). In *CDLA/2462/2003*, the Commissioner has reiterated the point that representatives may also be witnesses.

> "8. Tribunals operate less formally than courts. They do not operate rights of audience. They allow, of course, professional legal representation. But they also allow lay representation and assistance from anyone whom the claimant wishes to assist in presenting a case to a tribunal. Given that breadth of representation, it is inevitable that the roles of representative and witness cannot be separated in the way that they would in a court. The same person may wish to put the claimant's case and give evidence in support of that case. The tribunal must take care to distinguish evidence from representation so that the former's provenance is known and can be the subject of questioning by the tribunal and other parties. But, subject to the practicalities of the way in which the taking of evidence is handled, there is no objection in principle to the same person acting in different capacities as a witness and as a representative. Nor is there any reason in principle why the probative value of evidence should depend upon whether or not it came from a representative."
>
> . . .
>
> 13. I emphasise that I am concerned here with a representative who wanted to give evidence from his own knowledge. I am not concerned with the different circumstance of a representative who wants to make a statement of the claimant's evidence to the appeal tribunal. Some tribunals refuse a representative the chance to do this. They insist on hearing the evidence from the claimant, allowing the representative to supplement the tribunal's questions to ensure that all the evidence is elicited from the claimant. That is a matter that is within the chairman's control of the procedure under regulation 49(1). Nothing I have written above affects the use of that power by [a] chairman to control the way that the claimant's own evidence is presented."

The possible conflict of interest where a person employed by a local authority represents a claimant in a housing benefit case where the same local authority is a party was considered in *CSHC/729/2003*. The Commissioner commended the practice of the representative concerned in drawing claimants' attention to the potential conflict. The Commissioner reserved the question whether he or a tribunal had any power to prevent a representative chosen by a claimant from acting. It is suggested that, in the absence of misconduct by the representative, there is no such power, although he could ensure that the claimant had made an informed choice.

Para. (11)

2.488 In *R(DLA) 3/06*, the Tribunal of Commissioners allowed an appeal against a decision of a tribunal who had drawn an adverse inference against a 12-year old claimant, alleged to have learning difficulties and behavioural problems, because her foster parent and appointee had failed to arrange for her to give evidence to the tribunal despite a summons. The Tribunal of Commissioners gave the following general guidance about child witnesses.

> "(i) A tribunal should have proper regard to the wishes of a child of sufficiently mature years and understanding who wishes to give evidence in a DLA claim made on his behalf. However, a tribunal should be very cautious before requiring any child to give evidence, and should only call for a child to give evidence if it is satisfied that a just decision cannot otherwise be made. Before reaching such a conclusion, the tribunal should consider first all the other available evidence, and then ask itself whether any necessary additional evidence can be obtained

from another source, for example, a health visitor, social worker, teacher, family member or friend, to avoid the need for the child to be called at all.

"(ii) In any event, a tribunal should be very slow to exercise its power to require a child to give evidence if that child's parent or carer takes the view that for the child to give evidence may be detrimental to the child's welfare, particularly if there is evidence from a competent professional that to do so might be harmful. It would be wholly exceptional for it to be appropriate for a tribunal to call a child in such circumstances.

"(iii) Even if it is those representing the child, rather than the tribunal, who wish the child to give evidence, as *Brown v Secretary of State for the Home Department* (LTA 97/6885/J) indicates, a tribunal has power to disallow the child from giving evidence if it is against the child's interests to do so. If it is proposed that the child gives evidence, the tribunal must consider whether it is in that child's interests to do so.

"(iv) The tribunal should bear in mind that the mere presence of a child at a hearing is unlikely to give a reliable indication of the effect of a child's disability in normal circumstances.

"(v) Where a decision is taken to call a child to give evidence, after submissions from interested persons (including the parents or carers of the child) a tribunal should give consideration to precisely how that evidence will be taken, so that the interests and welfare of the child are maintained, giving any directions that are appropriate. In doing so the tribunal will bear in mind that a child may perceive what is said at a tribunal hearing very differently from an adult. It will be necessary for the tribunal to identify any matters that the child ought not to hear (e.g. it will not generally be appropriate for a child to hear criticism of those responsible for his or her care) and questions that the child ought not to be asked (e.g. it will not generally be appropriate to question a child about his or her own care needs).

"(vi) In addition, where a child is to be called to give evidence, the tribunal will need to give consideration to practical matters such as the geography of the hearing room, having an appropriate adult in close attendance, whether any of the tribunal (including the chairman) should be selected because of experience in dealing with child witnesses and even (in appropriate cases) taking such steps as taking the child's evidence by video link if available, giving directions where appropriate."

Manner of providing expert assistance

50.—(1) Where an appeal tribunal require one or more experts to provide assistance to it in dealing with a question of fact of special difficulty under section 7(4), such an expert shall, if the chairman, or in the case of a tribunal with only one member, that member, so requests, attend at the hearing and give evidence and if the chairman or member sitting alone considers it appropriate, the expert shall enquire into and provide a written report on the question.

(2) A copy of any written report received from an expert in accordance with paragraph (1) shall be supplied to every party to the proceedings.

DEFINITIONS

"appeal"—see reg.1(3).
"party to the proceedings"—*ibid.*

GENERAL NOTE

The expert may assist the tribunal as a witness, which implies that the parties may cross-examine him or her. There is no provision for an expert to sit as an assessor.

Social Security and Child Support (Decisions and Appeals) Regs 1999

Postponement and adjournment

1.491   **51.**—(1) Where a person to whom notice of an oral hearing is given wishes to request a postponement of that hearing he shall do so in writing to the clerk to the appeal tribunal stating his reasons for the request, and the clerk to the appeal tribunal may grant or refuse the request as he thinks fit or may pass the request to a legally qualified panel member who may grant or refuse the request as he thinks fit.

(2) Where the clerk to the appeal tribunal or the panel member, as the case may be, refuses a request to postpone the hearing he shall—
  (a) notify in writing the person making the request of the refusal; and
  (b) place before the appeal tribunal at the hearing both the request for the postponement and notification of its refusal.

(3) A panel member or the clerk to the appeal tribunal may of his own motion at any time before the beginning of the hearing postpone the hearing.

(4) An oral hearing may be adjourned by the appeal tribunal at any time on the application of any party to the proceedings or of its own motion.

(5) [1 . . .]

AMENDMENT

1. Social Security and Child Support (Decisions and Appeals) (Miscellaneous Amendments) Regulations 2002 (SI 2002/1379), reg.15 (May 20, 2002).

DEFINITIONS

"appeal tribunal"—see s.39(1) of the Social Security Act 1998.
"clerk to the appeal tribunal"—see reg.1(3).
"legally qualified panel member"—*ibid.*
"panel member"—*ibid.*
"party to the proceedings"—*ibid.*

GENERAL NOTE

2.492   The distinction between a postponement and an adjournment is that the former occurs before the beginning of the hearing and the latter occurs once the hearing has begun, although an application for an adjournment may be made right at the beginning of a hearing. In *CDLA/3680/1997*, the Commissioner said that "[w]here an application for a postponement is refused—or no reply is received to such an application—it is incumbent on the claimant to take all possible steps to appear, or to have someone appear on his or her behalf, before the tribunal in order to assist the tribunal in considering whether there should be an adjournment". A representative should be ready to argue the case as well as possible if the application for an adjournment is refused.

This regulation is concerned only with the postponement or adjournment of oral hearings. There is no express power to adjourn a paper hearing but such a power is to be implied (see *CDLA/1552/1998* and also the note to reg.39).

In *CSDLA/90/1998*, the Commissioner was highly critical of a local authority representative who had represented a claimant before a tribunal on an application for an adjournment. The claimant had had a prior engagement and the Commissioner found that the representative had indicated to her that she need not attend the tribunal hearing without asking her why the other engagement should take priority. When the tribunal refused to adjourn the hearing the representative had withdrawn. The Commissioner said that the nature of the other engagement should have been explained to the tribunal, that it was not for a representative to tell a claimant not to attend a hearing (because a tribunal were not bound to grant an adjournment merely because the claimant was not there) and that a representative who wished to withdraw should obtain the leave of the tribunal to do so. The claimant had been entitled to expect her representative to argue her case on the basis of the evidence available to him and doing so would not have prevented him from arguing on appeal that the tribunal had erred in refusing the adjournment.

The power to postpone or adjourn proceedings must not be used arbitrarily or capriciously and, in particular, must not be used in order to defeat the general purpose of the legislation, but otherwise there is a complete discretion so long as it is exercised judicially (*CIS/2292/2000*, citing *Jacobs v Norsalta Ltd* [1977] I.C.R. 189). Nonetheless, in *CIS/2292/2000*, a tribunal erred in rejecting an application for an adjournment made by the representative of a claimant who was in prison, in circumstances where the claimant's oral evidence had an important part to play. In both *CIB/1009/2004* and *CIB/2058/2004*, Commissioners have emphasised that the inquisitorial approach of tribunals is not a complete substitute for representation and have cited *R. v Social Security Commissioner, Ex p. Bibi* (unreported, May 23, 2000) in which Collins J said that, although there is no absolute right to representation, there is an absolute right to be dealt with fairly and that it was hardly unreasonable for a person to wish to be represented by the particular solicitor with whom she had been dealing. Therefore, a claimant's desire to be represented, or to be represented by a particular person, is a factor that ought to be given proper weight in considering whether or not to grant an adjournment. As to the balancing exercise itself, in *CIB/1009/2004* the Commissioner said—

"13. A tribunal will always require to be persuaded that an adjournment is necessary – because there is always a potential disadvantage in adjourning a case – but the arguments against an adjournment in tribunal proceedings in a social security case may not be quite the same as those applicable in adversarial proceedings in the courts. In particular, the interests of the parties are not usually as closely balanced. In an ordinary social security case, where the Secretary of State does not provide a representative or have witnesses in attendance, there is very little disadvantage to the Secretary of State in granting the claimant an adjournment. It is usually the claimant himself who suffers the principal disadvantage of delay. If the claimant judges that disadvantage to be less than the disadvantage of proceeding without representation, a tribunal should not too readily substitute its own judgment on the relative weight of those two factors. The main consideration for the tribunal will therefore be whether the adjournment can be justified in the light of the substantial cost of a further hearing and the delay in the determination of another case whose place the adjourned hearing will take. Thus the interests of taxpayers and claimants in general need to be balanced against the interests of the particular appellant.

14. If the claimant is to blame for need to request an adjournment, his interests are likely to be given correspondingly less weight. A claimant's interests may also be given less weight where his representative's fault has led to the request for an adjournment. By agreeing to act for a claimant, a representative takes some responsibility for the case and tribunals are entitled to exert pressure on representatives to behave properly. However, in an environment where most representatives are not qualified lawyers and where most claimants are not paying for the services of their representatives, some care must be taken not to cause injustice to a claimant by visiting upon him the sins of his representative. The tribunal's response must be proportionate, having regard to the consequences for the claimant of possibly losing his appeal."

In *CSDLA/90/1998*, the Commissioner also held that, when representation is undertaken by a local authority, the claimant is entitled to be fully represented by the authority until disposal of the appeal and the local authority must, if necessary, arrange representation through their legal department in order to avoid a postponement or an adjournment of a hearing. In *CIB/1009/2004*, a Commissioner disagreed with that approach and said that a local authority was entitled to limit the power of representatives to call upon other resources of the authority when a particular representative was unavailable due to illness. However, he went on to say that a representative should make reasonable efforts to secure alternative representation, even if that meant cancelling some other appointments, and that that implied that a request for an adjournment due to the non-availability of a representative should contain a clear indication that consideration had been given to the possibility of someone else representing the claimant. In the absence of such an explanation, the tribunal might be entitled to infer that the reasonable efforts had not been made to find alternative representation. However, a failure by a representing authority to make reasonable efforts to secure alternative representation should not have led to a refusal of an adjournment, when further efforts might not have made any difference, the claimant himself was blameless, a lot of money was at stake and the case was not straightforward so that an experienced representative might have assisted the tribunal to reach a conclusion favourable to the claimant.

In *Evans v Secretary of State for Social Security* (reported as *R(I) 5/94*), a medical appeal tribunal disagreed with the opinions of two consultants. The Court of Appeal held that, where a tribunal proposed to put a different interpretation on the same clinical findings from that put by another expert, "fairness points to the need for an adjournment so that, where possible, the tribunal's provisional view can be brought to the attention of the claimant's own advisers". A similar approach has been taken by Park J when hearing an appeal from a Pensions Appeal Tribunal (*Butterfield v Secretary of State for Defence* [2002] EWHC 2247 (Admin)). He said that, when a medically qualified member of a tribunal is the only person present with specialist medical knowledge and he perceives a possible medical objection to the claimant's case that has not been pointed out before, he must draw it to the claimant's attention and it may be necessary to offer the claimant an adjournment so that he has a realistic opportunity to consider the point "however inconvenient and irksome that may be". This makes clear what was probably meant in *Evans*. There need not always be an adjournment but the tribunal's provisional view should be put to the claimant and the claimant should expressly be *offered* an adjournment.

There is no general rule that an appeal to a tribunal should be postponed while related criminal proceedings are pending (*CIS/1216/2005*, against which an appeal has been brought). The wishes of the parties will be relevant but will not be determinative. Often a claimant will not wish an appeal to be heard while criminal proceedings are pending lest anything he says at the tribunal hearing is used against him in the criminal trial. However, another claimant may prefer an appeal to be heard first because a finding that he or she was entitled to benefit is likely to undermine a prosecution for obtaining the same benefit by deception.

Adjournments are sometimes necessary because a member of the tribunal is obliged to stand down to avoid an appearance of bias (see the annotation to s.14 of the Social Security Act 1998). In *CCS/1876/2006*, the Commissioner suggested that there might be occasions when it was prudent for a member of a tribunal to stand down in order to strengthen a party's confidence in the fairness of the procedures, even if there was no strict legal duty to do so, but he did acknowledge that the expense of an adjournment had to be kept in mind.

At a hearing following an adjournment, a tribunal may be constituted by one or more members who sat on the earlier tribunal and one or more who did not, if no evidence was taken before the adjournment. If evidence was taken before the adjournment, the tribunal should generally be either entirely the same or entirely differently constituted and, in the latter case, must have a complete rehearing, although they are entitled to accept the recorded evidence of a witness who gave evidence at the first hearing provided the rules of natural justice are not infringed (*R(U) 3/88*).

In fact the practice of the Appeals Service requires a chairman to indicate whether any evidence has been heard at an adjourned hearing and, if it has, the clerk will always arrange for the tribunal to consist either of entirely the same

(SI 1999/991, reg.51)

members or entirely different members. This avoids the risk of subconscious being carried over from one hearing to the other or of a member remembering evidence from the first hearing that does not appear in the record of proceedings (see *CDLA/2429/2004*).

A decision to adjourn is appealable only if it disposes of the substantive issues before the tribunal and either makes the outcome of the case before the tribunal inevitable or prevents a final decision from being made (*CDLA/557/2001*). Otherwise, the parties must wait until the final decision is made and appeal against that decision. A legally qualified panel member should not subvert a decision of a tribunal to adjourn for a medical report by immediately directing that the case be relisted without the report (*CSDLA/866/2002*). A refusal to adjourn is not itself appealable (*Carpenter v Secretary of State for Work and Pensions* [2003] EWCA Civ 33 (reported as *R(IB) 6/03*)) but an unfair refusal to adjourn may make the final decision of the tribunal erroneous in point of law so that an appeal may be brought against that final decision (*R. v Medical Appeal Tribunal (Midland Region) Ex p. Carrarini* [1966] 1 W.L.R. 883 (also reported as an appendix to *R(I) 13/65*).

That was the position in *CM/449/1990*, where the claim was made on behalf of a child with severe learning difficulties. His mother had written as soon as she was given notice of the hearing to apply for an adjournment on the ground that her son was away in short-term care. The tribunal refused the adjournment and dismissed the appeal, saying that they were not prepared to grant it "due to the high incidence of requests for adjournments". The Commissioner allowed the claimant's appeal on the ground that no reasonable tribunal could have refused the request for an adjournment and also on the ground that the tribunal had based their decision entirely on a wholly irrelevant consideration. It may be arguable that the Commissioner went too far in holding that the prevalence of requests for adjournments can never be a factor to be taken into account in considering such a request, but even if that is right, such a consideration cannot prevail without any regard at all being had to the particular facts and circumstances of the individual case.

Physical examinations at oral hearings

52. For the purposes of section 20(3) an appeal tribunal may not carry out a physical examination except in a case which relates to—
  (a) the extent of a person's disablement and its assessment in accordance with section 68(6) of, and Schedule 6 to, the Contributions and Benefits Act;
  (b) the extent of a person's disablement and its assessment in accordance with section 103 of that Act;
  (c) diseases or injuries prescribed for the purposes of section 108 of that Act.

2.493

DEFINITIONS

"appeal tribunal"—see s.39(1) of the Social Security Act 1998.
"the Contributions and Benefits Act"—see s.84 of the Social Security Act 1998.

GENERAL NOTE

For the meaning of "physical examination", see the note to s.20(3) of the Social Security Act 1998. See reg.41 for the circumstances in which a tribunal may refer a claimant for medical examination.

2.494

Social Security and Child Support (Decisions and Appeals) Regs 1999

Chapter V

Decisions of Appeal Tribunals and Related Matters

Appeal tribunal decisions

Decisions of appeal tribunals

53.—(1) Every decision of an appeal tribunal shall be recorded in summary by the chairman, or in the case of an appeal tribunal which has only one member, by that member.

(2) The decision notice specified in paragraph (1) shall be in such written form as shall have been approved by the President and shall be signed by the chairman, or in the case of an appeal tribunal which has only one member, by that member.

(3) As soon as may be practicable after an appeal or referral has been decided by an appeal tribunal, a copy of the decision notice [³ . . .] shall be sent or given to every party to the proceedings who shall also be informed of—

(a) his right under paragraph (4); and

[¹ (b) except in the case of an appeal under the Vaccine Damage Payments Act, the conditions governing appeals to a Commissioner.]

[² (4) [³ Subject to paragraph (4A),] a party to the proceedings may apply in writing to the clerk to the appeal tribunal for a statement of the reasons for the tribunal's decision within one month of the sending or giving of the decision notice to every party to the proceedings or within such longer period as may be allowed in accordance with regulation 54 and following that application the chairman, or in the case of a tribunal with only one member, that member shall record a statement of the reasons and a copy of that statement shall be given to every party to the proceedings as soon as may be practicable.]

[³ (4A) Where—

(a) the decision notice is corrected in accordance with regulation 56; or

(b) an application under regulation 57 for the decision to be set aside is refused for reasons other than a refusal to extend the time for making the application,

the period specified in paragraph (4) shall run from the date on which notice of the correction or the refusal of the application for setting aside is sent to the applicant.]

(5) If the decision is not unanimous, the decision notice specified in paragraph (1) shall record that one of the members dissented and the statement of reasons referred to in paragraph (4) shall include the reasons given by the dissenting member for dissenting.

Amendments

1. Social Security and Child Support (Decisions and Appeals), Vaccine Damage Payments and Jobseeker's Allowance (Amendment) Regulations 1999 (SI 1999/2677), reg.10 (October 18, 1999).

2. Social Security and Child Support (Decisions and Appeals) (Miscellaneous Amendments) Regulations 2002 (SI 2002/1379), reg.16 (May 20, 2002).

3. Social Security, Child Support and Tax Credits (Miscellaneous Amendments) Regulations 2005 (SI 2005/337), reg.2(10) (March 18, 2005).

(SI 1999/991, reg.53)

DEFINITIONS

"appeal tribunal"—see s.39(1) of the Social Security Act 1998.
"clerk to the appeal tribunal"—see reg.1(3).
"Commissioner"—see s.39(1) of the Social Security Act 1998 and reg.57B.
"party to the proceedings"—see reg.1(3).
"President"—*ibid.*
"the Vaccine Damage Payments Act"—see s.84 of the Social Security Act 1998.

GENERAL NOTE

Para. (1)

Where the Secretary of State's decision is defective in form but the tribunal agrees with its substance, it is not necessary for the tribunal to reformulate the Secretary of State's decision in the tribunal's decision notice unless the decision as expressed by the Secretary of State is wrong in some *material* respect (e.g. it states an incorrect ground of supersession) or there is likely to be some practical benefit to the claimant or to the adjudication process in future in reformulating the decision *(R(IB) 2/04* at para.82). On the other hand, attempting to reformulate the decision may serve to focus the tribunal's mind on the correct issues and so it may have a value. Where a statement of reasons is requested under para.(4), the statement should explain what the decision under appeal should have been even if the decision notice does not.

Where an appeal is against an "outcome decision" expressed in terms of a claimant's entitlement to benefit, a decision notice "should make it absolutely clear whether the tribunal has made an outcome decision (subject, in some cases, to the precise amount being calculated by the Secretary of State) or has remitted the final decision on entitlement to the Secretary of State" *(CIS/624/2006,* in which it was suggested that the President of appeal tribunals might wish to consider whether the form of decision notice usually issued in income support and similar cases should be altered to assist chairmen with that task).

2.496

Para. (2)

The form of decision notice currently approved by the President does not have a special space for reasons to be given but there is nothing forbidding a chairman from including brief reasons in the decision notice and it is suggested that it is good practice to do so (although differing views have been expressed by Commissioners on this issue, see *CIB/4497/1998* and *CSDLA/551/1999*). Apart from anything else, an unsuccessful party is more likely to ask for a statement of reasons under para.(4) if no reasons at all are given for a decision, especially if it arises at a "paper hearing". There being no duty to include any reasons at all in a decision notice, where some reasons are given but are inadequate, the consequence is not to render the tribunal's decision erroneous in point of law. The remedy is to apply for a proper statement of reasons under para.(4) *(CIB/4497/1998)*. Such a statement cures any inadequacy in reasons given in a decision notice *(CSDLA/531/2000, CIS/2345/2001)*. However, if the reasons in the full statement are inconsistent with the reasons given in a decision notice, the decision of the tribunal will be set aside as erroneous in point of law *(CCR/3396/2000, CIS/2345/2001)*.

2.497

Para. (4)

A refusal to adjourn is not a "decision" for which a statement of reasons may be required under this paragraph, although an unexplained refusal to adjourn may make a final decision erroneous in point of law unless an explanation that is not perverse may be inferred from the circumstances *(Carpenter v Secretary of State for Work and Pensions* [2003] EWCA Civ 33 (reported as *R(IB) 6/03)*).

The new version of this paragraph was inserted largely to reverse the effect of *R(IB) 4/02*. As an application for a statement of reasons is now to be sent to the clerk (rather than the chairman), reg.2(a) applies so that the application is "sent"

2.498

Social Security and Child Support (Decisions and Appeals) Regs 1999

when it is received by the clerk. The statement must be sent to all the parties and not just the party who requested it.

In *CH/2553/2005*, the clerk did not receive the request for a statement of reasons and the applicant failed to chase up the request until the absolute time-limit for applying for an extension of time under reg.54 had expired. It was held that the chairman was under no *duty* to issue a statement of reasons. It was also held that a chairman has the *power* to issue a statement of reasons without a request but that, if he or she does so after the time within which a request may be made, the statement is not treated as one and so does not start time running for the purposes of the time-limit for applying for leave to appeal. The Commissioner declined to say whether, and in what circumstances, such a statement of reasons could be challenged for inadequacy.

A chairman's power to write a statement of reasons survives the termination of his or her appointment to the panel. The statement must at least be adopted by the chairman (or possibly another member) of the tribunal who heard the appeal. Therefore a statement written by a regional chairman in the erroneous belief that it could not be written by the chairman who heard the appeal because her appointment had come to an end, was not valid (*CIS/2132/1998*).

It is usually an error of law to fail to issue a statement of reasons when a request is made within the prescribed time and there are occasions when an application for leave to appeal should be treated as such a request *(R(IS) 11/99)*. An application for leave to appeal received within the time allowed for asking for a statement of reasons is, in practice, treated as a request for such a statement. In *CDLA/5793/1997*, it had been held that such a request was implied "whenever the claimant's application for leave to appeal raises an issue that is not fully explained in the summary grounds issued as part of a decision notice or by the other documents in the case". However, although they commended the practice of treating an application for leave received within one month of the issue of a decision notice as an application for a statement of reasons, a Tribunal of Commissioners in Northern Ireland has emphasised in *R3/02(IB)* that there is no rule of law requiring a legally qualified panel member to do so. In both *R(IS) 11/99* and *R3/02(IB)*, it is stated that there are occasions when an error of law can be demonstrated without there being a statement of reasons and that a Commissioner can determine an appeal in those circumstances, although it is obviously not possible to challenge a tribunal's decision on the grounds of inadequacy of reasoning in circumstances where there is no written statement of reasons. Furthermore, a tribunal's decision will not be erroneous in law for breach of the duty to imposed by this paragraph if the decision notice issued under para.(1) in fact contains all that would be required in a full statement of reasons *(R(IS) 11/99)*, or if the two documents read together provide an adequate statement between them (*CIS/2345/2001*). The practice of some chairmen of stating that the summary reasons on a decision notice amount to a full statement of reasons has been frowned upon, on the basis that such summary reasons are more likely to contain errors than fuller statements produced in response to a request. In *CSDLA/551/1999*, the Commissioner went as far as to say that it was of no effect and that a separate statement of reasons was required in all cases, but that is not the conventional view and is inconsistent with what was said in *R(IS) 11/99*.

Long decisions need to be properly organised. In *Jasim v Secretary of State for the Home Department* [2006] EWCA Civ 342, the Court of Appeal commented on the "unmanageable length" of some paragraphs in a decision of the Asylum and Immigration Tribunal, one of which ran for almost three pages of single-spaced type. It was suggested that the use of shorter paragraphs, with sub-paragraphs and cross-headings where appropriate, was a useful aid not just to the reader but also to the writer.

Unlike its predecessors, this paragraph includes no express duty to record the tribunal's findings but this makes no practical difference because it is necessary to record a tribunal's findings on any matters in dispute as part of the explanation for its decision (*R(I) 4/02* and also *R2/01(IB)*, a decision of a Tribunal of

Commissioners in Northern Ireland). Indeed, it has been said in *Evans* (below) that there are occasions when a record of the tribunal's findings provides a complete explanation for the decision.

In *CDLA/1807/2003*, the tribunal chairman produced two statements of reasons for the tribunal's decision, the second because he had forgotten he had already written a statement. The reasons differed. The Commissioner commented that the reasons should be a statement of the *tribunal's* reasons and not the chairman's later rationalisation of the conclusion reached by the tribunal and that at least one of the statements plainly did not accurately reflect the tribunal's reasons. He set aside the tribunal's decision. Inexplicable inconsistency between the decision notice and the statement of reasons led to an appeal being allowed in *CCR/3396/2000*.

The inadequacy of statements of reasons is probably the most common ground upon which tribunals' decsions are set aside by Commissioners. The superficiality of many submissions made by both claimants' representatives and the Secretary of State's representatives on this issue has been the subject of adverse comment by Commissioners (see, for example, *CIB/4497/1998* in which it was said that there is no simple formula for writing reasons for a decision).

In *Re Poyser and Mills' Arbitration* [1964] 2 Q.B. 467, 478, Megaw J. said:

"Parliament provided that reasons shall be given, and in my view that must be read as meaning that proper, adequate reasons must be given. The reasons that are set out must be reasons that will not only be intelligible, but which deal with the substantial points that have been raised."

In *R(A) 1/72*, the Chief Commissioner, considering an appeal from a delegated medical practioner acting on behalf of the Attendance Allowance Board, said:

"The obligation to give reasons for the decision in [a case involving a conflict of evidence] imports a requirement to do more than only to state the conclusion, and for the determining authority to state that on the evidence the authority is not satisfied that the statutory conditions are met, does no more than this. It affords no guide to the selective process by which the evidence has been accepted, rejected, weighed or considered, or the reasons for any of these things. It is not, of course, obligatory thus to deal with every piece of evidence or to over elaborate, but in an administrative quasi-judicial decision the minimum requirement must at least be that the claimant, looking at the decision should be able to discern on the face of it the reasons why the evidence has failed to satisfy the authority. For the purpose of the regulation which requires the reasons for the review decision to be set out, a decision based, and only based, on a conclusion that the total effect of the evidence fails to satisfy, without reasons given for reaching that conclusion, will in many cases be no adequate decision at all."

In *R. (Asha Foundation) v Millennium Commission* [2003] EWCA Civ 66 (*The Times*, January 24, 2003), the Court of Appeal considered the approach Sedley J. had taken in *R. v Higher Education Funding Council Ex p. Institute of Dental Surgery* [1994] 1 W.L.R. 242 to the question of whether there was a duty to give any reasons at all and held that, where there is a duty to give reasons, the same approach should be taken to the question whether reasons were adequate. Sedley J.'s approach required the balancing of a number of considerations, which might vary from case to case. He said:

"The giving of reasons may among other things concentrate the decision-maker's mind on the right questions; demonstrate to the recipient that this is so; show that the issues have been conscientiously addressed and how the result has been reached or alternatively alert the recipient to a justiciable flaw in the process.

On the other side of the argument, it may place an undue burden on decision-makers; demand an appearance of unanimity where there is diversity; call for the articulation of sometimes inexpressible value judgments; and offer an invitation to the captious to comb the reasons for previously unsuspected grounds of challenge."

It was acknowledged in *Baron v Secretary of State for Social Services* (reported as an appendix to *R(M) 6/86*) that there are limits to the extent to which a tribunal can be expected to give reasons for decisions on matters of judgment, such as the distance a claimant could walk without having to stop or the extent of breathlessness and pain which caused him to stop. Assessments of disablement also give rise to difficult judgments. In *CI/636/1993*, the Commissioner said:

> "Whether or how far the duty in law to give reasons for their decision extends beyond saying that the particular percentage arrived at is in the medical judgment of the tribunal a fair one on these particular facts must depend on the nature of the individual case and the issues that have been raised in it. It seems to me that the position is correctly summarised by the Commissioner in *R(I) 30/61* at paragraph 8: there may well be cases where a mere statement that the tribunal makes an assessment at a particular percentage is in itself a sufficient record, since it implies that they think that is a fair assessment; but in other cases findings of fact and an explanation of reasons will be needed to show that evidence they have accepted or rejected as justifying the making of a smaller or larger assessment, since otherwise the claimant will be left guessing as to the basis on which the decision has been arrived at. And in a case where specific submissions backed with expert medical evidence have been addressed to them on the basis of assessment to be used, it will normally be an error of law for the tribunal simply to state their conclusion in the form of a percentage without making it clear to what extent and for what reasons they are accepting or rejecting the suggested basis, since they will not have carried out the general duty to give reasons on a material issue raised before them: see *R(I) 18/61* para.13."

In many cases it will be obvious from a finding as to the claimant's loss of faculty what the resulting disablement must have been but in others it is necessary for a tribunal to make specific findings as to the resulting disabilities (*CI/343/1988*). In *CI/1802/2001*, it was again stressed that a decision assessing the extent of a claimant's disablement is likely to be inadequate if the tribunal have not explained the factual basis of their decision.

> "This can often be simply expressed. In many cases it will be enough to say that the evidence given by the claimant about the effect of a particular accident or disease on his or her daily life has been accepted. In some cases, where the claimant's evidence is for some reason found to be unreliable, it may be that the tribunal will state that it felt able to accept only those disabilities which in its expert opinion were likely to flow from problems disclosed on clinical examination. Other cases may need more detail."

However, where a tribunal assesses disablement for the purpose of determining entitlement to disablement benefit and the claimant is not suffering from an injury specified in Sch.2 of the Social Security (General Benefit) Regulations 1982, it is not necessary for the statement of reasons to refer to the prescribed degrees of disablement set against the injuries in that Schedule even though reg.11(8) of those Regulations suggests that the Schedule may act as a general guide to the assessment of disablement (*R(I) 1/04*). See, also, the decision of the Tribunal of Commissioners in *R(I) 2/06*, where the same approach was taken and *CI/1802/2001* was approved.

Resorting to describing a Benefits Agency Medical Service doctor as "independent" as a reason for preferring his evidence to medical evidence obtained on behalf of the claimant was described as "irrational" in *CIB/563/2001*, given that the Benefits Agency Medical Service doctor was trained and paid by one of the parties to the proceedings. In any event, that reason was inadequate because the doctor acting on behalf of the claimant had recorded different clinical findings and there was no suggestion that he did not conduct a full examination or failed to take account of the claimant's history.

A Tribunal of Commissioners in Northern Ireland has held in *R 3/01 (IB)* that there is no universal obligation on an appeal tribunal to explain an assessment of credibility. It will usually be sufficient to say that a witness is not believed or is exaggerating. It is the decision that has to be explained. A tribunal is not obliged to give reasons for its reasons. There may be situations when a further explanation will be required but the only standard is that the reasons should explain the decision.

In the same case, it was held that a tribunal must record their findings on every descriptor of the all work test that is in issue and those raised by clear implication but that there is no universal rule that individual reasons must be given for the selection of a particular descriptor. The reasons given must explain why the tribunal reached the decision they did but need not always explain why it did not reach any different conclusion. However, it is suggested that there *is* a need to explain why a *specific* contention advanced by a party has not been accepted, at least where the contention is a major part of that party's case. It was said in *Flannery v Halifax Estate Agencies Ltd* [2001] 1 W.L.R. 377, CA, that, where there is expert evidence and analysis advanced by both parties, a statement of reasons must "enter into the issues" in order to explain why the unsuccessful party's evidence has failed to prevail. However, in *English v Emery Reimbold & Strick Ltd.* [2002] EWCA Civ 605; [2002] 1 W.L.R. 2409, the Court of Appeal sought to discourage the "cottage industry" of applications inspired by *Flannery* and followed *Eagil Trust Co Ltd v Pigott-Brown* [1985] 3 All E.R. 119, 122 in which Griffiths L.J. had stressed that there was no duty on a judge in giving his reasons to deal with every argument presented to him. The Court also said that, while a judge will often need to refer to a piece of evidence or to a submission which he has accepted or rejected, provided the reference is clear, it may be unnecessary to detail, or even summarise, the evidence or submission in question.

> "The essential requirement is that the terms of the judgment should enable the parties and any appellate tribunal readily to analyse the reasoning that was essential to the Judge's decision."

Where a tribunal has rejected a claimant's account as to how he came by an injury, it is not bound to make any finding as to how he did come by it, where that would be no more than speculation (*AJ (Cameroon) v Secretary of State for the Home Department* [2007] EWCA Civ 373). However, there will, of course, be cases where a tribunal's finding that the injury was due to a different cause is the explanation for rejecting the claimant's case. In *CCS/1626/2002*, the Commissioner said that a person could hardly complain about the adequacy of findings of fact or reasoning lying behind an estimate of income when the need to make an estimate was due to that person's failure to provide better evidence. In *R(I) 3/03*, a Tribunal of Commissioners criticised the Secretary of State for supporting, by reference to an occasional infelicitous word in a statement of reasons, an unrealistic argument advanced by a claimant to the effect that a tribunal had overlooked a basic proposition of law. They said that there are some propositions of law, such as the nature of the civil burden and standard of proof, that are of such fundamental importance in the work of tribunals that it is almost inconceivable that tribunals will have overlooked them and that it should therefore be assumed that they have understood them unless there is something to show otherwise in the substance of what a tribunal has decided.

Specific guidance as to the approach to be taken in medical cases before appeal tribunals has been given by the Court of Appeal in *Evans v Secretary of State for Social Services* (reported as *R(I) 5/94*) where it was said:

> "1. The decision should record the medical question or questions which the tribunal is required to answer. Provided the questions are set out and the answers are directed to the questions it should then be possible for the parties to know the issues to which the tribunal have addressed themselves.
> 2. In cases where the tribunal have medically examined the claimant they should record their findings. These findings by themselves may be sufficient to demonstrate the reason why they have reached a particular conclusion.

3. Where, however, the clinical findings do not point to some obvious diagnosis it may be necessary to give a short explanation as to why they have made one diagnosis rather than another. Such an explanation will be important in cases where the tribunal's diagnosis differs from a reasoned diagnosis of another qualified practitioner who has examined the claimant on an earlier occasion.

4. A decision on a question of causation may pose particular difficulties when one is examining the adequacy of the reasons for a decision. In some cases it may be sufficient for the tribunal to record that it was not satisfied that the present condition was caused by the relevant trauma. Where, however, a claimant has previously been in receipt of some benefit or allowance (particularly if paid over a long period of time) and there is no question of malingering or bad faith then . . . the tribunal should go further than merely to state a conclusion. If one accepts that the underlying principle is fairness the claimant should be given some explanation, which may be very short, to enable him or his advisors to know where the break in causation has been found. Thus it may well be that the claimant will wish to reapply and for this purpose fairness requires that, if possible, he should be told why his claim has failed."

That was in the context of decisions of a medical appeal tribunal who had jurisdiction in respect of certain issues only, including the "medical questions" in respect of mobility allowance and the "disablement questions" in respect of disablement benefit. The reference to "the medical question or questions" must be read against that background and must therefore be taken to refer to the *legal* issues as much as the medical issues in a case.

In *CDLA/5419/1999*, it is pointed out that the fact that a claimant is unsuccessful does not always imply rejection of the medical evidence advanced by him or her. In that case, the claimant's doctor said that the claimant required attention but he did not specify how much. The tribunal accepted that the claimant required some attention but found that it was not sufficient to qualify for disability living allowance. The Commissioner said that the doctor's evidence had therefore not supported the element of the claimant's case upon which she failed and that, in the circumstances of the case, there had been no duty to refer to the doctor's evidence at all. A similar point has been made by a Tribunal of Commissioners in Northern Ireland (*R2/04(DLA)*) and by the Court of Appeal in Northern Ireland (*Quinn v Department for Social Development* [2004] NICA 22). In the former case, however, the Tribunal of Commissioners added that, "where it is evident that the claimant attaches great significance to a letter or report, it may be prudent for a tribunal to say, briefly, that it has read the document but derived no assistance from it" and it may be helpful to say why if the relevance or value of the evidence is likely to be controversial. In *R(M) 1/96*, the Commissioner held that the fact of a previous award does not raise any presumption in the claimant's favour or result in the need for consistency having to be treated as a separate issue on a renewal claim. However, he said that the requirement for a tribunal to give reasons for its decision means that it is usually necessary for a tribunal to explain why it is not renewing a previous award, unless that is obvious from their findings. That approach was applied by the Court of Appeal in Northern Ireland in *Quinn*. The Court also accepted that, in the circumstances of that particular case, there had been no need for the tribunal to refer to a medical report obtained for the purpose of determining the previous claim. Similarly, in *R. (Viggers) v Pensions Appeal Tribunal* [2006] EWHC 1066 (Admin), a Pensions Appeal Tribunal was held to have erred when it did not even mention that it was making a much lower assessment of disablement than the Veterans Agency Medical Services, let alone refer to any evidence in the papers including the reasoned opinion of the VAMS' medical adviser. "If they were going to differ, and differ so markedly, from the opinion of the VAMS, the basis of that disagreement required, in my judgment, to be spelt out."

In *Baron v Secretary of State for Social Services* (reported as an appendix to *R(M) 6/86*), it was said that:

"The overriding test must always be: is the tribunal providing both parties with the materials which will enable them to know that the tribunal has made no error of law in reaching its findings of fact?"

The approach taken in social security cases is not very different from that taken in other areas of public law. In the context of planning, Lord Brown of Eaton-under-Heywood summarised the effect of case law in *South Bucks DC v Porter* (No.2) [2004] UKHL 33 [2004] 1 W.L.R. 1953 at [36]:

"The reasons for a decision must be intelligible and they must be adequate. They must enable the reader to understand why the matter was decided as it was and what conclusions were reached on the 'principal important controversial issues', disclosing how any issue of law or fact was resolved. Reasons can be briefly stated, the degree of particularity required depending entirely on the nature of the issues falling for decision. The reasoning must not give rise to a substantial doubt as to whether the decision-maker erred in law, for example by misunderstanding some relevant policy or some other important matter or by failing to reach a rational decision on relevant grounds. But such adverse inference will not readily be drawn. The reasons need refer only to the main issues in the dispute, not to every material consideration. They should enable disappointed developers to assess their prospects of obtaining some alternative development permission, or, as the case may be, their unsuccessful opponents to understand how the policy or approach underlying the grant of permission may impact upon future such applications. Decision letters [which contain statements of reasons] must be read in a straightforward manner, recognising that they are addressed to parties well aware of the issues involved and the arguments advanced. A reasons challenge will only succeed if the party aggrieved can satisfy the court that he has genuinely been substantially prejudiced by the failure to provide an adequately reasoned decision".

The European Court of Human Rights has taken much the same approach as the United Kingdom's courts. In *Hirvisari v Finland* 2001, it was said:

"Although Article 6(1) obliges courts to give reasons for their decisions, it cannot be understood as requiring a detailed answer to every argument. Thus, in dismissing an appeal, an appellate court may, in principle, simply endorse the reasons for the lower court's decision . . . A lower court or authority in turn must give such reasons as to enable the parties to make effective use of any existing rights of appeal."

Standard form decisions have been frowned upon in *CI/5199/1998* and *CIB/4497/1998*, not on grounds of principle but because they tend to be used not only when appropriate but also when the circumstances of the case make it inappropriate.

In *R(IS) 5/04*, it was held that a delay in providing reasons did not necessarily render a decision erroneous in point of law. The Commissioner said that a delay in providing reasons may itself amount to a breach of Article 6 of the European Convention on Human Rights (although, if the tribunal's decision was not flawed in any other respect, the remedy for such a breach would presumably be an award of damages by a court) and she also held that a delay may be relevant on an appeal because it may indicate that the reasons are unreliable. However, in the particular case before her, where the statement of reasons had been requested on July 1, 2002 and was not sent to the parties until October 29, 2002, the Commissioner found there to have been no error of law. The Court of Appeal has since taken the same approach in relation to delays in the promulgation of decisions by employment tribunals. Delay may give rise to the state's liability to pay compensation to the victim of the delay but, where an appeal against the tribunal's decision lies only on a point of law, it is not enough to claim that the decision is "unsafe" because of the delay. However, there may be exceptional cases in which unreasonable delay in promulgating a decision can properly be treated as a serious procedural error or material irregularity giving rise to a question of law if there is a real risk that, due to the delayed decision, the party complaining was deprived of the substance of his right to a fair trial under Art. 6 of the Convention. It is necessary

Social Security and Child Support (Decisions and Appeals) Regs 1999

to consider whether the delay has caused the tribunal to reach a wrong finding or to overlook or forget evidence (*Bangs v Connex South Eastern Ltd* [2005] EWCA Civ 14, in which it was held that there had been no error of law despite the fact that the tribunal's decision was not promulgated until a year after the hearing ended.) Effectively, delay is merely a factor to be borne in mind when assessing the adequacy of a statement of reasons.

In *Barke v SEETEC Business Technology Centre Ltd* [2005] EWCA Civ 578, the Court of Appeal approved the practice in the employment appeal tribunal of sifting appeals and inviting employment tribunals to supplement their reasons when the reasons appear to be inadequate. This is done to save the costs of an appeal and of a rehearing where the reasons can adequately be supplemented, although it was recognised in *Barke* that it will not always be appropriate if, for example "the inadequacy of reasoning is on its face so fundamental that there is a real risk that supplementary reasons will be reconstructions of proper reasons, rather than the unexplained actual reasons for the decision". It was also said that the employment appeal tribunal "should always be alive to the danger that an employment tribunal might tailor its response to a request for explanations or further reasons (usually subconsciously rather than deliberately) so as to put the decision in the best possible light". In *Hatungimana v Secretary of State for the Home Department* [2006] EWCA Civ 231, the Court of Appeal declined to apply *Barke* on an appeal from the Asylum and Immigration Tribunal, stressing that the procedural rules of that tribunal were different from those governing employment tribunals. In *CA/4297/2004*, a Commissioner had already distinguished *Barke* and held that a salaried chairman, considering an application for leave to appeal under reg.58(6)(a), had been wrong to ask the fee-paid chairman of the tribunal to supplement his statement of reasons for the tribunal's decision and that the fee-paid chairman had had no power to do so. There are substantial practical arguments against the course taken by the salaried chairman in the case before the Commissioner because some substantial delay was caused as the claimant had to be given the opportunity to comment on the supplemented statement. The Commissioner pointed out that appeals to Commissioners are usually dealt with speedily without oral hearings and that the cost and length of rehearings before tribunals are relatively modest. That is quite apart from the danger referred to by the Commissioner of a fee-paid chairman being led into introducing reasoning on issues that were not in fact considered by the whole tribunal. However, it is arguable that the Commissioner went too far in suggesting that reasons can never be supplemented when an application is made for leave to appeal. What might have been permissible would have been for the salaried chairman to have referred the application to the fee-paid chairman for determination, with an indication that he might feel able to answer the grounds of appeal. A modest expansion of reasons when leave to appeal is being refused (or granted) may be acceptable in some cases (e.g. *R(M) 2/78*). It will be for the Commissioner to consider whether the reasons are reliable against the background of the case.

Para. (5)

2.499   A decision will be set aside by a Commissioner if there has been a failure to include reasons for dissent (*CDLA/572/2001*).

Late applications for a statement of reasons of tribunal decision

2.500   **54.**—(1) The time for making an application for [¹. . .] the statement of the reasons for a tribunal's decision may be extended where the conditions specified in paragraphs (2) to (8) are satisfied [¹, subject to [² regulation 53(4A)], but no application shall in any event be brought more than three months after the date of the sending or giving of the notice of the decision of the appeal tribunal.

(2) An application for an extension of time under this regulation shall be made in writing and shall be determined by a legally qualified panel member.

(SI 1999/991, reg.54)

(3) An application under this regulation shall contain particulars of the grounds on which the extension of time is sought, including details of any relevant special circumstances for the purposes of paragraph (4).

(4) The application for an extension of time shall not be granted unless the panel member is satisfied that it is in the interests of justice for the application to be granted.

(5) For the purposes of paragraph (4) it is not in the interests of justice to grant the application unless the panel member is satisfied that—
  (a) the special circumstances specified in paragraph (6) are relevant to the application; or
  (b) some other special circumstances are relevant to the application, and as a result of those special circumstances it was not practicable for the application to be made within the time limit specified in regulation 53(4).

(6) For the purposes of paragraph (5)(a), the special circumstances are that—
  (a) the applicant or a [1 . . .] or dependant of the applicant has died or suffered serious illness;
  (b) the applicant is not resident in the United Kingdom; or
  (c) normal postal services were adversely disrupted.

(7) In determining whether it is in the interests of justice to grant the application, the panel member shall have regard to the principle that the greater the amount of time that has elapsed between the expiration of the time within which the application for a copy of the statement of reasons for a tribunal's decision is to be made and the making of the application for an extension of time, the more compelling should be the special circumstances on which the application is based.

(8) In determining whether it is in the interests of justice to grant the application, no account shall be taken of the following—
  (a) that the person making the application or any person acting for him was unaware of, or misunderstood, the law applicable to his case (including ignorance or misunderstanding of the time limits imposed by these Regulations); or
  (b) that a Commissioner or a court has taken a different view of the law from that previously understood and applied.

(9) An application under this regulation for an extension of time which has been refused may not be renewed.

(10) The panel member who determines the application shall record a summary of his [1 determination] in such written form as has been approved by the President.

(11) As soon as practicable after the [1 determination] is made a copy of the decision shall be sent or given to every party to the proceedings.

(12) Any person who under paragraph (11) receives a copy of the [1 determination] may, within one month of the decision being sent to him, apply in writing for a copy of the reasons for that decision and a copy shall be supplied to him.
  [1 (1)[2 . . .]]

AMENDMENTS

1. Social Security and Child Support (Decisions and Appeals) (Miscellaneous Amendments) Regulations 2002 (SI 2002/1379), reg.17 (May 20, 2002).

Social Security and Child Support (Decisions and Appeals) Regs 1999

2. Social Security, Child Support and Tax Credits (Miscellaneous Amendments) Regulations 2005 (SI 2005/337), reg.2(11) (March 18, 2005).

DEFINITIONS

"appeal tribunal"—see s.39(1) of the Social Security Act 1998.
"Commissioner"—*ibid.* and see reg.57B.
"legally qualified panel member"—see reg.1(3).
"panel member"—*ibid.*
"partner"—*ibid.*
"party to the proceedings"—*ibid.*
"President"—*ibid.*

Record of tribunal proceedings

2.501 55.—(1) A record of the proceedings at an oral hearing, which is sufficient to indicate the evidence taken, shall be made by the chairman, or in the case of an appeal tribunal which has only one member, by that member, in such medium as he may direct.
[1 (2) The clerk to the appeal tribunal shall preserve—
(a) the record of proceedings;
(b) the decision notice; and
(c) any statement of the reasons for the tribunal's decision,
for the period specified in paragraph (3).
(3) That period is six months from the date of—
(a) the decision made by the appeal tribunal;
(b) any statement of reasons for the tribunal's decision;
(c) any correction of the decision in accordance with regulation 56;
(d) any refusal to set aside the decision in accordance with regulation 57; or
(e) any determination of an application under regulation 58 for leave to appeal against the decision,
or until the date on which those documents are sent to the office of the Social Security and Child Support Commissioners in connection with an appeal against the decision or an application to a Commissioner for leave to appeal, if that occurs within the six months.
(4) Any party to the proceedings may within the time specified in paragraph (3) apply in writing for a copy of the record of proceedings and a copy shall be supplied to him.]

AMENDMENT

1. Social Security, Child Support and Tax Credits (Miscellaneous Amendments) Regulations 2005 (SI 2005/337), reg.2(12) (March 18, 2005).

DEFINITIONS

"appeal tribunal"—see s.39(1) of the Social Security Act 1998.
"clerk to the appeal tribunal"—see reg.1(3).
"party to the proceedings"—*ibid.*

GENERAL NOTE

Para. (1)

2.502 The opening words of the regulation show that the "record of proceedings" is a note of the evidence and submissions received at the hearing. This is often taken to refer to the oral evidence and submissions but it probably extends to at least a record of what written evidence was before the tribunal which may in turn imply a duty on someone to keep a copy of that evidence. In practice, the Tribunals Service usually

(SI 1999/991, reg.55)

keeps the whole file for six months from the last action on the file, which complies with the duty however the regulation is construed.

Where an appeal is based on what happened at a hearing, a Commissioner will be slow to go behind a full record of proceedings (*CS/343/1994*) but will admit evidence if it is necessary to do so where a full and particularised allegation is made that the conduct of the hearing led to a breach of the rules of natural justice (*R(M)1/89*). A Commissioner may obtain statements from those present at the hearing, including the members of the tribunal, but it will not be necessary to obtain statements from members of the tribunal if the appellant's case is supported by other evidence, such as the record of proceedings and the statement of reasons, unless the case involves an allegation of personal misconduct that it would be unfair to find proved without the person concerned having had the opportunity of commenting (*CDLA/5574/2002*).

However, it is not just in cases where procedural impropriety is alleged that a record of proceedings is an important document. Because a statement of reasons ought to deal with the principal points raised by the parties but a tribunal is not always required to consider points that have not been explicitly raised and because a tribunal may have an investigatory role, the record of proceedings may be an important document in a case where it is suggested that the statement of reasons is inadequate or that the tribunal failed to ask questions about a particular issue. It may, however, be supplemented. In *CH/2484/2006*, the Deputy Commissioner said—

> "I appreciate that a record of proceedings is not a complete *verbatim* note and that it is possible for points to be omitted, but if an appellant to the Commissioner wishes to base a submission on the overlooking of evidence or submissions and the evidence or submission are not recorded in the record, it seems to me to be necessary as a general rule for it to equip itself with evidence (such as a statement by someone who was present) that that piece of evidence or submission was in fact made. It should also raise the matter with the other side in advance, so as to avoid surprise and facilitate agreement on the position if possible."

In that case, the local authority was the appellant. Where a claimant is an appellant and the Secretary of State was not present at the hearing before the tribunal, the Secretary of State will not be in a position to dispute a statement by the claimant as to what occurred at that hearing. As suggested above, it will be open to a Commissioner to seek the views of the tribunal but he or she will not be obliged to do so.

Paras (2) and (3)

Until these Regulations came into force in 1999, a record of proceedings had to be kept for 18 months. The duty to keep the other documents was introduced in 2005 and makes it unnecessary for a person seeking leave to appeal to a Commissioner to supply copies with the application. The reduction of the period for keeping the record of proceedings (and in practice the whole tribunal file) to six months may appear undesirable but it is arguable that the Deputy Commissioner went too far in *CSIB/439/2004* in suggesting, obiter, that it might breach the right to a fair hearing guaranteed by Art.6 of the European Convention on Human Rights. All parties should have had copies of the decision notice and any statement of reasons and would have had six months in which to ask for a copy of the record of proceedings and, if a party has destroyed his own copies of documents or failed to ask for a record of proceedings, it is not clear that he should be able to complain that the tribunal has destroyed its copies of the documents. The effect of the six-month period is that it remains necessary for an applicant to provide the documents required to support a very late application for leave to appeal.

2.503

Para. (4)

The duty to provide a record of proceedings is a duty to provide one that is comprehensible without some other person's assistance (*CIB/3013/1997*) in order that people may understand what happened on the hearing on the appeal (*CDLA/4110/1997*), so that providing an illegible document is not sufficient. A failure to comply with this duty will not always render the tribunal's decision erroneous in point of law

2.504

Social Security and Child Support (Decisions and Appeals) Regs 1999

but it will do so if, in a particular case, it is necessary to have regard to the evidence given at the hearing or to any contention put forward at the hearing in order to decide whether some other ground of appeal is made out (*CDLA/1389/1997*). It may be thought that the obvious course of action if an illegible copy of a record of proceedings is produced is to ask the chairman to provide a legible version, if that is still practical.

Correction of accidental errors

2.505   **56.**—(1) The clerk to the appeal tribunal [¹ or a legally qualified panel member] may at any time correct accidental errors in [² the notice of any decision] of an appeal tribunal made under a relevant enactment, the Child Support Act or the Vaccine Damage Payments Act.

[² (2) A correction made to a decision notice shall be deemed to be part of the decision notice and written notice of the correction shall be given as soon as practicable to every party to the proceedings.]

(3) In this regulation and regulation 57, "relevant enactment" has the same meaning as in section 28(3).

AMENDMENTS

1. Social Security and Child Support (Miscellaneous Amendments) Regulations 2000 (SI 2000/1596), reg.30 (June 19, 2000).
2. Social Security, Child Support and Tax Credits (Miscellaneous Amendments) Regulations 2005 (SI 2005/337), reg.2(13) (March 18, 2005).

DEFINITIONS

"appeal tribunal"—see s.39(1) of the Social Security Act 1998.
"the Child Support Act"—see s.84 of the Social Security Act 1998.
"clerk to the appeal tribunal"—see reg.1(3).
"legally qualified panel member"—*ibid.*
"party to the proceedings"—*ibid.*
"relevant enactment"—by virtue of para.(3), see s.28(3) of the Social Security Act 1998.
"the Vaccine Damage Payments Act"—see s.84 of the Social Security Act 1998.

GENERAL NOTE

2.506   Regulation 56 allows correction only of accidental errors, "such as a typing mistake or misspelling of a name or an omission about which both sides if asked, would agree" (*CI/3887/1999*). It cannot be used to remove an error of law on an issue central to an appeal. Indeed, the regulation has now been amended to make it clear that it applies only to decision notices. It may still be permissible to correct a minor slip in a statement of reasons (see reg.57A(3)) but any such correction will not affect time limits. If a legally qualified panel member realises, after a decision has been issued, that there is an obvious and fundamental error of law in the decision, a party may be invited to apply for leave to appeal so that the decision may be set aside under s.13 of the Social Security Act 1998 and a rehearing directed.

Note that the time for applying for a statement of reasons of a tribunal's decision is now extended by reg.53(4A) in a case where there is a correction. A correction is effective only when notice is given as required by para.(2). If notice is not given, the date from which time for appealing runs is left in abeyance (*CI/3887/1999*). Strictly speaking, an application for leave to appeal against a decision lapses if the decision is corrected and a new application may be required, although a pending application may be treated as being an application against the new decision, at any rate by a Commissioner (*CSI/74/1991*).

A decision is only effective when it is sent out (*R(I) 14/74*). Until then, it may be altered informally. Even if an oral "decision" has been given, the case may be

(SI 1999/991, reg. 56)

recalled by the tribunal before it is sent out, if it appears to them that they have made a serious mistake (*CI/141/1987*, applying *Re Harrison's Settlement* [1955] Ch. 260). Generally it would then be necessary to have a rehearing.

Setting aside decisions on certain grounds

57.—(1) On an application made by a party to the proceedings, a decision of an appeal tribunal made under a relevant enactment, the Child Support Act or the Vaccine Damage Payments Act, may be set aside by a legally qualified panel member in a case where it appears just to set the decision aside on the ground that—
  (a) a document relating to the proceedings in which the decision was made was not sent to, or was not received at an appropriate time by, a party to the proceedings or the party's representative or was not received at an appropriate time by the person who made the decision;
  (b) a party to the proceedings in which the decision was made or the party's representative was not present at a hearing relating to the proceedings.
(2) In determining whether it is just to set aside a decision on the ground set out in paragraph (1)(b), the panel member shall determine whether the party making the application gave notice that he wished to have an oral hearing, and if that party did not give such notice the decision shall not be set aside unless [¹. . .] that member is satisfied that the interests of justice manifestly so require.
[¹ (3) An application under this regulation shall—
  (a) be made within one month of the date on which—
    (i) a copy of the decision notice is sent or given to the parties to the proceedings in accordance with regulation 53(3); or
    (ii) the statement of the reasons for the decision is given or sent in accordance with regulation 53(4),
    whichever is the later;
  (b) be in writing and signed by a party to the proceedings or, where the party has provided written authority to a representative to act on his behalf, that representative;
  (c) contain particulars of the grounds on which it is made; and
  (d) be sent to the clerk to the appeal tribunal.]
(4) Where an application to set aside a decision is entertained under paragraph (1), every party to the proceedings shall be sent a copy of the application and shall be afforded a reasonable opportunity of making representations on it before the application is determined.
[² (4A) Where a legally qualified panel member refuses to set aside a decision he may treat the application to set aside the decision as an application under regulation 53(4) for a statement of the reasons for the tribunal's decision, subject to the time limits set out in regulation 53(4) and (4A).]
(5) Notice in writing of a determination on an application to set aside a decision shall be sent or given to every party to the proceedings as soon as may be practicable and the notice shall contain a statement giving the reasons for the determination.
[¹(6) The time within which an application under this regulation must be made may be extended by a period not exceeding one year where the conditions specified in paragraphs (7) to (11) are satisfied.
(7) An application for an extension of time shall be made in accordance with paragraph (3)(b) to (d), shall include details of any relevant special

2.507

circumstances for the purposes of paragraph (9) and shall be determined by a legally qualified panel member.

(8) An application for an extension of time shall not be granted unless the panel member is satisfied that—
   (a) if the application is granted there are reasonable prospects that the application to set aside will be successful; and
   (b) it is in the interests of justice for the application for an extension of time to be granted.

(9) For the purposes of paragraph (8) it is not in the interests of justice to grant an application for an extension of time unless the panel member is satisfied that—
   (a) the special circumstances specified in paragraph (10) are relevant to that application; or
   (b) some other special circumstances exist which are wholly exceptional and relevant to that application,
and as a result of those special circumstances, it was not practicable for the application to set aside to be made within the time limit specified in paragraph (3)(a).

(10) For the purposes of paragraph (9)(a) the special circumstances are that—
   (a) the applicant or a partner or dependant of the applicant has died or suffered serious illness;
   (b) the applicant is not resident in the United Kingdom; or
   (c) normal postal services were disrupted.

(11) In determining whether it is in the interests of justice to grant an application for an extension of time, the panel member shall have regard to the principle that the greater the amount of time that has elapsed between the expiry of the time within which the application to set aside is to be made and the making of the application for an extension of time, the more compelling should be the special circumstances on which the application for an extension is based.

(12) An application under this regulation for an extension of time which has been refused may not be renewed.]

AMENDMENTS

1. Social Security and Child Support (Decisions and Appeals) (Miscellaneous Amendments) Regulations 2002 (SI 2002/1379), reg.18 (May 20, 2002).
2. Social Security, Child Support and Tax Credits (Miscellaneous Amendments) Regulations 2005 (SI 2005/337), reg.2(14) (March 18, 2005).

DEFINITIONS

"appeal tribunal"—see s.39(1) of the Social Security Act 1998.
"the Child Support Act"—see s.84 of the Social Security Act 1998.
"clerk to the appeal tribunal"—see reg.1(3).
"legally qualified panel member"—*ibid*.
"panel member"—*ibid*.
"partner"—*ibid*.
"party to the proceedings"—*ibid*.
"relevant enactment"—by virtue of reg.56(3), see s.28(3) of the Social Security Act 1998.
"the Vaccine Damage Payments Act"—see s.84 of the Social Security Act 1998.

(SI 1999/991, reg.57)

GENERAL NOTE

Para. (1)

Regulation 10(1)(c) of the Social Security (Adjudication) Regulations 1995 provided for a third ground for setting aside when "the interests of justice so require" which had been held to be limited to procedural errors and mishaps, being valid under the forerunner of para.1(a) of Sch.5 to the Social Security Act 1998 rather than the forerunner of s.28 (*R(U) 3/89*). It seems odd that that ground should have been dropped when s.13 of the Social Security Act 1998 has so expanded the grounds upon which a decision may be set aside. Section 13(2) is not a complete substitute because there are cases when there has been a procedural slip and the interests of justice might require a decision to be set aside even though, strictly speaking, there has been no breach of the rules of natural justice and the tribunal's decision is not erroneous in point of law. The most obvious example is where a tribunal has quite properly decided to proceed with a case in the unexplained absence of a material witness and it subsequently transpires that the witness had a very good reason for not appearing and for not informing the tribunal or the party intending to call him or her. However, if a power to set aside a decision to remedy an obvious unfairness may be regarded as a "procedural safeguard", such a power may be implied notwithstanding its absence from the statutory scheme (see *per* Lord of Harwich in *Lloyd v McMahon* [1987] A.C. 625 at 702–3). Section 28(2) of the 1998 Act appears to anticipate the existence of implied powers of this nature. The loss of reg.10(1)(c) of the 1995 Regulations may therefore be immaterial. On the other hand, the Court of Appeal has doubted the existence of an inherent power in a statutory tribunal to rescind or review its own decisions *Akewushola v Secretary of State for the Home Department* [2000] 1 W.L.R. 2295 and Newman J has held that there is no such power (*Secretary of State for Defence v President of the Pensions Appeal Tribunals (England and Wales)* [2004] EWHC 141 (Admin)).

Setting aside under reg.57 is appropriate where a claimant has not received notice of a hearing that has been properly sent (*R(SB) 19/83*). In *R(SB) 55/83*, it was held that that was the only remedy available to a claimant in those circumstances and that there was no basis upon which a Commissioner could allow an appeal. That approach has been rejected in *CDLA/5413/1999* where it is held that a decision of a tribunal is erroneous in law where notice of a hearing has not been received by a party even though there may have been no breach of the rules of natural justice by the tribunal. See also *CIB/303/1999*. In *CIB/5227/1999*, it was pointed out that it was necessary to explain fully the circumstances of the case when making an application for a decision to be set aside. In that case, as in *CDLA/5413/1999*, the reason that the claimant had not received notice of the hearing was that none had been sent because the claimant had not received the clerk's direction requiring him to state whether he wished there to be an oral hearing (see, now, reg.39(1)).

In *CSB/15394/1996* and *CSB/574/1997*, a tribunal refused to set aside a decision on the ground that the claimant's case for the setting aside amounted to an allegation that there had been a breach of the rules of natural justice which was an error of law so that an appeal to a Commissioner was the appropriate course for the claimant to take. The Commissioner hearing the appeal disagreed with that approach. He pointed out that most grounds for setting aside would also be proper grounds for appeal and that the regulation existed to provide an expeditious alternative to an appeal. On the other hand, in *CSDLA/303/1998*, the Commissioner held that a claimant was not entitled to raise by way of appeal an issue of fact determined under the forerunner of this regulation. The tribunal considering the application for setting aside had found as a fact that a fax allegedly sent to the Independent Tribunal Service had not in fact been sent. The Commissioner held that that question of fact could not be considered on an appeal because "there could be no question of unfairness arising as the claimant had been provided with the remedy of seeking set aside". It is not recorded whether or not the claimant was offered an oral hearing of the application for setting aside, which would have been

2.508

unusual. It may still be arguable that a finding made on such an application without an oral hearing is not sufficient to remove a Commissioner's jurisdiction to consider the same issue on an appeal.

In *CG/2973/2004*, the Commissioner held a tribunal decision to be erroneous in point of law because medical evidence sent by the claimant in support of an application for an adjournment had not been received by the tribunal. He also held that the fact that the claimant had unsuccessfully tried to have the decision set aside on the same ground did not prevent her from taking the point on appeal to a Commissioner. He observed that the chairman who had refused to set the decision aside had done so on the basis that her presence could not have made any difference to the outcome of her hearing. The case is therefore distinguishable from *CSDLA/303/1998*. The fact that the applicant's presence would not have made any difference is a matter that can legitimately be taken into account when considering whether "it appears just to set the decision aside" and it would also be relevant to the question whether there had been a breach of the rules of natural justice, but the Commissioner disagreed with the chairman's view of the possible importance of the claimant's evidence.

An appeal against *CG/2973/2004* was dismissed by the Court of Appeal (*Levy v Secretary of State for Work and Pensions* [2006] EWCA Civ 890 (reported as *R(G) 2/06*)), but the relevance of the claimant's application under reg.57 was not the subject of argument in the Court of Appeal.

Tribunals are entitled to take a robust approach to the non-appearance of parties and to proceed to hear cases in their absence, but a necessary concomitant of such a robust approach must be a greater preparedness to set aside decisions under reg.57(1(b) (*Cooke v Glenrose Fish Co* [2004] I.C.R. 1188).

Paragraph (1) specifically provides that, even where the conditions of sub-para. (a) or (b) are satisfied, a decision need be set aside only if it is "just". This is consistent with the European Convention on Human Rights. Under the Convention, a person who did not receive notice of a hearing is not entitled as of right to have the decision set aside, unless he has a real prospect of success on a rehearing (*Akram v Adam* [2004] EWCA Civ 1601; [2005] 1 W.L.R. 2762).

If a case is reheard by a differently constituted tribunal, it is usual for the decision that has been set aside to be included in the papers. That is not inappropriate. Even if their findings of fact cannot be relied upon, issues identified by the first tribunal may well be of assistance to the new tribunal, although it must be careful not to be influenced by the discredited findings (*Swash v Secretary of State for the Home Department* [2006] EWCA Civ 1093; [2007] 1 W.L.R. 1264). There may, however, be special circumstances in which the legally qualified panel member setting the first decision aside considers that the interests of justice require the case to be heard by a tribunal that has not seen that decision and he or she will be able to issue appropriate directions to ensure that that happens (*ibid.*).

[¹ Provisions common to regulations 56 and 57

57A.—(1) [² . . .]

(2) There shall be no appeal against a correction made under regulation 56 or a refusal to make such a correction or against a determination given under regulation 57.

(3) Nothing in this Chapter shall be construed as derogating from any power to correct errors or set aside decisions which is exercisable apart from these Regulations.]

AMENDMENTS

1. Social Security and Child Support (Decisions and Appeals) (Miscellaneous Amendments) Regulations 2002 (SI 2002/1379), reg.19 (May 20, 2002).

2. Social Security, Child Support and Tax Credits (Miscellaneous Amendments) Regulations 2005 (SI 2005/337), reg.2(15) (March 18, 2005).

(SI 1999/991, reg.57AA)

[¹ Service of decision notice by electronic mail

57AA. For the purposes of the time limits in regulations 53 to 57, a properly addressed copy of a decision notice sent by electronic mail is effective from the date it is sent.]

AMENDMENT

1. Social Security, Child Support and Tax Credits (Miscellaneous Amendments) Regulations 2005 (SI 2005/337), reg.2(16) (March 18, 2005).

[¹ Interpretation of Chapter V

57B.—(1) In Chapter V, except in regulations 58 and 58A—
"Commissioner" includes Child Support Commissioner;
"decision" includes a determination on a referral.
(2) In Chapter V—
"decision notice" has the meaning given in regulation 53(1) and (2).]

AMENDMENT

1. Social Security, Child Support and Tax Credits (Miscellaneous Amendments) Regulations 2005 (SI 2005/337), reg.2(17) (March 18, 2005).

DEFINITION

"Commissioner"—see s.39(1) of the Social Security Act 1998.

Applications for leave to appeal to a Commissioner (not including child support)

Application for leave to appeal to a Commissioner from an appeal tribunal

58.—(1) [³ Subject to paragraph (1A),] an application for leave to appeal to a Commissioner from a decision of an appeal tribunal under [² section 13 of the 1997 Act or under] section 12 or 13 shall—
(a) be [² sent to the clerk to the appeal tribunal within the period of one month of the date of the applicant being sent] a written statement of the reasons for the decision against which leave to appeal is sought; and
[³ (b) be in writing and signed by the applicant or, where he has given written authority to a representative to make the application on his behalf, by that representative;
(c) contain particulars of the grounds on which the applicant intends to rely;
(d) contain sufficient particulars of the decision of the appeal tribunal to enable the decision to be identified; and
(e) if the application is made late, contain the grounds for seeking late acceptance.
(1A) Where after the written statement of the reasons for the decision has been sent to the parties to the proceedings—
(a) the decision notice is corrected in accordance with regulation 56; or
(b) an application under regulation 57 for the decision to be set aside is refused for reasons other than a refusal to extend the time for making the application,
the period specified in paragraph (1)(a) shall run from the date on which notice of the correction or the refusal of the application for setting aside is sent to the applicant.]

(2) Where an application for leave to appeal to a Commissioner is made by the Secretary of State [¹or the Board], the clerk to an appeal tribunal shall, as soon as may be practicable, send a copy of the application to every other party to the proceedings.

(3) [² . . .]

[² (4) A person determining an application for leave to appeal to a Commissioner shall record his determination in writing and send a copy to every party to the proceedings.]

(5) Where there has been a failure to apply for leave to appeal within the period of time specified in paragraph (1)(a) [³ 01 (1A)] but an application is made within one year of the last date for making an application within that period, a legally qualified panel member may, if for special reasons he thinks fit, accept and proceed to consider and determine the application.

[² (6) Where an application for leave to appeal against a decision of an appeal tribunal is made—
(a) if the person who constituted, or was the chairman of, the appeal tribunal when the decision was given was a fee-paid legally qualified panel member, the application may be determined by a salaried legally qualified panel member; or
(b) if it is impracticable, or it would be likely to cause undue delay, for the application to be determined by whoever constituted, or was the chairman of, the appeal tribunal when the decision was given, the application may be determined by another legally qualified panel member.]

AMENDMENTS

1. Tax Credits (Decisions and Appeals) (Amendment) Regulations 1999 (SI 1999/2570), reg.27 (October 5, 1999). Note that amendments made by these regulations only have effect with respect to tax credit (reg.1(2) of the Amendment Regulations).

2. Social Security and Child Support Decisions and Appeals) (Miscellaneous Amendments) Regulations 2002 (SI 2002/1379), reg.20, with effect from May 20, 2002.

3. Social Security, Child Support and Tax Credits (Miscellaneous Amendments) Regulations 2005 (SI 2005/337), reg.2(18) (March 18, 2005).

DEFINITIONS

"the 1997 Act"—see reg.1(3).
"appeal tribunal"—see s.39(1) of the Social Security Act 1998.
"the Board"—see reg.1(3).
"clerk to the appeal tribunal"—*ibid*.
"Commissioner"—see s.39(1) of the Social Security Act 1998.
"legally qualified panel member"—see reg.1(3).
"party to the proceedings"—*ibid*.

GENERAL NOTE

Para.(1)

2.513 No provision is made for an appeal to be brought against a decision when there is no statement of reasons. In practice, if the application is made within the time for requesting a statement of reasons, the application will be treated as such a request. The problems arise where the application is received too late and no statement of reasons is issued. In *R(IS) 11/99*, it was held that a tribunal chairman had no jurisdiction under the previous legislation to consider an application for leave to appeal if there was no full statement of the tribunal's decision. It was also held that a

(SI 1999/991, reg. 58)

Commissioner did have jurisdiction, but that was doubted in *CIS/4437/1998*. Under the new legislation the position is clearer. A panel member cannot grant leave to appeal if there is no written statement of reasons (because the date of issue of such a statement is the date from which time runs) but, under reg.9 of the Social Security Commissioners (Procedure) Regulations 1999, an application may be made to a Commissioner not only when one has been "refused" by a panel member but also when one has been "rejected" (e.g. for want of jurisdiction) (*CSDLA/536/1999*).

An application may be made by fax (*CDLA/4895/2001*). It is no longer necessary to send a copy of the statement of reasons with the application but it is necessary to ensure that the application enables the decision being challenged to be identified. The tribunal's reference number should be sufficient but, where there the applicant has had more than one case in the previous year, it may still be a good idea to send the statement of reasons so that there is no doubt as to the decision being challenged.

Para. (5)

There is a broad discretion to extend the time for appealing where that is necessary to enable justice to be done. The approach of the Court of Appeal in *R. v Secretary of State for the Home Department Ex p. Mehta* [1975] 1 W.L.R. 1087 was followed in *R(M) 1/87* and it was held that it was wrong to consider only whether there were special reasons for the delay in applying for leave to appeal. In *CCS/2064/1999*, it was suggested that relevant factors included the strength of the grounds of appeal, the amount of money involved, whether the decision affected current entitlement, whether there was an adequate alternative remedy, the difficulties that the lapse of time might create for making any further findings of fact and the way in which the parties had conducted the case, including their respective contributions to delay. However, in *R(Howes) v Social Security Commissioner* [2007] EWHC 559 (Admin), Black J, in rejecting an argument that deciding whether there were special reasons required consideration of the factors listed in r.3.9 of the Civil Procedure Rules 1998 (SI 1998/3182), also disapproved of judge-made lists of relevant considerations and said that "[t]he concept of special reasons is a broad and flexible one and the factors that are relevant will be dependent upon the circumstances of the individual case". The amount of delay is likely to be relevant in most cases but, in *CSDLA/71/1999*, the Commissioner made it plain that "special reasons" for admitting a late application for leave to appeal would not necessarily be found merely because the application was made only two or three days late, even if the applicant had an arguable case on the merits. In that case, the applicant was not helped by the fact that the original explanation for the delay advanced by his representative turned out not to be true and the Commissioner refused leave to appeal.

2.514

Para. (6)

The new version of this paragraph legitimises the practice of all applications for leave to appeal being considered by full-time legally-qualified panel members.

2.515

[¹ Appeal to a Commissioner by a partner

58A. A partner within the meaning of section 2AA(7) of the Administration Act (full entitlement to certain benefits conditional on work-focused interview for partner) may appeal to a Commissioner under section 14 from a decision of an appeal tribunal in respect of a decision specified in section 2B(2A) and (6) of the Administration Act.]

2.516

AMENDMENT

1. Social Security, Child Support and Tax Credits (Miscellaneous Amendments) Regulations 2005 (SI 2005/337), reg.2(19) (March 19, 2005).

Social Security and Child Support (Decisions and Appeals) Regs 1999

DEFINITIONS

"the Administration Act"—see reg.1(3).
"appeal tribunal"—*ibid.*
"Commissioner"—see s.39 of the Social Security Act 1998.

GENERAL NOTE

2.517 This regulations, made under s.14(3)(b) of the Social Security Act 1998, is necessary because a partner does not fall within the term "claimant" in s.14(3)(b).

PART VI

REVOCATIONS

Revocations

2.518 **59.**—(1) The Regulations listed in column (2) of Schedule 4 are hereby revoked to the extent specified in column (3) of that Schedule.

(2) Notwithstanding their revocation for particular purposes, the Regulations listed in column (2) of Schedule 4 shall continue to have full effect up to and including November 28, 1999 in relation to any benefit to which these Regulations do not apply for the time being by virtue of regulation 1(2).

(3) So much of any document as refers expressly or by implication to any regulation revoked by paragraph (1) shall, in so far as the context permits, for the purposes of these Regulations be treated as referring to the corresponding provision of these Regulations.

SCHEDULE 1

2.519 PROVISIONS CONFERRING POWERS EXERCISED IN MAKING THESE REGULATIONS

Column (1) Provision		Column (2) Relevant Amendments
Vaccine Damage Payments Act 1979	Section 4(2) and (3)	The Act, Section 46
Child Support Act 1991	Section 7A(1)	The Act, Section 47
	Section 16(6)	The Act, Section 40
	Section 20(5) and (6)	The Act, Section 42
	Section 28ZA(2)(b) and (4)(c)	The Act, Section 43
	Section 28ZB(6)(c)	The Act, Section 43
	Section 28ZC(7)	The Act, Section 44
	Section 28ZD(1) and (2)	The Act, Section 44
	Section 46B	The Act, Schedule 7, paragraph 44
	Section 51(2)	The Act, Schedule 7, paragraph 46
	Schedule 4A, paragraph 8	The Act, Schedule 7, paragraph 53
Social Security Administration Act 1992	Section 5(1)(hh)	The Act, Section 74
	Section 159	The Act, Schedule 7, paragraph 95

(SI 1999/991, Sch.1)

Column (1) Provision		Column (2) Relevant Amendments
	Section 159A	The Act, Schedule 7, paragraph 96
Pension Schemes Act 1993	Section 170(3)	The Act, Schedule 7, paragraph 131
Social Security (Recovery of Benefits) Act 1997	Section 10	The Act, Schedule 7, paragraph 149
	Section 11(5)	
Social Security Act 1998	Section 6(3)	
	Section 7(6)	
	Section 9(1), (4) and (6)	
	Section 10(3) and (6)	
	Section 11(1)	
	Section 12(2) and (3), (6) and (7)	
	Section 14(10)(a) and (11)	
	Section 16(1) and Schedule 5	
	Section 17	
	Section 18(1)	
	Section 20	
	Section 21(1) to (3)	
	Section 22	
	Section 23	
	Section 24	
	Section 25(3)(b) and (5)(c)	
	Section 26(6)(c)	
	Section 28(1)	
	Section 31(2)	
	Section 79(1) and (3) to (7)	
	Section 84	
	Schedule 1, paragraphs 7, 11 and 12	
	Schedule 2, paragraph 9	
	Schedule 3, paragraphs 1, 4 and 9	

SCHEDULE 2   **Regulation 27**

DECISIONS AGAINST WHICH NO APPEAL LIES

Child benefit

1. A decision of the Secretary of State as to whether an educational establishment be recognised for the purposes of Part IX of the Contributions and Benefits Act.

2. A decision of the Secretary of State to recognise education provided otherwise than at a recognised educational establishment.

3. A decision of the Secretary of State made in accordance with the discretion conferred upon him by the following provisions of the Child Benefit (Residence and Persons Abroad) Regulations 1976—

(a) regulation 2(2)(c)(iii) (decision relating to a child's temporary absence abroad);

(b) regulation 7(3) (certain days of absence abroad disregarded).

4. A decision of the Secretary of State made in accordance with the discretion conferred upon him by regulation 2(1) or (3) of the Child Benefit (General) Regulations 1976 (provisions relating to contributions and expenses in respect of a child).

Claims and payments

[5 **5.** A decision, being a decision of the Secretary of State unless specified below as a decision of the Board, under the following provisions of the Claims and Payments Regulations—

[8 (a) regulation 4(3) or (3B) (which partner should make a claim for income support or jobseeker's allowance);]

(b) [8 . . .];

[8 (bb) regulation 4D(7) (which partner should make a claim for state pension credit);]

2.520

2.521

Social Security and Child Support (Decisions and Appeals) Regs 1999

    (c) [⁸ . . .];
    (d) [⁸ . . .];
    (e) [⁸ . . .];
    (f) regulation 7 (decision by the Secretary of State or the Board as to evidence and information required);
    (g) regulation 9 and Schedule 1 (decision by the Secretary of State or the board as to interchange of claims with claims for other benefits);
    (h) regulation 11 (treating claim for maternity allowance as claim for incapacity benefit);
    (i) regulation 15(7) (approving form of particulars required for determination of retirement pension questions in advance of claim);
    (j) regulations 20 to 24 (decisions by the Secretary of State or the Board as to the time and manner of payments);
    (k) regulation 25(1) (intervals of payment of attendance allowance and disability living allowance where claimant is expected to return to hospital);
    (l) regulation 26 (manner and time of payment of income support);
    (m) regulation 26A (time and intervals of payment of jobseeker's allowance);
[⁷ (mm) regulation 26B (payment of state pension credit);]
    (n) regulation 27(1) and (1A) (decision by the Board as to manner and time of payment of tax credits);
    (o) regulation 30 (decision by the Secretary of State or the Board as to claims or payments after death of claimant);
    (p) regulation 30A (payment of arrears of joint-claim jobseeker's allowance where nominated person can no longer be traced);
    (q) regulation 31 (time and manner of payment of industrial injuries gratuities);
    (r) regulation 32 (decision by the Secretary of State or the Board where person unable to act);
    (s) regulation 33 (appointments by the Secretary of State or the Board where person unable to act);
    (t) regulation 34 (decision by the Secretary of State or the Board as to paying another person on a beneficiaries behalf);
    (u) regulation 34A(1) (payment, out of benefit, of mortgage interest to qualifying lender);
    (v) regulation 35(2) (payment to third person of maternity expenses or expenses for heating in cold weather);
    (w) regulation 36 (decision by the Secretary of State or the Board to pay partner as alternative payee);
    (x) regulation 38 (decision by the Secretary of State or the Board as to the extinguishment of right to payment of sums by way of benefit where payment not obtained within the prescribed period, except a decision under paragraph (2A) (payment requested after expiration of prescribed period));
    (y) regulations 42 to 46 (mobility component of disability living allowance and disability living allowance for children;
    (z) regulation 47(2) and (3) (return of instruments of payment etc. to the Secretary of State or the Board).]

Contracted out pension schemes

2.522   **6.** A decision of the Secretary of State under section 109 of the Pension Schemes Act 1993 or any Order made under it (annual increase of guaranteed minimum pensions).

Decisions depending on other cases

2.523   **7.** A decision of the Secretary of State under section 25 or 26 (decisions and appeals depending on other cases).

Deductions

2.524   **8.** A decision which falls to be made by the Secretary of State under the Fines (Deductions from Income Support) Regulations 1992, other than [¹ a decision whether benefit is sufficient for a deduction to be made].

    9.—(1) Except in relation to a decision to which sub-paragraph (2) applies, any decision of the Secretary of State under the Community Charges (Deductions from Income Support) (No.2) Regulations 1990, the Community Charges (Deductions from Income Support) (Scotland) Regulations 1989 or the Council Tax (Deductions from Income Support) Regulations 1993.

    (2) This sub-paragraph applies to a decision—
        (a) whether there is an outstanding sum due of the amount sought to be deducted;

(SI 1999/991, Sch.2)

   (b) whether benefit is sufficient for a deduction to be made; and
   (c) on the priority to be given to any deduction.

European Community regulations

10. An authorization given by the Secretary of State in accordance with article 22(1) or (1) of Council Regulation (EEC) No.1408/71 on the application of social security schemes to employed persons, to self-employed persons and to members of their families moving within the Community.   2.525

Expenses

11. A decision of the Secretary of State whether to pay expenses to any person under section 180 of the Administration Act.   2.526

Guardian's allowance

12. A decision of the Secretary of State relating to the giving of a notice under regulation 5(8) of the Social Security (Guardian's Allowance) Regulations 1975 (children whose surviving parents are in prison or legal custody).   2.527

Income support

13. A decision of the Secretary of State [³...] made in accordance with paragraph (1) or (2) of regulation 13 (income support and social fund determinations on incomplete evidence).   2.528

[6 State pension credit

13A. A decision of the Secretary of State made in accordance with paragraph (1) or (3) of regulation 13 in relation to state pension credit (determination on incomplete evidence).]   2.529

Industrial injuries benefit

14. A decision of the Secretary of State relating to the question whether—   2.530
   (a) disablement pension be increased under section 104 of the Contributions and Benefits Act (constant attendance); or
   (b) disablement pension be further increased under section 105 of the Contributions and Benefits Act (exceptionally severe disablement);
and if an increase is to be granted or renewed, the period for which and the amount at which it is payable.

15. A decision of the Secretary of State under regulation 2(2) of the Social Security (Industrial Injuries and Diseases) Miscellaneous Provisions Regulations 1986 as to the length of any period of interruption of education which is to be disregarded.

16. A decision of the Secretary of State to approve or not to approve a person undertaking work for the purposes of regulation 17 of the Social Security (General Benefit) Regulations 1982.

17. A decision of the Secretary of State as to how the limitations under Part VI of Schedule 7 to the Contributions and Benefits Act on the benefit payable in respect of any death are to be applied in the circumstances of any case.

Invalid vehicle scheme

18. A decision of the Secretary of State relating to the issue of certificates under regulation 13 of, and Schedule 2 to, the Social Security (Disability Living Allowance) Regulations 1991.   2.531

Jobseeker's allowance

19.—(1) A decision of the Secretary of State under Chapter IV of Part II of the Jobseeker's Allowance Regulations as to the day and the time a claimant is to attend at a job centre.   2.532

(2) A decision of the Secretary of State as to the day of the week on which a claimant is required to provide a signed declaration under regulation 24(10) of the Jobseeker's Allowance Regulations.

(3) A decision of the Secretary of State [³...] made in accordance with regulation 15 (Jobseeker's allowance determinations on incomplete evidence).

[⁵ Loss of Benefit for Breach of Community Order

19A. A decision of the Secretary of State that a relevant benefit shall not be payable or shall be reduced in accordance with a determination of a court made under section 62(1) of the Child Support, Pensions and Social Security Act 2000 where the only ground of appeal is that the court's determination was made in error.]   2.533

Social Security and Child Support (Decisions and Appeals) Regs 1999

Payments on account, overpayments and recovery

2.534　20. A decision of the Secretary of State under the Social Security (Payments on account, Overpayments and Recovery) Regulations 1988, except a decision of the Secretary of State under the following provisions of those Regulations—
  (a) regulation 3(1)(a) to offset any interim payment made in anticipation of an award of benefit;
  (b) regulation 4(1) as to the overpayment of an interim payment;
  (c) regulation 5 as to the offsetting of a prior payment against a subsequent award;
  (d) regulation 11(1) as to whether a payment in excess of entitlement has been credited to a bank or other account;
  (e) regulation 13 as to the sums to be deducted in calculating recoverable amounts;
  (f) regulation 14(1) as to the treatment of capital to be reduced;
  (g) regulation 19 determining a claimant's protected earnings; and
  (h) regulation 24 whether a determination as to a claimant's protected earnings is revised or superseded.

Persons abroad

2.535　21. A decision of the Secretary of State made under—
  (a) regulation 2(1)(a) of the Social Security Benefit (Persons Abroad) Regulations 1975 whether to certify that it is consistent with the proper administration of the Contributions and Benefits Act that a disqualification under section 113(1)(a) of that Act should not apply;
  (b) regulation 9(4) or (5) of those Regulations whether to allow a person to avoid disqualification for receiving benefit during a period of temporary absence from Great Britain longer than that specified in the regulation.

Reciprocal Agreements

2.536　22. A decision of the Secretary of State made in accordance with an Order made under section 179 of the Administration Act (reciprocal agreements with countries outside the United Kingdom).

Social fund awards

2.537　23. A decision of the Secretary of State under section 78 of the Administration Act relating to the recovery of social fund awards.

Suspension

2.538　24. A decision of the Secretary of State relating to the suspension of a relevant benefit or to the payment of such a benefit which has been suspended under Part III.

Up-rating

2.539　25. A decision of the Secretary of State relating to the up-rating of benefits under Part X of the Administration Act.

[²26. Any decision treated as a decision of the Secretary of State whether or not to waive or defer a work-focused interview.]

Loss of Benefit

2.540　[⁴ 27. A decision of the Secretary of State that a sanctionable benefit as defined in section 7(8) of the Social Security Fraud Act 2001 is not payable, or is to be reduced, pursuant to section 7, 8 or 9 of that Act as a result of convictions for one or more benefit offences in each of two sets of proceedings, one offence being committed within 3 years of conviction for another, where the only ground of appeal is that any of the convictions was erroneous.]

AMENDMENTS

1. Social Security Act 1998 (Commencement No.12 and Consequential and Transitional Provisions) Order 1999 (SI 1999/3178), art.3(19) and Sch.19, para.2 (November 29, 1999).

2. Social Security (Work-focused Interviews) Regulations 2000 (SI 2000/897), reg.16(5) and Sch.6, para.7 (April 3, 2000).

(SI 1999/991, Sch. 2)

3. Social Security and Child Support (Miscellaneous Amendments) Regulations 2000 (SI 2000/1596), reg.34 (June 19, 2000).
4. Social Security (Loss of Benefit) Regulations 2001 (SI 2001/4022), reg.21 (April 1, 2002).
5. Social Security and Child Support (Decisions and Appeals) (Miscellaneous Amendments) Regulations 2002 (SI 2002/1379), reg.21 (May 20, 2002).
6. State Pension Credit (Consequential, Transitional and Miscellaneous Provisions) Regulations 2002 (SI 2002/3019), reg.21 (April 7, 2003).
7. State Pension Credit (Decisions and Appeals – Amendments) Regulations 2003 (SI 2003/1581), reg.2 (June 18, 2003).
8. Social Security, Child Support and Tax Credits (Decisions and Appeals) Regulations 2004 (SI 2004/3368), reg.2(9) (December 21, 2004).

DEFINITIONS

"the Administration Act"—see s.84 of the Social Security Act 1998.
"the Claims and Payments Regulations"—see reg.1(3).
"the Contributions and Benefits Act"—see s.84 of the Social Security Act 1998.
"decision"—see reg.27(2).
"the Jobseeker's Allowance Regulations"—see reg.1(3).
"relevant benefit"—see s.39(1) of the Social Security Act 1998.
"state pension credit"—see reg.1(3).
"work-focused interview"—*ibid.*

GENERAL NOTE

Before December 21, 2004, para.5(a) to (e) had the effect that decisions under regs 4, 4A, 4D and 6 of the Social Security (Claims and Payments) Regulations 1987 as to whether a claim had been properly made were unappealable and that was also the effect of the original form of para.5 that was replaced from May 20, 2002. Now the only decisions under those regulations that are not appealable are decisions as to which of two partners should make claims where the partners do not agree.

If reg.27 is made under s.12(2) of the Social Security Act 1998, it is arguable that much of Sch.2 to the Regulations is ultra vires, having regard to s.12(3). It is not easy to see why, for instance, a decision of the Secretary of State that an educational establishment be recognised for the purposes of child benefit or to recognise education provided otherwise than at such a recognised establishment (paras 1 and 2 of Sch.2) is not a decision "that relates to the conditions of entitlement" to child benefit. The fact that a large element of discretion is involved is not material. There is no reason in principle why such a discretion should not be exercised by a tribunal. There may be sound reasons for restricting the rights of appeal in cases where there is a large element of pure discretion, so that any challenge has to be by way of application for revision under s.9 or for judicial review, and, of course, there was no right of appeal under the old legislation, but it is arguable that neither of those considerations carries much weight against the clear language of s.12(3). On the other hand, it is arguable that reg.27 is made under para.9 of Sch.2 to the Act, which is in much broader terms than s.12. Both regulation-making powers are to be found in Sch.1 to the Regulations. What the point is in having s.12(2) qualified by s.12(3) when there is the broader unqualified power in the same Act is unclear but an argument that a broad power should be regarded as qualified by the scope of the narrower power found little sympathy in *R. v Secretary of State for Social Security, Ex p. Moore, The Times*, March 9, 1993.

The question of the validity of this Schedule has been considered in four Commissioners' decisions without any very clear resolution of these issues. In the first two cases, the Schedule was held to be valid as far as it affected the individual cases, but different grounds were given. In *CJSA/69/2001*, the Commissioner considered that this Schedule was made under s.12(2) of the 1998 Act but held that para.5 was intra vires insofar as it then prohibited any appeal against a decision by the Secretary

2.541

of State under reg.4 of the Social Security (Claims and Payments) Regulations 1987 that a claim was to be treated as not made until the claimant provided his P45. He pointed out that s.12(3) applies only in respect of a benefit for which a claim has been validly made. However, he declined to determine whether or not the claim *had* been validly made, accepting the submission of the Secretary of State that a right of appeal could arise only after the Secretary of State had decided that a claim had been validly made and that it was beyond the power of a tribunal to consider whether the condition of reg.4(1B)(b) of the 1987 Regulations (or reg.4(1B)(d) which might have been more relevant) was met. It is suggested that an alternative construction of s.12(3) would be that it is necessary for there to be a right of appeal against any decision as to whether or not a claim was valid. *CF/3565/2001*, decided a few days later by a different Commissioner who was apparently unaware of the approach taken in *CJSA/69/2001*, concerned a decision of the Secretary of State not to recognise education provided otherwise than at a recognised educational establishment, which the Commissioner held to fall within para.2 of this Schedule. The Commissioner held that this Schedule was validly made under s.12(1)(a) of, and para.9 of Sch.2 to, the 1998 Act. In fact, as was noted in *CJSA/69/2001*, s.12(1) is not listed in Sch.1 to the Regulations as being a power under which the Regulations were made, doubtless because it does not independently confer any power to make regulations. Curiously, the Commissioner in *CJSA/69/2001* stated that Sch.3 was also not listed in Sch.1 to the Regulations when it is, although it is not clear why the Commissioner mentioned it at all as it is irrelevant. Even more curiously, he did not mention para.9 of Sch.2, which *does* confer the relevant power to make regulations relied upon in *CF/3565/2001* and is also listed in Sch.1 to the Regulations. Equally, the Commissioner deciding *CF/3565/2001* did not consider the argument that the Schedule might have been made under s.12(2) of the 1998 Act. He did however reject a broader argument that the Schedule was ultra vires because it was inconsistent with the European Convention on Human Rights. He held, applying *R. (Alconbury Developments Ltd) v Secretary of State for the Environment, Transport and the Regions* [2001] UKHL 23; [2001] 2 W.L.R. 1389, that judicial review was an adequate remedy in the case before him, although he left open the question whether the Schedule would be ultra vires for the purposes of other cases.

In *R(IS) 6/04*, the Commissioner again had a challenge to para.5 in its first form and the question was whether an appeal lay against the Secretary of State's decision that the claimant had not complied with the prescribed requirements for making a valid claim. The Commissioner considered it unnecessary to say how the regulation-making power in para.9 of Sch.2 to the Act should be construed or whether para.5 of Sch.2 to the Regulations had been made under that power because he agreed with the construction of s.12 applied in *CJSA/69/2001* so that, even applying the approach more favourable to the claimant, he considered that para.5 was validly made when the Regulations first came into force. However, he held the absence of a right of appeal to be incompatible with Art.6 of the European Convention on Human Rights and so disapplied the paragraph insofar as it was necessary to do so to ensure that a claimant was entitled to appeal against a decision as to whether or when a claim had been validly made in accordance with the prescribed requirements. This restored the position to what it had been before the Social Security Act 1998 had come into force (*R(U) 9/60*). The Secretary of State withdrew an appeal to the Court of Appeal and subsequently amended para.5(a) in order to provide a right of appeal against a decision that a claim had not been validly made. It does not necessarily follow, however, that he accepted that the Commissioner's decision as to the application of Art. 6 of the Convention was correct. Indeed, in *R(H) 3/05*, leading counsel for one of the claimants acknowledged that the reasoning in *R(IS) 6/04* had been overtaken by that in *Runa Begum v Tower Hamlets London (First Secretary of State intervening)* [2003] UKHL 5; [2003] 2 A.C. 430 in which it was held by the House of Lords that there was no breach of Art. 6 of the Convention where an appeal from a local authority's decision in respect of their duties to homeless people lay only on a point of law. One possible inference to be drawn from the House of Lords' decision is that judicial review of the unappealable decisions listed in Sch.2 of these Regulations, or the similar provisions relating to housing benefit and council tax benefit in issue in *R(H)3/05*, is an adequate remedy under the Convention. However, counsel submitted that the House of Lords' conclusion in *Runa Begum*, that there was no unfairness in not having an appeal on a point of fact, was reached against the background of a system of internal review by a different officer of appropriate seniority, whereas, in housing benefit and council tax cases, such system of internal review as there had formerly been had been replaced by an appeal to a tribunal, which is the procedure available in other social security cases. In the absence of as sophisticated a system of review as there was in *Runa Begum*, he argued, there had to be a right of appeal on questions of fact. It was unnecessary for the Tribunal of Commissioners to express a view on that argument and they did not do so.

The fourth case in which an ultra vires challenge to Sch.2 was raised is *Campbell v Secretary of State for Work and Pensions* [2005] EWCA Civ 989, where the Court of Appeal agreed with a Tribunal of Commissioners that a decision under the Convention on Social Security between Great Britain and Jamaica was a decision on payability rather than entitlement, because the convention was given force by the Social Security (Jamaica) Order 1997 which was made under s.179 of the Social Security Administration Act 1992. Section 12(3) of the Social Security Act 1998 therefore did not come into play and the decision was unappealable by virtue of para.22 of Sch.2 to the Regulations, read with para.9 of Sch.2 to the Act.

In this Schedule, "decision" includes determinations embodied in or necessary to a decision (see reg.27(2)).

SCHEDULE 3   Regulations 1(3) and 35

QUALIFICATIONS OF PERSONS APPOINTED TO THE PANEL

Legal Qualifications

1. Persons who—   2.542
   (a) have a general qualification (construed in accordance with section 71 of the Courts and Legal Services Act 1990); or
   (b) are advocates or solicitors in Scotland.

Medical Qualifications

2. [2 . . .] registered medical practitioners, where—   2.543
   [2 (a) the practitioner is a citizen of an EEA state and his name appears on a medical specialist register maintained in an EEA state in accordance with the Medical Directive, or he is a Swiss citizen with equivalent qualifications; or]
   (b) the practitioner holds a vocational training certificate or a certificate of acquired rights in an EEA State other than the United Kingdom which must in his case be recognised in the United Kingdom by virtue of the Medical Directive (whether or not as read with the EEA Agreement) or by virtue of an enforceable community right; or
   (c) [2 (c) the practitioner does not satisfy the requirements of sub-paragraph (a) or (b) above, but has not less than 10 years experience in clinical practice, or as a medical disability analyst in disciplines which are the same or similar to those undertaken by practitioners to whom those sub-paragraphs apply.]

3. In paragraph 2 above and in this paragraph—

"EEA Agreement" means the Agreement of the European Economic Area signed at Oporto on May 2, 1992 as adjusted by the Protocol signed at Brussels on March 17, 1993;
"EEA State" means a state which is a contracting party to the EEA Agreement;
"Medical Directive" means Council Directive 93/16/EEC of April 5, 1993 to facilitate the free movement of doctors and the mutual recognitions of their diplomas, certificates and other evidence of formal qualifications, as amended by Council Directive 97/50/EC of October 6, 1997 [2 or any directive which replaces Directive 93/16/EEC];
"Vocational training certificate" means a diploma, certificate or other evidence of formal qualifications awarded on completion of a course of specific training in general medical practice and referred to in article 30 of the Medical Directive.

Social Security and Child Support (Decisions and Appeals) Regs 1999

Financial Qualifications

2.544　　4. Accountants who are members of—
　　　　(a) the Institute of Chartered Accountants in England and Wales;
　　　　(b) the Institute of Chartered Accountants in Scotland;
　　　　(c) the Institute of Chartered Accountants in Ireland;
　[¹(cc) the Institute of Certified Public Accountants in Ireland;]
　　　　(d) the Association of Chartered Certified Accountants;
　　　　(e) the Chartered Institute of Management Accountants; or
　　　　(f) the Chartered Institute of Public Finance and Accountancy.

Disability Qualifications

2.545　　5. Persons, other than registered medical practitioners, who are experienced in dealing with the needs of disabled persons—
　　　　(a) in a professional or voluntary capacity; or
　　　　(b) because they are themselves disabled.

AMENDMENTS

1. Social Security and Child Support (Decisions and Appeals) (Miscellaneous Amendments) Regulations 2002 (SI 2002/1379), reg.22 (May 20, 2002).
2. Social Security, Child Support and Tax Credits (Miscellaneous Amendments) Regulations 2005 (SI 2005/337), reg.2(20) (March 19, 2005).

DEFINITIONS

"EEA agreement"—see para.(3).
"EEA state"—*ibid*.
"Medical Directive"—*ibid*.
"Vocational training certificate"—*ibid*.

GENERAL NOTE

2.546　　For the role played by panel members with each type of qualification, see reg.36.

Para.1

2.547　　Any person on the roll of solicitors has a "general qualification", even if he or she does not have a practising certificate, and so does any barrister, even if the exercise of his or her rights of audience is curtailed because of the regulations of the Bar Council (*CIS/1344/2004*).

[¹SCHEDULE 3A]　　　　　　　　　　　　　　Regulation 7(1)(a)

DATE FROM WHICH SUPERSEDINL DECISION TAKES EFfECT WHERE A CLAIMANT IS IN RECEIPT OF INCOME SUPPORT OR JOBSEEKER'S ALLOWANCE.

Income Support

2.548　　1. Subject to paragraphs 2 to 6, where the amount of income support payable under an award is changed by a superseding decision made on the ground of a change of circumstances, that superseding decision shall take effect—
　　　　(a) where income support is paid in arrears, from the first day of the benefit week in which the relevant change of circumstances occurs or is expected to occur; or
　　　　(b) where income support is paid in advance, from the date of the relevant change of circumstances, or the day on which the relevant change of circumstances is expected to occur, if either of those days is the first day of the benefit week and otherwise from the next following such day, and
for the purposes of this paragraph any period of residence in temporary accommodation under arrangements for training made under section 2 of the Employment and Training Act 1973 or section 2 of the Enterprise and New Towns (Scotland) Act 1990 for a period which is expected to last for seven days or less shall not be regarded as a change of circumstances.

(SI 1999/991, Sch. 3A)

2. In the cases set out in paragraph 3, the superseding decision shall take effect from the day on which the relevant change of circumstances occurs or is expected to occur.

3. The cases referred to in paragraph 2 are where—
   (a) income support is paid in arrears and entitlement ends, or is expected to end, for a reason other than that the claimant no longer satisfies the provisions of section 124(1)(b) of the Contributions and Benefits Act;
   [²(aa) income support is being paid from 8th April 2002 to persons who, immediately before that day, had a preserved right for the purposes of the Income Support Regulations;]
   (b) a child or young person referred to in regulation 16(6) of the Income Support Regulations (child in care of local authority or detained in custody) lives, or is expected to live, with the claimant for part only of the benefit week;
   (c) [⁵ . . .]
   (d) a person referred to in paragraph 1, 2, 3 or 18 of Schedule 7 to the Income Support Regulations—
      (i) ceases, or is expected to cease, to be a patient; or
      (ii) a member of his family ceases, or is expected to cease, to be a patient, in either case for a period of less than a week;
   (e) a person referred to in paragraph 8 of Schedule 7 to the Income Support Regulations—
      (i) ceases to be a prisoner; or
      (ii) becomes a prisoner;
   (f) a person to whom section 126 of the Contributions and Benefits Act (trade disputes) applies—
      (i) becomes incapable of work by reason of disease or bodily or mental disablement; or
      (ii) enters the maternity period (as defined in section 126(2) of that Act) or the day is known on which that person is expected to enter the maternity period;
   (g) during the currency of the claim, a claimant makes a claim for a relevant social security benefit—
      (i) the result of which is that his benefit week changes; or
      (ii) under regulation 13 of the Claims and Payment Regulations and an award of that benefit on the relevant day for the purposes of that regulation means that his benefit week is expected to change;
   [⁷ (h) regulation 9 of the Social Security (Disability Living Allowance) Regulations 1991 (persons in certain accommodation other than hospitals) applies, or ceases to apply, to the claimant for a period of less than one week.]

4. A superseding decision made in consequence of a payment of income being treated as paid on a particular day under regulation 31(1)(b) [⁴ (2) or (3)] or 39C(3) of the Income Support Regulations (date on which income is treated as paid) shall take effect from the day on which that payment is treated as paid.

5. Where—
   (a) it is decided upon supersession on the ground of a relevant change of circumstances [⁵ or change specified in paragraph 12 and 13] that the amount of income support is, or is to be, reduced; and
   (b) the Secretary of State certifies that it is impracticable for a superseding decision to take effect from the day prescribed in the preceding paragraphs of this Schedule (other than where paragraph 3(g) or 4 applies),
that superseding decision shall take effect—
      (i) where the relevant change has occurred, from the first day of the benefit week following that in which that superseding decision is made; or
      (ii) where the relevant change is expected to occur, from the first day of the benefit week following that in which that change of circumstances is expected to occur.

6. Where—
   (a) a superseding decision ("the former supersession") was made on the ground of a relevant change of circumstances in the cases set out in paragraphs 3(b) to (g); and
   (b) that superseding decision is itself superseded by a subsequent decision because the circumstances which gave rise to the former supersession cease to apply ("the second change"),
that subsequent decision shall take effect from the date of the second change.

Jobseeker's Allowance

7. Subject to paragraphs 8 to 11, where a decision in respect of a claim for jobseeker's allowance is superseded on the ground that there has been or there is expected to be, a

Social Security and Child Support (Decisions and Appeals) Regs 1999

relevant change of circumstances, the supersession shall take effect from the first day of the benefit week (as defined in regulation 1(3) of the Jobseeker's Allowance Regulations) in which that relevant change of circumstances occurs or is expected to occur.

2.555 8. Where the relevant change of circumstances giving rise to the supersession is that—
(a) entitlement to jobseeker's allowance ends, or is expected to end, for a reason other than that the claimant no longer satisfies the provisions of section 3(1)(a) [² or 3A(1)(a)] of the Jobseekers Act; or
[³ (aa) jobseeker's allowance is being paid from 8th April 2002 to persons who, immediately before that day, had a preserved right for the purposes of the Jobseeker's Allowance Regulations;]
(b) a child or young person who is normally in the care of a local authority or who is detained in custody lives, or is expected to live, with the claimant for a part only of the benefit week; or
(c) [⁵ . . .]
(d) the partner of the claimant or a member of his family ceases, or is expected to cease, to be a hospital in-patient for a period of less than a week; [² or,
(e) a joint-claim couple ceases to be [⁶ couple]],
the supersession shall take effect from the date that the relevant change of circumstances occurs or is expected to occur.

2.556 9. Where the relevant change of circumstances giving rise to a supersession is any of those specified in paragraph 8, and, in consequences of those circumstances ceasing to apply, a further superseding decision is made, that superseding decision shall take effect from the date that those circumstances ceased to apply.

2.557 10. Where, under the provisions of regulation 96 or 102C(3) of the Jobseeker's Allowance Regulations, income is treated as paid on a certain date and that payment gives rise, or is expected to give rise, to a relevant change of circumstance resulting in a supersession, that supersession shall take effect from that date.

2.558 11. Where a relevant change of circumstances [⁵ or change specified in paragraphs 12 and 13] occurs which results, or is expected to result, in a reduced award of jobseeker's allowance then, if the Secretary of State is of the opinion that it is impracticable for a supersession to take effect in accordance with [⁵ paragraph 12 or] the preceding paragraphs of this Schedule, the supersession shall take effect from the first day of the benefit week following that in which the relevant change of circumstances occurs.]

[⁵*Changes other than changes of circumstances*]

2.559 12. Where an amount of income support or jobseeker's allowance payable under an award is changed by a superseding decision specified in paragraph 13 the superseding decision shall take effect—
(a) in the case of a change in respect of income support, from the day specified in paragraph 1(a) or (b) for a change of circumstances; and
(b) in the case of a change in respect of jobseeker's allowance, from the day specified in paragraph 7 for a change of circumstances.
13. The following are superseding decisions for the purposes of paragraph 12—
(a) a decision which supersedes a decision specified in regulation 6(2)(b) to (ee); and
(b) a superseding decision which would, but for paragraph 12, take effect from a date specified in regulation 7(5) to (7), (12) to (16), (18) to (20), (22), (24) and (33).]

AMENDMENTS

1. Social Security and Child Support (Miscellaneous Amendments) Regulations 2000 (SI 2000/1596), reg.35 (June 19, 2000).

2. Social Security Amendment (Joint Claim) Regulations 2001 (SI 2001/518), reg.4(c) (March 19, 2001).

3. Social Security Amendment (Residential Care and Nursing Homes) Regulations 2002 (SI 2002/398), reg.3 (April 8, 2002).

4. Social Security (Working Tax Credit and Child Tax Credit) (Consequential Amendments) (No.3) Regulations 2003 (SI 2003/1731), reg.5 (August 8, 2003).

5. Social Security, Child Support and Tax Credits (Miscellaneous Amendments) Regulations 2005 (SI 2005/337), reg.2(21) (March 19, 2005).

6. Civil Partnership (Consequential Amendments) Regulations 2005 (SI 2005/2878), reg.8(4) (December 5, 2005).

(SI 1999/991, Sch. 3A)

7. Social Security (Miscellaneous Amendments) (No. 3) Regulations 2006 (SI 2006/2377), reg. 3(3) (October 2, 2006).

DEFINITIONS

"the Claims and Payments Regulations"—see reg.1(3).
"the Contributions and Benefits Act"—see s.84 of the Social Security Act 1998.
"the Income Support Regulations"—see reg.1(3).
"the Jobseekers Act"—see s.84 of the Social Security Act 1998.
"the Jobseeker's Allowance Regulations"—see reg.1(3).
"a joint-claim couple"—*ibid.*
"superseding decision"—see para.13.

GENERAL NOTE

Paragraphs 12 and 13 have the effect that any change to an existing award of income support or jobseeker's allowance takes place from the start of a benefit week.

2.560

[¹ SCHEDULE 3B

DATE ON WHICH CHANGE OF CIRCUMSTANCES TAKES EFFECT WHERE CLAIMANT ENTITLED TO STATE PENSION CREDIT

1. Where the amount of state pension credit payable under an award is changed by a superseding decision made on the ground that there has been a relevant change of circumstances, that superseding decision shall take effect from the following days—
   (a) for the purpose only of determining the day on which an assessed income period begins under section 9 of the State Pension Credit Act, from the day following the day on which the last previous assessed income period ended; and
   (b) except as provided in the following paragraphs, from the day that change occurs or is expected to occur if either of those days is the first day of a benefit week but if it is not from the next following such day.

2.561

2. Subject to paragraph 3, where the relevant change is that the claimant's income (other than deemed income from capital) has changed, the superseding decision shall take effect on the first day of the benefit week in which that change occurs or if that is not practicable in the circumstances of the case, on the first day of the next following benefit week.

2.562

3. Paragraph 2 shall not apply where the only relevant change is that working tax credit under the Tax Credits Act 2002 becomes payable or becomes payable at a higher rate.

2.563

4. A superseding decision shall take effect from the day the change of circumstances occurs or is expected to occur if—
   (a) the person ceases to be or becomes a prisoner, and for this purpose "prisoner" has the same meaning as in regulation 1(2) of the State Pension Credit Regulations; or
   (b) whilst entitled to state pension credit a claimant is awarded another social security benefit and in consequence of that award his benefit week changes or is expected to change.

2.564

[² 5. In a case where the relevant circumstance is that the claimant ceased to be a patient, if he becomes a patient again in the same benefit week, the superseding decision in respect of ceasing to be a patient shall take effect from the first day of the week in which the change occured.]

2.565

6. In paragraph 5, "patient" means a person (other than a prisoner) who is regarded as receiving free in-patient treatment within the meaning of the Social Security (Hospital In-Patients) Regulations 1975.]

2.566

[³ 7. Where an amount of state pension credit payable under an award is changed by a superseding decision specified in paragraph 8 the superseding decision shall take effect from the day specified in paragraph 1(b).

2.567

8. The following are superseding decisions for the purposes of paragraph 7—
   (a) a decision which supersedes a decision specified in regulation 6(2)(b) to (ee) and (m); and
   (b) a superseding decision which would, but for paragraphs 2 and 7, take effect from a date specified in regulation 7(5) to (7), (12) to (16) and (29C).]

2.568

AMENDMENTS

1. State Pension Credit (Consequential, Transitional and Miscellaneous Provisions) Regulations 2002 (SI 2002/3019), reg.22 (April 7, 2003).

Social Security and Child Support (Decisions and Appeals) Regs 1999

2. State Pension Credit (Transitional and Miscellaneous Provisions) Amendment Regulations 2003 (SI 2003/2274), reg.5(4) (October 6, 2003).

3. Social Security (Miscellaneous Amendments) (No.2) Regulations 2006 (SI 2006/832), reg.5(4) (April 10, 2006).

DEFINITIONS

"assessed income period"—see reg.1(3).
"patient"—see para.6.
"state pension credit"—*ibid.*
"State Pension Credit Act"—*ibid.*
"State Pension Credit Regulations"—*ibid.*

GENERAL NOTE

2.569   The misspelling of what should read as "occurred" in para.5 occurs in the Queen's Printer's copy of the statutory instrument.

SCHEDULE 4   **Regulation 59**

2.570   [REVOCATIONS]

Column 1 Statutory Instrument Number	Column 2 Statutory Instrument	Column 3 Provision Revoked
1979/432	The Vaccine Damage Payments Regulations 1979	Part III
1992/2641	The Child Support Appeal Tribunals (Procedure) Regulations 1992	The whole Regulations
1995/311	The Social Security (Incapacity for Work) (General) Regulations 1995	Regulations 19 and 20 to 22
1995/1801	The Social Security (Adjudication) Regulations 1995	The whole Regulations
1996/182	The Social Security (Adjudication) and Child Support Amendment Regulations 1996	Regulation 2
1996/425	The Social Security (Industrial Injuries and Diseases) (Miscellaneous Amendments) Regulations 1996	Regulation 2
1996/1518	The Social Security (Adjudication) Amendment Regulations 1996	The whole Regulations
1996/2306	The Social Security (Claims and Payments and Adjudication) Amendment Regulations 1996	Regulations 8 and 9
1996/2450	The Social Security (Adjudication) and Child Support Amendment (No.2) Regulations 1996	Regulations 2 to 13
1996/2659	The Social Security (Adjudication Amendment (No.2) Regulations 1996	The whole Regulations
1997/65	The Income-Related Benefits and Jobseeker's Allowance (Miscellaneous Amendments) Regulations 1997	Regulation 16
1997/793	The Social Security (Miscellaneous Amendments) (No.2) Regulations 1997	Regulations 1(2)(a) and 8 to 17
1997/810	The Social Security (Industrial Injuries) (Miscellaneous Amendments) Regulations 1997	Regulations 2, 3 and 4
[[1]1997/955]	The Social Security (Adjudication) and Commissioners Procedure and Child	In regulation 1(2), the definition of "the Adjudication Regulations"

(SI 1999/991, Sch. 4)

Column 1 Statutory Instrument Number	Column 2 Statutory Instrument	Column 3 Provision Revoked
	Support Commissioners (Procedure) Amendment Regulations 1997	and regulation 2 to 6
1997/1839	The Social Security (Attendance Allowance and Disability Living of "the Adjudication Allowance) (Miscellaneous Regulations" and regulation 4 Amendments) Regulations 1997	In regulation 1(2) the definition of "the Adjudication Regulations" and regulation 4
1997/2237	The Social Security (Recovery of Benefits) (Appeals) Regulations 1997	The whole Regulations
1997/2305	The Social Security (Miscellaneous Amendments) (No.4) Regulations 1997	Regulation 4

AMENDMENT

1. Social Security and Child Support (Decisions and Appeals) Amendment (No.2) Regulation 1999 (SI 1999/1623), reg.7 (July 5, 1999).

The Social Security (General Benefit) Regulations 1982

(SI 1982/1408) (AS AMENDED)

ARRANGEMENT OF REGULATIONS

PART I

General

1. Citation, commencement and interpretation.
2. Exceptions from disqualification for imprisonment etc.
3. Suspension of payment of benefit during imprisonment etc.
4. Interim payments by way of benefit under the Act.

2.571

The Secretary of State for Social Services, in exercise of the powers conferred upon him by sections 50(4), 56(7), 57(5), 58(3), 60(4) and (7), 61(1), 62(2), 67(1), 68(2), 70(2), 72(1) and (8), 74(1), 81(6), 82(5) and (6), 83(1), 85(1), 86(2) and (5), 90(2), 91(1), 119(3) and (4) and 159(3) of, and paragraphs 2, 3 and 6 of Schedule 8, paragraphs 1 and 8 of Schedule 9 and Schedule 14 of the Social Security Act 1975 and of all other powers enabling him in that behalf, hereby makes the following regulations, which only consolidate the regulation hereby revoked, and which accordingly, by virtue of paragraph 20 of Schedule 3 to the Social Security Act 1980, are not subject to the requirements of section 10 of that Act for prior reference to the Social Security Advisory Committee and, by virtue of section 141(2) and paragraph 12 of Schedule 16 of the Social Security Act 1975, do not require prior reference to the Industrial Injuries Advisory Council:—

The Social Security (General Benefit) Regulations 1982

Part I

General

Citation, commencement and interpretation

2.572
1.—(1) These regulations may be cited as the Social Security (General Benefit) Regulations 1982 and shall come into operation on 4th November, 1982.
(2) In these regulations, unless the context otherwise requires—
"the Act" means the Social Security Act 1975;
[³ 'bereavement benefit' means a benefit referred to in section 20(1)(ea) of the Social Security Contributions and Benefits Act 1992;]
"the Child Benefit Act" means the Child Benefit Act 1975;
"child benefit" means benefit under Part I of the Child Benefit Act;
[¹ "determining authority" means, as the case may require, the Secretary of State, an appeal tribunal constituted under section 7 of the Social Security Act 1998, the Chief or any other Social Security Commissioner appointed under Schedule 4 to that Act, or a tribunal consisting of any three or more such Commissioners constituted in accordance with section 16(7) of that Act;]
"entitled to child benefit" includes treated as so entitled;
"industrial injuries benefit" means [². . .] disablement benefit and industrial death benefit payable under section 50 of the Act;
"parent" has the meaning assigned to it by section 24(3) of the Child Benefit Act;
[⁴ "shared additional pension" means a shared additional pension under section 55A of the Social Security Contributions and Benefits Act 1992;]
"standard rate of increase" means the amount specified in Part IV or Part V of Schedule 4 to the Act as the amount of an increase of the benefit in question for an adult dependant;
"the Workmen's Compensation Act" means the Workmen's Compensation Acts 1925 to 1945, or the enactments repealed by the Workmen's Compensation Act 1925 or the enactments repealed by the Workmen's Compensation Act 1906;
and other expressions have the same meanings as in the Act.
(3) Unless the context otherwise requires, any reference in these regulation—
(a) to a numbered section is to the section of the Act bearing that number;
(b) to a numbered regulation is a reference to the regulation bearing that number in these regulations and any reference in a regulation to a numbered paragraph is a reference to the paragraph of that regulation bearing that number.

Amendments

1. The Social Security Act 1998 (Commencement No.8, and Savings and Consequential and Transitional Provisions) Order 1999 (SI 1999/1958), Sch.5 (July 4, 1999).
2. The Social Security (Abolition of Injury Benefit) (Consequential) Regulations 1983 (SI 1983/186), reg.13 (April 6, 1983).
3. The Social Security (Benefits for Widows and Widowers) (Consequential Amendments) Regulations 2000 (SI 2000/1483), reg.8 (April 9, 2001).
4. The Social Security (Shared Additional Pension) (Miscellaneous Amendments) Regulations 2005 (SI 2005/1551) (July 6, 2005).

(SI 1982/1408, reg. 2) (as amended)

Exceptions from disqualification for imprisonment etc.

2.—(1) The following provisions of this regulation shall have effect to except benefit from the operation of [section 113(1)(b) of the Social Security Contributions and Benefits Act 1992] which provides that (except where regulations otherwise provide) a person shall be disqualified for receiving any benefit and an increase of benefit shall not be payable in respect of any person as the beneficiary's [[8] spouse or civil partner], for any period during which that person is undergoing imprisonment or detention in legal custody (hereinafter in this regulation referred to as "the said provisions").

(2) The said provisions shall not operate to disqualify a person for receiving [[1]incapacity benefit], [[2]attendance allowance, disability living allowance], widow's benefit, [[6] bereavement benefit,] child's special allowance, maternity allowance, [[7] a shared additional pension] retirement pension of any category, age addition, [[3]severe disablement allowance], [[4]. . .disablement benefit], [[5]. . .reduced earnings allowance, retirement allowance] or industrial death benefit or to make an increase of benefit not payable in respect of a person as the beneficiary's [[8] spouse or civil partner], for any period during which that person is undergoing imprisonment or detention in legal custody in connection with a charge brought or intended to be brought against him in criminal proceedings, or pursuant to any sentence or order for detention made by a court in such proceedings, unless, in relation to him, a penalty is imposed at the conclusion of those proceedings or, in the case of default of payment of a sum adjudged to be paid on conviction, a penalty is imposed in respect of such default.

(3) The said provisions shall not operate to disqualify a person for receiving any benefit (not being a guardian's allowance or death grant), or to make an increase of benefit not payable in respect of a person as the beneficiary's [[8] spouse or civil partner], for any period during which that person is undergoing detention in legal custody after the conclusion of criminal proceedings if it is a period during which he is liable to be detained in a hospital or similar institution in Great Britain as a person suffering from mental disorder unless—

[[9] (a) he is detained or liable to be detained under section 45A of the Mental Health Act 1983 (hospital and limitation directions) or section 59A of the Criminal Procedure (Scotland) Act 1995 (hospital direction); or

(b) he is detained or liable to be detained under section 47 of the Mental Health Act 1983 (removal to hospital of persons serving sentences of imprisonment, etc.) or section 136 of the Mental Health (Care and Treatment) (Scotland) Act 2003 (transfer of prisoners for treatment for mental disorder).]

(4) Where, as respects a person in relation to whom [[9] paragraph (3)(a) or (b)] is satisfied, a certificate given by or on behalf of the Secretary of State [[9] or Scottish Ministers] shows the earliest date on which that person would have been expected to be discharged from the detention pursuant to the said sentence or order if he had not been transferred to a hospital or similar institution, the said conditions shall be deemed not to be satisfied in relation to that person as from the day next following that date.

(5) The said provisions shall not operate to disqualify a person for receiving a guardian's allowance or death grant.

The Social Security (General Benefit) Regulations 1982

[5(6) Subject to paragraph (7), the said provisions shall not operate to disqualify a person for receiving disablement benefit, other than any increase of that benefit, for any period during which he is undergoing imprisonment or detention in legal custody.]

(7) The amount payable by virtue of the last preceding paragraph by way of any disablement pension or pensions in respect of any period, other than a period in respect of which that person is excepted from disqualification by virtue of the provisions of paragraph (3) of this regulation, during which that person is and has continuously been undergoing imprisonment or detention in legal custody, shall not exceed the total amount payable by way of such pension or all such pensions for a period of one year.

(8) For the purposes of this regulation—
   (a) "court" means any court in the United Kingdom, the Channel Islands or the Isle of Man or in any place to which the Colonial Prisoners Removal Act 1884 applies or any naval court-martial, army court-martial or air force court-martial within the meaning of the Courts-Martial (Appeals) Act 1968, or the Courts-Martial Appeal Court;
   (b) "hospital or similar institution" means any place (not being a prison, a detention centre, a Borstal institution, a young offenders institution or a remand centre, and not being at or in any such place) in which persons suffering from mental disorder are or may be received for care or treatment;
   (c) "penalty" means a sentence of imprisonment, Borstal training or detention under section 53 of the Children and Young Persons Act 1933 or under section 57(3) of the Children and Young Persons (Scotland) Act 1937 or under section 208(3) and 416(4) of the Criminal Proceedings (Scotland) Act 1975 or an order for detention in a detention centre;
   (d) in relation to a person who is liable to be detained in Great Britain as a result of any order made under the Colonial Prisoners Removal Act 1884, references to a prison shall be construed as including references to a prison within the meaning of that Act;
   (e) [9. . .]
   (f) [9. . .]
   (g) criminal proceedings against any person shall be deemed to be concluded upon his being found insane in those proceedings so that he cannot be tried or his trial cannot proceed.

(9) Where a person outside Great Britain is undergoing imprisonment or detention in legal custody and, in similar circumstances in Great Britain, he would have been excepted, by the operation of any of the preceding paragraphs of this regulation, from disqualification under the said provisions (referred to in paragraph (1)) for receiving the benefit claimed, he shall not be disqualified for receiving that benefit by reason only of his said imprisonment or detention.

(10) Paragraph (9) applies to increases of benefit not payable under the said provisions as it applied to disqualification for receiving benefit.

AMENDMENTS

1. The Social Security (Incapacity Benefit) (Consequential and Transitional Amendments and Savings) Regulations 1995 (SI 1995/829), reg. 16 (April 13, 1995).

2. The Disability Living Allowance and Disability Working Allowance (Consequential Provisions) Regulations 1991 (SI 1991/2742), reg.11 (April 6, 1992).

3. The Social Security (Severe Disablement Allowance) Regulations 1984 (SI 1984/1303), reg.11 (November 29, 1984).

4. The Social Security (Abolition of Injury benefit) (Consequential) Regulations 1983 (SI 1983/186), reg.13 (April 6, 1983).

5. The Social Security (Industrial Injuries and Diseases) (Miscellaneous Amendments) Regulations 1996 (SI 1996/425), reg.4 (March 24, 1996).

6. The Social Security (Benefits for Widows and Widowers) (Consequential Amendments) Regulations 2000 (SI 2000/1483), reg.6 (April 9, 2001).

7. The Social Security (Shared Additional Pension) (Miscellaneous Amendments) Regulations 2005 (SI 2005/1551) (July 6, 2005).

8. The Social Security (Civil Partnership) (Consequential Amendments) Regulations 2005 (SI 2005/2878) (December 5, 2005).

9. The Social Security (Hospital In-Patients) Regulations 2005 (SI 2005/3360), reg.3 (April 10, 2006).

Definitions

"the Act": reg.1.
"benefit": C & BA 1992, s.122.
"court": para.(8)(a).
"Great Britain": by Art.1 of the Union with Scotland Act 1706, this means England, Scotland and Wales.
"hospital or similar institution": para.(8)(b).
"penalty": para.(8)(c).
"the said provisions": para.(1).

General Note

Persons who can bring themselves within the terms of this regulation can escape the disqualification from benefit provided for in s.113(1)(b) of the Contributions and Benefits Act. Different rules apply to different benefits.

Under para.(2) the disqualification applies in cases of imprisonment in connection with criminal proceedings where such penalty is imposed at the conclusion of proceedings. Imprisonment outside the exercise of criminal jurisdiction does not disqualify from benefit: *R(S)8/79*. It is now established that "penalty" in this paragraph includes the imposition of a suspended sentence and that a suspended sentence amounts to a sentence of imprisonment: *R(S)1/71*.

Paragraph (3) deals with the transfer of offenders from prison to hospital as mental patients under the mental health legislation. The disqualification in such circumstances exists only for the length of the original sentence: *R(P)2/57* reversing *R(S)9/56*. Provision is made for the Secretary of State to issue a certificate which is conclusive as to the earliest date on which the original sentence would come to an end had the person not been transferred to hospital.

References to the Mental Health Act 1959 should now be read as references to the Mental Health Act 1983.

Suspension of payment of benefit during imprisonment etc.

3.—(1) Subject to the following provisions of this regulation, the payment to any person of any benefit—
  (a) which is excepted from the operation of [section 113(1)(b) of the Social Security Contributions and Benefits Act 1992] by virtue of the provisions of regulation 2(2), (5) and (6) or by any of those paragraphs as applied by regulation 2(9); or

2.574

2.575

(b) which is payable otherwise than in respect of a period during which he is undergoing imprisonment or detention in legal custody;

shall be suspended while that person is undergoing imprisonment or detention in legal custody.

(2) Paragraph (1) shall not operate to require the payment of any benefit to be suspended while the beneficiary is liable to be detained in a hospital or similar institution as defined in regulation 2(8)(b) during a period for which in his case, benefit to which regulation 2(3) applies is or would be excepted from the operation of the said [section 113(1)] by virtue of the provision of regulation 2(3).

(3) A guardian's allowance or death grant, or any benefit to which paragraph (1)(b) applies may nevertheless be paid while the beneficiary is undergoing imprisonment or detention in legal custody to any person appointed for the purpose by the Secretary of State to receive and deal with any sums payable on behalf of the beneficiary on account of that benefit, and the receipt of any person so appointed shall be a good discharge to the Secretary of State and the National Insurance Fund for any sum so paid.

(4) Where, by virtue of this regulation, payment of benefit under [Part V of the Social Security Contribution and Benefits Act 1992] is suspended for any period, the period of suspension shall not be taken into account in calculating any period under the provisions of regulation 22 of the Social Security (Claims and Payments) Regulations 1979 (extinguishment of right to sums payable by way of benefit which are not obtained within the prescribed time).

Interim payments by way of benefit under the Act

2.576

4.—(1) Where, under arrangements made by the Secretary of State with the consent of the Treasury, payment by way of benefit has been made pending determination of a claim for it without due proof of the fulfilment of the relevant conditions or otherwise than in accordance with the provisions of the Act and orders and regulations made under it, the payment so made shall, for the purposes of those provisions, but subject to the following provisions of this regulation, be deemed to be a payment of benefit duly made.

(2) When a claim for benefit in connection with which a payment has been made under arrangements such as are referred to in paragraph (1) above is determined by a determining authority—
  (a) if that authority decides that nothing was properly payable by way of the benefit in respect of which the payment was made or that the amount properly payable by way of that benefit was less than the amount of the payment, it may, if appropriate, direct that the whole or part of the overpayment be treated as paid on account of benefit (whether benefit under the Act or the Supplementary Benefits Act 1976) which is properly payable, but subject as aforesaid shall require repayment of the overpayment; and
  (b) if that authority decides that the amount properly payable by way of the benefit in respect of which the payment was made equals or exceeds the amount of that payment, it shall treat that payment as paid on account of the benefit properly payable.

(3) Unless before a payment made under arrangements such as are mentioned in paragraph (1) above has been made to a person that person had been

(SI 1982/1408, reg.4) (as amended)

informed of the effect of sub-paragraph (a) of paragraph (2) above as it relates to repayment of an overpayment, repayment of an overpayment shall not be required except where the determining authority is satisfied that[1] he, or any person acting for him, has, whether fraudulently or otherwise, misrepresented or failed to disclose any material fact and that the interim payment has been made in consequence of the misrepresentation or failure.]

(4) An overpayment required to be repaid under the provisions of this regulation shall, without prejudice to any other method of recovery, be recoverable by deduction from any benefit then or thereafter payable to the person by whom it is to be repaid or any persons entitled to receive his benefit on his death.

AMENDMENT

1. The Social Security (Payments on account, Overpayment and Recovery) Regulations 1987 (SI 1987/491), reg.19 (April 6, 1987).

GENERAL NOTE

This regulation has not been repealed by the Overpayments Regulations because its provisions will still be needed for cases where the relevant determination was made before April 6, 1987. As time passes the provision will fall into disuse, and will in due course be revoked.

The Social Security (Incapacity Benefit Work-focused Interviews) Regulations 2003

(SI 2003/2439)

ARRANGEMENT OF REGULATIONS

1. Citations and commencement
2. Interpretation
3. Requirement for a relevant person entitled to a specified benefit to take part in an interview
4. Continuing entitlement to a specified benefit dependent upon an interview
5. The interview
6. Waiver of requirement to take part in an interview
7. Deferment of requirement to take part in an interview
8. Exemptions
9. Taking part in an interview
10. Failure to take part in an interview
11. Good cause
12. Appeals
13. Amendment to the Income Support (General) Regulations 1987 *(omitted)*
14. Amendment to the Housing Benefit (General) Regulations 1987 *(omitted)*
15. Amendment to the Council Tax Benefit (General) Regulations 1992 *(omitted)*
16. Amendment to the Jobseeker's Allowance Regulations 1996 *(omitted)*
17. Amendment to the Social Security (Jobcentre Plus Interviews) Regulations 2002 *(omitted)*

The Social Security (Incapacity Benefit Work-focused Interviews) Regs 2003

SCHEDULE

GENERAL NOTE

2.579   This new set of work-focused interview regulations joins the following work-focused interview regulations currently in force:
The Social Security (Work-focused Interviews for Lone Parents) and Miscellaneous Amendments Regulations 2000 (SI 2000/1926).
The Social Security (Jobcentre Plus Interviews) Regulations 2002 (SI 2002/1703).
All the work-focused interview regulations are designed to encourage those claiming benefit to return to work. This new scheme is introduced following the Green Paper, *Pathways to Work. Helping People into Employment,* Cm 5690 (November 2002). A claimant already caught by the existing regulations will be exempt from an interview under the new regulations. The scheme originally applied only to new claimants aged between 18 and 60 claiming a specified benefit, but the amendments extend the scheme to existing claimants. For existing claimants there is a lighter touch in that only three, rather than six, interviews are required.
The scheme introduced by these regulations follows the pattern set by the earlier regulations but has three stages: the initial interview, a boosted interview, and a follow up stage. Claimant are obliged not just to attend an interview, but to 'take part in' an interview; this involves answering specified questions, participating in discussion, and assisting the interview in the completion of an action plan. Failure to do so can result in a penalty deduction equal to 20 per cent of the applicable amount for a single adult claimant.

2.580   The Secretary of State for Work and Pensions, in exercise of the powers conferred upon him by sections 123(1)(a), (d) and (e), 136(3) and (5)(b), 137(1) and 175(3) and (4) of the Social Security Contributions and Benefits Act 1992, sections 2A(1), (3) to (6) and (8), 2B(6) and (7), 189(4) to (6) and (7A) and 191 of the Social Security Administration Act 1992 and sections 12(1) and (4)(b), 35(1) and 36(2) and (4) of the Jobseekers Act 1995 and of all other powers enabling him in that behalf, after consultation with the Council on Tribunals in accordance with section 8(1) of the Tribunals and Inquiries Act 1992 and in respect of provisions in these Regulations relating to housing benefit and council tax benefit with organisations appearing to him to be representative of the authorities concerned and after reference to the Social Security Advisory Committee, hereby makes the following Regulations:

Citation and commencement

2.581   1. These Regulations may be cited as the Social Security (Incapacity Benefit Work-focused Interviews) Regulations 2003 and shall come into force on 27th October 2003.

Interpretation

2.582   2. In these Regulations—
"benefit week" means any period of seven days corresponding to the week in respect of which the relevant specified benefit is due to be paid;
"interview" means a work-focused interview with a relevant person who has claimed a specified benefit and which is conducted for any or all of the following purposes—

(SI 2003/2439, reg. 2)

   (a) assessing that relevant person's prospects for existing or future employment (whether paid or voluntary);
   (b) assisting or encouraging that relevant person to enhance his prospects of such employment;
   (c) identifying activities which that relevant person may undertake to strengthen his existing or future prospects of employment;
   (d) identifying current or future employment, training or rehabilitation opportunities suitable to that relevant person's needs;
   (e) identifying educational opportunities connected with the existing or future employment prospects or needs of that relevant person;

"officer" means a person who is an officer of, or who is providing services to or exercising functions of, the Secretary of State;

"personal capability assessment" means the assessment defined in Part III of the Social Security (Incapacity for Work) (General) Regulations 1995 (personal capability assessment);

"relevant decision" has the meaning given by section 2B(2) of the Social Security Administration Act 1992 (supplementary provisions relating to work-focused interviews);

[2 "relevant person" means—
   (a) a person to whom paragraph (b) does not apply and who—
      (i) resides in an area identified in—
         (aa) Part 1 of the Schedule to these Regulations and who makes a claim for a specified benefit on or after 27th October 2003,
         (bb) Part 2 [3 or Part 6] of that Schedule and who makes such a claim on or after 5th April 2004,
         (cc) Part 3 of that Schedule and who makes such a claim on or after 31st October 2005,
         (dd) Part 4 of that Schedule and who makes such a claim on or after 24th April 2006, or
         (ee) Part 5 of that Schedule and who makes such a claim on or after 30th October 2006; or
      [4 (ff) Part 7 of that Schedule and who makes a claim on or after 29th December 2006 at an office of the Department for Work and pensions which is designated by the Secretary of State as a Pathways to Work office; or]
      (ii) resides in an area identified in—
         (aa) Part 1 of the Schedule to these Regulations and who made a claim for a specified benefit on or after 27th October [3 1997] but before 27th October 2003, or
         (bb) Part 2 of that Schedule and who made such a claim on or after 5th April [3 1998] but before 5th April 2004, [3 or
         (cc) Part 6 of that Schedule and who made such a claim before 5th April 2004,]
and who is entitled to a specified benefit under that claim; or
   (b) a person who would fall within both heads (i) and (ii) of paragraph (a) and who—
      (i) does not make a claim for a specified benefit on or after 7th February 2005, or
      (ii) makes a claim for a specified benefit on or after 7th February 2005;]

The Social Security (Incapacity Benefit Work-focused Interviews) Regs 2003

"specified benefit" means—
- (a) incapacity benefit;
- (b) income support where paragraph 7 (persons incapable of work) of Schedule 1B to the Income Support (General) Regulations 1987 applies;
- [2 (c) income support where paragraph 24 or 25 (persons appealing against a decision which embodies a determination that they are not incapable of work) of Schedule 1B to the Income Support (General) Regulations 1987 applies; or]
- (d) severe disablement allowance.

AMENDMENTS

1. The Social Security (Incapacity Benefit Work-focused Interviews) Amendments Regulations 2005 (SI 2005/3), reg.2 (February 7, 2005).
2. The Social Security (Incapacity Benefit Work-focused Interviews) Amendment (No.2) Regulations 2005 (SI 2005/2604) (October 31, 2005).
3. The Social Security (Incapacity Benefit Work-focused Interviews) Amendment Regulations 2006 (SI 2006/536) (April 3, 2006).
4. The Social Security (Incapacity Benefit Work-focused Interviews) Amendment (No.2) Regulations 2006 (SI 2006/3088) (December 29, 2006).

[1 **Persons who move home**

2A. —(1) This regulation applies to a person who, on or after 29th December 2006,—
- (a) ceases to reside in an area identified in one of the Parts of the Schedule to these Regulations, and
- (b) immediately begins residing in an area identified in a different Part of that Schedule ("the new area").

(2) Where paragraph (4) or (5) applies, the person shall be treated as continuing to fall within whichever of paragraphs (a)(i), (a)(ii), (b)(i) or (b)(ii) of the definition of "relevant person" he fell within before he began residing in the new area.

(3) Where neither paragraph (4) nor (5) applies, the person shall cease to be a relevant person.

(4) This paragraph applies where paragraph (a)(i) or (b)(i) of the definition of "relevant person" applies to the person and the new area is an area identified in—
- (a) Parts 1 to 6 of that Schedule, or
- (b) Part 7 of that Schedule and his award of a specified benefit is administered in respect of the new area from an office of the Department for Work and Pensions which is designated by the Secretary of State as a Pathways to Work office.

(5) This paragraph applies where—
- (a) paragraph (a)(ii) or (b)(ii) of the definition of "relevant person" applies to the person, and
- (b) the new area is an area identified in Part 1, 2 or 6 of that Schedule.]

AMENDMENT

1. The Social Security (Incapacity Benefit Work-focused Interviews) Amendment (No.2) Regulations 2006 (SI 2006/3088) (December 29, 2006).

(SI 2003/2439, reg. 3)

Requirement for a relevant person entitled to a specified benefit to take part in an interview

3.—(1) Subject to [1 paragraphs (2) and (2A) below and regulations 6 to 8] a relevant person who—
   (a) is entitled to a specified benefit; and
[1 (b) has attained the age of 18 but has not attained the age of 60—
      (i) in respect of a relevant person to whom paragraph (a)(i) or (b)(i) of the definition of "relevant person" applies, on the day on which he makes his claim for that specified benefit; or
      (ii) in respect of a relevant person to whom paragraph (a)(ii) or (b)(ii) of the definition of "relevant person" applies, on 7th February 2005,]
   shall be required to take part in an interview as a condition of his continuing to be entitled to the full amount of the specified benefit which is payable to him.

(2) A relevant person who
   (a) has taken part in an interview under paragraph (1) above by virtue of—
      (i) being; or
      (ii) having been,
   entitled to a specified benefit; and
   (b) becomes entitled to—
      (i) another specified benefit; or
      (ii) the same specified benefit where sub-paragraph (a)(ii) applies; and
   (c) has not—
      (i) been engaged in remunerative work; or
      (ii) made a claim for a jobseeker's allowance,
   after having been entitled to the specified benefit referred to in sub-paragraph (a) above and before becoming entitled to the specified benefit referred to in sub-paragraph (b) above,
shall not be required to take part in a further interview under paragraph (1) above.

[1 (2A) A relevant person who becomes entitled to two or more specified benefits and has not taken part in an interview under paragraph (1) above by virtue of that entitlement—
   (a) is only required to take part in one interview under that paragraph; and
   (b) that interview counts for the purposes of all those benefits.]

[1 (3) An officer shall arrange for the interview referred to in paragraph (1) above to take place—
   (a) in respect of a relevant person to whom paragraph (a)(i) or (b)(i) of the definition of "relevant person" applies, after the expiry of eight weeks after the date the claim for a specified benefit is made or as soon as is reasonably practicable thereafter; or
   (b) in respect of a relevant person to whom paragraph (a)(ii) or (b)(ii) of the definition of "relevant person" applies, on a date the officer determines.]

2.583

AMENDMENT

1. The Social Security (Incapacity Benefit Work-focused Interviews) Amendments Regulations 2005 (SI 2005/3), reg.2 (February 7, 2005).

Continuing entitlement to a specified benefit dependent upon an interview

4.—(1) Subject to paragraph (2) below and regulations 6 to 8 a relevant person who—
   (a) has taken part in an interview under regulation 3;
   (b) is entitled to a specified benefit; and
   (c) has not attained the age of 60,

shall be required to take part in [¹ a sequence of further interviews as provided for by paragraph (1A) below], each at, or as soon as is reasonably practicable after, the expiry of one month from the day he last took part in an interview, the day he was treated under regulation 6 as having complied with such a requirement to take part in an interview or, as the case may be, the day a relevant decision was made under regulation 9(4), as a condition of his continuing to be entitled to the full amount of the specified benefit which is payable to him.

[¹ (1A) A relevant person to whom—
   (a) paragraph (a)(i) or (b)(i) of the definition of "relevant person" applies shall be required to take part in a sequence of five further interviews;
   (b) paragraph (a)(ii) or (b)(ii) of the definition of "relevant person" applies shall be required to take part in a sequence of two further interviews.]

(2) A relevant person who—
   (a) has taken part in one or more interviews under paragraph (1) above by virtue of—
      (i) being; or
      (ii) having been,
      entitled to a specified benefit; and
   (b) becomes entitled to—
      (i) another specified benefit; or
      (ii) the same specified benefit where sub-paragraph (a)(ii) applies; and
   (c) has not—
      (i) been engaged in remunerative work; or
      (ii) made a claim for a jobseeker's allowance,
      after having been entitled to the specified benefit referred to in sub-paragraph (a) above and before becoming entitled to the specified benefit referred to in sub-paragraph (b) above,

shall be required to continue to take part in the sequence of interviews in accordance with paragraph (1) until he has taken part in a total of five [¹ or, as the case may be, two] such interviews.

(3) Subject to regulations 6 and 7, where a relevant person—
   (a) has taken part in the five [¹ or, as the case may be, two] further interviews referred to in paragraph (1) above;
   (b) is entitled to a specified benefit; and
   (c) has not attained the age of 60,

he shall be required to take part in an interview as a condition of his continuing to be entitled to the full amount of the specified benefit which is payable to him where any of the circumstances specified in paragraph (6) below apply or where paragraph (7) below applies.

(4) Subject to regulations 6 and 7, where a relevant person—

(SI 2003/2439, reg. 4)

(a) has had the requirement to take part in [¹ the five or, as the case may be, two] interviews referred to in paragraph (1) above waived in accordance with regulation 6;
(b) is entitled to a specified benefit; and
(c) has not attained the age of 60,

he shall be required to take part in an interview as a condition of his continuing to be entitled to the full amount of the specified benefit which is payable to him where any of the circumstances specified in paragraph (6) below apply or where paragraph (7) below applies.

(5) Subject to regulations 6 and 7, where—
[¹ (a) a relevant person falls within paragraph (a)(i) or (b)(i) of the definition of "relevant person";
(aa) regulation 8 applies to the relevant person;]
(b) the relevant person is entitled to a specified benefit; and
(c) the relevant person has not attained the age of 60,

he shall be required to take part in an interview as a condition of his continuing to be entitled to the full amount of the specified benefit which is payable to him where any of the circumstances specified in paragraph (6) below apply or where paragraph (7) below applies.

(6) The circumstances specified in this paragraph are those where—
(a) it is determined in accordance with a personal capability assessment that a relevant person is incapable of work and therefore, continues to be entitled to a specified benefit;
(b) a relevant person's entitlement to a carer's allowance ceases whilst his entitlement to a specified benefit continues;
(c) a relevant person becomes engaged or ceases to be engaged in part-time work; or
(d) a relevant person has been undergoing education, training or a rehabilitation programme arranged by an officer and that education, training or rehabilitation programme comes to an end.

(7) A requirement to take part in an interview arises under this paragraph where a relevant person has not been required to take part in an interview under paragraphs (3) to (5) above for at least 36 months from the date he last took part in an interview.

AMENDMENT

1. The Social Security (Incapacity Benefit Work-focused Interviews) Amendments Regulations 2005 (SI 2005/3), reg.2 (February 7, 2005).

The interview

5.—(1) The officer shall inform a relevant person who is required to take part in an interview of the time and place of the interview.

(2) An officer shall conduct the interview.

(3) The officer may determine that an interview is to take place in the relevant person's home where it would, in the officer's opinion, be unreasonable to expect that relevant person to attend elsewhere because that relevant person's personal circumstances are such that attending elsewhere would cause him undue inconvenience or endanger his health.

2.585

Waiver of requirement to take part in an interview

6.—(1) A requirement imposed by these Regulations to take part in an interview shall not apply where an officer determines that an interview would not be—
   (a) of assistance to the relevant person concerned; or
   (b) appropriate in the circumstances.

(2) A relevant person in relation to whom a requirement to take part in an interview has been waived under paragraph (1) above shall be treated for the purposes of—
   (a) regulation 3 or 4; and
   (b) entitlement to a specified benefit,
as having complied with that requirement in respect of that interview.

Deferment of requirement to take part in an interview

7.—(1) An officer may determine, in the case of a relevant person, that the requirement to take part in an interview shall be deferred at the time the requirement to take part in an interview arises or applies because an interview would not at that time be—
   (a) of assistance to that relevant person; or
   (b) appropriate in the circumstances.

(2) Where the officer determines in accordance with paragraph (1) above that the requirement to take part in an interview shall be deferred, he shall also determine when that determination is made, the time when the requirement to take part in an interview is to apply in the relevant person's case.

(3) Where a requirement to take part in an interview has been deferred in accordance with paragraph (1) above, then until—
   (a) a determination is made under regulation 6(1);
   (b) the relevant person takes part in an interview; or
   (c) a relevant decision has been made in relation to that relevant person in accordance with regulation 9(4),
that relevant person shall be treated for the purposes of entitlement to a specified benefit as having complied with that requirement.

Exemptions

[1 **8.** A relevant person to whom—
   (a) paragraph (a)(i) or (b)(i) of the definition of "relevant person" applies, shall be exempt form the requirement to take part in any interview under regulation 4(1);
   (b) paragraph (a)(ii) or (b)(ii) of the definition of "relevant person" applies, shall be exempt from the requirement to take part in any interview under regulation 3(1) or 4, if, on the day on which the requirement to take part in that interview arises or applies, the relevant person is treated as incapable of work in accordance with the provisions of regulation 10 of the Social Security (Incapacity for Work) (General) Regulations 1995 (certain persons with a severe condition to be treated as incapable of work).]

AMENDENT

1. The Social Security (Incapacity Benefit Work-focused Interviews) Amendments Regulations 2005 (SI 2005/3), reg.2 (February 7, 2005).

(SI 2003/2439, reg. 9)

Taking part in an interview

9.—(1) The officer shall determine whether a relevant person has taken part in an interview.

(2) A relevant person shall be regarded as having taken part in an interview referred to in regulation 3 if—
  (a) he attends for the interview at the place and time notified to him by the officer;
  (b) he participates in discussions with the officer in relation to the relevant person's employability, including any action the relevant person and the officer agree is reasonable and they are willing to take in order to help the relevant person enhance his employment prospects;
  (c) he provides answers (where asked) to questions and appropriate information about—
    (i) details of and the level to which he has pursued any educational qualifications;
    (ii) his employment history;
    (iii) his aspirations for future employment;
    (iv) any vocational training he has undertaken;
    (v) any skills he has acquired which fit him for employment;
    (vi) any vocational training or skills which he wishes to undertake or acquire;
    (vii) any paid or unpaid employment he is engaged in;
    (viii) the extent to which his medical condition, in his opinion, restricts his ability to obtain or puts him at a disadvantage in obtaining employment;
    (ix) his work related abilities; and
    (x) any caring or childcare responsibilities he has; and
  (d) he assists the officer in the completion of an action plan which records the matters discussed in relation to sub-paragraph (b) above.

(3) A relevant person shall be regarded as having taken part in any one of the interviews referred to in regulation 4 if—
  (a) he attends for the interview at the place and time notified to him by the officer;
  (b) he participates in discussions with the officer—
    (i) in relation to the relevant person's employability or any progress he might have made towards obtaining employment;
    (ii) about any action the relevant person or the officer might have taken as a result of the matters discussed in relation to paragraph (2)(b) above;
    (iii) about how, if at all, the action plan referred to in paragraph (2)(d) above should be amended; and
    (iv) in order to consider any of the programmes and support available to help the relevant person obtain employment;
  (c) he provides answers (where asked) to questions and appropriate information about—
    (i) the content of any report made following his personal capability assessment, insofar as that report relates to the relevant person's capabilities and employability; and
    (ii) his opinion as to the extent to which his medical condition restricts his ability to obtain employment; and

(d) he assists the officer in the completion of any amendment of the action plan referred to in paragraph (2)(d) above in light of the matters discussed in relation to sub-paragraph (b) above and the information provided in relation to sub-paragraph (c) above.

(4) Where an officer determines that a relevant person has failed to take part in an interview and good cause has not been shown for that failure within five working days of the day on which the interview was to take place, a relevant decision shall be made for the purposes of section 2B of the Social Security Administration Act 1992.

Failure to take part in an interview

10.—(1) A relevant person in respect of whom a relevant decision has been made in accordance with regulation 9(4) shall, subject to paragraph (12) below, suffer the consequences specified in paragraph (2) below.

(2) The consequences specified in this paragraph are, subject to paragraphs (3) and (4) below, that the relevant person's benefit shall be reduced as from the first day of the next benefit week following the day a relevant decision was made, by a sum equal to 20 per cent. of the amount applicable on the date the first reduction commences in respect of a single claimant for income support aged not less than 25.

(3) Benefit reduced in accordance with paragraph (2) above shall not be reduced below ten pence per week.

(4) Where two or more specified benefits are in payment to a relevant person, a reduction made in accordance with paragraph (2) above shall be applied, except in a case to which paragraph (5) below applies, to the specified benefits in the following order of priority—

(a) income support;
(b) incapacity benefit;
(c) severe disablement allowance.

(5) Where the amount of the reduction is greater than some, but not all, of the specified benefits listed in paragraph (4) above, the reduction shall be made against the first benefit in that list which is the same as, or greater than, the amount of the reduction.

(6) For the purpose of determining whether a specified benefit is the same as, or greater than, the amount of the reduction for the purposes of paragraph (5) above, ten pence shall be added to the amount of the reduction.

(7) In a case where the whole of the reduction cannot be applied against any one specified benefit because the amount of no one benefit is the same as, or greater than, the amount of the reduction, the reduction shall be applied against the first benefit in payment in the list of priorities in paragraph (4) above and so on against each benefit in turn until the whole of the reduction is exhausted or, if this is not possible, the whole of the specified benefits are exhausted, subject in each case to ten pence remaining in payment.

(8) Where the rate of any specified benefit payable to a relevant person changes, the rules set out above for a reduction in the benefit payable shall be applied to the new rates and any adjustments to the benefits against which the reductions are made shall take effect from the beginning of the first benefit week to commence for that relevant person following the change.

(9) Paragraph (1) above shall apply to a relevant person each time a relevant decision is made in accordance with regulation 9(4) in respect of him.

(SI 2003/2439, reg.10)

(10) Where a relevant person whose benefit has been reduced in accordance with paragraph (2) above subsequently takes part in an interview, the whole of the reduction shall cease to have effect on the first day of the benefit week in which the requirement to take part in an interview was met.

(11) For the purposes of determining the amount of any benefit payable, a relevant person shall be treated as receiving the amount of any specified benefit which would have been payable but for a reduction made in accordance with paragraph (2) above.

(12) The consequences specified in paragraph (2) above shall not apply to a person who—
  (a) brings new facts to the notice of the Secretary of State within one month of the date on which a relevant decision was notified to him and—
     (i) those facts could not reasonably have been brought to the Secretary of State's notice within five working days of the day on which the interview was to take place; and
     (ii) those facts show that he had good cause for his failure to take part in the interview;
  (b) is no longer required to take part in an interview as a condition for continuing to be entitled to the full amount of the specified benefit which is payable to him apart from these Regulations; or
  (c) attains the age of 60.

Good cause

11. Matters to be taken into account in determining whether a relevant person has shown good cause for his failure to take part in an interview include—
  (a) that the relevant person misunderstood the requirement to take part in the interview due to any learning, language or literacy difficulties of the relevant person or any misleading information given to the relevant person by the officer;
  (b) that the relevant person was attending a medical or dental appointment, or accompanying a person for whom the relevant person has caring responsibilities to such an appointment, and that it would have been unreasonable, in the circumstances, to rearrange the appointment;
  (c) that the relevant person had difficulties with his normal mode of transport and that no reasonable alternative was available;
  (d) that the established customs and practices of the religion to which the relevant person belongs prevented him from attending on the day or at the time fixed for the interview;
  (e) that the relevant person was attending an interview with an employer with a view to obtaining employment;
  (f) that the relevant person was pursuing employment opportunities as a self-employed earner;
  (g) that the relevant person or a dependant of his or a person for whom he provides care suffered an accident, sudden illness or relapse of a physical or mental health condition;
  (h) that the relevant person was attending the funeral of a relative or close friend on the day fixed for the interview;
  (i) that a disability from which the relevant person suffers made it impossible for him to attend at the time fixed for the interview.

2.591

The Social Security (Incapacity Benefit Work-focused Interviews) Regs 2003

Appeals

2.592   **12.**—(1) This regulation applies to any relevant decision under regulation 9(4) or any decision made under section 10 of the Social Security Act 1998 (decisions superseding earlier decisions) superseding such a relevant decision.

(2) This regulation applies whether the decision is as originally made or as revised under section 9 of the Social Security Act 1998 (revision of decisions).

(3) In the case of a decision to which this regulation applies, the relevant person in respect of whom the decision was made shall have a right of appeal under section 12 of the Social Security Act 1998 (appeal to appeal tribunal) to an appeal tribunal.

Regs 13-17 omitted.

SCHEDULE

PART I

2.593   1. For the purposes of regulation 2 the areas are—
   (a) the areas of—
   Amber Valley Borough Council;
   Bolsover District Council excluding the postcode districts of S43 4, NG19 7 and S80 4;
   Chesterfield Borough Council;
   Derby City Council;
   Derbyshire Dales District Council excluding the postcode districts of S32 and S33;
   Erewash Borough Council;
   High Peak Borough Council excluding the postcode districts of S32 and S33;
   North East Derbyshire District Council excluding the postcode districts of S12 3A, S12 3B, S12 3D, S12 3E, S12 3F, S12 3G, S12 3H, S12 3J, S12 3L, S12 3U, S12 3XA, S12 3XB, S12 3XE, S12 3XH, S12 3XL, S12 3XQ, S17 3 and S11 7;
   South Derbyshire District Council;
   (b) the following postcode districts—
   CF31;
   CF32 excluding the following parts: CF32 OP, CF32 OQ, CF32 OR, CF32 OS, CF32 OTA, CF32 OTB, CF32 OTD, CF32 OTE, CF32 OTF, CF32 OTH, CF32 OTL, CF32 OTN;
   CF33 excluding the following parts: CF33 6PS, CF33 6PT, CF33 6PU, CF33 6RA, CF33 6RB, CF33 6RD, CF33 6RL;
   CF34;
   CF35 excluding the following parts: CF35 5AB, CF35 5AD, CF35 5AE, CF35 5AF, CF35 5AG, CF35 5AH, CF35 5AL, CF35 5AN, CF35 5AR, CF35 5AS, CF35 5AY, CF35 5BA, CF35 5BB, CF35 5BD, CF35 5BE, CF35 5BG, CF35 5BH, CF35 5BJ, CF35 5BL, CF35 5BN, CF35 5BP, CF35 5BQ, CF35 5BW, CF35 5BY, CF35 5BZ, CF35 5DA, CF35 5DD, CF35 5DE, CF35 5DF, CF35 5DG, CF35 5DH, CF35 5DL, CF35 5DN, CF35 5DP, CF35 5DR, CF35 5DS, CF35 5DT, CF35 5DU, CF35 5DW, CF35 5DY, CF35 5EA, CF35 5EB, CF35 5ED, CF35 5EE, CF35 5EF, CF35 5EG, CF35 5HY, CF35 5RG, CF35 5RH, CF35 5S;
   CF36 to CF45;
   CF72 8 excluding the following parts: CF72 8JU to CF72 8JZ;
   CF72 9;
   CF15 7 excluding the following parts: CF15 7A, CF15 7H, CF15 7JL to CF15 7JZ, CF15 7L, CF15 7NH to CF15 7NX, CF15 7UG to CF15 7UW, CF15 7W to CF15 7Z;
   FK20 8SB;
   G78;
   G82 5BT, G82 5EN, G82 5EP, G82 5ER to G82 5ET, G82 5EW to G82 5EZ, G82 5HB, G82 5HD to G82 5HH, G82 5HL, G82 5HN, G82 5HQ, G82 5HW, G82 5JH,

(SI 2003/2439, Sch.)

G82 5JJ, G82 5JQ, G82 5JT, G82 5JU, G82 5JW to G82 5JZ, G82 5L, G82 5N, G82 5P to G82 5Q, G82 5Y;
G83 7A, G83 7B, G83 7DA, G83 7DB, G83 7DD to G83 7DH, G83 7DJ, G83 7DL, G83 7DN, G83 7DP to G83 7DU, G83 7DW, G83 7E, G83 7Y, G83 8NT, G83 8NU, G83 8NX to G83 8NZ, G83 8PA, G83 8PB, G83 8PD to G83 8PG, G83 8RA, G83 8RB, G83 8RD to G83 8RH, G83 8RQ, G83 8SZ, G83 8T, G83 8W;
G84;
PA1;
PA2 0, PA2 6 to PA2 8B, PA2 8D, PA2 8E, PA2 8H, PA2 8J, PA2 8L, PA2 8N, PA2 8P to PA2 8T, PA2 8UD, PA2 8UE, PA2 8UG, PA2 8UJ, PA2 8UL, PA2 8UQ, PA2 8UT, PA2 8UU, PA2 8UW to PA2 8UY, PA2 8W, PA2 8Y, PA2 9;
PA3 1 to PA3 4;
PA4 to PA10;
PA11 3A, PA11 3B, PA11 3D, PA11 3E, PA11 3H to PA11 3J, PA11 3L, PA11 3NA, PA11 3NB, PA11 3ND to PA11 3NG, PA11 3NL, PA11 3NN, PA11 3NP to PA11 3NR, PA11 3NT, PA11 3NU, PA11 3NW to PA11 3NZ, PA11 3PA, PA11 3PB, PA11 3PD to PA11 3PH, PA11 3PJ, PA11 3PL, PA11 3PN, PA11 3PP to PA11 3PU, PA11 3PW to PA11 3PZ, PA11 3QA, PA11 3QB, PA11 3QD to PA11 3QH, PA11 3QJ, PA11 3QL, PA11 3QN, PA11 3QP to PA11 3QT, PA11 3QW to PA11 3QZ, PA11 3RA, PA11 3RB, PA11 3RD, PA11 3RE, PA11 3RG, PA11 3RH, PA11 3RL, PA11 3RN, PA11 3RP to PA11 3RU, PA11 3RX to PA11 3RZ, PA11 3SA, PA11 3SB, PA11 3SD to PA11 3SH, PA11 3SJ, PA11 3SL, PA11 3SN, PA11 3SP to PA11 3SU, PA11 3SW to PA11 3SZ, PA11 3T, PA11 3Y;
PA12;
PA13 4A, PA13 4B, PA13 4D, PA13 4E, PA13 4H, PA13 4J, PA13 4L, PA13 4N, PA13 4PA, PA13 4PB, PA13 4PD to PA13 4PH, PA13 4PJ, PA13 4PL, PA13 4PN, PA13 4PP to PA13 4PU, PA13 4PW to PA13 4PZ, PA13 4Q to PA13 4T, PA13 4W, PA13 4Y, PA13 4Z;
PA14 5, PA14 6A, PA14 6B, PA14 6D, PA14 6E, PA14 6H, PA14 6J, PA14 6L, PA14 6N, PA14 6PA, PA14 6PB, PA14 6PD to PA14 6PH, PA14 6PJ, PA14 6PL, PA14 6PN, PA14 6PP to PA14 6PT, PA14 6PW, PA14 6Q to PA14 6TA, PA14 6TD, PA14 6TE, PA14 6TG, PA14 6TH, PA14 6TJ, PA14 6TL, PA14 6TN, PA14 6TP, PA14 6TR, PA14 6TS, PA14 6U, PA14 6WA, PA14 6WD to PA14 6WF, PA14 6X, PA14 6YA, PA14 6YB, PA14 6YD to PA14 6YH, PA14 6YJ, PA14 6YL, PA14 6YN, PA14 6YP to PA14 6YU, PA14 4YW to PA14 6YZ;
PA15;
PA16;
PA18 to PA33;
PA34 4, PA34 5A, PA34 5B, PA34 5D, PA34 5E, PA34 5H to PA34 5J, PA34 5N to PA34 5P, PA34 5QA, PA34 5QD, PA34 5QE, PA34 5R to PA34 5T, PA45 5UG to PA34 5UJ, PA34 5UL, PA34 5UN, PA34 5UQ, PA34 5Y;
PA35 to PA37;
PA38 4BA, PA38 4BB, PA38 4BD, PA38 4BE, PA38 4BG, PA38 4BH, PA38 4BJ, PA38 4BL, PA38 4BN, PA38 4BQ, PA38 4DB, PA38 4DD to PA38 4DH, PA38 4DJ, PA38 4DL, PA38 4DN, PA38 4DP to PA38 4DR;
PA41 to PA49;
PA60 to PA78.

Part II

2. For the purposes of regulation 2 the areas are— 2.594
(a) the areas of—
Basildon District Council;
Braintree District Council;
[²Brentwood District Council];
Castle Point District Council;
Chelmsford Borough Council;
Colchester Borough Council;
Epping Forest District Council;
Harlow District Council;
Maldon District Council;

The Social Security (Incapacity Benefit Work-focused Interviews) Regs 2003

[² . . .];
Rochford District Council;
[² . . .];
Southend on Sea Borough Council;
[² . . .];
[² . . .];
Tendring District Council;
Thurrock Borough Council;
Uttlesford District Council;
[² . . .];
(b) the following postcode districts—
BB1—BB12;
BB18;
[²DH2];
[²DH3];
DH9 0RY, DH9 0RZ, DH9 0SA;
NE8;
NE9 5, NE9 6, NE9 7A, NE9 7B, NE9 7D, NE9 7E, NE9 7H, NE9 7J, NE9 7L, NE9 7NA, NE9 7NB, NE9 7ND, NE9 7QA, NE9 7QB, NE9 7QD to NE9 7QF, NE9 7SP, NE9 7T, NE9 7UA, NE9 7UB, NE9 7UD, NE9 7UP, NE9 7US to NE9 7UU, NE9 7UX, NE9 7UY, NE9 7W, NE9 7XA, NE9 7XB, NE9 7XD to NE9 7XH, NE9 7XJ, NE9 7XL, NE9 7XN, NE9 7XP to NE9 7XU, NE9 7XY, NE9 7YA, NE9 7YB, NE9 7YD to NE9 7YH, NE9 7YJ, NE9 7YL, NE9 7YN, NE9 7YP, NE9 7YS;
NE10;
NE11;
NE15 8NR;
NE16 3, NE16 4, NE16 5A, NE16 5B, NE16 5D, NE16 5EB, NE16 5ED to NE16 5EF, NE16 5EH, NE16 5EL, NE16 5EN, NE16 5EP to NE16 5EU, NE16 5EW, NE16 5EX, NE16 5H, NE16 5J, NE16 5L, NE16 5N, NE16 5P to NE16 5U, NE16 5W to NE16 5Z, NE16 6AA, NE16 6AB, NE16 6AD, NE16 6AE, NE16 6BE, NE16 6BG, NE16 6NU, NE16 6NX, NE16 6PA, NE16 6PB, NE16 6PD to NE16 6PG;
NE17 7AA, NE17 7AB, NE17 7AD to NE17 7AH, NE17 7AJ, NE17 7AN, NE17 7AP, NE17 7AQ, NE17 7AR, NE17 7AS, NE17 7AW, NE17 7AZ, NE17 7BA, NE17 7BB, NE17 7BD, NE17 7BP, NE17 7BS to NE17 7BU, NE17 7BX to NE17 7BZ, NE17 7D, NE17 7E, NE17 7HA, NE17 7HB, NE17 7HD, NE17 7HE, NE17 7HS, NE17 7HU, NE17 7HX to NE17 7HZ, NE17 7J, NE17 7L, NE17 7QE, NE17 7TE, NE17 7TF to NE17 7TH, NE17 7TJ, NE17 7TL;
NE36 0E, NE36 0H, NE36 0J, NE36 0L, NE36 0N, NE36 0P to NE36 0U, NE36 0W, NE36 0Y, NE37 3JB;
NE39 1, NE39 2;
NE40;
NE41 8JD, NE41 8JE, NE41 8JG, NE41 8JH, NE41 8JJ, NE41 8JL, NE41 8JN, NE41 8JQ, NE41 8JW;
NE42 5NL, NE42 5NN, NE42 5NP, NE42 5NR, NE42 5NW;
NE82;
NE85 2NE;
NE98 1B, NE98 1X, NE98 1YL;
OL12 8AA to ZZ;
OL13;
SR5 1RP;
SR6 7A, SR6 7B, SR6 7D, SR6 7E, SR6 7H, SR6 7J, SR6 7L, SR6 7NA, SR6 7ND to SR6 7NH, SR6 7NJ, SR6 7NN, SR6 7NP to SR6 7NT, SR6 7NW, SR6 7NZ, SR6 7P to SR6 7T, SR6 7W to SR6 7Y.

[¹ PART III

2.595   **3.** For the purposes of regulation 2 the areas are—
(a) the areas of—
Cumbria County Council;
Darlington Borough Council;
Glasgow City Council;
Hartlepool Borough Council;
Middlesbrough Borough Council;

(SI 2003/2439, Sch.)

Redcar and Cleveland Borough Council;
Stockton Borough Council; and
(b) the following postcode districts—
FY1 to FY8;
L39;
L40;
LA1 to LA6;
PR1 to PR7;
PR9;
PR25;
PR26;
WN8.

PART IV

4. For the purposes of regulation 2 the areas are— 2.596
(a) the areas of—
Barnsley Metropolitan Borough Council;
City of Sunderland Council;
Chester-le-Street District Council;
Doncaster Metropolitan Borough Council;
Durham City Council;
East Dunbartonshire Council;
Easington District Council;
North Lanarkshire Council;
Rotherham Metropolitan Borough Council;
Sedgefield Borough Council;
South Lanarkshire Council; and
(b) the following postcode districts—
CF33 6PS to CF33 6PU, CF33 6RA to CF33 6RD, CF33 6RL;
CH41 to CH49;
CH60 to CH63;
DH6 0;
DH7 0;
DH8 0, DH8 5 to DH8 9;
DH9 6 to DH9 9;
DL2 3;
DL11;
DL12 0, DL12 8, DL12 9;
DL13 1 to DL13 5;
DL14 0, DL14 6 to DL14 9;
DL15 0, DL15 8, DL15 9;
[² G13 0, G13 4;
G14 0;
G60;
G63 0;
G81 1 to G81 6;
G82 1 to G82 5;
G83 0, G83 8, G83 9;]
L1 to L9;
L11 to L13;
L15 to L19;
L24 to L27;
M1 to M9;
M11 to M23;
M27;
M28;
M30 to M33;
M38;
M40;
M41;
M44;
M50;

The Social Security (Incapacity Benefit Work-focused Interviews) Regs 2003

M60;
M90;
NE16 6;
SA1 to SA8;
SA9 2;
SA10 6 to SA10 9;
SA11 1 to SA11 5;
SA12 6 to SA12 9;
SA13 1 to SA13 3;
SA14 to SA18;
SA19 2, SA19 6 to SA19 9;
SA20 0, SA20 1, SA20 6;
SA31 to SA39;
SA41 to SA48;
SA61 to SA73;
SY23 to SY25;
WA13 9SR to WA13 9UZ, WA13 9WA, WA13 9WX to WA13 9WZ;
WA14;
WA15.

PART V

2.597 5. For the purposes of regulation 2 the areas are—
(a) the areas of—
Halton Borough Council;
Knowsley Metropolitan Borough Council;
Newcastle Borough Council;
St Helens Council;
Sefton Council;
Stafford Borough Council;
Stoke on Trent City Council; and
(b) the following postcode districts—
B74 3;
B75 5RY to B75 5SZ;
B77 1 to B77 5;
B78 2, B78 3;
B79 0, B79 7 to B79 9;
CF37 4HN, CF37 4HP, CF37 4HR, CF37 4HW;
CF46 5, CF46 6;
CF47 0, CF47 8, CF47 9;
CF48 1 to CF48 4;
CF81 8JA to CF81 8ZY, CF81 9;
CF82 7, CF82 8;
CF83 1 to CF83 4, CF83 8;
DE13 0, DE13 7 to DE13 9;
DE14 1 to DE14 3;
DE15 0, DE15 9;
NP11 3 to NP11 7;
NP12 0 to NP12 3;
NP13 1 to NP13 3;
NP22 3 to NP22 5;
NP23 4 to NP23 8;
NP24 6;
SK11 0;
SK17 0;
ST7 3, ST7 4;
ST8 to ST10;
ST13;
ST14 5, ST14 7, ST14 8;
ST17;
ST18;
ST19 5, ST19 9;
TF10 9BJ, TF10 9BL, TF10 9BX, TF10 9BZ;

(SI 2003/2439, Sch.)

TF11 8J to TF11 8N;
WS3 5;
WS6;
WS7;
WS11 to WS13;
WS14 0, WS14 9;
WS15;
WV6 7EY;
WV10 7, WV10 8Q;
WV11 2.]

[² Part VI

6. For the purposes of regulation 2 the areas are the areas of—
Mendip District Council;
Sedgemoor District Council;
South Somerset District Council;
Taunton Deane Borough Council;
West Somerset District Council.]

[³ Part 7

7. For the purposes of regulation 2, the areas are any area not included in Parts 1 to 6.]

Amendments

1. The Social Security (Incapacity Benefit Work-focused Interviews) Amendment (No.2) Regulations 2005 (SI 2005/2604) (October 31, 2005).
2. The Social Security (Incapacity Benefit Work-focused Interviews) Amendment Regulations 2006 (SI 2006/536) (April 3, 2006).
3. The Social Security (Incapacity Benefit Work-focused Interviews) Amendment (No.2) Regulations 2006 (SI 2006/3088) (December 29, 2006).

The Social Security (Jobcentre Plus Interviews) Regulations 2002

(SI 2002/1703) (as amended)

Arrangement of Regulations

1. Citation and amendment
2. Interpretation and application
3. Requirement for person claiming a specified benefit to take part in an interview
4. Continuing entitled to specified benefit dependent on an interview
5. Time when interview is to take place
6. Waiver of requirement to take part in an interview
7. Deferment of requirement to take part in an interview
8. Exemptions
9. Claims for two or more specified benefits
10. The interview
11. Taking part in an interview
12. Failure to take part in an interview
13. Circumstances where regulation 12 does not apply
14. Good cause
15. Appeals

2.598

2.599

16. Revocations and transitional provision
17. Amendments to regulations

The Secretary of State for Work and Pensions, in exercise of the powers conferred upon him by sections 2A(1), (3) to (6) and (8), 2B(6) and (7), 5(1)(a) and (b), 6(1)(a) and (b), 7A, 189(1), (4) and (5) and 191 of the Social Security Administration Act 1992 and section 68 of, and paragraphs 3(1), 4(4), 6(8), 20(3) and 23(1) of Schedule 7 to, the Child Support, Pensions and Social Security Act 2000, and of all other powers enabling him in that behalf, after consultation with the Council on Tribunals in accordance with section 8(1) of the Tribunals and Inquiries Act 1992 and in respect of provisions in these Regulations relating to housing benefit and council tax benefit with organisations appearing to him to be representative of the authorities concerned, and after agreement by the Social Security Advisory Committee that proposals in respect of these Regulations should not be referred to it, hereby makes the following Regulations:

Citation and commencement

2.600

1. These Regulations may be cited as the Social Security (Jobcentre Plus Interviews) Regulations 2002 and shall come into force on 30th September 2002.

Interpretation and application

2.601

2.—(1) In these Regulations, unless the context otherwise requires—
"the 1998 Act" means the Social Security Act 1998;
"benefit week" means any period of seven days corresponding to the week in respect of which the relevant specified benefit is due to be paid;
[³. . .]
"the Careers Service" means—
(a) in England and Wales, a person with whom the Secretary of State or, as the case may be, the National Assembly for Wales, have made arrangements under section 10(1) of the Employment and Training Act 1973 or a local education authority to whom a direction has been given by the Secretary of State or the National Assembly for Wales under section 10(2) of that Act;
(b) in Scotland, a person with whom the Scottish Ministers have made arrangements under section 10(1) of the Employment and Training Act 1973 or any education authority to whom a direction has been given by the Scottish Ministers under section 10(2) of that Act;
"the Connexions Service" means a person of any description with whom the Secretary of State has made an arrangement under section 114(2)(a) of the Learning and Skills Act 2000 and section 10(1) of the Employment and Training Act 1973 and any person to whom he has given a direction under section 114(2)(b) of the Learning and Skills Act 2000 and section 10(2) of the Employment and Training Act 1973;
"interview" means a work-focused interview with a person who has claimed a specified benefit and which is conducted for any or all of the following purposes—
(a) assessing that person's prospects for existing or future employment (whether paid or voluntary);

(SI 2002/1703, reg.2) (as amended)

   (b) assisting or encouraging that person to enhance his prospects of such employment;
   (c) identifying activities which that person may undertake to strengthen his existing or future prospects of employment;
   (d) identifying current or future employment or training opportunities suitable to that person's needs; and
   (e) identifying educational opportunities connected with the existing or future employment prospects or needs of that person;

[³ "lone parent" has the meaning it bears in regulation 2(1) of the Income Support (General) Regulations 1987;]

"officer" means a person who is an officer of, or who is providing services to or exercising functions of, the Secretary of State;

[³ "relevant benefit" means income support other than income support where one of the following paragraphs of Schedule 1B to the Income Support (General) Regulations 1987 applies—
   (a) paragraph 7 (persons incapable of work), or
   (b) paragraph 24 or 25 (persons appealing against a decision which embodies a determination that they are not incapable of work);]

[³ "specified benefit" means income support, incapacity benefit and severe disablement allowance;]

[³ "specified person" means—
(a) a lone parent, or
(b) a person who claims—
   (i) incapacity benefit,
   (ii) income support where paragraph 7 (persons incapable of work) of Schedule 1B to the Income Support (General) Regulations 1987 applies,
   (iii) income support where paragraph 24 or 25 (persons appealing against a decision which embodies a determination that they are not incapable of work) of Schedule 1B to the Income Support (General) Regulations 1987 applies, or
   (iv) severe disablement allowance.]

(2) For the purposes of these Regulations—
(a) a person shall be deemed to be in remunerative work where he is in remunerative work within the meaning prescribed in [⁴ regulation 6 of the Housing Benefit Regulations 2006]; but
(b) a person shall be deemed not to be in remunerative work where—
   (i) he is not in remunerative work in accordance with subparagraph (a) above; or
   (ii) he is in remunerative work in accordance with sub-paragraph (a) above and is not entitled to income support but would not be prevented from being entitled to income support solely by being in such work; and
(c) a person shall be deemed to be engaged in part-time work where he is engaged in work for which payment is made but he is not engaged or deemed to be engaged in remunerative work.

(3) Except in a case where regulation 16(2) applies [⁵ . . .] regulations 3 to 15 apply in respect of a person who makes a claim for a specified benefit on or after 30th September 2002 at an office of the Department for Work and Pensions which is designated by the Secretary of State as a Jobcentre Plus Office or at an office of a relevant authority (being a person within section 72(2) of the Welfare Reform and Pensions Act 1999) which displays the **one** logo.

The Social Security (Jobcentre Plus Interviews) Regulations 2002

(4) Where a claim for benefit is made by a person ("the appointee") on behalf of another, references in these Regulations to a person claiming benefit shall be treated as a reference to the person on whose behalf the claim is made and not to the appointee.

(5) In these Regulations, unless the context otherwise requires, a reference—

(a) to a numbered regulation is to a regulation in these Regulations bearing that number;

(b) in a regulation to a numbered paragraph or sub-paragraph is to the paragraph or sub-paragraph in that regulation bearing that number;

(c) to a numbered Schedule is to the Schedule to these Regulations bearing that number.

AMENDMENTS

1. The Social Security Amendment (Carer's Allowance) Regulations 2002 (SI 2002/2497), Sch.2 (October 28, 2002).

2. Social Security (Working Neighbourhoods) Regulations 2004 (SI 2004/959), reg.26(2) (April 26, 2004).

3. The Social Security (Work-focused Interviews) Amendment Regulations 2005 (SI 2005/2727) (October 31, 2005).

4. The Housing Benefit and Council Tax Benefit (Consequential Provisions) Regulations 2006 (SI 2006/217), Sch.2, para.21 (March 6, 2006).

5. The Social Security (Working Neighbourhoods) Miscellaneous Amendment Regulations 2006, (SI 2006/909) (April 24, 2006).

Requirement for person claiming a specified benefit to take part in an interview

2.602　**3.**—(1) Subject to regulations 6 to 9, a person who—

[¹ (a) either—

　(i) makes a claim for a relevant benefit, or

　(ii) is entitled to a specified benefit other than a relevant benefit;]

[¹ (b) on the day on which he [claims a specified benefit], has attained the age of 16 but has not attained the age of 60; and]

(c) is not in remunerative work,

is required to take part in an interview.

(2) An officer shall, except where paragraph (3) applies, conduct the interview.

(3) An officer may, if he considers it appropriate in all the circumstances, arrange for a person who has not attained the age of 18 to attend an interview with the Careers Service or with the Connexions Service.

AMENDMENT

1. The Social Security (Work-focused Interviews) Amendment Regulations 2005 (SI 2005/2727) (October 31, 2005).

Continuing entitlement to specified benefit dependent on an interview

2.603　**4.**—(1) Subject to regulations 6 to 9, a person who has not attained the age of 60 and who is entitled to a specified benefit, shall be required to take part in an interview as a condition of his continuing to be entitled to the full amount of benefit which is payable apart from these Regulations where paragraph (2) applies and—

(SI 2002/1703, reg. 4) (as amended)

 (a) in the case of a lone parent who has attained the age of 18 and who is neither claiming incapacity benefit nor severe disablement allowance, [⁴ paragraph (3), (38), (3D), (3F), or (3H)] applies; or

 (b) in any other case, any of the circumstances specified in paragraph (4) apply or where paragraph (5) applies.

(2) This paragraph applies in the case of a person who has taken part in an interview under regulation 3 or who would have taken part in such an interview [⁴ but for—

 (i) the requirement being waived in accordance with regulation 6;

 (ii) the requirement being deferred in accordance with regulation 7;

 (iii) the requirement not arising because the person was at the time of the claim for the specified benefit subject to provisions within the Social Security (Working Neighbourhoods) Regulations 2004[13] by virtue of regulation 2(3) of those Regulations; or

 (iv) the person being required to take part in an interview under the Social Security (Quarterly Work-focused Interviews for Certain Lone Parents) Regulations 2004.]

(3) This paragraph applies at the times specified in paragraph (3A) where the young child condition is not satisfied (see paragraph (5B)) and where the lone parent—

 (a) last took part,

 (b) last failed to take part, or

 (c) was last treated as having taken part,

in a relevant interview on a date or after 30th April 2006 but before 30th October 2006.

(3A) Paragraph (3) first applies one year after that date, and it applies again every six months after the day on which it first applies.

(3B) This paragraph applies at the times specified in paragraph (3C) where the young child condition is not satisfied and where the lone parent—

 (a) last took part,

 (b) last failed to take part, or

 (c) was last treated as having taken part,

in a relevant interview on a date that was not on or after 30th April 2006 but before 30th October 2006.

(3C) Paragraph (3B) first applies six months after that date, and it applies again every six months after the day on which it first applies.

(3D) This paragraph applies at the times specified in paragraph (3E) where the young child condition is satisfied and where the interview that the lone parent—

 (a) last took part in,

 (b) last failed to take part in, or

 (c) was last treated as having taken part in,

was the first relevant interview.

(3E) Paragraph (3D) first applies six months after the date of that first interview, and it applies again upon each anniversary of the date of that first interview.

(3F) This paragraph applies at the times specified in paragraph (3G) where the young child condition is satisfied and where the interview that the lone parent—

 (a) last took part in,

 (b) last failed to take part in, or

The Social Security (Jobcentre Plus Interviews) Regulations 2002

(c) was last treated as having taken part in,
was the second relevant interview.

(3G) Paragraph (3F) first applies six months after the date of that second interview, and it applies again upon each anniversary of the date on which it first applies.

(3H) This paragraph applies at the times specified in paragraph (3I) where the young child condition is satisfied and where the interview that the lone parent—
  (a) last took part in,
  (b) last failed to take part in, or
  (c) was last treated as having taken part in,
was not the first or second relevant interview.

(3I) Paragraph (3H) first applies one year after the date of that interview, and it applies again upon each subsequent anniversary of that date.]

(4) The circumstances specified in this paragraph are those where—
  (a) it is determined in accordance with a personal capability assessment that a person is incapable of work and therefore, continues to be entitled to a specified benefit;
  (b) a person's entitlement to an [1 carer's allowance] ceases whilst entitlement to [3a] specified benefit continues;
  (c) a person becomes engaged or ceases to be engaged in part-time work;
  (d) a person has been undergoing education or training arranged by the officer and that education or training comes to an end; and
  (e) a person who has not attained the age of 18 and who has previously taken part in an interview, attains the age of 18.

(5) A requirement to take part in an interview arises under this paragraph where a person has not been required to take part in an interview by virtue of paragraph (4) for at least 36 months.

[4 (5A) In this regulation, "relevant interview" means an interview under—
  (a) the Social Security (Working Neighbourhoods) Regulations 2004,
  (b) the Social Security (Quarterly Work-focused Interviews for Certain Lone Parents) Regulations 2004, or
  (c) these Regulations,
in relation to the lone parent's current claim.

(5B) For the purposes of this regulation, the young child condition is satisfied where the lone parent is responsible for and living in the same household as—
  (a) a single child aged under 5, or
  (b) more than one child where the youngest is aged under 5.]

(6) [3 . . .].

AMENDMENTS

1. The Social Security Amendment (Carer's Allowance) Regulations 2002 (SI 2002/2497), Sch.2 (October 28, 2002).
2. Social Security (Working Neighbourhoods) Regulations 2004 (SI 2004/959), reg.26 (April 26, 2004).
3. The Social Security (Work-focused Interviews) Amendment Regulations 2005 (SI 2005/2727) (October 31, 2005).
4. The Social Security (Work-focused Interviews for Lone Parents) Amendment Regulations 2007 (SI 2007/1034) (April 30, 2007).

(SI 2002/1703, reg.5) (as amended)

Time when interview is to take place

5. An officer shall arrange for an interview to take place as soon as reasonably practicable after—
[¹ (a) the expiry of eight weeks after the date the claim for a specified benefit, other than a relevant benefit, is made;
(aa) the claim for a relevant benefit is made;]
(b) the requirement under regulation 4(1) arises; or,
(c) in a case where regulation 7(1) applies, the time when that requirement is to apply by virtue of regulation 7(2).

AMENDMENT

1. The Social Security (Work-focused Interviews) Amendment Regulations 2005 (SI 2005/2727) (October 31, 2005).

Waiver of requirement to take part in an interview

6.—(1) A requirement imposed by these Regulations to take part in an interview shall not apply where an officer determines that an interview would not—
(a) be of assistance to the person concerned; or
(b) be appropriate in the circumstances.
(2) A person in relation to whom a requirement to take part in an interview has been waived under paragraph (1) shall be treated for the purposes of—
(a) regulation 3 or 4; and
(b) any claim for, or entitlement to, a specified benefit,
as having complied with that requirement.

Deferment of requirement to take part in an interview

7.—(1) An officer may determine, in the case of any particular person, that the requirement to take part in an interview shall be deferred at the time the claim is made or the requirement to take part in an interview arises or applies because an interview would not at that time—
(a) be of assistance to that person; or
(b) be appropriate in the circumstances.
(2) Where the officer determines in accordance with paragraph (1) that the requirement to take part in an interview shall be deferred, he shall also determine when that determination is made, the time when the requirement to take part in an interview is to apply in the person's case.
(3) Where a requirement to take part in an interview has been deferred in accordance with paragraph (1), then until—
(a) a determination is made under regulation 6(1);
(b) the person takes part in an interview; or
(c) a relevant decision has been made in relation to that person in accordance with regulation 11(4),
that person shall be treated for the purposes of any claim for, or entitlement to, a specified benefit as having complied with that requirement.

Exemptions

8.—(1) Subject to paragraph (2), persons who, on the day on which the claim for a specified benefit is made or the requirement to take part in an interview under regulation 4 or 7(2) arises or applies—

2.604

2.605

2.606

2.607

The Social Security (Jobcentre Plus Interviews) Regulations 2002

(a) are engaged in remunerative work; or
(b) are claiming, or are entitled to, a jobseeker's allowance, shall be exempt from the requirement to take part in an interview.

(2) Paragraph (1)(b) shall not apply where—

(a) a joint-claim couple (as defined for the purposes of section 1(4) of the Jobseekers Act 1995) have claimed a jobseeker's allowance; and

(b) a member of that couple is a person to whom regulation 3D(1)(c) of the Jobseeker's Allowance Regulations 1996 (further circumstances in which a joint-claim couple may be entitled to a jointclaim jobseeker's allowance) applies.

[1 (3) A person who, on the day on which the claim for a specified benefit is made or the requirement to take part in an interview under regulation 4 or 7(2) arises or applies is—

(a) required to take part in an interview; or
(b) not required to take part in an interview by virtue of—
(i) a waiver of a requirement; or
(ii) a deferment of an interview,

under the Social Security (Incapacity Benefit Work-focused Interviews) Regulations 2003 [2 or regulation 2A [3 or 2B] of the Social Security (Work-focused Interviews for Lone Parents) and Miscellaneous Amendments Regulations 2000] shall be exempt from the requirement to take part in an interview.]

AMENDMENTS

1. The Social Security (Incapacity Benefit Work-focused Interviews) Regulations 2003 (SI 2003/2439) (October 27, 2003).
2. The Social Security (Work-focused Interviews) Amendment Regulations 2005 (SI 2005/2727) (October 31, 2005).
3. The Social Security (Work-focused Interviews for Lone Parents) Amendment Regulations 2007 (SI 2007/1034) (April 30, 2007).

Claims for two or more specified benefits

2.608　**9.** A person who would otherwise be required under these Regulations to take part in interviews relating to more than one specified benefit—

(a) is only required to take part in one interview; and
(b) that interview counts for the purposes of all those benefits.

The interview

2.609　**10.**—(1) The officer shall inform a person who is required to take part in an interview of the place and time of the interview.

(2) The officer may determine that an interview is to take place in the person's home where it would, in his opinion, be unreasonable to expect that person to attend elsewhere because that person's personal circumstances are such that attending elsewhere would cause him undue inconvenience or endanger his health.

Taking part in an interview

2.610　**11.**—(1) The officer shall determine whether a person has taken part in an interview.

(SI 2002/1703, reg.11) (as amended)

[² (2) A person who has not taken part in an interview under these Regulations before 31st October 2005 shall be regarded as having taken part in his first interview under these Regulations if—
  (a) he attends for the interview at the place and time notified to him by the officer;
  (b) where he is a specified person, he participates in discussions with the officer in relation to the specified person's employability, including any action the specified person and the officer agree is reasonable and they are willing to take in order to help the specified person enhance his employment prospects;
  (c) he provides answers (where asked) to questions and appropriate information about—
    (i) the level to which he has pursued any educational qualifications;
    (ii) his employment history;
    (iii) any vocational training he has undertaken;
    (iv) any skills he has acquired which fit him for employment;
    (v) any paid or unpaid employment he is engaged in;
    (vi) any medical condition which, in his opinion, puts him at a disadvantage in obtaining employment;
    (vii) any caring or childcare responsibilities he has;
    (viii) his aspirations for future employment;
    (ix) any vocational training or skills which he wishes to undertake or acquire; and
    (x) his work related abilities; and
  (d) where he is a specified person, he assists the officer in the completion of an action plan which records the matters discussed in relation to sub-paragraph (b) above.

(2A) A person who has taken part in an interview under these Regulations before 31st October 2005 shall be regarded as having taken part in his first interview under these Regulations after 30th October 2005 if—
  (a) he attends for the interview at the place and time notified to him by the officer;
  (b) where he is a specified person, he participates in discussions with the officer in relation to the specified person's employability, including any action the specified person and the officer agree is reasonable and they are willing to take in order to help the specified person enhance his employment prospects;
  (c) he participates in discussions with the officer—
    (i) in relation to the person's employability or any progress he might have made towards obtaining employment; and
    (ii) in order to consider any of the programmes and support available to help the person obtain employment;
  (d) he provides answers (where asked) to questions and appropriate information about—
    (i) the content of any report made following his personal capability assessment, insofar as that report relates to the person's capabilities and employability;
    and
    (ii) his opinion as to the extent to which his medical condition restricts his ability to obtain employment; and

(e) where he is a specified person, he assists the officer in the completion of an action plan which records the matters discussed in relation to sub-paragraph (b) above.

(2B) A person shall be regarded as having taken part in any subsequent interview under these Regulations if—
  (a) he attends for the interview at the place and time notified to him by the officer;
  (b) he participates in discussions with the officer—
    (i) in relation to the person's employability or any progress he might have made towards obtaining employment; and
    (ii) in order to consider any of the programmes and support available to help the person obtain employment;
  (c) where he is a specified person, he participates in discussions with the officer—
    (i) about any action the specified person or the officer might have taken as a result of the matters discussed in relation to paragraphs (2)(b) or (2A)(b) above; and
    (ii) about how, if at all, the action plan referred to in paragraphs (2)(d) or (2A)(e) above should be amended;
  (d) he provides answers (where asked) to questions and appropriate information about—
    (i) the content of any report made following his personal capability assessment, insofar as that report relates to the person's capabilities and employability;
    and
    (ii) his opinion as to the extent to which his medical condition restricts his ability to obtain employment; and
  (e) where he is a specified person, he assists the officer in the completion of any amendment of the action plan referred to in paragraphs (2)(d) or (2A)(e) above in light of the matters discussed in relation to sub-paragraphs (b) and (c) above and the information provided in relation to sub-paragraph (d) above.]

[1 (3) A person who, on the day on which the claim for a specified benefit is made or the requirement to take part in an interview under regulation 4 or 7(2) arises or applies is—
  (a) required to take part in an interview; or
  (b) not required to take part in an interview by virtue of—
    (i) a waiver of a requirement; or
    (ii) a deferment of an interview,
under the Social Security (Incapacity Benefit Work-focused Interviews Regulations 2003 shall be exempt from the requirement to take part in an interview.]

(4) Where an officer determines that a person has failed to take part in an interview and good cause has not been shown for that failure within five working days of the day on which the interview was to take place, a relevant decision shall be made for the purposes of section 2B of the Social Security Administration Act 1992.

AMENDMENTS

1. The Social Security (Incapacity Benefit Work-Focused Interviews) Regulations 2003 (SI 2003/2439), reg.17 (October 27, 2003).

(SI 2002/1703, reg.11) (as amended)

2. The Social Security (Work-focused Interviews) Amendment Regulations 2005 (SI 2005/2727) (October 31, 2005).

Failure to take part in an interview

12.—(1) A person in respect of whom a relevant decision has been made in accordance with regulation 11(4) shall, subject to paragraph (12), suffer the consequences set out below.

(2) Those consequences are—
 (a) where the interview arose in connection with a claim for a [² relevant benefit], that the person to whom the claim relates is to be regarded as not having made a claim for a [² relevant benefit];
 (b) where an interview which arose in connection with a claim for a [² relevant benefit] was deferred and benefit became payable by virtue of regulation 7(3), that the person's entitlement to that benefit shall terminate from the first day of the next benefit week following the date on which the relevant decision was made;
 (c) where the claimant has an award of benefit and the requirement for the interview arose under regulation 4, [² or by virtue of the claimant falling within regulation 3(1)(a)(ii),] the claimant's benefit shall be reduced as from the first day of the next benefit week following the day the relevant decision was made, by a sum equal (but subject to paragraphs (3) and (4)) to 20 per cent. of the amount applicable on the date the deduction commences in respect of a single claimant for income support aged not less than 25.

(3) Benefit reduced in accordance with paragraph (2)(c) shall not be reduced below ten pence per week.

(4) Where two or more specified benefits are in payment to a claimant, a deduction made in accordance with this regulation shall be applied, except in a case to which paragraph (5) applies, to the specified benefits in the following order of priority—
 (a) income support;
 (b) incapacity benefit;
 (c) [²...];
 (d) [²...];
 (e) severe disablement allowance.

(5) Where the amount of the reduction is greater than some (but not all) of the specified benefits listed in paragraph (4), the reduction shall be made against the first benefit in that list which is the same as, or greater than, the amount of the reduction.

(6) For the purpose of determining whether a specified benefit is the same as, or greater than, the amount of the reduction for the purposes of paragraph (5), ten pence shall be added to the amount of the reduction.

(7) In a case where the whole of the reduction cannot be applied against any one specified benefit because no one benefit is the same as, or greater than, the amount of the reduction, the reduction shall be applied against the first benefit in payment in the list of priorities at paragraph (4) and so on against each benefit in turn until the whole of the reduction is exhausted or, if this is not possible, the whole of the specified benefits are exhausted, subject in each case to ten pence remaining in payment.

(8) Where the rate of any specified benefit payable to a claimant changes, the rules set out above for a reduction in the benefit payable shall be

2.611

applied to the new rates and any adjustments to the benefits against which the reductions are made shall take effect from the beginning of the first benefit week to commence for that claimant following the change.

(9) Where a claimant whose benefit has been reduced in accordance with this regulation subsequently takes part in an interview, the reduction shall cease to have effect on the first day of the benefit week in which the requirement to take part in an interview was met.

(10) For the avoidance of doubt, a person who is regarded as not having made a claim for any benefit because he failed to take part in an interview shall be required to make a new claim in order to establish entitlement to any specified benefit.

(11) For the purposes of determining the amount of any benefit payable, a claimant shall be treated as receiving the amount of any specified benefit which would have been payable but for a reduction made in accordance with this regulation.

(12) The consequences set out in this regulation shall not apply in the case of a person who brings new facts to the notice of the Secretary of State within one month of the date on which the decision was notified and—
  (a) those facts could not reasonably have been brought to the Secretary of State's notice within five working days of the day on which the interview was to take place; and
  (b) those facts show that he had good cause for his failure to take part in the interview.

(13) In paragraphs (2) and (12), the "decision" means the decision that the person failed without good cause to take part in an interview.

AMENDMENTS

1. The Social Security Amendment (Carer's Allowance) Regulations 2002 (SI 2002/2497), Sch.2 (October 28, 2002).
2. The Social Security (Work-focused Interviews) Amendment Regulations 2005 (SI 2005/2727) (October 31, 2005).

Circumstances where regulation 12 does not apply

2.612   **13.** The consequences of a failure to take part in an interview set out in regulation 12 shall not apply where—
  (a) he is no longer required to take part in an interview as a condition for continuing to be entitled to the full amount of benefit which is payable apart from these Regulations; or
  (b) the person attains the age of 60.

Good cause

2.613   **14.** Matters to be taken into account in determining whether a person has shown good cause for his failure to take part in an interview include—
  (a) that the person misunderstood the requirement to take part in the interview due to any learning, language or literacy difficulties of the person or any misleading information given to the person by the officer;
  (b) that the person was attending a medical or dental appointment, or accompanying a person for whom the claimant has caring responsibilities to such an appointment, and that it would have been unreasonable, in the circumstances, to rearrange the appointment;

(c) that the person had difficulties with his normal mode of transport and that no reasonable alternative was available;
(d) that the established customs and practices of the religion to which the person belongs prevented him attending on that day or at that time;
(e) that the person was attending an interview with an employer with a view to obtaining employment;
(f) that the person was actually pursuing employment opportunities as a self-employed earner;
(g) that the person or a dependant of his or a person for whom he provides care suffered an accident, sudden illness or relapse of [1 a physical or mental health condition];
(h) that he was attending the funeral of a close friend or relative on the day fixed for the interview;
(i) that a disability from which the person suffers made it impracticable for him to attend at the time fixed for the interview.

AMENDMENT

1. The Social Security (Work-focused Interviews) Amendment Regulations 2005 (SI 2005/2727) (October 31, 2005).

Appeals

15.—(1) This regulation applies to any relevant decision made under regulation 11(4) or any decision under section 10 of the 1998 Act superseding such a decision.

(2) This regulation applies whether the decision is as originally made or as revised under section 9 of the 1998 Act.

(3) In the case of a decision to which this regulation applies, the person in respect of whom the decision was made shall have a right of appeal under section 12 of the 1998 Act to an appeal tribunal.

Revocations and transitional provision

16.—(1) Subject to paragraph (2), the Social Security (Work-focused Interviews) Regulations 2000 ("the 2000 Regulations") and the Social Security (Jobcentre Plus Interviews) Regulations 2001 ("the 2001 Regulations") are hereby revoked to the extent specified in Schedule 1.

(2) Notwithstanding paragraph (1), both the 2000 Regulations (except for regulations 4, 5 and 12(2)(a) and (b)) and the 2001 Regulations (except for regulations 3 and 11(2)(a) and (b)) [2 . . .] shall continue to apply as if these Regulations had not come into force for the period specified in paragraph (3) in the case of a person who, on the day before the day on which these Regulations come into force, is both a relevant person and entitled to a specified benefit for the purposes of those Regulations.

(3) The period specified for the purposes of paragraph (2) shall be the period beginning on the day on which these Regulations come to force and ending on the day on which the person—
(a) ceases to be a relevant person for the purposes of the 2000 Regulations or, as the case may be, the 2001 Regulations;
(b) is not entitled to any specified benefit for the purposes of those Regulations; or
(c) attains the age of 60,
whichever shall first occur.

The Social Security (Jobcentre Plus Interviews) Regulations 2002

AMENDMENTS

1. Social Security (Working Neighbourhoods) Regulations 2004 (SI 2004/959), reg.26(4) (April 26, 2004).
2. The Social Security (Working Neighbourhoods) Miscellaneous Amendment Regulations 2006, (SI 2006/909) (April 24, 2006).

Amendments to regulations

2.616   *Omitted*

2.617   *Schedules 1 and 2 omitted.*

The Social Security (Jobcentre Plus Interviews for Partners) Regulations 2003

(SI 2003/1886)

ARRANGEMENT OF REGULATIONS

2.618
1. Citation and commencement
2. Interpretation and application
3. Requirement for a partner to take part in an interview as a cpondition of a specified benefit continuing to be paid at full amount.
4. Time when interview is to take place
5. Waiver of requirement to take part in an interview
6. Deferment of requirement to take part in an interview
7. Exemption
8. Claims for two or more specified benefits.
9. The interview.
10. Taking part in an interview.
11. Failure to take part in an interview.
12. Circumstances where regulation 11 does not apply.
13. Good cause.
14. Appeals
15. *Omitted.*

GENERAL NOTE

2.619   These controversial regulations extend the scheme of work-focused interviews to the partners of claimants, and cover five benefits: income support, income-based jobseeker's allowance, incapacity benefit, severe disablement allowance and carer's allowance. The pattern follows that to be found in the earlier regulations relating to work-focused interviews in other contexts. But those regulations apply only where the claim was made after the commencement date of the regulations where both the partners are between the ages of 18 and 60; these regulations apply whenever benefit is in payment and whenever the claim is through a Jobcentre Plus office. A further distinction is that the interview under these regulations is a once and for all interview without there being provisions for follow-up interviews. Failure to participate results in a deduction equal to 20 per cent of the single adult applicable amount for income support. Both partners have an independent right of appeal, so that both can, in principle, appeal against the same decision.

(SI 2003/1886)

Whereas a draft of this instrument was laid before Parliament in accordance with section 190(1) of the Social Security Administration Act 1992 and approved by resolution of each House of Parliament;

Now, therefore, the Secretary of State for Work and Pensions, in exercise of the powers conferred upon him by sections 2AA(1) and (4) to (7), 2B(6), 189(1) and (4) to (6) and 191 of the Social Security Administration Act 1992 and of all other powers enabling him in that behalf, after consultation with the Council on Tribunals in accordance with section 8(1) of the Tribunals and Inquiries Act 1992, by this instrument, which contains only regulations made by virtue of, or consequential upon, section 2AA of the Social Security Administration Act 1992 and which is made before the end of the period of 6 months beginning with the coming into force of that provision, hereby makes the following Regulations:

Citation and commencement

1. These Regulations may be cited as the Social Security (Jobcentre Plus Interviews for Partners) Regulations 2003 and shall come into force on 12th April 2004.

Interpretation and application

2.—(1) In these Regulations—
"the 1998 Act" means the Social Security Act 1998;
"benefit week" means any period of seven days corresponding to the week in respect of which the relevant specified benefit is due to be paid;
"claimant" means a claimant of a specified benefit who has a partner to whom these Regulations apply;
[² "couple" means—
   (a) a man and woman who are married to each other and are members of the same household;
   (b) a man and woman who are not married to each other but are living together as husband and wife;
   (c) two people of the same sex who are civil partners of each other and are members of the same household; or
   (d) two people of the same sex who are not civil partners of each other but are living together as if they were civil partners,
and for the purposes of paragraph (d), two people of the same sex are to be regarded as living together as if they were civil partners if, but only if, they would be regarded as living together as husband and wife were they instead two people of the opposite sex;]
"interview" means a work-focused interview with a partner which is conducted for any or all of the following purposes—
   (a) assessing the partner's prospects for existing or future employment (whether paid or voluntary);
   (b) assisting or encouraging the partner to enhance his prospects of such employment;
   (c) identifying activities which the partner may undertake to strengthen his existing or future prospects of employment;
   (d) identifying current or future employment or training opportunities suitable to the partner's needs; and
   (e) identifying educational opportunities connected with the existing or future employment prospects or needs of the partner;

2.620

2.621

The Social Security (Jobcentre Plus Interviews for Partners) Regs 2003

"officer" means a person who is an officer of, or who is providing services to or exercising functions of, the Secretary of State;

"partner" means a person who is a member of the same couple as the claimant, or, in a case where the claimant has more than one partner, a person who is a partner of the claimant by reason of a polygamous marriage, but only where—

(a) the claimant has been awarded a specified benefit at a higher rate referable to that partner; and

(b) both the partner and the claimant have attained the age of 18 but have not attained the age of 60;

"polygamous marriage" means any marriage during the subsistence of which a party to it is married to more than one person and the ceremony of marriage took place under the law of a country which permits polygamy;

"specified benefit" means a benefit to which section 2AA applies.

(2) [³ . . .] Regulations 3 to 13 apply to a partner in circumstances where on or after 12th April 2004 the claimant's award of a specified benefit is being administered from an office of the Department for Work and Pensions which is designated by the Secretary of State as a Jobcentre Plus Office and the claimant has been continuously entitled to the benefit for 26 weeks or longer.

AMENDMENTS

1. Social Security (Working Neighbourhoods) Regulations 2004 (SI 2004/959), reg.27(2) (April 26, 2004).

2. The Civil Partnership (Pensions, Social Security and Child Support) (Consequential etc. Provisions) Order 2005 (SI 2005/2877) (December 5, 2005).

3. The Social Security (Working Neighbourhoods) Miscellaneous Amendment Regulations 2006, (SI 2006/909) (April 24, 2006).

Requirement for partner to take part in an interview as a condition of a specified benefit continuing to be paid at full amount

2.622   **3.**—(1) Subject to regulations 5 to 8, a partner to whom these Regulations apply is required to take part in an interview as a condition of the claimant continuing to be paid the full amount of a specified benefit which is payable apart from these Regulations.

(2) Where a requirement to take part in an interview arises under paragraph (1), a requirement to take part in an interview shall also apply to any other specified benefit in payment to the claimant at a higher rate referable to his partner on the date set for the interview and notified to the partner in accordance with regulation 9(1).

Time when interview is to take place

2.623   **4.** An officer shall arrange for an interview to take place as soon as reasonably practicable after—

(a) the requirement under regulation 3(1) arises; or

(b) in a case where regulation 6(1) applies, the time when that requirement is to apply by virtue of regulation 6(2).

Waiver of requirement to take part in an interview

2.624   **5.**—(1) A requirement imposed by these Regulations to take part in an interview shall not apply where an officer determines that an interview would not—

(SI 2003/1886, reg. 5)

(a) be of assistance to the partner concerned; or
(b) be appropriate in the circumstances.

(2) A partner in relation to whom a requirement to take part in an interview has been waived under paragraph (1) shall be treated for the purposes of regulation 3 as having complied with that requirement.

Deferment of requirement to take part in an interview

6.—(1) An officer may determine, in the case of any particular partner, that the requirement to take part in an interview shall be deferred at the time that the requirement to take part in it arises or applies because an interview would not at that time—
(a) be of assistance to the partner concerned; or
(b) be appropriate in the circumstances.

(2) Where the officer determines in accordance with paragraph (1) that the requirement to take part in an interview shall be deferred, he shall also, when that determination is made, determine the time when the requirement to take part in an interview is to apply in the partner's case.

(3) Where a requirement to take part in an interview has been deferred in accordance with paragraph (1), then until—
(a) a determination is made under regulation 5(1);
(b) the partner takes part in an interview; or
(c) a relevant decision has been made in accordance with regulation 10(3),

the partner shall be treated for the purposes of regulation 3 as having complied with that requirement.

Exemption

7. A partner who, on the day on which the requirement to take part in an interview arises or applies under regulation 3(1) or 6(2), is in receipt of a specified benefit as a claimant in his own right shall be exempt from the requirement to take part in an interview under these Regulations.

Claims for two or more specified benefits

8. A partner who would otherwise be required under these Regulations to take part in interviews relating to more than one specified benefit—
(a) is only required to take part in one interview during any period where the claimant is in receipt of two or more specified benefits concurrently; and
(b) that interview counts for the purposes of each of those benefits.

The interview

9.—(1) An officer shall inform a partner who is required to take part in an interview of the date, place and time of the interview.

(2) The officer may determine that an interview is to take place in the partner's home where it would, in his opinion, be unreasonable to expect the partner to attend elsewhere because the partner's personal circumstances are such that attending elsewhere would cause him undue inconvenience or endanger his health.

(3) An officer shall conduct the interview.

The Social Security (Jobcentre Plus Interviews for Partners) Regs 2003

Taking part in an interview

2.629   **10.**—(1) The officer shall determine whether a partner has taken part in an interview.

(2) A partner shall be regarded as having taken part in an interview if and only if—

(a) he attends for the interview at the place and time notified to him by the officer; and

(b) he provides answers (where asked) to questions and appropriate information about—

   (i) the level to which he has pursued any educational qualifications;
   (ii) his employment history;
   (iii) any vocational training he has undertaken;
   (iv) any skills he has acquired which fit him for employment;
   (v) any paid or unpaid employment he is engaged in;
   (vi) any medical condition which, in his opinion, puts him at a disadvantage in obtaining employment; and
   (vii) any caring or childcare responsibilities he has.

(3) Where an officer determines that a partner has failed to take part in an interview and good cause has not been shown either by the partner or by the claimant for that failure within five working days of the day on which the interview was to take place, a relevant decision shall be made for the purposes of section 2B of the Social Security Administration Act 1992 and the partner and the claimant shall be notified accordingly.

Failure to take part in an interview

2.630   **11.**—(1) Where a relevant decision has been made in accordance with regulation 10(3), subject to paragraph (11), the specified benefit payable to the claimant in respect of which the requirement for the partner to take part in an interview under regulation 3 arose shall be reduced, either as from the first day of the next benefit week following the day on which the relevant decision was made, or, if that date arises five days or less after the day on which the relevant decision was made, as from the first day of the second benefit week following the date of the relevant decision.

(2) The deduction made to benefit in accordance with paragraph (1) shall be by a sum equal (but subject to paragraphs (3) and (4)) to 20 per cent. of the amount applicable on the date the deduction commences in respect of a single claimant for income support aged not less than 25.

(3) Benefit reduced in accordance with paragraph (1) shall not be reduced below ten pence per week.

(4) Where two or more specified benefits are in payment to a claimant, in relation to each of which a requirement for the partner to take part in an interview had arisen under regulation 3, a deduction made in accordance with this regulation shall be applied, except in a case to which paragraph (5) applies, to those benefits in the following order of priority—

(a) an income-based jobseeker's allowance;
(b) income support;
(c) incapacity benefit;
(d) severe disablement allowance;
(e) carer's allowance.

(5) Where the amount of the reduction is greater than some (but not all) of those benefits, the reduction shall be made against the first benefit in the

(SI 2003/1886, reg.11)

list in paragraph (4) which is the same as, or greater than, the amount of the reduction.

(6) For the purpose of determining whether a benefit is the same as, or greater than, the amount of the reduction for the purposes of paragraph (5), ten pence shall be added to the amount of the reduction.

(7) In a case where the whole of the reduction cannot be applied against any one benefit because no one benefit is the same as, or greater than, the amount of the reduction, the reduction shall be applied against the first benefit in the list of priorities at paragraph (4) and so on against each benefit in turn until the whole of the reduction is exhausted or, if this is not possible, the whole of those benefits are exhausted, subject in each case to ten pence remaining in payment.

(8) Where the rate of any specified benefit payable to a claimant changes, the rules set out above for a reduction in the benefit payable shall be applied to the new rates and any adjustments to the benefits against which the reductions are made shall take effect from the beginning of the first benefit week to commence for that claimant following the change.

(9) Where the partner of a claimant whose benefit has been reduced in accordance with this regulation subsequently takes part in an interview, the reduction shall cease to have effect on the first day of the benefit week in which the requirement to take part in an interview was met.

(10) For the purposes of determining the amount of any benefit payable, a claimant shall be treated as receiving the amount of any specified benefit which would have been payable but for a reduction made in accordance with this regulation.

(11) Benefit shall not be reduced in accordance with this regulation where the partner or the claimant brings new facts to the notice of the Secretary of State within one month of the date on which the decision that the partner failed without good cause to take part in an interview was notified and—
   (a) those facts could not reasonably have been brought to the Secretary of State's notice within five working days of the day on which the interview was to take place; and
   (b) those facts show that he had good cause for his failure to take part in the interview.

Circumstances where regulation 11 does not apply

12. The reduction of benefit to be made under regulation 11 shall not apply as from the date when a partner who failed to take part in an interview ceases to be a partner for the purposes of these Regulations or is no longer a partner to whom these Regulations apply under the provisions within regulation 2(2).

2.631

Good cause

13. Matters to be taken into account in determining whether the partner or the claimant has shown good cause for the partner's failure to take part in an interview include—
   (a) that the partner misunderstood the requirement to take part in an interview due to any learning, language or literacy difficulties of the partner or any misleading information given to the partner by the officer;
   (b) that the partner was attending a medical or dental appointment, or accompanying a person for whom the partner had caring responsibilities

2.632

The Social Security (Jobcentre Plus Interviews for Partners) Regs 2003

to such an appointment, and that it would have been unreasonable, in the circumstances, to rearrange the appointment;
(c) that the partner had difficulties with his normal mode of transport and that no reasonable alternative was available;
(d) that the established customs and practices of the religion to which the partner belongs prevented him attending on that day or at that time;
(e) that the partner was attending an interview with an employer with a view to obtaining employment;
(f) that the partner was actually pursuing employment opportunities as a self-employed earner;
(g) that the partner, claimant or a dependant or a person for whom the partner provides care suffered an accident, sudden illness or relapse of a chronic condition;
(h) that he was attending the funeral of a close friend or relative on the day fixed for the interview;
(i) that a disability from which the partner suffers made it impracticable for him to attend at the time fixed for the interview.

Appeals

2.633 **14.**—(1) This regulation applies to any relevant decision made under regulation 10(3) or any decision under section 10 of the 1998 Act superseding such a decision.

(2) This regulation applies whether the decision is as originally made or as revised under section 9 of the 1998 Act.

(3) In the case of a decision to which this regulation applies, the partner in respect of whom the decision was made and the claimant shall each have a right of appeal under section 12 of the 1998 Act to an appeal tribunal.

Amendments to the Social Security and Child Support (Decisions and Appeals) Regulations 1999

2.634 **15.** *Omitted*

The Social Security (Loss of Benefit) Regulations 2001

(SI 2001/4022)

2.635 *Made*   *18th December 2001*
Coming into force   *1st April 2002*

Whereas a draft of this instrument was laid before Parliament in accordance with section 11(3) of the Social Security Fraud Act 2001, section 80(1) of the Social Security Act 1998 and section 5A(3) of the Pensions Appeal Tribunals Act 1943 and approved by resolution of each House of Parliament.

Now, therefore, the Secretary of State, in exercise of the powers conferred by sections 7(3) to (6), 8(3) and (4), 9(2) to (5), 10(1) and (2) and 11(1) of the Social Security Fraud Act 2001, section 189(4) of the Social Security Administration Act 1992, sections 79(4) and 84 of, and paragraph 9 of Schedule 2 to, the Social Security Act 1998 and section 5A(2) of the

(SI 2001/4022)

Pensions Appeal Tribunals Act 1943, and of all other powers enabling him in that behalf, by this Instrument, which is made before the end of the period of 6 months beginning with the coming into force of sections 7 to 13 of the Social Security Fraud Act 2001 and which contains only regulations made by virtue of, or consequential upon, those sections, hereby makes the following Regulations:

PART I

GENERAL

Citation, commencement and interpretation

1.—(1) These Regulations may be cited as the Social Security (Loss of Benefit) Regulations 2001 and shall come into force on 1st April 2002.

(2) In these Regulations, unless the context otherwise requires—
"the Act" means the Social Security Fraud Act 2001;
"the Benefits Act" means the Social Security Contributions and Benefits Act 1992;
"the Council Tax Benefit Regulations" means the Council Tax Benefit Regulations 2006;
[[1] "the Council Tax Benefit (State Pension Credit) Regulations" means the Council Tax Benefit (Persons who have attained pensionable age for state pension credit) Regulations 2006;
"the Housing Benefit Regulations" means the Housing Benefit Regulations 2006;
"the Housing Benefit (State Pension Credit) Regulations" means the Housing Benefit (Persons who have attained pensionable age for state pension credit) Regulations 2006;]
"the Income Support Regulations" means the Income Support (General) Regulations 1987;
"the Jobseekers Act" means the Jobseekers Act 1995;
"the Jobseeker's Allowance Regulations" means the Jobseeker's Allowance Regulations 1996;
"claimant" in a regulation means the person claiming the sanctionable benefit referred to in that regulation;
"disqualification period" means the period in respect of which the restrictions on payment of a relevant benefit apply in respect of an offender in accordance with section 7(6) of the Act and shall be interpreted in accordance with regulation 2; and
"offender" means the person who is subject to the restriction in the payment of his benefit in accordance with section 7 of the Act.

(3) Expressions used in these Regulations which are defined either for the purposes of the Jobseekers Act or for the purposes of the Jobseeker's Allowance Regulations shall, except where the context otherwise requires, have the same meaning as for the purposes of that Act or, as the case may be, those Regulations.

(4) In these Regulations, unless the context otherwise requires, a reference—

2.636

The Social Security (Loss of Benefit) Regulations 2001

(a) to a numbered regulation is to the regulation in these Regulations bearing that number;
(b) in a regulation to a numbered paragraph is to the paragraph in that regulation bearing that number.

AMENDMENT

1. Housing Benefit and Council Tax Benefit (Consequential Provisions) Regulations 2006 (SI 2006/217), Sch.2, para.20(2) (March 6, 2006).

Disqualification period

2.—(1) Subject to paragraph (2), the first day of the disqualification period for the purpose of section 7(6) of the Act shall be—
  (a) [1 subject to sub-paragraph (c),] where, on the determination day—
    (i) the offender is in receipt of a sanctionable benefit;
    (ii) the offender is a member of a joint-claim couple which is in receipt of a joint-claim jobseeker's allowance; or
    (iii) the offender's family member is in receipt of income support, jobseeker's allowance [2, state pension credit], housing benefit or council tax benefit,
  the day which is 28 days after the determination day;
  (b) where sub-paragraph (a) does not apply, the day which is 28 days after the first day after the determination day on which the Secretary of State decides to award—
    (i) a sanctionable benefit to the offender;
    (ii) a joint-claim jobseeker's allowance to a joint-claim couple of which the offender is a member; or
    (iii) [1 income support [2 jobseeker's allowance or state pension credit]] to an offender's family member.
[1(c) where the only sanctionable benefits which the offender or, as the case may be, the offender's family member, is in receipt of are housing benefit or council tax benefit or both of them, the day which is 28 days after the first day after the determination day on which the Secretary of State is notified by the relevant authority that the offender or an offender's family member is in receipt of either or both of those benefits or, as the case may be, has been awarded either or both of those benefits and in this sub-paragraph, "relevant authority" means the relevant authority administering the offender's or the offender's family member's housing benefit or council tax benefit.]

(2) For the purposes of [1 paragraph] (1), the first day of the disqualification period shall be no later than 3 years and 28 days after the date of the conviction of the offender for the benefit offence in the later proceedings referred to in section 7(1) of the Act and section 7(9) of the Act (date of conviction and references to conviction) shall apply for the purposes of this paragraph as it applies for the purposes of section 7 of the Act.

(3) In this regulation, "the determination day" means the day on which the Secretary of State determines that a restriction under—
  (a) section 7 of the Act would be applicable to the offender were he in receipt of a sanctionable benefit;
  (b) section 8 of the Act would be applicable to the offender were he a member of a joint-claim couple which is in receipt of a joint-claim jobseeker's allowance; or

(SI 2001/4022, reg. 2)

(c) section 9 of the Act would be applicable to the offender's family member were that member in receipt of income support, jobseeker's allowance [², state pension credit], housing benefit or council tax benefit.

AMENDMENTS

1. Social Security (Loss of Benefit) Amendment Regulations 2002 (SI 2002/486), reg.2 (April 1, 2002).
2. State Pension Credit Regulations 2002 (SI 2002/1792), regs 25(2) and 26(2)(i) (October 6, 2003).

PART II

REDUCTIONS

Reduction of income support

3.—(1) Subject to paragraphs (2) to (4), any payment of income support which falls to be made to an offender in respect of any week in the disqualification period, or to an offender's family member in respect of any week in the relevant period, shall be reduced—
   (a) where the claimant or a member of his family is pregnant or seriously ill, by a sum equivalent to 20 per cent.;
   (b) where the applicable amount of the offender used to calculate that payment of income support has been reduced pursuant to regulation 22A of the Income Support Regulations (appeal against a decision embodying an incapacity for work determination), whether or not the appeal referred to in that regulation is successful, by a sum equivalent to 20 per cent;
   (c) in any other case, by a sum equivalent to 40 per cent.,
of the applicable amount of the offender in respect of a single claimant for income support on the first day of the disqualification period or, as the case may be, on the first day of the relevant period, and specified in paragraph 1(1) of Schedule 2 to the Income Support Regulations.

(2) Payment shall not be reduced under paragraph (1) to below 10 pence per week.

(3) A reduction under paragraph (1) shall, if it is not a multiple of 5p, be rounded to the nearest such multiple or, if it is a multiple of 2.5p but not of 5p, to the next lower multiple of 5p.

(4) A payment of income support shall not be reduced as provided in paragraph (1) in respect of any week in the disqualification period in respect of which that payment of income support is subject to a restriction imposed pursuant to section 62 or 63 of the Child Support, Pensions and Social Security Act 2000 (loss of benefit provisions).

(5) Where the rate of income support payable to an offender or an offender's family member changes, the rules set out above for a reduction in the benefit payable shall be applied to the new rate and any adjustment to the reduction shall take effect from the first day of the first benefit week to start after the date of the change.

(6) In this regulation, "benefit week" shall have the same meaning as in regulation of 2(1) of the Income Support Regulations.

2.638

The Social Security (Loss of Benefit) Regulations 2001

[¹ **Reduction in state pension credit**

3A.—(1) Subject to the following provisions of this regulation, state pension credit shall be payable in the case of an offender for any week comprised in the disqualification period or in the case of an offender's family member for any week comprised in the relevant period, as if the rate of benefit were reduced—
    (a) where the offender or the offender's family member is pregnant or seriously ill, by 20 per cent. of the relevant sum; or
    (b) where sub-paragraph (a) does not apply, by 40 per cent. of the relevant sum.
(2) In paragraph (1), the "relevant sum" is the amount applicable—
    (a) except where sub-paragraph (b) applies, in respect of a single claimant aged not less than 25 under paragraph 1(1) of Schedule 2 to the Income Support Regulations; or
    (b) if the claimant's family member is the offender and the offender has not attained the age of 25, the amount applicable in respect of a person of the offender's age under paragraph 1(1) of Part I of that Schedule,
on the first day of the disqualification period or, as the case may be, on the first day of the relevant period.
(3) Payment of state pension credit shall not be reduced under this regulation to less than 10 pence per week.
(4) A reduction under paragraph (1) shall, if it is not a multiple of 5 pence, be rounded to the nearest such multiple or, if it is a multiple of 2.5 pence but not of 5 pence, to the next lower multiple of 5 pence.
(5) Where the rate of state pension credit payable to an offender or an offender's family member changes, the rules set out above for a reduction in the credit payable shall be applied to the new rate and any adjustment to the reduction shall take effect from the first day of the first benefit week to start after the date of change.
(6) In paragraph (5), "benefit week" has the same meaning as in regulation 1(2) of the State Pension Credit Regulations 2002.
(7) A person of a prescribed description for the purposes of the definition of "family" in section 137(1) of the Benefits Act as it applies for the purpose of this regulation is—
    (a) a person who is an additional spouse for the purposes of section 12(1) of the State Pension Credit Act 2002 (additional spouse in the case of polygamous marriages);
    (b) a person aged 16 or over who is treated as a child for the purposes of section 142 of the Benefits Act.]

AMENDMENT

1. State Pension Credit Regulations 2002 (SI 2002/1792), reg.25(3) (October 6, 2003).

Reduction of joint-claim jobseeker's allowance

4. In respect of any part of the disqualification period when section 8(2) of the Act does not apply, the reduced rate of joint-claim jobseeker's allowance payable to the member of that couple who is not the offender shall be—
    (a) in any case in which the member of the couple who is not the offender satisfies the conditions set out in section 2 of the Jobseekers

(SI 2001/4022, reg. 4)

Act (contribution-based conditions), a rate equal to the amount calculated in accordance with section 4(1) of that Act;
(b) in any case where the couple are a couple in hardship for the purposes of regulation 11, a rate equal to the amount calculated in accordance with regulation 16;
(c) in any other case, a rate calculated in accordance with section 4(3A) of the Jobseekers Act save that the applicable amount shall be the amount determined by reference to paragraph 1(1) of Schedule 1 to the Jobseeker's Allowance Regulations as if the member of the couple who is not the offender were a single claimant.

PART III

HARDSHIP

Meaning of "person in hardship"

5.—(1) In this Part of these Regulations, a "person in hardship" means, for the purposes of regulation 6, a person, other than a person to whom paragraph (3) or (4) applies, where—
(a) she is a single woman who is pregnant and in respect of whom the Secretary of State is satisfied that, unless a jobseeker's allowance is paid, she will suffer hardship;
(b) he is a single person who is responsible for a young person and the Secretary of State is satisfied that, unless a jobseeker's allowance is paid, the young person will suffer hardship;
(c) he is a member of [² a couple] where—
   [² (i) at least one member of the couple is a woman who is pregnant; and]
   (ii) the Secretary of State is satisfied that, unless a jobseeker's allowance is paid, the woman will suffer hardship;
(d) he is a member of a polygamous marriage and—
   (i) one member of the marriage is pregnant; and
   (ii) the Secretary of State is satisfied that, unless a jobseeker's allowance is paid, that woman will suffer hardship;
(e) he is a member of [² a couple] or of a polygamous marriage where—
   (i) one or both members of the couple, or one or more members of the polygamous marriage, are responsible for a child or young person; and
   (ii) the Secretary of State is satisfied that, unless a jobseeker's allowance is paid, the child or young person will suffer hardship;
(f) he has an award of a jobseeker's allowance which includes or would, if a claim for a jobseeker's allowance from him were to succeed, have included in his applicable amount a disability premium and the Secretary of State is satisfied that, unless a jobseeker's allowance is paid, the person who would satisfy the conditions of entitlement to that premium would suffer hardship;
(g) he suffers, or his partner suffers, from a chronic medical condition which results in functional capacity being limited or restricted by physical impairment and the Secretary of State is satisfied that—

2.641

The Social Security (Loss of Benefit) Regulations 2001

    (i) the suffering has already lasted, or is likely to last, for not less than 26 weeks; and

    (ii) unless a jobseeker's allowance is paid to that person, the probability is that the health of the person suffering would, within 2 weeks of the Secretary of State making his decision, decline further than that of a normally healthy adult and that person would suffer hardship;

(h) he does, or his partner does, or in the case of a person who is married to more than one person under a law which permits polygamy, at least one of those persons does, devote a considerable portion of each week to caring for another person who—

    (i) is in receipt of an attendance allowance or the care component of disability living allowance at one of the two higher rates prescribed under section 72(4) of the Benefits Act;

    (ii) has claimed either attendance allowance or disability living allowance, but only for so long as the claim has not been determined, or for 26 weeks from the date of claiming, whichever is the earlier; or

    (iii) has claimed either attendance allowance or disability living allowance and has an award of either attendance allowance or the care component of disability living allowance at one of the two higher rates prescribed under section 72(4) of the Benefits Act for a period commencing after the date on which that claim was made,

and the Secretary of State is satisfied, after taking account of the factors set out in paragraph (5), in so far as they are appropriate to the particular circumstances of the case, that the person providing the care will not be able to continue doing so unless a jobseeker's allowance is paid to the offender;

(i) he is a person or is the partner of a person to whom section 16 of the Jobseekers Act applies by virtue of a direction issued by the Secretary of State, except where the person to whom the direction applies does not satisfy the requirements of section 1(2)(a) to (c) of that Act;

(j) he is a person—

    (i) to whom section 3(1)(f)(iii) of the Jobseekers Act (persons under the age of 18) applies, or is the partner of such a person; and

    (ii) in respect of whom the Secretary of State is satisfied that the person will, unless a jobseeker's allowance is paid, suffer hardship; or

(k) he is a person—

    (i) who, pursuant to the Children Act 1989, was being looked after by a local authority;

    (ii) with whom the local authority had a duty, pursuant to that Act, to take reasonable steps to keep in touch; or

    (iii) who, pursuant to that Act, qualified for advice and assistance from a local authority,

but in respect of whom head (i), (ii) or (iii) above, as the case may be, had not applied for a period of 3 years or less as at the date on which he complies with the requirements of regulation 9; and

    (iv) who, as at the date on which he complies with the requirements of regulation 9, is under the age of 21.

(SI 2001/4022, reg. 5)

(2) Except in a case to which paragraph (3) or (4) applies, a person shall, for the purposes of regulation 7, be deemed to be a person in hardship where, after taking account of the factors set out in paragraph (5) in so far as they are appropriate to the particular circumstances of the case, the Secretary of State is satisfied that he or his partner will suffer hardship unless a jobseeker's allowance is paid to him.

(3) In paragraphs (1) and (2), a person shall not be deemed to be a person in hardship—
  (a) where he is entitled, or his partner is entitled, to income support or where he or his partner fall within a category of persons prescribed for the purpose of section 124(1)(e) of the Benefits Act;
  (b) during any period in respect of which it has been determined that a jobseeker's allowance is not payable to him pursuant to section 19 of the Jobseekers Act (circumstances in which a jobseeker's allowance is not payable); or
  (c) during any week in the disqualification period in respect of which he is subject to a restriction imposed pursuant to section 62 or 63 of the Child Support, Pensions and Social Security Act 2000 (loss of benefit provisions).

(4) Paragraph (1)(h) shall not apply in a case where the person being cared for resides in a [¹ care home, an Abbeyfield Home or an independent hospital].

(5) Factors which, for the purposes of paragraphs (1) and (2), the Secretary of State is to take into account in determining whether the person is a person in hardship are—
  (a) the presence in that person's family of a person who satisfies the requirements for a disability premium specified in paragraphs 13 and 14 of Schedule 1 to the Jobseeker's Allowance Regulations or for a disabled child premium specified in paragraph 16 of that Schedule to those Regulations;
  (b) the resources which, without a jobseeker's allowance, are likely to be available to the offender's family, the amount by which these resources fall short of the amount applicable in his case in accordance with regulation 10 (applicable amount in hardship cases), the amount of any resources which may be available to members of the offender's family from any person in the offender's household who is not a member of his family and the length of time for which those factors are likely to persist;
  (c) whether there is a substantial risk that essential items, including food, clothing, heating and accommodation, will cease to be available to that person or a member of his family, or will be available at considerably reduced levels and the length of time those factors are likely to persist.

(6) In determining the resources available to that person's family under paragraph (5)(b), any training premium or top-up payment paid pursuant to the Employment and Training Act 1973 shall be disregarded.

AMENDMENTS

1. Social Security (Care Homes and Independent Hospitals) Regulations 2005 (SI 2005/2687), reg.15(2) (October 24, 2005).
2. Civil parnership (Pensions, Social Security and Child Support) (Consequential etc. Provisions) Order 2005 (SI 2005/2877), Sch.3, para.34(2) (December 5, 2005).

Circumstances in which an income-based jobseeker's allowance is payable to a person who is a person in hardship

2.642   **6.**—(1) This regulation applies to a person in hardship within the meaning of regulation 5(1) and is subject to the provisions of regulations 8 and 9.

(2) An income-based jobseeker's allowance shall be payable to a person in hardship even though section 7(2) of the Act prevents payment of a jobseeker's allowance to the offender or section 9 of the Act prevents payment of a jobseeker's allowance to an offender's family member but the allowance shall be payable under this paragraph only if and so long as the claimant satisfies the conditions for entitlement to an income-based jobseeker's allowance.

Further circumstances in which an income-based jobseeker's allowance is payable to a person who is a person in hardship

2.643   **7.**—(1) This regulation applies to a person in hardship within the meaning of regulation 5(2) and is subject to the provisions of regulations 8 and 9.

(2) An income-based jobseeker's allowance shall be payable to a person in hardship even though section 7(2) of the Act prevents payment of a jobseeker's allowance to the offender or section 9 of the Act prevents payment of a jobseeker's allowance to an offender's family member but the allowance shall not be payable under this paragraph—
  (a) where the offender is the claimant, in respect of the first 14 days of the disqualification period;
  (b) where the offender's family member is the claimant, in respect of the first 14 days of the relevant period,
and shall be payable thereafter only if and so long as the claimant satisfies the conditions for entitlement to an income-based jobseeker's allowance.

Conditions for payment of income-based jobseeker's allowance

2.644   **8.**—(1) An income-based jobseeker's allowance shall not be payable in accordance with regulation 6 or 7 except where the claimant has—
  (a) furnished on a form approved for the purpose by the Secretary of State or in such other form as he may in any particular case approve, a statement of the circumstances he relies upon to establish entitlement under regulation 5(1) or, as the case may be, 5(2); and
  (b) signed the statement.

(2) The completed and signed form shall be delivered by the claimant to such office as the Secretary of State may specify.

Provision of information

2.645   **9.** For the purpose of section 7(4)(b) of the Act, the offender, and for the purpose of section 9(4)(b) of the Act, the offender or any member of his family, shall provide to the Secretary of State information as to the circumstances of the person alleged to be in hardship.

Applicable amount in hardship cases

2.646   **10.**—(1) The weekly applicable amount of a person to whom an income-based jobseeker's allowance is payable in accordance with this Part shall be

(SI 2001/4022, reg.10)

reduced by a sum equivalent to 40 per cent. or, in a case where the claimant or any other member of his family is either pregnant or seriously ill, 20 per cent. of the following amount—
  (a) where the claimant is a single claimant aged not less than 18 but less than 25 or a member of a couple or polygamous marriage where one member is aged not less than 18 but less than 25 and the other member or, in the case of a polygamous marriage each other member, is a person under 18 who is not eligible for an income-based jobseeker's allowance under section 3(1)(f)(iii) of the Jobseekers Act or is not subject to a direction under section 16 of that Act, the amount specified in paragraph 1(1)(d) of Schedule 1 to the Jobseeker's Allowance Regulations;
  (b) where the claimant is a single claimant aged not less than 25 or a member of a couple or a polygamous marriage (other than a member of a couple or polygamous marriage to whom sub-paragraph (a) applies) at least one of whom is aged not less than 18, the amount specified in paragraph 1(1)(e) of Schedule 1 to the Jobseeker's Allowance Regulations.

(2) A reduction under paragraph (1) shall, if it is not a multiple of 5p, be rounded to the nearest such multiple or, if it is a multiple of 2.5p but not of 5p, to the next lower multiple of 5p.

PART IV

HARDSHIP FOR JOINT-CLAIM COUPLES

Application of Part and meaning of "couple in hardship"

11.—(1) This Part of these Regulations applies in respect of any part of the disqualification period when section 8(2) of the Act would otherwise apply.

2.647

(2) In this Part of these Regulations, a "couple in hardship" means, for the purposes of regulation 13, a joint-claim couple, other than a couple to whom paragraph (4) or (5) applies, who are claiming a jointclaim jobseeker's allowance jointly where at least one member of that couple is an offender and where—
  (a) [¹ care home, an Abbeyfield Home or an independent hospital] and the Secretary of State is satisfied that, unless a joint-claim jobseeker's allowance is paid, she will suffer hardship;
  (b) one or both members of the couple are members of a polygamous marriage, one member of the marriage is pregnant and the Secretary of State is satisfied that, unless a joint-claim jobseeker's allowance is paid, she will suffer hardship;
  (c) the award of a joint-claim jobseeker's allowance includes, or would, if a claim for a jobseeker's allowance from the couple were to succeed, have included in their applicable amount a disability premium and the Secretary of State is satisfied that, unless a joint-claim jobseeker's allowance is paid, the member of the couple who would have caused the disability premium to be applicable to the couple would suffer hardship;

The Social Security (Loss of Benefit) Regulations 2001

(d) either member of the couple suffers from a chronic medical condition which results in functional capacity being limited or restricted by physical impairment and the Secretary of State is satisfied that—
  (i) the suffering has already lasted or is likely to last, for not less than 26 weeks; and
  (ii) unless a joint-claim jobseeker's allowance is paid, the probability is that the health of the person suffering would, within two weeks of the Secretary of State making his decision, decline further than that of a normally healthy adult and the member of the couple who suffers from that condition would suffer hardship;

(e) either member of the couple, or where a member of that couple is married to more than one person under a law which permits polygamy, one member of that marriage, devotes a considerable portion of each week to caring for another person who—
  (i) is in receipt of an attendance allowance or the care component of disability living allowance at one of the two higher rates prescribed under section 72(4) of the Benefits Act;
  (ii) has claimed either attendance allowance or disability living allowance, but only for so long as the claim has not been determined, or for 26 weeks from the date of claiming, whichever is the earlier; or
  (iii) has claimed either attendance allowance or disability living allowance and has an award of either attendance allowance or the care component of disability living allowance at one of the two higher rates prescribed under section 72(4) of the Benefits Act for a period commencing after the date on which that claim was made,
  and the Secretary of State is satisfied, after taking account of the factors set out in paragraph (6) in so far as they are appropriate to the particular circumstances of the case, that the person providing the care will not be able to continue doing so unless a joint-claim jobseeker's allowance is paid; or

(f) section 16 of the Jobseekers Act applies to either member of the couple by virtue of a direction issued by the Secretary of State, except where the member of the joint-claim couple to whom the direction applies does not satisfy the requirements of section 1(2)(a) to (c) of that Act;

(g) section 3A(1)(e)(ii) of the Jobseekers Act (member of joint-claim couple under the age of 18) applies to either member of the couple and the Secretary of State is satisfied that unless a jointclaim jobseeker's allowance is paid, the couple will suffer hardship; or

(h) one or both members of the couple is a person—
  (i) who, pursuant to the Children Act 1989, was being looked after by a local authority;
  (ii) with whom the local authority had a duty, pursuant to that Act, to take reasonable steps to keep in touch; or
  (iii) who, pursuant to that Act, qualified for advice or assistance from a local authority,
  but in respect of whom head (i), (ii) or (iii) above, as the case may be, had not applied for a period of 3 years or less as at the date on which the requirements of regulation 15 are complied with; and

(SI 2001/4022, reg.11)

    (iv) who, as at the date on which the requirements of regulation 15 are complied with, is under the age of 21.

(3) Except in a case to which paragraph (4) or (5) applies, a joint-claim couple shall, for the purposes of regulation 14, be deemed to be a couple in hardship where the Secretary of State is satisfied, after taking account of the factors set out in paragraph (6) in so far as they are appropriate to the particular circumstances of the case, that the couple will suffer hardship unless a joint-claim jobseeker's allowance is paid.

(4) In paragraphs (2) and (3), a joint-claim couple shall not be deemed to be a "couple in hardship"—

(a) where one member of the couple is entitled to income support or falls within a category of persons prescribed for the purposes of section 124(1)(e) of the Benefits Act; or

(b) during a period in respect of which it has been determined that both members of the couple are subject to sanctions for the purposes of section 20A of the Jobseekers Act (denial or reduction of joint-claim jobseeker's allowance).

(5) Paragraph (2)(e) shall not apply in a case where the person being cared for resides in a [² care home, an Abbeyfield Home or an independent hospital].

(6) Factors which, for the purposes of paragraphs (2) and (3), the Secretary of State is to take into account in determining whether a joint-claim couple will suffer hardship are—

(a) the presence in the joint-claim couple of a person who satisfies the requirements for a disability premium specified in paragraphs 20H and 20I of Schedule 1 to the Jobseeker's Allowance Regulations;

(b) the resources which, without a joint-claim jobseeker's allowance, are likely to be available to the joint-claim couple, the amount by which these resources fall short of the amount applicable in their case in accordance with regulation 16 (applicable amount of joint-claim couple in hardship cases), the amount of any resources which may be available to the joint-claim couple from any person in the couple's household who is not a member of the family and the length of time for which those factors are likely to persist;

(c) whether there is a substantial risk that essential items, including food, clothing, heating and accommodation, will cease to be available to the joint-claim couple, or will be available at considerably reduced levels, the hardship that will result and the length of time those factors are likely to persist.

(7) In determining the resources available to the offender's family under paragraph (6)(b), any training premium or top-up payment paid pursuant to the Employment and Training Act 1973 shall be disregarded.

AMENDMENTS

1. Social Security (Care Homes and Independent Hospitals) Regulations 2005 (SI 2005/2687), reg.15(3) (October 24, 2005).

2. Civil Partnership (Pensions, Social Security and Child Support) (Consequential etc. Provisions) Order 2005 (SI 2005/2877), Sch.3, para.34(3) (December 5, 2005).

Circumstances in which a joint-claim jobseeker's allowance is payable where a joint-claim couple is a couple in hardship

2.648

12.—(1) This regulation applies where a joint-claim couple is a couple in hardship within the meaning of regulation 11(2) and is subject to the provisions of regulations 14 and 15.

(2) A joint-claim jobseeker's allowance shall be payable to a couple in hardship even though section 8(2) of the Act prevents payment of a joint-claim jobseeker's allowance to the couple or section 8(3) of the Act reduces the amount of a joint-claim jobseeker's allowance payable to the couple but the allowance shall be payable under this paragraph only if and for so long as—
  (a) the joint-claim couple satisfy the other conditions of entitlement to a joint-claim jobseeker's allowance; or
  (b) one member satisfies those conditions and the other member comes within any paragraph in Schedule A1 to the Jobseeker's Allowance Regulations (categories of members not required to satisfy conditions in section 1(2B)(b) of the Jobseekers Act).

Further circumstances in which a joint-claim jobseeker's allowance is payable to a couple in hardship

2.649

13.—(1) This regulation applies to a couple in hardship falling within regulation 11(3) and is subject to the provisions of regulations 14 and 15.

(2) A joint-claim jobseeker's allowance shall be payable to a couple in hardship even though section 8(2) of the Act prevents payment of a joint-claim jobseeker's allowance to the couple or section 8(3) of the Act reduces the amount of a joint-claim jobseeker's allowance payable to the couple but the allowance—
  (a) shall not be payable under this paragraph in respect of the first 14 days of the prescribed period; and
  (b) shall be payable thereafter only where the conditions of entitlement to a joint-claim jobseeker's allowance are satisfied or where one member satisfies those conditions and the other member comes within any paragraph in Schedule A1 to the Jobseeker's Allowance Regulations (categories of members not required to satisfy conditions in section 1(2B)(b) of the Jobseekers Act).

Conditions for payment of a joint-claim jobseeker's allowance

2.650

14.—(1) A joint-claim jobseeker's allowance shall not be payable in accordance with regulation 12 or 13 except where either member of the couple has—
  (a) furnished on a form approved for the purpose by the Secretary of State or in such other form as he may in any particular case approve, a statement of the circumstances he relies upon to establish entitlement under regulation 11(2) or, as the case may be, 11(3); and
  (b) signed the statement.

(2) The completed and signed form shall be delivered by a member of the couple to such office as the Secretary of State may specify.

Provision of information

2.651

15. For the purposes of section 8(4)(b) of the Act, a member of the couple shall provide to the Secretary of State information as to the circumstances of the alleged hardship of the couple.

(SI 2001/4022, reg.16)

Applicable amount of joint-claim couple in hardship cases

16.—(1) The weekly applicable amount of a couple to whom a joint-claim jobseeker's allowance is payable in accordance with this Part shall be reduced by a sum equivalent to 40 per cent. or, in a case where a member of the joint-claim couple is either pregnant or seriously ill or where a member of the joint-claim couple is a member of a polygamous marriage and one of those members is either pregnant or seriously ill, 20 per cent of the following amount—

(a) where one member of the joint-claim couple or of the polygamous marriage is aged not less than 18 but less than 25 and the other member or, in the case of a polygamous marriage, each other member, is a person under 18 to whom section 3A(1)(e)(ii) of the Jobseekers Act applies or is not subject to a direction under section 16 of that Act, the amount specified in paragraph 1(1)(d) of Schedule 1 to the Jobseeker's Allowance Regulations;

(b) where one member of the joint-claim couple or at least one member of the polygamous marriage (other than a member of a couple or polygamous marriage to whom sub-paragraph (a) applies) is aged not less than 18, the amount specified in paragraph 1(1)(e) of Schedule 1 to the Jobseeker's Allowance Regulations.

(2) A reduction under paragraph (1) shall, if it is not a multiple of 5p, be rounded to the nearest such multiple or, if it is a multiple of 2.5p but not of 5p, to the next lower multiple of 5p.

2.652

PART V

HOUSING BENEFIT AND COUNCIL TAX BENEFIT

17. *Omitted.* 2.653
18. *Omitted.* 2.654

PART VI

DEDUCTIONS FROM BENEFITS AND DISQUALIFYING BENEFITS

Social security benefits not to be sanctionable benefits

19. The following social security benefits are to be treated as a disqualifying benefit but not a sanctionable benefit—

(a) constant attendance allowance payable under article 14 of the Naval, Military and Air Forces Etc. (Disablement and Death) Service Pensions Order 1983 ("the Order") or article 14 or 43 of the Personal Injuries (Civilians) Scheme 1983 ("the Scheme");

(b) exceptionally severe disablement allowance payable under article 15 of the Order or article 15 or 44 of the Scheme;

(c) mobility supplement payable under article 26A of the Order or article 25A or 48A of the Scheme;

2.655

The Social Security (Loss of Benefit) Regulations 2001

(d) constant attendance allowance and exceptionally severe disablement allowance, payable under sections 104 and 105 respectively of the Benefits Act where a disablement pension is payable under section 103 of that Act; and

(e) a bereavement payment payable under section 36 of the Benefits Act.

Deductions from benefits

20. Any restriction in section 7, 8 or 9 of the Act shall not apply in relation to payments of benefit to the extent of any deduction from the payments which falls to be made under regulations made under section 5(1)(p) of the Social Security Administration Act 1992 for, or in place of, child support maintenance and for this purpose, "child support maintenance" means such maintenance which is payable under the Child Support Act 1991.

Part VII

Other Amendments

21. *Omitted.*
22. *Omitted.*

Social Security (Medical Evidence) Regulations 1976

(SI 1976/615) (as amended)

Arrangement of Regulations

1. Citation, commencement and interpretation.
2. Evidence of incapacity for work and confinement.
3. *Revoked.*
4. *Revoked.*
5. Self-certificate for first seven days of a spell of incapacity for work.

Schedules

Schedule 1
  Part I:—Rules
  Part II:—Form of Doctor's Statement
  Part III:—The Notes
Schedule 1A
  Part I: Rules
  Part II: Form of Special Statement
Schedule 1B
  Part I: Rules
  Part II: Form of Doctor's Statement
Schedule 2
Part I Rules
Part II Form of Certificate

(SI 1976/615) (as amended)

The Secretary of State for Social Services, in exercise of powers conferred upon him by section 115(1) of, and Schedule 13 to, the Social Security Act 1975 and of all other powers enabling him in that behalf, after reference to the National Insurance Advisory Committee hereby makes the following regulations:

Citation, commencement, and interpretation

1.—(1) These regulations may be cited as the Social Security (Medical Evidence) Regulations 1976, and shall come into operation on 4th October,
(2) In these regulations, unless the context otherwise requires—
"the Act" means the Social Security Act 1975;
[¹ "the Contributions and Benefits Act" means the Social Security Contributions and Benefits Act 1992;
"the all work test" means the test provided for in section 171C of the Contributions and Benefits Act;]
[² "registered midwife" means a midwife who is registered as a midwife with the United Kingdom Central Council for Nursing, Midwifery and Health Visiting under the Nurses, Midwives and Health Visitors Act 1979;
"doctor" means a registered medical practitioner;]
"signature" means, in relation to any statement or certificate given in accordance with these regulations, the name by which the person giving that statement or certificate, as the case may be, is usually known (any name other than the surname being either in full or otherwise indicated) written by that person in his own handwriting; and "signed" shall be construed accordingly.
(3) Any reference in these regulations to any provisions made by or contained in any enactment or instrument shall, except in so far as the context otherwise requires, be construed as a reference to that provision as amended or extended by any enactment or instrument and as including a reference to any provision which it re-enacts or replaces, or which may re-enact or replace it, with or without modification.
(4) The rules for the construction of Acts of Parliament contained in the Interpretation Act 1889 shall apply in relation to this instrument and in relation to the revocation effected by it as if this instrument, the regulations revoked by it and regulations revoked by the regulations so revoked were Acts of Parliament, and as if each revocation were a repeal.

2.660

AMENDMENTS

1. The Social Security (Medical Evidence) Amendment Regulations 1994 (SI 1994/2975), reg.2 (April 13, 1995).
2. The Social Security (Medical Evidence) Amendment Regulations 1987 (SI 1987/409), reg.2 (April 6, 1987).

Evidence of incapacity for work and confinement

2.—(1) [¹ Subject to regulation 5] [³ where a person claims he is entitled to any benefit, allowance or advantage (other than industrial injuries benefit or statutory sick pay), and his entitlement to that benefit, allowance or advantage depends on his being incapable of work, then in respect of each day until he has been assessed for the purposes of the [⁵ personal capability assessment], he shall provide evidence of such incapacity]—

2.661

[³(a) by means of a certificate in the form of a statement in writing given by a doctor in accordance with the rules set out in Part I of Schedule 1 to these Regulations on the form set out in Part II of that Schedule; or
(b) where a doctor—
   (i) has not given a statement under sub-paragraph (a) of this paragraph since the patient was examined and wishes to give such a statement but more than one day has passed since the examination; or
   (ii) advises that the patient should refrain from work on the basis of a written report from another doctor,
by means of a special statement given in accordance with the rules set out in Part I of Schedule 1A to these Regulations on the form set out in Part II of that Schedule;] or
[²](c) [⁵ where the question of whether a person is capable or incapable of work fulls to be determined in accordance with the personal capability assessment] and the Secretary of State so requests, a statement in writing given by a doctor in accordance with the rules set out in Part I of Schedule 1B to these Regulations on the form set out in Part II of that Schedule; or
(d) where it would be unreasonable to require a person to provide a statement [⁴ in accordance with sub-paragraphs (a) to (c),] such other evidence as may be sufficient to show that he should refrain [⁴ (or should have refrained)] from work by reason of some specific disease or bodily or mental disablement.]

(2) Every person to whom paragraph (1) applies [² who has not been assessed for the purposes of the all work test] shall, before he returns to work, furnish evidence of the date on which he will become fit to resume work either in accordance with rule 10 of Part I of Schedule 1 to these regulations, or by such other means as may be sufficient in the circumstances of the case.

[⁶ (3) Every woman who claims maternity benefit shall furnish evidence—
(a) where the claims is made in respect of expectation of confinement, that she is pregnant and as to the stage which she has reached in her pregnancy; or
(b) where the claim is made by virtue of the fact of confinement, that she has been confined;
and shall furnish such evidence by means of a maternity certificate given by a doctor or by as registered midwife [not earlier than the beginning of the 20th week before the week in which she is expected to be confined] in accordance with the rules set out in Part I of Schedule 2 to these regulations in the appropriate form set out in Part II of that Schedule or by such other means as may be sufficient in the circumstances of any particular case.]

AMENDMENTS

1. The Social Security (Medical Evidence, Claims and Payments) Amendments Regulations 1982 (SI 1982/699), reg.2 (June 14, 1982).
2. The Social Security (Medical Evidence) Amendment Regulations 1994 (SI 1994/2975), reg.2 (April 13, 1995).
3. The Social Security (Medical Evidence) Amendment Regulations 1992 (SI 1992/2471), reg.3 (March 9, 1992).
4. The Social Security (Incapacity for Work) Miscellaneous Amendments Regulations 1995 (SI 1995/987), reg.4 (April 13, 1995.)
5. The Social Security (Incapacity) Miscellaneous Amendments Regulations 2000 (SI 2000/590), reg.6 (April 3, 2000).

(SI 1976/615, reg.2) (as amended)

6. The Social Security (Medical Evidence) and Statutory Maternity Pay (Medical Evidence) (Amendment) Regulations 2001 (SI 2001/2931), reg.2 (September 28, 2001).

GENERAL NOTE

In *CSIS/065/1991*, the Commissioner ruled that the reference in the regulation to "such other means as may be sufficient in the particular circumstances of any particular case" meant that evidence of incapacity need not be in the form of a medical certificate. This means that medical certificates other than in the form set out in the Schedule may be acceptable as well as evidence from the claimant himself or herself (para.14). Whether such evidence is sufficient is a matter for determination by the decision-maker or tribunal. Failure to consider this issue will be an error of law.

In *CIB/17533/1996* the Commissioner addressed an issue which was being argued by a number of representatives, namely that there was no jurisdiction to make an all work test determination where the adjudication officer had requested the claimant to obtain the special Form Med. 4 and this form was not available to the adjudication officer when the decision was made. Form Med. 4 is the special form which specifically directs doctors to consider capacity for *all* work in certifying incapacity for work. The Commissioner concludes that "the somewhat legalistic proposition that a decision by an adjudication officer made without a form MED4 is a nullity or is erroneous in law cannot in my view be sustained" (para.8 of Common Appendix).

2.662

Regulation 3 revoked by The Social Security (Claims and Payments) Regulations 1979 (SI1979/628), reg.32 (July 9, 1979).

2.663

Regulation 4 revoked by The Social Security (Medical Evidence, Claims and Payments) Amendments Regulations 1982 (SI1982/699), reg.2 (June 14, 1982).

2.664

[¹Self-certificate for first 7 days of a spell of incapacity for work

5.—[²(1)[³ The evidence of incapacity required for the purposes of determining entitlement to a benefit, allowance or advantage referred to in regulation 2(1)]—
  (a) for a spell of incapacity which lasts less than 8 days, or
  (b) in respect of any of the first 7 days of a longer spell of incapacity;
may consist of a self certificate instead of a certificate in the form of a statement in writing given by a doctor in accordance with regulation 2(1).]
(2) For the purpose of this regulation:
  a "self-certificate" means a declaration made by the claimant in writing, in a form approved for the purpose by the Secretary of State, that he has been unfit for work from a date or for a period specified in the declaration and may include a statement that the claimant expects to continue to be unfit for work on days subsequent to the date on which it is made";
  [³ "spell of incapacity" has the meaning given to it by section 171B(3) of the Contributions and Benefits Act.]]

2.665

AMENDMENTS

1. The Social Security (Medical Evidence, Claims and Payments) Amendments Regulations 1982 (SI 1982/699), reg.2 (June 14, 1982).
2. The Social Security (Medical Evidence, Claims and Payments) Amendment Regulations 1989 (SI 1989/1686), reg.2 (October 9, 1989).
3. The Social Security (Medical Evidence) Amendment Regulations 1994 (SI 1994/2975), reg.2 (April 13, 1995).

Social Security (Medical Evidence) Regulations 1976

SCHEDULE 1   **Regulation 2(1)**

Part I

Rules

2.666

1. In these rules, unless the context otherwise requires—

"claimant" means the person in respect of whom a statement is given in accordance with these rules;
"doctor" means a registered medical practitioner not being the claimant;
"doctor's statement" means a statement given in accordance with these rules;
"2 weeks" means any period of 14 consecutive days.

2. The doctor's statement shall be in the form set out in Part II of this Schedule.

[¹3. Where the claimant—
  (a) is on the list of a person providing primary medical services under the National Health Service Act 1977 or the National Health Service (Scotland) Act 1978 and is being attended by a doctor performing such services; or
  (b) is on the list of a doctor, or list held jointly by two or more doctors performing personal medical services in connection with a pilot scheme under the National Health Service (Primary Care) Act 1997 and is being attended by such a doctor,
the doctor's statement shall be on the form provided by the Secretary of State for he purpose and shall be signed by the attending doctor.]

4. In any other case, the doctor's statement shall be either on a form provided by the Secretary of State for the purpose or in a form substantially to the like effect, and shall be signed by the doctor attending the claimant.

5. Every doctor's statement shall be completed in ink or other indelible substance, and shall contain the following particulars—
  (a) the claimant's name;
  (b) the date of the examination on which the doctor's statement is based;
  (c) the diagnosis of the claimant's disorder in respect of which the doctor is advising the claimant to refrain from work or, as the case may be, which has caused the claimant's absence from work;
  (d) the date on which the doctor's statement is given;
  (e) the address of the doctor.
and shall bear, opposite the words "Doctor's signature," the signature of the doctor making the statement written after there have been entered the claimant's name and the doctor's diagnosis.

6. Subject to rules 7 and 8 below, the diagnosis of the claimant's disorder in respect of which the doctor is advising the claimant to refrain from work or, as the case may be, which has caused the claimant's absence from work shall be specified as precisely as the doctor's knowledge of the claimant's condition at the time of the examination permits.

7. Where, in the doctor's opinion, a disclosure to the claimant of the precise disorder would be prejudicial to his well-being, the diagnosis may be specified less precisely.

8. In the case of an initial examination by a doctor in respect of a disorder stated by the claimant to have caused incapacity for work, where—
  (a) there are no clinical signs of that disorder, and
  (b) in the doctor's opinion, the claimant need not refrain from work,
instead of specifying a diagnosis "unspecified" may be entered.

9. A doctor's statement must be given on a date not later than one day after the date of the examination on which it is based, and no further doctor's statement based on the same examination shall be furnished other than a doctor's statement by way of replacement of an original which has been lost or mislaid, in which case it shall be clearly marked "duplicate."

10. Where, in the doctor's opinion, the claimant will become fit to resume work on a day not later than 2 weeks after the date of the examination on which the doctor's statement is based, the doctor's statement shall specify that day.

11. Subject to rules 12 and 13 below, the doctor's statement shall specify the minimum period during which, in the doctor's opinion, the claimant should, by reason of his disorder, refrain from work.

12. The period specified shall begin on the date of the examination on which the doctor's statement is based and shall not exceed 6 months unless the claimant has, on the advice of a doctor, refrained from work for at least 6 months immediately preceding that date.

13. Where—

(SI 1976/615, Sch.1) (as amended)

(a) the claimant has, on the advice of a doctor, refrained from work for at least 6 months immediately preceding the date of the examination on which the doctor's statement is based, and

(b) in the doctor's opinion, it will be necessary for the claimant to refrain from work for the foreseeable future, instead of specifying a period, the doctor may, having regard to the circumstances of the particular case, enter the words "until further notice."

14. The Notes set out in Part III of this Schedule shall accompany the form of doctor's statement provided by the Secretary of State.

15. A doctor may, having regard to the circumstances of the particular case, indicate on the doctor's statement that the claimant should be considered for vocational rehabilitation.

PART II

FORM OF DOCTOR'S STATEMENT   2.667

DOCTOR'S STATEMENT

In confidence to

Mr./Mrs./Miss ....

I examined you today/yesterday and advised you that:

(a) you need not refrain from work

(b) you should refrain from work

for ....

OR until ....

Diagnosis of your disorder causing absence from work ....

Doctor's remarks

Doctor's signature

Date of signing

Recommendation for vocational rehabilitation

PART III

THE NOTES   2.668

The following notes shall accompany the form of doctor's statement provided by the Secretary of State—

On the doctor's statement—

(1) After the words "you should refrain from work for", the period entered must not exceed 6 months unless the patient has, on the advice of a doctor, already refrained from work for a continuous period of 6 months.

(2) After the words "you should refrain from work until"—
 (a) if the patient is being given a date when he can return to work the date entered should not be more than 2 weeks after the date of the examination;
 (b) if the patient has already been incapable of work for at least 6 months and recovery of capacity for work in the foreseeable future is not expected "further notice" may be entered.

AMENDMENT

1. General Medical Services and Personal Medical Services Transition and Consequential Provisions Order 2004 (SI 2004/865), Sch.1 (April 1, 2004).

Social Security (Medical Evidence) Regulations 1976

SCHEDULE 1A   **Regulation 2(1)**

Part I

RULES

2.669   1. In these rules, unless the context otherwise requires—

"claimant" means the person in respect of whom a statement is given in accordance with these rules;
"doctor" means a registered medical practitioner not being the claimant;
"special statement" means the form prescribed in Part II of this Schedule.

2. Where a doctor advises a claimant to refrain from work on the basis of a written report which he has received from another doctor or where a doctor has not issued a statement since the claimant was examined and he wishes to issue a statement more than a day after the examination he shall use the special statement.

3. The special statement shall be completed in the manner described in paragraph 5 of Part I to Schedule 1.

4. Subject to rules 5 and 6 below, the diagnosis of the claimant's disorder in respect of which the doctor is advising the claimant to refrain from work or as the case may be, which has caused the claimant's absence from work shall be specified as precisely as the doctor's knowledge of the claimant's condition permits.

5. Where, in the doctor's opinion, a disclosure to the claimant of the precise disorder would be prejudicial to his well being, the diagnosis may be specified less precisely.

6. In a case of a disorder stated by the claimant to have caused incapacity for work, where—
   (a) no clinical signs have been found of that disorder, and
   (b) in the doctor's opinion, the claimant need not refrain from work, instead of specifying a diagnosis "unspecified" may be entered.

7. Part B of the special statement must only be given on a date not later than one month after the date of the written report on which the special statement is based and that part shall only be used where the claimant is being advised to refrain from work for a specified period of not more than one month.

Part II

2.670   **FORM OF SPECIAL STATEMENT**

FOR SOCIAL SECURITY AND   Special Statement
STATUTORY SICK PAY   by the Doctor
PURPOSES ONLY

In confidence to

Mr./Mrs./Miss/Ms ....

(A) I have examined you on the   (B) I have not examined you but, on the
                                             basis of a recent written report from—
following dates .... Doctor ....(Name if known)
.... of ....
....
and advised you that you should   .... (Address)
refrain from work   I have advised you that should refrain

From .... to ....   from work for/until ....

Diagnosis of your disorder
causing absence from work ....

(SI 1976/615, Sch.1A) (as amended)

Doctor's remarks

Doctor's signature

Date of signing

The special circumstances in which this form may be used are described in the handbook "Medical Evidence for Social Security and Statutory Sick Pay purposes".

AMENDMENT

1. The Social Security (Miscellaneous Provisions) Amendments Regulations 1992 (SI 1992/247), reg.3 (March 9, 1992).

SCHEDULE 1B   Regulation 2(1)(c)

PART I

RULES

1. In these rules, unless the context otherwise requires—

"claimant" means the person in respect of whom a statement is given in accordance with these rules;
"doctor" means a registered medical practitioner not being the claimant;
"all work test statement" means a statement given by a doctor in accordance with these rules.

2. Where the Secretary of State has requested that the claimant provide an all work test statement, that statement shall be provided in the form prescribed in Part II of this Schedule notwithstanding that the claimant has already provided a statement in accordance with Schedule 1 or 1A.

3. The all work test statement shall be completed in accordance with rules 3, 4, 5 [² and 9 to 13] of Part I to Schedule 1.

4. Subject to rule 5 below, the diagnosis of—
   (a) the disorder in respect of which the doctor is advising the claimant to refrain from work or, as the case may be, which has caused the claimant's absence from work; and
   (b) any other condition which could affect the claimant's capacity for work, shall be specified as precisely as the doctor's knowledge of the claimant's condition at the time of the examination permits.

5. Where, in the doctor's opinion, a disclosure to the claimant of the precise disorder would be prejudicial to his well being, the diagnosis may be specified less precisely.

6. The notes set out in Part III of this Schedule shall accompany the form of doctor's statement provided by the Secretary of State.

2.671

Social Security (Medical Evidence) Regulations 1976

Part II

2.672 **FORM OF DOCTOR'S STATEMENT**

THIS STATEMENT SHOULD <u>NOT</u> BE USED FOR PEOPLE CLAIMING STATUTORY SICK PAY FROM THEIR EMPLOYER.

Doctor's Statement

In confidence to
Mr/Mrs/Miss/Ms ....

Note for Doctor—We are making an assessment of your patient's eligibility for incapacity Benefit and other state benefits under the terms of the all work test. Please complete the following boxes.

Main diagnosis (*be as precise as possible*) ....

Other diagnoses ....

Doctor's remarks
(Including comments on the disabling effects of the condition, treatment and progress—accuracy and detail will avoid requests for completion of a medical report).

Note for Doctor—While the all work test is being carried out, we need evidence that your patient should refrain from <u>his usual occupation</u>. Please provide the following information (which will not be part of the [3 perpetual capability assessment).

I am issuing the following statement based upon the current guidance to certifying medical practitioners. I examined you today/yesterday and advised you that:

(a) You need not refrain from your usual occupation

(b) You should refrain from your usual occupation

for (*insert period*) ....

OR until ....

Doctor's signature

Date of signing

Form Med 4

Part III

The Notes

The following notes shall accompany the form of doctor's statement provided by the Secretary of State:

2.673 1. After the words on the doctor's statement "you should refrain from your usual occupation"—
  (i) if the patient is being given a date when he can return to work, the date entered should not be more than 2 weeks after the date on which the statement is issued;
  (ii) if recovery of capacity for work in the foreseeable future is not expected, "further notice" may be entered.

742

(SI 1976/615, Sch.1B) (as amended)

2. The "remarks" box should be used to provide additional information; including further details of diagnosed conditions, the disabling effect of such conditions, and notes on the patient's treatment and progress. Accuracy and detail will avoid requests for completion of a medical report.

3. The "remarks" box should also be used to state whether or not the patient is able to travel a reasonable distance to a medical examination as a result of his condition. If no entry is made, it will be assumed that the patient can travel.

4. This form of doctor's statement should not be used where the patient is claiming statutory sick pay from their employer. Form Med 3 should be used for that purpose.

AMENDMENTS

1. The Social Security (Medical Evidence) Amendment Regulations 1994 (SI 1994/2975), reg.3 (April 13, 1995).

2. The Social Security (Incapacity for Work) Miscellaneous Amendments Regulations 1995 (SI 1995/987), reg.4 (April 13, 1995).

3. The Social Security (Incapacity) Miscellaneous Amendments Regulations 2000 (SI 2000/590), reg.6 (April 3, 2000).

[1]SCHEDULE 2   Regulation 2(3)

PART I

RULES

1. In these rules any reference to a woman is a reference to the woman in respect of whom a maternity certificate is given in accordance with these rules.

2. A maternity certificate shall be given by a doctor or registered midwife attending the woman and shall not be given by the woman herself.

3. The maternity certificate shall be on a form provided by the Secretary of State for the purpose and the wording shall be that set out in the appropriate part of the form specified in Part II of this Schedule.

4. Every maternity certificate shall be completed in ink or other indelible substance and shall contain the following particulars—
   (a) the woman's name;
   (b) the week in which the woman is expected to be confined or, if the maternity certificate is given after confinement, the date of that confinement and the date the confinement was expected to take place [2 . . .];
   (c) the date of the examination on which the maternity certificate is based;
   (d) the date on which the maternity certificate is signed; and
   (e) the address of the doctor or where the maternity certificate is signed by a registered midwife the personal identification number given to her by the United Kingdom Central Council for Nursing, Midwifery and Health Visiting ("UKCC") on her registration in Part 10 of the register maintained under section 10 of the Nurses, Midwives and Health Visitors Act 1979 and the expiry date of that registration,

and shall bear opposite the word "Signature", the signature of the person giving the maternity certificate written after there has been entered on the maternity certificate the woman's name and the expected date or, as the case may be, the date of the confinement.

5. After a maternity certificate has been given, no further maternity certificate based on the same examination shall be furnished other than a maternity certificate by way of replacement of an original which has been lost or mislaid, in which case it shall be clearly marked "duplicate".

Social Security (Medical Evidence) Regulations 1976

[²]PART II

FORM OF CERTIFICATE

2.676 MATERNITY CERTIFICATE

Please fill in this form in ink

Name of patient

Fill in this part if you are giving the certificate before the confinement Do not fill this in more [³ than 20 weeks] before the week the baby is expected.

I certify that I examined you on the date given below. In my opinion you can expect to have your baby in the week that includes ..../.........../........
Week means a period of 7 days starting on a Sunday and ending on a Saturday.

Fill in this part if you are giving the certificate after the confinement.
I certify that I attended you in connection with the birth which took place on

......./.........../........ when you were delivered of a child [ ] children. In my opinion your baby was expected in the week that includes ..../.........../........

Date of examination ..../.........../........

Date of signing ..../.........../........

Signature

Registered midwives

Please give your UKCC Personal Identification Number and the expiry date of your registration with the UKCC.

Doctors
Please stamp your name and address here if the form has not been stamped by the [³ Primary Care Trust or Local Health Board in whose medical performers list you are included (or, in Scotland, by the Health Board in whose primary medical services performers list you are included)] in whose medical list you are included.

AMENDMENTS

  1. The Social Security (Medical Evidence) Amendment Regulations 1987 (SI 1987/409), reg.4 (April 6, 1987)
  2. The Social Security (Miscellaneous Provisions) Amendment Regulations 1991 (SI 1991/2284), reg.21 (November 1, 1991)
  3. General Medical Services and Personal Medical Services Transition and Consequential Provisions Order 2004 (SI 2004/865), Sch.1 (April 1, 2004).

(SI 2001/3252)

The Social Security (Notification of Change of Circumstances) Regulations 2001

(SI 2001/3252)

Made	26th September 2001
Laid before Parliament	2nd October 2001
Coming into force	18th October 2001

ARRANGEMENT OF REGULATIONS

1. Citation and commencement
2. Notification for purpose of sections 111A and 112 of the Social Security Administration Act 1992
3. Change affecting jobseeker's allowance
4. Change affecting housing benefit or council tax benefit
5. Change affecting other benefit payment or advantage.

2.677

GENERAL NOTE

Section 16 of the Social Security Fraud Act 2001 (c.11), which came fully into force on October 18, 2001, amends the Administration Act 1992 to create new offences relating to failure to notify a change of circumstances, which affects entitlement to benefit. The requirements of the offences under the amended provisions of the Administration Act (which are not reproduced in Vol.III) are, broadly, fourfold (1) there has been a change of circumstances affecting entitlement to benefit, (2) the change is not excluded by regulations from changes which are required to be notified, (3) the person knows that the change affects entitlement to benefit, and (4) the person dishonestly fails to give a prompt notification in the prescribed manner to the prescribed person. These regulations set out the matter prescribed by the statute for the purposes of the criminal offences. The explanatory note to the regulations indicates that they are intended to mirror the existing requirements prescribed for the purposes of claims and payments under ss.5 and 6 of the Administration Act. The regulations are reproduced here so that those dealing with questions arising in the appeal tribunals and elsewhere in relation to claims for benefit are aware of the existence of these requirements under the criminal law. They may be referred to in overpayment cases.

The Secretary of State for Work and Pensions, in exercise of the powers conferred on him by ss.111A(1A), (1B), (1D) and (1E), 112(1A) to (1D), 189(1), (3) and (4) and 191 of the Social Security Administration Act 1992 and of all other powers enabling him in that behalf, and after consultation in respect of provisions of these Regulations relating to housing benefit and council tax benefit with organisations appearing to him to be representative of the authorities concerned, by this Instrument, which is made before the end of the period of 6 months from the coming into force of s.16 of the Social Security Fraud Act 2001, hereby makes the following Regulations:

2.678

Citation and commencement

1. These Regulations may be cited as the Social Security (Notification of Change of Circumstances) Regulations 2001 and shall come into force on 18th October 2001.

2.679

The Social Security (Notification of Change of Circumstances) Regs 2001

Notification for purposes of sections 111A and 112 of the Social Security Administration Act 1992

2.680   **2.** Regulations 3 to 5 below prescribe the person to whom, and manner in which, a change of circumstances must be notified for the purposes of sections 111A(1A) to (1G) and 112(1A) to (1F) of the Social Security Administration Act 1992 (offences relating to failure to notify a change of circumstances).

Change affecting jobseeker's allowance

2.681   **3.**—(1) Where the benefit affected by the change of circumstances is a jobseeker's allowance, notice must be given [1 . . .] to the Secretary of State [1 . . .] at the office that the claimant is required to attend in accordance with a notification given to him under regulation 23 of the Jobseeker's Allowance Regulations 1996—
[1 (a) in writing or by telephone (unless the Secretary of State determines in any particular case that notice must be in writing or may be given otherwise than in writing or by telephone); or
 (b) in writing if in any class of case he requires written notice (unless he determines in any particular case to accept notice given otherwise than in writing).]
(2) In this regulation "Secretary of State" includes a person designated as an employment officer by an order made by the Secretary of State under section 8(3) of the Jobseekers Act 1995.

AMENDMENT

1. The Social Security (Miscellaneous Amendments) (No.2) Regulations 2006 (SI 2006/832), reg.2 (April 10, 2006).

Change affecting housing benefit or council tax benefit

2.682   **4.**—(1) Where the benefit affected by the change of circumstances is housing benefit or council tax benefit, notice must be given or sent in writing to the relevant authority at—
  (a) the designated office; or
  (b) in a case where notification at another office is permitted under [1 regulation 88 of the Housing Benefit Regulations 2006, regulation 69 of the Housing Benefit (Persons who have attained the qualifying age for state pension credit) Regulations 2006, regulation 74 of the Council Tax benefit Regulations 2006 or regulation 59 of the Council Tax benefit (persons who have attained the qualifying age for state pension credit) Regulations 2006] (duty to notify changes for claims and payments purposes), that other office.
(2) In this regulation "designated office" and "relevant authority" have the same meaning as in the [1 Housing Benefit Regulations 2006, Housing Benefit (Persons who have attained the qualifying age for state pension credit) Regulations 2006, Council Tax benefit regulations 2006, and Council Tax benefit (Persons who have attained the qualifying age for state pension credit) Regulations 2006].

AMENDMENT

1. The Housing Benefit and Council Tax Benefit (Consequential Provisions) Regulation 2006 (SI 2006/217), Sch.2, para.19 (March 6, 2006).

(SI 2001/3252, reg.4)

Change affecting other benefit payment or advantage

5.—(1) Where the benefit or other payment or advantage affected by the change of circumstances is not a jobseeker's allowance, housing benefit or council tax benefit, notice must be given [³. . .] to the Secretary of State [³ at the appropriate office—
  (a) in writing or by telephone (unless the Secretary of State determines in any particular case that notice must be in writing or may be given otherwise than in writing or by telephone); or
  (b) in writing if in any class of case he requires written notice (unless he determine in any particular case to accept notice given otherwise than in writing)]

[² (1ZA) Where this paragraph applies, where the notice in writing referred to in paragraph (1) is given or sent by an electronic communication that notice must be given or sent in accordance with the provisions set out in Schedule 9ZC to the Social Security (Claims and Payments) Regulations 1987 (electronic communication). (1ZB) Paragraph (1ZA) applies in relation to carer's allowance.]

[¹ (1A) The reference in paragraph (1) to notice "in writing" includes where that notice relates to child benefit, notice given or sent in accordance with Schedule 9C to the Social Security (Claims and Payments) Regulations 1987 (electronic communication).]

(2) In this regulation "the appropriate office" has the same meaning as in the Social Security (Claims and Payments) Regulations 1987.

AMENDMENTS

1. The Social Security (Electronic Communications) (Child Benefit) Order 2002 (SI 2002/1789), art.8 (October 28, 2002). These regulations are revoked with effect from December 1, 2003 by the Social Security (Electronic Communications) (Carer's Allowance) Order 2003, SI 2003/2800, reg.4.
2. The Social Security (Electronic Communications) (Carer's Allowance) Order 2003, SI 2003/2800, reg.3, (December 1, 2003).
3. The Social Security (Notification of Change of Circumstances) Regulations 2003, SI 2003/3209, reg.3 (January 6, 2004).

Social Security (Payments on Account, Overpayments and Recovery) Regulations 1988

(SI 1988/664) (AS AMENDED)

ARRANGEMENT OF REGULATIONS

PART I

GENERAL

1. Citation, commencement and interpretation.

Social Security (Payments on Account, etc.) Regulations 1988

PART II

INTERIM PAYMENTS

2. Making of interim payments.
3. Bringing interim payments into account.
4. Recovery of overpaid interim payments.

PART III

OFFSETTING

5. Offsetting prior payment against subsequent award.
6. Exception from offset of recoverable overpayment.

PART IV

PREVENTION OF DUPLICATION OF PAYMENTS

7. Duplication and prescribed income.
8. Duplication and prescribed payments.
9. Duplication and maintenance payments.
10. Conversion of payments made in a foreign currency.

PART V

DIRECT CREDIT TRANSFER OVERPAYMENTS

11. Recovery of overpayments by automated or other direct credit transfer.

PART VI

REVISION OF DETERMINATION AND CALCULATION OF AMOUNT RECOVERABLE

12. Circumstances in which determination need not he revised.
13. Sums to be deducted in calculating recoverable amounts.
14. Quarterly diminution of capital resources.

PART VII

THE PROCESS OF RECOVERY

15. Recovery by deduction from prescribed benefits.
16. Limitations on deductions from prescribed benefits.
17. Recovery from couples.

(SI 1988/664) (as amended)

PART VIII

RECOVERY BY DEDUCTIONS FROM EARNINGS FOLLOWING TRADE DISPUTE

18. Recovery by deductions from earnings.
19. Award and protected earnings.
20. Service and contents of deduction notices.
21. Period for which deduction notice has effect.
22. Effect of deduction notice.
23. Increase of amount of award on appeal or otherwise.
24. Notice of variation of protected earnings.
25. Power to serve further deduction notice on resumption of employment.
26. Right of Secretary of State to recover direct from claimant.
27. Duties and liabilities of employers.
28. Claimants to give notice of cessation or resumption of employment.
29. Failure to notify.

PART IX

REVOCATIONS, TRANSITIONAL PROVISIONS AND SAVINGS

30. Revocations.
31. Transitional provisions and savings.

Whereas a draft of the following Regulations was laid before Parliament in accordance with the provisions of section 83(3)(b) of the Social Security Act 1986 and approved by resolution of each House of Parliament.

Now, therefore, the Secretary of State for Social services, in exercise of the powers conferred upon him by sections 23(8), 27, 51(1)(t) and (u), 55, 83(1), 84(1) and 89 of that Act and all other powers enabling him in that behalf, by this instrument, which contains only regulations made under the sections of the Social Security Act 1986 specified above and provisions consequential on those sections and which is made before the end of a period of 12 months from the commencement of those sections, makes the following Regulations:

PART I

GENERAL

Citation, commencement and interpretation

1.—(1) These regulations may be cited as the Social Security (Payments on account, Overpayments and Recovery) Regulations 1988 and shall come into force on 6th April 1988.

(2) In these Regulations, unless the context otherwise requires—

"the Act" means the Social Security Act 1986;

[¹⁰ "the Administration Act" means the Social Security Administration Act 1992;]

[⁵"adjudicating authority" means, as the case may require, the Secretary of State, an appeal tribunal constituted under Chapter 1 of Part I of the

2.685

Social Security (Payments on Account, etc.) Regulations 1988

Social Security Act 1998, the Chief or other Commissioner, or a tribunal consisting of any three or more Commissioners constituted in accordance with section 16(7) of that Act]

[6"adjudicating authority" means, as the case may require, the Board, an officer of the Board, an appeal tribunal constituted under section 7 of the Social Security Act 1998, the Chief Social Security Commissioner or any other Social Security Commissioner, or a tribunal of three or more such Commissioners constituted in accordance with section 16(7) of that Act]

"benefit" means [9 a jobseeker's allowance, state pension credit and] any benefit under the Social Security Act 1975 [SSCBA, Parts II to V], child benefit, family credit, income support and [1any social fund payment under sections 32(2)(a) and 32(2A) of the Act [SSCBA, s.138(1)(a) and (2)] [3and any incapacity benefit under sections 30A(1) and (5) of the Contributions and Benefits Act]];

[8 "bereavement benefit" means a benefit referred to in section 20(1)(ea) of the Contributions and Benefits Act;

"bereavement payment" means the sum specified in Part II of Schedule 4 to the Contributions and Benefits Act and referred to in section 36 of that Act;]

[6"the Board" means the Commissioners of Inland Revenue]

"child benefit" means benefit under Part I of the Child Benefit Act 1975 [SSCBA, Part IX];

"the Claims and Payments Regulations" means the Social Security (Claims and Payments) Regulations 1987;

[3"the Contributions and Benefits Act" means the Social Security Contributions and Benefits Act 1992;]

[2"disability living allowance" means a disability living allowance under section 37ZA of the Social Security Act 1975 [SSCBA, s.71];

[7 "disabled person's tax credit" means a disabled person's tax credit under section 129 of the Contributions and Benefits Act and, in relation to things done, or falling to be done, prior to 5th October 1999, shall include a reference to disability working allowance;] [7. . .]

"guardian's allowance" means an allowance under section 38 of the Social Security Act 1975 [SSCBA, s.77];

"income support" means income support under Part II of the Act [SSCBA, Part VII] and includes personal expenses addition, special transitional addition and transitional addition as defined in the Income Support (Transitional) Regulations 1987;

"Income Support Regulations" means the Income Support (General) Regulations 1987;

[4 "Jobseeker's Allowance Regulations" means the Jobseeker's Allowance Regulations 1996;]

"severe disablement allowance" means an allowance under section 36 of the Social Security Act 1975 [SSCBA, s.68].

[9 "state pension credit" means the benefit payable under the State Pension Credit Act 2002;

"the State Pension Credit Regulations" means the State Pension Credit Regulations 2002]

[7 "start notification" means a notification of entitlement to tax credit furnished to an employer by the Board, referred to in section 6(2)(a) of the Tax Credits Act 1999;

(SI 1988/664, reg.1) (as amended)

"tax credit" means working families' tax credit or disabled person's tax credit;

"working families' tax credit" means working families' tax credit under section 128 of the Contributions and Benefits Act and, in relation to things done, or falling to be done, prior to 5th October 1999 shall include a reference to family credit.]

(3) Unless the context otherwise requires, any reference in these regulations to a numbered Part or regulation is a reference to the Part or regulation bearing that number in these Regulations and any reference in a regulation to a numbered paragraph is a reference to the paragraph of that regulation bearing that number.

AMENDMENTS

1. The Social Security (Payments on account, Overpayments and Recovery) Amendments Regulations 1989 (SI 1989/136), reg.3 (February 27, 1989).

2. The Disability Living Allowance and Disability Working Allowance (Consequential Provisions) Regulations 1991 (SI 1991/2742), reg.15 (April 6, 1992).

3. The Social Security (Incapacity Benefit) (Consequential and Transitional Amendments and Savings) Regulations 1995 (SI 1995/829), reg.21(2) (April 13, 1995).

4. The Social Security and Child Support (Jobseeker's Allowance) (Consequential Amendments) Regulations 1996 (SI 1996/1345), reg.23(2) (October 7, 1996).

5. The Tax Credits (Payments on Account, Overpayments and Recovery) (Amendment) Regulations 1999 (SI 1999/2571), reg.3 (October 5, 1999).

6. For tax credits purposes only these words substituted by The Tax Credits (Payments on Account, Overpayments and Recovery) (Amendment) Regulations 1999 (SI 1999/2571), reg.3 (October 5, 1999).

7. The Tax Credits (Payments on Account, Overpayments and Recovery) (Amendment) Regulations 1999 (SI 1999/2571), reg.3 (October 5, 1999).

8. The Social Security (Benefits for Widows and Widowers) (Consequential Amendments) Regulations 2000 (SI 2000/1483), reg.10 (April 9, 2001).

9. State Pension Credit (Consequential, Transitional and Miscellaneous Provisions) Regulations 2002 (SI 2002/3019), reg.24 (October 6, 2003).

10. The Social Security, Child Support and Tax Credits (Miscellaneous Amendments) Regulations 2005 (SI 2005/337), reg.10 (March 18, 2005).

PART II

INTERIM PAYMENTS

Making of interim payments

2.—(1) [³Subject to paragraph (1A),] the Secretary of State may, in his discretion, [⁴ the Board may in their discretion] make an interim payment, that is to say a payment on account of any benefit to which it appears to him [⁴ them] that a person is or may be entitled [⁶ (or, where subparagraph (a) applies, entitled apart from satisfying the condition of making a claim)], in the following circumstances—

(a) a claim for that benefit has not been made in accordance with the Claims and Payments Regulations and it is impracticable for such a claim to be made immediately [⁶, including where it is impracticable to satisfy immediately the national insurance number requirements in section 1(1A) and (1B) of the Administration Act]; or

2.686

Social Security (Payments on Account, etc.) Regulations 1988

 (b) a claim for that benefit has been so made, but it is impracticable for it or [⁵ an] application or appeal which relates to it to be determined immediately; or

 (c) an award of that benefit has been made but it is impracticable for the beneficiary to be paid immediately, except by means of an interim payment.

[⁶ (1A) Paragraph (1) shall not apply pending the determination of an appeal.]

 (2) [¹Subject to paragraph (3)] on or before the making of an interim payment the recipient shall be given notice in writing of his liability under this Part to have it brought into account and to repay any overpayment.

 (3) Where the recipient of an interim payment of disability living allowance—

 (a) is terminally ill within the meaning of [section 66(2) of the Social Security Contributions and Benefits Act 1992]; or

 (b) had an invalid carriage or other vehicle provided by the Secretary of State under section 5(2)(a) of the National Health Service Act 1977 and Schedule 2 to that Act or under section 46 of the National Health Service (Scotland) Act 1978,

the requirement to give notice in paragraph (2) of this regulation shall be omitted.

[²(4) Where an interim payment of income support is made because a payment to which the recipient is entitled by way of child support maintenance under the Child Support Act 1991, or periodical payments under a maintenance agreement within the meaning of section 9(1) of that Act or under a maintenance order within the meaning of section 107(15) of the Social Security Administration Act 1992, has not been made, the requirement in paragraph (2) of this regulation to give notice shall be omitted.]

AMENDMENTS

1. The Disability Living Allowance and Disability Working Allowance (Consequential Provisions) Regulations 1991 (SI 1991/2742), reg.15 (April 6, 1992).

2. The Social Security (Payments on account, Overpayments and Recovery) Amendment Regulations 1993 (SI 1993/650), reg.2 (April 5, 1993).

3. The Social Security (Persons from Abroad) Miscellaneous Amendments Regulations 1996 (SI 1996/30), reg.10 (February 5, 1996).

4. For tax credits purposes only The Tax Credits (Payments on Account, Overpayments and Recovery) (Amendment) Regulations 1999 (SI 1999/2571), reg.4 (October 5, 1999).

5. The Social Security Act 1998 (Commencement No.9, and Savings and Consequential and Transitional Provisions) Order 1999 (SI 1999/2422), Sch.8 (September 6, 1999).

6. The Social Security, Child Support and Tax Credits (Miscellaneous Amendments) Regulations 2005 (SI 2005/337), reg.10 (March 18, 2005).

GENERAL NOTE

2.687 Interim payments are made at the discretion of the Secretary of State. Thus there is no right of appeal and any refusal can only be challenged (other than by making further representations) by judicial review. The test under para.(1) is not whether it is "clear" that the person will qualify for a particular benefit, but whether it appears to the Secretary of State that he "is or may be entitled" to that benefit (*R. v Secretary of State for Social Security Ex p. Sarwar, Getachew and Urbanek* (1995) 7 Admin. L.R. 781). Thus the Secretary of State can decide to make interim payments even where entitlement to, for example, income support is not certain.

(SI 1988/664, reg.2) (as amended)

Interim payments are recoverable if the person is subsequently found not to be entitled to the benefit claimed (see reg.4).

The introduction of an habitual residence rule for income support from August 1, 1994 (see the additional definition of "person from abroad" in reg.21(3) of the Income Support Regulations) focussed fresh attention on this regulation. Most claimants who fail the test were not eligible for urgent cases payments under reg.70(3) of the Income Support Regulations, even before the February 1996 changes, and so face a delay of what can be several months until their appeal is heard without any benefit. This led to many claimants asking for interim payments pending the hearing of their appeals which in a few cases at least were paid. But this in turn precipitated the introduction of para.(1A).

Under para.(1A), in force from February 5, 1996, an interim payment will not be made if an appeal is pending unless the Secretary of State considers that there *is* entitlement to benefit. (See *R. v Secretary of State for Social Security Ex p. Grant* (High Court, July 31, 1997.)) This change is apparently to restore the original policy intention that interim payments could be made where entitlement was clear but the amount of benefit due was not (para.46 of the DSS Explanatory Memorandum to the Social Security Advisory Committee (Cm.3062/1996)). But the wording of para.(1)(b) and the first part of reg.4(3)(ii) somewhat belies this. Moreover, if the case involves a point of Community law (as, e.g. an appeal concerning the habitual residence test may do), para.(1A) could be in breach of Community law in so far as it prevents the Secretary of State from having the power to grant interim relief (see *Factortame Ltd v Secretary of State for Transport (No.2)* [1991] 1 A.C. 603, [1991] 1 All E.R. 70).

In a ruling made in the appeal *CDLA/913/1994*, reported as *R(DLA) 4/99* and *R(DLA) 5/99* the Commissioner held that he had no jurisdiction to order interim payment of benefit where a question had been referred to the European Court of Justice for a preliminary ruling. The case in which the question arose was concerned with entitlement, not payment, and to make such an order would go beyond what was required by Community law. The Commissioner left it open whether there was jurisdiction to make an interim or provisional award of benefit in such circumstances, since he was satisfied that, even if such a power exists, he would not exercise his discretion to make an award.

That ruling was challenged by way of judicial review. In *R. v Social Security Commisioner Ex p. Snares* [1997] C.O.D. 403, Popplewell J. rejected the challenge. He decided that the exercise of discretion by the Commissioner could not be impugned. Unfortunately, however, Popplewell J. did not adopt the distinction made by the Commissioner between an award of entitlement and an order for payment and tended to run the two issues together. If it had been necessary to the determination, he would have regarded the question of the interim remedies available pending a ruling by the Court of Justice as not *acte claire* and would have made a further reference to the Court of Justice.

Bringing interim payments into account

[¹3. [²Subject to paragraph (2)] where it is practicable to do so and, where notice is required to be given under regulation 2(2), such notice has been given—
  (a) any interim payment, other than an interim payment made in the circumstances mentioned in regulation 2(4),—
    (i) which was made in anticipation of an award of benefit shall be offset by the adjudicating authority in reduction of the benefit to be awarded; and
    (ii) whether or not made in anticipation of an award, which is not offset under sub-paragraph (i) shall be deducted by the Secretary of State from—

2.688

Social Security (Payments on Account, etc.) Regulations 1988

    (a) the sum payable under the award of benefit on account of which the interim payment was made; or

    (b) any sum payable under any subsequent award of the same benefit to the same person; and

(b) any interim payment made in the circumstances mentioned in regulation 2(4) shall be offset by the Secretary of State against any sum received by him in respect of arrears of child support maintenance payable to the person to whom the interim payment was made.]

[²(2) Where the interim payment in paragraph (1)(a) is a payment on account of tax credit, paragraph (1)(a), but not paragraph (1)(b), shall apply with the modification that, for the words "Secretary of State" there is substituted the word "Board".]

AMENDMENTS

1. The Social Security (Payments on account, Overpayments and Recovery) Amendment Regulations 1993 (SI 1993/650), reg.2 (April 5, 1993).
2. The Tax Credits (Payments on Account, Overpayments and Recovery) (Amendment) Regulations 1999 (SI 1999/2571), reg.5 (October 5, 1999).

Recovery of overpaid interim payments

2.689   **4.**—(1) Where the adjudicating authority has determined that an interim payment has been overpaid in circumstances which fall within paragraph (3) and [¹where notice is required to be given under regulation 2(2), such notice has been given], that authority shall determine the amount of the overpayment.

(2) The amount of the overpayment shall be recoverable by the Secretary of State, by the same procedures and subject to the same conditions as if it were recoverable under section 53(1) of the Act [SSAA, s.71(1)].

(3) The circumstances in which an interim payment may be determined to have been overpaid are as follows—

(a) an interim payment has been made under regulation 2(1)(a) or (b) but—
    (i) the recipient has failed to make a claim in accordance with the Claims and Payments Regulations as soon as practicable, or has made a claim which is either defective or is not made on the form approved for the time being by the Secretary of State and the Secretary of State has not treated the claim as duly made under regulation 4(7) of the Claims and Payments Regulations; or
    (ii) it has been determined that there is no entitlement on the claim, or that the entitlement is less than the amount of the interim payment or that benefit is not payable; or
    (iii) the claim has been withdrawn under regulation 5(2) of the Claims and Payments Regulations; or

(b) an interim payment has been made under regulation 2(1)(c) which exceeds the entitlement under the award of benefit on account of which the interim payment was made[¹; or

(c) an interim payment of income support has been made under regulation 2(1)(b) in the circumstances mentioned in regulation 2(4).]

(4) For the purposes of this regulation a claim is defective if it is made on the form approved for the time being by the Secretary of State but is not completed in accordance with the instructions on the form.

(SI 1988/664, reg. 4) (as amended)

[²(5) Where the interim payment in paragraph (1)(a) is a payment on account of tax credit, paragraph (1)(a), but not paragraph (1)(b), shall apply with the modification that, for the words "Secretary of State" there is substituted the word "Board".]

AMENDMENTS

1. The Social Security (Payments on account, Overpayments and Recovery) Amendment Regulations 1993 (SI 1993/650), reg.2 (April 5, 1993).
2. The Tax Credits (Payments on Account, Overpayments and Recovery) (Amendment) Regulations 1999 (SI 1999/2571), reg.5 (October 5, 1999).

PART III

OFFSETTING

Offsetting prior payment against subsequent award

5.—(1) Subject to [² paragraphs (1A) [⁷, (2A) and (6)] and] regulation 6 (exception from offset of recoverable overpayment), any sum paid in respect of a period covered by a subsequent determination in any of the cases set out in paragraph (2) shall be offset against arrears of entitlement under the subsequent determination and, except to the extent that the sum exceeds the arrears, shall be treated as properly paid on account of them.

[²(1A) In paragraph (1) the reference to "any sum paid" shall, in relation to tax credit, include a reference to any amount or calculation of tax credit payable in respect of a period to the date of subsequent determination, which is included in a start notification given by the Board to an employer, and for the payment of which the employer remains responsible.]

(2) Paragraph (1) applies in the following cases—

[⁶ *Case 1: Payment pursuant to a decision which is revised or superseded, or overturned on appeal*
Where a person has been paid a sum by way of benefit [or by way of a shared additional pension under section 55A of the Social Security Contributions and Benefits Act 1992] pursuant to a decision which is subsequently revoked under section 9 of the Social Security Act 1998, superseded under Section 10 of that Act or overturned on appeal.]

Case 2: Award or payment of benefit in lieu
Where a person has been paid a sum by way benefit under the original award and it is subsequently determined, . . ., that another benefit should be awarded or is payable in lieu of the first.

Case 3: Child benefit and severe disablement allowance
Where either—
  (a) a person has been awarded and paid child benefit for a period in respect of which severe disablement allowance [⁴ or incapacity benefit for persons incapacitated in youth in accordance with section 30(A)(1)(b) and (2A) of the Contributions and Benefits Act] is subsequently determined to be payable to the child concerned, or
  (b) severe disablement allowance [⁴ or incapacity benefit for persons incapacitated in youth in accordance with section 30(A)(1)(b) and (2A) of the Contributions and Benefits Act] is awarded and paid for

2.690

a period in respect of which child benefit is subsequently awarded to someone else, the child concerned in the subsequent determination being the beneficiary of the original award.

Case 4: Increase of benefit for dependant

Where a person has been paid a sum by way of an increase in respect of a dependent person under the original award and it is subsequently determined that that other person is entitled to benefit for that period, or that a third person is entitled to the increase for that period in priority to the beneficiary of the original award.

Case 5: Increase of benefit for partner

Where a person has been paid a sum by way of an increase in respect of a partner (as defined in regulation 2 of the Income Support Regulations) and it is subsequently determined that that other person is entitled to benefit for that period.

[² (2A) In paragraph (2), Case 2 shall not apply where either—
(a) the sum paid under the original award, or
(b) the subsequent decision on the revision, supersession or appeal,
referred to in the Case (but not both) is or relates to tax credit.]

(3) Where an amount has been deducted under regulation 13(b) (sums to be deducted in calculating recoverable amounts) an equivalent sum shall be offset against any arrears of entitlement of that person under a subsequent award of [⁵ income support, state pension credit and] [¹, or incomebased jobseeker's allowance] for the period to which the deducted amount relates.

(4) Where child benefit which has been paid under an award in favour of a person (the original beneficiary) is subsequently awarded to someone else for any week, the benefit shall nevertheless be treated as properly paid if it was received by someone other than the original beneficiary, who—
   (a) either had the child living with him or was contributing towards the cost of providing for the child at a weekly rate which was not less than the weekly rate under the original award, and
   (b) could have been entitled to child benefit in respect of that child for that week had a claim been made in time.

(5) Any amount which is treated, under paragraph (4), as properly paid shall be deducted from the amount payable to the beneficiary under the subsequent award.

[⁷ (6) Subject to regulation 6, any sums under—
   (a) Schedule 5 or 5A to the Contributions and Benefits Act (pension increases or lump sum where entitlement to retirement pension or shared additional pension is deferred); or
   (b) Schedule 1 to the Social Security (Graduated Retirement Benefit) Regulations 2005 (increases or lump sum where entitlement to greaduate retirement benefit is deferred),
Paid pursuant to a decision which is subsequently revised under section 9 of the Social Security Act 1998, superseded under section 10 of that Act or overturned on appeal, shall be offset against any sums due under the subsequent determination and, except to the extent that the sum exceeds the amount now due, shall be treated as properly paid on account of it.]

AMENDMENTS

1. The Social Security and Child Support (Jobseeker's Allowance) (Consequential Amendments) Regulations 1996 (SI 1996/1345), reg.23(5) and (6) (October 7, 1996).

(SI 1988/664, reg.5) (as amended)

2. The Tax Credits (Payments on Account, Overpayments and Recovery) (Amendment) Regulations 1999 (SI 1999/2571), reg.7 (October 5, 1999).

3. The Social Security Act 1998 (Commencement No.11 and Transitional Provisions) Order 1999 (SI 1999/2860), Sch.4 (October 18, 1999).

4. The Social Security (Incapacity Benefits) Miscellaneous Amendments Regulations 2000 (SI 2000/3120), reg.5 (April 6, 2001).

5. State Pension Credit (Consequential, Transitional and Miscellaneous Provisions) Regulations 2002 (SI 2002/3019), reg.24 (October 6, 2003).

6. The Social Security (Shared Additional Pension) (Miscellaneous Amendments) Regulations 2005 (SI 2005/1551) (July 6, 2005).

7. The Social Security (Deferral of Retirement Pensions etc.) Regulations 2006 (SI 2006/516) (April 6, 2006).

GENERAL NOTE

This regulation contains important powers to deal with cases where a subsequent award of one benefit replaces an earlier award of a different benefit. It enables the benefit originally awarded to be treated as paid on account of the benefit subsequently awarded. The circumstances in which the power is available are spelled out in the five cases listed in the regulation. Tribunals may need to refer to this power when the result of their decision is to substitute one benefit for another which has already been awarded.

In *Brown v Secretary of State for Work and Pensions* [2006] EWCA Civ 89, reported as *R(DLA) 2/07*, the Court of appeal, interpreting reg. 5(1) ruled that where payments of disability living allowance had been suspended because there has been an overpayment, and a new decision made, payments subsequently awarded could not be offset against the irrecoverable overpayment, since the amount of payments would vary depending on how long it took for the new decision to be reached.

The Department has issued fresh guidance following this case, which can be found at Memo DMG 17/07.

2.691

Exception from offset of recoverable overpayment

6. No amount may be offset under regulation 5(1) which has been determined to be a recoverable overpayment for the purposes of section 53(1) of the Act [SSAA, s.71(1)].

2.692

PART IV

PREVENTION OF DUPLICATION OF PAYMENTS

Duplication and prescribed income

7.—[¹ (1) For the purposes of section 74(1) of the Social Security Administration Act 1992 (⁴income support, state pension credit and] [³ and income-based jobseeker's allowance] and other payments), a person's prescribed income is—
 (a) income required to be taken into account in accordance with Part V of the Income Support Regulations [³or, as the case may be, Part VIII of the Jobseeker's Allowance Regulations] [⁴ or Part II of the State Pension Credit Regulations], except for the income specified in sub-paragraph (b); and]
[²(b) income which, if it were actually paid, would be required to be taken into account in accordance with Chapter VIIA of Part V of the Income Support Regulations [³or, as the case may be, Chapter VIII of Part VIII of the Jobseeker's Allowance Regulations] (child support

2.693

757

Social Security (Payments on Account, etc.) Regulations 1988

maintenance); but only in so far as it relates to the period beginning with the effective date of the maintenance assessment under which it is payable, as determined in accordance with regulation 30 of the Child Support (Maintenance Assessment Procedure) Regulations 1992, and ending with the first day which is a day specified by the Secretary of State under regulation 4(1) of the Child Support (Collection and Enforcement) Regulations 1992 as being a day on which payment of child support maintenance under that maintenance assessment is due.]

(2) The prescribed date in relation to any payment of income prescribed by [¹paragraph (1)(a)] is—
  (a) where it is made in respect of a specific day or period, that day or the first day of the period;
  (b) where it is not so made, the day or the first day of the period to which it is fairly attributable.

[²(3) Subject to paragraph (4), the prescribed date in relation to any payment of income prescribed by paragraph (1)(b) is the last day of the maintenance period, determined in accordance with regulation 33 of the Child Support (Maintenance Assessment Procedure) Regulations 1992, to which it relates.

(4) Where the period referred to in paragraph (1)(b) does not consist of a number of complete maintenance periods the prescribed date in relation to income prescribed by that sub-paragraph which relates to any part of that period which is not a complete maintenance period is the last day of that period.]

AMENDMENTS

1. The Social Security (Payments on account, Overpayments and Recovery) Amendment Regulations 1993 (SI 1993/650), reg.2, as amended by The Social Security (Miscellaneous Provisions) Amendment Regulations 1993 (SI 1993/846), reg.4 (April 5, 1993).
2. The Social Security (Payments on account, Overpayments and Recovery) Amendment Regulations 1993 (SI 1993/650), reg.2, as amended by The Social Security (Miscellaneous Provisions) Amendment Regulations 1993 (SI 1993/846), reg.4 (April 5, 1993).
3. The Social Security and Child Support (Jobseeker's Allowance) (Consequential Amendments) Regulations 1996 (SI 1996/1345), reg.23(3) (October 7, 1996).
4. State Pension Credit (Consequential, Transitional and Miscellaneous Provisions) Regulations 2002 (SI 2002/3019), reg.24 (October 6, 2003).

GENERAL NOTE

2.694

See the notes to s.74(1) of the Administration Act.

Under s.54 of the Child Support Act 1991 "maintenance assessment" means an assessment of maintenance made under that Act, including, except where regulations prescribe otherwise, an interim assessment. Under reg.30 of the Child Support (Maintenance Assessment Procedure) Regulations 1992, the effective date of a new assessment is usually, when the application was made by the person with care of the child, the date on which a maintenance enquiry form was sent to the absent parent or, where the application was made by the absent parent, the date on which an effective maintenance form was received by the Secretary of State. Arrears will inevitably accrue while the assessment is being made. In the meantime income support or income-based JSA can be paid in full to the parent with care. When the arrears are paid, the amount of "overpaid" income support or JSA is recoverable under s.74(1) of the Administration Act.

(SI 1988/664, reg.7) (as amended)

See the notes to reg.60C of the Income Support (General) Regulations for the interaction with payments of other arrears of child support maintenance, which are excluded from the operation of s.74(1). Note also s.74A of the Administration Act and regs 55A and 60E of the Income Support Regulations and regs 119 and 127 of the Jobseeker's Allowance Regulations.

Duplication and prescribed payments

8.—(1) For the purposes of section [⁸ 74(2) of the Administration Act] (recovery of amount of benefit awarded because prescribed payment not made on prescribed date), the payment of any of the following is a prescribed payment—

(a) any benefit under the Social Security Act 1975 [SSCBA, Parts II to V] other than any grant or gratuity or a widow's payment;
(b) any child benefit;
(c) any family credit;
(d) any war disablement pension or war widow's pension which is not in the form of a gratuity and any payment which the Secretary of State accepts as analogous to any such pension;
(e) any allowance paid under the Job Release Act 1977;
(f) any allowance payable by or on behalf of [²Scottish Enterprise Highlands and Islands Enterprise or] [¹the Secretary of State] to or in respect of a person for his maintenance for any period during which he is following a course of training or instruction provided or approved by [²Scottish Enterprise Highlands and Islands Enterprise or] [¹the Secretary of State]
(g) any payment of benefit under the legislation of any member State other than the United Kingdom concerning the branches of social security mentioned in Article 4(1) of Regulation (EEC) No.1408/71 on the application of social security schemes to employed persons, to self-employed persons and to members of their families moving within the Community, whether or not the benefit has been acquired by virtue of the provisions of that Regulation;
[³. . .]

[⁶ (i) any bereavement benefit other than a bereavement payment.]
[⁸ (j) any contribution-based jobseeker's allowance within the meaning of section 1(4) of the Jobseekers Act.]
[⁹ (k) payments under the Financial Assistance Scheme Regulations 2005.]

(2) The prescribed date, in relation to any payment prescribed by paragraph (1) is the date by which receipt of or entitlement to that benefit would have to be notified to the Secretary of State if it were to be taken into account in determining, whether [⁵by way of revision or supersession], the amount of or entitlement to [⁷ income support, a state pension credit] [⁴, or income-based jobseeker's allowance].

2.695

AMENDMENTS

1. Employment Act 1989, Sch.5, paras 1 and 4 (November 16, 1989).
2. The Enterprise (Scotland) Consequential Amendments Order 1991 (SI 1991/387), art.14 (April 1, 1991).
3. The Tax Credits (Payments on Account, Overpayments and Recovery) (Amendment) Regulations 1999 (SI 1999/2571), reg.8 (October 5, 1999).
4. The Social Security and Child Support (Jobseeker's Allowance) (Consequential Amendments) Regulations 1996 (SI 1996/1345), reg.23(5) and (6) (October 7, 1996).

5. The Social Security Act 1998 (Commencement No.11 and Transitional Provisions) Order 1999 (SI 1999/2680), Sch.4 (October 18, 1999).
6. The Social Security (Benefits for Widows and Widowers) (Consequential Amendments) Regulations 2000 (SI 2000/1483), reg.10 (April 9, 2001).
7. State Pension Credit (Consequential, Transitional and Miscellaneous Provisions) Regulations 2002 (SI 2002/3019), reg.24 (October 6, 2003).
8. The Social Security, Child Support and Tax Credits (Miscellaneous Amendments) Regulations 2005 (SI 2005/337), reg.10 (March 18, 2005).
9. The Social Security (Payments on account, Overpayments and Recovery) Amendment Regulations 2005 (SI 2005/3476) (January 19, 2006).

GENERAL NOTE

2.696 See the notes to s.74(2) of the Administration Act.

R(IS)14/94 concerned an overpayment of income support which arose from the award of invalid care allowance. The claimant was an elderly widow, whose daughter was her appointee. Income support was paid to the widow. The daughter was in receipt of invalid care allowance in respect of her mother. Recovery was sought under s.27 of the Social Security Act 1986 (now s.74 of the Administration Act) from the widow.

The claimant argued that the words in reg.8(2) "taken into account" meant that only the claimant's resources and requirements were to be considered. The Commissioner rejects such a narrow reading of the words and says that "the words 'into account' should be given a wide interpretation and in the context include 'take notice of'."

Duplication and maintenance payments

2.697 **9.** For the purposes of section 27(3) of the Act [SSAA, s.74(3)] (recovery of amount of benefit awarded because maintenance payments not made), the following benefits are prescribed—
(a) child benefit;
(b) increase for dependants of any benefit under the Social Security Act 1975 [SSCBA, Parts II to V];
(c) child's special allowance under section 31 of the Social Security Act 1975 [SSCBA, s.56]; and
(d) guardian's allowance.

GENERAL NOTE

2.698 See the notes to s.74(3) of the Administration Act.

Conversion of payments made in a foreign currency

2.699 **10.** Where a payment of income prescribed by regulation 7(1), or a payment prescribed by regulation 8(1), is made in a currency other than sterling, its value in sterling, for the purposes of section 27 of the Act [SSAA, s.74] and this Part, shall be determined, after conversion by the Bank of England, or by [¹any institution which is authorised under the Banking Act 1987], as the net sterling sum into which it is converted, after any banking charge or commission on the transaction has been deducted.

AMENDMENT

1. The Social Security (Payments on Account, Overpayments and Recovery) (Amendment) Regulations 1988 (SI 1988/688), reg.2(2) (April 11, 1988).

(SI 1988/664, reg.11) (as amended)

PART V

DIRECT CREDIT TRANSFER OVERPAYMENTS

Recovery of overpayments by automated or other direct credit transfer

11.—(1) [¹ Subject to paragraph (4)] where it is determined by the adjudicating authority that a payment in excess of entitlement has been credited to a bank or other account under an arrangement for automated or other direct credit transfer made in accordance with regulation 21 of the Claims and Payments Regulations and that the conditions prescribed by paragraph (2) are satisfied, the excess, or the specified part of it to which the Secretary of State's certificate relates, shall be recoverable under this regulation.

(2) The prescribed conditions for recoverability under paragraph (1) are as follows—
(a) the Secretary of State has certified that the payment in excess of entitlement, or a specified part of it, is materially due to the arrangements for payments to be made by automated or other direct credit transfer; and
[² (b) notice of the effect to which this regulation would have, in the event of an overpayment, was given to the beneficiary or to a person acting form his—
   (i) in writing, where the claim was made in writing; or
   (ii) either orally or in writing, where the claim was made by telephone
before he agreed to the arrangement.]

(3) Where the arrangement was agreed to before April 6, 1987 the condition prescribed by paragraph (2)(b) need not be satisfied in any case where the application for benefit to be paid by automated or other direct credit transfer contained a statement, or was accompanied by a written statement made by the applicant, which complied with the provisions of regulation 16A(3)(b) and (8) of the Social Security (Claims and Payments) Regulations 1979 or, as the case may be, regulation 7(2)(b) and (6) of the Child Benefit (Claims and Payments) Regulations 1984.

[¹ Where the payment mention in paragraph (1) is a payment of tax credit, paragraphs (1) and (2) shall apply with the modifications that—
(a) in paragraph (1) for the words "Secretary of State" there is substituted the words "Board's", and
(b) in paragraph (2) for the words "Secretary of State" there is substituted the word "Board".]

2.700

AMENDMENTS

1. The Tax Credits (Payments on Account, Overpayments and Recovery) (Amendment) Regulations 1999 (SI 1999/2571), reg.9 (October 5, 1999).
2. The Social Security (Claims and Payments and Payments on account, Overpayments and Recovery) Amendment Regulations 2005 (SI 2005/34), reg.3 (May 2, 2005).

Social Security (Payments on Account, etc.) Regulations 1988

Part VI

Calculation of Amount Recoverable

Circumstances in which determination need not be revised

2.701   **12.** [² Section 71(5) or (5A) of the Administration Act] (recoverability dependent on reversal, variation, revision [¹ or supersession] of determination) shall not apply where the fact and circumstances of the misrepresentation or non-disclosure do not provide a basis for [¹ the decision pursuant to which the payment was made to be revised under section 9 of the Social Security Act 1998 or superseded under section 10 of that Act.]

Amendments

1. The Social Security Act 1998 (Commencement No.9, and Savings and Consequential and Transitional Provisions) Order 1999 (SI 1999/2422), Sch.8 (September 6, 1999).
2. The Social Security, Child Support and Tax Credits (Miscellaneous Amendments) Regulations 2005 (SI 2005/337), reg.10 (March 18, 2005).

General Note

2.702   See the notes to s.71(5A) of the Administration Act.

Sums to be deducted in calculating recoverable amounts

2.703   **13.**—[² Subject to paragraph (2)] in calculating the amounts recoverable under section 53(1) of the Act [SSAA, s.71(1)] or regulation 11, where there has been an overpayment of benefit, the adjudicating authority shall deduct—
  (a) any amount which has been offset under Part III;
  (b) any additional amount of income support [³ or state pension credit] [¹, or income-based jobseeker's allowance] which was not payable under the original, or any other, determination, but which should have been determined to be payable—
    (i) on the basis of the claim as presented to the adjudicating authority, or
    (ii) on the basis of the claim as it would have appeared had the misrepresentation or non-disclosure been remedied before the determination;
but no other deduction shall be made in respect of any other entitlement to benefit which may be, or might have been, determined to exist.
[² (2) Paragraph (1) shall apply to tax credit only where both—
  (a) The overpayment of benefit referred to in paragraph (1), and
  (b) The amount referred to in sub-paragraph (a) of that paragraph,
Are tax credit, and with the modification that sub-paragraph (b) of that paragraph is omitted.]

Amendments

1. The Social Security and Child Support (Jobseeker's Allowance) (Consequential Amendments) Regulations 1996 (SI 1996/1345), reg.23(5) and (6) (October 7, 1996).
2. The Tax Credits (Payments on Account, Overpayments and Recovery) (Amendment) Regulations 1999 (SI 1999/2571), reg.11 (October 5, 1999).
3. State Pension Credit (Consequential, Transitional and Miscellaneous Provisions) Regulations 2002 (SI 2002/3019), reg.24 (October 6, 2003).

(SI 1988/664, reg.13) (as amended)

GENERAL NOTE

See the notes to s.71(1) and (2) of the Administration Act, 1992 for important case law affecting this provision.

In *CP/5257/1999* the Commissioner interpreted the poorly drafted reg.13 by holding that:
(a) the regulation is not limited to overpayments of income support or income-based jobseeker's allowance, but covers overpaid benefit other than these two benefits; and
(b) the regulation only applies where the benefit sought to be offset is income support or income-based jobseeker's allowance.

In *CIS/1777/2000* a different Commissioner said,

"[Regulation 13] was amended to include a reference to income-based jobseeker's allowance when that benefit was introduced in 1996. I do not read the provision as authorising the deduction from an overpayment of jobseeker's allowance that would have been paid if a claim for that benefit has been made rather than a claim for income support. Head (i) refers to the claim as presented—the claim as presented was for income support. Head (ii) refers to the claim as it would have appeared if the facts had been correctly represented—if the facts had been correctly known, the claim would have appeared as a claim for income support to which the claimant was not entitled. The claimant might have been advised by the Department of Social Security to make a claim for an income based jobseeker's allowance, but that would have been a different claim—there is no power for the Secretary of State to treat a claim for income support as a claim for income based jobseeker's allowance in the alternative under Schedule 1 to the Social Security (Claims and Payments) Regulations 1987." (para.9)

The interpretation of the regulation was revisited in *CIS/2291/2001* following the 1999 amendments. The Commissioner concludes,

"17. Although the wording is particularly obscure for such an important and potentially severe rule, the effect is clear. Anyone who is working or capable of work so as to exclude them from income support must claim jobseeker's allowance. If they do not, and they continue to receive income support, they risk losing both the income support actually received and the jobseeker's allowance they might have received.
18. Regulation 13 does not contain any discretion. That rests with the Secretary of State in deciding whether and how to collect any overpayment. No doubt the Secretary of State will take into account whether the public purse has in reality lost the sum claimed as overpaid or some other amount."

In *CDLA/3768/2002*, the Commissioner said,

"15. . . . the decision maker acting for the Secretary of State [in presenting the case to the tribunal] should first consider whether any amount has been offset under Part III (regulations 5 and 6 of the Social Security (Payments on Account, Overpayments and Recoveries) Regulations 1988. This may call for further enquiry, bearing in mind always that it is for the Secretary of State to meet any problems arising from conflicts of evidence or absence of proof of any relevant issue . . .
16. The other issues that regulation 13(1) requires the decision maker and tribunal to identify and deduct is:

'any additional amount of income support or income-based jobseeker's allowance which was not payable under the original or any other determination, but which should have been determined to be payable on the basis of the claim as presented to the adjudicating authority or on the basis of the claim as it would have appeared had the misrepresentation or nondisclosure been remedied before the determination'.

Social Security (Payments on Account, etc.) Regulations 1988

I have removed the punctuation for the reasons given in *CIS/2291/2001*. Regulation 13(1) then emphasises that no other deduction shall be made for any other actual or hypothetical entitlement."

The Administrative Court in *Larusai v Secretary of State for Work and Pensions*, [2003] EWHC 371 (Admin) was called upon to consider the relationship of benefits administered by the Department and tax credits administered by the Board of Inland Revenue in relation to the offsetting of benefits where there are recoverable overpayments of benefits administered by the Department. The claimant had been overpaid income support which was recoverable, but argued that a notional entitlement to working families tax credit should be set off against the overpayment notwithstanding the absence of such a provision in reg.13. The claimant argued that the Secretary of State in exercising his discretion as to the amount of the recoverable overpayment had acted unlawfully in failing to deduct a notional amount of working families tax credit from the overpayment. The decision was never likely to require the Secretary of State to exercise his discretion in the way for which the claimant argued, but the decision is interesting for the way in which the Administrative Court responded to the claimant's arguments:

(1) The claimant argued that the Secretary of State's approach in treating tax credits as different from benefits administered by the Department and so precluding any discretionary offset of working families tax credit was irrational. The Court did not accept this, seeing nothing irrational in attempts to change the perception of claimants about the difference between benefits which required a person to be out of work and those which were payable to people in work.

(2) The claimant argued that the policy of the Secretary of State had departed from its own guidelines in pursuing a policy of exercising its discretion only in "exceptional circumstances". The Court concluded that this was a matter of phraseology and did not render the policy unlawful.

(3) The claimant argued that the decision to recover the whole of the overpaid income support without deduction of a notional entitlement to working families tax credit constituted a penal sanction (it appears that the claimant would have been entitled to something in the order of £2,000 by way of working families tax credit). Since the policy in reg.13 was to secure full recovery subject to the specified offsets and since the notional amount of working families tax credit did not constitute a debt by the Department to the claimant, it could not be said that there was anything which could be characterised as a penal sanction; there was no basis for the claimant's argument.

(4) The Court said that an argument based on the Government securing a windfall equal to the notional amount of the working families tax credit was misconceived. It "misrepresents the structural position, as well as the law, to describe this as "a windfall to the State."' (para.30).

(5) The claimant raised the question of hardship resulting from the requirement to repay overpaid benefit. The Court simply notes that the Secretary of State has been provided with full details of the claimant's circumstances, that there is inevitably an element of hardship when overpaid benefit is recovered, but that it "is not for this court, unless it is satisfied that there has been an unlawful exercise of discretion, to form a view about the financial margins with which this case, or any case, might give rise to." (para.32).

See also *Department for Work and Pensions v Richards*, [2005] EWCA Crim 491.

Public Records Act 1958

2.705   *R(IS) 1/05* gives guidance on the significance of the Public Records Act 1958 to the retention of documents by the Department, and the onus of proof where a claimant asserts that there has been an underpayment of benefit in the past which reduces the amount of a recoverable overpayment. The overpayment at issue in this case had arisen as a result of admitted false statements made by the claimant which resulted in the award of income support. The point of contention was whether the claimant could offset the substantial overpayment by underpayments of benefit in circumstances where many of the relevant documents had long since been destroyed by the Department under its document retention policy.

The requirements of the Public Records Act 1958 were seen as something of a red herring, and the Commissioner has little time for them, noting, "It is difficult to believe that these elaborate procedures [in the 1958 Act] were ever intended to apply to social security claim forms". In fairness, the claimant's representative had abandoned this point in arguing the case before the Commissioner.

The onus of proof in cases such as this was a rather more substantial point, particularly in the light of the House of Lords in *Kerr v Department for Social Development* [2004] UKHL 23 (see para.1.373.1 of Vol.III). The Commissioner sees no real difference in the views expressed by Lady Hale in *Kerr* and the long-established wisdom that "if a particular matter relates to the qualifying conditions of entitlement it is a claimant who must bear the consequences of ignorance; however, if what is in issue constitute an exception to such conditions, then the Department bears the burden of establishing that factor which operates to disentitled the claimant". (para.43). The issue which arises under reg.13 is distinct from the recovery of the overpayment; it is not necessarily related to the period which is covered by the s.71 revision or supersession nor to the same benefit the subject of recovery. The Commissioner concludes,

"If, as is trite law, one who submits an initial claim for benefit has the burden of showing that its qualifying conditions are met, it can hardly be the case that one who must pay benefit back because it has been demonstrated that she should never have had it, has an easier task in establishing a similar entitlement to offset against the proven debt. In my judgement, nothing in principle or on account of the statutory language or from the structure of the overpayment scheme or to further its consistency can justify such a departure from what is usual and right." (para.47.)

Quarterly diminution of capital resources

14.—(1) For the purposes of section 53(1) of the Act [SSAA, s.71(1)], where income support [4 or state pension credit] [2, or income-based jobseeker's allowance] [1, working families tax credit or disabled pension's tax credit] has been overpaid in consequence of a misrepresentation as to the capital a claimant possesses or a failure to disclose its existence, the adjudicating authority shall treat that capital as having been reduced at the end of each quarter from the start of the overpayment period by the amount overpaid by way of income support[2, or income-based jobseeker's allowance] [1, working families tax credit or disabled pension's tax credit] within that quarter.

(2) Capital shall not be treated as reduced over any period other than a quarter or in circumstances other than those for which paragraph (1) provides.

(3) In this regulation—

"a quarter" means a period of 13 weeks starting with the first day on which the overpayment period began and ending on the 90th consecutive day thereafter.

"overpayment period" is a period during which income support [4 or state pension credit] [3or an income-based jobseeker's allowance,] [1 working families tax credit or disabled pension's tax credit] is overpaid in consequence of a misrepresentation as to capital or a failure to disclose its existence.

Amendments

1. The Tax Credits (Payments on Account, Overpayments and Recovery) (Amendment) Regulations 1999 (SI 1999/2571), reg.12 (October 5, 1999).
2. The Tax Credits (Payments on Account, Overpayments and Recovery) (Amendment) Regulations 1999 (SI 1996/2571), reg.23(5) and (6) (October 7, 1996).
3. The Social Security (Jobseeker's Allowance and Payments on account) (Miscellaneous Amendments) Regulations 1996 (SI 1996/2519), reg.3(2) (October 7, 1996).
4. State Pension Credit (Consequential, Transitional and Miscellaneous Provisions) Regulations 2002 (SI 2002/3019), reg.24 (October 6, 2003).

General Note

See the notes to s.71(1) and (2) of the Administration Act.

Part VII

The Process of Recovery

Recovery by deduction from benefits

15.—(1) Subject to regulation 16, where any amount is recoverable under sections 27 or 53(1) of the Act [SSAA, ss.74 or 71(1)], or under these Regulations, that amount shall be recoverable by the Secretary of State from any of the benefits prescribed by the next paragraph, to which the person from whom [¹the amount is determined] to be recoverable is entitled.

(2) The following benefits are prescribed for the purposes of this regulation—
  (a) subject to paragraphs (1) and (2) of regulation 16, any benefit under the Social Security Act 1975 [SSCBA, Parts II to V];
  (b) subject to paragraphs (1) and (2) of regulation 16, any child benefit;
  (c) [⁵. . .]
  (d) subject to regulation 16, any income support [⁶ or state pension credit], [⁴or a jobseeker's allowance].
  [²(e) [⁵. . .];
  [³(f) any incapacity benefit.]

Amendments

1. The Social Security (Payments on account, Overpayments and Recovery) Amendments Regulations 1988 (SI 1988/688), reg.2(3) (April 11, 1988).
2. The Disability Living Allowance and Disability Working Allowance (Consequential Provisions) Regulations 1991 (SI 1991/2742), reg.15 (April 6, 1992).
3. The Social Security (Incapacity Benefit) (Consequential and Transitional Amendments and Savings) Regulations 1991 (SI 1995/829), reg.21(3) (April 13, 1995).
4. The Social Security (Jobseeker's Allowance and Payments on account) (Miscellaneous Amendments) Regulations 1996 (SI 1996/2519), reg.3(3) (October 7, 1996).
5. The Social Security (Jobseeker's Allowance and Payments on account) (Miscellaneous Amendments) Regulations 1996 (SI 1996/2519), reg.13 (October 5, 1999).
6. State Pension Credit (Consequential, Transitional and Miscellaneous Provisions) Regulations 2002 (SI 2002/3019), reg.24 (October 6, 2003).

(SI 1988/664, reg.16) (as amended)

Limitations on deductions from prescribed benefits

16.—(1) Deductions may not be made from entitlement to the benefits prescribed by paragraph (2) except as a means of recovering an overpayment of the benefit from which the deduction is to be made.

(2) The benefits [¹prescribed] for the purposes of paragraph (1) are guardian's allowance, [². . .] and child benefit.

(3) Regulation 15 shall apply without limitation to any payment of arrears of benefit other than any arrears caused by the operation of [¹² regulation 20 of the Social Security and Child Support (Decisions and Appeals) Regulations 1999 (making of payments which have been suspended)]

(4) Regulation 15 shall apply to the amount of [⁵benefit] to which a person is presently entitled only to the extent that there may, subject to paragraphs 8 and 9 of Schedule 9 to the Claims and Payments Regulations, be recovered in respect of any one benefit week—
  (a) in a case to which paragraph (5) applies, not more than the amount there specified; and
  (b) in any other case, 3 times 5 per cent of the personal allowance for a single claimant aged not less than 25, that 5 per cent being, where it is not a multiple of 5 pence, rounded to the next higher such multiple.

[⁶(4A) Paragraph (4) shall apply to the following benefits—
  (a) income support;
  (b) an income-based jobseeker's allowance;
  (c) where, if there was no entitlement to a contribution-based jobseeker's allowance, there would be entitlement to an income-based jobseeker's allowance at the same rate, a contribution-based jobseeker's allowance.]

[¹¹ (d) state pension credit.]

[⁹ (5) Where a person responsible for the misrepresentation or failure to disclose a material fact has, by reason thereof—
  (a) been found guilty of an offence whether under statute or otherwise; or
  (b) made an admission after caution of deception or fraud for the purpose of obtaining benefit; or
  (c) agreed to pay a penalty under section 115A of the Social Security Administration Act 1992 and the agreement has not been withdrawn,
the amount mentioned in paragraph (4)(a) shall be 4 times 5 per cent. of the personal allowance for a single claimant aged not less than 25, that 5 per cent. being, where it is not a multiple of 10 pence, rounded to the nearest 10 pence or, if it is a multiple of 5 pence but not of 10 pence, the next higher multiple of 10 pence.]

[⁶(5A) Regulation 15 shall apply to an amount of a contribution-based jobseeker's allowance, other than a contribution-based jobseeker's allowance to which paragraph (4) applies in accordance with paragraph (4A)(c), to which a person is presently entitled only to the extent that there may, subject to paragraphs 8 and 9 of Schedule 9 to the Claims and Payments Regulations be recovered in respect of any one benefit week a sum equal to one third of the age-related amount applicable to the claimant under section 4(1)(a) of the Jobseekers Act 1995.

(5B) For the purposes of paragraph (5A) where the sum that would otherwise fall to be deducted includes a fraction of a penny, the sum to be deducted shall be rounded down to the nearest whole penny.]

Social Security (Payments on Account, etc.) Regulations 1988

(6) [⁵ Where—
(a) in the calculation of the income of a person to whom income support is payable, the amount of earnings or other income falling to be taken into account is reduced by paragraphs 4 to 9 of Schedule 8 to the Income Support Regulations (sums to be disregarded in the calculation of earnings) or paragraphs 15 and 16 of Schedule 9 to those Regulations (sums to be disregarded in the calculation of income other than earnings); or
(b) in the calculation of the income of a person to whom income-based jobseeker's allowance is payable, the amount of earnings or other income falling to be taken into account is reduced by paragraphs 5 to 12 of Schedule 6 to the Jobseeker's Allowance Regulations (sums to be disregarded in the calculation of earnings) or paragraphs 15 and 17 of Schedule 7 to those Regulations (sums to be disregarded in the calculation of income other than earnings),
[¹¹ or
(c) in the calculation of the income of a person to whom state pension credit is payable, the amount of earnings or other income falling to be taken into account is reduced in accordance with paragraph 1 of Schedule 4 (sums to be disregarded in the calculation of income other than capital), or Schedule 6 (sums disregarded from claimant's earnings) to the State Pension Credit Regulations,]
the weekly amount] applicable under paragraph (4) may be increased by not more than half the amount of the reduction, and any increase under this paragraph has priority over any increase which would, but for this paragraph, be made under paragraph 6(5) of Schedule 9 to the Claims and Payments Regulations.

(7) Regulation 15 shall not be applied to a specified benefit so as to reduce the benefit in any one benefit week to less than 10 pence.

(8) In this regulation—
[⁹ 'admission after caution' means—
(i) in England and Wales, an admission after a caution has been administered in accordance with a Code issued under the Police and Criminal Evidence Act 1984;
in Scotland, an admission after a caution has been administered, such admission being duly witnessed by two persons;]
"benefit week" means the week corresponding to the week in respect of which the benefit is paid;
[¹¹ "personal allowance for a single claimant aged not less than 25" means—
(a) in the case of a person who is entitled to either income support or state pension credit, the amount for the time being specified in paragraph 1(1)(e) of column (2) of Schedule 2 to the Income Support Regulations; or
(b) in the case of a person who is entitled to income-based jobseeker's allowance, the amount for the time being specified in paragraph 1(1)(e) of column (2) of Schedule 1 to the Jobseeker's Allowance Regulations;]
"specified benefit" means—
(a) a jobseeker's allowance;
(b) income support when paid alone or together with any incapacity benefit, retirement pension or severe disablement allowance in a combined payment in respect of any period;

(SI 1988/664, reg.16) (as amended)

(c) if incapacity benefit, retirement pension or severe disablement allowance is paid concurrently with income support in respect of any period but not in a combined payment, income support and such of those benefits as are paid concurrently;
(d) state pension credit when paid alone or together with any retirement pension, incapacity benefit or severe disablement allowance in a combined payment in respect of any period; and
(e) if retirement pension, incapacity benefit or severe disablement allowance is paid concurrently with state pension credit in respect of any period but not in a combined payment, state pension credit and such of those benefits as are paid concurrently, but does not include any sum payable by way of child maintenance bonus in accordance with section 10 of the Child Support Act 1995 and the Social Security (Child Maintenance Bonus) Regulations 1996.]
but does not include any sum payable by way of child maintenance bonus in accordance with section 10 of the Child Support Act 1995 and the Social Security (Child Maintenance Bonus) Regulations 1996.]

AMENDMENTS

1. The Social Security (Payments on account, Overpayments and Recovery) Amendments Regulations 1988 (SI 1988/688), reg.2(4) (April 11, 1988).
2. The Disability Living Allowance and Disability Working Allowance (Consequential Provisions) Regulations 1991 (SI 1991/2742), reg.15 (April 6, 1992).
3. The Social Security (Incapacity Benefit) (Consequential and Transitional Amendments and Savings) Regulations 1995 (SI 1995/829), reg.21(4) (April 13, 1995).
4. The Social Security (Claims and Payments, etc.) Amendment Regulations 1996 (SI 1996/672), reg.4 (April 4, 1996).
5. The Social Security and Child Support (Jobseeker's Allowance) (Consequential Amendments) Regulations 1996 (SI 1996/1345), reg.23(4) (October 7, 1996).
6. The Social Security (Jobseeker's Allowance and Payments on account) (Miscellaneous Amendments) Regulations 1996 (SI 1996/2519), reg.3(4) (October 7, 1996).
7. The Social Security (Child Maintenance Bonus) Regulations 1996 (SI 1996/3195), reg.16(3) (April 7, 1997).
8. The Social Security (Miscellaneous Amendments) Regulations 1997 (SI 1997/454), reg.8(10) (April 6, 1997).
9. The Social Security (Payments on Account, Overpayment and Recovery) Amendment Regulations 2000 (SI 2000/2336), reg.2, (October 2, 2000).
10. The Social Security (Claims and Payments and Miscellaneous Amendments) (No.2) Regulations 2002 (SI 2002/2441), reg.134, (October 23, 2002).
11. State Pension Credit (Consequential, Transitional and Miscellaneous Provisions) Regulations 2002 (SI 2002/3019), reg.24 (October 6, 2003).
12. The Social Security, Child Support and Tax Credits (Miscellaneous Amendments) Regulations 2005 (SI 2005/337) reg.10 (March 18, 2005).

Recovery from couples

17. In the case of an overpayment of income support [3 or state pension credit] [2, or income-based jobseeker's allowance] [1, family credit or disability working allowance] to one of [4 a couple], the amount recoverable by deduction, in accordance with regulation 15, may be recovered by deduction from income support [3 or state pension credit] [2, or income-based jobseeker's allowance] [1, family credit or disability working allowance] payable to either of them, provided that the two of them are [4 a couple] at the date of the deduction.

2.710

Social Security (Payments on Account, etc.) Regulations 1988

AMENDMENTS

1. The Disability Living Allowance and Disability Working Allowance (Consequential Provisions) Regulations 1991 (SI 1991/2742), reg.15 (April 6, 1992).
2. The Social Security and Child Support (Jobseeker's Allowance) (Consequential Amendments) Regulations 1996 (SI 1996/1345), reg.23(5) and (6) (October 7, 1996).
3. State Pension Credit (Consequential, Transitional and Miscellaneous Provisions) Regulations 2002 (SI 2002/3019), reg.24 (October 6, 2003).
4. The Civil Partnership (Pensions, Social Security and Child Support) (Consequential etc. Provisions) Order 2005 (SI 2005/2877) (December 5, 2005).

PART VIII

RECOVERY BY DEDUCTIONS FROM EARNINGS FOLLOWING TRADE DISPUTE

Recovery by deductions from earnings

2.711   **18.**—(1) Any sum paid to a person on an award of income support made to him by virtue of section 23(8) of the Act [SSCBA, s.127] (effect of return to work after a trade dispute) shall be recoverable from him in accordance with this Part of these Regulations.

(2) In this Part, unless the context otherwise requires—

"available earnings" means the earnings, including any remuneration paid by or on behalf of an employer to an employee who is for the time being unable to work owing to sickness, which remain payable to a claimant on any pay-day after deduction by his employer of all amounts lawfully deductible by the employer otherwise than by virtue of a deduction notice;

"claimant" means a person to whom an award is made by virtue of section 23(8) of the Act [SSCBA, s.127];

"deduction notice" means a notice under regulation 20 or 25;

"employment" means employment (including employment which has been suspended but not terminated) in remunerative work, and related expressions shall be construed accordingly;

"pay-day" means an occasion on which earnings are paid to a claimant;

"protected earnings" means protected earnings as determined by an adjudicating authority, in accordance with regulation 19(2), under regulation 19(1)(a) or 24;

"recoverable amount" means the amount (determined in accordance with regulation 20(3) or (5) or regulation 25(2)(a)) by reference to which deductions are to be made by an employer from a claimant's earnings by virtue of a deduction notice;

"repaid by the claimant" means paid by the claimant directly to the Secretary of State by way of repayment of income support otherwise recoverable under this Part of these Regulations.

(3) Any notice or other document required or authorised to be given or sent to any person under the provisions of this Part shall be deemed to have been given or sent if it was sent by post to that person in accordance with paragraph (6) of regulation 27 where that regulation applies and, in any other case, at his ordinary or last known address or in the case of an employer at the last place of business where the claimant to which it

(SI 1988/664, reg.18) (as amended)

relates is employed, and if so sent to have been given or sent on the day on which it was posted.

Award and protected earnings

19.—(1) Where an adjudicating authority determines that a person claiming income support is entitled by virtue of section 23(8) of the Act [SSCBA, s.127] (effect of return to work after a trade dispute) and makes an award to him accordingly he shall determine the claimant's protected earnings (that is to say the amount below which his actual earnings must not be reduced by any deduction made under this Part).

(2) The adjudicating authority shall include in his decision—
(a) the amount of income support awarded together with a statement that the claimant is a person entitled by virtue of section 23(8) of the Act [SSCBA, s.127] and that accordingly any sum paid to him on that award will be recoverable from him as provided in this Part;
(b) the amount of the claimant's protected earnings, and
(c) a statement of the claimant's duty under regulation 28 (duty to give notice of cessation or resumption of employment).

[¹(3) The protected earnings of the claimant shall be the sum determined by—
(a) taking the sum specified in paragraph (4),
(b) adding the sum specified in paragraph (5), and
(c) subtracting from the result any child benefit which falls to be taken into account in calculating his income for the purposes of Part V of the Income Support Regulations.]

(4) The sum referred to in paragraph (3)(a) shall be the aggregate of the amounts calculated under regulation 17(a) to (d), 18(a) to (e), 20 or 21, as the case may be, of the Income Support Regulations.

(5) The sum referred to in paragraph (3)(b) shall be £27 except where the sum referred to in paragraph (3)(a) includes an amount calculated under regulation 20 in which case the sum shall be £8.00.

AMENDMENT

1. The Social Security (Payments on account, Overpayments and Recovery) Amendments Regulations 1988 (SI 1988/688), reg.2(5) (April 11, 1988).

Service and contents of deduction notices

20.—(1) Where the amount of income support has not already been repaid by the claimant, the Secretary of State shall serve a deduction notice on the employer of the claimant.

(2) A deduction notice shall contain the following particulars—
(a) particulars enabling the employer to identify the claimant;
(b) the recoverable amount;
(c) the claimant's protected earnings as specified in the notification of award.

(3) Subject to paragraph (5) the recoverable amount shall be—
(a) the amount specified in the decision as having been awarded to the claimant by way of income support; reduced by
(b) the amount (if any) which has been repaid by the claimant before the date of the deduction notice.

(4) If a further award relating to the claimant is made the Secretary of State shall cancel the deduction notice (giving written notice of the

cancellation to the employer and the claimant) and serve on the employer a further deduction notice.

(5) The recoverable amount to be specified in the further deduction notice shall be the sum of—
  (a) the amount determined by applying paragraph (3) to the further award; and
  (b) the recoverable amount specified in the cancelled deduction notice less any part of that amount which before the date of the further notice has already been deducted by virtue of the cancelled notice or repaid by the claimant.

Period for which deduction notice has effect

21.—(1) A deduction notice shall come into force when it is served on the employer of the claimant to whom it relates and shall cease to have effect as soon as any of the following conditions is fulfilled—
  (a) the notice is cancelled by virtue of regulation 20(4) or paragraph (2) of this regulation;
  (b) the claimant ceases to be in the employment of the person on whom the notice was served;
  (c) the aggregate of—
     (i) any part of the recoverable amount repaid by the claimant on or after the date of the deduction notice, and
     (ii) the total amount deducted by virtue of the notice,
  reaches the recoverable amount;
  (d) there has elapsed a period of 26 weeks beginning with the date of the notice.

(2) The Secretary of State may at any time give a direction in writing cancelling a deduction notice and—
  (a) he shall cause a copy of the direction to be served on the employer concerned and on the claimant;
  (b) the direction shall take effect when a copy of it is served on the employer concerned.

Effect of deduction notice

22.—(1) Where a deduction notice is in force the following provisions of this regulation shall apply as regards any relevant pay-day.

(2) Where a claimant's earnings include any bonus, commission or other similar payment which is paid other than on a day on which the remainder of his earnings is paid, then in order to calculate his available earnings for the purposes of this regulation any such bonus, commission or other similar payment shall be treated as being paid to him on the next day of payment of the remainder of his earnings instead of on the day of actual payment.

(3) If on a relevant pay-day a claimant's available earnings—
  (a) do not exceed his protected earnings by at least £1, no deduction shall be made;
  (b) do exceed his protected earnings by at least £1, his employer shall deduct from the claimant's available earnings one half of the excess over his protected earnings,
so however that where earnings are paid other than weekly the amount of the protected earnings and the figure of £1 shall be adjusted accordingly, in particular—

(SI 1988/664, reg.22) (as amended)

(c) where earnings are paid monthly, they shall for this purpose be treated as paid every five weeks (and the protected earnings and the figure of £1 accordingly multiplied by five);

(d) where earnings are paid daily, the protected earnings and the figure of £1 shall be divided by five,

and if, in any case to which sub-paragraph (c) or (d) does not apply, there is doubt as to the adjustment to be made this shall be determined by the Secretary of State on the application of the employer or the claimant.

(4) Where on a relevant pay-day earnings are payable to the claimant in respect of more than one pay-day the amount of the protected earnings and the figure of £1 referred to in the preceding paragraph, adjusted where appropriate in accordance with the provisions of that paragraph, shall be multiplied by the number of pay-days to which the earnings relate.

(5) Notwithstanding anything in paragraph (3)—

(a) the employer shall not make a deduction on a relevant pay-day if the claimant satisfies him that up to that day he has not obtained payment of the income support to which the deduction notice relates;

(b) the employer shall not on any relevant pay-day deduct from the claimant's earnings by virtue of the deduction notice an amount greater than the excess of the recoverable amount over the aggregate of all such amounts as, in relation to that notice, are mentioned in regulation 21(1)(c)(i) and (ii); and

(c) where the amount of any deduction which by this regulation the employer is required to make would otherwise include a fraction of 1p, that amount shall be reduced by that fraction.

(6) For the purpose of this regulation "relevant pay-day" means any pay-day beginning with—

(a) the first pay-day falling after the expiration of the period of one month from the date on which the deduction notice comes into force; or

(b) if the employer so chooses, any earlier pay-day after the notice has come into force.

Increase of amount of award on appeal or [¹ otherwise]

23. If the amount of the award is increased, whether on appeal or [¹ otherwise], this Part shall have effect as if on the date on which the amount of the award was increased—

(a) the amount of the increase was the recoverable amount; and

(b) the claimant's protected earnings [¹, where a notice of variation of protected earnings is given under regulation 24, were the earnings stated in the notice]

2.716

AMENDMENT

1. The Social Security Act 1998 (Commencement No.12, and Consequential and Transitional Provisions) Order 1999 (SI 1999/3178), Sch.9 (November 29, 1999).

[¹ Notice of variation] of protected earnings

[¹ . . .] **24.**—(1) [¹ . . .]

[¹ (2) The Secretary of State shall give a claimant's employer written notice varying the deduction notice where a decision as to a claimant's protected earnings is revised or superseded.]

(3) Variation of a deduction notice under paragraph (2) shall take effect either from the end of the period of 10 working days beginning with the day

2.717

on which notice of the variation is given to the employer or, if the employer so chooses, at any earlier time after notice is given.

AMENDMENT

1. The Social Security Act 1998 (Commencement No.12 and Consequential and Transitional Provisions) Order 1999 (SI 1999/3178), Sch.9 (November 29, 1999).

Power to serve further deduction notice on resumption of employment

2.718   **25.**—(1) Where a deduction notice has ceased to have effect by reason of the claimant ceasing to be in the employment of the person on whom the notice was served, the Secretary of State may, if he thinks fit, serve a further deduction notice on any person by whom the claimant is for the time being employed.

(2) Notwithstanding anything in the foregoing provisions of these Regulations, in any such deduction notice—
  (a) the recoverable amount shall be equal to the recoverable amount as specified in the previous deduction notice less the aggregate of—
     (i) the total of any amounts required to be deducted by virtue of that notice, and
     (ii) any additional part of that recoverable amount repaid by the claimant on or after the date of that notice,
or, where this regulation applies in respect of more than one such previous notice, the aggregate of the amounts as so calculated in respect of each such notice;
  (b) the amount specified as the claimant's protected earnings shall be the same as that so specified in the last deduction notice relating to him which was previously in force or as subsequently [¹ varied].

AMENDMENT

1. The Social Security Act 1998 (Commencement No.12 and Consequential and Transitional Provisions) Order 1999 (SI 1999/3178), Sch.9 (November 29, 1999).

Right of Secretary of State to recover direct from claimant

2.719   **26.** Where [¹, at any time, it is not practicable for the Secretary of State] by means of a deduction notice, to effect recovery of the recoverable amount or of so much of that amount as remains to be recovered from the claimant, the amount which remains to be recovered shall, by virtue of this regulation, be recoverable from the claimant by the Secretary of State.

AMENDMENT

1. The Social Security Act 1998 (Commencement No.12 and Consequential and Transitional Provisions) Order 1999 (SI 1999/3178), Sch.9 (November 29, 1999).

Duties and liabilities of employers

2.720   **27.**—(1) An employer shall keep a record of the available earnings of each claimant who is an employee in respect of whom a deduction notice is in force and of the payments which he makes in pursuance of the notice.

(2) A record of every deduction made by an employer under a deduction notice on any pay-day shall be given or sent by him to the Secretary of State, together with payment of the amount deduced, by not later than the 19th day of the following month.

(3) Where by reason only of the circumstances mentioned in regulation 22(5)(a) the employer makes no deduction from a claimant's weekly earnings on any pay-day he shall within 10 working days after that pay-day give notice of that fact to the Secretary of State.

(4) Where a deduction notice is cancelled by virtue of regulation 20(4) or 21(2) or ceases to have effect by virtue of regulation 21(1) the employer shall within 10 working days after the date on which the notice is cancelled or, as the case may be, ceases to have effect—
  (a) return the notice to the Secretary of State and, where regulation 21(1) applies, give notice of the reason for its return;
  (b) give notice, in relation to each relevant pay-day (as defined in regulation 22(6)), of the available earnings of the claimant and of any deduction made from those earnings.

(5) If on any pay-day to which regulation 22(3)(b) applies the employer makes no deduction from a claimant's available earnings, or makes a smaller deduction than he was thereby required to make, and in consequence any amount is not deducted while the deduction notice, or any further notice which under regulation 20(4) cancels that notice, has effect—
  (a) the amount which is not deducted shall, without prejudice to any other method of recovery from the claimant or otherwise, be recoverable from the employer by the Secretary of State; and
  (b) any amount so recovered shall, for the purposes of these Regulations, be deemed to have been repaid by the claimant.

(6) All records and notices to which this regulation applies shall given or sent to the Secretary of State, on a form approved by him, at such office of the [¹Department of Social Security] as he may direct.

AMENDMENT

1. The Transfer of Functions (Health and Social Security) Order 1988 (SI 1988/1843), art.3(4) (November 28, 1988).

Claimants to give notice of cessation or resumption of employment

28.—(1) Where a claimant ceases to be in the employment of a person on whom a deduction notice relating to him has been duly served knowing that the full amount of the recoverable amount has not been deducted from his earnings or otherwise recovered by the Secretary of State, he shall give notice within 10 working days to the Secretary of State of his address and of the date of such cessation of employment.

(2) Where on or after such cessation the claimant resumes employment (whether with the same or some other employer) he shall within 10 working days give notice to the Secretary of State of the name of the employer and of the address of his place of employment.

Failure to notify

29. If a person fails to comply with any requirement under regulation 27 or 28 to give notice of any matter to the Secretary of State he shall be guilty of an offence and liable on summary conviction to a fine not exceeding—
  (a) for any one offence, level 3 on the standard scale; or
  (b) for an offence of continuing any such contravention, £40 for each day on which it is so continued.

The Social Security Act 1998 (Prescribed Benefits) Regulations 2006

(SI 2006/2529)

Made 14th September 2006
Laid before Parliament 21st September 2006
Coming into force 16th October 2006

The Secretary of State for Work and Pensions makes the following Regulations in exercise of the powers conferred by sections 8(3)(h), 79(1) and 84 of the Social Security Act 1998.

In accordance with section 173(1)(b) of the Social Security Administration Act 1992, the Secretary of State has obtained the agreement of the Social Security Advisory Committee that proposals in respect of these Regulations need not be referred to it.

Citation and commencement

1. —(1) These Regulations may be cited as the Social Security Act 1998 (Prescribed Benefits) Regulations 2006 and shall come into force on 16th October 2006.

Prescribed benefits

2. The benefits prescribed for the purposes of section 8(3)(h) of the Social Security Act 1998 (decisions by Secretary of State) are—
 (a) the following benefits under the Social Security Act 1975—
  (i) sickness benefit under section 14;
  (ii) unemployment benefit under section 14;
  (iii) invalidity pension under section 15;
  (iv) invalidity allowance under section 16;
  (v) attendance allowance under section 35; and
  (vi) mobility allowance under section 37A;
 (b) supplementary benefit under the Supplementary Benefit Act 1976.

GENERAL NOTE

Except for attendance allowance, the benefits listed are benefits that had been abolished before the Social Security Act 1998 Act came into force and are therefore not within the scope of s.8(3)(a) to (g) of that Act. Attendance allowance has presumably been included from an abundance of caution because it is now payable only to people over the age of 65, whereas until 1992 it was payable to younger people. The need for this provision was revealed by *CDLA/2999/2004*, in which it was held that, because the transitional provision made when the 1998 Act came into force relies on the concept of a "relevant benefit" as defined by s.8(3), there was no power to make a supersession decision under s.10 of the 1998 Act in respect of mobility allowance, with the consequence that an overpayment of mobility allowance could not be recovered under s.71 of the Social Security Administration Act 1992. It is not entirely clear why the scope of s.8(3) of the 1998 Act has not been made precisely the same as the scope of s.71 of the 1992 Act (see para. 4(1) of Sch. 10 to the 1992 Act) but perhaps it was thought unlikely that any wider prescription would be required in practice. It is doubtful that the omission of the second "s" from the short title of the Supplementary Benefits Act 1976 is significant.

(SI 2004/2244)

The Social Security (Quarterly Work-focused Interviews for Certain Lone Parents) Regulations 2004

(SI 2004/2244)

Made   30th August 2004
Coming into force in accordance with regulation 1

ARRANGEMENT OF REGULATIONS

1. Citation, amendment and interpretation.
2. Requirement for a relevant person to take part in an interview.
3. Waiver of requirement to take part in an interview.
4. Deferment of requirement to take part in an interview.
5. The interview.
6. Taking part in an interview.
7. Failure to take part in an interview.
8. Good cause.
9. Appeals.
10. *Amends the Work-focused Interviews for Lone Parents Regulations 2000.*
Schedule

GENERAL NOTE

These regulations provide for certain lone parents living in the Extended Schools Childcare Pilot areas to attend mandatory work focused interviews on a quarterly basis. The purpose of the childcare schemes is said to be to provide high quality affordable childcare. The regulations apply to lone parents in the designated areas who have been in receipt of income support for twelve months, who are aged between 18 and 60 and whose youngest child is at least 12 years old. The regulations essentially come into force on September 30, 2004 but detailed commencement provisions are to be found in reg.1.

There are some stylistic differences in drafting in these regulations compared with other regulations on work-focused interviews, but these appear not to be intended to give rise to any difference of treatment or approach. Some of the changes are clearly for the avoidance of doubt. An example is the provisions on deferment which make clear that there must be a determination of a future date on which liability to take part in an interview will arise. As with other regulations on work-focused interviews, there is an appeal against any decision that a person has failed to attend an interview without good cause for that failure.

The Secretary of State for Work and Pensions, in exercise of the powers conferred upon him by s.2A(1)(b), (3)(b) to (f), (4)(b), (5)(a) and (b), (6) and (8), 2B(6) to (8), 189(4) to (6) and (7A) and 191 of the Social Security Administration Act 1992 and of all other powers enabling him in that behalf, after consultation with the Council on Tribunals in accordance with s.8(1) of the Tribunals and Inquiries Act 1992 and after agreement by the Social Security Advisory Committee that proposals in respect of these Regulations should not be referred to it, hereby makes the following Regulations:

Citation, commencement and interpretation

1.—(1) These Regulations may be cited as the Social Security (Quarterly Work-focused Interviews for Certain Lone Parents) Regulations 2004.

(2) These Regulations shall come into force—
  (a) in respect of a lone parent—
    (i) who resides in an education authority area or a local education authority area identified in the Schedule to these Regulations;
    (ii) who has been entitled to a specified benefit for not less than 12 months immediately prior to 30th September 2004; and
    (iii) whose youngest child, for whom the lone parent is responsible and who is a member of the lone parent's household, is at least 12 years old on 30th September 2004,
on 30th September 2004;
  (b) in respect of a lone parent—
    (i) who resides in an education authority area or a local education authority area identified in that Schedule;
    (ii) who after 30th September 2004 reaches the first anniversary of his entitlement to a specified benefit; and
    (iii) whose youngest child, for whom the lone parent is responsible and who is a member of the lone parent's household, reaches the age of 12 years after 30th September 2004,
on the date of that first anniversary or the date that child reaches the age of 12 years, whichever is the later.

(3) In these Regulations—
"benefit recipient" means a person who—
  (a) has not attained the age of 60; and
  (b) is entitled to a specified benefit at a higher rate referable to his partner;
"benefit week" means any period of seven days corresponding to the week in respect of which income support is due to be paid;
"education authority" means an education authority described in section 135(1) of the Education (Scotland) Act 1980 and "education authority area" shall be construed in accordance with the provisions of that section;
"interview" means a work-focused interview with a relevant person conducted for any or all of the following purposes—
  (a) assessing that person's prospects for existing or future employment (whether paid or voluntary);
  (b) assisting or encouraging that person to enhance his prospects of such employment;
  (c) identifying activities which that person may undertake to strengthen his existing or future prospects of employment;
  (d) identifying current or future employment or training opportunities suitable to that person's needs; and
  (e) identifying educational opportunities connected with the existing or future employment prospects or needs of that person;
"local education authority" means a local education authority described in section 12 of the Education Act 1996 (local education authorities and their areas) and "local education authority area" shall be construed in accordance with the provisions of that section;
"lone parent" means a person who has no partner and who is responsible for, and a member of the same household as, a child;
"officer" means a person who is an officer of, or who is providing services to or exercising functions of, the Secretary of State;
"partner" means a person who is a member of the same couple as a benefit recipient, or, in a case where a benefit recipient has more than one

(SI 2004/2244, reg.3)

partner, a person who is a partner of the benefit recipient by reason of a polygamous marriage;

"polygamous marriage" means any marriage during the subsistence of which a party to it is married to more than one person and the ceremony of marriage took place under the law of a country which permits polygamy;

[1 "relevant person" means a person—
 (a) to whom paragraph (2)(a) or (b) applies; and
 (b) who has attained the age of 18 but not attained the age of 60; [and
 (c) who—
    (i) is nor required to take part in an interview under regulation 2A of the Social Security (Work-focused Interviews for Lone Parnets) and Miscellaneous Amendments Regulations 2000; or
    (ii) has not had such a requirement waived or deferred under regulations 5 or 6 of those Regulations;]

"specified benefit" means income support other than income support which is awarded where—
 (a) paragraph 7 of Schedule 1B to the Income Support (General) Regulations 1987 (prescribed categories of person—persons incapable of work) applies;
 (b) paragraph 24 or 25 of Schedule 1B to the Income Support (General) Regulations 1987 (prescribed categories of person—persons appealing against a decision which embodies a determination that they are not incapable of work) applies.

AMENDMENT

1. The Social Security (Work-focused Interviews) Amendment Regulations 2005 (SI 2005/2727) (October 31, 2005).

Requirement for a relevant person to take part in an interview

2.—(1) Subject to regulations 3 and 4, a relevant person shall be required to take part in an interview as a condition of that person continuing to be entitled to the full amount of a specified benefit which is payable apart from these Regulations.

(2) A relevant person shall first be required to take part in an interview under paragraph (1) as soon as is reasonably practicable after the date these Regulations come into force in respect of that person.

(3) Subject to regulations 3 and 4, a requirement under paragraph (1) shall arise at intervals of not less than 13 weeks beginning with—
 (a) the day on which the relevant person last took part in an interview in accordance with this regulation;
 (b) the day he was treated under regulation 3 as having complied with such a requirement; or
 (c) the day a relevant decision was made in accordance with regulation 6(3),

whichever is the later, as a condition of his continuing to be entitled to the full amount of a specified benefit which is payable apart from these Regulations.

Waiver of requirement to take part in an interview

3.—(1) A requirement imposed by these Regulations to take part in an interview shall not apply where an officer determines that an interview would not be—

(a) of assistance to the relevant person; or
(b) appropriate in the circumstances.
(2) A relevant person in relation to whom a requirement to take part in an interview has been waived under paragraph (1) above shall be treated for the purposes of regulation 2 as having complied with that requirement in respect of that interview.

Deferment of requirement to take part in an interview

4.—(1) An officer may determine, in the case of a relevant person, that the requirement under regulation 2 to take part in an interview shall be deferred at the time the requirement to take part in an interview arises or applies because an interview would not at that time be—
(a) of assistance to that relevant person; or
(b) appropriate in the circumstances.
(2) Where an officer determines in accordance with paragraph (1) that the requirement to take part in an interview shall be deferred, he shall also determine when that determination is made, the time when the requirement to take part in an interview is to apply in the relevant person's case.
(3) Where a requirement to take part in an interview has been deferred in accordance with paragraph (1) then until—
(a) a determination is made under regulation 3(1);
(b) the relevant person takes part in an interview; or
(c) a relevant decision has been made in relation to that relevant person in accordance with regulation 6(3),
that relevant person shall be treated for the purposes of his continuing to be entitled to the full amount of a specified benefit which is payable apart from these Regulations as having complied with that requirement.

The interview

5.—(1) An officer shall inform the relevant person who is required to take part in an interview of the date, time and place of the interview.
(2) An officer may determine that an interview is to take place in the relevant person's home where it would, in the officer's opinion, be unreasonable to expect that relevant person to attend elsewhere because that person's personal circumstances are such that attending elsewhere would cause him undue inconvenience or endanger his health.
(3) An officer shall conduct the interview.

Taking part in an interview

6.—(1) An officer shall determine whether a relevant person has taken part in an interview.
[1 (2) A relevant person who has not taken part in an interview under these Regulations before 31st October 2005 shall be regarded as having taken part in his first interview under these Regulations if—
(a) he attends for the interview at the place and time notified to him by the officer;
(b) he participates in discussions with the officer in relation to the relevant person's employability, including any action the relevant person and the officer agree is reasonable and they are willing to take in order to help the relevant person enhance his employment prospects;

(SI 2004/2244, reg. 6)

    (c) he provides answers (where asked) to questions and appropriate information about—
        (i) the level to which he has pursued any educational qualifications;
        (ii) his employment history;
        (iii) any vocational training he has undertaken;
        (iv) any skills he has acquired which fit him for employment;
        (v) any paid or unpaid employment he is engaged in;
        (vi) any medical condition which, in his opinion, puts him at a disadvantage in obtaining employment;
        (vii) any caring or childcare responsibilities he has;
        (viii) his aspirations for future employment;
        (ix) any vocational training or skills which he wishes to undertake or acquire; and
        (x) his work related abilities; and
    (d) he assists the officer in the completion of an action plan which records the matters discussed in relation to sub-paragraph (b) above.

(2A) A relevant person who has taken part in an interview under these Regulations before 31st October 2005 shall be regarded as having taken part in his first interview under these Regulations after 30th October 2005 if—
    (a) he attends for the interview at the place and time notified to him by the officer;
    (b) he participates in discussions with the officer in relation to the relevant person's employability, including any action the relevant person and the officer agree is reasonable and they are willing to take in order to help the relevant person enhance his employment prospects;
    (c) he participates in discussions with the officer—
        (i) in relation to the relevant person's employability or any progress he might have made towards obtaining employment; and
        (ii) in order to consider any of the programmes and support available to help the relevant person obtain employment;
    (d) he provides answers (where asked) to questions and appropriate information about—
        (i) the content of any report made following his personal capability assessment, insofar as that report relates to the relevant person's capabilities and employability; and
        (ii) his opinion as to the extent to which his medical condition restricts his ability to obtain employment; and
    (e) he assists the officer in the completion of an action plan which records the matters discussed in relation to sub-paragraph (b) above.

(2B) A relevant person shall be regarded as having taken part in any subsequent interview under these Regulations if—
    (a) he attends for the interview at the place and time notified to him by the officer;
    (b) he participates in discussions with the officer—
        (i) in relation to the relevant person's employability or any progress he might have made towards obtaining employment;
        (ii) about any action the relevant person or the officer might have taken as a result of the matters discussed in relation to paragraphs (2)(b) or (2A)(b) above;
        (iii) about how, if at all, the action plan referred to in paragraphs (2)(d) or (2A)(e) above should be amended; and

Social Security (Quarterly Work-focused Interviews) Regs 2004

        (iv) in order to consider any of the programmes and support available to help the relevant person obtain employment;
    (c) he provides answers (where asked) to questions and appropriate information about—
        (i) the content of any report made following his personal capability assessment, insofar as that report relates to the relevant person's capabilities and employability; and
        (ii) his opinion as to the extent to which his medical condition restricts his ability to obtain employment; and
    (d) he assists the officer in the completion of any amendment of the action plan referred to in paragraphs (2)(d) or (2A)(e) above in light of the matters discussed in relation to sub-paragraph (b) above and the information provided in relation to sub-paragraph (c) above.]

    (3) Where an officer determines that a relevant person has failed to take part in an interview and good cause has not been shown by the relevant person for that failure within five working days of the day on which the interview was to take place, a relevant decision shall be made for the purposes of section 2B of the Social Security Administration Act 1992 and the relevant person shall be notified accordingly.

AMENDMENT

1. The Social Security (Work-focused Interviews) Amendment Regulations 2005 (SI 2005/2727) (October 31, 2005).

Failure to take part in an interview

2.734   **7.**—(1) Where a relevant decision has been made in accordance with regulation 6(3), subject to paragraphs (2) and (7), the specified benefit payable to the relevant person shall be reduced as from the first day of the next benefit week following the day a relevant decision was made, by a sum equal to 20 per cent. of the amount applicable on the date the first reduction commences in respect of a single claimant for income support aged not less than 25.

    (2) The specified benefit reduced in accordance with paragraph (1) shall not be reduced below ten pence per week.

    (3) Where the rate of the specified benefit payable to a relevant person changes, the reduction described in paragraph (1) shall be applied to the new rates and any adjustments to the specified benefit against which the reduction is made shall take effect from the beginning of the first benefit week to commence for that relevant person following the change.

    (4) Paragraph (1) shall apply to a relevant person each time a relevant decision is made in accordance with regulation 6(3) in respect of the relevant person.

    (5) Where a relevant person whose specified benefit has been reduced in accordance with paragraph (1) subsequently takes part in an interview, the whole of the reduction shall cease to have effect on the first day of the benefit week in which the requirement to take part in an interview was met.

    (6) Where paragraph (4) applies, for the purposes of determining the amount of the specified benefit payable a relevant person shall be treated as receiving the amount of the specified benefit which would have been payable but for a reduction made in accordance with paragraph (1).

    (7) The specified benefit shall not be reduced in accordance with paragraph (1) where the relevant person brings new facts to the notice of the

(SI 2004/2244, reg. 7)

Secretary of State within one month of the date on which a relevant decision was notified to him and—
   (a) those facts could not reasonably have been brought to the Secretary of State's notice within five working days of the day on which the interview was to take place; and
   (b) those facts show that the relevant person had good cause for his failure to take part in the interview.

(8) Where a reduction of specified benefit has been made in accordance with paragraph (1) the whole of that reduction shall cease to have effect on the date when the relevant person—
   (a) is no longer required to take part in an interview as a condition for continuing to be entitled to the full amount of the specified benefit which is payable to the relevant person apart from these Regulations; or
   (b) attains the age of 60.

Good cause

8. Matters to be taken into account in determining whether a relevant person has shown good cause for the relevant person's failure to take part in an interview include— 2.735
   (a) that the relevant person misunderstood the requirement to take part in the interview due to any learning, language or literacy difficulties of the relevant person or any misleading information given to him by an officer;
   (b) that the relevant person was attending a medical or dental appointment, or accompanying a person for whom the relevant person has caring responsibilities to such an appointment, and that it would have been unreasonable in the circumstances to rearrange the appointment;
   (c) that the relevant person had difficulties with his normal mode of transport and that no reasonable alternative was available;
   (d) that the established customs and practices of the religion to which the relevant person belongs prevented him from attending on the day or at the time or place fixed for the interview;
   (e) that the relevant person was attending an interview with an employer with a view to obtaining employment;
   (f) that the relevant person was pursuing employment opportunities as a self-employed earner;
   (g) that the relevant person or a dependant or a person for whom the relevant person provides care suffered an accident, sudden illness or relapse of a physical or mental health condition;
   (h) that the relevant person was attending the funeral of a close relative or close friend on the day fixed for the interview;
   (i) that a disability of the relevant person made it impracticable for him to attend at the time fixed for the interview.

Appeals

9.—(1) This regulation applies to any relevant decision under regulation 6(3) or any decision made under section 10 of the Social Security Act 1998 (decisions superseding earlier decisions) superseding such a relevant decision. 2.736

(2) This regulation applies whether the decision is as originally made or as revised under section 9 of the Social Security Act 1998 (revision of decisions).

(3) In the case of a decision to which this regulation applies, the relevant person in respect of whom the decision was made shall have a right of appeal under section 12 of the Social Security Act 1998 (appeal to appeal tribunal) to an appeal tribunal.

SCHEDULE

1. For the purposes of regulation 1(2)—
   (a) the local education authority areas are Bradford, Greenwich, Haringey, Leicester, Leicestershire, Lewisham, Sandwell and Torfaen;
   (b) the education authority areas are Aberdeenshire and Fife.

The Employment Protection (Recoupment of Jobseeker's Allowance and Income Support) Regulations 1996

(SI 1996/2349)

Made	10th September 1996
Laid before Parliament	11th September 1996
Coming into force	7th October 1996

2.737 The Secretary of State in exercise of the powers conferred on him by section 16 and section 41(4) of the Industrial Tribunals Act 1996, section 58(1) of the Social Security Administration Act 1992, and of all other powers enabling him in that behalf, and after reference to the Social Security Advisory Committee in so far as is required by section 172 of the Social Security Administration Act 1992, and after consultation with the Council on Tribunals, in so far as is required by section 8 of the Tribunals and Inquiries Act 1992, hereby makes the following Regulations:—

PART I

INTRODUCTORY

Citation and Commencement

2.738 **1.** These Regulations may be cited as the Employment Protection (Recoupment of Jobseeker's Allowance and Income Support) Regulations 1996 and shall come into force on 7th October 1996.

Interpretation

2.739 **2.**—(1) In these Regulations, unless the context otherwise requires, the following expressions have the meanings hereby assigned to them respectively, that is to say—
"the 1992 Act" means the Trade Union and Labour Relations (Consolidation) Act 1992;
"the 1996 Act" means the Employment Rights Act 1996;
"prescribed element" has the meaning assigned to it in Regulation 3 below and the Schedule to these Regulations;

(SI 1996/2349, reg.2)

"protected period" has the same meaning as in section 189(5) of the 1992 Act;

"protective award" has the same meaning as in section 189(3) of the 1992 Act;

"recoupable benefit" means any jobseeker's allowance or income support as the case may be, which is recoupable under these Regulations;

"recoupment notice" means a notice under these Regulations;

"Secretary of the Tribunals" means the Secretary of the Central Office of the [1 Employment] Tribunals (England and Wales) or, as the case may require, the Secretary of the Central Office of the [1 Employment] Tribunals (Scotland) for the time being;

(2) In the Schedule to these Regulations references to sections are references to sections of the 1996 Act unless otherwise indicated and references in column 3 of the table to the conclusion of the tribunal proceedings are references to the conclusion of the proceedings mentioned in the corresponding entry in column 2.

(3) For the purposes of these Regulations (and in particular for the purposes of any calculations to be made by an [1 employment tribunal] as respects the prescribed element) the conclusion of the tribunal proceedings shall be taken to occur—

(a) where the [1 employment tribunal] at the hearing announces the effect of its decision to the parties, on the date on which that announcement is made;

(b) in any other case, on the date on which the decision of the tribunal is sent to the parties.

(4) References to parties in relevant [1 employment tribunal] proceedings shall be taken to include references to persons appearing on behalf of parties in a representative capacity.

(5) References in these Regulations to anything done, or to be done, in, or in consequence of, any tribunal proceedings include references to anything done, or to be done, in, or in consequence of any such proceedings as are in the nature of a review, or re-hearing or a further hearing consequent on an appeal.

AMENDMENT

1. Employment Rights (Dispute Resolution) Act 1998, s.1(2)(a) (August 1, 1998).

PART II

INDUSTRIAL TRIBUNAL PROCEEDINGS

Application to payments and proceedings

3.—(1) Subject to paragraph (2) below these Regulations apply— 2.740

(a) to the payments described in column 1 of the table contained in the Schedule to these Regulations, being, in each case, payments which are the subject of [1 employment tribunal] proceedings of the kind described in the corresponding entry in column 2 and the prescribed element in relation to each such payment is so much of the relevant monetary award as is attributable to the matter described in the corresponding entry in column 3; and

(b) to payments of remuneration in pursuance of a protective award.

(2) The payments to which these Regulations apply by virtue of paragraph (1)(a) above include payments in proceedings under section 192 of the 1992 Act and, accordingly, where an order is made on an employee's complaint under that section, the relevant protective award shall, as respects that employee and to the appropriate extent, be taken to be subsumed in the order made under section 192 so that the provisions of these Regulations relating to monetary awards shall apply to payments under that order to the exclusion of the provisions relating to protective awards, but without prejudice to anything done under the latter in connection with the relevant protective award before the making of the order under section 192.

AMENDMENT

1. Employment Rights (Dispute Resolution) Act 1998, s.1(2)(a) (August 1, 1998).

Duties of the [1 employment tribunals] and of the Secretary of the Tribunals in respect of monetary awards

4.—(1) Where these Regulations apply, no regard shall be had, in assessing the amount of a monetary award, to the amount of any jobseeker's allowance or any income support which may have been paid to or claimed by the employee for a period which coincides with any part of a period to which the prescribed element is attributable.

(2) Where the [1 employment tribunal] in arriving at a monetary award makes a reduction on account of the employee's contributory fault or on account of any limit imposed by or under the 1992 Act or 1996 Act, a proportionate reduction shall be made in arriving at the amount of the prescribed element.

(3) Subject to the following provisions of this Regulation it shall be the duty of the [1 employment tribunal] to set out in any decision which includes a monetary award the following particulars—
  (a) the monetary award;
  (b) the amount of the prescribed element, if any;
  (c) the dates of the period to which the prescribed element is attributable;
  (d) the amount, if any, by which the monetary award exceeds the prescribed element.

(4) Where the [1 employment tribunal] at the hearing announces to the parties the effect of a decision which includes a monetary award it shall inform those parties at the same time of the amount of any prescribed element included in the monetary award and shall explain the effect of Regulations 7 and 8 below in relation to the prescribed element.

(5) Where the [1 employment tribunal] has made such an announcement as is described in paragraph (4) above the Secretary of the Tribunals shall forthwith notify the Secretary of State that the tribunal has decided to make a monetary award including a prescribed element and shall notify him of the particulars set out in paragraph (3) above.

(6) As soon as reasonably practicable after the Secretary of the Tribunals has sent a copy of a decision containing the particulars set out in paragraph (3) above to the parties he shall send a copy of that decision to the Secretary of State.

(7) In addition to containing the particulars required under paragraph (3) above, any such decision as is mentioned in that paragraph shall contain a

statement explaining the effect of Regulations 7 and 8 below in relation to the prescribed element.

(8) The requirements of paragraphs (3) to (7) above do not apply where the tribunal is satisfied that in respect of each day falling within the period to which the prescribed element relates the employee has neither received nor claimed jobseeker's allowance or income support.

AMENDMENT

1. Employment Rights (Dispute Resolution) Act 1998, s.1(2)(a) (August 1, 1998).

Duties of the [¹ employment tribunals] and of the Secretary of the Tribunals in respect of protective awards

5. (1) Where, on a complaint under section 189 of the 1992 Act, an [¹ employment tribunal]—
   (a) at the hearing announces to the parties the effect of a decision to make a protective award; or
   (b) (where it has made no such announcement) sends a decision to make such an award to the parties; the Secretary of the Tribunals shall forthwith notify the Secretary of State of the following particulars relating to the award—
      (i) where the [¹ employment tribunal] has made such an announcement as is described in paragraph (1)(a) above, the date of the hearing or where it has made no such announcement, the date on which the decision was sent to the parties;
      (ii) the location of the tribunal;
      (iii) the name and address of the employer;
      (iv) the description of the employees to whom the award relates; and
      (v) the dates of the protected period.
(2)(a) Where an [¹ employment tribunal] makes such an announcement as is described in paragraph (1)(a) above in the presence of the employer or his representative it shall advise him of his duties under Regulation 6 below and shall explain the effect of Regulations 7 and 8 below in relation to remuneration under the protective award.
   (b) Without prejudice to (a) above any decision of an [¹ employment tribunal] to make a protective award under section 189 of the 1992 Act shall contain a statement advising the employer of his duties under Regulation 6 below and an explanation of the effect of Regulations 7 and 8 below in relation to remuneration under the protective award.

AMENDMENT

1. Employment Rights (Dispute Resolution) Act 1998, s.1(2)(a) (August 1, 1998).

Duties of the employer to give information about protective awards

6.—(1) Where an [¹ employment tribunal] makes a protective award under section 189 of the 1992 Act against an employer, the employer shall give to the Secretary of State the following information in writing—
   (a) the name, address and national insurance number of every employee to whom the award relates; and
   (b) the date of termination (or proposed termination) of the employment of each such employee.

The Employment Protection (Recoupment of JSA and IS) Regulations 1996

(2) Subject to paragraph (3) below the employer shall comply with paragraph (1) above within the period of ten days commencing on the day on which the [¹ employment tribunal] at the hearing announces to the parties the effect of a decision to make a protective award or (in the case where no such announcement is made) on the day on which the relevant decision is sent to the parties.

(3) Where, in any case, it is not reasonably practicable for the employer to comply with paragraph (1) above within the period applicable under paragraph (2) above he shall comply as soon as reasonably practicable after the expiration of that period.

AMENDMENT

1. Employment Rights (Dispute Resolution) Act 1998, s.1(2)(a) (August 1, 1998).

PART III

RECOUPMENT OF BENEFIT

Postponement of Awards

2.744

7.—(1) This Regulation shall have effect for the purpose of postponing relevant awards in order to enable the Secretary of State to initiate recoupment under Regulation 8 below.

(2) Accordingly—
 (a) so much of the monetary award as consists of the prescribed element;
 (b) payment of any remuneration to which an employee would otherwise be entitled under a protective award, shall be treated as stayed (in Scotland, sisted) as respects the relevant employee until—
  (i) the Secretary of State has served a recoupment notice on the employer; or
  (ii) the Secretary of State has notified the employer in writing that he does not intend to serve a recoupment notice.

(3) The stay or sist under paragraph (2) above is without prejudice to the right of an employee under section 192 of the 1992 Act to present a complaint to an [¹ employment tribunal] of his employer's failure to pay remuneration under a protective award and Regulation 3(2) above has effect as respects any such complaint and as respects any order made under section 192(3) of that Act.

AMENDMENT

1. Employment Rights (Dispute Resolution) Act 1998, s.1(2)(a) (August 1, 1998).

Recoupment of Benefit

2.745

8.—(1) Recoupment shall be initiated by the Secretary of State serving on the employer a recoupment notice claiming by way of total or partial recoupment of jobseeker's allowance or income support the appropriate amount, computed, as the case may require, under paragraph (2) or (3) below.

(2) In the case of monetary awards the appropriate amount shall be whichever is the less of the following two sums—

(SI 1996/2349, reg. 8)

  (a) the amount of the prescribed element (less any tax or social security contributions which fall to be deducted therefrom by the employer); or
  (b) the amount paid by way of or paid as on account of jobseeker's allowance or income support to the employee for any period which coincides with any part of the period to which the prescribed element is attributable.

(3) In the case of remuneration under a protective award the appropriate amount shall be whichever is the less of the following two sums—
  (a) the amount (less any tax or social security contributions which fall to be deducted therefrom by the employer) accrued due to the employee in respect of so much of the protected period as falls before the date on which the Secretary of State receives from the employer the information required under Regulation 6 above; or
  (b) the amount paid by way of or paid as on account of jobseeker's allowance or income support to the employee for any period which coincides with any part of the protected period falling before the date described in (a) above.

(4) A recoupment notice shall be served on the employer by post or otherwise and copies shall likewise be sent to the employee and, if requested, to the Secretary of the Tribunals.

(5) The Secretary of State shall serve a recoupment notice on the employer, or notify the employer that he does not intend to serve such a notice, within the period applicable, as the case may require, under paragraph (6) or (7) below, or as soon as practicable thereafter.

(6) In the case of a monetary award the period shall be—
  (a) in any case in which the tribunal at the hearing announces to the parties the effect of its decision as described in Regulation 4(4) above, the period ending 21 days after the conclusion of the hearing or the period ending 9 days after the decision has been sent to the parties, whichever is the later; or
  (b) in any other case, the period ending 21 days after the decision has been sent to the parties.

(7) In the case of a protective award the period shall be the period ending 21 days after the Secretary of State has received from the employer the information required under Regulation 6 above.

(8) A recoupment notice served on an employer shall operate as an instruction to the employer to pay, by way of deduction out of the sum due under the award, the recoupable amount to the Secretary of State and it shall be the duty of the employer to comply with the notice. The employer's duty under this paragraph shall not affect his obligation to pay any balance that may be due to the employee under the relevant award.

(9) The duty imposed on the employer by service of the recoupment notice shall not be discharged by payment of the recoupable amount to the employee during the postponement period or thereafter if a recoupment notice is served on the employer during the said period.

(10) Payment by the employer to the Secretary of State under this Regulation shall be a complete discharge in favour of the employer as against the employee in respect of any sum so paid but without prejudice to any rights of the employee under Regulation 10 below.

(11) The recoupable amount shall be recoverable by the Secretary of State from the employer as a debt.

The Employment Protection (Recoupment of JSA and IS) Regulations 1996

GENERAL NOTE

2.746 When assessing compensation, an employment tribunal must make a gross award, ignoring any jobseeker's allowance or income support paid to the employee during the relevant period, (reg.4(1)) and must give the Secretary of State details of the award (regs 4 and 5). The award is then postponed under reg.7 to allow the Secretary of State to recoup under reg.8 from the employer the amount of jobseeker's allowance and income support paid to the employee during the relevant period. The relevant period is the period in respect of which compensation for loss of pay or arrears of pay is awarded but ends at the date of the employment tribunal's decision if the award covers a period in the future (reg.3 and Sch. and see *Homan v A1 Bacon Co Ltd* [1996] I.C.R. 721). The Secretary of State serves a recoupment notice on the employer who must pay the recoupable amount to the Secretary of State, by way of deduction out of the sum due under the award, and then pay the balance of the award to the employee (reg.8(8)). An employee may give notice to the Secretary of State that he does not accept the amount specified in the recoupment notice (reg.10(1)) and may appeal to an appeal tribunal against any decision of the Secretary of State in response to such a notice (reg.10(2B)).

Order made in secondary proceedings

2.747 **9.**—(1) In the application of any of the above provisions in the case of—
(a) proceedings for an award under section 192 of the 1992 Act; or
(b) proceedings in the nature of a review, a re-hearing or a further hearing consequent on an appeal,
it shall be the duty of the [1 employment tribunal] or, as the case may require, the Secretary of State, to take the appropriate account of anything done under or in consequence of these Regulations in relation to any award made in the original proceedings.
(2) For the purposes of this Regulation the original proceedings are—
(a) where paragraph (1)(a) above applies the proceedings under section 189 of the 1992 Act; or
(b) where paragraph (1)(b) above applies the proceedings in respect of which the re-hearing, the review or the further hearing consequent on an appeal takes place.

AMENDMENT

1. Employment Rights (Dispute Resolution) Act 1998, s.1(2)(a) (August 1, 1998).

PART IV

DETERMINATION [2 . . .] OF BENEFIT RECOUPED

Provisions relating to determination of amount paid by way of or paid as on account of benefit

2.748 **10.**—(1) Without prejudice to the right of the Secretary of State to recover from an employer the recoupable benefit, an employee on whom a copy of a recoupment notice has been served in accordance with Regulation 8 above may, within 21 days of the date on which such notice was served on him or

(SI 1996/2349, reg.10)

within such further time as the Secretary of State may for special reasons allow, give notice in writing to the Secretary of State that he does not accept that the amount specified in the recoupment notice in respect of jobseeker's allowance or income support is correct.

[² (2) Where an employee has given notice in writing to the Secretary of State under paragraph (1) above that he does not accept that an amount specified in the recoupment notice is correct, the Secretary of State shall make a decision as to the amount of jobseeker's allowance or, as the case may be, income support paid in respect of the period to which the prescribed element is attributable or, as appropriate, in respect of so much of the protected period as falls before the date on which the employer complies with Regulation 6 above.

(2A) The Secretary of State may revise either upon application made for the purpose or on his own initiative a decision under paragraph (2) above.

(2B) The employee shall have a right of appeal to an appeal tribunal constituted under Chapter I of Part I of the 1998 Act against a decision of the Secretary of State whether as originally made under paragraph (2) or as revised under paragraph (2A) above.

(2C) The Social Security and Child Support (Decisions and Appeals) Regulations 1999 shall apply for the purposes of paragraphs (2A) and (2B) above as though a decision of the Secretary of State under paragraph (2A) above were made under section 9 of the 1998 Act and any appeal from such a decision were made under section 12 of that Act.

(2D) In this Regulation "the 1998 Act" means the Social Security Act 1998.

(3) Where the Secretary of State recovers too much money from an employer under these Regulations the Secretary of State shall pay to the employee an amount equal to the excess.]

(4) In any case where, after the Secretary of State has recovered from an employer any amount by way of recoupment of benefit, the decision given by the [¹ employment tribunal] in consequence of which such recoupment took place is set aside or varied on appeal or on a re-hearing by the industrial tribunal, the Secretary of State shall make such repayment to the employer or payment to the employee of the whole or part of the amount recovered as he is satisfied should properly be made having regard to the decision given on appeal or re-hearing.

AMENDMENTS

1. Employment Rights (Dispute Resolution) Act 1998, s.1(2)(a) (August 1, 1998).
2. The Social Security Act 1998 (Commencement No.12 and Consequential and Transitional Provisions) Order 1999 (SI 1999/3178) (November 29, 1999).

GENERAL NOTE

The jurisdiction of the Secretary of State and the tribunal is confined to the question of the amount of jobseeker's allowance or income support paid in respect of the relevant period. In *R(JSA) 3/03*, it was held that no reduction could be made to the recoupable amount to take account of the loss of tax credits caused by the loss of employment. Presumably the loss of such benefits can be claimed from the employer as a head of compensation (see *Neal v Bingle* [1998] Q.B. 466). The Commissioner also held that s.14 of the Social Security Act 1998 provided a right of appeal to a Social Security Commissioner against a decision of an appeal tribunal under para.(2B).

2.749

The Employment Protection (Recoupment of JSA and IS) Regulations 1996

Revocation and Transition Provision

2.750   **11.** *Omitted.*

SCHEDULE   Regulation 3

2.751   TABLE RELATING TO MONETARY AWARDS

Column 1 **Payment**	Column 2 **Proceedings**	Column 3 **Matter to which prescribed element is attributable**
1. Guarantee payments under section 28.	1. Complaint under section 34.	1. Any amount found to be due to the employee and ordered to be paid under section 34(3) for a period before the conclusion of the tribunal proceedings.
2. Payments under any collective agreement having regard to which the appropriate Minister has made an exemption order under section 35.	2. Complaint under 2. section 35(4).	Any amount found to be due to the employee and ordered to be paid under section 34(3), as applied by section 35(4), for a period before the conclusion of the tribunal proceedings.
3. Payments of remuneration in respect of a period of suspension on medical grounds under section 64 and section 108(2).	3. Complaint under section 70.	3. Any amount found to be due to the employee and ordered to be paid under section 70(3) for a period before the conclusion of the tribunal proceedings.
4. Payments of remuneration in respect of a period of suspension on maternity grounds under section 68.	4. Complaint under section 70.	4. Any amount found to be due to the employee and ordered to be paid under section 70(3) for a period before the conclusion of the tribunal proceedings.
5. Payments under an order for reinstatement under section 114(1).	5. Complaint of unfair dismissal under section 111(1).	5. Any amount ordered to be paid under section 114(2)(a) in respect of arrears of pay for a period before the conclusion of the tribunal proceedings.
6. Payments under an order for re-engagement under section 117(8).	6. Complaint of unfair dismissal under section 111(1).	6. Any amount ordered to be paid under section 115(2)(d) in respect of arrears of pay for a period before the conclusion of the tribunal proceedings.
7. Payments under an award of compensation for unfair dismissal in cases falling under section 112(4) (cases where no order for reinstatement or re-engagement has been made).	7. Complaint of unfair dismissal under section 111(1).	7. Any amount ordered to be paid and calculated under section 123 in respect of compensation for loss of wages for a period before the conclusion of the tribunal proceedings.
8. Payments under an award of compensation	8. Proceedings in respect of non-compliance with order.	8. Any amount ordered to be paid and calculated

(SI 1996/2349, Sch.)

Column 1 Payment	Column 2 Proceedings	Column 3 Matter to which prescribed element is attributable
for unfair dismissal under section 117(3) where reinstatement order not complied with.		under section 123 in respect of compensation for loss of wages for a period before the conclusion of the tribunal proceedings.
9. Payments under an award of compensation for unfair dismissal under section 117(3) where re-engagement order not complied with.	9. Proceedings in respect of non-compliance with order.	9. Any amount ordered to be paid and calculated under section 123 in respect of compensation for loss of wages for a period before the conclusion of the tribunal proceedings.
10. Payments under an interim order for reinstatement under section 163(4) of the 1992 Act.	10. Proceedings on an application for an order for interim relief under section 161(1) of the 1992 Act.	10. Any amount found to be due to the complainant and ordered to be paid in respect of arrears of pay for the period between the date of termination of employment and the conclusion of the tribunal proceedings.
11. Payments under an interim order for re-engagement under section 163(5)(a) of the 1992 Act.	11. Proceedings on an application for an order for interim relief under section 161(1) of the 1992 Act.	11. Any amount found to be due to the complainant and ordered to be paid in respect of arrears of pay for the period between the date of termination of employment and the conclusion of the tribunal proceedings.
12. Payments under an order for the continuation of a contract of employment under section 163(5)(b) of the 1992 Act where employee reasonably refuses re-engagement.	12. Proceedings on an application for an order for interim relief under section 161(1) of the 1992 Act.	12. Any amount found to be due to the complainant and ordered to be paid in respect of arrears of pay for the period between the date of termination of employment and the conclusion of the tribunal proceedings.
13. Payments under an order for the continuation of a contract of employment under section 163(6) of the 1992 Act where employer fails to attend or is unwilling to reinstate or re-engage.	13. Proceedings on an application for an order for interim relief under section 161(1) of the 1992 Act.	13. Any amount found to be due to the complainant and ordered to be paid in respect of arrears of pay for the period between the date of termination of employment and the conclusion of the tribunal proceedings.
14. Payments under an order for the continuation of a contract of employment under sections 166(1) and (2) of the 1992 Act where reinstatement or re-engagement order not complied with.	14. Proceedings in respect of non-compliance with order.	14. Any amount ordered to be paid to the employee by way of compensation under section 166(1)(b) of the 1992 Act for loss of wages for the period between the date of termination of employment and the conclusion of the tribunal proceedings.

The Employment Protection (Recoupment of JSA and IS) Regulations 1996

Column 1	Column 2	Column 3
Payment	Proceedings	Matter to which prescribed element is attributable
15. Payments under an order for compensation under sections 166(3)–(5) of the 1992 Act where order for the continuation of contract of employment not complied with.	15. Proceedings in respect of non-compliance with order.	15. Any amount ordered to be paid to the employee by way of compensation under section 166(3)–(4) of the 1992 Act for loss of wages for the period between the date of termination of employment and the conclusion of the tribunal proceedings.
16. Payments under an order under section 192(3) of the 1992 Act on employer's default in respect of remuneration due to employee under protective award.	16. Complaint under section 192(1) of the 1992 Act.	16. Any amount ordered to be paid to the employee in respect of so much of the relevant protected period as falls before the date of the conclusion of the tribunal proceedings.

The Social Security (Recovery of Benefits) Regulations 1997

(SI 1997/2205)

ARRANGEMENT OF REGULATIONS

2.752

1. Citation, commencement and interpretation.
2. Exempted trusts and payments.
3. Information to be provided by the compensator.
4. Information to be provided by the injured person.
5. Information to be provided by the employer.
6. Provision of information.
7. Application for a certificate of recoverable benefits.
8. Payments into court.
9. Reduction of compensation: complex cases.
10. Structured settlements.
11. Adjustments.
12. Transitional provisions.

The Secretary of State for Social Security, in exercise of the powers conferred by section 189(4), (5) and (6) of the Social Security Administration Act 1992 and sections 4(9), 14(2), (3) and (4), 16(1) and (2), 18, 19, 21(3), 23(1), (2), (5) and (7), 29 and 32 of, and paragraphs 4 and 8 of Schedule 1 to, the Social Security (Recovery of Benefits) Act 1997, and of all other powers enabling her in that behalf, hereby makes the following Regulations:

Citation, commencement and interpretation

2.753

1.—(1) These Regulations may be cited as the Social Security (Recovery of Benefits) Regulations 1997 and shall come into force on 6th October 1997.
(2) In these Regulations—
"the 1992 Act" means the Social Security Administration Act 1992;
"the 1997 Act" means the Social Security (Recovery of Benefits) Act 1997;
"commencement day" means the day these Regulations come into force;

(SI 1997/2205, reg.1)

"compensator" means a person making a compensation payment;
"Compensation Recovery Unit" means the Compensation Recovery Unit of the Department of Social Security at [¹ Durham House, Washington, Tyne and Wear, NE38 7SP].

(3) A reference in these Regulations to a numbered section or Schedule is a reference, unless the context otherwise requires, to that section of or Schedule to the 1997 Act.

AMENDMENT

1. Social Security (Recovery of Benefits) (Miscellaneous Amendments) Regulations 2000 (SI 2000/3030), reg.2 (December 4, 2000).

DEFINITION

"compensation payment"—see s.1(4) of the Social Security (Recovery of Benefits) Act 1997.

Exempted trusts and payments

2.—(1) The following trusts are prescribed for the purposes of paragraph 4 of Schedule 1—

(a) the Macfarlane Trust established on 10th March 1988 partly out of funds provided by the Secretary of State to the Haemophilia Society for the relief of poverty or distress among those suffering from haemophilia;

(b) the Macfarlane (Special Payments) Trust established on 29th January 1990 partly out of funds provided by the Secretary of State, for the benefit of certain persons suffering from haemophilia;

(c) the Macfarlane (Special Payments) (No.2) Trust established on 3rd May 1991 partly out of funds provided by the Secretary of State, for the benefit of certain persons suffering from haemophilia and other beneficiaries;

(d) the Eileen Trust established on 29th March 1993 out of funds provided by the Secretary of State for the benefit of persons eligible for payment in accordance with its provisions;

[¹(e) a trust established out of funds provided by the Secretary of State in respect of persons who suffered, or who are suffering, from variant Creutzfelt-Jakob disease for the benefit of persons eligible for interim payments in accordance with its provisions;

(f) a trust established out of funds provided by the Secretary of State in respect of persons who suffered, or who are suffering, from variant Creutzfelt-Jakob disease for the benefit of persons eligible for payments, other than interim payments, in accordance with its provisions;]

[⁴ (g) the UK Asbestos Trust established on 10th October 2006, for the benefit of certain persons suffering from asbestos-related diseases;

(h) the EL Scheme Trust established on 23rd November 2006, for the benefit of certain persons suffering from asbestos-related diseases.]

(2) The following payments are prescribed for the purposes of paragraph 8 of Schedule 1—

(a) any payment to the extent that it is made—
   (i) in consequence of an action under the Fatal Accidents Act 1976; or

2.754

The Social Security (Recovery of Benefits) Regulations 1997

(ii) in circumstances where, had an action been brought, it would have been brought under that Act;
(b) any payment to the extent that it is made in respect of a liability arising by virtue of section 1 of the Damages (Scotland) Act 1976;
(c) any payment made under the Vaccine Damage Payments Act 1979 to or in respect of the injured person;
(d) any award of compensation made to or in respect of the injured person under the Criminal Injuries Compensation Act 1995 or by the Criminal Injuries Compensation Board under the Criminal Injuries Compensation Scheme 1990 or any earlier scheme;
(e) any compensation payment made by British Coal in accordance with the NCB Pneumoconiosis Compensation Scheme set out in the Schedule to an agreement made on the 13th September 1974 between the National Coal Board, the National Union of Mine Workers, the National Association of Colliery Overmen Deputies and Shot-firers and the British Association of Colliery Management;
(f) any payment made to the injured person in respect of sensorineural hearing loss where the loss is less than than 50 dB in one or both ears;
(g) any contractual amount paid to an employee by an employer of his in respect of a period of incapacity for work;
(h) any payment made under the National Health Service (Injury Benefits) Regulations 1995 or the National Health Service (Scotland) (Injury Benefits) Regulations 1974;
(i) any payment made by or on behalf of the Secretary of State for the benefit of persons eligible for payment in accordance with the provisions of a scheme established by him on 24th April 1992 or, in Scotland, on 10th April 1992.
[2 (j) any payment made from the Skipton Fund, the ex-gratia payment scheme administered by the Skipton Fund Limited, incorporated on 25th March 2004, for the benefit of certain persons suffering from hepatitis C and other persons eligible for payments in accordance with the scheme's provisions.]
[3 (k) any payment made from the London Bombings Relief Charitable Fund, the company limited by guarantee (number 5505072) and registered charity of that name established on 11th July for the purpose of (amongst other things) relieving sickness, disability or financial need of victims (including families or dependants of victims) of the terrorist attacks carried out in London on 7th July 2005.]

AMENDMENTS

1. Social Security Amendment (Capital Disregards and Recovery of Benefits) Regulations 2001 (SI 2001/1118), reg.4 (April 12, 2001).
2. Social Security (Miscellaneous Amendments) (No.2) Regulations 2004 (SI 2004/1141), reg.7 (May 12, 2004).
3. Income-related Benefits (Amendment) (No.2) Regulations 2005 (SI 2005/3391), reg.6 (December 12, 2005).
4. Social Security (Recovery of Benefits) Amendment) Regulations 2007 (SI 2007/357, reg.2 (March 12, 2007).

DEFINITIONS

"compensation payment"—see s.1(4) of the Social Security (Recovery of Benefits) Act 1997.
"payment"—see s.29 of the Social Security (Recovery of Benefits) Act 1997.

(SI 1997/2205, reg.3)

Information to be provided by the compensator

3.—The following information is prescribed for the purposes of section 23(1):
  (a) the full name and address of the injured person;
  (b) where known, the date of birth or national insurance number of that person, or both if both are known;
  (c) where the liability arises, or is alleged to arise, in respect of an accident or injury, the date of the accident or injury;
  (d) the nature of the accident, injury or disease; and
  (e) where known, and where the relevant period may include a period prior to 6th April 1994, whether, at the time of the accident or injury or diagnosis of the disease, the person was employed under a contract of service, and, if he was, the name and address of his employer at that time and the person's payroll number.

2.755

DEFINITION

"injured person"—see s.1(4) of the Social Security (Recovery of Benefits) Act 1997.

Information to be provided by the injured person

4. The following information is prescribed for the purposes of section 23(2):
  (a) whether the accident, injury or disease resulted from any action taken by another person, or from any failure of another person to act, and, if so, the full name and address of that other person;
  (b) whether the injured person has claimed or may claim a compensation payment, and, if so, the full name and address of the person against whom the claim was or may be made;
  (c) the amount of any compensation payment and the date on which it was made;
  (d) the listed benefits claimed, and for each benefit the date from which it was first claimed and the amount received in the period beginning with that date and ending with the date the information is sent;
  (e) in the case of a person who has received statutory sick pay during the relevant period and prior to 6th April 1994, the name and address of any employer who made those payments to him during the relevant period and the dates the employment with that employer began and ended; and
  (f) any changes in the medical diagnosis relating to the condition arising from the accident, injury or disease.

2.756

DEFINITIONS

"compensation payment"—see s.1(4) of the Social Security (Recovery of Benefits) Act 1997.
"injured person"—ibid.
"listed benefit"—see s.29 of the Social Security (Recovery of Benefits) Act 1997.

Information to be provided by the employer

5. The following information is prescribed for the purposes of section 23(5):
  (a) the amount of any statutory sick pay the employer has paid to the injured person since the first day of the relevant period and before 6th April 1994;

2.757

The Social Security (Recovery of Benefits) Regulations 1997

(b) the date the liability to pay such statutory sick pay first arose and the rate at which it was payable;
(c) the date on which such liability terminated; and
(d) the causes of incapacity for work during any period of entitlement to statutory sick pay during the relevant period and prior to 6th April 1994.

DEFINITION

"injured person"—see s.1(4) of the Social Security (Recovery of Benefits) Act 1997.

Provision of information

2.758   **6.** A person required to give information to the Secretary of State under regulations 3 to 5 shall do so by sending it to the Compensation Recovery Unit not later than 14 days after—
(a) where he is a person to whom regulation 3 applies, the date on which he receives a claim for compensation from the injured person in respect of the accident, injury or disease;
(b) where he is a person to whom regulation 4 or 5 applies, the date on which the Secretary of State requests the information from him.

DEFINITIONS

"Compensation Recovery Unit"—see reg.1(2).

Application for a certificate of recoverable benefits

2.759   **7.**—(1) The following particulars are prescribed for the purposes of section 21(3)(a) (particulars to be included in an application for a certificate of recoverable benefits):
(a) the full name and address of the injured person;
(b) the date of birth and, where known, the national insurance number of that person;
(c) where the liability arises or is alleged to arise in respect of an accident or injury, the date of the accident or injury;
(d) the nature of the accident, injury or disease;
(e) where the person liable, or alleged to be liable, in respect of the accident, injury or disease, is the employer of the injured person, or has been such an employer, the information prescribed by regulation 5.

(2) An application for a certificate of recoverable benefits is to be treated for the purposes of the 1997 Act as received by the Secretary of State on the day on which it is received by the Compensation Recovery Unit, or if the application is received after normal business hours, or on a day which is not a normal business day at that office, on the next such day.

DEFINITIONS

"the 1997 Act"—see reg.1(2).
"Compensation Recovery Unit"—ibid.
"injured person"—see s.1(4) of the Social Security (Recovery of Benefits) Act 1997.
"recoverable benefit"—ibid.

Payments into court

2.760   **8.**—(1) Subject to the provisions of this regulation, where a party to an action makes a payment into court which, had it been paid directly to

another party to the action ("the relevant party"), would have constituted a compensation payment—
 (a) the making of that payment shall be treated for the purposes of the 1997 Act as the making of a compensation payment;
 (b) a current certificate of recoverable benefits shall be lodged with the payment; and
 (c) where the payment is calculated under section 8, the compensator must give the relevant party the information specified in section 9(1), instead of the person to whom the payment is made.

(2) The liability under section 6(1) to pay an amount equal to the total amount of the recoverable benefits shall not arise until the person making the payment into court has been notified that the whole or any part of the payment into court has been paid out of court to or for the relevant party.

(3) Where a payment into court in satisfaction of his claim is accepted by the relevant party in the initial period, then as respects the compensator in question, the relevant period shall be taken to have ended, if it has not done so already, on the day on which the payment into court (or if there were two or more such payments, the last of them) was made.

(4) Where, after the expiry of the initial period, the payment into court is accepted in satisfaction of the relevant party's claim by consent between the parties, the relevant period shall end, if it has not done so already, on the date on which application to the court for the payment is made.

(5) Where, after the expiry of the initial period, payment out of court is made wholly or partly to or for the relevant party in accordance with an order of the court and in satisfaction of his claim, the relevant period shall end, if it has not done so already, on the date of that order.

(6) In paragraphs (3), (4) and (5), "the initial period" means the period of 21 days after the receipt by the relevant party to the action of notice of the payment into court having been made.

(7) Where a payment into court is paid out wholly to or for the party who made the payment (otherwise than to or for the relevant party to the action) the making of the payment into court shall cease to be regarded as the making of a compensation payment.

(8) A current certificate of recoverable benefits in paragraph (1) means one that is in force as described in section 4(4).

GENERAL NOTE

See the note to s.16(1) and (2) of the Social Security (Recovery of Benefits) Act 1997, under which this regulation is made.

Reduction of compensation: complex cases

9.—(1) This regulation applies where—
 (a) a compensation payment in the form of a lump sum (an "earlier payment") has been made to or in respect of the injured person; and
 (b) subsequently another such payment (a "later payment") is made to or in respect of the same injured person in consequence of the same accident, injury or disease.

(2) In determining the liability under section 6(1) arising in connection with the making of the later payment, the amount referred to in that subsection shall be reduced by any amount paid in satisfaction of that liability as it arose in connection with the earlier payment.

(3) Where—

(a) a payment made in satisfaction of the liability under section 6(1) arising in connection with an earlier payment is not reflected in the certificate of recoverable benefits in force at the time of a later payment, and
(b) in consequence, the aggregate of payments made in satisfaction of the liability exceeds what it would have been had that payment been so reflected,

the Secretary of State shall pay the compensator who made the later payment an amount equal to the excess.

(4) Where—
(a) a compensator receives a payment under paragraph (3), and
(b) the amount of the compensation payment made by him was calculated under section 8,

then the compensation payment shall be recalculated under section 8, and the compensator shall pay the amount of the increase (if any) to the person to whom the compensation payment was made.

(5) Where both the earlier payment and the later payment are made by the same compensator, he may—
(a) aggregate the gross amounts of the payments made by him;
(b) calculate what would have been the reduction made under section 8(3) if that aggregate amount had been paid at the date of the last payment on the basis that—
   (i) so much of the aggregate amount as is attributable to a head of compensation listed in column (1) of Schedule 2 shall be taken to be the part of the gross amount which attributable to that head, and
   (ii) the amount of any recoverable benefits shown against any head in column (2) of that Schedule shall be taken to be the amount determined in accordance with the most recent certificate of recoverable benefits;
(c) deduct from that reduction calculated under sub-paragraph (b) the amount of the reduction under section 8(3) from any earlier payment; and
(d) deduct from the latest gross payment the net reduction calculated under sub-paragraph (c) (and accordingly the latest payment may be nil).

(6) Where the Secretary of State is making a refund under paragraph (3), he shall send to the compensator (with the refund) and to the person to whom the compensation payment was made a statement showing—
(a) the total amount that has already been paid by that compensator to the Secretary of State;
(b) the amount that ought to have been paid by that compensator; and
(c) the amount to be repaid to that compensator by the Secretary of State.

(7) Where the reduction of a compensation payment is recalculated by virtue of paragraph (4) or (5) the compensator shall give notice of the calculation to the injured person.

GENERAL NOTE

2.762   This regulation is made under ss.18(1) to (3) and 19 of the Social Security (Recovery of Benefits) Act 1997 and is concerned with cases where more than one lump-sum compensation payment is made to a victim in respect of a single accident, injury or disease. (Structured settlements involving periodical payments are dealt with in reg.10). Regulation 9 covers cases where the same compensator makes more than one lump-sum payment and also cases where different compensators make payments because they all contributed to the accident, injury or disease. However, it makes no attempt at apportionment of liability for recoverable benefits between different compensators. It is concerned only to ensure that there is not double recovery and it does not even attempt that in a case where benefit has been paid as a result of two different injuries each attributable to a different accident. See *R(CR)2/04* and the note to s.1 of the Act for the way that liability is attributed in such a case. Where two compensators are liable in respect of the same accident, injury or disease, the one making the first compensation payment is likely to have the greater liability to the Secretary of State and must seek a contribution from the other so that they each bear a fair share of the liability for benefits.

Paragraph (2) simply provides that when a second compensation payment is made, the Secretary of State should not recover benefits that were recovered when the earlier payment was made. Paragraph (3) provides for a refund to the compensator if benefits are erroneously recovered for a second time. Paragraph (4) provides that, where the compensator has reduced under s.8 of the Act the amount of compensation paid to the victim (in effect recovering from the victim the benefits that the victim had received and the compensator had to pay to the Secretary of State), he must recalculate the s.8 reduction in the light of a refund under para.(3) and pay the appropriate amount, if any, to the victim. Where the same compensator made both the compensation payments, he may aggregate them for the purpose of recalculating the appropriate s.8 reduction under para.(4) (para.(5)). Paragraphs (6) and (7) require the victim to be told by the Secretary of State about any refund under para.(3) and by the compensator about any recalculation under paras (4) and (5).

Structured settlements

10.—(1) This regulation applies where—
(a) in final settlement of an injured person's claim, an agreement is entered into—
  (i) for the making of periodical payments (whether of an income or capital nature); or
  (ii) for the making of such payments and lump sum payments; and
(b) apart from the provisions of this regulation, those payments would fall to be treated for the purposes of the 1997 Act as compensation payments.

(2) Where this regulation applies, the provisions of the 1997 Act and these Regulations shall be modified in the following way—
(a) the compensator in question shall be taken to have made on that day a single compensation payment;
(b) the relevant period in the case of the compensator in question shall be taken to end (if it has not done so already) on the day of settlement;
(c) payments under the agreement referred to in paragraph (1)(a) shall be taken not to be compensation payments;
(d) paragraphs (5) and (7) of regulation 11 shall not apply.

(3) Where any further payment falls to be made to or in respect of the injured person otherwise than under the agreement in question, paragraph (2) shall be disregarded for the purpose of determining the end of the relevant period in relation to that further payment.

(4) In any case where—
(a) the person making the periodical payments ("the secondary party") does so in pursuance of arrangements entered into with another ("primary party") (as in a case where the primary party purchases an annuity for the injured person from the secondary party), and
(b) apart from those arrangements, the primary party would have been regarded as the compensator,

The Social Security (Recovery of Benefits) Regulations 1997

then for the purposes of the 1997 Act, the primary party shall be regarded as the compensator and the secondary party shall not be so regarded.

(5) In this regulation "the day of settlement" means—
(a) if the agreement referred to in paragraph (1)(a) is approved by a court, the day on which that approval is given; and
(b) in any other case, the day on which the agreement is entered into.

General Note

2.764
This regulation is made under s.8(4) to (6) of the Social Security (Recovery of Benefits) Act 1997.

Where a final settlement is reached in the form of an agreement that involves the making of periodical payments (whether of a capital or income nature and whether or not they are combined with sum lump sums), the compensator is treated as having made a compensation payment on the day the agreement is reached. That is when the "relevant period" under s.3 of the Act is taken to have ended and when the compensator becomes liable to make a payment to the Secretary of State under s.6. Further payments under the agreement (by whomever they are made (see para.(4)) do not count as compensation payments (para.(2)(c)) but any payments outside it will (para.(3)) and reg.9 will apply to them.

Adjustments

2.765
11.—(1) Where the conditions specified in subsection (1) and paragraphs (a) and (b) of subsection (2) of section 14 are satisfied, the Secretary of State shall pay the difference between the amount that has been paid and the amount that ought to have been paid to the compensator.

(2) Where the conditions specified in subsection (1) and paragraphs (a) and (b) of subsection (3) of section 14 are satisfied, the compensator shall pay the difference between the total amounts paid and the amount that ought to have been paid to the Secretary of State.

(3) Where the Secretary of State is making a refund under paragraph (1), or demanding payment of a further amount under paragraph (2), he shall send to the compensator (with the refund or demand) and to the person to whom the compensation payment was made a statement showing—
(a) the total amount that has already been paid to the Secretary of State;
(b) the amount that ought to have been paid; and
(c) the difference, and whether a repayment by the Secretary of State or a further payment to him is required.

(4) This paragraph applies where—
(a) the amount of the compensation payment made by the compensator was calculated under section 8; and
(b) the Secretary of State has made a payment under paragraph (1).

(5) Where paragraph (4) applies, the amount of the compensation payment shall be recalculated under section 8 to take account of the fresh certificate of recoverable benefits and the compensator shall pay the amount of the increase (if any) to the person to whom the compensation payment was made.

(6) This paragraph applies where—
(a) the amount of the compensation payment made by the compensator was calculated under section 8;
(b) the compensator has made a payment under paragraph (2); and
(c) the fresh certificate of recoverable benefits issued after the review or appeal was required as a result of the injured person or other person to whom the compensation payment was made supplying to the

(SI 1997/2205, reg.11)

compensator information knowing it to be incorrect or insufficient with the intent of enhancing the compensation payment calculated under section 8, and the compensator supplying that information to the Secretary of State without knowing it to be incorrect or insufficient.

(7) Where paragraph (6) applies, the compensator may recalculate the compensation payment under section 8 to take account of the fresh certificate of recoverable benefits and may require the repayment to him by the person to whom he made the compensation payment of the difference (if any) between the payment made and the payment as so recalculated.

GENERAL NOTE

This is a key provision. Paragraphs (1) to (3) simply provide for the appropriate refund or demand for further payment to be made by the Secretary of State following a review or appeal. Of more practical importance are paras (4) and (5) requiring that, where there is a refund, the compensator must recalculate any reduction in a compensation payment made under s.8 of the Social Security (Recovery of Benefits) Act 1997 and pay the amount of any increase in the compensation payment to the claimant. That means that a compensator does not have any practical interest in challenging a certificate for recoverable benefits insofar as he has reduced the claimant's compensation to take account of the benefits (*R(CR) 2/03*). Unfortunately, it appears that these paragraphs are overlooked even by experienced insurance companies with the result that they retain money due to claimants. Paragraphs (6) and (7) make similar provision for cases where there is a demand for a further payment, only in those circumstances they have the effect that the claimant may have to make a further payment to the compensator. They operate only if the claimant knowingly supplied incorrect, or insufficient, information to the compensator and the compensator innocently passed it on to the Secretary of State.

2.766

Transitional provisions

12.—(1) In relation to a compensation payment to which by virtue of section 2 the 1997 Act applies and subject to paragraph (2), a certificate of total benefit issued under Part IV of the 1992 Act shall be treated on or after the commencement date as a certificate of recoverable benefits issued under the 1997 Act and the amount of total benefit treated as that of recoverable benefits.

2.767

(2) Paragraph (1) shall not apply to a certificate of total benefit which specifies an amount in respect of disability living allowance without specifying whether that amount was, or is likely to be, paid wholly by way of the care component or the mobility component or (if not wholly one of them) specifying the relevant amount for each component.

[1(3) Any appeal under section 98 of the 1992 Act made on or after 6th October 1997 which has not been determined before 29th November 1999 shall be referred to an appeal tribunal constituted in accordance with paragraph (3I) below.

(3A) Any appeal duly made before 6th October 1997 which has not been referred to a medical appeal tribunal or a social security appeal tribunal shall be referred to and determined by an appeal tribunal constituted in accordance with paragraph (3I) below.

(3B) Any appeal duly made before 6th October 1997 and referred to a medical appeal tribunal shall be determined by an appeal tribunal constituted in accordance with paragraph (3I) below which shall determine all issues.

(3C) Any appeal duly made before 6th October 1997 and referred to a social security appeal tribunal shall be determined by an appeal tribunal

803

which shall consist of a legally qualified panel member and in making its determination, the appeal tribunal shall be bound by any decision of a medical appeal tribunal to which a question under section 98(5) of the 1992 Act was referred.

(3D) An appeal tribunal constituted in accordance with paragraph (3I) below shall completely rehear any appeal made under section 98 of the 1992 Act which stands adjourned immediately before 29th November 1999.

(3E) Where a Commissioner holds that the decision of a medical appeal tribunal or a social security appeal tribunal on an appeal made before 6th October 1997 was erroneous in law and refers the case to an appeal tribunal, that appeal tribunal shall be constituted in accordance with paragraph (3I) below and shall determine all issues in accordance with the Commissioner's direction.

(3F) Regulation 11 of the Social Security (Recoupment) Regulations 1990 ("the 1990 Regulations") and regulation 12 of those Regulations shall have effect in relation to any appeal under section 98 of the 1992 Act made on or after 6th October 1997 with the modification that for the word "chairman" in each place in which it occurs there were substituted the words "legally qualified panel member".

(3G) Regulation 13 of the 1990 Regulations shall have effect in relation to any appeal under section 98 of the 1992 Act made on or after 6th October 1997.

(3H) Any other transitional question arising from an appeal made under section 98 of the 1992 Act in consequence of the coming into force of the Social Security and Child Support (Decisions and Appeals) Regulations 1999 ("the 1999 Regulations") shall be determined by a legally qualified panel member who may for this purpose give such directions consistent with these regulations as are necessary.

(3I) For the purposes of paragraphs (3) to (3B) and (3E) above an appeal tribunal shall be constituted under Chapter I of Part I of the Social Security Act 1998 as though the appeal were made under section 11(1)(b) of the 1997 Act.

(3J) In this regulation, "legally qualified panel member" has the meaning it bears in regulation 1(3) of the 1999 Regulations.]

(4) Paragraph (5) applies where—
(a) an amount has been paid to the Secretary of State under section 82(1)(b) of the 1992 Act,
(b) liability arises on or after the commencement day to make a payment under section 6(1), and
(c) the compensation payments which give rise to the liability to make both payments are to or in respect of the same injured person in consequence of the same accident, injury or disease.

(5) Where this paragraph applies, the liability under section 6 shall be reduced by the payment (or aggregate of the payments, if more than one) described in paragraph (4)(a).

(6) Where—
(a) a payment into court has been made on a date prior to the commencement day but the initial period, as defined in section 93(6) of the 1992 Act, in relation to that payment, expires on or after the commencement day; and
(b) the payment into court is accepted by the other party to the action in the initial period,

that payment into court shall be treated as a compensation payment to which the 1992 Act, and not the 1997 Act, applies.

(7) Where a payment into court has been made prior to the commencement day, remains in court on that day and paragraph (6) does not apply, that payment into court shall be treated as a payment to which the 1997 Act applies, but paragraph (1) (b) and (c) of regulation 8 shall not apply.

AMENDMENT

1. Social Security Act 1998 (Commencement No.12 and Consequential and Transitional Provisions) Order 1999 (SI 1999/3178), Art.3(17) and Sch.17 (November 29, 1999).

GENERAL NOTE

This regulation has been amended in such a way that it now makes transitional provision not only for the coming into force of the Social Security (Recovery of Benefits) Act 1997 but also for the coming into force of the Social Security Act 1998.

The Social Security (Work-focused Interviews for Lone Parents) and Miscellaneous Amendments Regulations 2000

(SI 2000/1926)

ARRANGEMENT OF REGULATIONS

1. Citation, commencement and interpretation
2. Requirement for lone parents claiming or entitled to income support to take part in an interview
3. Taking part in an interview
4. Circumstances where requirement to take part in an interview does not apply
5. Deferment of requirement to take part in an interview
6. Waiver
7. Consequence of failure to take part in an interview
8. Reduction of income support
9. Appeals
10. Amendments to Regulations (*not reproduced*)

Schedule 1: Areas where these regulations come into force on 30th October 2000 in respect of lone parents who are not entitled to income support
Schedule 2 *omitted*

The Secretary of State for Social Security, in exercise of the powers conferred upon him by sections 123(1)(d) and (e) and 137(1) of the Social Security Contributions and Benefits Act 1992 and sectons 2A(1), (3)(b) to (f), (4), (5)(a) and (b), (6), (7) and (8), 2B(2), (6) and (7), 2C, 189(4) to (7A) and 191 of the Social Security Administration Act 1992 and of all other powers enabling him in that behalf, after consultation with the Council on Tribunals in accordance with section 8(1) of the Tribunals and Inquiries Act 1992 and in respect of provisions in these Regulations relating to housing benefit and council tax benefit with organisations appearing to him to be representative of the authorities concerned and after agreement by the Social Security Advisory Committee that proposals in respect of these

The Social Security (Work-focused Interviews) Regulations 2000

Regulations should not be referred to it, hereby makes the following Regulations:

Citation, commencement and interpretation

2.770
1.—(1) These Regulations may be cited as the Social Security (Work-focused Interviews for Lone Parents) and Miscellaneous Amendments Regulations 2000.

(2) This Regulation and paragraphs 2 to 5 of Schedule 2 and regulation 10 in so far as it relates to those paragraphs shall come into force on 14th August 2000.

(3) Regulations 2 to 9, paragraph 1 of Schedule 2 and regulation 10 in so far as it relates to that paragraph shall—
- (a) come into force on 30th October 2000 in respect of lone parents who on that date—
    - (i) live in an area identified in Schedule 1: and
    - (ii) are not entitled to income support;
- (b) subject to sub-paragraph (a), come into force on 30th April 2001 in respect of lone parents who on that date—
    - (i) are not entitled to income support; or
    - (ii) are entitled to income support and are not—
        - (aa) responsible for; and
        - (bb) living in the same household as,
    a child under the age of 13;
- (c) subject to the preceding sub-paragraphs, come into force on 1st April 2002 in respect of lone parents who on that date are entitled to income support and are not—
    - (i) responsible for; and
    - (ii) living in the same household as,
    a child under the age of 9;
- (d) subject to the preceding sub-paragraphs, where a lone parent—
    - (i) is responsible for and living in the same household as a child whose 13th birthday occurs in the period beginning on 1st May 2001 and ending on 31st March 2002; and
    - (ii) is not on the date of the 13th birthday responsible for and living in the same household as a younger child,
    come into force in respect of that lone parent on the date of that child's 13th birthday;
- (e) subject to the preceding sub-paragraphs, where a lone parent—
    - (i) is responsible for and living in the same household as a child whose 9th birthday occurs in the period beginning on 2nd April 2002 and ending on 6th April 2003; and
    - (ii) is not on the date of the 9th birthday responsible for and living in the same household as a younger child,
    come into force in respect of that lone parent on the date of that child's 9th birthday; and
- [1 (f) subject to the preceding sub-paragraphs, come into force on 7th April 2003 in respect of lone parents who on that date are entitled to income support and are not responsible for and living in the same household as a child under the age of 5 years and 3 months;
- [3 (g) subject to the preceding sub-paragraphs, come into force on 5th April 2004 in respect of a lone parent who on that date is entitled to income

(SI 2000/1926, reg. 1)

support and is responsible for an living in the same household as a child.]
come into force in respect of that lone parent on the date that child reaches the age of 5 years and 3 months.]

(4) In these Regulations, unless the context otherwise requires—

"the 1998 Act" means the Social Security Act 1998;

"benefit week" means any period of seven days corresponding to the week in respect of which income support is due to be paid;

"lone parent" has the meaning it bears in regulation 2(1) of the Income Support (General) Regulations 1987;

"interview" means a work-focused interview with a lone parent conducted for any or all of the following purposes—
  (a) assessing that person's prospects for existing or future employment (whether paid or voluntary);
  (b) assisting or encouraging that person to enhance his prospects of such employment;
  (c) identifying activities which that person may undertake to strengthen his existing or future prospects of employment;
  (d) identifying current or future employment or training opportunities suitable to that person's needs; and
  (e) identifying educational opportunities connected with the existing or future employment prospects or needs of that person; and

"officer" means an officer of, or providing services to, the Secretary of State.

(5) In these Regulations, unless the context otherwise requires, a reference—
  (a) to a numbered regulation is to a regulation in these Regulations bearing that number;
  (b) in a regulation to a numbered paragraph or sub-paragraph is to the paragraph or sub-paragraph in that regulation bearing that number;
  (c) to a numbered Schedule is to the Schedule to these Regulations bearing that number.

AMENDMENTS

1. The Social Security (Work-focused Interviews for Lone Parents) Amendment Regulations 2002 (SI 2002/670), reg.2 (April 8, 2002).

2. The Social Security (Work-focused Interviews for Lone Parents) Amendment Regulations 2003 (SI 2003/400), reg.2 (April 7, 2003).

3. The Social Security (Miscellaneous Amendments) Regulations 2004 (SI 2004/565), reg.7 (April 5, 2004).

[¹ General requirement for lone parents claiming or entitled to income support to take part in an interview

2.—(1) Subject to this regulation and regulations 2A, 2B and 4 to 6, a lone parent is required to take part in an interview if he falls within any of paragraphs to (4).

(2) A lone parent falls within this paragraph if he makes a claim for income support in respect of himself.

(3) A lone parent falls within this paragraph if he is entitled to income support and has not taken part or been required to take part in a relevant interview.

2.771

(4) A lone parent falls within this paragraph if he is entitled to income support and has—
  (a) taken part,
  (b) failed to take part, or
  (c) been treated as having taken part,
in a relevant interview.

(5) Where a lone parent falls within paragraph (4) the requirement to take part in an interview arises at the times set out in paragraph (6), except where the young child condition is satisfied (see paragraph (9)) in which case the requirement arises at the times set out in paragraph (7).

(6) The requirement arises (where the young child condition is not satisfied)—
  (a) where the lone parent—
    (i) last took part,
    (ii) last failed to take part, or
    (iii) was last treated as having taken part,
in a relevant interview on a date on or after 30th April 2006 but before 30th October 2006, one year after that date, and it arises again every six months after it first arises; or
  (b) where the lone parent does not fall within sub-paragraph (a), every six months after the date on which he—
    (i) last took part,
    (ii) last failed to take part, or
    (iii) was last treated as having taken part,
in a relevant interview.

(7) The requirement arises (where the young child condition is satisfied)—
  (a) here the interview that the lone parent—
    (i) last took part in,
    (ii) last failed to take part in, or
    (iii) was last treated as having taken part in,
was the first relevant interview, six months after the date of that first interview, and it arises again upon each anniversary of that date;
  (b) here the interview that the lone parent—
    (i) last took part in,
    (ii) last failed to take part in, or
    (iii) was last treated as having taken part in,
was the second relevant interview, six months after the date of that second interview, and it arises again upon each anniversary of the day on which it first arises;
  (c) in any other case, on each anniversary of the date of the interview that the lone parent—
    (i) last took part in,
    (ii) last failed to take part in, or
    (iii) was last treated as having taken part in.

(8) In this regulation, "elevant interview"means an interview under—
  (a) the Social Security (Working Neighbourhoods) Regulations 2004
  (b) the Social Security (Quarterly Work-focused Interviews for Certain Lone Parents) Regulations 2004, or
  (c) these Regulations,
in relation to the lone parent's current claim.

(9) For the purposes of this regulation, the young child condition is satisfied where the lone parent is responsible for and living in the same household as—

(a) a single child aged under 5, or

(b) more than one child where the youngest is aged under 5.

(10) Where a determination has been made in relation to a lone parent under regulation 6(1) (waiver) or (as the case may be) under a corresponding provision of the Regulations referred to in paragraph (8)(a) or (b), he is to be treated for the purposes of paragraph (3) as if he has not taken part or been required to take part in a relevant interview.

AMENDMENT

1. Inserted by The Social Security (Work-focused Interviews for Lone Parents) Amendment Regulations 2007, (SI 2007/1034) (April 30, 2007).

[¹ Requirement for specified lone parents to take part in an interview

2A.—(1) In this regulation, "specified lone parent" means a lone parent who—

(a) is responsible for and living in the same household as—
   (i) a single child aged 14 or 15, or
   (ii) more than one child where the youngest is aged 14 or 15, and
(b) has been continuously entitled for at least 12 months to income support other than—
   (i) income support where paragraph 7 (persons incapable of work) of Schedule 1B to the Income Support (General) Regulations 1987(a) applies, or
   (ii) income support where paragraph 24 or 25 (persons appealing against a decision which embodies a determination that they are not incapable of work) of Schedule 1B to the Income Support (General) Regulations 1987(b) applies.

(2) Subject to paragraph (3) and regulations 4 to 6, a specified lone parent is required to take part in an interview.

(3) Where a lone parent has taken part in an interview under regulation 2 [² or 2B], a requirement shall not arise under paragraph (2) until the expiry of 13 weeks from the day of that interview.

(4) Subject to regulations 4 to 6, a specified lone parent is required to take part in a further interview after the expiry of 13 weeks from the day on which—

(a) he last took part in an interview;
(b) he last failed to take part in an interview; or
(c) a determination was made under regulation 6 with effect that he is to be treated as having taken part in an interview.

(5) [² . . .]

(6) A specified lone parent who—

(a) is required to take part in an interview under this regulation, or
(b) has had a requirement to take part in an interview under this regulation waived or deferred,

is not required to take part in an interview under regulation 2 unless he ceases to be a specified lone parent.

(7) For the avoidance of doubt, the words "lone parent" in the other provisions of these Regulations includes specified lone parents.]

AMENDMENTS

1. The Social Security (Work-focused Interviews) Amendment Regulations 2005 (SI 2005/2727) (October 31, 2005).

The Social Security (Work-focused Interviews) Regulations 2000

2. The Social Security (Work-focused Interviews for Lone Parents) Amendment Regulations 2007, (SI 2007/1034) (April 30, 2007).

[¹ Requirement for certain lone parents in certain areas to take part in an interview

2B. —(1) This regulation applies to a lone parent who—
 (a) is responsible for and living in the same household as—
  (i) a single child aged 11, 12 or 13, or
  (ii) more than one child where the youngest is aged 11, 12 or 13;
 (b) has been continuously entitled to income support for at least 12 months; and
 (c) resides in an area specified in Schedule 3 to these Regulations.
(2) Subject to regulations 4 to 6, a lone parent to whom this regulation applies is required to take part in an interview every 13 weeks after he—
 (a) last took part in an interview,
 (b) last failed to take part in an interview, or
 (c) was last treated as having taken part in an interview.
(3) A lone parent who—
 (a) is required to take part in an interview under this regulation, or
 (b) has had a requirement to take part in an interview under this regulation waived or deferred,
is not required to take part in an interview under regulation 2 unless he ceases to fall within this regulation.]

AMENDMENT

1. Inserted by The Social Security (Work-focused Interviews for Lone Parents) Amendment Regulations 2007, (SI 2007/1034) (April 30, 2007).

[¹ The interview

2C. —(1) An interview under these Regulations shall take place as soon as is reasonably practicable after the date on which the requirement to take part in the interview arises.
(2) An officer shall inform the lone parent of the place and time of the interview.
(3) An officer may determine that an interview is to take place in the lone parent's home where it would, in the opinion of the officer, be unreasonable to expect that lone parent to attend elsewhere because that lone parent's personal circumstances are such that attending elsewhere would—
 (a) cause him undue inconvenience, or
 (b) endanger his health.

AMENDMENT

1. Inserted by The Social Security (Work-focused Interviews for Lone Parents) Amendment Regulations 2007, (SI 2007/1034) (April 30, 2007).

Taking part in an interview

3.—(1) An officer shall determine whether a lone parent has taken part in an interview.
[¹ (2) Subject to regulations 5(2) and 6(2), a lone parent who has not taken part in an interview under these Regulations before 31st October

(SI 2000/1926, reg. 3)

2005 shall be regarded as having taken part in his first interview under these Regulations if—
(a) he attends for the interview at the place and time notified to him by the officer;
(b) he participates in discussions with the officer in relation to the lone parent's employability, including any action the lone parent and the officer agree is reasonable and they are willing to take in order to help the lone parent enhance his employment prospects;
(c) he provides answers (where asked) to questions and appropriate information about—
  (i) the level to which he has pursued any educational qualifications;
  (ii) his employment history;
  (iii) any vocational training he has undertaken;
  (iv) any skills he has acquired which fit him for employment;
  (v) any paid or unpaid employment he is engaged in;
  (vi) any medical condition which, in his opinion, puts him at a disadvantage in obtaining employment;
  (vii) any caring or childcare responsibilities he has;
  (viii) his aspirations for future employment;
  (ix) any vocational training or skills which he wishes to undertake or acquire; and
  (x) his work related abilities; and
(d) he assists the officer in the completion of an action plan which records the matters discussed in relation to sub-paragraph (b) above.

(2A) Subject to regulations 5(2) and 6(2), a lone parent who has taken part in an interview under these Regulations before 31st October 2005 shall be regarded as having taken part in his first interview under these Regulations after 30th October 2005 if—
(a) he attends for the interview at the place and time notified to him by the officer;
(b) he participates in discussions with the officer in relation to the lone parent's employability, including any action the lone parent and the officer agree is reasonable and they are willing to take in order to help the lone parent enhance his employment prospects;
(c) he participates in discussions with the officer—
  (i) in relation to the lone parent's employability or any progress he might have made towards obtaining employment; and
  (ii) in order to consider any of the programmes and support available to help the lone parent obtain employment;
(d) he provides answers (where asked) to questions and appropriate information about—
  (i) the content of any report made following his personal capability assessment, insofar as that report relates to the lone parent's capabilities and employability; and
  (ii) his opinion as to the extent to which his medical condition restricts his ability to obtain employment; and
(e) he assists the officer in the completion of an action plan which records the matters discussed in relation to sub-paragraph (b) above.

(2B) Subject to regulations 5(2) and 6(2), a lone parent shall be regarded as having taken part in any subsequent interview under these Regulations if—
(a) he attends for the interview at the place and time notified to him by the officer;

The Social Security (Work-focused Interviews) Regulations 2000

(b) he participates in discussions with the officer—
  (i) in relation to the lone parent's employability or any progress he might have made towards obtaining employment;
  (ii) about any action the lone parent or the officer might have taken as a result of the matters discussed in relation to paragraph (2)(b) or (2A)(b) above;
  (iii) about how, if at all, the action plan referred to in paragraphs (2)(d) or (2A)(e) above should be amended; and
  (iv) in order to consider any of the programmes and support available to help the lone parent obtain employment;
(c) he provides answers (where asked) to questions and appropriate information about—
  (i) the content of any report made following his personal capability assessment, insofar as that report relates to the lone parent's capabilities and employability; and
  (ii) his opinion as to the extent to which his medical condition restricts his ability to obtain employment; and
(d) he assists the officer in the completion of any amendment of the action plan referred to in paragraphs (2)(d) or (2A)(e) above in light of the matters discussed in relation to sub-paragraph (b) above and the information provided in relation to sub-paragraph (c) above.]

AMENDMENT

1. The Social Security (Work-focused Interviews) Amendment Regulations 2005 (SI 2005/2727) (October 31, 2005).

[¹ Circumstances where requirement to take part in an interview does not apply

4.—(1) Regulation 2 shall not apply where the lone parent—
(a) has attained the age of 60;
(b) has not attained the age of 18; or
(c) is—
  (i) required to take part in an interview, or
  (ii) not required to take part in an interview by virtue of—
    (aa) a waiver of a requirement, or
    (bb) a deferment of an interview, under the Social Security (Work-focused Interviews) Regulations 2000, the Social Security (Jobcentre Plus Interviews) Regulations 2001, the Social Security (Jobcentre Plus Interviews) Regulations 2002, [³ or the Social Security (Incapacity Benefit Work-focused Interviews) Regulations 2003.]
(2) [². . .]
[³ (3) Regulations 2A and 2B shall not apply where the lone parent—
(a) has attained the age of 60, or
(b) has not attained the age of 18.
(4) Regulation 2B shall not apply where the lone parent is—
(a) required to take part in an interview, or
(b) not required to take part in an interview by virtue of—
  (i) a waiver of a requirement, or
  (ii) a deferment of an interview,
under the Social Security (Incapacity Benefit Work-focused Interviews) Regulations 2003.]

(SI 2000/1926, reg. 4)

AMENDMENTS

1. The Social Security (Work-focused Interviews) Amendment Regulations 2005 (SI 2005/2727) (October 31, 2005).
2. The Social Security (Working Neighbourhoods) Miscellaneous Amendment Regulations 2006, (SI 2006/909) (April 24, 2006).
3. The Social Security (Work-focused Interviews for Lone Parents) Amendment Regulations 2007, (SI 2007/1034) (April 30, 2007).

Deferment of requirement to take part in an interview

5.—(1) A requirement by virtue of these Regulations to take part in an interview shall not apply to a person until a date determined by an officer where he determines that an interview would not [^{1} until] that time be—
(a) of assistance to that person; or
(b) appropriate in the circumstances.

(2) Except for the purpose of [^{2} regulations [^{3} 2, 2A and 2B], where an officer has made a decision under paragraph (1), the person to whom that decision relates shall be treated for the purposes of any claim for, or entitlement to, income suppport as having complied with the requirement to take part in an interview until an officer decides whether that person took part in the interview which had been deferred under paragraph (1).

2.777

AMENDMENTS

1. The Social Security (Claims and Information and Work-focused Interviews for Lone Parents) Amendment Regulations 2001 (SI 2001/1189), reg.3 (April 23, 2001).
2. The Social Security (Work-focused Interviews) Amendment Regulations 2005 (SI 2005/2727) (October 31, 2005).
3. The Social Security (Work-focused Interviews for Lone Parents) Amendment Regulations 2007, (SI 2007/1034) (April 30, 2007).

Waiver

6.—(1) A requirement imposed by these Regulations to take part in an interview shall not apply if an officer determines that an interview would not be—
(a) of assistance to the lone parent; or
(b) appropriate in the circumstances.

(2) A person in relation to whom a requirement to take part in an interview has been waived under paragraph (1) shall be treated for the purposes of—
(a) [^{1} regulations 2 and 2A]; and
(b) any claim for, or entitlement to, income support,
as having complied with that requirement.

2.778

AMENDMENT

1. The Social Security (Work-focused Interviews) Amendment Regulations 2005 (SI 2005/2727) (October 31, 2005).

Consequence of failure to take part in an interview

7.—(1) Subject to paragraphs (2) and (5) and regulations 5 and 6, the consequences specified in paragraphs (3) and (4) ensue if a person does not—
(a) take part in any interview when required to do so; and

2.779

The Social Security (Work-focused Interviews) Regulations 2000

    (b) show good cause for not taking part in an interview before the end of five working days following the day on which the interview was to take place.

  (2) In a case where within one month of the date on which the decision was notified to a lone parent that he failed without good cause to take part in an interview—

    (a) he brings new facts to the notice of an officer which could not reasonably have been brought to an officer's notice within five working days of the day on which the interview was to take place; and

    (b) those facts show that he had good cause for his failure to take part in the interview

paragraph (1)(b) shall apply with the modification that for the words "five working days following" there were substituted the words "one month of".

  (3) A person to whom paragraph (1) and—

    (a) regulation [² 2(2)] applies shall be regarded as not having made a claim for income support; or

    (b) regulation [² 2(3) or (4), 2A or 2B] applies shall have his income support reduced in accordance wtih regulation 8.

  (4) Where an interview which arose in connection with a claim was deferred and benefit became payable in accordance with regulation 5(2), the person's entitlement to income support shall terminate as from the first day of the next benefit week following the date the decision was made that the person failed without good cause to take part in an interview.

  (5) For the purposes of this regulation and regulation 8(1), matters to be taken into account in determining whether a person has shown good cause for his failure to take part in an interview include—

    (a) that the lone parent misunderstood the requirement to take part in the interview due to any learning, language or literacy difficulties of the lone parent or any misleading information given to him by an officer;

    (b) that the lone parent was attending a medical or dental appointment, or accompanying someone for whom he has caring responsibilities to such an appointment, and that it would be unreasonable, in the circumstances, to have rearranged that appointment;

    (c) that the lone parent had difficulties with his normal mode of transport and that no reasonable alternative was available;

    (d) that the established customs and practices of the religion to which that lone parent belongs prevented him attending at the time and place for the interview notified to him by an officer;

    (e) that the lone parent was attending an interview with an employer with a view to obtaining employment;

    (f) that the lone parent was pursuing employment opportunities as a self-employed earner;

    (g) that a dependant of the lone parent or someone for whom the lone parent provides care suffered an accident, sudden illness or relapse of [¹ a physical or mental health condition];

    (h) that the lone parent was attending a funeral of a close friend or relative on the day fixed for the interview; and

    (i) that a disability from which the lone parent suffers made it impracticable for him to attend at the time fixed for the interview.

  (6) For the avoidance of doubt, a person who is regarded as not having made a claim for income support because he failed to take part in

(SI 2000/1926, reg. 7)

an interview shall be required to make a new claim for income support in order to establish entitlement to that benefit.

AMENDMENTS

1. The Social Security (Work-focused Interviews) Amendment Regulations 2005 (SI 2005/2727) (October 31, 2005).
2. The Social Security (Work-focused Interviews for Lone Parents) Amendment Regulations 2007, (SI 2007/1034) (April 30, 2007).

Reduction of income support

8.—(1) Subject to paragraphs (2) and (3), any payment of income support which falls to be made to a person after the date on which an officer decided under these Regulations that that person had not—
(a) taken part; and
(b) shown good cause for not taking part,
in an interview shall be reduced as from the first day of the next benefit week following the date the decision was made, by a sum equal to 20 per cent of the income applicable (specified in Part I of Schedule 2 to the Income Support (General) Regulations 1987) on the date the deduction commences in respect of a single claimant for income support aged not less than 25.

(2) Payment shall not be reduced under paragraph (1) below 10 pence per week.

(3) A reduction under this regulation shall cease to have effect as regards a person from whichever is the earlier of—
(a) the date on which that person attains the age of 60;
(b) the date on which that person ceased to be a lone parent; and
(c) the first day of the benefit week in which that person meets the requirement to take part in an interview.

(4) Where the rate of income support payable to a person changes, the rules set out above for a reduction in the benefit payable shall be applied to the new rates and any adjustments to the reduction shall take effect from the beginning of the first benefit week to commence for that person following the change.

2.780

Appeals

9.—(1) This regulation applies to any relevant decision made under these Regulations or any decision under section 10 of the 1998 Act (decisions superseding earlier decisions) superseding such a decision.

(2) This regulation applies—
(a) whether the decision is as originally made or as revised under section 9 of the 1998 Act (revision of decisions); and
(b) as if any decision made, superseded or revised otherwise than by the Secretary of State was a decision made, superseded or revised by him.

(3) In the case of a decision to which this regulation applies, the person in respect of whom the decision was made shall have a right of appeal under section 12 of the 1998 Act (appeal to appeal tribunal) to an appeal tribunal.

2.781

The Social Security (Work-focused Interviews) Regulations 2000

2.782   SCHEDULE 1   **Regulation 1(3)(a)**

AREAS WHERE THESE REGULATIONS COME INTO FORCE ON 30TH OCTOBER 2000 IN RESPECT OF LONE PARENTS WHO ARE NOT ENTITLED TO INCOME SUPPORT

For the purposes of regulation 1(3)(a), the areas are—
(a) the areas of Shropshire County Council and Telford Wrekin District Council; and
(b) the following postcode districts—
DH2 1AA to DH2 1BO
DH2 1XA to DH2 1XQ
DH3 1 and DH3 2
NE8 and NE9
NE10 0
NE10 8 and NE10 9
NE11
NE16 3 to NE16 5
NE16 6NX to NE16 6PE
NE16 8
NE17 7AA to NE17 7HE
NE17 7HG to NE17 7LM
NE17 7TA to NE17 7ZZ
NE21 1
NE21 4 to NE21 6
NE31 1 to NE31 5
NE32 2 to NE32 4
NE33
NE34 0
NE34 6 to NE34 9
NE35 1 and NE35 9
NE36 0 and NE36 1
NE39
NE40 3 to NE40 4
NE42 5 to NE42 6
NE43 7
SR6 7.
(c) The area of Five Council excluding the following postcode districts—
DD 6 8 and DD 6 9
KY 14 6
KY 16 0
KY 16 9.

AMENDMENT

1. The Social Security (Work-focused Interviews for Lone Parents) Amendment Regulations 2002 (SI 2002/670), reg.2 (April 8, 2002).

2.783   *Schedule 2 omitted.*

[[1] SCHEDULE 3]   **Regulation 2B(1)**

2.784   For the purposes of regulation 2B, the areas are the areas of—
Barnet London Borough Council;
Bexley London Borough Council;
Blaby District Council;
Cardiff Council;
Charnwood Borough Council;
City of Bradford Metropolitan District Council;
Dudley Metropolitan Borough Council;
East Lothian Council;
Edinburgh City Council;
Enfield London Borough Council;
Greenwich London Borough Council;

(SI 2000/1926, Sch.3)

Harborough District Council;
Hinckley and Bosworth Borough Council;
Leicester City Council;
Leicestershire County Council;
Lewisham London Borough Council;
Melton Borough Council;
Midlothian Council;
North West Leicestershire District Council;
Oadby and Wigston Borough Council;
Sandwell Metropolitan Borough Council;
Scottish Borders Council;
Vale of Glamorgan Council;
West Lothian Council.]

AMENDMENT

1. Inserted by The Social Security (Work-focused Interviews for Lone Parents) Amendment Regulations 2007, (SI 2007/1034) (April 30, 2007).

The Social Security (Working Neighbourhoods) Regulations 2004

(SI 2004/959)

These regulations are revoked with effect from April 24, 2006 by The Social Security (Working Neighbourhoods) Miscellaneous Amendments Regulations 2006 (SI2006/909), subject to savings for its provisions which amend other regulations. There are also transitional provisions in reg. 4, but these expired on October 31, 2006 at the latest. 2.785

SECTION B

CHILD BENEFIT AND GUARDIAN'S ALLOWANCE

Note

Administration and Adjudication

The administration and adjudication of claims to child benefit and guardian's allowance has been transferred to Her Majesty's Revenue and Customs, but for an interim period of unspecified duration the administration and adjudication of these claims will remain with the social security adjudicating authorities. Nevertheless, a separate set of administration and adjudication regulations has been produced which came into effect on April 7, 2003. These mirror, but do not always exactly replicate, the administration and adjudication regulations which apply more generally and are reproduced earlier in this volume. Users of this volume are advised to check the annotations to the corresponding provisions of the more generally applicable regulations where no specific annotation is provided to regulations reproduced in this part of the book.

The Child Benefit and Guardian's Allowance (Administration) Regulations 2003

(SI 2003/492)

Made 5th March 2003
Laid before Parliament 5th March 2003
Coming into force 7th April 2003

ARRANGEMENT OF REGULATIONS

PART I

GENERAL

1. Citation, commencement and effect
2. Interpretation
3. Use of electronic communications
4. Notification for purposes of sections 111A and 112 of the Administration Act and sections 105A and 106 of the Administration (NI) Act

PART II

CLAIMS AND AWARDS

5. Making a claim
6. Time within which claims to be made
7. Evidence and information
8. Amending claims
9. Withdrawing claims
10. Defective applications
11. Claims for child benefit treated as claims for guardian's allowance and vice versa
12. Advance claims and awards
13. Date of entitlement under an award for the purposes of payability
14. Effective date of change of rate
15. Duration of claims and awards

PART III

PAYMENTS

16. Manner of payment
17. Direct credit transfers
18. Time of payment
19. Persons who may elect to have child benefit paid weekly

20. Elections for weekly payment by persons to whom child benefit was payable for a period beginning before and ending after 15th March 1982
21. Manner of making elections under regulations 19 and 20
22. Interim payments
23. Information to be given and changes to be notified
24. Fractional amounts of benefit or allowance
25. Payments to persons under the age of 18 years
26. Extinguishment of right to payment if payment is not obtained within the prescribed period

Part IV

Third Parties

27. Persons who may act on behalf of those unable to act
28. Appointment of persons to act on behalf of those unable to act
29. Persons who may proceed with a claim made by a person who has died
30. Persons who may receive payments which a person who has died had not obtained
31. Person who may make a claim on behalf of a person who has died
32. Regulations 29, 30 and 31: supplementary
33. Payment to one person on behalf of another
34. Payment to partner as alternative payee

Part V

Overpayments and Recovery

35. Recovery of overpayments by direct credit transfer
36. Circumstances in which determination need not be reversed, varied, revised or superseded
37. Calculating recoverable amounts
38. Offsetting prior payments of child benefit and guardian's allowance against arrears payable by virtue of a subsequent determination
39. Offsetting prior payments of income support or jobseeker's allowance against arrears of child benefit or guardian's allowance payable by virtue of a subsequent determination
40. Exception from offset of recoverable overpayment
41. Bringing interim payments into account
42. Recovery of overpaid interim payments

Part VI

Revocations and Transitional Provisions

43. Revocations
44. Transitional provisions

(SI 2003/492)

Schedule 1

Powers Exercised in Making These Regulations

Schedule 2

Electronic Communications

Part I General

1. Introduction
2. Interpretation
3. Scope of this Schedule

Part II General

4. Use of electronic communications by the Board
5. Restrictions on the use of electronic communications by persons other than the Board
6. Use of intermediaries

Part III Evidential Provisions

7. Effect of delivering information by means of electronic communications
8. Proof of content
9. Proof of identity of sender or recipient
10. Information delivered electronically on another's behalf
11. Proof of delivery of information
12. Use of unauthorised means of electronic communications

Schedule 3

Revocations

The Commissioners of Inland Revenue, in exercise of the powers conferred upon them by the provisions set out in Schedule 1, hereby make the following Regulations:

Part I

General

Citation, commencement and effect

1.—(1) These Regulations may be cited as the Child Benefit and Guardian's Allowance (Administration) Regulations 2003 and shall come into force on 7th April 2003 immediately after the commencement of

The Child Benefit and Guardian's Allowance (Administration) Regs 2003

section 50 of the Tax Credits Act 2002 for the purposes of entitlement to payment of child benefit and guardian's allowance.

(2) These Regulations have effect only in relation to—
(a) child benefit and guardian's allowance under the Contributions and Benefits Act; and
(b) child benefit and guardian's allowance under the Contributions and Benefits (NI) Act.

Interpretation

2.788
2. In these Regulations—
"the adjudicating authority" means—
(a) the Board;
(b) an appeal tribunal constituted under Chapter 1 of Part 1 of the Social Security Act 1998 or Chapter 1 of Part 2 of the Social Security (Northern Ireland) Order 1998; or
(c) a Commissioner within the meaning of section 39(1) of that Act or to whom an appeal lies under Article 15 of that Order;
"the Administration Act" means the Social Security Administration Act 1992;
"the Administration (NI) Act" means the Social Security Administration (Northern Ireland) Act 1992;
"appropriate office" means—
(a) in relation to child benefit or guardian's allowance under the Contributions and Benefits Act—
(i) as regards the Board, the Child Benefit Office, Waterview Park, Washington, Tyne and Wear or [1 any Enquiry Centre maintained by the Board];
(ii) as regards a relevant authority, any office of the Department for Work and Pensions which is designated by the Secretary of State as a Jobcentre Plus Office;
(b) in relation to child benefit or guardian's allowance under the Contributions and Benefits (NI) Act—
(i) as regards the Board, the Child Benefit Office (Northern Ireland), Windsor House, Bedford Street, Belfast or [1 any Enquiry Centre maintained by the Board];
(ii) as regards a relevant authority, any office of the Social Security Agency of the Department for Social Development in Northern Ireland;
[1 (c) in relation to child benefit or guardian's allowance under either of those Acts, as regards the Board, Comben House, Farriers Way, Netherton, Merseyside;]
"the approved form" has the meaning given by regulation 5(1)(a);
"the Board" means the [1 Commissioners for Her Majesty's Revenue and Customs];
"the Contributions and Benefits Act" means the Social Security Contributions and Benefits Act 1992;
"the Contributions and Benefits (NI) Act" means the Social Security Contributions and Benefits (Northern Ireland) Act 1992;
"interim payment" has the meaning given by regulation 22(1);
"married couple" means a man and a woman who are married to each other and are neither—
(a) separated under a court order, nor

(SI 2003/492, reg. 2)

(b) separated in circumstances in which the separation is likely to be permanent;

"partner" means a member of a married or an unmarried couple;

"relevant authority" means—
  (a) in relation to child benefit or guardian's allowance under the Contributions and Benefits Act, the Secretary of State or a person providing services to the Secretary of State;
  (b) in relation to child benefit or guardian's allowance under the Contributions and Benefits (NI) Act, the Department for Social Development in Northern Ireland or a person providing services to that Department;

"unmarried couple" means a man and a woman who are not a married couple but are living together as husband and wife;

"writing" includes writing produced by electronic communications used in accordance with Schedule 2.

AMENDMENT

1. The Child Benefit and Guardian's Allowance (Miscellaneous Amendments) Regulations 2006 (SI 2006/203) (April 10, 2006).

Use of electronic communications

3. Schedule 2 (the use of electronic communications) has effect.   2.789

Notification for purposes of sections 111A and 112 of the Administration Act and sections 105A and 106 of the Administration (NI) Act

4.—(1) This regulation prescribes the person to whom, and manner in which, a change of circumstances must be notified for the purposes of sections 111A(1A) to (1G) and 112(1A) to (1F) of the Administration Act and sections 105A(1A) to (1G) and 106(1A) to (1F) of the Administration (NI) Act (offences relating to failure to notify a change of circumstances).   2.790

(2) Notice of the change of circumstances must be given to the Board, or, where relevant, a relevant authority, in writing (except where they determine or it determines, in any particular case, that they or it will accept a notice other than in writing) by delivering or sending it to an appropriate office.

PART II

CLAIMS AND AWARDS

Making a claim

5.—(1) A claim for child benefit or guardian's allowance must be made to the Board or a relevant authority in writing—   2.791
  (a) on a form for the time being approved by the Board ("the approved form") which has been completed in accordance with the instructions on it; or
  (b) in such other manner as the Board may accept as sufficient in the circumstances of the particular case.

(2) The person making the claim must deliver or send it to an appropriate office.

The Child Benefit and Guardian's Allowance (Administration) Regs 2003

(3) Subject to regulation 10, the claim is made on the date on which it is received by the appropriate office.

Time within which claims to be made

2.792 [¹ **6.**—(1) The time within which a claim for child benefit or guardian's allowance is to be made is 3 months beginning with any day on which, apart from satisfying the conditions for making the claim, the person making the claim is entitled to the benefit or allowance.

(2) Paragraph (1) shall not apply where—
- (a) a person has been awarded child benefit or guardian's allowance while he was present and residing in great Britain, or Northern Ireland;
- (b) at a time when payment of the award has not been suspended or terminated (under regulations 18 to 20 of the Child Benefit and Guardian's Allowance (Decisions and Appeals) Regulations 2003 or otherwise), he take up residence in Northern Ireland, or Great Britain as the case may be ("the new country of residence"); and
- (c) a new claim for that benefit or allowance is made in the new country of residence, for a period commencing on the later of—
  - (i) the date of the change of residence referred to in sub-paragraph (b), or
  - (ii) the date on which, apart from satisfying the conditions for making the claim, the person became entitled to the benefit or allowance under the legislation of the new country of residence.]
- [² (d) a person who has claimed asylum and, on or after 6th April 2004, makes a claim for that benefit or allowance and satisfies the following conditions—
  - (i) the person is notified that he has been recorded as a refugee by the Secretary of State; and
  - (ii) he claims that benefit or allowance within 3 months of receiving that notification.

(3) In a case falling within paragraph (2)(d) the person making the claim shall be treated as having made it on the date when he submitted his claim for asylum.]

AMENDMENTS

1. The Child Benefit and Guardian's Allowance) (Administration) (Amendment No.3) Regulations 2003 (SI 2003/2107), reg.6 (September 3, 2003).
2. The Child Benefit and Guardian's Allowance (Miscellaneous Amendments) Regulations 2004 (SI 2004/761), reg.2 (April 6, 2004).

GENERAL NOTE

2.793 The social security systems of Great Britain and Northern Ireland are formally separate, though in many respects—and certainly in relation to child benefit and guardian's allowance—identical. A problem arose that claimants moving from Great Britain to Northern Ireland (and the reverse) often continued to cash their Great Britain child benefit. This amendment replaces the three month limit on back-dating of benefit to an unlimited period where such a situation has arisen, so that entitlements can be 'balanced out'.

Evidence and information

2.794 **7.**—(1) A person making a claim for child benefit or guardian's allowance must furnish such certificates, documents, information and evidence in connection with the claim, or any question arising out of it, as may be required by the Board.

(2) A person required under paragraph (1) to furnish certificates, documents, information and evidence must do so—
   (a) within one month of being required by the Board to do so; or
   (b) within such longer period as the Board may consider reasonable.

[¹ (3) If a person is required, by virtue of paragraph (1) to furnish a certificate of a [² the birth or adoption of a child or qualifying young person], the certificate so produced must be either an original certificate or a copy authenticated in such manners as would render it admissible in proceedings in any court in the jurisdiction in which the copy was made.]

AMENDMENTS

1. Child Benefit and Guardian's Allowance (Administration) (Amendment) Regulations 2004 (SI 2004/1240) (May 1, 2004).
2. The Child Benefit and Guardian's Allowance (Miscellaneous Amendments) Regulations 2006 (SI 2006/203) (April 10, 2006).

GENERAL NOTE

This provision would appear to reflect the rather more legalistic approach the Board of Inland Revenue adopt to some issues, since the Department for Work and Pensions never seem to have felt the need for such a provision.

Amending claims

8.—(1) A person who has made a claim for child benefit or guardian's allowance may amend it by giving to the Board or a relevant authority notice in writing in accordance with paragraph (2).

(2) A notice under paragraph (1) must be delivered or sent to an appropriate office at any time before a determination has been made on the claim.

(3) The Board may treat a claim amended in accordance with this regulation as if it had been so amended when first made.

Withdrawing claims

9.—(1) A person who has made a claim for child benefit or guardian's allowance may withdraw it by giving notice in writing to the Board or a relevant authority.

(2) A notice of withdrawal given in accordance with paragraph (1) has effect when it is received by an appropriate office.

Defective applications

10.—(1) If an appropriate office receives a defective application, the Board or the relevant authority may refer it back to the person making it or supply him with the approved form for completion.

(2) Where—
(a) in accordance with paragraph (1), a defective application has been referred back, or an approved form supplied, to a person; and
(b) a claim is received by an appropriate office—
   (i) within the period of one month beginning with the date on which the defective application was referred back or the approved form was supplied; or

(ii) within such longer period as the Board may consider reasonable, the claim shall be treated as having been made on the date on which the appropriate office received the defective application.

(3) "Defective application" means an intended claim which—

(a) is made on an approved form which has not been completed in accordance with the instructions on it; or

(b) is in writing but is not made on the approved form.

Claims for child benefit treated as claims for guardian's allowance and vice versa

2.799   **11.**—(1) Where it appears to the Board that a person who has made a claim for child benefit in respect of a child [¹ or qualifying young person] may be entitled to guardian's allowance in respect of the same child [¹ or qualifying young person], the Board may treat, either in the alternative or in addition, the claim as being a claim for guardian's allowance by that person.

(2) Where it appears to the Board that a person who has made a claim for guardian's allowance in respect of a child [¹ or qualifying young person] may be entitled to child benefit in respect of the same child [¹ or qualifying young person], the Board may treat, either in the alternative or in addition, the claim as being a claim for child benefit by that person.

AMENDMENT

1. The Child Benefit and Guardian's Allowance (Miscellaneous Amendments) Regulations 2006 (SI 2006/203) (April 10, 2006).

Advance claims and awards

2.800   **12.**—(1) This regulation applies where a person who has made a claim for child benefit or guardian's allowance does not satisfy the requirements for entitlement on the date on which the claim is made.

(2) If the Board are of the opinion that, unless there is a change of circumstances, the person will satisfy those requirements for a period beginning with a date ("the relevant date") not more than 3 months after the date on which the claim is made, they—

(a) may treat the claim as if made for a period beginning with the relevant date; and

(b) may award the benefit or allowance accordingly, subject to the condition that the person satisfies the requirements for entitlement when the benefit or allowance becomes payable under the award.

(3) If the requirements for entitlement are found not to have been satisfied on the relevant date, a decision under paragraph (2)(b) to award benefit may be revised under—

(a) in relation to child benefit and guardian's allowance under the Contributions and Benefits Act, section 9 of the Social Security Act 1998;

(b) in relation to child benefit and guardian's allowance under the Contributions and Benefits (NI) Act, Article 10 the Social Security (Northern Ireland) Order 1998.

Date of entitlement under an award for the purposes of payability

2.801   **13.**—(1) This regulation applies where child benefit or guardian's allowance is awarded for a period of a week or weeks and the earliest date on which entitlement would commence is not a Monday.

(2) For the purposes of determining the day from which the benefit or allowance is to become payable, entitlement shall be treated as beginning on the Monday next following the earliest date referred to in paragraph (1).

Effective date of change of rate

14. Where a change in the rate of child benefit or guardian's allowance would take effect, but for this regulation, on a day which would not be the appropriate pay day for the benefit or allowance, the change shall take effect from the appropriate pay day next following.

Duration of claims and awards

15.—(1) Subject to paragraphs (2) and (3), a claim for child benefit or guardian's allowance shall be treated as made for an indefinite period and any award shall be made for an indefinite period.

(2) If it would be inappropriate to treat a claim as made and to make an award for an indefinite period (for example, where a relevant change of circumstances is reasonably to be expected in the near future), the claim shall be treated as made for a definite period which is appropriate in the circumstances and any award shall be made for that period.

(3) In any case where benefit or allowance is awarded in respect of days subsequent to the date on which the claim was made, the award shall be subject to the condition that the person by whom the claim was made satisfies the requirements for entitlement.

Part III

Payments

Manner of payment

16.—(1) Subject to regulation 17, child benefit or guardian's allowance shall be paid by means of an instrument of payment or by such other means as appears to the Board to be appropriate in the circumstances of the particular case.

(2) If a person entitled to child benefit is also entitled to guardian's allowance, the allowance shall be paid in the same manner as that in which the child benefit is paid under this regulation.

(3) Instruments of payment which have been issued by the Board remain their property.

(4) A person who has an instrument of payment must on ceasing to be entitled to the benefit or allowance to which the instrument relates, or when required to do so by the Board, deliver it to the Board or such person as the Board may direct.

Direct credit transfers

17.—(1) The Board may make an arrangement with a person claiming, or entitled to, child benefit or guardian's allowance for the payment of the benefit or allowance by way of direct credit transfer in accordance with paragraphs (2) to (4).

(2) The direct credit transfer shall be into a bank account or other account—
  (a) in the name of—
    (i) the person entitled to the benefit or allowance,
    (ii) that person's partner, or
    (iii) a person acting on behalf of that person; or
  (b) in the joint names of the person entitled to benefit and—
    (i) that person's partner, or
    (ii) a person acting on that person's behalf.
(3) Subject to paragraph (4), the benefit or allowance shall be paid within seven days of the last day of each successive period of entitlement.
(4) The Board may make a particular payment by direct credit transfer otherwise than is provided by paragraph (3) if it appears to them appropriate to do so for the purpose of—
  (a) paying any arrears of benefit or allowance, or
  (b) making a payment in respect of a terminal period of an award for any similar purpose.
(5) Where an arrangement is made under paragraph (1)—
  (a) in relation to child benefit, any guardian's allowance to which the person entitled to the child benefit is entitled shall be paid in the same manner as the child benefit;
  (b) in relation to guardian's allowance, the child benefit to which the person entitled to the guardian's allowance is entitled shall be paid in the same manner as the guardian's allowance.
(6) An arrangement made under paragraph (1) may be terminated—
  (a) by the person entitled to benefit, or by a person acting on behalf of that person, giving a notice in writing to the Board; or
  (b) by the Board if the arrangement seems to them to be no longer appropriate to the circumstances of the particular case.
(7) A person giving a notice under paragraph (6)(a) must deliver or send it to an appropriate office as regards the Board.

Time of payment

18.—(1) Subject to paragraphs (2) to (4), child benefit and guardian's allowance shall be paid in accordance with an award as soon as reasonably practicable after the award has been made.
(2) Child benefit shall be paid—
  (a) if a person entitled to it makes an election under regulation 19 or 20, weekly beginning with the first convenient date after the election has been made;
  (b) in any other case, in the last week of each successive period of four weeks of the period of entitlement.
(3) Where benefit is paid at four-weekly intervals in accordance with paragraph (2)(b), the Board must arrange for it to be paid weekly if they are satisfied that payment at intervals of four weeks is causing hardship.
(4) If a person who has made a claim for child benefit is also entitled to guardian's allowance, the allowance shall be paid at the same intervals as the child benefit.
(5) The Board must take steps to notify persons to whom child benefit or guardian's allowance is payable of the arrangements they have made for payment in so far as those arrangements affect those persons.

(SI 2003/492, reg.19)

Persons who may elect to have child benefit paid weekly

19.—(1) A person may make an election under this regulation to have child benefit paid weekly if—
(a) he is a lone parent; or
(b) he or his partner is receiving—
  (i) income support; or
  (ii) an income-based allowance payable under Part 1 of the Jobseekers Act 1995 or Part 2 of the Jobseekers (Northern Ireland) Order 1995.

(2) "Lone parent" means a person who has no partner and is entitled to child benefit in respect of a child [¹ or qualifying young person] for whom he is responsible.

(3) A person making an election under this regulation—
(a) must furnish, in such manner and at such times as the Board may determine, such certificates, documents, other information or facts as the Board may require which may affect his right to receive payment of the benefit weekly; and
(b) as soon as reasonably practicable after any change of circumstances which he might reasonably be expected to know might affect that right, must notify the Board in writing of that change in accordance with paragraph (4).

(4) A notification under paragraph (3)(b) must be delivered or sent to an appropriate office as regards the Board.

AMENDMENT

1. The Child Benefit and Guardian's Allowance (Miscellaneous Amendments) Regulations 2006 (SI 2006/203) (April 10, 2006).

Elections for weekly payment by persons to whom child benefit was payable for a period beginning before and ending after 15th March 1982

20.—(1) This regulation applies to a person to whom child benefit is payable for an uninterrupted period beginning before and ending after 15th March 1982.

(2) A person to whom this regulation applies may make an election to have the benefit paid weekly after 15th March 1982 if—
(a) he makes it before the end of the period of 26 weeks beginning with the day on which benefit was payable for the first four weeks in respect of which arrangements for four-weekly payment were made;
(b) in the case of benefit under the Contributions and Benefits Act, he was absent from Great Britain on 15th March 1982 for any of the reasons specified in paragraph (3) and he makes the election before the end of the period of 26 weeks beginning with the first week in respect of which benefit became payable to him in Great Britain on his return; or
(c) in the case of benefit under the Contributions and Benefits (NI) Act, he was absent from Northern Ireland on 15th March 1982 for any of the reasons specified in paragraph (3) and he makes the election before the end of the period of 26 weeks beginning with the first week in respect of which benefit became payable to him in Northern Ireland on his return.

The Child Benefit and Guardian's Allowance (Administration) Regs 2003

(3) The reasons specified in this paragraph are that the person—
(a) was a serving member of the forces;
(b) was the spouse of such a serving member; or
(c) was living with such a serving member as husband or wife.
(4) "Serving member of the forces" means a person, other than one mentioned in Part 2 of Schedule 6 to the Social Security (Contributions) Regulations 2001, who, being over the age of 16 years, is a member of any establishment or organisation specified in Part 1 of that Schedule (being a member who gives full pay service) but does not include any such person while absent on desertion.

Manner of making elections under regulations 19 and 20

2.809

21.—(1) This regulation applies to elections under regulations 19 and 20.
(2) An election—
(a) must be made by notice in writing to the Board; and
(b) must be delivered or sent to an appropriate office as regards the Board.
(3) An election is made on the date on which it is received by the appropriate office.
(4) Where a person has made an election, child benefit is payable weekly so long as—
(a) he remains continually entitled to it; and
(b) in the case of an election under regulation 19, the conditions specified in paragraph (1)(a) or (b) of that regulation continue to be satisfied.
(5) A person who has made an election may cancel it at any time by giving to the Board a notice in writing which must be sent or delivered to an appropriate office as regards the Board.
(6) The Board must give effect to a notice given in accordance with paragraph (5) as soon as reasonably practicable after receiving it.

Interim payments

2.810

22.—[¹ (1) If the condition in any sub-paragraph of paragraph (1A) is satisfied, the Board may make a payment on account ("an interim payment") of any child benefit or guardian's allowance to which it appears to them that a person—
(a) is or may be entitled, were a claim made,
(b) where sub-paragraph (a) of paragraph (1A) applies, would or might be entitled, were a claim made,
(c) where sub-paragraph (b) of that paragraph applies, would or might be entitled, were the national insurance number condition satisfied.
(1A) The conditions are that—
(a) a claim for benefit or allowance has not been made in accordance with these Regulations and it is impracticable for such a claim to be made immediately;
(b) a claim has been made in accordance with these Regulations, the conditions of entitlement are satisfied other than the national insurance number condition, and it is impracticable for that condition to be satisfied immediately;
(c) a claim for the benefit or allowance has been so made but it is impracticable for it, or an application or appeal relating to it, to be determined immediately;

(d) an award of the benefit or allowance has been made but it is impracticable for the person entitled to it to be paid immediately other than by means of an interim payment.]

(2) Paragraph (1) does not apply pending the determination of an appeal [¹ . . .]

(3) On or before the making of an interim payment, the Board must give the person to whom payment is to be made notice in writing of his liability under regulations 41 and 42 to have it brought into account and to repay any overpayment.

[¹ (4) In this regulation "the national insurance number condition" means the condition imposed—
(a) in Great Britain by section 13(1A) and (1B), of the Administration Act (requirement for claim to be accompanied by details of national insurance number);
(b) in Northern Ireland, by section 11(1A) and (1B) of the Administration (NI) Act.]

AMENDMENT

1. The Child Benefit and Guardian's Allowance (Miscellaneous Amendments) Regulations 2005 (SI 2005/343), reg.8 (March 18, 2005).

Information to be given and changes to be notified

23.—(1) This regulation applies to any person entitled to child benefit or guardian's allowance and any person by whom, or on whose behalf, payments of such benefit or allowance are receivable.

(2) A person to whom this regulation applies must furnish in such manner and at such times as the Board may determine such information or evidence as the Board may require for determining whether a decision on an award—
(a) in relation to benefit or allowance under the Contributions and Benefits Act, should be revised under section 9 or superseded under section 10 of the Social Security Act 1998;
(b) in relation to benefit or allowance under the Contributions and Benefits (NI) Act, should be revised under Article 10 or superseded under Article 11 of the Social Security (Northern Ireland) Order 1998.

(3) A person to whom this regulation applies must furnish in such manner and at such times as the Board may determine such information and evidence as the Board may require in connection with the payment of the benefit or allowance.

(4) A person to whom this regulation applies must notify the Board or a relevant authority of any change of circumstances which he might reasonably be expected to know might affect—
(a) the continuance of entitlement to the benefit or allowance; or
(b) the payment of it,
as soon as reasonably practicable after the change occurs.

(5) A notification under paragraph (4)—
(a) must be given by notice in writing or orally; and
(b) must be sent, delivered or given to the appropriate office.

Fractional amounts of benefit or allowance

24. Where the amount of any child benefit or guardian's allowance payable includes a fraction of a penny, that fraction—

The Child Benefit and Guardian's Allowance (Administration) Regs 2003

(a) if it is less than a half, shall be disregarded;
(b) if it is a half or more, shall be treated as a whole penny.

Payments to persons under the age of 18 years

25. Where a sum of child benefit or guardian's allowance is paid to a person under the age of 18 years (whether on his own behalf or on behalf of another), either of the following is a sufficient discharge to the Board for the sum paid—
(a) a direct credit transfer under regulation 17 into the person's account;
(b) the receipt by the person of a payment made by some other means.

Extinguishment of right to payment if payment is not obtained within the prescribed period

26.—(1) The right to payment of any sum of child benefit or guardian's allowance shall be extinguished if payment of that sum is not obtained within the period of 12 months from the date on which the right is treated as having arisen.

(2) Subject to paragraph (5), the right to payment of a sum is treated as having arisen—
(a) if the Board have given or sent an instrument of payment in respect of the sum to the person to whom it is payable or have sent such an instrument to a place approved by them for collection by that person—
  (i) on the date of the instrument, or
  (ii) if a replacement instrument of payment has been so given or sent, on the date of the last such instrument;
(b) in relation to any sum to which sub-paragraph (a) does not apply, if the Board have given or sent a notice (orally or in writing) that the sum is available for collection—
  (i) on the date of the notice, or
  (ii) if more than one such notice has been given or sent, on the date of the first notice;
[1 (bb) in relation to any sum which the person entitled to it and the Board have arranged to be paid by way of direct credit transfer into a bank or other account, on the due date for payment of such a sum;]
(c) in relation to any sum to which [1 none of the preceding sub-paragraphs applies], on such date as the Board may determine.

(3) The giving or sending by the Board of an instrument of payment under sub-paragraph (a) of paragraph (2), or a notice under sub-paragraph (b) of that paragraph, shall be effective even if the sum contained in the instrument, or the notice, is more or less than the sum which the person concerned has the right to receive.

(4) The date of an instrument of payment is—
(a) the date of issue of that instrument; or
(b) if later, the earliest date specified in the instrument on which payment may be obtained.

(5) Where a question arises as to whether a right to payment of a sum has been extinguished under this regulation, the period of 12 months referred to in paragraph (1) shall be extended to the date on which the Board decide the question, and the right shall be treated for the purposes of this regulation as having arisen on that date, if the Board are satisfied that—

(a) a notice in writing requesting payment of the sum was first received by them after the expiration of the period of 12 months from the date on which, ignoring this paragraph, the right would be treated as having arisen;
(b) from a day within that period until the date on which the notice in writing was given there was good cause for not giving the notice; and
(c) no payment of the sum has been made by way of direct credit transfer in accordance with regulation 17 and—
   (i) no instrument of payment has been given or sent to the person to whom the sum is payable; or
   (ii) any such instrument has been produced to them and no replacement instrument of payment has been given or sent to that person.

(6) This regulation has effect in relation to a person authorised or appointed to act on behalf of a person entitled to child benefit or guardian's allowance in the same manner as it has effect in relation to such a person.

AMENDMENT

1. The Child Benefit and Guardian's Allowance (Miscellaneous Amendments) Regulations 2005 (SI 2005/343), reg.9 (March 18, 2005).

PART IV

THIRD PARTIES

Persons who may act on behalf of those unable to act

27.—(1) Anything required by these regulations to be done by or to any person who is for the time being unable to act may be done by or to—
(a) in England and Wales, a receiver appointed by the Court of Protection with power to claim, or, as the case may be, receive, the benefit or allowance on behalf of the person;
(b) in Scotland, [1 guardian acting or appointed under the Adults with Incapacity (Scotland) Act 2000] who is administering the estate of the person;
(c) in Northern Ireland, a controller appointed by the High Court, with power to claim, or, as the case may be, receive, the benefit or allowance on behalf of the person; or
(d) a person appointed under regulation 28(2) to act on behalf of the person.

(2) Where a sum of child benefit or guardian's allowance is paid to a receiver or other person mentioned in paragraph (1)(a), (b), (c) or (d), either of the following is a sufficient discharge to the Board for the sum paid—
(a) a direct credit transfer under regulation 17 into the person's account;
(b) the receipt by the person of a payment made by some other means.

AMENDMENT

1. The Child Benefit and Guardian's Allowance (Miscellaneous Amendments) Regulations 2005 (SI 2005/343), reg.10 (March 18, 2005).

Appointment of persons to act on behalf of those unable to act

28.—(1) This regulation applies where—
(a) a person is for the time being unable to act;
(b) the person is, or is alleged to be, entitled to child benefit or guardian's allowance (whether or not a claim for the benefit or allowance has been made by him or on his behalf); and
(c) no receiver or other person mentioned in regulation 27(1)(a), (b) or (c) has been appointed in relation to the person.

(2) The Board may appoint a person who—
(a) has applied in writing to them to act on behalf of the person who is unable to act, and
(b) if a natural person, is over the age of 18 years,
to exercise, on behalf of the person who is unable to act, any right relating to child benefit or guardian's allowance to which that person may be entitled and to receive and deal on his behalf with any sums payable to him in respect of the benefit or allowance.

(3) Where an appointment has been made under paragraph (2)—
(a) the Board may at any time revoke it; and
(b) the person appointed may resign from the appointment after having given one month's notice in writing to the Board of his intention to do so.

(4) An appointment made under paragraph (2) shall terminate when the Board are notified that a receiver or other person mentioned in regulation 27(1)(a), (b) or (c) has been appointed.

Persons who may proceed with a claim made by a person who has died

29.—(1) The Board may appoint such person as they think fit to proceed with a claim for child benefit or guardian's allowance [1, and to deal with any issue related to the revision of, supersession of, or appeal in connection with a decision on, that claim] which has been made by a person who has died.

(2) Subject to regulation 32(2), the Board may pay or distribute any sum payable under an award on a claim proceeded with under paragraph (1) to or among—
(a) persons over the age of 16 years claiming as personal representatives, legatees, next of kin or creditors of the person who has died; and
(b) if the person who has died was illegitimate, any other persons over that age.

(3) "Next of kin" means—
(a) in England and Wales, and in Northern Ireland, the persons who would take beneficially on an intestacy;
(b) in Scotland, the persons entitled to the moveable estate of the deceased on intestacy.

(4) Where a sum is paid under paragraph (2) to a person, either of the following is a sufficient discharge to the Board for the sum paid—
(a) a direct credit transfer under regulation 17 into the person's account;
(b) the receipt by the person of a payment made by some other means.

(5) If the Board consider that a sum or part of a sum which may be paid or distributed under paragraph (2) is needed for the benefit of a person under the age of 16 years, they may obtain a good discharge for that sum

by paying it to a person over that age whom they are satisfied will apply the sum for the benefit of the person under that age.

(6) Regulation 26 (extinguishment of right) applies to a payment or distribution made under paragraph (2).

AMENDMENT

1. The Child Benefit and Guardian's Allowance (Miscellaneous Amendments) Regulations 2005 (SI 2005/343), reg.11 (March 18, 2005).

Persons who may receive payments which a person who has died had not obtained

30.—(1) This regulation applies where a person who has died had not obtained at the date of his death a sum of child benefit or guardian's allowance which was payable to him.

(2) Subject to regulation 32(2), the Board may, unless the right to payment had already been extinguished at the date of death, pay or distribute the sum to or amongst the persons mentioned in regulation 29(2)(a) and (b).

(3) Regulation 26 (extinguishment of right) applies to a payment or distribution made under paragraph (2), except that, for the purposes of paragraph (1) of that regulation, the period of 12 months shall be calculated from the date on which the right to payment is treated as having arisen to the person to whom the payment or distribution is made (and not from the date on which that right is treated as having arisen in relation to the person who has died).

Person who may make a claim on behalf of a person who has died

31.—(1) If the conditions specified in paragraph (2) are satisfied, a claim may be made in the name of a person who has died for any child benefit or guardian's allowance to which he would have been entitled if he had claimed it in accordance with these Regulations.

(2) Subject to paragraph (3), the following conditions are specified in this paragraph—
  (a) within 6 months of the date of death an application must have been made in writing to the Board for a person, whom the Board think fit to be appointed to make the claim, to be so appointed;
  (b) a person must have been appointed by the Board to make the claim; and
  (c) the person so appointed must have made the claim not more than 6 months after the appointment.

(3) Subject to paragraphs (4) and (5), if the Board certify that to do so would be consistent with the proper administration of the Contributions and Benefits Act, the period of 6 months mentioned in paragraph (2)(a) or (c) shall be extended by such period (not exceeding 6 months) as may be specified in the certificate.

(4) If a certificate given under paragraph (3) specifies a period by which the period of 6 months mentioned in paragraph (2)(a) shall be extended, the period of 6 months mentioned in paragraph (2)(c) shall be shortened by a period corresponding to the period so specified.

(5) No certificate shall be given under paragraph (3) which would enable a claim to be made more than 12 months after the date of death. For the

The Child Benefit and Guardian's Allowance (Administration) Regs 2003

purposes of this paragraph, any period between the date on which the application for a person to be appointed to make the claim is made and the date on which that appointment is made shall be disregarded.

(6) A claim made in accordance with this regulation shall be treated for the purposes of these Regulations as if it had been made on the date of his death by the person who has died.

Regulations 29, 30 and 31: supplementary

2.820   **32.**—(1) The Board may dispense with strict proof of the title of a person claiming in accordance with regulation 29, 30 or 31.

(2) Neither paragraph (2) of regulation 29 nor paragraph (2) of regulation 30 applies unless written application for payment of the sum under that paragraph is made to the Board within 12 months from the date of death or such longer period as the Board may allow.

Payment to one person on behalf of another

2.821   **33.**—(1) Subject to paragraph (2), the Board may direct that child benefit or guardian's allowance shall be paid, wholly or in part, to another natural person on behalf of the person entitled to it.

(2) The Board may not make a direction under paragraph (1) unless they are satisfied that it is necessary for protecting the interests of—
   (a) the person entitled to the benefit or allowance; or
   (b) any child [1 or qualifying young person] in respect of whom the benefit or allowance is payable.

AMENDMENT

1. The Child Benefit and Guardian's Allowance (Miscellaneous Amendments) Regulations 2006 (SI 2006/203) (April 10, 2006).

Payment to partner as alternative payee

2.822   **34.**—(1) Subject to paragraph (2), where a member of a married couple or an unmarried couple is entitled to child benefit or guardian's allowance, the Board may make arrangements whereby that benefit or allowance, as well as being payable to the person entitled to it, may, in the alternative, be paid to that person's partner on behalf of that person.

(2) Paragraph (1) does not apply to guardian's allowance where a wife has elected that the allowance is not to be paid to her husband in accordance with regulation 10 of the Guardian's Allowance (General) Regulations 2003 (prescribed manner of making an election under section 77(9) of the Contributions and Benefits Act and section 77(9) of the Contributions and Benefits (NI) Act).

PART V

OVERPAYMENTS AND RECOVERY

Recovery of overpayments by direct credit transfer

2.823   **35.**—(1) If the adjudicating authority determines that—

(a) a payment of child benefit or guardian's allowance in excess of entitlement has been credited to a bank account or other account under an arrangement for direct credit transfer made in accordance with regulation 17; and
(b) the conditions specified in paragraph (2) are satisfied,
the excess, or the specified part of it to which the certificate referred to in sub-paragraph (a) of that paragraph relates, shall be recoverable.
(2) The following conditions are specified in this paragraph—
(a) the Board must have certified that the payment in excess of entitlement, or a specified part of it, is materially due to the arrangement for payments to be made by direct credit transfer; and
(b) subject to paragraph (3), notice of the effect which this regulation would have, in the event of an overpayment, must have been given in writing to the person entitled to the benefit or allowance, or to a person acting in his behalf, before he agreed to the arrangement.

(3) In the case of an arrangement relating to child benefit which was agreed to before 6th April 1987, the condition specified in paragraph (2)(b) need not be satisfied in any case where the application for the benefit to be paid by direct credit transfer contained a statement, or was accompanied by a written statement made by the applicant, which complied with the provisions specified in paragraph (4).

(4) The provisions specified in this paragraph are—
(a) in relation to child benefit under the Contributions and Benefits Act, regulation 7(2)(b) and (6) of the Child Benefit (Claims and Payments) Regulations 1984;
(b) in relation to child benefit under the Contributions and Benefits (NI) Act, regulation 7(2)(b) and (6) of the Child Benefit (Claims and Payments) Regulations (Northern Ireland) 1985.

Circumstances in which determination need not be reversed, varied, revised or superseded

36.—(1) This regulation applies where, whether fraudulently or otherwise, a person has misrepresented, or failed to disclose, material facts which do not provide a basis for the determination in pursuance of which an amount of child benefit or guardian's allowance was paid—
(a) in relation to benefit or allowance under the Contributions and Benefits Act, to be revised under section 9 or superseded under section 10 of the Social Security Act 1998;
(b) in relation to benefit or allowance under the Contributions and Benefits (NI) Act, to be revised under Article 10 or superseded under Article 11 of the Social Security (Northern Ireland) Order 1998.

(2) Where this regulation applies—
(a) in relation to an amount mentioned in paragraph (1) relating to child benefit or guardian's allowance under the Contributions and Benefits Act, neither subsection (5) nor (5A) of section 71 of the Administration Act (recoverability dependent on reversal, variation, revision or supersession of determination) applies;
(b) in relation to an amount mentioned in paragraph (1) relating to child benefit or guardian's allowance under the Contributions and Benefits (NI) Act, neither subsection (5) nor (5A) of section 69 of the

Administration (NI) Act (recoverability dependent on reversal, variation, revision or supersession of determination) applies.

Calculating recoverable amounts

2.825   37. Where there has been an overpayment of child benefit or guardian's allowance, in calculating the amounts recoverable under section 71(1) of the Administration Act, section 69(1) of the Administration (NI) Act or regulation 35, the adjudicating authority must deduct any amount which is offset under regulation 38.

Offsetting prior payments of child benefit and guardian's allowance against arrears payable by virtue of a subsequent determination

2.826   **38.**—(1) Subject to regulation 40, in either of the cases specified in paragraphs (2) and (3)—
  (a) a sum of child benefit paid for a period covered by a subsequent determination shall be offset against any arrears of entitlement to the benefit payable for that period by virtue of the subsequent determination;
  (b) a sum of guardian's allowance paid for a period covered by a subsequent determination shall be offset against any arrears of entitlement to the allowance payable for that period by virtue of the subsequent determination, and, except to the extent that it exceeds them, the sum so paid shall be treated as properly paid on account of the arrears.
(2) The case specified in this paragraph is where a person has been paid a sum pursuant to a determination which subsequently—
  (a) is revised under section 9 or superseded under section 10 of the Social Security Act 1998;
  (b) is revised under Article 10 or superseded under Article 11 of the Social Security (Northern Ireland) Order 1998; or
  (c) is overturned on appeal.
(3) The case specified in this paragraph is where a person has been paid a sum for a period by way of an increase in respect of a dependent person and it is subsequently determined that—
  (a) the dependent person is entitled to the benefit or allowance for that period; or
  (b) a third person is entitled to the increase for that period in priority to the person who has been paid.
(4) Where child benefit which has been paid under an award in favour of a person ("the first claimant") is subsequently awarded to another ("the second claimant") for any week, the benefit shall nevertheless be treated as properly paid if it was received by someone (other than the first claimant) who—
  (a) had [¹ the child or qualifying young person] living with him or was contributing towards the cost of providing for [¹ the child or qualifying young person] at a weekly rate which was not less than the weekly rate under the original award; and
  (b) could have been entitled to child benefit in respect of [¹ that child or qualifying young person] for that week had a claim been made in time.
(5) Any amount which is treated under paragraph (4) as properly paid shall be deducted from the amount payable to the second claimant under the subsequent award.

(SI 2003/492, reg.38)

AMENDMENT

1. The Child Benefit and Guardian's Allowance (Miscellaneous Amendments) Regulations 2006 (SI 2006/203) (April 10, 2006).

Offsetting prior payments of income support or jobseeker's allowance against arrears of child benefit or guardian's allowance payable by virtue of a subsequent determination

39.—(1) This regulation applies where—
(a) a person has been paid a sum by way of income support or jobseeker's allowance; and
(b) it is subsequently determined that—
  (i) child benefit or guardian's allowance should be awarded or is payable in lieu of the income support or jobseeker's allowance; and
  (ii) the income support or jobseeker's allowance was not payable.

(2) Subject to regulation 40, any sum of income support or jobseeker's allowance in respect of the period covered by the subsequent determination—
(a) shall be offset against any arrears of entitlement to the child benefit or guardian's allowance payable for that period by virtue of that determination; and
(b) except to the extent that it exceeds them, the sum so paid shall be treated as properly paid on account of the arrears.

Exception from offset of recoverable overpayment

40. No amount may be offset under regulation 38(1) or 39(2) which has been determined to be a recoverable overpayment for the purposes of section 71(1) of the Administration Act or section 69(1) of the Administration (NI) Act.

Bringing interim payments into account

41.—(1) Subject to paragraph (2), if it is practicable to do so—
(a) any interim payment made in anticipation of an award of child benefit or guardian's allowance shall be offset by the adjudicating authority in reduction of the benefit or allowance to be awarded;
(b) any interim payment (whether or not made in anticipation of an award) which is not offset under sub-paragraph (a) shall be deducted by the Board from—
  (i) the sum payable under the award of benefit or allowance on account of which the interim payment was made; or
  (ii) any sum payable under any subsequent award of the benefit or allowance to the same person.

(2) Paragraph (1) does not apply unless the Board have given the notice required by regulation 22(3).

Recovery of overpaid interim payments

42.—(1) Subject to paragraph (2), if the adjudicating authority, in the circumstances specified in either of paragraphs (3) and (4), has determined that an interim payment has been overpaid, it shall determine the amount of the overpayment.

The Child Benefit and Guardian's Allowance (Administration) Regs 2003

(2) Paragraph (1) does not apply unless the Board have given the notice required by regulation 22(3).

(3) The circumstances specified in this paragraph are where an interim payment has been made under regulation 22(1)(a) and (b) and—
  (a) the recipient has failed to make a claim in accordance with these Regulations as soon as practicable;
  (b) the recipient has made a defective application and the Board have not treated the claim as duly made under regulation 10;
  (c) it has been determined that—
    (i) there is no entitlement on the claim;
    (ii) the entitlement is less than the amount of the interim payment; or
    (iii) the benefit or allowance on the claim is not payable; or
  (d) the claim has been withdrawn.

(4) The circumstances specified in this paragraph are where an interim payment has been made under regulation 22(1)(c) which exceeds the entitlement under the award of benefit on account of which the interim payment was made.

(5) The amount of any overpayment determined under paragraph (1) shall be recoverable by the Board in the same manner as it would be if it were recoverable under—
  (a) in relation to child benefit or guardian's allowance under the Contributions and Benefits Act, section 71(1) of the Administration Act;
  (b) in relation to child benefit or guardian's allowance under the Contributions and Benefits (NI) Act, section 69(1) of the Administration (NI) Act.

Part VI

Revocations and Transitional Provisions

Revocations

2.831   43. The subordinate legislation specified in column (1) of Parts 1 and 2 of Schedule 3, in so far as it relates to child benefit or guardian's allowance, is revoked to the extent mentioned in column (3) of that Schedule.

Transitional provisions

2.832   44.—(1) Anything done or commenced under any provision of the instruments revoked by regulation 43, so far as relating to child benefit or guardian's allowance, is to be treated as having been done or as being continued under the corresponding provision of these Regulations.

(2) The revocation by regulation 43 of an instrument which itself revoked an earlier instrument subject to savings does not prevent the continued operation of those savings, in so far as they are capable of continuing to have effect.

(3) "Instrument" includes a Statutory Rule of Northern Ireland.

(SI 2003/492, Sch.1)

SCHEDULE 1

Preamble

POWERS EXERCISED IN MAKING THESE REGULATIONS

1. The following provisions of the Administration Act—   2.833
   (a) section 5(1)(a), (b), (c), (d), (g), (h), (hh), (i), (j), (k), (l), (m), (p), (q) and (r) and (2)(a) and (g);
   (b) section 7(1), (2) and (3)(a);
   (c) section 71(4), (5), (5A), (6), (7) and (11)(a) and (f);
   (d) section 111A(1A), (1B), (1D) and (1E);
   (e) section 112(1A) to (1D);
   (f) section 189(1), (4), (5) and (6);
   (g) section 191.
2. The following provisions of the Administration (NI) Act—   2.834
   (a) section 5(1)(a), (b), (c), (d), (g), (h), (hh), (i), (j), (k), (l), (m), (n), (q), (r), (s) and (t) and (2)(a) and (g);
   (b) section 69(4), (5), (5A), (6), (7) and (11)(a) and (f);
   (c) section 105A(1A), (1B), (1D) and (1E);
   (d) section 106(1A) to (1D);
   (e) section 165(1), (4), (5), (6) and (11A);
   (f) section 167(1).
3. Sections 9(1) and 84 of the Social Security Act 1998.
4. Articles 2(2) and 10(1) of the Social Security (Northern Ireland) Order 1998.
5. Sections 132 and 133(1) and (2) of the Finance Act 1999.
6. Sections 50(1) and (2)(b) and (d) and 54(2) of the Tax Credits Act 2002.

Regulation 3

SCHEDULE 2

ELECTRONIC COMMUNICATIONS

PART I

GENERAL

Introduction

1. This Schedule supersedes the Social Security (Electronic Communications) (Child Benefit) Order 2002 which was made under section 8 of the Electronic Communications Act 2000.   2.835

Interpretation

2.—(1) In this Schedule—   2.836
  "electronic communications" includes any communications by means of a telecommunication system (within the meaning of the Telecommunications Act 1984);
  "official computer system" means a computer system maintained by or on behalf of the Board—
    (a) to send or receive information; or
    (b) to process or store information.
(2) References in this Schedule to the delivery of information and to information shall be construed in accordance with section 132(8) of the Finance Act 1999.

Scope of this Schedule

3. This Schedule applies to the delivery of information to or by the Board, the delivery of which is authorised or required by these Regulations.   2.837

PART II

GENERAL

Use of electronic communications by the Board

4. The Board may only use electronic communications in connection with the matters referred to in paragraph 3 if—   2.838
   (a) the recipient has indicated that he consents to the Board using electronic communications in connection with those matters; and
   (b) the Board have not been informed that that consent has been withdrawn.

The Child Benefit and Guardian's Allowance (Administration) Regs 2003

Restrictions on the use of electronic communications by persons other than the Board

2.839   **5.**—(1) A person other than the Board may only use electronic communications in connection with the matters referred to in paragraph 3 if the conditions specified in subparagraphs (2) to (5) are satisfied.

(2) The first condition is that the person is for the time being permitted to use electronic communications for the purpose in question by an authorisation given by means of a specific or general direction of the Board.

(3) The second condition is that the person uses—
  (a) an approved method for authenticating the identity of the sender of the communication;
  (b) an approved method of electronic communications; and
  (c) an approved method for authenticating any information delivered by means of electronic communications.

(4) The third condition is that any information sent by means of electronic communications is in an approved form (including the manner in which the information is presented).

(5) The fourth condition is that the person maintains such records in written or electronic form as may be specified in a specific or general direction given by the Board.

(6) "Approved" means approved for the purposes of this Schedule, and for the time being, by means of a specific or general direction given by the Board.

Use of intermediaries

2.840   **6.** The Board may use intermediaries in connection with—
  (a) the delivery of information by means of electronic communications in connection with the matters referred to in paragraph 3; and
  (b) the authentication or security of anything transmitted by any such means, and may require other persons to use intermediaries in connection with those matters.

PART III

EVIDENTIAL PROVISIONS

Effect of delivering information by means of electronic communications

2.841   **7.**—(1) Information which is delivered by means of electronic communications shall be treated as having been delivered in the manner or form required by any provision of these Regulations if, but only if, all the conditions imposed by—
  (a) this Schedule,
  (b) any other applicable enactment (except to the extent that the condition thereby imposed is incompatible with this Schedule); and
  (c) any specific or general direction given by the Board,
  are satisfied.

(2) Information delivered by means of electronic communications shall be treated as having been delivered on the day on which the last of the conditions imposed as mentioned in sub-paragraph (1) is satisfied.
This is subject to the following qualifications.

(3) The Board may by a general or specific direction provide for information to be treated as delivered upon a different date (whether earlier or later) than that given by sub-paragraph (2).

(4) Information shall not be taken to have been delivered to an official computer system by means of electronic communications unless it is accepted by the system to which it is delivered.

Proof of content

2.842   **8.**—(1) A document certified by an officer of the Board to be a printed-out version of any information delivered by means of electronic communications under this Schedule on any occasion shall be evidence, unless the contrary is proved, that that information—
  (a) was delivered by means of electronic communications on that occasion; and
  (b) constitutes the entirety of what was delivered on that occasion.

(2) A document purporting to be a certificate given in accordance with sub-paragraph (1) shall be presumed to be such a certificate unless the contrary is proved.

Proof of identity of sender or recipient

2.843   **9.** The identity of—
  (a) the sender of any information delivered to an official computer system by means of electronic communications under this Schedule, or
  (b) the recipient of any information delivered by means of electronic communications from an official computer system,

(SI 2003/492, Sch.2)

shall be presumed, unless the contrary is proved, to be the person recorded as such on an official computer system.

Information delivered electronically on another's behalf
10. Any information delivered by an approved method of electronic communications on behalf of any person shall be deemed to have been delivered by him unless he proves that it was delivered without his knowledge or connivance.

2.844

Proof of delivery of information
11.—(1) The use of an authorised method of electronic communications shall be presumed, unless the contrary is proved, to have resulted in the delivery of information—
   (a) in the case of information falling to be delivered to the Board, if the delivery of the information has been recorded on an official computer system;
   (b) in the case of information falling to be delivered by the Board, if the despatch of the information has been recorded on an official computer system.

(2) The use of an authorised method of electronic communications shall be presumed, unless the contrary is proved, not to have resulted in the delivery of information—
   (a) in the case of information falling to be delivered to the Board, if the delivery of the information has not been recorded on an official computer system;
   (b) in the case of information falling to be delivered by the Board, if the despatch of the information has not been recorded on an official computer system.

(3) The time of receipt of any information sent by an authorised means of electronic communications shall be presumed, unless the contrary is proved, to be that recorded on an official computer system.

2.845

Use of unauthorised means of electronic communications
12.—(1) Sub-paragraph (2) applies to information which is required to be delivered to the Board in connection with the matters mentioned in paragraph 3.

(2) The use of a means of electronic communications, for the purpose of delivering any information to which this paragraph applies, shall be conclusively presumed not to have resulted in the delivery of that information, unless—
   (a) that means of electronic communications is for the time being approved for delivery of information of that kind; and
   (b) the sender is approved for the use of that means of electronic communications in relation to information of that kind.

2.846

Regulation 43

SCHEDULE 3

REVOCATIONS

PART I

REVOCATIONS APPLICABLE TO GREAT BRITAIN

2.847

Column (1)	Column (2)	Column (3)
Subordinate legislation revoked	*References*	*Extent of revocation*
The Social Security (Claims and Payments) Regulations 1987	SI 1987/1968	The whole of the Regulations.
The Social Security (Claims and Payments) Amendment Regulations 1988	SI 1988/522	The whole of the Regulations.
The Social Security (Payments on account, Overpayments and Recovery) Regulations 1988	SI 1988/664	The whole of the Regulations.
The Social Security (Payments on account, Overpayments and Recovery) Amendment Regulations 1988	SI 1988/688	The whole of the Regulations.
The Social Security (Common Provisions) Miscellaneous	SI 1988/1725	In regulation 1(2), the definitions of "the Claims and Payments

Column (1)	Column (2)	Column (3)
Subordinate legislation revoked	References	Extent of revocation
Amendment Regulations 1988		Regulations" and "the Payments on account, Overpayment and Recovery Regulations". Regulations 3 and 4.
The Social Security (Claims and Payments and Payments on account, Overpayments and Recovery) Amendment Regulations 1989	SI 1989/136	The whole of the Regulations.
The Social Security (Abolition of Earnings Rule) (Consequential) Regulations 1989	SI 1989/1642	Regulation 2.
The Social Security (Medical Evidence, Claims and Payments Amendment Regulations 1989	SI 1989/1686	In regulation 1(2), the definition of "the Claims and Payments Regulations". Regulations 3 to 9.
The Social Security (Claims and Payments) Amendment Regulations 1990	SI 1990/725	The whole of the Regulations.
The Social Security (Attendance Allowance and Claims and Payments) Amendment Regulations 1990	SI 1990/1871	Regulation 3.
The Social Security (Miscellaneous Provisions) Amendment Regulations 1990	SI 1990/2208	In regulation 1(2), the definition of "Claims and Payments Regulations". Regulations 7 to 16.
The Enterprise (Scotland) Consequential Amendments Order 1991	SI 1991/387	Article 14.
The Social Security (Miscellaneous Provisions) Amendment Regulations 1991	SI 1991/2284	In regulation 1(2), the definition of "the Claims and Payments Regulations". Regulations 5 to 20.
The Social Security (Claims and Payments) Amendment Regulations 1991	SI 1991/2741	The whole of the Regulations.
The Disability Living Allowance and Disability Working Allowance (Consequential Provisions) Regulations 1991	SI 1991/2742	In regulation 1(3), the definition of "the Payments on account, Overpayments and Recovery Regulations". Regulation 15.
The Social Security (Miscellaneous Provisions) Amendment Regulations 1992	SI 1992/247	Regulation 1(2). Regulations 9 to 17.
The Social Security (Claims and Payments) Amendment Regulations 1992	SI 1992/1026	In regulation 2, the definition of "the Claims and Payments Regulations". Regulations 3 to 6. The Schedule.
The Social Security (Miscellaneous Provisions) Amendment (No.2) Regulations 1992	SI 1992/2595	In regulation 1(2), the definition of "Claims and Payments Regulations". The whole of Part 2.

(SI 2003/492, Sch.3)

Column (1)	Column (2)	Column (3)
Subordinate legislation revoked	*References*	*Extent of revocation*
The Social Security Benefits (Amendments Consequential Upon the Introduction of Community Care Regulations 1992	SI 1992/3147	In Schedule 1, paragraph 8. The Social Security (Claims and Payments) Amendment Regulations 1993 S.I. 1993/478 The whole of the Regulations.
The Deductions from Income Support (Miscellaneous Amendment) Regulations 1993	SI 1993/495	In regulation 1(2), "the Claims and Payments Regulations". Regulation 2.
The Social Security (Payments on account, Overpayments and Recovery) Amendment Regulations 1993	SI 1993/650	The whole of the Regulations.
The Social Security (Miscellaneous Provisions) Amendment Regulations 1993	SI 1993/846	Regulation 4.
The Social Security (Claims and Payments) Amendment (No.2) Regulations 1993	SI 1993/1113	The whole of the Regulations.
The Social Security (Claims and Payments) Amendment (No.3) Regulations 1993	SI 1993/2113	Regulation 3.
The Social Security (Claims and Payments) Amendment Regulations 1994	SI 1994/2319	The whole of the Regulations.
The Social Security (Claims and Payments) Amendment (No.2) Regulations 1994	SI 1994/2943	The whole of the Regulations.
The Social Security (Claims and Payments) Amendment (No.3) Regulations 1994	SI 1994/2944	The whole of the Regulations.
The Social Security (Claims and Payments) Amendment (No.4) Regulations 1994	SI 1994/3196	The whole of the Regulations.
The Social Security (Incapacity Benefit) (Consequential and Transitional Amendments and Savings) Regulations 1995	SI 1995/829	In regulation 1(2), the definition of "the Payments on account, Overpayments and Recovery Regulations". Regulation 21.
The Social Security (Income Support and Claims and Payments) Amendment Regulations 1995	SI 1995/1613	Regulation 3. Schedule 2.
The Income-related Benefits Schemes and Social Security (Claims and Payments) (Miscellaneous Amendments) Regulations 1995	SI 1995/2303	In regulation 1(7), the definition of "the Claims and Payments Regulations". Regulation 10.
The Social Security (Income Support, Claims and Payments and Adjudication) Amendment Regulations 1995	SI 1995/2927	Regulation 1(2)(b). Regulation 3.
The Social Security (Claims and Payments) Amendment Regulations 1995	SI 1995/3055	The whole of the Regulations.
The Social Security (Persons from Abroad) Miscellaneous Amendments Regulations 1996	SI 1996/30	In regulation 1(2), the definition of "the Payments on account, Overpayments and Recovery Regulations".

The Child Benefit and Guardian's Allowance (Administration) Regs 2003

Column (1)	Column (2)	Column (3)
Subordinate legislation revoked	References	Extent of revocation
The Social Security (Industrial Injuries and Diseases) (Miscellaneous Amendments) Regulations 1996	SI 1996/425	Regulation 10. Regulation 3.
The Child Support (Maintenance Assessments and Special Cases) and Social Security (Claims and Payments) Amendment Regulations 1996	SI 1996/481	In regulation 1(2), the definition of "Claims and Payments Regulations". Regulations 5 and 6.
The Social Security (Claims and Payments Etc.) Amendment Regulations 1996	SI 1996/672	Regulation 2. Regulation 4.
The Social Security and Child Support (Jobseeker's Allowance) (Consequential Amendments) Regulations 1996	SI 1996/1345	Regulation 23.
The Social Security (Disability Living Allowance and Claims and Payments) Amendment Regulations 1996	SI 1996/1436	Regulation 3.
The Social Security (Claims and Payments) (Jobseeker's Allowance Consequential Amendments) Regulations 1996	SI 1996/1460	The whole of the Regulations.
The Child Benefit, Child Support and Social Security (Miscellaneous Amendments) Regulations 1996	SI 1996/1803	In regulation 1(4), the definition of "the Claims and Payments Regulations". Regulations 18 to 21.
The Social Security (Claims and Payments and Adjudication) Amendment Regulations 1996	SI 1996/2306	In regulation 1(2), the definition of "the Claims and Payments Regulations". Regulations 2 to 7.
The Social Security (Jobseeker's Allowance Consequential Amendments) (Deductions) Regulations 1996	SI 1996/2344	Regulation 25.
The Income Support and Social Security (Claims and Payments) (Miscellaneous Amendments) Regulations 1996	SI 1996/2431	Regulation 7.
The Social Security (Jobseeker's Allowance and Payments on Account) (Miscellaneous Amendments) Regulations 1996	SI 1996/2519	Regulation 3.
The Social Security (Claims and Payments) Amendment (No.2) Regulations 1996	SI 1996/2988	The whole of the Regulations.
The Social Security (Child Maintenance Bonus) Regulations 1996	SI 1996/3195	Regulation 16(2) and (3).
The Social Security (Social Fund and Claims and Payments) (Miscellaneous Amendments) Regulations 1997	SI 1997/792	Regulation 8.
The Social Security (Miscellaneous Amendments) (No.2) Regulations 1997	SI 1997/793	Regulation 1(2)(b). Regulations 2 to 7.

(SI 2003/492, Sch.3)

Column (1)	Column (2)	Column (3)
Subordinate legislation revoked	*References*	*Extent of revocation*
The Social Security and Child Support (Miscellaneous Amendments) Regulations 1997	SI 1997/827	Regulation 7.
The Social Security (Claims and Payments and Adjudication) Amendment No.2 Regulations 1997	SI 1997/2290	In regulation 1(2), the definition of "the Claims and Payments Regulations". Regulations 5 and 6.
The Social Security (Miscellaneous Amendments) (No.4) Regulations 1997	SI 1997/2305	Regulation 5.
The Social Security (Claims and Payments) (Amendment) Regulations 1997	SI 1997/3034	The whole of the Regulations.
The Social Security (Miscellaneous Amendments) (No.4) Regulations 1998	SI 1998/1174	Regulation 8(3).
The Social Security (Claims and Payments) Amendment Regulations 1998	SI 1998/1381	The whole of the Regulations.
The Social Security (Claims and Payments) Amendment (No.2) Regulations 1998	SI 1998/3039	The whole of the Regulations.
The Social Security Act 1998 (Commencement No.7 and Consequential and Transitional Provisions) Order 1999	SI 1999/1510 (C.43)	Article 4.
The Social Security Act 1998 (Commencement No.8, and Savings and Consequential and Transitional Provisions) Order 1999	SI 1999/1958 (C.51)	Article 4(9) and (10). Schedules 9 and 10.
The Social Security (Claims and Payments) Amendment Regulations 1999	SI 1999/2358	The whole of the Regulations.
The Social Security Act 1998 (Commencement No.9, and Savings and Consequential and Transitional Provisions) Order 1999	SI 1999/2422 (C.61)	Article 3(8) and (9). Schedules 7 and 8.
The Social Security (Miscellaneous Amendments) (No.2) Regulations 1999	SI 1999/2556	Regulation 7.
The Social Security and Child Support (Tax Credits) Consequential Amendments Regulations 1999	SI 1999/2566	Regulation 4.
The Social Security Act 1998 (Commencement No.11, and Savings and Consequential and Transitional Provisions) Order 1999	SI 1999/2860 (C.75)	Article 3(3) and (4). Schedules 3 and 4.
The Social Security (Claims and Information) Regulations 1999	SI 1999/3108	Regulation 5. In Schedule 3, paragraph 2.
The Social Security Act 1998 (Commencement No.12 and Consequential and Transitional Provisions) Order 1999	SI 1999/3178 (C.81)	Article 3(6) and (9). Schedule 6.

The Child Benefit and Guardian's Allowance (Administration) Regs 2003

Column (1)	Column (2)	Column (3)
Subordinate legislation revoked	*References*	*Extent of revocation*
The Social Security (Immigration and Asylum) Consequential Amendments Regulations 2000	SI 2000/636	Schedule 9. In regulation 1(3), the definition of "the Claims and Payments Regulations".
The Social Security (Claims and Payments) Amendment Regulations 2000	SI 2000/1366	Regulation 5. The whole of the Regulations.
The Social Security (Benefits for Widows and Widowers) (Consequential Amendments) Regulations 2000	SI 2000/1483	Regulations 9 and 10.
The Social Security and Child Support (Miscellaneous Amendments) Regulations 2000	SI 2000/1596	In regulation 1(2), the definition of "the Claims and Payments Regulations". Regulation 3.
The Social Security (Work-focussed Interviews for Lone Parents) and Miscellaneous Amendments Regulations 2000	SI 2000/1926	In regulation 10, the words "The Social Security (Claims and Payments) Regulations 1987,". In Schedule 2, paragraph 1.
The Social Security (Joint Claims: Consequential Amendments) Regulations 2000	SI 2000/1982	Regulation 2.
The Social Security (Payments on account, Overpayments and Recovery) Amendment Regulations 2000	SI 2000/2336	The whole of the Regulations.
The Social Security (Incapacity Benefit) Miscellaneous Amendments Regulations 2000	SI 2000/3120	Regulation 3. Regulation 5.
The Social Security (Claims and Payments) Amendment Regulations 2001	SI 2001/18	The whole of the Regulations.
The Social Security (Miscellaneous Amendments) Regulations 2001	SI 2001/488	Regulation 11.
The Social Security Amendment (Joint Claims) Regulations 2001	SI 2001/518	Regulation 5.
The Social Security (Jobcentre Plus Interviews) Regulations 2001	SI 2001/3210	In regulation 15, the words "The Social Security (Claims and Payments) Regulations 1987,". In Schedule 2, paragraph 1.
The Social Security (Notification of Change of Circumstances) Regulations 2001	SI 2001/3252	Regulation 5.
The Social Security (Claims and Payments) Amendment Regulations 2002	SI 2002/355	The whole of the Regulations.
The Social Security Amendment (Residential Care and Nursing Homes) Regulations 2002	SI 2002/398	Regulation 2.
The Social Security (Claims and Payments and Miscellaneous	SI 2002/428	Regulations 1(2), 2 and 3.

(SI 2003/492, Sch.3)

Column (1)	Column (2)	Column (3)
Subordinate legislation revoked	References	Extent of revocation
Amendments) Regulations 2002 The Social Security (Jobcentre Plus Interviews) Regulations 2002	SI 2002/1703	In Schedule 2, paragraph 1.
The Social Security (Claims and Payments) Amendment (No.2) Regulations 2002	SI 2002/1950	The whole of the Regulations.
The Social Security (Claims and Payments and Miscellaneous Amendments) (No.2) Regulations 2002	SI 2002/2441	The whole of the Regulations.
The Social Security (Claims and Payments and Miscellaneous Amendments) (No.3) Regulations 2002	SI 2002/2660	Regulation 2.

PART II

REVOCATIONS APPLICABLE TO NORTHERN IRELAND

Omitted 2.848

The Child Benefit and Guardian's Allowance (Administrative Arrangements) Regulations 2003

(SI 2003/494)

Made 5th March 2003
Laid before Parliament 5th March 2003
Coming into force 7th April 2003

ARRANGEMENT OF REGULATIONS

1. Citation and commencement 2.849
2. Interpretation
3. Provision of information or evidence to relevant authorities
4. Giving information or advice by relevant authorities
5. Recording, verification and holding, and forwarding, of claims etc. received by relevant authorities

The Commissioners of Inland Revenue, in exercise of the powers conferred upon them by sections 58 and 65(1), (2), (7) and (9) of the Tax Credits Act 2002, hereby make the following Regulations:

Citation and commencement

1. These Regulations may be cited as the Child Benefit and Guardian's Allowance (Administrative Arrangements) Regulations 2003 and shall 2.850

851

The Child Benefit and Guardian's Allowance (Arrangements) Regs 2003

come into force on 7th April 2003 immediately after the Child Benefit and Guardian's Allowance (Administration) Regulations 2003.

Interpretation

2.851   **2.** In these Regulations—
"the Board" means the [[1] Commissioners for the Majesty's Revenue and Customs];
"defective application" has the meaning given by regulation 10(3) of the principal Regulations;
"the principal Regulations" means the Child Benefit and Guardian's Allowance (Administration) Regulations 2003;
"relevant authority" means—
(a) the Secretary of State;
(b) the Department for Social Development in Northern Ireland; or
(c) a person providing services to the Secretary of State or that Department.

AMENDMENT

1. The Child Benefit and Guardian's Allowance (Miscellaneous Amendments) Regulations 2006 (SI 2006/203) (April 10, 2006).

Provision of information or evidence to relevant authorities

2.852   **3.**—(1) Information or evidence relating to child benefit or guardian's allowance which is held—
(a) by the Board; or
(b) by a person providing services to the Board, in connection with the provision of those services,
may be provided to a relevant authority for the purposes of, or for any purposes connected with, the exercise of that relevant authority's functions under the principal Regulations.
(2) Information or evidence relating to child benefit and guardian's allowance may be provided to a relevant authority by persons other than the Board (whether or not persons by whom claims or notifications relating to child benefit or guardian's allowance are or have been made or given).

Giving of information or advice by relevant authorities

2.853   **4.** A relevant authority to which a claim or notification is or has been made or given by a person in accordance with the principal Regulations may give information or advice relating to child benefit and guardian's allowance to that person.

Recording, verification and holding, and forwarding, of claims etc. received by relevant authorities

2.854   **5.**—(1) A relevant authority may record and hold—
(a) claims and notifications received by virtue of the any of the principal Regulations; and
(b) information or evidence received by virtue of regulation 3(2).

(SI 2003/494, reg. 5)

(2) Subject to paragraphs (3) and (4), a relevant authority or a person providing services to the Board must forward to the Board such a claim or notification, or such information or evidence, as soon as reasonably practicable after being satisfied that it is complete.

(3) Before forwarding a claim or notification in accordance with paragraph (2), a relevant authority must verify whether the details of the claim or notification are consistent with any details held by it which have been provided in connection with a relevant claim for benefit that relates to—
  (a) the person by whom the claim for child benefit or guardian's allowance is or has been made; or
  (b) [¹ the child or qualifying young person in respect to whom] the child benefit or guardian's allowance is payable.

(4) Before forwarding a claim in accordance with paragraph (2), a relevant authority must verify that—
  (a) any national insurance number provided in respect of the person by whom the claim is made exists and has been allocated to that person;
  (b) the matters verified in accordance with sub-paragraph (a) accord with—
    (i) its own records; or
    (ii) in the case of a person providing services to the Secretary of State or the Department for Social Development in Northern Ireland, records held by the Secretary of State or that Department.

(5) Before forwarding a claim in accordance with paragraph (2), a relevant authority may verify the existence of any original document provided by the person making the claim which is required to be returned to him.

(6) If a relevant authority cannot locate any national insurance number in respect of a person by whom such a claim is made, it must forward to the Board or a person providing services to the Board the claim.

(7) "National insurance number" means the national insurance number allocated within the meaning of—
  (a) regulation 9 of the Social Security (Crediting and Treatment of Contributions, and National Insurance Numbers) Regulations 2001; or
  (b) regulation 9 of the Social Security (Crediting and Treatment of Contributions, and National Insurance Numbers) Regulations (Northern Ireland) 2001.

(8) "Claim for benefit" means a claim for—
  (a) a benefit in relation to which—
    (i) the Secretary of State has functions under the Social Security Contributions and Benefits Act 1992; or
    (ii) the Department for Social Development in Northern Ireland has functions under the Social Security Contributions and Benefits (Northern Ireland) Act 1992; or
  (b) a jobseeker's allowance under—
    (i) the Jobseekers Act 1995; or
    (ii) the Jobseekers (Northern Ireland) Order 1995.

AMENDMENT

1. The Child Benefit and Guardian's Allowance (Miscellaneous Amendments) Regulations 2006 (SI 2006/203) (April 10, 2006).

The Child Benefit and Guardian's Allowance (Decisions and Appeals) Regulations 2003

(SI 2003/916)

Made   27th March 2003
Coming into force   7th April 2003

ARRANGEMENT OF REGULATIONS

PART 1

GENERAL

2.855

1. Citation, commencement and effect
2. Interpretation
3. Service of notices or documents
4. Use of electronic communications

PART 2

REVISION OF DECISIONS

5. Revision of decisions within a prescribed period or on an application
6. Late applications for revision of decisions
7. Procedure for revision of decisions on an application
8. Revision of decisions against which there has been an appeal
9. Revision of decisions against which no appeal lies
10. Revision of decisions arising from official error etc.
11. Revision of decisions following the award of another relevant benefit
12. Date as from which revised decisions take effect

PART 3

SUPERSEDING DECISIONS

13. Cases and circumstances in which superseding decisions may be made
14. Procedure for making superseding decisions on an application
15. Interaction of revisions and superseding decisions
16. Date as from which superseding decisions take effect
17. Effective date for late notifications of change of circumstances

PART 4

SUSPENSION AND TERMINATION

18. Suspension in prescribed cases
19. Provision of information or evidence

(SI 2003/916)

20. Termination in cases of failure to furnish information or evidence
21. Making of payments which have been suspended

Part 5

Other Matters

22. Decisions involving issues that arise on appeal in other cases
23. Appeals involving issues that arise on appeal in other cases

Part 6

Rights of Appeal and Procedure for Bringing Appeals

24. Other persons with a right of appeal
25. Decisions against which no appeal lies
26. Notice of decision against which appeal lies
27. Appeals against decisions which have been revised
28. Time within which an appeal is to be brought
29. Late appeals
30. Interests of justice
31. Making of appeals and applications
32. Discontinuing action on appeals
33. Death of a party to an appeal

Part 7

Revocations, Transitional Provisions and Consequential Amendments

34. Revocations
35. Transitional provisions
36. Consequential amendments to the Decisions and Appeals Regulations
37. Consequential amendments to the Decisions and Appeals (NI) Regulations

SCHEDULE 1

POWERS EXERCISED IN MAKING THESE REGULATIONS

SCHEDULE 2

DECISIONS AGAINST WHICH NO APPEAL LIES

PART 1

DECISIONS MADE UNDER PRIMARY LEGISLATION

PART 2

DECISIONS MADE UNDER SECONDARY LEGISLATION

PART 3

OTHER DECISIONS

Whereas a draft of this instrument was laid before Parliament in accordance with section 80(1) of the Social Security Act 1998 and Article 75(1A) of the Social Security (Northern Ireland) Order 1998 and approved by resolution of each House of Parliament;

Now, therefore, the Commissioners of Inland Revenue, in exercise of the powers conferred upon them by the provisions set out in Schedule 1 and, in accordance with section 8 of the Tribunals and Inquiries Act 1992, after consultation with the Council on Tribunals, hereby make the following Regulations:

PART 1

GENERAL

Citation, commencement and effect

1.—(1) These Regulations may be cited as the Child Benefit and Guardian's Allowance (Decisions and Appeals) Regulations 2003 and shall come into force on 7th April 2003 immediately after the commencement of section 50 of the Tax Credits Act 2002 for the purposes of entitlement to payment of child benefit and guardian's allowance.

(2) These Regulations have effect only in relation to—
(a) child benefit and guardian's allowance under the Contributions and Benefits Act; and

(b) child benefit and guardian's allowance under the Contributions and Benefits (NI) Act.

Interpretation

2.—(1) In these Regulations—
"the 1998 Act" means the Social Security Act 1998;
"the Administration Act" means the Social Security Administration Act 1992;
"the Administration (NI) Act" means the Social Security Administration (Northern Ireland) Act 1992;
"the Administration Regulations" means the Child Benefit and Guardian's Allowance (Administration) Regulations 2003;
"appeal tribunal" means—
  (a) in relation to child benefit or guardian's allowance under the Contributions and Benefits Act, an appeal tribunal constituted under Chapter 1 of Part 1 of the 1998 Act;
  (b) in relation to child benefit or guardian's allowance under the Contributions and Benefits (NI) Act, an appeal tribunal constituted under Chapter 1 of Part 2 of the 1998 Order;
"the appropriate office" means—
  (a) in relation to child benefit or guardian's allowance under the Contributions and Benefits Act, the Child Benefit Office, Waterview Park, Washington, Tyne and Wear;
  (b) in relation to child benefit or guardian's allowance under the Contributions and Benefits (NI) Act, the Child Benefit Office (Northern Ireland), Windsor House, Bedford Street, Belfast;
  (c) any Inland Revenue Enquiry Centre;
"the Board" means the Commissioners of Inland Revenue;
"claimant" means a person who has claimed child benefit or guardian's allowance and includes, in relation to an award or decision, a beneficiary under the award or a person affected by the decision;
"clerk to the appeal tribunal" means—
  (a) in relation to child benefit or guardian's allowance under the Contributions and Benefits Act, a clerk assigned to the appeal tribunal in accordance with regulation 37 of the Decisions and Appeals Regulations;
  (b) in relation to child benefit or guardian's allowance under the Contributions and Benefits (NI) Act, a clerk assigned to the appeal tribunal in accordance with regulation 37 of the Decisions and Appeals Regulations (NI);
"Commissioner" means—
  (a) in relation to child benefit or guardian's allowance under the Contributions and Benefits Act, the Chief Social Security Commissioner or any other Social Security Commissioner appointed under the 1998 Act and includes a tribunal of three or more Commissioners constituted under section 16(7);
  (b) in relation to child benefit or guardian's allowance under the Contributions and Benefits (NI) Act, the Chief Social Security Commissioner or any other Social Security Commissioner appointed under the 1998 Order and includes a tribunal of two or more Commissioners constituted under Article 16(7);

"the Contributions and Benefits Act" means the Social Security Contributions and Benefits Act 1992;

"the Contributions and Benefits (NI) Act" means the Social Security Contributions and Benefits (Northern Ireland) Act 1992;

"the Decisions and Appeals Regulations" means the Social Security and Child Support (Decisions and Appeals) Regulations 1999;

"the Decisions and Appeals Regulations (NI)" means the Social Security and Child Support (Decisions and Appeals) Regulations (Northern Ireland) 1999;

"family" has—
  (a) in relation to child benefit and guardian's allowance under the Contributions and Benefits Act, the meaning given by section 137 of that Act;
  (b) in relation to child benefit and guardian's allowance under the Contributions and Benefits (NI) Act, the meaning given by section 133 of that Act;

"legally qualified panel member" means—
  (a) in relation to child benefit or guardian's allowance under the Contributions and Benefits Act, a panel member who satisfies the requirements of paragraph 1 of Schedule 3 to the Decisions and Appeals Regulations;
  (b) in relation to child benefit or guardian's allowance under the Contributions and Benefits (NI) Act, a panel member who satisfies the requirements of paragraph 1 of Schedule 2 to the Decisions and Appeals Regulations (NI);

"the Northern Ireland Department" means the Department for Social Development in Northern Ireland;

"the 1998 Order" means the Social Security (Northern Ireland) Order 1998;

"panel" means the panel constituted under section 6 or Article 7;

"panel member" means a person appointed to the panel;

"party to the proceedings" means the Board and any other person who—
  (a) is one of the principal parties for the purposes of sections 13 and 14 or Articles 14 and 15; or
  (b) has a right of appeal to an appeal tribunal under section 12(2) or Article 13(2);

"relevant benefit" means child tax credit under the Tax Credits Act 2002 and—
  (a) in relation to child benefit or guardian's allowance under the Contributions and Benefits Act, any of the benefits mentioned in section 8(3);
  (b) in relation to child benefit or guardian's allowance under the Contributions and Benefits (NI) Act, any of the benefits mentioned in Article 9(3);

"superseding decision" has the meaning given by regulation 13(1);

"writing" includes writing produced by electronic communications used in accordance with regulation 4.

(2) In these Regulations—
(a) a reference to a numbered section without more is a reference to the section of the 1998 Act bearing that number;
(b) a reference to a numbered Article without more is a reference to the Article of the 1998 Order bearing that number.

(SI 2003/916, reg.2)

GENERAL NOTE

"the Board"
The definition of "the Board" must be read in the light of the Commissioners for Revenue and Customs Act 2005. Section 5(2)(a) vests all the functions of the former Commissioners of Inland Revenue in the Commissioners for Her Majesty's Revenue and Customs and s.4(1) provides that the Commissioners and the officers of Revenue and Customs may together be referred to as Her Majesty's Revenue and Customs.

Service of notices or documents

3.—(1) Where, under any provision of these Regulations—
(a) a notice or other document is required to be given or sent to the clerk to the appeal tribunal or the Board, the notice or document is to be treated as having been so given or sent on the day that it is received by the clerk or the Board;
(b) a notice (including notification of a decision of the Board) or other document is required to be given or sent to any person other than clerk to the appeal tribunal or the Board, the notice or document is, if sent by post to that person's last known address, to be treated as having been given or sent on the day that it was posted.

(2) In these Regulations, "the date of notification", in relation to a decision of the Board, means the date on which notification of the decision is treated under paragraph (1)(b) as having been given or sent.

2.858

DEFINITIONS

"the Board"—see reg.2(1).
"clerk to the appeal tribunal"—*ibid.*

GENERAL NOTE

Paragraph (1)
See the note to reg.2 of the Social Security and Child Support (Decisions and Appeals) Regulations 1999 to which this is equivalent.

2.859

Paragraph (2)
This has the effect that whenever the phrase "the date of notification" is used in subsequent provisions in these Regulations, it refers to the date on which notification of a decision of the Board is treated under para.(1)(b) as having been given or sent.

2.860

Use of electronic communications

4.—(1) Schedule 2 to the Administration Regulations (the use of electronic communications) applies to the delivery of information to or by the Board which is authorised or required by these Regulations in the same manner as it applies to the delivery of information to or by the Board which is authorised or required by the Administration Regulations.

(2) References in paragraph (1) to the delivery of information shall be construed in accordance with section 132(8) of the Finance Act 1999.

2.861

DEFINITIONS

"the Administration Regulations"—see reg.2(1).
"the Board"—*ibid.*

Child Benefit & Guardian's Allowance (Decisions & Appeals) Regs 2003

PART 2

REVISION OF DECISIONS

Revision of decisions within a prescribed period or on an application

5.—(1) Subject to paragraph (3), if the conditions specified in paragraph (2) are satisfied—
- (a) a decision under section 8 or 10 may be revised by the Board under section 9; and
- (b) a decision under Article 9 or 11 may be revised by them under Article 10.

(2) The conditions specified in this paragraph are that—
- (a) the Board commence action leading to the revision within one month of the date of notification of the decision; or
- (b) subject to regulation 6, an application for the revision was received by the Board at the appropriate office—
   - (i) within one month of the date of notification of the decision;
   - (ii) if a written statement of the reasons for the decision requested under regulation 26(1)(b) was provided within the period specified in paragraph (i), within 14 days of the expiry of that period; or
   - (iii) if such a statement was provided after the period specified in paragraph (i), within 14 days of the date on which the statement was provided.

(3) Paragraph (1) does not apply in respect of a relevant change of circumstances which occurred since the decision [[1] had effect (or, in the case of an advance award under regulation 12 of the Child Benefit and Guardian's Allowance (Administration) Regulations 2003 (advance claims and awards), was made)] or where the Board have evidence or information which indicates that a relevant change of circumstances will occur.

AMENDMENT

1. Child Benefit and Guardian's Allowance (Miscellaneous Amendments) Regulations 2005 (SI 2005/343), reg.3 (March 18, 2005).

DEFINITIONS

"the appropriate office"—see reg.2(1).
"the Board"—*ibid.*
"the date of notification"—see reg.3(2).

GENERAL NOTE

This regulation provides for revision of a decision where the Board or the claimant takes action within one month of the date of notification of the decision. It is equivalent to reg.3(1) and (9)(a) of the Social Security and Child Support (Decisions and Appeals) Regulations 1999. The time for making an application may be extended if a request for reasons has been made promptly (para.(2)(b)(ii) and (iii)) or where the conditions of reg.6 are met. The time for appealing against a decision is extended if an application is made for revision, so that the claimant is not prejudiced by first having sought a revision (see reg.28(2)).

Late applications for revision of decisions

6.—(1) The Board may extend the time limits specified in regulation 5(2)(b)(i) to (iii) if the first and second conditions are satisfied.

(2) The first condition is that an application for an extension of time must be made to the Board by the claimant or a person acting on his behalf.

(3) The second condition is that the application for the extension of time must—
  (a) contain particulars of the grounds on which the extension is sought;
  (b) contain sufficient details of the decision which it is sought to have revised so as to enable it to be identified; and
  (c) be made within 13 months of the latest date by which the application for revision should have been received by the Board in accordance with regulation 5(2)(b).

(4) An application for an extension of time must not be granted unless the Board are satisfied that—
  (a) it is reasonable to grant it;
  (b) the application for revision has merit; and
  (c) special circumstances are relevant to the application for an extension of time as a result of which it was not practicable for the application for revision to be made within the time limits specified in regulation 5(2)(b)(i) to (iii).

(5) In determining whether it is reasonable to grant an application for an extension of time, the Board must have regard to the principle that the greater the amount of time that has elapsed between the expiration of the time limits specified in regulation 5(2)(b)(i) to (iii) and the making of the application, the more compelling the special circumstances mentioned in paragraph (4)(c) should be.

(6) In determining whether it is reasonable to grant an application for an extension of time, the Board must take no account of the following—
  (a) that the applicant or any person acting for him was unaware of, or misunderstood, the law applicable to his case (including being unaware of, or misunderstanding, the time limits imposed by these Regulations); or
  (b) that a Commissioner or a court has taken a different view of the law from that previously understood and applied.

(7) An application for an extension of time which has been refused may not be renewed.

DEFINITIONS

"the Board"—see reg.2(1).
"claimant"—*ibid*.
"Commissioner"—*ibid*.

GENERAL NOTE

This is equivalent to reg.4 of the Social Security and Child Support (Decisions and Appeals) Regulations 1999.

Procedure for revision of decisions on an application

7.—(1) The Board may treat—
  (a) an application for a decision under section 10 as an application for a revision under section 9;

Child Benefit & Guardian's Allowance (Decisions & Appeals) Regs 2003

(b) an application for a decision under Article 11 as an application for a revision under Article 10.

(2) Paragraph (3) applies where, in order to consider all the issues raised by an application for such a revision, the Board require further evidence or information from the applicant.

(3) Where this paragraph applies, the Board must notify the applicant that further evidence or information is required and—
  (a) if the applicant provides relevant further evidence or information within one month of the date of notification or such longer period of time as the Board may allow, the decision may be revised;
  (b) if the applicant does not provide such evidence or information within that time, the decision may be revised on the basis of the application.

DEFINITIONS

"the Board"—see reg.2(1).
"the date of notification"—see reg.3(2).

GENERAL NOTE

Paragraph (1)

2.866 This is equivalent to reg.3(10) of the Social Security and Child Support (Decisions and Appeals) Regulations 1999 and provides for an application for a superseding decision to be treated as an an application for revision. Reg.14(1) makes provision for an application for a revision to be treated as an application for superseding decision.

Paragraphs (2) and (3)

2.867 These are equivalent to reg.3(2) of the Social Security and Child Support (Decisions and Appeals) Regulations 1999.

Revision of decisions against which there has been an appeal

2.868 **8.**—(1) In the circumstances prescribed by paragraph (2), any of the following decisions may be revised by the Board at any time—
  (a) a decision under section 8 or 10;
  (b) a decision under Article 9 or 11.

(2) The circumstances prescribed by this paragraph are circumstances where there is an appeal to an appeal tribunal against the decision within the time prescribed by regulation 28, or in a case to which regulation 29 applies within the time prescribed by that regulation, but the appeal has not been determined.

(3) If—
  (a) the Board make one of the following decisions ("the original decision")—
    (i) a decision under section 8 or 10 or one under section 9(1) revising such a decision; or
    (ii) a decision under Article 9 or 11 or one under Article 10(1) revising such a decision;
  (b) the claimant appeals to an appeal tribunal against the original decision;
  (c) after the appeal has been made, but before it results in a decision by the appeal tribunal, the Board make a second decision which—
    (i) supersedes the original decision in accordance with section 10 or Article 11; or

(SI 2003/916, reg.8)

(ii) decides a further claim for child benefit or guardian's allowance by the claimant; and
(d) the Board would have made their second decision differently if, at the time they made it, they had been aware of the decision subsequently made by the appeal tribunal,

the second decision may be revised by the Board at any time.

DEFINITIONS

"appeal tribunal"—see reg.2(1).
"the Board"—*ibid.*
"claimant"—*ibid.*

GENERAL NOTE

This is equivalent to reg.3(5A) of the Social Security and Child Support (Decisions and Appeals) Regulations 1999 and enables a decision made while an appeal to a tribunal is pending to be revised in the light of the tribunal's decision.

2.869

Revision of decisions against which no appeal lies

9.—(1) In the case prescribed by paragraph (2), any of the following decisions may be revised by the Board at any time—
(a) a decision under section 8 or 10;
(b) a decision under Article 9 or 11.
(2) The case prescribed by this paragraph is the case of decisions which—
(a) are specified in—
(i) Schedule 2 to the 1998 Act; or
(ii) Schedule 2 to the 1998 Order; or
(b) are prescribed by regulation 25 (decisions against which no appeal lies).

2.870

DEFINITION

"the Board"—see reg.2(1).

GENERAL NOTE

This is equivalent to reg.3(8) of the Social Security and Child Support (Decisions and Appeals) Regulations 1999.

2.871

Revision of decisions arising from official error etc.

10.—(1) In the circumstances prescribed by paragraph (2), any of the following decisions may be revised by the Board at any time—
(a) a decision under section 8 or 10;
(b) a decision under Article 9 or 11.
(2) The circumstances prescribed by this paragraph are circumstances where the decision—
(a) arose from an official error; or
(b) was made in ignorance of, or was based upon a mistake as to, some material fact and, as a result of that ignorance of, or mistake as to, that fact, is more advantageous to the claimant than it would otherwise have been.
(3) "Official error" means an error made by—
(a) an officer of the Board acting as such, which no person outside the Inland Revenue caused or to which no such person materially contributed; or

2.872

(b) a person employed by a person providing services to the Board and acting as such which no other person who was not so employed caused or to which no such other person materially contributed,

but does not include an error of law which is shown to have been an error by virtue of a subsequent decision of a Commissioner or the court.

DEFINITIONS

"the Board"—see reg.2(1).
"claimant"—*ibid*.
"Commissioner"—*ibid*.
"Inland Revenue", by virtue of s.39(2) of the Social Security Act 1998, see s.191 of the Social Security Administration Act 1992.
"official error"—see para.(3).

GENERAL NOTE

2.873 This is equivalent to reg.3(5) of the Social Security and Child Support (Decisions and Appeals) Regulations 1999. For the interpretation of the definition of "official error", see the note to reg.1(3) of the 1999 Regulations.

Revision of decisions following the award of another relevant benefit

2.874 **11.**—(1) In the circumstances prescribed by paragraph (2), any of the following decisions may be revised by the Board at any time—
(a) a decision under section 8 or 10;
(b) a decision under Article 9 or 11.
(2) The circumstances prescribed by this paragraph are circumstances where—
(a) the decision awards child benefit or guardian's allowance to a person; and
(b) an award of another relevant benefit, or of an increase in the rate of another relevant benefit, is made to that person or a member of his family for a period which includes the date on which the decision took effect.

DEFINITIONS

"the Board"—see reg.2(1).
"family"—*ibid*.
"relevant benefit"—*ibid*.

GENERAL NOTE

2.875 This is equivalent to reg.3(7) of the Social Security and Child Support (Decisions and Appeals) Regulations 1999. A decision may be revised where a later decision in respect of a relevant benefit affects entitlement under the earlier decision from the date it took effect. If the later decision affects entitlement under the earlier decision from a later date, the earlier decision is superseded under reg.13(2)(e) instead of being revised.

Date as from which revised decisions take effect

2.876 **12.** If the Board decide that—
(a) on a revision under section 9, the date as from which the decision under section 8 or 10 took effect was erroneous; or
(b) on a revision under Article 10, the date as from which the decision under Article 9 or 11 took effect was erroneous,

the revision shall take effect as from the date from which the decision would have taken effect had the error not been made.

Definition

"the Board"—see reg.2(1).

General Note

This is equivalent to reg.5 of the Social Security and Child Support (Decisions and Appeals) Regulations 1999 and provides the exception to the general rule imposed by s.9(3) of the Social Security Act 1998 that a revision is effective from the same date as the decision being revised. The exception is where a ground for the revision is that the effective date of the original decision was wrong.

Part 3

Superseding Decisions

Cases and circumstances in which superseding decisions may be made

13.—(1) Subject to regulation 15, the Board may make a decision under section 10 or Article 11 ("a superseding decision"), either on their own initiative or on an application received by them at an appropriate office, in any of the cases and circumstances prescribed by paragraph (2).

(2) The cases and circumstances prescribed by this paragraph are cases and circumstances where the decision to be superseded is—
  (a) a decision in respect of which—
      (i) there has been a relevant change of circumstances since it [¹ had effect (or, in the case of an advance award under regulation 12 of the Child Benefit and Guardian's Allowance (Administration) Regulations 2003 (advance claims and awards), was made)]; or
      (ii) it is anticipated that there will be such a change;
  (b) a decision (other than one to which sub-paragraph (d) refers)—
      (i) which was erroneous in point of law, or was made in ignorance of, or was based upon a mistake as to, some material fact; and
      (ii) in relation to which an application for a superseding decision was received by the Board, or a decision by the Board to act on their own initiative was taken, more than one month after the date of notification of the decision to be superseded or after the expiry of such longer period of time as may have been allowed under regulation 6;
  (c) a decision of an appeal tribunal or a Commissioner which—
      (i) was made in ignorance of, or was based upon a mistake as to, some material fact;
      (ii) in a case to which subsection (5) of section 26 applies, was dealt with in accordance with subsection (4)(b) of that section; or
      (iii) in a case to which paragraph (5) of Article 26 applies, was dealt with in accordance with paragraph (4)(b) of that Article;

Child Benefit & Guardian's Allowance (Decisions & Appeals) Regs 2003

  (d) a decision—
    (i) specified in Schedule 2 to the 1998 Act;
    (ii) specified in Schedule 2 to the 1998 Order; or
    (iii) prescribed by regulation 25 (decisions against which no appeal lies); or
  (e) a decision where—
    (i) the claimant has been awarded entitlement to child benefit or guardian's allowance; and
    (ii) subsequent to the first day of the period to which that entitlement relates, the claimant or a member of his family becomes entitled to, or to an increase in the rate of, another relevant benefit.

AMENDMENT

1. Child Benefit and Guardian's Allowance (Miscellaneous Amendments) Regulations 2005 (SI 2005/343), reg.4 (March 18, 2005).

DEFINITIONS

"appeal tribunal"—see reg.2(1).
"appropriate office"—*ibid*.
"the Board"—*ibid*.
"claimant"—*ibid*.
"Commissioner"—*ibid*.
"the date of notification"—see reg.3(2).
"family"—see reg.2(1).
"relevant benefit"—*ibid*.
"superseding decision"—see para.(1).

GENERAL NOTE

Paragraph (1)

2.879   This is equivalent to reg.6(1) of the Social Security and Child Support (Decisions and Appeals) Regulations 1999. See the note to that provision. One difference is the use of the phrase "superseding decision" instead of "supersession" but this seems to be only a matter of style.

Paragraph (2)

2.880   This is equivalent to reg.6(2)(a) to (e) of the 1999 Regulations, the other sub-paragraphs of reg.6(2) of the 1999 regulations not being relevant to child benefit or guardian's allowance.

The context, as well as a comparison with the 1999 Regulations, makes it clear that the "decision" in subpara.(b) refers only to decisions of the Board. Decisions of tribunals and Commissioners fall to be superseded on the ground of ignorance of, or mistake as to, a material fact only under subpara.(c). Subpara.(b)(ii) prevents any overlap with reg.5. In subpara.(d) "decision" also refers only to decisions of the Board, because the relevant decisions do not fall within the jurisdiction of appeal tribunals or Commissioners but, in subparas (a) and (e), "decision" includes decisions of appeal tribunals and Commissioners.

Subparagraph (e) provides for supersession only where the later decision affects entitlement under the earlier decision from a date later than the date from which the earlier decision was effective. If the later decision has effect from the date from which the earlier decision was effective, revision under reg.11 is appropriate if the earlier decision was a decision of the Board. If the earlier decision was a decision of an appeal tribunal or Commissioner, it is not clear that there will always be grounds for supersession, save under subpara.(a)(i), which is unlikely to produce the appropriate degree of backdating.

(SI 2003/916, reg.13)

A superseding decision is effective from the date it is made (s.10(5) of the Social Security Act 1998), save where reg.16 provides otherwise.
See further the note to reg.6 of the 1999 Regulations.

Procedure for making superseding decisions on an application

14.—(1) The Board may treat—
(a) an application for a revision under section 9 as an application for a decision under section 10;
(b) an application for a revision under Article 10 as an application for a decision under Article 11.

(2) Paragraph (3) applies where, in order to consider all the issues raised by an application for a superseding decision, the Board require further evidence or information from the applicant.

(3) Where this paragraph applies, the Board must notify the applicant that further evidence or information is required and—
(a) if the applicant provides further relevant evidence or information within one month of the date of notification or such longer period of time as the Board may allow, the decision to be superseded may be superseded;
(b) if the applicant does not provide such evidence or information within that period, the decision to be superseded may be superseded on the basis of the application.

DEFINITIONS

"the Board"—see reg.2(1).
"the date of notification"—see reg.3(2).
"superseding decision"—by virtue of reg.2(1), see reg.13(1).

GENERAL NOTE

Paragraph (1)

This is equivalent to reg.6(5) of the Social Security and Child Support (Decisions and Appeals) Regulations 1999. It permits an application for revision to be treated as an application for supersession. Reg.7(1) permits an application for supersession to be treated as an application for revision. See the note to s.12 of the Social Security Act 1998 for a discussion of the question whether, on appeal, a tribunal may treat a superseding decision as a refusal to revise or a revision as a refusal to supersede.

Paragraphs (2) and (3)

These are equivalent to reg.6(4) of the 1999 Regulations.

Interaction of revisions and superseding decisions

15.—(1) This regulation applies to any decision in relation to which circumstances arise in which the decision may be revised under section 9 or Article 10.

(2) A decision to which this regulation applies may not be superseded by a superseding decision unless—
(a) circumstances arise in which the Board may revise the decision in accordance with Part 2;
and

(b) further circumstances arise in relation to the decision which—
  (i) are not specified in any of the regulations in Part 2; but
  (ii) are prescribed by regulation 13(2) or are ones where a superseding decision may be made in accordance with regulation 14(3).

DEFINITIONS

"the Board"—see reg.2(1).
"superseding decision"—by virtue of reg.2(1), see reg.13(1).

GENERAL NOTE

2.885 This is equivalent to reg.6(3) of the Social Security and Child Support (Decisions and Appeals) Regulations 1999.

Date as from which superseding decisions take effect

2.886 **16.**—(1) This regulation prescribes cases or circumstances in which a superseding decision shall take effect as from a prescribed date other than the date on which it was made or, where applicable, the date on which the application for it was made.

(2) If a superseding decision is made on the basis that—
(a) there has been a relevant change of circumstances since the decision to be superseded had effect [¹ (or, in the case of an advance award, was made)]; or
(b) it is anticipated there will be such a change,
it shall take effect as from the earliest date prescribed by paragraphs (3) to (8).

(3) In any case where the superseding decision is advantageous to the claimant and notification of the change was given in accordance with any enactment or subordinate legislation under which that notification was required, the date prescribed by this paragraph is—
(a) if the notification was given within one month of the change occurring or such longer period as may be allowed under regulation 17, the date the change occurred or, if later, the first date on which the change has effect; or
(b) if the notification was given after the period mentioned in subparagraph (a), the date of notification of the change.

(4) In any case where the superseding decision is advantageous to the claimant and is made on the Board's own initiative, the date prescribed by this paragraph is the date on which the Board commenced action with a view to the supersession.

(5) In any case where the superseding decision is not advantageous to the claimant, the date prescribed by this paragraph is the date of the change.

(6) Decisions which are advantageous to claimants include those mentioned in regulation 27(5).

(7) If—
(a) the Board supersede a decision made by an appeal tribunal or a Commissioner in accordance with paragraph (i) of regulation 13(2)(c); and
(b) as a result of the ignorance or mistake referred to in that paragraph, the decision to be superseded was more advantageous to the claimant than it would otherwise have been,

the superseding decision shall take effect as from the date on which the decision of the appeal tribunal or the Commissioner took, or was to take, effect.

(8) If the Board supersede a decision made by an appeal tribunal or a Commissioner in accordance with paragraph (ii) or (iii) of regulation 13(2)(c), the superseding decision shall take effect as from the date on which it would have taken effect had it been decided in accordance with the determination of the Commissioner or the court in the appeal referred to in section 26(1)(b) or Article 26(1)(b).

(9) If a superseding decision is made in consequence of a decision which is a relevant determination for the purposes of section 27 or Article 27, it shall take effect as from the date of the relevant determination.

[^{1} (9A) Where—
(a) a Commissioner or the court determines an appeal as mentioned in section 27(1)(a) or Article 27(1)(a) ("the relevant determination") and the Board make a decision of the kind specified in section 27(1)(b) or Article 27(1)(b);
(b) there is an appeal against the relevant determination;
(c) after the Board's decision, payment is suspended in accordance with regulation 18(1) and (3)(b); and
(d) on appeal the court reverses the relevant determination in whole or in part,

a consequential decision by the Board under section 10 or Article 11 which supersedes the earlier decision referred to in sub-paragraph (a) above shall take effect from the date on which that earlier decision took effect.

In this paragraph "the court" has the meaning given in section 27 or Article 27 (as the case requires).]

(10) If the Board supersede a decision in accordance with subparagraph (e) of regulation 13(2), the superseding decision shall take effect as from the date on which entitlement arises—
(a) to the other relevant benefit referred to in paragraph (ii) of that sub-paragraph; or
(b) to an increase in the rate of that benefit.

AMENDMENT

1. Child Benefit and Guardian's Allowance (Miscellaneous Amendments) Regulations 2005 (SI 2005/343), reg.5 (March 18, 2005).

DEFINITIONS

"appeal tribunal"—see reg.2(1).
"the Board"—*ibid*.
"claimant"—*ibid*.
"Commissioner"—*ibid*.
"prescribed"—see s.84 of the Social Security Act 1998.
"relevant benefit"—see reg.2(1).
"superseding decision"—by virtue of reg.2(1), see reg.13(1).

GENERAL NOTE

This is equivalent to reg.7(1) to (7) and (33) of the Social Security and Child Support (Decisions and Appeals) Regulations 1999. See the notes to reg.7 of the 1999 Regulations. (The other provisions of reg.7 of the 1999 Regulations have no relevance to child benefit or guardian's allowance.)

2.887

Effective date for late notifications of change of circumstances

17.—(1) For the purposes of paragraph (3) of regulation 16, the Board may allow a longer period of time than the period of one month mentioned in sub-paragraph (a) of that paragraph for the notification of a change of circumstances if the first and second conditions are satisfied.

(2) The first condition is that an application for the purposes of regulation 16(3) must be made by the claimant or a person acting on his behalf.

(3) The second condition is that the application for the purposes of regulation 16(3) must—
   (a) contain particulars of the relevant change of circumstances and the reasons for the failure to notify the change on an earlier date; and
   (b) be made within 13 months of the date on which the change occurred.

(4) An application under this regulation must not be granted unless the Board are satisfied that—
   (a) it is reasonable to grant it;
   (b) the change of circumstances notified by the applicant is relevant to the decision which is to be superseded; and
   (c) special circumstances are relevant to the application as a result of which it was not practicable for the applicant to notify the change of circumstances within one month of the change occurring.

(5) In determining whether it is reasonable to grant an application for the purposes of regulation 16(3), the Board must have regard to the principle that the greater the amount of time that has elapsed between the date one month after the change of circumstances occurred and the date the application is made, the more compelling the special circumstances mentioned in paragraph (4)(c) should be.

(6) In determining whether it is reasonable to grant an application for the purposes of regulation 16(3), the Board must take no account of the following—
   (a) that the applicant or any person acting for him was unaware of, or misunderstood, the law applicable to his case (including being unaware of, or misunderstanding, the time limits imposed by these Regulations); or
   (b) that a Commissioner or a court has taken a different view of the law from that previously understood and applied.

(7) An application for the purposes of regulation 16(3) which has been refused may not be renewed.

DEFINITIONS

"the Board"—see reg.2(1).
"claimant"—*ibid*.
"Commissioner"—*ibid*.

GENERAL NOTE

This is equivalent to reg.8 of the Social Security and Child Support (Decisions and Appeals) Regulations 1999.

(SI 2003/916, reg.18)

Part 4

Suspension and Termination

Suspension in prescribed cases

18.—(1) The Board may suspend payment of child benefit or guardian's allowance, in whole or in part, in the circumstances prescribed by paragraph (2) or (3).

(2) The circumstances prescribed by this paragraph are circumstances where it appears to the Board that—
  (a) an issue arises as to whether the conditions for entitlement to the benefit or allowance are or were fulfilled;
  (b) an issue arises as to whether a decision relating to an award of the benefit or allowance should be—
    (i) revised under section 9 or Article 10; or
    (ii) superseded under section 10 or Article 11;
  (c) an issue arises as to whether any amount paid or payable to a person by way of, or in connection with a claim for, the benefit or allowance is recoverable under—
    (i) section 71 of the Administration Act;
    (ii) section 69 of the Administration (NI) Act; or
    (iii) regulations made under either of those sections;
  (d) the last address notified to them of a person who is in receipt of the benefit or allowance is not the address at which that person is residing; or
  (e) the details of a bank account or other account which has been notified to them and to which payment of the benefit or allowance by way of a credit is to be made to a person are incorrect.

(3) The circumstances prescribed by this paragraph are where—
  (a) an appeal is pending against a decision of an appeal tribunal, a Commissioner or a court; or
  (b) an appeal is pending against a decision given in a different case by a Commissioner or a court (whether or not relating to child benefit or guardian's allowance) and it appears to the Board that, if the appeal were to be determined in a particular way, an issue would arise as to whether the award of child benefit or guardian's allowance should be revised or superseded.

(4) For the purposes of section 21(3)(c) and Article 21(3)(c), the prescribed circumstances are circumstances where an appeal tribunal, a Commissioner or a court has made a decision and the Board—
  (a) are awaiting receipt of the decision or, in the case of an appeal tribunal decision, are considering whether to apply for a statement of the reasons for it;
  (b) in the case of an appeal tribunal decision, have applied for, and are awaiting receipt of, such a statement; or
  (c) have received the decision, or, in the case of an appeal tribunal decision, such a statement, and are considering—
    (i) whether to apply for leave to appeal; or
    (ii) where leave to appeal has been granted, whether to appeal.

2.890

(5) In the circumstances prescribed by paragraph (4), the Board must give written notice, as soon as reasonably practicable, to the person in respect of whom payment has been or is to be suspended of their proposal—
- (a) to make a request for a statement of the reasons for an appeal tribunal decision;
- (b) to apply for leave to appeal; or
- (c) to appeal.

DEFINITIONS

"the Administration Act"—see reg.2(1).
"the Administration (NI) Act"—*ibid*.
"appeal tribunal"—*ibid*.
"the Board"—*ibid*.
"Commissioner"—*ibid*.
"prescribed"—see s.84 of the Social Security Act 1998.

Provision of information or evidence

2.891 **19.**—(1) This regulation applies where the Board require information or evidence for a determination whether a decision awarding child benefit or guardian's allowance should be—
- (a) revised under section 9 or Article 10; or
- (b) superseded under section 10 or Article 11.

(2) A person to whom this paragraph applies must—
- (a) supply the information or evidence within—
   - (i) the period of one month beginning with the date on which the notification under paragraph (4) was sent to him; or
   - (ii) such longer period as he satisfies the Board is necessary in order to enable him to comply with the requirement; or
- (b) satisfy the Board within the period of time specified in subparagraph (a)(i) that—
   - (i) the information or evidence required of him does not exist; or
   - (ii) it is not possible for him to obtain it.

(3) A person to whom paragraph (2) applies is any of the following—
- (a) a person in respect of whom payment of the benefit or allowance has been suspended in the circumstances prescribed by regulation 18(2);
- (b) a person who has made an application for the decision to be revised or superseded;
- (c) a person who fails to comply with the provisions of regulation 23 of the Administration Regulations in so far as they relate to information, facts or evidence required by the Board.

(4) The Board must notify a person to whom paragraph (2) applies of the requirements of that paragraph.

(5) The Board may suspend the payment of benefit or allowance, in whole or in part, to a person falling within paragraph (3)(b) or (c) who fails to satisfy the requirements of paragraph (2).

DEFINITIONS

"the Administration Regulations"—see reg.2(1).
"the Board"—*ibid*.

(SI 2003/916, reg.20)

Termination in cases of failure to furnish information or evidence

20.—(1) Subject to paragraph (3), this regulation applies where—
(a) a person whose benefit or allowance has been suspended under regulation 18 subsequently fails to comply with a requirement for information or evidence under regulation 19 and more than one month has elapsed since the requirement was made; or
(b) a person's benefit or allowance has been suspended under regulation 19(5) and more than one month has elapsed since the first payment was so suspended.

(2) The Board must decide that the person ceases to be entitled to the benefit or allowance from the date on which payment was suspended except where entitlement to the benefit or allowance ceases on an earlier date.

(3) This regulation does not apply where benefit or allowance has been suspended in part under regulation 18 or 19.

DEFINITION

"the Board"—see reg.2(1).

Making of payments which have been suspended

21.—(1) Payment of benefit or allowance suspended in accordance with regulation 18 or 19 must be made in any of the circumstances prescribed by paragraphs (2) to (5).

(2) The circumstances prescribed by this paragraph are circumstances where—
(a) in a case to which regulation 18(2)(a), (b) or (c) applies, the Board are satisfied that—
  (i) the benefit or allowance suspended is properly payable; and
  (ii) no outstanding issues remain to be resolved;
(b) in a case to which regulation 18(2)(d) applies, the Board are satisfied that they have been notified of the address at which the person is residing;
(c) in a case to which regulation 18(2)(e) applies, the Board are satisfied that they have been notified of the correct details of the bank account or other account to which payment of the benefit or allowance by way of a credit is to be made to the person.

(3) The circumstances prescribed by this paragraph are circumstances where, in a case to which regulation 18(3)(a) applies, the Board—
(a) in the case of a decision of an appeal tribunal, do not apply for a statement of the reasons for that decision within the period of one month specified in—
  (i) in relation to child benefit and guardian's allowance under the Contributions and Benefits Act, regulation 53(4) of the Decisions and Appeals Regulations;
  (ii) in relation to child benefit and guardian's allowance under the Contributions and Benefits (NI) Act, regulation 53(4) of the Decisions and Appeals Regulations (NI);
(b) in the case of a decision of an appeal tribunal, a Commissioner or a court—
  (i) do not make an application for leave to appeal within the time prescribed for the making of such an application; or

(ii) where leave to appeal is granted, do not make the appeal within the time prescribed for the making of it;
(c) withdraw an application for leave to appeal or the appeal; or
(d) are refused leave to appeal in circumstances where it is not open to them to renew the application, or to make a further application, for such leave.

(4) The circumstances prescribed by this paragraph are circumstances where, in a case to which regulation 18(3)(b) applies, the Board, in relation to the decision of the Commissioner or the court in the different case—
(a) do not make an application for leave to appeal within the time prescribed for the making of such an application;
(b) where leave to appeal is granted, do not make the appeal within the time prescribed for the making of it;
(c) withdraw an application for leave to appeal or the appeal; or
(d) are refused leave to appeal in circumstances where it is not open to them to renew the application, or to make a further application, for such leave.

(5) The circumstances prescribed by this paragraph are circumstances where, in a case to which paragraph (5) of regulation 19 applies, the Board are satisfied that—
(a) the benefit or allowance suspended is properly payable; and
(b) the requirements of paragraph (2) of that regulation have been satisfied.

DEFINITIONS

"appeal tribunal"—see reg.2(1).
"the Board"—*ibid*.
"Commissioner"—*ibid*.
"the Contributions and Benefits Act"—*ibid*.
"the Contributions and Benefits (NI) Act"—*ibid*.
"the Decisions and Appeals Regulations"—*ibid*.
"the Decisions and Appeals (NI) Regulations"—*ibid*.

PART 5

OTHER MATTERS

Decisions involving issues that arise on appeal in other cases

2.894

22.—(1) A case which satisfies the condition specified in paragraph (2) is a prescribed case for the purposes of section 25(3)(b) and Article 25(3)(b) (prescribed cases and circumstances in which a decision may be made on a prescribed basis).

(2) The condition specified in this paragraph is that the claimant would be entitled to the benefit or allowance to which the decision which falls to be made relates, even if the appeal in the other case referred to in section 25(1)(b) or Article 25(1)(b) were decided in a way which is the most unfavourable to him.

(3) For the purposes of subsection (3)(b) of section 25 and paragraph (3)(b) of Article 25, the prescribed basis on which the Board may make the decision is as if—

(a) the appeal in the other case which is referred to in subsection (1)(b) of that section, or paragraph (1)(b) of that Article, had already been determined; and
(b) that appeal had been decided in a way which is the most unfavourable to the claimant.

(4) For the purposes of subsection (5)(c) of section 25 and paragraph (5)(c) of Article 25 (prescribed circumstances in which, for the purposes of the section or the Article, an appeal is pending against a decision), the prescribed circumstances are circumstances where the Board—
(a) certify in writing that they are considering appealing against that decision; and
(b) consider that, if such an appeal were to be determined in a particular way—
    (i) there would be no entitlement to the benefit or allowance in a case to which subsection (1)(a) of that section, or paragraph (1)(a) of that Article, refers; or
    (ii) the appeal would affect the decision in that case in some other way.

DEFINITIONS

"the Board"—see reg.2(1).
"claimant"—*ibid*.
"prescribed"—see s.84 of the Social Security Act 1998.

Appeals involving issues that arise on appeal in other cases

23. For the purposes of subsection (6)(c) of section 26 and paragraph (6)(c) of Article 26 (prescribed circumstances in which an appeal against a decision which has not been brought, or an application for leave to appeal has not been made, but the time for so doing has not yet expired, is pending for the purposes of the section or the Article), the prescribed circumstances are circumstances where the Board—
(a) certify in writing that they are considering appealing against that decision; and
(b) consider that, if such an appeal were already determined, it would affect the determination of the appeal described in subsection (1)(a) of that section or paragraph (1)(a) of that Article.

DEFINITION

"the Board"—see reg.2(1).

PART 6

RIGHTS OF APPEAL AND PROCEDURE FOR BRINGING APPEALS

Other persons with a right of appeal

24. For the purposes of section 12(2) and Article 13(2), the following persons are prescribed—

(a) any person appointed by the Board under regulation 28(1) of the Administration Regulations to act on behalf of another who is unable to act;
(b) any person appointed by the Board under regulation 29(1) of those regulations to proceed with the claim of a person who has made a claim for benefit or allowance and subsequently died;
(c) any person who, having been appointed by the Board under paragraph (2) of regulation 31 of those regulations to claim on behalf of a deceased person, makes a claim in accordance with that regulation.

DEFINITIONS

"the Administration Regulations"—see reg.2(1).
"prescribed"—see s.84 of the Social Security Act 1998.

GENERAL NOTE

2.897 See the note to reg.25 of the Social Security and Child Support (Decisions and Appeals) Regulations 1999.

Decisions against which no appeal lies

2.898 **25.**—(1) Subject to paragraph (2), for the purposes of section 12(2) and Article 13(2), the decisions set out in Schedule 2 are prescribed as decisions against which no appeal lies to an appeal tribunal.
(2) Paragraph (1) shall not have the effect of prescribing any decision that relates to the conditions of entitlement to child benefit or guardian's allowance for which a claim has been validly made or for which no claim is required.
(3) In this regulation and Schedule 2, "decision" includes any determination embodied in or necessary to a decision.

DEFINITIONS

"appeal tribunal"—see reg.2(1).
"prescribed"—see s.84 of the Social Security Act 1998.

GENERAL NOTE

2.899 Paragraph (2) reiterates what is said in s.12(3) of the Social Security Act 1998. As para.9 of Sch.2 to the Act is not listed among the powers exercised in making these Regulations (see Sch.1), Sch.2 to these Regulations must be made under s.12. For the implication of that, see the note to Sch.2 to the Social Security and Child Support (Decisions and Appeals) Regulations 1999.

Notice of decision against which appeal lies

2.900 **26.**—(1) A person with a right of appeal under the 1998 Act, the 1998 Order or these Regulations against a decision of the Board must—
(a) be given written notice of the decision against which the appeal lies;
(b) be informed that, in a case where that written notice does not include a statement of the reasons for that decision, he may, within one month of the date of notification of that decision, request that the Board provide him with a written statement of the reasons for that decision; and
(c) be given written notice of his right of appeal against that decision.

(SI 2003/916, reg.26)

(2) If the Board are requested under paragraph (1)(b) to provide a written statement of the reasons for the decision, they [¹ shall provide the statement within 14 days of receipt of the request or as soon as practicable afterwards].

AMENDMENT

1. Child Benefit and Guardian's Allowance (Miscellaneous Amendments) Regulations 2005 (SI 2005/343), reg.6 (March 18, 2005).

DEFINITIONS

"the 1998 Act"—see reg.2(1).
"the Board"—*ibid.*
"the 1998 Order"—*ibid.*

GENERAL NOTE

See the note to reg.28 of the Social Security and Child Support (Decisions and Appeals) Regulations 1999.

2.901

Appeals against decisions which have been revised

27.—(1) This regulation applies where—

2.902

(a) a decision—
  (i) under section 8 or 10 is revised under section 9; or
  (ii) under Article 9 or 11 is revised under Article 10, before an appeal against that decision is determined; and
(b) the decision as revised is not more advantageous to the appellant than the decision before it was revised.

(2) The appeal shall not lapse and is to be treated as though it had been brought against the decision as revised.

(3) The appellant shall have a period of one month from the date of notification of the decision as revised to make further representations as to the appeal.

(4) After the expiration of the period specified in paragraph (3), or within that period if the appellant consents in writing, the appeal shall proceed unless, in the light of the further representations from the appellant, the Board further revise their decision and that decision is more advantageous to the appellant than the decision before it was revised.

(5) Decisions which are more advantageous to the appellant include those in consequence of which—

(a) child benefit or guardian's allowance paid to him is greater or is awarded for a longer period;
(b) the amount of benefit or allowance in payment would have been greater but for the operation of—
  (i) any provision of the Administration Act or the Administration (NI) Act; or
  (ii) any provision of the Contributions and Benefits Act, or any provision of the Contributions and Benefits (NI) Act, restricting or suspending the payment of, or disqualifying a claimant from receiving, some or all of the benefit or allowance;
(c) a denial or disqualification for the receiving of benefit or allowance is lifted wholly or in part;
(d) a decision to pay benefit or allowance to a third party is reversed;

(e) benefit or allowance paid is not recoverable under—
   (i) section 71 of the Administration Act or section 69 of the Administration (NI) Act; or
   (ii) regulations made under either of those sections;
(f) the amount of benefit or allowance paid which is recoverable as mentioned in sub-paragraph (e) is reduced; or
(g) a financial gain accrues or will accrue to the appellant in consequence of the decision.

DEFINITIONS

"the Administration Act"—see reg.2(1).
"the Administration (NI) Act"—*ibid*.
"the Board"—*ibid*.
"claimant"—*ibid*.
"the Contributions and Benefits Act"—*ibid*.
"the Contributions and Benefits (NI) Act"—*ibid*.
"the date of notification"—see reg.3(2).
"writing"—see reg.2(1).

GENERAL NOTE

2.903   Like reg.30 of the Social Security and Child Support (Decisions and Appeals) Regulations 1999, this provides an exception to the general rule that an appeal lapses when the decision under appeal is revised (see s.9(6) of the Social Security Act 1998 and the note to s.9(5)).

Time within which an appeal is to be brought.

2.904   **28.**—(1) Subject to the following provisions of this Part, where an appeal lies from a decision of the Board to an appeal tribunal, the time within which that appeal must be brought is—
(a) within one month of the date of notification of the decision against which the appeal is brought;
(b) if a written statement of the reasons for that decision is requested and provided within the period mentioned in sub-paragraph (a), within 14 days of the expiry of that period; or
(c) if a written statement of the reasons for that decision is requested but is not provided within the period mentioned in sub-paragraph (a), within 14 days of the date on which the statement is provided.
(2) If the Board—
(a) revise a decision under section 9 or Article 10;
(b) make a superseding decision; or
(c) following an application for a revision [¹ under regulation 5], do not revise a decision under section 9 or Article 10,
the period of one month specified in paragraph (1) shall begin to run from the date of notification of the revision or supersession or the date the Board issue a notice that they are not revising the decision.
(3) If a dispute arises as to whether an appeal was brought within the time limit specified in this regulation, the dispute must be referred to, and be determined by, a legally qualified panel member.
(4) The time limit specified in this regulation for bringing an appeal may be extended in accordance with regulation 29.

(SI 2003/916, reg.28)

AMENDMENT

1. Child Benefit and Guardian's Allowance (Decisions and Appeals) (Amendment) Regulations 2004 (SI 2004/3377), reg.2(2) (December 21, 2004).

DEFINITIONS

"appeal tribunal"—see reg.2(1).
"the Board"—*ibid.*
"the date of notification"—see reg.3(2).
"legally qualified panel member"—see reg.2(1).
"superseding decision"—by virtue of reg.2(1), see reg.13(1).

GENERAL NOTE

This is equivalent to reg.31 of the Social Security and Child Support (Decisions and Appeals) Regulations 1999. The amendment deliberately introduces the anomaly, identified in *R(IS) 15/04* (subsequently approved by the Court of Appeal in *Beltekian v Westminster City Council* [2004] EWCA Civ 1784 (reported as *R(H) 8/05*)) in the context of reg.31 of the 1999 Regulations, that a refusal to revise where the application for revision was made otherwise than under reg.5 is not appealable if the decision being revised was given more than thirteen months earlier. The justification that has been advanced is that the claimant will have had more than thirteen months in which to challenge the original decision. Consistency with that argument would suggest that, say, "official error" should be a ground of supersession with limited backdating. It is also odd that there is a right of appeal where it is said that a revision does not lead to a high enough award but there is no right of appeal if there is a refusal to revise at all.

Late appeals

29.—(1) The time within which an appeal must be brought may be extended in accordance with this regulation, but no appeal shall in any event be brought more than one year after the expiration of the last day for appealing under regulation 28.

(2) An application for an extension of time under this regulation must—
 (a) be made in accordance with regulation 31; and
 (b) be determined by a legally qualified panel member except where the Board consider that the application satisfies paragraph (5)(b).

(3) If the Board consider that an application under this regulation satisfies paragraph (5)(b), they may grant it.

(4) An application under this regulation must contain particulars of the grounds on which the extension of time is sought, including details of any relevant special circumstances specified in regulation 30(2).

(5) An application under this regulation must not be granted unless-
 (a) the panel member is satisfied that if the application is granted, there are reasonable prospects that the appeal will be successful; or
 (b) the panel member is satisfied, or the Board are satisfied, that it is in the interests of justice for the application to be granted (see generally regulation 30).

(6) An application under this regulation which has been refused may not be renewed.

(7) The panel member who determines an application under this regulation must record a summary of his decision in such written form as has been approved by the President.

2.905

2.906

(8) "The President" means—
(a) in relation to child benefit or guardian's allowance under the Contributions and Benefits Act, the President of appeals tribunals appointed under section 5;
(b) in relation to child benefit or guardian's allowance under the Contributions and Benefits (NI) Act, the President of appeals tribunals appointed under Article 6.

(9) As soon as practicable after the decision is made a copy of the decision must be sent or given to every party to the proceedings.

DEFINITIONS

"the Board"—see reg.2(1).
"the Contributions and Benefits Act"—*ibid*.
"the Contributions and Benefits (NI) Act"—*ibid*.
"legally qualified panel member"—*ibid*.
"the President"—see para.(8).

GENERAL NOTE

2.907 This is equivalent to reg.32(1) to (4) and (9) to (11) of the Social Security and Child Support (Decisions and Appeals) Regulations 1999. See reg.30 for provisions equivalent to reg.32(5) to (8) of the 1999 Regulations.

Paragraph (3)
2.908 See the note to reg.32(2) of the 1999 Regulations.

Interests of justice

2.909 **30.**—(1) For the purposes of paragraph (5)(b) of regulation 29, it is not in the interests of justice to grant an application under that regulation unless the panel member is satisfied, or the Board are satisfied, that—
(a) the special circumstances specified in paragraph (2) are relevant to the application; or
(b) some other special circumstances exist which are wholly exceptional and relevant to the application,
and, as a result of those special circumstances, it was not practicable for the appeal to be brought within the time limit specified in regulation 28.

(2) The special circumstances specified in this paragraph are that—
(a) the applicant or a partner or dependant of the applicant has died or suffered serious illness;
(b) the applicant is not resident in the United Kingdom; or
(c) normal postal services were disrupted.

(3) "Partner" means—
(a) where a person is a member of a married couple or an unmarried couple, the other member of that couple; or
(b) where a person is polygamously married to two or more members of his household, any such member.

(4) In determining whether it is in the interests of justice to grant an application under regulation 29, the panel member or the Board must have regard to the principle that the greater the amount of time that has elapsed between the expiration of the time within which the appeal is to be brought under regulation 28 and the making of the application, the more

compelling the special circumstances mentioned in paragraph (1) should be.

(5) In determining whether it is in the interests of justice to grant an application under regulation 29, the panel member or the Board must take no account of the following—
  (a) that the applicant or any person acting for him was unaware of or misunderstood the law applicable to his case (including ignorance or misunderstanding of the time limits imposed by these Regulations); or
  (b) that a Commissioner or a court has taken a different view of the law from that previously understood and applied.

DEFINITIONS

"the Board"—see reg.2(1).
"Commissioner"—*ibid.*
"partner"— see para.(3).

GENERAL NOTE

This is equivalent to reg.32(5) to (8) of the Social Security and Child Support (Decisions and Appeals) Regulations 1999.

2.910

Paragraph (5)
See the notes to reg.32(8) of the 1999 Regulations.

2.911

Making of appeals and applications

31.—(1) Subject to the following provisions of this regulation, an appeal, or an application for an extension of time for making an appeal, to an appeal tribunal must—
  (a) be in writing—
    (i) on a form approved for the purpose by the Board ("the approved form"); or
    (ii) in such other format as the Board may accept as sufficient for the purpose;
  (b) be signed by—
    (i) the person who has a right of appeal under section 12(2) or Article 13(2); or
    (ii) if that person has provided written authority to a representative to act on his behalf, that representative;
  (c) be sent or delivered to an appropriate office;
  (d) contain particulars of the grounds on which it is made; and
  (e) contain sufficient particulars of the decision or the subject of the application, to enable that decision or subject to be identified.

(2) An approved form which is not completed in accordance with the instructions on it—
  (a) subject to paragraph (3), does not satisfy the requirements of paragraph (1), and
  (b) may be returned by the Board to the sender for completion in accordance with those instructions.

(3) If the Board are satisfied that an approved form, although not completed in accordance with the instructions on it, includes sufficient

2.912

information to enable the appeal or application to proceed, they may treat it as satisfying the requirements of paragraph (1).

(4) If an appeal or application made in writing otherwise than on the approved form includes sufficient information to enable the appeal or application to proceed, the Board may treat it as satisfying the requirements of paragraph (1).

(5) If an appeal or application made in writing otherwise than on the approved form does not include sufficient information to enable the appeal or application to proceed, the Board may request further information in writing from the appellant or applicant.

(6) If an appellant or applicant to whom an approved form is returned, or from whom further information is requested, duly completes and returns the form or sends the further information and that form or further information is received by the Board—
- (a) within 14 days of the date on which the form was returned to him by them, the time for making the appeal shall be extended by 14 days from the date on which the form was returned;
- (b) within 14 days of the date on which the further information was requested by them, the time for making the appeal shall be extended by 14 days from the date of the request;
- (c) within such longer period as they may direct, the time for making the appeal shall be extended by a period equal to that longer period.

(7) If an appellant or applicant to whom an approved form is returned, or from whom further information is requested, does not complete and return the form or send further information within the period of time specified in paragraph (6), the Board must forward a copy of the appeal or application, together with any other relevant documents or evidence, to a legally qualified panel member who must—
- (a) determine whether the appeal or application satisfies the requirement of paragraph (1), and
- (b) inform the appellant or applicant and the Board of his determination.

(8) If—
- (a) an approved form is duly completed and returned or further information is sent after the expiry of the period of time specified in paragraph (6); and
- (b) no determination has been made under paragraph (7) at the time the form or the further information is received by the Board,

the Board must forward the duly completed form or further information to the legally qualified panel member who must take into account any further information or evidence set out in that form or the further information.

DEFINITIONS

"appeal tribunal"—see reg.2(1).
"appropriate office"—*ibid*.
"the approved form"—see para.(1)(a)(i).
"the Board"—see reg.2(1).
"legally qualified panel member"—*ibid*.

GENERAL NOTE

2.913 This is equivalent to reg.33(1) to (9) of the Social Security and Child Support (Decisions and Appeals) Regulations 1999.

(SI 2003/916, reg.32)

Discontinuing action on appeals

32. The Board may discontinue action on an appeal to an appeal tribunal if—
   (a) the appeal has not been forwarded to the clerk to an appeal tribunal or to a legally qualified panel member; and
   (b) the appellant or an authorised representative of the appellant has given written notice that he does not wish the appeal to continue.

DEFINITIONS

"appeal tribunal"—see reg.2(1).
"the Board"—*ibid*.
"clerk to the appeal tribunal"—*ibid*.
"legally qualified panel member"—*ibid*.

GENERAL NOTE

This is equivalent to reg.33(10) of the Social Security and Child Support (Decisions and Appeals) Regulations 1999.

Death of a party to an appeal

33.—(1) In any proceedings, on the death of a party to those proceedings (other than a member of the Board), the Board may appoint such person as they think fit to proceed with the appeal in the place of such deceased party.

(2) A grant of probate, confirmation or letters of administration to the estate of the deceased party, whenever taken out, shall have no effect on an appointment made under paragraph (1).

(3) If a person appointed under paragraph (1) has, prior to the date of such appointment, taken any action in relation to the appeal on behalf of the deceased party, the effective date of appointment by the Board shall be the day immediately prior to the first day on which such action was taken.

DEFINITION

"the Board"—see reg.2(1).

GENERAL NOTE

This is equivalent to reg.34 of the Social Security and Child Support (Decisions and Appeals) Regulations 1999.

Part VII

Revocations, Transitional Provisions and Consequential Amendments

Revocations

34. The following provisions are hereby revoked—
(a) in so far as they relate to child benefit or guardian's allowance under the Contributions and Benefits Act, Parts 2, 3 and 4 of, and Schedule 2 to, the Decisions and Appeals Regulations;
(b) in so far as they relate to child benefit or guardian's allowance under the Contributions and Benefits (NI) Act, Parts 2, 3 and 4 of, and Schedule 1 to, the Decisions and Appeals Regulations (NI).

DEFINITIONS

"the Contributions and Benefits Act"—see reg.2(1).
"the Contributions and Benefits (NI) Act"—*ibid.*
"the Decisions and Appeals Regulations"—*ibid.*
"the decision and Appeals (NI) Regulations"—*ibid.*

Transitional provisions

35. Anything done or commenced under any provision revoked by regulation 34, so far as relating to child benefit or guardian's allowance, is to be treated as having been done or as being continued under the corresponding provision of these Regulations.

36. *Omitted.*
37. *Omitted.*

SCHEDULE 1   **Preamble**

POWERS EXERCISED IN MAKING THESE REGULATIONS

1. Section 5(1)(hh) of the Administration Act.
2. Section 5(1)(hh) of the Administration (NI) Act.
3. The following provisions of the 1998 Act—
(a) section 9(1), (4) and (6);
(b) section 10(3) and (6);
(c) section 12(2), (3), (6) and (7);
(d) section 16(1) and paragraphs 1 to 4 and 6 of Schedule 5;
(e) section 21;
(f) section 22;
(g) section 23;
(h) section 25(3)(b) and (5)(c);
(i) section 26(6)(c);
(j) section 79(1), (2A) and (4) to (7);
(k) section 84.
4. The following provisions of the 1998 Order—
(a) Article 2(2);
(b) Article 10(1), (4) and (6);
(c) Article 11(3) and (6);
(d) Article 13(2), (3), (6) and (7);
(e) Article 16(1) and paragraphs 1 to 4 and 6 of Schedule 4;
(f) Article 21;

(g) Article 22;
(h) Article 23;
(i) Article 25(3)(b) and (5)(c);
(j) Article 26(6)(c);
(k) Article 74(1) and (3) to (6).

5. Sections 132 and 133(1) and (2) of the Finance Act 1999. 2.926
6. The following provisions of the Tax Credits Act 2002— 2.927
   (a) section 50(1) and (2)(e) and (f);
   (b) section 54(2);
   (c) paragraphs 15 and 19 of Schedule 4.

DEFINITIONS

"the 1998 Act"—see reg.2(1).
"the Administration Act"—*ibid.*
"the Administration (NI) Act"—*ibid.*
"the 1998 Order"—*ibid.*

SCHEDULE 2 Regulation 25

DECISIONS AGAINST WHICH NO APPEAL LIES

PART I

DECISIONS MADE UNDER PRIMARY LEGISLATION

1. A decision of the Board whether to recognise, for the purposes of Part 9 of the Contributions and Benefits Act or Part 10 of the Contributions and Benefits (NI) Act— 2.928
   (a) an educational establishment; or
   (b) education provided otherwise than at a recognised educational establishment.
2. A decision of the Board whether to pay expenses to any person under— 2.929
   (a) sections 180 and 180A of the Administration Act; or
   (b) section 156 of the Administration (NI) Act.
3. A decision of the Treasury relating to the up-rating of child benefit or guardian's allowance under— 2.930
   (a) Part 10 of the Administration Act; or
   (b) Part 9 of the Administration (NI) Act.
4. A decision of the Board under— 2.931
   (a) section 25 or 26; or
   (b) Article 25 or 26.

PART II

DECISIONS MADE UNDER SECONDARY LEGISLATION

5. A decision of the Board relating to— 2.932
   (a) the suspension of child benefit or allowance under Part 4; or
   (b) the payment of such a benefit or allowance which has been so suspended.
6. A decision of the Board under any of the following provisions of the Administration Regulations— 2.933
   (a) [1 . . .]
   (b) regulation 7 (decision as to evidence and information required);
   (c) [1 . . .]
   (d) regulation 11 (decision as to claims for child benefit treated as claims for guardian's allowance and vice versa);
   (e) regulation 18 (decision as to the time of payments);
   (f) regulation 19 (decision as to elections to have child benefit paid weekly);
   (g) regulation 23 (decision as to information to be given);
   (h) regulation 26 (decision as to extinguishment of right to payment if payment is not obtained within the prescribed period) other than a decision under paragraph (5) (decision as to payment request after expiration of prescribed period);
   (i) regulation 28 (decision as to appointments where person unable to act);

Child Benefit & Guardian's Allowance (Decisions & Appeals) Regs 2003

  (j) regulations 29 to 32 (decisions as to claims or payments after death of claimant);
  (k) regulation 33 (decision as to paying a person on behalf of another);
  (l) regulation 34 (decision as to paying partner as alternative payee);
  (m) Part 5 other than a decision under—
    (i) regulation 35(1) (decision as to whether a payment in excess of entitlement has been credited to a bank or other account);
    (ii) regulation 37 (decision as to the sums to be deducted in calculating recoverable amounts);
    (iii) regulation 38 (decision as to the offsetting of a prior payment of child benefit or guardian's allowance against arrears of child benefit or guardian's allowance payable by virtue of a subsequent determination);
    (iv) regulation 39 (decision as to the offsetting of a prior payment of income support or jobseeker's allowance against arrears of child benefit or guardian's allowance payable by virtue of a subsequent determination);
    (v) regulation 41(1) (decision as to bringing interim payments into account);
    (vi) regulation 42(1) (decision as to the overpayment of an interim payment).

2.934 7. A decision of the Board made in accordance with the discretion conferred upon them by the following regulations of the Child Benefit (General) Regulations 2003—
  (a) regulation 4(1) or (4) (provisions relating to contributions and expenses in respect of a child);
  (b) regulation 24(1)(c) or 28(1)(c) (decisions relating to a child's temporary absence abroad).

2.935 8. A decision of the Board relating to the giving of a notice under regulation 8(2) of the Guardian's Allowance (General) Regulations 2003 (children whose surviving parents are in prison or legal custody).

2.936 9. A decision of the Board made in accordance with an Order made under—
  (a) section 179 of the Administration Act (reciprocal agreements with countries outside the United Kingdom); or
  (b) section 155 of the Administration (NI) Act (reciprocal agreements with countries outside the United Kingdom).

Part III

Other Decisions

2.937 10. An authorization given by the Board in accordance with Article 22(1) or 55(1) of Council Regulation (EEC) No.1408/71 on the application of social security schemes to employed persons, to self-employed persons and to members of their families moving within the Community.

Amendments

1. Child Benefit and Guardian's Allowance (Decisions and Appeals) (Amendment) Regulations 2004 (SI 2004/3377), reg.2(3) (December 21, 2004).

Definitions

  "the Administration Act"—see reg.2(1).
  "the Administration (NI) Act"—*ibid.*
  "the Administration Regulations"—*ibid.*
  "the Board"—*ibid.*
  "the Contributions and Benefits Act"—*ibid.*
  "the Contributions and Benefits (NI) Act"—*ibid.*

General Note

2.938 See the notes to reg.25 of these Regulations and Sch.2 to the Social Security and Child Support (Decisions and Appeals) Regulations 1999.

PART III

EUROPEAN COMMUNITY LAW

European Communities Act 1972

(1972 C.28) (AS AMENDED)

ARRANGEMENT OF SECTIONS REPRODUCED

1. Short title and interpretation
2. General implementation of Treaties
3. Decisions on, and proof of, Treaties and Community instruments, etc.

PART I

GENERAL PROVISIONS

Short title and interpretation

1.—(1) This Act may be cited as the European Communities Act 1972.
(2) In this Act [¹ . . .]—
"the Communities" means the European Economic Community, the European Coal and Steel Community and the European Atomic Energy Community;
"the Treaties" or "the Community Treaties" means, subject to subsection (3) below, the pre-accession treaties, that is to say, those described in Part I of Schedule 1 to this Act, taken with—
 (a) the treaty relating to the accession of the United Kingdom to the European Economic Community and to the European Atomic Energy Community, signed at Brussels on the 22nd January 1972; and
 (b) the decision, of the same date, of the Council of the European Communities relating to the accession of the United Kingdom to the European Coal and Steel Community; [² and
 (c) the treaty relating to the accession of the Hellenic Republic to the European Economic Community and to the European Atomic Energy Community, signed at Athens on 28th May 1979; and
 (d) the decision, of 24th May 1979, of the Council relating to the accession of the Hellenic Republic to the European Coal and Steel Community;] [³ and
 (e) the decisions of the Council of 7th May 1985, 24th June 1988, [¹¹ . . .] 31st October 1994, [¹¹ and 29th September 2000,] on the Communities' system of own resources; and]
 (f) [³ . . .]; [⁴ and
 (g) the treaty relating to the accession of the Kingdom of Spain and the Portuguese Republic to the European Economic Community and to the European Atomic Energy Community, signed at Lisbon and Madrid on 12th June 1985; and

(h) the decision, of 11th June 1985, of the Council relating to the accession of the Kingdom of Spain and the Portuguese Republic to the European Coal and Steel Community;] [and
(i) [^{1} ...]; [^{5} and
(j) the following provisions of the Single European Act signed at Luxembourg and The Hague on 17th and 28th February 1986, namely Title II (amendment of the treaties establishing the Communities) and, so far as they relate to any of the Communities or any Community institution, the preamble and Titles I (common provisions) and IV (general and final provisions);] [^{6} and
(k) Titles II, III and IV of the Treaty on European Union signed at Maastricht on 7th February 1992, together with the other provisions of the Treaty so far as they relate to those Titles, and the Protocols adopted at Maastricht on that date and annexed to the Treaty establishing the European Community with the exception of the Protocol on Social Policy on page 117 of Cm 1934] [^{7} and
(l) the decision, of 1st February 1993, of the Council amending the Act concerning the election of the representatives of the European Parliament by direct universal suffrage annexed to Council Decision 76/787 Euratom of 20th September 1976] [^{8} and
(m) the Agreement on the European Economic Area signed at Oporto on 2nd May 1992 together with the Protocol adjusting that Agreement signed at Brussels on 17th March 1993] [^{9} and
(n) the treaty concerning the accession of the Kingdom of Norway, the Republic of Austria, the Republic of Finland and the Kingdom of Sweden to the European Union, signed at Corfu on 24th June 1994;] [^{10} and
(o) the following provisions of the Treaty signed at Amsterdam on 2nd October 1997 amending the Treaty on European Union, the Treaties establishing the European Communities and certain related Acts
  (i) Articles 2 to 9,
  (ii) Article 12, and
  (iii) the other provisions of the Treaty so far as they relate to those Articles,
and the Protocols adopted on that occasion other than the Protocol on Article J.7 of the Treaty on European Union]
[^{12} and
(p) the following provisions of the Treaty signed at Nice on 26th February 2001 amending the Treaty on European Union, the Treaties establishing the European Communities and certain related Acts—
  (i) Articles 2 to 10, and
  (ii) the other provisions of the Treaty so far as they relate to those Articles,
and the Protocols adopted on that occasion;]
and any other treaty entered into by any of the Communities, with or without any of the member States, or entered into, as a treaty ancillary to any of the Treaties, by the United Kingdom; [^{13} and
(q) the treaty concerning the accession of the Czech Republic, the Republic of Estonia, the Republic of Cyprus, the Republic of Latvia, the Republic of Lithuania, the Republic of Hungary, the

Republic of Malta, the Republic of Poland, the Republic of Slovenia and the Slovak Republic to the European Union, signed at Athens on 16th April 2003;]
and any expression defined in Schedule 1 to this Act has the meaning there given to it.

[[14] and

(r) the treaty concerning the accession of the Republic of Bulgaria and Romania to the European Union, signed at Luxembourg on 25th April 2005;]

(3) If Her Majesty by Order in Council declares that a treaty specified in the Order is to be regarded as one of the Community Treaties as herein defined, the Order shall be conclusive that it is to be so regarded; but a treaty entered into by the United Kingdom after the 22nd January 1972, other than a pre-accession treaty to which the United Kingdom accedes on terms settled on or before that date, shall not be so regarded unless it is so specified, nor be so specified unless a draft of the Order in Council has been approved by resolution of each House of Parliament.

(4) For purposes of subsections (2) and (3) above, "treaty" includes any international agreement, and any protocol or annex to a treaty or international agreement.

AMENDMENTS

1. Interpretation Act 1978, s.25(1).
2. European Communities (Greek Accession) Act 1979, s.1.
3. European Communities Act 1995, s.1.
4. European Communities (Spanish and Portuguese Accession) Act 1985, s.1.
5. European Communities (Amendment) Act 1986, s.1.
6. European Communities (Amendment) Act 1993, s.1.
7. European Parliamentary Elections Act 1993, s.3.
8. European Economic Area Act 1993, s.1.
9. European Union (Accessions) Act 1994, s.1.
10. European Communities (Amendment) Act 1998, s.1.
11. European Communities (Finance) Act 2001, s.1 (December 4, 2001).
12. European Communities (Amendment) Act 2002, s.1 (February 26, 2002).
13. European Union (Accessions) Act 2003, s.1 (November 13, 2003).
14. European Union (Accessions) Act 2006 c.2 (February 16, 2006).

GENERAL NOTE

The Member States
The Member States of the European Union are:

Austria	France	Italy	Spain
Belgium	Germany	Luxembourg	Sweden
Denmark	Greece	Netherlands	United Kingdom
Finland	Ireland	Portugal	

From May 1, 2004, the following ten countries are members of the European Union:

Czech Republic	Cyprus	Estonia	Latvia
Lithuania	Hungary	Malta	Poland
Slovakia	Slovenia		

From January 1, 2007, Bulgaria and Romania became Member States of the European Union, but see The Social Security (Bulgaria and Romania) Amendment Regulations 2006 (SI 2006/3341), effective from January 1, 2007, which deal with the consequences of membership for the entitlement of nationals of these countries to income-related benefits.

There are three additional countries which with the Member States form the countries of the European Economic Area; they are
Iceland   Liechtenstein   Norway
Community social security law generally applies to nationals of the Member States and of the additional countries of the European Economic Area "EEA", since the social security rules are extended to their nationals by the EEA Treaty. For this reason the term "EEA country" or countries is frequently used to describe those countries whose nationals are beneficiaries of the Community rules on social security.

In addition, nationals of Switzerland are covered by the rules in Reg.1408/71 with effect from June 1, 2002, and from June 1, 2003, third country nationals who have been lawfully resident in two Member States are covered by the co-ordinating regulation under Regulation 859/2003/EC, which is reproduced later in this volume.

The treaties

3.4   The key treaty for social security purposes is the European Community Treaty ("EC Treaty") formerly the European Economic Community Treaty (or "EEC Treaty"). There is now a European Union governed by the Treaty on European Union (or Maastricht Treaty). This has been amended by the Treaty of Amsterdam and now consists of three pillars: the European Communities, Common Foreign and Security Policy, and Police and Judicial Cooperation in Criminal Matters.

The EC Treaty began life as the EEC Treaty. The EC Treaty has been amended many times. The Treaty on European Union was signed at Maastricht on February 7, 1992, and is often referred to as the Maastricht Treaty.

Renumbering and citation of the treaties

3.5   The Treaty of Amsterdam, which entered into force in May 1999 amended both the EC Treaty and the Treaty on European Union (the "TEU"). It renumbered both treaties. This has presented the potential for confusion, since there will be a long transitional period during which two sets of numbering will be encountered in the literature.

The convention has emerged of citing either the old number in parentheses, or, where more appropriate, the new number is parentheses. So, for example, the general prohibition on discrimination on grounds of nationality was originally in Art.6 of the EC Treaty, but this has been renumbered as Art.13. So it would now be cited Art.13 (ex 6) EC. But if reference to the original version is more appropriate, then it would be cited Art.6 (now 13) EC.

The Treaty on European Union is cited as follows: Art.6 TEU. The conventions which apply to citation of the EC Treaty in its original and renumbered form equally apply to the renumbering of this treaty, but note that this treaty was originally structured around letters and numbers rather than just numbers. For example, Art.6 (ex F) TEU, or Art.F (now 6) TEU.

General implementation of Treaties

3.6   **2.**—(1) All such rights, powers, liabilities, obligations and restrictions from time to time created or arising by or under the Treaties, and all such remedies and procedures from time to time provided for by or under the Treaties, as in accordance with the Treaties are without further enactment to be given legal effect or used in the United Kingdom shall be recognised and available in law, and be enforced, allowed and followed accordingly; and the expression "enforceable Community right" and similar expressions shall be read as referring to one to which this subsection applies.

(2) Subject to Schedule 2 to this Act, at any time after its passing Her Majesty may by Order in Council, and any designated Minister or department may by regulations, make provision—

(1972 c. 28, s. 2) (as amended)

(a) for the purpose of implementing any Community obligation of the United Kingdom, or enabling any such obligation to be implemented, or of enabling any rights enjoyed or to be enjoyed by the United Kingdom under or by virtue of the Treaties to be exercised; or

(b) for the purpose of dealing with matters arising out of or related to any such obligation or rights or the coming into force, or the operation from time to time, of subsection (1) above;

and in the exercise of any statutory power or duty, including any power to give directions or to legislate by means of orders, rules, regulations or other subordinate instrument, the person entrusted with the power or duty may have regard to the objects of the Communities and to any such obligation or rights as aforesaid.

In this subsection "designated Minister or department" means such Minister of the Crown or government department as may from time to time be designated by Order in Council in relation to any matter or for any purpose, but subject to such restrictions or conditions (if any) as may be specified by the Order in Council.

(3) There shall be charged on and issued out of the Consolidated Fund or, if so determined by the Treasury, the National Loans Fund the amounts required to meet any Community obligation to make payments to any of the Communities or member States, or any Community obligation in respect of contributions to the capital or reserves of the European Investment Bank or in respect of loans to the Bank, or to redeem any notes or obligations issued or created in respect of any such Community obligation; and, except as otherwise provided by or under any enactment—

(a) any other expenses incurred under or by virtue of the Treaties or this Act by any Minister of the Crown or government department may be paid out of moneys provided by Parliament; and

(b) any sums received under or by virtue of the Treaties or this Act by any Minister of the Crown or government department, save for such sums as may be required for disbursements permitted by any other enactment, shall be paid into the Consolidated Fund or, if so determined by the Treasury, the National Loans Fund.

(4) The provision that may be made under subsection (2) above includes, subject to Schedule 2 to this Act, any such provision (of any such extent) as might be made by Act of Parliament, and any enactment passed or to be passed, other than one contained in this Part of this Act, shall be construed and have effect subject to the foregoing provisions of this section; but, except as may be provided by any Act passed after this Act, Schedule 2 shall have effect in connection with the powers conferred by this and the following sections of this Act to make Orders in Council and regulations.

(5) [^{1} . . .] and the references in that subsection to a Minister of the Crown or government department and to a statutory power or duty shall include a Minister or department of the Government of Northern Ireland and a power or duty arising under or by virtue of an Act of the Parliament of Northern Ireland.

(6) A law passed by the legislature of any of the Channel Islands or of the Isle of Man, or a colonial law (within the meaning of the Colonial Laws Validity Act 1865) passed or made for Gibraltar, if expressed to be passed or made in the implementation of the Treaties and of the obligations of the United Kingdom thereunder, shall not be void or inoperative

by reason of any inconsistency with or repugnancy to an Act of Parliament, passed or to be passed, that extends to the Island or Gibraltar or any provision having the force and effect of an Act there (but not including this section), nor by reason of its having some operation outside the Island or Gibraltar; and any such Act or provision that extends to the Island or Gibraltar shall be construed and have effect subject to the provisions of any such law.

AMENDMENT

1. Northern Ireland Constitution Act 1973, s.41.

MODIFICATION

The operation of this section is modified in relation to Scotland by the Scotland Act 1998, s.15 and Sch.8 and the Scotland Act 1998 (Transfer of Functions to the Scottish Ministers etc.) Order 1999, (SI 1999/1750), and in relation to Northern Ireland by the Northern Ireland Act 1998 and the Northern Ireland Assembly Act 1973.

GENERAL NOTE

The binding nature of Community law

3.7　European Community law is binding on United Kingdom courts and tribunals by virtue of this section. Any rule of law qualifying as "an enforceable Community right" is to be given legal effect in the law of the United Kingdom. Whenever there is a clash between United Kingdom law and European Community law, the rule of European Community law is to prevail: see s.2(4).

Community legislation

3.8　European Community law takes a variety of forms but the forms most likely to be met in tribunals and before the Commissioners are *regulations* and *directives*. Art.249 (ex 189) EC provides that regulations are to have the force of law in all the Member States without further implementation, whereas directives are addressed to Member States and require conversion (if necessary) into national law.

Regulations retain their Community character and are binding in all Member States in exactly the same way as that Member State's primary legislation. Individuals may rely on the provisions of regulations by citing them just as if they were statutory provisions emanating from the United Kingdom Parliament. Indeed, they may be regarded as superior to national legislation since no national legislature can alter the form of a Community regulation.

Directives are a form of legislation which is intended to enable Community law to be enacted in each Member State in the manner which best fits the legal traditions of that Member State. So the obligation is to achieve the result required by the directive, but the choice of form and method is for each Member State to select. There is a requirement that each Member State to whom a directive is addressed must notify the Commission of the national law which implements the requirements of the directive.

Every piece of secondary legislation must find its authority in a provision of the EC Treaty. This is known as the legal basis or legal base for the measure. Legal base is important because the provision of the EC Treaty under which it is made will set out the decision-making procedure to be followed. This has generated disputes between the institutions, where an institution takes the view that the secondary legislation should have been made under a Treaty provision which requires its greater involvement in that procedure than under the provision under which the Council has adopted it.

The two most important doctrines developed in the case law of the Court of Justice of the European Communities (hereafter "Court of Justice") are:

(1972 c.28, s.2) (as amended)

- the supremacy of Community law
- the direct effect of Community law.

Supremacy

The supremacy of Community law requires that any conflict between a rule of Community law and a rule of national law must be decided in favour of the rule of Community law. See Case C-213/89 *R. v Secretary of State for Transport Ex p. Factortame* [1990] E.C.R. I-2433; [1991] 3 C.M.L.R. 589. Note the requirements of the doctrine as re-affirmed in this case, which involved a procedural rule in English law which operated as a barrier to a remedy under Community law; significantly, it involved the non-application of a United Kingdom statute.

3.9

Direct effect

A helpful distinction drawn by some authorities is between direct applicability and direct effect.

3.10

Direct applicability refers to the *status* of the source of a rule of Community law, and refers to those sources which are automatically law in the national legal orders of all the Member States. Treaty articles have this character, as do regulations. It is not open to a Member State to interfere with the direct application of a regulation in the national legal order. This preserves the Community nature of the source of obligation throughout all the Member States. If you know that an article of a particular regulation gives you a right in your own national legal order, you can be sure that the same right is provided in all the national legal orders under the same article of the same regulation. The only difference is that it will be in another official language of the Community.

The attribute of direct applicability is a feature of the supremacy of Community law.

Note that in some areas the Member States have transferred sole competence to legislate to the Community; one purpose for such transfers of sovereignty is to ensure the uniform application of law throughout the Community. This is sometimes called the doctrine of *pre-emption*. The effect is that once an area is occupied by Community law, Member States cannot legislate in that area.

Direct effect refers to the *content* of a rule, and describes its capacity to give rise to rights for individuals which they can plead before national courts, and which national courts must recognise.

Just as it is the case that not every provision of national law gives rise to rights for individuals, so too it is the case that not every provision of Community law gives rise to direct effect. It is necessary to consider the scope and wording of any provision in order to determine whether it is capable of giving rise to direct effect.

Where the status of the provision of Community law in issue is one which has the attribute of direct applicability, it is simply a matter of interpretation to determine whether direct effect arises. So, in the case of Treaty articles and regulations, the requirements for direct effect are that the rule in question:

- is sufficiently clear and precise; and
- is unconditional.

The direct effect of directives has given rise to particular problems, since Art.249 (ex 189) EC provides that directives are:

- addressed to the Member States; and
- are binding as to the result to be achieved; but
- leave the choice of form and methods to the national authorities of the Member States.

All directives give Member States a time limit within which to implement the requirements of the directive. They are obliged to inform the Commission of the action taken to implement the directive. Failure to implement a directive by the deadline is likely to result in action being taken by the Commission to bring the

Member State before the Court of Justice under Art.226 (ex 169) EC for failing to fulfil its obligations under the EC Treaty.

Proper and complete implementation of a directive results in individuals acquiring rights under the implementing national law.

It is now accepted that, where the deadline for implementation has passed without the directive's being implemented or without its being implemented properly, a directive can give rise to direct effect where it contains an obligation as to the result to be achieved which meets the requirements for direct effect set out above, *provided that* the party against whom the right is asserted is the State or "an emanation of the State". This is called a vertical relationship, and so vertical direct effect of directives is said to be permitted. Note particularly the definition of what constitutes an emanation of the State in Case C-188/89 *Foster v British Gas* [1990] E.C.R. I-3313; [1990] 2 C.M.L.R. 833.

However, the Court of Justice has ruled that the direct effect of directives does not arise where the right is being asserted against another private party. This is called a horizontal relationship, and so horizontal direct effect of directives is said not to be possible. There are a number of reasons for this:

1. To do so would impose an insuperable burden on private parties. Whereas it is justifiable to refuse to permit the State and its emanations from being able to plead the State's wrongdoing to avoid its liabilities, it would be wrong to impose a similar burden on a private party.

2. Directives are addressed to Member States. To allow the horizontal direct effect of directives would be to remove the distinction between regulations and directives. It would also provide an incentive for Member States not to implement directives, since they would take effect in any event after the expiry of the time for implementation.

The doctrine of indirect effect

3.11 To mitigate the harshness of a rule relating to the direct effect of directives as between private parties, the Court of Justice has imposed obligations on national authorities and national courts to interpret national law compatibly with the requirements of directives so far as it is possible to do so. This obligation flows from the duty of solidarity to be found in Art.10 (ex 5) EC.

State liability for breaches of Community law

3.12 The Court of Justice has developed rules which ensure the effective enjoyment of Community rights for individuals. The Court has even fashioned the requirement for a remedy where a Member State has failed either wholly or in part to implement a directive, and the relationship between the parties is a horizontal one. However, the remedy is available wherever there has been a breach of Community law of sufficient seriousness to engage the remedy.

Under the *Francovich* line of cases, courts in the Member States are obliged to compensate individuals who have suffered loss as a result of infringements of Community law by Member States. Three conditions for liability are required:

- the rule of Community law grants rights to individuals and the content of those rights is clearly identifiable;

- the breach by the Member State is sufficiently serious to trigger liability for loss;

- there is a direct causal link between the breach of the rule by the Member State and the loss suffered by the individuals concerned.

This important remedy has been refined in subsequent case law. This is helpfully summarised in the decision of the House of Lords of October 28, 1999 in *R. v Secretary of State for Transport Ex p. Factortame Ltd (No.5)*, HL, [1999] 3 W. L. R. 1062; [1999] 4 All E.R. 906; [1999] 3 C. M. L. R. 597.

The Community law doctrine of the effective enjoyment of Community rights

The case law has established that national law must afford the same remedies in relation to the enforcement of Community law as are available for the enforcement of national law. This has come to be known as the doctrine of the effective enjoyment of Community rights and operates on the basis of two principles: see for example, Case C-312/93 *Peterbroeck* v *Belgium* [1995] ECR I-4599, paragraph 12).

3.13

The principle of *equivalence* requires that the conditions laid down by national law for the pursuit of Community rights are not discriminatory by comparison with those relating to domestic claims. The principle of *effectiveness* requires that any restrictions imposed must not be such as to render the reliance on Community rights virtually impossible or excessively difficult. The doctrine applies regardless of the course of the Community right on which the individual is relying: it may be a Treaty provision, regulation or directive, or indeed any other instrument having legal effect. The case law of the Court of Justice on the application of this doctrine to national time limits has proved difficult.

The issue first arose in the context of Ireland's failure fully to implement Dir.79/7. In Case 286/85 *McDermott* v *Minister for Social Welfare* [1987] E.C.R. 1453; [1987] 2 C.M.L.R. 607, the Court of Justice ruled that Art.4(1) of Dir.79/7 could be relied on by individuals as from December 23, 1984. In Case 208/90 *Emmott* v *Minister for Social Welfare and Attorney General* [1991] E.C.R. I-4269, the Court of Justice ruled as incompatible with Community law a limitation period operative under national law which had the effect of completely defeating the claimant's reliance on Community law entitlements. The case arose in the context of failures by the Irish Government to implement the requirements of Directive 79/7 on equal treatment of men and women in matters pertaining to social security. Mrs Emmott sought payment of her disability benefit at the same rate paid to married men. Ultimately she began judicial review proceedings but the national authorities pleaded that her application was time-barred since the time limit was three months from the date when the grounds of the application first arose. This completely defeated her claim. The Court of Justice ruled that where directives had not been properly implemented by a Member State, that State could not rely on national rules on time limits to defeat entirely a claim arising from the Member State failure.

The scope of that decision has been clarified in later case law. In Case C-338/91 *Steenhorst Neerings* [1993] E.C.R. I-5475, the Court of Justice ruled that national provisions which simply limit the period prior to the date of claim for which benefit entitlement may be claimed were not inconsistent with Community law.

In *Steenhorst Neerings*, the Court of Justice said:

"21. It should be noted first that, unlike the rule of domestic law fixing time-limits for bringing actions, the rule described in the question referred for a preliminary ruling in this case does not affect the right of individuals to rely on Directive 79/7 in proceedings before the national courts against a defaulting Member State. It merely limits the retroactive effect of claims made for the purpose of obtaining the relevant benefits.

22. The time-bar resulting from the expiry of the time-limit for bringing proceedings serves to ensure that the legality of administrative decisions cannot be challenged indefinitely. The judgment in Emmott indicates that that requirement cannot prevail over the need to protect the rights conferred on individuals by the direct effect of provisions in a directive so long as the defaulting Member State responsible for those decisions has not properly transposed the provisions into national law.

23. On the other hand, the aim of the rule restricting the retroactive effect of claims for benefits for incapacity for work is quite different from that of a rule imposing mandatory time-limits for bringing proceedings. As the Government of the Netherlands and the defendant in the main proceedings explained in their written observations, the first type of rule, of which examples can be found in other social security laws in the Netherlands, serves to ensure sound administration, most

importantly so that it may be ascertained whether the claimant satisfied the conditions for eligibility and so that the degree of incapacity, which may well vary over time, may be fixed. It also reflects the need to preserve financial balance in a scheme in which claims submitted by insured persons in the course of a year must in principle be covered by the contributions collected during that same year.

24. The reply to the first question must therefore be that Community law does not preclude the application of a national rule of law whereby benefits for incapacity for work are payable not earlier than one year before the date of claim, in the case where an individual seeks to rely on rights conferred directly by Article 4(1) of Directive 79/7 with effect from 23 December 1984 and where on the date the claim for benefit was made the Member State concerned had not yet properly transposed that provision into national law."

The ruling in *Steenhorst Neerings* was followed in Case C-410/92 *Johnson v Chief Adjudication Officer* [1994] E.C.R. I-5483, where the Court said:

"26. However, it is clear from the judgment in *Steenhorst-Neerings* that the solution adopted in *Emmott* was justified by the particular circumstances of that case, in which a time-bar had the result of depriving the applicant of any opportunity whatever to rely on her right to equal treatment under the directive.

27. The Court pointed out in *Steenhorst-Neerings* (paragraph 20) that in *Emmott* the applicant in the main proceedings had relied on the judgment of the Court in Case 286/85 *McDermott v Minister for Social Welfare* [1987] E.C.R. 1453 in order to claim entitlement by virtue of Article 4(1) of Directive 79/7, with effect from 23 December 1984, to invalidity benefits under the same conditions as those applicable to men in the same situation. The administrative authorities had then declined to adjudicate on her claim since Directive 79/7 was the subject of proceedings pending before a national court. Finally, even though Directive 79/7 had still not been correctly transposed into national law, it was claimed that the proceedings she had brought to obtain a ruling that her claim should have been accepted were out of time.

28. In contrast, the rule at issue in *Steenhorst-Neerings* did not affect the right of individuals to rely on Directive 79/7 in proceedings before the national courts against a defaulting Member State but merely limited to one year the retroactive effect of claims for benefits for incapacity for work.

29. The Court concluded (paragraph 24) that Community law did not preclude the application of a national rule of law whereby benefits for incapacity for work were payable not earlier than one year before the date of claim, in the case where an individual sought to rely on rights conferred directly by Article 4(1) of Directive 79/7 with effect from 23 December 1984 and where on the date the claim for benefit was made the Member State concerned had not yet properly transposed that provision into national law.

30. In the light of the foregoing, the national rule which adversely affects Mrs Johnson's action before the Court of Appeal is similar to that at issue in *Steenhorst-Neerings*. Neither rule constitutes a bar to proceedings; they merely limit the period prior to the bringing of the claim in respect of which arrears of benefit are payable."

Walker-Fox v Secretary of State for Work and Pensions [2005] EWCA Civ 1441, reported as *R(IS) 3/06* is the appeal against the decision in *CIS/0488/2004*. The judgment contains a detailed discussion of the authorities; in particular, the Court of Appeal was keen to limit the situations in which the *Emmott* case would apply to circumstances close to the situation which arose in that case. In allowing the Secretary of State's appeal the Court of Appeal considered that the Deputy Commissioner had erred in confusing "the *making* of a claim with the *outcome* of a claim. The real question is whether it was virtually impossible or excessively difficult to *make* the claim" (para.46 of the judgment). The Court of Appeal concluded that it was not.

Interim relief

3.14   A Commissioner has for the first time had to consider whether Community law principles on effective enjoyment of Community rights requires the grant of interim

(1972 c.28, s.2) (as amended)

relief in a case where payments of disability living allowance were stopped when the claimant moved to Spain and where a Commissioner had referred questions to the Court of Justice under Art.234 (ex 177) EC. In *R(DLA) 4/99* and *R(DLA) 5/99* the Commissioner does not directly answer the question since he proceeds on the assumption that there might be such a power but does not consider that the claimant's case met the necessary threshold of being "strongly arguable" as distinct from being merely "arguable". Despite this conclusion the decision raises many of the difficult issues which would arise if the Commissioners were to have such a power. It could well follow that tribunals enjoyed a similar power. A particular difficulty is that tribunals and the Commissioners are concerned with entitlement, whereas the mechanics of payment are matters for the Secretary of State alone. Such a distinction of role (which has, of course, for many purposes been removed by the Social Security Act 1998 without removing all the possible problems) might not be able to survive an onslaught relying on European authority on remedies before national judicial bodies.

The appellant in the case sought a judicial review of the Commissioner's decision in *R. v Social Security Commissioner Ex p. Snares* [1997] C.O.D. 403, Divisional Court of QBD, March 24, 1997, reported as *R(DLA) 4/99*. The Divisional Court concluded that the Commissioner could not be faulted in the way he had exercised any discretion he had in the case. The case does not advance matters beyond what the Commissioner said. The trend of the case law of the Court of Justice is, however, that European Community law requires national judicial authorities to have the power to give legal effect to rights arising under Community law. An example of where this might be problematic is the absence of any power for tribunals or the Commissioners to award interest on late benefit or costs: see *R(FC)2/90*.

Decisions on, and proof of, Treaties and Community instruments, etc

3.—(1) For the purposes of all legal proceedings any question as to the meaning or effect of any of the Treaties, or as to the validity, meaning or effect of any Community instrument, shall be treated as a question of law (and, if not referred to the European Court, be for determination as such in accordance with the principles laid down by and any relevant [¹ decision of the European Court or any court attached thereto)].

(2) Judicial notice shall be taken of the Treaties, of the Official Journal of the Communities and of any decision of, or expression of opinion by, the European Court [¹ or any court attached thereto] on any such question as aforesaid; and the Official Journal shall be admissible as evidence of any instrument or other act thereby communicated of any of the Communities or of any Community institution.

(3) Evidence of any instrument issued by a Community institution, including any judgment or order of the European Court [¹ or any court attached thereto], or of any document in the custody of a Community institution, or any entry in or extract from such a document, may be given in any legal proceedings by production of a copy certified as a true copy by an official of that institution; and any document purporting to be such a copy shall be received in evidence without proof of the official position or handwriting of the person signing the certificate.

(4) Evidence of any Community instrument may also be given in any legal proceedings—
  (a) by production of a copy purporting to be printed by the Queen's Printer;
  (b) where the instrument is in the custody of a government department (including a department of the Government of Northern Ireland), by production of a copy certified on behalf of the department to be a true

3.15

copy by an officer of the department generally or specially authorised so to do;

and any document purporting to be such a copy as is mentioned in paragraph (b) above of an instrument in the custody of a department shall be received in evidence without proof of the official position or handwriting of the person signing the certificate, or of his authority to do so, or of the document being in the custody of the department.

(5) *Omitted.*

AMENDMENT

1. European Communities (Amendment) Act 1986, s.2.

GENERAL NOTE

3.16   Questions as to the meaning and effect of the treaties and of any Community legislation are questions of law. Where such questions are decided by national courts or tribunals, they are to be decided in accordance with principles laid down in any decision of the Court of Justice or Court of First Instance. In deciding such questions, judicial notice is to be taken of the treaties and secondary legislation as well as of decisions of the Community courts.

Extracts from the EC Treaty

PART I

PRINCIPLES

Article 2 (ex 2) EC

3.17   The Community shall have as its task, by establishing a common market and an economic and monetary union and by implementing common policies or activities referred to in Articles 3 and 4, to promote throughout the Community a harmonious, balanced and sustainable development of economic activities, a high level of employment and of social protection, equality between men and women, sustainable and non-inflationary growth, a high degree of competitiveness and convergence of economic performance, a high level of protection and improvement of the quality of the environment, the raising of the standard of living and quality of life, and economic and social cohesion and solidarity among Member States.

Article 3 (ex 3) EC

3.18   1. For the purposes set out in Article 2, the activities of the Community shall include, as provided in this Treaty and in accordance with the timetable set out therein:
   (a) the prohibition, as between Member States, of customs duties and quantitative restrictions on the import and export of goods, and of all other measures having equivalent effect;

Article 3

(b) a common commercial policy;
(c) an internal market characterised by the abolition, as between Member States, of obstacles to the free movement of goods, persons, services and capital;
(d) measures concerning the entry and movement of persons as provided for in Title IV;
(e) a common policy in the sphere of agriculture and fisheries;
(f) a common policy in the sphere of transport;
(g) a system ensuring that competition in the internal market is not distorted;
(h) the approximation of the laws of Member States to the extent required for the functioning of the common market;
(i) the promotion of coordination between employment policies of the Member States with a view to enhancing their effectiveness by developing a coordinated strategy for employment;
(j) a policy in the social sphere comprising a European Social Fund;
(k) the strengthening of economic and social cohesion;
(l) a policy in the sphere of the environment;
(m) the strengthening of the competitiveness of Community industry;
(n) the promotion of research and technological development;
(o) encouragement for the establishment and development of trans-European networks;
(p) a contribution to the attainment of a high level of health protection;
(q) a contribution to education and training of quality and to the flowering of the cultures of the Member States;
(r) a policy in the sphere of development cooperation;
(s) the association of the overseas countries and territories in order to increase trade and promote jointly economic and social development;
(t) a contribution to the strengthening of consumer protection;
(u) measures in the spheres of energy, civil protection and tourism.

2. In all the activities referred to in this Article, the Community shall aim to eliminate inequalities, and to promote equality, between men and women.

GENERAL NOTE

The Court has frequently found its inspiration for an interpretation of a particular provision of the Treaty or of secondary legislation by reference to the objectives of the Community as set out in Arts 2 and 3: for example, Case 53/81 *Levin v Staatssecretaris van Justitie* [1982] E.C.R. 1035 (para.15 of the judgment), though the terms of these articles are not sufficiently precise to give rise to direct effect: Case 126/86 *Giménez Zaera v Instituto Nacional de la Seguridad Social* [1987] E.C.R. 3697 (para.11 of judgment in relation to Art.2).

3.19

Article 5 (ex 3b) EC

The Community shall act within the limits of the powers conferred upon it by this Treaty and of the objectives assigned to it therein.

In areas which do not fall within its exclusive competence, the Community shall take action, in accordance with the principle of subsidiarity, only if and insofar as the objectives of the proposed action cannot be sufficiently achieved by the Member States and can therefore, by reason of the scale or effects of the proposed action, be better achieved by the Community.

3.20

General Note

3.21 Note that Community law on social security only seeks to co-ordinate the different social security systems of the Member States (plus the three EEA countries). There has been no attempt to date to harmonise social entitlements in the Member States, though there are provisions requiring that there be no discrimination on grounds of sex in the application of the social security rules of the Member States: see Dir.79/7 reproduced below.

Article 10 (ex 5) EC

3.22 Member States shall take all appropriate measures, whether general or particular, to ensure fulfilment of the obligations arising out of this Treaty or resulting from action taken by the institutions of the Community. They shall facilitate the achievement of the Community's tasks. They shall abstain from any measure which could jeopardise the attainment of the objectives of this Treaty.

General Note

3.23 This article is sometimes referred to as establishing the principle of "solidarity" under which Member States undertake a legal obligation to further Community objectives. It has been used as the basis for the obligation to interpret national law compatibly with Community law: see Case 14/83 *Von Colson and Kamann v Land Nordrhein Westfalen* [1984] E.C.R. 1891; [1986] 2 C.M.L.R. 430; Case C-106/89 *Marleasing SA* [1990] E.C.R. I-4135; [1992] 1 C.M.L.R. 305; and Case C-168/95 *Criminal Proceedings against Arcaro* [1996] E.C.R. I-4705.

Article 12 (ex 6) EC

3.24 Within the scope of application of this Treaty, and without prejudice to any special provisions contained therein, any discrimination on grounds of nationality shall be prohibited.

The Council, acting in accordance with the procedure referred to in Article 251, may adopt rules designed to prohibit such discrimination.

General Note

3.25 This is the general statement of non-discrimination on grounds of nationality, which applies wherever the provisions of the treaty apply. In Case C-85/96 *Martinez Sala v Freistaat Bayern* [1998] E.C.R. I-2691, it was held that a person lawfully resident in Germany could rely on the principle of non-discrimination to gain access to social security benefits in Germany notwithstanding that she was not a worker within Art.49 (now 39) EC(see below). A crucial aspect of the case which is not fully explained is what constitutes lawful residence in a Member State. See also the case law discussed in the annotations to Art.18 EC below.

Article 13 (ex 6a) EC

3.26 [[1] 1.] Without prejudice to the other provisions of this Treaty and within the limits of the powers conferred by it upon the Community, the Council,

Article 13

acting unanimously on a proposal from the Commission and after consulting the European Parliament, may take appropriate action to combat discrimination based on sex, racial or ethnic origin, religion or belief, disability, age or sexual orientation.

[¹ 2. By way of derogation from paragraph 1, when the Council adopts Community incentive measures, excluding any harmonisation of the laws and regulations of the Member States, to support action taken by the Member States in order to contribute to the achievement of the objectives referred to in paragraph 1, it shall act in accordance with the procedure referred to in Article 251.]

AMENDMENT

1. Treaty of Nice, Art.2(2) (February 1, 2003).

Article 14 (ex 7a) EC

1. The Community shall adopt measures with the aim of progressively establishing the internal market over a period expiring on December 31 1992, in accordance with the provisions of this Article and of Articles 15, 26, 47(2), 49, 80, 93 and 95 and without prejudice to the other provisions of this Treaty.

2. The internal market shall comprise an area without internal frontiers in which the free movement of goods, persons, services and capital is ensured in accordance with the provisions of this Treaty.

3. The Council, acting by a qualified majority on a proposal from the Commission, shall determine the guidelines and conditions necessary to ensure balanced progress in all the sectors concerned.

3.27

PART II

CITIZENSHIP OF THE UNION

Article 17 (ex 8) EC

1. Citizenship of the Union is hereby established. Every person holding the nationality of a Member State shall be a citizen of the Union. Citizenship of the Union shall complement and not replace national citizenship.

2. Citizens of the Union shall enjoy the rights conferred by this Treaty and shall be subject to the duties imposed thereby.

3.28

GENERAL NOTE

The allocation of nationality to individuals is a matter for each Member State to determine, subject to very limited intervention by Community law. These qualifications mean that it will not be open to a Member State to deny that an individual has the nationality of a Member State even though certain rules of its own civil justice system operate in a way which does not recognise the nationality. An example is the Case C-369/90 *Micheletti*, [1992] E.C.R. I-4239. Micheletti held both Argentinean and Italian nationality. Prior to moving to Spain, he had been resident in Argentina for some time. Under certain Spanish rules, this meant that he was treated as an Argentinian national and his Italian nationality was not recognised.

3.29

Extracts from the EC Treaty

He was refused a residence permit on this basis. The Court of Justice ruled that it was not open to a Member State could not use its internal law on nationality to deny recognition to a dual national of the nationality of another Member State. Nor is it necessary to have a passport as evidence of the holding of the nationality of a Member State if the nationality can be established by other means: see Case C-376/89 *Giagounidis*, [1991] E.C.R. I-1069.

The laws of the Member States govern changes of nationality just as they govern the attribution of nationality.

Article 18 (ex 8a) EC

3.30 [¹ **1.** Every citizen of the Union shall have the right to move and reside freely within the territory of the Member States, subject to the limitations and conditions laid down in this Treaty and by the measures adopted to give it effect.

2. If action by the Community should prove necessary to attain this objective and this Treaty has not provided the necessary powers, the Council may adopt provisions with a view to facilitating the exercise of the rights referred to in paragraph 1. The Council shall act in accordance with the procedure referred to in Article 251.

3. Paragraph 2 shall not apply to provisions on passports, identity cards, residence permits or any other such document or to provisions on social security or social protection.]

AMENDMENT

1. Treaty of Nice, Art.2(3) (February 1, 2003).

GENERAL NOTE

3.31 There is now a line of cases which suggests that entitlement to social benefits in a Member State may flow from the holding of citizenship of the Union coupled with lawful residence in a Member State. The Court is beginning to repeat, rather like a mantra, that citizenship of the Union is 'destined to be the fundamental status of nationals of the Member States, enabling those who find themselves in the same situation to receive the same treatment in law irrespective of their nationality, subject to such exceptions as are expressly provided for': see, for example, Case C-209/03 *Bidar* [2005] Q.B. 812, ECJ, para.31 of the judgment.

In Case C-85/96 *Martínez Sala*, [1998] E.C.R. I-2691, Maria Martínez Sala, a Spanish national lawfully resident in Germany, found herself in need of financial support from the State. The Court of Justice rules that the prohibition of discrimination on grounds of nationality applied in this case and that she was entitled to obtain social assistance on the same basis as German nationals.

Case C-184/99 *Grzelczyk*, [2001] E.C.R. I-6193, concerned a French student undertaking higher education in Belgium. For the first three years of the course, he managed to maintain himself, but ran into financial difficulties in his fourth year of study and sought help from the State. The referring court did not regard Grzelczyk as a worker and so he could derive no help from the provisions applicable to workers. He appeared to be a student; the Directive on the free movement of students, expressly provides that they are not entitled to maintenance grants from the State as a matter of Community law entitlement, though this was without prejudice to their entitlement to social security on the same basis as nationals of the State of residence. Nevertheless the Court of Justice ruled that Grzelczyk was lawfully resident in Belgium as a student by reason of being a citizen of the Union and was entitled to receive the same support that would be afforded to a Belgian student in the same circumstances by reason of the operation of Article 12 EC.

Article 18

Case C-138/02 *Collins* [2005] Q.B. 145, concerned a man who came to the United Kingdom to look for work. He held the nationality of the United States and Ireland. Though he had worked in the United Kingdom many years before, the gap meant that he could not be considered to be a worker. He was subject to the requirement that he show habitual residence in the United Kingdom before he could become entitled to income-based jobseeker's allowance. The Court of Justice recognised that it was legitimate to impose a requirement that the person seeking the benefit had established a genuine link with the employment market of the State in which he was seeking an unemployment benefit. Furthermore, a residence-based test was not, of itself, inappropriate provided that its scope and application were clear and proportionate to establish the necessary link. See para.3.57 below for a brief discussion of the decision of the Commissioner following the ruling of the Court of Justice, and the appeal against that decision in *Collins v Secretary of State for Work and Pensions*, reported as *R(JSA) 3/06*.

Case C-456/02 *Trojani* [2004] All E.R. (EC) 1065, takes this further. Trojani was a single man of French nationality. He clearly fell on hard times. He was living in a Salvation Army hostel in Belgium under an arrangement where he undertook various jobs for the hostel as part of a personal rehabilitation scheme, in exchange for which he received board and lodging and an allowance of €25.00 per week. He claimed the minimex (the minimum subsistence allowance in Belgium). His claim was refused on the grounds that he was not a Belgian national. Trojani brought proceedings before the Labour Court in Brussels to challenge this refusal. That Court referred questions to the Court of Justice. The Court advised that Trojani did not appear to be a worker because of the nature of his commitment to the hostel where he lived. The second one essentially concerned the possible entitlement of Trojani to the minimex as a person exercising his right to reside in Belgium as a citizen of the European Union. The Advocate General concluded that it was open to Belgium to deny Trojani a right of residence because he did not have the means to support himself. The Court was a little more circumspect. Referring to the ruling in the *Baumbast* case, the Court indicates that it would not be disproportionate to deny Trojani a right of residence on the basis that he did not have the means to be self-sufficient. In other words, he had no *Community* right to reside. But the Court went on to note that he may have a right to reside under *national law*, since he had been issued with a residence permit under national law by the municipal authorities in Brussels. The Court made three points (at paras 41–6 of its judgment):

(1) Social assistance falls within the scope of the EC Treaty.

(2) A citizen of the Union who is not economically active may rely on the prohibition of discrimination on grounds of nationality where he has been "lawfully resident" in the host Member State "for a certain time or possesses a residence permit" (para.43).

(3) Restricting entitlement to social assistance to the nationals of the host Member State constitutes discrimination on grounds of nationality contrary to Article 12 EC.

It would follow that, if the national court concludes that Trojani was "lawfully resident" in Belgium under *national law*, then the prohibition of discrimination in Community law would be engaged, and the restriction of entitlement to the minimex to Belgian nationals in the circumstances of this case would breach the equality provisions of the EC Treaty.

The dramatic impact of the citizenship provisions is also illustrated by the judgment of the Court of Justice in case C-209/03 *Bidar*, Judgment of March 15, 2005. This case concerned a claim for a student loan by a French national who had come to the United Kingdom some years earlier and had completed his secondary education here. The Court of Justice recalled what it described as "settled case-law" (para.32 of the judgment) that a citizen of the European Union lawfully resident in the territory of the host Member Staste can rely on Article 12 EC in all situations which fall within the material scope of the EC Treaty. Prior to this case, the award of financial support to students for their living expenses, whether in the form of grants or loans, had been considered to be outside the material scope of the EC Treaty. But the Court says that developments in Community law, especially the introduction of citizenship of the Union called for a change in that position. Such matters are now to be treated as within the scope of the EC Treaty for all the reasons set out in the judgment. The Court of Justice went on to rule that the application of the prohibition of discrimination meant that a person lawfully resident in the host Member State who has received a substantial part of his secondary education in that Member State and so has established a genuine link with the society of that State must be treated in the same manner as a national of that State.

Considerable substance is given to the citizenship approach to the right to move and reside in a Member State other than that of a person's own nationality in Dir. 2004/38/EC, which is reproduced at para.3.60 of this Volume.

Courts and tribunals in England and Wales seem to be taking a narrow view of the right to reside flowing from Art.18 EC. So in *Ali v Secretary of State for the Home Department* [2006] EWCA Civ 484, the Court of Appeal ruled that the right to reside under Art.18 EC was not an unfettered right, that a parent could not claim a derivative right to reside by reason of a five-year-old child of that person being in primary education in the United Kingdom, and that a spouse (a Dutch national residing in the United Kingdom) who has not worked in the United Kingdom was not a worker under Community law.

CIS/3573/2005, decided by a Tribunal of Commissioners, concerned a Swedish national born in Somalia who had come to live in the United Kingdom. She had not worked in the United Kingdom, and claimed income support. The Tribunal of Commissioners said,

> "31. Both the treaty of Rome, as amended, and EEC Directive 90/364 make it entirely clear that national governments are entitled to restrict the right to residence of European Union nationals and to restrict any social assistance to them, even if they are, in fact, resident under a lawful right of entrance and no steps have been taken for their removal. Mr Knafler submitted that the reality of the situation is that no steps will ever be taken to remove the claimant as, even if she were removed, she would have an immediate right of re-entry. However, in our view having a right of re-entry is somewhat different to fulfilling conditions for social assistance."

It should, however, be noted that the claimant in this case is likely in a relatively short period of time to meet the habitual residence test if she remains in the United Kingdom.

In case *C-406/04, De Cuyper*, [2006] ECR I-6947, the Court of Justice ruled that freedom of movement and residence, conferred on citizens of the Union under Article 18 EC, does not preclude a residence clause, which is imposed on an unemployed person over 50 years of age who is exempt from the requirement of providing that he is available for work, as a condition for the retention of his entitlement to unemployment benefit. De Cuyper, a Belgian national, was born in 1942. He was no longer required to 'submit to the local control procedures' in connection with his entitlement to unemployment benefit because he was over 50 years of age. Following a routine check, it was established that he spent considerable periods each year living in France. He was subsequently refused unemployment benefit. The Court of Justice concluded that the benefit in question was an unemployment benefit (as distinct from a pre-retirement benefit) and that, although the restriction on his right of movement if he was to remain entitled to unemployment benefit was a restriction on his right to free movement, the requirement for residence was objectively justifiable having regard to the need to monitor the employment and family situation of unemployed persons. There was no less restrictive measure capable of meeting the monitoring requirement.

Case C-520/04 *Turpeinen* [2006] ECR I-10685, ruled that Art. 18 EC outlaws national legislation under which the income tax charged on a retirement pension paid by an institution of the Member State concerned to a person in another Member State exceeds the tax charged on a pension payable to a resident of the Member State concerned, where that pension constitute al or nearly all of the person's income.

A series of cases decided by a Tribunal of Commissioners (*CIS/3573/2005; CPC/2920/2005; CIS/2559/2005; CIS/2680/2005; and CH/2484/2005*) has determined that non economically active nationals of the Member States (and of the EEA countries) do not acquire a right to reside under Community law and any discrimination which arises as a consequence of such nationals being required to establish a right to reside is objectively justified and proportionate. A memorandum (Memo DMG Vol 2 01/06) from the Department for Work and Pensions indicates that the changes consequent upon the entry into force of Directive 2004/38/EC (the "Citizenship Directive") do not alter the position. That proposition may be questionable, since it is based on the (unspoken) premise that the Citizenship Directive is purely a consolidating measure, when it is at least arguable that it develops the rights attached to Citizenship of the Union, and introduces a new Community right of permanent residence.

The decisions of the Tribunal of Commissioners have been largely upheld by the Court of Appeal in *Abdirahman v Secretary of State for Work and Pensions, Abdirahman v Leicester City Council and Secretary of State for Work and Pensions*, and *Ullusow v Secretary of State for Work and Pensions* [2007] EWCA Civ 657. On the European points raised in argument, the Court of Appeal concluded that the rights claimed by the claimants were not within the scope of application of the EC Treaty, and so the prohibition of discrimination in Art. 12 EC did not apply. They further held that the claimants had no "right to reside" under national law, and so neatly side-stepped the possible consequences of the decision of the Court of Justice in *Trojani*, which had ruled that equal treatment was required where a person had a right to reside in the country under national law (in that case, Trojani held a residence permit—of course, there is no direct equivalent under United Kingdom law). Of particular significance is that the Court of Appeal considered that the relevant Directive was Dir. 90/364/EEC, which has been repealed by the Citizenship Directive. The Court of Appeal also ruled that the requirement that a claimant has the 'right to reside' as a precondition to entitlement to benefit was not incompatible with European Community Law.

In *Zalewska v Department of Social Development*, Judgment of Northern Ireland Court of Appeal of May 9, 2007, the Northern Ireland Court of Appeal has dismissed an appeal from the decision of the Commissioner in *C 6/05-06*, in essence, to similar effect, though this case concerned the rights of nationals from some of the new Member States which joined in May 2004. The Court concluded that the Acts of Accession by which the new Member States joined the European Union permitted Member States to derogate from the Community provisions in Art. 39 EC. During the transitional period, the rights of nationals of the designated new Member States arose solely under national law. The steps taken by the United Kingdom were reasonable and proportionate under the permitted derogations and so did not go beyond what was permitted. Leave to appeal to the House of Lords has been refused by the NI Court of Appeal, but the application is likely to be renewed before the House of Lords.

In *CIS/3875/2005* the Commissioner found that a French national could not claim a right to reside in Community law based on his being a recipient of services. It may be significant that the Commissioner did not consider the *Carpenter* case (C-60/00 *Carpenter v Secretary of State for the Home Department* [2002] ECR I-6279.). See also *CIS/3182/2005* which concerned a Dutch national who had worked for about six weeks before giving up work because she was pregnant. The Commissioner concluded that she had no right to reside under the United Kingdom regulations.

See also *CH/3314/2005* and *CIS/3315/2005* which concerned a person who claimed to be seeking work, but who had worked from mid-July to mid-October

2004; the Commissioner ruled that she nevertheless had no 'right to reside' in the United Kingdom.

CH/1400/2006 concerned a woman who was a Slovenian national. She had entered the United Kingdom with her three children in September 2003. She began a postgraduate course in contemporary cinema culture in September 2004. In July 2005 she applied for housing benefit, and had appealed against its refusal. The tribunal had held that she had a right to reside under Community law as a person receiving services, namely the education on the course on which she was enrolled at the time of her claim. The Commissioner allowed the local authority's appeal on the grounds that the claimant was a person from abroad. In coming to that conclusion, he relied on Case 263/86 *Humbel* [1988] ECR 5365, and Case C-109/92, *Wirth*, [1993] ECR I-6447 in concluding that the provision of education was not the provision of services. It is certainly possible to read paragraphs 18 and 19 of the Luxembourg Court's ruling in *Wirth* as *not applying* to the provision of a course in a University where a student is paying (as in this case) full cost fees because she has the status of an overseas student. The Commissioner went on to consider whether the claimant had a right to reside as a student under the terms of the Students Directive (Directive 93/96/EEC) but concluded that this Directive required a student to have "sufficient resources to avoid becoming a burden on the social assistance system of the host Member State". However, in coming to that conclusion the Commissioner does not refer to Case C-184/99 *Grzelczyk* where the Court accepted that, in the case of students, what was required was an assurance of sufficient resources, which may be frustrated by the passage of time, and which does not preclude access to national assistance. The Commissioner also rejected a final argument based on Regulation 1408/71. It seems that no argument was presented based upon Case C-456/02 *Trojani* on the grounds that the claimant was lawfully resident in the United Kingdom, and on these grounds alone was entitled to equal treatment.

In *W (China) and X (China) v Secretary of State for the Home Department* [2006] EWCA Civ 1494, rather surprisingly, distinguished the decision of the Court of Justice in the *Chen* case (Case C-200/02, *Zhu and Chen*, [2004] ECR I-9925) in which it had held that third country nationals who were the parents of a Union citizen—in this case a baby born in Northern Ireland who thereby became entitled to Irish citizenship—had a right to reside in a Member State since otherwise the entitled of the child to reside would be rendered nugatory. The Court of Appeal indicated disagreement with the decision in the *Chen* case on the grounds that certain matters were not argued. In approaching the case in the way it did, the Court of Appeal focused exclusively on the technical requirements of Directive 90/364, giving it a priority which the Court of Justice had not, and arguably failed to give sufficient weight to the growing case law on rights flowing from Union citizenship provided in the Treaty.

In Case C-1/05 *Yunying Jia v Migrationsverket*, Judgment of January 9, 2007, the Court of Justice ruled,

"Article 1(1)(d) of Council Directive 73/148/EEC of 21 May 1973 on the abolition of restrictions on movement and residence within the Community for nationals of Member States with regard to establishment and the provision of services is to be interpreted to the effect that 'dependent on them' means that members of the family of a Community national established in another Member State within the meaning of Article 43 EC need the material support of that Community national or his or her spouse in order to meet their essential needs in the State of origin of those family members or the State from which they have come at the time when they apply to join that Community national. Article 6(b) of that directive must be interpreted as meaning that proof of the need for material support may be adduced by any appropriate means, while a mere undertaking from the Community national or his or her spouse to support the family members concerned need not be regarded as establishing the existence of the family members' situation of real dependence."

Article 19

Article 19 (ex 8b) EC

1. Every citizen of the Union residing in a Member State of which he is not a national shall have the right to vote and to stand as a candidate at municipal elections in the Member State in which he resides, under the same conditions as nationals of that State. This right shall be exercised subject to detailed arrangements adopted by the Council, acting unanimously on a proposal from the Commission and after consulting the European Parliament; these arrangements may provide for derogations where warranted by problems specific to a Member State.
2. Without prejudice to Article 190(4) and to the provisions adopted for its implementation, every citizen of the Union residing in a Member State of which he is not a national shall have the right to vote and to stand as a candidate in elections to the European Parliament in the Member State in which he resides, under the same conditions as nationals of that State. This right shall be exercised subject to detailed arrangements adopted by the Council, acting unanimously on a proposal from the Commission and after consulting the European Parliament; these arrangements may provide for derogations where warranted by problems specific to a Member State.

Article 20 (ex 8c) EC

Every citizen of the Union shall, in the territory of a third country in which the Member State of which he is a national is not represented, be entitled to protection by the diplomatic or consular authorities of any Member State, on the same conditions as the nationals of that State. Member States shall establish the necessary rules among themselves and start the international negotiations required to secure this protection.

Article 21 (ex 8d) EC

Every citizen of the Union shall have the right to petition the European Parliament in accordance with Article 194.
Every citizen of the Union may apply to the Ombudsman established in accordance with Article 195.
Every citizen of the Union may write to any of the institutions or bodies referred to in this Article or in Article 7 in one of the languages mentioned in Article 314 and have an answer in the same language.

Article 22 (ex 8e) EC

The Commission shall report to the European Parliament, to the Council and to the Economic and Social Committee every three years on the application of the provisions of this Part. This report shall take account of the development of the Union.
On this basis, and without prejudice to the other provisions of this Treaty, the Council, acting unanimously on a proposal from the Commission and after consulting the European Parliament, may adopt provisions to strengthen or to add to the rights laid down in this Part, which it shall recommend to the

Member States for adoption in accordance with their respective constitutional requirements.

TITLE III

FREE MOVEMENT OF PERSONS, SERVICES AND CAPITAL

CHAPTER I

WORKERS

Article 39 (ex 48) EC

3.36 **1.** Freedom of movement for workers shall be secured within the Community.

2. Such freedom of movement shall entail the abolition of any discrimination based on nationality between workers of the Member States as regards employment, remuneration and other conditions of work and employment.

3. It shall entail the right, subject to limitations justified on grounds of public policy, public security or public health:
  (a) to accept offers of employment actually made;
  (b) to move freely within the territory of Member States for this purpose;
  (c) to stay in a Member State for the purpose of employment in accordance with the provisions governing the employment of nationals of that State laid down by law, regulation or administrative action;
  (d) to remain in the territory of a Member State after having been employed in that State, subject to conditions which shall be embodied in implementing regulations to be drawn up by the Commission.

4. The provisions of this Article shall not apply to employment in the public service.

GENERAL NOTE

3.37 The activities of the Community include an internal market characterised by the abolition, as between Member States, of obstacles to the free movement of goods, persons, services and capital: Art.3 (ex 3) EC. Free movement of persons is generally regarded as encompassing workers, establishment, and services under Arts 39 (ex 48) to 55 (ex 66). EC Directives grant rights of free movement for students and retired persons, provided they are not a burden on the social assistance schemes of the Member State of residence, and for persons of independent means. Article 18 (ex 8a) EC recognises these rights as incidents of European citizenship.

Beneficiaries of the rules are nationals of the Member States. Companies or firms must meet both a nationality and "residence" test; they must, under Art.48 (ex 58) EC be formed under the law of a Member State and have their registered office, central administration or principal place of business within the Community. To claim the rights accorded by Community law, there must generally be some activity which engages the Community rules: Case 175/78 *Saunders* [1979] E.C.R. 1129; Case C-41/90 *Höfner v Macrotron* [1991] E.C.R. I-1979. So-called reverse discrimination is permitted. But the rights deriving from Community law can be pleaded against the State of which the person is a national if there is some connecting factor to the situations contemplated by Community law: Cases C-332/90 & C-132/93 *Volker Steen* [1992] E.C.R. I-341 and [1994] E.C.R. I-2715.

Community law defines a worker as someone obliged to provide services for another, in return for reward, and subject to the direction and control of that other person: Case 66/85 *Lawrie-Blum* [1986] E.C.R. 2121. Workers include those in low-paid, part-time work, provided that their work is effective and genuine and not on such a small scale as to be regarded as purely marginal and ancillary: Case 53/81 *Levin* [1982] E.C.R. 1035, though in applying this test account need only be taken of the pattern of work in the Member State of residence: Case C-357/89 *Raulin* [1992] E.C.R. I-1027.

A person does not cease to be a worker for the purposes of Art.39 simply by ceasing to be employed. So a German worker whose employment ended not long after it had started when she suffered a back injury did not, by that reason alone, cease to be a worker: *CIS/3890/2005*. Note that Art.7(3)(a) of the Citizenship Directive expressly provides that a person temporarily unable to work by reason of illness or accident retains the status of a worker. Furthermore, Art.17(1)(b) affords a right of permanent residence to those who become permanently incapacitated for work after a continuous period of residence in the host Member State for two years.

In case C-258/04 *Ioannidis*, [2005] ECR I-8275, the Court avoided ruling on the interpretation of Articles 12, 17 and 18 EC, but did rule that it is contrary to Art.39 EC and Art. 7(2) of reg. 1612/68 for a member state to refuse to grant a tideover allowance to a national of another Member State seeking their first employment, who is not the dependent child of a migrant worker residing in the Member State granting the allowance, solely on the ground that the claimant completed their secondary education in another Member State.

Work or employment should be distinguished from establishment (governed by Arts 43–48 EC) which includes self-employment, the setting up of agencies, branches and subsidiaries, and activities by companies or firms. A modest continuing presence will constitute establishment: Case 205/84 *Commission v Germany* [1986] E.C.R. 3755. Freedom of movement (governed by Arts 49–55 EC) also exists for both providers and recipients of services: Case 186/87 *Cowan* [1989] E.C.R. 195. Services are activities provided for remuneration. Education principally financed by public funds is not a service: Case C-109/93 *Wirth* [1993] E.C.R. I-6447.

Where Community law applies, there is a prohibition on any form of discrimination based on nationality. A breach of Community law could flow from a non-discriminatory provision which has the effect of hindering free movement: Case C-415/93 *Bosman* [1995] E.C.R. I-4921.

Those within the Community provisions have a right of entry and residence in the Member State which are elaborated in Dir.2004/38/EC, reproduced at para.3.60 of this Volume. There are rights for both the economic factor and members of their families. Nonnational spouses are treated as if they were nationals of a Member State: Case 131/85 *Gül* [1986] E.C.R. 1573. Council Reg.1612/68 [1968–69] O.J. Spec. Ed. 475 spells out the rights of workers and their families. There is a right to remain after a period of economic activity in a Member State.

Note that certain persons whose circumstances do not bring themselves within the Treaty rules on free movement of workers may have an independent right to reside in a Member State other than that of their nationality under Article 18 EC, which was held in Case C-413/99 *Baumbast and R v Secretary of State for the Home Department*, Judgment of September 17, 2002, [2002] E.C.R. I-7091, to be directly effective as regards Mr Baumbast.

Work seekers enjoy a limited right of entry and residence, but not other social rights accorded to those who have found work: Case 316/85 *Lebon* [1987] E.C.R. 2811. Note that the citizenship line of cases discussed in the annotations to Art.18 may require some reconsideration of the law as stated in *Lebon*. Those now in the position of Lebon who are lawfully resident in the host Member State and have the necessary link with the host Member State are entitled to be treated equally with nationals of that State even though they are not workers.

Failure to recognise qualifications, and regulation of the activity by the host State have generated much case law in relation to establishment and services. Equality of treatment with nationals is required, but where there are harmonising directives, those prevail. Among the most important are the Mutual Recognition Dirs 89/48 [1989] O.J. L19/16 and 92/51 [1992] O.J. L209/25. But even in the absence of harmonising directives, the equal treatment provisions of the Treaty give rise to an obligation to consider the equivalence of qualifications and schemes of regulation. In all cases there is an obligation to give reasons for any refusal to recognise qualifications, which must be susceptible of challenge in the Member State to test the compatibility of the decision with the requirements of Community law: Case 226/86 *Heylens* [1987] E.C.R. 4097.

National rules regulating economic activity can only be applied where they can be justified by imperative reasons relating to the public interest, where they apply equally to all persons engaged in that activity in the Member State, where there are no applicable safeguards applied in the home State, where the controls are objectively necessary, and where the measures imposed are the least restrictive to secure the legitimate objective: Case C-106/91 *Ramrath* [1992] E.C.R. I-3351.

The rights are subject to exceptions and limitations. Limitations may be imposed on grounds of public policy, public health and public security under Arts 39(3) (ex 48(3)), 46(1) (ex 56(1)) and 55 (ex 66) EC, spelled out in Dir.2004/38/EC. The public policy ground requires the presence of a genuine and sufficiently serious threat to the requirements of public policy affecting one of the fundamental interests of society: Case 30/77 *Bouchereau* [1977] E.C.R. 1999. The genuineness of the limitation is tested by looking at the regulation of the objectionable conduct within the State: Joined Cases 115 & 116/81 *Adoui and Cornuaille* [1982] E.C.R. 1665.

Article 39(4) (ex 48(4)) EC excludes employment in the public service. A functional test has been adopted for identifying such employment: it must involve the exercise of powers conferred by public law, and responsibility for safeguarding the interests of either central and local government: Case 149/79 *Commission v Belgium* [1980] E.C.R. 3881 and [1982] E.C.R. 1845. Articles 45 (ex 55) and 55 (ex 66) EC exclude from the rights of establishment and services activities connected with the exercise of official authority. Again a functional approach is adopted: Case 2/74 *Reyners* [1974] E.C.R. 631.

Whenever adverse decisions are taken in respect of entry and residence, there are due process guarantees in Chapter VI at Dir.2004/38/EC).

Enlargement, free movement and access to social security benefits

3.38   Ten new States joined the European Union on May 1, 2004, but there are detailed Treaties of Accession with these ten new Member States. In relation to the law of the internal market relating to workers, establishment and services, there will be transitional periods over which the full application of the Treaty rules will be phased in. The Europe Agreements, which paved the way for membership, did not give a right of access to the labour markets of the Member States for nationals of the applicant countries. The result is that virtually all nationals from the new Member States who were, prior to May 1, 2004, workers in the territories of the 15 existing Member States were there as a result of the application national immigration rules or of the provisions of bilateral agreements between the countries in question. Those lawfully resident in one of the Member States acquired rights under the Europe Agreements, and from May 1, 2004 will acquire rights under the EC Treaty.

In the past, it has been common to have transitional periods for the implementation. These have been followed by, or coupled with, a period during which safeguard measures may be taken if there is serious or persistent disruption of the labour market as a result of the exercise of the free movement rights. In the case of the accession of Spain and Portugal, a transitional period of seven to ten years for the free movement of workers was agreed, though the full operation of the Treaty provisions was achieved after six years. Transitional periods for the right of establishment, and

Article 39

freedom of movement to provide services have not been applied on past enlargements. This is largely accounted for by provisions in agreements prior to accession which have paved the way for free movement in these sectors. There are, however, special rules in relation to posting of workers from Germany and Austria.

The 2004 enlargement has been accompanied by a very high level of concern about the potential of labour migration to disturb the labour markets of some Member States. Such concerns have flowed from geographic proximity, (leading to a prediction that labour migration will be concentrated in the so-called "front-line" Member States) considerable variations in earnings levels, differential levels of unemployment, and a concern that there will be a greater propensity for labour migration than with earlier enlargements.

It is important to realise that the transitional period covers only the right of movement for the purposes of employment. There will be an immediate right to move for the purposes of study or residence.

The arrangements for the 2004 enlargement are as follows. Until May 1, 2006, the current Member States may choose to apply national rules to the admission of workers from the new Member States (except Cyprus and Malta, whose nationals will enjoy full Community law rights from May 1, 2004). After this two-year period, the Commission will report on migration patterns and the current Member States will be required to define their position from May 1, 2006. The expectation is that some of the alarmist talk about labour migration will not materialise and that it will be possible to move to the application of Community rules on the free movement of workers. Those countries which did so would be able to apply safeguard measures for a period of three years in the event of their experiencing serious and unexpected disturbances of the labour market. On previous enlargements, similar safeguard measures have been available, but they have never been invoked.

From May 1, 2009, those current Member States still applying national rules would be called upon to open up their labour markets subject to the possibility of seeking safeguard measures to address serious and unexpected disturbances of the labour market. From May 1, 2011, Community rules will apply to movement of workers to all current Member States.

Free movement of workers who are nationals of the current Member States to the new Member States will take effect under the same transitional arrangements, though it is likely that some Member States will choose to apply a very liberal regime from the date of enlargement. There is a seven-year safeguard provision written into the Treaty of Accession for Malta.

Finally, there is a standstill clause, under which no Member State may introduce measures more restrictive than those in place immediately prior to May 1, 2004. There will also be a Community preference in the labour market for nationals of the new Member States over nationals from countries which are not members of the EU.

What does this mean for entitlement to benefits under UK law? The position will be complex, since the first task will be to determine the status of the claimant under the EC Treaty. Government concerns about so-called "benefit tourism" ("safeguarding the UK's social security system from the possibility of exploitation") have led to the introduction of amendments to the habitual residence test in order to avoid this phenomenon. These are to be found in the Social Security (Habitual Residence) Amendment Regulations 2004 (SI 2004/1232), which were made on April 28, 2004, laid before Parliament on April 30, 2004, and entered into force on May 1, 2004), which will need to be read with the Accession (Immigration and Worker Registration) Regulations 2004 (SI 2004/1219) which also entered into force on May 1, 2004. The regulations provide that for the purposes of entitlement to income support, income-based jobseeker's allowance, council tax benefit, housing benefit, and State pension credit, a person will not be treated as habitually resident in the UK, the Channel Islands, the Isle of Man or the Republic of Ireland—a condition of entitlement to these benefits—unless they have a "right to reside" in the UK, the Channel Islands, the Isle of Man or the Republic of Ireland.

Extracts from the EC Treaty

The position in relation to nationals of the new Member States would accordingly appear to be as follows:

1. A distinction is made between nationals of Cyprus and Malta, who will enjoy full Treaty rights from May 1, 2004 and nationals of the remaining eight Member States. Nationals of Cyprus and Malta will accordingly be treated in exactly the same way as nationals of existing EEA countries.
2. Claims to disability living allowance and attendance allowance for those resident in the United Kingdom will not be restricted. There is already a residence test for entitlement to these benefits.
3. For the eight countries of central and eastern Europe who are joining (referred to in DWP jargon as "A8 nationals"), there will be a distinction between those in employment and those in self-employment. The Government has indicated if those admitted under the right of establishment cease their occupational activity, they will not be eligible for benefit. That is a controversial proposition under Community law.
4. Access to means-tested benefits will only be available for those who meet the new habitual residence test which includes a requirement that the person enjoys a "right to reside". Those who do not meet the habitual residence test are treated as "persons from abroad" under the various regulations regardless of their nationality.
5. Nationals of the eight affected new Member States who come to the United Kingdom to work will be required to register with the Home Office as soon as they take up employment. The requirement to register will cease once the person has been working (periods of self-employment will not count as working) in the United Kingdom while holding a valid worker's registration scheme certificate for a continuous period of 12 months.
6. The combined effect of the habitual residence test and the requirement for registration would seem to mean that a registered worker who becomes unemployed before they have accrued their 12 months registration will not be eligible for benefit.
7. Access to contribution-based benefits will not be affected and entitlement will arise once the requisite contribution record has been established.
8. Co-ordination of social security under Regulation 1408/71 applies to all new Member States with effect from May 1, 2004.

The following background documentation sets out the thoughts behind the new legislation and the response of the Social Security Advisory Committee to it:

— Note from the Social Security Advisory Committee, March 23, 2004 on the Social Security (Habitual Residence) Amendment Regulations.

— Consultation on the Social Security (Habitual Residence) Amendment Regulations 2004: Supplemental Information to Explanatory Memorandum: The Draft Accession (Immigration and Worker Registration) Regulations 2004.

— Press release: April 30, 2004, Department for Work and Pensions: "Regulations to protect benefit system and welcome workers".

— The Report of the Social Security Advisory Committee dated April 22, 2004 on the proposals referred to them in respect of these Regulations, Cm. 6181.

In *Secretary of State for the Home Department v Limbuela, Tesema and Adam*, [2004] EWCA Civ 540, the Court of Appeal ruled that the refusal to provide State support for three asylum seekers who had not applied for asylum within three days of their arrival in the United Kingdom under s.55 of the Nationality, Immigration and Asylum Act 2002 engaged their Convention rights under Article 3. The appeal of

Article 39

the Secretary of State against the decision of the Court of Appeal has been dismissed by a unanimous House of Lords, [2005] UKHL 66. For a discussion of the potential impact of the new rules on A8 nationals and some issues relating to their compatibility with Community law, see *R. (on the application of H and D) v Secretary of State for Work and Pensions* [2004] EWHC 1097 Admin. This is the decision of Collins J on the application for judicial review of the new regulations. Collins J dismissed the application in so far as it related to compatibility with Community law since he regarded the matter as covered by the derogation from the full application of the provisions on the free movement of workers. Collins J refers to what was at the time the pending appeal in *Limbuela* as possibly being determinative of the human rights arguments raised in the application.

Article 40 (ex 49) EC

The Council shall, acting in accordance with the procedure referred to in Article 251 and after consulting the Economic and Social Committee, issue directives or make regulations setting out the measures required to bring about freedom of movement for workers, as defined in Article 39, in particular: 3.39

(a) by ensuring close cooperation between national employment services;
(b) by abolishing those administrative procedures and practices and those qualifying periods in respect of eligibility for available employment, whether resulting from national legislation or from agreements previously concluded between Member States, the maintenance of which would form an obstacle to liberalisation of the movement of workers;
(c) by abolishing all such qualifying periods and other restrictions provided for either under national legislation or under agreements previously concluded between Member States as imposed on workers of other Member States conditions regarding the free choice of employment other than those imposed on workers of the State concerned;
(d) by setting up appropriate machinery to bring offers of employment into touch with applications for employment and to facilitate the achievement of a balance between supply and demand in the employment market in such a way as to avoid serious threats to the standard of living and level of employment in the various regions and industries.

Article 41 (ex 50) EC

Member States shall, within the framework of a joint programme, encourage the exchange of young workers. 3.40

Article 42 (ex 51) EC

The Council shall, acting in accordance with the procedure referred to in Article 251, adopt such measures in the field of social security as are necessary to provide freedom of movement for workers; to this end, it shall make arrangements to secure for migrant workers and their dependants: 3.41

(a) aggregation, for the purpose of acquiring and retaining the right to benefit and of calculating the amount of benefit, of all periods taken into account under the laws of the several countries;
(b) payment of benefits to persons resident in the territories of Member States.

The Council shall act unanimously throughout the procedure referred to in Article 251.

General Note

3.42 Article 42 EC provides for the co-ordination of social security rules in the Member States (extended to the EEA countries by the EEA Agreement) in order to minimise a potential barrier to the free movement of workers. Co-ordination requires co-operation between the Member States to provide interchange between different national social security systems. The Court of Justice has frequently drawn attention to the distinction between harmonisation and co-ordination and noted that the substantive and procedural differences between the social security systems of the Member States remain unaffected by Art.42 and its secondary legislation: Case 41/84 *Pinna* [1986] E.C.R. 1 at 24–5. But it has also been established that those exercising the right of freedom of movement should not lose advantages in the field of social security; this has come to be known as the *Petroni* principle: Case 24/75 *Petroni* [1975] E.C.R. 1149, para.13 of judgment.

Three general principles emerge from the complex rules of co-ordination which can be found in Reg.1408/71 and the case law:

1. A national of a Member State (or EEA country) is not to be disqualified from entitlement to benefits on the grounds of nationality or on a change of country or residence within the European Union (or EEA).

2. A national of a Member State (or EEA country) may become entitled to a benefit by having contributions or qualifying periods of employment in one Member State (or EEA country) aggregated with those arising in another Member State (or EEA country).

3. A national of a Member State (of EEA country) should not be better off in relation to entitlement to benefits by reason of his or her exercise of rights to move freely between Member States (or EEA countries).

Note that Regulation 1408/71 is due to be replaced by the "simplified" social security regulation, probably some time in 2007: see Regulation 883/2004/EC of April 29, 2004 on the coordination of social security systems [2004] OJ L200/1, correcting OJ L166/1.

Section 4

The Court of Justice

Article 220 (ex 164) EC

3.43 [¹ The Court of Justice and the Court of First Instance, each within its jurisdiction, shall ensure that in the interpretation and application of this Treaty the law is observed.

In addition, judicial panels may be attached to the Court of First Instance under the conditions laid down in Article 225a in order to exercise, in certain specific areas, the judicial competence laid down in this Treaty.]

Article 220

AMENDMENT

1. Treaty of Nice, Art.2(26) (February 1, 2003).

Article 225 (ex 168a) EC

[¹ **1.** The Court of First Instance shall have jurisdiction to hear and determine at first instance actions or proceedings referred to in Articles 230, 232, 235, 236 and 238, with the exception of those assigned to a judicial panel and those reserved in the Statute for the Court of Justice. The Statute may provide for the Court of First Instance to have jurisdiction for other classes of action or proceeding.

Decisions given by the Court of First Instance under this paragraph may be subject to a right of appeal to the Court of Justice on points of law only, under the conditions and within the limits laid down by the Statute.

2. The Court of First Instance shall have jurisdiction to hear and determine actions or proceedings brought against decisions of the judicial panels set up under Article 225a.

Decisions given by the Court of First Instance under this paragraph may exceptionally be subject to review by the Court of Justice, under the conditions and within the limits laid down by the Statute, where there is a serious risk of the unity or consistency of Community law being affected.

3. The Court of First Instance shall have jurisdiction to hear and determine questions referred for a preliminary ruling under Article 234, in specific areas laid down by the Statute.

Where the Court of First Instance considers that the case requires a decision of principle likely to affect the unity or consistency of Community law, it may refer the case to the Court of Justice for a ruling.

Decisions given by the Court of First Instance on questions referred for a preliminary ruling may exceptionally be subject to review by the Court of Justice, under the conditions and within the limits laid down by the Statute, where there is a serious risk of the unity or consistency of Community law being affected.]

3.44

AMENDMENT

1. Treaty of Nice, Art.2(31), (February 1, 2003).

[¹*Article 225a*

The Council, acting unanimously on a proposal from the Commission and after consulting the European Parliament and the Court of Justice or at the request of the Court of Justice and after consulting the European Parliament and the Commission, may create judicial panels to hear and determine at first instance certain classes of action or proceeding brought in specific areas.

The decision establishing a judicial panel shall lay down the rules on the organisation of the panel and the extent of the jurisdiction conferred upon it.

Decisions given by judicial panels may be subject to a right of appeal on points of law only or, when provided for in the decision establishing the

3.45

Extracts from the EC Treaty

panel, a right of appeal also on matters of fact, before the Court of First Instance.

The members of the judicial panels shall be chosen from persons whose independence is beyond doubt and who possess the ability required for appointment to judicial office. They shall be appointed by the Council, acting unanimously.

The judicial panels shall establish their Rules of Procedure in agreement with the Court of Justice. Those Rules shall require the approval of the Council, acting by a qualified majority.

Unless the decision establishing the judicial panel provides otherwise, the provisions of this Treaty relating to the Court of Justice and the provisions of the Statute of the Court of Justice shall apply to the judicial panels.]

AMENDMENT

1. Inserted by the Treaty of Nice, Art.2(32) (February 1, 2003).

Article 226 (ex 169) EC

3.46   If the Commission considers that a Member State has failed to fulfil an obligation under this Treaty, it shall deliver a reasoned opinion on the matter after giving the State concerned the opportunity to submit its observations.

If the State concerned does not comply with the opinion within the period laid down by the Commission, the latter may bring the matter before the Court of Justice.

Article 227 (ex 170) EC

3.47   A Member State which considers that another Member State has failed to fulfil an obligation under this Treaty may bring the matter before the Court of Justice.

Before a Member State brings an action against another Member State for an alleged infringement of an obligation under this Treaty, it shall bring the matter before the Commission.

The Commission shall deliver a reasoned opinion after each of the States concerned has been given the opportunity to submit its own case and its observations on the other party's case both orally and in writing.

If the Commission has not delivered an opinion within three months of the date on which the matter was brought before it, the absence of such opinion shall not prevent the matter from being brought before the Court of Justice.

Article 228 (ex 171) EC

3.48   1. If the Court of Justice finds that a Member State has failed to fulfil an obligation under this Treaty, the State shall be required to take the necessary measures to comply with the judgment of the Court of Justice.

Article 228

2. If the Commission considers that the Member State concerned has not taken such measures it shall, after giving that State the opportunity to submit its observations, issue a reasoned opinion specifying the points on which the Member State concerned has not complied with the judgment of the Court of Justice.

If the Member State concerned fails to take the necessary measures to comply with the Court's judgment within the time limit laid down by the Commission, the latter may bring the case before the Court of Justice. In so doing it shall specify the amount of the lump sum or penalty payment to be paid by the Member State concerned which it considers appropriate in the circumstances.

If the Court of Justice finds that the Member State concerned has not complied with its judgment it may impose a lump sum or penalty payment on it.

This procedure shall be without prejudice to Article 227.

Article 230 (ex 173) EC

[¹ The Court of Justice shall review the legality of acts adopted jointly by the European Parliament and the Council, of acts of the Council, of the Commission and of the ECB, other than recommendations and opinions, and of acts of the European Parliament intended to produce legal effects vis-à-vis third parties.

It shall for this purpose have jurisdiction in actions brought by a Member State, the European Parliament, the Council or the Commission on grounds of lack of competence, infringement of an essential procedural requirement, infringement of this Treaty or of any rule of law relating to its application, or misuse of powers.

The Court of Justice shall have jurisdiction under the same conditions in actions brought by the Court of Auditors and by the ECB for the purpose of protecting their prerogatives.

Any natural or legal person may, under the same conditions, institute proceedings against a decision addressed to that person or against a decision which, although in the form of a regulation or a decision addressed to another person, is of direct and individual concern to the former.

The proceedings provided for in this article shall be instituted within two months of the publication of the measure, or of its notification to the plaintiff, or, in the absence thereof, of the day on which it came to the knowledge of the latter, as the case may be.]

3.49

AMENDMENT

1. Treaty of Nice, Art.2(34) (February 1, 2003).

3.50

Article 231 (ex 174) EC

If the action is well founded, the Court of Justice shall declare the act concerned to be void.

In the case of a regulation, however, the Court of Justice shall, if it considers this necessary, state which of the effects of the regulation which it has declared void shall be considered as definitive.

Extracts from the EC Treaty

Article 234 (ex 177) EC

3.51   The Court of Justice shall have jurisdiction to give preliminary rulings concerning:
(a) the interpretation of this Treaty;
(b) the validity and interpretation of acts of the institutions of the Community and of the ECB;
(c) the interpretation of the statutes of bodies established by an act of the Council, where those statutes so provide.

Where such a question is raised before any court or tribunal of a Member State, that court or tribunal may, if it considers that a decision on the question is necessary to enable it to give judgment, request the Court of Justice to give a ruling thereon.

Where any such question is raised in a case pending before a court or tribunal of a Member State against whose decisions there is no judicial remedy under national law, that court or tribunal shall bring the matter before the Court of Justice.

GENERAL NOTE

3.52   Any national court or tribunal can refer questions on the interpretation of the ECTreaty, and on the validity and interpretation of Community legislation to the Court of Justice under Art.234 (ex 177) EC. The objective of the procedure is a partnership between national courts and tribunals and the Court of Justice to ensure the uniform application in all Member States of Community law.

Courts other than final appeal courts have a *discretion* to make a reference, whereas final appeal courts have a *duty* to refer questions for consideration by the Court of Justice where answers to those questions are necessary to enable the national court to determine the question before it.

The effect of a court or tribunal seeking a ruling is that the national proceedings stand adjourned pending the receipt of the ruling of the Court of Justice. The case is then relisted for determination before the national court or tribunal in the light of the ruling of the Court of Justice on the point of Community law. The Court of Justice is careful not to determine the point arising under national law.

It is an error of law for a tribunal to fail to address a point of European Community law raised in the course of an appeal: *R(SB)6/91*, para.5, and *R(S)2/93*.

Care should be taken whenever a tribunal is called upon to decide an issue involving a national of an EEA country. If a case involves a national of an EEA country, inquiry should be made to determine whether the provisions of European Community law apply to that person and assist in qualifying them for benefit. Failure to do so is an error of law: *CIS/771/1997*.

The Court of Justice has stressed in Case 166/73 *Rheinmühlen* [1974] E.C.R. 33 at 38, that the objective of the preliminary ruling procedure is a partnership between national courts and tribunals and the Court of Justice with a view to ensuring the uniform application of Community law in all the Member States.

Under the procedure, the Court of Justice advises on the meaning of Community law put to it by a national court or tribunal. The discretion as to whether a reference is made is a wide one, and may be exercised by the court or tribunal of its own notion or on application for the court or tribunal to consider doing so by the parties. The leading case of the Court of Justice on the exercise of the discretion to refer is Joined Cases 36 & 71/80 *Irish Creamery Milk Suppliers Association v Ireland* [1981] E.C.R. 735. The principles laid down in this case have been approved in Case 72/83 *Campus Oil v Minister for Industry and Energy* [1984] E.C.R. 2727; and Case 14/86 *Pretore di Salo v Persons Unknown* [1987] E.C.R. 2545. The following points emerge from this line of cases:

1. It is for the national court or tribunal to decide at what stage of proceedings it is appropriate for a preliminary ruling to be requested.
2. In order to assist the Court of Justice, it is essential for the national court or tribunal to define the legal context in which the reference is made.
3. This suggests that in some cases it might well be appropriate for the facts in the case to be established and for questions of purely national law to be settled at the time of the reference.
4. Attempts to fetter or limit the discretion of the national court or tribunal are inconsistent with Community law.
5. The discretion to refer is that of the national court or tribunal and not that of the parties.

Practice in English courts and tribunals has been influenced by the guidelines expressed by Lord Denning in *Bulmer v Bollinger (No.2)* [1974] Ch 401, but these are not binding on any court or tribunal and aspects of them are inconsistent with statements of the Court of Justice. Distilling a considerable body of case law and adding points specific to the social security jurisdictions, the following factors are relevant in the determination by a tribunal or Commissioner of the exercise of the discretion to refer questions to the Court of Justice, namely whether:

1. a serious point of Community law arises in the case which has been fully argued by the parties;
2. the relevant facts have been found or are substantially agreed;
3. the point of law will be substantially determinative of the case;
4. there is any Community authority precisely or closely in point;
5. there is any Commissioners' authority addressing the point of Community law; and
6. it seems certain that at some stage in the life of the case, it will have to be referred to the Court of Justice.

The expense and delay caused by an inappropriate reference will be issues every tribunal and Commissioner will consider. The factors set out above are consistent with Community law on the exercise of the discretion to refer. The absence of full argument on the Community point—from both the claimant and the Secretary of State—(and full argument is likely to be rare in tribunals) suggests that caution should be the order of the day before the tribunals. On the other hand, tribunals should not be inhibited from making a reference if the relevant facts have been found, if the point has been fully argued, if the tribunal concludes that the appeal turns on the proper interpretation of a point of Community law, if there is no relevant authority which suggests that the question of interpretation is free from doubt, and if it seems certain that at some stage a reference will need to be made to resolve the question. It is probably fair to say that such circumstances will not be common place in the tribunals.

The Court of Justice has itself issued guidance for national courts and tribunals on the making of references and this is reproduced at the end of the annotations to this Article.

Although there are prescribed forms of order for references from the High Court, the Court of Justice does not make any formal requirements as to form. The tribunal (or Commissioner) is responsible for drafting the questions it wishes to refer. The question should be couched in terms which pose a general question of law rather than the specific issues raised in the case. The questions should be self-contained and self-explanatory, since they will be notified to the Commission, Council and the Member States under Art.20 of the Statute of the Court. These may choose within two months of the notification to submit written observations on the questions raised. Though the only requirement is the formulation of questions for the Court of Justice, it will be helpful to the Court to provide the following further information:

1. the facts of the case;
2. the relevant provisions of United Kingdom law;
3. the relevant provisions of Community law;
4. a summary of the contentions of the parties on the question or questions referred;
5. if necessary, the reasons why the answers to the questions referred are considered necessary to decide the case.

A ruling given by the Court of Justice is binding on the national court or tribunal as to the interpretation of the Community law in question. It will also bind future courts or tribunal determining similar questions: see s.3(1), European Communities Act 1972.

In *CIS/501/1993* the Commissioner had to consider whether he had jurisdiction to consider the validity of a reference to the Court of Justice made by a tribunal. The Commissioner, of course, only has jurisdiction when there is a "final" decision of a tribunal. The question was whether a reference could be regarded as a final decision. The Commissioner relied on RSC Ord.114, r.6 and *R. v International Stock Exchange of the United Kingdom and the Republic of Ireland Ltd Ex p. Else (1982) Ltd* [1993] Q.B. 534 in holding that an order referring questions to the Court of Justice is to be treated as a final decision against which appeal will lie. He then set aside the decision to refer since the answer to the question posed was clearly not "necessary" to enable the tribunal to resolve the issue before it. The Commissioner also makes reference to the guidelines set down by the Court of Appeal in *Bulmer*. Those guidelines are, as noted above, not wholly consistent with statements made by the Court of Justice and care should be taken in relying exclusively upon them without referring to the relevant decisions of the Court of Justice and subsequent decisions of the United Kingdom courts: see generally A. Arnull, "References to the European Court" (1990) 15 E.L.Rev. 375.

The Court of Justice guidance is as follows:

Court of Justice of the European Communities

NOTE FOR GUIDANCE ON REFERENCES BY NATIONAL COURTS FOR PRELIMINARY RULINGS

3.53 The development of the Community legal order is largely the result of cooperation between the Court of Justice of the European Communities and national courts and tribunals through the preliminary ruling procedure under Article 177 of the EC Treaty and the corresponding provisions of the ECSC and Euratom Treaties.[1]

In order to make this co-operation more effective, and so enable the Court of Justice better to meet the requirements of national courts by providing helpful answers to preliminary questions, this Note for Guidance is addressed to all interested parties, in particular to all national courts and tribunals.

It must be emphasised that the Note is for guidance only and has no binding or interpretative effect in relation to the provisions governing the preliminary ruling procedure. It merely contains practical information which, in the light of experience in applying the preliminary ruling procedure, may help to prevent the kind of difficulties which the Court has sometimes encountered.

Article 234

1. Any court or tribunal of a Member State may ask the Court of Justice to interpret a rule of Community law, whether contained in the Treaties or in acts of secondary law, if it considers that this is necessary for it to give judgement in a case pending before it.

   Courts or tribunals against whose decisions there is no judicial remedy under national law must refer questions of interpretation arising before them to the Court of Justice, unless the Court has already ruled on the point or unless the correct application of the rule of Community law is obvious.[2]

2. The Court of Justice has jurisdiction to rule on the validity of acts of the Community institutions. National courts or tribunals may reject a plea challenging the validity of such an act. But where a national court (even one whose decision is still subject to appeal) intends to question the validity of a Community act, it must refer that question to the Court of Justice.[3]

   Where, however, a national court or tribunal has serious doubts about the validity of a Community act on which a national measure is based, it may, in exceptional cases, temporarily suspend application of the latter measure or grant other interim relief with respect to it. It must then refer the question of validity to the Court of Justice, stating the reasons for which it considers that the Community act is not valid.[4]

3. Questions referred for a preliminary ruling must be limited to the interpretation of a provision of Community law, since the Court of Justice does not have jurisdiction to interpret national law or assess its validity. It is for the referring court or tribunal to apply the relevant rule of Community law in the specific case pending before it.

4. The order of the national court or tribunal referring a question to the Court of Justice for a preliminary ruling may be in any form allowed by national procedural law. Reference of a question or questions to the Court of Justice generally involves a stay of the national proceedings until the Court has given its ruling, but the decision to stay proceedings is one which is for the national court alone to take in accordance with its own national law.

5. The order for reference containing the question or questions referred to the Court will have to be translated by the Court's translators into the other official languages of the Community. Questions concerning the interpretation or validity of Community law are frequently of general interest and the Member States and Community institutions are entitled to submit observations. It is therefore desirable that the reference should be drafted as clearly and precisely as possible.

6. The order for reference should contain a statement of reasons which is succinct but sufficiently complete to give the Court, and those to whom it must be notified (the Member States, the Commission and in certain cases the Council and the European Parliament), a clear understanding of the factual and legal context of the main proceedings.[5]

   In particular, it should include:

   - a statement of the facts which are essential to a full understanding of the legal significance of the main proceedings;
   - an exposition of the national law which may be applicable;
   - a statement of the reasons which have prompted the national court to refer the question or questions to the Court of Justice; and
   - where appropriate, a summary of the arguments of the parties.

   The aim should be to put the Court of Justice in a position to give the national court an answer which will be of assistance to it. The order for reference should also be accompanied by copies of any documents needed for a proper understanding of the case, especially the text of the applicable national

7. A national court or tribunal may refer a question to the Court of Justice as soon as it find that a ruling on the point or points of interpretation or validity is necessary to enable it to give judgment. It must be stressed, however, that it is not for the Court of Justice to decide issues of fact or to resolve disputes as to the interpretation or application of rules of national law. It is therefore desirable that a decision to refer should not be taken until the national proceedings have reached a stage where the national court is able to define, if only as a working hypothesis, the factual and legal context of the question; on any view, the administration of justice is likely to be best served if the reference is not made until both sides have been heard.[6]

8. The order for reference and the relevant documents should be sent by the national court directly to the Court of Justice, by registered post, addressed to: The Registry, Court of Justice of the European Communities, L-2925. Telephone (352) 43031. The Court Registry will remain in contact with the national court until judgment is given, and will send copies of the various documents (written observations, Report for the Hearing, Opinion of the Advocate General). The Court will also send its judgment to the national court. The Court would appreciate being informed about the application of its judgment in the national proceedings and being sent a copy of the national court's final decision.

9. Proceedings for a preliminary ruling before the Court of Justice are free of charge. The Court does not rule on costs.

FOOTNOTES

1. A preliminary ruling is also provided for by protocols to several conventions concluded by the Member States, in particular the Brussels Convention on Jurisdiction and the Enforcement of Judgments in Civil and Commercial Matters.

2. Judgment in Case 283/81 *CILFIT v Ministero della Sanita* [1982] E.C.R. 3415.

3. Judgment in Case 314/85 *Firma Foto-Frost v Hauptzollamt Lübeck-Ost* [1987] E.C.R. 4199.

4. Judgments in Joined Cases C-143/88 & C-92/89 *Zuckerfabrik Süerdithmarschen and Zuckerfabrik Soest* [1991] E.C.R. I-415 and in Case C-465/93 *Atlanta Fruchthandelsgesellschaft* [1995] E.C.R. I-3761.

5. Judgment in Joined cases C-320/90, C-321/90 & C-322/90 *Telemarsicabruzzo* [1993] E.C.R. I-393.

6. Judgments in Case 70/77 *Simmenthal v Amministrazione delle Finanze dello Stato* [1978] E.C.R. 1453.

PART VI

GENERAL AND FINAL PROVISIONS

Article 308 (ex 235) EC

3.54   If action by the Community should prove necessary to attain, in the course of the operation of the common market, one of the objectives of

Article 308

the Community and this Treaty has not provided the necessary powers, the Council shall, acting unanimously on a proposal from the Commission and after consulting the European Parliament, take the appropriate measures.

GENERAL NOTE

This provision is sometime referred to as the "reserve power", since it gives the Community a power to take action in the absence of a specific authority to do so in the Treaty where action is necessary to attain one of the objectives of the Community. The power has been used in relation to certain social security measures, for example, Dir.79/7 (see below).

3.55

Regulation (EEC) No 1612/68 of the Council of 15 October 1968 on Freedom of Movement for Workers within the Community

[1968] O.J. L257/2

TITLE I OMITTED

TITLE II:

EMPLOYMENT AND EQUALITY OF TREATMENT

Article 7

1. A worker who is a national of a Member State may not, in the territory of another Member State, be treated differently from national workers by reason of his nationality in respect of any conditions of employment and work, in particular as regards remuneration, dismissal, and should he become unemployed, reinstatement or reemployment;
2. He shall enjoy the same social and tax advantages as national workers.
3. He shall also, by virtue of the same right and under the same conditions as national workers, have access to training in vocational schools and retraining centres.
4. Any clause of a collective or individual agreement or of any other collective regulation concerning eligibility for employment, employment, remuneration and other conditions of work or dismissal shall be null and void in so far as it lays down or authorises discriminatory conditions in respect of workers who are nationals of the other Member States.

3.56

GENERAL NOTE

If a national of a Member State is a worker within the meaning of the Regulation, then Art.7(2) is often a better passport to entitlement to a social security benefit than the co-ordinating rules in Reg.1408/71. A worker is entitled to be treated in exactly the same way as someone in a similar position who is a national of the Member State. See, for examples, *R(IS)4/98* and *R(IS)12/98*.

For a review of some of the authorities, see the commentary on reg.21 of the Income Support (General) Regulations 1987 in Volume II of this series.

3.57

Regulation (EEC) No 1612/68

In *CJSA/4065/1999* the Commissioner referred questions to the Court of Justice. On March 23, 2004 the Court delivered its judgment in Case C-138/02 *Collins v Secretary of State for Work and Pensions* [2005] Q.B. 145. The case concerns Mr Collins who holds both Irish and American nationality. He had spent about ten months working in the UK after spending a semester as a student here. In 1998 he returned to the UK to look for work and shortly afterwards claims an income-based jobseeker's allowance. This was refused because he was not regarded as being habitually resident in the UK. The Advocate General and the Court have used different reasoning in reaching essentially the same conclusion.

The Advocate General begins his Opinion by recalling the rights of citizens of the Union under Art.39 EC, but also notes that a person must have the status of actually being a "worker" (as distinct from a "work seeker") before he or she can rely on Art.7(2) of Regulation 1612/68. The Advocate General goes on to note that the habitual residence test is, in principle, indirectly discriminatory since it is easier for UK nationals to fulfil the requirement than nationals of other Member States. However, the Advocate General considers that a condition as to residence which makes it possible to ascertain the degree of connection with the State and the links which the claimant has with the domestic employment market may be justified in order to avoid the movement of persons with the purpose of taking advantage of non-contributory benefits and to prevent abuses. The Advocate General accordingly proposes that the answer to the questions posed by the Commissioner should that Community law as it now stands does not require that an income-based social security benefit be provided to a citizen of the Union who seeks work in a Member State with whose employment market he lacks any connection or link.

The Court concludes that a person in Collins' situation is not a "worker" for the purposes of Title II of Regulation 1612/68, although it is for the national adjudicating authorities to determine whether the term "worker" as used in the national legislation is to be understood in the same sense. Furthermore, Collins does not have a right to reside in the UK solely on the basis of Council Directive 68/360. Finally, the Court concludes,

> "... the right to equal treatment laid down in Art.48(2) (now 39(2)) of the Treaty, read in conjunction with Arts 6 (now 12) and 8 (now 17) of the Treaty, does not preclude legislation which makes entitlement to a jobseeker's allowance conditional on a residence requirement, in so far as that requirement may be justified on the basis of objective considerations that are independent of nationality of the persons concerned and proportionate to the legitimate aim of the national provisions". (para.73).

CJSA/4065/1999, decision of March 4, 2005, is the Commissioner's decision on the reference in *Collins*. On the status of Collins as a worker for the purposes of Regulation 1612/68 in the JSA Regulations, the Commissioner had this to say:

> "In my judgment, the reference in regulation 85(4) of the JSA Regulations to a 'workers for the purposes of [Regulation 1612/68]' must have been intended to have a narrower effect than a reference to a person within the scope of application of the Regulation as a whole. By 'worker' is meant a person who falls within the Community concept of worker in relation to the parts of Regulation 1612/68 that expressly confer entitlements on people in their capacity as workers, rather than in their capacity as nationals of a Member State. That restricts the meaning on the reference in the JSA Regulations to persons who are workers for the purposes of Title II of Part I of Regulation 1612/68. The meaning does not extend to persons who are entitled to assistance under Title I of Part I (in particular Article 5) or who fall only within the broader sense of 'worker' mentioned in paragraph 32 of the ECJ's judgment." (para.16).

The Commissioner then turns to the Court of Justice's conclusions on Community law requirements in relation to justification for the requirement to establish habitual

Article 7

residence, and finds that the test of justification and proportionality is met by the habitual residence test as a condition of entitlement to a meanstested jobseeker's allowance. However, he adds a proviso: for the application of the requirement for any day to be proportionate in any particular case, the answer to the question, "Has the point been reached that the relevant national authority has become satisfied of the genuineness of the claimant's search for work?" must be in the negative. The Commissioner's decision is largely upheld by the Court of Appeal in *Collins v Secretary of State for Work and Pensions* [2006] EWCA Civ 376. However, the Court of Appeal concludes that the Commissioner erred in concluding that in order to render the habitual residence test compatible with Community law it was necessary to introduce the proviso set out above. The result is that the habitual residence test alone is, in the view of the Court of Appeal, sufficient to secure compatibility with Community law on access to a jobseekers allowance.

In Case C-413/01 *Ninni-Orasche v Bundesminister für Wissenschaft, Verkehr und Kunst,* Judgment of November 6, 2003 [2004] All E.R. (EC) 765, the Court was considering a reference from *Verwaltungsgerichthof,* Austria concerning an Italian national, Franca Ninni-Orasche, who had been married to an Austrian national since January 1993 and had been resident in Austria since November 1993. Ninni-Orasche had been employed as a waitress between July 6 and September 25, 1995; she also had some duties as a cashier and in relation to stock control. She was also undertaking part-time study and subsequently passed examinations qualifying her for admission to an Austrian university. She was refused financial support for her studies. The question was whether she was a worker for the purposes of Art.39 EC, and more particularly Regulation 1612/68, since she would then appear potentially to be entitled to financial support for her studies under Art.7(2) of the Regulation (provided other conditions were satisfied). The Court concluded that the short-term work Ninni-Orasche had undertaken qualified her as a worker under Art.39 EC "provided that the activity performed as an employed person is not purely marginal or ancillary" (para.32). This is an issue to be determined by the national courts. Furthermore, a person would not be treated as voluntarily unemployed merely because the initial contract of employment was for a fixed term which has expired.

Note also the citizenship line of cases discussed in the annotations to Art.18 of the EC Treaty above.

There is an argument that child trust contributions under the Child Trust Funds Act 2004 fall within the scope of Art.7(2), which would mean that the exclusion of payment to children in respect of whom child benefit is paid under the application of Community law but who do not reside in the United Kingdom might not survive legal scrutiny. See annotations to s.2 of the Child Trust Funds Act 2004 in Vol.IV.

Article 42

1. *Omitted.*
2. This regulation shall not affect measures taken in accordance with Article 51 of this Treaty.
3. *Omitted.*

3.58

GENERAL NOTE

Following the amendment of the EC Treaty, Art.51 is now Art.42 EC and refers to the adoption of measures in the field of social security.

In *C50/90-00 (DLA)* a Commissioner in Northern Ireland concluded that the effect of Art.42(2) can be to preclude the application of Art.7(2) where the matter is governed by Regulation 1408/71 (a regulation made under Art.51 (now 42) EC).

3.59

The case concerned a claimant for a disability living allowance on the basis of Community law; the claimant was at all relevant times resident in Ireland. She later claimed a disability living allowance in Northern Ireland where she worked, arguing that Art.7(2) meant that the residence and presence conditions could not be applied to her. The Commissioner upholds the decision of the tribunal that she could not maintain the Art.7(2) right since disability living allowance was a benefit falling within Art.10a of Regulation 1408/71, which alone applied to her situation. She says,

"28. It does not appeal to me that Article 42(2) can be given anything other than its plain meaning, i.e. that Regulation (EEC)1612/68 is not to affect measures taken under Article 51. The provisions of that regulation cannot have any effect on such measures".

In *CIS/825/2001* a Commissioner in England, while not dissenting from the decision of the Commissioner in Northern Ireland, disagrees with the reasoning, since it is too wide. The Commissioner in England says,

"43. I conclude from both the specific comments of the Court in *EC Commission v French Republic* and from the absence of the point being taken by or to the Court in other cases that the 'plain meaning' attached to Article 42(2) in C 50/99-00 (DLA) is too wide. The right granted by Article 7(2) of Regulation 1612/68 is a fundamental aspect of the freedom of movement of workers—and, perhaps it should now be said, of European citizens. It is one of the essential aspects of the freedom granted by Article 39 (formerly Article 48) of the Treaty, securing the freedom of movement of workers. Regulation 1408/71 is about coordinating social security systems under Article 42 (formerly 51) of the Treaty by adopting 'such measures as are necessary to provide freedom of movement of workers'. Those Articles pursue parallel aims, and I do not readily read a final provision in Regulation 1612/68 as undercutting those parallel aims so as to reduce a worker's rights under Article 7 of that Regulation unless there is clear reason to do so. The reason to do so, as the European Court reflects, is that there is some provision of Regulation 1408/71 in application which provides a benefit to a worker in a different way to Regulation 1612/68 but, by reason of the purposes of those Regulations, to the same end. In other words, it is an example of what used to be given the Latin tag *specialia generalibus derogant*—a specific rule derogates from a general rule. But, in this context, both rules are concerned with granting rights and not restricting them".

In *Secretary of State for Work and Pensions v Bobezes* [2005] EWCA Civ 111, (the appeal against the Commissioner's decision in *CIS/825/2001*) reported as *R(IS) 6/05*, the Court of Appeal alluded to the question of whether Art.42 precluded the application of Art.7 of Regulation 1612/68 to the claimant's case. Lord Slynn said:

"15. Despite all these arguments based on the European Court's authorities the real point for the purpose of this case is that, when considering whether there is discrimination against Mr Bobezes in the application of . . . the United Kingdom Regulation, there is no difference between Article 3 [of Regulation 1408/71] and Article 7 [of Regulation 1612/68] . . . . Both unequivocally prohibit the different treatment of migrant workers and national workers in the grant and payment of the allowance. . . Despite the Secretary of State's argument [that it was essential for the court to decide under which of the two regulations the matter had to be resolved] I do not consider that it would be appropriate in the circumstances for the court to review all the authorities and to express an opinion on what is at best a theoretical question with no consequences for the parties to this appeal."

Directive 2004/38/EC of the European Parliament and of the Council of 29 April 2004 on the right of citizens of the Union and their family members to move and reside freely within the territory of the Member States amending Regulation (EEC) No 1612/68 and repealing Directives 64/221/EEC, 68/360/EEC, 72/194/EEC, 73/148/EEC, 75/34/EEC, 75/35/EEC, 90/364/EEC, 90/365/EEC and 93/96/EEC

[2004] OJ L229/35 CORRIGENDUM [2005] OJ L197/34

Date for implementation: April 30, 2006

The European Parliament and the Council of the European Union

Having regard to the Treaty establishing the European Community, and in particular Articles 12, 18, 40, 44 and 52 thereof,
Having regard to the proposal from the Commission,
Having regard to the opinion of the European Economic and Social Committee,
Having regard to the opinion of the Committee of the Regions,
Acting in accordance with the procedure laid down in Article 251 of the Treaty,
Whereas:

(1) Citizenship of the Union confers on every citizen of the Union a primary and individual right to move and reside freely within the territory of the Member States, subject to the limitations and conditions laid down in the Treaty and to the measures adopted to give it effect.

(2) The free movement of persons constitutes one of the fundamental freedoms of the internal market, which comprises an area without internal frontiers, in which freedom is ensured in accordance with the provisions of the Treaty.

(3) Union citizenship should be the fundamental status of nationals of the Member States when they exercise their right of free movement and residence. It is therefore necessary to codify and review the existing Community instruments dealing separately with workers, self employed persons, as well as students and other inactive persons in order to simplify and strengthen the right of free movement and residence of all Union citizens.

(4) With a view to remedying this sector-by-sector, piecemeal approach to the right of free movement and residence and facilitating the exercise of this right, there needs to be a single legislative act to amend Council Regulation (EEC) No 1612/68 of 15 October 1968 on freedom of movement for workers within the Community, and to repeal the following acts: Council Directive 68/360/EEC of 15 October 1968 on the abolition of restrictions on movement and residence within the Community for workers of Member States and their families, Council Directive 73/148/EEC of 21 May 1973 on the abolition of restrictions on movement and residence within the Community for nationals of Member States with regard to establishment and the provision of services, Council Directive 90/364/EEC of 28 June 1990 on the right of residence (8), Council Directive 90/365/EEC of 28 June 1990 on the right

of residence for employees and self-employed persons who have ceased their occupational activity (9) and Council Directive 93/96/EEC of 29 October 1993 on the right of residence for students.

(5) The right of all Union citizens to move and reside freely within the territory of the Member States should, if it is to be exercised under objective conditions of freedom and dignity, be also granted to their family members, irrespective of nationality. For the purposes of this Directive, the definition of "family member" should also include the registered partner if the legislation of the host Member State treats registered partnership as equivalent to marriage.

(6) In order to maintain the unity of the family in a broader sense and without prejudice to the prohibition of discrimination on grounds of nationality, the situation of those persons who are not included in the definition of family members under this Directive, and who therefore do not enjoy an automatic right of entry and residence in the host Member State, should be examined by the host Member State on the basis of its own national legislation, in order to decide whether entry and residence could be granted to such persons, taking into consideration their relationship with the Union citizen or any other circumstances, such as their financial or physical dependence on the Union citizen.

(7) The formalities connected with the free movement of Union citizens within the territory of Member States should be clearly defined, without prejudice to the provisions applicable to national border controls.

(8) With a view to facilitating the free movement of family members who are not nationals of a Member State, those who have already obtained a residence card should be exempted from the requirement to obtain an entry visa within the meaning of Council Regulation (EC) No 539/2001 of 15 March 2001 listing the third countries whose nationals must be in possession of visas when crossing the external borders and those whose nationals are exempt from that requirement (1) or, where appropriate, of the applicable national legislation.

(9) Union citizens should have the right of residence in the host Member State for a period not exceeding three months without being subject to any conditions or any formalities other than the requirement to hold a valid identity card or passport, without prejudice to a more favourable treatment applicable to job-seekers as recognised by the case-law of the Court of Justice.

(10) Persons exercising their right of residence should not, however, become an unreasonable burden on the social assistance system of the host Member State during an initial period of residence. Therefore, the right of residence for Union citizens and their family members for periods in excess of three months should be subject to conditions.

(11) The fundamental and personal right of residence in another Member State is conferred directly on Union citizens by the Treaty and is not dependent upon their having fulfilled administrative procedures.

(12) For periods of residence of longer than three months, Member States should have the possibility to require Union citizens to register with the competent authorities in the place of residence, attested by a registration certificate issued to that effect.

(13) The residence card requirement should be restricted to family members of Union citizens who are not nationals of a Member State for periods of residence of longer than three months.

(14) The supporting documents required by the competent authorities for the issuing of a registration certificate or of a residence card should be comprehensively specified in order to avoid divergent administrative practices or interpretations constituting an undue obstacle to the exercise of the right of residence by Union citizens and their family members.

(15) Family members should be legally safeguarded in the event of the death of the Union citizen, divorce, annulment of marriage or termination of a registered partnership. With due regard for family life and human dignity, and in certain conditions to guard against abuse, measures should therefore be taken to ensure that in such circumstances family members already residing within the territory of the host Member State retain their right of residence exclusively on a personal basis.

(16) As long as the beneficiaries of the right of residence do not become an unreasonable burden on the social assistance system of the host Member State they should not be expelled. Therefore, an expulsion measure should not be the automatic consequence of recourse to the social assistance system. The host Member State should examine whether it is a case of temporary difficulties and take into account the duration of residence, the personal circumstances and the amount of aid granted in order to consider whether the beneficiary has become an unreasonable burden on its social assistance system and to proceed to his expulsion. In no case should an expulsion measure be adopted against workers, self-employed persons or job-seekers as defined by the Court of Justice save on grounds of public policy or public security.

(17) Enjoyment of permanent residence by Union citizens who have chosen to settle long term in the host Member State would strengthen the feeling of Union citizenship and is a key element in promoting social cohesion, which is one of the fundamental objectives of the Union. A right of permanent residence should therefore be laid down for all Union citizens and their family members who have resided in the host Member State in compliance with the conditions laid down in this Directive during a continuous period of five years without becoming subject to an expulsion measure.

(18) In order to be a genuine vehicle for integration into the society of the host Member State in which the Union citizen resides, the right of permanent residence, once obtained, should not be subject to any conditions.

(19) Certain advantages specific to Union citizens who are workers or self-employed persons and to their family members, which may allow these persons to acquire a right of permanent residence before they have resided five years in the host Member State, should be maintained, as these constitute acquired rights, conferred by Commission Regulation (EEC) No 1251/70 of 29 June 1970 on the right of workers to remain in the territory of a Member State after having been employed in that State (1) and Council Directive 75/34/EEC of 17 December 1974 concerning the right of nationals of a Member State to remain in the territory of another Member State after having pursued therein an activity in a self-employed capacity.

(20) In accordance with the prohibition of discrimination on grounds of nationality, all Union citizens and their family members residing in a Member State on the basis of this Directive should enjoy, in that Member State, equal treatment with nationals in areas covered by the Treaty, subject to such specific provisions as are expressly provided for in the Treaty and secondary law.

(21) However, it should be left to the host Member State to decide whether it will grant social assistance during the first three months of

residence, or for a longer period in the case of job-seekers, to Union citizens other than those who are workers or self-employed persons or who retain that status or their family members, or maintenance assistance for studies, including vocational training, prior to acquisition of the right of permanent residence, to these same persons.

(22) The Treaty allows restrictions to be placed on the right of free movement and residence on grounds of public policy, public security or public health. In order to ensure a tighter definition of the circumstances and procedural safeguards subject to which Union citizens and their family members may be denied leave to enter or may be expelled, this Directive should replace Council Directive 64/221/EEC of 25 February 1964 on the coordination of special measures concerning the movement and residence of foreign nationals, which are justified on grounds of public policy, public security or public health.

(23) Expulsion of Union citizens and their family members on grounds of public policy or public security is a measure that can seriously harm persons who, having availed themselves of the rights and freedoms conferred o them by the Treaty, have become genuinely integrated into the host Member State. The scope for such measures should therefore be limited in accordance with the principle of proportionality to take account of the degree of integration of the persons concerned, the length of their residence in the host Member State, their age, state of health, family and economic situation and the links with their country of origin.

(24) Accordingly, the greater the degree of integration of Union citizens and their family members in the host Member State, the greater the degree of protection against expulsion should be. Only in exceptional circumstances, where there are imperative grounds of public security, should an expulsion measure be taken against Union citizens who have resided for many years in the territory of the host Member State, in particular when they were born and have resided there throughout their life. In addition, such exceptional circumstances should also apply to an expulsion measure taken against minors, in order to protect their links with their family, in accordance with the United Nations Convention on the Rights of the Child, of 20 November 989.

(25) Procedural safeguards should also be specified in detail in order to ensure a high level of protection of the rights of Union citizens and their family members in the event of their being denied leave to enter or reside in another Member State, as well as to uphold the principle that any action taken by the authorities must be properly justified.

(26) In all events, judicial redress procedures should be available to Union citizens and their family members who have been refused leave to enter or reside in another Member State.

(27) In line with the case-law of the Court of Justice prohibiting Member States from issuing orders excluding for life persons covered by this Directive from their territory, the right of Union citizens and their family members who have been excluded from the territory of a Member State to submit a fresh application after a reasonable period, and in any event after a three year period from enforcement of the final exclusion order, should be confirmed.

(28) To guard against abuse of rights or fraud, notably marriages of convenience or any other form of relationships contracted for the sole purpose of enjoying the right of free movement and residence, Member States should have the possibility to adopt the necessary measures.

(29) This Directive should not affect more favourable national provisions.

(30) With a view to examining how further to facilitate the exercise of the right of free movement and residence, a report should be prepared by the Commission in order to evaluate the opportunity to present any necessary proposals to this effect, notably on the extension of the period of residence with no conditions.

(31) This Directive respects the fundamental rights and freedoms and observes the principles recognised in particular by the Charter of Fundamental Rights of the European Union. In accordance with the prohibition of discrimination contained in the Charter, Member States should implement this Directive without discrimination between the beneficiaries of this Directive on grounds such as sex, race, colour, ethnic or social origin, genetic characteristics, language, religion or beliefs, political or other opinion, membership of an ethnic minority, property, birth, disability, age or sexual orientation.

Have Adopted this Directive

GENERAL NOTE

The Citizenship Directive was a long time in the making. The initial proposal was made in 2001 and the Directive entered into force on April 30, 2006. It repeals and re-enacts nine directives, and amends one regulation. A further regulation will be repealed by the Commission. 3.61

There were more than two years of negotiations about the Directive before it was adopted in 2004, and a further two years was allowed for its implementation. This suggests that it is more than mere consolidation of the secondary legislation to be found in the repealed legislative measures.

Note that The Immigration (European Economic Area) Regulations 2006 (SI 2006/1003) implement in United Kingdom law the requirements of the Directive.

The thrust of the Citizenship Directive can explored under a number of headings.

Integrating the rules on free movement

The existing piecemeal approach to the regulation of rights of entry and residence is replaced with a single instrument which sets out rights of exit and entry, the right to reside, and an elaboration of the circumstances in which a person can be removed from the territory of a Member State other than that of their nationality. There are two remaining regulations which are likely to be central to the movement of persons. First, Regulation 1612/68 remains which sets out specific arrangements to facilitate the free movement of workers. Secondly, Regulation 1408/71/EEC is unaffected. This seeks to co-ordinate the social security systems of the Member States so that they are not an obstacle to the free movement of persons. 3.62

Regulation 1251/70/EEC on the right of workers to remain in the territory of a Member State after having been employed in that State is not repealed by the Citizenship Directive. It is a regulation of the Commission which could not be repealed by the European Parliament and the Council. It is to be repealed by the Commission.

Extending the concept of the family

Under the previous regime, the family of a worker for Community purposes included the spouse, children under the age of 21, and children over the age of 21 together with relatives in the ascending line of the worker and spouse who are actually dependent on the worker. Family members need not be citizens of the Union, 3.63

though many will be. This list is extended by Art.2(2) of the Citizenship Directive to include:

> "the partner with whom the Union citizen has contracted a registered partnership, on the basis of the legislation of a Member State, if the legislation of the host Member State treats registered partnerships as equivalent to marriage and in accordance with the conditions laid down in the relevant legislation of the host Member State;"

This extends the notion of spouse to include the recognition of unmarried partner status in the legislation of the Member States. The language is clearly broad enough to encompass same-sex relationships, but there is a requirement that the host Member State treats such partnerships as equivalent to marriage in the same circumstances. There is also the limitation that the registered partnership on which the mover is depending arises under the law of one of the Member States.

Article 3 of the Citizenship Directive which defines the beneficiaries of the rules in the Directive refers to the definitions in Art.2, but goes on to incorporate an obligation to "facilitate" entry and residence for other persons including "the partner with whom the Union citizen has a durable relationship, duly attested." Some substance is given to the concept of facilitation by the last sentence of Art.3:

> "The host Member State shall undertake an extensive examination of the personal circumstances and shall justify denial of entry or residence to these people."

The outcome is a complex definition of family. The inclusion of registered partners is bound to give rise to difficulty.

There are sure to be references to the Court of Justice on the extended concept of the family for the purposes of rights of free movement.

A new right of permanent residence

3.64 A continuing right of residence under the old regime required repeated renewal of residence permits, or the completion of periods of economic activity which led to a right to remain after completion of a period of economic activity. The new regime is far simpler. A continuous period of five years residence entitles citizens of the Union and their families to a right of permanent residence under Art.16 of the Citizenship Directive. This is not conditional on any particular activity or possession of a particular level of resources. The right of permanent residence is only lost after absence from the host Member State for "a period exceeding two consecutive years".

Reducing bureaucracy

3.65 Citizens of the Union will no longer need to obtain residence permits. Simple registration (if required by the host Member State) is all that can be required. A registration certificate will be issued where registration is required. A residence card is introduced for family members who are not themselves citizens of the Union.

Tighter controls on deportation

3.66 The Commission considers that expulsion of citizens of the Union does not have a place in the area of freedom, security and justice, being built in Europe. So, the Citizenship Directive reduces the scope for Member States to rely on the derogations in the EC Treaty on grounds of public policy, public security and public health in deporting nationals of other Member States. Once a person has acquired a right of permanent residence, then *serious* grounds of public policy or public security will alone justify expulsion. Once a person has resided in the host Member State for a period of 10 years, then only *imperative* ground of public security will justify expulsion.

In any case where expulsion is contemplated on grounds of public policy or public security, the host Member State shall take account of considerations such as how long the individual concerned has resided on its territory, his/her age, state of health, family and economic situation, social and cultural integration into the host Member State and the extent of his/her links with the country of origin.

Equal treatment

3.67 The prohibition of discrimination on grounds of nationality in matters within the scope of the EC Treaty has always been a foundational principle of the Community and Union. In the early days of the Community, the prohibition of discrimination belonged to the market integration model, and was targeted at removing obstacles to economic activity. That approach had to develop organically as social integration became a stronger feature of the ever-closer union of peoples envisaged by the EC Treaty. Now the prohibition of discrimination has become attached to citizenship of the Union, and its constitutional status has been confirmed. Advocate General Jacobs said in his Opinion in Case C-274/96, *Bickel and Franz* [1998] E.C.R. I-7637:

> "Freedom from discrimination on grounds of nationality is the most fundamental right conferred by the Treaty and must be seen as a basic ingredient of Union citizenship."

Taken without any qualifications, this would mean that any citizen of any Member State present in a state other than that of his or her own nationality must be treated in exactly the same manner as nationals of the host State in the same situation. Any difference of treatment would need to be objectively justified on grounds which did not relate to the nationality of the individual. Such a proposition concerns Member States particularly in relation to access to public benefits. While Member States are generally very welcoming of self-sufficient, healthy nationals of other Member States coming to work, study or live, concerns soon emerge with the prospect of the mover needing the support of the State for financial assistance or medical assistance.

Article 24(1) of the Citizenship Directive provides:

> "Subject to such specific provisions as are expressly provided for in the Treaty and secondary law, all Union citizens residing on the basis of this Directive in the territory of the host Member State shall enjoy equal treatment with the nationals of that Member State within the scope of the Treaty. The benefit of this right shall be extended to family members who are not nationals of a Member State and who have the right of residence or permanent residence."

Article 24(2) excludes entitlement to equal treatment in access to social assistance for those with the right of residence for up to three months or longer period as work seekers. It also excludes from equal treatment in access to financial support for studies (other than for those who had and retain economically active status as workers, or self-employed persons) those present for less than five years.

CHAPTER I

GENERAL PROVISIONS

Article 1

Subject

3.68 This Directive lays down:
(a) the conditions governing the exercise of the right of free movement and residence within the territory of the Member States by Union citizens and their family members;

Directive 2004/38/EC

(b) the right of permanent residence in the territory of the Member States for Union citizens and their family members;
(c) the limits placed on the rights set out in (a) and (b) on grounds of public policy, public security or public health.

GENERAL NOTE

3.68.1 See discussion at para.3.31 above of a series of cases which considered the requirement that person must have a "right to reside" in the United Kingdom as a condition of entitlement to certain benefits.

Article 2

Definitions

For the purposes of this Directive:

3.69 1. "Union citizen" means any person having the nationality of a Member State;
2. "family member" means:
(a) the spouse;
(b) the partner with whom the Union citizen has contracted a registered partnership, on the basis of the legislation of a Member State, if the legislation of the host Member State treats registered partnerships as equivalent to marriage and in accordance with the conditions laid down in the relevant legislation of the host Member State;
(c) the direct descendants who are under the age of 21 or are dependants and those of the spouse or partner as defined in point (b);
(d) the dependent direct relatives in the ascending line and those of the spouse or partner as defined in point (b);
3. "host Member State" means the Member State to which a Union citizen moves in order to exercise his/her right of free movement and residence.

Article 3

Beneficiaries

3.70 1. This Directive shall apply to all Union citizens who move to or reside in a Member State other than that of which they are a national, and to their family members as defined in point 2 of Article 2 who accompany or join them.
2. Without prejudice to any right to free movement and residence the persons concerned may have in their own right, the host Member State shall, in accordance with its national legislation, facilitate entry and residence for the following persons:
(a) any other family members, irrespective of their nationality, not falling under the definition in point 2 of Article 2 who, in the country from which they have come, are dependants or members of the household of the Union citizen having the primary right of residence, or where serious health grounds strictly require the personal care of the family member by the Union citizen;

Article 3

(b) the partner with whom the Union citizen has a durable relationship, duly attested.

The host Member State shall undertake an extensive examination of the personal circumstances and shall justify any denial of entry or residence to these people.

CHAPTER II

RIGHT OF EXIT AND ENTRY

Article 4

Right of exit

1. Without prejudice to the provisions on travel documents applicable to national border controls, all Union citizens with a valid identity card or passport and their family members who are not nationals of a Member State and who hold a valid passport shall have the right to leave the territory of a Member State to travel to another Member State.

2. No exit visa or equivalent formality may be imposed on the persons to whom paragraph 1 applies.

3. Member States shall, acting in accordance with their laws, issue to their own nationals, and renew, an identity card or passport stating their nationality.

4. The passport shall be valid at least for all Member States and for countries through which the holder must pass when travelling between Member States. Where the law of a Member State does not provide for identity cards to be issued, the period of validity of any passport on being issued or renewed shall be not less than five years.

Article 5

Right of entry

1. Without prejudice to the provisions on travel documents applicable to national border controls, Member States shall grant Union citizens leave to enter their territory with a valid identity card or passport and shall grant family members who are not nationals of a Member State leave to enter their territory with a valid passport.

No entry visa or equivalent formality may be imposed on Union citizens.

2. Family members who are not nationals of a Member State shall only be required to have an entry visa in accordance with Regulation (EC) No.539/2001 or, where appropriate, with national law. For the purposes of this Directive, possession of the valid residence card referred to in Article 10 shall exempt such family members from the visa requirement.

Member States shall grant such persons every facility to obtain the necessary visas. Such visas shall be issued free of charge as soon as possible and on the basis of an accelerated procedure.

3. The host Member State shall not place an entry or exit stamp in the passport of family members who are not nationals of a Member State provided that they present the residence card provided for in Article 10.

4. Where a Union citizen, or a family member who is not a national of a Member State, does not have the necessary travel documents or, if required, the necessary visas, the Member State concerned shall, before turning them back, give such persons every reasonable opportunity to obtain the necessary documents or have them brought to them within a reasonable period of time or to corroborate or prove by other means that they are covered by the right of free movement and residence.

5. The Member State may require the person concerned to report his/her presence within its territory within a reasonable and non-discriminatory period of time. Failure to comply with this requirement may make the person concerned liable to proportionate and non-discriminatory sanctions.

GENERAL NOTE

Regulation 539/2001/EC does not apply to the United Kingdom.

CHAPTER III

RIGHT OF RESIDENCE

Article 6

Right of residence for up to three months

1. Union citizens shall have the right of residence on the territory of another Member State for a period of up to three months without any conditions or any formalities other than the requirement to hold a valid identity card or passport.

2. The provisions of paragraph 1 shall also apply to family members in possession of a valid passport who are not nationals of a Member State, accompanying or joining the Union citizen.

Article 7

Right of residence for more than three months

1. All Union citizens shall have the right of residence on the territory of another Member State for a period of longer than three months if they:
   (a) are workers or self-employed persons in the host Member State; or
   (b) have sufficient resources for themselves and their family members not to become a burden on the social assistance system of the host Member State during their period of residence and have comprehensive sickness insurance cover in the host Member State; or
   (c) — are enrolled at a private or public establishment, accredited or financed by the host Member State on the basis of its legislation

Article 7

or administrative practice, for the principal purpose of following a course of study, including vocational training; and
— have comprehensive sickness insurance cover in the host Member State and assure the relevant national authority, by means of a declaration or by such equivalent means as they may choose, that they have sufficient resources for themselves and their family members not to become a burden on the social assistance system of the host Member State during their period of residence;

or
(d) are family members accompanying or joining a Union citizen who satisfies the conditions referred to in points (a), (b) or (c).

2. The right of residence provided for in paragraph 1 shall extend to family members who are not nationals of a Member State, accompanying or joining the Union citizen in the host Member State, provided that such Union citizen satisfies the conditions referred to in paragraph 1(a), (b) or (c).

3. For the purposes of paragraph 1(a), a Union citizen who is no longer a worker or self-employed person shall retain the status of worker or self-employed person in the following circumstances:
  (a) he/she is temporarily unable to work as the result of an illness or accident;
  (b) he/she is in duly recorded involuntary unemployment after having been employed for more than one year and has registered as a jobseeker with the relevant employment office;
  (c) he/she is in duly recorded involuntary unemployment after completing a fixed-term employment contract of less than a year or after having become involuntarily unemployed during the first twelve months and has registered as a jobseeker with the relevant employment office. In this case, the status of worker shall be retained for no less than six months;
  (d) he/she embarks on vocational training. Unless he/she is involuntarily unemployed, the retention of the status of worker shall require the training to be related to the previous employment.

4. By way of derogation from paragraphs 1(d) and 2 above, only the spouse, the registered partner provided for in Article 2(2)(b) and dependent children shall have the right of residence as family members of a Union citizen meeting the conditions under 1(c) above. Article 3(2) shall apply to his/her dependent direct relatives in the ascending lines and those of his/her spouse or registered partner.

Article 8

Administrative formalities for Union citizens

1. Without prejudice to Article 5(5), for periods of residence longer than three months, the host Member State may require Union citizens to register with the relevant authorities.

2. The deadline for registration may not be less than three months from the date of arrival. A registration certificate shall be issued immediately, stating the name and address of the person registering and the date of the registration. Failure to comply with the registration requirement may

3.76

render the person concerned liable to proportionate and non-discriminatory sanctions.

3. For the registration certificate to be issued, Member States may only require that

— Union citizens to whom point (a) of Article 7(1) applies present a valid identity card or passport, a confirmation of engagement from the employer or a certificate of employment, or proof that they are self-employed persons,
— Union citizens to whom point (b) of Article 7(1) applies present a valid identity card or passport and provide proof that they satisfy the conditions laid down therein,
— Union citizens to whom point (c) of Article 7(1) applies present a valid identity card or passport, provide proof of enrolment at an accredited establishment and of comprehensive sickness insurance cover and the declaration or equivalent means referred to in point (c) of Article 7(1).

Member States may not require this declaration to refer to any specific amount of resources.

4. Member States may not lay down a fixed amount which they regard as "sufficient resources", but they must take into account the personal situation of the person concerned. In all cases this amount shall not be higher than the threshold below which nationals of the host Member State become eligible for social assistance, or, where this criterion is not applicable, higher than the minimum social security pension paid by the host Member State.

5. For the registration certificate to be issued to family members of Union citizens, who are themselves Union citizens, Member States may require the following documents to be presented:

(a) a valid identity card or passport;
(b) a document attesting to the existence of a family relationship or of a registered partnership;
(c) where appropriate, the registration certificate of the Union citizen whom they are accompanying or joining;
(d) in cases falling under points (c) and (d) of Article 2(2), documentary evidence that the conditions laid down therein are met;
(e) in cases falling under Article 3(2)(a), a document issued by the relevant authority in the country of origin or country from which they are arriving certifying that they are dependants or members of the household of the Union citizen, or proof of the existence of serious health grounds which strictly require the personal care of the family member by the Union citizen;
(f) in cases falling under Article 3(2)(b), proof of the existence of a durable relationship with the Union citizen.

Article 9

Administrative formalities for family members who are not nationals of a Member State

1. Member States shall issue a residence card to family members of a Union citizen who are not nationals of a Member State, where the planned period of residence is for more than three months.

Article 9

2. The deadline for submitting the residence card application may not be less than three months from the date of arrival.

3. Failure to comply with the requirement to apply for a residence card may make the person concerned liable to proportionate and non-discriminatory sanctions.

Article 10

Issue of residence cards

1. The right of residence of family members of a Union citizen who are not nationals of a Member State shall be evidenced by the issuing of a document called "Residence card of a family member of a Union citizen" no later than six months from the date on which they submit the application. A certificate of application for the residence card shall be issued immediately.

2. For the residence card to be issued, Member States shall require presentation of the following documents:
  (a) a valid passport;
  (b) a document attesting to the existence of a family relationship or of a registered partnership;
  (c) the registration certificate or, in the absence of a registration system, any other proof of residence in the host Member State of the Union citizen whom they are accompanying or joining;
  (d) in cases falling under points (c) and (d) of Article 2(2), documentary evidence that the conditions laid down therein are met;
  (e) in cases falling under Article 3(2)(a), a document issued by the relevant authority in the country of origin or country from which they are arriving certifying that they are dependants or members of the household of the Union citizen, or proof of the existence of serious health grounds which strictly require the personal care of the family member by the Union citizen;
  (f) in cases falling under Article 3(2)(b), proof of the existence of a durable relationship with the Union citizen.

Article 11

Validity of the residence card

1. The residence card provided for by Article 10(1) shall be valid for five years from the date of issue or for the envisaged period of residence of the Union citizen, if this period is less than five years.

2. The validity of the residence card shall not be affected by temporary absences not exceeding six months a year, or by absences of a longer duration for compulsory military service or by one absence of a maximum of 12 consecutive months for important reasons such as pregnancy and childbirth, serious illness, study or vocational training, or a posting in another Member State or a third country.

Article 12

Retention of the right of residence by family members in the event of death or departure of the Union citizen

3.80
1. Without prejudice to the second subparagraph, the Union citizen's death or departure from the host Member State shall not affect the right of residence of his/her family members who are nationals of a Member State.

Before acquiring the right of permanent residence, the persons concerned must meet the conditions laid down in points (a), (b), (c) or (d) of Article 7(1).

2. Without prejudice to the second subparagraph, the Union citizen's death shall not entail loss of the right of residence of his/her family members who are not nationals of a Member State and who have been residing in the host Member State as family members for at least one year before the Union citizen's death.

Before acquiring the right of permanent residence, the right of residence of the persons concerned shall remain subject to the requirement that they are able to show that they are workers or self-employed persons or that they have sufficient resources for themselves and their family members not to become a burden on the social assistance system of the host Member State during their period of residence and have comprehensive sickness insurance cover in the host Member State, or that they are members of the family, already constituted in the host Member State, of a person satisfying these requirements. "Sufficient resources" shall be as defined in Article 8(4).

Such family members shall retain their right of residence exclusively on a personal basis.

3. The Union citizen's departure from the host Member State or his/her death shall not entail loss of the right of residence of his/her children or of the parent who has actual custody of the children, irrespective of nationality, if the children reside in the host Member State and are enrolled at an educational establishment, for the purpose of studying there, until the completion of their studies.

Article 13

Retention of the right of residence by family members in the event of divorce, annulment of marriage or termination of registered partnership

3.81
1. Without prejudice to the second subparagraph, divorce, annulment of the Union citizen's marriage or termination of his/her registered partnership, as referred to in point 2(b) of Article 2 shall not affect the right of residence of his/her family members who are nationals of a Member State. Before acquiring the right of permanent residence, the persons concerned must meet the conditions laid down in points (a), (b), (c) or (d) of Article 7(1).

2. Without prejudice to the second subparagraph, divorce, annulment of marriage or termination of the registered partnership referred to in point 2(b) of Article 2 shall not entail loss of the right of residence of a

Article 13

Union citizen's family members who are not nationals of a Member State where:
- (a) prior to initiation of the divorce or annulment proceedings or termination of the registered partnership referred to in point 2(b) of Article 2, the marriage or registered partnership has lasted at least three years, including one year in the host Member State; or
- (b) by agreement between the spouses or the partners referred to in point 2(b) of Article 2 or by court order, the spouse or partner who is not a national of a Member State has custody of the Union citizen's children; or
- (c) this is warranted by particularly difficult circumstances, such as having been a victim of domestic violence while the marriage or registered partnership was subsisting; or
- (d) by agreement between the spouses or partners referred to in point 2(b) of Article 2 or by court order, the spouse or partner who is not a national of a Member State has the right of access to a minor child, provided that the court has ruled that such access must be in the host Member State, and for as long as is required.

Before acquiring the right of permanent residence, the right of residence of the persons concerned shall remain subject to the requirement that they are able to show that they are workers or self-employed persons or that they have sufficient resources for themselves and their family members not to become a burden on the social assistance system of the host Member State during their period of residence and have comprehensive sickness insurance cover in the host Member State, or that they are members of the family, already constituted in the host Member State, of a person satisfying these requirements. "Sufficient resources" shall be as defined in Article 8(4).

Such family members shall retain their right of residence exclusively on personal basis.

Article 14

Retention of the right of residence

1. Union citizens and their family members shall have the right of residence provided for in Article 6, as long as they do not become an unreasonable burden on the social assistance system of the host Member State.

2. Union citizens and their family members shall have the right of residence provided for in Articles 7, 12 and 13 as long as they meet the conditions set out therein.

In specific cases where there is a reasonable doubt as to whether a Union citizen or his/her family members satisfies the conditions set out in Articles 7, 12 and 13, Member States may verify if these conditions are fulfilled. This verification shall not be carried out systematically.

3. An expulsion measure shall not be the automatic consequence of a Union citizen's or his or her family member's recourse to the social assistance system of the host Member State.

4. By way of derogation from paragraphs 1 and 2 and without prejudice to the provisions of Chapter VI, an expulsion measure may in no case be adopted against Union citizens or their family members if:
- (a) the Union citizens are workers or self-employed persons, or

(b) the Union citizens entered the territory of the host Member State in order to seek employment. In this case, the Union citizens and their family members may not be expelled for as long as the Union citizens can provide evidence that they are continuing to seek employment and that they have a genuine chance of being engaged.

Article 15

Procedural safeguards

3.83   1. The procedures provided for by Articles 30 and 31 shall apply by analogy to all decisions restricting free movement of Union citizens and their family members on grounds other than public policy, public security or public health.
2. Expiry of the identity card or passport on the basis of which the person concerned entered the host Member State and was issued with a registration certificate or residence card shall not constitute a ground for expulsion from the host Member State.
3. The host Member State may not impose a ban on entry in the context of an expulsion decision to which paragraph 1 applies.

CHAPTER IV

RIGHT OF PERMANENT RESIDENCE

Section I

Eligibility

Article 16

General rule for Union citizens and their family members

3.84   1. Union citizens who have resided legally for a continuous period of five years in the host Member State shall have the right of permanent residence there. This right shall not be subject to the conditions provided for in Chapter III.
2. Paragraph 1 shall apply also to family members who are not nationals of a Member State and have legally resided with the Union citizen in the host Member State for a continuous period of five years.
3. Continuity of residence shall not be affected by temporary absences not exceeding a total of six months a year, or by absences of a longer duration for compulsory military service, or by one absence of a maximum of 12 consecutive months for important reasons such as pregnancy and childbirth, serious illness, study or vocational training, or a posting in another Member State or a third country.

Article 16

4. Once acquired, the right of permanent residence shall be lost only through absence from the host Member State for a period exceeding two consecutive years.

Article 17

Exemptions for persons no longer working in the host Member State and their family members

1. By way of derogation from Article 16, the right of permanent residence in the host Member State shall be enjoyed before completion of a continuous period of five years of residence by:
  (a) workers or self-employed persons who, at the time they stop working, have reached the age laid down by the law of that Member State for entitlement to an old age pension or workers who cease paid employment to take early retirement, provided that they have been working in that Member State for at least the preceding twelve months and have resided there continuously for more than three years. If the law of the host Member State does not grant the right to an old age pension to certain categories of self-employed persons, the age condition shall be deemed to have been met once the person concerned has reached the age of 60;
  (b) workers or self-employed persons who have resided continuously in the host Member State for more than two years and stop working there as a result of permanent incapacity to work. If such incapacity is the result of an accident at work or an occupational disease entitling the person concerned to a benefit payable in full or in part by an institution in the host Member State, no condition shall be imposed as to length of residence;
  (c) workers or self-employed persons who, after three years of continuous employment and residence in the host Member State, work in an employed or self-employed capacity in another Member State, while retaining their place of residence in the host Member State, to which they return, as a rule, each day or at least once a week.
  For the purposes of entitlement to the rights referred to in points (a) and (b), periods of employment spent in the Member State in which the person concerned is working shall be regarded as having been spent in the host Member State.
Periods of involuntary unemployment duly recorded by the relevant employment office, periods not worked for reasons not of the person's own making and absences from work or cessation of work due to illness or accident shall be regarded as periods of employment.

2. The conditions as to length of residence and employment laid down in point (a) of paragraph 1 and the condition as to length of residence laid down in point (b) of paragraph 1 shall not apply if the worker's or the self-employed person's spouse or partner as referred to in point 2(b) of Article 2 is a national of the host Member State or has lost the nationality of that Member State by marriage to that worker or self-employed person.

3. Irrespective of nationality, the family members of a worker or a self-employed person who are residing with him in the territory of the host

Member State shall have the right of permanent residence in that Member State, if the worker or self-employed person has acquired himself the right of permanent residence in that Member State on the basis of paragraph 1.

4. If, however, the worker or self-employed person dies while still working but before acquiring permanent residence status in the host Member State on the basis of paragraph 1, his family members who are residing with him in the host Member State shall acquire the right of permanent residence there, on condition that:
   (a) the worker or self-employed person had, at the time of death, resided continuously on the territory of that Member State for two years; or
   (b) the death resulted from an accident at work or an occupational disease; or
   (c) the surviving spouse lost the nationality of that Member State following marriage to the worker or self-employed person.

Article 18

Acquisition of the right of permanent residence by certain family members who are not nationals of a Member State

3.86 Without prejudice to Article 17, the family members of a Union citizen to whom Articles 12(2) and 13(2) apply, who satisfy the conditions laid down therein, shall acquire the right of permanent residence after residing legally for a period of five consecutive years in the host Member State.

Section II

Administrative formalities

Article 19

Document certifying permanent residence for Union citizens

3.87 1. Upon application Member States shall issue Union citizens entitled to permanent residence, after having verified duration of residence, with a document certifying permanent residence.

2. The document certifying permanent residence shall be issued as soon as possible.

Article 20

Permanent residence card for family members who are not nationals of a Member State

3.88 1. Member States shall issue family members who are not nationals of a Member State entitled to permanent residence with a permanent residence card within six months of the submission of the application. The permanent residence card shall be renewable automatically every 10 years.

Article 20

2. The application for a permanent residence card shall be submitted before the residence card expires. Failure to comply with the requirement to apply for a permanent residence card may render the person concerned liable to proportionate and non-discriminatory sanctions.

3. Interruption in residence not exceeding two consecutive years shall not affect the validity of the permanent residence card.

Article 21

Continuity of residence

For the purposes of this Directive, continuity of residence may be attested by any means of proof in use in the host Member State. Continuity of residence is broken by any expulsion decision duly enforced against the person concerned.

3.89

Chapter V

Provisions Common to the Right of Residence and the Right of Permanent Residence

Article 22

Territorial scope

The right of residence and the right of permanent residence shall cover the whole territory of the host Member State. Member States may impose territorial restrictions on the right of residence and the right of permanent residence only where the same restrictions apply to their own nationals.

3.90

Article 23

Related rights

Irrespective of nationality, the family members of a Union citizen who have the right of residence or the right of permanent residence in a Member State shall be entitled to take up employment or self-employment there.

3.90.1

Article 24

Equal treatment

1. Subject to such specific provisions as are expressly provided for in the Treaty and secondary law, all Union citizens residing on the basis of this Directive in the territory of the host Member State shall enjoy equal treatment with the nationals of that Member State within the scope of the Treaty. The benefit of this right shall be extended to family members who are not nationals of a Member State and who have the right of residence or permanent residence.

3.91

2. By way of derogation from paragraph 1, the host Member State shall not be obliged to confer entitlement to social assistance during the first three months of residence or, where appropriate, the longer period provided for in Article 14(4)(b), nor shall it be obliged, prior to acquisition of the right of permanent residence, to grant maintenance aid for studies, including vocational training, consisting in student grants or student loans to persons other than workers, self-employed persons, persons who retain such status and members of their families.

Article 25

General provisions concerning residence documents

3.92
1. Possession of a registration certificate as referred to in Article 8, of a document certifying permanent residence, of a certificate attesting submission of an application for a family member residence card, of a residence card or of a permanent residence card, may under no circumstances be made a precondition for the exercise of a right or the completion of an administrative formality, as entitlement to rights may be attested by any other means of proof.

2. All documents mentioned in paragraph 1 shall be issued free of charge or for a charge not exceeding that imposed on nationals for the issuing of similar documents.

Article 26

Checks

3.93
Member States may carry out checks on compliance with any requirement deriving from their national legislation for non nationals always to carry their registration certificate or residence card, provided that the same requirement applies to their own nationals as regards their identity card. In the event of failure to comply with this requirement, Member States may impose the same sanctions as those imposed on their own nationals for failure to carry their identity card.

CHAPTER VI

RESTRICTIONS ON THE RIGHT OF ENTRY AND THE RIGHT OF RESIDENCE ON GROUNDS OF PUBLIC POLICY, PUBLIC SECURITY OR PUBLIC HEALTH

Article 27

General principles

3.94
1. Subject to the provisions of this Chapter, Member States may restrict the freedom of movement and residence of Union citizens and their family

Article 27

members, irrespective of nationality, on grounds of public policy, public security or public health. These grounds shall not be invoked to serve economic ends.

2. Measures taken on grounds of public policy or public security shall comply with the principle of proportionality and shall be based exclusively on the personal conduct of the individual concerned. Previous criminal convictions shall not in themselves constitute grounds for taking such measures. The personal conduct of the individual concerned must represent a genuine, present and sufficiently serious threat affecting one of the fundamental interests of society. Justifications that are isolated from the particulars of the case or that rely on considerations of general prevention shall not be accepted.

3. In order to ascertain whether the person concerned represents a danger for public policy or public security, when issuing the registration certificate or, in the absence of a registration system, not later than three months from the date of arrival of the person concerned on its territory or from the date of reporting his/her presence within the territory, as provided for in Article 5(5), or when issuing the residence card, the host Member State may, should it consider this essential, request the Member State of origin and, if need be, other Member States to provide information concerning any previous police record the person concerned may have. Such enquiries shall not be made as a matter of routine. The Member State consulted shall give its reply within two months.

4. The Member State which issued the passport or identity card shall allow the holder of the document who has been expelled on grounds of public policy, public security, or public health from another Member State to re-enter its territory without any formality even if the document is no longer valid or the nationality of the holder is in dispute.

Article 28

Protection against expulsion

1. Before taking an expulsion decision on grounds of public policy or public security, the host Member State shall take account of considerations such as how long the individual concerned has resided on its territory, his/her age, state of health, family and economic situation, social and cultural integration into the host Member State and the extent of his/her links with the country of origin.

2. The host Member State may not take an expulsion decision against Union citizens or their family members, irrespective of nationality, who have the right of permanent residence on its territory, except on serious grounds of public policy or public security.

3. An expulsion decision may not be taken against Union citizens, except if the decision is based on imperative grounds of public security, as defined by Member States, if they:
   (a) have resided in the host Member State for the previous 10 years; or
   (b) are a minor, except if the expulsion is necessary for the best interests of the child, as provided for in the United Nations Convention on the Rights of the Child of 20 November 1989.

3.95

Directive 2004/38/EC

Article 29

Public health

3.96
1. The only diseases justifying measures restricting freedom of movement shall be the diseases with epidemic potential as defined by the relevant instruments of the World Health Organisation and other infectious diseases or contagious parasitic diseases if they are the subject of protection provisions applying to nationals of the host Member State.
2. Diseases occurring after a three-month period from the date of arrival shall not constitute grounds for expulsion from the territory.
3. Where there are serious indications that it is necessary, Member States may, within three months of the date of arrival, require persons entitled to the right of residence to undergo, free of charge, a medical examination to certify that they are not suffering from any of the conditions referred to in paragraph 1. Such medical examinations may not be required as a matter of routine.

Article 30

Notification of decisions

3.97
1. The persons concerned shall be notified in writing of any decision taken under Article 27(1), in such a way that they are able to comprehend its content and the implications for them.
2. The persons concerned shall be informed, precisely and in full, of the public policy, public security or public health grounds on which the decision taken in their case is based, unless this is contrary to the interests of State security.
3. The notification shall specify the court or administrative authority with which the person concerned may lodge an appeal, the time limit for the appeal and, where applicable, the time allowed for the person to leave the territory of the Member State. Save in duly substantiated cases of urgency, the time allowed to leave the territory shall be not less than one month from the date of notification.

Article 31

Procedural safeguards

3.98
1. The persons concerned shall have access to judicial and, where appropriate, administrative redress procedures in the host Member State to appeal against or seek review of any decision taken against them on the grounds of public policy, public security or public health.
2. Where the application for appeal against or judicial review of the expulsion decision is accompanied by an application for an interim order to suspend enforcement of that decision, actual removal from the territory may not take place until such time as the decision on the interim order has been taken, except:

Article 31

- where the expulsion decision is based on a previous judicial decision; or
- where the persons concerned have had previous access to judicial review; or
- where the expulsion decision is based on imperative grounds of public security under Article 28(3).

3. The redress procedures shall allow for an examination of the legality of the decision, as well as of the facts and circumstances on which the proposed measure is based. They shall ensure that the decision is not disproportionate, particularly in view of the requirements laid down in Article 28.

4. Member States may exclude the individual concerned from their territory pending the redress procedure, but they may not prevent the individual from submitting his/her defence in person, except when his/her appearance may cause serious troubles to public policy or public security or when the appeal or judicial review concerns a denial of entry to the territory.

Article 32

Duration of exclusion orders

1. Persons excluded on grounds of public policy or public security may submit an application for lifting of the exclusion order after a reasonable period, depending on the circumstances, and in any event after three years from enforcement of the final exclusion order which has been validly adopted in accordance with Community law, by putting forward arguments to establish that there has been a material change in the circumstances which justified the decision ordering their exclusion. The Member State concerned shall reach a decision on this application within six months of its submission.

2. The persons referred to in paragraph 1 shall have no right of entry to the territory of the Member State concerned while their application is being considered.

3.99

Article 33

Expulsion as a penalty or legal consequence

1. Expulsion orders may not be issued by the host Member State as a penalty or legal consequence of a custodial penalty, unless they conform to the requirements of Articles 27, 28 and 29.

2. If an expulsion order, as provided for in paragraph 1, is enforced more than two years after it was issued, the Member State shall check that the individual concerned is currently and genuinely a threat to public policy or public security and shall assess whether there has been any material change in the circumstances since the expulsion order was issued.

3.100

Chapter VII

Final Provisions

Article 34

Publicity

3.101 Member States shall disseminate information concerning the rights and obligations of Union citizens and their family members on the subjects covered by this Directive, particularly by means of awareness-raising campaigns conducted through national and local media and other means of communication.

Article 35

Abuse of rights

3.102 Member States may adopt the necessary measures to refuse, terminate or withdraw any right conferred by this Directive in the case of abuse of rights or fraud, such as marriages of convenience.

Any such measure shall be proportionate and subject to the procedural safeguards provided for in Articles 30 and 31.

Article 36

Sanctions

3.103 Member States shall lay down provisions on the sanctions applicable to breaches of national rules adopted for the implementation of this Directive and shall take the measures required for their application. The sanctions laid down shall be effective and proportionate. Member States shall notify the Commission of these provisions not later than 30 April 2006 and as promptly as possible in the case of any subsequent changes.

Article 37

More favourable national provisions

3.104 The provisions of this Directive shall not affect any laws, regulations or administrative provisions laid down by a Member State which would be more favourable to the persons covered by this Directive.

Article 38

Repeals

3.105 1. Articles 10 and 11 of Regulation (EEC) No 1612/68 shall be repealed with effect from 30 April 2006.

Article 38

2. Directives 64/221/EEC, 68/360/EEC, 72/194/EEC, 73/148/EEC, 75/34/EEC, 75/35/EEC, 90/364/EEC, 90/365/EEC and 93/96/EEC shall be repealed with effect from 30 April 2006.

3. References made to the repealed provisions and Directives shall be construed as being made to this Directive.

Article 39

Report

No later than 30 April 2008 the Commission shall submit a report on the application of this Directive to the European Parliament and the Council, together with any necessary proposals, notably on the opportunity to extend the period of time during which Union citizens and their family members may reside in the territory of the host Member State without any conditions. The Member States shall provide the Commission with the information needed to produce the report.

Article 40

Transposition

1. Member States shall bring into force the laws, regulations and administrative provisions necessary to comply with this Directive by 30 April 2006. When Member States adopt those measures, they shall contain a reference to this Directive or shall be accompanied by such a reference on the occasion of their official publication. The methods of making such reference shall be laid down by the Member States.

2. Member States shall communicate to the Commission the text of the provisions of national law which they adopt in the field covered by this Directive together with a table showing how the provisions of this Directive correspond to the national provisions adopted.

Article 41

Entry into force

This Directive shall enter into force on the day of its publication in the *Official Journal of the European Union*.

Article 42

Addresses

This Directive is addressed to the Member States.
Done at Strasbourg, 29 April 2004.

Council Regulation (EEC) No 1408/71

Council Regulation (EEC) No 1408/71 on the application of social security schemes to employed persons, to self-employed persons and to members of their families moving within the Community

TEXT AS AMENDED BY COUNCIL REGULATION (EC) 118/97 OF DECEMBER 2, 1996

[1997] OJ L28/4 (AS FURTHER AMENDED)

CONTENTS

TITLE I: GENERAL PROVISIONS (ARTICLES 1 TO 12)

TITLE II: DETERMINATION OF THE LEGISLATION APPLICABLE (ARTICLES 13 TO 17A)

TITLE III: SPECIAL PROVISIONS RELATING TO THE VARIOUS CATEGORIES OF BENEFITS

Chapter 1: Sickness and maternity

Section 1: Common provisions (Article 18)
Section 2: Employed or self-employed persons and members of their families (Articles 19 to 24)
Section 3: Unemployed persons and members of their families (Article 25)
Section 4: Pension claimants and members of their families (Article 26)
Section 5: Pensioners and members of their families (Articles 27 to 34)
Section 6: Miscellaneous provisions (Article 35)
Section 7: Reimbursement between institutions (Article 36)

Chapter 2: Invalidity

Section 1: Employed or self-employed persons subject only to legislations under which the amount of invalidity benefits is independent of the duration of periods of insurance (Articles 37 to 39)
Section 2: Employed or self-employed persons subject either only to legislations under which the amount of invalidity benefit depends on the duration of periods of insurance or residence or to legislations of this type and of the type referred to in Section 1 (Article 40)
Section 3: Aggravation of invalidity (Article 41)
Section 4: Resumption of provision of benefits after suspension or withdrawal—Conversion of invalidity benefits into old-age benefits. Recalculation of benefits granted under Article 39 (Articles 42 and 43)

Chapter 3: Old age and death (pensions) (Articles 44 to 51)

Chapter 4: Accidents at work and occupational disease

Section 1: Right to benefits (Articles 52 to 59)
Section 2: Aggravation of an occupational disease for which the benefit has been awarded (Article 60)

Section 3: Miscellaneous provisions (Articles 61 and 62)
Section 4: Reimbursements between institutions (Article 63)

Chapter 5: Death grants (Articles 64 to 66)

Chapter 6: Unemployment benefits

Section 1: Common provisions (Articles 67 and 68)
Section 2: Unemployed persons going to a Member State other than the competent State (Articles 69 and 70)
Section 3: Unemployed persons who, during their last employment, were residing in a Member State other than the competent State (Article 71)
Chapter 7: Family benefits (Articles 72 to 76)
Chapter 8: Benefits for dependent children of pensioners and for orphans (Articles 77 to 79)

TITLE IV: ADMINISTRATIVE COMMISSION ON SOCIAL SECURITY FOR MIGRANT WORKERS (ARTICLES 80 AND 81)

TITLE V: ADVISORY COMMITTEE ON SOCIAL SECURITY FOR MIGRANT WORKERS (ARTICLES 82 AND 83)

TITLE VI: MISCELLANEOUS PROVISIONS (ARTICLES 84 TO 93)

TITLE VII: TRANSITIONAL AND FINAL PROVISIONS (ARTICLES 94 TO 98).

ANNEXES

Annex I: Persons covered by the Regulation
Annex II: Special schemes for self-employed persons excluded from the scope of the Regulation pursuant to the fourth subparagraph of Article 1 (j)—Special childbirth allowances excluded from the scope of the Regulation pursuant to Article 1 (u)—Special non-contributory benefits within the meaning of Article 4 (2b) which do not fall within the scope of Regulation
Annex IIa: Special non-contributory benefits
Annex III: Provisions of social security conventions remaining applicable notwithstanding Article 6 of the Regulation—Provisions of social security conventions which do not apply to all persons to whom the Regulation applies
Annex IV: Legislations referred to Article 37 (1) of the Regulation under which the amount of invalidity benefits is independent of the length of periods of insurance—Special schemes for self-employed persons within the meaning of Articles 38 (3) and 45 (3) of Regulation (EEC) No 1408/71—Cases referred to in Article 46 (1) (b) of the Regulation where the calculation of benefit in accordance with Article 46 (2) of the Regulation may be waived—Benefits and agreements referred to in Article 46b (2) of the Regulation
Annex V: Concordance between the legislation of Member States on conditions relating to the degree of invalidity
Annex VI: Special procedures for applying the legislations of certain Member States
Annex VII: Instances in which a person shall be simultaneously subject to the legislation of two Member States

Annex VIII: Schemes that provide only for family allowances or supplementary or special allowances for orphans.

GENERAL NOTE

3.111 A consolidated version of Reg.1408/71 was passed in December 1996. The version of the regulation printed here is based on that text. Amendments made prior to December 1996 are not noted, but the text has been updated to take account of subsequent amendments of the Regulation and annotated to show the source of those amendments in the same manner as for United Kingdom statutory material.

It is important to realize that the Regulation is concerned with the co-ordination of social security schemes and not with the harmonization of the social security laws of the Member States. The Court of Justice has consistently stressed this distinction in its judgments on provisions of Regulation 1408/71. So, for example, in Joined Cases C-393 and C-394/99 *Hervein and Lorthiois*, [2002] E.C.R. I-2829, the Court said:

> ". . . the system put in place by Regulation No 1408/71 is merely a system of coordination. . . .
> . . . it . . . does not follow from [Articles 39 and 43 of the Treaty] that, in the absence of harmonisation of the social security legislation, neutrality as regard the complexity, for the persons concerned, of the administration of their social security cover will be guaranteed in all circumstances." (paras 52 and 58 of the judgment.)

The purpose of the Regulation is to build bridges in order to connect different social security schemes so that those moving within the EEA are not disadvantaged as a result of exercising their rights of free movement. However, notwithstanding this important distinction between co-ordination and harmonisation, there are certainly adaptive pressures on Member States as a result of the requirements of co-ordination of benefit schemes which tend to pull Member State policy closer together.

See http://europa.eu.int/comm/employment_social/social_security_schemes/index_en.htm for useful information from the European Commission on the coordination of social security schemes.

The scheme of co-ordination applies to the Member States, to the three countries which together with the Member States form the European Economic Area (Iceland, Liechtenstein and Norway), and to Switzerland.

From April 1, 2006 a protocol entered into force which extents the Agreement on the Free Movement of Persons between the EU and Switzerland to the 10 Member States which joined the European Union on May 1, 2004.

Regulation 883/2004/EC—the "simplified" regulation

3.112 A new "simplified" regulation has been produced on the coordination of social security, which is expected to come into force some time in 2007: see Regulation 883/2004/EC of April 29, 2004 on the coordination of social security schemes, [2004] OJ L200/1, correcting OJ L166/1. Work is currently under way on the preparation of an updated version of the implementing regulation. The new regulation is not merely a consolidating measure, since it adds new benefits (pre-retirement benefits) to those which are coordinated among the Member States.

The Council of the European Union

3.113 *Having regard* to the Treaty establishing the European Community, and in particular Articles 51 and 235 thereof,
Having regard to the proposal from the Commission,
Having regard to the opinion of the European Parliament,

Council Regulation (EEC) No 1408/71

Having regard to the opinion of the Economic and Social Committee,

Whereas the provisions for co-ordination of national social security legislations fall within the framework of freedom of movement for workers who are nationals of Member States and should contribute towards the improvement of their standard of living and conditions of employment;

Whereas freedom of movement for persons, which is one of the cornerstones of the Community, is not confined to employed persons but also extends to self-employed persons in the framework of the freedom of establishment and the freedom to supply services;

Whereas the considerable differences existing between national legislations as regards the persons to whom they apply make it preferable to establish the principle that the Regulation applies to all persons insured under social security schemes for employed persons and for self-employed persons or by virtue of pursuing employment or self-employment;

Whereas it is necessary to respect the special characteristics of national social security legislations and to draw up only a system of coordination;

Whereas it is necessary, within the framework of that co-ordination, to guarantee within the Community equality of treatment under the various national legislations to workers living in the Member States and their dependants and their survivors;

Whereas the provisions for coordination must guarantee that workers moving within the Community and their dependants and their survivors retain the rights and the advantages acquired and in the course of being acquired;

Whereas these objectives must be attained in particular by aggregation of all the periods taken into account under the various national legislations for the purpose of acquiring and retaining the right to benefits and of calculating the amount of benefits, and by the provision of benefits for the various categories of persons covered by the Regulation regardless of their place of residence within the Community;

Whereas employed persons and self-employed persons moving within the Community should be subject to the social security scheme of only one single Member State in order to avoid overlapping of national legislations applicable and the complications which could result therefrom;

Whereas the instances in which a person should be subject simultaneously to the legislation of two Member States as an exception to the general rule should be as limited in number and scope as possible;

Whereas with a view to guaranteeing the equality of treatment of all workers occupied on the territory of a Member State as effectively as possible, it is appropriate to determine as the legislation applicable, as a general rule, that of the Member State in which the person concerned pursues employment of self-employment;

Whereas in certain situations which justify other criteria of applicability, it is possible to derogate from this general rule;

Whereas certain benefits foreseen under national laws may fall simultaneously within social security and social assistance, because of the personal scope of their application, their objectives and their manner of application, it is necessary to lay down a system of coordination, which takes into account the special characteristics of the benefits concerned, that should be included in the Regulation in order to protect the interests of migrant workers in accordance with the provisions of the Treaty;

Whereas such benefits should be granted, in respect of persons falling within the scope of this Regulation, solely in accordance with the legislation of the country of residence of the person concerned or of the members of his or her family, with such aggregation of periods of residence completed in any other Member State as is necessary and without discrimination on grounds of nationality;

Whereas it is necessary to lay down specific rules, in particular in the field of sickness and unemployment, for frontier workers and seasonal workers, taking account of the specific nature of their situation;

Whereas in the field of sickness and maternity benefits, it is necessary to guarantee the protection of persons living or staying in a Member State other than the competent Member State;

Whereas the specific position of pension claimants and pensioners and the members of their families calls for the provisions governing sickness insurance to adapted to their situation;

Whereas for invalidity benefits a system of coordination should be drawn up which respects the specific characteristics of national legislations; whereas it is therefore necessary to make a distinction between legislations under which the amount of invalidity benefit is independent of the length of insurance and legislations under which the amount depends on the aforementioned length;

Whereas the differences between the schemes in the Member States call for the adoption of rules of coordination which are applicable in the case of aggravation of invalidity;

Whereas it is expedient that a system for the award of old-age benefits and survivors benefits be worked out where the employed or self-employed person has been subject to the legislation of one or more Member States;

Whereas there is a need to determine the amount of a pension calculated in accordance with the method used for aggregation and pro rata calculation and guaranteed by Community law where the application of national legislation, including provisions concerning reduction, suspension or withdrawal, is less favourable than the aforementioned method;

Whereas, to protect migrant workers and their survivors against an excessively stringent application of the national provisions concerning reduction, suspension or withdrawal, it is necessary to include provisions laying down strict rules for the application of these provisions;

Whereas, in respect of benefits for accidents at work and occupational diseases, it is necessary, for the purpose of affording protection, that rules be laid down covering the situation of persons residing or staying in a Member State other than the competent Member State;

Whereas it is necessary to lay down specific provisions for death grants;

Whereas, in order to secure mobility of labour under improved conditions, it is necessary henceforth to ensure closer coordination between the unemployment insurance schemes and the unemployment assistance schemes of all the Member States;

Whereas it is therefore particularly appropriate, in order to facilitate search for employment in the various Member States, to grant to an unemployed worker, for a limited period, the unemployment benefits provided for by the legislation of the Member State to which he was last subject;

Whereas, with a view to determining the legislation applicable to family benefits, the criterion of employment ensures equal treatment between all workers subject to the same legislation;

Whereas, in order to avoid unwarranted overlapping of benefits, there is a need to provide for rules of priority in the case of overlapping of the right to family benefits under the legislation of the competent State and under the legislation of the country of residence of the members of the family;

Whereas the legislations of the Member States differ from each other and are specific in nature, it is considered necessary to draw up specific rules for the coordination of the national schemes providing benefits for dependent children of pensioners and for orphans;

Whereas it is necessary to establish an Administrative Commission consisting of a government representative from each of the Member States, charged in particular with dealing with all administrative questions or questions of interpretation arising from the provisions of this Regulation, and to further cooperation between the Member States;

Whereas it is desirable, within the framework of an Advisory Committee, to have the representatives of workers and employers examine the issues treated by the Administrative Commission;

Whereas it is necessary to lay down special provisions which correspond to the special characteristics of the national legislations in order to facilitate the application of the rules of co-ordination.

Has Adopted this Regulation

Title I

General Provisions

Article 1

Definitions

For the purpose of this Regulation: 3.114
(a) *employed person* and *self-employed person* mean respectively:
   (i) [¹ any person who is insured, compulsorily or on an optional continued basis, for one or more of the contingencies covered by the branches of a social security scheme for employed or self-employed persons or by a special scheme for civil servants;]
   (ii) any person who is compulsorily insured for one or more of the contingencies covered by the branches of social security dealt with in this Regulation, under a social security dealt with in this Regulation, under a social security scheme for all residents or for the whole working population, if such person:
      — can be identified as an employed or self-employed person by virtue of the manner in which such scheme is administered or financed, or,
      — failing such criteria, is insured for some other contingency specified in Annex I under a scheme for employed or self-employed persons, or under a scheme referred to in (iii),

either compulsorily or on an optional continued basis, or, where no such scheme exists in the Member State concerned, complies with the definition given in Annex I;
   (iii) any person who is compulsorily insured for several of the contingencies covered by the branches dealt with in this Regulation, under a standard social security scheme for the whole rural population in accordance with the criteria laid down in Annex I;
   (iv) any person who is voluntarily insured for one or more of the contingencies covered by the branches dealt with in this Regulation, under a social security scheme of a Member State for employed or self-employed persons or for all residents or for certain categories of residents:
— if such person carries out an activity as an employed or self-employed person, or
— if such person has previously been compulsorily insured for the same contingency under a scheme for employed or self-employed persons for the same Member State;

(b) *frontier worker* means any employed or self-employed person who pursues his occupation in the territory of a Member State and resides in the territory of another Member State to which he returns as a rule daily or at least once a week; however, a frontier worker who is posted elsewhere in the territory of the same or another Member State by the undertaking to which he is normally attached, or who engages in the provision of services elsewhere in the territory of the same or another Member State, shall retain the status of frontier worker for a period not exceeding four month, even if he is prevented, during that period, from returning daily or at least once a week to the place where he resides;

(c) *seasonal worker* means any employed person who goes to the territory of a Member State other than the one in which he is resident to do work there of a seasonal nature for an undertaking or an employer of that State for a period which may on no account exceed eight month, and who stays in the territory of the said State for the duration of this work; work of a seasonal nature shall be taken to mean work which, being dependent on the succession of the seasons, automatically recurs each year;

[² (ca) *student* means any person other than an employed or self-employed person or a member of his family or survivor within the meaning of this Regulation who studies or receives vocational training leading to a qualification officially recognised by the authorities of a Member State, and is insured under a general social security scheme or a special social security scheme applicable to students;]

(d) *refugee* shall have the meaning assigned to it in Article 1 of the Convention of the Status of Refugees, signed at Geneva on 28 July 1951;

(e) *stateless person* shall have the meaning assigned to it in Article 1 of the Convention on the Status of Stateless Persons, signed in New York on 28 September 1954;

(f) (i)   *member of the family* means any person defined or recognized as a member of the family or designated as a member of the household by the legislation under which benefits are provided or, in the cases referred to in Articles 22(1)(a) and 31, by the legislation of the Member State in whose territory such person resides;

Article 1

where, however, the said legislations regard as a member of the family or a member of the household only a person living under the same roof as the [² employed or self-employed person or student], this condition shall be considered satisfied if the person in question is mainly dependent on that person. [³ Where the legislation of a Member State does not enable members of the family to be distinguished from the other persons to whom it applies, the term 'member of the family shall have the meaning given in Annex I.]

(ii) where, however, the benefits concerned are benefits for disabled persons granted under the legislation of a Member State to all nationals of that State who fulfil the prescribed conditions, the term "member of the family" means at least the spouse of an [² employed or self-employed person or student] and the children of such person who are either minors or dependent upon such person;

(g) *survivor* means any person defined or recognized as such by the legislation under which the benefits are granted; where, however, the said legislation regards as a survivor only a person who was living under the same roof as the deceased, this condition shall be considered satisfied if such person was mainly dependent on the deceased;

(h) *residence* means habitual residence;

(i) *stay* means temporary residence;

(j) *legislation* means in respect of each Member State statutes, regulations and other provisions and all other implementing measures, present or future, relating to the branches and schemes of social security covered by Article 4(1) and (2) or those special non-contributory benefits covered by Article 4(2a).

The term excludes provisions of existing or future industrial agreements, whether or not they have been the subject of a decision by the authorities rendering them compulsory or extending their scope. However, in so far as such provisions:

(i) serve to put into effect compulsory insurance imposed by the laws and regulations referred to in the preceding subparagraph; or

(ii) set up a scheme administered by the same institution as that which administers the schemes set up by the laws and regulations referred to in the preceding subparagraph,

the limitation on the term may at any time be lifted by a declaration of the Member State concerned specifying the schemes of such a kind to which this Regulation applies. Such a declaration shall be notified and published in accordance with the provisions of Article 97.

The provisions of the preceding subparagraph shall not have the effect of exempting from the application of this Regulation the schemes to which Regulation No 3 applied.

The term "legislation" also excludes provisions governing special schemes for self-employed persons the creation of which is left to the initiatives of those concerned or which apply only to a part of the territory of the Member State concerned, irrespective of whether or not the authorities decided to make them compulsory or extend their scope. The special schemes in question are specified in Annex II;

Council Regulation (EEC) No 1408/71

[¹ (ja) *special scheme of civil servants* means any social security scheme which is different from the general social security scheme applicable to employed persons in the Member States concerned and to which all, or certain categories of, civil servants or persons treated as such are directly subject;]

(k) *social security convention* means any bilateral or multilateral instrument which binds or will bind two or more Member States exclusively, and any other multilateral instrument which binds or will bind at least two Member States and one or more other States in the field of social security, for all or part of the branches and schemes set out in Article 4(1) and (2), together with agreements, of whatever kind, concluded pursuant to the said instruments;

(l) *competent authority* means, in respect of each Member State, the Minister, Ministers or other equivalent authority responsible for social security schemes throughout or in any part of the territory of the State in question;

(m) *Administrative Commission* means the commission referred to in Article 80;

(n) *institution* means, in respect of each Member State, the body or authority responsible for administering all or part of the legislation;

(o) *competent institution* means:
  (i) the institution with which the person concerned is insured at the time of the application for benefit;
    or
  (ii) the institution from which the person concerned is entitled or would be entitled to benefits if he or a member or members of his family were resident in the territory of the Member State in which the institution is situated; or
  (iii) the institution designated by the competent authority of the member State concerned; or
  (iv) in the case of a scheme relating to an employer's liability in respect of the benefits set out in Article 4(1), either the employer or the insurer involved or, in default thereof, a body or authority designated by the competent authority of the Member State concerned;

(p) *institution of the place of residence* and *institution of the place of stay* means respectively the institution which is competent to provide benefits in the place where the person concerned resides and the institution which is competent to provide benefits in the place where the person concerned is staying, under the legislation administered by that institution or, where no such institution exists, the institution designated by the competent authority of the Member State in question;

(q) *competent State* means the Member State in whose territory the competent institution is situated;

(r) *periods of insurance* means periods of contribution or period of employment or self-employment as defined or recognized as periods of insurance by the legislation under which they were completed or considered as completed, and all periods treated as such, where they are regarded by the said legislation as equivalent to periods of insurance; [¹ periods completed under a special scheme for civil servants are also considered as periods of insurance;]

Article 1

(s) *periods of employment* and *periods of self-employment* means periods so defined or recognized by the legislation under which they were completed, and all periods treated as such, where they are regarded by the said legislation as equivalent to periods of employment or of self-employment; [¹ periods completed under a special scheme for civil servants are also considered as periods of insurance;]

(sa) *periods of residence* means periods as defined or recognized as such by the legislation under which they were completed or considered as completed;

(t) *benefits* and *pensions* mean all benefits and pensions, including all elements thereof payable out of public funds, revalorization increases and supplementary allowances, subject to the provisions of Title III, as also lump-sum benefits which may be paid in lieu of pensions, and payments made by way of reimbursement of contributions;

(u) (i) the term *family benefits* means all benefits in kind or in cash intended to meet family expenses under the legislation provided for in Article 4(1)(h), excluding the special childbirth or adoption allowances referred to in Annex II;

(ii) *family allowances* means periodical cash benefits granted exclusively by reference to the number and, where appropriate, the age of members of the family;

(v) *death grants* means any once-for-all payment in the event of death exclusive of the lump-sum benefits referred to in subparagraph (t).

AMENDMENTS

1. Regulation 1606/98/EC, [1998] OJ L209/1 (October 25, 1998).
2. Regulation 307/99/EC, [1999] OJ L38/1 (May 1, 1999).
3. Regulation 1290/97/EC, [1997] OJ L176/1 (October 4, 1997).

GENERAL NOTE

Article 1 contains crucial definitions in the application of the co-ordinating rules it contains. These are autonomous concepts under Community law and are to be applied from a Community perspective.

Two particularly important definitions are those of "residence" and "stay". Residence is defined as habitual residence which is similar to but not necessarily identical to the concept adopted in United Kingdom regulations as a condition of entitlement to benefit. Residence is contrasted with stay which is temporary residence in a Member State; residence here probably means presence since holidays abroad constitute a stay in another Member State.

3.115

Definition of employed or self-employed person

In a closely reasoned decision, the Commissioner in *R(IS) 1/06* held that, in order to be within the personal scope of the Regulation in relation to a claim for a means-tested benefit, it was not enough to have been insured against some of the risks envisaged by the Regulation, there was a need to be an employed or self-employed person as defined by the Regulation. A claimant who had received benefits in another Member State on the basis of residence alone could not bring herself within the definition of being an employed or self-employed person. One way of establishing the status of an employed or self-employed person is to have made contributions as a person falling within such a category of contributors. In the case before the Commissioner there was, however, nothing to in the administration or financing of the Dutch social security scheme to identify the claimant as an employed or self-employed person.

3.116

Council Regulation (EEC) No 1408/71

[¹*Article 2*

Persons covered

3.117
1. This Regulation shall apply to employed and self-employed persons and to students who are or have been subject to the legislation of one or more Member States and who are nationals of one of the Member States or who are stateless persons or refugees residing within the territory of one of the Member States, as well as to members of their families and their survivors.

2. This Regulation shall apply to the survivors of employed or self-employed persons and of students who have been subject to the legislation of one or more Member States, irrespective of the nationality of such persons, where their survivors are nationals of one of the Member States, or stateless persons or refugees residing within the territory of one of the Member States.]

AMENDMENT

1. Regulation 307/99/EC, [1999] OJ L38/1 (May 1, 1999).

GENERAL NOTE

3.118
The latest amendment brings students into the framework of the Regulation, though they must have been subject to the legislation of one or more Member States in their own right in order to fall within the scope of the Regulation by reason of their student status.

Note that the Regulation applies to both employed and self-employed persons. It also covers their families who have rights as such and not simply derivative rights flowing from the work of another member of their family: Case C-308/93 *Cabanis-Issarte* [1996] E.C.R. I-2097. In order to be a beneficiary of the rules in the Regulation, a person must be a national of an EEA country.

Article 3

Equality of treatment

3.119
1. Subject to the special provisions of this Regulation, persons [¹ . . .] to whom this Regulation applies shall be subject to the same obligations and enjoy the same benefits under the legislation of any Member State as the nationals of the State.

2. The provisions of paragraph 1 shall apply to the right to elect members of the organs of social security institutions or to participate in their nomination, but shall not affect the legislative provisions of any Member State relating to eligibility or methods of nomination of persons concerned to those organs.

3. Save as provided in Annex III, the provisions of social security onventions which remain in force pursuant to Article 7.2(c) [¹ . . .], shall apply to all persons to whom this Regulation applies.

AMENDMENT

1. Regulation 647/2005/EC, [2005] OJ L117/1 (May 5, 2005).

Article 3

GENERAL NOTE

The obligation in this article is central to the system of co-ordination established by the regulation. Equality of treatment is a foundational principle of the Community which is set out in Art.12 (ex 6) EC. The prohibition is restated in Art.39(2) (ex 48(2)) EC on the free movement of workers; the co-ordination of social security is part of the chapter on the free movement of workers. The requirement of equal treatment has been given a broad interpretation by the Court of Justice, which has consistently stated that it covers not only overt forms of discrimination but also covert forms of discrimination under which certain requirements and conditions which are not on their face based on nationality in effect operate to discriminate between nationals of the EEA countries: see Case 237/78 *Toia* [1979] E.C.R. 2645.

3.120

In Case C-346/05 *Chateignier*, [2006] ECR I-10951, the Court of Justice ruled:

"Article 39(2) EC and Article 3(1) of Council Regulation (EEC) No 1408/71 of 14 June 1971 . . . are to be interpreted as precluding national legislation under which the competent institution of the Member State of residence denies unemployment benefits to a national of another Member State on the ground that, on the date when the benefit claim was submitted, the person concerned had not completed a specified period of employment in that Member State of residence, whereas there is no such requirement for nationals of that Member State."

Article 2 of Reg.1408/71 brings refugees, as defined in Art.1, within its personal scope. Article 3(1) provides that those within the personal scope of the Regulation are entitled to the same rights as nationals of the Member State in which they are resident. But note that "resident" is defined in Art.1 as "habitual residence".

In *CF/3662/1999* a person seeking asylum sought to rely on this provision to obtain a right of entry and residence in the United Kingdom. The Commissioner dismissed the appeal on the authority of *Krasniqi v Chief Adjudication Officer* (reported as *R(IS) 15/99* to the effect that a claimant who has no connection with any Member State of the European Union other than the United Kingdom cannot rely on Reg.1408/71. That decision is found to be entirely consistent with authority from the Court of Justice of the European Communities in Joined Cases C-95/99–C-98/99 *Khalil v Bundesanstalt für Arbeit* [2001] ECR I-7413.

The issue of discrimination prohibited by Art.3 was discussed in *Secretary of State for Work and Pensions v Bobezes*, [2005] EWCA Civ 111, reported as *R(IS) 6/05*. The claimant was a Portuguese national who had been a worker in the United Kingdom who had become permanently incapable of work. He was in receipt of income support including an allowance for a child. When the child when to visit her grandmother in Portugal from August to November 1998, the decision maker concluded that there was no entitlement to the child allowance on the grounds of absence from Great Britain for more than four weeks. The claimant argued that he had been the victim of discrimination prohibited by Community law in that, had the child gone to stay with a grandparent in Great Britain, there would have been a continuing entitlement to the allowance. There was discussion in the Court of Appeal as to whether Art.7(2) of Reg.1612/68 applied or Art.3 of Reg.1408/71. The Court of Appeal declines to resolve the question of the relationship of these two provisions and proceeds on the basis that the claimant could rely on Art.3 of Reg.1408/71.

The key question then addressed concerned proof of discrimination. The Secretary of State argued that the claimant must produce statistical evidence to show the claimed discrimination, while the claimant argued that he had to do no more than show that the requirements of the United Kingdom legislation were intrinsically more likely to affect essentially migrant workers. The Court of Appeal concludes that adjudicating authorities should take a "broad approach and to find that indirect discrimination is liable to affect a significant number of migrant workers on the ground of nationality without statistical proof being available." (para.24 of judgment). Lord Slynn said that the proper approach was to compare the children of migrant workers with British children whose families are normally resident here.

Council Regulation (EEC) No 1408/71

Article 4

Matters covered

3.121

1. This Regulation shall apply to all legislation concerning the following branches of social security:
   (a) sickness and maternity benefits;
   (b) invalidity benefits, including those intended for the maintenance or improvement of earning capacity;
   (c) old-age benefits;
   (d) survivors' benefits;
   (e) benefits in respect of accidents at work and occupational diseases;
   (f) death grants;
   (g) unemployment benefits;
   (h) family benefits.

2. This Regulation shall apply to all general and special social security schemes, whether contributory or non-contributory, and to schemes concerning the liability of an employer or shipowner in respect of the benefits referred to in paragraph 1.

[² **2a.** This Article shall apply to special non-contributory cash benefits which are provided under legislation which, because of its personal scope, objectives and/or conditions for entitlement has characteristics both of the social security legislation referred to in paragraph 1 and of social assistance.

"Special non-contributory cash benefits" means those:
   (a) which are intended to provide either:
       (i) supplementary, substitute or ancillary cover against the risks covered by the branches of social security referred to in paragraph 1, and which guarantee the persons concerned a minimum subsistence income having regard to the economic and social situation in the Member State concerned;
           or
       (ii) solely specific protection for the disabled, closely linked to the said person's social environment in the Member State concerned,
       and
   (b) where the financing exclusively derives from compulsory taxation intended to cover general public expenditure and the conditions for providing and for calculating the benefits are not dependent on any contribution in respect of the beneficiary. However, benefits provided to supplement a contributory benefit shall not be considered to be contributory benefits for this reason alone;
       and
   (c) which are listed in Annex IIa.]

2b. This Regulation shall not apply to the provisions in the legislation of a Member State concerning special non-contributory benefits, referred to in Annex II, Section III, the validity of which is confined to part of its territory.

3. The provisions of Title III of this Regulation shall not, however, affect the legislative provisions of any Member State concerning a shipowner's liability.

4. This Regulation shall not apply to social and medical assistance, to benefit schemes for victims of war or its consequences, [¹ . . .].

AMENDMENTS

1. Regulation 1606/98/EC, [1998] OJ L209/1 (October 25, 1998).

Article 4

2. Regulation 647/2005/EC, [2005] OJ L117/1 (May 5, 2005).

GENERAL NOTE

The Regulation applies to all legislation governing benefits protecting against the eight named risks. These social risks are those identified in ILO Convention 102. It does not matter whether the specified benefits are provided under contributory or non-contributory schemes. Special non-contributory benefits are also covered where they provide supplementary, substitute or ancillary cover against the social risk set out in the article, or are specific protection for disabled people. The Article provides an exhaustive list of the branches of social security governed by the Regulation. The Article applies to all legislation concerning the specified branch of social security; legislation is defined in very broad terms in Art.1, and the Court of Justice has described the definition as "remarkable for its breadth": Case 87/76 *Bozzone* [1977] E.C.R. 687.

3.122

Whether a particular benefit falls within the scope of these eight branches of social security as well as whether any of the exceptions applies is determined in accordance with Community law, and not simply the classification of a benefit under the national scheme. The Court of Justice has consistently said that whether a benefit is within the material scope of the Regulation "rests entirely on the factors relating to each benefit, in particular its purpose and the conditions for its grant": Case 9/78 *Gillard* [1978] E.C.R. 1661, para.12 of the judgment. The fact that the benefit has a dual purpose does not exclude it from the material scope of the Regulation.

In Case C-160/96 *Molenaar* [1998] E.C.R. I-843, the Court of Justice ruled that care insurance was a benefit intended to supplement sickness insurance and so constituted a sickness benefit for the purpose of Regulation 1408/71. This was taken further in Joned Cases C-502/01 and C-31/02 *Gaumain-Cerri* and *Barth*, Judgment of July 8, 2004, where the Court ruled that the payment of old-age insurance in respect of carers of a person in receipt of care insurance also constituted a sickness benefit.

Note that the United Kingdom, after much argument, eventually conceded that winter fuel payments are an old-age benefit within the material scope of Regulation 1408/71. For background and discussion of the implications, see *Secretary of State for Work and Pensions v Walker-Fox* [2005] EWCA Civ. 1441, reported as *R(IS) 3/06*, and *R(IS) 8/06*.

It is possible that issues will arise as to whether child trust contributions under the Child Trust Funds Act 2004 constitute family benefits within Regulation 1408/71, since s.2 of the Act excludes payment of the contribution where child benefit is in payment under the coordination rules, but the child is not resident in the United Kingdom.

Social assistance is excluded from the scope of the Regulation together with medical assistance, and schemes for war victims.

The distinction between social insurance and social assistance used to be more clear cut than it is today. Social insurance as originally conceived related to insurance-based schemes in respect of certain risk against which workers or their employers would insure; it also included provision for what might be regarded as the certainties of life: birth, old age and death. By contrast social assistance is support provided by the State at its discretion on the basis of need. There is also a third group of benefits which are provided on the basis of need, but are a matter of legal entitlement and not discretion. Considerable debate still surrounds the true nature of benefits like income support in the United Kingdom which are means tested but are paid as a matter of legal right to those who meet closely specified conditions of entitlement and at a rate also set out in regulations. In *Perry v Chief Adjudication Officer*, [1999] 2 C.M.L.R. 439, reported as *R(IS)4/99*, the Court of Appeal held that income support was not a special non contributory benefit (see Art.10a below) within the meaning of the Regulation, but this decision must now be read in the light of Case C-90/97 *Swaddling v Adjudication Officer* [1999] E.C.R. I-1075; [1999] 2 C.M.L.R. 679, reported as *R(IS)6/99*, in which the Court of Justice ruled that income support is a special non-contributory benefit within the meaning of the Regulation.

In *CIB/4243/1999*, the Commissioner held that short-term incapacity benefit whether paid at the lower or the higher rate is a sickness benefit for the purposes of Reg.1408/71, while long-term incapacity benefit is an invalidity benefit for the purposes of the Regulation (para.17).

Article 5

Declarations by the Member States on the scope of this Regulation

3.123 The Member States shall specify the legislation and schemes referred to in Article 4(1) and (2), the special non-contributory benefits referred to in Article 4(2a), the minimum benefits referred to in Article 50 and the benefits referred to in Articles 77 and 78 in declarations to be notified and published in accordance with Article 97.

General Note

3.124 Little assistance is provided by reference to declarations made by Member States, since they are not always kept up to date. The United Kingdom declaration is certainly out of date.

Article 6

Social security conventions replaced by this Regulation.

3.125 Subject to the provisions of Articles 7, 8 and 46(4) this Regulation shall, as regards persons and matters which it covers, replace the provisions of any social security convention binding either;
  (a) two or more Member States exclusively, or
  (b) at least two Member States and one or more other States, where settlement of the cases concerned does not involve any institution of one of the latter States.

Relevant Provisions of the Implementing Regulation

Art.5, Reg. 574/72/EEC.

Relevant Decisions of the Administrative Commission

Recommendation No 22 of June, 18 2003 concerning the *Gottardo* judgment, according to which the advantages enjoyed by a state's own nationals under a bilateral convention on social security with a non-member country must also be granted to workers who are nationals of other Member States, [2003] OJ L326/35.

General Note

3.126 This article gives priority to the provisions of the Regulation over social security conventions concluded between the Member States. This has given rise to some complex and difficult case law. The essential question was whether advantages arising under the existing conventions were lost when the Regulation came into force, and whether this was compatible with the EC Treaty provisions. In its first decision on this issue in Case 82/72 *Walder*, [1973] E.C.R. 599, the Court ruled that the provisions of Article 6 were mandatory and did not allow for exceptions which were not expressly set out in the Regulation. Case 227/89 *Rönfeldt*, [1991] E.C.R. I-323 concerned a German national who had from 1941 to 1957, and so prior to the entry into force of Regulation 1408/71 (or its predecessor), worked in Germany

Article 6

before moving to Denmark and working there until 1971 when he returned to Germany. Retirement pension ages were 65 in Germany and 67 in Denmark; in Germany an early retirement pension could be claimed at 63 provided that a person had completed 35 years of insurance. Rönfeldt claimed an early retirement pension but was refused since the German authorities took the view that contributions paid in Denmark could not be taken into account in Germany until the claimant reached the Danish retirement age of 67. The Court noted that Art.45 of the Regulation to take insurance periods completed in other Member States into account in determining whether a person has acquired, retained or recovered a right to benefit, but Art.46 does not require contributions paid elsewhere to be taken into account in calculating the amount of a benefit. This was in contrast to the requirements of a convention between Germany and Denmark. The Court then ruled that it was incompatible with the provisions of the EC Treaty on free movement of workers to deprive a person of advantages which they had acquired under a convention.

The judgment presented very significant problems of administration for the Member States since it would mean that in very many cases multiple computations would be needed because of the number of bilateral and multilateral treaties in existence. The Court clarified its judgment in the *Rönfeldt* case in Case 475/93 *Thévenon and Speyer* [1995] E.C.R. I-3813. The Court explained that the rule in the *Rönfeldt* case only applied where a right to freedom of movement had been exercised prior to the entry into force; it did not apply where the right of free movement was first exercised after Regulation 1408/71 had replaced the provisions of the bilateral convention. The *Rönfeldt* exception applied only to those who had already accrued certain rights under the bilateral convention. It did not preserve the more beneficial rule in the convention for those first exercising their right of free movement under the regime set in place by Regulation 1408/71. The consequence is that it is not a requirement for institutions in the Member States to investigate in every claim whether a person might have a more advantageous position under a bilateral or multilateral convention. In Case C-113/96 *Gómez Rodríguez*, [1998] E.C.R. I-2482, ruled that a comparison of rights had to be made only once: at the first determination of benefit entitlement within the terms of Regulation 1408/71. In Case C-75/99 *Thelen*, [2000] E.C.R. I-9399 and Case C-277/99 *Kaske,* [2000] E.C.R. I-1261, the Court ruled that the only purpose of the *Rönfeldt* exception was to preserve entitlement to an established social right which was not part of Community law at the time when the national of a Member State relying on it had such an entitlement. The *Rönfeldt* exception was based on a person's legitimate expectation that accrued rights would not be lost.

Article 7

International provisions not affected by this Regulation

1. This Regulation shall not affect obligations arising from: 3.127
  (a) any convention adopted by the International Labour Conference which, after ratification by one or more Member States, has entered into force;
  (b) the European Interim Agreements on Social Security of 11 December 1953 concluded between the Member States of the Council of Europe.

2. The provisions of Article 6 notwithstanding, the following shall continue to apply:
  (a) the provision of the Agreements of 27 July 1950 and 30 November 1979 concerning social security for Rhine boatmen;
  (b) the provisions of the European Convention of 9 July 1956 concerning social security for workers in international transport;

[¹ (c) certain provisions of social security conventions entered into by the Member States before the date of application of this Regulation provided that they are more favourable to the beneficiaries or if they arise from specific historical circumstances and their effect is limited in time if these provisions are listed in Annex III.]

AMENDMENT

1. Regulation 647/2005/EC, [2005] OJ L117/1 (May 5, 2005).

RELEVANT PROVISIONS OF THE IMPLEMENTING REGULATION

Art.5, Reg. 574/72/EEC.

GENERAL NOTE

3.128   Art.3(3) and Annex III provide exceptions to the operation of certain provisions of this article.

Article 8

Conclusion of conventions between Member States

3.129   **1.** Two or more Member States may, as need arises, conclude conventions with each other based on the principles and in the spirit of this Regulation.

2. Each Member State shall notify, in accordance with the provisions of Article 97(1), any convention concluded with another member State under the provisions of paragraph 1.

GENERAL NOTE

3.130   Art.3(3) and Annex III provide exceptions to the operation of certain provisions of this article.

Article 9

Admission to voluntary or optional continued insurance

3.131   **1.** The provisions of the legislation of any Member State which make admission to voluntary or optional continued insurance conditional upon residence in the territory of that State shall not apply to persons resident in the territory of another Member State, provided that at some time in their past working life they were subject to the legislation of the first State as employed or as self-employed persons.

2. Where under the legislation of a Member State, admission to voluntary or optional continued insurance is conditional upon completion of periods of insurance, the periods of insurance or residence completed under the legislation of another Member State shall be taken into account, to the extent required, as if they were completed under the legislation of the first State.

RELEVANT PROVISIONS OF THE IMPLEMENTING REGULATION

Art.6, Reg.574/72/EEC.

Article 9a

Article 9a

[¹ **Prolongation of the reference period**

If the legislation of a Member State subordinates recognition of entitlement to a benefit to the completion of a minimum period of insurance during a determined period preceding the contingency insured against (reference period) and lays down that periods during which benefits were paid under the legislation of that Member State or periods devoted to child-rearing in the territory of that Member State shall extend this reference period, the periods during which invalidity or old age pensions or sickness, unemployment, industrial accidents at work or occupational disease benefits were paid under the legislation of another Member State and periods devoted to child-rearing in the territory of another Member State shall also extend this reference period.]

3.132

AMENDMENT

1. Regulation 647/2005/EC, [2005] OJ L117/1 (May 5, 2005).

Article 10

Waiving of residence clauses—Effect of compulsory insurance on reimbursement of contributions

1. Save as otherwise provided in this Regulation invalidity, old-age or survivors' cash benefits, pension for accidents at work or occupational diseases and death grants acquired under the legislation of one or more Member States shall not be subject to any reduction, modification, suspension, withdrawal or confiscation by reason of the fact that the recipient resides in the territory of a Member State other than that in which the institution responsible for payment is situated.

3.133

The first subparagraph shall also apply to lump-sum benefits granted in cases of remarriage of a surviving spouse who was entitled to a survivors' pension.

2. Where under the legislation of a Member State reimbursement of contributions is conditional upon the person concerned having ceased to be subject to compulsory insurance, this condition shall not be considered satisfied as long as the person concerned is subject to compulsory insurance [¹ . . .] under the legislation of another Member State.

AMENDMENT

1. Regulation 307/99/EC, [1999] OJ L38/1 (May 1, 1999).

GENERAL NOTE

This article and Art.10a deal with the exportability of benefits. They set out the general rules on which a benefit acquired in one EEA country may continue in payment where the beneficiary moves to another EEA country. Though issues remain as to the classification of certain benefits, those rules seem fairly clear. Member States tend to argue that benefits are social assistance and are not capable of exportation. So in Case 139/82 *Piscitello* [1983] E.C.R. 1427, the Italian Government argued that the *pensione sociale* was social assistance, but the Court concluded that it was a benefit

3.134

analogous to an old age pension and so Paolo Piscitello could take it with her when she moved from Italy to Belgium to join members of her family living there.

The exportability of sickness and maternity, and unemployment benefits applies only to a very limited extent, since the Member States are extremely cautious about losing the ability to monitor the genuineness of the claim or the claimant's continuing job search activities. The putting together of sickness and maternity benefits is unfortunate in this regard.

The concern of the Member States that certain individuals would tour the Member States collecting the most favourable benefit entitlements and exporting them to where they wanted to live led to a new regime being introduced for what are called special non-contributory benefits. Such benefits are under Art.10a payable only in the territory of the Member State to those resident there. Special non-contributory benefits must be listed in Annex IIa of the Regulation. Though payability is linked to residence, the process of acquisition is not tied to a single Member State.

See *Harris v Secretary of State for Social Security*, reported as *R(DLA)2/99* concerning a disability living allowance.

Entitlement to export those benefits which were excluded from the exportability rules in Art.10 continued for those who already had an entitlement as at the date Art.10a was introduced into the Regulation, that is, June 1, 1992 (see Reg.1247/93/EEC[1992] O.J. L136/1). DLA is a single benefit, and so the addition of a care component where a mobility component is already in payment prior to the date of this change does not result in the loss of the protected exportability of the benefit: see *CDLA/402/2003*.

On the exportability of winter fuel payments, see *CIS/488/2004* and *CIS/1491/2004*. In *CIS/1491/2004* the Commissioner had to consider whether there was an entitlement to winter fuel payments by a person born in 1928 whose residence in Great Britain had ended before the introduction of winter fuel payments. The Commissioner concluded that the payments are not a supplement to retirement pension, but are a separate and free-standing form of old age benefit. It was not accordingly contrary to Community law to condition entitlement to such a benefit on residence in Great Britain. Since the claimant could not secure entitlement to a winter fuel payment, it followed that he could not export that to which he was not entitled. Article 10 only permits the export of a benefit to another Member State after entitlement to it has been acquired. That was not the case here.

Article 10a

Special non-contributory benefits

3.135 [¹ **1.** The provisions of Article 10 and of Title III shall not apply to the special non-contributory cash benefits referred to in Article 4(2a). The persons to whom this Regulation applies shall receive these benefits exclusively in the territory of the Member State in which they reside and under the legislation of that State, in so far as these benefits are mentioned in Annex IIa. Benefits shall be paid by, and at the expense of, the institution of the place of residence.]

2. The institution of a Member State under whose legislation entitlement to benefits covered by paragraph 1 is subject to the completion of periods of employment, self-employment or residence shall regard, to the extent necessary, periods of employment, self-employment or residence completed in the territory of any other Member State as periods completed in the territory of the first Member State.

3. Where entitlement to a benefit covered by paragraph 1 but granted in the form of a supplement is subject, under the legislation of a Member State, to receipt of a benefit covered by Article 4 (1) (a) to (h), and no such benefit is due under that legislation, any corresponding benefit granted under the legislation of any other Member State shall be treated as a benefit granted under the legislation of the first Member State for the purposes of entitlement to the supplement.

4. Where the granting of a disability or invalidity benefit covered by paragraph 1 is subject, under the legislation of a Member State, to the condition that the disability or invalidity should be diagnosed for the first time in the territory of that Member State, this condition shall be deemed to be fulfilled where such diagnosis is made for the first time in the territory of another Member State.

AMENDMENT

1. Regulation 647/2005/EC, [2005] OJ L117/1 (May 5, 2005).

RELEVANT DECISIONS OF THE ADMINISTRATIVE COMMISSION

Decision No. 151 of 22 April, 1993 concerning the application of Article 10a of Regulation (EEC) No. 1408/71 and of Article 2 of Regulation (EEC) No. 1247/92, [1994] OJ L244/1.

Decision No. 153 of 13 May, 1993 on the implementation of Article 10a of Regulation (EEC) No. 1408/71 and of Article 2 of Regulation (EEC) No. 1247/92, [1994] OJ L244/19.

GENERAL NOTE

The concept of special non-contributory benefits was introduced into Regulation 1408/71 by Regulation 1247/92/EEC, [1992] OJ L/136/1. Such benefits are benefits which provide "supplementary, substitute or ancillary cover" in respect of the risks set out in Art.4, or "solely as specific protection for the disabled" (see Art. 4(2a) above). By an amendment in 2005 additional qualifying words were added which refer to minimum subsistence income benefits and qualify the benefits for disabled people by referring to their being "closely linked to the said person's social environment in the Member State concerned."

The significance of the designation of a benefit as a special non-contributory benefit is *not* that it is taken outside the scope of Regulation 1408/71 completely, but that it is payable only on the territory of the competent State. The United Kingdom's list of benefits included in Annex IIa has always been among the longer lists of such benefits.

The nature of disability living allowance was considered in Case C-20/96 *Snares v The Adjudication Officer* [1997] E.C.R. I-6057, reported as *R(DLA)5/99*, and of attendance allowance in Case C-297/96 *Partridge v The Adjudication Officer* [1998] E.C.R. I-1467, reported as *R(A) 1/99*. The Court of Justice took the view that the listing of the benefit in Annex IIa must be accepted as establishing the nature of the benefit; the absence of a revised declaration under Art.5 did not prejudice this position. The result was the same in *Partridge*.

It was accepted in the Court of Appeal in *Perry v Chief Adjudication Officer*, reported as *R(IS)4/99* that income support is a special non-contributory benefit. This was confirmed in a ruling from the Court of Justice in *Swaddling v Adjudication Officer*, reported as *R(IS)6/99*, but that ruling also indicated the effect of the benefit remaining one within the scope of Regulation 1408/71 for other purposes.

Though it is a precondition for claiming that a benefit is a special non-contributory benefit that it is listed in Annex IIa, that is not conclusive as to its status. It remains open to the Court of Justice to determine that the benefit is a supplement to one of the benefits within the material scope of the Regulation: Case C-215/99 *Jauch* [2001] E.C.R. I-1901, and Case C-43/99 *Leclere* [2001] E.C.R. I-4265. This case rather took the Member States by surprise, since they had assumed that inclusion in Annex IIa was conclusive. But the Court ruled that it must examine in cases where the issue arose whether a benefit genuinely qualified as a special non-contributory benefit; specification in

3.136

Annex IIa was not conclusive. The fallout from the decision in *Jauch and Leclere* is that claims that benefits are special non-contributory benefits can now subject to more detailed enquiry if that matter comes before the Court of Justice.

In Case C-160/02 *Skalka*, [2004] ECR I-5613 the Court had to consider the status of a supplementary pension in Austria, which was listed in Annex IIa. In essence this is a topping up pension to bring a pensioner's income up to a certain level. It was, however, only payable to people habitually resident in Austria. Skalka was an Austrian national who had retired early and moved to Spain. The Court accepted that it was a special non-contributory benefit. There was clear evidence that the benefit was non-contributory. In para.22 the Court said:

"22. A special benefit within the meaning of Article 4(2a) of Regulation No 1408/71 is defined by its purpose. It must either replace or supplement a social security benefit and be by its nature social assistance justified on economic and social grounds and fixed by legislation setting objective criteria (see to that effect Case C-20/96 *Snares* [1997] ECR I-6057, paragraphs 33, 42 and 43, Case C-297/96 *Partridge* [1998] ECR I-3467, paragraph 34, and Case C-43/99 *Leclère and Deaconescu* [2001] ECR I-4265, paragraph 32).

26. As all the interveners have stated, the Austrian compensatory supplement tops up a retirement pension or an invalidity pension. It is by nature social assistance in so far as it is intended to ensure a minimum means of subsistence for its recipient where the pension is insufficient. Its grant is dependent on objective criteria defined by law. Consequently, it must be classified as a 'special benefit' within the meaning of Regulation No 1408/71."

In Case C-286/03 *Silvia Hosse*, [2006] ECR I-1771, the Grand Chamber of the Court of Justice was faced with a reference concerning a German care allowance. It was regional benefit, but that did not prove to be material to the Court's ruling. The Court noted that the Community institutions were entitled to legislate for certain exceptions to the principle of exportability of social security benefits, but recapitulated its earlier case law on the classification of benefits. The Court then explained why the German benefit was not a special non-contributory benefit:

"36. The scheme of Regulation No 1408/71 shows that the concept of 'social security benefit' within the meaning of Article 4(1) and the concept of 'special non-contributory benefit' within the meaning of Article 4(2a) and (2b) of the regulation are mutually exclusive. A benefit which satisfies the conditions of a 'social security benefit' within the meaning of Article 4(1) of Regulation No 1408/71 therefore cannot be analysed as a 'special non-contributory benefit".

37. A benefit may be regarded as a social security benefit in so far as it is granted to the recipients, without any individual and discretionary assessment of personal needs, on the basis of a legally defined position and relates to one of the risks expressly listed in Article 4(1) of Regulation No 1408/71 (see, inter alia, Case 249/83 *Hoeckx* [1985] ECR 973, paragraphs 12 to 14; Case C-78/91 *Hughes* [1992] ECR I-4839, paragraph 15; Case C-160/96 *Molenaar* [1998] ECR I-843, paragraph 20; and *Jauch*, paragraph 25).

38. It follows that benefits which are granted objectively on the basis of a legally defined position and are intended to improve the state of health and life of persons reliant on care have the essential purpose of supplementing sickness insurance benefits, and must be regarded as 'sickness benefits' within the meaning of Article 4(1)(a) of Regulation No 1408/71 (*Molenaar*, paragraphs 24 and 25, and *Jauch*, paragraph 28).

39. A care allowance such as that granted under the SPGG is intended to compensate, in the form of a flat-rate contribution, for the additional expenditure resulting from the recipients' condition of reliance on care, in particular the cost of the assistance it is necessary to provide them with.

40. The amount of such a care allowance depends of the degree of reliance on care. It corresponds to the time spent on care, expressed in terms of hours

per month. Assessment of reliance on care is regulated in detail in a measure laying down a classification according to degrees of reliance. The other income of the person reliant on care has no effect on the amount of the care allowance.

41. The allowance is paid to persons who do not receive any pension under the Federal provisions. Those persons are essentially members of the families of socially insured persons, recipients of social assistance, disabled workers, and persons receiving pensions from the provinces and municipalities.

42. Consequently, while a care allowance such as that at issue in the main proceedings may have a different system from that applicable to the German benefits of insurance against reliance on care at issue in *Molenaar* and the Austrian federal care allowance at issue in *Jauch*, it none the less remains of the same kind as those benefits.

43. Moreover, as the Court observed in *Jauch*, the conditions for the grant of care allowance and the way in which it is financed cannot have the intention or the effect of changing the character of care allowance as analysed in the *Molenaar* and *Jauch* judgments. The fact that the grant of the benefit is not necessarily linked to payment of a sickness insurance benefit or a pension awarded on a basis other than sickness insurance cannot therefore change that analysis.

44. In those circumstances, even if they have their own particular characteristics, such benefits must be regarded as sickness benefits within the meaning of Article 4(1)(a) of Regulation No 1408/71.

45. In the light of the above factors, one of the conditions necessary for Article 4(2b) of Regulation No 1408/71 to apply, namely the classification of the benefit in question as a 'special benefit', is not satisfied. There is thus no longer any need to consider whether the other conditions laid down in that article are satisfied."

Case C-154/05 *Kersbergen-Lap and Dams-Schipper* [2006] ECR I-6249, raised the question of whether an incapacity benefit for disabled young people who had never worked constituted a special non-contributory benefit. Two recipients of the benefit had moved to France and Germany respectively, and the payment of the benefit had been stopped. It was again easy to conclude that the benefit was non-contributory, and as in the earlier cases the focus was on whether the benefit was special. The Third Chamber concluded:

"30. A special benefit within the meaning of Article 4(2a) of Regulation No 1408/71 is defined by its purpose. It must either replace or supplement a social security benefit and be by its nature social assistance justified on economic and social grounds and fixed by legislation setting objective criteria (see Case C-160/02 *Skalka* [2004] ECR I-5613, paragraph 25, and case-law cited).

31. As was pointed out by the Netherlands Government, the Wajong benefit is a replacement allowance intended for those who do not satisfy the conditions of insurance for obtaining invalidity benefit under Article 4(1)(b) of Regulation No 1408/71. By guaranteeing a minimum income to a socially disadvantaged group (disabled young people), the Wajong benefit is by its nature social assistance justified on economic and social grounds. Moreover, it is granted according to objective criteria defined by law.

32. With regard to the fact that the benefit at issue in the main proceedings is granted without any means test or needs assessment being carried out, as was pointed out by the Commission, the majority of disabled young people would not have sufficient means of subsistence if they did not receive that benefit.

33. Further, that benefit is closely linked to the socio-economic situation in the Netherlands since it is based on the minimum wage and the standard of living in that Member State. The Court has in the past accepted that the grant of benefits closely linked with the social environment may be made subject to a condition of residence in the State of the competent institution (see, to that effect, Case 313/86 *Lenoir* [1988] ECR 5391, paragraph 16; Case C-20/96 *Snares* [1997] ECR I-6057, paragraph 42; and Case C-43/99 *Leclerc and Deaconescu* [2001] ECR I-4265, paragraph 32).

34. It follows that a benefit under the Wajong must be classified as a special benefit within the meaning of Regulation No 1408/71."

Case C-265/05 *José Perez Naranjo* Judgment of January 16, 2007, concerned a supplementary old-age allowance payable in France. Perez Naranjo was a Spanish national who had worked in France but then return to Spain. Since November 1991 he has been in receipt of a French old-age pension. His claim for the supplementary allowance was refused. In this case the Grand Chamber quickly concluded that the benefit was a special benefit; it was similar to both social security and social assistance, and so had a mixed character which meant it had to be regarded as a special benefit (para.35 of the Judgment). The question of whether it was contributory was rather more complex and required an examination of the financing of the benefit. It is acknowledged that this is an enquiry which might better be resolved following consideration in the national courts (para.36). In connection with this enquiry the Court observes that it is necessary to consider whether there is an identifiable link between the supplementary allowance and the general social contribution on earned income and substitute income. In a steer to the national court, the Grand Chamber says,

" . . . even if the part of the general social contribution based on earned income and substitute income must be regarded as a contribution rather than financing from public resources, the link between that contribution and the supplementary allowance is not sufficiently identifiable for that allowance to be classified as a contributory benefit." (para.52).

The issue of what are genuinely special non-contributory benefits remains a particularly hot topic, and there is an important case pending before the Court of Justice. The context in which the matter is being raised is perhaps unusual. The Commission has brought an action (Case C-299/05) against the European Parliament and the Council seeking the annulment of provisions in amendments to Annex IIa which include, inter alia, the United Kingdom benefits of attendance allowance, carer's allowance and disability living allowance. The Commission argues that these are not special non-contributory benefits and have no place in Annex IIa (whose benefits can be territorial only, by virtue of Art.10a). See [2005] OJ C243/9. The Advocate General delivered her Opinion in this case on May 3, 2007, and invited the Court to rule that all three designated benefits in issue in the case do not constitute special non-contributory benefits. The Court is not, of course, obliged to follow the Opinion of the Advocate General. The Court's decision is awaited.

Article 11

Revalorization of benefits

3.137   Rules for revalorization provided by the legislation of a Member State shall apply to benefits due under that legislation taking into account the provisions of this Regulation.

GENERAL NOTE

3.138   "Revalorization" would appear to refer to uprating of benefits.

Article 12

Prevention of overlapping of benefits

3.139   1. This Regulation can neither confer nor maintain the right to several benefits of the same kind for one and the same period of compulsory insurance.

Article 12

However, this provision shall not apply to benefits in respect of invalidity, old age, death (pensions) or occupational disease which are awarded by the institutions of two or more Member States, in accordance with the provisions of Articles 41, 43(2) and (3), 46, 50 and 51 or Article 60(1)(b).

2. Save as otherwise provided in this Regulation, the provisions of the legislations of a Member State governing the reduction, suspension or withdrawal of benefits in cases of overlapping with other social security benefits or any other form of income may be invoked even where such benefits were acquired under the legislation of another Member State or where such income was acquired in the territory of another Member State.

3. The provisions of the legislation of a Member State for reduction, suspension or withdrawal of benefit in the case of a person in receipt of invalidity benefits or anticipatory old-age benefits pursuing a professional or trade activity may be invoked against such person even though he is pursuing his activity in the territory of another Member State.

4. An invalidity pension payable under Netherlands legislation shall, in case where the Netherlands institution is bound under the provisions of Article 57(5) or 60(29)(b) to contribute also to the cost of benefits for occupational disease granted under the legislation of another Member State, be reduced by the amount payable to the institution of the other Member State which is responsible for granting the benefits for occupational disease.

RELEVANT PROVISIONS OF THE IMPLEMENTING REGULATION

Arts 7–10a, Reg.574/72/EEC.

GENERAL NOTE

Article 12 contains the Community rules on overlapping benefits, which provide the authority for national systems to adjust national benefit by reason of entitlement to a benefit in another EEA country which is awarded by reason of the application of the Community co-ordination rules. Article 12 lays down a number principles relating to overlapping of benefits: 3.140

(1) Regulation 1408/71 can neither confer nor maintain the right to several benefits *of the same kind* for one and the same period of compulsory insurance.

(2) The rules apply only to short-term benefits since the rules on aggregation and apportionment which apply to long-term benefits achieve the same effect without the need for rules relating to the overlapping of benefits.

(3) The rules only apply where acquisition of a benefit arises through the application of the Community rules.

See also Arts 7–10a of Reg.574/72 reproduced below.

TITLE II

DETERMINATION OF THE LEGISLATION APPLICABLE

Article 13

General rules

[¹**1.** Subject to Articles 14c and 14f, persons to whom this Regulation applies shall be subject to the legislation of a single Member State only.   3.141

That legislation shall be determined in accordance with the provisions of this Title.]

2. Subject to Articles 14 to 17:
(a) a person employed in the territory of one Member State shall be subject to the legislation of that State even if he resides in the territory of another Member State or if the registered office or place of business of the undertaking or individual employing him is situated in the territory of another Member State;
(b) a person who is self-employed in the territory of one Member State shall be subjected to the legislation of that State even if he resides in the territory of another Member State;
(c) a person employed on board a vessel flying the flag of a Member State shall be subject to the legislation of the State;
(d) civil servants and persons treated as such shall be subject to the legislation of the Member State to which the administration employing them is subject;
(e) a person called up or recalled for service in the armed forces, or for civilian service, of a Member State shall be subject to the legislation of that State. If entitlement under that legislation is subject to the completion of periods of insurance before entry into or after release from such military or civilian service, periods of insurance completed under the legislation of any other Member State shall be taken into account, to the extent necessary, as if they were periods of insurance completed under the legislation of the first State. The employed or self-employed person called up or recalled for service in the armed forces or for civilian service shall retain the status of employed or self-employed person;
(f) a person to whom the legislation of a Member State ceases to be applicable, without the legislation of another Member State becoming applicable to him in accordance with one of the rules laid down in the aforegoing subparagraphs or in accordance with one of the exceptions or special provisions laid down in Articles 14 to 17 shall be subject to the legislation of the Member State in whose territory he resides in accordance with the provisions of that legislation alone.

AMENDMENTS

1. Regulation 1606/98/EC, [1998] OJ L209/1 (October 25, 1998).

RELEVANT PROVISIONS OF THE IMPLEMENTING REGULATION

Art.10b, Reg.574/72/EEC.

GENERAL NOTE

3.142   Title II of Reg.1408/71 provides a complete system of the conflict of laws for answering questions concerning both jurisdiction and the choice of law to apply to any situation involving an international element between EEA countries. The basic proposition is that persons to whom the regulation applies are at any given time subject to the legislation of a single EEA country only, which will normally apply its own social security laws to the matter subject to the co-ordinating rules in the Regulation. The starting point to which there are exceptions is that priority is given to the place of employment or self-employment. There are, however, very many special situations where this rule is displaced.

CF/1727/2006 contains guidance on the procedure for obtaining a formal decision of the National Insurance Contributions Office as to a person's liability to pay national insurance contributions. That is important for Regulation 1408/71, since it will also determine which law is applicable to a claim for child benefit.

Both employed (Art.13(2)(a)) and self-employed (Art.13(2)(b)) persons who live in one EEA country but work in another EEA country are subject, for any given claim, to the legislation of the EEA country in which they work. This rule applies even if the registered office of centre of administration of an employer is in a different EEA country. The Court of Justice has even applied the provisions of Title II by analogy where a situation arises which is not covered directly by its provisions. So in Case 60/93 *Aldewereld* [1994] E.C.R. I-2991, a question arose as to whether a Dutch national recruited by a company established in Germany and sent to work in Thailand was covered by the legislation of The Netherlands or Germany. The Court concluded that there was a sufficient link with Community law for Community law to apply, and that there was a real and substantial link with Germany in relation to the employment. Aldewereld should accordingly be treated as a person employed in Germany, and the provisions of German social security law would apply to his liability to pay social security contributions.

Determining the location of self employment may be more complex than determining the location of employment. Given the varied nature of self employment, careful enquiry may be needed in order to determine whether there is a separation of the place of residence and the place of the self employment, especially where the activity is conducted from him. For example, a person who moves to Spain to live there, but who continues his self-employment as a business adviser advising only clients in the United Kingdom may well continue to be self-employed in the United Kingdom.

The Court has interpreted the rules on the applicable legislation in order to ensure that practical effect is given to the scheme in the Regulation. The facts of Case 196/90 *De Paep* [1991] E.C.R. I-4815, were rather unusual. Mrs De Paep owned a vessel on which her husband and son were employed. Following damage to the vessel, it was declared unseaworthy. Despite this it was sailed across the Channel from Belgium to the United Kingdom. During this passage, the vessel was shipwrecked, and the husband and son were lost at sea. Under Belgian law on employment contracts for seamen, contracts of employment automatically terminate when a vessel is declared unseaworthy. The effect in law was that the husband and son were technically not employed on the vessel when it sank. Nor were they flying on a vessel carrying the flag of Belgium (the vessel was registered in the United Kingdom). The Court ruled that neither condition precluded the legislation of Belgium from applying to the claim made by Madeleine De Paep for an annuity by way of compensation for loss sustained as a result of accidents at work following the death of her son. The Court said:

". . . according to the case-law of the Court the provisions of Title II of Regulation No. 1408/71 . . . constitute a complete and uniform system of conflict rules . . . and that those provisions are intended not only to prevent the simultaneous application of a number of national legislative systems and the complications which might ensue, but also to ensure that the persons covered by Regulation No 1408/71 are not left without social security cover because there is no legislation applicable to them. In particular, the conditions concerning the right of a person to become affiliated to a social security scheme may not have the effect of excluding from the scope of the legislation at issue persons to whom it applies pursuant to Regulation No 1408/71 . . . {" (para.18 of the judgment).

Article 13(2)(f)

Article 13(2)(f) resolves an uncertainty that had arisen from the decision of the Court of Justice in Case 302/84 *Ten Holder*, [1986] E.C.R. 1821, in which had suggested that the legislation of the place where a person last worked was applicable to them forever thereafter until such time as the person undertook further employment or self-employment. The Court, however, mitigated its decision in two subsequent cases: Case C-140/88 *Noij*, [1991] E.C.R. I-387, and Case C-245/88 *Daalmeijer*, [1991] ECR I-555, ruling that a person who had ceased all work and moved country became subject to the legislation of the State of residence.

3.143

The application of the principle in Art.13(2)(f) appears to have become more sweeping than might first have been expected. One of the questions which arose in Case C-275/96 *Kuusijärvi*, [1998] E.C.R. I-3419, was whether the exception applied where a person had permanently ceased all occupational activity, or whether it also applied where a person had ceased occupational activity in circumstances where it might reasonable be expected that he or she would resume occupational activities at some time in the future. In its judgment the Court ruled that Art.13(2)(f) also applied in the latter situation. This would appear to permit Member States to draft their social security legislation in such a way that they can impose a residence requirement for continued entitlement to benefit acquired in that State.

See Art.89 and paras 18 to 20 of Annex VI for special provisions applicable in the United Kingdom on the application of the rule in Art.13(2)(f).

Students

3.144 Note that there are no rules in Title II relating to the applicable legislation for students (who do not fall within any of the other rules). This suggests that, for the purposes of the Regulation, they may be subject to the social security systems of two Member States, or fall outside the social security system of any Member State.

Article 14

Special rules applicable to persons, other than mariners, engaged in paid employment

3.145 Article 13(2)(a) shall apply subject to the following exceptions and circumstances:
1. (a) A person employed in the territory of a Member State by an undertaking to which he is normally attached who is posted by that undertaking to the territory of another Member State to perform work there for that undertaking shall continue to be subject to the legislation of the first Member State, provided that the anticipated duration of that work does not exceed 12 months and that he is not sent to replace another person who has completed his term of posting.
   (b) if the duration of the work to be done extends beyond the duration originally anticipated, owing to unforeseeable circumstances, and exceeds 12 months, the legislation of the first Member State shall continue to apply until the completion of such work, provided that the competent authority of the Member State in whose territory the person concerned is posted or the body designated by that authority gives its consent; such consent must be requested before the end of the initial 12 month period. Such consent cannot, however, be given for a period exceeding 12 months.
2. A person normally employed in the territory of two or more Member States shall be subject to the legislation determined as follows:
   (a) A person who is a member of the travelling or flying personnel of an undertaking which, for hire or reward or on its own account, operates international transport services for passengers or goods by rail, road, air or inland waterway and has its registered office or place of business in the territory of a Member State shall be subject to the legislation of the latter State, with the following restrictions:
      (i) where the said undertaking has a branch or permanent representation in the territory of a Member State other than that in

Article 14

which it has its registered office or place of business, a person employed by such branch or permanent representation shall be subject to the legislation of the Member State in whose territory such branch or permanent representation is situated;
  (ii) where a person is employed principally in the territory of the Member State in which he resides, he shall be subject to the legislation of that State, even if the undertaking which employs him has no registered office or place of business or branch or permanent representation in that territory.
(b) A person other than that referred to in (a) shall be subject:
  (i) to the legislation of the Member State in whose territory he resides, if he pursues his activity partly in that territory or if he is attached to several undertakings or several employers who have their registered offices or places of business in the territory of different Member States;
  (ii) to the legislation of the Member State in whose territory is situated the registered office or place of business of the undertaking or individual employing him, if he does not reside in the territory of any of the Member States where he is pursuing his activity.
3. A person who is employed in the territory of one Member State by an undertaking which has its registered office or place of business in the territory of another Member State and which straddles the common frontier of these States shall be subject to the legislation of the Member State in whose territory the undertaking has its registered office or place of business.

RELEVANT PROVISIONS OF THE IMPLEMENTING REGULATION

Arts 11 and 12a, Reg.574/72/EEC.

RELEVANT DECISIONS OF THE ADMINISTRATIVE COMMISSION

Decision No 126 of 17 October, 1985 concerning the application of Article 14(1)(a), 14a(1)(a), 14b(1) and (2) of Regulation (EEC) No 1408/71, [1986] OJ C141/3.

Decision No 148 of 25 June, 1992 concerning the use of the certificate concerning the applicable legislation (Form E101) where the period of posting does not exceed three months, [1993] OJ C22/124.

Decision No 181 of 13 December, 2000 concerning the interpretation of Articles 14(1), 14a(1) and 14b(1) and (2) of Council Regulation (EEC) No 1408/71 on the legislation applicable to posted workers and self-employed workers temporarily working outside the competent State, [2001] OJ L329/73.

GENERAL NOTE

Article 14 deals with two very different sets of circumstances. The first concerns the posting of workers by an enterprise in circumstances where the affiliation to the home social security system is maintained. Similar rules also apply to self employed persons temporarily working in a Member State other than that to which they are affiliated for social security purposes under Art.14a. The rules set out below are essentially applied by analogy to the situation of self employed persons. The second concerns the determination of the applicable legislation where a person has two or more employments in different Member States. There is also a third rule concerning enterprises which 'straddle' frontiers; this probably concerns only one or two agricultural enterprises on the borders of Member States.   **3.146**

The rules on posted workers
On the posting of workers, see also Decision No 181 of the Administrative Commission of December 13, 2000, [2000] OJ L329/73, and *Practical Guide for*   **3.147**

981

the Posting of Workers in the Member States of the European Union and the European Economic Area and in Switzerland, issued by the Administrative Commission: *http://europa.eu.int/comm/employment_social/social_security_schemes/docs/posting_en.pdf*

There are four conditions which must be satisfied for the posting rules to apply: (1) affected workers must be sent to work abroad by an undertaking to which they are normally attached; (2) the workers must be performing work abroad for the undertaking that sent them abroad; (3) the anticipated duration of the posting must not initially exceed 12 months, though in the circumstances set out in the article, this can be extended to 24 months; and (4) the posting must not be for the purpose of replacing another posted worker. It is important that there is, throughout the posting, a direct relationship between the undertaking and the posted worker.

Such a direct relationship will be present when the following features will be present: (a) a contractual relationship continues to exist between employer and employee; (b) the power to terminate that contract remains with the posting undertaking; (c) the nature of the work undertaken by the posted worker must be determinable by the posting undertaking; and (d) the obligation with regard to the remuneration of the worker rests with the undertaking which concluded the contract, irrespective of who actually makes the payment of that remuneration.

Some of the guidance flows from the decision of the Court of Justice in Case C-202/97 *Fitzwilliam Executive Search Ltd*, [2002] ECR I-883. This case concerned the activities of Fitzwilliam in placing workers both in Ireland in the Netherlands in the agricultural and horticultural sectors. The company recruited workers in order for them to be posted. Its turnover in the Netherlands came to exceed that in Ireland. The Dutch authorities took the view that workers engaged by Fitzwilliam in order to be posted to the Netherlands were subject to Dutch law and required to pay Dutch social security contributions. The question which arose in the reference made by the Dutch courts was whether workers recruited for the purpose posting to another Member State were within the posting rules in Article 14. The Court decided that, for Article 14 to apply, the undertaking in question must normally carry on its activities in the sending State, which meant that it habitually carries on significant activities in that State. Performance of management activities which are purely internal in that State cannot justify the use of the posting provisions. The following are considered in Decision No 181 and the Guide to be helpful indicators of the significance of the activities carried out in the sending State: (a) the place where the undertaking has its registered office and administration; (b) the number and nature of its staff there; (c) the place of recruitment of the posted worker; (d) the place where the majority of contracts are concluded; (e) the law applicable to the contracts signed by the undertaking with its clients and with its workers; and (f) turnover in the sending State and in the Member State(s) to which the workers are sent. The Guide indicates that habitual performance of the activities will be met if the activity has been carried out for four months or more; in the case of lesser periods a case-by-case consideration having regard to all the circumstances is required.

A person's status as a posted worker is attested by the issue in the sending State of Form E101 which certifies that the holder is subject to the legislation of the issuing State and so is exempt from the application of the legislation of the receiving State. Case C-178/97 *Barry Banks*, [2000] ECR I-2005 concerned a refusal by the Belgian authorities to accept the validity of a Form E101 issued by the United Kingdom authorities (for which provision is made in Arts 11 and 11a of Regulation 574/72). Banks was an opera singer who undertook short term contracts singing in Brussels. The Belgian authorities took the view that Banks and his colleagues were employed in Belgium, but they held Forms E101 certifying that they were self-employed persons in the United Kingdom. The Court of Justice ruled that, as long as it had not been withdrawn or declared invalid, the Form E101 certificate is binding on the competent institution of the place where the worker or self employed person goes. That institution may refer the matter back to the certifying institution for investigation if it suspects fraud, but otherwise must accept the exemption from its own legislation.

Article 14

These decisions have been affirmed in Case C-2/05 *Herbosch Kiere NV* [2006] ECR I-1079.

Note that longer periods of exemption may be secured by an agreement between two Member States under Art.17.

Article 14a

Special rules applicable to persons, other than mariners, who are self-employed

Article 13(2)(b) shall apply subject to the following exceptions and circumstances:

1. (a) A person normally self-employed in the territory of a Member State and who performs work in the territory of another Member State shall continue to be subject to the legislation of the first Member State, provided that the anticipated duration of the work does not exceed 12 months.

(b) If the duration of the work to be done extends beyond the duration originally anticipated, owing to unforeseeable circumstances, and exceeds 12 months, the legislation of the first Member State shall continue to apply until the completion of such work, provided that the competent authority of the Member State in whose territory the person concerned has entered to perform the work in question or the body appointed by that authority gives its consent; such consent must be requested before the end of the initial 12-month period, Such consent cannot, however, be given for a period exceeding 12 months.

2. A person normally self-employed in the territory of two or more Member States shall be subject to the legislation of the Member State in whose territory he resides if he pursues any part of his activity in the territory of that Member State. If he does not pursue any activity in the territory of the Member State in which he resides, he shall be subject to the legislation of the Member State in whose territory he pursue his main activity. The criteria used to determine the principal activity are laid down in the Regulation referred to in Article 98.

3. A person who is self-employed in an undertaking which has its registered office or place of business in the territory of one Member State and which straddles the common frontier of two Member States shall be subject to the legislation of the Member State in whose territory the undertaking has its registered office or place of business.

4. If the legislation to which a person should be subject in accordance with paragraph 2 or 3 does not enable that person, even on a voluntary basis, to join a pension scheme, the person concerned shall be subject to the legislation of the other Member State which would apply apart from these particular provisions, or should the legislations of two or more Member States apply in this way, he shall be subject to the legislation decided on by common agreement amongst the Member States concerned or their competent authorities.

Relevant Provisions of the Implementing Regulation

Arts 11a and 12a, Reg.574/72/EEC.

3.148

Council Regulation (EEC) No 1408/71

RELEVANT DECISIONS OF THE ADMINISTRATIVE COMMISSION

Decision No 126 of 17 October, 1985 concerning the application of Article 14(1)(a), 14a(1)(a), 14b(1) and (2) of Regulation (EEC) No 1408/71, [1986] OJ C141/3.

Decision No 181 of 13 December, 2000 concerning the interpretation of Articles 14(1), 14a(1) and 14b(1) and (2) of Council Regulation (EEC) No 1408/71 on the legislation applicable to posted workers and self-employed workers temporarily working outside the competent State, [2001] OJ L329/73.

GENERAL NOTE

3.149   See annotations to Art.14 for comment on the provisions concerning "posting" of self employed persons.

Article 14b

Special rules application to mariners

3.150   Article 13(2)(c) shall apply subject to the following exceptions and circumstances:

1. A person employed by an undertaking to which he is normally attached, either in the territory of a Member State or on board a vessel flying the flag of a Member State, who is posted by that undertaking on board a vessel flying the flag of another Member State to perform work there for that undertaking shall, subject to the conditions provided in Article 14(1), continue to be subject to the legislation of the first Member State.

2. A person normally self-employed, either in the territory of a Member State or on board a vessel flying the flag of a Member State and who performs work on his own account on board a vessel flying the flag of another Member State shall, subject to the conditions provided in Article 14a(1), continue to be subject to the legislation of the first Member State.

3. A person who, while not being normally employed at sea, performs work in the territorial waters or in a port of a Member State on a vessel flying the flag of another Member State within those territorial waters or in that port, but is not a member of the crew of the vessel, shall be subject to the legislation of the first Member State.

4. A person employed on board a vessel flying the flag of a Member State and remunerated for such employment by an undertaking or a person whose registered office or place of business is in the territory of another Member State shall be subject to the legislation of the latter State if he is resident in the territory of that State; the undertaking or person paying the remuneration shall be considered as the employer for the purpose of the said legislation.

RELEVANT PROVISIONS OF THE IMPLEMENTING REGULATION

Art.11a, Reg.574/72/EEC.

RELEVANT PROVISIONS OF THE ADMINISTRATIVE COMMISSION

Decision No 126 of 17 October, 1985 concerning the application of Article 14(1)(a), 14a(1)(a), 14b(1) and (2) of Regulation (EEC) No 1408/71, [1986] OJ C141/3.

Decision No 181 of 13 December, 2000 concerning the interpretation of Articles 14(1), 14a(1) and 14b(1) and (2) of Council Regulation (EEC) No 1408/71 on the legislation applicable to posted workers and self-employed workers temporarily working outside the competent State, [2001] OJ L329/73.

Article 14c

Article 14c

Special rules applicable to persons who are simultaneously employed in the territory of one Member State and self-employed in the territory of another Member State

A person who is simultaneously employed in the territory of one Member State and self-employed in the territory of another Member State shall be subject:
(a) save as otherwise provided in subparagraph (b) to the legislation of the Member State in the territory of which he is engaged in paid employment or, where he pursues such an activity in the territory of two or more Member States, to the legislation determined in accordance with Article 14(2) or (3);
(b) in the cases mentioned in Annex VII:
— to the legislation of the Member State in the territory of which he is engaged in paid employment, that legislation having been determined in accordance with the provisions of Article 14(2) or (3), where he pursues such an activity in the territory of two or more Member States,
and
— to the legislation of the Member State in the territory of which he is self-employed, that legislation having been determined in accordance with Article 14a(2), (3) or (4), where he pursues such an activity in the territory of two or more Member States.

RELEVANT PROVISIONS OF THE IMPLEMENTING REGULATION

Art.12a, Reg.574/72/EEC.

Article 14d

Miscellaneous provisions

[1 1. The person referred to in Article 14(2) and (3), Article 14a(2), (3) and (4), Article 14c(a) and Article 14e shall be treated, for the purposes of application of the legislation laid down in accordance with these provisions, as if he pursued all his professional activity or activities in the territory of the Member State concerned.]

2. The person referred to in Article 14c(b) shall be treated, for the purposes of determining the rates of contributions to be charged to self-employed workers under the legislation of the Member State in whose territory he is self-employed, as if he pursued his paid employment in the territory of the Member State concerned.

3. The provisions of the legislation of a Member State under which a pensioner who is pursuing a professional or trade activity is not subject to compulsory insurance in respect of such activity shall also apply to a pensioner whose pension was acquired under the legislation of another Member State, unless the person concerned expressly asks to be so subject by applying to the institution designated by the competent authority of the first Member State and named in Annex 10 to the Regulation referred to in Article 98.

[¹*Article 14e*]

Special rules applicable to persons insured in a special scheme for civil servants who are simultaneously employed and/or self-employed in the territory of one or more other Member States

3.153 A person who is simultaneously employed as a civil servant or a person treated as such and insured in a special scheme for civil servants in one Member State and who is employed and/or self-employed in the territory of one or more other Member States shall be subject to the legislation of the Member State in which he is insured in a special scheme for civil servants.]

AMENDMENT

1. Regulation 1606/98/EC, [1998] OJ L209/1 (October 25, 1998).

RELEVANT PROVISIONS OF THE IMPLEMENTING REGULATION

Art.12b, Reg.574/72/EEC.

[¹*Article 14f*]

Special rules applicable to civil servants simultaneously employed in more than one Member State and insured in one of these States in a special scheme

3.154 A person who is simultaneously employed in two or more Member States as a civil servant or person treated as such and insured in at least one of those Member States in a special scheme for civil servants shall be subject to the legislation of each of these Member States.]

AMENDMENT

1. Regulation 1606/98/EC, [1998] OJ L209/1 (October 25, 1998).

RELEVANT PROVISIONS OF THE IMPLEMENTING REGULATION

Art.12b, Reg.574/72/EEC.

Article 15

Rules concerning voluntary insurance or optional continued insurance

3.155 1. Articles 13 to 14d shall not apply to voluntary insurance or to optional continued insurance unless, in respect of one of the branches referred to in Article 4, there exists in any Member State only a voluntary scheme of insurance.

Article 15

2. Where application of the legislations of two or more Member States entails overlapping of insurance:
— under a compulsory insurance scheme and one or more voluntary or optional continued insurance schemes, the person concerned shall be subject exclusively to the compulsory insurance scheme;
— under two or more voluntary or optional continued insurance schemes, the person concerned may join only the voluntary or optional continued insurance scheme for which he has opted.

3. However, in respect of invalidity, old age and death (pensions), the person concerned may join the voluntary or optional continued insurance scheme of a Member State, even if he is compulsorily subject to the legislation of another Member State, to the extent that such overlapping is explicitly or implicitly admitted in the first Member State.

Article 16

Special rules regarding persons employed by diplomatic missions and consular posts, and auxiliary staff of the European Communities

1. The provisions of Article 13 (2) (a) shall apply to persons employed by diplomatic missions and consular posts and to the private domestic staff of agents of such missions or posts.

2. However, employed persons covered by paragraph 1 who are nationals of the Member State which is the accrediting or sending State may opt to be subject to the legislation of that State. Such right of option may be renewed at the end of each calendar year and shall not have retrospective effect.

3. Auxiliary staff of the European Communities may opt to be subject to the legislation of the Member State in whose territory they are employed, to the legislation of the Member State to which they were last subject or to the legislation of the Member State whose nationals they are, in respect of provisions other than those relating to family allowances, the granting of which is governed by the conditions of employment applicable to such staff. This right of option, which may be exercised once only, shall take effect from the date of entry into employment.

RELEVANT PROVISIONS OF THE IMPLEMENTING REGULATION

Arts 13 and 14, Reg.574/72/EEC.

RELEVANT DECISIONS OF THE ADMINISTRATIVE COMMISSION

Decision No 89 of 20 March, 1973 concerning the interpretation of Article 16(1) and (2) of Council Regulation (EEC) No 1408/71 relating to persons employed by diplomatic missions and consular posts, [1974] OJ C86/7.

Article 17

Exceptions to Articles 13 to 16

Two or more Member States, the competent authorities of these States or the bodies designated by these authorities may by common agreement

Council Regulation (EEC) No 1408/71

provide for exceptions to the provisions of Articles 13 to 16 in the interest of certain categories of persons or of certain persons.

RELEVANT PROVISIONS OF THE IMPLEMENTING REGULATION

Arts 11, 11a, Reg.574/72/EEC.

RELEVANT DECISIONS OF THE ADMINISTRATIVE COMMISSION

Recommendation No 16 of 12 December, 1984 concerning the conclusion of Agreement pursuant to Article 17 of Council Regulation (EEC) No 1408/71, [1985] OJ C273/3.

GENERAL NOTE

3.158   This provision was used in Case 101/83 *Brusse* [1984] E.C.R. 2223 to "rescue" a claimant from a long gap in his contribution record in the United Kingdom. The terms of the agreement covered a period before the UK was a Member State of the European Community but was expressly made under Art.17 in relation to the period from January 1, 1973 (when the UK acceded). The Court of Justice ruled that agreements under Art.17 could be retrospective; the test was whether the agreement was in the interests of the worker concerned. This approach was confirmed in Case C-454/93 *van Gestel* [1995] E.C.R. I-1707. The scope of agreements under Art.17 is accordingly very wide, provided that the parties are satisfied that the terms of the agreement are in the interests of certain persons or categories of persons.

Article 17a

Special rules concerning recipients of pensions due under the legislation of one or more Member State

3.159   The recipient of a pension due under the legislation of a Member State or of pensions due under the legislation of several Member States who resides in the territory of another Member State may at his request be exempted from the legislation of the latter State provided that he is not subject to that legislation because of the pursuit of an occupation.

GENERAL NOTE

3.160   This provision requires the pensioner to trigger the exemption by applying for it.

Article 18

Title III

Special Provisions Relating to the Various Categories of Benefits

Chapter 1

Sickness and Maternity

Section 1

Common Provisions

Article 18

Aggregation of periods of insurance, employment or residence

1. The competent institution of a Member State whose legislation makes the acquisition, retention or recovery of the right to benefits conditional upon the completion of periods of insurance, employment or residence shall, to the extent necessary, take account of periods of insurance, employment or residence completed under the legislation of any other Member State as if they were periods completed under the legislation which it administers.

2. The provisions of paragraph 1 shall apply to seasonal workers, even in respect of periods prior to any break in insurance exceeding the period allowed by the legislation of the competent State, provided, however, that the person concerned has not ceased to be insured for a period exceeding four months.

3.161

Relevant Provisions of the Implementing Regulation

Arts 15 and 16, Reg.574/72/EEC.

General Note

Where the person claiming a sickness benefit has been employed or self-employed and falls ill in a Member State while not working, then the competent State will be the Member State in which that person was last insured as an employed or self employed person.

3.162

The determination of the applicable legislation in relation to entitlement to sickness benefits was considered by the Court of Justice of the European Communities in Case 150/82 *Coppola v Insurance Officer*, [1983] E.C.R. 43. The Court ruled:

"11. By virtue of [Article 13(2)(a)], and in the absence of contrary provisions referring to the particular type of benefit in question, only the legislation of the State in whose territory the worker is employed is therefore applicable. Although that provision does not expressly mention the case of a worker who is not employed when he seeks sickness benefit, it is appropriate to interpret it as meaning that, where necessary, it refers to the legislation of the State in whose territory the worker was last employed.

12. It follows from the fact that, by virtue of Article 13(2)(a), the legislation of only one Member State is applicable, that the institution or institutions of a single Member State, namely the State in whose territory the worker is or was last employed, must be considered competent for the purpose of the application of Article 18(1). . . ."

Note that Article 89 and Annex VI contains special rules relating to the determination of the applicable law where there has been a change of the applicable law arising under Art.13(2)(f): see para.20 of Section Y of Annex VI reproduced below.

See *R(IB)1/02* for an example of the application of the aggregation principles. Periods of receipt of sickness benefit in another Member State assisted the claimant in qualifying for entitlement to long-term incapacity benefit.

SECTION 2

EMPLOYED OR SELF-EMPLOYED PERSONS AND MEMBERS OF THEIR FAMILIES

Article 19

Residence in a Member State other than the competent State—General rules

3.163   1. An employed or self-employed person residing in the territory of a Member State other than the competent State, who satisfies the conditions of the legislation of the competent State for entitlement to benefits, taking account where appropriate of the provisions of Article 18, shall receive in the State in which he is resident:
  (a) benefits in kind provided on behalf of the competent institution by the institution of the place of residence in accordance with the provisions of the legislation administered by that institution as though he were insured with it;
  (b) cash benefits provided by the competent institution in accordance with the legislation which it administers. However, by agreement between the competent institution and the institution of the place of residence, such benefits may be provided by the latter institution on behalf of the former, in accordance with the legislation of the competent State.

2. The provisions of paragraph 1 shall apply by analogy to members of the family who reside in the territory of a Member State other than the competent State in so far as they are not entitled to such benefits under the legislation of the State in whose territory they reside.

Where the members of the family reside in the territory of a Member State under whose legislation the right to receive benefits in kind is not subject to condition of insurance or employment, benefits in kind which they receive shall be considered as being on behalf of the institution with which the employed or self-employed person is insured, unless the spouse or the person looking after the children pursues a professional or trade activity in the territory of the said Member State.

Article 19

RELEVANT PROVISIONS OF THE IMPLEMENTING REGULATION

Arts 17 and 18, Reg.574/72/EEC.

GENERAL NOTE

Chapter 1 of Title III applies both to benefits in kind (medical treatment, provision of medication and the such like) as well as to benefits in cash (sums to offset the loss of income which usually accompanies sickness). Benefits in kind are the responsibility of the Department of Health and are outside the scope of this work, though there is an exceptionally lively and topical case law on these matters. Much of the case law relating to sickness benefits relates to benefits in kind.

3.164

The provisions of Chapter 1 need to be read carefully to ensure that the correct rules are applied where benefits in cash are in issue.

Case C-215/90 *Chief Adjudication Officer* v *Twomey* [1992] E.C.R. I-1823, reported as *R(S) 3/92*, determined that Art.19 applies to nationals of a Member State who, after being in paid employment in one Member State, go to live in another Member State where they fall ill, even though they have not worked there before falling ill.

Article 20

Frontier workers and members of their families—Special rules

A frontier worker may also obtain benefits in the territory of the competent State. Such benefits shall be provided by the competent institution in accordance with the provisions of the legislation of that State, as though the person concerned where resident in that State. Members of his family may receive benefits under the same conditions; however, receipt of such benefits shall, except in urgent cases, be conditional upon an agreement between the States concerned or between the competent authorities of those States or, in its absence, on prior authorization by the competent institution.

3.165

RELEVANT PROVISIONS OF THE IMPLEMENTING REGULATION

Art.19, Reg.574/72/EEC.

RELEVANT DECISIONS OF THE ADMINISTRATIVE COMMISSION

Decision No 116 of 15 December, 1982 concerning the granting of benefits in kind provided for in Article 17(7) and Article 60(6) of Regulation (EEC) No 574/72 and the concepts of urgency within the meaning of Article 20 of Regulation (EEC) No 1408/71 and of extreme urgency within the meaning of Articles 17(7) and 60(6) of regulation (EEC) No 574/72, [1983] OJ C193/8. Decision No 135 of 1 July, 1987 concerning the granting of benefits in kind provided for in Article 17(7) and Article 60(6) of Regulation (EEC) No 574/72 and the concepts of urgency within the meaning of Article 20 of Regulation (EEC) No 1408/71 and of extreme urgency within the meaning of Articles 17(7) and 60(6) of Regulation (EEC) No 574.72, [1988] OJ C64/5.

Article 21

Stay in or transfer of residence to the competent State

1. The employed or self-employed person referred to in Article 19 (1) who is staying in the territory of the competent State shall receive benefits in accordance with the provisions of the legislation of that State as though he were resident there, even if he has already received benefits for the same case of sickness or maternity before his stay.

2. Paragraph 1 shall apply by analogy to the members of the family referred to in Article 19 (2).

However, where the latter reside in the territory of a Member State other than the one in whose territory the employed or self-employed person resides, benefits in kind shall be provided by the institution of the place of stay on behalf of the institution of the place of residence of the persons concerned.

3. Paragraphs 1 and 2 shall not apply to frontier workers and the members of their families.

4. An employed or self-employed person and members of his family referred to in Article 19 who transfer their residence to the territory of the competent State shall receive benefits in accordance with the provisions of the legislation of that State even if they have already received benefits for the same case of sickness or maternity before transferring their residence.

RELEVANT PROVISIONS OF THE IMPLEMENTING REGULATION

Art.19a, Reg.574/72/EEC.

Article 22

Stay outside the competent State—Return to or transfer of residence to another Member State during sickness or maternity—Need to go to another Member State in order to receive appropriate treatment

1. An employed or self-employed person who satisfies the conditions of the legislation of the competent State for entitlement to benefits, taking account where appropriate of the provisions of Article 18, and:

[¹ (a) whose condition requires benefits in kind which become necessary on medical grounds during a stay in the territory of another Member State, taking into account the nature of the benefits and the expected length of the stay;]

or

(b) who, having become entitled to benefits chargeable to the competent institution, is authorized by that institution to return to the territory of the Member State where he resides, or to transfer his residence to the territory of another Member State;

or

(c) who is authorized by the competent institution to go to the territory of another Member State to receive there the treatment appropriate to his condition,

Article 22

shall be entitled:
(i) to benefits in kind provided on behalf of the competent institution by the institution of the place of stay or residence in accordance with the provisions of the legislation which it administers, as though he were insured with it; the length of the period during which benefits are provided shall be governed, however, by the legislation of the competent State;
(ii) to cash benefits provided by the competent institution in accordance with the provisions of the legislation which it administers. However, by agreement between the competent institution and the institution of the place of stay or residence, such benefits may be provided by the latter institution on behalf of the former, in accordance with the provisions of the legislation of the competent State.

[¹ **1a.** The Administrative Commission shall establish a list of benefits in kind which, in order to be provided during a stay in another Member State, require, for practical reasons, a prior agreement between the person concerned and the institution providing the care;]

2. The authorization required under paragraph 1 (b) may be refused only if it is established that movement of the person concerned would be prejudicial to his state of health or the receipt of medical treatment.

The authorization required under paragraph 1 (c) may not be refused where the treatment in question is among the benefits provided for by the legislation of the Member State on whose territory the person concerned resided and where he cannot be given such treatment within the time normally necessary for obtaining the treatment in question in the Member State of residence taking account of his current state of health and the probable course of the disease.

[¹ **3.** Paragraphs 1, 1a and 2 shall apply by analogy to members of the family of an employed or self-employed person.]

However, for the purpose of applying paragraph 1 (a) and (c) (i) to the members of the family referred to in Article 19 (2) who reside in the territory of a Member State other than the one in whose territory the employed or self-employed person resides:
(a) benefits in kind shall be provided on behalf of the institution of the Member State in whose territory the members of the family are residing by the institution of the place of stay in accordance with the provisions of the legislation which it administers as if the employed or self-employed person were insured there. The period during which benefits are provided shall, however, be that laid down under the legislation of the Member State in whose territory the members of the family are residing;
(b) the authorization required under paragraph 1 (c) shall be issued by the institution of the Member State in whose territory the members of the family are residing.

4. The fact that the provisions of paragraph 1 apply to an employed or self-employed person shall not affect the right to benefit of members of his family.

AMENDMENT

1. Regulation 631/2004/EC, [2004] OJ L100/1 (June 1, 2004).

Council Regulation (EEC) No 1408/71

RELEVANT PROVISIONS OF THE IMPLEMENTING REGULATION

Arts 21–24, Reg.574/72/EEC.

RELEVANT DECISIONS OF THE ADMINISTRATIVE COMMISSION

Decision No 74 of 22 February, 1973 concerning the provision of medical care in cases of temporary stay under Article 22(1)(a)(i) of Regulation (EEC) No 1408/71 and Article 21 of Regulation (EEC) No 574/72, [1973] OJ C75/4.

Decision No 138 of 17 February, 1989 concerning the interpretation of Article 22(1)(c)(i) of Regulation (EEC) No 1408/71 in the case of organ transplants or other forms of surgery requiring tests on biological samples while the person concerned is not present in the Member State where the tests are carried out, [1989] OJ C287/3.

Decision No 175 of 23 June, 1999 on interpretation of the concept of "benefits in kind" in the event of sickness or maternity pursuant to Article 19(1) and (2), Article 22, Article 22a, Article 22b, Article 25(1), (3) and (4), Article 26, Article 28(1), Article 28a, Article 29, Article 31, Article 34a and Article 34b of Council Regulation (EEC) No 1408/71 and on calculation of the amounts to be refunded under Articles 93, 94 and 95 of Regulation (EEC) No 574/72 as well as the advances to be paid pursuant to Article 102(4) of the same Regulation, [2000] OJ L47/32.

Decision No 194 of 17 December, 2003 conerning the uniform application of Article 22(1)(a)(i) of Council Regulation (EEC) No 1408/71 in the Member State of stay, [2004] OJ L104/127.

Decision No 195 of 23 March, 2004 on the uniform application of Article 22(1)(a)(i) of Regulation (EEC) No 1408/71 as regards health care in conjunction with pregnancy and childbirth, [2004] OJ L160/134.

Decision No 196 of 23 March, 2004 pursuant top Article 22(1a), [2004] OJ L160/136.

GENERAL NOTE

3.168 Where cash benefits are in issue, they are to be awarded by the competent institution in the competent State in accordance with its own legislation, subject to any agreement for them to be paid in the State of stay or residence on behalf of the institution of the competent State.

R(S) 2/94 concerned an earlier form of wording in this Article, but the proposition for which it stands remains pertinent. Although a person is entitled to cash benefits for the period during which that person's condition necessitates benefits in kind, that period is to be interpreted as meaning the period of medical treatment at hospital and not the subsequent period during which the person is not at hospital but is taking prescribed medication. Since the claimant was only at the hospital for one day, that day fell within the first three days of an interruption of employment and so sickness benefit was not payable for that day.

Article 22a

Special rules for certain categories of persons

3.169 Notwithstanding Article 2 of the Regulation, Article 22(1)(a) and (c) shall also apply to persons who are nationals of a Member State and are insured under the legislation of a Member State and to the members of their families residing with them.

RELEVANT DECISIONS OF THE ADMINISTRATIVE COMMISSION

Decision No 174 of 20 April, 1999 concerning the interpretation of Article 22a of Regulation (EEC) No 1408/71, [2000] OJ L47/30.

Article 22a

Decision No 175 of 23 June, 1999 on interpretation of the concept of "benefits in kind" in the event of sickness or maternity pursuant to Article 19(1) and (2), Article 22, Article 22a, Article 22b, Article 25(1), (3) and (4), Article 26, Article 28(1), Article 28a, Article 29, Article 31, Article 34a and Article 34b of Council Regulation (EEC) No 1408/71 and on calculation of the amounts to be refunded under Articles 93, 94 and 95 of Regulation (EEC) No 574/72 as well as the advances to be paid pursuant to Article 102(4) of the same Regulation, [2000] OJ L47/32.

Article 22b

Employment in a Member State other than the competent State—Stay in the State of employment

[^{1} . . .] 3.170

AMENDMENT

1. Regulation 631/2004/EC, [2004] OJ L100/1 (June 1, 2004).

Article 22c

Studies in a Member State other than the competent State—stay in the State where the studies are pursued

[^{1} . . .] 3.171

AMENDMENT

1. Regulation 307/99/EC, [1999] OJ L38/1 (May 1, 1999).

Article 23

Calculation of cash benefits

1. The competent institution of a Member State whose legislation provides that the calculation of cash benefits shall be based on average earnings or on average contributions, shall determine such average earnings or contributions exclusively by reference to earnings or contributions completed under the said legislation. 3.172

2. The competent institution of a Member State whose legislation provides that the calculation of cash benefits shall be based on standard earnings, shall take account exclusively of the standard earnings or, where appropriate, of the average of standard earnings for the periods completed under the said legislation.

[^{1} **2a.** The provisions of paragraphs 1 and 2 shall also apply where the legislation applied by the competent institution provides for a specific reference period and this period coincides, where appropriate, with the whole or part of the periods completed by the person concerned under the legislation of one or more other Member States.]

3. The competent institution of a Member State under whose legislation the amount of cash benefits varies with the number of members of the family, shall also take into account the members of the family of the person concerned who are resident in the territory of another Member State as if they were resident in the territory of the competent State.

AMENDMENT

1. Regulation 647/2005/EC, [2005] OJ L117/1 (May 5, 2005).

RELEVANT PROVISIONS OF THE IMPLEMENTING REGULATION

Art.25, Reg.574/72/EEC.

Article 24

Substantial benefits in kind

3.173   **1.** Where the right of an employed or self-employed person or a member of his family to a prosthesis, a major appliance or other substantial benefits in kind has been recognized by the institution of a Member State before he becomes insured with the institution of another Member State, the said employed of self-employed person shall receive such benefits at the expense of the first institution, even if they are granted after he becomes insured with the second institution.

2. The Administrative Commission shall draw up the list of benefits to which the provisions of paragraph 1 apply.

RELEVANT DECISIONS OF THE ADMINISTRATIVE COMMISSION

Decision No 115 of 15 December, 1982 concerning the granting of prostheses, major appliances and other substantial benefits in kind provided for in Article 24(2) of regulation (EEC) No 1408/71 of the Council, [1983] OJ C193/7.

SECTION 3

UNEMPLOYED PERSONS AND MEMBERS OF THEIR FAMILIES

Article 25

3.174   [¹ **1.** An unemployed person who was formerly employed or self-employed and to whom the provisions of Article 69(1) of Article 71(1)(b)(ii), second sentence apply and who satisfies the conditions laid down in the legislation of the competent State for entitlement to benefits in kind and cash benefits, taking account where necessary of the provisions of Article 18, shall receive for the period of time referred to in Article 69(1)(c):
   (a) benefits in kind which become necessary on medical grounds for this person during his stay in the territory of the Member State where he is seeking employment, taking account of the nature of the benefits and the expected length of the stay. These benefits in kind shall be provided on behalf of the competent institution by the institution of the Member State in which the person is seeking employment, in

Article 25

accordance with the provisions of the legislation which the latter institution administers, as if he were insured with it;
(b) cash benefits provided by the competent institution in accordance with the provisions of the legislation which it administers. However, by agreement between the competent institution and the institution of the Member State in which the unemployed person seeks employment, benefits may be provided by the latter institution on behalf of the former institution in accordance with the provisions of the legislation of the competent State. Unemployment benefits under Article 69(1) shall not be granted for the period during which cash benefits are received.

1a. Article 22(1a) shall apply by analogy.]

2. A totally unemployed person who was formerly employed and to whom the provisions of Article 71(1)(a)(ii) or the first sentence of Article 71(1)(b)(ii) apply, shall receive benefits in kind and in cash in accordance with the provisions of the legislation of the Member State in whose territory he resides, as though he had been subject to that legislation during his last employment, taking account where appropriate of the provisions of Article 18; the cost of such benefits shall be met by the institution of the country of residence.

3. Where an unemployed person satisfies the conditions of the legislation of the Member State which is responsible for the cost of unemployment benefits for entitlement to sickness and maternity benefits, taking account where appropriate of the provisions of Article 18, the members of his family shall receive these benefits, irrespective of the Member State in whose territory they reside or are staying. Such benefits shall be provided:
  (a) with regard to the benefits in kind, by the institution of the place of residence or stay in accordance with the provisions of the legislation which it administers, on behalf of the competent institution of the Member State which is responsible for the cost of unemployment benefits;
  (b) with regard to cash benefits, by the competent institution of the Member State which is responsible for the cost of unemployment benefits, in accordance with the legislation which it administers.

4. Without prejudice to any provisions of the legislation of a Member State which permit an extension of the period during which sickness benefits may be granted, the period provided for in paragraph 1 may, in cases of force majeure, be extended by the competent institution within the limit fixed by the legislation administered by that institution.

AMENDMENT

1. Regulation 631/2004/EC, [2004] OJ 100/1 (June 1, 2004).

RELEVANT PROVISIONS OF THE IMPLEMENTING REGULATION

Arts 26 and 27, Reg.574/72/EEC.

RELEVANT DECISIONS OF THE ADMINISTRATIVE COMMISSION

Decision No 175 of 23 June, 1999 on interpretation of the concept of "benefits in kind" in the event of sickness or maternity pursuant to Article 19(1) and (2), Article 22, Article 22a, Article 22b, Article 25(1), (3) and (4), Article 26, Article 28(1), Article 28a, Article 29, Article 31, Article 34a and Article 34b of Council Regulation (EEC) No 1408/71 and on calculation of the amounts to be refunded under Articles 93, 94 and 95 of Regulation (EEC) No 574/72 as well as the advances to be paid pursuant to Article 102(4) of the same Regulation, [2000] OJ L47/32.

Article 25a

Contributions payable by wholly unemployed persons

3.175   The institution which is responsible for granting benefits in kind and cash benefits to the unemployed persons referred to in Article 25(2) and which belongs to a Member State whose legislation provides for deduction of contributions payable by unemployed persons to cover sickness and maternity benefits shall be authorized to make such deductions in accordance with the provisions of its legislation.

SECTION 4

PENSION CLAIMANTS AND MEMBERS OF THEIR FAMILIES

Article 26

Right to benefits in kind in cases of cessation of the right to benefits from the institution which was last competent

3.176   1. An employed or self-employed person, members of his family or his survivors who, during the investigation of a claim for pension, cease to be entitled to benefits in kind under the legislation of the Member State last competent, shall nevertheless receive such benefits under the following conditions: benefits in kind shall be provided in accordance with the provisions of the legislation of the Member State in whose territory the person or persons concerned reside, provided that they are entitled to such benefits under that legislation or would be entitled to them under the legislation of another Member State if they were residing in the territory of that State, taking account where appropriate of the provisions of Article 18.

2. A pension claimant who is entitled to benefits in kind under the legislation of a Member State which obliges the person concerned to pay sickness insurance contributions himself during the investigation of his pension claim shall cease to be entitled to benefits in kind at the end of the second month for which he has not paid the contributions due.

3. Benefits in kind provided in accordance with the provisions of paragraph 1 shall be chargeable to the institution which has collected contributions in accordance with the provisions of paragraph 2; where no contributions are payable under the provisions of paragraph 2, the institution responsible for the cost of the benefits in kind after awarding the pension in accordance with the provisions of Article 28 shall refund the amount of the benefits provided to the institution of the place of residence.

RELEVANT PROVISIONS OF THE IMPLEMENTING REGULATION
Art.28, Reg.574/72/EEC.

Article 26

Relevant Decisions of the Administrative Commission

Decision No 175 of 23 June, 1999 on interpretation of the concept of "benefits in kind" in the event of sickness or maternity pursuant to Article 19(1) and (2), Article 22, Article 22a, Article 22b, Article 25(1), (3) and (4), Article 26, Article 28(1), Article 28a, Article 29, Article 31, Article 34a and Article 34b of Council Regulation (EEC) No 1408/71 and on calculation of the amounts to be refunded under Articles 93, 94 and 95 of Regulation (EEC) No 574/72 as well as the advances to be paid pursuant to Article 102(4) of the same Regulation, [2000] OJ L47/32.

Section 5

Pensioners and Members of their Families

Article 27

Pensions payable under the legislation of several State where there is a right to benefits in the country of residence

A pensioner who is entitled to draw pensions under the legislation of two or more Member States, of which one is that of the Member State in whose territory he resides, and who is entitled to benefits under the legislation of the latter Member State, taking account where appropriate of the provisions of Article 18 and Annex VI, shall, with the members of his family, receive such benefits from the institution of the place of residence and at the expense of that institution as though the person concerned were a pensioner whose pension was payable solely under the legislation of the latter Member State.

3.177

Article 28

Pensions payable under the legislation of one or more States, in cases where there is no right to benefits in the country of residence

1. A pensioner who is entitled to a pension under the legislation of one Member State or to pensions under the legislation of two or more Member States and who is not entitled to benefits under the legislation of the Member State in whose territory he resides shall nevertheless receive such benefits for himself and for members of his family, in so far as he would, taking account where appropriate of the provisions of Article 18 and Annex VI, be entitled thereto under the legislation of the Member State or of at least one of the Member States competent in respect of pensions if he were resident in the territory of such State. The benefits shall be provided under the following conditions:
   (a) benefits in kind shall be provided on behalf of the institution referred to in paragraph 2 by the institution of the place of residence as though the person concerned were a pensioner under the legislation of the State in whose territory he resides and were entitled to such benefits;

3.178

(b) cash benefits shall, where appropriate, be provided by the competent institution as determined by the rules of paragraph 2, in accordance with the legislation which it administers. However, upon agreement between the competent institution and the institution of the place of residence, such benefits may be provided by the latter institution on behalf of the former, in accordance with the legislation of the competent State.

2. In the cases covered by paragraph 1, the cost of benefits in kind shall be borne by the institution as determined according to the following rules:

(a) where the pensioner is entitled to the said benefits under the legislation of a single Member State, the cost shall be borne by the competent institution of that State;

(b) where the pensioner is entitled to the said benefits under the legislation of two or more Member States, the cost thereof shall be borne by the competent institution of the Member State to whose legislation the pensioner has been subject for the longest period of time; should the application of this rule result in several institutions being responsible for the cost of benefits the cost shall be borne by the institution administering the legislation to which the pensioner was last subject.

RELEVANT PROVISIONS OF THE IMPLEMENTING REGULATION

Art.29, Reg.574/72/EEC.

RELEVANT DECISIONS OF THE ADMINISTRATIVE COMMISSION

Decision No 175 of 23 June, 1999 on interpretation of the concept of "benefits in kind" in the event of sickness or maternity pursuant to Article 19(1) and (2), Article 22, Article 22a, Article 22b, Article 25(1), (3) and (4), Article 26, Article 28(1), Article 28a, Article 29, Article 31, Article 34a and Article 34b of Council Regulation (EEC) No 1408/71 and on calculation of the amounts to be refunded under Articles 93, 94 and 95 of Regulation (EEC) No 574/72 as well as the advances to be paid pursuant to Article 102(4) of the same Regulation, [2000] OJ L47/32.

Article 28a

Pensions payable under the legislation of one or more of the Member States other than the country of residence where there is a right to benefits in the latter country

3.179 Where the pensioner entitled to a pension under the legislation of one Member State, or to pensions under the legislations of two or more Member States, resides in the territory of a Member State under whose legislation the right to receive benefits in kind is not subject to conditions of insurance or employment, nor is any pension payable, the cost of benefits in kind provided to him and to members of his family shall be borne by the institution of one of the Member States competent in respect of pensions, determined according to the rules laid down in Article 28(2), to the extent that the pensioner and members of his family would have been entitled to such benefits under the legislation administered by the said institution if they resided in the territory of the Member State where that institution is situated.

Article 28a

RELEVANT PROVISIONS OF THE IMPLEMENTING REGULATION

Art.29, Reg.574/72/EEC.

RELEVANT DECISIONS OF THE ADMINISTRATIVE COMMISSION

Decision No 175 of 23 June, 1999 on interpretation of the concept of "benefits in kind" in the event of sickness or maternity pursuant to Article 19(1) and (2), Article 22, Article 22a, Article 22b, Article 25(1), (3) and (4), Article 26, Article 28(1), Article 28a, Article 29, Article 31, Article 34a and Article 34b of Council Regulation (EEC) No 1408/71 and on calculation of the amounts to be refunded under Articles 93, 94 and 95 of Regulation (EEC) No 574/72 as well as the advances to be paid pursuant to Article 102(4) of the same Regulation, [2000] OJ L47/32.

Article 29

Residence of members of the family in a State other than the one in which the pensioner resides—Transfer of residence to the State where the pensioner resides

1. Members of the family of a pensioner entitled to a pension under the legislation of one Member State or to pensions under the legislation of two or more Member States who reside in the territory of a Member State other than the one in which the pensioner resides shall, where he is entitled to benefits under the legislation of one Member State, receive benefits as though the pensioner were resident in the same territory as themselves. Benefit shall be provided under the following conditions:

[¹ (a) benefits in kind shall be provided by the institution of the place of residence of the members of the family in accordance with the provisions of the legislation which that institution administers, the cost being borne by the institution determined in accordance with the provisions of Article 27 or Article 28(2); if the place of residence is situated in the competent Member State, benefits in kind shall be provided, and the cost borne, by the competent institution;]

(b) cash benefits shall, where appropriate, be provided by the competent institution as determined by the provisions of Article 27 or 28(2), in accordance with the provisions of the legislation which it administers. However, upon agreement between the competent institution and the institution of the place of residence of the members of the family, such benefits may be provided by the latter institution on behalf of the former, in accordance with the provisions of the legislation of the competent State.

2. Members of the family referred to in paragraph 1 who transfer their residence to the territory of the Member State where the pensioner resides, shall receive:

(a) benefits in kind under the provisions of the legislation of that State, even if they have already received benefits for the same case of sickness or maternity before transferring their residence;

(b) cash benefits provided where appropriate by the competent institution determined by the provisions of Article 27 or 28(2), in accordance with the legislation which it administers. However, upon agreement between the competent institution and the institution of the place of residence of the pensioner, such benefits may be provided

3.180

by the latter institution on behalf of the former, in accordance with the provisions of the legislation of the competent State.

AMENDMENT

1. Regulation 1223/98/EC, [1998] OJ L168/1 (January 1, 1998, but in relation to France January 1, 2002).

RELEVANT PROVISIONS OF THE IMPLEMENTING REGULATION

Art.30, Reg.574/72/EEC.

RELEVANT DECISIONS OF THE ADMINISTRATIVE COMMISSION

Decision No 175 of 23 June, 1999 on interpretation of the concept of "benefits in kind" in the event of sickness or maternity pursuant to Article 19(1) and (2), Article 22, Article 22a, Article 22b, Article 25(1), (3) and (4), Article 26, Article 28(1), Article 28a, Article 29, Article 31, Article 34a and Article 34b of Council Regulation (EEC) No 1408/71 and on calculation of the amounts to be refunded under Articles 93, 94 and 95 of Regulation (EEC) No 574/72 as well as the advances to be paid pursuant to Article 102(4) of the same Regulation, [2000] OJ L47/32.

Article 30

Substantial benefits in kind

3.181   The provisions of Article 24 shall apply by analogy to pensioners.

[¹ *Article 31*

Stay of the pensioner and/or members of his family in a State other than the State in which they reside

3.182   1. A pensioner entitled to a pension or pensions under the legislation of one Member State or to pensions under the legislation of to or more Member States who is entitled to benefits under the legislation of one of those States shall, with members of his family who are staying in the territory of a Member State other than the State in which they reside, receive:
  (a) benefits in kind which become necessary on medical grounds during a stay in the territory of the Member State other than the State of residence, taking into account the nature of the benefits and the expected length of the stay. These benefits in kind shall be provided by the institution of the place of stay, in accordance with the provisions of the legislation which it administers, on behalf of the institution of the place of residence of the pensions or of the members of his family;
  (b) cash benefits provided, where appropriate, by the competent institution as determined by Article 27 or 28(2), in accordance with the provisions of the legislation which it administers. However, upon agreement between the competent institution and the institution of the place of stay, these benefits may be provided by the latter institution on behalf of the former, in accordance with the provisions of the legislation of the competent State.

Article 31

2. Article 22(1a) shall apply by analogy.]

AMENDMENT

1. Regulation 631/2004/EC, [2004] OJ L100/1 (June 1, 2004).

RELEVANT PROVISIONS OF THE IMPLEMENTING REGULATION

Art.31, Reg.574/72/EEC.

RELEVANT PROVISIONS OF THE ADMINISTRATIVE COMMISSION

Decision No 175 of 23 June, 1999 on interpretation of the concept of "benefits in kind" in the event of sickness or maternity pursuant to Article 19(1) and (2), Article 22, Article 22a, Article 22b, Article 25(1), (3) and (4), Article 26, Article 28(1), Article 28a, Article 29, Article 31, Article 34a and Article 34b of Council Regulation (EEC) No 1408/71 and on calculation of the amounts to be refunded under Articles 93, 94 and 95 of Regulation (EEC) No 574/72 as well as the advances to be paid pursuant to Article 102(4) of the same Regulation, [2000] OJ L47/32.

Article 32

[. . .] 3.183

Article 33

Contributions payable by pensioners

1. The institution of a Member State which is responsible for payment of a pension and which administers legislation providing for deductions from pensions in respect of contributions for sickness and maternity shall be authorized to make such deductions, calculated in accordance with the legislation concerned, from the pension payable by such institution, to the extent that the cost of the benefits under Article 27, 28, 28a, 29, 31 and 32 is to be borne by an institution of the said Member State.

2. Where, in the cases referred to in Article 28a, the acquisition of benefits in respect of sickness and maternity is subject to the payment of contributions or similar payments under the legislation of a Member State in whose territory the pensioner in question resides, by virtue of such residence, these contributions shall not be payable.

3.184

GENERAL NOTE

In Case C-50/05 *Nikula* [2006] ECR I-7029, the Court of Justice ruled that Art.33(1) does not preclude the inclusion, in the basis of calculation in determining sickness insurance contributions in the Member State of residence, of pensions paid by the institutions of another Member State, provided that the sickness insurance contributions do not exceed the amount of pension paid in then Member State of residence. But Art. 39 EC does preclude the amount of pensions received from institutions of another Member State being taken into account if contributions have already been paid in the other State out of the income from work received in that State. It is for the person concerned to prove that the earlier contributions were in fact paid.

3.184.1

Council Regulation (EEC) No 1408/71

Article 34

General provisions

3.185
1. For the purposes of Articles 28, 28a, 29 and 31, a pensioner who is in receipt of two or more pensions due under the legislation of a single Member State shall be regarded as a pensioner entitled to draw a pension under the legislation of one Member State, within the meaning of these provisions.

2. Articles 27 to 33 shall not apply to a pensioner or to members of his family who are entitled to benefits under the legislation of a Member State as a result of pursuing a professional or trade activity. In such a case, the person concerned shall, for the purposes of the implementation of this chapter, be considered as an employed or self-employed person or as a member of an employed or self-employed person's family.

[1 SECTION 5A

PERSONS WHO STUDY OR RECEIVE VOCATIONAL TRAINING AND MEMBERS OF THEIR FAMILIES

Article 34a

Special provisions for students and members of their families

3.186
[2 Articles 18, 19, 22(1)(a) and (c) and (1a), 22(2), second subparagraph, 22(3), 23, and 24 and Sections 6 and 7 shall apply by analogy to students and to members of their families, as required.]

AMENDMENTS

1. Regulation 307/99/EC, [1999] OJ L38/1 (May 1, 1999).
2. Regulation 631/2004/EC, [2004] OJ L100/1.

RELEVANT DECISIONS OF THE ADMINISTRATIVE COMMISSION

Decision No 175 of 23 June 1999 on interpretation of the concept of "benefits in kind" in the event of sickness or maternity pursuant to Article 19(1) and (2), Article 22, Article 22a, Article 22b, Article 25(1), (3) and (4), Article 26, Article 28(1), Article 28a, Article 29, Article 31, Article 34a and Article 34b of Council Regulation (EEC) No 1408/71 and on calculation of the amounts to be refunded under Articles 93, 94 and 95 of Regulation (EEC) No 574/72 as well as the advances to be paid pursuant to Article 102(4) of the same Regulation, [2000] OJ L47/32.

Article 34b

Common provisions

3.187
[1 . . .]

AMENDMENT

1. Regulation 631/2004/EC, [2004] OJ L100/1.

Article 35

Section 6

Miscellaneous Provisions

Article 35

Scheme applicable where there are a number of schemes in the country of residence or stay—Previous illness—Maximum period during which benefits are granted

1. Subject to paragraph 2, where the legislation of the country of stay or residence contains several sickness or maternity insurance schemes, the provisions applicable under Article 19, 21(1), 22, 25, 26, 28(1), 29(1) or 31 shall be those of the scheme covering manual workers in the steel industry. Where, however, the said legislation includes a special scheme for workers in mines and similar undertakings, the provisions of such scheme shall apply to that category of workers and members of their families provided the institution of the place of stay or residence to which application is made is competent to administer such scheme.

2. [² . . .].

3. Where, under the legislation of a Member State, the granting of benefits is conditional upon the origin of the illness, that conditions [¹ shall not apply to persons] to whom this Regulation applies, regardless of the Member State in whose territory they reside.

4. Where the legislation of a Member State fixes a maximum period for the granting of benefits, the institution which administers that legislation may, where appropriate, take account of the period during which the benefits have already been provided by the institution of another Member State for the same case of sickness or maternity.

3.188

Amendments

1. Regulation 307/99/EC, [1999] OJ L38/1 (May 1, 1999).
2. Regulation 647/2005/EC, [2005] OJ L117/1 (May 5, 2005).

Relevant Provisions of the Implementing Regulation

Arts 32–24, Reg.574/72/EEC.

Section 7

Reimbursement Between Institutions

Article 36

1. Benefits in kind provided in accordance with the provisions of this chapter by the institution of one Member State on behalf of the institution of another Member State shall be fully refunded.

3.189

2. The refunds referred to in paragraph 1 shall be determined and made in accordance with the procedure provided for by the implementing Regulation referred to in Article 98, either on production of proof of actual expenditure or on the basis of lump-sum payments.

In the latter case, the lump-sum payments shall be such as to ensure that the refund is as close as possible to actual expenditure.

3. Two or more Member States, or the competent authorities of those States, may provide for other methods of reimbursement or may waive all reimbursement between institutions under their jurisdiction.

Chapter 2

Invalidity

Relevant Provisions of the Implementing Regulation

Provisions relating to administrative checks and medical examinations can be found in Arts 51–2, and on payment of benefits in Arts 53–59, Reg.574/72/EEC.

General Note

3.190 Whereas the Regulation adopts an approach to short-term benefits which results generally in one Member State being responsible for the payment of such benefits, such an approach is applied less easily to long-term benefits, since, under such a system, a Member State may become liable to pay a long-term benefit for a substantial period without having received contributions to support that benefit. The general approach to long-term benefits is that each Member State pays its proportionate share of the pension. The position becomes more complicated in the case of invalidity pensions, since the Member State take two fundamentally different approaches to invalidity benefits. Some Member States operate invalidity benefits in much the same way as they operate old age benefits. These are known as Type B schemes. Other Member States have schemes under which invalidity benefit is paid on fixed scales (which may be related to the level of previous earnings) which are not tied to periods of insurance, though there may be a requirement for a minimum period of insurance. These schemes are known as Type A schemes. The United Kingdom scheme is a Type A scheme. Co-ordination of Type A and Type B schemes presents particular difficulties. The effect of the provisions of the Regulation can be summarised as follows:

1. Claimant insured in a single country.	Entitled to invalidity benefits calculated in accordance with the legislation of that country.
2. Claimant insured in more than one country where the amount of the invalidity benefit is determined by reference to the length of insurance periods.	Entitled to invalidity benefits from each country in accordance with the periods of insurance. The calculation is as for retirement pensions.
3. Claimant insured in more than one country where the amount of the invalidity benefit is independent of the length of insurance periods.	Entitled to invalidity benefits from the country in which the claimant became an invalid (even if this is lower than the benefits paid in any of the other countries where the claimant has been insured).

Article 36

4. Claimant first insured in a country where the amount of the invalidity benefit depends on the length of insurance periods and then in a country where the amount of invalidity benefit is independent of the length of insurance periods.	Entitled to invalidity benefit from the first country in accordance with the periods of insurance, and an invalidity benefit from the second country which may be reduced to take account of the benefit received from the first country.
5. Claimant first insured in a country where the amount of the pension is independent of the length of insurance periods and then in a country where the amount of invalidity benefit depends on the length of insurance periods.	Entitled to invalidity benefit from the first country and an invalidity benefit from the second country in accordance with the periods of insurance.

SECTION 1

EMPLOYED PERSONS OR SELF-EMPLOYED PERSONS SUBJECT ONLY TO LEGISLATION UNDER WHICH THE AMOUNT OF INVALIDITY BENEFITS ITS INDEPENDENT OF THE DURATION OF THE PERIODS OF INSURANCE

Article 37

General provisions

1. An employed person or a self-employed person who has been successively or alternately subject to the legislation of two or more Member States and who has completed periods of insurance exclusively under legislation according to which the amount of invalidity benefits is independent of the duration of periods of insurance shall receive benefits in accordance with Article 39. This Article shall not affect pension increases or supplements in respect of children, granted in accordance with Chapter 8.

2. Annex IV, part A, lists legislations of the kind mentioned in paragraph 1 which are in force in the territory of each of the Member States concerned.

RELEVANT PROVISIONS OF THE IMPLEMENTING REGULATION

Arts 35, 39, 40, and 41–50 of Reg.5764/72/EEC.

Article 38

Consideration of periods of insurance or of residence completed under the legislation to which an employed person or a self-employed person was subject for the acquisition, retention or recovery of the right to benefits

1. Where the legislation of a Member State makes the acquisition, retention or recovery of the right to benefits, under a scheme which is not a special

3.191

3.192

scheme within the meaning of paragraph 2 or 3, subject to the completion of periods of insurance or of residence, the competent institution of that Member State shall take account, where necessary, of the periods of insurance or of residence completed under the legislation of any other Member State, be it under a general scheme or under a special scheme and either as an employed person or as a self-employed person. For that purpose, it shall take account of these periods as if they had been completed under its own legislation.

2. Where the legislation of a Member State makes the granting of certain benefits conditional upon the periods of insurance having been completed only in a occupation which is subject to a special scheme for employed persons or, where appropriate, in a specific employment, periods completed under the legislation of other Member States shall be taken into account for the granting of these benefits only if completed under a corresponding scheme or, failing that, in the same occupation or, where appropriate, in the same employment.

If, account having been taken of the periods thus completed, the person concerned does not satisfy the conditions for receipt of these benefits, these periods shall be taken into account for the granting of the benefits under the general scheme or, failing that, under the scheme applicable to manual or clerical workers, as the case may be, subject to the condition that the person concerned has been affiliated to one or other of these schemes.

3. Where the legislation of a Member State makes the granting of certain benefits conditional upon the period of insurance having been completed only in a occupation subject to a special scheme for self-employed persons, periods completed under the legislation of other Member States shall be taken into account for the granting of these benefits only if completed under a corresponding scheme or, failing that, in the same occupation. The special schemes for self-employed persons referred to in this paragraph are listed in Annex IV, part B, for each Member State concerned.

If, account having been taken of the periods thus completed, the person concerned does not satisfy the conditions for receipt of these benefits, these periods shall be taken into account for the granting of the benefits under the general scheme or, failing that, under the scheme applicable to manual or clerical workers, as the case may be, subject to the condition that the person concerned has been affiliated to one or other of these schemes.

RELEVANT PROVISIONS OF THE IMPLEMENTING REGULATION

Arts 15, and 35, Reg.574/72/EEC.

Article 39

Award of benefits

1. The institution of a Member State whose legislation was applicable at the time when incapacity for work followed by invalidity occurred shall determine, in accordance with that legislation, whether the person concerned satisfies the conditions for entitlement to benefits, taking account, where appropriate, of Article 38.

Article 39

2. A person who satisfies the conditions referred to in paragraph 1 shall receive the benefits only from the said institution, in accordance with the provisions of the legislation which it administers.

3. A person who is not entitled to benefits under paragraph 1 shall receive the benefits to which he is still entitled under the legislation of another Member State taking account, where appropriate, of Article 38.

4. If the legislation referred to in paragraph 2 or 3 provides that the amount of the benefits shall be determined taking into account the existence of members of the family other than the children, the competent institution shall also take into consideration those members of the family of the person concerned who are residing in the territory of another Member State, as if they were residing in the territory of the competent State.

5. If the legislation referred to in paragraph 2 or 3 lays down provisions for the reduction, suspension or withdrawal of benefits in the case of overlapping with other income or with benefits of a different kind within the meaning of Article 461(2), Article 46a(3) and Article 46c(5) shall apply *mutatis mutandis*.

6. A wholly unemployed employee to whom Article 71(1)(a)(ii) or the first sentence of Article 71(1)(b)(ii) applies shall receive the invalidity benefits provided by the competent institution of the Member State in whose territory he resides, in accordance with the legislation which it administers, as though he had been subject to that legislation during his last employment, account being taken, where appropriate, of Article 38 and/or Article 25(2). The institution of the country of residence shall be responsible for paying these benefits.

Where that institution applies legislation providing for deduction of contributions payable by unemployed persons to cover invalidity benefits, it shall be authorized to make such deductions in accordance with the provisions of its legislation.

If the legislation which that institution administers provides for the calculation of benefits to be based on wages or salaries, the institution shall take into account the wages or salaries received in the last country of employment and in the country of residence in accordance with the legislation which it administers. Where no wage or salary has been received in the country of residence, the competent institution shall refer, as necessary and in accordance with the rules laid down in its legislation, to the salaries received in the last country of employment.

Relevant Provisions of the Implementing Regulation

Arts 35, and 38 of Reg.5764/72/EEC.

Section 2

Employed Persons or Self-employed Persons Subject Either Only to Legislation Under Which the Amount of Invalidity Benefit Depends on the Duration of Periods of Insurance or Residence or the Legislation of This Type and of the Type Referred to in Section 1

Article 40

General provisions

1. An employed person or a self-employed person who has been successively or alternately subject to the legislation of two or more Member States, of which at least one is not of the type referred to in Article 37(1), shall receive benefits under the provisions of Chapter 3, which shall apply *mutatis mutandis*, taking into account the provisions of paragraph 4.

2. However, an employed or self-employed person who suffers incapacity for work leading to invalidity while subject to a legislation listed in Annex IV, part A, shall receive benefits in accordance with the provisions of Article 37 (1) on the following conditions:

— that he satisfies the conditions of that legislation or other legislations of the same type, taking account where appropriate of Article 38, but without having recourse to periods of insurance completed under legislations not listed in Annex IV, part A, and

— that he does not satisfy the conditions required for the acquisition of the right to invalidity benefits under a legislation not listed in Annex IV, part A, and

— that he does not assert any claims to old-age benefits, account being taken of the second sentence of Article 44(2).

3. (a) For the purpose of determining the right to benefits under the legislation of a Member State, listed in Annex IV, part A, which makes the granting of invalidity benefits conditional upon the person concerned having received cash sickness benefits or having been incapable or work during a specified period, where an employed person or a self-employed person who has been subject to that legislation suffers incapacity for work leading to invalidity while subject to the legislation of another Member State, account shall be taken of the following, without prejudice to Article 37(1):

  (i) any period during which, in respect of that incapacity for work, he has, under the legislation of the second Member State, received cash sickness benefits, or, in lieu thereof, continued to receive a wage or salary;

  (ii) any period during which, in respect of the invalidity which followed that incapacity for work, he has received benefits within the meaning of this Chapter 2 and of Chapter 3 that follows, of the Regulation granted in respect of invalidity under the legislation of the second Member State.

Article 40

as if it were a period during which cash sickness benefits were paid to him under the legislation of the first Member State or during which he was incapable or working within the meaning of that legislation.
(b) The right to invalidity benefits under the legislation of the first Member State shall be acquired either upon expiry of the preliminary period of compensation for sickness, as required by that legislation, or upon expiry of the preliminary period of incapacity of work as required by that legislation, but not before:
   (i) the date of acquisition of the right to invalidity benefits referred to in subparagraph (a)(ii) under the legislation of the second Member State,
   or
   (ii) the day following the last day on which the person concerned is entitled to cash sickness benefits under the legislation of the second Member State.

4. A decision taken by an institution of a Member State concerning the degree of invalidity of a claimant shall be binding on the institution of any other Member State concerned, provided that the concordance between the legislation of these States on conditions relating to the degree of invalidity is acknowledged in Annex V.

RELEVANT PROVISIONS OF THE IMPLEMENTING REGULATION

Arts 35, 36, 37, 40, and 41–50 of Reg.5764/72/EEC.

RELEVANT DECISIONS OF THE ADMINISTRATIVE COMMISSION

Decision No 132 of 23 April, 1987 concerning the interpretation of Article 40(3)(a)(ii) of Council Regulation (EEC) No 1408/71 of 14 June, 1971.

GENERAL NOTE

In *R(IB) 1/02* the Commissioner ruled that short-term incapacity benefit (whether paid at the lower or higher rate) is a sickness benefit within the meaning of Article 4, and long-term incapacity benefit is an invalidity benefit which is not subject to contribution requirements but to the receipt for the specified period of short-term incapacity benefit. The Commissioner notes that the provision of the Regulation on invalidity benefit do not use the concept of the competent State; entitlement to invalidity benefit in the United Kingdom can arise where the claimant has received sickness benefit for 364 days in another Member State, since the claimant's entitlement to sickness benefit in another Member State is to be treated as entitlement in the United Kingdom. The facts of *CIB/4471/2000* were much more complex. The claimant had worked and paid social security contributions successively in the United Kingdom, Belgium and Italy. Following an injury suffered at work in Italy, the claimant had moved to Belgium. He sought to claim invalidity benefits in Belgium and the United Kingdom. There appears to have been considerable difficulty in obtaining official information about the benefit position in Italy and Belgium. The Commission again notes that the claimant would become entitled to invalidity benefit in the United Kingdom (his claim pre-dated the introduction of incapacity benefit) if he could establish that he had received sickness benefit for 168 days in another Member State. It transpired that he was paid the equivalent of statutory sick pay by his employer in Italy for less than the requisite period, and so his claim for United Kingdom invalidity benefit could not succeed. Note that an employer paying sickness benefit under a statutory scheme can be the competent institution within the meaning of the Regulation: Case C-45/90 *Paletta* [1992] E.C.R. I-3423, paras 19–24 of the judgment).

3.195

Section 3

Aggravation of Invalidity

Article 41

1. In the case of aggravation of an invalidity for which an employed person or a self-employed person is receiving benefits under the legislation of a single Member State, the following provisions shall apply:
    (a) if the person concerned has not been subject to the legislation of another Member State since receiving benefits, the competent institution of the first State shall grant the benefits, taking the aggravation into account, in accordance with the provisions of the legislation which it administers;
    (b) if the person concerned has been subject to the legislation of one or more of the other Member States since receiving benefits, the benefits shall be granted to him, taking the aggravation into account, in accordance with Article 37(1) or 40(1) or (2), as appropriate;
    (c) if the total number of the benefit or benefits payable under subparagraph (b) is lower than the amount of the benefit which the person concerned was receiving at the expense of the institution previously liable for payment, such institution shall pay him a supplement equal to the difference between the two amounts;
    (d) if, in the case referred to in subparagraph (b), the institution responsible for the initial incapacity is a Dutch institution, and if:
        (i) the illness which caused the aggravation is the same as the one which gave rise to the granting of benefits under Dutch legislation,
        (ii) this illness is an occupational disease within the meaning of the legislation of the Member State to which the person concerned was last subject and entitles him to payment of the supplement referred to in Article 60(1)(b), and
        (iii) the legislation or legislations to which the person concerned has been subject since receiving benefits is or are listed in Annex IV, part A,
    the Dutch institution shall continue to provide the initial benefit after the aggravation occurs, and the benefit due under the legislation of the last Member State to which the person concerned was subject shall be reduced by the amount of the Dutch benefit;
    (e) if, in the case referred to in subparagraph (b), the person concerned is not entitled to benefits at the expense of an institution of another Member State, the competent institution of the first State shall grant the benefits, according to the provisions of the legislation of the State, taking into account the aggravation and, where appropriate, Article 38.
2. In the case of aggravation of an invalidity for which an employed person or a self-employed person is receiving benefits under the legislation of two or more Member States, the benefits shall be granted to him, taking the aggravation into account, in accordance with Article 40(1).

Article 41

RELEVANT PROVISIONS OF THE IMPLEMENTING REGULATION

Arts 35, 36, and 37 of Reg.5764/72/EEC.

SECTION 4

RESUMPTION OF PROVISION OF BENEFITS AFTER SUSPENSION OR WITHDRAWAL—CONVERSION OF INVALIDITY BENEFITS INTO OLD-AGE BENEFITS—RECALCULATION OF BENEFITS GRANTED UNDER ARTICLE 39

Article 42

Determination of the institution responsible for the provision of benefits where provision of invalidity benefits is resumed

1. If provision of benefits is to be resumed after suspension, such provision shall, without prejudice to Article 43, be the responsibility of the institution or institutions which were responsible for provision of the benefits at the time of their suspension.

2. If, after withdrawal of benefits, the condition of the person concerned warrants the granting of further benefits, they shall be granted in accordance with Article 37(1) or Article 40(1) or (2), as appropriate.

RELEVANT PROVISIONS OF THE IMPLEMENTING REGULATION

Arts 35, 36, and 37 of Reg.5764/72/EEC.

Article 43

Conversion of invalidity benefits into old-age benefits— Recalculation of benefits granted under Article 39

1. Invalidity benefits shall be converted into old-age benefits, where appropriate, under the condition laid down by the legislation or legislations under which they were granted, and in accordance with Chapter 3.

2. Where a person receiving invalidity benefits can establish a claim to old-age benefits under the legislation of one or more Member States, in accordance with Article 49, any institution which is responsible for providing invalidity benefits under the legislation of a Member State shall continue to provide such a person with the invalidity benefits to which he is entitled under the legislation which it administers until the provisions of paragraph 1 become applicable as regards that institution or so long as the person concerned fulfils the conditions for such benefits.

3. Where invalidity benefits granted in accordance with Article 39 under the legislation of a Member State are converted into old-age benefits and where the person concerned does not yet satisfy the conditions required by one or more national legislations to receive these benefits, the person concerned shall receive, from this or these Member States, from the date of the conversion, invalidity benefits granted in accordance with Chapter 3 as if that Chapter had been applicable at the time when his incapacity for work leading to invalidity occurred, until the person concerned satisfies the qualifying conditions for old-age benefit laid down by the national legislations concerned or, where such conversion is not provided for, as long as he has a right to invalidity benefits under the legislation or legislations concerned.

4. The invalidity benefits provided under Article 39 shall be recalculated pursuant to Chapter 3 as soon as the beneficiary satisfies the qualifying conditions for invalidity benefits laid down by a legislation not listed in Annex IV, part A, or as soon as he receives old-age benefits under the legislation of another Member State.

RELEVANT PROVISIONS OF THE IMPLEMENTING REGULATION

Arts 36 and 37 of Reg.5764/72/EEC.

[¹ SECTION 5

PERSONS COVERED BY A SPECIAL SCHEME FOR CIVIL SERVANTS

Article 43a

1. The provisions of Articles 37, 38(1), 39 and Sections 2, 3 and 4 shall apply by analogy to persons covered by a special scheme for civil servants.

2. However, if the legislation of a Member State makes the acquisition, liquidation, retention or recovery of the rights to benefit under a special scheme for civil servants subject to the condition that all periods of insurance have been completed under one or more special schemes for civil servants in that Member State, or are regarded by the legislation of that Member State as equivalent to such periods, account shall be taken only of the periods which can be recognised under the legislation in that Member State.

If, account having been taken of the periods thus completed, the person concerned does not satisfy the conditions for the receipt of these benefits, these periods shall be taken into account for the granting of the benefits under the general scheme or, failing that, the scheme applicable to manual or clerical workers, as the case may be.

3. Were, under the legislation of a Member State, benefits are calculated on the basis of the last salary or salaries received during a reference period, the competent institution of that State shall take into account for the purposes of the calculation only those salaries, duly revalued, received during the period for which the person concerned was subject to that legislation.]

AMENDMENT

1. Regulation1606/98/EC, [1998] OJ L209/1 (October 25, 1998).

RELEVANT PROVISIONS OF THE IMPLEMENTING REGULATION

Arts 36 and 37 of Reg.5764/72/EEC.

Article 43a

CHAPTER 3

RELEVANT PROVISIONS OF THE IMPLEMENTING REGULATION

Provisions relating to administrative checks and medical examinations can be found in Arts 51–2, and on payment of benefits in Arts 53–59, Reg.574/72/EEC.

OLD AGE AND DEATH (PENSIONS)

Article 44

General provisions for the award of benefits where an employed or self-employed person has been subject to the legislation of two or more Member States

1. The rights to benefits of an employed or self-employed person who has been subject to the legislation of two or more Member States, or of his survivors, shall be determined in accordance with the provisions of this Chapter.

2. Save as otherwise provided in Article 49, the processing of a claim for an award submitted by the person concerned shall have regard to all the legislations to which the employed or self-employed person has been subject. Exception shall be made to this rule if the person concerned expressly asks for postponement of the award of old-age benefits to which he would be entitled under the legislation of one or more Member States.

[[1] 3. This chapter shall not apply to increases in or supplements to pensions in respect of children or to orphans' pensions to be granted in accordance with the provisions of Chapter 8.]

AMENDMENT

1. Regulation 1399/99/EC, [1999] OJ L164/1 (September 1, 1999).

RELEVANT PROVISIONS OF THE IMPLEMENTING REGULATION

Arts 36 and 37 of Reg.5764/72/EEC.

RELEVANT DECISIONS OF THE ADMINISTRATIVE COMMISSION

Recommendation No 23 of 29 October, 2003 on the processing of pension claims, [2004] OJ L104/125.

3.200

Article 45

Consideration of periods of insurance or of residence completed under the legislations to which an employed person or self-employed person was subject, for the acquisition, retention or recovery of the right to benefits

1. Where the legislation of a Member State makes the acquisition, retention or recovery of the right to benefits, under a scheme which is not a special scheme within the meaning of paragraph 2 or 3, subject to the completion of periods of insurance or of residence, the competent institution of that Member State shall take account, where necessary, of the periods of insurance or of residence completed under the legislation of any other Member State, be it under a general scheme or under a special scheme and either as an employed person or a self-employed person. For that purpose, it shall take account of these periods as if they had completed under its own legislation.

2. Where the legislation of a Member State makes the granting of certain benefits conditional upon the periods of insurance having been completed only in an occupation which is subject to a special scheme for employed persons or, where appropriate, in a specific employment, periods completed under the legislation of other Member States shall be taken into account for the granting of these benefits only if completed under a corresponding scheme or, failing that, in the same occupation or, where appropriate, in the same employment. If, account having been taken of the periods thus completed, the person concerned does not satisfy the conditions for receipt of these benefits, these periods shall be taken into account for the granting of the benefits under the general scheme or, failing that, under the scheme applicable to manual or clerical workers, as the case may be, subject to the condition that the person has been affiliated to one or other of these schemes.

3. Where the legislation of a Member State makes the granting of certain benefits conditional upon the periods of insurance having been completed only in an occupation subject to a special scheme for self-employed persons, periods completed under the legislations of other Member States shall be taken into account for the granting of these benefits only if completed under a corresponding scheme or, failing that, in the same occupation. The special schemes for self-employed persons referred to in this paragraph are listed in Annex IV, part B, for each Member State concerned. If, account having been taken of the periods referred to in this paragraph, the person concerned does not satisfy the conditions for receipt of these benefits, these periods shall be taken into account for the granting of the benefits under the general scheme or, failing this, under the scheme applicable to manual or clerical workers, as the case may be, subject to the condition that the person concerned has been affiliated to one or other of these schemes.

4. The periods of insurance completed under a special scheme of a Member State shall be taken into account under the general scheme or, failing that, under the scheme applicable to manual or clerical workers, as the case may be, of another Member State for the acquisition, retention or recovery of the right to benefits, subject to the condition that the person

Article 45

concerned has been affiliated to one or other of these schemes, even if these periods have already been taken into account in the latter State under a scheme referred to in paragraph 2 or in the first sentence of paragraph 3.

5. Where the legislation of a Member State makes the acquisition, retention or recovery of the right to benefits conditional upon the person concerned being insured at the time of the materialization of the risk, this condition shall be regarded as having been satisfied in the case of insurance under the legislation of another Member State, in accordance with the procedures provided in Annex VI for each Member State concerned.

6. A period of full employment of a worker to whom Article 81(1)(a)(ii) or (b)(ii), first sentence, applies shall be taken into account by the competent institution of the Member State in whose territory the worker concerned resides in accordance with the legislation administered by that institution, as if that legislation applied to him during his last employment.

Where that institution applies legislation providing for deduction of contributions payable by unemployed persons to cover old age pensions and death, it shall be authorized to make such deductions in accordance with the provisions of its legislation.

If the period of full unemployment in the country of residence of the person concerned can be taken into account only if contribution periods have been completed in that country, this condition shall be deemed to be fulfilled if the contribution periods have been completed in another Member State.

RELEVANT PROVISIONS OF THE IMPLEMENTING REGULATION

Arts 15, 36 and 37 of Reg.574/72/EEC.

RELEVANT DECISIONS OF THE ADMINISTRATIVE COMMISSION

Decision No 81 of 22 February, 1973 concerning aggregation of insurance periods completed in a given occupation in application of Article 45(2) of Regulation (EEC) No 1408/71, [1973] OJ C 75/11.

Decision No 134 of 1 July, 1987 concerning the interpretation of Article 45(2) of Regulation (EEC) No 1408/71 relating to aggregation of insurance periods completed in an occupation subject to a special scheme in one or more Member States, [1988] OJ C64/4.

Decision No 136 of 1 July, 1987 concerning the interpretation of Article 45(1) to (3) of Council Regulation (EEC) No 1408/71 with regard to the taking into account of insurance periods completed under the legislations of other Member States for the acquisition, retention or recovery of the right to benefits, [1988] OJ C64/7.

Article 46

Award of benefits

1. Where the conditions required by the legislation of a Member State for entitlement to benefits have been satisfied without having to apply Article 45 or Article 40(3), the following rules shall apply:

(a) the competent institution shall calculate the amount of the benefit that would be due:

(i) on the one hand, only under the provisions of the legislation which it administers;

(ii) on the other hand, pursuant to paragraph 2;

(b) the competent institution may, however, waive the calculation to be carried out in accordance with (a)(ii) if the result of this calculation, apart from differences arising from the use of round figures, is equal to or lower than the result of the calculation carried out in accordance with (a)(i), in so far as that institution does not apply any legislation containing rules against overlapping as referred to in Articles 46b and 46c or if the aforementioned institution applies a legislation containing rules against overlapping in the case referred to in Article 46c, provided that the said legislation lays down that benefits of a different kind shall be taken into consideration only on the basis of the relation of the periods of insurance or of residence completed under that legislation alone to the periods of insurance or of residence required by that legislation in order to qualify for full benefit entitlement.

Annex IV, part C, lists for each Member State concerned the cases where the two calculations would lead to a result of this kind.

2. Where the conditions required by the legislation of a Member State for entitlement to benefits are satisfied only after application of Article 45 and or Article 40(3), the following rules shall apply:

(a) the competent institution shall calculate the theoretical amount of the benefit to which the person concerned could lay claim provided all periods of insurance and/or of residence, which have been completed under the legislation of the Member States to which the employed person or self-employed person was subject, have been completed in the State in question under the legislation which it administers on the date of the award of the benefit. If, under this legislation, the amount of the benefit is independent of the duration of the periods completed, the amount shall be regarded as being the theoretical amount referred to in this paragraph;

(b) the competent institution shall subsequently determine the actual amount of the benefit on the basis of the theoretical amount referred to in the preceding paragraph in accordance with the ratio of the duration of the periods of insurance or of residence completed before the materialization of the risk under the legislation which it administers to the total duration of the periods of insurance and of residence completed before the materialization of the risk under the legislations of all the Member States concerned.

3. The person concerned shall be entitled to the highest amount calculated in accordance with paragraphs 1 and 2 from the competent institution of each Member State without prejudice to any application of the provisions concerning reduction, suspension or withdrawal provided for by the legislation under which this benefit is due.

Where that is the case, the comparison to be carried out shall relate to the amounts determined after the application of the said provisions.

4. When, in the case of invalidity, old-age or survivor's pensions, the total of the benefits due from the competent institutions of two or more Member States under the provisions of a multilateral social security convention referred to in Article 6 (b) does not exceed the total which would be due from such Member States under paragraphs 1 to 3, the person concerned shall benefit from the provisions of this Chapter.

Article 46

RELEVANT PROVISIONS OF THE IMPLEMENTING REGULATION

Arts 36 and 37 of Reg.5764/72/EEC.

RELEVANT DECISIONS OF THE ADMINISTRATIVE COMMISSION

Decision No 91 of 12 July, 1973 concerning the interpretation of Article 46(3) of Council Regulation (EEC) No 1408/71 relating to the award of benefits due under paragraph 1 of the said Article.

GENERAL NOTE

This article is at the heart of the treatment of entitlement to old age pensions where a person has contribution records in more than one Member State. Article 45 contains the basic aggregation rule requiring the competent institution of a Member State to take account of period of insurance, employment or self-employment completed in another Member State as if they had been completed there. In Case 2/72 *Murru* [1972] E.C.R. 333, the Court of Justice ruled that a period of unemployment could be assimilated to a period of employment under Community rules if the legislation of the country under which the period of unemployment had been completed so provided. Periods are aggregated under Community rules even where they would not be aggregated under the legislation of the State of the competent institution: Joined Cases 113–114/92 and 156/92 *Fabrizii* [1993] E.C.R. I-6707.

3.203

Article 46 sets out the basis for determining the award of benefits. Each Member State to whose legislation the claimant has been subject must undertake the following computation. Periods of less than one year are generally ignored: Art.48. First it calculates the pension entitlement to which claimant would be entitled if that country applies only its own legislation.

Next, the first step in the second calculation is taken: regard is had to the total period to be taken into account under the legislation of all the relevant countries. Each country then determines the amount of pension to which that would give entitlement: this is known as the "theoretical amount". The second step in the second calculation is to calculate what proportion of the theoretical amount the ratio of years completed in the country doing the calculation to the total years bears. This is called the "actual amount". So in the case of a claim who had spent ten years out of 40 years taken into account under the legislation of the country in question, the actual amount would be one quarter of the theoretical amount. But the actual amount is not what the claimant necessarily receives since this must first be compared with the amount calculated solely under the legislation of the country of claim. The higher of these two amounts is awarded. Each country to whose legislation the claimant has been subject makes this calculation and awards a pension on the basis of the calculation. So the pensioner will receive a pension made up of contributions from each of the Member State's to whose legislation he has been subject.

An example might make this all rather less abstract. Suppose that a worker has worked continuously for 40 years, spending 15 years in Ireland, 8 years in the United Kingdom, and 17 years in the Netherlands. First, each country calculates the claimant's pension entitlement based on the years of work in that country. There would be a problem in the United Kingdom, since ten years of contributions are needed for the award of a retirement pension for someone with a working life of 40 years. But each country must then compute the theoretical amount on the assumption that the whole of the claimant's working life had been in that State. This would produce entitlement to a full pension in the United Kingdom. But the claimant is only entitled to a pro rata pension for the years actually worked in the United Kingdom. On this basis the claimant would be entitled to a 20 per cent retirement pension from the United Kingdom. Since this is higher than the nil entitlement under the first calculation, the United Kingdom would be required to pay him or her a one-fifth retirement pension. The other countries involved would undertake the same calculation.

Note that if the claimant had completed ten years in the United Kingdom, there would be an entitlement to a one-quarter pension under both calculations.

See Article 50 for a provision guaranteeing a minimum pension. The purpose is to ensure a basic standard of living where a person has a series of relatively short periods of employment of self employment in several Member States.

The specific rules on the overlapping of benefits in Articles 46a, 46b and 46c display characteristics of technicality and complexity, and are not always easy to understand. But note that they do not apply to benefits calculated in accordance with Article 46(2). This means that the individual pro rata pensions calculated in accordance with the formula in Article 46 are protected against the rules on the overlapping of benefits.

Article 46a

General provisions relating to reduction, suspension or withdrawal applicable to benefits in respect of invalidity, old age or survivors under the legislations of the Member States

3.204

1. For the purposes of the Chapter, overlapping of benefits of the same kind shall have the following meaning: all overlapping of benefits in respect of invalidity, old age and survivors calculated or provided on the basis of periods of insurance and/or residence completed by one and the same person.

2. For the purposes of this Chapter, overlapping of benefits of different kinds means all overlapping of benefits that cannot be regarded as being of the same kind within the meaning of paragraph 1.

3. The following rules shall be applicable for the application of provisions on reduction, suspension or withdrawal laid down by the legislation of a Member State in the case of overlapping of a benefit in respect of invalidity, old age or survivors with a benefit of the same kind or a benefit of a different kind or with other income:

(a) account shall be taken of the benefits acquired under the legislation of another Member State or of other income acquired in another Member State only where the legislation of the first Member State provides for the taking into account of benefits or income acquired abroad;

(b) account shall be taken of the amount of benefits to be granted by another Member State before deductions of taxes, social security contributions and other individual levies or deductions;

(c) no account shall be taken of the amount of benefits acquired under the legislation of another Member State which are awarded on the basis of voluntary insurance or continued optional insurance;

(d) where provisions on reduction, suspension or withdrawal are applicable under the legislation of only one Member State on account of the fact that the person concerned receives benefits of a similar or different kind payable under the legislation of other Member States or other income acquired within the territory of other Member States, the benefit payable under the legislation of the first Member State may be reduced only within the limit of the amount of the

Article 46a

benefits payable under the legislation or the income acquired within the territory of other Member States.

RELEVANT PROVISIONS OF THE IMPLEMENTING REGULATION

Arts 36 and 37 of Reg.5764/72/EEC.

Article 46b

Special provisions applicable in the case of overlapping of benefits of the same kind under the legislation of two or more Member States

1. The provisions on reduction, suspension or withdrawal laid down by the legislation of a Member State shall not be applicable to a benefit calculated in accordance with Article 46(2).
2. The provisions on reduction, suspension or withdrawal laid down by the legislation of a Member State shall apply to a benefit calculated in accordance with Article 46(1)(a)(i) only if the benefit concerned is:
   (a) either a benefit, which is referred to in Annex IV, part D, the amount of which does not depend on the length of the periods of insurance of residence completed,
   or
   (b) a benefit, the amount of which is determined on the basis of a credited period deemed to have been completed between the date on which the risk materialized and a later date. In the latter case, the said provisions shall apply in the case of overlapping of such a benefit:
      (i) either with a benefit of the same kind, except where an agreement has been concluded between two or more Member States providing that one and the same credited period may not be taken into account two or more times;
      (ii) or with a benefit of the type referred to in (a).

The benefits referred to in (a) and (b) and agreements are mentioned in Annex IV, part D.

3.205

RELEVANT PROVISIONS OF THE IMPLEMENTING REGULATION

Arts 36 and 37 of Reg.5764/72/EEC.

Article 46c

Special provisions applicable in the case of overlapping of one or more benefits referred to in Article 46a(1) with one or more benefits of a different kind or with other income, where two or more Member States are concerned

1. If the receipt of benefits of a different kind or other income entails the reduction, suspension or withdrawal of two or more benefits referred to in Article 46(1)(a)(i), the amounts which would not be paid in strict application of the provisions concerning reduction, suspension or

3.206

withdrawal provided for by the legislation of the Member States concerned shall be divided by the number of benefits subject to reduction, suspension or withdrawal.

2. Where the benefit in question is calculated in accordance with Article 46(2), the benefit or benefits of a different kind from other Member States or other income and all other elements provided for by the legislation of the Member State for the application of the provisions in the respect of reduction, suspension or withdrawal shall be taken into account in proportion to the periods of insurance and/or residence referred to in Article 46(2)(b), and shall be used for the calculation of the said benefit.

3. If the receipt of benefits of a different kind or of other income entails the reduction, suspension or withdrawal of one or more benefits referred to in Article 46(1)(a)(i), and of one or more benefits referred to in Article 46(2), the following rules shall apply:
   (a) where in a case of a benefit or benefits referred to in Article 46(1)(a)(i), the amounts which would not be paid in strict application of the provisions concerning reduction, suspension or withdrawal provided for by the legislation of the Member States concerned shall be divided by the number of benefits subject to reduction, suspension or withdrawal;
   (b) where in a case of a benefit or benefits calculated in accordance with Article 46(2), the reduction suspension or withdrawal shall be carried out in accordance with paragraph 2.

4. Where, in the case referred to in paragraphs 1 and 3(a), the legislation of a Member State provides that, for the application of provisions concerning reduction, suspension or withdrawal, account shall be taken of benefits of a different kind and/or other income and all other elements in proportion to the periods of insurance referred to in Article 46(2)(b), the division provided for in the said paragraphs shall not apply in respect of that Member State.

5. All the above mentioned provisions shall apply *mutatis mutandis* where the legislation of one or more Member States provides that the right to a benefit cannot be acquired in the case where the person concerned is in receipt of a benefit of a different kind, payable under the legislation of another Member State, or of other income.

RELEVANT PROVISIONS OF THE IMPLEMENTING REGULATION

Arts 36 and 37 of Reg.5764/72/EEC.

Article 47

Additional provisions for the calculation of benefits

1. For the calculation of the theoretical and pro rata amounts referred to in Article 46 (2), the following rules shall apply:
   (a) where the total length of the periods of insurance and of residence completed before the risk materialized under the legislations of all the Member States concerned is longer than the maximum period required by the legislation of one of these States for receipt of full benefit, the competent institution of that State shall take into

Article 47

consideration this maximum period instead of the total length of the periods completed; this method of calculation must not result in the imposition on that institution of the cost of a benefit greater than the full benefit provided for by the legislation which it administers. This provisions shall not apply to benefits, the amount of which does not depend on the length of insurance;

(b) the procedure for taking account of overlapping periods is laid down in the implementing Regulation referred to in Article 98;

(c) where, under the legislation of a Member State, benefits are calculated on the basis of average earnings, an average contribution, an average increase or on the relation which existed, during the periods of insurance, between the claimant's gross earnings and the average gross earnings of all insured persons other than apprentices, such average figures or relations shall be determined by the competent institution of that State solely on the basis of the periods of insurance completed under the legislation of the said State, or the gross earnings received by the person concerned during those periods only;

(d) where, under the legislation of a Member State, benefits are calculated on the basis of the amount of earnings, contributions or increases, the competent institution of the State shall determine the earnings, contributions and increases to be taken into account in respect of the periods of insurance or residence completed under the legislation of other Member States on the basis of the average earnings, contributions or increases recorded in respect of the periods of insurance completed under the legislation which it administers;

(e) where, under the legislation of a Member State, benefits are calculated on the basis of standard earnings or a fixed amount, the competent institutions of that State shall consider the standard earnings or the fixed amount to be taken into account by it in respect of periods of insurance or residence completed under the legislations of other Member States as being equal to the standard earnings or fixed amount or, where appropriate, to the average of the standard earnings or the fixed amount corresponding to the periods of insurance completed under the legislation which it administers;

(f) where, under the legislation of a Member State, benefits are calculated for some periods on the basis of the amount of earnings and, for other periods, on the basis of standard earnings or a fixed amount, the competent institution of that State shall, in respect of periods of insurance or residence completed under the legislations of other Member States, take into account the earnings or fixed amounts determined in accordance with the provisions referred to in (d) or (e) or, as appropriate, the average of these earnings or fixed amounts, where benefits are calculated on the basis of standard earnings or a fixed amount for all the periods completed under the legislation which it administers, the competent institution shall consider the earnings to be taken into account in respect of the periods of insurance or residence completed under the legislations of other Member States as being equal to the national earnings corresponding to the standard earnings or fixed amounts;

(g) where, under the legislation of a Member State, benefits are calculated on the basis of average contributions, the competent institution shall determine that average by reference only to those periods of insurance completed under the legislation of the said State.

2. The provisions of the legislation of a Member State concerning the revalorization of the factors taken into account for the calculation of benefits shall apply, as appropriate, to the factors to be taken into account by the competent institution of that state, in accordance with paragraph 1, in respect of the periods of insurance or residence completed under the legislation of other Member States.

3. If, under the legislation of a Member State, the amount of benefits is determined taking into account the existence of members of the family other than children, the competent institution of that State shall also take into consideration those members of the family of the person concerned who are residing in the territory of another Member State as if they were residing in the territory of the competent State.

4. If the legislation which the competent institution of a Member State administers requires a salary to be taken into account for the calculation of benefits, where the first and second subparagraphs of Article 45(6) have been applied, and if, in this Member State, only periods of full unemployment with benefit in accordance with Article 71(1)(a)(ii) or the first sentence of Article 71(1)(b)(ii) are taken into consideration for the payment of pensions, the competent institution of that Member State shall pay the pension on the basis of the salary it used as the reference for providing that unemployment benefit in accordance with the legislation which it administers.

RELEVANT PROVISIONS OF THE IMPLEMENTING REGULATION

Arts 36, 37, and 38 of Reg.5764/72/EEC.

Article 48

Periods of insurance or of residence of less than one year

1. Notwithstanding Article 46(2), the institution of a Member State shall not be required to award benefits in respect of periods completed under the legislation it administers which are taken into account when the risk materializes, if:

— the duration of the said periods does not amount to one year,

and

— taking only these periods into consideration, no right to benefit is acquired by virtue of the provisions of that legislation.

2. The competent institution of each of the Member States concerned shall take into account the periods referred to in paragraph 1, for the purposes of applying Article 46(2) excepting subparagraph (b).

3. If the effect of applying paragraph 1 would be to relieve all the institutions of the Member States concerned of their obligations, benefits shall be awarded exclusively under the legislation of the last of those States whose conditions are satisfied, as if all the periods of insurance and residence completed and taken into account in accordance with Article 45(1) to (4) had been completed under the legislation of that State.

Article 48

RELEVANT PROVISIONS OF THE IMPLEMENTING REGULATION

Arts 36 and 37 of Reg.5764/72/EEC.

RELEVANT DECISIONS OF THE ADMINISTRATIVE COMMISSION

Decision No 79 of 22 February, 1973 concerning the interpretation of Article 48(2) of Regulation (EEC) No 1408/71 relating to the aggregation of insurance periods and periods treated as such for the purposes of invalidity, old age and death, [1973] OJ C75/9.

Article 49

Calculation of benefits where the person concerned does not simultaneously satisfy the conditions laid down by all the legislations under which periods of insurance or of residence have been completed or when he has expressly requested a postponement of the award of old-age benefits

1. If, at a given time, the person concerned does not satisfy the conditions laid down for the provisions of benefits by all the legislations of the Member States to which he has been subject, taking into account where appropriate Article 45 and/or Article 40(3), but satisfies the conditions or one or more of them only, the following provisions shall apply:
   (a) each of the competent institutions administering a legislation whose conditions are satisfied shall calculate the amount of the benefit due, in accordance with Article 46;
   (b) however:
      (i) if the person concerned satisfies the conditions of at least two legislations without having recourse to periods of insurance or residence completed under the legislations whose conditions are not satisfied, these periods shall not be taken into account for the purposes of Article 46(2) unless taking account of the said periods makes it possible to determine a higher amount of benefit;
      (ii) if the person concerned satisfies the conditions of one legislation only without having recourse to periods of insurance or residence completed under the legislations whose conditions are not satisfied, the amount of the benefit due shall, in accordance with Article 46(1)(a)(i), be calculated only in accordance with the provisions of the legislation whose conditions are satisfied, taking account of the periods completed under that legislation only, unless taking account of the periods completed under the legislations whose conditions are not satisfied makes it possible, in accordance with Article 46(1)(a)(ii), to determine a higher amount of benefit.
   The provisions of this paragraph shall apply mutatis mutandis where the person concerned has expressly requested the postponement of the award of old-age benefits, in accordance with the second sentence of Article 44(2).
2. The benefit or benefits awarded under one or more of the legislations in question, in the case referred to in paragraph 1, shall be recalculated automatically in accordance with Article 46, as and when the conditions required

3.209

by one or more of the other legislations to which the person concerned has been subject are satisfied, taking into account, where appropriate, Article 45 and taking into account once again, where appropriate, paragraph 1. This paragraph shall apply mutatis mutandis where a person requests the award of old-age benefits acquired under the legislation of one or more Member States which had until than been postponed in accordance with the second sentence of Article 44(2).

3. A recalculation shall automatically be made in accordance with paragraph 1, without prejudice to Article 40(2), where the conditions required by one or more of the legislations concerned are no longer satisfied.

RELEVANT PROVISIONS OF THE IMPLEMENTING REGULATION

Arts 36 and 37 of Reg.5764/72/EEC.

RELEVANT DECISIONS OF THE ADMINISTRATIVE COMMISSION

Decision No 96 of 15 March, 1974 concerning the revision of rights to benefit pursuant to Article 49(2) of Council Regulation (EEC) No 1408/71.

Article 50

Award of a supplement where the total of benefits payable under the legislations of the various Member States does not amount to the minimum laid down by the legislation of the State in whose territory the recipient resides

3.210   A recipient of benefits to whom this Chapter applies may not, in the State in whose territory he resides and under whose legislation a benefit is payable to him, be awarded a benefit which is less than the minimum benefit fixed by that legislation for a period of insurance or residence equal to all the periods of insurance or residence equal to all the periods of insurance taken into account for the payment in accordance with the preceding Articles. The competent institution of that State shall, if necessary, pay him throughout the period of his residence in its territory a supplement equal to the difference between the total of the benefits payable under this Chapter and the amount of the minimum benefit.

RELEVANT PROVISIONS OF THE IMPLEMENTING REGULATION

Arts 36 and 37 of Reg.5764/72/EEC.

RELEVANT DECISIONS OF THE ADMINISTRATIVE COMMISSION

Decision No 105 of 19 December, 1975 on the implementation of Article 50 of Regulation (EEC) No 1408/71, [1976] OJ C117/3.

Article 51

Revalorization and recalculation of benefits

3.211   1. If, by reason of an increase in the cost of living or changes in the level of wages or salaries or other reasons for adjustment, the benefits of the States

Article 51

concerned are altered by a fixed percentage or amount, such percentage or amount must be applied directly to the benefits determined under Article 46, without the need for a recalculation in accordance with that Article.

2. On the other hand, if the method of determining benefits or the rules for calculating benefits should be altered, a recalculation shall be carried out in accordance with Article 46.

RELEVANT PROVISIONS OF THE IMPLEMENTING REGULATION

Arts 36 and 37 of Reg.5764/72/EEC.

[Article 51a

Persons covered by a special scheme for civil servants

1. The provisions of Article 44, 45(1), (5) and (6) and Articles 46 to 51 shall apply by analogy to persons covered by a special scheme for civil servants.

2. However, if the legislation of a Member State makes the acquisition, liquidation, retention or recovery of the rights to benefits under a special scheme for civil servants subject to the condition that all periods of insurance have been completed under one or more special schemes for civil servants in that Member State, or are regarded by the legislation of that Member State as equivalent to such periods, account shall be taken only of the periods which can be recognised under the legislation in that Member State.

If, account having been taken of the periods thus completed, the person concerned does not satisfy the conditions for the receipt of these benefits, these periods shall be taken into account for the granting of the benefits under the general scheme or, failing that, the scheme applicable to manual or clerical workers, as the case may be.

3. Where, under the legislation of a Member State, benefits are calculated on the basis of the last salary or salaries received during a reference period, the competent institution of that State shall take into account for the purposes of the calculation only those salaries, duly revalued, received during the period or periods for which the person concerned was subject to that legislation.

AMENDMENT

1. Regulation 1606/98/EC, [1998] OJ L209/1 (October 25, 1998).

CHAPTER 4

ACCIDENTS AT WORK AND OCCUPATIONAL DISEASES

RELEVANT PROVISIONS OF THE IMPLEMENTING REGULATION

Provisions relating to administrative checks and medical examinations can be found at Art.76, and on payment of pensions at Art.77, Reg.574/72/EEC.

3.212

3.213

Council Regulation (EEC) No 1408/71

GENERAL NOTE

3.214 Chapter 4 of Title III contains provisions covering accidents at work and occupational diseases. Though these provisions are detailed and substantial, they appear to give rise to fewer difficulties than certain other types of benefit. This may, in part, be because the EEA countries do not make entitlement to benefits for accidents at work and occupational diseases conditional upon the completion of particular periods of insurance. So, the provisions of Chapter 4 do not need to deal with rules of aggregation.

It will be recalled that under Title II the competent State is normally the State in which the claimant is working. Articles 52 to 56 provide modifications to that rule. Article 52, reflecting the approach adopted in relation to sickness benefits, provides that persons habitually resident in a country other than that in which they work are to receive benefits in the State in which they reside. The distinction familiar from the sickness benefit rules between benefits in kind and cash benefits is repeated. Benefits in kind are provided on behalf of the competent State in accordance with the legislation of the country of residence as if the beneficiary were insured there. They are re-imbursed by the competent State. Cash benefits are, however, provided by the competent institution in accordance with the legislation of the competent State.

Frontier workers, presumably by reason of their likely proximity to the country in which they work, may also obtain benefits in the territory of the competent State: Art.53. Article 54 provides for generous treatment of those who are temporarily residing in the competent State or who transfer their permanent residence to the competent State. Article 55 contains provisions which apply to those who sustain an accident at work or contract an occupational disease:

- who are staying in the territory of an EEA country other than the competent State; or

- who have become entitled to benefits chargeable to the competent institution and are authorised to return to the country of their residence or to transfer their residence to another EEA country; or

- who are authorised by the competent institution to go to another EEA country for treatment appropriate to their condition.

These groups are entitled to benefits in kind in accordance with the legislation of the country of stay or residence, and cash benefits in accordance with the legislation of the competent State. There are limitations on the refusal of authority to move in Article 55(2). Finally, Article 56 provides that an accident while travelling which occurs in the territory of a State other than the competent State is deemed to have occurred in the territory of the competent State.

It is in the nature of some occupational diseases that they develop as a result of prolonged exposure to a particular environment. Article 57 deals with situations where the claimant has been exposed to the same risk in several EEA countries. In such cases, the starting point is that benefits are to be awarded exclusively under the legislation of the last of those countries whose conditions of entitlement are satisfied. So, if a claimant does not meet the conditions of entitlement in the last country, that country is required to forward to application to the next country in line to see whether the conditions of entitlement are met there. Paragraphs (2) to (5) add glosses to this rule. Any condition that the disease was first diagnosed on the territory of that country are to be read as a condition that the disease first arose in any EEA country: Case 28/85 *Deghillage* [1986] E.C.R. 991.

Similarly time limits are liberated from any territorial constraints; activities pursued in other EEA countries are to be treated as activities pursued in the country of claim. Article 57(5) contains a special rule where the occupational disease is sclerogenic pneumoconiosis, under which the costs of the benefits are to be shared between the countries where the claimant pursued an activity likely to have caused the disease.

Article 51a

Article 58 deals with the calculation of cash benefits. If the national scheme meets the cost of taking the injured or sick persons to hospital or to their home, Article 59(1) contains provisions for authorising the cost of taking persons sustaining an accident at work or suffering an occupational disease to hospital or to the place of residence in their country of residence. The provision presumably refers to a move either home or to a hospital near home after initial treatment; otherwise the provision produces the odd result that initial hospitalisation which is likely to be required in an emergency would require prior authorisation. No authorisation is needed if the person is a frontier worker. Article 59(2) contains corresponding provisions for the transport of a body of a person killed in an accident at work to 'the place of burial' in the country of residence. Presumably this provision would also apply where the method of disposal of the body was cremation, though the article refers only to burial.

Where there is a subsequent aggravation of the injury or disease, little difficult arises if the person has not been engaged in an occupation likely to cause aggravation of the disease in another country. The first country continues to have jurisdiction over the matter: Art.60(1)(a). But where there has been some engagement in an occupation likely to cause an aggravation in another country, the first country continues to be liable for the benefits under its own legislation for the disease ignoring the aggravation, while the second country is required to pay a supplement which is the difference between the amount it would have awarded if the disease had first occurred under its own legislation and the amount of benefit to which there is entitlement under its own legislation having regard to the aggravation: Art.60(1)(b). The two awards from different countries do not overlap: Art.60(1)(c).

Section 3 of Chapter 4 contains a number of detailed rules which accommodate a variety of special features which exist in the legislation of some EEA countries. The provisions are detailed and specific.

SECTION 1

RIGHT TO BENEFITS

Article 52

Residence in a Member State other than the competent State—General rules

An employed or self-employed person who sustains an accident at work or contracts an occupational disease, and who is residing in the territory of a Member State other than the competent State, shall receive in the State in which he is residing:
  (a) benefits in kind, provided on behalf of the competent institution by the institutions of his place of residence in accordance with the provisions of the legislation which it administers as if he were insured with it;
  (b) cash benefits provided by the competent institution in accordance with the provisions of the legislation which it administers. However, by agreement between the competent institution and the institution of the place of residence, these benefits may be provided by the latter institution on behalf of the former in accordance with the legislation of the competent State.

3.215

Council Regulation (EEC) No 1408/71

RELEVANT PROVISIONS OF THE IMPLEMENTING REGULATION

3.216   Arts 60–61, and 65–66, Reg.574/72/EEC.

Article 53

Frontier workers—Special rule

A frontier worker may also obtain benefits in the territory of the competent State. Such benefits shall be provided by the competent institution in accordance with the provisions of the legislation of that State, as if the person concerned were residing there.

RELEVANT PROVISIONS OF THE IMPLEMENTING REGULATION

Arts 60–61, and 65–66, Reg.574/72/EEC.

Article 54

Stay in or transfer of residence to the competent State

3.217   1. An employed or self-employed person covered by Article 52 who is staying in the territory of the competent State shall receive benefits in accordance with the provisions of the legislation of that State, even if he has already received benefits before his stay. This provision shall not, however, apply to frontier workers.

2. An employed or self-employed person covered by Article 52 who transfers his place of residence to the territory of the competent State shall receive benefits in accordance with the provisions of the legislation of that State, even if he has already received benefits before transferring his residence.

RELEVANT PROVISIONS OF THE IMPLEMENTING REGULATION

Arts 65–66, Reg.574/72/EEC.

Article 55

Stay outside the competent State—Return to or transfer of residence to another Member State after sustaining an accident or contracting an occupational disease—Need to go to another Member State in order to receive appropriate treatment

3.218   1. An employed or self-employed person who sustains an accident at work or contracts an occupational disease and:
    (a) who is staying in the territory of a Member State other than the competent State;
        or
    (b) who, after having become entitled to benefits chargeable to the competent institution, is authorized by that institution to return to the

Article 55

territory of the Member State where he is resident, or to transfer his place of residence to the territory of another Member State; or
(c) who is authorized by the competent institution to go to the territory of another Member State in order to receive there the treatment appropriate to his condition;

shall be entitled:
    (i) to benefits in kind provided on behalf of the competent institution by the institution of the place of stay or residence in accordance with the provisions of the legislation administered by that institution as though he were insured with it, the period during which benefits are provided shall, however, be governed by the legislation of the competent State;
    (ii) to cash benefits provided by the competent institution in accordance with the legislation which it administers. However, by agreement between the competent institution and the institution of the place of say or residence, those benefits may be provided by the latter institution on behalf of the former institution, in accordance with the legislation of the competent State.

2. The authorization required under paragraph 1(b) may be refused only if it is established that movement of the person concerned would be prejudicial to his state of health or to the medical treatment being given.

The authorization required under paragraph 1(c) may not be refused where the treatment in question cannot be given to the person concerned in the territory of the Member State in which he resides.

RELEVANT PROVISIONS OF THE IMPLEMENTING REGULATION

Arts 62–66, Reg.574/72/EEC.

Article 56

Accidents while travelling

An accident while travelling which occurs in the territory of a Member State other than the competent State shall be deemed to have occurred in the territory of the competent State.

3.219

RELEVANT PROVISIONS OF THE IMPLEMENTING REGULATION

Arts 65–66, Reg.574/72/EEC.

Article 57

Benefits for an occupational disease where the person concerned has been exposed to the same risk in several Member States

1. When a person who has contracted an occupational disease has, under the legislation of two or more Member States, pursued an activity which by its nature is likely to cause that disease, the benefits that he or his survivors may claim shall be awarded exclusively under the legislation of the last of

3.220

those States whose conditions are satisfied, taking into account, where appropriate, paragraphs 2 to 5.

2. If, under the legislation of a Member State, the granting of benefits in respect of an occupational disease is subject to the condition that the disease in question was first diagnosed within its territory, such condition shall be deemed to be satisfied if the disease was first diagnosed in the territory of another Member State.

3. If, under the legislation of a Member State, the granting of benefits in respect of an occupational disease is subject to the condition that the disease in question was diagnosed within a specific time limit following cessation of the last activity which was likely to cause such a disease, the competent institution of that State, when checking the time at which such activity was pursued, shall take into account, to the extent necessary, similar activities pursued under the legislation of any other Member State, as if they had been pursued under the legislation of the first State.

4. If, under the legislation of a Member State, the granting of benefits in respect of an occupational disease is subject to the condition that an activity likely to cause the disease in question was pursued for a certain length of time, the competent institution of the State shall take into account, to the extent necessary, periods during which such activity was pursued under the legislation of any other Member State, as if it had been pursued under the legislation of the first State.

5. In cases of sclerogenic pneumoconiosis, the cost of cash benefits, including pensions, shall be divided among the competent institutions of the Member States in whose territory the person concerned pursued an activity likely to cause the disease. This division shall be carried out on the basis of the ratio which the length of the periods of old-age insurance or residence referred to in Article 45(1) completed under the legislation of each of the States bears to the total length of the periods of old-age insurance or residence completed under the legislation of all the States at the dates on which the benefits commenced.

6. The Council shall determine unanimously, on a proposal from the Commission, the occupational diseases to which the provisions of paragraph 5 shall be extended.

RELEVANT PROVISIONS OF THE IMPLEMENTING REGULATION

Arts 67–69, and 75 Reg.574/72/EEC.

RELEVANT DECISIONS OF THE ADMINISTRATIVE COMMISSION

Decision No 85 of 22 February, 1973 concerning the interpretation of Article 57(1) of Regulation (EEC) No 1408/71 and Article 67(3) of Regulation (EEC) No 574/72 relating to the determination of the applicable legislation and the institution competent for the award of benefits in respect of occupation diseases, [1973] OJ C75/17.

Article 58

Calculation of cash benefits

1. The competent institution of a Member State whose legislation provides that the calculation of cash benefits shall be based on average earnings

Article 58

shall determine such average earnings exclusively by reference to earnings confirmed as having been paid during the periods completed under the said legislation.

2. The competent institution of a Member State whose legislation provides that the calculation of cash benefits shall be based on standard earnings shall take account exclusively of the standard earnings, or where appropriate, of the average of standard earnings for the periods completed under the said legislation.

3. The competent institution of a Member State whose legislation provides that the amount of cash benefits shall vary with the number of members in the family shall take into account also the members of the family of the person concerned who are residing in the territory of another Member State, as if they were residing in the territory of the competent State.

RELEVANT PROVISIONS OF THE IMPLEMENTING REGULATION

Art.70, Reg.574/72/EEC.

GENERAL NOTE

In Case C-205/05 *Nemec*, [2006] ECR I-10745, the Court of Justice ruled: 3.222

"Article 58(1) of Regulation (EEC) No 1408/71 . . . interpreted in accordance with the objective set out in Article 42 EC, requires that, in a situation such as that in the main proceedings, calculation of the 'average wage or salary', within the meaning of the first of those two provisions, takes into account the pay that the person concerned could reasonably have earned, given his subsequent employment record, had he continued to work in the Member State in which the competent institution is situated."

Article 59

Costs of transporting a person who has sustained an accident at work or is suffering from an occupational disease

1. The competent institution of a Member State whose legislation provides for meeting the costs of transporting a person who has sustained an accident at work or is suffering from an occupational disease, either to his place of residence or to a hospital, shall meet such costs to the corresponding place in the territory of another Member State where the person resides, provided that that institution gives prior authorization for such transport, duly taking into account the reasons justifying it. Such authorization shall not be required in the case of a frontier worker.   3.223

2. The competent institution of a Member State whose legislation provides for the costs of transporting the body of a person killed in an accident at work to the place of burial shall, in accordance with the provisions of the legislation which it administers, meet such costs to the corresponding place in the territory of another Member State, where the person was residing at the time of the accident.

Council Regulation (EEC) No 1408/71

SECTION 2

AGGRAVATION OF AN OCCUPATIONAL DISEASE FOR WHICH THE BENEFIT HAS BEEN AWARDED

Article 60

3.224
1. In the event of aggravation of an occupational disease for which an employed or self-employed person has received or is receiving benefit under the legislation of a Member State, the following rules shall apply:
    (a) if the person concerned has not, while in receipt of benefits, been engaged in an occupation under the legislation of another Member State likely to cause or aggravate the disease in question, the competent institution of the first Member State shall be bound to meet the cost of the benefits under the provisions of the legislation which it administers taking into account the aggravation;
    (b) if the person concerned, while in receipt of benefits, has pursued such an activity under the legislation of another Member State, the competent institution of the first Member State shall be bound to meet the cost of the benefits under the legislation which it administers without taking the aggravation into account. The competent institution of the second Member State shall grant a supplement to the person concerned, the amount of which shall be equal to the difference between the amount of benefits due after the aggravation and the amount which would have been due prior to the aggravation under the legislation which it administers if the disease in question had occurred under the legislation of that Member State;
    (c) if, in the case covered by subparagraph (b), an employed or self-employed person suffering from sclerogenic pneumoconiosis or from a disease determined under Article 57(6) is not entitled to benefits under the legislation of the second Member State, the competent institution of the first Member State shall be bound to provide benefits under the legislation which it administers, taking the aggravation into account. The competent institution of the second Member State shall, however, meet the cost of the difference between the amount of cash benefits, including pensions, due from the competent institution of the first Member State, taking the aggravation into account, and the amount of the corresponding benefits which were due prior to the aggravation;
    (d) the provisions for reduction, suspension or withdrawal laid down by the legislation of a Member State shall not apply to persons receiving benefits awarded by institutions of two Member States in accordance with subparagraph (b).
2. In the event of aggravation of an occupational disease giving rise to the application of the provisions of Article 57(5), the following provisions shall apply:
    (a) the competent institution which granted the benefits in accordance with the provisions of Article 57(1) shall be bound to provide benefits under the legislation which it administers taking the aggravation into account;

Article 60

(b) the cost of cash benefits, including pensions, shall continue to be divided between the institutions which shared the costs of former benefits in accordance with the provisions of Article 57(5). Where, however, the person has again pursued an activity likely to cause or to aggravate the occupational disease in question, either under the legislation of one of the Member States in which he had already pursued an activity of the same nature or under the legislation of another Member State, the competent institution of such State shall meet the cost of the difference between the amount of benefits due, taking account of the aggravation, and the amount of benefits due prior to the aggravation.

RELEVANT PROVISIONS OF THE IMPLEMENTING REGULATION
Art.71, Reg.574/72/EEC.

SECTION 3

MISCELLANEOUS PROVISIONS

Article 61

Rules for taking into account the special features of certain legislations

1. If there is no insurance against accidents at work or occupational diseases in the territory of the Member State in which the person concerned happens to be, or if such insurance exists but there is no institution responsible for providing benefits in kind, those benefits shall be provided by the institution of the place of stay or residence responsible for providing benefit in kind in the event of sickness.

2. Where the legislation of the competent State makes wholly cost-free benefits in kind conditional upon use of the medical service organized by the employer, benefits in kind provided in the cases referred to in Articles 52 and 55(1) shall be deemed to have been provided by such a medical service.

3. Where the legislation of the competent State includes a scheme relating to the obligations of the employer, benefits in kind provided in the case referred to in Articles 52 and 55(1) shall be deemed to have been provided at the request of the competent institution.

4. Where the nature of the scheme of the competent State relating to compensation for accidents at work is not that of compulsory insurance, the provision of benefits in kind shall be made directly by the employer or by the insurer involved.

5. Where the legislation of a Member State provides expressly or by implication that accidents at work or occupational diseases which have occurred or have been confirmed previously shall be taken into consideration in order to assess the degree of incapacity, to establish a right to any benefit, or to determine the amount of benefit, the competent institution

of that Member State shall also take into consideration accidents at work or occupational diseases which have occurred or have been confirmed previously under the legislation of another Member State as if they had occurred or had been confirmed under the legislation which it administers.

6. Where the legislation of a Member State provides expressly or by implication that accidents at work or occupational diseases which have occurred or have been confirmed subsequently shall be taken into consideration in order to assess the degree of incapacity, to establish the right to any benefit, or to determine the amount of such benefit, the competent institution of that Member State shall also take into consideration accidents at work or occupational diseases which have occurred or have been confirmed subsequently under the legislation of another Member State, as if they had occurred or had been confirmed under the legislation which it administers, but only where:

(a) no compensation is due in respect of the accident at work or the occupational disease which had occurred or had been confirmed previously under the legislation which it administers;
and

(b) no compensation is due by virtue of the legislation of the other Member State under which the accident at work or the occupational disease occurred or was confirmed subsequently, account having been taken of the provisions of paragraph 5, in respect of that accident at work or that occupational disease.

RELEVANT PROVISIONS OF THE IMPLEMENTING REGULATION

Arts 72–3, Reg.574/72/EEC.

Article 62

Scheme applicable where there are several schemes in the country of stay or residence—Maximum duration of benefits

1. If the legislation of the country of stay or residence has several insurance schemes, the provisions applicable to employed or self-employed persons covered by Article 52 or 55(1) shall be those of the scheme for manual workers in the steel industry. However, if that legislation includes a special scheme for workers in mines and similar undertakings, the provisions of that scheme shall apply to that category of workers where the institution of the place of stay or residence to which they submit their claim is competent to administer that scheme.

2. If the legislation of a Member State fixes a maximum period during which benefits may be granted, the institution which administers that legislation may take into account any period during which the benefits have already been provided by the institution of another Member State.

RELEVANT PROVISIONS OF THE IMPLEMENTING REGULATION

Art.74, Reg.574/72/EEC.

Article 63

SECTION 4

REIMBURSEMENTS BETWEEN INSTITUTIONS

Article 63

1. The competent institution shall be obliged to reimburse the amount of benefits in kind provided on its behalf in accordance with the provisions of Articles 52 and 55(1).
2. The reimbursements referred to in paragraph 1 shall be determined and made in accordance with the procedures laid down by the implementing Regulation referred to in Article 98, on proof of actual expenditure.
3. Two or more Member States, or the competent authorities of such States, may provide for other methods of reimbursement or waive reimbursement between the institutions coming under their jurisdiction.

3.227

[¹ SECTION 5

STUDENTS

Article 63a

The provisions of Sections 1 to 4 shall apply by analogy to students.]

3.228

AMENDMENT

1. Regulation 307/99/EC, [1999] OJ L38/1 (May 1, 1999).

CHAPTER 5

DEATH GRANTS

Article 64

Aggregation of periods of insurance or residence

The competent institution of a Member State whose legislation makes the acquisition, retention or recovery of the right to death grants subject to the completion of periods of insurance or residence shall take account, to the extent necessary, of periods of insurance or residence completed under the legislation of any other Member State as though they had been completed under the legislation which it administers.

3.229

Relevant Provisions of the Implementing Regulation
Arts 15, and 78–9, Reg.574/72/EEC.

Article 65

Right to grants where death occurs in, or where the person entitled resides in, a Member State other than the competent State

3.230
1. When an employed or self-employed person, a pensioner or a pension claimant, or a member of his family, dies in the territory of a Member State other than the competent State, the death shall be deemed to have occurred in the territory of the competent State.
2. The competent institution shall be obliged to award death grants payable under the legislation which it administers, even if the person entitled resides in the territory of a Member State other than the competent State.
3. The provisions of paragraphs 1 and 2 shall also apply when the death is the result of an accident at work or an occupational disease.

Relevant Provisions of the Implementing Regulation
Arts 78–79, Reg.574/72/EEC.

Article 66

Provision of benefits in the event of the death of a pensioner who had resided in a Member State other than the one whose institution was responsible for providing benefits in kind

3.231
In the event of the death of a pensioner who was entitled to a pension under the legislation of one Member State, or to pensions under the legislations of two or more Member States, when such pensioner was residing in the territory of a Member State other than the one whose institution was responsible for providing him with benefits in kind under the provisions of Article 28, the death grants payable under the legislation administered by that institution shall be provided by that institution at its own expense as though the pensioner had been residing in the territory of the Member State of that institution at the time of his death.

The provisions of the preceding paragraph shall apply by analogy to the members of the family of a pensioner.

[¹Article 66a

Students

3.232
The provisions of Articles 64 to 66 shall apply by analogy to students and to the members of their family.]

Amendment

1. Regulation 307/99/EC, [1999] OJ L38/1 (May 1, 1999).

Article 67

CHAPTER 6

UNEMPLOYMENT BENEFITS

SECTION 1

COMMON PROVISIONS

Article 67

Aggregation of periods of insurance or employment

1. The competent institution of a Member State whose legislation makes the acquisition, retention or recovery of the right to benefits subject to the completion of periods of insurance shall take into account, to the extent necessary, periods of insurance or employment completed as an employed person under the legislation of any other Member State, as though they were periods of insurance completed under the legislation which it administers, provided, however, that the periods of employment would have been counted as periods of insurance had they been completed under that legislation.

2. The competent institution of a Member State whose legislation makes the acquisition, retention or recovery of the right to benefits subject to the completion of periods of employment shall take into account, to the extent necessary, periods of insurance or employment completed as an employed person under the legislation of any other Member State, as though they were periods of employment completed under the legislation which it administers.

3. Except in the cases referred to in Article 71(1)(a)(ii) and (b)(ii), application of the provisions of paragraphs 1 and 2 shall be subject to the condition that the person concerned should have completed lastly:

— in the case of paragraph 1, periods of insurance,

— in the case of paragraph 2, periods of employment,

in accordance with the provisions of the legislation under which the benefits are claimed.

4. Where the length of the period during which benefits may be granted depends on the length of periods of insurance or employment, the provisions of paragraph 1 or 2 shall apply, as appropriate.

RELEVANT PROVISIONS OF THE IMPLEMENTING REGULATION

Arts 15, and 80, Reg.574/72/EEC.

GENERAL NOTE

The provisions of Reg.1408/71 dealing specifically with unemployment benefit demonstrate an overly cautious view by the Member States of the motives of unemployed persons moving between the Member States. Provision is made in Art.67 for

3.233

3.234

periods of employment or insurance to be aggregated in order to determine entitlement to unemployment benefits. But there is a sting in the tail of the provision. Aggregation is only possible under the legislation of the country in which the person claiming "lastly" completed periods of insurance or employment. The result is, for example, that a British national living and working in Germany who becomes unemployed cannot return to the United Kingdom and claim jobseeker's allowance on the basis of contributions to the German scheme, because he or she will not have lastly completed a period of insurance in the United Kingdom unless they could bring themselves within the scope of Art.71: see below. This territorial limitation on aggregation seems unnecessarily restrictive, and has been the subject of criticism: See, for example, Wikeley, N., *"Migrant Workers and Unemployment Benefit in the European Community"* [1988] J.S.W.L. 300.

The severity of the rule is illustrated in Case C-62/91 Gray v *Adjudication Officer* [1992] E.C.R. I-2737. Gray, a British national, had lived and worked in Spain running a restaurant from 1971 to 1990. He returned to the United Kingdom after selling the business without having registered as unemployed in Spain. He claimed unemployment benefit in the United Kingdom, and appealed the refusal to award him the benefit to the Bognor Regis social security appeal tribunal. It was argued by the adjudication officer that there was no entitlement in the United Kingdom because the claimant was last insured in Spain. Furthermore since he had not registered as unemployed in Spain, no question could arise as to any entitlement under Art.69. The tribunal also concluded that the claimant had been habitually resident in Spain and so could not take the benefit of the rules in Article 71. The lay members of the tribunal (the lawyer chairman of the tribunal considered that the provisions were consistent with the Treaty rules) clearly saw an injustice and felt that certain provisions of Arts 67 and 69 militated against the Treaty rules on free movement of persons. They clearly insisted (as they were entitled to) that a reference be made concerning the validity of the provisions in question. The Court, however, concluded that there was no factor of such a kind as to affect the validity of the provisions in issue. Both conferred on workers rights which they would not otherwise enjoy.

Article 68

Calculation of benefits

3.235
1. The competent institution of a Member State whose legislation provides that the calculation of benefits should be based on the amount of the previous wage or salary shall take into account exclusively the wage or salary received by the person concerned in respect of his last employment in the territory of that State.

However, if the person concerned had been in his last employment in that territory for less than four weeks, the benefits shall be calculated on the basis of the normal wage or salary corresponding, in the place where the unemployed person is residing or staying, to an equivalent or similar employment to his last employment in the territory of another Member State.

2. The competent institution of a Member State whose legislation provides that the amount of benefits varies with the number of members of the family, shall take into account also members of the family of the person concerned who are residing in the territory of another Member State, as though they were residing in the territory of the competent State. This provision shall not apply if, in the country of residence of the members of the family, another person is entitled to unemployment benefits for the calculation of which the members of the family are taken into consideration.

Article 68

RELEVANT PROVISIONS OF THE IMPLEMENTING REGULATION

Arts 81–82, Reg.574/72/EEC.

RELEVANT DECISIONS OF THE ADMINISTRATIVE COMMISSION

Decision No 83 of 22 February 1973 concerning the interpretation of Article 68(2) of Regulation (EEC) No 1408/71 and of Article 82 of regulation (EEC) No 574/72 relating to increases in unemployment benefit for dependent members of the family, [1973] OJ C75/14.

GENERAL NOTE

Article 68(1) provides that where unemployment benefit is linked to a previous wage or salary, the salary or wages to be taken into account are those in respect of the last employment in that State: Case 67/79 *Fellinger* [1980] E.C.R. 535. However, where the amount of benefit varies with the number of members of the family, members of the family residing in another EEA country are to be treated as residing in the competent State.

3.236

SECTION 2

UNEMPLOYED PERSONS GOING TO A MEMBER STATE OTHER THAN THE COMPETENT STATE

Article 69

Conditions and limits for the retention of the right to benefits

1. An employed or self-employed person who is wholly unemployed and who satisfies the conditions of the legislation of a Member State for entitlement to benefits and who goes to one or more other Member States in order to seek employment there shall retain his entitlement to such benefits under the following conditions and within the following limits:
   (a) Before his departure, he must have been registered as a person seeking work and have remained available to the employment services of the competent State for at least four weeks after becoming unemployed, However, the competent services or institutions may authorize his departure before such time has expired.
   (b) He must register as a person seeking work with the employment services of each of the Member States to which he goes and be subject to the control procedure organized therein. This condition shall be considered satisfied for the period before registration if the person concerned registered within seven days of the date when he ceased to be available to the employment services of the State he left. In exceptional cases, this period may be extended by the competent services or institutions.
   (c) Entitlement to benefits shall continue for a maximum period of three months from the date when the person concerned ceased to be available to the employment services of the State which he left, provided that the total duration of the benefits does not exceed the duration of

3.237

the period of benefits he was entitled to under the legislation of that State. In the case of a seasonal worker such duration shall, moreover, be limited to the period remaining until the end of the season for which he was engaged.

2. If the person concerned returns to the competent State before the expiry of the period during which he is entitled to benefits under the provisions of paragraph 1(c), he shall continue to be entitled to benefits under the legislation of that State; he shall lose all entitlement to benefits under the legislation of the competent State if he does not return there before the expiry of that period. In exceptional cases, this time limit may be extended by the competent services or institutions.

3. The provisions of paragraph 1 may be invoked only once between two periods of employment.

4. [1 . . .]

AMENDMENT

1. Regulation 647/2005/EC, [2005] OJ L117/1 (May 5, 2005).

RELEVANT PROVISIONS OF THE IMPLEMENTING REGULATION

Art.83, Reg.574/72/EEC.

RELEVANT DECISIONS OF THE ADMINISTRATIVE COMMISSION

Recommendation No 21 of 28 November 1996 concerning the application of Article 69(1)(a) of Regulation (EEC) No 1408/71 to unemployed persons accompanying their spouses employed in a Member State other than the competent State, [1997] OJ C67/3.

GENERAL NOTE

3.238
Article 69 provides a limited right to export unemployment benefit for up to three months where the person goes to another EEA country for the purpose of seeking work. Strict conditions surround the right to export the benefit, and failure to return to the competent State within the three-month period normally results in the loss of all entitlement to benefits under the legislation of the competent State. The right to export unemployment benefit can only be exercised once in any period of unemployment. Under Art.70 benefits are paid by the unemployment benefit institution in the place to which the person goes but are to be reimbursed by the competent State. Because of the limitation on aggregation, the rules in Art.71 take on extra significance and have been the subject of many references to the Court of Justice. They provide exceptions to the rule that the competent State is that in which the claimant lastly worked, and permit claims in the EEA country in which persons are habitually resident where that country is different from that in which they worked. There are separate rules for frontier workers and others.

In Joined Cases 41, 121 & 796/79 *Testa, Maggio and Vitale* [1980] E.C.R. 1979, the validity of Art.69(2) of Reg.1408/71 was questioned in circumstances where each of three Italian nationals lost the residual entitlement to unemployment benefit in Germany when they did not return within three months to Germany from an authorised stay in Italy in order to look for work there. In two of the cases, the later return was explained by an intervening illness. The Court had little difficulty in concluding that there was nothing to impugn the validity of the provisions of Art.69(2) which provided that all entitlement to unemployment benefit would cease if the beneficiary did not return to the competent State before the expiry of the authorised period of absence. There was, according to the Court, a

Article 69

clear advantage to the person in that they were, during their period of absence abroad, exempt from the controls applicable in the competent State (even though they would be subject to the controls in the country to which they went). The only glimmer of hope related to the Court's advice on how the discretion to extend the period in exceptional cases should be applied: see also Case 139/78 *Coccioli* [1979] E.C.R. 991. First, retrospective applications for extensions of the period are admissible. Secondly, the competent institution in exercising its discretion must take account of the principle of proportionality in Community law. In each case, the institution must consider the extent to which the three-month period has been exceeded, the reasons for the delay in returning, and the seriousness of the legal consequences arising from the delay. This would, presumably, include consideration of the residual amount of benefit which might be forfeit if all entitlement were to cease.

The Commission's Proposal for a Council Regulation amending, for the benefit of unemployed workers, Reg.1408/71 on the application of social security schemes to employed persons and their families moving within the Community, 18 June 1980, [1980] O.J. C169/22, contained amendments which would not deprive workers of entitlement to any residual period of entitlement in the territory of the Member State they left. The proposals have not been implemented.

Article 69(1)(a)
In C-215/00 *Rydergård* [2002] E.C.R. I–1817, the Court ruled that the period of four weeks referred to in Art.69(1)(a) need not be completed without a break. Short breaks—for example, where the claimant moved to a child caring benefit because her child was ill for just a few days—would not cause the four week qualifying period to start to run all over again.

Article 70

Provision of benefits and reimbursements

1. In the cases referred to in Article 69 (1), benefits shall be provided by the institution of each of the States to which an unemployed person goes to seek employment.

The competent institution of the Member State to whose legislation an employed or self-employed person was subject at the time of his last employment shall he obliged to reimburse the amount of such benefits.

2. The reimbursements referred to in paragraph 1 shall be determined and made in accordance with the procedure laid down by the implementing Regulation referred to in Article 98, on proof of actual expenditure, or by lump sum payments.

3. Two or more Member States, or the competent authorities of those States, may provide for other methods of reimbursement or payment, or may waive all reimbursement between the institutions coming under their jurisdiction.

3.239

Council Regulation (EEC) No 1408/71

SECTION 3

UNEMPLOYED PERSONS WHO, DURING THEIR LAST EMPLOYMENT, WERE RESIDING IN A MEMBER STATE OTHER THAN THE COMPETENT STATE

Article 71

3.240
1. An unemployed person who was formerly employed and who, during his last employment, was residing in the territory of a Member State other than the competent State shall receive benefits in accordance with the following provisions:
(a)(i) A frontier worker who is partially or intermittently unemployed in the undertaking which employs him, shall receive benefits in accordance with the provisions of the legislation of the competent State as if he were residing in the territory of that State; these benefits shall be provided by the competent institution.
  (ii) A frontier worker who is wholly unemployed shall receive benefits in accordance with the provisions of the legislation of the Member State in whose territory he resides as though he had been subject to that legislation while last employed; these benefits shall be provided by the institution of the place of residence at its own expense.
(b)(i) An employed person, other than a frontier worker, who is partially, intermittently or wholly unemployed and who remains available to his employer or to the employment services in the territory of the competent State shall receive benefits in accordance with the provisions of the legislation of that State as though he were residing in its territory; these benefits shall be provided by the competent institution.
  (ii) An employed person, other than a frontier worker, who is wholly unemployed and who makes himself available for work to the employment services in the territory of the Member State in which he resides, or who returns to that territory, shall receive benefits in accordance with the legislation of that State as if he had last been employed there; the institution of the place of residence shall provide such benefits at its own expense. However, if such an employed person has become entitled to benefits at the expense of the competent institution of the Member State to whose legislation he was last subject, he shall receive benefits under the provisions of Article 69. Receipt of benefits under the legislation of the State in which he resides shall be suspended for any period during which the unemployed person may, under the provisions of Article 69, make a claim for benefits under the legislation to which he was last subject.
2. An unemployed person may not claim benefits under the legislation of the Member State in whose territory he resides while he is entitled to benefits under the provisions of paragraph 1(a)(i) or (b)(i).

RELEVANT PROVISIONS OF THE IMPLEMENTING REGULATION
Art.84, Reg.574/72/EEC.

Article 71

RELEVANT DECISIONS OF THE ADMINISTRATIVE COMMISSION

Decision No 160 of 28 November 1995 concerning the scope of Article 71(1)(b)(ii) of Council regulation (EEC) No 1408/71 relating to the right to unemployment benefits of workers, other than frontier workers, who, during their last employment, were residing in the territory of a Member State other than the competent State, [1996] OJ L49/31.

GENERAL NOTE

Some of the rigours of the limited aggregation and exportability rules is moderated by the provisions of Art.71, which concern situations in which the claimant was residing, during their last period of work, in a country other than the competent State. Since the provisions of Art.71 are exceptions to the rules in Arts 67 and 69, the Court of Justice has said that they must be strictly interpreted: Case 76/76 *di Paolo* [1977] E.C.R. 315, paras 12 and 13 of the judgment.

3.241

The rules in Art.71(1)(a) concern frontier workers, who are defined by Art.1(b) as persons who work in one Member State and reside in a different Member State to which they return "as a rule daily or at least once a week." Note that there is specific provision made in Art.1(b) for posted frontier workers enabling them to retain the status of frontier worker for four months even where the posting prevents them from returning home at least once a week.

Under Art.71(1)(a)(i), frontier workers who are "partially or intermittently unemployed" receive unemployment benefits in accordance with the legislation of the competent State as though they were residing there. Under Art.71(1)(a)(ii), frontier workers who are "wholly unemployed" receive unemployment benefits in accordance with the legislation of the country in which they reside as though they had been subject to that legislation while working.

Article 71(1)(b) deals with workers other than frontier workers, and is rather more complex, since it permits a wholly unemployed worker to choose whether unemployment benefits are paid in the country of last employment or in the country of residence. Article 71(1)(b)(i) provides that workers who are "partially, intermittently or wholly unemployed" and who remain available for work in the territory of the competent State receive unemployment benefits in accordance with the provisions of the legislation of the competent State as though they resided there. Article 71(1)(b)(ii) provides that wholly unemployed workers may make themselves available to the employment office in the country of residence and receive unemployment benefits there as though they had been last employed there.

The references to residence in Art.71 refer to the concept of "habitual residence" which has a specific meaning in Community law. Workers, other than frontier workers, will only be able to take advantage of the more favourable rules on entitlement to unemployment benefit if they can show that they were habitually resident in a country other than that in which they worked. For a decision of a Social Security Commissioner holding that a determination by the Inland Revenue that a person is "ordinarily resident" in the United Kingdom for tax purposes "has no relevant whatsoever" in assessing whether a person is habitually resident here, see *R(U)4/86*. It may be putting it too strongly to say that it has no relevance whatsoever, but it is clearly not determinative of the question. It is not difficult to imagine the complexity of the circumstances presented in many cases, where, for example, the employment is of comparatively short duration, or where a family is split with certain family members remaining in one country while others live with the worker in the place of work. For a useful survey of the case-law on Art.71(1)(b)(ii), see the Advocate General's Opinion in Case 388/87 *Warmerdam-Steggerda*, [1989] E.C.R. 1203. Article 71(2) contains anti-overlapping provisions precluding the payment of unemployment benefits in the country of residence alongside payment of benefits under the legislation of the country of last employment.

The Court in *di Paolo* had indicated that the special rules in Art.71 were justified for certain categories of workers who retain close ties, in particular of a personal and

1045

vocational nature, with the country where they have settled and are habitually resident. There is in such cases the best possibility of finding new employment in that country. It is consistent with this principle to permit a person to change their habitual residence from the country of work to another country during the course of their employment.

In Case 236/87 *Bergemann* [1988] E.C.R. 5125 Anna Bergemann, a Dutch national living and working in the Netherlands, married and during a period of leave moved to Germany with her husband. She remained on leave from her employment until it ended and did not return to the Netherlands. The question arose as to whether Art.71(1)(b)(ii) applied to someone in her situation. Having regard to the justification set out above, the Court concluded that her move during a period of leave and the fact that she had not returned to work in the Netherlands did not preclude her being regarded as within the terms of the article.

Similarly, the Court had little difficulty in regarding a university employee who had undertaken a fixed term two year exchange with a university in another Member State and who returned home in the vacations as falling within the ambit of the provision: Case C-216/89 *Reibold* [1990] E.C.R. I-4163.

In such cases account should be taken of the duration and continuity of the residence of the persons concerned before they moved, of the length and purpose of their absence, of the nature of the work in the other EEA country, and of their intentions as ascertained from all the surrounding circumstances.

The circumstances presented in Case C-102/91 *Knoch* [1991] E.C.R. I-4341, were a little more complex. Doris Knoch was employed at the University of Bath as a language assistant for two years. At the end of her contract she claimed and was awarded unemployment benefit in England for the best part of July and August. She subsequently returned to Germany where she claimed unemployment benefit in December. The question arose as to whether she could claim in Germany after having claimed in England, and, if so, how the German authorities should deal with any unemployment benefit paid in England. The Court rules that, provided that Knoch was habitually resident in Germany during her employment in England, she was entitled to the benefit of the rules in Art.71. There was nothing in those rules which precluded a person first claiming under the legislation of the country where they were employed and subsequently in the country in which they were habitually resident. However, the benefits received would almost certainly overlap under the provisions of Art.12 of Reg.1408/71. It followed that in determining entitlement under the legislation of the country of residence, a deduction should be made of the benefit received in respect of the days for which unemployment benefit had been paid in the country of employment. Entitlement to unemployment benefit would, of course, be suspended for any period in which such a person exported their unemployment benefit entitlement in accordance with the rules in Art.69. Case C-287/92 *Toosey* [1994] E.C.R. I-279, reported as *R(S) 7/94*, concerned a British national who had last worked in the United Kingdom in 1964–65. She then moved to Belgium where she worked until 1982, when she became disabled. She subsequently moved back to the United Kingdom. She claimed severe disablement allowance, but was refused on the basis that she had not been resident in Great Britain for ten of the twenty years preceding her claim. The Court of Justice ruled that the determining factor as to whether Art.71 applied at all is the residence of the person concerned in a Member State other than that to whose legislation she was subject during her last employment. This meant that the first sentence of Art.71(1)(b)(ii) did not apply to a worker in the position of the claimant who was resident in the State of employment, that is, Belgium, when the incapacity for work followed by invalidity occurred.

Article 71a

[¹ SECTION 4

PERSONS COVERED BY A SPECIAL SCHEME FOR CIVIL SERVANTS

Article 71a

1. The provisions of Sections 1 and 2 shall apply to persons covered by a special unemployment scheme for civil servants.
2. The provisions of Section 3 shall not apply to persons covered by a special unemployment scheme for civil servants. An unemployed person who is covered by a special scheme for civil servants, who is partially or wholly unemployed, and who, during his last employment, was residing in the territory of a Member State other than the competent State, shall receive benefits in accordance with the provisions of the legislation of the competent State as if he were residing in the territory of that State; these benefits shall be provided by the competent institution at its expense.]

3.242

AMENDMENT

1. Regulation 1606/98/EC, [1998] OJ L209/1 (October 25, 1998).

CHAPTER 7

FAMILY BENEFITS

GENERAL NOTE

Where entitlement to benefits is conditional on the completion of periods of insurance, employment or self-employment, there is the usual requirement that such periods completed in the territory of an EEA country other than the competent State are to be treated as completed under the legislation of the competent State: Art.72. The normal rule is that entitlement to family benefits is determined in accordance with the law of the EEA country in which the claimant is employed or self-employed. Where the children reside in a different country, they are treated as residing in the EEA country where the claimant is in work: Art.73. Those who are wholly unemployed and come within the provisions of Article 71(1)(a)(ii) or 71(1)(b)(ii) are, however, entitled to benefits under the legislation of the country of their residence for the family members residing with them: Art.72a. Other unemployed persons are entitled to family benefits from the country responsible for their unemployment benefits: Art.74. There are a number of special situations which may need to be considered. Where entitlement arises under Arts 73 or 74, this is made subject to the provisions of the substantial Annex VI which sets out special procedures for applying the legislation of certain countries. Provision is made in Article 75 for payment to an institution or person actually maintaining the members of the family rather than to the claimant "if the family benefits are not used by the person to whom they should be provided for the maintenance of the members of the family."

The above rules are easy to understand. Complications, however, arise where entitlement to family benefits arises in more than one country. In the United Kingdom child benefit is normally payable to the mother (provided that she is responsible for

3.243

the maintenance of the children, which is presumed where the children are living with her), but this is not universally the case. Equally family benefits may be payable on the basis of residence rather than the completion of insurance periods. Finally, both parents may be working in different countries and have an entitlement by reason of their occupation. This situation can be illustrated by the facts of Case C-119/91 *McMenamin* [1992] E.C.R. I-6393. The family lived in Ireland, where the father worked. The mother was a frontier worker crossing into Northern Ireland each working day to teach there. The family claimed and received child benefits in Ireland. The mother claimed child benefits in Northern Ireland on the basis of her employment there. Since the effect of the provisions of chapter 7 of Title II was that her children were treated as residing in Northern Ireland, she met the conditions of entitlement to child benefits in Northern Ireland. Much of the case-law of the Court of Justice has been concerned with the application of provisions for dealing with the overlap of such benefits in such cases as this. The provisions of Regulation 1408/71 have been modified in this regard on many occasions.

The current position is governed by Article 76 of Regulation 1408/71 and Article 10 and 10a of Regulation 574/72. Article 76 deals with overlapping benefits where family benefits are provided by the country of residence in addition to the legislation of some other country. Where the benefits in the country of residence of the family members are provided:

- during the same period, and
- for the same family members, and
- by reason of the claimant carrying on an occupation,

benefits payable under the legislation of another country are suspended "up to the amount provided for in the legislation of the country of residence of the family members." In this way, the family gets the higher of the family benefits in the two countries, but the payment of those benefits may be apportioned between them. Article 76(2) effectively requires a claim to be made in the country where the family members resides, since the other country may suspend the benefits up to the amount provided in the legislation of the country of residence even if a claim for benefit there is not made. But it is clear that the provision will only apply where entitlement to the benefit exists: Case 134/77 *Ragazzoni* [1978] E.C.R. 963.

Article 10(1)(a) of Regulation 574/72 makes corresponding provision where entitlement is not subject to conditions of insurance, employment or self-employment. Again the effect is either that the higher of two benefits is alone payable, or that the lower benefits are topped up in the other country by the difference between that amount and the higher amount which it pays. The possible permutations are considerable, but the overall effect of chapter 7 of Title II is to produce a result which means that the family effectively gets the benefit of the most favourable regime among those countries to whose legislation it is subject.

Article 72

Aggregation of periods of insurance, employment or self-employment

3.244 Where the legislation of a Member State makes acquisition of the right to benefits conditional upon completion of periods of insurance, employment or self-employment, the competent institution of that State shall take into account for this purpose, to the extent necessary, periods of insurance, employment or self-employment completed in any other Member State, as if they were periods completed under the legislation which it administers.

Article 72

Relevant Provisions of the Implementing Regulation

Art.85, Reg.574/72/EEC.

Article 72a

Employed persons who have become fully unemployed

An employed person who has become fully unemployed and to whom Article 71(1)(a)(ii) or (b)(ii), first sentence, apply shall, for the members of his family residing in the territory of the same Member State as he, receive family benefits in accordance with the legislation of the State, as if he had been subject to that legislation during his last employment, taking account, where appropriate, of the provisions of Article 72. These benefits shall be provided by, and at the expense of, the institution of the place of residence.

Where that institution applies legislation providing for deduction of contributions payable by unemployed persons to cover family benefits, it shall be authorized to make such deductions in accordance with the provisions of its legislation.

Article 73

Employed or self-employed persons the members of whose families reside in a Member State other than the competent State

An employed or self-employed person subject to the legislation of a Member State shall be entitled, in respect of the members of his family who are residing in another Member State, to the family benefits provided for by the legislation of the former State, as if they were residing in that State, subject to the provisions of Annex VI.

Relevant Provisions of the Implementing Regulation

Art.86, Reg.574/72/EEC.

Relevant Decisions of the Administrative Commission

Decision No 142 of 13 February 1990 concerning the application of Articles 73, 74 and 75 of Regulation (EEC) No 1408/71, [1990] OJ C80/7.

Decision No 145 of 27 June 1990 concerning the payment of arrears of family benefits due to self-employed persons pursuant to Articles 73 and 74 of Regulation (EEC) No 1408/71, [1991] OJ C235/1.

General Note

In *CF/667/1997* the Commissioner at paras 19–25 examines the question which needs to be considered in determining the entitlement of parents, resident in France, to child benefit under United Kingdom law under Art.73 of the Regulation.

Article 74

Unemployed persons the members of whose families reside in a Member State other than the competent State

An unemployed person who was formerly employed or self-employed and who draws unemployment benefits under the legislation of a Member State shall be entitled, in respect of the members of his family residing in another Member State, to the family benefits provided for by the legislation of the former State, as if they were residing in that State, subject to the provisions of Annex VI.

Relevant Provisions of the Implementing Regulation

Art.88, Reg.574/72/EEC.

Relevant Decisions of the Administrative Commission

Decision No 142 of 13 February 1990 concerning the application of Articles 73, 74 and 75 of Regulation (EEC) No 1408/71, [1990] OJ C80/7.

Decision No 145 of 27 June 1990 concerning the payment of arrears of family benefits due to self-employed persons pursuant to Articles 73 and 74 of Regulation (EEC) No 1408/71, [1991] OJ C235/1.

Article 75

Provisions of benefits

1. Family benefits shall be provided, in the cases referred to in Article 73, by the competent institution of the State to the legislation of which the employed or self-employed person is subject and, in the cases referred to in Article 74, by the competent institution of the State under the legislation of which an unemployed person who was formerly employed or self-employed receives unemployment benefits. They shall be provided in accordance with the provisions administered by such institutions, whether or not the natural or legal person to whom such benefits are payable is residing or staying in the territory of the competent State or in that of another Member State.

2. However, if the family benefits are not used by the person to whom they should be provided for the maintenance of the members of the family, the competent institution shall discharge its legal obligations by providing the said benefits to the natural or legal person actually maintaining the members of the family, at the request of, and through the agency of, the institution of their place of residence or of the designated institution or body appointed for this purpose by the competent authority of the country of their residence.

3. Two or more Member States may agree, in accordance with the provisions of Article 8, that the competent institution shall provide the family benefits due under the legislation of those States or of one of those States to the natural or legal person actually maintaining the members of the family, either directly or through the agency of the institution of their place of residence.

Relevant Provisions of the Implementing Regulation

Art.86, Reg.574/72/EEC.

Relevant Decisions of the Administrative Commission

Decision No 142 of 13 February 1990 concerning the application of Articles 73, 74 and 75 of Regulation (EEC) No 1408/71, [1990] OJ C80/7.

Article 76

Article 76

Rules or priority in cases of overlapping entitlement to family benefits under the legislation of the competent State and under the legislation of the Member State of residence of the members of the family

1. Where, during the same period, for the same family member and by reason of carrying on an occupation, family benefits are provided for by the legislation of the Member State in whose territory the members of the family are residing, entitlement to the family benefits due in accordance with the legislation of another Member State, if appropriate under Article 73 or 74, shall be suspended up to the amount provided for in the legislation of the first Member State.

2. If an application for benefits is not made in the Member States in whose territory the members of the family are residing, the competent institution of the other Member State may apply the provisions of paragraph 1 as if benefits were granted in the first Member State.

3.250

RELEVANT DECISIONS OF THE ADMINISTRATIVE COMMISSION

Decision No 119 of 24 February 1983 concerning the interpretation of Article 76 and Article 79(3) of regulation (EEC) No 1408/71 and of Article 10(1) of Regulation (EEC) No 574/72 relating to the overlapping of family benefits and allowances, [1983] OJ C295/3.

Decision No 147 of 10 October 1990 concerning the application of Article 76 of regulation (EEC) No 1408/71, [1991] OJ C235/21.

[1 *Article 76a*

Students

The provisions of Article 72 shall apply by analogy to students.]

3.251

AMENDMENT

1. Regulation 307/99/EC, [1999] OJ L38/1 (May 1, 1999).

CHAPTER 8

BENEFITS FOR DEPENDENT CHILDREN OF PENSIONERS AND FOR ORPHANS

Article 77

Dependent children of pensioners

1. The term "benefits", for the purposes of this Article, shall mean family allowances for persons receiving pensions for old age, invalidity or an accident at work or occupational disease, and increases or supplements to such pensions in respect of the children of such pensioners, with the exception of

3.252

Council Regulation (EEC) No 1408/71

supplements granted under insurance schemes for accidents at work and occupational diseases.

2. Benefits shall be granted in accordance with the following rules, irrespective of the Member State in whose territory the pensioner or the children are residing:
- (a) to a pensioner who draws a pension under the legislation of one Member State only, in accordance with the legislation of the Member State responsible for the pension;
- (b) to a pensioner who draws pensions under the legislation of more than one Member State:
  - (i) in accordance with the legislation of whichever of these States he resides in provided that, taking into account, where appropriate, the provisions of Article 79(1)(a), a right to one of the benefits referred to in paragraph 1 is acquired under the legislation of that State;

    or
  - (ii) in other cases in accordance with the legislation of the Member State to which he has been subject for the longest period of time, provided that, taking into account, where appropriate, the provisions of Article 79(1)(a), a right to one of the benefits referred to in paragraph 1 is acquired under such legislation; if no right to benefit is acquired under that legislation, the conditions for the acquisition of such right under the legislations of the other Member States concerned shall be examined in decreasing order of the length of periods of insurance or residence completed under the legislation of those Member States.

RELEVANT PROVISIONS OF THE IMPLEMENTING REGULATION

Arts 90–92, Reg.574/72/EEC.

RELEVANT DECISIONS OF THE ADMINISTRATIVE COMMISSION

Decision No 150 of 26 June 1992 concerning the application of Articles 77, 78 and 79(3) of Regulation (EEC) No 1408/71 and of Article 10 of regulation (EEC) No 574/72, [1993] OJ C229/5.

GENERAL NOTE

3.253   In *R(F) 1/94* the Commissioner ruled that the pension which the pensioners must be in receipt of has to be a pension awarded on the grounds of old age, invalidity, industrial accident or occupational disease. It did not cover a Fire Brigade Medical Discharge pension. In *R(F) 1/98* the Commissioner concluded that war or service pensions are also generally outside the scope of pensions which bring Art.77 into play. The claimant was in receipt of a service pension and an invalidity pension, but the latter was not payable because it was wholly offset by the higher service pension that was in payment. The Commissioner added the following important rider to the proposition that war or service pensions are generally outside Art.77:

> "22. In my judgment therefore, a person 'draws a pension for invalidity' for the purposes of Art.77 so long as he has a present entitlement to it and in fact receives payment equal to or exceeding the amount of that entitlement, **either** by means of the general arrangements for payment of such benefit under the national social security scheme, **or** by receiving payment out of public funds under some other scheme which the terms of the social security scheme integrate with itself *pro tanto* by making the other payment in effect satisfy the social security entitlement.

Article 77

Whether this is viewed in strict analysis as the person 'drawing' the social security pension by another means or as the scheme that actually pays him being brought within the scope *ratione materiae of* the EEC Regulation to the limited extent to which it thus becomes integrated with the national social security scheme, does not seem to me greatly to matter."

Article 78

Orphans

[¹ **1.** The term "benefits", for the purposes of this Article, means family allowances and, where appropriate, supplementary or special allowances for orphans.]

2. Orphans' benefits shall be granted in accordance with the following rules, irrespective of the Member State in whose territory the orphan or the natural or legal person actually maintaining him is resident:
- (a) for the orphan of a deceased employed or self-employed person who was subject to the legislation of one Member State only in accordance with the legislation of that State;
- (b) for the orphan of a deceased employed or self-employed person who was subject to the legislation of several Member States:
    - (i) in accordance with the legislation of the Member State in whose territory the orphan resides provided that, taking into account, where appropriate, the provisions of Article 79(1)(a), a right to one of the benefits referred to in paragraph 1 is acquired under the legislation of that State;
    - (ii) in other cases in accordance with the legislation of the Member State to which the deceased had been subject for the longest period of time, provided that, taking into account, where appropriate, the provisions of Article 79(1)(a), the right to one of the benefits referred to in paragraph 1 is acquired under the legislation of that State; if no right is acquired under that legislation, the conditions for the acquisition of such right under the legislations of the other Member States shall be examined in decreasing order of the length of periods of insurance or residence completed under the legislation of those Member States.

However, the legislation of the Member State applicable in respect of provisions of the benefits referred to in Article 77 for a pensioner's children shall remain applicable after the death of the said pensioner in respect of the provisions of the benefits to his orphans.

3.254

AMENDMENT

1. Regulation 1399/99/EC, [1999] OJ L164/1 (September 1, 1999).

RELEVANT PROVISIONS OF THE IMPLEMENTING REGULATION

Arts 90–92, Reg.574/72/EEC.

RELEVANT DECISIONS OF THE ADMINISTRATIVE COMMISSION

Decision No 150 of 26 June 1992 concerning the application of Articles 77, 78 and 79(3) of Regulation (EEC) No 1408/71 and of Article 10 of regulation (EEC) No 574/72, [1993] OJ C229/5.

Council Regulation (EEC) No 1408/71

[¹ Article 78a

3.255 Orphans' pensions, except those granted under insurance schemes for accidents at work and occupational diseases, shall be treated as 'benefits' within the scope of Article 78(1) if the deceased was at any time covered by a scheme which provides only family allowances or supplementary or special allowances for orphans. These schemes are listed in Annex VIII.]

AMENDMENT

1. Regulation 1399/99/EC, [1999] OJ L164/1 (September 1, 1999).

Article 79

Provisions common to benefits for dependent children of pensioners and for orphans

3.256 1. Benefits, within the meaning of [¹ Articles 77, 78 and 78a], shall be provided in accordance with the legislation determined by applying the provisions of those Articles by the institution responsible for administering such legislation and at its expense as if the pensioner or the deceased had been subject only to the legislation of the competent State.
However:
(a) if that legislation provides that the acquisition, retention or recovery of the right to benefits shall be dependent on the length of periods of insurance, employment, self-employment or residence such length shall be determined taking into account, where appropriate, the provisions of Article 45 or, as the case may be, Article 72;
(b) if that legislation provides that the amount of benefits shall be calculated on the basis of the amount of the pension, or shall depend on the length of periods of insurance the amount of these benefits shall be calculated on the basis of the theoretical amount determined in accordance with the provisions of Article 46(2).

2. In a case where the effect of applying the rule laid down in Articles 77(2)(b)(ii) and 78(2)(b)(ii) would be to make several Member States competent, the length of the periods being equal, benefits within the meaning of Article [¹ 77, 78 or 78a], as the case may be, shall be granted in accordance with the legislation of the Member States to which the pensioner or the deceased was last subject.

3. The right to benefits due only under the national legislation or under the provisions of paragraph 2 and under [1 Articles 77, 78 and 78a] shall be suspended if the children become entitled to family benefits or family allowances under the legislation of a Member State by virtue of the pursuit of a professional or trade activity. In such a case, the persons concerned shall be considered as members of the family of an employed or self-employed person.

AMENDMENT

1. Regulation 1399/99/EC, [1999] OJ L164/1 (September 1, 1999).

Article 79

RELEVANT PROVISIONS OF THE IMPLEMENTING REGULATION

Arts 90–92, Reg.574/72/EEC.

RELEVANT DECISIONS OF THE ADMINISTRATIVE COMMISSION

Decision No 119 of 24 February 1983 concerning the interpretation of Article 76 and Article 79(3) of regulation (EEC) No 1408/71 and of Article 10(1) of Regulation (EEC) No 574/72 relating to the overlapping of family benefits and allowances, [1983] OJ C295/3.

Decision No 150 of 26 June 1992 concerning the application of Articles 77, 78 and 79(3) of Regulation (EEC) No 1408/71 and of Article 10 of regulation (EEC) No 574/72, [1993] OJ C229/5.

[¹ *Article 79a*

Provisions relating to benefits for orphans entitled to benefits under a special scheme for civil servants

1. Notwithstanding the provisions of [² Article 78a], orphans' pensions drawn under a special scheme for civil servants shall be calculated in accordance with the provisions of Chapter 3.

2. Where, in a case provided for in paragraph 1, periods of insurance, employment, self-employment or residence have been completed under a general scheme, then benefits due under that general scheme shall be paid in accordance with the provisions of Chapter 8 [² unless otherwise provided for in Article 44(3)]. Periods of insurance, self-employment or employment completed in accordance with the legislation of a special scheme for civil servants or periods which are regarded by the legislation of that Member State as equivalent to such periods, shall, where appropriate, be taken into account for the acquisition, retention or recovery of the rights to benefit in accordance with the legislation of the general scheme.]

AMENDMENTS

1. Regulation 1606/98/EC, [1998] OJ L209/1 (October 25, 1998).
2. Regulation 1399/99/EC, [1999] OJ L164/1 (September 1, 1999).

TITLE IV

ADMINISTRATIVE COMMISSION ON SOCIAL SECURITY FOR MIGRANT WORKERS

Article 80

Composition and working methods

1. There shall be attached to the Commission an Administrative Commission on Social Security for Migrant Workers (hereinafter called

Council Regulation (EEC) No 1408/71

"the Administrative Commission") made up of a government representative of each of the Member States, assisted, where necessary, by expert advisers. A representative of the Commission shall attend the meetings of the Administrative Commission in an advisory capacity.

2. The Administrative Commission shall be assisted in technical matters by the International Labour Office under the terms of the agreements concluded to that end between the European Community and the International Labour Organization.

3. The rules of the Administrative Commission shall be drawn up by mutual agreement among its members.

Decisions on questions of interpretation referred to in Article 81 (a) shall be unanimous. They shall be given the necessary publicity.

4. Secretarial services shall be provided for the Administrative Commission by the Commission.

Article 81

Tasks of the Administrative Commission

The Administrative Commission shall have the following duties:
   (a) to deal with all administrative questions and questions of interpretation arising from the provisions of this Regulation and subsequent Regulations, or from any agreement or arrangement concluded thereunder, without prejudice to the right of the authorities, institutions and persons concerned to have recourse to the procedures and tribunals provided for by the legislations of Member States, by this Regulation or by the Treaty;
   (b) to carry out all translations of documents relating to the implementation of this Regulation at the request of the competent authorities, institutions and tribunals of the Member States, and in particular translations of claims submitted by persons who may be entitled to benefit under the provisions of this Regulation;
   (c) to foster and develop cooperation between Member States in social security matters, particularly in respect of health and social measures of common interest;
   (d) [1 to foster and develop co-operation between Member States by modernizing procedures for exchange of information, in particular by adapting the information flow between institutions for the purpose of telematic exchange, taking account of the development of data processing in each Member State. The main aim of such modernization shall be to expedite the award of benefits.]
   (e) to assemble the factors to be taken into consideration for drawing up accounts relating to the costs to be borne by the institutions of the Member States under the provisions of this Regulation and to adopt the annual accounts between the said institutions;
   (f) to undertake any other function coming within its competence under the provisions of this and of subsequent Regulations or any agreement or arrangement made thereunder;
   (g) to submit proposals to the Commission for working out subsequent Regulations and for the revision of this and subsequent Regulations.

Article 81

AMENDMENT

1. Regulation 1290/97/EC, [1997] OJ L176/1 (October 4, 1997).

GENERAL NOTE

The Administrative Commission from time to time makes decisions on the interpretation and application of provisions of Regulation 1408/71 and Regulation 574/72. These are for guidance, but often provide very helpful guidance; they also often address concerns which have been expressed by Member States in the meetings of the Administrative Commission. The most important decisions are reported in the *Official Journal*.

3.260

TITLE V

ADVISORY COMMITTEE ON SOCIAL SECURITY FOR MIGRANT WORKERS

Article 82

ESTABLISHMENT, COMPOSITION AND WORKING METHODS

1. An advisory Committee on Social Security for Migrant Workers (hereinafter called "the Advisory Committee") is hereby established, with [^{1} 150] members comprising, from each Member State:
   (a) two representatives of the government, of whom one at least must be a member of the Administrative Commission;
   (b) two representatives of trade unions;
   (c) two representatives of employers' organizations.
   For each of the categories referred to above, an alternate member shall be appointed for each Member State.

3.261

2. Members of the Advisory Committee and their alternates shall be appointed by the Council which shall endeavour, when selecting representatives of trade unions and employers' organizations, to achieve an equitable representation on the Committee of the various sectors concerned.
   The list of members and their alternates shall be published by the Council in the *Official Journal of the European Communities*.

3. The term of office for members and alternates shall be two years. Their appointments may be renewed. On expiry of their term of office, members and alternates shall remain in office until they are replaced or until their appointments are renewed.

4. The Advisory Committee shall be chaired by a representative of the Commission. The chairman shall not vote.

5. The Advisory Committee shall meet at least once each year. It shall be convened by its chairman, either on his own initiative or on written application to him by at least one-third of the members. Such application must include concrete proposals concerning the agenda.

6. Acting on a proposal from its chairman, the Advisory Committee may decide, in exceptional circumstances, to take advice from any persons or representatives of organizations with extensive experience in social security matters. Furthermore, the Committee shall receive technical assistance from the International Labour Office under the same conditions as

the Administrative Commission, under the terms of the agreement concluded between the European Community and the International Labour Organization.

7. The opinions and proposals of the Advisory Committee must state the reasons on which they are based. They shall be delivered by an absolute majority of the votes validly cast.

The Committee shall, by a majority of its members, draw up its rules of procedure which shall be approved by the Council, after receiving the opinion of the Commission.

8. Secretarial services shall be provided for the Advisory Committee by the Commission.

AMENDMENT

1. Annex 2 of Treaty of Accession (May 1, 2004).

Article 83

Tasks of the Advisory Committee

3.262   The Advisory Committee shall be empowered, at the request of the Commission of the European Communities, of the Administrative Commission or on its own initiative:
(a) to examine general questions or questions of principle and problems arising from the implementation of the Regulations adopted within the framework of the provisions of Article 51 of the Treaty;
(b) to formulate opinions on the subject for the Administrative Commission and proposals for any revision of the Regulations.

TITLE VI

MISCELLANEOUS PROVISIONS

Article 84

Cooperation between competent authorities

3.263   1. The competent authorities of Member States shall communicate to each other all information regarding:
(a) measures taken to implement this Regulation:
(b) changes in their legislation which are likely to affect the implementation of this Regulation.

2. For the purposes of implementing this Regulation, the authorities and institutions of Member States shall lend their good offices and act as though implementing their own legislation. The administrative assistance furnished by the said authorities and institutions shall, as a rule, be free of charge. However, the competent authorities of the Member States may agree to certain expenses being reimbursed.

Article 84

3. The authorities and institutions of Member States may, for the purpose of implementing this Regulation, communicate directly with one another and with the persons concerned or their representatives.

4. The authorities, institutions and tribunals of one Member State may not reject claims or other documents submitted to them on the grounds that they are written in an official language of another Member State. They shall have recourse where appropriate to the provisions of Article 81(b).

5. (a) Where, under this Regulation or under the implementing Regulation referred to in Article 98, the authorities or institutions of a Member State communicate personal data to the authorities or institutions of another Member State, that communication shall be subject to the legal provisions governing protection of data laid down by the Member State providing the data.
Any subsequent transmission as well as the storage, alteration and destruction of the data shall be subject to the provisions of the legislation on data protection of the receiving Member State.
(b) The use of personal data for purposes other than those of social security shall be subject to the approval of the person concerned or in accordance with the other guarantees provided for by national legislation.

[¹*Article 84a*

Relations between the institutions and the persons covered by this Regulation

1. The institutions and persons covered by this Regulation shall have a duty of mutual information and cooperation to ensure the correct implementation of this Regulation.

The institutions, in accordance with the principle of good administration, shall respond to all queries within a reasonable period of time and shall in this connection provide the persons concerned with any information required for exercising the rights conferred on them by this Regulation.

The persons concerned shall inform the institution of the competent State and of the State of residence as soon as possible of any changes in their personal or family situation which affect their right to benefits under this Regulation.

2. Failure to respect the obligation of information referred to in paragraph 1, third subparagraph, may result in the application of proportionate measures in accordance with national law. Nevertheless, these measures shall be equivalent to those applicable to similar situations under domestic law and shall not make it impossible or excessively difficult in practice for claimants to exercise the rights conferred on them by this Regulation.

3. In the event of difficulties in the interpretation or application of this Regulation which could jeopardise the rights of a person covered by it, the institution of the competent State or of the State of residence of the person involved shall contact the institution(s) of the Member State(s) concerned. If a solution cannot be found within a reasonable period, the authorities concerned may call on the Administrative Commission to intervene.]

AMENDMENT

1. Regulation 631/2004/EC, [2004] OJ L100/1 (June 1, 2004).

Article 85

Exemptions from or reductions of taxes—Exemption from authentication

3.265　**1.** Any exemption from or reduction of taxes, stamp duty, notarial or registration fees provided for in the legislation of one Member State in respect of certificates or documents required to be produced for the purposes of the legislation of that State shall be extended to similar documents required to be produced for the purposes of the legislation of another Member State or of this Regulation.

2. All statements, documents and certificates of any kind whatsoever required to be produced for the purposes of this Regulation shall be exempt from authentication by diplomatic or consular authorities.

[1 **3.** An electronic message sent by an institution in conformity with the provisions of this Regulation and the implementing Regulation may not be rejected by any authority or institution of another Member State on the grounds that it was received by electronic means, once the receiving institution has declared its ability to receive electronic messages. Reproduction and recording of such messages shall be presumed to be a correct and accurate reproduction of the original document or recording of the information it relates to, unless there is proof to the contrary.

An electronic message shall be considered valid if the computer system on which the message is recorded contains the safeguards necessary in order to avoid any alteration, disclosure or access to the recording. It shall at any time be possible to reproduce the information recorded in directly legible form. When an electronic message is transferred from one social security institution to another, appropriate security measures shall be taken in accordance with the relevant Community provisions.]

AMENDMENT

1. Regulation 1290/97/EC, [1997] OJ L176/1 (October 4, 1997).

Article 86

Claims, declarations or appeals submitted to an authority, institution or tribunal of a Member State other than the competent State

3.266　**1.** Any claim, declaration or appeal which should have been submitted, in order to comply with the legislation of one Member State, within a specified period to an authority, institution or tribunal of that State shall be admissible if it is submitted within the same period to a corresponding authority, institution or tribunal of another Member State. In such a case the authority, institution, or tribunal receiving the claim, declaration or

Article 86

appeal shall forward it without delay to the competent authority, institution or tribunal of the former State either directly or through the competent authorities of the Member State concerned. The date on which such claims, declarations or appeals were submitted to the authority, institution or tribunal of the Second State shall be considered as the date of their submission to the competent authority, institution or tribunal.

2. Where a person entitled to do so under the legislation of a Member State has submitted to that State a claim for family benefits even though that State is not competent by priority right, the date on which that first application was made shall be considered as the date on which it was submitted to the competent authority, institution or tribunal, provided that a new application is submitted in the Member State which is competent by priority right by a person entitled to do so under the legislation of that State. The second application must be submitted within a period of one year after notification of the rejection of the first application or the cessation of payment of benefits in the first Member State.

GENERAL NOTE

This Article contains the important provision that a claim made to a State other than the competent State is to be forwarded to the competent State without delay and is to be treated by that State as a claim made in time if it was received within the relevant time limit in the first State.

3.267

Article 87

Medical examinations

1. Medical examinations provided for by the legislation of one Member State may be carried out at the request of the competent institution, in the territory of another Member State, by the institution of the place of stay or residence of the person entitled to benefits, under conditions laid down in the implementing Regulation referred to in Article 98 or, failing these, under conditions agreed upon between the competent authorities of the Member States concerned.

3.268

2. Medical examinations carried out under the conditions laid down in paragraph 1 shall be considered as having been carried out in the territory of the competent State.

Article 88

Transfers from one Member State to another of sums of money payable pursuant to this Regulation

Where appropriate, money transfers effected in accordance with this Regulation shall be made in accordance with the relevant agreements in force between the Member States concerned at the time of transfer. Where no such agreements are in force between two Member States, the competent authorities of the said States or the authorities responsible for

3.269

Article 89

Special procedures for implementing certain legislations

3.270   Special procedures for implementing the legislations of certain Member States are set out in Annex VI.

GENERAL NOTE

3.271   Note that there are special rules in Annex VI for determining the applicable legislation. So far as the United Kingdom is concerned, these contains multiple provisions including special rules where Article 13(2)(f) comes into play.

Article 90

3.272   [. . .]

Article 91

Contributions chargeable to employers or undertakings not established in the competent State

3.273   An employer shall not be bound to pay increased contributions by reason of the fact that his place of business or the registered office or place of business of his undertaking is in the territory of a Member State other than the competent State.

Article 92

Collection of contributions

3.274   **1.** Contributions payable to an institution of one Member State may be collected in the territory of another Member State in accordance with the administrative procedure and with the guarantees and privileges applicable to the collection of contributions payable to the corresponding institution of the latter State.

2. The procedure for the implementation of the provisions of paragraph 1 shall be governed, in so far as is necessary, by the implementing Regulation referred to in Article 98 or by means of agreements between Member States. Such implementing procedures may also cover procedures for enforcing payment.

Article 93

Rights of institutions responsible for benefits against liable third parties

1. If a person receives benefits under the legislation of one Member State in respect of an injury resulting from an occurrence in the territory of another State, any rights of the institution responsible for benefits against a third party bound to compensate for the injury shall be governed by the following rules:
   (a) Where the institution responsible for benefits is, by virtue of the legislation which it administers, subrogated to the rights which the recipient has against the third party, such subrogation shall be recognized by each Member State.
   (b) Where the said institution has direct rights against the third party, such rights shall be recognized by each Member State.
2. If a person receives benefits under the legislation of one Member State in respect of an injury resulting from an occurrence in the territory of another Member State, the provisions of the said legislation which determine in which cases the civil liability of employers or of the persons employed by them is to be excluded shall apply with regard to the said person or to the competent institution.

The provisions of paragraph 1 shall also apply to any rights of the institution responsible for benefit against an employer or the persons employed by him in cases where their liability is not excluded.

3. Where, in accordance with the provisions of Article 36(3) and/or Article 63(3), two or more Member States or the competent authorities of those States have concluded an agreement to waive reimbursement between institutions under their jurisdiction, any rights arising against a liable third party shall be governed by the following rules:
   (a) Where the institution of the Member State of stay or residence awards benefits to a person in respect of an injury which was sustained within its territory, that institution, in accordance with the legislation which it administers, shall exercise the right to subrogation or direct action against the third party liable to provide compensation for the injury.
   (b) For the purpose of implementing (a):
      (i) the person receiving benefits shall be deemed to be insured with the institution of the place of stay or residence, and
      (ii) that institution shall be deemed to be the debtor institution.
   (c) The provisions of paragraphs 1 and 2 shall remain applicable in respect of any benefits not covered by the waiver agreement referred to in this paragraph.

3.275

Council Regulation (EEC) No 1408/71

Title VII

Transitional and Final Provisions

Article 94

Transitional provisions for employed persons

1. No right shall be acquired under this Regulation in respect of a period prior to 1 October, 1972 or to the date of its application in the territory of the Member State concerned or in a part of the territory of that State.

2. All periods of insurance and, where appropriate, all periods of employment or residence completed under the legislation of a Member State before 1 October, 1972 or before the date of its application in the territory of that Member State or in a part of the territory of that State shall be taken into consideration for the determination of rights acquired under the provisions of this Regulation.

3. Subject to the provisions of paragraph 1, a right shall be acquired under this Regulation even though it relates to a contingency which materialized prior to 1 October, 1972 or to the date of its application in the territory of the Member State concerned or in a part of the territory of that State.

4. Any benefit which has not been awarded or which has been suspended by reason of the nationality or place of residence of the person concerned shall, on the application of the person concerned, be awarded or resumed with effect from 1 October, 1972 or the date of its application in the territory of the Member State concerned or in a part of the territory of that State, provided that the rights previously determined have not given rise to a lump sum payment.

5. The rights of a person to whom a pension was awarded prior to 1 October, 1972 or to the date of its application in the territory of the Member State concerned or in a part of the territory of that State may, on the application of the person concerned, be reviewed, taking into account the provisions of this Regulation. This provision shall also apply to the other benefits referred to Article 78.

6. If an application referred to in paragraph 4 or 5 is submitted within two years from 1 October, 1972 or from the date of its application in the territory of the Member State concerned, the rights acquired under this Regulation shall have effect from that date, and the provisions of the legislation of any Member State concerning the forfeiture or limitation of rights may not be invoked against the persons concerned.

The same provisions shall apply as regards the application of this Regulation in those territories which became a part of the Federal Republic of Germany on 3 October, 1990 provided that the application referred to in paragraph 4 or 5 is submitted within two years of 1 June, 1992.

7. If an application referred to in paragraph 4 or 5 is submitted after the expiry of the two-year period after 1 October, 1972 or following the date of its application in the territory of the Member State concerned, rights which have not been forfeited or which are not time barred shall have effect from

Article 94

the date on which the application was submitted, except where more favourable provisions of the legislation of any Member state apply.

The same provisions shall apply as regards the application of this Regulation in those territories which became a part of the Federal Republic of Germany on 3 October, 1990 provided that the application referred to in paragraph 4 or 5 is submitted after two years have elapsed from 1 June, 1992.

8. In case of sclerogenic pneumoconiosis, the provision of Article 57(5) shall apply to cash benefits for an occupational disease the expense of which, in the absence of agreement between the institutions concerned, could not be divided between those institutions before 1 October, 1972.

9. The family allowances received by employed persons employed in France or unemployed workers receiving unemployment benefits under French legislation in respect of the members of their families residing in another Member State on the date of 15 November, 1989 shall continue to be paid at the rates, within the limits and according to the procedures applicable on that date as long as their amount exceeds that of the benefits that would be due as from the date of 16 November, 1989 and as long as the persons concerned are subject to French legislation. Account shall not be taken of interruptions lasting less than one month nor of periods during which unemployment or sickness is drawn.

The procedure for implementing this paragraph and in particular the sharing of the cost of these allowances shall be determined by mutual agreement between the Member States concerned or by their competent authorities after the Administrative Commission has delivered an opinion.

10. The rights of persons to whom a pension was awarded prior to the entry into force of Article 45 (6) may be reviewed at their request subject to the provisions of Article 45 (6).

RELEVANT DECISIONS OF THE ADMINISTRATIVE COMMISSION

Decision No 75 of 22 February 1973 concerning the investigation of applications for review made under Article 94(5) of regulation (EEC) No 1408/71 by invalidity pensioners, [1973] OJ C75/5.

Decision No 146 of 10 October 1990 concerning the interpretation of Article 94(9) of regulation (EEC) No 1408/71, [1991] OJ C235/9.

Article 95

Transitional provisions for self-employed persons

1. No right shall be acquired under this Regulation in respect of a period prior to 1 July, 1982 or to the date of its implementation in the territory of the Member State concerned or in a part of the territory of that State.

2. All insurance periods and, where appropriate, all periods of employments, of self-employment or of residence completed under the legislation of a Member State before 1 July, 1982 or before the date of implementation of this Regulation in the territory of that Member State or in a part of the territory of that State shall be taken into consideration for the determination of rights acquired under this Regulation.

3. Subject to paragraph 1, a right shall be acquired under this Regulation even though it relates to a contingency which materialized prior to 1 July,

3.277

1982 or to the date of implementation of this Regulation in the territory of the Member State concerned or in a part of the territory of that State.

4. Any benefit which has not been awarded or which has been suspended by reason of the nationality or place of residence of the person concerned shall, on the application of the person concerned, be awarded or resumed with effect from 1 July, 1982 or from the date of implementation of this Regulation in the territory of the Member State concerned or in a part of the territory of that State, provided that the rights previously determined have not given rise to a lump-sum payment.

5. The rights of a person to whom a pension was awarded prior to 1 July, 1982 or to the date of implementation of this Regulation in the territory of the Member State concerned or in a part of the territory of that State may, on the application of the person concerned, be reviewed, taking into account this Regulation. This provision shall also apply to the other benefits referred to in Article 78.

6. If an application referred to in paragraph 4 or 5 is submitted within two years of 1 July, 1982 or of the date of implementation of this Regulation in the territory of the Member State concerned, the rights acquired under this Regulation shall have effect from that date, and the provisions of the legislation of any Member State concerning the forfeiture or limitation of rights may not be invoked against the persons concerned.

The same provisions shall apply as regards the application of this Regulation in those territories which became a part of the Federal Republic of Germany on 4 October, 1990 provided that the application referred to in paragraph 4 or 5 is submitted within two years of 1 June, 1992.

7. If an application referred to in paragraph 4 or 5 is submitted after the expiry of the two-year period from 1 July, 1982 or following the date of implementation of this Regulation in the territory of the Member State concerned, rights which have not been forfeited or are not barred by limitation shall have effect from the date on which the application was submitted, except where more favourable provisions of the legislation of any Member State apply.

The same provisions shall apply as regards the application of this Regulation in those territories which became a part of the Federal Republic of Germany on 3 October, 1990 provided that the application referred to in paragraph 4 or 5 is submitted after two years have elapsed from 1 June, 1992.

Article 95a

Transitional provisions for application of Regulation (EEC) No 1248/92 [1992] OJ L136/7

1. Under Regulation (EEC) No 1248/92 no right shall be acquired for a period prior to 1 June 1992.

2. All insurance periods or periods of residence completed under the legislation of a Member State before 1 June 1992 shall be taken into consideration for the determination of rights to benefits pursuant to Regulation (EEC) No 1248/92.

3. Subject to paragraph 1, a right shall be acquired under Regulation (EEC) No 1248/92 even though relating to a contingency which materialized prior to 1 June 1992.

Article 95a

4. The rights of a person to whom a pension was awarded prior to 1 June 1992 may, on the application of the person concerned, be reviewed, taking into account the provisions of Regulation (EEC) No 1248/92.

5. If an application referred to in paragraph 4 is submitted within two years from 1 June 1992 the rights acquired under Regulation (EEC) No 1248/92 shall have effect from that date, and the provisions of the legislation of any Member State concerning the forfeiture of limitation of rights may not be invoked against the persons concerned.

6. If the application referred to in paragraph 4 is submitted after the expiry of the two-year period after 1 June 1992, rights which have not been forfeited or not barred by limitation shall have effect from the date on which the application was submitted, except where more favourable provisions of the legislation of any Member State apply.

Article 95b

Transitional provisions for application of Regulation (EEC) No 1247/92 [1992] OJ L136/1

1. Regulation (EEC) No 1247/92 shall not provide any entitlement for periods prior to 1 June 1992.

2. The periods of residence and periods of employment or of self-employment completed on the territory of a Member State before 1 June 1992 shall be taken into consideration for the determination of rights acquired under the provisions of Regulation (EEC) No 1247/92.

3. Subject to paragraph 1, a right shall be acquired pursuant to Regulation (EEC) No 1247/92 even where it relates to a contingency that occurred before 1 June 1992.

4. All special non-contributory benefits which have not been awarded or which have been suspended by reason of the nationality of the person concerned shall, on the application of the person concerned, be awarded or resumed with effect from 1 June 1992, provided that the rights previously determined have not given rise to a lump-sum payment.

5. The rights of persons to whom a pension was awarded prior to 1 June 1992, may, on the application of the persons concerned, be reviewed, taking account of the provisions of Regulation (EEC) No 1247/92.

6. If an application referred to in paragraph 4 or 5 is submitted within two years from 1 June 1992, the rights acquired pursuant to Regulation (EEC) No 1247/92 shall have effect from that date, and the provisions of the legislation of any Member State concerning the forfeiture or limitation of rights may not be invoked against the persons concerned.

7. If an application referred to in paragraph 4 or 5 is submitted after the expiry of the two-year period after 1 June 1992, rights which have not been forfeited or which are not time-barred shall have effect from the date on which the application was submitted, except where more favourable provisions of the legislation of any Member State apply.

8. The application of Article 1 of Regulation (EEC) No 1247/92 may not result in the withdrawal of benefits which are awarded before 1 June 1992 by the competent institutions of the Member State under Title III of Regulation (EEC) No 1408/71 to which Article 10 of the latter Regulation is applicable.

9. The application of Article 1 of Regulation (EEC) No 1247/92 may not result in the rejection of an application for a special non-contributory benefit awarded as a supplement to a pension, which was submitted by the person concerned who had satisfied the conditions for the award of this benefit before 1 June 1992, even where the person concerned resides on the territory of a Member State other than the competent Member State, provided that the application for the benefit is submitted within a period of five years starting from 1 June 1992.

10. Notwithstanding the provisions of paragraph 1, any special non-contributory benefit, granted as a supplement to a pension, which has not been awarded or which has been suspended by reason of the residence of the person concerned on the territory of a Member State other than the competent Member State shall, on the application of the person concerned, be awarded or resumed with effect from 1 June 1992, in the first case from the date on which the benefit should have been awarded, and in the second case on the date of suspension of the benefit.

11. Where special non-contributory bencfits as referred to in Article 4 (2a) of Regulation (EEC) No 1408/71 may, during the same period and for the same person, be granted pursuant to Article 10a of that Regulation by the competent institution of the Member State in the territory of which that person is resident and pursuant to paragraphs 1 to 10 of this Article by the competent institution of another Member State, the person concerned may only aggregate those benefits up to the limit of the highest amount of the special benefit he could claim under one of the legislations in question.

12. The detailed rules of application of paragraph 11, and in particular the application, with regard to the benefits referred to in that paragraph, of the clauses for reduction, suspension or abolition provided for under the legislation of one or more Member States and the allocation of the differential additional amounts shall be set by decision of the Administrative Commission on Social Security for Migrant Workers and, where appropriate, by common accord of the Member States concerned or their competent authorities.

[¹*Article 95c*

Transitional provisions for application of Regulation (EC) 1606/98 [1998] OJ L209/1

1. No rights shall be acquired under Regulation (EC) No 1606/98 for any period prior to 25 October 1998.

2. Any period of insurance and, where appropriate, any period of employment, self-employment or residence completed under the legislation of a Member State before 25 October 1998 shall be taken into account for the determination of rights acquired in accordance with the provisions of Regulation (EC) No 1606/98.

3. Subject to the provisions of paragraph 1, a right shall be acquired under Regulation (EC) No 1606/98 even if it relates to a contingency arising prior to 25 October 1998.

4. Any benefit that has not been awarded or that has been suspended on account of the nationality or the residence of the person concerned shall, at the latter's request, be awarded or resumed from 25 October 1998, provided

Article 95c

that the rights for which benefits were previously awarded did not give rise to a lump-sum payment.

5. The rights of persons who prior to 25 October 1998, obtained the award of a pension may be reviewed at their request, account being taken of the provisions of Regulation (EC) No 1606/98. The provision shall also apply to the other benefits referred to in Articles 78 and 79 insofar as it applies to Articles 78 and 79a.

6. If the request referred to in paragraph 4 or 5 is lodged within two years from 25 October 1998, rights deriving from Regulation (EC) No 1606/98 shall be acquired from that date and the provisions of the legislation of any Member State on the forfeiture or lapse of rights may not be applied to the persons concerned.

7. If the request referred to in paragraph 4 or 5 is lodged after expiry of the period of two years following 25 October 1998, rights not forfeited or lapsed shall be acquired from the date of such request, subject to any more favourable provision of the legislation of any Member State.]

AMENDMENT

1. Regulation 1606/98/EC, [1998] OJ L209/1.

[¹*Article 95d*

Transitional provisions applicable to students

1. No rights shall be acquired under this Regulation by students, members of their families or their survivors for any period prior to 1 May 1999.

2. Any period of insurance and, where appropriate, any period of employment, self-employment or residence completed under the legislation of a Member State before 1 May 1999 shall be taken into account for the determination of rights acquired in accordance with the provisions of this Regulation.

3. Subject to the provisions of paragraph 1, a right shall be acquired under this Regulation even if it relates to a contingency arising prior to 1 May 1999.

4. Any benefit that has not been awarded or that has been suspended on account of the nationality or the residence of the person concerned shall, at the latter's request, be awarded or resumed from 1 May 1999, provided that the rights for which benefits were previously awarded did not give rise to a lump-sum payment.

5. If the request referred to in paragraph 4 is lodged within two years of 1 May 1999, rights deriving from this Regulation in favour of students, members of their families and their survivors shall be acquired from that date and the provisions of the legislation of any Member State on the forfeiture or lapse of rights may not be applied to the persons concerned.

6. If the request referred to in paragraph 4 is lodged after the expiry of the period of two years following 1 May 1999, rights not forfeited or lapsed shall be acquired from the date of such request, subject to any more favourable provisions of the legislation of any Member State.]

AMENDMENT

1. Regulation 307/99/EC, [1999] OJ L38/1 (May 1, 1999).

[¹*Article 95e*]

Transitional provisions for application of Regulation (EC) 1399/99 [1999] OJ L164/1

3.282   1. Regulation (EC) No 1399/1999 shall be applicable to rights of orphans where the parent under whom the orphan is entitled died after 1 September 1999.

2. Any period of insurance or residence completed under the legislation of a Member State before 1 September 1999 shall be taken into account for the determination of rights acquired in accordance with Regulation (EC) No 1399/1999.

3. The rights of orphans where the parent under whom they are entitled died before 1 September 1999 may be reviewed at their request in accordance with Regulation (EC) 1399/1999.

4. If the request referred to in paragraph 3 is lodged within two years from 1 September 1999, rights deriving from Regulation (EC) No 1399/1999 shall be acquired from that date and the provisions of any Member State on the forfeiture or lapse of rights may not be applied to the persons concerned.

5. If the request referred to in paragraph 3 is lodged after the expiry of the period of two years following 1 September 1999, rights not forfeited or lapsed shall be acquired from the date of such request, subject to any more favourable provisions of the legislation of any Member State.]

AMENDMENT

1. Regulation 1399/99/EC, [1999] OJ L164/1 (September 1, 1999).

[¹*Article 95f*]

Transitional provisions relating to Annex II, section I, under the headings "D. GERMANY" and "R. AUSTRIA"

3.283   1. Annex II, section I, under the headings "D. GERMANY" and "R. AUSTRIA", as amended by Regulation (EC) No 647/2005 of the European Parliament and of the Council of 13 April 2005 amending Council Regulations (EEC) No 1408/71 on the application of social security schemes to employed persons, to self-employed persons and to members of their families moving within the Community and (EEC) No 574/72 laying down the procedure for implementing Regulation (EEC) No 1408/71 (*), shall not establish any entitlement for the period prior to 1 January 2005.

2. Any period of insurance and, where appropriate, any period of employment, self-employment or residence under the legislation of a Member State prior to 1 January 2005 shall be taken into consideration in determining acquired rights in accordance with the provisions of this Regulation.

3. Subject to the provisions of paragraph 1, a right shall be acquired under this Regulation even where it relates to a contingency that occurred prior to 1 January 2005.

4. Any benefit that has not been awarded or that has been suspended on account of the nationality or the residence of the person concerned shall, at the latter's request, be awarded or resumed from 1 January 2005, provided

Article 95f

that the rights for which benefits were previously awarded did not give rise to a lump-sum payment.

5. The rights of persons to whom a pension was awarded prior to 1 January 2005 may, on the application of the persons concerned, be reviewed, taking account of the provisions of this Regulation. This shall also apply to other benefits pursuant to Article 78.

6. If an application referred to in paragraph 4 or 5 is submitted within two years from 1 January 2005, the rights acquired under this Regulation shall have effect from that date and the provisions of the legislation of any Member State concerning the forfeiture or limitation of rights may not be invoked against the persons concerned.

7. If the application referred to in paragraph 4 or 5 is submitted after the expiry of the two-year period after 1 January 2005, rights which have not been forfeited or barred by limitation shall have effect from the date on which the application was submitted, except where more favourable provisions of the legislation of any Member State apply.]

AMENDMENT

1. Regulation 647/2005/EC, [2005] OJ L117/1 (May 5, 2005).

[¹*Article 95g*

Transitional provisions relating to the deletion, in Annex IIa, of the entry relating to the Austrian care allowance (Pflegegeld).

In the case of applications for care allowances under Austrian federal law (Bundespflegegeldgesetz) submitted not later than 8 March 2001 on the basis of Article 10a(3) of this Regulation, this provision shall continue to apply as long as the beneficiary of the care allowance continues to reside in Austria after 8 March 2001.]

3.284

AMENDMENT

1. Regulation 647/2005/EC, [2005] OJ L117/1 (May 5, 2005).

Article 96

Agreements relating to reimbursement between institutions

The Agreements concluded pursuant to Articles 36(3), 63(3) and 70(3) before 1 July 1982 shall apply likewise to persons to whom the scope of the present Regulation was extended on that date, except in the event of an objection by one of the contracting Member States to these Agreements.

3.285

This objection shall be taken into account if the competent authority of that Member State informs the competent authority of the other Member State(s) concerned in writing before 1 October 1983. A copy of this communication shall be forwarded to the Administrative Commission.

Council Regulation (EEC) No 1408/71

Article 97

Notification pursuant to certain provisions

3.286   **1.** The notifications referred to in Articles 1(j), 5 and 8(2) shall be addressed to the president of the Council. They shall indicate the date of entry into force of the laws and schemes in question or, in the case of the notifications referred to in Article 1(j), the date from which this Regulation shall apply to the schemes mentioned in the declarations of the Member States.
2. Notifications received in accordance with the provisions of paragraph 1 shall be published in the *Official Journal of the European Communities*.

Article 98

Implementing Regulation

3.287   A further Regulation shall lay down the procedure for implementing this Regulation.

GENERAL NOTE

3.288   The implementing regulation is Regulation 574/72 reproduced below.

ANNEX I

PERSONS COVERED BY THE REGULATION

*Sections marked ** reordered by part 2.1(b)(ii) of Annex II of the Treaty of Accession with effect from 1 May, 2004.*

I. Employed persons and/or self-employed persons (Article 1(a)(ii) and (iii) of the Regulation)

3.289   A. BELGIUM

Does not apply.

[¹ B. CZECH REPUBLIC

Does not apply.]

**C. DENMARK

1. Any person who, from the fact of pursuing an activity as an employed person, is subject:
   (a) to the legislation on accidents at work and occupational diseases for the period prior to 1 September 1977;
   (b) to the legislation on supplementary pensions for employed persons (arbejdsmarkedets tillaegspension, ATP) for a period commencing on or after 1 September 1977, shall be considered as an employed person within the meaning of Article 1(a)(ii) of the Regulation.

Annex I

2. Any person who, pursuant to the law on daily cash benefits in the event of sickness or maternity, is entitled to such benefits on the basis of an earned income other than a wage or salary shall be considered a self-employed person within the meaning of Article 1(a)(ii) of the Regulation.

**D. GERMANY

If the competent institution for granting family benefits in accordance with Chapter 7 of Title III of the Regulation is a German institution, then within the meaning of Article 1(a)(ii) of the Regulation:
  (a) "employed person" means compulsorily insured against unemployment or any person who, as a result of such insurance, obtains cash benefits under sickness insurance or comparable benefits [² or any established civil servant in receipt of a salary in respect of his/her civil servant status which is at least equal to that which, in the case of an employed person, would result in compulsory insurance against unemployment;]
  (b) "self-employed person" means any person pursuing self-employment which is bound:
    — to join, or pay contributions in respect of, an old-age insurance within a scheme for self-employed persons,
    or
    — to join a scheme within the framework of compulsory pension insurance.

[¹ E. ESTONIA

Does not apply.]

**F. GREECE

1. Persons insured under the OGA scheme who pursue exclusively activities as employed persons or who are or have been subject to the legislation of another Member State and who consequently are or have been "employed persons" within the meaning of Article 1(a) of the Regulation are considered as employed persons within the meaning of Article 1(a)(iii) of the Regulation.
2. For the purposes of granting the national family allowance, persons referred to in Article 1(a)(i) and (iii) of the Regulation are considered as employed persons within the meaning of Article 1(a)(ii) of the Regulation.

**G. SPAIN

Does not apply.

**H. FRANCE

If a French institution is the competent institution for the grant of family benefits in accordance with Title III, Chapter 7 of the Regulation:
1. "employed person" within the meaning of Article 1(a)(ii) of the Regulation shall be deemed to mean any person who is compulsorily insured under the social security scheme in accordance with Article L311-2 of the Social Security Code and who fulfils the minimum conditions regarding work or remuneration provided for in Article L313-1 of the Social Security Code in order to benefit from cash benefits under sickness insurance, maternity and invalidity cover or the person who benefits from these cash benefits;

2. "self-employed person" within the meaning of Article 1(a)(ii) of the Regulation shall be deemed to mean any person who performs a self-employed activity and who is required to take out insurance and to pay old-age benefit contributions to a self-employed persons' scheme.

**I. IRELAND

1. Any person who is compulsorily or voluntarily insured pursuant to the provisions of [³ Sections 9, 21 and 49 of the Social Welfare (Consolidation) Act 1993] shall be considered an employed person within the meaning of Article 1(a)(ii) of the Regulation.

2. Any person who is compulsorily or voluntarily insured pursuant to the provisions of [³ Sections 17 and 21 of the Social Welfare (Consolidation) Act 1993] shall be considered a self-employed person within the meaning of Article 1(a)(ii) of the Regulation.

**J. ITALY

Does not apply.

[¹ K. CYPRUS

Does not apply.]

[¹ L. LATVIA

Does not apply.]

[¹ M. LITHUANIA

Does not apply.]

**N. LUXEMBOURG

Does not apply.

[¹ O. HUNGARY

Does not apply.]

[¹ P. MALTA

Any person who is a self-employed person or a self-occupied person within the meaning of the Social Security Act (Cap. 318) 1987 shall be considered as a self-employed person within the meaning of Article 1(a)(ii) of the Regulation.]

**Q. NETHERLANDS

Any person pursuing an activity or occupation without a contract of employment shall be considered a self-employed person within the meaning of Article 1(a)(ii) of the Regulation.

**R. AUSTRIA

Does not apply.

[¹ POLAND

Does not apply.]

Annex I

**T. PORTUGAL

Does not apply.

[¹ SLOVENIA

Does not apply.]

[¹ SLOVAKIA

Does not apply.]

**W. FINLAND

Any person who is an employed or self-employed person within the meaning of the legislation on the Employment Pensions Scheme shall be considered respectively as employed or self-employed with the meaning of Article 1(a)(ii) of the Regulation.

**X. SWEDEN

Any person who is an employed or self-employed person within the meaning of the legislation on work injury insurance shall be considered respectively as employed or self-employed with the meaning of Article 1(a)(ii) of the Regulation.

**Y. UNITED KINGDOM

Any person who is an "employed earner" or a "self-employed earner" within the meaning of the legislation of Great Britain or of the legislation of Northern Ireland shall be regarded respectively as an employed person or a self-employed person within the meaning of Article 1(a)(ii) of the Regulation. Any person in respect of whom contributions are payable as an "employed person" or a "self-employed person" in accordance with the legislation of Gibraltar shall be regarded respectively as an employed person or a self-employed person within the meaning of Article 1(a)(ii) of the Regulation.

II. Members of the family (Second sentence of Article 1(f) of the Regulation)

A. BELGIUM

Does not apply.

[¹ B. CZECH REPUBLIC

For the purpose of determining entitlement to benefits in kind pursuant to the provisions of Chapter 1 of Title III of the Regulation, the expression "member of the family" means a spouse and/or a dependent child as defined by the State Social Support Act No 117/1995 sb.]

**C. DENMARK

For the purpose of determining a right to sickness or maternity benefits in kind existing pursuant to Articles 22(1)(a) and 31 of the Regulation, the expression "member of the family" shall mean:
 1. the spouse of an employed person, a self-employed person or other entitled persons under the terms of the Regulation, in so far as they are not themselves entitled persons under the terms of the Regulation; or

2. a child under 18 years of age in the care of someone who is an entitled person under the terms of the Regulation.

**D. GERMANY

Does not apply.

[¹ E. ESTONIA

Does not apply.]

**F. GREECE

Does not apply.

**G. SPAIN

Does not apply.

**[⁴ H. FRANCE

For the purpose of determining entitlement to family allowances or family benefits, the term "member of the family" means any person mentioned in Article L 512-3 of the Social security Code.]

**I. IRELAND

In order to determine the right to benefits in kind for sickness and maternity in application of the Regulation, the term "member of the family" shall mean any person considered as being a dependent of an employed person or of a self-employed person for the application of the Health Acts of 1947 to 1970.

**J. ITALY

Does not apply.

[¹ K. CYPRUS

Does not apply.]

[¹ L. LATVIA

For the purpose of determining entitlement to benefits in kind pursuant to the provisions of Chapter 1 of Title III of the Regulation, "member of the family" means a spouse or a child under the age of 18.]

[¹ M. LITHUANIA

For the purpose of determining entitlement to benefits in kind pursuant to the provisions of Chapter 1 of Title III of the Regulation, "member of the family" means a spouse or a child under the age of 18.]

**N. LUXEMBOURG

Does not apply.

Annex I

[¹ O. HUNGARY

Does not apply.]

[¹ P. MALTA

Does not apply.]

**Q. NETHERLANDS

Does not apply.

**R. AUSTRIA

Does not apply.

[¹ S. POLAND

Does not apply.]

**T. PORTUGAL

Does not apply.

[¹ U. SLOVENIA

Does not apply.]

[¹ V. SLOVAKIA

For the purpose of determining entitlement to benefits in kind pursuant to the provisions of Chapter 1 of Title III of the Regulation, "member of the family" means a spouse and/or a dependent child as defined by the Act on child allowances and additional child allowances.]

**W. FINLAND

For the purpose of determining entitlement to benefits in kind pursuant to the provisions of Chapter 1 of Title III of the Regulation, "member of the family" means a spouse or a child as defined by the Sickness Insurance Act.

**X. SWEDEN

For the purpose of determining entitlement to benefits in kind pursuant to the provisions of Chapter 1 of Title III of the Regulation, "member of the family" means a spouse or a child under the age of 18.

**Y. UNITED KINGDOM

For the purpose of determining entitlement to benefits in kind the term "member of the family" means:

1. As regards the legislation of Great Britain and Northern Ireland:
(1) a spouse, provided that:
(a) that person, whether employed or self-employed, or another person entitled under the Regulation, is:
   (i) residing with the spouse; or
   (ii) contributing to the maintenance of the spouse;

and
(b) the spouse does not:
(i) have earnings as an employed or self-employed person or income as a person entitled under the Regulation; or
(ii) receive a social security benefit or pension based on the spouse's own insurance;
(2) a person having care of a child, provided that:
(a) the employed or self-employed person or person entitled under the Regulation is:
(i) living together with the person as though husband and wife; or
(ii) contributing to the maintenance of the person;
and
(b) the person does not:
(i) have earnings as an employed or self-employed worker or income as a person entitled under the Regulation; or
(ii) receive a social security benefit or pension based on that person's own insurance;
(3) a child in respect of whom that person, the employed or self-employed person, or another person entitled under the Regulation is or could be paid child-benefit.

2. As regard the legislation of Gibraltar:

any person regarded as a dependent within the meaning of the Group Practice Scheme Ordinance, 1973.

AMENDMENTS

1. Annex II of Treaty of Accession (May 1, 2004).
2. Regulation 1399/99/EC, [1999] OJ L164/1 (September 1, 1999).
3. Regulation 1223/98/EC, [1998] OJ L168/1 (July 1, 1998).
4. Regulation 1290/97/EC, [1997] OJ L176/1 (October 4, 1997).

ANNEX II

(Article 1(j) and (u) of the Regulation)

Sections marked ** *reordered by part 2.1(b)(ii) of Annex II of the Treaty of Accession with effect from 1 May, 2004.*
Only provisions relating to the United Kingdom have been reproduced.

I. Special schemes for self-employed persons excluded from the scope of the Regulation pursuant to the fourth subparagraph of Article 1(j)

3.291 **Y. UNITED KINGDOM

Does not apply.

Annex II

II. Special childbirth or adoption allowances excluded from the scope of the Regulation under the terms of Article 1(u)(i)

**Y. UNITED KINGDOM

None.

III. Special non-contributory benefits within the meaning of Article 4(2b) which do not fall within the scope of the Regulation

**Y. UNITED KINGDOM

None.

Annex IIa

Special Non-Contributory Benefits

(Article 10a of the Regulation)

*Sections marked ** reordered by part 2.1(b)(ii) of Annex II of the Treaty of Accession with effect from 1 May, 2004.*
Only provisions relating to the United Kingdom have been reproduced.

**Y. UNITED KINGDOM

[2 (a) State Pension credit (State Pension Credit Act 2002)
  (b) Income-based allowances for jobseekers (Jobseekers Act 1995, 28 June 1995, Sections 1, (2)(d)(ii) and 3, and Jobseekers (Northern Ireland) Order 1995 of 18 October 1995, Articles 3(2)(d)(ii) and 5)
  (c) Income Support (Social Security Act 1986 of 25 July 1986, Section 20 to 22 and Section 23, and Social Security (Northern Ireland) Order 1986 of 5 November 1986, Articles 21 to 24)
  (d) Disability Living Allowance (Disability Living Allowance and Disability Working Allowance Act 1991 of 27 June 1991, Section 1, and Disability Living Allowance and Disability Working Allowance (Northern Ireland) Order 1991 of 24 July 1991, Article 3)
  (e) Attendance Allowance (Social Security Act 1975 of 20 March 1975, Section 35, and Social Security (Northern Ireland) Act 1975 of 20 March 1975, Section 35)
  (f) Carer's Allowance (Social Security Act 1975 of 20 March 1975, Section 37, and Social Security (Northern Ireland) Act 1975 of 20 March 1975, Section 37).]

Amendments

1. Regulation 1386/2001/EC, [2001] OJ L187/1 (September 1, 2001) (*earlier replaced amendment*).
2. Regulation 647/2005/EC, [2005] OJ L117/1 (May 5, 2005).

Council Regulation (EEC) No 1408/71

GENERAL NOTE

3.295   The issue of what are genuinely special non-contributory benefits remains a live one. The context in which the matter is being raised is perhaps unusual. The Commission has brought an action (Case C-299/05) against the European Parliament and the Council seeking the annulment of provisions in amendments to Annex IIa which include, inter alia, the United Kingdom benefits of attendance allowance, carer's allowance and disability living allowance. The Commission argues that these are not special non-contributory benefits and have no place in Annex IIa (whose benefits can be territorial only, by virtue of Article 10a). See [2005] OJ C243/9.

ANNEX III

PROVISIONS OF SOCIAL SECURITY CONVENTIONS REMAINING APPLICABLE NOTWITHSTANDING ARTICLE 6 OF THE REGULATION—PROVISIONS OF SOCIAL SECURITY CONVENTIONS WHICH DO NOT APPLY TO ALL PERSONS TO WHOM THE REGULATION APPLIES

(Articles 7(2)(c) and 3(3) of the Regulation)

Sections marked ** reordered by part 2.1(b)(ii) of Annex II of the Treaty of Accession with effect from 1 May, 2004.
Only provisions relating to the United Kingdom have been reproduced.

General comments

3.296   1. In so far as the provisions contained in this Annex provide for references to the provisions of other conventions, those references shall be replaced by references to the corresponding provisions of this Regulation, unless the provisions of the conventions in question are themselves contained in this Annex.

2. The termination clause provided for in a social security convention, some of whose provisions are contained in this Annex, shall continue to apply as regards those provisions.

[² 3. Account being taken of the provisions of Article 6 of this Regulation, it is to be noted that the provisions of bilateral Conventions which do not fall within the scope of this Regulation and which remain in force between Member States are not listed in this Annex, inter alia, provisions providing for aggregation of insurance periods fulfilled in a third country.]

A. Provisions of social security conventions remaining applicable notwithstanding Article 6 of the Regulation. (Article 7(2)(c) of the Regulation)

3.297   **24. [² . . .]

[¹ 47. CZECH REPUBLIC—UNITED KINGDOM

None.]

**69. [² . . .]

**90. GERMANY—UNITED KINGDOM

[² (a) Article 7(5) and (6) of the Convention on social security of 20 April 1960 (legislation applicable to civilians serving the military forces);
(b) Article 5(5) and (6) of the Convention on unemployment insurance of 20 April 1960 (legislation applicable to civilians serving the military forces).]

[¹ 110. ESTONIA—UNITED KINGDOM

No convention.]

**129. [² . . .]

**147. [² . . .]

**164. [² . . .]

**180. IRELAND—UNITED KINGDOM

[² Article 8 of the Agreement of 14 September 1971 on social security (concerning the transfer and reckoning of certain disability credits);]

**195. [² . . .]

[¹ 209. CYPRUS—UNITED KINGDOM

None.]

[¹ 222. LATVIA—UNITED KINGDOM

No convention.]

[¹ 243. [² . . .]

**245. [² . . .]

[¹ 255. HUNGARY—UNITED KINGDOM

None.]

[¹ 264. MALTA—UNITED KINGDOM

None.]

**272. [² . . .]

**279. [² . . .]

[¹ 285. POLAND—UNITED KINGDOM

None.]

**290. PORTUGAL—UNITED KINGDOM

(a) Article 2 (1) of the Protocol on medical treatment of 15 November 1978.
(b) As regards Portuguese employed persons, and for the period from 22 October 1987 to the end of the transitional period provided for in Article 220(1) of the Act relating to the conditions of accession of Spain and Portugal: Article 26 of the Social Security Convention of 15 November 1978, as amended by the Exchange of Letters of 28 September 1987.

[¹ 294. SLOVENIA—UNITED KINGDOM

None.]

[¹ 297. SLOVAKIA—UNITED KINGDOM

None.]

**299. [² . . .]

**300. [² . . .]

B. Provisions of Conventions which do not apply to all persons to whom the Regulations applies Article 3(3) of the Regulation)

3.298   **24. [² . . .]

[¹ 47. CZECH REPUBLIC—UNITED KINGDOM

None.]

**69. [² . . .]

**90. [² . . .]

[¹ 110. ESTONIA—UNITED KINGDOM

No convention.]

**129. [² . . .]

**147. [² . . .]

Annex III

**164. [² . . .]

**180. [² . . .]

**195. [² . . .]

[¹ 209. CYPRUS—UNITED KINGDOM
None.]

[¹ 222. LATVIA—UNITED KINGDOM
No convention.]

[¹ 234. LITHUANIA—UNITED KINGDOM
No convention.]

**245. [² . . .]

[¹ 255. HUNGARY—UNITED KINGDOM
None.]

[¹ 264. MALTA—UNITED KINGDOM
None.]

**272. [² . . .]

**279. [² . . .]

[¹ 285. POLAND—UNITED KINGDOM
None.]

**290. [² . . .]

[¹ 294. SLOVENIA—UNITED KINGDOM
None.]

[¹ 297. SLOVAKIA—UNITED KINGDOM
None.]

**299. [² . . .]

**300. [² . . .]

AMENDMENTS

1. Annex II of the Treaty of Accession (May 1, 2004).
2. Regulation 647/2005/EC, [2005] OJ L117/1 (May 5, 2005).

Council Regulation (EEC) No 1408/71

ANNEX IV

(Articles 37(2), 38(3), 45(3), 46(1)(b) and 46b(2) of the Regulation)

Sections marked ** reordered by part 2.1(b)(ii) of Annex II of the Treaty of Accession with effect from 1 May, 2004.
Only provisions relating to the United Kingdom have been reproduced.

A. Legislations referred to in Article 37(1) of the Regulation under which the amount of invalidity benefits is independent of the length of periods of insurance

3.299   **Y. UNITED KINGDOM

(a) *Great Britain*
Sections 15 and 36 of the Social Security Act 1975.
Sections 14, 15 and 16 of the Social Security Pensions Act 1975.
(b) *Northern Ireland*
Sections 15 and 36 of the Social Security (Northern Ireland) Act 1975.
Articles 16, 17 and 18 of the Social security Pensions (Northern Ireland) Order 1975.

GENERAL NOTE

3.300   Sections 15 and 36 of the Social Security Act 1975 and sections 14, 15 and 16 of the Social Security Pensions Act 1975 have been repealed and re-enacted with effect from July 1, 1992 respectively in sections 33 and 68, and sections 33(3), 40 and 41 o the Social Security (Contributions and Benefits) Act 1992.

B. Special schemes for self-employed persons within the meaning of Articles 38(3) and 45(3) of Regulation No 1408/71

3.301   **Y UNITED KINGDOM

None.

C. Cases referred to in Article 46(1)(b) of the Regulation where the calculation of benefit in accordance with Article 46(2) of the Regulation may be waived

3.302   **Y. UNITED KINGDOM

All applications for retirement and widow's pension determined pursuant to the provisions of Title III, Chapter 3 of the Regulation, with the exception of those for which:
(a) during a tax year beginning on or after 6 April 1975:
   (i) the party concerned had completed periods of insurance, employment or residence under the legislation of the United Kingdom and of another Member State; and
   (ii) one (or more) of the tax years referred to in (i) was not considered a qualifying year within the meaning of the legislation of the United Kingdom;

(b) the periods of insurance completed under the legislation in force in the United Kingdom for the periods prior to 5 July 1948 would be taken into account for the purposes of Article 46(2) of the Regulation by application of the periods of insurance, employment or residence under the legislation of another Member State.

D. Benefits and agreements referred to in Article 46b(2) of the Regulation

1. Benefits referred to in Article 46b(2)(a) of the Regulation, the amount of which is independent of the length of periods of insurance or residence completed:
   (a) The invalidity benefits provided for by the legislations referred to in part A of this Annex.
   (b) The full Danish national old-age pension acquired after 10 years' residence by persons who will have been awarded a pension by 1 October 1989 at the latest.
   (c) The Spanish death allowances and survivors' pensions granted under the general and special schemes.
   (d) The widows' allowance under the widowhood insurance of the French general social security system or the agricultural workers' system.
   (e) The widowers' or widows' invalidity pension under the French general social security system or the agricultural workers' system, when calculated on the basis of the invalidity pension of a deceased spouse, paid in accordance with Article 46(1)(a)(i).
   (f) the Netherlands survivors' pension under the Law of 21 December 1995 on general insurance for surviving dependants.
   (g) Finnish national pensions determined according to the National Pensions Act of 8 June 1956 and awarded under the transitional rules of the National Pensions Act (547/93) and the additional amount of the child's pension in accordance with the Survivors' pension Act of 17 January 1969.
   (h) The full Swedish basic pension awarded under the basic pension legislation which applied before 1 January 1993 and the full basic pension awarded under the transitional rules to the legislation applying from that date.

2. Benefits referred to in Article 46b(2)(b) of the Regulation, the amount of which is determined by reference to a credited period deemed to have been completed between the date on which the risk materialized and a later date:
   (a) Danish early-retirement pensions, the amount of which is determined in accordance with legislation in force before 1 October 1984.
   (b) German invalidity and survivors' pensions, for which account is taken of a supplementary period, and German old-age pensions, for which account is taken of a supplementary period already acquired.
   (c) Italian pensions for total incapacity for work (inabilità).
   (d) Luxembourg invalidity and survivors' pensions.
   (e) Finnish employment pensions for which account is taken of future periods according to the national legislation.

3.303

Council Regulation (EEC) No 1408/71

(f) Swedish invalidity and survivors' pensions for which account is taken of a credited period of insurance and Swedish old-age pensions for which account is taken of credited periods already acquired.

3. Agreements referred to in Article 46b(2)(b)(i) of the Regulation intended to prevent the same credited period being taken into account two or more times:

Nordic Convention of 15 June 1992 on social security.

The Social Security Agreement of 28 April 1997 between the Federal Republic of Germany and Finland.

Annex V

Concordance Between the Legisllations of Member States on Conditions Relating to the Degree of Invalidity

(Article 40(4) of the Regulation)

3.304 *Omitted.*

Annex VI

Special Procedures for Applying the Legislations of Certain Member States

(Article 89 of the Regulation)

*Sections marked ** reordered by part 2.1(b)(ii) of Annex II of the Treaty of Accession with effect from 1 May, 2004.*
Only the section concerning the United Kingdom has been reproduced.

**Y. UNITED KINGDOM

3.305   **1.** When a person who is normally resident in Gibraltar, or who has been required, since he last arrived in Gibraltar, to pay contributions under the legislation of Gibraltar as an employed person, applies, as a result of incapacity to work, maternity or unemployment, for exemption from the payment of contributions over a certain period, and asks for contributions for that period to be credited to him, any period during which that person has been working in the territory of a Member State other than the United Kingdom shall, for the purposes of his application, be regarded as a period during which he has been employed in Gibraltar and for which he has paid contributions as an employed person in accordance with the legislation of Gibraltar.

2. Where, in accordance with United Kingdom legislation, a person may be entitled to a retirement pension if:

(a) the contributions of a former spouse are taken into account as if they were that person's own contributions, or
(b) the relevant contribution conditions are satisfied by that person's spouse or former spouse,

then provided, in each case, that the spouse or former spouse is or was an employed or self-employed person who had been subject to the legislation of two or more Member States, the provisions of Chapter 3 of Title III of the Regulation shall apply in order to determine entitlement under United Kingdom legislation. In this case, references in the said Chapter 3 to "periods of insurance" shall be construed as references to periods of insurance completed by:

[4 (i) a spouse or former spouse where a claim is made by:
— a married woman, or
— a person whose marriage has terminated otherwise than by the death of the spouse,

or

(ii) a former spouse, where a claim is made by:
— a widower who immediately before pensionable age is not entitled to widowed parent's allowance, or
— a widow who immediately before pensionable age is not entitled to widowed mother's allowance, widowed parent's allowance or widow's pension, or who is only entitled to an age-related widow's pension calculated pursuant to Article 46(2) of the Regulation, and for this purpose "age-related widow's pension" means a widow's pension payable at a reduced rate in accordance with section 39(4) of the Social Security Contributions and Benefits Act 1992.]

3. (a) If unemployed benefit provided under United Kingdom legislation is paid to a person pursuant to Article 71(1)(a)(ii) or (b)(ii) of the Regulation, then for the purpose of satisfying the conditions imposed by United Kingdom legislation in relation to child benefit concerning a period of presence within Great Britain or, as the case may be, Northern Ireland, periods of insurance, employment or self-employment completed by that person under the legislation of another Member State shall be regarded as periods of presence in Great Britain or, as the case may be, Northern Ireland.

(b) If, pursuant to Title II of the Regulation, excluding Article 13(2)(f), United Kingdom legislation is applicable in respect of an employment or self-employed person who does not satisfy the condition imposed by United Kingdom legislation in relation to child benefit concerning:
  (i) presence within Great Britain or, as the case may be, Northern Ireland, he shall be regarded, for the purpose of satisfying such condition, as being so present;
  (ii) a period of presence within Great Britain, or, as the case may be, Northern Ireland, periods of insurance, employment or self-employment completed by the said worker under the legislation of another Member State shall, for the purpose of satisfying such conditions, be regarded as periods of presence in Great Britain or, as the case may be, Northern Ireland.

(c) In respect of claims to family allowances under the legislation of Gibraltar the foregoing provisions of subparagraphs (a) and (b) shall apply by analogy.

Council Regulation (EEC) No 1408/71

4. The widow's payment provided under United Kingdom legislation shall be treated, for the purposes of Chapter 3 of the Regulation, as a survivor's pension.

5. For the purposes of applying Article 10a(2) to the provisions governing entitlement to attendance allowance, invalid care allowance and disability living allowance, a period of employment, self-employment or residence completed in the territory of a Member State other than the United Kingdom shall be taken into account insofar as is necessary to satisfy conditions as to presence in the United Kingdom, prior to the day on which entitlement to the benefit in question first arises.

6. In the event of an employed person subject to United Kingdom legislation being the victim of an accident after leaving the territory of one Member State while travelling, in the course of this employment, to the territory of another Member State, but before arriving there, his entitlement to benefits in respect of that accident shall be established:

(a) as if the accident had occurred within the territory of the United Kingdom,
and
(b) for the purpose of determining whether he was an employed earner under the legislation of Great Britain or the legislation of Northern Ireland or an employed person under the legislation of Gibraltar, by disregarding his absence from those territories.

7. The Regulation does not apply to those provisions of United Kingdom legislation which are intended to bring into force any social security agreement concluded between the United Kingdom and a third State.

8. For the purposes of Chapter 3 of Title III of the Regulation no account shall be taken of graduated contributions paid by the insured person under United Kingdom legislation or of graduated retirement benefits payable under that legislation. The amount of the graduated benefits shall be added to the amount of the benefit due under the United Kingdom legislation as determined in accordance with the said chapter. The total of these two amounts shall constitute the benefit actually due to the person concerned.

9. [. . .]

10. For the purpose of applying the Non-Contributory Social Insurance Benefit and Unemployment Insurance Ordinance (Gibraltar), any person to whom this Regulation is applicable shall be deemed to be ordinarily resident in Gibraltar if he resides in a Member State.

11. [[1] For the purposes of Articles 27, 28, 28a, 29, 30 and 31 of this Regulation, benefits payable outside the United Kingdom solely because of Article 95b(8) of the Regulation shall be considered as invalidity benefits.]

12. For the purpose of Article 10(1) of the Regulation any beneficiary under United Kingdom legislation who is staying in the territory of another Member State shall, during that stay, be considered as if he resided in the territory of that other Member State.

13.1. For the purpose of calculating an earnings factor with a view to determining the right to benefits under United Kingdom legislation, subject to point 15, each week during which an employed or self-employed person has been subject to the legislation of another Member State and which commenced during the relevant income tax year within the meaning of United Kingdom, legislation shall be taken into account in the following way:

(a) Periods between 6 April 1975 and 5 April 1987:

Annex VI

    (i) for each week of insurance, employment or residence as an employed person, the person concerned shall be deemed to have paid contributions as an employed earner on the basis of earnings equivalent to two-thirds of that year's upper earnings limit;

    (ii) for each week of insurance, self-employment or residence as a self-employed person the person concerned shall be deemed to have paid class 2 contributions as a self-employed earner.

(b) Periods from 6 April 1987 onwards:

    (i) for each week of insurance, employment or residence as an employed person, the person concerned shall be deemed to have received, and paid contributions as an employed earner, for, weekly earnings equivalent to two-thirds of that week's upper earnings limit;

    (ii) for each week of insurance, self-employment or residence as a self-employed person the person concerned shall be deemed to have paid class 2 contibutions as a self-employed earner.

(c) For each full week during which he has completed a period treated as a period of insurance, employment, self-employment or residence, the person concerned shall be deemed to have had contributions or earnings credited to him as appropriate, but only to the extent required to bring his total earnings factor for that tax year to the level required to make that tax year a reckonable year within the meaning of the United Kingdom legislation governing the crediting of contributions or earnings.

13.2. For the purposes of Article 46(2)(b) of the Regulation, where:

(a) if in any income tax year starting on or after 6 April 1975, an employed person has completed periods of insurance, employment or residence exclusively in a Member State other than the United Kingdom, and the application of paragraph 1(a)(i) or paragraph 1(b)(i) results in that year being counted as a qualifying year within the meaning of United Kingdom legislation for the purposes of Article 46(2)(a) of the Regulation, he shall be deemed to have been insured for 52 weeks in that year in that other Member State:

(b) any income tax year starting on or after 6 April 1975 does not count as a qualifying year within the meaning of United Kingdom legislation for the purposes of Article 46(2)(a) of the Regulation, any periods of insurance, employment or residence completed in that year shall be disregarded.

13.3. For the purpose of converting an earnings factor into periods of insurance the earnings factor achieved in the relevant income tax year within the meaning of United Kingdom legislation shall be divided by that year's lower earnings limit. The result shall be expressed as a whole number, any remaining fraction being ignored.

The figure so calculated shall be treated as representing the number of weeks of insurance completed under United Kingdom legislation during that year provided that such figure shall not exceed the number of weeks during which in that year that person was subject to that legislation.

14. In applying Article 40(3)(a)(ii), account shall only be taken of periods during which the employed or self-employed person was incapable of work within the meaning of United Kingdom legislation.

15.1. For the purpose of calculating, under Article 46(2)(a) of the Regulation, the theoretical amount of that part of the pension which consists of an additional component under United Kingdom legislation:
   (a) the expression "earnings, contributions or increases" in Article 47(1)(b) of the Regulation shall be construed as meaning surpluses in earnings factors as defined in the Social Security Pensions Act 1975 or, as the case may be, the Social Security Pensions (Northern Ireland) Order 1975;
   (b) an average of the surpluses in earnings factor shall be calculated in accordance with Article 47(1)(b) of the Regulation as construed in subparagraph (a) above by dividing the aggregated surpluses recorded under United Kingdom legislation by the number of income tax years within the meaning of United Kingdom legislation (including part income tax years) completed under that legislation since 6 April 1978 which occur within the relevant period of insurance.

15.2. The expression "periods of insurance or residence" in Article 46(2) of the Regulation shall be construed, for the purpose of assessing the amount of that part of the pension which consists of an additional component under United Kingdom legislation, as meaning periods of insurance or residence which have been completed since 6 April 1978.

16. An unemployed person returning to the United Kingdom after the end of the period of three months during which he continued to receive benefits under the legislation of the United Kingdom pursuant to Article 69(1) of the Regulation shall continue to be entitled to unemployment benefits by way of derogation from Article 69(2) if he satisfies the conditions in the aforementioned legislation.

17. For the purposes of entitlement to severe disablement allowance any employed or self-employed person who is, or has been, subject to United Kingdom legislation in accordance with Title II of the Regulation, excluding Article 13(2)(f):
   (a) shall, for the entire period during which he was employed or self-employed and subject to United Kingdom legislation whilst present or resident in another Member State, be treated as having been present or resident in the United Kingdom;
   (b) shall be entitled to have periods of insurance as an employed or self-employed person completed in the territory and under the legislation of another Member State treated as periods of presence or residence in the United Kingdom.

18. A period of subjection to United Kingdom legislation in accordance with Article 13(2)(f) of the Regulation may not:
   (a) be taken into account under that provision as a period of subjection to United Kingdom legislation for the purposes of Title III of the Regulation,
   nor
   (b) make the United Kingdom the competent State for the provision of the benefits provided for in Article 18, 38 or 39(1) of the Regulation.

19. Subject to any conventions concluded with individual Member States, for the purposes of Article 13(2)(f) of the Regulation and Article 10b of the Implementing Regulation, United Kingdom legislation shall cease to apply at the end of the day on the latest of the following three days to any person previously subject to United Kingdom legislation as an employed or self-employed person:

Annex VI

(a) the day on which residence is transferred to the other Member State referred to in Article 13(2)(f);
(b) the day of cessation of the employment or self-employment, whether permanent or temporary, during which that person was subject to United Kingdom legislation;
(c) the last day of any period of receipt of United Kingdom sickness or maternity benefit (including benefits in kind for which the United Kingdom is the competent State) or unemployment benefit which
   (i) began before the date of transfer of residence to another Member State or, if later,
   (ii) immediately followed employment or self-employment in another Member State while that person was subject to United Kingdom legislation.

20. The fact that a person has become subject to the legislation of another Member State in accordance with Article 13(2)(f) of the Regulation, Article 10b of the Implementing Regulation and point 19 above, shall not prevent:
(a) the application to him by the United Kingdom as the competent State of the provisions relating to employed or self-employed persons of Title III, Chapter 1 and Chapter 2, Section 1 or Article 40(2) of the Regulation if he remains and employed or self-employed person for those purposes and was last so insured under the legislation of the United Kingdom;
(b) his treatment as an employed or self-employed person for the purposes of Chapter 7 and 8 of Title III of the Regulation or Articles 10 or 10a of the Implementing Regulation, provided United Kingdom benefit under Chapter 1 of Title III is payable to him in accordance with paragraph (a).

[² 21. In the case of either students or members of their family or survivors of a student, Article 10a(2) of the Regulation shall not apply to benefits intended solely as specific protection for the disabled.]

22. [⁴ . . .]

AMENDMENTS

1. Regulation 1290/97/EC, [1997] OJ L176/1 (October 4, 1997).
2. Regulation 307/99/EC, [1999] OJ L307/99 (May 1, 1999).
3. Regulation 1399/99/EC, [1999] OJ L164/1 (September 1, 1999).
4. Regulation 647/2005/EC, [2005] OJ L117/1 (May 5, 2005).

[¹ ANNEX VII

INSTANCES IN WHICH A PERSON SHALL BE SIMULTANEOUSLY SUBJECT TO THE LEGISLATION OF TWO MEMBER STATES

(Article 14c(1)(b) of the Regulation)

1. Where he is self-employed in Belgium and gainfully employed in any other Member State.
2. Where a person is self-employed in the Czech Republic and gainfully employed in any other Member State.

Council Regulation (EEC) No 1408/71

3. Where a person resident in Denmark is self-employed in Denmark and gainfully employed in any other Member State.

4. For the agricultural accident insurance scheme and the old-age insurance scheme for farmers: where he is self-employed in farming in Germany and gainfully employed in any other Member State.

5. Where a person resident in Estonia is self-employed in Estonia and gainfully employed in any other Member State.

6. For the pension insurance scheme for self-employed persons: where he is self-employed in Greece and gainfully employed in any other Member State.

7. Where a person resident in Spain is self-employed in Spain and gainfully employed in any other Member State.

8. Where he is self-employed in France and gainfully employed in any other Member State, except Luxembourg.

9. Where he is self-employed in farming in France and gainfully employed in Luxembourg.

10. Where he is self-employed in Italy and gainfully employed in any other Member State.

11. Where a person resident in Cyprus is self-employed in Cyprus and gainfully employed in any other Member State.

12. Where a person is self-employed in Malta and gainfully employed in any other Member State.

13. Where he is self-employed in Portugal and gainfully employed in any other Member State.

14. Where a person resident in Finland is self-employed in Finland and gainfully employed in any other Member State.

15. Where a person is self-employed in Slovakia and gainfully employed in any other Member State.

16. Where a person resident in Sweden is self-employed in Sweden and gainfully employed in any other Member State.]

AMENDMENT

1. Annex II to the Treaty of Accession (May 1, 2004).

[¹ ANNEX VIII

SCHEMES THAT PROVIDE ONLY FOR FAMILY ALLOWANCES OR SUPPLEMENTARY OR SPECIAL ALLOWANCES FOR ORPHANS

(Article 78a of the Regulation)

Sections marked ** reordered by part 2.1(b)(ii) of Annex II of the Treaty of Accession with effect from 1 May, 2004.
Only provisions relating to the United Kingdom have been reproduced.

**Y. UNITED KINGDOM

1. Great Britain and Northern Ireland
Provisions under the Social Security Contributions and Benefits Act 1992 and the Social Security Contributions and Benefits (Northern Ireland)

Annex VIII

Act 1992, relating to child benefit (including any higher rates for lone parents); child dependency allowances paid to pensioners and guardian's allowance.

2. Gibraltar

Provisions under the Social Security (Open Long-Term Benefits Scheme) Ordinance 1997 and the Social Security (Closed Long-Term Benefits Scheme) Ordinance 1996 relating to child dependency increased paid to pensioners and guardian's allowance.

AMENDMENT

1. Regulation 1399/99/EC, [1999] OJ L164/1 (September 1, 1999).

Council Regulation (EEC) No 574/72 of 21 March 1972 Laying Down the Procedure for Implementing Regulation (EEC) No 1408/71 on the Application of Social Security Schemes to Employed Persons, to Self Employed Persons, to Self-employed Persons and to Their Families Moving within the Community

GENERAL NOTE

This is the implementing regulation which lays down detailed rules, generally but not exclusively, of an administrative nature. Reference is given in the annotations to Reg.1408/71 to the applicable provisions of this regulation.

3.308

CONTENTS

TITLE I: GENERAL PROVISIONS (ARTICLES 1 TO 4).

TITLE II: IMPLEMENTATION OF THE GENERAL PROVISIONS OF THE REGULATION (ARTICLES 5 TO 10A)

TITLE III: IMPLEMENTATION OF THE PROVISIONS OF THE REGULATION FOR DETERMINING THE LEGISLATION APPLICABLE (ARTICLES 10B TO 14).

TITLE IV: IMPLEMENTATION OF THE SPECIAL PROVISIONS OF THE REGULATION RELATING TO THE VARIOUS CATEGORIES OF BENEFITS

Chapter 1: General rules for the aggregation of periods (Article 15)
Chapter 2: Sickness and maternity (Articles 16 to 34)
Chapter 3: Invalidity, old-age and death (pensions) (Articles 35 to 59)
Chapter 4: Accidents at work and occupational diseases (Articles 60 to 77)
Chapter 5: Death grants (Articles 78, 79)
Chapter 6: Unemployment benefits (Articles 80 to 84)
Chapter 7: Family benefits (Articles 85 to 88)
Chapter 8: Benefits for dependent children of pensioners and for orphans (Articles 90 to 92)

Council Regulation (EEC) No 574/72

Title V: Financial Provisions (Articles 93 to 107)

Title VI: Miscellaneous Provisions (Articles 108 to 117)

Title VII: Transitional and Final Provisions (Articles 118 to 122)

Annexes

Annex 1: Competent authorities
Annex 2: Competent institutions
Annex 3: Institutions of the place of residence and institutions of the place of stay
Annex 4: Liaison bodies
Annex 5: Implementing provisions of bilateral conventions which remain in force
Annex 6: Procedure for the payment of benefits
Annex 7: Banks
Annex 8: Grant of family benefits
Annex 9: Calculation of the average annual cost of benefits in kind
Annex 10: Institutions and bodies designated by the competent authorities
Annex 11: Schemes referred to in Articles 35 (2) of the Regulation

The Council of the European Union

3.309 *Having regard* to the Treaty establishing the European Community, and in particular Articles 51 and 235 thereof,
Having regard to Regulation (EEC) No 1408/71 on the application of social security schemes to employed persons, to self-employed persons and to members of their families moving within the Community, and in particular Article 98 thereof,
Having regard to the proposal from the Commission,
Having regard to the opinion of the European Parliament,
Having regard to the opinion of the Economic and Social Committee,
Whereas there is a need to lay down the procedure for implementing Regulation (EEC) No 1408/71 adapted to the basic rules and to the experience gained in applying these texts over the years;
Whereas it is necessary, in particular, to specify the competent authorities and institutions in each Member State as well as the liaison bodies entitled to exchange information directly between themselves;
Whereas it is necessary to specify the documents to be furnished and to be completed by the persons concerned in order to obtain benefits;
Whereas it is necessary to specify in detail the procedure for implementing the provisions of Regulation (EEC) No 1408/71 concerning the determination of the legislation applicable as well as the provisions concerning the different categories of benefits;
Whereas it is also necessary to specify the conditions for the refund of benefits provided by the institution of one Member State on behalf of the institution of another Member State, and the duties of the Audit Board;
Whereas it is necessary to lay down the methods of application for the procedure to be followed for currency conversion within the framework of the European Monetary System;

Preamble

Whereas it is necessary, with a view to facilitating communication between the authorities and institutions of the Member State, to provide for the possibility of electronic data processing in connection with the application of Regulation (EEC) No 1408/71;

Whereas it should be made possible for Annexes 1, 4, 5, 6, 7 and 8 to Regulation (EEC) No 574/72 to be amended by means of a regulation adopted by the Commission at the request of the Member State or Member States concerned or their competent authorities and after consultation of the Administrative Commission; whereas the sole aim of amending these Annexes is to incorporate into a Community instrument decisions adopted by the Member State concerned or by their competent authorities,

Has Adopted this Regulation

Title I

General Provisions

Article 1

Definitions

For the purposes of this Regulation:
(a) "Regulation" means Regulation (EEC) No 1408/71;
(b) "implementing Regulation" means this Regulation;
(c) the definitions in Article 1 of this Regulation have the meaning assigned to them in the said Article.

3.310

Article 2

Printed model forms—Information on legislations—Guides

[¹ **1.** Models of the documents necessary for the application of the Regulation and of the implementing Regulation shall be drawn up by the Administrative Commission.

These documents may be transferred between institutions either in paper or other form or by means of telematic services as standardised electronic messages in accordance with Title Via. The exchange of information by means of telematic services shall be subject to agreement between the competent authorities or the bodies designated by the competent authorities of the sending Member State and those of the receiving Member State.]

2. For the benefit of the competent authorities of each Member State, the Administrative Commission may assemble information on the provisions which come within the scope of this Regulation.

3. The Administrative Commission shall prepare guides for the purpose of advising persons concerned of their rights and of the administrative formalities to be completed for the exercise of those rights.

3.311

Council Regulation (EEC) No 574/72

The Advisory Committee shall be consulted before such guides are drawn up.

AMENDMENT

1. Regulation 631/2004/EC, [2004] OJ L100/1 (June 1, 2004).

Article 3

Liaison bodies—Communications between institutions and between beneficiaries and institutions

3.312
1. The competent authorities may designate liaison bodies which may communicate directly with each other.

2. Any institution of a Member State, and any person residing or staying in the territory of a Member State, may make application to the institution of another Member State, either directly or through the liaison bodies.

3. Decisions and other documents emanating from an institution of a Member State and intended for persons residing or staying in the territory of another Member State may be communicated directly by registered letter with acknowledgement of receipt.

Article 4

Annexes

3.313
1. The competent authority or authorities of each Member State are listed in Annex I.

2. The competent institutions of each Member State are listed in Annex 2.

3. The institutions of the place of residence and the institutions of the place of stay of each Member State are listed in Annex 3.

4. The liaison bodies designated pursuant to Article 3(1) of the implementing Regulation are listed in Annex 4.

5. The provisions referred to in Articles 5, 53(3), 104, 105(2), 116 and 121 of the implementing Regulation are listed in Annex 5.

6. The procedure for the payment of benefits chosen by the institutions responsible for payment in each Member State, in accordance with Article 53(1) of the implementing Regulation, is listed in Annex 6.

7. The names and registered offices or place of business of the banks referred to in Article 55(1) of the implementing Regulation are listed in Annex 7.

8. The Member States to which the provisions of Article 10a(1)(d) of the implementing Regulation apply in their dealings with each other are listed in Annex 8.

9. The schemes to be taken into consideration when calculating the average annual cost of benefits in kind, in accordance with Articles 94(3)(a) and 95(3)(a) of the implementing Regulation, are listed in Annex 9.

10. Annex 10 lists the institutions or bodies designated by the competent authorities pursuant, in particular, to the following provisions:
   (a) Regulation: Article 14c, Article 14d(3) and 17;

Article 4

(b) implementing Regulation: Article 6(1), Article 8, Articles 10b, 11(1), 11a(1), 12a, 13(3) and (3), 14(1), (2) and (3), 38(1), 70(1), 80(2), 81, 82(2), 85(2), 86(2), 89(1), 91(2), 102(2), 109, 110, 113(2).

11. [¹ . . .]

AMENDMENT

1. Regulation 647/2005/EC, [2005] OJ L117/1 (May 5, 2005).

TITLE II

IMPLEMENTATION OF THE GENERAL PROVISIONS OF THE REGULATION

IMPLEMENTATION OF ARTICLES 6 AND 7 OF THE REGULATION

Article 5

Replacement by the implementing Regulation of arrangements for implementing conventions

The provisions of the implementing Regulation shall replace those of the arrangements for implementing the conventions referred to in Article 6 of the Regulation; they shall also replace the provisions relating to the implementation of the provisions of the conventions referred to in Article 7(2)(c) of the Regulation in so far as they are not listed in Annex 5.

3.314

IMPLEMENTATION OF ARTICLE 9 OF THE REGULATION

Article 6

Admission to voluntary or optional continued insurance

1. If, by virtue of Articles 9 and 15(3) of the Regulation, a person satisfies the conditions for admission to a voluntary or optional continued insurance in respect of invalidity, old age and death (pensions) in several schemes under the legislation of one Member State, and if he has not been subject to compulsory insurance under one of those schemes by virtue of his last employment or self-employment he may, under the said Articles, join the voluntary or optional continued insurance scheme specified by the legislation of that Member State or, failing that, the scheme of his choice.

3.315

2. In order to invoke the provisions of Article 9(2) of the Regulation, a person shall submit to the institution of the Member State in question a certified statement relating to the insurance periods or periods of residence completed under the legislation of any other Member State. Such certified statement shall be issued, at the request of the person concerned, by the institution or institutions who administer the legislation under which he has completed those periods.

Council Regulation (EEC) No 574/72

IMPLEMENTATION OF ARTICLE 12 OF THE REGULATION

Article 7

General rules on the application of the provisions designed to prevent overlapping

3.316   1. Where the benefits due under the legislation of two or more Member States are conditional upon mutual reductions, suspensions or withdrawals, the amounts which would not be paid in strict application of the provisions concerning reduction, suspension or withdrawal provided for by the legislation of the Member States concerned shall be divided by the number of benefits subject to reduction, suspension or withdrawal.

2. In order to implement Article 12(2), (3) and (4), Article 46a, Article 46b and Article 46c of the Regulation, the competent institutions concerned shall provide each other, at their own request, with all appropriate information.

Article 8

Rules applicable in the case of overlapping of rights to sickness or maternity benefits under the legislation of several Member States

3.317   1. If an employed or self-employed person or a member of his family is entitled to claim maternity benefits under the legislations of two or more Member States, those benefits shall be granted exclusively under the legislation of the Member State in whose territory the confinement took place or, if the confinement did not take place in the territory of one of these Member States, exclusively under the legislation of the Member State to which the employed or self-employed person was last subject.

2. If an employed or self-employed person is entitled to claim sickness benefits under the legislation of Ireland and the United Kingdom for the same period of incapacity for work, those benefits shall be granted exclusively under the legislation of the Member State to which the person concerned was last subject.

3. In the cases referred to in Article 14c(b) [[1] and 14f] of the Regulation, where the person in question or a member of his family is entitled to claim benefits in kind in respect of sickness or maternity under the two legislations in questions, the following rules shall be applicable:
   (a) Where at least one of those legislations stipulates that the benefits shall be awarded in the form of a reimbursement to the person entitled to benefit, this shall be the exclusive responsibility of the institution of the Member State in whose territory they have been awarded.
   (b) If the benefits have been awarded in the territory of a Member State other than the two Member States in question, they shall be the exclusive responsibility of the institution of the Member State to whose legislation the person in question is subject by virtue of his paid employment.

Article 8

AMENDMENT

1. Regulation 1606/98/EC, [1998] OJ L209/1 (October 25, 1998).

Article 8a

Rules applicable in the case of overlapping of rights to sickness benefits, benefits with respect to accidents at work or occupational disease under Greek legislation and the legislation of one or more other Member States

If during the same period an employed or self-employed person or member of his family is entitled to claim sickness benefits, benefits with respect to accidents at work or occupational disease under Greek legislation and under the legislation of one or more Member States, these benefits shall be granted exclusively under the legislation to which the person concerned was last subject.

3.318

Article 9

Rules applicable in the case of overlapping of rights to death grants under the legislation of several Member States

1. Where the death occurs in the territory of a Member State, the right to a death grant acquired under the legislation of that Member State only shall be maintained, whilst the right acquired under the legislation of any other Member State shall lapse.

3.319

2. Where the death occurs in the territory of one Member State when the right to a death grant has been acquired under the legislation of two or more other Member States, or where the death occurs outside the territory of the Member States and the said right has been acquired under the legislation of two or more Member States, only the right acquired under the legislation of the Member State to which the deceased person was last subject shall be maintained, whilst the right acquired under the legislation of any other Member State shall lapse.

[¹ **3.** By way of derogation from paragraphs 1 and 2, in the cases referred to in Articles 14c(b) or 14f of the Regulation, any entitlement to death grants acquired under the legislation of the Member States concerned shall be retained.

AMENDMENT

1. Regulation 1606/98/EC, [1998] OJ L209/1 (October 25, 1998).

Article 9a

Rules applicable in the case of overlapping of rights to unemployment benefits

3.320   If an employed or self-employed person, entitled to unemployment benefits under the legislation of a Member State to which he was subject during his last employment or self-employment pursuant to Article 69 of the Regulation, goes to Greece where he is also entitled to unemployment benefits by virtue of a period of insurance, employment or self-employment previously completed under Greek legislation, the right to benefits under Greek legislation shall be suspended for the period laid down in Article 69(1)(c) of the Regulation.

Article 10

Rules applicable in the case of overlapping of rights to family benefits or family allowances for employed or self-employed persons

3.321   1. (a) Entitlement to benefits or family allowances due under the legislation of a Member State, according to which acquisition of the right to those benefits or allowances is not subject to conditions of insurance, employment or self-employment, shall be suspended when, during the same period and for the same member of the family, benefits are due only in pursuance of the national legislation of another Member State or in application of Articles 73, 74, 77 or 78 of the Regulation, up to the sum of those benefits.
   (b) However, where a professional or trade activity is carried out in the territory of the first member State:
      (i) in the case of benefits due either only under national legislation of another Member State or under Articles 73 or 74 of the Regulation to the person entitled to family benefits or to the person to whom they are to be paid, the right to family benefits due either only under national legislation of that other Member State or under theses Articles shall be suspended up to the sum of family benefits provided for by the legislation of the Member State in whose territory the member of the family is residing. The cost of the benefits paid by the Member State in whose territory the member of the family is residing shall be borne by that Member State;
      (ii) in the case of benefits due either only under national legislation of another Member State or under Articles 77 or 78 of the Regulation, to the person entitled to these benefits or to the person to whom they are payable, the right to these family benefits or family allowances due either only under the national legislation of that other Member State or in application of those Articles shall be suspended; where this is the case, the person concerned shall be entitled to the family benefits or family allowances of the Member State in whose territory the children reside, the cost to be borne by that Member State, and, where appropriate, to benefits other than the family allowances

Article 10

referred to in Article 77 or Article 78 of the Regulation, the cost to be borne by the competent State as defined by those Articles.

2. If an employed person subject to the legislation of a Member State is entitled to family allowances by virtue of periods of insurance or employment previously completed under Greek legislation, this right shall be suspended where, during the same period and for the same member of the family, family benefits or allowance are due under the legislation of the first Member State pursuant to Articles 73 and 74 of the Regulation, up to the sum of those benefits.

3. Where family benefits are due, over the same period and for the same member of the family, from two Member States pursuant to Articles 73 and/or 74 of the Regulation, the competent institution of the Member State with legislation providing for the highest levels of benefit shall pay the full amount of such benefit and be reimbursed half this sum by the competent institution of the other Member State up to the limit of the amount provided for in the legislation of the latter Member State.

RELEVANT DECISIONS OF THE ADMINISTRATIVE COMMISSION

Decision No 119 of 24 February 1983 concerning the interpretation of Article 76 and Article 79(3) of regulation (EEC) No 1408/71 and of Article 10(1) of Regulation (EEC) No 574/72 relating to the overlapping of family benefits and allowances, [1983] OJ C295/3.

Decision No 150 of 26 June 1992 concerning the application of Articles 77, 78 and 79(3) of Regulation (EEC) No 1408/71 and of Article 10 of regulation (EEC) No 574/72, [1993] OJ C229/5.

Article 10a

Rules applicable where an employed or self-employed person is subject successively to the legislation of several Member States during the same period or part of a period

Where an employed or self-employed person has been subject successively to the legislation of two Member States during the period separating two dates for the payment of family benefits as provided for by the legislation of one or both of the Member States concerned, the following rules shall apply:

(a) The family benefits which the person concerned may claim by virtue of being subject to the legislation of each one of these States shall correspond to the number of daily benefits due under the relevant legislation. Where such legislation does not provide for daily benefits, the family benefits shall be granted in proportion to the length of time during which the person concerned has been subject to the legislation of each one of the Member States in relation to the period fixed by the legislation concerned.

(b) Where the family benefits have been provided by an institution during a period when they should have been provided by another institution, there shall be an adjustment of accounts between the said institutions.

(c) For the purposes of subparagraphs (a) and (b), where periods of employment or self-employment completed under the legislation of one Member State are expressed in units different from those which are used for the calculation of family benefits under the legislation of another Member State to which the person concerned has also been subject during the same period, the conversion shall be carried out in

accordance with the provisions of Article 15 (3) of the implementing Regulation.
(d) Notwithstanding the provisions of subparagraph (a) in respect of dealings between the Member States listed in Annex 8 to the implementing regulation, the institution bearing the costs of the family benefits by reason of the first employment or self-employment during the period concerned shall bear such costs throughout the entire current period.

TITLE III

IMPLEMENTATION OF THE PROVISIONS OF THE REGULATIONS FOR DETERMINING THE LEGISLATION APPLICABLE

IMPLEMENTATION OF ARTICLES 13 TO 17 OF THE REGULATION

Article 10b

Formalities pursuant to Article 13(2)(f) of the Regulation

3.323   The date and conditions on which the legislation of a Member State ceases to be applicable to a person referred to in Article 13(2)(f) of the Regulation shall be determined in accordance with that legislation. The institution designated by the competent authority of the Member State whose legislation becomes applicable to the person shall apply to the institution designated by the competent authority of the former Member State with a request to specify this date.

[¹*Article 10c*

Formalities laid down in the event of the application of Article 13(2)(d) of the Regulation to civil servants and persons treated as such

3.324   For the application of Article 13(2)(d), the institution designated by the competent authority of the Member State whose legislation is applicable shall issue a certificate stating that the civil servant or the person treated as such is subject to its legislation.]

AMENDMENT

1. Regulation 647/2005/EC, [2005] OJ L117/1 (May 5, 2005).

Article 11

Formalities in the case of the posting elsewhere of an employed person pursuant to Articles 14(1) and 14b(1) of the Regulation and in the case of Agreements concluded under Article 17 of the Regulation

3.325   1. The institutions designated by the competent authority of the Member State whose legislation is to remain applicable shall issue a certificate stating

Article 11

that an employed person shall remain subject to that legislation up to a specific date:
 (a) at the request of the employed person or his employer in cases referred to in Articles 14(1) and 14b(1) of the Regulation;
 (b) in cases where article 17 of the Regulation applies.
 2. The consent provided for in cases referred to in Articles 14(1)(b) and 14b(1) of the Regulation shall be requested by the employer.

Article 11a

Formalities pursuant to Articles 14a(1) and 14b(2) of the Regulation and in the case of Agreements concluded under Article 17 of the Regulation in the case of work carried out in the territory of a Member State other than that in which the person concerned is normally self-employed

1. The institution designated by the competent authority of the Member State whose legislation is to remain applicable shall issue a certificate stating that the self-employed person shall remain subject to that legislation up to a specified date:
 (a) at the request of the self-employed person in cases referred to in Articles 14a(1) and 14b(2) of the Regulation;
 (b) in cases where Article 17 of the Regulation applies.
 2. The consent provided for in cases referred to in Articles 14a(1) and 14b(2) of the Regulation shall be requested by the self-employed person.

3.326

Article 12

Special provisions concerning insurance of employed persons under the German social security scheme

Where, under the terms of Articles 13(2)(a), 14(1) and (2) or 14b(1) of the Regulation, or under an agreement concluded pursuant to Article 17 of the Regulation, German legislation applies to a person employed by an undertaking or employer whose registered office or place of business is not situated on German territory, and the person concerned has no fixed job on German territory, this legislation shall apply as if the person concerned were employed in his place of residence on German territory.

If the employed person has no residence on German territory, German legislation shall apply as if he were employed in a place for which the Allgemeine Ortskrankenkasse Bonn (Local General Sickness Fund of Bonn), Bonn, is competent.

3.327

Article 12a

[¹ Rules applicable in respect of the persons referred to in Article 14(2) and (3), Article 14a(2) to (4) and Article 14c of the Regulation who normally carry out an employed or self-employed activity in the territory of two or more Member States

For the application of the provisions of Article 14(2) and (3), Article 14a(2) to (4) and Article 14c of the Regulation, the following rules shall apply:]

3.328

Council Regulation (EEC) No 574/72

1. (a) A person who normally pursues his activity in the territory of two or more Member States or in an undertaking which has its registered office or place of business in the territory of one Member State and which straddles the common frontier of two Member States, or who is employed simultaneously in the territory of one Member State and self-employed in the territory of another Member State shall notify this situation to the institution designated by the competent authority of the Member State in the territory of which he resides.
   (b) Where the legislation of the Member State in the territory of which the person resides is not applicable to him, the institution designated by the competent authority of that Member State shall in turn notify the situation to the institution designated by the competent authority of the Member State whose legislation is applicable.

[¹ 1a. Where, in accordance with Article 14(2)(a) of the Regulation, a person who is a member of the travelling or flying personnel of an international transport undertaking is subject to the legislation of the Member State in whose territory the registered office or place of business of the undertaking, or the branch or permanent establishment employing him, is located, or where he resides and is predominantly employed, the institution designated by the competent authority of that Member State shall issue to the person concerned a certificate stating that he is subject to its legislation.]

2. (a) Where, in accordance with Article 14(2)(b)(i) or the first sentence of paragraph 2 of Article 14a of the Regulation, a person who is normally employed or self-employed in the territory of two or more Member States and who pursues part of his activity in the Member State in whose territory he resides is subject to the legislation of that Member State, the institution designated by the competent authority of that Member State shall issue to the person concerned a certificate stating that he is subject to its legislation and shall send a copy thereof to the institution designated by the competent authority of any other Member State:
      (i) in the territory of which the person concerned pursues a part of his activity,
      and/or
      (ii) if he is an employed person, in the territory of which an undertaking or an employer by whom he is employed has its registered office or place of business.
   (b) The latter institution shall, where necessary, send to the institution designated by the competent authority of the Member State whose legislation is applicable the information necessary to assess the contributions for which the employer or employers and/or the person concerned are liable by virtue of that legislation.

3. (a) Where, in accordance with Article 14(3) or 14a(3) of the Regulation, a person who is employed in the territory of one Member State by an undertaking which has its registered office or place of business in the territory of another Member State and which straddles the common frontier of those States, or who is self-employed in such an undertaking, is subject to the legislation of the Member State in whose territory the undertaking has its registered office or place of business, the institution designated by the competent authority of the latter Member State shall issue to the person concerned a certificate stating that he is subject to its legislation and shall send a copy thereof to the

Article 12a

institution designated by the competent authority of any other Member State:
  (i) in the territory of which the person concerned is employed or self-employed;
  (ii) in the territory of which the person concerned resides.
  (b) Paragraph 2 (b) above shall apply by analogy.
4. (a) Where, in accordance with Article 14(2)(b)(ii) of the Regulation, an employed person who does not reside in the territory of any of the Member States in which he is pursuing his activity is subject to the legislation of the Member State in whose territory is situated the registered office or place of business of the undertaking or individual employing him, the institution designated by the competent authority of the latter Member State shall issue to the employed person a certificate stating that he is subject to its legislation and shall send a copy thereof to the institution designated by the competent authority of any other Member State:
  (i) in the territory of which the employed person pursues a part of his activity;
  (ii) in the territory of which the employed person resides.
  (b) Paragraph 2(b) above shall apply by analogy.
5. (a) Where, in accordance with the provisions of the second sentence of paragraph 2 of Article 14a of the Regulation, a person who is normally self-employed in the territory of two or more Member States, but who does not pursue any part of his activity in the territory of the Member State in which he resides, is subject to the legislation of the Member State in whose territory he pursues his principal activity, the institution designated by the competent authority of the Member State in the territory of which he resides shall forthwith inform the institution designated by the competent authorities of the other Member States concerned.
  (b) The competent authorities of the Member States concerned or the institutions designated by those competent authorities shall by common agreement determine the legislation applicable to the person concerned, account being taken of the provisions of subparagraph (d) and, where appropriate, of the provisions of Article 14a(4) of the Regulation, within a period of not more than six months counting from the day on which the situation of the person concerned was notified to one of the institutions concerned.
  (c) The institution administering the legislation that has been determined as being applicable to the person concerned shall issue a certificate to that person showing that he is subject to that legislation and shall send a copy thereof to the other institutions concerned.
  (d) For the purpose of determining, in pursuance of the third sentence of Article 14a(2) of the Regulation, the principal activity of the person concerned, account shall be taken first and foremost of the locality in which the fixed and permanent premises from which the person concerned pursues his activities is situated. Failing this, account shall be taken of criteria such as the usual nature or the duration of the activities pursued, the number of services rendered and the income arising from those activities.
  (e) The institution concerned shall exchange all information necessary to determine both the principal activity of the person concerned and

the contributions payable under the legislation that has been determined as being applicable to him.

6. (a) Without prejudice to paragraph 5, and in particular to subparagraph (b) thereof, if an institution designated by the competent authority of the Member State whose legislation would be applicable by virtue of Article 14a(2) or (3) of the Regulation establishes that the provisions of paragraph 4 of the said Article apply in the case of the person concerned, it shall notify the competent authorities of the other Member States concerned or the institutions designated by those authorities; where necessary, the legislation to be applicable to the person concerned shall be decided on by common agreement.

(b) The information referred to in paragraph 2(b) above shall be sent by the other institutions concerned to the institutions designated by the competent authority of the Member State whose legislation is determined to be applicable.

7. (a) Where, in accordance with Article 14c(a) of the Regulation, a person who is employed simultaneously in the territory of one Member State, and is self-employed in the territory of another Member State, is subject to the legislation of the Member State in whose territory he is engaged in paid employment, the institution designated by the competent authority of the latter Member State shall issue to the employed person a certificate stating that he is subject to its legislation and shall send a copy thereof to the institution designated by the competent authority of any other Member State:

(i) in the territory of which that person is self-employed;
(ii) in the territory of which that person resides.

(b) Paragraph 2(b) above shall apply by analogy.

8. Where, in accordance with the provisions of Article 14, 14c(b) of the Regulation, a person who is simultaneously employed in the territory of one Member State and self-employed in the territory of another Member State is subject to the legislation of two Member States, the provisions of points 1, 2, 3 and 4 shall be applicable in respect of paid employment, and the provisions of points 1, 2, 3, 5 and 6 shall be applicable mutatis mutandis in respect of self-employment.

The institution designated by the competent authorities of the two Member States, whose legislation is determined to be applicable, shall inform each other accordingly.

AMENDMENT

1. Regulation 647/2005/EC, [2005] OJ L117/1 (May 5, 2005).

Article 12b

Rules applicable in respect of persons referred to in Article 14e or 14f of the Regulation

3.329

The provisions are Article 12a(1), (2), (3) and (4) shall apply by analogy to those persons covered by Articles 14e or 14f of the Regulation. In cases covered by Article 14f of the Regulation, the institution designated by the competent authorities of the Member States whose legislation is determined to be applicable shall inform each other accordingly.

Article 12b

AMENDMENT

1. Regulation 1606/98/EC, [1998] OJ L209/1 (October 25, 1998).

Article 13

Exercise of the right of option by persons employed by diplomatic missions and consular posts

1. The right of option provided for in Article 16(2) of the Regulation must be exercised in the first instance within the three months following the date on which the employed person was engaged by the diplomatic mission or consular post concerned, or on which he entered into the personal service of agents of such mission or post.

The option shall take effect on the date of entry into employment.

When the person concerned renews his right of option at the end of a calendar year, the option shall take effect on the first day of the following calendar year.

2. The person concerned who exercises his right of option shall inform the institution designated by the competent authority of the Member State for whose legislation he has opted, at the same time notifying his employer thereof. The said institution shall, where necessary, forward such information to all other institutions of the same Member State, in accordance with directives issued by the competent authority of that Member State.

3. The institution designated by the competent authority of the Member State for whose legislation the person concerned has opted shall issue to him a certificate testifying that he is subject to the legislation of that Member State while he is employed by the diplomatic mission or consular post in question or in the personal service of agents of such mission or post.

4. Where the person concerned has opted for German legislation to be applied, the provisions of that legislation shall be applied as though he were employed in the place where the German Government has its seat. The competent authority shall designate the competent sickness insurance institution.

Article 14

Exercise of right of option by auxiliary staff of the European Communities

1. The right of option provided for in Article 16(3) of the Regulation must be exercised at the time when the contract of employment is concluded. The authority empowered to conclude such contract shall inform the institution designated by the competent authority of the Member State for whose legislation the auxiliary staff member has opted. The said institution shall, where necessary, forward such information to all other institutions of the same Member State.

2. The institution designated by the competent authority of the Member State for whose legislation the auxiliary staff member has opted shall issue to him a certificate testifying that his is subject to the legislation of that Member State while he is employed by the European Communities as an auxiliary staff member.

3. The competent authorities of the Member States shall, where necessary, designate the competent institutions in respect of members of the auxiliary staff of the European Communities.

4. Where an auxiliary staff member, employed in the territory of a Member State other than Germany, has opted for German legislation to be applied, the provisions of that legislation shall be applied as though the auxiliary staff member were employed in the place where the German Government has its seat. The competent authority shall designate the competent sickness insurance institution.

TITLE IV

IMPLEMENTATION OF THE SPECIAL PROVISIONS OF THE REGULATION RELATING TO THE VARIOUS CATEGORIES OF BENEFITS

CHAPTER 1

GENERAL RULES FOR THE AGGREGATION OF PERIODS

Article 15

1. In the cases referred to in Articles 18(1), 38, 45(1) to (3), 64, and 67(1) and (2) of the Regulation, aggregation of periods shall be effected in accordance with the following rules:
   (a) To periods of insurance or residence completed under the legislation of one Member State shall be added periods of insurance or residence completed under the legislation of any other Member State, to the extent that this is necessary to have recourse thereto in order to supplement periods of insurance or residence completed under the legislation of the first Member State for the purpose of acquiring, retaining, or recovering the rights to benefits, provided that such periods of insurance or residence do not overlap. Where benefits in respect of invalidity, old age or death (pensions) are to be awarded by the institutions of two or more Member States in accordance with the provisions of Article 46(2) of the Regulation, each of the institutions concerned shall effect a separate aggregation, by taking into account the whole of the periods of insurance or residence completed by the employed or self-employed person under the legislations of all the Member States to which he has been subject, without prejudice, where appropriate, to the provisions of Article 45(2) and (3) and Article 47(1)(a) of the Regulation. Nevertheless, in the cases referred to in Article 14c(b) of the Regulation, the above mentioned institutions shall likewise take account, for the award of benefits, of the periods of insurance or of residence completed under an obligatory insurance scheme under the legislation of the two Member States in question which overlap each other.

Article 15

[¹ Nevertheless, in the cases referred to in Articles 14c(b) or 14f of the Regulation, the abovementioned institutions shall likewise take account, for the award of benefits, of the periods of insurance or of residence completed under an obligatory insurance scheme under the legislation of the Member States in question which overlap each other.]

(b) When a period of insurance or residence completed under compulsory insurance under the legislation of one Member State coincides with a period of insurance completed under voluntary or optional continued insurance under the legislation of another Member State, only the period completed under compulsory insurance shall be taken into account.

(c) When a period of insurance or residence, other than a period treated as such, completed under the legislation of one Member State coincides with a period treated as such under the legislation of another Member State, only the period other than a period treated as such shall be taken into account.

(d) Any period treated as such under the legislations of two or more Member States shall be taken into account only by the institution of the Member State under whose legislation the insured person was last compulsorily insured prior to the said period; where the insured person has not been compulsorily insured under the legislation of a Member State before the said period, the latter shall be taken into account by the institution of the Member State under whose legislation he was compulsorily insured for the first time after the said period.

(e) Where it is not possible to determine accurately the period of time in which certain periods of insurance or residence were completed under the legislation of one Member State, such periods shall be presumed not to overlap with periods of insurance or residence completed under the legislation of another Member State and shall, where advantageous, be taken into account.

(f) Where under the legislation of one Member State certain periods of insurance or residence are taken into account only if they have been completed within a specified time limit, the institution which administers such legislation shall:
   (i) only take into account periods of insurance or residence completed under the legislation of another Member State if they were completed within the said time limit,
   (ii) extend such a time limit for the duration of periods of insurance or residence completed wholly or partly within the said time limit under the legislation of another Member State, where the periods of insurance or residence involved under the legislation of the second Member State give rise only to the suspension of the time limit within which the periods of insurance or residence must be completed.

2. Periods of insurance or residence completed under the legislation of a Member State to which the Regulation does not apply, but which are taken into account under the legislation of that Member State to which the Regulation does apply, shall be considered as periods of insurance or residence to be taken into account for the purposes of aggregation.

3. When periods of insurance completed under the legislation of one Member State are expressed in units different from those used by the

Council Regulation (EEC) No 574/72

legislation of another Member State, the conversion necessary for the purposes of aggregation shall be carried out according to the following rules:
  (a) Where the person concerned is an employed person who has been subject to a six-day week or if he is self-employed:
      (i) one day shall be equivalent to eight hours and vice versa;
      (ii) six days shall be equivalent to one week and vice versa;
      (iii) 26 days shall be equivalent to one month and vice versa;
      (iv) three months or 13 weeks or 78 days shall be equivalent to one quarter and vice versa;
      (v) for the conversion of weeks into months and vice versa the weeks and months shall be converted into days;
      (vi) the application of the preceding rules shall not have the effect of producing, for the sum total of the periods of insurance completed during one calendar year, a total exceeding 312 days or 52 weeks or 12 months or four quarters.
  (b) If the person concerned is an employed person who has been subject to a five-day week:
      (i) one day shall be equivalent to nine hours and vice versa;
      (ii) five days shall be equivalent to one week and vice versa;
      (iii) 22 days shall be equivalent to one month and vice versa;
      (iv) three months or 13 weeks or 66 days shall be equivalent to one quarter and vice versa;
      (v) for the conversion of weeks into months and vice versa, the weeks and the months shall be converted into days;
      (vi) the application of the preceding rules shall not have the effect of producing, for the sum total of the periods of insurance completed during one calendar year, a total exceeding 264 days or 52 weeks or 12 months for four quarters.
  (c) If the person concerned is an employed person who has been subject to a seven-day week:
      (i) one day shall be equivalent to six hours and vice versa;
      (ii) seven days shall be equivalent to one week and vice versa;
      (iii) thirty days shall be equivalent to one month and vice versa;
      (iv) three months or 13 weeks or 90 days shall be equivalent to one quarter and vice versa;
      (v) for the conversion of weeks into months and vice versa, the weeks and the months shall be converted into days;
      (vi) the application of the preceding rules shall not have the effect of producing, for the sum total of the periods of insurance completed during one calendar year, a total exceeding 360 days or 52 weeks or 12 months for four quarters.

Where the periods of insurance completed under the laws of a Member State are expressed in months, the days which correspond to a fraction of a month, in accordance with the conversion rules set out in this paragraph, are considered as an entire month.

AMENDMENT

1. Regulation 1606/98/EC, [1998] OJ L209/1 (October 25, 1998).

RELEVANT DECISIONS OF THE ADMINISTRATIVE COMMISSION

Decision No 137 of 15 December 1988 concerning the application of Article 15(3) of regulation (EEC) No 574/72, [1989] OJ C140/3.

Article 16

CHAPTER 2

SICKNESS AND MATERNITY

IMPLEMENTATION OF ARTICLE 18 OF THE REGULATION

Article 16

Certification of periods of insurance

1. In order to invoke the provisions of Article 18 of the Regulation, an employed or self-employed person shall submit to the competent institution a certified statement specifying the periods of insurance completed under the legislation to which he was last subject.
2. This certified statement shall be issued at the request of the employed or self-employed person by the institution or institutions of the Member State to whose legislation he was last subject. If he does not submit the said certified statement, the competent institution shall obtain it from the institution or institutions concerned.
3. The provisions of paragraph 1 and 2 shall apply by analogy if it is necessary to take into account periods of insurance previously completed under the legislation of any other Member State in order to satisfy the conditions of the legislation of the competent State.

IMPLEMENTATION OF ARTICLE 19 OF THE REGULATION

Article 17

Benefits in kind in the case of residence in a Member State other than the competent State

1. In order to receive benefits in kind under Article 19 of the Regulation, an employed or self-employed person must register himself and the members of his family with the institution of his place or residence by submitting a certified statement testifying that he and the members of his family are entitled to the said benefits. This certified statement, based upon information supplied by the employer, where appropriate, shall be issued by the competent institution. If the employed or self-employed person or the members of his family do not submit the said certified statement the institution of the place of residence shall obtain it from the competent institutions.
2. That certified statement shall remain valid until the institution of the place of residence receives notification of its cancellation.
However, where the said certified statement has been issued by a German, French, Italian or Portuguese institution, it shall be valid only for a period of one year following the date on which it was issued and must be renewed every year.

Council Regulation (EEC) No 574/72

3. If the person concerned is a seasonal worker, the certified statement referred to in paragraph 1 shall be valid for the whole of the expected duration of the seasonal work, unless, in the meanwhile, the competent institution notifies the institution of the place of residence of its cancellation.

4. The institution of the place of residence shall inform the competent institution of every registration effected in accordance with the provisions of paragraph 1.

5. Upon each application for benefits in kind, the person concerned shall submit the supporting documents required for the granting of benefits in kind under the legislation of the Member State in whose territory he resides.

6. [^{1} . . .]

7. [^{1} . . .]

8. The employed or self-employed person or the members of his family shall inform the institution of the place of residence of any change in their situation which is likely to alter their entitlement to benefits in kind, in particular any cessation or change of the employment or self-employment of the person concerned or any transfer of residence or stay of the employed or self-employed person or of a member of his family. Likewise, should the employed or self-employed person cease to be insured or cease to be entitled to benefits in kind, the competent institution shall inform the institution of the place of residence accordingly. The institution of the place of residence may, at any time, request the competent institution to supply it with any information relating to the employed or self-employed person's insurance or to his entitlement to benefits in kind.

9. Two or more Member States or the competent authorities of those Member States may, having received the opinion of the Administrative Commission, agree on other implementing provisions.

AMENDMENT

1. Regulation 631/2004/EC, [2004] OJ L100/1 (June 1, 2004).

Article 18

Cash benefits in the case of residence in a Member State other than the competent State

1. In order to receive cash benefits under Article 19(1)(b) of the Regulation an employed or self-employed person shall, within three days of commencement of the incapacity for work, apply to the institution of the place of residence by submitting a notification of having ceased work, or, if the legislation administered by the competent institution or by the institution of the place of residence so provides, a certificate of incapacity for work issued by the doctor providing treatment for the person concerned.

2. Where the doctors providing treatment in the country of residence do not issue certificates of incapacity for work, the person concerned shall apply directly to the institution of the place of residence within the time limit fixed by the legislation which it administers.

That institution shall immediately have the incapacity for work medically confirmed and the certificate referred to in paragraph 1 drawn up. Such certificate shall state the probable duration of the incapacity and shall be forwarded to the competent institution forthwith.

Article 18

3. In cases where paragraph 2 does not apply, the institution of the place of residence shall, as soon as possible and in any event within the three days following the date on which the person concerned applied to it, have him medically examined as if he were insured with that institution. The report of the examining doctor shall indicate, in particular, the probable duration of the incapacity for work, and shall be forwarded to the competent institution by the institution of the place of residence within the three days following the date of the examination.

4. The institution of the place of residence shall subsequently carry out any necessary administrative checks or medical examination of the person concerned as if he were insured with that institution. As soon as it establishes that the person concerned is fit to resume work, it shall forthwith notify him and the competent institution accordingly, stating the date on which his incapacity for work ceased. Without prejudice to the provisions of paragraph 6, the notification to the person concerned shall be treated as a decision taken on behalf of the competent institution.

5. In all cases the competent institution shall reserve the right to have the person concerned examined by a doctor of its own choice.

6. If the competent institution decides to withhold the cash benefits because the person concerned has not completed the formalities laid down by the legislation of the country of residence, or if it establishes that the person concerned is fit to resume work, it shall notify the person concerned of its decision and shall simultaneously send a copy of such decision to the institution of the place of residence.

7. When the person concerned resumes work, he shall notify the competent institution accordingly, if such notification is required by the legislation administered by that institution.

8. The competent institution shall pay cash benefits by the appropriate method, in particular by international money order, and shall inform the institution of the place of residence and the person concerned accordingly. Where cash benefits are paid by the institution of the place of residence on behalf of the competent institution, the latter shall inform the person concerned of his rights and shall notify the institution of the place of residence of the amount of the cash benefits, the dates for payment, and the maximum period during which they should be granted, in accordance with the legislation of the competent State.

9. Two or more Member States, or the competent authorities of those Member States may, having received the opinion of the Administrative Commission, agree on other implementing provisions.

IMPLEMENTATION OF ARTICLE 20 OF THE REGULATION

Article 19

Special provisions for frontier workers and members of their families

In the case of frontier workers or members of their families, medicinal products, bandages, spectacles and small appliances may be issued, and laboratory analyses and tests carried out, only in the territory of the Member State in which they were prescribed, in accordance with the provisions of the legislation of that Member State, except where the legislation administered

3.336

APPLICATION OF THE SECOND INDENT OF ARTICLE 21(2) OF THE REGULATION

Article 19a

Benefits in kind in the event of a stay in the competent State—embers of the family resident in the Member State other than that in which the employed or self-employed person resides

3.337　**1.** In order to receive benefits in kind under the terms of Article 21 of the Regulation, members of the family shall present to the institution at the place of stay a certificate stating that they are entitled to the said benefits. This certificate, which shall be provided by the institution of the place of residence of the members of the family, if possible prior to their leaving the territory of the Member State on which they reside, shall, in particular, indicate where appropriate the maximum period for granting benefits in kind, as laid down by the legislation of that Member State. If the members of the family do not present the said certificate, the institution at the place of stay shall contact the institution of the place of residence in order to obtain it.

[¹ Article 17(9) of the implementing Regulation shall apply by analogy.]

AMENDMENT

1. Regulation 631/2004/EC, [2004] OJ L100/1 (June 1, 2004).

IMPLEMENTATION OF ARTICLE 22 OF THE REGULATION

Article 20

Benefits in kind in the case of a stay in a Member State other than the competent State—Special case of persons employed in international transport and members of their families

3.338　[¹ . . .]

AMENDMENT

1. Regulation 631/2004/EC, [2004] OJ L100/1 (June 1, 2004).

[¹*Article 21*

Benefits in kind in the case of a stay in a Member State other than the competent State

3.339　**1.** In order to receive benefits in kind under Article 22(1)(a)(i) of the Regulation, an employed or self-employed person shall submit to the care of the provider a document issued by the competent institution certifying

Article 21

that he is entitled to benefits in kind. That document shall be drawn up in accordance with Article 2. If the person concerned is not able to submit that document, he shall contact the institution of the place of stay which shall request from the competent institution a certified statement testifying that the person concerned is entitled to benefits in kind.

A document issued by the competent institution for entitlement to benefits in accordance with Article 22(1)(a)(i) of the Regulation, in each individual case concerned, shall have the same effect with regard to the care provider as national evidence of the entitlements of the person insured with the institution of the place of stay.

2. Article 17(9) of the implementing Regulation shall apply by analogy.]

AMENDMENT

1. Regulation 631/2004/EC, [2004] OJ L100/1 (June 1, 2004).

Article 22

Benefits in kind for employed or self-employed persons who transfer their residence or return to their country of residence, and for employed or self-employed persons authorized to go to another Member State for medical treatment

1. In order to receive benefits in kind under Article 22(1)(b)(i) of the Regulation, an employed or self-employed person shall submit to the institution of the place of residence a certified statement testifying that he is entitled to continue receiving the said benefits. The certified statement, which shall be issued by the competent institution, shall specify in particular, where necessary, the maximum period during which such benefits may continue to be provided, in accordance with the provisions of the legislation of the competent State. The certified statement may, at the request of the person concerned, be issued after his departure if, for reasons of force majeure, it cannot be drawn up beforehand.

[¹ **2.** Article 17(9) of the implementing Regulation shall apply by analogy.]

3. Paragraphs 1 and 2 shall apply by analogy in respect of the provisions of benefits in kind in the case referred to in Article 22(1)(c)(i) of the Regulation.

3.340

AMENDMENT

1. Regulation 631/2004/EC, [2004] OJ L100/1 (June 1, 2004).

Article 23

Benefits in kind for members of the family

The provisions of Article 21 or 22 of the implementing Regulation, as appropriate, shall apply by analogy in respect of the granting of benefits in kind to members of the family as provided for in Article 22(3) of the Regulation.

[¹ However, in the cases referred to in the second subparagraph of Article 22(3) of the Regulation, the institution of the place of residence and the

3.341

Council Regulation (EEC) No 574/72

legislation of the country of residence of the members of the family shall be considered, respectively, as the competent institution and as the legislation of the competent State for the purposes of Article 17(9), 21 and 22 of the implementing Regulation.]

AMENDMENT

1. Regulation 631/2004/EC, [2004] OJ L100/1 (June 1, 2004).

Article 24

Cash benefits for employed or self-employed persons in the case of a stay in a Member State other than the competent State

3.342 The provisions of Article 18 of the implementing Regulation shall apply by analogy in respect of the receipt of cash benefits under Article 22(1)(a)(ii) of the Regulation. However, without prejudice to the obligation to submit a certificate of incapacity for work, an employed or self-employed person who is staying in the territory of a Member State without pursing any employment or self-employment there, shall not be required to submit the notification of having ceased work referred to in Article 18(1) of the implementing Regulation.

IMPLEMENTATION OF ARTICLE 23(3) OF THE REGULATION

Article 25

Certified statement relating to the members of the family to be taken into account in the calculation of cash benefits

3.343 1. In order to receive benefits under the provisions of Article 23(3) of the Regulation, an employed or self-employed person shall submit to the competent institution a certified statement relating to the members of his family who are resident in the territory of a Member State other than that wherein the said institution is situated.

2. This certified statement shall be issued by the institution of the place of residence of the members of the family.

It shall be valid for the 12 months following the date of its issue.

It may be renewed; in such a case, it shall be valid from the date of its renewal.

The person concerned shall immediately notify the competent institution of any occurrence necessitating an amendment to the said certified statement. Such amendment shall take effect from the date of such occurrence.

3. In place of the certified statement provided for in paragraph 1, the competent institution may require the person concerned to produce recent civil status documents relating to the members of his family who are resident in the territory of a Member State other than that wherein the said institutions is situated.

Article 26

IMPLEMENTATION OF ARTICLE 25(1) OF THE REGULATION

Article 26

Benefits for unemployed persons who go to a Member State other than the competent State in order to seek employment there

[¹ 1. In order to receive benefits in cash and in kind under Article 25(1)(a) and (1a) of the Regulation, an unemployed person or a family member accompanying him shall submit to the care provider a document issued by the competent institution certifying that he is entitled to benefits in kind. That document shall be drawn up in accordance with the provisions of Article 2. If the person concerned is not able to submit that document, he shall contact the institution of the place of stay which shall request from the competent institution a certified statement testifying that the person concerned is entitled to benefits in kind.

A document issued by the competent institution for entitlement to benefits in accordance with Article 25(1)(a) of the Regulation, in each individual case concerned, shall have the same effect with regard to the care provider as national evidence of the entitlement of persons insured with the institution of the place to which the unemployed person has gone.

1a. In order to receive benefits in cash under Article 25(1)(b) of the Regulation for himself and for members of his family, an unemployed person shall submit to the insurance institution of the place where he has gone a certified statement for which, prior to his departure, he shall have applied to the competent insurance institution. If the unemployed person does not submit that certified statement, the institution of the place to which he has gone shall obtain it from the competent institution. That certified statement must testify the existence of the right to the benefits in question under the conditions set out in Article 69(1)(a) of the Regulation, indicate the duration of such right taking into account the provisions of Article 69(1)(c) of the Regulation and, in the case of incapacity for work or hospitalisation, specify the amount of cash benefits to be provided, where appropriate, by way of sickness insurance during the abovementioned period.]

2. The unemployment insurance institution of the place where the unemployed person has gone shall testify, on a copy of the certified statement referred to in Article 83 of the implementing Regulation which shall be sent to the sickness insurance institution of that same place, that the conditions laid down in Article 69(1)(b) of the Regulation have been fulfilled and shall specify the date from which they were fulfilled, and the date from which the unemployed person shall receive unemployment insurance benefits at the expense of the competent institution.

[¹ 3. Article 17(9) of the implementing Regulation shall apply by analogy.]

4. In order to receive the cash benefits provided for by the legislation of the competent State, the unemployed person shall, within three days, send a certificate of incapacity for him, to the sickness insurance institution of the place to which he has gone. He shall also state the date up to which he has received sickness insurance benefits and his address in the country where he is.

3.344

5. The sickness insurance institution of the place to which the unemployed person has gone shall, within three days, notify the competent sickness insurance institution, as well as the institution where the unemployed person is registered as seeking employment, of the date when the incapacity for work began and ended.

6. In the cases defined in Article 25(4) of the Regulation, the sickness insurance institution of the place to which the unemployed person has gone shall inform the competent sickness insurance institution and the competent unemployment insurance institution that it considers that the conditions justifying the extension of the period during which benefits in cash and in kind may be granted are satisfied, stating the grounds on which its opinion is based, and shall attach to the communication it sends to the competent sickness insurance institution a detailed report from the examining doctor on the condition of the patient, indicating the probable period during which the conditions for applying Article 25(4) of the Regulation will exist. The competent sickness insurance institution shall then take the decision as to the extension of the period during which benefits may be granted to the sick unemployed person.

7. The provisions of Article 18(2), (3), (4), (5), (6), (8) and (9) of the implementing Regulation shall apply by analogy.

AMENDMENT

1. Regulation 631/2004/EC, [2004] OJ L100/1 (June 1, 2004).

IMPLEMENTATION OF ARTICLE 25(3) OF THE REGULATION

Article 27

Benefits in kind for members of the family of unemployed persons in the case of residence in a Member State other than the competent State

3.345   The provisions of Article 17 of the implementing Regulation shall apply by analogy in respect of the granting of benefits in kind to the members of the family of unemployed persons when such members of the family are resident in the territory of a Member State other than the competent State.

At the time of the registration of the members of the family of unemployed persons receiving benefits under the provisions of Article 69(1) of the Regulation the certified statement referred to in Article 26(1) of the implementing Regulation must be produced. This certified statement shall be valid for the period of time during which the benefits may be granted under Article 69(1) of the Regulation.

Article 28

IMPLEMENTATION OF ARTICLE 26 OF THE REGULATION

Article 28

Benefits in kind for pension claimants and for members of their families

1. In order to receive benefits in kind in the territory of the Member State in which he resides, under Article 26(1) of the Regulation, a claimant and the members of his family shall register with the institution of the place of residence by submitting a certified statement testifying that he is entitled under the legislation of another Member State to the said benefits for himself and for the members of his family. This certified statement shall be issued by the institution of that other Member State which is responsible for benefits in kind.

2. The institution of the place of residence shall inform the institution which has issued the certified statement of every registration effected in accordance with paragraph 1.

3.346

IMPLEMENTATION OF ARTICLES 28 AND 28A OF THE REGULATION

Article 29

Benefits in kind for pensioners and members of their families who are not resident in a Member State under whose legislation they receive a pension and are entitled to benefits

1. In order to receive benefits in kind in the territory of the Member State in which he resides, under Articles 28(1) and 28a of the Regulation, a pensioner and the members of his family [[1] residing in the same Member State] shall register with the institution of the place of residence by submitting a certified statement testifying that he is entitled to the said benefits for himself and for the members of his family, under the legislation or one of the legislations under which a pension is payable.

2. This certified statement shall be issued, at the request of the pensioner, by the institution or one of the institutions responsible for payment of the pension or, where appropriate, by the institution empowered to determine entitlement to benefits in kind, as soon as the pensioner satisfies the conditions for acquisition of the right to such benefits. If the pensioner does not submit the certified statement, the institution of the place of residence shall obtain it from the institution or institutions responsible for payment of the pension, or, where appropriate, from the institution empowered to issue such certified statement. Whilst awaiting the receipt of this certified statement the institution of the place of residence may, in the light of the documentary evidence accepted by it, register the pensioner and the members of his family [[1] residing in the same Member State] provisionally. This registration shall bind the institution responsible for the payment of benefits in kind only if this latter institution has issued the certified statement provided for in paragraph 1.

3.347

3. The institution of the place of residence shall inform the institution which has issued the certified statement provided for in paragraph 2 of every registration effected in accordance with the provisions of the said paragraph.

4. When an application is made for benefits in kind it must be proved to the institution of the place of residence, by means of the receipt or the counterfoil of the money order of the last payment made, that the pensioner is still entitled to a pension.

5. The pensioner or the members of his family [¹ residing in the same Member State] shall inform the institution of the place of residence of any entitlement to benefits in kind, in particular any suspension or withdrawal of the pension and any transfer of their residence. The institutions responsible for the pension shall also inform the institution of the pensioners place of residence of any such change.

6. The Administrative Commission shall, to the extent necessary, fix the procedure for determining the institution which shall bear the cost of the payment of benefits in kind, in the case referred to in Article 28(2)(b) of the Regulation.

AMENDMENT

1. Regulation 1223/98/EC, [1998] OJ L168/1 (January 1, 1998 but for France 1 January 2002).

IMPLEMENTATION OF ARTICLE 29 OF THE REGULATION

Article 30

Benefits in kind for members of the family who are resident [¹ outside the competent Member State] in a Member State other than the State in which the pensioner is resident

1. In order to receive benefits in kind, in the territory of the Member State in which they reside, under Article 29(1) of the Regulation, the members of the family shall register with the institution of their place of residence by submitting the documentary evidence required by the legislation which that institution administers for the granting of such benefits to members of the family of a pensioner, together with a certified statement testifying that the pensioner is entitled to benefits in kind for himself and for the members of his family. [¹ This certified statement, which shall be issued by the institution or by one of the institutions responsible for paying the pension, or, where applicable, the institution empowered to decide on entitlement to benefits in kind, shall remain valid as long as the institution of the place of residence of the members of the family has not been notified of its cancellation. However, where the said certified statement has been issued by a German, French, Italian or Portuguese institution, it shall be valid only for a period of one year following the date on which it was issued and must be renewed every year. If the members of the family do not present a certified statement, the institution of the place of residence shall, in order to obtain it, contact the institution or institutions responsible for paying the pension or, where applicable, the institution empowered to do so.]

Article 30

2. When making an application for benefits in kind the members of the family shall submit to the institution of their place of residence the certified statement referred to in paragraph 1, if the legislation which that institution administers provides that such an application must be accompanied by evidence of entitlement to a pension.

[¹ **3.** The institution which has issued the certified statement, the institution of the place of residence shall, in order to obtain it, contact the institution or institutions responsible for paying the pension or, where applicable, the institution empowered to do so.]

4. The members of the family shall inform the institution of their place of residence of any change in their situation which is likely to alter their entitlement to benefits in kind, in particular any transfer of residence.

5. The institution of the place of residence shall inform the institution of which issued the statement referred to in paragraph 1 of any registration it has carried out, in accordance with the provisions of that paragraph.

AMENDMENT

1. Regulation 1223/98/EC, [1998] OJ L168/1 (January 1, 1998 but for France 1 January 2002).

IMPLEMENTATION OF ARTICLE 31 OF THE REGULATION

[¹*Article 31*

Benefits in kind for pensioners and members of their families staying in a Member State other than the one in which they reside

1. In order to receive benefits in kind under Article 31 of the Regulation, a pensioner shall submit to the care provider a document issued by the institution of the place of residence certifying that he is entitled to the benefits in kind. That document shall be drawn up in accordance with Article 2. If the person concerned is not able to submit that document, he shall contact the institution of the place of stay shall request from the institution of the place of residence a certified statement testifying that the person concerned is entitled to benefits in kind.

A document issued by the competent institution for entitlement to benefits is accordance with Article 31 of the Regulation, in each individual case concerned, shall have the same effect with regard to the care provider as national evidence of the entitlements of persons insured with the institution of the place of stay.

2. Article 17(9) of the implementing Regulation shall apply by analogy.

3. Paragraphs 1 and 2 shall apply by analogy in respect of the granting of benefits in kind to the members of the family covered by Article 31 of the Regulation. If these family members reside in the territory of a Member State other than that of the pensioner, the document referred to in paragraph 1 shall be issued by the institution of their place of residence.]

AMENDMENT

1. Regulation 631/2004/EC, [2004] OHJ L100/1 (June 1, 2004).

Council Regulation (EEC) No 574/72

IMPLEMENTATION OF ARTICLE 35(1) OF THE REGULATION

Article 32

Institution to which workers in mines and similar undertakings and members of their families may apply when staying or residing in a Member State other than the competent State

3.350 **1.** In the cases referred to in Article 35(1) of the Regulation and where, in the country of stay or residence, the benefits provided under the insurance scheme for sickness or maternity covering manual workers in the steel industry are equivalent to those provided under the special scheme for workers in mines and similar undertakings, workers belonging to the latter category and members of their families may apply to the nearest institution in the territory of the Member State in which they are staying or residing, specified in Annex 3 to the implementing Regulation, even if the latter is an institution of the scheme applicable to manual workers in the steel industry, which institution shall then provide such benefits.

2. Where the benefits provided under the special scheme for workers in mines and similar undertakings are more advantageous, such workers or the members of their families shall have the option of applying either to the institution responsible for the administration of that scheme, or to the nearest institution in the territory of the Member State in which they are staying or residing which administers the scheme for manual workers in the steel industry. In the latter case, the institution in question shall draw the attention of the person concerned to the fact that by applying to the institution responsible for the administration of the abovementioned special scheme, he will obtain more advantageous benefits; it must, furthermore, inform him of the name and address of such institution.

IMPLEMENTATION OF ARTICLE 35(2) OF THE REGULATION

Article 32a

3.351 [1 . . .]

AMENDMENT

1. Regulation 647/2005/EC, [2005] OJ L117/1 (May 5, 2005).

Article 33

IMPLEMENTATION OF ARTICLE 35(4) OF THE REGULATION

Article 33

Taking account of the period during which benefits have already been provided by the institution of another Member State

For the purposes of implementing the provisions of Article 35(4) of the Regulation, the institution of a Member State called upon to provide benefits may request the institution of another Member State to supply it with information relating to the period during which the latter institution has already provided benefits for the same case of sickness or maternity.

3.352

Article 34

Refund by the competent institution of one Member State of expenses incurred during a stay in another Member State

1. If it is not possible during an employed or self-employed person's stay in a Member State other than the competent State to complete the formalities provided for in Articles 20(1) and (4) and 21, 23 and 31 of the implementing Regulation, his expenses shall, upon his application, be refunded by the competent institution in accordance with the refund rates administered by the institution of the place of stay.

3.353

2. The institution of the place of stay shall, at the request of the competent institution, supply it with the necessary information about such rates. If the institution of the place of stay and the competent institution are bound by an agreement providing either that no refund, or that a lump-sum refund of benefits provided, in pursuance of Articles 22(1)(a)(i) and 31 of the Regulation, be made, the institution of the place of stay shall, in addition, be required to transfer to the competent institution the amount to be refunded to the person concerned in pursuance of the provisions of paragraph 1.

3. Where major expenses are involved, the competent institution may pay an appropriate advance to the person concerned as soon as that person submits to the said institution the claim for refund.

4. Notwithstanding paragraphs 1, 2 and 3, the competent institution may effect the reimbursement of expenses incurred in accordance with the rates it administers provided that it is possible to make a refund in accordance with these rates, that the expenses to be refunded do not exceed a level determined by the Administrative Commission and that the employed person or self-employed person or pensioner agrees to the application of this provision. In any case, the amount of reimbursement shall not exceed the amount of the expenses actually incurred.

[¹ **5.** If the legislation of the State of stay does not provide for rates of reimbursement, the competent institution may effect the reimbursement in accordance with the rates it administers, without the agreement of the person concerned being necessary. In no case shall the amount of reimbursement exceed the amount of the expenses actually incurred.]

Council Regulation (EEC) No 574/72

AMENDMENT

1. Regulation 1386/2001/EC, [2001] OJ L187/1 (September 1, 2001).

CHAPTER 3

INVALIDITY, OLD-AGE AND DEATH (PENSIONS)

SUBMISSION AND INVESTIGATION OF CLAIMS FOR BENEFITS

Article 35

Applications for invalidity benefits where an employed person or a self-employed person has been subject only to the legislations mentioned in part A of Annex IV to the Regulation and also in the case referred to in Article 40(2) of the Regulation

3.354

1. In order to receive benefits under Articles 37, 38 and 39 of the Regulation, including the cases referred to in Articles 40(2), 41(1) and 42(2) of the Regulation, an employed or self-employed person shall submit a claim either to the institution of the Member State to whose legislation he was subject at the time of occurrence of the incapacity for work followed by invalidity or the aggravation of such invalidity, or to the institution of the place of residence, which shall then forward the claim to the first institution, indicating the date on which it was submitted; this date shall be regarded as the date of the submission of the claim to the first institution. However, if sickness insurance cash benefits have been granted, the date on which such cash benefits ceased to be granted must, where appropriate, be regarded as the date of submission of the pension claim.

2. In the case referred to in Article 41(1)(b) of the Regulation, the institution with which the employed or self-employed person was last insured shall notify the amount and the operative date of the benefits due under the legislation which it administers to the institution initially responsible for payment of the benefits. With effect from that date, the benefits due prior to the aggravation of the invalidity shall be cancelled or reduced to an amount not exceeding the supplement referred to in Article 41(1) of the Regulation.

3. The provisions of paragraph 2 shall not apply in the case referred to in Article 41(1)(d) of the Regulation. In this case, the institution with which the claimant was last insured shall apply to the Netherlands institution in order to ascertain the amount due from that institution.

Article 36

Claims for old-age and survivors' benefits (excluding orphans' benefits) and invalidity benefits in cases not referred to in Article 35 of the implementing Regulation

1. In order to receive benefits under Articles 40 to 51 of the Regulation, except in the cases referred to in Article 35 of the implementing Regulation, the person concerned shall submit a claim to the institution of the place of residence in accordance with the procedure provided for by the legislation administered by that institution. If the employed or self-employed person has not been subject to that legislation, the institution of the place of residence shall forward the claim to the institution of the Member State to whose legislation he was last subject, indicating the date on which the claim was submitted. That date shall be regarded as the date on which the claim was submitted to the latter institution.

2. Where a claimant resides in the territory of a Member State to whose legislation the employed or self-employed person has not been subject, he may submit his claim to the institution of the Member State to whose legislation the employed or self-employed person was last subject.

3. Where a claimant resides in the territory of a State which is not a Member State, he shall submit his claim to the competent institution of that Member State to whose legislation the employed or self-employed person was last subject.

Should the claimant submit his claim to the institution of the Member State of which he is a national, the latter shall forward such claim to the competent institution.

4. A claim for benefits sent to the institution of one Member State shall automatically involve the concurrent award of benefits under the legislation of all the Member States in question whose conditions the claimant satisfies except where, under Article 44(2) of the Regulation, the claimant asks for postponement of any old-age benefits to which he would be entitled under the legislation of one or more Member States.

3.355

Article 37

Documents and information which should accompany claims to the benefits referred to in article 36 of the implementing Regulation

The submission of the claims referred to in Article 36 of the implementing Regulation shall be subject to the following rules:
(a) the claim must be accompanied by the required supporting documents and must be made on the form provided for by the legislation:
  (i) of the Member State on whose territory the claimant resides, in the case referred to in Article 36(1);
  (ii) of the Member State to which the employed or self-employed person was last subject, in the cases referred to in Article 36(2) and (3);
(b) the accuracy of the information supplied by the claimant must be established by official documents attached to the claim form, or

3.356

confirmed by the competent bodies of the Member State in whose territory the claimant resides;

(c) the claimant must indicate, in so far as is possible, either the institution or institutions administering insurance in respect of invalidity, old-age or death (pensions) of any Member State with which the employed or self-employed person has been insured, or in the case of an employed person the employer or employers for whom he has worked in the territory of any Member State, by producing any employment certificates which he may have in his possession;

(d) if, under Article 44(2) of the Regulation, the claimant asks for the postponement of the award of any old-age benefits to which he would be entitled under the legislation of one or more member States he must specify the legislation under which he is claiming benefits.

Article 38

Certified statements of the members of the family to be taken into account when establishing the amount of the benefit

1. In order to receive benefits under the provisions of Article 39(4) or 47(3) of the Regulation, the claimant shall submit a certified statement relating to the members of his family, his children excepted, who are residing in the territory of a Member State other than in which the institution responsible for the award of benefits is situated.

This certified statement shall be issued by the sickness insurance institution of the place of residence of the members of the family, or by another institution designated by the competent authority of the Member State in whose territory they are resident. The provisions of the second and third sub-paragraphs of Article 25(2) of the implementing Regulation shall apply by analogy.

In place of the certified statement provided for in the first sub-paragraph, the institution responsible for the award of benefits may require the claimant to supply recent civil status documents relating to the members of his family, his children excepted, who are residing in the territory of a Member State other than the State in which the said institution is situated.

2. In the case referred to in paragraph 1, if the legislation administered by the institution concerned requires that the members of the family should live under the same roof as the pensioner, the fact that the said members of the family who do not satisfy that condition are nevertheless mainly dependent on the claimant must be established by documents proving the regular transmission of part of the claimant's earnings.

Article 39

Article 39

Investigation of applications for invalidity benefits where an employed person or a self-employed person has been subject only to the legislations mentioned in part A of Annex IV to the Regulation

1. If an employed or self-employed person has submitted a claim for invalidity benefits, and the institution establishes that the provisions of Article 37(1) of the Regulation apply, that institution shall, where necessary, obtain from the institution with which the person concerned was last insured a certified statement of the periods of insurance completed by him under the legislation administered by the last institution.

2. Where it is necessary to take into account periods of insurance previously completed under the legislation of any other Member State in order to satisfy the conditions of the legislation of the competent State, the provisions of paragraph 1 shall apply by analogy.

3. In the case referred to in Article 39(3) of the Regulation, the institution which has investigated the claimant's case shall forward his file to the institution with which the person concerned was last insured.

4. Articles 41 to 50 of the implementing Regulation shall not apply to the investigation of claims referred to in paragraphs 1, 2 and 3.

3.358

Article 40

Determination of the degree of invalidity

In order to determine the degree of invalidity, the institution of the Member State shall take into consideration the documents and medical reports and the information of an administrative nature obtained by the institution of any other Member State. Each institution shall, however, retain the right to have the claimant examined by a doctor of its own choice except where the provisions of Article 40(4) of the Regulation apply.

3.359

INVESTIGATION OF CLAIMS FOR BENEFITS IN RESPECT OF INVALIDITY, OLD AGE AND SURVIVORS IN THE CASES REFERRED TO IN ARTICLE 36 OF THE IMPLEMENTING REGULATION

Article 41

Determination of the investigating institutions

1. Claims for benefit shall be investigated by the institution to which they have been sent or forwarded in accordance with the provisions of Article 36 of the implementing Regulation. This institution is hereinafter referred to as the "investigating institution".

3.360

Council Regulation (EEC) No 574/72

2. The investigating institution shall forthwith notify claims for benefits to all the institutions concerned on a special form, so that the claims may be investigated simultaneously and without delay by all these institutions.

Article 42

Forms to be used for the investigation of claims for benefits

3.361 1. When investigating claims for benefits the investigating institution shall use a form which will include, in particular, a statement and a summary of the periods of insurance or residence completed by the employed or self-employed person under the legislation of all the Member States concerned.
2. These forms, when forwarded to the institution of any other Member State, shall take the place of supporting documents.

Article 43

Procedure to be followed by the institution concerned in the investigation of a claim

3.362 1. The investigating institution shall enter on the form provided for in Article 42(1) of the implementing Regulation the periods of insurance or residence completed under the legislation which it administers and it shall forward a copy of that form to the institution administering insurance in respect of invalidity, old-age or death (pensions) of any Member State with which the employed or self-employed person has been insured enclosing, where appropriate, any employment certificates produced by the claimant.
2. Where only one other institution is involved, that institution shall complete the said form by indicating:
 (a) the periods of insurance or residence completed under the legislation which it administers;
 (b) the amount of benefit which the claimant could claim in respect of those periods of insurance or residence only;
 (c) the theoretical amount and the actual amount of benefits calculated in accordance with the provisions of Article 46(2) of the Regulation.
The form, thus completed, shall be returned to the investigating institution.
If a right to benefits is acquired taking into account only the periods of insurance or residence completed under the legislation administered by the institution of the second Member State, and if the amount of benefit corresponding to those periods can be determined without delay, whereas the calculation procedure referred to in subparagraph (c) requires an appreciably longer period of time, the form shall be returned to the investigating institution with the information referred to in subparagraphs (a) and (b); the information referred to in subparagraph (c) shall be forwarded to the investigating institution as soon as possible.
3. If two or more other institutions are involved, each one of those institutions shall complete the said form by indicating the periods of insurance or residence completed under the legislation which it administers, and shall return it to the investigating institution.

Article 43

If a right to benefits is acquired taking into account only the periods of insurance or residence completed under the legislation administered by one or more of those institutions, and if the amount of benefit corresponding to those periods can be determined without delay, the investigating institution shall be simultaneously notified of that amount and of the periods of insurance or residence; if the determination of the said amount involves some delay, the investigating institution shall be notified of that amount as soon as it has been determined.

On receipt of all the forms giving information concerning periods of insurance or residence and, where appropriate, the amount or amounts due under the legislation of one or more of the Member States concerned, the investigating institution shall forward a copy of the forms thus completed to each of the institutions concerned which shall specify thereon the theoretical amount and the actual amount of the benefits, calculated in accordance with the provisions of Article 46(2) of the Regulation, and shall return the form to the investigating institution.

4. As soon as the investigating institution, upon receipt of the information referred to in paragraphs 2 or 3, establishes the fact that the provisions of Article 40(2) or 48(2) or (3) of the Regulation should be applied, it shall inform the other institutions concerned accordingly.

5. In the case provided for in Article 37(d) of the implementing Regulation, the institutions of the Member States to whose legislation the claimant has been subject but to which he has applied for postponement of the award of the benefits shall enter on the form provided for in Article 42(1) of the implementing Regulation only the periods of insurance or residence completed by the claimant under the legislation which they administer.

Article 44

Institution empowered to take a decision relating to the degree of invalidity

1. Subject to the provisions of paragraphs 2 and 3, only the investigating institution shall be empowered to take the decision referred to in Article 40(4) of the Regulation concerning the degree of invalidity of the claimant. It shall take such a decision as soon as it is in a position to determine whether, taking account, where appropriate, of the provisions of Article 45 of the Regulation, the conditions for entitlement fixed by the legislation which it administers are fulfilled. It shall notify such decision forthwith to the other institutions concerned.

2. If, taking account of the provisions of Article 45 of the Regulation, the conditions for entitlement, other than those relating to the degree of invalidity, laid down by the legislation administered by the investigating institution are not fulfilled, that institution shall immediately notify the competent institution in respect of invalidity of the other Member State to whose legislation the employed or self-employed person was last subject. This institution shall, if the conditions for entitlement laid down by the legislation which it administers are fulfilled, be empowered to take the decision relating to the degree of invalidity of the claimant; it shall forthwith notify that decision to the other institutions concerned.

3. Where necessary, the matter may have to be referred back, under the same conditions, to the competent institution in respect of invalidity of the Member State to whose legislation the employed or self-employed person was first subject.

Article 45

Provisional payment of benefits and advance payments of benefits

1. If the investigating institution establishes that the claimant is entitled to benefits under the legislation which it administers without having recourse to periods of insurance or residence completed under the legislation of other Member States, it shall pay such benefits immediately on a provisional basis.
2. If the claimant is not entitled to benefits under paragraph 1 but, from information supplied to the investigating institution pursuant to Article 43(2) or (3) of the implementing Regulation, it transpires that a right to benefits is acquired under the legislation of another Member State taking into account only the periods of insurance or residence completed under that legislation, the institution which administers the said legislation shall pay such benefits on a provisional basis as soon as the investigating institution has informed it of its obligation to do so.
3. If, in the case referred to in paragraph 2, a right to benefits is acquired under the legislation of more than one Member State, taking into account only those periods of insurance or residence completed under each one of those legislations, the payment of benefits on a provisional basis shall be the responsibility of the institution which in the first place informed the investigating institution of the existence of such a right; it shall be the duty of the investigating institution to inform the other institutions concerned.
4. The institution required to pay benefits under paragraph 1, 2 or 3 shall forthwith inform the claimant of the fact, drawing his attention explicitly to the provisional nature of the measure taken and to the fact that is not open to appeal.
5. If no benefit is payable to the claimant on a provisional basis under paragraph 1, 2 or 3, but it transpires from information received that a right is acquired under Article 46(2) of the Regulation, the investigating institution shall pay him an appropriate recoverable advance, the amount of which shall be as close as possible to the amount he will probably be awarded under Article 46(2) of the Regulation.
6. Two Member States or the competent authorities or those member States may agree to apply other methods of payment of benefits on provisional basis in cases where only the institutions of those States are concerned. Any such agreements which are concluded on this subject shall be notified to the Administrative Commission.

Article 46

Amounts due for periods of voluntary insurance or optional continued insurance, which must not be taken into consideration under Article 15(1)(b) of the implementing Regulation.

For the calculation of the theoretical amount and of the actual amount of the benefit in accordance with Article 46(2)(a) and (b) of the Regulation, the rules laid down in Article 15(1)(b), (c) and (d) of the implementing Regulation shall be applicable.

The amount actually due, calculated in accordance with Article 46(2) of the Regulation, shall be increased by the amount which corresponds to the periods of voluntary or optional continued insurance, which have not been taken into account under Article 15(1)(b) of the implementing Regulation. This increase shall be calculated in accordance with the provisions of the Member State's legislation under which the periods of voluntary insurance or of optional continued insurance have been completed.

The comparison referred to in Article 46(3) of the Regulation must be made bearing the aforesaid increase in mind.

3.365

Article 47

Calculation of the amounts due corresponding to the periods of voluntary or optional continued insurance

In accordance with the legislation it applies, the institution of each Member State shall calculate the amount corresponding to the periods of voluntary or optional continued insurance which, under Article 46a(3)(c) of the Regulation, is not subject to the provisions for withdrawal, reduction or suspension of another Member State.

3.366

Article 48

Notification to the claimant of the decisions of the institutions

1. The final decision taken by each of the institutions concerned shall be notified to the investigating institution. Each of these decisions must specify the grounds and time-limits for appeal provided for by the legislation in question. When all these decisions have been received, the investigating institution shall communicate them to the claimant in his own language by means of a summarized statement to which the aforesaid decisions shall be appended. Periods allowed for appeals shall commence only on the date of receipt of the summarized statement by the claimant.

2. On dispatch to the claimant of the summarized statement provided for in paragraph 1, the investigating institution shall simultaneously forward a copy to each one of the institutions concerned, enclosing with it a copy of the decisions of the other institutions.

3.367

Article 49

Recalculation of benefits

3.368
1. For the purpose of implementing Article 43(3) and (4), Article 49(2) and (3) and Article 51(2) of the Regulation, the provisions of Article 45 of the implementing Regulation shall apply mutatis mutandis.

2. In the event of recalculation, withdrawal or suspension of a benefit, the institution which has taken such a decision shall immediately notify the person concerned and each of the institutions on which the person concerned has a claim, if necessary through the good offices of the investigating institution. The decision must specify the grounds and time-limits for appeal provided for by the legislation in question. Periods allowed for appeals shall commence only on the date of receipt of the decision by the person concerned.

Article 50

Measures designed to accelerate the award of benefits

3.369
1. (a) (i) Where an employed or self-employed person who is a national of one Member State becomes subject to the legislation of another Member State, the competent institution in respect of pensions of the latter Member State shall, using all the means at its disposal and at the time of registration of the person concerned, forward to the body designated by the competent authority of that same Member State, all information relating to the identification of the person concerned and the name of the said competent institution and the insurance number allotted by the latter.
(ii) Moreover, the competent institution referred to in subparagraph (i) shall also, as far as possible, forward to the body designated under the provisions of subparagraph (i) any other information which may facilitate and accelerate the award of the pensions.
(iii) Such information shall be forwarded, under conditions fixed by the Administrative Commission, to the body designated by the competent authority of the Member State concerned.
(iv) For the implementation of the provisions of subparagraphs (i), (ii) and (iii), stateless persons and refugees shall be deemed to be nationals of the member State to whose legislation they were first subject.
(b) The institutions concerned shall, at the request of the person concerned or of the institution with which he is currently insured, draw up his insurance history starting not later than one year before the date on which he will reach pensionable age.

2. The Administrative Commission shall fix the methods for implementing the provisions of paragraph 1.

RELEVANT DECISIONS OF THE ADMINISTRATIVE COMMISSION

Decision No 117 of 7 July 1982 concerning the conditions for implementing Article 50(1)(a) of Council Regulation (EEC) No 574/72 of 21 March 1972, [1983] OJ C238/3.

Article 50

Decision No 118 of 20 April 1983 concerning the conditions for implementing Article 50(1)(b) of Council Regulation (EEC) No 574/72 of 21 March 1972, [1983] OJ 306/2.

Decision No 192 of 29 October 2003 concerning the conditions for implementing Article 50(1)(b) of Council Regulation (EEC) No 574/72, [2004] OJ L104/114.

ADMINISTRATIVE CHECKS AND MEDICAL EXAMINATIONS

Article 51

1. When a person in receipt of benefits, in particular:

(a) invalidity benefits;
(b) old-age benefits awarded in the event of unfitness for work;
(c) old-age benefits awarded to elderly unemployed persons;
(d) old-age benefits awarded in the event of cessation of a professional or trade activity;
(e) survivors' benefits awarded in the event of invalidity or unfitness for work;
(f) benefits awarded on condition that the means of the recipient do not exceed a prescribed limit,

is staying or residing in the territory of a Member State other than the State in which the institution responsible for payment is situated, administrative checks and medical examinations shall be carried out, at the request of that institution, by the institution of the place of stay or residence of the recipient in accordance with the procedures laid down by the legislation administered by the latter institution. The institution responsible for payment shall, however, reserve the right to have the recipient examined by a doctor of its own choice.

2. If it is established that the recipient referred to in paragraph 1 is employed or self-employed or has means in excess of the prescribed limit while receiving benefits, the institution of the place of stay or residence shall send a report to the institution responsible for payment which has requested the check or examination. This report shall indicate in particular the nature of the employment or self-employment pursued by the person concerned, the amount of earnings or means which he has had during the last complete quarter, the normal earnings obtained in the same area by an employed person or a self-employed person at the same level as the person concerned in the occupation which he followed before becoming an invalid over a reference period to be determined by the institution responsible for payment and, where appropriate, the opinion of a medical expert on the state of health of the person concerned.

3.370

Article 52

When, after suspension of the benefits which he was receiving, the person concerned recovers his right to benefits whilst residing in the territory of a Member State other than the competent State, the institutions concerned

3.371

Council Regulation (EEC) No 574/72

shall exchange all relevant information with a view to the resumption of the provision of the said benefits.

PAYMENT OF BENEFITS

Article 53

Method of payment of benefits

3.372 *Omitted*

Article 54

Notification to the paying body of the detailed schedule of payments to be made

3.373 *Omitted*

Article 55

Payment of amounts due into the account of the paying body

3.374 *Omitted*

Article 56

Payment of amounts due by the paying body to persons entitled to benefits

3.375 *Omitted*

Article 57

Settlement of accounts in respect of the payment referred to in Article 56 of the implementing Regulation

3.376 *Omitted*

Article 58

Recovery of expenses incurred in the payment of benefits

3.377 *Omitted*

Article 59

Article 59

Notification of transfer of residence of the person entitled to benefits

When a person entitled to benefits due under the legislation of one or more Member States transfers his residence from the territory of one State to that of another State, he shall notify this fact to the institution or institutions responsible for the payment of such benefits and to the paying body.

3.378

CHAPTER 4

ACCIDENTS AT WORK AND OCCUPATIONAL DISEASES

IMPLEMENTATION OF ARTICLES 52 AND 53 OF THE REGULATION

Article 60

Benefits in kind in the case of residence in a Member State other than the competent State

1. In order to receive benefits in kind under Article 52(a) of the Regulation, an employed or self-employed person shall submit to the institution of the place of residence a certified statement testifying that he is entitled to such benefits in kind. This certified statement, based upon information supplied by the employer, where appropriate, shall be issued by the competent institution. Moreover, if the legislation of the competent State so provides, the employed or self-employed person shall submit to the institution of the place of residence a receipt from the competent institution of notification of an accident at work or of an occupational disease. If the person concerned does not submit such documents, the institution of the place of residence shall obtain them from the competent institution and, pending their arrival, it shall grant him the benefits in kind under sickness insurance, provided that he satisfies the conditions for entitlement thereto.

3.379

2. That certified statement shall remain valid until the institution of the place of residence receives notification of its cancellation.

However, when the said certified statement has been issued by a French institution, it shall be valid only for a year following the date of its issue, and must be renewed every year.

3. If the person concerned is a seasonal worker, the certified statement referred to in paragraph 1 shall be valid for the whole of the expected duration of the seasonal work unless, in the meanwhile, the competent institution notifies the institution of the place of residence of its cancellation.

4. Upon each application for benefits in kind, the person concerned shall submit the supporting documents for the granting of benefits in kind under the legislation of the Member State in whose territory he resides.

5. In the event of hospitalization the institution of the place of residence shall, within three days of becoming aware of the fact, notify the competent institution of the date of entry into hospital, the probable duration of hospitalization and the date of leaving hospital.

6. The institution of the place of residence shall notify the competent institution in advance of any decision relating to the granting of benefits in kind where the likely or actual cost exceeds a lump sum which is fixed and periodically reviewed by the Administrative Commission.

The competent institution shall have 15 days from the day on which such information is sent within which to raise any objection and to state the reasons on which such objection is based; if, at the end of that period, no such objection has been raised, the institution of the place of residence shall grant the benefits in kind. Where such benefits in kind have to be granted in a case of extreme urgency, the institution of the place of residence shall forthwith inform the competent institution thereof.

7. The person concerned shall inform the institution of the place of residence of any change in his situation which is likely to alter his entitlement to benefits in kind, in particular any cessation or change of employment or self-employment or any transfer of residence or stay. Likewise, should the person concerned cease to be insured or cease to be entitled to benefits in kind, the competent institution shall inform the institution of the place of residence accordingly. The institution of the place of residence may, at any time, request the competent institution to supply it with any information relating to the insurance of the person concerned or to his entitlement to benefits in kind.

8. In the case of frontier workers, medicinal products, bandages, spectacles and small appliances may be issued, and laboratory analyses and tests carried out, only in the territory of the Member State in which they were prescribed in accordance with the provisions of the legislation of that Member State.

9. Two or more Member State or the competent authorities of these Member States may, having received the opinion of the Administrative Commission, agree on other implementing provisions.

RELEVANT DECISIONS OF THE ADMINISTRATIVE COMMISSION

Decision No 116 of 15 December 1982 concerning the granting of benefits in kind provided for in Article 17(7) and Article 60(6) of Regulation (EEC) No 574/72 and the concepts of urgency within the meaning of Article 20 of Regulation (EEC) No 1408/71 and of extreme urgency within the meaning of Articles 17(7) and 60(6) of regulation (EEC) No 574/72, [1983] OJ C193/8.

Decision No 133 of 2 July 1987 concerning the application of Article 17(7) and 60(6) of Council Regulation (EEC) No 574/72, [1987] OJ C284/3.

Decision No 135 of 1 July 1987 concerning the granting of benefits in kind provided for in Article 17(7) and Article 60(6) of Regulation (EEC) No 574/72 and the concepts of urgency within the meaning of Article 20 of Regulation (EEC) No 1408/71 and of extreme urgency within the meaning of Articles 17(7) and 60(6) of Regulation (EEC) No 574/72, [1988] OJ C64/5.

Article 61

Article 61

Cash benefits other than pensions in the case of residence in a Member State other than the competent State

1. In order to receiver cash benefits other than pensions under Article 52(b) of the Regulation, an employed or self-employed person shall, within three days of commencement of the incapacity for work, apply to the institution of the place of residence by submitting a notification of having ceased work or, if the legislation administered by the competent institution or by the institution of the place of residence so provides, a certificate of incapacity for work issued by the doctor providing treatment for the person concerned.

2. If the doctors providing treatment in the country of residence do not issue certificates of incapacity for work, the person concerned shall apply directly to the institution of the place of residence within the time limit fixed by the legislation which it administers.

The institution shall immediately have the incapacity for work medically confirmed and the certificate referred to in paragraph 1 drawn up. Such certificate shall state the probable duration of the incapacity and shall be forwarded to the competent institution forthwith.

3. In case where paragraph 2 does not apply, the institution of the place of residence shall, as soon as possible and in any event within the three days following the date on which the person concerned applied to it, have him medically examined as if he were insured with that institution. The report of the examining doctor shall indicate, in particular, the probable duration of the incapacity for work, and shall be forwarded to the competent institution of the place of residence within the three days following the date of the examination.

4. The institution of the place of residence shall subsequently carry out any necessary administrative checks or medical examinations of the person concerned as if he were insured with that institution. As soon as it establishes that he is fit to resume work it shall forthwith notify the person concerned and the competent institution accordingly stating the date on which the incapacity for work ceased. Without prejudice to the provisions of paragraph 6, the notification to the person concerned shall be treated as a decision taken on behalf of the competent institution.

5. In all cases, the competent institution shall reserve the right to have the person concerned examined by a doctor of its own choice.

6. If the competent institution decides to withhold the cash benefits because the person concerned has not completed the formalities laid down by the legislation of the country of residence, or if it establishes that the person concerned is fit to resume work, it shall notify the person concerned of its decision and shall simultaneously send a copy of such decision to the institution of the place of residence.

7. When the person concerned resumes work, he shall notify the competent institution accordingly if such notification is required by the legislation administered by that institution.

8. The competent institution shall pay cash benefits by the appropriate method, in particular by international money order, and shall inform the institution of the place of residence and the person concerned accordingly.

Where cash benefits are paid by the institution of the place of residence on behalf of the competent institution, the latter shall inform the person concerned of his rights and shall notify the institution of the place of residence of the amount of the cash benefits, the dates for payment and the maximum period during which they should be granted, in accordance with the legislation of the competent State.

9. Two or more Member States or the competent authorities of those Member States may, having received the opinion of the Administrative Commission, agree on other implementing provisions.

IMPLEMENTATION OF ARTICLE 55 OF THE REGULATION

Article 62

Benefits in kind in the case of a stay in a Member State other than the competent State

3.381

1. In order to receive benefits in kind, a person employed in international transport covered by Article 14(2)(a) of the Regulation who, in the course of his employment, goes to the territory of a Member State other than the competent State, shall, as soon as possible, submit to the institution of the place of stay a special certified statement issued by the employer or by his agent during the current calendar month or during the two calendar months preceding its submission. Such certified statement shall state in particular the date from which the person concerned has been employed by the said employer and the name and address of the competent institution. If the person concerned has submitted such certified statement, he shall be presumed to have satisfied the conditions for acquisition of the right to benefits in kind. If the person concerned is unable to contact the institution of the place of stay before receiving medical treatment he shall nevertheless receive such treatment on presentation of the said certified statement as if he were insured with that institution.

2. The institution of the place of stay shall within three days inquire of the competent institution whether the person concerned satisfied the conditions for acquisition of the right to benefits in kind. The institution of the place of stay shall provide the benefits in kind until it receives a reply from the competent institution, but for not more than 30 days.

3. The competent institution shall send its reply to the institution of the place of stay within 10 days of the receipt of the request from that institution. If that reply is in the affirmative, the competent institution shall indicate, if necessary, the maximum period during which the benefits in kind may be granted, in accordance with the legislation which it administers, and the institution of the place of stay shall continue to provide the said benefits.

4. Benefits in kind provided by virtue of the presumption made in paragraph 1 shall be reimbursed as provided for in Article 36(1) of the Regulation.

5. In place of the certified statement provided for in paragraph 1 the employed person referred to in that paragraph may submit to the institution of the place of stay a certified statement as provided for in paragraph 6.

Article 62

6. In order to receive benefits in kind under Article 55(1)(a)(i) of the Regulation, except in cases where a presumption is made under paragraph 1, the employed or self-employed person shall submit to the institution of the place of stay a certified statement stating that he is entitled to benefits in kind. Such certified statement, which shall be issued by the competent institution, if possible before the person concerned leaves the territory of the Member State in which he resides, shall specify in particular, where necessary, the maximum period during which benefits in kind may be granted, in accordance with the legislation of the competent State. If the person concerned does not submit the said certified statement, the institution of the place of stay shall obtain it from the competent institution.

7. The provisions of Article 60(5), (6) and (9) of the implementing Regulation shall apply by analogy.

Article 63

Benefits in kind for employed or self-employed persons who transfer their residence or return to their country of residence, and for employed or self-employed persons authorized to go to another Member State for medical treatment

1. In order to receive benefits in kind under Article 55(1)(b)(i) of the Regulation, an employed or self-employed person shall submit to the institution of the place of residence a certified statement testifying that he is entitled to continue receiving the said benefits. This certified statement, which shall be issued by the competent institution, shall specify in particular, where necessary, the maximum period during which such benefits may continue to be provided, in accordance with the provisions of the legislation of the competent State. The certified statement may, at the request of the person concerned, be issued after his departure if, for reasons of force majeure, it cannot be draw up beforehand.

2. The provisions of Article 60(5), (6) and (9) of the implementing Regulation shall apply by analogy.

3. Paragraphs 1 and 2 shall apply by analogy in respect of the provision of benefits in kind in the case referred to in Article 55(1)(c)(i) of the Regulation.

3.382

Article 64

Cash benefits other than pensions in the case of a stay in a Member State other than the competent State

The provisions of Article 61 of the implementing Regulation shall apply by analogy in respect of the receipt of cash benefits, other than pensions, under Article 55(1)(a)(ii) of the Regulation.

However, without prejudice to the obligation to submit a certificate of incapacity for work, an employed or self-employed person who is staying in the territory of a Member State without pursuing any professional or trade activity there shall not be required to submit the notification of having ceased work referred to in Article 61(1) of the implementing Regulation.

3.383

Council Regulation (EEC) No 574/72

IMPLEMENTATION OF ARTICLES 52 TO 56 OF THE REGULATION

Article 65

Declarations, investigations and exchange of information between institutions to an accident at work sustained in, or an occupational disease contracted in, a Member State other than the competent State

3.384

1. When an accident at work is sustained in, or an occupational disease is diagnosed for the first time in, the territory of a Member State other than the competent State, a declaration of the accident at work or occupational disease must be made in accordance with the provisions of the legislation of the competent State without prejudice to any legal provisions in force in the territory of the Member State in which the accident at work was sustained or in which the occupational disease was first diagnosed, and which shall in such a case remain applicable. This declaration shall be sent to the competent institution and a copy shall be sent to the institution of the place of residence or to the institution of the place of stay.

2. The institution of the Member State in whose territory the accident at work was sustained or in which the occupational disease was first diagnosed, shall forward to the competent institution, in duplicate, the medical certificate drawn up in that territory and any relevant information which the latter institution may request.

3. If, in the case of an accident sustained while travelling in the territory of a Member State other than the competent State, there are grounds for holding an enquiry in the territory of the first Member State, an investigator may be appointed for that purpose by the competent institution, which shall so inform the authorities of that Member State. Those authorities shall assist the said investigator, in particular by appointing a person to assist him in the consultation of official reports and any other documents relating to the accident.

4. At the end of the treatment, a detailed report shall be forwarded to the competent institution together with medical certificates concerning the permanent consequences of the accident or disease, and in particular the present condition of the person concerned, and the recovery from the injuries or their consolidation. The relevant fees shall be paid by the institution of the place of residence or the institution of the place of stay, as the case may be, in accordance with the rate applied by the institution, but shall be chargeable to the competent institution.

5. The competent institution shall, on request, notify the institution of the place of residence or the institution of the place of stay, as the case may be, of the decision determining the date of recovery from the injuries or their consolidation and, where appropriate, the decision relating to the granting of a pension.

Article 66

Article 66

Disputes concerning the occupational nature of the accident or disease

1. When, in the cases referred to in Article 52 or 55(1) of the Regulation, the competent institution disputes the application of the legislation relating to accidents at work or occupational diseases, it shall forthwith notify that fact to the institution of the place of residence or institution of the place of stay which provided the benefits in kind; those benefits shall then be considered as coming under sickness insurance and shall continue to be provided thereunder upon presentation of the certificates or certified statements referred to in Articles 20 and 21 of the implementing Regulation.

2. When a final decision has been reached on this subject, the competent institution shall forthwith notify the fact to the institution of the place of residence or to the institution of the place of stay which provided the benefits in kind. Where the case is not one of an accident at work or an occupational disease that institution shall continue to provide the said benefits in kind under sickness insurance if the employed or self-employed person is entitled thereto. In other cases, the benefits in kind received by the person concerned under sickness insurance shall be considered as benefits for an accident at work or an occupational disease.

3.385

IMPLEMENTATION OF ARTICLE 57 OF THE REGULATION

Article 67

Procedure in the case of exposure to the risk of an occupational disease in several Member States

1. In the case covered by Article 57(1) of the Regulation, notification of the occupational disease shall be forwarded either to the competent institution in respect of occupational diseases of the Member State under whose legislation the person suffering from the disease last pursued an activity likely to cause the disease in question, or to the institution of the place of residence, which shall forward the notification to the said competent institution.

2. If the competent institution referred to in paragraph 1 ascertains that an activity which might cause the occupational disease in question was last pursued under the legislation of another Member State, it shall forward the notification and the accompanying documents to the corresponding institution of that Member State.

3. When the institution of the Member State under whose legislation the person suffering from the disease last pursued an activity which might cause the occupational disease in question ascertains that such person or his survivors do not satisfy the conditions of that legislation, taking into account the provisions of Article 57(2), (3) and (4) of the Regulation, the said institution shall:
  (a) forward, without delay, to the institution of the Member State under whose legislation the person suffering from the disease previously

3.386

pursued an activity which might cause the disease in question, the notification and all accompanying documents, including the findings and reports of the medical examinations arranged by the first institution, and a copy of the decision referred to under (b);

(b) simultaneously notify the person concerned of its decision, indicating in particular the reasons for the refusal of benefits, the grounds and time limits for appeal, and the date on which the file was forwarded to the institution referred to under (a).

4. Where necessary the case should be referred back, in accordance with the same procedure, to the corresponding institution of the Member State under whose legislation the person suffering from the disease first pursued the activity which might cause the occupational disease in question.

Article 68

Exchange of information between institutions in the event of an appeal against a decision to reject a claim—Payment of advances in the event of such an appeal

3.387

1. Where an appeal its lodged against a decision to reject a claim taken by the institution of one of the Member States under whose legislation the person suffering from the disease pursued an activity which might cause the occupational disease in question, that institution shall so inform the institution to which the notification has been forwarded in accordance with the procedure laid down in Article 67(3) of the implementing Regulation, and shall subsequently notify it of the final decision reached.

2. If the right to benefits was acquired under the legislation administered by the latter institution, taking into account the provisions of Article 57(2), (3) and (4) of the Regulation, that institution shall pay advances up to an amount to be determined, where necessary, after consultation with the institution against whose decision the appeal was lodged. The latter institution shall reimburse the amount of the advance paid if, as a result of the appeal, it is required to provide the benefits. That amount shall then be deducted from the total amount of the benefits due to the person concerned.

Article 69

Apportionment of the cost of cash benefits in cases of sclerogenic pneumoconiosis

3.388

The following rules shall apply for the implementation of Article 57(5) of the Regulation:

(a) the competent institution of the Member State under whose legislation cash benefits are granted pursuant to Article 57(1) of the Regulation (hereinafter called "the institution responsible for payment of cash benefits") shall use a form containing, in particular, a statement and summary of all periods of insurance (old-age insurance) or periods of residence completed by the person suffering from the disease under the legislation of each one of the Member States concerned;

Article 69

(b) the institution responsible for payment of cash benefits shall forward that form to all old-age insurance institutions of those Member States with which the person suffering from the disease was insured; each one of the said institutions shall enter on the form the periods of insurance (old-age insurance) or periods of residence completed under the legislation which it administers and shall return the form to the institution responsible for payment of cash benefits;

(c) the institution responsible for payment of cash benefits shall then apportion the costs between itself and the other competent institutions concerned; it shall notify the latter of such apportionment for their approval together with appropriate supporting evidence in particular as regards the total amount of cash benefits granted and the calculation of the percentages of the apportionment;

(d) to the end of each calendar year, the institution responsible for payment of cash benefits shall forward to each of the other competent institutions concerned a statement of cash benefits paid during the financial year under consideration, showing the amount due from each of them according to the apportionment provided for under (c); each one of those institutions shall refund the amount due to the institution responsible for payment of cash benefits as soon as possible, and within three months at the latest.

IMPLEMENTATION OF ARTICLE 58(3) OF THE REGULATION

Article 70

Certified statement relating to the members of the family to be taken into consideration when calculating cash benefits including pensions

1. In order to receive benefits under the provisions of Article 58(3) of the Regulation the claimant shall submit a certified statement relating to the members of his family who are residing in the territory of a Member State other than that in which the institution responsible for the award of cash benefits is situated.

This certified statement shall be issued by the sickness insurance institution of the place of residence of the member of the family or by another institution designated by the competent authority of the Member State in whose territory they are resident. The provisions of the second and third subparagraphs of Article 25(2) of the implementing Regulation shall apply by analogy.

In place of the certified statement provided for in the first subparagraph, the institution responsible for the award of cash benefits may require the claimant to produce recent civil status documents relating to member of his family who are residing in the territory of a Member State other than that in which the said institution is situated.

2. In the case referred to in paragraph 1, if the legislation administered by the institution concerned requires that the members of the family should live under the same roof as the claimant, the fact that the said member of the

family who do not satisfy that condition are nevertheless mainly dependent on the claimant must be established by documents proving the regular transmission of part of the claimant's earnings.

IMPLEMENTATION OF ARTICLE 60 OF THE REGULATION

Article 71

Aggravation of an occupational disease

1. In the cases covered by Article 60(1) of the Regulation, the claimant shall supply the institution of the Member State from which he is claiming rights to benefits with all information relating to benefits previously granted in respect of the occupational disease in question. That institution may apply to any other institution which has previously been competent in order to obtain any information which it considers necessary.

2. In the case covered by Article 60(1) of the Regulation, the competent institution required to pay the cash benefits shall notify the other institution concerned, for its approval, of the amount of costs to be borne by the latter institution as a result of the aggravation, together with appropriate supporting evidence. At the end of each calendar year, the first institution shall send the second institution a statement of the cash benefits paid during the financial year in question, showing the amount due from the latter institution which shall make the refund to the first institution as soon as possible, and within three months at the latest.

3. In the case referred to in the first sentence of Article 60(2)(b) of the Regulation, the institution responsible for payment of cash benefits shall notify the competent institutions concerned, for their approval, of the changes made in the previous apportionment of costs together with the appropriate supporting evidence.

4. In the case referred to in the second sentence of Article 60(2)(b) of the Regulation, the provisions of paragraph 2 shall apply by analogy.

IMPLEMENTATION OF ARTICLE 61(5) AND (6) OF THE REGULATION

Article 72

Assessment of the degree of incapacity in the case of an accident at work sustained previously or subsequently or an occupational disease diagnosed previously or subsequently

1. In order to asses the degrees of incapacity, to establish a right to any benefit, or to determine the amount of such benefit in the cases referred to in Article 61(5) and (6) of the Regulation, a claimant shall supply the competent institution of the Member State to whose legislation he was subject at the time when the accident at work was sustained or the occupational disease was first diagnosed, with all information on previous or subsequent

Article 72

accidents at work sustained or occupational diseases contracted by him when he was subject to the legislation of any other Member State, whatever the degree of incapacity caused by those previous or subsequent cases.

2. In accordance with the legislation which it administers in respect of the acquisition of the right to benefit, and the determination of the amount of benefit, the competent institution shall take into account the degree of incapacity caused by those previous or subsequent cases.

3. The competent institution may apply to any other institution which was previously or subsequently competent to obtain any information which it considers necessary.

When a previous or a subsequent incapacity for work was caused by an accident sustained while the person concerned was subject to the legislation of a Member State which makes no distinction as to the origin of the incapacity for work, the competent institution in respect of a previous or subsequent incapacity for work or the body designated by the competent authority of the Member State concerned shall, at the request of the competent institution of another Member State, supply information on the degree of the previous or subsequent incapacity for work and, as far as possible, any information which would make it possible to determine whether the incapacity was the result of an accident at work within the meaning of the legislation administered by the institution of the second Member State. Where such is the case, the provisions of paragraph 2 shall apply by analogy.

IMPLEMENTATION OF ARTICLE 61(1) OF THE REGULATION

Article 73

Institutions to which workers in mines and similar undertakings may apply when staying or residing in a Member State other than the competent State

1. In the cases referred to in Article 62(1) of the Regulation and where, in the country of stay or residence, the benefits provided under the insurance scheme for accidents at work and occupational disease covering manual workers in the steel industry are equivalent to those provided under the special scheme for workers in mines and similar undertakings, workers belonging to the latter category may apply to the nearest institution in the territory of the Member State in which they are staying or residing specified in Annex 3 of the implementing Regulation, even if the latter is an institution of the scheme applicable to manual workers in the steel industry, which institution shall then provide such benefits.

2. Where the benefits provided under the special scheme for workers in mines and similar undertakings are more advantageous, such workers shall have the option of applying either to the institution responsible for the administration of that scheme, or to the nearest institution in the territory of the Member State in which they are staying or residing, which administers the scheme for manual workers in the steel industry. In the latter case the institution in question shall draw the attention of the person

3.392

concerned to the fact that by applying to the institution responsible for the administration of the abovementioned special scheme, he will obtain more advantageous benefits; it must, furthermore, inform him of the name and address of such institution.

IMPLEMENTATION OF ARTICLE 62(2) OF THE REGULATION

Article 74

Taking account of the period during which benefits have already been provided by the institution of another Member State

3.393   For the purpose of Article 61(2) of the Regulation, the institution of a Member State called upon to provide benefits may request the institution of another Member State to supply it with information relating to the period during which the latter institution has already provided benefits for the same case of accident at work or occupational disease.

SUBMISSION AND INVESTIGATION OF PENSION CLAIMS, EXCLUDING PENSIONS IN RESPECT OF OCCUPATIONAL DISEASES COVERED BY ARTICLE 57 OF THE REGULATION

Article 75

3.394   **1.** In order to receive a pension or supplementary allowance under the legislation of a Member State, an employed or self-employed person or his survivors residing in the territory of another Member State shall make a claim either to the competent institution, or to the institution of the place of residence, which shall forward such claim to the competent institution. The submission of the claim shall be subject to the following rules:
(a) the claim must be accompanied by the required supporting documents and made on the form provided for by the legislation administered by the competent institution;
(b) the accuracy of the information supplied by the claimant must be established by official documents attached to the claim form, or confirmed by the competent bodies of the Member State in whose territory the claimant resides.

2. The competent institution shall notify the claimant of its decisions directly or through the liaison body of the competent State; it shall send a copy of that decision to the liaison body of the Member State in whose territory the claimant resides.

Article 76

ADMINISTRATIVE CHECKS AND MEDICAL EXAMINATIONS

Article 76

1. Administrative checks and medical examinations, including medical examinations provided for in the event of pensions being reviewed, shall be carried out at the request of the competent institution by the institution of the Member State in whose territory the person entitled to benefits happens to be, in accordance with the procedures laid down by the legislation administered by the latter institution. The competent institution shall, however, reserve the right to have the person entitled to benefits examined by a doctor of its own choice.

2. Any person drawing a pension for himself or for an orphan shall inform the institution responsible for payment of any change in his situation or in that of the orphan which is likely to modify the pension rights.

PAYMENT OF PENSIONS

Article 77

Payment of pensions due from the institution of one Member State to pensioners resident in the territory of another Member State shall be made in accordance with the provisions of Articles 53 to 58 of the implementing Regulation.

CHAPTER 5

DEATH GRANTS

IMPLEMENTATION OF ARTICLES 64, 65 AND 66 OF THE REGULATION

Article 78

Submission of a claim for a grant

In order to receive a death grant under the legislation of a Member State other than the State in whose territory he resides, the claimant shall submit his claim either to the competent institution or to the institution of the place of residence.

The claim must be accompanied by the supporting documents required by the legislation which the competent institution administers.

Council Regulation (EEC) No 574/72

The accuracy of the information supplied by the claimant must be established by official documents attached to the claim or confirmed by the competent bodies of the Member State in whose territory the claimant resides.

Article 79

Certified statement of periods

3.398　**1.** In order to invoke the provisions of Article 64 of the Regulation, a claimant shall submit to the competent institution a certified statement specifying the periods of insurance or residence completed by the employed or self-employed person under the legislation to which he was last subject.

2. This certified statement shall be issued, at the request of the claimant, by the sickness insurance or the old-age insurance institution, as the case may be, with which the employed or self-employed person was last insured. If the claimant does not submit the said certified statement, the competent institution shall obtain it from one or other of the aforementioned institutions.

3. The provisions of paragraphs 1 and 2 shall apply by analogy if, in order to satisfy the conditions of the legislation of the competent State, it is necessary to take into account periods of insurance or residence previously completed under the legislation of any other Member State.

CHAPTER 6

UNEMPLOYMENT BENEFITS

IMPLEMENTATION OF ARTICLE 67 OF THE REGULATION

Article 80

Certified statement of periods of insurance or employment

3.399　**1.** In order to invoke the provisions of Article 67(1), (2) or (4) of the Regulation, the person concerned shall submit to the competent institution a certified statement specifying the periods of insurance or employment completed previously as an employed person under the legislation to which he was last subject, together with any further information required by the legislation administered by that institution.

2. This certified statement shall be issued, at the request of the person concerned, either by the competent institution in respect of unemployment of the Member State to whose legislation he was last subject, or by another institution designated by the competent authority of the said Member State. If he does not submit the said certified statement, the competent institution shall obtain it from one or other of the aforementioned institutions.

3. The provisions of paragraphs 1 and 2 shall apply by analogy if, in order to satisfy the conditions of the legislation of the competent State, it is

Article 80

necessary to take into account periods of insurance or employment completed previously as an employed person under the legislation of any other Member State.

IMPLEMENTATION OF ARTICLE 68 OF THE REGULATION

Article 81

Certified statement for the calculation of benefits

Where the responsibility for the calculation of benefits rests upon an institution covered by Article 68(1) of the Regulation, and where a person has not pursued his last employment for at least four weeks in the territory of the Member State in which that institution is situated, he shall submit to the said institution a certified statement indicating the nature of the last employment pursued for at least four weeks in the territory of another Member State, and the branch of the economy in which that employment was pursued. If the person concerned does not submit this certified statement, the said institution shall obtain it either from the competent institution in respect of unemployment of the latter Member State with which he was last insured, or from another institution designated by the competent authority of that Member State.

3.400

Article 82

Certified statement relating to the members of the family to be taken into consideration for the calculation of benefits

1. In order to invoke the provisions of Article 68(2) of the Regulation, the person concerned shall submit to the competent institution a certified statement relating to the members of his family who are resident in the territory of a Member State other than the one in which the said institution is situated.

3.401

2. This certified statement shall be issued by the institution designated by the competent authority of the Member State in whose territory those members of the family reside. It must certify that the members of the family are not taken into consideration for the calculation of unemployment benefits due to another person under the legislation of the said Member State.

The certified statement shall be valid for the 12 months following the date of its issue. It may be renewed; in such case, it shall be valid from the date of its renewal. The person concerned shall immediately notify the competent institution of any occurrence necessitating an amendment to the said certified statement. Such amendment shall take effect from the date of such occurrence.

3. Where the institution issuing the certified statement referred to in paragraph 1 is not in a position to certify that the members of the family are not taken into consideration for the calculation of unemployment benefits due to another person under the legislation of the Member State in whose territory they reside, the person concerned shall, when submitting the certified statement to the competent institution, supplement the said certified statement by a declaration to that effect.

The provisions of the second subparagraph of paragraph 2 shall apply by analogy to that declaration.

IMPLEMENTATION OF ARTICLE 69 OF THE REGULATION

Article 83

Conditions and limits for the retention of the right to benefits when an unemployed person goes to another Member State

1. In order to retain the right to benefits, an unemployed person covered by Article 69(1) of the Regulation shall submit to the institution of the place to which he has gone a certified statement in which the competent institution shall certify that he is still entitled to benefits under the conditions laid down in paragraph 1(b) of the said Article. The competent institution shall specify in particular in this certified statement:
    (a) the amount of benefit to be paid to the unemployed person under the legislation of the competent State;
    (b) the date on which the unemployed person ceased to be available to the employment services of the competent State;
    (c) the time limit under Article 69(1)(b) of the Regulation for registration as a person seeking work in the Member State to which the unemployed person has gone;
    (d) the maximum period, in accordance with Article 69(1)(c) of the Regulation, during which the right to benefit may be retained;
    (e) facts which might alter entitlement to benefit.
2. An unemployed person who intends to go to another Member State in order to seek employment there shall before his departure, apply for the certified statement referred to in paragraph 1. If the unemployed person does not submit the said certified statement, the institution of the place to which he has gone shall obtain it from the competent institution. The employment services of the competent State must ensure that the unemployed person has been informed of his obligations under Article 69 of the Regulation and under this Article.
3. The institution of the place to which the unemployed person has gone shall notify the competent institution of the date on which the unemployed person registered and the date on which payment of benefits was commenced and shall pay out the benefits of the competent State in accordance with the procedure provided for by the legislation of the Member State to which the unemployed person has gone.

The institution of the place to which the unemployed person has gone shall carry out a check or arrange for one to be carried out as if it were dealing with an unemployed person entitled to benefits under the legislation which it administers. It shall inform the competent institution of any occurrence coming within paragraph 1(e) above as soon as the same comes to its knowledge and, in cases where the benefit has to be suspended

Article 83

or withdrawn, it shall immediately discontinue payment of the benefit. The competent institution shall forthwith inform it to what extent, and from what date, the unemployed person's entitlement to benefit is affected by that fact.

Payment of benefits may only be resumed, where appropriate, after receipt of such information. Where the benefit has to be reduced, the institution of the place to which the unemployed person has gone shall continue to pay him a reduced amount of benefit, subject to adjustment, after receipt of the reply from the competent institution.

4. Two or more Member States or the competent authorities of those Member States may, having received the opinion of the Administrative Commission, agree on other implementing provisions.

IMPLEMENTATION OF ARTICLE 71 OF THE REGULATION

Article 84

Unemployed persons who were formerly employed and who, during their last employment, were residing in a Member State other than the competent State

1. In the cases referred to in Article 71(1)(a)(ii) and in the first sentence of Article 71(1)(b)(ii) of the Regulation, the institution of the place of residence shall be considered to be the competent institution, for the purposes of implementing the provisions of Article 80 of the implementing Regulation.

2. In order to claim benefits under the provisions of Article 71(1)(b)(ii) of the Regulation, an unemployed person who was formerly employed shall submit to the institution of his place of residence, in addition to the certified statement provided for in Article 80 of the implementing Regulation, a certified statement from the institution of the Member State to whose legislation he was last subject, indicating that he has no right to benefits under Article 69 of the Regulation.

3. For the purposes of implementing the provisions of Article 71(2) of the Regulation, the institution of the place of residence shall ask the competent institution for any information relating to the entitlements, from the latter institution, of the unemployed person who was formerly an employed person.

3.403

Chapter 7

Family Benefits

Implementation of Article 72 of the Regulation

Article 85

Certified statement of periods of employment or self-employment

3.404   1. In order to invoke the provisions of Article 72 of the Regulation, a person shall submit to the competent institution a certified statement specifying the period of insurance, employment or self-employment completed under the legislation to which he was last subject.

2. That certified statement shall be issued, at the request of the person concerned, either by the competent institution in respect of family benefits of the Member State with which he was last insured, or by another institution designated by the competent authority of the said Member State. If he does not submit the said certified statement, the competent institution shall obtain it from one or other of the abovementioned institution unless the sickness insurance institution is able to forward him a copy of the certified statement provided for in Article 16(1) of the implementing Regulation.

3. The provisions of paragraphs 1 and 2 shall apply by analogy if, in order to satisfy the conditions of the legislation of the competent State, it is necessary to take into account periods of insurance, employment or self-employment completed previously under the legislation of any other Member State.

Implementation of Articles 73 and 75(1) and (2) of the Regulation

Article 86

3.405   1. In order to receive family benefits under Article 73 of the Regulation, an employed person shall submit a claim to the competent institution, where necessary through his employer.

2. In support of his claim, the employed person shall submit a certificate relating to members of his family residing in the territory of a Member State other than that in which the competent institution is situated. Such certificate shall be issued, either by the authorities competent in civil status matters in the country of residence of those members of the family, or by the competent institution in respect of sickness insurance in the place of residence of those members of the family, or by another institution designated by the competent authority of the Member State in whose territory those members of the family reside. Such a certificate must be renewed every year.

Article 86

3. Where the legislation of the competent State provides that the family benefits may or must be paid to a person other than the employed person, the latter shall also submit in support of his claim, information identifying the individual to whom the family benefits are to be paid in the country of residence (name, forename, full address).

4. The competent authorities of two or more Member States may agree on special procedures for the payment of family benefits, in particular with a view to facilitating the implementation of Article 75(1) and (2) of the Regulation. Such agreements shall be communicated to the Administrative Commission.

5. An employed person shall inform the competent institution where necessary through his employer:

— of any change in the situation of the members of his family which might alter entitlement to family benefits,

— of any change in the number of members of his family for whom family benefits are due,

— of any transfer of residence or stay of such members of the family,

— of any pursuit of a professional or trade activity by virtue of which family benefits are also due under the legislation of the Member State in whose territory the members of the family are resident.

Article 87

[. . .] 3.406

IMPLEMENTATION OF ARTICLE 74 OF THE REGULATION

Article 88

The provisions of Article 86 of the implementing Regulation shall apply by analogy to unemployed persons who where formerly employed or self-employed and who are covered by Article 74 of the Regulation. 3.407

Article 89

[. . .] 3.408

Council Regulation (EEC) No 574/72

CHAPTER 8

BENEFITS FOR DEPENDENT CHILDREN OF PENSIONERS AND FOR ORPHANS

IMPLEMENTATION OF ARTICLES 77, 78 AND 79 OF THE REGULATION

Article 90

3.409

1. In order to receive benefits under Article 77 or 78 of the Regulation, a claimant shall submit a claim to the institution of his place of residence, in accordance with the procedures laid down by the legislation administered by that institution.

2. If, however, the claimant does not reside in the territory of the Member State in which the competent institution is situated, he may submit his claim either to the competent institution or to the institution of his place of residence, which shall then forward the claim to the competent institution, indicating the date on which it was submitted. The date shall be considered as the date of submission of the claim to the competent institution.

3. If the competent institution referred to in paragraph 2 finds that there is no entitlement under the legislation which it administers, it shall forward the claim forthwith, together with all necessary documents and information, to the institution of the Member State to whose legislation the employed or self-employed person was subject for the longest period of time.

Where necessary the matter may have to be referred back, under the same conditions, to the institution of the Member State under whose legislation the person concerned completed the shortest of his periods of insurance or residence.

4. The Administrative Commission shall, where necessary, lay down any supplementary procedures required for the submission of claims for benefits.

Article 91

3.410

1. Payment of benefits due under Article 77 or 78 of the Regulation shall be made in accordance with the provisions of Articles 53 to 58 of the implementing Regulation.

2. The competent authorities of the Member States shall, where necessary, designate the competent institution for paying benefits due under Article 77 or 78 of the Regulation.

Article 92

3.411

Any person to whom benefits are paid under Article 77 or 78 of the Regulation for a pensioner's children or for orphans, shall inform the institution responsible for the payment of such benefits:

Article 92

- any change in the situation of the children or orphans that is likely to alter the entitlement to benefits,
- any modification in the number of children or orphans in respect of whom benefits are due,
- any transfer of residence of the children or orphans,
- of any pursuit of a professional or trade activity giving entitlement to family benefits or family allowances for such children or orphans.

TITLE V

FINANCIAL PROVISIONS

Title V omitted.

TITLE VI

MISCELLANEOUS PROVISIONS

Article 108

Proof of status of seasonal worker

In order to prove that he is a seasonal worker, the employed person covered by Article 1(c) of the Regulation shall be required to submit his contract of employment stamped by the employment services of the Member State in whose territory he has gone to work or has worked. If no seasonal employment contract is concluded in that Member State, the institution of the country of employment shall, where appropriate, issue, in the case of a claim for benefits, a certificate attesting that, on the basis of information supplied by the person concerned, the work which he is doing or has done is of a seasonal nature.

Article 109

Arrangement for payment of contributions

The employer who has no place of business in the Member State in whose territory the employed person is employed may agree with the latter that he shall assume the obligations of the employer with regard to the payment of contributions.

The employer shall notify the competent institution or, where necessary, the institution designated by the competent authority of the said Member State of any such arrangement.

Article 110

Mutual administrative aid relating to the recovery of benefits which were not due

3.415   If the institution of a Member State which provided benefits intends to take action against a person who has received benefits which were not due to him, the institution of the place of residence of such person, or the institution designated by the competent authority of the Member State in whose territory that person resides, shall lend its good offices to the first institution.

Article 111

Recovery by social security institutions of payments not due, and claims by assistance bodies

3.416   1. If, when awarding or reviewing benefits in respect of invalidity, old-age or death (pensions) pursuant to Chapter 3 of Title III of the Regulation, the institution of a Member State has paid to a recipient of benefits a sum in excess of that to which he is entitled, that institution may request the institution of any other Member State responsible for the payment of corresponding benefits to that recipient to deduct the amount overpaid from the arrears which it pays to the said recipient. The latter institution shall transfer the amount deducted to the creditor institution. Where the amount overpaid cannot be deducted from the arrears, the provisions of paragraph 2 shall apply.

2. When the institution of a Member State has paid to a recipient of benefits a sum in excess of that to which he is entitled that institution may, within the conditions and limits laid down by the legislation which it administers, request the institution of any other Member State responsible for the payment of benefits to that recipient to deduct the amount overpaid from the amounts which it pays to the said recipient. The latter institution shall make the deduction under the conditions and within the limits provided for such setting-off by the legislation which it administers, as if the sums had been overpaid by itself, and shall transfer the amount deducted to the creditor institution.

3. When a person to whom the Regulation applies has received assistance in the territory of a Member State during a period in which he was entitled to benefits under the legislation of another Member State, the body which gave the assistance may, if it is legally entitled to reclaim the benefits due to the said person, request the institution of any other Member State responsible for the payment of benefits in favour of that person to deduct the amount of the assistance paid from the amounts which the latter pays to the said person.

When a member of the family of a person to whom the Regulation applies has received assistance in the territory of a Member State during a period in which the said person was entitled to benefits under the legislation of another Member State in respect of the member of the family concerned, the body which gave the assistance may, if it is legally entitled to reclaim the benefits due to the said person in respect of the member of the family concerned, request the institution of any other Member State responsible for the payment of such benefits in favour of that person to deduct the

Article 111

amount of assistance paid from the amounts which the latter pays to the said person in respect of the member of the family concerned.

The institution responsible for payment shall make the deduction under the conditions and within the limits provided for such setting-off by the legislation which it administers, and shall transfer the amount deducted to the creditor body.

GENERAL NOTE

This is the provision dealing with recovery of overpayments as between EEA countries. Perhaps unsurprisingly, it has given rise to a number of Commissioners' decisions.

In *R(SB) 3/91* the Commissioner ruled that for Article 111 to apply, it was not necessary for the other State's benefit to have been awarded under Regulation 1408/71. It sufficed that the claimant was a person to whom the personal scope of Regulation 1408/71 applied. This did not require the person to have been a migrant worker.

In *R(IS) 6/02* the Commissioner ruled, confirming *CIS/12082/1996*, that nothing in Reg.1408/71 or Reg.574/72 precluded the application of s.74(2) of the Administration Act to the circumstances of the case. Furthermore supplementary benefit and income support were not to be regarded as supplements to old age pensions under Art.46 of Reg.1408/71; in so holding the Commissioner found that the benefit at issue in Case C-132/96 *Stinco* [1998] E.C.R. I-5225 could be distinguished. The Commissioner ruled:

> "In my judgment, a 'supplementary allowance' within Article 1(t) is one which has the specific connections with a specific social security benefit, as exemplified by the Italian supplement in *Stinco and Panfilo*. It does not extend to a general social benefit which may provide a practical supplement to recipients of specific social security benefits, but which provides an income to others in many different circumstances whose resources are inadequate for their needs." (para.23 of decision.)

In *Scrivner v Chief Adjudication Officer* [1990] 1 C.M.L.R. 637 reported as *R(SB) 1/91*, the Court of Appeal upheld the decision of the Commissioner to the effect that Art.111(3) only applies where a member of the claimant's family receives a benefit in their own right, and not where the claimant receives an additional amount of benefit because he has a family.

3.417

Article 112

When an institution has made payments which are not due, either directly or through another institution, and when their recovery has become impossible, the amounts in question shall remain finally chargeable to the first institution, save where the payment which was not due is the result of fraud.

3.418

Article 113

Recovery of benefits in kind provided but not due to persons employed in international transport

1. If the right to benefits in kind is not recognized by the competent institution, the benefits in kind which have been provided to a person employed in international transport by the institution of the place of stay by virtue of

3.419

Council Regulation (EEC) No 574/72

the presumption referred to in Article 20(1) or 62(1) of the implementing Regulation, shall be refunded by the competent institution.

2. Expenses incurred by the institution of the place of stay in respect of any person employed in international transport who has not previously applied to the institution of the place of stay and is not entitled to benefits in kind but has nevertheless received benefits in kind upon presentation of the certified statement referred to in Article 20(1) or 62(1) of the implementing Regulation, shall be refunded by the institution shown as competent in the said certified statement or by any other institution designated for that purpose by the competent authority of the Member State concerned.

3. The competent institution or, in the case referred to in paragraph 2, the institution shown as competent or the institution designated for that purpose shall debit the recipient of benefits with the value of the benefits in kind which were provided but were not due to him. The said institution shall notify these debits to the Audit Board referred to in Article 101(3) of the implementing Regulation which shall draw up a statement thereof.

Article 114

Provisional payments of benefits in cases of dispute over the legislation to be applied or the institution which should provide benefits

3.420   In the case of a dispute between the institutions or competent authorities of two or more Member States, either as to which legislation should apply under Title II of the Regulation, or as to which institution should provide the benefits, the person concerned who could claim benefits if there were no dispute shall provisionally receive the benefits provided for by the legislation administered by the institution of the place of residence or, if the person concerned does not reside in the territory of one of the Member States concerned, the benefits provided for by the legislation administered by the institution to which his claim was submitted in the first instance.

Article 115

Procedures for medical examinations carried out in a Member State other than the competent State

3.421   The institution of the place of stay or residence which is required under Article 87 of the Regulation to carry out a medical examination, shall act in accordance with the procedures laid down by the legislation which it administers.

In the absence of such procedures, it shall apply to the competent institution for information on the procedures to be applied.

Article 116

Article 116

Agreements relating to the recovery of contributions

1. Agreements concluded pursuant to Article 92(2) of the Regulation shall be entered in Annex 5 to the implementing Regulation.

2. Agreements concluded for the implementation of Article 51 of the Regulation shall continue to apply provided they are included in Annex 5 to the implementing Regulation.

3.422

[¹ TITLE VIA

PROVISIONS GOVERNING ELECTRONIC DATA PROCESSING]

Title VIa omitted.

3.423

AMENDMENT

1. Regulation 1290/97/EC, [1997] OJ L176/1 (October 4, 1997).

TITLE VII

TRANSITIONAL AND FINAL PROVISIONS

Article 118

Transitional provisions relating to pensions for employed persons

1. Where the contingency arises before 1 October 1972 or before the date of implementation of the implementing Regulation in the territory of the Member State concerned and the claim for pension has not been awarded before that date, such claim shall give rise to a double award, in as much as benefits must be granted, pursuant to such contingency, for a period prior to that date:
  (a) for the period prior to 1 October 1972 or to the date of implementation of the implementing Regulation in the territory of the Member State concerned, in accordance with the Regulation or agreements in force between the Member States concerned.
  (b) for the period commencing on 1 October 1972 or on the date of implementation of the implementing Regulation in the territory of the Member State concerned, in accordance with the Regulation.
However, if the amount calculated pursuant to the provisions referred to under (a) is greater than that calculated pursuant to the provisions referred to under (b), the person concerned shall continue to be entitled to the amount calculated pursuant to the provisions referred to under (a).

3.424

2. A claim for invalidity, old age or survivors' benefits submitted to an institution of a Member State from 1 October 1972 or from the date of implementation of the implementing Regulation in the territory of the Member State concerned, or in a part of the territory of that State, shall automatically necessitate the reassessment of the benefits which have been awarded for the same contingency prior to that date by the institution or institutions of one or more of the other Member States, in accordance with the Regulation; such reassessment may not give rise to any reduction in the amount of the benefit awarded.

Article 119

Transitional provisions relating to pensions for self-employed persons

3.425   1. Where the contingency arises before 1 July 1982 or before the date of implementation of the implementing Regulation in the territory of the Member State concerned and the claim for pension has not been awarded before that date, such claim shall give rise to a double award, in as much as benefits must be granted, pursuant to such contingency, for a period prior to that date:
   (a) for the period prior to 1 July 1982 or to the date of implementation of the implementing Regulation in the territory of the Member State concerned, in accordance with the Regulation or agreements in force between the Member States concerned before that date;
   (b) for the period commencing on 1 July 1982 or on the date of implementation of the implementing Regulation in the territory of the Member State concerned, in accordance with the Regulation.
However, if the amount calculated pursuant to the provisions referred to under (a) is greater than that calculated pursuant to the provisions referred to under (b), the person concerned shall continue to be entitled to the amount calculated pursuant to the provisions referred to under (a).

2. A claim for invalidity, old age or survivors' benefits submitted to the institution of a Member State from 1 July 1982 or from the date of implementation of the implementing Regulation in the territory of the Member State concerned, or in a part of the territory of that State, shall automatically necessitate the reassessment of the benefits that have already been awarded for the same contingency prior to that date by the institution or institutions of one or more of the other Member States, in accordance with the Regulation; such reassessment may not give rise to any reduction in the amount of benefit awarded.

Article 119a

Transitional provisions relating to pensions for the purpose of applying the last part of Article 15(1)(a) of the implementing Regulation

3.426   1. Where the date on which the contingency arises precedes 1 January 1987 and where the claim for a pension has not yet resulted in an award

before that date, such claim shall, in as much as benefits must be granted, pursuant to such contingency, for a period prior to the last-mentioned date, give rise to a double award:
  (a) for the period prior to 1 January 1987, in accordance with the provisions of the Regulation or of agreements in force between the Member States concerned;
  (b) for the period commencing on 1 January 1987, in accordance with the provisions of the Regulation.
If, however, the amount calculated in pursuance of the provisions referred to under (a) is greater than that calculated in pursuance of the provisions referred to under (b), the person concerned shall continue to be entitled to the amount calculated in pursuance of the provisions referred to under (a).

2. A claim for invalidity, old-age or survivors' benefits submitted to an institution of a Member State from 1 January 1987 shall automatically necessitate the reassessment, in accordance with the provisions of the Regulation, of the benefits which have been awarded for the same contingency prior to that date by the institution or institutions of one or more of the other Member States, without prejudice to the provisions of Article 3.

3. The rights of the persons concerned who obtained the award of pensions prior to 1 January 1987 in the territory of the Member State in question may be revised at their request in the light of the provisions of Council Regulation (EEC) No 3811/86.[1]

4. If the request referred to in paragraph 3 is submitted within one year following 1 January 1987, entitlement to rights under Regulation (EEC) No 3811/86 shall be acquired from 1 January 1987 or from the date of the entitlement to a pension where the last-mentioned date is subsequent to 1 January 1987; in such case the provisions of the legislation of any Member State with regard to the withdrawal or limitation of rights may not be relied upon as against the persons concerned.

5. If the request referred to in paragraph 3 is submitted after expiry of the period of one year following 1 January 1987, entitlement to rights acquired under Regulation (EEC) No 3811/86 which have not been withdrawn or in respect of which the period of limitation has not been exceeded shall be acquired from the date on which the request is submitted, unless more favourable provisions of the legislation of any of the Member States are applicable.

FOOTNOTE

1. OJ NO L355, 16.12.1986, p.5.

[[1]*Article 120*

Persons who study or receive vocational training

The provisions of this Regulation, with the exception of Article 10 and 10a, shall apply, where appropriate, by analogy to students.]

AMENDMENT

1. Regulation 307/99/EC, [1999] OJ L307/99 (May 1, 1999).

Council Regulation (EEC) No 574/72

Article 121

Supplementary implementing agreements

1. Two or more Member States or the competent authorities of those Member States may, where necessary, conclude agreements designed to supplement the administrative procedure for implementing the Regulation. Such agreements are listed in Annex 5 to the implementing Regulation.

2. Agreements similar to those referred to in paragraph 1, which are in force on the day preceding 1 October 1972, shall continue to apply provided they are included in Annex 5 to the implementing Regulation.

[¹*Article 122*

Special provisions concerning amendment of the Annexes

The Annexes to the implementing Regulation may be amended by a Commission Regulation at the request of the Member State or Member States concerned or their competent authorities, and after the unanimous opinion of the Administrative Commission has been obtained.]

AMENDMENT

1. Regulation 1399/99/EC, [1999] OJ L164/1.

ANNEX 1

COMPETENT AUTHORITIES

(Article 1(1) of the Regulation, and Articles 4(1) and 122 of the implementing Regulation)

** *Section numbering re-ordered by Annex II of the Treaty of Accession with effect from May 1, 2004.*
Only provisions concerning the United Kingdom have been reproduced.

**Y. UNITED KINGDOM

[¹ 1. Secretary of State for Work and Pensions, London]

1a. Secretary of State for Health, London

[² 1b. The Commissioners of the Inland Revenue or their official representative, London]

2. Secretary of State for Scotland, Edinburgh

3. Secretary of State for Wales, Cardiff

Annex 1

[¹ 4. Department for Social Development, Belfast; Department of Health and Social Services and Public Safety, Belfast]

[² 5. Principal Secretary, Social Affairs, Gibraltar.]

[² 6. Chief Executive of the Gibraltar Health Authority.]

AMENDMENTS

1. Regulation 185/2003/EC, [2003] OJ L271/3 (November 11, 2003).
2. Regulation 89/2001/EC, [2001] OJ L14/16 (February 6, 2001).

ANNEX 2

** *Section numbering re-ordered by Annex II of the Treaty of Accession with effect from May 1, 2004.*
Only provisions concerning the United Kingdom have been reproduced.

COMPETENT INSTITUTIONS

(Article 1(o) of the Regulation and Article 4(2) of the implementing Regulation)

**Y. UNITED KINGDOM

1. Benefits in kind

—Great Britain and Northern Ireland	Authorities which grant National Health Service Benefits
—Gibraltar	Gibraltar Health Authority

2. Cash benefits

—Great Britain	Department for Work and Pensions, London
—Northern Ireland	Department for Social Development, Belfast
—Gibraltar	Principal Secretary, Social Affairs, Gibraltar

3. Family benefits

—Great Britain	Inland Revenue, Child Benefit Office, Newcastle upon Tyne
	Inland Revenue, Tax Credit Office, Preston
—Northern Ireland	Inland Revenue, Tax Credit Office, Belfast
	Inland Revenue, Child Benefit Office (NI), Belfast
—Gibraltar	Principal Secretary, Social Affairs, Gibraltar

Council Regulation (EEC) No 574/72

ANNEX 3

INSTITUTIONS OF THE PLACE OF RESIDENCE AND INSTITUTIONS OF THE PLACE OF STAY

(Article 1(p) of the Regulation and Article 4(3) of the implementing Regulation)

3.432   ** *Section numbering re-ordered by Annex II of the Treaty of Accession with effect from May 1, 2004.*
Only provisions concerning the United Kingdom have been reproduced.

**Y. UNITED KINGDOM

1. Benefits in kind

—Great Britain and Northern Ireland	Authorities which grant National Health Service Benefits
—Gibraltar	Gibraltar Health Authority, 17 Johnstone's Passage, Gibraltar

2. Cash benefits (except for family benefits)

—Great Britain	Department for Work and Pensions, The Pension Service, International Pension Centre, Tyneview Park, Newcastle upon Tyne NE98 1BA
—Northern Ireland	Department for Social Development, Northern Ireland Social Security Agency, Network Support Branch, Overseas Benefit Unit, Block 2, Stormont Estate, Belfast BT4 3SJ
—Gibraltar	Department of Social Services, 23 Mackintosh Square, Gibraltar

3. Family benefits

For the purpose of applying Articles 73 and 74 of the Regulation:

—Great Britain	Inland Revenue, Child Benefit Office of Great Britain, Newcastle upon Tyne NE88 1AA
—Northern Ireland	Inland Revenue, Tax Credit Office, Dorchester House, Great Victoria Street, Belfast BT2 7WF Inland Revenue, Child Benefit Office (NI), Windsor House, 9-15 Bedford Street, Belfast BT2 7UW
—Gibraltar	Department of Social Services, 23 Mackintosh Square, Gibraltar

Annex 4

ANNEX 4

LIASION BODIES

(Articles 3(1), 4(4) and 122 of the implementing Regulation)

** *Section numbering re-ordered by Annex II of the Treaty of Accession with effect from May 1, 2004.*
Only provisions concerning the United Kingdom have been reproduced.

3.433

**Y. UNITED KINGDOM

Great Britain:

(a) contributions and benefits in kind for posted workers	Inland Revenue, Centre for Non Residents, Benton Park View, Newcastle upon Tyne NE98 1ZZ
(b) all other questions	Department for Work and Pensions, The Pension Service, International Pension Centre, Tyneview Park, Newcastle upon Tyne NE98 1BA

Northern Ireland:

(a) contributions and benefits in kind for posted workers	Inland Revenue, Centre for Non Residents, Benton Park View, Newcastle upon Tyne NE98 1ZZ
(b) all other questions	Department for Social Development, Northern Ireland Social Security Agency, Network Support Branch, Overseas Benefits Unit, Block 2, Stormont Estate, Belfast BT4 3SJ

Gibraltar: Department for Work and Pensions, The Pension Centre, International Pensions Centre, Tyneview Park, Newcastle upon Tyne NE98 1BA

Council Regulation (EEC) No 574/72

Annex 5

Implementing Provisions of Bilateral Conventions Which Remain in Force

(Articles 4(5), 5, 53(3), 104, 105(2), 116, 121 and 122 of the implementing Regulation)

** *Section numbering re-ordered by Annex II of the Treaty of Accession with effect from May 1, 2004.*
Only provisions concerning the United Kingdom have been reproduced.

General observations

I. Whenever the provisions set out in this Annex refer to the provisions of Conventions or of Regulations No 3, No 4 or No 36/63/EEC, those references shall be replaced by references to the corresponding provisions of the Regulation or of the implementing Regulation, unless the provisions of those Conventions remain in force by virtue of their inclusion in Annex II to the Regulation.

II. The denunciation clause contained in a Convention, certain provisions of which are included in this Annex, shall remain in force in respect of the said provisions.

**24. BELGIUM-UNITED KINGDOM

(a) The exchange of letters of 4 May and 14 June 1976 regarding Article 105(2) of the implementing Regulation (waiving of reimbursement of the costs of administrative checks and medical examinations).

(b) The exchange of letters of 18 January and 14 March 1977 regarding Article 36(3) of the Regulation (arrangement for reimbursement or waiving of reimbursement of the costs of benefits in kind provided under the terms of Chapter 1 of Title III of the Regulation) as amended by the exchange of letters of 4 May and 23 July 1982 (agreement for reimbursement of costs incurred under Article 22(1)(a) of the Regulation).

[¹ 47. CZECH REPUBLIC—UNITED KINGDOM

None.]

**69. DENMARK—UNITED KINGDOM

1. The exchange of letters of 30 March and 19 April 1977 as modified by an exchange of letters of 8 November 1989 and of 10 January 1990 shall be added in point 1 after 19 April 1977 regarding Articles 36(3), 63(3) and 70(3) of the Regulation and Article 105(2) of the implementing Regulation (waiving of reimbursement of the costs of:

(a) benefits in kind provided under the terms of Chapter 1 or 4 of Title III of the Regulation;

(b) [. . .]

Annex 5

(c) administrative checks and medical examinations referred to in Article 105 of the implementing Regulation).

2. The exchange of letters of 5 March and 10 September 1984 relating to the non-application to self-employed persons of agreements regarding the waiver of reimbursement of unemployment benefits paid pursuant to Article 69 of the Regulation, in dealings with Gibraltar.

90. GERMANY—UNITED KINGDOM

(a) Articles 8, 9, 25 to 27 and 29 to 32 of the Arrangement of 10 December 1964 on the implementation of the Agreement of 20 April 1960.

(b) The Agreement of 29 April 1977 concerning the waiving of the reimbursement of costs of benefits in kind for sickness, maternity, accidents at work and occupational diseases, costs of unemployment benefit and costs of administrative checks and medical examinations.

(c) The exchange of letters of 18 July and 28 September 1983 relating to the non-application to self-employed persons of agreements concerning the waiver of reimbursement of unemployment benefits paid pursuant to Article 69 of the Regulation, in dealings with Gibraltar.

[1 **110. ESTONIA—UNITED KINGDOM**

No convention.]

129. GREECE—UNITED KINGDOM

No convention.

[2 **147. SPAIN—UNITED KINGDOM**

The exchange of letters of 30 July and 26 September 1980 concerning reciprocal waiver of the reimbursement of unemployment benefits (Article 70(3) of the Regulation.]

164. FRANCE—UNITED KINGDOM

[2 (a) The Exchange of Letters of 25 March and 28 April 1997 regarding Article 105(2) of the implementing Regulation (waiving of reimbursement of the costs of administrative checks and medical examinations).

(b) The Agreement of 8 December 1998 on the specific methods of determining the amounts to be re-imbursed for benefits in kind pursuant to Regulation (EEC) No 1408/71 and (EEC) 574/72.

180. IRELAND—UNITED KINGDOM

Agreement of 8 November 2000 on the waiving of reimbursement of the costs of benefits in kind of sickness, maternity, accidents at work and occupational diseases, and the costs of administrative and medical controls.

195. ITALY—UNITED KINGDOM

The exchange of letters of 1 and 16 February 1995 concerning Articles 36(3) and 63(3) of the Regulation (reimbursement of waiving of reimbursement of expenditure for benefits in kind) and article 105(2) of the implementing Regulation (waiving of reimbursement of the costs of administrative checks and medical examinations).

[¹ 209. CYPRUS—UNITED KINGDOM

None.]

[¹ 222. LATVIA—UNITED KINGDOM

No convention.]

[¹ 234. LITHUANIA—UNITED KINGDOM

No convention.]

**245. LUXEMBOURG—UNITED KINGDOM

(a) The exchange of letters of 28 November and 18 December 1975 regarding Article 70(3) of the Regulation (waiving of reimbursement of benefits paid pursuant to Article 69 of the Regulation).
(b) The exchange of letters of 18 December 1975 and 20 January 1976 regarding Articles 36(3) and 63(3) of the Regulation and Article 105(2) of the implementing Regulation (waiving of reimbursement of costs of benefits in kind provided under the terms of Chapter 1 or 4 or Title III of the Regulation, and also of the costs entailed in administrative checks and medical examinations referred to in Article 105 of the implementing Regulation).
(c) The exchange of letters of 18 July and 27 October 1983 relating to the non-application of the agreement detailed at (a) to self-employed persons moving between Luxembourg and Gibraltar.

[¹ 255. HUNGARY—UNITED KINGDOM

None.]

[¹ 264. MALTA—UNITED KINGDOM

None.]

**272. NETHERLANDS—UNITED KINGDOM

(a) The second sentence of Article 3 of the Administrative Arrangement of 12 June 1956 on the implementation of the Convention of 11 August 1954.
(b) The exchange of letters of 25 April and 26 May 1986 concerning Article 36(3) of the Regulation (reimbursement or waiver of reimbursement of expenditure for benefits in kind), as amended.

**279. AUSTRIA—UNITED KINGDOM

(a) Article 18(1) and (2) of the Arrangement of 10 November 1980 for the implementation of the Convention on social security of 22 July 1980 as amended by Supplementary Arrangements No 1 of 26 March 1986 and No 2 of 4 June 1993 with regard to persons who cannot claim treatment under Chapter 1 of Title III of the Regulation.

Annex 5

(b) Article 18(1) of the said Arrangement with regard to persons who can claim treatment under Chapter 1 of Title III of the Regulation on the understanding that for Austrian nationals resident in the territory of Austria and for nationals of the United Kingdom resident in the territory of the United Kingdom (with the exception of Gibraltar) the relevant passport shall replace the form E 111 for all benefits covered by that form.

(c) Agreement of 30 November 1994 concerning the reimbursement of expenditure for social security benefits.

[¹ 285. POLAND—UNITED KINGDOM

None.]

**290. PORTUGAL—UNITED KINGDOM

Articles 3 and 4 of the Annex to the Administrative Arrangement of 31 December 1981 for the application of the Protocol on medical treatment of 15 November 1978.

[¹ 294. SLOVENIA—UNITED KINGDOM

None.]

[¹ 297. SLOVAKIA—UNITED KINGDOM

None.]

**299. FINLAND—UNITED KINGDOM

The exchange of letters of 1 and 20 June 1995 concerning Articles 36(3) and 63(3) of Regulation (EEC) No 1408/71 (reimbursement or waiving of reimbursement of the cost of benefits in kind) and Article 105(2) of Regulation (EEC) No 574/72 (waiving of reimbursement of the cost of administrative checks an medical examinations).

**300. SWEDEN—UNITED KINGDOM

The arrangement of 15 April 1997 concerning Article 36(3) and 63(3) of the Regulation (reimbursement or waiving of reimbursement of the cost of benefits in kind) and Article 105(2) of the implementing Regulation (waiving of refunds of the costs of administering checks and medical examinations).

AMENDMENTS

1. Annex II to the Treaty of Accession (May 1, 2004).
2. Regulation 89/2001/EC, [2001] OJ L14/16 (February 6, 2001).

Council Regulation (EEC) No 574/72

Annex 6

Procedure for the Payment of Benefits

(Articles 4(6), 53(1) and 122 of the Implementing Regulation)

** *Section numbering re-ordered by Annex II of the Treaty of Accession with effect from May 1, 2004.*
Only provisions concerning the United Kingdom have been reproduced.

General observation

3.435 Payments of arrears and other single payments shall in principle be made through the liaison bodies. Current and sundry payments shall be made in accordance with the procedure set out in this Annex.

**Y. UNITED KINGDOM

Direct payment.

Annex 7

Banks

(Articles 4(7), 55(3) and 122 of the implementing Regulation)

3.436 ** *Section numbering re-ordered by Annex II of the Treaty of Accession with effect from May 1, 2004.*
Only provisions concerning the United Kingdom have been reproduced.

**Y. UNITED KINGDOM

Great Britain
Bank of England, London
Northern Ireland
Northern Bank Limited, Belfast
Gibraltar
Barclays Bank, Gibraltar

Annex 8

[¹ ANNEX 8

GRANT OF FAMILY BENEFITS

(Articles 4(8), 10a(d) and 122 of the implementing Regulation)

Only provisions concerning the United Kingdom have been reproduced. Article 10a (d) of the implementing Regulation is applicable to:

A. Employed and self-employed persons

(a) with a reference period of one calendar month in dealings between
 — Belgium and the United Kingdom
 — the Czech Republic and the United Kingdom
 — Germany and the United Kingdom
 — Lithuania and the United Kingdom
 — Austria and the United Kingdom
 — Poland and the United Kingdom
 — Portugal and the United Kingdom
 — Slovenia and the United Kingdom
 — Slovakia and the United Kingdom
 — Finland and the United Kingdom
 — Sweden and the United Kingdom
(b) with a reference period of a quarter of a calendar year in dealings between:
[. . .]

B. Self-employed persons

With a reference period of a quarter of a calendar year in dealings between:
[. . .]

C. Employed persons

With a reference period of one calendar month in dealing between:
[. . .]

AMENDMENT

1. Annex II to the Treaty of Accession (May 1, 2004).

Council Regulation (EEC) No 574/72

ANNEX 9

CALCULATION OF THE AVERAGE ANNUAL COST OF BENEFITS IN KIND

3.438

(Articles 4(9), 94(3)(a) and 95(3)(a) of the implementing Regulation)

** *Section numbering re-ordered by Annex II of the Treaty of Accession with effect from May 1, 2004.*
Only provisions concerning the United Kingdom have been reproduced.

**Y. UNITED KINGDOM

The average annual cost of benefits in kind shall be calculated by taking into consideration the benefits provided by the National Health Service of the United Kingdom.

ANNEX 10

INSTITUTIONS AND BODIES DESIGNATED BY THE COMPETETENT AUTHORITIES

(Article 4(10) of the implementing Regulation)

3.439

** *Section numbering re-ordered by Annex II of the Treaty of Accession with effect from May 1, 2004.*
Only provisions concerning the United Kingdom have been reproduced.

**Y. UNITED KINGDOM

1. For the purposes of applying Articles 14c, 14d(3) and 17 of the Regulation and Articles 6(1), 11(1), 11a(1), 12a, 13(2) and (3), 14(1), (2) and (3), 80(2), 81, 82(2) and 109 of the implementing Regulation:

Great Britain:	Inland Revenue, Centre for Non-Residents, Benton Park View, Newcastle upon Tyne, NE98 1ZZ.
Northern Ireland:	Department for Social Development, Northern Ireland Social Security Agency, Network Support Branch, Overseas Benefits Unit, Block 2, Stormont Estate, Belfast BT4 3SJ, Inland Revenue, Centre for Non-Residents, Benton Park View, Newcastle upon Tyne, NE 98 1ZZ.

Annex 10

2. For the purposes of applying Articles 36 and 63 of the Regulation and Articles 8, 38(1), 70(1), 91(2), 102(2), 110 and 113(2) of the implementing Regulation:

Great Britain:	Department for Work and Pensions, The Pension Service, International Pension Centre, Tyneview Park, Newcastle upon Tyne NE98 1BA.
Northern Ireland:	Department for Social Development, Northern Ireland Social Security Agency, Network Support Branch, Overseas Benefits Unit, Block 2, Stormont Estate, Belfast BT4 3SJ

3. For the purposes of applying Articles 85(2), 86(2) and 89(1) of the implementing Regulation:

Great Britain:	Inland Revenue, Child Benefit Office of Great Britain, Newcastle upon Tyne, NE88 1AA, Inland Revenue, Tax Credit Office, Preston, PR1 0SB.
Northern Ireland:	Inland Revenue, Tax Credit Office, Dorchester House, Great Victoria Street, Belfast, BT2 7WF, Inland Revenue, Child Benefit Office (NI), Windsor House, 9–15 Bedford Street, Belfast, BT2 7UW.

ANNEX 11

[1 . . .]

3.440

AMENDMENT

1. Regulation 647/2005/EC, [2005] OJ L117/1 (May 5, 2005).

Council Regulation (EEC) No 574/72

Selected list of E-Forms

3.441 This is an unofficial list of E Forms used in connection with the administration of social security benefits under Regulation 1408/71. It is drawn from the list on the European Commission website.

E Form	Description
	Posting
E101	Certificate concerning applicable legislation
E102	Extension of term of posting or of activity as a self-employed person
	Health care sector
E104	Certificate concerning the aggregation of periods of insurance, employment or residence
E105	Certificate concerning the members of the family of an employed person or self-employed person to be taken into consideration for the calculation of cash benefits in the case of incapacity for work
E109	Certificate for the registration of members of the employed or self-employed person's family and the updating of lists
E112	Certificate concerning the retention of the right to sickness of maternity benefits currently being provided
E115	Claim for cash benefits for incapacity for work
E116	Medical report relating to incapacity for work (sickness, maternity, accident at work, occupational disease)
E117	Granting of cash benefits in the case of maternity and incapacity for work
E119	Certificate concerning the entitlement of unemployed persons and the members of their family to sickness and maternity insurance benefits
E121	Certificate for the registration of pensioners and the updating of lists
E124	Claim for death grant
	Pensions sector
E201	Certificate concerning the aggregation of periods or insurance or periods of residence
E202	Investigation of a claim for an old-age pension
E203	Investigation of a claim for a survivor's pension
E204	Investigation of a claim for an invalidity pension
E207	Information concerning the insured person's insurance history
E208	Determination of entitlement to pension
E209	Determination of pension amounts regarding the possible application of article 46(3) of Regulation
E210	Notification of decision concerning a claim for pension
E211	Summary of decisions
E212	Appeals and periods allowed for appeals
E213	Detailed medical report
E215	Administrative report on the position of a pensioner
E501	Request for information on insurance history of a worker
E504	Communication of insurance number of worker
E505	Certificate concerning the insurance history of a worker

Annex 11

E Form	Description
	Unemployment sector
E301	Certificate concerning the periods to be taken into account for the granting of unemployment benefits
E302	Certificate relating to members of the family of an unemployed person who must be taken into account for the calculation of benefits
E303/4	Certificate concerning retention of the right to unemployment benefits
	Family benefits
E401	Certificate concerning composition of a family for the purpose of granting of family benefits
E411	Request for information on entitlement to family benefits in the Member State of residence of the members of the family
	Non-contributory benefits
E601	Request for information concerning the amount of income received in a Member State other than the competent Member State
E602	Concerning the aggregation of periods of employment or self-employment or of residence

Relevant Decisions of the Administrative Commission

Decision No 76 of 22 February 1973 concerning the conditions for the use of Forms E402, E403 and E404, [1973] OJ C75/6

Council Regulation (EC) No 859/2003 of 14 May 2003 Extending the Provisions of Regulation (EEC) No 1408/71 and Regulation (EEC) No 574/72 to Nationals of Third Countries Who are not Already Covered by Those Provisions Solely on the Ground of Their Nationality

[2003] OJ L124/1

General Note

As the Preamble makes clear, for some years, there has been concern that nationals of countries other than EEA countries and Switzerland ("participating countries") were at a disadvantage in that there was no provision for the co-ordination of the social security rules of two or more participating countries for the benefit of third country nationals who had lawfully lived and worked in the EU. This regulation seeks to ameliorate their circumstances by extending, with effect from June 1, 2003, the provisions of Regulation 1408/71 to such third country nationals where they have had contact with two or more participating countries.

3.442

The Council of the European Union

Having regard to the Treaty establishing the European Community and in particular Article 63, point 4 thereof,

3.443

Having regard to the proposal from the Commission,[1]
Having regard to the opinion of the European Parliament,[2]
Whereas:

1. As its special meeting in Tampere on 15 and 16 October 1999, the European Council proclaimed that the European Union should ensure fair treatment of third-country nationals who reside legally in the territory of its Member States, grant them rights and obligations comparable to those of EU citizens, enhance non-discrimination in economic, social and cultural life and approximate their legal status to that of Member States' nationals.

2. In its resolution of 27 October 1999,[3] the European Parliament called for prompt action on promises of fair treatment for third-country nationals legally resident in the Member States and on the definition of their legal status, including uniform rights as close as possible to those enjoyed by the citizens of the European Union.

3. The European Economic and Social Committee has also appealed for equal treatment of Community nationals and third-country nationals in the social field, notably in its opinion of 26 September 1991 on the status of migrant workers from third countries.[4]

4. Article 6(2) of the Treaty on European Union provides that the Union shall respect fundamental rights, as guaranteed by the European Convention on the Protection of Human Rights and Fundamental Freedoms signed in Rome on 4 November 1950 and as they result from the constitutional traditions common to the Member States, as general principles of Community law.

5. This Regulation respects the fundamental rights and observes the principles recognised in particular by the Charter of Fundamental Rights of the European Union, in particular the spirit of its Article 34(2).

6. The promotion of a high level of social protection and the raising of the standard of living and quality of life in the Member States are objectives of the Community.

7. As regards the conditions of social protection of third-country nationals, and in particular the social security scheme applicable to them, the Employment and Social Policy Council argued in its conclusions of 3 December 2001 that the coordination applicable to third-country nationals should grant them a set of uniform rights as near as possible to those enjoyed by EU citizens.

8. Currently, Council Regulation (EEC) No 1408/71 of 14 June 1971 on the application of social security schemes to employed persons and their families moving within the Community,[5] which is the basis for the coordination of the social security schemes of the different Member States, and Council Regulation (EEC) No 574/72 of 21 March 1972, laying down the procedure for implementing Regulation (EEC) No 1408/71,[6] apply only to certain third-country nationals. The number and diversity of legal instruments used in an effort to resolve problems in connection with the coordination of the Member States' social security schemes encountered by nationals of third countries who are in the same situation as Community nationals give rise to legal and administrative complexities. They create major difficulties for the individuals concerned, their employers, and the competent national social security bodies.

9. Hence, it is necessary to provide for the application of the coordination rules of Regulation (EEC) No 1408/71 and Regulation (EEC) No 574/72 to third-country nationals legally resident in the Community who are not

currently covered by the provisions of these Regulations on grounds of their nationality and who satisfy the other conditions provided for in this Regulation; such an extension is in particular important with a view to the forthcoming enlargement of the European Union.

10. The application of Regulation (EEC) No 1408/71 and Regulation (EEC) No 574/72 to these persons does not give them any entitlement to enter, to stay or to reside in a Member State or to have access to its labour market.

11. The provisions of Regulation (EEC) No 1408/71 and Regulation (EEC) No 574/72 are, by virtue of this Regulation, applicable only in so far as the person concerned is already legally resident in the territory of a Member State. Being legally resident is therefore a prerequisite for the application of these provisions.

12. The provisions of Regulation (EEC) No 1408/71 and Regulation (EEC) No 574/72 are not applicable in a situation which is confined in all respects within a single Member State. This concerns, inter alia, the situation of a third country national who has links only with a third country and a single Member State.

13. The continued right to unemployment benefit, as laid down in Article 69 of Regulation (EEC) No 1408/71, is subject to the condition of registering as a job-seeker with the employment services of each Member State entered. Those provisions may therefore apply to a third-country national only provided he/she has the right, where appropriate pursuant to his/her residence permit, to register as a job-seeker with the employment services of the Member State entered and the right to work there legally.

14. Transitional provisions should be adopted to protect the persons covered by this Regulation and to ensure that they do not lose rights as a result of its entry into force.

15. To achieve these objectives it is necessary and appropriate to extend the scope of the rules coordinating the national social security schemes by adopting a Community legal instrument which is binding and directly applicable in every Member State which takes part in the adoption of this Regulation.

16. This Regulation is without prejudice to rights and obligations arising from international agreements with third countries to which the Community is a party and which afford advantages in terms of social security.

17. Since the objectives of the proposed action cannot be sufficiently achieved by the Member States and can therefore, by reason of the scale or effects of the proposed action, be better achieved at Community level, the Community may take measures in accordance with the principle of subsidiarity enshrined in Article 5 of the Treaty. In compliance with the principle of proportionality as set out in that Article, this Regulation does not go beyond what is necessary to achieve these objectives.

18. In accordance with Article 3 of the Protocol on the position of the United Kingdom and Ireland annexed to the Treaty on the European Union and to the Treaty establishing the European Community, Ireland and the United Kingdom gave notice, by letters of 19 and 23 April 2002, of their wish to take part in the adoption and application of this Regulation.

19. In accordance with Articles 1 and 2 of the Protocol on the position of Denmark annexed to the Treaty on the European Union and to the Treaty establishing the European Community, Denmark is not taking part in the adoption of this Regulation and is not therefore bound by or subject to it,

FOOTNOTES

1. OJ C 126 E, 28.5.2002, p.388.
2. Opinion of 21 November 2002.
3. OJ C 154, 5.6.2000, p.63.
4. OJ C 339, 231.12.1991, p.82.
5. OJ L 149, 5.7.1971, p.2; Regulation last amended by Regulation (EC) No 1386/2001 of the European parliament and of the Council (OJ L187, 10.7.2001, p.1).
6. OJ L 74, 27.3.1972, p.1; Regulation last amended by Commission Regulation (EC) No 410/2002 (OJ L 62, 5.3.2002, p.17).

Has Adopted this Regulation

Article 1

3.444 Subject to the provisions of the Annex to this Regulation, the provisions of Regulation (EEC) No 1408/71 and Regulation (EEC) No 574/72 shall apply to nationals of third countries who are not already covered by those provisions solely on the ground of their nationality, as well as to members of their families and to their survivors, provided they are legally resident in the territory of a Member State and are in a situation which is not confined in all respects within a single Member State.

GENERAL NOTE

3.445 This short article enfranchises third country nationals into the scheme for the co-ordination of social security found in the two principal regulations where they are not already within that scheme. Some third country nationals are already covered by the rules in Regulation 1408/71, namely, stateless persons, refugees and members of families and survivors of Community nationals in the circumstances set out in Regulation 1408/71.

The condition for third country nationals is that they are "lawfully resident" in the territory of a Member State. This phrase is not defined, but will have to be applied by national authorities in accordance with their immigration laws. The most likely way forward will be that Member States will regard as lawfully resident all those whose immigration status is compliant with national requirements. But see for discussion of the phrase in a different context, *Szoma v Secretary of State for Work and Pensions* [2005] UKML 64, reported as *R(IS) 2/01*, in which the House of Lords ruled that, under UK social security regulations and in the context of asylum seekers, persons subject to immigration control are lawfully present in the United Kingdom.

Note too that the extension of Regulation 1408/71 to third country nationals only relates to the co-ordination of schemes within the participating countries, and so has no application where the third country national has only had contact with the social security system of one Member State. So, for example, the regulation does not apply where an Australian national is living and working in the UK, and has had no contact with the social security system of any other Member State.

Article 2

3.446 1. This Regulation shall not create any rights in respect of the period before 1 June 2003.

2. Any period of insurance and, where appropriate, any period of employment, self-employment or residence completed under the legislation

Article 2

of a Member State before 1 June 2003 shall be taken into account for the determination of rights acquired in accordance with the provisions of this Regulation.

3. Subject to the provisions of paragraph 1, a right shall be acquired under this Regulation even if it relates to a contingency arising prior to 1 June 2003.

4. Any benefit that has not been awarded or that has been suspended on account of the nationality or the residence of the person concerned shall, at the latter's request, be awarded or resumed from 1 June 2003, provided that the rights for which benefits were previously awarded did not give rise to a lump-sum payment.

5. The rights of persons who prior to 1 June 2003, obtained the award of a pension may be reviewed at their request, account being taken of the provisions of this Regulation.

6. If the request referred to in paragraph 4 or paragraph 5 is lodged within two years from 1 June 2003, rights deriving from this Regulation shall be acquired from that date and the provisions of the legislation of any Member State on the forfeiture or lapse of rights may not be applied to the persons concerned.

7. If the request referred to in paragraph 4 or paragraph 5 is lodged after expiry of the deadline referred to in paragraph 6, rights not forfeited or lapsed shall be acquired from the date of such request, subject to any more favourable provisions of the legislation of any Member State.

GENERAL NOTE

This article deals with the temporal effect of the extension of the system of co-ordination to third country nationals. Rights may not be acquired prior to June 1, 2003, but periods of insurance or residence before that date may be taken into account in determining entitlement to a right accruing after June 1, 2003. So, periods of contribution prior to June 1, 2003 may be taken into account in determining whether there is entitlement to a benefit payable with effect from June 1, 2003 or later.

3.447

Article 3

This Regulation shall enter into force on the first day of the month following its publication in the Official Journal of the European Union.

This Regulation shall be binding in its entirety and directly applicable in the Member States in accordance with the Treaty establishing the European Community.

Done at Brussels, 14 May 2003.

3.448

ANNEX

SPECIAL PROVISIONS REFERRED TO IN ARTICLE 1

I. GERMANY

3.449

In the case of family benefits, this Regulation shall apply only to third-country nationals who are in possession of a residence permit meeting the definition in German law of the "Aufenthaltserlaubnis" or "Aufenthaltsberechtigung".

II. AUSTRIA

In the case of family benefits, this Regulation shall apply only to third-country nationals who fulfil the conditions laid down by Austrian legislation for permanent entitlement to family allowances.

Council Directive 79/7/EEC of December 19 1978 on the Progressive Implementation of the Principle of Equal Treatment for Men and Women in Matters of Social Security

[1979] OJ L6/24

THE COUNCIL OF THE EUROPEAN COMMUNITIES,

3.450 *Having regard* to the Treaty establishing the European Economic Community, and in particular Article 235 thereof,

Having regard to the proposal from the Commission,[1]

Having regard to the opinion of the European Parliament,[2]

Having regard to the opinion of the Economic and Social Committee,[3] whereas Article 1 (2) of Council Directive 76/207 of February 9 1976 on the implementation of the principle of equal treatment for men and women as regards access to employment, vocational training and promotion, and working conditions[4] provides that, with a view to ensuring the progressive implementation of the principle of equal treatment in matters of social security, the Council, acting on a proposal from the Commission, will adopt provisions defining its substance its scope and the arrangements for its application;

whereas the Treaty does not confer the specific powers required for this purpose;

whereas the principle of equal treatment in matters of social security should be implemented in the first place in the statutory schemes which provide protection against the risks of sickness, invalidity, old age, accidents at work, occupational diseases and unemployment, and in social assistance in so far as it is intended to supplement or replace the abovementioned schemes;

whereas the implementation of the principle of equal treatment in matters of social security does not prejudice the provisions relating to the protection of women on the ground of maternity;

whereas, in this respect, Member States may adopt specific provisions for women to remove existing instances of unequal treatment,

[1979] OJ L6/24

HAS ADOPTED THIS DIRECTIVE:

FOOTNOTES

1. [1977] O.J. C34/3.
2. [1977] O.J. C299/13.
3. [1977] O.J. C180/36.
4. [1976] O.J. L39/40.

GENERAL NOTE

The Community institutions recognised that moves to secure the principle of equal treatment for men and women would be incomplete without the inclusion of provisions dealing with social security. Directive 79/7 was made under Art.235 EC, and was part of the programme of legislation flowing from the commitment to equal pay for equal work to be found in Art.141 (ex 119) EC, rather than part of the programme for securing the free movement of workers.

Unfortunately a number of concepts in the directive have been interpreted slightly differently from what might be regarded as corresponding provisions of Reg.1408/71. Furthermore, the coverage of Dir.79/7 is not the same as that of Reg.1408/71 in terms of the benefits covered.

The Directive was required to be implemented in all the Member States from and including December 23, 1984.

Article 1

The purpose of this Directive is the progressive implementation, in the field of social security and other elements of social protection provided for in Article 3, of the principle of equal treatment for men and women in matters of social security, hereinafter referred to as "the principle of equal treatment".

Article 2

This Directive shall apply to the working population—including self-employed persons, workers and self-employed persons whose activity is interrupted by illness, accident or involuntary unemployment and persons seeking employment—and to retired or invalided workers and selfemployed persons.

GENERAL NOTE

Those within the personal scope of this Directive are not the same as those who are within the personal scope of Reg.1408/71. The Directive applies to the "working population". There is a link with employment (which includes selfemployment) related social security benefits in the Directive which makes it more limited than the concept of insured persons under Reg.1408/71.

The Court of Justice has given a very wide meaning to the term "working population", holding that it covers any worker, including those who are seeking work: Case C-280/94 *Van Damme* [1996] E.C.R. I-179. It extends to include someone who gives up work to care for a sick relative: Case 150/85 *Drake v Chief Adjudication Officer* [1986] E.C.R. 1995. But it does not include those who have never worked in a paid capacity: Joined Cases 48/88, 106/88 & 107/88 *Achterberg te Riele* [1989] E.C.R. 1963. Nor does it cover someone who gives up work to look after healthy children, since this is not one of the risks covered in Art.3: Case C-31/90 *Johnson v Chief Adjudication Officer (Johnson I)*, [1991] E.C.R. 3723, reported as *R(S) 1/95*.

In CG/5425/1995 the Commissioner held that the Directive did not apply to a woman who had last worked in 1949, and who claimed invalid care allowance to look after her mother in 1989. It is clear that there must be a causal link between giving up work and the incidence of one of the risks covered by Art.3.

Article 3

3.455   1. This Directive shall apply to:
(a) statutory schemes which provide protection against the following risks:
— sickness,
— invalidity,
— old age,
— accidents at work and occupational diseases,
— unemployment;
(b) social assistance, in so far as it is intended to supplement or replace the schemes referred to in (a).

2. This Directive shall not apply to the provisions concerning survivors' benefits nor to those concerning family benefits, except in the case of family benefits granted by way of increases of benefits due in respect of the risks referred to in paragraph 1(a).

3. With a view to ensuring implementation of the principle of equal treatment in occupational schemes, the Council, acting on a proposal from the Commission, will adopt provisions defining its substance, its scope and the arrangements for its application.

GENERAL NOTE

3.456   In Case 150/85 *Drake v Chief Adjudication Officer* [1986] E.C.R. 1995, the Court of Justice said that:

"Article 3(1) must be interpreted as including any benefit which in a broad sense forms part of one of the statutory schemes referred to or a social assistance provision intended to supplement or replace such a scheme." (para.21)

In case C-243/90 *R. v Secretary of State for Social Security Ex p. Smithson* [1992] E.C.R. I-467, the Court explained,

"In order to fall within the scope of the Directive, the benefit must be directly and effectively linked to the protection against one of the risks specified in Article 3(1)." (para.14)

R(A)2/94 holds that attendance allowance is an "invalidity benefit" within the meaning of Art.10 of Reg.1408/71. It follows that it also falls within the scope of this directive, as will disability living allowance. The position is not changed by the categorisation of those benefits as special non-contributory benefits which are not exportable under Reg.1408/71.

The Court of Justice has ruled that income support constitutes social assistance: Joined Cases C-63/91 & C-64/91 *Jackson and Cresswell v Chief Adjudication Officer* [1992] E.C.R. I-4737 (printed as appendix to *R(IS)10/91*). But discriminatory treatment may fall foul of Council Dir.76/207 on the implementation of the principle of equal treatment for men and women as regards access to employment, vocational training and promotion and working conditions, [1976] O.J. L39/40. A similar view has been taken in relation to family credit (now working families' tax credit), see Case C-116/94 *Meyers v Chief Adjudication Officer* [1995] E.C.R. I-2131, reported as *R(FC)2/98*.

Article 3

The classification of family credit (now working families' tax credit) proved to be somewhat problematic. It was classified as a family benefit for the purposes of Reg.1408/71: Case C-78/91 *Hughes v Chief Adjudication Officer* [1992] E.C.R. I-4839. However, it could arguably be regarded as having provided protection against the risk of unemployment through its role in topping up low pay.

In Case C-137/94 *R. v Secretary of State for Health Ex p. Richardson* [1995] E.C.R. I-3407, the Court ruled that free prescription charges fell within the material scope of the directive; it did not matter that these were regarded as a health benefit in the United Kingdom. In Case C-382/98 *R. v Secretary of State for Social Security Ex p. Taylor* judgment of December 16, 1999 [1999] E.C.R. I-8955, the Court ruled that winter fuel payments under the social fund were also within the material scope of the Directive.

In *Hockenjos v Secretary of State for Social Security*, Court of Appeal, May 2, 2001 [2001] EWCA Civ. 624, the Court of Appeal ruled that there is one statutory scheme for a jobseeker's allowance and that the benefit is one which provides protection against the risk of unemployment. Accordingly the benefit falls within the scope of Art.3 of the Directive.

In *CPC/4177/2005*, the Commissioner decided that state pension credit is a benefit falling within the scope of Directive 79/7.

See also *R(P) 1/95* and *R(P) 1/96*.

Article 4

1. The principle of equal treatment means that there shall be no discrimination whatsoever on ground of sex either directly, or indirectly by reference in particular to marital or family status, in particular as concerns:
— the scope of the schemes and the conditions of access thereto,
— the obligation to contribute and the calculation of contributions,
— the calculation of benefits including increases due in respect of a spouse and for dependants and the conditions governing the duration and retention of entitlement to benefits.

2. The principle of equal treatment shall be without prejudice to the provisions relating to the protection of women on the grounds of maternity.

3.457

GENERAL NOTE

The Court of Justice has ruled that Art.4 outlaws both direct and indirect forms of discrimination: Case 30/85 *Teuling* [1987] E.C.R. 2497, and Case C-226/91 *Molenbroek* [1992] E.C.R. I-5943.

3.458

The test to be applied was laid down in Case C-229/89 *Commission v Belgium* [1991] E.C.R. I-2205:

"Article 4(1) of Directive 79/7 precludes less favourable treatment from being accorded to a social group when it is shown to be made up of a much greater number of person or one or other sex, unless the provision ins question is 'based on objectively justified factors unrelated to any discrimination on grounds of sex'." (para.13)

Note that in *Blaik v Chief Adjudication Officer*, reported as *R(SB) 6/91*, the Court of Appeal decided that a difference of treatment accorded to a man and a woman on the ground of differing marital or family status (in the context of supplementary benefit) was not indirect discrimination within Art.4 and so did not breach Dir.79/7.

In *CIB/230/2000*, the Commissioner had to consider whether the provisions of regs 4 and 5 of the Overlapping Benefits Regulations resulted in discrimination prohibited by the Directive. The claimant had been in receipt of widow's pension since July 1995; she subsequently became entitled to incapacity benefit, but the adjudication officer decided that the benefit was not payable to her because it overlapped with widow's pension on the application of regs 4 and 5 of the Overlapping Benefits Regulations. The claimant argued that there was discrimination contrary to Dir.79/7/EEC relying on Case C-337/91 *A M van Gemert-Derks v Bestuur van de Nieuwe Industriële Bedrijfsvereniging* [1993] E.C.R. I-5435, which decided that, although survivors' benefits are outside the scope of the Directive, Art.4 precludes a national rule which withdraws from widows who are unfit for work the benefits applicable to that risk on their being granted a widow's pension, if that withdrawal is not the result of a voluntary renunciation by the beneficiary and is not applicable to widowers who are entitled to benefits for incapacity to work.

The Secretary of State argued before the Commissioner that (1) there was a difference between a withdrawal of benefit and an adjustment of the amount payable, and (2) it was essential that the withdrawl should involve a drop in income. The Commissioner rejected both those arguments. The Commissioner says that "what matters is the practical effect that the claimant was to receive nothing by way of incapacity benefit" (para.12). On the second issue, the Commissioner notes,

> "The principle was stated clearly and unequivocally in [*van Gemert-Derks*] that there is discrimination whenever women are deprived of a right to claim a benefit which men continue to receive in the same situation." (para.13.)

Addressing the issue in the case, the Commissioner says,

> "... if I had to, I would conclude that in the present case regulation 4(5) of the Overlapping Benefits Regulations, as applied to incapacity benefit and women in receipt or claiming widow's pension discriminated against women for the purposes of Directive 79/7. However, since below I have concluded that there is nevertheless objective justification for that discrimination, so that Article 4(1) of the Directive is not breached, I do not have to reach a final decision on this point." (para.20.)

Addressing the issue of objective justification, the Commissioner concluded that reg.4(5) of the Overlapping Benefits Regulations served the aim of co-ordinating the social security system, which is unrelated to any discrimination based on sex. So the Commissioner concludes that, if there was prima facie discrimination on grounds of sex contrary to Dir.79/7 in the application of reg.4(5) to the claimant, the discrimination was objectively justified (para.33).

In *Secretary of State for Social Security v Walter* [2001] EWCA Civ 1913; [2002] 1 C.M.L.R. 27 (reported as *R(JSA)3/02*) the Court of Appeal held that there was no breach of Dir.79/7 in the context of a claim by a student, whose studies were in suspense, and who had claimed a jobseeker's allowance. She challenged the regulations as directly discriminatory against pregnant women.

A Tribunal of Commissioners in *R(JSA)4/03* has held that the rule in reg.51(2)(c) of the Jobseeker's Allowance Regulations 1996 affects disproportionately more women than men and cannot be objectively justified. It is accordingly incompatible with Art.4 of Dir.79/7 and has no effect. Regulation 51(2)(c) provides that the number of hours persons or their partners are engaged in remunerative work is to be determined by disregarding those periods in which they are not required to work where they work at a school or other educational establishment or some other place of employment and the cycle of work consists of one year but with school holidays or similar vacations during which they do not work.

In *CJSA/4890/1998* the Commissioner ruled that reg.77(1), (2) and (3)(b) of the JSA Regulations on child additions and family premium discriminates unlawfully on grounds of sex. Statistical information had been presented to the Commissioner which showed that 92 per cent of men who shared the care of their children for at least 104 nights a year could not get child additions in income-based JSA because they did not receive child benefit as compared with eight per cent of women sharing care who could not get the addition for that reason.

Article 4

In *Hockenjos v Secretary of State for Social Security*, Judgment of December 21, 2004, [2004] EWCA Civ 1749, the Court of Appeal has allowed the claimant's appeal against the decision of the Commissioner in *CJSA/4890/2003* and dismissed the Department's cross appeal. It will be recalled that *Hockenjos v Secretary of State for Social Security* [2001] EWCA Civ 624 (and referred to in the annotations to Art.3) was the decision of the Court of Appeal determining that jobseeker's allowance was a benefit falling within the material scope of the Directive. This decision of the Court of Appeal deals with the substance of the claimant's claim to entitlement to additional amounts in respect of his children (the child premium) and to the family premium. Though he had shared care of the children, child benefit was paid to the children's mother which precluded payment of the additions to the claimant.

All three judges in the Court of Appeal reach the same conclusion by somewhat different lines of reasoning on the detail of the case. The Department conceded that the conditions of entitlement for child additions to a jobseeker's allowance, which linked these to entitlement to child benefit, were indirectly discriminatory, but argued that the discrimination could be objectively justified. The claimant was a man with shared care of his children following his separation from his wife. The Department argued that the link with entitlement to child benefit ensured consistency of decision-making. Scott Baker LJ, delivering the first judgment said:

> "45. According, in my judgment the position is this. The law is set out in the European Court's judgment in *Seymour-Smith*. The Secretary of State must first show that the discriminatory rule reflects a legitimate aim of social policy. Next he must show that the aim is unrelated to any discrimination based on sex and finally that he could reasonably consider that the means chosen are suitable for attaining that aim. Built into this final question is the balance between holding fast to the Community's fundamental principles on the one hand and the Member State's freedom to achieve its own social policy on the other."

Scott Baker L.J. concludes that regs 77(1), (2), (3) and (5) are discriminatory contrary to Article 4 of the Directive and have not been justified by the Secretary of State.

The question of the remedy to be applied once this conclusion was reached clearly troubled the Court of Appeal, and there was an ultimately fruitless excursion into the possible impact of the Apportionment Act 1870. The conclusion reached is that the proper remedy is for the whole allowance to be paid to the claimant in respect of each child, since both children met the test of being members of the claimant's household for whom he was responsible. This is because there is no provision in the jobseeker's allowance scheme permitting the splitting of the additions for children.

The alleged unlawful discrimination in *CIB/3933/2001* arose in the context of claims to for an increase of incapacity benefit for children. The parents were separated, but the children lived with their father for part of the week. He was refused an increase in his incapacity benefit for the children because he was not in receipt of child benefit for the children. He argued that the requirement that a person be in receipt of child benefit in order to be entitled to the increased constituted unlawful discrimination between men and women. The Commissioner accepted that men were more likely to be adversely affected by this requirement but that it was objectively justified on the grounds that, in most cases where parents are separated, it is mothers who undertake the greater proportion of the practical responsibility for caring for children of the family.

The alleged unlawful discrimination in *R(IB)5/04* arose in the context of the age requirements in relation to entitlement to an incapacity benefit. The claimant, a woman, became incapable of work when she was 64. If she had been a man, she would have paid contribution and would have been eligible to claim incapacity benefit at that age. The Commissioner felt bound by the decision in *Graham* to rule that the alleged discrimination was not unlawful under the provisions of the Directive. However, he stayed the case on the basis that proceeding might be brought to enable the claimant to pay contributions, but in the absence of such proceedings the appeal is to be treated as dismissed. The appeal was definitively dismissed on March 26, 2004 since the claimant had indicated that no such proceedings were to be brought.

In case C-423/04 *Richards v Secretary of State for Work and Pensions*, reported as *R(P) 1/07*, the Court of Justice has ruled that Art.4(1) of the Directive precludes legislation which denies a person, who has undergone male-to-female gender reassignment, enititlement to a retirement pension on the ground that she has not reached the age of 65, when she would have been entitled to such a pension at the age of 60 had she been held to be a woman as a matter of national law. This is the response to the Commissioner's reference in *CP/0428/2004*.

See now new Departmental Guidance in Memo DMG 06/07.

On the application of the principle established in *Richards* to a case in which the claimant had not be the date of the decision under appeal undergone gender reassignment surgery, see *CP/3485/2003* discussed in more detail at para. 1.120 in Volume I.

Article 5

3.459 Member States shall take the measures necessary to ensure that any laws, regulations and administrative provisions contrary to the principle of equal treatment are abolished.

Article 6

3.460 Member States shall introduce into their national legal systems such measures as art necessary to enable all persons who consider themselves wronged by failure to apply the principle of equal treatment to pursue their claims by judicial process, possibly after recourse to other competent authorities.

GENERAL NOTE

3.461 In Case C-66/95 *R. v Secretary of State for Social Security Ex p. Sutton* [1997] E.C.R. I-2163, the Court of Justice ruled that Art.6 required a judicial process which would ensure that those who had been wronged by discrimination prohibited by the directive could get the benefit to which they were entitled, but went on to rule that "the payment of interest on arrears of benefits cannot be regarded as an essential component of the right as so defined." (para.25.) Contrast certain decisions under the European Convention on Human Rights which seem to assume that just satisfaction under the Convention will require the payment of interest: see annotations to Art.41 ECHR.

Article 7

3.462 1. This Directive shall be without prejudice to the right of Member States to exclude from its scope:
(a) the determination of pensionable age for the purposes of granting old-age and retirement pensions and the possible consequences thereof for other benefits;
(b) advantages in respect of old-age pension schemes granted to persons who have brought up children; the acquisition of benefit entitlements

Article 7

following periods of interruption of employment due to the bringing up of children;
(c) the granting of old-age or invalidity benefit entitlements by virtue of the derived entitlements of a wife;
(d) the granting of increases of long-term invalidity, old-age, accidents at work and occupational disease benefits for a dependent wife;
(e) the consequences of the exercise, before the adoption of this Directive, of a right of option not to acquire rights or incur obligations under a statutory scheme.

2. Member States shall periodically examine matters excluded under paragraph 1 in order to ascertain, in the light of social developments in the matter concerned, whether there is justification for maintaining the exclusions concerned.

GENERAL NOTE

Cases involving the Directive frequently raise issues of the scope of the derogations to be found in this article. The Court of Justice always takes the view that exceptions should be strictly construed, whereas freedoms are to be liberally construed. 3.463

Article 7(1)(a)

In Case C-9/91 *R. v Secretary of State for Social Security Ex p. Equal Opportunities Commission* [1992] E.C.R. I-4297, the Court of Justice ruled that Art.7(1)(a) permitted a Member State which retained differential pensionable ages for men and women and in which pensions were funded from contributions to retain a system under which men continued to be contribute for five years longer than women in order to be entitled to the same basic pension and by requiring men who work until the age of 65 to pay contributions whereas a woman who chooses to work beyond the age of 60 is not required to continue to pay contributions. The difference in treatment must, however, be necessarily linked to the difference in the statutory pensionable age. 3.464

In Case C-328/91 *Thomas v Secretary of State for Social Security* [1993] E.C.R. I-1247, reported as *R(G) 2/94*, the Court of Justice was called upon to rule on the nature of non-contributory invalidity benefits having regard to whether the different entitlement of men and women were such as to have "possible consequences . . ." for the purposes of prescribing different pensionable ages within the meaning of Article 7(1)(a). The Court ruled that the situations envisaged by the words "possible consequences thereof for other benefits" were limited to the forms of discrimination which are necessarily and objectively linked to the difference in retirement age.

In Case C-92/94 *Secretary of State for Social Security v Graham* [1995] E.C.R. I-2521, reported as *R(S)2/95*, concerned entitlement to invalidity benefit and the differential requirements applied to men and women. Rose Graham was 58 when she ceased work after several years in self-employment. As a person within five years of pensionable age who was not entitled to the invalidity allowance component of invalidity benefit; when she reached the age of 60 her entitlement to an invalidity pension was limited to the amount of her retirement pension (a condition which does not apply to a man until the age of 65), and her retirement was taxable whereas invalidity pension was tax-free. The claimant argued that the differential treatment was neither necessarily nor objectively linked to the difference in retirement age. The Court is somewhat unsatisfactory reasoning holds that the differential treatment is within the exception having regard to the coherence of the social security system. It is estimated that there were almost 40,000 look-alike cases affected by the decision. Where there are appeals on the grounds of links between invalidity benefit or unemployment benefit (by analogy), they seem certain to fail.

By contrast in Case C-137/94 *R. v Secretary of State for Health Ex p. Richardson* [1995] E.C.R. I-3407, it was held that the discriminatory treatment of men and women in relation to the restriction of entitlement to free prescriptions to those over retirement age unlawfully discriminated against men, since there was no necessary or objective link to pensionable age in the case of this social benefit. See also Case C-382/98 *R. v Secretary of State for Social Security Ex p. Taylor*, judgment of December 16, 1999, [1999] E.C.R. I-8955, in which the Court ruled that the different conditions of entitlement for man and women to winter fuel payments under the social fund could not be justified under the derogations in this article.

In Case C-303/02 *Haackert v Pensionsversicherungsanstalt der Angestellten*, Judgment of March 4, 2004, the Court of Justice ruled that the exception in Art.7(1)(a) applied to early old-age pension schemes with different entitlement ages for men and women because of the close link with the age at which old-age pensions, which were not awarded early, would arise. In the circumstances of the case before the Court, the early old-age pension operated as a substitute for the old-age pension.

In *CIB/13368/1996* the Commissioner ruled that the claimant (and all women whose entitlement to incapacity benefit derives from industrial injury or prescribed disease) are entitled to continue to receive the benefit after the age of 60 and before reaching the age of 65 since there is a breach of the principle of equal treatment in the United Kingdom regulations which does not fall within the exemption in Art.7(1)(a) but this decision was set aside, by consent, in the Court of Appeal on June 20, 2000 in *Chief Adjudication Officer v Rowlands*, because it was accepted that, in the light of the decision of the Court of Justice in Case C-196/98 *Hepple v Adjudication Officer* judgment of May 23, 2000, [2000] E.C.R. I-3701, the Commissioner's decision could not be upheld. In *Hepple*, the Court of Justice ruled that, in relation to reduced earnings allowance, the age conditions were held to fall within the exception in Art.7(1)(a) in order to preserve coherence between the rules on reduced earnings allowance and the rules on old age pensions. The Court said that discrimination of the kind at issue in the main proceedings is objectively and necessarily linked to the difference between the retirement age for men and that for women, to that it is covered by the derogation for which Art.7(1)(a) of the Directive provides (para.34 of the judgment). A key issue in the case had been the permissibility of introducing age conditions which differ according to sex *after* the date for implementation of the Directive.

Article 7(1)(c)

3.465   In *R(P) 1/96* the Commissioner held that the question of whether United Kingdom contribution requirements breached the prohibition of discrimination in Dir.79/7 is a question of law and so was not be determined by the Secretary of State. The claimant, who had been married more than once, was arguing that the failure to take into account her first husband's contributions in determining her entitlement to a retirement pension constituted indirect discrimination against women. The Commissioner considered that such discrimination as there might bewas permitted by Art.7(1)(c).

Article 7(1)(d)

3.466   In Case C-420/92 *Bramhill v Chief Adjudication Officer* [1994] E.C.R. I-3191, reported as *R(P) 2/96*, the Court of Justice ruled that,

> "Article 7(1)(d) of Council Directive 79/7 . . . does not preclude a Member State which provided for increases in long-term old-age benefits in respect of a dependent spouse to be granted only to me from abolishing that discrimination solely with regard to women who fulfil certain conditions."

Article 7

Article 7(2)
This would appear to be insufficiently precise to give rise to direct effect, since the term "periodically" is so open-ended. It is also difficult to see what right an individual could claim as a result of any such review.

3.467

Article 8

1. Member States shall bring into force the laws, regulations and administrative provisions necessary to comply with this Directive within six years of its notification. They shall immediately inform the Commission thereof.

2. Member States shall communicate to the Commission the text of laws, regulations and administrative provisions which they adopt in the field covered by this Directive, including measures adopted pursuant to Article 7(2).

They shall inform the Commission of their reasons for maintaining any existing provisions on the matters referred to in Article 7(1) and of the possibilities for reviewing them at a later date.

3.468

General Note

The Directive was required to be implemented from and including December 23, 1984. Those of its provisions that meet the requirements for direct effect have so operated since that date.

3.469

Article 9

Within seven years of notification of this Directive, Member States shall forward all information necessary to the Commission to enable it to draw up a report on the application of this Directive for submission to the Council and to propose such further measures as may be required for the implementation of the principle of equal treatment.

3.470

Article 10

This Directive is addressed to the Member States.

3.471

A Select Bibliography on European Social Security Law

Migration and Social Security Handbook (3rd ed., CPAG, London, 2002)

European Commission, *Compendium of Community Provisions on Social Security 1995* (4th ed., Office for Official Publications of the European Communities, Luxembourg, 1995).

European Commission, *Judgments of the Court of Justice of the European Communities related to Social Security for Migrant Workers* (Office for Official Publications of the European Communities, Luxembourg, 1995).

A Select Bibliography on European Social Security Law

European Commission, *Your Social Security Rights when Moving within the European Union. A Practical Guide* (Office for Official Publications of the European Communities, Luxembourg, 1997).

Hervey, T, "Social Security" in T Hervey, *European Social Law and Policy* (Longman, London, 1998), ch.5.

Luckhaus, L, "European Social Security Law" in A Ogus and N Wikeley, *The Law of Social Security* (4th ed., Butterworths, London, 1995), ch.18.

Pennings, F, *Introduction to European Social Security Law* (4th ed., Intersentia, Antwerp, 2003).

White, R, *EC Social Security Law* (Longman, London, 1999).

PART IV

HUMAN RIGHTS LAW

Human Rights Act 1998

(1998 c.42)

ARRANGEMENT OF SECTIONS

Introduction 4.01

1. The Convention Rights
2. Interpretation of Convention Rights

Legislation

3. Interpretation of legislation
4. Declaration of incompatibility
5. Right of Crown to intervene

Public authorities

6. Act of public authorities
7. Proceedings
8. Judicial remedies
9. Judicial acts

Remedial action

10. Power to take remedial action

Other proceedings and rights

11. Safeguard for existing human rights
12. Freedom of expression
13. Freedom of thought, conscience and religion

Derogations and reservations

14. Derogations
15. Reservations
16. Period for which designated derogations have effect
17. Periodic review of designated reservations

Human Rights Act 1998

Judges of the European Court of Human Rights

18. Appointment to the European Court of Human Rights (*Omitted*)

Parliamentary procedure

19. Statements of compatibility

Supplemental

20. Orders etc. under this Act
21. Interpretation, etc.
22. Short title, commencement, application and extent

SCHEDULES

Schedule 1—The Articles
  Part I—The Convention
  Part II—The First Protocol
  Part III—The Sixth Protocol
Schedule 2—Remedial Orders
Schedule 3—Derogation and Reservation
  Part I—Derogation
  Part II—Reservation
Schedule 4—Judicial Pensions (*Omitted*)

GENERAL NOTE

4.02   This Act has been described as "the first historic step ... towards a constitutional Bill of Rights" (Lester, A and Pannick, D (ed.) *Human Rights Law and Practice* (Butterworths, London, 1999) at para.1.44. It followed a Labour consultation paper of December 1996 entitled *Bringing Rights Home*, a manifesto commitment by the Labour Party in 1997, and an October 1997 White Paper entitled *Rights Brought Home: The Human Rights Bill*, Cm.3782.

The Act entered into force on October 2, 2000: The Human Rights Act 1998 (Commencement No.2) Order 2000 (SI 2000/1851). The commencement of each section is noted in the annotation to each section.

The UK has been a party to the European Convention on Human Rights since September 23, 1953 and has recognised the right of individual petition under the Convention continuously since January 14, 1966. Until this Act come into force, rights accruing for individuals under the Convention could not be invoked directly to determine whether they have been victims of a violation of the rights protected by the Convention. Individuals within the jurisdiction could only use the "ordinary" law of the land to secure their rights. If they believed that these have been denied them by the State or a part of the State, and they have sought redress under the national legal order (exhausted domestic remedies in the language of the Convention), they have been able to make an application to the Commission of Human Rights (prior to November 1, 1998) and direct to the Court of Human Rights (from November 1, 1998) claiming to be victims of a violation of one of the rights protected. If the application is admitted, then the Court of Human Rights may adjudicate on the issue. The Convention organs, which are part of the Council of Europe, are located in Strasbourg; they should not be confused with the institutions of the European Union. The Court of Justice of the European Communities is located in Luxembourg.

Introduction

The Convention Rights

1.—(1) In this Act "the Convention rights" means the rights and fundamental freedoms set out in—
(a) Articles 2 to 12 and 14 of the Convention,
(b) Articles 1 to 3 of the First Protocol, and
[2 (c) Article 1 of the Thirteenth Protocol,]
as read with Articles 16 to 18 of the Convention.

(2) Those Articles are to have effect for the purposes of this Act subject to any designated derogation or reservation (as to which see sections 14 and 15).

(3) The Articles are set out in Schedule 1.

(4) The [¹ Secretary of State] may by order make such amendments to this Act as he considers appropriate to reflect the effect, in relation to the United Kingdom, of a protocol.

(5) In subsection (4) "protocol" means a protocol to the Convention—
(a) which the United Kingdom has ratified; or
(b) which the United Kingdom has signed with a view to ratification.

(6) No amendment may be made by an order under subsection (4) so as to come into force before the protocol concerned is in force in relation to the United Kingdom.

COMMENCEMENT

October 2, 2000: the Human Rights Act 1998 (Commencement No.2) Order 2000 (SI 2000/1851).

AMENDMENTS

1. The Secretary of State for Constitutional Affairs Order 2003 (SI 2003/1887) (August 19, 2003).
2. Human Rights Act 1998 (Amendment) Order 2004 (SI 2004/1574) (22 June, 2004)

GENERAL NOTE

The Preamble to the Act describes its objective as to give "further effect" to the rights and freedoms guaranteed by the European Convention on Human Rights. The further effect given to the rights encompassed by the Act is their effect within the national legal order, so that they can be invoked directly in proceedings before United Kingdom courts. This is the scheme of incorporation adopted for the United Kingdom. The late former President of the Court has expressed the advantages of incorporation as follows,

"It has in fact two advantages: it provides the national court with the possibility of taking account of the Convention and the Strasbourg case-law to resolve the dispute before it, and at the same time it gives the European organs an opportunity to discover the views of the national courts regarding the interpretation of the Convention and its application to a specific set of circumstances. The dialogue which thus develops between those who are called upon to apply the Convention on the domestic level and those who must do so on the European level is crucial for an effective protection of the rights guaranteed under the Convention." (Rolv Ryssdal, Speech at the ceremony for the 40th anniversary of the European Convention on Human Rights at Trieste, 18 December 1990, Council of Europe document Court (90) 318, 2.

Convention rights are defined in subs.(1) as Arts 2–12 and 14 of the Convention itself, together with certain articles of the First and Sixth Protocols as read with Arts 16–18 of the Convention. These articles are set out in Sch.1. Their effect is subject to the terms of any derogation under Art.15 of the Convention or any reservation filed by the UK Government. Derogations are governed in more detail by s.14, and reservations by s.15; the current derogations and reservation are set out in Sch.3. The Secretary of State is given power to amend the Act to give effect to rights contained in protocols to the Convention which have not yet been ratified by the UK. For example, the UK Government has indicated that consideration is being given to ratification of certain provisions of the Seventh Protocol, but not of the Fourth Protocol.

Convention rights as defined in s.1 do not include Art.1 which provides that parties to the Convention "shall secure to everyone within their jurisdiction the rights and freedoms" set out in Arts 2–18 of the Convention. Nor do they include Art.13 which gives a right to an effective remedy in the following terms:

"Everyone whose rights and freedoms as set forth in this Convention are violated shall have an effective remedy before a national authority notwithstanding that the violation has been committed by persons acting in an official capacity."

The incorporation of Art.1 among Convention rights named by the Act is probably not necessary since the purpose of the Act is to give effect to Convention rights within the national legal order. However, it should be noted that the rights given by the Convention are not linked in any way to the nationality of an individual; they are guaranteed to all within the UK's jurisdiction. This differs from many rights given by EU law where the beneficiaries are nationals of the Member States of the European Union.

The failure to include Art.13 among the Convention rights may be more problematic, though the Lord Chancellor stoutly argued that its inclusion was not necessary because the Act gives effect "to Article 13 by establishing a scheme under which Convention rights can be raised before out domestic courts": HL Vol.583 col.475 (November 18, 1997). In the Commons, the Home Secretary made a similar point. There is apparently some concern that inclusion of the article might lead all manner of courts and tribunals to "invent" new remedies for violation of Convention rights. The Act is cautious on the issue of remedies where a violation is found: see commentary to s.8. However, both the Lord Chancellor and the Home Secretary conceded that in considering any question of remedies, courts or tribunals may have regard to the terms of Art.13 under s.2 of the Act. However, situations may arise where the scheme of the Act arguably does not offer an effective remedy for the violation, though it should be noted that the nature and scope of the effectiveness of the remedy required under Art.13 has hardly been touched on in the Strasbourg case law.

An example might help to illustrate the possible lacuna. Suppose a claimant before an appeal tribunal succeeds in persuading the tribunal that there has been an excessive delay in giving judgment on an appeal; This would constitute a violation of Art.6(1), ECHR. In this type of case, the Court of Human Rights has often awarded some compensation for the delay, but an appeal tribunal has no power to award compensation, or interest on late benefit. This would leave the individual without a remedy unless the mere statement that there was a violation was considered sufficient in the circumstances of the case. Any claim for compensation would have to be the subject of separate (and wholly novel) proceedings in a different forum. It is at least arguable that making a person in this position go to two judicial bodies for a remedy for the same violation is a failure to provide an effective remedy.

(1998 c.42, s.2)

Interpretation of Convention rights

2.—(1) A court or tribunal determining a question which has arisen in connection with a Convention right must take into account any—
  (a) judgment, decision, declaration or advisory opinion of the European Court of Human Rights,
  (b) opinion of the Commission given in a report adopted under Article 31 of the Convention,
  (c) decision of the Commission in connection with Article 26 or 27(2) of the Convention, or
  (d) decision of the Committee of Ministers taken under Article 46 of the Convention,
whenever made or given, so far as, in the opinion of the court or tribunal, it is relevant to the proceedings in which that question has arisen.

(2) Evidence of any judgment, decision, declaration or opinion of which account may have to be taken under this section is to be given in proceedings before any court or tribunal in such manner as may be provided by rules.

(3) In this section "rules" means rules of court or, in the case of proceedings before a tribunal, rules made for the purposes of this section—
  (a) by [1 . . .] [2 the Lord Chancellor or] the Secretary of State, in relation to any proceedings outside Scotland;
  (b) by the Secretary of State, in relation to proceedings in Scotland; or
  (c) by a Northern Ireland department, in relation to proceedings before a tribunal in Northern Ireland—
    (i) which deals with transferred matters; and
    (ii) for which no rules made under paragraph (a) are in force.

4.05

COMMENCEMENT

October 2, 2000: The Human Rights Act 1998 (Commencement No.2) Order 2000 (SI 2000/1851).

AMENDMENTS

1. The Secretary of State for Constitutional Affairs Order 2003 (SI 2003/1887) (August 19, 2003).
2. The Transfer of Functions (Lord Chancellor and Secretary of State) Order 2005 (SI 2005/3429) (January 12, 2006).

GENERAL NOTE

Introduction
This section requires courts and tribunals to have regard to the Strasbourg case law, past, present and future, in deciding any question relating to a Convention right. Note that the Strasbourg case law is not binding. There are two reasons for this. First, it will not always be easy to transplant directly the point being made by the Strasbourg organ where the case involves the complexities of other legal systems. Secondly, the Convention sets a minimum standard; one possibly dramatic effect of incorporation is that the United Kingdom authorities will set a higher standard than the common European standard which is set by the Strasbourg organs.

The section refers to dispositions of three Strasbourg organs: the Commission, the Court and the Committee of Ministers. In order to understand the reasons for this, both the old and the new Strasbourg systems must be understood.

4.06

1197

The "old" system of protection

4.07 The Convention, in its original form, created two organs "to ensure the observance of the engagements undertaken by the High Contracting Parties": the European Commission of Human Rights and the European Court of Human Rights. The main function of these two organs, sometimes collectively referred to as the Strasbourg organs, (together with the Committee of Ministers discussed later) was to deal with applications made by States and by individuals alleging violations of the Convention. Under old Art.24, any State party to the Convention could refer to the Commission any alleged breach of the provisions of the Convention by another State party. Under old Art.25, the Commission could receive applications from any person, non-governmental organization, or group of individuals claiming to be the victim of a violation by one of the Member States of the rights set forth in the Convention and any relevant Protocols. The procedure differed depending on whether the application is made under Art.24 or 25; what follows describes the process in relation to individual applications under Art.25.

Once an application was registered, the Commission first considered, and issued a *decision* on, whether the application met the admissibility requirements. If it did not, that was an end of the matter. If the application was declared admissible, the Commission went on to conduct an investigation into the merits of the complaint and to consider whether there had been a violation of the Convention. The result was a *report* from the Commission expressing an *opinion* (which is not legally binding) as to whether or not there has been a violation. The report was communicated on a confidential basis to the applicant and to the State concerned and was delivered to the Committee of Ministers, the political organ of the Council of Europe. Throughout this time, attempts would have been made to secure a friendly settlement "on the basis of respect for human rights".

Final decisions on cases on which the Commission had reported and which had not resulted in a friendly settlement were made by the Committee of Ministers, or the Court of Human Rights. Recognition of the jurisdiction of the Court was technically voluntary under old Art.46 of the Convention. Within three months of the transmission of the Commission report to the Committee of Ministers, the application could be referred to the Court for determination by the Commission, the defendant State, or the State whose national was alleged to be the victim. The applicant had no standing to refer the application to the Court, unless the defendant State was a party to Protocol 9. Where this was so, the applicant could refer the matter to the Court, but (unless it was also referred to the Court by the Commission or a State) it first had to be submitted to a panel of three judges, who could decide unanimously that the application should not be considered by the Court because it did not raise a serious question affecting the interpretation or application of the Convention.

If the case was referred to the Court and heard by it, there was a full judicial procedure, and even where Protocol 9 had not been ratified, some accommodations were made which allowed limited participation by the applicant. The Courts at in plenary session or in Chambers of nine. Decisions were made by a majority of the judges present and voting, with the President enjoying a casting vote if this was necessary. Separate opinions could be attached to the judgment of the majority.

Those cases which were not referred to the Court within three months of transmission of the Commission's report to the Committee of Ministers were automatically referred to the Committee of Ministers for final decision. The practice of the Committee of Ministers in recent years was simply to endorse the Commission report without any further investigation of the merits of the case.

The use of a political organ was a compromise to ensure that all applications resulted in a final determination. In the early years, there were States which had not recognised the competence of the Court, and there have always been cases which no one has referred to the Court.

(1998 c.42, s.2)

The "new" system of protection
Protocol 11 has amended the Convention to make provision for a new wholly judicial system of determination of applications. The Commission and the Court have been replaced from November 1, 1998 by a new permanent Court, which handles both the admissibility and merits phases of application. The Court is also charged with seeking to secure friendly settlement of matters before it.

4.08

Individual applications are made to the Court under Art.34 and individuals have full standing before the Court. Complaints are initially considered by a three-judge committee which will consider whether the application meets the Convention's admissibility criteria, but it can only rule an application to be inadmissible if it is unanimous. These criteria have not changed and flow from the terms of Arts 34 and 35 and involve the consideration of nine questions:
1. Can the applicant claim to be a victim?
2. Is the defendant State a party to the Convention?
3. Have domestic remedies been exhausted?
4. Is the application filed within the six-month time-limit?
5. Is the application signed?
6. Has the application been brought before?
7. Is the application compatible with the Convention?
8. Is the application manifestly ill-founded?
9. Is there an abuse of the right of petition?

In recent years somewhere around one in four to one in seven applications has been declared admissible, though over the life of the Convention fewer than one in ten applications has progressed beyond the admissibility phase.

Those cases which are not ruled inadmissible by the three judge committee are put before a seven judge chamber of the Court, which will include the judge sitting in respect of the defendant State. The chamber will consider the written arguments of the parties, investigate the material facts if these are in contention, and hear oral argument. This stage of the proceedings concludes with a decision whether the complaint is admissible and whether a friendly settlement is possible. There follows a consideration of the merits. In some cases, no doubt the admissibility and merits phases will be joined.

Certain cases of special difficulty can be referred by a chamber to a Grand Chamber of 17 judges.

The Court has an advisory jurisdiction, but the procedure has not been used to date. Its limited focus means than it is unlikely ever to be used.

Which authorities are the most important?
Though the section requires courts and tribunals to have regard to authorities from all three Strasbourg organs, but there can be little doubt that the most important are the judgments of the Court of Human Rights.

4.09

Too great a reliance should not be placed on decisions on admissibility of any antiquity, since these have not always been fully reasoned and where the decision is to declare an application inadmissible are, by definition, not based on any comprehensive consideration of the merits. Furthermore the volume of such decisions has been such that the quality of the reasoning in admissibility decisions can be opaque. How much can be learned from a decision which outlines some facts as asserted in the application and then decides that the application is "manifestly ill-founded"? In many cases no observations had been sought from the respondent government.

Authorities on the interpretation of the concept of a "victim" of a violation of the Convention may be particularly persuasive, because of the drafting of s.7(7): see commentary to that section. The same view is taken of the concept of "just satisfaction" in s.8(3): see commentary to that section.

The relationship between Strasbourg judgments and national judgments
Kay v Lambeth LBC, Leeds CC v Price [2006] UKHL 10, [2006] 2 WLR 570 provides guidance for courts and tribunals when faced with a judgment of the Court of

Human Rights which conflicts with an earlier binding authority of a national court. Both Justice and Liberty were permitted to intervene in the case. The Court rejected the argument that a lower court could depart from what would otherwise be a binding precedent of a higher court where there was a later judgment of the Court of Human Rights which was clearly inconsistent with the judgment of the higher court. The effect of the House of Lords ruling is that the development of case law will be influenced by the judgments of the Court of Human Rights, but that legal certainty can only be maintained if conflicts between decisions of the Court of Human Rights and those of national courts are determined within the hierarchy of courts in the national legal order.

There are aftershocks of this decision in the social security context in the context of whether non-contributory benefits are 'possessions' within Article 1 of Protocol 1. So, for example, both *Couronne* and *CIS/1757/2006* (para.40) decide that they were bound to follow *Reynolds* and *Campbell R (H) 1/05* in the Court of Appeal to the effect that non-contributory benefits are not possessions, notwithstanding the decision of the Grand Chamber to the contrary in *Stec*. It is understood that CPAG are concerned about this approach and have raised the matter with the Department for Work and Pensions. There is certain to be further case law on this point in the social security context. In such litigation it would be argued that the special circumstances of the post-Court of Appeal litigation in *Reynolds* would provide grounds for *not* following the general rule laid down in *Price*.

Legislation

Interpretation of legislation

4.10   **3.**—(1) So far as it is possible to do so, primary legislation and subordinate legislation must be read and given effect in a way which is compatible with the Convention rights.

(2) This section—
  (a) applies to primary legislation and subordinate legislation whenever enacted;
  (b) does not affect the validity, continuing operation or enforcement of any incompatible primary legislation; and
  (c) does not affect the validity, continuing operation or enforcement of any incompatible subordinate legislation if (disregarding any possibility of revocation) primary legislation prevents removal of the incompatibility.

Commencement

October 2, 2000: The Human Rights Act 1998 (Commencement No.2) Order 2000 (SI 2000/1851).

General Note

4.11   There is a powerful new principle of statutory interpretation here: so far as it is *possible* to do so, primary and secondary legislation whenever enacted *must* be read in a way which is compatible with Convention rights whenever a question of Convention rights is in issue. The requirement applies to all users of the legislation; it does not apply solely to courts and tribunals, nor does it require that a public authority (see s.6) is a party to the issue raised.

The principle is clearly mandatory and strongly so. A judge writing in a journal has said that the section creates a rebuttable presumption in favour of an interpretation consistent with Convention rights: Lord Steyn, "Incorporation and Devolution—A Few Reflections on the Changing Scene" [1998] E.H.R.L.R. 153, at 155.

However, where primary legislation cannot be read compatibly with Convention rights, then a court or tribunal does not have the power to strike down or ignore the incompatible primary legislation. Certain courts may, however, declare the legislation incompatible with Convention rights. This preserves the sovereignty of Parliament and is one of the clever features of the Act that have enabled it to fit into the constitutional traditions of the UK.

Where secondary legislation cannot be read compatibly with Convention rights, two possibilities will arise. First, if the incompatibility of the secondary legislation is required by the primary legislation under which it is made, then the status of the secondary legislation is the same as that of incompatible primary legislation. Its validity, continuing operation and enforcement are unaffected. But if the incompatibility is not required by the primary legislation, then it cannot be said to be within the powers of the primary legislation under which it is enacted, and any court or tribunal (and seemingly anyone called on to interpret that legislation) can disregard it: its validity, continuing operation and enforcement will be affected.

To some extent, this obligation to force an interpretation from a statutory provision is not entirely new, since European Community law requires legislation implementing the requirements of Community law to be read, so far as it is possible to do so, in a manner which achieves the objectives of the EC Treaty: see the view taken in the House of Lords in *Webb v EMO Air Cargo (UK) Ltd* [1992] 2 All E.R. 929.

The application of the rule of interpretation in s.3 has now been the subject of comment in the highest courts of the United Kingdom.

The distinction between interpretation and legislation had been made by Lord Woolf C.J., in the Court of Appeal in *Poplar Housing and Regeneration Community Association Ltd v Donoghue* [2002] Q.B. 48,

> "It is difficult to overestimate the importance of section 3. It applies to legislation passed both before and after the Human Rights Act 1998 came into force. Subject to the section not requiring the court to go beyond what is possible, it is mandatory in its terms. . . . Now, when section 3 applies, the courts have to adjust their traditional role in relation to interpretation so as to give effect to the direction contained in section 3. It is as though legislation which predates the Human Rights Act 1998 and conflicts with the Convention has to be treated as being subsequently amended to incorporate the language of section 3. . . . Section 3 does not entitle the court to *legislate* (its task is still one of *interpretation*, but interpretation in accordance with the direction contained in section 3. . . .
>
> The most difficult task which courts face is distinguishing between legislation and interpretation. Here practical experience of seeking to apply section 3 will provide the best guide. However, if it is necessary in order to obtain compliance to radically alter the effect of the legislation this will be an indication that more than interpretation is involved."

In *R. v A (Complainant's Sexual History) (No. 2)* [2002] A.C. 45, the House of Lords has commented on the effect of the obligation in s.3 in the context of the interpretation of s.41 of the Youth Justice and Criminal Evidence Act 1999 in relation to the evidence which may be adduced in rape trials. Lord Steyn said,

> ". . . the interpretative obligation under section 3 is a strong one. It applies even if there is no ambiguity in the language in the sense of the language being capable of two different meanings. It is an emphatic adjuration by the legislature . . . Section 3 places a duty on the court to strive to find a possible interpretation compatible with Convention rights. Under ordinary methods of interpretation a court may depart from the language of the statute to avoid absurd consequences: section 3 goes much further. . . . Section 3 . . . requires a court to find an interpretation compatible with Convention rights if it is possible to do so. . . . In accordance with the will of Parliament as reflected in section 3 it will sometimes be necessary to

adopt an interpretation which linguistically may appear strained. The techniques to be used will not only involve the reading down of express language in a statute but also the implication of provisions. A declaration of incompatibility is a measure of last resort. It must be avoided unless it is plainly impossible to do so."

Lord Hope of Craighead said,

"The rule of construction which section 3 lays down is quite unlike any previous rule of statutory interpretation. There is no need to identify an ambiguity or absurdity. Compatibility with Convention rights is the sole guiding principle. That is the paramount object which the rule seeks to achieve. But the rule is only a rule of interpretation. It does not entitle the judges to act as legislators."

The Court also endorsed the distinction between interpretation and legislation identifed by Lord Woolf C.J. in the *Poplar Housing* case.

This point was also reiterated by the House of Lords in *Re S (FC); Re S and Re W* [2002] 2 All E.R. 192, where Lord Nicholls said,

"In applying section 3 courts must be ever mindful of this outer limit. The Human Rights Act reserves the amendment of primary legislation to Parliament. By this means the Act seeks to preserve parliamentary sovereignty. The Act maintains the constitutional boundary. Interpretation of statutes is a matter for the courts; the enactment of statutes, and the amendment of statutes, are matters for Parliament. . . . The area of real difficulty lies in identifying the limits of interpretation in a particular case. . . . For present purposes it is sufficient to say that a meaning which departs substantially from a fundamental feature of an Act of Parliament is likely to have crossed the boundary between interpretation and amendment. This is especially so where the departure has important practical repercussions which the court is not equipped to evaluate. In such a case the overall contextual setting may leave no scope for rendering the statutory provision Convention compliant by legitimate use of the process of interpretation."

In *Ghaidan v Godin-Mendoza*, [2004] UKHL 30, the House of Lords ruled that the policy reasons for giving a statutory tenancy to the survivor of a cohabiting heterosexual couple applied equally to the survivor of a cohabiting homosexual couple. In so holding, they interpreted para.2 and 3 of Sch.1 to the Rent Act 1977 to secure compatibility with Convention rights. This avoided less favourable treatment of homosexual couples in the enjoyment of their Convention rights under Art.8 ECHR which could not be objectively justified.

The case is important for its re-affirmation of the approach which should be adopted in reading and giving effect to primary and subordinate legislation in a way which is compatible with Convention rights. Significantly, the judges in the House of Lords did not attempt to write words into or delete words from the statutory provisions in issue, preferring simply to indicate what the substantive effect of those provisions should be (see opinion of Lord Nicholls at para.35). The task of interpretation under s.3 required courts, if necessary, to depart from the unambiguous meaning of a legislative provision in order to ensure respect for Convention rights. Lord Steyn said that declarations of incompatibility under s.4 were remedies of last resort, and that s.3 represents the principal remedial measure. Lord Steyn also indicated that there had been a tendency to concentrate too much on linguistic features of particular legislative provisions; what was required was a broad purposive approach concentrating on the Convention right in issue. Lord Rodger said,

"123. Attaching decisive importance to the precise adjustments required to the language of any particular provision would reduce the exercise envisaged by s.3(1) to a game where the outcome would depend in part on the particular turn of phrase chosen by the draftsman and in part on the skill of the court in devising brief formulae to make the provision compatible with Convention rights. The statute book is the work of many different hands in different parliaments over hundreds of years and, even today, two different draftsmen might choose different language to express the same proposition. In enacting s.3(1), it cannot have been the intention of parliament to place those asserting their rights at the mercy of the linguistic choices of the individual who happened to draft the provision in question. What matters is not so much the particular phraseology chosen by the draftsman as the substance of the measure which Parliament has enacted in those words. Equally, it cannot have been the intention of Parliament to place a premium on the skill of those called on to think up a neat way round the draftsman's language. Parliament was not out to devise an entertaining parlour game for lawyers, but, so far as possible, to make legislation operate compatibly with Convention rights. This means concentrating on matters of substance, rather than on matters of mere language.

124. Sometimes it may be possible to isolate a particular phrase which causes the difficulty and to read in words that modify it so as to remove the incompatibility. Or else the court may read in words that qualify the provision as a whole. At other times the appropriate solution may be to read down the provision so that it falls to be given effect in a way that is compatible with the Convention rights in question. In other cases the easiest solution may be to put the offending part of the provision into different words which convey the meaning that will be compatible with those rights. The preferred technique will depend on the particular provision and also, in reality, on the person doing the interpreting. This does not matter since they are simply different means of achieving the same substantive result. However, precisely because s.3(1) is to be operated by many others besides the courts, and because it is concerned with interpreting and not with amending the offending provision, it respectfully seems to me that it would be going too far to insist that those using the section to interpret legislation should match the standards to be expected of a parliamentary draftsman amending the provision: cf. *R. v Lambert* [2002] 2 A.C. 545 at 585, para.80, *per* Lord Hope of Craighead. It is enough that the interpretation placed on the provision should be clear, however it may be expressed and whatever the precise means adopted to achieve it."

The proper approach to the application of s.3 would appear in the light of all the authorities to involve a number of steps. First, it is necessary to identify the legislative provision which it is argued breaches Convention rights: see *R. v A (No. 2)* [2002] A.C. 45. Then consideration should be given to whether that provision involves a breach of Convention rights: see *Poplar Housing and Regeneration Community Association Ltd v Donoghue* [2002] Q.B. 48. If there is, then a s.3 interpretation is needed and the focus here should be on compatibility with the Convention right. This can be achieved by reading in Convention rights, that is, by implying words in the legislative provision to secure compatibility with Convention rights; or by reading down, that is, by applying a narrower interpretation in order to secure compatibility. But it is not necessary to specify the precise rewording of the provision: see *Ghaidan v Godin-Mendoza* above.

The limits of interpretation are reached where the required construction conflicts with the express words of a legislative provision: see *R. (Anderson) v Secretary of State for the Home Department* [2003] 1 A.C. 837. The same conclusion will be reached if there is a conflict with the legislative provision by necessary implication. Finally, the limits of construction are reached when the construction placed on the provision alters the statutory scheme in a fundamental way.

In *R(G) 2/04*, the reported decision in *CG/1467/2001*, the Commissioner, following the decision of the Court of Appeal in *R. (Hooper) v Secretary of State for Work and Pensions* [2003] 1 W.L.R 2623 in this respect—which was not in issue in the appeal to the House of Lords—that the words of the statute admitted of only one interpretation. The effect of this was to preclude a man from claiming widow's benefit in respect of a spouse who died before April 9, 2001. See annotations to Art.14 of the European Convention on Human Rights for more detail on this line of cases.

Declaration of incompatibility

4.—(1) Subsection (2) applies in any proceedings in which a court determines whether a provision of primary legislation is compatible with a Convention right.

(2) If the court is satisfied that the provision is incompatible with a Convention right, it may make a declaration of that incompatibility.

(3) Subsection (4) applies in any proceedings in which a court determines whether a provision of subordinate legislation, made in the exercise of a power conferred by primary legislation, is compatible with a Convention right.

(4) If the court is satisfied—
  (a) that the provision is incompatible with a Convention right, and
  (b) that (disregarding any possibility of revocation) the primary legislation concerned prevents removal of the incompatibility,
it may make a declaration of that incompatibility.

(5) In this section "court" means—
  (a) the House of Lords;
  (b) the Judicial Committee of the Privy Council;
  (c) the Courts-Martial Appeal Court;
  (d) in Scotland, the High Court of Justiciary sitting otherwise than as a trial court or the Court of Session;
  (e) in England and Wales or Northern Ireland, the High Court or the Court of Appeal.

(6) A declaration under this section ("a declaration of incompatibility")—
  (a) does not affect the validity, continuing operation or enforcement of the provision in respect of which it is given; and
  (b) is not binding on the parties to the proceedings in which it is made.

COMMENCEMENT

October 2, 2000: The Human Rights Act 1998 (Commencement No.2) Order 2000 (SI 2000/1851).

GENERAL NOTE

This section gives certain courts power to make declarations of incompatibility where primary or secondary legislation cannot be read compatibly with Convention rights. It is a discretionary power available to the higher courts only. It arises in any proceedings; there is again no requirement that one of the parties is a public authority. Neither appeal tribunals nor Commissioners have the power to make declarations of incompatibility.

It is perhaps unfortunate that the only routes to declarations of incompatibility in the social security jurisdiction are appeal from a Commissioner to the Court of Appeal, or taking judicial review proceedings in the High Court against a tribunal or a Commissioner.

The effect of a declaration of incompatibility is not to declare the legislation invalid, inoperative or unenforceable, and so does not give rise to any claim for damages for breach of the Human Rights Act: *Re K: A Child*, Court of Appeal, November 15, 2000 [2001] 2 All E.R. 719. The impeached provision will continue in full force and effect pending any amendment. The effect of a declaration of incompatibility is to put the Government on notice of the incompatibility. The Government may then choose to take the remedial action provided for in s.10 of and Sch.2 to the Act.

On July 10, 2003, the House of Lords ruled on the appeal in *Wilson v Secretary of State for Trade and Industry*, [2003] UKHL 40. They reversed the decision of the

Court of Appeal to make a declaration of incompatibility in respect of s.127 of the Consumer Credit Act 1974.

Wilson had borrowed £5,000 from First County Trust on the security of her BMW 318 convertible. The loan agreement added a £250 document fee to the £5,000 loan, thus mis-stating the amount of the loan as £5,250. In 1999 Wilson issued a claim in the county court, inter alia, for a declaration that the loan agreement was unenforceable because it did not contain all the prescribed terms. The county court ruled in the lender's favour, but this was reversed in the Court of Appeal, but adjourned to enable Convention rights arguments to be considered. The Secretary of State argued that the Court had no power to make a declaration of incompatibility because the agreement pre-dated October 2, 2000, the date the Human Rights Act 1998 entered into force. However, the Court said that the act which violated Convention rights was not the agreement but any order of the Court making the loan agreement unenforceable. They went on to make a declaration of incompatibility.

The House of Lords has ruled that the Human Rights Act 1998 is not to be applied retrospectively, and so there was no jurisdiction in the Court of Appeal to make the declaration of incompatibility. A statute concerned with Convention rights could not render acts unlawful which were lawful when they were undertaken, since this would impose retrospective liability.

Their Lordships did go on to consider whether the provisions of s.127 were compatible with Convention rights. The section imposed a mandatory sanction designed to ensure that lenders directed their minds to compliance with their obligations. It was a measure for the protection of the consumer, the weaker party in such transactions. This appeared to be in the view of the court not a violation of Convention rights in relation to the loans covered by the section (up to £25,000). In these circumstances there was no lack of proportionality in the sanction for failure to comply with the requirements of the legislation.

In *R(IS) 12/04* the Commissioner concludes that a tribunal's lack of power to make a declaration of incompatibility is not a good reason for not dealing fully with human rights issues raised before tribunals. The Commissioner notes that in some circumstances, tribunals do have the power to declare subordinate legislation to have been invalidly made. The tribunal's reasons were found to be inadequate because they had dismissed detailed human rights arguments on the basis that they could not make a declaration of inadmissibility under s.4.

In its admissibility decision of June 18, 2002 in *Hobbs v United Kingdom (App.63684/00)*, the Court of Human Rights ruled that a declaration of incompatibility is not an effective remedy within the meaning of Art.35 of the Convention for the purpose of the rule requiring an applicant to exhaust domestic remedies. The Court rejected the Government's invitation to reconsider this position in its admissibility decision of March 16, 2004 in *Walker v United Kingdom (App.37212/02)*. The Court was strongly influenced by the fact that a declaration of incompatibility was not binding on the parties.

Right of Crown to intervene

5.—(1) Where a court is considering whether to make a declaration of incompatibility, the Crown is entitled to notice in accordance with rules of court.

(2) In any case to which subsection (1) applies—
(a) a Minister of the Crown (or a person nominated by him),
(b) a member of the Scottish Executive,
(c) a Northern Ireland Minister,
(d) a Northern Ireland department,
is entitled, on giving notice in accordance with rules of court, to be joined as a party to the proceedings.

4.14

Human Rights Act 1998

(3) Notice under subsection (2) may be given at any time during the proceedings.

(4) A person who has been made a party to criminal proceedings (other than in Scotland) as the result of a notice under subsection (2) may, with leave, appeal to the House of Lords against any declaration of incompatibility made in the proceedings.

(5) In subsection (4)—

"criminal proceedings" includes all proceedings before the Courts-Martial Appeal Court; and

"leave" means leave granted by the court making the declaration of incompatibility or by the House of Lords.

COMMENCEMENT

October 2, 2000: The Human Rights Act 1998 (Commencement No.2) Order 2000 (SI 2000/1851).

Public authorities

Acts of public authorities

4.15
6.—(1) It is unlawful for a public authority to act in a way which is incompatible with a Convention right.

(2) Subsection (1) does not apply to an act if—
(a) as the result of one or more provisions of primary legislation, the authority could not have acted differently; or
(b) in the case of one or more provisions of, or made under, primary legislation which cannot be read or given effect in a way which is compatible with the Convention rights, the authority was acting so as to give effect to or enforce those provisions.

(3) In this section "public authority" includes—
(a) a court or tribunal, and
(b) any person certain of whose functions are functions of a public nature,

but does not include either House of Parliament or a person exercising functions in connection with proceedings in Parliament.

(4) In subsection (3) "Parliament" does not include the House of Lords in its judicial capacity.

(5) In relation to a particular act, a person is not a public authority by virtue only of subsection (3)(b) if the nature of the act is private.

(6) "An act" includes a failure to act but does not include a failure to—
(a) introduce in, or lay before, Parliament a proposal for legislation; or
(b) make any primary legislation or remedial order.

COMMENCEMENT

October 2, 2000: The Human Rights Act 1998 (Commencement No.2) Order 2000 (SI 2000/1851).

GENERAL NOTE

4.16
The obligation in s.6(1) is at the heart of the scheme of incorporation in the Act. It could be said that all the other provisions flow from the requirement that public

authorities of any kind act compatibly with Convention rights. Note that there is a "defence" in s.6(2) where there was a statutory requirement to act in a particular manner. Here there will, of course, be an incompatibility between the statutory provision and Convention rights.

The key concept in the section is that of a public authority. This includes courts and tribunals, but not either House of Parliament, and is extended to "any person certain of whose functions are functions of a public nature" The difficult two words become very difficult 12 words. Only "certain" of the authority's functions need be of a public nature, and there is no liability in respect of the exercise of their functions of a private nature.

The question of what constitutes a public authority is reminiscent of the definitional problem of determining what are "emanations of the State" for the purposes of the horizontal application of EC Directives. The test is certainly not the same, but the same difficulties will arise in determining those institutions at the margins of State power which constitute public authorities. The definition will require judicial interpretation, but it is clearly a functional test.

There is, however, no doubt that the Department and all its constituent parts constitute public authorities, as, of course, do the tribunals and other judicial bodies. All must act compatibly with Convention rights. This means that they must take up obvious Convention points even if they are not raised by the parties, since otherwise they would be acting unlawfully by acting in a manner which is not compatible with Convention rights.

In *Poplar Housing and Regeneration Community Association Ltd v Donoghue* [2002] Q.B. 48, the Court of Appeal provided some useful guidance on the definition of the notion of a public authority as defined in the section. The definition is to be given a generous interpretation. Hybrid bodies which exercised both public and private functions were public authorities only in relation to acts of a public nature and not acts of a private nature. But the fact that a public regulatory body supervised a body did not necessarily indicate that any act subject to supervision was an act of a public nature.

On the concept of "public authority" for the purposes of this Act, see also *Parochial Church Council of the Parish of Aston Cantlow and Wilmcote with Billesley, Warwickshire v Wallbank* [2003] UKHL 37; [2003] 3 W.L.R. 283; and *Hampshire County Council v Beer t/a Hammer Trout Farm* [2003] EWCA Civ 1056; [2004] 1 W.L.R. 233.

In the *Aston Cantlow* case, Lord Nicholls said,

"12. What, then, is the touchstone to be used in deciding whether a function is public for this purpose? Clearly there is no single test of universal application. There cannot be, given the diverse nature of governmental functions and the variety of means by which these functions are discharged today. Factors to be taken into account include the extent to which in carrying out the relevant function the body is publicly funded, or is exercising statutory powers, or is taking the place of central government or local authorities, or is providing a public service."

For a detailed consideration of the concept of "public authority" and the way in which the courts are approaching the determination of this issue, see generally *The Meaning of Public Authority under the Human Rights Act.* Seventh Report of the Joint Committee on Human Rights of Session 2003–04 HL Paper 39 HC 382, which can be found at http://www.publications.parliament.uk/pa/jt2003/04/jtselect/jtrights/39/39.pdf.

The Joint Committee expresses some concern about the way the courts are interpreting the concept, but commends the approach adopted by the House of Lords in the *Aston Cantlow* case.

The duty of courts to act compatibly and precedent

In *Leeds City Council v Price* [2006] UKHL 10, the House of Lords ruled that in almost all cases where there is a conflict between authorities of the Court of Human Rights in Strasbourg and of a superior court in the United Kingdom, an inferior court or tribunal in the United Kingdom should follow the decision of the national court. That is a controversial proposition, but the rule may well not apply if the point at issue is not in dispute between the parties. So, for example, in *Esfandiari* [2006] EWCA Civ 282, reported as *R(IS) 11/06*, neither party contested the proposition that all benefits count as possessions following the decision of the Court of Human Rights in *Stec*, even though an earlier Court of Appeal decision has ruled that means-tested benefits cannot be treated as "possessions" for the purpose of Art.1 of Protocol 1. This may simply be an illustration of the Court of Appeal not regarding the House of Lords ruling as applying to them, or, perhaps rather more likely, that there was recent and specific Strasbourg authority on the point. There is certainly authority that in such circumstances, any court or tribunal should not lightly depart from germane Strasbourg case law: see *Attorney General's reference No 4 of 2002* [2004] UKHL 43, at para.33; and *Anderson* [2002] UKHL 46, paras 17–18.

See further annotations to s.2 at para 4.09.

Section 6(2)
The proper interpretation of subs.(2) is discussed in the judgment of the House of Lords in *Hooper*, [2005] UKHL 29: see paras 2–6, 41–52, 62–83, 91–96, and 101–126.

Proceedings

4.17   **7.**—(1) A person who claims that a public authority has acted (or proposes to act) in a way which is made unlawful by section 6(1) may—
(a) bring proceedings against the authority under this Act in the appropriate court or tribunal, or
(b) rely on the Convention right or rights concerned in any legal proceedings,
but only if he is (or would be) a victim of the unlawful act.

(2) In subsection (1)(a) "appropriate court or tribunal" means such court or tribunal as may be determined in accordance with rules; and proceedings against an authority include a counterclaim or similar proceeding.

(3) If the proceedings are brought on an application for judicial review, the applicant is to be taken to have a sufficient interest in relation to the unlawful act only if he is, or would be, a victim of that act.

(4) If the proceedings are made by way of a petition for judicial review in Scotland, the applicant shall be taken to have title and interest to sue in relation to the unlawful act only if he is, or would be, a victim of that act.

(5) Proceedings under subsection (1)(a) must be brought before the end of—
(a) the period of one year beginning with the date on which the act complained of took place; or
(b) such longer period as the court or tribunal considers equitable having regard to all the circumstances,
but that is subject to any rule imposing a stricter time limit in relation to the procedure in question.

(6) In subsection (1)(b) "legal proceedings" includes—
(a) proceedings brought by or at the instigation of a public authority; and
(b) an appeal against the decision of a court or tribunal.

(7) For the purposes of this section, a person is a victim of an unlawful act only if he would be a victim for the purposes of Article 34 of the Convention if proceedings were brought in the European Court of Human Rights in respect of that act.

(8) Nothing in this Act creates a criminal offence.

(9) In this section "rules" means—

(a) in relation to proceedings before a court or tribunal outside Scotland, rules made by [^{1} . . .] [^{2} the Lord Chancellor or] the Secretary of State for the purposes of this section or rules of court,
(b) in relation to proceedings before a court or tribunal in Scotland, rules made by the Secretary of State for those purposes,
(c) in relation to proceedings before a tribunal in Northern Ireland—
  (i) which deals with transferred matters; and
  (ii) for which no rules made under paragraph (a) are in force, rules made by a Northern Ireland department for those purposes,

and includes provision made by order under section 1 of the Courts and Legal Services Act 1990.

(10) In making rules, regard must be had to section 9.

(11) The Minister who has power to make rules in relation to a particular tribunal may, to the extent he considers it necessary to ensure that the tribunal can provide an appropriate remedy in relation to an act (or proposed act) of a public authority which is (or would be) unlawful as a result of section 6(1), by order add to—
(a) the relief or remedies which the tribunal may grant; or
(b) the grounds on which it may grant any of them.

(12) An order made under subsection (11) may contain such incidental, supplemental, consequential or transitional provision as the Minister making it considers appropriate.

(13) "The Minister" includes the Northern Ireland department concerned.

COMMENCEMENT

October 2, 2000: The Human Rights Act 1998 (Commencement No.2) Order 2000 (SI 2000/1851).

AMENDMENTS

1. The Secretary of State for Constitutional Affairs Order 2003 (SI 2003/1887) (August 19, 2003).
2. The Transfer of Functions (Lord Chancellor and Secretary of State) Order 2005 (SI 2005/3429) (January 12, 2006).

GENERAL NOTE

Introduction
This section is full of difficulty. A person who believes that a public authority has acted unlawfully by not acting in a manner compatible with Convention rights may bring proceedings under s.7. Such a person must under subs. (7) show that they would be a victim for the purposes of Art.34 of the Convention if proceedings were brought before the Court of Human Rights in respect of the allegedly unlawful act.

The section refers to at least three different types of proceedings: (1) the so-called new "constitutional tort" under subs.(1)(a); (2) judicial review under subs.(3); and (3) "any legal proceedings" in subs.(1)(b).

Changes to the Civil Procedures Rules to accommodate these proceedings left a number of questions unanswered.

4.18

Standing to raise the complaint: the victim requirement
Under subs.(7) which applies to the whole section, only a person who can show that they would fall within the victim requirement under Art.34 of the Convention has standing to complain of the unlawful act by the public authority. The concept of "victim" is a particular concept under Convention case law, and for this reason the interpretative requirement to have regard to Convention case law must be particularly

4.19

strong since otherwise the specific reference to Art.34 in subs.(7) would be otiose. Article 34 has replaced Art.25 in the original version of the Convention prior to its amendment by Protocol 11.

Fortunately, the Strasbourg authorities—and here admissibility decisions of the Commission under the "old" system of protection (see commentary to s.2) will be particularly useful—have been generous in the matter of standing to make an application under the Convention.

The term "person" under the Convention (*personne physique* in the French text) clearly refers only to natural persons, but the Commission has accepted applications from corporate and unincorporated bodies whose rights under the Convention have been violated. So complaints have been accepted from companies, partnerships, trades unions, churches, political parties, and numerous other types of institution. It would seem that only public bodies themselves are excluded from the possibility of making an individual petition. Furthermore there are no restrictions on grounds of nationality, residence or any other status.

Standing has been extended to representative complaints, for example, by parents on behalf of children where that is appropriate, though there is no age limit for making an application: App.10929/84 *Nielsen v Denmark* (1986) 46 D.R. 55 and App.22920/93 *MB v United Kingdom* (1994) 77-A D.R. 42. Equally, there is no bar to application by persons under a disability: App.1572/62 *X v Austria* (1962) 5 Yearbook 238.

Associations have no standing to bring actions in a representative capacity: App.10581/83 *Norris and National Gay Federation v Ireland* (1984) 44 D.R. 132, though if they provide evidence that they are acting on behalf of specified individuals, the application may be accepted: App.10983/84 *Confédération des Syndicats médicaúx français et Fédération nationale des Infirmiers v France* (1986) 47 D.R. 225.

In some cases potential victims may make an application, such as in cases where covert surveillance might take place without any notification of the possibility to the individual: *Klass v Germany*, judgment of September 6, 1978, Series A No.28; (1979–80) 2 E.H.R.R. 214.

The Commission and the Court will not, however, countenance an application in the abstract as a means of testing the compatibility of provisions of a national legal order: App.9297/81 *X Association v Sweden* (1982) 28 D.R. 204. Drawing the distinction between potential victims and claims in the abstract is not always easy: see App.10039/82 *Leigh v United Kingdom* (1984) 38 D.R. 74.

In *Director General of Fair Trading v Proprietary Association of Great Britain*, Court of Appeal, July 26, 2001 [2001] EWCA Civ 1217 (sometimes referred to as *Re medicaments (No.4))*, the Court of Appeal made some passing, and inconclusive comments on the nature of the "victim requirement" under s.7. The Court expressly avoided dealing with the possible distinction between interest groups which are really associations of interested individuals which might be regarded as a group of individuals each of whom may be regarded as a victim and broader representative groups (examples given are Amnesty International or the Joint Council for the Welfare of Immigrants) which have special expertise but who cannot be classified as a collection of victims. The Court simply stated that each case must be decided in its own context.

Note the discussion of the victim requirement (particularly victim status and retrospectivity) in the judgment of the House of Lords in *Hooper* [2005] UKHL 29: see paras 53–9.

Subsection (1)(a): the new constitutional tort

4.20 A person who can show that they meet the victim test may bring proceedings against the authority "in the appropriate court or tribunal". This is to be determined in accordance with rules to be made, outside Scotland, by the Lord Chancellor or the Secretary of State. The Civil Procedure Rules simply map this action onto the existing division of responsibilities between the county courts and the High Court.

The time limits for such an action are, however, specified in subs.(5). The action is to be brought within one year of the date on which the act complained of took place or such longer period as the court or tribunal considers equitable having regard to all the circumstances. There is a proviso that both the one year time limit and any extension of it is to be without prejudice to any rule imposing a stricter time limit "in relation to the procedure in question." An example would be judicial review where the normal time limit is three months unless this is extended by the court. However, where an action is brought under a procedure with a longer limitation period, it would seem that the longer limitation period will apply; such proceedings would not, however, arise under subs.(1)(a) but presumably under subs.(1)(b).

Under s.9(1), where the unlawful act of which the applicant complains is a judicial act, it is stated that proceedings under s.7(1)(a) may be brought only by exercising a right of appeal, seeking judicial review against those bodies susceptible to judicial review, or "in such other forum as may be prescribed by rules."

Judicial review: subss (3) and (4)

Where the proceedings are by way of judicial review on the grounds that a public authority has acted unlawfully, the normal sufficient interest test of standing (which would permit action by a representative body or a pressure group) is replaced by a test that the applicant must satisfy the victim test in subs.(7).

4.21

Raising Convention rights in any legal proceedings: subs. (1)(b)

Convention rights may be raised in any legal proceedings, provided that the person can show that they would be a victim under Art.34 of the Convention. So a person bringing proceedings on a well-established cause of action can raise his or her Convention rights at any time. Indeed, the court or tribunal is under a duty by virtue of s.6(1) to take obvious Convention points since they are under a duty to act in a manner compatible with the Convention.

4.22

Apart from judicial review claims (which may be important if a person is seeking the possibility of a money remedy), Convention rights are most likely to be raised in the course of appeals to the appeal tribunals and before the Commissioners. The commentary to the Convention rights set out in Sch.1 gives some indication of the sorts of issues which might be raised under them.

In *CSIB/973/1999* a Scottish Commissioner warns of the need for responsible resort to the taking of human rights points. He complains of a point which was "in the nature of a wrap up omnibus ground of appeal placed before the Commissioners no doubt in the hope that there was something in the point." The Commissioner regrets the absence of rules setting out the manner in which human rights points are to be taken before the Commissioners. He goes on to indicate the content of those rules; this might assist those contemplating raising human rights points before both tribunals and Commissioners. The provision of the Convention which it is argued has been breached should be identified, together with the remedy sought in respect of the breach. The legal principles and authorities relied on and any error of law by the tribunal which it is asserted were made consequent on the breach should also be identified. Such points should be taken on proper notice so that both parties can research them and focus on them in their arguments to the adjudicating body. That is, no doubt, good advice, but the duty in s.6(1) on public authorities to act compatibly with Convention rights means that adjudicating bodies must themselves consider obvious points arising under the Convention even if they are not raised by the parties.

In *R(IS)12/04* the Commissioner reminds tribunals of the need to address fully arguments based on Convention rights in the following terms,

"13. Finally, it is necessary to consider the adequacy of the tribunal's reasons. I agree with the Secretary of State that a tribunal's lack of any power to make a declaration of incompatibility is not a good reason for not dealing fully with Human Rights issues, particularly since a tribunal may have power in some cases to declare subordinate legislation to have been invalidly made-see *Chief Adjudication Officer v Foster* [1993] 1 All ER 705. The claimant in this appeal clearly went to considerable trouble to set out his arguments under the Human Rights Act clearly and comprehensively in response to the chairman's direction, and I consider that he was entitled to a much fuller explanation of the tribunal's reasons for rejecting his arguments than the very short passage at the end of the statement of reasons set out above. The reasons for the tribunal's rejection of the claimant's discrimination arguments are not apparent from the statement, and I therefore consider that, in all the circumstances, the tribunal's reasons were inadequate."

The Court of Appeal in *R. (on the application of Hooper, Withey, Naylor and Martin v Secretary of State for Work and Pensions* [2003] EWCA Civ 813 addresses at paras 29–46 the question of when a person becomes a victim within the meaning of s.7, and did not find the application of Strasbourg case law to be satisfactory. The Strasbourg authorities appeared to provide that only when a man has made a claim to a benefit is he in a position to complain that he is not being treated in the same way as a woman, and so, only then, would become a victim for the purposes of Art. 34 of the Convention. The Court of Appeal describes as "unattractive" an argument raised by the United Kingdom Government before the Court of Human Rights in *White v United Kingdom* (App.53134/99), admissibility decision of June 7, 2001, that the claimant was not a victim because he had not claimed on the official form, notwithstanding that this was designed specifically for widows. Differing from the views expressed by Moses J in the court below, the Court of Appeal concludes that it is not necessary for the claim to be made in writing in order to constitute the applicant as a victim for the purpose of asserting his Convention rights. The Court of Appeal says, ". . . we can see no reason in principle why an oral claim, made and rejected, should not suffice to constitute a claim." Note, however, that the oral claim is not a perfected claim for the purposes of the Claims and Payments Regulations, simply for the purposes of giving a person standing to claim Convention rights as a victim of a violation of those rights. This aspect of the Court of Appeal's decision was accepted by the House of Lords, [2005] EWHL 29.

Judicial remedies

4.23   **8.**—(1) In relation to any act (or proposed act) of a public authority which the court finds is (or would be) unlawful, it may grant such relief or remedy, or make such order, within its powers as it considers just and appropriate.

(2) But damages may be awarded only by a court which has power to award damages, or to order the payment of compensation, in civil proceedings.

(3) No award of damages is to be made unless, taking account of all the circumstances of the case, including—
  (a) any other relief or remedy granted, or order made, in relation to the act in question (by that or any other court), and
  (b) the consequences of any decision (of that or any other court) in respect of that act,
the court is satisfied that the award is necessary to afford just satisfaction to the person in whose favour it is made.

(4) In determining—
  (a) whether to award damages, or
  (b) the amount of an award,
the court must take into account the principles applied by the European Court of Human Rights in relation to the award of compensation under Article 41 of the Convention.

(5) A public authority against which damages are awarded is to be treated—
  (a) in Scotland, for the purposes of section 3 of the Law Reform (Miscellaneous Provisions) (Scotland) Act 1940 as if the award were made in an action of damages in which the authority has been found liable in respect of loss or damage to the person to whom the award is made;
  (b) for the purposes of the Civil Liability (Contribution) Act 1978 as liable in respect of damage suffered by the person to whom the award is made.

(6) In this section—
"court" includes a tribunal;
"damages" means damages for an unlawful act of a public authority; and
"unlawful" means unlawful under section 6(1).

COMMENCEMENT

October 2, 2000: The Human Rights Act 1998 (Commencement No.2) Order 2000 (SI 2000/1851).

GENERAL NOTE

Section 8(1) grants a broad competence, but the nature of the remedies available will vary according to the forum. The relief, remedy or order open to the court or tribunal must be one already within its powers. So the Act gives no new competence to decision-making bodies to provide a remedy for a violation of a Convention right. The decision not to extend the powers of all courts and tribunals to include new remedies for violations of Convention rights was apparently motivated by a concern that there would be an explosion of damages awards in this area across a wide range of decision-making bodies. This was the same concern which led to the exclusion of Art.13 of the Convention from the incorporated rights. There is, accordingly, a wide but not unlimited range of remedies available for breaches of Convention rights.

The drafting of s.8 reveals a concern that damages for violations of Convention rights should be contained. Section 8(2) provides that damages for an unlawful act of a public authority under the Act may be awarded only by a court (or tribunal) which has power to award damages, or to order the payment of compensation, in civil proceedings. Furthermore, damages, though not the remedy of last resort, are circumscribed since they are not to be made unless the court is satisfied that the award is necessary to afford just satisfaction to the person in whose favour the award is made, having regard to all the circumstances of the case, and in particular any other remedy or relief granted and the consequences of any decision in respect of the breach of Convention rights: subs.(3). As noted above, decisions about the award of damages and the amount of damages are to be informed by reference to the case law of the Court of Human Right in awarding just satisfaction.

A number of observations need to be made about the structure of s.8. It assumes that the range of remedies currently available to United Kingdom courts will be adequate to remedy breaches of Convention rights. It seeks to discourage an explosion of damages awards. The Lord Chancellor indicated that the intent was to match the awards victims would get if they received just satisfaction under Art.41: HL Vol.582 col.1232, November 3, 1997. It establishes a system in which the luck of the forum will determine whether duplication of litigation will be needed to secure a money remedy. A good example would be an appeal heard by an appeal tribunal, which has no power to award damages, and it has been established that it has no power award interest on the late payment of benefit; This undoubtedly follows from the reasoning of the Social Security Commissioner in *R(FC)2/90*; see also the decision of the Court of Justice in *R. v Secretary of State for Social Security Ex p. Sutton* [1997] E.C.R. I-2163; [1997] 2 C.M.L.R. 382. Nor it seems would any other court. Yet the Court of Human Rights has awarded interest on the late payment of benefit: *Schuler-Zgraggen v Switzerland*, judgment of June 24, 1993, Series A, No.263; (1993) 16 E.H.R.R. 405. In the early days of Community law, an action for a declaration was one means of securing a judicial statement of an entitlement under Community law. This would seem to be the only route open within the national legal order to a victim who had only received social security benefit to which he or she was entitled some years late and who wished to raise the claim for interest on the late payment. Otherwise, such a person would have to raise the complaint that no interest was available before the Court in Strasbourg.

Perhaps the most pertinent point to make is that the deference to the provisions of the Convention on just satisfaction in the national legislation is misplaced. The provisions in Art.41 of the Convention on affording just satisfaction are a safety net

4.24

where the national legal order does not offer full compensation for the breach of the Convention.

The starting point is that the national legal order should determine what remedies are appropriate for breaches of the Convention. Such an obligation flows from Art.13 of the Convention. Indeed, it could be argued that the effect of s.8 replicates the failures of earlier years to recognise what was demanded by the Convention. It assumes that the current panoply of remedies available in the national legal order meets the requirements of the Convention. It also reveals a deep anxiety about damages as a remedy for breach of a Convention right.

The potential gap in remedies available can, however, be cured under the rule-making power in s.7(11) and (12) which enables additional powers to be given to tribunals to add to the remedies open to them, and to define the grounds on which any additional remedies may be granted.

Where the act complained of is a judicial act, damages as a remedy is limited to compensation for unlawful detention awarded in accordance with Art.5(5): s.9(3).

In *CSIS/460/2002*, the Commissioner makes some comments on the nature of remedies for a violation of Convention rights in the context of an argument that one remedy could be to order a permanent stay of the proceedings. The Commissioner concludes,

> "A tribunal has no power to impose a permanent stay of an appeal. There is no express statutory provision nor can one be implied by virtue of necessity. Mr Orr drew an analogy with an appeal abating. However that derives from a principle of common law and is not a stay by a court or tribunal. Where an appellant dies before the determination of the appeal, the appeal is not terminated by that fact. However, unless and until there is an appointment of someone to proceed with the appeal or there is a personal representative, then no-one is legally competent to take the appeal forward. In such circumstances, the appeal is considered as automatically 'abated', by which is meant suspended. It can nevertheless be revived by the appropriate procedure. Any statement by a tribunal or a Commissioner that an appeal has been abated is thus for clarification only. Abatement is therefore very different from the power to grant a permanent stay. Such a concept could in any event give no advantage to the respondent as it would leave outstanding the adverse decision. The Secretary of State is not legally obliged to contine the customary suspension of recovery procedures and would have no reason to do so if the appeal is permanently stayed." (para.49.)

See also discussion of remedies in *Dyer v Watson* [2002] 4 All E.R. 1, especially the analysis by Lord Millett at paras 128–133.

Judicial acts

4.25   **9.**—(1) Proceedings under section 7(1)(a) in respect of a judicial act may be brought only
   (a) by exercising a right of appeal;
   (b) on an application (in Scotland a petition) for judicial review; or
   (c) in such other forum as may be prescribed by rules.
   (2) That does not affect any rule of law which prevents a court from being the subject of judicial review.
   (3) In proceedings under this Act in respect of a judicial act done in good faith, damages may not be awarded otherwise than to compensate a person to the extent required by Article 5(5) of the Convention.
   (4) An award of damages permitted by subsection (3) is to be made against the Crown; but no award may be made unless the appropriate person, if not a party to the proceedings, is joined.
   (5) In this section—
       "appropriate person" means the Minister responsible for the court concerned, or a person or government department nominated by him;

(1998 c.42, s.9)

"court" includes a tribunal;
"judge" includes a member of a tribunal, a justice of the peace [¹ (or, in Northern Ireland, a lay magistrate)] and a clerk or other officer entitled to exercise the jurisdiction of a court;
"judicial act" means a judicial act of a court and includes an act done on the instructions, or on behalf, of a judge; and
"rules" has the same meaning as in section 7(9).

COMMENCEMENT

October 2, 2000: The Human Rights Act 1998 (Commencement No.2) Order 2000 (SI 2000/1851).

AMENDMENT

1. The Justice (Northern Ireland) Act 2002 (Commencement No.8) Order 2005 SR 2005/109, Art.2, Sch. (April 1, 2005).

Remedial action

Power to take remedial action

10.—(1) This section applies if—
(a) a provision of legislation has been declared under section 4 to be incompatible with a Convention right and, if an appeal lies—
  (i) all persons who may appeal have stated in writing that they do not intend to do so;
  (ii) the time for bringing an appeal has expired and no appeal has been brought within that time; or
  (iii) an appeal brought within that time has been determined or abandoned; or
(b) it appears to a Minister of the Crown or Her Majesty in Council that, having regard to a finding of the European Court of Human Rights made after the coming into force of this section in proceedings against the United Kingdom, a provision of legislation is incompatible with an obligation of the United Kingdom arising from the Convention.

(2) If a Minister of the Crown considers that there are compelling reasons for proceeding under this section, he may by order make such amendments to the legislation as he considers necessary to remove the incompatibility.

(3) If, in the case of subordinate legislation, a Minister of the Crown considers—
(a) that it is necessary to amend the primary legislation under which the subordinate legislation in question was made, in order to enable the incompatibility to be removed, and
(b) that there are compelling reasons for proceeding under this section,
he may by order make such amendments to the primary legislation as he considers necessary.

(4) This section also applies where the provision in question is in subordinate legislation and has been quashed, or declared invalid, by reason of incompatibility with a Convention right and the Minister proposes to proceed under paragraph 2(b) of Schedule 2.

(5) If the legislation is an Order in Council, the power conferred by subsection (2) or (3) is exercisable by Her Majesty in Council.

4.26

(6) In this section "legislation" does not include a Measure of the Church Assembly or of the General Synod of the Church of England.

(7) Schedule 2 makes further provision about remedial orders.

COMMENCEMENT

October 2, 2000: The Human Rights Act 1998 (Commencement No.2) Order 2000 (SI 2000/1851).

GENERAL NOTE

4.27   This section and Sch.2 make provision for a fast-track Parliamentary procedure to respond to a declaration of incompatibility by a court.

Other rights and proceedings

Safeguard for existing human rights

4.28   **11.**—A person's reliance on a Convention right does not restrict—
(a) any other right or freedom conferred on him by or under any law having effect in any part of the United Kingdom; or
(b) his right to make any claim or bring any proceedings which he could make or bring apart from sections 7 to 9.

COMMENCEMENT

October 2, 2000: The Human Rights Act 1998 (Commencement No.2) Order 2000 (SI 2000/1851).

GENERAL NOTE

4.29   The rights given to persons under s.7 to complain of unlawful acts by public authorities in acting in a manner incompatible with the Convention does not limit in any way existing rights under UK law. The new rights are additional to existing rights and not in substitution for them.

Freedom of expression

4.30   **12.**—(1) This section applies if a court is considering whether to grant any relief which, if granted, might affect the exercise of the Convention right to freedom of expression.

(2) If the person against whom the application for relief is made ("the respondent") is neither present nor represented, no such relief is to be granted unless the court is satisfied—
(a) that the applicant has taken all practicable steps to notify the respondent; or
(b) that there are compelling reasons why the respondent should not be notified.

(3) No such relief is to be granted so as to restrain publication before trial unless the court is satisfied that the applicant is likely to establish that publication should not be allowed.

(4) The court must have particular regard to the importance of the Convention right to freedom of expression and, where the proceedings relate to material which the respondent claims, or which appears to the court, to be journalistic, literary or artistic material (or to conduct connected with such material), to—

(a) the extent to which—
  (i) the material has, or is about to, become available to the public; or
  (ii) it is, or would be, in the public interest for the material to be published;
(b) any relevant privacy code.
(5) In this section—
"court" includes a tribunal; and
"relief" includes any remedy or order (other than in criminal proceedings).

COMMENCEMENT

October 2, 2000: The Human Rights Act 1998 (Commencement No.2) Order 2000 (SI 2000/1851).

GENERAL NOTE

This section is a response to concerns expressed by media interests that the Act would limit freedom of expression by giving priority to the development of privacy under Art.8 of the Convention. The section is not needed, since the Strasbourg case law makes it clear that a balance has to be struck between the privacy of the individual and the freedom of the press.

4.31

Freedom of thought, conscience and religion

13.—(1) If a court's determination of any question arising under this Act might affect the exercise by a religious organisation (itself or its members collectively) of the Convention right to freedom of thought, conscience and religion, it must have particular regard to the importance of that right.

(2) In this section "court" includes a tribunal.

4.32

COMMENCEMENT

October 2, 2000: The Human Rights Act 1998 (Commencement No.2) Order 2000 (SI 2000/1851).

GENERAL NOTE

This section was included in response to concerns expressed on behalf of religious groups that priority would be given to other provisions of the Convention than the provision on freedom of religion in Art.9 and that churches would find themselves being required in the name of human rights to do things contrary to their tenets. Like s.12, this section is not needed, since the Strasbourg case law makes it clear that a balance has to be struck between the pluralism of a modern democratic societies and respect for religious and personal beliefs.

4.33

Derogations and reservations

Derogations

14.—(1) In this Act "designated derogation" means—
[. . .[1]] any derogation by the United Kingdom from an Article of the Convention, or of any protocol to the Convention, which is designated for the purposes of this Act in an order made by the Secretary of State.
(2) [. . .[1]].
(3) If a designated derogation is amended or replaced it ceases to be a designated derogation.

4.34

(4) But subsection (3) does not prevent the [² Secretary of State] from exercising his power under subsection (1)[. . .¹] to make a fresh designation order in respect of the Article concerned.

(5) The [² Secretary of State] must by order make such amendments to Schedule 3 as he considers appropriate to reflect—

(a) any designation order; or
(b) the effect of subsection (3).

(6) A designation order may be made in anticipation of the making by the United Kingdom of a proposed derogation.

COMMENCEMENT

October 2, 2000: The Human Rights Act 1998 (Commencement No.2) Order 2000 (SI 2000/1851).

AMENDMENTS

1. The Human Rights Act (Amendment) Order 2001 (SI 2001/1216), art.2 (April 1, 2001).
2. The Secretary of State for Constitutional Affairs Order 2003 (SI 2003/1887) (August 19, 2003).

Reservations

4.35   15.—(1) In this Act "designated reservation" means—
(a) the United Kingdom's reservation to Article 2 of the First Protocol to the Convention; and
(b) any other reservation by the United Kingdom to an Article of the Convention, or of any protocol to the Convention, which is designated for the purposes of this Act in an order made by the Secretary of State.

(2) The text of the reservation referred to in subsection (1)(a) is set out in Part II of Schedule 3.

(3) If a designated reservation is withdrawn wholly or in part it ceases to be a designated reservation.

(4) But subsection (3) does not prevent the [¹ Secretary of State] from exercising his power under subsection (1)(b) to make a fresh designation order in respect of the Article concerned.

(5) The [¹ Secretary of State] must by order make such amendments to this Act as he considers appropriate to reflect—

(a) any designation order; or
(b) the effect of subsection (3).

COMMENCEMENT

October 2, 2000: The Human Rights Act 1998 (Commencement No.2) Order 2000 (SI 2000/1851).

AMENDMENT

1. The Secretary of State for Constitutional Affairs Order 2003 (SI 2003/1887) (August 19, 2003).

Period for which designated derogations have effect

4.36   16.—(1) If it has not already been withdrawn by the United Kingdom, a designated derogation ceases to have effect for the purposes of this Act— [. . .¹] at the end of the period of five years beginning with the date on which the order designating it was made.

(2) At any time before the period—
  (a) fixed by subsection (1) [. . .¹], or
  (b) extended by an order under this subsection,
comes to an end, the [² Secretary of State] may by order extend it by a further period of five years.

(3) An order under section 14(1)[. . .¹] ceases to have effect at the end of the period for consideration, unless a resolution has been passed by each House approving the order.

(4) Subsection (3) does not affect—
  (a) anything done in reliance on the order; or
  (b) the power to make a fresh order under section 14(1)[. . .¹].

(5) In subsection (3) "period for consideration" means the period of forty days beginning with the day on which the order was made.

(6) In calculating the period for consideration, no account is to be taken of any time during which—
  (a) Parliament is dissolved or prorogued; or
  (b) both Houses are adjourned for more than four days.

(7) If a designated derogation is withdrawn by the United Kingdom, the [² Secretary of State] must by order make such amendments to this Act as he considers are required to reflect that withdrawal.

COMMENCEMENT

October 2, 2000: The Human Rights Act 1998 (Commencement No.2) Order 2000 (SI 2000/1851).

AMENDMENTS

1. The Human Rights Act (Amendment) Order 2001 (SI 2001/1216), art.3 (April 1, 2001).
2. The Secretary of State for Constitutional Affairs Order 2003 (SI 2003/1887) (August 19, 2003).

Periodic review of designated reservations

17.—(1) The appropriate Minister must review the designated reservation referred to in section 15(1)(a)—
  (a) before the end of the period of five years beginning with the date on which section 1(2) came into force; and
  (b) if that designation is still in force, before the end of the period of five years beginning with the date on which the last report relating to it was laid under subsection (3).

(2) The appropriate Minister must review each of the other designated reservations (if any)—
  (a) before the end of the period of five years beginning with the date on which the order designating the reservation first came into force; and
  (b) if the designation is still in force, before the end of the period of five years beginning with the date on which the last report relating to it was laid under subsection (3).

(3) The Minister conducting a review under this section must prepare a report on the result of the review and lay a copy of it before each House of Parliament.

COMMENCEMENT

October 2, 2000: The Human Rights Act 1998 (Commencement No.2) Order 2000 (SI 2000/1851).

Judges of the European Court of Human Rights

4.38 *Section 18 omitted.*

Parliamentary procedure

Statements of compatibility

4.39 **19.**—(1) A Minister of the Crown in charge of a Bill in either House of Parliament must, before Second Reading of the Bill—
  (a) make a statement to the effect that in his view the provisions of the Bill are compatible with the Convention rights ("a statement of compatibility"); or
  (b) make a statement to the effect that although he is unable to make a statement of compatibility the government nevertheless wishes the House to proceed with the Bill.
(2) The statement must be in writing and be published in such manner as the Minister making it considers appropriate.

COMMENCEMENT

Section 19 entered into force on November 24, 1998: (SI 1998/2882).

GENERAL NOTE

4.40 Part of the scheme of the Act is to require improved pre-legislative scrutiny of legislation to ensure its compliance with Convention rights. The use of the section to date has been disappointing, since no reasoning is publicly available to elaborate a simple Ministerial statement that the provisions of a Bill are compatible with Convention rights.

Supplemental

4.41 *Section 20 omitted.*

Interpretation, etc.

4.42 **21.**—(1) In this Act—
  "amend" includes repeal and apply (with or without modifications);
  "the appropriate Minister" means the Minister of the Crown having charge of the appropriate authorised government department (within the meaning of the Crown Proceedings Act 1947);
  "the Commission" means the European Commission of Human Rights;
  "the Convention" means the Convention for the Protection of Human Rights and Fundamental Freedoms, agreed by the Council of Europe at Rome on 4th November 1950 as it has effect for the time being in relation to the United Kingdom;
  "declaration of incompatibility" means a declaration under section 4;
  "Minister of the Crown" has the same meaning as in the Ministers of the Crown Act 1975;
  "Northern Ireland Minister" includes the First Minister and the deputy First Minister in Northern Ireland;
  "primary legislation" means any—
    (a) public general Act;

(1998 c.42, s.21)

  (b) local and personal Act;
  (c) private Act;
  (d) Measure of the Church Assembly;
  (e) Measure of the General Synod of the Church of England;
  (f) Order in Council—
    (i) made in exercise of Her Majesty's Royal Prerogative;
    (ii) made under section 38(1)(a) of the Northern Ireland Constitution Act 1973 or the corresponding provision of the Northern Ireland Act 1998; or
    (iii) amending an Act of a kind mentioned in paragraph (a), (b) or (c);
and includes an order or other instrument made under primary legislation (otherwise than by the National Assembly for Wales, a member of the Scottish Executive, a Northern Ireland Minister or a Northern Ireland department) to the extent to which it operates to bring one or more provisions of that legislation into force or amends any primary legislation;
"the First Protocol" means the protocol to the Convention agreed at Paris on March 20 1952;
[1. . .]
"the Eleventh Protocol" means the protocol to the Convention (restructuring the control machinery established by the Convention) agreed at Strasbourg on May 11 1994;
[1 "the Thirteenth Protocol" means the protocol to the Convention (concerning the abolition of the death penalty in all circumstances agreed at Vilnius on 3rd May 2002;]
"subordinate legislation" means any—
  (a) Order in Council other than one—
    (i) made in exercise of Her Majesty's Royal Prerogative;
    (ii) made under section 38(1)(a) of the Northern Ireland Constitution Act 1973 or the corresponding provision of the Northern Ireland Act 1998; or
    (iii) amending an Act of a kind mentioned in the definition of primary legislation;
  (b) Act of the Scottish Parliament;
  (c) Act of the Parliament of Northern Ireland;
  (d) Measure of the Assembly established under section 1 of the Northern Ireland Assembly Act 1973;
  (e) Act of the Northern Ireland Assembly;
  (f) order, rules, regulations, scheme, warrant, byelaw or other instrument made under primary legislation (except to the extent to which it operates to bring one or more provisions of that legislation into force or amends any primary legislation);
  (g) order, rules, regulations, scheme, warrant, byelaw or other instrument made under legislation mentioned in paragraph (b), (c), (d) or (e) or made under an Order in Council applying only to Northern Ireland;
  (h) order, rules, regulations, scheme, warrant, byelaw or other instrument made by a member of the Scottish Executive, a Northern Ireland Minister or a Northern Ireland department in exercise of prerogative or other executive functions of Her Majesty which are exercisable by such a person on behalf of Her Majesty;
"transferred matters" has the same meaning as in the Northern Ireland Act 1998; and

"tribunal" means any tribunal in which legal proceedings may be brought.

(2) The references in paragraphs (b) and (c) of section 2(1) to Articles are to Articles of the Convention as they had effect immediately before the coming into force of the Eleventh Protocol.

(3) The reference in paragraph (d) of section 2(1) to Article 46 includes a reference to Articles 32 and 54 of the Convention as they had effect immediately before the coming into force of the Eleventh Protocol.

(4) The references in section 2(1) to a report or decision of the Commission or a decision of the Committee of Ministers include references to a report or decision made as provided by paragraphs 3, 4 and 6 of Article 5 of the Eleventh Protocol (transitional provisions).

(5) Any liability under the Army Act 1955, the Air Force Act 1955 or the Naval Discipline Act 1957 to suffer death for an offence is replaced by a liability to imprisonment for life or any less punishment authorised by those Acts; and those Acts shall accordingly have effect with the necessary modifications.

COMMENCEMENT

Section 21(5) entered into force on November 9, 1998. The remainder of the section entered into force on October 2, 2000: The Human Rights Act 1998 (Commencement No.2) Order 2000 (SI 2000/1851).

AMENDMENT

1. Human Rights Act 1998 (Amendment) Order 2004 (SI 2004/1574), Art.2(2) (June 22, 2004).

Short title, commencement, application and extent

4.43 22.—(1) This Act may be cited as the Human Rights Act 1998.

(2) Sections 18, 20 and 21(5) and this section come into force on the passing of this Act.

(3) The other provisions of this Act come into force on such day as the Secretary of State may by order appoint; and different days may be appointed for different purposes.

(4) Paragraph (b) of subsection (1) of section 7 applies to proceedings brought by or at the instigation of a public authority whenever the act in question took place; but otherwise that subsection does not apply to an act taking place before the coming into force of that section.

(5) This Act binds the Crown.

(6) This Act extends to Northern Ireland.

(7) Section 21(5), so far as it relates to any provision contained in the Army Act 1955, the Air Force Act 1955 or the Naval Discipline Act 1957, extends to any place to which that provision extends.

GENERAL NOTE

4.44 This section entered into force on November 9, 1998.

Subsection (4), which entered into force on November 9, 1998, provides that the lawfulness of an act of a public authority may be called into question in proceedings under s.7(1)(b) (any legal proceedings in which Convention rights are raised) whenever that act took place if those proceedings are begun by a public authority. In other words, it has a retrospective effect in this regard, but if the proceedings are brought other than by a public authority, no complaint can be made about an act of a public authority prior to the entry into force of s.7(1)(b).

(1998 c.42, s.22)

The issue of the possible retrospective application of the Human Rights Act 1998 in the context of tribunal decisions would appear to have been laid to rest; the position is neatly summarised in *R(IS)3/02*, where the Commissioner concludes,

"The effect and interaction of sections 3, 6, 7 and 22 of the Human Rights Act in relation to appeals from inferior tribunal decisions given before 2 October 2000 was much debated before me but the argument that Mr Cox [of Counsel] sought to advance in this appeal, that the 1998 Act had a retrospective effect extending even to turning past lawful decisions of courts and tribunals into unlawful ones in United Kingdom law from 2 October 2000 and to obliging appellate courts to reverse the effect retrospectively from that date onwards, has now conclusively been shown to be untenable: see *R v Lambert* [2001] 3 WLR 206, affirming what was said by Sir Andrew Morritt V-C in *Wilson v First County Trust Ltd (No.2)* [2001] 3 WLR 42, 51; and cf also the recent decision of the Tribunal of Scots Commissioners in case *CSDLA 1019/99*." (para.15.)

A tribunal sitting on or after October 2, 2000 on an appeal against a decision made before October 2, 2000 cannot consider Convention points, since s.12(8)(b) of the SSA 1998 confines the tribunal to the state of United Kingdom law at the time the decision was given, and cannot be interpreted in any other way. It might be observed, however, that there may be circumstances in which the Convention provides assistance in the interpretation of existing UK law without there being a situation in which a claimant can be said to be relying on Convention rights as provided by s.7 of the HRA 1998 *(CDLA/1338/2001)*.

See also *R(IS)6/04, CSIS/460/2002*, and *CCS/1306/2001*. The latter summarises at para.22 the case law on the extent to which Convention rights can be relied upon prior to October 2, 2000.

SCHEDULES

SCHEDULE 1

THE ARTICLES

PART I

THE CONVENTION

RIGHTS AND FREEDOMS

Article 2—Right to life

1. Everyone's right to life shall be protected by law. No one shall be deprived of his life intentionally save in the execution of a sentence of a court following his conviction of a crime for which this penalty is provided by law. 4.45
2. Deprivation of life shall not be regarded as inflicted in contravention of this Article when it results from the use of force which is no more than absolutely necessary:
   (a) in defence of any person from unlawful violence;
   (b) in order to effect a lawful arrest or to prevent the escape of a person lawfully detained;
   (c) in action lawfully taken for the purpose of quelling a riot or insurrection.

GENERAL NOTE

This article is unlikely to have much relevance in the social security jurisdiction. It is not a vehicle for arguing for a particular allocation of resources by the State. So arguments that without the payment of benefit, a person's life will be at risk and so the State cannot be said to be protecting by law everyone's right to life are destined to fail. This would appear to follow from those cases where the relatives of murder victims have sought to argue that the police failed to protect the victim: App.9837/82 *M v United Kingdom and Ireland* (1986) 47 D.R. 27. 4.46

Human Rights Act 1998

Article 3—Prohibition of torture

4.47 No one shall be subjected to torture or to inhuman or degrading treatment or punishment.

GENERAL NOTE

4.48 This article is concerned with conduct which attains at least a minimum level of severity. It is not concerned with anything which a person might find degrading. See *Ireland v United Kingdom*, judgment of January 18, 1978, Series A No.25; (1979–80) 2 E.H.R.R. 25, para.162 of the judgment, and *Tyrer v United Kingdom*, judgment of April 25, 1978, Series A No.26; (1979–80) 2 E.H.R.R.1, para.30 of the judgment. The effect of setting a high threshold is that trivial complaints, and even activity which is considered undesirable or illegal, will not fall within the scope of the article unless they cause sufficiently serious suffering or humiliation to the victim. The assessment of seriousness is relative. In its judgment in *Ireland v United Kingdom*, the Court suggested that the following factors are relevant in determining the existence of inhuman treatment: the duration of the treatment, its physical and mental effects, and the sex, age, and state of health of the victim. But it should also be remembered that the Convention is a "living instrument" whose standards are not set in stone; it receives a living interpretation and must be considered in the light of present day circumstances.

It follows that arguments, for example, that a medical examination in connection with a benefit claim was felt to be degrading or inhuman by the claimant will fall well below the threshold required to engage this article even where the doctor behaves improperly.

In *R. (on the application of Joanne Reynolds) v Secretary of State for Work and Pensions*, judgment of March 7, 2002, [2002] EWHC 426, it was argued that a failure to pay the claimant more than £41.35 per week by way of social security constituted degrading treatment. Wilson J. gives this argument short shrift, pointing out that "Article 3 proscribes ill-treatment of a depth which the level of payment to Ms Reynolds wholly fails to reach."

In *Secretary of State for the Home Department v Limbuela, Tesema and Adam* [2004] EWCA Civ 540, the Court of Appeal ruled that the refusal to provide State support for three asylum seekers, who had not applied for asylum within three days of their arrival in the United Kingdom under s.55 of the Nationality, Immigration and Asylum Act 2002, engaged their Convention rights under Art.3. Carnwath L.J. said that the case raised the question of the level of abject destitution to which such individuals must sink before their suffering reaches the minimum threshold for Art.3 to bite. Shelter was regarded as a basic amenity and the threat of not having access to shelter in the future could come within the ambit of inhuman and degrading treatment under Art.3. Laws L.J. dissented. Carnwath L.J. said,

> "118. . . . I acknowledge with gratitude the illumination provided by Laws L.J.'s powerful discussion of the scope of Art.3, and its application in the present context. As he says, the legal reality is a spectrum. At one end is state-authorised violence. At the other are to be found executive decisions in exercise of lawful policy objectives, which have consequences for individuals so severe that 'the court is bound to limit the State's right to implement the policy on Art.3 grounds'. I agree also with much of his analysis of the consequences of that distinction, and of the correct approach to the task of drawing the line in an individual case.
>
> 119. Laws L.J. accepts that Art.3 may be engaged by a particular 'vulnerability' in the individual, or external circumstances which make it impossible for him to find food and other basic amenities. Where, with respect, I part company from him is in his view that, on the evidence available to us, the judges were not entitled to find that such circumstances existed in the present cases. I would add that I find it diYcult not to regard shelter of some form from the elements at night (even if it is limited as it was in *T's* case) as a 'basic amenity', at least in winter and bad weather. . . ."

(1998 c.42, Sch.1)

The appeal of the Secretary of State against the decision of the Court of Appeal has been dismissed by a unanimous House of Lords, [2005] UKHL 66.

The judgment is important because it sets out circumstances within the context of State support for individuals which fall within the ambit of inhuman and degrading treatment in Art.3.

Article 4—Prohibition of slavery and forced labour

1. No one shall be held in slavery or servitude.
2. No one shall be required to perform forced or compulsory labour.
3. For the purpose of this Article the term "forced or compulsory labour" shall not include:
   (a) any work required to be done in the ordinary course of detention imposed according to the provisions of Article 5 of this Convention or during conditional release from such detention;
   (b) any service of a military character or, in case of conscientious objectors in countries where they are recognised, service exacted instead of compulsory military service;
   (c) any service exacted in case of an emergency or calamity threatening the life or well-being of the community;
   (d) any work or service which forms part of normal civic obligations.

4.49

GENERAL NOTE

Being required to be available for work as a condition of entitlement to benefit will not constitute forced or compulsory labour.

4.50

Article 5—Right to liberty and security

1. Everyone has the right to liberty and security of person. No one shall be deprived of his liberty save in the following cases and in accordance with a procedure prescribed by law:
   (a) the lawful detention of a person after conviction by a competent court;
   (b) the lawful arrest or detention of a person for non-compliance with the lawful order of a court or in order to secure the fulfilment of any obligation prescribed by law;
   (c) the lawful arrest or detention of a person effected for the purpose of bringing him before the competent legal authority on reasonable suspicion of having committed an offence or when it is reasonably considered necessary to prevent his committing an offence or fleeing after having done so;
   (d) the detention of a minor by lawful order for the purpose of educational supervision or his lawful detention for the purpose of bringing him before the competent legal authority;
   (e) the lawful detention of persons for the prevention of the spreading of infectious diseases, of persons of unsound mind, alcoholics or drug addicts or vagrants;
   (f) the lawful arrest or detention of a person to prevent his effecting an unauthorised entry into the country or of a person against whom action is being taken with a view to deportation or extradition.
2. Everyone who is arrested shall be informed promptly, in a language which he understands, of the reasons for his arrest and of any charge against him.
3. Everyone arrested or detained in accordance with the provisions of paragraph 1 (c) of this Article shall be brought promptly before a judge or other officer authorised by law to exercise judicial power and shall be entitled to trial within a reasonable time or to release pending trial. Release may be conditioned by guarantees to appear for trial.
4. Everyone who is deprived of his liberty by arrest or detention shall be entitled to take proceedings by which the lawfulness of his detention shall be decided speedily by a court and his release ordered if the detention is not lawful.
5. Everyone who has been the victim of arrest or detention in contravention of the provisions of this Article shall have an enforceable right to compensation.

4.51

GENERAL NOTE

There are two parts to the protections afforded by Art.5. First, it prohibits detention save in the exhaustive list of circumstances listed in para.(1). Secondly, it offers a set of procedural guarantees for those detained. Though the article refers to liberty and security of the person, the Strasbourg organs have not treated liberty and security as different concepts; there is no authority for arguing that security of the person refers to physical integrity independent of liberty. The article has little application in the field of social security.

4.52

Human Rights Act 1998

Article 6—Right to a fair trial

4.53   1. In the determination of his civil rights and obligations or of any criminal charge against him, everyone is entitled to a fair and public hearing within a reasonable time by an independent and impartial tribunal established by law. Judgment shall be pronounced publicly but the press and public may be excluded from all or part of the trial in the interest of morals, public order or national security in a democratic society, where the interests of juveniles or the protection of the private life of the parties so require, or to the extent strictly necessary in the opinion of the court in special circumstances where publicity would prejudice the interests of justice.

2. Everyone charged with a criminal offence shall be presumed innocent until proved guilty according to law.

3. Everyone charged with a criminal offence has the following minimum rights:
   (a) to be informed promptly, in a language which he understands and in detail, of the nature and cause of the accusation against him;
   (b) to have adequate time and facilities for the preparation of his defence;
   (c) to defend himself in person or through legal assistance of his own choosing or, if he has not sufficient means to pay for legal assistance, to be given it free when the interests of justice so require;
   (d) to examine or have examined witnesses against him and to obtain the attendance and examination of witnesses on his behalf under the same conditions as witnesses against him;
   (e) to have the free assistance of an interpreter if he cannot understand or speak the language used in court.

GENERAL NOTE

4.54   Article 6 is central to the scheme of protection in the Convention, and has generated the largest number of applications and judgments. Article 6 is an omnibus provision which contains a blueprint for what constitutes a fair trial. Accordingly, it warrants extensive treatment.

There is a discernible trend among some Commissioners to use the fair trial requirements embedded in Art.6 rather than the common law language of natural justice in deciding whether tribunal proceedings have been fair. A good example is *CJSA/5100/2001,* where the Commissioner said,

> "5. I chose to explain my decision in term's of the claimant's Convention right to a fair hearing under article 6(1) of the European Convention on Human Rights and Fundamental Freedoms. In particular, I rely on the equality of arms principle that has developed in the jurisprudence of the Strasbourg authorities as part of that right. It requires that the procedure followed by the tribunal must strike a fair balance between the parties so that none is at a disadvantage as against the others. . .
>
> 6. I could, no doubt, have reached the same conclusion under domestic principles of natural justice. However, the Human Rights Act 1998 provides a convenient opportunity for Commissioners to rebase their decisions on procedural fairness in fresh terms. In my view, this would be desirable. I am sure that tribunals are familiar with the principles of natural justice. However, increasingly the cases that come to me suggest that they are not applying them. If there is a common theme in those cases, it is that the tribunal has not provided a procedural balance between the parties. The introduction of the language of balance would provide a touchstone for tribunals."

The Commissioner in *CIB/2751/2002* agreed with those sentiments in the context of a case which had involved the refusal of a domiciliary hearing in joined appeals concerning entitlement to an incapacity benefit and a severe disablement allowance.

Does the resolution of social security disputes involve the determination of civil rights and obligations?

4.55   The first question which must be addressed is whether decision-making in social security constitutes "the determination of . . . civil rights and obligations". Answering this question requires detailed discussion of a line of Convention cases.

The formulation in Art.6 would seem to exclude the initial decisions by decision-makers since the article contemplates a situation in which there is a dispute. This is clearer from the French text, which refers to *contestations*. It cannot be said that there is a dispute when what is at issue is an initial determination of entitlement to benefit (see *Feldbrugge v The Netherlands*, judgment of May 29, 1986, Series A, No.99; (1986) 8 E.H.R.R. 425, para.25 of the judgment); the vast majority of such decisions are not the subject of appeal to a tribunal. But what of the tribunals? Are they determining civil rights and obligations? The essential question is whether Art.6 covers only private law rights to the exclusion of public law matters: a distinction which is much more formal in continental systems of law than in the United Kingdom's common law system.

It was not long before the issue came before the Court of Human Rights in the *Ringeisen* case (*Ringeisen v Austria (No. 1)*, judgment of July 16, 1971, Series A, No.13; (1979–80) 1 E.H.R.R. 455) after the majority of the Commission had concluded that Art.6 should be construed restrictively as including only those proceedings which are typical of relations between private individuals and as excluding those proceedings in which the citizen is confronted by those who exercise public authority. The Court took a different view. Article 6 covers all proceedings the result of which is decisive for the private rights and obligations of individuals, and neither the character of the legislation (whether, for example civil, commercial or administrative) nor that of the authority with jurisdiction over the dispute (whether, for example, court, tribunal or administrative body) are of great consequence. Since the decision in this case, the Court has adopted a liberal interpretation of the concept of civil rights and obligations.

Several cases have considered whether social security disputes involve the determination of civil rights and obligations.

The *Feldbrugge* case (*Feldbrugge v The Netherlands*, judgment of May 29, 1986, Series A, No.99; (1986) 8 E.H.R.R. 425) concerned a dispute over entitlement to a sickness allowance in The Netherlands. Mrs Feldbrugge had been registered as unemployed, but then ceased to register because she had become ill and did not consider herself fit for work. The Occupational Association (the body responsible for administering sickness allowance in The Netherlands) arranged for her to be medically examined by their consulting doctor, who concluded that she was fit for work. The sickness allowance was stopped. The claimant appealed to the Appeals Board and the President of the Appeals Board arranged for her to be seen by a gynaecologist who was one of the permanent medical experts attached to the Appeals Board. That doctor examined her and gave her an opportunity to comment. The doctor consulted another gynaecologist and two general practitioners (one of whom was the claimant's GP). They all agreed with the decision that the claimant was fit for work, but the permanent medical expert considered that an orthopaedic specialist should also be consulted. An orthopaedic surgeon examined the claimant who was again given an opportunity to comment. The three practitioners consulted by the gynaecologist were also consulted following this examination. The orthopaedic surgeon concluded in the light of all the medical findings that the claimant was fit for work in accordance with the initial contested decision. The President of the Appeals Board then ruled against the claimant, who filed an objection which raised the matter before the Appeals Board itself, which found the objection lacking in substance. An appeal to the Central Appeals Board was unsuccessful. Mrs Feldbrugge complained that she had not had a fair trial before the President of the Appeals Board in violation of Art.6(1). The Court had to face squarely the issue of whether the adjudication of the claimant's dispute was a matter concerning her civil rights and obligations. The Court weighed the features of the case which suggested that the matter was one of public law against the features which suggested that it was one of private law. The public law nature of the legislation on sickness allowances, the compulsory nature of insurance against illness, and the assumption by the State of responsibility for social protection had to be weighed against the personal and economic nature of the asserted right, its connection with the contract of employment, and affinities with insurance under the ordinary law. After weighing these interests, the Court ruled by a majority of ten votes to seven, that, taken together, the private law aspects of the sickness allowance scheme were "predominant" and the adjudication of Mrs Feldbrugge's claim was therefore covered by Art.6(1).

The *Deumeland* case (*Deumeland v Germany*, judgment of May 29, 1986, Series A, No.20; (1986) 8 E.H.R.R. 448), decided on the same day as the *Feldbrugge* case, concerned industrial injury pensions in Germany. The proceedings in Germany were extraordinarily protracted, and this was the substance of the applicant's complaint. Gerhard Deumeland had in January 1970 slipped on a snow covered pavement as he was coming home from an appointment with an ear-nose-and-throat specialist whom he had consulted on leaving his workplace. He died in March 1970, and his widow claimed a widow's supplementary pension on the basis that the death of Gerhard had been the consequence of an industrial accident. The first set of proceedings before the Berlin Social Security Court of Appeal lasted from June 1970 to December 1972. The outcome of these proceedings was a decision that the accident in question was neither an industrial accident nor an accident on the way to or from work. There was accordingly no entitlement to a widow's supplementary pension. Mrs Deumeland appealed to the Berlin Social Security Court of Appeal, where the first set of proceedings lasted from November 1972 to September 1973. These were unsuccessful. An appeal on a point of law was pursued before the Bundessozialgericht (Federal Social Security Court) which lasted from October 1973 to May 1975. In the course of these proceedings, the claimant challenged a judge for bias accusing him of delaying the proceedings. That challenge was not successful and the appeal decision was taken by a panel which included the unsuccessfully challenged judge. The decision of the Bundessozialgericht was to set aside the decision of the Berlin Social Security Court of Appeal and to remit the case for a fresh hearing.

4.56 The second set of proceedings before the Berlin Social Security Court of Appeal lasted from May 1975 to March 1979. In December 1976 during the course of these proceedings, Mrs Deumeland died and her son, Klaus, was allowed to continue the proceedings. The outcome was a decision that the claim to the widow's pension was unfounded. Klaus Deumeland sought to appeal to the Bundessozialgericht. Leave to appeal was eventually refused. Leave for a further appeal to the Bundesverfassungsgericht (Federal Constitutional Court) was refused by that Court, and a subsequent application to the Berlin Social Security Court of Appeal by Klaus Deumeland to have the proceedings reopened was not only unsuccessful but also resulted in his being fined DM800 for bringing vexatious proceedings. For reasons which are very similar to those in the *Feldbrugge* case, the Court, by a majority of 9 votes to 8, concluded that the proceedings of which the applicant complained had been concerned with the determination of civil rights and obligations.

The *Feldbrugge* and *Deumeland* cases had involved benefits which flowed from an insurance principle, and this feature might be seen as critical in drawing a distinction between social insurance and social assistance. The latter term refers to those benefits which fall outside the sphere of social insurance and involve the State stepping in to provide benefits for those who have no entitlement to insurance-based benefits, or whose entitlement is such that their income is below subsistence level. The distinction came before the Court in the *Salesi* case (*Salesi v Italy*, judgment of February 26, 1993, Series A, No.257-E (1998) 26 E.H.R.R. 187). Enrica Salesi had claimed a monthly disability allowance in the Lazio social security department, which had been refused. In February 1986, she brought proceedings against the Minister of the Interior before the pretore del lavoro (magistrates' court exercising their labour jurisdiction) in Rome seeking payment of the benefit. The Minister appealed against the decision of the pretore awarding the benefit, and the Rome District Court dismissed the appeal in May 1989. A subsequent appeal to the Court of Cassation was also dismissed. Even though the claimant was ultimately the winning party, she complained to the Commission alleging a violation of Art.6(1) by reason of the length of the proceedings.

The Court re-affirmed its decisions in *Feldbrugge* and *Deumeland* noting,

"... the development in the law that was initiated by those judgments and the principle of equality of treatment warrant taking the view that today the general rule is that Article 6(1) does apply in the field of social insurance."

The Court went on,

"In the present case, however, the question arises in connection with welfare assistance and not . . . social insurance. Certainly there are differences between the two, but they cannot be regarded as fundamental at the present stage of development of social security law. This justifies following, in relation to the entitlement to welfare allowances, the opinion which emerges from [the judgments in *Feldbrugge* and *Deumeland*] as regards the classification of the right to social insurance benefits, namely that State intervention is not sufficient to establish that Article 6(1) is inapplicable." (para.19 of the judgment.)

The Court concluded that there were no convincing reasons for distinguishing welfare benefits from the rights to social insurance benefits asserted in the earlier cases. The decision of the Court may be criticised for its poverty of reasoning, but nevertheless remains an authority for the extension of Art.6(1) to all disputes concerning social security benefits.

The *Schuler-Zgraggen* case (*Schuler-Zgraggen v Switzerland*, judgment of June 24, 1993, Series A, No.263; (1993) 16 E.H.R.R. 405) concerned a claim to an invalidity pension. The claimant had been employed and paid contributions into the federal invalidity insurance scheme. She contracted open pulmonary tuberculosis and applied for an invalidity pension. The Compensation Office awarded a half pension, which was subsequently increased to a full pension. In 1984 the applicant gave birth to a son. In 1985 she was required to undergo a medical examination by doctors appointed by the Invalidity Insurance Board. This resulted in a decision to terminate the award of the invalidity pension. The claimant appealed to the relevant Appeals Board. In the course of these proceedings she was refused a sight of her medical file which had been seen by the Appeals Board. The Board subsequently dismissed her appeal. The claimant lodged an appeal against this decision with the Federal Insurance Court, whose decision was to remit the case to the Compensation Office, whose reconsideration did not result in the award of a pension. The Court followed its earlier decisions in concluding that the proceedings in issue were concerned with the determination of civil rights and obligations. The Court also followed the decision in *Salesi* in virtually identical language,

"... the development in the law that was initiated by those judgments [in *Feldbrugge* and *Deumeland*] and the principle of equality of treatment warrant taking the view that today the general rule is that Article 6(1) does apply in the field of social insurance, including even welfare assistance." (para.46 of the judgment.)

The *Schouten and Meldrum* case (*Schouten and Meldrum v The Netherlands*, judgment of December 9, 1994, Series A, No.304; (1994) 19 E.H.R.R. 432) concerned the liability of persons in similar positions to employers to pay contributions to an occupational association in respect of physiotherapists who worked for them. This was the first case in which the Court had been called upon to determine an issue involving the payment of contributions under a social security scheme as distinct from disputes concerning entitlement to benefits. The Court took the view that the approach adopted in *Feldbrugge* and *Deumeland* was appropriate in the case of liability to pay contributions. The public law and private law aspects of the arrangements should be weighed to see whether one or the other were predominant. Using exactly the same factors as had been in issue in *Feldbrugge*, the Court concluded that the private law aspects were predominant and that Art.6(1) applied.

A challenge to the system of recovering State benefits from personal injury awards has also failed at the admissibility stage (App.2877/95, *Graeme Knightley v United Kingdom*, decision of September 4, 1997). See also *Stevens and Knight v United Kingdom*, decision of September 9, 1998, in which the Commission simply ignored arguments that the determination of claims to sickness benefit, statutory sick pay and invalidity benefit did not constitute the determination of civil rights and obligations.

These cases establish beyond a peradventure that adjudication of social security disputes involves the determination of civil rights and obligations to which the procedural guarantees of Art.6(1) apply: see also *CDLA/5413/1999*. They have been followed even in cases where the pensions of those employed in the public service were involved (*Lombardo v Italy*, judgment of November 26, 1992, Series A, No.249-B; (1996) 21 E.H.R.R. 188; and *Massa v Italy*, judgment of August 24, 1993, Series A, No.265-B; (1994) 18 E.H.R.R.266. It follows that the rules on what constitutes a fair trial apply to the proceedings of tribunals, the Commissioners and the courts when dealing with social security questions.

The Secretary of State made a concession in *Wood v Secretary of State for Work and Pensions* [2003] EWCA Civ 53 (see para.24) (reported as *R(DLA) 1/03*) which would appear to mean that all social security appeals involve the determination of civil rights and obligations and so attract the protection of Art.6. See also *R(IS)6/04*, but note para.68 of *R(H) 3/05*.

In a housing case, *Begum v Tower Hamlets LBC* [2003] UKHL 5, the House of Lords also took a broad view of what constitutes the determination of civil rights and obligations (without making any definitive ruling on what does and does not fall within this formulation in Art.6) and went on to make a number of pertinent comments on what constitutes independence and impartiality for the purposes of the article. A decision by a rehousing manager employed by a local authority reviewing a decision to offer a particular property to the applicant was held not to constitute an "independent and impartial" tribunal' for the purposes of Art.6, but a determination on review by the county court "on any point of law arising from the decision" which did not permit the making of fresh findings of fact did meet the requirements of Art.6.

What is a fair trial under Article 6(1)?

4.57
The Strasbourg organs have indicated that Art.6(1) demands not only an overall requirement of a fair hearing but also the presence of specific features in order for there to be a fair trial. The overall requirement has been summarised as follows,

> "The effect of Article 6(1) is, inter alia, to place the 'tribunal' under a duty to conduct a proper examination of the submissions, arguments and evidence adduced by the parties, without prejudice to its assessment of whether they are relevant to its decision." (*Kraska v Switzerland*, judgment of April 19, 1993, Series A, No.254-B; (1994) 18 E.H.R.R. 188, para.30 of the judgment.)

It is important that the general requirements for a fair trial are appreciated, since they continue to be developed in specific circumstances by the Strasbourg organs. Certain of the requirements are of a general nature, whereas others are more specifically stated in Art.6.

Four features *inherent* in the concept of a fair trial appear to have flowed from this general notion of a fair trial.

The first and perhaps most important is the concept of *égalité des armes*, which translates inelegantly into English as "equality of arms". In English law, it is an aspect of the requirement of natural justice. It requires that each party has a broadly equal opportunity to present a case in circumstances which do not place one of the parties as a substantial disadvantage as regards the opposing party (see *Dombo Beheer BV v The Netherlands*, judgment of October 27, 1993, Series A, No.274-A; (1994) 18 E.H.R.R. 213, para.33 of the judgment). In *CDLA/5413/1999*, the Commissioner expresses concern that the principle of equality of arms may be breached by the provisions of the Adjudication Regulations on notice, which provide that notice required to be given or sent by the Department are, if sent by post, deemed to be given on the day of posting, whereas notice required to be given by a claimant is only treated as given when it reaches the Department.

In an expansive reading of the Strasbourg case law, the Commissioner in *CDLA/2748/2002* draws on specific case law relating to criminal proceedings in

Art.6(3)(e) on the provision of interpretation and translation to suggest that Art.6 requires that effective and efficient interpretation and translation is a feature of tribunal adjudication where the claimant needs this. He says that "a failure of interpretation must therefore affect the fairness of the tribunal hearing." (para.11).

Secondly, there must be a judicial process, which requires each side to have the opportunity to have knowledge of and comment on the observations filed or evidence adduced by the opposing party (*Ruiz-Mateos v Spain*, judgment of June 23, 1993, Series A, No.262; (1993) 16 E.H.R.R. 505, para.63 of the judgment). Non-disclosure of material by one side to the other is likely to give rise to violations of this feature of a fair trial, as might issues of the circumstances in which evidence was acquired. In the *Feldbrugge* case, the applicant complained that she had not had a proper opportunity to present her case. The Court found that the proceedings before the President of the Appeals Board "were not attended to a sufficient degree, by one of the principal guarantees of a judicial procedure" (para.44 of the judgment) in that, although the applicant had been afforded the opportunity to comment on her condition during the medical examinations, she was neither able to present oral argument nor to file written pleadings before the President of the Appeals Board; nor was she able to consult the two reports of the consultants and to formulate objections to them.

Thirdly, there is a requirement for a reasoned decision, which is regarded as implicit in the notion of a fair trial. The level of reasoning need not be detailed. If a court gives reasons, then the requirement for a reasoned decision is prima facie met, but a decision which on its face shows that it was made on a basis not open to the judge cannot be said to be a reasoned decision (see *De Moor v Belgium*, judgment of June 23, 1994, Series A, No.292-A; (1994) 18 E.H.R.R. 372). For a case in which a violation of Art.6 was found because of the inadequacy of the reasons for rejecting certain medical evidence in a social security context, see *H.A.L. v Finland (App.38267/97)* Judgment of January 27, 2004. The introduction of short-form decisions in tribunals is unlikely to fall foul of this provision, since a party is entitled to a full statement of reasons on application within one month of the day on which the decision notice was notified to the parties. Decisions of the Commissioners are always given in full, except a decision made with the consent of the parties to set aside a tribunal decision and remit the case for a rehearing by the tribunal.

The final issue is whether a trial can be fair if there is no right of appearance in person. The law here remains in a state of development and the Court has yet to pronounce in detail on this in civil cases, but the Commission has held that in some cases a fair trial is only possible in the presence of the parties. An example would be a case where the personal character and manner of life of a party are directly relevant to the formation of the court's opinion on the point at issue. Custody disputes over children might be such cases (See App.434/58, *X v Sweden*, June 30, 1959, 2 Y.B. 354 at 370). Presence may need to be distinguished from participation. In the *Schuler-Zgraggen* case, the applicant had not availed herself of the opportunity to request a hearing, but nevertheless complained that the proceedings were unfair because the Federal Insurance Court had not ordered a hearing of its own motion. The Court accepted the arguments of the Government that purely written proceedings did not in the circumstances of this case prejudice the interests of the litigant. It was accepted that a written procedure would offer advantages of efficiency and speed which might be jeopardised if oral hearings became the rule. The Court concluded,

> "The Court reiterates that the public character of court hearings constitutes a fundamental principle enshrined in Article 6(1). Admittedly, neither the letter nor the spirit of this provision prevents a person from waiving of his own free will, either expressly or tacitly, the entitlement to have his case heard in public, but any such waiver must be made in an unequivocal manner and must not run counter to any important public interest." (para.58 of the judgment.)

These comments have relevance both for paper hearings before appeal tribunals and for procedure before the Commissioners (see below).

4.58 There are four *specific features* of a fair trial to be found on the face of Art.6.
First, trial must be before "an independent and impartial tribunal established by law." This requirement includes a subjective and an objective element. The subjective test involves an enquiry into whether the particular judge in the case was actually biased, or lacking in independence or impartiality. Propriety will be presumed in the absence of specific evidence of bias. The objective test involves determination of whether the court or tribunal offers guarantees sufficient to exclude any legitimate doubt about its impartiality or independence. This can include both specific difficulties caused by certain persons being involved in particular decisions, as well as what might be called structural problems with the forum for the resolution of the dispute. A good example of structural problems can be found in the English courts-martial cases, which have determined that the role (at the time) of the convening officer in the management of the prosecution case conflicted with his role as convenor of the court-martial, in particular his appointment of its members (who were subordinate in rank to himself and fell within his chain of command) (see *Findlay v United Kingdom*, judgment of February 25, 1997; (1997) 24 E.H.R.R. 221; and *Coyne v United Kingdom*, judgment of September 24, 1997, *The Times*, October 24, 1997, E.C.H.R.).

Tsfayo v United Kingdom (App. 60860) Judgment of November 14, 2006, is now largely of historical interest, but a violation of Article 6 was found on the grounds that the Housing Benefit Review Board was not an independent and impartial tribunal. However, the comments in the case on the relationship between appeals and other remedies are of considerable significance, and it was suggested that, for this reason, the United Kingdom would seek to have the case referred to the Grand Chamber. That does not appear to have happened.

Secondly, publicity is seen as one of the guarantees of the fairness of a trial, but the requirement for hearings to be in public is surrounded by a substantial list of circumstances in which the presumption of public hearings is displaced. It is now also clear that interlocutory matters do not have to be in public. So the Commission has rejected a complaint that interlocutory proceedings before a High Court Master in Chambers without elaborating its reasons violated Art.6: App.3860/68, *X v United Kingdom* (1970) 30 C.D. 70). A similar view would almost certainly be taken of proceedings for leave to appeal. As already noted, a written procedure may suffice provided that there are proper opportunities for requesting or ordering an oral hearing.

Thirdly, Art.6(1), on its face, requires that judgment is pronounced publicly, and this requirement is not expressed to be subject to the list of limitations which apply to a public trial. The leading case is *Pretto* (*Pretto and others v Italy*, judgment of December 8, 1983, Series A, No.71; (1984) 6 E.H.R.R. 182. The Court seems to have been very accommodating to a wide range of practice in this regard among the Contracting States, indicating that the form of publicity to be given to a judgment is to be assessed in the light of special features of particular proceedings. It certainly appears to be the case that nothing more than the formal disposition need be announced publicly, and it seems that the public availability of the outcome is as important as the matter being read out in open court. So in the *Pretto* case, the availability of the disposition in the court registry was considered to meet the requirements for public pronouncement of the judgment.

Lastly, under Art.6(1), litigants are entitled to judgment in a reasonable time. Complaints of violations of this requirement have been the single most numerous sort of alleged violation of the Convention. Such cases have rarely involved the United Kingdom (but see *Robins v United Kingdom*, judgment of September 23, 1997; (1998) 26 E.H.R.R. 527). Though the case law is voluminous, the principles can be stated quite simply. The first task is to determine the period or periods in issue, before moving on to consider the reasonableness of the length of the proceedings. The period in issue will include any appellate proceedings. In forming judgments on the reasonableness of the length of the proceedings, the following factors are relevant: the complexity of the case, the behaviour of the applicant, the conduct of the judicial authorities, and what is at stake for the applicant. However, backlogs of judicial business are not a defence to unreasonable delays. In *Deumeland*, the period in issue was

10 years, seven months and three weeks from the application to the Berlin Social Security Court to the rejection of the application to the Bundesverfassungsgericht. The claim to benefit involved a straightforward factual issue involving no great legal complexity, but the behaviour of Klaus Deumeland had protracted the proceedings. Detailed examination of the progress of the case through the various courts showed that the case had lain dormant before the Berlin Social Security Court for significant periods, and the period taken to resolve the second set of proceedings before the appellate body was excessive. There was a violation of the right to judgment within a reasonable time, but it is significant that the Court also finds that the mere declaration of a violation was in the circumstances of the case considered to be adequate just satisfaction under what is now Art.41 of the Convention. A delay of a little over six years in the *Salesi* case was also found to constitute a violation of Art.6(1). The reasonableness of the time taken to give judgment must be determined in each case in the light of its own particular circumstances.

The issue of judgment within a reasonable time in the social security context was raised in *R(IS)1/04*, where the claimant argued that the (it should be said typical) lengthy period before an overpayment decision is taken meant that there was a breach of Art.6. An overpayment decision was made on October 14, 2000 in respect of an overpayment which had arisen in 1994 and 1995. The Commissioner concludes that for the purposes of the measurement of time in the context of a complaint that judgment has not been given within a reasonable time, time started running on October 14, 2000, since it was at that point that a dispute arose; a different Commissioner in *R(IS)2/04* takes the same view at para.20. That was enough to dispose of the point since a tribunal determined the appeal in May 2001 which was manifestly within a reasonable time. The claimant had also sought to suggest that overpayment decisions were in the nature of criminal charges. The Commissioner, after careful consideration of the authorities, concludes that overpayment decisions involve the determination of civil rights and obligations and not the determination of a criminal charge (see paras 12–17).

See also *CIS/4220/2002*, which draws on the decision of the Court in *Dyer v Watson*, [2002] 4 All E.R. 1.

The Court of Human Rights has ruled, in *Bullerwell v United Kingdom* (App.48013/99), decision of December 12, 2002 (2003) 36 E.H.R.R. CD 76, ECHR, as inadmissible a complaint that judgment was not given in a reasonable time in an industrial injuries benefit case which involved four hearings by a medical appeal tribunal, three appeals to the Commissioner, and an application for judicial review which resulted in an unsuccessful appeal to the Court of Appeal. The outcome is unsurprising even though the first appeal was lodged in July 1991 and the trail of litigation ended in July 1998 when the House of Lords refused a petition for leave to appeal the refusal of leave to apply for judicial review. The Court applies its tried and tested methodology of considering the complexity of the case, the parties' conduct and that of the competent authorities, and the importance of what was at stake for the applicant in the litigation. There is nothing significant in the decision but it is an excellent example of the approach of the new Court to admissibility of complaints and contains a detailed and fair analysis of the course of these lengthy proceedings. There is one interesting comment on Commissioner's directions, as follows:

"On 7 May 1996 the applicant applied to the Commissioner for leave to appeal against the MAT's decision of 26 April 1996. Less than a month later the Commissioner made directions for the filing of observations by the Secretary of State, and, on 21 August 1996, just over a month after these observations were filed, leave to appeal was granted. Thereafter the Commissioner made a number of further directions for the determination of the appeal itself, but it was not until 15 January 1997 that he decided that it was necessary for the Secretary of State to file a written submission on the mean of the word 'diffuse'. Although it cannot be said that the period between 21 August 1996 and 15 January 1997 was one of judicial inactivity, the Court considers that time would have been saved if the

Commissioner had explicitly requested these observations from the Secretary of State at the outset." (p.13.)

This illustrates that the new Court is willing to look in considerable detail at the course of the proceedings as part of its examination of whether judgment has been given within a reasonable time. While it is important to remember that this is a decision on the admissibility of the complaint, it does suggest that a succession of small and unnecessary delays could accumulate into a sufficient lengthy period of delay for the Court to consider that there was a case to answer in relation to the length of proceedings.

The application of Article 6(1) to appeal proceedings

4.59 Article 6 does not require Contracting States to have a system of appeals from decisions at first instance in civil cases (*De Cubber v Belgium*, judgment of October 26, 1984, Series A, No.86; (1985) 7 E.H.R.R. 236, para.32 of the Judgment), but if the State does provide a system of appeals, it too must comply with the guarantees to be found in Art.6(1) (*Fejde v Sweden*, judgment of September 26, 1991, Series A, No.212-C; (1994) 17 E.H.R.R. 14, para.32 of the judgment). It follows that a defect at first instance might be corrected at the appellate stage of the proceedings. Where there is an appeal, the requirement to exhaust domestic remedies before a complaint can be made under the Convention means that it must be used, and it will then be the totality of the domestic proceedings which is considered by the Commission and Court. It will always be necessary to look at the character of the appellate proceedings to determine the extent to which they are able to remedy any deficiency at first instance. For example, the shortcoming identified in the *Feldbrugge* case could not be remedied on appeal, because the nature of the appeal was restricted to four very narrow grounds, none of which offered the opportunity for the applicant to participate to the extent required by Art.6 in the proceedings which determined her dispute.

A fair appeal is unlikely to be able to correct a defect arising from a structural problem in the first instance court or tribunal which results in its not being an independent and impartial tribunal (*De Cubber v Belgium*, judgment of October 26, 1984, Series A, No.86; (1985) 7 E.H.R.R. 236, para.33 of the judgment). There is a suggestion that the quashing by an appeal court on the specific ground that the first instance court or tribunal was not independent and impartial might have cured the defect, but this could amount to recognition that there was no right to a court in the particular instance. This is a right which the Court has read into Art.6.

There has been an ongoing debate in English law concerning the adequacy of judicial review as a remedy for what might be regarded as an earlier breach of Convention rights. In *CTC/0031/2006* the Commissioner considered this question in the context of an appeal concerning the backdating of a claim to Child Tax Credit. The Commissioner dismissed the appeal on the grounds that the acceptance of a 'manner' of claiming is an administrative act involving the exercise of discretion. Accordingly, judicial review was an adequate remedy and there was no basis for the argument that Article 6 ECHR required the recognition of a right to appeal to a tribunal on this question.

The right to a court

4.60 The Court has recognised that Art.6 must contain a right of access to a court for the determination of a particular issue. So the prohibition (at the time) in English Prison Rules on bringing a defamation action against a prison officer, who was alleged to have accused the prisoner wrongly of having assaulted him, violated this right (*Golder v United Kingdom*, judgment of February 21, 1975, Series A, No.18; (1979–80) 1 E.H.R.R. 524). A similar conclusion was reached in a case originating from Ireland where there was no procedure by which a father could challenge a decision of the authorities placing his daughter for adoption (*Keegan v Ireland*, judgment of May 26, 1994, Series A, No.290; (1994) 18 E.H.R.R. 342). The right might even include a right to some sort of representation in order to make the right effective. In the *Airey* case (*Airey v Ireland*, judgment of October 9, 1979, Series A, No.32;

(1998 c.42, Sch.1)

(1979–80) 2 E.H.R.R. 305), the applicant had been unable to find a lawyer to act for her because of her financial position and the absence of legal aid. She needed a separation order to protect her from her husband who was prone to violence towards her. The procedure was complex and not such as could be managed effectively by a litigant in person. The Court concluded that, in such circumstances, Art.6 requires the provision of legal assistance where "such assistance proves indispensable for an effective access to court." (para.26 of the judgment). The case is sometimes wrongly read too sweepingly as imposing an obligation on State to have a legal aid scheme, at least for complex litigation. The judgment is rather more limited; it will be necessary to look at the nature of the right being protected by the litigation, what is at stake for the applicant, and the complexity of the procedure before the particular decision-making body in making a judgment as to whether Art.6 requires a State to provide legal assistance.

In *CJSA/5101/2001* the claimant sought to rely on the *Airey* case to ground an entitlement to legal representation. The Commissioner stated,

> "The claimant has no right to legal representation under British law in a social security case, and the European Convention on Human Rights does not give him that right. I have no power under British law to grant him legal representation and the European Convention on Human Rights, again does not give me that power." (para.9).

Though undoubtedly correct in the circumstances of the case before him, it is not entirely inconceivable that a set of circumstances might arise in which the *Airey* test requiring legal assistance and possibly legal representation might arise in the future.

Legal aid for representation at oral hearings is now possible in England and Wales through the Community Legal Service established by the Access to Justice Act 1999. The Lord Chancellor has made directions which permit support to be provided for representation where one of four criteria is met:
1. The case must be of significant public interest.
2. The case must be of overwhelming importance for the claimant.
3. It is practically possible for the claimant to bring the proceedings.
4. A lack of public funding would lead to obvious unfairness.

It must follow that Commissioners should be alert to the need to consider the circumstances of claimants and should make directions which might lead to the grant of funded legal representation where one of the four criteria set out above is satisfied. The position in Scotland is more favourable; since December 2002, publicly-funded legal representation is available in all proceedings before the Commissioners sitting in Scotland.

Application to social security procedure

As noted above, initial decision-making on claims to benefit does not fall within Art.6, though appeals to the appeal tribunals and onward appeals to the Social Security Commissioners do attract the due process guarantees of Art.6. **4.61**

There have now been a number of cases in which English courts have had to consider the application of the requirement for a fair trial under Article 6 to proceedings arising in England. The state of the authorities is helpfully summarised by the Court of Appeal in *R. (on the application of Thompson) v The Law Society* [2002] EWCA Civ 167. Clarke L.J. delivering the judgment of the Court with which his colleagues agreed says,

> "The key point as a matter of principle is that the question whether the procedure satisfies article 6(1), where there is a determination of civil rights and obligations, must be answered by reference to the whole process. The question in each case is whether the process involves a court or courts having 'full jurisdiction to deal with the case as the nature of the decision requires'. There may be cases in which a

public and oral hearing is required at first instances and other cases where it is not, just as there may be cases in which the potential availability of judicial review will not be sufficient to avoid a breach of article 6(1)".

Procedure before the tribunals is unlikely to raise any difficulties under Art.6. It is just possible that an issue could arise from the introduction of paper hearings. However, paper hearings will only arise where the claimant does not ask for an oral hearing. There might be an arguable violation of Art.6 where a paper hearing proceeds in a case which is for particular reasons more appropriate for an oral hearing. Regulation 39(5) of the Decisions and Appeals Regulations provides a power for the chairman of an appeal tribunal of his or her own motion to direct an oral hearing of an appeal. A good example of an appeal which might not be appropriate for a paper hearing might be a case involving a substantial overpayment of benefit where the claimant maintained that disclosure had taken place. Here issues of credibility are raised which can best be resolved by seeing and hearing the claimant.

In *CDLA/5413/1999* the Commissioner concluded that the claimant had been denied a fair hearing when she had asked for an oral hearing and an appeal proceeded in her absence because the deemed notice of the hearing had never reached her. The Commissioner says,

"49. Rehearsing again the salient features of this case in the light of the above analysis [of the requirements of Art.6 ECHR], it is one where the claimant asked, in accordance with regulations, for an oral hearing. The hearing was to be before the only tribunal or court competent to give her case a full hearing as to issues of fact. It was a case in which her presence and evidence were clearly relevant to the issue before the tribunal. She was unrepresented. She was not present at the hearing. The Secretary of State was not represented. There was no clerk present. The tribunal heard the case, and in doing so both assumed it had the capacity to do so and that it did not need to adjourn. It did that because the claimant was assumed to know about the hearing because of the deemed notice provision. But the claimant did not know about the hearing through no fault of her own.
50. The question for me on those facts is whether there was a fair hearing of this case before the decision of the tribunal was made, in the judicial sense of 'fair hearing'. In my view there was not. This is because the claimant asked for an oral hearing and did not receive it. This was through no fault of her own but because of the operation, against her interests, of a rule of procedure that was not a 'fair balance' as between her and the other party to the appeal, the Secretary of State.
51. It does not matter whether that unfairness was the result of the decision of the tribunal itself to continue with the case or whether it was the result of some failure in the method by which the claimant was supposed to be given notice and for which the tribunal itself had no direct responsibility. The essential matter is that the decision under appeal was reached without the tribunal hearing the claimant and without if having any of the permissible grounds for not hearing her."

In *C5/05-06 (IB)*, a Commissioner in Northern Ireland set aside the decision of a tribunal where the claimant had asked for an oral hearing but did not attend. The claimant subsequently indicated that he had not received notification of the hearing, nor had his solicitors. The Commissioner, following *CDLA/5413/1999*, appears to consider that in such circumstances there had been a breach of Article 6.

Support for this view can now be found in the Strasbourg case law. In *Elo v Finland* (App. 30742/02) the Court of Human Rights was considering a complaint that the lack of an oral hearing before an Accident Board whose task was to determine the level of disability following an accident at work. The Court found no breach of Article 6. It stated the general proposition,

"... unless there are exceptional circumstances that justify dispensing with a hearing, the right to a public hearing under Article 6(1) implies a right to an oral hearing at least before one instance." (para.34).

(1998 c.42, Sch.1)

The Court went on:

"36. The Court reiterates that the character of the circumstances that may justify dispensing with an oral hearing essentially comes down to the nature of the issues to be decided by the competent national court not to the frequency with which such issues come before the courts. This does not mean that refusing to hold an oral hearing may be justified only in rare cases (see *Miller v Sweden*, No. 55853/00, § 29, 8 February 2005). Thus, the Court has recognised that disputes concerning benefits under social-security schemes are generally rather technical and their outcome usually depends on the written opinions given by medical doctors. Many such disputes may accordingly be better dealt with in writing than in oral argument. Moreover, it is understandable that in this sphere the national authorities should have regard to the demands of efficiency and economy. Systematically holding hearings could be an obstacle to the particular diligence required in social-security cases (see *Schuler-Zgraggen v Switzerland*, cited above, pp. 19–20, § 58).

37. Turning to the particular circumstances of the present case, the Court observes that the jurisdiction of the Accident Board and the Insurance Court was not limited to matters of law but also extended to factual issues. The issue before them was whether the applicant's injuries attained the category 7 disability on the scale of injuries and whether his injuries could have been assessed under the general title "the lower extremities as a whole" as alleged by the applicant. The question is whether hearing oral evidence from the applicant and the doctors treating him could have produced anything relevant and decisive which was not already encompassed in the written evidence and submissions. The Accident Board found an oral hearing manifestly unnecessary. Nor did the Insurance Court find an oral hearing necessary as the decisive factor for reaching a decision in the applicant's case was the medical opinions on the applicant's injuries.

38. The Court observes that under the Ministry's decision the personal circumstances of a claimant are not taken into account when assessing the disability category to be attributed. Thus the Accident's Board's and Insurance Court's assessments were entirely based on the medical evidence in the case, presented in the form of written medical certificates issued by the applicant's doctors. The medical certificates on which the applicant relied supported his claim. It does not appear that the doctors' opinions differed (see, *mutatis mutandis*, *Döry v Sweden*, cited above, § 42). The Court sees no reason to differ from the finding of the Insurance Court that the applicant's entitlement to compensation had to be based on the evaluation of the injuries sustained to his heels and ankles, which assessment could be made on the basis of the written medical evidence. Further, there is no indication that a hearing was needed in order to hear oral testimony (see *Ringel v Sweden* (dec.), No. 13599/03, 23 March 2004).

39. In these circumstances, it must be concluded that the dispute in the case concerned the correct interpretation of written medical evidence. The Court considers that the Accident Board and the Insurance Court could adequately resolve this issue on the basis of the medical certificates before them and the applicant's written submissions.

40. Having regard to the foregoing, the Court finds that there were circumstances which justified dispensing with a hearing in the applicant's case."

It will also be important to ensure that the requirements implicit in "égalité des armes" are always met; this will mean that the claimant always has the opportunity to respond to the case put forward on behalf of the Secretary of State, and that new evidence is not put before the tribunal at such a late stage that the claimant has no opportunity to comment upon it.

It has long been held that a tribunal must give both sides the opportunity to consider authorities raised by the other side, and, where the introduction of a new and key authority is introduced at a late stage, to consider an adjournment to enable the significance of the authority to be fully considered in the argument put to the tribunal. That requirement flowed from the requirements of natural justice. A case relating to the employment tribunals now makes the same point in relation to the requirements for a fair hearing under Article 6: see *Sheridan v Stanley Cole (Wainfleet) Ltd*, [2003] EWCA Civ 1046. The Court of Appeal stresses that the relevant authority must have a central role in shaping the decision for the requirement to bite. It had to have altered or affected the way the issues had been addressed to a significant extent. Again the notion of the fair-minded observer is called into play in that the authority will have had a major effect on the proceedings if a fair-minded observer would say that the case had been decided in a way which could not have been anticipated by a party fixed with such knowledge of the law and procedure as it would be reasonable to attribute to that party in all the circumstances.

It is possible that a claimant might take issue with the composition of a tribunal in which there is no guarantee that, for example, a medically qualified panel member is not also a member of the panel of examining medical practitioners used by the Benefits Agency. There would clearly be a breach of natural justice (and a violation of Art.6(1)) if a doctor who had examined a claimant sat on the tribunal which heard the appeal, but it is clear that this would be obvious from the papers and that the normal expectation is that the doctor would not sit. The requirement that an applicant must exhaust all domestic remedies before complaining of a breach of the Convention would mean that an applicant would need to pursue an appeal to the Social Security Commissioner, who would, in the face of the circumstances described, have no hesitation in setting the tribunal decision aside for breach of natural justice and remitting the case for an oral hearing before a properly constituted tribunal. In this way, a remedy would be provided for the breach of Art.6 in the domestic courts. However, where the objection related to the *possibility* of inclusion of a doctor on the tribunal who also conducted examinations for the Benefits Agency, it is difficult to see how a remedy could be provided by the tribunal. A claimant might find little sympathy given to the argument that he or she has no complaint about the impartiality of the specific member of the tribunal, but objects that a medical member might also be an examining medical practitioner for the Benefits Agency. There is something slightly odd about a tribunal holding in the abstract that it is not an independent and impartial tribunal. For this reason, it may well be that judicial review would be the proper route to raise such a challenge, although to be a victim for the purposes of the Convention, the claimant would of necessity also have an appeal to the tribunal.

4.62 The most significant decision applying Art.6 to tribunal practice and procedure is the decision of the Tribunal of Commissioners in *CSDLA/1019/1999*, (the *Gillies* case—reversed in the Court of Session, whose decision was upheld in the House of Lords, reported as *R(DLA) 5/06*) in which the practice of medical members of the tribunal also on occasion holding office as examining medical practitioners for the Department, though ultimately the decision is based upon common law tests of bias applying in Scotland. There is an indication that the present law in England and Wales would produce the same outcome. The decision of the Tribunal of Commissioners is that the presence on an appeal tribunal of a medical member of a disability appeal tribunal who regularly undertook work as an examining medical practitioner could give rise to a reasonable apprehension of bias on the part of an objective third party. This would taint the independence and impartiality of a tribunal on which that medical member sat.

In *CSDLA/91/2003* a Scottish Commissioner considered an argument that "the presence of an EMP on the tribunal compromised the appearance of independence of the tribunal." The Commissioner says,

> "12. What was struck down in the *Gillies* case, was a situation where a medical member sitting on a tribunal is also an EMP and where the report of another EMP was part of the evidence in the case. As the Tribunal said, what raises objective bias is the concern that an EMP member of a tribunal (see paragraph 80 of *CSDLA/1019/1999*:—
>
>> '. . . because of the substantial current involvement in the same role as the reporting doctor, may start with an inclination to accept that evidence rather than objectively viewing the competing version.'

13. The Tribunal of Commissioners gave no support to an argument that EMPs are intrinsically not independent of the Department. The Tribunal did not therefore suggest that the mere presence on a tribunal of an EMP as a member compromised the appearance of the independence of a tribunal. I disagree with what is said at page 732 of Volume III of the Social Security Legislation 2002:—

> 'The decision of the Tribunal of Commissioners is that the presence on an appeal tribunal of a medical member of a disability appeal tribunal who regularlay undertook work as an examining medical practitioner could give rise to a reasonable apprehension of bias on the part of an objective third party. That would taint the independence and impartiality of a tribunal on which that medical member sat.' "

It is quite correct that the detailed factual circumstances presented in *CSDLA/ 1019/1999* are as stated by the Commissioner; it is suggested, however, that the Commissioner's reading of the implications of the case is too narrow. It is at least arguable that *CSDLA/1019/1999* can be read as authority for the proposition cited (especially when the decision is read against the background of the approach of the Strasbourg organs to issues of bias). It is argued that it is difficult to see why objective bias might be present only where the report of another examining medical practitioner is before the tribunal. The reasonable apprehension of bias results from the presence on the tribunal of medical members who regularly provide reports for one of the parties to the proceedings. That seems to be intrinsic to the reasoning of the Tribunal in *CSDLA/1019/1999*. The Scottish Commissioner concludes,

> "14. In this appeal, there was no report by an EMP for consideration by the tribunal. Therefore, the presence on the tribunal of an EMP and the fact that, because this was a paper hearing the point could not be put to the claimant, is irrelevant. No issue arose of the member starting off with a prejudice in favour of any particular type of evidence which was before the tribunal."

The last sentence would seem to get close to confusing the distinction between subjective and objective bias which is at the heart of the Strasbourg approach to independence and impartiality under Art.6 ECHR. Subjective bias would be present where an issue arose as to a member "starting off with a prejudice in favour of any type of evidence", whereas objective bias would arise if there was the reasonable prospect of an impartial observer concluding that there *might* be bias in such circumstances (for the decision of the House of Lords upholding the Court of Session reversing *CSDLA/1019/1999* (*Gillies*) see below.)

Leave to appeal to the Court of Appeal was granted but not pursued in respect of *CI/4421/2000*, in which the Commissioner observes, having regard to various ways in which the Secretary of State might become involved in an appeal, "Taken together, those factors form a strong case that the appeal tribunal might appear not to be independent from the Secretary of State." (para.32.)

The formulation of the test of bias in United Kingdom law has been changed to take account of the case law of the European Court of Human Rights by the Court of Appeal in *Re Medicaments and Related Classes of Goods (No.2)* [2001] 1 W.L.R. 700. The key passage reads,

> "When the Strasbourg jurisprudence is taken into account, we believe that a modest adjustment of the test in *R v Gough* is called for, which makes it plain that it is, in effect, no different from the test applied in most of the Commonwealth and in Scotland. The court must first ascertain all the circumstances which have a bearing on the suggestion that the judge was biased. It must then ask itself whether those circumstances would lead a fair-minded and informed observer to conclude that there was a real possibility, or a real danger, the two being the same, that the tribunal was biased." (at 726–7.)

This formulation of the test of bias has now been approved by the House of Lords in *Magill v Weeks; Magill v Porter*, judgment of July 8, 2002, [2002] H.R.L.R. 16.

CI/5880/1999 and the Northern Ireland Tribunal of Commissioners' decision in *C28/001–01 (IB)(T)* establish that Art.6 of the European Convention does not require more in the way of reasons for decisions than well-established principles established over the year in Commissioners' decisions.

The discussion of bias has been advanced with the decision of the House of Lords in *Lawal v Northern Spirit Ltd*, [2003] UKHL 35, judgment of June 19, 2003. The House of Lords was considering the "systemic issue" of possible objective bias under a system which permitted counsel appointed as part-time judges of the Employment Appeal Tribunal (EAT) to appear on appeals before that court. Though the opinion of the House of Lords is couched very much in the context of the system of adjudication in employment cases, the broad approach is of more general application stressing the "indispensable requirement of public confidence in the administration of justice" which "requires higher standards today than was the case even a decade or two ago." (para.22.) The House of Lords re-affirms the test of bias set out in *Porter v Magill*: "The question is whether the fair-minded and informed observer, having considered the facts, would conclude that there was a real possibility that the tribunal was biased" The House of Lords says that it is unnecessary to delve into the characteristics to be attributed to the fair-minded and informed observer save that such an observe "will adopt a balanced approach." The conclusion is that the practice of permitting counsel appointed as part-time judges of the EAT to appear before it should be discontinued.

This more robust approach to the issue of objective bias is certain to influence developments in social security adjudication.

The House of Lords has upheld the decision of the Court of Session reversing the decision of the Tribunal of Commissioners in *Gillies v Secretary of State for Work and Pensions* [2006] UKHL 2. The Court of Session had concluded:

> "Having considered the factual circumstances we are of the view that the fact that Dr A. carried out examinations and provided reports for the Benefits Agency as an EMP would not be sufficient to raise in the mind of a reasonable and well-informed observed an apprehension as to his or her impartiality as a member of a disability appeal tribunal. The mere fact that the tribunal would require to consider and assess report of other doctors who acted as EMPs would not be such as to raise such an apprehension." (para.38.)

In coming to this decision, the Court of Session considered the decision of the House of Lords in *Lawal v Northern Spirit Ltd*, but appears to have distinguished it on the grounds that the circumstances before the House of Lords were that, in the Employment Appeal Tribunal, lay members "look to the judge for guidance on the law and can be expected to develop a fairly close relationship of trust and confidence with the judge". The Court of Session did not consider that the case before them involved any likelihood of deference, there being "no relationship of law to professional or of subordinate to superior" (para.37). The Court of Session appear to accept that the Tribunal of Commissioners identified the right test, but applied it incorrectly—and this constituted an error of law. The Court of Session took a different view on the application of the test; they were influenced by the argument that, taken too widely, an objection could be based simply on membership of a particular professional body: did pointing to a subset of certain professionals involve a distinction with real difference?

This leaves the authorities on bias in something of any unsatisfactory state. *Lawal v Northern Spirit Limited* would appear to be more in tune with the Strasbourg authorities in its approach to the issue of the possible perception of bias. It takes a broader view of the notion of the objective bystander; *Gillies* make distinctions which would probably be lost on the objective bystander. However, support for the approach adopted by the Court of Session can be found in the decision of the Administrative Court in *R. (on the application of PD) v Merseyside Care NHS Trust* [2003] EWHC 2469. This case concerned the possibility of objective bias resulting from the presence on a mental health review tribunal of a consultant psychiatrist employed by the health authority in a case where that authority had detained the patient. The consultant psychiatrist had had no contact with the patient or with the detaining hospital. There was absolutely no question of his having been *actually* biased. The Administrative Court considered that there were adequate safeguards to avoid any objective bystander apprehending the possibility of bias. The issue is not whether a professional is able to retain his or her independence in a particular set of circumstances, but whether an objective and fair-minded observer would be satisfied as to the independence and impartiality of that decision maker. The Administrative Court appears to have been partly influenced by the potential problems of finding a sufficient number of consultant psychiatrists to serve on the tribunals if consultant psychiatrists employed by the NHS Trust which had detained the patient whose appeal was being heard were excluded. That may be a less pressing issue in relation to medical members of the appeal tribunals. The decision of the Administrative Court was upheld in the Court of Appeal in even more trenchant terms: [2004] EWCA Civ 311. It is questionable whether resourcing issues are a legitimate consideration under the Strasbourg case law which has always rejected arguments based on practicalities in Contracting Parties' fulfilling their obligations under Art.6 (for example, in relation to the giving of judgment with a reasonable time where arguments about shortage of judicial resources have been given short shrift: see *Hentrich v France*, (1994) 18 E.H.R.R. 440, para.61 of the judgment).

The decision of the House of Lords in the *Gillies* case is considered in detail in the commentary on s.14 of the Social Security Act 1998, and that detail is not repeated here. The decision of the House of Lords is perhaps remarkable for the absence of a detailed focus on Art.6 of the Convention, preferring to root its decision in UK authorities on bias. The test which is applied is that of the "fair-minded and informed observer" who is neither complacent nor unduly sensitive or suspicious, and who is able to distinguish between what is relevant and what is not, and to be able to determine what weight should be given to those matters which are relevant.

The House of Lords did not consider the decision of the Court of Session on bias and medical members in *Secretary of State for Work and Pensions v Cunningham*, Court of Session, August 6, 2004, reported as *R(DLA) 7/04*. The Deputy Commissioner had ruled that a situation might well have arisen of a reasonable apprehension of bias in circumstances where an examining medical practitioner had sat as the medical member of a tribunal with the chairman at 22 tribunal sessions, with the disability member at 14 tribunal sessions, and with both the chairman and the disability member at three tribunal sessions. The Court of Session agreed. The facts before the Deputy Commissioner were said by the Court of Session to be "readily distinguishable" from those which arose in *Gillies*.

Counsel for the Secretary of State, were the Court to go against him (as it did), asked for clarification as to how far the decision depended on the frequency with which the doctor had sat with the other members of the tribunal. The Court of Session declined to go further than the obvious point that it might have made a difference if the doctor had sat only once with the other members some considerable time before the case in issue.

CDLA/2379/2005 concerned a claim that there was bias which would constitute a violation of Article 6 where the doctor had sat with the chairman of the tribunal on three previous occasions in a two year period. The Commissioner concluded, with some reservations, that, though there was no actual bias, there was the perception of bias. He had resolved these in favour of setting aside the decision since the Court of Appeal in *Locabail* had indicated that doubts should be resolved in favour of recusal, or, as in this case, setting the decision aside.

In an unreported decision in *Secretary of State for Work and Pensions v McNab*, the Court of Session on March 20, 2007, by consent, allowed the Secretary of State's appeal against the decision in *CSDLA/0364/2005* insofar as the decision relates to the composition of the tribunal. The apparent effect of this decision is that, where there has only been one prior sitting of the tribunal chair or carer member with a medical member who is also an examining medical practitioner, there will be no appearance of bias in the absence of other circumstances.

In its admissibility decision of April 8, 2003 in *Wingrave v United Kingdom (App.40029/02)*, the Court of Human Rights had declared inadmissible part of the claim (relating (1) to a breach of contract claim, (2) to the requirement to make a new claim at age 65 for disability living allowance, and (3) concerning the quality of her representation) but adjourned the issue concerning the length of the proceedings. The appeal had been twice remitted for rehearing by the Commissioners and had taken nearly five years to conclude. The decision on the admissibility of that complaint was adjourned by the Court of Human Rights in its decision of April 8, 2003. By a decision of May 18, 2004, the Court of Human Rights has declared this aspect of the complaint admissible.

Part of the decision of the Tribunal of Commissioners in *CIB/3645/2002* concerned an argument that the absence of a right of appeal in the social security legislation contravened the claimant's rights under Art.6 of the Convention. The Tribunal of Commissioners decided the decision that the claimant was, on not permanently incapacitated for work at the time of leaving Great Britain for Jamaica concerned the payability of benefit while the claimant was in Jamaica rather his entitlement to the benefit. The decision was accordingly not within the scope of s.12(3) of the Social Security Act 1998. Furthermore Art.6 was not relevant because Art.6 had "no part to play in the ambit of substantive rights, as opposed to procedural rights." (para.43), since Art.13(2) of the Social Security (Jamaica) Order 1997 (SI 1997/871) provided a subjective test, under which the Secretary of State determined whether benefit was to continue to be payable abroad if he considered the claimant likely to be permanently incapacitated for work when leaving Great Britain.

The Tribunal of Commissioners indicates that it has not come to this decision lightly and adds a rider in para.54 of its decision:

"Finally, we should make clear that our decision is limited to the issues before us. On the basis of the decision of Mr Commissioner Howell Q.C. *in CIB/3654/2002* [this appears to be an erroneous reference, which should be to *CIS/540/2002*, now reported as *R(IS) 6/04*], it may be arguable that that the Human Rights Act and Art.6 of the European Convention may require rights of appeal to be granted against decisions under reciprocal agreement provisions in respect of which rights of appeal had existed previously. There may also be other cases in which it may be arguable that para.22 of Sch.2 of the Decisions and Appeals Regulations does not restrict certain rights of appeal without deciding whether the provision is ultra vires (as found in CIB/3586/2000 (starred decision 15/00)). We express no view on the correctness of those decisions."

The claimant is appealing to the Court of Appeal under the name *Campbell v Secretary of State for Work and Pensions*. The appeal was dismissed on July 28, 2005, [2005] EWCA Civ. 989.

The presence on the adjudicating panel of a member who has drunk alcohol over lunch and falls asleep during the afternoon sitting and demonstrably fails to concentrate on the proceedings will render the proceedings unfair: see *Stansby v Datapulse* [2003] EWCA Civ 1951, an employment tribunal case. Arguments in multi-panel courts or tribunals that bias on the part of one of the members might be overlooked because they can be outvoted by the remaining members will not be regarded as sound: *Lodwick v London Borough of Southwark* [2004] EWCA Civ 306, a case in which alleged bias on the part of one member of an employment tribunal was in issue.

The tribunals are structured in such a way that claimants can appear in person. It is unlikely that the significant evidence that represented claimants do better than unrepresented ones (Genn, H. and Genn, Y., *The Effectiveness of Representation at Tribunals*, (Lord Chancellor's Department, London, 1989)) would persuade the Court of Human Rights that proceedings before the tribunals were such that the State was obliged to provide legal assistance.

Perhaps the tribunals are most at risk of complaints that judgment has not been given in a reasonable time, particularly where an appeal to the Commissioner has resulted in the setting aside of the decision and the remission of the case for a fresh hearing. Current delays both before the tribunals and the Commissioners can result in four or more years passing before a final decision is made. This could in a simple case be regarded as excessive under Art.6, particularly if the case had lain dormant for some time either in the Commissioner's office after the papers were ready for determination, or within the appeals service awaiting listing for the rehearing. The existence of backlogs and excessive workloads on the judiciary are not accepted as justifications for unreasonable delays. The Court has consistently stated that the Contracting States must organise their judicial systems in such a way that their tribunals can meet the requirement to give judgment within a reasonable time (see, for example, *Massa v Italy*, judgment of August 24, 1993, Series A, No.265-B; (1994) 18 E.H.R.R. 266, para.28 of the judgment).

Two particular aspects of procedure before the Commissioner might be problematic. The first relates to entitlement to an oral hearing. The Social Security Commissioners Procedure Regulations 1999 provide that, where a request is made for a hearing, the Commissioner "shall grant the request unless he is satisfied that the application or appeal can properly be determined without a hearing" (reg.23(2)). Most appeals to the Commissioner are determined without a hearing, but many applications for a hearing are refused. The standard reasons simply repeat the words of the regulation. Many appeals are pursued before the Commissioner without the benefit of expert advice and assistance. Since the appeal to the Commissioner lies only on a point of law, the underlying argument is that an unrepresented appellant is unlikely to be able in oral argument to advice the position established by the exchange of written arguments between adjudication officer and appellant. There is a provision that a Commissioner can of his or her own motion direct an oral hearing (reg.23(4)). It would be conceivable that an appellant might try to argue that the presumption in the regulation has effectively been reversed in practice, and that an oral hearing will only be granted if the appellant can show reasons why there should be one.

A second exposure under Art.6 of the Convention could result from argument that legal assistance is necessary to enable a person to pursue an appeal effectively before the Commissioner. For a case brought before the Strasbourg Court on the issue of judgment in a reasonable time in relation to a claim for a disability living allowance which was twice appealed to the Commissioners and which was found to be manifestly ill-founded, see *Wingrave v United Kingdom*, (App.40029/02), admissibility decisions at April 8, 2003 and May 18, 2004. The arguments that would be advanced by the appellant would be that the jurisdiction of the Social Security Commissioners is described by themselves as broadly equivalent to an appeal to the High Court and is available only on points of law. Furthermore, social security law is of great complexity and specialist assistance is needed to construct and argue legal points involved in appeals. The countervailing arguments would, no doubt, be that the Commissioners adopt an inquisitorial approach to the file, and considerable preparatory work is undertaken by legal officers to ensure that the file is complete before it is placed before a Commissioner for determination of the appeal. There is force in both arguments. Which would prevail if the matter came before the Court of Human Rights is hard to predict.

In *CDLA/1761/2002* the claimant raised an Art.6 issue in relation to the delay (of about six months) in producing the written statement of reasons for the tribunal's decision. The Commissioner did not need to address the argument in full, but rightly notes that Art.6 is concerned with the overall length of the proceedings and not with delays in relation to specific parts of the process.

CJSA/5100/2001 was an overpayments case. The claimant argued that a witness the Secretary of State intended to have give evidence at the tribunal (but who declined to attend) would not have been able to identify his wife as the person who had undertaken remunerative work. No further attempts were made to secure this evidence. In remitting the case for a rehearing, the Commissioner indicates that the language of "equality of arms" under the case law of the Court of Human Rights may be more helpful than the language of natural justice in ensuring fairness between the parties in a tribunal hearing:

> "5. I chose to explain my decision in terms of the claimant's Convention right to a fair hearing under Article 6(1) of the European Convention on Human Rights and Fundamental Freedoms. In particular, I rely on the equality of arms principle that has been developed in the jurisprudence of the Strasbourg authorities as part of that right. It requires that the procedure followed by the tribunal must strike a fair balance between the parties so that none is at a disadvantage as against the others: see paragraph 33 of the judgment of the ECHR in *Dombo Beheer BV v The Netherlands* (1993) 18 EHRR 213.
>
> 6. I could, no doubt, have reached the same conclusion under domestic principles of natural justice. However, the Human Rights Act 1998 provides a convenient opportunity for Commissioners to rebase their decisions on procedural fairness in fresh terms. In my view, this would be desirable. I am sure that tribunals are familiar with the principles of natural justice. However, increasingly the cases that come before me suggest that they are not applying them. If there is a common theme in those cases, it is that the tribunal had not provided a procedural balance between the parties. The introduction of the language of balance would provide a touchstone for tribunals.
>
> 7. I detect at least three factors that have contributed to the trend that I have observed. One factor is that the language of natural justice may have become stale to tribunals from over familiarity. A second factor is that the time between an appeal being lodged and being heard is now much shorter than it was. That will often be to the claimant's advantage. However, it is not an advantage if a claimant does not have time to prepare a case. The final factor, for which there is clear evidence across all regions of the Appeals Service, is the concern to avoid adjournments. This has led some tribunals to take an approach to hearings that is robust at the expense of fairness.
>
> 8. The new language would help to counter any staleness with the traditional language of natural justice. That language is the language of procedural fairness. There is nothing wrong with that. But it has led to an emphasis on the disposal of the case, with less concern than is appropriate on the procedure. The language of balance would provide criteria by which appropriate cases for adjournments could be identified and distinguished from inappropriate cases.
>
> 9. There are decisions on which this new approach could be built. I have used the language of equality of arms and balance when dealing with adjournments to allow a claimant to obtain medical evidence (*CIB/3427/2001*) and with the provision of evidence by the Secretary of State relating to earlier personal capability assessments (*CIB/3985/2001*). And Mr Commissioner Williams has used the same language when dealing with deemed notice provisions and the exercise of discretions (*CDLA/5413/1999*)."

In *CJSA/5101/2001* the Commissioner concluded (relying on the Court of Human Rights decision in the *Airey* case: see para.4.60 above) that Art.6 does not give any automatic entitlement to legal representation, though particular circumstances may result in the need for legal representation if there is to be a fair trial.

Article 6 does not require an appeal to the tribunal if there is another recognised remedy, such as judicial review, which provides the opportunity for a fair trial involving the determination of a person's civil rights and obligations: *CF/3565/2001*, paras 11–15.

CDLA/3432/2001 involved a challenge to the rules in regs 31 and 32 of the Social Security Commissioners Procedure Regulations limiting the grounds on which a Commissioner could set aside a decision of a Commissioner as being an interference with the rights in Art.6. The Commissioner rightly give such arguments short shrift, noting that they contribute to the rights enshrined in Art.6.

In *R. (on the application of Wall) v The Appeals Service and Benefits Agency* [2003] EWHC 465 Admin, the applicant raised three objections that proceedings before a tribunal had breached the requirements of Art.6. First, no or no sufficient reasons had been given for the tribunal's decision. Secondly, there was no oral hearing. Thirdly, the District Chairman who had heard his appeal had previously been involved in other decisions concerning the applicant's case. All three objections were dismissed. The first and second were rejected because Art.6 does not require that there is an oral hearing in every case, and that there were appropriate safeguards in striking out cases (this was such a case). In relation to the third objection, the Court observes that there needs to be something more than the mere involvement of a judge in a latter case where they have been involved in an earlier case in order to establish a lack of impartiality for Art.6 to be breached.

It is clear that a judicial process in social security decision-making which constitute bargaining with the claimant will not meet the requirements of a fair hearing under Art.6. As an illustration, see *CSDLA/606/2003* where the tribunal's record of proceedings tells it all,

Parties introduced.

Offer put to the appellant just to reinstate higher mobility

Told to think about it. 10 mins.

Put to appellant risk of losing all if goes ahead.

Told to think again. 5 mins later.

Has decided will accept offer (reproduced in para.7 of Commissioner's decision).

The Social Security Act 1998

A number of aspects of the Social Security Act 1998 would appear to leave open the possibility of challenge for compatibility with Convention rights.

One of the great achievements of the Office of the President of Social Security Appeal Tribunals (OPSSAT) and its successor, the Independent Tribunal Service (ITS), has been to emphasise the independence of the tribunals hearing appeals by claimants against decisions of adjudication officers in the Department of Social Security. That success has dramatically increased respect for the tribunals. Certain provisions of the Social Security Act 1998 at best undermine that independence, and at worst may leave the structure exposed to challenges under the Convention as not constituting independent and impartial tribunals. New "unified appeal tribunals" have replaced the tribunals which formed part of the ITS, which is itself abolished. Appointment to the panels is happily not a matter for the Secretary of State, but for the Lord Chancellor (or Lord Advocate in Scotland), though s.6 provides that the number of appointments and their terms and conditions are subject to the consent of the Secretary of State. Appeal tribunals may consist of one, two or three members and the requirements for a lawyer chairman of the tribunals goes.

The authority of the new tribunals is, however, undermined by the provision that the Secretary of State may supersede any decision of a tribunal or of a Social Security Commissioner (s.11(1)). That power is subject to provisions of the Decisions and Appeals Regulations, which broadly limit the exercise of the power to situations where there is a change of circumstances or new evidence comes to light. Formerly such limitations appeared in the primary legislation (s.35, Social Security Administration Act 1992), and it is disturbing to see that this practice has been discontinued.

Section 13(3) contains a bizarre provision (see commentary on it in this volume), which raises interesting questions about the relationship between the parties and the

4.63

tribunal, but, for the reasons set out in the commentary to the provision, it is unlikely to have real significance.

Section 26 would appear to be objectionable in that it enables the Secretary of State who is one of the parties to the dispute to direct the tribunal on the determination of the appeal. Such a provision must result in the tribunal not being independent and impartial, since it is a characteristic of an independent and impartial tribunal that it is not susceptible to instructions concerning the exercise of its judicial function (*Ettl v Austria*, judgment of April 23, 1987, Series A, No.117; (1988) 10 E.H.R.R. 255, para.38 of the judgment).

The Council on Tribunals has suggested that the proposed new structure for the tribunals could resemble the unsatisfactory system which was abandoned many years ago, and has suggested that the new arrangements are a cause for concern (*Annual Report of the Council on Tribunals for 1996/97*, (1997–98) H.C. 376). There may, accordingly, be challenges to the compatibility of the new structure with the requirement that tribunals are independent and impartial. The Secretary of State, who is a party to proceedings before the tribunals is also the paymaster and, in certain circumstances, is able to overrule their decisions. Their independence certainly appears less clear cut than that of their predecessors, which may well also be relevant were the matter to be considered by the Court of Human Rights.

The issue which faced the Tribunal of Commissioners in *R(IS)15/04* was whether there is a right of appeal against a decision taken by the Secretary of State not to revise a previous decision under reg.3(5)(a) of the Decisions and Appeal Regulations. The parties accepted that there was no such right under the provisions of national law, so the issue was whether one or more provisions of the European Convention required that there be such an appeal. An argument based on Art.6 failed. The Tribunal of Commissioners accepted that a decision whether or not to revise was a determination of a claimant's civil rights and obligations within Art.6, but that the process of judicial review taken together with the right to an appeal in relation to the original decision produced a situation in which there was no denial of access to a court. The alternative argument was based on Art.14 ECHR where the comparator was a person whom was within the scope of the Decisions and Appeal Regulations governing housing benefit and council tax benefit. Such a claimant, it was argued, would have a right of appeal. The Tribunal of Commissioners concluded that there was no right of appeal for a person in comparable circumstances under the housing benefit regime. Hence the claim to discrimination was not sustained.

Criminal charges

4.64 A question arises as to whether determinations of the Commissioners under the Forfeiture Act of 1982, of proceedings for penalty additions to overpayments under the Social Security Administration (Fraud) Act 1997, and of possible penalty proceedings under the Tax Credits Act 1999 constitute the determination of criminal charges under Art.6 and so attract the additional protections for such matters in the article. Though these matters are largely outside the ambit of these volumes, it may be helpful to express a view on this question.

The concept of a criminal charge is an autonomous one under the Convention, and so it is not the classification of the matter under national law which is determinative of the issue. National classification is not, however, wholly irrelevant since the Strasbourg organs have always regarded as a criminal charge something so considered by national law.

In other cases the following factors have been taken into account in making the determination: the nature of the "offence", the severity of the sanction imposed having regard in particular to any loss of liberty since this is a principal characteristic of criminal liability: see *Engel v The Netherlands*, judgment of June 8, 1976; Series A, No.22; (1979–80) 1 E.H.R.R. 647. Having regard to this case and to the judgment of the Court in *Ravnsborg v Sweden* (judgment of March 23, 1994, Series A, No.283-B; (1994) 18 E.H.R.R. 38), it is argued that such proceedings would not constitute the determination of a criminal charge. The essence of the penalty provision is civil rather than criminal in nature.

Article 7—No punishment without law

1. No one shall be held guilty of any criminal offence on account of any act or omission which did not constitute a criminal offence under national or international law at the time when it was committed. Nor shall a heavier penalty be imposed than the one that was applicable at the time the criminal offence was committed.

2. This Article shall not prejudice the trial and punishment of any person for any act or omission which, at the time when it was committed, was criminal according to the general principles of law recognised by civilised nations.

Article 8—Right to respect for private and family life

1. Everyone has the right to respect for his private and family life, his home and his correspondence.

2. There shall be no interference by a public authority with the exercise of this right except such as is in accordance with the law and is necessary in a democratic society in the interests of national security, public safety or the economic well-being of the country, for the prevention of disorder or crime, for the protection of health or morals, or for the protection of the rights and freedoms of others.

GENERAL NOTE

Introduction

Article 8 is one of the most open-ended provisions of the Convention and is not yet fully developed in its scope. The concept of private life is very wide and not easily contained within a single comprehensive definition. The article has encompassed such diverse matters as the interception of communications, various forms of surveillance, the collection and retention of personal data, the protection of the physical integrity of the individual, the preservation of family ties, harassment and nuisance affecting the home, and environmental protection. Like the series of articles which follows, the rights given in para.(1) are limited by the exceptions listed in para.(2). If there is an interference with one of the rights protected in the first paragraph, then it will be necessary to see whether this is justified under the limitations in the second paragraph. Here the Strasbourg organs have consistently required the interference to be (1) for one of the specified reasons; (2) in accordance with law; (3) necessary in a democratic society; and (4) proportionate in the sense that there is no other way of protecting the recognised interest which constitutes a lesser interference with the right.

Benefit and family life

Article 8 of the Convention guarantees respect, among other things, for family life, subject to the limitation contained in the article. Family life encompasses ties between near relatives, which certainly extends to children, parents and grandparents, though it is unclear how far it includes relationships between siblings, aunts and uncles. In general the Strasbourg organs have preferred relationships in the vertical line to those in the horizontal line.

In the *CG v Austia* (1737/90) case (the judgment is discussed in detail below), the applicant had complained that the refusal to award him the emergency assistance requested violated respect for his family life (presumably on the grounds that refusal of the assistance threatened the break up of, or hardship to, his family); the admissibility decision is not specific on the basis for declaring this part of his complaint admissible (see (1994) 18 E.H.R.R. CD51). Neither the Commission nor the Court found it necessary to consider this aspect of the complaint since they concluded that there was a violation of Art.14 read in conjunction with Art.1 of Protocol 1. Nevertheless, it remains open for the limits of the protection under Art.8 to be explored in the context of entitlements to social security. But it would be fair to say that there are few indications that the Strasbourg organs regard the Convention right here as including an obligation on the State to make payments to families for their support.

The Commission has held that there was no hindrance to family life where a wife was obliged to pay insurance contributions for her husband who was a house-husband, even though husbands did not have to pay contributions in respect of housewives. Since the matter could not be brought within Art.8, the question of discrimination under Art.14 (see below) could not be considered.

In *CJSA/935/1999* the Commissioner made some *obiter* comments on the rights of transsexuals to respect for their identity. The issue had arisen in the context of a claim that the use of the national insurance number in a jobseeker's agreement enabled the claimant's gender at birth to be identified. The decision contains a useful overview of some leading decisions in this area both under European Community law and under the European Convention on Human Rights.

For the latest summary of the position of transsexuals in the light of recent decisions of the Strasbourg Court, see the opinions of the House of Lords in *Bellinger v Bellinger* [2003] UKHL 21 (April 10, 2003).

But note the decision of the Court of Human Rights in *Grant v United Kingdom (App. 32570/03),* Judgment of May 23, 2006, which concerned a male-to-female transsexual who had been refused a pension on reaching the age of 60. Initial failures to secure the pension before reaching the age of 65 were re-opened following the grant of a gender recognition certificate under the Gender Recognition Act 2004. Grant succeeded in securing a judgment that the United Kingdom was in breach of Art.8 E.C.H.R. from July 2002 when the Court of Human Rights handed down its decision in *Goodwin v United Kingdom* (2002) 35 E.H.R.R. 447.

In *R(DLA) 4/02* the claimant argued that covert filming of the claimant in public places by the Department violated her Convention rights under Art.8. The Commissioner did not agree having regard to the balance which had to be struck between the interests of the individual and those of the community as a whole. In claiming benefit, the claimant had necessarily accepted a degree of interference with her private life. The covert filming had been limited to activities in public and was brief. The information gathered was used only for the purposes of considering the claimant's continuing entitlement to the benefit she had claimed.

It is clear from the decision of the Court of Appeal and House of Lords in *R. (on the application of Hooper, Withey, Naylor and Martin) v Secretary of State for Work and Pensions,* [2003] EWCA Civ 813, and [2005] UKHL 29, that benefits for widows and widowers fall within the ambit of Art.8. However, income support and income-based jobseeker's allowance schemes do not, according to the Court of Appeal, *per se* engage Art.8: see *Carson and Reynolds v The Secretary of State for Work and Pensions,* [2003] EWCA Civ 797.

Some helpful guidance on the application of Art.8 to covert filming is provided by the decision of the Employment Appeal Tribunal in *XXX v YYY and ZZZ,* April 9, 2003, EAT/0729 and EAT/0413/02. The issue before the employment tribunal related to claims of sex discrimination and victimisation by a nanny, who had been involved in a consensual sexual relationship with the father of the child for whom she was employed to care, which had broken down. The nanny made a covert video recording of events one morning involving herself and the father in the presence of the child; the recording depicts sexual advances made by the father to the nanny. The issue concerned the admissibility of this recording in the proceedings. The EAT was particularly concerned with the rights of the child under Art.8 of the Convention, but also recognised that Art.6 ECHR also came into play in that the applicant (the nanny) was arguing that the admission of the video recording was essential for her to be guaranteed a fair trial under that article. The guidance given by the EAT incorporates the guidance which had been contained in the judgment of the Court of Appeal in *Jones v University of Warwick* [2003] 1 W.L.R. 954, as follows:

"26. Mr Weir [Counsel for the Claimant] argues that unless it was *necessary* for the insurers to take the actions they did, the evidence must inevitably, at least in a case such as this, be held inadmissible. He submits that otherwise the court would be contravening the duty that it is under, pursuant to s.6 of the Human

Rights Act not to contravene Art.8. While the court should not ignore the contravention of Art.8, to adopt Mr Weir's approach would fail to recognise that the contravention would still remain that of the insurer's enquiry agent and not that of the court. The court's obligation under s.6 of the Human Rights Act is to 'not itself act in a way which is incompatible with a convention right' (see *Venables v News Group Newspapers Ltd* [2001] 2 W.L.R. 1038 at P.1048/9 paras 24–27).

27. As the Strasbourg jurisprudence makes clear, the Convention does not decide what is to be the consequence of evidence being obtained in breach of Art.8 (see *Schenk v Switzerland* [1988] 13 E.H.R.R. 242 and *PG and JH v United Kingdom* application no. 44787/98 ([2002] Crim. L.R. 308 para.76). This is a matter, at least initially, for the domestic courts. Once the court has decided the order, which it should make in order to deal with the case justly, in accordance with the overriding objectives set out in Part 1.1 of the CPR in the exercise of its discretion under Part 32.1, then it is required or it is necessary for the court to make that order. Accordingly if the court could be said to have breached Art.8.1 by making the order which it has decided the law requires, it would be acting within Art.8.2 in doing so.

28. That leaves the issue as to how the court should exercise its discretion in the difficult situation confronting the district judge and Judge Harris. The court must try to give effect to what are here the two conflicting public interests. The weight to be attached to each will vary according to the circumstances. The significance of the evidence will differ as will the gravity of the breach of Art.8, according to the facts of the particular case. The decision will depend on all the circumstances. Here, the court cannot ignore the reality of the situation. This is not a case where the conduct of the defendant's insurers is so outrageous that the defence should be struck out. The case, therefore, has to be tried. It would be artificial and undesirable for the actual evidence, which is relevant and admissible, not to be placed before the judge who has the task of trying the case. We accept Mr Owen's [Counsel for the defendants] submission that to exclude the use of the evidence would create a wholly undesirable situation. Fresh medical experts would have to be instructed on both sides. Evidence which is relevant would have to be concealed from them, perhaps resulting in a misdiagnosis; and it would not be possible to cross-examine the claimant appropriately. For these reasons we do not consider it would be right to interfere with the Judge's decision not to exclude the evidence."

In *R. (Smith) v Secretary of State for Defence and Secretary of State for Work and Pensions* [2004] EWHC 1797 (Admin), Wilson J. held that respect for private life under Art.8 encompasses respect for a person's need for financial support "when under as well as over the age of 60". The case concerned an argument by an ex-wife that she was entitled to payment of that part of a pension which was subject to a pension sharing order below the age of 60 since the pension was so payable to her former husband. The judge held that the provisions governing the payment to the ex-wife of the pension at the age of 60 did not breach her rights under Art.8,

> "One cannot say that the impugned provision challenges the principle that the claimant needs financial support before as well as after the age of 60. In making the provision the state has decreed only that provision carved out of pension rights should not result in payment earlier than what is presently regarded, in the context of state provision, as normal pensionable age. In other words pension credits are conferred so as to address later, rather than earlier, need; and, because of the delay in payment suffered by some pension credit members, the real amount of their pension is correspondingly increased. The impugned provision does not derogate from the duty of the divorce court under [the matrimonial legislation] to have regard to a spouse's likely needs prior to the age of 60 in deciding what, of any, order to make for her or his benefit by way of financial provision or property adjustment in addition to the pension sharing order." (para.21(b).)

In *C1/05-06 (WB), C2/05-06 (WB),* and *C3/05-06 (WB),* a Commissioner in Northern Ireland concluded that an absolute three months time limit for claiming widow's benefit does not violate Article 8. She said,

"17. . . . . I am doubtful that the three month time limit for claiming a benefit can in any way be linked to or have a "meaningful connection" with an Article 8 right in the absence of any Article 14 discrimination. However, even if a link exists, it is too tenuous to be within the ambit of the right. The right is not to the benefit but to the respect set out in Article 8. The time limit in no way violates that respect."

The Social Security Administration (Fraud) Act 1997

4.69 Section 14 of the Social Security Administration (Fraud) Act 1997 adds a s.122(1A) to the Social Security Administration Act 1992 making it an offence for a person, without reasonable excuse, to fail to notify a change of circumstances, or, knowingly, to cause or allow another person to fail to notify a change of circumstances which is required to be notified to the Benefits Agency, where the person knows that the other person is required to notify the change. The effect of this provision is that a welfare rights adviser might commit an offence if a client provides information which would have an effect on the award of a benefit and indicates that this information has not been disclosed to the Benefits Agency. If the adviser gave clear advice that there was a duty to disclose the information to the Benefits Agency, that would probably constitute reasonable excuse for not then themselves notifying the information. The provision is designed to catch those likely to benefit from the failure to disclose, such as fraudulent landlords receiving housing benefit.

The conflict faced by the adviser is clear. It is between confidentiality and the proper administration of the social security benefits schemes. It is not difficult to imagine claimants complaining that disclosure of the confidential information by the adviser was a breach of their private life. They could argue by analogy with the surveillance cases under the Convention that there was an interference with private life under Art.8 which would then need to be tested against the permitted limitations in para.(2) of the article. It would follow that if the claimant is to be protected, so too should the adviser who is exposed to possible prosecution, though the adviser would probably avoid the commission of the offence by advising that disclosure should be made by the claimant. This would, it is argued, result in the adviser having reasonable excuse for not making the disclosure.

The 1997 Act also contains (as does s.3 of the Social Security Act 1998) provisions on the exchange of information by Government departments which might be open to challenge for similar reasons. But such challenges would be highly speculative and would require development of the law protecting private life beyond that which is currently recognised in the case law of the Court.

Article 9—Freedom of thought, conscience and religion

4.70 1. Everyone has the right to freedom of thought, conscience and religion; this right includes freedom to change his religion or belief and freedom, either alone or in community with others and in public or private, to manifest his religion or belief, in worship, teaching, practice and observance.

2. Freedom to manifest one's religion or beliefs shall be subject only to such limitations as are prescribed by law and are necessary in a democratic society in the interests of public safety, for the protection of public order, health or morals, or for the protection of the rights and freedoms of others.

GENERAL NOTE

4.71 Reliance on this article to avoid the normal requirements, for example, to pay national insurance contributions are most unlikely to succeed. The Commission has held that a Dutch system of old-age pension insurance, alleged to interfere with the religious duty of caring for old people, did not violate the article: App.1497/62, *Reformed Church of X v The Netherlands* (1962) 5 Y.B. 286; and App.2065/63, *X v The Netherlands* (1965) 8 Y.B. 266.

(1998 c.42, Sch.1)

Article 10—Freedom of expression

4.72

1. Everyone has the right to freedom of expression. This right shall include freedom to hold opinions and to receive and impart information and ideas without interference by public authority and regardless of frontiers. This Article shall not prevent States from requiring the licensing of broadcasting, television or cinema enterprises.

2. The exercise of these freedoms, since it carries with it duties and responsibilities, may be subject to such formalities, conditions, restrictions or penalties as are prescribed by law and are necessary in a democratic society, in the interests of national security, territorial integrity or public safety, for the prevention of disorder or crime, for the protection of health or morals, for the protection of the reputation or rights of others, for preventing the disclosure of information received in confidence, or for maintaining the authority and impartiality of the judiciary.

Article 11—Freedom of assembly and association

4.73

1. Everyone has the right to freedom of peaceful assembly and to freedom of association with others, including the right to form and to join trade unions for the protection of his interests.

2. No restrictions shall be placed on the exercise of these rights other than such as are prescribed by law and are necessary in a democratic society in the interests of national security or public safety, for the prevention of disorder or crime, for the protection of health or morals or for the protection of the rights and freedoms of others. This Article shall not prevent the imposition of lawful restrictions on the exercise of these rights by members of the armed forces, of the police or of the administration of the State.

Article 12—Right to marry

4.74

Men and women of marriageable age have the right to marry and to found a family, according to the national laws governing the exercise of this right.

Article 14—Prohibition of discrimination

4.75

The enjoyment of the rights and freedoms set forth in this Convention shall be secured without discrimination on any ground such as sex, race, colour, language, religion, political or other opinion, national or social origin, association with a national minority, property, birth or other status.

GENERAL NOTE

Introduction

4.76

Article 14 prohibits discrimination on the grounds of sex, race, colour, language, religion, political or other opinion, national or social origin, association with a national minority, property, birth or other status. However, the protection is only applicable to the enjoyment of the rights and freedoms set forth in the Convention. It is the linking of Art.14 with another article of the Convention which gives it substance. In order to have effect, it does not have to be shown that there is a violation of the substantive article, (see *CP/5084/2001*) merely that the alleged discrimination operates in a field which is covered by the protections afforded by those provisions. Indeed the practice of the Court has been to decline to consider Art.14 in conjunction with another article if they find a violation of the article on its face. The article is likely to be a fruitful source of complaint in social security cases. Following the admissibility decision of the Grand Chamber in the *Stec* case (*Stec v United Kingdom* (Apps 65731/01 and 65900/01), admissibility decision of September 5, 2005), which ruled that both contributory and non-contributory social security benefits fall within the ambit of Art.1 of Protocol 1, it will be easy for claimants to establish that any claimed discrimination in the operation of the conditions of entitlement for the benefit can be contested under Art.14.

On August 22, 2006, the Court of Human Rights handed down its judgments in *Pearson v United Kingdom*, and *Walker v United Kingdom*. In both cases, the Court followed its decision in *Stec*, in ruling that differential State pensionable ages, and a requirement for men to continue to make national insurance contributions must be regarded as pursing a legitimate aim and as being reasonably and objectively justified.

In *Barrow v United Kingdom* (App. 42735/02), Judgment of August 22, 2006, the Court of Human Rights has also followed the judgment of the Grand Chamber in *Stec* in finding that the change from incapacity benefit to State retirement pension for a woman at the age of 60, which results in her receiving less money than a man in a similar position, does not breach either Article 1 of Protocol 1, nor Article 14 when read together with Article 1 of Protocol 1.

The Strasbourg appreciation

4.77 Where Art.14 is considered, the Court of Human Rights asks itself whether there is a difference of treatment between two groups which may properly be compared on one of the grounds mentioned (and the list is not closed by reason of the last two words referring to "other status"). The question in then asked whether that difference of treatment pursues a legitimate aim. Finally, the Court considers whether the means employed are proportionate to the legitimate aim pursued. In making this judgment, due regard will be had to the State's margin of appreciation, which will vary depending on the circumstances of each case. Where the discrimination is based on sex, there is little room for a margin of appreciation, but where broader policy issues are under consideration (such as housing allocation policies to ensure a supply of housing for poorer people), the margin of appreciation will be wider (see *Gillow v United Kingdom*, judgment of November 24, 1986, Series A, No.109; (1989) 11 E.H.R.R. 335, para.66 of the judgment).

For guidance on the Strasbourg approach to consideration of cases involving claims of sex discrimination in entitlement to social security benefits, see *Stec v United Kingdom* (Apps 67531/01 and 65900/01) admissibility decision of September 5, 2005. But for the approach of United Kingdom courts, see *Carson and Reynolds* [2005] UKHL 37 discussed below.

The ground of differentiation

4.78 There is considerable debate as to whether Art.14, permits any ground of differentiation to be used to bring a case within Art.14 or whether ground of differentiation must relate to personal characteristics. An example of the former would be differential treatment based on place of residence, whereas an example of the latter would be differential treatment based on ethnic origin. The short answer to this question is that the Strasbourg organs have not determined the answer to this question definitively; it is one of the troublesome aspects of Art.14. However, there is no direct authority which provides that the ground of differentiation must be based on a personal characteristic. The better view, therefore, is that there is no formal requirement flowing from the Strasbourg case law which requires that the party seeking to show discrimination falling within Art.14 is based upon a personal characteristic: see *Stubbings v United Kingdom* (Apps 22083/93 and 22095/93); (1997) 23 E.H.R.R. 213, where the differential treatment related to the legal system's approach to providing a remedy for psychological harm resulting from child abuse and other types of actionable wrong; and *National & Provincial Building Society v United Kingdom* (Apps 21319/93, 21449/93 and 21675/93), (1998) 25 E.H.R.R. 127, which concerned recovery of tax paid under invalidated tax regulations. It will, however, be easier to establish a situation as falling within Art.14 where the ground of differentiation is a personal characteristic. It is probably also true that different treatment which is based other than on a personal characteristic may be easier for the State to justify.

Although there is conflict in the English authorities on this issue, the balance seems now to be in favour of interpreting 'other status' in the article as meaning a personal characteristic: see *R v Chief Constable of South Yorkshire Police, Ex p. LS and Ex p. Marper* [2004] UKHL 39, paras 48–9, followed in *Taylor v Lancashire County Council and Secretary of State for Environment Food and Rural Affairs as intervenor* [2005] EWCA Civ 284, para.49. The comparison is said to be 'to do with who people are, not what their problem is.'

In *Barber v Secretary of State for Work and Pensions* [2002] EWHC 1915 (Admin), it was suggested that the difference in treatment must be based on a personal characteristic. This can be contrasted with *Wandsworth LBC v Michalak* [2002] EWCA Civ 271, (which concerned the arrangements for the assignment of, and succession to, tenancies), which suggest that the difference need not be based on personal characteristics in the strict sense. *Barber* has been followed by the Commissioner in *CIS/3280/2001*, where the differential treatment arose in relation to persons in local authority residential accommodation and persons in private residential accommodation in relation to entitlement to a funeral payment. The Commissioner concluded that the claimant was not able to show any discrimination based on her "status" for the purposes of the application of Art.14. See also *CJSA/232/2003* in respect of which the Commissioner has granted leave to appeal to the Court of Appeal where a different Commissioner comes to the same conclusion in dismissing an appeal based on an argument that the standard rate of interest for calculating mortgage interest payments as part of housing costs in relation to entitlement to income support was discriminatory contrary to Art.8 when read with Article 14. The Commissioner accepted that entitlement to housing costs could bring the claimant within the scope of the rights protected by Art.8.

The opinions of the House of Lords in *Carson and Reynolds* [2005] UKHL 39, paras 13 and 53–4, confirmed the importance of identifying a personal characteristic, but also indicated that this is to be interpreted broadly so that it does not simply encompass something a person is born with. So in *Francis v Secretary of State for Work and Pensions* [2005] EWCA Civ 1303, reported as *R(IS)* 6/06 the Court of Appeal affirmed the need to identify a personal characteristic but indicated that this need not be immutable and can be the result of the exercise of choice.

The importance of the prohibition of discrimination in the enjoyment of the rights protected by the Convention has already been mentioned. Furthermore the *Gaygusuz* case provides a clear example of the application of the provision in a social security context. (*Gaygusuz v Austria* (1997) 23 E.H.R.R. 364.) The key issue in the case proved to be a simple one. Gaygusuz was a Turkish national who had worked in Austria. He had paid contributions under the Austrian social security scheme, but had experienced periods of unemployment and periods when he was unfit for work. He applied for an advance on his retirement pension as a form of emergency assistance, but was refused because he was not an Austrian national. His attempts to redress his grievance using domestic procedures were unsuccessful and he complained to the Commission that there had been a violation of a number of articles of the Convention. Among his complaints was a complaint of a violation of Art.14 taken in conjunction with Art.1 of Protocol 1. The first question was whether the substance of the claim was a matter covered by the protection of property in Art.1 of Protocol 1, since otherwise Art.14 could have no application. Ultimately the Court concluded that Article 1 of Protocol 1 was engaged. The discrimination here was blatant. Nationals had an entitlement, and non-nationals did not. It is difficult to see how such discrimination might be justified. The Austrian government argued that there was a special responsibility on a State to care for its own nationals, and there were certain exceptions to the nationality condition (which had not assisted Gaygusuz). Neither the Court nor the Commission was persuaded by these arguments. There had been a violation because there was discrimination within Art.14 which was not capable of objective and reasonable justification. See also to the same effect *Poirrez v France* (App.40892/98), (2005) 40 E.H.R.R. 2, ECHR.

See also *Okpisz v Germany* (App.59140/00) (2006) 42 E.H.R.R. 33 ECHR, for an example of a case where discrimination on grounds of nationality (in relation to entitlement to family benefits) could not be justified.

The coupling of Art.14 and 1 of Protocol 1 opens up the possibility for case law development of the principle of equality in social security entitlement, but note that, on the United Kingdom authorities, only contributory benefits have been held to constitute possessions under Article 1 of Protocol 1. The adjudicating authorities have already had to wrestle with issues of discrimination flowing from Community law under the equal treatment directives, but that has focused on discrimination between men and women. Community rights are also linked in some cases to worker status under Community law. By contrast, there are no such limitations in relation to equal treatment under Art.14. In the *Van Breedam* case (App.11577, *Van Breedam v Belgium* (1989) 62 D.R. 109) the Commission ruled inadmissible an application concerning liability to pay supplementary social security contributions where the discrimination alleged was between painters and sculptors on the one hand and writers and musicians on the other in relation to the treatment of royalties as a basis for levying contributions. Although the application was ruled inadmissible, the Commission does not appear to question the legitimacy of the comparative groups put forward by the applicant, since the grounds of their decision are that there was a legitimate reason for the difference of treatment.

In the *Krafft and Rougeot* case (App.11543/85, *Krafft and Rougeot v France* (1990) 65 D.R. 51) the calculation of judicial pensions in France was in issue, and again the Commission did not appear to question the legitimacy of comparing the treatment of those appointed to judicial office from private practice and those appointed from within the court service. Again the difference of treatment was found to have a legitimate basis.

The Court of Human Rights has declared admissible a complaint by a man that it is a breach of Art.14 read with Art.1 of Protocol 1 to require a man to pay national insurance contributions beyond the age of 60 when the liability of a woman ceases: *Walker v United Kingdom* (App.37212/02), Decision of March 16, 2004.

The Court of Human Rights has declared admissible a complaint by a man that the differences in state pensionable age between men and women breach Art.1 of Protocol 1 when read in conjunction with Art.14: *Pearson v United Kingdom* (App.8374/03), Decision of April 27, 2004.

The Court of Human Rights has also declared admissible a complaint by a woman that it is a breach of Art.14 read with Art.1 of Protocol 1 in that her entitlement to incapacity benefit ceases at the age of 60 whereas a man in the same situation would continue to receive incapacity benefit until the age of 65. The applicant receives less by way of state retirement pension, to which she became entitled at the age of 60, than she previously received by way of incapacity benefit: *Barrow v United Kingdom* (App.42735/02), Decision of April 27, 2004.

But in *Stec v United Kingdom* (Apps 65731/01 and 65900/01), Judgment of April 12, 2006, the Court of Human Rights concluded that there was no breach of the Convention flowing from the conditions of entitlement to the now largely obsolete reduced earnings allowance and retirement allowance. Those benefits were linked to the normal State pension age of 60 for a woman and 65 for a man. The effect was that women transferred to the lower retirement allowance at age 60. In other cases, the ground of complaint related to the date at which the rate of reduced earnings allowance was frozen which, it was argued, discriminated unlawfully between men and women.

Does Art.14 cover indirect discrimination?

4.79 In *CH/5125, 5126, 5128, 5129* and *5130/2002* the Commissioner addresses at paras 36–55 of his decision the question of whether Art.14 covers indirect as well as direct discrimination. Though he was able to decide the appeals without reference to this issue, he sets out his reasoning on this important practical issue. His reasoning is summed up as follows:

"54. My conclusions on the indirect discrimination argument are these. I respectfully agree with what Sir Richard Tucker said in *Barber*. There is no decision that actually and expressly accepts that indirect discrimination is covered by article 14. I find that surprising. The text books accept that indirect discrimination is covered and cite some cases in support. However, my analysis of *Marckx* and the *Belgian Linguistic Case (No.2)* show that the passages cited do not support the proposition. There are, though, comments in other authorities that do support Mr Goudie's argument, both in the Strasbourg jurisprudence (*McShane*) and in the domestic law (*Marper*). The principle underlying *Thlimmenos* also supports Mr Goudie. Finally, there is no reason in principle why article 14 should not apply to indirect discrimination as well as any other form of discrimination, whether direct, intentional, unintentional or any other form that can exist. Under the Strasbourg jurisprudence, Convention rights have to be interpreted dynamically in accordance with current circumstances. Those circumstances include the various forms in which discrimination occurs in practice and which are controlled by legislation."

The appeal to the Court of Appeal against this decision under the name of *Campbell v South Northamptonshire DC and the Secretary of State for Work and Pensions* [2004] EWCA Civ 409, was dismissed. Permission to appeal to the House of Lords was refused by the Court of Appeal.

In *Esfandiari* [2006] EWCA Civ 282, the Court of Appeal was of the view that an indirect discrimination claim under Art.14 should be treated with some care because the case law is limited in this area. The key test will be whether the effects on the disadvantaged group are disproportionately prejudicial. In *CP/518/2003*, however, the Commission said that if the issue of indirect discrimination arose in the context of discrimination of grounds of sex, the weighty reasons would be required in order to justify the differential treatment.

The Michalak test

What came to be known as the *Michalak* test, from its adoption by the Court of Appeal in *Wandsworth London Borough Council v Michalak*, [2003] 1 W.L.R. 617, was a distillation of the questions it was said that the Convention organs ask themselves when examining a complaint under Art.14 enunciated in S Grosz, J Beatson and P Duffy, *Human Rights. The 1998 Act and the European Convention* (London, 2000), para.C14–08. The original four questions were expanded to five:

4.80

(1) Do the facts fall within the ambit of one or more of the Convention rights?

(2) Was there a difference in treatment in respect of that right between the complainant and others put forward for comparison?

(3) If so, was the difference in treatment on one or more of the proscribed grounds under Art.14?

(4) Were those others in an analogous situation?

(5) Was the difference in treatment objectively justified in the sense that it had a legitimate aim and bore a reasonable relationship of proportionality to that aim?

However, the framework questions did not seem to work in every situation and in *Ghaidan v Godin-Mendoza* [2004] UKHL 30; [2004] 3 W.L.R. 113, Baroness Hale sounded a warning:

"... the *Michalak* questions are a useful tool of analysis but there is a considerable overlap between them: in particular between whether the situations to be compared were truly analogous, whether the difference in treatment was based on a proscribed ground and whether it had an objective justification. If the situations were not truly analogous it may be easier to conclude that the difference was based on something other than a proscribed ground. The reasons why their situations are analogous but their treatment different will be relevant to whether the treatment is objective justified. A rigidly formulaic approach is to be avoided". (para.134.)

Without offering an alternative test, Lord Hoffmann in his judgment in the House of Lords in *Carson and Reynolds* [2005] UKHL 37, paras 28–33 expresses reservations about the *Michalak* test, and does not apply it in coming to his conclusions on the claims of the applicants in the case.

The influence of the *Michalak* test must be regarded as in decline, though it will remain ' a useful tool of analysis' for some time. It is most helpful as a checklist of issues which frequently arise in cases involving the need to apply Art.14.

Benefits for widows and widowers

It should first be noted that arguments based upon Art.14 by those who are unmarried and who are seeking equal treatment with those who are, or have been,

4.81

1255

married seem destined for failure. In *Shackell v United Kingdom, (App.45851/99)*, Decision on admissibility of April 27, 2000, the Court confirmed that the situations of married partners and unmarried cohabitees are not analogous. The Court said,

"The Court accepts that there may well now be increased social acceptance of stable personal relationships outside the traditional notion of marriage. However, marriage remains an institution which is widely accepted as conferring a particular status on those who enter it. The situation of the applicant [a woman whose partner had died] is therefore not comparable to that of a widow."

The Court went on to say that any distinctions would also be capable of objective justification,

"The Court considers that the promotion of marriage, by way of limited benefits for surviving spouses, cannot be said to exceed the margin of appreciation afforded to the respondent Government."

The application was accordingly found to be manifestly ill-founded. The Commissioner in *R(G)1/04* follows this decision and *CG/1259/2002* in refusing to regard widows and the partners of deceased men as in a comparable situation for the purposes of entitlement to widow's benefits.

For a case arising under the war pensions legislation which include provision for an "unmarried dependant living as a spouse", see *Secretary of State for Defence v Hopkins* [2004] EWHC 299 (Admin).

4.81A A series of cases before the Court of Human Rights show the potential application of Art.14 in conjunction with Art.8 and Art.1 of Protocol 1 for changing the shape of social security provision. In App.365789/97, *Cornwell v United Kingdom* and App.38890/97, *Leary v United Kingdom,* two widowers complained that they were not entitled to benefits which would have been available to them had they been widows. The UK Government did not contest the admissibility of either case (save in relation to one of the periods in respect of which Cornwell complained): see admissibility decisions of May 11, 1999 in both cases. The cases have been struck out of the Court's list on a friendly settlement being reached. The Government indicated that it would pay the applicants, on an extra-statutory basis, the amounts to which they would have been entitled had they been widows. The Government also drew attention to provisions in what are now ss.54–56 of the Welfare Reform and Pensions Act 1999 making provision for bereavement payments, allowances for bereaved spouses, and certain new pension arrangements, which avoid the discrimination which previously existed as between widows and widowers.

Willis v United Kingdom (App.36042/97), judgment of June 11, 2002, [2002] 35 E.H.R.R. 21 concerned a complaint by a man. The complainant argued that there was a breach Art.14 taken in conjunction with Art.8, and a branch of Art.14 when taken in conjunction with Art.1 of Protocol 1 of the Convention since, had he been a woman in a similar position, he would have been entitled to a widowed mother's allowance and widow's payment. He also complained in identical terms about his future non-entitlement to a widow's pension, and of a violation of Art.13. The Court of Human Rights held unanimously that—

(a) Article 14 taken in conjunction with Art.1 of Protocol 1 applied to the complainant's complaint concerning non-entitlement to a widow's payment and widowed mother's allowance, and that there had been a violation of Art.14 read together with Art.1 of Protocol 1;

(b) it was not necessary to consider the complaint under Art.14 taken together with Art.8;

(c) there had been no violation of Art.14 taken in conjunction with Art.8 or Art.1 of Protocol 1 in relation to the complaint concerning non-entitlement to a widow's pension;

(d) it was not necessary to consider whether Art.8 and Art.1 of Protocol 1 are applicable to the complaint concerning widow's pension

(e) it was not necessary to consider the case under Art.14 read together with Art.8 or Art.1 of Protocol 1 in relation to the complaint of discrimination suffered by the claimant's late wife; and
(f) there had been no violation of Art.13.

The Court ruled that a widow's payment and widowed mother's allowance, being contributory in nature, are capable of constituting a pecuniary right within the ambit of Art.1 of Protocol 1. This was all that was necessary in order to open the door to complaints of discrimination under Art.14. Consistently with its often stated case law, the Court said that "very weighty" reasons would be necessary to ground objective justification where the grounds of discrimination were sex. The Government had not advanced any arguments which met the requirements of objective and reasonable justification. There was a violation of Art.14 taken together with Art.1 of Protocol 1.

In relation to a widow's pension, the Court concluded that the claimant had not been treated any differently from a woman in an analogous situation. A widow in the claimant's position would not qualify for a widow's pension under the Contributions and Benefits Act 1992 until at least 2006 and might never qualify by reason of certain other statutory conditions. The Court accordingly concluded that no issue of discrimination as regards entitlement to a widow's pension arose on the facts of this case.

The Court sidesteps consideration of any violation of Art.14 read in conjunction with Art.8 in relation (a) to a widowed mother's allowance and widow's payment because it had concluded that there was a breach of Art.14 read in conjunction with Art.1 of Protocol 1, and (b) to a widow's pension because it had concluded that no issue of discrimination arose on the facts of the case.

The Court did not consider that any separate issues were raised by the complaint or discrimination raised in relation to the claimant's late wife.

Short shrift was given to the complaint of a violation of Art.13 since the Court recalled its well established case law that Art.13 does not go so far as to guarantee a remedy allowing a State's primary legislation to be challenged before a national authority on the grounds that it is contrary to the Convention.

The decision in *Willis* contradicts the decision of Moses J. in *Hooper* on the benefits being within the ambit of Art.1 of Protocol 1 because the contributions were those of another. There was a sufficient link through the system of contributions.

The long-awaited judgments of the Court of Human Rights in *Runkee and White v United Kingdom* (Apps 42949/98 and 53134/99) were handed down on May 10, 2007. This finally resolves the position in relation to the litigation concerning widowers' entitlements under the legislation in force prior to April 9, 2001. The Court ruled that there was no violation of Art. 14 taken in conjunction with Art. 1 of Protocol 1 in connection with non-entitlement to a widow's pension, but that there was a violation of Art. 14 taken in conjunction with Art.1 of Protocol 1. The Court further ruled that it was not necessary to consider either complaint under Art. 14 taken in conjunction with Art. 8.

The saga of the Government's response to the discrimination between men and women which occurred in relation to benefits for widows and widowers has now been considered by the House of Lords in *R v Secretary of State for Work and Pensions, Ex p. Hooper* [2005] UKHL 29. The four claimants were widowers, whose circumstances were such that, had they been widows, they would have been able to claim widow's benefits. At issue were widow's payments (the lump sum benefit of £1,000); widowed mother's allowance; and widow's pension. They claimed that this differential treatment of men and women who had lost their spouses constituted discrimination contrary to Art.14 when read with Art.8 or Art.1 of Protocol 1 with effect from 2 October 2000. The new scheme of bereavement benefits took effect in April 2001: widow's payment was replaced by a bereavement payment, widowed mother's allowance by a widowed parent's allowance, and widow's pension by a bereavement allowance. In both the Court of Appeal and the House of Lords, the Secretary of State conceded that all widow's benefits fall within the ambit of one or both of the substantive Convention articles on which the claimants relied.

The Secretary of State argued that the payment of widow's pension to women only could be objectively justified, whereas the application of s.6(2) of the Human Rights Act 1998 meant that the payment of widow's payment and widowed mother's allowance was not unlawful under s.6(1) of the Act.

Lord Hoffmann, giving the lead judgment of the House, first addressed objective justification for widow's pension. Lord Hoffman notes that widow's pension was never a means-tested benefit; it was predicated on the basis that older widows as a class were more likely to be in financial need than older widowers. Furthermore 'there has never been any social or economic justification for extending widow's pension to men under pensionable age'. Bearing these two considerations in mind, Lord Hoffmann offers a history of widow's pensions up to their abolitions and replacement with a 52 week bereavement allowance for both men and women whose spouses had died. Lord Hoffmann notes:

"So the question in the case of WP is not so much whether there was justification for not paying it to men as whether there was justification for not having moved faster in abolishing its payment to women." (para.17.)

The essence of the conclusion that there was objective justification can be found in paragraph 32:

"Once it is accepted that older widows were historically an economically disadvantaged class which merited special treatment but were gradually becoming less disadvantaged, the question of the precise moment at which such special treatment is no longer justified becomes a social and political question within the competence of Parliament."

The second argument put by the Secretary of State was that any unlawful discrimination arising from the non-payment of the equivalent of widow's payment and widowed mother's allowance to widowers was 'immunised' by the effect of s.6(2) of the 1998 Act. The argument of the widowers before the House of Lords was not that the payments to widows infringed their Convention rights; they also accepted that the Contributions and Benefits Act 1992 imposed no obligation on the Secretary of State to make payments to widowers, but they did argue that the Secretary of State 'could have made such payments by exercising the common law powers of the Crown as a corporation sole to make discretionary payments of funds under its control' (para.43). The failure to do so constituted a breach of their Convention rights. Lord Hoffman concludes that s.6(2)(b) applies to the circumstances of the case. Section 6(2)(b) assumes that the Secretary of State could have acted differently but excludes liability if the Minister was giving effect to a statutory provision which could not be read as Convention-compatible. That was the situation here; in paying widows but not widowers, the Secretary of State was giving effect to sections 36 and 37 of the Contributions and Benefits Act 1992, which could not be read as requiring payments to widowers.

The final complaint made by the widowers related to the differential treatment by the Government of those who had petitioned the Court of Human Rights before the Human Rights Act 1998 came into force and themselves. The petitioners to the Strasbourg Court had received payments in the friendly settlement of their cases, but those making claims after the entry into force of the 1998 Act had not. Lord Hoffmann is unimpressed with this claim which he says fails for three reasons. First, there is doubt about whether being a person who has started legal proceedings is a personal characteristic. Secondly, any discrimination there might be does not appear to come within the scope of the Convention. Thirdly, there would be objective justification for the differential treatment even if the first two hurdles could be cleared.

Note that in *R(G) 2/04*, the Commissioner rules on a point of interpretation on which he regarded himself as bound by the decision of the Court of Appeal in the *Hooper* litigation (which was not in issue in the appeal to the House of Lords in that litigation) that "no man who claims widow's benefit in respect of a spouse who died before April 9, 2001 is entitled under British social security legislation to any payment of widow's benefit." (para.2.)

The Carson and Reynolds litigation
The House of Lords has given judgment on the claim by Annette Carson that there is discrimination in breach of Convention rights in payment of contributory pensions to pensioners in some overseas countries without uprating of those pensions; and on the claim by Joanne Reynolds that the payment of jobseeker's allowance and income support to those under the age of 25 at a lower rate than those aged 25 or more constituted discrimination in breach of Convention rights: *R. v Secretary of State for Work and Pensions, Ex p. Carson, R. v Secretary of State for Work and Pensions, Ex p. Reynolds* [2005] UKHL 37. **4.82**

Lord Hoffmann and Lord Walker of Gestingthorpe give the lead judgments in a 4–1 decision that there is no breach of Convention rights in the *Carson* case and a unanimous decision that there is no breach of Convention rights in the *Reynolds* case.

Lord Hoffmann's judgment is intellectually seductive, but turns very much on the premise that "social security benefits are part of an intricate and interlocking system of social welfare which exists to ensure certain minimum standards of living for the people of this country" (para.18) which is, in turn linked to a certain extent to the tax system. Lord Hoffmann is "content to assume that Ms Carson's pension rights were a possession" (para.12). Likewise, he was content to accept that residence abroad constituted a personal characteristic and so constituted a "status" for the purpose of the application of Art.14.

Because of the interlocking nature of the system, and its relationship with the tax system, Lord Hoffmann concludes that the position of non-residents is materially and relevantly different from that of United Kingdom residents. (para.25). Once this is accepted, it is a matter for Parliament to determine the amount, if any, which she receives. Lord Hoffmann continues:

". . . in deciding what expatriate pensioners should be paid, Parliament must be entitled to take into account competing claims on public funds." (para.25.)

Lord Hoffmann took a similarly robust view of the distinction between payments to expatriate pensioners where there is a treaty (which frequently make provision for uprating of pensions) and those where there is no such treaty.

Without determining whether income support constitutes a possession for the purposes of Art.1 of Protocol 1, Lord Hoffmann concluded that the relative positions of those under and over the age of 25 are relevantly different. A line had to be drawn somewhere. So it followed that the claim of Ms Reynolds failed.

Lord Carswell dissented in relation to Ms Carson's appeal. Lord Carswell considers that contributors whose pensions are paid countries where pensions are uprated and contributors whose pensions are paid in countries where pensions are not uprated are in relevantly comparable situations. For Lord Carswell, some objective justification needs to be provided for the differential treatment of these groups. He was not persuaded that any of the arguments put forward constituted objective justification. He is clearly persuaded by the fact that all the pensioners have "duly paid the contributions required to qualify for their pensions". (para.98.)

It is understood that the issues raised in this litigation are the subject of an application to the Court of Human Rights in the pending case of *Jackson v United Kingdom*.

Further United Kingdom authorities
Commissioners have addressed a number of arguments based on Art.14 when read in conjunction with some other provision. **4.83**

In *CP/5084/2001* the argument was that the reduction in retirement pension which arises under the Hospital In-Patients Regulations constituted discrimination when read in conjunction with Art.1 of Protocol 1 (the right to property). The claimant sought to compare the position of (a) those in receipt of State retirement pension with those in hospital without any form of State benefit (in particular those with a private occupational pensions) and (b) those in receipt of a State retirement pension who are in hospital and those who are not. The Commissioner did not accept that the persons in these groups were in analogous positions. Technically, if this was the Commissioner's conclusion, he did not need to consider objective and reasonable justification, since that is only relevant if there are analogous situations. However, the Commissioner goes on to note that there was objective and reasonable justification for the reduction in retirement pension. The Commissioner does note that there is no reduction in such circumstances where the benefit is statutory sick pay, statutory maternity pay, maternity allowance or industrial injuries benefits, but does not consider the position if the claimant had chosen as a comparator those in receipt of such benefits. This could well be an appropriate comparator group, and it might well be difficult to show objective and reasonable justification for the differential treatment in these circumstances.

In *CIS/4769/2001* the Commissioner faced the argument that there was discrimination contrary to Art.14 when read in conjunction with Art.8 and 9 arising from the limitations on the expenses payable by way of funeral expenses under the social fund. The case was pursued by comparing the position of a national of an EEA country who was a migrant worker with a national of Pakistan. The Commissioner accepted that there might be indirect discrimination in relation to these comparator groups, which would therefore need to be objectively justified. The Commissioner identified the saving of cost and the saving of administrative complication as being capable of being objective justifications. The Commissioner, after lengthy consideration of all the arguments, concludes,

> "65. Parliament has taken a great deal of trouble in framing and reframing the regulations, to limit the expenditure of public money which, at least where indirect discrimination is concerned, is on the authorities within its legitimate functions. This is an area of economic and social policy where a balance has to be struck between equitable treatment and the efficient use of necessarily limited resources. Article 8 expressly requires the striking of such a balance. Article 9 does not, but my view of the evidence is that it is Article 8 consideration of family harmony which primarily motivated the appellant. I agree with the tribunal that the religious aspects were matters of expectation rather than necessity. The appellant has not fully persuaded me that there actually is indirect discrimination, and he has not persuaded me that, if there is, it is not objectively justified."

In *CG/2965/2002*, the Commissioner held that the male survivor of an unmarried couple was not entitled to a bereavement benefit. The different treatment of married and unmarried couples could be objectively justified by reference to the value of promoting married relationships (notwithstanding the review by the Government begun in November 2001 on whether to establish a scheme of civil partnerships outside marriage).

In *CG/734/2003* the Commissioner concluded that there was no breach of the Human Rights Act 1998 by reason of the differential treatment under the Computation of Earnings Regulations of weekly-paid and monthly-paid workers when calculating deemed periods of gainful employment for the purposes of entitlement to an invalid care allowance.

In *R(IS) 12/04* the Commissioner dismisses as without foundation and argument based on Art.1 of Protocol 1 and 14 ECHR that reg.42(2A) of the Income Support General Regulations breaches Convention rights in a case where a claimant aged 61 with a personal pension plan did not draw income from it and was deemed to have notional income from that plan which reduced his entitlement to income support. The argument was that reg.42(2A) interferes with a claimant's ability to leave funds in a pension scheme to accumulate and so hinders a claimant's ability to use and develop his property as he wishes. The provision, it was argued, "discriminates against men because the entitlement of women to a state retirement pension between the ages of 60 and 65 means that a smaller proportion of women than men are on income support, so that a greater proportion of men than women with person pension schemes have to draw income from those schemes before the age of 65". (para.7.)

In *Ghaidan v Godin-Mendoza* [2004] UKHL 30, the House of Lords ruled that the policy reasons for giving a statutory tenancy to the survivor of a cohabiting heterosexual couple applied equally to the survivor of a cohabiting homosexual couple. In so holding, they interpreted paras 2 and 3 of Sch.1 to the Rent Act 1977 to secure compatibility with Convention rights. This avoided less favourable treatment of homosexual couples in the enjoyment of their Convention rights under Art.8 ECHR which could not be objectively justified. There may well be implications flowing from this decision into other areas where homosexual couples are treated differently from heterosexual couples.

See also *Secretary of State for Work and Pensions v M; Langley v Bradford Metropolitan District Council and Secretary of State for Work and Pensions* [2004] EWCA Civ 1343; one case concerned the calculation of child support liability and the other a housing benefit case. In the M case, M was currently living in a same-sex relationship and the material regulations were treated as applying to her as they apply to members of heterosexual partnerships and marriages. In the *Langley* case, the claimant complained that she was not entitled to housing benefit because she was paying rent to a former cohabiting partner of the opposite sex, whereas she would not have been entitled had she been paying to a former cohabiting partner of the same sex. Her appeal had been dismissed by the Commissioner because there was no material similarity or analogy between her case and that of the comparator she put forward. The Court of Appeal disagrees with his reasoning, though the Court concludes for different reasons that there has been no breach of her Convention rights. The approach of the members of the Court differed in their approach.

Lord Justice Kennedy, who adopted the submission made to him by the Secretary of State, concluded that housing benefit falls outside the ambit of Art.8 (and so no argument under Art.14 could arise) because there is no obligation under Art.8 to provide the benefit and its provision is not the State's method of demonstrating respect for the home.

Lord Justice Neuberger was, however, prepared to accept that it is was arguable that the housing benefit scheme did fall within the ambit of Art.8, without deciding the point; though he did stress that the decision in *Douglas v North Tyneside MBC* [2003] EWCA Civ 1847 could be a substantial barrier to proving even this. However, Ms Langley was not entitled to succeed under Art.14 because, following the reasoning of the Court of Appeal at paragraphs [160]–[163] of *R. (Hooper) v Secretary of State for Work and Pensions* [2003] 1 W.L.R. 2623, compensating her would achieve no legitimate aim. Her complaint in truth was that reg.7(1)(c)(i) did not apply to same-sex partnerships, not that it does apply to opposite-sex partnerships. But once that point had been reached it would only compound the anomaly that same-sex partnerships fall outside the regulation by saying that opposite-sex partnerships should not fall within it, thus rendering the regulation of no effect whatsoever.

Lord Justice Sedley was much clearer in his view that the housing benefit scheme as a whole did come within the ambit of Art.8. He distinguished Lord Justice Laws' comment in *Reynolds* [2003] 3 All E.R. 577 that the income support scheme per se does not engage Art.8, by stressing that the housing benefit scheme is a discrete scheme with a particular purpose that does lie within the ambit of Art.8. However, for him the more precise question which needed to be asked here was whether reg.7(1)(c)(i) came within the ambit of Art.8. It was this particular regulation which Ms Langley was complaining of and its was only this regulation that she was arguing she was a "victim" of under s.7(1) of the Human Rights Act 1998. She was not a victim of the housing benefit scheme as a whole.

Viewed from this perspective the question for Lord Justice Sedley was whether the specific anti-abuse provision came within the ambit of Art.8 (respect for the home and family), which it did not. In order to rank as a victim Ms Langley would need to show that, if the regulation included same-sex partners, she would in some appreciable way be better off. That she plainly could not do. The only way she would be better off would be if there were no reg.7(1)(c)(i) at all. But in that circumstance what Ms Langley would be the victim of would not be the discriminatory element of the regulation but the regulation itself; of which no Convention complaint could be made.

The House of Lords found the issues just as difficult in the appeal in *Secretary of State for Work and Pensions v M* [2006] UKHL 11, although the brief summary which follows may not fully reflect the careful and detailed reflections on the questions before their Lordships. Lord Bingham did not consider that the circumstances presented by M were within the scope of family life or private life. Lord Nicholls found the link between the claims made and Art.8 too tenuous to provide the basis for a claim under Art.14 read in conjunction with Art.8. Lord Walker too considered that the scope of Art.8 was not yet such that the circumstances presented by M could be said to fall within its ambit. Lord Mance agreed with Lord Walker that a tenuous link between the child support regime and M's family life or private life is insufficient to bring the case within the ambit of Article 8. However, he notes the pace of change in the area of same-sex relationships of very recent effect whereas the Court was dealing with the position in 2001 and 2002. In contrast, Baroness Hale concluded that Art.8 was engaged, since there was a public law duty (as well as a private law duty) on parents to support their children; the State had stepped in to establish a child support scheme as one of its policies to support families. Dissenting from the majority, she went on to rule that this was a case of unjustified discrimination.

4.84 In *Douglas v North Tyneside MBC and Secretary of State for Education and Skills* [2003] EWCA Civ 1847, the claimant was above the upper age limit for eligibility for a student loan. He argued that there was unjustifiable discrimination on grounds of age in breach of Art.14 when read in conjunction with Art.2 of Protocol 1 on the right to education. The Court of Appeal ruled that tertiary education fell within the ambit of Art.2 of Protocol 1, and went on to consider the Art.14 complaint. The Court held that student loans were one step removed from the provision of education, and were not so closely related to the provision of education as to prevent the claimant from participating. So, although the provision of tertiary education was within the ambit of Art.2 of Protocol 1, the provision of student loans to support it was not. Had the Court concluded that it was, they would have held that the difference in treatment on grounds of age was justified. In delivering the judgment of the Court, Scott Baker L.J. said,

> "62. It is not for the courts to interfere with the Secretary of State's funding arrangements provided they are lawfully made and applied. Funding arrangements for further education fall within the general area where social and economic judgements are required that involve the allocation of finite resources and the balancing of competing claims. The courts in my judgment have to be careful when considering an issue of justification such as would arise in the present case were Art.2 to be engaged not to trespass into the discretionary area of resource allocation. That is an area that is not justiciable.
>
> 63. I find the following points compelling in favour of the Secretary of State's argument that the funding arrangement is justified:
>
> — Higher education is a scarce resource; it is not available to everybody, as is primary and secondary education.
> — The government is entitled to decide the priorities in the allocation of scarce resources.
> — The arrangements are entitled to treat older students differently on the ground that the scheme is a loan scheme and the money is expected to be repaid. It is a reasonable assumption that older students have less chance of being in a position to repay than younger students. (The obligation to repay the loan ceases at 65.)
> — The age cut-off is part of a larger picture on which a judgment is made.
> — There are other measures that may be available to assist a student who is ineligible by way of age for a loan. These are fee waiver and a hardship grant.

64. For these broad reasons, therefore, I am satisfied that the Secretary of State discharges the burden of justification."

R. (Smith) v Secretary of State for Defence and Secretary of State for Work and Pensions [2004] EWHC 1797 (Admin), concerned complaint by an ex-wife that there was a breach of Art.14 read in conjunction with Art.1 of Protocol 1 (or Art.8) where a pension payable to the pension holder was payable below the age of 60 but where the pension payable to the ex-wife following a pension sharing order did not take effect until she reached the age of 60. Wilson J. accepted that this was discrimination within Art.14 on grounds of both age and gender, he found that it was justified since the policy objective was to encourage ex-wives under the age of 60 to work until that age—a legitimate aim of the state—and that, if for some reason she could not do so, "she could reasonably expect the divorce court to oblige the ex-husband to provide her with support in respect of that period" (para.32).

In *Esfandiari v Secretary of State for Work and Pensions* [2006] EWCA Civ 282 (the appeals against *CIS/1870/2003; CIS/2302/2003; CIS/2305/2003* and *CIS/2624/2003*), reported as *R(IS) 11/06*, the Court of Appeal considered whether the funeral payments provisions which restrict the payment of funeral expenses where the funeral is held in the United Kingdom (or in certain cases another country within the European Economic Area) are compatible with the European Convention. The Court was unanimous in concluding that this was not a case of discrimination at all, but even if those migrants who wished to bury relatives in their country of origin were a group, then any differential treatment could easily be justified as matters where the State enjoyed a wide margin of appreciation is setting its policy. The Court of Appeal regards the different outcome in Community law as arising because of the special rights which migrant workers are accorded under the EC Treaty.

The Commissioner in *CSJSA/0125/2004* summarises the approach to be taken,

"The language of the articles is crucial. There are two essentials that have to be satisfied for the facts as established to fall within the ambit. First the matter relied upon must have a direct relationship to the substantive Convention right, in this case Art.8. Second the discrimination must be of the type provided for in Art.14 and not be discrimination of a sort not covered. On both these issues the claimant fails in this case.... Just because the Convention gives a right to respect for one's home does not mean that something which is indirectly related to the home, such as payments of interest of a heritably secured debt obtained for the purposes of purchasing the home, falls within the ambit of the Convention right provided by Art.8. In my view the provision of housing costs in respect of the payment of interest is too remote from the right secured by the Convention for it to fall within the ambit. Such provision falls outwith what Art.8 seeks to secure. Further and in any event for Art.8 to be engaged, where there is no positive obligation to provide state assistance, the discrimination asserted would have to be of the type set out in Art.14." (para.14.)

The "direct link" test espoused in this case is probably not good law in the light of the decision of the House of Lords in *M* and of the Court of Appeal in *Esfandiari*.

In *CIS/1616/2004*, the Commissioner dismissed an argument that an income support claimant who shares the care of a child with a local authority was in an analogous position to an income support claimant who shares parental responsibilities with an ex-partner. As a result, even assuming that Art.8 could be applied, there was no claim under Art.14 of the Convention. Nor did European Community law assist the claimant in this case.

In *Francis v Secretary of State for Work and Pensions* [2005] EWCA Civ 1303 (the appeal against *CIS/1965/2003*, reported as *R(IS) 6/06*), the Court of Appeal found that the refusal to award a maternity grant constituted discrimination contrary to Art.14 of the Convention. The Secretary of State had conceded that the circumstances presented by Ms Francis engaged Art.8 of the Convention. Ms Francis argued that her situation as a person with a residence order in respect of a child born to her sister was analogous to that of an adopter under the Adoption Act 1976. There was no objective justification for the difference in treatment.

In *R(IS) 12/06*, the Commissioner ruled that exclusion from entitlement to a severe disability premium of a claimant who is residing with and is a close relative of their landlord is not contrary to Art.14 when read with Art.1 of Protocol 1.

In *CP/518/2003*, the Commissioner, following *CP/5084/2001*, ruled that the reduction of retirement pension for a person receiving hospital in-patient treatment in accordance with the Hospital In-Patients Regulations 1975 (as amended) did not breach Art.14 when read in conjunction with Art.1 of Protocol 1.

In *R(P) 2/06* a Tribunal of Commissioners concluded that the United Kingdom rules preventing the payment of widows' benefits to widows of polygamous marriages in the circumstances of the cases before them did not fall foul of the prohibition of discrimination in Art.14 when read with Art.8. The Tribunal of Commissioners was unanimous as to the outcome, but one Commissioner's line of reasoning differs from that of his two colleagues.

In *H E Manning v Revenue and Customs Commissioners*, SpC552, decision of July 3, 2006, the Special Commissioner held, in the face of claims by a self-employed person that there was a breach of Article 14 read together with Article 1 of Protocol 1, that it was not discriminatory that national insurance contributions for the employed ceased at the age of 65 whereas Class 4 contributions for the self-employed ceased if the person had attained that age at the beginning of the tax year. The Special Commissioner noted that admissibility decisions of the European Commission of Human Rights had held that difference in treatment between the employed and self-employed was justified, and that any difference in treatment was wholly in favour of self-employed people.

R(G) 1/06 concerned entitlement of an elderly widower to a bereavement payment. Section 36(1)(a) of the Contributions and Benefits Act provides that, even where the contribution conditions are met, there is no entitlement to a bereavement payment when the bereaved party is over pensionable age at the time of the relevant death, and the spouse who has died was getting their own Category A retirement pension. The Commissioner explains the historical origins of this limiting condition. It was argued on behalf of the claimant that the restrictive condition operated to discriminate between deceased spouses who had or had not opted for a Category B rather than a Category A retirement pension, and that this was contrary to Article 14 when read with either Article 8 or Article 1 of Protocol 1. The Commissioner found that he could not interpret the relevant statutory provisions in a manner compatible with this interpretation. However, he was not persuaded that three was discrimination in breach of the Convention. He ruled,

> "28. . . . . In a system as complicated and interlocking as the insured benefits scheme under the United Kingdom social security system it is inevitable that differences of treatment, even anomalies and incongruities, may arise at the boundaries between one set of facts and another. Such things are inherent in the system but it is clear on the authority of the House of Lords in *R (Carson) v Secretary of State* [2005] UKHL 37, [2006] 1 AC 173 that the mere existence of such dividing lines, not raising questions of differential treatment between categories of human beings on the "suspect" grounds, such as sex, race, and so forth or otherwise offensive to accepted notions of the respect due to the individual, does not constitute unlawful discrimination in the human rights context.
>
> 29. The dividing lines drawn in a contributory insurance system between the benefits for those who are themselves just under or over pensionable age, those whose deceased partners happen to have just under or over the 25% level of contributions to qualify them for a Category A retirement pension (or for that matter those whose deceased partners had a 100% contribution record, or 99% or something less, on the alternative construction put forward), or those whose partners had or had not happened to elect under section 43 to forgo their own contributory pension benefit on their own contributions and receive a Category B pension on

their spouse's contributions instead, are all in my judgment squarely within the area that is left to be determined by the national legislation; and the same applies to deciding whether or in what way what may now be viewed largely as an historical anomaly in section 36(1)(a) should be eliminated. If the effect of the condition is now "incongruous" as suggested in the tribunal chairman's statement of reasons at pages 42 to 43 of file CG 1614/05, that is a matter those concerned for claimants in this position must take up in some other forum than this."

In *R (on the application of RJM) v Secretary of State for Work and Pensions* [2007] EWCA Civ 614, the claimant had mental health problems and was in receipt of income support including a disability premium. The disability premium was removed when the claimant was sleeping rough, since he was then without accommodation. The claimant argued that the removal of the disability premium constituted unlawful discrimination contrary to Article 14 when read with Article 1 of Protocol 1. He appeared to base his complaint on unwarranted distinctions between those with and without accommodation. The Court of Appeal ruled that being homeless was not a status analogous to the grounds covered by Art. 14; it was not a personal characteristic. Nor can it properly be said that a person without accommodation has a property status. But even if the applicant did have a status within Art. 14, the refusal to pay a disability premium to those who do not have accommodation is not unlawful under the Convention because the Secretary of State could justify their differential treatment.

The judgment also addresses the apparent conflict between some English authorities and the judgment of the Court of Human Rights in *Steç*, but the issue did not need to be resolved because the Secretary of State made a limited concession accepting that RJM's claim fell within the ambit of Art.1 of Protocol 1.

The precise scope of this concession has caused some concern, and it is understood that a Commissioner has issued directions in a case before him asking the Secretary of State to indicate how far the concession extended. It is clearly unsatisfactory if the Secretary of State is deciding whether or not to attack the application of the judgment in *Steç* because of the conflict with certain national authorities on a case by case basis.

In *Couronne v Secretary of State for Work and Pensions, Bontemps v Secretary of State for Work and Pensions* [2006] EWHC 1514 (Admin), it was argued that the refusal to award jobseekers allowance to British Citizens arriving from Mauritius (whose parents had been displaced from the Chagos Islands) constituted discrimination in breach of Article 14 when read with Article 8 and/or Article 1 of Protocol 1. It was argued, inter alia, that the comparator group (British Citizens of Irish ethnic origin are exempt from the habitual residence test, whereas the claimants were not. Bennett J concluded:

"96. In my judgment the aim of the habitual residence test is a legitimate one. Both the ECJ and the Court of Appeal have said so, at least in the context of community law. If the aim, as explained in the evidence, is to protect the British taxpayer from claims by persons who have no genuine or real intention of settling in the UK, if it has been the subject of wide debate and consultation, and if Parliament itself has debated the matter in 1999, it is a nonsense to suggest that the habitual residence test does not have a legitimate aim. The real complaint of the Claimants is, in my judgment, that the implementation of the habitual residence test in relation to the Chagossians, given their special history, is not a proportionate means of achieving the legitimate aim.

97. The word 'proportionate' to my mind imports the notion of a balanced response to a given situation. I do not see how it can be said that the inclusion of British citizens of Irish national or ethnic origin within the habitual residence test is not proportionate to the legitimate aim. The complaint of the Chagossians must be that they were not exempted from the scope of the habitual residence test, particularly in the light of their exile and being granted British citizenship. But that, with all due respect, is, as Mr Howell submitted, not the question. The question is whether the habitual residence test is a proportionate means of achieving a legitimate aim given

the particular disadvantage to which it is said to put other British citizens not of Irish national or ethnic origin only if an exception is made for the Chagossians. I am afraid that the brutal reality is that the Chagossians are seeking to be treated better than their comparator group and thus seeking a complete exemption from the habitual residence test. The argument as to exile (particularly as British citizens) has no relevance, because it is an exemption that they would have to seek even if the habitual residence test was framed solely in terms of habitual residence in the United Kingdom; and, as is apparent, the Claimants could not (and do not) object to a habitual residence test framed solely in those terms. The distinction made by the UK Government between the plight of the people of Montserrat and of the Chagossians is one about which argument will rage. But hard and difficult decisions have to be made. There may be no 'right' answer, only a least wrong one. The question is whether the refusal of the UK Government to exempt them from the habitual residence is a proportionate response. In my judgment it is . . . ."

Article 16—Restrictions on political activity of aliens

4.85 Nothing in Articles 10, 11 and 14 shall be regarded as preventing the High Contracting Parties from imposing restrictions on the political activity of aliens.

Article 17—Prohibition of abuse of rights

4.86 Nothing in this Convention may be interpreted as implying for any State, group or person any right to engage in any activity or perform any act aimed at the destruction of any of the rights and freedoms set forth herein or at their limitation to a greater extent than is provided for in the Convention.

Article 18—Limitation on use of restrictions on rights

4.87 The restrictions permitted under this Convention to the said rights and freedoms shall not be applied for any purpose other than those for which they have been prescribed.

PART II

THE FIRST PROTOCOL

Article 1—Protection of property

4.88 Every natural or legal person is entitled to the peaceful enjoyment of his possessions. No one shall be deprived of his possessions except in the public interest and subject to the conditions provided for by law and by the general principles of international law. The preceding provisions shall not, however, in any way impair the right of a State to enforce such laws as it deems necessary to control the use of property in accordance with the general interest or to secure the payment of taxes or other contributions or penalties.

GENERAL NOTE

Introduction

4.89 Article 1 of Protocol 1, as explained in the *Sporrong and Lönnroth* case (*Sporrong and Lönnroth v Sweden* (A/52); (1983) 5 E.H.R.R. 35), comprises three distinct rules. First, there is a right to peaceful enjoyment of possessions. Secondly, persons can only be deprived of their possessions subject to certain conditions; and, thirdly, States are entitled to control the use of property in accordance with the general interest.

The notion of a "possession" under the article has an autonomous meaning under the Convention. Certain rights and interests which constitute assets can be regarded as possessions. The law in this area is not entirely settled. It now seems clear that contributions to a pension fund (see below) may create a property right in an undefined part of the total fund. But where social security systems are involved, there is no entitlement to a specific sum by way of pension: see App.4288/69, *X v United Kingdom* (1970) 13 Y.B. 892.

It is unclear whether a legal claim can be a pecuniary right. One case concerning enforcement of an arbitration award suggested that an enforceable debt is a pecuniary right: *Stran Greek Refineries and Stratis Andreadis v Greece* (A/301–B); (1995) 19 E.H.R.R. 293. In another case a legitimate expectation that a claim would be dealt with in accordance with normal tort principles was treated as a pecuniary right: *Pressos Compania Naviera SA v Belgium* (1996) 21 E.H.R.R. 301, and contrast *National and Provincial Building Society v United Kingdom* (1998) 25 E.H.R.R. 127.

In *Stretch v United Kingdom* (App 44277/98), (2004) 38 E.H.R.R. 12 which concerned an option for renewal of a lease, the Court of Human Rights neatly summarises the present position as to what constitutes a 'possession' under this Article:

"The Court recalls that, according to the established case-law of the Convention organs, 'possessions' can be 'existing possessions' or assets, including claims, in respect of which the applicant can argue that he has at least a 'legitimate expectation' of obtaining effective enjoyment of a property right (see, inter alia, *Pine Valley Developments Ltd v Ireland*, cited above, § 51, *Pressos Compania Naviera S.A. v Belgium* Judgment of 20 November 1995, Series A no.332, p.21, § 31). By way of contrast, the hope of recognition of the survival of an old property right which it has long been impossible to exercise effectively cannot be considered as a 'possession' within the meaning of Article 1 of Protocol No.1, nor can a conditional claim which lapses as a result of the non-fulfilment of the condition (see the recapitulation of the relevant principles in *Malhous v the Czech Republic* (dec.), no. 33071/96, 13 December 2000, ECHR 2000-XII, with further references, in particular to the Commission's case-law; also *Prince Hans-Adam II v Germany* [GC], No. 42527/98, ECHR 2001-VIII, § 85, and *Nerva v the United Kingdom*, No. 42295/98, Judgment of 24 September 2002, § 43)." (para.32.)

Property rights and social security

Entitlements arising under pension and social security schemes have proved difficult to classify in relation to property rights; the position was for some time unclear. A distinction had been drawn in the case law between benefits which were paid on the basis of contributions, and those which were paid without reference to contributions. But the case law did not always seem to maintain this distinction. However, the admissibility decision of the Grand Chamber in the *Stec* case (*Stec v United Kingdom* (Apps 67531/01 and 65900/01), admissibility decision of September 5, 2005) has clarified matters.

4.90

In the *Stec* case, the Grand Chamber accepted that the existing case law was ambiguous on the significance of contributions in bringing a claim within the scope of Art.1 of Protocol 1 for the purpose of claiming discriminatory treatment which breached Art.14 of the Convention. The Grand Chamber lays down a new approach which is to be applied in future cases, relying on an interpretation which renders the rights in the Convention practical and effective rather than theoretical and illusory. The Grand Chamber also referred to the Court's case law under Art.6, which had brought disputes concerned all forms of social security within the scope of that article. The Court said:

"50. The Court's approach to Article 1 of Protocol No.1 should reflect the reality of the way in which welfare provision is currently organised within the Member States of the Council of Europe. It is clear that within those States, and within most individual States, there exists a wide range of social security benefits designed to confer entitlements which arise as of right. Benefits are funded in a large variety of ways: some are paid for by contributions to a specific fund; some depend on a claimant's contribution record; many are paid for out of general taxation on the basis of a statutorily defined status . . . Given the variety of funding methods, and the interlocking nature of benefits under most welfare systems, it appears increasingly artificial to hold that only benefits financed by contributions to a specific fund fall within the scope of Article 1 of Protocol No.1. Moreover, to exclude benefits paid for out of general taxation would be to disregard the fact that many claimants under this latter type of system also contribute to its financing, through the payment of tax.

51. In the modern, democratic State, many individuals are, for all or part of their lives, completely dependent for survival on social security and welfare benefits. Many domestic legal systems recognise that such individuals require a degree of certainty and security, and provide for benefits to be paid—subject to the fulfilment of the conditions of eligibility—as of right. Where an individual has an assertable right under domestic law to a welfare benefit, the importance of that interest should also be reflected by holding Article 1 of Protocol No.1 to be applicable."

The Court goes on to note that the bringing of social security fairly and squarely within the scope of Art.1 of Protocol 1 does not create any right to acquire property. However, if a State does create rights to social security benefits, the benefit schemes must be operated in a manner which is compatible with the prohibition of discrimination set out in Art.14.

Attempts have been made to argue that the suspension of retirement pension for those serving terms of imprisonment breached the property rights in Art.1 of Protocol 1, but the applications were declared inadmissible (Apps.27004/95, *Josef Szrabjer v United Kingdom*, and 27011/95, *Walter Clarke v United Kingdom*, decision of October 23, 1997) and invalidity benefit (App.27537/95, *George Carlin v United Kingdom*, decision of December 3, 1997). The public interest was served by avoiding a situation in which prisoners enjoyed the advantage of accumulating a lump sum by receiving a State benefit without any outgoing living expenses. Arguments based on discrimination between prisoners and non-prisoners were dismissed as a comparison of two different factual situations. Other comparisons were also found to be without merit. See also discussion of benefits for widowers in the commentary on Art.14 above.

See the comment on *Willis v United Kingdom* (App.36042/97), judgment of June 11, 2002 in para.4.78 above.

In *CP/4762/2001* the Commissioner found that the provisions under which a person became entitled to a retirement pension normally with effect from the Monday following their 65th birthday gives rise to no Convention issue either under Art.1 of Protocol 1, nor under that provision when read in conjunctions with Art.14 E.C.H.R.

In *CP/0281/2002*, the Commissioner ruled that there was no breach of Art.1 of Protocol 1 as a consequence of the requirement under the Pension Schemes Act 1993 that any additional pension is reduced by the amount of any guaranteed minimum pension payable to a person.

In *R. (Smith) v Secretary of State for Defence and Secretary of State for Work and Pensions* [2004] EWHC 1797 (Admin), Wilson J. held that a non-contributory pension under the Armed Forces Pension Scheme was a possession within the ambit of Art.1 of Protocol 1. This extended to the spouse of the pension holder following the making of a pension-sharing order. However, Art.1 of Protocol 1 does not guarantee a right to a pension of a particular amount, nor payment from a particular time. The remainder of the case principally concerned this article when read in conjunction with Art.14, and is discussed in the annotations to Art.14.

In *R(P) 1/06*, the Commissioner ruled that the three months time limit on the backdating of a claim for retirement pension did not constitute a deprivation of property contrary to Art. 1 of Protocol 1. Nor was there any question of a claim based on discrimination by reading Article 14 together with Art. 1 of Protocol 1.

In *C8/06-07(IB)* a Commissioner in Northern Ireland said,

"15. I consider there is no merit in the submission based on Article 1 of Protocol 1. There is no inbuilt Convention right to any State benefit. A State is not obliged to provide benefit. The right to benefit only arises when the conditions therefore (which are provided under domestic legislation) are satisfied. In this case they were not so satisfied. The claimant was not entitled to the benefit because he worked and his work did not fall within the categories of exempt work. The basic rule in relation to IB is that those who work are not entitled to it. The benefit is, after all, an incapacity for work benefit. There are exceptions to this basic rule but they relate only to certain categories of work. The relevant category here includes that the work be work of which the required notice is given. Working on the assumption that the domestic law requirement of written notice within 42 days is valid, there is no entitlement to IB if work is done which does not come within an exempt category. Article 1 of Protocol 1 is not therefore invoked, there being no property to enjoy. The claimant is not being asked to repay benefit incorrectly paid. His benefit entitlement is merely being determined according to the applicable statutory conditions of entitlement."

Although the application was declared admissible on other grounds, it seems implicit in the decision of the Court of Human Rights in *Meyne-Moskalczuk and others v The Netherlands* (App.53002/99), Decision of December 9, 2003, that entitlement to a pension arising following the making of a pension sharing order in matrimonial proceedings will give rise to a property right within Art.1 of Protocol 1.

Article 2—Right to education

No person shall be denied the right to education. In the exercise of any functions which it assumes in relation to education and to teaching, the State shall respect the right of parents to ensure such education and teaching in conformity with their own religious and philosophical convictions.

4.91

GENERAL NOTE

The full scope of this right is yet to be determined. The existing case law is mainly concerned with primary education, but the Commission has not ruled out the application of the provision to higher education (see, for example, *Sulak v Turkey* (1996) 84 D.R. 101). The confused state of the exclusion of students in fulltime higher education from entitlement to most social security benefits might well leave the United Kingdom exposed to challenge under this provision. On the assumption that the provision applies to higher education, it could be argued that students are currently required to abandon their courses completely in order to become eligible for certain social security benefits with the result that they lose entitlement to the balance of finance to support their studies if they wish to return to their courses later on. This could be argued to operate to deny them the right to an education.

4.92

In *Douglas v North Tyneside MBC and Secretary of State for Education and Skills* [2003] EWCA Civ 1847, the Court of Appeal ruled that tertiary education falls within the ambit of Art.2 of Protocol 1. The Court of Appeal held that, although there was no European or domestic authority establishing clearly that tertiary education falls within the ambit of Art.2 of Protocol 1, the Convention was a living instrument and the number of adults in higher education had grown. There was no principle that the article applied only to earlier stages of education, and so tertiary education falls within the ambit of the article. The case turned on the application of Art.14 when read in conjunction with Art.2 of Protocol 1, and is discussed in the update to the annotations on Art.14 above.

Article 3—Right to free elections

The High Contracting Parties undertake to hold free elections at reasonable intervals by secret ballot, under conditions which will ensure the free expression of the opinion of the people in the choice of the legislature.

4.93

PART III

ARTICLE 1 OF THE THIRTEENTH PROTOCOL

Omitted (concerns the abolition of the death penalty).

Schedule 2 omitted.

4.94

Human Rights Act 1998

Schedule 3

Derogation and Reservation

4.95   [. . .] gs

Part II

Reservation

4.96   At the time of signing the present (First) Protocol, I declare that, in view of certain provisions of the Education Acts in the United Kingdom, the principle affirmed in the second sentence of Article 2 is accepted by the United Kingdom only so far as it is compatible with the provision of efficient instruction and training, and the avoidance of unreasonable public expenditure.
Dated March 20, 1952. Made by the United Kingdom Permanent Representative to the Council of Europe.

General Note

4.97   The derogations of 1988 and 1989 in respect of Art.5(3) of the Convention were withdrawn by the Government on February 26, 2001. The amendments to the Act were made by The Human Rights Act (Amendment) Order 2001 (SI 2001/1216) which entered into force on April 1, 2001.
The derogation contained in the Human Rights Act (Designated Derogation) Order 2001 (SI 2001/3644) in force from November 13, 2001 contained derogations from the provisions of Art.5(1) to permit the detention of foreign nationals in the United Kingdom under the Anti-terrorism, Crime and Security Act 2001. That derogation has been withdrawn and effect is given to its withdrawal by the repeal of P I of Sch.3 to the Human Rights Act 1998 by the Human Rights Act 1998 (Amendment) Order 2005 (SI 2005/1071) with effect from April 8, 2005.

4.98   *Schedule 4 omitted.*

A Select Bibliography on Human Rights Law

The following material may be found to be helpful on the Human Rights Act 1998:
Baker, C. (ed.), *Human Rights Act 1998: A Practitioner's Guide* (Sweet & Maxwell, London, 1998): see particularly Ch.12 entitled "Social Security".
Grosz, S., Beatson, J. and Duffy, P., *Human Rights. The 1998 Act and the European Convention*, (Sweet & Maxwell, London, 2000).
Lester, A. and Pannick, D. (ed.) *Human Rights Law and Practice*, (Butterworths, London, 1999).
Starmer, K., *European Human Rights Law/The Human Rights Act 1998 and the European Convention on Human Rights* (Legal Action Group, London, 1999).
Wadham, J., Mountfield, H., Edmundson, A., and Gallagher, C., *Blackstone's Guide to the Human Rights Act 1998* (4th ed., Oxford University Press, 2007).

Three useful texts on the European Convention on Human Rights are:
Harris, D, O'Boyle, M and Warbrick, C, *Law of the European Convention on Human Rights* (Butterworths, London, 1995).
Ovey, C. and White, R., *The European Convention on Human Rights* (4th ed., Oxford University Press, Oxford, 2006).
Reid, K., *A Practitioner's Guide to the European Convention on Human Rights* (2nd ed., Sweet & Maxwell, London, 2004).

INDEX

This index has been prepared using Sweet and Maxwell's Legal Taxonomy. Main index entries conform to keywords provided by the Legal Taxonomy except where references to specific documents or non-standard terms (denoted by quotation marks) have been included. These keywords provide a means of identifying similar concepts in other Sweet & Maxwell publications and online services to which keywords from the Legal Taxonomy have been applied. Readers may find some minor differences between terms used in the text and those which appear in the index. Suggestions to *sweetandmaxwell.taxonomy@thomson.com*.

Abuse of rights
generally, 4.86
Accidents
Council Regulation
aggravation, 3.224
general note, 3.213–3.214
implementing regulations, 3.379–3.396
miscellaneous, 3.225–3.226
reimbursement between institutions, 3.227
rights to benefits, 3.215–3.223
students, 3.228
industrial injuries benefits
notification, 1.52–1.54
"Accommodation costs"
payment of benefit, 2.213
Adjudication (benefits)
introduction, 1.78
supplementary benefits, 1.237
Adjudication officers
transfer of functions, 1.336–1.337
Adjustment (benefits)
child benefit, 1.130–1.131
child maintenance, 1.120–1.121
income support, 1.113–1.119
overlapping benefits, 1.110–1.112
Administrative Commission on Social Security for Migrant Workers
generally, 3.258
tasks, 3.259–3.260
Advance claims
disability living allowance, 2.93–2.94
disability working allowance, 2.95–2.96
generally, 2.90–2.92
maternity allowance, 2.100
pension following deferment, for, 2.105–2.106
retirement pensions, 2.101–2.102
state pension credit, 2.99
Advisory bodies
Administrative Commission on Social Security for Migrant Workers

Advisory bodies—*cont.*
Administrative Commission on Social Security for Migrant Workers—*cont.*
generally, 3.258
tasks, 3.259–3.260
Advisory Committee on Social Security for Migrant Workers
generally, 3.261
tasks, 3.262
Industrial Injuries Advisory Council
cases where consultation not required, 1.209
functions, 1.208
generally, 1.207
Social Security Advisory Committee
cases where consultation not required, 1.209
functions, 1.208
generally, 1.205–1.206
Advisory Committee on Social Security for Migrant Workers
generally, 3.261
tasks, 3.262
Age
provision of information, 1.155–1.156
Age addition
claims for benefit, 2.36–2.37
imprisonment, 2.573–2.575
"Age-related benefits"
income support, 1.193–1.195
job-seeker's allowance, 1.196–1.197
Aggregation
accidents at work, 3.224
death grants, 3.229
family benefits, 3.244
general rules, 3.332
invalidity, 3.196
maternity, 3.161
sickness, 3.161
unemployment benefits, 3.233
Alienation (benefits)
generally, 1.222–1.224

1271

Index

Aliens
  human rights, 4.85
"All work test certificate"
  form, 2.672–2.673
  rules, 2.671
Alterations
  see **Amendments**
Alternative, payment in the
  claims for benefit
    generally, 2.84–2.85
    list of benefits, 2.178
Amendment of claim
  generally, 2.61–2.63
Amendments
  age-related benefits
    income support, 1.193–1.195
    job-seeker's allowance, 1.196–1.197
  component rates
    income support, 2.411
  income support
    age-related benefits, 1.193–1.195
    component rates, 2.411
    rates of benefit, 1.187–1.189
  job-seeker's allowance
    age-related benefits, 1.196–1.197
    rates of benefit1.190–1.191
  rates of benefit
    age-related benefits, 1.193–1.197
    child benefit, 1.182–1.186
    contributory benefits, 1.177–1.178
    income support, 1.187–1.189
    job-seeker's allowance, 1.190–1.191
    state pension credit, 1.192
Amsterdam Treaty
  see **Human rights**
"Another person on beneficiary's behalf"
  payment of benefits, 2.155
Appeal notices
  acknowledgment, 2.306–2.307
  case management directions, 2.314–2.316
  decisions
    correction of errors, 2.331
    forfeiture rule questions, 2.330
    generally, 2.328–2.329
    setting aside, 2.332–2.335
    supplementary, 2.336
  directions, 2.314–2.316
  generally, 2.300–2.301
  medical evidence, 2.318–2.319
  response to notice or reference
    generally, 2.310–2.311
    reply, 2.312–2.313
  time limits, 2.302–2.303
  withdrawal, 2.325–2.326
Appeals
  appeals tribunals, from
    see also Appeals (from appeals tribunal)
    generally, 1.397–1.410
    procedure, 1.413–1.422
  appeals tribunals, to
    see also Appeals (to appeals tribunal)
    appealable decisions, 2.430–2.431

Appeals—*cont.*
  appeals tribunals, to—*cont.*
    appellants, 2.428–2.429
    applications, 2.451–2.452
    choice of hearing, 2.465–2.466
    death of party, 2.453
    decisions, 2.497–2.511
    determination, 2.461–2.462
    directions, 2.465–2.466
    extension of time limits, 2.444–2.450
    generally, 1.374–1.391
    issues determinable by Revenue, 2.463–2.464
    late appeals, 2.444–2.450
    medical examinations, 2.469–2.472
    non-disclosure of medical evidence, 2.471–2.472
    oral hearings, 2.481–2.494
    record of proceedings, 2.501–2.504
    revision of decisions, 2.437–2.439
    striking out, 2.477–2.478
    time limits, 2.441–2.443
    unappealable decisions, 2.432–2.433, 2.520–2.541
    withdrawal, 2.467–2.468
    witness summons, 2.473–2.474
  certificates of recoverable benefit
    generally, 1.277–1.292
    Regulations, 2.436
  child benefit
    death of party, 2.916–2.917
    decisions, against, 2.900–2.901
    decisions against which no appeal lies, 2.898–2.899, 2.928–2.938
    discontinuance, 2.914–2.915
    general right, 2.896–2.897
    interests of justice, in, 2.909–2.911
    issues arising on appeal in other cases, 2.895
    late appeals, 2.906–2.911
    procedure, 2.912–2.913
    revised decisions, against, 2.902–2.903
    time limits, 2.904–2.905
  Commissioners, from
    application for leave to appeal, 2.337–2.338
    generally, 1.411–1.412
    guaranteed minimum pensions, 1.247–1.248
  Commissioners, to
    see also Appeals (to Commissioners)
    application for leave to appeal, 2.291–2.303
    decisions, 2.328–2.336
    generally, 1.397–1.410
    procedure, 1.413–1.422, 2.308–2.327
    references, 2.304–2.307
  guardian's allowance
    death of party, 2.916–2.917
    decisions, against, 2.900–2.901
    decisions against which no appeal lies, 2.898–2.899, 2.928–2.938
    discontinuance, 2.914–2.915

Appeals—*cont.*
guardian's allowance—*cont.*
general right, 2.896–2.897
interests of justice, in, 2.909–2.911
issues arising on appeal in other cases, 2.895
late appeals, 2.906–2.911
procedure, 2.912–2.913
revised decisions, against, 2.902–2.903
time limits, 2.904–2.905
incapacity benefit interviews, 2.592
jobcentre plus interviews
generally, 2.614
partners, for, 2.633
quarterly work-focused interviews for certain lone parents, 2.736
settlement by agreement, 1.2–1.8
work-focused interviews for lone parents, 2.781

Appeals (from appeals tribunal)
see also **Appeals (to Commissioners)**
errors of law, 1.400
findings of fact, 1.401
generally, 1.397–1.410
inadequate reasons, 1.403
materiality of errors, 1.405
misdirection of law, 1.402
natural justice, 1.404
partner, by, 2.516–2.517
perversity, 1.401
point of law, 1.400
precedent, 1.406
procedural irregularity, 1.404
procedure
generally, 1.413–1.422
regulations, 2.512–2.515
right to fair trial, 1.404

Appeals (to appeals tribunal)
appealable decisions
benefits, 1.516–1.524
contributions, 1.525–1.526
regulations, 2.430–2.431
appellants, 2.428–2.429
certificates of recoverable benefit
generally, 1.277–1.292
Regulations, 2.436
correction of errors
generally, 2.505–2.506
miscellaneous provisions, 2.509
death of party, 2.453
decisions
correction of errors, 2.505–2.506
generally, 2.497–2.499
late application for statement of reasons, 2.500
record of proceedings, 2.501–2.504
service by electronic mail, 2.510
setting aside, 2.507–2.508
definitions, 2.511
dependant upon appeal in other cases
generally, 1.444–1.451
regulations, 2.425
extension of time limits, 2.444–2.450

Appeals (to appeals tribunal)—*cont.*
generally, 1.374–1.391
guaranteed minimum pensions, 1.247–1.248
issues determinable by Revenue
generally, 1.437–1.438
regulations, 2.463–2.464
medical examinations
generally, 1.426–1.428
regulations, 2.469–2.470
non-disclosure of medical evidence, 2.471–2.472
oral hearings
adjournment, 2.491–2.492
choice of, 2.465–2.466
directions, 2.465–2.466
expert assistance, 2.489–2.490
physical examinations, 2.493–2.494
postponement, 2.491–2.492
procedure, 2.481–2.488
record of proceedings, 2.501–2.504
procedure
applications, 2.451–2.452
determination, 2.461–2.462
generally, 1.413–1.422
medical examinations, 2.469–2.472
oral hearings, 2.465–2.466
withdrawal, 2.467–2.468
witness summons, 2.473–2.474
record of proceedings, 2.501–2.504
recovery of benefit
generally, 1.277–1.281
reference of questions, 1.282–1.287
supplementary, 1.291–1.292
re-determination, 1.392–1.396
revision of decisions, 2.437–2.439
service by electronic mail, 2.510
setting aside decisions
generally, 2.507–2.508
miscellaneous provisions, 2.509
settlement by agreement, 1.2–1.8
statement of reasons
generally, 2.497–2.499
late application, 2.500
striking out
generally, 2.477–2.478
misconceived applications, 2.478
reinstatement, 2.479
time limits
extension, 2.444–2.450
generally, 2.441–2.443
unappealable decisions
generally, 1.504–1.515
regulations, 2.432–2.433, 2.520–2.541
withdrawal, 2.467–2.468
witness summons, 2.473–2.474

Appeals (from Commissioners)
application for leave to appeal, 2.337–2.338
generally, 1.411–1.412
guaranteed minimum pensions, 1.247–1.248

1273

Index

Appeals (to Commissioners)
  application for leave to appeal
    decisions, 2.328–2.336
    determination, 2.299
    directions, 2.314–2.316
    generally, 2.291–2.295, 2.512–2.515
    medical evidence, 2.318–2.319
    notice, 2.296–2.298
    withdrawal, 2.325–2.326
  correction of errors, 2.331
  decisions
    correction of errors, 2.331
    forfeiture rule questions, 2.330
    generally, 1.546–1.547, 2.328–2.329
    setting aside, 2.332–2.335
    supplementary, 2.336
  directions, 2.314–2.316
  forfeiture rule questions
    meaning, 2.283–2.284
    post-decision procedure, 2.330
  grounds
    errors of law, 1.400
    findings of fact, 1.401
    generally, 1.397–1.410
    inadequate reasons, 1.403
    materiality of errors, 1.405
    misdirection of law, 1.402
    natural justice, 1.404
    partner, by, 2.516–2.517
    perversity, 1.401
    point of law, 1.400
    precedent, 1.406
    procedural irregularity, 1.404
    right to fair trial, 1.404
  hearings
    generally, 2.322
    request for, 2.320–2.321
  irregularities, effect of, 2.327
  linked case notice, 2.317
  medical evidence, non-disclosure of, 2.318–2.319
  notice of appeal
    acknowledgment, 2.306–2.307
    decisions, 2.328–2.336
    directions, 2.314–2.316
    generally, 2.300–2.301
    medical evidence, 2.318–2.319
    reply to response, 2.312–2.313
    response, 2.310
    service, 2.288
    time limits, 2.302–2.303
    withdrawal, 2.325–2.326
  partner, by, 2.516–2.517
  procedure, 1.413–1.422
  recovery of benefit
    generally, 1.277–1.281
    reference of questions, 1.282–1.287
    supplementary, 1.291–1.292
  reference under Forfeiture Act 1982
    acknowledgment, 2.306–2.307
    decisions, 2.328–2.336
    directions, 2.314–2.316
    generally, 2.304–2.307

Appeals (to Commissioners)—*cont.*
  reference under Forfeiture Act 1982—*cont.*
    medical evidence, 2.318–2.319
    reply to response, 2.312–2.313
    response, 2.310
    withdrawal, 2.325–2.326
  reply to response, 2.312–2.313
  representation, 2.308–2.309
  request for hearings, 2.320–2.321
  response to notice or reference
    generally, 2.310–2.311
    reply, 2.312–2.313
  service of notices, 2.288
  setting aside decisions, 2.332–2.335
  transfer of proceedings, 2.286
  witness summons, 2.323–2.324

Appeals Tribunal
  see **Social Security and Child Support Appeals Tribunal**

Applications (permission to appeal)
  acknowledgment, 2.306–2.307
  courts, to, 2.337–2.338
  decisions
    correction of errors, 2.331
    forfeiture rule questions, 2.330
    generally, 2.328–2.329
    setting aside, 2.332–2.335
    supplementary, 2.336
  determination, 2.299
  directions, 2.314–2.316
  generally, 2.300–2.301
  medical evidence, 2.318–2.319
  notice, 2.296–2.298
  response to notice or reference
    generally, 2.310–2.311
    reply, 2.312–2.313
  time limits, 2.302–2.303
  withdrawal, 2.325–2.326

Appointments (third parties)
  claims for benefit, 2.153–2.160

Assembly
  see **Human rights**

Assessment of damages
  see **Measure of damages**

Assignment (benefits)
  generally, 1.222–1.224

Attendance allowance
  claims for benefit
    further claims, 2.97–2.98
    imprisonment, 2.573–2.575
    payment of benefit, 2.137

"Attendance in person"
  claims for benefit, 2.82–2.83

"Automated credit transfers"
  overpayment of benefits
    generally, 1.101
    regulations, 2.700
  payment of benefits, 2.131–2.132

Benefits fraud
  child support maintenance, 2.656
  council tax benefit, 2.654
  couple in hardship, 2.647

Index

Benefits fraud—*cont.*
deductions from benefits, 2.656
definitions
  couple in hardship, 2.647
  disqualification period, 2.637
  generally, 2.636
  person in hardship, 2.641
disqualification period, 2.637
disqualifying benefits, 2.655
hardship (jobseeker's allowance)
  applicable amount, 2.646
  circumstances of payment, 2.642–2.643
  conditions for payment, 2.644
  provision of information, 2.645
  relevant person, 2.641
hardship (joint-claim couples)
  applicable amount, 2.652
  circumstances of payment, 2.648–2.649
  conditions for payment, 2.650
  provision of information, 2.651
  relevant couple, 2.647
housing benefit, 2.653
income support, 2.638
joint-claim jobseeker's allowance
  generally, 2.640
  legislative basis, 1.571
legislative basis
  definitions, 1.576
  effect on members of offender's family, 1.572
  generally, 1.569–1.570
  joint-claim jobseeker's allowance, 1.571
  mitigation of provisions, 1.573
  regulations, 1.574
loss of benefit
  child support maintenance, 2.656
  council tax benefit, 2.654
  disqualification period, 2.637
  disqualifying benefits, 2.655
  hardship, 2.641–2.652
  housing benefit, 2.653
  income support, 2.638
  joint-claim jobseeker's allowance, 2.640
  state pension credit, 2.639
  person in hardship, 2.641
  state pension credit, 2.639
Bereavement benefits
claims for benefit
  late claims, 1.38–1.40
  work-focused interviews, 1.22
work-focused interviews, 1.22
Board of Inland Revenue
see **Inland Revenue**
Breach (community orders)
couple in hardship, 2.21
definitions
  couple in hardship, 2.21
  generally, 2.3–2.4
  person in hardship, 2.13–2.14
  prescribed payment, 2.5–2.6
  prescribed period, 2.7–2.8
general note, 2.2

Breach (community orders)—*cont.*
hardship (jobseeker's allowance cases)
  applicable amount, 2.20
  circumstances of payment, 2.15–2.17
  conditions for payment, 2.18
  provision of information, 2.19
  relevant person, 2.13–2.14
hardship (joint-claim couples)
  applicable amount, 2.26
  circumstances of payment, 2.22–2.23
  conditions for payment, 2.24
  provision of information, 2.25
  relevant couple, 2.21
income support, 2.9–2.10
information, 2.27–2.31
joint-claim jobseeker's allowance
  generally, 2.11–2.12
  legislative basis, 1.564
legislative basis
  appeals, 1.567
  general note, 1.561
  generally, 1.562–1.563
  joint-claim jobseeker's allowance, 1.564
  information, 1.565
  regulations, 1.566
loss of benefit
  definitions, 2.3–2.8
  general note, 2.2
  hardship, 2.7–2.26
  income support, 2.5–2.6
  information, 2.27–2.31
person in hardship, 2.13–2.14
prescribed payment, 2.5–2.6
prescribed period, 2.7–2.8

Carer's allowance
electronic communications
  claims for benefit, 2.55
  payment of benefit, 2.151
Category A retirement pensions
claims for benefit
  see also **Claims for benefit**
  advance claims, 2.101–2.102
  generally, 2.36–2.37
  gender recognition, 1.615–1.616
  imprisonment, 2.573–2.575
Category B retirement pensions
claims for benefit
  see also **Claims for benefit**
  advance claims, 2.101–2.102
  generally, 2.36–2.37
  gender recognition, 1.617–1.618
  imprisonment, 2.573–2.575
Category C retirement pensions
claims for benefit
  see also **Claims for benefit**
  advance claims, 2.101–2.102
  generally, 2.36–2.37
  gender recognition, 1.622–1.623
  imprisonment, 2.573–2.575
Category D retirement pensions
claims for benefit
  see also **Claims for benefit**

Index

Category D retirement pensions—*cont.*
claims for benefit—*cont.*
advance claims, 2.101–2.102
generally, 2.36–2.37
imprisonment, 2.573–2.575
Causation
overpayment of benefits, 1.99
Certificates of recoverable benefit
appeals to Commissioners, 1.288–1.290
appeals to tribunal
generally, 1.277–1.281, 2.436
reference of questions, 1.282–1.287
supplementary, 1.291–1.292
applications
generally, 1.261–1.263
regulations, 2.759
contents, 1.264–1.265
review
generally, 1.273–1.276
regulations, 2.398–2.399
supplementary, 1.291–1.292
Change of circumstances
council tax benefit, 2.682
housing benefit, 2.682
jobseeker's allowance, 2.681
notification requirement, 2.680
other benefits, 2.683
supercession of decisions, 2.396–2.397
Charges
generally, 1.222–1.224
Child benefit
administration and adjudication
arrangements, 2.852–2.854
appeals, 2.894–2.917
claims and payments, 2.791–2.822
decisions, 2.862–2.889
electronic communications, 2.835–2.846
overpayments, 2.823–2.830
suspension, 2.890–2.893
termination, 2.892
administrative arrangements
definitions, 2.851
legislative basis, 1.591–1.592
provision of information, 2.852–2.853
recording, etc. of claims, 2.854
alteration of rates of benefit, 1.182–1.186
appeals
death of party, 2.916–2.917
decisions, against, 2.900–2.901
decisions against which no appeal lies, 2.898–2.899, 2.928–2.938
discontinuance, 2.914–2.915
general right, 2.896–2.897
interests of justice, in, 2.909–2.911
issues arising on appeal in other cases, 2.895
late appeals, 2.906–2.911
procedure, 2.912–2.913
revised decisions, against, 2.902–2.903
time limits, 2.904–2.905

Child benefit—*cont.*
claims for benefit
see also **Claims for benefit**
advance claims, 2.800
amendment, 2.796
application, 2.791
defective applications, 2.798
duration, 2.803
effective date of change of rate, 2.802
electronic, 2.56
evidence, 2.794–2.795
generally, 1.67–1.69
holding, 2.854
information, 2.794–2.795
payability, 2.801
recording, 2.854
third parties, 2.817
time limits, 2.792–2.793
verification, 2.854
withdrawal, 2.797
decisions
definitions, 2.857
electronic communications, 2.861
issues arising on appeal in other cases, 2.894
no appeal lies, against which, 2.928–2.938
revision, 2.862–2.877
service of notices, 2.858–2.860
superseding, 2.878–2.889
suspension of award, 2.890–2.893
termination of award, 2.892
electronic communications
claims for benefit, 2.56
generally, 2.789, 2.861
miscellaneous provisions, 2.835–2.846
payment of benefit, 2.152
legislative basis
administrative arrangements, 1.591–1.592
functions of Board, 1.586
transfer of functions, 1.580–1.583
transitional provisions, 1.587–1.589
national insurance numbers, 2.790
overlapping benefit, 1.130–1.131
overpayment of benefits
calculation, 2.825
direct credit transfer, by, 2.823
generally, 1.109
interim payments, 2.829–2.830
offsetting, 2.826–2.828
prescribed payments, 2.695–2.698
payment of benefit
date of entitlement, 2.801
direct credit transfers, 2.805
effective date of change of rate, 2.802
election for weekly payment, 2.807–2.809
electronic, 2.152
extinguishment of right, 2.814
fractional amounts, 2.812
information, 2.811
interim payment, 2.810

1276

Index

Child benefit—*cont.*
payment of benefit—*cont.*
  method, 2.804
  person under 18 years, 2.813
  third parties, 2.818
  time, 2.806
provision of information
  by authorities, 2.853
  to authorities, 2.852
revision of appealed decisions
  appeal, against which an, 2.868–2.869
  application, on, 2.862–2.867
  award of other benefit, after, 2.874–2.875
  Board, by, 2.862–2.867
  effective date, 2.876–2.877
  error, arising from, 2.872–2.873
  interaction with superseding, 2.884–2.885
  no appeal lies, against which, 2.870–2.871
revision of decisions by Board
  generally, 2.862–2.864
  late applications, 2.864
  procedure, 2.865–2.867
revision of decisions on application
  generally, 2.862–2.864
  late applications, 2.864
  procedure, 2.865–2.867
superseding decisions
  effective date, 2.886–2.889
  interaction with revision, 2.884–2.885
  procedure, 2.881–2.883
  relevant cases and circumstances, 2.878–2.880
suspension
  generally, 2.890
  provision of information, 2.891
  subsequent payment, 2.893
termination, 2.892
third parties
  appointment, 2.816
  claims on behalf of deceased, 2.817
  persons who may act, 2.815
  receipt by partner, 2.822
  receipt on behalf of another, 2.821
  receipt on behalf of deceased, 2.818–2.820
transfer of functions
  Board, to, 1.582–1.583
  transitional provisions, 1.587–1.589
  Treasury, to, 1.580–1.581

Child Benefit and Guardian's Allowance (Administration) Regulations 2003
arrangement, 2.786
citation, 2.787
commencement, 2.787
definitions, 2.788
effect, 2.787
general provisions
  claims and awards, 2.791–2.803
  electronic communications, 2.789
  national insurance numbers, 2.790

Child Benefit and Guardian's Allowance (Administration) Regulations 2003—*cont.*
general provisions—*cont.*
  overpayments, 2.823–2.830
  payments, 2.804–2.814
  third parties, 2.815–2.822
revocations
  generally, 2.831
  schedule, 2.847–2.848
schedules
  electronic communications, 2.835–2.846
  powers exercised, 2.833–2.834
  revocations, 2.847–2.848
  transitional provisions, 2.832

Child Benefit and Guardian's Allowance (Administrative Arrangements) Regulations 2003
arrangement of, 2.849
citation, 2.850
commencement, 2.850
definitions, 2.851
general provisions, 2.852–2.854

Child Benefit and Guardian's Allowance (Decisions and Appeals) Regulations 2003
arrangement of, 2.855
citation, 2.856
commencement, 2.856
definitions, 2.857
effect, 2.856
general provisions
  appeals, 2.896–2.917
  electronic communications, 2.861
  other matters, 2.894–2.895
  revision of decisions, 2.862–2.877
  service of notices, 2.858–2.860
  superseding decisions, 2.878–2.889
  suspension, 2.890–2.893
  termination, 2.892
revocations, 2.918
schedules
  appeals, 2.928–2.938
  powers exercised, 2.922–2.927
  transitional provisions, 2.919

Child dependants
pensioners
  civil servants' special scheme, 3.257
  common provisions, 3.256
  generally, 3.252–3.253
  implementing regulation, 3.409–3.411

Child support
deductions from benefit
  arrears, 2.219
  generally, 2.158–2.159
  miscellaneous provisions, 2.237–2.245
loss of benefit, 2.656

Child support appeal tribunals
appointment panel
  generally, 1.345–1.346
  qualifications, 2.454, 2.542–2.547

1277

Index

Child support appeal tribunals—*cont.*
clerks
  functions, 2.460
  generally, 1.498
composition, 2.455–2.459
constitution, 1.347–1.349
decisions
  correction of errors, 2.505–2.506
  definitions, 2.511
  generally, 2.497–2.499
  late application for statement of reasons, 2.500
  record of proceedings, 2.501–2.504
  setting aside, 2.507–2.508
definition, 1.476
delegation of functions, 1.499
issues determinable by Revenue
  generally, 1.437–1.438
  regulations, 2.463–2.464
medical examinations
  generally, 1.426–1.428
  regulations, 2.469–2.470
officers, 1.496
oral hearings
  adjournment, 2.491–2.492
  choice of, 2.465–2.466
  directions, 2.465–2.466
  expert assistance, 2.489–2.490
  physical examinations, 2.493–2.494
  postponement, 2.491–2.492
  procedure, 2.481–2.488
  record of proceedings, 2.501–2.504
President
  functions, 1.497
  generally, 1.343–1.344
  remuneration, 1.495
  tenure of office, 1.494
procedure
  applications, 2.451–2.452
  determination, 2.461–2.462
  generally, 1.413–1.422
  medical examinations, 2.469–2.472
  oral hearings, 2.465–2.466
  withdrawal, 2.467–2.468
  witness summons, 2.473–2.474
remuneration, 1.495
staff, 1.496
striking out
  generally, 2.477–2.478
  misconceived applications, 2.478
  reinstatement, 2.479
unification, 1.341–1.342
withdrawal, 2.467–2.468
witness summons, 2.473–2.474
Child support officers
transfer of functions, 1.336–1.337
Child Support, Pensions and Social Security Act 2000
arrangement of sections, 1.560
general note, 1.561
general provisions, 1.562–1.567
"Child's special allowance"
imprisonment, 2.573–2.575

Children
notice of decision, 2.434–2.435
payment of benefit, 2.143
Christmas bonus
generally, 1.472–1.473, 1.505
Citizenship
Directive
  general note, 3.61–3.67
  operative provisions, 3.68–3.109
  recitals, 3.60
generally, 3A.28–3A.35
Civil partnerships
generally, 1.631–1.632
references to stepchildren, etc, 1.633–1.634
"Civil servants' special scheme"
dependent children of pensioners, 3.257
generally, 3.153–3.154
invalidity, 3.199
orphans, 3.257
pensions, 3.212
unemployment benefits, 3.242
Claims (benefits)
adjudication,
  see also **Adjudication (benefit)**
  introduction, 1.78
advance claims
  disability living allowance, 2.93–2.94
  disability working allowance, 2.95–2.96
  generally, 2.90–2.92
  maternity allowance, 2.100
  pension following deferment, for, 2.105–2.106
  retirement pensions, 2.101–2.102
  state pension credit, 2.99
age addition, 2.36–2.37
alternative, in the
  generally, 2.84–2.85
  list of benefits, 2.177
amendments, 2.61–2.63
attendance allowance
  further claims, 2.97–2.98
attendance in person, 2.82–2.83
bereavement benefits
  late claims, 1.38–1.40
  work-focused interviews, 1.22
carer's allowance
  electronic claims, 2.55
child benefit
  advance claims, 2.800
  amendment, 2.796
  application, 2.791
  defective applications, 2.798
  duration, 2.803
  effective date of change of rate, 2.802
  electronic claims, 2.56
  evidence, 2.794–2.795
  generally, 1.67–1.69
  holding, 2.854
  information, 2.794–2.795
  payability, 2.801
  recording, 2.854
  third parties, 2.817

Index

Claims (benefits)—*cont.*
  child benefit—*cont.*
    time limits, 2.792–2.793
    verification, 2.854
    withdrawal, 2.797
  cold weather payments, 2.103–2.104
  conditional entitlement
    generally, 1.34–1.35
    optional, 1.37
    supplementary provisions, 1.36
  council tax benefits, 1.47–1.51
  date of claim
    generally, 2.64–2.78
    tax credit, 2.66
  date of entitlement
    generally, 2.107–2.108
    state pension credit, 2.109
  disabled persons tax credit,
    initial claims, 1.61–1.62
    repeat claims, 1.61–1.62
  disability living allowance
    advance payments, 2.93–2.94
    further claims, 2.97–2.98
  disability working allowance
    advance payments, 2.95–2.96
  duration of award, 2.110–2.111
  electronic communications
    carer's allowance, 2.55
    child benefit, 2.56
    miscellaneous provisions, 2.246–2.259
  emergency payments, 1.76–1.77
  entitlement
    generally, 1.24–1.30
    retrospective effect, 1.31–1.33
  evidence, 2.80–2.81
  exemptions, 2.36–2.37
  forwarding, 2.54
  function sharing, 1.59
  further claims
    attendance allowance, 2.97–2.98
    disability living allowance, 2.97–2.98
  guardian's allowance
    advance claims, 2.800
    amendment, 2.796
    application, 2.791
    defective applications, 2.798
    duration, 2.803
    effective date of change of rate, 2.802
    evidence, 2.794–2.795
    holding, 2.854
    information, 2.794–2.795
    payability, 2.801
    recording, 2.854
    third parties, 2.817
    time limits, 2.792–2.793
    verification, 2.854
    withdrawal, 2.797
  holding information, 2.267
  incapacity benefit, 2.86
  income support
    exempt claims, 2.36–2.37
    generally, 2.38–2.52
    method, 2.41

Claims (benefits)—*cont.*
  industrial injuries benefits
    claimant obligations, 1.58–1.60
    medical examinations, 1.55–1.57
    notice of accident, 1.52–1.54
  information
    generally, 2.80–2.81
    local authorities, by, 2.268
  interchange of benefits
    generally, 2.84–2.85
    list of benefits, 2.178
  jobseeker's allowance
    exempt claims, 2.36–2.37
    generally, 2.38–2.52
    method, 2.43
    special provisions, 2.179
  local authorities
    child support, 2.266
    functions, 2.264
    holding information, 2.267
    provision of information, 2.268
    use and supply of information,
      2.273–2.277
    war pensions, 2.266
  maternity allowance
    advance claims, 2.100
    generally, 2.87–2.88
    maternity pay, 1.72–1.73
  method
    electronic claims, 2.55–2.56
    forwarding claims, 2.54
    further provisions, 2.53
    generally, 2.38–2.52
    state pension credit, 2.57–2.60
  mortgage interest, 1.74–1.75
  necessity
    generally, 1.24–1.30
    retrospective effect, 1.31–1.33
  One offices
    child benefit, 2.266
    generally, 2.53–2.54
    war pensions, 2.266
  pension following deferment, 2.105–2.106
  post-30th September 1990, 1.24–1.30
  pre-1st October 1990
    generally, 1.234–1.235
    introduction, 1.4
  provision of information
    generally, 2.80–2.81
    local authorities, by, 2.268
  Regulations
    advance claims, 2.90–2.106
    alternate claims, 2.84–2.85
    amendment, 2.61–2.63
    attendance in person, 2.82–2.83
    date of claim, 2.64–2.78
    date of entitlement, 2.107–2.109
    duration of award, 2.110–2.111
    electronic claims, 2.55–2.56
    evidence, 2.80–2.81
    exempt claims, 2.36–2.37
    forwarding claims, 2.54
    further provisions, 2.53

Index

Claims (benefits)—*cont.*
Regulations—*cont.*
generally, 1.43–1.45
information, 2.80–2.81
interchange of benefits, 2.84–2.85
making claims, 2.57–2.60
method, 2.38–2.52
One offices, 2.53–2.54
time of claim, 2.113–2.128
withdrawal, 2.61–2.63
work-focused interviews, 2.79
retirement pensions,
advance claims, 2.101–2.102
generally, 2.36–2.37
severe disablement allowance, 2.86
sharing of functions, 1.59
sick pay, 1.70–1.71
social fund, 1.63–1.66
state pension credit
advance claims, 2.99
after attaining qualifying age, 2.56
before attaining qualifying age, 2.55
date of claim, 2.56
general note, 2.67
generally, 2.54
statutory maternity pay, 1.72–1.73
statutory sick pay, 1.70–1.71
supplementary benefits, 1.237
time of claim
generally, 2.113–2.128
prescribed period, 2.181–2.182
war pensions, 2.266
widowed mother's allowance, 1.41–1.42
widow's benefit, 1.41–1.42
withdrawal of claim, 2.61–2.63
work-focused interviews for lone parents
conditional entitlement, 1.34–1.35
generally, 2.79
local authorities, by, 2.264
nature, 2.263
optional, 1.37
supplementary provisions, 1.36
working families tax credit, 2.41
Clerical errors
appeals procedure
generally, 2.505–2.506
miscellaneous provisions, 2.509
Commissioners procedure, 2.331
decisions
generally, 1.459–1.462
regulations, 2.400
Cold weather payments
claims for payment, 2.103–2.104
Commissioners of Social Security
see **Social Security Commissioners**
Community orders
couple in hardship, 2.21
definitions
couple in hardship, 2.21
generally, 2.3–2.4
person in hardship, 2.13–2.14
prescribed payment, 2.5–2.6
prescribed period, 2.7–2.8

Community orders—*cont.*
general note, 2.2
hardship (jobseeker's allowance cases)
applicable amount, 2.20
circumstances of payment, 2.15–2.17
conditions for payment, 2.18
provision of information, 2.19
relevant person, 2.13–2.14
hardship (joint-claim couples)
applicable amount, 2.26
circumstances of payment, 2.22–2.23
conditions for payment, 2.24
provision of information, 2.25
relevant couple, 2.21
income support, 2.9–2.10
information, 2.27–2.31
joint-claim jobseeker's allowance
generally, 2.11–2.12
legislative basis, 1.564
legislative basis
appeals, 1.567
general note, 1.561
generally, 1.562–1.563
joint-claim jobseeker's allowance, 1.564
information, 1.565
regulations, 1.566
loss of benefit
definitions, 2.3–2.8
general note, 2.2
hardship, 2.7–2.26
income support, 2.5–2.6
information, 2.27–2.31
person in hardship, 2.13–2.14
prescribed payment, 2.5–2.6
prescribed period, 2.7–2.8
Compensation
recovery of payments, 1.132
"Competent authorities"
co-operation between, 3.263
definition, 3.114
"Competent institution"
definition, 3.114
"Competent State"
definition, 3.114
"Component rates"
income support, 2.411
Computation (benefits)
alteration of rates of benefit
age-related benefits, 1.193–1.197
child benefit, 1.182–1.186
contributory benefits, 1.177–1.178
income support, 1.187–1.189
job-seeker's allowance, 1.190–1.191
up-rating of pensions, 1.179–1.181
Computers
decisions, 1.338–1.339
Conscience
see **Human rights**
Constant attendance allowance
payment of benefit, 2.137
Constitutional law
proceedings against public authorities, 4.20

1280

Index

"Consular staff"
Council Regulation, 3.156
Contracting out (pensions) (appeals)
decisions
 correction of errors, 2.505–2.506
 definitions, 2.511
 generally, 2.497–2.499
 late application for statement of reasons, 2.500
 record of proceedings, 2.501–2.504
 setting aside, 2.507–2.508
issues determinable by Revenue
 generally, 1.437–1.438
 regulations, 2.463–2.464
medical examinations
 generally, 1.426–1.428
 regulations, 2.469–2.470
oral hearings
 adjournment, 2.491–2.492
 choice of, 2.465–2.466
 directions, 2.465–2.466
 expert assistance, 2.489–2.490
 physical examinations, 2.493–2.494
 postponement, 2.491–2.492
 procedure, 2.481–2.488
 record of proceedings, 2.501–2.504
procedure
 applications, 2.451–2.452
 determination, 2.461–2.462
 generally, 1.413–1.422
 medical examinations, 2.469–2.472
 oral hearings, 2.465–2.466
 withdrawal, 2.467–2.468
 witness summons, 2.473–2.474
striking out
 generally, 2.477–2.478
 misconceived applications, 2.478
 reinstatement, 2.479
 withdrawal, 2.467–2.468
 witness summons, 2.473–2.474
"Contributions chargeable to employers"
collection, 3.274
generally, 3.273
Contributory benefits
alteration of rates of benefit, 1.177–1.178
claims for benefit
see also **Claims for benefit**
generally, 1.24–1.62
procedure, 2.32–2.128
payment of benefit, 2.129–2.150
Convention rights
see **Human rights**
"Correction of errors"
appeals procedure
 generally, 2.505–2.506
 miscellaneous provisions, 2.509
Commissioners procedure, 2.331
decisions
 generally, 1.459–1.462
 regulations, 2.400

Council Directive on Citizenship (2004/38)
general note, 3.61–3.67
operative provisions, 3.68–3.109
recitals, 3.60
Council Directive on Equal Treatment (79/7)
general note, 3.451
operative provisions, 3.451–3.471
recitals, 3.450
Council Regulation on application of social security schemes to employed and self-employed persons (1971)
Administrative Commission, 3.258–3.260
Advisory Committee, 3.261–3.262
annex
 application of national legislation, 3.305
 Conventions continuing to apply, 3.296–3.297
 family allowance schemes, 3.307
 miscellaneous, 3.299–3.303
 non-contributory benefits, 3.294–3.295
 person covered, 3.289–3.290
 simultaneous application of legislation, 3.306
 special schemes, 3.291–3.293
arrangement of regulations, 3.110
definitions, 3.114–3.116
determination of applicable legislation
 exceptions to rules, 3.157–3.158
 general rules, 3.141–3.144
 miscellaneous provisions, 3.152
 special rules, 3.145–3.160
extension Regulation (2003)
 annexes, 3.449
 general note, 3.442
 general provisions, 3.444–3.448
 recitals, 3.443
final provisions, 3.285–3.288
forms, 3.441
general note, 3.111–3.112
general provisions
 conclusion of conventions, 3.129–3.130
 declarations on scope, 3.123–3.124
 equality of treatment, 3.119–3.120
 international provisions not affected, 3.127–3.128
 matters covered, 3.121–3.122
 non-contributory benefits, 3.135–3.136
 optional continued insurance, 3.131
 overlapping benefits, 3.139–3.140
 persons covered, 3.117–3.118
 prolongation of reference period, 3.132
 revalorisation of benefits, 3.137–3.138
 social security conventions replaced, 3.125–3.126
 voluntary insurance, 3.131
 waiver of residence, 3.133–3.134
implementation Regulation (1972)
 annexes, 3.430–3.440
 arrangement of regulations, 3.308
 general note, 3.308

1281

Index

Council Regulation on application of social security schemes to employed and self-employed persons (1971)—*cont.*
implementation Regulation (1972)—*cont.*
general provisions, 3.310–3.409
miscellaneous provisions, 3.413–3.422
recitals, 3.309
transitional provisions, 3.424–3.429
miscellaneous provisions, 3.263–3.275
recitals, 3.113
special provisions
accidents at work, 3.213–3.228
death grants, 3.229–3.232
dependent children, 3.252–3.257
family benefits, 3.243–3.251
invalidity, 3.190–3.199
occupational diseases, 3.213–3.228
pensions, 3.200–3.212
sickness and maternity, 3.161–3.189
unemployment benefits, 3.233–3.242
transitional provisions, 3.276–3.284
Council Regulation on freedom of movement for workers (1968)
general provisions, 3.56–3.59
Council tax benefit
change of circumstances, 2.682
claims for benefit, 1.47–1.51
loss of benefit, 2.654
work-focused interviews, 1.22
"Couple in hardship"
reduction for breach of community order, 2.21
Court of Justice
see **European Court of Justice**
Court orders
see **Judgments and orders**

"Date of claim"
generally, 2.64–2.78
tax credit, 2.66
"Date of entitlement"
generally, 2.107–2.109
Death (claimants)
appeals procedure, 2.453
payment of benefit, 2.144–2.146
provision of information
generally, 1.155–1.156
notification, 1.157–1.158
"Death grants"
EC law
generally, 3.229–3.232
implementing regulation, 3.397–3.398
Decisions
alteration in component rates
income support, 2.411
appeals from appeals tribunal
generally, 1.397–1.410
procedure, 1.413–1.422
appeals to appeals tribunal
appealable decisions, 1.516–1.526, 2.430–2.431
appellants, 2.428–2.429

Decisions—*cont.*
appeals to appeals tribunal—*cont.*
certificates of recoverable benefit, 2.436
death of party, 2.453
decisions, 2.497–2.511
definitions, 2.511
dependant upon appeal in other cases, 1.444–1.451, 2.425
extension of time limits, 2.444–2.450
generally, 1.374–1.391
issues determinable by Revenue, 1.437–1.438, 2.463–2.464
late appeals, 2.444–2.450
medical examinations, 1.426–1.428, 2.469–2.470
non-disclosure of medical evidence, 2.471–2.472
oral hearings, 2.465–2.466, 2.481–2.494
procedure, 1.413–1.422, 2.451–2.452, 2.461–2.462
re-determination, 1.392–1.396
revision of decisions, 2.437–2.439
striking out, 2.477–2.478
time limits, 2.441–2.443
unappealable decisions, 1.504–1.515, 2.432–2.433, 2.520–2.541
withdrawal, 2.467–2.468
witness summons, 2.473–2.474
appeals from Commissioner, 1.411–1.412
appeals to Commissioner
applications for leave, 2.512–2.515
dependant upon appeal in other cases, 1.444–1.451, 2.424
generally, 1.397–1.410
issues determinable by Revenue, 1.437–1.438
medical examinations, 1.423–1.435
partner, by, 2.516–2.517
procedure, 1.413–1.422
unappealable decisions, 1.504–1.515
appeals tribunals
appointment panel, 1.345–1.346, 2.454, 2.542–2.547
clerks, 2.460
composition, 2.455–2.459
constitution, 1.347–1.349
definition, 1.476
President, 1.343–1.344
supplementary, 1.494–1.503
unification, 1.341–1.342
certificates of recoverable benefit
appeals, 2.436
review, 2.398–2.399
child benefit
definitions, 2.857
electronic communications, 2.861
issues arising on appeal in other cases, 2.894
no appeal lies, against which, 2.928–2.938
revision, 2.862–2.877
service of notices, 2.858–2.860

1282

Index

Decisions—*cont.*
child benefit—*cont.*
superseding, 2.878–2.889
suspension of award, 2.890–2.893
termination of award, 2.892
Christmas bonus, 1.472–1.473, 1.505
Commissioners, by
correction of errors, 2.331
forfeiture rule questions, 2.330
generally, 2.328–2.329
reference of issues to Board, 2.404–2.405
setting aside, 2.332–2.335
supplementary, 2.336
computer use, 1.338–1.339
correction of errors
generally, 1.459–1.462
regulations, 2.400
errors
restriction of benefit, 1.452–1.458
setting aside decisions, 1.459–1.462
failure to furnish information, 1.433–1.434
failure to submit to medical, 1.435–1.436
guardian's allowance
definitions, 2.857
electronic communications, 2.861
issues arising on appeal in other cases, 2.894
no appeal lies, against which, 2.928–2.938
revision, 2.862–2.877
service of notices, 2.858–2.860
superseding, 2.878–2.889
suspension of award, 2.890–2.893
termination of award, 2.892
incapacity for work
generally, 1.467–1.469
regulations, 2.401–2.403
income support
alteration in component rates, 2.411
incomplete evidence, 2.409
termination of award, 2.412
incomplete evidence
income support, 2.409
jobseeker's allowance, 2.413
social fund contributions, 2.409
industrial accidents
effect, 1.465–1.466
generally, 1.463–1.464
industrial diseases, 1.470–1.471
industrial injuries benefits
generally, 1.521
regulations, 2.406–2.407
information, use of, 1.340
jobseeker's allowance
alteration in component rates, 2.411
incomplete evidence, 2.413
termination of award, 2.412
medical examinations
appeal tribunal, for, 1.426–1.428, 2.469–2.470
failure to submit to, 1.435–1.436
Secretary of State, for, 1.423–1.425

Decisions—*cont.*
notice of decision, 2.434–2.435
pension credit, 1.523
pilot schemes, 1.481
procedure
finality of decisions, 1.418–1.421
generally, 1.413–1.417
matters arising, 1.422
medical examinations, 1.423–1.428
regulations, 1.536–1.542
recovery of benefits, 1.519–1.520
recrudescence of prescribed disease, 2.408
re-determination of appeals, 1.392–1.396
reference of issues to Revenue
appeals, 1.437–1.438
generally, 1.370–1.371
retirement pensions
period of deferment, after, 2.410
revision of decisions
appeals, 2.437–2.439
definitions, 2.391
effective date, 2.369–2.370
extension of time limits, 2.366–2.368
generally, 1.356–1.362
procedure, 2.349–2.364
Secretary of State, by
appeals, 1.374–1.412
dependant upon appeal in other cases, 1.439–1.443
generally, 1.350–1.355
industrial injuries benefits, 2.406–2.407
reference of issues to Revenue, 1.370–1.371
regulations, 1.372–1.373
review of decisions, 1.356–1.362
superseding earlier decisions, 1.363–1.369
service of notices, 2.346–2.348
setting aside decisions, 1.459–1.462
social fund determinations
incomplete evidence, 2.409
supersession of decisions
change of circumstances, 2.396–2.397
definitions, 2.391
effective date, 2.384–2.390
generally, 1.363–1.369
income support, 2.548–2.553
jobseekers' allowance, 2.554–2.560
procedure, 2.372–2.381
state pension credit, 2.561–2.569
suspension of benefit
failure to furnish information, 1.431–1.432, 2.419–2.420
failure to submit to medical, 1.435–1.436, 2.421–2.422
prescribed circumstances, 1.429–1.430, 2.415–2.416
provision of information, 2.417–2.418
recommencement of payments, 2.423
termination of benefit
failure to furnish information, 1.433–1.434, 2.419–2.420

1283

Decisions—*cont.*
  termination of benefit—*cont.*
    failure to submit to medical, 1.435–1.436, 2.421–2.422
    third parties, payments to, 1.518
    transfer of functions, 1.336–1.337
Declarations of incompatibility
see also **Human rights**
  generally, 4.12–4.13
  intervention by Crown, 4.14
  remedial action, 4.26–4.27
Deductions (benefits)
  loss of benefit, 2.656
Deductions (compensation)
  appeals to Commissioners, 1.288–1.290
  appeals to tribunal
    generally, 1.277–1.281
    reference of questions, 1.282–1.287
    supplementary, 1.291–1.292
  assessment of damages, 1.297–1.298
  certificates of recoverable benefit
    appeals, 1.277–1.292
    applications, 1.261–1.263
    contents, 1.264–1.265
    review, 1.273–1.276
  court orders, 1.293–1.294
  disregarded payments, 1.306–1.310
  income support
    additional amounts, 1.142–1.146
    diversion of arrested earnings, 1.150
    generally, 1.133–1.136
    recovery from liable person, 1.137–1.141
    transfer of orders, 1.142–1.146
  information, 1.312–1.316
  introduction, 1.256
  liability of compensator
    generally, 1.266–1.267
    overpayments, 1.304–1.305
    recovery procedure, 1.268–1.269
    wrongly-made payments, 1.306–1.310
  overpayments
    disregards, 1.306–1.310
    generally, 1.304–1.305
  payments into court, 1.295–1.296
  provision of information, 1.312–1.316
  recoverable benefits, 1.257–1.258
  recoverable payments
    exempt payments, 1.329
    generally, 1.257–1.258
    list, 1.332–1.334
    small payments, 1.330–1.331
  reduction of compensation payment
    complex cases, 1.299–1.303
    generally, 1.270–1.263
    lump sum payments, 1.299–1.301
    more than one person, payments by, 1.302–1.303
    periodical payments, 1.299–1.301
    supplementary, 1.272
  reference of questions, 1.282–1.287
  relevant cases, 1.255–1.256

Deductions (compensation)—*cont.*
  relevant payments
    exempt payments, 1.329
    generally, 1.257–1.258
    list, 1.332–1.334
    small payments, 1.330–1.331
  relevant period, 1.259–1.260
  review of certificates
    generally, 1.273–1.276
    supplementary, 1.291–1.292
Deferment (interviews)
  incapacity benefit interviews, 2.587
  jobcentre plus interviews
    generally, 2.625
    partners, for, 2.633
  work-focused interviews, 2.777
Deferment (pensions)
  advance claims, 2.105–2.106
  gender recognition, 1.620–1.621
Deferred pensions
  advance claims, 2.105–2.106
Delay
  payment of lump sums, 2.133
"Dependency benefits"
  claims for benefit
    see also **Claims for benefit**
    generally, 1.24–1.62
    procedure, 2.32–2.128
  payment of benefit, 2.129–2.150
Dependent children
see **Child dependants**
"Diplomatic staff"
  Council Regulation, 3.156
Direct credit transfers
  overpayment of benefits
    generally, 1.101
    regulations, 2.700
  payment of benefits, 2.131–2.132
Direct effect
  generally, 3.10
Direct payments
  accommodation costs, 2.213
  another person on beneficiary's behalf, to
    child benefit, 2.821
    generally, 2.155
    guardian's allowance, 2.821
  appointee, to, 2.153–2.154
  child benefit
    appointment, 2.816
    persons who may act, 2.815
    receipt by partner, 2.822
    receipt on behalf of another, 2.821
    receipt on behalf of deceased, 2.818–2.820
  child support, of
    arrears, 2.219
    generally, 2.158–2.159
    miscellaneous provisions, 2.237–2.245
    decisions, 1.518
  funeral providers, to, 2.158
  guardian's allowance
    appointment, 2.816

Index

Direct payments—*cont.*
guardian's allowance—*cont.*
  persons who may act, 2.815
  receipt by partner, 2.822
  receipt on behalf of another, 2.821
  receipt on behalf of deceased,
    2.818–2.820
hostels, to
  generally, 2.160
  miscellaneous, 2.214
housing costs, 2.212
loans, 2.220
maternity expenses, 2.158
maximum amounts, 2.221
mortgage lenders, to
  generally, 2.156–2.157
  miscellaneous, 2.224–2.236
partner, to
  child benefit, 2.822
  generally, 2.161–2.161
  guardian's allowance, 2.822
priority, 2.222–2.223
utility companies, to
  generally, 2.158
  miscellaneous, 2.216
  service charges, 2.215
  water charges, 2.217
Directives
Citizenship (2004/38)
  general note, 3.61–3.67
  operative provisions, 3.68–3.109
  recitals, 3.60
Equal Treatment (79/7)
  general note, 3.451
  operative provisions, 3.451–3.471
  recitals, 3.450
Disability living allowance
claims for benefit
  see also **Claims for benefit**
  advance payments, 2.93–2.94
  further claims, 2.92–2.98
EC Regulation
  aggravation, 3.196
  civil servant's special scheme, 3.199
  employees, 3.191–3.195
  general note, 3.190
  implementing regulations,
    3.354–3.378
  resumption after suspension,
    3.197–3.198
  self-employed, 3.191–3.195
imprisonment, 2.573–2.575
mobility component
  children, 2.169
  exempt cases, 2.168
  payment to Motability, 2.170–2.172
payment of benefit
  attendance allowance, 2.137
  Motability, to, 2.170–2.172
payment to Motability
  generally, 2.170
  restriction, 2.172
  termination, 2.171

Disability working allowance
claims for benefit
  see also **Claims for benefit**
  advance payments, 2.95–2.96
Disabled persons tax credit
claims for benefit
  see also **Claims for benefit**
  initial claims, 1.61–1.62
  repeat claims, 1.61–1.62
date of claim, 2.64
overpayment of benefits, 1.84
payment of benefit, 2.141
Disablement benefit
imprisonment, 2.573–2.575
Disclosure
overpayment of benefits
  generally, 1.93
  '*One*' office, at, 1.95
  recipients, 1.94
Discrimination
see also **Human rights**
Carson litigation, 4.82
developments in Canada, 4.83
generally, 4.75
ground of differentiation, 4.78
indirect discrimination, 4.79
introduction, 4.76
Michalak test, 4.80
Reynolds litigation, 4.82
UK authorities, 4.82–4.83
widowers' benefits, 4.81
widows' benefits, 4.81
Disqualification (benefits)
fraud on social security system
  period, 2.637
  relevant benefits, 2.655
imprisonment, 2.573–2.575
Duplication of payments
maintenance payments, 2.697–2.699
prescribed income, 2.693–2.694
prescribed payments
  foreign currency payments, 2.699
  generally, 2.695–2.696
Duration (awards)
generally, 2.110–2.111

EC law
binding nature, 3.7
Council Directives
  citizenship, 3.60–3.109
  direct effect, 3.10
  equal treatment, 3.450–3.471
  indirect effect, 3.11
  liability for breach, 3.12
Council Regulations
  application of social security schemes to
    employed and self-employed
    persons, 3.110–3.449
  freedom of movement of workers,
    3.56–3.59
EC Treaty
  citizenship, 3A.28–3A.35
  Court of Justice, 3A.43–3.53

Index

EC law—cont.
EC Treaty—cont.
final provisions, 3.54–3.55
freedom of movement, 3A.36–3A.42
principles, 3.17–3A.27
effective enjoyment of rights, 3.13
implementation of Treaties
direct effect, 3.10
generally, 3.6
indirect effect, 3.11
liability for breach, 3.12
supremacy, 3.9
interim relief, 3.13
proof of Treaties, 3.15–3.16
supremacy, 3.9
types, 3.8
EC Treaty
citation, 3.5
citizenship, 3A.28–3A.35
European Court of Justice
generally, 3A.43–3.52
guidance for references, 3.53
final provisions, 3.54–3.55
freedom of movement, 3A.36–3A.42
generally, 3.4
implementation, 3.6–3.13
operative provisions
citizenship, 3A.28–3A.35
Court of Justice, 3A.43–3.53
freedom of movement, 3A.36–3A.42
principles, 3.17–3A.27
proof, 3.15–3.16
principles, 3.17–3A.27
proof, 3.15–3.16
renumbering, 3.5
Education
see **Human rights**
Effective enjoyment of rights
EC law, 3.13
Electronic communications
carer's allowance
claims for benefit, 2.55
payment of benefit, 2.151
child benefit
claims for benefit, 2.56
generally, 2.789, 2.861
miscellaneous provisions, 2.835–2.846
payment of benefit, 2.152
claims for benefit
carer's allowance, 2.55
child benefit, 2.56
miscellaneous provisions, 2.246–2.259
guardian's allowance
generally, 2.789, 2.861
miscellaneous provisions, 2.835–2.846
payment of benefit
carer's allowance, 2.151
child benefit, 2.152
service of appeal decisions, 2.510
"Emergency payments"
claims for benefit, 1.76–1.77

Employees
accidents at work
aggravation, 3.224
general note, 3.213–3.214
implementing regulations, 3.379–3.396
miscellaneous, 3.225–3.226
reimbursement between institutions, 3.227
rights to benefits, 3.215–3.223
students, 3.228
Administrative Commission
generally, 3.258
tasks, 3.259–3.260
Advisory Committee
generally, 3.261
tasks, 3.262
aggregation of periods
accidents at work, 3.224
death grants, 3.229
family benefits, 3.244
general rules, 3.332
invalidity, 3.196
maternity, 3.161
sickness, 3.161
unemployment benefits, 3.233
child dependants
civil servants' special scheme. 3.257
common provisions, 3.256
generally, 3.252–3.253
implementing regulation, 3.409–3.411
civil servants special scheme
dependent children of pensioners, 3.257
generally, 3.153–3.154
invalidity, 3.199
orphans, 3.257
pensions, 3.212
unemployment benefits, 3.242
claims submitted to other authority, 3.266–3.267
competent authorities
co-operation between, 3.263
definition, 3.114
competent institution, 3.114
competent State, 3.114
conclusion of Conventions, 3.129–3.130
consular staff, 3.156
contributions chargeable to employers
collection, 3.274
generally, 3.273
co-operation between competent authorities, 3.263
Council Regulation
Administrative Commission, 3.258–3.260
Advisory Committee, 3.261–3.262
annexes, 3.289–3.307
arrangement of regulations, 3.110
definitions, 3.114–3.116
determination of applicable legislation, 3.141–3.160
extension of, 3.392–3.399
final provisions, 3.285–3.288

Index

Employees—*cont.*
Council Regulation—*cont.*
   general note, 3.111–3.112
   general provisions, 3.117–3.140
   implementation of, 3.308–3.440
   miscellaneous provisions, 3.263–3.275
   recitals, 3.113
   special provisions, 3.161–3.257
   transitional provisions, 3.276–3.284
death grants
   generally, 3.229–3.232
   implementing regulation, 3.397–3.398
declarations on scope, 3.123–3.124
definitions, 3.114–3.116
dependent children of pensioners
   civil servants' special scheme. 3.257
   common provisions, 3.256
   generally, 3.252–3.253
   implementing regulation, 3.409–3.411
determination of applicable legislation
   civil servants, 3.153–3.154
   consular staff, 3.156
   diplomatic staff, 3.156
   employed in one member state and self-employed in another, 3.151
   employed persons, 3.145–3.147
   exceptions to articles, 3.157–3.158
   general rules, 3.141–3.144
   implementing regulation, 3.323–3.331
   mariners, 3.150
   miscellaneous provisions, 3.152
   posted workers, 3.147
   recipients of pensions due in more than one member state, 3.159–3.160
   self-employed persons, 3.148–3.149
   special rules, 3.145–3.151
   students, 3.144
   voluntary insurance, 3.155
diplomatic staff, 3.156
employment and self-employment in more than one state, 3.151
employed person, 3.114
equality of treatment, 3.119–3.120
exemption from authentication, 3.265
exemption from fees, 3.265
family benefits
   generally, 3.243–3.251
   implementing regulation, 3.404–3.407
foreign nationals
   annexes, 3.399
   general note, 3.392
   general provisions, 3.394–3.398
   recitals, 3.393
frontier workers
   accidents at work, 3.216
   definition, 3.114
general note, 3.111–3.112
habitual residence, 3.114
international provision not affected
   generally, 3.127–3.128
   implementing regulation, 3.314
invalidity
   aggravation, 3.196

Employees—*cont.*
invalidity —*cont.*
   civil servant's special scheme, 3.199
   employees, 3.191–3.195
   general note, 3.190
   implementing regulations, 3.354–3.378
   resumption after suspension, 3.197–3.198
   self-employed, 3.191–3.195
mariners, 3.150
maternity
   aggregation rules, 3.161–3.162
   employees, 3.163–3.173
   frontier workers, 3.165
   implementing regulations, 3.333–3.353
   miscellaneous provisions, 3.188
   pension claimants, 3.176
   pensioners, 3.177–3.185
   reimbursement between institutions, 3.189
   self-employed, 3.163–3.173
   students, 3.186–3.187
   unemployed, 3.174–3.175
   vocational students, 3.186–3.187
matters covered, 3.121–3.122
medical examinations, 3.268
member of the family, 3.114
nationals of third countries
   annexes, 3.399
   general note, 3.392
   general provisions, 3.394–3.398
   recitals, 3.393
non-contributory benefits, 3.294–3.295
occupational diseases
   aggravation, 3.224
   general note, 3.213–3.214
   implementing regulations, 3.379–3.396
   miscellaneous, 3.225–3.226
   reimbursement between institutions, 3.227
   rights to benefits, 3.215–3.223
   students, 3.228
orphans
   civil servants' special scheme. 3.257
   common provisions, 3.256
   generally, 3.254–3.255
   implementing regulation, 3.409–3.411
overlapping benefits
   generally, 3.139–3.140
   implementing regulation, 3.316–3.321
pensions
   accidents at work, 3.396
   generally, 3.200–3.212
   implementing regulations, 3.354–3.378
periods of employment, 3.114
periods of insurance, 3.114
periods of residence, 3.114
persons covered
   annex, 3.289–3.290
   generally, 3.117–3.118
posted workers, 3.147
prolongation of reference period, 3.132
recipients of pensions due in more than one member state, 3.159–3.160

1287

Employees—*cont.*
refugee, 3.114
reimbursement between institutions
   agreements relating to, 3.285
   occupational diseases, 3.227
   sickness and maternity, 3.189
residence, 3.114
revalorization of benefits
   generally, 3.137–3.138
   pensions, 3.211
seasonal worker, 3.114
self-employed person, 3.114
sickness
   aggregation rules, 3.161–3.162
   employees, 3.163–3.173
   frontier workers, 3.165
   implementing regulations, 3.333–3.353
   miscellaneous provisions, 3.188
   pension claimants, 3.176
   pensioners, 3.177–3.185
   reimbursement between institutions, 3.189
   self-employed, 3.163–3.173
   students, 3.186–3.187
   unemployed, 3.174–3.175
   vocational students, 3.186–3.187
simultaneous employment and self-employment in more than one state, 3.151
social security conventions replaced
   generally, 3.125–3.126
   implementing regulation, 3.314
special non-contributory benefits, 3.135–3.136
special rules
   civil servants, 3.153–3.154
   consular staff, 3.156
   diplomatic staff, 3.156
   employed in one member state and self-employed in another, 3.151
   employed persons, 3.145–3.147
   mariners, 3.150
   miscellaneous provisions, 3.152
   posted workers, 3.147
   recipients of pensions due in more than one member state, 3.159–3.160
   self-employed persons, 3.148–3.149
   special rules, 3.145–3.151
   students, 3.144
   voluntary insurance, 3.155
stateless person, 3.114
stay, 3.114
students
   accidents at work, 3.228
   generally, 3.144
   sickness and maternity, 3.186–3.187
   transitional provisions, 3.283
survivor, 3.114
temporary residence, 3.114
third country nationals
   annexes, 3.399
   general note, 3.392

Employees—*cont.*
third country nationals—*cont.*
   general provisions, 3.394–3.398
   recitals, 3.393
   transfer of sums payable between member states, 3.269
unemployment benefits
   civil servants' special scheme, 3.242
   common provisions, 3.233–3.236
   implementing regulation, 3.399–3.403
   person going to other member state, 3.237–3.239
   person residing in other member state, 3.240–3.241
voluntary insurance
   applicable legislation, 3.155
   generally, 3.131
   implementing regulation, 3.315
   waiver of residence, 3.133–3.134
Employed earners
   see **Employees**
Employment Protection (Recoupment of Jobseeker's Allowance and Income Support) Regulations 1996
citation, 2.738
commencement, 2.738
definitions, 2.739
general provisions
   determination of benefit recouped, 2.748–2.749
   industrial tribunal proceedings, 2.740–2.743
   recoupment of benefit, 2.744–2.747
long title, 2.737
revocation, 2.750
schedule, 2.751
transitional provision, 2.750
Employment tribunal proceedings (recovery of benefits)
definitions, 2.739
determination of amount, 2.748–2.749
duties of employer. 2.743
duties of tribunals
   monetary awards, 2.741
   protective awards, 2.742
legislative basis
   further provisions, 1.252
   general note, 1.249
   general provisions, 1.250–1.251
postponement of award, 2.744
procedure, 2.745–2.746
relevant payments
   generally, 2.740
   table of monetary awards, 2.751
relevant proceedings, 2.740
secondary proceedings, 2.747
Employment Tribunals Act 1996
general note, 1.249
general provisions, 1.250–1.252
Equal treatment
general note, 3.451
operative provisions, 3.451–3.471
recitals, 3.450

Index

Equality
Council Regulation, 3.119–3.120
human rights, 4.84
Errors
appeals procedure
generally, 2.505–2.506
miscellaneous provisions, 2.509
correction
appeals procedure, 2.505–2.506
Commissioners procedure, 2.331
decisions, 1.459–1.462
decisions
generally, 1.459–1.462
regulations, 2.400
restriction of benefit, 1.452–1.458
setting aside decisions, 1.459–1.462
Error of law
appeals from appeal tribunal, 1.400
European Communities Act 1972
see also **EC law**
arrangement of sections, 3.1
citation, 3.2
commencement, 3.2
definitions, 3.2–3.5
general provisions
implementation of Treaties, 3.6–3.13
proof of Treaties, 3.14–3.15
European Convention on Human Rights
see also **Human rights**
First Protocol
education, 4.91–4.92
free elections, 4.93
property, 4.88–4.90
freedoms
assembly, 4.73
conscience, 4.70–4.71
expression, 4.72
religion, 4.70–4.71
thought, 4.70–4.71
prohibitions
abuse of rights, 4.86
discrimination, 4.75–4.83
forced labour, 4.49–4.50
punishment without law, 4.65
slavery, 4.49–4.50
torture, 4.47–4.48
protections
property, 4.88–4.90
restrictions
limitation on use, 4.87
political activity of aliens, 4.85
rights
education, 4.91–4.92
equality, 4.84
fair trial, 4.53–4.64
free elections, 4.93
liberty, 4.51–4.52
life, 4.45–4.46
marriage, 4.74
private life, 4.66–4.69
security, 4.51–4.52
Thirteenth Protocol, 4.94

European Court of Justice
generally, 3A.43–3.52
guidance for references, 3.53
Evidence
claims for benefit, 2.80–2.81
overpayment of benefits, 1.85
"Exchange of information"
overseas authorities, 1.216
Expression
see **Human rights**
Extensions of time
appeals procedure, 2.444–2.450
revision of decisions, 2.366–2.368
Extinguishment (benefits)
generally, 2.163–2.166

Failure to disclose
overpayment of benefits
generally, 1.93
material fact, 1.97
mental capacity, 1.96
missing documents, 1.98
suspension of benefit
generally, 1.431–1.432
regulations, 2.419–2.420
Failure to furnish information
see **Withholding information**
Failure to maintain
diversion of arrested earnings, 1.150
generally, 1.133–1.136
recovery of benefit
additional amounts, 1.142–1.146
generally, 1.137–1.141
transfer of orders, 1.142–1.146
reduction of income support, 1.147–1.149
"Failure to submit to medical"
suspension of benefit
generally, 1.435–1.436
regulations, 2.421–2.422
Fair trial
see **Human rights**
Family benefits
generally, 3.243–3.251
implementing regulation, 3.404–3.407
Family life
see **Human rights**
Forced labour
generally, 4.49
introduction, 4.50
Forfeiture Act 1982
arrangement of sections, 1.12
general provisions, 1.13–1.22
Forfeiture rule
acknowledgement, 2.306–2.307
application to benefits, 1.17–1.18
determination by Commissioner
further provisions, 2.305
generally, 1.17–1.18, 2.304
post-decision procedure, 2.330
procedure, 2.306–2.307
meaning, 1.13–1.14, 2.283–2.284
murderers, 1.19–1.20

Forfeiture rule—*cont.*
  notification, 2.306–2.307
  post-decision procedure, 2.330
"Fractional sums"
  payment of benefit, 2.142
Fraud
  see also **Loss of benefit**
  council tax benefit, 2.654
  deductions from benefits, 2.656
  definitions, 2.636–2.637
  disqualifying benefits, 2.655
  hardship, 2.641–2.652
  housing benefit, 2.653
  legislative basis, 1.568–1.574
  reductions, 2.638–2.640
Free elections
  see **Human rights**
Freedom of assembly and association
  generally, 4.73
Freedom of expression
  generally, 4.72
  miscellaneous provision, 4.30–4.31
Freedom of movement for workers
  generally, 3A.36–3A.42
  Regulation, 3.56–3.59
Freedom of peaceful assembly
  generally, 4.73
Freedom of thought, conscience and religion
  generally, 4.70
  introduction, 4.71
  miscellaneous provision, 4.32–4.33
Frontier workers
  accidents at work, 3.216
  definition, 3.114
Funding
  Commissioner's procedure, 2.289–2.290
Funeral expenses
  payment of benefit, 2.158
"Further claims"
  disability living allowance, 2.92–2.98

"Gender recognition"
  application of provisions, 1.605
  certification, 1.601
  definitions, 1.604
  general note, 1.603
  introductory, 1.606
  long-term incapacity benefit, 1.613–1.614
  occupational pensions
    equivalent benefits, 1.629–1.630
    general note, 1.626
    guaranteed minimum, 1.627–1.628
  retirement pensions
    Category A, 1.615–1.616
    Category B, 1.617–1.618
    Category C, 1.622–1.623
    deferment of, 1.620–1.621
    graduated, 1.624–1.625
    shared additional, 1.619
  widowed mother's allowance, 1.607–1.608
  widowed parent's allowance, 1.611–1.612
  widow's pension, 1.609–1.610

Gender Recognition Act 2004
  see also **Gender recognition**
  arrangement of sections, 1.599
  commencement, 1.600
  definitions, 1.604
  general note, 1.601
  general provisions, 1.602–1.603
  schedules, 1.605–1.630
Good cause
  extinguishment, 2.166
  incapacity benefit interviews, 2.591
  jobcentre plus interviews
    generally, 2.613
  partners, for, 2.632
  work-focused interviews for lone parents, 2.735
"Guaranteed minimum payments"
  decisions and appeals, 1.247–1.248
Guardian's allowance
  administration and adjudication
    arrangements, 2.852–2.854
  appeals, 2.894–2.917
  claims and payments, 2.791–2.822
  decisions, 2.862–2.889
  electronic communications, 2.835–2.846
  overpayments, 2.823–2.830
  suspension, 2.890–2.893
  termination, 2.892
  administrative arrangements
    definitions, 2.851
    legislative basis, 1.591–1.592
    provision of information, 2.852–2.853
    recording, etc. of claims, 2.854
  appeals
    death of party, 2.916–2.917
    decisions, against, 2.900–2.901
    decisions against which no appeal lies, 2.898–2.899, 2.928–2.938
    discontinuance, 2.914–2.915
    general right, 2.896–2.897
    interests of justice, in, 2.909–2.911
    issues arising on appeal in other cases, 2.895
    late appeals, 2.906–2.911
    procedure, 2.912–2.913
    revised decisions, against, 2.902–2.903
    time limits, 2.904–2.905
  claims for payment
    see also **Claims for benefit**
    advance claims, 2.800
    amendment, 2.796
    application, 2.791
    defective applications, 2.798
    duration, 2.803
    effective date of change of rate, 2.802
    evidence, 2.794–2.795
    holding, 2.854
    information, 2.794–2.795
    payability, 2.801
    recording, 2.854
    third parties, 2.817
    time limits, 2.792–2.793

Index

Guardian's allowance—*cont.*
claims for payment—*cont.*
  verification, 2.854
  withdrawal, 2.797
decisions
  definitions, 2.857
  electronic communications, 2.861
  issues arising on appeal in other cases, 2.894
  no appeal lies, against which, 2.928–2.938
  revision, 2.862–2.877
  service of notices, 2.858–2.860
  superseding, 2.878–2.889
  suspension of award, 2.890–2.893
  termination of award, 2.892
electronic communications
  generally, 2.789, 2.861
  miscellaneous provisions, 2.835–2.846
legislative basis
  administrative arrangements, 1.591–1.592
  functions of Board, 1.586
  transfer of functions, 1.580–1.583
  transitional provisions, 1.587–1.589
national insurance numbers, 2.790
overpayment of benefits
  calculation, 2.825
  direct credit transfer, by, 2.823
  interim payments, 2.829–2.830
  offsetting, 2.826–2.828
  prescribed payments, 2.695–2.698
payment of benefit
  date of entitlement, 2.801
  direct credit transfers, 2.805
  effective date of change of rate, 2.802
  election for weekly payment, 2.807–2.809
  extinguishment of right, 2.814
  fractional amounts, 2.812
  generally, 2.135
  information, 2.811
  interim payment, 2.810
  method, 2.804
  person under 18 years, 2.813
  third parties, 2.818
  time, 2.806
provision of information
  by authorities, 2.853
  to authorities, 2.852
revision of appealed decisions
  appeal, against which an, 2.868–2.869
  application, on, 2.862–2.867
  award of other benefit, after, 2.874–2.875
  Board, by, 2.862–2.867
  effective date, 2.876–2.877
  error, arising from, 2.872–2.873
  interaction with superseding, 2.884–2.885
  no appeal lies, against which, 2.870–2.871

Guardian's allowance—*cont.*
revision of decisions by Board
  generally, 2.862–2.864
  late applications, 2.864
  procedure, 2.865–2.867
revision of decisions on application
  generally, 2.862–2.864
  late applications, 2.864
  procedure, 2.865–2.867
superseding decisions
  effective date, 2.886–2.889
  interaction with revision, 2.884–2.885
  procedure, 2.881–2.883
  relevant cases and circumstances, 2.878–2.880
suspension
  generally, 2.890
  provision of information, 2.891
  subsequent payment, 2.893
  termination, 2.892
third parties
  appointment, 2.816
  claims on behalf of deceased, 2.817
  persons who may act, 2.815
  receipt by partner, 2.822
  receipt on behalf of another, 2.821
  receipt on behalf of deceased, 2.818–2.820
transfer of functions
  Board, to, 1.582–1.583
  transitional provisions, 1.587–1.589
  Treasury, to, 1.580–1.581

Habitual residence
Council Regulation, 3.114

Harassment
racial discrimination, 1.5

Hardship (loss of benefit)
jobseeker's allowance
  applicable amount, 2.646
  circumstances of payment, 2.642–2.643
  conditions for payment, 2.644
  provision of information, 2.645
  relevant person, 2.641
joint-claim couples
  applicable amount, 2.652
  circumstances of payment, 2.648–2.649
  conditions for payment, 2.650
  provision of information, 2.651
  relevant couple, 2.647

Hardship (reduction for breach of community order)
jobseeker's allowance
  applicable amount, 2.20
  circumstances of payment, 2.15–2.17
  conditions for payment, 2.18
  provision of information, 2.19
  relevant person, 2.13–2.14
joint-claim couples
  applicable amount, 2.26
  circumstances of payment, 2.22–2.23
  conditions for payment, 2.24
  provision of information, 2.25
  relevant couple, 2.21

Index

Heating
payment of benefit, 2.158
"Holding information"
local authorities, 2.267
Hostels
direct payments
generally, 2.160
miscellaneous, 2.214
Housing benefits
change of circumstances, 2.682
work-focused interviews, 1.22
"Housing costs"
payment of benefit, 2.212
Human rights
abuse of rights, 4.86
assembly and association, 4.73
conscience, thought and religion
generally, 4.70
introduction, 4.71
miscellaneous provision, 4.32–4.33
Convention rights
generally, 4.3–4.4
interpretation, 4.5–4.9
death penalty, 4.94
declarations of incompatibility
generally, 4.12–4.13
intervention by Crown, 4.14
remedial action, 4.26–4.27
derogations
duration, 4.36
generally, 4.34
periodic review, 4.37
withdrawal, 4.97
discrimination
Carson litigation, 4.82
developments in Canada, 4.83
generally, 4.75
ground of differentiation, 4.78
indirect discrimination, 4.79
introduction, 4.76
Michalak test, 4.80
Reynolds litigation, 4.82
UK authorities, 4.82–4.83
widowers' benefits, 4.81
widows' benefits, 4.81
ECHR judges, 4.38
education
generally, 4.91
introduction, 4.92
equality, 4.84
European Convention on Human Rights
Articles, 4.45–4.87
First Protocol, 4.88–4.93
Thirteenth Protocol, 4.94
existing human rights, safeguards for
conscience, freedom of, 4.32–4.33
expression, freedom of, 4.30–4.31
generally, 4.28–4.29
religion, freedom of, 4.32–4.33
thought, freedom of, 4.32–4.33
expression
generally, 4.72
miscellaneous provision, 4.30–4.31

Human rights—*cont.*
fair trial
generally, 4.54–4.64
introduction, 4.53
family life
generally, 4.66
introduction, 4.67–4.69
forced labour
generally, 4.49
introduction, 4.50
free elections, 4.93
freedom of assembly and association, 4.73
freedom of conscience, thought and religion
generally, 4.70
introduction, 4.71
miscellaneous provision, 4.32–4.33
freedom of expression
generally, 4.72
miscellaneous provision, 4.30–4.31
indirect discrimination, 4.79
interpretation of Convention rights
generally, 4.5
introduction, 4.6
new system of protection, 4.8–4.9
old system of protection, 4.7
judicial acts, 4.25
judicial remedies, 4.23–4.24
legislation
declaration of incompatibility, 4.12–4.13
interpretation, 4.10–4.11
intervention by Crown, 4.14
remedial action, 4.26–4.27
liberty
generally, 4.51
introduction, 4.52
life
generally, 4.45
introduction, 4.46
marriage, 4.74
no punishment without law, 4.65
Parliamentary procedure
statements of compatibility, 4.39–4.40
political activity of aliens, 4.85
private life, right to respect for
generally, 4.66
introduction, 4.67–4.69
proceedings
"any legal proceedings", 4.22
constitutional torts, 4.20
generally, 4.17–4.18
judicial review, 4.21
standing of claimant, 4.19
"victim" requirement, 4.19
prohibition of discrimination
Carson litigation, 4.82
developments in Canada, 4.83
generally, 4.75
ground of differentiation, 4.78
indirect discrimination, 4.79
introduction, 4.76

Index

Human rights—*cont.*
prohibition of discrimination—*cont.*
  Michalak test, 4.80
  Reynolds litigation, 4.82
  UK authorities, 4.82–4.83
  widowers' benefits, 4.81
  widows' benefits, 4.81
prohibition of forced labour
  generally, 4.49
  introduction, 4.50
prohibition of slavery
  generally, 4.49
  introduction, 4.50
prohibition of torture
  generally, 4.47
  introduction, 4.48
prohibition on abuse of rights, 4.86
property
  generally, 4.88
  introduction, 4.89–4.90
punishment without law, no, 4.65
public authorities' acts
  generally, 4.15–4.16
  judicial acts, 4.25
  judicial remedies, 4.23–4.24
  proceedings, 4.17–4.22
religion
  generally, 4.70
  introduction, 4.71
  miscellaneous provision, 4.32–4.33
remedial action, 4.26–4.27
reservations
  generally, 4.35
  text, 4.96
restriction on political activity of aliens, 4.85
right to education
  generally, 4.91
  introduction, 4.92
right to fair trial
  generally, 4.54–4.64
  introduction, 4.53
right to free elections, 4.93
right to liberty
  generally, 4.51
  introduction, 4.52
right to life
  generally, 4.45
  introduction, 4.46
right to marry, 4.74
right to respect for private and family life
  generally, 4.66
  introduction, 4.67–4.69
right to security
  generally, 4.51
  introduction, 4.52
safeguards for existing human rights
  conscience, freedom of, 4.32–4.33
  expression, freedom of, 4.30–4.31
  generally, 4.28–4.29
  religion, freedom of, 4.32–4.33
  thought, freedom of, 4.32–4.33

Human rights—*cont.*
security
  generally, 4.51
  introduction, 4.52
slavery
  generally, 4.49
  introduction, 4.50
statements of compatibility, 4.39–4.40
Thirteenth Protocol, 4.94
thought
  generally, 4.70
  introduction, 4.71
  miscellaneous provision, 4.32–4.33
torture
  generally, 4.47
  introduction, 4.48
Treaty of Amsterdam, 3.5

Human Rights Act 1998
arrangement of sections, 4.1
citation, 4.43
commencement, 4.43–4.44
definitions, 4.42
general note, 4.2
general provisions
  derogations, 4.34–4.37
  ECHR judges, 4.38
  legislation, 4.10–4.14
  other rights, 4.28–4.33
  Parliamentary procedure, 4.39–4.40
  public authorities, 4.15–4.25
  remedial action, 4.26–4.27
  reservations, 4.35
introductory provisions, 4.3–4.9
schedules
  derogations and reservations, 4.95–4.97
  European Convention, 4.45–4.94
  reservation, 4.96–4.97
supplementary provisions, 4.41

Imprisonment
disqualification from benefit, 2.573–2.575
suspension of benefit, 2.575

"Inalienability of benefit"
generally, 1.222–1.224

Incapacity benefit
claims for benefit
  see also **Claims for benefit**
  generally, 2.86
EC Regulation
  aggravation, 3.196
  civil servant's special scheme, 3.199
  employees, 3.191–3.195
  general note, 3.190
  implementing regulations, 3.354–3.378
  resumption after suspension, 3.197–3.198
  self-employed, 3.191–3.195
imprisonment, 2.573–2.575
payment of benefit, 2.136
provision of information
  employer, by, 1.166–1.167, 1.170–1.171

1293

Incapacity benefit—*cont.*
  work-focused interviews
    see also **Incapacity benefit (interviews)**
    generally, 1.22
    Regulations, 2.578–2.598
Incapacity benefit (interviews)
  appeals, 2.592
  consequence of failure to take part
    generally, 2.590
    good cause, 2.591
  deferment, 2.587
  definitions, 2.582
  exemptions, 2.588
  failure to take part
    generally, 2.590
    good cause, 2.591
  general note, 2.579–2.580
  general requirement, 2.583–2.584
  place and time, 2.585
  relevant areas, 2.593–2.598
  taking part, 2.589
  waiver, 2.586
Incapacity for work
  all work test
    forms, 2.672–2.673
    rules, 2.671
  forms
    all work test statement, 2.672–2.673
    general certificate, 2.667–2.668
    maternity certificate, 2.676
    special statement, 2.670
  general certificate
    forms, 2.667–2.668
    rules, 2.666
  generally, 2.661–2.662
  maternity certificate
    forms, 2.676
    rules, 2.674–2.675
  medical evidence
    forms and rules, 2.666–2.676
    generally, 2.661–2.664
    self-certification, 2.665
  rules
    all work test statement, 2.671
    general certificate, 2.666
    maternity certificate, 2.674–2.675
    special statement, 2.669
  self-certification, 2.665
  special statement
    forms, 2.670
    rules, 2.669
Income support
  alteration of rates of benefit
    age-related benefits, 1.193–1.195
    decisions, 2.411
    generally, 1.187–1.189
    termination of award, 2.412
  breach of community order, 2.5–2.6
  claims for benefit
    see also **Claims for benefit**
    exempt claims, 2.36–2.37
    generally, 2.38–2.52

Income support—*cont.*
  claims for benefit—*cont.*
    method, 2.41
  decisions
    alteration in component rates, 2.411
    incomplete evidence, 2.409
  failure to maintain
    additional amounts, 1.142–1.146
    diversion of arrested earnings, 1.150
    generally, 1.133–1.136
    recovery from liable person, 1.137–1.141
    reduction of income support, 1.147–1.149
    transfer of orders, 1.142–1.146
  liability to maintain, 1.136
  loss of benefit, 2.638
  overpayment of benefits
    generally, 1.109
    prescribed income, 2.693–2.694
  payment of benefit, 2.138
  personal representative, obligations of, 1.159–1.161
  recoupment in tribunal proceedings
    definitions, 2.739
    determination of benefit recouped, 2.748–2.749
    industrial tribunal proceedings, 2.740–2.743
    recoupment of benefit, 2.744–2.747
  reduction for breach of community order, 2.5–2.6
  supplementary benefits, and
    claims for benefit, 1.237
    generally, 1.221
    miscellaneous, 1.237
    overpayment of benefits, 1.237
    payment of benefit, 1.237
  termination of award, 2.412
  work-focused interviews, 1.22
"Incomplete evidence"
  income support, 2.409
  jobseeker's allowance, 2.413
  social fund contributions, 2.409
Indirect effect
  generally, 3.11
"Industrial accidents"
  effect, 1.465–1.466
  generally, 1.463–1.464
Industrial diseases
  Council Regulation
    aggravation, 3.224
    general note, 3.213–3.214
    implementing regulations, 3.379–3.396
    miscellaneous, 3.225–3.226
    reimbursement between institutions, 3.227
    rights to benefits, 3.215–3.223
    students, 3.228
  decisions, 1.470–1.471
Industrial death benefit
  imprisonment, 2.573–2.575

Index

Industrial Injuries Advisory Council
cases where consultation not required, 1.209
functions, 1.208
generally, 1.207

Industrial injuries benefits
accident notification, 1.52–1.54
claimant obligations, 1.58–1.60
claims for benefit
see also **Claims for benefit**
claimant obligations, 1.58–1.60
medical examinations, 1.55–1.57
notice of accident, 1.52–1.54
decisions
generally, 1.521
regulations, 2.406–2.407
medical examinations, 1.55–1.57
notification obligations, 1.52–1.54
payment of benefits, 2.148
provision of information, 1.166–1.167

"Industrial injuries gratuities"
payment of benefit, 2.148

Industrial tribunals (recovery of benefits)
definitions, 2.739
determination of amount, 2.748–2.749
duties of employer. 2.743
duties of tribunals
monetary awards, 2.741
protective awards, 2.742
legislative basis
further provisions, 1.252
general note, 1.249
general provisions, 1.250–1.251
postponement of award, 2.744
procedure, 2.745–2.746
relevant payments
generally, 2.740
table of monetary awards, 2.751
relevant proceedings, 2.740
secondary proceedings, 2.747

Information
provision
see also **Provision of information**
age, 1.155–1.156
claims for benefit, 2.80–2.81
death, 1.155–1.158
electronic communications, 2.151–2.152
incapacity benefit, 1.166–1.167, 1.170–1.171
industrial injuries benefits, 1.166–1.167
maintenance proceedings, 1.172
marriage, 1.155–1.156
maternity allowance, 1.166–1.167
payment of benefit, 2.149–2.152
personal representatives, by, 1.159–1.161
recovery of benefits, 1.312–1.316, 2.755–2.758
Secretary of State, by, 1.558–1.559
severe disablement allowance, 1.166–1.167, 1.170–1.171

Information—*cont.*
provision—*cont.*
statutory maternity pay, 1.168–1.171
statutory sick pay, 1.164–1.167
suspension of benefit, 2.417–2.418
use
decisions, 1.340
local authorities, 2.273–2.277

Inland Revenue
decisions by officers, 1.546–1.547

"Instruments of payment"
generally, 2.173

Insurance
Council Regulation
applicable legislation, 3.155
generally, 3.131
implementing regulation, 3.315

"Interchange of benefits"
claims for benefit
generally, 2.84–2.85
list of benefits, 2.178

Interim payments
benefit under Act, by way of, 2.576–2.577
bringing into account, 2.688
generally, 2.686–2.687
overpayment, 2.689

Invalid care allowance
work-focused interviews, 1.22

Invalidity benefits
Council Regulation
aggravation, 3.196
civil servant's special scheme, 3.199
employees, 3.191–3.195
general note, 3.190
implementing regulations, 3.354–3.378
resumption after suspension, 3.197–3.198
self-employed, 3.191–3.195

"Irrecoverable sums"
overpayments, 1.556–1.557

Irregularities
Commissioners procedure, 2.327

Jobcentre Plus (interviews)
appeals, 2.614
consequence of failure to take part
exempt circumstances, 2.612
generally, 2.611
good cause, 2.613
deferment of requirement, 2.606
definitions, 2.601
exempt persons, 2.607
general requirement, 2.602
multiple benefit claims, 2.608
partners, for
appeals, 2.633
date, place and time, 2.628
deferment, 2.625
definitions, 2.621
exemption, 2.626
failure to take part, 2.630–2.631
general note, 2.619

1295

Index

Jobcentre Plus (interviews)—*cont.*
partners, for—*cont.*
good cause, 2.632
multiple benefit claims, 2.627
requirement, 2.622
taking part, 2.629
time, 2.623
waiver, 2.624
place and time, 2.609
purpose, 2.603
relevant areas, 2.680
taking part, 2.610
timing, 2.604
waiver, 2.605
Jobseeker's allowance
alteration of rates of benefit
age-related benefits, 1.196–1.197
generally, 1.190–1.191
breach of community order, 2.11–2.12
change of circumstances, 2.681
claims for benefit
see also **Claims for benefit**
exempt claims, 2.36–2.37
generally, 2.38–2.52
method, 2.43
special provisions, 2.179
decisions
alteration in component rates, 2.411
incomplete evidence, 2.413
termination of award, 2.412
joint-claim jobseeker's allowance
generally, 2.11–2.12
legislative basis, 1.564
overpayment of benefits
generally, 1.107–1.108
prescribed income, 2.693–2.694
payment of benefit
generally, 2.139
untraceable person, 2.147
recoupment in tribunal proceedings
definitions, 2.739
determination of benefit recouped, 2.748–2.749
industrial tribunal proceedings, 2.740–2.743
recoupment of benefit, 2.744–2.747
reduction for breach of community order, 2.11–2.12
termination of award, 2.412
Judgments and orders
recovery of benefits, 1.293–1.294
Judicial acts
acts of public authorities, 4.25
"Judicial remedies"
acts of public authorities, 4.23–4.24
Judicial review
proceedings against public authorities, 4.21

Lay representatives
Commissioner's procedure, 2.308–2.309
Legal advice and funding
Commissioner's procedure, 2.289–2.290

Legal aid
Commissioner's procedure, 2.289–2.290
Legal representation
Commissioner's procedure, 2.308–2.309
Legislation
declaration of incompatibility, 4.12–4.13
interpretation, 4.10–4.11
intervention by Crown, 4.14
remedial action, 4.26–4.27
Liberty
see **Human rights**
Life
see **Human rights**
Limitation periods
overpayment of benefits, 1.82–1.83
Loans
deductions from benefit, 2.220
Local authorities
see also **Public authorities**
claims for payment
child support, 2.266
functions, 2.264
holding information, 2.267
provision of information, 2.268
use and supply of information, 2.273–2.277
war pensions, 2.266
Locus standi
proceedings against public authorities, 4.19
Lone parents
work-focused interviews
appeals, 2.781
consequence of failure to take part, 2.779–2.780
deferment of requirement, 2.777
definitions, 2.770
exempt persons, 2.776
general requirement, 2.771
relevant areas, 2.775–2.776
taking part, 2.775
waiver, 2.778
Long-term benefits
gender recognition, 1.613–1.614
payment of benefit, 2.134
Loss of benefit
breach of community order, for
see also **Loss of benefit (community orders)**
definitions, 2.2–2.8
hardship, 2.13–2.26
information, 2.27–2.31
legislative basis, 1.562–1.567
reduced amounts, 2.9–2.12
commission of benefits fraud, for
see also **Loss of benefit (benefits fraud)**
definitions, 2.636–2.637
hardship, 2.641–2.652
housing benefit, 2.653
income support, 2.638
joint-claim jobseeker's allowance, 2.640
legislative basis, 1.568–1.574
state pension credit, 2.639

Index

Loss of benefit (benefits fraud)
child support maintenance, 2.656
council tax benefit, 2.654
couple in hardship, 2.647
deductions from benefits, 2.656
definitions
  couple in hardship, 2.647
  disqualification period, 2.637
  generally, 2.636
  person in hardship, 2.641
disqualification period, 2.637
disqualifying benefits, 2.655
hardship (jobseeker's allowance)
  applicable amount, 2.646
  circumstances of payment, 2.642–2.643
  conditions for payment, 2.644
  provision of information, 2.645
  relevant person, 2.641
hardship (joint-claim couples)
  applicable amount, 2.652
  circumstances of payment, 2.648–2.649
  conditions for payment, 2.650
  provision of information, 2.651
  relevant couple, 2.647
housing benefit, 2.653
income support, 2.638
joint-claim jobseeker's allowance
  generally, 2.640
  legislative basis, 1.571
legislative basis
  definitions, 1.576
  effect on members of offender's family, 1.572
  generally, 1.569–1.570
  joint-claim jobseeker's allowance, 1.571
  mitigation of provisions, 1.573
  regulations, 1.574
person in hardship, 2.641
state pension credit, 2.639
Loss of benefit (community orders)
couple in hardship, 2.21
definitions
  couple in hardship, 2.21
  generally, 2.3–2.4
  person in hardship, 2.13–2.14
  prescribed payment, 2.5–2.6
  prescribed period, 2.7–2.8
general note, 2.2
hardship (jobseeker's allowance cases)
  applicable amount, 2.20
  circumstances of payment, 2.15–2.17
  conditions for payment, 2.18
  provision of information, 2.19
  relevant person, 2.13–2.14
hardship (joint-claim couples)
  applicable amount, 2.26
  circumstances of payment, 2.22–2.23
  conditions for payment, 2.24
  provision of information, 2.25
  relevant couple, 2.21
income support, 2.9–2.10
information, 2.27–2.31

joint-claim jobseeker's allowance
  generally, 2.11–2.12
  legislative basis, 1.564
legislative basis
  appeals, 1.567
  general note, 1.561
  generally, 1.562–1.563
  joint-claim jobseeker's allowance, 1.564
  information, 1.565
  regulations, 1.566
loss of benefit
  definitions, 2.3–2.8
  general note, 2.2
  hardship, 2.7–2.26
  income support, 2.5–2.6
  information, 2.27–2.31
person in hardship, 2.13–2.14
prescribed payment, 2.5–2.6
prescribed period, 2.7–2.8
"Lump sums"
delay in payment, 2.133

Maastricht Treaty
citation, 3.5
generally, 3.4
implementation, 3.6–3.14
proof, 3.15–3.16
renumbering, 3.5
Maintenance
provision of information, 1.172
Mariners
see **Seafarers**
Marriage
human rights, 4.74
provision of information, 1.155–1.156
"Material facts"
overpayment of benefits, 1.97
"Materiality of errors "
appeals from appeal tribunal, 1.405
Maternity allowance
claims for benefit
  see also **Claims for benefit**
  advance claims, 2.100
  generally, 2.87–2.88
  imprisonment, 2.573–2.575
  payment of benefit, 2.136
  provision of information, 1.166–1.167
Maternity benefits
Council Regulation
  aggregation rules, 3.161–3.162
  employees, 3.163–3.173
  frontier workers, 3.165
  implementing regulations, 3.333–3.353
  miscellaneous provisions, 3.188
  pension claimants, 3.176
  pensioners, 3.177–3.185
  reimbursement between institutions, 3.189
  self-employed, 3.163–3.173
  students, 3.186–3.187
  unemployed, 3.174–3.175
  vocational students, 3.186–3.187
self-employed persons, 3.118

1297

"Maternity expenses"
  payment of benefit, 2.158
Maternity pay
  claims for benefit
    see also **Claims for benefit**
    generally, 1.72–1.73
  medical evidence
    form, 2.676
    rules, 2.654–2.675
  provision of information
    employer, by, 1.170–1.171
    Secretary of State, by, 1.168–1.169
Measure of damages
  recovery of benefit, 1.297–1.298
Medical evidence
  Commissioners procedure, 2.318–2.319
Medical evidence (incapacity for work)
  all work test
    forms, 2.672–2.673
    rules, 2.671
  forms
    all work test statement, 2.672–2.673
    general certificate, 2.667–2.668
    maternity certificate, 2.676
    special statement, 2.670
  general certificate
    forms, 2.667–2.668
    rules, 2.666
  generally, 2.661–2.662
  maternity certificate
    forms, 2.676
    rules, 2.674–2.675
  medical evidence
    forms and rules, 2.666–2.676
    generally, 2.661–2.664
    self-certification, 2.665
  rules
    all work test statement, 2.671
    general certificate, 2.666
    maternity certificate, 2.674–2.675
    special statement, 2.669
  self-certification, 2.665
  special statement
    forms, 2.670
    rules, 2.669
Medical examinations
  appeals tribunal, for
    generally, 1.426–1.428
    regulations, 2.469–2.470
  Council Regulation, 3.268
  failure to submit to, 1.435–1.436
  industrial injuries benefits, 1.55–1.57
  Secretary of State, for, 1.423–1.425
  suspension of benefit
    generally, 1.435–1.436
    regulations, 2.421–2.422
Mental capacity
  overpayment of benefits, 1.96
Migrant workers
  general note, 3.111
Minors
  notice of decision, 2.434–2.435
  payment of benefit, 2.143

Misrepresentation
  overpayment of benefits
    fraudulently or otherwise, 1.91
    generally, 1.86
    material fact, 1.97
    mental capacity, 1.96
    misrepresents, 1.92
    missing documents, 1.98
"Missing documents"
  overpayment of benefits, 1.98
Mobility component
  payment of benefit
    children, 2.169
    exempt cases, 2.168
    payment to Motability, 2.170–2.172
  payment to Motability
    generally, 2.170
    restriction, 2.172
    termination, 2.171
"Monetary awards"
  recoupment in tribunal proceedings, 2.741
"Mortgage interest"
  claims for benefit, 1.74–1.75
  direct payments
    generally, 2.156–2.157
    miscellaneous, 2.224–2.236
Motability scheme
  direct payments
    generally, 2.170
    restriction, 2.172
    termination, 2.171
Movement of workers
  see **Freedom of movement for workers**
"Multiple benefit claims"
  jobcentre plus interviews
    generally, 2.608
    partners, for, 2.627
Murder
  forfeiture rule, 1.19–1.20

National insurance numbers
  application for, 1.218–1.219
  child benefit, 2.790
  guardian's allowance, 2.790
Natural justice
  appeals from appeal tribunal, 1.404
"Neglect to maintain"
  diversion of arrested earnings, 1.150
  generally, 1.133–1.136
  recovery of benefit
    additional amounts, 1.142–1.146
    generally, 1.137–1.141
    transfer of orders, 1.142–1.146
    reduction of income support, 1.147–1.149
No punishment without law
  generally, 4.65
Non-contributory benefits
  claims for benefit
    see also **Claims for benefit**
    generally, 1.24–1.62
    procedure, 2.32–2.128
  Council Regulation, 3.294–3.295
  payment of benefit, 2.129–2.150

Index

Non-disclosure
see **Failure to disclose**
Northern Ireland
co-ordination, 1.211
reciprocal arrangements, 1.212
Notice of appeal
see **Appeal notices**
Notification
industrial injuries benefits, 1.52–1.54

Occupational diseases
see **Industrial diseases**
Occupational pensions
gender recognition
equivalent benefits, 1.629–1.630
general note, 1.626
guaranteed minimum, 1.627–1.628
"Official error"
definition, 2.343
Offsetting
generally, 1.91
Regulations
exceptions, 2.692
generally, 2.690–2.691
Old age benefits
see **Pensions**
"One offices"
claims for benefit
child benefit, 2.266
generally, 2.53–2.54
war pensions, 2.266
disclosure, 1.95
"Optional continued insurance"
applicable legislation, 3.155
generally, 3.131
implementing regulation, 3.315
Oral hearings
appeals procedure
adjournment, 2.491–2.492
directions, 2.465–2.466
expert assistance, 2.489–2.490
physical examinations, 2.493–2.494
postponement, 2.491–2.492
procedure, 2.481–2.488
record of proceedings, 2.501–2.504
Orders
recovery of benefits, 1.293–1.294
Orphans
civil servants' special scheme. 3.257
common provisions, 3.256
generally, 3.254–3.255
implementing regulation, 3.409–3.411
"Out of jurisdiction appeal"
definition, 2.344
Overlapping benefits
child benefit, 1.130–1.131
Council Regulation
generally, 3.139–3.140
implementing regulation, 3.316–3.321
generally, 1.110–1.112
Overpayment of benefits
automated credit transfers
generally, 1.101

Overpayment of benefits—*cont.*
automated credit transfers—*cont.*
regulations, 2.700
calculation of amount, 1.100
causation, 1.99
child benefit
calculation, 2.825
direct credit transfer, by, 2.823
generally, 1.109
interim payments, 2.829–2.830
offsetting, 2.826–2.828
prescribed payments, 2.695–2.698
claimant's estate, 1.90
deduction from benefits
generally, 2.708
limitations, 2.709
direct transfers
generally, 1.101
regulations, 2.700
disclosure
generally, 1.93
'*One*' office, at, 1.95
recipients, 1.94
evidence, 1.85
failure to disclose
generally, 1.93
material fact, 1.97
mental capacity, 1.96
missing documents, 1.98
generally, 1.79–1.81
guardian's allowance
calculation, 2.825
direct credit transfer, by, 2.823
generally, 1.109
interim payments, 2.829–2.830
offsetting, 2.826–2.828
prescribed payments, 2.695–2.698
guide, 1.104
income support
generally, 1.113–1.119
prescribed income, 2.693–2.694
interim payments, 2.689
irrecoverable sums, 1.556–1.557
jobseeker's allowance
generally, 1.107–1.108
prescribed income, 2.693–2.694
limitation period, 1.82–1.83
misrepresentation
fraudulently or otherwise, 1.91
generally, 1.86
material fact, 1.97
mental capacity, 1.96
misrepresents, 1.92
missing documents, 1.98
Northern Ireland, 1.128–1.129
offsetting
generally, 1.91
regulations, 2.690–2.691
presentation of evidence, 1.85
recoverable amount
diminution of capital resources, 2.706–2.707
deductions, 2.703–2.705

1299

Index

Overpayment of benefits—*cont.*
  recoverable amount—*cont.*
    generally, 2.701–2.702
    introduction, 1.100
  recovery of benefits
    disregards, 1.306–1.310
    generally, 1.304–1.305
    jobseeker's allowance, 1.107–1.108
    limitation period, 1.82–1.83
    Northern Ireland, 1.128–1.129
    procedure, 2.708–2.722
  recovery from earnings after trade dispute
    cessation of employment, 2.721–2.722
    deduction notices, 2.713–2.719
    employer's duties, 2.720
    generally, 2.711
    increased awards, 2.716
    protected earnings, 2.712
    resumption of employment, 2.721–2.722
  recovery procedure
    couples, from, 2.710
    deduction from benefits, from, 2.708–2.709
    deduction from earnings after trade dispute, by, 2.711–2.722
  relevant person
    appointee, 1.82
    generally, 1.87
    spouses, 1.91
  requirements
    any person, 1.87
    appointees, 1.82
    automated credit transfers, 1.101
    causation, 1.99
    determination of amount, 1.100
    disclosure, 1.93–1.94
    failure to disclose, 1.93
    fraudulently or otherwise, 1.91
    generally, 1.86
    material fact, 1.97
    mental capacity, 1.96
    misrepresents, 1.92
    missing documents, 1.98
    tax credit, 1.102
  social fund
    generally, 1.105–1.106
    procedure, 1.123–1.127
  supplementary benefits, 1.237
  tax credit, 1.102
  variation of benefit, 1.84
"Overseas authorities"
  exchange of information with, 1.216

"Party to the proceedings"
  definition, 2.345
Payments
  another person on beneficiary's behalf, to, 2.155
  appointee, to, 2.153–2.154
  attendance allowance, 2.137
  carer's allowance
    electronic payments, 2.151

Payments—*cont.*
  child benefit
    date of entitlement, 2.801
    direct credit transfers, 2.805
    effective date of change of rate, 2.802
    election for weekly payment, 2.807–2.809
    electronic payments, 2.152
    extinguishment of right, 2.814
    fractional amounts, 2.812
    generally, 2.135
    information, 2.811
    interim payment, 2.810
    method, 2.804
    person under 18 years, 2.813
    third parties, 2.818
    time, 2.806
  child support payments
    generally, 2.158–2.159
    miscellaneous provisions, 2.237–2.245
  constant attendance allowance, 2.137
  death, 2.144–2.146
  delay
    lump sums, 2.133
  direct credit transfer, by
    generally, 2.131–2.132
    overpayment, 1.101, 2.700
  direct payment
    accommodation costs, 2.213
    another person on beneficiary's behalf, to, 2.155
    appointee, to, 2.153–2.154
    child support payments, of, 2.158–2.159, 2.237–2.245
    funeral providers, to, 2.158
    hostels, to, 2.160, 2.214
    housing costs, 2.212
    maternity expenses, 2.158
    maximum amounts, 2.221
    miscellaneous, 2.210–2.236
    mortgage lenders, to, 2.156–2.157, 2.224–2.236
    partner, to, 2.161
    priority, 2.222–2.223
    utility companies, to, 2.158, 2.215–2.217
  disability living allowance
    attendance allowance, 2.137
    mobility component, 2.170–2.172
  disabled persons' tax credit, 2.141
  duplication
    maintenance payments, 2.697–2.698
    prescribed income, 2.693–2.694
    prescribed payments, 2.695–2.696
  electronic communication, use of
    carer's allowance, 2.151
    child benefit, 2.152
    miscellaneous provisions, 2.246–2.259
  fractional sums, 2.142
  funeral expenses, 2.158
  guardian's allowance
    date of entitlement, 2.801
    direct credit transfers, 2.805

Index

Payments—*cont.*
  guardian's allowance—*cont.*
    effective date of change of rate, 2.802
    election for weekly payment, 2.807–2.809
    extinguishment of right, 2.814
    fractional amounts, 2.812
    generally, 2.135
    information, 2.811
    interim payment, 2.810
    method, 2.804
    person under 18 years, 2.813
    third parties, 2.818
    time, 2.806
  heating expenses, 2.158
  hostels, to person in, 2.160
  incapacity benefit, 2.136
  income support, 2.138
  industrial injuries gratuities, 2.148
  information required, 2.149–2.150
  instruments of payment, 2.173
  interim payments
    bringing into account, 2.688
    generally, 2.686–2.687
    overpayment, 2.689
  jobseeker's allowance
    generally, 2.139
    untraceable person, 2.147
  long term benefits, 2.134
  lump sums
    delay, 2.133
  maternity allowance, 2.136
  maternity expenses, 2.158
  method of payment
    generally, 2.129
    miscellaneous, 2.189–2.202
  mortgage payments, 2.156–2.157
  Motability, to
    generally, 2.170
    restriction, 2.172
    termination, 2.171
  off-setting
    exceptions, 2.692
    generally, 2.690–2.691
  partner, to, 2.161
  person aged 17 or under, 2.143
  residential accommodation, to person in, 2.160
  severe disablement allowance, 2.136
  state pension benefit, 2.140
  supplementary benefits, 1.237
  third parties
    accommodation costs, 2.213
    another person on beneficiary's behalf, to, 2.155
    appointee, to, 2.153–2.154
    funeral providers, to, 2.158
    hostels, to, 2.160, 2.214
    housing costs, 2.212
    maternity expenses, 2.158
    maximum amounts, 2.221
    miscellaneous, 2.210–2.236

Payments—*cont.*
  third parties—*cont.*
    mortgage lenders, to, 2.156–2.157, 2.224–2.236
    partner, to, 2.161
    priority, 2.222–2.223
    utility companies, to, 2.158, 2.215–2.217
  time of payment
    generally, 2.129
    long term benefits, 2.183–2.188
    miscellaneous, 2.173
  untraceable person, 2.147
  working families' tax credit, 2.141
Payment into court
  recovery of benefits
    generally, 1.295–1.296
    regulations, 2.760
Pension credit
  see **State pension credit**
Pension deferment
  see **Deferred pensions**
Pension Schemes Act 1993
  general provisions, 1.247–1.248
Pensions
  claims for benefit
    see also **Claims for benefit**
    advance claims, 2.101–2.102
    generally, 2.36–2.37
  Council Regulation
    accidents at work, 3.396
    generally, 3.200–3.212
    implementing regulations, 3.354–3.378
  gender recognition
    Category A, 1.615–1.616
    Category B, 1.617–1.618
    Category C, 1.622–1.623
    deferment, 1.620–1.621
    graduated, 1.624–1.625
    occupational pensions, 1.626–1.630
    widow's pension, 1.609–1.610
  guaranteed minimum payments, 1.247–1.248
  imprisonment, 2.573–2.575
Permission to appeal
  acknowledgment, 2.306–2.307
  courts, to, 2.337–2.338
  decisions
    correction of errors, 2.331
    forfeiture rule questions, 2.330
    generally, 2.328–2.329
    setting aside, 2.332–2.335
    supplementary, 2.336
  determination, 2.299
  directions, 2.314–2.316
  generally, 2.300–2.301
  medical evidence, 2.318–2.319
  notice, 2.296–2.298
  response to notice or reference
    generally, 2.310–2.311
    reply, 2.312–2.313
  time limits, 2.302–2.303
  withdrawal, 2.325–2.326

Index

Permission to appeal—*cont.*
joint-claim jobseeker's allowance
generally, 2.11–2.12
legislative basis, 1.564
"Person in hardship"
generally, 2.13–2.14
Personal representatives
information obligations, 1.159–1.161
"Persons aged 17 or under"
payment of benefit, 2.143
notice of decision, 2.434–2.435
Pilot schemes
generally, 1.481
"Point of law"
appeals from appeal tribunal, 1.400
appeals from Commissioner, 1.411–1.412
Political activity of aliens
see **Human rights**
Precedent
appeals from appeal tribunal, 1.406
"Prescribed benefits"
generally, 2.723–2.725
"Prescribed payment"
generally, 2.5–2.6
"Prescribed period"
generally, 2.7–2.8
Prisoners
disqualification from benefit, 2.573–2.575
suspension of benefit, 2.575
Private life
see **Human rights**
Procedural irregularity
appeals from appeal tribunal, 1.404
Protection of property
generally, 4.88
introduction, 4.89
social security, 4.90
Protective awards
recoupment in tribunal proceedings, 2.742
Public authorities
claims for payment
child support, 2.266
functions, 2.264
holding information, 2.267
provision of information, 2.268
use and supply of information, 2.273–2.277
war pensions, 2.266
generally, 4.15–4.16
human rights
generally, 4.15–4.16
judicial acts, 4.25
judicial remedies, 4.23–4.24
proceedings, 4.17–4.22
remedial action, 4.26–4.27
standing, 4.19
judicial acts, 4.25
judicial remedies, 4.23–4.24
proceedings
"any legal proceedings", 4.22
constitutional torts, 4.20
generally, 4.17–4.18

Public authorities—*cont.*
proceedings—*cont.*
judicial review, 4.21
standing of claimant, 4.19
"victim" requirement, 4.19
racial discrimination
exceptions, 1.7–1.10
generally, 1.5–1.6
meaning, 1.2
racial grounds, 1.4
victimisation, 1.3
remedial action, 4.26–4.27
standing, 4.19
"victim" requirement, 4.19
Punishment without law
see **Human rights**

"Quarterly work-focused interviews for certain lone parents"
appeals, 2.736
conduct of interview, 2.732
definitions, 2.728
failure to take part in interview, 2.734–2.735
general note, 2.727
good cause, 2.735
place and time of interview, 2.732
relevant education authorities, 2.736
requirement to take part
deferment, 2.731
general, 2.729
waiver, 2.730
taking part in interview
failure to take part, 2.734–2.735
generally, 2.733

Race discrimination
exceptions
decisions not to prosecute, 1.11
judicial acts, 1.8
immigration and nationality cases, 1.9–1.10
legislative acts, 1.8
generally, 1.6–1.17
harassment, 1.5
meaning, 1.2
racial grounds, 1.4
victimisation, by way of, 1.3
Race Relations Act 1976
arrangement of sections, 1.1
general provisions, 1.2–1.11
Reciprocal enforcement
exchange of information with overseas authorities, 1.216
Northern Ireland, 1.211–1.212
outside UK, 1.213–1.215
"Record of proceedings"
appeals procedure, 2.501–2.504
Recoupment in tribunal proceedings
see **Recovery of benefits**
Recovery of benefits
adjustments, 2.765–2.766
appeals to Commissioners, 1.288–1.290

1302

Index

Recovery of benefits—*cont.*
  appeals to tribunal
    generally, 1.277–1.281
    reference of questions, 1.282–1.287
    supplementary, 1.291–1.292
  assessment of damages, 1.297–1.298
  certificates of recoverable benefit
    appeals, 1.277–1.292
    applications, 1.261–1.263
    contents, 1.264–1.265
    regulations, 2.759
    review, 1.273–1.276
  compensation payments
    exempt payments, 1.329, 2.754
    generally, 1.257–1.258
    list, 1.332–1.334
    small payments, 1.330–1.331
  couples, from, 2.710
  court orders, 1.293–1.294
  deduction notices
    contents, 2.713
    duration, 2.714
    effect, 2.715
    further, 2.718
    service, 2.713
    variation, 2.716–2.717
  deductions from benefits, from, 2.708–2.709
  disregarded payments, 1.306–1.310
  earnings after trade dispute, from
    cessation of employment, 2.721
    deduction notices, 2.713–2.718
    employer's duties, 2.720
    failure to notify, 2.722
    generally, 2.711
    increased awards, 2.716
    protected earnings, 2.712
    resumption of employment, 2.721
  exemptions, 2.754
  general note, 1.254
  income support
    additional amounts, 1.142–1.146
    diversion of arrested earnings, 1.150
    generally, 1.133–1.136
    recovery from liable person, 1.137–1.141
    transfer of orders, 1.142–1.146
  information
    compensator, by, 2.755
    employer, by, 2.757
    generally, 1.312–1.316
    injured person, by, 2.756
    procedure, 2.758
  introduction, 1.132
  liability of compensator
    generally, 1.266–1.267
    overpayments, 1.304–1.305
    recovery procedure, 1.268–1.269
    wrongly-made payments, 1.306–1.310
  overpayments
    disregards, 1.306–1.310
    generally, 1.304–1.305

Recovery of benefits—*cont.*
  payments into court
    generally, 1.295–1.296
    regulations, 2.760
  provision of information
    compensator, by, 2.755
    employer, by, 2.757
    generally, 1.312–1.316
    injured person, by, 2.756
    procedure, 2.758
  recoverable benefits, 1.257–1.258
  recoverable payments
    exempt payments, 1.329
    generally, 1.257–1.258
    list, 1.332–1.334
    small payments, 1.330–1.331
  reduction of compensation payment
    complex cases, 1.299–1.303
    generally, 1.270–1.263
    lump sum payments, 1.299–1.301
    more than one person, payments by, 1.302–1.303
    periodical payments, 1.299–1.301
    supplementary, 1.272
  reference of questions, 1.282–1.287
  Regulations
    adjustments, 2.765–2.766
    exemptions, 2.754
    generally, 1.322
    payments into court, 2.760
    provision of information, 2.755–2.758
    structured settlements, 2.763–2.764
  relevant cases, 1.255–1.256
  relevant payments
    exempt payments, 1.329, 2.754
    generally, 1.257–1.258
    list, 1.332–1.334
    small payments, 1.330–1.331
  relevant period, 1.259–1.260
  review of certificates
    generally, 1.273–1.276
    supplementary, 1.291–1.292
  structured settlements, 2.763–2.764

Recovery of benefits (overpayment of benefits)
  disregards, 1.306–1.310
  earnings after trade dispute, from
    cessation of employment, 2.721–2.722
    deduction notices, 2.713–2.719
    employer's duties, 2.720
    generally, 2.711
    increased awards, 2.716
    protected earnings, 2.712
    resumption of employment, 2.721–2.722
  generally, 1.304–1.305
  jobseeker's allowance, 1.107–1.108
  limitation period, 1.82–1.83
  Northern Ireland, 1.128–1.129
  procedure
    couples, from, 2.710
    deduction from benefits, from, 2.708–2.709

Recovery of benefits (overpayment of benefits)—*cont.*
procedure—*cont.*
  deduction from earnings after trade dispute, by, 2.711–2.722
  recoverable amount
    capital resources, diminution of, 2.706–2.707
    deductions, 2.703–2.705
    generally, 2.701–2.702
"Recrudescence"
  prescribed disease decisions, 2.408
"Re-determination"
  appeals, 1.392–1.396
Reduced earnings allowance
  imprisonment, 2.573–2.575
"Reduction of benefits"
  breach of community orders
    definitions, 2.2–2.8
    hardship, 2.13–2.26
    information, 2.27–2.31
    legislative basis, 1.562–1.567
    reduced amounts, 2.9–2.12
  complex cases
    generally, 1.299–1.303
    lump sum payments, 1.299–1.301
    more than one person, payments by, 1.302–1.303
    periodical payments, 1.299–1.301
    regulations, 2.761–2.762
  generally, 1.270
  income support, 1.147–1.149
  supplementary, 1.272
References
  forfeiture rule
    see also **References (forfeiture rule)**
    generally, 2.306–2.319
  issues to Revenue
    appeals, 1.437–1.438
    generally, 1.370–1.371
References (forfeiture rule)
  acknowledgment, 2.306–2.307
  decisions
    correction of errors, 2.331
    forfeiture rule questions, 2.330
    generally, 2.328–2.329
    setting aside, 2.332–2.335
    supplementary, 2.336
  directions, 2.314–2.316
  Forfeiture Act 1982, under, 2.305
  medical evidence, 2.318–2.319
  response to notice or reference, generally, 2.310–2.311
  reply, 2.312–2.313
  withdrawal, 2.325–2.326
Registrar of births, deaths and marriages
  generally, 1.155–1.156
  notification of death, 1.157–1.158
Reimbursement
  between institutions
    agreements relating to, 3.285
    occupational diseases, 3.227
    sickness and maternity, 3.189

Religion
  see **Human rights**
Representation
  see **Lay representatives**
  see **Legal representation**
Residence
  Council Regulation, 3.114
Residential accommodation
  payment of benefit
    accommodation costs, 2.213
    person in accommodation, 2.160
Restriction on political activity of aliens
  generally, 4.85
Retirement pensions
  claims for benefit
    see also **Claims for benefit**
    advance claims, 2.101–2.102
    generally, 2.36–2.37
  gender recognition
    Category A, 1.615–1.616
    Category B, 1.617–1.618
    Category C, 1.622–1.623
    deferment, 1.620–1.621
    graduated, 1.624–1.625
    shared additional, 1.619
    occupational pensions, 1.626–1.630
    widow's, 1.609–1.610
  imprisonment, 2.573–2.575
"Revalorization"
  Council Regulation
    generally, 3.137–3.138
    pensions, 3.211
Revision
  appeals, 2.437–2.439
  child benefit
    appeal, against which an, 2.868–2.869
    application, on, 2.862–2.867
    award of other benefit, after, 2.874–2.875
    Board, by, 2.862–2.867
    effective date, 2.876–2.877
    error, arising from, 2.872–2.873
    interaction with superseding, 2.884–2.885
    no appeal lies, against which, 2.870–2.871
  definitions, 2.391
  effective date, 2.369–2.370
  extension of time limits, 2.366–2.368
  generally, 1.356–1.362
  guardian's allowance
    appeal, against which an, 2.868–2.869
    application, on, 2.862–2.867
    award of other benefit, after, 2.874–2.875
    Board, by, 2.862–2.867
    effective date, 2.876–2.877
    error, arising from, 2.872–2.873
    interaction with superseding, 2.884–2.885
    no appeal lies, against which, 2.870–2.871
  procedure, 2.339–2.364

Index

Right to education
generally, 4.91
introduction, 4.92
Right to fair hearing
appeals from appeal tribunal, 1.404
Right to fair trial
access to court, 4.60
appeals, 4.59
criminal charges, 4.64
generally, 4.53
independence of tribunals, 4.63
introduction, 4.54
meaning, 4.57–4.58
resolution of disputes, 4.55–4.56
social security procedure, 4.61–4.62
Right to free elections
generally, 4.93
Right to liberty and security
generally, 4.51
introduction, 4.52
Right to life
generally, 4.45
introduction, 4.46
Right to marry
generally, 4.74
Right to respect for private and family life
benefits, 4.68
fraud, 4.69
generally, 4.66
introduction, 4.67
Right to thought, conscience and religion
generally, 4.70
introduction, 4.71
miscellaneous provision, 4.32–4.33

Seafarers
Council Regulation, 3.150
Seasonal workers
Council Regulation, 3.114
Secretaries of State (decisions)
appeals to appeals tribunal
appealable decisions, 1.516–1.524, 2.430–2.431
appellants, 2.428–2.429
certificates of recoverable benefit, 2.436
death of party, 2.453
decisions, 2.497–2.508
definitions, 2.511
dependant upon appeal in other cases, 1.444–1.451, 2.425
extension of time limits, 2.444–2.450
generally, 1.374–1.391
issues determinable by Revenue, 1.437–1.438, 2.463–2.464
late appeals, 2.444–2.450
medical examinations, 1.426–1.428, 2.469–2.470
non-disclosure of medical evidence, 2.471–2.472
oral hearings, 2.465–2.466, 2.481–2.494

Secretaries of State (decisions)—*cont.*
appeals to appeals tribunal—*cont.*
procedure, 1.413–1.422, 2.451–2.452, 2.461–2.462
re-determination, 1.392–1.396
revision of decisions, 2.437–2.439
striking out, 2.477–2.478
time limits, 2.441–2.443
unappealable decisions, 1.504–1.515, 2.432–2.433, 2.520–2.541
withdrawal, 2.467–2.468
witness summons, 2.473–2.474
dependent upon appeal in other cases, 1.439–1.443
generally, 1.350–1.355
industrial injuries benefits
generally, 1.521
regulations, 2.406–2.407
reference of issues to HMRC
appeals, 1.437–1.438
generally, 1.370–1.371
regulations, 1.372–1.373
revision of decisions
appeals, 2.437–2.439
definitions, 2.391
effective date, 2.369–2.370
extension of time limits, 2.366–2.368
generally, 1.356–1.362
procedure, 2.339–2.364
superseding earlier decisions
change of circumstances, 2.396–2.397
definitions, 2.391
effective date, 2.384–2.390
generally, 1.363–1.369
income support, 2.548–2.553
jobseekers' allowance, 2.554–2.560
procedure, 2.372–2.381
state pension credit, 2.561–2.569
Security and liberty
see **Human rights**
"Self-certification"
medical evidence, 2.665
Self-employed workers
accidents at work
aggravation, 3.224
general note, 3.213–3.214
implementing regulations, 3.379–3.396
miscellaneous, 3.225–3.226
reimbursement between institutions, 3.227
rights to benefits, 3.215–3.223
students, 3.228
Administrative Commission
generally, 3.258
tasks, 3.259–3.260
Advisory Committee
generally, 3.261
tasks, 3.262
aggregation of periods
accidents at work, 3.224
death grants, 3.229
family benefits, 3.244

1305

Index

Self-employed workers—*cont.*
  aggregation of periods—*cont.*
    general rules, 3.332
    invalidity, 3.196
    maternity, 3.161
    sickness, 3.161
    unemployment benefits, 3.233
  civil servants special scheme
    dependent children of pensioners, 3.257
    generally, 3.153–3.154
    invalidity, 3.199
    orphans, 3.257
    pensions, 3.212
    unemployment benefits, 3.242
  claims submitted to other authority, 3.266–3.267
  competent authorities
    co-operation between, 3.263
    definition, 3.114
  competent institution, 3.114
  competent State, 3.114
  conclusion of Conventions, 3.129–3.130
  consular staff, 3.156
  contributions chargeable to employers
    collection, 3.274
    generally, 3.273
  co-operation between competent authorities, 3.263
  Council Regulation
    Administrative Commission, 3.258–3.260
    Advisory Committee, 3.261–3.262
    annexes, 3.289–3.307
    arrangement of regulations, 3.110
    definitions, 3.114–3.116
    determination of applicable legislation, 3.141–3.160
    extension of, 3.392–3.399
    final provisions, 3.285–3.288
    general note, 3.111–3.112
    general provisions, 3.117–3.140
    implementation of, 3.308–33.132
    miscellaneous provisions, 3.263–3.275
    recitals, 3.113
    special provisions, 3.161–3.257
    transitional provisions, 3.276–3.284
  death grants
    generally, 3.229–3.232
    implementing regulation, 3.397–3.398
  declarations on scope, 3.123–3.124
  definitions, 3.114–3.116
  dependent children of pensioners
    civil servants' special scheme. 3.257
    common provisions, 3.256
    generally, 3.252–3.253
    implementing regulation, 3.409–3.411
  determination of applicable legislation
    civil servants, 3.153–3.154
    consular staff, 3.156
    diplomatic staff, 3.156
    employed in one member state and self-employed in another, 3.151
    employed persons, 3.145–3.147

Self-employed workers—*cont.*
  determination of applicable legislation—*cont.*
    exceptions to articles, 3.157–3.158
    general rules, 3.141–3.144
    implementing regulation, 3.323–3.331
    mariners, 3.150
    miscellaneous provisions, 3.152
    posted workers, 3.147
    recipients of pensions due in more than one member state, 3.159–3.160
    self-employed persons, 3.148–3.149
    special rules, 3.145–3.151
    students, 3.144
    voluntary insurance, 3.155
  diplomatic staff, 3.156
  employment and self-employment in more than one state, 3.151
  employed person, 3.114
  equality of treatment, 3.119–3.120
  exemption from authentication, 3.265
  exemption from fees, 3.265
  family benefits
    generally, 3.243–3.251
    implementing regulation, 3.404–3.407
  frontier workers
    accidents at work, 3.216
    definition, 3.114
  general note, 3.111–3.112
  habitual residence, 3.114
  international provision not affected
    generally, 3.127–3.128
    implementing regulation, 3.314
  invalidity
    aggravation, 3.196
    civil servant's special scheme, 3.199
    employees, 3.191–3.195
    general note, 3.190
    implementing regulations, 3.354–3.378
    resumption after suspension, 3.197–3.198
    self-employed, 3.191–3.195
  mariners, 3.150
  maternity
    aggregation rules, 3.161–3.162
    employees, 3.163–3.173
    frontier workers, 3.165
    implementing regulations, 3.333–3.353
    miscellaneous provisions, 3.188
    pension claimants, 3.176
    pensioners, 3.177–3.185
    reimbursement between institutions, 3.189
    self-employed, 3.163–3.173
    students, 3.186–3.187
    unemployed, 3.174–3.175
    vocational students, 3.186–3.187
  matters covered, 3.121–3.122
  medical examinations, 3.268
  member of the family, 3.114
  nationals of third countries
    annexes, 3.399
    general note, 3.392

Self-employed workers—*cont.*
nationals of third countries—*cont.*
   general provisions, 3.394–3.398
   recitals, 3.393
non-contributory benefits, 3.294–3.295
occupational diseases
   aggravation, 3.224
   general note, 3.213–3.214
   implementing regulations, 3.379–3.396
   miscellaneous, 3.225–3.226
   reimbursement between institutions, 3.227
   rights to benefits, 3.215–3.223
   students, 3.228
orphans
   civil servants' special scheme. 3.257
   common provisions, 3.256
   generally, 3.254–3.255
   implementing regulation, 3.409–3.411
overlapping benefits
   generally, 3.139–3.140
   implementing regulation, 3.316–3.321
pensions
   accidents at work, 3.396
   generally, 3.200–3.212
   implementing regulations, 3.354–3.378
periods of employment, 3.114
periods of insurance, 3.114
periods of residence, 3.114
persons covered
   annex, 3.289–3.290
   generally, 3.117–3.118
posted workers, 3.147
prolongation of reference period, 3.132
recipients of pensions due in more than one member state, 3.159–3.160
refugee, 3.114
reimbursement between institutions
   agreements relating to, 3.285
   occupational diseases, 3.227
   sickness and maternity, 3.189
residence, 3.114
revalorization of benefits
   generally, 3.137–3.138
   pensions, 3.211
seafarers, 3.150
seasonal worker, 3.114
self-employed workers, 3.114
sickness
   aggregation rules, 3.161–3.162
   employees, 3.163–3.173
   frontier workers, 3.165
   implementing regulations, 3.333–3.353
   miscellaneous provisions, 3.188
   pension claimants, 3.176
   pensioners, 3.177–3.185
   reimbursement between institutions, 3.189
   self-employed, 3.163–3.173
   students, 3.186–3.187
   unemployed, 3.174–3.175
   vocational students, 3.186–3.187

Self-employed workers—*cont.*
simultaneous employment and self-employment in more than one state, 3.151
social security conventions replaced
   generally, 3.125–3.126
   implementing regulation, 3.314
special non-contributory benefits, 3.135–3.136
special rules
   civil servants, 3.153–3.154
   consular staff, 3.156
   diplomatic staff, 3.156
   employed in one member state and self-employed in another, 3.151
   employed persons, 3.145–3.147
   mariners, 3.150
   miscellaneous provisions, 3.152
   posted workers, 3.147
   recipients of pensions due in more than one member state, 3.159–3.160
   self-employed persons, 3.148–3.149
   special rules, 3.145–3.151
   students, 3.144
   voluntary insurance, 3.155
stateless person, 3.114
stay, 3.114
students
   accidents at work, 3.228
   generally, 3.144
   sickness and maternity, 3.186–3.187
   transitional provisions, 3.283
survivor, 3.114
temporary residence, 3.114
third country nationals
   annexes, 3.399
   general note, 3.392
   general provisions, 3.394–3.398
   recitals, 3.393
transfer of sums payable between member states, 3.269
unemployment benefits
   civil servants' special scheme, 3.242
   common provisions, 3.233–3.236
   implementing regulation, 3.399–3.403
   person going to other member state, 3.237–3.239
   person residing in other member state, 3.240–3.241
voluntary insurance
   applicable legislation, 3.155
   generally, 3.131
   implementing regulation, 3.315
waiver of residence, 3.133–3.134
Service
electronic mail
   appeals to appeals tribunals, 2.510
notices
   Commissioners procedure, 2.288
Setting aside
appeals
   generally, 2.507–2.508
   miscellaneous provisions, 2.509

1307

Index

Setting aside—*cont.*
  decisions
    generally, 1.459–1.462
    regulations, 2.332–2.335
Severe disablement allowance
  claims for benefit
    see also **Claims for benefit**
    generally, 2.86
  EC Regulation
    aggravation, 3.196
    civil servant's special scheme, 3.199
    employees, 3.191–3.195
    general note, 3.190
    implementing regulations, 3.354–3.378
    resumption after suspension, 3.197–3.198
    self-employed, 3.191–3.195
  imprisonment, 2.573–2.575
  payment of benefit, 2.136
  provision of information, 1.166–1.167, 1.170–1.171
  work-focused interviews, 1.22
Shared additional pensions
  gender recognition, 1.619
"Sharing of functions"
  claims for benefits, 1.59
Sick pay
  claims for benefit
    see also **Claims for benefit**
    generally, 1.70–1.71
  provision of information
    employer, by, 1.166–1.167
    Secretary of State, by, 1.164–1.165
Sickness benefits
  Council Regulations
    aggregation rules, 3.161–3.162
    employees, 3.163–3.173
    frontier workers, 3.165
    implementing regulations, 3.333–3.353
    miscellaneous provisions, 3.188
    pension claimants, 3.176
    pensioners, 3.177–3.185
    reimbursement between institutions, 3.189
    self-employed, 3.163–3.173
    students, 3.186–3.187
    unemployed, 3.174–3.175
    vocational students, 3.186–3.187
Slavery
  generally, 4.49
  introduction, 4.50
Social fund
  adjustment, 1.203–1.204
  allocations, 1.201–1.202
  claims for benefit
    see also **Claims for benefit**
    generally, 1.63–1.66
  decisions
    incomplete evidence, 2.409
    generally, 1.199–1.200
  overpayment of benefits
    generally, 1.105–1.106
    procedure, 1.123–1.127

Social fund officers
  transfer of functions, 1.336–1.337
Social Security Act 1998
  arrangement of sections, 1.335
  citation, 1.492
  commencement, 1.492–1.493
  definitions, 1.476–1.477, 1.489
  general provisions
    appeal tribunals, 1.341–1.349
    Christmas bonus, 1.472–1.473
    decision-making, 1.336–1.340
    error correction, 1.452–1.462
    incapacity for work, 1.467–1.469
    industrial accidents, 1.463–1.466
    industrial diseases, 1.470–1.471
    Inland Revenue appeals, 1.437–1.438
    medical examinations, 1.423–1.428
    procedure, 1.413–1.422
    Secretary of State appeals, 1.439–1.451
    social security appeals, 1.374–1.412
    social security decisions, 1.350–1.373
    suspension of benefits, 1.429–1.436
  miscellaneous provisions
    pilot schemes, 1.481
    regulations and orders, 1.483–1.485
    reports by SoS, 1.486
  recitals, 1.335
  schedules
    appeal tribunals, 1.494–1.503
    appealable decisions, 1.516–1.526
    Commissioners, 1.527–1.535
    excluded decisions, 1.504–1.515
    procedure, 1.536–1.543
Social Security Administration Act 1992
  arrangement of sections, 1.23
  citation, 1.233
  commencement, 1.233
  definitions, 1.231–1.233
  general provisions
    adjudication, 1.78
    adjustment of benefit, 1.110
    advisory bodies and consultation, 1.205–1.209
    claims for benefit, 1.24–1.77
    computation of benefit, 1.177–1.197
    enforcement, 1.121–1.153
    failure to maintain, 1.133
    information, 1.154–1.176
    overpayment of benefits, 1.79–1.109
    payment of benefit, 1.24–1.77
    reciprocal arrangements with other systems, 1.211–1.215
    recovery of benefit, 1.132
    social fund, 1.198–1.210
  miscellaneous provisions, 1.217–1.225
  schedules
    claims for benefit, 1.234–1.236
    supplementary benefit, etc., 1.237–1.238
  subordinate legislation, 1.226–1.230
Social Security Advisory Committee
  cases where consultation not required, 1.209

Index

Social Security Advisory Committee— *cont.*
functions, 1.208
generally, 1.205–1.206
Social Security and Child Support Appeals Tribunal
appointment panel
  generally, 1.345–1.346
  qualifications, 2.454, 2.542–2.547
clerks
  functions, 2.460
  generally, 1.498
composition, 2.455–2.459
constitution, 1.347–1.349
decisions
  correction of errors, 2.505–2.506
  definitions, 2.511
  generally, 2.497–2.499
  late application for statement of reasons, 2.500
  record of proceedings, 2.501–2.504
  setting aside, 2.507–2.508
definition, 1.476
delegation of functions, 1.499
issues determinable by Revenue
  generally, 1.437–1.438
  regulations, 2.463–2.464
medical examinations
  generally, 1.426–1.428
  regulations, 2.469–2.470
officers, 1.496
oral hearings
  adjournment, 2.491–2.492
  choice of, 2.465–2.466
  directions, 2.465–2.466
  expert assistance, 2.489–2.490
  physical examinations, 2.493–2.494
  postponement, 2.491–2.492
  procedure, 2.481–2.488
  record of proceedings, 2.501–2.504
President
  functions, 1.497
  generally, 1.343–1.344
  remuneration, 1.495
  tenure of office, 1.494
procedure
  applications, 2.451–2.452
  determination, 2.461–2.462
  generally, 1.413–1.422
  medical examinations, 2.469–2.472
  oral hearings, 2.465–2.466
  withdrawal, 2.467–2.468
  witness summons, 2.473–2.474
remuneration, 1.495
staff, 1.496
striking out
  generally, 2.477–2.478
  misconceived applications, 2.478
  reinstatement, 2.479
unification, 1.341–1.342
withdrawal, 2.467–2.468
witness summons, 2.473–2.474

Social Security (Breach of Community Order) Regulations 2001
citation, 2.2
commencement, 2.2
definitions
  generally, 2.2–2.2.1
  person in hardship, 2.13–2.14
  prescribed payment, 2.3–2.3.1
  prescribed period, 2.4–2.4.1
general note, 2.1.1
general provisions
  hardship, 2.7–2.26
  information, 2.27–2.31
  reduced amounts, 2.9–2.12
recitals, 2.1
Social Security (Claims and Information) Regulations 1999
arrangement of regulations, 2.260
citation, 2.261
commencement, 2.261
definitions, 2.262
general provisions, 2.263–2.278
Social Security (Claims and Payments) Regulations 1987
arrangement of regulations, 2.32
citation, 2.33
commencement, 2.33
definitions, 2.34–2.35
general provisions
  claims for benefits, 2.36–2.128
  disability living allowances, 2.167–2.172
  extinguishment of benefits, 2.163–2.166
  payment of benefit, 2.129–2.150
  third parties, 2.153–2.161
miscellaneous provisions
  payment of benefit, 2.173
  revocations, 2.174
  savings, 2.175–2.176
schedules
  child benefit, 2.203–2.209
  child support maintenance deductions, 2.237–2.245
  claims for benefits, 2.177–2.178
  deductions from benefit, 2.210–2.236
  electronic communication, use of, 2.246–2.259
  jobseeker's allowance, 2.179–2.179
  payment of benefit, 2.183–2.202
  time limits, 2.181–2.182
Social Security Commissioners
appeals from, 2.337–2.338
appeals to
  see also **Social Security Commissioners (appeals)**
  application for leave to appeal, 2.291–2.303
  decisions, 2.328–2.336
  procedure, 2.308–2.327
  recovery of benefit, 1.288–1.290
  references, 2.304–2.307
appointment, 1.527

1309

Index

Social Security Commissioners—*cont.*
  delegation of functions
    generally, 2.287
    supplementary, 1.530
  powers, 2.285
  recovery of benefits
    generally, 1.277–1.281
    reference of questions, 1.282–1.287
    supplementary, 1.291–1.292
  reference under Forfeiture Act 1982
    acknowledgment, 2.306–2.307
    decisions, 2.328–2.336
    directions, 2.314–2.316
    generally, 2.304–2.307
    medical evidence, 2.318–2.319
    reply to response, 2.312–2.313
    response, 2.310
    withdrawal, 2.325–2.326
  remuneration, 1.528
  tenure of office, 1.529

Social Security Commissioners (appeals)
  appeal notices
    acknowledgment, 2.306–2.307
    decisions, 2.328–2.336
    directions, 2.314–2.316
    funding of legal services, 2.289–2.290
    generally, 2.300–2.301
    medical evidence, 2.318–2.319
    reply to response, 2.312–2.313
    response, 2.310
    service, 2.288
    time limits, 2.302–2.303
    withdrawal, 2.325–2.326
  appeals from, 2.337–2.338
  appeals to
    application for leave to appeal, 2.291–2.303
    decisions, 2.328–2.336
    procedure, 2.308–2.327
    recovery of benefit, 1.288–1.290
    references, 2.304–2.307
  application for leave to appeal
    decisions, 2.328–2.336
    determination, 2.299
    directions, 2.314–2.316
    generally, 2.291–2.295
    medical evidence, 2.318–2.319
    notice, 2.296–2.298
    withdrawal, 2.325–2.326
  application for leave to appeal to courts, 2.337–2.338
  appointment, 1.527
  correction of errors, 2.331
  decisions
    correction of errors, 2.331
    forfeiture rule questions, 2.330
    generally, 1.546–1.547, 2.328–2.329
    setting aside, 2.332–2.335
    supplementary, 2.336
  delegation of functions
    generally, 2.287
    supplementary, 1.530

Social Security Commissioners (appeals)—*cont.*
  directions, 2.314–2.316
  forfeiture rule questions
    meaning, 2.283–2.284
    post-decision procedure, 2.330
  funding of legal services, 2.289–2.290
  hearings
    generally, 2.322
    request, 2.320–2.321
  irregularities, effect of, 2.327
  linked case notice, 2.317
  medical evidence, non-disclosure of, 2.318–2.319
  notice of appeal
    acknowledgment, 2.306–2.307
    decisions, 2.328–2.336
    directions, 2.314–2.316
    funding of legal services, 2.289–2.290
    generally, 2.300–2.301
    medical evidence, 2.318–2.319
    reply to response, 2.312–2.313
    response, 2.310
    service, 2.288
    time limits, 2.302–2.303
    withdrawal, 2.325–2.326
  powers, 2.285
  recovery of benefit
    generally, 1.277–1.281
    reference of questions, 1.282–1.287
    supplementary, 1.291–1.292
  reference under Forfeiture Act 1982
    acknowledgment, 2.306–2.307
    decisions, 2.328–2.336
    directions, 2.314–2.316
    generally, 2.304–2.307
    medical evidence, 2.318–2.319
    reply to response, 2.312–2.313
    response, 2.310
    withdrawal, 2.325–2.326
  remuneration, 1.528
  reply to response, 2.312–2.313
  representation, 2.308–2.309
  request for hearings, 2.320–2.321
  response to notice or reference
    generally, 2.310–2.311
    reply, 2.312–2.313
  service of notices, 2.288
  setting aside decisions, 2.332–2.335
  tenure of office, 1.529
  transfer of proceedings, 2.286
  witness summons, 2.323–2.324

Social Security Commissioners (Procedure) Regulations 1999
  arrangement of regulations, 2.279
  citation, 2.280
  commencement, 2.280
  definitions, 2.283–2.284
  general provisions
    appeals, 2.300–2.303
    applications for leave to appeal, 2.291–2.299
    decisions, 2.328–2.336

Index

Social Security Commissioners (Procedure) Regulations 1999—*cont.*
general provisions—*cont.*
further appeal, 2.337–2.338
generally, 2.285–2.288
procedure, 2.308–2.327
references, 2.304–2.306
revocation, 2.281
transitional provisions, 2.282
Social Security, etc. (Decisions and Appeals) Regulations 1999
arrangement of regulations, 2.339
citation, 2.340
commencement, 2.340
definitions, 2.340–2.345
general provisions
appeals, 2.424–2.517
miscellaneous issues, 2.398–2.413
revision of decisions, 2.349–2.371
supersession of decisions, 2.372–2.397
suspension of payment, 2.415–2.423
termination of payment, 2.415–2.423
revocations, 2.518
schedules
change of circumstances, 2.548–2.569
provisions conferring powers, 2.519
qualification of Tribunal members, 2.542–2.547
revocations, 2.570
unappealable decisions, 2.520–2.541
service of notices, 2.346–2.348
Social Security Fraud Act 2001
arrangement of regulations, 1.568
general provisions, 1.569–1.574
Social Security (General Benefit) Regulations 1982
arrangement of regulations, 2.571
citation, 2.572
commencement, 2.572
definitions, 2.572
general provisions, 2.573–2.577
Social Security (Incapacity Benefit Work-focused Interviews) Regulations 2003
arrangement of regulations, 2.578
citation, 2.581
commencement, 2.581
definitions, 2.582
general note, 2.579–2.580
general provisions, 2.583–2.592
schedule, 2.598
Social Security (Jobcentre Plus Interviews) Regulations 2002
amendments, 2.616
arrangement of regulations, 2.599
citation, 2.600
commencement, 2.600
definitions, 2.601
general provisions, 2.602–2.614
revocations, 2.615
schedules, 2.617
transitional provision, 2.615

Social Security (Jobcentre Plus Interviews for Partners) Regulations 2003
amendments, 2.634
arrangement of regulations, 2.618
citation, 2.620
commencement, 2.620
definitions, 2.621
general note, 2.619
general provisions, 2.622–2.633
Social Security (Loss of Benefit) Regulations 2001
amendments, 2.657–2.658
citation, 2.636
commencement, 2.636
definitions, 2.636–2.637
general provisions
council tax benefit, 2.654
deductions from benefits, 2.656
disqualifying benefits, 2.655
hardship, 2.641–2.652
housing benefit, 2.653
reductions, 2.638–2.640
recitals, 2.635
Social Security (Medical Evidence) Regulations 1976
arrangement of regulations, 2.659
citation, 2.660
commencement, 2.660
definitions, 2.660
general provisions, 2.661–2.665
schedules, 2.666–2.676
Social Security (Notification of Change of Circumstances) Regulations 2001
arrangement of regulations, 2.677
citation, 2.679
commencement, 2.679
general note, 2.678
general provisions, 2.680–2.683
Social Security (Payments on Account, Overpayments and Recovery) Regulations 1988
arrangement of regulations, 2.684
citation, 2.685
commencement, 2.685
definitions, 2.685
general provisions
calculation of recoverable amount, 2.701–2.707
duplication of payments, 2.693–2.699
interim payments, 2.686–2.689
offsetting, 2.690–2.692
overpayments, 2.700
recovery procedure, 2.708–2.722
Social Security (Quarterly Work-focused Interviews for Certain Lone Parents) Regulations 2004
arrangement of regulations, 2.726
citation, 2.728
commencement, 2.728
definitions, 2.728
general note, 2.727
general provisions, 2.729–2.736
schedule, 2.736

1311

Index

Social Security (Recovery of Benefits) Act 1997
application, 1.319–1.320
arrangement of sections, 1.253
citation, 1.327
commencement, 1.327–1.328
definitions, 1.321
extent, 1.327
general note, 1.254
general provisions
  appeals, 1.277–1.292
  certificates of recoverable benefit, 1.261–1.265
  complex cases, 1.299–1.303
  courts, 1.293–1.298
  liability of payer, 1.266–1.269
  reduction of payment, 1.270–1.272
  references, 1.282–1.292
  reviews, 1.273–1.292
introductory provisions, 1.255–1.260
miscellaneous provisions
  amendment of Schedule 2, 1.317
  Crown, 1.319–1.320
  disregard of compensation payments, 1.306–1.310
  Northern Ireland, 1.318
  overpaid amounts, 1.304–1.305
  provision of information, 1.312–1.316
  Regulations and orders, 1.322
schedules
  compensation payments, 1.329–1.334
  transitional provisions, 1.324–1.325
Social Security (Recovery of Benefits) Regulations 1997
arrangement of regulations, 2.752
citation, 2.753
commencement, 2.753
definitions, 2.753
general provisions
  adjustments, 2.765–2.766
  application for certificate, 2.759
  complex cases, 2.761–2.762
  exemptions, 2.754
  payments into court, 2.760
  provision of information, 2.755–2.758
  structured settlements, 2.763–2.764
transitional provisions, 2.767–2.768
Social Security, etc., (Transfer of Functions, etc.) Act 1999
arrangement of sections, 1.544
citation, 1.554
commencement, 1.554
definitions, 1.552–1.553
general provisions
  decisions and appeals, 1.545–1.550
miscellaneous provisions, 1.551
recitals, 1.544
Social Security (Work-focused Interviews for Lone Parents) and Miscellaneous Amendments Regulations 2000
arrangement of regulations, 2.769
citation, 2.770

Social Security (Work-focused Interviews for Lone Parents) and Miscellaneous Amendments Regulations 2000—*cont.*
commencement, 2.770
definitions, 2.770
general provisions, 2.771–2.781
schedules, 2.782–2.784
Social Security (Working Neighbourhoods) Regulations 2004
general note, 2.785
Standing
see **Locus standi**
State maternity allowance
see **Maternity allowance**
State pension credit
alteration of rates of benefit, 1.192
claims for benefit
  see also **Claims for benefit**
  advance claims, 2.99
  after attaining qualifying age, 2.56
  before attaining qualifying age, 2.55
  date of claim, 2.56
  general note, 2.57
  generally, 2.54
date of entitlement, 2.109
decisions, 1.523
loss of benefit, 2.639
payment of benefit, 2.140
"Statements of reasons"
appeals procedure
  generally, 2.497–2.499
  late application, 2.500
Statements of compatibility
human rights, 4.39–4.40
Statutory maternity pay
claims for benefit
  see also **Claims for benefit**
  generally, 1.72–1.73
  medical evidence
    form, 2.676
    rules, 2.654–2.675
  provision of information
    employer, by, 1.170–1.171
    Secretary of State, by, 1.168–1.169
Statutory sick pay
claims for benefit
  see also **Claims for benefit**
  generally, 1.70–1.71
Council Regulation
  aggregation rules, 3.161–3.162
  employees, 3.163–3.173
  frontier workers, 3.165
  implementing regulations, 3.333–3.353
  miscellaneous provisions, 3.188
  pension claimants, 3.176
  pensioners, 3.177–3.185
  reimbursement between institutions, 3.189
  self-employed, 3.163–3.173
  students, 3.186–3.187
  unemployed, 3.174–3.175

Index

Statutory sick pay—*cont.*
 Council Regulation—*cont.*
  vocational students, 3.186–3.187
  provision of information
   employer, by, 1.166–1.167
   Secretary of State, by, 1.164–1.165
Stepchildren
 civil partnerships, 1.633–1.634
Striking out
 appeals
  generally, 2.477–2.478
  misconceived applications, 2.478
  reinstatement, 2.479
Structured settlements
 recovery of benefits, 2.763–2.764
Students
 Council Regulation
  accidents at work, 3.228
  generally, 3.144
  sickness and maternity, 3.186–3.187
  transitional provisions, 3.283
Supersession
 child benefit
  effective date, 2.886–2.889
  interaction with revision, 2.884–2.885
  procedure, 2.881–2.883
  relevant cases and circumstances, 2.878–2.880
 definitions, 2.391
 effective date
  change of circumstances, 2.396–2.397
  generally, 2.384–2.390
  income support, 2.548–2.553
  jobseekers' allowance, 2.554–2.560
  state pension credit, 2.561–2.569
 generally, 1.363–1.369
 guardian's allowance
  effective date, 2.886–2.889
  interaction with revision, 2.884–2.885
  procedure, 2.881–2.883
  relevant cases and circumstances, 2.878–2.880
 procedure, 2.372–2.381
Supplementary benefits
 claims for benefit, 1.237
 generally, 1.221
 miscellaneous, 1.237
 overpayment of benefits, 1.237
 payment of benefit, 1.237
Suspension (benefits)
 child benefit
  generally, 2.890
  provision of information, 2.891
  subsequent payment, 2.893
 failure to furnish information
  generally, 1.431–1.432
  regulations, 2.419–2.420
 failure to submit to medical
  generally, 1.435–1.436
  regulations, 2.421–2.422
 guardian's allowance
  generally, 2.890
  provision of information, 2.891

Suspension (benefits)—*cont.*
 guardian's allowance—*cont.*
  subsequent payment, 2.893
 imprisonment, 2.575
 prescribed circumstances
  generally, 1.429–1.430
  regulations, 2.415–2.416
 provision of information, 2.417–2.418
 recommencement of payments, 2.423

Tax credits
 legislative basis, 1.578
 overpayment of benefits, 1.102
Tax Credits Act 2002
 arrangement of sections, 1.577
 definitions, 1.595–1.596
 general note, 1.578
 general provisions, 1.580–1.586
 schedules, 1.598
 supplementary provisions
  administrative arrangements, 1.591–1.592
  Parliamentary control of instruments, 1.594
  regulations and orders, 1.593
  transitional provisions, 1.587–1.589
Termination (benefits)
 child benefit, 2.892
 failure to furnish information, for
  child benefit, 2.892
  generally, 1.431–1.432
  guardian's allowance, 2.892
  regulations, 2.419–2.420
 failure to submit to medical, for
  generally, 1.435–1.436
  regulations, 2.421–2.422
  guardian's allowance, 2.892
Third parties
 claims by
  see also **Third party claims**
  generally, 2.817
  persons who may act, 2.815
 payments to
  see also **Direct payments**
  accommodation costs, 2.213
  another person on beneficiary's behalf, to, 2.155
  appointee, to, 2.153–2.154
  child benefit, 2.815–2.822
  decisions, 1.518
  funeral providers, to, 2.158
  guardian's allowance, 2.815–2.822
  hostels, to, 2.160
  housing costs, 2.212
  maternity expenses, 2.158
  maximum amounts, 2.221
  mortgage lenders, to, 2.156–2.157
  partner, to, 2.161–2.161
  priority, 2.222–2.223
  service charges, 2.215–2.216
  utility companies, to, 2.158
  water charges, 2.217

1313

Third party claims
child benefit
generally, 2.817
persons who may act, 2.815
guardian's allowance
generally, 2.817
persons who may act, 2.815
Thought, conscience and religion
see **Human rights**
Time limits
appeals procedure
extension, 2.444–2.450
generally, 2.441–2.443
claims for benefit
generally, 2.113–2.128
prescribed period, 2.181–2.182
payment of benefit
generally, 2.129
long term benefits, 2.183–2.188
miscellaneous, 2.173–2.176
Torture
generally, 4.47
introduction, 4.48
"Transfer of functions"
decisions, 1.336–1.337
Transfer of proceedings
Commissioners procedure, 2.286
Treaty of Amsterdam
generally, 3.5
Treaty on European Union
citation, 3.5
generally, 3.4
implementation, 3.6–3.14
proof, 3.15–3.16
renumbering, 3.5

Unemployment benefits
civil servants' special scheme, 3.242
common provisions, 3.233–3.236
implementing regulation, 3.399–3.403
person going to other member state, 3.237–3.239
person residing in other member state, 3.240–3.241
Untraceable persons
payment of benefits, 2.147
Uprating
Council Regulation
generally, 3.137–3.138
pensions, 3.211
Utilities
direct payments
generally, 2.158
miscellaneous, 2.216
service charges, 2.215
water charges, 2.217

Vaccine Damage Appeals Tribunal
see **Social Security and Child Support Appeals Tribunal**
Variation (benefits)
overpayment of benefits, 1.84

Victimisation
racial discrimination, 1.3
Victims
proceedings against public authorities, 4.19
Vocational training
Council Regulation
accidents at work, 3.228
generally, 3.144
sickness and maternity, 3.186–3.187
transitional provisions, 3.283
"Voluntary insurance"
Council Regulation
applicable legislation, 3.155
generally, 3.131
implementing regulation, 3.315

Waiver
incapacity benefit interviews, 2.586
jobcentre plus interviews
generally, 2.605
partners, for, 2.624
residence, 3.133–3.134
work-focused interviews for lone parents, 2.778
War pensions
claims for benefit, 2.266
Water charges
payment of benefit, 2.217
Welfare Reform and Pensions Act 1999
arrangement of sections, 1.555
general provisions, 1.556–1.559
Welsh language
duty to prepare schemes, 1.240–1.241
legal proceedings, in, 1.242
oaths and affirmations, 1.243–1.238
prescribed forms, 1.245–1.246
Welsh Language Act 1993
arrangement of sections, 1.239
general provisions, 1.240–1.246
Widowed mother's allowance
claims for benefit
see also **Claims for benefit**
generally, 1.41–1.42
gender recognition, 1.607–1.608
Widowed parent's allowance
gender recognition, 1.611–1.612
Widowers' benefits
discrimination, 4.81
Widows' benefits
claims for benefit
see also **Claims for benefit**
generally, 1.41–1.42
discrimination, 4.81
gender recognition, 1.609–1.610
imprisonment, 2.573–2.575
work-focused interviews, 1.22
Widow's pension
gender recognition, 1.609–1.610
Withdrawal
appeals procedure, 2.467–2.468
claims for benefit, 2.61–2.63

Index

Withholding information
suspension of benefit
  child benefit, 2.892
  generally, 1.433–1.434
  guardian's allowance, 2.892
  regulations, 2.419–2.420
Witness summonses
appeals procedure, 2.473–2.474
Commissioners procedure, 2.323–2.324
Work-focused interviews
definition, 2.340
Jobcentre Plus
  see also **Jobcentre Plus**
  appeals, 2.614
  deferment, 2.606
  definitions, 2.601
  exempt persons, 2.607
  failure to take part, 2.611–2.613
  general requirement, 2.602
  multiple benefit claims, 2.608
  place and time, 2.609
  purpose, 2.603
  relevant areas, 2.680
  taking part, 2.610
  timing, 2.604
  waiver, 2.605
Jobcentre Plus for partners
  appeals, 2.633
  deferment, 2.625
  definitions, 2.621
  exemption, 2.626
  failure to take part, 2.630–2.632
  general note, 2.619
  general requirement, 2.622
  multiple benefit claims, 2.627
  place and time, 2.628
  taking part, 2.629
  time, 2.623
  waiver, 2.624
incapacity benefit
  see also **Incapacity benefit**
  appeals, 2.592
  deferment, 2.587
  definitions, 2.582
  exemptions, 2.588
  failure to take part, 2.590–2.591
  general note, 2.579
  general requirement, 2.583–2.584
  place and time, 2.585
  relevant areas, 2.593–2.598
  taking part, 2.589
  waiver, 2.586
lone parents
  see also **Work-focused interviews (lone parents)**
  generally, 2.770–2.784
  quarterly interviews, 2.727–2.736
quarterly interviews for certain lone parents
  appeals, 2.736
  conduct of interview, 2.732
  definitions, 2.728
  failure to take part in interview, 2.734–2.735

Work-focused interviews—*cont.*
quarterly interviews for certain lone parents—*cont.*
  general note, 2.727
  good cause, 2.735
  place and time of interview, 2.732
  relevant education authorities, 2.736
  requirement to take part, 2.729–2.731
  taking part in interview, 2.733–2.735
taking part
  incapacity benefit interviews, 2.589–2.591
  jobcentre plus interviews, 2.611–2.614
  jobcentre plus interviews for partners, 2.630–2.633
  lone parents, 2.775–2.780
  working neighbourhoods, 2.785
Work-focused interviews (lone parents)
appeals, 2.781
claims for benefit
  conditional entitlement, 1.34–1.35
  generally, 2.79
  local authorities, by, 2.264
  nature, 2.263
  optional, 1.37
  supplementary provisions, 1.36
conduct of interview, 2.774
consequence of failure to take part
  generally, 2.779
  reduction of income support, 2.780
deferment, 2.777
definitions, 2.770
effect of failure to take part
  generally, 2.779
  reduction of income support, 2.780
exempt persons, 2.776
failure to take part
  generally, 2.779
  reduction of income support, 2.780
general requirement, 2.771
quarterly interviews
  appeals, 2.736
  conduct of interview, 2.732
  deferment of requirement, 2.731
  definitions, 2.728
  failure to take part in interview, 2.734–2.735
  general note, 2.727
  good cause, 2.735
  place and time of interview, 2.732
  relevant education authorities, 2.736
  requirement to take part, 2.729
  taking part in interview, 2.733

1315

Work-focused interviews (lone parents)—*cont.*
quarterly interviews—*cont.*
waiver of requirement, 2.730
relevant areas, 2.782–2.784
specified lone parents in certain areas to take part, 2.773
specified lone parents to take part, 2.772
taking part, 2.775
timing of interview, 2.774
waiver, 2.778

Working families' tax credit
claims for benefit
see also **Claims for benefit**
exempt claims, 2.36–2.37
generally, 2.38–2.52
method, 2.43
date of claim, 2.64
overpayment of benefits, 1.84
payment of benefit, 2.141
"Working neighbourhoods"
general note, 2.785